Manual of Accounting – IFRS for the UK 2013 Volume one

Global Accounting Consulting Services
PricewaterhouseCoopers LLP

Published by

Bloomsbury Professional

Bloomsbury Professional, an imprint of Bloomsbury Publishing Plc, Maxwelton House, 41–43 Boltro Road, Haywards Heath, West Sussex, RH16 1BJ

ISBN 978 1 78043 106 2

British Library Cataloguing-in-Publication Data.
A catalogue record for this book is available from the British Library.

Printed in Great Britain.
Typeset by YHT Ltd, 4 Hercies Road, Hillingdon, Middlesex UB10 9NA

Authors

The Manual of Accounting – IFRS for the UK is written by the Global Accounting Consulting Services team of PricewaterhouseCoopers LLP.

Writing team led by
Barry Johnson
Peter Holgate

Authors, contributors and reviewers

Andrea Allocco
John Althoff
Ariane Amiot
Michelle Amjad
Wayne Andrews
Carolyn Anthony
Jason Aeschliman
Jan Backhuijs
Gábor Balázs
Rod Balding
Scott Bandura
Andrea Bardens
Dieter Baumann
Erin Bennett
Catherine Benjamin
Dewald van den Berg
Nicole S Berman
Andreas Bödecker
Martin Boucher
Elizabeth Buckley
Claire Burke
Francoise Bussac
Holger Busack
Jill Butler
Beate Butollo
Michel Charbonneau
Tracy YH Chen
Voon Hoe Chen
Jo Clarke
Maria Constantinou
Erin Craike
Sergio Cravero
Sophie Cren
Howard Crossland
Tony de Bell
Adrian Dadd
Jens Otto Damgaard
Richard Davis
Sallie Deysel
Gayani Dias
Anita Dietrich
Lawrence Dodyk
Mary Dolson

Peter Eberli
Michele Embling
Hugo van den Ende
Ian Farrar
Tina Farington
Peter Feige
Regina Fikkers
Peter Flick
Michael Gaull
Judith Gehrer
Imre Guba
Menno ten Hacken
Gary Van Haren
Maarten Hartman
Margaret Heneghan
Peter Hogarth
Sue Horlin
Claire Howells
Agnes Hussherr
Doug Isaac
Claes Janzon
Udo Kalk-Griesan
Jayne Kerr
Yvonne Kam
Akhil Kapadiya
Hannah King
Hitoshi Kiuchi
Marie Kling
Sabine Koch
Eniko Konczol
Matthias Kroner
Sheetal Kumar
Margot Le Bars
Sumi Lee
Luis de Leon Ortiz
Eliza Li
Liina Link
Claude Lopater
Marian Lovelace
Moi Lre Kok
Tomas Konieczny
Gesa Mannigel
Joanna Malvern

David Maroun
Robert Marsh
Gabriela Martinez
David Mason
Avni Mashru
Jan McCahey
Helen McCann
John McDonnell
Holger Meurer
Michelle Millar
Janet Milligan
Marc Minet
Stuart Montgomery
Luis Montero
Steve Moseley
Armon Nakhai
Tasos Nolas
Renshia van Noordwyk
Michelle Orozco
Florence Ortega
Sebastian di Paola
Hari Patel
John Patterson
Moshe Peress
Peter Piga
Fabricio Pimenta
Djohan Pinnarwan
Olaf Pusch
Tom Quinn
Alfredo Ramirez
Niranjan Raman
Thomas Roberts
Craig Robichaud
Bernd Roese
Meina Rose
Galina Ryltsova
James Saloman
Darsen Samaroo
Cathy Samsel
Olivier Scherer
Peter Schlicksup
Iain Selfridge
Rich Sharko

Paul Shepherd
Leila Sijelmassi
Ada Siu
Cody Smith
Shelley So
Lihor Spazzoli
Magnus Sprenger
Dusty Stallings
Henrik Steffensen
Tue Stensgård Sørensen
Bjørn Einar Strandberg
Rika Suzuki,
Dennis Svensson
Jessica Taurae
Lyndsay Taylor
Laura Taylor
Richard Tattershall
Liza Thérache
Sandra Thompson
Steve Todd
Giovanni Andrea Toselli
Frank Traczewski
Folker Trepte
Sarah Troughton
Gail Tucker
Ago Vilu
Zubair Wadee
Simon Whitehead
Barbara Willis
Michelle Winarto
Helen Wise
Koon Min Wong
Katie Woods
Caroline Woodward
Simon Wray
Tak Yano
Elza Yuen
Milan Zeleny
Reto Zemp
Per-Ove Zetterlund
Karen Zhang

Foreword

By Hans Hoogervorst
Chairman
International Accounting Standards Board

Much of the work of practising accountants and standard-setters today is concerned with the global harmonisation of financial reporting. More than a hundred countries now require or permit the use of IFRSs, including the majority of G20 members.

In addition to the widespread use of the standards, the ongoing financial crisis has stress-tested modern financial reporting like never before. The associated economic difficulties have, in the last few years, put increased spotlight on accounting standards, especially those dealing with financial instruments. Policymakers have followed developments in financial reporting with keen interest. Difficult though these issues have been, they have at the same time underlined the immense need for and importance of truly global financial reporting standards. Developing and improving these standards is one of our main priorities.

Given the importance of global harmonisation, it is important that the interpretation and application of IFRS is consistent from country to country. IFRSs are principle-based standards that require judgement calls to be made by accounting professionals. Judgement is, of course, most likely to be sound when it is based on experience. In today's rapidly changing environment, I commend this IFRS Manual of Accounting, which gives preparers and practitioners the benefits of the extensive experience and professional judgement of PricewaterhouseCoopers.

October 2012

Preface

The Manual of Accounting – IFRS for the UK is a practical guide to International Financial Reporting Standards. This Manual covers diverse areas of accounting from the recognition and measurement of financial instruments to accounting for deferred taxation, business combinations and share-based payments. It explains in detail the rules that apply to preparing consolidated financial statements and considers the other statements that appear in annual reports such as cash flow statements. The views expressed in this Manual are based on the experience of the PricewaterhouseCoopers' UK Accounting Consulting Services team. The views expressed are a guide to applying IFRS rather than a set of definitive interpretations. The application of IFRS to a specific company is a matter of judgement given its particular facts and circumstances. Moreover, the application of IFRS might be influenced by the views of regulators.

Even in a work of this size it is not possible to cover every aspect of company reporting. For example, this Manual does not deal with the issues faced by specific industries, such as banks and insurance companies, although much of the advice given in the text will assist them. The reporting requirements that apply to interim financial statements are covered in our book Manual of Accounting – Interim and preliminary reporting for the UK.

We hope that finance directors, accountants, legal practitioners, company administrators, financial advisors and auditors will find this Manual useful.

Barry Johnson, Peter Holgate
PricewaterhouseCoopers LLP
London
October 2012

Contents

Contents

Volume two

International standards and interpretations

International standards

Interpretations

IFRIC 1	Changes in existing decommissioning, restoration and similar liabilities
IFRIC 2	Members' shares in co-operative entities and similar Instruments
IFRIC 3	Emission rights
IFRIC 4	Determining whether an arrangement contains a lease
IFRIC 5	Rights to interests arising from decommissioning, restoration and environmental rehabilitation funds
IFRIC 6	Liabilities arising from participating in a specific market – Waste electrical and electronic equipment
IFRIC 7	Applying the restatement approach under IAS 29 Financial reporting in hyper-inflationary economies
IFRIC 8	Scope of IFRS 2
IFRIC 9	Re-assessment of embedded derivatives
IFRIC 10	Interim financial reporting and impairment
IFRIC 11	IFRS 2 – Group and treasury share transactions
IFRIC 12	Service concession arrangements
IFRIC 13	Customer loyalty programmes
IFRIC 14	IAS 19 – The limit on a defined benefit asset, minimum funding requirements and their interaction
IFRIC 15	Agreements for the construction of real estate
IFRIC 16	Hedges of a net investment in a foreign operation
IFRIC 17	Distributions of non-cash assets to owners
IFRIC 18	Transfers of assets from customers
IFRIC 19	Extinguishing financial liabilities with equity instruments
IFRIC 20	Stripping costs in the production phase of a surface mine
SIC 7	Introduction of the euro
SIC 10	Government Assistance – No specific relation to operating activities
SIC 12	Consolidation – Special purpose entities
SIC 13	Jointly controlled entities – Non-Monetary contributions by venturers
SIC 15	Operating leases – Incentives
SIC 21	Income taxes – Recovery of revalued non-depreciable assets
SIC 25	Income taxes – Changes in the tax status of an entity or its shareholders
SIC 27	Evaluating the substance of transactions in the legal form of a lease
SIC 29	Service Concession Arrangements: Disclosures
SIC 31	Revenue – Barter transactions involving advertising services
SIC 32	Intangible assets – Web site costs

Abbreviations and terms used

AAPA	Association of Authorised Public Accountants
ABI	Association of British Insurers
AC	Appeal Cases, law reports
ACG	Audit Committees guidance
Accounts	financial statements
ADR	American depositary receipts
AESOP	all employee share ownership plan
the 1985 Act	the Companies Act 1985 (as amended by the Companies Act 1989)
the 1989 Act	the Companies Act 1989
the 2006 Act	the Companies Act 2006
ACCA	Association of Chartered Certified Accountants
ACT	advance corporation tax
AFS	available-for-sale
AG	Application Guidance
AGM	Annual General Meeting
AIC	Association of Investment Companies
AIM	Alternative Investment Market
AIMR	Alternative Investment Market Rules
AITC	Association of Investment Trust Companies
All ER	All England Law Reports
AMPS	auction market preferred shares
APB	Auditing Practices Board
APC	Auditing Practices Committee
App	Application note of a Financial Reporting Standard
App	Appendix
ARC	Accounting Regulatory Committee
ARSs	auction rate securities
ASB	Accounting Standards Board
ASC	Accounting Standards Committee
AVC	additional voluntary contribution
BBA	British Bankers' Association
BC	Basis for Conclusions (to an accounting standard)
BCLC	Butterworths Company Law Cases
BERR	Department for Business, Enterprise and Regulatory Reform (formerly the DTI and now BIS)
BEV	business enterprise value
BIS	Department for Business, Innovation and Skills (formerly BERR before that DTI)
BNA 1985	Business Names Act 1985
BOFI	banks and other financial industry entities
BVCA	British Venture Capital Association

Abbreviations and terms used

C	currency unit
CA85	the Companies Act 1985
CA06	the Companies Act 2006
CCA	current cost accounting
CCAB	Consultative Committee of Accountancy Bodies Limited
CC	The Combined Code – Principles of good governance and code of best practice
CC(CP)	Companies Consolidation (Consequential Provisions) Act 1985
CEO	chief executive officer
CESR	Committee of European Securities Regulators
CGAA	Co-ordinating Group on Audit and Accounting Issues
CGU	cash-generating unit
Ch	Chancery Division, law reports
Chp	Chapter
chapter (1)	'PricewaterhouseCoopers' Manual of accounting' – chapter (1)
CIF	cost, insurance, freight
CIMA	Chartered Institute of Management Accountants
CIPFA	Chartered Institute of Public Finance and Accountancy
CISCO	The City Group for Smaller Companies
Cmnd	Command Paper
CBO	collateralised bond obligation
CDO	collateralised debt obligation
CLO	collateralised loan obligation
CMO	collateralised mortgage obligation
CODM	chief operating decision maker
COSO	Committee of Sponsoring Organisations of the Treadway Commission
CPP	current purchasing power
CR	Report of the committee on The Financial Aspects of Corporate Governance (the 'Cadbury Report')
CSR	corporate social responsibility
CTD	cumulative translation difference
CUV	continuing use value
DCF	discounted cash flow
DG XV	Directorate General XV
the 7th Directive	EC 7th Directive on Company Law
DP	discussion paper
DRC	depreciated replacement cost
DTI	Department of Trade and Industry
DTR	Disclosure rules and transparency rules
EASDAQ	European Association of Securities Dealers Automated Quotation
EBIT	earnings before interest and tax
EBITDA	earnings before interest, tax, depreciation and amortisation
EC	European Community
ECU	European currency unit
ED	exposure draft
EEA	European Economic Area
EEE	electrical and electronic equipment

EFRAG	European Financial Reporting Advisory Group
EGM	extraordinary general meeting
EITF	Emerging Issues Task Force (US)
EPS	earnings per share
ESOP	employee share ownership plan
ESOT	employee share ownership trust
EU	European Union
EU 2005 Regulation	Regulation (EC) No 1606/2002 on the application of International Accounting Standards
EUV	existing use value
FASB	Financial Accounting Standards Board (US)
FEE	The European Federation of Accountants
FIFO	first-in, first-out
financial statements	Accounts
FLA	Finance and Leasing Association
FM	facilities management
FOB	free on board
FPI	foreign private investors (US-listed)
FRAG	Financial Reporting and Auditing Group of the ICAEW
Framework	Framework for the preparation and presentation of financial statements
FRED	Financial Reporting Exposure Draft
FRA	forward rate agreement
FRC	Financial Reporting Council
FRN	floating rate note
FRRP	Financial Reporting Review Panel
FRS	Financial Reporting Standard
FRSSE	Financial Reporting Standard for Smaller Entities
FSA	Financial Services Authority
FTSE	The Financial Times Stock Exchange
FVLCS	fair value less costs to sell
FVTPL	at fair value through profit or loss
GAAP	generally accepted accounting principles (and practices)
GAAS	generally accepted auditing standards
GB	Great Britain
GCFR	Going Concern and Financial Reporting – published by the joint working group of the Hundred Group of finance directors, ICAEW and ICAS
GRI guidelines	Global Reporting Initiative guidelines
HEFCE	Higher Education Funding Council for England
HMSO	Her Majesty's Stationery Office
HP	hire purchase
HMRC	HM Revenue & Customs
HR	human resources
IAASB	International Auditing and Assurance Standards Board
IAS	International Accounting Standard (see also IFRS)
IASB	International Accounting Standards Board
IASC	International Accounting Standards Committee

Abbreviations and terms used

IBF	Irish Bankers' Federation
IBNR	incurred but not reported
ICAEW	Institute of Chartered Accountants in England and Wales
ICAI	Institute of Chartered Accountants in Ireland
ICAS	Institute of Chartered Accountants of Scotland
ICFR	Internal Control and Financial Reporting – published by the joint working group of the Hundred Group of finance directors, ICAEW and ICAS
ICR	Industrial Cases Reports
ICSA	Institute of Chartered Secretaries and Administrators
ICTA	Income and Corporation Taxes Act 1988
IFAC	International Federation of Accountants
IFRIC	International Financial Reporting Interpretations Committee
IFRS	International Financial Reporting Standard (see also IAS)
IG	Implementation Guidance (to an accounting standard)
IGU	income-generating unit
IIMR	Institute of Investment Management and Research (see SIP)
IIR	internal rate of return
IIRC	International Integrated Reporting Committee
IoD	Institute of Directors
IOSCO	International Organisation of Securities Commissions
IPO	initial public offering
IPR&D	in-process research and development
IR	Statement on interim reporting issued by ASB
ISA	International Standard on Auditing
ISA (UK & Ire)	International Standard on Auditing (UK and Ireland)
ISDA	International Swap Dealers Association
ISP	internet service provider
IVSC	International Valuation Standards Committee
JWG	Joint Working Group
LIBID	London inter-bank bid rate
LIBOR	London inter-bank offered rate
LIFFE	the London International Financial Futures and Options Exchange
LIFO	last-in, first-out
LR	UK Listing Authority's Listing Rules
LTIP	long-term incentive plan
MAC	material adverse change clause
MBO	management buy-out
MD&A	management's discussion and analysis
MEEM	multi-period excess earnings method
MR	Master of the Rolls
NASDAQ	National Association of Securities Dealers Automated Quotations
NAPF	National Association of Pension Funds
NCI	non-controlling interest
NCU	national currency unit
NIC	national insurance contributions

OECD	Organisation for Economic Co-operation and Development
OEICs	open-ended investment companies
OFT	Office of Fair Trading
OFR	operating and financial review
OIAC	Oil Industry Accounting Committee
OTC	over-the-counter market
PA	preliminary announcement
para(s)	paragraph(s) of Schedules to the Companies Acts, or IFRSs or IASs or FRSs, or SSAPs, or FREDs, or EDs, or DPs, or text
PCAOB	Public Company Accounting Oversight Board (US)
PE	price-earnings
PHEI	previously held equity interest
PFI	Private Finance Initiative
PLUSR	Plus Rules for Issuers (for PLUS-quoted entities)
PPE	property, plant and equipment
PPERA	Political Parties, Elections and Referendums Act 2000
PPF	Pension Protection Fund
PRAG	Pensions Research Accountants Group
PS	Practice Statements
QC	Queen's Counsel
QCA	Quoted Companies Alliance
QUEST	qualifying employee share ownership trust
R&D	research and development
RCN	replacement cost new
RCNLD	replacement cost new less depreciation
RDG	regional development grant
Reg	regulation of a statutory instrument (for example, SI 1995/2092 Reg 5 = regulation 5 of The Companies (Summary Financial Statements) Regulations 1995)
RFR	relief-from-royalty
RICS	Royal Institution of Chartered Surveyors
ROI	return on investment
RS	Reporting Standard
SAC	the Standards Advisory Council
SAC	subjective acceleration clause
SAS	Statement of Auditing Standards
SC	Session Cases
Sch	Schedule to the Companies Act 1985 (eg CA85 4A Sch 85 = Schedule 4A, paragraph 85)
SDC	Standards Development Committee
SEC	Securities and Exchange Commission (US)
Sec(s)	Section(s) of the 1985 Act/Sections(s) of the 2006 Act
SEE	social, environmental and ethical
SERPS	State earnings related pension scheme
SFAC	Statement of Financial Accounting Concepts issued in the US
SFAS	Statement of Financial Accounting Standards issued in the US
SI	Statutory Instrument
SIC	Standing Interpretation Committee of the IASC (see IFRIC)

Abbreviations and terms used

SIP	Society of Investment Professionals (formerly IIMR)
SIPs	share incentive plans
SMEs	small and medium-sized entities
SOI	Statement of Intent
SoP	Statement of principles
SORIE	statement of recognised income and expense
SORP	Statement of Recommended Practice
SPE	special purpose entity
SPV	special purpose vehicle
SSAP	Statement of Standard Accounting Practice
Stock Exchange (or LSE)	the London Stock Exchange
STRGL	statement of total recognised gains and losses
TR	Technical Release of the ICAEW
TSR	total shareholder return
TUPE	Transfer of Undertakings (Protection of Employment) Regulations
UITF	Urgent Issues Task Force
UK	United Kingdom
UKCGC	UK Corporate Governance Code
US	United States of America
VAT	value added tax
VIU	value in use
VIE	variable interest entity
WACC	weighted average cost of capital
WARA	weighted average return analysis
WEEE	Waste electrical and electronic equipment
WLR	Weekly Law Reports
xBRL	extensible business reporting language

Chapter 1

Introduction, accounting principles and applicability of IFRS

Introduction, accounting principles and applicability of IFRS

Introduction

Financial reporting today

1.1 Recent years have seen major changes in financial reporting worldwide. While various trends can be identified (such as the emergence of narrative reporting including 'management commentary'), the single most important change is convergence around international financial reporting standards (IFRS). That is, gradually, 'national GAAP' is becoming rarer and in most countries it is being supplemented or replaced by the use of IFRS. The extent and manner of this varies from country to country. In some parts of the world IFRS has become or has replaced national GAAP, though often this involves making local adaptation so the result is not pure IFRS. In the EU, national GAAP remains, but EU-endorsed IFRS has been mandated for the consolidated financial statements of listed companies and is permitted in some countries for other contexts. Various countries are now looking at the new 'IFRS for SMEs' and wondering whether to implement that as a simplified alternative to full IFRS, in some cases as a replacement of national GAAP. The USA has for some years been engaged in a significant programme of work with the IASB to converge IFRS and US GAAP and this programme has been a major influence on the way in which IFRS has developed over the last decade or more.

1.2 Three major factors underlie these changes. First and most fundamentally, the case for harmonisation of financial reporting is compelling. Global businesses and international investors need to have accounting information that they can understand and compare when running businesses and making investment decisions. Despite the different histories and cultural backgrounds that have led to many national GAAPs, there is an overwhelming need for accounting principles to be harmonised worldwide.

1.3 Secondly, a suitable institutional framework has been in place. The International Accounting Standards Board (IASB) has been an effective and influential standard-setter in the global arena. This is despite the fact that the IASB has no formal power of its own. Any adoption or compliance with IFRS by jurisdictions, regulators or companies is of their own volition.

1.4 Thirdly, various territories and regions have adopted or mandated the use of IFRS. A major boost in this regard was the June 2002 European Commission Regulation that required all EU listed companies from 2005 to prepare their consolidated financial statements using IFRS, rather than national GAAP. IFRS or a local variant have been adopted in countries as diverse as Australia, Hong Kong, China, Central and Eastern Europe, including Russia, parts of the Middle East, Africa, the Caribbean and Canada. The current wave of transitioning territories includes South Korea and much of South America. In other countries such as Switzerland, Japan and India, IFRS is currently permitted and is used to varying degrees. The details vary, but the trend is clear and strong.

Global harmonisation — IFRS and US GAAP

1.5 Global harmonisation, then, is what the IASB is all about. But true global harmonisation would include not only the impressive array of countries just mentioned but also the USA. The IASB cannot claim to be *the* global standard setter as long as the FASB sets rules for the US markets.

1.6 Things started to change, first, with the IASB/FASB 'Norwalk Agreement' of 2002; and then with the announcement in July 2007 by the US SEC of two important initiatives relating to US GAAP and IFRS. The first was that, at the end of 2007, the SEC dropped the 'US GAAP reconciliation' – that is, the reconciliation required to be given by foreign private issuers (FPIs) from home country GAAP to US GAAP – as long at the FPI is using IFRS. These reconciliations w ere a cost and burden to FPIs and yet the general view was that hardly any use is made of them by investors or others. We should note, however, that the SEC said that the home country GAAP – the principal financial reporting convention – should be IFRS as issued by the IASB, not a variant of IFRS.

1.7 This alone was a big step, but the second part of the July 2007 announcement was, or seemed at the time, potentially more far-reaching. The second development was that the SEC proposed that IFRS might be permissible in the US markets as an alternative to US GAAP. The timescale, even at the time, was extended. They indicated that the decision might be confirmed in 2011, with implementation perhaps as soon as 2014, though potentially later, and subject to various conditions. For some while, a formal announcement from the SEC was expected. An SEC staff announcement in May 2011 apparently gave some clues. The staff outlined a possible approach, which was termed 'condorsement', evidently a mixture of convergence and endorsement. The SEC and FASB would remain in place with authority to set standards for the US markets, but US GAAP and IFRS would gradually converge such that, in time, the two would be similar or the same.

1.8 Following some delay, the SEC staff issued a paper in July 2012. Those who expected it to contain a recommendation or policy decision about the application of IFRS in the US markets were disappointed. The staff did indicate that IFRS is generally perceived to be of high quality but noted that there are areas where gaps remain. They also identified concerns about inconsistencies in the application of IFRS globally. The report states that adopting IFRS as authoritative guidance in the US is not supported by the vast majority of participants in the US capital markets. The chairman of the IFRS Foundation trustees expressed regret that the SEC report does not contain a recommended action plan on next steps.

1.9 Many questions arise from this:

- Will the USA ever adopt IFRS? Will they stick with US GAAP 'for ever', or will they adopt IFRS in say five or ten years' time? Will the two GAAPs gradually converge over an extended period?

- Will the IASB, with reduced focus on convergence with the US, be free to take a different route than it has followed in the last few years?

- What will be the nature and extent of the US's role in international standard-setting in future?

- What are the implications for countries that have yet to decide on following IFRS – principally Japan and India?

1.10 The US announcement certainly has implications for the IASB. The period from 2007 until 2012 was one of significant co-operation between the IASB and the FASB. They had frequent joint board meetings, and they adopted the same standards in some areas (for example, operating segments and business combinations) and worked jointly towards convergence on other subjects. Nevertheless, the boards did not always agree, as the variety of proposals on financial instruments show. The two boards were working towards agreed joint standards on revenue recognition, leasing and insurance, as well as on financial instruments. The objective had been to finish these converged standards by June 2011 – when Sir David Tweedie handed over to the new IASB chairman, Hans Hoogervorst. However, the complexities and disagreements were such that none of the four were finished and indeed the new IASB board decided to re-expose revenue and leasing. Hence the timescale for these projects has become drawn out. Indeed the new regime at the IASB seems to be characterised by less emphasis on convergence with the US, a less frenetic level of activity than obtained in early 2011 and by a more consultative approach, an early example of which is the IASB's July 2011 formal public consultation on its work programme.

1.11 It is instructive to look back at the recent period of close co-operation between the IASB and the FASB. In one sense, the goal of convergence of the two, and bringing the USA into the IFRS family seemed to have obvious merit – to be welcomed as the final stages of the global harmonisation of accounting. In practice, it is not so straightforward. Certainly, the Norwalk Agreement was strategically a highly important step to harmonise accounting around the world. For a year or two after the Agreement was made in 2002, it seemed so obviously right that to challenge its basis would have been heretical. Gradually since then, the view has started to change. As the world has seen more of the effects of harmonisation, it has begun to ask whether incorporating aspects of US GAAP into IFRS is actually the good idea that it seemed. This is not to say that harmonisation has been a one-way track. Indeed there are many examples where the FASB is changing its standards to adopt IFRS solutions. But despite that, there is a perception that IFRS is suffering from two things: first, the importing of specific US rules and secondly the adoption of US-style detailed prescription. The US has been setting detailed accounting rules for over 70 years and recent decades have witnessed more and more detailed rules being written in response to the combination of a complex business environment and a litigious society. US GAAP may not be perfect, but it does suit the US environment – where it is written essentially for listed (that is, SEC-registered) companies. Hence, a problem with IFRS/US GAAP harmonisation is that US GAAP is in danger of being exported, *via* IFRS, to many countries that have a different business environment from the USA's, have smaller economies and a smaller accounting infrastructure. In many of those countries IFRS is often being applied across the whole economy, not just to the listed sector. So, there is a potential problem of unsuitability of standards for the contexts in which they are being applied. It was important, therefore, for the IASB to remember that convergence with US GAAP, although an important objective, should not be carried out in such as way as to make its standards unsuitable for its widespread and varied constituency. With the SEC's announcement of July 2012, the IASB is now freer to make its own decisions.

1.12 In this context, the IASB's recent work on developing a form of IFRS for small and medium-sized entities (SMEs) is particularly important. The IFRS for SMEs was published in July 2009 and is intended, despite its somewhat inaccurate name, for those entities that are not publicly accountable. It is up to each country to decide whether to use IFRS for SMEs, and when; and to decide to whom it would apply or be available. In comparison with full IFRS, the IFRS for SMEs has somewhat simplified recognition and measurement rules and reduced disclosures. A number of territories have adopted full IFRS for the whole economy and are finding it overly complex for the non-publicly-accountable sector. Hence they have welcomed the IFRS for SMEs. Quite how many countries will adopt it is still emerging. But in principle it allows the IASB to offer to a vast number of companies world-wide a set of standards in a form that is suitable to their scale and sophistication. That is, some countries may not want to adopt, in place of national GAAP, the full rigours of IFRS, but may consider that IFRS for SMEs is suitable for the unlisted sector to which national GAAP often applies. So, while the world's listed and public interest companies will stay with, or adopt, full IFRS, there is likely to be a much bigger adoption, measured by number of companies, of IFRS for SMEs.

The EU and politics

1.13 The EU Regulation of 2002 required listed groups to prepare their consolidated financial statements using IFRS for periods commencing on or after 1 January 2005. The Regulation introduced a permissive regime for other entities. As noted above, this regulation was a major step for Europe and for the IASB – as well as being an encouragement for other territories to adopt IFRS. EU adoption of IFRS is good news for harmonisation, but with an important proviso. The EU needs to bring IFRSs into EU law and it cannot do so without a formal process of adoption. To achieve this, it has developed a complex 'endorsement mechanism'. This comprises the Commission; an official Accounting Regulatory Committee (ARC); and a private sector body – the European Financial Reporting Advisory Group (EFRAG) – which ensures that the IASB has a full understanding of the European viewpoint and advises the Commission and the ARC.

1.14 The endorsement mechanism is proving to be, at best, a mixed blessing. Most of the IASB's standards have been endorsed, though IAS 39 was not endorsed in full. After a lengthy process that owed more to politics than to accounting, a so-called 'carve-out' version of IAS 39 was approved. That is, the November 2004 EU-endorsed version of IAS 39 excluded a few paragraphs to which some EU banks objected. These paragraphs are a small part of only one standard, but politically they are highly significant, as they show that the IASB cannot take EU-endorsement for granted. Politically, the process is highly significant as it introduces the prospect that, with one or more future standards, there may emerge a more fundamental difference between EU IFRS and IFRS as promulgated by the IASB.

1.15 The second effect of the EU endorsement process is that it introduces delay and uncertainty. It has tended to take about a year, after a standard has been finalised by the IASB, for it to be endorsed by the EU. However, in the case of IFRS 9, issued in 2009, the endorsement process has still not started. This makes it difficult for companies to know whether a particular new or amended standard, or interpretation from the IFRS Interpretations Committee, will be endorsed and available to be applied at an imminent year end.

1.16 In a broader context, politics and accounting – for long only occasional bedfellows – have been interacting more since 2009. Specifically, the G20 heads of state and finance ministers have taken an interest in accounting, as part of their work on trying to stabilise the global financial system. They have put pressure on the IASB and the FASB to accelerate their work on improving and simplifying IAS 32 and IAS 39. A result of this is that the two boards are working hard on the reform of financial instrument accounting – but doing so in bits. Papers appear on fair value measurement; then on classification and measurement; then on impairment; then on hedge accounting; and so on. This is far from ideal, as the pieces of the jigsaw interact in complex ways. Certainly the process of improving these standards is taking longer than the G20 had in mind.

Preparers and users of financial statements

1.17 Looking back on first-time adoption in the EU and elsewhere, we can see that experience with the new IFRS information has been mixed. Some analysts were, inevitably, better prepared than others. Some company finance teams had prepared better than others. Some companies were affected more fundamentally than others. Companies are required by the first-time adoption rules in IFRS 1 to publish reconciliations of profit and net assets as between national GAAP and IFRS. For many companies, the aspects of converting to IFRS that had the biggest numerical impact on profit measurement were goodwill (no longer having an amortisation charge) and share-based payment (starting to have an IFRS 2 charge against profits). A lot of companies were affected by IASs 32 and 39 on financial instruments, especially in the banking and insurance sectors. Other subjects were more of a surprise. For example, there were more implementation problems and profit and balance sheet effects arising out of lease accounting and foreign currency rules than had been expected. All this is starting to read like history for countries that adopted IFRS in 2005. But countries in the current wave of transitioning territories are now encountering the same issues. They are, at least, better off in that they can learn from the experience of other countries and companies.

1.18 But an important distinction can be seen overall between the attitudes of preparers and users. The general experience with IFRS adoption has been that finance directors and other preparers were relatively negative towards IFRS in the sense that they saw considerable cost and work in performing the conversion; and they saw a result that was different rather than better. Users – fund managers, analysts and others – were more positive. They did not directly incur the costs and the work of conversion, though they did have to become familiar with a new GAAP. But they see the fruits of harmonisation much more than preparers do, as they are the beneficiaries of comparable information for the economy, or for the sector that they follow. A recent trend is that user groups are becoming much more involved in the standard-setting process. A leading example of this is the Corporate Reporting User Forum (CRUF).

1.19 This is not to say, however, that standard setters and companies are giving users exactly what they want. Accounting information is intended to be useful to users of financial statements in making economic decisions. But the recent and imminent reforms will bring new challenges as well as new information. Something of a polarity is already noticeable. Three examples illustrate this. First, standard-setters are promoting a broader notion of performance ('comprehensive income'), incorporating both transaction-based profits and a wider range of value changes than before. Both of those elements of performance will display volatility. At the same time, companies want to give analysts, and analysts seemingly want to receive, information that is (a) close to cash flows and (b) stable and useful as a predictor of future results. Hence the popularity of EBITDA and 'adjusted earnings' and 'adjusted EPS' of different types. Numbers like this are perfectly valid, but need to be placed in context: it is important that they are not given more prominence than the GAAP numbers.

1.20 A second example where standard-setters and users are not aligned is in the vexed area of fair value accounting. Some of the thinking and proposals by the IASB and FASB suggest that the standard-setters are pursuing a medium and longer-term agenda of more fair value information. Yet this is not necessarily what many users want. Certainly, users are interested in fair value information for many assets and liabilities, but this does not, from their point of view, need to be on the balance sheet: some can be given adequately in the footnotes. At an extreme, if all assets and liabilities, including inherent goodwill, were to be fair valued, the result might, in principle, be the value of the entity. But most users would baulk at this, saying that it is their job to value the entity and its shares, not the role of accounting information to do so. Of course, this extreme is highly unlikely to be reached in reality, due to limits on what assets and liabilities can be recognised and on what can be measured satisfactorily.

1.21   The third example is the extent of disclosure. The increasing level of disclosure required by IFRS, together with other factors, has led to annual reports becoming longer and longer. This is a concern to those who have to prepare financial statements. Conversely, analysts seem to want more and more information and new accounting standards push practice in the same direction. But the growing list of disclosures is a concern to the IASB and to many of its constituents. The IASB commissioned a study in 2011 that was carried out jointly by the Scottish and New Zealand Institutes of Chartered Accountants. The report – 'Losing the excess baggage – reducing disclosures in financial statements to what's important' – was published in August 2011. Their conclusion was that as much as 30% of the content of financial statements could be deleted without serious consequences. The IASB has indicated, following its 2011 agenda consultation, that it intends to add to its agenda a project to establish a disclosure framework, and various national and regional standard-setters or regulators are actively interested in the issue. Whether, following this activity, disclosures will be cut or whether the apparently inexorable trend will continue remains to be seen.

Accounting principles and applicability of IFRS

1.22   Here we introduce the concepts underlying accounting practices that are discussed in greater detail throughout this book as they relate to particular accounting issues and problems. These concepts are set out under IFRS in the IASB's 'Conceptual framework for financial reporting' issued in September 2010 (the Framework). It supersedes the 'Framework for the preparation and presentation of financial statements' (the Framework (1989)).

GAAP in the UK

The composition of GAAP in the UK

UK.1.22.1   The components of GAAP in the UK vary according to the type of company or entity. However, generally there are components that are mandatory (in law or in practice) and components that are not mandatory. The core mandatory components are set out in the following paragraphs.

UK.1.22.2   For those companies applying IFRS, GAAP in the UK is:

- The Companies Act 2006, insofar as it applies to entities adopting IFRS (see from para UK. 1.22.38).

- Accounting standards that have been adopted by the EU (see from para 1.36). These standards are some or all of the following:

  - International Accounting Standards (IASs).

- International Financial Reporting Standards (IFRSs).
- Interpretations that have been adopted by the EU. That is:
  - Interpretations developed originally by the Standing Interpretations Committee (SIC).
  - Interpretations issued by the International Financial Reporting Standards Interpretations Committee (IFRS IC).
- For listed companies, the Listing Rules and the Disclosure and Transparency Rules.

UK.1.22.3 The IASB has also published IFRS for Small and Medium-sized Entities (SMEs). This is a standalone suite of standards tailored for non publicly accountable entities as opposed to a standard within the sphere of the main IFRS framework. IFRS for SMEs is not currently available for UK companies preparing financial statements under IFRS. See further from paragraph 1.29.

UK.1.22.4 Other components of GAAP in the UK for those applying IFRS will be authoritative to varying degrees but non-mandatory. These include:

- The IASB's Framework. The Framework does not have the status of an accounting standard. Nevertheless, it is authoritative in two senses. First, it provides a frame of reference to guide the IASB in its development of standards. It should help guide companies and auditors as to the meaning and intention of individual standards if they are unclear. Secondly, the Framework provides a reference for the accounting treatment of transactions for which there is no specific GAAP.

- Statements issued by the ASB that are relevant for UK companies reporting under IFRS.

- Statements and recommendations from the professional bodies, such as ICAEW Technical Releases and accounting recommendations. Professional bodies' accounting-related statements are unlikely to address the interpretation of IFRS, but they will still be relevant in the context of company law issues.

- Established practice. Practices that are generally accepted, even though not codified in official literature, can be regarded as part of GAAP in the UK. An example of this is the guidance in this Manual of Accounting.

UK.1.22.5 UK Financial Reporting Standards (FRSs) and Statements of Standard Accounting Practice (SSAPs) do not apply to entities using IFRS. However, IAS 8 contains guidance on the selection of accounting policies. In the hierarchy of selection, management should first consider IFRSs and interpretations of IFRSs. If there is no standard or interpretation in the relevant area, management should develop a policy that addresses the decision-making needs of users and that is reliable. [IAS 8 para 10].

UK.1.22.6 In doing so, the entity should consider (in this order):

■ Requirements and guidance in other international standards and interpretations dealing with similar issues.

■ The content of the IASB's Framework (see from para 1.48).

[IAS 8 para 11].

UK.1.22.7 After referring to the items in paragraph UK.1.22.6, management may consider the pronouncements of other standard-setting bodies that use a similar conceptual framework to the IASB's, other accounting literature (such as this Manual of Accounting) and industry practices, as long as they do not conflict with the sources of guidance outlined in paragraph UK.1.22.6. [IAS 8 para 12].

UK.1.22.8 Some FRSs and SSAPs may address topics not covered by IFRSs and serve as a reference where IFRSs are silent.

UK.1.22.9 Certain industry groups in the UK develop Statements of Recommended Practice ('SORPs'). These give guidance on the application of accounting standards to specialised industries and non-profit-making sectors. SORPs cannot override the requirements of IFRS. However, the SORP may fit into the hierarchy for selecting accounting policies (see para UK.1.22.5) as additional guidance in areas that are not covered by IFRS, as long as that guidance does not contradict IFRS, interpretations of IFRSs or the Framework.

UK.1.22.10 The sectors for which SORPs are in issue are:

■ Authorised funds.

■ Charities.

■ Further and higher education institutions.

■ Insurance.

■ Investment trusts.

■ Local authorities.

■ Oil and gas.

■ Pension schemes.

■ Registered social landlords.

■ Unit trusts.

■ Leasing.

■ Open-ended investment companies (OEICs).

■ Limited liability partnerships.

UK.1.22.11 The output of the Financial Reporting Review Panel (FRRP), the enforcer of financial reporting in the UK, constitutes part of GAAP in the UK. The FRRP does not issue rules but announces its findings in relation to individual companies or groups and makes statements of more general application (see from para UK.1.22.65). These companies generally change their accounting practices or give additional disclosure, following discussion with the FRRP. The FRRP usually issues formal statements only where companies have deviated from existing requirements of UK company law or accounting standards. However, in some cases, the FRRP's views have added to, or modified, the previous understanding of UK GAAP and IFRS. Companies and auditors should take heed of the FRRP announcements.

Applicability of IFRS in the UK

EU Regulation on IFRS

UK.1.22.12 All listed companies in the EU (including banks and insurance companies) have been required to prepare consolidated financial statements under EU-adopted IFRS since financial years beginning on or after 1 January 2005 under the 'EU 2005 Regulation'. The Regulation permits Member States to extend the requirement to use IFRS to unlisted groups and to individual company financial statements (see from para UK.1.22.19 onwards) and the UK permits this.

UK.1.22.13 Listed companies in this context means any companies that, at the balance sheet date, have securities admitted to trading on a regulated market of any member state. Securities in this context include debt as well as shares.

UK.1.22.14 Regulated markets in the UK are the following:

- London Stock Exchange – Regulated Market
- The London Metal Exchange
- ICE Futures Europe
- SWX Europe Limited
- The London International Financial Futures and Options Exchange (LIFFE)
- EDX
- PLUS-listed Market

UK.1.22.15 AIM is not included in the above list, because it ceased to be a 'regulated market' in 2004. AIM companies are not subject to the EU 2005 Regulation that requires them to prepare financial statements under IFRS. However, the AIM rules require companies that have subsidiaries and are incorporated in any EEA member state, the Isle of Man or the Channel Islands to apply EU-adopted IFRS.

UK.1.22.16 The 2005 Regulation applies to the *consolidated* financial statements of entities with securities admitted to trading on a regulated market. Entities should first examine whether they are required to prepare consolidated financial statements under the 7th Directive, set out in UK law in sections 399 to 403 of the Companies Act 2006 and described in chapter 24. Entities that are not required to prepare such financial statements under EU law are outside the Regulation's scope. This is the case whether or not IFRS would require consolidated financial statements.

UK.1.22.17 The 7th Directive sets out certain exclusions from consolidation (transposed to UK law in sections 402 and 405 of the Companies Act 2006). However, these exclusions are not relevant to companies to whom the 2005 Regulation applies. Adopted IFRSs will set out the scope of the consolidated financial statements – that is, which entities should be included and how they should be accounted for. [EU clarification para 2.2.2(c)].

UK.1.22.18 The scope of the 2005 Regulation applies only to companies governed by a law of a Member State. This means that, for example, a US company that has a listing on the London Stock Exchange does not have to prepare consolidated financial statements under IFRS.

Extension of the EU Regulation

UK.1.22.19 The EU 2005 Regulation allows Member States to extend the requirement to use IFRS to unlisted groups and to individual company financial statements. All UK companies (except charitable companies) and building societies are permitted to use EU-adopted IFRS in their individual and/or consolidated financial statements. However, there are some restrictions and conditions:

- Once a company has prepared its financial statements under EU-adopted IFRS, it can revert to UK GAAP in a later financial year, if there is a *"relevant change in circumstance"*. A relevant change in circumstance occurs if the company becomes a subsidiary of an undertaking that is not preparing its individual financial statements under EU-adopted IFRS or if the company (or its parent) ceases to have its securities traded on a regulated market. [CA06 Sec 395(3)].

- The Companies and Limited Liability Partnerships (Accounts and Audit Exemptions and Change of Accounting Framework) Regulations 2012 (SI 2012 No. 2301) changed the law to allow a company to revert to UK GAAP in circumstances other than a *"relevant change in circumstance"*. The regulations provide that companies that prepare individual IFRS financial statements may switch to Companies Act financial statements for a reason other than a relevant change of circumstances provided they have not switched to Companies Act financial statements in the period of five years preceding the first day of the financial year in which they wish to implement the change of accounting framework. These regulations came into force on 1st October 2012 and apply to financial years ending on or after that date.

- A parent company may elect to prepare its individual financial statements under UK GAAP even if it uses EU-adopted IFRS in its consolidated financial statements.

- Where the parent company prepares group accounts, the directors of the parent company have a responsibility to ensure that all UK subsidiaries in the same group adopt the same accounting framework as each other, unless there are 'good reasons' not do so. The parent should ensure that all UK companies in the group use either EU-adopted IFRS or UK GAAP. However, where a parent adopts EU-adopted IFRS in both its consolidated financial statements and its individual financial statements, it will not be required to ensure that all its subsidiaries use EU-adopted IFRS too. [CA06 Sec 407(5)]. The Department for Business, Innovation and Skills (the BIS) issued guidance notes on these rules, including an explanation of when there might be 'good reasons' (see para UK.1.22.20).

- Building societies are subject to the same requirements as companies in that they have the option of adopting IFRS in their individual and consolidated financial statements.

- Charitable companies may not prepare financial statements under IFRS. IFRS does not specifically address charity sector transactions and the government believes that the direct application of IFRS without modification through a SORP might create 'interpretational issues'. In addition, there are no plans to permit unincorporated charities to use IFRS.

UK.1.22.20 The BIS has issued guidance to help companies apply these rules. These include an explanation of where there might be 'good reasons' for the directors not to prepare all the individual financial statements within a group by using the same accounting framework. The provision allows a degree of flexibility where there are genuine, including cost/benefit, grounds for not using the same framework. Such reasons include:

- An IFRS group acquires a subsidiary that does not use IFRS. In the year of acquisition, it might not be practicable for the newly-acquired subsidiary to move to IFRS straight away.

- A group might include subsidiaries that are themselves publicly traded. In this case, market pressures or regulatory requirements to use IFRS might come into play, without necessarily justifying a move to IFRS by the non-publicly traded subsidiaries.

- Where a subsidiary or a parent is planning to list and might wish to convert to IFRS in advance, but the rest of the group is not intending to list.

- The group might include small subsidiaries where the cost of moving to IFRS might outweigh the benefits.

If the parent's directors adopt a different framework for any entities within the group, they should be able to justify any inconsistency to shareholders, regulators or other interested parties.

UK.1.22.21 The BIS guidance does not mention tax as a 'good reason' for adopting a different framework for one or more UK subsidiaries within a group. In commercial terms tax is a business cost like any other. We have sought advice from legal counsel as to whether tax may be a good reason. The question is one of degree, depends on individual facts and circumstances, and the directors must weigh up various matters in reaching their conclusion.

UK.1.22.22 In the case of existing arrangements or structures, where a transition from UK GAAP to EU-adopted IFRS would result in a significant increase or potential volatility in taxable profits, or a significant acceleration of tax cash outflows, or introduce a significant new tax exposure, compared with the company continuing to use UK GAAP, the tax consequences may be a 'good reason' to keep one or more subsidiaries on UK GAAP. For example, a company's revenue recognition might be accelerated under IFRS, accelerating tax payments. 'Significant' in this context might be in absolute terms or relative to the company's size. A trivial tax effect should not be used as an excuse to keep a company on UK GAAP. Similarly, if, as a result of a company using EU-adopted IFRS, the group could no longer claim the benefits of existing tax planning (or the benefits would be significantly reduced or new tax risks would arise under EU-adopted IFRS such that the planning would not have been entered into with companies using EU-adopted IFRS) the tax effect of using EU-adopted IFRS may be a good reason for one or more subsidiaries to remain on UK GAAP. However, as noted above it is also necessary to weigh up other matters in reaching the conclusion on whether tax may be a good reason such as comparability with the rest of the group.

UK.1.22.23 In contrast, where the accounting frameworks of subsidiaries in a group are currently aligned, the burden of proof to justify departing from this situation is more onerous. The main purpose of having aligned accounting frameworks is to enable shareholders (amongst other interested parties) to understand the accounts and compare them with the accounts of other companies in the group. In considering whether there are good reasons to adopt different accounting frameworks, the directors must ask how obscure or difficult to understand different accounting frameworks would make the accounts in comparison to the rest of the group. Other factors include how certain it is that any tax planning arrangements put in place will lead to tax benefit, the size of any ensuing tax saving and reputational risk.

UK.1.22.24 Individual companies prepare either 'Companies Act individual financial statements' or 'IAS individual financial statements'. A group's consolidated financial statements are prepared as 'Companies Act consolidated financial statements' or 'IAS consolidated financial statements'. Schedules 1 and 6 of SI 2008/410, 'The Large and Medium-sized Companies and Groups (Accounts and Reports) Regulations 2008', apply to 'Companies Act individual financial statements' and 'Companies Act consolidated financial statements' respectively. Those schedules do not apply to 'IAS individual financial statements' or 'IAS consolidated financial statements'. However, the basic requirement to prepare financial statements, including the circumstances in which consolidated financial statement are required, as well as the requirements on audit, approval, distribution and filing, continue to apply to all companies (see from para UK.1.22.38).

UK.1.22.25 Although the government has allowed a free choice for companies over IFRS adoption, within the limits described, there are other parties (such as regulators) that may force adoption or limit it.

UK.1.22.26 The requirements and options to prepare financial statements under UK GAAP or IFRS are considered in the next section.

How to determine whether a UK group should comply with IFRS

UK.1.22.27 The diagram below explains which groups will have to apply IFRS in their consolidated financial statements and which groups can apply IFRS on a voluntary basis.

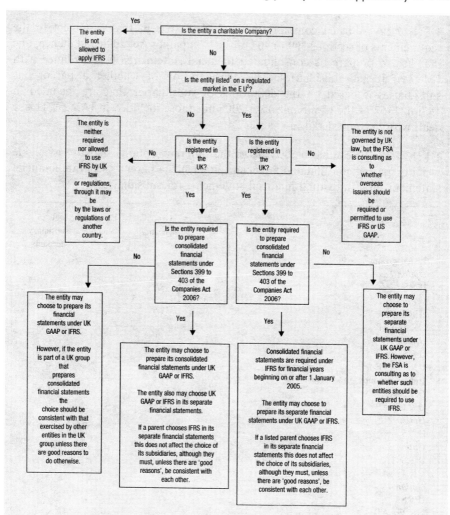

Notes:

1   Listed means any security admitted to trading on an EU regulated market. This includes both debt and equity securities.

2   EU regulated markets are as defined in the EU 2005 Regulation – see paragraph UK.1.22.14. A UK company with a security listed on any EU regulated market will be subject to the Regulation if it is required to prepare consolidated financial statements under UK law.

UK.1.22.28   Before it can be ascertained that the Regulation applies, and hence whether IFRS consolidated financial statements are required, it is first necessary to determine whether the entity is a parent that is required to prepare consolidated financial statements by sections 399 to 403 of the Companies Act 2006.

UK.1.22.29 A listed company will only be a parent that is subject to the requirements of sections 399 to 403 of the Companies Act 2006 and, hence, one that has to prepare its consolidated financial statements in accordance with IFRS, if it has subsidiaries. The consideration of whether a parent has subsidiaries is based on the definitions of subsidiaries that are included in section 1162 of the Companies Act 2006 not those included in IAS 27. This is dealt with in more detail in chapter 24.

UK.1.22.30 The table below shows the different options that are available when preparing consolidated financial statements, a parent's separate financial statements and individual financial statements for subsidiaries.

	Group accounts	Parent accounts	UK subsidiary accounts
Listed groups			
Option 1			
IFRS	✓	✓	✓
Option 2			
IFRS	✓	✓	
UK GAAP			✓
Option 3			
IFRS	✓		
UK GAAP		✓	✓
Unlisted groups			
Option 1			
UK GAAP	✓	✓	✓
Option 2			
IFRS	✓	✓	✓
Option 3			
IFRS	✓	✓	
UK GAAP			✓
Option 4			
IFRS	✓		
UK GAAP		✓	✓

Which accounting requirements apply?

UK.1.22.31 For a group that has to apply EU-adopted IFRS in its consolidated financial statements or has decided to use EU-adopted IFRS voluntarily, all of the IFRSs and interpretations of IFRSs that are adopted by the EU will apply (see para UK.1.22.32). However, as explained in paragraph UK.1.22.28 above, whether a company needs to prepare consolidated financial statements is determined by looking at the rules in the Companies Act 2006. Once it has been decided that consolidated financial statements are required under the Act, the rules in IAS 27 apply. In particular, the entities that should be treated as subsidiaries and consolidated are determined by looking at the rules in IAS 27, not those in the Companies Act. IAS 27's requirements are dealt with in detail in chapter 24.

UK.1.22.32 Some standards, or parts thereof, may not be adopted or may be rejected by the EU (see from para 1.40 for details of the endorsement process). A company may apply a non-adopted standard only if it is consistent with adopted standards and is consistent with the conditions set out in paragraph 10 of IAS 8 (see further chapter 4). [EU clarification para 2.1.3]. It is likely that, if a non-adopted standard replaces an existing standard, companies subject to the EU 2005 Regulation will not be able to apply it, as it will probably conflict with an existing adopted standard. If, however, a non-adopted standard deals with a subject area that is not covered by an adopted standard, then it may be that the use of paragraph 10 of IAS 8 will lead companies to use that standard in their IFRS financial statements. This is because the guidance in IAS 8 on selecting accounting policies leads entities towards using standards dealing with similar subjects and to using the Framework. The non-adopted standard will be a standard dealing with a similar subject and, in addition, will be consistent with the Framework. The standard may not be used if it is inconsistent with EU-adopted standards.

UK.1.22.33 The IASB issues standards with an effective date some time in the future. This should allow sufficient time for the standard to be endorsed. However, particularly where a company seeks to apply a standard early, it is possible that a standard will have been issued by the IASB before a company's year end, but endorsement by the EU occurs after the year end. The EU has confirmed that a standard endorsed after the balance sheet date but before the financial statements are signed may be used in those financial statements, provided both the standard and the Regulation introducing it permit early adoption.

UK.1.22.34 IFRIC interpretations may be used independently of the endorsement process, unless the interpretation is accompanied by a consequential amendment to a standard.

UK.1.22.35 If different international standards are adopted by the EU than the full set that has been issued by the IASB, or if there are delays in endorsing standards, EU entities will not necessarily be using all IFRSs. A standard may have been rejected or a standard that supersedes another may not yet have been adopted. The Accounting Regulatory Committee (ARC) recommends the following wording for use in the notes to the financial statements and in the audit report: *"in accordance with International Financial Reporting Standards as adopted by the EU"*; or *"in accordance with IFRSs as adopted by the EU"*. The use of the plural 'IFRSs' shows that IFRSs are endorsed one by one, rather than as a package. It also noted that the term 'as' is significant: it clarifies that the statement should be read as 'in the manner in which IFRSs have been adopted in the EU following the endorsement procedure' and not simply as 'IFRSs that have been adopted'.

UK.1.22.36 UK law cannot restrict companies' compliance with, or the choices they have in accounting for, certain items under adopted IFRSs. This includes restricting choices that are available within IFRS. Where IFRSs do not specify the accounting for particular transactions, paragraph 10 of IAS 8 directs entities to use judgement in developing accounting policies and gives guidance as to what should inform that judgement. UK law cannot restrict or hinder the requirement to apply judgement by specifying any particular treatment. [EU clarification para 3.1].

UK.1.22.37 Whilst Member States may not restrict choices that are available under IFRS, certain disclosures might be required in addition to those required by IFRS. The EU clarification states that additional disclosures may continue to apply to general purpose financial statements where the disclosures are outside the scope of endorsed IFRS. EU directives (as transposed into national law), Member States or regulatory authorities may require disclosures, including those to be given outside the financial statements and those to be given within the financial statements that cover subjects outside the scope of IFRS. These might relate to, for example, corporate governance or directors' remuneration by individual. [EU clarification para 4.1]. One example of a disclosure that has been retained in UK law to apply to companies preparing IFRS financial statements is employee costs. See from paragraph UK.1.22.38 for a description of the parts of UK law that will continue to apply to companies preparing IFRS financial statements.

What Companies Act requirements apply?

UK.1.22.38 The Companies Act 2006 was implemented in phases after receiving Royal Assent. The Act is fully implemented for accounting periods beginning on or after 6 April 2008. The Act extends GB company law to Northern Ireland; previously it required separate Northern Ireland legislation.

UK.1.22.39 Companies that are required to use EU-adopted IFRS, or that choose to use EU-adopted IFRS, prepare their financial statements in accordance with the requirements of IFRS, rather than the accounting requirements of the Companies Act 2006. Therefore, in broad terms, the requirements in SI 2008/410 relating to the form and content of accounts (in particular, the accounts formats in Schedules 1, 2, 3 and 6) no longer apply to companies using IFRS. However, the disclosure requirements in relation to staff costs from section 411 of the Companies Act 2006 is applicable to companies using IFRS to ensure that these disclosures continue to be given by all companies and groups.

UK.1.22.40 The basic requirement to prepare financial statements, including the circumstances in which consolidated financial statements are required, as well as the requirements on audit, approval, distribution and filing, continue to apply to all companies (see from para UK.1.22.43). Also, certain information required by the Companies Act 2006 to be included in the annual report and accounts will apply to companies using EU-adopted IFRS. Hence, for example, a listed company's consolidated financial statements will be required to include a directors' remuneration report and a directors' report (including a business review).

UK.1.22.41 The BIS has issued guidance notes ('Requirements under the Companies Act 2006 and application of the IAS Regulation') to help companies to apply the new rules. These include a summary of those provisions in the Companies Act 2006 that continue to apply to companies preparing financial statements under IFRS. These are listed in paragraph 9.22 of the guidance notes as follows[1]:

Companies Act 2006 Section	Requirement
386 to 389	Duty to keep accounting records.
390 to 392	A company's financial year and accounting reference periods.
393	Accounts to give a true and fair view.
394 to 397	Preparation of individual financial statements.
399, 403, 404 and 406	Preparation of consolidated financial statements.
407	Consistency of financial statements within group.
400 to 402	Exemption from requirement to prepare consolidated financial statements.
405 and 402	Subsidiary undertakings included in the consolidation.
408(1), (3) and (4)	Treatment of individual profit and loss account where consolidated financial statements are prepared.
409 to 413	Disclosure in notes to financial statements.
414, 450, 433, 436, 444, 445, 446 and 447	Approval and signing of financial statements.
415 to 419, 433 and 436	Directors' report.
420 to 422, 437, 438 and 447	Directors' remuneration report.
475, 495, 496, 497, 498, 503, 505 and 444	Auditors' report and duties of auditors.
423 to 425, 431 and 432	Persons entitled to receive or demand copies of accounts and reports.
430	Annual financial statements and reports to be made available on web site.
433 to 436	Requirements in connection with publication of financial statements.
437 and 438	Accounts and reports to be laid before company in general meeting.
441 to 453	Filing of accounts and reports with the registrar of companies.
442	Period allowed for laying and delivering accounts and reports.
454 to 461, 1126 and 1130	Revision of defective accounts and reports.
463	Liability for false or misleading statements in reports.
469	Preparation and filing of financial statements in Euros.
416(3), 417(1), 444(1)(3), 414(3), 419(2), 444(5) and 450(3)	Certain exemptions for small companies.
381 to 384, 465 to 467	Qualification of company as small or medium-sized, so far as applicable to exemptions from audit, from certain directors' report disclosures and for

	exemption from obligation to prepare consolidated financial statements.
426 to 429, 434(6) and 435(7)	Summary financial statements.
472	Notes to the financial statements.
385, 471, 472, 474, 1161, 1162 and 1173	Various definitions.

[1] This list only shows the sections in the Companies Act 2006 that are applicable to companies reporting under EU-adopted IFRS. It does not show applicable sections in other Parts of the Act, for instance, share capital and distributable profits, that continue to apply to all companies.

UK.1.22.42 The following paragraphs consider in more detail some of the sections of the Act that continue to apply to companies adopting IFRS (as well as applying to companies following UK GAAP).

The requirement to prepare financial statements

UK.1.22.43 The directors are required to prepare financial statements for the company for each financial year that are either in compliance with sections 394 and 395(1) of the Companies Act 2006 ('Companies Act individual financial statements') or in accordance with EU-adopted IFRS ('IAS individual financial statements'). Companies Act individual financial statements should comprise a balance sheet as at the last day of the financial year and a profit and loss account for the financial year. [CA06 Sec 396]. The balance sheet should give a true and fair view of the company's state of affairs as at the end of the financial year; and the profit and loss account should give a true and fair view of the company's profit or loss for the financial year. In addition, the financial statements should comply with SI 2008/410 as to form and content and additional information required.

UK.1.22.44 Companies preparing IAS individual financial statements are required to prepare financial statements in accordance with international accounting standards (and to state that they have done so in the notes to the financial statements). [CA06 Sec 397]. 'International accounting standards' means IFRS as endorsed by the EU (see from para 1.40). [CA06 Sec 474(1)].

UK.1.22.45 In addition, if at the end of the financial year the company is a parent company within the meaning of the Companies Act 2006, the directors should also prepare consolidated financial statements for the group for the year. [CA06 Sec 399(2)].

UK.1.22.46 Companies required to prepare consolidated financial statements under the Act that have any security listed on a regulated market within the EU (see para UK.1.22.12) are required to prepare those consolidated financial statements under EU-adopted IFRS (they will be 'IAS consolidated financial statements'). Companies that are not required to prepare consolidated IAS financial statements may choose to do so. These financial statements will also be prepared in accordance with EU-adopted IFRS. Where the directors of a parent company prepare IAS consolidated financial statements, they should state in the notes that the financial statements have been prepared in accordance with international accounting standards. [CA06 Secs 406, 474(1)].

UK.1.22.47 Companies that are parent companies and that do not prepare IAS consolidated financial statements are required to prepare 'Companies Act consolidated financial statements'. Such financial statements should give a true and fair view of the assets, liabilities, financial position and profit or loss for the financial year of the undertakings included in the consolidation as a whole, as far as concerns the parent company's members. They should also consist of a consolidated balance sheet dealing with the state of affairs of the parent company and its subsidiaries as at the last date of the financial year and a profit and loss account for the financial year. In addition, the financial statements should comply with SI 2008/410 as to form and content and additional information required. [CA06 Sec 404(1)(3)].

UK.1.22.48 Guidance on which companies are required to use IFRS and which companies may optionally use it is given in paragraph UK.1.22.27.

The true and fair requirement

UK.1.22.49 Section 393 of the Companies Act 2006 specifies that the directors must not approve the financial statements (either of an individual company or a group) unless they are satisfied that the financial statements give a true and fair view of the assets, liabilities, financial position and profit or loss. The auditor of a company must have regard to this requirement when carrying out the statutory audit. For companies using IFRS, this is supplemented by the requirement in IAS 1 that the *"financial statements shall present fairly the financial position, financial performance and cash flows of an entity"* (see further chapter 3). [IAS 1 para 15]. The IASB's framework (see para 1.50) notes that fair presentation and a true and fair view are equivalent. [Framework para BC3.44].

UK.1.22.50 The Act's requirements in relation to the true and fair override do not apply to companies preparing IFRS financial statements. IFRS requirements regarding overriding international standards are contained in IAS 1. This issue, in addition to discussion of the requirement in IAS 1 to present fairly, is covered in chapter 3.

Accounting concepts

UK.1.22.51 Certain basic accounting principles have been contained in the Act since 1981. However, most of these appear in IFRS and are dealt with in this chapter or in chapter 3. One concept that is covered by the Act, but which is not directly dealt with in the IASB's framework, is 'prudence' in the context of realisation. The concept of 'prudence and realisation' is covered in the following section.

Prudence and realisation

UK.1.22.52   The Companies Act 2006 is more restrictive than IFRS in terms of profits that may be included in the profit and loss account. Schedule 1 to SI 2008/410 states: *"...only profits realised at the balance sheet date shall be included in the profit and loss account"*. IFRS contains no such restriction and, therefore, there could be instances where unrealised profits might be included in the profit and loss account under IFRS, which the provisions of Schedule 1 to SI 2008/410 would not permit to be included. UK rules on distributions require that distributions may only be made out of realised profits. For this purpose, realised profits are defined as:

> *"Such profits ... of the company as fall to be treated as realised in accordance with principles generally accepted, at the time when the accounts are prepared, with respect to the determination for accounting purposes of realised profits..."* [CA06 Sec 853(4)(5)].

UK.1.22.53   Realisation is, therefore, an accounting rather than a legal concept. The effect of the above Schedule 1 requirement has been that generally, under UK GAAP, the profit and loss account has been made up of realised and, therefore, distributable profits. If the profit and loss account under IFRS includes unrealised profits it will be necessary to keep track of such profits and exclude them when considering profits available for distribution. Therefore, in the present legal and accounting framework, companies (and auditors) need guidance on determining realised profits because:

■   Directors need to know what profits recognised in the financial statements are realised so that they can determine the amount of profits available for lawful distribution.

■   The law assumes that accountants will be in a position to determine what is meant by realised.

UK.1.22.54   The ICAEW and ICAS have developed detailed guidance (Tech 02/10) on determining realised profits in the context of distributions under the Companies Act 2006. This is *de facto* GAAP on what constitutes a distributable profit. The concepts of 'realised' and 'distributable' profits' are considered in chapter 23.

UK.1.22.55   Unlike in UK GAAP, IFRS does not state that only realised profits can be recorded in the income statement. Many gains that would not, under UK thinking, fall to be treated as realised are recognised in the income statement, for instance, gains on revaluing investment properties.

Notwithstanding the presentation of realised profits under IFRS, the principles of section 853 of the Companies Act 2006 apply when determining the level of profits available for distribution.

The UK financial reporting environment

The Financial Reporting Council

UK.1.22.56 The Financial Reporting Council Limited (FRC) was established in 1990 along with two subsidiaries, the Accounting Standards Board Limited and the Financial Reporting Review Panel Limited. The purpose of these bodies was to provide an institutional framework to underpin financial reporting in the UK. The accountancy profession, the City and the government share in the funding of these bodies.

UK.1.22.57 The FRC's role is to promote high quality corporate governance and reporting to foster investment. It does this in two ways:

- In the area of codes and standards it:
    - sets relevant UK codes and standards and related guidance for governance, accounting, auditing and actuarial work;
    - influences codes and standards at international level, and
    - researches potential improvements in those areas:
- In the area of 'conduct' it:
    - Authorises Recognised Supervisory Bodies ('RSBs') and Recognised Qualifying Bodies ('RQBs') to approve accountants to carry out audits and to offer a recognised audit qualification respectively, and reviewing the way that the RSBs and RQBs discharge their responsibilities.
    - Oversees how the actuarial profession regulates its members.
    - Inspects and reports upon the quality of the work performed by auditors of public interest entities.
    - Reviews the reports and accounts of public interest entities to determine compliance with the applicable financial reporting framework.
    - Investigates possible misconduct by professional accountants and/ or actuaries and, where appropriate in the public interest, pursues disciplinary proceedings.

UK.1.22.57.1 The FRC Plan for 2011/12, published in April 2011, included a major project to work with the Government to ensure that the FRC has the powers and structure necessary to carry out its responsibilities and consult on any changes. Proposed changes were announced as a result of a joint consultation by the Department for Business, Innovation and Skills (BIS) and the FRC on reform.

UK.1.22.57.2 The proposals to reform the FRC were designed to achieve three principal objectives:

- To ensure the organisation is joined-up and streamlined, with an ability to focus on key strategic issues.

- To introduce an integrated and more efficient approach to the FRC's key regulatory roles – with a wider range of proportionate sanctions and greater independence from those it regulates.

- To develop the FRC's existing expertise and further enhance its standing and influence in international regulation.

UK.1.22.57.3 Under the new structure the strategic direction of the FRC and key decisions on standards and how the organisation discharges its responsibilities are taken by the Board. The Board is supported by three Committees: a Codes and Standards Committee ('CSC'), a Conduct Committee ('CC'), and an Executive Committee.

UK.1.22.57.4 Codes and Standards includes the areas covered by the Board's Corporate Governance Committee (CGU), the Accounting Council, the Audit and Assurance Council and the Actuarial Council (previously the Accounting Standards Board (ASB), the Auditing Practices Board (APB) and the Board for Actuarial Standards (BAS)). The Conduct Division of the FRC covers supervisory and disciplinary matters and encompassed the areas covered by the Financial Reporting Review Panel (FRRP), the Professional Oversight Board (POB), the Audit Inspection Unit (AIU) and the Accounting and Actuarial Disciplinary Board (AADB).

UK.1.22.57.5 The reform of the FRC required a change in the law and this was given parliamentary approval by the House of Commons and House of Lords in June 2012. The new organisational structure of the FRC, based around the two primary areas of 'Codes and Standards' and 'Conduct', is represented in the following diagram:

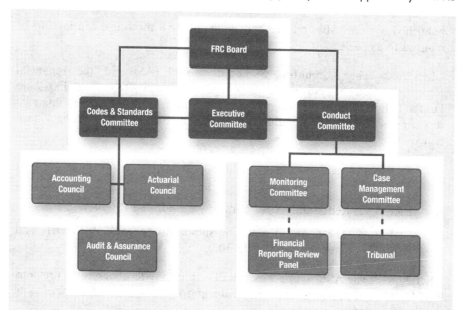

UK.1.22.58 The Chair and Deputy Chair of the FRC Board are appointed by the Secretary of State for Business, Innovation and Skills; other directors are appointed by the FRC Board.

UK.1.22.59 The FRC's previous six subsidiary operating boards have been replaced by a number of Councils which support the Committees and the Board. An exception to this is the Financial Reporting Review Panel (FRRP – see further para UK.1.22.65), which will continue to operate with only limited changes. In relation to codes, standard setting and policy questions the FRC will be advised by three Councils, on Accounting, on Audit and assurance and on Actuarial matters. The CC will be supported by two sub-committees – on its monitoring/supervisory work and on disciplinary matters.

The Accounting Council (formally the Accounting Standards Board)

UK.1.22.60 As discussed above, as part of the FRC reform, the Accounting Standards Board (ASB) has been replaced by the Accounting Council. Under the new FRC structure the Councils do not have power to set accounting standards and so the FRC became the prescribed body for issuing accounting standards (the standard-setting body for the purposes of section 461(1) of the Companies Act 2006). However, the EU 2005 Regulation overrides national law, so the IASB is the legal standard-setter for companies adopting IFRS, subject to EU endorsement (see from para UK.1.22.31). The FRC is now the body that sets accounting standards for UK entities that do not apply IFRS.

UK.1.22.61 As part of the transitional provisions anything done by the ASB or in the process of being done by the ASB in relation to accounting standards is treated as being done by, or continued by the FRC. Documents originally published by the ASB, and decisions taken at ASB meetings, continue to be referred to as such.

UK.1.22.62 The Accounting Standards Board (ASB) of the Financial Reporting Council previously published Financial Reporting Exposure Drafts (FREDs) setting out revised proposals for the future of financial reporting in the UK and Republic of Ireland. The following FREDs have been issued:

- FRED 46 'Application of financial reporting requirements' (draft FRS 100).

- FRED 47 'Reduced disclosure framework' (draft FRS 101).

- FRED 48 'The financial reporting standard applicable in the UK and Republic of Ireland' (draft FRS 102).

UK.1.22.63 The ASB issued these FREDs following feedback to its previous FREDs 43 to 45 and as a result the ASB is proposing significant changes to its previous proposals, including:

- Eliminating the tier system – previous proposals recommended the introduction of a tier system for financial reporting depending on an entity's status. The ASB has removed this recommendation and, consequently, the application of EU-adopted IFRS will not be extended beyond that required by law.

- Introducing accounting treatments permitted under current accounting standards – previously the ASB had sought to make minimal changes to the IFRS for SMEs. This decision has now been reviewed and the ASB is now proposing that where an accounting treatment is currently permitted in UK and Irish accounting standards and in International Accounting Standards it should be retained. As a consequence, the options to revalue land and buildings, capitalise borrowing costs and carry forward certain development expenses have been incorporated into FRED 48.

- Incorporating guidance for public benefit entities into FRED 48 – the ASB issued a separate exposure draft that addressed the needs of public benefit entities in March 2011, but it is now proposed that all accounting requirements be incorporated into the single standard.

UK.1.22.64 The ASB is proposing that the new standards will apply for accounting periods beginning on or after 1 January 2015, with early application to be permitted.

The Financial Reporting Review Panel

UK.1.22.65 The Financial Reporting Review Panel (FRRP) now sits below the Conduct Committee. Its role is to examine material departures from the Act's accounting requirements, including the accounting standards. The Companies Act 2006 provides for the Secretary of State to enquire into the accounts of companies and, where necessary, to apply for a court order requiring their revision. [CA06 Secs 455, 456]. The Secretary of State has the power to authorise others to apply to the Court. [CA06 Sec 457]. The Conduct Committee was given this authority by The Supervision of Accounts and Reports (Prescribed Body) and Companies (Defective Accounts and Directors' Reports) (Authorised Person) (S.I. 2012 No. 1439). Previously, the FRRP itself had been the authorised body. Pursuant to its Operating Procedures the Panel handles cases involving public and large private companies. [FRRP website 2012]. All other cases fall to the BIS. The following types of company fall within the FRRP's authority:

- Public limited companies, unless they are subsidiaries in small or medium-sized groups.

- Companies within a group headed by a public limited company.

- Any private company that does not qualify as small or medium-sized as defined by section 456 of the Companies Act 2006.

- Any private company within a group that does not qualify as small or medium-sized group.

[FRRP operating procedures para 11].

UK.1.22.65.1 As part of the wider changes to the FRC, changes were made to the operating procedures of the FRRP, based on the objectives of the reform. The key changes are to:

- Enable the Panel to share information received by the Panel with the AIU.

- Reserve the right of the Panel to make an announcement where, following its intervention, a company makes a significant change, whether corrective to, or clarifying, its financial or corporate reporting.

- Enable the Panel to release its own press announcement if the fact of a Panel enquiry has become public other than as a result of a Panel press notice.

UK.1.22.66 The FRRP does not routinely examine all the financial statements of the companies falling within its authority. It acts on matters drawn to its attention. It also selects financial statements on the basis of risk. It selects reports, *"by methods which take into account the Panel's assessment of the risk of non-compliance and the consequence of non-compliance and as a result of complaints"*. [FRRP operating procedures para 3]. It focuses on the financial statements in specific industries, following its risk-based assessment and after discussions with the FSA and the panel's Standing Advisory Group. The panel also conducts targeted reviews to check compliance with specific accounting requirements.

UK.1.22.67   The panel does not just focus on annual financial statements. It is now authorised to review compliance with the Act in respect of the directors' reports of large and medium-sized companies. The panel is also empowered to examine all financial information published by listed companies, including interim reports and preliminary announcements. The FRRP liaises with the FSA in this respect and has signed a memorandum of understanding with the FSA in order to facilitate co-operation and sharing of information.

UK.1.22.68   HM Revenue & Customs (HMRC) is permitted to disclose information to the FRRP that will assist the panel in its investigations. [CA06 Sec 458]. HMRC may only disclose information to the panel that relates to issues of apparent non-compliance with the Companies Act and accounting standards. It will discuss its concerns with the company and will tell the company that it is contacting the panel. There are no provisions for the panel to disclose any information to HMRC with regard to accounting, tax or any other issues.

UK.1.22.69   The FRRP normally attempts to seek a voluntary agreement with the company's directors about any necessary revisions to the financial statements in question. This allows the directors to follow the rules regarding the voluntary revision of defective financial statements, rather than those for revision by court order. [CA06 Sec 454]. However, if the FRRP cannot reach an agreement with the company's directors, it has authority from the Secretary of State for Business, Innovation and Skills to use the Act's powers to compel the revision of financial statements if the court finds that they are defective. [CA06 Sec 455]. It also has funds available to it to fund any legal proceedings. To date, all cases examined by the FRRP have been resolved without involving adjudication by the courts.

The international financial reporting structure

1.23   The current international financial reporting structure is represented in the following diagram:

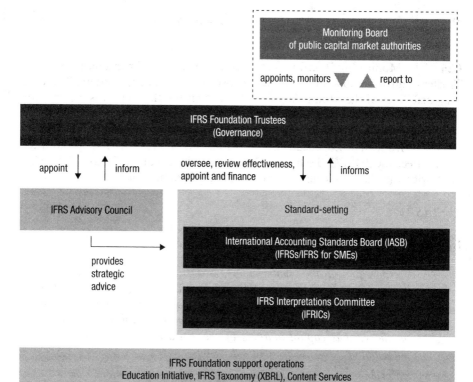

1.24 The trustees are responsible for governing the IFRS Foundation. The Trustees promote the work of the International Accounting Standards Board (IASB) and the rigorous application of IFRSs, but are not involved in any technical matters relating to the standards. This responsibility rests solely with the IASB. The Trustees' responsibilities include, but are not limited to:

- Appointing members of the IASB, the IFRS Interpretations Committee and the IFRS Advisory Council.

- Establishing and amending the operating procedures, consultative arrangements and due process for the IASB, the Interpretations Committee and the Advisory Council.

- Reviewing annually the IASB's strategy and assessing its effectiveness.

- Ensuring the financing of the IFRS Foundation and approving annually its budget.

1.25 In exercising their governance responsibilities, the Trustees may reconsider or amend the IASB's due process or recommend, for example, improvements to the IASB's outreach activities. In addition, the Constitution requires the Trustees to undertake a formal, public review of the structure of the IFRS Foundation, its governance arrangements and its effectiveness in fulfilling the organisation's objectives every five years. The Trustees are accountable to a Monitoring Board of public authorities.

1.26 The Monitoring Board was established to create a direct link between the Trustees and the public authorities who oversee the standard setters. The main responsibilities of the Monitoring Board are to ensure that the Trustees continue to discharge their duties as defined by the constitution and to approve the appointment and reappointment of Trustees. The Monitoring Board comprises members from the European Commission, the IOSCO Emerging Markets Committee, the IOSCO Technical Committee, the Japanese Financial Services Authority and the US Securities and Exchange Commission.

The IASB

1.27 The IASB's objectives are:

"*(a) to develop, in the public interest, a single set of high quality, understandable and enforceable global accounting standards that require high quality, transparent and comparable information in financial statements and other financial reporting to help participants in the various capital markets of the world and other users of the information to make economic decisions;*

(b) to promote the use and rigorous application of those standards;

(c) in fulfilling the objectives associated with (a) and (b), to take account of, as appropriate, the special needs of small and medium-sized entities and emerging economies; and

(d) to bring about convergence of national accounting standards and IFRSs to high quality solutions."

[Preface para 6].

1.28 The due process for international accounting standard-setting is as follows:

- Identifying and reviewing the issues related to the topic and considering the application of the Framework.

- Studying national accounting requirements and practice and exchanging views with national standard-setters.

- Consulting the IFRS Advisory Council (formerly the Standards Advisory Council) (see para 1.35) about the advisability of adding the topic to the IASB's agenda.

- Forming an advisory group to give advice to the IASB on the project.

- Publishing for public comment a discussion document.

- Publishing for public comment an exposure draft approved by at least nine votes of the IASB, including any dissenting opinions held by IASB members and a basis for conclusions.

- Considering all comments received within the comment period on discussion documents and exposure drafts.

- Considering the desirability of holding a public hearing or conducting field tests and, if considered desirable, holding such hearings and conducting such field tests.

- Approving a standard by at least nine votes of the IASB and including in the published standard any dissenting opinions and a basis for conclusions explaining the steps in the IASB's due process and how the IASB dealt with public comments on the exposure draft.

- Publishing within a standard a basis for conclusions, explaining, among other things, the steps in the IASB's due process and how the IASB dealt with public comments on the exposure draft and the dissenting view of any IASB member.

1.29 In July 2011 the IASB launched the first formal public agenda on its future work plan with comments being requested by 30 November 2011. There has not yet been an announcement on any changes to the IASB's agenda however a feedback statement is expected by the end of 2012.

1.29.1 The comment period for international exposure drafts is generally 90 days, although in exceptional circumstances this may be reduced. The IASB publishes all comment letters on its web site and explains how it has responded to comments in the basis for conclusions attached to published standards.

1.29.2 The IASB publishes two suites of standards – IFRSs and IFRSs for SMEs.

1.30 IFRSs are designed for the general purpose financial statements and other financial reporting of all profit-orientated entities. They may also be useful for non-profit orientated entities. General purpose financial statements give information about financial performance, position and cash flow that is useful for making economic decisions by a range of users, including shareholders, creditors, employees and the general public. A complete set of financial statements includes a balance sheet (statement of financial position), statement of comprehensive income, a statement of changes in equity, a cash flow statement, a list of accounting policies and notes to the financial statements. [Preface paras 9 to 11]. Any limitations on the scope of individual IFRSs are set out in the particular standards. [Preface para 16].

1.31 IFRS for SMEs was published in July 2009. The objective was to publish a separate standard to apply to the general purpose financial statements and other financial reporting of small and medium-sized entities, private entities and non publicly-accountable entities. IFRS for SMEs is not relevant to all entities and, therefore, its application is restricted. Section 1 of the IFRS for SMEs discusses the standard's scope. Key differences between IFRS and IFRS for SMEs are:

- The omission of certain standards not relevant to SMEs (such as earnings per share, segment reporting and interim reporting).

- The removal of certain policy choices available under IFRSs.

- The simplification of measurement requirements in some areas.

- Reductions in disclosure requirements.

- Simplification of language.

1.32 IFRSs apply from the date specified in the standard and transition provisions should be applied where appropriate. [Preface para 19]. The general policy of the IASB is to apply new standards retrospectively, to all relevant transactions whether they took place before or after the issue of the standard. This might have an effect on previously negotiated contracts or agreements; it is up to those who negotiate such contracts and agreements to make appropriate provisions for future changes. [Preface para 20]. In some specific circumstances, the IASB may specify that new standards are adopted prospectively. This is considered on a case by case basis.

The IFRS Interpretations Committee (formerly the International Financial Reporting Interpretations Committee)

1.33 The IFRS Interpretations Committee (IFRS IC), (formerly the International Financial Reporting Issues Committee or 'IFRIC') addresses emerging issues that require attention before an international standard can be amended or issued. It is a committee of the IASB whose duties include the interpretation of IFRSs, where conflicting or unsatisfactory interpretations have emerged, and to give timely guidance on issues that have not yet been addressed by IFRS. It does not issue standalone standards. Interpretations are, however, authoritative: IAS 1 states: *"International Financial Reporting Standards (IFRSs) are standards and Interpretations adopted by the International Accounting Standards Board (IASB)"*. [IAS 1 para 7]. All interpretations must be approved by at least nine votes of the IASB.

1.34 The IFRS Interpretations Committee handbook sets out how the requirements of transparency and consistency are applied in the seven stages of due process, as set out below:

- Identification of issues.

- Setting the agenda.

- IFRS IC meetings and voting.

- Development of a draft Interpretation.

- The IASB's role in the release of a draft interpretation.

- Comment period and deliberation.

- The IASB's role in an interpretation.

The IFRS Advisory Council (formerly the Standards Advisory Council)

1.35 The IFRS Advisory Council (formerly the Standards Advisory Council or 'SAC') provides a formal forum for those wider accountancy interests who may not be represented on the Board. The Advisory Council's role is to provide broad strategic advice on the IASB's agenda priorities and insight into the possible benefits and costs of particular projects. The Advisory Council must be consulted on any major projects that the IASB undertakes and on any changes to the Constitution.

Local adoption of IFRS

1.36 In some jurisdictions, the IASB's standards apply automatically; but in many jurisdictions they need to go through an endorsement process of some kind before they are brought into effect. Here we consider the endorsement process within the EU.

ARC and EFRAG

1.37 Before IFRSs can be used in the EU, they have to go through a process of adoption or endorsement. The EU adoption process involves various bodies considering every IFRS and interpretation. They then decide whether to include them in EU law. This process is complex and involves the European Commission (EC) and two tiers: a 'regulatory level' and an 'expert level'.

1.38 The 'regulatory level' – the Accounting Regulatory Committee (ARC) – comprises representatives of Member States and is chaired by the EC. It gives an opinion on whether a particular international standard should be adopted by the EU.

1.39 The 'expert level' — the European Financial Reporting Advisory Group (EFRAG) — is an independent private body that considers the standards from a European viewpoint. Its task is to provide, at the EC's request, advice on the technical soundness of new standards. It is composed of academics, analysts, auditors, industry representatives and users. Within EFRAG itself are two tiers, a Technical Expert Group and a Supervisory Board. The Technical Expert Group has various functions, one of the most significant being involvement at an early stage in the formation of IFRS. EFRAG co-ordinates European users, preparers, professionals and standard-setters so that there is a concerted European influence on international standard-setting.

Endorsement mechanism

1.40 Under the EU 2005 Regulation, in order for an international standard or interpretation to be adopted, it must be "*conducive to the European public good*". [Regulation Article 3]. In addition its application must result in a true and fair view and meet the criteria of understandability, relevance, reliability and comparability.

1.41 Some standards, or parts thereof, might not be adopted or might be rejected by the EU. To date this has happened only with certain narrow aspects of IAS 39 relating to hedge accounting that affects only a limited number of companies. The EU can reject a part of a standard where it deals with a distinct subject area. A company cannot apply a non-adopted standard if it is not consistent with adopted standards.

1.42 Once a standard or interpretation has been agreed and published by the IASB, the EU decides whether to make that standard mandatory in the EU. The decision is taken under the 'endorsement mechanism'.

1.43 The endorsement mechanism involves the following steps (IFRSs, amendments to IFRSs and IFRIC interpretations are referred to as 'standards'):

- A new standard issued by the IASB is assessed by EFRAG, which submits a technical recommendation to the EC and the ARC.

- The standard must be translated into the national languages of all of the Member States before it can be put to a vote.

- The EC has no power to amend the text of a standard, although it is of the view that it may delete parts of the text.

- The EC submits a proposal to the ARC, which has to pass a vote on whether the standard should be adopted or rejected. A majority is required. If there is no majority or the ARC votes in favour of rejection, the EC may return the issue to EFRAG or bring the matter before the Council of Ministers.

- The EC also submits its proposal to the European Parliament, which has three months in which to hold a vote. If no vote is held, the Parliament is deemed to have voted in favour of the EC's proposal.

- Once the EC and the European Parliament have approved the standard, a Regulation to that effect appears in the 'Official Journal of the European Union'. Three days later, the Regulation (and hence the standard) comes into European law. However, the standard's endorsement will have its own effective date from when it can be applied. In some situations, the Regulation may also state when an endorsed standard will come into effect.

The above process normally takes around 10 months, although the time may vary depending on how complex and controversial the issue is.

1.44 Companies may only use new standards that replace existing endorsed standards or amendments to endorsed standards if these have been endorsed.

1.45 If a new standard deals with an area not covered by existing endorsed standards, it may be possible to use it under the hierarchy rules for selecting accounting policies in IAS 8. However, this is only possible if the new standard does not conflict with or include any amendments to existing endorsed standards.

1.46 IFRIC interpretations may be adopted independently of the endorsement process, provided that they are not accompanied by a consequential amendment to a standard.

1.47 Endorsement is also an important consideration when preparing interim financial information. This is considered in chapter 31.

Framework for setting accounting standards

1.48 IFRS operates under the IASB's Conceptual Framework for financial reporting.

1.49 The IASB is currently reviewing its Framework and seeks to converge it with the conceptual framework of the US standard setter (the Financial Accounting Standards Board (FASB)). The project is being undertaken in phases. At the time of writing, chapters dealing with the objective of general purpose financial reporting (chapter 1) and qualitative characteristics of useful financial information (chapter 2) have been completed and an exposure draft has been published in relation to the reporting entity concept (chapter 1). Chapter 3 contains the remaining text of the Framework published in 1989.

1.50 The main sections of the IASB's Framework are:

- Foreword – including the status of the conceptual framework project.

- Introduction – including comments on the purpose and scope of the Framework.

- Objectives, usefulness and limitations of general purpose financial reporting – including information about a reporting entity's economic resources, claims and changes in resources and claims.

- The reporting entity – which is still to be added.

- Qualitative characteristics of useful financial information of relevance and faithful representation and the enhancing qualitative characteristics of comparability, verifiability, timeliness and understandability.

- The remaining text of the Framework (1989), not yet updated, including:

    - Underlying assumption – the going concern convention.

    - Elements of financial statements – including financial position (assets, liabilities and equity) and performance (income and expenses).

    - Recognition of elements – including probability of future benefit, reliability of measurement and recognition of assets, liabilities, income and expenses.

    - Measurement of elements – including an inconclusive discussion on historical cost and its alternatives.

- Concepts of capital and its maintenance – including a further inconclusive discussion on financial as opposed to physical capital maintenance.

- Approval of the Framework.

- Basis for conclusions.

- Table of concordance – reflecting how the contents of the Framework (1989) and the Framework correspond.

Introduction

1.51 The Framework reflects the concepts that underlie the preparation and presentation of financial statements for external users. Its purpose is to:

- Assist the IASB in the development of future international accounting standards and in its review of existing international accounting standards.

- Assist the IASB in promoting harmonising regulations, accounting standards and procedures relating to presenting financial statements by providing a basis for reducing the number of alternative accounting treatments permitted by international accounting standards.

- Assist national standard-setting bodies in developing national standards.

- Assist preparers of financial statements in applying international accounting standards and in dealing with topics that have yet to form the subject of an international accounting standard.

- Assist auditors in forming an opinion as to whether financial statements conform to international accounting standards.

- Assist users of financial statements in interpreting the information contained in financial statements prepared in conformity with international accounting standards.

- Provide those who are interested in the work of IASB with information about its approach to formulating international accounting standards.

1.52 The Framework is not a standard. It deals with general purpose financial reporting that is useful to a range of users. It identifies users as existing and potential investors, lenders, and other creditors. Other parties, such as employees, suppliers, customers, governments and their agencies, regulators and the public might find general purpose financial reports useful. However, general purpose financial reports are not primarily directed to these parties. [Framework para OB10].

1.53 The IASB has recognised that here may be a limited number of instances where the Framework is in conflict with an IFRS. An IFRS always prevails over the Framework.

The objective, usefulness and limitations of general purpose financial reporting

1.54 The IASB identifies the objective of general purpose financial reporting as being the provision of *"financial information about the reporting entity that is useful to existing and potential investors, lenders and other creditors in making decisions about providing resources to the entity. Those decisions involve buying, selling or holding equity and debt financial instruments, and providing or settling loans and other forms of credit"*. [Framework para OB2].

1.55 Decisions about buying, selling or holding equity and debt financial instruments as well as providing or settling loans and other forms of credit by existing and potential investors are dependent upon the returns expected to be generated by those instruments, namely, dividends, principal and interest repayments and market price increases. Expectations about returns are dependent upon an assessment of the amount, timing, and uncertainty of future net cash inflows. [Framework para OB3].

1.56 In order to assess the prospects for future net cash inflows, information is needed about *"the resources of the entity, claims against the entity and how efficiently and effectively the entity's management and governing board have discharged their responsibilities to use the entity's resources"*. [Framework para OB4]. Information about management's discharge of its responsibilities assists existing investors, lenders and other creditors who have the right to vote on or influence management's actions in making decisions.

- Information about the nature and amounts of economic resources and claims assists in identifying financial strengths and weaknesses. It supports the assessment of an entity's liquidity and solvency, its needs for additional financing and the likelihood of raising that finance. The distribution of future cash flows among those with existing claims against the entity can be estimated from information about the priority and payment terms of existing claims. [Framework para OB13].

- Changes in a reporting entity's economic resources and claims result from the entity's performance and from other events or transactions such as issuing debt or equity instruments. Users need to be able to distinguish between these changes in order to assess the potential for future cash flows. [Framework para OB15]. Financial performance information is essential to understand the return that is generated from the use of available resources. It provides insight into how well management has discharged its responsibilities to make efficient and effective use of resources. Information about the variability and components of return supports the assessment of the uncertainty of future cash flows.

- Accrual accounting shows the effects of transactions, events and circumstances on the economic resources and claims in the period in which those effects occur, irrespective of when the resulting cash receipts and payments take place. [Framework para OB17].

- Cash flow information during a period assists users in assessing the entity's ability to generate future net cash inflows. It shows how cash is obtained and spent including borrowings and repayment of debt, cash distributions to investors and other factors that might impact upon the entity's liquidity or solvency

1.57 The Framework identifies the primary users of general purpose financial reports, to whom the general purpose financial report are directed, as those existing and potential investors, lenders and other creditors who cannot require entities to provide information directly to them and, therefore, are obliged to rely on the general purpose financial reports for their information needs. [Framework para OB5].

1.58 General purpose financial reports are not designed to reflect the entity's value. They provide information to assist existing and potential investors, lenders and other creditors estimate the entity's value. [Framework para OB7].

1.59 The Framework establishes the concepts that underlie the estimates, judgements and models upon which financial reports are based. [Framework para OB11].

Underlying assumption

1.60 The Framework is based on a single assumption underlying financial statements, namely going concern. The Framework notes that financial statements are prepared on a basis that assumes an *"... entity is a going concern and will continue in operation for the foreseeable future".* [Framework para 4.1]. This is also addressed in IAS 1 and in chapter 3.

1.61 The Framework refers to accruals in such a way that reflects the shift in accounting thinking away from performance statement matching towards asset and liability definitions. It does not include any direct reference to matching and instead states that accruals accounting shows the effects of transactions, events and circumstances on the economic resources and claims in the period in which those effects occur, irrespective of when the resulting cash receipts and payments take place. [Framework para OB17]. This avoids the situations that could occur under the 'matching' view of accruals, where items appeared on the balance sheet that did not meet the definition of assets or liabilities.

Qualitative characteristics of useful financial information

1.62 In order for financial information to be useful, it must be relevant and faithfully represent what it purports to represent. The usefulness of financial information is enhanced if it is comparable, verifiable, timely and understandable. [Framework para QC4]. Relevance and faithful representation are considered to be the fundamental qualitative characteristics of financial information. [Framework para QC5]. Neither a faithful representation of an irrelevant phenomenon, nor an unfaithful representation of a relevant phenomenon helps users make good decisions. [Framework para QC17].

1.63 Transparency, high quality, internal consistency, true and fair view or fair presentation and credibility have been suggested as desirable qualitative characteristics of financial information. However, the IASB consider these to be *"different words to describe information that has the qualitative characteristics of relevance and representational faithfulness enhanced by comparability, verifiability, timeliness and understandability"*. [Framework para BC3.44].

1.64 Relevance suggests the ability to influence users' economic decisions by helping or confirming the evaluation of events of the past, present or future. [Framework para QC6]. Financial information is considered to be capable of making a difference to users' decisions if it has "predictive value, confirmatory value or both". [Framework para QC7]. Materiality is a subsidiary concept of relevance. Materiality depends on the size or amount of an item judged in relation to its circumstances (see para 1.79 below).

1.65 To be useful, information must not only present relevant effects of transactions and other events and conditions, but it must also faithfully represent the effects of transactions and other events and conditions that it purports to represent. To be a perfectly faithful representation, three characteristics would need to be present, namely, *completeness, neutrality*, and *freedom from error*. The IASB's objective is to maximise those qualities to the extent possible. [Framework para QC12].

1.66 'Completeness' refers to the inclusion of all information necessary for a user to understand the transactions and other events and conditions being depicted, including all necessary descriptions and explanations. In some instances *completeness* "may also entail explanations of significant facts about the quality and nature of the items, factors and circumstances that might affect their quality and nature, and the process used to determine the numerical depiction". [Framework para QC13].

1.67 'Neutrality' refers to a lack of bias in the selection or presentation of financial information. The financial information is not slanted, weighted, emphasised, de-emphasised or otherwise manipulated to increase the probability that the financial information will be received favourably or unfavourably by users. *Neutrality* does not mean information with no purpose or no influence on behaviour. [Framework para QC 14]. The characteristics of prudence and conservatism are excluded from faithful representation, because both are inconsistent with the concept of *neutrality*.

1.68 'Faithful' representation does not mean that the information is accurate in all respects. 'Free from error' means there are no errors or omissions in the description of the effects of transactions and other events and conditions, and the process used to produce the reported information has been selected and applied with no errors in the process. *"In this context, free from error does not mean perfectly accurate in all respects. For example, an estimate of an unobservable price* *or value cannot be determined to be accurate or inaccurate. However, a representation of that estimate can be faithful if the amount is described clearly and accurately as being an estimate, the nature and limitations of the estimating process are explained, and no errors have been made in selecting and applying an appropriate process for developing the estimate".* [Framework para QC15].

1.69 In the basis for conclusion the IASB indicated that substance over form was not considered a separate component of faithful representation, because it would be redundant. *"Faithful representation means that financial information represents the substance of an economic phenomenon rather than merely representing its legal form. Representing a legal form that differs from the economic substance of the underlying economic phenomenon could not result in a faithful representation."* [Framework para BC3.26].

1.70 The Framework suggests that the most effective and efficient way of applying the fundamental qualitative characteristics (relevance and faithful representation) would be:

- Identify the transactions and other events and conditions that have the potential to be useful to the users of the financial information.

- Identify the type of financial information about the transactions and other events and conditions that would be most relevant if it is available and can be faithfully represented. [Framework para QC18].

Enhancing qualitative characteristics

1.71 The Framework considers the qualitative characteristics of *comparability, verifiability, timeliness* and *understandability* enhance the usefulness of information that is relevant and faithfully represented. These characteristics may also help determine which of two ways should be used to depict a transaction or other event or condition if both are considered equally relevant and faithfully represented. [Framework para QC19].

1.72 The first, enhancing qualitative characteristic is *comparability*, over time and from one entity to another. This requires consistency, and the disclosure of accounting policies and any changes in them. It also requires disclosure of corresponding figures for previous periods. [Framework paras 20 to 25]. The Framework does not give primacy to either *comparability* within an entity or *comparability* between entities. IFRS 1 does make such a distinction in the context of first time adoption of IFRS; *comparability* within an entity's first IFRS financial statements is more important than *comparability* with entities already using IFRS (see chapter 3).

1.73 Consistency must not be confused with *comparability*. "Consistency refers to the use of the same methods for the same items, either from period to period within a reporting entity or in a single period across entities. *Comparability* is the goal, consistency helps to achieve that goal". [Framework para 22].

1.74 The enhancing qualitative characteristic of *verifiability* helps assure users that information faithfully represents the economic transactions and other events and conditions it purports to represent. It means that "different knowledgeable and independent observers could reach consensus, although not necessarily complete agreement, that a particular depiction is a faithful representation". [Framework paras QC26 to QC28].

1.75 *Timelines* refers to having information available in time to be capable of influencing decisions. [Framework para QC29]. Information that is not provided on a timely basis is less useful to users in their decision-making.

1.76 Classifying, characterising and presenting information clearly and concisely makes it *understandable*. [Framework QC30]. Some transactions and other events and conditions are inherently complex and it is not possible to make them easily understandable. Reports excluding such information might be easier to understand, however, they would then be incomplete and, consequently, potentially misleading. [Framework paras QC30 to QC32].

1.77 The cost of providing financial information that is both relevant and faithfully represents what it purports to represent is a constraint on the provision of useful financial information. Because of the inherent subjectivity, different individuals' assessments of the costs and benefits of reporting financial information varies, hence the IASB seeks to consider costs and benefits in relation to financial reporting in general terms and not solely in relation to individual reporting entities. [Framework paras QC35 to QC39].

1.78 The Framework does not directly address the true and fair view or fair presentation. However, it notes that where the qualitative characteristics above are applied along with appropriate accounting standards this normally results in financial statements that convey what is generally understood as a true and fair view of, or as presenting fairly such information. [Framework para BC 3.44]. The true and fair view and fair presentation are addressed in chapter 3.

Materiality

1.79 As noted in paragraph 1.64 above, materiality is a subsidiary concept of relevance. Materiality sets the threshold for determining whether an item is relevant. The definition of materiality in the Framework is:

> "*Information is material if omitting it or misstating it could influence the decisions that users make on the basis of financial information about a specific reporting entity. In other words, materiality is an entity-specific aspect of relevance based on the nature or magnitude, or both, of the items to which the information relates in the context of an individual entity's financial report*". [Framework para QC11].

1.80 The nature and materiality of the information affect its relevance; in some cases, the nature of information alone is sufficient to determine its relevance.

Determining whether information is material or not is a matter of professional judgement. The following items often qualify as material, regardless of their individual size:

- Related party transactions.

- A transaction or adjustment that changes a profit to a loss, and *vice versa*.

- A transaction or adjustment that takes an entity from having net current assets to net current liabilities, and *vice versa*.

- A transaction or adjustment that affects an entity's ability to meet analysts' consensus expectations.

- A transaction or adjustment that masks a change in earnings or other trends.

- A transaction or adjustment that concerns a segment or other portion of the entity's business that has been identified as playing a significant role in the entity's operations or profitability.

- A transaction or adjustment that affects an entity's compliance with loan covenants or other contractual requirements.

- A transaction or adjustment that has the effect of increasing management's compensation, for example by satisfying requirements for the award of bonuses.

- Changes in laws and regulations.

- Non-compliance with laws and regulations.

- Fines against the entity.

- Legal cases.

- Deterioration in relationships with individual or groups of key suppliers, customers or employees.

- Dependency on a particular supplier, customer or employee.

1.81 An item that is not material is not relevant, cannot influence a user's decisions and need not be reported in the financial information. If immaterial items are reported in financial information, they can interfere with decision-making, because excessive detail may obscure the relevant information. However, determining what is material is a matter of professional judgement, and it would be inappropriate to set fixed monetary limits or rules.

Elements of financial statements

1.82 Elements are the 'broad classes' that the financial effects of transactions and other events are grouped into in financial statements. [Framework para 4.2]. There are two main groups of elements. The first is associated with measuring an entity's financial position: assets, liabilities and equity. The second is those elements that relate to measuring an entity's performance: income and expenses. Within these main categories there are sub-classifications – for example, expenses by function or nature, and assets and liabilities by degree of liquidity.

1.83 All the other definitions rest on those for assets and liabilities. An asset is *"…a resource controlled by the entity as a result of past events and from which future economic benefits are expected to flow to the entity"*. [Framework para 4.4(a)].

1.84 The future economic benefits may come from assisting in production or in the direct increase of cash. The Framework emphasises economic substance over legal form and that not all assets and liabilities will meet the criteria for recognition (discussed in para 1.92 below).

> **Example – Asset held is controlled by another party**
>
> Entity A enters into a legal arrangement to act as trustee for entity B by holding listed shares on entity B's behalf. Entity B makes all investment decisions, and entity A will act according to entity B's instructions. Entity A will earn a trustee fee for holding the shares. Any dividends or profit/(loss) from the investments belong to entity B.
>
> Entity A should not recognise the listed shares as its asset even though it is in possession of the shares.
>
> Entity A does not control the investment's future economic benefits. Benefits from the investments flow to entity B and entity A earns a trustee fee for holding the shares regardless of how the shares perform. The listed shares do not, therefore, meet the criteria of an asset in entity A's balance sheet.

1.85 Assets will generally arise through the expenditure of cash. However, expenditure will not always result in an asset, even where it is expected that economic benefits will flow. This is generally because the entity making the expenditure will not control any expected benefits. The Framework makes a similar, less specific point: *"when an entity incurs expenditure, this may provide evidence that future economic benefits were sought but is not conclusive proof that an item satisfying the definition of an asset has been obtained"*. [Framework para 4.14].

> **Example 1 – Costs incurred do not meet the criteria for recognition as an asset**
>
> Entity C incurs start-up costs but has not met the criteria for recognising the costs of constructing an intangible asset contained in paragraph 45 of IAS 38. Entity C may have an expectation of benefits arising from its expenditure, as the activity may lead to an intangible asset and a further expectation that this will lead to economic benefits (profits) flowing to the entity.
>
> Until the development phase is entered, however, the entity does not have sufficient expectation or control of any economic benefits that might flow, and the expenditure does not meet the definition of an asset. [IAS 38 para 57(a)].

Example 2 – Costs incurred do not result in the control of a resource

Entity D is streamlining its operations. It decides to move one of its factories to Asia to reduce operating costs and is able to reduce future cash outflow significantly by doing so. Redundancy payments were made to employees currently working in the present factory as part of the relocation exercise.

The redundancy payments should not be recognised as an asset. The redundancy payment does not give entity D control over a resource, although it results in entity D reducing its future cash outflows. An asset should only be recognised if the entity controls certain resources.

Example 3 – Asset contributed by the government

Entity E receives a property from the government for the development of a leisure park as part of the government's efforts to increase tourism in the country. The property's fair value can be reliably measured and entity E has control over the leisure park's development and operation.

The grant of the property is a government grant; the property should, therefore, be measured at fair value. [IAS 20 para 23].

Entity E has control over the property from which future economic benefits are expected to flow to entity E when the leisure park is in operation. The property's value can also be reliably measured. The definition and recognition criteria of assets are both met.

The government grant should be presented in the balance sheet in accordance with IAS 20.

1.86 The IASB's definition of liability is *"a present obligation of the entity arising from past events, the settlement of which is expected to result in an outflow from the entity of resources embodying economic benefits"*. [Framework para 4.4(b)].

1.87 Obligations do not have to be legally binding, but they do not include future commitments. Liabilities include those provisions that require estimation. [Framework paras 4.15 to 4.19].

1.88 Equity is a residual item – that is the residual interest in the assets of the entity after deducting all its liabilities. [Framework para 4.4(c)]. However, it can be sub-classified into various types of capital and reserves. These can reflect legal restrictions or the differing rights of various owners.

1.89 The income and expense elements of performance are also measured in terms of assets and liabilities. Income is measured by increases in assets or decreases in liabilities other than those relating to equity participants. Expenses are the reverse. [Framework para 4.25].

1.90 Sub-components of income are:

■ Revenue from the entity's ordinary activities.

- Gains such as the disposal of fixed assets that may be ordinary or otherwise.

[Framework paras 4.29 and 4.30].

1.91 Income also includes unrealised gains, although these are not necessarily recognised in the income statement. Expenses include realised and unrealised losses. [Framework paras 4.33 to 4.35].

Recognition

1.92 The IASB's Framework calls for recognition of elements when:

- it is probable that any future economic benefit associated with the item will flow to or from the entity; and

- the item has a cost or value that can be measured with reliability

[Framework para 4.38].

An item might meet the definition of an asset but not the recognition criteria.

> **Example – Recognition of an asset is prohibited under a specific standard**
>
> Entity F is in the beverage business. Its brand is known throughout the world. The brand may be sold and has a market value.
>
> Management should not recognise the brand as an asset, although it meets the definition of one. Management is prohibited from recognising internally-generated brands, mastheads, publishing titles, customer lists and items similar in substance. [IAS 38 para 63]. The recognition criteria for intangible assets are more narrowly defined by IAS 38, limiting recognition to assets for which cost can be measured reliably, rather than cost or value. [IAS 38 para 21(b)]. The cost cannot be distinguished from the cost of developing the business as a whole. Such items are not recognised as intangible assets, as the cost cannot be reliably measured.
>
> When similar assets are acquired from a third party, the consideration given to acquire those assets is distinguishable from the general costs of developing the business as a whole and would, therefore, be recognised, as long as they also meet the criteria of control and the probable flow of future economic benefits.

1.93 IFRS does not define the meaning of 'probable'. The Framework states that *"the concept is in keeping with the uncertainty that characterises the environment in which an entity operates. Assessments of the degree of uncertainty attaching to the flow of future economic benefits are made on the basis of the evidence available when the financial statements are prepared. For example, when it is probable that a receivable owed by an entity will be paid, it is then justifiable, in the absence of any evidence to the contrary, to recognise the receivable as an asset".* [Framework para 4.40]. We consider that probable means 'more likely than not', that is a probability of more than 50%.

1.94 The second criterion for recognition is reliability. The Framework notes that estimates are an inherent part of financial reporting and that estimates in themselves do not undermine the reliability of financial information. Where an item has the characteristics of an element but does not meet the recognition criteria, disclosure in the notes may be appropriate. [Framework paras 4.41, 4.43].

1.95 The Framework takes an asset and liability approach rather than focusing on income and expenses. The recognition criterion for income and expenses is as follows: *"Income is recognised in the income statement when an increase in future economic benefits related to an increase in an asset or a decrease of a liability has arisen that can be measured reliably. This means, in effect, that recognition of income occurs simultaneously with the recognition of increases in assets or decreases in liabilities..."* [Framework para 4.47].

Example – Asset and liability approach

Entity G, a telecom entity, invoices its customers for call charges on a monthly basis. At the beginning of March, the total value of invoices that entity G sent out to its customers was C500,000. The invoices relate to calls customers made in February. The invoices are payable by the customers by the end of April.

Entity G should recognise income of C500,000 in the income statement at the end of February. A corresponding increase in assets (accounts receivable) should be recognised in the balance sheet.

Under accrual accounting the effects of transactions and other events are recognised when they occur. They are reported in the financial statements of the periods to which they relate. [Framework para OB17]. Revenue is not accelerated or deferred to match the timing of the receipt of cash or the raising of the invoices.

1.96 The recognition criterion for expenses is the mirror of the recognition criterion for income. Expenses should be recognised when incurred and when the expenditures produce no future economic benefits or when, and to the extent that, future economic benefits do not qualify, or cease to qualify, for recognition in the balance sheet as an asset. [Framework para 4.52]. The discussion on recognition of expenses covers matching: *"expenses are recognised in the income statement on the basis of a direct association between the costs incurred and the earning of specific items of income"*. However, matching is tightly circumscribed: *"the application of the matching concept under this Framework does not allow the recognition of items in the balance sheet which do not meet the definition of assets or liabilities"*. [Framework para 4.50]. Where the flow of economic benefits is unclear, expenses may have to be allocated on a rational basis – for example, when measuring the expense incurred when assets are used up (that is, depreciation). [Framework para 4.51].

Measurement of the elements

1.97 The Framework does not prescribe measurement bases. A number of different measurement bases are used in practice, including historical cost, current cost, realisable value and present value; most entities use historical cost. This is one part of the Framework that has not been changed to align with developments in accounting thinking. The IASB in particular has been an advocate of fair values (see para 1.107), but these are not referred to in the Framework.

Capital maintenance

1.98 Most entities adopt a financial concept of capital maintenance. As explained in paragraph 1.100, this concentrates on maintaining the financial capital that an entity's owners have invested. The selection of the appropriate concept of capital maintenance depends on the needs of users. The Board does not prescribe a particular model, except where there are unusual circumstances such as hyper-inflation.

Status of the Framework for UK companies

UK.1.98.1 The Framework is not an accounting standard and does not, therefore, need to be adopted into EU law.

Accounting conventions

1.99 All accounting systems depend on the capital maintenance concept adopted, the basis used to value assets and the unit of measurement used. The different options available for each of these components are considered in this section.

Capital maintenance concepts

1.100 Capital maintenance is central to the measurement of total accounting profit. Disregarding additions to capital or repayments of capital and distributions, accounting profit is the difference between a company's capital at the start of the period and at the end of the period. An entity can only be considered to have made a profit if it has increased its net assets, which are represented by its capital, above what is necessary to maintain its opening capital. Total accounting profit can, therefore, only be measured once a definition has been established as to what capital is to be maintained. [Framework paras 4.57 and 4.58].

1.101 There are two different concepts of capital maintenance: operating capital maintenance and financial capital maintenance. Operating capital maintenance, although it can be measured in a variety of different ways, generally seeks to ensure that the business' physical operating capacity is preserved. Financial capital maintenance attempts to conserve the value of the funds that shareholders have invested in the business. Financial capital maintained can either be the monetary value of capital attributable to shareholders or a value adjusted by a general purchasing power index to maintain capital as a fund of real purchasing power. [Framework para 4.59].

Example – Two concepts of capital maintenance

A sole trader starts a business buying and selling second-hand cars. In his first year of trading, he buys one car for C1,000 and sells it for C2,000. At the time he sells the car, the cost of buying an equivalent car is C1,200; general inflation between the dates of buying and selling is 10%. Under financial capital maintenance (in monetary terms and in real terms) and operating capital maintenance, the trader's income statement would be as follows:

Capital maintenance concepts	Financial capital maintenance		
	Monetary capital	General purchasing power	Operating capital maintenance
	C	C	C
Sales	2,000	2,000	2,000
Cost of sales	(1,000)	(1,000)	(1,200)
Operating profit	1,000	1,000	800
Inflation adjustment to opening capital	–	(100)	–
Total gains	1,000	900	800

Monetary financial capital maintenance, which is the most commonly used basis, takes no account of the effects of inflation. The profit of C1,000 is the amount in excess of the business's original capital. In column two, the inflation adjustment shows the effect of the general increase in prices on the opening financial capital of C1,000 and seeks to ensure that profit is measured only after preserving the opening capital in the business in terms of its general purchasing power. The profit of C900 leaves capital of C1,100 in the business to maintain its purchasing power.

Operating capital maintenance is concerned with preserving the productive capacity of the business. In this example, this is the trader's ability to replace the item of stock sold. Under operating capital maintenance, the trader has a profit of C800 and capital in the business of C1,200, which is sufficient to purchase a car to begin the next period's trade.

Valuation bases

1.102   The measurement of profit is also affected by the valuation basis chosen. There are a variety of valuation bases, including historical cost, current cost and market value or fair value. [Framework para 4.54 to 4.56].

Units of measurement

1.103   The unit of measurement affects how profit is determined. Reporting can be in nominal currency or in units of constant purchasing power. Financial statements for two different years may be denominated in nominal currency, but because of inflation, the purchasing power of this nominal currency is not the same. The use of a unit of constant purchasing power eliminates these difficulties in comparability. One method is the unit of current purchasing power. All non-monetary assets and liabilities relating to dates prior to the reporting date are restated by reference to movements in a general price index, such as the retail price index, into the value of the currency at the reporting date.

Conventions

1.104 Capital maintenance concepts, asset valuation bases and the units of measurement used can be combined in different ways to create different accounting conventions. The options outlined above would result in many different accounting conventions, but not all the combinations are sensible. The more common conventions are summarised below.

Historical cost convention

1.105 The historical cost convention values assets at their historical cost, uses financial capital maintenance and uses the nominal currency as its unit of measurement. However, when prices are rising, historical cost accounting may distort reported profits and balance sheet values. It is, therefore, less useful for making investment decisions or decisions about amounts to distribute. In the example in paragraph 1.101, if the trader had taken the profit of C1,000 for his own use, there would not be sufficient funds in the business for it to continue to trade at the same level.

Modified historical cost convention

1.106 Sometimes the historical cost convention is modified by the revaluation of certain non-current assets. Modified historical cost accounting uses financial capital maintenance and uses the nominal currency as its unit of measurement. But certain non-current assets, usually land and buildings, are included at a valuation above historical cost. This gives some indication of the value to the business of some of the assets employed. The unrealised gains as a result of revaluing assets are generally not recognised in the income statement. This suggests that the gain is an element of the capital of the business that must be retained in order to maintain the business' operating capacity, although no attempt is made to employ operating capital maintenance. In addition, not all companies revalue their assets and, in the past, not all companies that revalued their assets did so on a regular basis. Therefore, comparability between different companies is reduced. If valuations are allowed to become out of date, their usefulness as an indication of the value of the assets to the business diminishes. IAS 16, therefore, requires that where an entity adopts a policy of revaluation, these should be made with sufficient regularity to ensure that the carrying amount does not differ materially from that which would be determined using fair value at the balance sheet date.

Modified historical cost/Fair value convention

1.107 Recent years have seen the development of a system of accounting based on historical cost but an increasing number of assets (and a few liabilities) reported at fair value. Fair value is defined in IAS 39 as *"the amount for which an asset could be exchanged, or a liability settled, between knowledgeable, willing parties in an arm's length transaction"*. [IAS 39 para 9]. This definition will change slightly on adoption of IFRS 13, which defines fair value as *"the price that would be received to sell an asset or paid to transfer a liability in an orderly transaction between market participants at the measurement date"*. [IFRS 13 para 9].

1.108   Standards that incorporate the use of fair values include IAS 19, IAS 39, IAS 40, IAS 41, and IFRS 2. However, many assets such a property, plant and equipment, intangibles and inventories are generally recorded at historical cost, as are most liabilities. The system is, therefore, sometimes described as a 'mixed measurement model'.

1.109   The IASB has pioneered the use of fair value, as it argues that it gives more relevant information to users of accounts. There are major questions, however, as to how much further fair value can be used. A current discussion is whether it should be applied to all financial instruments; most commentators believe this would be a step too far.

Current purchasing power

1.110   The current purchasing power (CPP) convention also values assets at their historical cost and uses financial capital maintenance. CPP uses a unit of constant purchasing power rather than the nominal currency for measurement. All non-monetary items in the financial statements, including capital, are restated by reference to a general price index. This maintains capital in terms of what shareholders can do with their funds in the economy as a whole, but the general price index used may not move the same way as the input prices specific to the company. Therefore, the resulting asset values may bear no relationship to their current value to the business. In addition, the capital maintained may be either too much or too little to maintain the business's operating capacity. In the example in paragraph 1.101, the increase in the general price index was less than the increase specific to second-hand cars. If the trader had taken all the CPP profit out of the business, he would not have had sufficient capital to replace his stock.

1.111   An example of the use of CPP accounting is in hyper-inflationary economies. IAS 29 give guidance in this area.

Current cost accounting

1.112   Current cost accounting conventions value assets at their current value to the business. Although this is often combined with operating capital maintenance and measurement in nominal currency, it can also be combined with financial capital maintenance and units of constant purchasing power. As combining current costs with nominal currency usually results in useful information, the additional complexity introduced by using units of constant purchasing power is often not warranted except in trend information. Current cost operating profit shows the current trading margin achieved by the business, as it charges the costs incurred at the prices applying when the sales were made. In other words, it takes inflationary 'holding gains' out of the measurement of income. It gives an indication of the entity's ability to generate profits from its current operations and also maintains its current operating capacity. In the operating capital maintenance example in paragraph 1.101, the operating profit is lower than under financial capital maintenance. This allows sufficient capital to be retained to replace stock and continue trading and may also give a more forward-looking perspective on future profits.

Chapter 2

First-time adoption of IFRS

First-time adoption of IFRS

Introduction

2.1 This chapter deals with first-time adoption of IFRS. IFRS 1 is the accounting standard that deals with this issue. It covers the general approach to conversion and the areas where the rules for first-time adopters are different from those for entities already applying IFRS.

IFRS 1

Introduction

2.2 The underlying principle of IFRS 1 is retrospective application of those standards in force at the end of an entity's first IFRS reporting period. That is, entities should use the standards in force at the end of the latest period covered by their first IFRS financial statements in their opening IFRS balance sheet and throughout all periods presented in their first IFRS financial statements. For a company with a December year end applying IFRS for the first time in 2011, this means applying the standards in force as at 31 December 2011. IFRS 1 contains specific optional exemptions and some mandatory exceptions from this general requirement. These are explained from paragraph 2.30 below.

2.3 All guidance related to first-time adoption is contained within IFRS 1, except where it explicitly refers to other standards. The transitional rules of other standards do not apply to first-time adopters except where specified in IFRS 1; new standards generally include any necessary amendments to IFRS 1. [IFRS 1 para 9].

Objectives and scope

2.4 IFRS 1's objective is that an entity's first IFRS financial statements and any interim financial reports for part of the period covered by those first IFRS financial statements should contain high quality information that:

- Is transparent and comparable over all periods presented (see para 2.21).
- Gives a good starting point for using IFRS.
- Can be produced at a cost that does not exceed the benefit to users.

[IFRS 1 para 1].

2.5 IFRS 1 is applicable to all entities' first IFRS financial statements and to interim financial reports presented under IAS 34, for part of the period covered by its first IFRS financial statements. [IFRS 1 para 2]. Interim financial reporting for first-time adopters is explained from paragraph 2.207 below.

2.6 The term 'first IFRS financial statements' is defined in IFRS 1 as an entity's *"first annual financial statements in which an entity adopts International Financial Reporting Standards (IFRSs), by an explicit and unreserved statement of compliance with IFRSs"*. [IFRS 1 App A]. The standard further states that financial statements are first IFRS financial statements if an entity *"presented its most recent previous financial statements... in accordance with national requirements that are not consistent with IFRSs in all respects"*. [IFRS 1 para 3(a)(i)].

Repeated first-time application

2.7 Questions have been raised as to whether IFRS 1 could be applied by an entity more than once. For example, a listed entity may have previously transitioned to IFRS (and applied IFRS 1) as a result of local regulations requiring the application of IFRS. This entity may subsequently delist and elect to revert to its local GAAP (not consistent with IFRS). The question is: what accounting treatment should an entity apply when it subsequently adopts IFRS again (that is, what might be called 'repeated first-time application'). The definition in IFRS 1 (see para 2.6) suggests that an entity that undertakes repeated first-time application would have to apply IFRS 1 again.

2.8 However, in the 2011 annual improvements to IFRSs, the IASB created an alternative approach. The amendment requires an entity applying 'repeated first-time application' to choose between applying (a) IFRS 1 and (b) applying IFRS retrospectively (in accordance to IAS 8).

2.9 The amendment is applicable for annual periods beginning on or after 1 January 2013 with earlier application permitted. So, an entity applying 'repeated first-time application' prior to this date could not adopt the IAS 8 approach under the old rules, but could do so by electing to early adopt the amendment.

Repeated application in connection with an IPO

2.10 Local regulations of particular jurisdictions might require IFRS financial statements to be filed as part of special purpose financial statements or reports (usually in connection with IPOs). Consider the following example:

> **Example – Repeated first-time application in connection with an IPO**
>
> Group A moves to IFRS with a transition date of 1 January 2010. For the purposes of its statutory financial statements, group A's reporting date is 31 December 2011. When group A transitioned, it applied IFRS 1 and only prepared one year of comparative information. Shortly after transitioning to IFRS the group decides to IPO in

jurisdiction X. The regulator of jurisdiction X requires that the IPO document should include two years of comparative information (that is, from 1 January 2009).

We consider that group A can apply IFRS 1 again for the IPO submission. It is our view that there is a distinction between the statutory requirements in connection with filing of statutory financial statements and the requirements of a particular regulator in connection with filing a special purpose/pro forma document (in this case an IPO document). Preparation of an IPO document should not affect group A's statutory financial reporting, which will continue to treat 1 January 2010 as its transition date. For the purposes of the IPO document it is acceptable for group A to apply a transition date of 1 January 2009.

Within the IPO document group A applies IFRS 1 at 1 January 2009, but at 1 January 2010 reverts to the basis already established by applying IFRS 1 at the time of preparing the statutory financial statements. As necessary, adjustments are accounted for in retained earnings similar to a transition from previous GAAP to IFRS.

First IFRS financial statements

2.11   The other situations where an entity's financial statements are its first IFRS financial statements are where the most recent previous financial statements were presented:

> "(a) (ii)   in conformity with IFRSs in all respects, except that the financial statements did not contain an explicit and unreserved statement that they complied with IFRSs;
>
> (iii)   containing an explicit statement of compliance with some, but not all, IFRSs;
>
> (iv)   in accordance with national requirements inconsistent with IFRSs, using some individual IFRSs to account for items for which national requirements did not exist; or
>
> (v)   in accordance with national requirements, with a reconciliation of some amounts to the amounts determined under IFRSs."

[IFRS 1 para 3(a)(ii) to (v)].

2.12   Financial statements under IFRS are also an entity's first financial statements if, previously, the entity:

> "(b)   prepared financial statements in accordance with IFRSs for internal use only, without making them available to the entity's owners or any other external users;
>
> (c)   prepared a reporting package in accordance with IFRSs for consolidation purposes without preparing a complete set of financial statements as defined in IAS 1 Presentation of Financial Statements (as revised in 2007); or
>
> (d)   did not present financial statements for previous periods."

[IFRS 1 para 3(b) to (d)].

2.13 Financial reporting information prepared for group reporting purposes will generally not qualify as IFRS financial statements. This is either because they are not a complete set of financial statements under IAS 1, and/or because they do not contain an explicit and unreserved statement of compliance with IFRS. Therefore, even where entities have been preparing IFRS information for group reporting purposes, their initial financial statements when moving from national GAAP to IFRS will be their 'first IFRS financial statements' as defined by IFRS 1.

2.14 There may be some instances where an entity has more than one previous GAAP. See the following example:

> **Example – Entity has multiple previous GAAPs**
>
> For an entity that has historically been preparing financial statements using multiple GAAPs, none of which are IFRS, what is its previous GAAP for the purpose of its first set of IFRS financial statements?
>
> We believe there are several factors that should be assessed when determining previous GAAP, however, the literature in IFRS 1 does not dictate which previous GAAP to use. Judgement should be applied to determine which GAAP would be appropriate to deem as previous GAAP. The selected GAAP used should be clearly disclosed. A key factor to consider is which financial statements were made available to the entity's owners or other external users. Financial statements prepared under a previous GAAP for internal use only would likely not be an appropriate previous GAAP for IFRS 1.
>
> Other factors that should be assessed when determining an entity's previous GAAP include where the majority of users are located and which GAAP they have been using. Another factor is to consider what is triggering the use of IFRS and whether it is a mandatory or voluntary transition. Previous financial statements prepared for a specific purpose with limited circulation may not be an appropriate previous GAAP. Regulatory requirements may also impact the determination of previous GAAP.

2.15 IFRS 1 provides examples of situations in which IFRS 1 does not apply, that is, when financial statements are not an entity's first IFRS financial statements. These are when an entity:

"*(a) stops presenting financial statements in accordance with national requirements, having previously presented them as well as another set of financial statements that contained an explicit and unreserved statement of compliance with IFRSs;*

(b) presented financial statements in the previous year in accordance with national requirements and those financial statements contained an explicit and unreserved statement of compliance with IFRSs; or

(c) presented financial statements in the previous year that contained an explicit and unreserved statement of compliance with IFRSs, even if the auditors qualified their audit report on those financial statements."

[IFRS 1 para 4]

2.16 The scope of IFRS 1 states that the standard applies when an entity first adopts IFRSs. It does not apply when an entity has, in its most recent previous financial statements, presented an explicit and unreserved statement of compliance with IFRS, even if those financial statements were accompanied by an audit report that was qualified. [IFRS 1 para 4(c)]. As noted in paragraph 2.15, IFRS 1 paragraph 4 as well as the basis for conclusions is clear in requiring an explicit statement of compliance with all requirements of IFRS. [IFRS 1 para BC5]. We believe entities should carefully consider the appropriateness of making an explicit statement of compliance in cases where there is fundamental non-compliance with IFRS. An example is where a functional currency has been selected that does not comply with the requirements of IAS 21. We believe that making an explicit statement of compliance in such a case would violate the principal objectives of IFRS 1.

2.17 The above provisions can be illustrated by the following examples:

Example 1 – First IFRS financial statements: previously complied with some, but not all IFRS

Entity A prepares its financial statements in accordance with its previous GAAP, but is required to prepare financial statements in accordance with IFRS for the year ending 31 December 20X7. Entity A's national standard setter has adopted standards that are identical to almost all IFRSs, but has not adopted standards with the same provisions as IAS 32 or IAS 39. The accounting treatment applied to financial instruments under its previous GAAP is different to that outlined in IAS 32 and IAS 39.

Entity A has stated in its previous GAAP financial statements that they are prepared in accordance with IFRS, except for IAS 32 and IAS 39.

IFRS 1 is applied when an entity's financial statements contain an explicit and unreserved statement of compliance with IFRS. The statement in the previous GAAP financial statements that the entity complied with some, but not all IFRSs is not an explicit and unreserved statement of compliance. Thus, entity A's financial statements for the year ending 31 December 20X7 will be its first IFRS financial statements.

Example 2 – First IFRS financial statements: qualified audit opinion

Entity B prepares financial statements that contain an explicit and unreserved statement of compliance with IFRS. The auditors' report on the financial statements for the year ended 31 December 20X6 was qualified due to the lack of sufficient audit evidence to verify the inventory balances held at the balance sheet date.

Entity B's management has agreed to ensure that appropriate evidence is available for the year ending 31 December 20X7.

IFRS 1 is not applied when an entity previously prepared financial statements that contained an explicit statement of compliance with IFRS, but for which the auditors' report was qualified. Therefore, entity B's financial statements for the year ending 31 December 20X7 will not be its first IFRS financial statements.

Example 3 – First IFRS financial statements: no comparative information presented

Entity C applies IFRS in its financial statements for the first time for the year ended 31 December 20Y0. Previous financial statements were prepared in accordance with local GAAP. As a result of local regulation, entity C is not required to present comparative information, and as such, the financial statements for the year ended 31 December 20Y0 do not include comparatives. Subsequent financial statements, however, filed with local regulators are required to present comparative information.

The financial statements for the year ended 31 December 20Y0 would not constitute entity C's first IFRS financial statements. As no comparative information is provided, the management of entity C believes that it is unable to make an explicit and unreserved statement of compliance with IFRS. Entity C's financial statements for the year ended 31 December 20Y1 would be its first IFRS financial statements since comparative information will be presented. IFRS 1 would apply in these financial statements with the date of transition being 1 January 20Y0.

2.18   The context in which the financial statements are prepared is not relevant to deciding whether or not they are the first IFRS financial statements. A company has adopted IFRS once it has included an explicit and unreserved statement of compliance with IFRS in its financial statements.

Example – First IFRS financial statements: Initial public offering

Entity D is planning an initial public offering and is required to include financial statements covering the three years ended 31 December 20X7 in the offering circular. The listing regulations require financial statements prepared in accordance with IFRS.

Entity D has previously applied local GAAP and will apply IFRS for the first time in the financial statements included in the offering circular. The financial statements will include an explicit and unreserved statement of compliance with IFRS.

These financial statements will be the first IFRS financial statements, so entity D's date of transition will be 1 January 20X5, which is the beginning of the earliest period presented.

Recognition and measurement

2.19   The date of transition is the beginning of the earliest period for which an entity presents full comparative information under IFRS in its first IFRS financial statements. IFRS 1 requires an entity to prepare *and present* an opening balance sheet as a primary statement at the date of transition to IFRS. [IFRS 1 para 6; App A]. IFRS 1 does not require an entity to present an opening balance sheet in its interim financial report in the year of first-time adoption. However, this is good information for users and can be included in either the interim financial report or included in a previously issued transition document. Comparative periods are discussed in more detail in paragraph 2.187 below.

2.20   By way of illustration, Canadian publicly accountable entities are required to adopt IFRS under the Accounting Standards Board of Canada (AcSB)

'Implementation Plan for Incorporating International Financial Reporting Standards into Canadian GAAP' for financial years beginning on or after 1 January 2011. Entities are required to present, at a minimum, one year of comparative information. The relevant dates for these entities are shown below:

Year end	First IFRS financial statements required for year ending	Opening balance sheet prepared and *presented* at date of transition to IFRS of
31 December	31 December 2011	1 January 2010
31 March	31 March 2012	1 April 2010
30 June	30 June 2012	1 July 2010
30 September	30 September 2012	1 October 2010

Accounting policies

2.21 Comparability is one of the four main qualitative characteristics of financial statements under the Framework. The IASB considered how comparability should apply to those adopting IFRS for the first time. It decided to concentrate on achieving *"comparability over time within a first-time adopter's first IFRS financial statements and between different entities adopting IFRSs for the first time at a given date; achieving comparability between first-time adopters and entities that already apply IFRSs is a secondary objective".* [IFRS 1 para BC10].

2.22 Entities should, therefore, use the same accounting policies throughout their first IFRS financial statements and in their opening IFRS balance sheet. These accounting policies should be those complying with the accounting standards effective at the end of an entity's *first IFRS reporting period.* [IFRS 1 para 7]. An entity's *first IFRS reporting period* is the *"latest reporting period covered by an entity's first IFRS financial statements".* [IFRS 1 App A]. Some new accounting standards allow for prospective application by entities already using IFRS. Those adopting IFRS for the first time should use the current version of an IFRS throughout the periods presented in its first IFRS financial statements. Previous versions of standards cannot be applied. [IFRS 1 para 8].

2.23 IFRS 1 explains that the disclosures required when accounting policies are changed under IAS 8 are not required for a first-time adopter. [IFRS 1 para 27]. The IASB amended IFRS 1 in May 2010 to further clarify that IAS 8 also does not apply to changes made to accounting policies during the period of an entity's first IFRS financial statements. This would include a change in policy between publication of an entity's first IFRS interim report and the entity's first IFRS financial statements. However, an entity must explain the change in its first IFRS financial statements as required by paragraph 23 of IFRS 1 and provide updated reconciliations (see further para 2.196). This disclosure requirement also applies where an entity changes its use of the exemptions in IFRS 1 between the interim report and its first IFRS financial statements. [IFRS 1 para 32(c)]. The amendment is effective for periods beginning on or after 1 January 2011 with earlier application permitted. [IFRS 1 para 27A].

Example 1 – Standards in force at the end of the first IFRS reporting period not yet known

Entity A's management intends to present entity A's first IFRS financial statements for the year ending 31 December 20X7. The date of transition to IFRS is 1 January 20X6 and the opening IFRS balance sheet will be prepared and presented as at this date.

Entity A's management has begun to discuss the impact of IFRS on the financial statements with its bankers and major shareholders. Management completed its opening IFRS balance sheet as at 1 January 20X6 in July 20X6 and would like to present the balance sheet to its bankers in connection with ongoing discussions about loan finance.

The accounting policies used to prepare the opening IFRS balance sheet must comply with the standards in force at the end of the first IFRS reporting period, which is 31 December 20X7. Entity A's management does not know what standards will be in force at the end of the first IFRS reporting period, so it cannot be certain an opening balance sheet prepared in July 20X6 will comply with the applicable IFRSs. Management, therefore, cannot state that the opening balance sheet uses the IFRS accounting policies that will be applied in the financial statements for the year ending 31 December 20X7. Entity A should, therefore, disclose in the notes to the opening IFRS balance sheet that the opening IFRS balance sheet is prepared based on IFRSs issued and outstanding as of July 20X6, but that subsequent changes in IFRSs that are effective for the year ended 31 December 20X7 could result in a change to the opening balance sheet.

Entity A should, therefore, disclose in the notes to the opening IFRS balance sheet that the opening IFRS balance sheet is prepared based on IFRSs issued and outstanding as of July 20X6, but that subsequent changes in IFRSs that are effective for the year ended 31 December 20X7 could result in a change to the opening balance sheet.

Example 2 – Change in accounting policies during year of first time adoption

Entity B is a first-time adopter of IFRS and prepares its first IFRS financial statements for the year ending 31 December 20X7. It has already published its first interim results to 30 June 20X7 in accordance with IAS 34 and IFRS 1. The interim financial report included the reconciliations of both total comprehensive income and of equity that are required by paragraph 32 of IFRS 1.

Since issuing the interim financial report, entity B's management has concluded that one of entity B's accounting policy choices applied at the interim should be changed for the full year. Should entity B's management apply IAS 8 in the financial statements for the year ending 31 December 20X7?

No. The first annual IFRS financial statements are prepared in accordance with the specific requirements of IFRS 1. Subject to certain specified exemptions and exceptions, paragraph 7 of IFRS 1 requires that entity B uses the same accounting policies in its opening IFRS balance sheet and throughout all periods presented. This overrides IAS 8's provisions about changes in accounting policies. Paragraph 27 of

IFRS 1 also explains that IAS 8's requirements for disclosures about changes in accounting policies do not apply in an entity's first IFRS financial statements.

Entity B should include an explanation of the change in policy that it has made since the interim financial report in the notes to those financial statements in accordance with paragraph 27A of IFRS 1. The disclosure note is likely to include information similar to what IAS 8 would otherwise require to help users of the financial statements understand the changes that have been made. Entity B should also ensure that the reconciliations of total comprehensive income and of equity presented in the first IFRS financial statements in accordance with paragraph 24 of IFRS 1 are updated from those included in the interim financial report to reflect the amended accounting policy.

2.24   Where an IFRS is not mandatory at the end an entity's first IFRS reporting period, but it allows early adoption, that IFRS can be used in the entity's first IFRS financial statements. [IFRS 1 para 8].

UK.2.24.1   For early adoption of an IFRS, UK companies will also have to consider the implications of EU endorsement of the IFRS – this is dealt with in chapter 1.

UK.2.24.2   UK entities have been required by FRS 18 to apply the most appropriate accounting policy and the reasons why this policy was chosen may still be applicable when selecting policies under IFRS. There is no explicit requirement under IFRS to select the 'most appropriate' accounting policies, but this is implicit in the requirement for financial statements to present fairly the financial position, financial performance and cash flows of an entity, which involves providing the most relevant and reliable information to users. In many cases policies that were most appropriate under UK GAAP would be those that would give the most relevant and reliable information under IFRS. This is likely to be true especially because the conceptual frameworks of UK GAAP and IFRS are very close.

UK.2.24.3   A UK entity that has previously revalued a class of tangible fixed assets under FRS 15 is not, therefore, bound to carry on doing so under IAS 16, but it may consider that continuing the policy will give readers of its financial statements the most useful financial information.

UK.2.24.4   An area that might be considered more contentious than property, plant and equipment is that of investment properties. Under IAS 40 there are two options for measurement. An entity can adopt a fair (market) value model or a cost less depreciation model. Following the view that a move from one framework to another leads to a fresh start in the choice of accounting policies, a reporting entity may choose either of these models on adopting IFRS. However, IAS 40 states that *"it is highly unlikely that a change from the fair value model to the cost model will result in a more appropriate presentation"*. [IAS 40 para 31]. UK entities following SSAP 19, 'Accounting for investment properties' have been using a fair value model since 1981. We believe that, despite paragraph 31 of IAS 40, electing to adopt a cost-based measurement basis on first-time adoption of IFRS is acceptable in principle. The reason is that the change in policy has not been made within the IFRS framework and so for IFRS purposes the measurement basis on first-time adoption is the first measurement basis used by the reporting entity. Paragraph 31 of IAS 40 only applies to changes made within the IFRS reporting framework. Such entities will, however, need to consider what information is most useful in the context of the users of their financial statements. See further paragraph UK.2.216.126.

2.25 Entities do not have to base their choice of policies when first applying IFRS on the policies applied under their previous GAAP.

Initial recognition and measurement

2.26 The general principle applied to an entity's opening IFRS balance sheet is that items should be recognised and measured in accordance with the standards in force at the end of an entity's first IFRS reporting period. So, entities apply the following rules:

- Recognise all assets and liabilities whose recognition is required by IFRSs.
- Do not recognise items as assets or liabilities if IFRSs do not permit such recognition.
- Reclassify items that were recognised under previous GAAP as one type of asset, liability or component of equity, but that are a different type of asset, liability or component of equity under IFRSs.
- Apply IFRSs in measuring all recognised assets and liabilities.

[IFRS 1 para 10]

2.27 These recognition and measurement criteria are applied retrospectively.

UK.2.27.1 Some of the implications of this for UK companies include the following:

- Development costs that meet the definition of an intangible asset under IAS 38 must be recognised. See further paragraph UK.2.216.104.
- Deferred tax liabilities should be recognised on the basis of temporary differences rather than timing differences, meaning that, for example, deferred tax will be provided on past revaluations. See further paragraph UK.2.216.25.
- Deferred tax liabilities will have to be remeasured by removing the effect of discounting where this option has been taken under FRS 19. See further paragraph UK.2.216.24.
- All derivative financial instruments should be measured at fair value, in accordance with the requirements of IAS 39, which unlike FRS 26 applies to all companies.

2.28 Most changes made on adoption of IFRS should be dealt with as adjustments to retained earnings or another appropriate category of equity at the date of transition. [IFRS 1 para 11]. For example, the following adjustments should be made to a category of equity other than retained earnings:

- The difference between cost of available-for-sale investments and their fair value at the date of transition, less impairment losses since purchase.

- The result of remeasuring derivative financial instruments classified as cash flow hedges in accordance with IAS 39.

- The difference between cost of property, plant and equipment and fair value where the allowed alternative in IAS 16 is adopted.

There are limited circumstances in which adjustments on transition are made against goodwill. See further paragraph 2.72.

2.29 Entities will apply IAS 12 at the date of transition. There will also be deferred tax impacts from some of the other accounting policy changes that are made on transition to IFRS or on use of exemptions in IFRS 1. The implementation guidance to IFRS 1 notes that an entity should apply IAS 12 to temporary differences between the carrying amount of the assets and liabilities in its opening IFRS balance sheet and their tax bases. [IFRS 1 para IG5]. These deferred tax impacts should also be accounted for as part of the adjustments made on transition, against retained earnings or another appropriate category of equity. Again, in limited circumstances deferred tax is adjusted against goodwill. See further paragraph 2.72.

Exceptions to the retrospective application of other IFRSs

2.30 The general requirement of IFRS 1 is full retrospective application of all accounting standards effective at the end of an entity's first IFRS reporting period. IFRS 1 has two categories of exceptions to full retrospective application – mandatory exceptions and optional exemptions.

2.31 The exemptions and exceptions and their application are summarised below.

Mandatory exceptions from full retrospective application	Scope – exception applies to	Dealt with from
Estimates.	All estimates, unless the bases adopted are not compliant with IFRS.	Paragraph 2.32.
Derecognition of financial assets and liabilities.	All non-derivative financial assets and liabilities derecognised before the date of transition unless the entity decides to adjust retrospectively per paragraph B3 of IFRS 1.	Paragraph 2.38.
Hedge accounting.	All hedging relationships in existence from accounting periods beginning prior to adoption of IAS 39.	Paragraph 2.40.
Non-controlling interests.	All equity in a subsidiary not attributable, directly or indirectly, to a parent.	Paragraph 2.52.
Classification and measurement of financial assets	Classification and measurement of financial assets must be based on facts and circumstances existing at the transition date.	Paragraph 2.54.
Embedded derivatives	Embedded derivatives might need to be separated based on an assessment of the conditions at the later of the date it first became a party to the contract and any reassessment required by paragraph B4.3.11 of IFRS 9.	Paragraph 2.55.
Government loans	All government grants classified as financial liabilities per IAS 32. Apply IFRS 9 and IAS 20 requirements retrospectively for loans originated before the date of transition.	Paragraph 2.56.

Optional exemptions from full retrospective application	Scope – where exemption taken, it applies to	Dealt with from
Business combinations.	All business combinations prior to the transition date, or if choose to apply IFRS 3 to a combination prior to the transition date then exemption applies to all combinations prior to that one.	Paragraph 2.58.
Share-based payment transactions.	Equity instruments granted on or before 7 November 2002 or equity instruments granted after 7 November 2002 and vested by the date of transition.	Paragraph 2.99.
Insurance contracts.	All insurance contracts.	Paragraph 2.106.

Deemed cost.	Any tangible fixed asset, investment property and to a limited number of intangible assets.	Paragraph 2.107.
Leases.	All arrangements that contain a lease.	Paragraph 2.129.
Employee benefits.	All employee benefit plans.	Paragraph 2.132.
Cumulative translation differences.	All cumulative translation differences existing at the date of transition to IFRS.	Paragraph 2.138.
Investments in subsidiaries, jointly controlled entities and associates.	Any investments in subsidiaries, jointly controlled entities and associates in separate financial statements.	Paragraph 2.143.
Assets and liabilities of subsidiaries, associates and joint ventures.	All assets and liabilities of individual subsidiaries, associates and joint ventures whose transition date is different to the parent/ group.	Paragraph 2.146.
Compound financial instruments.	All compound financial instruments where the liability component has been settled by the date of transition to IFRS.	Paragraph 2.159.
Designation of previously recognised financial instruments.	Any financial instrument.	Paragraph 2.161.
Fair value measurement of financial assets or financial liabilities at initial recognition.	All relevant financial assets or financial liabilities.	Paragraph 2.166.
Decommissioning liabilities included in the cost of property, plant and equipment.	All decommissioning liabilities.	Paragraph 2.170.
Financial assets or intangible assets accounted for in accordance with IFRIC 12.	All relevant financial assets or intangible assets accounted for in accordance with IFRIC 12.	Paragraph 2.174.
Borrowing costs.	All borrowing costs.	Paragraph 2.176.
Transfers of assets from customers	Transfers of assets from customers in the scope of IFRIC 18.	Paragraph 2.179.
Severe hyper-inflation	Any entity with functional currency that was, or is, the currency of a hyper-inflationary economy.	Paragraph 2.181.
Joint arrangements	A first-time adopter may apply the transition provisions in IFRS 11 with certain exceptions.	Paragraph 2.182.
Stripping costs	First-time adopters may apply the transitional provisions set out in paragraphs A1 to A4 of IFRIC 20.	Paragraph 2.183.
Extinguishing financial liabilities with equity instruments	Extinguishing of financial liabilities within the scope of IFRIC 19.'	Paragraph 2.184.

Estimates

2.32   The first mandatory exception from full retrospective application of IFRS is in the area of estimates. The standard requires that:

> *"An entity's estimates in accordance with IFRSs at the date of transition to IFRSs shall be consistent with estimates made for the same date in accordance with previous GAAP (after adjustments to reflect any difference in accounting policies), unless there is objective evidence that those estimates were in error."* [IFRS 1 para 14].

2.33   Paragraph 17 of IFRS 1 clarifies that the same rule applies to the comparative period in an entity's first IFRS financial statements. That is, hindsight cannot be used either at the date of transition or at any point during the comparative period, including the end of the comparative year. If more information comes to light about estimates made under previous GAAP then it should be treated in the same way as non-adjusting events after the balance sheet date under IAS 10. [IFRS 1 para 15]. This applies unless the information shows that the previous estimate was in error.

2.34   Certain estimates may not have been required by a first-time adopter's previous GAAP (or at the date of the comparative balance sheet), but are required by IFRS. IFRS 1 requires entities to make those estimates on transition and to base those estimates on conditions that existed at the date of transition (or at the date of the comparative balance sheet). [IFRS 1 para 16]. Estimates should not be updated for conditions later than the date of transition to IFRS (or the date of the comparative balance sheet in the first IFRS financial statements). For example, an entity may have to fair value a particular asset when adopting IFRS that it did not have to fair value under its previous GAAP. Any estimates that are required to determine fair value should be based on conditions at the date of transition to IFRS (or the date of the comparative balance sheet) and not on later conditions. An entity may have to make an estimate on transition to IFRS 'as at' a date earlier than the date of transition to IFRS. In that case, the estimate should be based on conditions existing at that earlier date. This is illustrated by example 1 in paragraph 2.36.

2.35 The following decision chart summarises the guidance:

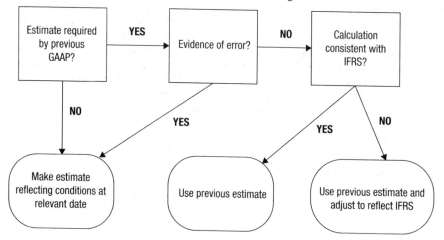

2.36 Situations where a calculation, or method of estimation, is not consistent with IFRS are not explicitly covered by IFRS 1. Paragraph 14 says that adjustments are only made in the case of errors or differences in policy, and not in cases of differences in methods of calculation. However, there is support in the implementation guidance of IFRS 1 for adjustments being made in cases where the calculation is not consistent with IFRS. *"...in some cases, an entity's depreciation methods and rates under previous GAAP may differ from those that would be acceptable under IFRSs (for example, if they were adopted solely for tax purposes and do not reflect a reasonable estimate of the asset's useful life). If those differences have a material effect on the financial statements, the entity adjusts accumulated depreciation in its opening IFRS balance sheet retrospectively so that it complies with IFRSs"*. [IFRS 1 para IG7]. Our view is, therefore, that where a method of estimation used under previous GAAP does not accord with that required by IFRS, the IFRS method of estimation should be used. The requirements are illustrated by the following examples.

UK.2.36.1 The implications of the guidance in IAS 39 with respect to impairment of financial assets for UK first-time adopters is discussed further in paragraph UK.2.216.122.

Example 1 – Estimates: compound financial instrument

Entity R issued a 10 year convertible bond on 31 July 20X3. It is convertible at the option of the holder from 1 January 20X7. Entity R has a date of transition to IFRS of 1 January 20X4.

Under previous GAAP the bond is recorded at its net proceeds. A finance charge is accrued at a constant rate on the carrying amount.

IAS 32 requires that a convertible bond should be split between its debt and equity components. [IAS 32 para 28]. Since the liability element of the instrument is still outstanding at entity R's date of transition, it cannot take the compound instruments exemption (described from para 2.159). On transition to IFRS, entity R must estimate the split of the compound financial instrument. This is an estimate that was not required under previous GAAP. Entity R should estimate the fair values of the components, using the guidance in paragraph 28 of IAS 32, as at 31 July 20X3. To select an appropriate discount rate, entity R should use the market conditions at 31 July 20X3, the date the instrument was issued. [IFRS 1 para IG36]. The cumulative finance costs should also be adjusted to the date of transition, based on the new carrying value of the debt. All adjustments should be reflected in retained earnings on transition to IFRS.

Example 2 – Estimates: legal provision

Entity S made a provision for C4m in its 31 December 20X3 previous GAAP financial statements for a litigation against the entity by one of its customers. This reflects conditions existing at that date: the possibility of litigation was uncertain; the claim was for damages of C8m, but the entity ascertained that the other party would probably settle for C4m without taking the case to court. A provision of C4m was made as a best estimate of the liability based on management's assessment and on advice from the company's lawyers.

Entity S's customer decided to take the case to court in 20X4. The case had not been heard by the time the 20X4 financial statements were approved. In its 20X4 financial statements the entity estimated that a provision of C5m best represented the most likely outcome and the provision was increased.

The case was settled in May 20X5 and entity S had to pay damages and costs of C5.5m.

Entity S prepares its first IFRS financial statements for the year to 31 December 20X5, presenting one year of comparative information. Its opening IFRS balance sheet is 1 January 20X4. The relevant standard under IFRS is IAS 37, which contains similar requirements in respect of such provisions to the equivalent standard in entity S's previous GAAP.

An estimate of the liability was required by entity S's previous GAAP and there is no evidence that its original estimate was in error. Therefore, in its opening IFRS balance sheet it should record a liability of C4m.

Similarly, the provision in entity S's balance sheet at 31 December 20X4 should remain at C5m, with C1m charged to the income statement in that period.

Entity S's 20X5 IFRS financial statements will reflect the outcome of the case, with a charge of C0.5m and settlement of the liability.

This is despite the fact that when the 20X5 first IFRS financial statements are prepared the outcome of the court case is known. Revisions to estimates are made prospectively whether an entity is moving to IFRS for the first time or not.

(See example 4 below for the scenario where a provision was not recognised under previous GAAP.)

Example 3 – Estimates: bad debt impairment

Entity T has consistently applied the following bad debt impairment method under its previous GAAP:

Debtors more than 60 days overdue 10%
Debtors more than 90 days overdue 25%
Debtors more than 180 days overdue 50%
Debtors more than 240 days overdue 100%

In addition to this, large balances are examined individually and allowances are made where management feel this is necessary.

Entity T adopts IFRS. An allowance to write down debtors to their recoverable amount was required under previous GAAP and is required under IFRS. Paragraph 59 of IAS 39 prescribes a detailed methodology for estimating impairment of financial assets.

The method required by IAS 39 to estimate the amount of impairment is different from that used by entity T under its previous GAAP. The allowance should, therefore, be updated for the IAS 39 methodology at the date of transition, with any adjustment made to retained earnings or another appropriate category of equity. Any assumptions should, however, stay the same. So if, for example, information available at the date of transition indicated that a particular debtor was unlikely to pay, then that information should be used in the opening IFRS balance sheet. This is the case even if the debtor subsequently did pay.

Example 4 – Estimates upon first time adoption of IFRS 1

The following example is based on IG example 1 in the implementation guidance to IFRS 1.

Entity U's first IFRS financial statements have a reporting date of 31 December 20X5 and include comparative information for one year as well as an opening balance sheet as at the date of transition to IFRS. In its previous GAAP financial statements for 31 December 20X3 and 20X4, entity U:

- Made estimates of accrued expenses and provisions at those dates.

- Accounted on a cash basis for a defined benefit pension plan.

- Did not recognise a provision for a court case arising from events that occurred in September 20X4. When the court case was concluded on 30 June 20X5, entity U was required to pay C1,000 and paid this on 10 July 20X5.

Application of requirements

In preparing its opening IFRS balance sheet at 1 January 20X4 and in its comparative balance sheet at 31 December 20X4, entity U:

(a)   Concludes that its estimates under previous GAAP of accrued expenses and provisions at 31 December 20X3 and 20X4 were made on a basis consistent with its accounting policies under IFRSs. Although some of the accruals and provisions turned out to be overestimates and others to be underestimates, entity U concludes that its estimates were reasonable and that, therefore, no error had occurred. Entity U, therefore, does not adjust the previous estimates for accrued expenses and provisions.

(b)   Makes estimates (in the form of actuarial assumptions) necessary to account for the pension plan under IAS 19. Entity U's actuarial assumptions at 1 January 20X4 and 31 December 20X4 do not reflect conditions that arose after those dates. For example:

    (i)   Discount rates at 1 January 20X4 and 31 December 20X4 for the pension plan and for provisions reflect market conditions at those dates.

    (ii)   Actuarial assumptions at 1 January 20X4 and 31 December 20X4 about future employee turnover rates do not reflect conditions that arose after those dates — such as a significant increase in estimated employee turnover rates as a result of a curtailment of the pension plan in 20X5.

(c)   The treatment of the court case at 31 December 20X4 depends on the reason why entity U did not recognise a provision under previous GAAP at that date.

Assumption 1 – Previous GAAP was consistent with IAS 37. Entity U concluded that the recognition criteria were not met. In this case, entity U's assumptions under IFRSs are consistent with its assumptions under previous GAAP. Therefore, entity U does not recognise a provision at 31 December 20X4. (See example 2 above for the scenario where a provision was recognised under previous GAAP.)

Assumption 2 – Previous GAAP was not consistent with IAS 37. Therefore, entity U develops estimates under IAS 37. Under IAS 37, an entity determines whether an obligation exists at the balance sheet date by taking account of all available evidence, including any additional evidence provided by events after the balance sheet date. Similarly, under IAS 10, the resolution of a court case after the balance sheet date is an adjusting event after the balance sheet date if it confirms that the entity had a present obligation at that date. In this instance, the resolution of the court case confirms that entity U had a liability in September 20X4 (when the events occurred that gave rise to the court case). Therefore, entity U recognises a provision at 31 December 20X4. Entity U measures that provision by discounting the C1,000 paid on 10 July 20X5 to its present value, using a discount rate that complies with IAS 37 and reflects market conditions at 31 December 20X4.

2.37   Estimates should be consistent with those made under previous GAAP *"after adjustments to reflect any difference in accounting policies"*. If, for example, an entity decides to adopt the revaluation model in IAS 16 for a class of property, plant and equipment it will do so from the date of transition as a change in accounting policy. Depending on whether the deemed cost exemption is applied, the entity may have to revalue its property, plant and equipment at the date of transition, resulting in a greater or lesser depreciation charge in the entity's first IFRS financial statements. This revaluation is part of the change in policy (to a revaluation basis) and should be accounted for retrospectively. The remaining useful economic lives of the class of property, plant and equipment are revised from 20X5, this should be accounted for prospectively and should not form part of the adjustment on transition to IFRS.

Derecognition

2.38 The mandatory exception from full retrospective application of the derecognition rules in IAS 39 applies to all financial assets and liabilities derecognised before 1 January 2004. [IFRS 1 App B para B2]. The exception requires first-time adopters to prospectively apply the derecognition criteria for non-derivative financial assets and liabilities per IAS 39 from 1 January 2004 onwards. This means that: (i) non-derivative financial assets and liabilities that were derecognised under previous GAAP before January 2004 will remain derecognised; therefore, those transactions would not have to be reconstructed; and (ii) non-derivative financial assets and liabilities that were derecognised under previous GAAP after 1 January 2004 will be recognised again in the financial statements of first time adopters, if they don't qualify for derecognition under IAS 39. Therefore, those transactions would have to be reconstructed using available information. The existing scope of this exception means that it is unlikely to be applicable for many current first time adopters. The IASB issued an amendment to IFRS 1 in December 2010 to replace the fixed date of 1 January 2004 with a reference to 'the date of transition to IFRSs', in order to provide relief to first-time adopters from having to reconstruct past transactions on transition. The effective date of the amendment is for annual periods beginning on or after 1 July 2011 with early adoption permitted.

2.39 However, an entity can elect to recognise non-financial assets and liabilities by reconstructing the related past transactions if the relevant information is available. More specifically, paragraph B3 of appendix B to IFRS 1 allows an entity to retrospectively apply the derecognition requirements in IAS 39 from a date of the entity's choosing, provided that such an entity has the information required by IAS 39 at the time of initially accounting for those transactions.

Hedge accounting

2.40 IFRS 1 includes a mandatory exception related to hedge accounting. Entities are unlikely to have adopted the criteria for documenting and testing hedges prior to preparing to adopt IFRS, even if those hedging strategies might be able to be used under IAS 39. [IFRS 1 para BC75]. Allowing entities to designate hedges retrospectively is open to abuse: designation (or not) might be driven by the impact on the income statement. IFRS 1, therefore, allows hedge accounting to be used only from the date that the designation and documentation of a hedge relationship is completed. The stages in the process can be illustrated in the flow chart below and are described in the paragraphs that follow.

First-time adoption of IFRS

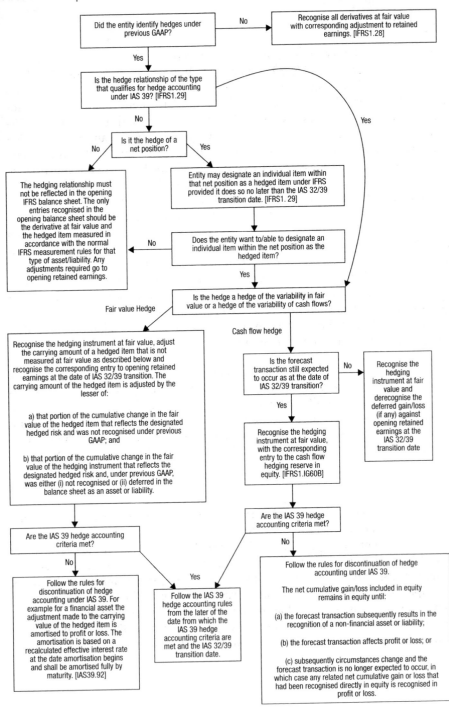

2.41 The first stage is to identify and fair value all derivative financial instruments and to remove all deferred losses and gains that arose on derivatives and were reported under previous GAAP as if they were assets or liabilities. [IFRS 1 App B para B4]. This should be done at the date of transition. The amounts that should be considered in this context include all amounts held on an entity's balance sheet in respect of derivative financial instruments, including those resulting from accrual accounting for derivatives under previous GAAP.

UK.2.41.1 In practical terms, UK entities required to apply the EU 2005 Regulation will already have applied FRS 29. Companies applying FRS 25 (IAS 32) will also have been disclosing fair values. They will, therefore, already have been calculating the fair value of derivative financial instruments for disclosure purposes though the fair value methodologies will have to be reviewed to ensure that they are consistent with IAS 39 and the values produced are reliable for measurement purposes. As regards deferred gains and losses, many UK entities that have not applied FRS 26 (IAS 39) did not carry separate amounts on the balance sheet in respect of most derivative financial instruments, except where the balance sheet date is not the same as the date on which the hedged transaction occurs. Whether the hedge accounting criteria are met at the date of transition, all deferred gains and losses must be removed from the balance sheet and all derivatives must be measured at fair value.

2.42 Entities should then consider whether the relationship that has been designated as a hedge under previous GAAP would qualify as a hedging relationship under IAS 39. Hedge accounting under IAS 39 is covered in chapter 6. Where an entity has a hedging relationship under previous GAAP that is a type that would not qualify as a hedge under IFRS, the elements of the relationship are accounted for under normal IFRS rules. So, for example, any derivative financial instruments forming part of the relationship will be measured at fair value with changes in fair value being recorded in comprehensive income. The only exception to this is for hedges of net positions. IFRS 1 states that in cases where a net position has been designated as a hedged item under previous GAAP, entities may designate individual items within that net position as hedged items under IFRS. [IFRS 1 App B para B5].

UK.2.42.1 One example of such a hedge occurs because of the treatment under IFRS of goodwill reported directly in reserves. Under UK GAAP, such goodwill may form part of the overall net investment that was hedged using the SSAP 20 cover method to the extent that it would not have been amortised had a policy of capitalisation and amortisation been followed. This is because the write off is a consequence of following an accounting policy, not because of the fact that the goodwill has lost its value. On first-time adoption of IFRS, goodwill that has been written off to reserves cannot be restated or recycled, either on transition or at any later date (see further para 2.75). Hedge accounting principles in IFRS require that the hedged item could affect profit or loss. Since the goodwill that is in reserves may never be capitalised or recycled on disposal then it will not affect profit or loss. For this reason goodwill written off to reserves cannot be subject to hedge accounting. Any portion of the hedging instrument that under UK GAAP was used to hedge the goodwill cannot be designated as a hedging instrument under IFRS. There is no effect at the point of transition, since amounts that have been recorded in reserves under the UK GAAP hedge would have to be recorded through the income statement under IFRS. Since all amounts are now in retained earnings at the date of transition 'reversal' of the hedge has no impact. It will only affect entities after transition. From this point, what was the hedging instrument (a foreign currency loan or a forward contract, for example) should be accounted for under normal IFRS rules.

2.43 Where the hedging relationship is of a type that would qualify under IAS 39, entities should make adjustments at the date of transition. In essence, the adjustments put entities in the position as if they had hedge accounted under IAS 39 up to the date of transition to IFRS. For fair value hedges, entities should adjust the carrying value of the hedged item. This adjustment results in the carrying amount of the hedged item reflecting the designated hedged risk. Entities must determine the cumulative change in the fair value of the hedged item reflecting the designated hedged risk that was not recognised under previous GAAP. This is compared to the cumulative change in the fair value of the hedging instrument reflecting the designated hedged risk that was either not recognised under previous GAAP or deferred as an asset or liability in the balance sheet. The adjustment to the carrying value of the hedged item should be the lower of these two amounts. [IFRS 1 para IG60A]. If some part of it had been previously recognised or deferred under previous GAAP then the difference should be adjusted on application of IAS 39.

Example – Fair value hedge accounting

Entity A prepares its first IFRS financial statements at 31 December 20X7 and its IFRS transition date is 1 January 20X6.

Entity A has a C100,000 5% fixed-rate loan asset that is hedged in a fair value hedge relationship under previous GAAP using a pay-fixed/receive-floating interest rate swap. The loan was accounted for at cost and the derivative was not recognised under previous GAAP. Entity A's management classifies the loan as 'loans and receivables' under IAS 39. The former hedge relationship is of a type that is permitted under IAS 39. At 1 January 20X6 the loan has an amortised cost of C100,000, the interest rate swap has a positive fair value of C5,100 and the negative fair value change of the loan attributable to the hedged risk is C4,900. Management has also prepared all the necessary designation and documentation that meets the IAS 39 requirements by 1 January 20X6. The hedge is expected to be highly effective.

Management should recognise the derivative at its fair value of C5,100 at 1 January 20X6, with the corresponding entry to retained earnings. The loan's carrying amount is adjusted by C4,900. This is the lesser of the change in fair value of the hedging instrument from the designated hedged risk and the change in the fair value of the hedged item from the designated hedged risk. [IFRS 1 para IG60A].

The changes in fair value of the derivative and the changes in fair value attributable to the hedged risk of the loan are recognised in the income statement in the following periods. [IAS 39 para 89].

2.44   Certain GAAPs may permit an assumption of no ineffectiveness or a short-cut method to evaluating hedge effectiveness if the critical terms of the hedging instrument and hedging item match. While the hedging relationship may qualify for hedge accounting under IAS 39, the documentation and effectiveness testing performed under the prior GAAP may not comply with IAS 39. Paragraph B6 of IFRS 1 indicates that if, before the date of transition, an entity had designated a transaction as a hedge but it did not meet the conditions in IAS 39, the entity should discontinue hedge accounting. Therefore, if IFRS compliant documentation and effectiveness testing is put in place as of, or prior to, the date of transition, hedge accounting could be continued.

2.45   The entity should record the cumulative change in fair value of the hedging instrument of a cash flow hedge as a separate component of other comprehensive income. IAS 39 requires the amounts recorded in the cash flow hedging reserve to be reclassified to the income statement in the period(s) the transaction affects profit or loss. The amount that is recorded in the cash flow hedging reserve at the transition date should reflect the extent that the transaction has not yet affected profit or loss. If some or all of the transaction had affected profit or loss prior to the transition date then the reserve should be adjusted at transition to reflect this, with the amount that would have been recorded in the income statement being transferred to the profit and loss reserve.

UK.2.46.1   Where a hedging instrument was terminated but the hedged item still exists under UK GAAP, the gain or loss arising on termination of the hedging instrument is generally deferred on the balance sheet and spread over what would have been the remaining period of the original hedge. Our view is that in such cases entities should also make the adjustments described in paragraphs 2.45 and 2.46 above and then apply the provisions in paragraphs 2.49 and 2.50 below.

Example – Cash flow hedge accounting

Entity B prepares its first IFRS financial statements to 31 December 20X7 and its IFRS transition date is 1 January 20X6.

Entity B has a floating rate loan asset that is hedged in a cash flow hedge relationship under previous GAAP, using a pay-floating/receive-fixed interest rate swap. Neither the loan nor the derivative was accounted for at fair value under previous GAAP. The loan is classified as a 'loans and receivables' under IFRS so the hedge relationship is of a type that qualifies for hedge accounting under IAS 39.

Management should measure the derivative at fair value (with the corresponding entry to the cash flow hedging reserve). The loan balance is not adjusted for the hedge relationship. The impact in equity is the fair value of the derivative. [IFRS 1 para IG60B].

The effective portion of subsequent changes in fair value of the derivative is recognised in other comprehensive income in the cash flow hedging reserve in the following periods and the ineffective portion of the changes in fair value of the derivative are recognised in the income statement. The amounts included in cash flow hedging reserve are subsequently included in the income statement in the same period or periods during which the forecast transaction affects profit or loss. [IAS 39 para 100].

2.46 For a hedge of a net investment the IFRS 1 exemption regarding cumulative translation differences (CTDs) are relevant. IFRS 1 provides relief from separately classifying CTDs prior to an entity's date of transition to IFRS and consequently reclassifying those differences to the income statement on disposal of the foreign operation (see further from para 2.138 below). Where the exemption is applied, CTDs prior to an entity's date of transition are recognised in retained earnings at the transition date. Paragraph D12 in Appendix D of IFRS 1 notes that the requirement of IAS 21 is that *"gains and losses on related hedges"* should be transferred to the income statement on disposal along with the CTDs. However, IFRS 1 does not specify whether entities are relieved from transferring any pre-transition gains and losses where the CTD exemption has been applied. Our view is that entities are exempt from transferring pre-transition translation differences on the hedging instrument to the income statement where the CTD exemption has been applied. Pre-transition gains and losses would, therefore, be recognised in retained earnings at the transition date. This avoids a mismatch in the income statement on disposal of reclassifying these translation differences whilst not recycling these hedged pre-transition CTDs. Since, however, the IAS 21 exemption applies only up to the date of transition to IFRS, entities should separately classify currency differences on hedging instruments from the date of transition to IFRS.

2.47 Once the adjustments described in paragraphs 2.45 and 2.46 above have been made, entities should consider whether the relationship that has been designated as a hedge under previous GAAP meets all the criteria for hedge accounting at the date of transition to IFRS. These are:

- There is formal designation and documentation of the hedging relationship and the entity's risk management objective and strategy for undertaking the hedge.

- The hedge is expected to be highly effective.

- For cash flow hedges, if the subject of the hedge is a forecast transaction it must be highly probable and should present an exposure to cash flow variations that could ultimately affect profit or loss.

- The effectiveness of the hedge can be reliably measured.

- Following the date of transition, the hedge is assessed on an ongoing basis and determined to be highly effective.

[IAS 39 para 88].

2.48   The entity can apply hedge accounting for the particular relationship under IAS 39 only if all of the above criteria are met.

> **Example – Hedging criteria under IAS 39**
>
> Entity C prepares its first IFRS financial statements to 31 December 20X7 and its IFRS transition date is 1 January 20X6.
>
> Entity C has a C100,000 5% fixed rate debt security that was hedged in a fair value hedge under previous GAAP with an interest rate swap. The debt security will be classified as available for sale (AFS) under IAS 39. There is an unrealised gain of C4,500 on the AFS and an unrealised loss on the swap of 5,000 at 1 January 20X6. Neither the gain nor the loss was recognised in the financial statements under previous GAAP. The change in the fair value of the AFS attributable to the change in interest rates (the hedged risk) is C4,800.
>
> What accounting entries should be recorded at 1 January 20X6 on the basis that the hedging relationship still qualifies for hedge accounting under IAS 39?
>
> The following entries are required at the transition date:
>
> | | | C | C |
> |---|---|---|---|
> | Dr | Opening retained earnings | 5,000 | |
> | | Cr   Derivative liability | | 5,000 |
> | To reflect the derivative at fair value | | | |
> | Dr | AFS Security | 4,500 | |
> | | Cr   Opening retained earnings | | 4,800 |
> | Dr | AFS reserve | 300 | |
>
> The carrying amount of the AFS is adjusted to reflect the full change in its fair value (that is, C4,500). This has two components: (a) the adjustment related to the hedged risk of C4,800; and (b) the remaining portion of the change in the fair value of the AFS (C300) in the AFS reserve.
>
> The net impact in equity is the difference between the change in the fair value of the AFS and the fair value of the derivative. [IFRS 1 para IG60A].
>
> The changes in the derivative's fair value are recognised in the income statement in the subsequent periods. The changes in fair value attributable to the hedged risk of the AFS also are recognised in the income statement. The changes in fair value attributable to remaining risks of the AFS are recognised in the AFS reserve. [IAS 39 para 89].

2.49   If any of the above criteria are not met, the entity should discontinue hedge accounting following the guidance in IAS 39. [IFRS 1 App B para B6]. IAS 39 requires hedge accounting to be discontinued prospectively where the hedge accounting criteria are not met. [IAS 39 para 91]. For a cash flow hedge that does not meet the criteria, the amount recorded in the cash flow hedging reserve at the transition date remains in equity until the forecast transaction occurs. [IAS 39 para 101].

2.50 Paragraph 91 of IAS 39 deals with discontinued fair value hedges. It gives the conditions where hedge accounting should be discontinued and states that hedge accounting should be discontinued prospectively. From the date of transition the hedged item will not be adjusted for the gain or loss on the hedged item attributable to the hedged risk, for financial assets or liabilities carried at cost or amortised cost. Any adjustments that had previously been made to the carrying value of a financial asset or liability for which the effective interest method is used should be amortised to the income statement, based on a recalculated effective interest rate. [IAS 39 para 92]. Available for sale financial assets will be measured at fair value from the date of transition to IFRS with gains and losses (excluding effective interest) recorded in other comprehensive income and not through the income statement. All derivatives will be measured at fair value through the income statement.

Example 1 – Discontinue fair value hedge accounting: loan

Entity D prepares its first IFRS financial statements at 31 December 20X7, and its IFRS transition date is 1 January 20X6.

Entity D had a 5% fixed-rate loan asset that was hedged in a fair value hedge relationship under previous GAAP using a pay-fixed/receive-floating cross currency interest rate swap. The loan was accounted for at cost and the derivative was not recognised under previous GAAP. Entity D's management will classify the loan as 'loans and receivables' under IAS 39. The former hedge relationship is of a type that is permitted under IAS 39.

At 1 January 20X6 the loan has an amortised cost of C100,000, the cross currency interest rate swap has a positive fair value of C5,000 and the negative fair value change of the loan attributable to the hedged risk is C3,000. Management does not expect the hedging relationship to be highly effective going forward.

Management should recognise the derivative at its fair value of C5,000 with the corresponding entry to retained earnings at the date of IFRS transition. The carrying amount of the loan is adjusted by C3,000. This represents the lower of that portion of the fair value change of the hedged item from the designated hedged risk and the fair value change of the hedging instrument from the designated hedged risk (C5,000). [IFRS 1 para IG60A].

Management should then discontinue hedge accounting. The C3,000 adjustment to the loan that was made on transition is amortised over the life of the loan using the effective interest rate method and the changes in fair value of the derivative continue to be recognised in the income statement. [IAS 39 para 92].

Example 2 – Discontinue fair value hedge accounting: AFS security

Entity E prepares its first IFRS financial statements to 31 December 20X7 and its IFRS transition date is 1 January 20X6.

Entity E (a C functional currency company) had a C100,000 5% fixed rate debt security that is hedged in a fair value hedge relationship under previous GAAP. The hedging instrument is a pay-fixed/receive-floating cross currency interest rate swap that was entered into when entity E bought the security. The security was accounted for at cost and the derivative was held off balance sheet under previous GAAP. Entity E will classify the security as AFS under IAS 39. The former hedge relationship is of a type that is permitted under IAS 39.

The cross currency interest rate swap has a negative fair value of C5,000 and the change in fair value of the AFS is a positive fair value of C3,000 at 1 January 20X6. The change in the fair value of the AFS attributable to the hedged risk is C3,500. Management does not expect the hedging relationship to be highly effective going forward. It will not meet the IAS 39 requirements for hedge accounting.

The following entries are recorded at the transition date:

		C	C
Dr	Opening retained earnings	5,000	
	Cr Derivative liability		5,000
To reflect the derivative at fair value			
Dr	AFS Security	3,000	
	Cr Opening retained earnings		3,500
Dr	AFS reserve	500	

The carrying amount of the AFS is adjusted to reflect the full change in its fair value (that is, C3,000). However, this comprises two components; the adjustment related to the hedged risk of C3,500 and the remaining portion of the fair value of the AFS (C500) in the AFS reserve.

The net impact in equity is the difference between the change in fair value of the AFS and the derivative's fair value. [IFRS 1 para IG60A].

The hedging relationship is discontinued from 1 January 20X6. Subsequent changes in the fair value of the AFS are reflected in the AFS reserve and the changes in the derivative's fair value are recognised in the income statement. The C3,500 transition adjustment is now amortised through the income statement using the effective interest method. The amount will be fully amortised by the security's maturity. [IAS 39 para 92].

2.51 Paragraph 101 of IAS 39 covers discontinued cash flow hedges and hedges of a net investment. There are five scenarios.

■ If the hedging instrument expires or is sold, terminated or exercised the cumulative gain or loss remains in other comprehensive income until the forecast transaction occurs. At this point paragraphs 97, 98 or 100 of IAS 39 apply. [IAS 39 para 101(a)]. Broadly, these state that the amounts deferred in equity are released to the income statement in the same period(s) that the hedged transaction affects profit or loss.

■ If the hedge no longer meets the criteria for hedge accounting the cumulative gain or loss remains separately recognised in other comprehensive income until the forecast transaction occurs. At this point paragraphs 97, 98 or 100 of IAS 39 apply. [IAS 39 para 101(b)]. Gains and losses on the hedging instrument arising from the date the hedge relationship fails are recognised directly in the income statement, under normal IAS 39 rules.

■ In cases where the forecast transaction is not highly probable but is expected to occur, the net cumulative gain or loss reclassified in other comprehensive income on application of IAS 39 remains there until either the forecast transaction results in the recognition of a non-financial asset or liability, the forecast transaction affects profit or loss or the forecast transaction is no longer expected to occur. The cumulative gain or loss is recognised in the income statement when one of the three possible outcomes occurs. [IFRS 1 para IG60B]. Gains and losses on the hedging instrument arising after the date on which the hedge relationship fails are recognised directly in the income statement, under normal IAS 39 rules.

■ If hedge accounting ceased because the forecast transaction that was hedged is no longer expected to occur, gains and losses deferred in other comprehensive income are recognised in the income statement immediately. [IAS 39 para 101(c)].

■ If the hedge designation is revoked the cumulative gain or loss remains in other comprehensive income until the forecast transaction occurs or is no longer expected to occur. When the transaction occurs; paragraphs 97, 98 or 100 of IAS 39 apply. If the transaction is no longer expected to occur the cumulative gain or loss deferred should be recognised in the income statement. [IAS 39 para 101(d)]. Gains and losses on the hedging instrument arising from the date on which the hedge relationship fails are recognised directly in the income statement, under normal IAS 39 rules.

Example 1 – Discontinue cash flow hedge accounting: loan

Entity F prepares its first IFRS financial statements to 31 December 20X7 and its IFRS transition date is 1 January 20X6.

Entity F has a floating rate loan asset that is hedged in a cash flow hedge relationship under previous GAAP, using a pay-floating/receive-fixed interest rate swap. Neither the loan nor the derivative was accounted for at fair value under previous GAAP. The loan is classified as a 'loans and receivables' under IFRS so the hedge relationship is of a type that qualifies for hedge accounting under IAS 39. However, the hedging relationship does not meet the hedge accounting criteria set out in IAS 39.

Management should measure the derivative at fair value (with the corresponding entry to cash flow hedging reserve). The loan balance is not adjusted for the hedge relationship. The impact in equity is the fair value of the derivative. [IFRS 1 para IG60B].

The hedging instrument is still held, but hedge accounting is no longer appropriate from the transition date. Any subsequent changes in the derivative's fair value are included in the income statement. The amounts included in other comprehensive income are reclassified to the income statement in the same period(s) during which the hedged item affects the income statement. [IAS 39 para 100].

Example 2 – Discontinue cash flow hedge accounting: Forecast transaction

Entity G prepares its first IFRS financial statements at 31 December 20X7 and its IFRS transition date is 1 January 20X6.

Entity G's management has designated a foreign currency forward contract as a cash flow hedge of a forecast transaction under previous GAAP. The foreign currency forward contract was designated as a hedge of a 20X6 forecast transaction under previous GAAP in June 20X4. By the transition date the transaction is no longer expected to occur.

Entity G must recognise the forward contract at fair value at 1 January 20X6. The forecast transaction is not expected to occur, so the corresponding entry on recognising the forward contract is to opening retained earnings rather than cash flow hedging reserve. Changes in the forward contract's fair value after 1 January 20X6 are recognised in the income statement.

Non-controlling interests

2.52 An entity must apply the following requirements of IAS 27 prospectively from the date of transition to IFRSs:

"*(a)   the requirement in [IAS 27] paragraph 28 that total comprehensive income is attributed to the owners of the parent and to the non-controlling interests even if this results in the non-controlling interests having a deficit balance;*

(b)   the requirements in [IAS 27] paragraphs 30 and 31 for accounting for changes in the parent's ownership interest in a subsidiary that do not result in a loss of control; and

(c)   the requirements in [IAS 27] paragraphs 34-37 for accounting for a loss of control over a subsidiary."

[IFRS 1 App B para B7].

2.53 However, if a first-time adopter elects to apply IFRS 3 retrospectively to past business combinations, it must restate all later business combinations and must also apply IAS 27 from that same date in accordance with paragraph C1 of IFRS 1. [IFRS 1 App B para B7].

Classification and measurement of financial assets

2.54 The IASB published IFRS 9 on classification and measurement of financial assets applicable for annual periods beginning on or after 1 January 2015 (after the IASB issued amendments in 2011) with earlier application permitted. IFRS 9 has two measurement categories: amortised cost and fair value. Where an entity applies IFRS 9 in its first IFRS financial statements, the classification and measurement guidance in paragraphs 4.1 to 4.4 of IFRS 9 must be applied based on facts and circumstance existing at the transition date. [IFRS 1 App B para B8].

Embedded derivatives

2.55 IFRS 9 requires an entity to assess whether an embedded derivative is required to be separated from the host contract and accounted for as a derivative when the entity first becomes a party to the contract. Subsequent re-assessment is prohibited unless there is a change in the contract's terms that significantly modifies the cash flows that otherwise would be required under the contract, in which case re-assessment is required. An entity determines whether a modification to cash flows is significant by considering the extent to which the expected future cash flows associated with the embedded derivative, the host contract or both have changed and whether the change is significant relative to the contract's previously expected cash flows.

2.55.1 A mandatory exception has been included in IFRS 1 in relation to embedded derivatives. A first-time adopter shall assess whether an embedded derivative is required to be separated from the host contract and accounted for as a derivative on the basis of the conditions that existed at the *later* of: (a) the date it first became a party to the contract and (b) the date a re-assessment is required by paragraph B4.3.11 of IFRS 9.

2.55.2 This exception is applicable to entities applying IFRS 9. IFRS 9 is applicable for annual periods beginning on or after 1 January 2015. Earlier application is permitted.

Government loans

2.56 IAS 20 requires that government loans with a below market rate of interest are measured at fair value on initial recognition. This raises practical issues for a first-time adopter as the general requirements in IFRS 1 to apply IFRSs retrospectively, may lead to an entity applying hindsight to derive a fair value at a date before the date of transition to IFRS.

2.56.1 Accordingly, there is now relief in paragraphs B10 and B 11 of IFRS 1 such that first-time adopters apply the requirements of IAS 20 prospectively to government loans existing at the date of transition to IFRS, unless the necessary information was obtained at the time of initially accounting for that loan. Consequently, if a first-time adopter did not, under its previous GAAP, recognise and measure a government loan in accordance with IAS 20, it uses the loan's previous GAAP carrying amount at the date of transition to IFRS as the loan's carrying amount in the opening IFRS statement of financial position. An entity applies IFRS 9 to the measurement of such loans after the date of transition to IFRS.

2.56.2 A further consequence of not applying IAS 20 and IFRS 9 retrospectively to government loans at the date of transition is that the corresponding benefit of the government loan at a below-market rate of interest is not recognised as a government grant.

2.56.3 A first-time adopter should classify all government loans received as a financial liabilities or an equity instruments in accordance with IAS 32.

Exemptions from full retrospective application

2.57 The general requirement of IFRS 1 is full retrospective application of all accounting standards effective at the end of an entity's first IFRS reporting period, whether those standards require prospective application or have specific transition rules. [IFRS 1 paras 7, 9]. IFRS 1 includes various targeted exemptions to this rule, where the IASB considered that retrospective application could prove to be too difficult or could result in a cost exceeding likely benefits to users. Any, all or none of these exemptions may be taken. The exemptions are not applied by analogy to other items. [IFRS 1 para 18]. Refer to the table in paragraph 2.31 above for a complete listing of all exemptions.

Business combinations

2.58 The exemption for business combinations is dealt with in Appendix C of IFRS 1 and may be complex to implement.

2.59 A revised version of IFRS 3 was published in 2008 and is effective for periods beginning on or after 1 July 2009. Furthermore, the revised version of IFRS 3 states that the standard can only be applied for reporting periods beginning on or after 30 June 2007. [IFRS 3 para 64]. This contrasts with IFRS 1, which allows an entity to restate past business combinations in accordance with IFRS 3 from any point in time. If a first-time adopter elects to apply IFRS 3 retrospectively to past business combinations, it must restate all later business combinations and must also apply IAS 27 from that same date. That date may be before a period beginning on or after 30 June 2007. [IFRS 1 App C para C1]. Paragraph 7 of IFRS 1 states an entity should use the same accounting policies in its opening balance sheet and throughout all periods presented. See the following example below.

> **Example – What version of IFRS 3 should a first-time adopter use if it chooses to restate business combinations prior to 30 June 2007 to IFRS?**
>
> An entity adopts IFRS for the first time in its financial statements prepared for the year ended 30 June 2010. The entity chooses to apply IFRS 3, and consequently IAS 27, to all business combinations arising on or after 1 July 2005. What version of IFRS 3 and IAS 27, should it use for business combinations that took place before and after 30 June 2007?
>
> IFRS 1 is clear that consistent accounting policies must be applied throughout all periods presented in an entity's first IFRS financial statements. The entity should not

apply different versions of IFRSs that were effective at earlier dates. [IFRS 1 para 8]. Thus, the entity would only apply the revised version of IFRS 3, and consequently IAS 27, for all business combinations and relevant transactions with non-controlling interests that took place on or after 1 July 2005. Business combinations prior to 1 July 2005 would not be restated.

2.60 The main provisions of the business combinations exemption are summarised in the table below:

	Provision	Adjustments made against	Dealt with from
Classification (as acquisition, merger, reverse acquisition)	■ Classification is the same as it was under previous GAAP.	■ Not applicable.	Paragraph 2.61.
Recognition ■ Assets and liabilities previously recognised in the business combination	■ Recognise all assets and liabilities in accordance with IFRS, except some financial assets and liabilities derecognised under previous GAAP, where the derecognition exception is applied. ■ Do not recognise assets and liabilities whose recognition is not permitted by IFRS.	■ Equity, except that, where an intangible asset is derecognised, it is adjusted against goodwill.	Paragraph 2.62.
■ Assets and liabilities not previously recognised in the business combination in consolidated balance sheet of the acquirer	■ Recognise assets and liabilities only if they would be recognised in accordance with IFRS in the financial statements of the acquired entity.	■ Equity, except where an intangible asset is recognised that had previously been subsumed within goodwill, which is adjusted against goodwill (as is related deferred tax and non-controlling interests).	Paragraph 2.64.

| Measurement | • Measure all assets and liabilities in accordance with IFRS.
• Where IFRS requires measurement at fair value, measure on this basis.
• For assets and liabilities measured at cost, the amount recorded on original combination is deemed cost for cost-based measurement.
• Assets and liabilities not previously recognised are measured on the basis IFRS would require in the financial statements of the acquired entity. | • Equity. | Paragraph 2.70. |

Classification

2.61 A first-time adopter may elect not to apply IFRS 3 retrospectively, that is, to business combinations that occurred before the date of transition to IFRS. The business combinations exemption applies to all transactions that meet the IFRS definition of a business combination (including business combinations outside the scope of IFRS 3, irrespective of its original classification under the entity's previous GAAP). If an entity decides to apply IFRS 3 to a business combination occurring before the transition date it must apply that standard as well as IAS 27 to all subsequent combinations. [IFRS 1 App C para C1]. Entities that choose to apply IFRS 3 to an earlier business combination must also apply IAS 36 and IAS 38 to those combinations.

Example 1 – IFRS 3 exemption from date prior to transition date

Entity V's management intends to present its first IFRS financial statements for the year ending 31 December 20Y0. The date of transition to IFRS is 1 January 20X9 and the opening IFRS balance sheet is prepared as at this date.

Entity V acquired at least one business every year from 20X0 to 20X9 and accounted for the business combinations in accordance with its previous GAAP. Entity V's management intends to apply the business combinations exemption in IFRS 1 and not restate any business combinations in the years from 20X0 to 20X6. However, entity V's management wants to restate the accounting entries it made in connection with the 20X7 business combination, but not restate the acquisitions made in 20X8 or 20X9.

Entity V's management can elect not to restate any business combinations before the date of transition to IFRS. However, if it elects to restate any business combination, then all subsequent business combinations must also be restated. Management must also restate the combinations in 20X8 if it elects to restate the acquisition in 20X7.

Management cannot avoid restating the business combination transaction in 20X9. This transaction took place in the period covered by the comparatives in the first IFRS financial statements. Entity V's management must, therefore, apply IFRS 3 to this business combination, because it is the business combination standard in force at the end of the first IFRS reporting period, 31 December 20Y0.

Example 2 – Business combination not included in the previous GAAP financial statements: restate in accordance with IFRS 3

Entity W's management presents entity W's first IFRS financial statements for the year ending 31 December 20X7. The date of transition to IFRS is 1 January 20X6 and the opening IFRS balance sheet is prepared as at this date.

Entity W acquired entity X. The agreement was signed in December 20X5 and was not subject to any approvals, so control passed to entity W in 20X5. The information necessary to complete the acquisition accounting required by entity W's previous GAAP was not available in January 20X6, so the acquisition was recognised for the first time in entity W's previous GAAP financial statements for the year ended 31 December 20X6. The impact of the acquisition is material.

This transaction was not included in the previous GAAP financial statements before the date of transition. The acquisition was not recognised under previous GAAP, but must be accounted for under IFRS. Entity W must recognise entity X's assets and liabilities at the transition date. The business combinations exemption could be applied allowing entity W to use the carrying values established under previous GAAP subject to any adjustments required by the exemption. The deemed goodwill is the difference at the date of transition between entity W's interest in the adjusted carrying amounts and the cost in entity W's separate financial statements of its investment in entity X.

Example 3 – IFRS 3 exemption: Business combination step acquisition

Entity Y prepares its first IFRS financial statements for the year ending 31 December 20Y0. The date of transition to IFRS is 1 January 20X9 and the opening IFRS balance sheet is prepared as at that date.

Entity Y has elected to apply the business combinations exemption, but to restate all business combinations occurring after 1 February 20X5.

Entity Y undertook a step acquisition of entity Z. It acquired: 13% interest on 31 March 20X3; 22% interest on 31 March 20X5; and a further 27% on 15 November 20X5, which was the final step in the acquisition.

The date of the acquisition of entity Y is 15 November 20X5, when the final purchase provided entity Y with control over entity Z.

The acquisition date of entity Z is after the restatement date of 1 February 20X5. Entity Y must, therefore, restate entity Y's acquisition in accordance with IFRS 3. However, the fact that the first step in entity Y's acquisition occurred on 31 March 20X3 does not affect other business combinations. Any acquisitions occurring between 31 March 20X3 and 1 February 20X5 do not need to be restated.

UK.2.61.1   For UK entities the key feature of this exemption is that business combinations occurring prior to the date of transition to IFRS that have been treated as mergers under FRS 6 or under SSAP 23 do not have to be restated as acquisitions.

Example 4 – IFRS 3 exemption: Business combination classification under previous GAAP

Entity F will prepare its first IFRS financial statements for the year ending 31 December 20X8. The date of transition to IFRS will be 1 January 20X7 and the opening IFRS balance sheet is prepared as at that date.

Entity F purchased some short-term contracts, internally-generated brand names, tangible assets and staff from a competitor in 20X6. The purchase was not classified as a business combination under entity F's previous GAAP. Management allocated the purchase price only to the tangible assets acquired in accordance with entity F's previous GAAP.

Should management make any adjustments to restate this transaction in connection with the opening IFRS balance sheet?

No. The business combinations exemption applies to all transactions that meet the IFRS definition of a business combination, irrespective of its original classification under the entity's previous GAAP. Although the transaction was not recognised as a business combination under entity F's previous GAAP, it would have been classified as one under IFRS. Entity F's management can, therefore, apply the business combinations exemption to this transaction and the transaction continues to be accounted for as the acquisition of assets. Entity F must, however, apply IAS 12 to the assets acquired and recognise any related deferred tax although the initial recognition exception may apply. See further chapter 13.

Recognition

2.62   The effect of the exemption in IFRS 1 is that business combinations prior to the transition date do not have to be restated. All the assets and liabilities pertaining to those combinations should be recognised and measured in accordance with IFRS. There are, however, certain exceptions to this as described below.

2.63   The recognition criteria for assets and liabilities *acquired and recognised* in past business combinations under the exemption are the same as those for other assets and liabilities of an entity adopting IFRS. However, the corresponding entries for any adjustments required on first-time adoption of IFRS are different in some cases. Recognised assets and liabilities both held generally and acquired in past business combinations should not be recognised in an entity's opening IFRS balance sheet if their recognition is not permitted by IFRS. The adjustment for derecognition is made to retained earnings or another appropriate category of equity apart from intangible assets acquired as part of a business combination. Any intangible asset recognised on a business combination under previous GAAP that cannot be recognised under IAS 38 should be adjusted against (that is, added to) goodwill. Any related deferred tax and non-controlling interest should also be adjusted against goodwill. [IFRS 1 App C para C4(c)].

UK.2.63.1 It is unlikely that, in practice, any such intangible assets would have been recognised in a business combination under UK GAAP, since the criteria in FRS 10 and IAS 38 are similar.

2.64 Where, on the other hand, an asset or liability has been *acquired, but not previously recognised* in a business combination, the recognition criteria are different from the normal recognition rules. The most common example is intangible assets that were not recognised under previous GAAP. These assets and liabilities should only be recognised on adoption of IFRS if they would have qualified for recognition in the separate balance sheet of the acquired entity under IFRS. [IFRS 1 App C para C4(f)]. All assets and liabilities recognised, excepting intangible assets (and related deferred tax and non-controlling interest), should be adjusted against retained earnings, or another appropriate category of equity. Where an intangible asset is recognised that was previously subsumed within goodwill then the adjustment should be made against goodwill. Related deferred tax and non-controlling interest should also be adjusted against goodwill. [IFRS 1 App C para C4(f), (g)(i)].

Example 1 – Recognition of intangible assets when using IFRS 3 exemption

Entity E prepares its first IFRS financial statements for the year ending 31 December 20X7. The date of transition to IFRS is 1 January 20X6 and the opening IFRS balance sheet is prepared as at that date.

Entity E acquired 80% of entity F in 20X2 and subsequently acquired the remaining 20% in 20X6. Entity E's management intends to apply the business combination exemption in IFRS 1 to the acquisition of entity F in 20X2.

Entity F owns a number of internally generated trademarks that are not recognised on its own IFRS balance sheet. The trademarks were not recognised on entity E's consolidated balance sheet immediately after the acquisition in 20X2.

The trademarks should not be recognised on entity E's IFRS consolidated balance sheet at the date of transition as they would not be recognised in F's own IFRS balance sheet. The purchase of the remaining 20% of the subsidiary after the date of transition does not alter this conclusion as this is a transaction with the non-controlling interest.

> **Example 2 – IFRS 3 exemption: Treatment of in-process research and development (IPR&D) costs**
>
> Prior to the IFRS transition date, entity A, a first-time adopter, acquired 100% of the outstanding shares of entity B. Entity B's identifiable assets included in-process research and development (IPR&D). Entity A assigned fair values to the IPR&D and, in accordance with its previous GAAP, expensed the assigned value immediately since the IPR&D had no alternative future use.
>
> Entity A elects to apply the business combinations exemption and will not go back and restate business combinations that occurred prior to the transition date.
>
> What should be done at the date of transition to IFRS?
>
> Assuming the IPR&D meets the IAS 38 criteria to qualify as an intangible asset under IFRS, entity A should reinstate the previously written-off IPR&D in its opening IFRS balance sheet. This adjustment is to opening retained earnings. [IFRS 1 App C para C4(e)].

2.65 Where an acquired entity has a separately acquired intangible asset that met the recognition criteria under IAS 38 but was expensed under previous GAAP, then this should be recognised as an asset on transition to IFRS. This is because if the acquired entity already used IFRS in its separate financial statements then the intangible asset would have been capitalised.

> **UK.2.65.1** There are two types of intangible asset that *will* be recognised on adoption of IFRS that may not have previously been recognised by UK entities. These are internally generated and acquired development costs. Where internally generated development costs meet the recognition criteria of IAS 38, which are similar to those of SSAP 13, 'Accounting for research and development', they *must* be capitalised. It may also be the case that a UK group has not recognised development costs on a business combination, as SSAP 13 gives entities the option of writing off such costs.

2.66 If an asset is recognised on transition under these requirements then it should be included in an entity's opening IFRS balance sheet at its acquisition date fair value as adjusted for any amortisation or impairment to the date of transition to IFRS.

2.67 An entity must recognise all assets and liabilities, other than intangibles, where IFRS requires their recognition, irrespective of whether or not they were acquired as part of a business combination. The criteria for recognition of most other assets and liabilities is the same whether they were acquired as part of a business combination, acquired directly by the reporting entity or internally generated.

2.68 For assets and liabilities that were not recognised on a business combination, but are subsequently recognised on adopting IFRS, the corresponding entry should be made to retained earnings or another appropriate category of equity. In the case of any intangible assets and related deferred tax and non-controlling interest, the corresponding adjustment should be made to goodwill. This is consistent with the treatment of assets and liabilities acquired in a combination that are derecognised on adoption of IFRS (see para 2.28). [IFRS 1 App C para C4(b)].

2.69   Any adjustments made to amounts recorded on past business combinations may also affect the measurement of deferred tax and non-controlling interest. Appropriate adjustments to these items should also be made on transition to IFRS. [IFRS 1 App C para C4(k)]. In addition to this, entities must ensure that IAS 12 is applied in respect of all consolidation adjustments that were made under previous GAAP. For example, where assets had been revalued to fair value on acquisition, deferred tax may not have been provided under previous GAAP, but provision is required by IAS 12. Similarly, a deferred tax provision is required in respect of temporary differences that have not been recognised by the acquired entity, prior to its acquisition, due to the initial recognition exception in IAS 12. Deferred tax that is related to the recognition of intangible assets is recognised against goodwill. All other deferred tax that is recognised, derecognised or remeasured as a result of past business combinations is adjusted against retained earnings or another appropriate category of equity.

Measurement

2.70   Assets and liabilities acquired in a business combination and recognised using the business combinations exemption explained in the paragraphs above are measured on the following basis:

- Some assets and liabilities are measured at fair value under IFRS. Such assets should be measured at fair value on transition to IFRS, whether they were acquired in a past business combination or not. [IFRS 1 App C para C4(d)]. Any adjustment arising from remeasurement should be made against retained earnings or another appropriate category of equity.

- Other assets and liabilities are measured on a cost basis under IFRS. The carrying value of an asset or liability immediately after a business combination is deemed cost for any cost-based measurement going forward from the date of the combination. [IFRS 1 App C para C4(e)]. This means that:

    - Previous GAAP fair value adjustments do not have to be revised. The fair value of an asset or liability recorded under previous GAAP on acquisition becomes its deemed cost for IFRS purposes even though the values determined may not comply with IFRS.

    - If the pooling of interests method was applied at the time of acquisition, the deemed cost will be the carrying value in the acquiree's books at the acquisition date.

    - The carrying value of the other tangible and intangible assets would not be adjusted unless:

- they were impaired in accordance with IAS 36; or
- the depreciation/amortisation charge since the acquisition date is materially different from the charge calculated in accordance with IFRS.

- Some assets and liabilities may not have been recognised on the acquisition under previous GAAP. These assets and liabilities should only be recognised if they would qualify for recognition in the acquired entity's separate IFRS balance sheet. [IFRS 1 App C para C4(f)].

Practical applications

2.71 The above provisions can be illustrated by the following examples:

Example 1 – First time adoption for business combinations: derecognition of liability

Country S's GAAP permitted provisions to be made on acquisition for restructuring costs as long as the plan had been made within six months of the acquisition. Entity A acquired entity B six months prior to transition to IFRS and made a provision for C1m, based on a plan that was formulated following the acquisition. Entity A's date of transition to IFRS occurs shortly before the plan is announced in detail to the acquired entity's employees.

The provision would not be permitted under IFRS 3, because there was no liability in the acquired entity at the date of acquisition. The liability of C1m is not recognised under IFRS (following para 2.63). Entity A should derecognise the liability, adjusting retained earnings on adopting IFRS.

Example 2 – First time adoption for business combinations: derecognition of intangible asset

Country T's GAAP required the recognition of a range of intangible assets on acquisition including an assembled workforce. Entity C had recognised an assembled workforce asset on acquisition of entity D.

The asset would not have been recognised on acquisition under IAS 38, as the standard specifies that an assembled workforce is not an identifiable intangible asset. This item should be derecognised with the corresponding entry being an adjustment to goodwill on adoption of IFRS.

Example 3 – First time adoption for business combinations: measurement of finance lease

Entity E acquired entity F and applied country U GAAP to the acquisition. In line with country U GAAP, entity E accounted for property finance leases of entity F as operating leases in its consolidated financial statements.

Entity E should capitalise the finance leases in its consolidated financial statements, as IAS 17 would require entity F to do so in its own separate financial statements. [IFRS 1 App C para C4(f)]. In accordance with IAS 17 entity E's management should record the building as an asset at the net present value of the minimum lease payments at the inception of the lease, less appropriate depreciation. Entity E should also record a finance lease liability at the net present value of the minimum lease payments at the inception of the lease; less capital repayments calculated using the rate of interest implicit in the lease. The difference between the amount recorded as property, plant and equipment and the amount recorded as finance lease liability should be included in retained earnings (following para 2.28 above).

Example 4 – First time adoption for business combinations: measurement of intangible assets

Country V's GAAP does not allow the recognition of intangible assets and, consequently, all are subsumed within goodwill. Entity G acquired entity H two years before transition to IFRS and accounted for the combination as an acquisition. In its consolidated financial statements entity G did not recognise intangibles in respect of entity H's internally generated brands or the costs of its separately acquired licences.

On transition to IFRS entity G should do the following with regard to these costs:

■ The brands should not be recognised, as they would not be recognised under IFRS in the individual financial statements of entity H. No adjustment is required (following para 2.64).

■ The separately acquired licences should be recognised as intangible assets in entity G's consolidated opening IFRS balance sheet in accordance with IAS 38. The adjustment to recognise this asset is made against goodwill, rather than retained earnings (following para 2.64).

Example 5 – First time adoption for business combinations: measurement of provisions

Entity I, recognised the expected costs of restructuring an acquired business, entity J, although it had not made the announcement necessary to create a legal or constructive obligation to complete the planned restructuring. Entity I also recognised a provision for the expected future losses of entity J's export division.

Entity I is not required to restate the purchase accounting entries made at the time entity J was acquired. However, entity I should consider whether any remaining balance in respect of the restructuring provision and the provision for future operating losses qualify for recognition at the date of transition to IFRS. Any provision that does not meet the IFRS recognition criteria at the date of transition to IFRS would not be recognised on the opening IFRS balance sheet, with a corresponding adjustment to retained earnings.

Goodwill

2.72   Where the IFRS 1 exemption for business combinations is used, goodwill in an entity's opening IFRS balance sheet should be stated at its carrying amount prior to the date of transition under that entity's previous GAAP, adjusted for only two things as described below.

■ Any previously recognised intangible assets that do not qualify for recognition under IFRS (see para 2.63), or any previously unrecognised intangible assets where recognition is required under IFRS (see para 2.64). Related adjustments to non-controlling interest and deferred tax should also be made against goodwill. [IFRS 1 App C para C4(g)(i)].

UK note – As stated at paragraph 2.63 above, it is unlikely that under UK GAAP any intangible assets will have been recognised on acquisition that are not allowed under IFRS, though the criteria for recognising development costs are slightly different under IAS 38 compared to SSAP 13, requiring the 'demonstration' of future benefits rather than SSAP 13's 'expectation' of future benefits. On the other hand, it may well be that development costs have not been recognised on a business combination, because it is a UK entity's policy to write off such costs. If they meet the recognition criteria of IAS 38 they should be recognised on transition and an adjustment made against goodwill. This only applies to any development costs that existed at the date of a business combination. Any other development costs that a group is required to recognised under IAS 38 should be adjusted against retained earnings.

■ Whether there is any indication of impairment or not, a first-time adopter should apply IAS 36 to test goodwill for impairment at the date of transition to IFRS, based on conditions at the transition date. Any impairment loss should be recorded in retained earnings (or revaluation reserve if required by IAS 36). [IFRS 1 App C C4(g)(ii)]. Paragraph C4(h)(ii) in Appendix C of IFRS 1 specifically states that goodwill under previous GAAP may not be restated to adjust any previous amortisation of goodwill. Our view is that it also cannot be restated to adjust any previous impairment of goodwill. Accordingly, the impairment review carried out on transition cannot result in an increase in the goodwill balance at the date of transition.

UK note – The requirement to perform an impairment review could prove costly for many UK entities and might be a reason why some may wish to not take the IFRS 1 exemption. However, several factors are likely to mitigate this:

■ IAS 36 requires annual impairment tests for all goodwill. There are no exemptions in IFRS 1 from applying IAS 36 and so an impairment test of goodwill would be required on transition to IFRS whether or not the IFRS 1 business combinations exemption is taken.

■ UK entities have been applying FRS 11 for some years and goodwill that has had an indication of impairment should have been tested for impairment under UK GAAP. There may be more work involved in carrying out a separate test at the transition date, and it may or may not result in adjustments to the carrying amounts of goodwill. Where it does lead to an adjustment, entities have the advantage of the adjustment being made against retained earnings. In such cases, however, entities will have to consider whether the adjustment on transition has been caused by moving to IFRS or whether an impairment existed under previous GAAP. As discussed in paragraph 2.201 below, these two types of adjustments have to be identified and disclosed separately.

- Where goodwill has been given an indefinite useful life or one greater than 20 years under UK GAAP it is already subject to an annual impairment test under FRS 11.

2.73 The previous version of IFRS 3 allowed a first-time adopter to adjust goodwill in respect of contingent consideration on a previous business combination where the contingency had since been resolved or where payment had become probable by the date of transition. If an amount had been recognised that was no longer probable or reliably measurable it was also adjusted against goodwill. This treatment was consistent with that applied by existing IFRS preparers under IFRS 3 (superseded). The ability for first-time adopters to adjust goodwill for contingent consideration was removed in the most recent version of IFRS 3. Existing IFRS preparers are permitted to adjust goodwill in line with IFRS 3 (superseded) for those business combinations accounted for under that standard. In May 2010, the IFRIC confirmed that the transition relief provided to existing IFRS preparers would not be extended to first-time adopters.

2.74 An example of a company that has adopted IFRS and recognised impairment losses on goodwill on transition is Amer Group Plc in Table 2.1.

Table 2.1 – Recognising impairment losses on goodwill on transition to IFRS

Amer Group Plc – Quarterly Report – 31 March 2004

TRANSITION TO IFRS: MAJOR CHANGES TO ACCOUNTING POLICIES AND FINANCIAL STATEMENTS REPORTED IN 2003 (extract)

5. GOODWILL, OTHER INTANGIBLE AND TANGIBLE LONG-TERM ASSETS

The major differences in accounting policies for goodwill, other intangible and tangible long-term assets between IFRS and FAS are included in two standards, IAS 36 and IFRS 3.

In accordance with IAS 36 the carrying amounts of assets are assessed on any indication of an impairment. If such an indication exists, a company should then estimate the recoverable amount of the asset. The recoverable amount is the higher of the asset's net selling price or value in use. An impairment loss is recognised when the recoverable amount of an asset is less than its carrying amount. At the date of transition of 1 January 2003 all goodwill, as well as intangible and tangible long-term assets of independent cash-generating units, were tested for possible impairments.

Impairment testing of goodwill at the date of transition

Goodwill is allocated to business segments. The recoverable amount of each segment's goodwill is calculated based on their discounted future cash flows. Future cash flows are based on the Amer Board's approved budgets and strategic plans for a period of the next three years. Forecasts for the following years are conservatively extrapolated based on the growth rate and profitability outlined in the approved plan. The discount rate is based on a long-term risk free market interest rate and a generally used standard risk premium.

As a result of the impairment tests, an impairment loss of EUR 19.1 million associated with Golf was recognised at the transition balance sheet of 1 January 2003.

Wilson Sporting Goods Co. and its subsidiaries were acquired in 1989. The goodwill generated at the time of the acquisition was not allocated to Wilson 's three business segments of Racquet Sports, Golf and Team Sports. According to IAS 14 (Segment Reporting) goodwill should be allocated to segments as a minimum requirement. If the total goodwill of the three Wilson segments would have been tested as a whole at the date of transition, the recoverable amount of goodwill would have been considerably higher than its carrying amount and no impairment loss would have been recognised.

The carrying amount of goodwill in each business segment at the date of transition of 1 January 2003 is (EUR million):

Racquet Sports	73.3
Golf	—
Team Sports	48.8
Winter Sports	11.7
Fitness Equipment	140.4
Sports Instruments	29.1
Total	303.3

The recoverable amount of goodwill in each segment except for Golf was significantly higher than its carrying amount at 1 January 2003.

Impairment tests for other intangible and tangible long-term assets

The recoverable amount of intangible and tangible long-term assets for each independent cash-generating unit is based on value-in-use calculations. Discounted future cash flows in these calculations cover the following five years and, similarly to the goodwill impairment testing, they are based on the approved budgets and strategic plans. Estimated net cash flow to be received for the disposal of the asset at the end of its useful life is used as a residual value in the calculations. The discount rate is based on a long-term risk free market interest rate and a generally used standard risk premium.

As a result of the impairment tests an impairment loss of EUR 16.0 million associated to the Golf Division's production plants was recognised at the transition balance sheet of 1 January 2003. This improves the Golf Division's results under IFRS in 2003 by EUR 2.5 million due to lower depreciation. However, a further impairment loss of EUR 4.1 million also associated with the Golf Division's production plants is included in the Group's 2003 results under IFRS. Applying both FAS and local accounting principles in 2002 and 2003's annual closings didn't lead to impairments of the Golf Division's long-term assets.

Recoverable amounts of long-term assets for all other independent cash-generating units except for Golf were significantly higher than their carrying amounts.

Revised standard for business combinations (IFRS 3)

In accordance with the new standard, IFRS 3, goodwill and other intangible long-term assets with indefinite useful lives should not be amortised. Instead these assets should be tested annually for impairment according to IAS 36. Retrospective cancellation of goodwill and other intangible assets' amortisation improves 2003 EBIT under IFRS by EUR 16.5 million.

Additionally, in conjunction with the transition to IFRS, the intangible long-term asset recognised in the acquisition of Atomic Austria GmbH in 1994 has now been reclassified to goodwill (EUR 10.3 million at 1 January 2003).

2.75 IFRS 1 does not allow goodwill that was previously written off to reserves under previous GAAP to be reinstated as an asset. In addition, when a subsidiary is subsequently disposed of, IFRS 1 does not permit the goodwill that was taken direct to reserves to be transferred to the income statement as part of the gain or loss on disposal. IFRS 1 does not allow a transfer to the income statement on impairment of the goodwill. Where goodwill has previously been written off to reserves then any adjustments that IFRS 1 requires to be made against goodwill will also go to reserves, that is, to retained earnings. [IFRS 1 App C para C4(i)].

2.76 Similar rules apply for associates and joint ventures. If the goodwill determined under previous GAAP was deducted from reserves and not included in the carrying amount of the associate, then such goodwill is not reinstated on transition to IFRS. This also applies when the associate is sold; the goodwill is not recycled back through the income statement.

> **Example – First-time adoption for business combinations: goodwill**
>
> The reporting date of an investor's first IFRS financial statements is 31 December 20X7. The investor presents comparatives for one year only as well as an opening balance sheet. Therefore, its date of transition to IFRS is 1 January 20X6. The investor has an associate that was acquired many years ago and goodwill arising on the acquisition of the associate was written off to reserves under previous GAAP. The associate was sold in June 20X6.
>
> In its opening balance sheet the goodwill arising on the acquisition of the associate would remain written off to reserves. The comparative income statement for the year ending 31 December 20X6 would show the gain or loss arising on the sale of the associate. The goodwill would be excluded from the calculation of the gain or loss on disposal.

2.77 IFRS 1 gives a further example of adjustments that cannot be made (by those using the exemption) against a previous GAAP goodwill balance. That is, goodwill should not be adjusted on transition to reverse any adjustments that IFRS 3 would not have permitted, but that had been made under a previous GAAP between the date of the business combination and the date of transition. [IFRS 1 App C para C4(h)(iii)]. For example, IFRS 3 allows a measurement period of a maximum of 12 months from the acquisition date to complete the accounting for a business combination. Within this period, adjustments may be made to goodwill as the fair values of assets and liabilities are finalised. [IFRS 3 para 45]. An entity's previous GAAP may have allowed a period greater than 12 months. Any adjustments to goodwill made under previous GAAP falling outside of the permitted measurement period under IFRS 3 would not be reversed on transition to IFRS.

Deferred tax

2.78 Where an entity takes the exemption from applying IFRS 3 to past business combinations, a number of deferred tax consequences arise in respect of those combinations. These are considered below.

2.79 The requirements of IAS 12 apply in the same way to all the assets and liabilities of a group. Temporary differences arise when the carrying amount of assets and liabilities acquired in a business combination are determined by reference to fair values at the date of exchange, but the tax bases of those assets and liabilities remain unchanged. Deferred tax should, therefore, be provided on the difference between the fair value and the tax base of all assets and liabilities acquired in a business combination. Even if an entity uses the exemption and does not have to restate past business combinations, it may still have to restate the deferred tax arising on those combinations. For example, if assets had been revalued to fair value on acquisition, but no deferred tax had been provided under previous GAAP, provision is required by IAS 12. This adjustment should be made on transition against retained earnings. (An adjustment is only made against goodwill in a few specified cases, see further para 2.72.)

UK.2.79.1 Normally, no deferred tax would have been provided on those temporary differences under FRS 19. The requirements of FRS 19 on a business combination are that deferred tax should be provided on timing differences as if those differences had arisen in the acquired entity. However, provision is required by IAS 12 and so even if the entity has used the business combinations exemption in IFRS 1, it will have to restate the deferred tax arising on those combinations.

2.80 Deferred tax consequences also arise on intangible assets that were recognised in past business combinations. Examples are given below and in Table 2.2.

Example – Deferred tax: intangible asset through acquisition

Entity A made an acquisition in 20X0. An intangible asset was recognised at that point and given an indefinite life. The intangible asset was not deductible for tax purposes. Under previous GAAP, such an asset did not create a temporary difference and no deferred tax arises, either on the asset's initial recognition or on impairment or disposal. Entity A will take advantage of the business combinations exemption. What is the treatment on adoption of IFRS?

Entity A must apply IAS 12 to all assets and liabilities acquired. Paragraph 22 of IAS 12 deals with temporary differences that arise on the initial recognition of an asset or liability. Recognition of a non-tax-deductible asset gives rise a temporary difference. When this occurs in a business combination paragraph 22(a) requires that a deferred tax liability is recognised, with the other side of the entry affecting goodwill (that is, increasing goodwill).

However, first-time adopters are bound by the rules in IFRS 1. Paragraph C4(g) in Appendix C of IFRS 1 states that only certain items can adjust previously recognised goodwill when the business combinations exemption is taken. Deferred tax arising on a previously recognised asset is not one of these items. On transition, entity A must recognise a deferred tax liability with the resulting debit being recorded in retained earnings or another category of equity. IFRS 1 overrides the requirement of IAS 12 in this respect.

Table 2.2 – Deferred tax on intangibles acquired before transition date

Unilever PLC – Report and accounts – 31 December 2005

35 First time adoption of International Financial Reporting Standards (extract)

Deferred tax

Under IFRSs deferred tax is recognised in respect of all taxable temporary differences arising between the tax base and the accounting base of balance sheet items. This means that deferred tax is recognised on certain temporary differences that would not have given rise to deferred tax under previous GAAP.

The additional deferred tax included in the balance sheet under IFRSs amounted to a net movement excluding reclassifications of €1 095 million as at 1 January 2004 and €1 068 million as at 31 December 2004. Included in these amounts is a deferred tax liability relating to intangible assets (trademarks and unpatented technologies) which were recognised at the time of the Bestfoods acquisition. As the Bestfoods acquisition was a share-based transaction, these intangible assets have a zero tax base. IAS 12 requires that a deferred tax liability amounting to €1 144 million as at 1 January 2004 and €1 071 million as at 31 December 2004 is recognised in respect of these intangible assets. Normally, recognition of this deferred tax liability would lead to a corresponding increase in goodwill, but under the exemption applied under IFRS 1 relating to business combinations Unilever is precluded from adjusting the carrying value of goodwill in respect of acquisitions prior to the transition date. Recognition of this new deferred tax liability under IFRSs therefore resulted in an equivalent reduction in equity at the transition date.

2.81 Goodwill from past business combinations may have been written off to reserves, but the carrying value of the goodwill is amortised for tax purposes. The goodwill may have a tax base, at the date of transition to IFRS, equal to the amount of tax deductions to be received in the future. The requirements of IAS 12 must be applied to the opening IFRS balance sheet. IAS 12 requires that a deferred tax asset should be recognised for all deductible temporary differences, as long as there will be sufficient taxable profits to recover the asset in future periods. IAS 12 does not provide a specific exemption from recognising deferred tax assets for tax-deductible goodwill written off directly to equity. Therefore, the deferred tax asset should be recognised, but the goodwill is not reinstated.

UK.2.81.1 Under FRS 19, the UK entity would have recognised a deferred tax liability equal to the amount of tax deductions received every year since acquisition. Suppose, for example, goodwill of £500,000 that is deductible for tax purposes at the rate of say 10% per annum, arose on an acquisition that took place on 1 January 1997, prior to the implementation date of FRS 10. The company decided not to reinstate the goodwill of £500,000 that was written off to reserves. In each year, following the acquisition, the company would have claimed a tax deduction of £50,000. Under FRS 19, the company would have recognised a deferred tax liability on the cumulative tax deduction available to 31 December 2003 of £105,000 (30% × 7 years @ £50,000). At 1 January 2004, the date of transition, the tax base of the goodwill is £150,000 (£500,000 — £350,000). A question arises as to whether it is appropriate to continue to recognise a deferred tax liability of £105,000 when the goodwill of £500,000 remains written off in reserves.

UK.2.81.2 In accordance with IFRS 1, the goodwill is not reinstated in the opening IFRS balance sheet, as the company did not recognise the goodwill as an asset under previous GAAP. However, a tax deduction of £150,000 is still available in respect of the goodwill at the date of transition. The difference between the tax base of the goodwill of £150,000 and its carrying value of nil creates a deductible temporary difference on which a deferred tax asset should be recognised (subject to meeting the recoverability test). This means that the company would have to reverse the deferred tax liability of £105,000 and, instead, recognise a deferred tax asset on the temporary difference of £150,000, that is, £45,000. The overall effect on opening retained earnings is a credit of £150,000. The deferred tax asset of £45,000 would be released to the profit and loss account over the remaining three year tax life of the goodwill.

2.82 Appendix C of IFRS 1 also sets out a number of other matters that apply to first-time adopters that do not apply IFRS 3 retrospectively to past business combinations. Consideration of these matters may well give rise to further deferred tax adjustments that should be recognised at the date of transition. Revisiting past business combinations may cause some practical issues for entities, particularly as differences between previous GAAP and IFRS would have existed for a number of years in respect of fair value adjustments made to fixed assets. All adjustments to deferred tax should be recorded in retained earnings or in another appropriate category of equity, apart from deferred tax related to an intangible asset that was previously subsumed within goodwill. In such cases the deferred tax should be adjusted against goodwill (see further para 2.72).

Foreign currency

2.83 IAS 21 made consequential amendments to IFRS 1. An entity does not have to apply IAS 21 retrospectively to fair value adjustments and goodwill arising in previous business combinations that occurred before the date of transition to IFRS. [IFRS 1 App C para C2]. The fair value adjustments and goodwill are treated as assets and liabilities of the acquiring entity. This means that they are either measured in the acquiring entity's functional currency at the transition date or they are treated as non-monetary foreign currency items from the acquiring entity's point of view, reported using the exchange rate applied under the entity's previous GAAP. Under the latter option, goodwill that has not been retranslated since acquisition can, using this exemption, remain at its carrying amount under previous GAAP at the date of transition to IFRS (subject to any adjustments as described in para 2.72 above). Like all goodwill it should be tested for impairment at the date of transition. [IFRS 1 App C para C4(g)(ii)]. From the date of transition to IFRS the goodwill is not retranslated under IFRS, but it is tested for impairment on an ongoing basis.

UK.2.83.1 This amendment will prove useful to those UK entities that did not in the past treat goodwill as a foreign currency asset. In the UK, prior to FRS 23, there have been two accepted treatments for goodwill arising on the acquisition of a foreign operation. One method is to translate goodwill at the date of acquisition and not subsequently retranslate it. It is not then included in the retranslation of the opening net assets on the grounds that it arises only on consolidation and is not part of the net assets of the foreign entity. The alternative method, and one which has become more common in practice (and is required by FRS 23), is to treat the goodwill as a foreign currency asset. Goodwill is then retranslated each period as part of the translation of the opening net investment. IAS 21 states that it is this second approach that should be adopted. [IAS 21 para 47]. Any UK entities that have adopted the former approach in respect of goodwill that has not been written off to reserves could have faced a practical issue: revisiting previous acquisitions to ascertain the translation rate at the date of acquisition. The amendment made by IAS 21 to IFRS 1 removes this problem.

UK.2.83.2 UK entities already treat fair value adjustments as adjustments to the assets and liabilities of the acquired entity and the exemption is not, therefore, necessary for such adjustments for UK groups.

2.84 The optional business combinations exemption is available to all business combinations (and transactions that would qualify as a business combination under IFRS 3) that occurred before the date of transition to IFRS. [IFRS 1 App C para C1]. If, however, the exemption is taken, there is a degree of choice: entities may apply it only to combinations that took place prior to a particular date and can restate all those that took place after that date in accordance with IFRS 3 (see further para 2.61). The provisions relating to the application of IAS 21 to goodwill and fair value adjustments are also contained within Appendix C of IFRS 1 and so apply to all business combinations that took place prior to an entity's date of transition to IFRS. Paragraph C2 in Appendix C of IFRS 1 provides that IAS 21 need not be applied to fair value adjustments and goodwill arising on business combinations that occurred prior to the date of transition to IFRS. If IAS 21 *is* applied, then it may be applied retrospectively to goodwill and fair value adjustments that arose in *either* all business combinations that occurred before the date of transition to IFRS, *or* to all business combinations that the entity chooses to restate to comply with IFRS 3 (see para 2.61). [IFRS 1 App C para C3].

2.85 Should an entity choose to apply IAS 21 to any goodwill or fair value adjustments from a past business combination, then the original foreign currency amount of goodwill should be established. Impairments and amortisation charges should be made by retranslating the impairment charge into the foreign currency at the rates on the dates to which the charges relate. The balance of goodwill in foreign currency will be carried forward at the date of transition to IFRS and, applying IAS 21, will continue to be retranslated.

Subsidiaries not previously consolidated

2.86 Paragraph C4(j) of Appendix C to IFRS 1 also contains guidance for situations where a subsidiary was not consolidated under an entity's previous GAAP. The Appendix notes the following examples of such situations.

- The entity was either not regarded as a subsidiary or there was an exemption from consolidation of that entity.

- The parent company did not prepare consolidated financial statements under local GAAP.

UK.2.86.1 An entity not being regarded as a subsidiary is unlikely to apply to many UK entities, as the definitions of subsidiary in FRS 2 and IAS 27 are similar.

UK.2.86.2 FRS 2 requires subsidiaries to be excluded from consolidation where there are severe long-term restrictions over the transfer of funds from subsidiary to parent. This exclusion is not contained in IAS 27, although it may be that such restrictions indicate that an entity does not control another and that it is, therefore, not a subsidiary and should not be consolidated. UK entities should, however, examine all subsidiaries that have been excluded from consolidation under UK GAAP on the basis of severe long-term restrictions to ascertain whether they nonetheless retain control and, hence, should consolidate the entity.

UK.2.86.3 Although the provisions of FRS 5 concerning quasi-subsidiaries and of SIC 12 regarding special purpose entities ('SPEs') are similar, entities should re-examine any entities that have not been consolidated to ensure that non-consolidation remains appropriate.

2.87 A subsidiary may have been excluded from consolidation where it has been acquired exclusively with a view to resale under previous GAAP. A subsidiary that meets the conditions in IFRS 5 to be classified as held-for-sale is consolidated and accounted for under IFRS 5. See chapter 26.

2.88 Where a first-time adopter has a subsidiary that has been acquired with a view to resale at the date of transition, then the subsidiary should be consolidated using the method set out in IFRS 5. Single line items of the subsidiary's assets (including goodwill) and liabilities are presented in the balance sheet. Paragraph C4(j) in Appendix C of IFRS 1 also applies, as follows: the subsidiary has not been consolidated under previous GAAP and so the assets and liabilities should, in principle, be restated under IFRS in order to calculate the deemed cost of goodwill. However, the method given in IFRS 5 for consolidating a subsidiary acquired exclusively with a view to resale is to fair value the liabilities and deduct this from the total cost in order to get a balancing assets and goodwill figure. A first-time adopter should, therefore, measure the liabilities of the previously unconsolidated subsidiary at the amounts that IFRS would require in the subsidiary's balance sheet. The difference between this and the cost of investment is recorded as the single figure of assets and goodwill. See chapter 26.

2.89   Where a first-time adopter has a subsidiary that was acquired with a view to resale but does not meet the conditions in IFRS 5 as held for sale, then the subsidiary should be consolidated using the method set out in IAS 27.

> **Example – First-time adoption: IFRS 5 held for sale criteria not met**
>
> Entity E prepares its first IFRS financial statements for the year ending 31 December 20X7. The date of transition to IFRS is 1 January 20X6 and the opening IFRS balance sheet is prepared as at that date.
>
> Entity E acquired a major competitor in 20X0 and used acquisition accounting under entity E's previous GAAP. Entity F, a subsidiary of the acquired entity, was not consolidated by entity E under its previous GAAP because entity E's management decided before the acquisition that entity F would be sold. Management recorded entity F at the expected sales proceeds and has not adjusted the carrying value since the acquisition. Management remains committed to selling entity F but has deferred pursuing an active plan to dispose of it and now considers that entity F, is unlikely to be sold in the next two years.
>
> Should management consolidate entity F on the opening IFRS balance sheet?
>
> Yes. There are no exemptions from applying the IAS 27 requirements. The only exemption permitted from IAS 27 is in respect of a subsidiary that, on acquisition, meets the criteria to be classified as held for sale in accordance with IFRS 5. Such a subsidiary is accounted for in accordance with IFRS 5. [IFRS 5 para BC53]. Entity F does not meet the IFRS 5 criteria because it has not been actively marketed since acquisition. Entity F should be consolidated.

2.90   Where a subsidiary has not been consolidated previously, but is required to be consolidated under IFRS, IFRS 1 does not require the parent entity to go back and apply IFRS 3 at the date of acquisition. The standard requires the parent entity to adjust the carrying amounts of the subsidiary's assets and liabilities in the consolidated financial statements to those that IFRS would require in the subsidiary's own separate balance sheet (see also para 2.64). The deemed cost of goodwill will then be the difference between the parent entity's interest in the adjusted carrying amounts of those net assets at the date of transition to IFRS and the cost of the investment in the parent entity's own financial statements. [IFRS 1 App C para C4(j)]. The parent entity does not have to fair value the subsidiary's assets and liabilities at the date of acquisition or at the date of transition to IFRS.

> **Example – Subsidiary not previously consolidated but required to be under IFRS**
>
> Entity G is a venture capital investor that acquired 60% of the voting shares in entity H in 20X1. Country X's previous GAAP does not require venture capital investors to consolidate subsidiaries. Entity G's management recorded the investment in entity H at fair value since acquisition, with changes in fair value recorded in the income statement.
>
> Entity G's management should restate entity H's assets and liabilities in accordance with IFRS as if entity H was adopting IFRS for the first time at the same date as entity G. The restated balance sheet is included in the consolidated opening balance sheet in accordance with IAS 27 requirements.
>
> The deemed cost of goodwill in respect of entity H is the difference between the cost of entity G's investment in entity H at the date of transition and its 60% share of entity H's net assets recorded on the opening IFRS balance sheet. The adjustments that entity G made under its previous GAAP to restate the investment to fair value at each balance sheet date are reversed with an adjustment against retained earnings.

2.91   A parent may have acquired a subsidiary and not previously consolidated it in line with requirements under its previous GAAP. On transition to IFRS, the parent recognises goodwill in those circumstances, which is measured in accordance with the requirements in paragraph 2.72. However, *"if the parent did not acquire the subsidiary in a business combination because it created the subsidiary, the parent does not recognise goodwill"*. [IFRS 1 para IG27(c)]. The parent entity will still have a cost of investment, because the subsidiary will have issued share capital to the parent entity on its formation. However, where the adjusted net assets of the subsidiary that was not purchased are less than the cost of investment in the parent entity's separate financial statements then the resulting debit adjustment does not create goodwill, but rather is a debit to retained earnings or another appropriate category of equity. However, where a subsidiary has not been consolidated under previous GAAP but it should have been, any adjustments made should be disclosed separately as a previous GAAP error (see para 2.201 below).

Associates and joint ventures

2.92   The business combinations exemption applies equally to acquisitions of investments in associates and joint ventures. [IFRS 1 App C para C5]. Entities taking advantage of the exemption will not have to revisit past acquisitions of associates and joint ventures and establish fair values and amounts of goodwill under IFRS. The requirements detailed from paragraph 2.58 should be applied.

2.93   There may be situations where an entity has been accounted for as an investment under previous GAAP and it is classified as an associate under IFRS. On transition, the investment is treated as an associate following the rules set out from paragraph 2.90 for subsidiaries that have not previously been consolidated. The entity should remeasure the assets and liabilities in the associate's separate balance sheet at the date of transition. Goodwill is calculated as the difference between this and the carrying amount in the investor's financial statements. It does not have to fair value the assets and liabilities of the associate. Any adjustment where the adjusted share of net assets is greater than the investing entity's investment carrying value, should be made against retained earnings or another appropriate category of equity.

2.94 An associate under previous GAAP may be a subsidiary for IFRS purposes. Goodwill and fair values may have already been calculated, although the calculations will have been on a previous GAAP basis and not on an IFRS basis. Our view is that the recognition and measurement provisions of the business combinations exemption apply in this case. Where the exemption is taken, the investing entity should account for the combination as the acquisition of a subsidiary under IFRS and make the adjustments required by paragraphs C4(b) to C4(f) in Appendix C of IFRS 1. Goodwill should not be adjusted, except for the items set out in paragraph B2(g) (see para 2.72). The entity cannot apply paragraph C4(j) in Appendix C of IFRS 1 and recalculate goodwill based on the parent entity's cost of investment and the subsidiary's carrying values of net assets.

UK.2.94.1 If a joint arrangement that is not an entity (a JANE) under UK GAAP would be a jointly controlled entity under IFRS, because it is, for example, housed in a partnership (see further para UK.2.216.88), then it should be accounted for as a jointly controlled entity (that is, proportionally consolidated or equity accounted). Goodwill would normally be nil in this situation as it is not generally recognised in JANE accounting under UK GAAP. However, some goodwill might arise if it needs to be adjusted for the items set out in paragraph C4(g) in Appendix C of IFRS 1 (see para 2.72 above).

2.95 Paragraph C5 in Appendix C of IFRS 1 notes that the date selected for applying the exemption to business combinations applies equally to acquisitions of investments in associates and interests in joint ventures. For example, if an entity chooses not to restate any business combinations prior to the transition date, it is then not permitted to restate any acquisitions of associates or joint ventures prior to the transition date. Entities may not choose different dates for different types of combinations.

Interaction of business combinations and employee benefits exemptions

2.96 The interaction of the different exemptions can be unclear. The following example illustrates how the business combinations exemption and that relating to employee benefits (see from para 2.132) work together.

Example – Business combinations exemption and employee benefits exemption

Management intends to present the first IFRS financial statements of entity B for the year ending 31 December 20X7. The date of transition to IFRS is 1 January 20X6. Entity B had reported under French GAAP. Entity B is the parent entity. Entity B acquired its subsidiary entity C in 20X4 and its subsidiary entity M in 20X5.

Entity B decided to apply the business combination exemption to the entity C acquisition, but not to the entity M acquisition.

Group B (the group) has three defined benefit pension plans:

Plan x – established by entity B, the parent entity, in 19X3.

Plan y – established by entity C in 19X5.

Plan z – established by entity M in 19X6.

Management decided not to use the employee benefits exemption in the first IFRS financial statements of the group. A 'corridor' approach will be applied under IFRS to unrecognised actuarial gains and losses.

How should management recognise actuarial gains and losses at the transition date?

The three defined benefit plans should each be analysed separately.

Plan x: This a defined benefit pension plan established by the parent. Plan x is not part of a previous business combination. The corridor approach should be applied from 19X3, the date the plan x was established.

Plan y: The group decided to use the business combinations exemption for entity C. All entity C's assets and liabilities should be accounted for according to the business combination exemption's requirements. The past acquisition accounted for under French GAAP is used as deemed cost under IFRS. The plan y obligation is not restated. The corridor approach should be applied from 20X4, the acquisition date.

Plan z: The group decided not to apply the business combinations exemption to entity M. Entity M's acquisition should be restated in accordance with IFRS 3. The plan z obligation should be restated in accordance with paragraph 108 of IAS 19: all cumulative gains and losses that arose before the acquisition date should be recognised at the acquisition date. The corridor approach should be applied from the acquisition date in 20X5.

If the above requirement appears to be burdensome and management still wish to apply the 'corridor' approach, they may consider application of the employee benefits exemption. However this exemption can only be used if it is applied to all of the Group's plans.

The following flow chart illustrates the interaction between the employee benefits exemption and the business combinations exemption:

First-time adoption of IFRS

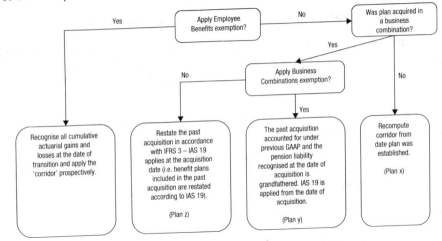

Interaction of business combinations and deemed cost exemption

2.97 The following example illustrates how the business combinations exemption and the deemed cost exemption (see from para 2.107) interact.

Example – Business combination and deemed cost exemptions

Entity R prepares its first IFRS financial statements for the year ending 31 December 20X7. The date of transition to IFRS is 1 January 20X6 and the opening IFRS balance sheet is prepared as at that date.

Entity R acquired entity S during 20X5. Entity S's balance sheet included property, plant and equipment, inventory and trade receivables. Entity R applied the pooling of interests method to account for the business combination and recorded the assets acquired using the book values recorded by entity S. There were no fair value adjustments.

Entity R intends to apply the business combinations exemption, so there will be no adjustments to the accounting treatment applied at the acquisition date. Entity R also intends to apply the deemed cost exemption and restate the property, plant and equipment to fair value at the date of transition to IFRS.

Can the deemed cost exemption be applied to the assets acquired in the business combination?

Yes. The deemed cost exemption does not exclude assets acquired in a business combination. The assets acquired in the business combination can be restated to fair value as deemed cost as permitted by IFRS 1.

Interaction of business combinations exemption and estimates exception

2.98 When a business combination occurs immediately prior to the date of transition to IFRS, it is possible that provisional fair values assigned to the acquired assets and assumed liabilities in the entity's financial statements at the date of transition may require adjustment in a later period. For instance, this will be necessary if the entity has not completed the process of gathering the information necessary for identifying and valuing acquired assets and assumed liabilities when it issued its previous GAAP financial statements. The following example illustrates our view on how the business combinations exemption and the mandatory exception relating to estimates (see from para 2.32) interact.

Example – Business combination exemption and estimates exception

Entity T acquired entity U on 30 November 20X5. Entity T did not have time to finalise its determination of the fair values of all of entity U's assets and liabilities by the time its 31 December 20X5 financial statements were authorised for issue, on 27 March 20X6. Under its local GAAP entity T was permitted to finalise the fair values in its consolidated financial statements for the year to 31 December 20X6. Any such adjustments were made against goodwill.

Entity T prepares its first IFRS financial statements for the year to 31 December 20X7, with one year of comparatives. Its date of transition to IFRS is 1 January 20X6. The finance director of entity T has read that estimates made under local GAAP cannot be amended on transition to IFRS, unless such estimates were made in error. Entity T will take advantage of the business combinations exemption in IFRS 1 and will not restate combinations that took place before its transition to IFRS. How does this affect the provisional fair value estimates on transition to IFRS?

Local GAAP required fair values at the acquisition date to be used. We believe that any adjustments to provisional fair value estimates represent a more precise determination of fair value. In other words, the provisional fair value estimates are intended to be temporary amounts recorded, pending the finalisation of the entity's estimate of fair value. Therefore, applying the business combinations exemption to this transaction means that the final fair value estimates established under local GAAP should be used as deemed cost at the date of the acquisition. This is provided that the estimated fair value in these circumstances would not be considered a revision of an estimate as contemplated in paragraph 14 of IFRS 1 and thus prohibited by this paragraph from being recognised in the opening IFRS balance sheet.

Another relevant aspect to consider in this situation is the recognition of allowed adjustments to goodwill in accordance with paragraph C4(g) of IFRS 1. There are two type of adjustments allowed by the standard (that is, intangibles that do not qualify for recognition and impairments of goodwill). (See para 2.72 above.) The adjustments to provisional values with a resulting adjustment to goodwill is not explicitly covered by paragraph C4(g) of IFRS 1. However, as mentioned above, we consider that the final fair values are a better representation of the amounts to be recorded as deemed cost as of the transition date. The provisional amounts at the date of acquisition do not represent the final amount that would have been recorded under previous GAAP.

Entity T should, therefore, reflect the revised fair values and goodwill that were recorded in its 20X6 local GAAP financial statements in its opening IFRS balance sheet at 1 January 20X6.

Share-based payment transactions

2.99 First-time adopters have various options when applying IFRS 2. These largely reflect the transitional provisions of that standard.

2.100 Broadly, the requirements of IFRS 2 are to be applied to grants of equity instruments made since ED 2 was issued (that is, 7 November 2002) and to liabilities in respect of cash-settled share-based payment transactions outstanding at the date of transition to IFRS. First-time adopters are encouraged, however, to apply IFRS 2's requirements to other transactions, although this option is somewhat restricted. The requirements for first-time adoption are illustrated in the table below.

Application of IFRS 2	Equity-settled transactions [IFRS 1 App D para D2].	Cash-settled transactions [IFRS 1 App D para D3].
Required	IFRS 2's requirements apply to all grants of shares, share options or other equity instruments made after 7 November 2002 that have not yet vested by the date of transition to IFRS. Modifications to the terms and conditions of a grant of equity instruments to which IFRS 2 has not been applied are dealt with in accordance with IFRS 2's requirements if that modification occurs after the date of transition to IFRS. This is the case even if the equity instrument in question was originally granted before 7 November 2002. For all grants of equity instruments to which IFRS 2 has not been applied, the information required by paragraphs 44 and 45 of IFRS 2 must still be disclosed.	IFRS 2's requirements apply to all liabilities arising from share-based payment transactions that exist at the date of transition to IFRS.
Encouraged	Apply IFRS 2's requirements to other grants of equity instruments only if the fair value of those instruments, determined at the measurement date as defined by IFRS 2 has previously been disclosed publicly.	

2.101 The application of the above requirements is illustrated in the following examples.

Example 1 – Unlisted entity with a June year end that adopts IFRS in 2008

Entity A has a June year end. Its first financial statements prepared in accordance with IFRS are for the year ending 30 June 2008. Hence, its date of transition to IFRS is 1 July 2006.

The requirements of IFRS 2 will apply to all grants of shares, share options or other equity instruments made after 7 November 2002 that have not yet vested by the date of transition to IFRS (1 July 2006).

Similarly, liabilities in respect of cash-settled transactions should be measured in accordance with the requirements of IFRS 2 if they have not been settled by 1 July 2006.

Example 2 – Modification of terms and conditions

Entity A (as described in example 1) made an award of share options to certain of its key management on 1 April 2002. Information in respect of the award is shown below:

- Number of awards – 100 (all of which are expected to vest).
- Number of options per award – 1,000.
- Exercise price – C1.20.
- Market price of shares at date of grant – C1.20.
- Fair value of option at date of grant – C0.60.
- Vesting period – 5 years.

Following a period of declining share prices, the exercise price of the options was reduced to C0.80 on 1 April 2005. The fair value of the original award on that date was C0.20 and the fair value of the re-priced option was C0.50.

As the original grant of options was made before 7 November 2002, entity A does not need to apply IFRS 2 to that grant. It must, however, account for the re-pricing in accordance with IFRS 2. The incremental fair value of each re-priced option is C0.30 (that is, $0.50 - 0.20$) so this amount is recognised over the remaining two years of the award. On the assumption that all of the awards do vest, the amount recognised in each accounting period will be as follows:

Year ending 31 December 2005 – C11,250 ($100 \times 1,000 \times 0.30 \times 9/12 \times \frac{1}{2}$)
Year ending 31 December 2006 – C15,000 ($100 \times 1,000 \times 0.30 \times \frac{1}{2}$)
Year ending 31 December 2007 – C3,750 ($100 \times 1,000 \times 0.30 \times 3/12 \times \frac{1}{2}$)

2.102 The requirement in paragraph D2 in Appendix D of IFRS 1 for previous public disclosure of the fair value of equity instrument granted will restrict the ability of companies to follow this route. One example of an entity that has previously disclosed the fair value of its employee options is BP plc as shown in Table 2.3 below.

Table 2.3 – Disclosure of fair value of employee share options

BP Plc – Annual Report – 31 December 2003

34 Employee share plans (extract)

BP does not recognize an expense in respect of share options granted to employees. If the fair value of options granted in any particular year is estimated and this value amortized over the vesting period of the options, an indication of the cost of granting options to employees can be made. The fair value of each share option granted has been estimated using a Black Scholes option pricing model with the following assumptions:

	2003	2002
Risk-free interest rate	3.5%	4.0%
Expected volatility	30%	26%
Expected life in years	1 to 5	1 to 5
Expected dividend yield	4.00%	3.75%
Weighted average fair value of options granted ($)	1.44	1.64

The additional expense that would have been recognized in 2003 on this basis would be $79 million ($90 million) and the impact on earnings per share would be 1 cent (1 cent).

2.103   Other companies with shares listed in the US may have disclosed the fair value of equity instruments granted in accordance with US GAAP for the purposes of US reporting.

Grants to which IFRS 2 does not apply

2.104   The disclosure requirements of paragraphs 44 and 45 of IFRS 2 apply to all grants of equity instruments to which the recognition and measurement requirements of IFRS 2 have not been applied. [IFRS 1 App D para D2]. These disclosures provide information that enables the users of the financial statements to understand the nature and extent of share-based payment arrangements that existed during the period.

2.105   IFRS 1 gives no guidance as to how to account for awards to which IFRS 2 has not been applied. An expense for such awards may have been recognised under previous GAAP. A question arises as to whether any previous GAAP expense recognised should be reversed in the absence of explicit guidance in IFRS 1. In most cases, since reversal of any such expense would only affect components of equity at the transition date, we believe that reversal of previous GAAP expense would not be required. Where previous GAAP expense has been capitalised as part of the cost of a self-constructed asset, an entity would need to consider whether the asset's carrying value complies with IAS 16. Specifically, paragraph 17(a) of IAS 16 permits directly attributable employee benefit expense to be capitalised as part of a self-constructed asset's cost. If expenses capitalised under previous GAAP are, in substance, materially the same as those permitted by IAS 16, we believe that reversal of those capitalised costs would not be required on transition.

Insurance contracts

2.106 IFRS 1 allows a first-time adopter to apply the transitional provisions of IFRS 4. [IFRS 1 App D para D4]. These are applied from the date and period that IFRS 4 is applied. The provisions give various reliefs from retrospective application of the standard. As some of the relief relates to periods beginning before 1 January 2005, they are unlikely to be applicable for many current first-time adopters. The one remaining relief that is most likely to be relevant is that IFRS 4 requires disclosure of claims development history that should go back to the period when the earliest material claim arose for which there is still uncertainty about the amount and the timing of payments, up to a maximum of ten years. The transitional provisions give relief from this requirement. First-time adopters need not give information about claims development that occurred more than five years before the end of the first financial year to which IFRS 4 is applied. In addition, if it is impracticable to give the information for claims development that happened before the beginning of the earliest period for which full comparative information complying with IFRS 4 is given, that fact should be disclosed. [IFRS 4 para 44].

Deemed cost

2.107 IAS 16 requires initial measurement of property, plant and equipment at cost (PPE). PPE includes assets that are held under a finance lease where initial recognition of PPE is required by IAS 17, but the subsequent measurement of such PPE is within IAS 16's scope. [IAS 16 para 4]. The exemption in IFRS 1 allows entities to use a value that is not depreciated cost in accordance with IAS 16 and IAS 23 as deemed cost on transition to IFRS. It is not necessary to apply the exemption to all assets or to a group of assets. For assets held under a finance lease, any revaluation to fair value would be a valuation of the right to use the asset (and not the asset itself) based on the remaining utility of the asset under the finance lease. There are three possible values that may be used as the basis of deemed cost at the date of transition. Any of these values may be applied to any individual item of PPE. These values are as follows:

■ A fair value at the date of transition to IFRS, that is, where an entity specifically fair values an asset at the date of transition.

■ A value of an item of property, plant and equipment that was revalued under a previous GAAP, at or before the date of transition to IFRS, where that revaluation was broadly comparable to either fair value or to cost (or depreciated cost) adjusted to reflect changes in a price index. The revaluation must have been recorded in the entity's previous GAAP financial statements. The revalued amount becomes deemed cost at the date of revaluation. If this was prior to the date of transition then depreciation should be applied from the date of revaluation up to the date of transition.

■ A deemed cost that was previously established using fair value at a particular 'event' date prior to transition, for example because of a privatisation or an IPO. An entity's previous GAAP may require an asset to be written down to its fair value when the asset's carrying amount is impaired. Provided the new carrying value of the impaired asset represented fair value, this value would qualify as an event-driven valuation. Like the revaluation under an entity's previous GAAP, this value is used as deemed cost at the date of that valuation, and should be depreciated up to the date of transition to IFRS (see para 2.118).

[IFRS 1 App D paras D5, D6, D8, IG9].

2.108 An entity may have previously revalued property, plant and equipment to fair value as well as adjusting the revalued amount in subsequent periods to reflect changes in a price index. The question arises as to whether the resulting carrying value at the date of transition could be considered deemed cost under the exemption. Paragraph BC47 of IFRS 1 further expands on the guidance in paragraph D6 to state that this exemption provides flexibility in moving to IFRS and is intended to be a cost-effective solution that uses information already available to the entity. On that basis, we believe that an entity may be able to treat the resulting carrying value at the date of transition as deemed cost.

2.109 Where a fair value has been established at a particular 'event date' in the context of paragraph D8 of IFRS 1, deemed cost is available for any asset or liability on a selective basis. However, the fair value must have actually been recorded in the entity's financial statements. A fair value adjustment that was not reflected in a subsidiary's own separate financial statements would not be a fair value that could be used by that subsidiary on transition to IFRS as 'deemed cost'. Furthermore, we believe that it would be inappropriate to recognise an asset or liability at the date of transition that was previously unrecognised, solely on the basis of the valuation event. Consistent with paragraph 10(b) of IFRS 1, we believe that this aspect of the exemption can only be applied if the asset or liability in question met the relevant recognition criteria in IFRS.

2.110 Local regulations may require entities to remeasure assets and liabilities to fair value on events such as a privatisation or an IPO and to recognise those revalued amounts as deemed cost under local GAAP. If such an event occurs after the date of transition to IFRS, IFRS 1 now permits entities to use these revalued amounts as deemed cost at the date the event occurs provided that its occurrence is during the period covered by the first IFRS financial statements. [IFRS App D para D8(b)]. Any resulting adjustment from the transition date to the event date would be recognised in retained earnings (or another appropriate category of equity) at the event date. At the date of transition, the assets and liabilities would either be measured at deemed cost using either fair value or revaluation as described above or in accordance with other applicable IFRSs.

2.111 As noted in paragraph 2.107, guidance under an entity's previous GAAP in respect of impairment may require an asset to be written down to its fair value and this value would qualify as an event-driven valuation. IFRS 1 permits an entity to recognise an event-driven valuation as deemed cost at the transition date, even if that valuation was performed after the transition date. However, where an entity identifies an impairment triggering event taking place after the transition date and the asset is written down to its fair value, we believe it would not be appropriate to recognise this fair value as deemed cost at the transition date. This is because the entity must use IAS 36 after its transition date and its previous GAAP is no longer applicable. Therefore, impairment of assets that result in the asset being written down to fair value under the previous GAAP would only qualify as an event-driven valuation if the impairment write-down occurred before the transition date.

2.112 IFRS 1 also provides specific relief in respect of oil and gas assets. Oil and gas assets in the development or production phase may have been accounted for using the full cost method. IFRS 1 states that on transition to IFRS, where an entity has applied full cost accounting under its previous GAAP, its oil and gas assets may be measured as follows:

- for exploration and evaluation assets, at the carrying value determined under the entity's previous GAAP; and

- for assets in the development and production phases, at the amount determined for the cost centre under the entity's previous GAAP allocated *pro rata* using reserves volumes or values at the transition date.

[IFRS 1 para D8A].

2.113 IFRS 1 is clear that this exemption may only be applied by entities that used the full cost method for accounting for oil and gas assets under their previous GAAP. If, however, an entity's previous GAAP resulted in oil and gas assets being accounted for in a manner generally consistent with IFRSs, then this exemption would not be available. [IFRS1 para BC 47E]. Where an entity applies the exemption, IFRS 1 also requires exploration and evaluation assets as well as assets in the development or production phases to be tested for impairment in accordance with IFRS 6 or IAS 36 as appropriate.

2.114 The IASB amended IFRS 1 to provide relief to entities that carry items of property, plant and equipment and intangible assets that are or were previously used in rate regulated activities. The amendment states that operations are considered to be subject to rate regulation if "*they provide goods or services to customers at prices (i.e. rates) established by an authorised body empowered to establish rates that bind the customers and that are designed to recover the specific costs the entity incurs in providing the regulated goods or services and to earn a specified return*". [IFRS 1 App D para D8B]. The specified return does not need to be of a fixed amount and may be stated as a minimum amount or a range.

2.115 The amendment permits a first-time adopter to use the previous GAAP carrying amount of such rate regulated assets as deemed cost at the date of transition to IFRS even if those assets would not qualify for recognition under IFRS. However, entities that use this exemption would be required to test these assets for impairment at the transition date in accordance with IAS 36. Furthermore, the amendment permits entities to choose the assets to which the exemption is applied. This is similar to the choice available in the deemed cost exemption for other types of assets. This amendment is effective for periods beginning on or after 1 January 2011 with earlier application permitted. When an entity applies this exemption in its IFRS financial statements, it is required to disclose the fact as well as the basis on which the carrying amounts were calculated under the entity's previous GAAP. [IFRS 1 para 31B].

2.116 Paragraph D5 in Appendix D of IFRS 1 does not set out detailed requirements under which fair value at the date of transition to IFRS should be determined. Entities that adopt a deemed cost have only to provide the limited disclosures required by paragraph 30 of IFRS 1. Methods and assumptions for determining the fair value, for example, do not have to be disclosed. Use of the deemed cost exemption is a cost-effective alternative approach for entities that do not perform a full retrospective application of the requirements of IAS 16 to their property, plant and equipment.

> **UK.2.116.1** Because of the different valuation bases for assets between current UK GAAP and IFRS, a previous valuation may not have been comparable to fair value. See further paragraph UK.2.216.32.

2.117 IAS 16 allows two measurement bases for classes of property, plant and equipment after initial measurement: cost or revaluation. [IAS 16 paras 15, 29]. As noted in paragraph 2.22 above an entity must use the same accounting policies throughout its first IFRS financial statements. For property, plant and equipment this means that it must choose a policy from the date of transition and apply that policy throughout its first IFRS financial statements. Entities are free to choose either measurement policy on adopting IFRS.

Assets measured at depreciated cost under IFRS

2.118 The deemed cost exemption means that where a class of property, plant and equipment is to be measured on a cost basis under IAS 16 then that class may comprise some or all of the following mix of measurements at an entity's date of transition to IFRS:

- Assets that were measured at depreciated historical cost under previous GAAP, stated at that depreciated historical cost.

- Assets that have been fair valued at the date of transition to IFRS stated at that fair value (using the first bullet in para 2.107 above).

- Assets that had been revalued some time ago under previous GAAP, whose values were frozen under that GAAP, stated at those frozen values depreciated to the date of transition (using the second bullet in para 2.107 above).

- Assets that had been revalued under previous GAAP, stated at those revalued amounts depreciated to the date of transition (using the second bullet in para 2.107 above).

- Assets that had been revalued in an event-driven revaluation, stated at those revalued amounts depreciated to the date of transition (using the third bullet in para 2.107 above).

2.119 Depreciation is based on original cost if an entity carries forward assets at depreciated cost under previous GAAP. If a deemed cost has been used then depreciation is based on that deemed cost. [IFRS 1 para IG9]. Assets should be stated at cost or deemed cost less accumulated depreciation in accordance with IAS 16 at the date of transition to IFRS. Management should not restate the carrying value of property, plant and equipment at the date of transition to IFRS to reflect revised useful lives. IFRS 1 requires that estimates made under previous GAAP are not revised unless there is evidence of an error or the estimates are not consistent with IFRS (see paras 2.32, 2.37).

2.120 Where an entity applied a policy of revaluing a class of fixed assets under its previous GAAP, IFRS 1 allows those values, on any particular asset, to be frozen and treated as deemed cost (less depreciation) on transition to IFRS. This should, however, be based on the latest valuation that took place under the previous GAAP in order to comply with paragraph D6 in Appendix D of IFRS 1. This is illustrated by the following example.

Example – Previous GAAP revaluation as a deemed cost

An entity prepares financial statements to a December year end. Under its previous GAAP it adopted a policy of revaluing its land and buildings. It carried out a full revaluation at 31 December 20X0 (valuing them at C1m), an interim valuation at 31 December 20X3 (valuing them at C2m), and another full valuation at 31 December 20X5 (valuing them at C2.5m). The land and buildings were stated at C1.8m in the financial statements immediately prior to revaluation at 31 December 20X5, having had C100,000 of depreciation charged in 20X4 and C100,000 charged in 20X5. The revaluations were equivalent to fair value.

The entity adopts IFRS for its financial statements to 31 December 20X6 and its date of transition is 1 January 20X5. It decides to take advantage of the deemed cost exemption with respect to the land and buildings. It will adopt a cost-based policy under IAS 16 and will use its valuation made under previous GAAP.

The entity cannot use the valuation of C2.5m at 31 December 20X5 as deemed cost at 1 January 20X5, as this valuation took place after its date of transition. Instead it should use the interim valuation at 31 December 20X3 as deemed cost for the land and buildings.

On the assumption that the previous GAAP depreciation was in compliance with IFRS, the carrying value at the entity's date of transition should be C1.9m, being the deemed cost of C2m adjusted for depreciation charged in 20X4 of C100,000.

In its opening IFRS balance sheet the land and buildings will be stated at:

	C'000
Cost	2,000
Accumulated depreciation	(100)
Net book value	1,900

Since the assets are now held on a deemed-cost basis under IFRS the entity's previously disclosed revaluation surplus will be transferred to retained earnings or another component of equity on transition to IFRS (see further para 2.125).

2.121   The deemed cost exemption allows previous GAAP revaluations to be used as deemed cost under IFRS, but only if those valuations were, at the time of the valuation, equivalent to fair value. In many cases the previous GAAP revaluation will be equivalent to fair value. However, in some cases valuations under previous GAAP will not be appropriate as they will not have been equivalent to fair value under IFRS.

2.122   Additionally, entities should ensure that the correct measurement under previous GAAP has been used: the valuation made under previous GAAP must be the fair value at the 'event' of privatisation or IPO. The deemed cost option requires only that a previous valuation was broadly comparable to fair value, or was based on depreciated cost adjusted to reflect changes to a price index.

Assets measured at revaluation under IFRS

2.123   IAS 16 allows, in addition to a cost-based policy, one based on revaluation. Classes of property, plant and equipment may be carried at fair value less depreciation. The carrying amounts at a balance sheet date should not be materially different from fair value at that date. [IAS 16 para 31]. IFRS 1's deemed cost exemption does not preclude assets in respect of which the exemption has been taken from being part of a class that is revalued under IAS 16. Entities should, however, ensure that values are 'current' so that they comply with IAS 16. An asset that is stated at depreciated cost or a deemed cost on transition to IFRS and is part of a class that is revalued on an ongoing basis under IAS 16 may have to be revalued at the date of transition to IFRS. If cost or deemed cost is materially different from fair value at the date of transition then the asset(s) should be revalued to fair value at that date. An entity that uses cost or a deemed cost based on a revaluation that took place sometime before transition, and then wishes to adopt a policy of revaluation, is likely to be required to revalue its assets at the date of transition to IFRS.

UK.2.123.1   The point regarding whether revaluations under UK GAAP are equivalent to fair value, noted at paragraph UK.2.116.1 above, is equally valid for assets where a UK GAAP valuation is carried forward to be used in a revalued class in IFRS.

2.124   Where an entity adopts the treatment of revaluation under IAS 16 it presents the cumulative revaluation surplus in other comprehensive income and accumulated in equity. [IAS 16 paras 39, 40]. IFRS 1 provides that the revaluation surplus at the date of transition to IFRS is the difference between the carrying amount of an asset and its cost or deemed cost. [IFRS 1 para IG10].

UK.2.124.1   Although it is not stated explicitly in IFRS 1, our view is that in cases where an asset has been revalued under previous GAAP and continues to be revalued under IFRS it has a cost rather than a deemed cost and the amount of the revaluation surplus disclosed should be based on the asset's original cost.

UK companies are required by law to disclose the cost of revalued assets and, therefore, they are able to carry forward any pre-existing revaluation reserve when moving to IFRS for those categories of asset that are to be revalued under IAS 16.

2.125   Where, however, an entity uses a revaluation as deemed cost at the date of transition in order to adopt a policy of cost under IFRS then any revaluation surplus previously disclosed in respect of that asset is transferred to another component of equity. Since there is no difference between the carrying amount of the asset and its deemed cost, the component of equity to which the surplus is transferred should not be described as a revaluation reserve.

UK.2.125.1   It should be noted that IFRS is not concerned with issues of realisation and the fact that a UK GAAP revaluation reserve is no longer disclosed under IFRS does not mean that it has become realised.

2.126   The above principles may be illustrated by the following example:

Example 1 – Assets measured at revaluation and depreciated cost under IFRS

Entity Q has four assets, each in a different class.

Assets 1 and 2 are revalued under previous GAAP. Assets 3 and 4 are not. Under previous GAAP, at 31 December 20X3, immediately prior to entity Q's date of transition to IFRS, its balance sheet (extract) is as follows:

	Asset 1 (valuation)	Asset 2 (valuation)	Asset 3 (cost)	Asset 4 (cost)	Total
Cost or revaluation	500	200	400	450	1,550
Accumulated depreciation	(100)	(50)	(200)	(170)	(520)
Net book value	400	150	200	280	1,030
Revaluation surplus	250	50	–	–	300

On adoption of IFRS entity Q decides that, under IFRS, it will:

- Continue to revalue asset 1. The fair value of asset 1 at the date of transition is not materially different from its carrying value under previous GAAP.

- Use the previous valuation of asset 2 as deemed cost, and adopt a policy of cost less depreciation under IFRS.

- Adopt a policy of revaluation for asset 3. The fair value of asset 3 at the entity's date of transition is 500.

- Continue to use a policy of cost less depreciation for asset 4.

All depreciation methods are already in accordance with those required by IAS 16.

First-time adoption of IFRS

The position on transition to IFRS at 1 January 20X4 is as follows:

	Asset 1 (valuation)	Asset 2 (cost)	Asset 3 (valuation)	Asset 4 (cost)	Total
Cost or revaluation	500	200	500	450	1,650
Accumulated depreciation	(100)	(50)	–	(170)	(320)
Net book value	400	150	500	280	1,330
Revaluation surplus	250	–	300	–	550
Adjustment to retained earnings	–	50	–	–	(50)

- The entity carries forward asset 1's previous GAAP cost and depreciation and continues to disclose a revaluation surplus of 250.

- Since the entity is adopting a policy of cost, then the previous valuation of 200 in respect of asset 2 becomes its deemed cost, depreciated by 50 to 150 at the date of transition. The previously disclosed revaluation surplus is transferred to retained earnings or another component of equity.

- Asset 3's fair value at the date of transition to IFRS is materially different from its carrying amount under previous GAAP. The asset should be revalued and stated at its fair value of 500 on the date of transition to IFRS. A revaluation surplus of 300 has been created on transition and should be separately presented.

- Asset 4 continues to be carried at cost less depreciation and the previous GAAP amounts should be carried forward into the entity's first IFRS financial statements.

Example 2 – Deemed cost exemption

Entity R prepares its first IFRS financial statements for the year ending 31 December 20X7. The date of transition to IFRS is 1 January 20X6 and the opening IFRS balance sheet is prepared as at that date.

Entity R operates a fleet of ships. The ships' engines are renewed every 10 years and under local GAAP the cost of renewal is charged to the income statement at the time of replacement. The vessels' original cost is depreciated over their estimated useful life of 30 years. Entity R's accounting records do not contain the information to identify the cost of engine renewals before 20X5.

The component approach required by IAS 16 should be applied prospectively from the date of transition to IFRS. Management should apply the deemed cost exemption to restate the vessels to fair value at the date of transition. The fair value should be analysed into the different significant components, for example engines and hulls. Management should depreciate each component over its remaining useful life.

There should be a corresponding adjustment to retained earnings and the amount of the adjustment disclosed in the first IFRS financial statements.

Example 3 – Deemed cost exemption: decommissioning obligation provisions

Entity S prepares its first IFRS financial statements for the year ending 31 December 20X7. The date of transition to IFRS is 1 January 20X6 and the opening IFRS balance sheet is prepared as at that date.

Entity S operates oil exploration and production facilities. There is a significant decommissioning obligation in connection with several oil wells, but entity T's previous GAAP did not require the obligation to be recognised.

Retrospective application of IAS 37 requires that management recognise the provision for decommissioning costs on the opening IFRS balance sheet. The provision should reflect the net present value of management's best estimate of the amount required to settle the obligation.

The obligation should be capitalised as a separate component of property, plant and equipment, together with the accumulated depreciation from the date the obligation was incurred to the transition date. The amount to be capitalised as part of the cost of the asset is calculated by discounting the liability back to the date the obligation initially arose using the best estimate of historical discount rates. The associated accumulated depreciation is calculated by applying the current estimate of the asset's useful life, using the entity's depreciation policy for the asset. [IFRS 1 para D21].

Any difference between the provision and the related component of property, plant and equipment, is adjusted against retained earnings.

Entity S's management could elect to apply the deemed cost exemption. Property, plant and equipment would be restated to fair value with a corresponding adjustment to retained earnings. Management would need to ensure that the fair value obtained was the gross fair value and not net of the decommissioning obligation. Management would recognise the provision for the decommissioning costs in accordance with IAS 37, but no cost in respect of the provision should be added to property, plant and equipment, but recognised in entity S's opening retained earnings.

Example 4 – Revaluation under previous GAAP as deemed cost when an entity's functional currency is different from the local reporting currency

How does an entity use a revaluation under previous GAAP as deemed cost when its functional currency is different to the local reporting currency at the transition date?

The entity first determines the date of the revaluation being used when using a previous GAAP revaluation as deemed cost in situations where the functional currency is different from the currency in which the revaluation was performed. IFRS 1 allows the entity to use a previous GAAP revaluation of an item of property, plant and equipment at, or before, the date of transition to IFRS (assuming certain conditions are met, see further para 2.107). Assuming the conditions are met, the functional currency cost is determined using the exchange rate as of the date of the revaluation. This date could be a date at or before the transition date. Note that further to an amendment to IFRS 1, the date of the revaluation may also occur during the first IFRS reporting period, see further paragraph 2.110.

Assets other than property, plant and equipment

2.127 The exemptions for fair value or deemed cost may also be applied to any investment property. [IFRS 1 App D para D7(a)]. This will only be appropriate in cases where an entity chooses to use the cost model for measurement of all of its investment properties under IAS 40. Therefore, the cost model under IAS 40 for first-time adopters may involve depreciating investment properties that have partly been restated to original cost or, where the deemed cost exemption has been used, have been stated at a revaluation at the date of transition or at an earlier date. The exemption may also be applied to any intangible assets that meet the recognition and revaluation criteria in IAS 38. [IFRS 1 App D para D7(b)]. The revaluation criteria in IAS 38 include the existence of an active market. IAS 38 discusses an active market stating that:

> *"It is uncommon for an active market with the characteristics described in paragraph 8 to exist for an intangible asset, although this may happen. For example, in some jurisdictions, an active market may exist for freely-transferable taxi licences, fishing licences or production quotas. However, an active market cannot exist for brands, newspaper mastheads, music and film publishing rights, patents or trademarks, because each such asset is unique. Also, although intangible assets are bought and sold, contracts are negotiated between individual buyers and sellers, and transactions are relatively infrequent. For these reasons, the price paid for one asset may not provide sufficient evidence of the fair value of another. Moreover, prices are often not available to the public."*

[IAS 38 para 78].

UK.2.127.1 Investment properties and first-time adoption are dealt with further in paragraph UK.2.216.126. The exemption for intangible assets will not apply to most intangibles recognised under UK GAAP. IAS 38's revaluation criteria are similar to FRS 10, which allows revaluation only where an intangible asset has a readily ascertainable market value and notes that most assets will not have such a value, though it could be that some operating licences, franchises and quotas might. Therefore, it is unlikely that UK entities will be able to apply a fair value as deemed cost to intangible assets on transition to IFRS.

2.128 Entities cannot use the deemed cost exemption for any assets or liabilities other than those stated in the above paragraphs. [IFRS 1 App D para D7].

Leases

2.129 IFRIC 4 deals with arrangements such as outsourcing, take or pay and the right to use capacity. It gives guidance on determining whether such arrangements are, or contain, leases, despite not having the legal form of a lease. If they fall within IFRIC 4 then they should be accounted for in accordance with IAS 17. Leasing, including the application of IFRIC 4, is dealt with in chapter 19.

2.130 The interpretation requires the assessment of whether or not an arrangement contains a lease to be carried out at the inception of the arrangement. It does, however, contain some transitional arrangements for existing users of IFRS so that, in the year of application, the assessment can be carried out based on facts existing at the start of the earliest comparative period rather than at inception. IFRS 1 was amended so that first-time adopters can determine whether or not an arrangement at the date of transition contains a lease on the basis of facts at that date. [IFRS 1 App D para D9].

2.131 Certain GAAPs, such as Canadian GAAP, contain guidance similar to IFRIC 4 within their framework. For first-time adopters transitioning from these GAAPs with existing leasing contracts accounted for in accordance with IFRIC 4, IFRS 1 provides additional relief. A re-assessment of the classification of those contracts according to IFRSs is not required when the same assessment has previously been made in accordance with their previous GAAP but at a date other than that required by other IFRSs. [IFRS 1 App D para D9A].

Employee benefits

2.132 IAS 19 allows entities to use a corridor approach to recognising actuarial gains and losses. This approach requires only a proportion of net actuarial gains and losses in excess of a limit of the greater of 10% of plan assets and plan liabilities to be recognised in the income statement. [IAS 19 para 92]. The transitional provisions of IAS 19 do not apply to first-time adopters of IFRS, in the same way that the transitional provisions of all other standards do not apply. [IFRS 1 para 9]. IFRS 1 allows entities to recognise all cumulative actuarial gains and losses at the date of transition on the balance sheet. The entity does not have to work out what it would have charged to the income statement in prior periods using the 'corridor approach', even if, after initial adoption of IFRS, it will use the 'corridor approach'. The exemption, if used, must be applied to all employee benefit plans. [IFRS 1 App D para D10].

2.133 If the exemption in IFRS 1 is taken, the entity should recognise the full net pension asset or liability (subject to the recognition criteria of IAS 19) on its balance sheet at the date of transition to IFRS. From this point onwards an entity may choose to adopt the 'corridor approach'. In an entity's first IFRS financial statements the entity must measure each defined-benefit plan at each balance sheet date. The defined-benefit obligation must be determined using the facts and circumstances and appropriate actuarial assumptions at each balance sheet date. An entity is permitted to obtain an actuarial valuation at one of these balance sheet dates and then roll the valuation forward or backward as appropriate. As part of that process, any material items arising between balance sheet dates must be reflected. [IFRS 1 para IG21].

2.134 The exemption does not apply to unrecognised past service costs. Accordingly, where benefit improvements have not yet vested, the net asset or liability recognised in respect of a defined benefit plan on first-time adoption of IFRS will not equate to the surplus or deficit in the plan. The accounting treatment of unvested past service costs is considered in chapter 11.

2.135 Swiss Post adopted IFRS for the first time in 2003 and applied the principles of IFRS 1 in so doing. It took advantage of the exemption described above and chose to follow the 'corridor' approach from then on, as illustrated in the following extract from its 2003 financial statements.

Table 2.4 – First-time adoption of IFRS

Swiss Post Group – financial statements – 31 December 2003

2 Accounting principles (extract)

As of 1 January 2003, the consolidated financial statements of Swiss Post have been prepared in accordance with International Financial Reporting Standards (hereinafter referred to as IFRS, formerly IAS). They also comply with the Postal Organization Act. The impact of the conversion from Swiss GAAP ARR (Accounting and Reporting Recommendations) to IFRS on consolidated equity and profit is disclosed in Note 3 (Impact of the change in accounting principles). Material differences compared with the accounting principles applied previously (Swiss GAAP ARR) are described below. The prior-year figures have been restated to conform to IFRS, thereby making a comparison between periods possible.

The consolidated balance sheet as at 31 December 2003 shows a negative equity position due to the recognition of a provision of CHF 3.7 billion for employee benefit obligations, recognized in accordance with IAS 19 as at 1 January 2002 (opening balance sheet as per IFRS). Funding of the shortfall by the Swiss Confederation was not prejudiced in any way as a result of these obligations being recognized in the balance sheet. On 29 October 2003, the Federal Council set out the principles according to which the problems associated with the pension funds of the Swiss Confederation and former government-owned enterprises would be solved. Based on the aforementioned principles, and in consultation with its pension fund, Swiss Post is examining measures to reduce its employee benefit obligations. Following the periodic review of the parameters on which IAS 19 calculations are based, assumptions regarding wage trends and pension indexation were adjusted effective 31 December 2003. However, this did not affect recognized employee benefit obligations and expenses provided for during 2003.

On 16 December 2003, the Federal Parliament reached a decision on the funding of the shortfall (calculated in accordance with federal legislation governing occupational retirement, survivors' and disability pension plans (BVG)) in the former Occupational Pension Plan for Special Services as part of the Swiss Confederation's budget proposals for 2004. In 2004, this shortfall will be funded by the Swiss Confederation, as a result of which it will be covered in accordance with the same principles which apply to the shortfall in the pension fund of the Confederation (PKB). This reduced the employee benefit obligations recognized in the consolidated balance sheet of Swiss Post by CHF 204 million as of 31 December 2003.

3 Impact of the change in accounting principles (extract)

In adopting IFRS as its accounting principles, Swiss Post prepared its financial statements as if IFRS had historically been applied. In each case, balance sheet items are restated by adjusting the opening value as at 1 January 2002 and taking the difference in the corresponding item to equity.

Consolidated equity as at 1 January 2002 and 31 December 2002 changed as follows as a result of adopting IFRS:

CHF m	31.12.2002	1.1.2002
Consolidated equity as stated in the annual report prepared in accordance with Swiss GAAP ARR	**2 290**	**2 085**
Adjusted (restated) items:		
a) Financial assets	732	22
b) Replacement capital expenditure for real estate	25	0
c) Restructuring provisions	32	35
d) Provisions for insurance risks	265	265
e) Provisions for employee benefit obligations	−3 669	−3 658
f) Provisions for long-term benefits due to employees and retirees	−423	−403
Other	4	11
Total	−3 034	3 728
Consolidated equity (restated) in accordance with IFRS	**−744**	**−1 643**

Group profit for 2002 changed as follows as a result of adopting IFRS:

CHF m	year 2002
Group profit as stated in the annual report prepared in accordance with Swiss GAAP ARR	**204**
Adjusted (restated) items:	
a) Profit/loss from financial services	21
b) Replacement capital expenditure for real estate	25
e) Pension expenses	−11
f) Staff costs	−20
Other	−8
Total	7
Group profit (restated) in accordance with IFRS	**211**

e) Employee benefit obligations

Employee benefit obligations were initially recognized in their entirety when the accounts were restated in accordance with IFRS as at 1 January 2002 . Of the CHF 3 713 million of employee benefit obligations disclosed, CHF 55 million of provisions were already recognized in the balance sheet prepared in accordance with Swiss GAAP ARR. The remaining CHF 3 658 million were recorded and charged to retained earnings as an adjustment to IFRS. Prepared in accordance with IFRS, the accounts for the 2002 financial year also contain plan amendment costs of around CHF 11 million, which were not recognized under Swiss GAAP ARR.

UK.2.135.1 This exemption is likely to prove very useful to UK companies that wish to use the corridor approach under IAS 19. As a result of FRS 17, a UK entity will have many of the numbers available that reflect the full market value of assets and actuarial value of liabilities of its defined benefit pension schemes. However, FRS 17 information will not have identified when actuarial gains and losses arose since plan inception, which is the starting point for being able to identify what might have been deferred and what might not.

2.136 The exemption is also useful for entities that do not choose the 'corridor' approach under IFRS. If an entity wishes to use the statement of comprehensive income option in IAS 19, then it must apply this method retrospectively, unless it takes advantage of the exemption in IFRS 1. One of the requirements of IAS 19 is that an entity discloses the cumulative amount of actuarial gains and losses recognised in other comprehensive income where the statement of comprehensive income approach has been applied. [IAS 19 para 120A(i)]. Therefore, to comply with this disclosure requirement, an entity would have to retrospectively determine the cumulative amount of actuarial gains and losses as at the transition date. In applying the exemption, an entity simply needs to account for the full net pension asset or liability on its balance sheet at the date of transition. Actuarial gains and losses arising from this point will be recorded through the statement of comprehensive income.

2.137   IAS 19 requires disclosure of the history of experience gains and losses. Paragraph 120A(p) of IAS 19 requires disclosure for the current annual period and the previous four annual periods of:

- the present value of the defined benefit obligation, the fair value of the defined benefit plan assets and the surplus or deficit in the plan, and

- the experience adjustments arising on:

    - the plan liabilities (expressed either as an amount or as a percentage of the plan liabilities at the balance sheet date); and

    - the plan assets (expressed either as an amount or as a percentage of the plan assets at the balance sheet date).

IFRS 1 states that this disclosure may be given as the amounts are determined for each accounting period prospectively from the transition date. [IFRS 1 App D para D11]. This applies whether or not the exemption in paragraph D10 in Appendix D relating to the 'corridor approach' is taken.

Cumulative translation differences

2.138   IAS 21, 'The effects of changes in foreign exchange rates', requires certain exchange differences arising on net investments in subsidiaries to be recognised in other comprehensive income and then recognised as income or expense on disposal of the foreign entity to which they relate. These are known as 'cumulative translation differences' (CTDs). [IFRS 1 App D para D12].

2.139   The IFRS 1 exemption on cumulative translation differences relieves entities from complying with certain requirements of IAS 21. Entities are not required to separately classify the CTD as other comprehensive income up to the date of transition and to transfer the CTD to the income statement on disposal of the related net investment. This relief is only for CTDs occurring up to the date of transition. Subsequently, CTDs must be recorded in accordance with IAS 21 and then transferred to the income statement as part of any gain or loss on disposal. If this exemption is taken, it applies to CTDs on all foreign operations. [IFRS 1 App D para D13].

2.140 CTDs in consolidated financial statements are those arising from applying the closing rate method. The differences are caused by retranslating a group's opening net investment (including monetary items that are in substance part of net investment) at closing rate, translating the income statement at average rates and retained earnings in the balance sheet at the closing rate.

2.141 The exchange differences arising on a foreign currency borrowing accounted for as a net investment hedge should be classified as other comprehensive income until disposal of the net investment. On disposal they should also be recognised as income or expenses on disposal of the investment.

UK.2.141.1 Under the UK standard SSAP 20, entities were required on consolidation to classify in equity the same exchange differences as those required to be classified in equity under IAS 21, but SSAP 20 did not require disclosure of these CTDs as a separate component of equity and does not permit recycling of these exchange differences to the income statement on disposal of the related foreign operation. Therefore, UK entities applying SSAP 20 will find the exemption useful on transition to IFRS.

UK.2.141.2 The UK standard FRS 23 contains the same requirement to track and recycle CTDs as IAS 21. However, FRS 23 contains transitional rules so that entities applying it can set CTDs to zero at the date of application and only track and recycle them from that point. UK companies will not have to recreate past CTDs on application of FRS 23. Therefore, entities moving to IFRS after applying FRS 23 will still find the IFRS 1 CTD exemption useful.

2.142 The CTD for a foreign operation is seldom easy to reconstruct. This is likely to be the case when:

- an investment has been held for a number of years and the calculation would require retrieval of profit for the year and average and closing exchange rates for many periods; or

- an entity's net investment has been built up in stages, with different amounts acquired in different periods at various exchange rates; or

- there are many separate foreign net investments within a group, thus many subsidiaries would lead to complex recalculations.

Investments in subsidiaries, jointly controlled entities and associates

2.143 When an entity prepares separate financial statements, IAS 27 requires it to account for its investment in subsidiaries, jointly controlled entities and associates either:

> *"(a) at cost; or*
>
> *(b) in accordance with IAS 39 Financial instruments: Recognition and measurement."*

[IFRS 1 App D para D14].

2.144 Where a first-time adopter elects to measure such investments at cost, it may use either cost determined in accordance with IAS 27 or deemed cost. The deemed cost is determined using either fair value in accordance with IAS 39 or the carrying amount under previous GAAP. [IFRS 1 App D para D15]. Where cost is determined in accordance with IAS 27, the standard requires all subsequent dividends to be presented as income in the investor's separate financial statements. [IAS 27 para 38A]. Hence, any dividends received by the investor would not be considered in establishing the cost of the investment in accordance with IAS 27.

2.145 If an entity uses a deemed cost in its opening IFRS balance sheet of its separate financial statements for an investment in a subsidiary, jointly controlled entity or associate, the entity's first IFRS separate financial statements should disclose:

> *"(a) the aggregate deemed cost of those investments for which deemed cost is their previous GAAP carrying amount;*
>
> *(b) the aggregate deemed cost of those investments for which deemed cost is fair value; and*
>
> *(c) the aggregate adjustment to the carrying amounts reported under previous GAAP."*

[IFRS 1 para 31].

Subsidiary, joint venture or associate adopts later than group

2.146 There are two options when an entity adopts IFRS at a date later than the group headed by its parent (or entity that has significant influence or joint control over it). It may measure its assets and liabilities at either:

> *"(a) the carrying amounts that would be included in the parent's consolidated financial statements, based on the parent's date of transition to IFRSs, if no adjustments were made for consolidation procedures and for the effects of the business combination in which the parent acquired the subsidiary; or*
>
> *(b) the carrying amounts required by the rest of this IFRS, based on the subsidiary's date of transition to IFRSs..."*

[IFRS 1 App D para D16].

2.147 With respect to the first of these options, a parent's consolidated financial statements may not contain an explicit and unreserved statement of compliance with IFRS, however, the accounting framework applied by the parent may be based on IFRS. For example, financial statements may be prepared in accordance with IFRS as adopted by the EU. In such a case, the question arises as to whether the parent is considered to have applied IFRS in order for a subsidiary to avail itself of this option.

2.148 We believe that the subsidiary would need to consider whether the parent's financial statements would comply with IFRS as issued by the IASB.

This would require an analysis of the parent's accounting policies to determine whether such compliance could be stated. Only relevant differences between the accounting framework applied by the parent and IFRS as issued IASB should be considered. For example, the framework applied may have different hedging requirements to IFRS as issued by the IASB. If the parent has no hedging relationships in place, then this area of difference is irrelevant. 'Dual compliance' by the parent is possible where an 'equivalent IFRS' (such as IFRS as adopted by the EU) is not identical to IFRS as issued by the IASB only if the parent is not affected by the difference(s). Where a subsidiary determines that its parent could assert compliance with IFRS as issued by the IASB, then we believe the first option noted in paragraph 2.146 would be available to the subsidiary.

2.149 A further note on the first option in paragraph 2.146 is that if the subsidiary was acquired after the parent's date of transition to IFRS, this option would not be available. This is because the *"carrying amount that would be included in the parent's consolidated financial statements, based on the parent's date of transition to IFRSs..."* simply would not exist. Since the parent did not have control over the subsidiary at its date of transition, the subsidiary was not included in the parent's consolidated financial statements at that date.

> **Example – Subsidiary is acquired after transition date of its parent**
>
> The parent and its group transitioned to IFRS on 1 January 20X5. The parent acquired 100% of a new subsidiary at 20 July 20X7 and on consolidation recognised the assets and liabilities of the subsidiary at fair value as required by IFRS 3. The subsidiary continued to apply its local GAAP and its accounting policy was to account for property, plant and equipment at cost.
>
> During year 20Y2, local regulations require the subsidiary to adopt IFRS with a transition date of 1 January 20Y1.
>
>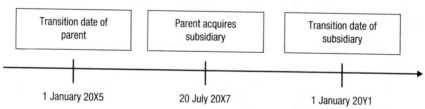
>
> As part of the transition exercise, the subsidiary intends to revalue its property, plant and equipment to fair value and elect the 'fair value as deemed cost' exemption in accordance with paragraph D5 in appendix D to IFRS 1. The subsidiary wishes to carry its property, plant and equipment at the same values as shown in the consolidated financial statements.
>
> The parent calculated the property, plant and equipment's fair value on the acquisition.
>
> The subsidiary cannot use this fair value on the transition to IFRS, as paragraph D16 in appendix D to IFRS 1 is clear that the measurement date has to be either: (a) the

parent's date of transition, or (b) the subsidiary's date of transition. As the subsidiary was acquired after the parent's date of transition to IFRS, option (a) is not available. The subsidiary was not included in the parent's consolidated financial statements at 1 January 20X5 and therefore such carrying amounts simply don't exist.

The subsidiary has to measure the assets based on fair value as deemed cost at its own transition date.

Paragraph D8 of appendix D to IFRS 1 (event driven revaluation at a date earlier or later than transition date) is not available as no such revaluation was recorded under previous GAAP at the time of acquisition.

The subsidiary will not be able to record its property, plant and equipment at the same values carried in the group consolidation if the subsidiary elects the 'deemed cost' exemption.

2.150 When a parent entity that prepares consolidated financial statements adopts IFRS for the first time it will require information from its subsidiary for those consolidated financial statements as at the date of transition. From this date the subsidiary will have to produce the information as if it had adopted IFRS for the first time from the parent's date of transition. The subsidiary may not ever have produced full IFRS financial statements. It makes sense that when the subsidiary moves to IFRS at a later date it has the option to use the same assumptions, exemptions and figures as it produced when its parent moved to IFRS.

2.151 Subsidiaries may wish to take the exemption and measure their assets and liabilities at the carrying amounts used in their parents' first IFRS financial statements. These carrying amounts are those before *"adjustments...made for consolidation procedures"*, for example, to eliminate intercompany profit in inventory, to align group accounting policies and any adjustments relating to the subsidiary's acquisition.

Example – Subsidiary adopts IFRS later than group: effect on goodwill

Entity O prepares its first IFRS financial statements for the year ending 31 December 20X7. The date of transition to IFRS is 1 January 20X6 and the opening IFRS balance sheet is prepared as at that date.

Entity O has made several acquisitions that were recorded using the purchase method under entity O's previous GAAP. Goodwill was recognised and amortised, so there is a balance of goodwill on entity O's previous GAAP balance sheet at 31 December 20X5.

Entity O was acquired by entity P in 20X3 and entity P deducted the resultant goodwill from equity in its consolidated financial statements in accordance with its previous GAAP. Entity P has adopted IFRS in 20X6 and its date of transition was 1 January 20X5. Entity P will not reinstate the goodwill deducted from equity on its opening IFRS balance sheet.

Can entity O apply the exemption in paragraph D16 in Appendix D of IFRS 1 and deduct the goodwill arising on its own acquisitions from equity so that the carrying amounts on entity O's IFRS opening IFRS balance sheet are the same as those of its parent, P?

No. The deduction of goodwill from equity by P on acquisition of entity O was a result of the requirements of entity P's previous GAAP. IFRS 1 requires that goodwill deducted from equity under previous GAAP should not be reinstated as an asset (see para 2.75).

The effects of entity P's acquisition of entity O are excluded from the exemption in paragraph D16 in Appendix D of IFRS 1. Entity O should include the goodwill carrying value from its own acquisitions on its opening IFRS balance sheet.

2.152 Where the subsidiary uses the group's date of transition as the basis of its own financial statements, IFRS 1 allows the subsidiary's assets and liabilities on its transition to be stated at *"the carrying amounts that would be included in the parent's consolidated financial statements,* based on *the parent's date of transition to IFRSs"*. [IFRS 1 App D para D16, emphasis added]. This is illustrated in the example below.

> **Example 1 – Subsidiary adopts IFRS later than group: measurement of assets and liabilities**
>
> Group M has a date of transition to IFRS of 1 January 20X6, producing its first IFRS financial statements for the year to 31 December 20X7
>
> On transition to IFRS, group M decides to use the deemed cost exemption and measures its buildings at their fair value at 1 January 20X6 of C1.2m, using these fair values as deemed cost. The buildings had previously been stated at a net book value of C400,000, being cost of C600,000 less depreciation of C200,000, at 31 December 20X5. One of the buildings, with a fair value of C450,000, a cost of C200,000 and a net book value of C150,000, was held in subsidiary N. The asset is being depreciated over 20 years and had 15 years remaining. Group M assesses that all of its buildings have a remaining useful economic life at the date of transition of 15 years.
>
> The country in which subsidiary N is located adopts IFRS for local statutory financial statements for financial years commencing on or after 1 January 20X6. Subsidiary N has a transition date of 1 January 20X7 and produces its first IFRS financial statements for the year to 31 December 20X8 with one year of comparatives. Subsidiary N was not able to revalue its property in its local financial statements. The net book values at 31 December 20X7 are as follows:

Year to	Subsidiary N (local GAAP)	Consolidation adjustment	N adjusted	Rest of group	Group M consolidated (IFRS)
	C'000	C'000	C'000	C'000	C'000
31 December 20X5	150[1]	300	450	750	1,200[2]
31 December 20X6	140	280[3]	420	700[4]	1,120
31 December 20X7	130	260	390	650	1,040

1 200-50
2 Deemed cost on transition
3 (450 – (450 ÷ 15)) –140
4 750 – (750 ÷ 15)

In its local GAAP financial statements at 31 December 20X7 subsidiary N has a net book value for the building of C130,000, represented by cost of C200,000 less 7 years of depreciation of C70,000.

When subsidiary N moves to IFRS in 20X8 it may use the exemption for the assets and liabilities of subsidiaries and, at its date of transition of 1 January 20X7, measure its building at the carrying amount that would be included in the consolidated financial statements based on the parent M's date of transition.

This means using the 'deemed cost' at the time of parent M's transition of C450,000 less depreciation of C30,000 to give a net book value of C420,000 in subsidiary N's own separate financial statements at 1 January 20X7.

The value in entity N's financial statements is the C420,000 'based on' the C450,000 value used in group M's consolidated financial statements at its date of transition, rather than the actual C450,000 'fair value as deemed cost' used in group M's consolidated financial statements.

Entity N should state the assets at a net book value of C420,000 at its date of transition of 1 January 20X7, being deemed cost of C450,000 less deprecation to date of C30,000. Our view is that the gross cost and depreciation (C450,000 and C30,000) should be reported in the subsidiary's own separate IFRS financial statements, and not a deemed cost of C420,000, as this provides more information to the users of the financial statements. At entity N's reporting date of 31 December 20X8 the building will be stated at cost of C450,000 less depreciation of C90,000, giving a net book value of C360,000.

The other option open to entity N in its own separate first IFRS financial statements is to use 1 January 20X7 as its transition date and use the deemed cost exemption. It could then fair value its buildings at the date of transition and either continue to value them going forward or treat this as deemed cost and adopt a cost less depreciation model.

Entity N could also choose to carry forward its previous cost and depreciation. The building will be stated at cost of C200,000 less depreciation of C80,000, giving a net book value of C120,000 at entity N's reporting date. This will result in a consolidation adjustment being required for the M group going forward.

The consolidation adjustment in this example reflects only the fair value adjustment to entity N's fixed assets on parent M's transition. This is not a consolidation adjustment that should be ignored for the purposes of the assets and liabilities of subsidiaries exemption, such as adjustments for the elimination of intra group profits.

Example 2 – Entity A creates a new entity (Newco) to be its parent

Entity A's date of transition to IFRS was 1 January 20X5, producing its first IFRS financial statements for the year to 31 December 20X6 with one year of comparatives. On 1 January 20X8 entity A created a new entity (Newco) which issued shares to entity A's shareholders so that it became the parent of entity A, its 100% subsidiary. The transaction was carried out as part of a capital restructuring of entity A.

Would the Newco be able to use 1 January 20X7 as its date of transition to IFRS and thus use the exemptions and exceptions under IFRS 1 for its first set of financial statements for the year ended 31 December 20X8?

No. In this situation, the Newco is simply a continuation of a previous reporting entity (entity A) and would use entity A's date of transition to IFRS of 1 January 20X5 as its own date of transition in accordance with paragraph D17 in Appendix D of IFRS 1. The assets and liabilities of the Newco will be those of entity A.

2.153   The second option given by the 'assets and liabilities of subsidiaries' exemption is that a subsidiary may use carrying amounts based on the subsidiary's own date of transition. This allows the subsidiary to adopt IFRS 1 independently of the group to which it belongs. The subsidiary may make its own choice from the exemptions available, at its own date of transition to IFRS.

2.154   The same exemption is available to associates or joint ventures that adopt IFRS at a date later than the entities that have significant influence or joint control over them. [IFRS 1 App D para D16]. This may give more options to associates or joint ventures where more than one party has significant influence or joint control or the investors or joint venturers have different transition dates.

Group adopts later than subsidiary, joint venture or associate

2.155   There are no similar options when a group becomes a first-time adopter later than its subsidiary, associate or joint venture. The standard sets out the carrying amounts for assets and liabilities that must be used. The entity, in its consolidated financial statements, should measure the assets and liabilities of the subsidiary, associate or joint venture at the *"same carrying amounts as in the financial statements of the subsidiary (or associate or joint venture), after adjusting for consolidation and equity accounting adjustments and for the effects of the business combination in which the entity acquired the subsidiary"*. [IFRS 1 App D para D17]. Once part of the group has moved to IFRS, the group as a whole should use the carrying amounts adopted by that subsidiary, associate or joint venture. With respect to determining whether subsidiaries have applied IFRS, see further guidance in paragraph 2.147 for the factors to consider.

2.156 It is necessary to establish which assets and liabilities existed at the date of acquisition and which assets and liabilities have since been acquired or assumed to determine the carrying amounts of assets or liabilities. The business combination exemption requirements are applied to the carrying amounts of assets and liabilities that existed at the date of acquisition. The adjustments required under this exemption are discussed from paragraph 2.58 onwards. The carrying amounts of assets and liabilities acquired or assumed after the subsidiary, associate or joint venture was acquired are measured at the same carrying amounts as in the subsidiary, associate or joint venture's own financial statements after adjusting for the effect of consolidation (and equity accounting adjustments). These might include accounting policy alignment, profits and losses included in assets. [IFRS 1 App D para D17, IG30].

> **Example – Group adopts IFRS later than associate**
>
> An investor acquired a 25% interest in an associate in 2001 for C200. The associate had net assets of C400 that principally comprised a property that had a fair value of C600. The investor calculated the goodwill arising on the acquisition of the associate based on this fair value. The goodwill arising was, therefore, C50. Since acquisition the associate acquired another property that cost C200. The associate adopts IFRS before the investor. The associate did not use the deemed cost exemption in its own IFRS financial statements and continues to recognise all property at historical cost. The associate has assets of C600 in its own IFRS financial statements (depreciation of these properties is ignored for the purposes of this example).
>
> The investor subsequently adopts IFRS. It takes advantage of the business combinations exemption and does not restate past business combinations. Therefore, the goodwill arising on the acquisition of the associate continues to be carried at C50. The investor bases its 25% share on net assets of C800, being C600 in respect of the fair value assigned to the property that the associate owned at date of acquisition and C200 in respect of the property subsequently purchased by the associate. For the property purchased after the date of acquisition, the investor must base its share on the carrying amount in the associate's own IFRS financial statements, that is C200. As the associate did not take advantage of the fair value deemed cost exemption and chose to continue with historical cost the investor must do the same.

Parent entities adopting earlier or later than the group

2.157 The rules are slightly different for parent entities. A parent entity that becomes a first-time adopter in its own separate financial statements at a different date than for its consolidated financial statements should use the same carrying amounts (except for consolidation adjustments) in both sets of financial statements. [IFRS 1 App D para D7]. The position in consolidated financial statements of a parent that moves to IFRS before the group does is the same as that for a subsidiary that moves before the group: the consolidated financial statements should use the measurements from the individual financial statements of the parent. However, the parent does not have the same option as a subsidiary that moves to IFRS later than the group in its own separate financial statements. It cannot adopt IFRS at its 'own' transition date, but rather has to base its measurements on those that the group used. With respect to determining whether the group has applied IFRS, see guidance in paragraph 2.147 for factors to consider.

2.158 The 'assets and liabilities of subsidiaries' exemption may interact with other exemptions in IFRS 1. Consider the following example:

Example 1 – Parent adopts IFRS later than subsidiary: property, plant, and equipment measurement

Group P is a large multi-national concern, and has operating subsidiaries in Europe, Asia and North America. It has been in existence for more than 60 years and has had a defined benefit pension plan in place for at least 20 years.

Subsidiary Q adopted IFRS in 20X1 in its own separate financial statements. The country of subsidiary Q's operation had previously introduced some IFRSs as part of its local GAAP. Subsidiary Q has been applying the requirements of IAS 19 and has used the corridor approach. On transition to IFRS subsidiary Q does not use the employee benefits exemption and continues to use the corridor approach in its first IFRS financial statements.

Group P adopts IFRS in 20X5. The group wishes to take the employee benefits exemption on transition and will use the corridor approach for accounting for actuarial gains and losses going forward. Group P notes that the exemption in paragraph D10 in Appendix D of IFRS 1 relating to employee benefits must, if it is taken, be applied to all employee benefit plans.

Since group P has adopted IFRS at a date later than that of its subsidiary Q, it should follow paragraph D17 in Appendix D of IFRS 1. The assets and liabilities of subsidiary Q must be measured at the same carrying amounts as in the separate financial statements of subsidiary Q subject to consolidation adjustments.

Taking these two exemptions together, the guidance in IFRS 1 would be applied as follows:

- group P must use the assets and liabilities as measured in subsidiary Q's separate financial statements;

- paragraph D17 permits group P to adjust the assets and liabilities of subsidiary Q for consolidation adjustments;

- group P elects to use the employee benefits exemption, which must be applied to all employee benefit plans within the group;

- group P must apply the exemption to subsidiary Q's pension plan to comply with the requirements of the employee benefits exemption; and

- the resulting adjustment to subsidiary Q's balance sheet is a consolidation adjustment as permitted by paragraph D17.

Example 2 – Parent adopts IFRS later than subsidiary: property, plant and equipment measurement

Entity C prepares its first IFRS financial statements for the year ending 31 December 20X7. The date of transition to IFRS is 1 January 20X6 and the opening IFRS balance sheet is prepared as at that date.

Entity C applies Dutch GAAP in its consolidated financial statements. It has subsidiaries throughout the world. Two of these, entity A in Barbados and entity B in Kenya, already apply IFRS in their local statutory financial statements.

The existence of subsidiaries that already apply IFRS restricts the exemptions available to entity C.

Entities A and B measured their property, plant and equipment in accordance with IAS 16. Entity C is not permitted to apply the deemed cost exemption and must use the amounts recorded by entities A and B in the consolidated opening IFRS balance sheet.

Entity C's management may elect to follow a different accounting policy from that applied by entities A and B, for example the revaluation model in IAS 16, but it must use the cost measurement that the subsidiaries recorded as a starting point.

Compound financial instruments

2.159   Under IAS 32 entities should split compound financial instruments into separate equity and liability components. [IAS 32 para 23]. IFRS 1 provides that if the liability component is no longer outstanding at the date of transition to IFRS a first-time adopter does not have to separate it from the equity component. [IFRS 1 App D para D18]. The reason for the exemption can be illustrated with the following example.

Example – Compound financial instruments

Entity A issued an instrument for net proceeds of C100m on 1 January 20X0. The main terms of the instrument were:

- The instrument's notional value of C100m bore a coupon of 7%, payable at the end of each year.
- Capital was repayable at the end of year five.
- Included in the debt instrument was an option for the holder of the instrument to convert, at any time in year five, into 400,000 entity A equity shares.

The instrument was not converted and the liability component is not outstanding at the date of transition.

Entity A determines, at the time of issuing the instrument, that the fair value of a similar instrument without the option to convert is C92m.

Under IAS 32, the two elements are recognised based on the fair value of an equivalent liability without an equity component, with the residual being the equity element. [IAS 32 para 28]. The instrument is, therefore, stated at C92m for the debt element and C8m for the equity element.

The instrument is accounted for as follows:

	1 January liability	Finance charge*	Payment	31 December liability	Equity (retained earnings)	Equity (shares to be issued)
20X0	(92.0)	(8.3)	7.0	(93.3)	8.3	(8.0)
20X1	(93.3)	(8.5)	7.0	(94.8)	16.8	(8.0)
20X2	(94.8)	(8.6)	7.0	(96.4)	25.4	(8.0)
20X3	(96.4)	(8.7)	7.0	(98.1)	34.1	(8.0)
20X4	(98.1)	(8.9)	107.0	(0.0)	43.0	(8.0)
		(43.0)	135.0			

* at an effective interest rate of 9.06%

Under IAS 32, by the end of the instrument's term, the cumulative amount in equity is a debit of C35m, representing the net of the finance cost of C43m (being C135m less C92m) and the equity proceeds of C8m.

Where entity A's previous GAAP did not require debt and equity elements to be split, it would have recorded the instrument at proceeds of C100 million and incurred a finance charge of C35 million. The result would have been a C35 million debit in the profit and loss reserve.

Where entity A applies the exemption, no adjustments are made to the C35 million debit in the profit and loss reserve. If IAS 32 had been applied, the only impact would be to split the net C35 million that is in equity into its components, being a C8 million credit and a C43 million debit.

2.160   Where the liability component is still outstanding at the date of transition to IFRS, a first-time adopter will have to separate it from the equity component. Compound instruments are bifurcated by first fair valuing the debt component, with the residual being equity. [IAS 32 para 31]. First-time adopters should use the date of issue of a compound instrument to measure the fair value of the liability, without the benefit of hindsight. This assessment should be based on the version of IAS 32 in force at the end of the entity's first IFRS reporting period. [IFRS 1 para IG36].

Example – Compound financial instruments: liability component outstanding at transition date

Entity G issued convertible debt on 1 January 20X1. The face value of the debt was 1,000 and it was issued at a discount of 150, incurring directly attributable transaction costs of 20. The debt carried a coupon of 8%, payable at the end of each year, and was convertible at the option of the holder into 500 shares from 1 January 20X7. The debt is repayable on 1 January 20X8 if the option has not been exercised.

Under previous GAAP the debt was recorded as a liability at 1 January 20X1 at 830 (850 less issue costs of 20) on issue and the finance cost is measured under the debt's term to 1 January 20X8 at a constant rate of 11.69%.

Entity G's date of transition to IFRS is 1 January 20X4. It adopts IAS 32 in the comparative period to its first IFRS reporting period to 31 December 20X5.

At entity G's date of transition, 1 January 20X4, the debt is stated at 887, calculated as follows:

	Balance b/f	finance cost 11.69%	Interest paid	Balance c/f
1 January 20X1	830	97)	(80)	847
1 January 20X2	847	99)	(80)	866
1 January 20X3	866	101) 297	(80)	887
1 January 20X4	887	104	(80)	911
1 January 20X5	911	106	(80)	937
1 January 20X6	937	110	(80)	967
1 January 20X7	967	113	(80)	1,000
1 January 20X8	1,000			
		730	560	

Entity G establishes that the fair value of similar fixed rate debt without an equity conversion option, issued by a similar company, was 800 on 1 January 20X1.

Applying IAS 32 to this instrument will result in the debt being stated at 852 at entity G's date of transition. This is the fair value of the debt at the date of its original issue (800), less the issue costs of 20, accounted for at the effective interest rate inherent in the debt of 12.97% up to the date of transition. The effective interest rate is applied in accordance with paragraph 47 of IAS 39 over the debt's expected life as illustrated in the table below. The difference between the proceeds of 850 and the fair value at the time of issue of 800, being 50, should be reclassified to equity on transition to IFRS. The actual fair value of the debt at the date of transition to IFRS is not relevant.

	Balance b/f	finance cost @ 12.97%	Interest Paid	Balance c/f
1 January 20X1	780	101)	(80)	801
1 January 20X2	801	104)	(80)	825
1 January 20X3	825	107) 312	(80)	852
1 January 20X4	852	111	(80)	883
1 January 20X5	883	114	(80)	917
1 January 20X6	917	119	(80)	956
1 January 20X7	956	124	(80)	1,000
1 January 20X8	1,000			
		780	560	

The entries required to restate the convertible debt from a previous GAAP basis to one compliant with IAS 32 on entity G's transition to IFRS are as follows:

Dr	Debt	35	
Dr	Equity – retained earnings	15	
	Cr Equity – equity instrument issued		50

The entries reflect the equity instrument that was issued on 1 January 20X1, with a deemed fair value of 50 at that time. The debit to equity – retained earnings adjustment of 15 represents the increase in cumulative finance costs under IFRS between issue and transition (312 versus 297).

UK.2.160.1 There are transition rules in relation to compound financial instruments in the presentation requirements of FRS 25 under UK GAAP similar to those of the IFRS 1 exemption. Entities can, therefore, avoid splitting the components of equity in respect of a compound instrument where the liability is no longer outstanding at the date of transition to FRS 26. If the date of transition to FRS 25 is different from a first-time adopter's date of transition to IFRS, then entities will still wish to use the IFRS 1 exemption. This is because if that exemption is not taken then the components of equity must be split retrospectively, that is, for all compound instruments ever issued. An entity cannot just go back to the date that FRS 25 was applied.

Designation of previously recognised financial instruments

2.161 IAS 39 allows a financial instrument to be designated as a financial asset or financial liability at 'fair value through profit or loss' (where permitted) or as 'available-for-sale' on initial recognition. Paragraph D19 in Appendix D of IFRS 1 allowed this designation to be made at the date of transition.

2.162 IAS 39 restricts the use of the option to designate a financial asset or financial liability as 'at fair value through profit or loss'. The conditions that are required to be met for the 'fair value option' to be used are any of the following: where the designation eliminates or significantly reduces an accounting mismatch; when a group of financial assets, financial liabilities or both are managed and their performance is evaluated on a fair value basis in accordance with a documented risk management or investment strategy; or when an instrument contains an embedded derivative that meets particular conditions. See further chapter 6.

2.163 The IASB has published IFRS 9 on the classification and measurement of financial assets, which applies for periods beginning on or after 1 January 2015 (after the IASB issued amendments in 2011) with earlier application permitted. IFRS 9 has two measurement categories: amortised cost and fair value. IFRS 9 removes the available for sale category for financial assets. An entity that is a first-time adopter and applies IFRS 9 can only apply the designation exemption to financial assets designated at fair value through profit or loss. Financial assets that are designated as amortised cost should be measured at transition using the effective interest method. If it is impracticable to retrospectively apply the effective interest method, an entity should use the fair value of the financial asset at the transition date as its amortised cost. [IFRS 1 App D para D19C].

2.164 Where a first-time adopter applies IFRS 9 and is considering designating a financial asset at fair value through profit or loss, the guidance in IFRS 9 would be referred to as opposed to IAS 39. Specifically, IFRS 9 has amended IFRS 1 as follows:

■ Any financial asset that meets the criteria for designation in IFRS 9 may be designated at fair value through profit or loss at the date of transition to IFRSs based on facts and circumstances existing at that date.

■ An equity investment that meets the criteria for designation in IFRS 9 may be designated at fair value through other comprehensive income at the date of transition to IFRSs based on facts and circumstances existing at that date.

[IFRS 1 App D paras D19A, D19B].

For designation of financial liabilities at fair value through profit or loss at the transition date, entities should continue to consider the guidance in IAS 39. [IFRS 1, App D para D19].

2.165 The IFRS 9 related amendments to IFRS 1 state that designation should be based on the facts and circumstances existing at the date of transition. It is not acceptable to designate retrospectively. Only facts and circumstances existing at the transition date are considered rather than those existing at the date the entity became a party to the contract. Whilst not explicitly stated in the guidance for designation of financial instruments in IFRS 1 prior to the amendment by IFRS 9, we believe that retrospective designation of any financial instrument on first-time adoption is inappropriate.

Fair value measurement of financial assets or financial liabilities at initial recognition

2.166 A limited amendment to IAS 39 was published in 2004. This amendment permits entities to measure their 'day one' profits (see further chapter 6) on initial recognition of financial instruments based on valuation techniques that only use observable market data or current market transactions in the same instrument either:

■ retrospectively;

■ prospectively for transactions entered into after 25 October 2002; or

■ prospectively for transactions entered into after 1 January 2004.

2.167 An amendment to IFRS 1 allows these requirements for the recognition of 'day one' profits to be applied either:

■ prospectively to transactions entered into after 25 October 2002; or

■ prospectively to transactions entered into after 1 January 2004.

[IFRS 1 App D para D20].

2.168 This is an optional exemption from full retrospective application, therefore, retrospective application is also available for first-time adopters.

2.169 The IASB issued an amendment to IFRS 1 in December 2010 to replace the fixed dates of 25 October 2002 and 1 January 2004 with references to 'the date of transition to IFRSs'. A similar amendment was also included for the derecognition exception (see further para 2.38). This amendment provides relief to first-time adopters from having to reconstruct past transactions on transition. The relief is available for annual periods beginning on or after 1 July 2011 with early adoption permitted.

Decommissioning liabilities included in the cost of property, plant and equipment

2.170 IFRIC 1 takes a prospective approach to changes in decommissioning liabilities. The change in liability is added to or deducted from the carrying value of the related asset (subject to not creating a negative asset) and the result is depreciated over the asset's remaining useful life. Under previous GAAP various methods may have been used to account for changes in such liabilities, some of which would not be compliant with IFRIC 1. The optional exemption from full retrospective application of IFRS allows entities to apply a short-cut method for liabilities in the scope of IFRIC 1.

2.171 First-time adopters may, applying the exemption, do the following:

■ Measure the liability in accordance with IAS 37.

■ To the extent the liability is within the scope of IFRIC 1, that is, it is a decommissioning, restoration or similar liability that is recognised both as part of the cost of an item of property, plant and equipment and as a liability under IAS 37, estimate the amount that would have been included in the cost of the related asset when the liability first arose. This is done by discounting the liability to that date using the entity's best estimate of the historical risk-adjusted discount rates that would have applied for that liability over the period since it was first incurred.

■ Calculate the accumulated depreciation on that discounted amount, as at the date of transition to IFRS, based on the current estimate of the useful life of the asset and using the depreciation policy adopted by the entity under IFRS.

[IFRS 1 App D para D21].

The resulting calculated amount is then added to the carrying value of the related asset.

2.172 An entity might use fair value as deemed cost and have decommissioning, restoration or similar liabilities within IFRIC 1's scope. To apply each exemption under IFRS 1, the entity would calculate the liability in accordance with IAS 37, state the asset at fair value and then record the difference in other comprehensive income. [IFRS 1 App D para D21].

2.173 IFRS 1 provides specific relief in respect of determining the deemed cost of oil and gas assets. Where an entity avails itself of this exemption, IFRS 1 provides specific guidance as to how the decommissioning liabilities exemption is applied; specifically an entity should:

■ Measure the liability in accordance with IAS 37.

■ Recognise the difference between that amount and the amount of the liability at the date of transition, determined under the entity's previous GAAP, in retained earnings.

[IFRS 1 App D para D21A].

UK.2.173.1 IAS 37 is almost identical to FRS 12 and all liabilities under UK GAAP should comply with the requirements of IAS 37. The issue then is how the other side of the adjustment to the liability was treated under UK GAAP. If entities did not apply the IFRIC 1 method, they should first reverse whatever adjustments were made when the estimate of the liability changed. The asset should now be adjusted, either in compliance with IFRIC 1 or using the exemption in paragraph 2.171. The only difference between the method allowed by the exemption and full retrospective application of IFRIC 1 is that the exemption allows use of estimates of useful economic life at the date of transition and the depreciation policy adopted under IFRS. In all other respects the exemption leads to an amount being added to the asset that is the same as that required by application of IFRIC 1. UK entities are, therefore, unlikely to get much benefit from applying the exemption.

Financial assets or intangible assets accounted for in accordance with IFRIC 12

2.174 IFRIC 12 applies to contractual arrangements whereby a private sector operator participates in the development, financing, operation and maintenance of infrastructure for public sector services. The interpretation must be applied for annual periods beginning on or after 1 January 2008.

2.175 An amendment to IFRS 1 allows a first-time adopter to apply the transitional provisions in IFRIC 12. [IFRS 1 App D para D22]. The transitional provisions are that IFRIC 12 should be applied retrospectively, unless it is impracticable. For further guidance see chapter 33.

Borrowing costs

2.176 IAS 23 was revised in March 2007. The option to expense borrowing costs that relate to qualifying assets, being assets that take a substantial period of time to get ready for use or sale, was removed. IAS 23 now requires such borrowing costs to be capitalised as part of the cost of the asset.

2.177 An amendment to IFRS 1 allows a first-time adopter to apply the transitional provisions set out in paragraphs 27 and 28 of the revised IAS 23. Any reference to the effective date in these paragraphs is interpreted as 1 January 2009 or the date of transition to IFRSs, whichever is later. [IFRS 1 App D para D23]. In practice, the amendments are applied prospectively to borrowing costs for which the commencement date for capitalisation is on or after 1 January 2009 or the date of transition to IFRSs if later. An alternative treatment permits an entity to designate any date before the effective date and apply the standard prospectively to borrowing costs relating to all qualifying assets for which the commencement date for capitalisation is on or after that date. [IAS 23 para 28]. For further guidance see chapter 16.

2.178   A question arises as to how borrowing costs capitalised under an entity's previous GAAP should be dealt with on transition to IFRS. The 2011 annual improvements allow an entity to apply IAS 23 to borrowing costs incurred from the transition date or from an earlier date as permitted by paragraph 28 of IAS 23. According to the amendment, an entity: (i) should not restate the borrowing cost component that was capitalised under previous GAAP and that was included in the carrying amount of assets at that date; and (ii) should account for borrowing costs incurred on or after that date in accordance with IAS 23, including those borrowing costs incurred on or after that date on qualifying assets already under construction. The amendment is applicable for annual periods beginning on or after 1 January 2013 with earlier application permitted.

Transfers of assets from customers

2.179   IFRIC 18 was issued in January 2009. The interpretation is specifically relevant for the utilities industry. It considers how an entity should account for assets received from a customer in return for connection to a network and/or ongoing access to goods or services.

2.180   An amendment to IFRS 1 allows a first-time adopter to apply the transitional provisions in IFRIC 18. [IFRS 1 App D para D24]. This means that IFRIC 18 may be applied prospectively from the date of transition to IFRS. In addition, an entity may designate any date before the date of transition and apply IFRIC 18 to all transfers of assets on or after that date. For further guidance see chapter 9.

Severe hyperinflation

2.181   In January 2011, the IASB amended IFRS 1 for entities that were unable to apply the requirements of IAS 29 for a period of time. [IFRS 1 App D para D26-D30]. These entities were unable to apply IAS 29, as the economy in which the entities operated was subject to severe hyper-inflation. The amendment states that the currency of a hyper-inflationary economy is subject to severe hyper-inflation when:

- a reliable general price index is not available to all entities with transactions and balances in the currency; and

■ exchangeability between the currency and a relatively stable foreign currency does not exist.

In order for an entity previously subject to severe hyper-inflation to resume preparing IFRS financial statements, IFRS 1's requirements should be considered. For further guidance see chapter 31.

Joint arrangements

2.182 A first-time adopter may apply the transition provisions in IFRS 11 (see chapter 28A) with the following exceptions:

■ When applying the transition provisions in IFRS 11, a first-time adopter applies these provisions at the date of transition to IFRS. This is consistent with the requirements for existing IFRS reporters to apply IFRS 11 from the beginning of the earliest period presented.

■ When changing from proportionate consolidation to the equity method, a first-time adopter tests for impairment the investment in accordance with IAS 36 as at the date of transition to IFRS, regardless of whether there is any indication that the investment may be impaired. Any resulting impairment is recognised as an adjustment to retained earnings at the date of transition to IFRS.

This exemption resulted from the issuance of IFRS 11 in May 2011. Entities are required to apply the amendments for annual periods beginning on or after 1 January 2013. Earlier application is permitted. [IFRS 11 App D paras D2-D4; IFRS 1 App D para D1(r)].

Stripping costs in the production phase of a surface mine

2.183 A first-time adopter may apply the transitional provisions set out in paragraphs A1 to A4 of IFRIC 20. In paragraph A1, reference to the effective date is interpreted as 1 January 2013 or the beginning of the first IFRS reporting period, whichever is later. This exemption resulted from the issuance of IFRIC 20 in October 2011 (for further details see paras A1 to A4 of appendix A to IFRIC 20).

Extinguishing financial liabilities with equity instruments

2.184 IFRIC 19 was issued in November 2009. The interpretation clarifies the accounting when an entity renegotiates the terms of its debt with the result that the liability is extinguished by the entity issuing its own equity instruments to the creditor. IFRIC 19 is effective for periods beginning on or after 1 July 2010 with earlier application permitted.

2.185 An amendment to IFRS 1 allows a first-time adopter to apply the transitional provisions in IFRIC 19. [IFRS 1 App D para D25]. This means that

IFRIC 19 is applied from the beginning of the earliest comparative period presented. For further guidance see chapter 31.

Presentation and disclosure

2.186 IFRS 1 states that there are no exemptions for first-time adopters from the presentation and disclosure requirements of other IFRSs. [IFRS 1 para 20]. Where there are disclosures that are different from, or additional to, those required by previous GAAP these will have to be given for all periods presented. So an entity with a December 20Y0 year end that presents one year of comparative information as well as presenting an opening balance sheet will need to have the information systems in place to be able to give full IFRS disclosures from the opening balance sheet date of 1 January 20X9 onwards.

Comparative information

2.187 Paragraph 38 of IAS 1 requires an entity to disclose comparative information in respect to the previous period for all reported amounts in the current period's financial statements. Thus, an entity must prepare and present at a minimum:

- Two balance sheets (three balance sheets for a first-time adopter).

- Two separate income statements (if presented).

- Two statements of comprehensive income.

- Two cash flow statements.

- Two statements of changes in equity.

- Related notes (including comparative information).

[IAS 1 paras 38, 39; IFRS 1 para 21].

2.188 A first-time adopter must now prepare *and present* an opening balance sheet. Therefore, a first-time adopter, at a minimum, will present three balance sheets in its first set of financial statements as well as two of each of the other statements listed above. The requirement to prepare and present the opening balance sheet also results in the need to include related footnote disclosure for the opening balance sheet. The annual improvements 2011 include a consequential amendment to IFRS 1 resulting from amendment to IAS 1. The amendment clarifies that comparative information for 'related notes' should also be presented. This is in line with our previous view; however the amendment is applicable for annual periods beginning on or after 1 January 2013. Earlier application is permitted. An example of a first-time adopter that has given an opening balance sheet is shown in Table 2.5.

Table 2.5 – Opening balance sheet presented by first-time adopter

Thomson Reuters Corporation – Annual report – 31 December 2009

THOMSON REUTERS CORPORATION

CONSOLIDATED STATEMENT OF FINANCIAL POSITION

(millions of U.S. dollars)	Notes	**December 31, 2009**	December 31, 2008	January 1, 2008
ASSETS				
Cash and cash equivalents	13	**1,111**	841	7,497
Trade and other receivables	14	**1,742**	1,818	1,581
Other financial assets	20	**76**	261	70
Prepaid expenses and other current assets	15	**734**	766	426
Current assets		**3,663**	3,686	9,574
Computer hardware and other property, net	16	**1,546**	1,556	731
Computer software, net	17	**1,495**	1,299	721
Other identifiable intangible assets, net	18	**8,694**	8,702	3,440
Goodwill	19	**18,130**	18,324	6,939
Other financial assets	20	**383**	286	511
Other non-current assets	21	**649**	627	488
Deferred tax	24	**13**	109	74
Total assets		**34,573**	34,589	22,478
LIABILITIES AND EQUITY				
Liabilities				
Current indebtedness	20	**782**	688	595
Payables, accruals and provisions	22	**2,651**	2,704	1,505
Deferred revenue		**1,187**	1,193	1,105
Other financial liabilities	20	**92**	60	29
Current liabilities		**4,712**	4,645	3,234
Long-term indebtedness	20	**6,821**	6,783	4,224
Provisions and other non-current liabilities	23	**1,878**	1,798	851
Other financial liabilities	20	**42**	222	–
Deferred tax	24	**1,785**	2,653	856
Total liabilities		**15,238**	16,101	9,165

Equity				
Capital	25	**10,177**	10,034	2,836
Retained earnings		**10,561**	10,650	10,476
Accumulated other comprehensive				
(loss) income		**(1,471)**	(2,268)	1
Total shareholders' equity		**19,267**	**18,416**	13,313
Non-controlling interests	31	**68**	72	–
Total equity		**19,335**	18,488	13,313
Total liabilities and equity		**34,573**	34,589	22,478

Contingencies (note 30)
The related notes form an integral part of these consolidated financial statements.

Notes to Consolidated Financial Statements (extract)

Basis of preparation (extract)

These consolidated financial statements represent the first annual financial statements of the Company and its subsidiaries prepared in accordance with International Financial Reporting Standards ("IFRS"), as issued by the International Accounting Standards Board ("IASB"). The Company adopted IFRS in accordance with IFRS 1, *First-time Adoption of International Financial Reporting Standards*. The first date at which IFRS was applied was January 1, 2008. In accordance with IFRS, the Company has:

- provided comparative financial information;
- applied the same accounting policies throughout all periods presented;
- retrospectively applied all effective IFRS standards as of December 31, 2009, as required; and
- applied certain optional exemptions and certain mandatory exceptions as applicable for first time IFRS adopters.

2.189 This comparative information must be presented in accordance with the policies in place for the first IFRS financial statements. These will be the policies and disclosures required by those standards in force at the end of an entity's first IFRS reporting period. [IFRS 1 para 7].

Other comparative information

2.190 An entity can elect to present additional years of comparative information in accordance with IFRS. This information might be required for regulatory purposes. When considering the presentation of comparatives in its first IFRS financial statements, an entity should consider any relief granted by regulators in respect of comparative information.

2.191 If a first-time adopter presents more than the required amount of comparative information, then periods prior to the immediate comparative period do not have to comply with IFRS. If a first time adopter elects to do this, however, that information should be prominently labelled as not being prepared under IFRS. The entity should disclose the nature of the main adjustments that would be required to make the information comply with IFRS. [IFRS 1 para 22]. The requirement is to disclose 'the nature' of the main adjustments, and not necessarily a quantification of them.

2.192 The impact on entities that are required to provide more, or choose to provide less, than the comparative information required under IFRS 1, as described in the preceding paragraphs, can be illustrated by the following examples:

> ### Example 1 – Presenting more than the IFRS 1 required comparative information
>
> New legislation will require entity A to prepare its consolidated financial statements for the year ending 31 December 20X9 in accordance with IFRS. Entity A's shares are registered with its national regulator, which requires two years of comparative financial information. The regulator requires that both comparative years are prepared in accordance with IFRS.
>
> IFRS 1 requires that one full year of comparative information as well as an opening balance sheet prepared in compliance with IFRS 1 is presented. However, an entity is permitted to present additional comparative financial information. The regulator requires an additional year of comparative information covering the year ending 31 December 20X7. The date of transition is the beginning of the earliest period for which full comparative information is given. This is the beginning of 20X7, so the date of transition to IFRS for entity A is 1 January 20X7.
>
> ### Example 2 – IFRS 1: presenting comparative information that is incomplete
>
> Entity B prepares its first IFRS financial statements for the year ending 31 December 20X9. There are significant differences between entity B's previous GAAP and IFRS. Entity B's management, therefore, plans to prepare its opening IFRS balance sheet at 1 January 20X9, so it has a starting point for its accounting under IFRS. The first IFRS financial statements will include one year of comparative information for the balance sheet, but due to the number of GAAP differences, management has opted not to present comparative information for the income statement and cash flow statement.
>
> IFRS 1 requires that one full year of comparative information, prepared in compliance with IFRS 1, is presented as well as an opening balance sheet. Entity B's management has decided not to present that information. This will mean that the financial statements are not compliant with IFRS as they will be unable to state explicit and unreserved compliance with IFRS (see further para 2.15).

Comparative information on the application of IFRS 9

2.193 The IASB issued IFRS 9 in November 2009. IFRS 9 amended IFRS 1 providing specific relief with respect to the comparative information where IFRS 9 is applied to periods beginning before 1 January 2012. Where the exemption is taken, the comparative information provided for items within IFRS 9's scope need not comply with IFRS 9. Relief is also provided from disclosures required by IFRS 7 for financial assets in IFRS 9's scope. Where this exemption is applied, the entity must adopt the following treatment:

- Apply the recognition and measurement guidance of its previous GAAP to comparative information related to financial assets within IFRS 9's scope.

■ Disclose the above fact as well as the basis used to prepare the comparative information.

■ Treat any adjustment between the application of IFRS 9 at the start of the first IFRS reporting period and the end of the comparative period as arising from a change in accounting policy.

■ Provide additional disclosures required by IAS 1 when compliance with the specific requirements in IFRSs is insufficient to enable users to understand the impact of particular transactions on the entity's financial position and financial performance (see further chapter 4).

[IFRS 1 App E para E2].

Disclosures about financial instruments

2.194   The IASB issued an amendment to IFRS 1 following the amendments to IFRS 7. The amendment to IFRS 7 requires enhanced fair value measurement and liquidity risk disclosures. For existing IFRS preparers, the transitional arrangements do not require comparative information for the disclosures required by the amendment in the first year of application. The amendment to IFRS 1 extends this transitional relief to first-time adopters. [IFRS 1 App E para E3]. The amendment applies to periods beginning on or after 1 July 2010 with earlier application permitted. For details of the amended disclosures required by IFRS 7, see further chapter 6.

Five year summaries

2.195   Many listed entities give five-year historical summaries of key financial data. IFRS 1 does not require historical summaries to comply with IFRSs. [IFRS 1 para 22]. The IASB decided not to require historical summaries to be restated, because it felt the cost of doing so would outweigh the benefits to users. Although IFRS 1 does not require historical summaries to be restated, it does require disclosure of the main adjustments that would make the data comply with IFRS. The entity should also *"label the previous GAAP information prominently as not being prepared under IFRSs"*. [IFRS 1 para 22(a)]. Like other comparative information not presented under IFRS (see further para 2.191), the nature of the main adjustments that would be required to comply with IFRS should be disclosed, but they do not have to be quantified. [IFRS 1 para 22(b)]. An example of disclosure is Table 2.6.

Table 2.6 –Transition to IFRS, historical summaries

Alliance UniChem PLC – Report and accounts – 31 December 2005

Five-year summary (extract)

The figures for 2004 and 2005 are extracted from this Annual Report and thus prepared under IFRS. The figures for 2001, 2002 and 2003 are UK GAAP figures presented in the same format as the 2004 and 2005 figures. The principal differences between UK GAAP and IFRS are described in note 50 to the financial statements which provides an explanation of the transition to IFRS.

Group income statements – year ended 31 December	UK GAAP 2001 £million	UK GAAP 2002 £million	UK GAAP 2003 £million	IFRS 2004 £million	IFRS 2005 £million
Revenue	7,089.4	7,771.6	8,799.3	8,898.4	9,171.2
Operating profit before amortisation of goodwill including: Share of associates' operating profit	198.1	227.0	263.1	289.7	331.8
Less: share of associates' operating profit	(17.4)	(21.5)	(36.8)	(46.1)	(70.8)
Operating profit before amortisation of goodwill	180.7	205.5	226.3	243.6	261.0
Costs in relation to proposed merger	–	–	–	–	(3.8)
Share of associates' post tax earnings	9.4	14.8	27.0	34.0	45.3
Profit on disposal of businesses	–	–	–	19.2	7.8
(Amounts written off)/profit on disposal of investments	–	–	–	(1.9)	2.1
Amortisation of goodwill	(10.7)	(12.2)	(13.3)	–	–
Profit from operations	179.4	208.1	240.0	294.9	312.4

Reconciliations

2.196 IFRS 1 requires the following reconciliations between previous GAAP and IFRS. These form part of the standard's overall requirement for explanation of the transition to IFRS. This is that *"an entity shall explain how the transition from previous GAAP to IFRSs affected its reported financial position, financial performance and cash flows"*. [IFRS 1 para 23]. The disclosures an entity should give are as follows:

"(a) reconciliations of its equity reported in accordance with GAAP to its equity in accordance with IFRSs for both of the following dates:

(i) the date of transition to IFRSs; and

(ii) the end of the latest period presented in the entity's most recent annual financial statements in accordance with previous GAAP;

(b) a reconciliation to its total comprehensive income in accordance with IFRSs for the latest period in the entity's most recent annual financial

statements. The starting point for that reconciliation shall be total comprehensive income in accordance with previous GAAP for the same period or, if an entity did not report such a total, profit or loss under previous GAAP; and

(c) if the entity recognised or reversed any impairment losses for the first time in preparing its opening IFRS statement of financial position, the disclosures that IAS 36 Impairment of Assets *would have required if the entity had recognised those impairment losses or reversals in the period beginning with the date of transition to IFRSs."*

[IFRS 1 para 24].

2.197 An entity that is preparing its first IFRS financial statements for the year to 31 December 20Y0, with one year of comparative information as well as presenting its opening balance sheet, will disclose reconciliations for: equity, that is net assets, at 1 January 20X9 and 31 December 20X9; and comprehensive income for the year to 31 December 20X9.

UK.2.197.1 It is worth noting what information needs to be reconciled. Consider the following example.

Example – Reconciliations required for first IFRS financial statements

Entity H has a December year end. It has published interim financial statements as at 30 June 2004. In these statements the entity has restated the balance sheet to present an investment in own shares as a deduction in arriving at shareholders' funds in accordance with UITF 38, 'Accounting for ESOP trusts'. When preparing the opening balance sheet reconciliation for inclusion in the first IFRS financial statements, should this be based on the figures included in the financial statements to 31 December 2003 as they were originally published, or should they take account of the reclassification of the investment in own shares under UITF 38?

In producing these reconciliations the entity should use the December 2003 figures as adjusted for the restatement caused by UITF 38. This will allow the users of financial statements to determine what the differences are that have been caused by moving from UK GAAP to IFRS, which is the purpose of these reconciliations, rather than also including accounting policy changes that have occurred under UK GAAP.

2.198 The reconciliations should give enough information to enable users to understand the material adjustments to the income statement and balance sheet and, if one was presented, to the cash flow statement. [IFRS 1 para 25]. In practice, this may require significant disclosure of adjustments to the financial statements for accounting policy differences.

2.199 For an entity with a December 20Y0 year end that presents two years of comparative information as well as an opening balance sheet (see further para 2.191 above), the standard would require the following:

- reconciliation of equity at 1 January 20X8 (date of transition) and 31 December 20X9 (end of last period presented under previous GAAP); and

- reconciliation of comprehensive income for the year to 31 December 20X9 (the period last presented under previous GAAP).

This leaves a gap in the reconciliations. Users of the financial statements would benefit if entities gave additional reconciliations of equity at 31 December 20X8 and of comprehensive income for the year to 31 December 20X8.

2.200 The implementation guidance to IFRS 1 includes an example of the reconciliations required. Examples of companies giving the disclosures required by IFRS 1 are Thomson Reuters Corporation (see Table 2.7) and Eastern Platinum Limited (see Table 2.8), both of Canada. For the first example, only the required reconciliations have been reproduced and more detailed (line-by-line) reconciliations that were also provided have not been reproduced.

Table 2.7 – Transition to IFRS, reconciliations under IFRS 1

Thomson Reuters Corporation – Annual report – 31 December 2009

NOTE 34: TRANSITION TO IFRS

These consolidated financial statements represent the first annual financial statements of the Company and its subsidiaries prepared in accordance with IFRS, as issued by the IASB. The Company adopted IFRS in accordance with IFRS 1, First-time Adoption of International Financial Reporting Standards. The first date at which IFRS was applied was January 1, 2008 ("Transition Date"). In accordance with IFRS, the Company has:

- provided comparative financial information;

- applied the same accounting policies throughout all periods presented;

- retrospectively applied all effective IFRS standards as of December 31, 2009, as required, and

- applied certain optional exemptions and certain mandatory exceptions as applicable for first time IFRS adopters.

The Company's consolidated financial statements were previously prepared in accordance with Canadian GAAP.

Initial elections upon adoption

Set forth below are the IFRS 1 applicable exemptions and exceptions applied in the conversion from Canadian GAAP to IFRS.

IFRS Exemption Options

1. **Business combinations** – IFRS 1 provides the option to apply IFRS 3, Business Combinations, retrospectively or prospectively from the Transition Date. The retrospective basis would require restatement of all business combinations that occurred prior to the Transition Date. The Company elected not to retrospectively apply IFRS 3 to business combinations that occurred prior to its Transition Date and such business combinations have not been restated. Any goodwill arising on such business combinations before the Transition Date has not been adjusted from the carrying value previously determined under Canadian GAAP as a result of applying these exemptions. Further, the Company did not early adopt IFRS 3 Revised and instead has adopted that standard upon its effective date which, for the Company, was January 1, 2010.

2. **Employee benefits** – IFRS 1 provides the option to retrospectively apply the corridor approach under IAS 19, Employee Benefits, for the recognition of actuarial gains and losses, or recognize all cumulative gains and losses deferred under Canadian GAAP in opening retained earnings at the Transition Date. The Company elected to recognize all cumulative actuarial gains and losses that existed at its Transition Date in opening retained earnings for all of its employee benefit plans.

3. **Currency translation differences** – Retrospective application of IFRS would require the Company to determine cumulative currency translation differences in accordance with IAS 21, The Effects of Changes in Foreign Exchange Rates, from the date a subsidiary or equity method investee was formed or acquired. IFRS 1 permits cumulative translation gains and losses to be reset to zero at transition date. The Company elected to reset all cumulative translation gains and losses to zero in opening retained earnings at its Transition Date.

4. **Share-based payments** – IFRS 2, Share-based Payments, encourages application of its provisions to equity instruments granted on or before November 7, 2002, but permits the application only to equity instruments granted after November 7, 2002 that had not vested by the Transition Date. The Company elected to avail itself of the exemption provided under IFRS 1 and applied IFRS 2 for all equity instruments granted after November 7, 2002 that had not vested by its Transition Date. Further, the Company applied IFRS 2 for all liabilities arising from share-based payment transactions that existed at its Transition Date. As a result of the transition method elected, the Company reversed the historical Canadian GAAP share-based compensation charges impacting shareholders' equity from retained earnings to capital.

5. **Borrowing costs** – IAS 23, Borrowing Costs, requires an entity to capitalize the borrowing costs related to all qualifying assets for which the commencement date for capitalization is on or after January 1, 2009. Early adoption is permitted. The Company elected not to early adopt this policy. Therefore, borrowing costs prior to January 1, 2009 are expensed.

IFRS Mandatory Exceptions

Set forth below are the applicable mandatory exceptions in IFRS 1 applied in the conversion from Canadian GAAP to IFRS.

1. **Hedge accounting** – Hedge accounting can only be applied prospectively from the Transition Date to transactions that satisfy the hedge accounting criteria in IAS 39, Financial Instruments: Recognition and Measurement, at that date. Hedging relationships cannot be designated retrospectively and the supporting documentation cannot be created retrospectively. As a result, only hedging relationships that satisfied the hedge accounting criteria as of its Transition Date are reflected as hedges in the Company's results under IFRS. All derivatives, whether or not they meet the IAS 39 criteria for hedge accounting, were fair valued and recorded in the statement of financial position.

2. **Estimates** – Hindsight is not used to create or revise estimates. The estimates previously made by the Company under Canadian GAAP were not revised for application of IFRS except where necessary to reflect any difference in accounting policies.

Reconciliations of Canadian GAAP to IFRS

IFRS 1 requires an entity to reconcile equity, comprehensive income and cash flows for prior periods. The Company's first time adoption of IFRS did not have an impact on the total operating, investing or financing cash flows. The following represents the reconciliations from Canadian GAAP to IFRS for the respective periods noted for equity, earnings and comprehensive income:

Reconciliation of Equity

(in millions of U.S. dollars)
As of

	December 31, 2008	January 1, 2008
Shareholders' equity under Canadian GAAP	20,126	13,571
Differences increasing (decreasing) reported shareholders' equity:		
1. Business combinations	(1,166)	–
2. Employee benefits	(773)	(320)
3. Share-based compensation	(50)	(5)
4. Revenue	3	4
5. Derivative instruments and hedging activities	14	(2)
6. Impairments	1	–
7. Income taxes	165	65
8. Non-controlling interest	168	–
Total equity under IFRS	18,488	13,313

Reconciliation of Earnings

(in millions of U.S. dollars)
For the year to date period ended

	December 31, 2008
Net earnings under Canadian GAAP	1,405
Differences in GAAP increasing (decreasing) reported earnings:	
1. Business combinations	(121)
2. Employee benefits	33
3. Share-based compensation	(20)
4. Revenue	(1)
5. Derivative instruments and hedging activities	–
6. Impairments	1
7. Income taxes	27
8. Foreign currency translation adjustments	(17)
9. Non-controlling interest	14
Net earnings under IFRS	1,321

Reconciliation of Comprehensive Income

(in millions of U.S. dollars)
For the year to date period ended

	December 31, 2008
Comprehensive loss under Canadian GAAP	(857)
Differences in GAAP (increasing) decreasing reported comprehensive loss:	
Differences in net earnings, net of tax	(84)
Unrealized cash flow hedges	16
Foreign currency translation adjustments to equity	(40)
Foreign currency translation adjustments to earnings	17
Actuarial losses on pension plans, net of tax	(389)
Comprehensive loss under IFRS	(1,337)

Changes in accounting policies

In addition to the exemptions and exceptions discussed above, the following narratives explain the significant differences between the previous historical Canadian GAAP accounting policies and the current IFRS accounting policies applied by the Company. Only the differences having an impact on Thomson Reuters are described below. The following is not a complete summary of all of the differences between Canadian GAAP and IFRS. Relative to the impacts on

Thomson Reuters, the descriptive caption next to each numbered item below corresponds to the same numbered and descriptive caption in the tables above, which reflect the quantitative impacts from each change. Unless a quantitative impact was noted below, the impact from the change was not material to Thomson Reuters.

1. BUSINESS COMBINATIONS

As stated in the section entitled "IFRS Exemption Options," the Company applied the exemption in IFRS 1 for business combinations. Consequently, business combinations concluded prior to January 1, 2008 have not been restated and the carrying amount of goodwill under IFRS as of January 1, 2008 is equal to the carrying amount under Canadian GAAP as of that date. The IFRS adjustments below relate to acquisitions occurring on or after January 1, 2008.

Measurement of Purchase Price

Canadian GAAP – Shares issued as consideration are measured at their market price a few days before and after the date the parties reached an agreement on the purchase price and the proposed transaction was announced.

IFRS – Shares issued as consideration are measured at their market value at the acquisition closing date. As a result, goodwill and equity were reduced by $979 million relative to the re-measurement of the shares issued as consideration for the Reuters acquisition.

Acquisition-related costs

Canadian GAAP – If certain conditions are met, the costs of a plan (1) to exit an activity of an acquired company, (2) to involuntarily terminate employees of an acquired company, or (3) to relocate employees of an acquired company are liabilities assumed in the purchase and are included in the allocation of the acquisition cost.

IFRS – Restructuring provisions are only included as part of the acquired liabilities when the acquiree has recognized an existing liability for restructuring in accordance with applicable IFRS standards. As a result, restructuring provisions recorded as part of the purchase price allocation under Canadian GAAP are charged to earnings under IFRS.

Adjustment to Purchase Price Allocation

Canadian GAAP – Initial purchase price allocations are subsequently adjusted through goodwill prospectively as changes in estimates. Further, while Canadian GAAP does not impose a time limit for the completion of the allocation process, in practice the process is considered final by the end of the fiscal year in which the acquisition occurred.

IFRS – If the initial accounting for a business combination can only be determined provisionally, subsequent adjustments to the allocation may be recognized if they occur within 12 months of the acquisition date. After 12 months, adjustments are recognized through income. The adjustments made as a result of finalizing the provisional accounting are retrospectively recognized from the acquisition date. As a result, adjustments to depreciation and amortization are retrospectively recorded to reflect the final purchase accounting.

See also the discussion below for differences in accounting for income taxes in business combinations affecting goodwill and intangible assets.

2. EMPLOYEE FUTURE BENEFITS

As stated in the section entitled "IFRS Exemption Options," the Company elected to recognize all cumulative actuarial gains and losses that existed at the Transition Date in opening retained earnings for all of its employee benefit plans.

Actuarial Gains and Losses

Canadian GAAP – Actuarial gains and losses that arise in calculating the present value of the defined benefit obligation and the fair value of plan assets are recognized on a systematic and consistent basis, subject to a minimum required amortization based on a "corridor" approach. The "corridor" was 10% of the greater of the accrued benefit obligation at the beginning of the year and the fair value of plan assets at the beginning of the year. This excess of 10% is amortized as a component of pension expense on a straight-line basis over the expected average service life of active participants. Actuarial gains and losses below the 10% corridor are deferred.

IFRS – The Company elected to recognize all actuarial gains and losses immediately in a separate statement of comprehensive income without recycling to the income statement in subsequent periods. As a result, actuarial gains and losses are not amortized to the income statement but rather are recorded directly to comprehensive income at the end of each period. As a result, the Company adjusted its pension expense to remove the amortization of actuarial gains and losses. The impact from unamortized actuarial losses was not separately measured as of the adoption date. Unamortized net actuarial losses disclosed as of December 31, 2007 were $255 million, including a significant portion of which were measured as of September 30, 2007. This amount is indicative of the impact from actuarial losses as of the adoption date of January 1, 2008.

Measurement Date

Canadian GAAP – The measurement date of the defined benefit obligation and plan assets can be a date up to three months prior to the date of the financial statements, provided the entity adopted this practice consistently from year to year. The Company measured the defined benefit obligation and plan assets for certain plans as of September 30.

IFRS – An entity is required to determine the present value of the defined benefit obligation and the fair value of plan assets with sufficient regularity such that the amounts recognized in the financial statements do not differ materially from the amounts that would be determined at the end of the reporting period. As a result, on transition to IFRS, the Company re-measured its defined benefit obligations and plan assets as of the end date of each period, which impacted the calculation of pension expense.

Fair Value of and Expected Return on Plan Assets

Canadian GAAP – The expected return on plan assets is the product of the expected long-term rate of return on plan assets and a market-related fair value of plan assets. The market-related fair value recognized changes in the fair value of plan assets over a five year period.

IFRS – The expected return on plan assets is product of the expected long-term rate of return on plan assets and a fair value of plan assets at the end of the reporting period. As a result, the Company adjusted its pension expense to reflect an expected return on plan assets using the fair value of its plan assets at the end of each period.

Accrued Benefit Asset

Canadian GAAP – When a defined benefit plan gives rise to an accrued benefit asset, a valuation allowance is recognized for any excess of the accrued benefit asset over the expected future benefit. The accrued benefit asset is presented in the statement of financial position net of the valuation allowance. A change in the valuation allowance is recognized in earnings for the period in which the change occurs.

IFRS – Similar to Canadian GAAP, IFRS limits the recognition of the net benefit asset under certain circumstances to the amount that is recoverable. Since the Company has elected to recognize all actuarial gains and loss in other comprehensive income, changes in valuation allowance are recognized in other comprehensive income in the period in which the changes occurred. As a result, the Company adjusted its pension expense to reflect this treatment.

3. **SHARE BASED COMPENSATION**

IFRS 2 is effective for the Company as of January 1, 2008 and is applicable to stock options and grants that are unvested at that date. The transition rules in IFRS 1 and IFRS 2 as applied by the Company result in the following:

- Stock options and share grants prior to November 7, 2002 are not taken into account for IFRS 2;

- Stock options and share grants subsequent to November 7, 2002 are only taken into account if they have not vested as at January 1, 2008; and,

- From January 1, 2008, all stock options, share grants and other share-based payments will be expensed in accordance with the policy stated in note 1.

Recognition of Expense

Canadian GAAP – For grants of share-based awards with graded vesting, the total fair value of the award is recognized on a straight-line basis over the employment period necessary to vest the award.

IFRS – Each tranche in an award with graded vesting is considered a separate grant with a different vesting date and fair value. Each grant is accounted for on that basis. As a result, the Company adjusted its expense for share-based awards to reflect this difference in recognition.

Forfeitures

Canadian GAAP – Forfeitures of awards are recognized as they occur.

IFRS – An estimate is required of the number of awards expected to vest, which is revised if subsequent information indicates that actual forfeitures are likely to differ from the estimate. As a result, the Company adjusted its expense to reflect this difference.

Cash-Settled Share Based Payments

Canadian GAAP – A liability for stock appreciation rights is accrued based upon the intrinsic value of the award with changes recognized in the income statement each period.

IFRS – An entity must measure the liability incurred at fair value by applying an option pricing model. Until the liability is settled, the fair value of the liability is re-measured at each reporting date, with changes in fair value recognized as the awards vest. Changes in fair value of vested awards are recognized immediately in earnings. As a result, the Company adjusted expenses associated with stock appreciation rights to reflect the changes of the fair values of these awards.

Measurement of Deferred Tax Assets

Canadian GAAP – A deferred tax asset is recognized for share-based awards based upon the cumulative amount of compensation cost recognized for an award.

IFRS – The deferred tax asset for a deductible temporary difference is based on an estimate of the future tax deduction. For share-based payment awards, future tax deductions are generally measured by reference to the intrinsic value of the vested award at the end of the reporting period. If the estimated future tax deduction exceeds the amount of the related cumulative compensation expense, the excess of the associated deferred tax is recognized directly in equity. If no or a reduced tax deduction is anticipated because the fair value of the shares has declined, the deferred tax asset is wholly or partly reversed to income or equity as appropriate depending on how the asset was originally recorded. As a result, the Company adjusted the deferred tax associated with share-based awards to reflect changes in the stock price.

4. REVENUE

Multi-component Arrangements

Canadian GAAP – Vendor specific objective evidence ("VSOE") for the undelivered element in a multi-component arrangement has to exist in order to recognize revenue for the delivered elements.

IFRS – Revenue is allocated and recognized for each element if fair value can be reliably measured, provided that stand alone value exists from a customer perspective. As a result, the Company recognized revenue earlier than under Canadian GAAP in certain instances.

Completed Contract Accounting

Canadian GAAP – In certain circumstances, revenue for various arrangements is recognized on a completed contract basis.

IFRS – The completed contract basis of accounting is not permitted. The percentage of completion basis is used unless one specific act is much more significant than any other, in which case the recognition of revenue is postponed until the significant act has been completed. As a result, for arrangements which did not have a significant act, the Company recognized revenue on a percentage of completion basis under IFRS.

5. DERIVATIVE INSTRUMENTS AND HEDGING ACTIVITIES

The Company has prospectively applied hedge accounting to those hedging relationships that satisfied the hedge accounting criteria of IAS 39 at its Transition Date in accordance with the transition requirement of IFRS.

Hedge Accounting

Canadian GAAP – If certain conditions are met, the "short cut method" and the "critical terms match" method can be used for the assessment and measurement of ineffectiveness and, for certain hedges, an assumption of no ineffectiveness can be made.

IFRS – IFRS does not permit the use of the short cut method nor the critical terms match method for the assessment and measurement of effectiveness in a hedging relationship. Ineffectiveness must be measured at each reporting period throughout the life of the hedging relationship. As a result, the Company measured ineffectiveness at each reporting period and recognized related amounts in earnings.

Credit Risk

Canadian GAAP – Prior to 2009, there was no explicit guidance related to incorporating credit risk into the fair values of derivatives. On January 20, 2009, the Emerging Issues Committee ("EIC") issued Abstract 173, Credit Risk and the Fair Value of Financial Assets and Financial Liabilities ("EIC 173"), which clarified that an entity's own credit risk and the credit risk of the counterparty should be taken into account when determining the fair value of financial assets and financial liabilities, including derivative instruments. This Abstract is to be applied retrospectively, without restatement of prior periods, to all financial assets and liabilities measured at fair value in interim and annual financial statements for periods ending after January 20, 2009. The Company adopted this standard as of January 1, 2009.

IFRS – Non-performance risk is required to be considered when determining the fair value of a financial asset or liability, which would include an entity's own credit risk for financial liabilities, including derivatives. Although the guidance in Canadian GAAP and IFRS are aligned as of January 1, 2009 with regard to the consideration of non-performance risk in computing the fair value of derivative instruments, the Company adjusted the value of certain instruments for reporting periods prior to January 1, 2009.

6. IMPAIRMENTS

Assets Held for Sale

Canadian GAAP – Assets held for sale are measured at the lower of their carrying amount or fair value less costs to sell. The carrying amount for determining impairment includes cumulative translation adjustments.

IFRS – Assets held for sale are also measured at the lower of their carrying amount or fair value less costs to sell, but the carrying value used in the calculation excludes cumulative translation adjustments. As a result of this change in measurement methodology, the Company calculated a higher impairment for a pre-existing impairment event. There were no new impairment events identified as a result of adopting IFRS.

Recoverable Amount

Canadian GAAP – A recoverability test is performed by first comparing the undiscounted expected future cash flows to be derived from the asset to its carrying amount. If the asset does not recover its carrying value, an impairment loss is calculated as the excess of the asset's carrying amount over its fair value.

IFRS – The impairment loss is calculated as the excess of the asset's carrying amount over its recoverable amount, where recoverable amount is defined as the higher of the asset's fair value less costs to sell and its value-in-use. Under the value-in-use calculation, the expected future cash flows from the asset are discounted to their net present value. As a result of the change in measurement methodology, the Company recognized additional impairments under IFRS as the carrying amount of assets held for sale was in excess of their fair value less cost to sell or value-in-use.

Reversal of Impairment

Canadian GAAP – Reversal of impairment losses is not permitted.

IFRS – Reversal of impairment losses is required for assets other than goodwill if certain criteria are met. As a result, the Company reversed certain impairments recognized under IFRS reflecting changes in expected cash flows. However, these reversals were not material.

7. INCOME TAXES

Intercompany Transactions

Canadian GAAP – Recognition of a deferred tax asset or liability for a temporary difference arising from intercompany transactions is prohibited. Such temporary differences may arise when the tax base of the asset in the buyer's jurisdiction differs from the carrying amount of the asset in the consolidated financial statements. Further, cash tax paid or recovered as a result of a transfer of an asset is recorded as a deferred tax asset or liability in the financial statements and recognized through tax expense when the asset leaves the Company or is otherwise utilized.

IFRS – There are no such exceptions under IFRS. Therefore, deferred tax is recognized for temporary differences arising on intercompany transactions measured at the tax rate of the buyer, and cash tax paid or recovered on intercompany transactions is recognized in the period incurred. As a result, the Company reversed certain tax deferrals on intercompany transactions.

Deferred Tax Assets of an Acquired Company Not Previously Recognized

Canadian GAAP – Previously unrecognized deferred tax assets of an acquired company are recognized as part of the cost of the acquisition when such assets are more likely than not to be realized as a result of a business combination. If an unrecognized deferred tax asset becomes realizable subsequent to the acquisition date, such benefit is also recognized through goodwill. The acquirer recognizes deferred tax assets that become realizable as a result of the acquisition as part of the cost of the acquisition.

IFRS – Previously unrecognized deferred tax assets of an acquired company are recognized as part of the cost of the acquisition if realization is more likely than not as a result of the business combination. If an unrecognized deferred tax asset becomes realizable subsequent to the acquisition date, the tax benefit is recognized in the income statement and a corresponding amount of goodwill is recognized as an operating expense. The acquirer recognizes deferred tax assets that become realizable as a result of the acquisition through earnings. As a result, the Company recognized deferred tax assets that become realizable as a result of the acquisition in earnings.

Accounting for Uncertainty in Income Tax Positions

Canadian GAAP – Benefits for uncertain tax positions are determined by reference to a two step process. First, the Company determines whether it is more likely than not that an uncertain tax position will be sustained upon examination. Where the position meets that criterion of likelihood, the amount of benefit is measured as the largest amount of benefit that is greater than 50% likely of being realized. Where the criterion of likelihood is not met, no benefit is recognized for the uncertain tax position. Additionally, under Canadian GAAP, uncertain tax positions were evaluated based solely on the technical merits of the positions. Liabilities were recorded where the technical merits were uncertain and the tax examination was not finalized.

IFRS – The provision for uncertain tax positions is a best estimate of the amount expected to be paid based on a qualitative assessment of all relevant factors, including the status of the tax authority examination. Uncertain tax positions were not evaluated solely on the technical merits of the position. As a result, the Company reduced its liability for uncertain tax positions.

Accounting for Uncertainty in Income Taxes in Business Combinations

Canadian GAAP – Changes to provisions for uncertain tax position relating to pre-acquisition periods are adjusted through the purchase price allocation, first reducing goodwill and intangible assets associated with the business combination and, only after exhausting those amounts, reducing income tax expense.

IFRS – Changes to pre-acquisition provisions for uncertain tax positions beyond 12 months of the acquisition date are recorded to the income statement. As a result, the Company adjusted its tax expense to reflect this difference.

Recognition of Deferred Tax Assets on Tax Deductible Goodwill in Business Combinations

Canadian GAAP – When the tax base of tax deductible goodwill exceeds its carrying value, no deferred tax asset is recognized in respect of that excess.

IFRS – Deferred tax assets are recognized in respect of all deductible temporary differences, subject to the usual assessment of recoverability.

Income Tax Effect of Other Reconciling Differences between Canadian GAAP and IFRS

Differences for income taxes include the effect of recording, where applicable, the deferred tax effect of other differences between Canadian GAAP and IFRS.

8. FOREIGN CURRENCY TRANSLATION ADJUSTMENT

As noted in the section entitled "IFRS Exemption Options," the Company has applied the one-time exemption to set the foreign currency cumulative translation adjustment ("CTA") to zero as of January 1, 2008. The cumulative translation adjustment balance as of January 1, 2008 of $280 million was recognized as an adjustment to retained earnings. The application of the exemption had no impact on net equity. Additionally, deferred foreign currency gains and losses on loans repaid that are reclassified into earnings from CTA will differ under IFRS due to the IFRS 1 election to reset the CTA balance at the Transition Date.

Presentation Reclassifications

1. RECLASSIFICATION OF SOFTWARE AMORTIZATION AND DEPRECIATION

Canadian GAAP – Amortization of external use computer software is included in cost of sales and amortization of internal use software is included in depreciation.

IFRS – Amortization of all computer software is presented separately on the face of the income statement.

2. DISCLOSURE OF EQUITY METHOD INVESTEES

Canadian GAAP – The share of profit or loss from equity method investees is presented as part of "Other income (expense)" in the income statement.

IFRS – A separate disclosure on the face of the income statement is required for the Company's share of profit or loss from equity method investees.

3. GAIN/LOSS ON SALE OF BUSINESS

Canadian GAAP – A gain or loss on disposal of a businesses or property is not a component of operating profit and is presented in other income and expense.

IFRS – A gain or loss from disposal of business or property is a component of the operating profit and is included in "Other operating gains and losses" in the income statement.

4. TAX RECLASSIFICATION

Interest Expense and Uncertain Tax Positions

Canadian GAAP – Interest expense payable on tax audit settlements is presented as part of tax expense.

IFRS – Interest expense payable on tax audit settlements is presented as part of interest expense.

Deferred Tax

Canadian GAAP – Deferred taxes are split between current and non-current components on the basis of either (1) the underlying asset or liability or (2) the expected reversal of items not related to an asset or liability.

IFRS – All deferred tax assets and liabilities are classified as non-current.

5. NON-CONTROLLING INTERESTS

Non-controlling Interest in Consolidated Subsidiary

Canadian GAAP – Non-controlling interests in the equity of a consolidated affiliate are classified as a separate component between liabilities and equity in the statement of financial position and as a component of net earnings within the income statement.

IFRS – Non-controlling interests are classified as a component of equity separate from the equity of the parent and are not included in net earnings, but rather presented as an allocation of net earnings.

As part of the adoption of IFRS, the term "minority interest" has been replaced with "non-controlling interests" in accordance with IAS 1.

Sale of Non-controlling Interest in a Consolidated Subsidiary

Canadian GAAP – In January 2008, the Company sold a non-controlling interest in a consolidated subsidiary. The gain on this sale was deferred because the fair value of all related future performance obligations could not be reliably measured.

IFRS – Under IFRS, there is greater flexibility to determine fair value and allocate consideration to multiple components. As a result, the gain on sale of the non-controlling interest was able to be reliably measured. The Company elected to treat this transaction as though it were with an equity participant. Accordingly, this gain was recognized in equity.

6. DISCONTINUED OPERATIONS

Canadian GAAP – To qualify as a discontinued operation an entity may not have any significant continuing involvement in the operations of the entity after the disposal transaction. Additionally, dispositions of entities are classified as discontinued operations, if certain criteria are met.

IFRS – Continuing involvement with a sold entity does not preclude presentation as a discontinued operation. Additionally, only disposals of significant operations, such as a segment, meet the IFRS requirements to present the results as discontinued operations. As a result, one entity that had been classified as a discontinued operation was reclassified to continuing operations under IFRS.

Restated Thomson Reuters financial statements

The following are reconciliations of the financial statements previously presented under Canadian GAAP to the amended financial statements prepared under IFRS.

Reconciliation of Consolidated Statement of Financial Position as of January 1, 2008

> (not reproduced in this extract)

Reconciliation of Consolidated Income Statement for the Year Ended December 31, 2008

> (not reproduced in this extract)

Reconciliation of Consolidated Statement of Comprehensive Income for the Year Ended December 31, 2008

> (not reproduced in this extract)

Reconciliation of Consolidated Statement of Financial Position as of December 31, 2008

> (not reproduced in this extract)

Table 2.8 – Transition to IFRS, reconciliations under IFRS 1

Eastern Platinum Limited – Annual report – 31 December 2009

Notes to the consolidated financial statements

(Expressed in thousands of U.S. dollars, except number of shares and per share amounts)

25. IFRS

IFRS 1 *First-time Adoption of International Financial Reporting Standards* sets forth guidance for the initial adoption of IFRS. Under IFRS 1 the standards are applied retrospectively at the transitional statement of financial position date with all adjustments to assets and liabilities taken to retained earnings unless certain exemptions are applied. The Company has applied the following exemptions to its opening statement of financial position dated January 1, 2008:

(a) Business Combinations

IFRS 1 indicates that a first-time adopter may elect not to apply IFRS 3 *Business Combinations* retrospectively to business combinations that occurred before the date of transition to IFRS. The Company has taken advantage of this election and has applied IFRS 3 to business combinations that occurred on or after January 1, 2008.

(b) Cumulative translation differences

IFRS 1 allows a first-time adopter to not comply with the requirements of IAS 21 *The Effects of Changes in Foreign Exchange Rates* for cumulative translation differences that existed at the date of transition to IFRS. The Company has chosen to apply this election and has eliminated the cumulative translation difference and adjusted retained earnings by the same amount at the date of transition to IFRS. If, subsequent to adoption, a foreign operation is disposed of, the translation differences that arose before the date of transition to IFRS will not affect the gain or loss on disposal.

(c) Share-based payment transactions

IFRS 1 encourages, but does not require, first-time adopters to apply IFRS 2 *Share-based Payment* to equity instruments that were granted on or before November 7, 2002, or equity instruments that were granted subsequent to November 7, 2002 and vested before the later of the date of transition to IFRS and January 1, 2005. The Company has elected not to apply IFRS 2 to awards that vested prior to January 1, 2008, which have been accounted for in accordance with Canadian GAAP.

(d) IAS 27 – Consolidated and Separate Financial Statements

In accordance with IFRS 1, if a company elects to apply IFRS 3 *Business Combinations* retrospectively, IAS 27 *Consolidated and Separate Financial Statements* must also be applied retrospectively. As the Company elected to apply IFRS 3 prospectively, the Company has also elected to apply IAS 27 prospectively.

(e) IAS 23 – Borrowing Costs

In accordance with IFRS 1, the Company has elected to prospectively apply IAS 23 effective January 1, 2009.

IFRS 1 also outlines specific guidelines that a first-time adopter must adhere to under certain circumstances. The Company has applied the following guidelines to its opening statement of financial position dated January 1, 2008:

(f) Assets and liabilities of subsidiaries and associates

In accordance with IFRS 1, if a parent company adopts IFRS subsequent to its subsidiary or associate adopting IFRS, the assets and the liabilities of the subsidiary or associate are to be included in the consolidated financial statements at the same carrying amounts as in the financial statements of the subsidiary or associate. The Company's principal operating subsidiary, Barplats Investments Limited, adopted IFRS in 2005.

(g) Estimates

In accordance with IFRS 1, an entity's estimates under IFRS at the date of transition to IFRS must be consistent with estimates made for the same date under previous GAAP, unless there is objective evidence that those estimates were in error. The Company's IFRS estimates as of January 1, 2008 are consistent with its Canadian GAAP estimates for the same date.

IFRS employs a conceptual framework that is similar to Canadian GAAP. However, significant differences exist in certain matters of recognition, measurement and disclosure. While adoption of IFRS has not changed the Company's actual cash flows, it has resulted in changes to the Company's reported financial position and results of operations. In order to allow the users of the financial statements to better understand these changes, the Company's Canadian GAAP statement of operations, statement of comprehensive income, statement of financial position and statement of cash flows for the year ended December 31, 2008 have been reconciled to IFRS, with the resulting differences explained.

(h) Revenue and interest income

The Company settles its metal sales three or five months, depending on the type of metal, following the physical delivery of the concentrates. The present value of sales revenue expected to be received in three or five months is recognized on the date of sale. The difference between the present value and the future value is recognized as interest revenue over the term of settlement. In its Canadian GAAP financial statements for the year ended December 31, 2008, the Company recorded the future value as sales revenue, as opposed to recognizing the difference between the present value and the future value as interest revenue over the term of settlement. The difference in the treatment of revenue results in a timing difference in the recognition of income and is not material to these financial statements.

(i) Property, plant and equipment

Due to the adjustments to the provision for environmental rehabilitation discussed in Note 25(k), the cost of property, plant and equipment is different in accordance with IFRS than in accordance with Canadian GAAP. As a result, even though depreciation is calculated in the same manner, the amount of depreciation differs.

(j) Share-based payments

IFRS

- Each tranche of an award with different vesting dates is considered a separate grant for the calculation of fair value, and the resulting fair value is amortized over the vesting period of the respective tranches.

- Forfeiture estimates are recognized in the period they are estimated, and are revised for actual forfeitures in subsequent periods.

Canadian GAAP

- The fair value of stock-based awards with graded vesting are calculated as one grant and the resulting fair value is recognized on a straight-line basis over the vesting period.
- Forfeitures of awards are recognized as they occur.

(k) Provision for environmental rehabilitation

IFRS

- The provision for environmental rehabilitation must be adjusted for changes in the discount rate.

Canadian GAAP

- The provision for environmental rehabilitation is not adjusted for changes in the discount rate.

(l) Deferred tax asset/liability

IFRS

- All deferred tax assets and liabilities must be classified as non-current.

Canadian GAAP

- Deferred tax assets and liabilities are classified as current or non-current as appropriate.

(m) Other comprehensive income (loss)

Other comprehensive income (loss) consists of the change in the cumulative translation adjustment ("CTA"). Due to other IFRS adjustments, the balances that are used to calculate the CTA are different in accordance with IFRS than in accordance with Canadian GAAP. As a result, CTA and other comprehensive income (loss) are different in accordance with IFRS than in accordance with Canadian GAAP.

(n) Impairment

IFRS– If indication of impairment is identified, the asset's carrying value is compared to the asset's discounted cash flows. If the discounted cash flows are less than the carrying value, the asset is impaired by an amount equal to the difference between the discounted cash flows and the carrying value.

Canadian GAAP — If indication of impairment is identified, the asset's carrying value is compared to the asset's undiscounted cash flows. If the undiscounted cash flows are less than the carrying value, the asset is impaired by an amount equal to the difference between the discounted cash flows and the carrying value.

The Company completed an impairment review of its assets at January 1, 2008 and concluded that the assets were not impaired in accordance with IFRS. At December 31, 2008, the carrying value of the Kennedy's Vale mineral property was less than the property's undiscounted cash flows, but greater than the property's discounted cash flows. As a result, the mineral property was concluded to be impaired in accordance with IFRS, but not impaired in accordance with Canadian GAAP. An impairment of $297.3 million and an income tax recovery of $71.5 million have been recorded relating to the Kennedy's Vale impairment.

(o) Presentation

The presentation in accordance with IFRS differs from the presentation in accordance with Canadian GAAP.

The January 1, 2008 Canadian GAAP statement of financial position has been reconciled to IFRS as follows:

		January 1, 2008		
		Canadian GAAP	Effect of transition to IFRS	IFRS
Assets				
Current assets				
Cash and cash equivalents	$	18,818	$ –	$ 18,818
Short-term investments		171,038	–	171,038
Trade and other receivables	(f)(h)	33,157	(597)	32,560
Inventories		6,888	–	6,888
		229,901	(597)	229,304
Property, plant and equipment	(f)(i)(k)	813,461	1,929	815,390
Refining contract		18,467	–	18,467
Other assets		1,247	–	1,247
		$ 1,063,076	$ 1,332	$ 1,064,408
Liabilities				
Current liabilities				
Accounts payable and accrued liabilities		$ 22,967	$ –	$ 22,967
Current portion of finance leases	(o)	–	748	748
Current portion of long-term liability		3,837	–	3,837
Deferred tax	(l)	6,416	(6,416)	–
		33,220	(5,668)	27,552
Provision for environmental rehabilitation	(f)(k)	2,889	3,335	6,224
Capital leases and other long-term liabilities	(o)	9,127	(9,127)	–
Finance leases	(o)	–	5,057	5,057
Loans	(o)	–	3,322	3,322
Deferred tax liabilities	(l)	143,616	6,416	150,032
		188,852	3,335	192,187
Equity				
Issued capital		868,045	–	868,045
Equity-settled employee benefits reserve		27,428	–	27,428
Currency translation adjustment	(b)	23,481	(23,481)	–
Deficit		(68,132)	21,747	(46,385)
Capital and reserves attributable to equity shareholders of the Company		850,822	(1,734)	849,088
Non-controlling interest		23,402	(269)	23,133
		874,224	(2,003)	872,221
		$ 1,063,076	$ 1,332	$ 1,064,408

The Canadian GAAP income statement and statement of comprehensive income for the twelve months ended December 31, 2008 have been reconciled to IFRS as follows:

First-time adoption of IFRS

	Note	12 months ended December 31, 2008		
		Canadian GAAP	Effect of transition to IFRS	IFRS
Revenue	(h)	$ 116,198	$ (1,517)	$ 114,681
Cost of operations				
Production costs		79,961	–	79,961
Depletion and depreciation	(i)	14,599	63	14,662
		94,560	63	94,623
Mine operating earnings		21,638	(1,580)	20,058
Expenses				
Impairment	(n)	–	297,285	297,285
General and administrative	(f)	19,411	30	19,441
Share-based payments	(j)	4,290	335	4,625
		23,701	297,650	321,351
Operating loss		(2,063)	(299,230)	(301,293)
Other income (expense)				
Interest income	(h)	7,081	1,863	8,944
Finance costs	(k)	(3,551)	(174)	(3,725)
Foreign exchange gain		(2,155)	–	(2,155)
Loss before income taxes		(688)	(297,541)	(298,229)
Deferred income tax recovery	(n)	13,623	71,490	85,113
Net profit (loss) for the year		$ 12,935	$ (226,051)	$ (213,116)
Attributable to				
Non-controlling interest		$ (3,429)	$ (306)	$ (3,735)
Equity shareholders of the Company		$ 16,364	$ (225,745)	$ (209,381)
Net profit (loss) for the year		$ 12,935	$ (226,051)	$ (213,116)

	Note	12 months ended December 31, 2008		
		Canadian GAAP	Effect of transition to IFRS	IFRS
Net profit (loss) for the year		$ 12,935	$ (226,051)	$ (213,116)
Other comprehensive loss – currency translation adjustment	(m)	(197,052)	27,475	(169,577)
Exchange differences on translating non-controlling interest	(o)	–	(7,396)	(7,396)
Comprehensive loss		$ (184,117)	$ (205,972)	$ (390,089)
Attributable to				
Non-controlling interest	(o)	(3,429)	(7,702)	(11,131)
Equity shareholders of the Company	$	(180,688)	$ (198,270)	$ (378,958)

The Canadian GAAP statement of financial position at December 31, 2008 has been reconciled to IFRS as follows:

		December 31, 2008		
	Note	Canadian GAAP	Effect of transition to IFRS	IFRS
Assets				
Current assets				
Cash and cash equivalents		$ 25,806	$ –	$ 25,806
Short-term investments		35,257	–	35,257
Trade receivables	(h)	9,556	(125)	9,431
Inventories		3,881	–	3,881
Deferred tax asset	(l)	1,178	(1,178)	–
		75,678	(1,303)	74,375
Property, plant and equipment	(i)(k)(n)	783,039	(277,566)	505,473
Refining contract		12,493	–	12,493
Other assets		1,017	–	1,017
		$ 872,227	$ (278,869)	$ 593,358
Liabilities				
Current liabilities				
Accounts payable and accrued liabilities		$ 36,729	–	$ 36,729
Current portion of finance leases		649	–	649
Current loans	(o)	2,972	247	3,219
		40,350	247	40,597
Non-current liabilities				
Non-current liabilities rehabilitation	(k)	2,846	2,752	5,598
Finance leases	(o)	3,261	(247)	3,014
Deferred tax liabilities	(l)(n)	117,234	(81,620)	35,614
		163,691	(78,868)	84,823
Equity				
Issued capital		890,049	–	890,049
Equity-settled employee benefits reserve	(j)	31,491	336	336
Currency translation adjustment	(m)	(173,571)	3,994	(169,577)
Deficit		(51,768)	(203,998)	(255,766)
Capital and reserves attributable to equity shareholders of the Company		696,201	(199,668)	496,533
Non-controlling interest		12,335	(333)	12,002
		708,536	(200,001)	508,535
		$ 872,227	$ (278,869)	$ 593,358

The reconciliation of the statement of cash flows for the twelve months ended December 31, 2008:

First-time adoption of IFRS

	Note	December 31, 2008 (12 months)		
		Canadian GAAP	Effect of transition to IFRS	IFRS
Operating activities				
Net profit (loss) for the year		$ (688)	$ (297,541)	$ (298,229)
Adjustments to net profit (loss) for non-cash items				
Depreciation	(i)	14,877	(215)	14,662
Refining contract amortization		1,353	–	1,353
Impairment	(n)	–	297,285	297,285
Share-based payments	(j)	4,290	335	4,625
Interest income	(o)	–	(8,944)	(8,944)
Finance costs	(o)	2,845	880	3,725
Foreign exchange loss	(o)	5,731	(3,576)	2,155
Net changes in non-cash working capital items				
Trade receivables	(h)	10,765	3,266	14,031
Inventories		1,391	–	1,391
Accounts payable and accrued liabilities		12,962	–	12,962
Cash generated from operations		53,526	(8,510)	45,016
Adjustments to net profit for cash items				
Realized foreign exchange gain	(o)	–	(1,157)	(1,157)
Interest income received	(o)	–	10,028	10,028
Finance costs paid	(o)	–	(375)	(375)
Net operating cash flows		53,526	(14)	53,512
Investing activities				
Acquisitions, net of cash acquired		(39,589)	–	(39,589)
Maturity of short-term investments	(o)	119,318	42	119,360
Purchase of other assets	(o)	–	(42)	(42)
Property, plant and equipment expenditures		(143,373)	–	(143,373)
Net investing cash flows		(63,644)	–	(63,644)
Financing activities				
Common shares issued for cash, net of share issue costs		22,004	–	22,004
Repayment of short-term debt	(o)	(892)	892	–
Other long-term liabilities	(o)	(3,411)	(898)	(4,309)
Net financing cash flows		17,701	(6)	17,695
Effect of exchange rate changes on cash and cash equivalents		(595)	20	(575)
Increase in cash and cash equivalents		6,988	–	6,988
Cash and cash equivalents, beginning of year		18,818	–	18,818
Cash and cash equivalents, end of year		$ 25,806	$ –	$ 25,806

GAAP errors

2.201 Paragraph 26 of IFRS 1 requires any errors in previous GAAP to be separately identified and disclosed in the reconciliation between previous GAAP and IFRS. Correction of prior period errors is dealt with in detail in chapter 3.

Designation of financial assets or financial liabilities

2.202 Entities may designate a previously recognised financial asset and/or liability as a financial asset or financial liability at fair value through profit or loss (where permitted), or as available-for-sale at the date of transition. If an entity elects to do this, it should disclose the fair value of financial assets or financial liabilities designated into each category at the date of designation and should also disclose their previous classification and carrying amounts prior to designation. Similar disclosures are also required where an entity applies IFRS 9 and elects to designate a previously recognised financial asset at fair value through profit or loss. [IFRS 1 paras 29, 29A].

Use of fair value as deemed cost

2.203 If an entity has used fair value as deemed cost for any item of property, plant and equipment, for an investment property or for an intangible asset then it should disclose, for each line item in the opening IFRS balance sheet, the aggregate of those fair values and the adjustments that were made to the carrying amounts under previous GAAP. [IFRS 1 para 30].

Use of deemed cost for investments in subsidiaries, jointly controlled entities and associates

2.204 If an entity has used deemed cost for any investment in a subsidiary, jointly controlled entity, or associate in its separate financial statements (see para 2.143) then it should disclose:

- the aggregate deemed cost of those investments where deemed cost is their previous GAAP carrying amount;

- the aggregate deemed cost of those investments where deemed cost is fair value; and

- the aggregate adjustment to the carrying amounts reported under previous GAAP.

[IFRS 1 para 31].

Use of deemed cost for oil and gas assets

2.205 If an entity has used the deemed cost exemption for oil and gas assets as outlined in paragraph 2.112, it should disclose that fact as well as the basis on which previous GAAP carrying amounts have been allocated. [IFRS 1 para 31A].

Use of deemed cost for operations subject to rate regulation

2.206 An entity, taking advantage of the deemed cost exemption for operations subject to rate regulation, as discussed in paragraph 2.114, it should disclose the fact and the basis on which previous GAAP carrying amounts have been calculated. [IFRS 1 para 31B]

Interim financial reports

2.207 IFRS 1 does not require entities applying IFRS for the first time to produce interim financial statements. However, where interim financial statements are presented in accordance with IAS 34 covering part of the period presented in an entity's first IFRS financial statements, IFRS 1 applies to those interims. [IFRS 1 para 2(b)]. Interim financial statements are dealt with in detail in Manual of Accounting – Interim financial reporting. If an entity does apply the provisions of IAS 34 for its interim financial report, IFRS 1 requires additional disclosures to those already required by IAS 34. Specifically, IFRS 1 states that:

> *"Each such interim financial report shall, if the entity presented an interim financial report for the comparable interim period of the immediately preceding financial year, include:*
>
> *(i)   a reconciliation of its equity in accordance with previous GAAP at the end of that comparable interim period to its equity under IFRSs at that date; and*
>
> *(ii) a reconciliation to its total comprehensive income in accordance with IFRSs for that comparable interim period (current and year to date). The starting point for that reconciliation shall be total comprehensive income in accordance with previous GAAP for that period or, if an entity did not report such a total, profit or loss in accordance with previous GAAP."*

[IFRS 1 para 32(a)].

2.208 A December year end entity adopting IFRS in 20Y0 and using IAS 34 for the interim period to 30 June 20Y0 would present a reconciliation from previous GAAP to IFRS of equity at 30 June 20X9 and comprehensive income for the six months to 30 June 20X9.

2.209 IFRS 1 requires entities presenting interim financial information under IAS 34 also to give the reconciliations required in their first IFRS financial statements. These are equity at the date of transition and the end of the last period presented under previous GAAP, and comprehensive income for the last year presented under previous GAAP (see para 2.196). If an entity presented a statement of cash flows under its previous GAAP, it should also explain, in a narrative, or by reconciliation, any material adjustments to the statement of cash flows. The reconciliations should be in sufficient detail so that users can understand material adjustments, and any previous GAAP errors should be clearly identified. [IFRS 1 para 32(b)]. If the reconciliations described in this paragraph are in another document (for example, if the entity presented them in its last previous GAAP financial statements) then the interim financial statements should cross-refer to that document. In cases where interim financial reports are the first financial reports in which an entity presents IFRS information, this will potentially result in a considerable amount of additional disclosures and explanations compared to standard interim financial reports.

2.210   A first-time adopter is required to present its opening IFRS balance sheet (see further para 2.188) in its first IFRS financial statements. It is not explicit that this requirement extends to condensed interim financial statements published in the year of IFRS adoption that are prepared in accordance with IAS 34. [IAS 34 para 8; IAS 1 para BC33]. Nevertheless, an entity may wish to consider whether disclosing such information would be helpful to the users of the financial statements. Any national regulatory requirements in an entity's local territory that require presentation of an opening IFRS balance sheet in the interim financial statements should also be considered.

2.211   An amendment to IFRS 1 requires disclosure where an entity changes its accounting policies or its use of exemptions in IFRS 1. The disclosures noted in paragraph 2.23 are also required in an entity's interim report. This would apply when an entity publishes interim reports on a quarterly basis and a change in policy or use of an exemption arises between the issuance of the various interim reports.

Example 1 – Reconciliations required for first IFRS interim financial statements

A company has a 31 March year end. Its annual financial statements for the year ended 31 March 20X7 and its interim financial report for the six months ended 30 September 20X6 were prepared in accordance with its previous GAAP. The company is adopting IFRS for its financial statements for the year to 31 March 20X8 and is preparing its interim financial report in accordance with IAS 34 for the six month period to 30 September 20X7. What reconciliations are required by IFRS 1 to be presented in the interim financial report?

IFRS 1 requires the following reconciliations to be presented:

- A reconciliation between equity reported under previous GAAP and equity reported under IFRS at:

    - The date of transition to IFRS – 1 April 20X6.

    - The end of the corresponding interim period – 30 September 20X6.

    - The end of the latest period in the most recent annual financial statements – 31 March 20X7.

- A reconciliation of the comprehensive income reported under previous GAAP to the comprehensive income reported under IFRS for:

    - The corresponding interim period – six months ended 30 September 20X6.

- ■ The latest period in the most recent annual financial statements – year ended 31 March 20X7.

- ■ An explanation of material adjustments to the cash flow statement for the year to 31 March 20X7.

Example 2 – Reconciliations required when an issuer does not begin using IFRS in a quarterly report

A regulator may not permit an issuer to begin using IFRS in a quarterly report, thus, in the year of adoption, an entity would file its quarterly financial statements in accordance with its previous GAAP and would then file its annual report in accordance with IFRS. Another scenario would be for the entity to first restate its prior year financial statements in accordance with IFRS.

Under either scenario, the adoption methodology would result in the first IFRS financial statements being issued in an annual report.

Is the entity required to include interim reconciliations as contemplated in IFRS 1, paragraph 32, in its initial interim financial report prepared in accordance with IFRS?

No. Reconciliations are not required since the initial interim financial report prepared under IFRS will be presented after an entity has prepared its first IFRS annual financial statements. Specifically, as the first IFRS interim financial report is issued after the first annual IFRS financial statements, the interim financial report is not, by definition, part of the period covered within the first IFRS financial statements.

2.212 Any errors that were made under previous GAAP are required by IFRS 1 to be separately identified in the reconciliations outlined in paragraph 2.209 above. [IFRS 1 para 26]. Although this requirement does not specifically extend to the reconciliations of equity and income at the corresponding interim date in the prior year (see para 2.207) we consider that such disclosure should be made so that all reconciliations presented are consistent.

2.213 Where an entity prepares more than one interim financial report during the period covered by its first set of IFRS financial statements (for example, if it prepares quarterly reports in accordance with IAS 34), then reconciliations should be included in each interim financial report in respect of the comparable interim period of the immediately preceding financial year. For instance, when preparing interim financial statements for the second quarter of the year (for example, the second quarter in 2010), the entity would include the reconciliations required by IFRS 1 relating to the same comparative quarter of the immediately preceding year (for example, second quarter in 2009). There should also be a reference to the reconciliation in the preceding published interim report (for example, the first quarter of 2011). Users of financial statements would be able to obtain additional information from any previous interim reports by looking at the reference. The amount of comparative disclosures provided would vary according to each reporting entity and its particular regulatory environment. Therefore, entities should assess if more information, including reconciliations from previous quarter(s), would need to be provided in addition to the minimum requirements for comparative information.

2.214   If an interim financial report is produced under IAS 34 for a period covered by an entity's first IFRS financial statements then the comparative interim period should be restated to comply with IFRS. [IFRS 1 para IG37].

2.215   IFRS 1 notes that the disclosures required by IAS 34 are based upon an assumption that users will have had access to the reporting entity's last annual financial statements. However, if those statements did not disclose facts that are material to understanding the present interim period, then these disclosures should be given. First-time adopters must disclose events and transactions material to understanding the transition, unless these have been disclosed in the last annual report. [IFRS 1 para 33]. Such disclosures are likely to include at least a description of the new accounting policies adopted and their effect on the financial statements. The necessary level of disclosure in an interim financial report in the year of transition will vary entity by entity.

2.216   The level of disclosure in an interim financial report in the year of transition where there are many differences from previous GAAP is illustrated in the example below.

Example – Year of transition to IFRS: interim financial report disclosures with many differences from previous GAAP

A multi-national group has major business lines in the production of steel and assorted consumer durable products, banking and lease financing. It operates on a global scale with production units throughout Europe, South America and parts of Asia, two new factories in Eastern Europe, banking subsidiaries in Europe, the US and the Middle East and lease financing operations throughout Europe and parts of Africa. The group includes 150 subsidiaries, all of which were consolidated under its previous GAAP.

The main GAAP differences are in the recognition and measurement of financial instruments, lease accounting and construction contracts, but there are many more differences that affect different entities within the group. In addition, there are key presentation changes such as the need for expanded segment reporting and changes in the classification of issued financial instruments that will affect the financial statements. The entity is proposing to take advantage of all relevant exemptions from full retrospective adoption of IFRS available to it in IFRS 1. What level of disclosure may be required in the notes to the interim financial report in the year of transition?

It is likely that the minimum disclosure requirements for an IFRS interim financial report will not be sufficient. The financial statements presented in accordance with IFRS will differ significantly from those previously presented in accordance with previous GAAP, with significant changes to the presentation, recognition, measurement and disclosure of items. The information necessary in addition to the minimum requirements will, therefore, be substantial and may well be nearly as extensive as a full set of annual financial statements.

Summary financial statements

UK.2.216.1 In the UK, the Companies Act 2006 permits, in certain circumstances, summary financial statements to be sent to a company's members, instead of the company's full financial statements. [CA06 Sec 426]. A summary financial statement means a statement that is derived from the company's annual financial statements and (in the case of a quoted company) the directors' remuneration report. The detailed requirements on form and content are set out in statutory instrument, 'The Companies (Summary Financial Statement) Regulations 1995' (SI 1995/2092), which was amended, with effect from 1 October 2005, by statutory instrument 'The Companies (Summary Financial Statement) (Amendment) Regulations 2005' (SI 2005/2281) so as to permit IFRS reporters to prepare summary financial statements.

UK.2.216.2 The statutory instrument on summary financial statements does not give specific direction or make specific reference to any reconciliations required for the first year of IFRS reporting. However, our view is that entities will need to give reconciliations from UK GAAP to IFRS that are sufficient to make the summary information disclosed understandable. We believe that this is best achieved by following the requirements of paragraph 39 of IFRS 1 (see para 2.196). For a first-time adopter with a year end of 31 December 20X7, this would mean reconciling equity on the date of transition (1 January 20X6) and at 31 December 20X6 from UK GAAP to IFRS and similarly reconciling its profit or loss for the year ended 31 December 20X6.

Practical applications of first-time adoption

UK.2.216.3 This section sets out the significant first-time adoption issues for UK entities moving to IFRS. It is not a list of differences between existing UK GAAP and IFRS and, in particular, does not cover areas where IFRS requires fewer or similar disclosures. IFRS 1 includes detailed implementation guidance explaining how IFRS 1's requirements interact with the requirements of some other IFRSs. The guidance focuses on those IFRSs that are most likely to involve questions that are specific to first-time adopters. [IFRS 1 para IG1].

IAS 1, Presentation of financial statements

UK.2.216.4 The formats set out in IFRS for the income statement are not as detailed or rigid as those for UK GAAP in Schedule 1 to SI 2008/410, 'The Large and Medium-sized Companies and Groups (Accounts and Reports) Regulations 2008' and in FRS 3,. Instead IAS 1 contains a minimum list of specific line items, as follows:

- Revenue.

- Finance costs.

- Share of the after-tax profit or loss of associates and joint ventures accounted for using the equity method.

- Tax expense.

- A single amount comprising the total of (i) the post-tax profit or loss of discontinued operations and (ii) the post tax gain or loss recognised on the measurement to fair value less costs to sell or on the disposal of the assets or disposal group(s) constituting the discontinued operation.

- Profit or loss.

- Each component of other comprehensive income classified by nature (excluding amounts in the bullet point directly below).

- Share of the other comprehensive income of associates and joint ventures accounted for using the equity method.

- Total comprehensive income.

[IAS 1 para 82].

On the face of the income statement the following should be disclosed:

- Profit or loss attributable to non-controlling interest.

- Profit or loss attributable to owners of the parent.

[IAS 1 para 83].

UK.2.216.5 Entities applying IAS 1 will produce an income statement that in many respects is no different to that given under existing UK GAAP. The main differences relate to exceptional and extraordinary items. IAS 1 does not contain the concept of 'super-exceptional' items, the three specific items that are separately disclosed below operating profit under the UK standard FRS 3. Although IAS 1 does not allow a separate line item for extraordinary items it does require separate disclosure *"when items of income and expense are material"*. [IAS 1 para 97]. This is broader than the current UK definition of exceptional items contained in FRS 3. These are *"material items which derive from events or transactions that fall within the ordinary activities of the reporting entity and which individually or, if of a similar type, in aggregate, need to be disclosed by virtue of their size or incidence if the financial statements are to give a true and fair view"*. [FRS 3 para 5]. However, the list of examples of such items given in IAS 1 is not dissimilar to those that might be considered exceptional in current UK GAAP: asset write-downs; restructuring; disposals of assets and investments; discontinued operations; litigation settlements; and other reversals of provisions. [IAS 1 para 98]. This area is dealt with more fully in chapter 4.

UK.2.216.6 The issue of balance sheet presentation is similar to that of the income statement for first time adopters. IAS 1 specifies a list of items that should be presented in the balance sheet. The minimum items are given below.

(a) Property, plant and equipment.

(b) Investment property.

(c) Intangible assets.

(d) Financial assets (excluding amounts shown under (e), (h) and (i)).

(e) Investments accounted for using the equity method.

(f) Biological assets.

(g) Inventories.

(h) Trade and other receivables.

(i) Cash and cash equivalents.

(j) The total of assets classified as held-for-sale and assets included in disposal groups classified as held-for-sale in accordance with IFRS 5.

(k) Trade and other payables.

(l) Provisions.

(m) Financial liabilities (excluding amounts shown under (k) and (l)).

(n) Liabilities and assets for current tax, as defined in IAS 12.

(o) Deferred tax liabilities and assets.

(p) Liabilities included in disposal groups classified as held for sale in accordance with IFRS 5.

(q) Non-controlling interests, presented within equity.

(r) Issued capital and reserve attributed to owners of the parent.

[IAS 1 para 54].

UK.2.216.7 The presentation of the balance sheet is, again, not significantly different to that under current UK GAAP. The presentation in IAS 1 is less rigid in terms of the line items required and the order that they should be presented in than those in Schedule 1 to SI 2008/410, 'The Large and Medium-sized Companies and Groups (Accounts and Reports) Regulations 2008'. However, the order is similar, with assets and liabilities being split between current and non-current.

UK.2.216.8 To comply with IAS 1, an entity's first financial statements must include at least three balance sheets, two statements of comprehensive income, two separate income statements (if presented), two statements of cash flows and two statements of changes in equity and related notes, including comparative information. [IFRS 1 para 21]. Many listed entities give five year historical summaries of key financial data. In the UK this information has been given voluntarily; it has never been either a Companies Act or a Listing Rule requirement. Where an entity presents a historical summary showing information about a period earlier than the prior year, IFRS 1 does not require the entity to comply with the recognition and measurement requirements of IFRS in respect of those periods. It may be that an entity presents comparative information under both UK GAAP (as previously presented), as well as the comparative information required by IAS 1. As noted in paragraph 2.195, where an entity's financial statements contain historical summaries or comparative information under previous GAAP, an entity should:

■ Identify prominently the non-IFRS information as not being prepared under IFRS.

■ Disclose the nature of the adjustments that would be required to comply with IFRS. (The entity need not disclose the quantity of those adjustments.)

[IFRS 1 para 22].

IAS 2, Inventories

UK.2.216.9 IAS 2 has similar recognition and measurement requirements to those contained in SSAP 9, 'Stocks and long-term contracts'. One area where new information will be required on transition to IFRS is to meet the disclosure requirements of the standard. IAS 2 requires the carrying amount of inventories carried at fair value less costs to sell to be disclosed and it also requires disclosure of the amount of any reversal of a write down, with an explanation for this. [IAS 2 paras 36(c), (f), (g)]. SSAP 9 requires neither of these disclosures and entities will have to find ways of obtaining this information if it is not recorded under UK GAAP. Although IAS 2 does not require inventories to be classified between raw materials, work in progress, finished goods and payments on account, it does require disclosure of *"the total carrying amount of inventories and the carrying amount in classifications appropriate to the entity"*. [IAS 2 para 36(b)]. Entities may wish to use the move to IFRS to consider the categorisation that gives the most useful information to readers of the financial statements.

IAS 7, Cash flow statements

UK.2.216.10 There are two main presentational differences between IAS 7 and FRS 1. The first is that the cash flows reported under IAS 7 relate to movements in cash and cash equivalents, whereas FRS 1 requires reporting of the movement in cash, being cash in hand and deposits repayable on demand less overdrafts. Cash equivalents are defined as *"short-term, highly liquid investments that are readily convertible to known amounts of cash and which are subject to an insignificant risk of changes in value"*. [IAS 7 para 6].

UK.2.216.11 In FRS 1 there is a category labelled 'management of liquid resources'. Liquid resources are defined as *"current asset investments held as readily disposable stores of value. A readily disposable investment is one that: (a) is disposable by the reporting entity without curtailing or disrupting its business; and is either: (b)(i) readily convertible into known amounts of cash at or close to its carrying amount, or (b)(ii) traded in an active market"*. [FRS 1 para 2]. The definition is substantially the same as that of cash equivalents in IAS 7, and the amounts that form part of cash equivalents for IAS 7 will generally be included in the category of 'liquid resources' in an FRS 1 cash flow statement. Under both standards the short-term characteristic is generally taken to mean a maturity of three months or less from the date of acquisition of the instrument.

UK.2.216.12 The key difference between the application of the definitions of 'cash' and 'liquid resources' in the UK and of 'cash and cash equivalents' is that of intention. Under FRS 1 all overdrafts are part of cash. Under IAS 7, the classification of bank overdrafts (and other very short-term borrowings) depends on their use within the entity: *"in some countries, bank overdrafts which are repayable on demand form an integral part of an entity's cash management. In these circumstances, bank overdrafts are included as a component of cash and cash equivalents. A characteristic of such banking arrangements is that the bank balance often fluctuates from being positive to overdrawn"*. [IAS 7 para 8]. UK entities, on moving to IFRS, should, therefore, look closely at their financing arrangements. It may be that bank overdrafts are viewed as a form of finance rather than as a cash management tool. Where this is the case the overdrafts should be part of financing cash flows rather than cash and cash equivalents. In many cases, however, overdrafts are part of an entity's cash management system and the bank balance fluctuates from being positive to overdrawn. In such cases overdrafts are part of cash and cash equivalents. There may also be some reasonably short-term investments that are investing in nature rather than being related to cash management. Entities, therefore, need to look carefully at their cash management and financing strategies and practices when adopting IFRS so that the correct items are included in cash and cash equivalents.

UK.2.216.13 The other main difference between IAS 7 and FRS 1 is that IAS 7 has three categories (operating, investing and financing activities) in its format whereas FRS 1 has nine. The international standard with its various options of presenting cash flows is more flexible than the UK standard and, as a result, there is a diversity of presentations in practice. UK companies making the transition to international standards may find this confusing. It is quite likely that UK companies may begin a process of experimentation by retaining some of the features of FRS 1, such as voluntarily presenting a reconciliation to net debt. The transition for UK entities should be relatively straightforward, since it involves combining information that is, under FRS 1, separately collected and presented. One single amount in UK cash flow statements that might be split under IFRS is taxation. IAS 7 requires that cash flows in relation to taxation on income should be classified and separately disclosed under operating activities in the cash flow statement, unless they can be specifically attributed to financing or investing activities. [IAS 7 para 35].

UK.2.216.14   However, it may be inappropriate and rather misleading to require allocation of tax flows between the three economic activities. A payment of UK corporation tax in an entity involves only one cash flow that is arrived at by applying the rate of corporation tax to the entity's total income. The total income is the result of aggregation of taxable income arising from all sources, including chargeable capital gains. The taxation rules under which taxable total income is calculated do not easily lend themselves to subdivision between operating, investing and financing activities. Consequently, any allocation that attempts to segregate the taxation cash flows in this manner may result in the reporting of hypothetical figures in the cash flow statement. We would therefore expect that taxation cash flows would not be split by those adopting IFRS and would be reported under the operating activities heading.

UK.2.216.15   The cash flows arising from dividends and interest receipts and payments should be classified in the cash flow statement under the activity appropriate to their nature. In most cases this will be relatively straightforward. IAS 7 gives an explicit choice in respect of interest and dividends. Interest and dividends received may be classified within operating or investing activities. Interest and dividends paid may be classified as operating or financing activities. The standard permits companies to show dividends paid in operating activities, because this allows users to determine the ability of an entity to pay dividends out of operating cash flows. [IAS 7 para 34]. Nevertheless, it is likely that most UK companies would categorise interest paid in operating and dividends paid to parent and minority shareholders in financing on the grounds that, although both are payments to providers of capital, interest paid is contractual and has to be paid when due, whereas dividends are discretionary and payments may vary according to the amount legally available for distribution, the cash available and the dividend policy of the entity.

UK.2.216.16   One further key difference between IAS 7 and FRS 1 is the scope: FRS 1 exempts entities that are 90% owned from presenting a cash flow statement, as long as the consolidated financial statements in which the subsidiary is included are publicly available. IAS 7 has no such exemption: all entities preparing financial statements under IFRS are required to produce a cash flow statement. UK entities that adopt IFRS that have previously been able to use the exemption in FRS 1 may not have prepared individual cash flow information previously. This will now be required under IAS 7.

IAS 8, Accounting policies, changes in accounting estimates and errors

UK.2.216.17 IAS 8 contains requirements for the treatment of changes in estimates and errors. These are similar to those in FRS 18, except that IAS 8 does not make a distinction between fundamental and other errors, and requires all material errors to be corrected by a prior period adjustment. [IAS 8 para 42]. This may affect first-time adopters, and care should be taken. Adjustments that relate to the prior year when adopting IFRS that are not related to changes in accounting policy will fall into three categories:

- Errors in applying UK GAAP.

- Errors that arose in situations where information later came to light that should have been available when the financial statements were prepared. For example, an asset with a significant book value had been stolen prior to a year end, but this had not been noticed.

- Changes that came to light only in retrospect because more information became available. For example, a provision had been made for a court case that was subsequently settled in an entity's favour.

UK.2.216.18 The first category is a previous GAAP error and should be dealt with in the reconciliation between UK GAAP and IFRS, but labelled as a UK GAAP error and not as a GAAP difference. This follows the requirements of paragraph 41 of IFRS 1. The second type of error is one that is not covered by IFRS 1, but does fall to be treated by the requirements of IAS 8. If the error is material then it should be corrected by a prior period adjustment. In an entity's first IFRS financial statements such a prior period adjustment will form a separate component of the reconciliations between equity and income under UK GAAP to IFRS. Although IAS 8 does not require such a reconciliation, there would be a gap in the IFRS 1 reconciliation without the error being shown. It should be clearly labelled as an error and the entity should also make the disclosures required by paragraph 49 of IAS 8. The third category is dealt with by IFRS 1's guidance on estimates. Where the provision was based upon the best information available at the time no adjustment is made to the comparative period in the entity's first IFRS financial statements. Where it was not, amounts should be adjusted accordingly and the treatment should be the same as for the second type of error above. [IFRS 1 para 14].

IAS 10, Events after the balance sheet date

UK.2.216.19 FRS 21 (IAS 10), which is applicable for accounting periods beginning on or after 1 January 2005, is largely identical to IAS 10 and so where FRS 21 was applicable there will be no issues for UK entities in respect of this standard when adopting IFRS.

UK.2.216.20 Entities adopting IFRS do not fully apply the requirements of IAS 10 on transition, because the rules in IFRS 1 on estimates override certain of IAS 10's requirements. IFRS 1 requires that estimates made on transition to IFRS (and at the end of any comparative periods) are consistent with those of an entity's previous GAAP, even if post-balance sheet information would have led to an adjustment of an amount. This is the case unless an estimate was made in error. [IFRS 1 para 14]. Therefore, the receipt of new information after the date of transition is to be treated in the same way as non-adjusting events after the balance sheet date under IAS 10. See further paragraph 2.32 onwards.

IAS 11, Construction contracts

UK.2.216.21   There are differences between IAS 11 and SSAP 9 in respect of construction contracts, but these are not so great that they should cause entities particular issues on transition to IFRS. The measurement rules are largely the same and the additional items that require disclosure should be readily available to most entities, such as the amount of retentions and the amount of contract revenue recognised in the period.

UK.2.216.22   One area where there is a difference between existing UK GAAP and IFRS is that of pre-contract costs. In the UK, this is dealt with in UITF Abstract 34, 'Pre contract costs'. UITF Abstract 34 precludes pre-contract costs from being capitalised before it is virtually certain that a contract can be obtained and the contract is expected to result in future net cash inflows. Any costs incurred before the contract is virtually certain should be expensed and should not be recapitalised. [UITF 34 para 15]. IAS 11, however, states that costs incurred in securing a contract should be included in the cost of the contract when it is probable that the contract can be obtained. [IAS 11 para 21]. 'Probable' is not defined in IAS 11, but it is reasonable to assume that it is a lower hurdle than 'virtually certain'. Entities applying IAS 11 for the first time should examine costs that were expensed under UITF Abstract 34 and consider whether they qualify as assets under IAS 11.

IAS 12, Income taxes

UK.2.216.23   IAS 12 encompasses the requirements of both FRS 16 and FRS 19. The requirements in respect of current tax are close to those of FRS 16. Accounting for deferred tax is, however, quite dissimilar. The approach is conceptually different, with IAS 12 taking a balance sheet approach that is based on temporary differences between the accounting and tax bases of assets and liabilities. UK entities will be required to adapt to a new mindset when considering deferred tax under IFRS. The implementation guidance to IFRS 1 notes that an entity should apply IAS 12 to temporary differences between the carrying amount of the assets and liabilities in its opening IFRS balance sheet and their tax bases. [IFRS 1 para IG5]. What this means in practice for a UK entity preparing its first IFRS financial statements with a reporting date of 31 December 20X7 is that the entity must:

- Apply IAS 12's requirements in preparing its opening IFRS balance sheet at 1 January 20X6, the date of transition to IFRS, and throughout all periods presented in its first IFRS financial statements.

- Measure current and deferred tax assets and liabilities in its opening balance sheet with reference to the tax laws and tax rates that had been enacted or substantively enacted at 1 January 20X6. See further paragraph UK.2.216.29.

- Reflect any adjustments arising as a result of adopting IAS 12 for the first time, such as recognition and measurement differences, as an adjustment to opening reserves at 1 January 20X6, unless IFRS 1 specifically requires another treatment, for example, in respect of business combinations.

Specific implementation issues are summarised below.

Discounting

UK.2.216.24   IAS 12 does not allow entities to discount deferred tax assets or liabilities, whereas FRS 19 does. For some industries, such as utilities and life insurance entities, the effect of discounting is material to say the least. Undoing the effect of discounting on liabilities will affect opening reserves on transition.

Revaluation of assets

UK.2.216.25   One area that will give rise to significant adjustments is where an entity has a policy of revaluing its investment properties and property, plant and equipment. Under FRS 19 deferred tax is provided only if the asset is revalued to fair value in each period with changes in fair values reported in the profit and loss account or if the company has entered into a binding agreement to sell the revalued asset, has recognised the gain or loss on sale and does not expect to obtain rollover relief. Similarly, where a fixed asset has been sold no deferred tax should be provided where it is more likely than not that the taxable gain will be rolled over. In such cases there is no liability. [FRS 19 paras 12 to 15]. Under IAS 12 revaluations create temporary differences and deferred tax must be provided. [IAS 12 para 20]. UK entities will need to provide additional deferred tax on revaluation of assets to the extent not previously recognised under FRS 19. This also applies to situations where the revalued amounts are treated as 'deemed cost' at the date of transition in accordance with IFRS 1 (see para 2.107). Furthermore, the measurement of deferred tax balances should reflect the manner in which the entity expects to recover the carrying amount of the revalued asset at the date of transition. The charge relating to deferred tax liabilities will be recognised either in retained earnings or in the revaluation reserve as appropriate.

Acquisitions undertaken in prior periods

UK.2.216.26   Another area that may give rise to additional deferred tax liabilities is in respect of acquisitions undertaken in prior periods. Under IFRS 1, an entity is allowed to take the exemption from applying IFRS 3 to past business combinations. Where this is the case, however, a number of deferred tax consequences arise in respect of those combinations.

Other adjustments that may arise on transition

UK.2.216.27   In addition to the principal adjustments dealt with above, some of the other adjustments that may arise on transition are noted below:

- Recognition of deferred tax liabilities in respect of compound financial instruments accounted for in accordance with IAS 32, where the liability element is still outstanding at the date of transition and where the tax base is not split in a similar manner to the accounting carrying amounts.

- Reassessment of deferred tax balances in respect of intra-group transactions.

- Recognition of deferred tax effects arising from translating the carrying amounts and tax bases of non-monetary assets of foreign branches having the same functional currency as the parent.

UK.2.216.28   It is unlikely that UK entities would need to reassess their deferred tax balances arising from the initial recognition exception, except where they relate to business combinations. This is because under FRS 19 such temporary differences would have been treated as permanent differences and no deferred tax would have been provided. Similarly, no adjustments are expected to arise from reassessment of deferred tax assets existing at the date of transition since the recognition criteria for the deferred tax assets under FRS 19 and IAS 12 are similar.

Tax rates

UK.2.216.29   The implementation guidance to IFRS 1 notes that *"under IAS 12 the measurement of current and deferred tax reflects tax rates and tax laws that have been enacted or substantively enacted by the balance sheet date"*. Following guidance on estimates in IFRS 1, *"an entity accounts for the effect of changes in tax rates and tax laws when those changes are enacted or substantively enacted"*. [IFRS 1 para IG6]. This means that if tax rates change in 20X7, a

20X7 first time-adopter does not adjust tax amounts for this change in its 20X6 comparatives.

IAS 16, Property, plant and equipment

UK.2.216.30 IFRS 1 permits an entity to elect to measure an item of property, plant and equipment at the date of transition to IFRS at its fair value and use that fair value as its deemed cost at that date. In addition, a first-time adopter may elect to use a revaluation made under its previous GAAP of an item of property, plant and equipment at, or before, the date of transition to IFRS as deemed cost at the date of the revaluation, if the revaluation was broadly comparable to (a) fair value or (b) cost or depreciated cost under IFRS, adjusted to reflect, for example, changes in a general or specific price index. [IFRS 1 App D paras D5, D6]. The deemed cost exemption and issues arising from its application are considered in detail in paragraph 2.107 onwards. Other application issues are discussed in the following paragraphs.

Revaluations

UK.2.216.31 Like FRS 15, IAS 16 allows an entity to adopt a policy of revaluation for a particular class or classes of fixed asset. [IAS 16 paras 29, 34]. IAS 16 requires a different basis of valuation, however. Valuation should be at fair value, which is defined as *"the amount for which an asset could be exchanged between knowledgeable, willing parties in an arm's length transaction"*. [IAS 16 para 6]. Under FRS 15 assets are valued using a current value to the business model. This is defined as the lower of replacement cost and recoverable amount. Recoverable amount is the higher of net realisable value and value in use. [FRS 15 paras 2, 43]. This is illustrated in the following diagram:

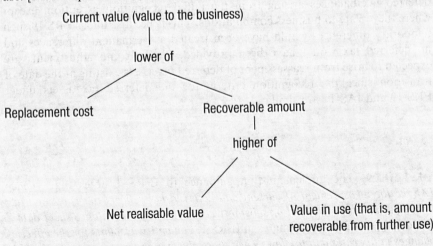

UK.2.216.32 Tangible fixed assets other than properties are valued under FRS 15 on a market value basis, where possible. Where market value is not obtainable, assets should be valued on the basis of depreciated replacement cost. [FRS 15 para 59]. Market value is equivalent to fair value under IAS 16. Properties, on the other hand, are valued differently under the two standards. Under both standards, specialised properties are valued at depreciated replacement cost. [IAS 16 para 33; FRS 15 para 53(b)]. However, FRS 15 requires non-specialised properties to be valued on the basis of existing use value (EUV). [FRS 15 para 53(a)]. This may be significantly different from fair value in some cases. Consider, for example, an entity that owns an eighty year old warehouse in a city centre by a riverside. On an EUV basis this may have a relatively low value, particularly if it does not have modern facilities such as overhead cranes. The warehouse may have potential for residential development and its fair value could be significantly higher than its EUV. FRS 15 does not allow the higher value for alternative use to be reflected in an entity's balance sheet if the warehouse were being used in the business as a warehouse. UK entities cannot, therefore, assume that their FRS 15 valuations are equivalent to IAS 16 values. Where there are significant differences an entity has the following options on transition to IFRS.

- If a policy of revaluation is to be used under IAS 16 for the class of assets that includes the asset with a significantly higher fair value compared to EUV, that asset will have to be revalued to its fair value at the date of transition. This will be necessary in order to ensure that, as required by IAS 16 paragraph 31, the carrying amount of the class at the balance sheet date is not materially different from the fair value (see also para 2.123 above).

- If a policy of revaluation is not to be applied to the class of assets to which the asset belongs, the asset may be restated to its original cost (less accumulated deprecation) at the date of transition to IFRS. Estimates of useful economic life on transition to IFRS should be consistent with those made under UK GAAP. [IFRS 1 para 14].

- Entities may also take advantage of the exemption contained in IFRS 1 (see para 2.107). The asset can be restated to fair value at the date of transition, with this value used as deemed cost. The other option in IFRS 1 of using a previous valuation as deemed cost is unlikely to be available, since the revaluation, when it was made, had to be broadly comparable to fair value or to cost adjusted for a general or specific price index. EUV does not meet either of these criteria where it is significantly different from fair value.

Residual values

UK.2.216.33 Under IAS 16, residual values are based on prices current at the balance sheet date, whereas under previous UK GAAP residual values were based on prices at the date of acquisition or later revaluation.

UK.2.216.34 Changes to residual value are accounted for prospectively. [IAS 16 para 46]. The estimation technique is different to that applied under the UK standard FRS 15. In such a situation, as described in paragraph 2.36, first-time adopters should adjust the residual values of their assets at the date of transition to IFRS and then use the amended depreciation that this implies from the date of transition.

Example – Residual values accounted for prospectively

Entity A bought an asset on 1 January 20X1, costing £100,000. The asset's useful economic life was 10 years and its residual value at the time of purchase was £10,000. Depreciation of £9,000 per year is charged. Under UK GAAP the asset had been depreciated for three years up to entity A's date of transition of 1 January 20X4. The carrying value of the asset was £73,000.

On transition to IFRS entity A establishes that the residual value of the asset at 1 January 20X4 is £17,000. The depreciation charge should be adjusted to £8,000 in 20X4. This is calculated as follows:

	£
Carrying value	73,000
Residual value	(17,000)
Amount to be depreciated	56,000
Depreciation period	7 years
Charge per year	8,000

Renewals accounting

UK.2.216.35 One significant issue in adopting IAS 16 concerns renewals accounting. Typically used in industries such as water, where there exists a large, often old, infrastructure, this method of approximating depreciation was a pragmatic solution allowed by FRS 15. The renewals method requires that major components and assets within an infrastructure system or grid (such as a transmission system) with determinable economic lives should be separately identified and depreciated over the economic life. The remaining system infrastructure or network asset is deemed to be not separately identifiable and no useful life can be reliably estimated. The annual expected maintenance expenditure is deemed to be equivalent to a depreciation charge for those parts of the system and is described in the income statement as depreciation. The cost of any identifiable assets is capitalised and depreciated. Renewals accounting is not acceptable under IAS 16, which requires the cost or fair value of fixed assets to be depreciated over the expected useful life. In many cases the actual cost of infrastructure assets is not known, through a combination of the assets being very old and the entities having been in the public sector where fixed assets were not recorded. The deemed cost exemption in IFRS 1 (see para 2.107 above) grants some relief to first-time adopters. Entities will be allowed to record fixed assets at fair value at the date of transition, with the fair value becoming deemed cost but there may be some practical difficulties in valuing the entire infrastructure network and in then establishing an appropriate residual value and depreciable life.

Changes in decommissioning and restoration liabilities

UK.2.216.36 The implications of IFRIC 1 for first-time adopters of IFRS are considered from paragraph 2.170.

Comparatives

UK.2.216.37 IFRS 1 does not make any exceptions to the general rule that comparatives should be presented in accordance with the new standard on first adoption. Accordingly a company that adopts IAS 16 in the financial statements for the year ended 31 December 20X7 should present comparative information prepared under IAS 16 for the year ended 31 December 20X6 in those financial statements. For the majority of UK companies that already comply with FRS 15, there should not be major changes to comparatives in view of the general similarity of FRS 15 to IAS 16. However, one important change is that the table of movements in cost and depreciation must be given for both the current and the prior period. This differs from present UK GAAP, where only the movements for the current period need be disclosed.

IAS 17, Leases

UK.2.216.38 IAS 17 has the same finance/operating classification basis for leases as the UK standard SSAP 21, 'Leases and hire purchase contracts'. *"A finance lease is a lease that transfers substantially all the risks and rewards incidental to ownership of an asset. Title may or may not eventually be transferred"*. [IAS 17 para 4]. The definition in SSAP 21 is almost identical. However, there is a rebuttable presumption in SSAP 21 that, where the present value of the lease payments amounts to substantially all of the fair value of the leased asset (normally 90% or more), the lease is a finance lease. [SSAP 21 para 15]. There is no such presumption in IAS 17. However, the international standard does provide the user with additional guidance on lease classification. Given the similarities in definitions, UK entities adopting IAS 17 should not encounter significant differences in lease classification. However, an exception to this is the classification of property leases, which is discussed further in paragraph UK.2.216.40 below. Despite the similarities, entities should examine those leases whose classification was considered borderline under UK GAAP.

UK.2.216.39 Lessees and lessors should classify leases as operating leases or finance leases on the basis of circumstances existing at the inception of the lease unless, since inception of the lease, the lessee and the lessor have agreed to change the provisions of the lease, in a manner that would have resulted in a different classification under IAS 17. [IFRS 1 para IG14]. In which case, the terms of the new agreement are used in determining the classification of the lease. Changes in estimates (for example, changes in estimates of the economic life or of the residual value of the leased property) or changes in circumstances (for example, default by the lessee) since the inception of the lease would not give rise to a new classification. In cases where a lease is reclassified this would result in an adjustment to retained earnings on transition to IFRS. The implementation guidance to IFRS 1 notes that in cases where an agreement has been revised in a way that would result in a different classification under IAS 17 the *"revised agreement is considered as a new agreement over its term"*. [IFRS 1 para IG14].

Property leases

UK.2.216.40 Leases of property can be viewed as two leases – a lease of a building and a lease of the land on which the building is sited. Under SSAP 21, there is no requirement to split property leases in this way. However, IAS 17 requires entities to make this split and classify the two components separately as either a finance or as an operating lease. [IAS 17 para 15A]. The split will be based upon the relative fair values of the two leasehold interests. It will only be possible to avoid making this split if it can be clearly demonstrated that, at inception, the land element of the lease is immaterial. It is likely that entities will require professional help in valuing the two components. It should be noted that, if the split cannot be made, IAS 17 requires the whole of the lease to be treated as a finance lease (unless it is clear that both elements are operating leases). [IAS 17 para 16]. In most cases, the land element of a lease will be classified as an operating lease. This is because land has an indefinite useful life and it is, therefore, unlikely that a lease will pass substantially all the risks and rewards of land ownership to the lessee. This means that under most property leases, lessors will have an asset of the land on their balance sheet. However, it is the element of the lease relating to the building that is likely to cause most problems for UK lessees and lessors. On many medium to long-term leases it will be more difficult to argue, once the land is taken out of the equation, that the lease does not transfer substantially all the risks and rewards of ownership of the building to the lessee. Consequently, some leases that are classified as operating leases under UK GAAP will have to be reclassified as finance leases as regards the buildings element. This could have a significant impact on the gearing, interest cost, depreciation and return on capital of the entities affected.

Example – Property leases: split between land and building

Company A entered into a 35 year lease of a property 15 years ago. Under UK GAAP, the whole of the property was classified as an operating lease. The principal terms of the lease are as follows:

Lease term	35 years
Total annual rentals payable in advance	£2.5m
Annual rentals in respect of building	£1.444m
Annual rentals in respect of the land	£1.056m
Fair value of building at inception of lease	£20m
Present value of lease payments in respect of the building	£20m
Interest rate implicit in building lease	7%

Company A is now adopting IFRS and, as required by IAS 17 has split the lease of the property into a lease of land and a lease of the building. Total rentals in respect of the property have been split between the land and the building based upon the relative fair values of the leasehold interest in the land and the leasehold interest in the building. [IAS 17 para 16]. The lease of the land has been classified as an operating lease. However, the lease of the building has been determined to be a finance lease as the minimum lease payments in respect of the building equal substantially all the fair value of the building at inception of the lease. How should this lease be reflected in the financial statements of company A on first-time adoption of IFRS?

There is no exemption under IFRS 1 in respect of accounting for leases. Therefore, the basic principle of full retrospective adoption must be applied. Company A's management must go back 15 years to the lease's inception and determine the amounts to be included in the financial statements in respect of the building.

IAS 17 requires that, on initial recognition, a lessee under a finance lease recognises assets and liabilities equal to the fair value of the leased property or, if lower, the present value of the minimum lease payments. [IAS 17 para 20]. Therefore, at the lease's commencement, company A would capitalise £20m in respect of the building and recognise a finance lease creditor for the same amount. This should be based upon values at the inception of the lease.

The building would then be depreciated on a straight-line basis over the lease term. This means that at the end of year 15, the building would have a carrying value of £11.43m (£20m — £20m × 15/35).

The finance lease creditor will accrue interest at the interest rate implicit in the lease and rentals paid in respect of the building will be applied in reducing the outstanding liability (similar to the calculation of the amortised cost of a financial liability). At the end of year 15, the outstanding balance of the finance lease creditor is calculated to be £16.35m.

Rental payments of £1.056m made in respect of the land will be recognised as an expense on a straight-line basis over the lease term. [IAS 17 para 35].

Therefore, the entries required to recognise the reclassification of the building lease on first-time adoption of IFRS are as follows:

Dr	Property plant and equipment — Cost	£20m	
Dr	Opening reserves	£4.92m	
	Cr Finance lease creditor		16.35m
	Cr Accumulated depreciation		£8.57m

The debit to opening reserves equals the difference between the finance lease creditor and the carrying value of the building at the date of transition to IFRS.

The amounts charged to the income statement under UK GAAP and IFRS can be reconciled as follows:

Amount charged to income under UK GAAP
Operating lease rentals (£2.5m x 15)   £37.50m

Amount charged to income under IFRS
Operating lease rentals for the land   £15.84m
(£1.056m x 15)
Depreciation   £8.57m
Interest charged on the finance lease creditor £18.01m
                                                        £42.42m

Difference (debit to opening reserves)   £4.92m

UK.2.216.41 It is interesting to consider how the requirement to split leases between land and buildings interacts with the deemed cost exemption (see further from para 2.107). Consider the following example.

Example – Property leases: split between land and building in relation to deemed cost exemption

Entity Q paid a £1m leasehold premium for a 40 year lease on a property in July 2002. This has been capitalised as a tangible fixed asset under UK GAAP and has been revalued up to £1.8m by 1 July 2004, which is entity Q's date of transition to IFRS.

At its date of transition, entity Q determines that the relative fair values of the initial leasehold interests were £800,000 for the building and £200,000 for the land. Entity Q wishes to take advantage of the deemed cost exemption and use the revalued amount of £1.8m as the cost of the leasehold interests at the date of transition. Based on the initial split of fair values the amounts in its final UK GAAP balance sheet at 30 June 2004 in relation to the building and the land are £1.44m and £360,000 respectively. Entity Q determines that the property element is a finance lease under IAS 17 and that the land is held under an operating lease. It proposes that the £1.44m is held in property, plant and equipment and that the £360,000 is held as a prepayment on adoption of IFRS. Is this proposal acceptable?

No. Entity Q is correct to split the leasehold interest. However, the deemed cost exemption is available to items of property, plant and equipment and not to prepayments. The building asset may, therefore, be stated at £1.44m and this can be used as its cost going forward under IFRS. The prepayment, however, must be restated to original cost (estimated at £200,000) and an adjustment is required on transition that will result in a debit of £160,000 to the revaluation reserve.

Lessor accounting

UK.2.216.42 The main measurement difference between IAS 17 and SSAP 21 is in the measurement of finance leases by lessors. Under IFRS a finance lease debtor is recognised at an amount equal to the net investment in the lease. This is the gross investment in the lease less unearned finance income. Gross investment in the lease is the aggregate of the minimum lease payments under a finance lease from the standpoint of the lessor and any unguaranteed residual value accruing to the lessor. [IAS 17 paras 36, 4]. In effect, the net investment method takes account only of the direct cash flows in the lease arrangement. The recognition of finance income should reflect a constant periodic rate of return on the lessor's net investment outstanding in respect of the finance lease. [IAS 17 para 39]. Under SSAP 21, on the other hand, total gross earnings under a finance lease should normally be allocated to accounting periods to give a constant rate of return on the lessor's net cash investment in the lease. The net cash investment represents the total cash invested after taking into account all of the cash flows associated with the lease. [SSAP 21 paras 39, 3]. It differs, therefore, from the amount of the net investment in the lease as it takes account of other cash flows, for example tax. This difference had more significance when UK entities could receive 100% capital allowances on certain fixed assets. However, it is likely that this could be a significant difference on transition to IFRS and entities should rebase their finance leases to the net investment method on transition to IFRS, with any differences from current carrying amounts treated as an adjustment to retained earnings.

Lease incentives

UK.2.216.43 A further area that may cause UK entities difficulty on transition to IFRS is the treatment of operating lease incentives. Under UK GAAP operating lease incentives should be spread on a straight line basis over the period until it is expected that market rates will prevail. UITF Abstract 12, 'Lessee accounting for reverse premiums and similar incentives', applied to lessees only and was effective for accounting periods ending on or after 23 December 1994 (including corresponding amounts for the immediately preceding period) in respect of lease agreements commencing in the current or the preceding accounting period. UITF Abstract 28 superseded UITF Abstract 12, 'Operating lease incentives', which applies the same treatment to lessors and was effective for financial statements relating to accounting periods ending on or after 22 September 2001 (including corresponding amounts for the immediately preceding period) in respect of lease agreements commencing in the current or the preceding accounting period. Neither abstract was fully retrospective. Operating lease incentives are dealt with in IFRS by SIC 15. The period of spreading for operating lease incentives may be different from that in UITF Abstract 28: SIC 15 requires incentives to be spread, by the lessor, *"over the lease term, on a straight-line basis unless another systematic basis is representative of the time pattern over which the benefit of the leased asset is* *diminished''*, or, in the case of the lessee, *"over the lease term, on a straight-line basis unless another systematic basis is representative of the time pattern of the lessee's benefit from the use of the leased asset"*. [SIC 15 paras 4, 5].

UK.2.216.44   There are two issues for UK first-time adopters. This first is that the transitional rules in SIC 15 do not apply to first-time adopters. These allowed the interpretation to be adopted prospectively for leases beginning on or after 1 January 1999. UK entities adopting IFRS will have to apply the provisions of SIC 15 to all operating leases that are in existence at the date of transition to IFRS, however long those leases have been running. [IFRS 1 para IG16]. Since the UITF Abstracts were not retrospective the information on incentives to sign leases that were entered into a number of years ago may be difficult to obtain. The second issue is that in the UK, where operating leases frequently have rent reviews to market rent, the period of spreading of a lease incentive is, in accordance with UITF 28, the period ending on the commencement of the market rent. Under IFRS, however, lease incentives must be spread over the lease term and in almost all cases straight-line will be the appropriate spreading method.

IAS 18, Revenue

UK.2.216.45   IFRS 1 does not contain any specific exemptions in respect of IAS 18. In the UK, Application note G to FRS 5 is the first accounting standard issued on revenue. It was applicable for financial years ending on or after 23 December 2003 and, therefore, will have been adopted by all entities prior to making the transition to IFRS. Prior to the issue of an accounting standard dealing with revenue in the UK, IAS 18 had been seen as useful guidance for UK practitioners and best practice was often in accordance with the international standard. In any case, compliance with Application note G to FRS 5 prior to first-time adoption of IFRS means that applying IAS 18 will not present entities making the transition to IFRS with any significant difficulties. In most cases the two standards are compatible and consistent.

IAS 19, Employee benefits

UK.2.216.46   The treatment of defined benefit plans under IAS 19 is in many respects the same as under FRS 17. Assets are measured at fair value (in December 2006, the ASB published an amendment to FRS 17, which amended paragraph 16 of the standard to replace 'mid-market value' with 'current bid price' (for valuing quoted securities), bringing alignment with IAS 19 in this area); liabilities are measured using the projected unit method and discounted at a high quality corporate bond rate (specified as AA in FRS 17). The main area of difference is in the treatment of actuarial gains and losses. These may, to an extent, be deferred under IAS 19 using the 'corridor approach'. Under this approach, actuarial gains and losses are recognised in the income statement under IAS 19, over a period representing the expected average remaining working lives of employees participating in the plan. Any deferred actuarial gains and losses are carried on the balance sheet as part of the net pension asset or liability. However, IAS 19 also contains an option for entities to recognise actuarial gains and losses in full as they arise, outside profit or loss, in other comprehensive income. This means that defined benefit plans may be treated in a similar way to UK GAAP (as represented by FRS 17). This option in IAS 19 is popular in the UK. The treatment of actuarial gains and losses is considered further in chapter 11.

UK.2.216.47 If the corridor approach is used, then as noted in paragraph 2.132 above, IFRS 1 gives an exemption so that entities need not go back and retrospectively determine how much of any actuarial gains and losses would have been deferred and may instead apply the 'corridor approach' on a prospective basis from the date of transition.

UK.2.216.48 A further issue for first-time adopters is potentially that of group pension plans. Under FRS 17, group pension plans are a type of multi-employer scheme from the perspective of the individual entities in the group. An entity can treat its participation in a group defined benefit plan as if it were a defined contribution plan in certain circumstances. [FRS 17 para 12]. On 7 December 2006, the ASB published an amendment to FRS 17. The multi-employer exemption for group pension schemes remains available under FRS 17, where certain conditions are met, but the disclosure requirements have been amended. In particular, companies that are unable to identify their share of the underlying assets and liabilities in a multi-employer scheme are required to disclose the reason why sufficient information is not available to account for the scheme as a defined benefit scheme. Under IAS 19, schemes between entities under common control are not multi-employer plans. Instead, IAS 19 includes specific rules in respect of group schemes. If there is a contractual agreement or stated policy for charging the net defined benefit cost for a group plan as a whole to the individual group entities, those group entities should recognise the cost so charged. Otherwise, the net defined benefit cost should be recognised in the financial statements of the group entity that is legally the sponsoring employer for the plan (with the other group entities accounting for the plan as if it were a defined contribution plan). [IAS 19 paras 34, 34A]. This could be a significant issue for individual entities that adopt IFRS. The IAS 19 rules for group schemes are considered further in chapter 11.

UK.2.216.49 Measuring the assets and liabilities, in particular the liabilities, of defined benefit pension plans is dependent on various assumptions. A UK entity first-time adopting IFRS will have reported FRS 17 numbers at both the beginning and the end of its comparative period when it first reports under IFRS. The application guidance to IFRS 1 notes that *"an entity's actuarial assumptions at the date of transition to IFRSs are consistent with actuarial assumptions made for the same date under previous GAAP..."* [IFRS 1 para IG19]. This follows the prohibition from using hindsight in estimates contained within IFRS 1 (see para 2.32). The same applies to estimates of market values and rates: these should be consistent with those made under UK GAAP for the purposes of FRS 17, unless there is objective evidence of error. The impact of revisions to actuarial assumptions made after the date of transition to IFRS is an actuarial gain or loss of the period in which the revisions are made. [IFRS 1 para IG19].

UK.2.216.50   The implementation guidance in IFRS 1 gives some relief from the number of actuarial valuations that entities have to carry out. An entity's first IFRS financial statements will contain measurements of employee benefits at three different dates: the date of transition, the date of the comparative balance sheet and the reporting date. Rather than require separate full actuarial valuations at each of these dates, paragraph IG21 of IFRS 1 notes that entities may roll forward and/or back full actuarial valuations, reflecting events between the valuation dates and the roll back dates. This is in line with the requirements of paragraph 57 of IAS 19 for entities using IFRS on an ongoing basis.

IAS 20, Accounting for government grants and disclosure of government assistance

UK.2.216.51   Government grants are recognised and measured in the same way in IFRS as in UK GAAP and first-time adopters should not encounter issues in this area. The only real difference is in the area of presentation. IAS 20 allows grants in respect of fixed assets either to be shown separately as deferred income or to be deducted from the cost of the asset. Although SSAP 4 also permits both treatments the standard says that in Counsel's opinion the option to deduct government grants from the cost of fixed assets is not available to companies governed by the requirements of the Companies Act 2006 Schedule 1 to SI 2008/410, 'The Large and Medium-sized Companies and Groups (Accounts and Reports) Regulations 2008' does not apply to companies applying IFRS (see further chapter 1) and, therefore, the option to deduct such grants from the cost of the related asset will be available to UK entities adopting IFRS.

IAS 21, The effects of changes in foreign exchange rates

UK.2.216.52   For foreign currency transactions one of the main transition issues that UK entities are likely to encounter concerns hedging transactions. SSAP 20 allowed transactions to be translated at a rate specified in a matching or related forward contract. The item translated could be, for example, a sale and debtor, a fixed asset or the purchase of an item of inventory. [SSAP 20 para 46]. IAS 21 requires all transactions to be translated at the rate of exchange ruling at the date of the transaction. Subsequent to this, monetary items, and non-monetary items that are carried at fair value, are retranslated at closing rates or rates applicable when the fair values were determined. [IAS 21 para 23]. Translating an item at the contracted rate under the terms of a relevant contract is a form of hedge accounting that is not permitted under IAS 39. IAS 39 details strict criteria that must be fulfilled before hedge accounting can be applied and specifies the appropriate accounting treatment for the hedged item and hedging instrument where hedge accounting is permitted.

UK.2.216.53 Foreign operations are dealt with in IAS 21 in a similar way to SSAP 20. Although there is no equivalent to SSAP 20's temporal method, it is likely that many operations that have been accounted for using the temporal method under SSAP 20 will have a functional currency that is the same as their parent's (see para UK.2.216.55 below). In such cases, the result in the parent's consolidated financial statements will be the same as if the temporal method had been used, since the foreign operation will first report in its functional currency (which would be the same as its parent's functional currency) before being consolidated. For other foreign entities, that are largely independent of the parent, the closing rate method is used by both standards. Whereas SSAP 20 allowed both average and closing rate for translation of the profit and loss account under the closing rate method, IAS 21 requires use of the exchange rate at the transaction date, which may be approximate to the average rate. [IAS 21 paras 39(b), 40]. Any UK entities that used the closing rate for translating the income statements of foreign operations would, therefore, have to adjust their comparatives in their first IFRS financial statements, with the difference being taken to opening equity. This will form part of the cumulative translation difference arising pre-IFRS adoption. As discussed in paragraph 2.138 above, one of the exemptions in IFRS 1 from full retrospective application is in respect of the cumulative translation difference. Entities are not required to separately classify and disclose the accumulated translation differences that have been taken to reserves on the translation of foreign operations before the date of transition to IFRS. This must, however, be done from the date of transition to IFRS.

UK.2.216.54 Furthermore, the requirement to retranslate goodwill and fair value adjustments as if they are assets and liabilities of the acquired entity, considered in paragraph 2.83 onwards, does not have to be applied retrospectively to business combinations that occurred before the date of transition to IFRS. Therefore, these goodwill and fair value adjustments are already expressed in the acquiring entity's functional currency or they are non-monetary foreign currency items from the acquiring entity's point of view, reported using the exchange rate applied under the entity's previous GAAP.

UK.2.216.55 IAS 21 states that an entity should determine its functional currency and measure its results and financial position in that currency. Functional currency is defined as *"the currency of the primary economic environment in which the entity operates"*. [IAS 21 para 8]. The standard goes on to give guidance as to the factors that will determine an entity's functional currency, including the currency in which sales prices are denominated and the currency in which costs are denominated. [IAS 21 para 9]. Under the UK standard SSAP 20 an entity was required to prepare its financial statements in its local currency, and to translate the results of foreign operations that have been prepared in their local currencies. The definition of local currency is *"the currency of the primary economic environment in which [an entity] operates and generates net cash flows"*. [SSAP 20 para 39]. In principle, therefore, the move from SSAP 20 to IAS 21 should not cause difficulties in this respect for UK entities, as the definitions are close. However, entities should examine their foreign operations.

UK.2.216.56 As noted in paragraph UK.2.216.55 above, UK entities applying SSAP 20 were required to present their financial statements in their local currency. Although IAS 21 requires that entities measure their results and position in their functional currencies, they may choose to present their financial statements in a different currency. Broadly, the method of translation is that assets and liabilities for all balance sheets should be translated at the closing rate existing at the date of each balance sheet presented and income and expense items for all periods presented should be translated at transaction rates (or average rates as an approximation). Exchange differences resulting from retranslation should be taken to equity. First-time adopters may, therefore, choose to present their financial statements in a currency other than their local (or functional) currency. This would generally only be the case where more useful information would result.

UK.2.216.57 The net investment rules of IAS 21 were moved to IAS 39 as part of the improvements project. First-time adoption issues regarding hedging are dealt with later in this chapter (see para UK.2.216.123 onwards).

UK.2.216.58 There is one additional disclosure in IAS 21 for which UK entities that have applied SSAP 20 will have to ensure they have the systems in place to collect the information. IAS 21 requires the total amount of exchange differences included in profit or loss for the period to be disclosed. SSAP 20, on the other hand, required disclosure only of the exchange differences included in the profit and loss account that have arisen on foreign currency borrowings less deposits.

UK.2.216.59 As noted above, SSAP 20 has been replaced in the UK by FRS 23 (IAS 21). Entities will apply FRS 23 when they apply FRS 26 (IAS 39). Application of these standards is dealt with in the Manual of Accounting – UK GAAP. FRS 23 is identical to IAS 21 and UK entities applying FRS 23 when they make the transition to IFRS will face no differences. The foreign currency-related exemptions, dealing with goodwill and CTDs (see para 2.138) will remain available to those that have applied FRS 23 under UK GAAP. Although there are transitional rules in FRS 23 giving similar exemptions, these may be from a different (earlier) date than the date of transition to IFRS and so entities will still wish to use the exemptions as at the date of transition. This is because the only alternative to using the IFRS 1 exemption is full retrospective application, rather than using the exemptions as at the date of adopting FRS 23. This is illustrated in the following example.

> **Example – Cumulative translation differences (CTDs) exemption**
>
> Entity P applies FRS 23 for its accounting period beginning on 1 January 2007. At that time it applies paragraph 59A and decides to set all cumulative translation differences to zero at 1 January 2007. It will track them from that date.
>
> Entity P adopts IFRS for its financial year beginning on 1 January 2009. Can it use the accumulated translation differences that are recorded in its UK GAAP financial statements at its transition date, which is 1 January 2008?
>
> No, it cannot. When IFRS is adopted there are two options: IAS 21 can be applied retrospectively, in which case the CTDs will have to be reconstructed from the dates of the overseas acquisitions. Alternatively, entity P can take advantage of the exemption in paragraph 22 of IFRS 1 and set CTDs to zero as at the date of transition, 1 January 2008. There is no option to use the CTDs that it has been recording under UK GAAP since 1 January 2007.

IAS 23, Borrowing costs

UK.2.216.60 In March 2007 a revised IAS 23 was issued. The main change from the previous version is the removal of the option of immediately expensing borrowing costs that relate to qualifying assets, being assets that take a substantial period of time to get ready for use or sale. The revised standard, therefore, represents a significant difference from UK requirements where a policy of capitalisation has not been adopted under UK GAAP.

UK.2.216.61 IAS 23 is wider in scope than the equivalent UK requirements set out in FRS 15, covering any asset that takes a substantial period of time to get ready for its intended use or sale. SSAP 9, although not explicit, would allow some interest on borrowings financing long-term contracts to be capitalised. In practice the requirements are likely to be applied to similar assets.

UK.2.216.62 First-time adopters will have an implementation issue in respect of the amount of interest capitalised. Where specific borrowing costs are capitalised, the amount of borrowing costs eligible for capitalisation under IAS 23 on an asset is the actual borrowing costs incurred on total borrowing in respect of the asset during the period, less any investment income on the temporary investment of those borrowings (that is, the net interest on total specific borrowings is capitalised). [IAS 23 para 12]. FRS 15 requires the capitalisation of interest incurred on specific borrowings based on the actual expenditures incurred to date on the asset (that is, gross interest payable is capitalised, but interest on 'excess' (or unspent) borrowings is ignored). [FRS 15 para 22]. Because FRS 15 only allows interest on specific borrowings to be capitalised to the extent of the expenditure on the asset there is no need to offset investment income on any unspent borrowings: the interest on unspent borrowings has not been capitalised. UK entities should revisit all borrowing costs capitalised to ensure that the correct amount of interest has been included in the cost of the asset. It may be that the 'net' amount of interest is not significantly different to the 'gross' amount, but this must be ascertained.

UK.2.216.63 IAS 23 contains transitional provisions permitting prospective adoption. [IFRS 1 App D para D23]. However, in situations where a deemed cost has been established for an asset, and used at the date of transition (see para 2.107), then any borrowing costs incurred prior to measurement of the asset should be included in the asset's deemed cost on transition to IFRS. [IFRS 1 paras IG25, IG9].

UK.2.216.64 IFRS 1 allows a first-time adopter to apply the transitional provisions in the revised IAS 23. For further guidance refer to paragraph 2.177.

IAS 24, Related party disclosures

UK.2.216.65 The definitions in IAS 24 and FRS 8 of related parties and of the transactions that need to be disclosed are similar and so adopting this standard should not cause difficulties for most UK entities already making disclosures under FRS 8. The main issues for UK first-time adopters relate to the standard's scope and the entities that will have to apply it. FRS 8 provides that wholly-owned subsidiary undertakings do not have to disclose transactions with members of the group or with any investees qualifying as related parties, provided that the consolidated financial statements in which that subsidiary is included are publicly available. [FRS 8 para 3(c)]. IAS 24 does not contain such an exemption and all subsidiaries that adopt IFRS will have to apply the standard's requirements fully. There is also no exemption from disclosure in the parent entity's separate financial statements of transactions with other group members. The information should in principle be available to subsidiaries, since it is required in order to prepare the consolidation (so that transactions and balances can be cancelled out), but entities adopting IFRS will still need to ensure that it is collected from the date of transition.

UK.2.216.66 One disclosure that is required by IAS 24, but not specifically by FRS 8 is: the terms and conditions of amounts due to or from related parties, together with the nature of the consideration and details or any guarantees given or received. [IAS 24 para 17(b)]. Entities will need to ensure that they have the systems in place to collect the relevant information. There are other differences in the definitions of related parties and in the disclosures, but this is the main one that IAS 24, adds to the requirements that are already in FRS 8. One disclosure that was within the pre-improved IAS 24 but that has now been removed is the requirement to disclose pricing policies for related party transactions. Instead, the standard provides that *"disclosures that related party transactions were made on terms equivalent to those that prevail in arm's length transactions are made only if such terms can be substantiated"*. [IAS 24 para 21].

IAS 26, Accounting and reporting by retirement benefit plans

UK.2.216.67   This standard is outside the scope of this chapter.

IAS 27, Consolidated and separate financial statements

UK.2.216.68   Although there are subtle differences between FRS 2 and IAS 27 in some of the provisions that explain how an entity might be controlled, they generally should not affect significantly the companies that are consolidated by UK groups on their transition to IFRS. However, some groups might find that the entities that they are required to consolidate do change significantly on transition to IFRS, because they have interests in a number of entities that are affected by these subtle differences. These differences are considered in detail in chapter 24.

Definition of subsidiary

UK.2.216.69   IAS 27's definition of subsidiary is based on control, defined as *"the power to govern the financial and operating policies of an entity so as to obtain benefits from its activities"*. [IAS 27 para 4]. Control is presumed to exist where more than half the voting power of an entity is owned (as in paragraph 14(a) of FRS 2). Control also exists when there is ownership of less than half the voting power, but also any one of the following:

- Power over more than half of the voting rights by virtue of an agreement with other investors (equivalent to FRS 2 para 14(d)).

- Power to govern the entity's financial and operating policies of the entity under a statute or an agreement (equivalent to FRS 2 para 14(c)).

- Power to appoint or remove the majority of the members of the board of directors or equivalent governing body and that board of directors or equivalent governing body controls the entity (equivalent to FRS 2 para 14(b)).

- Power to cast the majority of votes at meetings of the board of directors or equivalent governing body.

[IAS 27 para 13].

UK.2.216.70   IAS 27 does not include an equivalent to paragraph 14(e) of FRS 2. This now states that a parent-subsidiary relationship exists when an entity has the power to exercise, or actually exercises, dominant influence or control or when it and the subsidiary undertaking are managed on a unified basis. In our view the conditions in paragraph 14(e) are evidence of control and any entities consolidated in both previous and current UK GAAP using this paragraph will also be consolidated under IAS 27. Additionally, SIC 12 provides that SPEs should be consolidated where the substance of the relationship is that an entity controls the SPE. [SIC 12 para 8]. This is equivalent to the rules in FRS 5 concerning quasi-subsidiaries.

UK.2.216.71 One subtle difference between IFRS and UK GAAP concerns the treatment of options. IAS 27 states that the existence and effect of potential voting rights that are currently exercisable (or convertible) should be considered, in addition to the factors described in paragraph 13 of IAS 27, when assessing whether an entity controls another entity. [IAS 27 para 14]. The UK position is that the options are taken into account in determining whether any party has a majority of the voting rights only when the option has been exercised. However, in practice other factors, such as dominant influence, may well make the decision to consolidate the same under both sets of accounting standards. It is likely, therefore, that the same entities will require consolidation under IFRS as under UK GAAP.

Exemptions

UK.2.216.72 IAS 27 also deals with parents that need not prepare consolidated financial statements. The exemptions are different in IAS 27 from those contained in FRS 2. However, both standards preclude entities that have publicly traded securities from taking an exemption from preparing consolidated financial statements. Therefore, all entities that are required to adopt IFRS by the EU 2005 Regulation will be required to prepare consolidated financial statements under IFRS. For entities that do not have any listed securities, which voluntarily adopt IFRS, there may be differences between those that are required to consolidate under current UK GAAP and those that are required to consolidate under IFRS. Under IAS 27 a parent need not present consolidated financial statements if all of the following conditions are met:

- It is wholly-owned, or the owners of the minority have been informed and do not object to non-preparation of consolidated financial statements.

- Its debt or equity securities are not publicly traded.

- It is not in the process of issuing securities in public securities markets.

- Its immediate or ultimate parent publishes consolidated financial statements that comply with IFRS.

[IAS 27 para 10].

UK.2.216.73 IAS 27 deals with subsidiaries that should be excluded from consolidation. This is covered from paragraph 2.86. How a group should deal with transition where parent entities and subsidiaries have different dates of transition is covered from paragraph 2.146.

Separate financial statements

UK.2.216.74 The standard also covers the treatment of subsidiaries in a parent company's separate financial statements. Under UK GAAP, this issue is not dealt with in FRS 2, and such investments are accounted for under the Companies Act 2006, being held either at cost or at a market value or directors' valuation under the Act's alternative accounting rules. [SI 2008/410 1 Sch 32(3)(a)(b)]. IAS 27 requires investments in subsidiaries (and jointly controlled entities and associates) to be accounted for, by class, at either cost or in accordance with IAS 39. [IFRS 1 App D para D14].

UK.2.216.75 In the UK, companies are often eligible for merger relief or group reconstruction relief if they issue shares to acquire other companies. [CA06 Secs 612, 611]. This relief allows the investing company to ignore some or all of the premium on the shares issued and hence to record the investment in the subsidiary at the nominal value of the shares issued (plus a minimum premium amount where group reconstruction relief is used). IAS 27 previously required investments to be recorded at cost (that is fair value at the date of acquisition) or at fair value under IAS 39. Hence companies that made use of merger relief or group reconstruction relief and had in the past recorded their investments at nominal value (plus minimum premium value, if any) would have had to restate those investments to cost in their separate financial statements on transition to IFRS. However, an amendment was issued in May 2008 that enables first time adopters instead to elect to use a deemed cost of either fair value or the carrying amount under previous accounting practice to measure the initial cost of investments. [IFRS 1 App D para D15]. See further paragraph 2.143 onwards.

UK.2.216.76 Also prior to the amendment to IFRS 1 and IAS 27 (described in para UK.2.216.75), distributions out of pre-acquisition profits were required under IAS 27 to be deducted from the cost of investment shown in a company's separate financial statements. Under UK GAAP, such dividends have been allowed to be taken directly to the profit and loss account and then an impairment test made on the carrying amount of the investment to determine whether it needs to be written down. This treatment was not acceptable under the previous IAS 27 and hence such dividends had to be adjusted back to the cost of investment. The amendment removes the definition of the cost method from IAS 27 and replaces it with a requirement to present dividends as income in the separate financial statements of the investor. [IAS 27 para 38A]. It is also necessary to consider impairment implications in accordance with IAS 36.

Disclosure

UK.2.216.77 The Companies Act 2006 includes extensive disclosures that are required to be given about subsidiaries, associates, joint ventures and other significant investments. [SI 2008/410 4 Sch 16,17,19]. These continue to be required in IFRS consolidated and separate financial statements. In addition, IAS 27 requires similar information to be given. There are two concessions from these disclosures given in the Companies Act 2006. These apply where the disclosures required by the Act are 'seriously prejudicial' to the entity's business and the Secretary of State has agreed to the non-disclosure and where the information to be given is excessive, in which case the information may be given only for the principal subsidiaries, associates and joint ventures. However, there is no equivalent exemption in IAS 27. Hence where a company has previously used the 'seriously prejudicial' exemption to exclude disclosing certain information, if this information is required by IAS 27 then the exemption can no longer be used for that information. However, where a company has given information for its principal subsidiaries, associates and joint ventures only, we consider that it would be acceptable to continue this type of disclosure under IAS 27.

IAS 28, Investments in associates

Business combinations exemption

UK.2.216.78 As set out in paragraph 2.58 onwards, an entity is not required to *restate* business combinations that were recognised before the date of transition to IFRS. Management can elect to restate a previous business combination, but if it does so it must also restate all later business combinations [IFRS 1 App C para C1]. IFRS 1 specifically states that the exemption for past business combinations also applies to past acquisitions of associates. [IFRS 1 App C para C5].

UK.2.216.79 Therefore, an investor does not have to fully restate the past acquisition of an associate before the date of transition, if an earlier business combination has not been restated. If the investor takes advantage of this exemption certain adjustments may still be required in determining the carrying value of the associate to be included in the opening balance sheet. Being allowed not to restate past acquisitions of associates does not mean that all the assets and liabilities pertaining to these acquisitions on which the investor's share is based should remain or be stated at their previous carrying value under UK GAAP. This is because, as a general principle, whether the business combinations exemption is taken or not, the equity accounted amounts included in a group's balance sheet in respect of associates should be measured in accordance with IFRS on transition. The business combination exemption and examples of adjustments that would be required are dealt with in detail from paragraph 2.58 onwards.

UK.2.216.80 IFRS 1 requires the resulting goodwill to be tested for impairment. However, as discussed in chapter 27, goodwill relating to an associate is included in its carrying value and is not regarded as a separate asset. Therefore, the entire carrying value of the associate should be tested for impairment in accordance with IAS 36 at the date of transition to IFRS.

Net liabilities

UK.2.216.81 It may be that the adjustments required to the assets and liabilities on which the investors share is based, result in the associate having net liabilities or that the associate continues to have net liabilities. The required accounting for an associate with net liabilities is different under UK GAAP from that required by IFRS. In most cases under UK GAAP, an investor continues to use the equity method even if this results in an interest in net liabilities. This is different from IFRS, as once an investor's interest in an associate is reduced to nil recognition of losses usually stops. Adjustments that arise as a result of the investor's share of losses ceasing to be recognised are taken to retained earnings.

Not equity accounted under previous GAAP

UK.2.216.82 There may be some entities that are classified as associates under IAS 28 that were not under FRS 9. This is because, although the definitions are similar in both standards, IAS 28 defines significant influence as *"the power to participate in the financial and operating policy decisions of the investee…"*. [IAS 28 para 2]. If an investor elected to be passive, significant influence would still exist as long as the investor had the power to participate in policy decisions when it so wished. FRS 9, on the other hand, requires the actual exercise of significant influence. UK entities adopting IFRS should, therefore, look closely at the relationships they have with those entities that are not classified as associates, because there is no significant influence (but there is a participating interest). However, as FRS 9 itself points out *"This difference may have a limited effect in practice because the best evidence of an entity's ability to exercise significant influence is the fact that it is exercising such an influence"*. [FRS 9 App II para 2].

UK.2.216.83 Should there be any such entities, that are classified as associates under IFRS but not UK GAAP, then first-time adopters may elect to apply the business combinations exemption. The associate will be accounted for under paragraphs C4(j) and C5 of Appendix C of IFRS 1 – *"in accordance with its previous GAAP, the first-time adopter may not have [included an associate] acquired in a past business combination (for example, because the [investor] did not regard it as [an associate] under previous GAAP…"*. In its consolidated financial statements, the investing entity should account for the associate that was an investment under UK GAAP by first adjusting the carrying amounts of the associate's assets and liabilities to the amounts that IFRS would require in the associate's separate balance sheet at the investor's date of transition to IFRS. The deemed cost of goodwill is then the difference, at the date of transition to IFRS, between the investing entity's share of those adjusted carrying amounts and the cost of investment in the investor's separate balance sheet. [IFRS 1 App C para C4(j)]. See also paragraph 2.93 above.

An investor becomes a first-time adopter at a different date from its associate

UK.2.216.84 The required accounting when an investor becomes a first-time adopter of IFRS earlier or later than its associate is considered further from paragraph 2.155.

IAS 29, Financial reporting in hyper-inflationary economies

UK.2.216.85 The main impact of entities adopting IFRS that have subsidiaries operating in hyper-inflationary economies is that the UK guidance in UITF 9, 'Accounting for operations in hyper-inflationary economies', allows a choice of methods whereas IAS 29 does not. It only allows the method whereby the financial statements are restated to reflect the impact of price changes. Entities that have used the approach of adopting a stable currency under UK GAAP will not be allowed to do this on adopting IFRS.

UK.2.216.86 IAS 29 has been incorporated into UK GAAP, as FRS 24 (IAS 29) applicable when FRS 26 is applied. UK companies that have followed FRS 24 will have no changes to account for on adoption of IFRS.

IAS 31, Interests in joint ventures

UK.2.216.87 The provisions of IAS 31 need, in the main, not cause too much difficulty for UK first-time adopters. Although the main permitted treatment for jointly controlled entities (JCEs) is proportionate consolidation, the equity method is also permitted. [IAS 31 paras 30, 38]. Jointly controlled assets and operations are accounted for by incorporating into its consolidated (and separate) financial statements the assets and liabilities, or share thereof, that the venturer controls, similar to the treatment of a joint arrangement that is not an entity (a JANE) under FRS 9.

Business combinations exemption

UK.2.216.88 As set out in paragraph 2.58 onwards, an entity is not required to *restate* business combinations that were recognised before the date of transition to IFRS. Management can elect to restate a previous business combination, but if it does so it must also restate all later business combinations. [IFRS 1 App C para C1]. IFRS 1 specifically states that the exemption for past business combinations also applies to past acquisitions of joint ventures. [IFRS 1 App C para C5].

UK.2.216.89   If the venturer takes advantage of this exemption, certain adjustments may still be required in determining the share of assets and liabilities (proportionate consolidation) or share of net assets (equity method) of the jointly controlled entity to be included in the opening balance sheet. Being allowed not to restate past acquisitions of JCEs does not mean that all the assets and liabilities pertaining to these acquisitions on which the venturer's proportionately consolidated or equity accounted share is based should remain or be stated at their previous carrying value under UK GAAP. This is because, as a general principle, whether the business combinations exemption is taken or not, the proportionately consolidated or equity accounted amounts included in a group's balance sheet in respect of JCEs should be measured in accordance with IFRS on transition. The business combination exemption and examples of adjustments that would be required are dealt with in detail from paragraph 2.58 onwards.

UK.2.216.90   IFRS 1 requires the resulting goodwill to be tested for impairment. This is only applicable for JCEs that are proportionately consolidated. This is because under the equity method goodwill relating to a JCE is included in its carrying value and is not regarded as a separate asset. Therefore, the entire carrying value of the JCE should be tested for impairment in accordance with IAS 36 at the date of transition to IFRS.

Not proportionately consolidated or equity accounted under previous GAAP

UK.2.216.91   There may, however, be some differences in classification for first-time adopters. This is because a jointly controlled entity in IAS 31 does not have to be carrying on a business of its own, as a joint venture does in FRS 9. Thus, any JANE that is housed in a legal entity will be a JCE under IFRS and not a jointly controlled operation or an interest in jointly controlled assets. This could change the presentation of the consolidated financial statements of many first-time adopters, particularly where the equity method is used and not the proportionate consolidation method. In such cases entities will be able to apply paragraph B2(j) of the business combinations exemption in IFRS 1. This means that they will not have to revisit the combination and calculate fair values. Instead the combination should be accounted for as a JCE from the date of transition. The carrying amount of the JCE's assets and liabilities are adjusted to the amount that IFRS would require in the JCE's own separate balance sheet at the venturer's date of transition to IFRS. The deemed cost of goodwill is the difference, at the date of transition, between the venturer's share of those adjusted carrying amounts and the cost of investment in the venturer's separate balance sheet. [IFRS 1 para C4(j)]. The JCE will be proportionately consolidated or equity accounted, depending on the venturer's accounting policy in its consolidated financial statements. See further paragraph 2.93.

A venturer becomes a first-time adopter at a different date to its jointly controlled entity

UK.2.216.92 The required accounting when a venturer becomes a first-time adopter of IFRS earlier or later than its jointly controlled entity is considered further from paragraph 2.155.

Jointly controlled operations and assets

UK.2.216.93 Jointly controlled assets and operations are accounted for by the venturer by incorporating into its consolidated or economic entity and separate financial statements the assets and liabilities, or share thereof, that the venturer controls. This is similar to the treatment of a JANE under FRS 9. Therefore, unless the JANE is housed in a legal entity (in which case it is a jointly controlled entity under IAS 31), the accounting remains the same on first-time adoption, subject to any adjustments required to ensure measurement is on an IFRS basis.

IAS 32, Financial instruments: Presentation

UK.2.216.94 Exemptions and exceptions in IFRS relating to financial instruments are dealt with in the following paragraphs:

- Paragraph 2.38 – Derecognition.
- Paragraph 2.40 – Hedge accounting.
- Paragraph 2.159 – Compound financial instruments.
- Paragraph 2.161 – Designation of previously recognised financial instruments.
- Paragraph 2.166 – Fair value measurement on initial recognition.
- Paragraph 2.193 – Exemption from restating comparatives.

IAS 33, Earnings per share

UK.2.216.95 FRS 22 (IAS 33), which has an effective date of accounting periods beginning on or after 1 January 2005, is almost identical to IAS 33. FRS 22 applies to entities whose ordinary shares or potential ordinary shares are publicly traded or who are in the process of issuing such shares or potential shares in public markets. [FRS 22 para 2]. Any such entities moving to IFRS after 2005 should have no transition issues when applying IAS 33.

IAS 34, Interim financial reporting

UK.2.216.96 Interim financial reporting is dealt with from paragraph 2.207.

IAS 36, Impairment of assets

UK.2.216.97 IAS 36 is similar to the UK standard FRS 11, but there are some differences. Issues that first-time adopters will face are discussed in the following paragraphs:

- Where an acquired business has been merged with existing operations, FRS 11 requires entities to calculate the internally generated goodwill at the time of the merger and to allocate subsequent impairments pro-rata between the two amounts of goodwill. [FRS 11 para 50]. IAS 36 does not require this. The result is that the impairment charge under UK GAAP is higher than under IFRS, as the notional net assets including goodwill, against which their recoverable amount is measured, is greater. On transition to IFRS it, therefore, might appear that entities could have to restate goodwill to reverse previous impairments charged under FRS 11 that would not have been required under IFRS. However, we do not believe that this adjustment is allowed since Appendix C of IFRS 1 specifically requires that the carrying amount of goodwill on transition should be the amount stated under an entity's previous GAAP adjusted only for two specific items (see further para 2.72 above), none of which is reversals of previously charged impairments.

- The allocation of impairment losses between the two standards is different: FRS 11 allocates them to goodwill, intangible assets and then tangible fixed assets. [FRS 11 para 48]. IAS 36 allocates them first to goodwill and then pro-rata to intangible and tangible fixed assets. [IAS 36 para 88]. FRS 11 is also more restrictive in the circumstances under which it permits the reversal of impairment losses on intangible assets. Some reallocations of impairment charges may need to be made on transition to IFRS.

- IAS 36 requires impairment losses on assets that have been revalued to be charged directly to the revaluation reserve relating to the particular assets and for any impairment loss that is greater than the revaluation reserve to be charged to the income statement. [IAS 36 para 60]. For revalued assets, FRS 11 states that charges should be made against the revaluation reserve until the asset value reaches depreciated historical cost, except in the case of revalued assets where the impairment is caused by a clear consumption of economic benefits, when it should be charged to the profit and loss account. [FRS 11 para 63]. UK entities that have made charges to the profit and loss account under UK GAAP for impairment of revalued assets may have to transfer the charge to the revaluation reserve in the comparative period in their first IFRS financial statements.

■ Cash generating units (CGUs) under IAS 36 are similar to income generating units under FRS 11. There are two methods for allocating goodwill to income generating units (IGUs) under UK GAAP for the purpose of impairment testing. Under the first method goodwill is allocated to individual IGUs. [FRS 11 para 34]. The second approach acceptable under UK GAAP allows the purchased goodwill component to be reviewed for impairment at a higher level of aggregation. IGUs can be combined if they were purchased as part of the same investment and are involved in similar parts of the business for the purpose of testing goodwill for impairment. [FRS 11 para 34]. In any case goodwill is allocated to the IGUs that have been purchased as part of the acquisition to which the goodwill belongs. Under IAS 36, however, goodwill is allocated to the acquirer's cash-generating units that are expected to benefit from the business combination's synergies, whether or not other assets or liabilities are assigned to those units. There may, therefore, be some different allocations of goodwill under IFRS, for new acquisitions and for ones that took place before the entity adopted IFRS.

UK.2.216.98   UK entities should be aware that IFRS 8 may change the way that we look at cash generating units. This may trigger potential impairments under IAS 36 that would not have been recognised prior to IFRS 8.

UK.2.216.99   As noted in paragraph 2.196, first-time adopters should disclose any impairment losses recognised or reversed in the opening IFRS balance sheet as if the impairment or reversal was recognised in accordance with IAS 36. These disclosures are detailed in paragraphs 113 to 119 in IAS 36.

UK.2.216.100   As noted in paragraph 2.72, all goodwill must be tested for impairment at the date of transition to IFRS. The goodwill test on first-time adoption may prove to be a large piece of work for many UK entities, particularly where entities have not had experience in performing impairment tests, because a policy of goodwill amortisation over 20 years or less has been followed, and there have not been any trigger events that would require a full impairment test to be performed. Following transition, goodwill must be tested at least annually under IAS 36. [IAS 36 para 90]. The indicators of impairment for assets other than goodwill and the requirements for testing CGUs are similar to those contained in FRS 11 and should not cause significant issues for first-time adopters.

IAS 37, Provisions, contingent liabilities and contingent assets

UK.2.216.101 Like the standards on impairment, the international and UK standards on provisions were developed contemporaneously. There are no substantive differences between IAS 37 and its UK equivalent, FRS 12, and so there should be no impact on first-time adoption by UK companies.

UK.2.216.102 How IFRIC 1 applies to first-time adopters is considered from paragraph 2.170.

UK.2.216.103 IFRIC 5 requires entities to account for their rights to reimbursements from such funds, or account for them in accordance with IAS 27, IAS 28 or IAS 31 if appropriate. Entities should separately account for their decommissioning liability. This interpretation affects a limited number of companies in the UK, but it may well prescribe a different treatment to that applied under UK GAAP. Affected entities may have to change their accounting treatment, but this should not cause significant transition difficulties.

IAS 38, Intangible assets

UK.2.216.104 IAS 38 is comparable in many respects to the UK standard, FRS 10. This section considers the different types of intangible asset within IAS 38's scope.

Internally generated intangible assets

UK.2.216.105 One significant difference between IFRS and UK GAAP noted in paragraph UK.2.65.1 above, dealing with the exemption for business combinations, is that IAS 38 requires the capitalisation of development costs, whereas SSAP 13 permits but does not require it. First-time adopters should examine development costs incurred but previously written off and must capitalise projects that meet the criteria in IAS 38 on transition to IFRS. The amount reinstated as an intangible asset should reflect the original cost less amortisation up to the date of transition. However, preparers should not use hindsight to capitalise intangible assets that would not have qualified for recognition at the date of transition, and in addition no amounts that were incurred before the recognition criteria are met should be retrospectively capitalised. [IFRS 1 para IG46]. UK entities should also, as well as examining SSAP 13 development costs that were written off as a matter of policy under UK GAAP, consider the scope of IAS 38. Although it has similar recognition criteria to SSAP 13, it covers all internally generated intangible assets. 'Development costs' refers to the development phase of the cost of internally generated intangible assets. It does not, however, allow the capitalisation of brands, mastheads and similar because they cannot be distinguished from development of the business as a whole. It may be, then, that more intangible assets will be capitalised on transition to IFRS because of this difference in scope, though this is likely to be limited since there is a restriction on brands etc. The other factor mitigating against more internally generated intangibles being recognised on transition to IFRS is that by their nature intangible assets tend to be unique and it is often difficult to demonstrate economic benefits until a relatively late stage of development.

Intangible assets acquired in a business combination

UK.2.216.106 For first-time adopters, intangible assets acquired in a business combination are dealt with from paragraph 2.64 above. Where such assets have been recognised in a business combination under FRS 10 it is likely that they would also meet the recognition criteria under IAS 38. Where such assets have not been recognised on acquisition they would be recognised on transition to IFRS only if they meet the criteria for recognition as assets that were internally generated by the acquired entity (in other words, recognition is not generally required). [IFRS 1 App C para C4(f)]. For example, a customer list created by the acquired entity may not have been recognised by the acquirer in a pre-transition combination. Even though it may meet the recognition criteria for an intangible asset acquired in a business combination under IFRS 3 and IAS 38, the list is not recognised as an asset on transition to IFRS. This is because the list was *internally generated* by the acquired entity and would not meet the recognition criteria in that entity.

UK.2.216.107 There is a much wider diversity of types of intangible asset that are likely to meet the recognition criteria for recognition in a business combination under IFRS 3 than under previous UK GAAP. However, few of them would meet the recognition criteria for recognition as internally generated intangibles in the acquired entity. Therefore, this provision of IFRS 1 is unlikely to require significant adjustments on transition to IFRS by UK companies. One significant exception for some companies may be in respect of development costs that meet the criteria for recognition in the acquired entity – see paragraph UK.2.216.106 above. Where, an intangible asset that was previously subsumed within goodwill by the acquirer meets the recognition criteria in the acquired entity and *is* recognised on transition then the adjustment should be made against goodwill (see para 2.72). [IFRS 1 App C para C4(g)].

Separately acquired intangible assets

UK.2.216.108 Separately acquired intangible assets are recognised on the basis of the criteria in IAS 38. It is likely that most purchased intangible assets recognised under UK GAAP would also be recognised under IAS 38, since the criteria are very similar. It is also likely that any intangibles that have been purchased by UK entities would also have been capitalised, in accordance with

FRS 10, which requires that separately acquired intangible assets are recorded at cost on acquisition. [FRS 10 para 9]. This is the same as the IAS 38 requirement. However, FRS 10 excludes research and development costs from its scope, whereas IAS 38 includes such costs in its scope. This means that a UK company may have written off acquired individual development projects on acquisition because FRS 10 did not apply and because the company took a lead from SSAP 13, which gives a choice between capitalising or expensing such costs immediately. On transition to IFRS such a company would have to reinstate such costs as an asset on transition to IFRS and amortised based on evidence existing at the date of transition to IFRS (following the principle outlined in paragraph 16 of IFRS 1).

Recognition on transition

UK.2.216.109   There are, therefore, at least two significant categories of intangible asset that are likely to be recognised on adoption of IFRS that may not have previously been recognised by UK entities. These are internally generated development costs and acquired development costs. Where internally generated development costs meet the recognition criteria of IAS 38, which are similar to those of SSAP 13, 'Accounting for research and development', they must be capitalised. It may also be the case that a UK group has not recognised development costs obtained by a separate acquisition or as part of a business combination, as SSAP 13 gives entities the option of writing off such costs.

Estimates including residual values

UK.2.216.110   If a UK entity makes changes in estimates of residual values or of useful lives at the date of transition, the amortisation charge for periods after the date of transition is adjusted to reflect the effect of the change in estimate in accordance with IAS 8. It is unlikely that UK companies would have to make major changes to useful lives or residual values on transition as the rules relating to these are similar to UK GAAP. One difference between FRS 10 and IAS 38 is that under FRS 10 residual value is based on prices at the date of acquisition or later revaluation of an asset, whereas under IAS 38 residual value is based on prices at the balance sheet date. However, under IAS 38 this has less relevance for intangible assets than for tangible assets, because the residual value for intangibles should generally be assumed to be nil, except in certain limited circumstances, such as a committed sale or an active market for the asset. [IAS 38 para 100].

IAS 39, Financial instruments: Recognition and measurement

UK.2.216.111   Exemptions and exceptions in IFRS relating to financial instruments are dealt with in the following paragraphs:

- Paragraph 2.38 – Derecognition.

- Paragraph 2.40 – Hedge accounting.

- Paragraph 2.159 – Compound financial instruments.

- Paragraph 2.161 – Designation of previously recognised financial instruments.

- Paragraph 2.166 – Fair value measurement on initial recognition.

UK.2.216.112 Where a UK entity has previously not adopted FRS 26, IAS 39 is one of the most challenging international standards for the entity to adopt. This is not because there are a lot of particular first-time adoption issues, but rather because the accounting is so different from that under pre-FRS 26 UK GAAP. The issues, exemptions and exceptions related to designation and hedging are dealt with from paragraphs 2.161 and 2.40 respectively. IFRS 1 states that *"an entity recognises and measures all financial assets and financial liabilities in its opening IFRS balance sheet in accordance with IAS 39, except as specified in paragraphs 27-30 of the IFRS, which address derecognition and hedge accounting, and paragraph 36A, which permits an exemption from restating comparative information"*. [IFRS 1 para IG52]. One of the main challenges in adopting IAS 39 is to embed the systems and procedures allowing it to operate the standard's requirements on a day to day basis. The main requirements of the standard are summarised in the paragraphs that follow.

UK.2.216.113 Many of IAS 39's requirements have been introduced into UK GAAP *via* FRS 26 (IAS 39). The application of this standard to UK companies is dealt with in the Manual of Accounting – UK GAAP. This standard, and how entities using it make the transition from UK GAAP to IFRS, is not dealt with further in this chapter. The following paragraphs deal with issues arising on transition to IFRS for UK entities that have not adopted FRS 26.

Recognition

UK.2.216.114 Financial assets or liabilities should be recognised when the entity becomes a party to the contractual provisions of the instrument. [IAS 39 para 14]. See further chapter 31.

Derecognition

UK.2.216.115 The derecognition rules in IAS 39 are primarily focused on risks and rewards, with a subsequent control test. [IAS 39 para 20]. For entities not applying FRS 26, FRS 5's derecognition criteria are risks and rewards based and so UK companies moving to IFRS will be familiar with applying of IAS 39's derecognition criteria. One important point that will impact UK entities is that there is no concept of linked presentation in IFRS. All UK entities that used such a presentation under UK GAAP should examine the detailed agreements and consider whether they will be required to present separate gross assets and liabilities or, in probably very rare circumstances, be able to derecognise parts of assets and liabilities. This will have to be dealt with on a case-by-case basis.

Measurement

UK.2.216.115 Financial instruments are categorised and the categories drive their measurement subsequent to initial recognition. The requirements as they apply to financial assets and liabilities that are not involved in hedging relationships (including derivative financial instruments) are summarised in the table below:

Financial assets	Measurement	Change in carrying amount
At fair value through profit or loss	Fair value	Income statement
Held to maturity	Amortised cost	Amortised to income statement
Loans and receivables	Amortised cost	Amortised to income statement
Available for sale	Fair value	Equity (except for impairment charges, foreign exchange, interest and dividends, which are recorded in the income statement)

Financial liabilities	Measurement	Change in carrying amount
At fair value through profit or loss	Fair value	Income statement
Other	Amortised cost	Amortised to income statement

Derivative financial instruments are categorised as 'at fair value through profit or loss' (unless they are accounted for as effective hedging instruments or are financial guarantee contracts). Where permitted by IAS 39, a financial asset or financial liability may be designated on initial recognition as a financial asset or financial liability at fair value through profit or loss (see also the exemption described in para 2.161).

[IAS 39 paras 9, 46, 47, 55].

UK.2.216.117 There are various significant challenges for first-time adopters with regard to financial instrument measurement. The first is to select the appropriate categorisation for assets and liabilities. As described in paragraph 2.161, classification may be determined at an entity's date of transition to IFRS, or at the start of its first IFRS reporting period. To some extent classification is driven by the substance of the instrument or by the entity's intentions: loans and receivables are non-derivative financial assets with fixed or determinable payments that are not quoted in an active market; held to maturity investments must have fixed or determinable payments and a fixed maturity and the entity must have a positive intent and ability to hold them until maturity. [IAS 39 para 9]. However, in certain circumstances, IAS 39 permits designation of a financial asset or liability as 'at fair value through profit or loss' (see further chapter 31).

UK.2.216.118 Notwithstanding the choice available to entities under IAS 39, initial designation is important for two reasons. In the first place it drives subsequent measurement and presentation of measurement changes. Entities should consider the effect that their choice of designation will have on the financial statements and how this will be explained to readers of the financial statements. This is a significant difference from the pre-FRS 26 UK measurement system that was largely cost-based, with many derivative financial instruments not appearing on the balance sheet at all. Initial designation is also important, because it affects how assets and liabilities are treated after they are classified. Once a financial asset or liability has been classified as a financial asset or liability at fair value through profit or loss it cannot later be reclassified. [IAS 39 para 50]. In addition, the strict tainting rules in the standard mean that no asset may be classified as held to maturity if, during the current financial year or during the preceding two years the reporting entity has sold, transferred, or exercised a put option on more than an insignificant amount of held to maturity investments before maturity. [IAS 39 paras 9, 52]. This is a group-wide restraint. An infringement by an insignificant subsidiary will render the entire group unable to hold financial assets as held to maturity for two years. Entities should, therefore, ensure, on transition to IFRS, that they believe they will be able to meet the criteria for all assets that they wish to classify as held to maturity. In practice it may be the case that few assets are classified as held to maturity. An important part of the conversion to IFRS in respect of financial instrument accounting is designation of financial assets and liabilities and modelling of the effect of different classifications. Classification is also important when considering hedge accounting (see further para UK.2.216.123 below).

UK.2.216.119 The second significant measurement challenge for first-time adopters of IFRS is the requirement to measure at fair value. In theory this should not be an issue, at least for those entities with listed securities, because such entities have been required to disclose fair values of financial instruments under FRS 29. The incorporation of these fair values into entities' balance sheets and income statements will, however, give added impetus to ensuring that fair value measurements are reliable. Entities should also ensure that fair value methodologies are IAS 39 compliant.

UK.2.216.120 All financial instruments are required to be initially measured at the fair value of the consideration given or received. Transaction costs are included in the initial measurement of fair value, except for financial assets and liabilities held at fair value through profit or loss. For these assets and liabilities transaction costs are recorded in the income statement. [IAS 39 para 43]. This means that, in principle, all financial assets and liabilities should be discounted to their present value. This principle applies to interest-free loans (where the loan has a term) and to debtors and creditors. This has not commonly been part of pre-FRS 26 UK GAAP and may prove a significant change for some entities, though materiality considerations will still apply under IFRS.

Fair value accounting

UK.2.216.121 Increasing use of fair values, including the fair valuing of derivatives that were off balance sheet under pre-FRS 26 UK GAAP, will inevitably lead to increased volatility in financial statements. Hedge accounting can be used to mitigate volatility, but the difficulties involved in obtaining hedge accounting can mean that some entities may choose to accept at least a degree of unpredictability. Turnover, profit, finance costs, net assets and reserves can all be affected. This in turn will have an effect on key performance indicators and on many financial covenants – including earnings per share, gearing, interest cover, dividend cover, margins, reward schemes. A key part of the process of moving to IFRS is the identification and management of these issues and risks.

Impairment

UK.2.216.122 IAS 39 introduces detailed rules in respect of impairment of financial assets. UK entities have been impairing such assets for many years: where companies apply UK GAAP, the Companies Act 2006 requires investments to be written down for permanent diminutions in value and requires debtors to be stated at the lower of cost and net realisable value. [CA85 4 Sch 19(1), 23; SI 2008/410 1 Sch 19(1), 24]. It does not, however, specify how entities should go about measuring financial asset diminutions (though some financial assets, such as investments in subsidiaries, are within the scope of FRS 11). IAS 39 specifies that entities should first assess whether there is any objective evidence that an asset or group of assets is impaired. This might be, for example, financial difficulty of the issuer, breach of contract or the recognition of an impairment loss in the prior period. [IAS 39 paras 58, 59]. Assets carried at amortised cost should then be measured at their expected future cash flows discounted at the financial instrument's original effective interest rate. [IAS 39 para 63]. Individually significant assets should be considered separately, with specific amounts written off. [IAS 39 para 64]. The requirement in respect of individually significant assets should not be very different from current practice. The real difference is for collective assets that are not individually significant, for example a large group of debtors. IAS 39 goes into some detail as to how impairment should be calculated for such assets. They should be grouped with other assets that have similar risk characteristics. This grouping might be, for example, all debtors from a particular country within a range of credit ratings. Historical loss data must be used to predict expected cash flows, or 'peer group experience' used if no historical data is available. [IAS 39 paras AG87 to AG92]. The standard introduces a good deal more rigour than is required by pre-FRS 26 UK GAAP and entities will have to develop robust methodologies on transition to IFRS. As noted above in paragraph 2.32 above when discussing estimates, hindsight should not be used on transition to IFRS.

Hedge accounting

UK.2.216.123   Hedge accounting is one of the most difficult areas of IAS 39. In part this is because the standard is rule-based and can be difficult to interpret. But in the main it is because hedge accounting is difficult to achieve under international accounting standards. The rules that allow an entity to apply hedge accounting are onerous because it is a break from the normal way of accounting under IAS 39: entities must, in effect, prove that they deserve the right to hedge account. Hedge accounting for first-time adopters has been discussed more fully when dealing with the mandatory exceptions from full retrospective application of IFRS from paragraph 2.40 above. From the point at which first-time adopters are able to hedge account they will have to comply with the strict rules of IAS 39. This will involve, for many entities, considerably more rigour in designating, documenting and measuring the effectiveness of hedges. Hedges that have been accounted for in a certain way under pre-FRS 26 UK GAAP, and which have been seen as economically successful, will have to be assessed on a case by case basis as to whether they qualify for hedge accounting under IAS 39. For those hedges that would qualify, entities should consider their strategies carefully, taking into account the amount of time and effort involved on the one hand and income statement volatility arising from not hedge accounting on the other.

Embedded derivatives

UK.2.216.124   An embedded derivative is a component of a combined contract that also includes a non-derivative host contract with the effect that some or all of the cash flows on the combined instrument vary in a way similar to a stand-alone derivative. IAS 39 requires embedded derivatives that meet the definition of a derivative to be separated from the host contract and accounted for as derivatives, that is at fair value through profit or loss, if (a) the economic characteristics of the embedded derivatives are not closely related to those of the host contract, (b) a separate instrument with the same terms as the embedded derivative would meet the definition of a derivative and (c) the combined instrument is not measured at fair value through profit or loss. [IAS 39 para 11].

UK.2.216.125   Embedded derivatives can appear in all sorts of contracts that an entity is party to, and assessing whether the derivative is closely related to the host contract is not always straightforward. Inflation-linked rentals are closely related to lease contracts, for example, whilst fixed rate debt extension options generally are not. Paragraphs AG27 to AG33 give additional guidance in this area. It is likely to prove a challenging area for first-time adopters. Embedded derivatives are dealt with in detail in chapter 31.

IAS 40, Investment property

UK.2.216.126 The main difference between IAS 40 and the equivalent UK standard, SSAP 19, 'Accounting for investment properties', is that IAS 40 allows a choice of measurement bases. Under IAS 40 an entity can choose, for all investment property, the fair value model or depreciated cost. [IAS 40 para 30]. This differs from the treatment required by SSAP 19, which requires investment properties to be carried at open market value and does not permit such property to be carried at depreciated historical cost. When the fair value model is applied under IAS 40, the carrying amount is not depreciated and the gain or loss arising from a change in the fair value is recognised in the income statement. [IAS 40 para 35]. Again, this differs from SSAP 19 where a revaluation gain or loss is recognised in the STRGL, unless it is a permanent deficit (or its reversal) that should be recognised in the profit and loss account. As discussed in paragraph 2.25 above, where IFRS allows a choice of policy, entities first-time adopting are free to choose which to adopt. UK entities may, therefore, choose to apply the cost model in IAS 40 when they move to IFRS. In addition to this, the deemed cost exemption (see para 2.107 above) allows such entities the choice of either restating investment property to original depreciated cost or of freezing the carrying amount under UK GAAP and using this as deemed cost. Although there is a free choice, as pointed out in paragraph 2.25, preparers will consider which measurement base gives the most relevant and reliable information to users of the financial statements. It may be difficult to argue that moving to a cost measurement basis provides users with more relevant and reliable information, particularly when they have seen investment property measured at open market value under SSAP 19 for a number of years. IAS 40 itself does not see moving from fair value to cost within the IFRS framework as being a move to a preferable accounting policy. [IAS 40 para 31].

UK.2.216.127 For UK companies applying IAS 40 for the first time there should be no major problems in determining fair values, as the existing SSAP 19 requirement is to carry investment property at open market value. The most significant effect for UK companies is likely to be deferred tax as disclosed in Table UK.2.8.1. IAS 12 is dealt with in chapter 13.

Table UK.2.8.1 – Disclosure of implications of first-time adoption of IFRS for UK investment property company

The British Land Company PLC – Annual report and accounts – 31 March 2004

Financial Review (extract)
Accounting issues

International Accounting Standards (IAS) will be applied, as required for all European Union listed companies, for our financial year ending 31 March 2006. The Group continues its preparations, which include changes to systems and methodologies, and will give further guidance on the accounting impact in due course.

The underlying performance of the business including cash flows will, of course, be unaffected. The reported results will however look significantly different and the accounting net asset value will be significantly lower than that shown under the Group's existing accounting policies. The five major areas identified to date where IAS differs from UK GAAP affecting British Land are as follows:

- UK GAAP does not permit deferred tax to be recognised where a business is not obliged to pay more tax at a future date. IAS on the other hand requires provision for all taxable and deductible differences between book values for tax purposes and accounting book values that are not 'permanent' timing differences. The effect of this change will be to reduce net assets.

  The most significant such difference for British Land are the base costs for tax purposes of its properties and investments, including shares in joint ventures, and the accounting book values which include material revaluation adjustments. Tax payments will arise only if British Land sells those assets and the amount of tax crystallised will reflect the price received at the time, the structure of the transaction, any tax benefits available such as loss relief and benefits derived from the tax position of the purchaser or of the Group at that time. None of these mitigating factors are accurately quantifiable where no transaction is in contemplation and negotiation, accordingly the provision to be booked under IAS will not represent an amount which the company expects to pay. IAS does not permit the deferred tax provision to be discounted to present value.

  The disclosures in note 7 to the financial statements show the calculation of the tax payable assuming all properties and investments are sold at the amount at which they are carried in the balance sheet, including trading and development surpluses but without regard to future events or tax planning.

- The definitions of finance and operating leases are different between UK GAAP and IAS. Most of the Group's leases will be unaffected. In the case of head leases on the Group's leasehold properties, IAS will require a financial liability and corresponding asset to be recognised in the balance sheet. Currently the financial effect of head leases is reflected by our valuers as a reduction from their valuations. The net asset effect of this change is not expected to be material.

- British Land uses derivatives to manage its interest rate risk. A description of financing policy and risk management is shown in the section Business Opportunity and Business Risk Management. In accordance with UK GAAP British Land's derivatives are not valued when they are hedges and any income or costs are recognised in the profit and loss account consistently with the underlying hedged transaction. IAS requires all derivatives to be carried at their fair values in the balance sheet and, where the related debt is not carried at market value, this could reduce or increase reported net assets. Hedge accounting whereby profits and losses are matched with those of the underlying (instrument or) cash flow is subject to restrictive tests under IAS and as a result there may be more earnings volatility. The European Union has yet to ratify the use of the International Financial Reporting

Standard covering hedge accounting (IAS 39) and there is uncertainty whether amendments may arise to IAS 39 as a result of the ratification process.

- Unlike UK GAAP which requires proposed final dividends to be accrued, IAS only permits recognition of the liability to pay a final dividend when this has been approved by the shareholders. This will lead to an increase in net asset value.

- IAS will require a portion of the Group's irredeemable convertible bonds to be recognised as equity. This will lead to an increase in net asset value.

IAS 41, Agriculture

UK.3.328 IAS 41 prescribes the accounting treatment, financial statement presentation and disclosures related to agricultural activity, IAS 41's basic principle is that biological assets are measured at fair value less estimated point-of-sale costs. Similarly, agricultural produce should be measured at fair value less estimated point-of-sale costs at the point of harvest. Gains or losses arising on re-measuring fair value are recognised in the income statement in the period in which they arise. There is no equivalent standard in UK GAAP for the accounting treatment related to agricultural activity, as defined in IAS 41. For further guidance on IAS 41 refer to chapter 32.

IFRS 2 to IFRS 7

UK.2.216.129 These standards are dealt with by specific exemptions and exceptions in IFRS 1. They are covered in the following paragraphs:

- IFRS 2 – paragraph 2.99.

- IFRS 3 – paragraph 2.58.

- IFRS 4 – paragraph 2.106.

IFRS 8 Operating segments

UK.2.216.130 In November 2006, the IASB issued IFRS 8 which replaces IAS 14 and aligns segment reporting with the requirements of the US standard SFAS 131.

UK.2.216.131 The scope of IFRS 8 and SSAP 25 differs. IFRS 8 applies to entities whose equity and debt securities are publicly traded or in the process of being so. SSAP 25 applies to public companies, banking and insurance companies and groups and certain other large entities.

UK.2.216.132 The requirements of IFRS 8 are significantly different to those of SSAP 25. IFRS 8 uses a 'management approach' under which segmental information is presented on the same basis as that used for internal reporting purposes. The approach in IFRS 8 differs from the risk/returns approach of SSAP 25. The 'management approach' in IFRS 8 applies to both the identification of segments and the amounts reported. The amounts reported may be non-GAAP. An explanation of the basis on which the information is prepared and a reconciliation to the amount recognised in the financial statements is required. The disclosure requirements of IFRS 8 are more extensive than those required in SSAP 25. Information will have to be disclosed under IFRS 8 that management might previously have preferred to keep private: there is no 'seriously prejudicial' exemption from disclosure.

UK.2.216.133   IFRS 1 does not make any exception for IFRS 8 to the general rule that comparative figures should be presented in accordance with IFRS 1.

Chapter 3

Accounting policies, accounting estimates and errors

Accounting policies, accounting estimates and errors

Introduction

3.1 This chapter covers the requirements of IAS 8, which deals with the accounting for accounting policies, accounting estimates and errors. Other aspects of reporting performance are covered by IAS 1 and IFRS 5, which are dealt with in chapters 4 and 26 respectively.

Objective and scope

3.2 IAS 8 prescribes criteria for selecting and applying accounting policies. It also deals with the accounting treatment and disclosure requirements of changes in accounting policies, accounting estimates and corrections of prior period errors. The standard aims to improve the relevance, reliability and comparability of financial statements. Disclosure requirements for accounting policies, except for those relating to changes in accounting policies, are set out in IAS 1 (see chapter 4). [IAS 8 paras 1, 2]. The tax effects of correcting prior period errors and changes in accounting policies are accounted for and disclosed in accordance with IAS 12 (see chapter 13). [IAS 8 paras 3, 4].

Selecting and applying accounting policies

General rules

3.3 Accounting policies are the specific principles, bases, conventions, rules and practices applied by an entity in preparing and presenting financial statements. [IAS 8 para 5]. The preparation of financial statements is based on certain general principles, for example, they are normally prepared on a going concern basis, on the accruals basis and under the historical cost convention (or historical cost convention modified by the revaluation of certain assets). There are general rules that apply to the recognition of the elements of financial statements such as income, expenses, assets, liabilities and equity. Assets, for example, are recognised when it is probable that the future economic benefits will flow to the entity and the asset has a cost or value that can be reliably measured.

3.4 The IASB's Framework sets out the objectives of financial statements and the concepts that underlie their preparation for external users. The Framework discusses the elements of financial statements in detail and the recognition criteria to be applied to those elements. For this reason, entities should not develop their own general principles for preparing their financial statements, insofar as they should generally use the going concern basis, recognise assets and liabilities only when they meet the definitions in the Framework, and so on.

3.5 The Framework sets out two fundamental qualitative characteristics of financial statements that are needed if the financial information is to be useful: namely, relevance and faithful representation. Materiality is a sub-principle of relevance. Characteristics of faithful representation are for information to be complete, neutral and free from error. Furthermore the usefulness of financial information is enhanced if it is comparable, verifiable, timely and understandable. [Framework paras QC4 to QC32]. These fundamental and enhancing qualitative characteristics are considered further in chapter 1.

3.6 One of the Framework's purposes is to assist the IASB in developing and reviewing existing international financial reporting standards (IFRSs). It is also intended to assist the IASB in promoting harmonisation of regulations by providing a basis for reducing the number of alternative accounting treatments permitted by international financial reporting standards.

3.7 Using the Framework as a basis, the IASB has adopted a large number of standards and interpretations that lay down either single accounting policies to be applied in complying with the standard or, in a few cases, alternative accounting policies that may be followed. As a result, selection of accounting policies by entities is largely pre-determined by existing standards.

Accounting policies contained in standards and interpretations

3.8 IAS 8 requires that where a standard or interpretation applies to a transaction, other event or condition, an entity should determine the accounting policy or policies to be applied to that item by reference to the requirements of that standard or interpretation. [IAS 8 para 7]. The standard notes that IFRSs are sometimes accompanied by guidance to assist entities in applying their requirements. All guidance will state whether it is an integral part of the IFRS and, therefore, forms parts of the requirements of the standard or interpretation. Guidance that is not integral is merely useful when applying the IFRS. [IAS 8 para 9]. In addition, standards include paragraphs in bold type and plain type. The paragraphs have equal authority, although the paragraphs in bold type indicate the main principles. [Preface to IFRSs para 14].

3.9 IAS 8 notes that IFRS sets out accounting policies that the IASB considers will result in financial statements that contain relevant and reliable information about the transactions, other events and conditions to which they apply. [IAS 8 para 8]. (The Framework has replaced 'reliable' with 'faithful representation', but IAS 8 has not yet been amended to reflect this.) Of the enhancing qualitative characteristics in the Framework (see para 3.5 above), understandability and comparability should follow automatically because standards (and the accounting policies they prescribe) ought to be understandable and, by definition, should promote comparability.

3.10 Where an accounting standard permits an entity to adopt one of two alternative accounting treatments, it is important that the entity clearly indicates the alternative that has been adopted (and which should be applied consistently, unless a standard permits otherwise). Examples of standards that have alternatives include IAS 16 and IAS 19. IAS 16 permits an entity to adopt either an historical cost policy or a revaluation policy for selected classes of assets (see chapter 16). IAS 19 permits a choice of policy for the presentation of pension cost where the profit or loss expense can be one total or can be split between operating and financing (see further chapter 11).

Materiality

3.11 IAS 8 notes that policies need not be applied where the effect of applying them is immaterial. [IAS 8 para 8]. This complements the statement in IAS 1 that disclosures required by IFRS need not be made if the information is immaterial. [IAS 1 para 31].

3.12 IAS 8 defines 'material' as it applies to omissions and misstatements (see para 3.66 onwards). The definition is *"Omissions or misstatements of items are material if they could, individually or collectively, influence the economic decisions that users make on the basis of the financial statements. Materiality depends on the size and nature of the omission or misstatement judged in the surrounding circumstances. The size or nature of the item, or a combination of both, could be the determining factor"*. [IAS 8 para 5]. The definition is consistent with the definition of materiality in the Framework (as a sub-principle of relevance) and so may also be applied to the application of accounting policies, particularly as non-application of a policy will often result in an omission or misstatement in any case.

3.13 In applying the definition of materiality, an entity should consider the characteristics of the users of the financial statements. The Framework states that financial reports are prepared for users who have a reasonable knowledge of business and economic activities and who review and analyse the information diligently. [Framework para QC32]. Consideration of materiality, therefore, needs to take account of how the economic decisions of such users would reasonably be expected to be influenced. [IAS 8 para 6]. In our view, reasonable knowledge of accounting would include the knowledge that financial statements are normally prepared on a going concern and accruals basis and a basic knowledge of the structure, content and purpose of the statement of comprehensive income, balance sheet, cash flow statement and statement of changes in equity.

3.14 Also, in relation to materiality, the standard notes that it is inappropriate to make or leave uncorrected, immaterial departures from IFRS to achieve a particular presentation of an entity's financial position, financial performance or cash flows. [IAS 8 para 8]. This statement implies that a departure that achieves a particular presentation can be immaterial. However, if that particular presentation is different from the presentation that would be achieved through compliance with the standard, it may be likely to influence the economic decisions of a user and hence be material. Examples of such departures would include situations where a small uncorrected error could trigger a breach of borrowing covenants or an employee share option award. Accordingly, even departures that appear to be relatively immaterial because of their size should be considered carefully.

3.15   We consider that a standard should be applied unless it is judged that the effects are clearly immaterial. This judgement will require an appropriate analysis, which should take into consideration classification, recognition, measurement and disclosure issues. Arguments that it is impracticable to apply a standard, or that amounts cannot be determined, are rarely reasons for considering the effect to be immaterial, because in the absence of quantification it is generally not possible to judge materiality.

Policies not contained in standards and interpretations

3.16   Where there is no standard or interpretation that specifically applies to a transaction, other event or condition, companies should use their judgement to develop and apply an accounting policy that is both relevant and reliable to the users. Reliability means that the financial statements should:

■   Faithfully represent the financial position, financial performance and cash flows.

■   Reflect the economic substance of transactions, other events and conditions, and not merely the legal form.

■   Be neutral, that is, free from bias.

■   Be prudent.

■   Be complete in all material respects.

[IAS 8 para 10].

3.17   In the absence of a standard or interpretation, management will usually seek out other guidance to assist them in exercising their judgement to develop and apply an accounting policy. IAS 8 recognises and requires this. It states that management should refer to the following sources and consider their applicability in the order in which they are set out below:

■   Requirements in international financial reporting standards and interpretations that deal with similar and related issues.

■   The definitions, recognition criteria and measurement concepts for assets, liabilities, income and expenses in the Framework.

[IAS 8 para 11].

3.18   The IASB is continually reviewing its existing standards and developing new guidance on issues as they arise, either through specific projects or through IFRS IC interpretations. Specific guidance on new issues is, therefore, sometimes not available from existing standards or is awaiting a consensus from IFRS IC. Nevertheless, principles and guidance from existing standards can often be useful in determining the appropriate accounting treatment on new issues where the features of a new type of transaction are similar to those covered by an existing standard. In addition, proposals in exposure drafts and guidance in new standards that are not yet effective may also be helpful when considering the accounting for transactions not fully addressed by existing standards. However, care should be taken when considering using proposals in exposure drafts or guidance in new standards for which early adoption is not permitted.

3.19   The IFRS IC published an agenda decision in March 2011 that considered the question of whether it could be appropriate to apply only certain aspects of an IFRS being analogised to, or whether the entire IFRS being analogised to would need to be applied. The IFRS IC observed that when management develops an accounting policy through analogy to an IFRS dealing with similar and related matters, it needs to use its judgement in applying all aspects of the IFRS that are applicable to the particular issue.

3.20   In addition, the standard suggests, but does not require, that management consider the most recent pronouncements by other standard-setters that use a similar conceptual framework as that set out in the IASB's Framework for developing accounting standards, other accounting literature and accepted industry practices, to the extent that they do not conflict with the IASB's standards and interpretations and the IASB's Framework. [IAS 8 para 12].

UK.3.20.1   An example in the UK where the directors, in preparing financial statements under IFRS, have had regard to a pronouncement by another standard setter (in this case, the Urgent Issues Task Force of the UK Accounting Standards Board) is given in Table UK.3.1.

Table UK.3.1 – Use of pronouncements by other standard setters

BT Group plc – Annual report & Form 20F – 31 March 2011

23. Retirement benefit plans (extract)

Principal assumptions used to measure BTPS liabilities (extract)

The rate of inflation influences the assumptions for salary and pension increases. In assessing the appropriate assumption for pension increases, management have considered the announcement in July 2010 by the UK Government that the Consumer Prices Index (CPI), rather than the Retail Prices Index (RPI), will be used as the basis for determining the rate of inflation for the statutory minimum rate of revaluation and indexation of occupational pension rights. Under the scheme rules the Government's decision has the following impact with effect for increases after 1 April 2011:

- members who commenced employment prior to 1 April 1986 – CPI will be used to revalue preserved pensions of deferred members and for the rate of inflationary increase applied to pensions in payment

- members who commenced employment on or after 1 April 1986 – CPI will be used to revalue preserved pensions of deferred members and RPI will continue to be used for inflationary increases to pensions in payment.

The Government's decision does not affect the accrual of benefits for employees while they are active members of the scheme for whom benefits accrue on a CARE basis that is linked to RPI.

The assumption for RPI has been assessed by reference to yields on long-term fixed interest and index-linked Government bonds and has regard to Bank of England published inflationary expectations. CPI is assessed at a margin below RPI taking into account long-term trends. The impact of using CPI instead of RPI is to reduce BTPS liabilities at 31 March 2011 by £3.5bn. In determining the most appropriate manner by which to reflect the impact of the change on the scheme liabilities, the directors have had regard to the UITF Abstract 48 "Accounting implications of the replacement of the Retail Prices Index with the Consumer Prices Index for retirement benefits" issued by the Urgent Issues Task Force of the UK Accounting Standards Board in December 2010. The Abstract states that, where the obligation is to pay pensions with increases based on a general measure of inflation rather than a measure linked specifically to RPI, a change in the inflation assumption represents an actuarial gain or loss rather than a cost relating to past service of employees. Accordingly, the gain on re-measurement of the liabilities of the BTPS to reflect CPI as the inflation measure is recorded as an actuarial gain in comprehensive income in 2011.

3.21 Sometimes, where IFRS does not give adequate guidance, entities look to other GAAPs. Specific industry guidance exists under US GAAP, for example, in the motion picture and television industries, which is sometimes referred to by entities in developing their accounting policies under IFRS. Entities may also be more inclined to refer to US GAAP where they have a US listing or significant US shareholders. It should be noted, however, that the application of a US GAAP treatment is appropriate only where that treatment is consistent with the principles underlying IFRS. Care should be taken when applying rules contained in US GAAP or any other GAAP, as they carry a risk of divergence from the principles of IFRS.

UK.3.21.1 In the UK, Statements of recommended practice (SORPs) are a valuable source of guidance that supplement UK standards and assist in developing accounting policies. SORPs have been developed to provide guidance for particular industry sectors, such as investment trusts, oil and gas, insurance and leasing. There is no IFRS equivalent to the SORPs so, for UK companies applying IFRS, the guidance in the existing UK SORPs may be applied in the same way as another GAAP; that is, only where the guidance is consistent with the principles of IFRS.

Consistency

3.22 Entities should apply their accounting policies consistently, unless a standard permits otherwise (see para 3.23). Generally, if a standard permits or requires different accounting policies to be applied to different categories of items, an entity should select an appropriate policy for each category and apply those policies consistently within each of the categories. [IAS 8 para 13]. For example, IAS 16 permits a policy of revaluation to be adopted for a class of property, plant and equipment, whilst at the same time another class may be measured at historical cost. The principle of consistency requires that, where an entity adopts different policies for different classes of property, plant and equipment, the policy adopted for each class should be applied consistently to all assets included in that class and from one accounting period to the next.

3.23 In some circumstances, accounting standards may permit entities to apply different accounting policies for similar items. An example is where an entity acquires less than 100% of a business. Under IFRS 3, an entity has a choice, on a transaction-by-transaction basis, regarding how it measures the non-controlling interest. See further chapter 25.

Issues for groups

3.24 Questions may arise as to whether IFRS makes it necessary for consistent accounting policies to be adopted in consolidated financial statements as compared to the individual financial statements of the parent or subsidiaries reporting under IFRS.

UK.3.24.1 The issue of whether companies within a group should have consistent accounting policies when they are all reporting under IFRS may be distinguished from a situation (as in the UK) where legislation permits entities to use UK GAAP for the parent and subsidiary individual financial statements, with IFRS being used only for the consolidated financial statements. In such situations, the use of UK GAAP for the parent and subsidiaries will clearly mean that the policies will not be consistent in many cases with the IFRS policies used in the consolidated financial statements.

3.25 For consolidated financial statements, IAS 27 (or IFRS 10) requires uniform accounting policies to be used for like transactions and other events in similar circumstances. Where any members of the group have adopted different accounting policies in their individual financial statements, appropriate consolidation adjustments should be made to achieve uniformity. [IAS 27 paras 24, 25; IFRS 10 paras 19, B87]. See further chapter 24. A similar requirement to use uniform accounting policies applies for equity-accounted investments. [IAS 28 para 26; IAS 28R para 35].

3.26 However, IFRS does not require the accounting policies of individual financial statements of the parent and its subsidiaries to be the same as those applied in the group's consolidated financial statements. For each entity that reports individually under IFRS, IAS 8 requires management to go through the same accounting policy selection process as for the consolidated financial statements and each entity should select accounting policies that enable its financial statements to give a fair presentation. The factors that the entity's management would take into account in determining the accounting policies for the group's consolidated financial statements would generally also apply to the individual entities. Accordingly, in most cases it would be reasonable to expect that the same accounting policies would be selected for the group, the parent and the subsidiaries reporting under IFRS.

3.27   There may be special reasons for adopting different policies across a group. The particular circumstances and cost-benefit considerations may vary significantly between different reporting entities and their users. As an example, comparability of accounting policies across a group of companies might be highly desirable and useful to the shareholders and potential investors of a listed company. Additionally, if a group also reports under US GAAP, management may wish to minimise the differences between its consolidated IFRS figures and its US GAAP figures. Whereas, comparability might be less of an issue for the users of the individual entities' financial statements, so other factors such as the effect of different accounting policies on subsidiaries' distributable profits, the level of non-controlling interest or regulatory considerations may weigh more heavily in the selection of their accounting policies.

3.28   Deciding to adopt consistent or different policies in the individual financial statements of the parent or its subsidiaries may involve the judgements of different boards of directors. Where different policies are adopted, an entity should be able to justify this with sound business or commercial reasons.

Changes in accounting policies

3.29   A change in accounting policy should be made only if:

■   the change is required by a standard or an interpretation; or

■   if the change will result in the financial statements providing reliable and more relevant information about the effects of transactions, other events or conditions on the entity's financial position, financial performance or cash flows.

[IAS 8 para 14].

3.29.1   A voluntary change in accounting policies does not involve a free choice for management. The new policy has to be justified in line with the second bullet point above. In addition, some regulators might require independent confirmation that the new policy is preferable to the old one, where the change does not result from a new or amended accounting standard.

3.30   In accordance with the principle of consistency (see para 3.22), an entity should apply the same accounting policy from one period to the next, unless a change in policy meets one of the two conditions specified above. This is because users of the financial statements need to be able to compare the financial statements of an entity over time in order to appreciate trends in its financial position, financial performance and cash flows. [IAS 8 para 15].

3.31 Changes in accounting policies may be categorised according to the three basic processes applied in the preparation of financial statements, namely, (i) recognition, (ii) measurement bases and (iii) presentation.

3.32 Changes in recognition policies would include, for instance:

- Changing revenue recognition regarding the sale of goods and services.
- Changing from recognising actuarial gains and losses on defined benefit pension plans under the 'corridor approach' (spreading in income statement, as previously permitted by IAS 19) to recognising in full as they arise in the statement of comprehensive income. See further chapter 11.

3.33 Changes in policies related to measurement bases would include for example a change from measuring a class of property, plant and equipment at depreciated historical cost to a policy of regular revaluation (note that this is dealt with prospectively as a revaluation, rather than retrospectively – see para 3.44 below).

3.34 A change in the classification of an item within the balance sheet, income statement or cash flow statement often represents a change in accounting policy related to presentation, except where driven by a change in circumstances (discussed further below).

3.35 IAS 8 notes that the introduction of an accounting policy to account for transactions or events that are different in substance from those previously occurring (that is, where circumstances have changed), is not a change of accounting policy. Similarly, adopting an accounting policy for events or transactions that did not occur previously or that were immaterial in the prior year is not a change of accounting policy and would be applied prospectively. [IAS 8 para 16]. For example, when there is a change in an entity's functional currency, IAS 21 requires the entity to account for this prospectively by translating all items into the new functional currency using the exchange rate at the date of the change (see further chapter 7). A change in functional currency is not a change in accounting policy as it arises as a result of a change to the entity's underlying transactions, events and conditions. [IAS 21 paras 35 to 37].

3.36 Another situation involving a change in circumstances occurs where there is a change in use of an existing asset. This is illustrated in the following example.

Example – Change in use of an existing asset

Entity A owns an office building that it has previously used for its own administrative purposes. Accordingly, the building has been classified as property, plant and equipment and carried at depreciated historical cost. During the current year, management moved the workforce to a new building and leased the old building to a third party. Accordingly, the old building was reclassified as investment property and carried at fair value.

The adoption of an accounting policy for events or transactions that differ in substance from previously occurring events or transactions is not a change in accounting policy. [IAS 8 para 16]. The change represents a change in use of the property and so no restatement of the comparative amounts should be made. [IAS 40 para 61]. The different accounting treatment applied to the same property in the current and prior years is appropriate, because the building was used for different purposes in the two years.

However, it should be noted that where a change in accounting policy is made to revalue the property under IAS 16, without a change in use, specific rules in IAS 8 apply – see paragraph 3.44 below.

3.37   Changes in accounting policy are made on the initial application of a standard or interpretation or may be made on some other voluntary basis. The requirements of IAS 8 differ between these two circumstances and are considered below.

Applying changes in accounting policies

General rules

3.38   A change in accounting policy that is made on the initial application (including early adoption) of an IFRS or interpretation should be accounted for in accordance with the specific transitional provisions of that standard or interpretation, if any. In the absence of any specific transitional provisions, the change should be accounted for in the same way as other voluntary changes in accounting policy described in paragraph 3.39 below. Early adoption of a new standard or interpretation is not classed as a voluntary change and so any specific transitional provisions in that new standard or interpretation should be applied. [IAS 8 paras 19, 20].

3.39   Specific transitional provisions are often included in new or revised IFRSs to allow prospective, rather than retrospective, application of the standard. This is sometimes because it would be impracticable to obtain the information necessary to restate comparatives. It may also be unduly onerous to apply a new accounting treatment on some past transactions (for example, business combinations).

3.40   On occasions, if there is no relevant IFRS, an entity may adopt the provisions of the most recent accounting standard or pronouncement issued by another standard-setter (although any transitional provisions in that standard or pronouncement cannot be used under IFRS). If an entity has used an accounting standard or pronouncement issued by another standard-setter and the standard or pronouncement is subsequently amended, the entity should determine whether the financial information prepared in accordance with the amended pronouncement provides reliable and more relevant information. If that is the case and the entity decides to follow the amended pronouncement, the change is accounted for under IAS 8 as a voluntary change in accounting policy. [IAS 8 para 21].

3.41 Voluntary changes of accounting policy and the adoption of new accounting standards or interpretations where there are no specific transitional rules, including changes in presentation, should be applied retrospectively, except to the extent that it is impracticable to determine either the period-specific effects or the cumulative effect of the change (see from para 3.98 below). All comparative amounts should be adjusted to show the results and financial position of prior periods as if the new accounting policy had always applied. [IAS 8 paras 22, 23]. 'Retrospective application' is defined in IAS 8 as *"applying a new accounting policy to transactions, other events and conditions as if that policy had always been applied"*. [IAS 8 para 5]. The adjustment to all periods prior to those presented should be reported as an adjustment to the opening balance of each affected component of equity (for example, retained earnings) for the earliest period presented. In addition, when an entity applies its changes in accounting policy retrospectively, IAS 1 requires the presentation of an additional balance sheet as at the start of the preceding period (see further paras 3.110, 3.110.1 and 3.112). The presentation in the statement of changes in equity of a prior period adjustment for a change in accounting policy is considered further in chapter 4.

3.42 For example, if a policy change is made in 20X7, and financial statements are presented for the year ended 31 December 20X7 with comparatives for the year ended 31 December 20X6, the comparatives for the year ended 31 December 20X6 are adjusted. The cumulative adjustment for years preceding 20X6 is then made to the balance of retained earnings and other equity components that may be affected, at 1 January 20X6. Any other information in respect of prior periods presented with the financial statements (for example, historical summaries) is also restated as far back as is practicable. [IAS 8 para 26]. See also paragraphs 3.110 and 3.110.1.

3.43 An example of a change in accounting policy on initial application of a standard or interpretation is given in Table 3.2. The extract includes the additional balance sheet required by IAS 1 (see para 3.110).

Table 3.2 – Prior year adjustment for change in accounting policy

China Mobile Limited – Annual report and accounts – 31 December 2009

Consolidated Balance Sheet

as at 31 December 2009

(Expressed in Renminbi)	Note	As at 31 December 2009 *RMB million*	As at 31 December 2008 *RMB million* (restated)	As at 1 January 2008 *RMB million* (restated)
Non-current assets				
...				
Deferred tax assets	21	**8,939**	7,614	6,121
...				
		464,013	418,257	356,534
Current assets				
...				
		287,355	240,170	207,635
Current liabilities				
...				
Deferred revenue	30	**35,573**	32,930	30,070
Accrued expenses and other payables	32	**69,335**	57,437	47,318
...				
		209,805	183,559	157,719
Non-current liabilities				
...				
		(33,929)	(34,217)	(34,301)
NET ASSETS		**507,634**	440,651	372,149
CAPITAL AND RESERVES				
...				
TOTAL EQUITY		**507,634**	440,651	372,149

[Note: the full balance sheet has not been reproduced in this extract.]

Notes to the financial statements (extract)

2 Changes in accounting policies (extract)

(ii) IFRIC/HK(IFRIC) Interpretation 13, *Customer loyalty programmes*
The Group has launched a Reward Program to its customers, which provides customers the option of electing to receive free telecommunications services or other gifts. The level of point reward earned by customers under the Reward Program varies depending on the customers' services consumption, years in services and payment history.

In prior years, the Group accounted for the obligation to provide free or discounted services or goods offered to the customers under the Reward Program using the incremental costs method. The estimated incremental cost to provide free or discounted services or goods was recognized as expenses and accrued as a current liability when customers were entitled to bonus points. When customers redeemed awards or their entitlements expired, the incremental cost liability was reduced accordingly to reflect the outstanding obligations.

With effect from 1 January 2009, as a result of adoption of IFRIC/HK(IFRIC) Interpretation 13, the point reward is accounted for as a separately identifiable component of the sales transactions in which the points are granted. The consideration received in relation to the sales transactions is allocated to points reward by reference to the estimated fair value of the points as revenue and is deferred until such reward is redeemed by the customers or the points expired.

The new accounting policy has been adopted retrospectively and the comparative amounts have been restated.

The effect on the consolidated balance sheet as at 1 January 2008 is an increase in deferred tax assets, an increase in deferred revenue, a decrease in accrued expenses and other payables and a decrease in net assets of RMB676,000,000, RMB6,308,000,000, RMB3,542,000,000 and RMB2,090,000,000, respectively.

The effect on the consolidated balance sheet as at 31 December 2008 is an increase in deferred tax assets, an increase in deferred revenue, a decrease in accrued expenses and other payables and a decrease in net assets of RMB730,000,000, RMB6,841,000,000, RMB3,855,000,000 and RMB2,256,000,000, respectively.

The effect on the Group's consolidated statement of comprehensive income for the year ended 31 December 2008 is an decrease in operating revenue, operating expenses, taxation and profit for the year of RMB533,000,000, RMB313,000,000, RMB54,000,000 and RMB166,000,000, respectively. The effect on the basic earnings per share and diluted earnings per share for the year ended 31 December 2008 is a decrease of RMB0.01 and RMB0.01, respectively.

The effect on the consolidated balance sheet as at 31 December 2009 is a decrease in deferred tax assets, a decrease in deferred revenue, an increase in accrued expenses and other payables and an increase in net assets of RMB724,000,000, RMB6,095,000,000, RMB3,146,000,000 and RMB2,225,000,000, respectively, had the previous accounting policy still been applied in the current year.

The effect on the Group's consolidated statement of comprehensive income for the year ended 31 December 2009 is a decrease in operating revenue, operating expenses, taxation and profit for the year of RMB746,000,000, RMB709,000,000, RMB6,000,000 and RMB31,000,000, respectively. The effect on the basic earnings per share and diluted earnings per share for year ended 31 December 2009 is a decrease of RMB0.002 and RMB0.002, respectively, had the previous accounting policy still been applied in the current year.

3.44   IAS 8 sets out the rules for accounting for changes in accounting policy, but makes a specific exception for a change in policy to measure property, plant and equipment or intangible assets at a revalued amount for the first time. IAS 8 states that the initial adoption of a policy to carry assets at revalued amounts in accordance with IAS 16 or IAS 38 is a change in accounting policy. However, such a change should be treated as a revaluation in accordance with IAS 16 or IAS 38, rather than in accordance with IAS 8. Therefore, the change is not accounted for retrospectively by restating comparatives. [IAS 8 paras 17, 18]. This means that the change in policy is accounted for as a revaluation in the year, rather than by means of a prior year adjustment.

UK.3.44.1   In the UK, restatement of the financial statements for prior years does not mean that the actual financial statements that were issued, approved and filed for those prior financial years have to be withdrawn and amended. The withdrawal of financial statements is governed by The Companies

(Revision of Defective Accounts and Reports) Regulations 2008. See paragraph UK.3.89.2.

3.45 A restatement of the financial statements for prior years by means of a prior year adjustment does not necessarily mean that the actual financial statements that were approved and issued for those prior financial years have to be withdrawn and amended.

Accounting for tax effects of a prior year adjustment

3.46 As seen in the example in Table 3.2, where a change in accounting policy requires adjustment of prior year amounts, the taxation effects of the change in accounting policy are treated as part of the prior year adjustment. Depending on the tax requirements in each territory, these may affect current or deferred taxes and may warrant resubmission of prior year tax returns.

3.47 Paragraph 22 of IAS 8 states that, where a change in accounting policy is applied retrospectively, an entity adjusts the opening balance of each affected component of equity for the earliest prior period presented and the other comparative amounts are disclosed as if the new accounting policy had always been applied. This adjustment consists of the direct effects of the change and the related income tax effect. Therefore, the tax effect of a change in accounting policy is part of the adjustment to opening retained earnings and should not be included as a component of the current period's tax expense.

3.48 For example, assume that an entity has a change in accounting policy that results in an increase in prior year income. Such a change may also have resulted in a change in the amount of taxable temporary differences as at the prior year balance sheet date, resulting in a change in the deferred tax balance. The change in deferred tax balances will be reflected as part of the prior year adjustment.

3.49 The IASB's 'Guidance on implementing IAS 8' contains an example of a change of policy that is applied retrospectively and shows the tax effects included in the prior year adjustment.

Changes to prior period adjustments recognised in interims

3.50 In a situation where an entity issues financial reports for an interim period in which a change in accounting policy has occurred, IAS 34 requires the comparative figures included in the interim financial report to be restated (see further Manual of Accounting – Interim financial reporting). [IAS 34 para 43].

3.51 Paragraph 28 of IAS 34 states that the frequency of an entity's reporting (annual, half-yearly, or quarterly) should not affect the measurement of its annual results. However, regardless of whether recognised at the interim or at the year end, the adjustments to the prior period comparatives are made with reference to the information available at the end of the relevant period, irrespective of any subsequent change in knowledge, events or availability of information. This is in line with paragraph 53 of IAS 8, which does not permit the use of hindsight when applying a new accounting policy.

> **Example – Subsequent adjustment of deferred tax asset recognised in a prior period adjustment**
>
> A company has changed its accounting policy for revenue recognition since the publication of its annual financial statements. The change in policy was accounted for in the entity's half-year interim financial statements, by means of a prior period adjustment. As stated in paragraph 3.46 above, when a prior period adjustment is recognised for a change in accounting policy, any tax impact should also be recognised. In this example, profits that were recognised under the old accounting policy but not the new one had already been taxed and as a result a deferred tax asset was created and recognised as part of the prior year adjustment as it was considered recoverable at the prior year balance sheet date.
>
> In the second half of the current year, management's assessment of forecast profits was reduced such that the recoverability of the deferred tax asset is no longer fully supportable. Therefore, in the annual financial statements, the deferred tax asset should be reduced. The write off of the deferred tax asset is treated as an expense in the second half of the current year and is recognised in the income statement as opposed to recognising it as part of the prior year restatement. If the write-off in the annual financial statements is significant, disclosure of the adjustment would be required in accordance with paragraph 26 of IAS 34 (see further Manual of Accounting – Interim financial reporting).

Changes in accounting estimates

3.52 Owing to the inherent uncertainties in business activity, preparing financial statements is not an exact science and involves making numerous estimates. Estimates involve judgements based on the latest available, reliable information. They are applied, for example, in determining an allowance for doubtful debts, provisions for slow-moving or obsolete inventory, the useful lives of property, plant and equipment and intangible assets, fair values of financial assets and financial liabilities, recoverability of deferred tax assets, actuarial assumptions relating to defined benefit pension schemes, warranty provisions, impairment provisions and so on. [IAS 8 para 32].

3.53 The use of reasonable estimates is an essential part of the preparation of financial statements and does not undermine their reliability. [IAS 8 para 33]. However, the degree of reliability of estimates can vary according to the nature of the item to which the estimate is applied or market conditions. For example, estimates of the useful lives of property, plant and equipment tend to change infrequently. On the other hand estimates of the expected rate of return on assets in a defined benefit pension scheme may change each year, or more frequently if applicable (for instance, in interim financial reports), particularly where markets are volatile. Additionally, some types of estimates have greater effect than others on financial statements.

3.53.1 In general, the same estimation techniques should be applied in preparing the interim financial report as are applied in preparing the annual financial statements. However, appendix C to IAS 34 (which accompanies, but is not part of the standard) notes some examples of situations where less rigorous estimates may be used at the interim date than would be required at the year end: these are covered in the Manual of Accounting – Interim financial reporting.

3.54 Because of the importance of estimates and judgements in the preparation of financial statements, IAS 1 requires disclosure in annual financial statements of key assumptions concerning the future and other key sources of estimation uncertainty at the balance sheet date that carry significant risk of causing a material adjustment to the carrying amount of assets and liabilities within the next financial year. In respect of the assets and liabilities concerned, entities are required to disclose their nature and carrying amounts at the balance sheet date. IAS 1 also requires disclosure of the judgements that management has made in applying the accounting policies with the most significant effect on the amounts recognised in the financial statements. [IAS 1 paras 122, 125]. Further details of these requirements are given in chapter 4.

3.55 Accounting estimates should be distinguished from accounting policies, because the effect of a change in an estimate is reflected in the current and sometimes future periods' statement of comprehensive income, whereas a change in accounting policy generally requires adjustment of previously reported amounts. Accounting policies are defined as: *"The specific principles, bases, conventions, rules and practices applied by an entity in preparing and presenting financial statements"*. [IAS 8 para 5].

3.56 Accounting estimates are not specifically defined in IAS 8, although a change in accounting estimates is defined as: *"... an adjustment of the carrying amount of an asset or a liability, or the amount of the periodic consumption of an asset, that results from the assessment of the present status of, and expected future benefits and obligations associated with, assets and liabilities. Changes in accounting estimates result from new information or new developments and, accordingly, are not corrections of errors"*. [IAS 8 para 5].

3.57 IAS 8 notes that sometimes it is difficult to distinguish a change in an accounting estimate from a change in accounting policy. In such cases, the change is treated as a change in an accounting estimate. The standard notes, particularly, that a change in the measurement basis, for example a change from carrying assets at historical cost to carrying them at fair value, is a change in accounting policy, not a change in an accounting estimate (see further para 3.44 for the accounting treatment for such change). [IAS 8 para 35]. In addition, the property, plant and equipment standard notes that a change in depreciation method is a change in estimate and not a change in accounting policy. [IAS 16 para 61].

3.58 Changes in accounting estimates may occur as a result of changes in the circumstances on which the estimate was based or because of new information, more experience or subsequent developments. Changes in accounting estimates do not, by their nature, relate to prior periods and are not the corrections of errors. [IAS 8 para 34].

3.59 The standard requires, except to the extent referred to in the following paragraph, the effect of a change in an accounting estimate to be recognised prospectively (that is, from the date of change) by including it in profit or loss in:

- the period of the change, if the change affects that period only; or
- the period of the change and future periods, if the change affects both.

[IAS 8 paras 36, 38].

3.60 In some circumstances, changes in estimate may impact both assets and liabilities, or relate to an equity item rather than impacting profit or loss. In such circumstances, the change is recognised by adjusting the carrying amount of the related assets and liabilities or the item of equity in the period of the change. [IAS 8 para 37]. Where the corresponding adjustments to an asset, a liability or an item of equity are not equal, the difference would generally be adjusted to profit or loss.

3.61 The effect of the interrelation of the rules in the two paragraphs above may be illustrated as follows. An entity may have estimated the amount of a liability that was covered by insurance at C1 million, but subsequently revises that estimate to C1.5 million. Initially it may have set up a liability for C1 million and an asset for the reimbursement right of C1 million. When it revises the estimate of the liability it increases it to C1.5 million, but if the insurance recovery is capped at C1.25 million the entity only increases the reimbursement right asset to C1.25 million. The increase in the estimate of the liability to C1.25 million gives rise to a corresponding increase in the estimate of the reimbursement right (debit reimbursement right 0.25m, credit liability 0.25m). The remaining increase in the liability (0.25m) is charged to the income statement.

3.62 An example of a change in estimate that affects a liability and an item of equity would be a revision of an estimate of tax payable on foreign exchange differences recognised in other comprehensive income, with a corresponding adjustment to the tax liability. An example that affects only an asset and equity would be revision to the estimate of the fair value of an asset (for example, an item of property, plant and equipment) when the revaluation surpluses in respect of such assets are required to be recognised in other comprehensive income.

3.63 An example of a change in accounting estimate that would affect the current period profit and loss and that would not affect future periods' profit and loss is a change in the allowance for doubtful debts. On the other hand, a change in the estimate of the useful life of an item of property, plant and equipment would affect both the current and future periods, because the depreciation charge is affected for both current and future periods until the end of the useful life. [IAS 8 para 38].

3.64 The effect of a change in accounting estimate reflected in the income statement should be included under the same line item in the income statement as was used previously for the estimate (see the example below). This ensures that the financial statements remain comparable from one period to the next.

Example – Subsequent recoverability of a bad debt

In 20X1, an entity recognised an allowance for impairment of a trade receivable from a customer who was in financial difficulties. The customer's financial position improved following a restructuring and in 20X3 the receivable was paid. The entity had recognised the impairment allowance in 20X1 within selling expenses in its income statement.

The entity should recognise the reversal of the impairment allowance against selling expenses. The reversal of the allowance should be included in the line in the income statement against which the original allowance was charged.

Recognising the effect of a change in an accounting estimate may have a material effect on the entity's income statement, in which case paragraph 97 of IAS 1 requires its nature and amount to be disclosed separately either on the face of the income statement or in the notes, to explain the entity's performance for the period.

In addition, for changes in accounting estimates, IAS 8 requires disclosure (unless it is impracticable) of the nature and amount of the change that affects the current period or that is expected to have an effect in future periods – see paragraph 3.122. [IAS 8 paras 39, 40].

3.65 Examples of revisions of estimates are given in Tables 3.3 and 3.4 below.

Table 3.3 – Change in accounting estimates (extract)

Magyar Telekom Telecommunications Plc – Annual report – 31 December 2008

12. Property, plant and equipment (extract)
The reviews of the useful lives of property, plant and equipment during 2008 affected the lives of a large number of assets including primarily the telecommunications equipment of both the fixed line and mobile operations. The revision results in the following change in the original trend of depreciation.

In HUF millions	2008	2009	2010	2011	After 2011
Increase/(decrease) in depreciation	(7,147)	(7,771)	(2,048)	1,374	15,592

> **Table 3.4 – Change of estimate of residual values of aircraft**
>
> **TUI Travel Plc – Annual report – 30 September 2008**
>
> **10. Property, plant and equipment (extract)**
>
> **Changes in estimates**
>
> During the year ended 30 September 2008, the Group reviewed the residual value of its remaining owned aircraft and the estimated useful economic lives of these aircraft. As a result the expected residual values of certain assets have been revised downwards. The effect of these changes on depreciation expense, recognised in cost of sales, in the year and in future years is an increase in the annual charge of £5.2m.

Errors

3.66   Errors may occur in the recognition, measurement, presentation or disclosure of elements of financial statements. IAS 8 states that financial statements do not comply with IFRS if they contain *material* errors. Nor do they comply if they contain immaterial errors that have been made intentionally to achieve a particular presentation of an entity's financial position, financial performance or cash flows. [IAS 8 para 41]. Generally, IAS 8 requires that adjustments to correct material errors are made retrospectively by amending comparatives and restating retained earnings at the beginning of the earliest period presented (see further para 3.80 onwards).

UK.3.66.1   Note that IAS 8 requires that *material* prior period errors should be corrected by restating prior period amounts. This is much broader than the UK GAAP rule in FRS 3, under which only 'fundamental' errors are corrected by means of a prior year adjustment.

Determining materiality

3.67   The term 'material' is defined in the standard and is discussed from paragraph 3.11 above. As noted in that discussion, to the extent that intentional errors are made in order to *"influence the economic decisions that users make on the basis of the financial statements"*, they would be material.

3.68   Generally, where a prior period error impacts any component of the financial statement being presented, the reporting entity evaluates whether the error is material and warrants adjusting the financial statements retrospectively. Materiality should not be assessed solely against a single measure such as the profit for the year or retained earnings, but rather against the financial statements as a whole. The error should be corrected, in accordance with paragraph 42 of IAS 8 (see para 3.80) by retrospectively adjusting the prior period financial statements. This is achieved by adjusting the comparative information for the periods affected that are included in the current period's financial statements. A restatement of the comparatives for prior years does not necessarily mean that the actual financial statements that were approved and issued for those prior financial years have to be withdrawn and amended. Management also needs to be aware of any specific regulatory requirements. For instance, SEC registrants reporting under IFRS also need to be aware of the requirements of SAB 108 (see below).

3.69 In September 2006, guidance was issued in the US by the SEC in respect of the correction of accounting errors. Staff Accounting Bulletin 108 ('SAB 108'), 'Considering the effects of prior year misstatements when quantifying misstatements in current year financial statements', requires the quantification of financial statement errors under US GAAP based on the effect of applying both the iron-curtain and the roll-over methods (see para 3.70 below) on each of the entity's primary statements (and related disclosures). This is referred to as the 'dual approach'. Prior to the introduction of SAB 108, entities applying US GAAP had the choice of adopting either the 'iron-curtain' or the 'roll-over' method.

3.70 The iron-curtain method quantifies an error as the amount by which the balance sheet is misstated and so focuses on the effect of correcting the period-end balance sheet, with less emphasis on the effects of reversing prior year errors on the income statement. The roll-over method quantifies an error as the amount by which the income statement is misstated and so focuses on the impact of a misstatement on the current year income statement, which can lead to the accumulation of misstatements in the balance sheet.

3.71 SAB 108 is not mandatory for financial statements prepared in accordance with IFRS. However, the SEC staff has made it clear that it does not expect differences between US GAAP and IFRS to arise as a result of SAB 108 and, accordingly, SEC registrants are encouraged to apply SAB 108 to assess the impact of misstatement reporting under IFRSs. The dual approach in SAB 108 is considered an acceptable approach for determining whether an error is material under IFRS.

[The next paragraph is 3.73.]

Identifying prior period errors

3.73 From time to time, material errors are discovered that relate to one or more prior periods for which financial statements have already been issued. If this happens, such material errors are corrected by adjusting the comparative information for the periods affected that are included in the current period's financial statements. [IAS 8 para 41].

3.74 'Prior period errors' are defined in IAS 8 as:

"… omissions from, and misstatements in, the entity's financial statements for one or more prior periods arising from a failure to use, or misuse of, reliable information that:

(a)   was available when financial statements for those periods were authorised for issue; and

(b) could reasonably be expected to have been obtained and taken into account in the preparation and presentation of those financial statements.

Such errors include the effects of mathematical mistakes, mistakes in applying accounting policies, oversights or misinterpretations of facts, and fraud."

[IAS 8 para 5].

3.75   As noted in the definition, determining whether or not there has been an error in a prior period requires that reliable information was available or could have reasonably been obtained at the time when the error was made. The term 'reliability' has been replaced in the Framework by the term 'faithfully represents' and this is one of the fundamental qualitative characteristics of financial statements that is discussed in the Framework. As noted in paragraph 3.5 above, reference is made, under the heading of 'faithful representation' to 'complete, neutral and free from error'. [Framework paras QC12 to QC16]. In respect of the latter, the Framework states that:

"Faithful representation does not mean accurate in all respects. Free from error means there are no errors or omissions in the description of the phenomenon, and the process used to produce the reported information has been selected and applied with no errors in the process. In this context, free from error does not mean perfectly accurate in all respects. For example, an estimate of an unobservable price or value cannot be determined to be accurate or inaccurate. However, a representation of that estimate can be faithful if the amount is described clearly and accurately as being an estimate, the nature and limitations of the estimating process are explained, and no errors have been made in selecting and applying an appropriate process for developing the estimate."

[Framework para QC15].

(As noted in para 3.9, although the Framework has replaced 'reliability' with 'faithful representation', IAS 8 has not yet been amended to reflect this.)

3.76   In most straightforward situations, reliable information will have been available *"when financial statements for those periods were authorised for issue"*. For example, where an error involves the under-accrual of a significant item of expense, evidence in the form of an invoice or creditor's statement may have been available, but was overlooked.

3.77   In other less straightforward situations, such as deliberate manipulation of results or fraud, it may be more difficult to establish whether reliable information existed at the time when the financial statements were issued, particularly where management was involved in carrying out the manipulation or fraud. The reason why such situations cause difficulty is because there may have been deliberate suppression or destruction of reliable information or false and unreliable information may have been created in order to conceal or justify the incorrect accounting.

UK.3.77.1 In the UK, when fraud is discovered auditors sometimes add a statement in their report that a company has failed to keep proper accounting records. Such failure to keep proper accounting records by definition implies an absence of reliable information.

3.78 Correction of prior period errors is sometimes only possible by using reliable information that emerges in subsequent periods and by reconstructing accounting records for the period concerned. For example, a fraud may be discovered after the issuance of two years of financial statements containing errors arising from the fraud. Management may have been involved and may have deliberately destroyed or falsified accounting records to cover up the fraud. Subsequently, it may be possible to reconstruct the records from information provided by management and by other sources such as suppliers and debtors.

3.78.1 The question is whether the above definition of prior period errors allows such an approach, using information that comes to light after the financial statements have been issued. We believe that it should.

3.79 We consider that even where a fraud has been perpetrated in a prior year by senior management and information has been suppressed or falsified such that proper accounting records were not kept, the error would usually still qualify as a prior period error under the definition above. This would be so even if the effect of the error cannot be quantified except by using relevant information that emerges in a future year (such as the fact that the fraud took place and details of what falsifications were perpetrated) and by reconstructing in that future year the accounting records relating to the earlier period. This is because, in many situations, reliable information will have existed in the prior year and a reasonable person, not involved in making the error, would have obtained and used that information (or if it was already available, would not have suppressed or destroyed it).

Correction of prior period errors

3.80 Except where it is impracticable (see para 3.83), a material prior period error should be corrected by retrospective restatement in the first financial statements issued following the discovery of the error. Retrospective restatement is defined as "... *correcting the recognition, measurement and disclosure of amounts of elements of financial statements as if a prior period error had never occurred*". Such restatement is achieved by:

- restating comparative amounts for the prior periods presented in which the error occurred; or

- if the error occurred before the earliest prior period presented in the financial statements, restating the opening balances of assets, liabilities and equity for the earliest prior period presented.

[IAS 8 paras 5, 42].

3.81 The restatement of financial statements for a material prior period error is treated in a manner similar to a change in accounting policy. The nature of the error should be disclosed as set out in paragraph 3.124 onwards (examples of disclosure are given in Tables 3.9 and 3.10 below). In addition, the presentation of an additional balance sheet as at the start of the preceding period is generally required (refer to paras 3.125 and 3.125.1).

3.82 The presentation in the statement of changes in equity of a prior period adjustment for a material error is considered further in chapter 4.

3.83 To the extent that it is impracticable to determine either the period-specific effects or the cumulative effects of a prior period error, retrospective restatement is not required. [IAS 8 para 43]. This might apply, for example, if records necessary to quantify the effect of the error have not been retained and cannot be recreated.

3.84 Where it is impracticable to determine the period-specific effects of an error on comparative information for one or more prior periods presented in the financial statements the entity should restate the opening balances of assets, liabilities and equity for the earliest period for which retrospective restatement is possible. This could, in an extreme case, be the current period if the period-specific effect cannot be determined for earlier periods. [IAS 8 para 44]. The effect on the financial statements where it is impracticable to determine the period-specific effects of a prior period error is treated in a manner similar to a change in accounting policy. This is illustrated in the example in paragraph 3.98 below.

3.85 Where it is impracticable to determine the cumulative effect of an error, as at the beginning of the current accounting period presented, an entity should adjust the comparative information to correct the error prospectively from the earliest practicable date. It, therefore, disregards the portion of the cumulative restatement of assets, liabilities and equity arising before that date. [IAS 8 paras 45, 47]. The effect on the financial statements where it is impracticable to determine the cumulative effects of a prior period error on all periods presented is treated in a manner similar to a change in accounting policy. This is illustrated in the example in paragraph 3.98 below.

3.86 The correction of a prior period error is excluded from the income statement for the period in which the error is discovered. [IAS 8 para 46]. However, if there is a correction, to the extent that the amount attributable to a prior period cannot be determined, it is included in the current period income statement (because, for example, it might just as easily relate to the current period). This means that assets, liabilities and equity for prior periods may be partially adjusted as indicated by paragraph 47 of IAS 8, but will be fully adjusted and corrected by the end of the current period.

3.87 Information presented in the form of an historical summary should also be adjusted by restatement from the earliest date practicable. [IAS 8 para 46].

3.88 The above paragraphs explain what entities should do when it is impracticable to restate retrospectively for the correction of a prior period error. They do not explain how to decide whether or not it is actually impracticable. The standard gives additional guidance on this and the guidance is discussed further from paragraph 3.98.

3.89 The correction of errors should be distinguished from changes in accounting estimates. As previously noted, accounting estimates are, by their nature, approximations that may need to be revised when additional information becomes available. They are necessary because of the inherent uncertainty over the monetary amounts to be attributed to items when applying an entity's accounting policies. As such they represent the result of management's best judgement under the prevailing circumstances and with the latest information. Errors, on the other hand, result from the deliberate or accidental misuse of or disregard for information that is available or that should be available. An example of an estimate given in the standard is a gain or loss recognised on the outcome of a contingency that could not previously be estimated reliably. Such a gain or loss does not constitute the correction of an error. [IAS 8 para 48].

UK.3.89.1 In the UK, restatement of the financial statements for prior years does not necessarily mean that the actual financial statements that were issued, approved and filed for those prior financial years have to be withdrawn and amended.

UK.3.89.2 In the UK there are provisions in the Companies Act 2006 that permit directors to voluntarily revise financial statements that have been laid before members and filed. The rules are set out in The Companies (Revision of Defective Accounts and Reports) Regulations 2008 (SI 2008/373). However, if errors have been corrected by way of a prior year adjustment in the latest financial statements, earlier years' financial statements are normally not revised. Paradoxically, if such earlier years' financial statements were revised under the provision of the 2006 Act, the revised financial statements would become the statutory financial statements for the year or years in question. It would then not be necessary to have a prior year adjustment for a material prior period error in the current year's financial statements, as the comparatives would have been amended to accord with the revised figures for that year filed at Companies House in accordance with the Act. See chapter 3 of the Manual of Accounting – Other statutory requirements for further guidance on revising financial statements.

3.90 Disclosure requirements in respect of prior year adjustments for material prior period errors are addressed in paragraph 3.124.

IFRS IC agenda decisions

3.91 The IFRS IC reviews newly-identified financial reporting issues not specifically addressed in IFRSs or issues where unsatisfactory or conflicting interpretations have developed, or seem likely to develop in the absence of authoritative guidance, with a view to reaching a consensus on the appropriate treatment. When issues are submitted for consideration, the IFRS IC decides whether to add the issue to its agenda. In some instances, the IFRS IC may decline to add an issue to its agenda. The reasons for this could be:

- The matter is the subject of a proposed standard (or proposed changes to an existing standard), so it is more efficient for the IASB to deal with the issue in the changes to the standard.

- The subject is so complex that IFRS IC cannot address it in a reasonable period of time.

- The standard seems clear so there should be little or no diversity in practice.

3.92 The reasons for not adding an item to the IFRS IC agenda are published on the IASB's web site as a record of decisions taken. That record does not form part of IFRSs. However, where the IFRS IC have considered a possible agenda item, but the record of the decision indicates that they feel that the treatment required by the standard is clear, the publication of the decision can have implications for entities that have previously applied a different interpretation in their accounting treatment.

3.93 As IFRS IC rejection decisions do not form part of IFRS, there has been debate in the accounting profession as to whether the third category in paragraph 3.91 above should be considered to require a change in accounting treatment to conform with the spirit of the rejection and, if so, whether the change should be regarded as a change in accounting policy or the correction of an error. While the accounting for restatement due to changes in accounting policy and changes in respect of errors is the same under IAS 8, there could be differing consequences depending on the regulatory environment and so companies need to give careful consideration to how the changes are described.

3.94 If the IFRS IC has considered whether a particular issue should be added to its agenda, this indicates that there has been some variety as to the appropriate accounting treatment. Therefore, subject to the specific facts, a working assumption might be that an accounting policy applied in the previous financial statements, prior to an IFRS IC rejection note, was based on a reasonable interpretation of the relevant standard at the time the accounting policy was selected, considering the available IFRS guidance at that time.

3.95 As IFRS IC rejection notes often provide clarification of the standards, there is an expectation on the part of stakeholders in IFRS that IFRS IC rejection notes will be carefully considered by preparers in determining their accounting policies. In the case of a change in a previous accounting treatment following the issue of an IFRS IC rejection note, a company should apply IAS 8 and provide proper and sufficient disclosure of the reasons for the change, having regard to the particular facts and circumstances of the individual case. Where it is not immediately clear whether the change resulting from the IFRS IC rejection is a change in accounting policy or the correction of an error, it may be acceptable, at least for a reasonable period following the publication of the IFRS IC rejection note, not to be explicit in distinguishing between a change in accounting policy and the correction of an error in the disclosure. Appropriate disclosure of the facts should be given (including reference to the IFRS IC rejection note). Wording on the change in accounting treatment could be along the following lines:

> *"The group previously accounted for [explanation of previous accounting practice]. Following the IFRS IC agenda decision on [subject matter] in [date], the group has reconsidered its accounting treatment. The group has adopted the treatment set out in the IFRS IC agenda decision [description of the new treatment]. This change in accounting treatment has been accounted for retrospectively and comparative information has been restated. [Disclose details of the effect.]".*

3.96 Consideration needs to be given to regulators' views. In particular, describing the restatement as a 'change in accounting treatment' may be viewed as unclear and regulators might insist (and auditing standards in some territories might require) that a restatement be described as either a change of accounting policy or correction of an error. In such cases, judgement will be needed to determine the nature of the change. In our view, for example, it would generally be appropriate to refer to a change in accounting policy when the prior treatment was widespread (for example, within a particular country or industry).

[The next paragraph is 3.98.]

Impracticability of retrospective application or restatement and application of hindsight

3.98 As noted previously, in certain limited circumstances, full retrospective application or restatement may not be practicable. To the extent that it is impracticable to determine either the period-specific effects for any reported period or the cumulative effects of changing an accounting policy or the correction of material prior period errors, full retrospective application of the new policy or correction of the prior period error is not required.

3.99 'Impracticable' is defined in IAS 8 in the following terms:

"Applying a requirement is impracticable when the entity cannot apply it after making every reasonable effort to do so. For a particular prior period, it is impracticable to apply a change in an accounting policy retrospectively or to make a retrospective restatement to correct an error if:

(a)   the effects of the retrospective application or retrospective restatement are not determinable;

(b)   the retrospective application or retrospective restatement requires assumptions about what management's intent would have been in that period; or

(c)   the retrospective application or retrospective restatement requires significant estimates of amounts and it is impossible to distinguish objectively information about those estimates that:

i.   provides evidence of circumstances that existed on the date(s) as at which those amounts are to be recognised, measured or disclosed; and

ii.   would have been available when the financial statements for that prior period were authorised for issue from other information"

[IAS 8 paras 5, 52].

3.100   The standard notes that one circumstance that might give rise to impracticability is where data may not have been collected in the prior period in a way that enables retrospective application of a new accounting policy or retrospective restatement of a prior period error and where it may not be practicable to create, or recreate, the information. [IAS 8 para 50].

3.101   Significant estimates are often required when adjusting comparative information for prior periods. This does not in itself prevent reliable adjustments or correction of the comparative amounts. [IAS 8 para 53]. When making estimates, the basis of the estimation should reflect the circumstances that existed in the prior period. However, with the passage of time, it becomes increasingly difficult to define those circumstances. In addition, with the passage of time, the estimates are increasingly likely to be unduly influenced by knowledge of events and circumstances that have arisen since that prior period. However, the basis of making estimates related to prior periods remains the same as for that for the current period, that is, the estimates reflect the circumstances that existed when the transaction, other event or condition occurred. [IAS 8 para 51].

3.102   The definition of 'impracticable' reproduced above requires information to (i) have been available at the time of issue of the prior period's financial statements and (ii) that gives evidence of circumstances that existed at the time when the transaction, other event or condition existed. Such information should be capable of being distinguished from other information, such as information that only became available after the financial statements for that period had been issued. The standard notes that, for some types of estimates, such as an estimate of a fair value measurement that is not based on an observable price or observable inputs (or, for entities applying IFRS 13, that uses significant unobservable inputs), it is not possible to distinguish these different sorts of information. This is presumably because such valuations would be highly subjective and it would be impossible to reliably recreate the subjective considerations that would have been taken into account when making the original estimate in the earlier period. Where it is not practicable to distinguish the type of information that was available and needed to recreate the circumstances in the earlier period from other information, retrospective application or restatement is not practicable. [IAS 8 para 52].

3.103   Use of hindsight is not permitted when applying a new accounting policy or correcting prior period errors, either to second guess management's intentions in the earlier period or in estimating amounts recognised, measured or disclosed in the prior period. The standard gives as an example of the former restriction, a correction of an error in the measurement of held to maturity investments and points out that a decision by management in a subsequent period not to hold the investments to maturity should not be taken into account in making the correction. Similarly, it gives as an example the correction of a prior period error in calculating an employee healthcare liability and points out that information about an unusually severe influenza epidemic in a later period should not be taken into account in making the correction to the earlier period's financial statements. [IAS 8 para 53].

3.104   Where full retrospective application is impracticable, an entity would account for the retrospective application or restatement in one of two ways described below, depending on whether it is impracticable to determine the period-specific effects of the change (see para 3.105) or whether it is impracticable to determine the cumulative effect of the change (see para 3.108).

3.105   The first approach applies where it is impracticable to determine the period-specific effects of a change on comparative information for one or more periods presented in the financial statements. Where this is the case, the new policy is applied retrospectively from the beginning of the earliest reported period for which it is possible to do so – this may be one of the reported prior periods (if there is more than one) or the current period. [IAS 8 para 24].

3.106   The standard explains that retrospective application to a particular prior period is not practicable unless the entity can determine the cumulative effect on the amounts in both the opening and closing balance sheets for that period. This is simply because the effect on the prior period's income statement will normally be the difference between the cumulative effect at the end and the cumulative effect at the beginning of the period. If one of these is not known the effect on the income statement (and, therefore, the effect on opening or closing equity) of that prior period cannot be determined.

3.107   The example below, illustrates the accounting where it is impracticable to determine the period-specific effects of a change on comparative information for one or more periods presented in the financial statements.

Example – Impracticable to determine the period-specific effects of a change in accounting policy (or correction of a material prior period error)

An entity changes its accounting policy during 20X7. The change affects net assets and expenses in all periods presented and is assumed to be consistent with the requirements of paragraph 14 of IAS 8. The entity reports current period financial information and comparative information for two prior periods.

The entity's accounting records do not enable it to determine the adjustments for all the periods being reported. Instead, the entity can determine the increase in net assets at the beginning of the current period (and the end of the previous period) and at the beginning of the previous period, as follows:

	20X7 C'000	20X6 C'000	20X5 C'000	Pre-20X5 C'000
At 1 January	800	600		
Net adjustment for the year	400	200		
At 31 December	1,200	800	600	

Full retrospective application of the policy to all periods presented is impracticable, because the period-specific effect of the change in 20X5 is not known. In accordance with IAS 8, the new policy is applied as at the start of the earliest period for which retrospective application is possible, that is 1 January 20X6. The adjustments made in the financial statements for 31 December 20X7 for the change in accounting policy are as follows:

	20X7 C'000	20X6 C'000	20X5 C'000
Adjustment to opening net assets and opening equity	800	600	–
Adjustment to prior period income statement		(200)	–

3.108 Where it is impracticable to determine the cumulative effect of retrospective application or restatement to all prior periods, an entity should adjust the comparative information from the earliest practicable date. [IAS 8 para 25]. The standard explains that this means that the portion of the cumulative adjustment before that date is disregarded. An accounting policy may be changed even if it is impracticable to apply it retrospectively (that is, to adjust figures) for *any* prior period. [IAS 8 para 27]. It would, however, be rare that a company would voluntarily adopt an accounting policy that it could not apply retrospectively because the lack of comparability would make the information less relevant.

Disclosures

Changes in accounting policy

3.109   For changes in accounting policy on initial application of a standard or interpretation that has an effect on current or prior periods, or that may have an effect on future periods, the following information should be disclosed. Where it is impracticable to determine the effect on one or more prior periods and, thus, certain of the information cannot be disclosed, the relevant disclosures in the last bullet point below should also be given to explain why that other information is omitted.

- The title of the standard or interpretation.

- The nature of the change in policy.

- Where applicable, the fact that the policy has been changed in accordance with the transitional provisions of the standard or interpretation.

- A description of those transitional provisions, including, as applicable, those that have an effect on current and prior periods and those that will have an effect on future periods.

- The amount of the adjustments for the current period (see para 3.110.2 below) and for each prior period presented, to the extent that it is practicable. The adjustments to be disclosed are those for each financial statement line item that is affected and, if IAS 33 applies to the entity, the adjustments for basic and diluted earnings per share.

- For each component of equity, the effects of changes in accounting policies, disclosed for each prior period and the beginning of the period (required by IAS 1 paras 106(b), 110). This is discussed further in chapter 4.

- The amount of the adjustments relating to periods prior to the earliest period presented in the financial statements, to the extent practicable.

- If retrospective application is required by IAS 8, but has not been practicable for a prior period presented in the financial statements, or for earlier periods, details of the circumstances that gave rise to the impracticability and a description of how and from when the change in policy has been applied.

[IAS 8 para 28].

3.110   Prior to the improvement referred to in paragraph 3.110.1 below, where an entity has applied an accounting policy retrospectively, it presents an additional balance sheet and related notes as of the beginning of the earliest comparative period. [IAS 1 para 10(f)]. IAS 1 is currently silent on whether the additional balance sheet is required when the change in the accounting policy has no impact on that balance sheet. However, in our view, entities may choose to omit the additional balance sheet if there is no impact on that balance sheet and this fact is disclosed. See further chapter 4.

3.110.1 In 'Annual improvements to IFRSs' issued in May 2012, the IASB amended the requirements in IAS 1 relating to the additional balance sheet. Where an entity has applied an accounting policy retrospectively and this has a material effect on the information in the balance sheet at the beginning of the preceding period, it is required to present that balance sheet. However, under the amended standard, which applies for annual periods beginning on or after 1 January 2013, the entity need not present the related notes to the additional balance sheet. [IAS 1 paras 40A, 40C]. The amendment clarifies that the additional balance sheet is given as at the beginning of the preceding period regardless of whether an entity's financial statements present comparative information for earlier periods.

3.110.2 In May 2012, the IASB tentatively agreed to remove the requirement to disclose the current period effect of a new accounting policy when the change is a result of changes in IFRSs. This would differ from a voluntary change in accounting policy (see para 3.112 below) where the requirement to disclose the current period effect of the change would be retained. The IASB also tentatively agreed to decide on a case-by-case basis whether additional disclosures are needed when transitional provisions for a new or amended IFRS do not require retrospective application. The IASB is developing an exposure draft proposing amendments to IAS 8.

3.111 Examples of disclosure of a change in policy on initial application of a standard or interpretation are given in Table 3.2 (see para 3.43 above) and, with transitional provisions on initial application, in Table 3.7 below.

3.112 For voluntary changes in accounting policy that have an effect on current or prior periods, or that may have an effect on future periods, the following information should be disclosed. Where it is impracticable to determine the effect on one or more prior periods and, thus, certain of the information cannot be disclosed, the relevant disclosures in the last bullet point below should also be given to explain why that other information is omitted.

- The nature of the change in policy.

- The reason why the new policy gives information that is reliable and more relevant than that given by the previous policy.

- The amount of the adjustments for the current period and for each prior period presented, to the extent that it is practicable. The adjustments to be disclosed are those for each financial statement line item that is affected and, if IAS 33 applies to the entity, the adjustments for basic and diluted earnings per share.

- For each component of equity, the effects of changes in accounting policies, disclosed for each prior period and the beginning of the period (required by IAS 1 paras 106(b), 110). This is discussed further in chapter 4.

- The amount of the adjustments relating to periods prior to the earliest period presented in the financial statements, to the extent practicable.

- If retrospective application has not been practicable for a prior period presented in the financial statements, or for earlier periods, details of the circumstances that gave rise to the impracticability and a description of how and from when the change in policy has been applied.

[IAS 8 para 29].

In addition, where an entity has applied an accounting policy retrospectively, it presents an additional balance sheet (see paras 3.110 and 3.110.1 above). Prior to the improvement referred to in paragraph 3.110.1 applying, IAS 1 is silent on whether the additional balance sheet is required when the change in the accounting policy has no impact on that balance sheet. However, in our view, entities may choose to omit the additional balance sheet if there is no impact on that balance sheet and this fact is disclosed. See further chapter 4.

3.113   An example of a voluntary change in accounting policy is shown in Table 3.6.

Table 3.6 – Disclosure of voluntary change in accounting policy

Rockhopper Exploration plc – Annual report – 31 March 2010

1 ACCOUNTING POLICIES (extract)

1.4 CHANGE IN ACCOUNTING POLICY

(i) Oil and gas assets
In the year, the group has changed its oil and gas assets accounting policy from a full cost policy to a successful efforts policy. Under the full cost method, all expenditure incurred in connection with and directly attributable to oil and gas assets was capitalised. Under the successful efforts policy geological and geophysical costs are expensed immediately to the income statement, and the costs of unsuccessful prospects are expensed in the income statement in the period in which they are determined to be unsuccessful.

The group believes the successful efforts policy provides reliable and more relevant information.

In accordance with IAS8 (Accounting Policies, Changes in Accounting Estimates and Errors) the change has been made retrospectively and the comparatives have been restated accordingly.

The tables below show the impact of the change in accounting policy:

LOSS BEFORE INCOME TAXES	2010 $'000	2009 $'000
Loss before change in accounting policy	(7,052)	(4,450)
Exploration expenses written off	(644)	(692)
Loss after change in accounting policy	(7,696)	(5,142)
Loss per share: cents (basic and diluted)		
As reported before change in accounting policy	(6.10)	(5.58)
Adjustment due to change in accounting policy	(0.55)	(0.87)
Restated after change in accounting policy	(6.65)	(6.45)

ASSETS	2010	2009	2008
	$'000	$'000	$'000
Intangible exploration and evaluation assets before change in accounting policy	41,637	26,843	25,942
Adjustment due to change in accounting policy	(644)	(692)	(24,389)
Cumulative effect from prior years	(25,081)	(24,389)	–
	15,912	1,762	1,553

CONSOLIDATED SHAREHOLDERS EQUITY	2010	2009	2008
	$'000	$'000	$'000
Consolidated shareholders equity before change in accounting policy	105,273	32,195	28,461
Adjustment due to change in accounting policy	(644)	(692)	(24,389)
Cumulative effect from prior years	(25,081)	(24,389)	–
	79,548	7,114	4,072

GROUP STATEMENT OF CHANGES IN EQUITY (extract)
FOR THE YEAR ENDED 31 MARCH 2010

	Share capital	Share premium	Share based remuneration	Merger reserve	Foreign currency translation reserve	Retained losses restated*	Total equity restated*
	$'000	$'000	$'000	$'000	$'000	$'000	$'000
Balance at 1 April 2008	1,330	28,597	1,371	(243)	4,123	(6,717)	28,461
Effect of change in accounting policy*	–	–	–	–	–	(24,389)	(24,389)
Balance at 1 April 2008 (restated)	1,330	28,597	1,371	(243)	4,123	(31,106)	4,072
Total comprehensive income for the year						(5,142)	
Exercise of share options **						57	
[Other movements in the year not reproduced]							
Balance at 31 March 2009	1,420	36,210	1,795	(243)	4,123	(36,191)	7,114
Total comprehensive income for the year						(7,696)	
Exercise of share options **						360	
[Other movements in the year not reproduced]							
Balance at 31 March 2010	2,966	113,874	2,355	(243)	4,123	(43,527)	79,548

* See change in accounting policy note 1.4.

** Editorial note: The adjustment shown relates to a transfer from the share-based remuneration reserve. Other movements in the statement of changes in equity are not reproduced for the purpose of this example.

GROUP BALANCE SHEET AS AT 31 MARCH 20

	Notes	31 March 2010 $'000	31 March 2009 restated* $'000	31 March 2008 restated* $'000
ASSETS				
Intangible exploration and evaluation assets	10	15,912	1,762	1,553
Property, plant and equipment	11	48	20	6
Other receivables	12	170	54	35
Payments on account	13	14,049	–	–
Restricted cash	14	35,955	251	–
Cash and cash equivalents	15	14,485	6,136	3,525
TOTAL ASSETS		80,619	8,223	5,119
LIABILITIES				
Other payables	16	1,071	1,109	1,047
TOTAL LIABILITIES		1,071	1,109	1,047
EQUITY				
Share capital	17	2,966	1,420	1,330
Share premium	18	113,874	36,210	28,597
Share based remuneration	18	2,355	1,795	1,371
Merger reserve	18	(243)	(243)	(243)
Foreign currency translation reserve	18	4,123	4,123	4,123
Retained losses	18	(43,527)	(36,191)	(31,106)
ATTRIBUTABLE TO THE EQUITY SHAREHOLDERS OF THE COMPANY		79,548	7,114	4,072
TOTAL LIABILITIES AND EQUITY		80,619	8,223	5,119

* See change in accounting policy, note 1.4.

3.114 The standard does not require the disclosures in the above paragraphs 3.109 and 3.112 to be repeated in subsequent years' financial statements. [IAS 8 paras 28, 29].

3.115 An example of disclosure of a change in policy is given in Table 3.7 below. The company has adopted a number of standards and the disclosure includes setting out the treatment now adopted, which effectively discloses how the company has dealt with the transitional provisions of IAS 23 (applied from 1 January 2008 and, therefore, no effect on the balance sheet at the commencement of the earliest period presented) and of the other standards adopted where relevant. In this extract, a balance sheet at the start of the earliest period presented is disclosed in accordance with IAS 1 as the changes to presentation of derivatives and a change in accounting for revenue affect that statement (see paras 3.110 and 3.112 above).

Table 3.7 – Disclosure of transitional provisions on adopting a new standard

Centrica plc – Annual report – 31 December 2009

Group Balance Sheet

31 December	Notes	2009 £m	2008 (restated) (i),(ii),(iii) £m	2007 (restated) (ii),(iii) £m
Non-current assets				
Goodwill	15	**2,088**	1,510	1,074
Other intangible assets	16	**734**	671	465
Property, plant and equipment[(i)]	18	**6,059**	4,689	3,910
Interests in joint ventures and associates	19	**2,422**	330	285
Deferred tax assets	27	**534**	311	27
Trade and other receivables	21	**143**	34	33
Derivative financial instruments[(ii)]	22	**316**	869	496
Securities	29	**176**	35	39
Retirement benefit assets	36	**–**	73	152
		12,472	8,522	6,481
Current assets				
Inventories	20	**382**	412	241
Current tax assets	27	**69**	39	40
Trade and other receivables	21	**4,181**	5,335	3,423
Derivative financial instruments[(ii)]	22	**492**	1,156	592
Securities	29	**74**	63	50
Cash and cash equivalents	24	**1,294**	2,939	1,130
		6,492	9,944	5,476
Assets of disposal groups classified as held for sale	38	**478**	–	–
Total assets		**19,442**	18,466	11,957
Current liabilities				
Trade and other payables[(iii)]	25	**(3,955)**	(4,395)	(3,400)
Current tax liabilities		**(184)**	(357)	(274)
Bank overdrafts, loans and other borrowings	26	**(86)**	(330)	(221)
Derivative financial instruments[(ii)]	22	**(1,744)**	(2,670)	(694)
Provisions for other liabilities and charges	28	**(193)**	(29)	(140)
		(6,162)	(7,781)	(4,729)
Net current assets		**330**	2,163	747
Non-current liabilities				
Trade and other payables	25	**(82)**	(67)	(20)
Bank overdrafts, loans and other borrowings	26	**(4,594)**	(3,218)	(1,793)
Derivative financial instruments[(ii)]	22	**(1,006)**	(1,529)	(823)
Deferred tax liabilities	27	**(1,179)**	(448)	(596)
Retirement benefit obligations	36	**(565)**	(186)	(55)
Provisions for other liabilities and charges	28	**(1,249)**	(865)	(581)
		(8,675)	(6,313)	(3,868)
Liabilities of disposal groups classified as held for sale	38	**(350)**	–	–
Net assets		**4,255**	4,372	3,360

Accounting policies, accounting estimates and errors

(i) Restated to capitalise borrowing costs on adoption of IAS 23 (Amendment), as explained in note 2.

(ii) Restated to classify the non-current portions of derivative financial instruments from current assets and liabilities to non-current assets and liabilities, as explained in note 2.

(iii) Restated to reflect the change in British Gas Services Limited's revenue recognition policy, as explained in note 2.

31 December	Notes	2009 £m	2008 (restated) (i),(ii) £m	2007 (restated) (ii) £m
Equity				
Called up share capital	30	**317**	315	227
Share premium account		**778**	729	685
Retained earnings (i),(ii)		**3,103**	2,759	1,301
Accumulated other comprehensive (loss)/ income	31	**(587)**	(40)	546
Other equity	32	**581**	549	542
Total shareholders' equity		**4,192**	4,312	3,301
Minority interests in equity	33	**63**	60	59
Total minority interests and shareholders' equity		**4,255**	4,372	3,360

(i) Restated to capitalise borrowing costs on adoption of IAS 23 (Amendment), as explained in note 2.

(ii) Restated to reflect the change in British Gas Services Limited's revenue recognition policy, as explained in note 2.

Notes to the financial statements (extract)

2. Summary of significant accounting policies (extract 1)

(a) Standards, amendments and interpretations effective in 2009 (extract)

At the date of authorisation of these consolidated Financial Statements, the following standards and amendments to existing standards were effective for the current period:

- IAS 23 (Amendment), Borrowing Costs, effective from 1 January 2009. The Amendment requires an entity to capitalise borrowing costs directly attributable to the acquisition, construction or production of a qualifying asset (one that takes a substantial period of time to get ready for use or sale) as part of the cost of that asset. The option of immediately expensing such borrowing costs was removed. The Group adopted IAS 23 (Amendment) retrospectively and applied a commencement date of 1 January 2008 for qualifying projects. The adoption of IAS 23 (Amendment) has resulted in an increase to the closing net book value of property, plant and equipment and an increase to deferred tax liabilities at 31 December 2009 amounting to £43 million (2008: £9 million) and £10 million respectively, and a reduction to interest expense and increase to the tax charge for the period amounting to £34 million (2008: £9 million) and £10 million respectively. The impact on deferred tax liabilities and the related taxation charge in 2008 was not material. The resulting impact on both basic and diluted earnings per share for 2009 was an increase of 0.5p (2008: 0.2p).

- 'Improvements to IFRSs' contains amendments to various existing standards, most being effective from 1 January 2009. One of these improvements envisions that not all derivative financial instruments be classified as current. The Group has classified those derivatives held for the purpose of Energy Procurement and Treasury Management as current or non-current based on expected settlement dates. Where the derivative is held for proprietary energy trading, it remains classified as current. The Group adopted this improvement with effect from 1 January 2009, prior to which all derivatives held for trading under IAS 39 were classified as current irrespective of settlement date. This change in presentation has resulted in recognition of non-current derivative financial assets of £316 million, current derivative financial assets of £492 million, non-current derivative financial liabilities of £1,006 million and current derivative financial liabilities of £1,744 million at 31 December 2009. The impact on comparatives has been to report an increase in non-current derivative financial assets of £674 million (2007: £424 million), a decrease in current derivative financial assets of £564 million (2007: £322 million), an increase in non-current derivative financial liabilities of £1,372 million (2007: £812 million) and a decrease in current derivative financial liabilities of £1,262 million (2007: £710 million).

2. Summary of significant accounting policies (extract 2)

(e) British Gas Services Limited – revenue recognition

Within British Gas Services Limited (BGSL), included within the Downstream UK – Residential services segment, revenue on fixed fee service contracts has been recognised on a straight-line basis over the contract period. Annual contracts were divided into 12 equal amounts which were taken to income each month. The whole of the first month's income was recorded in the calendar month of the sale or renewal.

Standard insurance accounting practice is to recognise revenue with regard to the incidence of risk over the period of cover. If there is a marked unevenness in the incidence of risk over the period of cover, a basis which reflects the profile of risk should be used. Whilst BGSL is not an insurer, its products have some similarities to insurance products for accounting purposes and the Directors consider that the accounting recognition of income should be undertaken on a similar basis. This is consistent with the Group's strategy and the Group has announced plans to convert many of BGSL's products to insurance products over the next two years and to effect this plan has created British Gas Insurance Limited (BGIL) which in 2009 received regulatory approval from the Financial Services Authority to sell insurance products. While income in BGSL has been accrued on a straight-line basis, the workload undertaken under the contracts is significantly higher in the winter. BGSL has therefore moved to recognising revenue, still over the contract period, but in line with the workload and the risk under the contracts. In making the change the deferred income has been calculated with reference to the number of days remaining in the contract period to reflect the point at which contracts are entered into more precisely.

The impact of the new policy is to reduce revenue in 2009 by £2 million (2008: £2 million) and brought forward reserves by £30 million, with an offsetting £31 million credit to deferred income. A corporation tax adjustment has been applied as a result, with a total £9 million reduction in the tax creditor by way of a decreased 2008 tax charge of £1 million and an increase to the brought forward reserves of £8 million.

Interim reporting and prior year restatement

3.116 As discussed in paragraphs 3.110 and 3.112, where an entity applies an accounting policy retrospectively or makes a retrospective restatement or reclassification, IAS 1 requires the presentation of an additional balance sheet as at the beginning of the preceding period. Where an entity publishes full financial statements for the interim period that reflect such a retrospective change, this additional statement is required. However, where an entity publishes condensed interim financial statements, there is no requirement to present this additional balance sheet. [IAS 1 para BC33]. See further chapter 4.

New or revised accounting standards not yet effective

3.117 Where a new standard or interpretation has been published, but has not yet come into effect, IAS 8 requires entities that have not applied the standard or interpretation early to make certain disclosures. These are the fact that the standard or interpretation has not been applied and disclosure of information that is known or that can be reliably estimated and that is relevant to assessing the possible impact of the new standard or interpretation on the entity's financial statements in the period of initial application. [IAS 8 para 30].

3.118   In making the disclosures referred to above, an entity should consider disclosing:

- The title of the new standard or interpretation.

- The nature of the future change in policy or policies.

- The date by which the standard or interpretation should be applied.

- The date from which the entity intends to apply the standard or interpretation.

- A discussion of the impact that initial application is expected to have on the financial statements or, if the impact is not known or cannot be estimated on a reasonable basis (for example, if an analysis by management is still in progress), a statement of that fact.

[IAS 8 para 31].

3.119   In our view, entities should make these disclosures even if the new accounting pronouncement is issued after the balance sheet date, but before the date of authorisation of the financial statements.

3.120   Our view is that disclosure under IAS 8 is not necessary in respect of standards and interpretations that are clearly not applicable to the entity (for example, industry-specific standards) or that are not expected to have a material effect on the entity. Instead, disclosure should be given in respect of the developments that are, or could be, significant to the entity. Management will need to apply judgement in determining whether a standard is expected to have a material effect. The assessment of materiality should consider the impact both on previous transactions and financial position and on reasonably foreseeable future transactions. For pronouncements where there is an option that could have an impact on the entity, the management expectation on whether the entity will use the option should be disclosed. The aim of the disclosure is to enable the user to assess the possible impact of the new standard or interpretation on the entity's financial statements and not to provide a general update on accounting developments.

3.121   An example of disclosure is given in Table 3.8.

Table 3.8 – Disclosure of impact of future accounting standards

BT Group plc – Annual report – 31 March 2012

Notes to the consolidated financial statements (extract)

Accounting standards, interpretations and amendments not yet effective
Certain new standards, interpretations and amendments to existing standards have been published that are mandatory for the group's accounting periods beginning on 1 April 2013. Those which are considered to be relevant to the group's operations are set out below.

Amendments to IAS 19 'Employee Benefits'
These amendments are intended to provide a clearer indication of an entity's obligations resulting from the provision of defined benefit pension plans and how those obligations will affect its financial position, financial performance and cash flow. The amendments include:

- The removal of the options to defer recognition of actuarial gains and losses and for alternative presentation of gains and losses by requiring immediate recognition of actuarial gains or losses in full in other comprehensive income and the inclusion of service and finance costs and plan administration costs in the income statement;

- The replacement of the expected return on pension plan assets and interest expense on pension plan liabilities with a single net interest component calculated on the net defined benefit liability or asset using the discount rate used to determine the defined benefit obligation; and

- Additional disclosures to explain the characteristics of a company's defined benefit plans, the amounts recognised in the financial statements and the risks arising from defined benefit plans.

IAS 19 requires retrospective adoption and therefore prior periods will be restated. The group estimates the impact on 2012 had the amendments applied would have been to increase operating costs by approximately £30m and reduce the net finance income on pensions, reported as a specific item, by approximately £295m, with compensating adjustments in other comprehensive income leaving equity unchanged. The group will also be required to make additional narrative disclosures.

Other new standards and amendments
The impact of the following new standards, amendments and interpretations which are effective from 1 April 2013 is under review, but the group does not currently expect any of these changes to have a significant impact on the group's results or financial position.

- Amendments to IFRS 7 'Financial Instruments: Disclosures'

- IFRS 9 'Financial Instruments'

- IFRS 10 'Consolidated Financial Statements'

- IFRS 11 'Joint Arrangements'

- IFRS 12 'Disclosure of Interests in Other Entities'

- IFRS 13 'Fair Value Measurement'

- Amendment to IAS 1 'Presentation of Items of Other Comprehensive Income'

- Amendments to IAS 32 'Financial Instruments: Presentation' and

- Improvements to IFRS 2011.

3.121.1 In May 2012, the IASB discussed the requirement to disclose the possible impact of forthcoming IFRSs that are not yet effective and tentatively agreed to retain this. However, the IASB tentatively decided to modify IAS 8 to require this disclosure only for IFRSs that were issued by the end of the reporting period and is developing an exposure draft.

Changes in accounting estimates

3.122 For changes in accounting estimates, an entity should disclose the nature and amount of the change that affects the current period or that is expected to have an effect in future periods. The only exception is where it is impracticable to estimate the effect on future periods. Where the effect on future periods is not disclosed because it is impracticable, that fact should be disclosed. [IAS 8 paras 39, 40]. Examples of disclosure are given in Tables 3.3 and 3.4.

3.123 There is an additional disclosure in respect of changes in estimates in IAS 34. Under IAS 34, where an estimate of an amount reported in an interim period is changed significantly during the final interim period of the financial year, but a separate financial report is not published for that final interim period, the nature and amount of that change in estimate should be disclosed in a note to the annual financial statements for that financial year. [IAS 34 para 26].

Prior period errors

3.124 For prior period errors, the following information should be disclosed. Where it is impracticable to determine the effect on one or more prior periods and, thus, certain of the information cannot be disclosed, the relevant disclosures in the last bullet point below should also be given to explain why that other information is omitted.

- The nature of the prior period error.

- The amount of the corrections for each prior period presented, to the extent that it is practicable. The corrections to be disclosed are those for each financial statement line item that is affected and, if IAS 33 applies to the entity, the adjustments for basic and diluted earnings per share.

- For each component of equity, the effects of corrections of errors, disclosed for each prior period and the beginning of the period (required by IAS 1 paras 106(b), 110). This is discussed further in chapter 4.

- The amount of the correction at the beginning of the earliest prior period presented.

- If retrospective restatement is impracticable for a particular prior period, details of the circumstances giving rise to the impracticability and a description of how and from when the error has been corrected.

Subsequent financial statements need not repeat these disclosures.

[IAS 8 para 49].

3.125 Prior to the improvement referred to in paragraph 3.125.1 below, where an entity makes a retrospective restatement of items in its financial statements or when it reclassifies items in its financial statements, it should present an additional balance sheet and related notes as of the beginning of the earliest comparative period. [IAS 1 para 10(f)]. However, in our view, companies may choose to omit the additional balance sheet if there is no impact on that balance sheet and this fact is disclosed. See further chapter 4.

3.125.1 In the 'Annual improvements to IFRSs' issued in May 2012, the IASB amended the requirements in IAS 1 relating to the additional balance sheet. Where an entity makes a retrospective restatement of items in its financial statements or when it reclassifies items in its financial statements, and this has a material effect on the information in the balance sheet at the beginning of the preceding period, it is required to present that balance sheet. However, under the amended standard, which applies for annual periods beginning on or after 1 January 2013, the entity need not present the related notes to the additional balance sheet. [IAS 1 paras 40A, 40C]. The amendment clarifies that the additional balance sheet is given as at the beginning of the preceding period regardless of whether an entity's financial statements present comparative information for earlier periods.

3.126 Subsequent financial statements need not repeat these disclosures. An example of disclosure is provided in Table 3.9. However, note that there is no effect on EPS in this example (and therefore no disclosure of any effect on EPS) as the adjustments do not affect the consolidated income statement. A further example is given in Table 3.10, but in this example no balance sheet is given as at the beginning of the earliest period presented, because there is no effect on that balance sheet and this fact is stated.

Table 3.9 – Disclosure of impact of error

The Weir Group plc – Report and accounts – 1 January 2010

Consolidated Balance Sheet (extract)

	Notes	1 January 2010 £m	26 December 2008 (as restated – note 2) £m	28 December 2007 (as restated – note 2) £m
ASSETS				
. . .				
LIABILITIES				
. . .				
Non-current liabilities				
Interest-bearing loans & borrowings	20	**174.2**	242.6	217.0
Derivative financial instruments	30	**31.0**	70.1	5.1
Provisions	22	**36.7**	36.4	22.6
Deferred tax liabilities	23	**60.4**	63.0	51.0
Retirement benefit plan deficits	24	**71.0**	29.9	8.6
Total non-current liabilities		**373.3**	442.0	304.3
Total liabilities		**809.1**	1,060.5	681.9
NET ASSETS		**742.4**	696.9	539.4
CAPITAL & RESERVES				
Share capital		**26.6**	26.6	26.5
Share premium		**38.0**	38.0	37.7
Treasury shares		**(7.9)**	(7.9)	(9.3)
Capital redemption reserve		**0.5**	0.5	0.5
Foreign currency translation reserve		**64.0**	76.9	0.2
Hedge accounting reserve		**0.6**	(8.3)	3.5
Retained earnings		**620.4**	570.9	479.8
Shareholders equity		**742.2**	696.7	538.9
Non-controlling interest		**0.2**	0.2	0.5
TOTAL EQUITY		**742.4**	696.9	539.4

[Note: the full balance sheet has not been reproduced in this extract.]

Consolidated Statement of Changes in Equity (extract)
for the 53 weeks ended 1 January 2010

	Share capital £m	Share premium £m	Treasury shares £m	Capital redemption reserve £m	Foreign currency translation reserve £m	Hedge accounting reserve £m	Retained earnings £m	Attributable to equity holders of the company £m	Non-controlling interest £m	Total equity £m
At 28 December 2007 (as previously reported – note 2)	26.5	37.7	(9.3)	0.5	0.2	3.5	485.6	544.7	0.5	545.2
Impact of restatement (note 2)	–	–	–	–	–	–	(5.8)	(5.8)	–	(5.8)
At 28 December 2007 (as restated – note 2)	26.5	37.7	(9.3)	0.5	0.2	3.5	479.8	538.9	0.5	539.4

[Movements in the year not reproduced]

At 26 December 2008 (as restated – note 2)	26.6	38.0	(7.9)	0.5	76.9	(8.3)	570.9	696.7	0.2	696.9
At 26 December 2008 (as previously reported – note 2)	26.6	38.0	(7.9)	0.5	76.9	(8.3)	581.8	707.6	0.2	707.8
Impact of restatement (note 2)	–	–	–	–	–	–	(10.9)	(10.9)	–	(10.9)
At 26 December 2008 (as restated – note 2)	26.6	38.0	(7.9)	0.5	76.9	(8.3)	570.9	696.7	0.2	696.9

[Movements in the year and the closing balances not reproduced]

[Note: the full statement of changes in equity has not been reproduced in this extract.]

Notes to the Group Financial Statements (extract)

2. Accounting policies (extract)

While updating the valuation of the Group's retirement benefit plans for the purposes of the Group's 2009 interim condensed financial statements, the qualified actuary who advises the Company identified an error in their model used to calculate the actuarial valuation of the Group's UK retirement benefit plans for the periods ended 28 December 2007 and 26 December 2008.

The impact of this was to understate the retirement benefit plan deficits on a cumulative basis by £8.1m at 28 December 2007 and £15.2m at 26 December 2008. There was also a corresponding overstatement of net deferred tax liabilities of £2.3m and £4.3m at those respective period ends.

The impact on the Consolidated Statement of Comprehensive Income was to increase actuarial losses on defined benefit plans by £7.1m and to decrease tax on items taken directly to equity by £2.0m in the 52 weeks ended 26 December 2008.

There was no material impact on the Consolidated Income Statement. The net impact was to overstate Group net assets by £5.8m and £10.9m at 28 December 2007 and 26 December 2008 respectively. All affected balances and amounts have been restated in these financial statements. To this effect, the Consolidated Statement of Comprehensive Income, Consolidated Balance Sheet, Consolidated Statement of Changes in Equity and affected notes present restated comparative information for the 52 weeks ended 26 December 2008. In addition, as required by IAS1, the Consolidated Balance Sheet and affected notes also present restated comparative information for the 52 weeks ended 28 December 2007.

Table 3.10 – Correction of prior period error

Primary Health Properties PLC – Annual report – 31 December 2009

2 Accounting policies (extract)

Restatement

During the year it was established that a swap interest accrual of £895,000 had been omitted from the 31 December 2008 accounts. The prior year balances have been restated to correct this error. The December 2008 trade and other payables balances has been increased by £895,000 and the bank swap interest income figure has been decreased by the same amount. As a result of the above adjustment, the 31 December 2008 basic loss per share figure increased from 68.5p per share to 71.2p per share and the adjusted earnings per share figure reduced from 18.8p to 16.2p. The retained earnings decreased from £27.7million to £26.8million. In addition £457,000 of bank charges previously recognised in administrative expenses has been reclassified as finance costs. There is no impact on the financial statements for the year ended 31 December 2009. The Directors have not presented a third column on the Group Balance Sheet because the restatement does not have an impact on the opening 2008 reserves.

Chapter 4

Presentation of financial statements

Presentation of financial statements

Introduction

4.1 Guidance on the overall structure of financial statements, including minimum requirements for each primary statement (statement of financial position, statement of comprehensive income, statement of changes in equity and statement of cash flows) and notes to the financial statements, is provided by IAS 1. These requirements are supplemented by the specific requirements of other accounting standards. IAS 1 applies to all entities reporting under IFRS, including those that present consolidated financial statements in accordance with IAS 27, (or IFRS 10) and those that present separate financial statements in accordance with IAS 27 (or IAS 27 (revised 2011)). [IAS 1 para 4].

4.2 The current version of IAS 1 formed part of a larger project that was being undertaken jointly by the IASB and the FASB. This project aimed to establish a common, high quality standard for the presentation of information in the financial statements, including the classification and display of line items and the aggregation of line items into subtotals and totals. IAS 1 was the first phase of the project and its requirements on the presentation of the statement of comprehensive income are similar (but not identical) to those of FASB Accounting Standards Codification ASC 220, 'Comprehensive income'. The future of the project is awaiting the outcome of the IASB's consultation on its future agenda.

4.3 The IASB issued 'Presentation of items of other comprehensive income (Amendments to IAS 1)' in June 2011. This is intended to highlight the importance that the IASB places on presenting profit or loss and other comprehensive income together and with equal prominence, although these can still be presented in separate statements (see further paras 4.11.2 and 4.101.1 onwards). The amendment requires items of other comprehensive income to be grouped into those that will be reclassified subsequently to profit or loss and those that will not be reclassified (see para 4.201.3). The amendment is effective for annual periods beginning on or after 1 July 2012, with earlier application permitted.

4.3.1 The IASB issued 'Annual improvements to IFRSs' in May 2012. This clarifies the requirements in IAS 1 for providing comparative information: when an entity provides financial statements beyond the minimum comparative information requirements (see para 4.49.1); and for the opening statement of financial position when an entity changes accounting policies, or makes retrospective restatements or reclassifications in accordance with IAS 8 (see para 4.46.1), including removal of the requirement to disclose related notes (see para 4.48.1.1). The amendment is effective for annual periods beginning on or after 1 January 2013, with early adoption permitted.

IFRS and UK law

UK.4.3.1 For EU regulated-market companies that prepare consolidated financial statements, an EU Regulation requires the use of EU-adopted IFRS in those financial statements. EU Regulations pass directly into UK law; UK legislation was not required to impose the requirement for IFRS on regulated-market companies' consolidated financial statements. However, the EU IFRS Regulation allows Member States to permit or require the adoption of IFRS by unlisted companies and in individual financial statements. The UK government brought in this Member State option on a permissive basis.

UK.4.3.2 The Companies Act 2006 and its supporting regulations, 'The Large and Medium-sized Companies and Groups (Accounts and Reports) Regulations 2008' (SI 2008/410) and 'The Small Companies and Groups (Accounts and Directors' Report) Regulations 2008' (SI 2008/409) prescribe the format of individual company and consolidated group financial statements. The formats set out in the legislation do not apply to companies preparing their financial statements in accordance with EU-adopted IFRS although there are certain disclosures required by law regardless of the accounting framework selected (for example, staff costs, directors' emoluments). In addition to prescribing the line items that should be disclosed by UK GAAP reporters in the balance sheet and profit and loss account, the law requires that they are presented in a certain order. Individual line items should be presented under IAS 1 and these are broadly similar to those set out in the legislation, but the order in which they appear is not mandated. Both listed and unlisted companies, except charitable companies, may use EU-adopted IFRS but, if they do not, they should prepare their financial statements in accordance with the formats set out in the legislation. The use of IFRS is only mandatory in the consolidated financial statements of regulated market companies.

UK.4.3.3 'EU regulated-market companies' are those whose securities are admitted to trading on a 'regulated market' in any EU Member State. The 'Alternative Investment Market' (AIM) is not a regulated market. Even though not required by law, the AIM rules mandate the application of EU-adopted IFRS for consolidated financial statements of AIM companies incorporated in an EEA member state. AIM companies incorporated in an EEA member state that are not parent companies and, therefore, do not prepare consolidated financial statements, have a choice and can either prepare their financial statements in accordance with EU-adopted IFRS or in accordance with the accounting and company legislation and regulations applicable in the AIM company's country of incorporation.

UK.4.3.4 Under IAS 1, financial statements cannot be described as complying with IFRS unless they comply with all of the IFRS standards and all IFRIC interpretations (see para 4.18). The EU has not adopted IAS 39 in its entirety (see further chapter 6). Many companies will be able to comply with both IAS 39 and EU-adopted IAS 39 but, for some companies, there will be a conflict between the two versions of the standard. Such companies will be required by the law to comply with EU-adopted IAS 39. They would not, therefore, be able to include a statement of compliance with IFRS in their financial statements, but will be able to include a statement of compliance with EU-adopted IFRS.

Objective and scope

4.4   IAS 1 aims to enhance the quality of financial statements by:

- Setting minimum requirements for the presentation of primary statements.

- Setting minimum requirements for notes to financial statements.

- Requiring full compliance with all applicable standards and interpretations, except in extremely rare cases.

- Providing practical guidance on issues such as going concern, consistency, materiality and comparative information.

4.5   IAS 1 states: *"This Standard prescribes the basis for presentation of general purpose financial statements to ensure comparability both with the entity's financial statements of previous periods and with the financial statements of other entities. It sets out overall requirements for the presentation of financial statements, guidelines for their structure and minimum requirements for their content."* [IAS 1 para 1].

4.6   The standard applies to all general purpose financial statements prepared under IFRS. [IAS 1 para 2]. General purpose financial statements are those intended to meet the needs of users who are not in a position to require an entity to prepare reports tailored to their particular information needs. [IAS 1 para 7]. IAS 1 applies to all types of entity and applies both to consolidated financial statements and to separate financial statements as defined in IAS 27. [IAS 1 para 4]. IAS 1 does not govern the structure and content of condensed interim financial information prepared under IAS 34. The 'overall considerations' set out in paragraphs 15 to 35 of IAS 1 are applicable to both annual financial statements and interim financial reports. [IAS 1 para 4]. These paragraphs deal with, for example, fair presentation, going concern, accruals basis of accounting, materiality and aggregation and offsetting, being the overall principles for preparing and presenting financial information, derived largely from the IASB's 'Conceptual framework for financial reporting'.

4.7   IAS 1 applies to all entities. Although IAS 1 is intended to be sufficiently flexible for it to be used by all entities, there is recognition that certain non-profit entities may have to amend the descriptions used for the line items or for the financial statements themselves. [IAS 1 para 5]. Likewise, the presentation of members' or unitholders' interests in the financial statements will need to be adapted for entities that do not have equity, as defined in IAS 32 or whose share capital is not equity. [IAS 1 para 6].

UK.4.7.1 In the UK there is no equivalent accounting standard on presentation but the form and content of UK GAAP company financial statements is laid down by UK company law derived from the EU 4th and 7th Directives. For other types of entities where there is no authoritative guidance, the formats in company law have generally been used as a guideline for preparing their financial statements. Such entities may also look to IAS 1 as being equally, if not more, persuasive evidence of best practice.

UK.4.7.2 IAS 1 applies to separate financial statements (as defined in IAS 27) and to consolidated financial statements prepared under IFRS. [IAS 1 para 4]. 'Separate' financial statements are equivalent to 'individual' financial statements, as referred to in the Companies Act 2006. In the UK, the parent's individual financial statements are required by law to be presented with the consolidated financial statements. However, most companies take advantage of the exemption in section 408(3) of the 2006 Act from publishing the parent's individual profit and loss account within the group financial statements (see para UK.4.246.13 for the application of this exemption under IFRS). The individual profit and loss account should still be prepared and approved by the board, but it need not form part of the published annual financial statements.

UK.4.7.3 All UK companies, except charitable companies, are permitted, but not required, to prepare financial statements under the EU IFRS Regulation. Parent companies, including the parent company of a listed group, applying IFRS in their consolidated financial statements are permitted to apply UK GAAP in the parent's separate financial statements. However, not applying the Regulation to the separate financial statements would mean that group financial statements and parent financial statements, although presented together, would be prepared on a different basis, possibly creating different gains and losses and different carrying values for assets and liabilities.

UK.4.7.4 Where a group prepares its consolidated financial statements under IFRS, the company may prefer to present its parent company financial statements on the same basis. As a concession contained in the law, this does not trigger a need to prepare all the UK subsidiaries' financial statements under IFRS too, although all the UK subsidiaries will be required to adopt the same accounting framework as each other, unless there are good reasons for not doing so, or unless the parent is not required to prepare group financial statements.

UK.4.7.5 The parent and its subsidiaries are separate legal persons with limited liability and distributable profits and, accordingly, separate financial statements are required to allow users to understand their individual financial positions. Under UK law, a company that is required to prepare group financial statements is not permitted to publish its individual financial statements without also publishing with them its group financial statements. [CA06 Sec 434(2)]; that is, the group financial statements and the individual financial statements cannot be published in separate documents. Whilst the requirement to publish individual financial statements is necessary to recognise the separate legal status of the parent, most users of the group financial statements are concerned primarily with the group's position, rather than the individual positions of the companies comprising the group.

UK.4.7.6   Under UK GAAP, group and company balance sheets (and notes thereto) are often presented alongside each other in a four-column format. Clearly, it would be undesirable, and potentially misleading, to use this form of presentation when the separate and consolidated financial statements have been prepared under different accounting frameworks. In such cases, a preferable approach would be to publish the separate and consolidated financial statements in separate sections of the financial statements document.

Purpose of financial statements

4.8   IAS 1 defines the objective of financial statements: *"…The objective of financial statements is to provide information about the financial position, financial performance and cash flows of an entity that is useful to a wide range of users in making economic decisions. Financial statements also show the results of management's stewardship of the resources entrusted to it. ….."*. [IAS 1 para 9].

4.9   The objective is met by providing information on assets, liabilities, equity, income and expenses (including gains and losses), contributions by and distributions to owners in their capacity as owners and cash flows. Although financial statements are an historical record and not a forecast, the standard recognises that financial statements have a predictive value in that past performance can be an indicator of likely future performance.

Responsibility for financial statements

4.10   IAS 1 excludes any mention of the responsibility for preparing and presenting the financial statements. However, as discussed in chapter 22, IAS 10 requires entities to disclose who authorised the issuance of the financial statements. [IAS 10 para 17].

UK.4.10.1   In the UK, the responsibility for company financial statements is included in legislation, with directors having a legal obligation to prepare and approve financial statements. The requirements for other entities are governed by their constitution or deed of trust or other governing instrument. Responsibility is a legal concept, not an accounting one.

Complete set of financial statements

4.11 A complete set of IFRS financial statements comprises the following statements, all of which should be presented with equal prominence:

- A statement of financial position as at the end of the period.

- A statement of comprehensive income for the period.

- A statement of changes in equity for the period.

- A statement of cash flows for the period.

- Notes, comprising a summary of significant accounting policies and other explanatory information.

- A statement of financial position as at the beginning of the earliest comparative period when an entity applies an accounting policy retrospectively or makes a retrospective restatement of items in its financial statements, or where it reclassifies items in its financial statements.

[IAS 1 para 10, 11].

4.11.1 In the 'Annual improvements to IFRSs' issued in May 2012, the IASB amended paragraph 10 of IAS 1 to add a reference to presenting comparative information in respect of the preceding period. The amendment also changed the wording in the last bullet point above to refer to a statement of financial position as at the beginning of the preceding period, rather than the earliest comparative period. See further para 4.46.1.

4.11.1.1 Entities can choose whether to present the statement of comprehensive income as a single statement, or as two statements, presenting the components of profit or loss as an income statement immediately followed by a statement of comprehensive income presenting the total profit or loss for the period and the individual items of other comprehensive income (that is, the items of income and expense that are not recognised in profit or loss). [IAS 1 para 12]. The key point is that all income and expenses should be included in a 'performance statement', rather than just being shown in the statement of changes in equity. The statement of comprehensive income is discussed from paragraph 4.100.

4.11.2 As noted in paragraph 4.3, the IASB issued 'Presentation of items of other comprehensive income (Amendments to IAS 1)' in June 2011. This requires financial statements to include a 'statement of profit or loss and other comprehensive income' for the period. The standard notes that a single statement can be presented with profit or loss and other comprehensive income presented in two sections. Alternatively, the profit or loss section can be given in a separate statement of profit or loss, which is similar to the existing requirement in IAS 1. The amendment to the standard specifies that, in a single statement, the sections are presented together with the profit or loss section presented first followed directly by the other comprehensive income section. It also clarifies that if a separate statement of profit or loss is presented, this should immediately precede the statement presenting comprehensive income. [IAS 1 (revised) para 10A]. In addition, the amendment to the standard notes that an entity may use other titles for the statement(s), such as 'statement of comprehensive income' (which is the terminology used in this chapter, together with 'income statement', where this is separately presented). See also paragraph 4.101.1 onwards.

4.12   The title of the primary statements reflects the function of those statements, as described in the IASB Framework. Nevertheless, an entity is permitted to use titles for the statements other than those used in IAS 1. An entity can, for example, continue to present a 'balance sheet' rather than a 'statement of financial position', should it wish to do so. However, it is important that the titles used are not misleading.

4.13   Paragraph 7 of IAS 1 defines 'notes'. It states: *"Notes contain information in addition to that presented in the statement of financial position, statement of comprehensive income, statement of changes in equity and statement of cash flows. Notes provide narrative descriptions or disaggregations of items presented in those statements and information about items that do not qualify for recognition in those statements"*.

4.14   IAS 1 requires that all entities prepare a statement of cash flows and IAS 7 sets out the detailed requirements for presentation and disclosure. There are no exemptions from the requirement to prepare a cash flow statement; for example, all the subsidiaries within a group should prepare a cash flow statement. (See chapter 30.)

4.15   IAS 1 indicates that entities should clearly identify the financial statements and distinguish them from other information in the same published document. [IAS 1 para 49]. IAS 1 recognises that many entities produce, outside the financial statements, a financial review by management. [IAS 1 para 13]. Some entities also provide additional reports and statements (for example, environmental reports and value added statements) as well as other financial data, within documents containing their financial statements. IAS 1 neither encourages nor discourages entities to prepare such additional reports and information, although they do not form part of the financial statements. This fact should be clear from the presentation and disclosures accompanying such information.

4.15.1   Reports and statements presented outside financial statements are outside the scope of IFRS. [IAS 1 para 14]. However, it is worth noting that IFRS 7 permits certain disclosures (such as the nature and extent of risks arising from financial instruments and the entity's approach to managing those risks) to be presented in statements such as a separate management commentary or business review accompanying the financial statements, provided that these disclosures are incorporated by a cross-reference in the financial statements to that other statement. [IFRS 7 App B para 6].

UK.4.15.2 In the UK, the Companies Act 2006 requires directors to include in their report a review of the business of the company and its subsidiaries. [CA06 Sec 417(1)]. This information is often given as part of an operating and financial review (OFR). There is no requirement for an entity to prepare an operating and financial review, although many UK listed and public interest entities produce one voluntarily; the ASB has, therefore, issued a reporting statement, 'Operating and financial review'. Although non-mandatory, the ASB's statement is recommended for quoted companies and any other companies preparing an OFR. The statutory business review and the OFR are covered in chapters 2 and 3 of the Manual of Accounting – Narrative Reporting.

4.15.2 In December 2010, the IASB published a practice statement, 'Management commentary', which provides non-mandatory guidance for the presentation of such a commentary where entities elect to include one or are required to do so by local regulators. Detailed guidance on the management commentary is given in a separate chapter.

General features

Fair presentation

4.16 IAS 1 states that: *"Financial statements shall present fairly the financial position, financial performance and cash flows of an entity. Fair presentation requires the faithful representation of the effects of transactions, other events and conditions in accordance with the definitions and recognition criteria for assets, liabilities, income and expenses set out in the Framework. The application of IFRSs, with additional disclosure when necessary, is presumed to result in financial statements that achieve a fair presentation"*. [IAS 1 para 15]. IFRS is defined as standards and interpretations adopted by the IASB. These comprise International Financial Reporting Standards and International Accounting Standards together with interpretations issued by the IFRS IC (or its predecessor bodies). [IAS 1 para 7]. An entity whose financial statements comply with IFRS should disclose that fact in the notes. [IAS 1 para 16].

4.17 Although disclosure additional to that set out in specific IFRS is recommended where it is necessary to enable the users of the financial statements to understand transactions or events of the reporting entity (see para 4.19), disclosure or explanation is not a substitute for proper accounting. [IAS 1 para 18].

4.18 IAS 1 requires an *"explicit and unreserved statement of compliance"* in the notes to the financial statements. Entities cannot state that their financial statements are IFRS-compliant if they do not comply with all the requirements of IFRS. [IAS 1 para 16]. It had been the practice of some entities to state that their financial statements were 'based on' international accounting standards or were 'in compliance with the accounting requirements' of those standards. That is, some entities had been selective in their application of IFRS requirements, reducing the reliability and understandability of the financial statements and thereby undermining users' ability to compare the financial position of different entities. Financial statements either comply with IFRS or they do not; there is no middle ground.

UK.4.18.1 The Basis for Conclusions on the IASB's Framework notes that a 'fair presentation' is equivalent to a 'true and fair view'. [Framework para BC3.44]. In countries that have adopted EU 4th and 7th Directives, including the UK, there is a legal requirement for local GAAP financial statements to give a true and fair view. Similarly, the EU IFRS Regulation that requires regulated-market companies to prepare their consolidated financial statements under IFRS sets out a basic principle that, for the EU to adopt an international accounting standard, it is necessary that its application results in a true and fair view of the financial position and performance of an entity. In the UK, to make the position clear, section 393 of the Companies Act 2006 includes a specific requirement that the financial statements give a true and fair view, regardless of the accounting framework selected. For companies applying EU-adopted IFRS, the form and content of the financial statements is not determined by the schedules in the statutory instruments supporting the 2006 Act (see para 4.3.2), but by IFRS and any additional provisions set out elsewhere in the Act. The requirement for financial statements to give a true and fair view exists for all UK companies but the accounting standards and law relevant to meeting this requirement vary according to the accounting framework applied.

4.19 IAS 1 states that, in virtually all circumstances, a fair presentation is achieved by compliance with applicable IFRSs.

"A fair presentation also requires an entity:

(a) to select and apply accounting policies in accordance with IAS 8, 'Accounting policies, Changes in Accounting Estimates and Errors'. IAS 8 sets out a hierarchy of authoritative guidance that management considers in the absence of a Standard or an Interpretation that specifically applies to an item.

(b) to present information, including accounting policies, in a manner that provides relevant, reliable, comparable and understandable information.

(c) to provide additional disclosures when compliance with the specific requirements in IFRSs is insufficient to enable users to understand the impact of particular transactions, other events and conditions on the entity's financial position and financial performance."

[IAS 1 para 17].

Fair presentation and true and fair overrides

4.20   Under IFRS, there is a basic principle that a fair presentation is achieved if financial statements are prepared in compliance with each applicable standard and interpretation. However, an entity is required to depart from the specific requirements of an IFRS in the extremely rare circumstances in which management concludes that compliance with the specific requirement would be so misleading that it would conflict with the objective of financial statements set out in the Framework, if the relevant regulatory framework requires or otherwise does not prohibit such a departure. [IAS 1 para 19]. An item is only considered to conflict with this objective if it does not represent faithfully the transactions, other events and conditions it purports to, or could reasonably be expected to, represent. Consequently, a departure from IFRS will be necessary only when the treatment required by an IFRS is clearly inappropriate and thus a fair presentation cannot be achieved either by applying the IFRS or through additional disclosure alone. Such departures are very rare indeed and should be handled with care. The situation where the regulatory framework prohibits a departure in such circumstances is discussed in paragraph 4.24.

UK.4.20.1   UK company law includes requirements on the presentation of financial statements under UK GAAP, but also includes a number of rules on the measurement of certain items within such statements. It is these measurement rules that have most commonly been the source of true and fair overrides in the UK, because those rules sometimes conflict with accounting treatments prescribed or required by accounting standards. Such overrides do not arise for those companies applying EU-adopted IFRS, because the parts of the law, in which these measurement rules appear, do not apply to them. In the UK, the regulatory framework has never been a barrier to financial statements giving a fair presentation. UK law has an overriding requirement that financial statements shall give a true and fair view and it, therefore, requires a company to depart from the law if this is necessary for the financial statements to give a true and fair view.

4.21   IAS 1 requires that:

"When an entity departs from a requirement of an IFRS in accordance with paragraph 19, it shall disclose:

(a)   *that management has concluded that the financial statements present fairly the entity's financial position, financial performance and cash flows;*

(b)   *that it has complied with applicable IFRSs, except that it has departed from a particular requirement to achieve a fair presentation;*

(c)   *the title of the IFRS from which the entity has departed, the nature of the departure, including the treatment that the IFRS would require, the reason why that treatment would be so misleading in the circumstances that it would conflict with the objective of financial statements set out in the Framework, and the treatment adopted; and*

(d)   for each period presented, the financial effect of the departure on each item in the financial statements that would have been reported in complying with the requirement."

[IAS 1 para 20].

4.22   In departing from IFRS, an entity should consider the objective of the standard or interpretation in question and determine why the objective is not met or is not relevant in its particular circumstances. It should also consider how its own circumstances differ from other entities that comply with the relevant IFRS requirement. Where other entities in similar circumstances comply with the requirement, there is a rebuttable presumption that the entity's compliance with the requirement would not be so misleading that it would conflict with the objective of financial statements set out in the Framework. [IAS 1 para 24]. Because fair presentation overrides of IFRS are rarely justified, IAS 1 requires extensive disclosures in the event of a departure from the requirements of IFRS. These disclosures enable users to calculate the adjustments that would be necessary to comply with IFRS in full. Users will then be in a position to derive IFRS-compliant financial statements if they wish to do so.

4.23   It may be that a departure from a requirement of a standard or an interpretation affects more than a single financial year. For example, if an entity departs from a requirement in respect of the measurement of assets or liabilities, in the following period there will be a consequential effect on the measurement of changes in assets and liabilities. In the first year of departure from the standard or interpretation, the entity should give the disclosures set out in paragraphs 4.21(a) to (d) above. In the following period, where the prior year departure affects amounts recognised in that period, the entity should give the disclosures shown in paragraphs 4.21(c) and (d). [IAS 1 paras 20, 21].

4.24   IAS 1 envisages the possibility that an override will be required to achieve a fair presentation, but that the regulatory framework within which the entity operates prohibits such a departure from IFRS. In these circumstances, the entity would be required to reduce the perceived misleading aspects of compliance through disclosures. The entity would disclose the title of the standard or interpretation in question, the nature of the relevant requirement and the reason that compliance with that requirement would be so misleading that it would conflict with the objective of financial statements, together with, for each period presented, the adjustments to each item in the financial statements that would be necessary to give a fair presentation. [IAS 1 para 23]. While the circumstances in which it will be necessary to depart from IFRS are rare, the circumstances in which such a departure will be necessary but prohibited by the regulatory authorities, will be rarer still.

Going concern

4.25 Financial statements are normally prepared on the assumption that the entity is a going concern and will continue in operation for the foreseeable future. [Framework para 4.1]. Therefore, for the financial statements to be prepared on a going concern basis, the entity should have neither the intention nor the need to liquidate or cease its operations in the foreseeable future. Management is required to assess, at the time of preparing the financial statements, the entity's ability to continue as a going concern and this assessment should cover the entity's prospects for at least 12 months from the end of the reporting period. [IAS 1 paras 25, 26]. The 12 month period for considering the entity's future is a minimum requirement; an entity cannot, for example, prepare its financial statements on a going concern basis if it intends to cease operations 18 months from the end of the reporting period. The existence of significant doubts about the entity's ability to continue as a going concern is not sufficient reason to depart from preparing financial statements on a going concern basis; financial statements should be prepared on a going concern basis unless management intends either to liquidate the entity or to cease trading, or has no realistic alternative but to do so. [IAS 1 para 25].

UK.4.25.1 The FRC in its guidance issued on going concern and liquidity risk for directors of UK companies in 2009 notes that neither UK GAAP nor IFRS specifies a maximum period that should be considered by the directors as part of their assessment of going concern. UK GAAP requires that disclosure should be made where the review period is less than 12 months from the date of approval of the financial statements. UK companies will generally adopt a review period of not less than 12 months from the date of approval of annual and half-yearly financial statements but, in rare cases, when they do not, this fact should be explained. Directors of companies in the UK applying this guidance when preparing IFRS financial statements should also make this disclosure, bearing in mind the IAS 1 requirement that the assessment should cover a period of at least 12 months from the end of the reporting period.

4.26 In many cases, the assessment of the entity's status as a going concern will be a simple matter. A profitable entity with no financing problems will almost certainly be a going concern. In other cases, management may need to consider very carefully the entity's ability to meet its liabilities as they fall due. Detailed cash flow and profit forecasts may be required before management can be satisfied that the entity is a going concern. Where there are significant doubts about the entity's ability to continue as a going concern, details of those uncertainties should be disclosed even if the financial statements continue to be prepared on a going concern basis. [IAS 1 para 25]. (See also para 4.227.) The disclosures should:

- adequately describe the principal events or conditions that give rise to the significant doubt on the entity's ability to continue in operation and management's plans to deal with these events or conditions; and

- state clearly that there is a material uncertainty related to events or conditions which may cast significant doubt on the entity's ability to continue as a going concern and, therefore, that it may be unable to realise its assets and discharge its liabilities in the normal course of business.

4.26.1 The latter bullet point was confirmed by an agenda decision published in July 2010 by the IFRS IC in response to a request for guidance on the disclosure requirements for uncertainties relating to an entity's ability to continue as a going concern. The IFRS IC noted that the application of the disclosure requirements in paragraph 25 of IAS 1 requires the exercise of professional judgement. The IFRS IC also noted that, for the disclosure of "*material uncertainties*" to be useful, it should identify that the disclosed uncertainties may cast significant doubt upon the entity's ability to continue as a going concern.

4.26.1.1 Further, events that occur after the reporting period may indicate that the entity is no longer a going concern. In a situation where management believed at the year end that the entity was a going concern, but their post-year end assessment leads them to conclude that it is not, any financial statements that are prepared after that assessment (including the financial statements in respect of which management are making the assessment) should not be prepared on a going concern basis. The carrying value of the assets and liabilities would be assessed accordingly. This is consistent with IAS 10 which requires a fundamental change to the basis of accounting where the going concern assumption is no longer appropriate. [IAS 10 para 14]. See chapter 22.

4.26.2 An example of a situation where disclosure of an uncertainty is required is given below. A further example of disclosure of an uncertainty where shareholder approval is required for a fundraising and restructuring of debt is given in Table 4.1 below.

Example – Uncertainty about the entity being a going concern

An entity has incurred losses during the last four years and its current liabilities exceed its total assets. The entity was in breach of its loan covenants and has been negotiating with the related financial institutions in order to keep them supporting its business. These factors raise significant doubt that the entity will be able to continue as a going concern. How should management disclose uncertainties that affect the entity's ability to continue as a going concern?

Management should state clearly that there is a material uncertainty related to events or conditions which may cast significant doubt on the entity's ability to continue as a going concern and, therefore, that it may be unable to realise its assets and discharge its liabilities in the normal course of business. They should describe the events and conditions that give rise to the material uncertainty as well as the actions proposed to address the situation. This disclosure should preferably be made in the same note where the basis for preparation of the financial statements is described. Management should also disclose the possible effects on the financial position, or that it is impracticable to measure them. Additionally, management should state whether or not the financial statements include any adjustments that result or might result in the future from the outcome of these uncertainties.

UK.4.26.3 For companies with a Premium Listing of equity shares in the UK, the requirement in the UK Corporate Governance Code for directors to confirm that the going concern basis is appropriate has, in effect, changed it from a presumption to an explicit statement for listed companies. Code provision C.1.3 says that *"the directors should report that the business is a going concern, with supporting assumptions or qualifications as necessary"*. This requirement is also contained in the Listing Rules. [LR 9.8.6 R (3)].

Table 4.1 – Uncertainty about the entity's ability to continue as a going concern

Premier Foods plc – Report and accounts – 31 December 2008

Notes to the financial statements (extract)

2.1 Basis of preparation (extract)

The Group consolidated financial statements have been prepared on the going concern basis, which assumes that the Group will continue to be able to meet its liabilities as they fall due for the foreseeable future.

Following the acquisition of RHM plc in March 2007, the Group has undertaken an extensive integration and restructuring programme, which has been delivered against a substantially more challenging trading, economic and credit environment. In view of the volatile operating conditions and the Group's significant level of leverage following the acquisitions of Campbell's and RHM plc, the Board and its advisors have spent recent months examining ways of accelerating the reduction of Group debt in order to establish additional financial headroom and a more appropriate long-term capital structure.

Following discussions with the Group's lending banks and considering the potential for the credit environment to remain difficult, the Board has concluded that raising additional equity combined with a renegotiated agreement with the Group's lending banks and an agreement with the Trustees of the Group's UK Defined Benefit Plans would provide a more appropriate capital structure, and achieve an increase in financial headroom given the more challenging trading environment. Further details on the equity raising, amended agreement with the lending banks and the agreement reached with the Trustees are shown in note 34.

This approach aims to minimise the quantum of new equity capital that needs to be raised whilst providing the Group with the appropriate comfort regarding its future liquidity and covenant headroom.

The amended agreement with the lending banks and the agreement with the Trustees are both conditional on the equity raising. The proposed equity raising requires that a resolution be passed by Shareholders at an Extraordinary General Meeting in order to proceed and in order for the amended terms under the Group's Term and Revolving Credit Facilities to take effect.

In the event that the resolution is not passed, the amended Term and Revolving Credit Facilities Agreement will not become effective. The Group would be required to re-enter negotiations with its lending banks. Should these further negotiations prove unsuccessful then the Group may have insufficient liquidity shortly thereafter in April or May 2009 and/or would face being unable to meet its financial covenants.

The Board has concluded that the resolution to be passed by Shareholders at the General Meeting in order for the placing and open offer and the firm placing to proceed such that the equity proceeds are received on 27 March 2009 in line with the timetable set out in the Prospectus for the Placing and Open Offer and Firm Placing, represents a material uncertainty that casts significant doubt upon the Group's ability to continue as a going concern. However, after considering the uncertainties described above the Board has a reasonable expectation that the Group will be successful in obtaining the necessary resolution and for this reason believes it is appropriate to continue to adopt the going concern basis in preparing the annual report and accounts. The financial statements do not include the adjustments that would result if the Group was unable to continue as a going concern.

34. Post balance sheet events (extract)

Financing Arrangements

On 12 January 2009, the Group arranged a £60m working capital facility to provide additional working capital headroom to 31 March 2009. As a consequence the total available debt facility during this period is £1,990m.

On 5 March 2009, the Group announced revised financing arrangements including a proposed share issuance and proposed changes to lending agreements to provide greater covenant and liquidity headroom and to extend the maturity of the facility. These revised financing arrangements require the approval of ordinary shareholders at an extraordinary general meeting scheduled for 23 March 2009.

With regards the lending agreements, the Group announced amendments to its Term and Revolving Credit Facilities. These amendments included a rephasing of the facilities to provide additional liquidity and covenant headroom to an extended maturity date in December 2013. The total facility as at 31 March 2009 will be £1,930m and will be amortised by £100m in April 2009. The facility will then be amortised by £50m in December 2009 and then in June and December of each year until December 2013 when the facility matures

As part of the amendment process the covenant schedule for the Group has been reset. The two covenants which the Group is required to meet are calculated and tested on a 12 month rolling basis at the half year and full year each year. For the next 12 months, those tests are as follows:

	June 2009	December 2009
Net Debt/EBITDA	5.00:1	4.75:1
EBITDA/Cash Interest	2.00:1	2.00:1

For the purposes of the covenant calculation net debt is defined as net borrowings and amounts guaranteed under standby letters of credit but excluding any financial indebtedness in relation to arrangements under its debtor securitisation programme and any items relating to its subsidiary Citadel Insurance Company Limited. EBITDA is defined as profit before tax excluding exceptional items, movement on the fair valuation of financial instruments, pension financing credit/charge, expenses relating to employee share incentive schemes and cash interest, which is defined to be net interest excluding the amortisation of debt issuance costs, exceptional write-off of financing costs, unwind of discount on provisions, securitisation interest and fair value adjustments for interest hedging instruments.

With regards to the proposed share issue, the Group proposes to raise approximately £404m, before expenses, through the issue of 1,553,416,776 new ordinary shares. This will be structured as a placing and open offer of 1,055,756,006 new ordinary shares at a price of 26 pence per share, and a firm placing of 497,660,770 new ordinary shares at a price of 26 pence per share. Subject to the approval of shareholders at the extraordinary general meeting, the Company expects to receive the proceeds on approximately 27 March 2009.

Pensions

The Group has agreed new arrangements with its four main Pension Schemes (RHM Pension Scheme, Premier Foods Pension Scheme, Premier Ambient Products Pension Scheme and Premier Grocery Products Pension Scheme) regarding deficit payments. The key terms of this agreement relate to providing greater certainty on deficit payments by fixing the deficit payments from 2009 to 2013 and agreeing that any incremental deficits arising from the 2010 and 2013 valuations will be recovered over a 12 year period. The new arrangements are conditional on the share placing and new financing arrangements.

4.27 Where financial statements are not prepared on a going concern basis, the financial statements should disclose that fact together with the reasons why the entity is no longer considered a going concern. Details of the new basis of accounting adopted should be also disclosed. [IAS 1 para 25].

4.28 The going concern assumption is reflected in the Framework as an underlying assumption normally made in preparing financial statements. This assumption, therefore, underlies the principles used to determine the amounts recognised and measured in financial statements as set out in IFRS. Hence, both assets and liabilities are usually recorded on the basis that their carrying amounts will be recovered or discharged in the normal course of business. For example, the carrying values of property, plant and equipment (such as depreciated cost or recoverable amount) reflect costs or values that the business expects to recover from future cash flows relating to their continued use and ultimate disposal. If, however, the business is not a going concern, these bases may not be appropriate.

4.28.1 In circumstances where the going concern basis of accounting is not considered appropriate, IFRS does not prescribe the basis of accounting under which financial statements should be prepared. While this may be assumed in many cases to be a liquidation or break-up basis, this will not be the case in all circumstances. For example, an entity may be placed in administration, with liquidation/break-up being one of the possible outcomes. Further, the basis of accounting in many respects might be mandated by the administrator. Therefore, if the relevant legislation permits it, the financial statements might be prepared on a basis other than IFRS, including advancing the timing of recognising provisions and reflecting impairments for post balance sheet events. Policies related to these matters should be set out in the notes and, as noted in paragraph 4.18, the entity would not be able to state that the financial statements are IFRS-compliant if they do not comply with all the requirements of IFRS.

4.29 If an entity is not a going concern, but is preparing its financial statements under IFRS, the measurement of assets and liabilities may be affected by changes in judgements that can arise when the going concern assumption ceases to be valid. For example, estimates of recoverable amounts of assets may require revision, potentially resulting in the recognition of impairments to the carrying value of some assets. However, in such circumstances, it would not be appropriate to recognise the expected profit on the intended disposal of assets, either as a reduction in the amounts recognised as impairments or provisions or as uplifts in the carrying value of the relevant assets (although some entities might revalue property, plant and equipment in accordance with previously established accounting policies in the normal way). Certain contracts may be regarded as onerous, requiring a provision. Provisions should not be made in respect of executory contracts (unless onerous) or restructuring costs that do not qualify as obligations under IAS 37 at the balance sheet date.

4.30 In some situations, the effect on the statement of financial position of ceasing to regard the business as a going concern may be negligible. Nevertheless, IAS 1 requires the financial statements to disclose that the entity is no longer regarded as a going concern. Unless there is a statement to the contrary, IFRS allows a reader to *presume* that an entity is carrying on business as a going concern. Consequently, where necessary, the entity should state that it has prepared its financial statements on a non-going concern basis, even if the effect of doing so has not been significant.

4.30.1 The determination of going concern should be made for each reporting entity. In many cases, a going concern basis *may not* be considered appropriate for an individual subsidiary, while the going concern basis *may* remain appropriate for the subsidiary's parent and for the group as a whole. Irrespective of the basis of accounting applied by a subsidiary, the going concern principles of IFRS are applied in the group's consolidated financial statements if the group itself is a going concern. This might result in recognition and measurement differences between the consolidated financial statements and the subsidiary's individual financial statements. For example, some subsidiary financial statements might be prepared on a basis other than IFRS (see para 4.28.1) and adjusted to reflect restructuring provisions arising after the balance sheet date, whereas these would not be reflected in the consolidated financial statements unless IAS 37's requirements have been met. Each situation should be evaluated on the basis of its facts and circumstances. It is important to determine whether adjustments that are reflected in the subsidiary's financial statements relate to conditions at the balance sheet date. If this is the case, the adjustments would be expected to result in similar measurements if both sets of financial statements are prepared in accordance with IFRS.

Accruals basis of accounting

4.31 Under the accruals basis of accounting, revenue and costs are recognised as they are earned or incurred rather than when the cash is received or paid. The accruals basis should be used in preparing the financial statements, except for cash flow information. [IAS 1 para 27].

4.32 The elements of financial statements (assets, liabilities, equity, income and expenses) should be recognised only when they meet the definitions and recognition criteria in the IASB's Framework. [IAS 1 para 28]. Entities frequently incur expenditure to provide future economic benefits to the entity, but these costs do not always meet the definition or recognition criteria of an asset. For example, start-up costs should not be capitalised or deferred just because management expects that revenues will be generated in the future. [IAS 38 para 69].

Materiality and aggregation

4.33 Each material class of similar items should be presented separately in the financial statements. Items of a dissimilar nature or function should be presented separately, unless they are immaterial. [IAS 1 para 29]. An immaterial line item is aggregated with other items either on the face of the primary statements or in the notes. An item that is not sufficiently material to warrant separate presentation on the face of the financial statements may nevertheless be sufficiently material that it should be presented separately in the notes. IFRS disclosure requirements only apply to material items. [IAS 1 paras 29 to 31]. Similarly, accounting policies in IFRSs need not be applied when the effect of applying them is immaterial. [IAS 8 para 8]. IAS 1 paragraph 7 gives a definition of 'material':

> *"Omissions or misstatements of items are material if they could, individually or collectively, influence the economic decisions that users make on the basis of the financial statements. Materiality depends on the size and nature of the omission or misstatement judged in the surrounding circumstances. The size or nature of the item, or a combination of both, could be the determining factor".*

4.34   According to the IASB's Framework, financial reports are prepared for users who have a reasonable knowledge of business and economic activities and who review and analyse the information diligently. [Framework para QC32]. Therefore, materiality is assessed against the decision-making of reasonably knowledgeable individuals. The concept of materiality is discussed further in chapter 3.

UK.4.34.1   The FRC discussion paper 'Cutting clutter', published in April 2011, drew attention to the need to focus on key messages in corporate reports and for these not to be obscured by unnecessary detail. In its 2011 report, the FRRP noted that some boards do not appear to apply a materiality threshold, or consider what is material by nature, when preparing their financial statements, because clearly immaterial or irrelevant detail is often disclosed. The FRRP noted that this can lead a user to conclude that the directors consider such amounts to be material and that all amounts greater than this have been disclosed. The FRRP encourages boards to use their judgment to determine and apply a quantitative threshold and qualitative assessment for materiality in relation to disclosures as part of their financial statements preparation process. It notes that a more rigorous approach might result in financial statements that are more meaningful, focused and relevant to users because inconsistencies and superfluous material will have been avoided.

Offsetting/netting

4.35   Offsetting or netting of assets and liabilities and of income and expenses is permitted when expressly required or permitted by an accounting standard. Otherwise, offsetting is prohibited because it detracts from giving users a full and proper understanding of the transactions, and of other events and conditions that have occurred. [IAS 1 paras 32, 33].

4.36   IAS 18 applies to the sale of goods and services and to income arising from the use by others of an entity's assets. It would not, therefore, apply to income arising from activities that are incidental to the main revenue-generating activities of the entity. It is not appropriate to net expenses against income recorded under IAS 18. This prohibition differs from the accounting where an entity is acting as an agent, in which case it presents commission revenue on a net basis rather than the gross inflows and outflows arising from the agency arrangement (see chapter 9).

4.36.1 Furthermore, expenses may be netted against income where that income does not fall within the scope of IAS 18, provided that this presentation reflects the substance of the transaction or other event and the income and expenses are related. [IAS 1 para 34]. In addition, gains and losses arising from groups of similar transactions are not reported on a net basis, unless they are immaterial. Finance revenue should not be offset against finance costs. See paragraph 4.147 for more details.

> **Example – Acceptability of offsetting income and expenses**
>
> A property investment and management entity owns a number of properties and leases them to tenants on operating leases, which include the provision of management services. The management services include cleaning, repairs to the fabric of the building, maintenance of heating, air conditioning and plumbing systems, maintenance of public areas such as the main entrance, provision of general security and upkeep of the gardens surrounding the properties. The entity engages a number of different service providers to provide the cleaning, security, plumbing, gardening and other services.
>
> The costs of the management services are recharged monthly to each tenant in proportion to the amount of space they occupy subject to an upper limit. Expenditures over the upper limit must be agreed in advance by the tenants or borne by the entity. The property management services represent approximately 20% of the rental costs and the entity earns an additional fee for the management services provided. In reporting its revenue, can the entity offset the amounts paid to the service providers from the amounts received from tenants?
>
> No, the property management revenues and costs should be presented gross in the statement of comprehensive income. The entity is a property investment entity and, therefore, providing management services is part of its main revenue-generating activities. Although different sub-contractors provide different elements of the service, the provision of such services is integral to the rental of the properties to the tenants. The entity is responsible for ensuring that the services provided meet the service level agreement with the tenants and carries the risk of non-payment in the event that a tenant fails to pay.

4.37 Items that would not be considered to be offsetting of assets and liabilities include:

- Accumulated depreciation of property plant and equipment.
- Impairment provisions.
- Accumulated amortisation of intangible assets.
- Provisions for inventory obsolescence.
- Provisions for bad debts.

4.38 Items that would be considered to be acceptable offsetting of income and expenses include:

- Income and related expenses on transactions that do not generate revenue and are incidental to the main revenue generating activities (where that presentation reflects the substance of the transaction or event):

  - Disposal proceeds and carrying value on disposal of non-current investment and operating assets.

  - Expenditure and related reimbursement under a contractual agreement (for example, a supplier's warranty agreement).

- Gains and losses arising from a group of similar items unless material, where separate presentation is required:

  - Foreign exchange gains and losses.

  - Gains and losses arising on financial instruments held for trading.

- Netting of the components of defined benefit pension cost (for example, current service cost, past service cost). (The components and the line items in which they are included are disclosed separately in the notes.)

- Defined benefit plan expenses may be presented net of amounts recognised for a reimbursement.

- Expense relating to a provision may be presented net of amounts recognised for a reimbursement.

Example – Presentation and calculation of gains arising on the sale of property plant and equipment

An entity is involved in manufacturing. During the period it sells one of its buildings and recognises a gain on the sale. How should management present the gain on sale of the building in the statement of comprehensive income?

Management should present the gain by netting the sale income with the carrying amount of the building and other related expenses. The gain on this transaction should be presented within operating profit (where operating profit is voluntarily disclosed). Proceeds or gains should not be classified as revenue.

Management should aggregate the gain, if appropriate, with amounts of a similar nature or function, for instance other gains or losses on sale of other property, plant and equipment. However, the gain or loss should be presented separately when the size, nature or incidence is such that separate disclosure is required. [IAS 1 para 97].

4.39 Where an entity has set up a provision for future expenditure, the provision will be released when the expenditure is incurred. To ensure that line items reflect the true cost of particular expenses or functions over time, the release of the provision should be included in the same line item as the original statement of comprehensive income charge that set up the provision.

Example – Treatment of the release of an onerous contract provision

In year 1, an entity creates a provision of C100,000 for an onerous lease contract on a disused distribution warehouse. The contract has one year outstanding at the year end and the entity includes the charge in distribution costs which then total C500,000. The distribution costs in year 2, before the release of the provision, are C400,000 which includes the rental charges on the disused warehouse. How should the entity deal with the release of the onerous contract provision in year 2?

In year 2, the entity should release the provision of C100,000 in the distribution costs line; distribution costs will then be shown as C300,000. The release of the provision should be disclosed in the notes to the financial statements. [IAS 37 para 84(c)]. By releasing the provision in distribution costs, the year 2 distribution costs presented represent only those costs incurred in year 2. The cost of the onerous lease was effectively incurred in year 1 when the lease became onerous, not when the rental obligations were paid to the lessor. In addition the total distribution costs for years 1 and 2 together are C800,000; if the provision had been released on a separate line, the distribution costs would have been artificially inflated to C900,000.

4.40   Offsetting of financial assets and liabilities is considered further in chapter 6. IAS 12 contains rules relating to the offsetting of tax items; this is considered in chapter 13. IAS 20 discusses the presentation of government grants related to assets; this is considered in chapter 9.

Frequency of reporting

4.41   Paragraph 36 of IAS 1 requires that financial statements are presented at least annually. When an entity changes the end of its reporting period and presents financial statements that are longer or shorter than one year, the entity should disclose the reason for using a period other than one year and disclose the fact that the comparative amounts are not comparable. Some entities prepare financial statements for a 52 week period (rather than an exact year) and this is permitted by paragraph 37 of IAS 1.

UK.4.41.1   In the UK there are legal restrictions on a company's ability to extend its reporting period. These are discussed further in chapter 3 of the Manual of Accounting – Other statutory requirements.

Comparative information

4.42   IAS 1 requires an entity to present comparative information in respect of the preceding period for all amounts reported in the current period's financial statements. This should include comparative information for narrative and descriptive information if it is relevant to understanding the current period's financial statements. [IAS 1 para 38].

4.42.1   In the 'Annual improvements to IFRSs' issued in May 2012, the IASB has clarified that an entity presents, as a minimum, two statements of financial position, two statements of comprehensive income, two separate statements of profit or loss (if presented), two statements of cash flows and two statements of changes in equity, and related notes. [IAS 1 para 38A]. The amended standard sets out the requirements for providing comparative information when an entity provides financial statements beyond these minimum comparative requirements (see para 4.49.1). It also includes amended requirements for the opening statement of financial position when an entity changes accounting policies, or makes retrospective restatements or reclassifications (see para 4.46.1). The amendments are effective for annual periods beginning on or after 1 January 2013, with early adoption permitted.

4.43 An exemption from the requirement to present comparative numerical information is sometimes given in accounting standards for reconciliations of opening and closing positions. For example, IAS 37 requires a reconciliation of the opening and closing provisions, but does not require the disclosure of a comparative reconciliation. [IAS 37 para 84]. On the other hand, under IAS 16 and IAS 38 full comparative information on the movements in opening and closing positions is required. Similarly, no exemption exists for the statement of changes in equity and, therefore, entities usually present a reconciliation of the opening and closing positions for the comparative period, immediately followed by a reconciliation of the opening and closing positions for the current period. Paragraph 4.215 shows an example of such a presentation.

4.44 Comparative narrative information need not be given if the information is no longer relevant. Where a legal dispute was outstanding at the previous balance sheet date and has still not been resolved, the financial statements for the current period should disclose details of that dispute and of the steps that have been taken to resolve the dispute. [IAS 1 para 40, IAS 1 (amended) para 38(b)]. If a legal dispute is settled during the year, it may be that the result of the dispute will need to be disclosed if it is considered that the related income or expense is of such size or nature that its separate disclosure is necessary to explain the entity's performance for the period (see para 4.162).

4.45 If the presentation or classification of items is changed, the comparative figures should also conform to the new presentation. The entity should disclose the nature and amounts of each item or class of items that is reclassified and the reasons for the restatement of the comparative information (see also para 4.54). [IAS 1 para 41]. Table 4.1.1 is an example of a change in presentation with a change in comparatives. The improvement to IAS 1 in May 2012 clarifies that this disclosure also applies as at the beginning of the preceding period.

4.46 In addition to these requirements (prior to the improvement referred to in paragraph 4.46.1) IAS 1 currently requires an entity to present a statement of financial position as at the beginning of the earliest comparative period when the entity applies an accounting policy retrospectively or makes a retrospective restatement (that is, when it makes a prior period adjustment for an error) or when it reclassifies items in its financial statements. Where entities present only two periods of information, this statement of financial position is presented in addition to those at the end of each of the two periods. [IAS 1 para 39]. The requirement for comparative information for the other primary statements is unchanged by such prior period adjustments and reclassifications. Therefore, an entity that makes such a prior period adjustment or reclassification will present, as a minimum, three statements of financial position, two of each of the other statements, and related notes.

4.46.1 The improvement to IAS 1 in May 2012 amended the requirements relating to the additional statement of financial position. Where an entity applies an accounting policy retrospectively, makes a retrospective restatement of items or reclassifies items in its financial statements and this has a material effect on the information in the statement of financial position at the beginning of the preceding period, it is required to present that statement. The amendment clarifies that the additional statement of financial position is given as at the beginning of the preceding period regardless of whether an entity's financial statements present comparative information for earlier periods. So, the entity presents three statements of financial position as at:

■ the end of the current period;

■ the end of the preceding period; and

■ the beginning of the preceding period.

[IAS 1 paras 40A, 40B, 40D].

4.47 Entities may make reclassifications or restatements that do not impact on the statement of financial position. An initial reading of paragraph 39 of IAS 1 (prior to the improvement referred to above) would suggest that a statement of financial position as at the beginning of the earliest comparative period should be presented in addition to the statements of financial position as at the end of the current period and as at the end of the previous period, even if none of the statements of financial position are impacted by the reclassification. However, entities are not required to provide a specific disclosure required by an IFRS if the information is not material. [IAS 1 para 31]. As discussed from paragraph 4.33, the materiality of an omission is measured against its ability to influence the economic decisions of the users of the financial statements. In our view, the omission of the statement of financial position as at the beginning of the earliest comparative period, where the restatement or reclassification does not affect the earliest statement of financial position and that fact is stated, is not material and is therefore permitted. Indeed, it could be argued that, in such circumstances, it is preferable to omit that statement of financial position to avoid unnecessary 'clutter' that might dilute the important messages of the financial statements. This view is consistent with the amended standard under which the concept of materiality is considered in determining whether a statement of financial position has to be presented for the beginning of the preceding period (see para 4.46.1). An example of such circumstances and disclosure is given in Table 4.1.A.

Table 4.1.A – Change in policy not affecting any statement of financial position

Tomkins plc – Annual report – 2 January 2010

2. Principal accounting policies (extract)

A. Basis of preparation (extract)

At the beginning of 2009, the Group adopted the following accounting pronouncements that are relevant to its operations, none of which had any significant impact on its results or financial position:

- IAS 1 Revised (2007) 'Presentation of Financial Statements'.

- IAS 23 Revised (2007) 'Borrowing Costs'.

- Amendments to IFRS 2 'Share-based Payment – Vesting Conditions and Cancellations'.

- Amendments to IFRS 7 'Financial Instruments: Disclosures – Improving Disclosures about Financial Instruments'.

- 'Improvements to IFRSs 2008', except where adoption of an improvement is not permitted without also adopting IAS 27 Revised (2008) 'Consolidated and Separate Financial Statements'.

- IFRIC 16 'Hedges of a Net Investment in a Foreign Operation'.

Retrospective application of the amendment to IFRS 2 had the effect of increasing administrative expenses by $0.5 million to $513.3 million in 2008 and by $0.3 million to $500.9 million in 2007, and there was a corresponding increase in the credit to equity in relation to share-based incentives (there were no tax effects). In 2008, the loss per share from continuing operations was increased by 0.05 cents to 7.34 cents. In 2007, basic earnings per share from continuing operations were reduced by 0.04 cents to 33.72 cents and diluted earnings per share from continuing operations were reduced by 0.03 cents to 33.34 cents. Prior year balance sheets were not affected by this change of accounting policy.

4.48 A similar argument can be made under the current version of IAS 1 in respect of the notes to the additional comparative statement of financial position. The requirement to present this additional statement, when the entity has made a restatement or reclassification, extends to the related notes. [IAS 1 para 39]. However, many of the notes to the statement of financial position will be unaffected by the restatement or reclassification. In our view, in such cases, it is sufficient for an entity to present only the notes to that additional statement that have been impacted by the restatement or reclassification, provided that the entity states in its financial statements that the other notes have not been impacted by the restatement or reclassification. The omission of the other notes to the additional statement is in our view, not material and is, therefore, permitted.

4.48.1 Judgement is required in determining if notes can be omitted. The pervasiveness and materiality of the adjustments should be considered. Full disclosure of all of the notes is required only when the restatement impacts most of the line items – for example, when a subsidiary is consolidated. It is only acceptable to present no additional notes when all of the information about the affected line items is presented in the disclosure required by IAS 8 about the effect of the restatement. A range of approaches between these extremes may be acceptable, based on the specific facts and circumstances: judgement will be required in each case.

4.48.1.1 The improvement to IAS 1 in May 2012 removed the requirement to present related notes to the opening statement of financial position. Under the amended standard, when an entity is required to present an additional statement of financial position under paragraph 40A of IAS 1 (that is, when it applies an accounting policy retrospectively, makes a retrospective restatement of items or reclassifies items), it has to disclose the information required by paragraphs 41 to 44 of IAS 1 for reclassifications (see paras 4.45 and 4.54) and by IAS 8 (see chapter 3). However, it need not present the related notes to the opening statement of financial position as at the beginning of the preceding period. [IAS 1 para 40C]. This contrasts with the position where an entity chooses to present additional comparative information, where related notes are required (see para 4.49.1).

4.48.2 The omission of certain notes under both the current and amended versions of IAS 1 does not extend to companies reporting a third statement of financial position as required by IFRS 1. Full comparative notes should be provided by first-time adopters, as no IFRS financial statements are available for the comparative period. See further chapter 2.

4.48.3 Entities may make restatements that do not impact the prior period's opening statement of financial position. An example is where provisional fair values are finalised for a business combination that occurred during the comparative period. Where the opening balances of the prior period are not affected because the adjustments occurred during the period, our view (which is in line with the amended standard) is that the opening statement of financial position and related notes may be omitted. A statement should be made explaining why the opening statement of financial position has been omitted.

> **Example – Business combinations and additional statements of financial position**
>
> A pet food manufacturer acquired a competitor in December 20X8 and accounted for the business combination under IFRS 3 on a provisional basis in its 31 December 20X8 annual financial statements. The business combination accounting was finalised in 20X9 and the provisional fair values were updated. As a result, the 20X8 comparatives were adjusted in the 20X9 annual financial statements. Does the restatement require an opening balance sheet (that is, an additional balance sheet) as of 1 January 20X8 under IAS 1?
>
> In our view, an additional statement of financial position is not required for the reasons explained above, that is, the acquisition had no impact on the entity's financial position at 1 January 20X8.

4.49 Some entities (SEC registrants, for example) present more than the minimum required under IFRS for comparative periods for certain statements. For example, an entity may present a comparative statement of financial position for only the previous period but comparative income statements for the previous two periods, which is permissible under IAS 1. The presentation of an additional comparative period for one statement does not trigger a requirement to present additional comparative periods for the other statements.

4.49.1 This is confirmed in the improvement to IAS 1 in May 2012. Under the amended standard, an entity might present a third statement of comprehensive income; presenting the current period, the preceding period and one additional comparative period. Where an entity chooses to do so, it is required to present, in the notes to the financial statements, the comparative information related to that additional statement of comprehensive income. [IAS 1 paras 38C, 38D]. However, the entity is not required to present a third statement of financial position, a third statement of cash flows or a third statement of changes in equity. The IASB decided that where an entity chooses to disclose additional information, full notes for that information are needed to ensure that the additional information is balanced and results in financial statements that achieve a fair presentation. [IAS 1 para BC32F].

4.50 Prior to the improvement referred to in paragraph 4.46.1, the additional statement of financial position presented on restatement or reclassification is presented as at *"the beginning of the earliest comparative period"*. [IAS 1 para 39]. Where an entity presents an unequal number of different types of primary statement, it may not always be obvious which period is the earliest comparative period. For example, an entity may present a statement of comprehensive income for the year 20X3 with comparatives for 20X2 and 20X1 along with a statement of financial position as at the end of 20X3 with a comparative statement as at the end of 20X2 only. If the earliest comparative period is taken to refer to all primary statements, the earliest comparative period would be 20X1, the earliest period for which the statement of comprehensive income is presented. The additional statement of financial position would then be presented as at the end of 20X0 (that is, the beginning of 20X1); the financial statements would therefore include statements of financial position as at the end of 20X3, 20X2 and 20X0 which is not a sensible presentation. If, on the other hand, the earliest comparative period is taken to refer to the statement of financial position only, as might be inferred from the fact that the additional presentation requirement is in respect of that statement, the earliest comparative period would be 20X2 and the additional statement of financial position would be presented as at the end of 20X1. The financial statements would then include statements of financial position as at the end of 20X3, 20X2 and 20X1, giving a continuous track record of statements of financial position. In our view, the latter approach is the most appropriate. However, preparers should also consider the position of their applicable regulators in this respect.

4.50.1 As explained in paragraph 4.46.1, the IASB has amended the requirements in IAS 1 relating to the additional statement of financial position. The amendment clarifies that the additional statement of financial position is given as at the beginning of the preceding period regardless of whether an entity's financial statements present comparative information for earlier periods.

4.51 Where it is impracticable to restate the comparative figures, then the entity should disclose the reason for not restating and the nature of the adjustments that would have been made if it had been practicable to do so. [IAS 1 para 42]. Applying a requirement is 'impracticable' when the entity cannot apply it after making every reasonable effort to do so. [IAS 1 para 7]. It is recognised that in some cases, such as when the data for the previous period has not been and cannot be collected in such a way as to permit reclassification, it will be necessary to depart from the normal rule and not reclassify. [IAS 1 para 43].

Consistency of presentation

4.52   IFRS requires entities to present the financial statements in a consistent manner. IAS 1 states:

> *"An entity shall retain the presentation and classification of items in the financial statements from one period to the next unless:*
>
> *(a)   it is apparent, following a significant change in the nature of the entity's operations or a review of its financial statements, that another presentation or classification would be more appropriate having regard to the criteria for selection and application of accounting policies in IAS 8; or*
>
> *(b)   an IFRS requires a change in presentation."*

[IAS 1 para 45].

4.53   Once management has selected a particular presentation, they should use it consistently. Most companies will seldom have good reason to change their presentation and, therefore, they should give careful consideration to the presentation that they wish to adopt when they prepare their first set of financial statements after incorporation or on transition to IFRS. Unless a standard or interpretation requires a change in presentation, an entity may only change its presentation if the changed presentation provides reliable and more relevant information; that is, the new presentation should be an improvement on the previous presentation. Just as entities should not change an accounting policy to another acceptable, but not improved, accounting policy, they should not change presentation to another acceptable, but not improved presentation. To ensure comparability, entities should only change to a presentation that is likely to continue to be used in future periods. [IAS 1 para 46].

4.54   Where an entity changes its presentation or classification of items, the notes to the financial statements should disclose the nature, amount of, and reason for the reclassification. [IAS 1 para 41]. As noted above, in the rare circumstances when it is impracticable to restate the corresponding amounts, disclosures are still required in these cases. (See further para 4.51.) The requirement for a statement of financial position to be presented as at the beginning of the earliest comparative period when items are reclassified is discussed in paragraph 4.46 above. This is further clarified by the improvement to IAS 1 in May 2012 (effective for annual periods beginning on or after 1 January 2013, with early adoption permitted), which clarifies that the disclosure in paragraph 41 of IAS 1 includes the beginning of the preceding period.

4.55 Table 4.1.1 illustrates the disclosure relating to a change of classification of certain revenue and costs in the income statement and of items in the statement of financial position, including the presentation of a statement of financial position as at the beginning of the earliest comparative period.

Table 4.1.1 — Change in presentation/classification

Fiat S.p.A. – Annual report – 31 December 2009

CONSOLIDATED STATEMENT OF FINANCIAL POSITION[(*)] (extract)

(€ million)	Note	At 31 December 2009	At 31 December 2008	At 1 January 2008
ASSETS				
Intangible assets	(14)	7,199	7,048	6,523
Property, plant and equipment	(15)	12,945	12,515	11,212
Investment property		–	–	10
Investments and other financial assets:	(16)	2,159	2,177	2,214
Investments accounted for using the equity method		1,884	1,899	1,930
Other investments and financial assets		275	278	284
Leased assets	(17)	457	505	396
Defined benefit plan assets		144	120	31
Deferred tax assets	(11)	2,580	2,386	1,892
Total Non-current assets		**25,484**	**24,751**	**22,278**
Inventories	(18)	8,748	11,438	10,024
Trade receivables	(19)	3,649	4,390	4,384
Receivables from financing activities	(19)	12,695	13,136	12,268
Current tax receivables	(19)	674	770	1,153
Other current assets	(19)	2,778	2,600	2,291
Current financial assets		899	967	1,016
Current investments		46	26	22
Current securities	(20)	217	177	291
Other financial assets	(21)	636	764	703
Cash and cash equivalents	(22)	12,226	3,683	6,639
Total Current assets		**41,669**	**36,984**	**37,775**
Assets held for sale	(23)	82	37	83
TOTAL ASSETS		**67,235**	**61,772**	**60,136**

SIGNIFICANT ACCOUNTING POLICIES (extract)

Accounting principles, amendments and interpretations adopted from 1 January 2009 (extract)

Improvement to IAS 16 – Property, Plant and Equipment

The improvement to IAS 16 – *Property, Plant and Equipment* requires an entity that in the course of its ordinary activities routinely sells items of property, plant and equipment that it has held for rental to others, to transfer such assets to inventories when they cease to be rented and become held for sale. As a consequence, the proceeds from the sale of such assets shall be recognised as revenue. Payments made to manufacture or acquire assets held for rental to others or those received from the subsequent sale of such assets are considered to arise from operating activities for the purposes of the Statement of cash flows.

Until 31 December 2008 the Group classified as Inventories leased assets that ceased to be rented under operating leases and were held for sale. When these assets were sold on a final basis, however, the Group recognised any gains or losses on disposal as Other income (expenses). Additionally, in the Statement of cash flows the Group classified cash flows arising from the manufacture, acquisition or disposal of the assets held for rental under operating leases as cash flows from (used in) investment activities. The Group also followed the accounting treatment used for leased assets for assets of the Trucks and Commercial Vehicles Sector sold under a buy-back commitment; at the end of the buy-back agreement term, however, these assets remained classified as Property, plant and equipment and any gains or losses on disposal were recognised as Other income (expenses). Cash flows arising from these assets were classified as cash flows from (used in) operating activities in the Statement of cash flows.

The Group adopted the amendment to IAS 16 retrospectively on 1 January 2009. As the method of measuring leased assets and assets sold under buy-back commitments was the same as that used for measuring inventory, the application of the new accounting treatment did not lead to any effect on Equity at 1 January 2008 or 31 December 2008, and on the Profit of 2008. Applying the amendment did however require certain items in the Statement of financial positions at 1 January 2008 and 31 December 2008 to be reclassified and certain items in the Income statement for 2008 and the Statement of cash flows for 2008 presented as comparative to be recalculated.

In further detail, the effects arising on the Statement of financial position presented for comparative purposes are as follows:

(€ million)	At 31 December 2008	At 1 January 2008
Property, plant and equipment		
As previously reported	12,607	11,246
Reclassification to Inventory for assets sold under buy-back commitments and held for sale	(92)	(34)
Amount after the reclassification	**12,515**	**11,212**

(€ million)	At 31 December 2008	At 1 January 2008
Inventory	11,346	9,990
As previously reported		
Reclassification from property, plant and equipment for assets sold under buy-back commitments and held for sale	92	34
Amount after the reclassification	**11,438**	**10,024**

The effects on the Income statement presented for comparative purposes are as follows:

(€ million)	2008
Net revenues	
As previously reported	59,380
Recognition of the proceeds from the sale of assets under buy-back commitments and leased assets	184
Amount as restated	**59,564**

(€ million)	2008
Cost of sales	49,423
As previously reported	
Change in Inventory for assets sold under buy-back commitments and leased assets	189
Amount as restated	**49,612**

(€ million)	2008
Other income (expenses)	
As previously reported	(23)
Reversal of gains from the sale of assets under buy-back commitment and leased assets	(18)
Reversal of losses from the sale of assets under buy-back commitment and leased assets	23
Amount as restated	**(18)**

The effects on the Statement of cash flows presented as comparative figures are as follows:

(€ million)	2008
Cash flows from (used in) operating activities	
As previously reported	384
Reclassification from Cash flows from (used in) investment activities	(218)
Amount after the reclassification	**166**

(€ million)	2008
Cash flows from (used in) investment activities	(6,310)
As previously reported	
Reclassification to Cash flows from (used in) operating activities	218
Amount after the reclassification	**(6,092)**

Structure and content

4.56 IAS 1 requires certain disclosures to be made on the face of the primary statements; other required disclosures may be made in the notes or on the face of the financial statements, unless another standard specifies otherwise. [IAS 1 paras 47, 48].

Identification

4.57 As noted in paragraph 4.15, IAS 1 requires the financial statements to be identified and distinguished from other information in the same published document. It is important for users of financial statements to understand the information that is presented in accordance with IFRS and other information that is supplementary to those financial statements. [IAS 1 paras 49, 50]. It is also important for the audited IFRS-compliant financial statements to be distinguished from unaudited information that may or may not be in compliance with IFRS. The use of alternative measures of performance, often referred to as 'non-GAAP measures', has been of concern to many financial statement readers, particularly regulators in North America and Europe. At times, such measures appear to give a more flattering picture of the entity's performance than the profit determined in accordance with IFRS. Entities should exercise care when presenting alternative performance measures in their published documents to ensure they are distinguished from the financial statements themselves. See also from paragraph 4.238.

4.58 IAS 1 also contains the following requirements:

"An entity shall clearly identify each financial statement and the notes. In addition, an entity shall display the following information prominently, and repeat it when necessary for the information presented to be understandable:

(a) *the name of the reporting entity or other means of identification, and any change in that information from the end of the preceding reporting period;*

(b) *whether the financial statements are of an individual entity or a group of entities;*

(c) *the date of the end of the reporting period or the period covered by the set of financial statements or notes;*

(d) *the presentation currency, as defined in IAS 21; and*

(e) *the level of rounding used in presenting amounts in the financial statements."*

[IAS 1 para 51].

4.59 Entities should determine the best way of presenting the information to meet the overall objective of clarity. The above requirements are usually met by presenting appropriate headings for items such as pages, statements and columns, but where financial statements are presented electronically, a different approach may be required. [IAS 1 para 52]. Also, entities may make their financial statements clearer by presenting the information in thousands or millions of the presentation currency. This is permitted as long as the level of rounding is stated and material information is not omitted. [IAS 1 para 53].

Statement of financial position (balance sheet)

Face of the statement of financial position

4.60 In financial statements complying with IFRS, as a minimum, the following items should be disclosed on the face of the statement of financial position (also known as the balance sheet):

- Property, plant and equipment.
- Investment property.
- Intangible assets.
- Financial assets (excluding amounts shown under other categories).
- Investments accounted for using the equity method.
- Biological assets.
- Inventories.
- Trade and other receivables.
- Cash and cash equivalents.
- The total of assets classified as held for sale and assets included in disposal groups classified as held for sale in accordance with IFRS 5.

- Trade and other payables.

- Provisions.

- Financial liabilities (excluding amounts shown under other categories).

- Liabilities and assets for current tax, as defined in IAS 12.

- Deferred tax liabilities and deferred tax assets, as defined in IAS 12.

- Liabilities included in disposal groups classified as held for sale in accordance with IFRS 5.

- Non-controlling interest, presented within equity.

- Issued capital and reserves attributable to owners of the parent.

[IAS 1 para 54].

4.61 Most entities preparing IFRS financial statements are required to present the face of the statement of financial position differentiating between current and non-current assets and between current and non-current liabilities, but IAS 1 does not prescribe the order or format in which such items are to be presented. Under IFRS, deferred tax assets and liabilities may not be classified as current. [IAS 1 para 56]. See the paragraphs starting at paragraph 4.65 for more details.

UK.4.61.1 The UK company law formats for individual and consolidated financial statements do not apply to those companies that elect to prepare IFRS financial statements. UK GAAP reporters may use a balance sheet presentation very similar to that of UK IFRS reporters. However, the company law formats do not permit UK GAAP reporters to present non-current debtors, stocks or deferred tax assets outside the current assets category. IAS 1 does not prescribe the order in which the above items appear. [IAS 1 para 57]. Additional line items, headings and sub-totals are required by IAS 1 when they are relevant to an understanding of the entity's financial position. [IAS 1 para 55]. Although the legislation requires that sub-totals are given for certain items (for example, fixed assets), it does not require the balance sheet total to be struck in a particular place.

4.62 IAS 1 requires the presentation of a minimum number of line items but it contains no requirements or recommendations on sub-totalling or balance sheet totals. Companies may present a total for net assets and show this as equal to the total of capital and reserves and non-controlling interest. Many companies show assets equal in total to liabilities plus capital and reserves.

4.63 The line items set out in paragraph 4.60 form the minimum content for the face of the statement of financial position. Nevertheless, entities should insert additional line items when required to do so by other IFRS or when the size, nature or function of an item or aggregation of similar items is such that separate presentation is relevant to an understanding of an entity's financial position. [IAS 1 para 55, 57(a)]. The descriptions of the line items and the order in which they are shown may be adapted according to the entity's nature and its transactions. Financial institutions, for example, would amend the descriptions of line items to provide information that is relevant to the operations of financial institutions. [IAS 1 para 57(b)]. Therefore, management should, to a large extent, exercise judgement in determining the most appropriate form of presentation and whether additional line items are shown separately, but in exercising that judgement they should consider the following factors:

- The nature and liquidity of the assets. For example, because of the difference in their nature, goodwill and other intangible assets would normally be presented separately on the face of the statement of financial position.

- The function of the assets.

- The nature, timing and amounts of liabilities. In most cases, this will lead, for example, to the separate presentation of interest bearing and non-interest bearing liabilities.

[IAS 1 para 58].

4.64 IAS 1 takes the view that the use of different measurement bases for assets or liabilities is indicative of a difference in their nature or function. For example, under IAS 16 property, plant and equipment may be carried at cost or at a revalued amount. Where entities choose to carry some of these assets at cost and some at revalued amounts, it is presumed that the choice of different measurement bases has been made because these assets have different natures or functions. Accordingly, the assets carried at cost should be shown separately from assets carried at revalued amounts on the face of the balance sheet. [IAS 1 para 59]. Historically, under IFRS, many preparers have included all property, plant and equipment at cost and, therefore, property, plant and equipment has usually appeared as a single line item on the face of the statement of financial position in IFRS financial statements.

Current/non-current classification

4.65 IAS 1 states that an entity shall present current and non-current assets, and current and non-current liabilities, as separate classifications on the face of the statement of financial position, except when a presentation based on liquidity provides information that is reliable and is more relevant. When that exception applies, all assets and liabilities should be presented broadly in order of liquidity. [IAS 1 para 60].

4.66 The IAS 1 guidance on the current/non-current distinction indicates that separate classification of current and non-current assets and liabilities is useful when an entity supplies goods or services within a clearly identifiable operating cycle, *"by distinguishing the net assets that are continuously circulating as working capital from those used in the entity's long term operations"*. [IAS 1 para 62]. An operating cycle is *"the time between the acquisition of assets for processing and their realisation in cash or cash equivalents"*. [IAS 1 para 68]. Companies are required under IAS 1 to present a current/non-current classified statement of financial position unless they judge a 'liquidity-based statement of financial position' 'more relevant'. Whether an entity presents a current/non-current classified statement of financial position is largely dependent on the industry in which it operates and, consequently, a current/non-current classified statement of financial position has become an expected form of presentation for certain types of entity.

4.67 Most industrial and retail entities would present a current/non-current classified statement of financial position because significant amounts of their assets and liabilities would be realised or settled within a relatively short period. On the other hand, depending on the nature of their business, some property developers may be less likely to use a current/non-current classified statement of financial position (as their assets and liabilities may be realised or settled over a long period, sometimes over several years), unless a clearly identifiable operating cycle exists. Although it is common practice to consider a normal operating cycle to be a year, the period of one year after the reporting period is not an inflexible cut-off point for determining the current/non-current status of assets and liabilities. An asset recoverable within the normal operating cycle of more than one year is still a current asset under IAS 1; a liability to be settled within the normal operating cycle of more than one year is a current liability (see paras 4.72 and 4.82). Nevertheless, companies need to determine whether a current/non-current classified statement of financial position gives the most relevant presentation. In situations where the operating assets and liabilities are recovered or settled over very long periods, a liquidity presentation may be more appropriate. For example, while a property development entity may have a clearly identifiable operating cycle, in some cases, it may not be sensible to present development properties (held as inventory) and debtors as current assets if the development properties are only likely to be realised several years after the reporting period.

4.68 Even where assets and liabilities are readily realisable or capable of immediate settlement, a classified statement of financial position may not be the most useful form of presentation. For example, investment companies would typically have such assets and liabilities but the timing of their realisation or settlement is dependent not just on their liquidity, but on investment managers' judgements on, for example, expected movements in market prices. The distinction between current and non-current items is not particularly meaningful in such cases. The standard specifically states that for some entities, such as financial institutions, a 'liquidity-based statement of financial position' will be more relevant because the entity does not supply goods or services within a clearly identifiable operating cycle. [IAS 1 para 63].

4.69 Whether an entity presents a current/non-current classified or a liquidity-based statement of financial position, it is nevertheless required to make additional disclosures in respect of each asset and liability line item that combines amounts expected to be recovered or settled within 12 months with those expected to be recovered or settled after 12 months. In such circumstances, the entity should disclose the amounts that are expected to be recovered or settled within 12 months of the reporting period and the amounts expected to be recovered or settled after more than 12 months. [IAS 1 para 61]. Such information is considered useful in assessing the liquidity and solvency of an entity. [IAS 1 para 65]. Depending on the entity's operating cycle an asset or liability may be current even where it is expected to be recovered or settled after more than 12 months from the end of the reporting period. See paragraphs 4.72 and 4.82. The standard uses the terms 'current' and non-current' but permits the use of alternative descriptions as long as the meaning is clear. [IAS 1 para 67]. An example of disclosure is given in Table 4.2

Table 4.2 – Current/non-current distinction and disclosure of amounts due after 1 year

EADS N.V. – Report and accounts – 31 December 2011

Significant accounting policies (extract)

Current and non-current assets and liabilities —

The classification of an asset or liability as a current or non-current asset or liability in general depends on whether the item is related to serial production or subject to long-term production. In case of serial production, an asset or liability is classified as a non-current asset or liability when the item is realised or settled respectively after 12 months after the reporting period, and as current asset or liability when the item is realised or settled respectively within 12 months after the reporting period. In case of construction contracts, an asset or liability is classified as non-current when the item is realised or settled respectively beyond EADS' normal operating cycle; and as a current asset or liability when the item is realised or settled in EADS' normal operating cycle. However, current assets include assets – such as inventories, trade receivables and receivables from PoC – that are sold, consumed and realised as part of the normal operating cycle even when they are not expected to be realised within 12 months after the reporting period. Trade payables are equally part of the normal operating cycle and are therefore classified as current liabilities.

19 Trade receivables (extract)

Trade receivables at 31 December 2011 and 2010 consist of the following:

In € million	31st December 2011	31st December 2010
Receivables from sales of goods and services	6,765	6,953
Allowance for doubtful accounts	(366)	(321)
Total	6,399	6,632

The trade receivables decrease by €-233 million mainly caused by Astrium (€-669 million) and Airbus (€-179 million), partly compensated by an increase at Eurocopter (€+527 million) and Cassidian (€+76 million).

Trade receivables are classified as current assets. As of 31 December 2011 and 2010, respectively, € 668 million and € 383 million of trade receivables are not expected to be collected within one year.

4.70 IAS 1 states that it may be appropriate for some entities to present some of their assets and liabilities using the current/non-current classification and other assets and liabilities in order of liquidity. [IAS 1 para 64]. The standard states that this mixed basis of presentation might arise when an entity has diverse operations. However, guidance is not given on how this mixed presentation might be adopted. For the most part, entities (or groups of entities) do not have operations that are so diverse that a departure from the normal presentation bases would be justified. IAS 27 does not permit a subsidiary to be excluded from consolidation because its activities are dissimilar from those of the other entities within the group, but instead requires groups to provide relevant information through disclosure of segmental information (see chapter 10). [IAS 27 para 17]. Although adopting a mixed basis of presentation is not equivalent to non-consolidation, the presentation problem that is caused by diverse operations should, in most cases, be addressed by segmental reporting without having to resort to a mixed presentation. It is important that the principle of full consolidation in IAS 27 (or IFRS 10) is not undermined by mixed presentation. Similarly, it is important that the line items in the balance sheet of an individual entity should reflect the entirety of that type of asset or liability. In the exceptional cases where a mixed presentation is appropriate, assets and liabilities should be accorded a prominence appropriate to their size and nature, rather than to the business or operation from which they are derived. An asset or liability is not less significant just because it arises in a business that is not the main activity of the entity or group.

4.71 Table 4.3 shows an example of a current/non-current classified statement of financial position. Table 4.4 shows an example of a liquidity-based statement of financial position.

Table 4.3 – Current/non-current classified statement of financial position

adidas AG – Annual Report – 31 December 2011

adidas AG Consolidated Statement of Financial Position (IFRS) (€ in millions)

	Note	Dec. 31, 2011	Dec. 31, 2010	Change in %
ASSETS				
Cash and cash equivalents	4	906	1,156	(21.6)
Short-term financial assets	5	465	233	99.1
Accounts receivable	6	1,707	1,667	2.4
Other current financial assets	7	304	197	54.6
Inventories	8	2,482	2,119	17.1
Income tax receivables	33	77	71	8.8
Other current assets	9	469	390	20.6
Assets classified as held for sale	10	25	47	(46.9)
Total current assets		**6,435**	**5,880**	**9.4**
Property, plant and equipment	11	963	855	12.7
Goodwill	12	1,580	1,539	2.7
Trademarks	13	1,503	1,447	3.8
Other intangible assets	13	160	142	12.1
Long-term financial assets	14	97	93	4.5
Other non-current financial assets	15	42	54	(22.3)
Deferred tax assets	33	493	508	(2.8)
Other non-current assets	16	107	100	6.1
Total non-current assets		**4,945**	**4,738**	**4.4**
Total assets		**11,380**	**10,618**	**7.2**
LIABILITIES AND EQUITY				
Short-term borrowings	17	289	273	5.9
Accounts payable		1,886	1,694	11.4
Other current financial liabilities	18	56	123	(54.1)
Income taxes	33	252	265	(4.9)
Other current provisions	19	507	470	7.9
Current accrued liabilities	20	990	842	17.6
Other current liabilities	21	301	241	24.4
Liabilities classified as held for sale	10	0	0	(27.7)
Total current liabilities		**4,281**	**3,908**	**9.5**

Long-term borrowings	17	991	1,337	(25.9)
Other non-current financial liabilities	22	6	15	(57.4)
Pensions and similar obligations	23	205	180	14.1
Deferred tax liabilities	33	430	451	(4.6)
Other non-current provisions	19	55	29	91.3
Non-current accrued liabilities	20	45	39	11.6
Other non-current liabilities	24	36	36	0.3
Total non-current liabilities		**1,768**	**2,087**	**(15.3)**
Share capital		209	209	–
Reserves		770	563	37.0
Retained earnings		4,348	3,844	13.1
Shareholders' equity	25	**5,327**	**4,616**	**15.4**
Non-controlling interests	26	4	7	(38.2)
Total equity		**5,331**	**4,623**	**15.3**
Total liabilities and equity		**11,380**	**10,618**	**7.2**

Rounding differences may arise in percentages and totals.
The accompanying notes are an integral part of these consolidated financial statements.

Table 4.4 – Liquidity-based statement of financial position
HSBC Holdings plc – Annual Report – Year ended 31 December 2011
Consolidated balance sheet at 31 December 2011

	Notes	2011 US$m	2010 US$m
ASSETS			
Cash and balances at central banks		129,902	57,383
Items in the course of collection from other banks		8,208	6,072
Hong Kong Government certificates of indebtedness		20,922	19,057
Trading assets	15	330,451	385,052
Financial assets designated at fair value	19	30,856	37,011
Derivatives	20	346,379	260,757
Loans and advances to banks		180,987	208,271
Loans and advances to customers		940,429	958,366
Financial investments	21	400,044	400,755
Assets held for sale		39,558	1,991
Other assets	27	48,699	41,260
Current tax assets		1,061	1,096
Prepayments and accrued income		10,059	11,966
Interests in associates and joint ventures	23	20,399	17,198
Goodwill and intangible assets	24	29,034	29,922
Property, plant and equipment	25	10,865	11,521
Deferred tax assets	10	7,726	7,011
Total assets		2,555,579	2,454,689

LIABILITIES AND EQUITY

Liabilities

Hong Kong currency notes in circulation		**20,922**	19,057
Deposits by banks		**112,822**	110,584
Customer accounts		**1,253,925**	1,227,725
Items in the course of transmission to other banks		**8,745**	6,663
Trading liabilities	28	**265,192**	300,703
Financial liabilities designated at fair value	29	**85,724**	88,133
Derivatives	20	**345,380**	258,665
Debt securities in issue	30	**131,013**	145,401
Liabilities of disposal groups held for sale	31	**22,200**	86
Other liabilities	31	**27,967**	27,964
Current tax liabilities		**2,117**	1,804
Liabilities under insurance contracts issued	32	**61,259**	58,609
Accruals and deferred income		**13,106**	13,906
Provisions	33	**3,324**	2,138
Deferred tax liability	10	**1,518**	1,093
Retirement benefit liabilities	7	**3,666**	3,856
Subordinated liabilities	34	**30,606**	33,387
Total liabilities		**2,389,486**	2,299,774
Equity			
Called up share capital	39	**8,934**	8,843
Share premium account		**8,457**	8,454
Other equity instruments		**5,851**	5,851
Other reserves		**23,615**	25,414
Retained earnings[5]		**111,868**	99,105
Total shareholders' equity		**158,725**	147,667
Non-controlling interests	38	**7,368**	7,248
Total equity		**166,093**	154,915
Total equity and liabilities		**2,555,579**	2,454,689

The accompanying notes on pages 291 to 413, 'Critical accounting policies' on pages 38 to 42, the audited sections of 'Risk' on pages 98 to 210 and the audited sections of 'Capital' on pages 211 to 217 form an integral part of these financial statements.

Current assets

4.72   IAS 1 defines current assets:

"An entity shall classify an asset as current when:

(a)   *it expects to realise the asset, or intends to sell or consume it, in its normal operating cycle;*

(b)   *it holds the asset primarily for the purpose of trading;*

(c)   *it expects to realise the asset within twelve months after the reporting period; or*

(d)   *the asset is cash or a cash equivalent (as defined in IAS 7) unless the asset is restricted from being exchanged or used to settle a liability for at least twelve months after the reporting period.*

The entity shall classify all other assets as non-current."

[IAS 1 para 66].

4.73 An operating cycle is *"the time between the acquisition of assets for processing and their realisation in cash or cash equivalents"*. Where the normal operating cycle cannot be identified, it is assumed to have a duration of 12 months. [IAS 1 para 68].

Receivables and inventories

4.74 A current asset is, therefore, not necessarily one that is recoverable within 12 months of the reporting period. Where the entity's operating cycle is such that inventory or trade receivables are normally not realised in cash within 12 months, they will still be treated as a current asset.

> **Example – Classification based on normal operating cycle**
>
> An entity produces airplanes. The length of time between first purchasing raw materials to make the planes and the date the entity completes the production and delivery is 10 months. The entity receives payment for the planes 6 months after delivery.
>
> (a) How should the entity show its inventory and trade receivables in its classified statement of financial position?
>
> The time between the first purchase of goods and the realisation of those goods in cash is 16 months (10 months + 6 months). The age of inventory held by the entity at the year end will range between zero months to 10 months, and once the goods are delivered, it will take a further 6 months to receive payment. All of the inventory should be classified as a current asset, even though some of the inventory will not be realised in cash within 12 months of the reporting period. This is because the inventory is realised in the entity's normal operating cycle, as envisaged by IAS 1 paragraph 66(a). However, the expected date of recovery of the inventory should be disclosed by the entity. The trade receivables will be realised in cash within 12 months of the reporting period and are, therefore, included as a current asset as we would expect.
>
> (b) Would the answer be different if the production time was 14 months and the time between delivery and payment was a further 15 months?
>
> No. The inventory and trade receivables should still be classified as a current asset. In this case, the inventory is, on average, older but nevertheless it is realised in cash in the entity's normal operating cycle. Similarly, the trade receivables are realised in cash as part of the operating cycle and should be classified as a current asset, even though they will not be realised in cash within 12 months of the reporting period. In addition to disclosing the expected date of recovery of the inventory, the maturity date of the trade receivables, a financial asset, will require disclosure under IFRS 7.

4.75 The classification of receivables should reflect the commercial reality of the situation. In most cases this will also be reflected in the transaction's legal terms. However, arrangements between related parties, particularly those between companies that are members of the same group, are often such that either legal terms are not specified or they are specified in a way that is different from the parties' intentions.

> **Example – Classification of an inter-company receivable due on demand**
>
> A parent provides a loan to a subsidiary. Interest of 8% is paid annually. The loan is repayable on demand. How should the loan receivable be classified in the parent's statement of financial position?
>
> Ordinarily, financial assets due on demand are current assets. However, the demand feature may be primarily a form of protection or a tax-driven feature of the loan and it may be the expectation and intention of both parties that the loan will remain outstanding for the foreseeable future. If this is the case, the instrument is, in substance, long-term in nature and should be classified as a non-current asset. If there is an intention that the loan will be repaid within 12 months of the reporting period, it should be classified as a current asset.

Cash and cash equivalents

4.76   Cash and cash equivalents are defined in IAS 7 as follows:

> "*Cash* comprises cash on hand and demand deposits. Cash equivalents *are short-term, highly liquid investments that are readily convertible to known amounts of cash and which are subject to an insignificant risk of changes in value.*"

[IAS 7 para 6].

4.76.1   Questions often arise regarding the classification of relatively liquid investments, such as commercial paper, eurobonds and deposits. Paragraph 7 of IAS 7 states that cash equivalents are held for the purpose of meeting short-term cash commitments, rather than for investment or other purposes. An investment generally qualifies as a cash equivalent when it has a short maturity of, say, three months or less from the date of acquisition (see chapter 30). To the extent that investments meet the definition of cash equivalents, they should be included in the heading 'cash and cash equivalents'. To the extent that they do not, they should be shown as financial assets. In the case of deposits not qualifying as cash equivalents, a separate heading may be used.

4.77   Current assets should exclude cash and cash equivalents that are restricted from being exchanged or used to settle a liability for at least 12 months after the reporting period. However, the existence of currency restrictions in a foreign jurisdiction would not necessarily preclude the classification of cash as current. See chapter 30.

Other financial assets

4.78   The current/non-current classification of other financial assets (including derivatives) is considered in chapter 6.

Assets held for disposal

4.79 Where a decision has been made to dispose of assets originally classified as non-current assets and they are expected to be realised within one year of the reporting period, they should be reclassified as current assets. IFRS 5 requires that assets held for disposal are not depreciated. Entities are required to present a non-current asset classified as held for sale and the assets of a disposal group classified as held for sale separately from other assets in the statement of financial position. [IFRS 5 para 38]. See chapter 26 for further detail on the criteria that must be met before assets are classified as held for sale.

Tax assets

4.80 Deferred tax assets should not be classified as current, regardless of the period over which they are expected to be recovered (see chapter 13). [IAS 1 para 56]. Some entities adopting current/non-current classified statements of financial position have shown deferred tax assets and deferred tax liabilities as separate categories; that is, they have shown deferred tax assets as neither current nor non-current, with the same approach adopted for liabilities. In our view, this is an incorrect interpretation of the requirements of IAS 1. IAS 1 states that a mixed presentation may be appropriate in certain circumstances, for example, an entity with diverse operations. [IAS 1 para 64]. However, deferred tax assets and liabilities arise in the financial statements of most entities, and in our view, it is not the standard's intention that the use of mixed presentation would be available or appropriate to all entities. Mixed presentation is discussed further in paragraph 4.70 above.

4.81 Other tax assets should be classified as current where they are expected to be realised within one year of the reporting period; otherwise they should be shown as non-current assets. [IAS 1 para 66(c)].

Current liabilities

4.82 IAS 1 defines current liabilities as follows:

> *"An entity shall classify a liability as current when:*
> *(a) it expects to settle the liability in the entity's normal operating cycle;*
> *(b) it holds the liability primarily for the purpose of trading;*
> *(c) the liability is due to be settled within twelve months after the reporting period; or*
> *(d) it does not have an unconditional right to defer settlement of the liability for at least twelve months after the reporting period (see paragraph 73). Terms of a liability that could, at the option of the counterparty, result in its settlement by the issue of equity instruments do not affect its classification.*

An entity shall classify all other liabilities as non-current."
[IAS 1 para 69].

4.82.1 Paragraph 69(d) of IAS 1 states that "... *terms of a liability that could, at the option of the counterparty, result in its settlement by the issue of equity instruments do not affect its classification*". This clarifies that conversion features that are at the holder's discretion do not impact the classification of the liability component of a convertible instrument. See further chapter 6.

4.83 Where it is expected that the liability will be settled within the entity's normal operating cycle, the liability should be classified as current even if, at the end of the reporting period, the entity has the right to defer payment until a later date. A current liability is not necessarily one that is settled within one year of the reporting period. Certain liabilities (such as trade payables and some accruals for employee and other operating costs) are incurred as part of the business' normal operating cycle and, as noted in paragraph 4.67 above, it may be that this operating cycle is longer than 12 months. Where an entity's operating cycle is not clearly identifiable, it is assumed to have a duration of 12 months. [IAS 1 para 70]. Where a liability is due to be settled within 12 months of the reporting period, it should be shown as a current liability, unless allowed otherwise under paragraph 73 of IAS 1 (see para 4.85 below). Examples of current liabilities would include some financial liabilities held for trading in accordance with IAS 39, loans repayable on demand, bank overdrafts and the current element of provisions, long-term loans, dividends payable, income taxes and other non-trade payables. Financial liabilities that provide long-term financing and are not due to be settled within one year of the end of the reporting period are classified as non-current liabilities (subject to para 4.84 below). [IAS 1 para 71].

> **Examples – Classification of warranty and environmental provisions**
>
> How should an entity classify the following liabilities and provisions in its statement of financial position?
>
> (a) Warranty provisions – The classification will depend on the warranty's terms. Warranties that guarantee product performance for a 12 month period are classified as current liabilities. Where the warranty covers a longer period, the provision should be split into its current and non-current elements, giving consideration to the length of the normal operating cycle.
>
> (b) Provision for environmental liabilities – This type of provision is unlikely to be part of a single operating cycle. Therefore, the provision should be split into its current and non-current elements, depending on the likely timing of the expenditure to meet the environmental obligation.

Borrowings and covenant compliance

4.84 IAS 1 states:

> "*An entity classifies its financial liabilities as current when they are due to be settled within twelve months after the reporting period, even if:*
>
> *(a) the original term was for a period longer than twelve months; and*

   *(b)   an agreement to refinance, or to reschedule payments, on a long-term
        basis is completed after the reporting period and before the financial
        statements are authorised for issue."*

[IAS 1 para 72].

4.84.1   An entity classifies a liability as current if it does not have the unconditional right to defer its settlement for at least 12 months after the end of the reporting period. [IAS 1 para 69(d)].

4.84.2   The IFRS IC published an agenda decision in November 2010 on the classification of a liability as current or non-current when the liability is not scheduled for repayment within 12 months of the end of the reporting period, but may be callable by the lender at any time without cause. The IFRS IC confirmed that under paragraph 69(d) of IAS 1, a liability is classified as a current liability if the entity does not have the unconditional right at the reporting date to defer settlement for at least 12 months after the reporting period. This is the case for a liability that can be called by the lender at any time without cause; so such a liability should be classified as current.

4.84.3   Some loan agreements include a change of control clause under which a borrowing becomes repayable if there is a change of control event. This raises the question as to whether the borrowing is required to be classified as a current liability under paragraph 69(d) of IAS 1 if an entity is unable to prevent a controlling shareholder selling its shares to a third party, even if there is no expectation that a change of control might happen within 12 months. Our view is that a change of control clause does not result in classification as a current liability if there has been no change of control event at the end of the reporting period. In this respect, we consider that a change of control clause is similar in substance to a loan covenant (see para 4.86 below). IAS 1 requires classification as a current liability if there is an actual breach at the balance sheet date, but not if there is only a potential breach. Therefore, a borrowing is not classified as current if the counter-party does not have a right as of the balance sheet date to demand repayment within 12 months of that date.

4.84.4   Many loan agreements include 'Material Adverse Change Clause' (MAC) and 'Subjective Acceleration Clause' (SAC) clauses under which the lender can call the borrowing based on subjective criteria. As above, this raises the question of whether the borrowing is required to be classified as a current liability under paragraph 69(d) of IAS 1. Each clause should be analysed individually as at the balance sheet date. If the lender has the right to call the loan at the balance sheet date, because the MAC or SAC has occurred, the loan should be classified as current. If the lender does not have the right at the balance sheet date to call the loan for at least 12 months based on the circumstances at the balance sheet date, the loan should be classified as non-current. We believe that these clauses are often similar to loan covenants and entities would follow similar guidance (see para 4.86 below).

4.85 A rescheduling or refinancing of debt that is at the discretion of the lender and occurs after the reporting period does not alter the liability's condition at the balance sheet date. Such rescheduling or refinancing is regarded as a non-adjusting post balance sheet event and it is not taken into account in determining the current/non-current classification of the debt. On the other hand, where, at the balance sheet date, the refinancing or rescheduling is fully at the discretion of the borrowing entity as a result of arrangements in force with the lender, and the borrowing entity is able to and intends to elect to roll over an obligation for at least a further year, the obligation may be classified as non-current even if it would otherwise be due in less than a year. The entity must have full discretion to roll the obligation over; the potential for a refinancing alone would not be sufficient to classify an obligation as non-current. [IAS 1 para 73].

4.85.1 IAS 1 does not specify that a refinancing or roll over must be completed with the same lender as the one that provided the obligation being refinanced, but it emphasises the timing of settlement and the obligation to settle as key to determining the classification of a liability. Where a refinancing requires borrowing from new parties and settlement with different existing lenders, the ability to refinance should not impact the classification of the liability in the balance sheet. This is illustrated in the example below.

> **Example – Classification of bank debt**
>
> An entity has an outstanding borrowing under a term loan facility with a bank that is due to be repaid six months after the end of the reporting period. Prior to the end of the reporting period, the entity and the lender agree a new facility that expires in three years, and into which the entity is able to roll the outstanding balance of its existing borrowing. The entity intends to roll over the existing borrowing into the new loan facility when the borrowing matures and to maintain the outstanding balance of the new facility for the duration of the new facility.
>
> (a) How should this borrowing be shown in the entity's statement of financial position?
>
> The borrowing should be classified as non-current. Although the loan is due for repayment within six months after the end of the reporting period, the entity has the ability and intent to roll this obligation over into the new loan facility. The substance is, therefore, that the debt does not require settlement until the new three year committed facility expires.
>
> (b) Would the answer be different if the existing loan and new facility were with different banks?
>
> Yes. Although the entity may have the ability to refinance the loan under a facility that has been agreed at the balance sheet date, refinancing of the loan in this circumstance would require its settlement (in substance and fact) concurrent with a new borrowing. The new borrowing could not be viewed as an extension of the existing loan; the loan should, therefore, be classified as current in the entity's balance sheet. However, the circumstances and availability of the new facility are likely to warrant disclosure.

4.85.2 The IFRS IC discussed this issue in November 2010 and January 2011. Those discussions indicate agreement with the position noted above and that there is no diversity in practice in this area. The IFRS IC did, however, recommend that the IASB amend the wording of paragraph 73 of IAS 1 through annual improvements to address circumstances where an existing loan facility is renegotiated with the same lender, but on different terms. The IASB issued an improvements exposure draft in May 2012 proposing to amend IAS 1 in this respect. The IASB noted that if an entity expects (and has the discretion) to refinance an existing loan on substantially different terms, classification of the loan as non-current at the balance sheet date is not consistent with the derecognition guidance for financial liabilities in IAS 39 (see chapter 6). The IASB therefore proposes to amend paragraph 73 of IAS 1 to clarify that for an existing loan that is due within 12 months of the balance sheet date to be classified as non-current, an entity must expect (and have the discretion) to refinance the loan for at least 12 months after the reporting period with the same lender, on the same or similar terms. In the IASB's view, terms are similar if the amendment of the terms would be expected to result in no substantial change to the rights and obligations of the parties to the loan facility.

4.85.3 An entity might enter into a factoring arrangement that involves it transferring its rights to cash to be collected from receivables to a third party (the factor) in exchange for an upfront cash payment. The accounting for these arrangements is dealt with in chapter 6. Where the entity continues to recognise the factored receivables under IAS 39, the finance received from the factor is recorded as a liability. The terms of the factoring arrangement need to be considered to determine how the liability should be classified in the statement of financial position.

> **Example – classification of liability from debt factoring arrangement**
>
> Consider whether a factoring obligation in respect of receivables is presented as current or non-current in two scenarios: (1) when the entity is required to pass through collected receivables and repurchase receivables on a monthly basis; and (2) when the entity offsets new draw downs with collections and makes a net payment only if there are insufficient receivables.
>
> *Fact pattern 1:*
>
> - Entity A enters into a 5 year debtors factoring facility where it sells eligible debtors. The credit terms of the debtors are 30 days.
>
> - Eligible debtors are legally valid debtors that do not exceed 90 days outstanding.
>
> - The debtors are not derecognised on the basis that the entity remains exposed to substantially all of the risks and rewards.
>
> - Collections from debtors must be passed through to the debt factor when collected. These collections can be netted against draw downs for the sale of new debtors. As a result, the net cash inflow and outflow each period is small.
>
> - Debtors not paid within 90 days are 'sold' back to the entity.

Fact pattern 2:

- Entity B enters into a 5 year term loan whereby funds can be drawn down provided that the principal outstanding does not exceed eligible debtors.

- Eligible debtors are legally valid debtors that do not exceed 90 days outstanding.

- Entity B is required to repay the shortfall if there is any breach of the covenant (that is, if debtors exceeds borrowings).

In both scenarios, the entity is required to sell the receivables each period. For the resulting obligation, the entity does not have the right to defer payment to the factor. An entity classifies a liability as current if it does not have the unconditional right to defer its settlement for at least 12 months after the end of the reporting period (see para 4.84.1). If an entity does not have discretion to refinance or roll over a liability for at least 12 months after the balance sheet date under an existing loan facility (in this case, the factoring arrangement), it classifies the liability as current. [IAS 1 paras 69(d), 73]. Therefore, the borrowings arising under both factoring arrangements above should be presented as current liabilities in the statement of financial position.

4.86 It is common practice for financial institutions to include borrowing covenants in the terms of loans. Under some borrowing covenants a loan, which would otherwise be long-term in nature, becomes immediately repayable if certain items related to the borrower's financial condition or performance are breached. Typically, these items are measures of liquidity or solvency based on ratios derived from the entity's financial statements. Where these types of breaches occur prior to the end of a reporting period, the borrowings should be classified as a current liability unless a sufficient waiver of the covenant is granted by the lender, such that the borrowing does not become immediately repayable. Where the borrower has breached a covenant of this nature by the end of the reporting period and the lender agrees, after the reporting period but before authorisation of the financial statements, not to require immediate repayment of the loan, the agreement of the lender is generally regarded as a non-adjusting post balance sheet event. This is because at the end of the reporting period, the agreement of the lender had not been obtained and the condition of the borrowing at that time was that it was immediately repayable. [IAS 1 para 74].

4.86.1 Some borrowings may include 'cross default' clauses, such that the terms of the borrowing are assessed, at least in part, against compliance with covenants of another borrowing. Once the related borrowing covenant is breached, the borrowing with the 'cross default' clause, and any similarly linked borrowings, may become immediately repayable and classified as a current liability. Table 4.5 is an example of disclosure of a breach of covenant during the reporting period and events subsequent to the end of the reporting period.

Table 4.5 – Breach of covenant resulting in loans restated as current at period end, post balance sheet reduction of debt

Interactive Prospect Targeting Holdings plc – Annual report – 31 December 2008

20. Borrowings

2008	2007	
	£'000	£'000
Secured borrowing at amortised cost		
Bank loans	**6,961**	4,797
Amount due for settlement within 12 months	**6,961**	800
Amount due for settlement after 12 months	–	3,997

The Group has a bank loan of €7.2m (2007: €6.5m). The loan of €6.5m was under an arrangement dated 13 June 2007. A restructuring fee of €0.65m was added on 26 September 2008.

As part of the loan restructure, certain conditions were due to be fulfilled by 15 December 2008. The Group failed to fulfil some of these conditions and on 29 December 2008 received formal notification from Barclays that the Group was in default under the terms of the restructuring. Barclays confirmed to the Group that it had no current intention of enforcing its rights or taking any immediate action in respect of the breaches under the terms of the restructuring, but it reserved the right to do so. The repayments were due in four equal instalments of €1.625m payable on 31 October 2009, 30 April 2010, 31 October 2010 and 30 April 2011. The rescheduling fee of €0.65m is payable on 31 October 2011. The loan bore interest at 5% above Euribor payable six monthly in arrears, the first payment to be made on 30 April 2009. Following the NP6 settlement disclosed in note 32, a total of €3.25m has been repaid, reducing the principal loan amount to €3.9m. As a result of this reduction the interest rate on the outstanding debt has been reduced from 5% to 2.5% above Euribor. The Barclays indebtedness remains in default and the Board is actively working to repay the full amount of the remaining debt as quickly as possible, with the intention that it should be repaid from the proceeds of sale of Directinet and Netcollections. Due to the loan covenants being in breach during the year, the bank loan was subsequently repayable on demand and has therefore been classified as current.**32. Events after the balance sheet date (extract)**

On 16 April 2009, NP6 including its subsidiary MailPerformance UK Limited was sold to Lerinardh SAS, a private equity backed vehicle of the previous owners. Lerinardh paid the Group £2.9m in cash and has undertaken to pay 50% of any supplementary capital gain if within six months it sells all or part of its shares in NP6. The settlement removed all claims that the vendors may have against the Group, including the release of a provision for £2.4m made in the Group accounts for the 2008 earn out.

4.86.2 There may be a period between the measurement date of the covenants and the date at which the borrower needs to report any breach to the bank. If the covenant test date is at or before the end of the reporting period, the fact that the borrower need not report the breach until after the period end does not indicate that the covenant has not been breached. Classification of the borrowing as a current liability would be required.

Example – Covenant breach reported after period end

An entity has a long-term loan with a bank. The terms of the loan require quarterly testing of certain covenant ratios. The bank requires the entity to file covenant compliance certificates within 60 days of the measurement date of the covenants. The entity's year end is 31 December 20X8. The entity was within the acceptable parameters based on the calculation of the ratios for the third quarter – that is, 30 September 20X8. The covenant testing date in the fourth quarter is 31 December 20X8. The financial results were finalised in January 20X9. Based on these, the entity was in breach of its covenants at 31 December 20X8. The entity is due to file the covenant compliance certificates on 2 March 20X9, which will show the breach. The entity believes that the breach in covenant does not occur until the filing date, as this is the date at which the bank would call the loan in the absence of any remedy. How should the loan balance be classified at year end?

Although reporting of the breach was not required until after the end of the reporting period, the entity was in effect in breach of its covenants at 31 December 20X8. This is the case even though the reported financial figures were not finalised until January. The entity did not have the unconditional right to defer settlement of the loan for at least 12 months after the end of the reporting period: the loan balance should, therefore, be re-classified as current.

4.87   Following a breach of a borrowing covenant, lenders often agree to a period of grace during which the borrower may rectify the breach. The lender agrees not to demand repayment during this time, but if the breach is not rectified, the debt becomes immediately repayable at the end of the period of grace. If, before the balance sheet date, the lender has agreed to such a period of grace and that period ends at least 12 months after the balance sheet date, the liability should be shown as non-current. [IAS 1 para 75]. If the breach of the borrowing covenant occurs after the balance sheet date, the liability is still shown as non-current, unless the breach was so serious that the financial statements could no longer be prepared on a going concern basis. The presentation of the loan is dictated by the condition of the loan as at the balance sheet date. Events after that date may give evidence of that condition, but they do not change it. This is consistent with IAS 10.

4.87.1   In contrast, some borrowing agreements include a period of grace, the effect of which is that the borrower does not lose the unconditional right to defer payment of the liability until the period of grace has expired. In this case, where the breach does not occur until this later date, the entity continues to present the borrowings as non-current.

Example – Borrowing agreement includes a period of grace

A term loan agreement includes a provision that the borrower must sell a foreign branch of its operations by 31 December 20X9. However, the agreement states that the borrower is permitted an additional 2 months to complete the sale if it is not able to sell the branch by that date. The borrower has not been able to find a buyer by 31 December 20X9. In its financial statements for the period ended 31 December 20X9, how will the borrowings be classified?

The entity should continue to classify the loan balance as non-current, as the agreement allows for a period of grace such that the actual breach of the loan conditions does not occur until 2 months after the end of the reporting period. The entity should consider the impact of the potential breach and the appropriateness of including disclosure on this item in the financial statements.

4.87.2   Table 4.5.1 illustrates a situation where a period of grace has been given but that does not extend for at least 12 months after the end of the reporting period. The relevant borrowings have, therefore, been reclassified as current liabilities.

Table 4.5.1 – Reclassification of borrowings – waiver less than 12 months

SAS AB – Annual report – 31 December 2009

Note 1 ● Significant accounting policies (extract)

As a direct consequence of its operating results for the year ended December 31, 2009, the Group would not have satisfied certain of the financial covenants included in the terms of its credit facilities, and as a result, has renegotiated the terms of four of its credit facilities. The amendments to the credit facilities, which are contingent upon raising at least MSEK 4,000 in net proceeds in the rights issue by the Group, would extend the repayment dates of the credit facilities to 2013 and modify the financial covenants. The lenders have granted a waiver for compliance with certain of the covenants included in the terms of these facilities until the earlier of when all the terms for the amendments are met, or until May 14, 2010. As the amendments to the credit facilities are contingent on the rights issue, and the waiver is only through May 14, 2010, MSEK 2,485 of the Group's borrowings have been classified as current liabilities in the consolidated balance sheet of the Group as of December 31, 2009. As result of the classification of these borrowings as current liabilities, the balance sheet as of December 31, 2009 reflects current liabilities in excess of current assets of MSEK 5,178.

4.88   The standard's approach to breaches of borrowing covenants focuses on the legal rights of the entity. However, in situations where the entity has the discretion to roll over or refinance loans, the entity's expectations on the timing of settlement also play a part in deciding the liability's classification.

UK.4.88.1   Where an entity experiences a downturn in trading results, in addition to the impact of these results on banking covenants, management should also consider if there is an impact on the entity's borrowing powers. For example, a company's Articles of Association may contain a borrowing restriction that requires the directors to restrict borrowings to a multiple of capital and reserves (as defined in the Articles). A significant loss might, therefore, affect the amount of any new borrowing that the company can take out or affect the roll-over of existing borrowings. If management considers that the company may breach (or has breached) the borrowing powers in its Articles it should discuss remedies (for example, ratification by shareholders) with its legal advisors.

4.89   Although events after the reporting period may not alter the classification of a liability, they may require disclosure as a non-adjusting event. IAS 1 paragraph 76 states that, in respect of loans classified as current liabilities, the following events should be disclosed as non-adjusting events in accordance with IAS 10, if they occur between the end of the reporting period and the date of authorisation of the financial statements:

- Refinancing on a long-term basis.

- Rectification of a breach of a long-term loan agreement.

- The granting by the lender of a period of grace to rectify a breach of a long-term loan agreement ending at least twelve months after the reporting period.

4.90   IAS 1 does not specify any disclosures for non-adjusting post balance sheet events (that is, events occurring after the end of the reporting period) in respect of loans classified as non-current liabilities. However, IAS 10 states:

> "If non-adjusting events after the reporting period are material, non-disclosure could influence the economic decisions that users make on the basis of the financial statements. Accordingly, an entity shall disclose the following for each material category of non-adjusting event after the balance sheet date:
>
> (a)   the nature of the event; and
>
> (b)   an estimate of its financial effect, or a statement that such an estimate cannot be made."

[IAS 10 para 21].

4.91   In the case of non-current liabilities, non-adjusting post balance sheet events requiring disclosure would also include breaches of loan agreements occurring between the end of the reporting period and the date of authorisation of the financial statements. See chapter 22.

Tax liabilities

4.92   As for deferred tax assets discussed in paragraph 4.80, deferred tax liabilities should be classified as non-current, regardless of the period over which the temporary differences are expected to reverse (see chapter 13). [IAS 1 para 56]. Other tax liabilities should be classified as current where they are due to be settled within one year of the end of the reporting period; otherwise they should be shown as non-current liabilities. [IAS 1 para 69(c)].

Convertible debt

4.93   The current/non-current classification of convertible debt is considered in chapter 6.

Other financial liabilities

4.93.1 The current/non-current classification of other financial liabilities (including derivatives) is considered in chapter 6.

Notes to the statement of financial position

4.94 IAS 1 requires entities to disclose, either on the face of the statement of financial position or in the notes, further sub-classifications of the line items presented, classified in a manner appropriate to the entity's operations. [IAS 1 para 77].

4.95 The level of this sub-classification depends on the size, nature and function of the items involved and on any specific requirements in other standards and interpretations. IAS 1 gives examples of items that require sub-classification:

- Property, plant and equipment should be shown by class. [IAS 16 para 73].

- Trade receivables, receivables from related parties, prepayments and other amounts should be shown separately.

- Inventories should be shown by class. Common classifications are merchandise, production supplies, materials, work in progress and finished goods. [IAS 2 para 37].

- Provisions for employee benefits should be shown separately from other provisions.

- Equity capital and reserves should be disaggregated into classes such as paid-in capital, share premium and reserves.

[IAS 1 para 78].

4.96 Paragraph 79 of IAS 1 has specific disclosure requirements in respect of each class of share capital and on the nature and purpose of each reserve within equity. In addition, disclosures are required relating to entities' management of their capital resources. Paragraph 79 and the capital disclosure requirements are dealt with in detail in chapter 23.

4.97 Where an entity, such as a partnership or trust, does not have share capital, it should disclose, for each category of equity interest, information equivalent to that required by IAS 1 for share capital (see chapter 23). [IAS 1 para 80].

4.98 IAS 1 requires that if an entity has reclassified certain items between financial liabilities and equity, it must disclose the amounts reclassified into and out of each category (financial liabilities or equity), and the timing and reason for that classification. These disclosures apply to the following types of instruments (which are discussed further in chapter 6):

- a puttable financial instrument classified as an equity instrument; or

■ an instrument that imposes on the entity an obligation to deliver to another party a pro rata share of the net assets of the entity only on liquidation and classified as an equity instrument (for example, some shares issued by limited life entities).

IAS 1 para 80A].

4.99 Other notes to the financial statements are considered from paragraph 4.218.

[The next paragraph is 4.101.]

Statement of comprehensive income

4.101 IAS 1 requires entities to present a 'statement of comprehensive income', setting out all items of income and expense (that is, all non-owner changes in equity) and gives entities a choice as to whether they present comprehensive income within a single statement or in two statements. [IAS 1 para 81]. A single statement contains all items of income and expense. Under the two statement approach, items of comprehensive income are divided between a separate income statement and a separate statement of comprehensive income. Where a two statement approach is adopted, the income statement is displayed immediately before the statement of comprehensive income. [IAS 1 para 12]. Under IAS 1, entities are not permitted to exclude certain income and expenses ('other comprehensive income') from any performance statement by including them directly in the statement of changes in equity (see para 4.209). IAS 1 sets out additional disclosure requirements in respect of 'other comprehensive income' whichever of the two approaches the entity adopts. These are described in paragraph 4.201 below.

4.101.1 As noted in paragraph 4.11.2, IAS 1 has been amended to require that financial statements include a 'statement of profit or loss and other comprehensive income' for the period. This may be presented as a single statement of profit or loss and other comprehensive income, with profit or loss and other comprehensive income presented in two sections. The sections are presented together, with the profit or loss section presented first followed directly by the other comprehensive income section. However, consistent with the existing requirement in IAS 1, an entity may present the profit or loss section in a separate statement of profit or loss. If so, the separate statement of profit or loss should immediately precede the statement presenting comprehensive income. [IAS 1 (revised) para 10A].

4.101.2 The amendment to the standard notes that if an entity presents a separate statement of profit or loss, it does not present the profit or loss section in the statement presenting comprehensive income. [IAS 1 (revised) para 81A]. This means that the line items in the statement of profit or loss (or the income statement) are not reproduced in the separate statement of comprehensive income. Instead, as at present and as shown in the amended illustrative examples to IAS 1 (revised), the separate statement of comprehensive income begins with the profit for the period.

4.101.3 In addition, the amendment to the standard notes that an entity may use other titles for the statement(s), such as 'statement of comprehensive income' which is the terminology used in this chapter, together with 'income statement' where this is separately presented. The amendment is effective for annual period beginning on or after 1 July 2012, with earlier application permitted.

Face of the statement of comprehensive income

4.102 In financial statements complying with IFRS, as a minimum, the following items should be disclosed on the face of the statement of comprehensive income under IAS 1:

(a)   Revenue.

(b)   Finance costs.

(c)   Share of profits and losses of associates and joint ventures accounted for using the equity method.

(d)   Tax expense.

(e)   A single amount comprising the total of:

  (i)   the post-tax profit or loss of discontinued operations; and

  (ii)   the post-tax gain or loss recognised on the measurement to fair value less costs to sell or on the disposal of the assets or disposal group(s) constituting the discontinued operation.

(f)   Profit or loss.

(g)   Each component of other comprehensive income classified by nature.

(h)   Share of other comprehensive income of associates and joint ventures accounted for using the equity method.

(i)   Total comprehensive income.

(j)   Allocations of profit or loss for the period:

  (i)   Profit or loss attributable to non-controlling interests.

  (ii)   Profit or loss attributable to owners of the parent.

(k)   Allocations of total comprehensive income for the period:

  (i)   Total comprehensive income attributable to non-controlling interests.

  (ii)   Total comprehensive income attributable to owners of the parent.

[IAS 1 paras 82, 83].

An entity may present items (a) to (f) and (j) above in a separate income statement. [IAS 1 para 84].

4.102.1   In addition, paragraph 33(d) of IFRS 5 requires disclosure of the amount of income from continuing operations and from discontinued operations attributable to owners of the parent. These disclosures may be presented either in the notes or in the statement of comprehensive income. See further chapter 26.

4.102.2   Paragraphs 82 and 83 have been amended by the IASB to clarify the requirements for the separate sections of 'profit or loss' and 'other comprehensive income. The main change is to replace items (g) and (h) above with a new requirement for items of other comprehensive income, classified by nature, to be grouped into those that will be reclassified subsequently to profit or loss when specific conditions are met, and those that will not be reclassified to profit or loss (see para 4.201.3). The amendment is effective for annual periods beginning on or after 1 July 2012, with earlier application permitted.

4.103   The implementation guidance accompanying IAS 1 gives examples of the statement of comprehensive income, showing the statement of comprehensive income as a single statement and the alternative approach showing two statements, the income statement and a separate statement of comprehensive income. These examples are reproduced in part below. The examples show components of other comprehensive income presented before any tax effect with the tax on other comprehensive income presented separately. As discussed from paragraph 4.202, entities may alternatively present each component of other comprehensive income net of tax.

'Single statement' approach

XYZ group – Statement of comprehensive income for the year ended 31 December 20X7 (extract)

(illustrating the presentation of comprehensive income in one statement and the classification of expenses within profit by function)

(in thousands of currency units)

	20X7	20X6
Revenue	390,000	355,000
Cost of sales	(245,000)	(230,000)
Gross profit	145,000	125,000
Other income	20,667	11,300
Distribution costs	(9,000)	(8,700)
Administrative expenses	(20,000)	(21,000)
Other expenses	(2,100)	(1,200)
Finance costs	(8,000)	(7,500)
Share of profit of associates	35,100	30,100
Profit before tax	161,667	128,000
Income tax expense	(40,417)	(32,000)
Profit for the year from continuing operations	121,250	96,000
Loss for the year from discontinued operations	–	(30,500)
Profit for the year	121,250	65,500
Other comprehensive income**:		
Exchange differences on translating foreign operations	5,334	10,667
Available-for-sale financial assets	(24,000)	26,667
Cash flow hedges	(667)	(4,000)
Gains on property revaluation	933	3,367
Actuarial gains (losses) in defined benefit pension plans	(667)	1,333
Share of other comprehensive income of associates	400	(700)
Income tax relating to components of other comprehensive income	4,667	(9,334)
Other comprehensive income for the year, net of tax	(14,000)	28,000
Total comprehensive income for the year	107,250	93,500
Profit attributable to:		
Owners of the parent	97,000	52,400
Non-controlling interest	24,250	13,100
	121,250	65,500
Total comprehensive income attributable to:		
Owners of the parent*	85,800	74,800
Non-controlling interest	21,450	18,700
	107,250	93,500

4055

Earnings per share
(not included in this example – see chapter 14)

* In addition, paragraph 33(d) of IFRS 5 requires disclosure of the amount of income from continuing operations and from discontinued operations attributable to owners of the parent. These disclosures may be presented either in the notes or in the statement of comprehensive income.

Alternatively, components of other comprehensive income could be presented in the statement of comprehensive income net of tax:

Other comprehensive income for the year, after tax**:	20X7	20X6
Exchange differences on translating foreign operations	4,000	8,000
Available-for-sale financial assets	(18,000)	20,000
Cash flow hedges	(500)	(3,000)
Gains on property revaluation	600	2,700
Actuarial gains (losses) in defined benefit pension plans	(500)	1,000
Share of other comprehensive income of associates	400	(700)
Other comprehensive income for the year, net of tax	(14,000)	28,000

** This statement of comprehensive income is based on IAS 1 prior to its amendment effective for annual periods beginning on or after 1 July 2012. The amendment requires items of other comprehensive income to be grouped into those that will be reclassified subsequently to profit or loss and those that will not be reclassified (see para 4.201.3).

'Two statement' approach

XYZ group – Income statement for the year ended 31 December 20X7 (extract)

(illustrating the presentation of comprehensive income in two statements and the classification of expenses within profit by nature)

(in thousands of currency units)

	20X7	20X6
Revenue	390,000	355,000
Other income	20,667	11,300
Changes in inventories of finished goods and work in progress	(115,100)	(107,900)
Work performed by the entity and capitalised	16,000	15,000
Raw material and consumables used	(96,000)	(92,000)
Employee benefits expense	(45,000)	(43,000)
Depreciation and amortisation expense	(19,000)	(17,000)
Impairment of property, plant and equipment	(4,000)	–
Other expenses	(6,000)	(5,500)
Finance costs	(15,000)	(18,000)
Share of profit of associates	35,100	30,100
Profit before tax	161,667	128,000
Income tax expense	(40,417)	(32,000)
Profit for the year from continuing operations	121,250	96,000
Loss for the year from discontinued operations	–	(30,500)
Profit for the year	121,250	65,500

Profit attributable to:		
Owners of the parent	97,000	52,400
Non-controlling interest	24,250	13,100
	121,250	65,500

Earnings per share
(not included in this example – see chapter 14)

XYZ group – Statement of comprehensive income for the year ended 31 December 20X7

(illustrating the presentation of comprehensive income in two statements)

(in thousands of currency units)

	20X7	20X6
Profit for the year	121,250	65,500
Other comprehensive income*:		
Exchange differences on translating foreign operations	5,334	10,667
Available-for-sale financial assets	(24,000)	26,667
Cash flow hedges	(667)	(4,000)
Gains on property revaluation	933	3,367
Actuarial gains (losses) in defined benefit pension plans	(667)	1,333
Share of other comprehensive income of associates	400	(700)
Income tax relating to components of other comprehensive income	4,667	(9,334)
Other comprehensive income for the year, net of tax	(14,000)	28,000
Total comprehensive income for the year	107,250	93,500
Total comprehensive income attributable to:		
Owners of the parent**	85,800	74,800
Non-controlling interest	21,450	18,700
	107,250	93,500

*   This statement of comprehensive income is based on IAS 1 prior to its amendment effective for annual periods beginning on or after 1 July 2012. The amendment requires items of other comprehensive income to be grouped into those that will be reclassified subsequently to profit or loss and those that will not be reclassified (see para 4.201.3).

** In addition, paragraph 33(d) of IFRS 5 requires disclosure of the amount of income from continuing operations and from discontinued operations attributable to owners of the parent. These disclosures may be presented either in the notes or in the statement of comprehensive income.

4.103.1   Table 4.5.2 below is an example of a single statement approach in practice.

Table 4.5.2 – Single statement of comprehensive income (extract)
AstraZeneca PLC – Annual report – 31 December 2011
Consolidated Statement of Comprehensive Income
for the year ended 31 December

	Notes	2011 $m	2010 $m	2009 $m
Revenue	1	**33,591**	33,269	32,804
Cost of sales		**(6,026)**	(6,389)	(5,775)
Gross profit		**27,565**	26,880	27,029
Distribution costs		**(346)**	(335)	(298)
Research and development	2	**(5,523)**	(5,318)	(4,409)
Selling, general and administrative costs	2	**(11,161)**	(10,445)	(11,332)
Profit on disposal of subsidiary	2.22	**1,483**	–	–
Other operating income and expense	2	**777**	712	553
Operating profit	2	**12,795**	11,494	11,543
Finance income	3	**552**	516	462
Finance expense	3	**(980)**	(1,033)	(1,198)
Profit before tax		**12,367**	10,977	10,807
Taxation	4	**(2,351)**	(2,896)	(3,263)
Profit for the period		**10,016**	8,081	7,544
Other comprehensive income:				
Foreign exchange arising on consolidation		**(60)**	26	388
Foreign exchange differences on borrowings forming net investment hedges		**24**	101	(68)
Amortisation of loss on cash flow hedge		**2**	1	1
Net available for sale gains taken to equity		**31**	4	2
Actuarial loss for the period	18	**(741)**	(46)	(569)
Income tax relating to components of other comprehensive income	4	**198**	(61)	192
Other comprehensive income for the period, net of tax		**(546)**	25	(54)
Total comprehensive income for the period		**9,470**	8,106	7,490
Profit attributable to:				
Owners of the Parent		**9,983**	8,053	7,521
Non-controlling interests		**33**	28	23
Total comprehensive income attributable to:				
Owners of the Parent		**9,428**	8,058	7,467
Non-controlling interests		**42**	48	23
Basic earnings per $0.25 Ordinary Share	5	**$7.33**	$5.60	$5.19
Diluted earnings per $0.25 Ordinary Share	5	**$7.30**	$5.57	$5.19
Weighted average number of Ordinary Shares in issue (millions)	5	**1,361**	1,438	1,448
Diluted weighted average number of Ordinary Shares in issue (millions)	5	**1,367**	1,446	1,450
Dividends declared and paid in the period	21	**3,752**	3,494	3,026

All activities were in respect of continuing operations. $m means millions of US dollars.

Editorial note: The statement of comprehensive income is based on IAS 1 prior to its amendment effective for annual periods beginning on or after 1 July 2012. The amendment requires items of other comprehensive income to be grouped into those that will be reclassified subsequently to profit or loss and those that will not be reclassified (see para 4.201.3).

4.103.2 Table 4.5.3 below is an example of a statement of comprehensive income for an entity using the 'two statement' approach, which reflects the amendments to IAS 1 referred to in paragraph 4.102.2: this extract presents separately the items that may be reclassified to profit or loss and the items that will not be reclassified. The extract is taken from a half year report, but this is similar to the statement that would be presented in an annual report.

Table 4.5.3 – Amcor Limited – Half year report – 31 December 2011

Consolidated Statements of Comprehensive Income
For the six months ended 31 December 2011

$ million	2011	2010
Profit for the financial period	215.6	236.3
Other comprehensive income/(loss)		
Items that may be reclassified subsequently to profit or loss:		
Cash flow hedges		
Effective portion of changes in fair value of cash flow hedges	2.3	(2.8)
Net change in fair value of cash flow hedges reclassified to profit or loss	1.8	2.3
Net change in fair value of cash flow hedges reclassified to non-financial assets	(0.3)	0.1
Tax on cash flow hedges	(1.2)	1.7
Exchange differences on translating foreign operations		
Exchange differences on translation of foreign operations	(60.4)	(551.4)
Net investment hedge of foreign operations	31.5	210.6
Exchange differences on translating foreign operations reclassified to profit or loss	–	1.8
Share of associates exchange fluctuation reserve	3.5	(3.0)
Tax on exchange differences on translating foreign operations	1.0	(29.7)
Items that will not be reclassified to profit or loss:		
Retained earnings		
Actuarial (loss)/gain on defined benefit plans	(15.4)	32.0
Tax on actuarial (losses)/gains on defined benefit plans	6.5	(10.0)
Other comprehensive loss for the financial period, net of tax	(30.7)	(348.4)
Total comprehensive income/(loss) for the financial period	184.9	(112.1)
Total comprehensive income/(loss) attributable to:		
Owners of Amcor Limited	171.5	(113.4)
Non-controlling interest	13.4	1.3
	184.9	(112.1)

Profit or loss for the period

4.104 All items of income and expense recognised in a period should be included in the profit or loss for the period, unless a standard or interpretation requires or permits otherwise. [IAS 1 para 88]. Items of income and expense excluded from the profit or loss for the period (for example, foreign currency gains and losses arising on translation of a foreign operation) are recognised as other comprehensive income in the statement of comprehensive income. These are addressed from paragraph 4.201.

4.105 IAS 1 does not require entities to disclose results from operating activities. IAS 1 – Basis for conclusions indicates that the IASB decided against requiring disclosure of 'operating profit' as the term was undefined. [IAS 1 BC55]. However, it is recognised that entities will often present such a measure, and the standard emphasises that where an entity does so, it should ensure the amount disclosed *"... is representative of activities that would normally be regarded as 'operating'...".* The Board indicated that it would be misleading and undermine the comparability of financial statements if items of an operating nature, such as impairments and restructuring costs, were excluded from operating profit, where such a measure is presented. [IAS 1 BC56]. Entities should, therefore, exercise care to ensure all operating type items are appropriately included when presenting a measure that is intended to represent operating activity.

4.106 Some entities provide measures of performance other than the profit or loss for the period or the other sub-totals or line items required by IAS 1 on the face of its primary statements. Such alternative performance measures (often referred to as 'non-GAAP' measures) are discussed from paragraph 4.238.

4.107 Profit or loss from associates and joint ventures is presented net of their related tax. Although the tax treatment of the profit or loss of associates and joint ventures is not explicit in the above list, the footnote to the 'share of profits in associates' line item in the statement of comprehensive income shown in the 'Guidance on implementing IAS 1' states: *"this means the share of associates' profit attributable to owners of the associates, that is, it is after tax and non-controlling interests in the associates".* See also paragraph 4.119 on the presentation of profit or loss from associates and joint ventures.

4.108 IAS 1 requires that companies present the total profit and total comprehensive income allocated between the non-controlling interest and the parent's owners; this is intended to ensure that the non-controlling interest is not presented as if it is an expense. Companies should ensure that the presentation of non-controlling interest in the statement of comprehensive income does not imply that it is an expense. For example, a presentation that shows an amount for non-controlling interest deducted from profit to arrive at profit attributable to owners implies that the non-controlling interest is an expense. The required presentation is consistent with the statement of financial position presentation required by IAS 27 (or IFRS 10), which requires that non-controlling interest is presented within equity, rather than as a liability. [IAS 1 BC59].

[The next paragraph is 4.113.]

Additional line items, headings and sub-totals

4.113 IAS 1 states: *"Because the effects of an entity's various activities, transactions and other events differ in frequency, potential for gain or loss and predictability, disclosing the components of financial performance assists users in understanding the financial performance achieved and in making projections of future financial performance ..."* [IAS 1 para 86]. As with the statement of financial position, additional line items, headings and sub-totals should be shown on the face of the statement of comprehensive income when such presentation is relevant to understanding the entity's financial performance. [IAS 1 para 85]. Relevance is one of the qualitative characteristics of useful financial information in the IASB Framework which states: *"Relevant financial information is capable of making a difference in the decisions made by users. Information may be capable of making a difference in a decision even if some users choose not to take advantage of it or are already aware of it from other sources"*. [Framework para QC6].

4.114 Clearly, the use of additional line items, headings and sub-totals must be subject to some restrictions. A purist approach would be to present only 'pure GAAP' information and require users of financial statements to interpret that information in isolation. In practice, however, this may be unnecessarily restrictive because, in some instances, there is a mismatch between the presentation and disclosure requirements of the accounting standards and the message that companies want to deliver or the information that analysts and other users wish to receive. The IASB's Framework recognises that financial statements should aim to meet the needs of investors and are prepared for *"users who have a reasonable knowledge of business and economic activities and who review and analyse the information diligently"*. [Framework para QC32]. The European Securities and Markets Authority (ESMA, formerly the Committee of European Securities Regulators (CESR) recommendation on alternative performance measures (see para 4.239) also recognises that such measures can provide investors with appropriate additional information if properly used and presented (see above). However, regulators in other jurisdictions may take a more restrictive view and, therefore, regulated companies should exercise caution where departing from a 'standard' presentation.

4.115 Management needs to exercise judgement in determining whether additional line items or sub-totals are necessary, subject to the overriding IAS 1 requirement to present information in a manner that provides relevant, reliable, comparable and understandable information. [IAS 1 para 17]. Different managements may take different views of the best way to present information. There may be several methods of presentation that are equally valid, just as there may be more than one acceptable accounting policy for a transaction.

4.116 However, the IASB's Framework states that if financial information is to be useful, it must be relevant and faithfully represent what it purports to represent. Characteristics of faithful representation are for information to be complete, neutral and free from error. [Framework paras QC4, QC12]. The apparent flexibility in IAS 1 can, therefore, only be used to enhance users' understanding of the GAAP-compliant numbers. It cannot be used to detract from the GAAP numbers. Non-GAAP information should not be given greater prominence in the financial statements than GAAP information. Non-GAAP alternative performance measures are addressed from paragraph 4.238.

4.117 Set out below are overall principles, including those contained within the ESMA (formerly CESR) recommendation of alternative performance measures (see para 4.239), that entities should apply when presenting additional line items, headings and sub-totals within the statement of comprehensive income (or, if presented, the separate income statement).

- Terms used for additional line items, columns and sub-totals should generally be terms recognised in IFRS. If this is not the case, care should be taken to define clearly the terms used to refer to these additional line items, sub-totals or columns.

- Items may be segregated (for example, by use of columns or sub-totals), but only where they are different in nature or function from other items in the statement (for example, share-based payments that form part of the remuneration of employees should be included in employee benefits expense, not shown in a different part of the statement).

- Additional line items, columns and sub-totals:

  - should only be presented when they are used internally to manage the business and are therefore relevant to an understanding of performance.

  - may be used, but only if they do not detract from the defined IFRS measures by introducing bias or by over-crowding the statement.

  - should never be given greater prominence that the defined IFRS measures.

- Each additional line item or column:

  - should contain all the revenue or expense that relates to the particular line item or column inserted.

  - should contain only revenue or expense that is revenue or expense of the entity itself (see para 4.120).

  - should only be used for material items where the entity's performance cannot be explained adequately by disclosure in the notes alone.

- It is generally not permissible to mix natural and functional classifications of expenses where the natural and functional categories of expenses overlap. However, see from paragraph 4.137 for discussion of where a mixed presentation may be considered acceptable.

- Various presentations will be acceptable individually, but consideration should be given to the aggregate effect of these presentations, so that the overall message of the statement is not distorted or confused.

- The presentation method should generally be consistent from year to year. Where another presentation method would be more appropriate, having regard to the criteria for selection and application of accounting policies in IAS 8 the presentation method should be changed. Otherwise changes should not be made unless there is a significant change in the entity's operations or a change in IFRS requiring a presentation change.

- The presentation method should comply with any local regulatory rules.

Additionally, the above guidance is also applicable in the circumstance where an entity concludes that the presentation of non-GAAP measures on the face of its statement is beneficial to understanding its performance and such presentation is not otherwise prohibited by applicable regulation (for example, the SEC). See from paragraph 4.238.

4.117.1   Entities are prohibited from showing any items of income and expense as extraordinary, either on the face of the statement of comprehensive income or in the notes. [IAS 1 para 87]. See paragraph 4.179.

Re-ordering of line items

4.118   In addition to recognising that additional line items might be appropriate, IAS 1 indicates that entities should re-order the line items and amend the descriptions of those items where this is necessary to explain the elements of performance. [IAS 1 para 86]. Therefore, the ordering and description of line items should not generally be amended, unless it is necessary; that is, entities do not have complete freedom on the ordering and description of line items. The line items of the statement of comprehensive income (or, if presented, separate income statement) would, therefore, normally be presented in the order set out in paragraph 4.102 above. However, it is generally acceptable and common practice to present finance cost as the last item before pre-tax profit, thereby separating financing activities from the activities that are being financed, so that the result before deducting interest cost is the pre-tax result from all the activities other than financing. Additionally, as discussed below, an entity may apply a different positioning in respect of 'share of profits from associates' when an alternative presentation is the most relevant to its business activities. In any event, entities are always governed by the overall requirement for a 'fair presentation'. The entity should consider the materiality and the nature and function of the items concerned. [IAS 1 para 86]. Offset of income and expenses is prohibited, except in the circumstances described in paragraph 4.38.

4.119   Normally, the share of profit of associates is shown after finance costs; this recognises that the share of profits from associates arises from what is essentially an investing activity, rather than part of the group's operating activities. However, where associates (and joint ventures) are an integral vehicle for the conduct of the group's operations and its strategy, it may be more appropriate to show finance costs after the share of profit of associates and joint ventures. In such cases, it may be appropriate either to insert a sub-total 'profit before finance costs' or to include the share of profits from associates and joint ventures in arriving at operating profit (if disclosed). It would not, however, be appropriate to include the share of associates and joint ventures within 'revenue' (and, therefore, within 'gross profit'). The share of associates and joint ventures does not represent a 'gross inflow of economic benefits' that is part of the definition of 'revenue' in IAS 18 rather, it is in the nature of a net gain.

4.120 Under the equity method of accounting, the revenue, operating profit, finance costs and tax of the associate or joint venture are not income or expenses of the group even though they affect the 'overall return' on the group's investment. Items such as 'share of associates' revenue', 'share of associates' operating profit', 'share of associates' finance costs', 'share of associates' tax' are not components of the group's own revenue and expenses but the 'share' of items that appear in another entity's financial statements. Presenting these items within the group's statement of comprehensive income would be inconsistent with the statement of financial position treatment. Where a group conducts a significant proportion of its business through associates or joint ventures and it wishes to highlight that fact to the reader of the statement of comprehensive income, it may choose to give additional financial information, outside the statement itself, as, say, a footnote to the statement with a cross-reference to further information contained in the notes to the financial statements. In any case, for each associate and joint venture that is material to the reporting entity, IFRS 12, which is effective for annual periods beginning on or after 1 January 2013, requires disclosure of summarised financial information about the associate or joint venture (see chapter 27). [IFRS 12 para 21]. In addition to the requirement in IFRS 12, there may be regulatory requirements to provide further information.

4.121 Of course, the position is different when the group elects under IAS 31 to account for a joint venture using proportional consolidation. In that case, for accounting purposes, the group is deemed to 'own' a share of each line item appearing in the statement of financial position of the joint venture and to share in revenue and expense of the joint venture appearing in its statement of comprehensive income. In accounting for a joint venture, groups should either equity account or proportionally consolidate, not mix the two treatments; it is not permissible to partially proportionally consolidate in the statement of comprehensive income whilst using 'pure equity accounting' in the statement of financial position.

4.122 In the following example, the entity, which is an investment management entity, has amended the descriptions and order of the line items to fit the nature of its business:

Table 4.6 – Amended descriptions and line items – separate income statement

BB Biotech AG – Annual Report – 31 December 2011

Consolidated statement of comprehensive income for the year ended December 31 (in CHF 1 000)

	Notes	2011	2010
Operating income			
Interest income		16	68
Dividend income		4 876	1 488
Other income		–	22
		4 892	**1 578**
Operating expenses			
Losses from marketable securities	4	52 839	129 630
Finance expenses	6	161	6 039
Foreign exchange losses net		91	2 957
Administrative expenses	9	4 586	4 962
Other expenses	10	6 266	4 284
		69 943	**147 872**
Operating income before tax	12	**(65 051)**	**(146 294)**
Tax expenses	7	(87)	(54)
Net loss for the year		**(65 138)**	**(146 348)**
Total comprehensive income for the year		**(65 138)**	**(146 348)**
Loss and diluted loss per share in CHF	11	(4.55)	(9.27)
Average outstanding shares	11	14 318 228	15 794 606

Sub-headings

4.123 Sub-headings should be used with care. In particular, it is important that the meaning of the sub-heading is clear; this may be achieved by including a definition of the sub-heading in the notes to the financial statements. In addition, extraordinary items are prohibited and entities should ensure that the presentation does not undermine this prohibition. As discussed above, where an entity discloses a figure for operating profit, this measure should include all operating items. [IAS 1 para BC56]. Earnings before interest and tax (EBIT) may be an appropriate sub-heading to show on the face of the statement of comprehensive income. This line item usually distinguishes between the pre-tax profits arising from operating items and those arising from financing activities. However, care is needed where such measures are presented, as the calculation and definition of such a measure may vary between entities and may impair comparability without clear disclosure. For instance, some groups exclude income from associates from EBIT, in which case EBIT is not equivalent to pre-tax profits before financing and may not be directly comparable to other entities using the same or a similar term. An example of a group that uses EBIT as a sub-heading is given in Table 4.7 below.

Table 4.7 – Earnings before interest and tax/Function of expense method

Metro AG – Annual Report – 31 December 2011

Income statement

for the financial year from 1 January to 31 December 2011 (extract)

€ million	Note no.	2010	2011
Net sales	1	**67,258**	**66,702**
Cost of sales		−52,865	−52,700
Gross profit on sales		**14,393**	**14,002**
Other operating income	2	1,627	1,690
Selling expenses	3	−12,173	−11,928
General administrative expenses	4	−1,585	−1,587
Other operating expenses	5	−51	−64
Earnings before interest and taxes EBIT		**2,211**	**2,113**
Result from associated companies		0	1
Other investment result	6	15	41
Interest income	7	112	133
Interest expenses	7	−718	−713
Other financial result	8	10	−102
Net financial result		**−581**	**−640**
Earnings before taxes EBT		**1,630**	**1,473**
Income taxes	10	−694	−732
Net profit for the period		**936**	**741**

4.124 Earnings before interest, tax, depreciation and amortisation (EBITDA) is a measure that many financial analysts use. It is sometimes described as 'cash earnings', a misnomer since the assets being depreciated or amortised have often been acquired for cash. EBITDA will also include many non-cash charges (for example, charges for expenses settled through shares) and is often impacted by previously established accruals and provisions (for example, unwinding of onerous lease provisions). Furthermore, EBITDA is not always defined consistently (for example, some entities include EBITDA from associates or other adjustments in the measure).

4.125 Where permitted by local practice and not otherwise prohibited by applicable regulation, some companies disclose EBITDA on the face of the statement of comprehensive income (or, if presented, the separate income statement). It is arguable whether this is desirable or whether EBITDA would be more appropriately disclosed in the Operating and financial review (OFR) or Management Discussion and Analysis (MD&A), or alternatively in a footnote to the financial statements. See from paragraph 4.238. However, subject to any regulatory limitations, we believe it may be acceptable for companies to show EBITDA on the face of the statement, provided the method for determining the measure is clear, and the presentation does not detract from the defined IFRS measures, either by implying that EBITDA is the 'real' profit or by overcrowding the statement so that the reader cannot determine easily the entity's IFRS performance. EBITDA should be given no more prominence than the disclosure of total profit. The following example shows the presentation of EBITDA on the face of the statement for an entity presenting its expenses by nature.

Example – EBITDA (nature of expense method)

	20X5	20X4
Revenue	xxx	xxx
Other income	xxx	xxx
Changes in inventories of finished goods and work in progress	(xxx)	xxx
Work performed by the entity and capitalised	xxx	xxx
Raw material and consumables used	(xxx)	(xxx)
Employee benefits expense	(xxx)	(xxx)
Other expenses	(xx)	(xx)
Earnings before interest, taxes, depreciation and amortisation	xxx	xxx
Depreciation of property, plant and equipment	(xxx)	(xxx)
Amortisation of intangible assets	(xxx)	(xxx)
Operating profit	xxx	xxx
Finance costs	(xxx)	(xxx)
Share of profit of associates	xxx	xxx
Profit before tax	xxx	xxx

Analysis of nature and function of expenses is discussed from paragraph 4.128 below.

This example shows a sub-total for operating profit. It could be misleading for depreciation and amortisation to be shown alongside finance costs and share of profits of associates without a sub-total in between. The presentation of EBITDA implies that the group is categorising its income and expenses; it may, therefore, be helpful to make it clear that depreciation and amortisation are part of its operating result, rather than part of the same category as finance costs.

4.126 As shown above, where an entity presents its expenses by nature, it is possible for EBITDA to be presented as a sub-total within the statement of comprehensive income. The presentation of EBITDA within the financial statements can be more problematic when an entity presents its expenses by function; it will not be possible to show depreciation and amortisation as line items in arriving at operating profit, because depreciation and amortisation are types of expense, not functions of the business. For example, 'cost of sales' and 'distribution expenses' generally both include depreciation. In such circumstances, some entities have undertaken to insert supplemental information on the face of their statement of comprehensive income (or, if presented, the separate income statement), which analyses the operating profit total between EBITDA, and depreciation and amortisation. This supplemental information is generally in the form of an added box within the statement so that the line items required under the function of expense approach are still properly reported. However, this type of presentation may be cumbersome and those companies wishing to disclose EBITDA may find it preferable to do so in the notes to the financial statements or in the accompanying OFR or MD&A. See from paragraph 4.238 on the use of alternative performance measures.

4.127 Similar arguments can be made for the use of other sub-totals as can be made for EBITDA. The key consideration is the impression that the reader will form of the entity's performance. Entities should not carve up the statement of comprehensive income (or, if presented, separate income statement) so as to show their performance in the most flattering light, as this would be misleading. The purpose of a sub-total or additional column is to separate items of income or expense that are different in nature or function from other items in the statement. It is not appropriate to use a sub-total to imply that, for example, a charge for employee expense arising from a share based payment is less a charge on operating profit than the charge for a cash-based salary.

Analysis of expenses: classification by nature or function

4.128 Entities should present an analysis of expenses using a classification based on either the nature of expenses or their function within the entity, whichever provides information that is reliable and more relevant. [IAS 1 para 99]. The sub-classification is given to highlight components of financial performance that may differ in terms of frequency, potential for gain or loss and predictability. [IAS 1 para 101]. The choice of type of analysis will depend on industry practice and the nature of the entity. The line items listed in paragraph 4.102 are the mandatory minimum requirements for presentation on the face of the statement of comprehensive income, but IAS 1 encourages entities to present the additional analysis of expenses on the face of the statement. Those entities that do not provide this analysis on the face of the statement should do so in the notes. [IAS 1 para 100].

4.129 Under the 'nature of expense' method, expenses are classified according to their nature (for example, depreciation, purchases of materials, transport costs, employee benefits and advertising costs) and are not reallocated among various functions within the entity. [IAS 1 para 102]. An entity involved in providing services is likely to analyse expenses under this method. In some jurisdictions, changes in finished goods and work in progress has traditionally been presented immediately following revenue (see Table 4.8 below). In such cases, care should be taken in the presentation to ensure that such amounts would not be regarded as revenue.

4.130 IAS 1 sets out an example of a classification using the nature of expense method as follows:

Revenue		X
Other income		X
Changes in inventories of finished goods and work in progress	X	
Raw materials and consumables used	X	
Employee benefits expense	X	
Depreciation and amortisation expense	X	
Other expenses	X	
Total expenses		(X)
Profit		X

[IAS 1 para 102].

4.130.1 Table 4.8 below illustrates the presentation under the nature of expense method.

Table 4.8 – Nature of expense method

Deutsche Lufthansa AG – Annual Report – 31 December 2011

Consolidated income statement (extract)
for the financial year 2011

in €m	Notes	2011	2010
Traffic revenue	3	23,779	21,466
Other revenue	4	4,955	4,993
Total revenue		**28,734**	**26,459**
Changes in inventories and work performed by entity and capitalised	5	139	165
Other operating income	6	2,324	2,610
Cost of materials and services	7	− 16,731	− 14,700
Staff costs	8	− 6,678	− 6,491
Depreciation, amortisation and impairment	9	− 1,722	− 1,654
Other operating expenses	10	− 5,293	− 5,003
Profit/loss from operating activities		**773**	**1,386**
Result of equity investments accounted for using the equity method	11	− 20	46
Result of other equity investments	11	91	57
Interest income	12	190	197
Interest expenses	12	− 478	− 543
Other financial items	13	− 110	− 9
Financial result		**− 327**	**− 252**
Profit/loss before income taxes		**446**	**1,134**

4.131 The implementation guidance accompanying IAS 1 gives a further example of an income statement with expenses classified by nature. In addition to the line items shown above, this example includes 'work performed by the entity and capitalised' as a line item. Such presentation is necessary where an entity adopts a natural analysis of expenses and presents its operating expenses on a 'gross' basis, before the deduction of any amounts capitalised. For example, in that case, the line item 'raw materials and consumables used' will be the total of all raw materials used even if those raw materials are used to construct property, plant and equipment ('PPE'). An entity that uses C1000 of raw materials of which C100 is capitalised will show, as separate line items, C1000 as 'raw materials and consumables used' and C100 as 'work performed by the entity and capitalised'. (The capitalised raw materials will affect the depreciation charge and/or profit or loss on disposal of PPE in due course.)

4.132   The example given in the implementation guidance in respect of the functional analysis of expenses does not include a line item for 'work performed by the entity and capitalised'. When operating expenses are presented by function, the amounts should be shown 'net' of any expenses capitalised, to show the amounts attributable to the particular function. In the example above, C900 would be included within cost of sales (or whichever other function used the raw materials that were not capitalised), but the C100 would not be presented within a separate line in the statement of comprehensive income. A functional analysis shows the costs allocated to each function; it does not show the 'gross' amounts of each type of expense less allocations of those expenses. This approach is extended to the presentation of costs that are, for example, 'allocated' to PPE or capitalised as development costs.

4.133   When the nature of expense method is used and finance costs are capitalised, we believe it most appropriate for the statement of comprehensive income (or, if presented, separate income statement) to present finance costs net of the amount capitalised, with the gross amount of finance costs and the amount capitalised disclosed in the notes to the financial statements if not otherwise presented separately on the face of the statement. This is because many financial statement users will derive an operating profit measure from the items presented in the statement, and there is a strong argument that, to ensure comparability across entities, the measure of operating profit should not be impacted by the choice of expense analysis (by nature or function). The presentation of finance costs on a gross basis accompanied by the inclusion of capitalised finance costs within an amalgamated total of 'work performed by the entity and capitalised' would increase the measure of operating profit that would be presented in or derived from the statement of an entity using the nature of expense method as compared with an entity that presents finance costs on a net basis. There is, however, some diversity in practice in this regard.

4.134   Under the function of expense or 'cost of sales' method, expenses are classified according to their function as part of cost of sales, distribution or administrative expenses. As a minimum, entities using this method of analysis should distinguish 'cost of sales' from other expenses. The standard states that this method can provide more relevant information, but the allocation of the costs can be arbitrary and requires considerable judgement. [IAS 1 para 103]. In many cases, costs are allocated to each function of the business for internal reporting purposes and the allocation of costs in the financial statements could be performed on the same basis. The 'cost of sales' method is commonly used by manufacturers and retailers.

4.135 IAS 1 sets out an example of a classification using the cost of sales method as follows:

Revenue	X
Cost of sales	X
Gross profit	X
Other income	X
Distribution costs	(X)
Administrative expenses	(X)
Other expenses	(X)
Profit	X

[IAS 1 para 103].

4.136 Within a functional analysis of expenses, costs directly associated with generating revenues should be included in cost of sales. Cost of sales should include direct material and labour costs but will also include indirect costs that can be directly attributed to generating revenue. These indirect costs will include, for example, depreciation of assets used in production. In our view, impairment charges should be classified according to how the depreciation or amortisation of the particular asset is classified.

4.136.1 Table 4.9 illustrates the presentation for the function of expense method.

Table 4.9 – Function of expense method

Hengxin Technology Ltd – Annual report – 31 December 2011

Consolidated Statement of Comprehensive Income

Financial year ended 31 December 2011

	Note	Group 2011 RMB'000	2010 RMB'000
Revenue	21	1,419,327	1,183,131
Cost of sales		(1,157,224)	(961,470)
Gross profit		262,103	221,661
Other operating income	22	7,405	15,292
Distribution and selling expenses		(62,522)	(55,841)
Administrative expenses		(41,108)	(36,256)
Other operating expenses	23	(27,147)	(10,404)
Finance costs	24	(13,203)	(9,723)
Profit before income tax	25	125,528	124,729
Income tax	26	(23,279)	(22,174)
Net profit for the year		102,249	102,555
Other comprehensive income:			
Exchange differences on translation		(290)	(20)
Total comprehensive income for the year		101,959	102,535
Earnings per share (RMB cents)			
– basic	27	26.4	30.4
– diluted	27	26.4	30.4

4.137 Entities should not generally mix functional and natural classifications of expenses by excluding certain expenses (for example, inventory write-downs, employee termination benefits and impairment charges) from the functional classifications to which they relate (see also para 4.138). However, mixing function and nature and the inclusion of additional line items in the statement of comprehensive income (or, if presented, the separate income statement) may be acceptable if all of the following criteria are met:

- The presentation of the income statement is neutral (free of bias). [Framework para QC14]. A biased presentation (for example, a presentation that gives undue prominence to certain line items) is not acceptable.

- The breakdown of expenses by nature required by paragraph 104 of IAS 1 is disclosed in the notes.

- The presentation is applied consistently and explained in the accounting policies.

A mixed presentation should not have the effect of understating cost of sales and overstating gross profit. For example, depreciation should generally be included in cost of sales in a business where depreciation is clearly linked to the cost of goods sold, such as a manufacturing business. It may be appropriate to exclude depreciation from cost of sales in a business where it is not closely linked to the cost of goods sold. Cost of sales should be clearly labelled as excluding depreciation in these circumstances, and a gross profit sub-total should not be reported. In determining the most appropriate presentation, management should have regard to the views of local regulators and whether they would permit the mixing of functional and natural items.

Example – Mix of expenses by function and nature

Entity A has six subsidiaries, the largest of which, entity B, represents 40% of the group's results. Entity B represents a separate business segment. All entities in the group present a functional analysis of expenses in their separate IFRS financial statements, except for entity B, which presents an analysis by the nature of expenses. As a functional analysis of entity B's expenses has not been prepared, entity A's management would like to present the consolidated income statement on a split-method basis, with entity B's results presented using a natural analysis and the rest of the group's results presented on a functional basis. Entity A's management argues that entity B's business represents a different segment and is not comparable with the rest of the group. Can management mix different analysis of expenses in the group's statement of comprehensive income?

The subsidiaries' results should be presented on a consistent basis in the consolidated income statement. Therefore, management cannot generally adopt a mix of the two types of analysis in the group's financial statements. Management should choose which format, function or nature, is most appropriate for the consolidated financial statements. The results of all entities within the group should be prepared on the chosen basis, which will require part of the group to prepare, for consolidation purposes, additional analysis to that used in their separate financial statements so that the aggregate disclosures in the consolidated financial statements are presented on a consistent basis. However, see paragraph 4.137 above for the circumstances in which some mixing of expenses by nature and function may be acceptable.

4.138 A collection of expenses of one or more natures is not necessarily the expenses of a function of the business. For example, the aggregate of restructuring costs (such as redundancy payments, inventory write-downs) and the aggregate of occupancy costs (rent, property insurance) should not normally be shown as a single line in a functional analysis, because neither restructuring nor occupancy are functions of the business (see also para 4.168). Under a functional analysis, an entity discloses the combined cost of performing a particular activity (for example, administration or distribution) in pursuit of its business objectives.

4.139 In practice, entities have a degree of choice between the two methods, but they need to choose the method that provides the most relevant information. [IAS 1 para 99]. Where the functional analysis is chosen, entities should also disclose additional information on the nature of expenses. This is because information on the nature of expenses is useful in predicting future cash flows. [IAS 1 paras 104, 105]. This additional information should, to fulfil the objective of assisting in predicting cash flows, disclose, by nature, details of all of the entity's expenses. IAS 1 specifically requires that depreciation, amortisation and employee benefits expense are disclosed.

Classification of expenses

4.140 Cost of sales will normally include:

- Opening (less closing) inventories.

- Direct materials.

- Other external charges (such as the hire of plant and machinery or the cost of casual labour used in the productive process).

- Direct labour.

- All direct production overheads, including depreciation and indirect overheads that can reasonably be allocated to the production function.

- Amortisation of development expenditure previously capitalised as an intangible asset.

- Cash discounts received on 'cost of sales' expenditure (this is not an offsetting, but an effective reduction in the purchase price of an item).

- Inventory write-downs.

4.141 Distribution costs are generally interpreted more widely than the name suggests and often include selling and marketing costs. Items normally included in this caption comprise:

- Payroll costs of the sales, marketing and distribution functions.

- Advertising.

- Salespersons' travel and entertaining.

- Warehouse costs for finished goods.

- Transport costs arising on the distribution of finished goods.

- All costs of maintaining sales outlets.

- Agents' commission payable.

4.142 Administrative expenses will normally include:

- The costs of general management.

- All costs of maintaining the administration buildings.

- Professional costs.

4.143 In some specific instances, the above analyses may not be appropriate, depending on the nature of the business. For example, in the context of a mail order entity, agents' commission payable may be regarded as a cost of sale rather than as a distribution cost. Likewise, certain transportation costs may be regarded as a cost of sale rather than a distribution cost (see further chapter 20).

4.144 The way in which an entity analyses its costs will depend very much on the nature of its business. Where an entity incurs significant operating expenses that it considers do not fall under any one of the headings 'cost of sales', 'distribution costs' and 'administrative expenses', there is nothing to prevent the entity including an additional item for these expenses (see para 4.158). The overriding consideration is that an entity should analyse its operating expenses consistently from year to year and in a manner that provides the most relevant information. Where an entity includes in any line item an estimate of an expense and, in a subsequent year, that estimate is shown to be in excess of the actual expense, the reversal of the 'excess expense' should be recognised in the same line item as the original expense estimate (see para 4.39). This principle is included as a specific requirement in IAS 2, which requires that *"the amount of any reversal of any write-down of inventories, arising from an increase in net realisable value, shall be recognised as a reduction in the amount of inventories recognised as an expense in the period in which the reversal occurs"*. [IAS 2 para 34].

[The next paragraph is 4.146.]

4.146 Finance costs will normally include:

- Interest payable on bank overdrafts and current and non-current borrowings. [IFRS 7 para 20].

- Unwinding of discounts on provisions. [IAS 37 para 60].

- Finance charges in respect of finance leases. [IAS 17 para 25].

- Dividends on preference shares classified as debt. [IAS 32 paras 35, 40].

- Amortisation of discounts and premiums on debt instruments that are liabilities . [IAS 39 paras 9, 47].

- Foreign exchange losses on foreign currency borrowings (see para 4.149 below).

- Changes in the fair value of certain derivative financial instruments (see para 4.151 below).

- Interest on tax payable where the interest element can be identified separately (see chapter 13).

4.147 Finance income (see para 4.148) should not be netted against finance costs. This does not preclude an entity from presenting finance income followed by finance costs and a sub-total (for example, 'net finance costs') on the face of the statement of comprehensive income (or, if presented, the income statement). However, where earning interest income is part of the entity's main business objectives, rather than an incidental benefit, that interest income should be included within the main 'revenue' heading. For example, a retailer that earns interest income from offering extended credit arrangements should include this interest income in its main 'revenue' heading. Similarly, a diversified conglomerate which has a financing business should include its finance income in the main 'revenue' heading.

4.148 IAS 1 requires an entity to present finance costs on the face of the statement of comprehensive income, but it does not require the separate presentation of finance income. The classification of finance income will depend on an entity's accounting policy for such items. For instance, entities may take the view that finance income, to the extent it is not included in the main 'revenue' heading, is most appropriately included as 'other operating income' or as separate line items in arriving at operating profit (if disclosed). Alternatively, entities may consider it appropriate to include finance income that arises from treasury activity (for example, income on surplus funds invested for the short term) outside operating profit whilst including other types of finance income as operating items. Although entities have some discretion in the way in which finance income is included in the statement of comprehensive income, the presentation policy adopted should be applied consistently and disclosed if material.

4.148.1 In addition, finance income normally includes items such as:

- Interest income on cash and cash equivalents. [IFRS 7 para 20].

- Unwinding of discounts on financial assets.

4.149 The classification of foreign exchange gains and losses requires judgement. Foreign exchange gains and losses that relate to borrowings and cash and cash equivalents would logically be classified as part of finance income/finance cost with all other foreign exchange gains and losses that are recognised in the statement of comprehensive income (or, if presented, the separate income statement) generally classified as 'other operating gains/losses', 'other operating income and expense' or similar line items. Alternatively, in some cases, entities may have an accounting policy where all foreign exchange gains and losses are presented either in 'other operating gains/losses' (or similar line items) or in 'finance income'/'finance cost', if such a policy is appropriate in the circumstances. Foreign currency exchange differences, including those on trade receivables (and unbilled revenue), should not be presented as part of revenue. Where the exchange gains or losses arise on a borrowing in a foreign currency undertaken to hedge a net investment in a foreign subsidiary, exchange differences are generally recognised in other comprehensive income in the consolidated financial statements and reclassified from equity when the group disposes of the net investment. [IAS 21 para 32; IAS 39 para 102]. Accounting for the disposal of a foreign operation that was hedged is dealt with in chapter 6. Accounting for full and partial disposals of a foreign operation is dealt with in chapter 7. In cases where exchange differences are reclassified to profit or loss as part of a disposal or partial disposal, they will generally be recorded in the same line in which the gain or loss on disposal is recognised – that is, 'other income' or 'other expenses'.

4.149.1 An entity may repurchase its own debt at an amount that reflects the debt's value in the market. The resulting difference arising between the carrying amount of the debt extinguished and the consideration paid is recognised in the statement of comprehensive income (or separate income statement if presented) in accordance with IAS 39. IAS 39 does not specify where the resultant gain or loss should be presented within the income statement. However, paragraph 15 of IAS 1 requires "*faithful representation of the effects of transactions*". For an entity that is not a financial institution, a debt-buy back transaction is in the nature of a financing activity (not an operating activity), as it changes the entity's borrowings. Hence, in our view, the gain or loss arising on extinguishing the debt should be recorded in the income statement under finance income or finance cost, respectively.

4.149.2 Depending on an entity's policy for presenting such items, other income (or other expenses, as appropriate) may include:

- Interest income on investments.

- Dividend income.

- Fair value gains and losses on financial assets at fair value through profit or loss.

- Gains and losses on trading derivatives.

4.150 Borrowing costs directly attributable to the acquisition, construction or production of qualifying assets are required to be capitalised as part of the asset's cost (see chapter 16). [IAS 23 para 8]. A qualifying asset is an asset that necessarily takes a substantial period of time to get ready for its intended use or sale. [IAS 23 para 5].

Derivative gains and losses

4.151 IAS 39 requires all derivatives to be measured at fair value in the statement of financial position, with changes in fair value being accounted for through profit or loss, except for derivatives that qualify as effective hedging instruments in a cash flow or a net investment hedge. There is limited guidance in the standards on the 'income statement geography' of derivative gains and losses. Entities, therefore, have some flexibility in how these items are presented. The line item in which such fair value changes are included will depend on the nature and purpose of the derivative and on the entity's presentation policy. The presentation policy should be described clearly, based on the entity's risk management policy and applied consistently.

4.152 The results of derivatives that are designated and effective hedges are included in the same line item as the impact of the related hedged item. Even a derivative that is an effective hedge will often have an ineffective element and the presentation of the gain or loss attributable to this hedge ineffectiveness should be consistent with the entity's policy on presenting the results of trading derivatives (see para 4.153).. This may mean that the results of the hedge ineffectiveness are included in the same line item as the impact of the related hedged item. For example, in the case of a hedge of fuel cost by an airline, if the hedge is 85% effective (and the other criteria for hedge accounting are met), the 15% ineffective element of the gain or loss is included in profit or loss and could be included in cost of sales. If the hedge is 70% effective (and, therefore, does not qualify for hedge accounting), 100% of the gain or loss is included in the profit or loss and could also be included in cost of sales. However, where derivatives are used to hedge revenue, the ineffective portion of the changes to the derivatives' fair value should not be included in revenue, as this does not relate to the goods or services delivered.

4.153 The results of trading derivatives and derivatives that are not designated and effective hedges are usually most appropriately shown within 'other operating gains and losses', or 'other operating income and expense', or as a separate line item, if the amount is significant. However, it may be appropriate to determine the classification of each major type of trading derivative (and derivatives that are not designated and effective hedges) separately. For instance, an entity might establish an accounting policy where all interest rate derivatives, whether taken out for trading/speculative or hedging purposes, would fall to be included in finance costs. In other words, the results of certain derivatives that do not meet the criteria for hedge accounting may be included in the same line item as the results of those derivatives that do so qualify, subject to the classification being in accordance with the entity's presentation policy. On the other hand, gains and losses on commodity derivatives should not be classified as part of finance cost as they do not relate to financing activities. Derivative gains and losses do not meet the definition of revenue and should not be reported as such, unless the derivatives are used to hedge revenue (in which case the effective portion of the changes to the derivatives' fair value can be included in revenue).

4.154 Derivatives that do not meet the criteria for hedge accounting (say, because the entity has failed to prepare formal documentation setting out the hedging relationship and the entity's risk management objective) but are nonetheless regarded by management as acting as hedges, are sometimes referred to as 'economic hedges'. It is not appropriate to divide similar types of 'non-designated' derivatives into two groups, 'economic hedges' and 'non-economic hedges', and to present their results in different places in the statement of comprehensive income, since the distinction between 'economic hedges' and 'non-economic hedges' is not recognised in IFRS. Consistent with paragraph 4.153, derivative gains or losses should not be included in revenue unless the derivatives are used to hedge revenue.

4.155 Where fair value gains and losses are presented separately in arriving at profit or loss, it is not appropriate to 'recycle' those gains and losses to other parts of profit or loss when they are realised. This is not to be confused with the reclassification of certain components of other comprehensive income (that is, certain income and expenses not dealt with in profit or loss). See paragraph 4.205.

Adaptation and additional line items

4.156 Many companies have adapted the descriptions and presentations shown in IAS 1 or have chosen to present additional items.

4.157 For example, while IAS 1 refers to 'distributions costs' and 'administrative expenses' other similar adaptations might include:

- Selling and distribution costs.
- Marketing, selling and distribution costs.
- Distribution costs, including marketing.
- Administrative and selling expenses.
- Selling and general administration expenses.

4.158 Additional line items should be inserted where this will make the entity's results more understandable. This objective will not be achieved where the addition of line items results in a cluttered statement of comprehensive income that obscures the entity's performance. Additional line items should only be inserted in respect of a material item or a combination of items that is material. Additional line items, where used, should generally be inserted beside other items that are similar in nature or function. Companies will need to ensure that each line item contains all the revenue or expense that relates to that particular line item.

4.159 Examples of additional items in a functional analysis of expenses include:

- Product support costs.
- Research and development.

- Public relations costs.

- Exploration costs.

4.160 Examples of additional items in a natural analysis of expenses include:

- Insurance costs.

- Occupancy costs.

- Professional fees.

- Abortive acquisition costs.

[The next paragraph is 4.162.]

Material and exceptional items

4.162 Paragraph 97 of IAS 1 requires *"when items of income and expense are material, an entity shall disclose their nature and amount separately"*. Materiality is defined in IAS 1 which states that either the size or the nature of an item, or a combination of both, could determine whether that item is material. That is, materiality of a transaction is determined, not just by its size, but also by its qualitative aspects. [IAS 1 para 7].

4.163 IAS 1 states that circumstances that may give rise to separate disclosure of items include:

- Writing down inventories to net realisable value, or impairments of property, plant and equipment, as well as the reversal of such write downs or impairments.

- Restructuring provisions or their reversal.

- Disposals of items of property, plant and equipment.

- Disposals of investments.

- Discontinued operations.

- Litigation settlements.

- Other reversals of provisions.

[IAS 1 para 98].

4.164 Disclosure of such information should be made on the face of the statement of comprehensive income (or, if presented, the separate income statement) *via* additional line items or headings if such presentation is relevant to understanding the entity's financial performance. [IAS 1 para 85]. Otherwise, these items should be disclosed in the notes to the financial statements. In relation to discontinued operations, IAS 1, in fact, requires that the net profit or loss attributable to discontinued operations and the re-measurement of assets, on the disposal of the assets or disposal groups constituting the discontinued operation, should be shown on the face of the statement of comprehensive income (or, if presented, the separate income statement). [IAS 1 para 82, IFRS 5 para 33].

4.165 IAS 1 does not include a specific name for the types of item that it says should be separately disclosed. The term 'exceptional items', used in some jurisdictions, is used in this chapter to refer to those items within profit or loss for which IAS 1 requires separate disclosure. The term 'exceptional items' should not be confused with the term 'extraordinary items'; the concept of 'extraordinary items' does not exist in IFRS and all items of income and expense, including exceptional items, are, therefore, deemed to arise from ordinary activities. Those companies that choose to disclose a category 'exceptional items' in their IFRS financial statements should ensure that the notes to the financial statements include a definition of this term; this is particularly important because the term 'exceptional item' is not defined within IFRS. The term will be unfamiliar to some users of the financial statements and may not be comparably applied across different companies. Similarly, where an entity uses any other term not defined in IFRS (for example, 'significant items' or 'unusual items', terms familiar to some users), a definition should be given in the notes to the financial statements or as a footnote to the statement of comprehensive income. Typically, companies include the definition of such terms in their principal accounting policies, as illustrated in Table 4.11. The presentation and definition of these items should be applied consistently from year to year. Additionally, some regulators may take a restrictive view of the suitability of presentation and definition of terms such as 'exceptional' or 'unusual' and regulated companies will need to consider these constraints.

Table 4.11 – Definition of exceptional items

Capital Shopping Centres Group PLC – Annual Report – 31 December 2011

2 Accounting policies – Group and Company (extract)

Exceptional items

Exceptional items are those items that in the Directors' view are required to be separately disclosed by virtue of their size or incidence to enable a full understanding of the Group's financial performance.

UK.4.165.1 Under UK GAAP, FRS 3 defines exceptional items as *"Material items which derive from events or transactions that fall within the ordinary activities of the reporting entity and which individually or, if of a similar type, in aggregate, need to be disclosed by virtue of their size or incidence if the financial statements are to give a true and fair view"*. [FRS 3 para 5].

UK.4.165.2 Whilst the UK standard does not refer to 'nature', the Financial Reporting Review Panel concluded in one case that the payment of fines was an important matter that ought to be brought specifically to the attention of the users of the financial statements. The Panel argued that the nature and circumstances of the fines concerned made them material even though, as the preparer of the financial statements argued, the amounts involved were not material. Certainly, this Panel decision has dissuaded companies from failing to make disclosure of transactions or events, purely on the basis of their monetary size. So, to that extent, the UK standard's definition of exceptional items would imply that 'material' includes items that are unusual by their nature and it is thus consistent with the IAS 1 description. The UK standard makes it clear that similar items should be aggregated in determining whether they need to be disclosed and that would also apply under IAS 1. [IAS 1 para 29].

4.166 Entities sometimes show 'operating profit before exceptional items', 'exceptional items' and 'operating profit'. This may be acceptable provided that (i) it does not clutter the statement of comprehensive income (or, if presented, the separate income statement) such that it dilutes clarity, and (ii) it does not undermine the expense analysis required, by excluding amounts that would otherwise be included therein. Headings such as 'underlying business performance' (or similar) should not normally be used to describe 'operating profit before exceptional items' as these types of heading tend to imply that the exceptional item has not arisen from the entity's ordinary activities. In addition, 'operating profit before exceptional items' should not receive more prominence than 'operating profit' by, say, being shown in bold print. In determining the most appropriate presentation, companies should have regard to the views of local regulators; it may be that the local regulator would not permit the use of the term 'exceptional item' or the presentation of the sub-total 'operating profit before exceptional items'.

4.167 In an analysis of expenses by nature, care should be taken to ensure that each class of expenses contains all items related to that class. An exceptional restructuring cost may, for example, include redundancy payments (an employee benefit cost), inventory write-downs (changes in inventory) and impairments in property, plant and equipment. It would not normally be acceptable to show restructuring costs as a separate line item in an analysis of expenses by nature where there is an overlap with other line items (see para 4.137). Nevertheless, it may sometimes be possible to present line items that do not create such an 'overlap', but this will depend on the nature of each of the costs. For example, payments made in a litigation settlement might be included as exceptional costs, if this cost did not form a component of any of the other categories.

4.168 When using the 'function of expense' method, the exceptional items should be included within the function to which they relate (see also paras 4.138 and 4.170). However, it will still be possible to show exceptional items separately on the face of the statement of comprehensive income (or, if presented, the separate income statement) by using a 'boxed presentation' under which the operating profit is analysed into 'operating profit before exceptional items' and 'exceptional items'. This form of presentation could also be used when a 'nature of expense' presentation is adopted. The objective of analysing the entity's expenses will need to be balanced against the objective of clarity in reporting; in many cases, analysis of expenses beyond the main categories set out in IAS 1 is best disclosed in the notes to the financial statements where accompanying narrative reporting can provide a fuller understanding of the amounts reported. A 'boxed presentation' may not, therefore, be the most suitable disclosure method. Entities that do adopt a 'boxed presentation' approach should avoid the overuse of boxes. For example, it is undesirable for an entity to analyse both 'operating profit' and 'profit before tax' into its non-exceptional and exceptional components. Such a presentation tends to clutter the primary statement presentation and also means that the exceptional item is reported more than once, giving the exceptional item more prominence than any other income or expense.

4.169 Paragraph 98 of IAS 1 states that restructuring cost provisions, and reversals thereof, are examples of items that would require separate disclosure on the face of the statement of comprehensive income or in the notes. For the reasons discussed above, in most cases, it will be difficult to give this disclosure on the face of the statement by use of additional line items. A columnar presentation (as in the example in para 4.173) is a possibility, but many entities will be able to explain their performance by giving the relevant disclosure in the notes.

UK.4.169.1 The examples below show some acceptable forms of presentation.

Example 1 – Exceptional items – function of expense method and boxed presentation of operating profit

	20X5	20X4
Revenue	xxx	xxx
Cost of sales	(xxx)	(xxx)
Gross profit	xxx	xxx
Other income	xxx	xxx
Distribution costs	(xxx)	(xxx)
Administrative expenses	(xxx)	(xxx)
Other expenses	(xxx)	(xxx)
Operating profit	xxx	xxx
Analysed as:		
Operating profit before exceptional items	xxx	xxx
Exceptional items	(xxx)	(xxx)
Operating profit	xxx	xxx
Finance costs	(xxx)	(xxx)
Share of profit of associates	xxx	xxx
Profit before tax	xxx	xxx

4.170 When using the 'function of expense' method, the exceptional items should be included within the function to which they relate. In our view, 'administrative expenses' and 'exceptional administrative expenses' should not be shown as separate line items without a sub-total, because the 'administrative expenses' line item would not contain all the expenses that relate to the administration function. Alternatively it is possible to show exceptional items separately on the face of the statement of comprehensive income (or, if presented, separate income statement) by, for example, disclosing the related amounts in brackets for each line item affected, or by using a 'boxed presentation' (addressed in para 4.126) under which the relevant expense item is analysed on the face of the statement into its exceptional and non-exceptional components. This form of presentation could also be used when a 'nature of expense' presentation is adopted.

4.171 It is acceptable to insert an additional line item in respect of an exceptional item provided that it is inserted in an appropriate place and provided that each line item expense includes all items related to that category. Where an entity is presenting a functional analysis of expenses, it is unlikely, in absence of a 'boxed presentation', to be able to insert an additional line item to deal with an exceptional item, because there is unlikely to be an exceptional function of the business; business functions tend to be the same from year to year. An entity may insert a new category of function in certain circumstances (for example, research and development), but this would not be described as 'exceptional' or in any way imply that it was a 'one-off' cost.

4.172 Where an exceptional item is shown as a separate line item on the face of the statement of comprehensive income, it should be shown next to the item that is closest to it in nature or function. For example, an exceptional impairment in the value of property, plant and equipment should generally be shown either above or below depreciation expense in a 'nature of expense' analysis. Care should be taken to ensure that each class of expenses includes all expenses, exceptional and non-exceptional, that relate to that class.

4.173 In some circumstances, entities have elected to employ multi-columnar formats in their income statement presentations to facilitate a better understanding of operating results and to highlight the impact of exceptional type items – for example, charges resulting from a major restructuring, particularly where these items impact multiple line items. Where management adopts such an approach and uses a separate column to segregate the impact of exceptional type items, it should exercise care to ensure that the presentation does not imply that the columnar results presented before exceptional items are the 'real' results. In particular, the 'before exceptionals' column should never be given greater prominence than the 'after exceptionals', or total column. Further, as explained above, headings such as 'underlying business performance' should not be used to refer to 'operating activity before exceptionals' as these types of headings may imply that the exceptional items have not arisen from an entity's ordinary activities.

Example – Exceptional items (columnar presentation – single year illustrated)

	20X5 Before exceptional items	20X5 Exceptional items	20X5 Total
Revenue	xxx		xxx
Cost of sales	(xxx)	(xxx)	(xxx)
Gross profit	xxx	(xxx)	xxx
Other income	xxx	xxx	xxx
Distribution costs	(xxx)	(xxx)	(xxx)
Administrative expenses	(xxx)	(xxx)	(xxx)
Other expenses	(xxx)		(xxx)
Finance costs	(xxx)		(xxx)
Share of profit of associates	xxx		xxx
Profit before tax	xxx	(xxx)	xxx
Income tax expense	(xxx)	xxx	(xxx)
Profit for the period	xxx	(xxx)	xxx

4.174 A columnar approach to the presentation of exceptional items may be a suitable form of presentation when there is more than one exceptional item or where a single exceptional event or transaction affects more than one line item. It is, of course, highly unlikely that there will be exceptional items relating to all line items as shown above.

4.175 A columnar presentation causes difficulties in presenting prior year exceptional items. Where there are prior year exceptional items, a six-column approach will be necessary if prior year results are to be presented consistently with current year results. This will often give a less clear presentation than would be achieved by presenting additional line items for exceptional items, but a failure to analyse the prior year into three columns could be taken to mean that there were no prior year exceptional items. In addition, if management is inserting additional columns because such a presentation is relevant to understanding the entity's performance, it follows that such a presentation should also be relevant to the comparative period. There will, therefore, be a trade off between 'cluttering' the statement of comprehensive income and giving the most relevant information. Management will have to exercise judgement as to which is the dominant factor in deciding the presentation and, in many cases, it will be more appropriate to make additional disclosures in the notes, rather than to crowd the statement with several columns. This is particularly the case where more than one prior period is included for comparative purposes. In addition, certain regulators may object to such presentations.

4.176 Where a six-column presentation is used, the three columns relating to the current period should be presented side by side, as should the three columns relating to the prior period; the current year 'before exceptionals' column should not be presented next to the 'before exceptionals' for the prior period. This is because the purpose of the columnar presentation is to analyse a particular year's performance; presenting the 'before exceptionals' column for the current period next to the 'before exceptionals' column for the prior period implies that the 'before exceptional' results are the 'core' results and are indicative of a trend in performance. Table 4.12 is an example of a six-column presentation.

Table 4.12 – Income statement columnar presentation

Elementis plc – Annual report and accounts 2011

Consolidated income statement (extract)
for the year ended 31 December 2011

	Note	2011 Before exceptional item $million	Exceptional items (note 5) $million	After exceptional items $million	2010 Before exceptional items $million	Exceptional items (note 5) $million	After exceptional items $million
Revenue	2	760.5	–	760.5	697.4	–	697.4
Cost of sales		(473.6)	–	(473.6)	(445.0)	–	(445.0)
Gross profit		286.9	–	286.9	252.4	–	252.4
Distribution costs		(82.7)	–	(82.7)	(82.8)	–	(82.8)
Administrative expenses		(67.1)	27.5	(39.6)	(67.3)	–	(67.3)
Operating profit	2	137.1	27.5	164.6	102.3	–	102.3
Finance income	3	2.6	–	2.6	0.4	–	0.4
Finance costs	4	(5.2)	–	(5.2)	(6.7)	–	(6.7)
Profit before income tax		134.5	27.5	162.0	96.0	–	96.0
Tax	6	(39.7)	1.8	(37.9)	(27.7)	5.8	(21.9)
Profit for the year		94.8	29.3	124.1	68.3	5.8	74.1
Attributable to:							
Equity holders of the parent		94.8	29.3	124.1	68.3	5.8	74.1
Non-controlling interests		–	–	–	–	–	–
		94.8	29.3	124.1	68.3	5.8	74.1

4.177 The columnar presentation described above should not be confused with a columnar reconciliation from a local GAAP to IFRS, which some entities may wish to report. For example, some companies prepare multi-columnar GAAP reconciliations that present a middle column containing the difference between, say, the local GAAP and IFRS (with the other columns containing the local GAAP totals and IFRS totals respectively). Such reconciliations are not acceptable on the face of the statement of comprehensive income, but are appropriate in the notes to the financial statements where the reconciling items can be fully explained in narrative form.

4.178 A columnar presentation should not be used to sideline or downgrade a collection of unrelated items from the statement of comprehensive income. However, this does not preclude an entity from showing separately an individual revenue or expense, or a group of related revenues and expenses, that arises as a result of a particular international accounting standard, provided that:

■ the items included in a separate column are different in nature or function from items included elsewhere; and

■ each column contains the total revenue or expense that relates to those particular items.

4.179 Where presented separately, these items should generally be included in operating activity, unless they relate to finance costs, share of profits or losses of associates and joint ventures, or the total profit or loss attributable to discontinued operations. With the exception of share of profits or losses of associates and joint ventures and of the total profit or loss attributable to discontinued operations (see para 4.107), they should not be presented net of tax. As noted in paragraph 4.117.1, exceptional items should not be presented in a way that implies they are extraordinary. Extraordinary items are prohibited under IFRS; it is, therefore, particularly important that the presentation of exceptional items should not undermine this prohibition.

4.180 In the case of profits and losses from sales of property, plant and equipment, separate disclosure is usually given, often on the face of the statement of comprehensive income (or, if presented, separate income statement). This is because the format headings in IAS 1 do not specifically cater for such profits and losses where they arise in continuing operations. However, such profits and losses should be shown in arriving at operating profit, or before finance costs if operating profit is not disclosed, unless the disposal is attributable to a discontinued operation requiring separate disclosure. [IAS 1 para 82].

4.181 The following examples consider the presentation in the statement of comprehensive income of exceptional type items related to (i) other income; (ii) a financial guarantee given on disposal of a business; and (iii) the sale of a subsidiary.

Example 1 – Compensation for loss of revenue

Entity A operates under the terms of a government licence in a regulated industry in country X. The entity received C3m from the government as compensation for loss of income that the entity suffered, because the licence agreement was modified. The original licence granted entity A exclusive rights to operate in country X and the modification allowed competition from locally-owned businesses. Receipt of the payment was unconditional and, accordingly, was recognised by entity A on receipt in the statement of comprehensive income (or, if presented, separate income statement). The compensation represents approximately 30% of the current year profit before tax. How should the compensation be presented in entity A's statement of comprehensive income?

Entity A should recognise the compensation from the government as 'other income'. The nature and size of the income is such that management should disclose it in a separate line on the face of the statement. Where operating profit is being disclosed, this line should normally be presented within operating profit; otherwise, it should be disclosed in the operating line items appearing before 'finance costs'.

Example 2 – Financial guarantee given on disposal of business

A manufacturing entity sold a business on 31 December 20X1, the last day of the accounting period. The business that was sold leased certain properties. The lessor has recourse to the entity under the terms of the lease for the unpaid rentals for a specified period of the lease. The entity recognised the recourse arrangement as a financial guarantee and recorded the liability at its fair value of C100,000 at the date of disposal, reducing the gain on disposal shown in the statement of comprehensive income (or, if presented, separate income statement) from C900,000 to C800,000. The financial liability was remeasured in accordance with IAS 39 at 31 December 20X2 and was stated at C80,000 in the statement of financial position at that date. The purchaser of the business defaulted on the last lease payment due in the specified period which has now expired and accordingly, in 20X3, the entity was been called upon to pay C85,000. How should the entity present the changes in the carrying value of the financial guarantee and the loss arising on the default in the statement of comprehensive income?

We consider that the financial guarantee was an intrinsic part of the disposal transaction and that subsequent adjustments to its carrying value should be dealt with in the same line of the statement in which the gain on disposal was shown in the earlier year, whether this be as part of continuing or discontinued operations. In 20X2, the entity should record C20,000 (C100,000 — C80,000) as a gain on disposal. In 20X3, the entity should record C5,000 (C85,000 — C80,000) as a loss on disposal. The overall gain/loss on disposal of the business over the three years is therefore C815,000, being the C900,000 'pre-guarantee gain' less C85,000 paid out under the guarantee. This properly reflects the overall profitability of the disposal transaction.

Financial guarantees are discussed further in chapters 6 and 21.

Example 3 – Gain on sale of subsidiary

Entity A had a foreign subsidiary, B, which it sold during the period. The gain on disposal of subsidiary B represents 80% of the group's profit for the year. How should the gain on disposal be treated in entity A's consolidated financial statements?

In its consolidated financial statements, entity A should present the gain on disposal of this subsidiary separately on the face of the entity's statement of comprehensive income (or, if presented, separate income statement). The separate presentation is required because of the nature and size of the amounts involved. The positioning within the statement will depend on whether the subsidiary is a discontinued operation under IFRS 5.

Continuing operation – Where the disposal of a subsidiary does not qualify as a discontinued operation under IFRS 5, the gain or loss on disposal will normally be shown within operating profit if this is disclosed, or in the line items before finance costs if it is not (as shown below). However, where it is clear that the disposal is a one-off transaction (that is, it is not expected that the entity will have a similar transaction in the future and there is no history of having similar transactions in the past), the gain or loss on disposal may be shown after operating profit but before finance costs.

	20X5 Total	20X4
Revenue	xxx	xxx
Cost of sales	(xxx)	(xxx)
Gross profit	xxx	xxx
Other income	xxx	xxx
Distribution costs	(xxx)	(xxx)
Administrative expenses	(xxx)	(xxx)
Other expenses	(xxx)	(xxx)
Gain on disposal of subsidiary B	xxx	xxx
Finance costs	(xxx)	(xxx)
Share of profit of associates	xxx	xxx
Profit before tax	xxx	xxx
Income tax expense	(xxx)	(xxx)
Profit for the period	xxx	xxx

Discontinued operation – Where the disposal of a subsidiary qualifies as a discontinued operation under IFRS 5, the gain on disposal should be included in the profit or loss on discontinued operations presented separately in accordance with paragraph 82 of IAS 1. IAS 1 requires disclosure, on the face of the statement of comprehensive income, of *"a single amount comprising the total of (i) the post-tax profit or loss of discontinued operations and (ii) the post-tax gain or loss recognised on measurement to fair value less costs to sell or on disposal of the assets or disposal group(s) constituting the discontinued operation"*, an example of which is shown below:

	20X5	20X4
Revenue	xxx	xxx
Cost of sales	(xxx)	(xxx)
Gross profit	xxx	xxx
Other income	xxx	xxx
Distribution costs	(xxx)	(xxx)
Administrative expenses	(xxx)	(xxx)
Other expenses	(xxx)	(xxx)
Finance costs	(xxx)	(xxx)
Share of profit of associates	xxx	xxx
Profit before tax	xxx	xxx
Income tax expense	(xxx)	(xxx)
Profit from continuing operations, net of tax	xxx	xxx
Profit from discontinued operation, net of tax	xxx	–
Profit for the period	xxx	xxx

4.182 As stated above, IAS 1 requires disclosure, on the face of the statement of comprehensive income, of *"a single amount comprising the total of (i) the post-tax profit or loss of discontinued operations and (ii) the post-tax gain or loss recognised on measurement to fair value less costs to sell or on disposal of the assets or disposal group(s) constituting the discontinued operation".* Further analysis of this single amount is required, but may be given either on the face of the statement or within the notes. Where an entity elects to give the disclosure on the face of the statement of comprehensive income, this disclosure should be presented in a separate section of the statement and not mingled with the results of continuing operations. In particular, it is not permissible to show, for example, total revenue as the sum of revenue from continuing and discontinued operations. Under IFRS, 'revenue' is revenue from continuing operations only. IAS 1 prescribes a position in the statement of comprehensive income for discontinued operations; entities are not permitted to promote elements of that disclosure to a higher position in the statement.

Example – Discontinued operations analysed on the face of the income statement

	20X5	20X5	20X4	20X4
Continuing operations:				
Revenue		xxx		xxx
Cost of sales		(xxx)		(xxx)
Gross profit		xxx		xxx
Other income		xxx		xxx
Distribution costs		(xxx)		(xxx)
Administrative expenses		(xxx)		(xxx)
Other expenses		(xxx)		(xxx)
Finance costs		(xxx)		(xxx)
Share of profit of associates		xxx		xxx
Profit before tax		xxx		xxx
Income tax expense		(xxx)		(xxx)
Profit from continuing operations		xxx		xxx
Discontinued operations:				
Revenue	xxx		xxx	
Expenses	(xxx)		(xxx)	
Profit before tax	xxx		xxx	
Income tax expense	(xxx)		(xxx)	
Gain on disposal of discontinued operation	xxx		xxx	
Income tax expense	(xxx)	xxx	(xxx)	xxx
Profit for the period		xxx		xxx

4.183 IFRS 3 requires an acquirer to disclose the amount of the acquiree's revenue and profit or loss since acquisition date that has been included in the consolidated statement of comprehensive income for the period, unless it is impracticable to do so. [IFRS 3 para B64(q)(i)]. However, there is no requirement to give this disclosure on the face of the statement of comprehensive income and, indeed, presentations that segregate the results of the acquired business from those of the 'original group' on the face of the statement can be problematic. The purpose of this disclosure is to show the impact of an acquisition on the group's results in the period of the acquisition.

4.184   Where there have been acquisitions in both the current and prior years, a columnar presentation of the results of the acquired business and the 'original group' would, because of the requirement to show comparatives, result in showing three columns in each year with no current year column being comparable to its prior year counterpart. The 'original group' column would be comparable with neither the comparative 'original group' column nor the comparative 'total' column. We consider, therefore, that, in such circumstances, the additional 'original group' and 'acquisition' columns would not assist in the provision of reliable and relevant information and should not, therefore, be given. However, where there were no acquisitions in the previous period and the acquired business has little or no impact on the original group, the problems outlined above would not arise. Nevertheless, companies should consider the desirability of such a presentation where there are likely to be acquisitions in future periods, necessitating a change in presentation from year to year. In our view, the requirement for consistency in presentation would outweigh the desirability of such analysis of results on the face of the statement of comprehensive income. Only where acquisitions are rare is a columnar presentation likely to be of any benefit.

4.184.1   Further guidance on business combinations and presentation in the statement of comprehensive income is given in chapter 25.

Notes to the statement of comprehensive income

Analysis of expenses between continuing and discontinued operations

4.185   IAS 1 and various other accounting standards require entities to disclose information about the amounts included in profit or loss. Where an entity has only continuing operations, the position is straightforward and the amount disclosed in the notes to the statement of comprehensive income for each category of expense is the total amount charged to the statement for that year. Where the entity has discontinued operations, part of each category of expense will be included in the 'discontinued operations section' of the statement with the remaining part being included within continuing operations.

4.186   In 'Improvements to IFRSs' issued in April 2009, the IASB amended IFRS 5 to clarify the disclosure requirements in respect of held for sale and discontinued operations. Paragraph 5B of IFRS 5 states:

"This IFRS specifies the disclosures required in respect of non-current assets (or disposal groups) classified as held for sale or discontinued operations. Disclosures in other IFRSs do not apply to such assets (or disposal groups) unless those IFRSs require:

(a) specific disclosures in respect of non-current assets (or disposal groups) classified as held for sale or discontinued operations; or

(b) disclosures about measurement of assets and liabilities within a disposal group that are not within the scope of the measurement requirement of IFRS 5 and such disclosures are not already provided in the other notes to the financial statements.

Additional disclosures about non-current assets (or disposal groups) classified as held for sale or discontinued operations may be necessary to comply with the general requirements of IAS 1, in particular paragraphs 15 and 125 of that Standard."

4.187 Therefore, in general, disclosure requirements in other standards do not apply to discontinued operations, unless specifically stated in that other standard, or where assets and liabilities in a discontinued operation are not within IFRS 5's scope for measurement. An example of a specific disclosure in another standard is paragraph 68 of IAS 33, which requires an entity to disclose the amount per share for discontinued operations.

4.188 Note that IFRS 5 states that additional disclosures about non-current assets (or disposal groups) classified as held for sale or discontinued operations may be necessary to comply with the general requirements of IAS 1 – in particular, paragraph 15 (fair presentation) and paragraph 125 (estimation uncertainty) of that standard.

4.189 The disclosure requirements for discontinued operations are dealt with in chapter 26.

UK.4.189.1 As discussed below, UK company law requires disclosure of employee costs and numbers. Since UK law does not recognise the distinction between continuing and discontinued operations, it follows that the legal disclosure requirements apply to the total operations of the company.

Employee benefits expense

4.190 Where an entity chooses to report expenses according to their nature, employee benefits expense is shown on the face of the statement of comprehensive income (or, if presented, separate income statement) (see para 4.129). If a functional analysis of expenses is shown, employee benefits expense should be disclosed in the notes to the financial statements (see para 4.139). Paragraph 105 of IAS 1 states that 'employee benefits' has the same meaning as in IAS 19. Employee benefits are defined in IAS 19 as: *"all forms of consideration given by an* *entity in exchange for service rendered by employees"*. [IAS 19 para 7]. (The definition has been amended in IAS 19 (revised) to make it clear that it includes consideration given for the termination of employment. [IAS 19 (revised) para 8].) Consideration given through share-based payments is dealt with in IFRS 2. See chapter 12 for more details.

4.191   IAS 19 states:

"Employee benefits include:

(a)   *short-term employee benefits, such as wages, salaries and social security contributions, paid annual leave and paid sick leave, profit sharing and bonuses (if payable within twelve months of the end of the period) and non-monetary benefits (such as medical care, housing, cars and free or subsidised goods or services) for current employees;*

(b)   *post-employment benefits such as pensions, other retirement benefits, post-employment life insurance and post-employment medical care;*

(c)   *other long-term employee benefits, including long-service leave or sabbatical leave, jubilee or other long-service benefits, long-term disability benefits and, if they are not payable wholly within twelve months after the end of the period, profit sharing, bonuses and deferred compensation; and*

(d)   *termination benefits"*.

[IAS 19 para 4].

4.191.1   For entities applying IAS 19 (revised), which is effective for annual periods beginning on or after 1 January 2013, this states:

"Employee benefits include:

(a)   *short-term employee benefits, such as the following, if expected to be settled wholly before twelve months after the end of the annual reporting period in which the employees render the related services:*
  (i)   *wages, salaries and social security contributions;*
  (ii) *paid annual leave and paid sick leave;*
  (iii) profit-sharing and bonuses; and
  (iv) non-monetary benefits (such as medical care, housing, cars and free or subsidised goods or services) for current employees;

(b)   *post-employment benefits, such as the following:*
  (i)   *retirement benefits (eg pensions and lump sum payments on retirement); and*
  (ii) *other post-employment benefits, such as post-employment life insurance and post-employment medical care;*

(c)   *other long-term employee benefits, such as the following:*
  (i)   *long-term paid absences such as long-service leave or sabbatical leave;*

(ii) jubilee or other long-service benefits; and
(iii) long-term disability benefits; and

(d)   termination benefits.

[IAS 19 (revised) para 5].

4.192   The IAS 1 requirement is for the disclosure of the total amount of employee benefit expense recognised in profit or loss. Other standards, IAS 19 in particular, contain requirements for the disclosure of the individual elements of employee benefit expense listed in paragraph 4.191 (a) to (d) and other matters related to the employee benefits. Disclosure of the number of employees is not an IFRS requirement but it is a legal disclosure requirement in many countries (for example, EU Member States).

UK.4.192.1   Although the number of employees is not a disclosure requirement under IFRS, the Companies Act 2006 require the average number of employees to be disclosed. This disclosure should be both in total and by category of employee with the categories being determined by the directors, having regard to the manner in which the company's activities are organised. [CA06 Sec 411]. Various types of disclosure have been adopted by companies, including by geographical region and by business segment. See from paragraph UK.4.193.1.

UK.4.192.2   Under UK law, employees are individuals the entity employs under contracts of service. [CA06 Sec 411]. A contract of service (or a contract of employment as it is also called) is an agreement under which the employer agrees to employ the employee for a wage or a salary in return for the employee's labour. This agreement should be made in writing. However, self-employed persons are not employed by the company, but merely have contracts to perform specific services for that company. The costs of self-employed people should normally be excluded from employee benefits expense, because their contracts will be contracts *for services*. Examples of such persons are consultants and contractors. The same approach is appropriate under IFRS, except in respect of directors and key management, as discussed in paragraph 4.194.

UK.4.192.3   In summary, the legal requirement in section 411 of the Companies Act 2006 is that either the profit and loss account format or the notes should disclose, in aggregate, each of the following amounts:

■   The wages and salaries that were either paid to employees or are payable to them, in respect of the financial year in question.

■   Social security costs that the company has incurred on behalf of its employees. For this purpose, social security costs are any contributions the company makes to any social security or pension scheme, or fund or arrangement that the State runs. These costs will include the employer's national insurance contributions.

- Other pension costs the company has incurred on behalf of employees. For this purpose, pension costs include:

  - Any costs incurred by a company in respect of any non-State occupational pension scheme that is established to provide pensions for employees or past employees.

  - Any sums the company has set aside for the future payment of pensions directly to current and former employees.

  - Any amounts the company has paid in respect of pensions, without those amounts having first been so set aside.

- Pension costs will, therefore, include the cost in respect of the company's participation in any pension scheme other than the State scheme.

UK.4.192.4 Schedule 10 to SI 2008/410, the 'Large and Medium-sized Companies and Groups (Accounts and Reports) Regulations 2008' (regulations which support 2006 Act), says that wages and salaries should be determined by reference to either the payments the company makes or the costs it incurs in respect of all persons it employs. [SI 2008/410 10 Sch 14(3)]. There is no definition in the legislation of 'costs incurred'. Although it is likely that a strict interpretation of this term would include the money value of benefits in kind, as in the case of directors' remuneration under Schedule 5 to SI 2008/410, in practice, companies have, in the past, sometimes charged the cost of staff benefits to other items in the profit and loss account and not to staff costs. There is no requirement in IFRS to disclose short-term employee benefits expense, but total employee benefits expense should be disclosed; employee benefits are defined in IAS 19 as set out in paragraph 4.191 above. Since the definition of employee benefits expense in IAS 19 specifically includes non-monetary benefits, it is not acceptable, under IFRS, to exclude benefits in kind from employee benefits expense.

4.193 Some companies have adopted profit sharing schemes for their employees. Amounts provided under such schemes are sometimes shown separately as additional items in the analysis of employee benefits expense.

Number of employees

UK.4.193.1 In addition to requiring that the notes to the profit and loss account should disclose employee costs, legislation requires that the notes should include information in respect of the number of employees.

UK.4.193.2 The two disclosures that the notes should contain in connection with the number of employees are:

- The average number of employees in the financial year. The number should be calculated by:

- Ascertaining the number of persons employed under contract of service, whether full-time or part-time, for each month in the year.

- Adding together all the monthly numbers.

- Dividing the resulting total by the number of months in the financial year.

The average number of employees includes persons who work wholly or mainly overseas, as well as persons who work in the UK.

- The average number of employees by category. This number should be calculated by applying the same method of calculation as outlined above to each category of employees. For this purpose, the categories of persons employed are to be such categories as the directors select, having regard to the way in which the company's activities are organised.

[CA06 Sec 411].

UK.4.193.3 Because the guidance on how to select categories is rather vague, directors of companies have chosen a variety of different categories. Methods have included splitting between part-time employees and full-time employees; between hourly-paid, weekly-paid and salaried staff; between production, sales and administration staff; and between staff employed in different geographical areas.

UK.4.193.4 There is no exemption from disclosure where (for example) a company is a wholly-owned subsidiary.

Directors and other key management personnel

4.194 Directors and other key management personnel who have a contract of service (that is, an employment contract) with the entity are clearly 'employees' under IFRS. In some cases, personnel may have a contract of service with one group entity whilst providing services to another group entity, with or without a recharge of the costs of their employment. These situations are considered in paragraph 4.199. In other cases, employees may not have a formal contract of service but the nature of their relationship with the entity is such that they are, in substance, employees and the cost of their services should, therefore, be included in 'employee benefits expense'.

4.195 The position is less clear when considering directors and key personnel where the legal status of their relationship with the entity is other than that of an employee. This might be the case where, for example, the entity engages a non-executive director and pays his 'service entity' for his services, the director providing similar services to a number of companies. IAS 19 states: *"For the purpose of this Standard, employees include directors and other management personnel"*. [IAS 19 para 6; IAS 19 (revised) para 7]. This could be interpreted as requiring all costs of engaging directors and key management, whether under employment contracts or otherwise, to be included in employee benefits expense.

With this interpretation, the employee benefits expense disclosable under IFRS would, in some cases, be a larger amount than the staff costs arising on employment contracts. The most important consideration is the transparency of the disclosure and its consistency year to year.

4.196   In any event, IFRS requires additional disclosure in respect of directors and key management. Regardless of the disclosure within employee benefits expense, payments made to directors and key management should be disclosed in the notes under IAS 24.

UK.4.196.1   In addition, company law sets out separate disclosure requirements concerning directors' emoluments and transactions and other arrangements involving directors. Company law also sets out disclosure requirements for a directors' remuneration report by quoted companies. These disclosures are considered in chapters 5 and 6 of the Manual of Accounting – Narrative Reporting.

Practical problems relating to employee benefits expense

4.197   In practice, there may be problems in deciding on the employees to include in employee benefits expense (and numbers, if disclosed). One of the most frequent problems arises where employees clearly work for one entity, but their contracts of service are with another entity (for example, the holding entity). Also, further complications arise when that other entity pays the wages and salaries of these employees. In such situations, if entities disclosed only the cost of those individuals they employ, it could lead to the disclosure of misleading information in the financial statements. Accordingly, an entity may need to give additional information to enable its financial statements to give a fair presentation.

4.198   Some of the more common problems that arise in this respect are considered in paragraph 4.199. These examples deal with the disclosure of both employee benefits expense and employee numbers. There is no requirement under IFRS to disclose employee numbers but entities may do so voluntarily, or to meet local legal requirements.

4.199   Some of the more common problems that arise in group situations are considered in the examples that follow:

Example 1 – Contracts of service with another group entity

Employees work full time for, and are paid by, a subsidiary entity, but their contracts of service are with the parent entity.

It would be misleading if there were no disclosure of employee benefits expense in the subsidiary entity's financial statements. Consequently, the wages and salaries that the subsidiary entity pays to those employees should be disclosed as 'employee benefits expense' in its financial statements. The notes to the subsidiary entity's financial statements should explain that those staff have contracts of service with another group entity. They should also explain why their remuneration and number (if provided) are disclosed in the financial statements.

The parent entity's consolidated financial statements normally will not be affected, because they will show the employee benefits expense of the group as a whole. If the parent entity is also preparing separate IFRS financial statements, then the parent entity's financial statements should explain that certain employees, having service contracts with the entity, work for and are paid for wholly by a subsidiary entity. The employee benefits expense should be disclosed and the entity may disclose the number of employees.

Similarly, if the contracts of service are with a fellow subsidiary entity, then that fellow subsidiary entity should disclose in the notes to its financial statements that certain employees, having service contracts with the entity, work for and are paid for wholly by a fellow subsidiary entity. The employee benefits expense should be disclosed and the entity may disclose the number of employees.

Where the parent (or fellow subsidiary) prepares a 'nature of expense' statement of comprehensive income, the employee benefits expense shown on the face of the statement will be the cost to that parent (or fellow subsidiary) of its employees. In the circumstances described above, this will be less than the amounts paid to the persons with whom it has contracts of service. This should be explained in the notes to the financial statements.

Example 2 – Subsidiary entity incurs management charge

Employees work full time for the subsidiary entity, but they are not paid by the subsidiary entity and they do not have service contracts with it. However, the subsidiary entity bears a management charge for their services from the entity that pays the employees and it can ascertain the proportion of the management charge that relates to employee benefits expense.

Again, in this situation it could be misleading if the subsidiary entity's financial statements disclosed no information about employee costs. Accordingly, where the information is available, it might be appropriate to disclose the proportion of the management charge that relates to employee benefits expense in the subsidiary entity's financial statements as employee benefits expense. In such circumstances, the notes to the financial statements should explain that the employees do not have contracts of service with the entity, and they should also explain why their costs and numbers (if provided) are disclosed in the financial statements.

For the reasons outlined in example 1 above, the parent entity's consolidated financial statements should not be affected. If the contracts of service are with, and the employees are paid by, the parent entity, and the parent is preparing separate IFRS financial statements, then the parent's financial statements should disclose the employee benefits expense and may disclose employee numbers in respect of all its employees and give details regarding the employee benefits expense that is recharged to the subsidiary and may disclose the number of employees that work for that subsidiary. If the contracts of service are with, and the employees are paid by, a fellow subsidiary entity then that fellow subsidiary's financial statements should disclose the employee benefits expense and may disclose employee numbers in respect of all its employees and give details regarding the employee costs that are recharged to the fellow subsidiary and may disclose the number of employees that work for that fellow subsidiary.

Example 3 – Subsidiary entity incurs non-specific management charge

The facts are the same as in example 2 except that the subsidiary entity is unable to break down the management charge and ascertain the part of it that relates to employee benefits expense.

In this situation, for the same reason as explained in example 2, the parent entity's consolidated financial statements will be unaffected. The notes to the subsidiary entity's financial statements should explain that the employees' contracts of service are with the parent entity and that their remuneration is included in the parent entity's financial statements. The notes should also explain that the management charge that the parent entity makes includes the cost of these employees, but that it is not possible to ascertain separately the element of the management charge that relates to employee benefits expense. If the parent is preparing separate financial statements and the parent pays the employees, the parent entity's separate financial statements should disclose the employees' remuneration in its employee benefits expense. The notes may disclose the number of employees involved and should explain that employees work for a subsidiary entity and that the entity recharges the cost of their employment to that subsidiary as part of a management charge.

If the employees' contracts of service are with a fellow subsidiary, rather than with the parent entity, and that fellow subsidiary also pays the employees, the fellow subsidiary's financial statements should disclose the employees' remuneration in its employee benefits expense. The notes may disclose the number of employees involved and should explain that employees work for a fellow subsidiary entity and that the entity recharges the cost of their employment to that fellow subsidiary as part of a management charge.

Example 4 – Subsidiary entity does not incur management charge

The facts are the same as in example 2 above, except that no management charge is made for the employees' services. This will often apply where staff work either full-time or part-time for small companies.

Under IAS 24 a related party transaction is a *"transfer of resources, services or obligations between a reporting entity and a related party, regardless of whether a price is charged"*. [IAS 24 para 9]. In this situation, even though no management charge is made, the subsidiary is receiving the benefit of the employees' services, paid for by another group entity, a related party. The notes to the subsidiary entity's financial statements should explain that the entity is not charged for the services provided by the employees that work for it. If appropriate, the notes should also indicate that the expense of these employees is included in the parent entity's consolidated financial statements and, where the information is available, it might be appropriate to disclose the amount of that expense.

Once again, if it is the parent entity that employs and pays the employees, its separate financial statements should include the cost of these employees in its employee benefits expense. If appropriate, the notes to the financial statements should explain that these employees work for a subsidiary entity, but that no management charge is made for their services to that entity. If it is a fellow subsidiary that employs and pays the employees, its financial statements should include the cost of these employees in its employee benefits expense. If appropriate, the notes to the financial statements should explain that these employees work for a fellow subsidiary entity, but that no management charge is made for their services to that entity. The number of employees involved may be disclosed in the parent's separate financial statements, or fellow subsidiary's financial statements, as appropriate.

Disclosures by groups

UK.4.199.1 Where a parent company prepares group financial statements, employee costs and numbers should be disclosed in respect of the consolidated group.

UK.4.199.2 Under Part 15 of the Companies Act 2006, where a parent company prepares group financial statements, a parent company is no longer required to present particulars of employee costs and numbers for the company. This is the case regardless of whether the parent company takes the exemption from presenting its own profit and loss account. [CA06 Sec 408].

Depreciation and amortisation

4.200 Where an entity presents a functional analysis of expenses it should also separately disclose depreciation and amortisation expense. [IAS 1 para 104]. This is a requirement not just of IAS 1 but also of IAS 16 and IAS 38. [IAS 16 para 73, IAS 38 para 118]. In addition, IAS 36 requires the disclosure of amounts charged to profit or loss for the period in respect of impairment losses and amounts credited to profit or loss for the period in respect of reversals of impairment losses. Both amounts charged and amounts credited to profit or loss should be disclosed separately from those charged and credited direct to equity. [IAS 36 para 126].

Other comprehensive income

4.201 As stated in paragraph 4.104, all items of income and expense recognised in a period should be included in profit or loss for the period, unless a standard or interpretation requires or permits otherwise. [IAS 1 para 88].The statement of comprehensive income presents all items of income and expense recognised in a period. Items of income and expense that are not taken to profit or loss but are shown in the statement of comprehensive income as 'other comprehensive income' will, therefore, include the following:

- Revaluation gains and losses on property, plant and equipment (IAS 16).

- Revaluation gains and losses on intangible assets (IAS 38).

- Gains and losses on re-measuring available-for sale financial assets (IAS 39).

- The portion of gains and losses on hedging instruments that are effective cash flow hedges (IAS 39).

- Foreign currency exchange gains and losses arising on translation of the net investment in a foreign operation in the consolidated financial statements when the foreign operation is a subsidiary (IAS 21).

- Foreign exchange differences arising on translation of an entity's results and financial position from functional currency to presentation currency if different (IAS 21).

- Actuarial gains and losses on defined benefit pension schemes under IAS 19 (or remeasurements of defined benefit plans under IAS 19 (revised)).

- The current and deferred tax charges or credits in respect of items taken to other comprehensive income (IAS 12).

4.201.1   In addition, IFRS 5 requires an entity to present separately any cumulative income or expense recognised in other comprehensive income relating to a non-current asset or disposal group classified as held for sale. [IFRS 5 para 38]. See further chapter 26.

4.201.2   The presentation of the group's share of associates and joint ventures' changes in other comprehensive income is dealt with in chapter 27.

4.201.3   For annual periods beginning on or after 1 July 2012, IAS 1 requires the other comprehensive income section to present line items for amounts of other comprehensive income in the period, classified by nature (including share of the other comprehensive income of associates and joint ventures accounted for using the equity method) and grouped into those that, in accordance with other IFRSs:

(a)   will not be reclassified subsequently to profit or loss; and

(b)   will be reclassified subsequently to profit or loss when specific conditions are met.

[IAS 1 (revised) para 82A].

4.201.4   Reclassification adjustments are considered further in paragraph 4.205 onwards. An example of the new disclosure is given in Table 4.5.2 in paragraph 4.103.2 above.

Tax on other comprehensive income

4.202   IAS 1, partly by amending IAS 12 clarifies and expands the requirements for the presentation of the tax related to items included in the statement of comprehensive income or taken direct to equity. Current and deferred tax should be dealt with in profit or loss, unless it relates to items dealt with in other comprehensive income or items taken directly to equity, in which case the tax related to those items should be recognised in other comprehensive income or in equity, as appropriate. [IAS 12 para 61A]. IAS 1 also requires that an entity should disclose the amount of income tax relating to each component of other comprehensive income (that is, income and expense not dealt with in profit or loss), including reclassification adjustments, either in the statement of comprehensive income or in the notes. [IAS 1 para 90]. Components of other comprehensive income may be presented on the face of the statement of comprehensive income net of the related tax effects or before the related tax effects with one amount shown for the aggregate amount of income tax relating to those components. [IAS 1 para 91].

4.202.1 IAS 1 has been amended to require that if an entity presents items of other comprehensive income before related tax effects with the aggregate tax shown separately, it should allocate the tax between the items that might be reclassified subsequently to the profit or loss section and those that will not be reclassified. [IAS 1 para 91]. The amendment is effective for annual periods beginning on or after 1 July 2012, with earlier application permitted. An example of the new disclosure is given in Table 4.5.2 in paragraph 4.103.2 above.

4.203 Whether the entity presents components of other comprehensive income net or gross of tax, the entity should disclose the tax effect of each component of other comprehensive income in the notes, to the extent the disclosure is not made on the face of the statement of comprehensive income. The illustrative example of this disclosure contained in the implementation guidance accompanying the standard is reproduced below.

XYZ Group

Disclosure of tax effects relating to each component of other comprehensive income

Notes
Year ended 31 December 20X7

	20X7			20X6		
	Before-tax amount	Tax (expense) benefit	Net-of-tax amount	Before-tax amount	Tax (expense) benefit	Net-of-tax amount
Exchange differences on translating foreign operations	5,334	(1,334)	4,000	10,667	(2,667)	8,000
Available-for-sale financial assets	(24,000)	6,000	(18,000)	26,667	(6,667)	20,000
Cash flow hedges	(667)	167	(500)	(4,000)	1,000	(3,000)
Gains on property revaluation	933	(333)	600	3,367	(667)	2,700
Actuarial gains (losses) in defined benefit pension plans	(667)	167	(500)	1,333	(333)	1,000
Share of other comprehensive income of associates	400	–	400	(700)	–	(700)
	(18,667)	4,667	(14,000)	37,334	(9,334)	28,000

Note: This illustrative example is based on IAS 1 prior to its amendment effective for annual periods beginning on or after 1 July 2012. The amendment requires items of other comprehensive income to be grouped into those that will be reclassified subsequently to profit or loss and those that will not be reclassified (see para 4.201.3).

4.204 The presentation and disclosure requirements for the tax effects of other comprehensive income are, therefore, more onerous than those applying to items dealt with in profit and loss. The tax effect of profit or loss items is disclosed in aggregate and there is no requirement to disclose the tax effect of individual items except indirectly to the extent they affect the reconciliations required by IAS 12. IAS 1 imposes more demanding disclosure requirements in respect of items not dealt with in profit or loss because the tax rates applying to those items are often different from those applying to profit or loss items, resulting in requests for more information from users of financial statements. An example that discloses the tax effects (and in addition the non-controlling interest effects) is given in Table 4.13.1.

Table 4.13.1 – Disclosure of tax effects on components of comprehensive income

Sasol Limited – Annual report – 30 June 2011

statement of comprehensive income
for the year ended 30 June

	Note	2011 Rm	2010 Rm	2009 Rm
Profit for year		**20 220**	16 387	13 715
Other comprehensive income, net of tax	44	**(1 943)**	(777)	(2 881)
Effect of translation of foreign operations	44	**(2 031)**	(802)	(2 485)
Effect of cash flow hedges	44	**111**	13	(497)
Investments available-for-sale	44	**–**	4	–
Tax on other comprehensive income	44	**(23)**	8	101
Total comprehensive income		**18 277**	15 610	10 834
Attributable to				
Owners of Sasol Limited		**17 849**	15 171	10 796
Non-controlling interests in subsidiaries		**428**	439	38
		18 277	15 610	10 834

Notes to the financial statements (extract)

for the year ended 30 June

	Note	2011 Rm	2010 Rm	2009 Rm
44 Other comprehensive income				
Components of other comprehensive income				
Effect of translation of foreign operations		**(2 031)**	(802)	(2 485)
Effect of cash flow hedges		**111**	13	(497)
gains/(losses) on effective portion of cash flow hedges		**107**	13	(430)
losses/(gains) on cash flow hedges transferred to hedged items		**4**	–	(67)
Gain on fair value of investments		**–**	4	–
Tax on other comprehensive income	22	**(23)**	8	101
Other comprehensive income for year, net of tax		**(1 943)**	(777)	(2 881)

The components of other comprehensive income can be reclassified subsequently to the income statement.

	Gross Rm	Tax Rm	Non-controlling interest Rm	Net Rm
Tax and non-controlling interest on other comprehensive income				
2011				
Effect of translation of foreign operations	**(2 031)**	–	**3**	**(2 028)**
Gain on effective portion of cash flow hedges	**107**	**(22)**	**(5)**	**80**
Loss on cash flow hedges transferred to hedged items	**4**	**(1)**	–	**3**
Other comprehensive income	**(1 920)**	**(23)**	**(2)**	**(1 945)**
2010				
Effect of translation of foreign operations	(802)	–	–	(802)
Gain on effective portion of cash flow hedges	13	9	7	29
Gain on fair value of investments	4	(1)	–	3
Other comprehensive income	(785)	8	7	(770)
2009				
Effect of translation of foreign operations	(2 485)	1	3	(2 481)
Losses on effective portion of cash flow hedges	(430)	89	26	(315)
Gain on cash flow hedges transferred to hedged items	(67)	10	–	(57)
Gain on fair value of investments	–	1	–	1
Other comprehensive income	(2,982)	101	29	(2,852)

Reclassification ('recycling') adjustments

4.205 IAS 1 requires an entity to disclose, either in the statement of comprehensive income or in the notes, 'reclassification adjustments' (also commonly referred to as 'recycling adjustments'), that relate to components of other comprehensive income. [IAS 1 para 92]. Reclassification adjustments are amounts previously recognised in other comprehensive income that are reclassified to profit or loss to comply with another accounting standard. They arise, for example, on disposal of a foreign operation (as required by IAS 21), on derecognition of available-for-sale financial assets and when a hedged forecast transaction affects profit or loss (as required by IAS 39). [IAS 1 para 95]. Under these accounting standards, unrealised gains may have been recognised in the current or previous periods. On reclassifying these unrealised gains to profit and loss, it is necessary to deduct them from 'other comprehensive income', otherwise they will be 'double-counted' in total comprehensive income. [IAS 1 para 93].

4.205.1 As noted in paragraph 4.201.3, IAS 1 has been amended, effective for annual periods beginning on or after 1 July 2012. The amendment requires items of other comprehensive income, classified by nature, to be grouped into those that will be reclassified subsequently to profit or loss when specific conditions are met and those that will not be reclassified to profit or loss.

4.206 An entity may present reclassification adjustments in the statement of comprehensive income or in the notes. Where the entity elects to disclose the reclassification adjustments in the notes, the amounts presented in the statement of comprehensive income as components of other comprehensive income should be after any related reclassification adjustments. [IAS 1 para 94]. The illustrative example of disclosure of reclassification adjustments contained in the implementation guidance accompanying the standard is reproduced below.

XYZ Group

Disclosure of components of other comprehensive income

Notes

Year ended 31 December 20X7

	20X7		20X6	
Exchange differences on translating foreign operations		5,334		10,667
Available-for-sale financial assets:				
Gains arising during the year	1,333		30,667	
Less: Reclassification adjustments for gains included in profit or loss	(25,333)	(24,000)	(4,000)	26,667
Cash flow hedges:				
Gains (losses) arising during the year	(4,667)		(4,000)	
Less: Reclassification adjustments for gains (losses) included in profit or loss	3,333		—	
Less: Adjustments for amounts transferred to initial carrying amount of hedged items	667	(667)	—	(4,000)
Gain on property revaluation		933		3,367
Actuarial gains (losses) in defined benefit pension plans		(667)		1,333
Share of other comprehensive income of associates		400		(700)
		(18,667)		37,334
Income tax relating to components of other comprehensive income		4,667		(9,334)
Other comprehensive income for the year		(14,000)		28,000

* This illustrative example is based on IAS 1 prior to its amendment effective for annual periods beginning on or after 1 July 2012. The amendment requires items of other comprehensive income to be grouped into those that will be reclassified subsequently to profit or loss and those that will not be reclassified (see para 4.201.3).

4.206.1 Table 4.13.1 in paragraph 4.204 shows an example of cash flow hedge gains being reclassified to profit or loss for the period. Table 4.13.2 below shows reclassification adjustments and tax as well as the share of other comprehensive income related to joint ventures and associates in the statement of comprehensive income. The note to the financial statements makes clear that 'derivative financial instruments' represent cash flow hedges.

Table 4.13.2 – Statement of comprehensive income

ArcelorMittal S.A. – Annual report – 31 December 2010

**Consolidated Statements of Comprehensive Income
ArcelorMittal and Subsidiaries**

(millions of U.S. dollars, except share and per share data)

	Year ended December 31, 2009[1]	Year ended December 31, 2010
Net income (including non-controlling interests)	**114**	**3,005**
Available-for-sale investments:		
Gain (loss) arising during the period net of tax (expense) benefit of (3) and (22) for 2009 and 2010, respectively	22	80
Reclassification adjustments for (gain) loss included in the statement of operations net of tax expense of nil and 41 for 2009 and 2010, respectively	(8)	(79)
	14	1
Derivative financial instruments:		
(Loss) gain arising during the period net of tax (expense) benefit of (34) and 89 for 2009 and 2010, respectively	59	(188)
Reclassification adjustments for (gain) loss included in the statement of operations net of tax expense (benefit) of 208 and 159 for 2009 and 2010, respectively	(590)	(392)
	(531)	(580)
Exchange differences arising on translation of foreign operations (net of tax (expense) benefit of (352) and (123) for 2009 and 2010, respectively)	3,100	(1,856)
Share of other comprehensive income (loss) related to associates and joint ventures	473	201
Total other comprehensive income (loss)	**3,056**	**(2,234)**
Total other comprehensive income (loss) attributable to:		
Equity holders of the parent	2,628	(2,310)
Non-controlling interests	428	76
	3,056	(2,234)
Total comprehensive income	**3,170**	**771**
Total comprehensive income attributable to:		
Equity holders of the parent	2,785	606
Non-controlling interests	385	165
Total comprehensive income	**3,170**	**771**

1 As required by IFRS 3, the 2009 information has been adjusted retrospectively for the finalization in 2010 of the allocation of purchase price of acquisitions made in 2009 (see note 3).

Editorial note: The statement of comprehensive income is based on IAS 1 prior to its amendment effective for annual periods beginning on or after 1 July 2012. The amendment requires items of other comprehensive income to be grouped into those that will be reclassified subsequently to profit or loss and those that will not be reclassified (see para 4.201.3).

4.207 Reclassification adjustments do not arise on changes in revaluation surplus (recognised in accordance with IAS 16 or IAS 38) or on actuarial gains and losses on defined benefit pension schemes (recognised in accordance with IAS 19). These components are recognised in other comprehensive income, but are not reclassified to profit or loss in subsequent periods. [IAS 1 para 96]. However, changes in revaluation surplus may be transferred to retained earnings as the asset is used or when it is derecognised; such transfers would be shown in the statement of changes in equity. Under IAS 19, actuarial gains and losses are reported in retained earnings in the period that they are recognised. For entities applying IAS 19 (revised), which is effective for annual periods beginning on or after 1 January 2013, amounts recognised in other comprehensive income (that is, remeasurements of defined benefit plans) are not reclassified to profit or loss in a subsequent period, but may be transferred within equity. [IAS 19 (revised) para 122].

Dividends

4.208 The amounts of dividends recognised as distributions to equity holders, and the related amount of dividends per share, should be disclosed either on the face of the statement of changes in equity, or in the notes. [IAS 1 para 107]. The 'Basis for conclusions' accompanying IAS 1 states that an entity should not present dividends in the statement of comprehensive income, because that statement presents items of performance and not owner changes in equity. [IAS 1 para BC75]. In addition, entities should disclose, in the notes, dividends proposed or declared after the end of the reporting period, and the related amount per share. Cumulative preference dividends not recognised should also be disclosed. [IAS 1 para 137]. The requirements for disclosure of dividends are dealt with in detail in chapter 23.

UK.4.208.1 In addition to IAS 1's requirement regarding dividends, the Listing Rules for listed companies require particulars to be disclosed of any arrangements under which a shareholder has either waived or agreed to waive any dividends. [LR 9.8.4 R (12)].

Statement of changes in equity

4.209 The statement of changes in equity presents all changes in equity – both (a) those relating to performance and (b) owner changes in equity, that is, transactions and events that increase or decrease equity, but are not part of performance. An example of the latter is the raising of new equity from shareholders. Other examples are given in paragraph 4.212 below. The requirement for a statement of changes in equity is in paragraph 106 of IAS 1. This requires the statement of changes in equity to include the following information:

■ Total comprehensive income for the period, showing separately the total amounts attributable to the parent's owners and to non-controlling interests.

■ For each component of equity, the effects of retrospective application or retrospective restatement recognised in accordance with IAS 8.

■ For each component of equity, a reconciliation between the carrying amount at the beginning and the end of the period, separately disclosing changes resulting from:

(i)   profit or loss;

(ii)   other comprehensive income (see para 4.209.1 below); and

(iii) transactions with owners in their capacity as owners, showing separately contributions by and distributions to owners and changes in ownership interests in subsidiaries that do not result in a loss of control.

[IAS 1 para 106].

4.209.1   For each component of equity, the analysis of other comprehensive income by item can be presented either in the statement of changes in equity or disclosed within the notes. [IAS 1 paras 106, 106A, 139F].

4.210   Examples of components of equity are: each class of contributed equity, the accumulated balance of each class of comprehensive income and retained earnings. [IAS 1 para 108].

4.211   The increase in the entity's net assets during the accounting period will be represented by the change in the entity's equity over that period. The overall change in equity is the sum of all income and expenses (whether those items are recognised in profit or loss or in other comprehensive income) and transactions with owners, such as share issues and dividend payments. [IAS 1 para 109].

4.212   The statement of changes in equity, therefore, includes the following:

■ Share issues and redemptions.

■ Purchase and sale of treasury shares.

■ Equity component of convertible bonds issued.

■ Dividends on instruments classified as equity.

- Credit entries reflecting the issue of equity instruments in connection with an equity-settled share-based payment arrangement (see chapter 12).

- Transactions with non-controlling interests that do not result in a change of control (chapter 24).

4.212.1 The presentation of the group's share of associates and joint ventures' changes in equity is dealt with in chapter 27.

4.213 Comparative information is required for all amounts reported in the financial statements, unless a standard or interpretation permits or requires otherwise. [IAS 1 para 38]. There is no exemption from the requirement to give comparative information for the statement of changes in equity (see para 4.42).

4.214 Retrospective application of accounting policies and error corrections are addressed in chapter 3 and from paragraph 4.45. IAS 8 requires that, unless another standard or interpretation requires otherwise, all changes in accounting policy and all corrections of errors are, where practicable, dealt with retrospectively (where the effect is material). Where retrospective adjustments affect the opening balance of net assets in the earliest comparative period presented, this retrospective adjustment is made against the balance of retained earnings, unless an alternative treatment is required or permitted by another standard or interpretation. The statement of changes in equity should disclose separately the adjustment to each component of equity arising from changes in accounting policy and from correction of errors. These adjustments are disclosed for each prior period and the beginning of the period. [IAS 1 para 110]. (IAS 1 imposes additional requirements in respect of comparative balance sheet information. See para 4.46).

4.215 An example of a statement of changes in equity is given in Table 4.14 below.

Table 4.14 – Statement of changes in equity

IMI plc – Annual report – 31 December 2011

Consolidated statement of changes in equity
for the year ended 31 December 2011

	Share capital	Share premium account	Capital redemption reserve	Hedging reserve	Translation reserve	Retained earnings	Total parent equity	Non-controlling interests	Total equity
	£m	£m	£m	£m	£m	£m	£m	£m	£m
As at 1 January 2010	84.9	166.6	7.9	7.4	41.1	91.9	399.8	2.2	402.0
Profit for the year						224.7	224.7	1.7	226.4
Other comprehensive income				(4.7)	15.7	(21.3)	(10.3)	0.3	(10.0)
Total comprehensive income				(4.7)	15.7	203.4	214.4	2.0	216.4
Issue of share capital	0.1	1.5					1.6		1.6
Dividends paid						(70.9)	(70.9)	(0.5)	(71.4)
Share based payments (net of tax)						10.3	10.3		10.3
Shares acquired for employee share scheme trust						(29.5)	(29.5)		(29.5)
Investment in partnership by UK Pension Fund								48.6	48.6
Income earned by partnership								(2.2)	(2.2)
At 31 December 2010	85.0	168.1	7.9	2.7	56.8	205.2	525.7	50.1	575.8

Changes in equity in 2011									
Profit for the year						200.4	200.4	3.3	203.7
Other comprehensive income				1.4	(9.8)	(68.1)	(76.5)	0.4	(76.1)
Total comprehensive income				1.4	(9.8)	132.3	123.9	3.7	127.6
Issue of share capital	–	1.2					1.2		1.2
Dividends paid						(88.8)	(88.8)		(88.8)
Share based payments (net of tax)						10.6	10.6		10.6
Shares acquired for employee share scheme trust						(7.8)	(7.8)		(7.8)
Income earned by partnership								(4.4)	(4.4)
At 31 December 2011	85.0	169.3	7.9	4.1	47.0	251.5	564.8	49.4	614.2

4.216 An illustrative example showing how the effects of a change in accounting policy is presented in a statement of changes in equity (by restating the opening balance) is given below.

Statement of changes in equity for the year ended 31 December 20X0

Attributable to owners of the parent

	Share capital	Share premium	Other reserves 1	Retained earnings	Total	Non-controlling interest	Total equity
	C'000	C'000	C'000	C'000	C'000	C'000	C'000
Balance at 1 January 20X9	20,000	10,424	6,364	48,070	84,858	1,400	86,258
Changes in accounting policy	–	–	–	400	400	100	500
Restated balance at 1 January 20X9	20,000	10,424	6,364	48,470	85,258	1,500	86,758

[Movements in the year and the closing balances not reproduced]
Balance as at 31 December 20X9

[Movements in the year and the closing balances not reproduced]
Balance as at 31 December 20X0

[Note: the full statement of changes in equity has not been reproduced in this example.]

1 Individual reserves can be grouped into 'other reserves' in the statement of changes in equity if these are similar in nature and can be regarded as a component of equity. If the individual reserves are not shown on the face of the statement of changes in equity, an analysis should be given in the notes.

Statement of cash flows

4.217 A statement of cash flows is required in all financial statements prepared to comply with IFRS. There are no exemptions from the requirement to prepare a statement of cash flows. A statement of cash flows is considered to be useful in providing users of financial statements with a basis to assess an entity's ability to generate cash, and the needs of the entity in utilising those cash flows. [IAS 1 para 111]. The requirements for statements of cash flows are considered in chapter 30.

Notes to the financial statements

Structure

4.218 The notes to the financial statements should be presented in a systematic manner and should disclose the following:

- Basis of preparation and accounting policies adopted in the preparation of the financial statements.

- Information required by IFRS that is not presented in the primary statements.

- Additional information that is not presented in the primary statements, but is relevant to an understanding of those statements.

[IAS 1 para 112].

4.219 Each item in the primary statements should be cross-referenced to any related information in the notes. [IAS 1 para 113]. The notes will contain more detailed analysis of amounts shown on the face of the primary statements as well as narrative information. They will address disclosure requirements of other standards and interpretations and will contain any other information that is necessary to achieve a fair presentation of the financial statements.

4.220 Disclosures are normally presented in the notes in the following order:

- Statement of compliance with IFRS (see para 4.16).

- Information about the basis of preparation and the specific accounting policies selected and applied for significant transactions and events. This may be presented as a separate component of the financial statements. [IAS 1 para 116].

- Information relating to line items presented on the face of the financial statements. Each financial statement item should be cross-referenced to the appropriate note. Such notes should, as far as possible, follow the order of the items in the financial statements.

- Other disclosures including contingencies, contractual commitments and other financial disclosures, as well as non-financial disclosures.

[IAS 1 para 114].

4.221 Typically, the notes to the financial statements will be presented in the order of the primary statement line items to which they relate. Nevertheless, it will be necessary or preferable to vary the ordering in some cases. IAS 1 cites the example of the disclosure of information on changes in fair value being combined with the disclosure of information on maturities of financial instruments even though one relates to the statement of comprehensive income and the other to the statement of financial position. [IAS 1 para 115].

Accounting policies, judgements and estimates

4.222 Entities should disclose, in a summary of significant accounting policies, the measurement basis and each specific accounting policy that is relevant to understanding the financial statements. [IAS 1 para 117]. This may be presented as a separate component of the financial statements. [IAS 1 para 116]. Where more than one measurement basis (historical cost, net realisable value, fair value or recoverable amount) is used in the financial statements, entities should indicate the categories of assets and liabilities to which each measurement basis is applied. [IAS 1 para 118]. The entity should disclose the accounting policies that it considers will assist users in understanding the financial statements. This will be particularly important where no policy is prescribed or where alternative policies are allowed, so that users can make proper comparisons of the financial statements of different entities. [IAS 1 para 119]. For example, an entity with investment properties should disclose whether it applies the fair value or cost model under IAS 40. Even where an accounting policy is mandated by a standard or interpretation, it should still be disclosed if it has a significant impact on the entity's financial statements. Entities might disclose accounting policies related to the following:

- Revenue recognition.

- Consolidation principles.

- Business combinations.

- Application of the equity method of accounting for investments in associates and joint ventures.

- Joint ventures.

- Share-based payments.

- Earnings per share.

- Depreciation and amortisation of tangible and intangible assets.

- Capitalisation of borrowing costs and other expenditure.

- Construction contracts.

- Investment properties.

- Derivative financial instruments and hedging.

- Other financial instruments and investments.

- Impairment of assets.

- Leases.

- Inventories.

- Taxes, including deferred taxes.

- Provisions.

- Employee benefit costs.

- Functional currency and presentation currency.

- Foreign currency translation and hedging.

- Government grants.

4.223 Clearly, entities should only disclose accounting policies that are relevant to them. An entity with no transactions, assets or liabilities in foreign currencies would obviously not disclose a policy on foreign currency translation; on the other hand, an entity with significant foreign operations or transactions would be expected to disclose its policy on the recognition of foreign exchange gains and losses. [IAS 1 para 120]. An accounting policy may still be significant because of the entity's operations even though the amounts shown for the current and prior periods are not material. [IAS 1 para 121].

4.224 IAS 1 requires that the financial statements disclose the judgements, apart from those involving estimations (see para 4.227), that management has made in the process of applying the accounting policies and that have the most significant effect on the amounts recognised in those financial statements. [IAS 1 para 122]. Examples of judgements made by management, given in IAS 1, include:

- Whether financial assets are held-to maturity investments.

- When substantially all the significant risks and rewards of ownership of financial assets and lease assets are transferred to other entities.

- Whether, in substance, particular sales of goods are financing arrangements and, therefore, do not give rise to revenue.

[IAS 1 para 123].

4.224.1 In addition, paragraph 123 of IAS 1 includes, as an example of a judgement made by management, whether the substance of the relationship between an entity and a special purpose entity indicates that the special purpose entity is controlled by the entity. This example has been removed by IFRS 10 and is replaced by a specific disclosure requirement in IFRS 12. See chapter 24.

4.225 The disclosure requirements in IAS 1 have the effect of requiring management to justify the view they have taken on some items. This is already done to a limited extent by other standards. IAS 40, for example, requires disclosure of the criteria by which management have distinguished investment property from owner-occupied property and from property held for sale, when classification of the property is difficult. Likewise, IAS 27 currently requires an entity to disclose the reasons why the entity's ownership interest does not constitute control, in respect of an investee that is not a subsidiary even though more than half of its voting or potential voting power is owned directly or indirectly through subsidiaries. [IAS 1 para 124]. For entities applying IFRS 12, there is a more explicit requirement for an entity to disclose the judgements it has made in determining whether it controls another entity. However, IAS 1 fills a gap by placing a general obligation on management to disclose the judgements made where there are no specific requirements in other standards. In this respect, the IAS 1 requirement is an aid to increasing the transparency of financial statements.

4.226 Similarly, these requirements might be relevant in lease accounting. Under the current rules in IAS 17, a lease is either an operating lease, where the leased asset and lease liability are off balance sheet, or a finance lease, where both leased asset and lease liability are shown on balance sheet. The judgement as to which category applies to a specific lease depends on management's assessment of whether the risks and rewards of ownership have been transferred to the lessee. In some cases, the required classification will be clear and no additional disclosure will be required under IAS 1. However, in some cases, the classification will not be so obvious. Operating leases are not always fundamentally different from finance leases; the change in one term of a lease could transfer it from one classification to another. Indeed, lease arrangements are sometimes constructed so that they marginally meet the definition of a particular type of lease. Paragraph 122 of IAS 1 requires disclosure of the judgements made in such cases, thereby making the accounting more transparent.

4.227 IAS 1 requires that *"an entity shall disclose information about the assumptions it makes about the future, and other major sources of estimation uncertainty at the end of the reporting period, that have a significant risk of resulting in a material adjustment to the carrying amounts of assets and liabilities within the next financial year. In respect of those assets and liabilities, the notes shall include details of: (a) their nature; and (b) their carrying amount as at the end of the reporting period".* [IAS 1 para 125].

4.228 The nature and extent of the information provided will vary according to the nature of the assumption and other circumstances, but there is an overriding requirement that the information should be provided in a way that helps users of the financial statements to understand the judgements made by management where there is estimation uncertainty. IAS 1 gives the following examples of the types of disclosure:

- Nature of the assumption or other estimation uncertainty.
- Sensitivity of carrying amounts to the methods, assumptions and estimates underlying their calculation, including the reasons for the sensitivity.
- Expected resolution of an uncertainty and the range of possible outcomes within the next financial year in respect of the carrying amounts of the asset and liabilities affected.
- Explanation of changes made to past assumptions concerning those assets and liabilities, if the uncertainty remains unresolved.

[IAS 1 para 129].

4.229 The disclosures required in respect of estimation uncertainty do not relate to those required in respect of significant judgements in applying accounting policies. [IAS 1 para 132]. The estimation uncertainty disclosures deal with situations where the entity has incomplete or imperfect information, often relating to the future. On the other hand, an entity may have complete information but still have to exercise judgement in applying accounting policies. For example, an entity may have complete knowledge of its ownership and voting rights in another entity but, in complex situations, it will still have to exercise judgement to determine whether it has control of that entity.

4.230 In many cases, the disclosure of estimation uncertainty is required by other standards. Areas that could require disclosure in respect of estimation uncertainty include the following:

- Recoverable amount of property, plant and equipment. [IAS 1 para 126].

- Fair value of revalued items of property, plant and equipment. [IAS 16 para 77(c); IFRS 13 para 93].

- Effect of technological obsolescence on inventories. [IAS 1 para 126].

- Significant assumptions applied in estimating fair values of financial assets and financial liabilities that are carried at fair value. [IFRS 7 para 27; IFRS 13 para 93].

- Major assumptions about future events affecting classes of provisions. [IAS 37 para 85(b)].

- Principal actuarial assumptions used at the balance sheet date in respect of defined benefit pension plans. [IAS 19 para 120A(n)]. (Significant actuarial assumptions used to determine the present value of the defined benefit obligation. [IAS 19 (revised) para 144].)

- Recoverable amount of trade receivables.

- Recoverability of deferred tax assets. [IAS 12 para 82].

4.231 Disclosure of estimation uncertainty is only required where there is a significant risk of material adjustment to the carrying amount of asset and liabilities within the next financial year. It may be that management makes estimates in respect of material amounts in the financial statements, but this does not necessarily mean that there is a significant risk of material adjustment. Material adjustments are most likely to arise in difficult, subjective or complex judgements. As the number of variables and assumptions increases, so the judgements become more complicated and the potential for future material adjustment increases accordingly. [IAS 1 para 127].

4.232 Where assets and liabilities are carried at fair value and this fair value is based on a recently observed market price (or, for entities applying IFRS 13, a quoted price in an active market for an identical asset or liability), there is little estimation uncertainty. Although the market value of those assets and liabilities may change in the next financial year, they may still be valued accurately as at the balance sheet date. It is not the purpose of IAS 1 to require identification of assets and liabilities that may be subject to significant market fluctuations in the following year. Only where the fair value as at the balance sheet date is subject to estimation uncertainty would IAS 1 require disclosure. [IAS 1 para 128]. IFRS 13 includes specific disclosure requirements in respect of fair value measurements for assets and liabilities that are measured at fair value (which will replace the disclosure requirements in IFRS 7 in respect of fair value measurements of each class of financial assets or financial liabilities) (see chapter 6).

4.232.1 IAS 1 also makes it clear that entities are not required to disclose budget information or forecasts in making the required disclosures. [IAS 1 para 130].

4.233 The standard restricts the disclosures to those that have a significant risk of material adjustment *within the next financial year*. The IASB considered that the longer the future period to which the disclosures relate, the greater the number of items that would qualify for disclosure and the less specific the disclosures tha could be made about particular assets and liabilities. A longer period than the next financial year might obscure the most relevant information with other disclosures. [IAS 1 BC84]. However, the assessment of the carrying amount of assets and liabilities is not based solely on expectations for the following financial year, but on the full amount of time in which the asset will be recovered or the liability settled. Therefore, a material adjustment to the carrying amount of an asset or liability could occur in the following financial year as a result of a reappraisal in that period of the recoverability of an asset or settlement of a liability over a much longer period. Entities will, therefore, need to take care that they do not narrow their disclosures excessively.

4.234 When it is impracticable to disclose the extent of the possible effects of an assumption or another source of estimation uncertainty at the balance sheet date, IAS 1 requires that *"... the entity discloses that it is reasonably possible, based on existing knowledge, that outcomes within the next financial year that are different from the assumption could require a material adjustment to the carrying amount of the asset or liability affected. In all cases, the entity discloses the nature and carrying amount of the specific asset or liability (or class of assets or liabilities) affected by the assumption"*. [IAS 1 para 131]. Note that 'impracticable' is defined in paragraph 7 of IAS 1 (see para 4.52).

4.235 Table 4.15 is an example of disclosure of judgements made in applying accounting policies and sources of estimation uncertainty.

Stolt-Nielsen Limited – Annual Report – 30 November 2011

Notes to the Consolidated Financial Statements (extract)

2. Significant Accounting Policies (extract)

Critical Accounting Estimates and Judgements

In connection with the preparation of the consolidated financial statements, management has made assumptions and estimates about future events, and applied judgements that affect the reported amounts of assets, liabilities, revenue, expenses and the related disclosures. The assumptions, estimates and judgements are based on historical experience, current trends and other factors that management believes to be relevant at the time the consolidated financial statements are prepared. On a regular basis, management reviews the accounting policies, assumptions, estimates and judgements to ensure that the financial statements are presented fairly and in accordance with International Financial Reporting Standards as adopted by the European Union ("IFRS") and IFRIC Interpretations. Critical accounting estimates and judgements are those that have a significant risk of having a material impact on the consolidated financial statements. Management believes the following areas are the more significant judgements and estimates used in the preparation of the Consolidated Financial Statements:

Description	Judgements and Uncertainties	Effect if Actual Results Differ From Assumptions
Voyage revenue and costs The Group generates a majority of its revenues through its tanker segment from the transportation of liquids by sea and inland water under contracts of affreightment or through contracts on the spot market. Tankers follow the percentage of completion method with operating revenue and expenses recognised on each voyage leg. This recognition is based on "budgeted voyage legs" that are reviewed and updated annually. After the voyage legs have begun they are updated for actual results and the latest updated estimates.	In applying the percentage of completion method, the revenues and expenses for voyages still in progress at the end of the reporting period are estimated and prorated over the period of the voyage leg. A voyage comprises one or more "voyage legs." For each voyage leg, estimates are made of revenue and related costs based on available actual information, current market parameters such as fuel cost and customer contract portfolios, and relevant historical data such as port costs. Revenue and cost estimates are updated continually through the voyage to account for changes in voyage patterns, to include the most up-to-date data and to finalise revenues and expenses.	The accrued voyage and prepaid voyage expense accounts are used to adjust revenues billed and vendor invoices received to the appropriate amounts to be recognised based on the percentage of completion method of accounting. Management does not believe there would be a material change if the percentage of completion method was based upon criteria other than voyage legs. However, if actual results are not consistent with estimates or assumptions, revenues or costs may be over- or under-stated. At November 30, 2011 and 2010, the accrued voyage expense account was $71.4 million and $64.1 million, respectively, in which $44.4 million and $23.7 million related to the deferral of revenues. Prepaid expenses included $17.0 million and $19.1 million of prepaid invoices for voyages in progress

Description	Judgements and Uncertainties	Effect if Actual Results Differ From Assumptions
		applicable to periods subsequent to November 30, 2011 and 2010, respectively.

Depreciation and Residual Values

The Group records the value of the ships at cost less accumulated depreciation and any impairment charges. The cost of the ships includes the contract price, pre-delivery costs incurred during the construction of new buildings, capitalised interest and any material expenses incurred upon acquisition such as initial repairs, improvements and delivery expenses to prepare the ship for its initial voyage.

Ships are depreciated on a straight-line basis over the ships' estimated useful lives, after reducing for the estimated residual values.

Depreciation is based on the cost of the different components of the ships less their residual values and the estimated useful lives for similar ships in the industry. The key judgements and estimates involved are:

- Estimated useful lives of the components of the ships which range from an estimated 12.5 to 30 years. However, actual lives of the components of parcel tankers or barges may be different depending on many factors such as quality of maintenance and repair and the type of product carried by the ships or barges and this may result in a shorter or longer life.
- Residual values are difficult to estimate given the long lives of ships and barges, the uncertainty as to future economic conditions and the future price of steel, which is considered as the main determinant of the residual price. The Group currently estimates residual value annually based upon the average steel price for the last three years and the estimated light displacement tonnage of the fleet.

If the estimated economic useful life is incorrect, or circumstances change such that the estimated economic useful life has to be revised, an impairment loss or additional depreciation expense could result in future periods.

A decrease in the useful life of the ship or barge or fall in the residual value would have the effect of increasing the annual depreciation charge and potentially resulting in an impairment loss.

If the residual value is over estimated, it would reduce the annual depreciation and overstate the value of the assets.

See Note 15 for further details.

Impairment of Ships

The Tanker fleet is reviewed for impairment whenever events or changes in circumstances indicate the

The carrying values of the ships in the Tanker and AGHL fleets may not represent their fair market value at any point in time

If actual results are not consistent with the estimates and assumptions used in estimating future cash flows and asset fair values while

Description	**Judgements and Uncertainties**	**Effect if Actual Results Differ From Assumptions**
carrying amount of the fleet may not be recoverable.	since the market prices of second-hand ships tend to fluctuate with changes in freight rates and the cost of new buildings. Both charter rates and new building costs tend to be cyclical in nature.	evaluating impairment, then the Group may be exposed to future losses that could be material.

Management measures the recoverability of an asset by comparing its carrying amount to the higher of its fair value less costs to sell or future discounted cash flows that the asset is expected to generate over its remaining useful life. If an asset is considered to be impaired, impairment is recognised in an amount equal to the excess of the carrying value of the asset over its recoverable value.

In order to assess impairment, estimates and assumptions regarding expected cash flows are made which require considerable judgement and are based upon existing contracts, historical experience, discount rates, financial forecasts and industry trends and conditions.

Impairment tests have been carried out in 2011 which resulted in no impairment being necessary. A projected 5% decrease in the deep sea and regional fleets' tanker trading gross margins assumed in the discounted cash flow models used in the impairment testing would result in a decrease in the present value of the tanker fleet of ships by approximately $187 million. The result is still higher than net book value and would not result in an impairment of the ships.

The Tanker ships are tested for impairment on a fleet basis as that is the lowest level in which the cash flows are independent of other cash-generating units.

An increase of 2% in the weighted average cost of capital used in the present value calculation would result in the decrease in present value of the deep sea and regional fleets of ships by approximately $250 million which would not result in an impairment of the ships.

AGHL Impairment Review
AGHL is the Group's joint venture providing transportation services in the LPG market. The LPG market has been very volatile and, as such, has been reviewed for impairment in 2011 by management. As its main assets are Very Large Gas Carriers, the methodology of testing is the same as used for the Tanker fleet. The value assigned to the key assumption in the impairment model, freight rate per ton, was $65/ton.

For AGHL, the recoverable amount of the plant, property and equipment exceeded its carrying amount by $83 million. A consistent reduction in trading gross margins of approximately 17.5% from the assumptions used would result in the recoverable amount being equal to its carrying amount.

Investments in Joint Ventures and Associates

The consolidated financial statements include the Group's accounts and all other entities in which the Group has a controlling financial interest, except where the control over the

There are a number of areas where significant judgement is exercised to establish whether an entity needs to be consolidated or reported under the equity method of accounting. In order to

If the judgement applied in determining the accounting treatment of an entity is incorrect or the fact pattern on which it is based changes, such entities may need to be consolidated or result in

Description	Judgements and Uncertainties	Effect if Actual Results Differ From Assumptions
operations is limited by significant participating interests held by another investor in such operations.	establish whether an entity is a consolidated subsidiary, a joint venture or an associate, key areas of judgement include:	unexpected losses being reflected on the consolidated financial statements.

Where the Group does not have control, either because of significant participating interests by other parties or presence of only significant influence or where there is joint control over an entity, the entity is accounted for using the equity method.

Controlling financial interest in an entity is evaluated first by considering whether the entity is a special purpose entity ("SPE"), a joint venture or an associate under IFRS.

- Qualitative analysis of an entity including review of, among other factors, its capital structure, contractual terms, which interests create or absorb variability, related party relationships and design of the entity.
- Rights of partners regarding significant business decisions, including disposals and acquisitions of assets.
- Board and management representation.
- Ability to make financing decisions.
- Operating and capital budget approvals and contractual rights of other parties.

The exercise of judgement on these areas determines whether a particular entity is consolidated or accounted for under the equity method.

For example, it is possible that an investment is accounted for as a joint venture or associate using the equity method despite having an ownership interest exceeding 50 percent where it does not exercise direct or indirect control over the investee. To the extent that the Group is deemed to control these entities, the entities would have to be consolidated. This would affect the balance sheet, income statement, statement of cash flows and debt covenants.

See Note 16 for further details.

Biological Assets

All mature turbot weighing more than 300 grams and mature sturgeon weighing more than 3 kilos are held at fair value less costs to sell and costs related to packaging. Gains and losses from changes in fair value are recognised in the income statement. Fair value is based upon observed prices for harvested fish, reduced for harvesting costs and freight costs.

Determination of fair value requires significant judgement which includes the:

- Market price at the balance sheet date which is often volatile and cyclical.
- Volume of biomass.
- Volume of mature biomass.
- Average weight of mature biomass.
- Estimated current mortality.
- Future mortality during harvesting and quality of the fish.

The Group's net earnings can fluctuate due to the fair value adjustments on the biological assets at each balance sheet date.

A small change in assumption, such as price, can have a significant change on the valuation. For example, based upon November 30, 2011 turbot volumes, a change in the price of EUR 1 per kilo would have an impact on the turbot valuation of EUR 2.0 million.

See Note 13 for further details.

Description	Judgements and Uncertainties	Effect if Actual Results Differ From Assumptions
	For sturgeon, the gender of the fish and the quantity of the caviar produced is also uncertain.	

Goodwill Impairment Testing

Goodwill is tested for impairment on an annual basis based upon the cash-generating unit for which the goodwill is assigned. The Group's goodwill relates to the Tank Container and Terminal segments.

For the Tank Container segment, the impairment test involves determining the recoverable amount of the Tank Container segment. The recoverable amount is based upon the higher of the segment's value in use or the segment's fair value less costs to sell. The Tank Container segment used the latter method and estimated the fair value by multiplying the segment's 2011 estimated earnings before depreciation, amortisation, interest and taxes ("EBITDA") by a multiple. The result of this calculation was $273 million higher than the net assets of the segment.

The EBITDA was chosen in estimating fair value for the impairment testing based upon historical experience.

For the Terminal segment, the goodwill relates to the acquisition of Marstel Holdings Pty Limited, including its subsidiaries ("Marstel") which was completed on October 4, 2011. The cash-generating units have been identified to be the Australia and New Zealand regions within the Terminal segment. As the acquisition occurred in the fourth quarter of 2011,

Impairment testing for goodwill is an area involving management judgement to assess whether the carrying value of assets can be supported by either fair value less costs to sell or value in use. For the fair value less costs to sell method, judgement is required in determining the multiple used. Value in use is calculated using the net present value of future cash flows derived from such assets using cash flow projections which have been discounted at an appropriate rate. In calculating the net present value of the future cash flows, certain assumptions are required to be made in respect of highly uncertain matters including management's expectations of:

- growth in EBITDA, calculated as adjusted operating profit before depreciation and amortisation;
- timing and quantum of future capital expenditures;
- long-term growth rates; and
- selection of discount rates to reflect the risks involved.

The Group prepares a formal five year management plan for each of its businesses, which are used in the value in use calculations.

Fair value less costs to sell is calculated based on current market price, binding sale agreement or any other

If the judgement applied in determining the recoverable amount of goodwill is incorrect or the fact pattern on which it is based changes, this could result in unexpected losses being reflected in the consolidated financial statements.

Based upon the 2011 EBITDA, the multiplier would have had to be reduced by approximately 50% in order for the Tank Container segment's recoverable value to equal its carrying amount. See Note 17 for further details related to goodwill.

Description	**Judgements and Uncertainties**	**Effect if Actual Results Differ From Assumptions**

impairment testing has not been performed.

method permitted under IFRS.

Changing the assumptions selected by management, in particular the discount rate and growth rate assumptions used in the cash flow projections, could significantly affect the Group's impairment evaluation and hence results. Further, the Group's review includes the key assumptions related to sensitivity in the cash flow projections.

Pensions and Other Postretirement Benefits

The Group sponsors defined benefit pension plans and a supplemental executive retirement plan covering eligible employees. Net periodic pension costs and accumulated benefit obligations are determined in accordance with IAS 19, "Employee Benefits," using a number of assumptions including the discount rate, the rate of compensation increases, retirement ages, mortality rates and expected long-term return on plan assets. These assumptions have a significant impact on the amounts reported. The Group's pension cost consists of service costs, interest costs, amortisation of prior service costs or benefits, expected returns on plan assets and, in part, on a market-related valuation of assets.

The Group also provides post-retirement benefits to eligible retired employees and their spouses. The post-retirement programme provides limited health care benefits. This plan is not funded.

Management considers a number of factors in developing the pension assumptions, including an evaluation of relevant discount rates, expected long-term returns on plan assets, plan asset allocations, mortality, expected changes in wages and retirement benefits, analyses of current market conditions and input from actuaries and other consultants.

Costs of the plans are based on actuarially determined amounts and are accrued over the period from the date of hire to the full eligibility date of employees who are expected to qualify for these benefits.

A 0.25% point increase (decrease) in the discount rate assumption would result in a decrease (increase) in net periodic service cost component of $0.2 million.

A 0.25% point increase (decrease) in the discount rate assumption for the defined benefit obligation would result in a decrease of $7.4 million and an increase of $7.8 million in the defined benefit obligation.

The effect of a 1% change in the assumed healthcare cost trends on the accumulated postretirement benefit obligation at the end of 2011 would be an approximate $1.6 million increase or an approximate $1.3 million decrease and the effect on the aggregate of the service cost and interest cost of the net periodic benefit cost for 2011 would be an approximate $0.1 million increase or decrease.

If more than one of these assumptions were changed simultaneously, the cumulative impact would not necessarily be the same as if

Description	Judgements and Uncertainties	Effect if Actual Results Differ From Assumptions
		only one assumption were changed in isolation.
		See Note 23 for further details.

Capital disclosures

4.236 IAS 1 requires entities to disclose information that will enable users of its financial statements to evaluate the entity's objectives, policies and processes for managing capital. These disclosure requirements are dealt with in chapter 23.

Other disclosures

4.237 The following information should be included in the financial statements, or included in other information published with them:

- The entity's domicile and legal form, its country of incorporation and address of the registered office (or principal place of business if different from the registered office).

- A description of the nature of the entity's operations and principal activities.

- The name of the entity's parent and the name of its ultimate parent (see chapter 29).

- If it is a limited life entity, information regarding the length of its life.

[IAS 1 para 138].

Alternative performance measures

4.238 Some companies provide measures of performance other than the profit or loss for the period or other sub-totals or line items that IAS 1 requires an entity to present on the face of its primary statements. In response to concerns that such alternative performance measures (often referred to as 'non-GAAP' measures) may lead to presentations that are misleading, regulators in various jurisdictions have issued guidance or rules related to their use. While other regulators may have their own guidance and rules regarding the use of non-GAAP measures, guidance and requirements issued by the European Securities and Markets Authority (ESMA, formerly the Committee of European Securities Regulators (CESR)) and the US Securities and Exchange Commission (SEC) are notable. For instance, in November 2005, ESMA issued a recommendation on disclosure of alternative performance measures that were defined as including 'operating earnings', 'cash earnings', 'earnings before one-time charges', 'EBITDA – earnings before interest, taxes, depreciation, and amortisation' (see para 4.125) and similar terms denoting adjustments to line items of the income statement, statement of financial position or statement of cash flows. This ESMA recommendation applies to the financial performance figures of listed companies in whatever manner they are provided to the financial markets; it, therefore, covers annual reports (including the 'front half'), interim reports and earnings announcements. It does not apply to prospectuses, as these are the subject of separate guidance.

4.239 The ESMA recommendation on alternative performance measures recognises that such measures can provide investors with appropriate additional information if properly used and presented. It, therefore, makes the following recommendations:

- ESMA believes that issuers should always follow the qualitative characteristics in the IASB's Framework (see chapter 1) for the preparation and presentation of financial information, including the preparation of alternative performance measures.

- Issuers should define the terminology used and the basis of calculation adopted (that is, defining the components included in an alternative performance measure). Clear disclosure is key to the understandability of any alternative performance measure and its relevance. Where relevant, investors should be made aware of the fact that alternative performance measures are not prepared in accordance with the accounting standards applied to audited financial statements. Alternative performance measures should be given meaningful names reflecting their basis of preparation in order to avoid misleading messages.

- Where possible, issuers should present alternative performance measures only in combination with defined measures (for example GAAP measures). Furthermore, issuers should explain the differences between both measures. This might be through a reconciliation of figures to provide investors with enough information to fully understand the entity's results and financial position.

- Comparatives should be provided for any alternative performance measure presented.

- Alternative performance measures should be presented consistently over time.

- To ensure that investors are not misled, alternative performance measures should not be presented with greater prominence than defined GAAP measures. Where alternative performance measures are derived from audited financial statements and resemble defined performance measures, but do not actually have the characteristics of the defined measures (such characteristics include being audited, based on an identified reporting framework, consistent and comparable with performance measures of other enterprises), ESMA recommends that defined measures should be given greater prominence than the alternative performance measures.

- Issuers may internally use alternative performance measures for measuring and controlling the entity's profitability and financial position. Generally, issuers explain this as the reason for presenting alternative performance measures to investors. ESMA expects issuers to give an explanation of the internal use of alternative performance measures in order to make investors understand the relevance of this information. This explanation is useful only when presented in direct relation to the alternative performance measures.

[ESMA (formerly CESR) Recommendation on Alternative Performance Measures].

UK.4.239.1 The FRRP in its 2010 annual report commented on the characteristics of good financial reporting. With reference to alternative performance measures, they indicated that highlighted or adjusted figures, key performance indicators (KPIs) and non-GAAP measures referenced in the business review should be clearly reconciled to the figures in the financial statements with any adjustments clearly explained.

4.240 In the US, in January 2003, the SEC issued rules ('FRR-65') setting out conditions for use of non-GAAP financial measures. In connection with these rules, the SEC adopted a disclosure regulation, Regulation G, which requires public companies that disclose material information that includes a non-GAAP financial measure to include in such a release a presentation of the most directly comparable GAAP financial measure and reconciliation of the non-GAAP financial measure to that most directly comparable GAAP financial measure. The SEC also set out additional rules on the inclusion of the non-GAAP financial measures in Commission filings in amendments to Item 10 of Regulation S-K, which restricted the use and presentation of such measures in SEC filings.

4.240.1 In January 2010, the SEC updated its guidance relating to non-GAAP measures. The rules on non-GAAP measures (that is, Regulation G and Item 10(e) of Regulation S-K) remain unchanged. The updated guidance encourages companies to be consistent in all of their communications on how they portray their businesses to investors and removed certain constraints that were viewed as discouraging companies from disclosing important non-GAAP measures in their SEC filings, particularly measures that exclude recurring items.

4.241 In addition to restrictions on the types of non-GAAP measure that may be disclosed and additional disclosure requirements that apply when such measures are used in an entity's annual report, interim report or earnings announcements, regulators may have their own rules on the positioning of such measures. For example, SEC regulations specifically prohibit the use of such disclosures on the face of the income statement. In such cases, it is important to determine whether a particular measure or disclosure is, in fact, 'non-GAAP'. IAS 1 requires the inclusion of additional line items and sub-totals on the face of the income statement where these are relevant to an understanding of an entity's financial performance. This flexibility recognises that it is not practical for the standard setters to devise a comprehensive list of line items to cover every type of income or expense that an entity may receive or incur and that is relevant to a user's understanding of the financial statements. Therefore, the fact that a line item is not defined in IFRS does not necessarily mean it is a non-GAAP item. Similarly, the use of additional sub-totals or columnar presentations that are relevant to an understanding of the entity's performance does not represent 'non-GAAP' measures or disclosures, provided such sub-totals (or columns) are labelled appropriately and do not detract from or contradict the IFRS defined measures. However, where a performance measure is disclosed, other than as a sub-total, and that measure is selective in the income and expenses included within it on a basis not commonly recognised in IFRS, it is likely to be considered 'non-GAAP'.

4.242 As noted in paragraph 4.116, the apparent flexibility in IAS 1 on the use of additional line items in the financial statements can only be used to enhance users' understanding of the GAAP-compliant numbers. It cannot be used to detract from the GAAP numbers. Therefore, where it is considered appropriate to include such measures, they should not be given greater prominence in the financial statements than GAAP information. Non-GAAP information is more often disclosed outside the financial statements, for example, within the Management commentary, Operating and financial review (OFR) or Management Discussion and Analysis (MD&A), but even then, it should be disclosed alongside the GAAP information, be clearly labelled and not given undue prominence. Regulators may place restrictions on the type or location of 'non-GAAP' disclosures. Management and auditors will have to exercise judgement to decide those presentations that are acceptable, being free from bias, and those that are not. For example, some entities choose to present gross sales and sales taxes separately on the face of the income statement to arrive at the revenue of the entity. Paragraph 8 of IAS 18 states that revenue excludes amounts collected on behalf of third parties, such as sales taxes. The line described as 'gross sales' is, therefore, not the entity's revenue number. Moreover, we consider that the disclosure is potentially misleading. Where, for example, the government increases the rate of VAT in a period, the disclosure of gross sales would imply a growth in revenue that does not exist. Similar presentation issues arise in respect of excise duties and these are discussed in chapter 9.

4.243 The guidance set out in paragraph 4.117 above is applicable in the circumstance where an entity includes non-GAAP measures on the face of its statement of comprehensive income because it concludes that it is beneficial to understanding its performance and such presentation is not prohibited by applicable regulation (for example, the SEC).

Interim and preliminary results statements

4.244 The requirements related to interim financial reporting under IFRS are set out in IAS 34 and addressed more fully in Manual of Accounting – Interim financial reporting. The overall considerations set out in IAS 1 (fair presentation, going concern, accruals basis, consistency, materiality and aggregation, and offsetting) apply to interim financial statements prepared in accordance with IAS 34. [IAS 1 para 4]. If an entity publishes full financial statements for the interim period, the form and content of those financial statements has to comply with IAS 1. [IAS 34 para 9]. If an entity publishes condensed financial information, IAS 34 requires the format of each of the condensed primary statements to be consistent with the format of the entity's most recent annual financial statements, except as noted below.

4.245 The disclosure of each of the main headings and sub-totals used should be consistent with those used in the most recent annual financial statements and selected explanatory notes. [IAS 34 para 10]. However, IAS 34 requires that changes in accounting policies (which includes changes in presentation) that are applied in the annual financial statements are also applied in the interim financial statements. [IAS 34 para 28].

4.246 As addressed from paragraph 4.46, when the entity applies an accounting policy retrospectively or makes a retrospective restatement or reclassification, IAS 1 (prior to its amendment in May 2012 – see para 4.46.1) requires the presentation of an additional statement of financial position and related notes as at the beginning of the earliest comparative period. (Following the amendment, which applies for annual periods beginning on or after 1 January 2013, the requirement is to present an additional statement of financial position at the beginning of the preceding period: also, the related notes need not be presented.) Where an entity publishes full financial statements for the interim period that reflect such a retrospective change, it should also publish this additional statement of financial position if amounts disclosed therein are impacted by the changes; if not impacted, it discloses this fact. However, where an entity is merely publishing condensed interim financial statements, there is no requirement to present this additional statement of financial position, although entities may wish to consider whether such information would be material to understanding the change. [IAS 1 para BC33].

UK.4.246.1 There is a similar consistency requirement in the Listing Rules. For UK listed companies, interim reports and preliminary statements should also be presented in a form that includes the items that are disclosable under the Listing Rules. Manual of Accounting – Interim financial reporting considers current requirements for interim reporting and preliminary announcements by listed companies.

Summary financial statements

UK.4.246.2 The detailed requirements relating to summary financial statements, including the procedures that have to be followed, are dealt with in chapter 3 of the Manual of Accounting – Other statutory requirements.

Listed companies' historical summaries

UK.4.246.3 There is no requirement for a company to include a historical summary of information in its annual report and accounts, but many companies do so. In the UK, this practice arose because the chairman of the Stock Exchange wrote to all UK listed companies in 1964 recommending that they should include a ten-year historical summary in their annual report and accounts. Disclosure of a historical summary in annual report and accounts has never become a Listing Rule requirement, but it has become well established practice, although most companies give a historical summary for a shorter period such as five years.

UK.4.246.4 There is no set format for historical summaries, but the type of information that listed companies normally have given in them is as follows:

Balance sheet

- Tangible assets.
- Other assets.
- Net borrowings.
- Capital and reserves.
- Non-controlling interests.

Profit and loss account

- Turnover.
- Operating profit.
- Interest.
- Profit on ordinary activities before taxation.
- Taxation.
- Profit after taxation.
- Non-controlling interests and preference dividends.
- Ordinary dividends and retained earnings.

Statistical information

- Earnings per share.
- Dividends per ordinary share.
- Dividend cover.
- Return on capital employed.

UK.4.246.5 The historical summary will normally show the actual figures that were reported for each year. However, in certain situations, the reported figures for earlier years may need to be adjusted. The circumstances where adjustments may be necessary are as follows:

- Where there is a change in accounting policy, IAS 8 requires the comparative figures for the preceding period to be restated if this is necessary to ensure that the reported figures for each year are stated on a consistent basis. In historical summaries, the figures for earlier years would usually be restated if it is practical to do so; it should also be made clear which figures have been restated. If the figures have not been restated, then this fact should be disclosed. On first application of IFRS, entities are not required under IFRS 1 to restate all comparative information to comply with IFRS. Where an entity presents historical summaries for periods before the first period for which full comparative information under IFRS is presented, there is no requirement to restate these earlier periods. [IFRS 1 para 22]. A five year record may, therefore, only have been restated to comply with IFRS for some comparative periods, depending on the date of first adoption of IFRS. The IASB decided not to require companies to restate the historical summary because, for some companies, the cost of doing so would exceed the benefits. Nevertheless, prior period information is only valuable where it is comparable and many companies may, therefore, choose to restate the historical summary if it is possible to do so without incurring excessive cost or creating a significant delay to the publication of the annual report and accounts. Where there are significant differences in accounting policy between the periods, the whole rationale for presenting a non-mandatory historical summary is undermined. First-time adoption of IFRS is discussed further in chapter 2.

- Where an operation is discontinued in a financial year, IFRS 5 requires the comparative statement of comprehensive income figures to be adjusted so that the disclosures relate to all operations that have been discontinued by the balance sheet date of the latest period presented. In historical summaries, the figures for each previous year would usually also be adjusted where it is feasible to do so; thus the results attributable to continuing operations would relate to operations that are currently continuing.

- Where errors have been corrected by a prior year adjustment, then the historical summary should be changed and again it should be made clear which figures have been restated.

- Earnings per share figures that are reported should be amended to reflect any:

    - New equity shares that have been issued by capitalising reserves.

    - Equity shares that have been split into shares of a lower nominal value.

- New equity shares that have been issued by way of rights issues.

- The earnings per share figures should be adjusted in the ways explained in chapter 14.

- Dividends per share should also be adjusted where there have been changes in the number of equity shares in issue due to capitalisation of reserves, a rights issue, or a split in the nominal value of shares in issue.

Publication of unaudited information

UK.4.246.6 Where a listed company publishes unaudited financial information in a class 1 circular or prospectus or publishes a profit forecast or profit estimate, the Listing Rules impose additional disclosure requirements in the company's next published annual report and accounts. The Listing Rules do not specify the section of the annual report and accounts in which the additional disclosures should be given, but require the following:

(a) The unaudited financial information, profit forecast or profit estimate previously published.

(b) The actual figures for the same period covered by the information reproduced under (a) above.

(c) An explanation of the difference between (a) and (b), if there is a difference of 10% or more between them.

[LR 9.2.18 R, LR 13.5.36 R].

UK.4.246.7 The above disclosure requirements do not apply to:

- *Pro forma* financial information prepared in accordance with Annex 1 and Annex 2 of the PD Regulation ('Regulation 809/2004 of the European Commission').

- Any preliminary statements of annual results or half-yearly or quarterly reports that are reproduced with the unaudited information.

- Any additional analysis of financial information that is set out in a financial information table in a class 1 circular.

[LR 9.2.19 G, LR 13.5.36 R].

UK law format for small companies

UK.4.246.8 On implementing the Member State options available under the EU IFRS Regulation, the UK government did not require unlisted companies to prepare financial statements under IFRS. The Companies Act 2006 also exempts small companies from certain disclosure requirements that relate to the annual financial statements and directors' report that are prepared for shareholders. The 2006 Act also permits abbreviated financial statements to be filed with the Registrar for small and medium-sized companies and it exempts small groups from preparing consolidated financial statements. A small company that elects to use IFRS is permitted to omit its profit and loss account (and supporting notes) from its published financial statements. It may also take advantage of the exemptions in relation to the directors' report, the requirement to prepare consolidated financial statements and the statutory audit. However, small companies that elect to prepare their financial statements under IFRS are not able to prepare abbreviated financial statements, because the form and content of such financial statements is set out in legislation that is not applicable to companies that prepare IFRS financial statements. The thresholds (turnover, balance sheet total and employee numbers) for determining small company status apply, but are based on equivalent items derived from IFRS financial statements.

Companies Act 2006

Accounting framework

UK.4.246.9   In the UK, the form and content of company and group financial statements is governed by UK law and UK accounting standards. An EU Regulation has determined that all EU regulated-market companies are required to report under EU-adopted IFRS in their consolidated financial statements. For those companies to which the EU IFRS Regulation applies, the format and content of their financial statements is governed by that EU Regulation and IFRS.

UK.4.246.10   The EU Regulation has direct legal effect in all EU countries and further legislation is not required to implement its requirement for IFRS *consolidated* financial statements for regulated-market companies. The options available to Member States under the Regulation relate to the *individual* financial statements of all companies and the *consolidated* financial statements of unlisted companies. In most cases, UK companies have a free choice as to whether they prepare their *individual* financial statements under IFRS or under UK GAAP. Similarly, UK companies whose securities are not traded on a regulated market may prepare their *consolidated* financial statements under UK GAAP. However, the government has imposed some restrictions and conditions. These are dealt with in detail in chapter 1.

UK.4.246.11   Individual companies will prepare either 'Companies Act individual financial statements' or 'IFRS individual financial statements'. A group's consolidated financial statements are prepared as 'Companies Act consolidated financial statements' or 'IFRS consolidated financial statements'. The requirements on the form and content of financial statements set out in the 2006 Act and its supporting regulations apply to 'Companies Act individual financial statements' and 'Companies Act consolidated financial statements' respectively. These parts of the legislation do not apply to 'IFRS individual financial statements' or 'IFRS consolidated financial statements'. However, the basic requirement to prepare financial statements, including the circumstances in which consolidated financial statements are required, as well as the requirements on audit, approval, distribution and filing, apply to all companies. See further chapter 1.

UK.4.246.12 The legal disclosure requirements in relation to staff costs are contained in the main body of the Acts to ensure that these disclosures continue to be given by all companies and groups. For financial years beginning on or after 6 April 2008, the 2006 Act creates an additional disclosure requirement, for all companies and groups, in respect of off balance sheet arrangements. Also, certain information outside the scope of IFRS and required by the 2006 Act to be included in the annual report and accounts, such as detailed information on directors' remuneration, will not be affected by the adoption of IFRS.

Parent's profit and loss account

UK.4.246.13 IAS 1 specifies the components of a complete set of financial statements prepared under IFRS and one of these components is a statement of comprehensive income (which may be presented as a single statement or as two statements: an income statement (or profit and loss account) and a statement of comprehensive income). Under UK law, when a parent company prepares consolidated financial statements in accordance with the 2006 Act, it is not required, subject to certain requirements, to publish its own profit and loss account and related notes. [CA06 Sec 408(3)]. This exemption continues to be available to parent companies that prepare their individual financial statements in accordance with EU-adopted IFRS. However, according to the guidance notes issued by the Department for Business, Innovation and Skills (BIS), this exemption does not extend to the statement of cash flows or statement of changes in equity; these primary statements are required in the parent's individual financial statements prepared under EU-adopted IFRS. The BIS guidance notes do not refer to IAS 1 and its requirement to present a statement of comprehensive income. However, applying the logic outlined in the guidance notes, the Act's exemption would apply to the whole performance statement where the single-statement approach is adopted. It does not make sense that the Act's exemption should apply differently depending on whether the one or two statement approach is used. Therefore, it follows that a parent company would also be exempt from publishing the statement of comprehensive income (that is, the primary statement presenting components of other comprehensive income) where the two-statement approach is adopted.

Off-balance sheet arrangements

UK.4.246.14 Following the transposition into UK law of the requirements of the EU Corporate Reporting Directive (2006/46/EC) ('the Directive'), the Companies Act 2006 requires the disclosure of 'off-balance sheet arrangements'. However, small companies are entirely exempt from the requirement and medium-sized companies may limit the disclosure to information about the nature and business purpose of such arrangements.

UK.4.246.15 The premise underlying the new disclosure requirement is that certain arrangements a company undertakes may have a material impact on the company but may not be included in the company's balance sheet. Consequently, if a company is or has been party to arrangements that are not reflected in its balance sheet, and the risks or benefits are material, the company should disclose:

- the nature and business purpose of the arrangements; and

- the financial impact of the arrangements on the company, to the extent necessary for enabling the company's financial position to be assessed.

[CA06 Sec 410A].

UK.4.246.16 When the company belongs to a group, the financial position of the group as a whole may also be affected. Consequently, aggregated disclosures have to be made in the notes to the consolidated financial statements.

UK.4.246.17 Application guidance from the BIS draws attention to Recital (9) to the Directive which states:

'Such off-balance-sheet arrangements could be any transactions or agreements which companies may have with entities, even unincorporated ones that are not included in the balance sheet. Such off-balance sheet arrangements may be associated with the creation or use of one or more Special Purpose Entities (SPEs) and offshore activities designed to address, inter alia, economic, legal, tax or accounting objectives. Examples of such off-balance-sheet arrangements include risk and benefit-sharing arrangements orobligations arising from a contract such as debt factoring, combined sale and repurchase agreements, consignment stock arrangements, take or pay arrangements, securitisation arranged through separate companies and unincorporated entities, pledged assets, operating leasing arrangements, outsourcing and the like. Appropriate disclosure of the material risks and benefits of such arrangements that are not included in the balance sheet should be set out in the notes to the accounts or the consolidated accounts.'

UK.4.246.18 The term 'arrangements' is undefined. Although Recital (9) to the Directive gives some examples of 'arrangements', the first sentence is very broad and could capture all executory contracts. The examples are not an exclusive list. Consequently, there is a danger that some companies may innocently provide unstructured disclosures covering large volumes of information (for example, purchase orders), that are really intended to be outside the scope (if that were made clear) of the legislation. Such a company would nevertheless appear to be compliant with the legislation.

UK.4.246.19 The issue has been raised with the UITF and, although the UITF is not authoritative for IFRS reporters, its view is relevant in interpreting a legal requirement that applies to both IFRS and UK GAAP reporters. The UITF recognised the concern regarding the lack of clarity in the disclosure requirement but stated that it could not issue an Abstract in absence of a definition of 'arrangement'. The UITF stated:

> "(i) when a company provides disclosures, it should consider the types of transactions envisaged by the EC (as quoted above) and the aim of the legislation;(ii) the disclosure requirement applies only where, at the balance sheet date, the risks or benefits arising from arrangements are material;(iii) disclosure need only be given to the extent necessary for enabling the financial position of the company to be assessed; and(iv) some accounting standards already require some disclosures that address items not necessarily included in the balance sheet but companies will need to consider whether arrangements outside the scope of those standards will require disclosure."

UK.4.246.20 We consider that, in the main, IFRS goes well beyond the minimum requirements of the law in ensuring that assets and liabilities are not inappropriately excluded from the balance sheet. It also imposes disclosure requirements on some types of arrangements, which are not included in the balance sheet, such as operating leases and contingent liabilities. Therefore, in most cases, compliance with IFRS should be sufficient to ensure compliance with the law. However, accounting standards do not necessarily provide for all circumstances and, as such, entities should consider making disclosures where, for example, they have had discussions with their auditors about off-balance sheet implications of transactions that their companies undertake or whether entities should be consolidated. In this respect, compliance with the requirements in IAS 1 to disclose critical accounting estimates and judgements should assist in formulating an appropriate disclosure that meets the legal requirement (see from paragraph 4.205).

UK.4.246.21 Furthermore, the experience from the 'credit crunch' of recent years and the ensuing problems with liquidity in the markets has highlighted concerns about latent risks and exposures that had not previously been considered an issue. Concerns have focused on, amongst others, unconsolidated Special Purpose Entities, liquidity facilities, loan commitments, guarantees and derivatives. In meeting the disclosure requirement on off-balance sheet arrangements, entities may need to consider a broader concept of financial impact of its off-balance sheet arrangements, in terms of, for example, liquidity, capital resources and credit risk. An example of disclosure of off balance sheet arrangements is Table UK.4.1.

UK.4.246.21.1 An example of disclosure of off balance sheet arrangements is table UK.4.1.

Table UK.4.1 – Disclosure of off balance sheet arrangements

BHP Billiton Plc – Annual report – 30 June 2011

3 Operating and financial review and prospects (extract)

3.8 Off-balance sheet arrangements and contractual commitments

Information in relation to our material off-balance sheet arrangements, principally contingent liabilities, commitments for capital expenditure and other expenditure and commitments under leases at 30 June 2011 is provided in note 21 'Contingent liabilities' and note 22 'Commitments' to the financial statements.

We expect that these contractual commitments for expenditure, together with other expenditure and liquidity requirements will be met from internal cash flow and, to the extent necessary, from the existing facilities described in section 3.7.3.

21 Contingent liabilities

Contingent liabilities at balance date, not otherwise provided for in the financial statements, are categorised as arising from:

	2011 US$M	2010 US$M
Jointly controlled entities		
Bank guarantees[a]	12	7
Actual or potential litigation[b]	1,384	878
Other	1	–
	1,397	885
Subsidiaries and jointly controlled assets (including guarantees)		
Bank guarantees[a]	1	1
Actual or potential litigation[c]	693	455
Other[a]	4	3
	698	459
Total contingent liabilities	2,095	1,344

(a) The Group has entered into various counter-indemnities of bank and performance guarantees related to its own future performance in the normal course of business.

(b) Actual or potential litigation amounts relate to a number of actions against the Group, none of which are individually significant and where the liability is not probable and therefore the Group has not provided for such amounts in these financial statements. Additionally, there are a number of legal claims or potential claims against the Group, the outcome of which cannot be foreseen at present, and for which no amounts have been included in the table above.

---

22 Commitments

	2011 US$M	2010 US$M
Capital expenditure commitments not provided for in the financial statements		
Due not later than one year	5,307	4,311
Due later than one year and not later than two years	1,419	491
Due later than two years and not later than three years	531	171
Due later than three years and not later than four years	35	16
Due later than four years and not later than five years	1	–
Total capital expenditure commitments	7,293	4,989
Lease expenditure commitments		
Finance leases		
Due not later than one year	88	95
Due later than one year and not later than two years	54	60
Due later than two years and not later than three years	50	51
Due later than three years and not later than four years	51	49
Due later than four years and not later than five years	46	49
Due later than five years	93	140
Total commitments under finance leases	382	444
Future financing charges	(93)	(111)
Right to reimbursement from joint venture partner	(97)	(108)
Finance lease liability	192	225
Operating leases[a]		
Due not later than one year	861	695
Due later than one year and not later than two years	640	580
Due later than two years and not later than three years	453	601
Due later than three years and not later than four years	208	255
Due later than four years and not later than five years	192	98
Due later than five years	1,197	830
Total commitments under operating leases	3,551	3,059
Other expenditure commitments[b]		
Due not later than one year	3,473	2,793
Due later than one year and not later than two years	1,486	1,291
Due later than two years and not later than three years	947	1,111
Due later than three years and not later than four years	564	768
Due later than four years and not later than five years	546	444
Due later than five years	2,059	1,923
Total commitments for other expenditure	9,075	8,330

(a) Operating leases are entered into as a means of acquiring property, plant and equipment. Rental payments are generally fixed, but with inflation escalation clauses on which contingent rentals are determined. Certain leases contain extension and renewal options.

(b) Other expenditure commitments include the supply of goods and services, royalties, exploration expenditure and chartering costs.

Other disclosures

UK.4.246.22 Whether adopting IFRS or continuing to adopt UK GAAP, company law requires companies to disclose considerable detail about their ultimate holding company, investments in subsidiaries and other related undertakings. These disclosure requirements are set out in statutory instruments supporting the 2006 Act, in Schedule 4 to the Large and Medium-sized Companies and Groups (Accounts and Reports) Regulations 2008 ('SI 2008/410') and in Schedule 2 to the Small Companies and Groups (Accounts and Directors' Report) Regulations 2008 ('SI 2008/409'). These disclosure requirements are set out in chapter 24.

UK.4.246.23 Schedules 5 and 8 to SI 2008/410 and Schedule 3 to SI 2008/409, set out the disclosure requirements concerning directors' remuneration. In addition, section 413 of the 2006 Act sets out disclosure requirements for certain transactions and other arrangements involving directors. These disclosures, which are required regardless of the accounting framework adopted, are considered in chapters 5 and 6 of the Manual of Accounting – Narrative Reporting.

Auditors' remuneration

UK.4.246.24 The Companies Act 2006 requires separate disclosure of the amounts of remuneration receivable by a company's auditors, in their capacity as auditors and also in respect of services other than audit. The legal requirements are set out in The Companies (Disclosure of Auditor Remuneration and Liability Limitation Agreements) Regulations 2008 (SI 2008/489).

UK.4.246.24.1 The 2008 Regulations have been revised by The Companies (Disclosure of Auditor Remuneration and Liability Limitation Agreements) (Amendment) Regulations 2011 (SI 2011/2198). The amendments apply for financial years beginning on or after 1st October 2011 (with early adoption permitted from 1 October 2011 for financial years beginning before that date).

UK.4.246.25 The analysis of fees receivable by auditors should be given in the notes to the financial statements. Disclosure is required of the amount of:

- Fees payable to the company's auditor for the statutory audit of the company's annual financial statements. Under the 2011 revised regulations, this disclosure also includes fees payable to associates of the company's auditors (as defined in the regulations).

- Fees payable to the company's auditor and its associates for the audits of the company's 'associates' (which includes its subsidiaries in this context) and for other services provided to the company and its associates (analysed between specified types of service). The types of other services required to be disclosed have been amended in the 2011 revised regulations.

- Fees payable to the company's auditor and its associates for audit and other services (analysed by specified type of services) supplied to the company's associated pension schemes. In respect of other services, this is irrespective of whether or not the company's auditor or any of its associates are the auditors of the pension schemes. [SI 2008/489 Reg 5].

UK.4.246.26 Remuneration includes payments in respect of expenses and benefits in kind. The nature and estimated money value of benefits in kind should be disclosed. [SI 2008/489 Reg 5].

UK.4.246.27 The disclosure requirements apply irrespective of the accounting framework (IFRS or UK GAAP) used in preparing the financial statements and apply to all financial statements (individual and consolidated), except that the disclosures in respect of fees for 'other services' are not required to be given by:

- A small or medium-sized company as defined by the Companies Act 2006.

- A small or medium-sized group.

- A subsidiary company in its individual financial statements, whose parent is required to, and does, prepare consolidated financial statements in accordance with the Companies Act 2006 and the subsidiary company is included in the consolidation.

- A parent company in its individual financial statements, where the company to required to, and does, prepare consolidated financial statements in accordance with the Companies Act 2006.

[SI 2008/489 Regs 4,5,6].

UK.4.246.28 Guidance on the 2008 Regulations is given in Technical Release 06/06 (revised), 'Disclosure of auditor remuneration', published by the ICAEW. The requirements for the disclosure of auditor remuneration are dealt with in chapter 4 of the Manual of Accounting – Other statutory requirements.

Chapter 5

Fair value

Fair value

Introduction

5.1 The IASB issued IFRS 13 in May 2011 as a common framework for measuring fair value when required or permitted by another IFRS. The standard is effective for annual periods beginning on or after 1 January 2013. Early adoption is permitted.

5.2 IFRS 13 defines fair value as: *"The price that would be received to sell an asset or paid to transfer a liability in an orderly transaction between market participants at the measurement date"*. [IFRS 13 para 9]. The key principle is that fair value is the exit price from the perspective of market participants who hold the asset or owe the liability at the measurement date. It is based on the perspective of market participants rather than just the entity itself, so fair value is not affected by an entity's intentions towards the asset, liability or equity item that is being fair valued.

5.3 This key principle is unlikely to result in significant valuation changes for assets, as most entities should already be applying this principle in practice. However, as this is a new standard, differences to previous practice may emerge as management applies the standard for the first time.

5.4 It is likely that some entities will see differences in the measurement of liabilities as previous practice has often been to measure liabilities based on the value to settle the liability with the counterparty rather than on the value to transfer the liability to a third party.

5.5 A fair value measurement requires management to determine four aspects: the particular asset or liability that is the subject of the measurement (consistent with its unit of account); the highest and best use for a non-financial asset; the principal (or, in its absence, the most advantageous) market; and the valuation technique. [IFRS 13 App B para B2].

5.6 IFRS 13 addresses how to measure fair value, but does not stipulate when fair value can or should be used.

5.7 The issue of when fair value should be used as a measurement basis in IFRS is controversial; hence the IASB did not introduce any new requirements to perform fair value measurements as a result of issuing IFRS 13. On the contrary, the IASB considered whether each use of the term fair value in IFRS was consistent with an exit price definition. Where this was not the case, the IASB made either scope changes to IFRS 13 or used another measurement basis in other IFRSs as appropriate.

Scope

5.8   IFRS 13 applies to all fair value measurements or disclosures that are either required or permitted by other standards, except:

■   share-based payments under IFRS 2;

■   leases under IAS 17; and

■   measures that are similar to but are not fair value, including the net realisable value measure in IAS 2, and the value-in-use measure in IAS 36.

[IFRS 13 para 6].

5.9   For the following items, the measurement requirements of IFRS 13 apply, but the disclosure requirements do not:

■   defined benefit plan assets measured at fair value under IAS 19;

■   retirement benefit plan investments measured at fair value under IAS 26; and

■   impaired assets measured at fair value less costs to sell under IAS 36.

[IFRS 13 para 7].

These standards already contain requirements to disclose how fair value has been measured. IFRS 13 added further disclosure requirements to IAS 36 when recoverable amount is based on fair value.

5.10   IFRS 13 applies to initial and subsequent measurements at fair value. [IFRS 13 para 8].

5.11   The term 'fair value' is used throughout IFRSs; given that there are so few scope exclusions, IFRS 13 is pervasive.

Measurement

5.12   IFRS 13 stipulates the following factors that should be considered in fair value measurement:

■   the asset or liability [IFRS 13 paras 11 to 14];

■   the transaction [IFRS 13 paras 15 to 21];

■   market participants [IFRS 13 paras 22 to 23]; and

■   the price [IFRS 13 paras 24 to 26].

5.13   In addition; there are considerations that are specific to:

■   non-financial assets;

- liabilities;

- equity; and

- financial instruments.

The asset or liability

Characteristics

5.14   A fair value measurement relates to a particular asset or liability. It should, therefore, incorporate the asset or liability's specific characteristics if market participants consider these characteristics when pricing the asset or liability. These characteristics could include condition, location and restrictions, if any, on sale or use as of the measurement date. [IFRS 13 para 11].

Unit of account

5.15   Under IFRS 13, fair value measurement may be applied to a stand-alone asset or liability (for example, an equity security, investment property, an intangible asset or a warranty liability) or a group of related assets and/or liabilities (for example, a business), depending on the circumstances. Determining how fair value measurement applies depends on the unit of account. The unit of account is determined based on the level at which the asset or liability is aggregated or disaggregated in accordance with the IFRS requirements applicable to the particular asset or liability being measured; it is not generally determined by IFRS 13 itself. The standard allows an exception when an entity manages a group of financial assets and liabilities on the basis of its net exposure to market risks or credit risks. See paragraph 5.149 below.

The transaction

5.16   Fair value measurement in IFRS 13 assumes that the asset or liability is exchanged in an orderly transaction between market participants under current market conditions at the measurement date. [IFRS 13 para 15].

5.17   Under IFRS 13, management determines fair value based on a transaction that would take place in the principal market or, in its absence, the most advantageous market. [IFRS 13 para 16]. If there is a principal market, the price in that market must be used even if prices in other markets are more advantageous. The reference transactions may be actual or hypothetical.

Principal market

5.18   The principal market is the market with the greatest volume and level of activity for the asset or liability. [IFRS 13 App A]. To determine the principal market, management needs to evaluate the level of activity in various different markets. However, the entity does not have to undertake an exhaustive search of all possible markets in order to identify the principal or most advantageous market; it should take into account all information that is readily available. In the absence of evidence to the contrary, the market in which an entity normally transacts is presumed to be the principal market, or the most advantageous market in the absence of a principal market. The entity's principal market is the market that it has access to that has the greatest volume and level of activity for the asset or liability, even if the prices in other markets are more advantageous. [IFRS 13 para 18].

5.19 An entity may have a number of different activities that use different markets for the same assets. There is no need to identify one principal, or most advantageous, market for the whole entity; each different business unit within the entity may have its own principal or most advantageous market. [IFRS 13 para 19].

Most advantageous market

5.20 The most advantageous market is the market that maximises the amount that would be received to sell the asset or minimises the amount that would be paid to transfer the liability, after taking into account transaction costs and transport costs. [IFRS 13 App A].

5.21 To determine the most advantageous market, management evaluates all potential markets in which it could reasonably expect to sell the asset or transfer the liability. For non-financial assets, identifying potential markets will be based on the 'highest and best use' valuation premise, from the perspective of market participants. [IFRS 13 para 31]. In order to determine the highest and best use of a non-financial asset (see para 5.41), the reporting entity may need to consider multiple markets.

5.22 In practice, most non-financial assets are already employed in their 'highest and best use', so this requirement is not as onerous as it may seem.

> **Example – Principal or most advantageous market**
>
> In a territory there are two available markets for soya bean:
>
> (a)   Export; this is the market where the higher prices would be available for the producer, but there are limitations in the volumes that can be sold in this market because the government sets a limit on the volume of exports and each producer needs to get an authorisation to export its production.
>
> (b)   Domestic: the prices are lower in this market as compared to the export market, but there are no restrictions in terms of volume (other than the demand of the product by purchasers).
>
> Producers intend to sell all of the production they can in the export market and, when they do not have any further authorisation to export, they sell the remaining production in the domestic market.
>
> Therefore, the most advantageous market is the export market, as this is the one that gives the higher benefits to the producers. But in terms of volume, the domestic market is the principal market for the producers and therefore is the one which should be used to determine fair value.

Market accessibility

5.23 In evaluating the principal or most advantageous markets, IFRS 13 restricts the eligible markets to only those that the entity can access at the measurement date. As different reporting entities may have access to different markets, the principal or most advantageous markets could vary between reporting entities. [IFRS 13 para 19].

5.24 Although an entity must be able to access the market, it does not need to be able to sell the particular asset or transfer the particular liability on the measurement date to be able to measure fair value on the basis of the price in that market. [IFRS 13 para 20].

> **Example – Accessing the principal market**
>
> A commodities trader has a reporting date of 31 December 20X0, which falls on a Saturday. The commodities trader holds commodity X for which it has access to both retail and wholesale markets. The principal market is the wholesale market, because that is the market with the greatest volume and level of activity for the commodity. However, the retail market selling prices are usually higher. The wholesale market only trades on weekdays, whereas the retail market trades also on Saturdays.
>
> The commodities trader is not allowed to use the higher retail price as the fair value of the commodities merely because the wholesale (principal) market does not trade on the measurement date.

No observable market

5.25 There may be no known or observable market for an asset or liability. For example, there may be no specific market for the sale of a cash generating unit or intangible asset. In such cases, the management should first identify potential market participants (for example, strategic and financial buyers) and then develop a hypothetical market based on the expected assumptions of those market participants.

Market participants

5.26 IFRS 13 emphasises that a fair value measurement should be based on the assumptions of market participants (that is, it is not an entity-specific measurement). [IFRS 13 para 22]. Market participants are buyers and sellers in the principal (or most advantageous) market for the asset or liability that are:

- *Independent.* The transaction counterparties are not related parties as defined in IAS 24. However, this does not preclude related-party transaction prices from being used as valuation inputs if there is evidence that the transactions were on market terms.

- *Knowledgeable.* Transaction counterparties have a reasonable understanding about the asset or liability and the transaction using all available information, including information that might be obtained through due diligence efforts that are usual and customary.

- *Able to transact in the asset or liability.*

- *Willing to transact in the asset or liability.* Transaction counterparties are motivated but not forced or otherwise compelled to transact.

[IFRS 13 App A].

5.27   Market participants seek to maximise the fair value of an asset or minimise the fair value of a liability in a transaction to sell the asset or to transfer the liability in the principal (or most advantageous) market for the asset or liability. [IFRS 13 para 22].

5.28   The entity is not required to identify specific market participants; instead it should develop a profile of potential market participants. The profile should consider factors specific to the asset or liability, the principal (or, in its absence, the most advantageous) market for the asset or liability, and market participants with whom the entity would transact in that market.

5.29   In the absence of an observable market, fair value is determined by considering the characteristics of market participants who would enter into a hypothetical transaction for the asset or liability. [IFRS 13 para 23(c)].

5.30   Determining who potential market participants are is a critical step in determining fair value due to the emphasis on the use of market participant assumptions. Identifying market participants may be straightforward if there is general knowledge of the types of participants in a particular market. In certain other cases, management may need to make assumptions about the type of market participants that may be interested in a particular asset or liability. Market participants can include strategic and financial investors. Strategic investors are typically those in the same or similar industries whilst financial investors are typically private equity or sovereign wealth funds.

5.31   Key considerations in developing market participant assumptions may include the specific location, condition and other characteristics of the asset or liability (for example, assumed growth rates, whether certain synergies are available to all market participants, and risk premium assumptions). For example, there may be no apparent exit market for customer relationship intangible assets. In this case, management may consider whether there are strategic buyers in the marketplace that would benefit from the customer relationships that are being valued. Most entities seek to build up their customer base as they grow their businesses, so the entity can look to potential participants in its industry that may be seeking additional growth and from there determine a hypothetical group of market participants.

The price

5.32   Under IFRS 13, fair value is based on the exit price (the price that would be received to sell an asset or would be paid to transfer a liability), not the transaction price or entry price (the price that was paid for the asset or that was received to assume the liability). [IFRS 13 para 24] Conceptually, entry and exit prices are different. The exit price concept is based on current expectations about the sale or transfer price from the perspective of market participants.

5.33   The IASB deliberated carefully before arriving at the conclusion to use an exit price. There are arguments against the use of exit prices. For example, one might argue that the exit price is not relevant when an entity intends to use an asset rather than sell it.

5.34   However, even if an entity intends to use the asset, exit price is still appropriate in a fair value measurement. This is because the exit price reflects expectations about future cash flows by selling it to a market participant that would use it in the same way. This is because a market participant will only pay for benefits that it expects to generate from the asset's use or sale. [IFRS 13 para BC39]. A similar logic applies to liabilities, in that a market participant would reflect expectations about cash outflows necessary to fulfil an obligation. [IFRS 13 para BC40].

5.35   The IASB did a standard-by-standard review to assess whether exit price was the interpretation taken in those circumstances where 'fair value' is mentioned in IFRSs. The intention was that if the exit price was not the interpretation, the IASB would change the term 'fair value' to something else. [IFRS 13 para BC41]. This review led the IASB to conclude that a current entry price and current exit price should be equal if they relate to the same asset or liability on the same date in the same form in the same market. The IASB did not therefore consider it necessary to make a distinction between a current entry price and a current exit price in IFRSs with a market-based measurement objective (that is, fair value); instead it decided to retain the term fair value and define it as a current exit price. [IFRS 13 para BC44].

5.36   The IASB has scoped out of this guidance those IFRSs where fair value measurement requirements are inconsistent with exit price. [IFRS 13 para BC45]. (See para 5.8 above.)

5.37   Fair value takes account of any restrictions on the sale or use of an asset, if those restrictions relate to the asset rather than to the holder of the asset and a market participant would take those restrictions into account in determining the price that he is prepared to pay.

Example 1 – Restriction on the sale of an equity instrument

This example has been reproduced from paragraph IE28 of IFRS 13.

> "*An entity holds an equity instrument (a financial asset) for which sale is legally or contractually restricted for a specified period. (For example, such a restriction could limit sale to qualifying investors.) The restriction is a characteristic of the instrument and, therefore, would be transferred to market participants. In that case the fair value of the instrument would be measured on the basis of the quoted price for an otherwise identical unrestricted equity instrument of the same issuer that trades in a public market, adjusted to reflect the effect of the restriction. The adjustment would reflect the amount market participants would demand because of the risk relating to the inability to access a public market for the instrument for the specified period. The adjustment will vary depending on all the following:*
>
> *(a)   the nature and duration of the restriction;*
>
> *(b)   the extent to which buyers are limited by the restriction (for example, there might be a large number of qualifying investors); and*
>
> *(c)   qualitative and quantitative factors specific to both the instrument and the issuer.*"

Example 2 – Restrictions on the use of an asset

This example has been reproduced from paragraph IE29 of IFRS 13.

> "*A donor contributes land in an otherwise developed residential area to a not-for-profit neighbourhood association. The land is currently used as a playground. The donor specifies that the land must continue to be used by the association as a playground in perpetuity. Upon review of relevant documentation (for example, legal and other), the association determines that the fiduciary responsibility to meet the donor's restriction would not be transferred to market participants if the association sold the asset, that is, the donor restriction on the use of the land is specific to the association. Furthermore, the association is not restricted from selling the land. Without the restriction on the use of the land by the association, the land could be used as a site for residential development. In addition, the land is subject to an easement (that is, a legal right that enables a utility to run power lines across the land). Following is an analysis of the effect on the fair value measurement of the land arising from the restriction and the easement:*
>
> *(a)   Donor restriction on use of land. Because in this situation the donor restriction on the use of the land is specific to the association, the restriction would not be transferred to market participants. Therefore, the fair value of the land would be the higher of its fair value used as a playground (that is, the fair value of the asset would be maximised through its use by market participants in combination with other assets or with other assets and liabilities) and its fair value as a site for residential development (that is, the fair value of the asset would be maximised through its use by market participants on a stand-alone basis), regardless of the restriction on the use of the land by the association.*

(b) *Easement for utility lines. Because the easement for utility lines is specific to (i.e. a characteristic of) the land, it would be transferred to market participants with the land. Therefore, the fair value measurement of the land would take into account the effect of the easement, regardless of whether the highest and best use is as a playground or as a site for residential development."*

5.38 These examples illustrate two points:

- Entity-specific restrictions (that is, donor restriction) do not affect fair value; asset-specific restrictions (that is, easement for utility lines) do affect fair value.

- Restrictions that are easily circumvented (that is, by selling the land) are unlikely to affect fair value.

5.39 IFRS 13 prohibits adjustment of fair value for transaction costs, which are accounted for in accordance with other IFRSs. However, transaction costs do not include transport costs under IFRS 13. Fair value should be adjusted for transport costs if location is a characteristic of the asset (for example, a commodity). [IFRS 13 para 25].

Transaction costs

5.40 IFRS 13 prohibits adjusting the fair value for transaction costs (see para 5.39 above), but it does require such transaction costs to be considered in determining the most advantageous market. Transaction costs are defined as:

"The costs to sell an asset or transfer a liability in the principal (or most advantageous) market for the asset or liability that are directly attributable to the disposal of an asset or the transfer of a liability and meet both of the following criteria:

(a) They result directly from and are essential to that transaction.

(b) They would not have been incurred by the entity had the decision to sell the asset or transfer the liability not been made (similar to costs to sell, as defined in IFRS 5)."

[IFRS 13 App A].

Example – The impact of transport costs and transaction costs on fair value

An entity has an asset that is sold in two different markets with similar volume of activities but with different prices. The entity enters into transactions in both markets and can access the price in those markets for the asset at the measurement date. There is no principal market for the asset.

	Market A	Market B
Price	27	25
Transport costs	(3)	(2)
	24	23
Transaction costs	(3)	(1)
Net amount received	21	22

In market A, the price that would be received is C27; transaction costs in that market are C3; and the costs to transport the asset to that market are C3 (that is, the net amount that would be received in market A is C21).

In market B, the price that would be received is C25; transaction costs in that market are C1; and the costs to transport the asset to that market are C2 (that is, the net amount that would be received in market B is C22).

If market A had been the principal market for the asset (that is, the market with the greatest volume and level of activity for the asset), the asset's fair value would be measured using the price that would be received in that market, after taking into account transport costs (C24). The same applies for market B (C23).

As a principal market for the asset does not exist, the fair value of the asset would be measured using the price in the most advantageous market. The most advantageous market is the market that maximises the amount that would be received to sell the asset, after taking into account transaction costs and transport costs (that is, the net amount that would be received in the respective markets).

The entity would maximise the net amount that would be received for the asset in market B (C22). So the fair value of the asset is measured using the price in that market (C25), less transport costs (C2), resulting in a fair value measurement of C23.

Considerations specific to non-financial assets: highest and best use

5.41 IFRS 13 requires the fair value of a non-financial asset to be measured based on its highest and best use from a market participant's perspective. [IFRS 13 para 27]. This requirement does not apply to financial instruments, liabilities or equity. This concept of 'highest and best use' is not new to IFRS valuations, although it has not explicitly been part of IFRS literature. Before IFRS 13, the basis of conclusions in IAS 40, in discussing the fair valuation of investment properties made reference to the International Valuation Standards

(IVS), which include this as a general valuation concept. The specific inclusion of this concept in IFRS, therefore, aligns IFRS with valuation practices.

5.42 Under IFRS 13, the highest and best use takes into account the asset's use that is:

- *physically possible* - takes into account the physical characteristics that market participants would consider (for example, property location or size);

- *legally permissible* - takes into account the legal restrictions on the asset's use that market participants would consider (for example, planning or zoning regulations); and

- *financially feasible* - takes into account whether an asset's use generates adequate income or cash flows to produce an investment return that market participants would require. This should incorporate the costs of converting the asset to that use.

5.43 Highest and best use is determined from the perspective of market participants. [IFRS 13 para 29]. It does not matter whether the entity intends to use the asset differently. For example, the entity could have made a defensive acquisition of a competing brand that it does not intend to use, in order to maintain or promote the competitive position of its own brand. Despite its intentions, the entity measures the fair value of the competing brand assuming its highest and best use by market participants. [IFRS 13 para 30].

5.44 When determining highest and best use, management should include all costs that market participants would incur in the circumstances. For example, if a parcel of land is currently used for farming, the fair value (assuming the highest and best use is to continue to use it for farming) should reflect the benefits of continuing to operate the land for farming, including any tax credits that could be realised by market participants. However, if it is determined that market participants would consider an alternative use for the land to be its highest and best use (for example, commercial or residential use), the fair value should include all costs (for example, legal costs, viability analysis, traffic studies), associated with re-zoning the land to the market participant's intended use. In addition, demolition and other costs associated with preparing the land for a different use should be included in the estimate of fair value. This concept is illustrated in example 2 in paragraph IE8 of IFRS 13. An effort to re-zone land contains an element of uncertainty related to whether the proposed re-zoning obtains approval. The land's fair value should, therefore, reflect this uncertainty. Re-zoning should not be considered if it is not feasible or it is unlikely to succeed.

5.45 However, IFRS 13 allows management to presume that its current use of an asset is the highest and best use, unless market or other factors suggest otherwise. [IFRS 13 para 29].

5.46 The IASB concluded that an entity that seeks to maximise the value of its assets would use those assets at their highest and best use; it would, therefore, be necessary for management to consider alternative uses of those assets only if there was evidence that the current use of the assets is not their highest and best use. In many cases, it would be unlikely for an asset's current use not to be its highest and best use. The most common examples are described in paragraphs IE7 to IE9 of IFRS 13 and include assets being held defensively and land.

5.47 The highest and best use of a non-financial asset may be on a stand-alone basis or may be achieved in combination with other assets and/or liabilities. In the latter case:

■ Fair value is based on the use of the asset in such an asset/liability group. It is assumed that the asset would be used within such a group and that the other assets and liabilities would be available to market participants.

■ The asset/liability group cannot include liabilities that are used to fund assets outside the asset/liability group.

■ Assumptions about highest and best use should be consistent for all non-financial assets in such an asset/liability group.

■ The fair value measurement assumes that the asset is sold consistent with the unit of account, and not as a group, because the market participant is assumed to have the other assets.

[IFRS 13 paras 31, 32].

5.48 When the highest and best use is in an asset/liability group, the synergies associated with the asset/liability group may be factored into the fair value of the individual asset in a number of ways, depending on circumstances.

■ Direct adjustments to fair value might be appropriate *"if the asset is a machine and the fair value measurement is determined using an observed price for a similar machine (not installed or otherwise configured for use), adjusted for transport and installation costs so that the fair value measurement reflects the current condition and location of the machine (installed and configured for use)"*. [IFRS 13 App B para B3(b)].

■ Adjustment to market participant assumptions might be appropriate *"for example, if the asset is work in progress inventory that is unique and market participants would convert the inventory into finished goods, the fair value of the inventory would assume that market participants have acquired or would acquire any specialised machinery necessary to convert the inventory into finished goods"*. [IFRS 13 App B para B3(c)].

■ Adjustment via the valuation technique might be appropriate *"when using the multi-period excess earnings method to measure the fair value of an intangible asset because that valuation technique specifically takes into account the contribution of any complementary assets and the associated liabilities in the group in which such an intangible asset would be used"*. [IFRS 13 App B para B3(d)].

- Allocation of fair value adjustments to individual assets might be appropriate *"in more limited situations, when an entity uses an asset within a group of assets, the entity might measure the asset at an amount that approximates its fair value when allocating the fair value of the asset group to the individual assets of the group. That might be the case if the valuation involves real property and the fair value of improved property (i.e. an asset group) is allocated to its component assets (such as land and improvements)"*. [IFRS 13 App B para B3(e)].

Considerations specific to liabilities and equity

Transfer of liabilities

5.49 Paragraph 34 of IFRS 13 stipulates (emphasis added): *"A fair value measurement assumes that a financial or non-financial liability or an entity's own equity instrument (for example, equity interests issued as consideration in a business combination) is transferred to a market participant at the measurement date. The transfer of a liability or an entity's own equity instrument assumes the following:*

(a) *A* liability would remain outstanding *and the market participant transferee would be required to fulfil the obligation. The* liability would not be settled *with the counterparty or otherwise extinguished on the measurement date.*

(b) *An entity's* own equity instrument would remain outstanding *and the market participant transferee would take on the rights and responsibilities associated with the instrument. The* instrument would not be cancelled *or otherwise extinguished on the measurement date"*.

5.50 The transfer concept for liabilities clarifies the previous IFRS definition of fair value (for example, in IAS 32, IAS 41, and IFRS 5), which required fair value for liabilities to be *"the amount for which a liability could be* settled, *between knowledgeable willing parties…"*. As liabilities could be 'settled' by extinguishing them or transferring them to another party, it was not clear whether settlement value referred to transfer value or the extinguishment value. IFRS 13 clarifies that the fair value is the transfer value rather than the extinguishment value. Thus the application of IFRS 13 may result in a change in practice for some entities.

5.51 Extinguishment value is generally not the transfer value. In some instances, an additional risk premium above the expected payout may be required because of uncertainty about the ultimate amount of the liability (for example, asbestos liabilities and performance guarantees). The risk premium paid to a third party may differ from the settlement value that the direct counterparty would be willing to accept. In addition, the party assuming a liability may have to incur certain costs to manage the liability or may require a profit margin.

5.52 In practice, there may be significant differences between the settlement value and the transfer value. Among the differences is the impact of credit risk, which is often not considered in the settlement of a liability. See further discussion in paragraphs 5.133 to 5.136.

Liability and equity instruments held by other parties as assets

5.53 In comparison to assets, observable active markets for liabilities and equities are much less likely to exist due to contractual and legal restrictions on liability and equity transfers. Even for quoted debt or equity securities, the market serves as an exit mechanism for the counterparty security holders rather than for the issuer. As a result the quoted price reflects the exit price for the investor rather than the issuer. IFRS 13 distinguishes such situations from the situation in which an exit market exists directly for the liability or equity instrument. When a quoted transfer price is not available for the issuer but the instrument is held by another party as an asset, management should measure fair value from the asset holder's perspective. [IFRS 13 para 37].

5.54 The IASB decided to use the fair value from the investor's perspective to measure the liability's fair value when there is no active market for the liability transfer. The IASB believes that the fair value from the viewpoints of investor and issuer should be the same in an efficient market, otherwise arbitrage would result. [IFRS 13 para BC89].

5.55 The IASB considered whether these different viewpoints could result in different fair values because the asset is liquid but the liability is not. The asset holder could easily sell the asset to another party, whereas the liability issuer will usually find it more difficult to transfer the liability to another party. In the end, the IASB decided that there was no conceptual reason why a different fair value should result, given that both parties are measuring the same instrument with identical contractual terms in the same market.

5.56 In such cases, the fair value of the liability or equity instrument is derived by:

(a) Using the quoted price in an active market for the identical item held by another party as an asset (for example, actively-quoted debt security prices).

(b) Using other observable inputs if the price in (a) is not available, such as the quoted price in an inactive market for the identical item held by another party as an asset (for example, quoted debt security prices in less active markets).

(c) Using another valuation technique if the observable inputs in (a) and (b) are not available, such as:

 (i) *an income approach* — this approach uses a present value technique that takes into account the future cash outflows that a market participant would expect to receive from holding the liability or equity instrument as an asset.

(ii) *a market approach* — under this approach, fair value is determined using quoted prices for similar liabilities or equity instruments held by other parties as assets.

Further discussion on the application of this concept to financial liabilities is in paragraph 5.132.

Liabilities not held by other parties as assets

5.58 There are certain liabilities that are not held by another party as an asset. An example is a decommissioning liability. [IFRS 13 App B para B31]. In such cases, the liability's fair value would have to be measured from the perspective of a market participant to whom the liability would be transferred. If a market is not available for the liability, a valuation technique is required to measure the liability's fair value. [IFRS 13 para 40].

5.59 These valuation techniques can include a present value technique that considers either:

■ the future cash outflows that a market participant would expect to incur in fulfilling the obligation, including the compensation that a market participant would require for taking on the obligation; or

■ the amount that a market participant would receive to enter into or issue an identical liability, using the assumptions that market participants would use when pricing the identical item (for example, having the same credit characteristics) in the principal market (or, in its absence, the most advantageous market).

[IFRS 13 para 41].

5.60 When using such present value calculations, the calculations should reflect the future cash outflows that market participants would expect to incur in fulfilling the obligation. These cash outflows should include:

■ market participants' expectations about the costs of fulfilling the obligation; and

■ the compensation that a market participant would require, which should include a return for:

   ■ *undertaking the activity* — the market participant would expect a compensation for fulfilling the obligation, as the participant will use valuable resources for this purpose; and

   ■ *assuming the risk associated with the obligation* - for assuming the obligations, the market participant would usually require a risk premium to compensate for the risk that actual cash outflows might differ from those expected.

Such risk premiums can be included by adjusting either the cash flows or the discount rate. However, the risk should not be double-counted (for example, by adjusting both cash flows and discount rate for the same risk). [IFRS 13 App B para B33].

5.61 Non-financial liabilities may not have a contractual rate of return or an observable market yield. When measuring such liabilities at fair value, the various components of return will sometimes be indistinguishable (for example, when using the price a third-party contractor would charge on a fixed fee basis). In other cases, the various components may require separate estimation (for example, when using the price a third-party contractor would charge on a cost plus basis). [IFRS 13 App B para B32]. Illustrative example number 11 to the standard shows how the fair value of such a liability may be measured. [IFRS 13 IE 35 to 39].

5.62 The above requirements appear complicated. However, the overriding objective is to determine what a potential market participant would require as compensation to take on the liability. For example, assume a factory is built on leased land that has to be returned to the owner in five years' time without the factory building. The decommissioning liability would be the liability associated with the costs of tearing down the factory and making good the land. The decommissioning liability's fair value might simply be the market rate that a demolition services provider would charge in order to agree, today, to take down the factory in five years' time. The above requirements are aimed at determining this amount.

Non-performance risk

5.63 IFRS 13 requires the liability's fair value to reflect the effect of non-performance risk, which is the risk that an entity will not fulfil an obligation. Non-performance risk includes the effect of credit risk, as well as any other factors that influence the likelihood of fulfilling the obligation. This applies to both financial and non-financial liabilities. [IFRS 13 para 42].

5.64 Before IFRS 13 was issued, there were different interpretations about how an entity's own credit risk should be reflected in a liability's fair value using the settlement notion in the previous definition of fair value. It is unlikely that the counterparty would accept an amount different from the contractual amount as settlement of the obligation if the entity's credit standing changed; consequently, those using the counterparty settlement interpretation of fair value did not find a significant impact from changes in their own credit risk when fair valuing their liabilities. The requirement to include non-performance risk, including credit risk, could result in a change for entities that have not included own credit risk in the fair value of their financial or non-financial liabilities previously (for example, derivative financial liabilities or acquired decommissioning liabilities).

5.65 IFRS 13 assumes that non-performance risk is the same before and after the transfer of the liability. This concept assumes that the liability would transfer to a credit-equivalent entity. [IFRS 13 para 42]. For further discussion of this in relation to financial instruments please refer to paragraphs 5.133 to 5.136.

5.66 The basis for conclusions sets out why this is the case. It states that although such an assumption is unlikely to be realistic for an actual transaction (because in most cases the reporting entity transferor and the market participant transferee are unlikely to have the same credit standing), it is necessary because:

■ A market participant taking on the obligation would not enter into a transaction that changes the non-performance risk associated with the liability without reflecting that change in the price.

■ Without specifying the credit standing of the entity taking on the obligation, there could be fundamentally different fair values for a liability depending on an entity's assumptions about the characteristics of the market participant transferee.

■ Those who might hold the entity's obligations as assets would consider the effect of the entity's credit risk and other risk factors when pricing those assets.

[IFRS 13 para BC94].

5.67 The level of non-performance risk imputed into the fair value should be consistent with the unit of account. For example, in determining the liability's fair value, the effect of third-party credit enhancements should be excluded if the credit enhancement is accounted for separately from the liability. [IFRS 13 para 44].

5.68 The reason for excluding a third-party credit enhancement is that the liability issuer does not get the benefit of the third-party credit enhancement whereas the asset holder does. The issuer has to pay the entire liability unless it goes bankrupt, irrespective of the third-party credit enhancement. So, in certain circumstances, the asset holder is allowed to consider the enhancement in its fair value, whereas the liability issuer is not. However, IFRS 13 does not specify whether the credit enhancement should or should not be accounted for separately from the liability. That is determined based on other IFRSs (see para 5.128 and para 39(b) of IFRS 13).

Shareholders' equity

5.69 The principles in IFRS 13 also apply to shareholders' equity. An example of this is when equity interests are issued as consideration in a business combination. The valuation model of instruments classified within shareholders' equity became consistent with the requirements for measuring the fair value of liabilities. The guidance specified that an entity should measure the fair value of its own equity instruments from the perspective of a market participant who holds the instrument as an asset. Similar to the application to liabilities, when equity instruments are not held by other parties as assets, an entity should use a valuation technique using market participant assumptions.

Valuation techniques

5.70 IFRS 13 describes three main approaches to measuring the fair value of assets and liabilities: the market approach, the income approach, and the cost approach. These approaches apply to both financial instruments and non-financial items.

General principles for selecting valuation techniques

5.71 The valuation technique selected should:

■ Be appropriate in the circumstances. [IFRS 13 paras 61, 62].

■ Be a technique for which sufficient data is available. [IFRS 13 para 61].

■ Maximise the use of relevant observable inputs and minimise the use of unobservable inputs. [IFRS 13 para 61].

■ Be consistent with the objective of estimating the price at which an orderly transaction to sell the asset or to transfer the liability would take place between market participants at the measurement date under current market conditions. [IFRS 13 para 62].

5.72 Examples of markets in which inputs might be observable include exchange markets, dealer markets, brokered markets and principal-to-principal markets, which are explained in paragraph B34 of IFRS 13:

"(a) Exchange markets – *In an exchange market, closing prices are both readily available and generally representative of fair value. An example of such a market is the London Stock Exchange.*

(b) Dealer markets – *In a dealer market, dealers stand ready to trade (either buy or sell for their own account), thereby providing liquidity by using their capital to hold an inventory of the items for which they make a market. Typically bid and ask prices (representing the price at which the dealer is willing to buy and the price at which the dealer is willing to sell, respectively) are more readily available than closing prices. Over-the-counter markets (for which prices are publicly reported) are dealer markets. Dealer markets also exist for some other assets and liabilities, including some financial instruments, commodities and physical assets (for example, used equipment).*

(c) Brokered markets – *In a brokered market, brokers attempt to match buyers with sellers but do not stand ready to trade for their own account. In other words, brokers do not use their own capital to hold an inventory of the items for which they make a market. The broker knows the prices bid and asked by the respective parties, but each party is typically unaware of another party's price requirements. Prices of completed transactions are sometimes available. Brokered markets include electronic communication networks, in which buy and*

sell orders are matched, and commercial and residential real estate markets.

(d) Principal-to-principal markets – *In a principal-to-principal market, transactions, both originations and resales, are negotiated independently with no intermediary. Little information about those transactions may be made available publicly.*"

5.73 It may be appropriate to use multiple valuation techniques; in which case, the reasonableness of the results of the various measurement techniques will have to be evaluated, and a point within that range will have to be selected that is most representative of fair value in the circumstances. [IFRS 13 para 63].

5.74 Valuation techniques should be applied consistently, unless alternative techniques provide an equally or more representative indication of fair value. This applies as well to the weights given to multiple valuation techniques when multiple techniques are used. Any changes are regarded as changes in accounting estimates, although the IAS 8 disclosures are not required. [IFRS 13 para 66]. The following events may necessitate changes in techniques/weights:

■ new markets develop;

■ new information becomes available;

■ information previously used is no longer available;

■ valuation techniques improve; or

■ market conditions change.

[IFRS 13 para 65].

Types of valuation technique

5.75 The three types of valuation technique described in the standard are discussed below:

Market approach

5.76 IFRS 13 defines this as "*A valuation technique that uses prices and other relevant information generated by market transactions involving identical or comparable (i.e. similar) assets, liabilities, or a group of assets and liabilities, such as a business*". [IFRS 13 App A]. Examples include:

■ Valuation techniques using market multiples derived from comparable transactions. [IFRS 13 App B para B6].

■ Matrix pricing – a mathematical technique used principally to value some types of financial instruments, such as debt securities, without relying exclusively on quoted prices for the specific securities, but rather relying on the securities' relationship to other benchmark quoted securities. [IFRS 13 App B para B7].

5.77 The market approach may be appropriate for certain assets. For example, some unquoted equity securities may be fair valued using earnings per share multiples derived from comparable quoted equity securities and land and buildings may be fair valued by references to prices achieved in sales of comparable properties.

Income approach

5.78 IFRS 13 defines this as "*Valuation techniques that convert future amounts (e.g., cash flows or income and expenses) to a single current (i.e. discounted) amount. The fair value measurement is determined on the basis of the value indicated by current market expectations about those future amounts*". [IFRS 13 App A]. Examples include:

■ Present value techniques (see paras 5.80 to 5.83 below).

■ Multi-period excess earnings method (MEEM).

■ Option pricing models. These include the Black-Scholes-Merton formula and binomial models that incorporate present value techniques and reflect both the time value and an option's intrinsic value.

Cost approach

5.79 IFRS 13 defines this as "*A valuation technique that reflects the amount that would be required currently to replace the service capacity of an asset (often referred to as current replacement cost)*". [IFRS 13 App A]. This assumes that fair value is the cost to acquire or construct a substitute asset of comparable utility, adjusted for obsolescence (including physical deterioration, functional (technological) obsolescence and economic (external) obsolescence). [IFRS 13 App B para B9]. The following flow diagram illustrates the application of the cost approach:

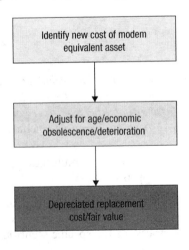

5.79.1 In our view, the cost approach should only be used when the other approaches are not available or produce unreasonable results.

Application of present value techniques

5.80 As noted above, present value techniques are a type of income approach. IFRS 13 neither prescribes the use of one single specific present value technique nor limits the use of present value techniques to measure fair value, instead indicating that a reporting entity should use the appropriate technique based on facts and circumstances specific to the asset or liability being measured and the market in which they are transacted. However, paragraph B12 of IFRS 13 discusses the use of present value techniques in determining fair value.

5.81 In accordance with paragraph B13 of IFRS 13, the following key elements from the perspective of market participants should be captured in developing a fair value measurement using present value:

- an estimate of future cash flows;

- expectations about possible variations in the amount and timing of cash flows;

- the time value of money based on the risk-free rate for monetary assets with maturity dates or durations that coincide with the period covered by the cash flows and pose neither uncertainty in timing nor risk of default to the holder (that is, a 'risk-free' interest rate);

- a risk premium due to uncertainty and illiquidity;

- other factors that market participants would take into account in the circumstances; and

- for a liability, the risk of non-performance, including the reporting entity's own credit risk.

5.82 Paragraph B14 of IFRS 13 goes on to discuss general principles that govern the application of all present value techniques.

- Cash flows and discount rates should reflect assumptions that market participants would use when pricing the asset or liability.

- Cash flows and discount rates should take into account only the factors attributable to the asset or liability being measured.

- To avoid double counting or omitting the effects of risk factors, discount rates should reflect assumptions that are consistent with those inherent in the cash flows. For example, a discount rate that reflects the uncertainty in expectations about future defaults is appropriate if using contractual cash flows of a loan (that is, a discount rate adjustment technique). That same rate should not be used if using expected (that is, probability-weighted) cash flows (that is, an expected present value technique) because the expected cash flows already reflect assumptions about the uncertainty in future defaults; instead, a discount rate that is commensurate with the risk inherent in the expected cash flows should be used.

- Assumptions about cash flows and discount rates should be internally consistent. For example, nominal cash flows, which include the effect of inflation, should be discounted at a rate that includes the effect of inflation. The nominal risk-free interest rate includes the effect of inflation. Real cash flows, which exclude the effect of inflation, should be discounted at a rate that excludes the effect of inflation. Similarly, after-tax cash flows should be discounted using an after-tax discount rate. Pre-tax cash flows should be discounted at a rate consistent with those cash flows.

- Discount rates should be consistent with the underlying economic factors of the currency in which the cash flows are denominated.

5.83 Projected cash flows are subject to specific (or unsystematic) risk and to systematic risk. Specific risk is risk that only a single entity or industry is subject to and can usually be eliminated, or at least substantially reduced, by diversification. Systematic risk is risk arising from general market, economic or political risk and cannot be reduced by diversification. In practice, adjusting the cash flows to reflect systematic risk is often difficult. In most instances, therefore, the discount rate that is applied to cash flows would incorporate systematic, or non-diversifiable risk, which would often be represented by a weighted-average cost of capital that would be required by a marketplace participant.

Fair value at initial recognition

5.84 Transaction prices may not equal fair value. Fair value under IFRS 13 is based on an exit price concept. Transaction prices are not always representative of exit prices, although in many cases they are. [IFRS 13 paras 57, 58].

5.85 In determining whether a transaction price is representative of fair value, management should consider factors specific to the transaction and the asset or liability, as well as whether any of the conditions below are applicable. [IFRS 13 para 59]. The transaction price might not represent fair value on initial recognition if any of the following conditions exist:

- The transaction is between related parties. However, such a transaction may be considered in a fair value measurement if there is evidence that it was conducted at market terms.

- The transaction takes place under duress or the price is forced upon the seller (for example, due to financial difficulty).

- The unit of account in the transaction is different from the asset or liability to be fair valued. For example:

    - the asset or liability being fair valued is only one of the elements in the transaction (for example, in a business combination);

- the transaction includes unstated rights and privileges (for example, financial guarantees) that are measured separately in accordance with another IFRS; or

- the transaction price includes transaction costs.

- The transaction does not take place in the principal or most advantageous market – for example, a retail market price would not represent fair value for a dealer if the dealer's principal or most advantageous market is the dealer market.

[IFRS 13 App B para B4].

5.86 One common criticism of IAS 39 is its treatment of the difference between fair value and transaction price upon initial recognition, commonly referred to as 'day-one profit or loss'. IAS 39 prohibits immediate recognition of day-one profit or loss in the income statement unless specific criteria are met. Unfortunately, IFRS 13 does not address this criticism. IFRS 13 states that "*If another IFRS requires or permits an entity to measure an asset or a liability initially at fair value and the transaction price differs from fair value, the entity shall recognise the resulting gain or loss in profit or loss unless that IFRS specifies otherwise*". Entities will, therefore, still be prohibited from recognising a day-one profit or loss under IAS 39 (or IFRS 9) unless the fair value of that instrument is evidenced by comparison with other observable current market transactions in the same instrument (that is, without modification or repackaging) or based on a valuation technique whose variables include only data from observable markets. [IAS 39 para AG76]. See also paragraph 5.159. This remains a key difference with US GAAP.

Valuation premiums and discounts

5.87 Valuation adjustments such as premiums and discounts may be necessary to reflect certain characteristics of the asset or liability being fair valued. Examples are control premiums or non-controlling interest discounts. There are two caveats to consider when including such adjustments:

- adjustments are not permitted for premiums or discounts that are inconsistent with the unit of account for the asset or liability being measured; and

- adjustments are permitted only when they reflect a characteristic of an asset or liability (for example, control premium). Adjustments are not permitted for premiums or discounts that reflect size as a characteristic of the entity's holding. Specifically, IFRS 13 prohibits adjustments for blockage factors that adjust the quoted price of an asset or a liability because the market's normal daily trading volume is not sufficient to absorb the quantity held by an entity. See also 'unit of account' above.

In all cases, if there is a quoted price in an active market (that is, a level 1 input) for an asset or a liability, management should use that price without adjustment when measuring fair value.

[IFRS 13 para 69].

Example 1 – Adjustments for size of holding

An entity has a holding of a share that is traded in an active market. If the entity sells its entire holding in a single transaction, the market's normal daily trading volume would not be sufficient to absorb the quantity held. That single transaction would affect the quoted price and result in the entity receiving a lower selling price. Should the entity adjust the fair value of that share to reflect this?

No. The unit of account based on other IFRS, is a single share based, not the overall holding. Therefore, the fair value of the asset or liability should be measured as the product of the quoted price for a single share and the quantity held by the entity. The same applies to a liability, or a position comprising a large number of identical assets or liabilities, such as a holding of financial instruments (unless the portfolio exception as described above in para 5.15 is applied to a net open position). [IFRS 13 para 80]. The same answer holds regardless of whether or not the security trades in an active market.

The flow chart below illustrates the above requirements.

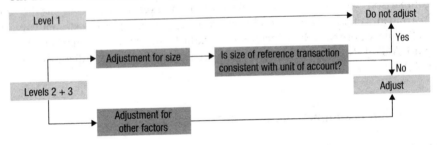

Example 2 – Adjustment for size of holding and other factors

Investor X holds a 10% investment in private entity Y. The investment is classified as an available-for-sale investment under IAS 39. Investor X fair values private company Y using a market multiple of comparable listed entity Z. Should this valuation be adjusted for:

■ Illiquidity of private entity Y's shares, as compared to listed entity Z?

■ The lower price investor X is likely get if investor X sold the entire 10% investment in a single transaction rather than if it sold its shares in entity Y in smaller batches?

Investor X should adjust for the private entity Y's illiquidity because this is a characteristic of private entity Y's shares. Private entity Y's shares are not listed; entity Z's shares are listed.

However, investor X should not adjust the valuation to reflect the likely outcome that if it sold all of its investment in private entity Y in a single transaction, it might receive a lower price. This is because the unit of account in IAS 39 is a single instrument. The fair value in IAS 39, therefore, reflects the fair value of each financial instrument in private entity Y.

Example 3 – Measuring the value of a listed associate

Entity C holds 25% of the equity of listed entity D which it treats as an associate under IAS 28 and equity accounts for the investment. In testing the investment for impairment, entity C wishes to use discounted cash flow methodology. Is this appropriate?

The investor may use discounted cash flow methodology to measure value in use under IAS 36 but must use the listed price multiplied by the number of shares held to measure fair value less costs to sell.

Example 4 – The unit of account based on other IFRSs

Entity A holds 100% of the shares in an unlisted entity B. Unlisted entity B is a cash-generating unit that is being tested for impairment under IAS 36, using the fair value less costs to sell (FVLCTS) method. Entity A fair values entity B using a market multiple of a comparable listed entity.

If entity A assumes the sale of unlisted entity B's shares in a single transaction, it is likely to receive a different price due to the size of the sale compared to selling the shares in smaller portions (say in units of 1,000 each time). For the purposes of determining FVLCTS, should entity A assume the sale of unlisted entity B's shares in a single or multiple transactions?

As the unit of account being fair valued is the cash-generating unit under IAS 36, the fair value that should be considered is the aggregate fair value of the CGU. Entity A should, therefore, assume the sale of unlisted entity B's shares in aggregate.

Example 5 – Application of premiums and discounts

Entity C holds 100% of the shares in entity D, which is a cash-generating unit being tested for impairment under IAS 36, using fair value less costs to sell. Entity C fair values entity D using a discounted cash flow method based on entity D's underlying cash inflows (for example, from sales) and outflows (for example, from expenses), and the industry cost of capital. Should entity C adjust the output of the discounted cash flow valuation model for a control premium?

Entity C should not make this adjustment. The control premium has already been imputed by the use of the business cash flows discounted at the weighted average cost of capital. This method of valuation implicitly assumes control. No further adjustment for control premium is required.

Fair value hierarchy

5.88 To increase consistency and comparability in fair value measurements and disclosures, IFRS 13 contains a fair value hierarchy equivalent to the hierarchy established under IFRS 7. The highest priority is given to level 1 inputs; level 3 inputs get the lowest priority. [IFRS 13 para 72].

5.89 A fair value measurement is categorised in its entirety in the same level of the fair value hierarchy as the lowest-level input that is significant to the entire measurement. An input is significant if that input can result in a significantly different fair value measurement. IFRS 13 requires consideration of factors specific to the asset or liability. [IFRS 13 para 73].

5.90 Determining the significance of a particular input to a fair value measurement is a matter of judgement. A starting point is to have a basic understanding of all of the inputs that factor into the fair value measurement, the relative significance of each of the inputs, and whether those inputs are externally verifiable or are derived through internal estimates.

5.91 There are no bright lines for determining significance; two different entities may reach different conclusions from the same fact pattern. We believe management should consider the impact of lower-level inputs on the fair value measurement at the time the measurement is made, as well as their potential impact on future movements in the fair value.

5.92 In assessing the significance of unobservable inputs to an asset or liability's fair value, management should:

- consider the sensitivity of the asset or liability's overall value to changes in the data; and

- re-assess the likelihood of variability in the data over the life of the asset or liability.

Additionally, we believe that the assessment should be performed on both an individual and an aggregate basis when more than one item of unobservable data (or more than one parameter) is used to measure the fair value of an asset or liability. This assessment will depend on the facts and circumstances specific to a given asset or liability and will require significant professional judgement.

5.93 Given the level of judgement that may be involved, management should document its rationale when it is not straightforward to determine the classification of inputs in the fair value hierarchy. In addition, it should develop and consistently apply a policy for determining significance.

5.94 Things that are not part of fair value, but which other literature requires management to include in measurement, are not considered when determining the hierarchical level – for example, costs to sell in a fair value less cost to sell valuation. [IFRS 13 para 73].

5.95 The fair value hierarchy ranks fair value measurements based on the type of inputs; it does not depend on the type of valuation techniques used. [IFRS 13 para 74].

5.96 Level 1 inputs are quoted prices (unadjusted) in active markets for identical assets or liabilities that the entity can access at the measurement date. [IFRS 13 para 76]. IFRS 13 highlights the following points in relation to level 1 inputs:

- The principal (or if unavailable, the most advantageous) market should be used. [IFRS 13 para 78].

- The transacting entity should be able to transact in the chosen market at measurement date. [IFRS 13 para 78].

- The quoted price should be used without adjustment whenever available, except in the following situations.

  - IFRS 13 provides a practical expedient for the fair value measurement of a large number of similar assets or liabilities (for example, debt securities) for which quoted prices in active markets are available but not readily accessible. A reporting entity may, therefore, measure fair value by using an alternative pricing method (for example, matrix pricing) instead of obtaining quoted prices for each individual security. If an alternative pricing method is used as a practical expedient, the resulting fair value measurement will be level 2.

  - In some situations, significant events (for example, principal-to-principal transactions, brokered trades and announcements) may occur after the close of a market but before the measurement date. When that is the case, a quoted market price may not be representative of fair value on the measurement date. Management should establish and consistently apply a policy for identifying and incorporating events that may affect fair value measurements. In addition, if management adjusts the quoted price, the resulting measurement will not be classified in level 1, but will be a lower-level measurement.

  - The measurement date, as specified in each accounting standard requiring or permitting fair value measurements, is the 'effective' valuation date. A valuation should, therefore, reflect only facts and circumstances available to market participants that exist on the specified measurement date (these include events occurring before the measurement date or that were reasonably foreseeable on that date) so that the valuation is appropriate for a transaction that would occur on that date. Changes in fair value after the measurement date are subsequent events and do not adjust the fair value but are only disclosed.

  - Consider an entity that is measuring the fair value of its quoted liability or equity instrument using the quoted price for the asset. [IFRS 13 para 79]. The quoted price may reflect factors that do not apply to the liability or equity instrument (see para 5.53 above). In such cases, the fair value should be adjusted for these factors, and the resulting fair value measurement would be classified in a lower level.

5.97   In certain situations, management may only have access to a single price source or quote. Apart from where the source is transactions on an exchange, a single source would not generally be a level 1 input, as a single market-maker would almost by definition suggest an inactive market. However, in some rare cases, a single market-maker dominates the market for a particular security such that trading in that security is active but all the activity flows through that market-maker. In those limited circumstances, a level 1 determination may be supported if the broker is standing ready to transact at that price.

5.98   In all cases other than the above fact pattern, management should determine if the single broker quote represents a level 2 or level 3 input. Key considerations in making this assessment include the following:

- Level 2: a single broker quote may be supported as a level 2 input if there is observable market information on comparables to support the single broker quote, and/or the broker stood willing to transact in the security at that price.

- Level 3: a single broker quotation is frequently a level 3 input if there are no comparables and the quote was provided as an indicative value with no commitment to actually transact at that price (for example, information obtained under an agreement to provide administrative pricing support to a fund for a security purchased from that broker). Such information will require additional follow-up or due diligence procedures when used in financial reporting.

Management should specifically consider the underlying facts associated with each valuation input in assessing the appropriate classification in the fair value hierarchy.

5.99   Level 2 inputs are inputs other than quoted prices included within level 1 that are observable for the asset or liability, either directly or indirectly. [IFRS 13 para 81]. Level 2 inputs include:

- Quoted prices for similar assets or liabilities in active markets.

- Quoted prices for identical or similar assets or liabilities in markets that are not active.

- Inputs other than quoted prices that are observable for the asset or liability, for example:

  - Interest rates and yield curves observable at commonly quoted intervals.

  - Implied volatilities.

  - Market-corroborated inputs.

[IFRS 13 para 82].

5.100   Paragraph B35 of IFRS 13 provides the following examples of level 2 inputs:

"*(a)*   Receive-fixed, pay-variable interest rate swap based on the London Interbank Offered Rate (LIBOR) swap rate. *A level 2 input would be the LIBOR swap rate if that rate is observable at commonly quoted intervals for substantially the full term of the swap.*

(b)   Receive-fixed, pay-variable interest rate swap based on a yield curve denominated in a foreign currency. *A level 2 input would be the swap rate based on a yield curve denominated in a foreign currency that is observable at commonly quoted intervals for substantially the full term of the swap. That would be the case if the term of the swap is 10 years and that rate is observable at commonly quoted intervals for 9 years, provided that any reasonable extrapolation of the yield curve for year 10 would not be significant to the fair value measurement of the swap in its entirety*

(c)   Receive-fixed, pay-variable interest rate swap based on a specific bank's prime rate. *A level 2 input would be the bank's prime rate derived through extrapolation if the extrapolated values are corroborated by observable market data, for example, by correlation with an interest rate that is observable over substantially the full term of the swap.*

(d)   Three-year option on exchange-traded shares. *A level 2 input would be the implied volatility for the shares derived through extrapolation to year 3 if both of the following conditions exist:*

   (i)   *Prices for one-year and two-year options on the shares are observable.*

   (ii)   *The extrapolated implied volatility of a three-year option is corroborated by observable market data for substantially the full term of the option.*

   In that case the implied volatility could be derived by extrapolating from the implied volatility of the one-year and two-year options on the shares and corroborated by the implied volatility for three-year options on comparable entities' shares, provided that correlation with the one-year and two-year implied volatilities is established.

(e)   Licensing arrangement. *For a licensing arrangement that is acquired in a business combination and was recently negotiated with an unrelated party by the acquired entity (the party to the licensing arrangement), a level 2 input would be the royalty rate in the contract with the unrelated party at inception of the arrangement.*

(f)   Finished goods inventory at a retail outlet. *For finished goods inventory that is acquired in a business combination, a level 2 input would be either a price to customers in a retail market or a price to retailers in a wholesale market, adjusted for differences between the condition and location of the inventory item and the comparable (i.e. similar) inventory items so that the fair value measurement reflects*

the price that would be received in a transaction to sell the inventory to another retailer that would complete the requisite selling efforts. Conceptually, the fair value measurement will be the same, whether adjustments are made to a retail price (downward) or to a wholesale price (upward). Generally, the price that requires the least amount of subjective adjustments should be used for the fair value measurement.

(g) Building held and used. *A level 2 input would be the price per square metre for the building (a valuation multiple) derived from observable market data, e.g. multiples derived from prices in observed transactions involving comparable (i.e. similar) buildings in similar locations.*

(h) Cash-generating unit. *A level 2 input would be a valuation multiple (e.g. a multiple of earnings or revenue or a similar performance measure) derived from observable market data, e.g. multiples derived from prices in observed transactions involving comparable (i.e. similar) businesses, taking into account operational, market, financial and non-financial factors.*"

5.101   IFRS 13 highlights the following points in relation to level 2 inputs:

- If the asset or liability has a specified (contractual) term, a level 2 input must be observable for substantially the full term of the asset or liability. [IFRS 13 para 82].

- Adjustments to level 2 inputs should include factors such as the condition and/or location of the asset or the liability on the measurement date and the volume and level of activity in the markets within which the inputs are observed. Adjustments are also required to the extent that inputs do not fully relate to items that are comparable to the asset or liability (including those factors in para 5.142). An adjustment that is significant to the fair value measurement may place the measurement in level 3 in the fair value hierarchy.

5.102   Certain inputs derived through extrapolation or interpolation may be corroborated by observable market data (for example, extrapolating observable one- and five-year interest rate yields to derive three-year yields) and would be considered a level 2 input.

Example 1 – Corroboration by market data

Assume that the Argentinean interest rate yield curve is correlated to the Chilean interest rate yield curve. Also assume that the Argentinean yield curve is observable for three years, but the Chilean yield curve is observable for only two years. Management could determine the third year of the Chilean yield curve based on the extrapolation of the Chilean yield curve from years one and two and the correlation of the third-year Argentinean yield curve. In this example, the Chilean yield for year three would be considered a level 2 input. However, extrapolating short-term data to measure longer term inputs may require assumptions and judgements that cannot be corroborated by observable market data and, therefore, may represent a level 3 input.

Example 2 – Corroboration by market data

How would the fair value measurement of a foreign exchange contract be classified in the fair value hierarchy if it is based on interpolated information?

Assume that the entity prepares its fair value measurement based on interpolation of observable market data. Key considerations in determining the appropriate classification within the fair value hierarchy include the following:

- A spot foreign exchange (FX) rate that can be observed through market data as being active is a level 1 input.

- A fair value measurement that can be interpolated using externally quoted sources would generally be a level 2 valuation. For example, assume that there are forward prices available for 30- and 60-day FX contracts that qualify as level 1 inputs and the entity is measuring a 50-day contract. If the price can be derived through simple interpolation, the resulting measurement is a level 2 valuation.

However, if the contract length is three years and prices are only available for the next two years, any extrapolated amount would be considered a level 3 valuation (on the assumption that this is significant to the valuation) if there was no other observable market information to corroborate the pricing inputs in the third year. Unlike the Chilean interest rates in example 1 above, which were corroborated by the Argentinean yield curve, the FX rate for the third year is not corroborated by any observable market information in this case.

5.103 Level 3 inputs are unobservable inputs for the asset or liability. [IFRS 13 para 86].

5.104 Paragraph B36 of appendix B to IFRS 13 provides the following examples of level 3 inputs:

"*(a) Long-dated currency swap. A level 3 input would be an interest rate in a specified currency that is not observable and cannot be corroborated by observable market data at commonly quoted intervals or otherwise for substantially the full term of the currency swap. The interest rates in a currency swap are the swap rates calculated from the respective countries' yield curves.*

(b) Three-year option on exchange-traded shares. A level 3 input would be historical volatility, i.e. the volatility for the shares derived from the shares' historical prices. Historical volatility typically does not represent current market participants' expectations about future volatility, even if it is the only information available to price an option.

(c) Interest rate swap. A level 3 input would be an adjustment to a mid-market consensus (non-binding) price for the swap developed using data that are not directly observable and cannot otherwise be corroborated by observable market data.

(d) *Decommissioning liability assumed in a business combination. A level 3 input would be a current estimate using the entity's own data about the future cash outflows to be paid to fulfil the obligation (including market participants' expectations about the costs of fulfilling the obligation and the compensation that a market participant would require for taking on the obligation to dismantle the asset) if there is no reasonably available information that indicates that market participants would use different assumptions. That level 3 input would be used in a present value technique together with other inputs, for example, a current risk-free interest rate or a credit-adjusted risk-free rate if the effect of the entity's credit standing on the fair value of the liability is reflected in the discount rate rather than in the estimate of future cash outflows.*

(e) *Cash-generating unit. A level 3 input would be a financial forecast (for example, of cash flows or profit or loss) developed using the entity's own data if there is no reasonably available information that indicates that market participants would use different assumptions.*"

5.105   IFRS 13 highlights the following points in relation to level 3 inputs:

■   Used only when observable inputs are not available. [IFRS 13 para 87].

■   A fair value measurement objective is to derive an exit price at the measurement date from the perspective of a market participant that holds the asset or owes the liability. Fair value measurements should, therefore, reflect the assumptions that market participants would use when pricing the asset or liability, including assumptions about risk. [IFRS 13 para 87].

■   Both the risk inherent in a particular valuation technique used to measure fair value (such as a pricing model) and the risk inherent in the inputs to the valuation technique should be considered. [IFRS 13 para 88].

■   Level 3 inputs should be developed using the best information available in the circumstances, which might include an entity's own data. However, the entity's own data should be adjusted if reasonably available information indicates that other market participants would use different data. For example, an entity should not factor in entity-specific synergies that are not available to market participants. An entity need not undertake exhaustive efforts to obtain information about market participant assumptions. [IFRS 13 para 89].

5.106   IFRS 13 permits the use of prices quoted by third parties (for example, pricing services and brokers), subject to the following:

■   The reporting entity should determine that these prices are developed in accordance with IFRS 13 requirements, including those requirements regarding significant decrease in the volume/level of activity. [IFRS 13 App B paras B45, B46].

- Less weight is placed on quotes that do not reflect the result of transactions. [IFRS 13 App B para B46].

- The nature of a quote (for example, whether it is an indicative price or a binding offer) should be considered; more weight is given to binding offers. [IFRS 13 App B para B47].

5.107   Many reporting entities obtain information from pricing services — such as Bloomberg, Interactive Data Corporation, Loan Pricing Corporation, Markit's Totem Service, broker pricing information and similar sources — for use as inputs in their fair value measurements. The information provided by these sources could be any level in the fair value hierarchy, depending on the source of the information for a particular security. Classification within the hierarchy is further discussed as follows:

Level 1 inputs

Generally, for a price or other input to qualify as level 1 in the fair value hierarchy, management should be able to obtain the price from multiple sources. Level 1 inputs relate to items traded on an exchange or an active index/market location.

Level 2 and level 3 inputs

In some cases, reporting entities may rely on pricing services or published prices that represent a consensus reporting of multiple brokers. It may not be clear if the prices provided can be transacted upon. In order to support an assertion that a broker quote or information obtained from a consensus pricing service represents a level 2 input, management should perform due diligence to understand how the price was developed, including understanding the nature and observability of the inputs used to determine that price. Additional corroboration could include:

- discussions with pricing services, dealers or other companies to obtain additional prices of identical or similar assets to corroborate the price;

- back-testing of prices to determine historical accuracy against actual transactions; or

- comparisons to other external or internal valuation model outputs.

The level of due diligence performed is highly dependent on the facts and circumstances, such as the type and complexity of the asset or liability being measured, as well as its observability and liquidity in the marketplace. Generally, the more unique the asset or liability being measured and the less liquid it is, the more due diligence will be necessary to corroborate the price in order to support classification as a level 2 input.

When performing due diligence, management should clearly document the assessment performed in arriving at its conclusions. Without additional supporting information, prices obtained from a single or multiple broker sources or a pricing service are indicative values or proxy quotes; we believe such information generally represents level 3 inputs.

Finally, management must have some higher-level (that is, observable) data to support classification of an input as level 2. A broker quote for which the broker does not stand ready to transact cannot be corroborated with an internal model populated with level 3 information, or with additional indicative broker quotes to support a level 2 classification. However, there may be other instances where pricing information can be corroborated by market evidence, resulting in a level 2 input.

Other considerations

5.108 Ultimately, it is management's responsibility to determine the appropriateness of its fair value measurements and their classification in the fair value hierarchy, including instances where pricing services are used. Therefore, reporting entities that use pricing services will need to understand how the pricing information has been developed and obtain sufficient information to be able to determine where instruments fall within the fair value hierarchy and that it was computed in a manner that represents an exit price.

> **Examples – Determining the hierarchy level for inputs**
>
> A pricing service could provide quoted prices for an actively traded equity security, which would be level 1 inputs if corroborated by the reporting entity. The same pricing service may also provide a corporate bond price based on matrix pricing, which may constitute a level 2 or level 3 input depending on the information used in the model.
>
> In another example, a reporting entity may obtain a price from a broker for a residential mortgage-backed security. The reporting entity may be fully aware of the depth and liquidity of the security's trading in the marketplace based on its historical trading experience. In addition, the pricing methodology for the security may be common and well understood (for example, matrix pricing) and, therefore, less due diligence may be required. However, a similar conclusion may not be appropriate in all instances (for example, a collateralised debt obligation that is not frequently traded and does not have liquidity in the marketplace).

Inactive markets and non-orderly transactions

Measuring fair value when the volume or level of activity has significantly decreased

5.109 The following flow chart highlights the considerations in determining the level of reliance on market prices:

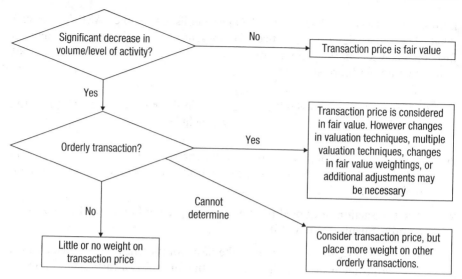

5.110 The following factors should be considered in determining whether there has been a significant decrease in the volume or level of activity (relative to the normal market activity):

■ There are few recent transactions.

■ Price quotations are not developed using current information.

■ Price quotations vary substantially either over time or among market-makers (for example, some brokered markets).

■ Indices that were previously highly correlated with the fair values of the asset or liability are demonstrably uncorrelated with recent indications of fair value for that asset or liability.

■ There is a significant increase in implied liquidity risk premiums, yields or performance indicators (such as delinquency rates or loss severities) for observed transactions or quoted prices when compared with the entity's estimate of expected cash flows, taking into account all available market data about credit and other non-performance risk for the asset or liability.

■ There is a wide bid-ask spread or significant increase in the bid-ask spread.

■ There is a significant decline in the activity of, or there is an absence of, a market for new issues (that is, a primary market) for the asset or liability or similar assets or liabilities.

■ Little information is publicly available (for example, for transactions that take place in a principal-to-principal market).

[IFRS 13 App B para B37].

5.111 Many of the factors noted above that are indicative of significant decreases in market volume and activity levels are also listed in a non-authoritative Expert Advisory Panel paper published by the IASB in October 2008. The paper describes practices for measuring the fair value of financial instruments when markets are no longer active and the fair value disclosures that could be made in those situations.

5.112 If there has been a significant decrease in the volume or level of activity, further analysis is needed. The entity may conclude that:

■ The transaction or quoted price still represents fair value. A decline in volume/activity, on its own, may not indicate that the quoted price does not represent fair value.

■ The transaction or quoted price does not represent fair value. In such cases, an adjustment is required if:

  ■ those prices are still used as the basis for measuring fair value and the adjustment may be significant to the fair value measurement; and

  ■ other circumstances necessitate the adjustment – for example, when a price for a similar asset requires significant adjustment to make it comparable to the asset being measured or when the price is stale.

■ The transaction is not orderly.

[IFRS 13 App B para B38].

5.113 When the decrease in volume/activity necessitates an adjustment, IFRS 13 requires the following:

■ Appropriate risk adjustments should be included for the uncertainty inherent in the cash flows, even when such adjustments are difficult to determine. [IFRS 13 App B para B39].

■ A change in valuation technique or the use of multiple valuation techniques may be appropriate in such situations. When multiple techniques result in a wide range of fair values resulting, further analysis may be required. [IFRS 13 App B para B40].

■ The objective of a fair value measurement remains the same — that is, to determine the price that would be received to sell an asset or paid to transfer a liability in an orderly transaction between market participants at the measurement date under current market conditions. [IFRS 13 App B para B41].

However, IFRS 13 does not specify a methodology for making such adjustments. [IFRS 13 App B para B39].

5.114 An entity's intention to hold an asset or settle a liability is not considered in measuring fair value, as fair value is a market-based measurement, not an entity-specific measurement. [IFRS 13 App B para B42].

Identifying transactions that are not orderly

5.115   It is not appropriate to conclude that all transactions in a market are not orderly simply due to a significant decrease in volume/level of activity. Indications that transactions are not orderly include:

- There was inadequate exposure to the market for a period before the measurement date to allow for marketing activities that are usual and customary for transactions involving such assets or liabilities under current market conditions.

- There was a usual and customary marketing period, but the seller marketed the asset or liability to a single market participant.

- The seller is in or near bankruptcy or receivership (that is, the seller is distressed).

- The seller was required to sell to meet regulatory or legal requirements (that is, the seller was forced).

- The transaction price is an outlier when compared with other recent transactions for the same or a similar asset or liability.

[IFRS 13 App B para B43].

5.116   IFRS 13 does not require exhaustive efforts to determine whether a transaction is orderly, but reasonably available information should not be ignored. If the entity is a party to a transaction, it is presumed to have sufficient information to conclude whether the transaction is orderly. [IFRS 13 App B para B44].

5.117   Little, if any, weight is given to the transaction price for transactions that are not orderly. The amount of weight placed on an orderly transaction price will depend on transaction volume, comparability of the transaction to the asset or liability being measured, proximity of the transaction to the measurement date and other facts and circumstances. If there is insufficient information to conclude whether or not a transaction is orderly, the transaction price is considered but given a lower weighting than prices from other, orderly, transactions. [IFRS 13 App B para B44].

Overall framework

5.118   The overall process for determining fair value under IFRS 13 may be illustrated by the following chart.

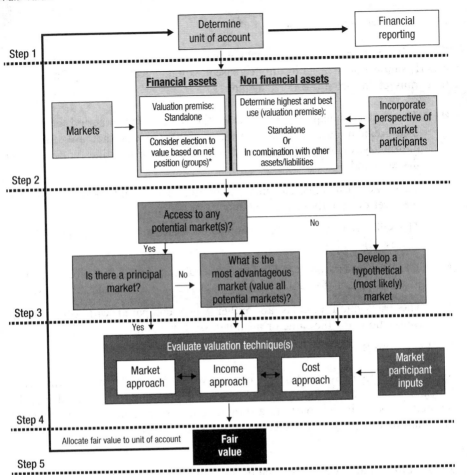

Disclosures

Disclosure objectives

5.119 IFRS 13 requires disclosure of sufficient information to help financial statement users to assess:

■ valuation techniques and inputs used to develop both recurring and non-recurring measurements of assets and liabilities carried at fair value after initial recognition; and

■ the effect on profit or loss or other comprehensive income of recurring level 3 fair value measurements.

[IFRS 13 para 91].

5.120 *Recurring fair value measurements* of assets or liabilities are those that other IFRSs require or permit in the statement of financial position at the end of each reporting period (for example, certain financial instruments in IAS 39, or biological assets in IAS 41).

5.121 *Non-recurring fair value measurements* of assets or liabilities are those that other IFRSs require or permit in the statement of financial position in particular circumstances (for example, when an entity measures an asset held for sale at fair value less costs to sell in accordance with IFRS 5).

5.122 Additional disclosures beyond the minimum requirements may be required to meet these objectives. The reporting entity should also consider:

■ the level of detail necessary;

■ the degree of emphasis on each requirement;

■ the degree of aggregation or disaggregation; and

■ whether or not additional information is needed to evaluate the quantitative disclosures.

[IFRS 13 para 92].

'Classes' of asset and liability

5.123 Similar to IFRS 7, IFRS 13 requires disclosures by 'classes of assets and liabilities'. Grouping assets and liabilities into classes is a judgemental exercise based on:

■ the nature, characteristics and risks of the asset or liability; and

■ the level of the fair value hierarchy within which the fair value measurement is categorised.

[IFRS 13 para 94].

5.124 In addition, IFRS 13 states that:

■ More classes may be required for level 3 fair value measurements as those fair values are exposed to more uncertainty and subjectivity.

■ IFRS 13 classes will often be more disaggregated than balance sheet line items.

■ Sufficient information should be provided to permit reconciliation to balance sheet line items.

■ If another IFRS specifies the classes, those classes may be used if they meet the above requirements (for example, IFRS 7).

[IFRS 13 para 94].

Minimum disclosures

5.125 The following are the minimum disclosures for each class of asset and liability measured at fair value after initial recognition:

(a) for recurring and non-recurring fair value measurements, the fair value measurement at the end of the reporting period (see example 1 below);

(b) for non-recurring fair value measurements, the reasons for the measurement;

(c) for recurring and non-recurring fair value measurements, the level in which they are categorised in the fair value hierarchy;

(d) for assets and liabilities held at the end of the reporting period that are measured at fair value on a recurring basis, the amounts of any transfers between level 1 and level 2, reasons for those transfers and the policy for determining when those transfers occur. Transfers into each level should be disclosed and discussed separately from transfers out of each level. For this disclosure and in ((h) below, the policy for determining timing of transfers between fair value levels should be consistently followed and disclosed. The policy should be consistent between transfers into and out of each level. Such transfers could be deemed to occur on the date of the event or change in circumstances that caused the transfer, the beginning of the reporting period or the end of the reporting period;

(e) for recurring/ non-recurring level 2 and 3 fair value measurements, a description of the valuation techniques and the inputs used;

(f) changes in valuation technique (for example, changing from market to income approach, or using additional valuation techniques) and reasons for the change;

(g) quantitative information about significant unobservable inputs used in level 3 fair values, unless those inputs are not developed by the reporting entity when measuring fair value (for example, when an entity uses unadjusted prices from prior transactions or third-party pricing information) and are not reasonably available to the reporting entity;

(h) for recurring level 3 fair values, a reconciliation from the opening to the closing balances, disclosing separately the following changes during the period:

- total gains/losses in profit or loss, and the line items in which they are recognised;

- total gains/losses in other comprehensive income, and the line items in which they are recognised;

- purchases, sales, issues and settlements (each disclosed separately);

- amounts of any transfers into and out of (inward and outward transfers separately disclosed) level 3, the reasons for those transfers, and the entity's policy for determining when transfers between levels are deemed to have occurred;

(i) for recurring level 3 fair values, amount of unrealised gains/losses in profit or loss, and the line items in which those unrealised gains/ losses are recognised;

(j) for recurring and non-recurring level 3 fair values, a description of valuation processes (including how an entity decides its valuation policies and procedures and analyses periodic changes in fair value measurements);

(k) for recurring level 3 fair values:

- a narrative description of the sensitivity to unobservable inputs that significantly affect the fair value;

- description of interrelationships between unobservable inputs and how these affect the sensitivity;

- if changing unobservable inputs to reasonably possible alternatives would change the fair values of financial assets and financial liabilities significantly, disclose:

    - that fact;

    - the effect of those changes; and

    - how the effect of a change to reflect a reasonably possible alternative assumption was calculated.

    Significance is judged with respect to profit or loss, and total assets or total liabilities, or, when changes in fair value are recognised in other comprehensive income, total equity;

(l) the fact that the highest and best use of a non-financial asset differs from current use, if this is the case, and the reason for such difference;

(m) an accounting policy decision to fair value financial assets and liabilities with offsetting positions on a net basis (see 'Offsetting positions in market or counterparty credit risk' above);

(n) for each class of assets and liabilities not measured at fair value but for which fair value is disclosed, the information required by above paragraphs (c), (e), (f) and (l) only;

(o) when a liability measured at fair value is issued with an inseparable third-party credit enhancement, the existence of that credit enhancement and whether it is reflected in the fair value of the liability; and

(p) the quantitative disclosures required above are presented in a tabular format unless another format is more appropriate.

[IFRS 13 paras 93-99].

5.126 The examples below have been reproduced from the illustrative examples included in the standard.

Example 1 — Fair value measurements at the end of the reporting

(C in millions)	Total	Fair value measurements at the end of the reporting period using			
Description	31 Dec 20X9	Quoted prices in active markets for identical assets (Level 1)	Significant other observable inputs (Level 2)	Significant unobservable inputs (Level 3)	Total gains (losses)
Recurring fair value measurements					
Trading equity securities[a]:					
Real estate industry	93	70	23		
Oil and gas industry	45	45			
Other	15	15			
Total trading equity securities	153	130	23	–	
Other equity securities[a]:					
Financial services industry	150	150			
Healthcare industry	163	110		53	
Energy industry	32			32	
Private equity fund investments[b]	25			25	
Other	15	15			
Total other equity securities	385	275	–	110	
Debt securities:					
Residential mortgage-backed securities	149		24	125	
Commercial mortgage-backed securities	50			50	
Collateralised debt obligations	35			35	
Risk-free government securities	85	85			
Corporate bonds	93	9	84		
Total debt securities	412	94	108	210	
Hedge fund investments:					
Equity long/short	55		55		
Global opportunities	35		35		
High-yield debt securities	90			90	
Total hedge fund investments	180	–	90	90	

	Fair value				
Derivatives:					
Interest rate contracts	57		57		
Foreign exchange contracts	43		43		
Credit contracts	38			38	
Commodity futures contracts	78	78			
Commodity forward contracts	20		20		
Total derivatives	236	78	120	38	
Investment properties:					
Commercial — Asia	31			31	
Commercial — Europe	27			27	
Total investment properties	58			58	
Total recurring fair value measurements	1,424	577	341	506	
Non-recurring fair value measurements					
Assets held for sale[c]	26		26		(15)
Total non-recurring fair value measurements	26		26		(15)

(a) On the basis of its analysis of the nature, characteristics and risks of the securities, the entity has determined that presenting them by industry is appropriate.
(b) On the basis of its analysis of the nature, characteristics and risks of the investments, the entity has determined that presenting them as a single class is appropriate.
(c) In accordance with IFRS 5, assets held for sale with a carrying amount of C35 million were written down to their fair value of C26 million, less costs to sell of C6 million (or C20 million), resulting in a loss of C15 million, which was included in profit or loss for the period.

(Note: A similar table would be presented for liabilities unless another format is deemed more appropriate by the entity.)

Example 2 – Valuation techniques and inputs [IFRS 13 paras IE63-IE64]

An entity might disclose the information in the table below for assets to comply with the requirement above to disclose the significant unobservable inputs used in the fair value measurement:

Quantitative information about fair value measurements using significant unobservable inputs (level 3)

(C in millions)

Description	Fair value at 31 Dec 20X9	Valuation technique(s)	Unobservable input	Range (weighted average)
Other equity securities:				
Healthcare industry	53	Discounted cash flow	Weighted average cost of capital	7%-16% (12.1%)
			Long-term revenue growth rate	2%-5% (4.2%)
			Long-term pre-tax operating margin	3%-20% (10.3%)
			Discount for lack of marketability [a]	5%-20% (17%)
			Control premium[a]	10%-30% (20%)
		Market-comparable companies	EBITDA multiple[b]	10-13 (11.3)
			Revenue multiple[b]	1.5-2.0 (1.7)
			Discount for lack of marketability[a]	5%-20% (17%)
			Control premium [a]	10%-30% (20%)
Energy industry	32	Discounted cash flow	Weighted average cost of capital	8%-12% (11.1%)
			Long-term revenue growth rate	3%-5.5% (4.2%)
			Long-term pre-tax operating margin	7.5%-13% (9.2%)
			Discount for lack of marketability[a]	5%-20% (10%)
			Control premium [a]	10%-20% (12%)
		Market-comparable companies	EBITDA multiple[b]	6.5-12 (9.5)
			Revenue multiple[b]	1.0-3.0 (2.0)
			Discount for lack of marketability[a]	5%-20% (10%)
			Control premium[a]	10%-20% (12%)
Private equity fund investments	25	Net asset value[c]	n/a	n/a

Debt securities:				
Residential mortgage-backed securities	125	Discounted cash flow	Constant pre-payment rate Probability of default Loss severity	3.5%-5.5% (4.5%) 5%-50% (10%) 40%-100% (60%)
Commercial mortgage-backed securities	50	Discounted cash flow	Constant pre-payment rate Probability of default Loss severity	3%-5% (4.1%) 2%-25% (5%) 10%-50% (20%)
Collateralised debt obligations	35	Consensus pricing	Offered quotes Comparability adjustments (%)	20-45 -10% to +15% (+5%)
Hedge fund investments:				
High-yield debt securities	90	Net asset value[c]	n/a	n/a
Derivatives:				
Credit contracts	38	Option model	Annualised volatility of credit[d] Counterparty credit risk[e] Own credit risk[e]	10%-20% 0.5%-3.5% 0.3%-2.0%
Investment properties:				
Commercial – Asia	31	Discounted cash flow	Long-term net operating income Cap rate	18%-32% (20%) 0.08-0.12 (0.10)
		Market-comparable approach	Price per square metre (USD)	$3,000-$7,000 ($4,500)
Commercial – Europe	27	Discounted cash flow	Long-term net operating income margin Cap rate	15%-25% (18%)0.06-0.10 (0.80)
		Market comparable approach	Price per square metre (EUR)	€4,000-€12,000 (€8,500)

(a) Represents amounts used when the entity has determined that market participants would take into account these premiums and discounts when pricing the investments.
(b) Represents amounts used when the entity has determined that market participants would use such multiples when pricing the investments.
(c) The entity has determined that the reported net asset value represents fair value at the end of the reporting period.
(d) Represents the range of the volatility curves used in the valuation analysis that the entity has determined market participants would use when the pricing contracts
(e) Represents the range of the credit default swap spread curves used in the valuation analysis that the entity has determined market participants would use when pricing the contracts.(Note: A similar table would be presented for liabilities unless another format is deemed more appropriate by the entity.)

In addition, an entity should provide additional information that will help users of its financial statements to evaluate the quantitative information disclosed. An entity might disclose some or all the following to comply with paragraph 92 of IFRS 13:

- The nature of the item being measured at fair value, including the characteristics of the item being measured that are taken into account in the determination of relevant inputs. For example, for residential mortgage-backed securities, an entity might disclose the following:

  - the types of underlying loans (for example, prime loans and sub-prime loans);

  - collateral;

  - guarantees or other credit enhancements;

  - seniority level of the tranches of securities;

  - the year of issue;

  - the weighted-average coupon rate of the underlying loans and the securities;

  - the weighted-average maturity of the underlying loans and the securities;

  - the geographical concentration of the underlying loans; and

  - information about the credit ratings of the securities.

- How third-party information such as broker quotes, pricing services, net asset values and relevant market data was taken into account when measuring fair value.

Example 3 – Reconciliation of fair value measurements categorised within level 3 of the fair value hierarchy [IFRS 13 paras IE61-62]

An entity might disclose the following for assets to comply with the above requirement to disclose the reconciliation:

| | Other equity securities | | Private equity fund | Debt securities | | Hedge fund investments | | Derivatives | Investment properties | | |
	Healthcare industry	Energy industry		Residential mortgage backed securities	Commercial mortgage backed securities	Collateralised debt obligations	High-yield debt securities	Credit contracts	Asia	Europe	Total
Opening balance:	49	28	20	105	39	25	145	30	28	26	495
Transfers into level 3				60(a)							60
Transfers out of level 3				(5)(b)							5
				(c)							
Total gains or losses for the period											
– Included in profit or loss			5	(23)	(5)	(7)	7	5	3	1	(14)
– Included in other comprehensive income	3	1									4
Purchases, issues, sales and settlements:											
– Purchases	1	3			16	17		18			55
– Issues											
– Sales				(12)							(74)
– Settlements							(62)		(15)		(15)
Closing balance:	53	32	25	125	50	35	90	38	31	27	506
Change in unrealised gains or losses for the period included in profit or loss for assets held at the end of the reporting period			5	(3)	(5)	(7)	(5)	2	3	1	(9)

(a) Transferred from level 2 to level 3 because of a lack of observable market data, resulting from a decrease in market activities for the securities.
(b) The entity's policy is to recognise transfers into and transfers out of level 3 as of the date of the event or change in circumstances that caused the transfer.
(c) Transferred from level 3 to level 2 because observable market data became available for the securities.(Note: A similar table would be presented for liabilities unless another format is deemed more appropriate by the entity.)

Gains and losses included in profit or loss for the period (above) are presented in financial income and in non-financial income as follows:

(C in millions)	Financial income	Non-financial income
Total gains or losses for the period included in profit or loss	(18)	4
Change in unrealised gains or losses for the period included in the profit or loss for assets held at the end of the reporting period	(13)	4

(Note: A similar table would be presented for liabilities unless another format is deemed more appropriate by the entity.)

Example 4 – Valuation processes [IFRS 13 para IE65]

An entity might disclose the following to comply with the requirement to disclose a description of the valuation processes used by the entity:

- for the group within the entity that decides the entity's valuation policies and procedures:

    - its description;

    - to whom that group reports; and

    - the internal reporting procedures in place (for example, whether and, if so, how pricing, risk management or audit committees discuss and assess the fair value measurements);

- the frequency and methods for calibration, back-testing and other testing procedures of pricing models;

- the process for analysing changes in fair value measurements from period to period;

- how the entity determined that third-party information, such as broker quotes or pricing services, used in the fair value measurement was developed in accordance with the IFRS; and

- the methods used to develop and substantiate the unobservable inputs used in a fair value measurement.

Example 5 – Information about sensitivity to changes in significant unobservable inputs [IFRS 13 para IE66]

An entity might disclose the following about its residential mortgage-backed securities to comply with the above requirement (that is, to provide a narrative description of the sensitivity of the fair value measurement to changes in significant unobservable inputs and a description of any interrelationships between those unobservable inputs):

The significant unobservable inputs used in the fair value measurement of the entity's residential mortgage-backed securities are prepayment rates, probability of default and loss severity in the event of default. Significant increases (decreases) in any of those inputs in isolation would result in a significantly lower (higher) fair value measurement. Generally, a change in the

> assumption used for the probability of default is accompanied by a directionally similar change in the assumption used for the loss severity and a directionally opposite change in the assumption used for prepayment rates.

Applying IFRS 13 to financial instruments

5.127 This section deals with issues arising from the specific application of IFRS 13 to financial assets and liabilities.

Unit of account

5.128 The unit of account is discussed in paragraph 5.15. For financial instruments, the unit of account under IAS 39/IFRS 9 is generally the standalone financial instrument. Consequently, in fair valuing financial instruments under IAS 39/IFRS 9, adjustments for premiums or discounts related to size as a characteristic of the reporting entity's holding are generally disallowed. However, there is an exception for a group of financial assets and financial liabilities with offsetting risks, which is discussed further below.

Determining the principal market and the most advantageous markets

5.129 Many financial instruments may be traded in multiple public markets, for example, securities listed on multiple exchanges. Determining the principal market and/or the most advantageous market may become more judgemental for such instruments. The principles in paragraphs 5.18 to 5.24 apply to all assets and liabilities.

> **Example – Most advantageous market for convertible debt**
>
> An entity holds a convertible debt that is carried at fair value. The convertible debt is not quoted in an active market, but the equity securities of the issuer are. In determining the convertible debt's fair value, it is necessary to consider both the redemption of the debt and the conversion into equity securities of the issuer. If the convertible debt is out of the money, the most advantageous market may be based on redemption of the debt for cash. If the convertible debt is in the money and can be exercised, the most advantageous market may be to assume conversion and sale of the underlying shares. However, an adjustment may be necessary to reflect the probability of exercise. The entity should also consider the convertible debt's value, which may be at a premium to the 'if converted' shares due to the combination of the convertible debt's yield and the option value of the conversion feature.

Liabilities

5.130 Most liabilities occur in the form of financial liabilities. This includes trade and other payables, borrowings, derivative liabilities, financial guarantee contracts, etc. Some liabilities are non-financial, for example, decommissioning and restoration liabilities, but this section focuses on financial liabilities. For non-financial liabilities see paragraphs 5.309 to 5.326.

5.131 Under IFRS 13, a liability's fair value is based on the price to transfer the obligation to a market participant at the measurement date, assuming that the liability will live on in its current form. As discussed in paragraphs 5.53 to 5.56, in the absence of an observable market for the transfer of a liability, paragraph 27 of IFRS 13 introduced the concept of considering the value of the corresponding asset held by a market participant when measuring the liability's fair value.

5.132 When valuing a liability by reference to the corresponding asset in its principal or most advantageous market, reporting entities should consider the following:

- Paragraph 45 of IFRS 13 clarifies that there should be no separate inputs or adjustments to existing inputs for restrictions on transfer of liabilities by the issuer of the liability in the measurement of the liability's fair value. This is in contrast to the fair value from the perspective of the asset holder, which must take into account any restriction on transfer of the asset by the asset holder. [IFRS 13 para 11(b)]. The Basis for Conclusions in paragraph BC 100 of IFRS 13 indicates that the Boards had two reasons for this guidance. First, restrictions on the transfer of a liability relate to the performance of the obligation, whereas restrictions on the transfer of an asset relate to marketability. Secondly, nearly all liabilities include a restriction on transfer, whereas most assets do not include a similar restriction. As a result, the effect of a restriction on transfer of a liability would theoretically be the same for all liabilities. This was consistent with prior practice for valuing liabilities based on a hypothetical transfer, but differs from the treatment of assets with restrictions.

- The fair value of the liability may not be the same as the fair value of the corresponding asset when the pricing includes a bid-ask spread. In such cases, the liability should be valued based on the price within the bid-ask spread that is most representative of fair value for the liability, which may not necessarily be the same as the price within the bid-ask spread that is most representative of fair value for the corresponding asset.

Example 1 – Liabilities and credit risk

Entity X and entity Y each enter into a contractual obligation to pay cash (C500) to entity Z in five years. Entity X has an AA credit rating and can borrow at 6%, and entity Y has a BBB credit rating and can borrow at 12%. Entity X will receive about C374 in exchange for its promise (the present value of C500 in five years at 6%). Entity Y will receive about C284 in exchange for its promise (the present value of C500 in five years at 12%). The fair value of the liability to each entity (that is, the proceeds) incorporates that entity's credit standing.

[IFRS 13 para IE32].

Example 2 – Debt obligation with quoted price (a market approach)

On 1 January 20X1 entity B issues at par a C2 million BBB-rated exchange-traded five-year fixed rate debt instrument with an annual 10% coupon. Entity B designated this financial liability as at fair value through profit or loss.

On 31 December 20X1 the instrument is trading as an asset in an active market at C929 per C1,000 of par value after payment of accrued interest. Entity B uses the quoted price of the asset in an active market as its initial input into the fair value measurement of its liability (C929 × (C2 million ÷ C1,000) = C1,858,000).

In determining whether the asset's quoted price in an active market represents the liability's fair value, entity B evaluates whether the asset's quoted price includes the effect of factors not applicable to the fair value measurement of a liability, for example, whether the quoted price of the asset includes the effect of a third-party credit enhancement if that credit enhancement would be separately accounted for from the perspective of the issuer. Entity B determines that no adjustments are required to the asset's quoted price. Accordingly, entity B concludes that the fair value of its debt instrument at 31 December 20X1 is C1,858,000. Entity B categorises and discloses the fair value measurement of its debt instrument within Level 1 of the fair value hierarchy.

[IFRS 13 paras IE40-IE42].

Example 3 – Debt obligation using present value technique

On 1 January 20X1 entity C issues at par in a private placement a C2 million BBB-rated five-year fixed rate debt instrument with an annual 10% coupon. Entity C designated this financial liability as at fair value through profit or loss.

At 31 December 20X1 entity C still carries a BBB credit rating. Market conditions, including available interest rates, credit spreads for a BBB-quality credit rating and liquidity, remain unchanged from the date the debt instrument was issued. However, entity C's credit spread has deteriorated by 50 basis points, because of a change in its risk of non-performance. After taking into account all market conditions, entity C concludes that if it was to issue the instrument at the measurement date, the instrument would bear a rate of interest of 10.5% or entity C would receive less than par in proceeds from the issue of the instrument.

For the purpose of this example, the fair value of entity C's liability is calculated using a present value technique. Entity C concludes that a market participant would use all the following inputs (consistently with paras B12–B30 of IFRS 13) when estimating the price the market participant would expect to receive to assume entity C's obligation:

- the terms of the debt instrument, including all the following:
    - coupon of 10%;
    - principal amount of C2 million; and
    - term of four years.

- the market rate of interest of 10.5% (which includes a change of 50 basis points in the risk of non-performance from the date of issue).

On the basis of its present value technique, entity C concludes that its liability's fair value at 31 December 20X1 is C1,968,641.

Entity C does not include any additional input into its present value technique for risk or profit that a market participant might require for compensation for assuming the liability. Because entity C's obligation is a financial liability, entity C concludes that the interest rate already captures the risk or profit that a market participant would require as compensation for assuming the liability. Furthermore, entity C does not adjust its present value technique for the existence of a restriction preventing it from transferring the liability.

[IFRS 13 paras IE43-IE47].

Transfer price versus settlement price

5.133   IFRS 13 requires liabilities to be fair valued based on transfer price. Fair value measurement based on a transfer price can differ significantly from a valuation based on settlement of a liability with the counterparty.

5.134   The value of a liability measured at fair value is the price that would be paid to transfer the liability to a third party. The amount that would be required to pay a third party (of equivalent credit or non-performance risk) to assume a liability may differ from the amount that a reporting entity would be required to pay its counterparty to extinguish the liability.

5.135   For example, a financial institution transferee may be willing to assume non-demand deposit liabilities for less than the principal amount due to the depositors, because of the relatively low funding cost of such liabilities. However, in other instances, an additional risk premium above the expected payout may be required because of uncertainty about the ultimate amount of the liability (for example, unit-linked liabilities). The risk premium paid to a third party may differ from the settlement amount the direct counterparty would be willing to accept to extinguish the liability. In addition, the party assuming a liability may have to incur certain costs to manage the liability or may require a profit margin.

5.136   These factors may cause the transfer amount to differ from the settlement amount. In measuring liabilities at fair value, the reporting entity must assume that the liability is transferred to a credit equivalent entity and that it continues after the transfer (that is, it is not settled). As such, it follows that the hypothetical transaction used for valuation is based on a transfer to a credit equivalent entity that is in need of funding and willing to take on the terms of the obligation.

Example – Difference between settlement and transfer value

Consider a debt obligation held by a bank with a face value of C100,000 and a market value of C95,000. For the purposes of this example, assume market interest rates are consistent with the amount in the note; however, there is a C5,000 discount due to market concerns about the risk of non-performance.

Settlement value

In the absence of exceptional circumstances, we would expect that the counterparty (counterparty A) would be required to pay the full face value of the note to settle the obligation, as the bank may not be willing to discount the note by the market discount or the credit risk adjustment. Therefore, the settlement value would be equal to the face amount of the note.

Transfer value

In order to calculate the transfer value, counterparty A must construct a hypothetical transaction in which another party (counterparty B), with a similar credit profile, is seeking financing on terms that are substantially the same as the note. Counterparty B could choose to enter into a new note agreement with the bank or receive the existing note from counterparty A in a transfer transaction. In this hypothetical transaction, counterparty B should be indifferent to obtaining financing through a new bank note or assumption of the existing note in transfer for a payment of C95,000. Therefore, the transfer value would be C95,000, C5,000 less than the settlement amount. In order to ensure compliance with IFRS 13, reporting entities must adopt an approach to valuing liabilities that incorporates the transfer concept. There is no exemption from or 'practical expedient' for this requirement. See also paragraphs 5.172 to 5.174.

Fair value of derivative liabilities and credit risk

5.137 The guidance in the previous section relating to fair values of liabilities also applies to derivative liabilities. The entity's own credit risk has to be incorporated into the derivative fair value when the derivative is in a liability position at the reporting date.

5.138 Prior to IFRS 13, IAS 39/IFRS 9 was silent on this issue, and in our view, a policy choice between either of the following approaches would be accepted prior to IFRS 13:

- Fair value based on a presumption that an entity has the practical ability to settle the liability in a way that enables it to realise gains and losses from changes in its own credit risk ('the full own credit risk approach').

- Fair value based on a 'close-out amount' that would be paid to the counterparty. This reflects the amount the entity would pay to settle the liability with the counterparty at the reporting date ('the counterparty close-out approach').

5.139 IFRS 13 prohibits the counterparty close-out approach. This means that under IFRS 13, an entity's own credit risk will impact hedge effectiveness for both cash flow and fair value hedge relationships.

Demand deposit liabilities

5.140 A demand deposit represents a promise by the deposit-taking institution to deliver cash either to the depositor or to third parties designated by the depositor. It imposes a contractual obligation that is a financial liability. A typical example is a current account in a bank. The current account holder can demand settlement at any time and the bank generally has the right to return the depositor's money at any time (even though that right is seldom exercised). It is often argued that the fair value of the financial liabilities with a demand feature is less than the demand amount, because not all depositors withdraw their money at the earliest opportunity. Often there is a core of deposits (withdrawals replaced by new deposits) that is left outstanding for long periods of time.

5.141 In developing IFRS 13, IASB confirmed the previous decision under IAS 39 that the fair value of a financial liability with a demand feature cannot be less than the amount payable on demand, discounted from the first date that the amount could be required to be repaid. [IFRS 13 paras 47, BC101]. In coming to this conclusion, the IASB noted that in many cases, the market price observed for such financial liabilities is the price at which they are originated between the customer and the deposit-taker, that is, the demand amount. Recognising such a financial liability at less than the demand amount will give rise to an immediate gain on the origination of such a deposit, which is inappropriate. [IFRS 13 para BC103].

Using quoted prices and observable inputs

5.142 A quoted asset price may have to be adjusted to derive the fair value of the corresponding liability or equity instrument if there are asset-specific factors that are not applicable to the liability or equity instrument. For example, a quoted debt security may be secured by a third-party guarantee. The quoted price of such a security would reflect the value of the guarantee. The issuer should exclude the effect of the guarantee from the quoted price if the issuer is measuring only the fair value of its own liability and the unit of account excludes the guarantee. [IFRS 13 para 39(b)]. See also paragraph 5.68. If management uses the quoted price for a similar (but not identical) debt or equity instrument to value its own debt, it would have to adjust for any differences in the characteristics between the debt or equity instruments. [IFRS 13 para 39(a)]. The price of the asset used to measure the fair value of the corresponding liability or equity instrument should not reflect the effect of a restriction preventing the asset's sale. [IFRS 13 para 39].

Application to intra-group financial guarantee contracts

5.143 The way in which the various valuation techniques in IFRS 13 can be applied to determine the fair value of an intra-group financial guarantee contract that is not negotiated in an arm's length transaction is considered in the paragraphs that follow.

References to market prices of similar instruments

5.144 An entity may be unable to identify a market price for financial guarantees identical to those that either it or a member of its group has issued. However, it may be possible to identify market prices for similar guarantees, credit default swaps or credit insurance products, the price of which could be adjusted. For example, parent P has guaranteed C100 million of five year debt issued by subsidiary S. It may be possible to identify credit insurance products issued by a bank relating to debt of this amount, maturity and credit quality. However, an adjustment may still be necessary, for example, to reflect liquidity aspects and differences between entity P's credit rating and that of the bank.

Interest rate differentials

5.145 Under this method, the entity calculates the value of the difference between the interest charged on the guaranteed loan and what would have been charged had the loan not been guaranteed. The premise is that the interest that the bank is willing to forego represents a 'price' that it is willing to pay for the guarantee. For example, parent P has guaranteed C100 million of five year debt issued by subsidiary S. Subsidiary S pays interest of X% on the debt. In the absence of the guarantee, the bank would impose an interest rate of Y%. Hence, the fair value of the guarantee represents the difference in the present value of the interest payments over the period of the guarantee.

5.146 This model is simple in principle, but presents practical problems when attempting to measure Y%. It is unlikely that the bank would provide a reliable estimate. Determining Y% requires an estimate of the credit spread (for example, above a base index such as LIBOR) appropriate to subsidiary S in isolation. This may prove difficult as, even without the guarantee, subsidiary S's credit rating will benefit from the entity being a member of parent P's group. Nevertheless, models based on determining a stand-alone credit rating for subsidiary S do exist and these should enable a reliable estimate to be made.

Discounted cash flow analysis (expected value)

5.147 Instead of considering the 'price' that a bank would pay for a guarantee, it might be possible to consider the 'price' that the issuer would demand for accepting the guarantee obligation. This can be estimated using a probability-adjusted discounted cash flow analysis. For example, parent P has guaranteed C100 million of five year debt issued by subsidiary S. The probability of default by subsidiary S is estimated at 0.04% (based on historical default rates amongst companies with the same credit rating as subsidiary S) and the loss in the event of default is estimated at 50% (based on subsidiary S's asset base and other collateral available to the bank). The expected value of the liability (its fair value) would, therefore, be C20,000.

5.148 Similar to the interest rate differential approach described above, this model is simple in principle, but presents practical problems when attempting to estimate the probability of default and the loss given default. Although data on these points is available, they rely on determining subsidiary S's credit rating as in the interest rate differential approach.

Offsetting positions in market or counterparty credit risk

5.149 IFRS 13 allows an exception whereby if an entity manages a group of financial assets and financial liabilities on the basis of its net exposure to either market risks or credit risks (as defined in IFRS 7), it can opt to measure the fair value of that group on the basis of the net position (that is, the net position is the unit of measurement for the purposes of the fair value measurement, rather than the individual financial assets and liabilities). [IFRS 13 para 48].

5.150 Although this exception is new, it was already a common valuation practice prior to IFRS 13. This new exception is not, therefore, expected to have a significant effect on existing valuation practices. This exception is permitted only if an entity:

■ manages the financial asset/liability group based on its net exposure to market/credit risk in accordance with its documented risk management or investment strategy;

■ provides information about the financial asset/liability group on a net basis to key management personnel as defined in IAS 24; and

■ measures those financial assets and liabilities at fair value in the statement of financial position on a recurring basis.

[IFRS 13 para 49].

5.151 Broad risk management strategies such as managing on the basis of value-at-risk may not be sufficient alone for a group to be eligible for the portfolio exception, because value-at-risk does not necessarily represent managing a portfolio to a net position.

5.152 Other conditions on the use of the exception are that it:

■ Applies only to financial assets and liabilities within the scope of IAS 39 and IFRS 9. [IFRS 13 para 52].

■ Applies only to financial assets and liabilities that are exposed to identical, or at least substantially similar, market risks. If the risks are not identical, the differences should be considered when allocating the group's fair value to component assets and liabilities. [IFRS 13 para 54].

■ Applies only to exposures of a similar duration. Paragraph 55 of IFRS 13 provides the following example: *"... an entity that uses a 12-month futures contract against the cash flows associated with 12 months' worth of interest rate risk exposure on a five-year financial instrument within a group made up of only those financial assets and financial liabilities measures the fair value of the exposure to 12-month interest rate risk on a net basis and the remaining interest rate risk exposure (i.e. years 2–5) on a gross basis".*

5.153 If the exception is applied, the fair value of the net position is measured using IFRS 13 principles. For example:

■ For market risks, fair value of the net position is the price within the bid-ask spread that is most representative of fair value in the entity's circumstances. [IFRS 13 para 53].

■ For credit risk, fair value of such a group should consider credit enhancements (such as master netting agreements and collateral requirements) and market participant expectations about the legal enforceability of such enhancements. [IFRS 13 para 56].

5.154 The above exception relates to *measurement* and does not permit net *presentation* of assets and liabilities within the group. Presentation is dealt with in other IFRSs. Where gross presentation is required, the fair value of the group should be allocated to the assets and liabilities within the group on a reasonable and consistent basis (for example, using the relative fair value approach). [IFRS 13 para 50].

5.155 The use of the exception, along with any policies for allocating bid-ask and credit adjustments, is regarded as an accounting policy decision that should be applied consistently from period to period for a given portfolio. [IFRS 13 para 51].

5.156 If an entity has a portfolio of financial assets and liabilities that qualify for the exception for the purposes of applying IFRS 13 (and only for the purpose of IFRS 13), the unit of measurement is the portfolio — that is, the net open risk or credit risk position. The portfolio, or net open position, becomes the asset or liability on which a reporting entity determines what a market participant would pay or expect to pay for it.

Example 1 – Applying the offsetting exception to equity securities

Entity X owns 50,000 shares of entity Y, and has entered into a forward contract to sell 25,000 of these shares 3 months later. Do the shares and forward contract qualify for the offsetting exception if the other criteria are met?

Yes, the shares and forward contract qualify for the offsetting exception as both relate to substantially the same risk. However, there could be an element of interest rate risk associated with the forward contract's fair value, arising from the fact that it can only be exercised 3 months later, which does not relate to the shares' fair value. This risk has to be taken into account in the fair value measurement of the shares and forward within the group. [IFRS 13 para 54].

Example 2 – Applying the offsetting exception to interest rate swaps

Entity B has $500m in 10 year pay 3 month LIBOR, receive fixed rate interest rate swaps (liability position) and $200m in 10 year receive 3 month LIBOR, pay fixed rate interest rate swaps (asset position). Can entity B elect the offsetting exception and adjust the bid-ask spread of the $500 million short position and the $200 million long position to a new bid-ask spread for the net short $300 million position based upon how market participants would price the net risk exposure at the measurement date?

Yes. These can qualify provided that the other criteria highlighted above are met.

Example 3 – Applying the offsetting exception to interest rate swaps with different maturities

Assume the same facts as above, except that the long position has a term to maturity of 12 years instead of 10 years. Can the interest rate swaps still qualify for the offsetting exception?

Provided that the other criteria are met, the offsetting criteria can be applied to the interest rate risks on the first 10 years. For the last 2 years, the interest rate risk exposure should be measured on a gross basis. [IFRS 13 para 55].

Fair value at initial recognition

5.157   Certain accounting standards require or permit an asset or a liability to be initially recognised at fair value. Paragraph 58 of IFRS 13 states that in many cases the transaction price equals fair value, such as when on the transaction date the transaction to buy an asset takes place in the market in which the asset would be sold. In determining whether a transaction price represents the fair value at initial recognition, a reporting entity should take into account factors specific to the transaction and to the asset or the liability. As discussed in paragraph B4 of IFRS 13, a transaction price may not represent the fair value of an asset or a liability at initial recognition if any of the following conditions exist:

■   the transaction is between related parties, although the price in a related party transaction may be used as an input into a fair value measurement if the reporting entity has evidence that the transaction was entered into at market terms;

■   the transaction takes place under duress or the seller is forced to accept the transaction price because of some urgency;

■   the unit of account represented by the transaction price is different from the unit of account for the asset or liability measured at fair value (for example, if the asset or liability is only one element in the transaction, such as in a business combination, if the transaction includes unstated rights and privileges that are measured separately, or if the transaction price includes transaction costs); or

■   the market in which the transaction takes place is different from the principal (or most advantageous) market (for example, a wholesale market versus a retail market).

5.158 For financial instruments, IAS 39/IFRS 9 indicates that when the transaction price differs from fair value, initial recognition of financial instruments should be based on the transaction price, adjusted to defer the difference between the fair value at initial recognition and the transaction price. [IAS 39 para AG76; IFRS 9 App B para B.5.1.2].

5.159 The only exception to the above occurs if the fair value is evidenced by comparison with other observable current market transactions in the same instrument, or it is based on a valuation technique whose variables include only data from observable markets. [IAS 39 para AG 76(a); IFRS 9 App B para B.5.1.2A(a)]. In such situations, the entity is required to use fair value. Consequently, the difference between the estimated fair value using a valuation technique and the transaction price results in the immediate 'day 1' recognition of a gain or loss. The IASB concluded that these conditions were necessary and sufficient to provide reasonable assurance that this fair value was genuine for the purposes of recognising up-front gains or losses.

> **Example – 'Day 1' gain or loss recognition**
>
> Entity A acquires a financial asset for C110, which is not quoted in an active market. The asset's fair value based on the entity's own valuation technique amounted to C115. However, that valuation technique does not solely use observable market data, but relies on some entity-specific unobservable inputs that approximate what market participants would consider in setting a price.
>
> The entity cannot recognise a 'day 1' profit of C5 and record the asset at C115. The use of unobservable entity-specific inputs to calculate a fair value that is different from the transaction price on 'day 1' is so subjective that its reliability is called into question. Hence, recognition of a 'day 1' gain or loss is not appropriate. Accordingly, the entity restricts its valuation to the transaction price and the asset is recorded at C110.

5.160 A question arises as to whether and how any gain or loss not recognised on 'day 1' should be recognised subsequently, or at all. An unrecognised 'day 1' gain or loss should be recognised after initial recognition only to the extent that it arises from a change in a factor (including time) that market participants would take into account when pricing the asset or liability. [IAS 39 para AG 76(b); IFRS 9 App B para B5.1.2A(b)]. It is not clear how the phrase *"a change in a factor (including time) that market participants would take into account when pricing the asset or liability"* should be interpreted. One interpretation is that a gain or loss should remain unrecognised until all market inputs become observable. Another interpretation is that it permits the recognition of a 'day 1' gain or loss in profit or loss on a systematic basis over time, even in the absence of any observable transaction data to support such a treatment. Indeed, during the IAS 39 exposure draft process, some interested parties asked the Board to clarify whether straight-line amortisation was an appropriate method of recognising the difference. The Board decided not to do this. It concluded that although straight-line amortisation may be an appropriate method in some cases, it is not appropriate in others. [IAS 39 para BC222(v)(ii)]. This would appear to suggest that an unrecognised 'day 1' gain or loss could be amortised either on a straight line basis or on another rational basis that reflects the nature of the financial instrument (for example, a non-linear amortisation for some option-based derivatives).

5.161 It should be noted that an unrecognised 'day 1' gain or loss is not separately identified in the balance sheet. However, IFRS 7 requires disclosure of the unrecognised amount, together with the change in the amount previously deferred, and the entity's accounting policy for determining when amounts deferred are recognised in profit or loss.

Fair value hierarchy

5.162 Paragraphs 5.88 to 5.108 discuss the fair value hierarchy. The discussion in this section focuses on certain specific aspects related to financial instruments.

Level 1 inputs

5.163 As discussed in paragraph 5.96, Level 1 inputs are quoted prices (unadjusted) for identical assets or liabilities in active markets. A quoted price for an identical asset or liability in an active market (for example, an equity security traded on the LSE) provides the most reliable fair value measurement and, if available, should be used to measure fair value in that particular market. However, if there are any adjustments to the quoted price, the whole valuation becomes Level 2 or below.

Level 1 inputs – Interaction with exemption on offsetting positions

Example – Valuation of offsetting positions in market risks

Entity A holds 10% of entity B's share capital. The shares are publicly traded in an active market. The currently quoted price is C100. Entity A has also entered into a short position on 5% of entity B's shares using derivatives, and has elected to measure the net exposure of 5% using the offsetting exemption in paragraph 48 of IFRS 13.

Entity A believes that the fair value of its 5% net position in entity B, if sold as a block, is greater than the quoted market price. Several independent estimates indicate that if entity A sold its net position as a block, it would be able to obtain a 5% premium above the quoted price.

Although entity A is valuing a net exposure, the published price quotation in an active market remains the best estimate of fair value. Therefore, entity A should continue to use the published price quotation to measure its net exposure.

Level 2 inputs – Similar but not identical instruments

Example – Valuation based on market price of a similar financial instrument

On 1 January 20X5, entity A acquires a bond issued by entity B through a private placement. The consideration paid and, therefore, the bond's fair value at initial recognition is C1 million. The entity classifies the bond as at fair value through profit or loss. The bond has no observable market price. At 31 December 20X5, the entity is able to identify actively traded corporate bonds that are similar to its bond.

As the bond being fair valued is not identical to the traded bonds, adjustments to the observable price of the traded bonds may be required. As the traded bonds are not identical, the measurement will be Level 2.

In carrying out the evaluation, the major elements of the two bonds that should be compared are as follows:

- The amount and timing of the contractual cash flows, including pre-payment expectations.

- The currency in which the bonds are payable.

- The credit risk rating and the factors on which changes in the credit risk rating are dependent. For example, the fair value of bonds issued by entities with different industry and geographical bases would be expected to respond differently to changes in the market factors.

- Any other term and conditions that could affect the bond's fair value.

Impact of selection of valuation technique on classification within fair value hierarchy

5.164 The IFRS 13 fair value hierarchy prioritises the inputs to the valuation techniques, not the valuation techniques themselves. Selecting the appropriate valuation technique(s) should be based on an assessment of the facts and circumstances specific to the asset or liability being measured. A reporting entity is required to use those valuation techniques that are appropriate in the circumstances and for which inputs are available without undue cost. However, a valuation technique using observable inputs should be prioritised over an approach populated with unobservable inputs.

Impact of valuation models on classification within the fair value hierarchy

5.165 Reporting entities commonly use proprietary models to calculate certain fair value measurements (for example, some long-term derivative contracts, impairments of financial instruments, and illiquid complex financial investments). Models may also be used to perform other fair value measurements, such as those required for asset retirement obligations or impairments of long-lived assets. The level within the fair value hierarchy is determined based on the characteristics of the inputs to the valuation, not on the model's methodology or complexity. However, certain valuations may require the use of complex models to develop forward curves and other inputs; therefore, the models and inputs are frequently inextricably linked.

5.166 The use of a model does not automatically result in a Level 3 fair value measurement. For example, a standard valuation model that uses all observable inputs is likely to result in a measurement that is classified as Level 2. However, to the extent that adjustments or interpolations are made to Level 2 inputs in an otherwise standard model, the measurement may fall into Level 3, depending on whether the adjusted inputs are significant to the measurement. Furthermore, if a reporting entity uses a valuation model that is proprietary and relies on unobservable inputs, the resulting fair value measurement will be categorised as Level 3.

5.167 For example, consider the measurement of a financial asset that is not actively traded. The valuation is performed using a proprietary model incorporating unobservable inputs. However, while the financial asset is not actively traded, assume the broker providing the inputs to be used in the model is standing ready to transact at the quoted price and/or sufficient corroborating data is obtained. Provided the model does not include management assumptions used to make adjustments to the data, it may be reasonable to conclude that the inputs, and thus the measurement, would be classified as a Level 2 fair value measurement. However, if the entity is required to develop a forward price curve, because the duration of the contract exceeds the length of time that observable inputs are available, or is otherwise required to make adjustments to observable data, the valuation is relying on Level 3 inputs and would be classified as a Level 3 fair value measurement if those inputs are significant to the overall fair value measurement.

Classification of funds invested only in actively-traded securities

5.168 Some reporting entities may invest in funds (an alternative investment) that invest primarily in exchange-traded equity securities. Such funds may not necessarily qualify for Level 1 classification in the fair value hierarchy.

5.169 The reporting entity should first determine the appropriate unit of account (that is, what is being measured). As further discussed in paragraph 14 of IFRS 13 the unit of account is determined based on other applicable IFRSs.

5.170 In most instances we would expect the unit of account for interests in mutual or alternative fund investments to be the interest in the investee fund itself, rather than the individual assets and liabilities held by the fund. The categorisation within the fair value hierarchy thus should be assessed based on the investment security in the fund itself and not the securities within the fund. The investment would be classified as Level 1 if the fair value measurement of the interest in the fund (not the underlying investments) was determined using observable inputs that reflect quoted prices (unadjusted) for identical assets in active markets. The assessment should be based on the individual facts and circumstances for each investment and reflect the considerations discussed in the earlier part of this section.

5.171 An investor cannot simply 'look through' an interest in an alternative investment to the underlying assets and liabilities to estimate fair value or to determine the classification of the fair value measurement within the fair value hierarchy in accordance with IFRS 13. Rather, the reporting entity should consider the inputs used to establish the fair value and whether they were observable or unobservable.

Inputs based on bid and ask prices

5.172   Bid and ask prices are common within markets for financial instruments. In these markets, dealers stand ready to buy at the bid price and sell at the ask price. If an input within the fair value measurement is based on bid prices and ask prices, the price within the bid-ask spread that is most representative of fair value in the circumstances is used to measure fair value. [IFRS 13 para 70].

5.173   This is one of the changes introduced by IFRS 13. Previously, IAS 39 required the use of bid prices for asset positions and ask prices for liability positions. These prices can still be used if they are most representative of fair value in the circumstances, but they are no longer required.

5.174   IFRS 13 does not preclude the use of mid-market pricing or other pricing conventions that are used by market participants as a practical expedient for fair value. Many reporting entities currently use or are contemplating the use of the mid-market convention as permitted by IFRS 13 because it simplifies some of the necessary calculations and allows use of the same quotes and prices when calculating the fair value of both assets and liabilities.

Change with respect to the use of the mid-market pricing convention

5.175   IFRS 13 provides the following guidance when considering use of a practical expedient for valuation when using inputs based on bid and ask prices:

> *"If an asset or liability measured at fair value has a bid price and an ask prices (for example, an input from a dealer market), the price within the bid-ask spread that is most representative of fair value in the circumstances shall be used to measure fair value, regardless of where in the fair value hierarchy the input falls (Level 1, 2, or 3). The use of bid prices for long positions (assets), and ask prices for short positions (liabilities) is permitted but not required.*
>
> *IFRS 13 does not preclude the use of mid-market pricing or other pricing conventions that are used by market participants as a practical expedient for fair value measurements within a bid-ask spread."*

[IFRS 13 paras 70, 71].

5.176   Given these alternatives, a reporting entity must adopt and consistently apply an accounting policy for pricing within the bid-ask spread. When developing its policy, a reporting entity will want to consider the practical and other implications of their possible choices.

5.177   The method of estimating fair value should generally be applied consistently.

Appropriateness of mid-market pricing convention

5.178 IFRS 13 indicates that pricing inputs with bid-ask spreads may be Level 1, 2, or 3 inputs; however, it does not specifically address when it is appropriate to use the mid-market practical expedient. Election of the mid-market practical expedient is presumed appropriate for pricing inputs within a bid-ask spread that fall within Level 1 of the fair value hierarchy (that is, unadjusted observable quoted prices for identical assets or liabilities). In these cases, a reporting entity does not need to evaluate mid-market pricing against expectations of where it actually would trade within the bid-ask range.

5.179 The mid-market practical expedient is appropriate for inputs from markets in which stand-ready, dealer-based bid-ask pricing exists. In addition, it may be applicable in other circumstances in which a bid-ask pricing protocol is used by market participants in valuation and measurement. Generally, the less observable the input, the less probable that it is subject to a bid-ask spread and, therefore, the less likely that use of a mid-market convention would be appropriate. For example, it may not be appropriate to apply a mid-market convention when the bid-ask spread is wide, indicating the inclusion of a pricing element other than transaction costs (for example, a liquidity reserve).

Example 1 – Treatment of bid-ask spread on initial recognition

An entity purchases an equity financial asset that it classifies as equity available-for-sale, paying the ask (offer) price of C104 and a brokerage commission of C3. The entity has established that mid-market prices are most representative of fair value. The entity uses the mid price to re-measure the financial asset and to recognise changes in fair value in other comprehensive income.

The following data is relevant:

Reference price	Acquisition	Balance sheet date
Bid price	C100	C110
Mid-market price	C102	C113
Ask or offer price	C104	C116

Financial assets classified as available-for-sale should be initially recognised at fair value, plus transaction costs paid to acquire the asset.

As stated above, the ask price represents the amount at which a dealer is willing to sell and, therefore, the price that the entity would have to pay to acquire the asset. The difference between the mid price that represents the asset's fair value and the ask price is a transaction cost. The commission paid to the broker is also a transaction cost.

Given the asset is classified as available-for-sale (that is, not at fair value through profit or loss) the transaction costs are included in the asset's initial carrying value. Therefore, the asset will be recorded at its fair value of C102 (mid price) plus the mid-ask spread (C2) plus commission (C3), a total of C107. At the balance sheet date, the asset will be valued at mid price (C113) at that date and any difference between this price and the amount recognised initially (C107) will be recorded in other comprehensive income.

Therefore, the appropriate accounting entries on initial recognition and at the balance sheet date are as follows:

	Dr C	Cr C
At acquisition		
Available-for-sale asset (mid price inclusive of transaction costs)	107	
Cash		107
At balance sheet date		
Available-for-sale asset	6	
Gain in other comprehensive income		6

If the asset is a debt instrument, the bid-ask spread, brokerage commission, and any premium, discount or other deferred fees and costs, are subsequently amortised and recognised as part of interest income over the asset's life using the effective interest method.

Example 2 – Treatment of bid-ask spread not included in initial carrying value of a financial asset

The facts are the same as in example 1 above, except that the entity classifies the financial asset as at fair value through profit or loss.

Financial assets classified as at fair value through profit or loss should be recognised initially at fair value. Transaction costs arising on a financial asset classified as at fair value through profit or loss (FVTPL) are immediately recognised in profit or loss and do not form part of the asset's initial carrying value. Hence, the asset is measured on initial recognition using the mid price (C102). At the balance sheet date, the asset will be valued at mid price (C113) at that date and any difference between this price and the amount recognised initially (C11) will be recorded in profit or loss.

The appropriate accounting entries on initial recognition and at the balance sheet date are as follows:

	Dr C	Cr C
At acquisition		
FVTPL asset (mid-price)	102	
Profit/loss (mid-ask spread of C2 + commission of C3)	5	
Cash		107
At balance sheet date		
FVTPL asset	11	
Profit/loss – fair value gain		11

Applying IFRS 13 to business combinations

5.180 IFRS 13 has widespread relevance to business combinations and asset acquisitions under IFRS 3. Fair values are required or permitted for the measurement of:

- consideration, including contingent consideration;

- any previously held equity interest;

- any non-controlling interest remaining after control is acquired (optional); and

- the identifiable assets acquired and liabilities assumed, including contingent liabilities.

Consideration

5.181 Consideration transferred is the sum of the acquisition date fair values of the assets transferred, the liabilities incurred by the acquirer to the former owners of the acquiree and the equity interests issued by the acquirer to the former owners of the acquiree (except for the measurement of share-based payment awards). Examples of consideration transferred include cash, other assets, contingent consideration, a subsidiary or a business of the acquirer transferred to the seller, common or preferred equity instruments, options, warrants and member interests of mutual entities. [IFRS 3 para 37].

5.182 Where consideration is other than cash, its fair value must be determined in accordance with IFRS 13.

5.183 Equity interests issued by the acquirer in a business combination may be either publicly traded or privately held. Where the shares are publicly traded, fair value will be the quoted share price on the acquisition date multiplied by the number of shares issued. [IFRS 13 para 69]. Where the acquirer issues unlisted shares as consideration, the fair value of the shares will be measured using valuation techniques, typically either the market or the income approach.

Contingent consideration

5.184 Recognising contingent consideration at fair value presents a number of measurement challenges. Entities will need to consider the key inputs of the arrangement and market participant assumptions when developing the assumptions used to determine the fair value. This will include the need to estimate the likelihood and timing of achieving the arrangement's relevant milestones. Entities will also need to exercise judgement when applying a probability assessment for each of the potential outcomes. On the acquisition date, the amount to be paid under the arrangement is uncertain and should be carefully considered. The fair value of liability classified contingent consideration will need to be updated each reporting period after the acquisition date. Changes in fair value measurements should consider the most current probability estimates and assumptions, including changes due to the time value of money.

5.185 Valuation methods for contingent consideration often range from discounted cash flow analyses and binomial models linked to discounted cash flow models, to the more intricate Monte Carlo simulations. The arrangement's terms and the payout structure will influence the type of valuation model used.

Example 1 – Cash settled contingent consideration – Liability classified

Entity A purchases entity B for C400 million. Entity A and entity B agree that if revenues of entity B exceed C250 million in the year following the acquisition date, entity A will pay C50 million to the former shareholders of entity B.

The arrangement requires entity A to pay cash. Therefore, entity A should measure the arrangement's fair value on the acquisition date and classify it as a liability. Any changes in the liability's fair value will be recognised in entity A's earnings until the arrangement is settled.

Entities would most likely consider a best estimate discounted cash flow methodology to measure the arrangement's fair value. A key determination for this approach is selecting a discount rate that best represents the risks inherent in the arrangement. In reality, there is more than one source of risk involved. For example, both projection risk (the risk of achieving the projected revenue level) and credit risk (the risk that the entity may not have the financial ability to make the arrangement payment) need to be considered.

Each of these risks may be quantifiable in isolation. But when the two risks exist in tandem, consideration should be given to factors such as the potential correlation between the two risks and the relative impact of each risk upon the realisation of the arrangement.

One alternative approach to determine the fair value of the cash settled contingent consideration would be to develop a set of discrete potential outcomes for future revenues. Some outcomes would show revenue levels above the C250 million performance target and some would be below. For those outcomes showing revenues above the C250 million threshold, a payout would result. For those below this threshold, there would be no payout.

Each of these discrete payout outcomes could then be assigned a probability and the probability-weighted average payout could be discounted based on market participant assumptions. For example, the following probability weighted alternative might be utilised in determining the fair value of the arrangement.

(in millions)

Outcome	Revenue level	Payout	Probability	Probability-weighted payout
1	C200	C0	10%	C0
2	225	0	15	0
3	250	0	15	0
4	275	50	40	20
5	300	50	20	10
		Total:	100%	C30
		Discount rate[1]		20%
		Fair value:		C25

1 A discount rate of 20% is used for illustrative purposes.

Example 2 – Share settled contingent consideration – Liability classified

Entity A purchases entity B by issuing 1 million equity shares in entity A to entity B's shareholders. At the acquisition date, entity A's share price is C40 per share. Entity A and entity B agree that if the shares of entity A are trading below C40 per share one year after the acquisition date, entity A will issue additional shares to entity B's former shareholders sufficient to protect against price declines below C40 million (that is, the acquisition date fair value of the 1 million shares issued).

The guarantee arrangement creates an obligation that entity A would be required to settle with a variable number of entity A's equity shares, the amount of which varies inversely to changes in the fair value of entity A's equity shares. For example, if entity A's share price decreases from C40 per share to C35 per share one year after the acquisition date, the amount of the obligation would be C5 million. Therefore, the guarantee arrangement would require liability classification on the acquisition date. Changes in the liability will be recognised in entity A's earnings until the arrangement is settled.

The best estimate or the probability-weighted approach will likely not be sufficient to value the share settled arrangement. In addition to the quantification of projection and credit risks, the modelling of entity A's share price is required. The following factors are relevant in performing a valuation for such arrangements:

■ Potential outcomes for entity A's financial results next year.

■ Potential outcomes for entity A's share price returns over the coming year.

■ Correlation of the distributions of the financial results and share price returns.

■ Potential outcomes for other market events that could impact the overall stock market.

■ Selection of an appropriate discount rate that adequately reflects all of the risks (for example, projection risk, share price return estimation risk, entity A's credit risk) not reflected in other assumptions of the valuation.

The contingent consideration arrangements illustrated in this example will likely require a valuation approach incorporating option pricing techniques to adequately incorporate these risks.

Example 3 – Share settled contingent consideration – Equity classified

Entity A acquires entity B in a business combination. The consideration transferred is 10 million entity A shares at the acquisition date and 2 million shares 2 years after the acquisition date if a performance target is met. The performance target is for entity B's revenues (as a wholly-owned subsidiary of entity A) to be greater than C500 million in the second year after the acquisition. The market price of entity A's shares is C15 at the acquisition date. Entity A's management assesses a 25% probability that the performance target will be met. A dividend of C0.25 per share is expected at the end of year 1 and 2, which the seller will not be entitled to receive.

The fair value is estimated at C7, 296,786 (see below). The fair value of the contingent consideration at the acquisition date in this example is based on the acquisition-date fair value of the shares and incorporates the probability that entity B will have revenues in 2 years greater than C500m. The value excludes the dividend cash flows in year 1 and 2 and incorporates the time value of money. The discount rate for the present value of dividends should be the acquirers cost of equity[1], because returns are available to equity holders from capital appreciation and dividends paid. Those earnings are all sourced from net income of the acquirer.

There are no remeasurements of the fair value in subsequent periods.

Revenue forecast (C millions)	A Probability	B Payment in shares	C Probability weighted number of shares
350	30%	0	
450	45%	0	
550	20%	2,000,000	400,000
650	5%	2,000,000	100,000
Total			500,000

C	Probability weighted shares	500,000
D	Share price	15
E	Probability weighted value	7,500,000
F	Acquirer's cost of equity	15%
G	Dividend year 1	125,000
G	Dividend year 2	125,000
H	Present value of dividend cash flow	203,214
I	Present value of contingent consideration	7,296,786

$$C = \text{sum of } (A \times B) \qquad G = 0.25 \times C \qquad I = E\text{-}H$$
$$E = C \times D \qquad H = G/(1+F) + G/(1+F)\hat{}2$$

[1]The required rate of return on dividends would likely be less than the cost of equity in many cases

5.186 As the examples illustrate, each arrangement has its own specific features requiring different modelling techniques and assumptions. Additionally, for liability classified contingent consideration, the valuation model will need to be flexible enough to handle changing inputs and assumptions that need to be updated each reporting period. The projected financial information used in valuing the contingent consideration arrangement should be consistent with the projected financial information used in valuing the intangible assets.

Valuing previously held equity interest

5.187 An acquirer should remeasure any previously held equity interest in the acquiree to fair value. [IFRS 3 para 42].

5.188 Previously held equity interest that has been measured at fair value as of each reporting date prior to the acquisition should be measured similarly as of the acquisition date.

5.189 The fair value of the previously held equity interest in a publicly traded entity should be based on the observable quoted market price without adjustment. [IFRS 13 para 69] This typically means that the previously held equity interest will be measured at a per share value close to that offered by the acquirer to obtain control. This is in line with the principle explained in paragraph BC384 of IFRS 3 that the acquirer exchanges its previously held equity interest for the controlling stake. At the acquisition date, the price at which the previously held shares could be sold to a market participant is the listed price.

5.190 However, the previously held equity interest in an entity that is not publicly traded will need to be measured using valuation techniques. Often the most practical approach is to derive the value of the previously held equity interest from the per share value of the consideration transferred to obtain control. If the previously held equity interest was previously an available for sale financial asset measured at fair value then the method previously used to measure fair value may be applied.

Valuing non-controlling interest

5.191 If an entity chooses to value the non-controlling interest (NCI) at fair value the measurement approach will depend on whether the NCI remains publicly traded or not. The fair value for NCI that remains publicly traded post acquisition should be determined using the NCI's quoted market price. [IFRS 13 para 69]. A reasonable method of estimating the fair value of the NCI, in the absence of quoted prices, is to gross up the fair value of the controlling interest for a control premium, where appropriate (see para 5.192 below). This method reflects the goodwill for the acquiree as a whole, in both the controlling interest and the NCI, which may be more reflective of the economics of the transaction. Use of both the market and income approaches should be considered, as they may provide further support for the fair value of the NCI.

5.192 When measuring the fair value of unlisted NCI entities need to consider the extent to which the NCI is expected to benefit from the synergies of the business combination. The price paid to obtain control typically includes a premium reflecting the synergies that the acquirer expects to achieve. If the NCI will also benefit from those synergies then the fair value measurement will include that premium. If the acquirer intends the synergies to be realised in another part of his group, in which the NCI have no participation, then the fair value of the NCI shares will not include the value of the synergies.

Measuring the fair value of the non-controlling interest — Market approach

5.193 Entities may need to consider using the market approach to value an NCI that is not publicly traded and for which the controlling interest value is not an appropriate basis for estimating fair value. The first step in applying this method is to identify publicly traded companies that are comparable to the acquiree. Pricing multiples of revenue or earnings are calculated from the guideline companies; these are analysed, adjusted, and applied to the revenue and earnings of the acquiree. Applying the pricing multiples to the acquiree's earnings results in the fair value of the acquiree on an aggregate basis. This is then adjusted to reflect the pro rata NCI ownership interest and control premium, if required, for any synergies from the acquisition that would be realised by the NCI. Similarly, the pricing multiples could be applied directly to the pro rata portion of the acquiree's earnings to estimate the fair value of the NCI. The following example illustrates this.

Example

Entity A acquires 350 shares, or 70%, of entity B, which is privately held, for C2,100 or C6.00 per share. There are 500 shares outstanding. The outstanding 30% interest in entity B represents the NCI that is required to be measured at fair value by entity A. At the acquisition date, entity B's most recent annual net income was C200. Entity A used the public entity market multiple method to measure the fair value of the NCI. Entity A identified three publicly traded companies comparable to entity B, which were trading at an average price-to-earnings multiple of 15. Based on differences in growth, profitability, liquidity and product differences, entity A adjusted the observed price-to-earnings ratio to 13 for the purposes of valuing entity B.

To measure the fair value of the NCI in entity B, entity A may initially apply the price-to-earnings multiple in the aggregate as follows:

Entity B net income	C200
Price-to-earnings multiple	13
Fair value of entity B	C2,600
Entity B NCI interest	30%
Fair value of entity B NCI	C780

Entities will have to understand whether the consideration transferred for the 70% interest includes a control premium paid by the acquirer and whether that control premium would extend to the NCI when determining its fair value. In this example, the fair value of entity B using the market approach is C2,600, which represents a minority interest value because the price-to-earnings multiple was derived from per-share prices (that is, excludes control). If it had been determined to be appropriate to include the control premium in the fair value estimate, grossing up the 70% interest yields a fair value for the acquiree as a whole of C3,000 (C2,100/0.70), compared to the C2,600 derived above, and a value for the NCI of C900.

Measuring the fair value of the non-controlling interest — Income approach

5.194 The income approach may be used to measure the NCI's fair value using a discounted cash flow analysis to measure the value of the acquired entity's whole business. The analysis performed as part of assigning the fair value to the assets acquired and liabilities assumed may serve as the basis for the fair value of the acquiree as a whole. Again, understanding whether a control premium exists and whether the NCI shareholders benefit from the synergies from the acquisition is critical in measuring the NCI's fair value.

5.195 If it is determined that a control premium exists and the premium would not extend to the NCI, there are two methods widely used to remove the control premium from the fair value of the business enterprise. One method is to calculate the pro rata NCI interest to the value of the business enterprise and apply a minority interest discount. Another method adjusts the projections used for the value of the business enterprise analysis to remove the economic benefits of control embedded in the projections.

Measuring the fair value of assets acquired and liabilities assumed

5.196 IFRS 3 requires the acquirer in a business combination to measure the assets acquired and liabilities assumed at fair value. These will normally include:

- Financial assets and liabilities (see paras 5.127 to 5.179).

- Inventory (see paras 5.198 to 5.206).

- Property, plant and equipment (see paras 5.207 to 5.221).

- Intangible assets (see paras 5.233 to 5.272).

- Non-financial liabilities including contingent liabilities (see paras 5.309 to 5.326).

Disclosures

5.197 The disclosure requirements of IFRS 13 do not apply to the fair values determined for acquisition accounting under IFRS 3. The fair value measurement standard disclosures only apply to assets and liabilities carried at fair value in the balance sheet after initial recognition.

Applying IFRS 13 to inventory

5.198 Most inventory is measured at the lower of cost and net realisable value under IAS 2 and is, therefore, outside IFRS 13's scope.

5.199 Agricultural produce at the point of harvest is measured at fair value less costs to sell and so is within IFRS 13's scope. [IAS 41 para 13]. The produce is transferred to inventory at fair value less costs to sell and this value becomes the 'cost' for measuring the inventory under IAS 2.

5.200 However, some entities that harvest agricultural produce and some that mine minerals have a policy of subsequently valuing their inventory at net realisable value. There may be a well-established practice in those industries of carrying inventories at net realisable value, because sale is assured under a forward contract or a government guarantee, or because there is an active market in the produce and a negligible risk that the produce will not be sold. This measure, whilst similar to fair value, is not within IFRS 13's scope (see para 5.8 above).

5.201 There are two categories of inventory to which IFRS 13 applies: the inventory of commodity broker-traders and inventory acquired in a business combination.

Inventory of commodity broker-traders

5.202 Broker-traders are those who trade in commodities on their own behalf or for others. Their inventories are normally traded in an active market and are purchased with a view to resale in the near future, generating a profit from fluctuations in price or broker-traders' margin. Industry practice is often to carry such inventories at fair value less costs to sell and so an entity may adopt this policy. Measurement of these inventories is, therefore, within IFRS 13's scope.

5.203 Entities with commodity inventory will measure fair value by reference to the market price for the item in the principal market. This will likely be a Level 1 measurement.

Inventory acquired in a business combination

5.204 IFRS 3 requires that inventory acquired in a business combination is measured at fair value. The fair value of finished goods inventory is measured by determining net realisable value (that is, estimated selling prices of the inventory, less the sum of (i) costs of disposal and (ii) a reasonable profit allowance for the selling effort) as this represents an exit price.

5.205 Work in progress inventory is measured similarly to finished goods inventory except that, in addition, the estimated selling price is adjusted for the costs to complete the manufacturing, and a reasonable profit allowance for the remaining manufacturing effort.

5.206 Raw material inventories are recorded at fair value and are generally measured based on the price that a market participant would pay currently for the inventory.

Applying IFRS 13 to property, plant and equipment

5.207   An entity will need to apply IFRS 13 to measure the fair value of property plant and equipment:

- when it chooses the revaluation model under IAS 16;

- when it acquires property plant and equipment in a business combination; or

- when it elects, on transition to IFRS, to take the fair value as deemed cost exemption in IFRS 1.

The principles in each case will be the same: to determine the price that a market participant would pay for the asset.

Measuring the fair value of land and buildings

5.208   The fair value of land and buildings is typically measured using the market approach or the income approach, because there is usually available market data for sales and rentals of land and buildings.

5.209   Fair value will reflect the highest and best use of the asset, which will usually be its existing use but may be for some other use. For example, if an entity owns a plot of land in a city centre on which it has a warehouse, the site may have potential for residential development. Its market value could be significantly higher than its value as an industrial site although the entity would have to incur costs, such as relocation or closure costs, in order to realise that value.

5.210   Illustrative example 2 in IFRS 13 explains how to deal with the value of land in such circumstances, but is silent on how the value of the building should be estimated if the entity continues to use it for something other than the highest and best use.

"An entity acquires land in a business combination. The land is currently developed for industrial use as a site for a factory. The current use of land is presumed to be its highest and best use unless market or other factors suggest a different use. Nearby sites have recently been developed for residential use as sites for high-rise apartment buildings. On the basis of that development, and recent zoning and other changes to facilitate that development, the entity determines that the land currently used as a site for a factory could be developed as a site for residential use (that is for high-rise apartment buildings) because market participants would take into account the potential to develop the site for residential use when pricing the land. The highest and best use of the land would be determined by comparing both of the following:

1. *the value of the land as currently developed for industrial use (that is the land would be used in combination with other assets, such as the factory, or with other assets and liabilities).*

2. *the value of the land as a vacant site for residential use, taking into account the costs of demolishing the factory and other costs (including the uncertainty about whether the entity would be able to convert the asset to the alternative use) necessary to convert the land to a vacant site (that is the land is to be used by market participants on a stand-alone basis).*

The highest and best use of the land would be determined on the basis of the higher of those values. In situations involving real estate appraisal, the determination of highest and best use might take into account factors relating to the factory operations, including its assets and liabilities."

[IFRS 13 paras IE 7, 8].

5.211 If an entity applies the revaluation model in IAS 16 and uses an asset under circumstances which are not the highest and best use for that asset, it must disclose that fact [IFRS 13 para 93(i)].

5.212 In the rare instances where an entity is valuing land and buildings for which there is no market data for sales or rentals, the depreciated replacement cost approach may be used to measure fair value. See paragraphs 5.213 to 5.221 below.

Measuring the fair value of plant and equipment

5.213 The fair value of plant and equipment is often measured using the replacement-cost method. This represents the highest value that a market participant would pay for an asset with similar utility. The cost approach is based on the principle of substitution. It uses the cost to replace an asset as an indicator of the fair value of that asset. To determine the appropriate substitute asset or asset group as a measure of fair value, the utility of the replacement asset is compared to the utility of the asset being measured. Comparable utility implies similar economic satisfaction, but does not necessarily require that the substitute asset is an exact duplicate of the asset being measured. The cost of an exact duplicate is referred to as reproduction cost. The substitute asset is perceived as equivalent if it possesses similar utility and, therefore, serves as a measure of fair value of the asset being valued.

5.214 Typically, the first step in the cost approach is to identify the asset's original cost, which represents the actual cost at the date of asset's manufacture and the corresponding first original in-service date. The next step is to adjust the original cost for changes in price levels between the asset's original in-service date and the date of the valuation to measure its replacement cost new (RCN). 'Replacement cost new' represents the indicated value of current labour and materials necessary to construct or acquire an asset of similar utility to the asset being measured.

5.215 Next, adjustments are made to 'replacement cost new' to represent any losses in value due to physical deterioration or functional obsolescence of the asset, which results in the value of replacement cost new less depreciation (RCNLD).

5.216 Physical deterioration represents the loss in value due to the decreased usefulness of a fixed asset as the asset's useful life expires. This can be caused by factors such as wear and tear, deterioration, physical stresses and exposure to various elements.

5.217 Excessive physical deterioration may result in an inability to meet production standards or result in higher product rejections as the tolerance on manufacturing equipment decreases. Higher than average maintenance expenditure requirements may also suggest higher levels of physical deterioration. However, below average maintenance expenditures may also indicate higher level of physical deterioration due to inadequate or deferred maintenance.

5.218 Functional obsolescence represents the loss in value due to the decreased usefulness of a fixed asset that is inefficient or inadequate relative to other more efficient or less costly replacement assets provided by new technological developments. Functional obsolescence is observed in several different forms. If the subject asset has excessive operating costs relative to a new asset, this may indicate a form of functional obsolescence. If in developing an asset's 'replacement cost new', that replacement cost is less than its reproduction cost, this may also be indicative of a form of functional obsolescence. The objective of the measurement is to identify the replacement cost of a modern equivalent asset.

5.219 Physical and functional obsolescence are direct attributes of the asset being valued. However, further adjustment may be necessary to 'replacement cost new less depreciation' for loss in value due to economic obsolescence to provide an indication of the fair value of the asset being measured.

5.220 Economic obsolescence represents the loss in value due to the decreased usefulness of a fixed asset caused by external factors, independent from the characteristics of the asset or how it is operated. Increased cost of raw materials, labour, or utilities that cannot be offset by an increase in price due to competition or limited demand; as well as a change in environmental or other regulations, inflation or high interest rates, may suggest the presence of economic obsolescence.

5.221 IFRS 13 permits the fair value of certain tangible assets to be measured using the replacement-cost method. However, there may be instances or industry practice where certain tangible assets are measured using an income or market approach. An example is the measurement of a power plant in the energy sector, which often has few, if any, intangible assets other than the embedded licence and so the cash flows from the plant reflect only the economic benefits generated by the plant and its embedded licence. Management should have regard to other IFRS to determine whether the assets measured together need to be accounted for separately. [IFRS 13 para 32]. This could result in a fair value measure above the replacement cost. In this situation, as replacement cost represents the highest price that a market participant would be prepared to pay; reporting entities should consider whether any of the difference is derived from or related to other assets included in the cash flows of the tangible assets, such as customer or contractual assets.

Applying IFRS 13 in impairment testing

5.222   The recoverable amount for impairment testing under IFRS is the higher of value in use and fair value less costs to sell. [IAS 36 para 6].

5.223   Value in use is not within IFRS 13's scope. [IFRS 13 para 6(c)].

5.224   Fair value less costs to sell is within the measurement scope of IFRS 13 but not within the disclosure scope of the standard. [IFRS 13 para 7(c)]. However, IFRS 13 introduced consequential amendments to IAS 36 that result in disclosures similar to those required by IFRS 13.

Measuring fair value less costs to sell

5.225   Very few assets (or businesses) tested for impairment under IAS 36 will be traded in an active market and be a Level 1 measurement. The asset most likely to meet the Level 1 criteria is an investment in an associate that is listed on an active market. The fair value of this asset will be measured using the quoted price multiplied by the number of shares held. For most other assets (or businesses) a valuation technique will be used to measure fair value.

5.226   In assessing fair value less costs to sell, there are a number of valuation methodologies that are used to assess the value of a business or an asset. More than one methodology is normally used to ensure that the valuations are cross checked and considered in light of all appropriate market evidence. See paragraph 5.73. (Note that, the replacement cost method is not appropriate for the purpose of impairment testing, as it does not reflect the economic benefits recoverable from use or disposal.) [IAS 36 para BCZ 29].

5.227   For some assets, particularly land and buildings, fair value may be measured by using the market approach as there is usually market data on sales or rentals. For many assets and businesses, however, an income approach will be appropriate.

Using the income approach for fair value less cost to sell

5.228   In practice, a first assessment of the valuation is performed using cash flows from management. There must be, where appropriate, market evidence to support the key assumptions underpinning the cash flow analysis; for example, growth rates may be considered by benchmarking to industry/analyst reports. If certain of the assumptions used are not those that a market participant would use, those cash flows must be adjusted to take into account the assumptions that are supported by market evidence.

5.229 The cash flows to be used in a discounted cash flow prepared to determine fair value less costs to sell will likely be different from those in a value in use calculation. Any differences in the assumptions in the cash flows used for the fair value less costs to sell compared to the cash flow forecasts used in the value in use analysis need to be considered for reasonableness. The assumptions could include restructurings, reorganisations or future investments (that would be excluded from a value in use calculation) if all rational market participants would be expected to undertake these expenditures and reorganisations in order to extract the best value from the purchase and, hence, they would have been factored into the acquisition price. In addition, as fair value less costs to sell is a post-tax measure, tax cash flows, whilst excluded from a VIU calculation, are included in the FVLCS calculation.

> **Example – Expenditure that rational market participants would expect**
>
> Entity S runs a number of casinos. It currently operates its head office function from two separate buildings in different locations as a result of historical acquisitions. The cost of exiting the smaller building is not considered to be significant.
>
> The annual goodwill impairment test is based on a fair value less cost to sell basis using a discounted cash flow model.
>
> The lease costs of the second premises should not be included in the cash flows. Operating a head office from two offices is considered unusual, and a buyer of the business would be likely to immediately cancel the second lease especially when the benefit outweighs the cost of exiting.
>
> Restructuring activities that are expected to enhance the value of a business are taken into account when determining fair value less costs to sell.

5.230 The discount rate applied to the market participant cash flows should reflect a market participant's required return on the investment. This may be, but is not always, the reporting entity's cost of capital. The discount rate should reflect the return required on the asset or business being tested for impairment in isolation. A group's cost of capital is the weighted average of the risks of the group and not the risk of the asset or business being tested for impairment.

5.231 If comparable transactions in similar assets or businesses are available, they should be used as market evidence. Consideration should be given to the comparability of the acquired asset/business to the asset/CGU being tested, for example, adjustments for factors such as size, growth expectations, profitability and risk will need to be considered. This evidence might arise in the implied multiple of earnings before interest, taxes, depreciation and amortisation

(EBITDA) or revenue that was paid in a comparable transaction, which when applied to the current model (and adjusted for points of difference) provides support for the valuation. For example, if there are a number of recent transactions in comparable entities where the price paid is six times EBITDA and management has produced a valuation that is ten times EBITDA, then the external data would appear not to support the assumptions made in the valuation. Care is needed in selecting comparable entities; risk profile and size may well be more important than geography. Care is also needed to avoid selection bias, if one transaction in ten provides some support for the EBITDA multiple, but the same transaction is regarded in the financial press as an over-payment and an isolated example, then it should not be used.

5.232   As a cross-check, it is useful to benchmark the fair value less costs to sell of a CGU to multiples implied by quoted comparable companies, although consideration will need to be given to comparability in terms of size, growth expectations, profitability, risk etc. In the unlikely event that a benchmark or comparable transactions do not exist, any possible external evidence (growth rates, industry trends, etc) is used to support the cash flow projections prepared by management.

Applying IFRS 13 to intangible assets

5.233   An entity will need to apply IFRS 13 to measure the fair value of intangible assets when:

- it applies the revaluation model under IAS 38; or
- it acquires intangible assets in a business combination.

Applying the revaluation model

5.234   Few intangible assets are traded in an active market. Where they are, fair value will be measured by reference to the quoted price of an identical asset and will be a Level 1 measurement.

Measuring the fair value of intangible assets acquired in a business combination

5.235   IFRS 3 requires entities to recognise, separately from goodwill, the identifiable intangible assets acquired in a business combination at their acquisition-date fair values. [IFRS 3 para 18]. When measuring the fair value of acquired intangible assets, the income, market, and cost approaches are generally considered. The income approach is most commonly used to value intangible assets acquired in a business combination given their unique nature. The valuation inputs used in the income approach should be developed based on market participant assumptions.

Income approach for intangible assets

5.236   The most common variations of the income approach, used in measuring an intangible asset's fair value, include:

- Multi-period excess earnings method.

- Relief-from-royalty method (RFR).

- Greenfield method.

- With and without method.

5.237   The cost savings and premium profit methods are other ways to value intangible assets but are used less frequently. The following paragraphs describe the most common variations of the income approach, as well as their common application to specific intangible assets.

The multi-period excess earnings method

5.238   The multi-period excess earning method (MEEM) is a commonly used method for measuring the fair value of intangible assets. The fundamental principle underlying the MEEM is to isolate the net earnings attributable to the asset being measured. Cash flows are generally used as a basis for applying this method. Specifically, an intangible asset's fair value is equal to the present value of the incremental after-tax cash flows (excess earnings) attributable solely to the intangible asset over its remaining useful life.

5.239   Intangible assets are generally used in combination with other tangible and intangible assets to generate income. The other assets in the group are often referred to as 'contributory assets', as they contribute to the realisation of the intangible asset's value. To measure the fair value of an intangible asset, its projected cash flows are isolated from the projected cash flows of the combined asset group over the intangible asset's remaining economic life. Both the amount and the duration of the cash flows are considered from a market participant's perspective.

5.240   The fair value measurement of an intangible asset starts with an estimate of the expected net income of a particular asset group. 'Contributory asset charges' or 'economic rents' are then deducted from the total net after-tax cash flows projected for the combined group to obtain the residual or 'excess earnings' attributable to the intangible asset. The contributory asset charges represent the charges for the use of an asset or group of assets (for example, working capital, fixed assets, trade names) and should be applied for all assets, excluding goodwill, that contribute to the realisation of cash flows for a particular intangible asset. The excess cash flows are then discounted to a net present value. The net present value of any tax benefits associated with amortising the intangible asset for tax purposes (where relevant) is added to arrive at the intangible asset's fair value.

5.241 The contributory asset charges are calculated using the assets' respective fair values and are conceptually based upon an 'earnings hierarchy' or prioritisation of total earnings ascribed to the assets in the group. The earnings hierarchy is the foundation of the MEEM in which earnings are first attributed to a fair return on contributory assets, such as investment in working capital and property, and plant and equipment. These are considered a pre-requisite to developing the ability to deliver goods and services to customers and thus their values are not included as part of the intangible asset's value.

5.242 The return or charge for each asset should be based upon comparable market rates, which reflect the amount market participants would charge for the use of the asset (that is, a 'market-derived rent'). In addition, contributory assets may benefit a number of intangible and other assets. The total return or charge earned by a particular asset should be distributed over the assets that benefit from its use. For example, in determining the fair value of intangible assets, a capital-intensive manufacturing business should have a higher contributory asset charge from fixed assets than that of a service business.

5.243 Terminal values are not appropriate in the valuation of a finite-lived intangible asset under the income approach. However, it is appropriate to add a terminal value to a discrete projection period for indefinite-lived intangible assets, such as some trade names.

5.244 The key assumptions of the MEEM, in addition to the projected cash flows over the asset's remaining useful life, are as follows and are discussed in the subsequent sections:

■ Discount rates, including reconciling rates of return.

■ Application of contributory asset charges.

■ Tax amortisation benefits.

Discount rates for intangible assets

5.245 An appropriate discount rate is an important factor in a multi-period excess earnings analysis, whether using expected (that is, probability adjusted) or conditional (that is, management's best estimate) cash flows. It is generally recognised by valuation practitioners that the total cash flows attributable to a group of assets can be disaggregated according to the varying levels of risk associated with the cash flows generated by the asset groups.

5.246 The discount rate should reflect the risks commensurate with the intangible asset's individual cash flow assumptions. Some intangible assets, such as order or production backlog, may be assigned a lower discount rate relative to other intangible assets, because the cash flows are more certain. Other intangible assets, such as technology-related and customer relationship intangible assets, are generally assigned higher discount rates, because the projected level of future earnings is deemed to have greater risk and variability. While discount rates for intangible assets could be higher or lower than the entity's WACC, they are typically higher than discount rates on tangible assets. The spectrum of risk is shown in the following diagram.

Spectrum of risk for intangible assets[1]

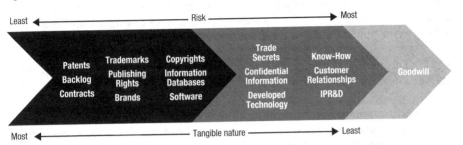

[1]Represents a general example of how risk could be assessed. Specific facts and circumstances should be evaluated.

5.247   The WACC represents the average expected return from the business (that is, all the assets and liabilities used collectively in generating the cash flows of the entire business) for a market participant investor, and includes an element to compensate for the average risk associated with potential realisation of these cash flows. The internal rate of return (IRR) represents the implied return from the transaction that may include acquirer-specific elements.

5.248   Conceptually, the WACC applicable for the acquiree should be the starting point for developing the appropriate discount rate for an intangible asset. The WACC and the IRR should be equal when the projected financial information (PFI) is market participant expected cash flows and the consideration transferred equals the fair value of the acquiree. However, circumstances arise in practice when the WACC and the IRR are not equal, creating the need for further analysis to determine the appropriate starting point for an intangible asset discount rate.

5.249   If a difference exists between the IRR and the WACC and it is driven by the cash flows (that is, optimistic or conservative bias rather than expected cash flows, while the consideration transferred is the fair value of the acquiree); best practice would be to use expected cash flows. If this is not possible, it may be necessary to consider the IRR as a starting point when considering adjustments to discount rates for intangible assets. However, in this situation it is important to assess whether the cash flows allocated to the individual intangible assets have been adjusted to eliminate the optimistic or conservative bias reflected in the overall business cash flows.

5.250   For example, if the IRR in a technology acquisition is higher than the WACC because the business cash flows include optimistic assumptions about revenue growth from selling products to future customers, adjustments must be made to the discount rate used to value the technology in the products that would be sold to both existing and future customers. However, if the revenue growth rate for the existing customer relationships does not reflect a similar level of growth or risk, then the discount rate for existing customer relationships should generally be based on the WACC without such adjustments.

5.251 If the difference between the IRR and the WACC is driven by the consideration transferred (that is, the transaction is a bargain purchase or includes entity specific synergies), then the WACC may be more applicable to use as the basis of the intangible assets' required returns. The relationship between the WACC and the IRR in certain circumstances impacts the selection of discount rates and is illustrated in the example below.

Example – Which discount rate to use

The projected financial information (PFI) represent market participant cash flows and consideration represents fair value.	WACC = IRR
Alternatively:	
The PFI is optimistic, therefore, WACC $\neq$ IRR	Adjust cash flows so WACC and IRR are the same
Consideration is a bargain purchase	Use WACC
PFI includes synergies not paid for	Use WACC
Consideration is not fair value, because it includes entity specific synergies	Use WACC

5.252 The WACC is generally the starting point for determining the discount rate applicable to an individual intangible asset. However, as discussed above, in certain circumstances the WACC may need to be adjusted if the cash flows do not represent market participant assumptions, for example because the information needed to adjust the cash flows is not available. Premiums and discounts are applied to the entity's WACC or IRR to reflect the relative risk associated with the particular tangible and intangible asset categories that comprise the group of assets expected to generate the projected cash flows. The range of discount rates assigned to the various tangible and intangible assets should reconcile, on a fair-value-weighted basis, to the entity's overall WACC. For example, working capital and fixed assets are generally assigned a lower required rate of return relative to a company's overall discount rate, whereas intangible assets and goodwill are assigned a higher discount rate. This is because achieving the lower levels of cash flows necessary to provide a 'fair' return on investment (ROI) on tangible assets is more certain than achieving the higher levels of cash flows necessary to provide a 'fair' ROI on intangible assets. Application of the concept is subjective and requires significant judgement.

Reconciliation of rates of return

5.253 The assignment of stratified rates to the various classes of assets is a challenging process, because there are few if any observable active markets for intangible assets. Nonetheless, companies should assess the overall reasonableness of the discount rate assigned to each asset by generally reconciling the discount rates assigned to the individual assets, on a fair-value-weighted basis, to the WACC of the acquiree (or the IRR of the transaction if the cash flows do not represent market participant assumptions). This reconciliation is often referred to as a 'weighted average return analysis' (WARA). The WARA is a tool to assess the reasonableness of the selected discount rates. Although goodwill is not explicitly valued by discounting residual cash flows, its implied discount rate should be reasonable, considering the facts and circumstances surrounding the transaction and the risks normally associated with realising earnings high enough to justify investment in goodwill. Determining the implied rate of return on goodwill is necessary to assess the reasonableness of the selected rates of return on the individual assets acquired. The rate of return should be consistent with the type of cash flows associated with the underlying asset; that is, the expected cash flows or conditional cash flows, as the rate of return may be different. Assets valued using expected cash flows would have a lower required rate of return than the same assets valued using conditional cash flows, because the latter cash flows include additional uncertainty.

5.254 The value of the assets used in the WARA should be adjusted to the extent the assets' value is not amortisable for tax purposes. Some transactions (for example, share acquisitions in some jurisdictions) do not result in a change in the tax basis of acquired assets or liabilities assumed. The following example shows a WARA reconciliation used to test the reasonableness of the discount rates applied to the individual assets.

Example – Weighted average return analysis

Entity A acquires entity B in a business combination for C400 million. Reconciling entity B's cash flows to the consideration transferred of C400 million results in an internal rate of return of 12.0%. Assume a 40.0% tax rate.

The WACC for comparable companies is 11.5%.

(C's in millions)

Assets	Fair value C	% of total %	After-tax discount rate %	Weighted average discount rates %
Working capital	30	7.5	4.0	0.3
Fixed assets	60	15.0	8.0	1.2
Patent	50	12.5	12.0	1.5
Customer relationships	50	12.5	13.0	1.6
Developed technology	80	20.0	13.0	2.6
Residual goodwill	130	32.5	15.0	4.9
Total	400	100.0		12.1

The discount rates selected for intangible assets in conjunction with the rates selected for other assets, including goodwill, results in a WARA of 12.1%, which approximates the comparable entity WACC and IRR of 11.5% and 12.0%, respectively. Therefore, the selected discount rates assigned to the assets acquired appear reasonable.

The rates used for contributory assets, which are working capital (4.0%) and fixed assets (8.0%), are generally consistent with after-tax observed market rates. In general, discount rates on working capital and fixed assets are derived assuming a combination of equity and debt financing. The cost of debt on working capital could be based on the company's short-term borrowing cost. The fixed asset discount rate may assume a greater portion of equity in its financing compared to working capital. The entity's overall borrowing cost for the debt component of the fixed asset discount rate would be used rather than a short-term borrowing cost as used for working capital.

The rates used to derive the fair value of the patent, customer relationships, and developed technology of 12.0%, 13.0%, and 13.0%, respectively, each represent a premium to the WACC (11.5%). The premium should be based on judgement and consistent with market participant assumptions. Certain intangible assets, such as patents and backlog contracts, are perceived to be less risky than other intangible assets, such as customer relationships, developed technology, and goodwill. Discount rates on lower-risk intangible assets may be consistent with the entity's WACC, whereas higher risk intangible assets may reflect the entity's cost of equity capital.

The implied discount rate for goodwill (15.0%) should, in most cases, be higher than the rates assigned to any other asset. Generally, goodwill has the most risk of all of the assets on the balance sheet; however, the implied rate of return should typically not be significantly higher than the rate of return on most other intangible assets. If the implied rate of return on goodwill is significantly different from the rates of return on the identifiable assets, the selected rates of return on the identifiable assets should be reconsidered.

Significant professional judgement is required to determine the discount rates that should be applied in performing WARA reconciliation. A selected rate of return on intangible assets greater than 14.0% would result in a lower fair value of the intangible assets and a higher implied fair value of goodwill (implying a lower rate of return on goodwill compared to other assets). This may suggest that the selected return on intangible assets is too high, because goodwill should conceptually have a higher rate of return than intangible assets.

Contributory asset charges

5.255   Cash flows associated with measuring the fair value of an intangible asset using the MEEM should be reduced or adjusted by contributory asset charges. The practice of taking contributory asset charges on assets, such as net working capital, fixed assets, and other identifiable intangible assets, is widely accepted among valuation practitioners. However, there are varying views related to which assets should be used to calculate the contributory asset charges. Some valuation practitioners have argued that goodwill in its entirety should be included as a contributory asset, presumably representing going concern value, institutional know-how, repeat patronage, and reputation of a business. A majority of valuation practitioners and accountants have rejected this view because goodwill is generally not viewed as an asset that can be reliably measured.

5.256 However, assembled workforce, as an element of goodwill, may be identifiable and reasonably measured, even though it does not meet the accounting criteria for separate recognition. As a result, an assembled workforce is typically considered a contributory asset, even though it is not recognised separately from goodwill. [IFRS 3 App B para B37]. It is rare to see a valuation of an intangible asset that includes a contributory asset charge for a portion of goodwill, with the exception of an assembled workforce. Improperly including a contributory asset charge will tend to understate the intangible asset's fair value and overstate goodwill. This is an evolving area; valuation practitioners are debating which other elements of goodwill might be treated in the same way as workforce and if such elements can be reasonably measured.

5.257 Another common practice issue in determining contributory asset charges is the inclusion of both returns 'on' and 'of' the contributory asset when the 'of' component is already reflected in the asset's cash flow forecast. For self-constructed assets, such as customer lists, the cost to replace them (that is, the return of value) typically is included in normal operating costs and, therefore, is already factored into the projected financial information (PFI) as part of the operating cost structure. Because this component of return is already deducted from the entity's revenues, the returns charged for these assets would include only the required return on the investment (that is, the profit element on those assets has not been considered) and not the return of the investment in those assets. The return of component encompasses the cost to replace an asset, which differs from the return on component, which represents the expected return from an alternate investment with similar risk (that is, opportunity cost of funds). Where returns of the asset are not included in the operating cost structure, a return on and a return of value would be charged.

5.258 The applied contributory asset charge may include both a return on and a return of component in certain circumstances. This may necessitate an adjustment to the cash flows used to value a particular intangible asset. For example, when a royalty rate is used as a technology contributory asset charge, the assumption is that the entity licenses its existing and future technology instead of developing it in house. If the cash flows were developed on the assumption that future technology will be developed in house, it would reflect cash expenditures for research and development. In this case, the cash flows used to value the individual intangible asset (for example, customer relationships) should be adjusted by eliminating the cash spent on research and development for future technology. This is because the royalty is the cost for licensing completed technology (whether current or future) from a third party. As a result, inclusion of cash spent on research and development in the cash flows results in double counting as there is no need to develop a technology in house when it is assumed to be licensed from a third party.

Tax amortisation benefits

5.259 The effect of income taxes should be considered when an intangible asset's fair value is estimated as part of a business combination. Generally, the tax amortisation benefit is applied when using the income approach and is not applied to the market approach. Market-based data used in the market approach is assumed to include the potential tax benefits resulting from obtaining a new tax basis.

5.260 Many business combinations result in the acquiring entity carrying over the acquiree's tax basis. As a result, the amounts recorded for financial reporting purposes will most likely differ from the amounts recorded for tax purposes. A deferred tax asset or deferred tax liability should generally be recognised for the effects of such differences. Although no 'step up' of the intangible asset's tax basis actually occurs, the estimation of fair value should still reflect hypothetical potential tax benefits as if it did. The tax benefits should reflect the tax legislation in the domicile where the asset is situated. However, if there are no tax benefits possible (that is, the tax legislation in the subject jurisdiction does not permit market participants to recognise a new tax basis under any circumstance), then the fair value of the assets should not include any tax benefits.

5.261 IFRS does not contain specific guidance with respect to applying the tax amortisation benefit. However, the asset's fair value is independent of the way an asset is acquired, alone or together with other assets in a business combination. An asset's fair value in a business combination normally reflects the price that would be paid for the individual asset if it was acquired separately. The tax amortisation benefit that would be available if the asset was acquired separately is reflected in the asset's fair value, if such a benefit would be available to more than one potential purchaser of the asset.

Relief-from-royalty method

5.262 The relief-from-royalty (RFR) method of the income approach is relatively specialised for use in measuring the fair value of those intangible assets that are often the subject of licensing, such as trade names, patents, and proprietary technologies.

5.263 The fundamental concept underlying this method is that in lieu of ownership, the acquirer can obtain comparable rights to use the subject asset via a licence from a hypothetical third-party owner. The asset's fair value is the present value of licence fees avoided by owning it (that is, the royalty savings). To appropriately apply this method, it is critical to develop a hypothetical royalty rate that reflects comparable comprehensive rights of use for comparable intangible assets. The use of observed market data, such as observed royalty rates in actual arm's length negotiated licences, is preferable to more subjective unobservable inputs.

5.264 Royalty rate selection requires judgement because most brands, trade names, trademarks and intellectual property have unique characteristics. The underlying technology or brand may have been licensed or sublicensed to third parties. The actual royalty rate charged by the entity for the use of the technology or brand to other parties is generally the best starting point for an estimate of the

Fair value

appropriate royalty rate. However, in the absence of actual royalty rate transactions, market-based royalty rates for similar products, brands, trade names, or technologies are used. Market rates are adjusted so that they are comparable to the subject asset being measured, and to reflect the fact that market royalty rates typically reflect rights that are more limited than those of full ownership. Market royalty rates can be obtained from various third-party data vendors and publications.

Example – The relief from royalty method

Entity A acquires technology from entity B in a business combination. Prior to the business combination, entity X was licensing the technology from entity B for a royalty of 5% of sales. The technology acquired from entity B is expected to generate cash flows for the next five years.

Entity A has determined the relief-from-royalty method is appropriate to measure the fair value of the acquired technology. The following is a summary of the assumptions used in the relief-from-royalty method:

Revenue: Represents the projected revenue expected from the technology over the period of expected cash flows, which is estimated to be five years.

Royalty rate: The royalty rate of 5% was based on the rate paid by entity X before the business combination, and is assumed to represent a market participant royalty rate. Actual royalty rates charged by the acquiree (that is, entity B) should be corroborated by other market evidence where available.

Discount rate: Based on an assessment of the relative risk of the cash flows and the overall entity's cost of capital, 15.0% is considered reasonable.

Tax amortisation benefits: Represents the present value of tax benefits generated from amortising the intangible asset. Based on the discount rate, tax rate, and a statutory 15-year tax life, the tax benefit was calculated to be 18.5% of the summation of present values.

	Year 1	Year 2	Year 3	Year 4	Year 5
Revenue	C10,000	C8,500	C6,500	C3,250	C1,000
Royalty rate	5.0%	5.0%	5.0%	5.0%	5.0%
Royalty savings	500	425	325	163	50
Income tax rate	40%	40%	40%	40%	40%
Less: Income tax expense	(200)	(170)	(130)	(65)	(20)
After-tax royalty savings	C300	C255	C195	C98	C30
Discount period[1]	0.5	1.5	2.5	3.5	4.5
Discount rate	15%	15%	15%	15%	15%
Present value factor[2]	0.9325	0.8109	0.7051	0.6131	0.5332
Present value of royalty savings[3]	C280	C207	C137	C60	C16
Sum of present values	C700				
Tax amortisation benefit[4]	129				
Fair value	C829				

[1] Represents a mid-period discounting convention, because cash flows are recognised throughout the year.

[2] Calculated as $1/(1+k)^t$, where k = discount rate and t = discount period.

[3] Calculated as the after-tax royalty savings multiplied by the present value factor.

[4] The tax amortisation benefit was calculated to be 18.5% of the summation of the present value of cash flows.

Greenfield method

5.265 The subject intangible asset is valued under the greenfield method using a hypothetical cash flow scenario of developing an operating business from an entity that at inception only holds the subject intangible asset. Consequently, this valuation method is most relevant for assets that are considered to be scarce or fundamental for the business even if they do not necessarily drive the excess returns that may be generated by the overall business. For example, the greenfield method is frequently used to value broadcasting licences. These assets are fundamental for a broadcasting business but do not necessarily generate excess returns for the business. Excess returns may be driven by the broadcasted content or technology.

5.266 This method considers the fact that the value of a business can be divided into three value categories, the 'going concern value', the value of the subject intangible asset, and the value of the excess returns driven by other assets. The going concern value is the value of having all necessary assets and liabilities assembled such that normal business operations can be performed. Under the greenfield method, the investments required to recreate the going concern value of the business (both capital investments and operating losses) are deducted from the overall business cash flows. This results in the going concern value being deducted from the overall business value. Similarly, the value of the excess returns driven by intangible assets other than the subject intangible asset is also excluded from the overall business cash flows by using cash flows providing only market participant or normalised levels of returns. The result of deducting the investment needed to recreate the going concern value and excluding the excess returns driven by other intangible assets from the overall business cash flows provides a value of the subject intangible asset, the third element of the overall business.

5.267 The greenfield method requires an understanding of how much time and investment it would take to grow the business considering the current market conditions. The expenses and capital expenditures required to recreate the business would be higher than the expense and capital expenditure level of an established business. In addition, the time to recreate or the 'ramp-up' period also determines the required level of investments (for example, to shorten the ramp-up period more investment would be required). In summary, the key inputs of this method are the time and required expenses of the ramp-up period, the market participant or normalised level of operation of the business at the end of the ramp-up period and the market participant required rate of return for investing in such a business (discount rate).

5.268 The tax amortisation benefit of the intangible asset should also be included in determining the value of the subject intangible asset.

With and without method

5.269 The value of the subject intangible asset under the with and without method is calculated by taking the difference between the business value estimated under two sets of cash flow projections:

■ The value of the business with all assets in-place at the valuation date.

■ The value of the business with all assets in-place except the subject intangible asset at the valuation date.

5.270 The fundamental concept underlying this method is that the value of the subject intangible asset is the difference between an established, on-going business and one where the subject intangible asset does not exist. If the subject intangible asset can be rebuilt or replaced in a certain period of time then the period of lost profit is limited to the time to rebuild. However, the incremental expenses required to rebuild the subject intangible asset also increase the difference between the scenarios and, therefore, the value of the subject intangible asset.

5.271 This valuation method is most applicable for assets that provide incremental benefits, either through higher revenues or lower cost margins, but where there are other assets that drive revenue generation. This method is sometimes used to value customer related intangible assets when the MEEM method is used to value another asset. Key inputs of this method are the assumptions of how much time and additional expenses are required to recreate the subject intangible asset, and the level of lost cash flows that should be assumed during this period. The expenses required to recreate the subject intangible asset should generally be higher than the expenses required to maintain its existing service potential. In addition, to shorten the time to recreate it would generally require a higher level of investment.

5.272 The tax amortisation benefit of the intangible asset should also be included in determining the value of the subject intangible asset.

Applying IFRS 13 to investment property

5.273 Under IAS 40 an entity may choose either the cost model for investment property or the fair value model. If an entity applies the fair value model, it is within the scope of IFRS 13.

5.274 Fair value for investment property is based on the property's highest and best use. [IFRS 13 para 27].

Example – Use of 'highest and best use' approach

An entity owns an investment property, which comprises land with an old warehouse on it. It has been determined that the land could be redeveloped into a leisure park. The land's market value would be higher if redeveloped than the market value under its current use. Management is unclear about whether the investment property's fair value should be based on the property's (land and warehouse) market value under its current use, or the land's potential market value if the leisure park redevelopment occurred.

The property's fair value should be based on the land's market value for its potential use. The 'highest and best use' is used as the most appropriate model for fair value. Using this approach the property's existing use value is not the only basis considered. Fair value is the highest value, determined from market evidence, by considering any other use that is financially feasible, justifiable and reasonably probable.

The highest and best use valuation assumes the site's redevelopment. This will involve demolishing the current warehouse and constructing a leisure park in its place. Therefore, none of the market value obtained for the land should be allocated to the building. The market value of the current building on the property's highest and best use (as a warehouse) is therefore zero. The building's current carrying amount should, therefore, be written down to zero.

Measuring fair value

5.275 An investment property's fair value is typically based either on the market approach by reference to sales in the market of comparable properties or the income approach by reference to rentals obtained from the subject property or similar properties. The cost approach is not appropriate for the fair value model under IAS 40.

5.276 Fair value reflects rental income from current leases and other assumptions that market participants make about future rental income, based on current conditions.

5.277 Fair value does not reflect the following factors to the extent that they would not be generally available to market participants:

- Additional value created by bringing together a number of properties in different locations and combining them into a portfolio of properties.

- Synergies between investment properties and other assets.

- Legal rights and restrictions that are specific to the present owner.

- Tax benefits or disadvantages that are specific to the present owner.

5.278 Fair value excludes any estimated price that is inflated or deflated by special terms such as unusual financing, sale and leaseback arrangements or special considerations or concessions granted by anyone associated with the sale.

Fair value

Fair value is determined without deduction for transaction costs that might be incurred on sale or other disposal.

5.279 A leased property interest is initially recognised at its fair value or, if lower, at the present value of the minimum lease payments. At acquisition and assuming that the lease has been negotiated at market rates, the fair value of such a leased property interest, net of all expected lease payments (including those relating to recognised liabilities), should be nil. This is because if the property interest is recorded at the present value of the minimum lease payments, the carrying amount of the property interest and of the related lease liability will be the same and the net amount will be nil. [IAS 40 para 41]. Normally, the fair value of the property interest will approximate to the present value of the minimum lease payments, since the minimum lease payments are discounted to present value using the interest rate implicit in the lease. [IAS 17 para 20]. This rate is defined in IAS 17 as the rate that, at inception of the lease, causes the present value of the minimum lease payments plus the unguaranteed residual value to equal the sum of the fair value of the leased asset plus any initial direct costs of the lessor. [IAS 17 para 4].

5.280 Where an entity has prepaid or accrued operating lease income in its balance sheet, it does not include the value of that income in the fair value of the related investment property, as the prepaid or accrued operating lease income is shown as a separate asset or liability. [IAS 40 para 50].

The market approach

5.281 The best evidence of fair value is usually provided by current prices in an active market for similar property in a similar location and condition and subject to similar lease terms and other conditions. Clearly, such conditions may not always be present and so an entity should take account of, and make allowances for, differences from the comparable properties in location, nature and condition of the property or in contractual terms of leases and other contracts relating to the property. For example, if the property is leased by the entity on a finance lease that contains restrictions on the uses to which a property may be put by present and future lessees, that could significantly affect its fair value, because it might restrict the entity's ability to obtain the optimum market rentals.

5.282 Where current prices in an active market are not available, entities should consider evidence from alternative sources, such as:

- Current prices in an active market for properties of a different nature, condition or location or that are subject to different lease or other contractual terms, adjusted to reflect the differences.

- Recent prices from transactions on less active markets, adjusted to reflect changes in economic conditions since the date of those transactions.

5.283 Using the market approach to measure the fair value of investment property is likely to be a Level 2 measurement.

The income approach

5.284 The fair value of an investment property may be measured using discounted cash flow projections based on reliable estimates of future rental income and expenditure, supported by the terms of existing lease and other contracts. Where practicable, external evidence should also be used, such as current market rents for properties of a similar nature, condition and location. Discount rates that reflect current market participant assessments of uncertainty regarding the amount and timing of cash flows should be used to discount the projected future cash flows.

5.285 Using the income approach to measure the fair value of investment property is likely to result in a Level 3 measurement as the most significant input will be the projected cash flows.

Disclosures

5.286 An entity that uses the fair value model for its investment property needs to comply with the disclosure requirements of IFRS 13 as well as the additional disclosures required by IAS 40.

5.285 An entity that uses the cost model in IAS 40 is required to disclose the fair value of its investment property [IAS 40 para 79(e)]. For this fair value which is disclosed only rather than being included in the balance sheet, IFRS 13 requires disclosure of:

- the level of the fair value hierarchy in which the measurement is classified;

- a description of the valuation technique and the inputs used; and

- if the asset is not being used for its highest and best use, a statement to that effect and the reason why.

[IFRS 13 para 97].

Applying IFRS 13 to biological assets

5.288 Biological assets are required by IAS 41 to be measured at fair value less costs to sell at both initial recognition and at each subsequent reporting date and so are within IFRS 13's scope for both measurement and disclosure.

The fair value hierarchy

5.289 An example of a Level 1 fair value measurement would be the price that could be obtained for a particular grade of maize that is actively traded on a commodities exchange.

5.290 A Level 2 fair value measurement would typically include a recent transaction price for the asset if there is no active market or market prices for similar assets, adjusted for the points of differences. It should however be noted that if adjustments made for points of differences are considered significant to the entire measurement, this may result in the fair value measurement being categorised as a Level 3 fair value measurement.

5.291 Level 3 fair value measurements are those that are based significantly on unobservable inputs. Common examples of such measurements are discounted cash flow analyses that use cash flows based judgements and assumptions made by management and are thus unobservable. A forester may, for example, perform a discounted cash flow analysis to arrive at the fair value of its forestry holdings. In performing the analysis, assumptions regarding growth, fires etc may need to be made based on the judgement, expectations and experience of management. The fair value measurement of the forestry assets will consequently be classified within Level 3 of the hierarchy.

Location of the asset

5.292 A biological asset's physical location is often one of the asset's critical characteristic (for example a commodity) and as a result transport costs are regularly incurred in an agricultural context as entities need to ensure that their agricultural produce is transported to its principal or most advantageous market. In such cases, paragraph 26 of IFRS 13 requires the fair value of those assets to be adjusted for transport costs.

5.293 Paragraph 28 of IFRS 13 specifies that fair value takes account of an asset's location and condition. Thus, transport costs impact the measurement of fair value. For example, the fair value of cattle at a farm is the price for the cattle in the principal market less the transport and other costs of getting the cattle from the farm to that market. This requirement to measure biological assets by taking transport costs into account when determining fair value as well as future costs to sell would most likely result in a loss on initial recognition of biological assets.

Example – Impact of transport costs on determining fair value

Entity A purchased cattle at an auction for C100,000 on 30 June 20X8. Costs of transporting the cattle back to the company's farm were C1,000. The company would have to incur similar transportation cost if it were to sell the cattle in the auction, in addition to an auctioneer's fee of 2% of sales price. Fair value less costs to sell is, therefore, C97,000 (C100,000 – C1,000 – C2,000), cash outflow equals C101,000, resulting in a loss on initial recognition of the cattle of C4,000 (C101,000 – C97,000).

By 31 December 20X8, the fair value of the cattle (taking into account its location and condition) had increased to C110,000 (that is, C110,000 is the market price net of costs of transporting the cattle to market). Hence, the cattle should be measured in entity A's financial statements at C107,800 (that is, C110,000 less the estimated auctioneer's fee of C2,200). The estimated costs of getting the cattle to the auction are not deducted as transport costs are taken into account in determining fair value.

Principal or most advantageous market

5.294 If there is a principal market for the asset, the fair value measurement represents the price in that market (whether that price is directly observable or estimated using another valuation technique), even if the price in a different market is potentially more advantageous at the measurement date. [IFRS 13 para 18]. In the absence of a principal market, the entity should use the price in the most advantageous market for the relevant asset.

5.295 The principal market for an entity's biological assets is defined as the market with the greatest volume and level of activity for the particular asset. Paragraph 17 of IFRS 13 clarifies that the market in which an entity would normally enter into a transaction to sell the asset, is presumed to be the principal market for that asset unless there is evidence to the contrary. See also paragraphs 5.18 to 5.22.

> **Example – Producer has access to more than one market**
>
> An entity is in the business of growing and harvesting sugar cane. Along with other local growers, it sells the harvested cane to the local mill. There are other mills located throughout the country. However, it is uneconomic to transport the sugar cane to other mills, although they often pay higher prices for the cane. Which market price should the entity use to establish fair value?
>
> IFRS 13 presumes that the market in which the entity would normally sell its assets is the principal market for those assets. Unless there is clear evidence to the contrary, the local market will be considered the principal market for the harvested sugar cane and the entity should use the local market price as the basis for determining fair value.

Market-based valuation techniques

5.296 Many biological assets have relevant market-determined prices or values available, as agricultural produce are often basic commodities that are traded actively. For example, there are usually market prices for calves and piglets, as there is an active market for these. Where there is an active market for a biological asset or agricultural produce, the quoted price in that market is the appropriate basis for determining the fair value of that asset.

5.297 Appendix A to IFRS 13 defines an active market as a market in which transactions for the asset or liability take place with sufficient frequency and volume to provide pricing information on an ongoing basis.

5.298 The nature of consumable biological assets and agricultural produce is such that an active market will normally exist. Some bearer biological assets (that is those producing multiple harvest), on the other hand, may seldom be sold so other techniques for measuring fair value may be necessary. If an active market does not exist, one or more of the following methods should be used to estimate fair value, if such data is available:

Fair value

- The most recent market transaction price, provided that there has not been a significant change in economic circumstances between the date of that transaction and the balance sheet date.

- Market prices for similar assets with adjustment to reflect differences.

- Sector benchmarks, such as the value of an orchard expressed per export tray, bushel or hectare and the value of cattle expressed per kilogram of meat.

5.299   Biological assets are often physically attached to land (for example, trees and vines). There may be no separate market for biological assets that are attached to the land, but an active market may exist for the combined assets, that is, for the biological assets, raw land and land improvements, as a package. An entity may use information regarding the combined assets to determine fair value for the biological assets. For example, the fair value of raw land and land improvements may be deducted from the fair value of the combined assets to arrive at the biological assets' fair value. [IAS 41 para 25].

Fair value in the absence of market-based prices or values

5.300   Where market-based prices or values are not available for a biological asset in its present location and condition, fair value should be measured on the basis of a valuation technique which is appropriate in the circumstances and for which sufficient data is available to measure fair value. The use of relevant observable inputs should be maximised whilst minimising the use of unobservable inputs. [IFRS 13 para 61]. An example of an appropriate valuation technique includes the use of present value techniques where the present value of expected net cash flows from the asset are discounted at a current market-based rate. [IFRS 13 App B para B13].

5.301   The fair value of bearer biological assets is generally determined through the use of a discounted cash flow method as a valuation technique, as market-determined prices or values are not available. The fair value of these assets is derived from the expected cash flows of the agricultural produce.

5.302   The cash flow model should include all directly attributable cash inflows and outflows and only those cash flows. The inflows will be the price in the market of the harvested crop for each crop over the asset's life. The outflows will be those incurred raising or growing the asset and getting it to market, for example, direct labour, feed, fertiliser and transport to market. The 'market' is where the asset will be sold. For some assets, this will be an actual market; for others, it may be the 'factory gate'.

5.303   Consistent with the objective of estimating fair value, the cash flows should be based as far as possible on market data. For example, while there is a market for fully grown salmon, there is no market for partly grown salmon. The fair value of a partly grown salmon is measured by projecting the cash flows from the sale of the salmon fully grown, less the cash outflows needed to grow the salmon to its marketable weight and discounting them to a present day value.

5.304 For purposes of estimating fair value of biological assets financing and taxation (where a pre-tax discount rate is used) cash flows are ignored. Any cash flows to be incurred in re-establishing biological assets after harvest are also excluded from the valuation (for example, the cost of re-planting a crop). A provision for re-planting may be required by IAS 37 once the biological asset is harvested but is not part of the asset's fair value as it is not a characteristic of the asset.

5.305 In the measurement of fair value an imputed contributory asset charge should be included where there are no cash flows associated with the use of assets essential to the agricultural activity, otherwise the fair value will be overstated. The most common example where this is necessary is where the land on which the biological asset is growing is owned by the entity. The cash flows should include a notional cash outflow for 'rent' of the land to be comparable with the asset of an entity that rents its land from a third party. The fair value of a biological asset is independent of the land on which it grows or lives. Examples where this approach is relevant include long-term biological assets, such as plantation forests, tea plantations and vineyards, but is also appropriate for some short-term assets.

> **Example 1 – Estimating fair value of short-lived assets in the absence of market-based prices or values**
>
> A quarterly reporting company with a December year end incurs costs in respect of sowing a wheat field for the quarter to June 20X8 of C900. Management expects to harvest the wheat at the end of November 20X8. The field is owned by the reporting entity and has an original cost of C2,000.
>
> Due to the lack of an active market for partly-grown wheat and very few sales of part-grown fields, there is no market-based fair value available. Consequently, for the purposes of preparing the financial statements, the wheat's fair value (excluding the land) should be based on the present value of the expected net cash flows. The relevant discount rate is 11%.
>
> Management's projections as at 30 June 20X8 of future cash flows are as follows:
>
> | Period | 3 months to Sept 20X8 | 3 months to Dec 20X8 | Total |
> |---|---|---|---|
> | Cash inflows | – | 4,000 | 4,000 |
> | Cash outflows[1] | (450) | (1,000) | (1,450) |
> | Net cash flows | (450) | 3,000 | 2,550 |
> | Discounted at 11% | (438) | 2,847 | 2,409 |
>
> [1] Included in the cash outflows is a contributory asset charge related to land and other assets recognised separately. This is not a 'true' cash flow in this case as there is no rental payable in this scenario. However, the charge is included in the valuation to ensure a consistent value to a situation where for example the land is rented.

Hence, the wheat field should be recognised at 30 June 20X8 at C4,409 (being C2,000 in respect of land and C2,409 in respect of part-grown wheat). A fair value gain of C2,409 and the operating costs incurred during the quarter should be recognised in the quarterly income statement. Alternative treatments of capitalising directly attributable costs as part of the biological asset are discussed in chapter 32.

In the three months ended 30 September 20X8, actual cash outflows amounted to C550 so this amount should be recognised as an operating expense. At 30 September 20X8 management's revised projections based on the then current trends for wheat prices for delivery in November 20X8 were as follows:

Period	3 months to Dec 20X8
Cash inflows	3,800
Cash outflows[1]	(1,000)
Net cash flows	2,800
Discounted at 11%	2,728

[1] Included in the cash outflows is a contributory asset charge related to land and other assets recognised separately.

Hence, the wheat should be measured at a fair value of C2,728. A fair value gain of C319 and the operating costs of C550 should be recognised in the quarterly income statement. The accounting treatment of the increase in fair value since the planting date is described in chapter 32.

At the point of harvest, the wheat is worth C4,700. The biological asset immediately before harvest should be measured at that amount with a fair value gain of C1,972 recognised in the income statement. At the date of harvest, the wheat's fair value is removed as a biological asset and classified as inventory, at C4,700 as its deemed cost. One method of presentation when the wheat is sold is for the entity to report revenue of C4,700 and a cost of sales (the deemed cost of inventory) of C4,700. Therefore, no gross profit is recognised if the harvested produce is immediately sold after harvest without adding value to the inventory by further processing.

In practice, alternative presentation methods could exist for different industries.

Example 2 – Estimating fair value of recurring harvest long-lived biological assets in the absence of market-based prices or values

Farmer S owns an apple orchard. As there is no active market for apple trees, farmer S performs a discounted cash flow calculation in order to estimate the fair value. For an orchard at the end of year 4, the calculation is illustrated as follows:

	Year 5	Year 6	Year 7	Year 23	Year 24
Cash-inflows	600	900	1,200	800	700
Cash-outflows	400	460	525	485	410
Contributory charge	50	70	95	80	45
Net flows	150	370	580	235	245

Discount rate	6%

Net fair value at end of year 4	5,842

Notes:

1. Cash flows for years 8-22 are assumed to be the same as for year 7.

2. Cash flows and discount rate do not include the effect of inflation, but are post-tax.

3. Contributory charge for land and other assets is included in the calculation to reflect an expense for assets owned and separately recognised.

4. Cash-outflows would include staff costs, water, electricity, fertilisers and other operating costs.

5. This valuation model includes further transformation of the asset (as the yield of the tree increases over years 5 and 6). Refer to chapter 32.

6. Apples that are on the tree at the date the valuation is performed are not valued separately as inventory, but form part of the valuation of the orchard.

For a non-recurring long-lived assets such as a forest, the calculation would be similar to this one except that there will be one cash-inflow at the end of the asset's life.

5.306 Sometimes, it is appropriate to adopt different valuation methods for different groups of assets. IAS 41 acknowledges that this may be helpful and gives the examples of assets grouped by age and quality. [IAS 41 para 15]. In its 2011 financial statements, Masonite (Africa) Limited grouped its standing timber according to age for the purpose of measuring fair value.

5.307 The purpose of a net present value calculation is to determine an estimate of the fair value of a biological asset in its present location and condition. An entity must, therefore, consider the present location and condition of the asset when determining an appropriate discount rate to be used and in estimating expected net cash flows. In determining the present value of expected net cash flows, an entity includes the net cash flows that market participants would use when pricing the asset in its principal or most advantageous market. [IFRS 13

App B para B14]. The following example considers the impact of additional biological transformation on the fair value estimation.

> **Example – Impact of additional biological transformation and future activities on fair value**
>
> An entity set up a coffee plantation incurring expenses of C1m. The coffee trees will take 3 to 5 years to mature and will then produce coffee berries for harvesting for approximately 20 years. During the period to maturity, the company will incur only maintenance costs. Thereafter, the entity will incur harvesting costs as well as maintenance costs. It will also receive revenues from the sale of the coffee berries.
>
> There is no market for recently planted coffee trees and there are no market-based data on the basis of which fair value could be estimated. Fair value is to be determined on the basis of the present value of future cash flows.
>
> The purpose of the net present value of expected net cash flows is to determine the fair value of the coffee trees in their present location and condition.
>
> It follows that an immature coffee tree is less valuable than a mature coffee tree that is high-yielding. This increase in value arising out of the biological transformation from an immature state to a mature state is exactly the sort of value change that IAS 41 would require to be recognised in the income statement (see chapter 32). The aim of the present value calculation is to derive as good an estimate of market value as possible; therefore, the value of the immature coffee trees should take account of the potential for future increases in yield. The risks associated with the future growth should be considered in estimating the expected net cash flows and determining an appropriate discount rate.

5.308   Occasionally, cost will approximate to fair value, particularly when:

- little biological transformation has taken place since the costs were originally incurred (for example, fruit tree seedlings planted immediately prior to a balance sheet date); or

- the impact of biological transformation on price is not expected to be material (for example, in respect of the initial growth in a 30-year pine plantation cycle).

[IAS 41 para 24].

Applying IFRS 13 to non-financial liabilities including contingent liabilities

5.309   Non-financial liabilities fall under IAS 37. The measurement basis in IAS 37 is not fair value and so non-financial liabilities are only within IFRS 13's scope when they are assumed in a business combination under IFRS 3. As a result, practical experience in this area is limited.

General principles for measuring non-financial liabilities

5.310 A liability is not considered merely a 'negative asset' when measuring fair value. The fair value of a liability under IFRS 13 relies on a transfer concept rather than settlement concept. Specifically, the fair value of a liability assumes the liability continues after transfer (in a credit-equivalent environment) and the transferor is completely relieved of its obligation after the transfer.

5.311 Paragraph 37 of IFRS 13 states that when there is no observable market price for the transfer of a liability and the identical liability is held by another party as an asset, a reporting entity should measure the liability's fair value from the perspective of a market participant that holds the identical liability as an asset at the measurement date. The standard suggests there is no conceptual reason why the liability value would diverge from the corresponding asset value in the same market. However, assets and liabilities typically trade in different markets (if they trade at all) and, therefore, may have different values. For example, the consumer who holds a vehicle warranty asset (the right to have his vehicle repaired) likely views the warranty asset in a much different way than the manufacturer who has a pool of warranty liabilities. They do not transact in the same market and would be unlikely to value the asset and liability in the same way. The valuation of liabilities under IFRS 13 is an evolving area.

5.312 An entity's non-financial liabilities are referred to as operating or performance obligations. Unlike debt, which requires only a cash transfer for settlement, satisfying a performance obligation may require the use of other operating assets. In addition, a performance obligation may mature simply by the passage of time (that is, non-contingent) or may depend on other (that is, contingent) events resulting in performance and other related risks.

5.313 A performance obligation may be contractual or non-contractual, which affects the risk that the obligation is satisfied and thus its fair value.

Measuring fair value

5.314 Since most non-financial liabilities are not traded in an active market, they are commonly valued using the income or cost approach.

5.315 Similar principles apply to using DCF to measure liabilities as when using the technique to measure assets. However it is important to recognise that there are differences, notably in how risk is dealt with.

5.316 When the fair value of an asset is being measured, the valuation considers the risk that the projected cash inflows will be less than expected and so increased risk reduces an asset's value. In contrast, when measuring a liability's fair value, the valuation considers the risk that the cash outflows will be greater than expected and increased risk increases the liability's value. If risk is reflected in the discount rate rather than by adjusting the cash flows, the rate increases when an asset is being valued and decreases when a liability is being valued.

5.317 IFRS 13 has clarified that the discount rate applied to projected cash flows for a non-financial liability includes an entity's own credit risk [IFRS 13 para 42]. This is an area where there was diversity in practice and so this clarification will be a change for some preparers. See also the discussion in paragraphs 5.133 to 5.136.

Deferred revenue

5.318 Deferred revenue in the context of a business combination represents an obligation to provide products or services to a customer when payment has been made in advance and delivery or performance has not yet occurred. Deferred revenue is a liability and represents a performance obligation. The deferred revenue amount recorded on the acquiree's balance sheet generally represents the cash received in advance, less the amount amortised for services performed to date, rather than a fair value amount.

5.319 The fair value of a deferred revenue liability typically reflects how much an acquirer has to pay a third party to assume the liability (that is, a transfer of the liability). Thus, the acquiree's recognised deferred revenue liability at the acquisition date is rarely the fair value amount that would be required to transfer the underlying contractual obligation.

5.320 Generally, there are two methods of measuring the fair value of a deferred revenue liability. The first method, commonly referred to as a bottom-up approach, measures the liability as the direct, incremental costs to fulfill the legal performance obligation, plus a reasonable profit margin if associated with goods or services being provided, and a premium for risks associated with price variability. Direct and incremental costs may or may not include certain overhead items, but should include costs incurred by market participants to service the remaining performance obligation related to the deferred revenue obligation. These costs do not include elements of service or costs incurred or completed prior to the consummation of the business combination, such as upfront selling and marketing costs, training costs and recruiting costs.

5.321 The reasonable profit margin should be based on the nature of the remaining activities and reflect a market participant's profit. If the profit margin on the specific component of deferred revenue is known, it should be used if it is representative of a market participant's normal profit margin on the specific obligation. If the current market rate is higher than the market rate that existed at the time the original transactions took place, the higher current rate should be used. The measurement of the fair value of a deferred revenue liability is generally performed on a pre-tax basis and, therefore, the normal profit margin should be on a pre-tax basis.

5.322 An alternative method of measuring the fair value of a deferred revenue liability (commonly referred to as a top-down approach) relies on market indicators of expected revenue for any obligation yet to be delivered. This approach starts with the amount that an entity would receive in a transaction, less the cost of the selling effort (which has already been performed) including a profit margin on that selling effort. This method is used less frequently, but is commonly used for measuring the fair value of remaining post-contract customer support for licensed software.

5.323   If deferred revenues exist at the time of the business combination, and intangible assets are valued using the income approach (for example, the relief from royalty method (RFR) or the multi-period excess earnings method (MEEM)), then adjustments may be required to the projections if they were prepared on an accrual basis. This will eliminate any revenues reflected in the projections that have already been received by the acquiree (that is, the acquired cash includes the deferred revenue amount). If the excess earnings method is used, the expenses and required profit on the expenses that are captured in valuing the deferred revenue are also eliminated from the projections. However, if cash based projected financial information (PFI) is used in the valuation and therefore acquired deferred revenues are not reflected in the PFI, then no adjustment is required in valuing intangible assets using the income approach.

Contingent liabilities

5.324   Valuing contingent liabilities is an area where there is limited practical experience and guidance.

5.325   IFRS 3 requires that an acquirer recognises, at fair value on the acquisition date, those contingent liabilities assumed that are reliably measurable present obligations. [IFRS 3 para 23]. IAS 37 defines contingent liabilities as either present or possible obligations. Present obligations are legal or constructive obligations that result from a past event. [IAS 37 para 10]. Possible obligations are obligations that arise from past events whose existence will be confirmed only by the occurrence or non-occurrence of one or more uncertain future events not wholly within an entity's control. [IAS 37 para 10].

5.326   Some variation of the income approach will most likely be used to estimate the fair value if fair value is determinable. A straightforward discounted cash flow technique may be sufficient in some circumstances while in other circumstances more sophisticated valuation techniques and models (for example, real options, option pricing, or Monte Carlo simulation) may be warranted.

Example – Valuing warranty liabilities

Assume that entity A is acquired in a business combination. Entity A is a manufacturer of computers and related products and provides a three year limited warranty to its customers related to the performance of its products. Expenses related to expected warranty claims are accrued based on the detailed analyses of past claims history for different products. Entity A's experience indicates that warranty claims increase each year of a contract based on the age of the computer components.

Entity A has three distinct computer products. One of its product lines (line 1) has significant new components for which there is little historical claims data, as well as other components for which historical claims data is available. Taking into account the liability's short-term nature and the expected cash flows over the warranty period, the acquirer determines that a 7% discount rate is applicable. In applying the acquisition method, the acquirer should calculate a fair value estimate for warranty claims related to lines 2 and 3 and to line 1, if determinable.

Cash flow models can be based on expected cash flows or conditional cash flows. Given the availability of historical claims data, the acquirer believes that the expected cash flow technique will provide a better measure of the warranty obligation.

To develop the probabilities needed to estimate expected cash flows, the acquirer evaluates entity A's historical warranty claims. This includes evaluating how the performance of the new components used in line 1 compares to the performance trends of the other components for which historical claims data is available.

The acquirer develops expected cash flows and a probability assessment for each of the various outcomes as shown below. The cash flows are based on different assumptions about the amount of expected service cost plus parts and labour related to a repair or replacement. The acquirer estimates the following outcomes for Line 1, each of which is expected to be payable over the three-year warranty period:

Warranty claims – expected cash flows

Product line 1	Probability	Year 1 C	Year 2 C	Year 3 C
Outcome 1	50%	3,000	6,000	12,000
Outcome 2	30%	8,000	14,000	20,000
Outcome 3	20%	12,000	20,000	30,000

In calculating the amount of the warranty obligation, the acquirer needs to estimate the level of profit a market participant would require to perform under the warranty obligations. The acquirer considers the margins for public companies engaged in the warranty fulfilment business as well as its own experience in arriving at a pre-tax profit margin equal to 5% of revenue[1].

The acquirer also needs to select a discount rate to apply to the probability weighted expected warranty claims for each year and discount them to calculate a present value. Because the expected claim amounts reflect the probability weighted average of the possible outcomes identified, the expected cash flows do not depend on the occurrence of a specific event. In this case, the acquirer determined that the discount rate is 7%[3].

The table below reflects the expected cash flows developed from the data in the previous table with the value of each outcome adjusted for the acquirer's estimate of the probability of occurrence.

Warranty claims – expected cash flows – probability adjusted

Product line 1	Year 1	Year 2	Year 3
	C	C	C
Outcome 1	1,500	3,000	6,000
Outcome 2	2,400	4,200	6,000
Outcome 3	2,400	4,000	6,000
Probability weighted	6,300	11,200	18,000
Pre-tax profit (5%)[1]	315	560	900
Warranty claim amount	6,615	11,760	18,900
Discount period[2]	0.5	1.5	2.5
Discount rate[3]	7%	7%	7%
Present value factor[4]	0.9667	0.9035	0.8444
Present value of warranty claims[5]	6,395	10,625	15,959
Estimated fair value[6] (rounded)	33,000		

[1] The expected payment should include a profit element required by market participants, which is consistent with the fair value transfer concept for liabilities. The profit element included here represents an assumed profit for this example and should only be viewed from the perspective of how to apply the profit element.

[2] A mid-year discounting convention was used based on the assumption that warranty claims occur evenly throughout the year.

[3] In practice, determining the discount rate can be a challenging process requiring a significant amount of judgement. The discount rate should consider a risk premium that market participants would consider when determining the fair value of a contingent liability. For performance obligations (for example, warranties, deferred revenues) determination of discount rates may be more challenging than for financial liabilities as assessment of non-performance risk component is not so readily obtainable as it may be for financial liabilities.

[4] Calculated as $1/(1+k)\hat{\ }t$, where k = discount rate and t = discount period.

[5] Calculated as the warranty claim amount multiplied by the present value factor.

[6] Calculated as the sum of the present value of warranty claims for years 1 through 3.

Chapter 6

Financial instruments

6.1 – Introduction, objectives and scope of IAS 32, IAS 39 and IFRS 7

6.1 – Introduction, objectives and scope of IAS 32, IAS 39 and IFRS 7

Introduction

Accounting for financial instruments

6.1.1 Financial markets have experienced, and continue to experience, significant developments since the 1980s. As foreign exchange rates, interest rates and commodity prices became increasingly volatile, a need arose to manage the commercial risks arising from the instability of these markets. Primary financial instruments, such as bonds and shares, that comprised much of the traditional financing and risk management activities, gave way to derivative products, such as futures, options, forward contracts and swaps, in managing risks. Entities were able to make substantial changes to their financial risk profile, virtually instantaneously, by entering into foreign exchange or interest rate swaps, or by acquiring options or forward contracts to hedge or take positions on future price movements. With the globalisation of financial markets, growth in international commerce, advancement in financial risk management and information technology, the development and use of cost effective innovative derivative products and complex financial instruments for managing risk and improving return on assets became commonplace.

6.1.2 However, it became apparent that this growth in the use of financial instruments had outstripped the development of guidance for their accounting. Traditional realisation and cost-based measurement concepts were no longer adequate to effectively portray their impact and risks, as some derivatives (for example, forward contracts and swaps) with no initial cost were simply not recognised until settlement, although some instruments with negative fair values were recorded as liabilities in the financial statements. Deficiencies in current accounting practices, inconsistent treatment of economically similar transactions and the lack of visibility in the financial statements caused difficulty for both preparers and users of financial statements. This resulted in an atmosphere of uncertainty, which many people believed might discourage the legitimate use of derivative instruments. Concern about inadequate accounting for derivatives was also heightened by the publicity surrounding large derivative-instrument losses at several companies. As a result, a pervasive need to develop a single, comprehensive standard for accounting and disclosure of financial instruments and hedging activities became important.

Development of financial instruments standards

6.1.3 In 1988, the International Accounting Standards Committee (IASC), the predecessor body of the IASB, started work developing a comprehensive standard on the recognition, measurement and disclosure of financial instruments. The first standard, IAS 32, was issued in 1995, followed by IAS 39 in March 1999. However, when the IASB was formed in 2001, it undertook a project to improve international standards inherited from the IASC. As a result, revised versions of IAS 32 and IAS 39 were issued in December 2003. Since then further amendments have been made to these standards, the principal one being the issue of a new standard, IFRS 7, in August 2005. As IFRS 7 includes all the disclosure requirements relating to financial instruments, the title of IAS 32 was amended to 'Financial instruments – Presentation'.

EU adoption

6.1.4 The EU Regulation required listed groups to prepare their consolidated financial statements using IFRS for periods commencing on or after 1 January 2005. For this to happen, IFRSs had to be brought into EU law through a complex endorsement mechanism. Although most of the IASB standards were endorsed, IAS 39 was not endorsed in full. Some aspects of IAS 39, namely the option to fair value all liabilities and certain aspects of hedge accounting that troubled banks and regulators, did not find favour with the EU and were removed. This 'carved out' version was endorsed by the EU in November 2004. The 'carve out' relating to the fair value option was removed as a result of a subsequent amendment to IAS 39 and endorsement by the EU in November 2005, but the one relating to hedge accounting remains with the result that there is still a difference between full IAS 39 and EU endorsed IAS 39.

The credit crisis and way forward

6.1.5 The credit crisis has highlighted the increasing complexity of financial instruments and their accounting. As a result, there has been pressure from the public, politicians and regulators to re-think and simplify the accounting for financial instruments. The IASB is keen to find a better accounting solution for financial instruments that will produce meaningful results without undue complexity and dependence on detailed rules.

6.1.6 As a first step in that process, the IASB and FASB identified three long-term projects relating to financial instruments: the replacement of IAS 39; derecognition; and financial instruments with characteristics of equity. IFRS 9 represents the first milestone in the IASB's planned replacement of IAS 39. It was published in November 2009 and replaces the multiple classification and measurement models for financial assets. In October 2010, the IASB published the classification and measurement model for financial liabilities. The IASB also continues to work on further stages of this standard, as described below.

6.1.6.1   IFRS 9 has been available for adoption since November 2009 but is not yet endorsed by the EU. In November 2011, the IASB tentatively decided to consider limited modifications to IFRS 9. In December 2011, the date for mandatory application of IFRS 9 was deferred to annual periods beginning on or after 1 January 2015. The IASB also amended the transition provisions to provide relief from restating comparative information and introduced new disclosures to help users of the financial statements understand the effect of moving to the IFRS 9 classification and measurement model.

6.1.6.2   Proposals for the second and third phases of the project continue to be developed. The project on derecognition was modified in June 2010 when the IASB decided to retain IAS 39's existing requirements on derecognition and these have been carried forward unchanged into IFRS 9. At the same time improvements to disclosure have been added into IFRS 7 (effective for annual periods beginning on or after 1 July 2011). Finally, work was suspended on the project on financial instruments with characteristics of equity along with a number of other projects in November 2010 to allow the IASB to concentrate on finalising other, more advanced/urgent projects (including phases 2 and 3 of IFRS 9).

6.1.7   In addition, the IASB published IFRS 13 in May 2011. It is effective for annual periods beginning on or after 1 January 2013. This standard will apply to any asset, liability or equity instrument that is measured at fair value or whose fair value is disclosed. Financial instruments will, therefore, commonly be measured in accordance with this standard. Chapter 5 sets out the guidance on measuring financial instruments at fair value in accordance with IFRS 13.

Objectives

6.1.8   IAS 32's objective is to establish principles for presenting financial instruments as financial liabilities or equity and for offsetting financial assets and financial liabilities. It applies to the classification of financial instruments, from the perspective of the issuer, into financial assets, financial liabilities and equity instruments. Furthermore, it deals with the classification of related interest, dividends, losses and gains; and the circumstances in which financial assets and liabilities should be offset. [IAS 32 para 2].

6.1.9   IAS 39's objective is to establish principles for recognising and measuring financial assets, financial liabilities and some contracts to buy or sell non-financial items. [IAS 39 para 1]. IAS 39 also deals with de-recognition of financial assets and financial liabilities and hedge accounting. Requirements for presenting and disclosing information about financial instruments set out in IAS 32 and IFRS 7 are designed to complement those principles.

6.1.10   IFRS 7's objective is to require entities to provide disclosures that enable users to evaluate:

- The significance of financial instruments for the entity's financial position and performance.

- The nature and extent of risks arising from financial instruments to which the entity is exposed during the period at the reporting date and how the entity manages these risks.

[IFRS 7 para 1].

Scope

6.1.11   Generally, IAS 32, IAS 39 and IFRS 7 have to be applied by all entities preparing their financial statements in accordance with IFRS and to all types of financial instruments, except for those specifically excluded from their scope [IAS 32 para 4; IAS 39 para 2; IFRS 7 para 3]. The definition of a financial instrument is broad and is discussed in chapter 4.

6.1.12   The scope of the three standards is very wide-ranging, but not identical. While IAS 32 and IAS 39 only deal with recognised financial instruments, IFRS 7 applies to both recognised as well as unrecognised financial instruments. Recognised financial instruments include financial assets and financial liabilities that are within IAS 39's scope. Unrecognised financial instruments include some financial instruments, for example, loan commitments that, although scoped out of IAS 39, are within IFRS 7's scope. [IFRS 7 para 4]. In other words, all financial instruments that are scoped out of IFRS 7 are also scoped out of IAS 39, but IAS 39 contains additional scope exclusions that go beyond IFRS 7 and IAS 32. [IAS 32 para 4; IFRS 7 para 3; IAS 39 para 2]. In general, items are scoped out of all the three standards if another standard is more prescriptive.

Interests in subsidiaries, associates and joint ventures

6.1.13   Interests in subsidiaries, associates and joint ventures that are accounted for using the cost method prescribed in IAS 27, IAS 28, and IAS 31, or that are accounted for in accordance with IFRS 5 [IAS 27 para 38; IAS 28 para 14; IAS 31 para 2(a)] are outside the scope of IAS 32, IFRS 7 and IAS 39.

6.1.14   However, such interests fall within the scope of the financial instrument standards in either of the following circumstances:

- The parent or the investor accounts for such interests in its separate financial statements in accordance with IAS 39 either as at fair value through profit or loss or as available for sale. [IAS 27 para 38]. In that situation, the interest in a subsidiary, associate or joint venture falls within IAS 32's and IFRS 7's scope. [IAS 32 para 4(a); IFRS 7 para 3(a)]. In addition, the disclosure requirements of IAS 27, IAS 28 and IAS 31 continue to apply.

- An interest in an associate or a joint venture that is scoped out of IAS 28 or IAS 31, because it is held by a venture capital organisation, mutual fund, unit trust and similar entity including an investment-linked insurance fund, that upon initial recognition is designated as at fair value through profit or loss (so called fair value option) or categorised as held for trading. [IAS 28 para 1, IAS 31 para 1]. In that situation, the investment is accounted for in accordance with IAS 39 and the disclosure requirements of IFRS 7, as well as of paragraph 37(f) of IAS 28 and of paragraphs 55 and 56 of IAS 31, apply.

6.1.15 Derivatives linked to interests in subsidiaries, associates and joint ventures fall within the scope of IAS 32, IFRS 7 and IAS 39, except where the derivative meets the definition of an equity instrument of the entity in IAS 32. In that situation, it is scoped out of IAS 39 and accounted for as equity in accordance with IAS 32; it is also scoped out of IFRS 7. [IAS 32 para 4(a); IFRS 7 para 3(a); IAS 39 para 2(a)].

6.1.16 An investor may, in addition to having a present ownership interest, hold share options in an investee (that is not presently a subsidiary) that, if exercised, give the investor voting power or reduce another party's voting power over the financial and operating policies of the investee (potential voting rights). Such potential voting rights that are currently exercisable and give access to the economic benefits would have been taken into account in establishing not only whether the investor has control, significant influence or joint control, but also in determining the share of the investment (economic interest) to be accounted for by consolidation, equity method or proportional consolidation. [IAS 27 paras 14, IG 4-5; IAS 28 para 8]. When instruments containing potential voting rights in substance currently give access to the economic benefits associated with an ownership interest and so affect the share of profits the investee accounts for when consolidating, proportionately consolidating or applying the equity method, the instrument is scoped out of IAS 39. [IAS 27 para IG 7]. This exclusion makes sense as it avoids double counting the same instrument twice, first by inclusion in the economic interest calculation and, secondly, by fair valuing the derivative through profit or loss. Therefore, in this situation, IAS 32 and IFRS 7 apply, but not IAS 39.

Employee benefit plans and share-based payments

6.1.17 Employee rights and obligations under employee benefit plans are financial instruments, because they are contractual rights or obligations that will result in the flow of cash to the past and present employees. However, as they are specifically accounted for under IAS 19, they are outside the scope of IAS 32, IFRS 7 and IAS 39. [IAS 32 para 4(b); IFRS 7 para 3(b); IAS 39 para 2(c)].

6.1.18 Similarly, share-based payment transactions to which IFRS 2 applies are outside the scope of IAS 32, IFRS 7 and IAS 39. However, IAS 32, IFRS 7 and IAS 39 apply to contracts to buy or sell non-financial items in share based payment transactions that can be settled net, unless they fall within the own use purchase and sale exception (see para 6.1.43 below). For example, if an entity enters into a contract to purchase a fixed quantity of a particular commodity in exchange for issuing a fixed number of own equity instruments that could be settled net in cash, the contract would fall within IAS 39's scope, unless it qualifies for the own use exception. [IAS 32 para 4(f)(i); IFRS 7 para 3(e); IAS 39 para 2(i)].

6.1.19 Furthermore, IAS 32 applies to treasury shares that are purchased, sold, issued or cancelled in connection with employee share option plans, employee share purchase plans and all other share-based payment arrangements. [IAS 32 paras 4(f)(ii), 33, 34].

Business combinations

6.1.20 In accordance with IFRS 3 'Business combinations', contracts for contingent consideration usually fall within the scope of IAS 32, IAS 39 and IFRS 7, provided they do not meet the definition of an equity instrument. [IFRS 3 paras 40 and 58]. However, from an acquirer's perspective only, contracts for contingent consideration in a business combination that occurred under IFRS 3 (superseded) – that is, those that occurred in annual periods starting prior to 1 July 2009 (or prior to an earlier date if IFRS 3 was adopted early), are still scoped out of IAS 32, IFRS 7 and IAS 39. From the perspective of the seller, all contracts for contingent consideration normally fall within the scope of IAS 39 as a financial asset (see also IFRS Manual of Accounting chapter 26).

6.1.21 Forward contracts between an acquirer and a vendor in a business combination to buy or sell an acquiree at a future date are scoped out of IAS 39, but not IFRS 7. [IAS 39 para 2(g)]. The scope exemption applies to both the acquirer and the seller. It applies only to forward contracts entered into before the acquisition date (that is, before the date the acquirer obtains control of the acquiree). The term of the forward contract should not exceed a reasonable period normally necessary to obtain any required approvals and to complete the transaction. The exemption in paragraph 2(g) should not be applied by analogy to investments in associates and other similar transactions, nor to combinations of put and call options that are in some ways similar to a forward (sometimes referred to as 'synthetic forwards').

Own equity instruments

6.1.22 Financial instruments issued by an entity, including options and warrants, that meet the definition of an equity instrument in IAS 32 or are required to be classified as equity in accordance with paragraphs 16A, 16B, 16C and 16D of IAS 32, are outside IAS 39's but inside IAS 32's scope. Such instruments, along with other equity accounts including retained earnings, represent the residual interest of the reporting entity and are, therefore, subject to different measurement considerations to those relevant to financial assets and financial liabilities. However, the holder (but not issuer) of such an instrument should apply IAS 39 unless it meets the exceptions discussed in paragraphs 6.1.16 to 6.1.19 above. [IAS 39 para 2(d)]. IFRS 7 deals with disclosures of financial instruments in general and doesn't scope out issuers' own equity instruments, for example, disclosure about compound financial instruments in paragraph 17 of

IFRS 7; although it does scope out instruments that are required to be classified as equity in accordance with paragraphs 16A, 16B, 16C and 16D of IAS 32. [IFRS 7 para 3(f)].

Rights and obligations under lease contracts

6.1.23   Finance lease contracts that give rise to financial assets for lessors and financial liabilities for lessees are financial instruments that are specifically dealt with in IAS 17. Therefore, they fall within the scope of IAS 32 and IFRS 7, but outside of IAS 39's scope, except as follows:

- Lease receivables are included in IAS 39's scope for derecognition and impairment purposes only.

- Finance lease payables are subject to IAS 39's derecognition provisions.

- Any derivatives embedded in lease contracts are also within IAS 39's scope.

[IAS 39 para 2(b)].

Rights and obligations under insurance contracts

6.1.24   An insurance contract is a contract under which one party (the insurer) accepts significant insurance risk from another party (the policyholder) by agreeing to compensate the policyholder if a specified uncertain future event (the insured event) adversely affects the policyholder. [IFRS 4 App A]. Principally, rights and obligations under insurance contracts are scoped out of IAS 32, IFRS 7 and IAS 39 and are accounted for under IFRS 4, because the policyholder transfers to the insurer significant insurance rather than financial risk. [IAS 32 para 4(d); IFRS 7 para 3(d); IAS 39 para 2(e)]. Financial risk is the risk of a possible future change in one or more of a specified interest rate, financial instrument price, commodity price, foreign exchange rate, index of prices or rates, credit rating or credit index or other variable, provided in the case of a non-financial variable that the variable is not specific to a party to the contract. [IFRS 4 App A]. If a financial instrument takes the form of an insurance contract, but involves the transfer of financial risks, as opposed to insurance risk, the contract would fall within the financial instrument standards. The distinction between insurance risk and other risks are set out in Appendix B to IFRS 4. [IFRS 4 App B paras 8-17]. IFRS 4 contains numerous examples of insurance contracts that fall within IFRS 4's scope and those that are not insurance contracts and may fall within the scope of IAS 32, IFRS 7 and IAS 39. [IFRS 4 App B paras 18-19] IFRS 7 provides disclosure only for those rights and obligations under insurance contracts that are also in IAS 39's scope. [IFRS 7 para 3(d)].

Contracts with discretionary participating features

6.1.25   Financial instruments that are within IFRS 4's scope, because they contain a discretionary participation feature are also scoped out of IAS 39. A discretionary participation feature is a contractual right to receive significant additional benefits, as a supplement to guaranteed benefits, whose amount or timing is at the issuer's discretion and that are contractually based on the performance of a specified pool of contracts, investment returns or profit or loss of the company, fund or other entity that issues the contract. [IFRS 4 App A]. However, these instruments are in IFRS 7's scope and subject to the requirements of IAS 32 except for those with respect to the distinction between financial liabilities and equity instruments. [IAS 32 para 4(e); IAS 39 para 2(e)].

Derivatives embedded in insurance contracts

6.1.26 Derivatives embedded in insurance contracts or in contracts containing discretionary participating features as discussed above are within the scope of IAS 32, IFRS 7 and IAS 39 if they require separation in accordance with IAS 39. [IAS 39 para 2(e); IAS 32 para 4(d) (e); IFRS 7 para 3((d); IFRS 4 paras 7, 34(d)]. For example, separate accounting would be required in circumstances where contractual payments embedded in a host insurance contract that is indexed to the value of equity instruments are not related to the host instrument, because the risks inherent in the host and the embedded derivative are dissimilar. [IAS 39 para AG 30(d)]. However, no separation is required if the embedded derivative itself is an insurance contract. [IAS 39 para 2(e); IFRS 4 para 7].

Financial guarantee contracts

6.1.27 Financial guarantee contracts (sometimes known as 'credit insurance') require the issuer to make specified payments to reimburse the holder for a loss it incurs if a specified debtor fails to make payment when due under a debt instrument's original or modified terms. [IAS 39 para 9]. That is, the holder is exposed to and has incurred a loss on the failure of the debtor to make payments. These contracts are often written by financial guarantee insurers in the form of insurance contracts, or they may be written by, banks and entities that do not operate as insurance entities, in other forms (for example, letter of credit, credit default contracts).

6.1.28 A contract that compensates the holder for more than the loss incurred does not meet the definition of a financial guarantee contract. For the definition to be met, the amount of reimbursement must be either less than the amount of the loss incurred or equal to the amount incurred in order to reimburse some or all of the loss the holder suffered because the debtor defaulted.

6.1.29 Contracts that provide compensation if another party fails to perform a contractual obligation, such as an obligation to construct a building, are performance guarantees. They do not transfer credit risk and, therefore, do not meet the definition of a financial guarantee contract. These type of guarantees are accounted for under IFRS 4 as insurance contracts.

6.1.30 The accounting treatment of a financial guarantee contract does not depend on its legal form or whether it is issued by a bank, insurance company or other entity. IAS 39 does not give any guidance on accounting for financial guarantee contracts from the holders' perspective. However, for the issuer, all contracts that meet the definition of a financial guarantee fall within IAS 39's scope and are accounted for by the issuer as financial liabilities. However, an option is available to insurers to continue to account for these contracts under IFRS 4 if they had met two conditions before IAS 39 was amended to include financial guarantees in its scope. These are that the issuer has:

■ previously *asserted* explicitly that it regards such contracts as insurance contracts; and

■ used accounting applicable to insurance contracts.

If these two conditions are met, the issuer may elect to apply either IFRS 4 or IAS 39 to such financial guarantee contracts. The issuer can make the election on a contract by contract basis, but the election for each contract is irrevocable. [IAS 39 paras 2(e), AG4]. Assertions that the issuer regards contracts as insurance can typically be found in business documentation, contracts, accounting policies, financial statements and communication with customers and regulators. [IAS 39 para AG 4A].

6.1.31 In contrast, some credit related guarantees do not, as a precondition for payment, require that the holder is exposed to, and has incurred a loss on, the failure of the debtor to make payments on the guaranteed asset when due. Such guarantees are not financial guarantee contracts as defined in paragraph 6.1.30 above and are not insurance contracts as defined in IFRS 4. Such guarantees are derivatives that must be accounted for as such under IAS 39. [IAS 39 para AG 4(b)]. However, a contract that requires an entity to make payments when the counterparty to a derivative contract fails to make a payment when due, is considered to meet the definition of a financial guarantee contract. This is because it is not the risk inherent in the derivative that is being guaranteed; it is the counterparty's credit risk that is being guaranteed in the event the counterparty defaults.

Example 1 – Credit related guarantee

A bank issues a credit-related guarantee contract (sometimes referred to as credit derivative) that provides for payment if the credit rating of a debtor falls below a particular level.

In this situation, the credit related contract will be accounted for as a derivative financial instrument under IAS 39, because the contract holder is not required to suffer a loss on a specified debt instrument – the bank will pay for the decrease in the credit worthiness of the debtor even if the debtor does not actually default. However, if the contract provides for payment only in the event that the entity suffers loss as a result of non-payment by the debtor, the contract would be a financial guarantee contract. Holders and issuers of credit derivatives will always account for them under IAS 39.

Example 2 – Residual value guarantee

An insurer is required to make payments to the insured party based on the fair value of a non-financial asset at a future date under a residual value guarantee contract.

In this situation, the risk of changes in the fair value of the non-financial asset is not a financial risk because the fair value reflects not only changes in market prices for such assets (a financial variable), but also the condition of the specific asset held (a non-financial variable). As the change in fair value of the non-financial asset is specific to the owner, it is not a derivative instrument and, therefore, the contract will be accounted for as an insurance contract in accordance with IFRS 4. However, if the contract compensates the insured party only for changes in market prices and not for changes in the condition of the specific non-financial asset held, the contract is a derivative and within IAS 39's scope. [IFRS 4, IG example 1.15, IAS 39 para AG 12A].

6.1.32   There is no exemption under IAS 39 for financial guarantee contracts issued between members of a group or entities under common control similar to those under US GAAP FIN 45. Such guarantees are inter-company transactions that are eliminated on consolidation. However, in the individual financial statements of the group member issuing the guarantee, the guarantee contract will need to be accounted for in accordance with IAS 39. This is considered further in chapter 9.

Example – Parent provides a comfort letter to a subsidiary

A subsidiary of a group takes out a loan with a bank. The parent provides a comfort letter to the subsidiary such that if the subsidiary fails to repay the loan to the bank when due, the parent will pay on its behalf.

The comfort letter simply constitutes an undertaking given by the parent to its subsidiary that, in the event the subsidiary fails to repay the loan to the bank when due, the parent will step in and discharge the subsidiary's debt. This is not a financial guarantee contract as the parent has not provided any guarantee to the bank (nor would the bank be able to enforce payment under what is effectively a private arrangement between the parent and its subsidiary) to repay the loan if the subsidiary defaults.

6.1.33   Intra-group guarantees also frequently cover other obligations, such as pension plan contributions, lease rentals and taxes. The issue is whether, in the group members' individual financial statements, such obligations are financial guarantee contracts or insurance contracts. As noted in paragraph 6.1.27 above, if a financial instrument takes the form of an insurance contract, but involves the transfer of financial risks, as opposed to insurance risk, the contract would fall within the scope of the financial instrument standards. It is, therefore, necessary to determine whether the risk transferred represents insurance risk or financial risk. The risk transferred in a guarantee of pension plan contributions, lease rentals and taxes is the risk that the subsidiary (or joint venture or associate) will not make a payment when due. The reasons for non-payment could vary widely and, whilst they might include some financial risk variables, it is likely that a significant part of the risk transferred will be operational (for example, cash flow difficulties or, at the extreme, bankruptcy). Hence, it appears that the significant risk transferred in a typical guarantee of pension plan contributions, lease rentals and taxes will be insurance risk. It is arguable, therefore, that guarantees of pension plan contributions, lease rentals and taxes should be treated as insurance contracts and accounted for accordingly.

6.1.34   Even though guarantees of pension plan contributions, operating lease rentals and taxes are insurance contracts within IFRS 4's scope, it is still necessary to consider whether they meet the definition of financial guarantee contracts within IAS 39's scope. The definition of a financial guarantee contract refers specifically to the terms of a debt instrument. Although the term 'debt instrument' is not specifically defined in IFRS, it is clear from the various references made in IAS 32 that a debt instrument is a type of loan, involving a borrower and a lender. It can be concluded, therefore, that pension plan contributions and tax liabilities are not debt instruments.

6.1.34.1   As regards leases, paragraph AG9 of IAS 32 states that *"a finance lease is regarded as primarily an entitlement of the lessor to receive, and an obligation of the lessee to pay, a stream of payments that are substantially the same as blended payments of principal and interest under a loan agreement. ... An operating lease, on the other hand, is regarded as primarily an uncompleted contract committing the lessor to provide the use of an asset in future periods in exchange for consideration similar to a fee for a service".* This analysis suggests that a finance lease resembles a debt instrument, while an operating lease does not. Guarantees of finance leases, but not operating leases, should therefore be included within IAS 39's definition of a financial guarantee contract. However, where operating leases fall within the definition of a financial instrument (that is, in respect of individual payments currently due and payable), the amounts represent a short-term term liability and should be included within IAS 39's definition of a financial guarantee.

6.1.35   Financial guarantee contracts fall within the scope of IAS 32 and IFRS 7 if they are accounted for in accordance with IAS 39. However, if the issuer elects to apply IFRS 4 to those contracts, the disclosure requirements of IFRS 4 and not IFRS 7 apply. [IAS 32 para 4(d); IFRS 7 para 3(d)]. The accounting treatment of financial guarantee contracts is considered further in chapter 9.

Weather derivatives

6.1.36   Some contracts require a payment based on climatic variables (sometimes described as weather derivatives) or on geological or other physical variables. For such contracts, payments are sometimes made on the amount of loss suffered by the entity and sometimes not. Prior to IAS 39's revision, all such contracts were scoped out of IAS 39 and treated as insurance contracts. However, following IFRS 4's publication, such contracts are accounted for as follows:

- Contracts that require a payment only if a particular level of the underlying climatic, geological, or other physical variables adversely affects the contract holder.

  These are insurance contracts as payment is contingent on changes in a physical variable that is specific to a party to the contract.

- Contracts that require a payment based on a specified level of the underlying variable regardless of whether there is an adverse effect on the contract holder.

These are derivatives and are within IAS 39's scope.

[IAS 39 para AG 1, IFRS 4 para BC 55].

Example – Weather derivatives

A farming entity in Punjab, a State in India, relies on the prospect of a good monsoon that would favourably impact its earnings for the season. A good monsoon in Punjab involves an average rainfall of about 400mm during the months of June, July and August. The entity enters into a contract with a counterparty that would pay a fixed sum of Rs1m if the entity suffers loss due to poor production caused by below average rainfall during the monsoon months. The premium paid on the contract is Rs50,000.

This is an example of a highly tailored or customised policy that provides the entity protection against an adverse impact on earnings due to poor production caused by poor monsoon in Punjab, irrespective of whether the rest of India has a good monsoon or not. Hence, the contract is an insurance contract and is scoped out of IAS 39. It should be noted that even if the farming entity's loss due to poor production is less than Rs1m, the entity would receive Rs1m as stipulated in the contract. The definition of an insurance contract does not limit the payment by the insurer to an amount equal to the financial impact of the adverse event. [IFRS 4 App para B13].

If, on the other hand, the sum of Rs1m was paid if the average rainfall was below 400mm during the months of June, July and August and it would be payable irrespective of whether the farming entity in Punjab had suffered any damage, the contract would be accounted for as a derivative instrument. This is because payment is made following the change in average rainfall which is a non-financial variable that is not specific to the holder of the contract and hence one of the variables considered in the definition of financial risk.

Loan commitments

6.1.37 Loan commitments are firm commitments to provide credit under pre-specified terms and conditions. [IAS 39 BC15]. They are usually entered into by financial institutions such as banks for providing loans to third parties at a specified rate of interest during a fixed period of time. Such a commitment is a derivative, since it has no initial net investment, it has an underlying variable (interest rate) and it will be settled at a future date. In effect, the lender has written an option that allows the potential borrower to obtain a loan at a specified rate.

6.1.38 The following loan commitments are within IAS 39's scope:

- Loan commitments that the entity designates as financial liabilities at fair value through profit or loss. This may be appropriate, for example, if the entity manages risk exposures related to loan commitments on a fair value basis. [IAS 39 para 4(a)].

- An entity that has a past practice of selling the assets resulting from its loan commitments shortly after origination should apply IAS 39 to all its loan commitments in the *same class*. The term 'same class' is not explained in the standard, but we believe that a commitment to provide borrowing facilities to a corporate entity is not in the same class as a commitment to provide residential mortgage loans, because of differing risk return profiles. [IAS 39 para 4(a)].

- Loan commitments that can be settled net in cash or by delivering or issuing another financial instrument. These loan commitments are derivatives. A loan commitment is not regarded as settled net merely because the loan is paid out in instalments (for example, a mortgage construction loan that is paid out in instalments in line with the progress of construction). [IAS 39 para 4(b)].

- Commitments to provide a loan at a below-market interest rate (see chapter 9). [IAS 39 para 4(c)].

6.1.39 Loan commitments that are not within IAS 39's scope should be accounted for in accordance with IAS 37. Where events make such a loan commitment an onerous contract, the contract falls within IAS 37's scope and a liability exists that should be recognised. However, all loan commitments, whether scoped in or out of IAS 39, are subject to IAS 39's derecognition provisions and to IFRS 7's disclosure requirements. [IAS 39 para 2(h); IFRS 7 para 4].

Contracts to buy or sell non-financial assets

6.1.40 Contracts to buy or sell non-financial items are, in general, not financial instruments. Many commodity contracts are of this type. However, if such contracts can be settled net in cash or by exchanging another financial instrument, they fall within the scope of IAS 32, IFRS 7 and IAS 39 as if they were financial instruments (derivatives). This is so, unless the contracts were entered into and continue to be held for the purpose of receipt or delivery of non-financial items to meet the entity's expected purchase, sale or usage requirements (often referred to as 'own use' purchase or sale exception). [IAS 32 paras 8-10; IFRS 7 para 5; IAS 39 para 5]. In other words, if the own use exception is met, the contract must not be accounted for as a derivative (that is, the application of the own use exception is not a choice).

Contracts that can be settled net

6.1.41 There are various ways in which a contract to buy or sell a non-financial asset can be settled net in cash, including when:

■ The terms of the contract permit either party to settle net in cash or another financial instrument or by exchanging financial instruments. Net settlement means that the entity will pay or receive cash (or an equivalent value in other financial assets) to and from the counterparty, equal to the net gain or loss on the contract on exercise or settlement.

■ The ability to settle the contract net is not explicitly stated in the contract, but the entity has a practice of settling similar contracts net in cash (whether with the counterparty, by entering into offsetting contracts or by selling the contract before its exercise or lapse). For example, a futures exchange permits an entity to enter into offsetting contracts that relieves the entity of its obligation to make or receive delivery of the non-financial asset.

■ For similar contracts, the entity has a practice of taking delivery of the underlying and selling it within a short period after delivery to generate a profit from short-term fluctuations in price or dealer's margin. An example is an exchange that offers a ready opportunity to sell the contract.

■ The non-financial asset that is the subject of the contract is readily convertible into cash.

[IAS 32 para 9; IAS 39 para 6].

6.1.42 Where the second and third bullet points above apply, the entity's activities make it clear that the contracts cannot qualify for 'normal' purchase or sale exception. Accordingly, such contracts are within the scope of the financial instrument standards. Other contracts that can be settled net should be evaluated to determine whether they qualify for the exception. For example, to qualify for the exception, a contract's terms must be consistent with the terms of an entity's normal purchases or sales; that is, the quantity specified in the contract must be expected to be used or sold by the entity over a reasonable period in the normal course of business. Other factors that may be relevant in determining whether or not the contract qualifies for the exception may include the locations to which delivery of the items will be made, the period of time between entering into the contract and delivery and the entity's prior practices with regard to such contracts.

Example – Forward contract to purchase a commodity

Entity XYZ enters into a fixed price forward contract to purchase one million kilograms of copper in accordance with its expected usage requirements. The contract permits XYZ to take physical delivery of the copper at the end of 12 months or to pay or receive a net settlement in cash, based on the change in fair value of copper.

The above contract needs to be evaluated to determine whether it falls within the scope of the financial instruments standards. The contract is a derivative instrument because there is no initial net investment, the contract is based on the price of copper and it is to be settled at a future date. However, if XYZ intends to settle the contract by taking delivery and has no history for similar contracts of settling net in cash, or of taking delivery of the copper and selling it within a short period after delivery for the purpose of generating a profit from short-term fluctuations in price or dealer's margin, the contract is not accounted for as a derivative under IAS 39. Instead, it is accounted for as an executory contract. [IAS 39 IG A1].

In the above example, it is possible for entity XYZ and the counterparty to reach different conclusions about whether the contract falls within IAS 39's scope. For example, a 'normal' sale by the counterparty may not be a 'normal' purchase by entity XYZ that would treat the contract as a derivative. This is one of the few areas of IAS 39 where a contract may be treated as a derivative by one party, but not be treated as a derivative by the other party.

Written options

6.1.43   A written option to buy or sell a non-financial item that can be settled net in accordance with paragraph 6.1.43 above cannot be considered to be entered into for the purpose of the receipt or delivery of the non-financial item in accordance with the entity's expected purchase, sale or usage requirements. This is because an option written by the entity is outside its control as to whether the holder will exercise or not. Such contracts are, therefore, always within the scope of IAS 32 and IAS 39. [IAS 32 para 10; IAS 39 para 7]. Volume adjustment features are also common, particularly within commodity and energy contracts and are discussed within chapter 5.

Royalty agreements

6.1.44   Although not specifically mentioned in IAS 39's scope section, the standard does not change the accounting treatment of royalty agreements which are based on the volume of sales or service revenues and that are accounted for in accordance with IAS 18. [IAS 39 para AG 2]. However, derivative contracts that are based on both sales volume and a financial variable (such as an exchange rate) are not excluded from IAS 39's scope, as set out in the example in chapter 4.

Rights to reimbursement receipts

6.1.45   Rights to receipts that reimburse expenditure required to settle a liability, provision for which is, or has been, made in accordance with IAS 37 are outside IAS 39's scope. [IAS 39 para 2(j)]. IAS 37 prescribes the required accounting. They, nevertheless, remain within the scope of IAS 32 and IFRS 7.

Structure of the chapters

6.1.46   Detailed discussion of accounting for financial instruments is structured around the following chapters:

- 6.2 – Nature and characteristics of financial instruments.

- 6.3 – Embedded derivatives in host contracts.

- 6.4 – Classification of financial instruments.

- 6.5 – Financial liabilities and equity.

- 6.6 – Recognition and derecognition of financial instruments.

- 6.7 – Measurement of financial instruments.

- 6.8 – Hedging and hedge accounting.

- 6.9 – Presentation and disclosure of financial instruments.

- 6.10 – IFRS 9.

- IFRS 13.

6.1.47 The above chapters address the requirements of IAS 32, IAS 39, IFRS 7, IFRS 9 and IFRS 13 as at 31 August 2012. All these standards are supplemented by application guidance that is an integral part of the standards and, where relevant, by illustrative examples that accompany them (which are not part of the standards). In addition, IAS 39 and IFRS 7 are supplemented by implementation guidance that is not part of the standards. Furthermore, as IAS 39 is largely based on the US standard FAS 133, the chapters that follow draw on the guidance of that standard where it is considered appropriate and necessary to do so.

6.2 – Nature and characteristics of financial instruments

6.2 – Nature and characteristics of financial instruments

Introduction

6.2.1 Financial instruments embrace a broad range of assets and liabilities. They include both primary financial instruments – financial assets such as cash, receivables and equity securities of another entity and financial liabilities such as debt – and derivative financial instruments such as financial options, forwards, swaps and futures. Derivative financial instruments are considered separately from paragraph 6.2.25 below.

Definitions relating to financial instruments

6.2.2 The definitions relating to financial instruments that appear in paragraph 11 of IAS 32 are common to three financial instrument standards, that is, IAS 32, IAS 39 and IFRS 7. The definitions also apply, unchanged, to IFRS 9, which will supersede IAS 39. The definitions are noted below.

6.2.3 A financial instrument is any contract that gives rise to a financial asset of one entity and a financial liability or equity instrument of another entity. The definitions of a financial asset and financial liability stated below include some derivative and non-derivative contracts that will or may be settled in the entity's own equity instruments. This is because a contract is not necessarily an equity instrument just because it may result in the receipt or delivery of the entity's own equity instruments, as discussed in chapter 6.5. [IAS 32 para 21].

6.2.4 A financial asset is any asset that is:

- Cash.

- An equity instrument of another entity.

- A contractual right:

    - to receive cash or another financial asset from another entity; or

    - to exchange financial assets or financial liabilities with another entity under conditions that are potentially favourable to the entity.

- A contract that will or may be settled in the entity's own equity instruments and is:

    - a non-derivative for which the entity is or may be obliged to receive a variable number of the entity's own equity instruments; or

- a derivative that will or may be settled other than by the exchange of a fixed amount of cash or another financial asset for a fixed number of the entity's own equity instruments. For this purpose the entity's own equity instruments do not include puttable instruments and obligations arising on liquidation that are classified as equity or instruments that are contracts for the future receipt or delivery of the entity's own equity instruments.

6.2.5 A financial liability is any liability that is:

- A contractual obligation:

  - to deliver cash or another financial asset to another entity; or

  - to exchange financial assets or financial liabilities with another entity under conditions that are potentially unfavourable to the entity.

- A contract that will or may be settled in the entity's own equity instruments and is:

  - a non-derivative for which the entity is or may be obliged to deliver a variable number of the entity's own equity instruments; or

  - a derivative that will or may be settled other than by the exchange of a fixed amount of cash or another financial asset for a fixed number of the entity's own equity instruments. For this purpose, rights, options or warrants to acquire a fixed number of the entity's own equity instruments for a fixed amount of any currency are equity instruments if offered on a pro rata basis to all of the entity's existing owners of the same class of equity instruments (see chapter 6.5). Also, for these purposes the entity's own equity instruments do not include puttable instruments and obligations arising on liquidation that are classified as equity or instruments that are themselves contracts for the future receipt or delivery of the entity's own equity instruments.

6.2.6 As an exception to the above, puttable instruments or instruments containing obligations arising on liquidation that would otherwise meet the definition of a financial liability are classified as equity instruments if they meet certain criteria. The criteria are discussed in detail in chapter 6.5.

[The next paragraph is 6.2.8.]

6.2.8 An equity instrument is any contract that evidences a residual interest in an entity's assets after deducting all of its liabilities. [IAS 32 para 11]. The term 'entity' includes individuals, partnerships, incorporated bodies and government agencies. [IAS 32 para 14]. Examples of equity instruments include non-puttable ordinary shares, some types of preference shares and share warrants or written call options that allow the holder to subscribe for or purchase a fixed number of non-puttable ordinary shares in the issuing entity in exchange for a fixed amount of cash or another financial asset.

Key features of the definitions

6.2.9   Some of the important concepts associated with the various terms that are included in the above definitions are considered below. An understanding of these concepts is particularly important and relevant in evaluating instruments that might qualify as financial instruments including derivatives.

Contractual basis

6.2.10   All financial instruments are defined by contracts. The rights or obligations that comprise financial assets or financial liabilities are derived from the contractual provisions that underlie them. The terms 'contract' and 'contractual' refer to an agreement between two or more parties that has clear economic consequences that the parties have little, if any, discretion to avoid, usually because the agreement is enforceable by law. Contracts defining financial instruments may take a variety of forms and need not be in writing. [IAS 32 para 13]. An example of an item that would not meet the definition of a financial instrument is an entity's tax liability, as it is not based on a contract between the entity and the tax authority, but arising through statute. Similarly, constructive obligations, as defined in IAS 37, do not arise from contracts and are not financial liabilities. [IAS 32 para AG 12]. On the other hand, a provision for an onerous contract (for example, provision for vacant leasehold property that is being sublet) is a financial liability as it arises from the unavoidable cost of meeting the obligations under the contract. Nevertheless, such provisions are scoped out of IAS 39 and are accounted for in accordance with IAS 37. [IAS 37 para 66].

6.2.11   A contractual right or contractual obligation to receive, deliver or exchange financial instruments is itself a financial instrument. This is evident from the definitions of financial assets and liabilities that include the terms financial assets and financial instruments within them. However, the terms are not circular. They envisage the possibility that a chain of contractual rights or contractual obligations may be established, but this chain must end ultimately with the receipt or payment of cash or to the acquisition or issue of an equity instrument. [IAS 32 para AG 7].

6.2.12   As the IAS 32 definitions require all financial instruments to be contracts, some question whether cash can be considered to be a contract. However, this concern is overcome because the definition of a financial asset stated in paragraph 6.2.4 above specifically states that cash is a financial instrument. IAS 32 application guidance also clarifies that currency (cash) is a financial asset because it represents the medium of exchange and is, therefore, the basis on which all transactions are measured and recognised in financial statements. A deposit of cash with a bank or similar financial institution is a financial asset because it represents the contractual right of the depositor to obtain cash from the institution or to draw a cheque or similar instrument against the balance in favour of a creditor in payment of a financial liability. [IAS 32 para AG 3]. On the other hand gold bullion is not a financial instrument like cash. It is a commodity. Although the bullion market is highly liquid, there is no contractual right to receive cash or another financial instrument inherent in bullion. [IAS 39 para IG B1].

6.2.13 Some common examples of financial instruments that give rise to financial assets representing a contractual right to receive cash in the future for the holder and corresponding financial liabilities representing a contractual obligation to deliver cash in the future for the issuer are as follows:

- Trade accounts receivable and payable.

- Notes receivable and payable.

- Loans receivable and payable.

- Bonds receivable and payable.

In each case, one party's contractual right to receive (or obligation to pay) cash is matched by the other party's corresponding obligation to pay (or right to receive). [IAS 32 para AG 4].

6.2.14 Another type of financial instrument is one for which the economic benefit to be received or given up is a financial asset other than cash. For example, a note payable in government bonds gives the holder the contractual right to receive and the issuer the contractual obligation to deliver government bonds, not cash. The bonds are financial assets because they represent obligations of the issuing government to pay cash. The note is, therefore, a financial asset of the note holder and a financial liability of the note issuer. [IAS 32 para AG 5].

Conditional (contingent) rights and obligations

6.2.15 The ability to exercise a contractual right or the requirement to satisfy a contractual obligation may be absolute, or it may be contingent on the occurrence of a future event. A note receivable or payable is an unconditional promise to pay, but a financial guarantee is a conditional financial instrument as it results in a contractual right of the lender to receive cash from the guarantor and a corresponding contractual obligation of the guarantor to pay the lender, if the borrower defaults. The contractual right and obligation exist because of a past transaction or event (assumption of the guarantee), even though the lender's ability to exercise its right and the requirement for the guarantor to perform under its obligation are both contingent on a future act of default by the borrower. [IAS 32 para AG 8].

6.2.16 Even though a contingent right and obligation can meet the definition of a financial asset and a financial liability, they are not always recognised in the financial statements. Some of these contingent rights and obligations may be insurance contracts within IFRS 4's scope, whilst others may be excluded from the standards' scope. [IAS 32 para AG 8].

6.2.17 Other contingencies that may require the payment of cash but do not as yet arise from a contract, such as a contingent receivable or payable for a court judgment, are not financial instruments. However, when those judgments become enforceable by a government or a court of law, and are thereby contractually reduced to fixed payment schedules, the judgment would be a financial instrument. When the parties agree to payment terms and those payment terms are reduced to a contract, then a financial instrument exists. Contrast this with a fine, which is not contractual.

Exchange under potentially favourable or unfavourable terms

6.2.18   The definitions of financial assets and financial liabilities make references to exchanges under conditions that are 'potentially favourable' or 'potentially unfavourable'. The meaning of these terms and the way they work in practice are best explained by means of an example.

> **Example – Exchange under potentially favourable or unfavourable terms**
>
> Entity A holds an option to purchase equity shares in a listed entity B for C5 per share at the end of a 90 day period.
>
> The above call option gives entity A a contractual right to exchange cash of C5 for an equity share in another entity and will be exercised if the market value of the share exceeds C5 at the end of the 90 day period. This is because as the terms will be favourable to entity A at the end of term, it will exercise the call option. Since entity A stands to gain if the call option is exercised, the exchange is potentially favourable to the entity. Therefore, the option is a derivative financial asset from the time the entity becomes a party to the option contract.
>
> On the other hand, if entity A writes an option under which the counterparty can force the entity to sell equity shares in the listed entity B for C5 per share at any time in the next 90 days, entity A has a contractual obligation to exchange equity shares in another entity for cash of C5 per share on potentially unfavourable terms if the holder exercises the option, because the market price per share exceeds the exercise price of C5 per share at the end of the 90 day period. Since entity A stands to lose if the option is exercised, the exchange is potentially unfavourable and the option is a derivative financial liability from the time the entity becomes a party to the option contract.

Comparison with non-financial assets and liabilities

6.2.19   As discussed above, financial instruments represent contractual rights or obligations to receive or pay cash or other financial assets. Non-financial items have a more indirect, non-contractual relationship to future cash flows.

6.2.20   The non-financial assets of a business (such as inventories, property, plant and equipment and intangibles) are inputs to some productive process. They are expected to contribute, along with other inputs, to the production and sale of goods or services. They must be used in a productive activity, and effectively transformed into goods or service, which must be sold, before there is any right to receive cash. Control of such physical and intangible assets creates an opportunity to generate an inflow of cash or another financial asset, but it does not give rise to a present right to receive cash or another financial asset. [IAS 32 para AG 10]. Even where physical assets, such as properties, are held as investments rather than as inventories, they are not financial instruments.

6.2.21　A contract to acquire or sell a non-financial asset at a specified price at a future date is not a financial instrument, because the contractual right of one party to receive a non-financial asset and the corresponding obligation of the other party do not establish a present right or obligation of either party to receive, deliver or exchange a financial asset. For example, contracts that provide for settlement only by the receipt or delivery of a non-financial item (for example, an option or forward contract on silver) are not financial instruments. Many commodity contracts are of this type. However, as stated in paragraph 6.1.40, contracts to buy or sell non-financial items that can be settled net or by exchanging financial instruments are treated as if they are financial instruments. [IAS 32 para AG 20]. For the same reasons as stated above, a firm commitment that involves the receipt or delivery of a physical asset is not a financial instrument. [IAS 32 para AG 21].

6.2.22　Another example is an operating lease to rent an office building. Under the lease, the lessor has committed to provide office space in future periods for consideration similar to a fee for a service. The contractual right of the lessee to receive the service and the corresponding obligation of the lessor do not establish a present right or obligation of either party to receive, deliver or exchange a financial asset until the service is delivered and amounts become due and payable. On the other hand, a finance lease is regarded as primarily an entitlement of the lessor to receive, and an obligation of the lessee to pay, a stream of payments that are substantially the same as a loan agreement. The lessor accounts for its investment in the amount receivable under the lease contract rather than the leased asset itself. [IAS 32 para AG 9]. Accordingly, an operating lease is not regarded as a financial instrument (except as regards individual payments currently due and payable), but a finance lease is regarded as one.

6.2.23　Assets (such as pre-paid expenses) for which the future economic benefit is the receipt of goods or services, rather than the right to receive cash or another financial asset, are not financial assets. Similarly, items such as deferred revenue and most warranty obligations are not financial liabilities, because the outflow of economic benefits associated with them is the delivery of goods and services, rather than a contractual obligation to pay cash or another financial asset. [IAS 32 para AG 11].

Identification of financial instruments

6.2.24　Paragraphs 6.2.10 to 6.2.23 considered some of the important concepts associated with the definitions relating to financial instruments supplemented, where necessary, with examples. For ease of understanding and as a practical aid, the table below provides a list of common balance sheet items and applies the concepts discussed above to determine whether the items meet the definition of a financial instrument. Paragraph references are included where applicable. The list is by no means exhaustive, but provides an aide-mémoire to help in identifying primary financial instruments. For the sake of completeness, the last two columns also establish whether the instruments so identified fall within or outside the scope of IAS 32, IFRS 7 or IAS 39/IFRS 9 discussed in detail from paragraph 6.1.11 above.

Balance sheet item	Financial instrument? Yes = ✓ No = ✗	Included within the scope of IAS 32 and IFRS 7 Yes = ✓ No = ✗	Included within the scope of IAS 39/ IFRS 9 Yes = ✓ No = ✗
Intangible assets	✗ – para 6.2.20	n/a	n/a
Property, plant and equipment	✗ – para 6.2.20	n/a	n/a
Investment property	✗ – para 6.2.20	n/a	n/a
Interests in subsidiaries (in separate financial statements), associates and joint ventures – accounted for under IAS 27, IAS 28 or IAS 31 respectively	✓ – para 6.1.13	✗ – para 6.1.13	✗ – para 6.1.13
Interests in subsidiaries (in separate financial statements), associates and joint ventures held for sale under IFRS 5	✓ – para 6.1.13	✗ – para 6.1.13	✗ – para 6.1.13
Interests in subsidiaries, associates and joint ventures – accounted for under IAS 39 in separate financial statements (in accordance with IAS 27 para 38(b))	✓ – para 6.1.13	✓ – para 6.1.14	✓ – para 6.1.14
Inter-company trading balances with subsidiaries, associates and joint ventures	✓ – para 6.2.13	✓	✓
Investments in other entities (available-for-sale and held for trading)	✓ – para 6.2.4	✓	✓
Inventories	✗ – para 6.2.20	n/a	n/a
Gross amount due from customers for construction contract work	✓ – para 6.9.38	✓	✓
Finance lease receivables (recognised by a lessor)	✓ – para 6.2.22	✓ – para 6.1.23	✗ – para 6.1.23
Trade receivables	✓ – para 6.2.13	✓	✓
Pre-payments – goods and services	✗ – para 6.2.23	n/a	n/a
Cash and cash equivalents	✓ – para 6.2.4	✓	✓

6.2 – Nature and characteristics of financial instruments

Trade payables	✓ – para 6.2.13	✓	✓
Contingent consideration in a business combination	✓ – para 6.1.20	✓ – para 6.1.20	✓ – para 6.1.20
Accruals – goods and services (settlement in cash)	✓ – para 6.2.13	✓	✓
Deferred income	✗ – para 6.2.23	n/a	n/a
Debt instruments	✓ – para 6.2.5	✓	✓
Derivative instruments	✓ – para 6.2.1	✓	✓
Net settled commodity-based contracts	✓ – para 6.1.40	✓ – para 6.1.40	✓ – para 6.1.40
Retirement benefit obligations	✓ – para 6.1.17	✗ – para 6.1.17	✗ – para 6.1.17
Provisions for constructive obligations (as defined in IAS 37)	✗ – para 6.2.10	n/a	n/a
Vacant leasehold property provision	✓ – para 6.2.10	✓	✗ – para 6.2.10
Warranty obligations (settled by delivery of goods or service)	✗ – para 6.2.23	n/a	n/a
Warranty obligations (settled by delivery of cash or other financial asset)	✓ – para 6.2.5	✓	✓
Financial guarantee contracts issued	✓ – para 6.2.15	✓ – para 6.1.30 (unless IFRS 4 applied)	✓ – para 6.1.30 (unless IFRS 4 applied)
Financial guarantee contracts held	✓ – para 6.2.15	✗ – para 6.7.60	✗ – para 6.7.60
Operating lease	✗ – para 6.2.22	n/a	n/a
Finance lease obligations	✓ – para 6.2.22	✓ – para 6.1.23	✗ – para 6.1.23
Dividend payable	note 1	note 1	note 1
Current and deferred tax	✗ – para 6.2.10	n/a	n/a
Redeemable preference shares (debt)	✓ – para 6.2.5	✓	✓
Entity's own equity shares	✓ – para 6.2.8	✓ – para 6.1.22	✗ – para 6.1.22
Employee share options	✓ – para 6.2.8	✗ – para 6.1.18	✗ – para 6.1.18
Other equity options over own equity shares	✓ – para 6.2.8	✓ – para 6.1.22	✗ – para 6.1.22
Non-controlling interest	✓ – note 2	✓ – note 2	note 2

Notes:

1 Dividend payable on the balance sheet is a financial liability when the dividend has been formally declared by the members in a general meeting and becomes a legal obligation of the entity to deliver cash to shareholders for the amount of the declared dividend. [IAS 32 para AG 13].

2 The non-controlling interest that may arise on consolidating a subsidiary is presented in the consolidated balance sheet within equity, separately from the equity of the owners of the parent. [IAS 27 (revised) para 27; IAS 32 para AG 29]. However, where the parent or any fellow subsidiary undertaking has an obligation to deliver cash or another financial asset in respect of a subsidiary's shares (for example, by virtue of a written put option), they are treated as financial liabilities in consolidated financial statements under IAS 32 and are in the scope of IAS 39. [IAS 32 paras AG 29 and AG 29A].

Derivative financial instruments

Introduction

6.2.25 Derivatives are financial instruments that derive their value from an underlying price or index, which could be for example, an interest rate, a foreign exchange rate or commodity price. Their primary purpose is to create rights and obligations that have the effect of transferring between the parties to the instrument one or more of the financial risks inherent in an underlying primary instrument. Consequently, they may be used for trading purposes to generate profits from risk transfers or they may be used as a hedging instrument for managing risks. Generally, there is no transfer of the underlying instrument between the parties either at inception or at maturity, but there are some exceptions.

6.2.26 A derivative instrument gives one party a contractual right to exchange financial assets or financial liabilities with another party under conditions that are potentially favourable, or a contractual obligation to exchange financial assets or financial liabilities with another party under conditions that are potentially unfavourable. Because the terms of the exchange are determined at inception, as prices in the financial markets change, those terms may become favourable or unfavourable (see para 6.2.18 above). Derivative instruments may either be free-standing or embedded in a financial instrument or in a non-financial contract (see chapter 6.3).

Definition

6.2.27 IAS 39 defines a derivative as a financial instrument or other contract with all of the following characteristics:

■ its value changes in response to the change in a specified interest rate, financial instrument price, commodity price, foreign exchange rate, index of prices or rates, credit rating or credit index, or other variable, provided in the case of a non-financial variable that the variable is not specific to a party to the contract (sometimes called the 'underlying');

- it requires no initial net investment or an initial net investment that is smaller than would be required for other types of contracts that would be expected to have a similar response to changes in market factors; and

- it is settled at a future date.

[IAS 39 para 9].

Key features of the definition

6.2.28 The characteristics referred to above make the definition of a derivative not only complex but fairly wide. For example, many contracts such as loan commitments (see para 6.1.37), certain contracts to buy or sell a non-financial item (see para 6.1.40) and regular way trades (see para 6.2.44 below) meet the definition of a derivative, in addition to the more commonly used and typical derivative instruments such as forwards, swaps, futures and options. Therefore, an understanding of these characteristics is particularly important and relevant in evaluating instruments that might qualify as, or contain, a derivative instrument. The paragraphs that follow examine some of the important concepts associated with these characteristics.

Underlying

6.2.29 As evident from the first characteristic stated in paragraph 6.2.27 above, an underlying is a variable, such as:

- An interest rate (for example, LIBOR).

- A security price (for example, the price of an XYZ entity equity share listed on a regulated market).

- A commodity price (for example, the price of a bushel of wheat).

- A foreign exchange rate (for example, €/$ spot rate).

- An index (for example, FTSE 100, a retail price index).

- A credit rating or a credit index (for example, Moody's credit rating).

- An insurance index or catastrophe-loss index.

- Non-financial variable (for example, a climatic or geological condition such as temperature, rainfall, or earthquake severity, or sales volume indices specifically created for settlement of derivatives).

6.2.30 Generally, an underlying may be any variable whose changes are observable or otherwise objectively verifiable. It may be the price or rate of an asset or liability that changes in response to changes in the market factors, but it is not the asset or the liability itself in most instances. The underlying will, therefore, generally be the referenced index that determines whether or not the derivative instrument has a positive or a negative value.

6.2.31 If the underlying is a non-financial variable as referred to in the last bullet point in paragraph 6.2.29 above, it must not be specific to a party to the contract in order for the derivative definition to be met. In other words, the terms of the contract must be sufficiently generic in nature to qualify as a derivative. For example, such variables might include an index of earthquake losses in a particular region or an index of temperatures in a particular city.

6.2.32 Examples of non-financial variables that are specific to a party to the contract and hence do not give rise to a derivative, include:

- the occurrence or non-occurrence of a fire that damages or destroys an asset of a party to the contract;
- EBITDA;
- revenue; or
- a measure of regulatory capital of a financial institution (for example, core tier 1 capital of a bank).

A change in the fair value of a non-financial asset is specific to the owner if the fair value reflects not only changes in market prices for such assets (a financial variable) but also the condition of the specific non-financial asset held (a non-financial variable). [IAS 39 para AG 12A]. Such contracts may fall to be treated as insurance contracts (see para 6.1.31 example 2).

6.2.33 A derivative instrument may have more than one underlying or variable. A typical example is a cross-currency interest rate swap that has one underlying based on a foreign exchange rate and another underlying based on an interest rate. A complex option may have two such variables, one based on an interest rate and the other based on the price of a commodity such as oil. Another example based on IAS 39's implementation guidance is given below.

> **Example – Foreign currency contract based on sales volume**
>
> Entity XYZ, whose functional currency is the US dollar, sells products in France denominated in euros. XYZ enters into a contract with an investment bank to convert euros to US dollars at a fixed exchange rate. The contract requires XYZ to remit euros based on its sales volume in France in exchange for US dollars at a fixed exchange rate of 1.20.
>
> The contract has two underlying variables (the foreign exchange rate and the volume of sales), no initial net investment – or an initial net investment that is smaller than would be required for other types of contracts that would be expected to have a similar response to changes in market factors – and a payment provision. If a contract has two or more underlyings and at least one of those underlyings is not a non-financial variable specific to a party to a contract, the entire contract is accounted for as a derivative (assuming the rest of the definition of a derivative is met).

> Therefore, the contact is a derivative even though one of the variables (sales volume) is a non-financial variable that is specific to a party to the contract. IAS 39 does not exclude from its scope derivatives that are based on sales volume. [IAS 39 para IG B8].

Notional amounts and payment provisions

6.2.34   A derivative usually has a notional amount, which is an amount of currency, a number of shares, a number of units of weight or volume or other units specified in the contract. However, a derivative instrument does not require the holder or writer to invest or receive the notional amount at the inception of the contract. The interaction of the notional amount and the underlying determines the settlement amount under a derivative instrument. The interaction may consist of a simple multiplication (for example, price × number of shares), or it may involve a formula that has leverage factors or other constants (for example, notional amount × interest rate where interest rate = 2.5 × LIBOR; the effect of any change in LIBOR is magnified by two and a half times).

6.2.35   Alternatively, a derivative could contain a 'payment provision' specifying a fixed payment or payment of an amount that can change (but not proportionally with a change in the underlying) as a result of some future event that is unrelated to a notional amount. For example, a contract may require a fixed payment of C1,000 if six month LIBOR increases by 100 basis points. Such a contract is a derivative even though a notional amount is not specified. [IAS 39 para AG 9]. Another example is where an entity receives C10 million if the share price of another entity decreases by more than 5% during a six month period, but pays C10 million if the share price increases by more than 5% during the same six month period. No payment is made if the share price is less than 5% up or down. This is a derivative contract where there is no notional amount to determine the settlement amount. Instead, there is a payment provision that is based on changes in the underlying.

Initial net investment

6.2.36   The second characteristic of a derivative instrument is that it has no initial net investment, or one that is *smaller* than would be required for other types of contracts that would be expected to have a similar response to changes in market factors. Professional judgement is required in interpreting the term in italic as it does not necessarily mean insignificant in relation to the overall investment. It is a relative measure and needs to be interpreted with care. This reflects the inherent leverage features typical of derivative instruments compared to the underlying instruments.

6.2.37   The following examples illustrate how initial net investment is determined in various circumstances:

Example 1 – No initial net investment of the notional amount

Forward based derivative contracts such as forward foreign exchange contracts and interest rate swaps are derivative instruments that typically do not require an initial net investment. This is because they are priced at-the-money at inception, which means that the fair value of the contracts is zero. If the fair value of the contract is not zero at inception (for example because they are 'off market' transactions), the contract is recognised as an asset or liability.

Under a forward foreign exchange contract the two parties agree to purchase or sell a foreign currency at a specified price, with delivery or settlement at a specified future date. Although the forward contract has a notional amount equal to the amount of the foreign currency, it does not require the holder or the writer to invest or receive the notional amount at the inception of the contract. Indeed, forward contracts do not have cash flows during the contract term. Settlement takes place at maturity of the contract.

Similarly, an interest rate swap may be viewed as a variation of a forward contract in which the two parties agree to exchange one set of interest cash flows calculated with reference to a fixed interest rate for another set of interest cash flows calculated with reference to a floating interest rate. No exchange of principal takes place. Typically, the rates are set so that the fair values of the fixed and floating legs are equal and opposite at inception with the result that the fair value of the swap on initial recognition is nil. As no money changes hands at inception, there is no initial net investment. Swap cash flows occur at regular intervals over the life of the swap contract based on a notional principal amount and fixed and floating rates specified in the swap.

Example 2 – Initial net investment less than the notional amount

Option contracts are derivative instruments that do require an initial net investment. An option is a contractual agreement that gives the buyer of the option the right, but not the obligation, to purchase (call) or sell (put) a specified security, currency or commodity (the underlying) at a specified price (exercise price) during a specified period of time (or on a specified date). For this right, the buyer pays a premium, which is the amount the seller requires to take on the risk involved in writing the option. Although this premium can be significant, it is often less than the amount that would be required to buy the underlying financial instrument to which the contract is linked. As such, the option fulfils the initial net investment criterion. [IAS 39 para AG 11].

On the other hand, if the option premium is so deep in-the-money at inception that the premium paid is close to making an investment in the underlying, then the option contract will fail the initial net investment criterion. In that situation, the instrument would not be accounted for as a derivative under IAS 39, but rather as an investment in the underlying asset itself.

Example 3 – Exchange of currencies

Some contracts may require a mutual exchange of currencies or other assets, in which case the net investment is the difference between the fair values of the assets exchanged. An example is a currency swap that requires the exchange of currencies at both inception and at maturity. The initial exchange of currencies at fair values in those arrangements (zero net investment) is not seen as an initial net investment. Instead, it is an exchange of one kind of cash for another kind of cash. [IAS 39 para AG 11].

Example 4 – Margin accounts

Many derivative instruments, such as futures contracts and exchange traded written options, require a margin payment – an initial amount that must be deposited before trading begins and which approximately equals the daily price fluctuation permitted for the contract being traded. Sometimes initial margin payments are set based on counterparty credit limits rather than by individual trade, but they are usually linked to trading volumes. Such payments are not part of the initial net investment. Rather, they are a form of collateral for the counterparty or clearing house to ensure that traders will perform on their contractual obligations. The initial margin may take the form of cash, securities or other specified assets, typically liquid assets. These are separate assets that are accounted for separately. [IAS 39 para IG B10]. Any variation in margin payments, which are generally made to reflect movements in the market prices of open trades, would be adjusted against the asset. See chapter 6.9 for consideration of balance sheet offset.

Example 5 – Pre-paid interest rate swap (fixed leg pre-paid)

Entity S enters into a C100m notional amount five-year pay-fixed, receive-variable interest rate swap. The interest rate of the variable part of the swap is reset on a quarterly basis to three month LIBOR. The interest rate of the fixed leg of the swap is 10% per year. At inception of the swap, Entity S pre-pays its fixed obligation of C50m (C100m × 10% × 5 years) discounted using market interest rates, while retaining the right to receive interest payments on the C100m reset quarterly based on three-month LIBOR over the life of the swap.

As stated in example 1 above at the money interest rate swap has a zero fair value at inception. Since entity S has pre-paid the fixed leg of the swap at inception at its fair value, the amount pre-paid is also equal to the fair value of the variable leg of the swap. This amount is however significantly less than the notional amount (C100m) on which the variable payments under the variable leg will be calculated. In other words, the initial net investment (the amount pre-paid of the present value of C50m) is still smaller than investing in a similar primary instrument (that is, C100m), such as a variable rate bond, that responds equally to changes in the underlying interest rate. Therefore, a pre-paid fixed leg swap fulfils the initial net investment criterion of IAS 39. Even though entity S has no future performance obligation, the ultimate settlement of the contract is at a future date and the value of the contract changes in response to changes in the LIBOR index. Accordingly, the contract is a derivative instrument.

On the other hand, if the fixed rate payment obligation is pre-paid subsequent to initial recognition, that is, during the term of the swap, then that would be regarded as a termination of the old swap and an origination of a new instrument that is evaluated under IAS 39. [IAS 39 para IG B4]. There is no explanation in the implementation guidance as to why this is so. Presumably this is because a significant fall in LIBOR between inception date and pre-payment date would cause the amount pre-paid (that is, the fair value of the fixed leg at the date of the pre-payment) to be significantly higher than the fair value of the fixed leg at date of inception. Therefore, the entity receiving the variable payments may not recover substantially all of its pre-paid investment under the contractual terms resulting in the termination of the old swap and the creation of a new instrument.

Example 6 – Pre-paid interest rate swap (floating leg pre-paid)

Entity S enters into a C100m notional amount five-year pay-variable, receive-fixed interest rate swap. The variable leg of the swap is reset on a quarterly basis to three-month LIBOR. The fixed interest payments under the swap are calculated as 10% times the swap's notional amount, that is, C10m per year. Entity S pre-pays its obligation under the variable leg of the swap at inception at current market rates, while retaining the right to receive fixed interest payments of 10% on C100m per year.

As stated in the previous example, the fair value of the fixed leg and the fair value of a floating leg are equal and offsetting so that the fair value of the interest rate swap at inception is zero. Since entity S has pre-paid the variable leg of the swap at inception at its fair value, the amount pre-paid, all else being equal, is also equal to the fair value of the fixed leg of the swap. That is, the initial net investment (the amount pre-paid) is equal to the present value of a fixed annuity of C10m per year over the swap's life. Thus, the initial net investment is equal to the investment required in a non-derivative contract that has a similar response to changes in market conditions. In other words, the amount pre-paid provides a return that is the same as that of an amortising fixed rate debt instrument of the amount of the pre-paid. For this reason, the instrument fails the initial net investment criterion of IAS 39. Therefore, the contract is not accounted for as a derivative. By discharging the obligation to pay variable interest rate payments, entity S in effect provides a loan to the counterparty. [IAS 39 para IG B5].

Example 7 – Pre-paid forward

Entity XYZ enters into a forward contract to purchase 1m entity T ordinary shares in one year. The current market price of entity T's shares is C50 per share; the one-year forward price of entity T's shares is C55 per share. XYZ is required to pre-pay the forward contract at inception with a C50m payment.

The initial investment in the forward contract of C50m is less than the notional amount applied to the underlying, 1m shares at the forward price of C55 per share, that is, C55m. However, the initial net investment *approximates* the investment that would be required for other types of contracts that would be expected to have a similar response to changes in market factors because entity T's shares could be purchased at inception for the same price of C50m. Accordingly, the pre-paid forward contract does not meet the initial net investment criterion of a derivative instrument. In this situation, the entity would record the investment itself as a non-derivative financial asset. [IAS 39 para IG B9].

It is not clear why the example in the implementation guidance uses the term 'approximate' when the initial net investment of C50m is equal to the amount that would be exchanged to acquire the asset relating to the underlying (market price of the share). Presumably the term is used to emphasise the point that the initial net investment test is a relative measure as indicated in paragraph 6.2.36 above and that a pre-payment amount of, for example, C42.5m (15% smaller than the original amount) may still meet the initial net investment criterion.

Settlement at a future date

6.2.38   The final part of the definition relates to settlement at a future date. All derivatives are settled at a future date. As explained in example 1 above, forward contracts are settled at a specified date in the future, whilst for an interest rate swap settlement occurs at regular intervals over the swap's life. An option is settled upon exercise or at maturity. Therefore, even if an option is expected not to be exercised, for example, because it is out-of-the-money and no additional exchange of consideration is expected to take place, the option still meets the settlement criterion, because expiry at maturity is a form of settlement. [IAS 39 para IG B7].

6.2.39   A derivative can be settled net in cash (that is, the entity has the right to receive or the obligation to pay a single net amount) or gross in cash/other financial asset (exchange of cash/other financial asset). Consider the following example:

> **Example – Interest rate swap with net or gross settlement**
>
> Entity ABC enters into an interest rate swap with a counterparty (XYZ) that requires ABC to pay a fixed rate of 8% and receive a variable amount based on three month LIBOR, reset on a quarterly basis. The fixed and variable amounts are determined based on a C100m notional amount. ABC and XYZ do not exchange the notional amount. ABC pays or receives a net cash amount each quarter based on the difference between 8% and three-month LIBOR. Alternatively, settlement may be on a gross basis.
>
> As the swap contract is settled on a periodical basis, each interest payment can be viewed as a series of forward contracts to exchange and receive cash on potentially favourable or unfavourable terms. The contract meets the definition of a derivative regardless of whether each interest payment is settled net or gross, because its value changes in response to changes in an underlying variable (LIBOR). There is no initial net investment and settlements occur at future dates. In other words, it makes no difference whether ABC and XYZ actually make the interest payment to each other (gross settlement). [IAS 39 para IG B3].

6.2.40   Settlement may also occur gross through physical delivery of the underlying financial item. An example is a forward contract to purchase C100 million of 5% fixed rate bond at a specified fixed date in the future. In this situation, at settlement date the entity would exchange cash for physical delivery of the bond (the underlying financial item) whose nominal value is equal to the notional amount of the contract and the market interest rate is the underlying. [IAS 39 para AG10].

Specific examples of derivative instruments

6.2.41   The key characteristics of a derivative contract were explained and illustrated above, where relevant, with examples. The following table provides typical examples of contracts that normally qualify as derivatives together with the relevant underlying, notional and settlement amounts.

Derivative	Underlying	Notional amount	Settlement amount
Stock options	Market price of share	Number of shares	(Market price at settlement – Strike Price) × Number of shares
Currency forward	Currency rate	Number of currency units	(Spot rate at settlement – Forward rate) × number of currency units
Commodity future	Commodity price per unit	Number of commodity units	Net settlement occurs daily and is determined by the change in the futures price and discounted to reflect the time to maturity
Interest rate swap	Interest rate index (receive 5% fixed and pay LIBOR)	Amounts in C 's	Net settlement occurs periodically throughout the contract's term based on the formula: (Current interest rate index – fixed rate specified in the contract) × Amounts in C's
Fixed payment contract	6 month LIBOR increases by 100 basis points	Not specified	Settlement amount based on payment provision in the contract.

Contracts to buy or sell non-financial items

6.2.42   An entity may also have a contract to buy or sell a non-financial item that can be settled net in cash or another financial instrument, or by exchanging financial instruments. Such contracts may fall within the definition of a derivative if they meet certain criteria (see further chapter 6.1). [IAS 39 para AG 10].

Contracts that are in substance derivatives

6.2.43   It is generally inappropriate to treat two or more separate financial instruments, such as an investment in a floating rate debt instrument and a floating to fixed interest rate swap with different counter parties, as a single combined instrument ('synthetic instrument' accounting), as discussed in chapter 11. [IAS 39 para IG C6]. However, as an exception to this, non-derivative transactions should be aggregated and treated as a derivative when, in substance, the transactions result in a derivative instrument. Indicators of this would include circumstances where the transactions:

- Are entered into at the same time and in contemplation of one another.

- Have the same counterparty.

- Relate to the same risk.

■ Have no substantive business purpose or there is no apparent economic need for structuring the transactions separately that could not also have been accomplished in a single transaction.

[IAS 39 para IG B6].

> **Example – In substance derivatives**
>
> Entity A makes a five-year fixed rate loan to entity B, while entity B at the same time makes a five-year variable rate loan for the same amount to entity A. There are no transfers of principal at inception of the two loans, since entities A and B have a netting agreement.
>
> The contractual effect is that the loans are, in substance, equivalent to an interest rate swap arrangement that meets the definition of a derivative – there is an underlying variable, no initial net investment and future settlement. The same answer would apply if entity A and entity B did not have a netting agreement, because the definition of a derivative instrument does not require net settlement. [IAS 39 para IG B6].

Regular way contracts

6.2.44 A regular way purchase or sale is a purchase or sale of a financial asset under a contract whose terms require delivery of the asset within the time frame established generally by regulation or convention in the marketplace concerned. [IAS 39 para 9]. Such contracts give rise to a fixed price commitment between trade date and settlement date that meets the definition of a derivative. However, because of the commitment's short duration, it is not recognised as a derivative financial instrument. Rather, IAS 39 provides for special accounting for such regular way contracts which is dealt with in chapter 6.6. [IAS 39 para AG 12].

Accounting for derivatives

6.2.45 The measurement requirements of IAS 39 require all derivatives to be measured at fair value on the balance sheet, with changes in fair value being accounted through profit or loss, except for derivatives that qualify as effective hedging instruments and derivatives that are linked to and must be settled by delivery of unquoted equity instruments whose fair value cannot be reliably measured. Measurement and hedging requirements are dealt with further in chapters 6.7 and 6.8 respectively.

6.3 – Embedded derivatives in host contracts

6.3 – Embedded derivatives in host contracts

Introduction

6.3.1 A derivative instrument that falls within IAS 39's scope need not be free-standing. Terms and conditions may be embedded in a financial instrument or non-financial contract (the 'host' contract) that behave like a free-standing derivative. These are referred to as embedded derivatives. The combination of the host contract and the embedded derivative is a 'hybrid instrument'.

6.3.2 An embedded derivative can arise from deliberate financial engineering, for example to make low interest-rate debt more attractive by including an equity-linked return. In other cases, they arise inadvertently through market practices and common contractual arrangements, such as leases and insurance contracts. Even purchase and sale contracts that qualify as executory contracts may contain embedded derivatives. In fact, they may occur in all sorts of contracts and instruments – the objective being to change the nature of cash flows that otherwise would be required by the host contract and effectively shift financial risks between the parties.

6.3.3 Analysing non-derivative financial instruments and executory contracts for potential embedded derivatives is one of the more challenging aspects of IAS 39. However, the challenge does not end there. As will be apparent later, a derivative identified in a host contract needs further evaluation to determine whether it should be accounted for separately as a stand-alone derivative at fair value. Not all embedded derivatives need to be accounted for separately from the host contract.

Definition and key characteristics

6.3.4 An embedded derivative is a component of a hybrid instrument that also includes a non-derivative host contract – with the effect that some of the cash flows of the hybrid instrument vary in a way similar to a stand-alone derivative. An embedded derivative causes some or all of the cash flows that otherwise would be required by the contract to be modified according to a specified interest rate, financial instrument price, commodity price, foreign exchange rate, index of prices or rates, credit rating or credit index, or other variable, provided in the case of a non-financial variable that the variable is not specific to a party to the contract. [IAS 39 para 10]. Variation of the cash flows over the contract's term is a critical indicator of the presence of one or more embedded derivatives. An example of a hybrid instrument is a loan that pays interest based on changes in the FTSE 100 index. The component of the contract that is to repay the principal amount is the host contract – this is the 'base state' with a pre-determined term and pre-determined cash flows. The component of the contract that is to pay interest based on changes in the FTSE 100 index is the embedded derivative – this component causes some or all of the cash flows of the host contract to change. The following diagram demonstrates this:

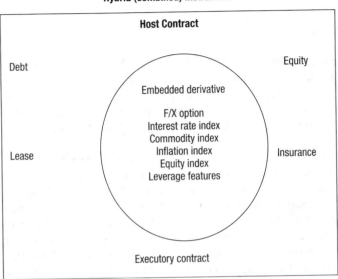

Hybrid (combined) instrument

6.3.5 A derivative that is attached to a financial instrument but is contractually transferable independently of that instrument, or has a different counterparty from that instrument, is not an embedded derivative, but a separate financial instrument [IAS 39 para 10]. An example is a bond with a detachable warrant. The owner of the bond-warrant package can exercise the warrant and buy shares for cash but keep the bond. This is unlike an owner of a convertible bond where the owner has to give up the bond in order to exercise the option.

Conditions for separation

6.3.6 Paragraph 11 of IAS 39 states that an embedded derivative should be separated from the host contract and accounted for as a derivative if all of the following three conditions are met:

- the economic characteristics and risks of the embedded derivative are not closely related to the economic characteristics and risks of the host contract;

- a separate instrument with the same terms as the embedded derivative would meet the definition of a derivative; and

- the hybrid instrument is not measured at fair value with changes in fair value recognised in profit or loss.

6.3.7 In relation to the third bullet point above, paragraph 11A of IAS 39 states that if a contract contains one or more embedded derivatives, an entity may designate the entire hybrid contract as a financial asset or financial liability at fair value through profit or loss unless:

- the embedded derivative(s) does not significantly modify the cash flows that otherwise would be required by the contract; or

- it is clear with little or no analysis when a similar hybrid instrument is first considered that separation of the embedded derivative(s) is prohibited, such as a pre-payment option embedded in a loan that permits the holder to pre-pay the loan for approximately its amortised cost.

6.3.8 The above requirements are summarised in the diagram below.

Questions that need to be asked

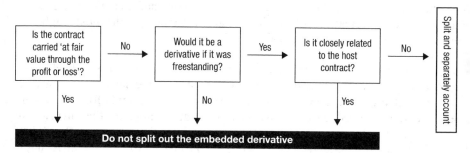

6.3.9 The rationale for the above requirements is to ensure that all the underlying risks in an instrument are properly reflected in the accounting. For instance, a debt host contract may contain an embedded derivative that exposes the contract to risks that are non-interest related. If there were no requirement to separate the non-interest related exposure from the host debt instrument, entities would be able to achieve an accounting result different from the accounting result achieved if it had issued two separate contracts with the same combined economic effect. Therefore, separation of the embedded derivative not only ensures that the accounting faithfully represents the contract's underlying nature and its exposure to various risks, but also achieves consistency in accounting compared with free-standing derivatives. However, measuring an embedded derivative separately from its host contract requires judgement, and sometimes such measurements may be difficult. Therefore, as a practical expedient IAS 39 provides that an embedded derivative need not be separated if it is regarded as closely related to its host contract.

6.3.10 Although the requirement to separate an embedded derivative from a host contract applies to both parties to a contract (that is, both the issuer and the holder of a hybrid instrument), the two parties to the contract might reach different accounting treatments when applying the decision tree in paragraph 6.3.8 above. For example, an equity conversion feature embedded in a convertible debt instrument denominated in the functional currency of the issuer is not closely related to the host debt instrument from the perspective of the holder of the instrument. However, from the issuer's perspective, the equity conversion option is an equity instrument and excluded from IAS 39's scope, provided it meets the conditions for classification as equity under IAS 32. [IAS 39 para AG 30(f)].

Interpretation of 'closely related'

6.3.11 Once an embedded derivative is identified, it is necessary to consider whether its economic characteristics and risks (that is, the factors that cause the derivative to fluctuate in value) are closely related to the economic characteristics and risks of the host contract. IAS 39 does not provide a definition of 'closely related'. Instead, the application guidance to the standard provides examples of situations where the embedded derivative is, or is not, closely related to the host contract. Those examples have an underlying theme. They tend to focus attention on the question of whether the underlying economic characteristics and risks of the embedded derivative behave in a manner similar to the host contract's economic characteristics and risks.

6.3.12 A key determinant in the closely related assessment process is likely to be risk. Risk in a derivative is determined by the underlying such as interest rate, foreign exchange, prices etc, and by any leverage in the formula for determining settlement. An embedded derivative such as a cap or floor on the interest rate (interest rate risk) that bears a close economic relationship to its host debt contract would be considered closely related. Conversely, when a derivative that is embedded in a debt instrument embodies an equity instrument's economic characteristics (for example, the derivative has a rate of return that is tied to the DAX 30 index), the economic characteristics of the derivative (equity-price risk) and host contract (interest rate risk) are different. In this situation, the embedded derivative would not be considered closely related to the host contract.

6.3.13 The following example illustrates how quantitative as well as qualitative factors should be taken into account in determining whether the economic characteristics and risks of an embedded derivative are closely related to those of the host contract.

> **Example – Electricity contract linked to coal prices**
>
> Entity A, an electricity provider, operates in a country where electricity is not traded on a market, and has a number of electricity contracts that have prices linked to coal prices. Management believes that, from a qualitative perspective, the electricity price is linked to the price of coal, as coal is a major input to the electricity generation process. A quantitative analysis reveals that electricity prices are not directly correlated with coal prices.
>
> A qualitative approach should be supported by quantitative analysis.
>
> Whilst coal is an important input in the production of electricity, the price of electricity is driven by many other factors and, therefore, it is important to assess the extent to which the economic characteristics and risks of coal are in practice closely related to those of electricity. A quantitative assessment of correlation may be relevant to this

determination and in this example may lead to the conclusion that the coal price is not closely related to the electricity price. The embedded derivative would, therefore, need to be separated.

Leverage embedded features in host contracts

6.3.14 Leverage embedded features can significantly modify some or all of the cash flows that otherwise would be required by the host contract. IAS 39 does not define the term 'leverage', although the term appears in several examples in paragraph AG33. In general, a hybrid instrument is said to contain embedded leverage features if some or all of its contractually required cash flows, determined by reference to changes in one or more underlyings, are modified in a manner that multiply or otherwise exacerbate the effect of those changes. An example of this would be a lease with payments linked to an inflation index multiplied by a factor of 2.5. The effect of leverage is only relevant for those embedded derivatives that would otherwise be 'closely-related' to the non-derivative host contract. This is because embedded derivatives that are not 'closely-related' would have to be separated out from the host contract in any event, irrespective of whether they are considered to be leveraged.

6.3.15 Although, in general, leverage has a multiplying effect, the standard does not quantify a numerical measure of leverage for closely related embedded derivatives although it does include the notion of at least doubling the holders interest rate of return in relation to embedded derivatives in which the underlying is an interest rate or an interest rate index (see para 6.3.31 below). In other words, although it may be clear that any embedded feature that leverages the exposure of the host contract to more than an insignificant amount would require separation, no guidance is given as to what would constitute an acceptable threshold. An example of this would be a contract for delivery of paper where the price is linked to a pulp index, transportation index and relevant inflation index where the indices are multiplied by percentages that reflect relative weighting of the cost factor in the production of paper. Such percentages would normally add up to 100%. To support the closely related assertion it has to be demonstrated that it was the normal way to price commercial contract in the market for paper at the time when the contract entered into. That could be done, for example, by reference to web sites of relevant industry associations, commodity or goods exchanges, etc. Therefore, judgement should be exercised after considering all relevant facts and circumstances that are specific to the situation.

Identifying the terms of embedded derivatives and host contracts

6.3.16 Because an assessment of whether an embedded derivative is 'closely related' to the host contract requires an understanding of the economic characteristics and risks of both the host contract and the derivative, it is necessary to consider the general principles that may be helpful in identifying the hosts and any derivatives that may be embedded in them.

6.3.17 Determining the type of host should not cause undue difficulty in practice as its economic characteristics and risks are readily transparent. Common host contracts that have derivatives embedded in them are given below:

- Debt instruments.

- Equity instruments.

- Leases.

- Executory contracts such as purchase and sales contracts.

- Insurance contracts.

The economic characteristics and risks of each of these contracts are considered in the application section below. Other hosts may exist, but as these are likely to be rare they are not considered in this chapter.

6.3.18 Searching for derivatives that may be embedded in the above hosts may be more challenging. Because few hybrid contracts actually use the term 'derivative', a thorough evaluation of a contract's terms must be performed to determine whether the contract contains an embedded derivative. Certain terms and phrases, however, may indicate the presence of an embedded derivative. Such terms and phrases may include:

- Pricing based on a formula.

- The right to purchase/sell additional units.

- Exchange/exchangeable into.

- Indexed to/adjusted by/referenced to.

- Premium/strike/limits.

- The right to cancel/extend/repurchase/return.

6.3.19 Another method of determining whether a contract has an embedded derivative is to compare the terms of a contract (such as interest rate, maturity date(s), cancellation provisions, etc) with the corresponding terms of a similar, non-complex contract. In other words, an entity should ascertain whether there are differences between typical market terms and the terms of the contract that is being evaluated. An investigation of differences may uncover an embedded derivative.

6.3.20 The following list illustrates how the nature of a host contract and embedded derivative may be determined:

Instrument	Host contract	Embedded derivative
Convertible bond	Debt instrument	Purchased call option on equity securities
Debt paying interest quarterly based on an equity index	Debt instrument	Four forward contracts p.a. on equity index
A two-year fixed-quantity sales contract including maximum and minimum pricing limits	Purchase contract	Commodity price collar
A two-year fixed-quantity sale contract of mobile phones denominated in GBP between a French seller and German buyer, both with euro functional currencies	Purchase contract	Foreign currency forward contract

Assessment of closely related criterion

6.3.21   It is clear that the assessment of the closely related criterion should be made when the contract is initially recognised, which is usually at inception of the contract. The question arises as to whether this initial assessment should be revisited during the contract's life. For example, an entity may determine, based on market conditions existing at the date of inception, that an embedded derivative in a host contract is closely related. Subsequently, market conditions change and the entity concludes that the embedded derivative is no longer closely related. The converse situation can also arise. The issue is in which circumstances the entity should make this re-assessment.

6.3.22   The above issue is addressed in IFRIC 9. IFRIC 9 re-confirms the treatment in IAS 39 that an entity should assess whether an embedded derivative is required to be separated from the host contract and accounted for as a derivative when the entity first becomes a party to the contract. This initial assessment is not revised, unless the contractual terms change and the change significantly modifies the expected future cash flows associated with the embedded derivative, the host contract or both relative to the previously expected cash flows on the contract. [IFRIC 9 para 7]. It follows that if the market conditions change and the market was the principal factor in determining whether the host contract and the embedded derivative are closely related, no re-assessment is required, unless the terms of the contracts are changed and the changes result in the revised expected cash flows being significantly different from the previously expected cash flows.

6.3.23   Furthermore, the IASB issued 'Amendments to International Accounting Standard 39 Financial instruments: Recognition and measurement – Embedded derivatives' in March 2009, which requires financial assets reclassified out of the fair value through profit or loss category (see chapter 6.4) to be assessed for embedded derivatives. The assessment is based on the circumstances that existed on the later date of (a) when the entity first became a party to the contract and (b) when a change in the terms of the contract significantly modifies the cash flows that otherwise would have been required under the contract. In the basis for conclusions to the amendment the board noted that, upon reclassification, the terms of any embedded derivative recognised, should not be different to those that would have been recognised at the relevant date for assessment of embedded derivatives.

6.3.24 Similarly, a first time adopter of IFRS should assess whether an embedded derivative is required to be separated from the host contract and accounted for as a derivative on the basis of the conditions that existed at the later of the date it first became a party to the contract and the date a re-assessment is required by the above paragraph. [IFRIC 9 para 8]. It follows that as the conditions existing at the date the entity first adopts IFRS are of no relevance to the assessment of whether the embedded derivative is closely related or not, there is no difference in treatment between a continuing IFRS reporter and a first time adopter of IFRS. [IFRS 1 para IG 55].

6.3.25 Paragraph 16 of IFRS 3 requires a company that acquires another company (the 'acquirer') to re-assess all contracts of the acquired entity for embedded derivatives at the acquisition date. The rationale for this approach is that all such contracts (to which the acquirer becomes a party as a result of the acquisition) should be accounted for in the same way as if the acquirer had taken them out individually at the time of acquisition. Generally this will result in more embedded derivatives being separated from host contracts in the group's consolidated financial statements, as compared with the acquired entity's stand-alone financial statements. This is because the embedded derivative guidance links some of the criteria for separating embedded derivatives to market conditions existing at initial recognition of the host contract. These separated embedded derivatives will be accounted for at fair value through profit or loss in the consolidated financial statements, after the acquisition (unless they are designated in a valid hedge relationship in accordance with IAS 39).

> **Example – Re-assessment of embedded derivative**
>
> A UK entity entered into an 'own use' long-term electricity purchase contract in the late 1980s. At that time, there was no market for electricity. However, prices for gas and electricity were linked and, there was high correlation between the two prices. Hence, the price of the electricity contract was linked to gas prices. However, following deregulation of the energy market in the UK in the mid 1990s, the prices of gas and electricity are no longer correlated. On transition to IFRS, the contract has a remaining maturity of two years.
>
> When considered at the date of transition to IFRS the price adjustment feature would have been regarded as closely related, reflecting market conditions prevailing at the date the contract was entered into. Given that there were no amendments to the terms of the contract, in accordance with paragraph 6.3.22 above, the initial assessment is not updated even though over time market conditions have changed and prices of gas and electricity are no longer correlated at the date of transition to IFRS.

On the other hand, if the entity entered into a similar contract after deregulation of the energy market, but before transition to IFRS, the price adjustment feature (electricity price in the contract is linked to gas prices and not market price of electricity) would not be regarded as closely related. Therefore, the embedded derivative would have to be separated and accounted for as a derivative at the date of transition to IFRS in accordance with paragraph 6.3.24 above.

Application of closely related criterion to different types of hosts

6.3.26 The application guidance to IAS 39 provides examples of situations where the embedded derivative is, or is not, closely related to the host contract. [IAS 39 paras AG30-AG33]. This guidance is not an exhaustive list of contract features or embedded derivatives but does contain many of the common features found in typical host contracts. Judgement will be required to analyse situations that are not included in the standard's examples. However, as determining what is closely related can prove challenging in practice, we have supplemented the standard's examples with additional examples where relevant. The following paragraphs deal with the application of the closely related criterion to different types of hosts and embedded derivatives.

Embedded derivatives in debt host contracts

6.3.27 The most common host for an embedded derivative is a debt contract. However, it is first necessary to identify the host debt in the hybrid instrument. The implementation guidance states that the terms of the host debt instrument should reflect the stated or implied substantive terms of the hybrid instrument. [IAS 39 para IG C1]. For example, if the terms indicate that the host instrument has a stated or predetermined maturity and pays a fixed, floating or zero-coupon rate of interest, then its economic characteristics and risks are those of a debt instrument.

6.3.28 In the absence of implied or stated terms, the entity makes its own judgement of the terms. However, in exercising such judgement, the entity should not seek out a component that is not specified in the contract. Nor should it establish the terms of the host debt instrument in a manner that would separate an embedded derivative that is not clearly present in the hybrid instrument, that is to say, it cannot create a cash flow that does not exist. For example, if a five-year debt instrument has fixed interest payments of C40,000 annually and a principal payment at maturity of C1 million multiplied by the change in an equity price index, it would be inappropriate to identify a floating rate host contract and an embedded equity swap that has an offsetting floating rate leg in lieu of identifying a fixed rate host. The host contract is a fixed rate debt instrument that pays C40,000 annually, because there are no floating interest rate cash flows in the hybrid instrument. [IAS 39 para IG C1].

6.3.29 The value of a debt instrument is determined by the interest rate that is associated with the contract. The interest rate stipulated in the debt instrument is usually a function of the following factors:

- Risk free interest rate.

- Credit risk.

- Expected maturity.

- Liquidity risk.

Thus, embedded derivatives that affect the yield on debt instruments because of any of the above factors would be considered to be closely related (unless they are leveraged or do not change in the same direction as interest rates and fail the test described in para 6.3.31. A detailed example is the inverse floater in example 3 of para 6.3.34 below). On the other hand, if the economic characteristics and risks of the embedded derivatives have features that are unrelated to interest rates (such as equity or commodity features), they would not be closely related to the debt host. Examples relating to the application of closely related criterion to a debt host and different embedded derivatives are considered in the following paragraphs.

Index linked interest payments

6.3.30 It is common for debt instruments to contain embedded interest rate indices that can change the amount of interest that would otherwise be paid or received. Typical interest rate indices are LIBOR and the prime rate index. More complex ones include leveraged interest rate indices, such as levered inverse floaters, range floaters, etc.

6.3.31 An embedded derivative in which the underlying is an interest rate or interest rate index that can change the amount of interest that would otherwise be paid or received on an interest-bearing host debt contract (or insurance contract) is closely related to the host contract unless:

- the combined instrument can be settled in such a way that the holder would not recover *substantially all* of its recognised investment; or

- the embedded derivative *could* at least double the holder's initial rate of return on the host contract *and could* result in a rate of return that is at least twice what the market return would be for a contract with the same terms as the host contract.

[IAS 39 para AG 33(a)].

Note that this assessment is made when the entity becomes party to the contract and on the basis of market conditions existing then (see para 6.3.22).

6.3.32 An example of an instrument meeting the first condition would be a bond callable by the issuer at an amount significantly lower than its issue price. Should the issuer decide to exercise the call option (that is, repurchase the bond) the holder would be required to sell it and, therefore, not recover substantially all of its recognised investment. The first condition that *"the holder would not recover substantially all of its recognised investment"* is not satisfied if the terms of the combined instrument permit, but do not require, the investor to settle the combined instrument in a manner that causes it not to recover substantially all of its recognised investment and the issuer has no such right (for example, a puttable debt instrument). An embedded interest rate derivative with such terms is regarded as closely related to the interest-bearing host contract. The condition that *"the holder would not recover substantially all of its recognised investment"* applies to situations in which the holder can be forced to accept settlement at an amount that causes the holder not to recover substantially all of its recognised investment. [IAS 39 para IG C10]. The term 'substantially all' is not defined in IAS 39 and, therefore, judgement should be exercised after considering all the relevant facts and circumstances that are specific to the situation.

6.3.33 The second condition has two parts and, therefore, both these parts should be met for the embedded derivative not to be considered closely related. So, for example, if the embedded derivative feature results in doubling the initial return under a possible future interest rate scenario no matter how remote, but, at the same time, that interest rate scenario would not result in a rate of return that is at least twice what the then-current market return would be for a contract that has the same terms as the host, then only one part of the condition would have been met and the embedded derivative would be regarded as closely related to the host.

6.3.34 The above provisions are intended to 'scope in' those embedded derivatives that cause the hybrid instrument to perform less like a debt instrument and more like a derivative (for example, hybrid instruments that are highly leveraged). The following examples illustrate the application of the above guidance to various interest rate index linked debt instruments.

Example 1 – Floating rate debt

Entity A takes out a floating rate loan with a bank. The contractually determined interest rate on the debt is six-month LIBOR plus two percentage points (assuming credit spread is two percentage points).

A plain vanilla floating rate instrument with a normal credit spread whose risk free interest rate component (for example, LIBOR) is periodically reset to market interest rate cannot contain an embedded derivative.

Example 2 – Floating rate debt with investor payment provision

Entity A issues a floating rate debt instrument with a face value of C50m. The contractually determined interest rate on the debt is six-month LIBOR. However, there is a provision that if six-month LIBOR increases by 200 basis points, the investor will pay C2m to the issuing company.

In this situation, the embedded derivative consists of a contingent payment provision that depends on LIBOR increasing by 200 basis points. The embedded derivative is not separated, because the investor will receive C50m and the C2m payment is not considered to reduce its initial investment substantially. Therefore, the first condition in paragraph 6.3.31 above is not met. Furthermore, there is no provision in the contract that causes the investor's yield to increase to at least twice the initial rate. Therefore, the second condition is not met. Accordingly, the embedded derivative is closely related to the debt host and no separation is necessary. The fact that LIBOR may increase by 200 basis points in a year is simply a condition that triggers the payment and is not relevant to determining whether the embedded derivative is closely related.

Example 3 – Leveraged inverse floater

Entity A takes out a loan with a bank. The contractually determined interest rate on the debt is calculated as $14.5\% - 2.5 \times$ three-month LIBOR (sometimes referred to as a leveraged inverse floater).

Three-month LIBOR at inception = 4% giving an initial yield of 4.5%.

The embedded derivative has an underlying that is highly leveraged such that there is the possibility of either a negative yield or a significantly higher than market yield. This is because, if under a future interest rate scenario three-month LIBOR increases to 8%, the yield would be negative, that is, -9.5% (14.5% – 24%) and the investor would not be able to recover substantially all of its recognised investment. Therefore, as the first condition in paragraph 6.3.31 above is satisfied, the embedded derivative is not closely related to the host contract and will be accounted for separately. In practice sometimes the yield will not be allowed to go negative. To prevent this happening, a floor is often imposed on the coupon rate.

Note that in this example there is no need to evaluate the second condition in paragraph 6.3.31 above. But if this condition were to be evaluated the result would be the same, that is, the embedded derivative would not be considered closely related to the host debt contract. This is because, for example, if under a future interest rate scenario, three-month LIBOR falls to 2%, the yield would be 9.5% (14.5% – 5%) which is more than twice the initial yield of 4.5%. Furthermore, the yield of 9.5% is also likely to be twice the *then* market yield for a contract with the same terms as the host.

Example 4 – Forward starting interest rate swap

Entity A issues a 8% fixed rate debt instrument that matures at the end of year 5. The entity has an option to convert the loan into a variable rate debt at LIBOR + 3% after two years. LIBOR at inception is 5%.

The embedded derivative included in the above debt host is an option on a forward starting interest rate swap that changes the fixed rate interest payments to floating rate after two years. In order to determine whether the option on the forward starting swap should be accounted for as a separate derivative, it is necessary to apply the second condition in paragraph 6.3.31 above.

Accordingly, if, under a future interest rate scenario (however remote), LIBOR increases to 14%, the increase would have the effect of more than doubling the initial return on the investment from 8% to 17% (14% + 3%). However, that interest rate scenario of 14% does not result in a market rate of interest that is twice the current market rate for a contract with the same terms as the host contract, which is only 17% assuming no change in credit rating. Therefore, as only one part of the second condition in paragraph 6.3.31 is satisfied, the embedded option on the forward starting interest rate swap is closely related to the debt host and no separation is permitted.

Inflation-linked interest and principal payments

6.3.35 There is often a close relationship between interest rates and inflation in an economy. The nominal rate of interest is often thought of as the real interest rate (the amount earned on a sum loaned or deposited in a bank) plus the rate of inflation. The more precise version that allows for the compounding effect is given by the following relationship know as the Fisher equation:

$$1 + n = (1 + r)(1 + i)$$

where:
n = nominal interest rate
r = real rate of interest
i = expected inflation rate

6.3.36 The above equation illustrates that the nominal interest rate reflects compensation to the lender for expected decreases, due to inflation, in the purchasing power of the principal and interest during the course of the loan. In other words, the nominal interest rate will vary directly with the expected rate of inflation, indicating that, in general, there is a strong correlation between the two.

6.3.37 A strong correlation is particularly true for a country whose interest and inflation rates are managed together as part of the country's monetary policy decisions. For example, the Bank of England in the UK, like the Federal reserve system in the US, is responsible for setting interest rates that are aimed at accommodating economic growth in an environment of stable prices. Consider, however, countries in the Eurozone where the interest rate is set by the European Central Bank (ECB). Although the ECB sets short-term interest rates aimed at maintaining inflation rates in the Eurozone below, but close to, two per cent (measured by year-on-year increase in the Harmonised Index of Consumer Prices) over the medium term, the inflation rate in a particular country within the Eurozone may be different from overall Eurozone inflation due to, for example, differences in national rates of growth, local market regulation, etc.

6.3.38 Therefore, where a company issues a debt instrument where the amount of interest or the principal to be repaid or both is linked to an inflation index, it would be necessary to perform a qualitative analysis to determine whether the underlying inflation index is closely related. A quantitative analysis may also provide useful evidence of correlation or otherwise, particularly in a changing economic environment. This analysis should be performed on a case by case basis and would include at least the following considerations:

- Demonstration, for example via a regression analysis, to support the contention that there is a long run statistically significant relationship between the interest rate for the maturity specified in the debt instrument and the inflation measure to which that debt's coupon is linked.

- The inflation index is a recognised measure of inflation in the economic environment in which the loan originates. If the inflation index relates to a different economy or is not one that is commonly used for the purpose of lending and borrowing, the underlying inflation index will not be regarded as closely related to the debt host. In the UK, inflation indices that are most commonly used are the retail price index and the consumer price index. Therefore, no other inflation indices will be appropriate where the bond is linked to UK inflation rate indices.

- The inflation adjustment is related to the same period that the coupon payments relate.

- The resulting real rate of return delivered by the inflation linked debt is itself a rate that would not be considered an embedded derivative under IAS 39 and is not dissimilar to market estimates of real rates at the time when the debt is issued.

- The inflation index is not leveraged in any way (see para 6.3.14-15 for discussion of the term leverage and examples in paras 6.3.34 and 6.3.71).

- A judgemental qualitative analysis supports the view that any short term deviations from the defined relationship are not indicative that the two measures are no longer closely related. For example, it is likely that short-term deviations between the two measures may indicate a disparity in a country whose interest and inflation rates are not managed together as part of the country's monetary policy decisions aimed at maintaining price stability.

- Where a quantitative analysis is performed this should demonstrate that the inflation index would not result in the rate of return on the debt instrument that would at least double the holder's initial rate of return on the instrument or at any point would not exceed twice what the market rate would be a contract with the same terms as the host debt instrument.

6.3.39 An entity issuing an inflation linked bond would need to perform the above analysis at inception to determine whether the inflation index is closely related to the host debt instrument. If the above conditions are not met, the embedded derivative would have to be separated from the host contract and accounted for as a derivative.

Example – Inflation-linked bond

A UK entity issues an inflation-linked sterling bond that pays a fixed interest of 5% per annum. The return of the principal amount is linked to UK Retail Price Index (RPI), which is a recognised headline measure of inflation in the economic environment in which the entity operates.

As the coupon on the bond is 5%, and the underlying principal of the bond is £100, the bond pays £5 interest per annum. If the inflation index increases to 10%, the principal of the bond would then increase to £110 and the interest payment increases to £5.50 (5% × C110).

In this example, as the principal payment is not leveraged and it is indexed to the headline measure of inflation in the economic environment in which the entity operates and, assuming the other indicators in the above paragraph are met, the inflation index is regarded as closely related to the host debt instrument.

Equity and commodity linked interest and principal payments

6.3.40   Equity-indexed interest or principal payments embedded in a host debt instrument or insurance contract – by which the amount of interest or principal is indexed to the value of equity instruments – are not closely related to the host instrument, because the risks inherent in the host and the embedded derivative are dissimilar. [IAS 39 para AG 30(d)]. Similarly, commodity-indexed interest or principal payments embedded in a host debt instrument or insurance contract – by which the amount of interest or principal is indexed to the price of a commodity (such as gold) – are not closely related to the host instrument, because the risks inherent in the host and the embedded derivative are dissimilar. [IAS 39 para AG 30(e)]. Therefore, where interest and principal payments in a debt instrument are indexed to an equity-index that is not specific to the entity, a commodity index or any other non-financial index, the embedded derivative must be accounted for separately.

Example 1 – Cash settled put option in a convertible bond

Entity A issues convertible bonds to entity H. The term of the bonds is 3 years and the par value is C2m. Each bond pays fixed interest annually at 6% a year and is convertible at any time by entity H until maturity into a fixed number of entity A's ordinary shares. Entity H also has the option to put the convertible bond back to entity A for cash at par at any time.

Entity A has determined that the market rate for a loan with comparable credit status and providing substantially the same cash flows on the same terms, but without the conversion option, is 7%.

Entity A's management should separate the convertible bond's equity and liability elements. [IAS 32 para 28]. The conversion option is an equity instrument of entity A provided it can only be settled by physical delivery of a fixed number of shares for a fixed amount of cash or other financial assets. It is not accounted for as a derivative. [IAS 39 para 2(d)].

Paragraph 49 of IAS 39 states that the fair value of a liability with a demand feature is not less than the amount payable on demand, discounted from the first date that the amount can be required to be paid. Hence entity A would record the liability at its nominal value with any residual consideration received being attributed to the equity component.

The option to put the convertible bond back to entity A for cash at par is an embedded derivative. This option is closely related to the host debt instrument, as the exercise price (par) is approximately equal to the bond's amortised cost before separating the equity element under IAS 32 in this example. [IAS 39 para AG30(g)].

Example 2 – Call option linked to an equity index

An entity issues a debt instrument at par with a term of five years. The debt is callable by the issuer 3 years after issue. If the debt is called, the holder will receive a sum that is the greater of the par value of the debt or the par value as adjusted by the percentage increase in the FTSE 100 index.

The embedded call option that is exercisable 3 years after the issue of the debt instrument is not closely related to the debt host as the payoff is indexed to an equity index. The equity linked feature provides an upside to the investor, which is linked to an index representing different risks from those of the ordinary debt instrument. Hence, the option should be separated from the host debt instrument and accounted for separately.

Example 3 – Payments linked to the price of a listed share

An entity issues a debt instrument at par with a term of five years. The debt is redeemable at par at any time. However, the loan agreement provides that during the term of the loan the entity will either receive or pay an amount based on the changes in the share price of an unrelated listed company A plc, the reference point being the market price of A plc at the date of issue of the debt instrument.

As the interest payments are based on the changes in the price of an equity instrument (equity risk), they are not closely related to the host debt instrument (characterised mainly by interest rate and credit risk). Therefore, the embedded equity linked amounts should be separated by both the issuer and the holder of the debt instrument and recorded on the balance sheet at fair value, with subsequent changes in fair value recognised in the income statement.

The answer would be the same if the interest or principal payments were linked to the movement in an equity index, such as S&P500 and even if they were linked to the market price of the entity's own shares because the entity's own shares are an example of an underlying that is a financial variable (see Chapter 6.2 for more details on the definition of a derivative) and the risks inherent in them are dissimilar to interest risk.

Example 4 – Equity linked bond with repayment floor

Entity A purchases a one-year debt instrument issued by bank B for its principal amount of C1,000 on the issue date. Bank B will make no interest payments during the life of the instrument. At maturity the holder will receive the principal amount plus any increase in the S&P 500 index since the issue date. The fair value of an at-the-money European option maturing in one year is C48 at issuance date.

Entity A classifies the debt instrument as held-to-maturity.

Management should recognise the hybrid instrument as a combination of a call option and a zero-coupon debt instrument. Entity A should first determine the option contract's fair value and strike price. [IAS 39 para AG 28].

Since the holder only receives increases in the value of the index since the issue date, the embedded option is at the money at the date of issue and its fair value consists only of its time value and no intrinsic value. Consequently, its fair value at the issue date is

C48 and the balance of the consideration given (C1000 – C48 = C952) is attributed to the carrying amount of the zero-coupon debt instrument.

The zero-coupon host contract should be recognised at amortised cost with interest accreted at the original effective interest rate of 5% to reach C1,000 at maturity. The option should be recognised at its fair value, initially C48 against the benchmark of C1,000, with subsequent gains or losses recognised in the income statement.

Example 5 – Commodity linked bond

A gold mining company issues a debt instrument with a face value of C10m and contingent interest payments in addition to a guaranteed minimum interest payment of 4% per annum. The contingent payments are linked to the price of gold such that an additional interest payment of 0.5% would be paid for every US$25 increase in gold price above US$260. The price of gold at issue date was US$310 per ounce. The market rate for a fixed interest loan without such additional features is 5%.

A commodity linked bond such as the one described above enables the issuer to reduce its financing cost by offering contingent payments to investors, whilst the investor is assured of a guaranteed minimum, but able to participate in any increase in the price of gold.

In this situation, the issuer would be viewed as having (a) issued a host debt instrument at a market rate of interest of 5%; and (b) purchased a swap contract to receive 1% fixed interest and pay a variable amount equal to the movement in the gold price above US$260. The swap contract is not closely related to the debt instrument as the factors that cause the swap to change in value (commodity price risk) are not the same as the factors that cause the debt host to change in value (interest rate risk).

Accordingly, the embedded swap contract should be separated from the host contract by both the issuer and the holder and recorded on the balance sheet at fair value, with subsequent changes in fair value recognised in the income statement.

6.3.41 Example 2 in the previous paragraph dealt with call options held by the issuer. A similar treatment arises in circumstances where the holder has the right to put the debt instrument back to the issuer in exchange for an amount of cash or other financial assets that varies on the basis of the change in an equity or commodity index that may increase or decrease. These instruments are commonly referred to as 'puttable instruments'. Unless the issuer on initial recognition designates the puttable instrument as a financial liability at fair value through profit or loss, it is required to separate an embedded derivative (that is, the indexed payment). [IAS 39 paras AG30(a), AG31].

Interest rate caps, floors and collars

6.3.42 Floating rate securities may have a maximum coupon that is paid at any reset date. The maximum coupon rate is called a cap. For example, suppose for a floating rate note with a coupon of three-month LIBOR + 50 basis points, there is a cap of eight per cent. If the three-month LIBOR at the coupon reset date is eight per cent, then the coupon rate would be eight and a half per cent. However, the cap would restrict the coupon rate to eight per cent. Therefore, a cap can be attractive to the issuing company as a protection against rises in interest rates. A cap can be thought of as an embedded option requiring no action by the issuer to be protected from a rise in interest rates. Effectively, the bondholder has granted to the issuer the right not to pay more interest than the cap. For the grant of this privilege, the issuer of the bond (the cap buyer) will have to pay a premium that will increase the overall cost of funds. If the relevant/market interest rate rises above the cap strike rate, then in effect payments are made by the cap seller to the cap buyer to compensate for the excess. This means that the cap is in-the-money whenever the strike rate is lower than the relevant/market rate of interest. It is out-of-the-money whenever the strike rate is above the relevant/market rate of interest.

6.3.43 In contrast, there could be a minimum coupon rate specified for a floating rate security. The minimum coupon rate is called a floor. If the coupon formula provides a coupon rate that is below the floor, the floor rate is paid instead. A floor is the mirror image of a cap. While a cap benefits the issuer if interest rates rise, a floor benefits the bondholder if interest rate falls. As with other options, the buyer must pay a premium to the issuer of the bond (the floor seller) that will reduce the issuer's overall cost of funds. If the coupon rate falls below the floor strike rate then payments are made by the seller to the buyer to compensate for the shortfall. This means that the floor is in-the-money whenever the strike rate is the above the relevant/market rate of interest. It is out-of-the-money whenever the strike rate is lower than the relevant/market rate of interest.

6.3.44 A floating rate security can have a cap and a floor. This feature is referred to as a collar. The buyer of a collar limits the maximum rate that he will pay and sets a minimum rate that he will pay and, therefore, will be exposed to interest rate movements within a range. Hence, as long as interest rates are within this band the buyer of the collar pays floating interest, no compensating payment is made or received by the buyer under the terms of the collar and the collar is said to be out-of-the-money.

6.3.45 An embedded floor or cap on the interest rate on a debt contract is closely related to the host contract, provided when the instrument is issued:

- the floor is at or below the market rate of interest (out-of-the-money); or

- the cap is at or above the market rate of interest (out-of-the-money); and

- the cap or floor is not leveraged in relation to the host contract.

[IAS 39 para AG 33(b)].

6.3.46 The assessment of whether the cap or floor is closely related to the host is made when the entity becomes party to the contract and is not subsequently revised unless the terms of the debt instrument are changed significantly (see para 6.3.22 above). An entity would become party to the contract when the debt is issued at inception, bought in the secondary market or on the date of a business combination in which the debt was acquired. It follows from the above that only in-the-money caps and floors when the entity becomes party to the contract or leverage provision would fail the closely related test. Therefore, an interest rate floor embedded in a variable rate debt instrument that was out-of-the-money when the debt instrument was initially recognised would not be separated from the host debt, even if interest rates subsequently fall so that the floor becomes in-the-money. Similar considerations apply to caps.

> **Example – Debt subject to an interest rate collar**
>
> Entity A has borrowed cash from a bank. The debt is interest-bearing at a variable rate, but within a collar. The variable rate on the date of inception of the loan was 7%, the floor was 5% and the cap was 9%.
>
> In this situation, the embedded derivative is a collar that modifies the cash flows of variable rate debt if the variable rate moves outside the range of the collar. IAS 39 does not specifically deal with collars in this context, although the guidance relating to caps and floors can be extended to collars. Since at the time when the variable rate debt instrument is issued, the interest rate is 7%, which is within the collar range, the collar is out-of-the-money. Hence, based on the guidance in paragraph 6.3.45 above, the embedded collar is regarded as closely related and separate accounting for the embedded derivative is prohibited.

Calls, puts and pre-payment options

6.3.47 The terms of a debt instrument may include an issuer call option (a callable bond), that is, a right of the issuer (but not the investor) to redeem the instrument early and pay a fixed price (generally at a premium over the par value). There may also be other pre-payment features that cause the whole or part of the outstanding principal to be repaid early. Adding call options and/or other pre-payment options should make it less attractive to buyers, since it reduces the potential upside on the bond. As interest rates go down and the bond price increases, the bonds are likely to be called back. Alternatively, the investor may have a put option to force early redemption of the outstanding principal. Such call option, put option and pre-payment features that are embedded in the debt host are derivatives.

6.3.48 The application guidance explains that these embedded derivatives are not closely related to the host debt contract, unless the option's exercise price is approximately equal on each exercise date to the host debt instrument's amortised cost or the exercise price of a pre-payment option reimburses the lender for an amount up to the approximate present value of lost interest for the remaining term of the host contract. [IAS 39 para AG 30(g)].

Example 1 – Calls and puts in debt instruments

An entity issues the following debt instruments:

■ 5 year zero coupon debt for proceeds of C7m with a face value of C10m; issue costs are insignificant. The debt is callable by the issuer at its amortised cost calculated on the basis of the effective interest rate method in the event of a change in tax legislation adversely affecting the tax deductions available to the issuer.

■ 5 year zero coupon debt for proceeds of C7m with a face value of C10m; issue costs are insignificant. The debt is puttable at its face value in the event of a change of control of the issuer.

In both scenarios above, the zero coupon debt will be recorded initially at its fair value of C7m, which is the consideration received. The debt will accrete to its final value of C10m at maturity in year 5. Therefore, between inception and maturity the debt's amortised cost will not be the same as its face value, except in the period close to maturity.

In the first scenario, if the debt is called by the issuer at its amortised cost, the call option does not accelerate the repayment of principal as the option's exercise price is the same as the debt's amortised cost (the exercise price is not fixed but variable), even though the debt was initially issued at a substantial discount. Therefore, in accordance with paragraph AG 30(g) of IAS 39, the call option is closely related to the debt host and would not be accounted for separately.

In the second scenario, if the debt is put back by the holder at its face value before maturity, the put option's exercise price of C10m (fixed at the outset) would not be the same as the debt's amortised cost at exercise date. Therefore, in accordance with paragraph AG 30(g) of IAS 39, the put option is not closely related to the debt host. This means that the put option must be separately accounted for.

Both debt instruments contain terms that allow the debts to be called or put back on the occurrence of a contingent event (adverse change in tax legislation or change in control). These terms (relating to factors other than interest rate risk and credit risk of the issuer) are not closely related to the debt hosts. However, determining whether the call or the put option is closely related to the host contract is based solely on the difference between the option's exercise price and the debt's amortised cost.

Example 2 – Pre-payment option in debt instruments

Entity A takes out a fixed rate loan with a bank for C1m. The loan is repayable in quarterly instalments. The debt contains a pre-payment option that may be exercised by entity A on the first day of each quarter. The exercise price is the remaining capital amount outstanding on the debt plus a penalty of C100,000.

At inception, entity A would record the financial liability at its fair value of C1m. As entity A makes repayments of capital to the bank, the amortised cost of the debt will change.

The exercise price of the pre-payment option at inception is C1m plus the penalty of C100,000. Whether the entity will exercise its option to pre-pay the loan early may depend on a number of reasons, but the level of interest rates is a critical variable. If there is a significant decline in interest rates, any potential gain from early pre-payment may well be more than the cost of the pre-payment (the penalty payable).

Given the penalty payable is fixed, the option's exercise price (outstanding principal + penalty) will always exceed the debt's amortised cost at each option exercise date as the loan is paid off in instalments. Hence, the pre-payment option is not closely related to the debt host and should be separately accounted for. The fair value of the option would need to be calculated and this will be a positive value to the entity as the value of the pre-payable bond = value of straight bond – value of pre-payment feature. If interest rates decline, the option's value will increase making it more attractive to the entity to repay the debt early.

Sometimes the pre-payment option's exercise price is a 'market adjusted value'. A market adjusted value is calculated by discounting the contractual guaranteed amount payable at the end of the specified term to present value using the current market rate that would be offered on a new loan having a maturity period equal to the remaining maturity period of the current loan. As a result, the adjustment necessary to arrive at the market adjusted value may be positive or negative, depending upon market interest rates at each option exercise date. In that situation, the pre-payment option enables the holder simply to cash out of the instrument at fair value at the date of pre-payment. Since the holder receives only the market adjusted value, which is equal to the fair value of the loan at the date of pre-payment, the pre-payment option has a fair value of zero at all times. In fact, on a stand-alone basis, a pre-payment option with a strike price equal to market value would not meet the definition of a derivative, so it cannot be an embedded derivative per IAS 39 paragraph 11.

6.3.49 Paragraph AG30(g) of IAS 39 contains another example of a pre-payment option which would be deemed to be closely related to the host contract. This states that if the pre-payment option reimburses the lender for an amount up to the approximate present value of lost interest for the host contract's remaining term it is closely related to the host contract. Lost interest is the product of the principal amount multiplied by the interest differential. The interest differential is the difference between the effective interest rate on the host contract less the effective interest rate that could be obtained by the lender if it invests the principal at the repayment date for the host contract's remaining term in a similar contract.

6.3.50 An embedded pre-payment option in an interest-only or principal-only strip (that is, an interest or principal cash flow stream that has been separated and payable at different dates) is closely related to the host contract provided the host contract:

- initially resulted from separating the right to receive contractual cash flows of a financial instrument that, in and of itself, did not contain an embedded derivative; and

- does not contain any terms not present in the original host debt contract.

[IAS 39 para AG 33(e)].

Term-extending options

6.3.51 Sometimes clauses are included in debt instruments that allow the issuer to extend the debt's term beyond its original maturity. An option or automatic provision to extend the remaining term to maturity of a debt instrument is not closely related to the host debt instrument, unless there is a concurrent adjustment to the approximate current market rate of interest at the time of the extension. [IAS 39 para AG 30(c)]. Thus, if there is no reset of interest rates at the time of the extension, the embedded derivative is not closely related to the debt host.

6.3.52 An alternative view is that the option to extend the term of the debt may be considered a loan commitment. Not all loan commitments fall within the scope of IAS 39, as set out in paragraphs 2(h) and 4 of IAS 39. In particular, only the following loan commitments are within the scope of IAS 39:

- Instruments that the entity designates as financial liabilities at fair value through profit or loss.

- Loan commitments that can be settled net in cash or by delivering or issuing another financial instrument.

- Commitments to provide a loan at a below-market interest rate.

Loan commitments that are not in the scope of IAS 39 do not meet the definition of a derivative, as all derivatives must be financial instruments within the scope of IAS 39. [IAS 39 paras 9, 11]. Hence, an option to extend the term of a debt instrument that is considered to be a loan commitment, that is, out of the scope of IAS 39 could not be an embedded derivative that needs to be assessed for separation (see para 6.3.6). The approach adopted (that is, whether to treat an option to extend the term of a debt instrument as only within the embedded derivatives requirements or as also within the requirements for loan commitments) is an accounting policy choice that should be applied consistently.

In March 2012, the IFRS IC considered whether term-extending options in fixed rate debt instruments should be separated from the host contract but decided not to add this issue to its agenda at this stage. If the Boards do not address the issue as part of their redeliberations on IFRS 9 then the IFRS IC may revisit it.

Example 1 – Term-extending options not reset to market rates

An entity issues 6% fixed rate debt that has a fixed term of 3 years. The entity is able to extend the debt before its maturity for an additional 2 year period at the same 6% interest.

In this example, as the entity is able to extend the debt's term at the same interest rate and there is no reset to current market rates, the term-extending option is not considered to be closely related to the debt host.

Such term-extending options could be valuable to an entity as it allows the issuer to refinance debt at the same interest rate when market rates are rising. Conversely, if market rates are falling, the entity would not exercise its option to extend. Therefore, the option is a derivative that would need to be accounted for separately at fair value through profit or loss, even though its value is closely related to interest rates that also affect the value of the underlying debt host.

The above treatment regarding term-extending options is justified, because otherwise such options could be used to circumvent the requirement to bifurcate a derivative in circumstances where the investor might not recover substantially all its initial recorded investment (see further para 6.3.31 above). Term-extending options in host debts typically involve postponement of the repayment of the principal and, even though such postponement does not cause the failure to recover substantially all of its initial recorded investment, it can significantly reduce the fair value of the recovery of that investment.

Alternatively, if the term-extending option was considered to be a loan commitment out of IAS 39's scope, it would not be separated from the host debt instrument.

Example 2 – Term-extending option reset to market rates

An entity issues a 6% fixed rate debt that has a fixed term of 3 years. The company is able to extend the debt before its maturity for an additional 2 year period, but the rate for the period of extension is the market rate at the time of the extension.

In this example, as the option to extend the term causes the interest rate to reset to current market rates, the option is regarded as closely related to the host debt. Common sense would also suggest such an option has no real value to the entity other than providing liquidity. This is because if the market interest rate at the time of extension is 8%, the entity cannot extend the term without paying an additional 2% interest anyway. On the other hand, if the market interest rate drops to 4%, the extension is equivalent to taking out a new loan at 4%.

6.3.53 If an entity issues a debt instrument and the holder of that debt instrument writes a call option on the debt instrument to a third party, the issuer regards the call option as extending the term to maturity of the debt instrument provided the issuer can be required to participate in or facilitate the remarketing of the debt instrument as a result of the call option being exercised. [IAS 39 para AG 30 (c)].

6.3.54 It is interesting to note that a bond that has a put option is economically no different to one that has a term-extending option, yet IAS 39 prescribes a different treatment for the derivatives embedded in them. Consider the following example:

Example – Comparison of put and extension option

An entity purchasers two bonds A and B with the following terms:

- Bond A has a stated maturity of 10 years, but the entity can put it back to the issuer at par after 3 years.

- Bond B has a stated maturity of 3 years, but after 3 years the entity can extend the maturity to 10 years (that is, 7 more years) at the same initial rate (that is, the interest rate is not reset to the interest rate at the date of extension).

Both bonds are issued by the same issuer at par and have a coupon rate of 6%.

Assume also that the following two scenarios exist at the end of year 3:

Scenario 1: For the issuer, the interest rate for 7 year debt is at 8%.

- The holder will put bond A back to the issuer and reinvest the par amount of the bond at 8%.

- The holder will not extend the maturity of bond B and, instead, will reinvest the principal at 8%.

Scenario 2: For the issuer, the interest rate for 7 year debt is at 4%.

- The holder will not put bond A back to the issuer and, instead, will continue to receive 6% for the next 7 years.

- The holder will extend the term of bond B and continue to receive 6% for the next 7 years.

As can be seen from the above, the entity is in the same position with respect to either Bond A or Bond B. However, IAS 39 prescribes a different treatment for the put and the term extension options embedded in Bond A and Bond B respectively.

As discussed in paragraph 6.3.48 above, the embedded put option derivative in Bond A is regarded as closely related to the Bond as the bond's amortised cost based on the effective interest rate at the end of three years is the same as par, which is also the put option's exercise price. This is because the expected cash flows would take into account the possibility of the debt being pre-paid early for the purposes of calculating the effective interest rate. [IAS 39 para 9]. Therefore, the embedded put option would not be recognised separately and fair valued.

On the other hand, the embedded term extension option is not regarded as closely related to the host debt, because under Bond B's terms the interest rates are not reset when the option is exercised. Therefore, the option would be separated and fair valued. Alternatively, if the embedded term extension option was considered to be a loan commitment outside IAS 39's scope, the option would not be separated, as it would not meet the definition of a derivative.

The above example illustrates that two instruments that are economically similar, but different in form by virtue of the way in which the terms of the embedded options are expressed, can lead to different accounting treatments for the embedded options.

To be able to rationalise the apparent conflict in accounting treatment between these two economically identical situations, it is necessary to consider the issuer's expectation of the instrument's life for the purposes of the effective interest rate calculation. Thus the issuer will not necessarily follow the legal form of the terms, but the economics in determining whether the instrument has a put option or a term extending option and thus the appropriate accounting treatment.

Credit sensitive payments and credit derivatives

6.3.55 IAS 39 does not deal specifically with payments based on the creditworthiness of the issuer of an instrument. However, as the stated in paragraph 6.3.29 above, the creditworthiness of the issuer is a key factor in setting the level of interest rate on the debt instrument. Thus, for debt instruments that provide for the interest rate to be reset in the event of a change in the issuer's published credit rating (say down from A to BBB) or a change in the issuer's creditworthiness, the embedded derivative would be closely related to the debt host, and so would not be separated from the host contract.

> **Example 1 – Credit sensitive payments**
>
> Entity A issues a bond with a coupon step-up feature that requires the issuer to pay an additional coupon to bondholders in the event of deterioration in the issuer's credit rating below a specified level. The coupon payable on the bond will return to the initial fixed rate in the event that the issuer's credit rating returns to the specified level.
>
> The coupon step-up clause meets the definition of a derivative as the value fluctuates in response to an underlying (in this case the credit rating); it requires no initial net investment and it is settled at a future date.
>
> The economic characteristics and risks of the embedded derivatives in both cases are closely related to the economic characteristics and risks of the host bond because:
>
> - both the embedded derivative and the host contract are driven by changes in the indications of the issuer's credit risk; and
>
> - such clauses do not transfer the credit risk to another party external to the original contractual relationships created by the debt instrument (see para 6.3.56 below).
>
> The embedded derivative is not accounted for separately from the host debt contract.

6.3.56 IAS 39 does, however, deal with credit derivatives that are embedded in host debt instruments. A credit derivative is a financial instrument designed to transfer credit risk from the person exposed to that risk to a person willing to take on that risk. The derivative derives its economic value by reference to a specified debt obligation, often described as the 'reference asset'.

6.3.57 Credit derivatives that are embedded in a host debt instrument and allow one party (the 'beneficiary') to transfer the credit risk of a particular reference asset, which it may not own, to another party (the 'guarantor') are not closely related to the host debt instrument. Such credit derivatives allow the guarantor to assume the credit risk associated with the reference asset without directly owning it. [IAS 39 AG30(h)].

> **Example – Credit-linked note**
>
> An investment bank issues a credit-linked note to another party (the investor) in return for a consideration equal to the par value of the note. The coupon on the note is linked to the credit risk of a portfolio of third party bonds (the reference assets). In economic terms, the credit-linked note comprises a fixed income instrument with an embedded credit derivative.
>
> The embedded credit derivative must be accounted for separately as it is linked to credit risks of debt instruments issued by third parties and not to the credit risk of the host debt instrument issued by the investment bank. The notion of an embedded derivative in a hybrid instrument refers to provisions incorporated into a single contract and not to provisions in separate contracts between different counterparties.

Equity conversion features

6.3.58 When an investor holds debt securities that are convertible into the issuer's equity shares at the investor's option, the equity conversion feature represents an embedded option written by the issuer on its equity shares. The embedded derivative is not closely related to the host debt instrument from the investor's perspective. [IAS 39 para IG C3]. From the issuer's perspective, the written equity conversion option is an equity instrument and excluded from IAS 39's scope provided it meets the conditions for that classification under IAS 32. [IAS 39 para AG 30(f)]. If, on the other hand, the debt instrument is convertible (or exchangeable) into shares of another entity, both the issuer and the holder would have to separate the embedded derivative from the host contract.

6.3.59 As the holder of a convertible bond is required to separate the embedded derivative, they are generally precluded from accounting for the debt host contract as a held-to-maturity investment. This is because classification as a held-to-maturity investment would be inconsistent with paying for the conversion feature – the right to convert into equity shares before maturity. However, the investor could classify the bond as an available-for-sale financial asset provided it is not purchased for trading purposes. If the bond is classified as available-for-sale (that is, fair value changes are recognised directly in equity until the bond is sold or impaired), the equity conversion option (the embedded derivative) is separated. The accounting for the holder, which is significantly different from the issuer as considered in chapter 6.5, is as follows:

- The embedded derivative's fair value (the equity conversion option from the issuer's perspective) is calculated first and comprises its time value and its intrinsic value, if any. The option has value on initial recognition even when it is out of the money.

After initial recognition, the embedded derivative is constantly remeasured at fair value at each balance sheet date and changes in the fair value are recognised in profit or loss, unless the option is part of a cash flow hedging relationship.

■ The carrying value of the host contract (the liability component from the issuer's perspective) is assigned the residual amount after deducting from the fair value of the instrument as a whole (the consideration paid to acquire the hybrid instrument) the amount separately determined for the embedded derivative.

If the convertible bond is measured at fair value with changes in fair value recognised in profit or loss, separating the embedded derivative from the host bond as illustrated above is not permitted. [IAS 39 para IG C3].

6.3.60 Another type of embedded derivative that is often found in practice relates to a type of funding provided by venture capital entities as illustrated in the example below.

> **Example – Equity kicker**
>
> A venture capital entity provides a subordinated loan that, in addition to interest and repayment of principal, contains terms that entitles the venture capital company to receive shares of the borrower free of charge or at a very low price (an 'equity kicker') in the event the borrower undergoes an IPO. As a result of this feature, the interest on the subordinated loan is lower than it would otherwise be.
>
> The 'equity kicker' meets the definition of a derivative even though the right to receive shares is contingent upon the future listing of the borrower. IAS 39 paragraph AG 9 states that a derivative could require a payment as a result of some future event that is unrelated to a notional amount. An 'equity kicker' feature is similar to such a derivative except that it does not give a right to a fixed payment, but an option right, if the future event occurs. Therefore, as the economic characteristics and risks of an equity return are not closely related to the economic characteristics and risks of a host debt instrument, the embedded derivative would be accounted for separately by the venture capital entity. [IAS 39 para IG C4].

Foreign currency features

6.3.61 An entity may issue debt in a currency other than its functional currency. Such a foreign currency loan is accounted for under IAS 21, 'The effects of changes in foreign exchange rates', which requires foreign currency gains and losses on monetary items to be recognised in profit or loss. As the foreign currency gains or losses are already recognised, a foreign currency derivative that may be embedded in such a host debt instrument is considered closely related and is not separated. This also applies to an embedded foreign currency derivative that provides a stream of principal or interest payments that are denominated in a foreign currency and embedded in a host debt instrument (for example, a dual currency bond). [IAS 39 para AG 33(c)].

Example – Dual currency bond

An entity with pound sterling as a functional currency issues a £10m debt instrument that provides for the annual payment of interest in euros and the repayment of principal in pound sterling.

This dual currency bond can be viewed as containing a foreign currency swap that converts the pound sterling interest payments to euro interest payments. As discussed above, this embedded swap is not accounted for separately as under IAS 21, any exchange gains and losses arising on the annual euro interest payments due to exchange rate changes are themselves reported in profit or loss. [IAS 21 para 28]. See also the example of the measurement of a dual currency bond in chapter 6.7.

6.3.62 Although many embedded foreign currency derivatives will not have to be separated from a foreign currency host debt instrument, some may. Consider the following examples:

Example 1 – Loan with foreign currency option

An entity issues a C10m loan at an above average market rate. The entity has the option to repay the loan at par for C10m or a fixed amount in a foreign currency, say €15m.

The debt instrument can be viewed as combining a loan at prevailing market interest rates and a foreign currency option. In effect, the issuer has purchased a foreign currency option that allows it to take advantage of changes in foreign currency exchange rates during the outstanding period of the loan. The premium for the option is paid as part of the higher interest cost. Similarly, the lender has written an option that exposes it to foreign currency risk. Because the borrower has the option of repaying the loan in its functional currency or in a foreign currency, the option is not closely related to the debt instrument (that is, it is not directly related to the currency of the loan or the interest rate that applies to that currency). The principle discussed in paragraph 6.3.61 above does not apply since application of IAS 21 rules for revaluing of monetary items would not lead to revaluation of the foreign currency option. Accordingly, the embedded foreign currency option should be separated from the host contract and accounted for separately by both parties to the contract. In contrast, if both the principal and the interest payments were made in a foreign currency (that is, if no optionality was involved), there would be no embedded derivative.

Example 2 – Interest payments linked to foreign currency exchange rates

An entity issues a £10m debt security at par. Quarterly interest payments, which are payable in pound sterling, are computed based on a formula that is linked to the £/€ exchange rate.

In this example, the quarterly interest is not denominated in foreign currency and, therefore, the principle discussed in paragraph 6.3.61 above does not apply. Since the formula for computing the interest payable on a sterling bond is linked to the £/€ exchange rate and not based on an interest rate or an index based on interest rates, an inflation index or the creditworthiness of the debtor, it is an embedded derivative that is not closely related to the sterling bond. Hence, it should be accounted for separately. The embedded derivative is a forward foreign exchange contract.

Embedded derivatives in equity host contracts

6.3.63   For embedded derivatives in an equity host contract, an analysis should first be performed to determine whether the host contract is an equity host. In carrying out this analysis, it is necessary to determine whether the host contract has any stated or pre-determined maturity and, if not, whether the residual interest represents a residual interest in the entity's net assets (see chapter 6.7). Generally, when a host contract encompasses a residual interest that involves the rights of ownership, it is an equity host. The value of an equity instrument is a function of the underlying equity price or index. Therefore, an embedded derivative would need to possess equity characteristics related to the same entity to be regarded as closely related. [IAS 39 para AG 27].

Calls and puts

6.3.64   A call option embedded in an equity instrument that enables the issuer to re-acquire that equity instrument at a specified price is not closely related to the host equity instrument from the holder's perspective. From the issuer's perspective, on the other hand, the call option is an equity instrument provided it meets the conditions for that classification under IAS 32, in which case it is excluded from IAS 39's scope. [IAS 39 para AG 30(b)].

6.3.65   A put option that requires the issuer to re-acquire an equity instrument at a specified price is similarly not closely related to the host contract from the holder's perspective. From the issuer's perspective, the put option is a written option that gives the counterparty the right to sell the issuer's own equity instrument to the entity for a fixed price. Under paragraph 23 of IAS 32, the issuer recognises a financial liability equal to the present value of the redemption amount (that is, the present value of the option's exercise price). See further chapter 6.5.

6.3.66   In the case of a puttable instrument that can be put back at any time for cash equal to a proportionate share of the entity's net asset value (such as units of an open-ended mutual fund or some unit-linked investment products), the effect of separating an embedded derivative and accounting for each component is to measure the combined instrument at the redemption amount that is payable at the balance sheet date if the holder exercised its right to put the instrument back to the issuer. [IAS 39 para AG 32]. This will apply to both the issuer and the investor in such an instrument, but for the issuer it is only relevant if the instrument is classified as a debt instrument in accordance with an amendment to IAS 32 and IAS 1, 'Puttable financial instruments and obligations arising on liquidation'.

6.3.67   The treatment of call and put options embedded in preference shares require careful consideration. This is because the terms of the preference share must be analysed first to determine whether the preference shares are more akin to an equity instrument or a debt instrument. Consider the following examples:

63029

Example 1 – Puttable preference shares

An entity issues C50m mandatorily redeemable preference shares at par with a fixed dividend of 8% per annum. The preference shares are puttable to the company for cash at par if market interest rate exceeds 12%.

The mandatorily redeemable preference shares (including fixed dividend) are a financial liability of the issuer and akin to a debt instrument. Furthermore, the embedded put option's exercise price, which is par, is approximately equal to the preference's shares amortised cost. Hence, the put option is considered closely related to the debt host.

Example 2 – Convertible preference shares

An entity issues C50m of irredeemable preference shares that give the holders a preferential right to return of capital in a winding up, but which are also convertible into a fixed number of ordinary shares at the holder's option. Any dividends paid in the year are at the discretion of the issuer.

As the preference shares are irredeemable and there is no obligation on the issuer to pay dividends, the shares are equity in nature. The conversion feature represents an embedded written call option on the company's ordinary shares, which on a free-standing basis would be an equity instrument of the entity. As both the embedded call option and the host are equity instruments, the entity does not account for the embedded option separately. Similarly, the investor would not have to account for the embedded option separately.

Embedded derivatives in lease host contracts

6.3.68 Embedded derivatives may be present in lease host contracts, whether the lease is an operating or a finance lease. The approach for determining whether an embedded derivative is closely related to a lease host is similar to the approach that is used for a debt host.

Inflation indexed rentals

6.3.69 An embedded derivative in a host lease contract is closely related to the host contract if the embedded derivative is an inflation-related index such as an index of lease payments to a consumer price index provided:

- the lease is not leveraged; and

- the index relates to inflation in the entity's own economic environment.

[IAS 39 para AG 33(f)].

6.3.70 The first bullet point makes it clear that an embedded inflation adjustment in the lease contract would not be closely related if it is considered to be leveraged. In determining whether inflation features embedded in lease contracts are leveraged, the guidance stated in paragraph 6.3.14-6.3.15 above should be followed. Generally, lease contracts often stipulate that payments will increase in line with inflation, in which case, the indexed linked lease payments would not be considered leveraged. Where this is not the case, an inflationary adjustment of greater than one would be considered sufficiently leveraged for the inflation feature to be accounted for separately. This is because, in practice, the market would expect the prices of goods and services to move in line with inflation, all other factors being equal. Therefore, any inflationary adjustments in a lease contract that increase the indexed cash flows by more than the normal rate of inflation are considered to be leveraged.

6.3.71   The second bullet point in paragraph 6.3.69 states that the index should relate to inflation in the entity's own economic environment. IAS 39 is silent as to whether this means the lessee's or the lessor's economic environment. It is reasonable to assume, however, that the economic environment that is most relevant to the lease contract is the one in which the leased asset is located, as the inflation index of that economic environment is the one that directly affects the lease rentals and, hence, the leased property's value. Consequently, the economic environment in which the lessee or the lessor operates is not relevant to the analysis.

Example 1 – Inflation linked rentals

A UK entity is the tenant in a 10 year lease of a property in the UK with rental payments in pound sterling that are contractually determined for the first year, but thereafter increase at a rate of one and a half times the change in UK RPI (Retail Price Index).

The future cash flows (the rental payments) will change in response to changes in the inflation index of France. The embedded inflation indexed payments are not leveraged and relate to the economic environment in which the leased asset is located. Therefore, the inflation adjustment is closely related to the lease contract and separation is not required.

Note: this is a lease payable in a currency that is not the functional currency of the UK lessee. Foreign currency features in lease contracts are discussed further from paragraphs 6.3.78 below.

Example 2 – Inflation linked rentals (leveraged)

A UK entity is the tenant in a 10 year lease of a property in the UK with rental payments in pound sterling that are contractually determined for the first year, but thereafter increasing at a rate of one and a half times the change in UK RPI (Retail Price Index).

The future cash flows (the rental payments) will change in response to changes in the UK RPI. Since the cash flows change by an amount in excess of the change in RPI, such cash flows are considered to be leveraged as discussed in paragraph 6.3.70 above. Therefore, the embedded inflation indexed payments would be accounted for separately.

A question arises as to whether the embedded derivative should be measured by reference to half times UK RPI or one and a half times UK RPI.

Some would favour the former treatment on the grounds that as the leverage portion of the embedded derivative is the amount over and above the change in the UK inflation index, this portion (half times RPI) should be accounted for separately as a derivative. On this basis, the host contract would contain the non-leveraged portion (one times RPI) that is considered to be closely related.

However, we consider that splitting the change in the fair value of an indexed linked derivative between a leveraged amount and a non-leveraged amount is not appropriate for the following reasons:

- A derivative has a single value and splitting a portion out in the above manner is not permitted under IAS 39.

- The leveraged and non-leveraged portions relate to the same risk and, since the inflation is leveraged overall, the entire link to RPI is no longer considered closely related.

- The separation creates cash flow patterns that are not evident in the lease contract because, in practice, the actual cash flows would consist of the minimum rentals plus amounts relating to the entire change in the inflation adjustment.

Therefore, the leveraged portion of the embedded derivative should be based on the total change in the UK inflation index, that is, one and a half times RPI, whilst the host would consist of a non-inflation linked lease rental contract.

Example 3 – Inflation linked rentals not related to the entity's economic environment

Facts are the same as in example 1 except that the inflation adjustment relates to a specified US annual inflation rate (for example, Retail Price Index, Consumer Price Index etc). The landlord is a US entity.

The future cash flows (the rental payments) will change in response to changes in the US inflation index. The embedded inflation indexed payments, although not leveraged, relate to a different economic environment to that in which the leased asset is located and the UK entity operates. Therefore, the inflation indexed payment is not closely related to the lease host contract and would be accounted for separately.

Example 4 – Upward only inflation-linked rentals

Entity A is a tenant in a 10 year UK property lease agreement. The rent for the first year is contractually determined at C100,000. The rental payments will change in line with an index of UK prices so if, at the end of year 1, the index had increased by 3%, the rent for year 2 would be C103,000. However, the lease provides that the rent may not be decreased. So if, during year 2, the index fell by 1%, the rent for year 3 would remain at C103,000. The index shows that UK prices are generally increasing at the inception of the lease (that is, there is UK inflation).

The rental payments are linked to an index. They follow that index while it is increasing, but do not follow it if it decreases. This feature is often known as 'upward only'. However, this lease contains a floor in the rental payments because of the upward-only feature, so it is necessary to identify whether the floor is in or out-of-the-money at the inception of the lease. Because the upward-only feature of the rent reviews means that the rentals can never fall below the floor, the floor is always out-of-the-money (not influencing the cash flows) both at inception (even where the relevant index is negative at the date of signing) and subsequently. Therefore, its presence does not alter the expected cash flows and so the derivative is closely related.

Contingent rentals based on related sales

6.3.72 Lease contracts may include contingent rentals that are based on certain related sales of the lessee. Such a contingent rental-related embedded derivative is considered to be closely related to the lease host contract and would not be accounted for separately. [IAS 39 para AG 33(f)].

Example – Lease rentals related to sales

A UK entity leases a property located in the UK. The rentals consist of a base rental of C10,000 plus 5% of the lessee's sales each month.

The rental payments will vary, depending on an underlying, being the entity's sales.

However, as stated above, the portion of the contingent rentals based on related sales is considered to be closely related to the host lease contract. Therefore, the sales related payments should not be separated.

Contingent rentals based on a variable interest rate

6.3.73 Where lease contracts include contingent rentals that are based on variable interest rates, the contingent rental-related embedded derivative is considered to be closely related to the lease host contract and would not be accounted for separately. [IAS 39 para AG 33(f)]. This is because a lease contract is akin to a debt instrument and, therefore, the obligation to make future payments for the use of the asset and the adjustment of those payments to reflect changes in a variable interest rate index such as the LIBOR are considered to be closely related.

Example – Lease rentals indexed to LIBOR

A UK entity leases a property located in the UK. The lease rentals are indexed to the UK LIBOR rate. The contract does not contain any leverage feature.

The embedded derivative does not need to be separated as the rentals are based on a variable interest rate index of the UK economy.

On the other hand, if the rentals were indexed to a variable interest rate of an economic environment that is different from the economic environment in which the leased asset is located, the related embedded derivative would not be regarded as closely related in the same way that a similarly indexed inflation payment would not be regarded as closely related (see para 6.3.69 above).

Purchase options in lease agreements

6.3.74 Often lease contracts include an option that allows the lessee to purchase the asset at the end of the lease term. Such a purchase option would not qualify as an embedded derivative for a number of reasons. First, the purchase option is based on a non-financial variable (the underlying price of the leased asset) that is specific to a party to the contract and, hence, currently fails the definition of a derivative. [IAS 39 para AG12A]. Secondly, in order to exercise the option, the lessee must pay the purchase price in cash and the lessor must physically deliver the leased asset (a non-financial asset). This constitutes gross settlement and, therefore, the option is not a financial instrument. However, if the terms in the contract allow either party to settle net in cash (considered unlikely) or the leased asset is readily convertible into cash (because an active trading market exists for the asset in question and, therefore, it is not specific to a party to the contract), the purchase option could qualify as a derivative (see chapter 6.1). [IAS 39 para 6].

Term extension or renewal options

6.3.75 A finance lease is viewed as being equivalent to debt for accounting and disclosure purposes. However, the right to extend the lease term is different from the right to extend the term of a debt instrument. The right to extend the lease is not a right to borrow funds for a further period as would be the case with a debt instrument; rather, the right to extend the lease is a right to use a non-financial asset for an additional period. Furthermore, under IAS 17 the extension term would either be included in the calculation of the minimum lease term if it is reasonably certain that, at the inception of the lease, the lessee will exercise the option; or the renewal would constitute a new lease because the leased asset and the corresponding liability (if either exists) would have been amortised to nil by the end of the original lease term. In either case, the renewal or the extension option would not meet the definition of a derivative, as it does not contain a net settlement provision.

Residual value guarantee in lease agreements

6.3.76 Where a lease includes a residual value guarantee, the lessee undertakes to make a payment if the residual value of the asset at the end of the lease falls below a pre-determined amount. A residual value guarantee does not meet the definition of a derivative because it has an underlying (price of the leased asset) that is specific to a party to the contract. Furthermore, under IAS 17, the gross value amount of any residual value guarantee is treated as part of the minimum lease payments and is accounted for as such. Therefore, it does not need to be accounted for under IAS 39.

Termination clause in lease agreements

6.3.77 Lease agreements are generally irrevocable, that is, the lessee is obliged to lease the asset during the non-cancellable period of the lease. However, the lease may contain an early termination clause that allows the lessee to terminate the contract, but only on the payment of a penalty. This penalty payment (sometimes referred to as the 'stipulated loss value') ensures that the lessor will be able to recover its remaining investment in the lease. This situation is similar in substance to a pre-payment option in a debt instrument, which is considered closely related in circumstances where the option's exercise price is approximately equal to the amortised cost of the debt instrument. See example 2 in paragraph 6.3.48 above. In that example, where the penalty payment clause had a 'market adjusted value' exercise price it had a fair value of zero, until the option was actually exercised.

Lease payments in foreign currencies

6.3.78 Finance lease contracts that give rise to financial assets in lessors and financial liabilities in lessees are financial instruments. Therefore, as a finance lease denominated in a foreign currency is similar in nature to a foreign currency loan, no separation of the embedded foreign currency derivative is required, because the foreign currency lease receivable and payable are monetary items that are accounted for in accordance with IAS 21. The guidance that applies to foreign currency loans is also applicable to foreign currency finance leases (see para 6.3.61), that is, the embedded derivative is not separated.

6.3.79 On the other hand, an operating lease is not regarded as a financial instrument. Therefore, an operating lease agreement that provides for payments in foreign currency may contain foreign currency embedded derivatives that may require separation. Paragraph AG33(d) of IAS 39 contains provisions that deal with embedded foreign currency derivatives in a host contract that is not a financial instrument. These are considered in paragraph 6.3.91 below. That guidance has been applied to the examples given below.

Example 1 – Operating lease rentals denominated in foreign currency

A UK company enters into an operating lease for a property in france with a European lessor that is denominated in euros. The functional currency of the lessee and the lessor are the pound sterling and the euro respectively.

Paragraph AG33(d) of IAS 39 provides that contracts, other than financial instruments, that specify payments denominated in the functional currency of any substantial party to the contract are closely related to the host contract.

In this example, the lease payments are denominated in the functional currency of the lessor – a substantial party to the contract. Therefore, the embedded derivative is closely related to the host contract and not separated. It is not appropriate to argue that because the payments are in a foreign currency and the UK lessee is exposed to currency risk there is an embedded foreign currency forward converting sterling payments to euros.

On the other hand, if the lease payments are denominated in a currency that is unrelated to either party's functional currency (for example, US dollars), the embedded foreign currency forward should be separated from the host contract and accounted for as a derivative. This applies to both parties to the contract.

Example 2 – Operating lease rentals denominated in foreign currency

On 1 June 20X2 entity A, a Russian oil refinery, entered into an arrangement with entity S to lease a building in Moscow for a 10-year period. The lease is classified as an operating lease. Entity A's management has determined its functional currency to be the US dollar.

Entity S is a property management and development entity located in Russia. Its management has determined its functional currency to be the Russian Rouble.

Entity S set the monthly lease repayments in Swiss francs to avoid exposure to any devaluation in the Russian Rouble and to obtain a natural hedge for the repayment of its Swiss franc denominated bonds.

As the Swiss franc is neither the functional currency of one of the substantial parties to the lease contract, nor a currency commonly used in Russia, nor the currency in which leases are routinely denominated in the world, the lease contract contains an embedded derivative that is not closely related to the host contract.

From entity S's perspective, the lease contract contains a series of embedded forward contracts to buy Swiss francs against Russian roubles. These embedded derivatives are not closely related to the host contract (lease contract denominated in Russian Rouble) and, therefore, should be accounted for separately. Entity S may however be able to use the separated forward contracts in a formal hedge of the cashflows on its Swiss franc bonds – see chapter 6.8 on hedging for more details of when this could be permissible.

From entity A's perspective, the lease contract contains a series of embedded forward contracts to sell Swiss francs against US dollars. These embedded derivatives are not closely related to the host contract (lease contract denominated in USD) and, therefore, should be accounted for separately.

Example 3 – Subsidiary's foreign currency lease payments guaranteed by parent

A major French operating subsidiary of a US parent enters into a lease with a Swiss company that requires lease payments in US dollars. The lease payments are guaranteed by the US parent. The functional currencies of the respective entities are their local currencies.

In this example, the substantial parties to the lease contract are the French lessee and the Swiss lessor. The guarantor is not a substantial party to the contract and, therefore, its functional currency is of no relevance to the analysis (see further para 6.3.92 below). Since the lease payments are made in US dollars, which is neither the functional currency of the lessee nor the lessor, the embedded foreign currency swap would need to be accounted for separately.

Embedded derivatives in executory contracts

6.3.80   Contracts to buy or sell a non-financial asset that qualify as executory contracts, including commitments (for example, take or pay contracts) that are entered into to meet the entity's expected purchase, sale or usage requirements and are expected to be settled by physical delivery, are not financial instruments.

Accordingly, they are scoped out of IAS 39 under the own use purchase or sale exception. [IAS 39 para 5]. However, even though such contracts are not financial instruments, they may contain embedded derivatives. Embedded derivatives may also be present in some service contracts.

6.3.81   IAS 39 contains little specific guidance relating to derivatives embedded in such contracts, except for features involving foreign currency. Therefore, it is necessary to consider carefully the economic characteristics and risks of such contracts in assessing whether embedded derivatives are present and, if so, whether they should be separately accounted for. Both quantitative and qualitative factors should be considered. Sometimes it may be possible to draw on the guidance discussed above for other host contracts. Indeed, it would not be unreasonable to do so, particularly for features such as pricing adjustments, inflation adjustments and caps, floors and collars on prices and quantities.

Price adjustment features

6.3.82   Normal purchase and sale contracts may contain price clauses that modify the contract's cash flows. In assessing the closely related criterion for the embedded derivative, it would be necessary to establish whether the underlying in a price adjustment feature incorporated into such a contract is related or unrelated to the cost or fair value of the goods or services being sold or purchased.

Example 1 – Price adjustment linked to market prices of goods purchased

An entity (whose functional currency is pound sterling) contracts to purchase 200 tonnes of aluminium from a UK supplier in 12 months' time. The aluminium is intended for use in the course of business. The purchase price will be the market price at the contract date plus an amount determined by a specified index of aluminium prices. The contract does not contain any leverage feature.

The future cash outflows are linked to movements in the market price for aluminium. The purpose of the embedded derivative is to ensure that the price paid for the aluminium is the market price at the date of purchase/supply rather than the date the two parties entered into the supply contract. This ensures that the seller passes any price risk to the entity. As the underlying is related to the price of the aluminium purchased, the derivative is closely related to the aluminium supply contract (host) and would not be accounted for separately.

Example 2 – Coal purchase contract linked to changes in the price of electricity

An entity enters into a coal purchase contract that includes a clause that links the price of coal to a pricing formula based on the prevailing electricity price at the date of delivery. The entity purchases the coal for its own use and there are no provisions to settle the contract net.

The coal purchase contract is the host contract. The pricing formula that changes the price risk from coal price to electricity price is the embedded derivative. Although coal may be used for the production of electricity, the underlying based on electricity prices is not pertinent to both the changes in the cost and the changes in the fair value of coal. Therefore, the embedded derivative (the electricity price adjustment) is not closely related to the host contract and should be accounted for separately.

Example 3 – Supply contract subject to multiple pricing adjustments

An entity has entered into a contract with a customer to sell 10,000 wooden chairs for a period of five years. The price per chair is contractually determined at C100 per chair for the first year and thereafter increases in line with changes in certain indices. 50% of the price of each chair is linked to an index of timber prices, 30% is linked to the UK wage inflation index. So if the timber index rises by 10% and the wage inflation index increases by 5%, the price for each chair will be C106.50 (being C50 × 1.1 + C30 × 1.05 + C20). The sales contract in its entirety does not meet the definition of a derivative as it will be settled by physical delivery in the normal course of business.

There are two embedded derivatives contained in this contract, because the price of chairs over the contract term is linked to the two indices (timber and wage inflation). The purpose of these embedded derivatives is to protect the entity's profit margin over the contract term by ensuring that changes in the prices of inputs are passed on to the end customer.

Although both indices are considered to be relevant and pertinent to the cost or fair value of the chairs being sold, they would be considered to be closely related to the host contract if, and only if, the entity can reliably demonstrate that the standard mix of direct material and direct labour for each chair produced is maintained.

If, however, the entity is unable to demonstrate reliably the clear linkage, then the embedded derivatives *may* be leveraged (because the percentage of the price linked to each index may not accurately reflect the cost structure). In other words, the magnitude of the price adjustment may cause the price of the host contract to increase by more than an insignificant amount (see para 6.3.15 above). In that situation, the indexed linked price adjustments would not be considered to be closely related.

6.3.83   Where a contract to buy or sell non-financial assets does not qualify for the own use purchase or sale exception, the entire contract would fall to be treated as if it were a financial instrument (and in most cases a derivative). In that situation, as the entire derivative contract would be accounted for at fair value through profit or loss, any derivatives embedded in such contracts would no longer need to be accounted for separately.

Example – Contract not qualifying for 'normal' purchase or sale exception

An entity enters into a forward contract to purchase 10,000 tonnes of coal. The contract does not qualify for the 'normal' purchase or sale exception as there is a provision in the contract for net settlement and the entity's past practice indicates that it will settle the contract net. Settlement is based on changes in the fair value of coal during the contract's term plus a payment provision based on a formula linked to prevailing electricity prices.

Given that the own use exception does not apply, the entire forward contract to purchase coal will be accounted for as a derivative in accordance with IAS 39 with gains and losses on the entire contract reported in the profit and loss account. Therefore, there is no need to identify separately the leverage payment provision as an embedded derivative.

Volume adjustment features

6.3.84 Many contracts for the supply of goods usually give the buyer the right to take either a minimum quantity of goods or any amount based on the buyer's requirements. A minimum annual commitment does not create a derivative as long as the entity expects to purchase all the guaranteed volume for its 'own use'. However, if it becomes likely that the entity will not take physical delivery of the product and, instead pay a penalty under the contract based on the market value of the product or some other variable, a derivative or an embedded derivative may well arise. In this situation, since physical delivery is no longer probable, the derivative would be recorded at the amount of the penalty payable. Changes in market price will affect the penalty's carrying value until the penalty is paid. On the other hand, if the amount of the penalty payable is fixed or pre-determined, there is no derivative as the penalty's value remains fixed irrespective of changes in the market value of the product. In other words, the entity will need to provide for the penalty payable once it becomes clear that non-performance is likely.

6.3.85 On the other hand, if the quantity specified in the contract is more than the entity's normal usage requirement and the entity intends to net settle part of the contract that it does not need in the normal course of the business, the contract will fail the 'own use' exemption. Chapter 6.1 sets out a number of ways in which the entity can settle the contract net. For example, the entity could take all the quantities specified in the contract and sell on the excess or it could enter into an offsetting contract for the excess quantity. In such situations, the entire contract falls within IAS 39's scope and should be marked-to-market.

6.3.86 From the supplier's perspective, however, the volume flexibility feature in the contract can be viewed in two ways. The first is to view the contract as a whole. The contract may include a written option for the element of volume flexibility. The whole contract should be viewed as one instrument and, if the item being supplied (electricity) is readily convertible to cash, entity A would be prevented from classifying the contract as 'own use' by paragraph 7 of IAS 39. This states that a written option on a non-financial item that is readily convertible to cash cannot be entered into for the purpose of the receipt or delivery of a non-financial item in accordance with the entity's expected purchase, sale or usage requirements. A second view is that the contract has two components, an 'own use' fixed volume host contract outside of IAS 39's scope for any contractually fixed volume element and an embedded written option potentially within IAS 39's scope for the volume flexibility element. The latter would be in IAS 39's scope if the item being supplied (electricity) is readily convertible to cash for the same reason as under the first view. In March 2010, the IFRS IC discussed the issue of volume flexibility and recognised that significant diversity exists in practice. However, the IFRS IC decided not to add the issue to its agenda because of the Board's project to develop a replacement for IAS 39.

6.3.87 As explained in section 6.1 of this financial instrument chapter, such written options have to be accounted for in accordance with IAS 39 if they can be 'settled net in cash'. 'Settled net in cash' in this context means either that the contract allows net settlement or the item that is the subject of the contract is readily convertible into cash.

6.3.88 Therefore, it is necessary to consider whether the contract contains a written option. A contract will not contain a true written option if the buyer did not pay any premium to receive the option. Receipt of a premium to compensate the supplier for the risk that the buyer may not take the optional quantities specified in the contract is one of the distinguishing features of a written option. [IAS 39 IG F1.3(a)(b)]. Therefore, it would be necessary to consider whether a net premium is received either at inception or over the contract's life in order to determine the accounting treatment. Any penalty payable for non-performance by the buyer may well amount to the receipt of a premium. If no premium can be identified, other terms of the contract may need to be examined to determine whether it contains a written option, in particular, whether the buyer is able to secure economic value from the option's presence. Contracts need to be considered on a case-by-case basis in order to determine whether they contain written options.

> **Example 1**
>
> Entity A, a car manufacturer enters into a contract to sell cars to entity B that is engaged in renting cars. The contracts provide for entity A to supply 50 cars of a specific model at a specified future date at a fixed price. Entity B has the option to take between 90% and 110% of the contract quantity. Available market information indicates that a similar contract for 50 cars but without volume flexibility would also be priced at the same fixed price specified in the contract. Entity B cannot monetise the value of the contract by selling on any excess cars in the market.
>
> The supply contract would not be considered a written option, as the pricing of the contract is the same as that for a similar contract with no volume flexibility. There is, therefore, no premium associated with the contract. Entity B cannot exercise any value from the option's presence; the contract is, therefore, not a written option and qualifies for the own-use exemption.
>
> **Example 2**
>
> Entity A, an electricity producer in the United Kingdom where there is an active electricity market, enters into a contract to sell electricity to entity B. The contracts provide for entity A to supply 100 units of electricity at a specified future date to entity B at a fixed price per unit. Entity B has the option to take between 90% and 110% of the contract quantity. The total quantity taken will be priced at C0.21 per unit. Available market information indicates that a similar contract for 100 units of electricity but without volume flexibility would be priced at C0.20 per unit. Entity B is also a supplier of electricity and can, therefore, monetise the contract's value by selling on any excess power into the market, that is, it can readily convert the electricity contract to cash.

The pricing of the contract is not the same as that for a similar contract without volume flexibility. The price per cubic meter includes a premium for the additional risk accepted by entity A in offering volume flexibility. The contract is, therefore, a written option and entity A cannot claim the own-use exemption. In that situation, the contract will be marked-to-market in accordance with IAS 39. As noted above entity A can view the contract in two ways:

- as a written option in its entirety and hence entity A cannot claim the own-use exemption. In that situation, the contract will be marked-to-market in accordance with IAS 39; or

- as a fixed volume contract for 90 units of electricity for C0.20 per unit for which the own use exemption could be claimed and a written option for 20 units at C0.21 per unit, which is within IAS 39's scope.

Inflation related features

6.3.89 It is not uncommon for purchase, sale or long-term service contracts to contain terms that are linked to an inflation index, particularly in periods of rising inflation. Inflation escalator clauses are included in such long-term contracts to protect the seller's margin in real terms. Although IAS 39 is silent on the treatment of inflationary adjustments in executory contracts, there is no reason, in principle, why the guidance on inflation adjustment features in lease host contracts would not be appropriate for such contracts. That guidance states that an embedded inflation-related index is closely related to the lease host contract if the index is not leveraged and it relates to inflation in the entity's own economic environment. [IAS 39 para AG 33(f)]. The application of this principle to lease contracts is considered from paragraphs 6.3.69 above. We believe similar considerations can be applied to purchase, sale and service contracts.

Example – Purchase contract linked to inflation

A UK entity contracts to purchase a fixed quantity of raw materials from a UK supplier in 12 months' time. The raw materials are intended for use in the entity's business. The purchase price will be the market price at the contract date plus an adjustment for UK RPI from the beginning of the contract. The contract does not contain any leverage feature.

The future cash flows are linked to an inflation index that is not leveraged and the index is in the local economic environment. Therefore, the embedded derivative is closely related to the host purchase contract.

If, on the other hand, the entity is unable to demonstrate that these goods are to be used in the course of its business, that is, the own use exception does not apply, the entire contract would be treated as a forward purchase contract that would fall to be settled net. In that situation, the forward purchase contract meets the definition of a derivative and, is itself, accounted for at fair value through profit or loss. So there is no need to account separately for any derivatives that may be embedded in it.

Caps, floors and collars

6.3.90 Contracts to buy or sell a non-financial asset may contain provisions that provide for payments to be made at the market price at the time of payment, but set an upper or lower limit or both on the final price to be paid or received. Such caps, floors or collars included in contracts are embedded derivatives. IAS 39 states that provisions included in a contract to purchase or sell an asset (for example, a commodity) that establish a cap and a floor on the price to be paid or received for the asset are closely related to the host contract if both the cap and floor were out-of-the-money and are not leveraged. [IAS 39 para AG 33(b)]. This guidance can be extended to a collar that would be closely related if it was out-of-the-money at inception (see para 6.3.44 above).

> **Example – Purchase contract with selling price subject to a cap and a floor**
>
> A manufacturer enters into a long-term contract to purchase a specified quantity of certain raw materials from a supplier. Under the contract, the supplier will provide the raw materials at the list price prevailing at the delivery date, but within a specified range. For example, the purchase price may not exceed C20 per kg or fall below C15 per kg. The current list price at inception of the contract is C18 per kg.
>
> From the manufacturer's perspective, the embedded derivatives contained in the purchase contracts are two options; a purchased call option with a strike price of C20 per kg and a written put with a strike price of C15 per kg. These options would each meet the definition of a derivative if they were free standing, because they have a notional amount (the fixed quantity to be purchased), an underlying (the price per kg), require no initial net investment and will be settled in the future.
>
> The economic characteristics and risks of the two options are closely related to the purchase contract, because the options are indexed to the asset's purchase price that is the subject of the contract and both the embedded cap (cap price of C20 is greater than current list price of C18) and the floor (floor price of C15 is lower than current list price of C18) are out-of-the-money at inception of the contract. Hence, the embedded derivatives are closely related and the host contract can be considered to be a purchase contract that requires delivery of the specified quantity of raw materials at a price equal to the current list price.

Foreign currency features

6.3.91 IAS 39 provides specific guidance for an embedded foreign currency derivative in a host contract that is not a financial instrument (such as a contract for the purchase or sale of a non-financial item where the price is denominated in a foreign currency). The embedded foreign currency derivative is closely related to the host contract provided it is not leveraged, does not contain an option feature and requires payments denominated in one of the following currencies:

■ The functional currency of any substantial party to that contract.

- The currency in which the price of the related goods or service that is acquired or delivered is routinely denominated in commercial transactions around the world (such as the US dollar for crude oil transactions).

- A currency that is commonly used in contracts to purchase or sell non-financial items in the economic environment in which the transaction takes place (for example, a relatively stable and liquid currency that is commonly used in local business transactions or external trade).

[IAS 39 para AG 33(d)].

6.3.92 The term 'substantial party' to the contract referred to in the first bullet point above is not explained in IAS 39. Generally, it is taken to mean a party that is acting as principal to the contract, that is, the buyer/seller. A bank that provides a guarantee on behalf of a local importer to a foreign supplier that the buyer will meet its payment obligations in foreign currency under the contract's terms is not a substantial party to the contract. Furthermore, the guarantor's functional currency is of no relevance in determining whether the payments denominated in the foreign currency are closely related to the contract.

6.3.93 A question also arises in practice as to the efforts one party to a contract needs to employ to determine the functional currency of its counterparty. Generally, there would be a rebuttable presumption that the local currencies of the economic environment in which the counterparties operate would be their functional currencies. In addition, the local currency is always presumed to be commonly used. Therefore, if the contract requires payment in either one of the two local currencies of the counterparties, the condition in the first bullet point above would be met. The position is less clear if payments are denominated in a currency that is not the local currency of either party to the contract. In that situation, the contracting parties would need to determine whether that currency is the functional currency of their counterparty. In practice, this determination should be made on the basis of all available evidence and reasonable assumptions about the counterparty. Furthermore, the guidance for determining functional currency in IAS 21 would need to be considered in determining the functional currency. An entity should not necessarily rely on a single indicator such as the currency in which the counterparty's sales are denominated. Rather, the entity should consider all relevant available information in determining the counterparty's functional currency.

Example 1 – Payments denominated in the functional currency of a party to the contract

A UK entity (whose functional currency is pound sterling) contracts to sell goods to a French purchaser whose functional currency is the euro. The contract will be fulfilled by the physical delivery of goods and payments by the French buyer would be made in euros.

In this example, the payment in euros exposes the UK entity to currency risk as the cash flows under the contract will vary with the £/€ exchange rate. The contract can be viewed as a host contract that is denominated in sterling containing an embedded foreign currency swap that converts payments in pound sterling to euros or an embedded foreign currency forward contract to sell pound sterling and buy euros. However, the embedded swap or the forward contract is not separated as the payments are denominated in the functional currency of the French buyer who is a substantial party to the contract.

Example 2 – Payments denominated in a third currency

A UK entity (whose functional currency is pounds sterling) contracts to sell goods to a Swiss purchaser whose functional currency is the Swiss francs. The contract will be fulfilled by the physical delivery of goods and payments by the Swiss buyer would be made in euros. The goods are not commonly priced in euros.

In this example, the payment and the receipt in euros exposes both the substantial parties to the contract to exchange risk. Since the contract requires that payments be denominated in euros, which is not the functional currency of either party to the transaction, the embedded derivative is not closely related and should be accounted for separately at fair value by both the Swiss buyer and the UK seller. From the UK seller's point of view the embedded derivative would be to buy euros and sell sterling. In the books of the Swiss buyer the embedded derivative would be to sell euros and buy Swiss francs. The nominal amount of the embedded forwards will be equal to the amount specified under the terms of the supply contract.

A particular issue arises in connection with the nature of the foreign currency embedded derivative in foreign currency purchase/sale contracts when the embedded derivative is required to be separated under paragraph AG 33(d). The issue is whether the embedded derivative is a forward contract that matures on the date on which goods are physically delivered, or on the date when cash settlement takes place.

Assume that the UK entity enters into the contract with the Swiss buyer to sell goods amounting to €100 on 1 March 20X6 for delivery on 30 June 20X6 and settlement on 31 July 20X6. The goods are not commonly priced in €. The UK entity's year end is 31 March 20X6. The following data is relevant.

Date	Event	Spot €/£	Forward €/£ (maturity June 20X6)	Forward €/£ (maturity July 20X6)
1 Mar 20X6	UK entity enters into a contract to sell goods for €100	0.70	0.725	0.72
31 Mar 20X6	UK entity's year end. Embedded derivative revalued	0.73	0.745	0.74
30 Jun 20X6	Goods delivered	0.75		0.77
31 Jul 20X6	Invoice amounting to €100 settled	0.78		

In this example, from the perspective of the UK seller, the firm commitment to sell goods is separated into two contracts – a host contact that is a firm commitment to sell goods in pound sterling and an embedded forward contract to buy euro and sell pound sterling with an inception date of 1 March 20X6. However, as stated above there is some debate regarding the deemed date of settlement/maturity of the embedded derivative.

Some take the view that the embedded derivative's settlement/maturity date is 30 June 20X6 when the goods are delivered. This is because the derivative that is embedded in the host firm commitment can no longer exist after that date as there is no host contract – the seller having fulfilled its commitment by delivering the goods to the customer. Following performance by the seller, the seller has an unconditional right to receive consideration from the customer. In other words, the embedded derivative is in the sales contract not in the receivable; the derivative being effectively settled by creation of a financial asset (receivable). Under this view, the accounting entries would be as follows:

Accounting for sale and embedded derivative

				Dr (Cr)		
		Sales	Debtors	Cash	Derivative	Profit and loss
Date	Transaction	£	£	£	£	£
1 Mar 20X6	Embedded derivative – nil fair value					
31 Mar 20X6	Change in fair value of embedded derivative – €100 @ (0.745 – 0.725) – ignoring discounting – there is a gain as, using the forward rate at the balance sheet date, to buy €100 would cost £74.5 compared to £72.5 using the contracted forward rate				2.0	(2.0)
30 Jun 20X6	Change in fair value of embedded derivative – €100 @ (0.75 – 0.745)				0.5	(0.5)
30 Jun 20X6	Recording sales at forward rate – 100 @ 0.725	(72.5)	72.5			
30 Jun 20X6	Embedded derivative settled against debtors		2.5		(2.5)	
31 Jul 20X6	Debtor carried at spot rate at 30 June 20X6 settled by receipt of €100 at spot rate – €100 @ 0.78		(75.0)	78		(3.0)
	Effect on profit or loss and balance sheet	(72.5)	–	78	–	(5.5)

Others take the view that the embedded derivative being a forward foreign exchange contract matures at the date of cash settlement on the grounds that the cash leg of the firm commitment is settled at that date. Under this view, the sale and the corresponding receivable are recognised in local currency using the forward rate when the goods are delivered, that is (C72). The embedded derivative and the debtor is settled when cash is received at 30 June 20X6 with any gain or loss arising on settlement recorded in profit or loss. Under this view, the accounting treatment would be as follows:

Accounting for sale and embedded derivative

				Dr (Cr)		
						Profit and
		Sales	Debtors	Cash	Derivative	loss
Date	Transaction	£	£	£	£	£
1 Mar 20X6	Embedded derivative – nil fair value					
31 Mar 20X6	Change in fair value of embedded derivative – €100 @ (0.74 – 0.72) – ignoring discounting – there is a gain as using the forward rate at the balance sheet date, to buy €100 would cost £74 compared to £72 using the contracted forward rate				2.0	(2.0)
30 Jun 20X6	Change in fair value of embedded derivative – €100 @ (0.77 – 0.74)				3.0	(3.0)
30 Jun 20X	Recording sales at forward rate – 100 @ 0.72	(72.0)	72.0			
31 Jul 20X6	Settlement date – receipt of €100 at spot rate – €100 @ 0.78		(72.0)	78	(5.0)	(1.0)
	Effect on profit and loss and balance sheet	(72.0)	–	78	–	(6.0)

Although both views can be sustained, in practice, entities generally tend to adopt the first treatment as they view these types of contract as inherent in future sales.

Example 3 – Payments denominated in the functional currency of a party to the contract, but the functional currency changes subsequently

A UK entity (whose functional currency is pound sterling) contracts to sell goods to a Japanese purchaser whose functional currency is the yen. The contract will be fulfilled by the physical delivery of goods and payments by the Japanese buyer would be made in yen. Subsequently, because of changes in economic circumstances, the functional currency of the Japanese buyer changes to US dollars.

The UK entity is required to assess whether the embedded derivative should be separated from the host sales contract and accounted for as a derivative when it first becomes a party to the contract. At the time the UK entity entered into the contract, the functional currency of the Japanese buyer was the yen. Therefore, no separation of the embedded derivative is required as yen is the functional currency of a substantial party to the contract. The issue is whether this initial assessment should be revisited following the change in the functional currency of the Japanese buyer.

As explained in paragraph 6.3.22 above, IFRIC 9 prohibits reassessment unless there is a change in the contract's terms that meet certain criteria . In such an instance, reassessment is required. In this situation, the contract terms remain unchanged, that is, the UK entity will still make payments in yen irrespective of the fact that the functional currency of the Japanese supplier has subsequently changed to US dollars. Therefore, the contract continues to be accounted for in the same manner as before, irrespective of the fact that the factors that led to the initial assessment have changed. However, any yen denominated contracts entered into with the Japanese buyer after it has changed its functional currency to US dollar would fail the closely related criterion, as they would not be in the functional currency of either party to the contract.

The above treatment also applies to the Japanese buyer even though it will be exposed to Yen/dollar currency risk when it makes payments under the contract. Such exchange gains and losses will fall to be accounted for in accordance with IAS 21. In other words, as long as the contract terms remain unchanged, the Japanese buyer cannot create an embedded currency exposure that did not exist at the date it became a party to the contract.

Example 4 – Option to make payments in alternative currencies

Facts are the same as in example 1 except that the contract contains an option to make payment in either euros or in Swiss francs.

In this example, the UK seller has written an option to receive payments in a currency that is not its functional currency and, therefore, exposes it to £/€ or £/Swiss Fr currency risk. Although euro is the functional currency of the other substantial party to the contract, there is no certainty at inception of the contract that settlement will be in euros. Hence, the foreign currency option is not closely related to the host.

Similarly, the French buyer has effectively purchased an option to make payments in its own functional currency (euros) or in a foreign currency (Swiss Fr) that exposes it to euros/Swiss Fr currency risk. Although the French buyer has the option to settle the contract in its own currency and eliminate any exchange risk, there is no certainty at inception of the contract that it would eventually exercise that option. Since the contract could also be settled in Swiss francs, the settlement can either be potentially favourable or unfavourable and is not closely related to the purchase contract.

Accordingly, the embedded option should be separated from the host contract and accounted for separately by both parties to the contract.

6.3.94 In relation to the second bullet point in paragraph 6.3.91 above, the currency in which the price of the related goods or services is routinely denominated in commercial transactions around the world is a currency that is used for similar transactions *all around the world*, not just in one local area. For example, if cross-border transactions in natural gas in North America are routinely denominated in US dollars and such transactions are routinely denominated in euros in Europe, neither the US dollar nor the euro is a currency in which natural gas is routinely denominated in commercial transactions around the world. [IAS 39 para IG C9]. Accordingly, apart from crude oil and some metals which are routinely denominated in US dollar in international commerce, very few items, if any, are likely to meet this requirement.

> **Example – Leveraged foreign currency provision**
>
> Entity A, whose functional currency is the euro, enters into a contract with entity B, whose functional currency is the Norwegian krone, to purchase oil in six months for US$10m. The host oil contract is not within IAS 39's scope, because it was entered into and continues to be for the purpose of delivery of a non-financial item in accordance with the entity's expected purchase, sale or usage requirements. The oil contract includes a leveraged foreign exchange provision that states that the parties, in addition to the provision of, and payment for, oil will exchange an amount equal to the fluctuation in the exchange rate of the US dollar and Norwegian krone applied to a notional amount of US$10m.
>
> In the example above, the payment provision under the host oil contract of US$10m can be viewed as a foreign currency derivative because the US dollar is neither entity A's nor entity B's functional currency. This foreign currency derivative would not be separated, however, because it follows from the second bullet point of paragraph 6.3.91 above that a crude oil contract that requires payment in US dollars is not regarded as a host contract with a foreign currency derivative.
>
> However, the leveraged foreign exchange provision that states that the parties will exchange an amount equal to the fluctuation in the exchange rate of the US dollar and Norwegian krone applied to a notional amount of US$10m is in addition to the required payment for the oil transaction. It is unrelated to the host oil contract and, therefore, should be separated from the host oil contract, and accounted for as an embedded derivative. [IAS 39 para IG C8].

6.3.95 The third bullet point in paragraph 6.3.91 refers to a currency that is *commonly used* in contracts to purchase or sell non-financial items in the economic environment in which the transaction takes place (for example, a relatively stable and liquid currency that is commonly used in local business transactions or external trade). This flexibility was added when IAS 39 was revised so that entities domiciled in small or developing economies may find it more convenient to denominate business contracts with entities from other small or developing economies in an internationally liquid currency (such as the US dollar or the euro) rather than the local currency of any parties to the contract.

6.3.96 Some have interpreted the 'commonly used' currency provision to be limited to those countries with small or developing economies and that do not have a currency that is freely convertible and able to be used in commercial transactions as set out in an example in the basis for conclusions in IAS 39. [IAS 39 para BC39]. However, others have noted that IAS 39 does not limit the application of this exception to only these territories, and so they have concluded that it also applies to contracts with entities in developed economies if the 'commonly used' criterion is met. For example, economic data supports that the US dollar is used in a wide variety of contracts by Canadian companies. It can, therefore, be argued that the US dollar is 'commonly used' in Canada even though it is not a small developing country. We see the merits of both points of view and, therefore, will accept either interpretation as an accounting policy election to be applied on a consistent basis.

6.3.97 The standard uses the term 'commonly used' to mean a currency that is relatively stable or liquid and that is commonly used in local business transactions or external trade. A currency is commonly used in local business transactions when monetary amounts are viewed by the general population not in terms of the local currency, but in terms of a relatively stable foreign currency and prices may be quoted in that foreign currency. [IAS 39 para BC40]. Indeed, undertaking business transactions in a stable or hard currency is fairly common for entities operating in a hyperinflationary economy as a protection against inflation. [IAS 29 para 3(b)]. It follows that the currency must be commonly used within the country, not just commonly used within a particular industry or particular market. This is an exemption to the general rule that foreign currency embedded derivatives need to be separated. The exemption's application should be supported by an appropriate analysis specific to the respective country.

6.3.98 Many countries around the world use more than one stable or liquid currency in undertaking local business transactions or external trade. Therefore, where such countries undertake transactions in those stable or liquid currencies rather than in their local currencies, the foreign currency derivative would be viewed as closely related to the host contract and would not be accounted for separately. This assessment should be a made on a country by country basis and be supported by a detailed analysis.

> **Example – Contract denominated in a currency commonly used in local business transactions**
>
> An entity located in a country with a hyper-inflationary economy contracts to purchase raw materials for use in its manufacturing process. The contract is denominated in US$, a stable currency, and not in the local currency, as most local transactions and external trade are undertaken in US$.

The embedded foreign currency derivative (denominated in a currency other than the local currency) does not need to be separated as the contract is denominated in a currency that is commonly used in the local economic environment.

If, however, the contract was priced in another international stable currency say the euro rather than the US$, and euro is not a currency that is commonly used in local business transactions, the embedded derivative (euro *versus* the entity's functional currency) would have to be separated.

Flow chart for identifying embedded derivatives in executory contracts

6.3.99   As stated previously, IAS 39 provides little or no guidance on derivatives that may be embedded in purchase, sale or service contracts. As identification of such embedded derivatives can be complex, the flow charts given below are to aid in the identification process. It should be noted that the flow chart has been constructed from the discussions undertaken above and is based on a simple executory contract to buy or sell a good, that is, does not need to be assessed for an embedded lease under IFRIC 4. In practice, such contracts may contain other terms and conditions whose interaction with the host is not obvious. Options that allow early termination of a contract by paying a penalty, options to change the quantities to be delivered and options to defer delivery are some examples of terms and condition that can be problematic and would require careful consideration.

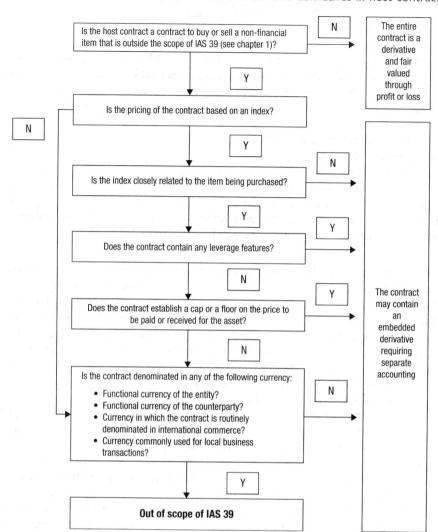

Is the host contract a contract to buy or sell a non-financial item that is outside the scope of IAS 39 (see chapter 1)? **N** → The entire contract is a derivative and fair valued through profit or loss

Y ↓

Is the pricing of the contract based on an index? — **N**

Y ↓

Is the index closely related to the item being purchased? **N** →

Y ↓

Does the contract contain any leverage features? **Y** →

N ↓

Does the contract establish a cap or a floor on the price to be paid or received for the asset? **Y** →

N ↓

Is the contract denominated in any of the following currency:

- Functional currency of the entity?
- Functional currency of the counterparty?
- Currency in which the contract is routinely denominated in international commerce?
- Currency commonly used for local business transactions?

N →

Y ↓

Out of scope of IAS 39

The contract may contain an embedded derivative requiring separate accounting

63051

Embedded derivatives in insurance contracts

6.3.100   In recent years, a growing number of complex insurance products have been developed and many of them may contain embedded derivatives. As stated in chapter 3, derivatives embedded in insurance contracts or in contracts containing discretionary participation features are within IAS 39's scope. A derivative embedded in an insurance contract is closely related to the host insurance contract if the embedded derivative and host insurance contract are so interdependent that an entity cannot measure the embedded derivative separately (that is, without considering the host contract). [IAS 39 para AG 33(h)]. However, if a policy combines a derivative instrument with an insurance contract thereby creating a hybrid instrument, the embedded derivative may have to be separated from the insurance contract in accordance with IAS 39, unless the embedded derivative itself is an insurance contract. [IFRS 4 para 7].

6.3.101   Contracts such as equity indexed annuities, equity indexed life insurance and embedded guarantees of minimum returns may contain embedded derivatives that are not closely related to the host insurance contract and will have to be separated and accounted for under IAS 39. Much of the guidance discussed above applies to embedded derivatives in insurance contracts as it does to any other contract. However, IFRS 4 paragraph 8 introduces a major exception to the principle of separation of embedded derivatives that are not closely related to the host contract. IFRS 4 permits an insurer to not separate a policyholder's embedded put option (also known as a cash surrender option) embedded in a host insurance contract when the option price is a fixed amount or a fixed amount and an interest rate. This exemption applies at all times even when the exercise price differs from the host insurance liability's carrying amount. The requirement to separate does, however, apply when the surrender value varies in response to a change in an equity or commodity price or index or a similar variable. [IFRS 4 para 8]. IFRS 4 paragraph 9 specifies that the same exemption applies to issuers of financial instruments with a discretionary participation feature. This area of accounting for embedded derivatives should always be considered in conjunction with IFRS 4. The implementation guidance to IFRS 4 contains many examples that illustrate the treatment of embedded derivatives contained in insurance contracts. [IFRS 4 paras IG 3, 4].

Accounting for embedded derivatives

6.3.102   On initial recognition, similar to all financial assets and liabilities, a financial instrument containing an embedded derivative is recognised at its fair value, that is, the fair value of the entire instrument. If the consideration paid / transaction price is not equal to the fair value of the instrument as a whole, then a day 1 gain or loss may arise. Whether such a gain or loss is recognised immediately within profit or loss depends on whether the conditions in paragraph AG76 of IAS 39 are met (as discussed in further detail in chapter 6.7). In summary, a day 1 gain or loss is recognised only when the fair value of the entire instrument is evidenced either by other observable current market transactions in the same instrument (without modification or packaging) or by a valuation technique whose variables include only data from observable markets.

6.3.103 When an embedded derivative is required to be separated from a host contract, the derivative element must be measured at fair value on the balance sheet, with changes in fair value being accounted for through profit or loss, consistent with the accounting for a freestanding derivative. At initial recognition of the embedded derivative, the embedded derivative's fair value must be determined before that of the host contract. Paragraph AG28 of IAS 39 states that *"The initial carrying amount of the host instrument is the residual after separating the embedded derivative"*. The host contract's carrying value at initial recognition is the difference between the fair value of the hybrid contract as a whole and the embedded derivative's fair value.

6.3.104 While a day 1 gain or loss may arise on the initial recognition of the entire instrument, if the criteria in paragraph AG76 of IAS 39 are met (see para 6.3.102), a day 1 gain or loss will not arise as a result of separating the embedded derivative from the host contract.

6.3.105 Published price quotations in an active market are normally the best evidence of fair value. Valuation techniques are used to determine the derivative's fair value if there is no active market for the embedded derivative. Valuing a derivative usually involves the exercise of judgement by management in making certain estimates such as the discount rate, extrapolation of future interest rates, foreign exchange rates and so on. The use of estimates for certain valuation parameters could be subjective, especially for long-term contracts that are common in the energy industry. Furthermore, certain embedded derivatives, in particular those arising from complex structured products, may contain several underlying variables making the valuation process complex.

6.3.106 If an entity is unable to determine reliably the fair value of an embedded derivative on the basis of its terms and conditions (for example, because the embedded derivative is based on an unquoted equity instrument), the embedded derivative's fair value is the difference between the fair value of the hybrid (combined) instrument and the host contract's fair value, if those can be determined reliably. [IAS 39 para 13]. If the entity is unable to determine the embedded derivative's fair value using this method either at initial recognition or at a subsequent financial reporting date, the entity should fair value the hybrid (combined) instrument and designate it as at fair value through profit or loss. [IAS 39 paras 12, 13]. Designation of financial instruments is discussed in chapter 6.4.

Example – Debt instrument that is exchangeable into shares of an unlisted entity

An entity issues a debt instrument that is exchangeable into shares of an unlisted entity whose fair value cannot be reliably measured. If the debt instrument is converted the unlisted equity investment would be recorded on the balance sheet at cost in accordance with paragraph 46(c) of IAS 39.

In this situation, the equity exchangeable feature is not closely related to the debt host and should be separated. However, although the equity instrument's fair value cannot be measured reliably, it would not be appropriate to measure the embedded derivative at cost. Instead, the entire combined contract is designated as a financial instrument at fair value through profit or loss. [IAS 39 para 12]. This presumes that the combined contract's fair value can be measured reliably.

However, the entity might conclude that the combined instrument's equity component may be sufficiently significant to preclude it from obtaining a reliable estimate of the fair value of the entire instrument. In that case, the combined instrument is measured at cost less impairment. [IAS 39 para IG C.11].

It should be noted that as the fair value of the embedded derivative that is linked to, and must be settled by delivery of, the above unlisted equity instrument cannot be measured, the embedded derivative cannot be designated as a hedging instrument. [IAS 39 para AG 96].

6.3.107 The requirement to identify an embedded derivative in a hybrid instrument, assess whether it should be separated from the host contract and, for those that do need to be separated, measure the derivatives at fair value at initial recognition and subsequently, can be complex or may result in less reliable measures than measuring the entire instrument at fair value through profit or loss.

6.3.108 Therefore, if a contract contains one or more embedded derivatives, an entity may designate the entire hybrid (combined) contract as a financial asset or financial liability at fair value through profit or loss, unless:

■ the embedded derivative(s) does not significantly modify the cash flows that otherwise would be required by the contract; or

■ it is clear with little or no analysis when a similar hybrid (combined) instrument is first considered that separation of the embedded derivative(s) is prohibited, such as a pre-payment option embedded in a loan that permits the holder to pre-pay the loan for approximately its amortised cost.

[IAS 39 para 11A].

The option to designate the entire instrument at fair value through profit or loss may be particularly helpful to banks and other entities that issue structured products containing several embedded derivatives

6.3.109 If an embedded derivative is separated, the host contract should be accounted for in accordance with IAS 39 if it is a financial instrument and in accordance with other appropriate standards if it is not a financial instrument.

IAS 39 does not address whether an embedded derivative should be presented separately on the face of the balance sheet. [IAS 39 para 11].

Separating a non-option-based embedded derivative

6.3.110   When separating a non-option-based embedded derivative, such as an embedded forward or swap, the standard requires the embedded derivative to be separated from its host contract on the basis of its stated or implied substantive terms, so as to result in it having a fair value of zero at initial recognition. [IAS 39 para AG 28]. If it were permitted to separate embedded non-option derivatives on other terms, a single hybrid instrument could be decomposed into an infinite variety of combinations of host instruments and embedded derivatives. However, as already explained in paragraph 6.3.28 above, an embedded derivative that is not already clearly present should not be separated, that is a cash flow that does not exist cannot be created (with exception of, for example, assuming a functional currency cash flow in an embedded FX forward contract). If the terms of an embedded forward contract were determined so as to result in a fair value other than zero at the inception of the hybrid instrument, that amount would essentially represent a borrowing or lending. Therefore, it is inappropriate to separate an embedded non-option derivative on terms that result in a fair value other than zero at the inception of the hybrid instrument. [IAS 39 paras IG C1, C2]. This means that the forward price assumed in the embedded derivative should generally be at market rates observed when the embedded derivative is separated.

> **Example – Separation of a non-option-based derivative to produce zero fair value at inception**
>
> Entity X advances C900 to entity Y for one year at 6% interest rate and concurrently enters into an equity-based derivative in which it will receive any increase or pay any decrease in the current market price (C100) of entity Z's equity shares. The current forward price for one year for entity Z's equity shares is C200. These two transactions (the loan and the derivative) can be bundled into a structured note that could have almost an infinite variety of terms. Three possible contractual terms for the structured note that would be purchased by entity X for C900 are shown below.
>
> ■ Entity X to receive at the end of the year C954 plus any excess (minus any shortfall) in the current market price of entity Z's equity shares over (or under) C200.
>
> ■ Entity X to receive at the end of the year C1,054 plus any excess (minus any shortfall) in the current market price of entity Z's equity shares over (or under) C300.
>
> ■ Entity X to receive at the end of the year C755 plus any excess (minus any shortfall) in the current market price of entity Z's equity shares over (or under) C1.
>
> All the above terms of the structured note will provide the same cash flows, given a specified market price of entity Z's shares. If the market price of entity Z's shares remains at C200 at the end of year 1, entity A will receive C954 under all the three

options. Similarly, if the market price of entity Z's shares increases to C306, entity A will receive C1,060 under all the options.

As is apparent, the difference in terms under the above three options are totally arbitrary, because those differences have no impact on the ultimate cash flows under the structured note. Thus those differences are not substantive and should have no influence on how the terms of the embedded derivatives are identified. Therefore, the hybrid instrument's separation into an embedded derivative and a host debt instrument should be the same for all the three options described above for the structured note.

That separation would generally result in the structured note being accounted for as a debt host contract with an initial carrying amount of C900 and a fixed annual interest rate of 6% and an embedded forward contract with C200 forward price, which results in an initial fair value of zero.

Separating an option-based embedded derivative

6.3.111 An embedded option-based derivative (such as an embedded put, call, cap, floor or swaption) is separated from its host contract on the basis of the option feature's stated terms. The initial host instrument's carrying amount is the residual amount after separating the embedded derivative. [IAS 39 para AG 28].

6.3.112 The implementation guidance explains that the economic behaviour of a hybrid instrument with an option-based embedded is fundamentally different from a non-option based derivative and depends critically on the strike price (or strike rate) specified for the option feature in the hybrid instrument.

6.3.113 If an entity were required to identify the terms of an embedded option-based derivative so as to achieve a fair value of the embedded derivative of zero, the strike price (or strike rate) generally would have to be determined so as to result in the option being infinitely out-of-the-money. This would imply a zero probability of the option feature being exercised. However, since the probability of the option feature in a hybrid instrument being exercised generally is not zero, it would be inconsistent with the likely economic behaviour of the hybrid instrument to assume an initial fair value of zero for the embedded derivative. Similarly, if an entity were required to identify the terms of an embedded option-based derivative so as to achieve an intrinsic value of zero for the embedded derivative, the strike price (or strike rate) would have to be assumed to equal the price (or rate) of the underlying variable at the initial recognition of the hybrid instrument. In this case, the option's fair value would consist only of time value. However, such an assumption would not be consistent with the likely economic behaviour of the hybrid instrument, including the probability of the option feature being exercised, unless the agreed strike price was indeed equal to the price (or rate) of the underlying variable at the initial recognition of the hybrid instrument. [IAS 39 para IG C.2].

6.3.114 Adjusting the strike price of an option-based embedded derivative, therefore, alters the nature of the hybrid instrument, whereas adjusting the strike price of a forward based embedded derivative does not necessarily alter the nature of the hybrid instrument. For example, if an option based embedded derivative is in-the-money, that intrinsic value does not represent a lending activity since the option may never be exercised (that is, it may expire out-of-the money due to a change in the underlying). Therefore, the separation of an option-based embedded derivative (including any embedded put, call, cap, floor, caption, floortion or swaption feature in a hybrid instrument) should be based on the stated terms of the option feature documented in the hybrid instrument. As a result, the embedded derivative would not necessarily have a fair value or intrinsic value equal to zero at the initial recognition of the hybrid instrument. [IAS 39 para IG C.2].

Multiple embedded derivatives

6.3.115 A host contract may contain more than one embedded derivative. Each derivative must be identified and assessed to see whether they warrant separate accounting. Separate accounting is required where the derivatives relate to different risk exposures and are readily separable and independent of each other. [IAS 39 para AG 29].

6.3.116 Where, however, it is not possible to value each embedded derivative separately because of inter-dependencies, they should be treated as a single compound embedded derivative and valued in accordance with the guidance discussed from paragraph 6.3.102 above. [IAS 39 para AG 29].

Example 1 – Callable convertible bond

An entity issues 20,000 callable convertible bonds at a total par value of C2 million. Each bond pays fixed interest and is convertible, at the holder's option, at any time up to maturity into the entity's ordinary shares. Each bond also contains an embedded call option that gives the bond's issuer the right to call and redeem the bond at any time before maturity.

The bond has two embedded options that are held by different parties. The bond's holder has the option to convert the bond into a specified number of shares. The issuer has the option to call back the bond and pay an amount generally at a premium over par value.

From the issuer's perspective, the equity conversion option is an equity instrument of the issuer and, therefore, it is outside IAS 39's scope. Under IAS 32, the issuer must separate the equity and the liability elements of the compound instrument. As far as the issuer's call option (the right to call and redeem the bond) is concerned, this must be valued separately (using an option pricing model) as it is distinct in character and risk from the written equity conversion option. This value is then included in the liability component before separating the equity component under IAS 32. The call option will need to be accounted for separately unless the option exercise price is approximately equal on each exercise date to the amortised cost of the host debt instrument or reimburses the lender for the present value of lost interest for the remainder of the host contract. [IAS 39 para AG 30(g); IAS 32 paras 31, IE 37].

From the holders' perspective, the purchased call option (to convert) and the written call (to redeem) are interlinked. This is because as the share price increases the issuer is likely to call the bond, thereby depriving the holder of the opportunity to make further returns on the bond. Although the optimal policy is to call the bond when its conversion price is equal to the call price, in practice, companies can establish a variety of call policies such as calling the instant the market value of the convertibles rises above the call price or waiting until the market value is well in excess of the call price. This interaction between the two options implies that they have to be valued together using an option pricing model. The single compound derivative is then accounted for separately from the host plain vanilla bond. Alternatively, the holder can designate the entire bond as at fair value through profit or loss as discussed in paragraph 6.3.108 above.

Example 2 – Bond with embedded forward and option features

An entity issues a debt instrument at par with a term of 5 years. The debt is callable 3 years after the issue. If the debt is called, the holder will receive an amount that is adjusted by the percentage change in the FTSE 100 index and that amount doubles if the FTSE 100 index exceeds a certain level.

In the above instrument, there are two embedded derivatives – a forward contract that pays double if the FTSE 100 index exceeds a certain level and an option that is linked to changes in the FTSE 100 index. It is not appropriate to separate both a forward and an option on the equity index, because those derivative features relate to the same risk exposure. Instead the forward and option elements are treated as a single compound, embedded derivative.

Embedded derivatives as hedging instruments

6.3.117 IAS 39 does not restrict the circumstances in which a derivative may be designated as a hedging instrument provided the hedge accounting criteria are met (subject to some limitations on written options). [IAS 39 para 72]. Therefore, embedded derivatives that are accounted for separately can be designated as hedging instruments, like any free standing derivatives, as long as the hedge accounting criteria are met. Hedge accounting is considered in chapter 6.8.

6.4 – Classification of financial instruments

6.4 – Classification of financial instruments

Introduction

6.4.1 IAS 39 classifies all financial assets and financial liabilities into specific categories. The need to classify financial instruments into specific categories arises from the mixed measurement model in IAS 39, under which some financial instruments are carried at amortised cost whilst others are carried at fair value. Consequently, a particular financial instrument's classification that is carried out at initial recognition drives the subsequent accounting treatment. IAS 39 prescribes four categories for financial assets and two categories for financial liabilities.

6.4.2 In November 2009, the IASB published the first part of IFRS 9, relating to classification and measurement of financial instruments. The new requirements are a fundamentally new approach to the classification and measurement of financial assets. IFRS 9 applies a consistent approach to classifying financial assets based on the entity's business model for managing the financial assets and the contractual cash flow characteristics of the financial assets, and replaces the numerous categories of financial assets in IAS 39 as shown in paragraph 6.4.3 below, each of which has its own classification criteria. The IASB updated IFRS 9 in October 2010 to include guidance on the classification of financial liabilities. The requirements in IAS 39 regarding the classification and measurement of financial liabilities have largely been retained. The criteria for classifying a financial liability 'at fair value through profit or loss' have not changed, with the exception that entities with financial liabilities designated at fair value through profit or loss recognise directly in other comprehensive income that part of the change in the fair value due to changes in the liability's credit risk. It is the IASB's intention that IFRS 9 will ultimately replace IAS 39 in its entirety. On 15 November 2011, the IASB decided to consider making limited modifications to IFRS 9 on an expedited basis to deal with specific application issues, interaction with the insurance project and to try to achieve convergence with proposals being developed by the FASB. IFRS 9 is dealt with in chapter 6.10.

Classification of financial assets

6.4.3 IAS 39 has four clearly defined categories of financial assets, as follows:

■ Financial assets 'at fair value through profit or loss'.

■ Held-to-maturity investments.

■ Loans and receivables.

■ Available-for-sale financial assets.

[IAS 39 para 9].

As stated above, the classification is important as it dictates how the financial assets and liabilities are subsequently measured in the financial statements. This classification is also relevant when looking at whether embedded derivatives need to be bifurcated (split). In the above list, the first and the last items are measured at fair value whilst the remaining two are measured at amortised cost.

Financial assets and liabilities at fair value through profit or loss

Definition

6.4.4   A financial asset or a financial liability can be classified as at fair value through profit or loss only if it meets of the following conditions:

- Upon initial recognition, it is designated by the entity as at fair value through profit or loss.

- It is classified as held-for-trading.

[IAS 39 para 9].

6.4.5   The fair value through profit or loss category incorporates items that are 'held-for-trading'. More significantly, it also gives entities the option to classify any financial instruments at fair value with all gains and losses taken to profit and loss in restricted circumstances (see further para 6.4.6).

Designation at fair value through profit or loss on initial recognition

6.4.6   An entity *may* designate a financial asset or a financial liability at fair value through profit or loss on initial recognition only in the following three circumstances:

- The designation eliminates or significantly reduces a measurement or recognition inconsistency (sometimes referred to as an 'accounting mismatch') that would otherwise arise (see para 6.4.9).

- A group of financial assets, financial liabilities or both is managed and its performance is evaluated on a fair value basis, in accordance with a documented risk management or investment strategy (see para 6.4.18).

- The item proposed to be designated at fair value through profit or loss is a hybrid contract that contains one or more embedded derivatives unless:

    - the embedded derivative(s) does not significantly modify the cash flows that otherwise would be required by the contract; or

    - it is clear with little or no analysis when a similar hybrid (combined) instrument is first considered that separation of the embedded derivative(s) is prohibited, such as a pre-payment option embedded in a loan that permits the holder to pre-pay the loan for approximately its amortised cost. [IAS 39 para 11A]. See further chapter 6.3.

[IAS 39 para 9].

6.4.7 The decision to designate a financial asset or a financial liability at fair value through profit or loss in the above situations is similar to an accounting policy choice where the policy selected is one that provides more relevant information. However, unlike an accounting policy choice, the above designation need not be applied consistently to all similar transactions. [IAS 39 para AG 4C]. In other words, the designation can be applied on an asset-by-asset or a liability-by-liability basis, with the result that different holdings of the same type of asset or liability may be accounted for differently, some using the fair value option and others not. For example, assume an entity expects to issue a number of similar financial liabilities amounting to C100 and expects to acquire a number of similar financial assets amounting to C50 that will be carried at fair value. Provided the criteria are satisfied, the entity may significantly reduce the measurement inconsistency by designating at initial recognition all of the assets but only some of the liabilities (for example, individual liabilities with a combined total of C45) as at fair value through profit or loss. The remaining liabilities amounting to C55 can still be carried at amortised cost.

6.4.8 The option can be applied only to whole instruments and not to portions, such as component of a debt instrument (that is, changes in value attributable to one risk such as interest rate risk and not credit risk); or proportions (that is, percentages). [IAS 39 para AG 4G]. This is because it may be difficult to isolate and measure the portion of a financial instrument if the portion is affected by more than one risk; the amount recognised in the balance sheet for that portion would be neither fair value nor cost; and the fair value adjustment for the portion may move the carrying amount of an instrument away from its fair value.

Accounting mismatch

6.4.9 IAS 39 imposes a mixed measurement model under which some financial instruments are measured at fair value and others at amortised cost; some gains and losses are recognised in profit or loss and others initially in other comprehensive income. This combination of measurement and recognition requirements can result in inconsistencies (sometimes referred to as an 'accounting mismatch') between the accounting for an asset (or group of assets) and a liability (or group of liabilities). An accounting mismatch occurs when assets and liabilities that are economically related (that is, share a risk) are treated inconsistently. This could occur where, in the absence of the fair value option, a financial asset is classified as available-for-sale (with most changes in fair value recognised directly in other comprehensive income), while a related liability is measured at amortised cost (with changes in fair value not recognised). In such circumstances, an entity may conclude that its financial statements would provide more relevant information if both the asset and the liability were classified as at fair value through profit or loss. [IAS 39 para AG 4D].

6.4.10 As explained above, the use of the fair value option may eliminate measurement anomalies for financial assets and liabilities that provide a natural offset of each other because they share the same risk, but where hedge accounting cannot be used because none of the instruments is a derivative. More importantly, even if some of the instruments are derivatives that could qualify for fair value hedge accounting, classification of both items at fair value through profit or loss achieves the same accounting result whilst avoiding the designation, tracking and assessing of hedge effectiveness that hedge accounting entails. It follows that the use of the fair value option as an alternative to hedge accounting can be of significant benefit to entities. However, such advantage also has a cost. Under the fair value option the entire change in fair value of the asset or liability would fall to be recognised in profit or loss, not simply the change in fair value attributable to the risk that is hedged by an offsetting derivative. As a result, the amount reported in profit or loss under the fair value option is unlikely to be the same as the change in fair value of the hedging derivative. This may lead to greater profit or loss volatility. Furthermore, hedge accounting can be revoked at any time, but the fair value option is irrevocable.

6.4.11 The IASB has not established a percentage, or a 'bright line', for interpreting 'significant' in the context of an accounting mismatch. However, the Basis for Conclusion makes it clear that an effectiveness test similar to that used for hedge accounting is not required to demonstrate that a reduction in an accounting mismatch is significant. [IAS 39 BC para 75B]. This means judgement is required to determine when the fair value option should be applied. In this regard, management should look at the objective of the proposed designation as 'at fair value through profit or loss'. Comparing the accounting impact – that is, the measurement basis and the recognition of gains and losses – of all relevant items (including, for example, any funding that it is not proposed to be designated at fair value through profit or loss) before and after the designation will give an indication of whether an accounting mismatch has been eliminated or significantly reduced.

6.4.12 Although it is necessary to demonstrate that there is an accounting mismatch, the extent of evidence needed to identify the accounting mismatch for which the fair value option is to be used need not be extensive. It may be possible to use the same evidence for a number of similar transactions, depending on the circumstances – for example, by identifying a particular kind of accounting mismatch that arises from one of the entity's chosen risk management strategies. It is not necessary to have the extensive documentation required for hedge accounting, but the entity does need to provide evidence that the fair value option was designated at inception. Also, IFRS 7 requires disclosure of the carrying amounts of assets and, separately, liabilities designated as 'at fair value through profit or loss'. The evidence must, therefore, include precise identification of the assets and liabilities to which the fair value option has been applied.

Example 1 – Fixed rate assets financed by fixed rate debentures

An entity is about to purchase a portfolio of fixed rate assets that will be financed by fixed rate debentures. Both financial assets and financial liabilities are subject to the same interest rate risk that gives rise to opposite changes in fair value that tend to offset each other.

In the absence of the fair value option, the entity may have classified the fixed-rate assets as available-for-sale with gains and losses on changes in fair value recognised in other comprehensive income and the fixed-rate debentures at amortised cost. Reporting both the assets and the liabilities at fair value through profit and loss corrects the measurement inconsistency and produces more relevant information. [IAS 39 para AG 4E(d)(i)].

Example 2 – Fixed rate bond converted to floating rate

An entity purchases a fixed rate bond and immediately enters into an interest rate swap to convert the fixed rate to floating rate.

Instead of claiming hedge accounting, the entity could designate the bond at fair value through profit or loss. Since both the bond and the swap will be measured at fair value through profit or loss, the entity achieves a similar accounting result to if fair value hedge accounting has been applied, but without the added burden of designating, assessing and measuring hedge effectiveness that hedge accounting entails.

It should be noted that the bond is fully fair valued for all risks and not just for the hedged interest rate risk that hedge accounting would require. Furthermore, the fair value option is irrevocable. Hedge accounting is revocable (see chapter 6.8).

Example 3 – Fixed rate loan offset by derivative liabilities

An entity is about to originate a 10-year fixed rate loan that, if not designated as at fair value through profit or loss, will be measured at amortised cost. The entity also has a nine-year derivative that it regards as related to, and shares the same risk as, the loan. The entity wishes to designate the asset as at fair value through profit or loss to eliminate the measurement and recognition inconsistency with the derivative.

Although, in this example, the relationship does not completely eliminate the economic exposure, the entity can still designate the asset at fair value through profit or loss. The difference in maturities does not prevent the entity from designating the asset at fair value through profit or loss, provided there is a perceived economic relationship between the asset and the derivative. The fair value option does not require the elimination of economic volatility; it requires the elimination or significant reduction of an accounting mismatch. In the above example, the asset is measured at amortised cost and the derivative is measured at fair value, hence the accounting mismatch. Secondly, there is a perceived economic relationship between the asset and liability – for example, they share a risk that gives rise to opposite changes in fair value that tend to offset.

Example 4 – Financing a group of loans with traded bonds

An entity is about to originate a specified group of loans to be financed by issuing traded bonds whose changes in fair value tend to offset each other. The entity expects to regularly buy and sell the bonds but rarely, if ever, to buy and sell the loans.

Reporting both the loans and the bonds at fair value through profit or loss eliminates the inconsistency in the timing of recognition of gains and losses that would otherwise result from measuring them both at amortised cost and recognising a gain or loss each time a bond is repurchased. [IAS 39 para AG 4E(d)(ii)].

> **Example 5 – Subsidiary's debt offset by interest rate swap with parent**
>
> A subsidiary is about to issue a liability to a third party and enter into a related interest rate swap with its parent. An accounting mismatch exists in the subsidiary's stand alone financial statements, and it intends to designate the liability as at fair value through profit or loss.
>
> Although it is appropriate for the subsidiary to designate the liability as at fair value through profit or loss in its individual financial statements, such designation is not possible in the consolidated financial statements. This is because the inter-company swap will be eliminated, and the 'mismatch' will not exist in the consolidated financial statements. However, if the parent can identify an external swap or other instrument that gives rise to an accounting mismatch on a consolidated basis, this may justify designating the liability as at fair value through profit or loss in the consolidated financial statements.

6.4.13 An accounting mismatch need not occur only between related financial assets and financial liabilities. It could also occur between a financial asset and a related liability or between a financial liability and a related asset. In both situations, the entity may use the fair value option on, respectively, the financial asset or financial liability, provided it concludes that the changes in fair value of both items are subject to the same risk and an accounting mismatch will be eliminated or significantly reduced by the designation.

> **Example – Financial assets offsetting insurance liabilities**
>
> An insurer holds financial assets whose fair value exposure offsets that of liabilities under insurance contracts that are measured using techniques that incorporate current market information. The financial assets are not held for trading and would not automatically be measured at fair value.
>
> Reporting both the insurance liabilities at a current value (as permitted by para 24 of IFRS 4) and the financial assets at fair value through profit or loss eliminates the inconsistency that would otherwise result from measuring the insurance liabilities at cost and the financial assets as available-for-sale or at amortised cost. [IAS 39 para AG 4E(b)].

6.4.14 Designations as at fair value through profit or loss should be made at initial recognition and once made are irrevocable. For practical purposes, the entity need not enter into all of the assets and liabilities giving rise to measurement or recognition inconsistency at exactly the same time. A reasonable delay is permitted provided that each transaction is designated as at fair value through profit or loss at its initial recognition and, at that time, any remaining transactions are expected to occur. [IAS 39 para AG 4F].

6.4.15 'Reasonable delay' should be assessed on a case-by-case basis, based as to what is reasonable in the circumstances. For example, a 'reasonable delay' could be a fairly short period in the case of entering into a derivative to offset some of the risks of an asset. A longer period could be justified if the delay arises from the need to assemble a portfolio of similar assets and arrange their funding. However, all financial assets and liabilities designated as at fair value through profit or loss must be accounted for on this basis from their initial recognition (and not only from the time any offsetting position is entered into).

6.4.16 It should be noted that if, for some reason, one of the offsetting instruments is derecognised, for instance, the fixed rate assets in example 1 or the interest rate swap in example 2 in paragraph 6.4.12 above, the other offsetting instrument – the fixed rate debentures in example 1 or the fixed rate bond in example 2 – would continue to be carried at fair value with gains and losses reported in profit or loss. This is because the designation at fair value through profit or loss at initial recognition is irrevocable, irrespective of whether the initial conditions that permitted the use of the option (to correct an accounting mismatch) still hold.

6.4.17 IFRS 7 also requires the entity to provide disclosures about financial assets and financial liabilities it has designated as at fair value through profit or loss, including how it has satisfied those conditions. For instruments that qualify for designation as at fair value through profit or loss in accordance with paragraph 6.4.9 above, the disclosure should include a narrative description of the circumstances underlying the measurement or recognition inconsistency that would arise. [IAS 39 para 9(b); IFRS 7 para B(5)]. See further chapter 6.9.

Group of financial assets and liabilities managed on a fair value basis

6.4.18 An entity may manage and evaluate the performance of a group of financial assets, financial liabilities or both in such a way that measuring that group at fair value through profit or loss results in more relevant information. Therefore, in order to designate financial instruments at fair value through profit or loss under the second criterion in paragraph 6.4.6 above, the designation should be based on the manner in which the entity manages and evaluates performance, rather than on the nature of those financial instruments. [IAS 39 para AG 4H]. An entity should designate all eligible financial instruments that are managed and evaluated together. [IAS 39 para AG 4J]. However, designation under this criterion must meet the following two requirements:

- The financial instruments are managed and performance evaluated on a fair value basis in accordance with a documented risk management or investment strategy.

- Information about the group is provided internally on that basis to the entity's key management as defined in IAS 24 (for example, the entity's board of directors and chief executive officer).

[IAS 39 para 9(b)(ii)].

6.4.19 The requirement that a group of financial assets and liabilities should be managed and performance evaluated on a fair value basis means that management should evaluate the portfolio on a full fair value basis and not on a risk-by-risk basis. For example, an entity that originates fixed interest rate loans and manages the interest rate risk of this portfolio based on the fair value attributable only to interest rate changes will be unable to use the fair value option. This is because the fair value concept is a broader notion than hedge accounting, such that evaluating the portfolio's performance for only some risks is not sufficient. Therefore, an entity's risk management policy and the resulting management information should look at the entire change in fair value and not for only some risks to justify the fair value option's use.

6.4.20 The required documentation of the entity's strategy need not be on an item-by-item basis, nor need it be in the level of detail required for hedge accounting. Documentation may be on a portfolio or group basis as long as it clearly identifies the items for which the fair value option is to be used. If the documentation relies on several other pre-existing documents, there needs to be an overall document that references these other documents and clearly demonstrates that the entity manages and evaluates the relevant financial assets or financial liabilities on a fair value basis. The documentation also needs to be sufficient to demonstrate that using the fair value option is consistent with the entity's risk management or investment strategy. In many cases, the entity's existing documentation, as approved by key management personnel, should be sufficient for this purpose. For example, if the performance management system for a group – as approved by the entity's key management personnel – clearly demonstrates that its performance is evaluated on a total return basis, no further documentation is required to demonstrate compliance with the above requirements. [IAS 39 para AG 4K].

6.4.21 As stated in paragraph 6.4.17 above, IFRS 7 requires the entity to provide disclosures about financial assets and financial liabilities it has designated as at fair value through profit or loss, including how it has satisfied those conditions. For instruments that qualify for designation as at fair value through profit or loss as a group of financial assets on liabilities, in accordance with paragraph 6.4.18 above, the disclosure should include a narrative description of how designation as at fair value through profit or loss is consistent with the entity's documented risk management or investment strategy. [IAS 39 para 9(b); IFRS 7 para B(5)]. See further chapter 6.9.

> **Example 1 – Portfolio of financial assets held by venture capital firms**
>
> A venture capital organisation invests in a portfolio of financial assets with a view to profiting from their total return in the form of interest or dividends and changes in fair value and evaluates its performance on that basis. Some investments meet the definition of associates and joint ventures, while others do not.
>
> IAS 28 and IAS 31 allow such investments to be measured at fair value through profit or loss rather than using equity accounting.
>
> The fair value option allows the other investments, which are also managed and evaluated on a total return basis, but which fall outside the scope of IAS 28 and IAS 31 to be measured at fair value through profit or loss if that is consistent with the

manner in which the entity manages and evaluates the performance of these investments. [IAS 39 para AG 4I(a)].

In other words, the entire portfolio can be measured at fair value through profit or loss provided the two requirements of paragraph 6.4.18 above are met.

Example 2 – Portfolio of financial assets held to back specific liabilities

An entity holds a portfolio of financial assets. The entity manages the portfolio so as to maximise its total return (that is, interest or dividends and changes in fair value) and evaluates its performance on that basis. The portfolio is held to back specific liabilities.

In this situation, the entity may designate the portfolio at fair value through profit or loss, because it is likely that the entity's strategy to maximise total return would be set by, and information about performance of the portfolio would be provided to, key management on a timely basis. This is so regardless of whether the entity also manages and evaluates the liabilities on a fair value basis. [IAS 39 para AG 4I(c)].

Exception

6.4.22 The fair value option is not available for investments in equity instruments that do not have a quoted market price in an active market and whose fair value cannot be reliably measured. [IAS 39 para 9]. Therefore, in the absence of a quoted market price in an active market, if the fair value of an equity investment is not reliably measurable, because the range of reasonable fair value estimates is significant and the probabilities of the various estimates within the range cannot be reasonably assessed, an entity is precluded from measuring the instrument at fair value. [IAS 39 paras AG 80, AG 81].

Held-for-trading

6.4.23 A financial asset is held-for-trading if it is:

- acquired or incurred principally for the purpose of selling or repurchasing it in the near-term;

- on initial recognition, part of a portfolio of identified financial instruments that are managed together and for which there is evidence of a recent actual pattern of short-term profit taking; or

- a derivative (except for a derivative that is a financial guarantee contract or a designated and effective hedging instrument).

[IAS 39 para 9].

6.4.24 Financial assets held-for-trading include:

- Debt and equity securities that are actively traded by the entity.

- Loans and receivables acquired by the entity with the intention of making a short-term profit from price or dealer's margin.

- Securities held under repurchase agreements.

Derivatives are always categorised as held-for-trading, unless they are accounted for as effective hedging instruments.

6.4.25 Trading generally reflects active and frequent buying and selling and financial instruments held-for-trading generally are used with the objective of generating a profit from short-term fluctuations in price or dealer's margin. [IAS 39 para AG 14]. Whether an entity holds financial assets to generate profit on short-term differences in prices must be assessed on the basis of the facts and circumstances surrounding the trading activity rather than on the individual transaction's terms. Evidence of this is based on the frequency of buying and selling, the turnover rate or average holding period of the financial assets included in the portfolio (portfolio churning). All available evidence should be considered to determine whether the entity is involved in trading activities.

6.4.26 Financial assets that are bought and held principally in a portfolio for the purpose of selling them in the near-term (thus held for only a short period of time) should be classified as trading at acquisition date. Although the term 'portfolio' is not explicitly defined in IAS 39, the context in which it is used suggests that a portfolio is a group of financial assets or financial liabilities that are managed together. Also the phrases 'selling them in the near-term' and 'held for only a short period of time' are not explained in IAS 39. Therefore, in practice, an entity should adopt a suitable definition of these phrases and apply them on a consistent basis to avoid any ambiguity. For example, it is likely that if a security was acquired with the intent of selling it within a few weeks or months, the security would be classified as held-for-trading. After being classified as held-for-trading, a single instrument in a portfolio may in fact be held for a longer period of time, as long as there is evidence of a recent actual pattern of short-term profit taking on financial instruments included in such a portfolio.

> **Example – Shares held-for-trading**
>
> An entity purchased quoted equity shares from the market with the intention of profiting from short-term price fluctuations. The entity held the shares for three years due to a large unexpected downturn in the stock market after which it sold the shares in a more buoyant market.
>
> Since management's intention at acquisition was to profit from short-term price fluctuations, the entity would have classified the shares as held-for-trading. The fact that after designation the shares were in fact held for a longer term, because the entity was unable to sell the shares at a loss in a bear market, would not frustrate the held-to-trading classification. Indeed, IAS 39 does not limit the period for which such an instrument can be held as long as the principal purpose at acquisition was to sell them in the near-term. Furthermore, as there is no definition of 'near-term' it is important for the entity to adopt a suitable definition and apply it consistently as explained in paragraph 6.4.25 above.

Held-to-maturity investments

Definition

6.4.27 Held-to-maturity investments are non-derivative financial assets with fixed or determinable payments and fixed maturity that an entity has the positive intention and ability to hold to maturity other than:

- Those that the entity upon initial recognition designates as at fair value through profit or loss.

- Those that the entity designates as available-for-sale.

- Those that meet the definition of loans and receivables.

[IAS 39 para 9].

6.4.28 For most financial assets, the standard regards fair value as a more appropriate measure than amortised cost. Classifying a security as held-to-maturity means that the enterprise is indifferent to future opportunities to profit from changes in the security's fair value and intends to accept the debt security's stipulated contractual cash flows, including the repayment of principal at maturity. The held-to-maturity category is, therefore, an exception. Consequently, its use is restricted to instruments that have specific terms and characteristics and by a number of detailed conditions, largely designed to test whether the entity has genuine intention and ability to hold those instruments to maturity. Also, significant penalties exist for entities that classify an instrument as held-to-maturity, but which is sold before maturity. These issues are considered below.

Fixed or determinable payments and fixed maturity

6.4.29 Instruments classified as held-to-maturity must have fixed or determinable payments and fixed maturity, which means that a contractual arrangement defines the amounts and dates of payments to the holder, such as interest and principal payments. Investments in equity shares have indefinite lives and, therefore, cannot be held-to-maturity financial assets. Other equity instruments, such as share options and warrants, cannot be classified as held-to-maturity because the amounts the holder receives may vary in a manner that is not predetermined. [IAS 39 para AG 17]. It follows that since held-to-maturity financial assets must have fixed maturity, it is mainly debt instruments that fall within this category. A mandatorily redeemable preference share is also, in substance, a debt instrument that may fall within this category.

6.4.30 The amount of determinable payment of principal or interest is normally established by reference to a source other than the financial instrument, and may involve a calculation. For example, floating rate interest on a financial instrument that is calculated from a reference interest rate such as the LIBOR or a bank's prime rate, and a principal amount that is linked to a price index such as the market price of a commodity like oil, are examples of determinable cash flows.

Example 1 – Floating rate note

Entity A purchases a note with variable interest rate and a fixed payment at maturity.

The floating rate note could qualify as a held-to-maturity investment since its payments are fixed (the principal) and the interest payments are specified by reference to a market or bench mark rate such as the LIBOR, which is determinable. A held-to-maturity classification for floating rate notes is, however, of little benefit, since its fair value will not change significantly in response to changes in interest rates.

Example 2 – Indexed linked principal payments

Entity A purchases a five-year equity-index-linked note with an original issue price of C10 at a market price of C12 at the time of purchase. The note requires no interest payments before maturity. At maturity, the note requires payment of the original issue price of C10 plus a supplemental redemption amount that depends on whether a specified share price index exceeds a predetermined level at the maturity date. If the share index does not exceed or is equal to the predetermined level, no supplemental redemption amount is paid. If the share index exceeds the predetermined level, the supplemental redemption amount equals the product of 1.15 and the difference between the level of the share index at maturity and the level of the share index when the note was issued divided by the level of the share index at the time of issue. Entity A has the positive intention and ability to hold the note to maturity.

The embedded equity feature is not closely related to the debt host and must be separated. Once the embedded derivative is fair valued and separated, the debt host can be classified as a held-to-maturity investment because it has a fixed payment of C10 and fixed maturity and entity A has the positive intention and ability to hold it to maturity. [IAS 39 para IG B13].

In this example, the purchase price of C12 is allocated between the host debt instrument and the embedded derivative. If, for instance, the fair value of the embedded equity feature at acquisition is C4, the host debt instrument is measured at C8 on initial recognition. In this case, the discount of C2 that is implicit in the host bond (principal of C10 minus the original carrying amount of C8) is amortised to profit or loss over the term to maturity of the note using the effective interest method.

Example 3 – Indexed linked interest

Entity A purchases a bond with a fixed payment at maturity and a fixed maturity date. The interest payments on the bond are indexed to the price of a commodity or equity and the entity has the positive intention and ability to hold the bond to maturity.

The commodity-indexed or equity-indexed interest payments result in an embedded derivative that is not closely related to the bond. Hence, it is necessary to separate the host debt investment (the fixed payment at maturity) from the embedded derivative (the index-linked interest payments).

Once the embedded derivative has been separated, the debt host can be classified as held-to-maturity as it has a fixed payment and a fixed maturity and entity A has the positive intention and ability to hold the bond to maturity. [IAS 39 para IG B14].

Example 4 – Perpetual debt instrument

Entity A purchases two perpetual debt instruments X and Y as follows:

- Instrument X pays an interest rate of 10% per annum for an indefinite period.
- Instrument Y pays an interest rate of 16% for the first 10 years and 0% in subsequent periods.

Entity A cannot classify instrument X that provides for interest payments for an indefinite period as held-to-maturity, because there is no maturity date. [IAS 39 para AG 17].

As far as instrument Y is concerned, it may be possible to argue from an economic perspective, that the instrument has a fixed maturity of 10 years. This is because the initial amount is amortised to zero over the first ten years using the effective interest method, since a portion of the interest payments represents repayments of the principal amount. The amortised cost is zero after year 10, because the present value of the stream of future cash payments in subsequent periods is zero (there are no further cash payments of either principal or interest in subsequent periods). Since the only cash flows under the terms are fixed interest payments over a period of 10 years, there is a strong argument to support held-to-maturity classification on the grounds that entity A has recovered all of its initial investment and the rights in the event of a liquidation has no value, notwithstanding that the terms do not specify a maturity date.

Intent to hold to maturity

6.4.31 A positive intent to hold financial assets to maturity is a much higher hurdle than simply having no present intention to sell. An entity does not have a positive intention to hold to maturity an investment in a financial asset with a fixed maturity if:

- The entity intends to hold the financial asset for an undefined period. In other words, as the entity has not actually defined a period, the positive intent to hold-to-maturity does not exist.

- The entity stands ready to sell the financial asset (other than if a situation arises that is non-recurring and could not have been reasonably anticipated by the entity) in response to changes in market interest rates or risks, liquidity needs, changes in the availability of and the yield on alternative investments, changes in financing sources and terms or changes in foreign currency risk. All these situations are indicative that the entity intends to profit from changes in the asset's fair value and has no intention of holding the financial asset to maturity.

- The issuer has a right to settle the financial asset at an amount significantly below its amortised cost. Where this is the case and the issuer is expected to exercise that right, the entity cannot demonstrate a positive intent to hold the financial asset to maturity. See further paragraph 6.4.33 below.

[IAS 39 para AG 16]

6.4.32 An entity's intention to hold a financial asset to maturity is not negated by unusual and unlikely events that could not be anticipated at the time of the original classification. For example, a disaster scenario that is only remotely possible, such as a run on a bank or a similar situation affecting an insurer, is not something that is assessed by an entity in deciding whether it has the positive intention and ability to hold an investment to maturity. [IAS 39 para AG 21].

6.4.33 A financial asset that is callable by the issuer would satisfy the criteria for classification as a held-to-maturity investment if the holder intends and is able to hold it until it is called or until maturity and the holder would recover substantially all of its carrying amount. This means that if the issuer can call the instrument at or above its carrying amount, the holder's original classification of the instrument as held-to-maturity is not invalidated because the call option, if exercised, would simply accelerate the asset's maturity. However, if the financial asset is callable on a basis that would result in the holder not recovering substantially all of its carrying amount, the financial asset cannot be classified as a held-to-maturity investment. Any premium paid and capitalised transaction costs should be considered in determining whether the carrying amount would be substantially recovered. [IAS 39 para AG 18]. If the issuer can call the instrument for an amount substantially different from its carrying amount, potentially, the embedded derivative should be separated (see chapter 6.3).

6.4.34 On the other hand, a financial asset that is puttable (that is, the holder has the right to require that the issuer repay or redeem the financial asset before maturity) cannot be classified as a held-to-maturity investment, because paying for a put feature in a financial asset is inconsistent with the positive intent to hold the financial asset until maturity. [IAS 39 para AG 19].

6.4.35 Similarly, an investment in a convertible bond that is convertible before maturity generally cannot be classified as a held-to-maturity investment, because that would be inconsistent with paying for the conversion feature – the right to convert into equity shares before maturity. [IAS 39 para IG C3]. By paying for the conversion feature in terms of a lower interest rate, the investor hopes to benefit from appreciation in value of the option embedded in the debt security. Therefore, in general, it is unlikely that the investor will be able to assert the positive intent and ability to hold a convertible debt security to maturity and forego the opportunity to profit by exercising the conversion option. Even if the convertible debt is separated into an equity option and a host debt instrument (see chapter 6.5), it generally still would be contradictory to assert the positive intent and ability to hold the debt host contract to maturity and forego the opportunity to exercise the conversion option. On the other hand, if the conversion option can only be exercised at maturity, it may be possible for the holder to demonstrate positive intent to hold the bond to maturity.

Ability to hold to maturity

6.4.36 It is not sufficient for the entity to demonstrate a positive intent to hold a financial asset to maturity; the entity must also demonstrate its ability to hold such an asset to maturity. An entity cannot demonstrate that ability if:

- it does not have the financial resources available to continue to finance the investment until maturity; or

- it is subject to an existing legal or other constraint that could frustrate its intention to hold the financial asset to maturity (although as noted in para 6.4.33 above, an issuer's call option does not necessarily frustrate this intention).

[IAS 39 para AG 23].

For example, it is unlikely that an open ended fund would be able to classify any financial asset as held-to maturity. Management might intend to hold the investments to maturity, but calls for redemption of shares or units could constrain the fund's ability to hold its investments to maturity.

6.4.37 An entity's intention and ability to hold debt instruments to maturity is not necessarily constrained if those instruments have been pledged as collateral or are subject to a repurchase agreement or securities lending agreement. However, an entity does not have the positive intention and ability to hold the debt instruments until maturity if it does not expect to be able to maintain or recover access to the instruments. [IAS 39 para IG B18].

> **Example 1 – Pledge of held-to-maturity assets as security**
>
> Entity A requires C18m of cash for its operating activities in 20X7. The entity's latest cash flow forecast indicates a C2m shortfall. The entity intends to raise the funds required by pledging its investments in bonds, which are classified as held-to-maturity, to a bank to obtain a banking facility.
>
> The bonds can continue to be classified as held-to-maturity provided that the entity is able to fulfil the conditions of the banking facility such that the bank will not exercise the pledge. Short-term liquidity problems do not necessarily undermine the entity's ability to hold the investments until maturity.

Assessment of held-to-maturity classification

6.4.38 An entity should assess its intention and ability to hold its held-to-maturity investments to maturity not only when those financial assets are initially recognised, but also at each subsequent balance sheet date. [IAS 39 para AG 25]. Because an entity is expected not to change its *intent* about a held-to-maturity security, the requirement to reassess the appropriateness of a security's classification would necessarily focus on the entity's *ability* to hold a security to maturity. Facts and circumstances may change that may cause the entity to lose its ability to hold a debt security to maturity. Unless those facts and circumstances fall within one of the exceptions discussed in paragraph 6.4.42 below, the entity would be forced to reclassify its held-to-maturity investments to available-for-sale.

The tainting rules

6.4.39 Because management should assert that the criteria for a held-to-maturity investment have been met for each investment, the sale, reclassification or exercise of a put option of certain held-to-maturity securities will call into question ('taint') management's intent to hold all securities in the held-to-maturity category. An entity should not classify any financial assets as held-to-maturity if the entity has, during the current financial year or during the two preceding financial years, sold or reclassified more than an insignificant amount of held-to-maturity investments before maturity. In other words, where an entity during the current financial year has sold or reclassified more than an insignificant amount of held-to-maturity investments before maturity (more than insignificant in relation to the total amount of held-to-maturity investments), it is prohibited from classifying any financial asset as held-to-maturity for a period of two years after the occurrence of this event. Furthermore, all the entity's held-to-maturity investments, not just investments of a similar type, should be reclassified into the available-for-sale category and measured at fair value (see para 6.4.77). In a sense, a penalty is imposed for a change in management's intention. When the prohibition ends (at the end of the second financial year following the tainting), the portfolio becomes 'cleansed', and the entity is once more able to assert that it has the intent and ability to hold debt securities to maturity. [IAS 39 paras 9, 54].

6.4.40 The tainting rules do not apply if only an insignificant amount of held-to-maturity investments is sold or reclassified. The standard does not define what an insignificant amount means, except that it should be measured by reference to the total amount of held-to-maturity investments. Therefore, judgement is needed to assess what is insignificant in each particular situation.

Example 1 – Application of the tainting rules

An entity's held-to-maturity portfolio consists of a mixture of sterling corporate bonds, treasury bonds and eurodollar bonds. The entity prepares its financial statements to 31 December 20X5. During September 20X5, the entity sold a certain eurodollar bond to realise a large gain.

The fact that the entity has sold one eurodollar investment (not considered insignificant in relation to the total held-to-maturity portfolio) does not mean that only the eurodollar sub-category has been tainted. The tainting rule is very clear. If an entity has sold or reclassified more than an insignificant amount of held-to-maturity investments, the entire portfolio and all remaining investments must be reclassified to the available-for-sale category. [IAS 39 para IG B20]. It follows that sub-classification of securities for the purpose of limiting the impact of sales or transfers of held-to-maturity securities is not acceptable practice.

The reclassification is recorded in the reporting period in which the sales occurred (that is, the year to 31 December 20X5). Furthermore, as explained in paragraph 6.4.39 above, the entity is prohibited from reclassifying any investments in the held-to-maturity category for two full financial years after 31 December 20X5. This means that any fixed interest securities acquired during 20X6 and 20X7, which could qualify for held-to-maturity classification, cannot be classified as such in those years. The earliest date that the entity is able to classify investments as held-to-maturity is 1 January 20X8 as shown in the diagram below:

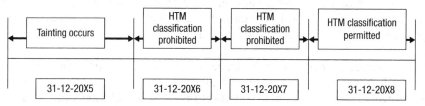

At 1 January 20X8 when the portfolio becomes cleansed, and it once again becomes appropriate to carry securities at held-to-maturity, the fair value of the affected securities on 1 January 20X8 becomes the new amortised cost. Furthermore, as tainting occurs in the year to 31 December 20X5, the held-to-maturity classification for the comparative period to 31 December 20X4 is not affected.

Example 2 – Regular disposal of small amounts of held-to-maturity securities

Entity X has a portfolio of financial investments that is classified as held-to-maturity. In the current period, it sold small amounts of investments from time to time.

Regular or systematic sales or transfers of immaterial amounts are indicative of management's intention not to hold financial assets to maturity. The tainting rules would apply and the entity should reclassify all its held-to-maturity investments as available-for-sale and measure them at fair value.

In addition, the entity may not create a sub-category of held-to-maturity in which to hold these investments. (The aim of this sub-categorisation would have been so that the sale of investments prior to maturity from that sub-category did not taint the entire held-to-maturity portfolio.)

Tainting in group situations

6.4.41 The tainting rules are designed to test an entity's assertion that it has the positive intent and ability to hold each security to maturity. The rules apply to all entities within a group. Therefore, if a subsidiary operating in a different legal or economic environment sells more than an insignificant amount of held-to-maturity investments, it would preclude the entire group from using the held-to-maturity category. This means that the entity would have to reclassify all its held-to-maturity investments in its consolidated financial statements, unless the sale qualifies for one of the exceptions noted in paragraph 6.4.42 below. [IAS 39 para IG B21]. Furthermore, at least two full financial years must pass before the entity can again classify financial assets as held-to-maturity in its consolidated financial statements. Sales between group entities generally would not taint the held-to-maturity classification at the group level, but may do so at the individual entity level. As the consequences of breaching the conditions are harsh, entities should carefully consider any plans to sell or transfer before classifying any asset to this category.

Exceptions to the tainting rules

6.4.42   There are a number of exceptions to the tainting rules. As already discussed in paragraph 6.4.39 above, a sale or reclassification of an insignificant amount of held-to-maturity investment would not result in tainting. Similarly, a sale or reclassification would not taint the rest of the portfolio if it was:

■   so close to maturity or the financial asset's call date (for example, less than three months before maturity) that changes in the market rate of interest would not have a significant effect on the financial asset's fair value;

■   made after the entity has collected substantially all of the financial asset's original principal through scheduled payments or pre-payments; or

■   due to an isolated event that is beyond the entity's control, is non-recurring and could not have been reasonably anticipated by the entity.

[IAS 39 para 9].

6.4.43   The conditions referred to in the first and second bullet points above relate to situations in which an entity can be expected to be indifferent whether to hold or sell a financial asset, because movements in interest rates after substantially all of the original principal has been collected or when the instrument is close to maturity will not have a significant impact on its fair value. Accordingly, in such situations, a sale would not affect reported net profit or loss and no price volatility would be expected during the remaining period to maturity. For example, if an entity sells a financial asset less than three months prior to maturity, that would generally qualify for use of this exception because the impact on the fair value of the instrument for a difference between the stated interest rate and the market rate generally would be small for an instrument that matures in three months relative to an instrument that matures in several years.

6.4.44   The term 'substantially all' in the second bullet point of paragraph 6.4.42 is not defined in IAS 39. The guidance to the previous version of IAS 39 stated that if an entity sells a financial asset after it has collected 90% or more of the financial asset's original principal through scheduled payments or pre-payments, this would generally qualify for this exception. However, if the entity has collected, say, only 10% of the original principal, that condition clearly is not met. Although the previous guidance has not been carried forward in the revised version, we believe that applying a 90% threshold as a rule of thumb to test whether 'substantially all' of the original principal has been collected is acceptable. Clearly, though, it cannot be applied as a hard-and-fast rule and cannot be applied to the derecognition criteria of IAS 39 (see chapter 6.6).

6.4.45   In relation to the last bullet point in paragraph 6.4.42 above, very few events would qualify as isolated events beyond the entity's control, that are non-recurring or reasonably unanticipated. A disaster scenario that is only remotely possible, such as a run on a bank or a similar situation affecting an insurer, would qualify as it is not something that would be assessed by an entity in deciding whether it has the positive intention and ability to hold an investment to maturity. [IAS 39 para AG 21]. The consequence is that if the sale or reclassification resulted from an event that is not isolated but within the entity's control or is potentially recurring or could have been anticipated at the date the held-to-maturity classification was made, this inevitably will cast doubt on the entity's intent and ability to hold a security to maturity. Consider the following example:

Example – Permitted sales

Entity X has a portfolio of financial assets that is classified as held-to-maturity. In the current period, at the direction of the board of directors, the senior management team has been replaced. The new management wishes to sell a portion of the held-to-maturity financial assets in order to carry out an expansion strategy designated and approved by the board.

A change in management is not identified under the standard as an instance where sales or transfers from held-to-maturity do not compromise the classification as held-to-maturity (see para 6.4.42 above).

Although the previous management team had been in place since the entity's inception and entity X had never before undergone a major restructuring, sales in response to a change in management would, nevertheless call into question entity X's intention to hold remaining held-to-maturity financial assets to maturity. [IAS 39 IG B16].

6.4.46 In addition to the above, the standard identifies some specific circumstances that may not have been anticipated at the time of the initial held-to-maturity classification and, therefore, would justify the sale of a security classified as held-to-maturity without calling into question management's intent to hold other debt securities to maturity in the future. Thus a sale or transfer of a held-to-maturity security due to one of the following circumstances would not result in tainting of a held-to-maturity portfolio.

- A significant deterioration in the issuer's credit worthiness (see para 6.4.47).

- Changes in tax laws (see para 6.4.50).

- Major business combination or disposition, such as a sale of a segment (see para 6.4.51).

- Changes in statutory or regulatory requirements (see para 6.4.53).

[IAS 39 para AG 22].

A significant deterioration in the issuer's creditworthiness

6.4.47 A sale due to a significant deterioration in the issuer's creditworthiness (evident by a downgrade in the issuer's credit rating by an external rating agency) might not raise a question about the entity's intention to hold other investments to maturity. However, the significance of deterioration in creditworthiness must be judged by reference to the credit rating at initial recognition. If the rating downgrade in combination with other information provides evidence of impairment (for example, if it becomes probable that all amounts due (principal and interest) will not be collected), the deterioration in creditworthiness often would be regarded as significant. Also, the significant deterioration must not have been reasonably anticipated when the entity classified the investment as held-to-maturity in order to meet the condition in IAS 39. A credit downgrade of a notch within a class or from one rating class to the immediately lower rating class could often be regarded as reasonably anticipated. Therefore, a sale triggered by such a downgrade would result in tainting of the held-to-maturity portfolio. Similarly, a sale as a result of the issuer's bankruptcy would be regarded as a permitted sale, but not one where the bankruptcy was anticipated at the acquisition date and the investor was, therefore, able to control the outcome. [IAS 39 para IG B15].

6.4.48 Where a credit rating is not available from an external rating agency to assess a decline in the issuer's creditworthiness, the entity is permitted to use its internal credit rating system to support the demonstration of significant deterioration in the issuer's creditworthiness. However, the internal credit rating system must be sufficiently robust to provide a reliable and objective measure of the issuer's credit rating and changes in those ratings on a consistent basis.

6.4.49 A sale following a significant deterioration in the issuer's creditworthiness should normally take place as soon as the entity becomes aware of the credit downgrade and not left until a later date. This is because if the sale or reclassification out of held-to-maturity category is not made immediately or shortly afterwards following the credit downgrade, it provides evidence that the entity is indifferent to the loss incurred in its held-to-maturity portfolio and intends to hold those investments to maturity. If, then a sale occurs many months after the credit downgrade, it is likely to be for reasons other than a credit downgrade.

Changes in tax laws

6.4.50 A sale following a change in tax law that eliminates or significantly reduces the tax-exempt status of interest on the held-to-maturity investment (but not a change in tax law that revises the marginal tax rates applicable to interest income) would not compromise the classification of held-to-maturity. This is because such a change was not contemplated at the time of the initial classification. On the other hand, if an entity undertakes a sale in anticipation of a change in the tax law that was not substantively enacted at the time of sale or reclassification, the entire held-to-maturity portfolio may well be tainted. Similarly, a sale as a result of change in tax law that revises the marginal tax rates for interest income will taint the entire held-to-maturity portfolio, since the change is likely to affect all debt instruments not simply the ones sold.

Major business combination or disposition

6.4.51 Following a business combination or disposal of a business segment, it may be necessary for the entity to sell or reclassify some of its own held-to-maturity securities in order to maintain the entity's existing interest rate risk position or credit risk policy that predated the business combination or disposal. In a business combination, it may also be necessary to sell some of the acquired entity's held-to-maturity securities, even though all of the acquired securities would be classified anew following such an acquisition. Although a business combination is an event that is within the entity's control, sales or reclassifications that are necessary to maintain the entity's existing interest rate risk position or credit risk policy arises as a direct consequence of the business combination or disposition and are not anticipated. Hence, such sales or reclassifications would not taint the entity's held-to-maturity portfolio.

6.4.52 On the other hand, sales of held-to-maturity securities to fund an acquisition that is within the entity's control would taint the portfolio. This is because such sales are not a consequence of the acquisition. Rather, as they have been made to fund the acquisition, they call into question the entity's intent and ability to hold the investment to maturity. Similarly, a sale in response to an unsolicited tender offer or a sale due to a change in the entity's business strategy would also taint the held-to-maturity portfolio. This is because such events are unlikely to fall into the category of isolated events that are beyond the entity's control, are non-recurring events and could not have been reasonably anticipated by the entity.

Changes in statutory or regulatory requirements

6.4.53 IAS 39 identifies the following situations where sale or reclassification out of the held-to-maturity category necessitated by changes in statutory or regulatory requirements would not call into question the entity's intent and ability to hold other investments to maturity.

- A change in statutory or regulatory requirements significantly modifying either what constitutes a permissible investment or the maximum level of particular types of investments, thereby causing an entity to dispose of a held-to-maturity investment.

- A significant increase in the risk weights of held-to-maturity investments used for regulatory risk-based capital purposes.

- A significant increase in the industry's regulatory capital requirements that causes the entity to downsize by selling held-to-maturity investments.

[IAS 39 para AG22(d-f)].

6.4.54 Sales of held-to-maturity securities resulting from statutory or regulatory requirements that affect the whole regulated industry as set out above are clearly isolated events beyond the entity's control, are non-recurring and could not have been reasonably anticipated by the entity.

6.4.55 In relation to the last situation in paragraph 6.4.53 above, if an entity is forced to downsize to comply with a significant increase in the industry's capital requirements, the sale of one or more held-to-maturity securities in connection with that downsizing would not call into question the classification of other held-to-maturity securities. Sometimes downsizing may be required to comply with a significant increase in *entity-specific* capital requirements imposed by regulators. In that situation, it may be difficult for the entity to demonstrate that the regulator's action could not have been reasonably anticipated at the time of the initial classification. Therefore, in this situation, the entity can avoid tainting only if it can demonstrate that the downsizing results from an increase in capital requirements, which is an isolated event that is beyond its control, is non-recurring and could not have been reasonably anticipated. [IAS 39 para IG B17].

6.4.56 It follows that blanket sales of held-to-maturity investments made as a matter of course to comply with regulatory capital requirements are not consistent with held-to-maturity accounting. For example, a sale of a held-to-maturity investment to realise gains to replenish regulatory capital depleted by a loan loss provision would taint the entire held-to-maturity portfolio, because realising such a gain is inconsistent with the held-to-maturity classification.

Decision tree for classifying financial assets as held-to-maturity

6.4.57 A decision tree for classifying financial assets as held-to-maturity is shown below.

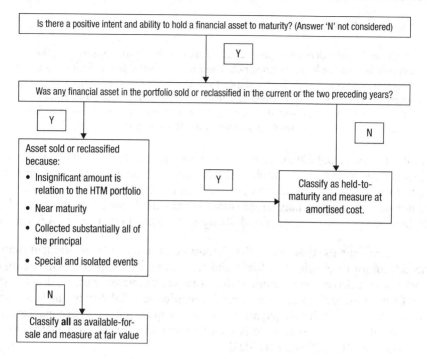

Loans and receivables

6.4.58 Loans and receivables are non-derivative financial assets with fixed or determinable payments that are not quoted in an active market other than:

- Those that the entity intends to sell immediately or in the near term, which should be classified as held-for-trading, and those that the entity upon initial recognition designates as at fair value through profit or loss.

- Those that the entity upon initial recognition designates as available-for-sale.

- Those for which the holder may not recover substantially all of its initial investment, other than because of credit deterioration, which should be classified as available-for-sale.

[IAS 39 para 9].

6.4.59 Loans and receivables typically arise when an entity provides money, goods or services directly to a debtor with no intention of trading the receivable. Examples include trade receivables, bank deposits and loan assets originated by the entity either directly or by way of syndication/participation arrangements. It also includes loans that are *purchased* in a secondary market that is not active and the loans are not quoted. Investments in debt securities that are quoted in a non-active market can also be classified as loans and receivables.

64023

Example – Bank deposits in other banks

Banks make term deposits with a central bank or other banks. Sometimes, the proof of deposit is negotiable, sometimes not. Even if negotiable, the depositor bank may or may not intend to sell it. Such a deposit meets the definition of loans and receivables, whether or not the proof of deposit is negotiable, unless the depositor bank intends to sell the instrument immediately or in the near term, in which case the deposit is classified as a financial asset held-for-trading. [IAS 39 para IG B23].

6.4.60 The principal difference between loans and receivables and other financial assets is that loans and receivables are not subject to the tainting provisions that apply to held-to-maturity investments. Consequently, loans and receivables that are not held-for-trading may be measured at amortised cost even if an entity does not have the positive intention and ability to hold the loan asset until maturity.

6.4.61 Instruments that meet the definition of an equity instrument under IAS 32 cannot be classified as loans and receivables by the holder. On the other hand, if a non-derivative instrument (for example, a preference share) that has the legal form of an equity instrument, but is recorded as a liability by the issuer and it has fixed or determinable payments and is not quoted in an active market, can be classified within loans and receivables by the holder, provided the definition is otherwise met. [IAS 39 para IG B22].

6.4.62 An interest acquired in a pool of assets that are not loans or receivables (for example, an interest in a mutual fund or a similar fund) cannot be classified as a loan or receivable. [IAS 39 para 9]. The consequence is that a purchase of a securitised asset that consists of a pool of loans and receivables that meets the definition of loans and receivables can be classified as loan and receivables by the holder. However, where an entity securitises its own portfolio of loans and receivables that were classified as loans and receivables before the securitisation and the derecognition provisions of IAS 39 apply, the securitisation may give rise to a new financial asset that is classified in accordance with the four categories of financial assets.

Debt instruments quoted in an active market

6.4.63 As stated in paragraph 6.4.58 above, an entity is not permitted to classify as a loan or receivable an investment in a debt instrument that is quoted in an active market. The IASB considered that the ability to measure a financial asset at amortised cost (as in the case of loans and receivables) is most appropriate when there is no liquid market for the asset. It is less appropriate to extend the category to debt instruments traded in liquid markets. Accordingly, for such investments an amortised cost basis of measurement is only permitted if the entity can demonstrate its positive intention and ability to hold the investments until maturity (see para 6.4.27 above). It is likely, therefore, that many originated and purchased investments in quoted bonds would be classified as available-for-sale.

Available-for-sale financial assets

6.4.64 Available-for-sale (AFS) financial assets are those non-derivative financial assets that are designated as available-for-sale or are not classified as:

- Loans and receivables.

- Held-to-maturity investments.

- Financial assets at fair value through profit or loss.

[IAS 39 para 9].

6.4.65 IAS 39 includes a degree of choice, on initial recognition to classify any non-derivative financial asset, except those held-for-trading or designated at fair value through profit or loss, as available-for-sale and, therefore, to measure it at fair value with changes in fair value recognised directly in other comprehensive income.

6.4.66 Examples of available-for-sale financial assets that are likely to be included in this category are:

- Equity investments that are not designated on initial recognition as at fair value through profit and loss.

- Financial assets that could have been classified as loans and receivables on initial recognition, but the holder chooses to designate on initial recognition as available-for-sale.

- Financial assets where the holder is unable to recover substantially all its initial investment, except through credit deterioration of the issuer.

- Puttable quoted debt securities that cannot be classified either as held-to-maturity because they are puttable (see para 6.4.34 above) or any quoted debt instrument that fails the held-to-maturity criteria (because they may be sold in response to liquidity needs (see para 6.4.39) or loans and receivables because they are quoted (see para 6.4.58)).

The main issue is, therefore, likely to focus on whether investments quoted in an active market should be classified as fair value through profit or loss or designated as available-for-sale on initial recognition.

> **Example – Balancing a portfolio**
>
> Entity A has an investment portfolio of debt and equity instruments. The documented portfolio management guidelines specify that the portfolio's equity exposure should be limited to between 30 and 50% of total portfolio value. The portfolio's investment manager is authorised to balance the portfolio within the designated guidelines by buying and selling equity and debt instruments.
>
> Whether entity A is permitted to classify the instruments as available-for-sale would depend on entity A's intentions and past practice. If the portfolio manager is

authorised to buy and sell instruments to balance the risks in a portfolio, but there is no intention to trade and there is no past practice of trading for short-term profit, the instruments can be classified as available-for-sale. If the portfolio manager actively buys and sells instruments to generate short-term profits, the financial instruments in the portfolio are classified as held-for-trading. [IAS 39 para IG B12].

Reclassification of assets between categories

6.4.67   Once a financial asset has been classified into a particular category on initial recognition, IAS 39 restricts the circumstances in which it is permissible or necessary to transfer that asset into another category. However, these rules were eased somewhat in October 2008 when the IASB amended IAS 39 to allow reclassification of certain financial assets out of a category requiring fair value measurement (that is, held-for-trading or available-for-sale) and into another category under limited circumstances (see paras 6.4.77 and 6.4.84). However, derivatives and financial assets designated as at fair value through profit or loss, as described in paragraph 6.4.6, are not eligible for this reclassification.

Transfer into and out of fair value through profit or loss

6.4.68   As explained in paragraph 6.4.6, entities are permitted to designate on initial recognition any financial asset or financial liability at fair value through profit and loss if it meets the criteria of paragraph 9 of IAS 39. However, to impose discipline on this approach, a financial asset or a financial liability that has been voluntarily designated cannot be transferred out of this category while it is held. A financial asset or a financial liability also cannot be reclassified or designated *into* this category after initial recognition. [IAS 39 para 50]. Such irrevocable designation at inception prevents 'cherry picking', as it is not known at initial recognition whether the asset's fair value will increase or decrease.

Transfer into and out of held-for-trading

6.4.69   After initial recognition, a financial asset may not be reclassified into the sub-category held-for-trading from another category. [IAS 39 para 50]. However, as mentioned in paragraph 6.4.67, from 1 July 2008, this requirement has been relaxed: a non-derivative financial asset can be reclassified out of the sub-category held-for-trading and into another category in the following circumstances:

- ■   If the financial asset meets the definition of loans and receivables at the date of reclassification and the entity at that date has the intent and ability to hold it for the foreseeable future or to maturity. [IAS 39 para 50D]. Note that a financial asset cannot meet the definition of loans and receivables if it is quoted in an active market (see para 6.4.63) or if it represents an interest in a pool of assets that are not themselves loans and receivables (see para 6.4.62).

- ■   For other financial assets (that is, those that do not meet the definition of loans and receivables) only in rare circumstances, provided that these financial assets are no longer held for the purpose of selling or repurchasing in the near term and meet the definition of the target category. [IAS 39 para 50B].

6.4.70 Paragraph BC104D of the Basis for Conclusions of the amendment to IAS 39 defines a rare circumstance as arising *"from a single event that is unusual and highly unlikely to recur in the near-term"*. In its press release announcing the publication of this amendment to IAS 39, the IASB indicated that the deterioration of the world's financial markets that occurred during the third quarter of 2008 was a possible example of 'a rare circumstance'.

6.4.71 At the date of reclassification, the fair value of any financial asset reclassified under these provisions becomes its new cost or amortised cost as applicable. Any gain or loss already recognised in profit or loss is not reversed. [IAS 39 paras 50C, 50F]. Guidance for the subsequent measurement of reclassified financial assets is provided in chapter 6.7.

6.4.72 Reclassification is not permissible for derivative financial assets. [IAS 39 para 50(a)]. However, this prohibition does not prevent a derivative that was initially classified as held-for-trading from being designated as a hedging instrument while it is held. Nor does it prevent a derivative that was designated as a hedging instrument from being classified as held-for-trading following revocation of the hedge. [IAS 39 para 50A].

6.4.73 Although reclassification does not imply any change to the financial instrument's terms, IFRIC 9 requires an entity to assess whether a contract contains an embedded derivative when it reclassifies a financial asset out of the sub-category of held-for-trading. [IFRIC 9 para 7]. Further guidance is provided in chapter 6.3.

Transfer into and out of loans and receivables

6.4.74 As explained in paragraphs 6.4.69 and 6.4.79, a non-derivative financial asset may be reclassified out of held-for-trading or available-for-sale and into loans and receivables if it meets the definition of loans and receivables and the entity has the ability and intention to hold it for the foreseeable future or until maturity.

6.4.75 Additionally, an entity can choose to designate a financial asset that satisfies the loans and receivables definition as available-for-sale only on initial recognition or on the date of transition to IFRS. If an asset is initially designated as a loan and receivable or has been reclassified as a loan and receivable per paragraph 6.4.69, it may not subsequently be re-designated as available-for-sale or held-for-trading.

6.4.76 However, different considerations apply if an asset that was initially classified as a loan and receivable becomes quoted in an active market such that the definition of loans and receivables is no longer met. This case is not specifically covered by IAS 39 and accordingly an entity has an accounting policy choice of reclassifying or not. The chosen policy should be applied consistently. So if an entity chooses reclassification as its accounting policy, it will need to reclassify all loans and receivables that become quoted in an active market as available-for-sale.

Transfer out of held-to-maturity into available-for-sale

6.4.77 Where, as a result of a change in intention or ability, it is no longer appropriate to classify an investment as held-to-maturity, it is reclassified as available-for-sale and remeasured at fair value. [IAS 39 para 51]. As explained in paragraph 6.4.39, a sale or reclassification calls into question management's intent and ability to hold financial assets to maturity and 'taints' the entire portfolio. Therefore, whenever sales or reclassification of more than an insignificant amount of held-to-maturity investments that do not meet any of the conditions of permitted sales set out in paragraph 6.4.42 occur, any remaining held-to-maturity investments are reclassified as available-for-sale. In such circumstances, the assets are remeasured to fair value, with any difference recognised in other comprehensive income. [IAS 39 para 52]. Guidance for the subsequent measurement of reclassified financial instruments is provided in chapter 6.7.

Transfer out of available-for-sale into held-to-maturity

6.4.78 An entity is allowed to reclassify a financial asset from available-for-sale to held-to-maturity, except in periods where the held-to-maturity category is tainted. For example, a quoted loan in an active market that was initially classified as available-for-sale may subsequently be reclassified to held-to-maturity category if the entity intends and has the ability to hold the loan to maturity. An instrument may be reclassified into the held-to-maturity category when the tainted held-to-maturity portfolio has been 'cleansed' at the end of the second financial year following the tainting (see para 6.4.39). In this case, the financial asset's carrying value, that is, its fair value at the date of reclassification, becomes the asset's new amortised cost. [IAS 39 para 54(a)]. Guidance for the subsequent measurement of reclassified financial assets is provided in chapter 6.7.

Transfer out of available-for-sale to loans and receivables

6.4.79 As mentioned in paragraph 6.4.74, an entity may reclassify a non-derivative financial asset from available-for-sale to loans and receivables if:

- the entity has the intention and ability to hold the asset for the foreseeable future or until maturity; and

- the asset meets the definition of loans and receivables. Note that a financial asset cannot meet the definition of loans and receivables if it is quoted in an active market (see para 6.4.63), if it represents an interest in a pool of assets that are not themselves loans and receivables (see para 6.4.62), or if the holder may not substantially recover all of its investment other than because of credit deterioration (see para 6.4.58).

[IAS 39 para 9,50C, 50E].

6.4.80 At the date of reclassification, the fair value of any financial asset reclassified under these provisions becomes its new cost or amortised cost as applicable. The treatment of any gain or loss already recognised in other comprehensive income depends on whether the asset has a fixed maturity. [IAS 39 paras 50C and 50F]. Further guidance on measurement is provided in chapter 6.7.

Summary

6.4.81 The reclassification requirements for financial assets described above are summarised in the following table:

From category	To category				
	Held-for-trading	Designated at fair value	Loans and receivables	Held-to-maturity	Available-for-sale
Held-for-trading		No	Yes (see paras 6.4.69-6.4.72)	Yes (see paras 6.4.69-6.4.72)	Yes (see paras 6.4.69-6.4.72)
Designated at fair value	No		No	No	No
Loans and receivables	No	No		No	Yes (see para 6.4.76)
Held-to-maturity	No	No	No		Yes (see para 6.4.77)
Available-for-sale	No	No	Yes (see para 6.4.79)	Yes (see para 6.4.78)	

Classification of financial liabilities

6.4.82 IAS 39 has two defined categories of financial liabilities, as follows:

- Financial liabilities 'at fair value through profit or loss'.
- Other financial liabilities (measured at amortised cost).

6.4.83 Like financial assets, a financial liability can be classified as at fair value through profit or loss only if it meets either of the following conditions:

- Upon initial recognition, it is designated by the entity at fair value through profit or loss.
- It is classified as held-for-trading.

[IAS 39 para 9].

Designation at fair value through profit or loss on initial recognition

6.4.84 The criteria for designation at fair value through profit are loss are the same for financial liabilities as for financial assets and are outlined in paragraph 6.4.6. An entity's ability to designate a financial instrument at fair value through profit or loss is an option. It does not restrict an entity's ability to measure a financial liability at amortised cost.

6.4.85 Where an entity takes the fair value option and measures its own debt at fair value using one of the situations mentioned in paragraph 6.4.6, changes in the entity's creditworthiness should be reflected in the fair value measurement of own debt instruments. This issue is addressed in chapter 6.7. However, the criteria in paragraph 6.4.6 do provide restrictions around the situations when an entity is able to designate its own financial liabilities at fair value through profit or loss, having been introduced in 2003 following controversy around the previous unrestricted fair value option in IAS 39.

Held-for-trading

6.4.86 A financial liability is held-for-trading if it is:

- acquired or incurred principally for the purpose of selling or repurchasing it in the near-term;

- part of a portfolio of identified financial instruments that are managed together and for which there is evidence of a recent actual pattern of short-term profit taking; or

- a derivative (except for a derivative that is a designated and effective hedging instrument).

[IAS 39 para 9].

6.4.87 Financial liabilities held-for-trading include:

- Derivative liabilities that are not accounted for as hedging instruments. For example, it will include derivatives with a negative fair value.

- Obligations to deliver financial assets borrowed by a short seller. A short sale is a transaction in which an entity sells securities it does not own, with the intention of buying securities on a future date to cover the sale. Securities borrowed are not recognised on the balance sheet, unless they are sold to third parties, in which case the obligation to return the securities is recorded as a trading liability and measured at fair value and any gains or losses are included in the income statement.

- Financial liabilities that are incurred with an intention to repurchase them in the near-term. For example, a quoted debt instrument that the issuer may buy back in the near-term depending on changes in its fair value.

- Financial liabilities that are part of a portfolio of identified financial instruments that are managed together and for which there is evidence of a recent pattern of short-term profit-taking.

The fact that a liability is incurred and used to fund trading activities does not mean that the liability is classified as held-for-trading.

[IAS 39 para AG 15].

Other financial liabilities

6.4.88 Financial liabilities that are not classified as at fair value through profit or loss would automatically fall into this category and are measured at amortised cost. Common examples are trade payables, borrowings and customer deposits.

Reclassification between categories

6.4.89 Reclassification of financial liabilities into or out of fair value through profit or loss is prohibited. However, as explained in paragraph 6.4.72, this prohibition does not apply to derivative financial liabilities that are designated or re-designated as hedging instruments.

Financial guarantee contracts

6.4.90 Financial guarantee contracts do not fit clearly into any category above if they were not initially classified as at fair value through profit or loss. They seem to form a separate category of their own. This is because subsequent measurement of these contracts, unless designated at inception as at fair value through profit or loss, is not consistent with that of the categories described above. Financial guarantee contracts are defined in chapter 6.1. Guidance for the measurement of financial guarantee contracts is provided in chapter 6.7.

6.5 – Financial liabilities and equity

6.5 – Financial liabilities and equity

Introduction

6.5.1 IAS 32 contains the principles for distinguishing between liabilities and equity issued by an entity. The substance of the contractual arrangement of a financial instrument, rather than its legal form, governs its classification. The overriding criterion is that if an entity does not have an unconditional right to avoid delivering cash or another financial asset to settle a contractual obligation, the contract is not an equity instrument.

6.5.2 IAS 32 should be applied by all entities to all types of financial instruments except those outside the standard's scope. The scope exemptions to IAS 32 are discussed in chapter 6.1. In practice, the more common and complex scope exemptions relate to contracts that fall within the scope of IFRS 2, IAS 19, or IFRS 4. Where the holder is an employee, director or provider of service to the entity, the contract should be carefully analysed to determine whether it is within the scope of IFRS 2, (see chapter 12) or IAS 19 (see chapter 11) or IAS 32. IFRS 2 may apply in situations that are not obvious. For example, IFRS 2 may apply where an entity issues warrants at an amount less than fair value. Refer to chapter 12 for additional guidance.

6.5.3 The IASB and the FASB have been working on a project to replace IAS 32 and converge IFRS and US GAAP for a number of years. The 'Financial instruments with characteristics of equity' project ('FICE') resulted in a discussion paper in 2008, but was put on hold in 2010. While any proposals could result in fundamental changes to the current model, the project is not expected to resume in the near future.

6.5.4 Classifying liability and equity instruments in accordance with IAS 32's rules is complex and requires the assessment of each component of an instrument's contractual terms. The impact of an incorrect classification on such issues as borrowings and other ratios (including debt covenants) and reported earnings can be highly significant to investors and other users of financial statements.

Principles for classifying financial liabilities and equity instruments

6.5.5 Before considering IAS 32's general principles for classifying a financial instrument as a financial liability or equity, it is appropriate to set out the standard's basic definitions of a financial liability and an equity instrument.

6.5.6 IAS 32 defines a financial liability as any liability that is:

- A contractual obligation

    - to deliver cash or another financial asset to another entity; or

    - to exchange financial assets or financial liabilities with another entity under conditions that are potentially unfavourable to the entity.

- A contract that will or may be settled in the entity's own equity instruments and is:

    - a non-derivative for which the entity is or may be obliged to deliver a variable number of the entity's own equity instruments; or

    - a derivative that will or may be settled other than by the exchange of a fixed amount of cash or another financial asset for a fixed number of the entity's own equity instruments. For this purpose the entity's own equity instruments do not include puttable instruments and obligations arising on liquidation that are classified as equity (as explained in para 6.5.29), rights issues denominated in a currency other than the functional currency of the issuer if they meet certain conditions (as explained in para 6.5.60) or instruments that are contracts for the future receipt or delivery of the entity's own equity instruments.

[IAS 32 para 11].

6.5.7 IAS 32 defines an equity instrument as any contract that evidences a residual interest in an entity's assets after deducting all of its liabilities. [IAS 32 para 11]. A residual interest is not necessarily a proportionate interest ranking *pari passu* with all other residual interests, for example, it may be an interest in a fixed amount of the entity's shares that may rank first in preference. For the purposes of determining whether a financial instrument is an equity instrument rather than a financial liability, the standard requires an issuer to apply the following expanded definition of an equity instrument that is essentially a converse of the above definition of a financial liability. Accordingly, an instrument is an equity instrument if, and only if, both of the conditions below are met:

- The instrument includes no contractual obligation:

    - to deliver cash or another financial asset to another entity; or

    - to exchange financial assets or financial liabilities with another entity under conditions that are potentially unfavourable to the entity.

- If the instrument will or may be settled in the issuer's own equity instruments, it is:

    - a non-derivative that includes no contractual obligation for the issuer to deliver a variable number of its own equity instruments; or

■ a derivative that will be settled only by the issuer exchanging a fixed amount of cash or another financial asset for a fixed number of its own equity instruments. For this purpose, rights and other issues denominated in any currency are equity instruments provided certain conditions are met (see further para 6.5.61). Also for this purpose, the issuer's own equity instruments do not include puttable instruments and obligations arising on liquidation that are classified as equity or instruments that are contracts for the future receipt or delivery of the issuer's own equity instruments.

A contractual obligation, including one arising from a derivative financial instrument, that will or may result in the future receipt or delivery of the issuer's own equity instruments, but does not meet both conditions above, is not an equity instrument. As an exception, an instrument that meets the definition of a financial liability is classified as an equity instrument if it has all the features and meets the conditions in the February 2008 amendment to IAS 32 (see para 6.5.34).

[IAS 32 para 16].

6.5.8 IAS 32 is a contract-based standard. 'Contract' or 'contractual' refers to an agreement between two or more parties that has clear economic consequences that the parties have little, if any, discretion to avoid, usually because the agreement is enforceable by law. Contracts, and thus financial instruments, may take a variety of forms and need not be in writing. [IAS 32 para 13]. Liabilities or assets that are not contractual (for example obligations established from local law or statute, such as income taxes) are not financial liabilities or financial assets. Similarly, constructive obligations, as defined in IAS 37, do not arise from contracts and are not financial liabilities. [IAS 32 para AG 12].

6.5.9 IAS 32 states that an issuer of a financial instrument should classify a financial instrument, or *its component parts,* on initial recognition as a financial liability, a financial asset or an equity instrument in accordance with the contractual arrangement's substance and the definitions of a financial liability, a financial asset and an equity instrument. [IAS 32 para 15]. The role of 'substance' in the classification of financial instrument should be restricted to considering the instrument's contractual terms. Anything that falls outside the contractual terms should not be considered for the purpose of assessing whether an instrument should be classified as a liability under IAS 32. Furthermore, in assessing the substance of the terms and conditions of a financial instrument, the impact of relevant local laws, regulations and the entity's governing charter in effect at the date of classification on those terms should also be considered, as noted in paragraph 6.5.28, but not expected future amendments to those laws, regulations and charter. [IFRIC 2 para 5].

6.5.10 A contractual financial obligation is necessary to classify a financial instrument as a liability. Such a contractual obligation could be established explicitly or could be indirectly established (see para 6.5.44). However, the obligation must be established through the terms and conditions of the financial instrument. As the IFRS IC agreed in March 2006, economic compulsion, by itself, does not result in a financial instrument being classified as a liability.

Example 1 – 'Step-up' instrument

An entity issues a non-redeemable callable bond where the fixed dividend of 5% can be deferred at the issuer's option. The instrument includes a 'step-up' dividend clause that would increase the dividend to 25% at a pre-determined date in the future unless the instrument had previously been called by the issuer.

This instrument includes no contractual obligation to pay the dividends or to call the instrument. Although there is an economic compulsion for the issuer to call the instrument on the date the dividend payment 'steps-up', there is no contractual obligation to do so. Therefore, the instrument would be classified as an equity instrument.

Example 2 – Discretionary dividends that have historically been paid each year.

An entity issues a non-redeemable callable subordinated bond with a fixed 6% coupon. The coupon can be deferred in perpetuity at the issuer's option. The issuer has a history of paying the coupon each year and the current bond price is predicated on the holders expectation that the coupon will continue to be paid each year. In addition the stated policy of the issuer is that the coupon will be paid each year, which has been publicly communicated.

Although there is both pressure on the issuer to pay the coupon, to maintain the bond price, and a constructive obligation to pay the coupon, there is no contractual obligation to do so. Therefore the bond is classified as an equity instrument.

6.5.11 Examining a financial instrument's component parts is key to correct classification. This is because debt instruments and shares come in many forms. They may be redeemable or non-redeemable. The returns may be mandatory or discretionary or may combine elements of both. Sometimes they may contain features (such as put and call options) that may or may not oblige the issuer to settle the instrument in cash or other financial assets. Consequently, it is necessary to examine the contractual terms of each component carefully, bearing in mind the definitions of a financial liability and an equity instrument, to determine whether they exhibit characteristics of a financial liability or equity. Once the characteristics of the individual components are determined, they can be combined to arrive at the overall assessment of whether the entire instrument is classified as a financial liability, or an equity instrument, or a compound instrument containing both liability and equity components.

6.5.12 Where an entity issues two or more instruments at (or nearly at) the same time to the same counterparty, the indicators outlined in IAS 39 must be considered when determining whether the contracts are linked and viewed as a single arrangement or as two separate contracts. Indicators that contracts are linked include:

- they are entered into at the same time and in contemplation of one another;

- they have the same counterparty;

- they relate to the same risk;

- there is no apparent economic need or substantive business purpose for structuring the transaction separately that would not also have been accomplished in a single transaction; and

- they cannot be transferred or redeemed separately.

[IAS 39 para IG B.6]

6.5.13 The general classification principles described above appear to be relatively simple, but the application in practice often presents difficulties. The contractual arrangement's substance and its legal form are commonly consistent, but not always. Since the contractual arrangement's substance rather than its legal form takes precedence, there could be situations where instruments that qualify as equity for regulatory or legal purposes are, on closer examination, liabilities for financial reporting purposes.

Reclassifications

6.5.14 Equity or liability classification is made by the entity on initial recognition in accordance with paragraph 15 of IAS 32. However, if the contractual terms and conditions are subsequently changed, it may result in derecognising of the original instrument (equity or liability) and the recognising of a new instrument (liability or equity). The accounting treatment for modifications of the contractual terms of financial liabilities, that may result in derecognising the liability and recognition of an equity instrument is dealt with in chapter 6.6.

6.5.15 The IFRS IC issued rejection wording in November 2006 that clarified the accounting treatment for transfers from equity to liability when the transfer is a result of a change in the instrument's contractual terms. This might be, for example a change in the contractual terms to require a coupon, which was previously at the discretion of the issuer, to be paid on the occurrence of a genuine contingent settlement event. The IFRS IC clarified that a financial liability is initially recognised at the time when the contractual terms are changed, irrespective of whether the change affects the contractual cash flows. The new liability is measured at fair value in accordance with paragraph 43 of IAS 39.

6.5.16 The IFRS IC also observed that the change in the instrument's terms gives rise to derecognising the original equity instrument. Paragraph 33 of IAS 32 states that no gain or loss is recognised in profit and loss on the purchase, sale, issue or cancellation of an entity's own equity instruments. The difference between the carrying amount of the equity instrument and the fair value of the newly-recognised financial liability is recorded in equity at the time the terms are changed. This applies even if the change in terms has no impact on the instrument's expected cash flows.

6.5.17 As far as reclassifications from financial liability to equity are concerned absent any modifications to the instrument's contractual terms and conditions, the guidance on reclassifications is less clear than the case where the contractual terms have changed. IAS 32 is silent on whether a re-assessment is required after initial recognition as paragraph 15 of IAS 32 only prescribes that an entity should classify the instrument, or its component parts, on initial recognition. Therefore, it is possible to argue that an instrument should not be reclassified after inception. On the other hand, paragraph 39 of IAS 39 states that an entity should remove a financial liability (or a part of a financial liability) from its balance sheet when, and only when, it is extinguished; that is when the obligation specified in the contract is discharged or cancelled or expires. Therefore, one could argue that if the contractual obligation that triggered liability classification terminates, then reclassification is appropriate because the obligation has been discharged or cancelled. Because of the lack of clarity in the literature, we believe that both treatments can be supported, and as a result an entity should determine an appropriate accounting policy and apply it consistently.

6.5.18 Consider the following example: An entity issues a 5 year convertible bond where the holder has the option to convert it into the issuers's equity shares after the first year, but where the conversion ratio is only fixed at the end of the first year at the lower of CU5 and 130% of the equity share price. As the number of shares the bond could be converted into is variable, on initial recognition the conversion option is recognised as a separate embedded derivative liability. However, at the end of year one, under the contract's original terms, the conversion ratio is fixed and, therefore, no longer meets the definition of a financial liability. In considering the guidance in IAS 32 above, the change in the conversion ratio from variable to fixed at the end of year 1 would not result in reclassification because the assessment would be based only on the terms at inception of the contract. Alternatively, in considering the guidance in IAS 39, the conversion option would be reclassified from a derivative liability to equity, because the obligation to deliver a variable number of shares upon conversion expires and the obligation to then deliver a fixed number of shares meets the definition of equity.

6.5.19 Reclassifications of puttable instruments and obligations arising on liquidation are dealt with from paragraph 6.5.40.

Contracts that are settled in cash or another financial assets

Contractual obligation to settle in cash or another financial assets

6.5.20 It is apparent from the above IAS 32 definitions of liability and equity instrument that the critical feature that distinguishes a liability from an equity instrument is the existence of a contractual obligation to deliver cash or another financial asset to the holder or to exchange a financial asset or financial liability with the holder under conditions that are potentially unfavourable to the issuer. In other words, if the issuer does not have an unconditional right to avoid delivering cash or another financial asset to settle a contractual obligation, the obligation meets the definition of a liability, with the limited exception of puttable instruments and obligations arising on liquidation that meet the strict criteria set out from paragraph 6.5.29.

6.5.21   An instrument that an issuer may be obliged to settle in cash or another financial instrument is a liability regardless of the manner in which it otherwise could be settled. For example, the obligation to deliver cash may cover the basic obligation either to repay the principal or interest/dividends or both. Also, the obligation need not be discharged in cash or another financial asset; it could be discharged by transfer of other kinds of assets in certain circumstances (for example, a property) as illustrated in paragraph 6.5.44 below. Indeed, in some circumstances it can even be settled by the issuer's own equity instruments. As long as the instrument involves a contractual unconditional obligation to deliver cash or another financial asset, that instrument (or component of the instrument) should be classified and accounted for as a liability (with the exception of certain puttable instruments and obligations arising on liquidation). Some examples of instruments that contain an obligation to transfer cash are considered below:

Example 1 – 6% mandatorily redeemable preference shares with mandatory fixed dividends

Preference share is the name given to any share that has some preferential rights in relation to other classes of shares, particularly in relation to ordinary shares. These preferential rights are of great variety, but refer normally to the right to a *fixed dividend*, although they could also refer to the right on winding up to receive a fixed part of the *capital* or otherwise to participate in the distribution of the company's assets (shares with such rights are often known as participating preference shares).

In determining whether a mandatorily redeemable preference share is a financial liability or an equity instrument, it is necessary to examine the particular contractual rights attaching to the instrument's principal and return components.

The instrument, in this example, provides for mandatory periodic fixed dividend payments and mandatory redemption by the issuer for a fixed amount at a fixed future date. Since there is a contractual obligation to deliver cash (for both dividends and repayment of principal) to the shareholder that cannot be avoided, the instrument is a financial liability in its entirety.

Example 2 – Non-redeemable preference shares with mandatory fixed dividends

When preference shares are non-redeemable, the appropriate classification is determined by the other rights that attach to them. Classification is based on an assessment of the contractual arrangement's substance and the definitions of a financial liability and an equity instrument. [IAS 32 para AG 26].

It is necessary to examine the particular contractual rights attaching to the instrument's principal and return components. In this example, the shares are non-redeemable and thus the amount of the principal has equity characteristics, but the entity has a contractual obligation to pay dividends that provides the shareholders with a lender's return. This obligation is not negated if the entity is unable to pay the dividends because of lack of funds or insufficient distributable profits. Therefore, the obligation to pay the dividends meets the definition of a financial liability. The overall classification is that the shares may be a compound instrument, which may require each component to be accounted for separately (see further para 6.5.91 below). It would be a compound instrument if the coupon was initially set at a rate other than the prevailing market rate (an 'off-market' rate) or the terms specified payment of discretionary dividends in addition to the fixed coupon. If the coupon on the preference shares was set at market rates at the date of issue and there were no provisions for the payment of discretionary dividends, the entire instrument would be classified as a financial liability, because the stream of cash flows is in perpetuity.

Example 3 – Perpetual debt

'Perpetual' debt instruments (such as 'perpetual' bonds, debentures and capital notes) normally provide the holder with the contractual right to receive payments on account of interest at fixed dates extending into the indefinite future. The holder either has no right to receive a return of principal or a right to a return of principal under terms that make it very unlikely or very far in the future.

In this example, the instrument is perpetual and non-redeemable, but the entity has a contractual obligation to deliver cash in the form of interest payments to perpetuity. The obligation to pay interest meets the definition of a financial liability. For example, an entity may issue a financial instrument requiring it to make annual payments in perpetuity equal to a stated interest rate of 8% applied to a stated par or principal amount of C1m. Assuming 8% to be the market rate of interest for the instrument when issued, the instrument is classified as a liability in its entirety at the net present value of the interest payments. In this situation, the instrument's holder and issuer have a financial asset and a financial liability, respectively. [IAS 32 para AG 6].

Example 4 – Zero coupon bond

A zero coupon bond is an instrument where no interest is payable during the instrument's life and that is normally issued at a deep discount to the value at which it will be redeemed. Although there are no mandatory periodic interest payments, the instrument provides for mandatory redemption by the issuer for a determinable amount at a fixed or determinable future date. Since there is a contractual obligation to deliver cash for the value at which the bond will be redeemed, the instrument is classified as a financial liability.

6.5.22 Paragraph 19 of IAS 32 states that a contractual obligation does not give rise to a financial liability if the entity has an unconditional right to avoid delivering cash or another financial asset in settlement of that obligation. Shareholders as a collective body make key decisions affecting an entity's financial position and performance over its life (for example regarding the distribution of dividends). Hence, their decisions have to be analysed from an accounting perspective. Shareholders can make decisions as part of the entity (as members of the entity's corporate governance structure) or they can be separate and distinct from the entity itself when making these decisions (as holders of a particular instrument). In light of the accounting principles under IAS 32, the role of shareholders – that is whether they are viewed as 'part of the entity' or as 'separate and distinct from the entity' – is critical in determining the classification of financial instruments where the entity's shareholders decide whether the entity delivers cash or another financial asset under those instruments.

6.5.23 Shares usually have voting rights leading to a two-fold role for a shareholder: (1) a holder of a financial instrument issued by the entity and (2) a member of the corporate governance structure of the entity. In other words, in addition to the contractual rights to cash flows (for example, dividends), the shareholder has a contractual right to participate in the decision-making process of the entity's governing body. Shareholder rights in relation to the entity's decision making process are generally exercised collectively in a general shareholder meeting (GSM). In many jurisdictions, corporate law stipulates that the GSM is one of the governing bodies of the entity and prescribes a specific process regarding how a GSM is to be held, who is entitled to propose an agenda item and how decisions are to be taken. In order to determine whether collective decisions of shareholders are decisions of the entity, it is necessary to determine whether these decisions are made as part of the entity's normal decision making process for similar transactions.

6.5.24 If the decisions are made as part of the entity's normal decision-making process for similar transactions, the shareholders are considered to be part of the entity. For example, if an entity's equity instruments embody a contractual obligation to pay cash, but the shareholders can as part of their normal decision making process for this type of transaction refuse to make such a cash payment, the shares would be classified as equity. The entity in this case has an unconditional right to avoid the payment of cash. [IAS 32 para 19].

6.5.25 If the decisions are not made as part of the entity's normal decision making process for similar transactions (for example, one shareholder or a class of shareholders can make the decision and this is not the process the entity generally follows to make financial decisions), the shareholders are viewed as separate and distinct from the entity. For example, if a single shareholder can make a decision that creates a contractual obligation for the issuer to pay cash for the entity's shares and such decisions normally require a majority of the shareholder votes, these shares would be classified as a liability. The entity in this case does not have an unconditional right to avoid payment of cash. See paragraph 6.5.76 for more examples.

Restriction on the ability to satisfy contractual obligations

6.5.26 A restriction on the ability of an entity to satisfy a contractual obligation, such as lack of access to foreign currency or the need to obtain approval for payment from a regulatory authority, does not negate the entity's contractual obligation or the holder's contractual right under the instrument. [IAS 32 para 19(a)]. For example, an obligation is not negated even if the instrument's terms are such that the amount payable on redemption is dependent on the company having sufficient distributable profits or reserves. A type of income bond where the bond is not redeemable by the issuer, but interest is payable only in the event that the issuer has sufficient distributable profits, is such an instrument. The bond would be classified as a liability because of the obligation to pay interest. The fact that the obligation to pay is dependent on the existence of profits makes the obligation contingent, but it does not remove the obligation (see further chapter 6.2).

Puttable instruments and obligations arising on liquidation

6.5.27 Other than those instruments that meet the criteria set out from paragraph 6.5.34 below, financial instruments that give the holder the right to put them back to the issuer for cash or another financial asset (a 'puttable instrument') are financial liabilities. For example, an entity that issues a preference share that is puttable by the holder at some future date would recognise a financial liability. The holder has a put option that requires the issuer to redeem the instrument for cash or another financial asset at some future date. Since the existence of an option for the holder to put the instrument back to the issuer for cash or another financial asset means that the issuer does not have an unconditional right to avoid delivering cash or cash equivalent, the puttable instrument meets the definition of a financial liability. This is the case whether or not the amount of cash or other financial assets to be delivered to the holder is fixed. Instruments that also give rise to a financial liability include obligations arising upon liquidation in finite life entities (except those meeting the criteria set forth in para 6.5.34), as noted in the example below.

> **Example – Obligation arising on the liquidation of the issuer**
>
> A limited partnership has a finite life of 25 years. The partnership's equity will be redeemed at the end of its term.
>
> In this situation, unless the criteria in paragraph 6.5.34 are met, the partnership's equity will be presented as a liability because the amount is payable only on liquidation and liquidation is certain (that is, not contingent) as the entity has a finite life.
>
> Even where a partnership has an indefinite life, if a partner's equity interest is redeemable upon a partner's death, that partner's equity interest should be classified as a liability, unless the criteria in paragraph 6.5.34 are met. This is because the redemption is based on an event that is certain to occur, although the partnership itself is not being liquidated.

6.5.28 Financial instruments that would be classified as equity if the holders did not have the right to request redemption are equity if the entity has the unconditional right to refuse redemption of the instrument. This is the case even if, in practice, the entity rarely does refuse a holder's request for redemption or if the unconditional right to refuse redemption arises from local law, regulation or the entity's governing charter rather than the terms of the instrument itself. Sometimes redemption is prohibited only if conditions, such as liquidity constraints, are met (or not met). In such cases, the entity still has an obligation in respect of the holder's redemption rights, as the conditions merely defer the payment of a liability already incurred. Alternatively, an unconditional prohibition may be partial. For example, a co-operative entity may be prohibited from redeeming its members' shares if redemption would cause the number of shares to fall below a specified level. In such circumstances, only members' shares in excess of the prohibition against redemption are liabilities. The number of shares or the amount of paid-in capital subject to a redemption prohibition may change over time. Such a change in the redemption prohibition leads to a transfer between financial liabilities and equity. The amount, timing and reason for the transfer should be separately disclosed. [IFRIC 2 paras 5-13].

6.5.29 In February 2008 the IASB published amendments to IAS 32 and IAS 1, 'Puttable financial instruments and obligations arising on liquidation' (the amendment). Some financial instruments, commonly issued by open-ended mutual funds, unit trusts, partnerships and some co-operative entities, allow the holder to 'put' the instrument – that is, require the issuer to redeem the instrument for cash or another financial asset – on terms that give the holder an equity-like return. Before the amendment, such financial instruments were classified as financial liabilities rather than equity, because of the contractual obligation for the issuer to deliver cash if the put is exercised by the holder, as discussed above.

6.5.30 The amendment introduces a limited exception to this rule. It requires financial instruments that would otherwise meet the definition of a financial liability to be classified as equity where certain strict criteria are met, as set out in paragraph 6.5.34. Those instruments addressed by the amendment are:

- Puttable financial instruments. A puttable instrument is defined as a financial instrument that gives the holder the right to put the instrument back to the issuer for cash or another financial asset or is automatically put back to the issuer on the occurrence of an uncertain future event or the death or retirement of the instrument holder. [IAS 32 para 11]. The amendment does not apply to instruments where the instrument holders can force liquidation only in their role as part of the entity's management (that is where they are members of the entity's corporate governance structure and are acting as such), rather than as individual holders of an instrument. See paragraph 6.5.22.

- Instruments, or components of instruments, that impose on the entity an obligation to deliver to another party a *pro rata* share of the entity's net assets only on liquidation. The obligation arises because liquidation is either certain to occur (such as in limited life entities) or is uncertain to occur but is at the option of the instrument holder. [IAS 32 para 16C]. In considering whether liquidation at the option of the instrument holder causes the instrument to be subject to the amendment it is necessary to consider whether liquidation arises from a shareholder acting in its instrument holder capacity or in its shareholder capacity. Only the former would be considered in the scope of paragraph 16C.

6.5.31 The amendment's scope is limited to non-derivative contracts. Derivative contracts (such as warrants) to be settled by the issue of a fixed number of puttable financial instruments or obligations arising on liquidation classified as equity under the amendment for a fixed amount of cash or other financial asset cannot be equity themselves. [IAS 32 para 11].

6.5.32 The amendment should not be used by analogy. [IAS 32 para 96B]. Furthermore, the classification of instruments under this exception should be restricted to the accounting for such an instrument under IAS 32, IAS 39, IFRS 7 and IAS 1. The instruments should not be considered an equity instrument under other guidance, in particular IFRS 2. [IAS 32 para 96C].

6.5.33 The concurrent amendment to IAS 1 requires disclosures about financial instruments classified as equity as a result of the amendment to IAS 32. Detail about these disclosures is given in chapter 23.

Criteria to be classified as equity

6.5.34 A non-derivative puttable instrument or obligation on liquidation (for example, arising in a limited life entity) is classified as equity only if all of the following criteria are met:

Criteria	Comment
1 The financial instrument is in the most subordinated class of instruments. That is, it: ■ has no priority over other claims to the entity's assets on liquidation; and ■ does not need to be converted to another instrument before it is in the most subordinated class. [IAS 32 paras 16A(b) and 16C(b)].	The instrument's claim on liquidation is assessed as if the entity were to liquidate on the date of classification. [IAS 32 para AG14B]. If an entity has two equally subordinated classes of instrument with different terms, neither can be classified as equity under the amendment. Additionally, if an open-ended investment fund has a small class of non-redeemable voting management shares that are the most subordinated, and a large class of non-voting investor shares that are puttable at fair value at the option of the holder, the investor shares are not the most subordinated class of instrument. Therefore, the non-voting investor shares cannot be classified as equity, regardless of the value or number of the management shares.

2 For puttable instruments, all instruments in its class should have identical features. [IAS 32 para 16A(c)].

   For obligations arising on liquidation, only the obligation on liquidation should be identical for all instruments in that class. [IAS 32 para 16C(c)].

To be considered identical, all puttable instruments in a class should, for example:

- have the same formula or other method to calculate the redemption price;
- rank equally on liquidation;
- have identical voting rights; and
- have all other features identical (for example, calls, management fees, currency of denomination).

For example, an open-ended fund has two sub-funds – sub-fund A and sub-fund B – and two classes of puttable shares – A shares and B shares – whose returns are based on the performance of sub-funds A and B respectively. The A and B shares are both the most subordinated class of shares in the fund's consolidated financial statements. However, neither are equity, as they do not have identical features because they carry rights to different sub-funds.

3 The instrument should entitle the holder to a *pro rata* share of the entity's net assets on liquidation. [IAS 32 paras 16A(a) and 16C(a)].

An instrument with a preferential right on liquidation is not an instrument with an entitlement to a *pro rata* share of the entity's net assets. So if a puttable instrument has a right to a fixed dividend on liquidation in addition to a share of the entity's net assets, but the other instruments in the class do not have the same right on liquidation, none of the shares in that class are equity. [IAS 32 para AG14C].

4 For puttable instruments only, the total expected cash flows attributable to the instrument over the instrument's life should be based substantially on the profit or loss, the change in recognised net assets, or the change in the fair value of entity over the instrument's life (excluding any effects of the instrument). [IAS 32 para 16A(e)].

Profit or loss and the change in recognised net assets should be measured in accordance with the relevant IFRSs and not any other GAAP. [IAS 32 para AG14E].

Cash flows attributable to the instrument over its life should be based on the profit or loss or change in the entity's net assets as a whole, not just part of the entity's business.

This condition would be met where the put is for cash equivalent to the entity's:

- fair value;
- IFRS book value of assets; or
- approximation to fair value using a formula based on net profit, for example, multiples of EBITDA, provided that the formula (for example, the multiple used) is reviewed regularly to ensure that it results in an approximate of fair value.

5 There are no other instruments that:
- substantially restrict or fix the return earned by the instrument holder; and
- have cash flows based substantially on profit or loss; the change in recognised net assets; or the change in the fair value of the entity over the instrument's life (excluding any effects of the instrument).

[IAS 32 paras 16B and 16D].

If an instrument provides a fixed or limited return because of the interaction with other instruments issued by the entity (for example, another instrument is participating in the share of net assets), it is not equity.

Non-financial contracts with the holder of the instrument should be ignored if those contracts have similar terms and conditions to an equivalent contract that might occur between a non-instrument holder and the entity. However, if the entity cannot determine that the non-financial contract with the puttable instrument holder is similar to an equivalent contract that might occur between a non-instrument holder and the issuing entity, it should not classify the puttable instrument as an equity instrument.

Examples of contracts entered into on normal commercial terms with unrelated parties that are unlikely to prevent puttable instruments from being classified as equity include:

- Instruments with cash flows substantially based on individual assets of the entity or on a percentage of revenue, such as commission arrangements.
- Employee profit-related performance bonuses.

■ Contracts requiring the payment of an insignificant percentage of profit for services rendered or goods provided. [IAS 32 para AG14J].

6 For puttable instruments only, the instrument should not contain any liability features, other than the put itself. [IAS 32 para 16A(d)].

For instruments containing obligations arising on liquidation there is no requirement for there to be no other contractual obligations, so the instrument may be compound (for example, a compound instrument where the liability component is extinguished over the instrument's life).

However, a puttable instrument cannot have another contractual obligation apart from the put itself and, hence, can never be a compound instrument.

For example, a puttable financial instrument that contains an obligation to either:

■ distribute current period profits on the demand of each holder based on a *pro rata* share of the entity's profits; or

■ distribute all taxable income as a requirement of the entity's constitution

cannot be classed as an equity instrument.

Transactions entered into by an instrument holder other than as owner of the entity

6.5.35   In certain situations the holder of a puttable instrument may enter into transactions with the entity in a role other than that of an owner. For example, a partner in a partnership may also provide management services to the entity or be remunerated for providing a financial guarantee for the partnership's debts. In other cases, rebates are given to the instrument holders based on their services rendered or business generated during the current and previous years. Such cash flows and contractual terms and conditions should be disregarded for the purposes of determining the classification of an instrument under all the criteria above, as long as they are similar to an equivalent transaction that might occur between a non-instrument holder and the issuing entity, that is, at arm's length. [IAS 32 para AG14I]. This is because such cash flows and contractual features are separate and distinct from the cash flows and contractual features of the puttable financial instrument.

Impact on consolidation

6.5.36 Instruments issued by a subsidiary that meet the criteria outlined above, and are, therefore, within the scope of the amendment at a separate or individual financial statements level, are not considered to be the most subordinated class from the group's perspective. [IAS 32 para BC 68]. Furthermore, the total expected cash flows over the life of a puttable financial instrument issued by a subsidiary will not be substantially based on the profit or loss or change in net assets of the whole group, but rather will be a subset of that group, being that of the subsidiary. Consequently, a puttable non-controlling interest is always classified as a liability on consolidation, even if it is classified as an equity interest in the subsidiary's own financial statements [IAS 32 para AG 29A].

6.5.37 Instruments issued by the parent that meet the criteria outlined above, and are, therefore, within the scope of the amendment at a separate financial statements level, in most cases will continue to be classified as equity at a consolidated financial statements level. Any non-controlling interest reflected at the group level does not generally meet the conditions in paragraph 16B of IAS 32 and, therefore, will generally not prevent such parent puttable instruments from being classified as equity on consolidation. This is because:

■ cash flows attributable to the non-controlling interest are based on a subset of the consolidated net assets, that is, net assets of the respective subsidiary, rather than consolidated net assets; and

■ in most cases the non-controlling interest will not have the effect of substantially restricting or fixing the residual return attributable to holders of the parent's puttable instruments.

[IAS 32 paras 16B, AG14J(a)].

6.5.38 If, however, the non-controlling interest meets the conditions in paragraph 16B of IAS 32 the parent's puttable instruments that meet the conditions for equity classification at a separate financial statements level are classified as a liability on consolidation. This will be the case when:

■ the subsidiary's net assets represent substantially all of the consolidated net assets such that the cash flows attributable to the non-controlling interest are substantially based on consolidated net assets; and

■ the non-controlling interest in the respective subsidiary is so significant that combined with the condition above it has the effect of substantially restricting or fixing the residual return attributable to holders of the parent's puttable instruments.

Judgement is applied to determine whether the subsidiary's net assets and the non-controlling interest in the respective subsidiary are so significant that the parent's puttable instruments classified as equity at a separate financial statements level are classified as a liability on consolidation.

6.5.39 The evaluation of instruments, or components of instruments, that impose on the entity an obligation to deliver to another party a *pro rata* share of the net assets of the entity only on liquidation will follow the criteria above related to the impact on consolidation as the requirements of paragraph 16D of IAS 32 are consistent with paragraph 16B.

Reclassification of puttable instruments and obligations arising on liquidation

6.5.40 Instruments will be in the scope of the amendment from the date when the instrument has all the features and meets the criteria set out above. This may not occur at the date of issue of the instrument, so it is necessary to reassess the classification if there is a change in relevant circumstances. For example, an entity may issue or redeem other instruments that change the most subordinated class of shares, which may require reclassification of some financial instruments from debt to equity or vice versa. [IAS 32 para 16E]. See chapter 23 for specific disclosure requirements on such a reclassification.

6.5.41 An entity should reclassify a financial instrument when appropriate, as follows:

■ Reclassify an equity instrument to a financial liability from the date the instrument ceases to have all the features required by the amendment. The financial liability is measured at the instrument's fair value at the date of reclassification. Any difference between the carrying value of the equity instrument and liability's fair value on the date of reclassification is recognised in equity.

■ Reclassify a financial liability as equity from the date the instrument has all the features required by the amendment. The equity instrument should be measured at the carrying value of the financial liability at the date of reclassification. [IAS 32 para 16F].

Own share buy-back programmes

6.5.42 During certain times of the year (for example, before an entity releases its results), listed companies are prohibited by certain local listing rules from buying their own shares in the market. The local listing rules may permit other arrangements to be entered into with independent third parties that result in the listed entity's shares being purchased on behalf of the listed entity, for example, by a bank. The contract requires the company to buy the shares the bank has purchased immediately after the prohibition period. For further details on own share buy-back programmes see chapter 23.

6.5.43 Own share buy-back programmes contain an obligation for an entity to purchase its own equity instruments for cash or another financial asset from the third party. This, therefore, gives rise to a financial liability for the present value of the redemption amount (for example, the present value of the forward repurchase price, option exercise price or other redemption amount). [IAS 32 para 23].

Absence of explicit obligations

6.5.44 IAS 32 states that the obligation to deliver cash or another financial asset need not be explicitly stated in the instrument. It may be established indirectly. However, the indirect obligation must be established through the terms and conditions of the financial instrument. [IAS 32 para 20]. IAS 32 clarifies the notion that an instrument may establish an obligation indirectly through its terms and conditions in two specific situations that are considered below.

6.5.45 First, a financial instrument may contain a non-financial obligation that must be settled if, and only if, the entity fails to make distributions or to redeem the instrument. If the entity can avoid a transfer of cash or another financial asset only by settling the non-financial obligation, the financial instrument is a financial liability. [IAS 32 para 20(a)].

> **Example – Settlement of obligation by transfer of non-cash asset**
>
> A property company raises C150m for constructing a number of properties. The loan has a maturity period of 5 years. The loan agreement stipulates that the property company must transfer to the lender one of its investment properties if it is unable to settle the loan for cash at maturity.
>
> In this agreement, if the property company is unable to settle the loan at maturity for cash, it is obliged to settle the obligation by transferring to the lender one of its other investment properties that, at the time of the settlement, may well be in excess of C150m. Therefore, an indirect financial obligation arises as the agreement contains a non-financial obligation that can be avoided only by making a transfer of cash. Hence, it is a financial liability.

6.5.46 The second situation is where a financial instrument is a financial liability if it provides that on settlement the entity will deliver either:

- cash or another financial asset; or
- its own shares whose value is determined to exceed substantially the value of the cash or other financial asset.

Although the entity does not have an explicit contractual obligation to deliver cash or another financial asset, the value of the share settlement alternative is such that the entity will have little choice but to redeem the obligation in cash. In any event, the holder has been guaranteed, in substance, receipt of an amount that is at least equal to the cash settlement option. Hence, the instrument is a financial liability.

[IAS 32 para 20(b)].

6.5.47 The IFRS IC clarified in March 2006 that where an instrument (the 'base' instrument) contains a clause that requires cash or other financial assets to be delivered on that base instrument if there is a contractual obligation to make payment on another (the 'linked') instrument, then the inclusion of this linker clause would establish an indirect obligation to deliver cash or another financial assets on the base instrument. As a result the IFRS IC agreed that the base instrument would be classified as a financial liability.

> **Example – Financial instrument ('base' instrument) linked to another (the 'linked') instrument**
>
> An entity issues non-redeemable callable preference shares (the 'base' instrument) with dividends that must be paid if interest is paid on another (the 'linked') instrument. The issuer must pay the interest on the 'linked' instrument that is also perpetual.
>
> In this example, the linkage to the linked instrument, on which there is a contractual obligation to pay interest, results in an indirect contractual obligation to pay dividends on the base instrument. If the linked instrument is callable by the issuer at any time, the issuer could avoid paying the dividends on base instrument. Therefore, until the linked instrument is called, a contractual obligation to pay dividends on the base instrument exists. If the present value of the expected dividend stream to perpetuity is equal to the whole principal of the financial instrument, the entire instrument would be classified as a liability. On the other hand, if the present value of the expected dividend stream is not equal to the whole principal of the financial instrument, the residual amount is attributable to the equity component.

6.5.48 Indirect obligations are considered part of the terms and conditions of a contract. A change to the indirect obligations of an instrument, which would include the repurchase by the entity of the 'linked' instrument in the above example, is, therefore, considered a change to the contract's contractual terms and conditions.

6.5.49 Whether changes to the terms of a 'base' liability that remove any contractual obligation to pay cash or transfer another financial asset result in extinguishment accounting are a matter of accounting policy choice as such changes are not specifically addressed in IAS 32 and such a transaction is not within IFRIC 19's scope. An entity can apply the same accounting treatment as when convertible debt is converted into shares (see para 6.5.96 below) where the existing debt's carrying value is transferred to equity and no gain or loss arises on conversion. Alternatively, the entity applies the extinguishment principles in chapter 6.6 where the existing instrument is derecognised and the new equity instruments issued are recognised at fair value. The difference would be recognised in profit or loss. [IAS 39 para 41].

Contracts settled in cash or other financial asset that are discretionary or at the option of the issuer

6.5.50 An equity instrument is any contract that evidences a residual interest in an entity's assets after deducting all of its liabilities. Therefore, only those instruments (or components of instruments) that do not meet the definition of a liability will be classified as equity. In other words, the entity must have an unconditional right to avoid delivery of cash or another financial asset. A typical example is an entity's non-puttable ordinary shares. The exception to this principle is when a puttable instrument or an obligation arising on liquidation meets the strict criteria in the February 2008 amendment to IAS 32 to be classified as equity (see para 6.5.34).

Payments that are discretionary or at the option of the issuer

6.5.51 If an instrument does not have a contractual (including contingent) obligation to deliver cash or another financial asset, it is classified as an equity instrument. Therefore, where payments of interest/dividends or the principal amount or both are discretionary in nature, equity treatment is appropriate for some or all of the instrument. For example, dividends payable on non-puttable ordinary shares depend on the entity's profitability. However, there is no compulsion on the directors to declare a dividend even though a past pattern of dividend payments may have created an expectation on the shareholders that a dividend will be declared and payable. Such discretionary payments do not create contractual obligations, because the directors cannot be required to deliver cash or another financial asset to the shareholders. Nevertheless, a liability must be recognised in respect of such non-puttable ordinary shares where the directors formally act to make a distribution and become legally obligated to the shareholders to do so. This may be the case following the declaration of a dividend, or when the entity is being wound up and any assets remaining after the satisfaction of liabilities become distributable to shareholders. [IAS 32 para AG 13]. Chapter 23 provides further guidance on the accounting for dividends.

> **Example – Non-redeemable preference shares with dividend payments linked to ordinary shares**
>
> An entity issues an non-redeemable preference shares on which dividends are payable only if the entity also pays a dividend on its ordinary shares ('dividend pusher').
>
> In this example, the dividend payments on the preference shares are discretionary and not contractual, because no dividends can be paid if no dividends are paid on the ordinary shares, which are an equity instrument. As the perpetual preference shares contain no contractual obligation ever to pay dividends and there is no obligation to repay the principal, they should be classified as equity in their entirety.
>
> Where the dividend payments are also cumulative, that is, if no dividends are paid on the ordinary shares, the preference dividends are deferred, the perpetual shares will be classified as equity only if the dividends can be deferred indefinitely and the entity does not have any contractual obligations whatsoever to pay those dividends.
>
> A liability for the dividend payable would be recognised once the dividend is declared.

6.5.52 The classification of an instrument as equity or a financial liability would not be impacted by, for example:

- A history of making distributions.

- An intention to make distributions in the future.

- A possible negative impact on price of the issuer's ordinary shares if distributions are not made (because of restrictions on paying dividends on the ordinary shares if dividends are not paid on the preference shares).

- The amount of the issuer's reserves.

- An issuer's expectation of a profit or loss for a period.

- An ability or inability of the issuer to influence the amount of its profit or loss for the period.

[IAS 32 para AG 26].

6.5.53 As explained in paragraph 6.5.27 unless, exceptionally, the criteria to be treated as equity in the February 2008 amendment to IAS 32 are met, where the holder has a put option that requires the issuer to redeem equity shares at some future date, the instrument (that is the equity shares and the put) is treated as a liability; the issuer cannot avoid settling the principal in cash. On the other hand, as discussed in chapter 6.3, if the issuer has an option to call or redeem what would be otherwise equity shares for cash at some future date, the instrument does not satisfy the definition of a financial liability as the issuer can avoid settling the principal in cash. This is because the issuer does not have a present obligation to transfer financial assets to the shareholders. In this case, redemption of the shares is solely at the issuer's discretion. An obligation may arise, however, when the issuer of the shares exercises its option, usually by formally notifying the shareholders of an intention to redeem the shares. [IAS 32 para AG 25].

6.5.54 The accounting treatment becomes more complex when the issuer has the option to avoid settling an instrument in cash through exercising an option to convert the instrument into a fixed number of equity shares, as illustrated below.

Example – Instrument convertible only at the option of issuer

An entity issues an instrument with the following terms

- The instrument has a stated 5% coupon that is mandatory.

- The issuer has an option to convert the instrument into a fixed number of its own shares at any time. The holder has no conversion option.

- The issuer has an option to redeem the instrument in cash at any time. The redemption price is the fair value of the fixed number of shares into which the instrument would have converted if it had been converted. The holder has no redemption option.

- The instrument has a 30 year stated maturity and, if not converted or redeemed previously, will be repaid in cash at maturity for its par value plus accrued but unpaid interest.

There are two valid views regarding the classification of the instrument by the issuer depending on analysis of the host contract (that is, liability host versus equity host). Therefore, we consider that an issuer has a policy choice between the following two treatments

(1)   The host contract can be viewed as an equity instrument, as the issuer has the ability to convert the instrument into a fixed number of its own shares at any time. It, therefore, has the ability to avoid making a cash payment or settling the instrument in a variable number of its own shares. Any feature that may have been considered to be an embedded derivative would not meet the definition of a derivative on a stand-alone basis given the ability to avoid payment. Hence, the issuer's conversion and redemption options would not be separated and the entire instrument would be classified as equity.

(2)   The issuer can classify this instrument as a liability, being a hybrid instrument comprised of:

(a)   a host liability component for the obligation to pay the mandatory coupons and to repay the instrument at maturity; and

(b)   an embedded derivative component for the entity's option to settle the instrument early in either a fixed number of its own shares or cash of an equivalent value. As these two early settlement mechanisms are interdependent, they are viewed as part of a single embedded derivative rather than as two separate embedded derivatives.

If option 2 is taken as a policy choice then the issuer has a second decision to make with regards measurement. On initial recognition either the fair value option can be taken in accordance with IAS 39 (as there is a significant embedded derivative) and the entire contract will be measured at fair value through profit or loss, or the issuer can value the host liability contract at amortised cost and separate the embedded derivative.

This policy choice would not be applicable where the conversion would result in issuing a number of shares that would substantially exceed the value of cash settlement. This is due to the fact there is an implicit obligation to settle in cash under paragraph 20(b)(ii) of IAS 32. While these circumstances are expected to be rare (and would need to be assessed as part of the contract at inception), paragraph 6.5.46 regarding implicit contractual terms should be considered in analysing the instrument.

6.5.55   Where a financial instrument only results in a contractual obligation for the issuer to deliver cash or other financial assets upon the occurrence of an uncertain future event, the instrument may still need to be classified as a financial liability from initial recognition if it meets the definition of a contingent settlement event. See paragraph 6.5.75 for more details.

Contracts that will or may be settled in an entity's own equity instruments

6.5.56   A contract is not an equity instrument solely because it may result in the receipt or delivery of the entity's own equity instruments. [IAS 32 para 21]. The classification of contracts that will or may be settled in the entity's own equity instruments is dependent on whether there is variability in either the number of own equity instruments delivered and/or variability in the amount of cash or other financial assets received, or whether both are fixed.

6.5.57 A contract that will be settled by the entity receiving (or delivering) a fixed number of its own equity instruments in exchange for a fixed amount of cash or another financial asset is an equity instrument. [IAS 32 para 22]. This is commonly referred to as the 'fixed for fixed' requirement. For example, an entity receives C100 upfront from the holder to issue 100 of the entity's own equity in three years time. This would meet the 'fixed for fixed' requirement as both the number of own equity shares delivered and the cash received is fixed when the financial instrument is initially recognised. The instrument would meet the definition of an equity instrument as the holder gets a residual interest in the entity. By fixing upfront the amount paid and the number of shares received the holder benefits from any upside and suffers the loss from any fall in the residual value of the entity.

6.5.58 However, an entity may have a contractual right or obligation to receive or deliver a number of its own shares or other equity instruments that varies so that the fair value of the entity's own equity instrument to be received or delivered equals the amount of the contractual right or obligation. Such a contract may be for a fixed amount or an amount that fluctuates in part or in full in response to changes in a variable. [IAS 32 para 21]. It would be inappropriate to account for such contracts as an equity instrument when an entity's own equity instruments are used 'as currency' as such a contract represents a right or obligation for a specified amount rather than a specified residual equity interest. Therefore, such a contract would be classified as a financial liability. The underlying variable can include the entity's own share price. [IAS 32 para AG 27(d)].

> **Example 1 – Own shares to the value of C1 million**
>
> An entity receives C1m in exchange for its promise that it will deliver its own equity shares in an amount sufficient to equal a value of C1m at a future date. If the share price at the date on delivery of the contract is C5, the entity would be required to issue 200,000 shares ie a total value of C1m.
>
> On the day the issuer delivers its own equity, the holder would be indifferent whether it received cash of C1m or shares to the value of C1m which it could sell and receive C1m in cash. Therefore, the entity is using its own equity as currency and as such the holder does not get a full residual interest. Hence the financial instrument is a liability.

Example 2 – Bermudan option with fixed but different strike prices

An entity issues an option to sell a fixed number of its own equity shares at a specified exercise price. The terms of the option state that the specified exercise price varies with the share price of the entity such that:

Share price	Conversion ratio
0-10C	10 shares at 1C per share
11-20C	10 shares at 1.5C per share

The variability in the exercise price, as a function of share price of the entity, results in a variable amount of cash for a fixed number of shares. The 'fixed for fixed' requirement is, therefore, violated. The option is, therefore, classified as a derivative financial liability and not as an equity instrument.

Example 3 – Call options where the underlying is an exchange ratio

Entities A, B and X are all listed companies. Entity A purchases an option to buy 5% of the share capital of entity X from entity B in return for entity A delivering its own equity shares to entity B. The exchange ratio is fixed when the option is written (for example, entity A pays 0.8 of entity A's own shares for the purchase of an option over 1 share of entity X).

This exchange ratio will violate the 'fixed for fixed' requirement. The fixed number of entity A's shares that entity A may issue is not equal to a fixed amount of cash, as the value of each share acquired in exchange can vary. Therefore, entity A must treat its purchased option as a derivative instrument under IAS 39.

6.5.59   The IASB was concerned that restricting the definition of an underlying variable could lead to structuring opportunities and abuse. Therefore, the standard requires that all forms of variability in either the own shares received or delivered, or the cash or another financial asset delivered or received, would result in financial asset or financial liability classification.

6.5.60   A contract that will be settled by an entity delivering a fixed number of its own equity instruments in exchange for a fixed amount of foreign currency (that is a currency other than the functional currency of the entity) is a financial liability. Apart from the exception described in paragraph 6.5.61, this is a liability because an obligation denominated in a foreign currency represents a variable amount of cash in the entity's functional currency. A foreign currency convertible bond (see example at para 6.5.105) is, therefore, a financial liability made up of two components. These components are: (1) a host bond denominated in the foreign currency (whose foreign exchange risk is accounted for under IAS 21) and (2) an embedded derivative which is a written option for the holder to exchange the foreign currency bond for a fixed number of functional currency denominated shares.

6.5.61   The IASB published an amendment to IAS 32, on the classification of rights issues, on 8 October 2009. The amendment addresses the accounting for rights issues (including rights, options and warrants) that are denominated in a currency other than the functional currency of the issuer. The amendment states that, if such rights are issued *pro rata* to an entity's existing shareholders for a fixed amount of any currency, they should be classified as equity, regardless of the currency in which the exercise price is denominated. This is a narrow amendment and should not be extended to other instruments by analogy (for example, warrants or rights issues on other than a *pro rata* basis and foreign currency denominated convertible bonds – see para 6.5.105). The amendment is effective for annual periods beginning on or after 1 February 2010. An example of an entity that has applied the amendment is shown in Table 6.5.1 below.

Table 6.5.1 – classification of rights issues

HSBC Holdings plc – Annual report – 31 December 2009

1 Basis of preparation (extract)

(a) Compliance with International Financial Reporting Standards (extract)

During 2009, HSBC adopted the following significant standards and amendments to standards:

- 'Classification of Rights Issues – Amendment to IAS 32', ('the amendment') which is effective for annual periods beginning on or after 1 February 2010, with early adoption permitted. HSBC has elected to adopt the amendment in advance of the effective date and, as required by IAS 8, has applied the amendment retrospectively. The amendment requires that rights issues, options or warrants to acquire a fixed number of the entity's own equity instruments for a fixed amount of any currency are equity instruments if the entity offers the rights issues, options or warrants pro rata to all of its existing owners of the same class of its own non-derivative equity instruments. The offer of rights by HSBC Holdings plc to its shareholders on 20 March 2009 was accounted for as an equity instrument, as required by the amendment, in the consolidated financial statements of HSBC and the separate financial statements of HSBC Holdings.

2 Summary of significant accounting policies (extract)

(ac) Rights issues

Rights issues to acquire a fixed number of the entity's own equity instruments for a fixed amount of any currency are equity instruments if the entity offers the rights issues pro rata to all of its existing owners of the same class of its own non-derivative equity instruments. On initial recognition, these rights are recognised in shareholders' equity and are not subsequently re-measured during the offer period. Following the exercise of the rights and the allotment of new shares, the cash proceeds of the rights issue are recognised in shareholders' equity. Incremental costs directly attributable to the rights issue are shown as a deduction from the proceeds, net of tax.

41 Rights issue (extract)

On 2 March 2009, HSBC Holdings announced its proposal to raise £12.5 billion (US$17.8 billion), net of expenses, by way of a fully underwritten rights issue. Under the proposal, HSBC offered its shareholders the opportunity to acquire 5 new ordinary shares for every 12 ordinary shares at a price of 254 pence per new ordinary share. For shareholders on the Hong Kong and Bermuda Overseas Branch Registers this offer was expressed in Hong Kong dollars and US dollars, respectively, fixed at published exchange rates on 27 February 2009. The proposal was subject to authorisation by the shareholders which was obtained at a general meeting held on 19 March 2009. The offer period commenced on 20 March 2009 and closed for acceptance on 3 April 2009. Dealing in the new shares began on 6 April 2009.

For details of called-up share capital and other equity instruments see Note 37.

6.5.62 Some financial instruments (denominated in the same currency as the issuer's functional currency) may be settled in a variable number of own equity instruments but also include a cap or floor or both (that is, a collar) that limits that variability. The existence of the cap, floor or collar does not change the instrument's classification from being a financial liability, as it is settled in a variable number of shares. However, it is necessary to determine whether the cap, floor or collar represents an embedded derivative and, if so, whether it is required to be separated out from the host instrument, as discussed in the examples below.

> **Example 1 – Instruments that are settled in a variable number of shares but subject to a cap**
>
> An entity issues an instrument that is settled at the end of the year by delivering equity shares to the value of C100. The fair value of the shares at the date of issue is C10. The instrument also contains a cap that limits the number of shares that the entity is required to deliver to 20 shares in order to prevent excessive dilution of the existing shareholders through the issue of new shares.
>
> There are two acceptable views on how the cap should be accounted for. Therefore, the issuer has an accounting policy choice between the following two treatments.
>
> *View 1 – The contract is a non-derivative liability to deliver a variable number of shares*
> The contract is an obligation to issue a variable number of shares to the value of *100*. The entire instrument is a liability on the grounds that the 'fixed for fixed' requirement in paragraph 16(b)(i) of IAS 32 is not met for the instrument as a whole, because the instrument will be settled in a variable number of shares. The number of shares to be issued is dependent on the share price at the date of settlement and is, therefore, variable.
>
> Paragraph 25 of IAS 32 further supports this view, because the movement in share price that determines the number of shares to be delivered under the contract (that is, to the value of 100) is outside the control of the issuer and the holder.
>
> *View 2 – Contract contains a debt host with a purchased put*
> The host instrument is an obligation to deliver a *variable number of shares* which is a liability. The instrument also contains an embedded derivative whose effect is to cap the amount of shares the entity will have to deliver according to the debt host, so that, overall, the issuer does not deliver shares in excess of the cap. This embedded derivative can be viewed as a purchased put that will be net share settled (that is, the number of shares to be delivered under the put will vary depending on the share price so that the overall contract results in the delivery of the capped number of shares).
>
> As the cap is not closely related to the debt host (it is linked to movements in the share price), the embedded cap would need to be bifurcated and accounted for at fair value through profit and loss (assuming the fair value option is not used for the entire contract).

Example 2 – Instruments that are settled in a variable number of shares but subject to a cap and floor (that is, a collar)

An entity issues an instrument that is settled at the end of the year by delivering equity shares to the value of C100. The fair value of the shares at the date of issue is C10. The instrument also contains:

- A cap that limits the number of shares that the entity is required to deliver to 20 shares.
- A floor that requires the entity to deliver a minimum of 5 shares.

The instrument is viewed as an obligation to deliver a variable number shares which is a liability. The instrument also contains both a purchased put and a written call that are net settled. The purchased put and the written call are within the scope of IAS 39, because they result in an exchange of a variable number of shares. Assuming that the fair value option is not used for the entire contract, the cap and floor should be bifurcated as embedded derivatives, because they are not closely related to the debt host (the underlying of these embedded derivatives is the share price). However, because the cap and floor are linked to the same risk exposure (that is, the share price) and are interdependent, they must be bundled together and bifurcated as a single compound embedded derivative in accordance with IAS 39 paragraph AG 29.

6.5.63 A single instrument should not be separated into a number of different instruments in order to satisfy the 'fixed for fixed' requirement where otherwise it would result in variability in either own equity, cash or another financial asset, if accounted for as a single instrument. For example, variability resulting from interdependent profit levels.

Example – Contingent consideration varies with time and performance conditions

Entity A acquires entity B and the contingent consideration payable to the seller is based on the following terms:

- If a performance target of profits of C100m is achieved by entity B in year 1, 100 additional shares will be issued to the seller.

- If a performance target of profits of C200m is achieved by entity B by the end of year 2 (cumulative of year 1 and year 2), 150 more shares will be issued to the seller.

- Entity B must meet the performance target in year 1 in order to be eligible to earn the additional shares in year 2 (that is, it is not possible to only receive 150 shares)

Where there are multiple contingent events it must be determined whether the unit of account is the overall contract or separate contracts within that overall contract. In order to be assessed as separate contracts they must be readily separable and independent of each other and relate to different risk exposures. In this example the periods are not readily separable or independent of each other as the delivery of shares in year 2 depends on the profits and delivery of shares in year 1. This is considered as one overall contract that results in a variable number of shares. It fails the 'fixed for fixed' requirement and is classified as a liability not equity.

6.5.64 In November 2009 the IFRS IC discussed whether a type of instrument where the exercise price is pre-determined at inception and only varies over time met the fixed for fixed condition and would, therefore, be classified as equity. The IFRS IC acknowledged there is diversity in practice in accounting for such instruments, but rejected issuing interpretive guidance due to the longer term debt-equity project that is in progress.

6.5.65 In the light of the IFRS IC discussions and diversity in practice, our view is that an entity may determine that such an instrument, where the exercise price is pre-determined at inception and only varies over time, meets the fixed for fixed condition and is classified as equity. If the strike price is not pre-determined at inception but determinable based on variables, such as the share price for example, the fixed for fixed condition would not be met. An entity may also determine that such an instrument where the exercise price is pre-determined at inception and only varies over time is a financial liability on the basis that the pre-determination of the exercise price introduces some variability that fails the fixed for fixed criterion.

6.5.66 An entity's decision as to whether the fixed for fixed condition is met when the strike price is pre-determined at inception and only varies over time is an accounting policy decision that should be applied consistently and disclosed appropriately.

6.5.67 An entity that previously considered that the fixed for fixed condition was not met may continue with its existing policy or may change its policy by following the guidance for changes in accounting policy as discussed in chapter 3.

Example – Variation in the cash received due to step-up adjustments

Entity A (US dollar functional currency) writes an option to entity B (not an employee) that enables entity B to buy 1 share of entity A on the following terms:

- If the option is exercised in year 1 the strike price is $1.
- If the option is exercised in year 2 the strike price is $2.
- If the option is exercised in year 3 the strike price is $3.

Entity A has a policy choice, which should be applied consistently.

Entity A may consider that the instrument is an equity instrument, because the exercise price is pre-determined and varies only with time. It, therefore, can be considered as meeting the condition that a fixed number of equity instruments will be issued for a fixed price.

On the other hand, entity A may consider that the instrument is a derivative financial liability. Entity A may consider that the different strike prices introduce variability such that a fixed number of shares will not be issued for a fixed amount of cash.

6.5.68 Complexity arises in practice when applying the principles for settlement in an entity's own equity instruments. Although IAS 32 states that variability in either the entity's own equity delivered or cash or another financial asset received results in a financial liability, not all forms of variability do in fact violate the 'fixed for fixed' requirement, including the example of a pre-determined price that only varies over time in paragraph 6.5.67 above. Another example is an adjustment to the conversion ratio of a convertible bond triggered by a stock split. For example the original conversion ratio is 1 share for every £1 (with a notional value of £2), however, upon a stock split each share now has a notional value of £1. It would, therefore, be necessary to adjust the conversion ratio to 2 shares for every £1 in order to maintain the relative economic rights of the shareholders and bondholders. Although the adjustment results in variability in the number of own equity delivered, the fact that this variability serves to maintain the relative economic rights of the shareholders and bondholders results in no violation of the 'fixed for fixed' requirement. Conversely, a contract to issue a fixed percentage number of an entity's equity instruments at a future date for a fixed amount of cash is not an equity instrument. This is because the entity's capital structure could change before the shares are issued, through share issues or repurchases, and so the number of shares that will be issued for the fixed amount of cash is variable.

6.5.69 Where variability is caused by the inclusion of an anti-dilution clause, such as the stock split clause outlined above, this will not result in a violation of the 'fixed for fixed' requirement provided, firstly the relative rights of the shareholders and bondholders are maintained, and secondly the instrument would otherwise meet the 'fixed for fixed' requirement. Other examples of anti-dilutive clauses are adjustments made for the payment of dividends and bonus issues, where new shares are issued to the entity's shareholders for no additional consideration through a capitalisation of reserves.

6.5.70 However, there are other 'anti-dilution' adjustments that may violate the 'fixed for fixed' requirement as seen in the example below for an adjustment for the issuance of shares at a market price that is below the strike price:

> **Example – Changes in conversion ratio upon the issuance of shares at a market price (below the strike price)**
>
> An entity issues warrants that permit the holders to buy 100 shares of its ordinary shares for $10 per share. The warrants have a 10 year term and are exercisable at any time. However, the terms of the warrants specify that if the entity subsequently issues ordinary shares at the then current market price for an amount of less than $10 per share, the strike price of the warrants is reduced to equal the issuance price of those shares.
>
> Does this adjustment to the strike price of the warrants violate the 'fixed for fixed' requirement in paragraph 16b(ii) of IAS 32?
>
> This adjustment to reduce the strike price for shares subsequently issued at a market price (but below the strike price) violates the 'fixed for fixed' requirement. This

adjustment does not preserve the economic rights of the warrant holders relative to the ordinary shareholders. This is because the adjustment effectively provides a form of compensation to the warrant holder if there is a subsequent issuance of shares at a market price that is not provided to the ordinary shareholders.

6.5.70.1 On the other hand, when an entity issues further shares at a strike price below the market price (most commonly seen through a rights issue), careful consideration needs to be given for whether all shareholders (both existing and new) are equally compensated and therefore whether the 'fixed for fixed' requirement is violated.

> **Example – Change in conversion ratio upon a rights issue**
>
> A convertible bond provides for a change to the conversion ratio upon a rights issue. Does an adjustment to the conversion ratio upon a rights issue violate the 'fixed for fixed' requirement in paragraph 16(b)(ii) of IAS 32?
>
> A rights issue is typically made up of two components: a bonus issue of nil paid ordinary shares, and the issue of new ordinary shares at market price.
>
> An adjustment for the bonus issue component of a rights issue preserves the relative rights of the convertible bondholders relative to the ordinary shareholders (that is, it maintains their relative ownership interests). Therefore, the adjustment to the conversion ratio is compensating the bondholder based on how the discount has diluted the total shares in issue. Hence, it does not violate the 'fixed for fixed' requirement.
>
> However, an adjustment for the second component – the issue of new ordinary shares at market price – does not preserve the economic position of the convertible bondholders and the ordinary shareholders relative to each other. An adjustment for this new share issue component at market price does not, therefore, meet the 'fixed for fixed' requirement. Furthermore, if the adjustment compensates for both components of the rights issue (the bonus issue and the issuance at market price), the adjustment will not meet the 'fixed for fixed' requirement.

6.5.71 A common adjustment in convertible bonds is the inclusion of a change of control clause. The clause adjusts the otherwise fixed for fixed conversion ratio upon a change of control event. The purpose of the adjustment is to compensate the bondholder for the loss of optionality either through a stated compensation amount or via a formula. As this change in control adjustment is not compensation that relates to the issuance of the equity shares but rather is compensation for the loss of optionality, it does not affect the relative rights of the shareholders and bondholders and does not result in a violation of the 'fixed for fixed' requirement.

6.5.72 The table below sets out the classification in various scenarios where a fixed or variable monetary obligation (not indexed to the entity's own share price) is settled in a fixed number or variable number of the entity's own shares. Instruments classified as financial liabilities under IAS 32, will require further analysis under IAS 39 to determine whether any embedded derivatives require to be bifurcated.

Contract settled in the equity's own shares	Monetary value of consideration[1]	Number of equity shares	Classification
Scenario 1	Fixed	Variable	Financial liability
Scenario 2	Variable	Variable	Financial liability
Scenario 3	Variable	Fixed	Financial liability
Scenario 4	Fixed in a currency other than the entity's functional currency[2]	Fixed	Financial liability
Scenario 5	Fixed	Fixed	Equity

1 in the functional currency of the issuer.

2 subject to the exception discussed from paragraph 6.5.61.

6.5.73 IAS 32 does not deal with the option to exchange a fixed number of one kind of the entity's own equity for a fixed number of a different kind of equity. An example is an option for a minority shareholder to exchange its holding of shares in a subsidiary for a fixed number of equity shares in the parent. Both legs of the contract are a fixed number of shares and in both cases the shares are a residual interest in some or all of the entity, that is equity. The contract does not violate the part of the definition of a financial liability in paragraph 11(b)(i) of IAS 32 because, although it is a non-derivative contract, it does not oblige the entity to deliver a variable number of its own equity instruments and hence the entity is not using its own equity instruments as 'currency'. From the perspective of the parent in preparing its separate financial statements, the contract is a derivative as it is over an asset (investment in its subsidiary), rather than an equity instrument.

6.5.74 A contract that will be settled in cash or another financial asset as opposed to the delivery of shares is a financial asset or financial liability even if the amount of cash or another financial asset that will be received or delivered is based on changes in the market price of the entity's own equity. An example is a net cash-settled share option. [IAS 32 para AG 27(c)]. Derivatives on own shares are considered further from paragraph 6.5.110 below.

Contingent settlement provisions

6.5.75 The obligation to deliver cash or financial assets need not be certain of occurring, it may be contingent on the occurrence or non-occurrence of uncertain future events (or on the outcome of uncertain circumstances) that are beyond the control of both the issuer or the holder of the instrument. Examples of such uncertain future events may include, but are not limited to:

- Changes in stock market index or consumer price index.

- Changes in interest rates or exchange rates.

- Changes in tax laws or other regulatory requirements.

- Changes in the issuer's key performance indicators such as revenue, net income or debt-to-equity ratios.

6.5.76   In accordance with IAS 32 paragraph 25, the instrument is a financial liability in the circumstances specified above. This is because at the time of the initial recognition, the issuer does not have an unconditional right to avoid delivering cash or another financial asset (or otherwise to settle it in such a way that it would be a financial liability) as it does not control the final outcome. A transfer of economic benefits as a result of a past event (the issue of the instrument) cannot be avoided depending on the outcome of the future event. Such financial instruments should, therefore, be classified as a financial liability.

Example 1 – Change of control events

A contract between entity A and a third party contains a requirement for entity A to make payments to the third party on a change of control of entity A. For example, where entity A may be taken over by entity B and where entity B is not connected to entity A.

The change of control event is outside the control of both the entity and the third party provided that it needs not to be agreed by the entity at a general meeting, as discussed in paragraphs 6.5.22-6.5.25. This will be the case if a purchaser could approach individual shareholders and buy their shares. Payments to a third party that are contingent on a change of control event are, therefore, financial liabilities when no agreement by a general meeting is required.

Example 2 – Shares with an obligation to pay out a percentage of profits

A bond includes an obligation to pay out a fixed 10% of profits each year and is mandatorily redeemable at par after 20 years.

The instrument has two liability components, a contractual obligation to redeem the instrument at par after 20 years and a contractual obligation to pay 10% of profits until redemption. The latter is a financial liability because, although the payment depends on the entity making profits (an uncertain future event), the future profits are outside the control of both the issuer and holder, but if profits are made the issuer cannot avoid making the payment, hence it meets the definition of a contingent settlement event. The 10% obligation does not meet the definition of an embedded derivative as the entity's profit is a non-financial variable that is specific to a party to the contract. [IAS 39 para 9].

Example 3 – mandatorily redeemable where an IPO does not occur

An undated cumulative bond, whose interest payments are at the discretion of the entity absent an IPO, contains a clause that states that the instrument (including all unpaid cumulative interest) will become mandatorily payable if there is not an IPO by the end of three years from the instrument's issuance date. Although it may be within the entity's control to determine whether the IPO is attempted, market and regulatory forces determine whether any attempt is successful (that is, whether the market will accept an IPO and whether all regulatory approvals will be obtained). These forces are beyond the control of the entity, therefore redemption upon an IPO event not occurring meets the definition of a contingent settlement event and results in the bond being classified as a financial liability from inception.

6.5.77   Where the event is within the control of the issuer but not the holder, it is possible for the issuer to avoid the event occurring and hence avoid settling the instrument, hence the event would not meet the definition of a contingent settlement event. For example an undated cumulative bond whose interest payments are at the discretion of the entity that contains a clause that states that the instrument (including all unpaid cumulative interest) will become mandatorily payable if a successful IPO occurs. As outlined in example 3 above, it is within an entity's control to determine whether an IPO is attempted and, hence, the entity can avoid a successful IPO taking place. Therefore, the clause does not meet the definition of a contingent settlement provision and results in the bond being classified as an equity instrument from inception.

6.5.78   Contingent settlement provisions sometimes exist within the terms of convertible loan instruments. When a convertible instrument must be settled in its entirety in cash at its fair value on the occurrence of a contingent settlement event (for example, a change in tax law; default on the instrument) that is outside the control of both the issuer and the holder, the whole instrument, including the option to convert, is treated as a financial liability. The option to convert is a (derivative) liability under paragraph 16(b)(ii) and paragraph 26 of IAS 32 because the conversion feature is not always settled by exchanging a fixed amount of cash for a fixed number of its own equity instruments. See paragraph 6.5.95 for instruments that have contingent settlement provisions and both liability and equity components.

6.5.79   Cash settlement of one financial instrument can be contingent upon the default of another financial instrument as discussed below.

> **Example – Instruments that are redeemable on default on another instrument ('cross default clauses')**
>
> An entity has issued two instruments. The first instrument is mandatorily redeemable and pays a mandatory fixed coupon and is therefore classified as a financial liability in accordance with IAS 32. The second instrument has no mandatory payments other than it is mandatorily redeemable if there is an event of default on the first instrument.
>
> The event of default on the first instrument is a contingent settlement provision that makes the second instrument a financial liability of the issuer under paragraph 25 of IAS 32. Whether or not an entity defaults on the payment related to an instrument depends, in part, on whether it has adequate resources to make the payments when contractually due. The availability of adequate resources depends primarily on the future revenue and income of the entity. Paragraph 25 of IAS 32 is clear that revenues and net income are not within the entity's control. Therefore, mandatory redemption in the event of default meets the definition of a genuine contingent settlement provision, which results in the second instrument being classified as a financial liability.

6.5.80   There are three exceptions where uncertain events outside the control of the issuer would not meet the definition of a contingent settlement event. These are where:

- The part of the contingent settlement provision that could require settlement in cash or another financial asset (or otherwise in such a way that it would be a financial liability) is not *genuine* (see para 6.5.81). [IAS 32 para 25].

- The issuer can be required to settle the obligation in cash or another financial asset (or otherwise to settle it in such a way that it would be a financial liability) only in the event of liquidation of the issuer (see para 6.5.83). [IAS 32 para 25].

- A third exception is introduced by the amendment to IAS 32 for puttable instruments and obligations arising on liquidation, as discussed from paragraph 6.5.29.

Settlement terms that are not genuine

6.5.81   The standard explains that a contingent settlement provision in a contract is not genuine if it requires settlement in cash only on the occurrence of an event that is extremely rare, highly abnormal and very unlikely to occur. In that situation, the contingent settlement provisions are not taken into account in the instrument's classification. Thus, a contract that requires settlement in cash or a variable number of the entity's own shares only on the occurrence of an event that is extremely rare, highly abnormal and very unlikely to occur is an equity instrument. Similarly, if settlement in a fixed number of an entity's own shares may be contractually precluded in circumstances that are outside the control of the entity, those circumstances can be ignored if there is no genuine possibility that they will occur. In that situation, the instrument continues to be classified as an equity instrument and not as a financial liability. [IAS 32 para AG 28].

6.5.82   In practice, terms are included in a contract for a purpose that is likely to have commercial effect. Therefore, it would be unusual to include settlement terms in a contract that are contingent on an event that is extremely rare, highly abnormal and very unlikely to occur. If such ineffective terms are included, it should be concluded that the terms are not genuine and should be ignored in determining the instrument's classification. However, 'not genuine' should not be equated to 'remote'. The IASB makes it clear in the Basis for conclusions to IAS 32 that it is not appropriate to disregard events that are merely 'remote'. The specific facts and circumstances would need to be considered.

Example 1 – Settlement terms based on increase in an index

An entity issues an instrument that is redeemable in cash if the FTSE 100 triples within a two week period.

In general, it is not for the entity to speculate whether an index will behave in a certain manner that may or may not trigger redemption of the instrument. As the entity will be unable to avoid a settlement in cash if the index reaches that level, the instrument should be treated as a financial liability.

However, in this situation, the tripling of the FTSE 100 within such a short period of time is extremely rare, highly abnormal and unlikely to occur. Furthermore, in practice, an investor is highly unlikely to advance funds on such redemption terms. Clearly the terms are artificial and not genuine and should be ignored for classification purposes.

Example 2 – Settlement terms based on changes in regulation

A bank issues an instrument that is redeemable in cash if the banking regulator changes the instrument's current classification from tier 1 capital to tier 2 capital in the future.

Whether the contingency in this example is genuine would depend upon the specific facts and circumstances. In some jurisdictions, the industry regulator has a history of applying such changes always prospectively and grandfathering existing instruments under their original classification. In that situation, a regulatory change would not affect the classification of an instrument that is currently outstanding and, consequently, the contingency would be regarded as not genuine.

Settlements that arise only on liquidation

6.5.83 Obligations to deliver cash or other financial assets that are contingent only on the issuer's liquidation should be ignored. This is rather obvious because different rights and obligations associated with the instruments come into effect at liquidation that would not otherwise be triggered during the ordinary course of business and, hence, would be inconsistent with the going concern assumption. A contingent settlement provision that provides for payment in cash or another financial asset only on the entity's liquidation is similar to an equity instrument that has priority in liquidation. Such a provision should, therefore, be ignored in classifying the instrument. However, if the instrument is redeemable on the occurrence of an event that may ultimately lead to eventual liquidation (for example, the entity becomes insolvent, goes into receivership or administration which is beyond the control of the entity), the instrument should still be classified as a financial liability.

Derivative financial instruments with settlement options

6.5.84 Sometimes a derivative contract may contain settlement options that give either party a choice over how it is settled (for example, the issuer or the holder can choose to settle the contract net in cash, or by exchanging shares for cash). IAS 32 states that when a derivative financial instrument gives one party a choice over how it is settled, it is a financial asset or a financial liability, unless all of the settlement alternatives would result in it being an equity instrument. [IAS 32 para 26].

6.5.85 An example of a derivative financial instrument with a settlement option that is a financial liability is an option for an entity to buy its own shares from a third party that the entity can decide to settle net in cash or by exchanging its own shares for cash. Forward and option contracts to buy or sell an entity's own equity instruments that contain settlement options are discussed in paragraph 6.5.118 below. Also, some contracts to buy or sell a non-financial item (not for 'own use') in exchange for the entity's own equity instruments are financial assets or financial liabilities and not equity instruments, if they can be settled either by delivery of the non financial item or net in cash or another financial instrument. [IAS 32 para 27]. Where the settlement option is contingent on a future event occurring, it will still fall under the settlement option accounting in accordance with paragraph 26 of IAS 32 from initial recognition, as discussed in paragraph 6.5.102.

Shares issued by subsidiaries

6.5.86 Normally equity shares issued by subsidiaries to persons outside the group are classified as non-controlling interests in the consolidated financial statements in accordance with IAS 1 and IAS 27. When classifying a financial instrument (or a component of it) in consolidated financial statements, an entity should consider all the terms and conditions agreed between group members and the instrument holders in determining whether the group as a whole has an obligation to deliver cash or another financial asset in respect of the instrument, or to settle it in a manner that results in liability classification.

6.5.87 For example, a member of the group might give a guarantee to pay amounts in respect of those shares, such as dividends or amounts due on their redemption; or another group member might undertake to purchase the shares in the event that the subsidiary issuing them fails to make the expected payments. Where this is so, the outside shareholders will look to the guarantor if the subsidiary has defaulted.

6.5.88 Consequently, in such a situation, the subsidiary may appropriately classify the instrument without regard to these additional terms in its separate financial statements. However, in the consolidated financial statements, the effect of other agreements between group members and the instrument holders means that the group as a whole is unable to avoid the transfer of economic benefits. Therefore, where such an obligation or settlement provision exists from the perspective of the group, the instrument (or the component of it that is subject to the obligation) is classified as a financial liability in the consolidated financial statements. [IAS 32 para AG 29].

Compound financial instruments

Introduction

6.5.89 Not all financial instruments are either liability or equity. Some, known as compound instruments contain elements of both in a single contact. A compound financial instrument is a non-derivative financial instrument that, from the issuer's perspective, contains both a liability and an equity component. [IAS 32 paras 28, AG 30]. Typical examples of such instruments are:

- A mandatorily redeemable preference share provides that dividend payments can be made at the issuer's discretion before the redemption date. Such an instrument contains a liability component (issuer's contractual obligation to deliver cash or another financial asset for payment of the redemption amount) and an equity component (the holder's right to receive dividends if declared). [IAS 32 para AG 37].

- A bond that is convertible into a fixed number of equity shares at the holder's option. From the issuer's perspective, such an instrument comprises two components: a financial liability (issuer's contractual obligation to deliver cash or another financial asset for payment of interest and principal, if not converted) and an equity instrument (a written call option granting the holder the right, for a specified period of time, to convert it into a fixed number of the entity's ordinary shares). The economic effect of issuing such an instrument is substantially the same as issuing simultaneously a debt instrument with an early settlement provision and warrants to purchase ordinary shares, or issuing a debt instrument with detachable share purchase warrants. [IAS 32 para 29]. If the issuer call option is contingent on a future event, it should still be for accounted for as a call option from initial recognition. For example:

Example – Provisional issuer call option to redeem at par

Company A issues a convertible bond that, if converted, converts into a fixed number of equity shares. The bond also contains a provisional call option that gives the issuer the option to redeem the bond at par if the share price is 130% of the conversion price for at least 20 days.

The convertible bond is a compound financial instrument with a debt host and equity conversion option. As the issuer call option is to redeem the bonds at par, it does not result in the conversion option having a cash settlement alternative. The conversion option is not, therefore, accounted for as an embedded derivative in accordance with paragraph 26 of IAS 32.

In respect of the issuer call option, the value of any derivative feature (such as a call option) embedded in a compound financial instrument, (other than the equity component) is included in the liability component. [IAS 32 para 31]. The call option is, therefore, considered part of the liability and not the equity component. The assessment of whether the call or put option is closely related to the host debt contract from the issuer's perspective is made before separating the equity element under IAS 32. [IAS 39 para AG 30(g)].

Separation of a compound financial instrument on initial recognition

6.5.90 The issuer of a non-derivative financial instrument should first evaluate the financial instrument's terms to determine whether it contains both a liability and an equity component. This evaluation should be done in accordance with the contractual arrangement's substance and the definition of a financial liability, financial asset and an equity component. If such components are identified, the issuer should account for the components separately as financial liabilities, financial assets or equity instruments. [IAS 32 para 28]. The liability and the equity components must be presented separately on the balance sheet. [IAS 32 para 29].

6.5.91 The above approach is often described as 'split accounting'. Split accounting is applied by the issuer of the financial statement to measure the liability and the equity components upon initial recognition of the instrument. The method, illustrated by reference to a convertible bond that is the most common form of a compound financial instrument, but which is equally applicable to other forms of compound financial instruments, allocates the fair value of the consideration for the compound instrument into its liability and equity components, as follows:

- The fair value of the consideration in respect of the liability component is measured first, at the fair value of a similar liability (including any embedded non-equity derivative features such as an issuer's call option to redeem the bond early) that does not have any associated equity conversion option. This becomes the liability component's carrying amount at initial recognition.

  In practice, the liability component's initial carrying value is determined by discounting the contractual stream of future cash flows (interest and principal) to the present value at the current rate of interest applicable to instruments of comparable credit status and providing substantially the same cash flows on the same terms, but without the equity component (the equity conversion option).

  The value of any embedded non-equity derivative features is separately determined and included in the liability component.

- The equity component (the equity conversion option) is assigned the residual amount after deducting from the fair value of the instrument as a whole the amount separately determined for the liability component.

  The equity component is excluded from IAS 39's scope and is never remeasured after initial recognition.

Since the sum of the carrying amounts assigned to the liability and equity components on initial recognition is always equal to the consideration received, which, in most circumstances is equal to the fair value of the instrument as a whole, no gain or loss arises from initially recognising the instrument's components separately in the above manner.

[IAS 32 paras 31, AG 31].

6.5.92 The requirement to separate the liability and the equity components of a single compound financial instrument in the above manner is consistent with the requirements for initial measurement of a financial liability in IAS 39 and the definitions in IAS 32 and the Framework of an equity instrument as a residual interest. Furthermore, the approach removes the need to estimate inputs to, and apply, complex option pricing models to measure the equity component of some compound financial instruments. [IAS 32 paras BC 29-30].

6.5.93 Once a compound financial instrument has been separated into its liability and equity components on initial recognition, the classification of the liability and equity components is not revised as a result of a change in the likelihood that a conversion option will be exercised, even when the option's exercise may appear to have become economically advantageous to some holders. This is because the entity's contractual obligation to make future payments remains outstanding until it is extinguished through conversion, the instrument's maturity or some other transaction. [IAS 32 para 30].

Example – Separation of a convertible bond

An entity issues 600,000 convertible bonds at the start of year 1. The bonds have a 3-year term, and are issued at par with a face value of C100 per bond, resulting in total proceeds of C60m, which is also the fair value of the bonds. Interest is payable annually in arrears at a nominal annual interest rate of 6%. Each C100 nominal bond is convertible at any time up to maturity into 25 ordinary shares. When the bonds are issued, the prevailing market interest rate for similar debt without conversion options is 9%. The entity incurs an issue cost of 1% on the nominal value of the bond amounting to C600,000.

As explained in paragraph 6.5.91 above, the liability component is measured first by discounting the contractually determined stream of future cash flows (interest and principal) to present value using a discount rate of 9%, the market interest rate for similar bonds having no conversion rights, as shown below.

	C
PV of interest payable at the end of year 1 – 3,600,000/1.09	3,302,752
PV of interest payable at the end of year 2 – 3,600,000/(1.09)^2	3,030,048
PV of interest payable at the end of year 3 – 3,600,000/(1.09)^3	2,779,861
PV of principal of C60,000,000 payable at the end of three years – 60,000,000/(1.09)^3	46,331,009
Total liability component	55,443,670
Total equity component (residual)*	4,556,330
Fair value of bonds	60,000,000

* The equity component is a written call option that allows the holder to call for the shares on exercise of the conversion option at any time before maturity (American option). Since equity is a residual, application of complex option pricing models are not necessary to determine the equity component. Instead, the difference between the bond's proceeds and the liability component's fair value of the liability component as computed above – the residual – is assigned to the equity component.

In accordance with IAS 32, the issue cost of C600,000 will need to be allocated between the liability and the equity components in proportion to the allocation of the proceeds as shown below:

	Equity component	Liability component	Total
	C	C	C
Gross proceeds allocated as above	4,556,330	55,443,670	60,000,000
Issue cost	(45,563)	(554,437)	(600,000)
Net proceeds	4,510,767	54,889,233	59,400,000

The amount credited to equity of C4,510,767 is not subsequently remeasured.

The liability component will be classified under IAS 39 either as a financial liability at fair value through profit or loss or as another liability measured at amortised cost using the effective interest rate method. If classified as a financial liability at fair value through profit or loss, the liability component will be initially recognised at C55,443,670 and the issue cost of C554,437 allocated to the liability component will be immediately expensed to the income statement. However, under the latter classification, the liability component will be initially recognised net of issue cost at C54,889,233. [IAS 39 para 43]. It will accrete to its final redemption amount of C60,000,000 at the end of year 3 at an effective interest rate of 9.38837% as shown below:

Year	Opening liability	Interest @ 9.38837%	Cash paid	Closing liability
	C	C	C	C
1	54,889,233	5,153,205	(3,600,000)	56,442,438
2	56,442,438	5,299,025	(3,600,000)	58,141,464
3	58,141,464	5,458,536	(63,600,000)	–
Total finance cost		15,910,767		

Total finance cost consists of:	
Interest payments	10,800,000
Issue cost allocated to liability component	554,437
Discount (representing gross proceeds allocated to equity component)	4,556,330
	15,910,767

Separation of a compound instrument containing non-equity derivatives

6.5.94 As explained above, a non-derivative compound financial instrument must be separated into its equity and liability components. In a convertible bond, the equity component arises from the embedded option to convert the liability into the issuer's equity. However, a convertible bond may also contain other non-equity derivative features such as a call, put or pre-payment option. The way in which a compound financial instrument with multiple derivative features is separated into its constituent parts is set out below:

■ First, the value of non-equity derivatives must be included in the liability component. [IAS 32 para 31]. This means that the liability component is established by measuring a bond's fair value with similar terms, credit status and containing similar non-equity derivative features, but without the equity conversion feature.

■ Secondly, the equity component is then arrived at by deducting the fair value attributable to the bond as determined above from the compound instrument's fair value.

■ Thirdly, given that the liability component contains the non-equity derivative features, it is necessary to assess whether such embedded derivative features are closely related to the host debt contract. In a convertible bond with a call option for example, that assessment will involve determining whether the call option's exercise price is approximately equal to the sum of the debt and the equity components, which is equal to the convertible bond's par value. This assessment is made before separating the equity element as determined above (see chapter 6.3). [IAS 39 para AG 30(g)]. If the bond is callable at par, the embedded call option is closely related to the host debt instrument. The embedded call option is not bifurcated (split out) and the liability component is determined as indicated above. If, on the other hand, the bond is callable at the carrying value of the liability component, the embedded call option is not closely related to the debt host. In that situation, the embedded call option is separated out of the liability component and accounted for separately. Separating the embedded derivative from the liability component does not affect the amount determined for the equity component as noted in bullet point two above.

■ Finally, the sum of the carrying amounts assigned to the various components as indicated above on initial recognition must always be equal to the compound instrument's fair value as a whole. No gain or loss should arise from initially recognising the instrument's components separately. [IAS 32 para 31].

Example – Separation of a callable convertible bond

An entity issues 600,000 callable convertible bonds at the beginning of year 1. The bonds are issued at par with a face value of C100 per bond, giving total proceeds of C60m, which is also the bond's fair value. The bonds are convertible by the holder into a fixed number of shares at any time after the first anniversary of its issue. Furthermore, the bonds do not have a fixed maturity; instead the issuer can call/redeem the bond at any time at the fixed stated principal amount of the bond.

The following information is relevant:

	Cm
Value of a straight bond without a call or equity conversion feature (plain vanilla)	57
Value of issuer call option in a similar bond without an equity conversion option based on an option pricing model (derivative asset)	2

As explained above, the value of the call option (the non-equity derivative) of C2m must be included in the liability component. In this situation, the inclusion results in the value of a callable bond without the equity conversion feature (the liability component) to be less than the value of a plain vanilla bond. This is because the issuer's right to call the bond in the event that interest rates go up and bond price increases makes the value of a callable bond less attractive to the holder than a plain vanilla bond.

Value of callable bond (the liability component)	55
Value of equity component (the conversion option) = residual	5
Fair value of bond = consideration received	60

As the liability component contains the call option, it is now necessary to assess whether the call option is closely related to the host debt instrument. In this situation, the call option's exercise price is set at C60m, the fixed stated principal of the bond. Therefore, at each exercise date, the option's exercise price of C60m is likely to be approximately equal to the amortised carrying amount of the bond plus the equity conversion option. Therefore, the call option is closely related to the host debt instrument. As a result, the call option is not separately accounted for, but remains part of the liability component. [IAS 39 AG 30(g)(i)].

The liability component of C55m will be subsequently measured in accordance with its classification under IAS 39 either as a financial liability at fair value through profit or loss or as another liability measured at amortised cost using the effective interest rate method. Although, in this situation, the bond can be called by the issuer at any time or converted by the holder at any time after the first anniversary of its issue, the liability component of C55m is not automatically accreted to its redemption amount of C60m by the end of year 1. This is because the effective interest rate method requires the entity to discount the cash flows over the instrument's expected life, taking into account all the financial instrument's contractual terms including pre-payment, call and similar options [IAS 39 para 9]. This period may well be a period greater than one year.

On the other hand, if the call option's exercise price were set at an amount that is not approximately equal to the debt instrument's amortised carrying amount or not set to reimburse the lender for the approximate present value of lost interest for the remaining terms of the host contract, the call option would fall to be accounted for separately [IAS 39 AG30(g)]. In that situation (assuming the call does not constitute a cash settlement alternative of the conversion option, per para 6.5.84), the proceeds of the converted bond would be allocated as follows:

	Dr Cm	Cr Cm
Cash	60	
Derivative asset (issuer call option)	2	
Host debt instrument		57
Equity component (written equity call option)		5

As can be seen from the above, the separation of the call option asset affects the value of the liability and not the equity component. The derivative asset will be fair valued at each subsequent balance sheet date until the option is exercised. The liability component would be amortised over its expected life (determined without reference to the call option to avoid double counting) under the effective interest method as stated above.

Instruments containing liability and equity components and contingent settlement provisions

6.5.95 The ability to convert a host instrument into own equity of the entity may be contingent on an uncertain future event. Where the uncertain future event meets the definition of a contingent settlement event as defined as in paragraph 6.5.75, the classification of the conversion option on initial recognition depends on whether the conversion option meets or violates the 'fixed for fixed' requirement if the uncertain future event occurs. Where the conversion option meets the 'fixed for fixed' requirement there are two acceptable views as to how to account for the instrument.

Example 1 – Contingently convertible bond

Entity A issues a contingently convertible bond repayable in 5 years; the debt host becomes convertible into common shares of entity A at a fixed ratio of 1:1.25 only if the contingent event occurs. The contingent event meets the definition of a contingent settlement event in accordance with paragraph 25 of IAS 32 and is 'genuine' – for example, a change in control event. There are no adjustments to the conversion ratio upon the contingent event occurring, and there are no other put or call options.

There are two views as to how to account for such an instrument. For debt instruments that contain contingent conversion features, it is not clear whether entities should first apply the rules for compound financial instruments (in IAS 32 para 28, see further from para 6.5.89) or the rules for contingent settlement provisions (in IAS 32 para 25, see further from para 6.5.75). Applying the rules for compound financial instruments first would result in an instrument being separated into its equity and liability components, because the instrument contains both. Applying the rules for contingent settlement provisions first would result in an instrument being recognised entirely as a financial liability, because paragraph 25 of IAS 32 states that such an instrument 'is a liability'. One of these views should be selected by an entity as a matter of accounting policy and applied consistently.

View 1 – compound financial instrument

The instrument contains both debt and equity components and so paragraph 28 of IAS 32 applies. The instrument is first separated into its component parts, namely a debt host and equity conversion option. The fact that the option is only contingently convertible will not cause liability classification of the conversion option under paragraph 25 of IAS 32 provided that, upon occurrence of the contingent event, it would be settled in such a way as to require classification as equity. If the contingent event were to occur in the example above, the conversion to own shares would still satisfy the 'fixed for fixed' requirement in paragraph 16(b)(ii) of IAS 32. The conversion option is classified as an equity component, resulting in a compound financial instrument.

View 2 – instrument is a liability

The instrument contains a contingent settlement feature (see further para 6.5.75). On the non-occurrence of the contingent event, interest is paid and the principal is repaid. According to paragraph 25 of IAS 32, an instrument containing a contingent settlement provision 'is a financial liability' and so the instrument is accounted for as a liability in its entirety. The instrument contains a debt host and an embedded derivative for the conversion option, which should be separated as it is not closely related to the debt host.

Conversion at or before maturity

6.5.96 The terms of a convertible instrument may require or allow the instrument to be converted into the entity's ordinary shares either at, or any time before, maturity. IAS 32 states that on conversion of a convertible instrument at maturity, the entity derecognises the liability component and recognises it as equity. The original equity component remains in equity. There is no gain or loss on conversion at maturity. [IAS 32 para AG 32].

Example – Conversion at maturity

The facts are the same as the example in paragraph 6.5.93 above, except that the bond is converted at the end of its three-year term.

The amortised cost of the bond will be stated at C60m at maturity after the last payment of interest has been made. As the bond is converted, the entity will issue 15m (600,000 × 25) of C1 nominal value. The liability component will be derecognised and transferred to equity. The accounting entries would be as follows:

	Dr Cm	Cr Cm
Liability	60	
Share capital		15
Reserves (a component of equity)		45

The amount that was previously recognised in equity, that is, C5 remains in equity.

6.5.97 The guidance included in paragraph AG 32 of IAS 32 as discussed above deals with conversion at maturity. However, the contractual terms of some convertible instruments allow for the conversion before the instrument's final maturity date. There is no specific guidance in IAS 32 as to what should be the accounting treatment if the holder elects to convert the bond early. However, as the instrument 'matures' on the date that the holder converts in accordance with the instrument's contractual terms, the guidance in IAS 32 paragraph AG 32 is relevant. Therefore, where a convertible debt is converted before maturity, the amount recognised in equity in respect of the shares issued should be the amount at which the liability for the debt is stated as at the date of conversion.

Example – Before maturity conversion of a convertible bond with an American conversion option

Convertible bonds with American options (those that give the holder the right to exercise the option at any time) are regularly converted before the loan's original maturity. To the extent that the carrying amount at the conversion date is not equal to the principal amount converted this should be accounted for in accordance with paragraph AG 32 of IAS 32, as the word 'maturity' means any date when the holder converts in accordance with the instrument's contractual terms. As an American option allows for conversion at any time before the expiry date, the conversion date will be the maturity date. As such, there is no gain or loss on conversion with American options. During the life of the host bond, expectations about early conversion should not be taken into account when estimating the cash flows used to apply the effective interest rate. The early conversion option is a characteristic of the equity component (the conversion option) not of the host liability. The estimated cash flows used to apply the effective interest rate method are, therefore, the contractual cash flows based on the contractual final maturity of the host liability (assuming there are no other puts or calls).

Mandatorily convertible instruments

6.5.98 A convertible bond may contain terms that *compel* the holder to convert the bond rather than being at the holder's option. Depending on the terms, the number of shares issued on conversion may be either variable or fixed. To the extent that the mandatorily convertible bond can only be settled by the issue of a variable amount of ordinary shares calculated to equal a fixed amount in the issuer's functional currency (that is, there is a repayment of principal), the instrument is a liability. To the extent that the mandatorily convertible bond can only be settled by the issue of a fixed number of ordinary shares, that part of the instrument is an equity component. Some mandatorily convertible instruments pay no interest or pay interest only if an ordinary dividend is paid (discretionary). This type of instrument has no liability component. Others pay interest until the bond is converted, in which case the issuer allocates part of the consideration received equal to the liability component. This is measured at the present value of the interest payments, discounted at the market rate of interest for a similar instrument with a similar credit status that has no conversion option. The balance of the consideration is allocated to the equity component as illustrated below.

> **Example – Mandatorily convertible bonds**
>
> An entity issues 600,000 convertible bonds at the start of year 1. The bonds have a 3-year term, and are issued at par with a face value of C100 per bond, resulting in total proceeds of C60m, which is also the bond's fair value. Interest is payable annually in arrears at a nominal annual interest rate of 6%. Each C100 nominal bond is mandatorily convertible at the end of the 3 year term into 25 ordinary shares. When the bonds are issued, the prevailing market interest rate for similar debt without conversion options is 9%. The entity incurs issue cost of 1% on the nominal value of the bond amounting to C600,000.
>
> As explained in the above paragraph, the liability component is measured first by discounting the contractually determined stream of future cash flows (interest only) to present value using a discount rate of 9%, the market interest rate for similar bonds having no conversion rights, as shown below.

	C
PV of interest payable at the end of year 1 – C3,600,000/1.09	3,302,752
PV of interest payable at the end of year 2 – C3,600,000/(1.09)^2	3,030,048
PV of interest payable at the end of year 3 – C3,600,000/(1.09)^3	2,779,860
Total liability component	9,112,660
Total equity component (residual)*	50,887,340
Total proceeds of the bond issue	60,000,000

* The difference between the proceeds of the bond and the fair value of the liability component as computed above (the residual) is assigned to the equity component.

In accordance with IAS 32, the issue cost of C600,000 will need to be allocated between the liability and the equity components in proportion to the allocation of the proceeds as shown below:

	Equity component	Liability component	Total
	C	C	C
Gross proceeds allocated as above	50,887,340	9,112,660	60,000,000
Issue cost	(508,873)	(91,127)	(600,000)
Net proceeds	50,378,467	9,021,533	59,400,000

The amount credited to equity of C50,378,467 is not subsequently remeasured.

The liability component of C9,021,533 will be measured subsequently at amortised cost using the effective interest rate method. As the interest payments on the bonds will reduce the liability component to zero, the effective interest rate in this situation is that rate of interest which discounts the three interest payments of C3,600,000 per year to its present value of C9,021,533. This rate amounts to 9.5659% as shown below:

Year	Opening liability	Interest @ 9.5659%	Cash paid	Closing liability
	C	C	C	C
1	9,021,533	862,990	(3,600,000)	6,284,523
2	6,284,523	601,171	(3,600,000)	3,285,694
3	3,285,694	314,306	(3,600,000)	–
Total finance cost		1,778,467		

When the bond is converted, the entity issues 15 million shares of C1 each. The original equity component of C50,378,467 effectively becomes the consideration for these shares. Where relevant, this amount would be allocated between share capital and share premium as follows:

	C
Share capital – 15 million shares of C1 each	15,000,000
Share premium	35,378,467
Original equity component	50,378,467

In other words, a mandatorily convertible instrument issued in the functional currency of the issuer is effectively a forward contract to issue or to deliver a fixed number of shares for which the consideration has been received in advance. Contrast this with the situation of an instrument that is convertible at any time before maturity (a written call option) discussed in paragraph 6.5.93 above.

Early redemption or repurchase

6.5.99 An entity may redeem or repurchase a convertible instrument before maturity, for example through negotiations with the bondholders, without affecting the conversion rights. When an entity extinguishes a convertible instrument before maturity through an early redemption or repurchase in which the original conversion privileges are unchanged, the entity should allocate the redemption consideration paid (including any transaction costs) to the instrument's liability and equity components at the date of repurchase or redemption. In making this allocation, the entity should use the same methodology (using current market data) that was used in the original allocation of proceeds received from the convertible instrument's issue between the separate components on initial recognition. [IAS 32 para AG 33].

6.5.100 Once the allocation of the consideration has been made, any resulting gain or loss is treated in accordance with accounting principles applicable to the related component, as follows:

- The difference between the consideration allocated to the liability component and its carrying value is recognised in profit or loss.

- The amount of consideration relating to the equity component is recognised in equity.

[IAS 32 para AG 34].

Example – Early redemption of a convertible bond

The facts are the same as the example in paragraph 6.5.93 above, except that on the first day of year 2, the entity makes a tender offer to the bondholders to repurchase the bond for its fair value at that date of C63m, which the bondholders accept. At the date of repurchase, the entity could have issued a non-convertible bond with a two-year term bearing an interest rate of 7%. The transaction cost of redeeming the bonds amounted to C200,000.

The carrying value of the liability component prior to redemption at the end of year 1 as calculated previously amounts to C56,442,438. The original equity component amounts to C4,510,767.

As explained above, the repurchase price is allocated between the liability component and the equity component on the same basis used in the original allocation process. This means the fair value of the liability component is measured first by discounting the remaining stream of future cash flows (interest and principal) to present value at the beginning of year 2, using a discount rate of 7%, the market interest rate for similar bonds having no conversion rights, as shown below.

	C
PV of interest payable at the end of year 2 – C3,600,000/1.07	3,364,486
PV of interest payable at the end of year 3 – C3,600,000/$(1.07)^2$	3,144,379
PV of principal of C60,000,000 payable at the end year 3 – C60,000,000 / $(1.07)^2$	52,406,324
Total liability component	58,915,189
Total equity component (residual)*	4,084,811
Total consideration payable on repurchase of bonds	63,000,000

* The difference between the consideration payable and the liability component's fair value as computed above is assigned to the equity component.

In accordance with IAS 32, the redemption cost of C200,000 will need to be allocated between the liability and the equity components in proportion to the allocation of the consideration as shown below:

	Equity component	Liability component	Total
	C	C	C
Consideration allocated as above	4,084,811	58,915,189	63,000,000
Redemption cost	12,968	187,032	200,000
Total	4,097,779	59,102,221	63,200,000

Difference arising on repurchase is as follows:

Consideration inclusive of costs as above	4,097,779	59,102,221	63,200,000
Carrying value prior to redemption as stated above	4,510,767	56,442,438	60,953,205
	412,988	(2,659,783)	(2,246,795)

The accounting entries in respect of the repurchase of the bond are as follows:

	Dr	Cr
	C	C
Bond Liability	56,442,438	
Debt Settlement expense (income statement)	2,659,783	
Cash		59,102,221

To record the repurchase of the liability component and the loss arising thereon

	Dr	Cr
Equity	4,097,779	
Cash		4,097,779

To record the cash paid on the repurchase of the equity component

The resulting balance of C412,988 relating to the equity component can be transferred to a different line item in equity, for example, retained earnings.

Modification of terms to induce early conversion

6.5.101 An entity may amend the terms of a convertible instrument to induce early conversion, for example by offering a more favourable conversion ratio or paying other additional consideration in the event of conversion before a specified date. In that situation, the entity should recognise a loss, at the date the terms are amended, calculated as the difference between:

■ the fair value of the consideration the holder receives on the instrument's conversion under the revised terms; and

■ the fair value of the consideration the holder would have received under the original terms.

[IAS 32 para AG 35].

Example – Early conversion of a convertible bond

The facts are the same as the example in paragraph 6.5.93 above, except that on the first day of year 2, the entity modifies the convertible instrument's terms to induce the bondholders to convert the bond within 60 days. Each C100 nominal bond is now convertible into 30 ordinary shares rather than the 25 ordinary shares under the original terms. The market value of the entity's shares at the date of the amendment is C5 per share.

As explained above, the loss arising on increasing the conversion ratio is calculated as follows:

	Cm
Fair value of consideration receivable under the new terms:	
Number of bonds (600,000) x Conversion ratio (30) x C5	90
Fair value of consideration receivable under the original terms:	
Number of bonds (600,000) x Conversion ratio (25) x C5	75
Value of additional shares issuable on conversion recognised in profit or loss	15

On the date of conversion, the entity issues 18m shares instead of 15m under the original conversion terms. Therefore, the consideration received for the 18m shares comprises the carrying value of the bond of C56,442,438 plus C15m (the market value of 3m shares @ C5 per share).

The accounting entries to record the early conversion are as follows:

	Dr	Cr
Bond liability	56,442,438	
Profit or loss (fair value of 3m shares @ C5 per share)	15,000,000	
Equity (issue of 18m shares)		71,442,438

Settlement options

6.5.102   In some instances, a convertible instrument may contain a settlement option that allows the issuer either to deliver a fixed number of shares when the bondholders exercise their rights to convert or deliver cash equal to the fair value of those shares at the date of conversion. Consistent with paragraph 6.5.84, where a convertible instrument contains such a cash settlement option, the conversion option is not an equity instrument, even though it is indexed to the market price of the entity's shares. Rather, it is an embedded derivative (effectively a written call option issued by the entity over its own shares) that is not closely related to the debt host. This means that instead of accounting for the conversion right as an equity instrument, the entity would account for the conversion right as a financial liability (a derivative) at fair value, with changes in fair value recognised in profit or loss. The effect of fair valuing the derivative means that gains and losses based on the entity's own share price would be reported in the profit or loss. This is also the case where the cash settlement option is contingent on a future event happening.

> **Example – Contingent settlement options**
>
> An entity has issued convertible bonds whose terms include a clause giving the issuer the option to redeem in cash the bonds at their fair market value in the event of the occurrence of an uncertain future event instead of issuing a fixed number of equity shares.
>
> The conversion option is a derivative. The terms of the convertible bond give the issuer the option to redeem the bonds for cash at their fair market value contingent upon a future event. On the occurrence of the uncertain future event there is a settlement alternative for the equity conversion option, as it can be settled at fair value, either in shares or in cash – that is, there is a net cash settlement option. An equity conversion option for which either party has a choice of settlement in cash or shares is a financial liability. [IAS 32 para 26]. Paragraph 26 of IAS 32 overturns the usual principle that something that is in the control of an issuer is not an obligation. This right of choice of settlement is contingent upon a future event in the example above, but the equity conversion option must still be accounted for as an embedded derivative in accordance with paragraph 26 of IAS 32.

6.5.103   When the holder exercises its right to convert and the entity chooses to settle its obligation by issuing a fixed number of shares, the liability's carrying value together with the derivative's fair value is derecognised and transferred to equity as the share issue is treated as an equity transaction. Note that the derivative should be marked to market through profit or loss immediately prior to conversion such that the time value of money on the option is captured in the income statement. Alternatively, the entity may record the shares at fair value and the difference between the fair value of the shares and the carrying value of the liability plus the fair value of the derivative is recognised in profit or loss. The same accounting treatment is achieved if the entity chooses the cash alternative as the amount of the cash consideration that is equal to the fair value of the shares at the date of conversion will be applied to extinguish the liability and the derivative instruments with any difference taken to profit or loss. Either method is acceptable, but it is an accounting policy choice that should be disclosed and applied consistently.

Convertible bond denominated in a foreign currency

6.5.104 It is not uncommon for an entity to issue a convertible bond that is denominated in a currency other than its functional currency, as discussed in paragraph 6.5.60. For example, an entity whose functional currency is the Swiss franc may issue a euro denominated convertible bond that can be converted into a fixed number of its own Swiss franc denominated equity instruments. In this case, the instrument comprises a host debt instrument denominated in a foreign currency and a written option to exchange a fixed number of the entity's own equity instruments for a fixed amount of cash that is denominated in a foreign currency.

6.5.105 In April 2005, the IFRS IC considered the accounting for a foreign currency convertible bond and stated that a fixed amount of foreign currency constitutes a variable amount of cash in the entity's functional currency. This position has not changed as a result of the IAS 32 amendment for the classification of rights issues discussed in paragraph 6.5.61. Therefore, foreign-currency-denominated-convertible bonds that will be settled by an entity delivering a fixed number of its own equity instruments in exchange for a fixed amount of foreign currency fail the 'fixed for fixed' requirement. The whole of the convertible bond is classified as a financial liability under IAS 32 and is subject to IAS 39 for recognition and measurement. The embedded written option's value changes in response to changes in the values of entity's equity and foreign exchange movements. Therefore, it is not a closely related embedded derivative, because the risks inherent in the derivative (equity risk) and in the debt host are dissimilar. [IAS 39 para AG 30(d)]. If the host debt is carried at amortised cost it will be subject to the translation rules of IAS 21, and the embedded derivative liability will be separated and fair valued through profit or loss.

Example – Convertible debt denominated in a foreign currency

On 1 January 20X5 a company with C functional currency issued 36,000 convertible bonds at par with a face value of US$1,000 per bond, giving total proceeds of US$36m. The bonds carry a coupon rate of 4% per annum payable in arrears. Each $1,000 bond is convertible, at the holder's discretion, at any time prior to maturity on 31 December 20X9, into 100 ordinary shares of C1 nominal.

The following information is relevant:

	Spot rate	Fair value of embedded derivative*
1 January 20X5	C1 = US$1.80	C3m
31 December 20X5	C1 = US$1.75	C4m
Average rate for the year	C1 = US$1.775	

* In accordance with paragraph AG 28 of IAS 39, the embedded derivative's fair value (the written option) must be determined first at inception of the contract. In this instance, the embedded derivative is indexed to both the share price denominated in C and the C/US$ exchange rate. Generally, where the derivatives relate to different risk exposures and are readily separable and independent of each other, they should be valued and accounted for separately. [IAS 39 para AG 29]. However, in this case, the exercise price of the equity conversion option is denominated in US$, but the underlying share is traded in C. Therefore, it is not possible to separate the equity price risk from the foreign currency risk and value each component separately, because the two are interdependent. In that situation, they should be bundled together and treated as a single compound derivative. [IAS 39 para AG 29]. On this basis, the fair value of the embedded derivative at initial recognition, calculated using an option pricing model, amounted to C3m and C4m respectively at 1 January 20X5 and 31 December 20X5.

As explained above, as the issuer's functional currency is C and the convertible bonds are denominated in US dollars, the conversion option is not an equity instrument, but an embedded derivative that is not closely related to the host debt instrument, because the risks inherent in the derivative (equity risk) and the host are dissimilar. Therefore, the conversion option should be separated and classified as a derivative liability.

The carrying value of the host contract at initial recognition is the difference between the consideration received of C20m ((US$36m @ 1.8) and the fair value of the embedded derivative of C3m, that is, C17m or US$30.6m (C17m @1.8).

The host foreign currency debt of US$30.6m will be measured subsequently at amortised cost using the effective interest rate method and then retranslated at each subsequent reporting date at the closing US$/C exchange rate. The company will pay 4% interest per annum on US$36m, that is, US$1.44m each year for the next 4 years and a principal amount of US$36m at the end of year 4, if the debt is not converted. The effective interest rate that discounts the interest and principal payments to its present value of US$30.6m is 8.5883% as shown below:

	Opening liability	Interest @ 8.5883%	Cash paid	Closing liability
	$'000	$'000	$'000	$'000
Year 1	30,600	2,628	(1,440)	31,788
Year 2	31,788	2,730	(1,440)	33,078
Year 3	33,078	2,841	(1,440)	34,479
Year 4	34,479	2,961	(37,440)	0

The interest payable in US$ is recorded in the profit or loss at the average rate ruling during the year. The closing liability is translated at the spot rate at the balance sheet. Any exchange difference arising is recognised in profit or loss as part of finance cost. Therefore, the amortised cost of the host foreign currency debt instrument at 31 December 20X5 would be calculated as follows:

		C'000
Opening liability	US$30,600,000 @ 1.8	17,000
Interest cost (profit or loss)	US$2,628,000 @ 1.775	1,481
Cash paid	US$1,440,000 @ 1.75	(823)
Exchange difference (profit or loss)*		507
Closing liability	US$31,788 @ 1.75	18,165

* The exchange difference comprises the exchange difference on the opening liability of C486 (US$30,600 @ [1.75-1.8]) and the exchange difference on the interest cost between closing rate and average rate of C21 (US$2,628 @ [1.775-1.8]).

At 31 December 20X5, the fair value of the embedded derivative liability is C4m. The increase in fair value results in a loss of C1m, which is recognised in profit or loss.

The foreign currency convertible bond is reported and presented in the financial statements as follows:

Income statement for the year ended 31 December 20X5	C'000
Other gains and (losses)	
Derivative instrument	(1,000)
Finance cost	
Interest expense	(1,481)
Foreign exchange difference	(507)
	(1,988)

Balance sheet	31 Dec 20X5 C'000	1 Jan 20X5 C'000
Current liabilities		
Borrowings	18,165	17,000
Derivative on convertible bond	4,000	3,000
	22,165	20,000

Alternatively, the foreign exchange difference may be presented in other gains and losses. Similarly, the bond and the derivative can be presented as a single number on the balance sheet. The classification of the host debt as a current or non-current liability is considered in chapter 6.9.

6.5.106   If a subsidiary issues a convertible bond that (if converted) converts into the parent's shares, the currency that should be looked to in determining whether the 'fixed for fixed' requirement in IAS 32 is met depends on the specific circumstances. For the purposes of the group's consolidated financial statements, a group should look to either the functional currency of the parent (into whose shares the bond is convertible), or that of the subsidiary (whose liability will be extinguished if the bond is converted). The choice to look to the functional currency of the subsidiary or the parent is a policy choice and should be applied on a consistent basis to all similar instruments. The IFRS IC decided to give no guidance on this issue. In the subsidiary's individual financial statements, the convertible is classified as a financial liability in its entirety, as the conversion option relates to the parent's shares and not the subsidiary's equity. In this case, under IAS 39 the conversion option is an embedded derivative, which should be separated, as it is not closely related to the debt host.

Preference shares with various rights

6.5.107   Preference shares come with various rights. They may be redeemable at the option of the holder or the issuer, mandatorily redeemable or non-redeemable. Dividends on such shares may be either fixed or payable at the issuer's discretion or their payments may be linked to payments on another instrument. IAS 32 requires the classification of preference shares to be based on an assessment of the contractual arrangement's substance and the definitions of a financial liability and an equity instrument. [IAS 32 paras AG 25, AG 26].

6.5.108 Because preference shares are relatively common, we summarise below, for ease of understanding and as a practical aid, the appropriate classification of preference shares for various combinations of redemption and dividend rights. It is assumed that the criteria for equity classification in the 2008 amendment to IAS 32 for puttable financial instruments and obligations arising on liquidation summarised in paragraph 6.5.34 have not been met.

Classification of preference shares

Terms		Classification	
Redemption of principal	**Payment of dividends (assume all at market rates)**	**Type of Instrument**	**Reasons**
Non-redeemable	Discretionary	Equity	There is no contractual obligation to pay cash. Any dividends paid are recognised in equity (see para 6.5.83).
	Non-discretionary	Liability	Liability component is equal to the present value of the dividend payments to perpetuity. Assuming the dividends are set at market rates, the proceeds will be equivalent to the fair value (at the date of issue) of the dividends payable to perpetuity. Therefore, the entire proceeds are classified as a liability.
Redeemable at the issuer's option at some future date.	Discretionary	Equity	There is no contractual obligation to pay cash. An option to redeem the shares for cash does not satisfy the definition of a financial liability. Any dividends paid are recognised in equity (see para 6.5.52).
	Non-discretionary	Liability with an embedded call option derivative	Liability component equal to the present value of the dividend payments to perpetuity. Assuming the dividends are set at market rates, the proceeds will be equivalent to the fair value (at the date of issue) of the dividends payable to perpetuity.

Terms		Classification	
Redemption of principal	**Payment of dividends (assume all at market rates)**	**Type of Instrument**	**Reasons**
			Therefore, the entire proceeds are classified as a liability. In addition, because the entire instrument is classified as a liability, the issuer call option to redeem the shares for cash is an embedded derivative (an asset). The embedded derivative may have to be accounted for separately, unless the option's exercise price is approximately equal on each exercise date to the instrument's amortised cost (see para 6.5.91).
Mandatorily redeemable at a fixed or determinable amount at a fixed or future date	Discretionary	Compound	Liability component is equal to the present value of the redemption amount. Equity component is equal to proceeds less liability component. Any dividends paid are related to the equity component and are recognised in equity (see para 6.5.123). It should be noted, however, that if any unpaid dividends are added to the redemption amount, then the whole instrument is a financial liability. [IAS 32 para AG 37].
	Non-discretionary	Liability	The entity has an obligation to pay cash in respect of both principal and dividends.
Redeemable at the holder's option at some future date.	Discretionary	Compound	Liability component equal to the present value of the redemption amount (on the basis that the criteria in the 2008 amendment to IAS 32 have not been met (see para 6.5.34)). Equity component is equal to proceeds less liability component (see para 6.5.80). Any dividends paid are related to the equity component and are recognised in equity (see para 6.5.123).

Terms		Classification	
Redemption of principal	Payment of dividends (assume all at market rates)	Type of Instrument	Reasons
			It should be noted, however, that if any unpaid dividends are added to the redemption amount, then the whole instrument is a financial liability. [IAS 32 para AG 37].
	Non-discretionary	Liability with an embedded put option derivative	There is a contractual obligation to pay cash in respect of both the principal and dividend. In addition, because the entire instrument is classified as a liability, the embedded put option to redeem the shares for cash is an embedded derivative. The embedded derivative may have to be accounted for separately unless the option's exercise price is approximately equal on each exercise date to the instrument's amortised cost (see chapter 6.3).

6.5.109 In the above table, dividend payments need not be a fixed percentage of the preference shares' nominal value. In some circumstances, the payment of dividends may be based on a fixed percentage of profits, for example, 10% of profits made each year. Such dividends are not an embedded derivative because they are based on a non-financial variable that is specific to one party to the contract (see further chapter 6.2). To the extent that the distribution based on a percentage of profits is non-discretionary and cannot be avoided, such payments give rise to a liability treatment on day one, even though the payments are contingent on the issuer making profits (see para 6.5.75 above).

Derivatives over own equity instruments

6.5.110 An entity may enter into a derivative contract for the purchase or sale of its own equity instruments. Depending upon the nature of the contract (forward based or option based) and the settlement terms (for example, gross or net in cash) in particular, such contracts may be accounted for as equity instruments, financial liabilities or as derivative assets and liabilities.

Contracts accounted for as equity instruments

6.5.111 A derivative contract that will be settled by the entity receiving or delivering a fixed number of its own equity instruments in exchange for a fixed amount of cash or another financial asset is an equity instrument. [IAS 32 paras 22, AG 27(a)]. An example is an issued share option that gives the counterparty a right to buy a fixed number of the entity's shares for a fixed price. The contract's fair value may change due to variation in the share price and market interest rates. However, provided that such changes in the contract's fair value do not affect the amount of cash or other financial assets to be paid or received, or the number of equity instruments to be received or delivered, on the contract's settlement, the contract is treated as an equity instrument. [IAS 32 para 22].

6.5.112 Any consideration received (such as the premium received for a written option or warrant on the entity's own shares) on a derivative contract that is an equity instrument is added directly to equity. Any consideration paid (such as the premium paid for a purchased option) is deducted directly from equity. Changes in an equity instrument's fair value are not recognised in the financial statements. [IAS 32 para 22].

6.5.113 The following examples illustrate the accounting treatment discussed above where an entity enters into derivative contracts to receive or deliver a fixed amount of its own shares in exchange for a fixed amount of cash at some future date.

Example 1 – Purchased call option to receive a fixed number of own shares for a fixed sum [IAS 32 para IE 15]

On 1 February 20X5, an entity purchases a call option for C5,000 under which it has the right but not the obligation to acquire 1,000 of its own shares for cash at the option's exercise of C102 per share. The option will be gross settled in that the entity will take delivery of the shares and pay the exercise price of C102,000 (C102 × 1,000) on the fixed maturity date of 31 January 20X6.

The following information is given:

	Market price per share	Fair value of option
	C	C
At 1 February 20X5	100	5,000
At 31 December 20X5	104	3,000
At 31 January 20X6	104	2,000

The accounting entries from inception to settlement of the contract are as follows:

At 1 February 20X5	Dr	Cr
Equity	C5,000	
Cash		C5,000

At inception of the contract, the entity would record the premium paid for the right to receive a fixed amount of its own shares in one year for a fixed price. As the contract meets the definition of an equity instrument, the premium is charged directly to equity as discussed above.

At 31 December 20X5

No entry is made on 31 December because no cash is paid or received. As the option contract meets the definition of an equity instrument, it is not subsequently re-measured as explained in paragraph 6.5.112. Therefore, the option's fair value is not relevant.

At 31 January 20X6	Dr	Cr
Equity	C102,000	
Cash		C102,000

The entity exercises the call option on the exercise date as it is in the money (exercise price of C102 per share < market price of C104 per share). As the contract is settled gross, the entity takes delivery of 1,000 of its own shares and pays a fixed amount of C102,000 to the counterparty that is recognised directly in equity. Hence, the total amount debited to equity in relation to the purchase is C107,000.

Example 2 – Written call option to deliver a fixed number of own shares for a fixed sum [IAS 32 para IE 20]

On 1 February 20X5, an entity writes a call option for C5,000 under which it has an obligation to sell 1,000 of its own shares for cash at a fixed price of C102 per share, if the counterparty exercises the option. The option will be gross settled in shares in that the entity will deliver its own shares and receive the exercise price of C102,000 (C102 × 1,000) on the fixed maturity date of 31 January 20X6.

The following information is given:

	Market price per share	Fair value of option
	C	C
At 1 February 20X5	100	5,000
At 31 December 20X5	104	3,000
At 31 January 20X6	104	2,000

The accounting entries from inception to settlement of the contract are as follows:

At 1 February 20X5	Dr	Cr
Cash	C5,000	
Equity		C5,000

At inception of the contract, the entity would record the premium received in exchange for the obligation to deliver a fixed amount of its own shares in one year for a fixed price. As the contract meets the definition of an equity instrument, the premium is credited directly to equity as discussed above.

At 31 December 20X5

No entry is made on 31 December because no cash is paid or received. As the option contract meets the definition of an equity instrument, it is not subsequently re-measured as explained in paragraph 6.5.95. Therefore, the option's fair value is not relevant.

At 31 January 20X6	**Dr**	**Cr**
Cash	C102,000	
Equity		C102,000

The counterparty exercises the call option on the exercise date as it is in the money (exercise price of C102 per share < market price of C104 per share). Therefore, the entity is obliged to deliver 1,000 of its own shares in exchange for C102,000 in cash. Hence, the total amount credited to equity in relation to the sale is C107,000.

Example 3 – Purchased put option to deliver a fixed number of own shares for a fixed sum
[IAS 32 para IE 25]

On 1 February 20X5, an entity purchases a put option for C5,000 under which it has the right to sell 1,000 of its own shares for cash at a fixed price of C98 per share, if the entity exercises the put option. The option will be gross settled in that the entity will deliver its own shares and receive the exercise price of C98,000 (C98 × 1,000) on the fixed maturity date of 31 January 20X6.

The following information is given:

	Market price per share	**Fair value of option**
	C	**C**
At 1 February 20X5	100	5,000
At 31 December 20X5	95	4,000
At 31 January 20X6	95	3,000

The accounting entries from inception to settlement of the contract are as follows:

At 1 February 20X5	**Dr**	**Cr**
Equity	C5,000	
Cash		C5,000

At inception of the contract, the entity would record the premium paid received in exchange for the obligation to deliver a fixed amount of its own shares in one year for a fixed price. As the contract meets the definition of an equity instrument, the premium is credited directly to equity as discussed above.

At 31 December 20X5

No entry is made on 31 December because no cash is paid or received. As the option contract meets the definition of an equity instrument, it is not subsequently re-measured as explained in paragraph 6.5.112. Therefore, the option's fair value is not relevant.

At 31 January 20X6	**Dr**	**Cr**
Cash	C98,000	
Equity		C98,000

The entity exercises the put option on the exercise date as it is in the money (exercise price of C98 per share > market price of C95 per share). Therefore, the counterparty is obliged to deliver C98,000 in cash to the entity in exchange for 1,000 shares. Hence, the total amount credited to equity is C93,000.

Example 4 – Forward contract to sell a fixed number of own shares for a fixed sum
[IAS 32 para IE 10]

On 1 February 20X5, an entity enters into a forward sale contract under which it has an obligation to sell 1,000 of its own shares for cash at a fixed price of C104 per share on 31 January 20X6.For simplicity, it is assumed that no dividends are paid on the underlying shares (that is the 'carry return' is zero) so that the present value of the forward price equals the spot price when the fair value of the forward contract is zero. The fair value of the forward has been computed as the difference between the market share price and the present value of the fixed forward price.

The following information is given:

	Market price per share	Fair value of forward
	C	C
At 1 February 20X5	100	Nil
At 31 December 20X5	110	(6,300)
At 31 January 20X6	106	(2,000)

The present value of the forward price on 1 February 20X5 is C100 per share.

The accounting entries from inception to settlement of the contract are as follows:

At 1 February 20X5

At inception of the contract, no entries are made as no cash is paid or received for the forward contract – it has an initial fair value of zero. As the entity enters into a forward contract to deliver a fixed number of its own shares in exchange for a fixed amount of cash or another financial asset, the forward contract meets the definition of an equity instrument because it cannot be settled otherwise than through the delivery of shares in exchange for cash.

At 31 December 20X5

No entry is made on 31 December because no cash is paid or received. As the forward contract meets the definition of an equity instrument, it is not subsequently re-measured as explained in paragraph 6.5.112. Therefore, the contract's fair value is not relevant.

At 31 January 20X6	**Dr**	**Cr**
Cash	C104,000	
Equity		C104,000

The entity settles the forward contract by delivery of 1,000 of its own shares and receives cash of C104,000 in exchange.

Contracts accounted for as financial liabilities

6.5.114 The above circumstances deal with derivative contracts that require gross physical settlement in shares for a fixed amount of cash at some future date. These physically settled contracts are treated as equity instruments. However, a contract that contains an obligation for an entity to purchase its own equity instruments for cash or another financial asset gives rise to a financial liability for the present value of the redemption amount (for example, for the present value of the forward repurchase price, option exercise price or other redemption amount). This is the case even if the contract itself is an equity instrument. When the financial liability is recognised initially under IAS 39, its fair value (the present value of the redemption amount) is reclassified from equity. Subsequently, the financial liability is measured in accordance with IAS 39. If the contract expires without delivery, the carrying amount of the financial liability is reclassified to equity. [IAS 32 para 23]. Paragraph 23 of IAS 32 has been amended by IFRS 13 to remove the reference to initial recognition of the instrument at fair value in accordance with IAS 39. The revised guidance clarifies that the obligation is initially measured at the present value of the redemption amount. This amendment is applicable from when entities adopt IFRS 13.

Example 1 – Forward contract to purchase a fixed number of own shares for a fixed sum [IAS 32 para IE 5]

On 1 February 20X5, an entity enters into a forward purchase contract under which it has the obligation to acquire 1,000 of its own shares for cash at a fixed price of C104 per share on 31 January 20X6.

For simplicity, it is assumed that no dividends are paid on the underlying shares (that is the 'carry return' is zero) so that the present value of the forward price equals the spot price of the entity's shares when the fair value of the forward contract is zero. The fair value of the forward has been computed as the difference between the market share price and the present value of the fixed forward price.

The following information is given:

	Market price per share	Fair value of forward
	C	C
At 1 February 20X5	100	Nil
At 31 December 20X5	110	6,300
At 31 January 20X6	106	2,000

The present value of the forward price on 1 February 20X5 is C100 per share.

The accounting entries from inception to settlement of the contract are as follows:

At 1 February 20X5	Dr	Cr
Equity	C100,000	
Liability		C100,000

As the entity enters into a forward contract to purchase a fixed number of its own shares in exchange for a fixed amount of cash or another financial asset, the forward contract meets the definition of an equity instrument, because it cannot be settled otherwise than through the delivery of shares in exchange for cash. Furthermore, at inception of the contract the entity has an obligation to pay C104,000 in cash in one year's time. Therefore, in accordance with paragraph 6.5.114, the entity recognises a liability for the redemption amount of C104,000 payable in one year at its present value of C100,000.

At 31 December 20X5	Dr	Cr
Interest expense	C3,660	
Liability		C3,660

As the liability needs to be accreted to its final redemption amount of C104,000, the entity recognises interest expense to 31 December in accordance with the effective interest rate method.

At 31 January 20X6	Dr	Cr
Interest expense	C340	
Liability		C340

The entity recognises interest expense to 31 January with the result that the liability is stated at its redemption amount.

	Dr	Cr
Liability	C104,000	
Cash		C104,000

The entity settles its obligation under the forward contract to purchase its own shares for cash of C104,000.

It should be noted that whilst an entity is required to recognise a liability at inception for a forward purchase of its own shares, there is no equivalent requirement to recognise an asset for a forward sale of its own shares, even though the two contracts are economically the 'mirror image' of each other (see example 4 in para 6.5.113 above). This is because in the former situation the shares that are the subject of a forward purchase cease to be equity until acquired as the entity has an obligation to pay cash. In a forward sale, the equity shares continue to be equity until sold.

6.5.115 An entity's contractual obligation to purchase its own equity instruments gives rise to a financial liability for the present value of the redemption amount even if the obligation to purchase is conditional on the counterparty exercising a right to redeem. An example is a written put option that gives the counterparty the right to sell an entity's own equity instruments to the entity for a fixed or variable price. Written puts that give the owners of a non-controlling interest the right to sell their shares to an entity are within the scope of paragraph 23 of IAS 32. For more detail on accounting for written puts over non-controlling interests see chapter 24.

Example 2 – Written put option to purchase a fixed number of own shares for a fixed sum [IAS 32 para IE 30]

On 1 February 20X5, an entity writes a put option for C5,000 under which it has the obligation to purchase 1,000 of its own shares for cash at a fixed price of C98 per share, if the counterparty exercises the put option. The option will be gross settled in that the entity will purchase its own shares and pay the exercise price of C98,000 (C98 × 1,000) on the fixed maturity date of 31 January 20X6.

The following information is given:

	Market price per share	Fair value of option
	C	C
At 1 February 20X5	100	5,000
At 31 December 20X5	95	4,000
At 31 January 20X6	95	3,000

The present value of the option's exercise price on 1 February 20X5 is C95 per share

The accounting entries from inception to settlement of the contract are as follows:

At 1 February 20X5	**Dr**	**Cr**
Cash	C5,000	
Equity		C5,000

At inception of the contract, the entity would record the premium received in exchange for the obligation to deliver a fixed amount of its own shares in one year for a fixed price. As the contract meets the definition of an equity instrument, the premium is credited directly to equity.

	Dr	**Cr**
Equity	C95,000	
Liability		C95,000

Furthermore, at inception of the contract the entity has an obligation to pay C98,000 in cash in one year's time. Therefore, as stated in the above paragraph, the entity recognises the obligation's present value to pay C98,000 in one year's time, that is, C95,000 as a liability.

At 31 December 20X5	**Dr**	**Cr**
Interest expense	C2,750	
Liability		C2,750

As the liability needs to be accreted to its final redemption amount of C98,000, the entity recognises interest expense to 31 December in accordance with the effective interest rate method.

At 31 January 20X6	**Dr**	**Cr**
Interest expense	C250	
Liability		C250

The entity recognises interest expense to 31 January with the result that the liability is stated at its redemption amount of C98,000.

	Dr	**Cr**
Liability	C98,000	
Cash		C98,000

On the same date, the counterparty exercises the put option as it is in the money (exercise price of C98 per share > market price of C95 per share). The entity settles its obligation under the put option by taking delivery of 1,000 of its own shares and paying cash of C98,000 to the counterparty.

If, on the other hand, the contract expires unexercised, the liability of C98,000 is reclassified to equity.

Contracts accounted for as derivative assets or liabilities

6.5.116   All other contracts on own equity that are not physically settled gross in shares for a fixed sum are treated as derivatives and accounted for as derivative assets or liabilities in accordance with IAS 39. These include contracts that are:

- Settled net in cash (or other financial assets). [IAS 32 para AG 27(c)]. Settled net in cash means that the party with a loss delivers to the party with a gain a cash payment equal to the gain and no shares are exchanged.

- Settled net in the entity's own shares. [IAS 32 para AG 27(c)]. Settled net in shares means that the party with a loss delivers to the party with a gain shares with a current fair value equal to the gain. In other words, the entity's own shares are used as a settlement currency.

- Settled net in cash or net in shares at the option of the entity or the counterparty (see para 6.5.84).

6.5.117   The following examples illustrate the accounting treatment discussed above where an entity enters into derivative contracts on an entity's own equity instruments that require settlement either net in cash or net in shares.

> **Example 1 – Forward purchase contract on own shares settled net in cash or net in shares** [IAS 32 paras IE 3, IE 4]
>
> On 1 February 20X5, an entity enters into a forward purchase contract under which it has the obligation to acquire 1,000 of its own shares at a fixed price of C104 per share on 31 January 20X6.
>
> In scenario 1, the contract can only be settled net in cash (no choice by either party).
>
> In scenario 2, the contract can only be settled net in shares (no choice by either party).
>
> For simplicity, it is assumed that no dividends are paid on the underlying shares (that is the 'carry return' is zero) so that the present value of the forward price equals the spot price of the entity's shares when the fair value of the forward contract is zero. The fair value of the forward has been computed as the difference between the market share price and the present value of the fixed forward price.
>
> The following information is given:
>
> | | Market price per share C | Fair value of forward C |
> |---|---|---|
> | At 1 February 20X5 | 100 | Nil |
> | At 31 December 20X5 | 110 | 6,300 |
> | At 31 January 20X6 | 106 | 2,000 |
>
> The present value of the forward price on 1 February 20X5 is C100 per share.
>
> The accounting entries from inception to settlement of the contract in the two scenarios (settled net in cash or net in shares) are as follows:

At 1 February 20X5

The price per share when the contract is agreed on 1 February 20X5 is C100, which is also the market price of the shares at that date. No entry is required, because the derivative's fair value is zero and no cash is paid or received. This applies whether the forward purchase contract is settled net in cash or net in shares.

At 31 December 20X5	**Dr**	**Cr**
Forward asset	C6,300	
Gain in profit or loss		C6,300

On 31 December 20X5, the market price per share has increased to C110 and, as a result, the forward contract's fair value has increased to C6,300. The increase in the contract's fair value is recognised in profit or loss.

At 31 January 20X6	**Dr**	**Cr**
Loss in profit or loss	C4,300	
Forward asset		C4,300

On 31 January 20X6, the market price per share has decreased to C106. The fair value of the forward contract is C2,000 [1,000 * (C106-C104)]. The decrease in the fair value on the forward contract from C6,300 to C2,000 is recognised in profit or loss.

Scenario 1 – Settled net in cash	**Dr**	**Cr**
Cash	C2,000	
Forward asset		C2,000

On the same day, the contract is settled net in cash. The entity has an obligation to deliver C104,000 in cash, being the settlement amount of the contract, to the counterparty. The counterparty has an obligation to deliver cash equal to the fair value of 1,000 shares at the date, that is C106,000 (1,000 × C106) to the entity. So the counterparty pays the net amount of C2,000 to the entity.

Scenario 2 – Settled net in shares	**Dr**	**Cr**
Equity	C2,000	
Forward asset		C2,000

If the contract is settled net in shares, the entity has an obligation to deliver C104,000 worth of its own shares to the counterparty. The counterparty has an obligation to deliver C106,000 (1,000 × C106) worth of the entity's shares to the entity. So the counterparty delivers the net amount of C2,000 worth of the entity's shares to the entity, that is, 18.9 shares (C2,000/C106). The settlement in shares is accounted for as an equity transaction.

Example 2 – Written call option on own shares settled net in cash or net in shares [IAS 32 paras IE 18, IE 19]

On 1 February 20X5, an entity writes a call option for C5,000 under which it has an obligation to sell 1,000 of its own shares at a fixed price of C102 per share, if the counterparty exercises the call option. The option will be settled on the fixed maturity date of 31 January 20X6.

In scenario 1, the contract can only be settled net in cash (no choice by either party).

In scenario 2, the contract can only be settled net in shares (no choice by either party).

The following information is given:

	Market price per share	Fair value of option
	C	C
At 1 February 20X5	100	5,000
At 31 December 20X5	104	3,000
At 31 January 20X6	104	2,000

The accounting entries from inception to settlement of the contract in the two scenarios (settled net in cash or net in shares) are as follows:

At 1 February 20X5	Dr	Cr
Cash	C5,000	
Call option obligation		C5,000

At inception of the contract, the entity would record the premium received under the contract in both scenarios.

At 31 December 20X5	Dr	Cr
Call option obligation	C2,000	
Gain in profit or loss		C2,000

On 31 December 20X5, the fair value of the call option obligation has fall to C3,000. The decrease in the fair value of the obligation is recognised as a gain in profit or loss.

At 31 January 20X6	Dr	Cr
Call option obligation	C1,000	
Gain in profit or loss		C1,000

On 31 January 20X6, the fair value of the call option obligation has fallen further to C2,000. The decrease in the fair value is recognised as a gain in profit or loss.

Scenario 1 – Settled net in cash	Dr	Cr
Call option obligation	C2,000	
Cash		C2,000

If the contract is settled net in cash, the entity has an obligation to deliver C104,000 in cash, being the fair value of the 1,000 shares on 31 January 20X6, to the counterparty. The counterparty has an obligation to deliver cash equal to the option's exercise price of C102,000 to the entity. So the entity pays the net amount of C2,000 to the counterparty.

Scenario 2 – *Settled net in shares*	**Dr**	**Cr**
Call option obligation	C2,000	
Equity		C2,000

If, the contract is settled net in shares, the entity has an obligation to deliver C104,000 worth of its own shares to the counterparty. The counterparty has an obligation to deliver C102,000 worth of the entity's shares to the entity. So the entity delivers the net amount of C2,000 worth of its own shares to the counterparty, that is, 19.2 shares (C2,000/C104). The settlement in shares is accounted for as an equity transaction.

Issuer or holder's settlement options

6.5.118   The examples above deal with situations where the settlement of the derivative contracts on own equity, either net in cash or net in shares, was dictated by the contractual terms (no choice). Sometimes such derivative contracts may contain settlement options that give either party a choice over how it is settled (for example, the issuer or the holder can choose to settle the contract net in cash, or net in shares or by exchanging shares for cash). As explained in paragraph 6.5.84 above, when a derivative financial instrument gives one party a choice over how it is settled, it is a financial asset or a financial liability unless all of the settlement alternatives would result in it being an equity instrument. [IAS 32 para 26].

Treatment of interest, dividends, gains and losses

6.5.119   The general principle of IAS 32 is that the treatment of interest, dividends, losses and gains follows the classification of the related instrument. Therefore, where such items relate to equity instruments, they are included in equity. On the other hand, if they relate to instruments that are classified as financial liabilities, they are included in profit or loss. IAS 32, therefore, requires that:

■   Interest, dividends, losses and gains relating to a financial instrument or a component that is a financial liability should be recognised as income or expense in profit or loss.

■   Distributions to holders of an equity instrument should be debited by the entity directly to equity, net of any related income tax benefit.

[IAS 32 para 35].

6.5.120   It follows from the above requirement that dividend payments on preference shares that are classified wholly as liabilities are included in calculating amortised cost and, hence, recognised as expenses in the same way as interest on a bond. They may be presented in the income statement either with interest on other liabilities or as a separate item. The standard notes that in some circumstances, it may be desirable to disclose interest and dividends separately in the income statement, because of the differences between interest and dividends with respect to matters such as tax deductibility. Disclosure of interest and dividends is subject to the requirements of IAS 1 and IFRS 7. Disclosures of the tax effects should be made in accordance with IAS 12. [IAS 32 para 40].

6.5.121 Gains and losses associated with redemptions or refinancings of financial liabilities are recognised in profit or loss. Similarly, gains and losses related to changes in the carrying amount of a financial liability are recognised in profit or loss. This is so even when they relate to an instrument that includes a right to the residual interest in the entity's assets in exchange for cash or another financial asset (for example, units in mutual funds that are puttable – see para 6.5.27 above). Under IAS 1, the entity presents any gain or loss arising from remeasurement of such an instrument separately on the face of the income statement when it is relevant in explaining the entity's performance. [IAS 32 para 41]. IAS 32 contains examples of income statement presentation where an entity has little or no equity. [IAS 32 paras IE 32-IE 33].

6.5.122 Redemptions or refinancings of equity instruments are recognised in equity. Changes in the fair value of an equity instrument are not recognised in the financial statements. [IAS 32 para 36].

6.5.123 The application of the principle in paragraph 6.5.119 above to compound financial instruments requires any payments relating to the liability component to be reported in profit or loss and any payments relating to the equity component to be reported in equity. An example is mandatorily redeemable preference shares with discretionary dividend payments. Such an instrument is a compound financial instrument, with the liability component being the present value of the redemption amount. The unwinding of the discount on this component is recognised in profit or loss and classified as interest expense. Any dividends paid relate to the equity component and are recognised as a distribution of profit or loss. A similar treatment applies if the redemption was not mandatory but at the option of the holder, or if the preference shares were mandatorily convertible into a variable number of ordinary shares calculated to equal a fixed amount or an amount based on changes in an underlying variable (for example, a commodity). However, if any unpaid dividends are added to the redemption amount, the entire instrument is a liability. In such a case, any dividends are classified as interest expense that will be accounted for in accordance with the effective interest method. [IAS 32 para AG 37].

> **Example – Premium payable on the cancellation of the conversion option in a convertible bond**
>
> An entity has issued a convertible bond, which is classified as a compound instrument (liability host bond and an equity conversion option). The entity decides after issue to cancel the conversion option in order to remove the dilution effect on its share capital. The issuer will have to pay the bondholder a premium to compensate for giving up its conversion rights, which is likely to be greater than the fair value of the conversion option to incentivise the bondholder to accept the change in terms. Provided that the terms of the liability component of the bond remain unchanged, the premium paid to cancel the equity conversion option is a payment for an own equity instrument. The premium paid is, therefore, debited to equity, as for any repurchase of an entity's own equity instruments.

Treatment of transaction costs of equity instruments

6.5.124 An entity typically incurs various costs in issuing or acquiring its own equity instruments. Those costs might include registration and other regulatory fees, underwriting costs and brokerage fees, amounts paid to lawyers, accountants, investment bankers and other professional advisers, fees and commissions paid to agents, brokers, and dealers, printing costs and stamp duties. Most such costs are transaction costs, that is, incremental costs that are directly attributable to the equity transaction that otherwise would have been avoided had the equity instruments not been issued. Transaction costs arising on the issue of equity instruments, however, do not include indirect costs, such as the costs of management time and administrative overheads, or allocations of internal costs that would have been incurred had the equity instruments not been issued. Nor do they include costs of researching different types of equity instruments or of ascertaining the suitability or feasibility of particular equity instruments. Generally, costs for marketing an IPO, including the 'road show', do not meet the definition of a transaction cost. Marketing costs primarily relate to the marketing of the entity itself. Therefore in most situations marketing costs for an IPO do not meet the definition of directly attributable and therefore are expensed through profit or loss.

6.5.125 IAS 32 requires that transaction costs of an equity transaction should be accounted for as a deduction from equity, net of any related income tax benefit. [IAS 32 para 35]. This treatment is based on the view that the transaction costs incurred are a necessary part of completing the equity transaction and form an integral part of it. Linking the equity transaction and costs of the transaction reflects the net proceeds received from the transaction in equity. This approach achieves a result which is consistent with paragraph 6.5.119 above, which states that a financial instrument's classification in the balance sheet determines whether interest, dividends, losses and gains relating to that instrument are reported in the income statement. As a result, losses relating to a financial instrument classified as the issuer's equity are reported by the issuer as movements in equity.

6.5.125.1 Qualifying transaction costs are often incurred in anticipation of an issuance of equity instruments and may cross reporting periods. For example, transaction costs may be incurred before an entity's year end but the issuance of the equity instruments does not occur until after the year end. It is unclear whether paragraph 35 of IAS 32 applies when the equity instrument has not yet been recognised. As such, management may choose to either record these costs as a deduction from equity or to defer the costs on the balance sheet until the equity instrument is recognised. This is a policy choice that should be applied consistently. Where the latter treatment is adopted, deferred costs are subsequently reclassified as a deduction from equity when the equity instruments are recognised. If the equity instruments are not subsequently issued, for example because the equity transaction is abandoned, the transaction costs should be recognised as an expense under both approaches.

6.5.126 Transaction costs that relate to the issue of a compound financial instrument are allocated to the instrument's liability and equity components in proportion to the allocation of proceeds (see example in para 6.5.93). See Chapter 6.7 for more discussion on transaction costs.

6.5.127 Transaction costs that relate jointly to more than one transaction (for example, costs of a concurrent offering of some shares and a stock exchange listing of other shares) are allocated to those transactions using a basis of allocation that is rational and consistent with similar transactions. [IAS 32 para 38]. This situation often arises when an entity undertakes an initial public offering (IPO) of its shares. As a result of the IPO, new shares are issued to investors to raise additional capital and, along with existing shares, subsequently become listed on a stock exchange. Costs incurred in listing existing shares on a stock exchange are not transaction costs relating to the issue of an equity instrument. This is because these costs are simply incurred to make the existing shares more marketable and are not related to the equity instrument's issue. In some situations, the existing shares may be included in a 'secondary offering' (that is, a sale of shares by existing shareholders as opposed to the company itself). As the cash generated from the sale of secondary shares is given to the selling shareholders, rather than the company, any costs incurred are not equity transaction costs. Therefore, these costs should be charged to the income statement. On the other hand, costs incurred in issuing new shares to raise capital ('primary offering') in an IPO are transaction costs of equity instrument and, as explained above, fall to be charged to equity. In practice, entities would need to identify the costs that are specifically attributable to the issue of new shares. All other costs of the IPO that would not have been incurred had the IPO not taken place should be allocated between the new shares and old shares on some reasonable basis, for example, in the ratio of old to new shares. It follows from the above that any costs incurred by the company in a 'secondary offering' of its own shares are not equity transaction costs. Accordingly, those costs should be charged to profit or loss.

6.5.128 The amount of transaction costs accounted for as a deduction from equity in the period is disclosed separately under IAS 1. The related amount of income taxes recognised directly in equity is included in the aggregate amount of current and deferred income tax credited or charged to equity that is disclosed under IAS 12. [IAS 32 para 39; IAS 12 para 81(a)].

Treasury shares

6.5.129 When an entity purchases its own shares and holds them in treasury ('treasury shares'), IAS 32 requires the following:

- The amount paid for the treasury shares is deducted from equity. This is because an entity's own equity instruments are not recognised as a financial asset regardless of the reason for which they are acquired. However, where an entity holds its own equity on behalf of others, for example, a financial institution holding its own equity on behalf of a client, there is an agency relationship and as a result those holdings are not included in the entity's balance sheet.

■ No gain or loss should be recognised in profit or loss on the purchase, sale, issue or cancellation of an entity's own equity instruments. This is because the acquisition and subsequent resale of treasury shares are transactions with entity's owners rather than a gain or loss to the entity.

■ Consideration paid or received for the purchase or sale of an entity's own equity instruments should be recognised directly in equity.

[IAS 32 paras 33, AG 36].

6.5.130   IAS 32 notes that own equity instruments may be acquired and held by the entity or by other members of the consolidated group (that is, the parent and its subsidiaries, but excluding the group's associates and joint ventures). [IAS 32 para 33]. Therefore, the above accounting applies to all interests in own equity instruments held by a company and, in consolidated financial statements, the parent's shares held by subsidiaries. In the latter case, this applies to all such shareholdings, including those held by subsidiaries that carry on a business of dealing in securities. However, in the individual financial statements of a subsidiary that holds shares in its parent, such shares are treated as an asset; that is, 'treasury shares' accounting does not apply as these are not 'own shares' for the subsidiary itself.

Example – Purchase of own shares held in treasury

Entity A (a listed company) has in issue 1,000,000 C1 ordinary shares originally issued at a premium of C9. It buys back 20,000 shares when their market value is C40 per share. The purchase is made out of retained profits and the entity holds the shares in treasury. In this situation, the entity does not reduce its issued share capital, but instead will reduce its retained profits by the consideration paid for the shares (that is, 20,000 × C40 = C800,000), as shown below.

It should be noted that this treatment only applies in the UK and the treatment in other jurisdictions may be different.

	Before purchase C'000	Purchase C'000	After purchase C'000
Net assets other than cash	20,000	20,000	
Cash	5,000	(800)	4,200
	25,000	(800)	24,200
Share capital	1,000	1,000	
Share premium	9,000	9,000	
Capital	10,000	10,000	
Retained profits	15,000	(800)	14,200
	25,000	(800)	24,200

As can be seen from the above example, the entire consideration paid for the purchase is recognised directly in equity (retained profits).

In the notes to the financial statements, entity A should explain that 20,000 C1 ordinary shares with an aggregate nominal value of C20,000 were purchased during the period and are held in treasury and that retained profits have been reduced by C800,000, being the consideration paid for these shares.

As stated in paragraph 6.5.125 above, the costs of an equity transaction should be accounted for as a deduction from equity. [IAS 32 para 35]. Therefore, expenses directly relating to the treasury share purchase should be treated as part of the overall cost of purchase and like the purchase cost itself should be recognised directly in equity (retained profits) and shown in the statement of changes in equity.

6.6 – Recognition and derecognition

6.6 – Recognition and derecognition

Introduction

6.6.1 Previous chapters have dealt with what qualifies as financial assets and financial liabilities. The next step in the accounting is to determine when financial assets and financial liabilities should be recognised, that is, included in an entity's balance sheet. Conversely, it is also necessary to know when a financial asset or financial liability should be derecognised, that is, when a previously recognised financial asset or financial liability should be removed from an entity's balance sheet.

6.6.2 As explained in chapter 6.2, the rights or obligations that comprise financial assets or financial liabilities are derived from the contractual provisions that underlie them. As a result, an entity only recognises a financial asset or a financial liability at the time it becomes a party to a contract. [IAS 39 para 14]. That is the point at which it has the contractual rights or contractual obligations. As the above discussion suggests, recognition issues for financial assets and financial liabilities tend to be straightforward. They are dealt with in paragraphs 6.6.6 to 6.6.24 below.

6.6.3 Conversely, when considering whether to cease recognising (derecognise) a financial asset or a financial liability, an entity needs to consider whether it still has that asset or liability. In other words, the entity needs to determine whether the rights or obligations contained in the original asset or liability cease to be contractual rights or obligations.

6.6.4 Derecognition issues for financial instruments are generally far from straightforward, except where relatively simple financial instruments and transactions are involved. The derecognition requirements in IAS 39 are complex as a result. These issues for financial instruments are discussed from paragraph 6.6.25 for financial assets and paragraph 6.6.163 for financial liabilities respectively.

6.6.5 In March 2009, the IASB issued the exposure draft 'Derecognition: Proposed amendments to IAS 39 and IFRS 7'. The exposure draft proposed an approach intended to reduce the complexity of the current requirements and the resulting difficulty in applying them in practice. It also introduced new disclosure requirements. However, the exposure draft did not attract significant support. In June 2010, the IASB decided to defer work on a new standard to concentrate on other more urgent projects, while focusing on improving and converging disclosure requirements. As a consequence, the IASB issued an amendment to IFRS 7 in October 2010 requiring greater disclosure of transferred financial assets. This is discussed further in chapter 6.9. Meanwhile, the existing IAS 39 recognition and derecognition requirements have been incorporated, unchanged, into IFRS 9.

Initial recognition

General principles

6.6.6   Under IAS 39 an entity is required to recognise a financial asset or liability on its balance sheet when, and only when, it becomes a party to the instrument's contractual provisions. [IAS 39 para 14].

Application of the general principles

6.6.7   Examples of situations where an entity becomes a party to the contractual provisions of a financial instrument are many and varied. Some of these situations are considered in the paragraphs that follow.

Unconditional receivables and payables

6.6.8   Unconditional receivables and payables are recognised as assets or liabilities when the entity becomes a party to the contract and, as a consequence, has a legal right to receive or a legal obligation to pay cash. [IAS 39 para AG 35(a)].

Forwards and options

6.6.9   When an entity becomes a party to a forward contract that falls within IAS 39's scope, it becomes exposed to risks and benefits at the contract commitment date, rather than on the date on which settlement takes place. At the commitment date, the fair values of the right and obligation are often equal, so that the net fair value of the forward contract is zero. If the net fair value of the right and obligation is not zero at inception, the contract is recognised as an asset or liability. [IAS 39 para AG 35(c)]. A forward contract that has a zero fair value at inception may become a net asset or liability in the future depending on the value of the underlying instrument or commodity that is the subject of the forward.

6.6.10   Similarly, option contracts that fall within IAS 39's scope are recognised as assets or liabilities when the holder or writer become a party to the contract. [IAS 39 para AG 35(d)]. Evidence that a recognisable event arises when the entities become parties to the contract lies in the fact that the option holder usually pays, and the option writer usually receives, a premium for the contract, which indicates that the rights and obligations undertaken by each party have value at that date.

Firm commitments to buy or sell non-financial assets

6.6.11 When an entity enters into a firm commitment to purchase a non-financial asset in the future, it does not have the contractual rights that comprise the asset. This means that the entity cannot use that asset, or sell it, or pledge it as collateral until the contract matures and the underlying asset is acquired. Therefore, assets to be acquired and liabilities to be incurred as a result of a firm commitment to purchase or sell goods or services are generally not recognised as assets or liabilities until at least one of the parties has performed under the agreement. For example, an entity that receives a firm order does not generally recognise an asset for the consideration to be received (and the entity that places the order does not recognise a liability for the consideration to be paid) at the time of the commitment but, rather, delays recognition until the ordered goods or services have been shipped, delivered or rendered. Another example is given in paragraph 6.6.102.

6.6.12 However, as stated in chapter 6.1 above, contracts to buy or sell non-financial assets that can be settled net or by exchanging financial instruments are treated as if they are financial instruments, that is, derivatives unless they were entered into and continued to be held to meet the entity's normal purchase, sale or usage requirements. Therefore, the net fair value of the contract itself is recognised as an asset or liability at the commitment date.

6.6.13 Also, if a previously unrecognised firm commitment is designated as a hedged item in a fair value hedge, IAS 39 requires that any change in the net fair value attributable to the hedged risk is recognised as an asset or liability after the inception of the hedge (see chapter 6.8). Some argue that it is conceptually incorrect to recognise an asset or liability for a firm commitment because it has been hedged. The IASB explains in the Basis of Conclusions that the only difference between a firm commitment that is not hedged and a one that is hedged is that the latter is re-measured for changes in the hedged fair value while the former is measured at its historical cost of zero. Accordingly, there is no fundamental difference in concept as far as recognition is concerned. [IAS 39 paras AG35(b), BC152].

Planned future transactions

6.6.14 As stated in paragraph 6.6.6 above, a financial asset or a liability should not be recognised before an entity becomes a party to the contract. It follows that planned future transactions, no matter how likely, cannot give rise to financial assets and liabilities because the entity has not become a party to a contract. [IAS 39 para AG 35(e)]. Such future transactions are future events to be recognised in the future periods when contractual rights are acquired or obligations incurred.

Regular way transactions

6.6.15 A regular way purchase or sale is a purchase or sale of a financial asset under a contract whose terms require delivery of the asset within the *time frame* established generally by regulation or convention in the *marketplace* concerned. [IAS 39 para 9]. Marketplace is not limited to a formal stock exchange or organised over-the-counter market. Rather, it means the environment in which the financial asset is customarily exchanged. An acceptable time frame in such a marketplace would be the period reasonably and customarily required for the parties to complete the transaction, prepare, and execute closing documents. [IAS 39 para IG B28].

6.6.16 In many regulated financial markets, a settlement mechanism will exist under which transactions in financial instruments (particularly quoted equities and bonds) entered into on a particular date are settled a few days after this transaction date. The date on which the transaction is entered into is called the 'trade date'. It is the date on which the entity commits to purchase or sell an asset. The date on which the transaction is settled by delivery of the underlying asset is called the 'settlement date'. For example, the standard settlement periods on the London Stock Exchange for equity market securities and wholesale gilts are trade date plus 3 business days $(T+3)$ and trade date plus 1 business day $(T+1)$ respectively. A contract with an individual or through a broker to buy or sell a financial asset that is normally traded on a regulated financial market, but with a settlement period that differs from that established by regulation in that financial marketplace, does not qualify as a regular way transaction. [IAS 39 para IG B29, B30].

6.6.17 A regular way purchase or sale that gives rise to a fixed price commitment between trade date and settlement date is a derivative – a forward contract. Therefore, in accordance with the principle explained in paragraph 6.6.9, a regular way purchase or sale would fall to be recognised as a forward contract at the commitment date (that is, trade date). However, because of the short duration of the commitment, such contracts are not recognised as derivative financial instruments under IAS 39. Instead, IAS 39 provides for special accounting for such regular way contracts, as discussed from paragraph 6.6.19 below. [IAS 39 para AG12]. This exception is a practical expedient to prevent the recognition of derivatives for short periods where the marketplace mechanism prevents settlement at the trade or commitment date. Furthermore, the exception also removes a potential distortion that would occur by recognising changes in fair value of the asset between trade and settlement date through profit or loss, when such changes in fair value after settlement date would either not be recognised at all (where the financial asset is classified as a held-to-maturity asset), or recognised in other comprehensive income (where the financial asset is classified as available-for-sale).

6.6.18 The regular way exception requires that the transaction will be settled by physical delivery of the financial instrument within the normal market time frame. Therefore, where a contract permits net settlement in cash or other financial assets equivalent to the change in the contract's fair value, it does not qualify as a regular way transaction. Such a contract is accounted for as a derivative in the period between trade and settlement date. [IAS 39 para AG 54]. Contracts that are settled outside the normal market time frame, whether settled net in cash or gross, will always be accounted for as derivatives.

Trade date versus settlement date accounting

6.6.19 IAS 39 provides that a regular way purchase or sale of financial assets should be recognised and derecognised, as applicable, using trade date accounting or settlement date accounting. Either method is acceptable, but it is an accounting policy choice that should be disclosed and applied consistently for all purchases and sales that belong to the same category of financial assets as set out in chapter 6.4. For this purpose assets that are held for trading form a separate category from assets designated at fair value through profit and loss. [IAS 39 para AG 53].

6.6.20 Where an entity adopts trade date accounting (the date on which an entity commits itself to purchase or sell an asset), the accounting treatment is as follows:

■ In respect of a purchase of a financial asset, the asset received and the liability to pay for it are recognised on the trade date. After initial recognition, the financial asset is subsequently measured either at amortised cost or at fair value depending on its initial classification as explained in chapter 6.7.

■ In respect of a sale of a financial asset, the asset is derecognised and the receivable from the buyer for the payment together with any gain or loss on disposal are recognised on the trade date.

IAS 39 notes that, generally, interest does not start to accrue on the asset and corresponding liability until settlement date when title passes.

[IAS 39 para AG 55].

6.6.21 Where an entity adopts settlement date accounting (the date that an asset is delivered to or by an entity), the accounting treatment is as follows:

■ In respect of a purchase of a financial asset, the asset is recognised on the day it is received by the entity. Any change in the asset's fair value to be received during the period between the trade date and the settlement date is accounted for in the same way as the acquired asset. In other words:

■ for assets carried at cost or amortised cost, the change in value is not recognised;

■ for assets classified as financial assets at fair value through profit or loss, the change in value is recognised in profit or loss; and

■ for available-for-sale assets, the change in value is recognised in other comprehensive income.

■ In respect of a sale of a financial asset, the asset is derecognised and the receivable from the buyer for the payment together with any gain or loss on disposal are recognised on the day that it is delivered by the entity. Any change in the fair value of the asset between trade date and settlement date is not recognised, as there is an agreed upon sale price at the trade date, making subsequent changes in fair value irrelevant from the seller's perspective. In other words, the seller's right to changes in the fair value ceases on the trade date.

[IAS 39 para AG 56].

6.6.22 The following examples illustrate the application of trade date and settlement date accounting to the various categories of financial asset identified by IAS 39. These examples are based on those included in IAS 39's implementation guidance. [IAS 39 paras IG D2.1, D2.2].

Example 1 – Regular way purchase of a financial asset

On 29 December 20X5, an entity commits to purchase a financial asset for C1,000, which is its fair value on commitment (trade) date. Transaction costs are immaterial. On 31 December 20X5 (financial year-end) and on 4 January 20X6 (settlement date) the fair value of the asset is C1,002 and C1,003, respectively. The amounts to be recorded for the asset will depend on how it is classified and whether trade date or settlement date accounting is used, as shown in the two tables below.

Trade date accounting			
Details	**Held-to-maturity investments – carried at amortised cost**	**Available-for-sale assets – remeasured to fair value with changes in other comprehensive income**	**Assets at fair value through profit or loss – remeasured to fair value with changes in profit or loss**
29 December 20X5	C	C	C
Dr Financial asset	1,000	1,000	1,000
Cr Liability for payment	(1,000)	(1,000)	(1,000)
To record asset and liability for payment			
31 December 20X5			
Dr Financial asset	–	2	2
Cr Other comprehensive income	–	(2)	–
Cr Income statement	–	–	(2)
To recognise change in fair value			
4 January 20X6			
Dr Financial asset	–	1	1
Cr Other comprehensive income	–	(1)	–
Cr Income statement	–	–	(1)
To recognise change in fair value			

4 January 20X6
Dr Liability for payment	1,000	1,000	1,000
Cr Cash	(1,000)	(1,000)	(1,000)

To record settlement of liability

Asset's carrying value at 4 January 20X6	1,000	1,003	1,003

Settlement date accounting

29 December 20X5
No entries are recorded at the commitment date

	–	–	–

31 December 20X5
Dr Financial asset	–	2	2
Cr Other comprehensive income	–	(2)	–
Cr Income statement	–	–	(2)

To recognise change in fair value

4 January 20X6
Dr Financial asset	–	1	1
Cr Other comprehensive income	–	(1)	–
Cr Income statement	–	–	(1)

To recognise change in fair value

4 January 20X6
Dr Financial asset	1,000	1,000	1,000
Cr Cash	(1,000)	(1,000)	(1,000)

To record the asset's purchase at the contracted cash amount plus changes in fair value since trade date.

Asset's carrying value at 4 January 20X6	1000	1003	1003

Example 2 – Regular way sale of a financial asset

On 29 December 20X5 (trade date) an entity enters into a contract to sell a financial asset for its current fair value of C1,010. The asset was acquired one year earlier for C1,000 and its amortised cost is C1,000. On 31 December 20X5 (financial year-end), the fair value of the asset is C1,012. On 4 January 20X6 (settlement date), the fair value is C1,013. The amounts to be recorded will depend on how the asset is classified and whether trade date or settlement date accounting is used as shown in the two tables below (any interest that might have accrued on the asset is disregarded).

Trade date accounting **Date**	Held-to-maturity investments - carried at amortised cost C	Available- for-sale assets – remeasured to fair value with changes in other comprehensive income C	Assets at fair value through profit or loss - remeasured to fair value with changes in profit or loss C
Carrying value prior to 29 December 20X5	1,000	1,010	1,010
29 December 20X5			
Dr Receivable	1,010	1,010	1,010
Cr Asset	(1,000)	(1,010)	(1,010)
Dr Other comprehensive income		10	–
Cr Profit or loss	(10)	(10)	–

To record disposal of the asset and 'recycling' of cumulative gain from other comprehensive income to profit or loss on disposal of the available-for-sale asset on trade date.

31 December 20X5
A change in the fair value of a financial asset that is sold on a regular way basis is not recorded in the financial statements between trade date and settlement date because the seller's right to changes in the fair value ceases on the trade date.

4 January 20X6			
Dr Cash	1,010	1,010	1,010
Cr Receivable	(1,010)	(1,010)	(1,010)

To record settlement of sales contract

Settlement date accounting			
29 December 20X5			
Carrying value prior to 29 December 20X5	1,000	1,010	1,010

31 December 20X5

A change in the fair value of a financial asset that is sold on a regular way basis is not recorded in the financial statements between trade date and settlement date, even if the entity applies settlement date accounting, because the seller's right to changes in the fair value ceases on the trade date.

4 January 20X6

Dr Cash	1,010	1,010	1,010
Cr Asset	(1,000)	(1,010)	(1,010)
Dr Other comprehensive income		10	–
Cr Profit or loss	(10)	(10)	–

To record the disposal of the asset and 'recycling' of cumulative gain on the available-for-sale asset recognised in other comprehensive income to profit or loss on settlement date.

In summary, regular way sale is accounted for as a sale on trade date if trade date accounting is used and on settlement date if settlement date accounting is used.

6.6.23 It should be noted that the above requirements apply only to transactions in financial assets. IAS 39 does not contain any specific requirements about trade date accounting and settlement date accounting for transactions in financial instruments that are classified as financial liabilities. This means that the general recognition and derecognition requirements for financial liabilities in IAS 39 apply. [IAS 39 para IG B32]. Under IAS 39, liabilities are recognised on the date the entity 'becomes a party to the contractual provisions of the instrument' (see para 6.6.6 above). Financial liabilities are derecognised only when they are extinguished, that is, when the obligation specified in the contract is discharged or cancelled or expires (see further para 6.6.164 below).

Exchange of non-cash financial assets

6.6.24 Sometimes an entity may enter into a regular way transaction to sell a non-cash financial asset not for cash, but in exchange for another non-cash financial asset. In this situation, a question arises as to whether any change in fair value of the financial asset to be received should be recognised between trade and settlement date in circumstances where the entity adopts settlement date accounting for the financial asset to be disposed of. The answer depends on the classification of the asset to be received in exchange and whether the entity uses trade date or settlement date accounting for purchases or sales of assets in that category. Consider the following example:

Example – Regular way sale of a financial asset for non-cash consideration

On 29 December 20X5 (trade date) entity A enters into a contract to sell note receivable A, which is carried at amortised cost, in exchange for bond B, which will be classified as held for trading and measured at fair value. Both assets have a fair value of C1,010 on 29 December, while the amortised cost of note receivable A is C1,000. Entity A uses settlement date accounting for loans and receivables and trade date accounting for assets held for trading.

On 31 December 20X5 (financial year-end), the fair value of note receivable A is C1,012 and the fair value of bond B is C1,009. On 4 January 20X6, the fair value of note receivable A is C1,013 and the fair value of bond B is C1,007.

The following entries are made:

	Dr C	Cr C
29 December 20X5		
Bond B	1,010	
Liability for payment		1,010
To record the purchase of bond B on the trade date as per entity's policy of using trade date accounting for assets held for trading.		
31 December 20X5		
Profit or loss	1	
Bond B		1
To record the change in fair value of bond B from C1,010 to C1,009.		
4 January 20X6		
Liability for payment	1,010	
Note receivable A		1,000
Profit or loss		10
To record the disposal of note receivable A and the resultant gain on sale in exchange for bond B on settlement date.		
Profit or loss	2	
Bond B		2
To record the change in fair value of bond B from C1,009 to C1,007.		

Derecognition of financial assets

Introduction

6.6.25 It is fairly common for entities to raise finance by selling financial assets, such as portfolios of trade receivables, loans, etc. No special problem arises where a transferor sells financial assets for cash or other assets, with no continuing involvement with the asset sold or with the transferee. The accounting for such transactions as sales with corresponding derecognition of the asset is well established. At the other extreme is a transfer of a financial asset where the buyer has an unconditional right and obligation to return the asset at the original price, usually with interest as in a repurchase transaction. Again, the accounting in this situation is fairly straightforward. The transaction is treated as a financing, with both the asset and the liability on balance sheet, because the risk and rewards of ownership of the asset have not been transferred.

6.6.26 Problems begin to surface, however, when transfers are undertaken between the above two extremes in circumstances where the seller retains certain interests in the assets transferred. Examples include transfers that are subject to recourse and agreements to acquire the transferred asset or make additional payments that reflect the performance of the transferred asset.

Requirements in IAS 39 for derecognition

6.6.27 IAS 39 contains one set of requirements that apply to the derecognition of all financial assets, from the simple maturity of an instrument to the more complex securitisation transactions. The standard provides a flow chart (below) that summarises IAS 39's requirements for evaluating whether, and to what extent, a financial asset is derecognised. Every transaction should be analysed using the strict sequence set out in the flow chart. Most importantly, there are two separate approaches to derecognition under IFRS: the 'risks and rewards' approach and the 'control' approach. The control approach is only used where the risks and rewards approach does not provide a clear answer. Hence the risks and rewards approach should be evaluated first. A detailed explanation of these two approaches and each step of the flow chart follows.

6.6.28 For analysis purposes and ease of reference, each step has a number and refers to a particular step in the diagram. For example, if step 6 = Yes, this means that the entity has transferred substantially all the risks and rewards of ownership. Similarly, if step 6 = No and step 7 = No, this means that the entity has neither transferred nor retained substantially all of the risks and rewards of ownership. This notation is used throughout the remainder of the chapter.

6.6 – Recognition and derecognition

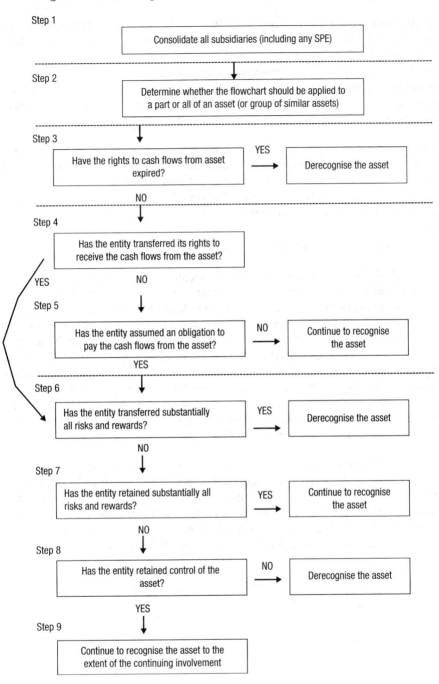

Consolidate all subsidiaries including any SPEs (step 1)

6.6.29 Many entities establish special purpose entities (SPEs), trusts, partnerships, etc. to acquire financial assets before these financial assets, or a portion thereof, are transferred to third-party investors. The transfer of financial assets to such an entity might qualify as a legal sale. However, if the substance of the relationship between the transferor and the SPE indicates that the transferor controls the SPE, the transferor should consolidate the SPE. The first step is to determine what is the reporting entity that is considering whether to derecognise the financial asset – that is, whether it is the consolidated or the individual entity. If it is the consolidated entity, the entity should first consolidate all subsidiaries, including any special purpose entities, in accordance with IAS 27 and SIC 12 (or IFRS 10 if applicable). It should then apply the derecognition analysis to the resulting group. (Note that an entity preparing separate financial statements will not need to consider this step.) [IAS 39 para 15].

6.6.30 Step 1, therefore, ensures that the derecognition analysis produces the same answer regardless of whether the entity transfers financial assets, or a portion thereof, directly to third party investors or through a consolidated SPE or trust that obtains the transferred assets and, in turn, transfers them directly to third party investors. [IAS 39 para BC64].

6.6.31 A variety of factors needs to be evaluated to determine whether the substance of the relationship between an entity and an SPE indicates the entity controls the SPE such that the SPE is consolidated. Indicators of control provided in SIC 12 paragraph 10 are:

■ In substance, the activities of the SPE are being conducted on the entity's behalf according to its specific business needs, so that the entity obtains benefits from the SPE's operation;

■ In substance, the entity has the decision-making powers to obtain the majority of the benefits of the SPE's activities or, by setting up an 'autopilot' mechanism, the entity has delegated these decision-making powers;

■ In substance, the entity has rights to obtain the majority of the SPE's benefits and, therefore, may be exposed to risks incidental to the SPE's activities; or

■ In substance, the entity retains the majority of the residual or ownership risks related to the SPE or its assets in order to obtain benefits from its activities.

6.6.32 The decision to consolidate an SPE always depends on specific facts and circumstances; if those change, entities will need to re-assess their consolidation decisions. This is especially relevant in difficult market conditions where companies might need to step in to support SPEs when there was previously no contractual obligation to do so. These issues are considered further in chapter 24.

6.6.32.1 On the other hand, the IAS 39 derecognition criteria are not applicable to financial assets held by operating subsidiaries that cease to be consolidated by the group though loss of control under IAS 27 (or IFRS 10). [However where special purpose entities (SPEs) are used to transfer financial assets, the substance of the transaction should be considered to determine whether it is appropriate to look through the SPE to the underlying assets.]

Determine whether the flow chart applies to all or part of an asset (step 2)

6.6.33 The next step (step 2 in the diagram in para 6.6.27 above) is to determine whether the analysis should be applied to a part of a financial asset (or part of a group of similar financial assets) or to a financial asset in its entirety (or a group of similar assets in their entirety). The standard stipulates that the derecognition rules should be applied to a part of a financial asset (or part of a group of similar financial assets) if, and only if, the part being considered for derecognition meets one of the following three conditions:

- The part comprises only specifically identified cash flows from a financial asset (or a group of similar financial assets).

- The part comprises only a fully proportionate (*pro rata*) share of the cash flows from a financial asset (or a group of similar financial assets).

- The part comprises only a fully proportionate (*pro rata*) share of specifically identified cash flows from a financial asset (or a group of similar financial assets). For example, if an entity enters into an arrangement in which the counterparty obtains the rights to a 90% share of interest cash flows from a financial asset (the specifically identified part), the derecognition rules are applied to that 90% of those interest cash flows. If there is more than one counterparty, it is not necessary for each counterparty to have a proportionate share of the specifically identified cash flows provided that the transferring entity retains a fully proportionate share.

[IAS 39 para 16(a)].

6.6.34 The above criteria must be applied strictly to determine whether the derecognition rules should be applied either to the whole asset, or to only a part of the asset. The meaning of 'a group of similar assets' is considered further from paragraph 6.6.56 below.

6.6.35 If it is not possible to identify a part, the derecognition rules must be applied to the financial asset in its entirety (or to the group of similar financial assets in their entirety). [IAS 39 para 16(b)]. Consider the examples below.

Example 1 – Sale of the first or the last specified amount of cash flows from a financial asset

An entity originates a portfolio of similar five-year interest-bearing loans of C1m. It then enters into an agreement with a counterparty. It agrees to pay the counterparty the first C0.9m of cash collected from the portfolio plus interest, in exchange for an upfront cash payment from the counterparty. The entity retains the rights to the last C0.1m plus interest, representing a subordinated interest in the portfolio. In this situation, the entity (transferor) cannot apply the derecognition requirements to part of the asset. This is because:

■ the first C0.9m of cash flow represents neither a specifically identifiable cash flow nor a fully proportionate (*pro rata*) share of all or part of the cash flows from the asset (it is not possible to identify which loans in the portfolio the first C0.9m cash flows will arise from); and

■ any credit losses are borne in the first instance by the entity (transferor) and are not shared proportionally between the parties.

As a result, the derecognition rules must be applied to the whole asset. On the other hand, if the arrangement resulted in the transfer of 90% of all cash flows from the asset, the derecognition rules would have been applied only to the proportion transferred, that is, 90%.

Example 2 – Sale of an asset subject to a guarantee

An entity enters into an arrangement to transfer the rights to 90% of the cash flows of a group of receivables, but provides a guarantee to compensate the buyer for any credit losses up to 8% of the principal amount of the receivables.

In this situation, although the transferor has transferred 90% of all cash flows from the asset, the existence of the guarantee means that the transferor has an obligation that could involve it in repaying some of the consideration received. Therefore, the derecognition requirements must be applied to the asset in its entirety and not just to the proportion of cash flows transferred.

Example 3 – Sale of an asset for part of its life

An entity enters into an arrangement to transfer the rights to 100% of the cash flows (interest and principal) arising in the last four years of a fixed rate loan receivable with an original maturity of 10 years. The principal is payable in a lump sum in year 10. In other words, the entity retains the right to interest cash flows for the first six years.

In this situation, it is clear that the entity has transferred the rights to the last 4 years of cash flows that represent specifically identifiable cash flows (the last 4 years of interest cash flows + principal cash flow). Therefore, in accordance with paragraph 6.6.33 above, the derecognition rules should be applied to this identifiable portion.

> ### Example 4 – Sale of a right to receive dividends or sale of shares but retained rights to dividends
>
> Entity A has a holding of shares in entity X (an available for sale financial asset). Entity A transfers to entity B the right to receive dividends paid on those shares in the next year.
>
> In this situation, the dividends for the next year are specifically identifiable cash flows and the derecognition rules should be applied to the dividend strip.
>
> Similarly, if entity A had transferred its holding of shares to entity B and retained the right to receive dividends for the next year, the cash flows arising on the transferred asset from the second year to perpetuity are also specifically identifiable cash flows. Therefore, the derecognition rules would be applied to only that part of the asset.

6.6.36 Once it has been established that the derecognition rules should be applied to the whole asset (or a group of similar assets) or to the qualifying part or portion identified in step 2 above, the remaining steps of the flow chart should be applied to that whole or part identified. This is referred to as 'the financial asset' in the paragraphs that follow. [IAS 39 para 16(b)].

Determine whether the rights to the cash flows from the asset have expired (step 3)

6.6.37 Once the entity has determined at what level (entity or consolidated) it is applying the derecognition requirements and to what identified asset (individual, group or component) those requirements apply, it can start assessing whether derecognition of the asset is appropriate. Step 3 considers whether the contractual rights to the cash flows from the financial asset have expired. If they have, the financial asset is derecognised. [IAS 39 para 17(a)]. This would be the case, for example, when a loan is extinguished, in the normal course, by payment of the entire amount due, thereby discharging the debtor from any further obligation. Another example is where a right from a purchased financial option is extinguished as a result of the contractual terms expiring without the holder requiring the writer to deliver or purchase the underlying financial asset.

Renegotiated loan assets

6.6.37.1 Derecognition at this step is usually obvious and requires little or no analysis, however, the situation can be more complex when an instrument's contractual terms are changed, for example when renegotiations result in modifications to the terms of a financial asset. The following discussion focuses on amendments to the original contractual terms of a financial asset, and therefore is not necessarily relevant to other events such as an expiry of certain contract terms or changes to legislation that has consequences for instruments drawn up under that specific territory's laws.

6.6.37.2 Events leading up to the modification or exchange of financial assets could be indicators of impairment, particularly when the borrower is in financial difficulty. In such circumstances the lender should first consider whether there has been objective evidence of impairment (except for assets held at FVTPL) and if so an impairment loss should be recognised as discussed in chapter 6.7. Regardless of whether an impairment is booked, it is then necessary to consider whether the financial asset should be derecognised in full or in part. That is, whether the revised terms give rise to the expiry of all or part (see step 2 above) of the contractual rights to the cash flows from the financial asset.

6.6.37.3 IAS 39 has specific requirements for when modifications to, and exchanges of, financial liabilities with the existing lender should be treated as extinguishments, as noted in paragraph 6.6.180. The overriding principle is that financial liabilities should be derecognised when the revised terms are substantially different. There is, however, no equivalent guidance in IAS 39 for the derecognition of renegotiated financial assets. It is therefore a matter of interpretation as to what is regarded as an expiry of the contractual cash flows. A sensible approach is to apply, by analogy, a similar principle to that applied to modifications and exchanges of financial liabilities between the same counterparties. Consequently, substantial modifications to the original cash flows that are in substance akin to an expiry of those cash flows would result in derecognition of the financial asset (or part thereof) and the recognition of a new financial asset on the revised terms.

6.6.37.4 Judgment is required in assessing whether a change in the contractual terms (such as a change in the currency or the remaining term of the loan) is substantial enough to represent an expiry of the original instrument (or a part thereof). This involves considering qualitative factors, as noted in paragraph 6.6.37.6 below. When considering a change in the contractual terms it may be necessary to consider how the cash flows under the revised terms compare with the cash flows under the original terms of the loan but based on expected cash flows used for impairment testing, rather than the full contractual cash flows. For example, if a borrower is in financial difficulties, the revised terms may simply reflect the borrower's ability to pay the original contractual cash flows, as already reflected in the lender's impairment assessment. In such circumstances and in the absence of any other factors, this may indicate that there is not, in substance, an expiry of the original cash flows.

6.6.37.5 The requirements in IAS 39 for assessing whether modified financial liabilities are derecognised include a prescriptive quantitative test (the '10% test') that compares the present value of the cash flows under the revised and original terms, as discussed in paragraph 6.6.181. [IAS 39 para AG62]. However, whilst applying a similar principle, for financial assets there is no requirement to use a similar quantitative test. Indeed the derecognition criteria for financial assets and liabilities are different, which can lead to asymmetrical accounting. Whilst it would be inappropriate to conclude that a financial asset should continue to be recognised based solely on the outcome of such a quantitative test, there is nothing to preclude such a test being included as one of the indicators to judge the extent of changes in cash flows, alongside other qualitative factors, such as those noted in the following paragraph.

6.6.37.6 Some, but not necessarily all, of the qualitative factors to consider when making such judgements on a change in contractual terms are discussed below. Any assessment would need to consider all relevant factors in aggregate and the conclusions reached will depend upon the specific facts and circumstances of each case.

Factors to consider	Comment
Restructuring of loan to recover expected principal/interest when borrower is in financial difficulties, eg interest payment holidays. (Such restructurings are sometimes referred to as forbearance.)	This could cover a range of circumstances. For example, a loan restructuring may defer some payments to cover a borrower's short term financial difficulties, such as a relatively short interest payment holiday where the foregone interest is capitalised. This may not be considered a significant change that represents an expiry of the cash flows, particularly when cash flows under the renegotiated arrangement largely reflect the cash flows the borrower is likely to be able to pay under the original terms. However the financial asset should be assessed for impairment.
	On the other hand, a wider complex restructuring of one instrument into a series of different instruments with different terms, maturities and cash flow profiles that significantly alters the expected future cash flows could be seen as an expiry of the cash flows, resulting in derecognition. This is consistent with the draft rejection wording issued by the IFRS IC after its May 2012 meeting in respect of a narrow fact pattern concerning renegotiated Greek sovereign debt. The scenario that the IFRS IC considered involved multiple debt holders, with original debts on different terms, all receiving the same renegotiated packages.
Insertion of substantial new terms, such as a profit share/equity incentive.	This could cover a variety of circumstances. However, the inclusion of new terms, such as a profit share, that significantly alters the expected future cash flows, including potentially the variability of those cash flows, may lead to full or partial derecognition of the original asset. For example the expected cash flows under the original and modified contracts may be similar at the date of renegotiation but the risk profile of those cash flows could have altered significantly if there is now potential for an upside that is greater than the original contractual cash flows. However if a reasonable range of variability points to the fact that the likely potential upside is simply a mechanism for recovering the original loan and not much more, then derecognition may not be appropriate.
Significant extension of term of loan when borrower is not in financial difficulty	This is similar to the example in paragraph 6.6.37.7 below.

Changes in interest rate.	Changes in interest rate could be to reflect current market conditions, or possibly moving from fixed to floating or vice versa. Whether they are significant enough to be treated as an expiry of cash flows will depend upon the circumstances. For example, the assessment may be influenced by the maturity of the instrument (how much of the expected cash flows relate to interest payments which have been varied, rather than principal, which has not) and the economic environment (the expected stability in interest rates over the instrument's remaining term).
Insertion of collateral/ other security and/or credit enhancements that affect the credit risk associated with the loan.	This depends upon the circumstances but often would not be considered an expiry of the cash flows: for example, if the value of collateral has fallen and additional collateral is added to prevent a covenant breach. If the renegotiated loan asset continues to be recognised, then the lender may need to consider whether any previous impairment should be reversed.
Changes to loan covenants to prevent breach of loan terms that do not change the amounts to be paid or their timing.	Short term waivers of loan covenants are unlikely to be considered significant where they enable the loan to be repaid as originally scheduled.
Change in the payor, for example a holding company taking on its subsidiary's liability due to a change in the credit quality of one of the parties.	Significant differences between the credit quality of the subsidiary and the holding company could, in the absence of an intra-group cross guarantee, give rise to significantly different cash flows after the transfer than expected beforehand and that may be considered an expiry of the cash flows. Generally if the new payor is a third party then the original debt has expired and derecognition is appropriate.
Change in denomination of the currency of the debt instrument.	Unless the two currencies were pegged, a change in currency would generally indicate an expiry of cash flows of the existing loan, as the revised loan is subject to influence from a different country's economy.

6.6.37.7   Below is an example where derecognition is considered appropriate.

Example – Derecognition of financial asset due to modification of cash flows

Bank A has entered into a 10 year loan arrangement with borrower B (classified either as available-for-sale debt or loans and receivables). The loan accrues interest at 4%.

At the end of year 8, as a result of an arm's length renegotiation, the remaining maturity has been modified from 2 years to 12 years and the coupon revised to 6% to maturity. Borrower B is not in any financial difficulty and there is no objective evidence of impairment.

In this situation, bank A has surrendered its rights to the 4% coupon for the next two years and the principal repayment in two years' time; the rights to these cash flows have expired and, hence, should be derecognised. A new 12 year loan and receivable should be recognised at fair value upon renegotiation, comprising a new principal payment in 12 years and 6% interest coupons for the next 12 years.

Determine whether the entity has transferred the cash flows from the asset or assumed an obligation to pay the cash flows from the asset (steps 4 and 5)

6.6.38 If the contractual rights to the cash flows have not expired, an entity derecognises the financial asset only when, amongst other criteria, it 'transfers' the cash flows from the asset. IAS 39 identifies two ways in which a transfer can be achieved. An entity 'transfers' a financial asset if, and only if, it either:

■ transfers the contractual rights to receive the financial asset's cash flows. [IAS 39 para 18(a)]. See step 4 in the diagram in paragraph 6.6.27 and paragraph 6.6.39 below; or

■ retains the contractual rights to receive the financial asset's cash flows, but assumes a contractual obligation to pay the cash flows to one or more recipients, in what is often referred to as a 'pass-through arrangement'. [IAS 39 para 18(b)]. See step 5 in the diagram in paragraph 6.6.27 and paragraph 6.6.47 below.

Transfer of contractual rights to receive cash flows

6.6.39 IAS 39 does not explain what is meant by the phrase *"transfers the contractual rights to receive the cash flows of the financial asset"*. A literal reading of the words would suggest that the phrase would apply to an asset's legal sale or a legal assignment of the rights to the cash flows from the asset. For example, an entity that has sold a financial asset (such as a legal sale of a bond) has transferred its rights to receive the cash flows from the asset. In this situation, the transferee has unconditional, presently exercisable rights to all the future cash flows. The transfer then has to be assessed in Step 6 in the diagram in paragraph 6.6.27 to determine whether it meets the derecognition criteria (see para 6.6.57 below).

6.6.40 On the other hand, consider an entity that enters into an arrangement with a bank whereby the bank manages the entity's securities. The entity transfers the securities into a safe custody account of the bank. The bank receives a management fee for its service, with the entity still making the decisions as to which securities will be sold and when. Such a transfer of securities to a custodian is not a transfer under paragraph 18(a) of IAS 39. The bank does not have the rights to the cash flows of the transferred securities and simply acts as the entity's agent.

6.6.41 Some types of financial asset (for example, a receivable or a portfolio of receivables), cannot be 'sold' in the same way as other types (for example, a bond), but they can be transferred by means of a novation or an assignment as explained in paragraph 6.6.114 below. Both novation and assignment will generally result in the transfer of contractual rights to receive the financial asset's cash flows. However, any further conditions or obligations placed upon the transferor in an assignment need to be considered and may impact this assessment.

6.6.42 Sometimes transfers of financial assets are made subject to certain conditions. Conditions attached to a transfer could include provisions relating to the existence and value of transferred cash flows at the date of transfer or conditions relating to the asset's future performance. Examples of such provisions include warranties relating to a transferred loan (for example, that the borrower met the specified lending criteria when the loan was advanced and is not in arrears at the date of transfer) or to its future performance (for example, that all repayments will be made when due). In our view, such conditions would not affect whether the entity has transferred the contractual rights to receive cash flows (under IAS 39 para 18(a)). Consider the various examples in 6.6.45. However, the existence of conditions relating to the asset's future performance might affect the conclusion related to the transfer of risks and rewards (see para 6.6.64), as well as the extent of any continuing involvement by the transferor in the transferred asset (see para 6.6.78).

6.6.43 In some instances, following the transfer of the contractual rights to receive a financial asset's cash flows, the transferor may continue to administer or provide servicing on the transferred asset. For example, a transferor may transfer all rights to cash flows, but continues to collect cash flows on behalf of the transferee in a capacity as an agent, rather than for its own benefit. This could occur where the original asset counterparties are notified that their obligation has been legally transferred to the transferee and are requested to pay the cash flows into a bank account for the transferee's benefit. In this case, the transferor continues to act purely as an agent in managing the collection of the transferee's cash flows. Determining whether the contractual rights to cash flows have been transferred is not affected by the transferor retaining the role of an agent to administer collection and distribution of cash flows. Therefore, retention of servicing rights by the entity transferring the financial asset does not in itself cause the transfer to fail the requirements in paragraph 18(a) of IAS 39. This would also apply in a scenario where the servicer co-mingled cash collections from the transferred assets with its own assets.

6.6.44 Where a receivable is transferred, in some instances, the original debtor may have the right to offset amounts that it owes to the transferor against any receivables due from the transferor. For example, entities Q and R owe each other amounts that are subject to a legal right of set off. Entity R sells its receivables from entity Q to entity S and agrees with entity S that if entity Q exercises its right of set off on the transferred receivable, entity R will make an equivalent payment to entity S. Such an arrangement (two-party offset) would not cause a transfer of the receivable to fail the requirements in paragraph 18(a) of IAS 39. The payment made by the transferor to the transferee if the right of offset is exercised, merely transfers to the transferee the value the transferor obtained when its liability to the original debtor was extinguished. Such rights of offset would also not impact the risks and rewards test (see further para 6.6.57 below). However, some offset arrangements involve three parties. In such an arrangement, a third party (for example, a sub-contractor who performed some of the services that gave rise to the receivable) has a right to offset amounts it is owed by the transferor against the transferred receivable. As a result, the third party has the unilateral ability to extinguish the contractual rights to receive cash flows from the original debtor. In our view, such an arrangement precludes the transfer from meeting the requirements of paragraph 18(a).

6.6.45 An entity may transfer receivables in respect of which it may subsequently issue credit notes. An example includes a situation where an entity's customer qualifies for a volume discount that is included in the general sales conditions between the entity and its customer. Such credit notes may be used against any existing or future invoice. Contractual credit notes issued by a transferor do not preclude a transfer of contractual rights to receive cash flows from an asset (that is, the original receivable). Such credit notes relate to the relationship between the transferor and its customer and not to the contract that is the receivable. They would, therefore, not preclude a transfer of the original receivable (for example, if the receivable was subsequently part of a debt factor arrangement) from meeting the criterion in paragraph 18(a). In a similar manner, normal warranties (a warranty provided on sale of goods that allows the customer to return the goods if faulty in a stated time period for a full refund) would also not preclude a transfer of the receivable from meeting the criterion in paragraph 18(a), because they relate to the business risk of the underlying transaction, which affects the existence of the receivable, rather than the financial risks associated with the receivable. For the same reasons, these conditions are also not taken into account for the risks and rewards test (see further from para 6.6.57).

6.6.46 Some transfers may include an option or a commitment for the transferor to repurchase the assets. These are often included for good business reasons, such as to enable the transferor to repurchase a receivable in a change of circumstances, for example, a change in tax laws. Such options do not prevent a transfer of the contractual rights to receive the cash flows from an asset, but do need to be considered when applying the risks and rewards test (see further from para 6.6.57 and the examples in IAS 39 para AG 51).

Assumption of obligations to pay cash flows to others (pass-through arrangements)

6.6.47 If there is no transfer of contractual rights under paragraph 18(a) of IAS 39 an entity should determine if there is an obligation to pass on the cash flows of the financial asset under a pass-through arrangement. (see step 5 in the diagram in para 6.6.27). Such pass-through arrangements arise where the entity continues to collect cash receipts from a financial asset (or more typically a pool of financial assets), but assumes an obligation to pass on those receipts to another party that has provided finance in connection with the financial asset. They are common in securitisations and sub-participation arrangements (see further para 6.6.104 below). The entity could be the financial asset's originator, or it could be a group that includes a consolidated special purpose entity that has acquired the financial asset from the originator and passes on cash flows to unrelated third party investors. For example, a transferor that is a trust or SPE may issue beneficial interests in the underlying financial assets to investors but continue to own those financial assets.

6.6.48 Under IAS 39, all of the following conditions have to be met by the entity (transferor) to conclude that such pass-through arrangements meet the criteria for a transfer. (Note that an eventual recipient is any party that may receive cash flows from the assets, excluding the transferor. Most often, they are the noteholders that have invested in a group of securitised assets, but they can also be swap counterparties or credit insurers that have an interest in the assets.)

■ The entity has no obligation to pay amounts to the eventual recipients, unless it collects equivalent amounts from the original asset. Short-term advances by the entity to the eventual recipients with the right of full recovery of the amount lent plus accrued interest from the amounts eventually payable to the eventual recipients at market rates do not violate this condition.

■ The entity is prohibited by the transfer contract's terms from selling or pledging the original asset other than as security to the eventual recipients for the obligation to pay them cash flows.

■ The entity has an obligation to remit any cash flows it collects on behalf of the eventual recipients without material delay. In addition, the transferor is not entitled to reinvest such cash flows, except in cash or cash equivalents as defined in IAS 7, 'Cash flow statements', during the short settlement period from the collection date to the date of required remittance to the eventual recipients, with any interest earned on such investments being passed to the eventual recipients.

[IAS 39 paras 19(a)-(c)].

The financial assets remain on the balance sheet if any one of these conditions is not met. If a transfer meets the pass-through requirements, the transferor is deemed to have transferred the asset. However, the transferor will still then need to assess whether it has transferred sufficient risks and rewards associated with the asset to achieve derecognition. These pass-through conditions follow from the Framework's definitions of assets and liabilities.

6.6.49 The first condition ensures that the transferor is not obliged to transfer funds to the transferee that it has not collected, that is, it is not required to fund payments to the eventual recipients. This means that the transferee must bear the late payment risk. However, short-term advances made by the transferor in periods where there are shortfalls in collection due to late payments from the asset or differences in the dates of collection from the assets and payments to the eventual recipients will not prevent the transaction from being treated as a transfer provided:

■ the short-term advances are made at market rates; and

- those advances plus any accrued interest are recoverable by deduction from the amounts eventually payable to the eventual recipients, or otherwise recoverable in full in the event that cash flows from the assets are insufficient.

6.6.50 The above conditions are necessary to ensure that derecognition is not prevented simply because a short-term cash flow is provided to the transferee. This would not be the case and derecognition would be prevented if the transferor was obliged to provide short-term loans at below market rates of interest or interest free loans because in such a case, the transferor, and not the transferee, would bear the slow-payment risk. Consider the examples below.

Example 1 – Fixed payments

Manufacturer D offers a financing scheme for the sale of its office furnishing products. A customer has the option to pay the purchase price and accrued interest in fixed monthly instalments over a maximum period of 24 months. Entity D agrees to pay to bank E every month a pre-determined amount of cash equal to the instalments due from its customers in exchange for an upfront cash payment. The payment of a fixed amount of cash does not qualify as a pass-through arrangement, because the amounts entity D is obliged to pay to bank E are not dependent on actual cash collections from its customers/receivables. Entity D is obliged to pay a pre-determined amount of cash calculated at the outset of the contract even if it has not collected the cash from its customers.

Example 2 – One party assumes a contractual obligation to pay cash flows from a financial asset to another party

Entity F enters into an arrangement with factor G. Entity F agrees to pass on the cash flows it collects from specified trade receivables to entity G for an upfront payment. Entity F has to transfer the collected cash flows within two working days. Entity F has no obligation to transfer cash to entity G, unless it collects equivalent amounts from the trade receivables; and it is prohibited by the arrangement's terms with entity F from selling or pledging the trade receivables to a third party. The three conditions for a pass-through arrangement are met in this scenario, because entity F:

- retains the contractual rights to receive the financial asset's cash flows, but assumes an obligation to pass on the cash flows from the underlying assets without material delay;

- cannot sell or pledge the asset; and

- has no obligation to make payments, unless it collects equivalent amounts from the asset.

Example 3 – Credit enhancements

Entity H sells C10,000 of receivables to a consolidated SPE for an up-front cash payment of C9,000 and a deferred payment of C1,000. The SPE issues notes of C9,000 to investors. Entity H will only receive the deferred payment of C1,000 if sufficient cash flows from the receivables remain after paying amounts due to investors. This provides credit enhancement to the noteholders in the form of over-collateralisation –

that is, entity H suffers the first loss on the transferred assets up to a specified amount. Such a transaction that provides credit enhancement *via* over-collateralisation may result in the entity meeting the pass-though requirements, provided these requirements are not failed due to other features in the arrangement.

Example 4 – Loan sub-participations

Bank I originates a large loan for a corporate client. Bank I agrees with other banks that in return for an upfront cash payment, bank I will pass on a percentage of all payments of principal and interest collected on the original loan to the participating banks as soon as they are received from the corporate client. The arrangement is non-recourse – that is, bank I has no obligation to pay the other banks, unless it collects equivalent amounts from the corporate loan. Bank I also cannot sell or pledge the loan. The transaction meets the requirements for a pass-through arrangement for the same reasons as discussed in example 3 above.

Example 5 – Pre-funded liquidity reserve

In a securitisation transaction, the SPE (a consolidated subsidiary of the transferor) is required to maintain a liquidity reserve to enable timely payments to be made to noteholders in the event of delayed receipts from the original assets. The transferor (entity A) has pre-funded this reserve by contributing cash or other assets to the SPE when establishing the SPE. If used, the reserve can be recovered only *via* the retention of future cash flows from the transferred assets.

By establishing a pre-funded liquidity reserve, entity A now has an obligation to pay amounts to eventual recipients that were not collected from the original asset. The transaction does not meet the pass-through requirement in paragraph 19(a) of IAS 39, because the amounts paid do not represent allowable short-term advances with a full right of recovery, they may be outstanding for some time and there is no right of recovery in the event of insufficient cash flows from the original asset. Similarly, the transaction would also fail the pass-through requirements if entity A had provided a firm commitment to advance cash to the SPE when required (rather than pre-funding the reserve), which can be recovered only *via* retention of future cash flows from the transferred assets. In this case, entity A can be obliged to pay amounts to eventual recipients that were not collected from the original asset, and those amounts are not short-term advances with a full right of recovery.

On the other hand, consider a situation where the liquidity reserve in the SPE was not pre-funded or committed to by entity A, but is created out of 'excess' cash flows collected from the transferred assets over and above those required to pay noteholders or other eventual recipients. It is contractually specified which cash flows are considered to be 'excess' cash flows. When the notes issued by the SPE are fully repaid at the end of the arrangement, entity A is entitled to the remaining balance of the reserve fund. Such a transaction may meet the pass-through requirements. This is because entity A is not paying the eventual recipients any amounts other than those collected from the original asset, because the fund is created through the cash flows from the transferred assets. Therefore, this meets the requirements of paragraph 19(a). In addition, as any amounts due to entity A (transferor) that are held in this reserve fund are not 'collected on behalf of eventual recipients', and therefore are not subject to the 'material delay' requirement of paragraph 19(c) of IAS 39. The purpose of setting up the fund is to make sure the cash is passed to eventual recipients without material delay once amounts become due to those eventual recipients. Also note that in this example, even though the pass-through requirements are met, the risks and rewards analysis should be applied to the transferred financial asset in its entirety, as there is not a transfer of a fully proportionate share of the cash flows; the transferor retains the most residual interest in cash flows from the asset in this arrangement, which affects the risks and rewards analysis.

Example 6 – Revolving structure

An entity sets up a programme to sell specified short-term receivables (such as trade receivables or credit card receivables) originated over five years to a consolidated special purpose entity (SPE). The SPE issues long-term notes to investors. As cash flows are collected on the receivables, those amounts are used by the SPE to purchase new receivables from the entity. At the end of five years, collections from the receivables are used to repay the principal of the long-term notes rather than being invested in new receivables.

Such an arrangement will fail the third condition in paragraph 6.6.48 because the arrangement involves a material delay before the original collection of cash is remitted. Furthermore, the nature of the new assets typically acquired means that most revolving arrangements involve reinvestment in assets that would not qualify as cash or cash equivalents.

6.6.51 The second condition regarding the transferor's ability to sell or pledge the financial assets highlights that the transferor does not control access to the future economic benefits associated with the transferred cash flows and, therefore, may not have an asset.

6.6.52 The third condition ensures that the transferor does not have use of, or benefit from, the cash it collects on the transferee's behalf and is required to remit them 'without material delay'. Again, this condition helps ensure the transferor has no asset. Immaterial delay is permitted for practical reasons. 'Without material delay' is not defined in the standard so judgment is required in making this assessment. The underlying facts and circumstances need to be reviewed carefully to assess whether the time interval between collection of the cash flows and their remittance to eventual recipients is reasonable in relation to the timing of payments on the underlying assets and market practices. For example, in some pass-through arrangements, such as securitisation of a portfolio of a large number of receivables (for example, credit card balances where customers often pay off the outstanding balance on a range of days each month), it is often not practical for the entity to transfer the relatively small amount of cash collected from individual accounts as and when they arise. Instead, for administrative convenience, the contractual arrangement may provide for their remittance to be made in bulk on a weekly, monthly or quarterly basis. In such situations, a remittance period of three months or less is generally acceptable, as in most securitisations interest is paid on a quarterly basis.

6.6.53 The third condition not only prohibits the transferor from reinvesting the cash flows received in the short settlement period between collection and remittance, but also restricts any investment made for the transferee's benefit to cash or cash equivalents as defined in IAS 7. This means that the transferor is not allowed to invest the funds in other high yielding medium-term investments for the benefit of the transferee or utilise the funds in generating further assets for securitisations (see below). Furthermore, the transferor is not permitted to retain any interest from such short-term highly liquid investments. All such interest received (but no more) must be remitted to the transferee as they arise. In practice, the funds are often paid into a trustee bank account for the transferee's benefit.

6.6.54 These pass-through tests are strict and some securitisation arrangements may well fail them.

6.6.55 The effect of meeting all the three pass-through conditions in paragraph 6.6.48 above is that the entity does not have an asset or a liability as defined in the Framework. The entity does not have an asset because it does not have the rights to control or benefit from the cash flows arising from the asset (second and third conditions). It follows that it also does not have a liability. Rather, in these situations, the entity acts more as an agent of the eventual recipient, merely collecting cash on its behalf, rather than as the asset's owner. Accordingly, if the conditions are met, the arrangement is treated as a transfer and considered for derecognition (that is, subject to the risk and rewards and control tests – see below). Conversely, if the conditions are not met, the entity acts more as the asset's owner with the result that the asset should continue to be recognised.

6.6.56 In the above discussions reference was made to the cash flows from the 'original asset'. An issue that arises in practice is what may be included in the 'original asset'? For example, it is not uncommon for an entity that originates loans and receivables to enter into contracts with third parties to mitigate some of the risks of the underlying assets, such as credit insurance, interest rate swaps etc. If those loans/receivables are later transferred together with the third party contracts to a buyer, the question arises as to what should be regarded as the 'original asset'. Consider the example below.

> **Example – Original assets (contracts between the vendor and a consolidated special purpose entity (SPE))**
>
> Entity A (the transferor) sells assets (for example, loans) to a consolidated SPE. The SPE issues notes to investors that are secured on those assets. Entity A then enters into derivatives (for example, interest rate swaps) and guarantees with the SPE to mitigate some of the risk on the assets for the noteholders. Cash flows to the noteholders that come from the transferor in relation to the derivatives or guarantees are not considered to be cash flows from the original asset. Therefore the arrangement does not meet the requirements of paragraph 19(a).
>
> The situation would have been different if entity A above had entered into derivatives or guarantees with a third party to mitigate the risks relating to the loans. Entity A then transfers the loans and the related third party contracts to a consolidated SPE. The SPE issues notes to investors that are secured on those loans. In such a case, our view is that the original asset can be interpreted to mean:

- all related contracts, including insurance contracts, guarantees and derivatives (for example, purchased options and swaps), transferred with the loans/receivables in a single transaction that share and mitigate some of the risks on the loans because those are the cash flows that will be paid to eventual recipients. Under this view, the related contracts would still meet the requirements of paragraph 19(a) above; or

- only the transferred loans/receivables themselves, in which case the arrangement would not meet the requirements of paragraph 19(a) as described above.

An entity should choose one of these two approaches as its accounting policy and apply it consistently. Furthermore, when performing a risks and rewards analysis (see para 6.6.57 below), the net cash flows of the transferred asset should be determined consistently with the policy chosen for determining the original asset.

6.6.56.1 The pass-through tests in paragraph 19 of IAS 39 may not be met immediately at the date the transfer arrangement is entered into. However, if they are all met after a passage of time, the transferred financial assets should be assessed for derecognition and a risks and rewards assessment carried out at that subsequent date. Consider the example below:

> **Example – Derecognition of loans when pass-through conditions are not met immediately at transaction date**
>
> On 1 January 20X1, bank A entered into a contract to sell a portfolio of recently originated mortgage loans to a specialised mortgage bank, B. Bank A continued to hold legal rights to the cash flows from the loans. Management concluded that bank A transferred substantially all the risks and rewards of the loans to bank B, subject to bank B having the right to sell back to bank A any loan on which any payment default occurs on or before 28 February 20X1. This fails the pass-through test because bank A has an obligation to pay amounts to bank B in excess of cash flows collected from the borrowers. [IAS 39 para 19(a)]. All other pass-through conditions in paragraph 19 of IAS 39 have been met.
>
> The loans will be regarded for accounting purposes as being transferred to bank B when the right to sell back any defaulted loans expires. The risks and rewards test will be performed when the transfer conditions are met, on 1 March 20X1. If the risks and rewards test is met at that date, this will result in the derecognition of the loans on 1 March 20X1 (as in this example).

Perform risk and rewards analysis (steps 6 and 7)

6.6.57 Once an entity has established that it has transferred a financial asset, either by transferring the contractual rights to receive the cash flows or under a qualifying pass-through arrangement, it carries out the risks and rewards test. This test begins in Step 6 in the diagram in paragraph 6.6.27 and requires the entity to evaluate whether it has:

- transferred substantially all the financial asset's risks and rewards of ownership (see para 6.6.58);

- retained substantially all the risks and rewards of ownership (see para 6.6.67); or

- neither transferred nor retained substantially all the risks and rewards of ownership. If this is the case, the entity should perform a control analysis (see Step 8 in the diagram in para 6.6.27 and para 6.6.70) to ascertain which party has control of the asset. [IAS 39 para 20].

Determine whether substantially all the risks and rewards of ownership have been transferred

6.6.58 If the entity transfers substantially all the risks and rewards of ownership of the asset, the entity must derecognise the financial asset as shown in step 6 in the diagram in paragraph 6.6.27 above. It may also have to recognise separately as assets and liabilities any rights and obligations created or retained in the transfer (see also para 6.6.136 below). [IAS 39 para 20(a)].

6.6.59 Examples of transactions that transfer substantially all the risks and rewards of ownership include:

- An unconditional sale of a financial asset. This is the most obvious example.

- A sale of a financial asset, together with an option to repurchase the financial asset at its fair value at the time of repurchase. In this situation, the entity is no longer exposed to any value risk (potential for gain and exposure to loss) on the transferred asset, which is borne by the buyer. The ability for the seller to buy the asset back at its fair value at the date of repurchase is economically no different from buying a new asset.

- A sale of a financial asset together with a put or call option that is deeply out of the money (that is, an option that is so far out of the money it is highly unlikely to go into the money before expiry). In this situation, the seller has no substantial risks and rewards, because there is no real possibility that the call or put option will be exercised. As the option has little or no value, such a sale is economically little different from an unconditional sale.

- The sale of a fully proportionate share of the cash flows from a larger financial asset in an arrangement that meets the pass-through conditions addressed in paragraph 6.6.48 above.

[IAS 39 paras 21, AG39].

6.6.60 If an entity determines that, as a result of the transfer, it has transferred substantially all the risks and rewards of ownership of the transferred asset, it does not recognise the transferred asset again in a future period, unless it re-acquires the transferred asset in a new transaction. [IAS 39 para AG41]. The risks and rewards to be considered in this derecognition step include interest rate risk, credit risk, foreign exchange risk, equity price risk, late payment risk and prepayment risk; depending on the particular asset that is being considered for derecognition. For example, in the case of short-term trade receivables, the main risks to consider are likely to be credit risk and late payment risk and perhaps foreign currency risk if they have been transacted in a foreign currency. In the case of mortgages, the key risks to consider are likely to be interest rate risk, credit risk and, in the case of fixed rate mortgages, prepayment risk.

6.6.61   In addition, as discussed in paragraph 6.6.42 above, sometimes transfers of financial assets are made subject to certain conditions. These conditions should be assessed to determine whether they should be taken into account for a risks and rewards analysis. Such conditions could include warranties (for example, the customers can return goods within a certain period if faulty) and credit notes given when customers qualify for volume discounts. In our view, such conditions should not be taken into account for the risks and rewards analysis. This is because warranties relate to the asset's condition at the date of sale and to whether a valid receivable exists rather than to risks and benefits in relation to its future performance. Similarly, contractual credit notes relate to the overall contractual relationship between the seller and its customer and not to the contract that is the receivable.

6.6.62   Two-party offset arrangements are also not factored into the risks and rewards analysis. An example of such an arrangement is when entities Q and R owe each other amounts and these amounts are subject to a legal right of set-off. Entity R sells its receivables due from entity Q to entity S and agrees with entity S that if entity Q exercises its right of set-off on a transferred receivables that entity R will make an equivalent payment to entity S. This is because the payment made by the seller (entity R) to the buyer (entity S), if the right of offset is exercised, merely transfers to the buyer the value the seller obtained when its receivable from the debtor was extinguished.

6.6.63   On the other hand, an option or commitment to repurchase a transferred asset on a change in circumstance (for example, a change in tax law/regulation) is taken into account in the risks and rewards analysis. A common example is where an entity has sold receivables to a factor. Within the terms of the sale agreement, if there is a change in the tax law/regulation, the entity has the option (or is committed) to repurchase the transferred assets from the factor at par. Risks and rewards are measured as an entity's exposure to variability in cash flows from the transferred asset. If the entity may (or may have to) repurchase the transferred asset for other than its fair value, it has retained some of the risks and rewards. The extent of risks and rewards retained depends on how likely the entity is to repurchase the receivables. The implications of options (and commitments) to repurchase at par value for transfers and continuing involvement are discussed in paragraph 6.6.78 below.

6.6.64   Determining whether the entity has transferred substantially all the risks and rewards of ownership will often be readily apparent from the terms and conditions of the transfer. Where this is not so obvious, the entity needs to undertake an evaluation. That evaluation requires the entity to compute and compare its exposure to the variability in the present value of the transferred asset's future net cash flows before and after the transfer. The net cash flows of the transferred assets should be determined consistently with the 'original asset', as discussed in the example in paragraph 6.6.56. If the entity considers the original asset as a combination of the loan portfolio and related derivatives, the post-transfer cash flows will be the seller's residual cash flows, taking into accounts all the payments to and from the recipients (noteholders derivative counterparties, etc.). The computation and comparison should be made using as the discount rate an appropriate current market interest rate. All reasonably possible variability in net cash flows (as to amounts and timing) should be considered, and greater weight should be given to those outcomes that are more likely to occur, that is, the amounts and timing need to be probability weighted. [IAS 39 para 22].

6.6.65 If, as a result of the contractual arrangements, the entity's exposure to such variability is no longer *significant in relation to the total variability* in the present value of the future net cash flows associated with the financial asset, the entity is regarded as having transferred substantially all the financial asset's risks and rewards of ownership. [IAS 39 para 21]. It should be noted that the computational comparison for derecognition is a relative and not an absolute test. That is, the extent to which the variability in the amounts and timing of the transferred asset's net cash flows is significant is measured in relation to the total variability. In other words, derecognition is not achieved solely if the entity's remaining exposure to an asset's risks and rewards is small in absolute terms, as noted in the example in paragraph 6.6.69.

6.6.66 IAS 39 does not provide any guidance as to what is meant by 'significant' as referred to in the above paragraph when comparing the difference between the present value of the cash flows from the financial asset before the transfer with the present value of the cash flow after the transfer. Therefore, judgement is needed to assess what is significant in each particular situation. A numerical computation is not necessarily required – often it will be obvious whether the entity has transferred substantially all the risks and rewards of ownership. [IAS 39 para 22]. In other cases it will be less clear and a computation will be required. There is limited guidance in the standard as to how to perform such a computation of the entity's exposure to the variability in the present value of the future net cash flows before and after the transfer. This can be done in a number of ways, but the example below illustrates one possibility.

> **Example – Variability in the amounts and timing of cash flows**
>
> An entity sells a portfolio of short term 30 day receivables with a nominal value of C1 billion to a third party. The entity guarantees first losses on the portfolio up to 1.25% of the loan volume. The average loss on similar receivables over the last 10 years amounts to 2%.
>
> In this example, the expected losses are C20m and the entity has guaranteed C12.5m. It might, therefore, appear that, as the entity has guaranteed 62.5% of all the expected losses, it has retained substantially all the risks and rewards of ownership. This is not so as the calculation cannot be done in this manner. The test looks to who absorbs variability in the asset's cash flows, rather than who has most of the expected losses. By giving a guarantee the entity has effectively retained a subordinated interest in the

receivables. If the subordinated retained interest absorbs all of the likely variability in net cash flows, the entity would retain the risks and rewards of ownership and continue to recognise the receivables in their entirety. However, this is not the case in this example. Therefore, in order to perform a risk and rewards analysis, it is necessary to determine the variability in the amounts and timing of the cash flows both before and after the transfer on a present value basis. One way to determine this is outlined below:

- The first step is to model different scenarios of cash flows from the C1 billion receivables portfolio that reflects the variability in the amounts and timing of cash flows before the transfer as discussed in paragraph 6.6.59 above.

- For each scenario, the present value of the cash flows is calculated by using an appropriate current market interest rate as stated in paragraph 6.6.59 above.

- Probabilities are then assigned to each scenario considering all reasonably possible variability in net cash flows, with greater probability weighting given to those outcomes that are more likely to occur.

- An expected variance is then calculated that reflects the cash flows' total variability in the amounts and timing.

The above steps are repeated for cash flows that remain after the transfer.

Finally, the expected variance after the transfer is compared with the variance before the transfer to determine whether there has been a significant change in the amounts and timing of cash flows as a result of the transfer. If the change is not significant, it can be concluded that there has been no substantial transfer of the risks and rewards of ownership. If the change is significant, it can be concluded that the risks and rewards of ownership have been substantially transferred.

An illustration of the modelling discussed above is shown below. For illustrative purposes, only six scenarios are included in this example. In practice, more scenarios may be required in order to adequately model the variability in net cash flows of the asset.

Pre-transfer Scenarios	PV of future cash flows	Probability %	Expected PV	Variability in PV	Probability weighted	Expected Variability
	1	2	3 = 1*2	4 = 1− $\sum$3	5 = 2*4	
Low loss	990,000	15.00	148,500	11,050	1,658	1,658
Normal loss and few pre-payments	985,000	20.00	197,000	6,050	1,210	1,210
Normal loss	980,000	35.00	343,000	1,050	368	368
Normal loss and many pre-payments	970,000	25.00	242,500	−8,950	−2,238	2,238
High loss	960,000	4.50	43,200	−18,950	−853	853
Very high loss	950,000	0.50	4,750	−28,950	−145	145
		100.00	978,950	−38,700	0	6,472

Post-transfer Scenarios	PV of future cash flows	Probability %	Expected PV	Variability in PV	Probability weighted	Expected Variability
	1	2	3 = 1*2	4 = 1– $\sum$3	5 = 2*4	
Low loss	10,000	15.00	1,500	-2,125	-319	319
Normal loss and few pre-payments	12,500	20.00	2,500	375	75	75
Normal loss	12,500	35.00	4,375	375	131	131
Normal loss and many pre-payments	12,500	25.00	3,125	375	94	94
High loss	12,500	4.50	563	375	17	17
Very high loss	12,500	0.50	63	375	2	2
		100.00	12,125	−250	0	638

The relative variability retained after the transfer = 638/6,472 = 9.86%. This implies that the entity has transferred substantially all of the risks and rewards of ownership of the receivables.

It should be noted that, in the above example, the cash flows' present value with their associated probabilities constitutes a discrete random variable, for which it is possible to derive an absolute value for the variability as indicated above. A better measure would be to calculate the standard deviation. However, in this example, that would also produce the same conclusion. In practice, however, the calculation may not be so simple and specialist advice should be taken.

Determine whether substantially all the risks and rewards of ownership have been retained

6.6.67   If the entity retains substantially all the risks and rewards of ownership of the asset, the entity continues to recognise the asset as shown in step 7 in the diagram in paragraph 6.6.27. [IAS 39 para 20(b)].

6.6.68   IAS 39 provides the following examples of transactions where substantially all the risks and rewards of ownership has been retained:

■ A sale and repurchase transaction where the repurchase price is a fixed price or the sale price plus a lender's return (for example, a repo or securities lending agreement).

■ A sale of a financial asset together with a total return swap that transfers the market risk exposure through the swap back to the entity.

■ A sale of a financial asset together with a deep in-the-money put or call option (that is an option that is so far in-the-money that it is highly likely to be exercised before expiry).

■ A sale of short-term receivables in which the entity guarantees to compensate the transferee for all credit losses which are likely to occur.

[IAS 39 para AG 40].

6.6.69   In the above examples it is clear that the entity has retained substantially all the risks and rewards of ownership. Where it is unclear whether the entity has retained (or transferred) substantially all the risks and rewards of ownership, it must evaluate the variability of the transferred asset's cash flows before and after the transfer as discussed in paragraph 6.6.58 above. If this comparison shows that the entity's exposure to the variability in the present value of the future net cash flows (discounted at the appropriate current market interest rate) from the financial asset does not change *significantly* as a result of the transfer, the entity is regarded as having retained substantially all the risks and rewards of the asset's ownership. [IAS 39 para 21]. Sometimes it can be difficult to perform a quantitative analysis of risks and rewards. Consider the following example.

Example – Determining a transfer of risks and rewards in a factoring arrangement with recourse

Entity A transfers a portfolio of trade receivables to a factor. The factor assumes the default risk of the transferred receivables, whereas entity A retains the late payment risk by paying interest on overdue amounts to the factor based on LIBOR plus a margin. The trade receivables transferred have a history of no defaults and no late payment since the start of the business relationship between entity A and the customers.

As noted in paragraph 6.6.65, the risks and rewards test should consider whether entity A's retained risks and rewards after the transfer (that is, the variability due to late payment risk) is no longer significant in relation to the total risks and rewards associated with the financial asset before the transfer (that is, taking into account both the risk of default and the risk of late payment). It is a relative rather than an absolute test. The lack of observed defaults and late payments does not justify an assumption that there are no risks attached to the receivables transferred to the factor. There are small, as yet unobserved, default and late payment risks attached to the receivables. In the absence of any observable data the risks and rewards test should be performed by looking to both qualitative and quantitative factors. The objective is to gain insight into the economics of the default and the late payment risks so as to be able to assess their relative significance.

Qualitative questions to be addressed could include:

■ How are late payment and default risk managed by entity A? The amount of resources entity A devotes to managing a risk might indicate the relative importance it attaches to that risk.

■ If the factor is in general unwilling to assume late payment risk, why is this?

■ If the factor is willing to assume the late payment risk as well as the default risk it has actually assumed, what price would/does it charge?

In addition to completing the risks and rewards analysis, entity A should consider quantitative aspects, including using index information of peers or industries to approximate the default risk and the late payment risk inherent in the portfolio of receivables transferred to the factor. Using this information may make the result of the risks and rewards analysis clear.

In other cases, it might be necessary to build a model that encompasses all the data and information gathered and, therefore, come up with a numerical computation of risks and rewards. The modelling of risks and rewards irrespective of any observable data is a challenging task and will be subject to simplifications and assumptions.

To the extent that the qualitative factors indicate that a significant risk has been retained, the entity should be able to demonstrate objectively that the late payment risk is not significant in order to achieve derecognition. Such a quantitative analysis should use data that is relevant to the receivables being factored.

Perform control analysis (steps 8 and 9)

Determine whether control of the asset has been retained

6.6.70 If the entity (transferor) has neither transferred nor retained substantially all the risks and rewards of ownership of the transferred financial asset – in other words it has retained some risks and rewards but has not substantially all of them – it is in a middle ground in which the risks and rewards analysis does not provide a clear answer. Hence, the transferor has to determine whether it has retained control of the asset (see step 8 in the diagram in para 6.6.27 above).

■ If the transferor has not retained control, it must derecognise the financial asset and recognise separately as assets or liabilities any rights and obligations created or retained in the transfer.

■ If the entity has retained control, it must continue to recognise the financial asset to the extent of its continuing involvement in the financial asset (see para 6.6.78).

[IAS 39 para 20(c)].

6.6.71 Control, in this context does not have the same meaning as in IAS 27, 'Consolidated and separate financial statements', that is, the power to govern the financial and operating policies of an entity so as to obtain benefits from its activities. In the context of derecognition, control is based on whether the transferee has the *practical ability* to sell the transferred asset. This looks to what the transferee can do with the asset, not what the transferor can do. This is a different concept of control that tries to identify whether the transferor continues to be exposed to the variability in the cash flows of the particular asset that was the subject of the transfer as opposed to having risks of a general nature, similar to a derivative. Therefore, where the transferee has the practical ability to sell the transferred asset, it follows that the transferee has control over the asset and the entity has lost control. On the other hand, if the transferee does not have the practical ability to sell the transferred asset, then the entity has retained control of the transferred asset. [IAS 39 paras 23, AG42].

Practical ability to sell the transferred asset

6.6.72 IAS 39 explains that the transferee has the 'practical ability' to sell the transferred asset if:

- the transferee can sell the asset in its entirety to an unrelated third party; and
- the transferee is able to exercise that ability *unilaterally* and *without imposing additional restrictions.*

The above conditions should be evaluated by considering what the transferee is able to do in practice, not what contractual rights it has with respect to the transferred asset (or indeed what contractual prohibition exists).

[IAS 39 paras 23, AG43].

6.6.73   In the context of the first condition above, the transferee will have the practical ability to sell the transferred asset if there is an active market in that asset, because the transferee could repurchase the transferred asset in the market if it needs to return the asset to the entity. [IAS 39 para AG42]. For example, the transferor may transfer a security with an option attached that allows the entity to repurchase it from the transferee at some future date. If the security is one in which an active market exists, the transferee may well sell the security to a third party, knowing that it will be easy to obtain a replacement asset and fulfil its obligation if the transferor exercises the option. The concept of control focuses on what the transferee is able to do in practice. Therefore, in this case, it is important that such an active market exists. The fact that the transferee may be unlikely to sell the transferred asset is of no relevance as long as it has the practical ability to do so. Conversely, if there is no market, the transferee is unable to ensure that it can fulfil its obligation to return the asset to the transferor if it sells the asset with no right to repurchase it. Hence in this case, even if the transferee has a contractual right to dispose of the transferred asset, that right will have little practical effect if there is no market for the transferred asset. [IAS 39 para AG43(a)].

6.6.74   In the context of the second condition above, the transferee should also be able to exercise its ability to transfer the asset independent of the actions of others and without having to impose additional restrictions or 'strings' to the transfer. [IAS 39 para AG43(b)(i)]. If the transferor has imposed obligations on the transferee concerning the servicing of a loan asset, the transferee would need to attach a similar provision to any transfer that it makes to a third party. Such 'additional restrictions' or 'strings' impede the asset's free transfer and fail the 'practical ability' to sell test.

> **Example – Sale of loan portfolio with credit default guarantee**
>
> Entity O sells a portfolio of loans to bank N for cash. The loans have an average historical loss ratio of 5%. Entity O guarantees credit default losses on the transferred assets of up to 4% as part of the arrangement. The terms of the guarantee specify that the holder of the guarantee can only claim under the guarantee if it holds the guaranteed loans. The credit default guarantee means that control has not been transferred. Bank N would lose the value of the credit default protection if it sold the transferred asset without also selling the credit default guarantee to the new buyer. In practice, bank N would only sell the transferred asset if it also sold the credit default protection to the buyer. However, giving such credit default protection is the insertion of an additional feature and, therefore, fails the control test.

6.6.75 Where the transferor writes a put option or provides a guarantee of the original asset, the transfer will also often fail the control test. In such situations, the transferee has effectively obtained two assets: the original asset that is the subject of the transfer, and the put option or the guarantee. Selling the transferred asset on its own invalidates the remaining asset, as the transferee immediately loses any ability to realise its value. In the absence of an active market, the transferee will only be able to realise the asset's value by selling a similar guarantee or put option with the assets. Put another way, if the put option or guarantee is valuable enough for significant risk to be retained by the transferor, it precludes the transfer of control. That is, it will be so valuable to the transferee that the transferee would not, in practice, sell the transferred asset to a third party without attaching a similar option or guarantee, or otherwise mirroring the conditions attached to the original transfer. As the transferee is constrained from selling the asset without attaching additional restrictions, the 'practical ability' to sell test fails, with the result that control of the transferred asset is retained by the transferor. [IAS 39 para AG44].

6.6.76 If the transferee has the practical ability to sell the transferred asset, the transferee has control over the asset. Hence the transferor has lost control and derecognises the asset. On the other hand, if the transferee does not have the practical ability to sell the transferred asset, the transferor has retained control of the transferred asset and continues to recognise the asset to the extent of its continuing involvement.

6.6.77 The 'control' concept is important because it helps determine how the transferor's remaining interest in the asset will be presented. If the transferor has retained control, it still has an interest in the specific assets that have been transferred. It should, therefore, continue to show that interest on the balance sheet, gross of any related liability. If control has been lost, the transferor still shows its remaining economic interest on the balance sheet, but presented net. This recognises that the transferor's interest is a net exposure (that is, more akin to a derivative) rather than an interest directly related to the specific assets that have been transferred.

Continuing involvement in transferred asset

6.6.78 The continuing involvement approach applies if the entity has neither transferred nor retained substantially all the risks and rewards of ownership and control has not passed to the transferee. Under the continuing involvement approach, the entity continues to recognise part of the asset. That part represents the extent of its continuing exposure to the risks and rewards of the financial asset. That is, the continuing involvement includes both obligations to support the risks arising from the asset's cash flows (for example, if a guarantee has been provided) and the right to receive benefits from these cash flows. In these circumstances a related liability is recognised, as well as part of the original asset.

6.6.79 Warranties, contractual credit notes and two-party offset arrangements are not taken into account in measuring an entity's continuing involvement for the reasons discussed in paragraphs 6.6.45, 6.6.61 and 6.6.62. On the other hand, options or commitments to repurchase the transferred assets on a change in circumstances – for example, a change in tax law/regulation – should be taken into account in measuring the entity's continuing involvement. For example, an entity has sold receivables to a factor. Within the terms of the sale agreement, if there is a change in the tax law/regulation, the entity has the option (or commitment) to repurchase the transferred assets from the factor at par. Such right (or commitment) is related specifically to a particular receivable and, therefore, should be taken into account in measuring the entity's continuing involvement. If the option (or commitment) is to repurchase any receivable, the continuing involvement asset would be the entire group of receivables – that is, no derecognition would be achieved. Continuing involvement is addressed further from paragraph 6.6.145.

Accounting by transferee

6.6.80 Although transferees are required to follow the recognition principles discussed from paragraph 6.6.6 above, it is important to note that the accounting treatment between the transferor and the transferee is intended to be symmetrical. Therefore, to the extent that a transfer of a financial asset does not qualify for derecognition, the transferee does not recognise the transferred asset as its asset. The transferee derecognises the cash or other consideration paid and recognises a receivable from the transferor. If the transferor has both a right and an obligation to re-acquire control of the entire transferred asset for a fixed amount (such as under a repurchase agreement), the transferee may classify it's receivable as a 'loan and receivable'. [IAS 39 para AG 50]. Similarly, if a transfer of a financial asset qualifies for derecognition, the transferor will treat it as a sale and the transferee will treat it as a purchase.

Disclosure

6.6.81 IFRS 7 sets out specific disclosure requirements for transfers that do not qualify for derecognition; these are addressed in chapter 6.9. However, paragraph 118 of IAS 1 also requires an entity to disclose the significant accounting policies that are relevant to an understanding of the financial statements. It requires an entity to disclose the judgements that management has made in the process of applying the entity's accounting policies and that have the most significant effect on the amounts recognised in the financial statements. This will include any significant accounting policy choices and judgements it has made in relation to derecognition, for example:

- What the entity regards as a transfer of contractual rights for the purposes of paragraph 18(a) IAS 39 as discussed in paragraph 6.6.39 above.

- What the entity regards as the 'original asset' for the purpose of paragraphs 19(a) and 20 of IAS 39 as discussed in paragraph 6.6.56 above.

For transfers that fail to qualify for derecognition, where relevant, an entity might also disclose that the assets are pledged against the related liability. In addition, the entity will maintain the same classification as it had prior to the failed derecognition. The current or non-current classification of the associated liability depends on the earliest date it is due to be settled. Generally, its classification will be the same as that of the asset. However, in the case of a revolving structure, the receivables that failed the derecognition test might be classified as current, whereas the notes to the investors may be non-current if they are not due to be settled within the next 12 months. In a securitisation of long-term assets funded by short-term commercial paper issuances, the converse could arise.

Practical application of the derecognition criteria

6.6.82   Having discussed the criteria for derecognition, it is necessary to consider how they can be applied to various types of transfers of financial assets that are often found in practice. Such transfers include repurchase agreements and stock lending agreements, factoring arrangements, securitisation transactions, loan transfers and transfers involving derivatives. Descriptions of these common types of transfers and the consequences of applying the derecognition criteria are considered below. The accounting treatment of transfers that qualify for derecognition, those that fail derecognition and those that continue to be recognised to the extent of the continuing involvement are considered from paragraph 6.6.129 below.

Repurchase and stock lending agreements

6.6.83   Repurchase agreements, commonly referred to as 'repos', are transactions involving the legal sale of a financial asset with a simultaneous agreement to repurchase it at a specified price at a fixed future date. In a typical repurchase agreement, an entity might sell a security such as a government bond to a third party in return for a cash consideration that is then reinvested in other assets that earn a return. At the specified date, the transferor repurchases that security. Financial institutions and other entities normally enter into these agreements because they provide liquidity and the opportunity to earn excess returns on the collateral. The main features of such agreements will usually be:

- The sale price – this may be the market value at the date of sale or another agreed price.

- The repurchase price – this may be fixed at the outset, vary with the period for which the asset is held by the buyer, or be the market price at the time of repurchase.

- The nature of the repurchase agreement – this may be an unconditional commitment for both parties, a call option exercisable by the seller, a put option exercisable by the buyer or a combination of put and call options.

- Other provisions – these may include, amongst others, the term of the agreement (overnight, short-term or longer), the buyer's ability to return a similar but not identical security to that which was sold; the buyer's ability to sell the security to a third party, the seller retaining access to any increase in to the asset's value (subject to the buyer receiving a lender's return) from a future sale to a third party and the seller providing any protection against loss through the operation of guarantees.

6.6.84 Entities may also enter into stock lending (sometimes referred to as securities lending) transactions. These transactions are initiated by broker-dealers and other financial institutions to cover a short sale or a customer's failure to deliver securities sold. In a typical stock lending agreement, the transferor/lender transfers a security to the transferee/borrower for a short period of time. The borrower is generally required to provide 'collateral' to the lender, commonly cash but sometimes other securities or a standby letter of credit, with a value slightly higher than the value of the security borrowed. If the collateral is cash, the lender earns a return and if it is other than cash, the lender receives a fee. At a specified date, the borrower returns the security to the lender.

6.6.85 Although the motivation to enter into a securities lending transaction is different from a repurchase agreement and the transactions may differ in form and sometimes risk protection, they are similar in substance. IAS 39, therefore, does not distinguish between the two types in determining whether the transferred asset qualifies for derecognition. [IAS 39 para AG 51(a)-(c)].

6.6.86 The application of the derecognition principles to repurchase and stock lending transactions will obviously depend upon the transaction's nature and specific characteristics. However, some of the typical features that are found in such transactions and how they should be evaluated for derecognition purposes are considered below.

Requirement for a transfer

6.6.87 In repurchase and stock lending agreements there is typically a legal sale of the underlying assets. Hence, the transferor has transferred the contractual rights to receive the cash flows of the financial assets and there is a transfer that meets IAS 39 paragraph 18(a) (step 4 in the diagram in 6.6.27 = yes).

Repurchase price

6.6.88 A repurchase agreement will require the transferor to repurchase the transferred asset at a particular price. Such price may be fixed at the outset or be the market price at the time of the repurchase. Depending on the pricing arrangement, the analysis would be as follows:

■ If the financial asset is loaned or sold under an agreement to repurchase the transferred asset at fair value at the date of repurchase, the transferred asset is derecognised. This is because the transferor has transferred substantially all the risk and rewards of ownership of the transferred asset (step 6 in the diagram in para 6.6.27 = Yes). [IAS 39 para AG 51(j)].

- If the financial asset is loaned or sold under an agreement to repurchase the asset at a fixed price or at a price that provides a lender's return on the sale price, the transferred asset is not derecognised. This is because the transferor retains substantially all the risks and rewards of ownership of the transferred asset (step 7 in the diagram in para 6.6.27 = Yes). [IAS 39 para AG 51(a)].

Agreement to return substantially the same asset

6.6.89   A repurchase or stock lending agreement may require the transferor to accept back assets that are substantially the same as those initially transferred. The term 'substantially the same' is not defined in the standard. However, it is generally taken to mean that the financial assets returned or repurchased must be identical in form and type and have identical maturities and contractual interest rates, so as to provide the same rights as the asset transferred. As there is no economic difference between the asset initially transferred and the asset to be re-acquired, the analysis would be the same as indicated above.

Agreement to substitute a similar asset with equal fair value

6.6.90   A repurchase or stock lending agreement may give the transferee the right to substitute a similar asset of equal fair value at the repurchase date. In this case, there is no economic difference in substance between returning the original asset or a similar asset of equal fair value. Depending on the repurchase price, the analysis would be identical to that discussed in the above paragraph. [IAS 39 para AG 51(c)].

Right of first refusal to repurchase at fair value

6.6.91   If an entity sells a financial asset and retains only a right of first refusal to repurchase the transferred asset at fair value if the transferee subsequently intends to sell it, the entity derecognises the asset because it has transferred substantially all the risks and rewards of ownership (step 6 in the diagram in para 6.6.27 = Yes). [IAS 39 para AG 51(d)]. This situation is effectively no different in substance to the situation described in the first bullet point in paragraph 6.6.88 above. Although not dealt with in the standard, if the right of first refusal to repurchase the transferred asset is at a price other than the asset's fair value at the date of repurchase (for example, a price pre-determined at inception), the analysis would be similar to the transferor having a call option. This situation is described in paragraph 6.6.123 below.

Transferee's right to pledge

6.6.92   A repurchase or securities lending agreement may give the transferee the right to sell or pledge the transferred asset during the term of the repurchase agreement. In this situation, if the transferor continues to recognise the asset, it should reclassify the asset on its balance sheet, for example, as a loaned asset or repurchase receivable. [IAS 39 para AG 51(a)].

6.6.93 Generally, the transferee's right to sell or pledge the transferred asset effectively indicates that the transferee has control of the asset and thus if some significant risks and rewards are transferred, derecognition is appropriate. For control to pass to the transferee, the right to sell or pledge must have economic substance without any 'strings' attached, as explained in paragraphs 6.6.75 and 6.6.76 above.

Wash sales

6.6.94 A 'wash sale' (sometimes referred to as a 'bed and breakfast' transaction) is the repurchase of a financial asset shortly after it has been sold. Such a transaction involves contracting to sell the financial asset to a third party with no express contract to buy it back. Therefore, such a repurchase does not preclude derecognition provided that the original sale transaction met the derecognition requirements. In other words, the sale and the repurchase transactions are viewed as two separate transactions under IAS 39. Since the time interval between sale and repurchase can be very short, it is unlikely that the transferor would benefit or suffer from any changes in asset values. Therefore, such transactions are normally undertaken to crystallise a capital gain or capital loss for taxation purposes or to convert unrealised revaluation gains on investments into realised gains so that they can be used for distribution by way of dividends to shareholders. However, if an agreement to sell a financial asset is entered into concurrently with an agreement to repurchase the same asset at a fixed price or the sale price plus a lender's return, then the asset is not derecognised. [IAS 39 para AG 51(e)].

Security given as collateral

6.6.95 In the sale and repurchase agreements discussed above, the sale price was assumed to be satisfied in cash. A variant often found in practice is that the sale consideration is satisfied by the transfer of another security rather than in cash. For example, assume that entity A sells security X subject to a repurchase agreement to entity B. The sale consideration is met by entity B transferring security Y. Such a transaction involves two transfers and two transferors so the requirement relating to the accounting treatment relating to transfers of financial assets will need to be applied twice – transfer of security X by entity A and transfer of security Y by entity B.

6.6.96 Each transferor will first apply the derecognition criteria discussed above to its own security – a risks and rewards approach first followed by the control approach if the risks and rewards approach is found not to be conclusive. It will then apply the derecognition criteria to the asset received as consideration from the point of view of the counterparty. If the counterparty would continue to recognise the asset under IAS 39 it is not recognised by the entity. [IAS 39 para AG50].

Linkage of transactions into a derivative

6.6.97   In some cases, an entity may enter into two or more transactions relating to the same asset at (or about) the same time. The issue arises as to whether these transactions should be accounted for separately, or aggregated and accounted for as a single transaction. As set out in paragraph 6.2.43, certain linked non-derivative transactions should be aggregated and treated as a derivative when, in substance, the transactions result in a derivative instrument.

> **Example – purchase plus repo**
>
> Entity A purchases a sovereign bond at fair value from entity B. At the same time entity A enters into a sale and repurchase agreement (repo) of the bond with entity B. Under the repo, entity A sells the bond back to entity B and agrees to buy it back from entity B on a specified future date at a specified price. The net effect of the two transactions is that no cash or bonds are exchanged between entity's A and B at inception.
>
> During the term of the transaction, entity A will pay to entity B interest on the notional financing under the repo and entity B will pay to entity A any interest coupons received on the bond (though these amounts may be rolled into the repurchase price and paid at the end of the repo). On maturity of the repo, entity B will deliver the bond to entity A in return for cash equal to the pre-agreed price.
>
> The cash flows of this transaction are consistent with the cash flows of a total return swap with physical settlement at the swap's maturity. If the two interest payments are rolled up and paid at the end of the term of the repo, the cash flows are similar to a forward contract to buy the bond.
>
> The definition of a derivative in IAS 39 paragraph 9 is met as the value of the transaction moves in response to the change in the fair value of the bond, the initial net investment is small and the transaction will be settled at a future date.
>
> The indicators of when non-derivative transactions should be treated as a derivative [IAS 39 para IG B6] are met as the transactions are entered into at the same time and in contemplation of each other, both relate to the same risk as they relate to the same bond and both are with the same counterparty, entity B. There is also no apparent economic need or substantive business purpose for the transactions to be structured separately.
>
> Hence, the above transactions should be accounted for together, as a derivative.

Factoring arrangements

6.6.98   A factoring transaction involves a transferor transferring its rights to some or all of the cash collected from some financial asset (usually receivables) to a third party (the factor) in exchange for a cash payment. Factoring of receivables is a well established method of obtaining finance, sales ledger administration services or protection from bad debts. Factoring arrangements may take various forms, but some of the principal features are as follows:

- The cash payment – this may be fixed at the outset or vary according to the actual period the receivables remain unpaid (late payment risk). Sometimes the factor may provide a credit facility that allows the seller to draw up to a fixed percentage of the face value of the receivables transferred.

- The nature of the agreement – may be a clean sale without recourse (the transferor has no obligations to make good any shortfall on the transferred assets) or may be more complex with various recourse provisions.

- Other provisions – these may include, amongst others, any representations or warranties provided by the transferor regarding the receivables' quality/condition at the point of transfer, servicing arrangements (whether the transferor will continue to manage the receivables or management will be taken over by the factor), or any credit protection facility (insurance cover) provided by the factor that may limit or eliminate the extent to which the factor has recourse to the seller.

Factoring without recourse

6.6.99 In a non-recourse factoring arrangement, the transferor does not provide any guarantee about the receivables' performance. In other words, the transferor assumes no obligations whatsoever to repay any sums received from the factor regardless of the timing or the level of collections from the underlying debts. In that situation, the entity has transferred substantially all the risks and rewards of ownership of the receivables and derecognises the receivables in their entirety (step 6 in the diagram in para 6.6.27 = yes). The accounting treatment of receivables subject to non-recourse factoring is considered in the second example in paragraph 6.6.132 below. In some situations, the transferor may continue to service the receivables for which it may receive a fee. The accounting treatment for a sale of receivables with servicing retained that is not subject to recourse and when the transferor has no residual interest in the receivables is considered in paragraph 6.6.139 below.

Requirement for a transfer

6.6.100 In most factoring arrangements, the factored receivables are assigned to the factor. In most cases, the transferor has transferred the contractual rights to receive the financial asset's cash flows and there is a transfer that meets IAS 39 paragraph 18(a) (step 4 in the diagram in para 6.6.27 = yes). However, this may not be the case if there are three party offset rights – see paragraph 6.6.44 above.

Factoring with recourse

6.6.101 In a factoring of receivables with recourse, the transferor provides the factor with full or limited recourse. The transferor is obligated under the terms of the recourse provision to make payments to the factor or to repurchase receivables sold under certain circumstances. These recourse provisions may take the form of guarantees by the seller for non-payment (bad debt credit risk) up to a certain limit or full default amount, a call option by the transferor (for example, to repurchase defaulted receivables), a put option by the factor for any defaulted assets or the seller agreeing to pay interest to the buyer for any overdue receivables (late payment risk). In some cases, they result in the transferor retaining substantially all the risks and rewards of ownership of the receivables with the effect that the entity continues to recognise the factored receivables (step 7 in the diagram in para 6.6.27 = yes). In other cases, the recourse provisions result in the transferor retaining some, but not substantially all, risks and rewards, in which case the control test must be considered. In most factoring arrangements that are subject to recourse, the transferee is precluded from selling the receivables, which means that the transferor continues to control them (step 8 in the diagram in para 6.6.27 = yes) and continuing involvement accounting may apply. Examples dealing with the accounting treatment of receivables subject to factoring with recourse can be found under paragraphs 6.6.141 and 6,6.151 below.

6.6.102   In some transactions, the contract requires the customer to pay part or all of the consideration before the entity provides any goods or services. The entity may factor the rights to these future cash flows before the goods or services have been provided and the related receivable recognised. For example, an entity may factor a future operating lease receivable. If an entity factors such unrecognised receivables, then the entity should recognise the factoring arrangement as financing, that is, the entity should recognise a liability for the amounts received from the factor, as there is no asset to derecognise.

> **Example – Factor of advance payments**
>
> Consider a five-year maintenance contract with payments to be billed annually in advance or an operating lease contract with rentals due quarterly in advance. Such contracts give rise to the question of when should a financial asset for the amounts due under the contract be recognised, since the entity has a contractual right to receive cash from when the contract is signed even though it has provided no goods or services at that time. In our view, no asset should be recognised until at least one of the parties has performed under the contract (see para 6.6.11). Such an arrangement comprises two elements. The first element is the sale of goods or services, which is an executory contract and hence is not recognised until the goods or services are delivered. The second element is a loan commitment (being the agreement by the customer to pay in advance, which is outside the scope of IAS 39. [IAS 39 para 2(h)]. Hence, no financial asset is recognised for either of the elements prior to performance or drawdown of the upfront payment.
>
> When the entity receives a payment before it has delivered the goods or services, it should recognise a non-financial liability that is presented in the balance sheet as revenue received in advance. However, if the entity factors the future cash inflows before recognising the receivable (that is, before the goods and services have been delivered), then the entity should recognise a financial liability for the amounts received from the factor.

Factoring receivables already subject to credit insurance

6.6.103   In some instances an entity may have already obtained credit insurance for a portfolio of receivables prior to factoring them. On factoring the factor becomes the beneficiary of the credit insurance. The question arises as to what is the 'original asset' for the purpose of the derecognition criteria: is it only the receivables or the receivables plus the credit insurance? In the absence of guidance within IAS 39 the term 'original asset' can be interpreted to mean either:

- all related contracts, including purchased options, swaps and insurance contracts, transferred with the loans/receivables in a single transaction that share and mitigate some of the risks on the loans because those are the cash flows that will be paid to the factor; or

- only the transferred loans/receivables themselves.

An entity must choose one of these two approaches as its accounting policy and apply it consistently throughout the derecognition assessment. For the above factoring transaction, the latter approach is more likely to result in derecognition. This is because the asset is viewed as uninsured receivables that are likely to have significant credit risk. Since this credit risk is transferred to the factor, it is more likely that the transaction will pass the risks and rewards test (that is, it is more likely that step 6 in the diagram in para 6.6.27 = yes). Under the first approach, the asset is viewed as credit insured receivables that are likely to have lower credit risk. Thus, any risk retained by the seller (other than that covered by the credit insurance) will be relatively more significant (that is, it is more likely that step 6 in the diagram in para 6.6.27 = no).

It should be noted that there is a separate question as to whether the credit insurance contract has been transferred, that will depend on the facts and circumstances.

Securitisations

6.6.104 Securitisation is a method of raising finance, first used by originators of mortgage loans, through a sale of a block or pool of loans, typically to a subsidiary or a thinly capitalised vehicle specially set up for the purpose – a special purpose entity (SPE). The SPE finances the purchase by issuing loan notes or other marketable debt instruments to outside investors that are often secured on the SPE's assets. This process is known as securitisation and is also referred to as asset backed finance. Also other pools of debts, such as credit card receivables, leases, hire purchase loans and trade debtors are securitised in a similar way to mortgages. This kind of SPE structure, that isolates the assets legally from the transferor and its creditors ('ring-fence') to avoid any consequences from bankruptcy, enables the originator to raise funds at competitive rates. The following outlines a typical securitisation transaction:

- The assets to be securitised are transferred by an originator/transferor to an SPE for an immediate cash payment.

- The SPE finances the transfer by issuing loan notes to investors. The SPE 's shares or residual beneficial interests, if any, are usually held by a party other than the originator (charitable trusts have often been used for this purpose). In addition, the major financial and operating policies are usually predetermined to a greater or lesser extent by the agreements that establish the securitisation (in other words, the SPE operates on so-called 'autopilot').

■ Because the SPE 's business activities are constrained and its ability to incur debt is limited, it faces the risk of a shortfall of cash below what it is obligated to pay investors. Arrangements are, therefore, made to protect the investors from losses occurring on the assets by a process termed 'credit enhancement'.

A commonly used form of credit enhancement occurs *via* the issue of subordinated debt (perhaps to the transferor) and other forms of equity-like claims that have the effect of dividing the risk of loss on the underlying assets ('tranching').

Credit enhancement may take a variety of other forms, including over-collateralisation (the aggregate value of assets transferred exceeds the consideration provided by the SPE), third party guarantee of the issuer's obligations (securities backed by a letter of credit), or third party credit insurance. All the arrangements provide a cushion against losses up to some limit.

■ The transferor is often granted rights to cash remaining from the transferred assets after payment of amounts due on the loan notes and other expenses of the issuer. These rights are generally intended, at least in part, to compensate the transferor for assuming some of the risk of credit or other losses. The mechanisms used to achieve this include servicing or other fees, deferred sale consideration, 'super interest' on amounts owed to the transferor (for example, subordinated debt), dividend payments and swap payments.

■ Cash accumulation from the assets (for example, from mortgage redemptions) is either used to redeem the loan notes or reinvested in other more liquid assets until the loan notes are repaid. Any surplus cash usually accrues to the transferor as noted above.

■ The transferor may continue to service the assets (for example, collect amounts from the borrower, set interest rates, etc) for which it may receive a 'servicing fee'. Often, the surplus cash mentioned above is extracted by an adjustment to the service fee.

6.6.105 In many situations, the SPE will be no more than an extension of the originator rather than an economic entity in its own right and, therefore, will be consolidated under SIC 12 (step 1 in the diagram in para 6.6.27). In that situation, the right to receive the cash flows from the asset will remain with the group (step 4 in the diagram in para 6.6.27 = no). However, the group may assume an obligation to pass-through the cash flows from the transferred asset to the investors that meets all the three conditions set out in paragraph 6.6.48 above (step 5 in the diagram in para 6.6.27 = yes). Nevertheless, the group may retain substantially all the risk and rewards of ownership of the securitised assets, because of credit enhancement measures described above. The IASB recognises that many securitisations may fail to qualify for derecognition either because one or more of the three pass-through conditions are not met, as in securitisation arrangements involving 'revolving structures' (see paragraph 6.6.54 above) or because the entity has retained substantially all the risks and rewards of ownership. [IAS 39 para BC 63].

Subordinated retained interests and credit guarantees

6.6.106 As discussed in paragraph 6.6.104 above, an entity may provide the transferee with credit enhancement by subordinating some or all of its interest retained in the transferred asset. Alternatively, an entity may provide the transferee with credit enhancement in the form of a credit guarantee that could be unlimited or limited to a specified amount. Although such credit enhancement techniques are often used in securitisation transactions, they could also be used in other forms of transfers of financial assets.

6.6.107 The provision of a credit guarantee by the entity will cause the pass-through tests of IAS 39 to be failed (see step 5 in the diagram in para 6.6.27) and, therefore, will prevent derecognition for transactions in which the pass-through tests are applied. This is because any payments made by the transferor under the guarantee are not cash flows from the original asset and, therefore, the existence of a credit guarantee fails the condition in paragraph 19(a) of IAS 39 (see further para 6.6.48 above). However, the retention of a subordinated interest in the transferred asset does not, in itself, cause the pass-through tests to be failed as it does not require the entity to make payments other than out of collections on the transferred assets. However, the retention of a subordinated interest is likely to result in the transferor retaining some of the risks and rewards of the asset.

6.6.108 In some securitisation structures an entity may retain an interest in the transferred assets in the form of the right to any 'excess spread'. The excess spread is generally any cash left in the SPE after paying the noteholders their interest and principal and after any costs incurred by the SPE. Again the retention of such an interest does not cause the pass-through test to be failed where the SPE is consolidated, but is likely to result in the transferor retaining at least some of the risks and rewards of the assets.

6.6.109 If an entity has either transferred the contractual rights of the asset or assumed an obligation to pay the cash flows to others that meets the pass-through tests, but still retains substantially all the risks and rewards of ownership of the transferred asset, the asset continues to be recognised in its entirety (step 7 in the diagram in para 6.6.27 = yes). However, if the entity retains some, but not substantially all, of the risks and rewards of ownership and has retained control (step 8 in the diagram in para 6.6.27 = yes), derecognition is precluded to the extent of the amount of cash or other assets that the entity could be required to pay under the subordination or credit guarantee agreement. [IAS 39 para AG 51(n)]. The accounting treatment of continuing involvement through a guarantee is considered in paragraph 6.6.151 below. The accounting treatment of a subordinated retained interest is considered in paragraph 6.6.144 below.

Removal of accounts provisions

6.6.110 Securitisations are sometimes carried out on terms that contain a provision that enables a transferor to call back some of the assets securitised at a subsequent date, subject to some restrictions. Such provisions are referred to as 'removal of accounts' provisions (ROAPs). Some ROAPs may allow the transferor unilaterally to specify the assets that may be removed; others may specify that the identification of assets for removal is done randomly or by the transferee. Such provisions are included for good business reasons. For example, the transferor may wish to protect the credit rating of a securitisation vehicle in the event of default of one of the securitised assets or may desire the ability to repurchase assets associated with operations to be discontinued or exited.

6.6.111 The ROAP described above is effectively a call option enabling the transferor to insist on a return of some of the transferred assets. This means that the transferor has retained control over the transferred assets, provided the transferee does not have the practical ability to sell the assets (which is usually the case in a securitisation). Therefore, if such a provision results in the entity neither retaining nor transferring substantially all the risks and rewards of ownership (step 8 in the diagram in para 6.6.27 = Yes), derecognition is precluded only to the extent of the amount subject to call/repurchase. For example, if the carrying amount and proceeds from the transfer of loan assets are C100,000 and any individual loan could be called back, but the aggregate amount of loans that could be repurchased could not exceed C10,000, C90,000 of the loans would qualify for derecognition. [IAS 39 para AG 51(l)].

Swaps

6.6.112 In a securitisation involving fixed rate assets, the transferor may enter into an interest rate swap with the SPE. Under the swap's terms, the transferor may undertake to receive the fixed rate interest on the transferred assets and pay a variable rate to the SPE, such that the SPE can pay variable rate interest to noteholders. If the SPE does not fall to be consolidated, then such a swap would not prevent derecognition provided the payments on the swap are not conditional on payments being made on the transferred asset. [IAS 39 para AG 51(p)]. The swap may, however, result in the retention of some risks of the asset's rewards, for example, if the terms cause some late payment risk to be retained.

6.6.113 If, however, the SPE is consolidated and the pass-through tests apply, the swap would prevent derecognition (see step 5 in the diagram in para 6.6.27). This is because the swap results in the transferor having an obligation to pay amounts to the eventual recipients (investors in the notes) even if it does not collect equivalent amounts from the assets. The swap may require a net payment to the SPE (that is then passed to noteholders) if interest rates rise so that the interest due on the notes exceeds that due on the assets. Hence, the pass-through test in IAS 39 paragraph 19(a) is failed and derecognition is precluded.

Loan transfers

6.6.114   As explained in paragraph 6.6.41, some kinds of financial assets cannot be sold in the same way as other assets. However, they can be transferred to third parties in return for an immediate cash payment. The transfer may be of the whole of a single loan, part of a loan, or of all or part of a portfolio of similar loans. The methods by which the benefits and risks of loans can be transferred vary between jurisdictions. As highlighted below and in the examples in paragraphs 6.6.180 and 6.6.184, from the issuer's perspective it is necessary to assess whether the loan transfer, regardless of its form, results in the borrower being legally released from its obligations under the existing loan to determine whether the loan has been extinguished. Common loan transfer methods include those described below, although there may be variations across different jurisdictions.

■   Novation

   Under a novation, typically the rights and obligations of the original lender (the transferor) under the loan agreement are cancelled and replaced by new ones whose main effect is to change the lender's identity. The transferor is released from its obligations to the borrower.

   Such a novation, therefore, will result in the transfer of the contractual rights to receive the financial asset's cash flows. Therefore, in the absence of any side agreements, such as a guarantee or other form of recourse arrangement, a forward purchase arrangement or option, the transferor will derecognise the loan in its entirety.

■   Assignment

   Under an assignment, the original lender's (the transferor's) rights to the future cash flows under the loan agreement, but not obligations (for example, warranty obligations to repair faulty goods) are typically transferred to the third party (the assignee). There are generally two types of assignments – assignments where the lender is required to give notice to the borrower (in some jurisdictions these are known as legal or open assignments) and assignments where no notice is required to be given to the borrower (in some jurisdictions these are known as equitable or silent assignments).

   Where the lender is required to give notice in writing to the borrower, and in the absence of any side agreements between the transferor and the transferee, the transferee normally acquires a direct legal claim on the future cash flows under the loan agreement.

   Where notice is not required to be given to the borrower, as the borrower is not aware that the lender has transferred its rights to the cash flows to another party, there is doubt as to whether the transferee has obtained the unconditional contractual rights to the cash flows of the transferred asset. In general, whether the contractual rights to the cash flows have been unconditionally transferred under such an assignment would depend on the law of the country that governs the assignment.

Both types of assignment are subject to equitable rights arising before notice is received. For example, a right of set-off held by the borrower against the lender will be good against the assignee for any transactions undertaken before the borrower receives notice of the assignment.

Assignments may or may not leave the transferor with continuing involvement in the loans depending on whether there are any residual interests, recourse provisions, buyback provisions, etc. The issues that arise in assignments are very similar to debt factoring and securitisations, most of which involve an assignment.

- Sub-participation

Under a sub-participation, the lender enters into a non-recourse back-to-back arrangement with a third party (the sub-participant) and, in exchange for a cash receipt of an amount equal to the whole or fully proportionate part of the loan, passes on the cash flows (both interest and principal) collected on the loan to the sub-participant. Typically all the contractual rights and obligations legally remain with the transferor.

Like assignments, sub-participation may or may not leave the transferor with continuing involvement in the loans depending on whether there are any residual interests, recourse provisions, buyback provisions, etc. Provided the sub-participation meets all the three pass-through conditions discussed in paragraph 6.6.48 above, there is no recourse to the transferor and the transferor does not retain any significant risks and rewards of ownership of the loans, derecognition is appropriate.

Loan syndications

6.6.115   Sometimes, a single lender may not be able to fund a large loan required by a borrower. In those situations, it is quite common for a group of lenders to fund the loan jointly. This is usually accomplished by a syndication under which several lenders share in lending to a single borrower, but each syndicate member lends a specific amount to the borrower and has the right to repayment from the borrower. Such a loan syndication is not a transfer of financial assets. Accordingly, each lender in the syndication should account for the amounts it is owed by the borrower.

6.6.116   In some loan syndications, the lead lender may advance funds to the borrower and transfer a fully proportionate share of the loan to different lenders. The borrower makes repayments directly to a lead lender who then distributes the collections to the other syndicate lenders in proportion to the amount lent. This situation is no different in substance to a sub-participation discussed above. Derecognition of the loans transferred to the different lenders would be appropriate if the lead lender is simply functioning as an agent, all the syndicate lenders have fully proportionate shares of the total lending and all the pass-through conditions and risks and rewards conditions are met.

Transfers involving derivatives

6.6.117 Transfers of financial assets often include derivatives, either explicitly or implicitly. Common derivatives that are found in transfer arrangements are put and call options, forward sale or repurchase contracts and swap agreements. Derivative instruments normally require exercise by one of the parties to the contract. In some instances, exercise of the derivative may be automatic, for example, where a transferor enters into a forward agreement to repurchase a transferred asset at a pre-determined price. In other instances, the exercise may be conditional on the occurrence of a particular event, for example, where the transferee has the right to put back to the transferor receivables that remain uncollectible.

6.6.118 In some circumstances, the existence of derivatives may not prevent derecognition, for example, if the pre-determined price mentioned in the first example above is set at market price at repurchase date. In other circumstances, derivatives may well prevent a transferor from derecognising a financial asset, thereby precluding sale treatment. Derivatives may also constrain a transferee's practical ability to sell the transferred asset, even if there is no legal constraint, with the result that the transferor retains control over the transferred asset. Any derivative that serves as an impediment to the transferee from realising the economic benefits inherent in the transferred asset should be carefully analysed to determine whether or not the transferor has retained control of the transferred asset.

6.6.119 Where the presence of a derivative prevents a transferor from derecognising a financial asset, the transferor's contractual rights or obligations related to the transfer are not accounted for separately as derivatives if recognising both the derivative and either the transferred asset or the liability arising from the transfer would result in recognising the same rights or obligations twice. [IAS 39 para AG 49].

6.6.120 It follows that the identification and evaluation of such derivatives is crucial to the derecognition analysis. Examples of transfers involving derivatives and the implications of the presence of the derivatives as regards derecognition are considered below. The accounting for transfers including derivatives that result in continued recognition to the extent of the entity's continuing involvement in the transferred asset are considered from paragraph 6.6.153 below.

Transfers subject to deep out-of-the-money option

6.6.121 A financial asset that is transferred subject only to a deep out-of-the-money put option held by the transferee or a deep out-of-the-money call option held by the transferor is derecognised. As a deep-out-of-the-money option is very unlikely to become in-the-money at the exercise date, the transferor is deemed to have transferred substantially all the risks and rewards of ownership (step 6 in the diagram in para 6.6.27 = yes). [IAS 39 para AG 51(g)].

6.6.122 If, due to subsequent events or changes in market conditions, it becomes probable that a deep out-of-the-money put or call option is likely to be exercised at the exercise date, the change in the option's probability being exercised would not result in the re-recognition of the financial asset that has previously been derecognised. This is consistent with the requirements in the standard that where an entity determines that, as a result of the transfer, it has transferred substantially all the risks and rewards of ownership, the entity does not recognise the transferred asset again in a future period, unless it re-acquires the transferred asset in a new transaction. [IAS 39 para AG 41]. Instead, the option would be accounted for as a derivative at fair value with the increase in its fair value reflected in profit or loss.

Transfer of readily obtainable assets subject to at-the-money call option

6.6.123 A financial asset that is readily obtainable in the market and transferred subject to the transferor holding a call option that is neither deeply in-the-money nor deeply out-of-the-money is derecognised. This is because the entity has neither retained nor transferred substantially all the risks and rewards of ownership and has not retained control (step 8 in the diagram in para 6.6.27 = no). [IAS 39 para AG 51(h)]. Although the option's existence means that the transferor has a continuing involvement in the asset, the fact that the asset is readily obtainable in the market means that the call option has no practical effect in creating any constraints on the transferee's practical ability to sell the asset. This is because if the transferred asset has been sold by the transferee and the transferor exercises the call option, the transferee will be able to fulfil its obligation by purchasing a replacement asset from the market. Therefore, the transferor retains no control over the transferred asset and derecognition of the transferred asset is appropriate. The transferor will account for the call option as a derivative at fair value with changes in fair value reflected in profit or loss.

6.6.124 Although not specifically dealt with in the standard, a readily obtainable financial asset that is transferred subject to the transferee holding a put option that is neither deeply in-the-money nor deeply out-of-the-money at the date of transfer is similarly derecognised for the reasons stated above. In this situation, if the transferee decides to exercise its rights under the put, the transferee would be able to meet its obligation by purchasing the asset from the market.

Transfer of assets subject to a fair value put or call option or a forward repurchase agreement

6.6.125 A transfer of a financial asset that is subject only to a put or call option or a forward repurchase agreement that has an exercise or repurchase price equal to the fair value of the financial asset at the time of repurchase results in derecognition, because of the transfer of substantially all the risks and rewards of ownership. [IAS 39 para AG 51(j)].

Transfer of assets subject to interest-rate swaps

6.6.126 An entity may transfer a fixed rate financial asset to a transferee and enter into an interest rate swap with the transferee to receive a fixed interest rate and pay a variable interest rate based on a notional amount that is equal to the principal amount of the transferred financial asset. The interest rate swap does not preclude derecognition of the transferred asset provided the payments on the swap are not conditional on payments being made on the transferred asset. [IAS 39 AG 51(p)].

Call and put options that are deeply in-the-money

6.6.127 If a transferred financial asset can be called back by the transferor and the call option is deeply in-the-money, the transfer does not qualify for derecognition. This is because the transferor has retained substantially all the risks and rewards of the asset's ownership by virtue of the fact that the call option is so valuable that its exercise appears virtually assured at inception. As explained in paragraph 6.6.119, a call option retained by the transferor that prevents the transfer from being accounted for as a sale is not separately recognised as a derivative asset. The accounting treatment is similar to sale and repurchase transactions considered in paragraph 6.6.142 below. Similarly, if the financial asset can be put back by the transferee and the put option is deeply in-the-money, the transfer does not qualify for derecognition because the transferor has retained substantially all the risks and rewards of ownership. Again the put option is not recognised separately, as to do so would result in double counting the same obligation. [IAS 39 para AG 51(f)].

Total return swaps

6.6.128 An entity may sell a financial asset to a transferee and enter into a total return swap with the transferee, whereby all of the cash flows from the underlying asset plus any increases and less any decreases in the underlying asset's fair value are remitted to the entity in exchange for a fixed or variable rate payment. In such a case, derecognition of all of the asset is prohibited. [IAS 39 para AG 51(o)].

Accounting treatment

6.6.129 The accounting treatment can be fairly complex, particularly in respect of transfers in which the entity (transferor) has continuing involvement in the transferred asset.

Transfers that qualify for derecognition

6.6.130 Where an entity determines that a transfer of a financial asset qualifies as a transfer and qualifies for derecognition because either:

- the entity has transferred substantially all the risks and rewards of ownership of the asset (step 6 in the diagram in para 6.6.27 = yes); or

- the entity has neither transferred nor retained substantially all the risks and rewards of ownership of the asset, and no longer retains control of the asset (step 8 in the diagram in para 6.6.27 = no),

the transferred asset is derecognised in its entirety and any new financial assets obtained, financial liabilities assumed and any servicing obligations are recognised at fair value. [IAS 39 para 25]. It should be noted that the phrase *"in its entirety"* includes part of a financial asset (or part of a group of similar financial assets) to which the derecognition tests have been applied as explained in paragraph 6.6.33 above.

6.6.131 On derecognition of a financial asset in its entirety, the difference between the carrying amount and the sum of:

- the consideration received (including any new assets obtained less any new liabilities assumed); and

- any cumulative gain or loss that had been recognised in other comprehensive income;

is recognised in profit or loss. The recycling of the cumulative gain or loss that had been recognised in other comprehensive income occurs on the derecognition of an available-for-sale financial asset.

[IAS 39 para 26].

6.6.132 There may also be instances where, following the financial asset's derecognition, a new financial asset is obtained or a new financial liability is assumed. As noted above, any new asset is part of the proceeds of sale. Any liability assumed, even if it is related to the transferred asset, is a reduction of the sales proceeds.

> **Example 1 – Derecognition of whole of a financial asset in its entirety**
>
> Entity A holds a small number of shares in entity B. The shares are classified as available-for-sale. On 31 March 20X6, the shares' fair value is C120 and the cumulative gain recognised in other comprehensive income is C20. On the same day, entity B is acquired by entity C, a large quoted entity. As a result, entity A receives shares in entity C with a fair value of C130.
>
> In this situation, the transfer of the shares in entity B qualifies for derecognition in their entirety as the entity no longer retains any risk and rewards of ownership. In addition, the transfer results in entity A obtaining a new financial asset, that is, shares in entity C that should be recognised at fair value as stated in paragraph 6.6.130 above. The gain on disposal, calculated in accordance with paragraph 6.6.131 above, is as follows:

	C
Proceeds received (fair value of cash or other securities received)	130
+ Fair value of any new financial asset acquired in the transfer	–
– Fair value of any new liability assumed in the transfer	–
Net proceeds	130
Carrying amount of the whole financial asset transferred	(120)
Gain or (loss) arising on derecognition	10
Amount recycled from other comprehensive income	20
Gain or (loss) recognised in profit or loss	30

The accounting entries to record the transfer are shown below:

	Dr C	Cr C
Fair value of shares in entity C acquired	130	
Carrying value of shares in entity B disposed of		120
Other comprehensive income ('recycling' of cumulative gain)	20	
Gain on disposal		30

Example 2 – Factoring without recourse

Entity A (the transferor) holds a portfolio of receivables with a carrying value of C1m. It enters into a factoring arrangement with entity B (the transferee) under which it transfers the portfolio to entity B in exchange for C900,000 of cash. Entity B will service the loans after their transfer and debtors will pay amounts due directly to entity B. Entity A has no obligations whatsoever to repay any sums received from the factor and has no rights to any additional sums regardless of the timing or the level of collection from the underlying debts.

In this example, entity A has transferred its rights to receive the cash flows from the asset *via* an assignment to entity B (step 4 in the diagram in para 6.6.27 = yes). Furthermore, as entity B has no recourse to entity A for either late payment risk or credit risk, entity A has transferred substantially all the risks and rewards of ownership of the portfolio (step 6 in the diagram in para 6.6.27 = yes). Hence, entity A derecognises the entire portfolio. The difference between the carrying value of C1m and cash received of C900,000, that is, the entire discount of C100,000 is recognised immediately as a financing cost in profit or loss.

The accounting that would apply if entity A continued to service the receivables is dealt with from paragraph 6.6.136 below.

Transferred asset is part of a larger asset

6.6.133   Where an entity transfers an asset that is part of a larger financial asset (for example, when an entity transfers interest only cash flows that are part of a debt instrument), and the part transferred qualifies for derecognition in its entirety, the previous carrying value of the larger financial asset is allocated between the part that continues to be recognised and the part that is derecognised.

The allocation is based on the relative fair values of those parts at the date of transfer. For this purpose, a retained servicing asset should be treated as part that continues to be recognised. The difference between the carrying amount allocated to the part derecognised and the sum of:

■ the consideration received for the part derecognised (including any new assets obtained less any new liabilities assumed); and

■ any cumulative gain or loss allocated to it that had been recognised in other comprehensive income;

is recognised in profit or loss. Any cumulative gain or loss that had been recognised in other comprehensive income is allocated between the part that continues to be recognised and the part that is derecognised, based on the relative fair values of those parts. The recycling of the cumulative gain or loss that had been recognised in other comprehensive income arises on derecognition of an available-for-sale financial asset.

[IAS 39 para 27].

6.6.134 In making an allocation of the previous carrying amount of a larger financial asset between the part transferred and the part that continues to be recognised, it is necessary to determine the fair value of the part that continues to be recognised. When the entity has a history of selling parts similar to the part that continues to be recognised or other market transactions exist for such parts, recent prices of actual transactions provide the best estimate of its fair value. When there are no price quotes or recent market transactions to support the fair value of the part that continues to be recognised, the best estimate of the fair value is the difference between:

■ the fair value of the larger financial asset as a whole; and

■ the consideration received from the transferee for the part that is derecognised.

[IAS 39 para 28].

6.6.135 In estimating the fair values of the part that continues to be recognised and the part that is derecognised, an entity should apply the fair value measurement requirements discussed in chapter 6.7. [IAS 39 para AG46].

Example – Derecognition of a part of a financial asset

On 1 April 20X2, an entity acquired corporate bonds at their face value of C5m. The bonds pay interest of 8% per annum in arrears and are redeemable at par at the end of year 10 on 31 March 20Y2.

On 31 March 20X6, when the current market rate of interest was 6%, the fair value of the bonds amounted to C5,491,732, consisting of the present value of the interest only strip of C1,966,930 and principal only strip of C3,524,802. On the same date, the entity unconditionally transferred its right to the principal only strip to a bank under a legal assignment for cash payment equal to its fair value without any recourse whatsoever. The entity retained the interest only strip (right to receive interest income on the bond at C400,000 per annum for the remaining 6 years).

In this example, the entity has transferred its rights to receive the principal cash flows to the bank *via* a legal assignment (step 4 in the diagram in para 6.6.27 = yes). Furthermore, as the entity has unconditionally sold its right to repayment when the bond matures on 31 March 20Y2 without recourse, it has transferred the risks and rewards attributable to the principal only strip that is part of a larger asset (step 6 in the diagram in para 6.6.27 = yes). Therefore, the entity can derecognise the principal only strip in its entirety.

In order to calculate the gain or loss on the principal only strip, it is necessary to allocate the carrying amount of C5m between the part sold and the part retained, based on their respective fair values as stated in paragraph 6.6.133 above. The allocation is shown below:

	Fair value	Percentage of fair value	Allocated carrying amount
	C	%	C
Principal only (PO) strip	3,524,802	64.1838	3,209,190
Interest only (IO) strip	1,966,930	35.8162	1,790,810
Total	5,491,732	100.0000	5,000,000

The accounting entries to record the part derecognised are as follows:

	Dr	Cr
	C	C
Cash received on sale of PO strip	3,524,802	
Carrying amount attributable to PO strip		3,209,190
Gain on sale of PO strip		315,612

If the bond had been classified as an available-for-sale financial asset, the bond would have been recorded at its fair value of C5,491,732 at 31 March 20X6. The amount credited to other comprehensive income would have amounted to C491,732. In that situation, it would be necessary to 'recycle' that portion of the fair value gain that is attributable to the principal only strip to the income statement. As stated in paragraph 6.6.133 above, this allocation should also be based on the relative fair values of the principal only and interest only strip. Accordingly, the portion of the gain recorded in other comprehensive income that is attributable to the principal only strip and fall to be recycled to the income statement amounts to C315,612 (64.1838% of C491,732).

The accounting treatment would be similar if, instead of unconditionally transferring the principal only strip at its fair value, the entity had transferred the interest only strip (the right to receive future interest income) at its fair value of C1,966,930 and retained the principal only strip. In that situation, a gain of C176,120 (C1,966,930 –

C1,790,810) would have arisen on the transfer if the asset was carried at amortised cost. On the other hand, if the asset was carried at fair value as available-for-sale, the 'recycled' gain to profit or loss would have amounted to C176,120 (35.8162% of C491,732).

Servicing assets and liabilities

6.6.136 Servicing is inherent in all loans and receivables. Servicing of mortgage loans, credit card receivables or other financial assets commonly includes, but is not limited to, collecting payments as they fall due, accounting for and remitting principal and interest payments to the transferee, monitoring non-performing loans/debtors, executing foreclosure if necessary and performing other administrative tasks. The service provider incurs the costs of servicing the assets often in return for a fee for performing the services.

6.6.137 Servicing rights do not meet the definition of a financial instrument because they represent a commitment to supply a service and can only be settled by the service delivery. However, since such servicing rights are, essentially, an expected stream of cash flows that results from a contractual agreement, they are so similar to financial instruments that they are recognised and initially measured on the same basis as financial assets and liabilities. Accordingly, where an entity transfers a financial asset in a transfer that qualifies for derecognition in its entirety and retains the right to service the financial asset for a fee, IAS 39 requires the entity to recognise either a servicing asset or a servicing liability for that servicing contract as follows:

- If the fee to be received is expected to be more than adequate compensation for the servicing, the entity should recognise a servicing asset for the servicing right. This asset should be recognised at an amount of the determined on the basis of the carrying amount of the larger financial asset as discussed in paragraph 6.6.133 above.

- If the fee to be received is not expected to compensate the entity adequately for performing the servicing, the entity should recognise a servicing liability for the servicing obligations at its fair value.

[IAS 39 para 24].

6.6.138 It follows from the above that where the benefits of servicing exactly compensates the service provider for its servicing responsibilities, there is no servicing asset or liability and the service contract's fair value is zero.

6.6.139 In some arrangements, an entity may retain the right to a part of the interest payments on transferred assets as compensation for servicing those assets. The part of the interest payments that the entity would give up upon termination or transfer of the servicing contract is allocated to the servicing asset or servicing liability. The part of the interest payments that the entity would not give up is an interest-only strip receivable. For example, if the entity would not give up any interest upon termination or transfer of the servicing contract, the entire interest spread is an interest-only strip receivable. For the purposes of applying the requirements of paragraph 6.6.133 above in respect of a transferred asset that is part of a larger financial asset, the fair values of the servicing asset and interest-only strip receivable are used to allocate the carrying amount of the receivable between the part of the asset that is derecognised and the part that continues to be recognised. If there is no servicing fee specified or the fee to be received is not expected to compensate the entity adequately for performing the servicing, a liability for the servicing obligation is recognised at fair value. [IAS 39 para AG 45].

Example 1 – Sale of receivable with servicing retained (servicing fee not specified in the contract)

Entity A owns a portfolio of loans with a carrying amount of C5m that yield 8% interest income. The loans are accounted for as loans and receivables at amortised cost.

The entity sells the entire portfolio to a bank for C5.25m without any recourse *via* a legal assignment. However, the entity agrees to service the portfolio over the remainder of its life for no additional payment and estimates that the amount that would fairly compensate it for servicing the portfolio is C200,000.

In this situation, as the entity transfers the entire portfolio including its right to receive future interest income on terms that qualify for derecognition under IAS 39, the entity would derecognise the carrying value of the portfolio of C5m. It would also recognise, in the absence of a servicing fee, a servicing liability of C200,000 in accordance with paragraph 6.6.137 above. The accounting entries to record the transfer are as follows:

	Dr C	Cr C
Cash	5,250,000	
Loans		5,000,000
Servicing liability		200,000
Gain on disposal		50,000

Example 2 – Sale of receivable with servicing retained (servicing fee specified in the contract)

The facts are the same as in example 1, except that entity A transfers the entire principal amount of the portfolio plus its right to receive interest income of 6% *via* a legal assignment for a consideration of C4,900,000 without any recourse. The entity retains the right to service the portfolio for which it will be compensated through a right to receive one-half of the interest income not sold (that is, 1% of the 2% future interest income retained). The remaining 1% is considered to be an interest-only strip retained by the entity A. At the date of transfer, the fair value of the interest-only strip is C275,000 and the fair value of the servicing asset is C75,000 (calculated as the present value of servicing fee receivable less a market fee for performing the service).

In this example, it is necessary to consider whether the criteria for derecognition should be applied to the portfolio of loans in its entirety or to separate portions (step 2 in the diagram in para 6.6.27). It is assumed that 75% (6% out of the 8%) of the interest cash flows transferred represents a full proportionate share of all the interest cash flows (see third bullet point of paragraph 6.6.33). This means that the entity will consider two portions of the whole portfolio, being 100% of the principal cash flows and 75% of the interest cash flows, separately for the purposes of derecognition.

Clearly, in this example, the rights to the cash flows have not expired as the loans still exist (step 3 in the diagram in para 6.6.27 = No) and so it is necessary to consider whether the entity has transferred its rights to receive the cash flows from the asset (step 4 in the diagram in para 6.6.27). However, the entity has legally assigned its rights to all of the principal cash flows and 6% of all the interest cash flows from the bond to the bank and, even though it has retained the rights to service the portfolio, this, in itself, does not prevent a transfer under paragraph 18(a) of IAS 39 (step 4 in the diagram in para 6.6.27 = Yes). Furthermore, as the transfer was made without any recourse, entity A has transferred substantially all the risks and rewards of those portions (step 6 in the diagram in para 6.6.27 = Yes). Therefore, entity A would derecognise the transferred portions.

In order to calculate the gain or loss arising on the transfer, the carrying amount of the financial asset (the portfolio of loans) of C5m should be allocated between the part sold and the part retained based on their relative fair values. In this regard, the servicing asset is allocated to the part that continues to be recognised as indicated in paragraph 6.6.133 above.

Interest sold/retained	Fair value	Percentage of fair value	Allocated carrying amount
	C	%	C
Loan sold (principal and 6% interest)	4,900,000	93.33	4,666,500
Interest-only strip retained	275,000	5.24	262,000
Servicing asset	75,000	1.43	71,500
Total	5,250,000	100.00	5,000,000

The gain arising on sale of the portion derecognised is the difference between the sales proceeds of C4,900,000 and the allocated carrying amount of C4,666,500, that is, C233,500. The retained interest in the transferred asset amounts to C333,500 (consisting of an interest-only-strip of C262,000 + servicing asset of C71,500).

Example 3 – Sale of listed debt securities subject to a call option

On 1 January 20X6, Bank A enters into an agreement to sell a portfolio of held for trading listed debt securities to an investment fund in exchange for a cash payment of C6m. The securities are subject to a call option that allows the bank to repurchase the securities for a price of C6.7m on 31 December 20X6. The securities' fair value at the date of transfer is C6.5m. The option's fair value is C0.5m. The investment fund has the practical ability to sell the securities to a third party.

The presence of the call option means that the bank has a continuing involvement in the transferred asset. However, as the securities are listed and the investment fund has the practical ability to sell the securities to a third party unilaterally and without imposing any conditions, the bank has not retained control of the securities. Accordingly the bank will derecognise the securities (step 8 in the diagram in para 6.6.27 = No), but record its rights under the call option separately.

Given that the call option's strike price (C6.7m) is more than the fair value of the underlying securities (C6.5m), the call option is out-of-the-money. Therefore, the fair value of the call option of C0.5m wholly relates to the time value of the option, which is also the premium paid by the bank.

Therefore, at the date of transfer, the company will record the following entries:

	Dr C	Cr C
Cash	6.0	
Trading portfolio		6.5
Derivative (call option)	0.5	

Bank A will recognise the call option at fair value through profit and loss.

Assume that at 31 December 20X6, the fair value of the securities increases to C7m and the bank exercises the option, Bank A will record the following entries:

	Dr C	Cr C
Derivative		0.2
Profit or loss	0.2	
Trading portfolio	7.0	
Cash		6.7
Derivative		0.3

As 31 December 20X6 is the call's expiry date, its time value at that date will be zero. The decline in the time value is included in the C 0.2 loss recognised in profit or loss.

Transfers that do not qualify for derecognition

6.6.140 Where a transfer does not result in the transferred asset's derecognition, the entity continues to recognise the transferred asset in its entirety and recognises a financial liability for the consideration received. [IAS 39 para 29]. The asset and the associated liability cannot be offset. In subsequent periods, the entity recognises any income on the transferred asset and any expense incurred on the financial liability. Again the entity cannot offset the income and the expense. [IAS 32 para 42, IAS 39 paras 29, 36]. This reflects the transaction's substance, which is accounted for as a collateralised borrowing.

6.6.141 It should be noted that the above treatment only applies when a financial asset is precluded from being derecognised in full (step 7 in the diagram in para 6.6.27 = yes). It does not apply in circumstances where a financial asset is not derecognised, because the entity has a continuing involvement in the financial asset (step 8 in the diagram in para 6.6.27 = yes). In those circumstances, special provisions apply and these are discussed from paragraph 6.6.145 below.

Example – Factoring with full recourse

Entity A (the transferor) holds a portfolio of receivables with a carrying value of C1m. It enters into a factoring arrangement with entity B (the transferee) under which it transfers the portfolio *via* an assignment to entity B in exchange for C900,000 of cash. All sums collected from debtors are paid by entity A to a specially nominated bank account opened by entity B (that is, entity A is only servicing the loans and has no right to the cash flows). Entity A agrees to reimburse entity B in cash for any shortfall between the amount collected from the receivable and the consideration of C900,000. Once the receivables have been repaid, any sums collected above C900,000 less interest on the initial payment until the date debtors pay, will be paid to entity A.

In this example, entity A has transferred its rights to receive the cash flows from the asset (step 4 in the diagram in para 6.6.27 = yes).

The next step is to consider whether entity A has transferred substantially all the risks and rewards of ownership of the receivables. Under the factoring arrangement, entity A's maximum possible exposure to entity B is to repay all of the consideration of C900,000 it has received. Although this situation is unlikely, it means that entity A has given a guarantee to compensate the transferee for all credit losses that are likely to occur. In addition, entity A receives the benefit of sums collected from debtors above C900,000. Consequently, entity A has retained both the credit and late payment risk associated with the receivables. Entity A has therefore retained substantially all the risk and rewards of ownership of the receivables and continues to recognise the receivables (step 7 in the diagram in para 6.6.27 = yes).

Entity A recognises the consideration received of C900,000 as a secured borrowing. The liability is measured at amortised cost with interest expense recognised over the period to maturity of the receivables in line with the interest rate charged by the factor.

Sale and repurchase agreements

6.6.142 The essential features of a sale and repurchase transaction are discussed from paragraphs 6.6.83 above. It is clear from the above discussions that a financial asset that is sold subject to the obligation to repurchase the same or a similar asset at a fixed price should not be derecognised. This is because the entity retains upside as well as downside exposure to gains and losses from the transferred asset. Therefore, the asset continues to be recognised in its entirety and the proceeds received are recognised as a liability. Similarly, the entity continues to recognise any income from the asset along with any expense incurred on the associated liability.

6.6.143 In some circumstances, a repurchase agreement may contain a provision that may allow the transferor to settle net in cash. That is, instead of taking physical delivery of the asset in consideration for paying the fixed price, the transferor settles the transaction net in cash by paying or receiving the difference between the fair value of the asset at the date of repurchase and the fixed repurchase price. The fact that the transferor is able to settle the transaction net in cash does not automatically mean that the transferor has lost control of the asset. [IAS 39 para AG 51(k)]. Also the transferor must still pass the 'risks and rewards' test (that is, to transfer substantially all risks and rewards), as well as the control test, before the transferor can derecognise the transferred asset. Examples of sale and repurchase transactions that are gross and net settled are considered below.

Example 1 – Sale and repurchase transaction (gross settled)

An entity purchases C10m, 10%, 5 year government bonds on 1 January 20X4 with semi-annual interest payable on 30 June and 31 December for C10.8m that results in a premium of C800,000. The entity classifies the bonds as held-to-maturity investments at amortised cost. The amortisation of the bonds to maturity using the effective interest method (see chapter 6.7) is shown below.

	Cash received	Interest income @ 4.013%	Carrying amount
1 Jan 20X4			10,800,000
1 Jul 20X4	500,000	433,408	10,733,408
1 Jan 20X5	500,000	430,735	10,664,143
1 Jul 20X5	500,000	427,956	10,592,099
1 Jan 20X6	500,000	425,064	10,517,163
1 Jul 20X6	500,000	422,057	10,439,220
1 Jan 20X7	500,000	418,929	10,358,149
1 Jul 20X7	500,000	415,676	10,273,825
1 Jan 20X8	500,000	412,292	10,186,117
1 Jul 20X8	500,000	408,772	10,094,889
31 Dec 20X8	500,000	405,111	10,000,000
	5,000,000	4,200,000	

On 1 July 20X5, the entity sells the bond at its fair value of C10.6m to a third party with an agreement to repurchase the bond on 1 July 20X6 for C10.65m.

As the repurchase price is fixed at the outset, the entity is precluded from derecognising the bond as discussed in paragraph 6.6.88 above (step 7 in the diagram in para 6.6.27 = Yes). The transferee will be entitled to receive the interest due on 1 Jan 20X6 and 1 July 20X6, that is, C1m that, together with the difference between the repurchase price and sale price of C50,000, represents a lender's return of 9.8943% per annum on the sale price. Therefore, the entity will continue to recognise the bond and the interest on it, as if it still held the bonds, as noted in paragraph 6.6.140 above.

It should be noted that although the repurchase agreement meets the definition of a derivative (it can be viewed as a forward contract), it is not separately recognised as a derivative and measured at fair value, because to do so would result in double counting of the same rights. Therefore, in this situation, the forward contract to repurchase the financial asset at a fixed price is not recorded as an asset (see further para 6.6.119 above).

The entity will also record a liability of C10.6m for the proceeds received. This liability accretes to the amount payable on repurchase of C10.65m at 1 July 20X6, using the effective interest method. The entity will continue to recognise a notional interest income in the periods to 1 Jan 20X6 and 1 July 20X6 and also account for an equal amount of notional interest paid to the third party. On 1 July 20X6 following repurchase of the bond by the entity, the liability of C10.65m will be eliminated as shown below:

	Liability Carrying value
Liability at 1 July 20X5	10,600,000
Interest payable for the half year to 31 December 20X5 @ 9.8943%	524,397
Notional cash paid to third party on 31 December 20X5*	(500,000)
Balance at 31 December 20X5	10,624,397
Interest payable for the half year to 30 June 20X6 @ 9.8943%	525,603
Notional cash paid to third party on 30 June 20X6*	(500,000)
Balance at 30 June 20X6	10,650,000
Liability repaid on 1 July 20X6 at repurchase price	(10,650,000)

* third party will receive interest directly from the bond as legal owner.

It may well be that the transferee is able to pledge or sell the bond during its period of ownership. In that situation, the transferor should reclassify the bond on its balance sheet as a loaned asset or repurchase receivable as explained in paragraph 6.6.92 above.

Example 2 – Sale and repurchase transaction (net settled in cash)

The facts are the same as in example 1 above, except that the repurchase contract is to be settled net in cash. The fair value of the asset at the settlement date amounts to C10.655m. This means that the entity will receive an additional C5,000 from the third party.

As explained above, the fact that the forward repurchase agreement requires net settlement does not automatically lead to derecognition. In this example, it is clear that the entity continues to recognise the asset as the net settlement price (being the difference between the fair value of the bond and the fixed price of C10.65m in the contract) reflects the movement in fair value of the bond. Hence the entity is still exposed to the risks and rewards of the bond for the term of the contract. As the entity will not physically get the bond back at the settlement date, the bond will be derecognised following receipt of the additional consideration of C5,000 at the settlement date. Therefore, it would not be appropriate to continue to classify the bond as held-to-maturity at amortised cost as in example 1. Instead, the entity would need to reclassify the bond as an available-for-sale financial asset at fair value at the sale date of 1 July 20X5. (Where an entity during the current financial year has sold or reclassified more than an insignificant amount of held-to-maturity investments before maturity (more than insignificant in relation to the total amount of held-to-maturity investments), it is prohibited from classifying any financial asset as held-to-maturity for a period of two years after the occurrence of this event, see further chapter 6.4.) The reclassification results in a gain to other comprehensive income as shown below:

Fair value of bond at 1 July 20X5	10,600,000
Amortised cost of bond at 1 July 20X5 as in example 1	10,592,099
Gain transferred to other comprehensive income following reclassification	7,901

Therefore, the entity will record the bond at its fair value of C10,600,000 and a corresponding liability of C10,600,000. The liability accretes to the repurchase price of C10,650,000 as shown in example 1.

At the settlement date of 1 July 20X6, immediately before derecognition the bond will be fair valued to C10,655,000 and a further gain of C5,000 will be recorded in other comprehensive income. As the contract will be net settled in cash, the bond is then derecognised, with the cumulative gain in other comprehensive income reclassified to profit or loss. Hence the entity will record the following entries:

	Dr C	Cr C
Liability	10,650,000	
Bond		10,655,000
Cash settlement	5,000	
Other comprehensive income – recycling of cumulative gain (7,901 + 5,000)	12,901	
Gain on disposal		12,901

The above example illustrates the point that although a forward repurchase agreement that requires net settlement in cash is economically equivalent to a deferred sale, the entity cannot derecognise the asset as the risks and rewards of ownership have been retained until settlement.

Subordinated retained interests and credit guarantees

6.6.144 An entity may provide the transferee with credit enhancement by subordinating some or all of its interest retained in the transferred asset. Alternatively, an entity may provide the transferee with credit enhancement in the form of a credit guarantee that could be unlimited or limited to a specified amount. If the entity retains substantially all the risks and rewards of ownership of the transferred asset, the asset continues to be recognised in its entirety. [IAS 39 para AG 51(n)].

> **Example – subordinated retained interest**
>
> Entity A originates a portfolio of 5 year interest-bearing loans of C10m. Entity A then enters into an agreement with entity B in which, in exchange for a cash payment of C9m, entity A agrees to pay to entity B the first C9m (plus interest) of cash collected from the loan portfolio. Entity A retains rights to the last C1m (plus interest). Expected collections on the loan portfolio are C9.5m and experience suggests that they are unlikely to be less than C9.3m.
>
> Entity A's retained interest in the cash flows from the loans is effectively subordinated. This is because if entity A collects, say, only C8m of its loans of C10m because some debtors default, entity A would have to pass on to entity B all of the C8m collected and keeps nothing for itself. On the other hand, if entity A collects C9.5m, it passes C9m to entity B and retains C0.5m.
>
> In this case, entity A retains substantially all the risks and rewards of ownership of the loans, because the subordinated retained interest absorbs all of the likely variability in net cash flows as discussed in paragraph 6.6.69. The loans continue to be recognised in their entirety even if the three pass-through conditions discussed in paragraph 6.6.48 are met, because derecognition is only achieved where, in addition, substantially all the risks and rewards of ownership are transferred. As derecognition is not achieved, the entire proceeds of C9m is recorded as a collateralised borrowing.

Continuing involvement in transferred assets

General

6.6.145 One of the most difficult derecognition issues relates to transfers of financial assets in which the transferor has some continuing interest in the asset. Examples include full or partial guarantees of the collectability of receivables, conditional or unconditional agreements to re-acquire the transferred assets and written or held options. The accounting treatment for some of these arrangements has been considered before in the context of failed derecognition through retention of risks and rewards. However, the accounting becomes complex when such arrangements give rise to continuing involvement accounting (that is, the transaction falls within the last box in the derecognition flow chart in para 6.6.27 above).

6.6.146 Under the derecognition criteria discussed above, when the entity transfers some significant risks and rewards and retains others and derecognition is precluded because the entity retains control of the transferred asset, the entity continues to recognise the asset to the extent of its continuing involvement. This should be measured in such a way that ensures that any changes in value of the transferred asset that are not attributed to the entity's continuing involvement are not recognised by the entity. It follows that the extent of the entity's continuing involvement in the transferred asset is the extent to which it is exposed to changes in the transferred asset's value. [IAS 39 para 30]. Measuring a financial asset in this manner may not be in accordance with the general measurement rules for financial assets, but is necessary to ensure that the accounting properly reflects the transferor's continuing involvement in the asset. IAS 39 contains detailed guidance on how to measure the asset when the continuing involvement takes the form of a guarantee or written or purchased options (including a cash-settled option or similar provision). These issues are considered from paragraphs 6.6.151 below.

Associated liability

6.6.147 When an entity continues to recognise an asset to the extent of its continuing involvement, the entity also recognises an associated liability. The associated liability is measured in such a way that the net carrying amount of the transferred asset and the associated liability is:

■ the amortised cost of the rights and obligations retained by the entity, if the transferred asset is measured at amortised cost; or

■ equal to the fair value of the rights and obligations retained by the entity when measured on a stand-alone basis, if the transferred asset is measured at fair value.

[IAS 39 para 31].

6.6.148 The above measurement basis may often result in a liability amount on initial recognition that is a 'balancing figure' that will not necessarily represent the proceeds received in the transfer. This is in contrast to the treatment for transfers that do not qualify for derecognition through retention of risks and rewards where the entire proceeds are accounted for as collateralised borrowing (see para 6.6.140 above). However, as explained in paragraph 6.6.146 above, special rules are necessary to account for transfers involving continuing involvement. The standard makes this clear by providing that *"despite the other measurement requirements in this standard"*, measuring the transferred asset and the associated liability in the manner described above reflects the rights and obligations that the entity has retained. [IAS 39 para 31].

Subsequent measurement

6.6.149 Subsequent to initial recognition, the fair value of the transferred asset and the associated liability should be accounted for consistently with each other in accordance with the general provisions of IAS 39 for measuring gains and losses. [IAS 39 para 33]. The requirement for consistent measurement means that designation of the associated liability at fair value through profit or loss is not available if the asset is measured at amortised cost. Also, the asset and the associated liability cannot be offset. [IAS 39 para 36].

6.6.150 The entity should continue to recognise any income arising on the transferred asset to the extent of its continuing involvement. It should also recognise any expense incurred on the associated liability. [IAS 39 para 32]. This requirement is comparable to the requirements for transfers that do not qualify for derecognition through retention of risks and rewards (see para 6.6.140 above). The income and the expense cannot be offset [IAS 39 para 36].

Continuing involvement through guarantees

6.6.151 An entity may provide a guarantee to pay for default losses on a transferred asset that prevents the transferred asset from being derecognised to the extent of the entity's continuing involvement. Assuming that the transferred asset was originally measured at amortised cost, the extent of the entity's continued involvement in the transferred asset, that is, the extent to which the entity continues to be exposed to the changes in the value of the transferred asset and the associated liability, is measured as follows:

■ The continuing involvement asset at the date of the transfer is measured at the lower of:

■ the carrying amount of the transferred asset; and

■ the maximum amount of the consideration received in the transfer that the entity could be required to repay ('the guarantee amount').

■ The associated liability is initially measured at the guarantee amount plus the fair value of the guarantee (which is normally the consideration received for the guarantee).

Subsequently, the initial fair value of the guarantee is recognised in profit or loss on a time proportion basis and the asset's carrying value is reduced by any impairment losses. If the guarantee is subsequently called, the liability is reduced by the cost of settlement. To the extent that the guarantee is not called and the entity is no longer exposed to the changes in the value of the transferred asset, that is the guarantee has lapsed unexercised, both the asset and the liability are reduced. [IAS 39 paras 30(a), AG48(a)].

Example 1 – Factoring with limited recourse (late payment risk retained)

Entity A (the transferor) holds a portfolio of trade receivables with a carrying value of C500m. Entity A enters into a factoring arrangement with entity B (the transferee) under which it transfers the portfolio to entity B in exchange for C490m of cash. Entity A transfers the credit risk, but retains the late payment risk up to a maximum of 180 days. After 180 days, the receivable is deemed to be in default and credit insurance takes effect. A charge is levied on the entity A for these late payments using a current rate of 6%. The fair value of the guarantee of late payment risk is C2m. Apart from late payment risk, entity A does not retain any credit or interest rate risk and does not carry out any servicing of the portfolio. There is no active market for the receivables.

In this example, entity A has transferred some but not all the risks and rewards of ownership – it has retained late payment risks, but has transferred credit risks (step 6 in the diagram in para 6.6.27 = No and step 7 = No). Furthermore, as there is no active market for the receivables, entity B does not have the practical ability to sell the transferred asset. Therefore, as entity B is constrained from selling the asset, the 'practical ability' test fails with the result that control of the transferred asset is retained by entity A. As a result of the above, entity A determines that it has a continuing involvement in the transferred receivables (step 8 in the diagram in para 6.6.27 = Yes).

Therefore, in accordance with paragraph 6.6.151 above, entity A measures the continuing involvement in the transferred asset at the lower of:

- the carrying amount of the transferred asset, that is, C500m; and

- the maximum amount of the consideration received in the transfer that entity A could be required to repay, that is, 6% on C500m for 180 days = 6% × 500 × 180/360 = C15m (the guaranteed amount).

Entity A will, therefore, record the continuing involvement asset at C15m.

Also in accordance with paragraph 6.6.151 above, entity A will measure the associated liability initially at the guarantee amount (C15m) + the fair value of the guarantee (C2m), a total of C17m. The associated liability is measured in such a way that the net carrying amount of the transferred asset and the associated liability is equal to the fair value of the guarantee.

Therefore, entity A would make the following entries at the date of transfer:

	Dr	Cr
Consideration received in cash	490	
Receivables transferred		500
Continued involvement in transferred asset	15	
Liability		17
Profit or loss – loss*	12	

*Consideration received of C490m – (consideration for guarantee C2m + carrying value of portfolio C500m). For illustration purposes, the above double entry shows a credit to receivables of C500m and a debit of C15m for the new continuing involvement asset. In practice, these entries would be combined, as the continuing involvement asset is a retained part of the transferred loans, not a new asset.

Entity A would make the following accounting entries subsequent to the date of transfer:

(i) To amortise the consideration for the guarantee over the period to which it relates (180 days):

	Dr	Cr
Liability	2	
Profit or loss		2

(ii) If the guarantee lapsed unexercised, the following entries would be made over the period for which late payment risk is retained as the maximum amount that entity A could be required to repay reduces due to timely payment on the receivables transferred:

	Dr	Cr
Continued involvement in transferred asset		15
Liability	15	

(iii) When late payment occurs, such that a charge is levied by entity B (taking an example charge of C4m), entity A would make the following entries:

Asset (to recognise the impairment of the continuing involvement asset)		4
Profit or loss	4	

(iv) The following entries would be made when a late payment charge is actually paid by entity A (taking an example of a charge of C4m):

Liability	4	
Cash		4

6.6.152   In some factoring transactions, the entity transfers receivables without receiving cash from the factor on the date of transfer and retains late payment risk. However, the entity has a right to draw down cash from the factor of up to a specified amount during the life of the factoring. In such a case, the entity should recognise a continuing involvement asset and liability for the late payment risk retained, calculated as explained in the example above. In addition, the entity should record a receivable from the factor, measured at the sum of the total fair value of the receivables at the date of transfer and the fair value of the late payment guarantee. This will give a similar accounting result as if cash of this amount had been received on the date of transfer.

Continuing involvement through options

6.6.153   As explained in paragraph 6.6.118 above, derivatives included in the transfer may constrain the transferee's practical ability to sell the transferred asset, even if there is no legal constraint, with the result that the transferor retains control over the transferred asset. In those circumstances, if the entity has neither transferred nor retained substantially all the risks and rewards of ownership of the transferred asset, the entity retains a continuing involvement in the transferred asset. For example, an entity may transfer a financial asset that is not readily obtainable in the market and holds a call option or writes a put option that is neither deeply in nor deeply out-of-the money at the date of transfer. [IAS 39 paras AG51(h)(i)].

6.6.154   When the entity's continuing involvement takes the form of a written or purchased option (or both) on the transferred asset, the extent of the entity's continuing involvement is the amount of the transferred asset that the entity may repurchase. However, in case of a put option on an asset written by the transferor that is measured by the transferor at fair value, the extent of the entity's continuing involvement is limited to the lower of the fair value of the transferred asset and the option exercise price. [IAS 39 para 30(b)]. This reflects the fact that the entity will not benefit from changes in the fair value above the option's exercise price. The manner in which the options are settled (physical or cash-settled) does not affect the measurement of the continuing involvement asset. [IAS 39 para 30(c)]. Depending on whether the transferred asset is measured at amortised cost or fair value, the associated liability is measured in accordance with paragraph 6.6.147 above as explained below.

Transfer of assets measured at amortised cost

6.6.155 Where a put option obligation written by an entity or call option right held by an entity prevents a transferred asset from being derecognised and the entity measures the transferred asset at amortised cost, the associated liability is measured at its cost (that is, the consideration received) adjusted for the amortisation of any difference between that cost and the amortised cost of the transferred asset at the option's expiration date. If the option is exercised, any difference between the associated liability's carrying amount and the exercise price is recognised in profit or loss. [IAS 39 para AG 48(b)].

Example – Asset measured at amortised cost subject to call option held by the transferor

Entity A has a portfolio of high yielding corporate bonds with an amortised carrying value of C102m. The bonds are not traded in the marketplace and are not readily obtainable. On 1 January 20X6, entity A sells the bonds to entity B for a consideration of C100m, but retains a call option to purchase the portfolio for C105m on 31 December 20X6. On that date, the amortised cost of the bonds will be C106m. The fair value of the bonds, at the date of transfer amounted to C104m.

The rights to receive cash flows from the asset have not expired (step 3 in the diagram in para 6.6.27 = no). However, entity A has transferred its right to receive cash flows (interest and principal on the bonds) to entity B (step 4 in the diagram in para 6.6.27 = yes). In this situation, the bonds are transferred, subject to a call option that is neither deeply in-the-money nor deeply out-of-the money (the option's exercise price is C105m compared to fair value of asset of C104m). The result is that the entity neither transfers nor retains substantially all the risks and rewards of ownership of the bonds (steps 6 and 7 in the diagram in para 6.6.27 = no). Furthermore, as the transferee does not have the practical ability to sell the bonds, derecognition of the bonds is precluded to the extent of the amount of the asset that is subject to the call option, because the entity has retained control of the asset (step 8 in the diagram in para 6.6.27 = yes).

As entity A has an option to buy back all of the bonds, it continues to recognise the bonds at their amortised cost, which will accrete from a carrying value of C102m to C106m at 31 December 20X6 using the effective interest rate method. The initial carrying amount of the liability is recorded at cost, that is, the consideration received of C100m. The liability is then accreted to C106m using the effective-interest rate method, which is the amortised cost of the transferred asset at the expiration date of the option (not the option's exercise price of C105m). As the asset is measured at amortised cost, the liability is also measured in a consistent manner as explained in paragraph 6.6.154 above.

Therefore, entity A would make the following entries:

	Dr C	Cr C
At 1 January 20X6 (date of transfer)		
Cash	100	
Associated liability		100
For the period to 31 December 20X6		
Bonds carried at amortised cost	4	
Income from bonds (106 – 102)		4
Interest on liability (106 – 100)	6	
Liability carried at amortised cost		6

At 31 December 20X6, entity A will exercise the option if the option exercise price of C105m is less than the fair value of the bonds. In that situation, entity A would record the following entries:

	Dr C	Cr C
Liability	106	
Cash (exercise price of option)		105
Gain on exercise of option		1

On the other hand, for example, if the strike price was C107m and the option lapses unexercised, both the asset and the liability are derecognised.

	Dr C	Cr C
Liability	106	
Carrying value of bond		106

A similar analysis would be carried out if, instead, of purchasing a call option, entity A wrote a put option that gave entity B the right to put the bonds back at 31 December 20X6.

Transfer of assets measured at fair value

6.6.156 Where a call option right held by the entity prevents a transferred asset from being derecognised and the entity measures the transferred asset at fair value, the transferred asset continues to be measured at fair value. This is because the call option gives the entity access to any increase in the asset's fair value. However, the measurement of the associated liability depends on whether the call option is in or at- the-money or out-of-the money, as described below.

- If the option is in or at-the-money, the associated liability is measured at the option's exercise price less the option's time value.

■ If the option is out-of-the money, the associated liability is measured at the fair value of the transferred asset less the option's time value.

The effect of the above measurement basis is to ensure that the associated liability is measured in such a way that the net carrying amount of the transferred asset and the associated liability is always equal to the fair value of the call option right. [IAS 39 para AG48(c)].

Example – Asset measured at fair value subject to call option held by the transferor

Entity A has 15% equity holding in entity B that was acquired some years ago for C40m. This holding is treated as an available-for-sale financial asset and the current fair value (and carrying value) is C104m. There is no active market in entity B's shares. On 1 January 20X6, entity A sells its 15% investment in entity B to bank C for a consideration of C100m, but retains a call option to purchase the investment for C105m on 31 December 20X7.

The rights to receive cash flows from the asset have not expired (step 3 in the diagram in para 6.6.27 = no). However, entity A has transferred its right to receive cash flows (dividends on the shares) from its investment to bank C (step 4 in the diagram in para 6.6.27 = yes), subject to a call option. The result is that the entity neither transfers nor retains substantially all the risks and rewards of ownership of the transferred asset (steps 6 and 7 in the diagram in para 6.6.27 = no). This is because:

■ entity A can exercise its call option so as to benefit from movements in the asset's fair value above the call option exercise price of C105m; and

■ entity A is not exposed to risk from decreases in the asset's market value below the call option exercise price.

With regard to the next question, whether entity A has retained control of its investment in entity B, this will depend upon whether bank C has the practical ability to sell the asset in its entirety to an unrelated third party, unilaterally and without imposing additional restrictions on the transfer. In this situation, there is no active market in entity B's shares, so a 15% stake is not readily obtainable in the market. The call option is neither deeply in-the-money nor deeply out-of-the-money (it is slightly out-of-the-money at inception as the option exercise price of C105m is more than the market value of the shares at C104m), but it is sufficiently valuable to prevent bank C from selling the asset immediately. These facts taken together lead to the conclusion that bank C does not have the practical ability to sell its investment in entity B. Consequently, entity A has retained control and derecognition is precluded to the extent of the amount of the asset that is subject to the call option (step 8 in the diagram in para 6.6.27 = yes).

Therefore, in accordance with paragraph 6.6.156, the entity continues to recognise the investment in entity B as an available-for-sale asset at fair value. At the date of transfer, the call option is out-of-the-money (option's exercise price of C105m is greater that the fair value of the asset at C104m). The premium paid on the option (all time value) is C4m (fair value of the asset of C104m less consideration received of C100m). As the option is out-of-the-money, IAS 39 requires the associated liability to be measured at the fair value of the transferred asset less the time value of the option as explained in the above paragraph. Therefore, the associated liability is recorded at

C104m – C4m = C100m, which is also equal to the consideration received. This ensures that the net amount of the transferred asset and the associated liability is equal to the fair value of the call option right. Therefore, entity A would make the following entries:

	Dr C	Cr C
At 1 January 20X6 (date of transfer)		
Cash	100	
Associated liability		100

Suppose that the asset's fair value increases to C106m at 31 December 20X6. The option is now in-the-money (exercise price of C105m < C106m) and its time value is C2m. In accordance with paragraph AG48(c) of IAS 39, the associated liability is measured at the option's exercise price (C105m) less the time value of the option (C2m) = C103m. This ensures that the net amount of the transferred asset (C106m) and the associated liability (C103m) is equal to the fair value of the call option right of C3m (intrinsic value of C1m + time value of C2m) as explained in paragraph 6.6.154 above.

	Dr C	Cr C
Entity A will record the following entries at 31 December 20X6		
Asset (increase in value from C104m to C106m)	2	
Liability (increase in value from C100m to C103m)		3
Other comprehensive income	1	

As the associated liability should be measured in a manner consistent with the available-for-sale asset in accordance with the general provisions of IAS 39 for measuring gains and losses as explained in paragraph 6.6.149 above, the movement in the liability is also recognised in other comprehensive income. The net loss of C1m recognised in other comprehensive income represents the fall in the value of the option from C4m to C3m.

It should be noted that to the extent that a transfer of a financial asset does not qualify for derecognition, the transferor's contractual rights or obligations related to the transfer are not accounted for separately as derivatives, since recognising both the derivative and the transferred asset would result in recognising the same rights twice. Therefore, entity A does not recognise the call option separately (see para 6.6.119 above).

Suppose that the fair value of the asset remains unchanged at 31 December 20X7. The entity will exercise the option as it is in-the-money. The accounting entries are as follows:

	Dr C	Cr C
Liability derecognised	103	
Other comprehensive income	2	
Cash paid		105

The overall loss of C3m over the two year period recognised in other comprehensive income represents the difference between the amount paid to re-acquire the asset for C105m and the consideration received on the transfer of C100m less the increase in the fair value of the asset of C2m (C106m – C104m) already recognised in other comprehensive income. It forms part of the cumulative net gain in other comprehensive income relating to the 15% equity holding in entity B. Suppose that the fair value of the asset falls to C103m at 31 December 20X7. In this situation, entity A will not exercise the option and will allow it to lapse. Both the transferred asset and the associated liability will be derecognised as shown below:

	Dr C	Cr C
Liability	103	
Asset		106
Other comprehensive income (recycling of cumulative gain C104m – C40m – C1m)	63	
Gain in profit or loss		60

The gain of C60m represents the net cash received of C60m (consideration received of C100m less original cost of C40m).

6.6.157 Where a put option written by an entity prevents a transferred asset measured at fair value from being derecognised, the transferred asset is measured at the lower of the fair value and the option exercise price. [IAS 39 para 30(b)]. This limitation is placed on the asset value because the entity has no right to the increase in the asset's fair value above the option exercise price. The associated liability is measured at the option's exercise price plus the time value of the option. This ensures that the asset's net carrying amount and the associated liability is always equal to the fair value of the put option obligation. [IAS 39 para AG48(d)]. The treatment is illustrated in the example given below.

Example – Asset measured at fair value subject to put option written by the transferor

Entity A has 15% equity holding in entity B that was acquired some years ago for C40m. This holding is treated as an available-for-sale financial asset and the current fair value at 1 January 20X6 (and carrying value) is C97m. There is no active market in entity B's shares.

On 1 January 20X6, entity A sells its investment in entity B to bank C for a consideration of C102m. However, entity A has granted a put option to bank C. Under the terms of the put option, bank C has the right to sell its investment in entity B back to entity A for C96m if the market value of its investment falls below C96m at any time in the next two years.

Entity A has transferred its right to receive cash flows (dividends on the shares) from its investment to bank C (step 4 in the diagram in para 6.6.27 = yes). However, in this situation, the investment is transferred, subject to a put option. The result is that the entity neither transfers nor retains substantially all the risks and rewards of ownership of the transferred asset (steps 6 and 7 in the diagram in para 6.6.27 = no). This is because:

- entity A is still exposed to movements in fair value below C96m, because if the fair value of the investment falls below C96m, bank C will put the investment back to company A for C96m; and

- entity A has not retained any benefit from increases in the market value of entity B.

With regard to the next question, whether entity A has retained control of its investment in entity B, this will depend upon whether bank C has the practical ability to sell the asset in its entirety to an unrelated third party, unilaterally and without imposing additional restrictions on the transfer. In this situation, there is no active market in entity B's shares, so a 15% stake is not readily obtainable in the market. The put option is neither deeply in-the-money nor deeply out-of-the money (it is slightly out-of-the-money at inception as the option exercise price of C96m is less than the market value of the shares at C97m), but it is sufficiently valuable to prevent bank C from selling the asset immediately. There would need to be a significant increase in the share's value to compensate bank C for the premium they have paid for the put option. These facts taken together lead to the conclusion that bank C does not have the practical ability to sell its investment in entity A. Consequently, entity A has retained control and derecognition is precluded to the extent of the amount of the asset that is subject to the put option (step 8 in the diagram in para 6.6.27 = yes).

Therefore, in accordance with the above paragraph, the entity recognises the investment in entity B at the lower of the fair value of the asset (C97m) and the option exercise price (C96m), that is, C96m, being the option's exercise price.

The premium received by entity A for writing the put option is C5m (consideration received of C102m less fair value of the asset of C97m). As the option is out-of-the-money, the entire premium represents the time value of the option. The associated liability is measured at the option exercise price (C96m) plus the time value of the option (C5m), that is, C101m, as explained in paragraph 6.6.157 above. This ensures that the net amount of the transferred asset (C96m) and the associated liability (C101m) is equal to the fair value of the put option obligation (C5m). Therefore, entity A would make the following entries:

	Dr C	Cr C
At 1 January 20X6 (date of transfer)		
Cash received	102	
Investment		1
Liability		101

Suppose that the fair value of the asset decreases to C94m at 31 December 20X6. The put option is now in-the-money (exercise price of C96m > C94m) and its time value is C2m. In accordance with the above paragraph 6.6.157 above, the asset is measured at the lower of the asset's fair value and the option's exercise price, that is, C94m, being the fair value of the asset. The associated liability is measured at the option's exercise price (C96m) plus the time value of the option (C2m), that is, C98m. This ensures that the net amount of the transferred asset (C94m) and the associated liability (C98m) is equal to the fair value of the put option obligation of C4m (intrinsic value of C2m + time value of C2m).

	Dr C	Cr C
Entity A will record the following entries at 31 December 20X6		
Asset (fall in value from C96m to C94m)		2
Liability (fall in value from C101m to C98m)	3	
Other comprehensive income		1

As the associated liability should be measured in a manner consistent with the available-for-sale asset in accordance with the general provisions of IAS 39 for measuring gains and losses as explained in paragraph 6.6.146 above, the movement in the liability is also recognised in other comprehensive income. The net gain of C1m represents the fall in the value of the put option obligation from C5m to C4m.

It should be noted that to the extent that a transfer of a financial asset does not qualify for derecognition, the transferor's contractual rights or obligations related to the transfer are not accounted for separately as derivatives, since recognising both the derivative and the transferred asset would result in recognising the same rights twice. Therefore, entity A does not recognise the put option separately (see para 6.6.119 above).

Suppose that the fair value of the asset remains unchanged at 31 December 20X7. Bank C decides to exercise the option as it is in-the-money. Entity A will have to re-acquire the asset at the put option price. The accounting entries are as follows:

	Dr C	Cr C
Liability derecognised	98	
Cash paid		96
Other comprehensive income		2

The overall gain of C3 recognised in other comprehensive income over the two year period represents the difference of C6m (consideration received of C102m less amount paid to re-acquire the asset for C96m) less C3m (fall in asset value from C97m at inception to C94m at exercise). It forms part of the cumulative net gain in other comprehensive income relating to the 15% equity holding in entity B.

Continuing involvement in a part of a financial asset

6.6.158 An entity may have a continuing involvement in only a part of a financial asset rather than the entire asset as discussed above. This situation may arise when an entity retains an option to repurchase part of a transferred asset, or retains a residual interest that does not result in the retention of substantially all the risks and rewards of ownership and the entity retains control. Where this is so, the entity allocates the financial asset's previous carrying amount between the part it continues to recognise under continuing involvement and the part it no longer recognises on the basis of the relative fair values of those parts on the date of transfer. [IAS 39 para 34].

6.6.159 The allocation exercise and the calculation of the gain or loss arising on the part of the asset that is no longer retained are carried out in a similar manner as described in paragraph 6.6.133 above. That is, the difference between the carrying amount allocated to the part that is no longer recognised and the sum of:

- the consideration received for the part no longer recognised; and

- any cumulative gain or loss allocated to it that had been recognised directly in other comprehensive income;

is recognised in profit or loss. Any cumulative gain or loss that had been recognised in other comprehensive income is allocated between the part that continues to be recognised and the part that is no longer recognised on the basis of the relative fair values of those parts. [IAS 39 para 34]. The recycling of the cumulative gain or loss that had been recognised in other comprehensive income relates to the part no longer recognised of an available-for-sale financial asset. In addition to the part retained, the entity continues to recognise its continuing involvement in the asset and the associated liability. The manner in which the above guidance is applied to continuing involvement in a part of a financial asset is illustrated in paragraph AG52 of IAS 39. Although that example is not presented here, the application illustrated in that example is best understood by reference to a securitisation transaction given below.

> **Example – Continuing involvement in a part of a financial asset**
>
> Entity A enters into a securitisation transaction in which it transfers a pool of receivables amounting to C1,000, but retains a subordinated interest of C100 in that pool.
>
> The terms of the securitisation arrangements show that the transaction is to be accounted for using the continuing involvement approach (which, *inter alia*, requires that the buyer assume significant risks and rewards).
>
> Under the continuing involvement approach, the seller typically recognises an asset of C200 and a liability of C100. This gives a net asset of C100 which might be expected as it represents the retained subordinated interest of C100. However, the gross numbers can be confusing to understand. AG52 analyses the transaction as comprising:
>
> - a retention of a non-subordinated 10% interest in the transferred assets; and
>
> - the subordination of that interest that is equivalent to the seller providing a credit guarantee.
>
> Both these elements result in continuing involvement and both need to be accounted for. The first element (the retention of a non-subordinated 10% interest) results in a continuing involvement asset of C100. In addition, the second element (the subordination of that interest which is equivalent to the seller providing a guarantee of the first C100 of losses) also results in a continuing involvement asset of C100, and a liability of C100 (being the maximum amount the entity may have to pay by losing the C100 asset recognised for the first element). Therefore, the seller will recognised a total continuing involvement asset of C200 and a liability of C100.

Measuring a financial asset in the above manner may not be in accordance with the general measurement rules for financial assets, but is necessary to ensure that the accounting properly reflects the transferor's continuing involvement in the asset.

Retained servicing

6.6.160 If a transaction is accounted for using continuing involvement and the transferor is required to service the assets without receiving adequate compensation for the service provided, a servicing liability should be recognised to the extent that the asset is derecognised, but no servicing liability should be recognised to the extent of the continuing involvement asset. For example, if the asset pre-transaction was C100 and the continuing involvement in the asset after the transaction was C60, the transferor would recognise a servicing liability for the C40 derecognised, but not for the C60 on the balance sheet. Servicing assets and liabilities are dealt with in detail from paragraph 6.6.136 above.

Accounting for collateral

6.6.161 A transfer of financial assets may require the transferor to provide non-cash collateral (such as a debt or equity instruments) to the transferee. If collateral is transferred to the transferee, the custodial arrangement is commonly referred to as a pledge. Transferees sometimes are permitted to sell or repledge (or otherwise transfer) collateral held under a pledge. The accounting for the collateral by the transferor and the transferee depends on whether the transferee has the right to sell or repledge the collateral and on whether the transferor has defaulted as shown in the table below.

Circumstance	Accounting by transferor	Accounting by transferee
Transferee has the right by contract or custom to sell or repledge the collateral.	The transferor reclassifies that asset in its balance sheet (for example, as a loaned asset, pledged equity instruments or repurchase receivable) separately from other assets that are not so encumbered. [IAS 39 para 37(a)]. This is because the transferor retains all the risks and rewards of ownership of the asset pledged as collateral and, therefore, cannot derecognise it under the normal rules for derecognition.	The transferee will not recognise the collateral as an asset. In the event that the transferee sells the collateral pledged to it, it recognises the proceeds from the sale and a liability measured at fair value for its obligation to return the collateral. [IAS 39 para 37(b)].
Transferor defaults under the terms of the contract and is no longer entitled to redeem the collateral.	Transferor derecognises the collateral. [IAS 39 para 37(c)].	Transferee recognises the collateral as its asset initially measured at fair value or, if it has already sold the collateral, derecognise its obligation to return the collateral. [IAS 39 para 37(c)].

All other situations not referred to above.	Transferor continues to recognise the collateral as its asset. [IAS 39 para 37(d)].	This is because the risks and rewards of ownership of the collateral have passed to the transferee.
		Transferee does not recognise the collateral as an asset. [IAS 39 para 37(d)].

Accounting by transferee

6.6.162 Transferees are required to follow the recognition principles discussed from paragraph 6.6.6 above. However the same asset should not be recognised by both the transferor and transferee at the same time. Therefore, to the extent that a transfer of a financial asset does not qualify for derecognition in the books of the transferor, the transferee does not recognise the transferred asset as its asset. Instead, the transferee derecognises the cash or other consideration paid and recognises a receivable from the transferor. If the transferor has both a right and an obligation to re-acquire control of the entire transferred asset for a fixed amount (such as under a repurchase agreement), the transferee may account for its receivable as a loan or receivable. [IAS 39 para AG 50].

Derecognition of financial liabilities

6.6.163 The derecognition rules for financial liabilities are somewhat different from those relating to financial assets. Whereas the derecognition rules for financial assets tend to focus on risks and rewards and may not lead to derecognition even though legal transfer has occurred, the derecognition rules for financial liabilities tend to focus on the legal release of the contractual obligations. Consequently, the IAS 39 provisions relating to derecognition of financial liabilities in whole or in part can be relatively straight forward and less subjective than those for derecognition of financial assets. The rules in IAS 39 deal with extinguishment of financial liabilities, their modification by lenders and the recognition and measurement of any gains or losses that arise from extinguishment and modification. These issues are considered in detail below.

Extinguishment of a financial liability

General principles

6.6.164 A financial liability (trading or other) is removed from the balance sheet when it is extinguished, that is when the obligation is discharged, cancelled or expired. [IAS 39 para 39]. This condition is met when the debtor either:

- discharges the liability (or part of it) by paying the creditor, normally with cash, other financial assets, goods or services; or

- is legally released from primary responsibility for the liability (or part of it) either by process of law or by the creditor.

[IAS 39 para AG 57].

6.6.165   The condition for extinguishment is also met if an entity repurchases a bond that it has previously issued, even if the entity is a market maker or intends to resell it in the near term. [IAS 39 para AG 58]. This is consistent with the treatment of treasury shares re-acquired by an entity, except that in the case of extinguishing a liability, any gain or loss that may arise is recognised (see para 6.6.177 below).

6.6.166   A financial liability may be converted into an equity instrument (for example, a convertible bond) or become an equity instrument without any change to its contractual terms (for example, through a lapse of certain terms). The treatment of such instruments is discussed in chapter 6.5.

Legal release by the creditor

6.6.167   It is clear from the general conditions that a debt is extinguished only if the debtor is legally released from its obligation by the creditor. This condition is met even if a creditor releases a debtor from its present obligation to make payments, but the debtor assumes a guarantee obligation to pay if the party assuming primary responsibility defaults. In this circumstance the debtor:

- recognises a new financial liability based on the fair value of its obligation for the guarantee; and

- recognises a gain or loss based on the difference between (i) any proceeds paid and (ii) the carrying amount of the original financial liability less the fair value of the new financial liability.

[IAS 39 para AG 63].

An example illustrating the above treatment is given below. Contrast this with in-substance defeasance discussed in paragraph 6.6.175 below.

> **Example – Transfer of debt obligation with legal release**
>
> Entity A transfers C100 million highly liquid government bonds into a trust that is owned by a registered charity. The trust does not fall to be consolidated by entity A. Those bonds will solely be used to repay entity A's issued C100 million fixed rate liability. The holders of the issued C100 million fixed rate liability have released entity A from its obligation to make payments. However, entity A enters into a guarantee arrangement whereby, if the trust does not make payments when due, then entity A will pay the debt holders.
>
> In this situation, derecognition of the fixed rate debt instruments is not precluded by virtue of the guarantee. Entity A has obtained legal release, which is a necessary and sufficient condition for the debt's derecognition, notwithstanding that entity A has given a guarantee to a third party.
>
> Entity A (the debtor) recognises a new financial liability based on the fair value of its obligation for the guarantee and recognises a gain or loss based on the difference between any proceeds paid and the carrying amount of the original financial liability less the fair value of the new financial liability. [IAS 39 para AG 63].

6.6.168 Sometimes, instead of providing a guarantee, the debtor may pay a third party to assume the obligations under the debt and obtain legal release from its creditor. In that situation, the second condition in paragraph 6.6.164 above is met and the debt is extinguished. However, if the debtor transfers its obligations under a debt to a third party and obtains legal release from the creditor, but undertakes to make payments to the third party so as to enable it to meet its obligation, the debtor recognises a new debt obligation to the third party. [IAS 39 para AG 60].

Supplier finance and reverse factoring

6.6.169 Some banks offer services to buyers of goods or services in order to facilitate payments of the trade payables arising from purchases from suppliers. Generally, the supplier delivers goods to the buyer and a trade payable is originated. These are commonly referred to as 'supplier finance' or 'reverse factoring arrangements'. The buyer selects payables to the supplier that it wishes to be subject to the reverse factoring or supplier finance arrangement and notifies the bank. Through some mechanism the supplier receives cash for its trade receivable. In some cases, a buyer enters into these contracts to obtain an early payment discount that it would otherwise not be in a position to obtain.

6.6.170 A buyer would not typically present liabilities payable to a financial institution as trade payables. Trade payables are generally understood to arise in the ordinary course of business with suppliers. When the original liability to a supplier has been extinguished in accordance with paragraph 6.6.164 above, the resulting new liability to the bank should be presented as bank financing or under another suitable heading rather than 'trade payables'. If the latter option is taken, the description of the chosen line item needs to be carefully considered to ensure that the entity's financial position is presented fairly and in a way that faithfully represents the effect of the transaction, as required by paragraph 15 of IAS 1 (revised). In particular, similar items should be presented together and should not be presented with dissimilar items, and the overall effect should not be misleading.

6.6.171 Another example is where the bank negotiates with the supplier directly, on the buyer's behalf. The bank agrees to pay the supplier before the legal due date to obtain an early payment discount. However, the bank's payment does not result in the legal settlement of the buyer's obligation under its trade payable. Rather, the supplier agrees to receive the amount from the buyer net of the early payment discount at the contractual due date and to reimburse the bank this same amount when it receives the payment from the buyer. Should the supplier fail to reimburse the bank, the buyer agrees to reimburse the bank. The bank charges a fee to the buyer, which effectively results in the bank and supplier sharing the benefit of the early payment discount. In such a case, as the buyer is not legally released from its original obligation, the buyer continues to recognise the trade payable to the supplier. However, it also recognises a guarantee obligation, initially measured at fair value, for its promise to reimburse the bank if the bank does not receive a reimbursement from the supplier.

6.6.172 In some circumstances, subsequent to the notification of selected receivables by the supplier, the bank offers the supplier a Receivables Purchase Agreement. Under this contract, the rights under the trade receivable are acquired from the supplier by the bank, but there is no legal release for the buyer from the payable. It is likely the buyer will be involved in some extent in such an arrangement. For example, the buyer agrees on changes in his rights under the original terms of the sale of goods – that is, he may no longer be eligible to offset the payable against credit notes received from the supplier, or the buyer may be restricted from making earlier direct payments to the supplier.

6.6.173 The rights of the trade receivable are transferred to the bank, but the buyer's obligation under the trade receivable is not legally extinguished. In such a case the buyer would need to consider whether the change to the terms of the trade payable is significant under paragraphs 40 and AG62 of IAS 39. If there is a significant change, the transfer is accounted for as an extinguishment – that is, the previous liability should be derecognised and replaced with a new liability to the bank. The effect of any additional restrictions imposed by the reverse factoring agreement on the buyer's rights will need careful consideration. For example, it may be the case that, as the buyer selects each payable at its sole discretion, it will only select those payables where from the buyer's perspective, the effect of any such restrictions on the rights and obligations is not significant. In contrast, it may be the case that all three, that is the buyer, bank and supplier, have agreed initially on a minimum amount of payables/receivables being refinanced by the bank, whereby the buyer has subsequently no further discretion to avoid the change in his rights even if the change might be significant to an individual payable.

6.6.174 The accounting for supplier finance and reverse factoring arrangements will depend on the exact facts and circumstances relating to them.

In-substance defeasance

6.6.175 In-substance defeasance is an arrangement whereby an entity makes a lump sum payment relating to its obligations to a third party (typically a trust). The trust then applies those funds and income thereon to discharge the entity's obligation to the lender. The entity has little or no right of access to the funds put in the trust. The trust does not assume any legal responsibility for the obligations and the lender is not a party to the in-substance arrangement. Some argue that as the entity has no right of access to those funds, it has effectively discharged its obligations to the lender. However, this view is inconsistent with the general rule in paragraph 6.6.164 above that a liability is not extinguished in the absence of a legal release. [IAS 39 para 63]. Therefore, in-substance defeasance arrangements do not result in derecognition of the liability.

Extinguishment through transfer of assets that fails derecognition

6.6.176 Sometimes an entity may transfer financial assets (other than cash) which the lender accepts as being in full and final settlement and thereby releases the debtor from its obligations. The entity derecognises the liability as the debt has been legally discharged. However, the financial assets transferred may fail the derecognition criteria, because either the entity has retained substantially all the risks and rewards of ownership or the entity has a continuing involvement in the transferred asset by virtue of retaining control. Therefore, where the derecognition criteria are not met, the transferred assets are not derecognised and the entity recognises a new liability relating to the transferred assets. [IAS 39 para AG 61].

Gain or loss arising on extinguishment

6.6.177 Where a financial liability (or part of a financial liability) is extinguished or transferred to another party, the entity should recognise any difference arising between the carrying amount of the financial liability (or part of the financial liability) extinguished or transferred and the consideration paid, including any non-cash assets transferred or liabilities assumed, in profit or loss. [IAS 39 para 41]. This applies even if the issuer of a debt instrument is a market maker in that instrument or intends to resell it in the near term. [IAS 39 para AG 58].

> **Example – Gain on extinguishment of debt in full**
>
> A bank has loaned C25m to a property investment company that invested the funds in residential properties consisting mainly of high quality apartments. However, as a result of a fall in occupancy rates, the entity is unable to meet its debt obligations. The entity successfully negotiated with the bank whereby the bank agreed to accept a property with a fair market value of C20m in full and final settlement of the C25m obligation. The property's carrying value was C21m.
>
> As a result of the negotiation, the loan is extinguished and the entity recognises a gain on the extinguishment as follows:
>
> | | Cm |
> |---|------|
> | Carrying value of liability | 25 |
> | Fair value of non-cash settlement | 20 |
> | Gain on extinguishment of debt | 5 |
> | | |
> | Carrying value of property | 21 |
> | Fair value of property transferred | 20 |
> | Loss on disposal | (1) |
>
> The gain on extinguishment of debt typically would be recorded in the income statement under finance income. The loss on disposal of the property would be charged against operating profits. It would not be appropriate to show a net gain of extinguishment of C4m in finance income.

6.6.178 If an entity repurchases only a part of a financial liability, the entity should allocate the previous carrying amount of the financial liability between the part that continues to be recognised and the part that is derecognised based on the relative fair values of those parts on the date of the repurchase. The difference between the carrying amount allocated to the part derecognised and the consideration paid, including any non-cash assets transferred or liabilities assumed, for the part derecognised is recognised in profit or loss. [IAS 39 para 42]. This means that the consideration paid for the repurchase is not simply set off against the original liability's carrying value, but a gain or loss is calculated based on the part derecognised as set out above.

Example – Derecognition of part of a liability

On 1 January 20X5, an entity issued 1 million 8% C100 nominal 10 year term bonds with interest payable each 30 June and 31 December. The bonds, which are traded in the market, were issued at par. Issue costs of C2m were incurred. Four years after the issue date, the entity repurchases 600,000 bonds at the then market value of C96 per C100 nominal. The amortised cost of the bond at 31 December 20X8 amounted to C98,655,495.The gain arising on repurchase is calculated as follows:

	C
Carrying value allocated to amount repurchased – 60% of C98,655,495	59,193,297
Amount paid on repurchase of 600,000 @ C96	57,600,000
Gain arising on repurchase	1,593,297

Exchange and modification of debt instrument

6.6.179 Entities frequently negotiate with lenders to restructure their existing debt obligations. There may be a variety of reasons for doing so, not necessarily when the entity is in financial difficulties. Such restructuring may result in a modification or an exchange of debt instruments with the lender that may be carried out in a number of ways. For instance, an entity may decide to take advantage of falling interest rates by cancelling its exposure to high-interest fixed-rate debt, pay a fee or penalty on cancellation and replace it with debt at a lower interest rate (exchange of old debt with new debt). Alternatively, the entity may seek to roll up the higher interest payments into a single payment that is payable on the loan's redemption or amend the amount payable on redemption (modification). Whether a modification or exchange of debt instruments represents a settlement of the original debt or merely a renegotiation of that debt determines the accounting treatment that should be applied by the borrower.

6.6.180 IAS 39 requires an exchange between an existing borrower and lender of debt instruments with substantially different terms to be accounted for as an extinguishment of the original financial liability and the recognition of a new financial liability. Similarly, a substantial modification of the terms of an existing financial liability or a part of it (whether or not attributable to the financial difficulty of the debtor) should be accounted for as an extinguishment of the original financial liability and the recognition of a new financial liability. [IAS 39 para 40]. Consider the examples below.

Example – Change in holders and repayment terms

An entity issued a five-year bond that is listed and traded on a stock exchange. In the following year, the entity proposes a modification of the bond's repayment terms, to extend the maturity. The proposed modification becomes effective if it achieves approval of more than 75% of the bondholders, in accordance with the terms set out in the offering circular. The dissenting bondholders are entitled to have their bonds purchased by the entity (or any other party) at fair value, being the market price immediately prior to the proposed modification being put to the bondholders for consideration. The entity appoints an investment bank to stand ready to acquire any bonds from dissenting bondholders and the bank will hold the bonds afterwards as principal. The proposed modification of the repayment terms was accepted by 80% of the bondholders. The dissenting 20% sell their bonds to an investment bank at fair value and 100% of the bonds are then modified

The first step is to determine whether the change in holder of 20% of the bonds to the investment bank from the dissenting bondholders gives rise to a legal release from primary responsibility for the liability. Depending on the legal jurisdiction, if the change in bondholder results in the legal release from primary responsibility for the original liability, those bonds are extinguished and should be derecognised in accordance with paragraph 39 of IAS 39, However, in many cases, a change in the holder of a security such as a bond does not result in the entity being legally released from the primary obligation under the liability. The term sheet for a security usually sets out the trading mechanism; in most cases, there is no new contract signed between the issuer and the new holder upon a transfer. In these circumstances, the acquisition of the bond by the investment bank from the dissenting bondholders is a transfer of an existing bond, not the issue of a new bond to a new lender. The transfer is not, therefore, considered to be a change in 'lender' before and after the transfer of the bonds.

The second step is to determine whether there has been an exchange or modification, under paragraph 40 of IAS 39 , between an existing borrower and lender with substantially different terms. As noted above, the transfer of the bonds does not represent a change in the lender; the modification in the bond's repayment terms is therefore considered to be between an existing borrower and lender for all of the outstanding bonds, rather than merely the 80% that accepted the modification of terms. The entity, therefore, applies paragraphs 40 and AG62 of IAS 39 to assess whether the change in repayment terms amounts to a substantial modification of the terms of an existing liability. Where the change is substantial, it is accounted for as an extinguishment of the original bond and the recognition of a new liability. Where the change in terms is not substantial, it is accounted for as a modification of the original financial liability.

6.6.181 The terms are substantially different if the discounted present value of the cash flows under the new terms, including any fees paid net of any fees received and discounted using the original effective interest rate, is at least 10% different from the discounted present value of the remaining cash flows of the original financial liability. [IAS 39 para AG 62].

6.6.182 The standard does not clarify whether the quantitative analysis outlined above is an example of a term that is substantially different or whether the analysis is the definition of substantially different. There is an accounting policy choice. Although it is clear that if the discounted cash flows change by at least 10%, the original debt should be accounted for as an extinguishment, there is nothing in the standard to suggest that the analysis should be restricted only to cash flow changes. Indeed, in order to meet the spirit of the standard, analysis of any modification of terms that are qualitative in nature may be performed. For example, qualitative changes in risk profile of the newly modified instrument compared to the original instrument may well indicate that the changes in terms are substantially different, as happens for example when contractual terms are changed so that the denomination of the original liability is changed to a different currency. In that situation, we believe it is acceptable to account for the substantial modification as an extinguishment, even though the above quantitative analysis may indicate a less than 10% cash flow change. Determining whether there is a substantial change in terms from a qualitative perspective is judgemental and will depend upon the specific facts and circumstances of each case. Similar qualitative factors to those given in paragraph 6.6.37.6 for modified financial assets may be relevant. These include, but are not limited to, the following:

- The currency that the debt instrument is denominated in.

- The interest rate (that is fixed *versus* floating rate).

- Conversion features attached to the instrument.

- Changes in covenants.

6.6.183 Alternatively, since the standard is unclear whether the 10% test is the definition of substantially different, a quantitative analysis could be performed to determine whether an exchange or a modification should be accounted for as an extinguishment. Under this alternative view, if the change in discounted cash flows is less than 10%, the exchange or modification would not be accounted for as an extinguishment. This alternative view is also acceptable if applied consistently and properly disclosed in the notes.

6.6.184 There is no guidance in the standard that assists in interpreting the terms 'existing borrower and lender' mentioned in paragraph 6.6.180 when looking at transactions where lending is *via* a syndicate of banks. In such cases, the borrower should determine in the first instance whether it has borrowed under one loan or under multiple loans. Sometimes syndicated loans are structured with one 'lead lender' signing the loan agreement. The agreement's substance rather than its legal form should dictate the accounting. Presented below are a number of factors that, individually or in combination, would tend to indicate that the borrower has borrowed under multiple loans:

- The borrower has the ability to selectively repay amounts on the loan to different members of the syndicate. In other words any payments made by the borrowers are not always split on a *pro rata* basis amongst all the syndicate members.

- The terms of the loan are not homogenous for various syndicate members.

- The borrower has the ability to selectively renegotiate portions of the loan with individual syndicate members or subsets of all the syndicate members.

- Individual syndicate members have the ability to negotiate their loan directly with the borrower without the approval of other syndicate members.

This is not an exhaustive list and, in most such arrangements, specific facts and circumstances will be necessary to determine the appropriate accounting. Consider the examples below.

Example 1 – Change of loan terms and change in interests within syndicate (single loan)

An entity signs a loan agreement that was negotiated with a syndicate of 20 banks that each have a 5% interest in the total amount borrowed. The entity has determined that it has borrowed under a single loan.

A year later, the borrower and the syndicate members agree to a change in the contract terms that have an impact of the future cash-flows (such as an extension of the maturity of the loan). In addition three banks sell their interest back to one of the existing syndicate members (bank A), so that bank A now has a 20% stake.

From the borrower's perspective, the loan is a single loan. Accordingly, since the modification is between an existing borrower and lender (the syndicate), the change to the terms of the loan would be evaluated on an aggregate basis to determine if the modification is an extinguishment or not. The transfer between syndicate members has no impact on the accounting by the borrower.

Example 2 – Multiple loans

An entity has a loan agreement signed by 20 banks, which are each determined to have granted separate loans to the borrower. Each of the 20 banks has a 5% stake in the total face amount of the loan. If new creditors join the group they must individually sign a new contract with the borrower. From the borrower's perspective, these are multiple loans and are accounted for as such.

Four of the banks transfer their 20% combined stake to another bank without any other change in the terms of the loan. It is necessary to determine whether the transfer is undertaken in a manner that results in the borrower being legally released from primary responsibility for the liability by the existing bank lender (further guidance on common methods of loan transfer is given in para 6.6.114). In this example, the new lender has to individually sign a new contract with the borrower and the borrower is legally released by the existing bank lender. The existing liability is therefore extinguished and this transaction is accounted for as an extinguishment of the four individual loans by the borrower and the recognition of a new loan liability. The bank to which the 20% stake is being transferred could be one within the original syndicate or one that was not previously a syndicate member.

However, consider a situation when bank A (a current syndicate member) sells a participation in its loan to bank B. In such a case, there would be no effect on the entity (borrower) unless the entity has been legally released from primary responsibility by bank A. In this example, bank A is still a creditor of the entity and bank B is a creditor of bank A.

On the other hand consider a situation where five of the banks in the above syndicate agree to extend the maturity of their loans. The remaining 15 institutions did not agree to the extension. The loans with the banks that agreed to the modification would be evaluated individually to determine if they were modified or extinguished. The loans to the banks that did not agree to the modification are unchanged and, therefore, do not need to be evaluated for modification or extinguishment.

If all the lenders agree to change terms of the loan that has an impact on its future cash flows, then in principle loans with each lender should be evaluated separately to determine if they have been extinguished or modified. If all the loans have homogenous terms, practically the same answer will be achieved if the loans are evaluated on an aggregate basis.

6.6.185 The liability being exchanged or modified might be only one component of a financial instrument. Where two or more components of a financial instrument are inter-dependent, a change to the terms of one component is likely to have repercussions on the other components. Each modification will need to be considered based on the specific facts and circumstances. Consider the examples below.

Example 1 – Extension of the term of a convertible bond when the conversion option is accounted for as an embedded derivative

Entity B issues a convertible bond in which the conversion option is accounted for as an embedded derivative (as it violates the fixed for fixed rule in IAS 32). Some time after issuance, the issuer and the holder renegotiate the terms of the convertible bond and agree to revised terms that include extending the bond's maturity and increasing the conversion ratio (where more ordinary shares of the issuer are to be delivered.)

From the issuer's perspective, the modification to the host contract and the derivative should be assessed together when applying the 10% test in paragraphs 40 and AG62 of IAS 39. This is because, in this case, the cash flows relating to the host debt and embedded derivative are interdependent. This is consistent with paragraph 40 of IAS 39, which states that *"a substantial modification of the terms of an existing financial liability or a part of it. . . . shall be accounted for as extinguishment of the original financial liability"*.

The term 'cash flow' in the 10% test of paragraph AG62 of IAS 39 includes the impact of settlement in a variable number of shares. One possible way of applying paragraph AG62 of IAS 39 is to assess the estimated cash flow as being the higher of the fair value of the share settlement at the date of the modification (using the current market share price) and the present value of cash flows attributable to the host. This approach reflects the optionality from the holder's perspective to choose the more valuable settlement option. Another way of determining the fair value of the share settlement in this approach is to use the forward price(s) of the entity's shares as at the estimated conversion date, and discounting to the modification date. Where the expected conversion date cannot be estimated reliably under this alternative, the contractual maturity date should be used. Other approaches might also be acceptable.

Example 2 – Exchange of a convertible instrument for debt

Entity A has issued two-year convertible debt for C100, in which the conversion option meets the 'fixed for fixed' test in IAS 32. It is, therefore, accounted for as an equity component (with a liability recognised for the debt component). At the end of year 1, the convertible debt has a fair value of C90 and the host debt component has a fair value of C85. Entity A agrees with the convertible debt holders to exchange their instrument for new non-convertible three-year debt with a fair value of C90.

Entity A has a policy choice as to whether a qualitative test is applied in addition to the 10% quantitative test when derecognising financial liabilities. If entity A considers both qualitative factors and the 10% quantitative test, either of the two approaches set out below (approaches A and B) may be applied to determine whether the liability component of the convertible bond should be derecognised. However, if entity A has a policy of only derecognising financial liabilities using the 10% quantitative test, only approach B below is applicable.

Approach A – qualitative assessment: extinguished in its entirety

From a qualitative perspective, provided the original conversion option was substantial (has not insignificant worth to the holder) at the date of the exchange, the new non-convertible debt instrument is substantially different from the convertible debt by virtue of it not being convertible. This is because the risk profile and related returns arising from the original conversion option are effectively terminated. The existing convertible debt should therefore be derecognised and the new debt recognised at its initial fair value of C90. This approach effectively applies the derecognition rules to the whole instrument (debt and equity component together).

A gain or loss is recognised on the extinguishment of the convertible bond in accordance with paragraph AG33 of IAS 32, being the difference between the carrying amount of that debt component and the allocated consideration paid to redeem it. The full consideration paid (in this case the C90 new debt issued) is allocated to the debt and equity components of the existing convertible instrument at the date of the transaction using the same allocation method as on initial recognition (that is, by fair valuing the liability and allocating the residual to the equity component). In this case, the new debt instrument is allocated to the debt and equity components of the convertible instrument using the same method – that is on an 85:5 basis.

The new debt allocated to extinguishing the equity conversion option of C5 (C90 × 5/90) does not result in a gain or loss. Rather, the difference between this amount and the carrying value of the conversion option is taken directly to equity.

Approach B – quantitative assessment: debt component subject to 10% test, equity component extinguished

Under this approach, the derecognition requirements in paragraphs 39 and 40 of IAS 39 are viewed as applying to financial liabilities only. Using the principle in paragraph AG33 of IAS 32, part of the new debt instrument replaces the debt component of the convertible instrument, and part replaces the equity component of the original instrument. The new debt instrument is, therefore, allocated to the debt and equity elements of the convertible instrument for the purpose of their separate derecognition assessments, using the same method as on initial recognition.

The derecognition test (quantitative only, or quantitative and qualitative, depending on entity A's policy) should be applied to the debt component only. In this example, applying the 10% test on this basis results in the entity continuing to recognise the old debt component. Equally, the terms of the debt component are not considered to be substantially modified from a qualitative perspective. The revision of the terms of the debt component is, therefore, treated as a modification in this example. Applying paragraph AG62 of IAS 39 results in spreading the difference due to the change in terms (using the same effective rate) over the remaining life of the new debt.

The remaining part of the new debt instrument extinguishes the conversion option, which does not give rise to a gain or loss. [IAS 32 para 33]. Rather, the difference between the amount of the new debt that extinguishes the conversion option, and the previous carrying value of the conversion option is taken directly to equity.

The combined result of the above two elements has the effect that, at the date of the exchange, part of the new debt is measured at its fair value (being the part that replaces the equity component); where there is no derecognition of the old debt component, part of the debt is measured at the amortised cost of the old debt component (the part that replaces the debt component of the original convertible).

If applying the derecognition criteria to the debt component results in derecognition of the existing old debt component, the gain or loss on derecognition is calculated in the same way as discussed in approach A above.

Debt to equity swaps

6.6.186 It is not uncommon for companies to replace their existing debt instruments with equity through renegotiations with their debt holders in order to reduce excessive interest burden. Debt for equity swaps are mostly carried out by companies that are in financial distress. Debt holders often agree to swap their loans for equity in the belief that if they take an equity stake in a troubled company, they will ultimately achieve a greater return.

6.6.187 IFRIC 19, 'Extinguishing financial liabilities with equity instruments', addresses the accounting treatment when an entity renegotiates the terms of its debt, with the result that the liability is extinguished by the debtor issuing its own equity instruments to the creditor (referred to as a 'debt for equity swap'). IFRIC 19 does not affect the investor's accounting. It also does not change the guidance for convertible bonds where extinguishing the liability by issuing equity shares is in accordance with its original terms (see chapter 6.5). Furthermore, IFRIC 19 does not apply to transactions with shareholders in their capacity as shareholders or transactions between entities under common control where there is a capital contribution (see para 6.6.195).

6.6.188 IFRIC 19 requires a gain or loss to be recognised in profit or loss when a financial liability is settled through the issuance of the entity's own equity instruments. The interpretation clarifies that the new equity instruments are treated as consideration paid for the extinguishment of a financial liability. The amount of the gain or loss recognised in profit or loss is therefore the difference between the carrying value of the financial liability (or part of a financial liability) extinguished and the fair value of the equity instruments issued, in accordance with paragraph 41 of IAS 39. The equity instruments issued are recognised and measured initially at fair value at the date the financial liability was extinguished. See the example below.

Example – Debt to equity swaps

An entity issued a debt instrument amounting to C50m repayable at par in year 10. Four years after issue it became clear that the entity was in financial difficulty and was unable to service its existing debt obligations. It therefore reached an agreement whereby the debt holders agreed to accept 5m equity shares of C1 each in full and final settlement of all amounts due under the debt instrument. The fair value of the equity shares issued in exchange was C25m.

As required by IFRIC 19, the new equity instrument is recorded at its fair value of C25m; and a gain is recognised on the extinguishment of the existing debt instrument. The accounting entries are as follows:

	Dr Cm	Cr Cm
Debt instrument	50	
Equity		25
Profit or loss – gain arising on extinguishment of debt		25

6.6.189 If the fair value of the equity instruments cannot be reliably measured, the fair value of the existing financial liability is used to measure the gain or loss. In measuring the fair value of a financial liability extinguished that includes a demand feature (for example a demand deposit), paragraph 49 of IAS 39 is not applied. [IFRIC 19 para 7]. Therefore, for the purposes of IFRIC 19, the fair value of a demand deposit may be determined to be less than the amount payable on demand, discounted from the first date that the amount could be required to be repaid.

6.6.190 If only part of the financial liability is extinguished, the entity assesses whether some of the consideration paid relates to a modification of the terms of the liability that remains outstanding. If part of the consideration paid does relate to a modification of the terms of the remaining part of the liability, the entity allocates the consideration paid between the part of the liability extinguished and the part of the liability that remains outstanding. The entity should consider all relevant facts and circumstances relating to the transaction in making this allocation. The consideration allocated to the remaining liability should form part of the assessment of whether the terms of the remaining liability have been substantially modified. If the remaining liability has been substantially modified, the entity accounts for the modification as an extinguishment of the original liability and the recognition of a new liability at fair value.

Example – Exchange of debt instrument for a modified debt instrument and equity shares

Entity C owes C500 to a lender, which is not a related party, but is unable to pay this liability in full. It renegotiates the debt with the lender which agrees to waive 80% of the liability (C400) in exchange for equity instruments in entity C with a fair value of C200. In addition, the terms of the remaining debt are modified to reset the interest rate and extend the term of the debt. The debt is carried at C500 prior to the renegotiation and its fair value is C300. The remaining debt has a fair value of C100 after renegotiation. The relative fair values of the instruments after the renegotiation are 33.3% liability (100/300) and 66.7% equity (200/300).

IFRIC 19 applies to 66.7% of the carrying value of the original liability (C500) that is extinguished by equity:

	Dr Cm	Cr Cm
Liability	333.3	
Equity		200.0
Profit or loss		133.3

The remaining 33.3% of the original liability (C166.7) is compared with the new liability to determine whether there has been a substantial modification of the remaining debt. If there is a substantial modification, additional journal entries are needed to recognise the extinguishment of the remaining debt:

	Dr Cm	Cr Cm
Liability (old)	167.7	
Liability (new)		100.0
Profit or loss		67.7

In a situation where there is a extinguishment of part of a debt by equity and a substantial modification of the remaining part of the debt, the total gain or loss on extinguishment is equal to the difference between the carrying value of the old liability and the total fair value of the new debt and equity (C500 – C300 = C200 in this example).

6.6.191 The amount of the gain or loss should be separately disclosed in the income statement or in the notes.

[The next paragraph is 6.6.195.]

Transactions involving entities within a group

6.6.195 Paragraph 3(a) of IFRIC 19 scopes out transactions between an entity and a lender, where the lender is also a direct or indirect shareholder and is acting in that capacity. In addition, IFRIC 19 does not apply to transactions where the lender and the entity are controlled by the same party or parties before and after the transaction and the substance of the transaction includes an equity distribution by, or contribution to, the entity. Transactions between entities within the same group should, therefore, be assessed to determine whether they are in or out of the scope of IFRIC 19.

6.6.196 An entity should assess the facts and circumstances to determine whether the lender is acting in its capacity as shareholder in the transaction or, for transactions between fellow subsidiaries, whether there is in substance a capital contribution or a distribution given (effectively *via* the parent). This might be the case where the debt for equity swap is structured as a capital contribution or where the subsidiary is, or subsidiaries are, 100% owned and the number of shares issued is not related to the fair value of the liability. In such a circumstance, it may not be appropriate to apply IFRIC 19 and recognise a gain or loss in the income statement based on the fair value of the equity instruments issued. Rather, the transaction could be accounted for either in full or in part as a capital contribution or distribution. In such circumstances, share capital would be measured as applicable under local law, the liability would be derecognised and the difference recorded in the equity of the borrower. The remainder of the transaction could then be accounted for in accordance with IFRIC 19.

6.6.197 On the other hand, an entity might determine that the transaction between group companies does not, in substance, include an equity distribution by, or contribution to, the entity. This might be the case, for example, when the subsidiary or subsidiaries are not 100% owned, the loan is on commercial terms and the number of shares issued to the other party is based on the fair value of the liability. In such a case, the subsidiary applies IFRIC 19 and recognises a gain or loss in the income statement for the difference between the carrying amount of the liability and the fair value of the shares.

Treatment of cost and fees incurred on debt restructuring

6.6.198 If an exchange of debt instruments or modification of terms is accounted for as an extinguishment, any costs or fees incurred are recognised as part of the gain or loss on the extinguishment. If the exchange or modification is not accounted for as an extinguishment, any costs or fees incurred adjust the liability's carrying amount and are amortised over the modified liability's remaining term. [IAS 39 para AG 62].

6.6.199 As the above paragraph refers to any cost or fees incurred, it would appear that IAS 39 does not distinguish between costs and fees payable to third parties, such as lawyers and accountants, and those payable directly to the lender. As these costs and fees are properly incurred in connection with the modification of the instrument's terms, it is appropriate to treat them as adjustments to future interest payments rather than costs and fees in the true sense of the term. Accordingly, if the fees paid to third parties are related directly to the modification, they should be recognised as part of the gain or loss if the modification is accounted for as an extinguishment. This is true even if the modification results in the issue of a new debt instrument. Only those costs that the issuer can demonstrate are incremental and directly related to the issue of the new debt instrument should be treated as costs of the new liability, rather than expensed as part of the gain or loss on the extinguishment of the existing instrument.

6.6.200   Where the modification of a financial liability is not accounted for as an extinguishment, the fees paid to third parties are adjusted against the existing liability's carrying value, together with other payments to the lender.

Example – Renegotiation of debt

A company borrowed C1m on 1 January 20X0 at a fixed rate of 9% per annum for 10 years. The company incurred issue costs of C100,000. Interest on the loan is payable yearly in arrears. As a result of deteriorating financial condition during 20X5, the company approached its bondholders for a modification of the bond's terms. The following terms were agreed with effect from 1 January 20X6 (all interest paid to date):

■   The interest rate is reduced to 7.5% payable yearly in arrears.

■   The original amount payable on maturity is reduced to C950,000.

■   The maturity of the loan is extended by two years to 31 December 20Y1.

■   Renegotiation fees of C30,000 are payable on 1 January 20X6.

The loan would be recorded initially at 1 January 20X0 at net proceeds of C900,000 and would be amortised using the effective interest rate (EIR) method discussed in chapter 6.7. The EIR is 10.6749% as shown below.

	Interest C 10.6749%	Payments C	Carrying value C
1 Jan 20X0			900,000
31 Dec 20X0	96,074	90,000	906,074
31 Dec 20X1	96,723	90,000	912,797
31 Dec 20X2	97,441	90,000	920,238
31 Dec 20X3	98,235	90,000	928,473
31 Dec 20X4	99,114	90,000	937,587
31 Dec 20X5	100,087	90,000	947,674
31 Dec 20X6	101,164	90,000	958,837
31 Dec 20X7	102,355	90,000	971,192
31 Dec 20X8	103,674	90,000	984,866
31 Dec 20X9	105,134	1,090,000	–

At 1 January 20X6, the remaining cash flows on the old debt comprise four annual interest payments of C90,000 and the C1m of principal payable at redemption. The present value of these remaining cash flows on that date amounts to C947,674 as shown above.

The present value of the cash flows under the revised terms discounted at the original EIR of 10.6749% is shown below:

		Cash Flows	Present value
1 Jan 20X6	Fees	30,000	30,000
31 Dec 20X6	Revised interest	75,000	67,766
31 Dec 20X7	Revised interest	75,000	61,230
31 Dec 20X8	Revised interest	75,000	55,324
31 Dec 20X9	Revised interest	75,000	49,988
31 Dec 20Y0	Revised interest	75,000	45,166
31 Dec 20Y1	Revised interest + principal	1,025,000	557,736
			867,210

The present value of C867,210 represents 91.5% of the present value of the old cash flows. As the difference in present values of C80,464 (947,674 – 867,210) is less than 10% of the present value of the old cash flows, the modification is not accounted for as extinguishment. The question arises as to how to account for the present value difference of C80,464 arising from the renegotiation. One approach would be to recognise the difference immediately in profit or loss by adjusting the previous carrying value of the liability from C947,674 to C867,210. Another approach would be to recognise the difference over the remaining life of the instrument by adjusting the effective interest rate so that the previous carrying value of C947,674 accretes to the redemption amount of C950,000 by 31 December 20Y1. There is support for both approaches in IAS 39 as explained below. The first approach is supported by paragraph AG 8 of IAS 39 that states:

> "If the entity revises its estimates of payments or receipts, the entity shall adjust the carrying value of the financial asset or financial liability (or group of financial instruments) to reflect actual and revised estimated cash flows. The entity recalculates the carrying value by computing the present value of estimated future cash flows at the financial instrument's original effective interest rate. The adjustment is recognised as income or expense in profit or loss." [IAS 39 para AG 8].

A renegotiation of an instrument's terms will change its contractual cash flows. This will also result in a change to the expected cash flows in most cases. Paragraph AG 8 can be read to apply to all cases in which cash flows are re-estimated, as there is nothing in that paragraph that limits it to cases when the cash flows are not renegotiated. The second approach is supported by paragraph AG 62 as discussed in paragraph 6.6.180 above. As the change in terms is not considered to be a substantial modification and, therefore, does not result in the extinguishment of the original liability, it is a more faithful representation to recognise any net gain or loss over the modified instrument's remaining life. This is further supported by the fact that, in the previous version of IAS 39, IGC 62-1 dealt with this issue and clearly favoured this treatment. There is nothing in the revised IAS 39 that indicates that the IASB intended a change to this treatment. Indeed, the table of concordance between the old and the new standard clearly indicates that IGC 62-1 is mapped into AG 62. Furthermore, it could be argued that paragraph AG 8 is not applicable, as a renegotiation that changes the instrument's terms and, hence, the future cash flows, is not the same as the entity revising its estimates. The effective interest rate that amortises the old carrying value, as adjusted for fees incurred of C30,000, is 8.6453% as shown below:

	Interest@ 8.6453%	Payments	Carrying value
			947,674
Fees paid			(30,000)
01 Jan 20X6			917,674
31 Dec 20X6	79,336	75,000	922,010
31 Dec 20X7	79,710	75,000	926,720
31 Dec 20X8	80,117	75,000	931,837
31 Dec 20X9	80,560	75,000	937,397
31 Dec 20Y0	81,040	75,000	943,437
31 Dec 20Y1	81,563	1,025,000	–

The treatment applied should be the one that is most appropriate to the particular facts and circumstances of the transaction being accounted for, reflecting the substance of the transaction. For example, if the renegotiation results in an immediate cash payment that includes a repayment of part of the principal, the recognition of a gain or loss would be more appropriate. This is because it would not be appropriate to spread forward a gain or loss that arises on a partial repayment by adjusting the EIR on the portion that continues to be recognised. Conversely, if an entity renegotiates to reduce the future interest payments on a loan in times of falling interest rates and partially compensates the lender by an immediate cash payment, the second method would be the more appropriate. This is because adjusting the EIR would best reflect the effect that the new interest rate environment has had on the remaining cash flows.

Other examples are given below:

Case A
An instalment loan is renegotiated to reduce the payments due in the remaining years of the loan in return for an immediate cash payment. In this case, the cash payment represents a re-payment of part of the liability. The first approach to recognise a gain or loss on the modification is, therefore, the most appropriate. It is not appropriate to spread forwards a gain or loss arising on a partial re-payment by adjusting the EIR on the portion that continues to be recognised.

Case B
An entity is close to breaching a loan covenant on a particular borrowing. It renegotiates the borrowing to remove the covenant in return for an immediate cash payment that reflects the different credit risk now associated with the loan. In this case, the second method to defer the loss over the remaining life of the loan is the most appropriate. The removal of the covenant results in a more risky loan that is appropriately reflected in a higher EIR.

Case C
An entity has had a fixed rate borrowing for some years, during which time interest rates have fallen. The entity renegotiates the borrowing to reduce the future interest

payments to the current market rate in return for an immediate cash payment. The cash payment does not fully compensate the lender for the lost future interest – that is, in economic terms, the effect of the fall in interest rates is shared between the parties to the loan. In this case, the second method is the most appropriate. Adjusting the EIR of the loan reflects the effect that the new interest environment has had on the remaining cash flows

6.6.201 Transaction costs are also likely to be incurred when an entity extinguishes a liability in exchange for equity instruments. IFRIC 19 does not specify how such costs should be accounted for. However, paragraph 5 of IFRIC 19 states that the issue of equity instruments to extinguish a liability is 'consideration paid' in accordance with IAS 39 paragraph 41 – that is IFRIC 9 considers a 'debt for equity swap' to be a liability extinguishment in accordance with IAS 39. Paragraph AG62 of IAS 39 notes that when an extinguishment of a liability occurs any costs or fees incurred are recognised as part of the gain or loss on extinguishment.

6.6.202 Paragraph 35 of IAS 32 requires transaction costs arising in respect of an equity transaction to be recognised as a component of equity to the extent they are incremental costs directly attributable to the equity transaction that would otherwise have been avoided. Such transaction costs that can be separately identified as relating solely to the issue of the new equity and not to the debt extinguishment should, therefore, be recognised in equity rather than profit or loss.

6.7 – Measurement of financial assets and liabilities

6.7 – Measurement of financial assets and liabilities

Introduction

6.7.1   An entity recognises a financial asset or a financial liability when it first becomes a party to the contractual rights and obligations in the contract. It is, therefore, necessary to measure those contractual rights and obligations on initial recognition. Under IAS 39, all financial instruments are measured initially by reference to their fair value, which is *normally* the transaction price, that is, the fair value of the consideration given or received. However, this will not always be the case.

6.7.2   Subsequent to initial recognition, IAS 39's measurement approach is best described as a 'mixed attribute' model with certain assets and liabilities measured at cost and others at fair value. The model depends upon an instrument's classification into one of the four categories of financial assets or one of the two categories of financial liabilities discussed in chapter 6.4. For example, depending on the nature of the instrument and management's intentions, a fixed interest security intended to be held-to-maturity would be measured at amortised cost and not at fair value. Notwithstanding this, as explained in chapter 6.4, the standard gives entities the option to classify financial instruments that meet certain special criteria at fair value with all gains and losses taken to profit and loss. The ability for entities to use the fair value option simplifies the application of IAS 39 by mitigating some anomalies that result from the use of the mixed measurement model.

6.7.3   This chapter deals with IAS 39's basic measurement requirements and addresses the concepts of fair value and amortised cost, including the use of the effective interest method and the standard's impairment model. However, the special form of accounting that applies when a financial asset or liability is designated by management in a hedging relationship is covered in chapter 6.8.

6.7.4   In November 2009 the IASB issued the first part of IFRS 9, relating to classification and measurement of financial instruments. The new requirements apply a consistent approach to classifying financial assets based on the entity's business model for managing the financial assets and the contractual cash flow characteristics of the financial asset and replace the numerous categories of financial assets in IAS 39. Financial assets will be measured at amortised cost or fair value and the fair value option is retained but the presentation of gains and losses is changed. The IASB updated IFRS 9 in October 2010 to include guidance on classification and measurement of financial liabilities and on derecognition of financial instruments. The classification and measurement of financial liabilities under IFRS 9 remains the same as under IAS 39 except where an entity has chosen to measure a liability at fair value through profit or loss (see para 6.7.155).

On 15 November 2011, the IASB tentatively decided to consider making limited modifications to IFRS 9 on an expedited basis to deal with specific application issues, interaction with the insurance project and convergence with the US-based FASB. A separate re-exposure draft 'Amortised cost and impairment of financial assets' is expected on the expected-loss impairment model and the IASB's tentative decisions to use a three bucket approach that determines the amount and timing of credit losses to be recognised. This model is expected to replace the numerous impairment methods in IAS 39 that arise from the different classification categories. It is the IASB's intention that IFRS 9 will ultimately replace IAS 39 in its entirety. IFRS 9 is dealt with in chapter 6.10.

6.7.5 In May 2011 the IASB issued IFRS 13. The standard provides a single source of fair value measurement guidance. It clarifies the definition of fair value, provides a framework for measuring fair value and requires disclosures for all assets and liabilities measured at fair value, on recurring (for example some financial instruments) or non-recurring (for example intangible assets acquired in a business combination) basis. The standard does not determine when fair value measurements are required. The measurement guidance in IFRS 13 will apply to all fair value measurements except for those within the scope of IFRS 2 or IAS 17, and certain other measurements that are required by other standards and are similar to, but are not, fair value. Disclosures are required for assets and liabilities measured at fair value with some exceptions. IFRS 13 amended IAS 39 and IFRS 9 to remove their guidance on fair value measurement. IFRS 13 is effective for annual periods beginning on or after 1 January 2013, with earlier application permitted, and it is applied prospectively as of the beginning of the annual period in which it is initially applied. IFRS 13 is dealt with in chapter 5. In this chapter, guidance on fair value measurements applies the requirements of IAS 39. Entities that have adopted IFRS 13 should refer to chapter 5 for the relevant fair value measurement guidance.

Initial measurement

Initial fair value

6.7.6 When a financial asset or financial liability is recognised initially, IAS 39 requires the entity to measure it at its 'fair value' plus, in certain situations, transaction costs (see para 6.7.13 below). [IAS 39 para 43]. The standard defines fair value as the amount for which an asset could be exchanged, or a liability settled, between knowledgeable willing parties in an arm's length transaction. [IAS 39 para 9]. The concept of fair value and requirements for determining the fair value of financial instruments are discussed in detail from paragraph 6.7.94 below.

6.7.7 Given that fair value is the price that arm's length market participants would pay or receive in a routine transaction under the market conditions at the date at which the asset or liability is to be measured for accounting purposes (the measurement date), it follows that a financial instrument's initial fair value will normally be the transaction price, that is, the fair value of the consideration given or received. [IAS 39 para AG 64].

6.7.8 In some circumstances the consideration given or received (say the face amount) may not necessarily be the financial instrument's fair value. For example, the fair value of a long-term note receivable that carries no interest is not equal to its face amount and, therefore, part of the consideration received is something other than its fair value. As the note receivable would have to be recorded initially at its fair value, its fair value has to be estimated. The instrument's fair value may be evidenced by comparison with other observable current market transactions in the same instrument (that is, without modification or repackaging) or based on a valuation technique whose variables include only data from observable markets. [IAS 39 para AG 76]. For a long-term loan or receivable with no stated interest, the fair value is normally arrived at by using a discounted cash flow valuation method. Under this method, the fair value can be estimated as the present value of all future cash receipts discounted using the prevailing market rate of interest for a similar instrument (similar as to currency, term, type of interest rate and other factors) with a similar credit rating issued at the same time. Any additional amount lent is an expense or a reduction of income, unless it qualifies for recognition as some other type of asset. [IAS 39 para AG 64].

6.7.9 A pragmatic measure, the standard permits short-term receivables and payables to be measured at the original invoice amount if the effect of discounting is immaterial. [IAS 39 para AG 79]. The IFRS IC also considered the accounting for extended payment terms, such as six-month's interest-free credit, and concluded that the accounting treatment under IAS 39 was clear. In such circumstances, the effect of the time value of money should be reflected when this is material. [IFRIC Update July 2004].

> **Example 1 – Interest free loan to a company**
>
> Entity A lends C1,000 to entity B for 5 years and classifies the asset under loans and receivables. The loan carries no interest. Instead, entity A expects other future economic benefits, such as an implicit right to receive goods or services at favourable prices.
>
> On initial recognition, the market rate of interest for a similar 5 year loan with payment of interest at maturity is 10% per year. The loan's initial fair value is the present value of the future payment of C1,000 discounted using the market rate of interest for a similar loan of 10% for 5 years, that is, C621.
>
> In this example, the consideration given of C1,000 is for two things – the fair value of the loan of C621 and entity A's right to obtain other future economic benefits that have a fair value of C379 (the difference between the total consideration given of C1,000 and the consideration given for the loan of C621).
>
> Entity A recognises the loan at its initial fair value of C621 that will accrete to C1,000 over the term of the loan using the effective interest method (see further para 6.7.67 below).

The difference of C379 is not a financial asset, since it is paid to obtain expected future economic benefits other than the right to receive payment on the loan asset. Entity A recognises that amount as an expense unless it qualifies for recognition as an asset under, say, IAS 38, or as part of the cost of investment in subsidiary, if entity B is a subsidiary of entity A.

Example 2 – Interest free loan to an employee

An entity grants an interest free loan of C1,000 to an employee for a period of two years. The market rate of interest to this individual for a two year loan with payment of interest at maturity is 10%.

The consideration given to the employee consists of two assets:

- The fair value of the loan, that is $C1,000/(1.10)^2 = C826$.

- The difference of C174 that is accounted for as employee compensation in accordance with IAS 19.

Example 3 – Interest free loan received from a government agency

An entity is located in an enterprise zone and receives an interest free loan of C500,000 from a government agency. The loan carries no interest and is repayable at the end of year three.

Loans received from a government that have a below-market rate of interest should be recognised and measured in accordance with IAS 39. The benefit of the below-market rate of interest should be measured as the difference between the initial carrying value of the loan determined in accordance with IAS 39 and the proceeds received. [IAS 20 para 10A].

So if the fair value is estimated at C450,000 under IAS 39, the loan would be recorded initially at its fair value of C450,000. The difference between the consideration received and the fair value of the loan, that is, C50,000, would fall to be accounted for as a government grant in accordance with IAS 20.

However, the IASB noted that applying IAS 39 to loans retrospectively may require entities to measure the fair value of loans at a past date. So the IASB decided that the amendment should be applied prospectively to government loans received in periods beginning on or after 1 January 2009.

6.7.10   In some circumstances, instead of originating an interest free loan, an entity may originate a loan that bears an off-market interest rate (for example, a loan that carries a higher or lower rate than the prevailing current market rate for a similar loan) and pays or receives an initial fee as compensation. In that situation, the entity still recognises the loan at its initial fair value, that is, net of the fee paid or received as illustrated below. The fee paid or received is amortised to profit or loss using the effective interest method. [IAS 39 para AG 65]. A similar requirement is included in IAS 18, where fees that are an integral part of a financial instrument's effective interest rate are generally treated as an adjustment to the effective interest rate. [IAS 18 para IE 14(a)].

Example – Off-market loan with origination fee

An entity originates a loan for C1,000 that is repayable in 5 year's time. The loan carries interest at 6%, which is less than the market rate of 8% for a similar loan. The entity receives C80 as compensation for originating a below market loan.

The entity should recognise the loan at its initial fair value of C920 (net present value of C60 of interest for 5 years and principal repayment of C1,000 discounted at 8%). This is equal to the net cash received (loan of C1,000 less origination fee of C80). The net amount of the loan of C920 accretes to C1,000 over the 5 year term using an effective interest of 8%.

In this example, the upfront fee received of C80 exactly compensates the entity for interest short fall of C20 for each of the next 5 years discounted at the market rate of 8%. Hence, no gain or loss arises on initial recognition.

6.7.11 A further exception to the general rule that the transaction price is not necessarily the financial instrument's initial fair value is of particular relevance to banking and insurance entities. Such entities often originate structured transactions and use models to estimate their fair values. Such models may show a 'day 1' gain (that is, the fair value exceeds the transaction price). However, IFRS permits departure from the transaction price only if fair value is evidenced by observable current market transactions in the same instrument or a valuation technique whose variables include only data from observable markets. As a result, an immediate 'day 1' gain is rarely recognised on initial recognition. This issue is considered further in paragraph 6.7.148 below.

Transaction costs

6.7.12 Transaction costs are incremental costs that are directly attributable to the acquisition or issue or disposal of a financial asset or financial liability. An incremental cost is one that would not have been incurred if the entity had not acquired, issued or disposed of the financial instrument. [IAS 39 para 9].

6.7.13 Transaction costs include fees and commissions paid to agents (including employees acting as selling agents), advisers, brokers and dealers, levies by regulatory agencies and securities exchanges and transfer taxes and duties. Transaction costs do not include debt premiums or discounts, financing costs or internal administrative or holding costs. [IAS 39 para AG 13].

6.7.14 The standard defines transaction costs to include internal costs, provided they are incremental and directly attributable to the acquisition, issue or disposal of a financial asset or financial liability. [IAS 39 para BC222(d)]. However, in practice, other than payments made to employees acting as selling agents (common in insurance contracts that fall to be accounted for under IAS 39 as financial instruments), salary costs of employees that would be incurred irrespective of whether the loan was granted are not incremental, nor are allocated indirect administrative costs or overheads.

6.7.15 The appendix to IAS 18 sets out a number of examples of financial services fees. IAS 18 distinguishes such fees between those that are an integral part of generating an involvement with the resulting financial instrument, those that are earned as services are provided and those that are earned on the execution of a significant act. Such fees may fall into two categories: fees associated with origination of a loan (loan origination fees) and fees associated with commitment to lend (commitment fees).

6.7.16 Loan origination fees may consist of:

- Fees that are charged to the borrower as 'pre-paid' interest or to reduce the loan's nominal interest rate (explicit yield adjustments).

- Fees to compensate the lender for origination activities such as evaluating the borrower's financial condition, evaluating and recording guarantees, collateral and other security arrangements, negotiating the instrument's terms, preparing and processing documents and closing the transaction.

- Other fees that relate directly to the loan origination process (for example, fees that are paid to the lender as compensation for granting a complex loan or agreeing to lend quickly).

6.7.17 Commitment fees are fees that are charged by the lender for entering into an agreement to make or acquire a loan. Sometimes they are referred to as facility fees for making a loan facility available to a borrower. The accounting treatment depends on whether or not it is probable that the entity will enter into a specific lending arrangement and whether the loan commitment is within IAS 39's scope. If it is probable that the entity will enter into the lending agreement and the loan commitment is not within IAS 39's scope, the commitment fee received is regarded as compensation for an ongoing involvement with the acquisition of a financial instrument and, together with the transaction costs (as defined in IAS 39), is deferred and recognised as an adjustment to the effective interest rate. If the commitment expires without the entity making the loan, the fee is recognised as revenue on expiry. [IAS 18 App para 14(a)(ii)]. On the other hand, if it is unlikely that a specific lending arrangement will be entered into and the loan commitment is outside IAS 39's scope, the commitment fee is recognised as revenue on a time proportion basis over the commitment period. Loan commitments that are within IAS 39's scope are accounted for as derivatives and measured at fair value. [IAS 18 App para 14(b)(ii); IAS 39 para 9].

6.7.18 The borrower's accounting mirrors that of the lender as discussed above. Therefore, to the extent there is evidence that it is probable that some or all of the facility will be drawn down, the facility fee is accounted for as a transaction cost under IAS 39. Where this is the case, the facility fee is deferred and treated as a transaction cost when draw-down occurs; it is not amortised prior to the draw-down. For example, draw-down might be probable if there is a specific project for which there is an agreed business plan. If a facility is for C20 million and it is probable that only C5 million of the facility will be drawn down, a quarter of the facility fee represents a transaction cost of the C5 million loan and is deferred until draw-down occurs. To the extent there is no evidence that it is probable that some or all of the facility will be drawn down, the facility fee represents a payment for liquidity services – that is, to secure the availability of finance on pre-arranged terms over the facility period. As such, to the extent draw down is not probable, the facility fee is capitalised as a prepayment for services and amortised over the period of the facility to which it relates. The availability of finance on pre-arranged terms provides benefit to an entity in a similar way to an insurance policy. If finance is needed in the future due to unforeseen events, the facility in place ensures that an entity can obtain this finance on known terms regardless of the economic environment in the future.

6.7.19 Direct loan origination costs relate to costs incurred by the entity for undertaking activities set out in the second bullet point of paragraph 6.7.16 above. Internal costs directly related to those activities should include only that portion of employee cost directly related to time spent performing those activities (see para 6.7.16 above).

6.7.20 It is apparent from the nature of the above fees that they are an integral part of generating an involvement with the resulting financial instrument and together with the related direct origination costs, are accounted for in a financial instrument's initial measurement as follows:

- When a financial asset or financial liability is recognised initially and not designated as at fair value through profit or loss, transaction costs (net of fees received) that are directly attributable to the acquisition or issue are added to the initial fair value. For financial assets, such costs are added to the amount originally recognised. For financial liabilities, such costs are deducted from the amount originally recognised. This applies to financial instruments carried at amortised cost and available-for-sale financial assets. [IAS 39 para 43].

- For financial instruments that are measured at fair value through profit or loss, transaction costs (net of any fees received or paid) are not added to or deducted from the initial fair value, but are immediately recognised in profit or loss on initial recognition.

- Transaction costs expected to be incurred on a financial instrument's transfer or disposal are not included in the financial instrument's measurement.

[IAS 39 para IG E1.1].

Example 1 – Initial measurement – transaction cost

An entity acquires an equity available-for-sale financial asset at its fair value of C100. Purchase commission of C2 is also payable. At the end of the entity's financial year, the asset's quoted market price is C105. If the asset were to be sold, a commission of C4 would be payable.

As the asset is not classified initially at fair value through profit or loss, the entity recognises the financial asset at its fair value that includes the purchase commission, that is, at C102. At the end of the entity's financial year, the asset is recorded at C105 without regard to the commission of C4 payable on sale. The change in fair value of C3 recognised in other comprehensive income includes the purchase commission of C2 payable at the acquisition date.

Example 2 – Allocation of transaction costs to a convertible instrument that contains a conversion option as an embedded derivative

An entity, with functional currency of C, issues a 5 year, euro-denominated convertible bond for C100. Transaction costs of C2 were incurred by the issuer. The host liability is to be accounted for at amortised cost. The fair value of the embedded derivative on initial recognition was C20.

Transaction costs relating to issuance of a convertible instrument for which the conversion feature is classified as an embedded derivative should be allocated to the host liability and the embedded conversion option in either of the following ways (that is, there is an accounting policy choice):

- Approach 1 – The convertible bond represents a liability in its entirety, as the conversion feature fails the fixed-for-fixed requirement for equity classification (see chapter 6.5). On initial recognition, the financial liability (that is, the entire instrument) should be recognised at fair value less transactions costs that are directly attributable to its issuance since the instrument is not at fair value through profit or loss. As the embedded derivative's fair value at initial recognition is C20, the host liability is initially recognised at C78 (C100 – C20 – C2) and there is no impact on profit or loss.

- Approach 2 – Under this approach, transaction costs are allocated to each component in proportion to the allocation of proceeds. Therefore, costs allocated to the embedded derivative are charged to profit or loss on initial recognition, and those allocated to the host contract are deducted from its initial carrying amount. Accordingly, the embedded derivative is recognised initially at C20, with (20/100) of the transaction costs (that is, C0.4) being recognised in profit or loss. The host liability is recognised initially at C78.4 (C100 – C20 – (80/100) × C2).

6.7.21 Entities may also receive fees for the provision of a service, such as loan servicing fee, or for the execution of a significant act such as placement fees for arranging a loan between two third parties and loan syndication fees. These fees are not integral to lending or borrowing and, therefore, cannot form part of the financial instrument's measurement.

6.7.22 The treatment of transaction costs on the subsequent measurement of available-for-sale financial assets is considered in paragraph 6.7.33 below and those carried at amortised cost are considered in paragraph 6.7.75 below.

Settlement date accounting for regular way transactions

6.7.23   When an entity uses settlement date accounting for an asset that is subsequently measured at cost or amortised cost, the asset is recognised initially at settlement date, but measured at the fair value on trade date. [IAS 39 para 44]. This is an exception to the general rule in paragraph 6.7.6 above that a financial asset should be recognised at its fair value on initial recognition. The accounting for regular way trades is considered in chapter 6.6.

Subsequent measurement of financial assets

General

6.7.24   As set out in chapter 6.4, financial assets are classified in one of four categories. Following their initial recognition, the classification determines how the financial asset is subsequently measured, including any profit or loss recognition. The following table summarises the requirements that are considered in detail in the remainder of this chapter.

Classification	Financial asset	Measurement basis	Changes in carrying amount	Impairment test (if objective evidence)
At fair value through profit or loss	Debt	Fair value	Profit or loss	No [5]
	Equity	Fair value	Profit or loss	No [5]
	Derivatives not designated as effective hedging instruments	Fair value	Profit or loss	–
Loans and receivables	Debt	Amortised cost	Profit or loss [3]	Yes
Held-to-maturity investments	Debt	Amortised cost	Profit or loss [3]	Yes
Available-for-sale financial assets	Debt	Fair value	OCI [2] Profit or loss [3]	Yes
	Equity	Fair value	OCI [2] Profit or loss [4]	Yes
	Equity [1]	Cost (fair value not reliably measurable)	Profit or loss [4]	Yes

1 Equity instruments that do not have any quoted market price in an active market and whose fair value cannot be reliably measured and derivative assets that are linked to and must be settled by delivery of such unquoted equity instruments.

2 Change in fair value including related foreign exchange differences other than those noted in note 3 or 4 below where relevant.

3 Interest calculated using the effective interest method, foreign exchange differences resulting from changes in amortised cost, impairment and reversal of impairment, where relevant, are taken to profit or loss.

4 Dividends and impairment are taken to profit or loss. Foreign exchange difference on (non-monetary) equity AFS investments taken to equity and recycled to profit or loss on disposal or impairment.

5 Any impairment will be taken though profit or loss as part of the change in fair value and so separate impairment testing is not necessary.

6.7.25 Financial assets that are designated as hedged items are subject to measurement under the hedge accounting requirements. These requirements apply in addition to, and may modify, the general accounting requirements that are discussed below. Hedge accounting is covered in chapter 6.8.

Financial assets at fair value through profit or loss

6.7.26 After initial recognition, financial assets falling within this category (including assets held-for-trading and derivative assets not designated as effective hedging instruments and assets designated on initial recognition at fair value through profit or loss) are measured at fair value, without the deduction of transaction costs that the entity may incur on sale or other disposal. [IAS 39 para 46]. Such transaction costs are future costs that relate to the sale or the disposal and have no relevance to determining fair value. Therefore, they are properly included in the period in which the sale or the disposal takes place.

6.7.27 The standard's requirements for determining the fair value of instruments that fall to be measured on this basis are considered from paragraph 6.7.94 below. Investments in equity instruments that do not have a quoted market price in an active market and whose fair value cannot be reliably measured and derivatives that are linked to and must be settled by delivery of such unquoted equity instruments, are measured at cost (see further para 6.7.140 below).[IAS 39 para 46(c)].

6.7.28 All gains and losses arising from changes in fair value of financial assets falling within this category are recognised, not surprisingly, in profit or loss. [IAS 39 para 55(a)]. This means that assets falling within this category are not subject to review for impairment as losses due to fall in value (including impairment) would automatically be reflected in profit or loss.

Loans and receivables

6.7.29 Loans and receivables, as defined in chapter 6.4, are measured at amortised cost using the effective interest method. [IAS 39 para 46(a)]. They are measured on this basis whether they are intended to be held-to-maturity or not. [IAS 39 para AG 68]. The amortised cost method of accounting is discussed from paragraph 6.7.67 below.

6.7.30 Gains and losses are recognised in profit or loss when loans and receivables are derecognised or impaired and throughout the amortisation process. Special rules apply for gain or loss recognition when loans and receivables are designated as hedged items. [IAS 39 para 56].

Held-to-maturity investments

6.7.31 Held-to-maturity investments are also measured at amortised cost using the effective interest method. Gains and losses are accounted for in the same way as loans and receivables. [IAS 39 para 46(b)].

Available-for-sale assets

6.7.32 Available-for-sale financial assets are measured at fair value. As with assets designated as at fair value through profit or loss, transaction costs that will be incurred on the sale or disposal of such assets are not deducted from the fair value. However, there is an exemption from measurement at fair value of an available-for-sale asset if its fair value cannot be measured reliably (see para 6.7.27 above). This exemption only applies to unquoted equity instruments and derivative contracts based on those instruments. These instruments are measured at cost. [IAS 39 para 46(c)].

6.7.33 As explained in paragraph 6.7.20 above, transaction costs that are directly attributable to the acquisition of an available-for-sale financial asset are added to the initial fair value. For available-for-sale financial assets, transaction costs are recognised in other comprehensive income as part of a change in fair value at the subsequent measurement. If an available-for-sale financial asset has fixed or determinable payments and does not have an indefinite life, the transaction costs are amortised to profit or loss using the effective interest method (see para 6.7.68 below). If an available-for-sale financial asset does not have fixed or determinable payments and has an indefinite life, the transaction costs are recognised in profit or loss when the asset is derecognised or becomes impaired and the cumulative gain or loss, including transaction costs, deferred in other comprehensive income is reclassified to profit or loss. [IAS 39 para AG 67].

6.7.34 All gains and losses arising from changes in fair value of available-for-sale financial assets are recognised directly in other comprehensive income except as follows:

- Interest calculated using the effective interest method is recognised in profit or loss (see further para 6.7.67 below). Dividends on an available-for-sale equity instruments are recognised in profit or loss when the entity's right to receive payment is established. [IAS 18 para 30(c)].

- Foreign exchange gains and losses on monetary financial assets are recognised in profit or loss (see further para 6.7.212 below).

- Impairment losses are recognised in profit or loss (see further para 6.7.201 below). Reversals of impairment of a debt instrument are also recognised in profit or loss, but reversals of impairment on equity instruments are not (see further para 6.7.204 below).

[IAS 39 para 55(b)].

6.7.35 When an available-for-sale financial asset is derecognised as a result of sale or is impaired, the cumulative gain or loss previously recognised in other comprehensive income is reclassified to profit or loss. [IAS 39 paras 55(b), 67]. For example, assume that an entity acquires an equity security for C500 that has a fair value at the end of the year of C600. A gain of C100 is recognised in other comprehensive income. In the following year, the entity sells the security for C550. In the year of sale, a profit of C50, being the difference between proceeds of C550 and original cost of C500 is recognised. This represents the difference between proceeds of C550 and previous carrying value of C600 (C50 loss) and the recycling to profit or loss of C100 gain previously recognised in other comprehensive income.

6.7.36 In the above example, a single security is used to illustrate the accounting for recycling. In practice, the entity may have acquired the same security in tranches at different dates and at different prices over a period of time. IAS 39 does not specify whether such fungible assets (or indeed any other fungible financial assets) should be considered individually or in aggregate, and, if in aggregate, which measurement basis (weighted average, first in first out (FIFO), specific identification) is appropriate for calculating the gain or loss on a partial disposal. This is in contrast to IAS 2, which specifies the use of weighted average or FIFO in most circumstances. In practice, entities may opt, as an accounting policy choice, for any one of the methods. The method used should be applied consistently for both impairment and disposal and disclosed.

6.7.37 It is conceivable that within a group, portfolios have a different nature – for example, an available-for-sale portfolio held for liquidity purposes *versus* an available-for-sale portfolio held for long-term strategic investment purposes. In this instance, it may be possible to justify using different cost formulae within an entity for the same securities. However, whatever cost formula is used, it should be used for both impairment and measurement of gains and losses on disposal.

6.7.38 The subsequent measurement of available-for-sale financial assets with fixed and determinable payments is complicated by the fact that fair value changes are recognised in other comprehensive income, but interest income is recognised in each period in profit or loss using the effective interest method. In order to ensure that the change in fair value is correctly calculated at the measurement date, it would be necessary to compare the instrument's clean price (the fair value of the instrument less accrued interest) with its amortised cost, also excluding accrued interest, at that date. Therefore, although the instrument is measured at fair value, the amortised cost must still be calculated using the effective interest method in order to determine interest income.

Example – Debt security classified as available-for-sale investment

On 1 January 20X5, an entity purchases 10% C10 million 5 year bonds with interest payable on 1 July and 1 January each year. The bond's purchase price is C10,811,100. The premium of C811,100 is due to market yield for similar bonds being 8%. Assuming there are no transaction costs, the effective interest rate is 8% (the effective interest method is discussed further in para 6.7.68 below).

The entity classifies the bond as available-for-sale. The entity prepares its financial statements at 31 March. On 31 March 20X5, the yield on bonds with similar maturity and credit risk is 7.75%. At that date, the fair value of this bond calculated by discounting 10 semi-annual cash flows of C500,000 and principal payment of C10 million at maturity at the market rate of 7.75% amounted to C11,127,710.

Since the bond is classified as available-for-sale, the bond will be measured at fair value with changes in fair value recognised in other comprehensive income.

At 1 January 20X5, the fair value of the bond is the consideration paid of C10,811,100 and the entry to record this is as follows:

	Dr C	Cr C
At 1 January 20X5		
Available-for-sale investment	10,811,100	
Cash		10,811,100

On 31 March 20X5, the entity will record interest income for the 3 months at the effective interest rate of 8%, that is, C10,811,100 × 8% × 3/12 = C216,222. Since the next coupon of C500,000 is due on 1 July 20X5, the entity will record a half-year interest accrual of C250,000. The difference of C33,778 between the interest income accrued and that recognised in the profit or loss represents the amortisation of the premium. The entry to record the interest income on 31 March 20X6 is as follows:

	Dr C	Cr C
At 31 March 20X5		
Available-for-sale investment (accrued interest)	250,000	
Available-for-sale investment (premium)		33,778
Profit or loss – interest income		216,222

The bond's amortised cost at 31 March 20X5 is, therefore, C10,777,322 (10,811,100 – 33,778)

The fair value of the bond at 31 March 20X5 is C11,127,710. This includes the accrued interest of C250,000. To calculate the clean price of the bond, the accrued income is deducted from the fair value. Therefore, the clean price of the bond is C10,877,710.

A comparison of the clean price of the bond and its amortised cost at 31 March 20X5 results in a gain as follows:

	C
Fair value of bond at 31 March 20X5 – clean price	10,877,710
Amortised cost of bond at 31 March 20X5	10,777,322
Change in value – Unrealised gain	100,388

The entry to record the gain at 31 March 20X5 is as follows:

	Dr	Cr
	C	C
At 31 March 20X5		
Available-for-sale investments	100,388	
Other comprehensive income		100,388

The movement in available-for-sale asset is shown below:

	C
At 1 Jan 20X5 – Fair value (inclusive of premium)	10,811,100
Accrued income (reflected in fair value)	250,000
Amortisation of premium	(33,778)
Fair value adjustment – gain	100,388
At 31 Mar 20X5 – Fair value	11,127,710

	C
Recognised in profit or loss – income	216,222
Recognised in other comprehensive income – gain	100,388
Total change in fair value	316,610

6.7.39 As stated in paragraph 6.7.34 above, dividends on an available-for-sale equity instrument are recognised in profit or loss when the entity's right to receive payment is established. The right to receive payment is established when the equity instrument's issuer declares a dividend or in the case of quoted equity securities, at the ex-dividend date. When a share goes ex-dividend shortly before the dividend payment is actually due, the price will drop (other things being equal) by the amount of the dividend. Therefore, depending upon the ex-dividend date (when the dividend income is recognised) and the payment date (when the receivable is settled), the realisation of part of the fair value through dividend payment will affect both profit or loss and equity as illustrated below.

Example – Dividend on available-for-sale investments

An entity acquires 1,000 quoted equity shares in another entity for C20,000. The shares are classified as available-for-sale. Just prior to the entity's year end of 31 December 20X5, the security goes ex-dividend following declaration of a dividend of C1.50 per share. At 31 December 20X5, the quoted ex-dividend price of the shares amounts to C21 per share. The entity receives payment of the dividend on 6 January 20X6.

At 31 December 20X5, the entity will recognise the dividend income in profit or loss and the change in the fair value of the shares in other comprehensive income as noted below:

	Dr C	Cr C
Dividend receivable	1,500	
Profit or loss – dividend income – 1,000 @ 1.50		1,500
Available-for-sale financial asset	1,000	
Other comprehensive income – 1,000 @ (21-20)		1,000

The shares' quoted price prior to the dividend adjustment would have been C22.50 giving a total fair value change of C2,500. However, as part of this change (C1,500) is realised as a result of the dividend income recognised in profit or loss; there is an equal and offsetting change in other comprehensive income.

Designation as hedged items

6.7.40 Financial assets that are designated as hedged items are subject to measurement under IAS 39's hedging accounting requirements. [IAS 39 para 46]. These special accounting rules generally override the normal accounting rules for financial assets. Hedge accounting is covered in chapter 6.8.

Reclassifications between categories

6.7.41 The amendment to IAS 39 issued in October 2008 allows reclassification of certain financial assets after initial recognition out of a category measured at fair value (that is, held-for-trading or available-for-sale) and into another category under limited circumstances (see chapter 6.4 and IAS 39 para 50 A-E). The tainting rules applicable to the held-to-maturity category remain unchanged.

6.7.42 When a financial asset is reclassified, the fair value at the date of reclassification becomes its new cost or amortised cost. [IAS 39 para 50 C and F]. Any gains or losses already recognised in profit or loss are not reversed. The new 'cost' is also used as the basis for assessing impairment in the future.

6.7.43 On reclassification, the effective interest rate is recalculated using the fair value at the date of reclassification. This new effective interest rate will be used to calculate interest income in future periods and considered as the original effective interest rate when measuring impairment.

6.7.44 For a financial asset denominated in a foreign currency that is reclassified to loans and receivables, the 'amortised cost' of the financial asset at the date of reclassification is calculated in the foreign currency and then translated at the spot rate to the functional currency at the date of reclassification. [IAS 39 para IG E3.4].

6.7.45 When an available-for-sale financial asset with fixed maturity is reclassified as held-to-maturity investment or loans and receivables, the fair value of the financial asset on that date becomes its new amortised cost. Any previous gain or loss on that asset that has been recognised directly in other comprehensive income is amortised to profit and loss over the investment's remaining life using the effective interest method. Any difference between the new amortised cost and the amount payable on maturity is also amortised in a similar manner, akin to the amortisation of a premium or a discount. If the financial asset is subsequently impaired, any gain or loss that has been recognised directly in other comprehensive income is recognised in profit or loss. [IAS 39 para 54(a)]. Essentially, interest income should not change as a result of reclassification and should continue to be based on the original amortisation schedule (that is, prior to reclassification). This is because the combination of the amortisation of the difference between the new amortised cost on the reclassified financial asset and the amount payable on maturity and the gain or loss to be amortised from other comprehensive income will result in the same net effective interest rate as originally determined prior to reclassification.

> **Example – Available-for-sale debt security reclassified to loans and receivables**
>
> On 1 January 20X9, an entity reclassifies a C9m bond from available-for-sale to loans and receivables. On the date of the reclassification, the bond's amortised cost is C9,198,571 and the original effective interest rate is 8.75%. The bond's fair value is C9,488,165, which becomes its new amortised cost. The excess of the new carrying amount over the amount receivable at maturity on 31 December 2X10 (that is C488,165) is amortised to profit or loss over the remaining term to give a new effective rate of 7% including interest coupons receivable, as shown below.
>
> In addition, the cumulative gain of C289,594 in other comprehensive income as at 31 December 20X8 (that is, the difference between the fair value of C9,488,165 and the amortised cost of C9,198,571) is also amortised to profit or loss during the remaining two years to maturity. The effect in profit or loss is the same as if the bond was classified as loans and receivables, as illustrated below:

	Cash received	Interest income @ 7%	New amortised co
	C	C	C
1 Jan 20X9			9,488,165
31 Dec 20X9	900,000	664,172	9,252,337
31 Dec 2 X10	9,900,000	647,663	–
		1,311,835	
Amortisation of gain in other comprehensive income in 20X9 and 2X10		289,594	
Total amount recognised in profit or loss		1,601,429	

If the C9m bonds had not been reclassified as available-for-sale, the total amount recognised in profit or loss would have been as follows:

	Cash received	Interest income @ 8.75%	Amortised cost
	C	C	C
31 Dec 20X8			9,198,571
31 Dec 20X9	900,000	804,876	9,103,447
31 Dec 20X10	9,900,000	796,553	
Total income from date of reclassification to maturity		1,601,429	

6.7.46 When a held-to-maturity investment is reclassified as available-for-sale, it should be remeasured at fair value at the date of reclassification. The difference between its previous carrying amount and fair value should be recognised in other comprehensive income. [IAS 39 paras 51, 52].

Example – Held-to-maturity investment reclassified as available-for-sale financial asset

On 1 January 20X0, an entity purchases 10% C10m 10 year bonds with interest payable annually on 31 December each year. The bond's purchase price is C10,811,100. This results in a bond premium of C811,100 and an effective interest rate of 8.75%. The bonds were classified by the entity as held-to-maturity.

On 31 December 20X5, when the bonds amortised cost and fair value amounted to C10,407,192 and C10,749,395 respectively, the entity sells C1m bonds and realises a gain as shown below:

	C
Fair value of C1m bond (10% of C10,749,395)	1,074,940
Carrying value of C1m bond (10% of C10,407,192)	1,040,719
Profit on disposal recognised in profit or loss	34,221

Since the entity has sold more than an insignificant amount of its held-to-maturity investments, the portfolio is tainted. As a result, the entity has to reclassify the remaining C9m bonds as available-for-sale assets. The difference between the carrying value of C9m bonds and their fair value is recognised in other comprehensive income as shown below:

	C
Fair value of C9m bond (90% of C10,749,395)	9,674,455
Carrying value of C9m bonds (90% of C10,407,192)	9,366,473
Gain on reclassification recognised in other comprehensive income	307,982

Even though the remaining investment is classified as available-for-sale, the entity will continue to recognise the interest income and the amortisation of the premium using the effective interest method in profit or loss and fair value changes in other comprehensive income, as illustrated in the example in paragraph 6.7.45. After the tainting period is over, the entity may reinstate the bonds again to held-to-maturity. This will happen after 31 December 20X7 (two full financial years following the partial disposal).

Settlement date accounting for regular way transactions

6.7.47 As stated in paragraph 6.7.23 above, when an entity uses settlement date accounting for an asset that is subsequently measured at cost or amortised cost, the asset is recognised initially at its fair value at trade date. Any subsequent change in fair value between trade date and settlement date is not recognised (other than impairment losses). For assets that are subsequently measured at fair value, any change in fair value between trade date and settlement date is recognised:

- In profit or loss for assets classified as at FVTPL.

- In other comprehensive income for assets classified as available-for-sale.

6.7.48 When assets measured at fair value are sold on a regular way basis, the change in fair value between trade date (the date the entity enters into the sales contract) and settlement date (the date proceeds are received) is not recorded because the seller's right to changes in fair value ceases on the trade date (see further chapter 6).

Negative fair values

6.7.49 The standard clarifies that if a financial instrument that was previously recognised as a financial asset is measured at fair value and its fair value falls below zero, it becomes a financial liability that should be measured as considered below. [IAS 39 para AG 66].

Subsequent measurement of financial liabilities

6.7.50 After initial recognition, an entity should measure financial liabilities, other than those described in paragraphs 6.7.52 to 6.7.66 below, at amortised cost using the effective interest method as discussed from paragraph 6.7.67 below. [IAS 39 para 47].

6.7.51 Where a financial liability is carried at amortised cost, a gain or loss is recognised in profit or loss when the financial liability is derecognised or through the amortisation process. [IAS 39 para 56].

Financial liabilities at fair value through profit or loss

6.7.52 After initial recognition, financial liabilities falling within this category (including liabilities held-for-trading and derivative liabilities not designated as hedging instruments) are measured at fair value. However, a derivative liability that is linked to and must be settled by delivery of an unquoted equity instrument whose fair value cannot be reliably measured should be measured at cost. [IAS 39 para 47(a)].

6.7.53 A change in a financial liability's fair value in this category that is not part of a hedging relationship should be recognised in the profit or loss for the period. [IAS 39 para 55]. The standard's requirements for determining the fair value of instruments that fall to be measured on this basis are considered from paragraph 6.7.94 below.

Financial liabilities arising on transfers of financial assets

6.7.54 Certain financial liabilities may arise when a transfer of a financial asset does not qualify for derecognition, or is accounted for using the continuing involvement approach. For example, a sale of an asset that is accompanied by the seller giving a guarantee of the asset's future worth may, depending on the substance, give rise to the asset's derecognition and recognition of a liability in respect of the guarantee or it may result in the asset not being derecognised and the proceeds being shown as a liability. Special rules apply for the measurement of the transferred asset and the associated liability so that these are measured on a basis that reflects the rights and obligations that the entity has retained. [IAS 39 paras 29, 31, 47(b)]. See further chapter 6.6.

Financial guarantee contracts

6.7.55 Financial guarantee contracts are defined in chapter 6.1. Financial guarantee contracts that are accounted for as financial liabilities under IAS 39 by the issuer are initially recognised at fair value. If the financial guarantee contract was issued to an unrelated party in a stand-alone arm's length transaction, its fair value at inception would likely be to equal the premium received, unless there was evidence to the contrary. [IAS 39 para AG4(a)].

6.7.56 In some circumstances, an issuer expects to receive recurring future premiums from an issued financial guarantee contract (for example, it issues a five year guarantee with annual premiums due at the start of each year). In that situation, an issue arises as to whether the issuer should recognise a receivable for the discounted value of the expected future premiums or should it recognise only the initial cash received (if any). As stated above, IAS 39 requires the financial guarantee contract to be initially recorded at fair value; that is likely to equal the premium received. By analogy with derivative contracts the fair value will take into account any future cash flows on the instrument including those relating to premiums receivable.

6.7.57 IAS 39 does not explicitly prohibit the recognition of a separate receivable for future premiums not yet due. This is evidenced by the basis for conclusions, paragraph BC 23D, which states that the IAS 39 requirement for initial recognition at fair value is consistent with US GAAP as represented by FIN 45 (FIN 45 requires recognition of a liability for the guarantee and a separate receivable for future premiums). Accordingly, entities are permitted to recognise a separate receivable. The entity should select a presentation policy and apply it consistently to all issued financial guarantee contracts.

6.7.58 Subsequent to initial recognition, an issuer accounts for financial guarantee contracts at the higher of:

■ the amount determined in accordance with IAS 37; and

■ the amount initially recognised (fair value) less, when appropriate, cumulative amortisation of the initial amount recognised in accordance with IAS 18.

[IAS 39 para 47(c)].

6.7.59 However, the above requirements do not apply:

■ if the financial guarantee contract was designated at fair value through profit or loss at inception. A contract designated at inception as at fair value through profit or loss is measured at fair value subsequently; or

■ if the financial guarantee contract was entered into or retained on transferring financial assets or financial liabilities to another party and prevented derecognition of the financial asset or resulted in continuing involvement (see chapter 6.6).

[IAS 39 para 47(a)(b), AG 4].

6.7.60 From the perspective of the holder the contract is outside IAS 39's scope. The holder's accounting treatment depends on whether the guarantee is purchased in the context of the origination of a debt instrument or is purchased to guarantee pre-existing debt instruments. In the first case the purchaser of the financial guarantee contract, who could be either the borrower or the lender, should amortise the cost of the guarantee using the effective interest rate method, unless the debt instrument is measured at fair value through profit and loss. In the second case the cost is recognised as a pre-payment asset and amortised over the shorter of the life of the guarantee and the expected life of the guaranteed debt instruments. The asset is tested for impairment under IAS 36. Lenders classify the amortisation and impairment charges as a reduction of interest income whilst borrowers treat it as an additional finance cost.

Intra-group financial guarantee contracts

6.7.61   As stated in chapter 6.1, intra-group financial guarantee contracts are not exempted from IAS 39's requirements and, on a stand-alone basis, will have to be measured in accordance with the standard. On a consolidation basis, the financial guarantee is not recognised as a separate contract, but is part of the group's liability to a third party (for example, a guarantee given by the parent to a subsidiary's bankers in the event the subsidiary fails to repay a loan to the bank when due). In the individual financial statements, the financial guarantee is recognised initially at fair value in accordance with IAS 39 (unless IFRS 4 applies).

6.7.62   Establishing such a fair value may be difficult if the financial guarantee contracts between related parties were not negotiated at arm's length and there are no comparable observable transactions with third parties. Given that intra-group guarantees are unlikely to be negotiated in a 'stand-alone arm's length transaction', fair value would have to be estimated. Paragraph 6.7.134 provides guidance on how to measure the fair value of intra-group financial guarantees.

6.7.63   As the fair value of an intra-group guarantee is unlikely to be equal to the fee charged, if any, the issuer would need to determine whether any difference should be treated as an expense or a capital contribution *via* an increase in investments in the subsidiary. This is an accounting policy choice. The method used should reflect the transaction's economic substance, be applied consistently to all similar transactions and be clearly disclosed in the financial statements. While each entity within a group can choose its own accounting policies, those policies must be aligned on consolidation.

6.7.64   Where a parent entity provides a guarantee to a bank that has advanced a loan to one of its subsidiaries, the subsidiary has obtained a benefit in that it would pay a lower rate of interest on the loan than it would have otherwise paid for an unguaranteed loan. The subsidiary could fair value the loan from the bank by reference to a normal market rate of interest it would pay on a similar but unguaranteed loan and take the benefit of the interest differential to equity as a capital contribution from the parent. Alternatively, the subsidiary could view the unit of account as being the guaranteed loan and therefore the fair value would be expected to be the face value of the proceeds the subsidiary receives. IAS 39 does not address the accounting for financial guarantees by the beneficiary and there is no requirement in IAS 24 to fair value non-arms length related party transactions. Therefore, there is an accounting policy choice as to whether a capital contribution is recognised in equity by the subsidiary for the benefit of the lower rate of interest on the loan than it would have otherwise paid for an unguaranteed loan. In practice, there is diversity on which accounting policy is applied, however, the majority of subsidiaries do not take the capital contribution to equity approach and instead recognise the fair value of the guaranteed loan.

Commitments to provide off-market loans

6.7.65   An entity may enter into a commitment to provide a loan at a below-market rate. After initial recognition at fair value, such a commitment is subsequently measured in the same way as a financial guarantee contract stated above. [IAS 39 para 47(d)].

Designation as hedged items

6.7.66   Financial liabilities that are designated as hedged items are subject to measurement under IAS 39's hedging accounting requirements. [IAS 39 para 47]. These special accounting rules generally override the normal accounting rules for financial liabilities. Hedge accounting is covered in chapter 6.8.

Amortised cost and the effective interest method

General

6.7.67   The amortised cost of a financial asset or financial liability is defined as the amount at which the financial asset or financial liability is measured at initial recognition minus principal repayments, plus or minus the cumulative amortisation using the 'effective interest method' of any difference between that initial amount and the amount payable at maturity and minus any reduction (directly or through the use of an allowance account) for impairment or uncollectibility. [IAS 39 para 9].

6.7.68   The effective interest method is a method of calculating the amortised cost of a financial asset or a financial liability (or group of financial assets or financial liabilities) and of allocating the interest income or interest expense over the relevant period. The method's principal features are as follows:

■   The effective interest rate is the rate that exactly discounts estimated future cash payments or receipts through the financial instrument's *expected life* or, when appropriate, a shorter period, to the net carrying amount of the financial asset or financial liability (see para 6.7.76 below). The effective interest rate is sometimes termed the level yield to maturity or to the next repricing date and is the internal rate of return of the financial asset or liability for that period. The internal rate of return can be calculated using a financial calculator, or the IRR function in a spreadsheet.

■   When calculating the effective interest rate, an entity should estimate cash flows considering all the financial instrument's contractual terms (for example, pre-payment, call and similar options), but should not consider future credit losses.

- The calculation should include all fees and points paid or received between parties to the contract that are an integral part of the effective interest rate, transaction costs, and all other premiums or discounts.

[IAS 39 para 9].

6.7.69 The effective interest rate method is grounded in historical transaction values, because its determination is based on the initial carrying amount of the financial asset or liability. Therefore, once determined it is not recalculated to reflect fair value changes in financial assets, for example, interest bearing available-for-sale assets due to changes in market interest rates. The effective interest method produces a periodic interest income or expense equal to a constant percentage of the carrying value of the financial asset or liability as illustrated in the example given in paragraph 6.7.78.

Estimation of cash flows

6.7.70 As noted in paragraph 6.7.68 above, the effective interest method uses a set of *estimated* future cash flows through the expected life of the financial instrument using all the financial instrument's contractual terms, rather than *contractual* cash flows. However, the financial instrument's expected life cannot exceed its contracted life. This applies not only to individual financial instruments, but to groups of financial instruments as well to achieve consistency of application. As the cash flows are often outlined in a contract or linked in some other way to the financial asset or financial liability in question, there is a presumption that the future cash flows can be reliably estimated for most financial assets and financial liabilities, in particular for a group of similar financial assets and similar financial liabilities. [IAS 39 para 9]. For example, for a portfolio of pre-payable mortgage loans, financial institutions often estimate pre-payment patterns based on historical data and build the cash flows arising on early settlement (including any pre-payment penalty) into the effective interest rate calculation.

6.7.71 However, in some rare cases it might not be possible to estimate reliably the cash flows of a financial instrument (or group of financial instruments). In those rare cases, the entity should use the contractual cash flows over the full contractual term of the financial instrument (or group of financial instruments). [IAS 39 para 9].

6.7.72 The standard requires that in estimating the future cash flows all the instrument's contractual terms, including pre-payment, call and similar options should be considered. [IAS 39 para 9]. Such pre-payment, call and put options, which are often embedded in the debt instruments, are derivatives. Therefore, as explained, in chapter 6.3, the entity must first determine whether such options need to be separately accounted for as embedded derivatives. Separate accounting for the embedded derivative will not be necessary if the option's exercise price is approximately equal to the instrument's amortised cost on each exercise date, or the exercise price reimburses the lender for an amount up to the approximate present value of the lost interest for the remaining term of the host contract, because in that situation the embedded derivative is regarded as closely related to the debt host. [IAS 39 para AG 30(g)].

6.7.73   Where a pre-payment, call or put option falls to be separately accounted for, its impact on estimating the future cash flows for the purposes of determining the effective interest rate should be ignored. Although this is not explained in the standard, it is rather obvious as to do otherwise would result in double counting the effects of the embedded derivative in profit or loss – first through the option's fair value movement and, secondly, through its effect on the effective interest rate. In practice, this means that if the option is regarded as closely related and not separately accounted for, the entity, in determining the instrument's expected life, needs to assess whether the option is likely to be exercised in estimating the future cash flows at inception. Furthermore, this assessment should continue in subsequent periods until the debt instrument is settled, because the likelihood of the option being exercised will affect the timing and amount of the future cash flows and will have an immediate impact in profit or loss. On the other hand, if the option is accounted for as a separate derivative, such considerations are not necessary as the likelihood of the option being exercised will be reflected in its fair value. In that situation, the effective interest rate is based on the instrument's contractual term. See further paragraph 6.7.84 below.

6.7.74   The standard also makes it clear that expected or future credit losses (defaults) should not be included in estimates of cash flows, because this would be a departure from the incurred loss model for impairment recognition. However, in some cases, financial assets are acquired at a deep discount that reflects incurred losses (for example, purchase of impaired debt). As such losses are already reflected in the price, they should be included in the estimated cash flows when computing the effective interest rate. [IAS 39 para AG 5]. Accordingly, the effective interest rate of the acquired distressed loan would be the discount rate that equates the present value of the expected cash flows (this would be less than the contractual cash flows specified in the loan agreement because of incurred credit losses) with the purchase price of the loan. The alternative of not including such credit losses in the calculation of the effective interest rate means that the entity would recognise a higher interest income than that inherent in the price paid.

Transaction costs and fees

6.7.75   Transaction costs and fees are discussed from paragraph 6.7.12 above. To the extent that they are integral to generating an involvement with a financial instrument, such costs and fees are included in the financial instrument's initial measurement. For financial instruments that are carried at amortised cost, such as held-to-maturity investments, loans and receivables, and financial liabilities that are not at fair value through profit or loss, transaction costs and fees are, therefore, included in calculating amortised cost using the effective interest method. This means that, in effect, they are amortised through profit or loss over the instrument's life (see para 6.7.68 above).

Amortisation period

6.7.76 Consistent with the estimated cash flow approach outlined from paragraph 6.7.70 above, the standard requires fees, points paid or received, transaction costs and other premiums or discount that are integral to the effective interest rate to be amortised over the instrument's expected life or, when applicable, a shorter period. A shorter period is used when the variable (for example, interest rates) to which the fee, transaction costs, discount or premium relates is repriced to market rates before the instrument's expected maturity. In such a case, the appropriate amortisation period is the period to the next such repricing date. [IAS 39 AG6]. The application of this requirement in the context of a floating rate instrument is considered in paragraph 6.7.84 below.

6.7.77 There is a presumption that the expected life of a financial instrument (or group of similar financial instruments) can be estimated reliably. However, in those rare cases when it is not possible to estimate reliably the expected life, the entity should use the full contractual term of the financial instrument (or group of financial instruments) as the amortisation period. [IAS 39 para 9]. The expected life cannot exceed the contractual term.

Illustrations of the effective interest rate method of amortisation

Fixed interest instruments

6.7.78 The examples that follow illustrate the application of the effective interest rate method of amortisation to fixed interest loans. In example 1, the fixed rate loan asset is repayable only at maturity (a similar example is given in IAS 39 para IG B26). In example 2, the fixed rate loan asset is repayable in equal annual instalments. In example 3, the loan's pre-determined rate of interest increases over the instrument's term ('stepped interest').

> **Example 1 – Fixed interest loan asset repayable at maturity**
>
> On 1 January 20X5, entity A originates a 10 year 7% C1m loan. The loan carries an annual interest rate of 7% payable at the end of each year and is repayable at par at the end of year 10. Entity A charges a 1.25% (C12,500) non-refundable loan origination fee to the borrower and also incurs C25,000 in direct loan origination costs.
>
> The contract specifies that the borrower has an option to pre-pay the instrument and that no penalty will be charged for pre-payment. At inception, the entity expects the borrower not to pre-pay.
>
> The initial carrying amount of the loan asset is calculated as follows:

	C
Loan principal	1,000,000
Origination fees charged to borrower	(12,500)
Origination costs incurred by lender	25,000
Carrying amount of loan	1,012,500

As explained in paragraph 6.7.72 above, it is first necessary to determine whether the pre-payment option should be separately accounted for. In this example, as the loan's principal amount is likely to be approximately equal to the loan's amortised cost at each exercise date, the borrower's option to pre-pay is closely related and not separately accounted for.

As the entity expects the borrower not to pre-pay, the amortisation period is equal to the instrument's full term. In calculating the effective interest rate that will apply over the term of the loan at a constant rate on the carrying amount, the discount rate necessary to equate 10 annual payments of C70,000 and a final payment at maturity of C1 million to the initial carrying amount of C1,012,500 is approximately 6.823%.

The carrying amount of the loan over the period to maturity will, therefore, be as follows:

	Cash in flows (coupon) C	Interest income @ 6.823% C	Amortisation of net fees C	Carrying amount C
1 Jan 20X5				1,012,500
31 Dec 20X5	70,000	69,083	917	1,011,588
31 Dec 20X6	70,000	69,025	975	1,010,613
31 Dec 20X7	70,000	68,959	1,041	1,009,572
31 Dec 20X8	70,000	68,888	1,112	1,008,460
31 Dec 20X9	70,000	68,812	1,188	1,007,272
31 Dec 20Y0	70,000	68,731	1,269	1,006,003
31 Dec 20Y1	70,000	68,644	1,356	1,004,647
31 Dec 20Y2	70,000	68,552	1,448	1,003,199
31 Dec 20Y3	70,000	68,453	1,547	1,001,652
31 Dec 20Y4	70,000	68,348	1,652	1,000,000
	700,000	687,500	12,500	
31 Dec 20Y4	Repayment of principal			(1,000,000)
31 Dec 20Y4	Carrying value of loan			Nil

As can be seen from the above, the effective interest income for the period is calculated by applying the effective interest rate of 6.823% to the loan's amortised cost at the end of the previous reporting period. The annual interest income decreases each year to reflect the decrease in the asset's carrying value as the initial net fee is amortised. Thus the difference between the calculated effective income for a given reporting period and the loan's coupon is the amortisation of the net fees during that reporting period. The loan's amortised cost at the end of the previous period plus amortisation in the current reporting period gives the loan's amortised cost at the end of the current period. By maturity date, the net fees received are fully amortised and the loan's carrying amount is equal to the face amount, which is then repaid in full.

Example 2 – Fixed interest loan asset repayable in equal annual instalments

On 1 January 20X5, entity A originates a 10 year 7% C1 million loan. The loan is repaid in equal annual payments of C142,378 through to maturity date at 31 December 20Y4. Entity A charges a 1.25% (C12,500) non-refundable loan origination fee to the borrower and also incurs C25,000 in direct loan origination costs.

The contract specifies that the borrower has an option to pre-pay the instrument and that no penalty will be charged for pre-payment. At inception, the entity expects the borrower not to pre-pay.

The initial carrying amount of the loan is calculated as follows:

	C
Loan principal	1,000,000
Origination fees charged to borrower	(12,500)
Origination costs incurred by lender	25,000
Carrying amount of loan	1,012,500

As in the previous example, the pre-payment option will not be separately accounted for. In calculating the effective interest rate that will apply over the term of the loan at a constant rate on the carrying amount, the discount rate necessary to equate 10 annual payments of C142,378 to the initial carrying amount of C1,012,500 is approximately 6.7322%. The carrying amount of the loan over the period to maturity will, therefore, be as follows:

	Cash in flows	Interest Income @ 6.7322%	Carrying amount
	C	C	C
1 Jan 20X5			1,012,500
31 Dec 20X5	142,378	68,164	938,286
31 Dec 20X6	142,378	63,167	859,075
31 Dec 20X7	142,378	57,835	774,531
31 Dec 20X8	142,378	52,143	684,296
31 Dec 20X9	142,378	46,068	587,987
31 Dec 20Y0	142,378	39,584	485,193
31 Dec 20Y1	142,378	32,664	375,479
31 Dec 20Y2	142,378	25,278	258,379
31 Dec 20Y3	142,378	17,395	133,396
31 Dec 20Y4	142,378	8,982	–
	1,423,780	411,280	

Example 3 – Fixed interest loan asset with interest step-up

On 1 January 20X5, entity A originates a 5 year debt instrument for C1million loan that is repayable at maturity. The contract provides for 5% interest in year 1 that increases by 2% in each of the following 4 years. Entity A also receives C25,000 in loan origination fees.

The loan's initial carrying amount is calculated as follows:

	C
Loan principal	1,000,000
Origination fees charged to borrower	(25,000)
Carrying amount of loan	975,000

In calculating the effective interest rate that will apply over the term of the loan at a constant rate on the carrying amount, the discount rate necessary to equate 5 annual step-up payments and a final payment at maturity of C1 million to the initial carrying amount of C925,000 is approximately 9.2934 %.

	Interest income @ 9.2934%	Cash in flows (coupon)	Carrying amount
	C	C	C
1 Jan 20X5			975,000
31 Dec 20X5	90,610	50,000	1,015,610
31 Dec 20X6	94,385	70,000	1,039,995
31 Dec 20X7	96,651	90,000	1,046,646
31 Dec 20X8	97,268	110,000	1,033,914
31 Dec 20X9	96,086	130,000	1,000,000
	475,000	450,000	

If the borrower were to repay the entire loan of C1 million early, say in 20X9, when the loan asset's carrying value is C1,033,914, the excess amount of C33,914 would have to be recognised in profit or loss. This effectively represents the excess income recognised in earlier periods that is now written back as shown below:

	C
Total income recognised to 31 Dec 20X8	378,914
Amortisation of fees	(25,000)
Cash received to 31 Dec 20X8	(320,000)
Excess income recognised prior to pre-payment by borrower in 20X9	33,914

Changes in estimated cash flows

6.7.79   As explained above, the cash flows that are discounted to arrive at the effective interest rate are estimated cash flows that are expected to occur over the instrument's expected life. However, in practice, actual cash flows rarely occur in line with expectations. There is usually variation in the amount, timing or both. Differences from the original estimates present a problem for the effective interest rate. If the variation is ignored, either the asset or liability will amortise before all of the cash flows occur, or a balance may remain after the last cash flow.

6.7.80   The standard, therefore, requires an entity to adjust the carrying amount of the financial asset or financial liability (or group of financial instruments) to reflect actual and revised estimated cash flows whenever it revises its cash flow estimates. The entity recalculates the carrying amount by computing the present value of estimated future cash flows at the financial instrument's original effective interest rate, or, when applicable, the revised effective interest calculated in accordance with IAS 39 paragraph 92 (see chapter 6.8). The adjustment is recognised in profit or loss as income or expense. [IAS 39 para AG 8].

Example – Changes in estimates of cash flows

The facts are the same as in example 1 in paragraph 6.7.78 above, except that on 1 January 20Y1, entity A revises its estimates of cash flows as it now expects that, because of a significant fall in interest rates during the previous period, the borrower is likely to exercise its option to pre-pay. Accordingly, entity A anticipates that 40% of the loan is likely to be repaid by the borrower in 20Y1, with the remaining 60% progressively at 20% in the following three years to maturity.

The revised cash flows are shown below. In accordance with paragraph 6.7.80 above, the opening balance at 1 January 20Y1 is adjusted. The adjusted amount is calculated by discounting the amounts the entity expects to receive in 20Y1 and subsequent years using the original effective rate of 6.823%. This results in the adjustment shown below. The adjustment is recognised in profit or loss in 20Y1.

		Carrying amount
1 Jan 20Y1	Opening amortised carrying amount before revision	1,006,003
	Adjustment for changes in estimate – profit or loss	2,563
1 Jan 20Y1	Adjusted amortised carrying amount after revision	1,003,440

	Opening amortised carrying amount	Interest income @ 6.823%	Cash in flows (coupon + repayment of principal)		Closing amortised carrying amount
	C	C	C		C
31 Dec 20Y1	1,003,440	68,465	70,000 +	400,000	601,905
31 Dec 20Y2	601,905	41,068	42,000 +	200,000	400,973
31 Dec 20Y3	400,973	27,358	28,000 +	200,000	200,331
31 Dec 20Y4	200,331	13,669	14,000 +	200,000	–

6.7.81   For financial assets reclassified in accordance with IAS 39 paragraphs 50B, D and E (see para 6.7.41), any increase in the estimates of expected future cash flows arising from recoveries is reflected by adjusting the effective interest rate prospectively, rather than as an adjustment to the carrying amount. Any increased recoverability of cash receipts is, therefore, spread over the debt instrument's remaining life. [IAS 39 para AG 8]. A decrease in the estimate of expected cash flows would be recorded as an impairment loss.

6.7.82   An increase in estimates of future cash receipts can be determined on a discounted or undiscounted basis. It is an accounting policy choice and should be applied consistently to all reclassified financial assets. Entities may determine whether there is a change in recoverable cash receipts on an undiscounted basis. In such a case, an entity adjusts effective interest rate for any increase in the total amount of undiscounted cash receipts it expects to recover, but not for a change in recoverable amount (that is, discounted) due only to changes in the timing or pattern of cash receipts. Entities may alternatively determine whether there is a change in recoverable cash receipts on a discounted basis. In such circumstances, an entity adjusts the effective interest rate if there is a change in the present value of the estimated cash receipts, thus taking into account timing and pattern of receipt as well as quantum. In both cases, the reference to 'recoverability' indicates that such cash receipts arise from a reversal of credit losses.

Example 1 – Increase in expected future cash flows arising from recoveries

An entity has reclassified a floating-rate financial asset to loans and receivables on 1 July 20X8. The loan was originally purchased for C100. At the date of reclassification, the fair value of the instrument had decreased substantially as a result of a decline in the creditworthiness of the counterparty to C80, and the entity expects to get undiscounted cash receipts of C90. At 31 December, the credit rating of the counterparty has increased (for example, because of government backing) and the entity now expects to get undiscounted cash receipts of C100. The entity should recalculate its effective interest rate prospectively to reflect those new cash receipts. The increase in expected future cash receipts should be reflected in a new effective interest rate.

Example 2 – Decrease in expected future cash flows arising from recoveries

An entity reclassified a fixed rate asset to loans and receivables on 1 July 20X8. The loan was originally purchased for C100. At the date of reclassification, the fair value of the instrument had decreased substantially as a result of a decline in the creditworthiness of the counterparty to C60, and the entity expects to get undiscounted cash receipts of C75. At 31 December 20X8, the recoverability of cash receipts has decreased further to C50. The amendment to paragraph AG 8 requires the effective interest rate to be adjusted only where there are increases in the estimates of future cash receipts. Decreases in estimates of future cash receipts do not result in a downwards adjustment to the effective interest rate. The reduction in estimated cash receipts at 31 December 20X8 will be reflected as an impairment loss in profit or loss measured in accordance with paragraph 63 of IAS 39 (see further para 6.7.173).

Example 3 – Increase in expected future cash flows arising from recoveries after impairment

An entity reclassified a fixed rate debt instrument to loans and receivables on 1 July 20X8. The loan was originally purchased for C100. At the date of reclassification, the instrument's fair value had decreased substantially as a result of a decline in the counterparty's creditworthiness to C60. At 31 December 20X8, the recoverability of cash receipts has decreased to C50, and the entity records an impairment loss. At 31 March 20X9, the recoverability of cash receipts has increased to C60. The entity should account for the increase in expected cash receipts as a reversal of the impairment recorded at 31 December 20X8 (see para 6.7.198).

6.7.83 When, subsequent to a reclassification, there is an increase in the cash flows expected to be recovered followed by a decrease in those expected cash flows, but the expected cash flows remain above the amount expected when the asset was reclassified (that is, there is not an impairment subsequent to reclassification), we consider that either of the following approaches would be acceptable:

■ Only increases in cash flows are dealt with by amending the effective interest rate prospectively. Any decreases, even those after an increase and still above the cash flows expected at the reclassification date, are accounted for by means of a cumulative catch up in accordance with IAS 39 paragraph AG8 (using, as the discount rate, the effective interest rate on the reclassified instrument that was determined after the prospective change in the effective interest rate due to an increase in the cash flows).

■ Increases and decreases above the level of cash flows expected on the reclassification date are dealt with prospectively by amending the effective interest rate. Any decreases below the cash flows expected on the reclassification date are accounted for by means of a cumulative catch-up in accordance with IAS 39 paragraph AG8, or as an impairment.

Issuer call option in debt instruments

6.7.84 The terms of a debt instrument may include an issuer call option, that is, a right of the issuer (but not the investor) to redeem the instrument early and pay a fixed price (generally at a premium over the par value). There may also be other pre-payment features that cause the whole or part of the outstanding principal to be repaid early. Adding call options and/or other pre-payment options should make the instrument less attractive to investors, since it reduces the potential upside on the bond. As market interest rates go down and the bond price increases (reflecting its above market interest rate), the bonds are likely to be called back. As explained in paragraph 6.7.72 above, such a call option embedded in the debt host is a derivative and would fall to be separately accounted for if its exercise price is not approximately equal to the debt host's amortised cost at each exercise date. Consider the example given below.

Example – Issuer call option in debt instrument

Entity A issues a fixed rate loan for C1m and incurs issue costs of C30,000 resulting in an initial carrying value of C970,000. The loan carries an interest rate of 8% per annum and is repayable at par at the end of year 10. However, under the contract, entity A can call the loan at any time after year 4 by paying a fixed premium of C50,000.

As explained in paragraph 6.7.72 above, it is first necessary to determine whether the call option is closely related to the host debt instrument. As the fixed premium is required to be paid whenever the call option is exercised after year 4, it may or may not be equal to the present value of any interest lost during the remaining term after exercise of the option. Furthermore, as the call option's exercise price is C1,050,000 (inclusive of the premium), it is unlikely to be approximately equal to the debt instrument's amortised cost in year 4, or at any time subsequently. Therefore, the call option has to be separated from the host debt contract and accounted for separately. This assumes that the expected life of the instrument is the full 10 year term. However, if the expected life is assumed to be 4 years, the 10 year loan with a call option after 4 years is economically equivalent to a 4 year loan with a 6 year extension option. Since there is no concurrent adjustment to the interest rate after 4 years, the term extension option would not be closely related and would need to be accounted for separately (see chapter 6.3). Therefore, in this case whatever way the loan and option are viewed, the embedded derivative is separated.

Even though the option is out of the money at inception, because the option's exercise price is greater than the debt instrument's carrying value, it has a time value. Suppose the option's fair value is C20,000 at inception. Since the value of a callable bond is equal to the value of a straight bond less the value of the option feature, the accounting entries at inception would be as follows:

	Dr C	Cr C
Embedded option (derivative asset)	20,000	
Cash	970,000	
Debt instrument (host)		990,000

Since the call option will be fair valued and accounted for separately with fair value movements taken to profit or loss, it has no impact on the entity's estimate of future cash flows as explained in paragraph 6.7.73 above and, accordingly, the amortisation period will be the debt host's period to original maturity. On this basis, the effective interest rate amounts to 8.15%. The amortisation schedule is shown below.

	Opening amortised cost	Interest expense @ 8.15%	Cash payments	Closing amortised cost
	C	C	C	C
Year 1	990,000	80,685	80,000	990,685
Year 2	990,685	80,741	80,000	991,427
Year 3	991,427	80,802	80,000	992,228
Year 4	992,228	80,867	80,000	993,095
Year 5	993,095	80,938	80,000	994,033
Year 6	994,033	81,014	80,000	995,047
Year 7	995,047	81,097	80,000	996,144
Year 8	996,144	81,186	80,000	997,330
Year 9	997,330	81,283	80,000	998,613
Year 10	998,613	81,387	1,080,000	–

The entity would recognise interest expense in profit or loss and the loan's amortised cost in the balance sheet each year in accordance with the above amortisation schedule.

In years 1 and 2, there is no change in interest rate since inception for an instrument of similar maturity and credit rating. The option's fair value (time value) at the end of year 2 is C10,000. The decrease in fair value of C10,000 since inception will be reported in profit and loss and the option will be recorded at C10,000 at the end of year 2.

At the end of year 3, interest rates have fallen and the option's fair value increases to C18,000. The increase in value of C8,000 will be recorded in profit or loss and the option will be recorded at its fair value of C18,000 at the end of year 3.

At the end of year 4, interest rates have fallen further. The option's fair value increases to C30,000 and the company decides to repay the loan at the end of year 4.

The accounting entries to reflect the change in the option's fair value and the loan's early repayment at the end of year 4 are as follows:

	Dr	Cr
	C	C
Embedded Option	12,000	
Profit or loss		12,000
Early repayment of loan		
Debt instrument (host)	993,095	
Embedded option (derivative asset)		30,000
Cash		1,050,000
Loss on derecognition of liability	86,905	

The loss of C86,905 in profit or loss reflects the fact that the fair value of the host contract has gone up in value as interest rates have fallen compared to its carrying value at amortised cost. The fair value of the host contract is actually C1,080,000, which is the option's fair value plus the fair value of the consideration given. The market rate of interest that discounts the interest payments of C80,000 for the next 6 years plus the principal repayment of C1,000,000 at maturity to the fair value of the host is 6.95%, indicating a significant fall in value compared to the instrument's stated interest rate of 8%.

Suppose that instead of an additional premium or penalty payable on early exercise, the option's exercise price is the fair value of the loan at each exercise date. In other words, the exercise price of the pre-payment option is a 'market adjusted value'. A market adjusted value is calculated by discounting the contractual guaranteed amount payable at the end of the specified term to present value using the current market rate that would be offered on a new loan with a similar credit rating and having a maturity period equal to the remaining maturity period of the current loan. As a result, the market adjusted value may be more or less than the loan principal, depending upon market interest rates at each option exercise date.

In that situation, the pre-payment option enables the issuer simply to pay off the loan at fair value at the pre-payment date. Since the holder receives only the market adjusted value, which is equal to the loan's fair value at the date of pre-payment, the pre-payment option (the embedded derivative) has a fair value of zero at all times. Since the pre-payment option, on a stand-alone basis, would not meet the definition of a derivative, it cannot be an embedded derivative, the loan is simply carried at its amortised cost as above, on the assumption that the loan is not going to be pre-paid. If, however, the entity expects to pre-pay the loan, the loan would be amortised over its expected life.

Floating rate instruments

6.7.85   As will be apparent from the above illustrations, the application of the effective interest rate method is relatively straight forward for fixed interest instruments with fixed terms. Indeed, it appears to be specifically designed for such instruments. However, the analysis is more complicated in the case of a financial instrument that provides for future cash flows that are determinable rather than fixed. Floating rate interest on a financial instrument that is linked to a reference rate such as **LIBOR** and a principal amount linked to a price index are examples of determinable cash flows. The apparent complication arises because, unlike fixed interest instruments where the effective interest rate generally stays constant over the instrument's term, for floating rate instruments, the periodic re-estimation of determinable cash flows to reflect movements in market rates of interest alters the instrument's effective yield.

6.7.86   However, although fluctuations in interest rates result in a change in the effective interest rate, there is usually no change in the instrument's fair value. Accordingly, where a floating rate instrument is acquired or issued and the amount at which it is recognised initially is equal to the principal receivable or payable at maturity, re-estimating the future interest payments normally has no significant effect on the carrying amount of the asset or liability. [IAS 39 para AG 7]. This means that the effective yield will always equal the rate under the interest rate formula (for example, LIBOR + 1%) in the instrument. The effect is that the carrying amount remains unchanged by the process, illustrated in paragraph 6.7.81 above, of re-estimating future cash flows and the effective interest rate. The result is that changes in LIBOR are reflected in the period in which the change occurs.

6.7.87   However, if a floating rate instrument is issued or acquired at a discount or premium, or the entity receives or incurs loan origination fees or costs, the question arises as to whether the premium or discount and other transaction fees or costs should be amortised over the period to the next repricing date, or over the instrument's expected life. The answer depends upon the nature of the premium or discount and its relationship with market rates.

- An amortisation period to the next repricing date should be used if the premium or discount on a floating rate instrument reflects interest that has accrued on the instrument since interest was last paid, or changes in market interest rate since the floating interest rate was reset to market rates. This is because the premium or discount relates to the period to the next interest reset date as, at that date, the variable to which the premium or discount relates (that is interest rates) is reset to market rates. In this case, the loan's fair value at the next repricing date will be its par value. This is illustrated in example 1 below.

- The instrument's expected life should be used as the amortisation period if the premium or discount results from changes in the credit spread over the floating rate specified in the instrument, or other variables that are not reset to market rates. In this situation, the date the interest rate is next reset is not a market-based repricing date of the entire instrument, since the variable rate is not adjusted for changes in the credit spread for the specific issue. This is illustrated in example 2 below.

[IAS 39 para AG 6].

Example 1 – Amortisation of discount over the period to the next repricing date

On 15 May 20X6, an entity acquires a C100 nominal 5 year floating rate bond that pays quarterly interest at 3 month LIBOR + 50 basis points for C99.25. LIBOR at the last reset date on 30 March 20X6 was 4.50% which determines the interest that would be paid on the bond on 30 June 20X6. On the purchase date, LIBOR was 4.75%. The discount of 0.75 (5.25% – 4.50%) is amortised to the next repricing date, that is, 30 June 20X6.

Example 2 – Amortisation of discount over the expected life of the instrument

A 20 year bond is issued at C100, has a principal amount of C100, and requires quarterly interest payments equal to current 3 month LIBOR plus 1% over the instrument's life. The interest rate reflects the market-based rate of return associated with the bond issue at issuance. Subsequent to issuance, the loan's credit quality deteriorates resulting in a rating downgrade. Therefore, the bond trades at a discount. Entity A purchases the bond for 95 and classifies it as held-to-maturity.

In this case, the discount of C5 is amortised to net profit or loss over the period to the bond's maturity and not to the next date interest rate payments are reset, as there is no adjustment to the variable rate as a result of the credit downgrade.

6.7.88 There is no specific guidance in the standard as to how transaction costs incurred in originating or acquiring a floating rate instrument should be amortised. Since such costs are sunk cost and are not subject to repricing, they will be amortised over the instrument's expected life. Any methodology that provides a reasonable basis of amortisation may be used. For example, entities may find it appropriate to amortise the fees and costs by reference to the interest rate at inception ignoring any subsequent changes in rates or to simply adopt a straight-line amortisation method.

Inflation linked bond

6.7.89 Entities sometimes issue or invest in debt instruments whose payments (principal and interest) are linked to the change in an inflation index of the period. Such an inflation-linked bond needs to be assessed to determine if the inflation-linking mechanism is a closely related embedded derivative that does not need to be recognised and measured separately under IAS 39. There are two possible approaches to account for changes in estimated future cash flows for an inflation-linked bond where the inflation linking mechanism has been found to be closely related.

- Applying the guidance in IAS 39 paragraph AG7, under which the bond is treated as a floating-rate debt instrument with the inflation link being part of the floating-rate mechanism. The EIR at initial recognition is determined as the rate that sets the estimated future cash flows to be paid on the bond, based on the expected level of the inflation index over the expected term of the bond to equal the fair value of the bond (usually the issue proceeds). However, if in subsequent periods there is a change in inflation expectations, the entity reflects these changes by adjusting both the expected future cash flows on the debt and the EIR. It follows that such changes in the entity's expectations of future inflation result in no adjustment to the carrying amount of the debt and no gain or loss.

- Applying the guidance in IAS 39 paragraph AG8 under which the EIR is determined at inception in the same way as above. However, if in subsequent periods there is a change in the level of the inflation expectations for the bond's remaining term, the entity revises its estimates of the future cash flows to be paid on the bond accordingly. It recalculates the bond's carrying amount by discounting the revised estimated cash flows using the original EIR. The resulting adjustment to the bond's carrying amount is recognised immediately in the income statement as a gain or loss. The result is that a gain or loss is recognised in the current period for changes in the entity's expectations of the future level of the inflation index.

6.7.90 Given that the standard is not clear as to how the EIR method applies for instruments with variable cash flows, the IFRIC was asked to provide guidance on how to apply the effective interest rate method to a financial instrument whose cash flows are linked to changes in an inflation index. [IFRIC update July 2008]. The IFRIC noted that paragraphs AG6-AG8 of IAS 39 provide the relevant application guidance. Judgement is required to determine whether an instrument is a floating rate instrument within the scope of paragraph AG7 or an instrument within the scope of paragraph AG8. In view of the existing application guidance in IAS 39, the IFRIC decided not to add this issue to its agenda. However, since the application of the effective interest rate method has widespread application in practice, the IFRIC has decided to refer the matter to the IASB.

6.7.91 Until such time as the IASB provides clarification, we believe an entity should make an accounting policy choice as to which method is acceptable and apply this method to all similar instruments. The way in which the above guidance should be applied is illustrated in the example given below.

Example – Inflation-linked bond

On 1 January 20X5, an entity invests in an inflation-linked bond for C100,000. The term of the bond is 5 years. The bond pays a fixed coupon of 5% per annum (real) at the end of each year on principal that is adjusted annually by the applicable year's percentage change in the consumer price index. The principal repayable at the end of year 5 is similarly adjusted for inflation.

Terms of the bond	
Proceeds received on 1 Jan 20X5	100,000
Fixed coupon @ 5% per annum (real interest rate)	5,000
Term	5 years
Principal and real interest adjusted annually for changes in the consumer price index	

Following are data of actual inflation rates and annual expected inflation rates on various dates

Annual expected percentage change in consumer price index

	1 Jan 20X5	1 Jan 20X6	1 Jan 20X7	1 Jan 20X8	1 Jan 20X9	Actual change
20X5	0.70%					1.20%
20X6	2.60%	1.40%				2.40%
20X7	2.80%	1.90%	1.70%			0%
20X8	2.80%	3.50%	2.10%	1.20%		3.40%
20X9	2.80%	3.50%	2.60%	1.60%	2.50%	2.50%

The expected inflation adjusted interest payments at the end of each year and the principal payment at the end of year 5 are shown below. The expected cash flows at the end of a year are calculated by multiplying the principal of C100,000 by the expected change in the consumer price index in that year. So at the beginning of 20X5, the principal at the end of 20X5 is expected to be C100,000 × 1.007 = C100,700. As the nominal coupon rate is 5%, the interest expected to be paid for 20X5 would be C5,035 (C100,700@5%). Similarly, at 1 Jan 20X6, the expected inflated adjusted principal at the end of year 20X6 would be C100,000 × 1.012 (the opening amount as adjusted by the actual increase in inflation during 20X5) × 1.014 (expected increase during 20X6) = C102,617 and the expected adjusted interest would be C5,131 (C102,617@5%).

Annual expected interest and principal cash flows						Actual inflation adjusted cash flows	
	1 Jan 20X5	1 Jan 20X6	1 Jan 20X7	1 Jan 20X8	1 Jan 20X9	Interest	Principal
20X5	5,035					5,060	
20X6	5,166	5,131				5,181	
20X7	5,311	5,228	5,270			5,181	
20X8	5,459	5,411	5,380	5,244		5,358	
20X9 – interest	5,612	5,601	5,520	5,328	5,492	5,492	
Principal	112,242	112,014	110,401	106,550	109,831		109,831
20X9	117,854	117,615	115,921	111,878	115,323	26,272	109,831

Note that the principal expected to be paid at the end of 20X9 is adjusted for expected changes in the index since 1 Jan 20X5. For example, the expected principal payable in 20X9 estimated at 1 Jan 20X5 = 100,000 × 1.007 × 1.026 × 1.028 × 1.028 × 1.028 = 112,242.

There are essentially two ways in which the bond could be amortised in accordance with the guidance provided in paragraph AG7 of IAS 39.

The first method views the EIR as a 'floating inflation adjusted rate' – similar to LIBOR. In this method, the finance cost recognised in profit or loss is the actual inflation adjusted interest paid during the year plus the actual increase in principal as adjusted for inflation during the year. So the carrying amount is equal to the inflation adjusted amount at the end of the period. This method is simple and is often used in practice.

Amortisation of bond based on AG7 – Method 1

	Opening balance	Finance cost	Cash flow	Closing balance
31 Dec 20X5	100,000	6,260	5,060	101,200
31 Dec 20X6	101,200	7,610	5,181	103,629
31 Dec 20X7	103,629	5,181	5,181	103,629
31 Dec 20X8	103,629	8,881	5,358	107,152
31Dec 20X9	107,152	8,171	115,323	0
		36,103	136,103	

The second method complies strictly with the guidance in paragraph AG7. In this method, the finance cost in each period is based on an adjusted EIR, calculated by discounting the expected cash flows to equal to the carrying amount at the beginning of each period. No further gain or loss arises.

Amortisation of bond based on AG7 – Method 2

	Opening balance	Finance cost @ adjusted EIR (see below)	Cash flow	Closing balance
31 Dec 20X5	100,000	7,408	5,060	102,348
31 Dec 20X6	102,348	7,496	5,181	104,662
31 Dec 20X7	104,662	7,172	5,181	106,653
31 Dec 20X8	106,653	5,235	5,358	106,530
31 Dec 20X9	106,530	8,793	115,323	0
		36,103	136,103	

Calculation of adjusted EIR based on expected cash flows

	EIR %	1 Jan 20X5	31 Dec 20X5	31 Dec 20X6	31 Dec 20X7	31 Dec 20X8	31 Dec 20X9
20X5	7.408	−100,000	5,035	5,166	5,311	5,459	117,854
20X6	7.324		−102,348	5,131	5,228	5,411	117,615
20X7	6.853			−104,662	5,270	5,380	115,921
20X8	4.908				−106,653	5,244	111,878
20X9	8.254					−106,530	115,323

The original effective interest rate at inception is 7.408%.

The way in which the bond would be amortised in accordance with the guidance provided in paragraph AG8 of IAS 39 is shown below. As the finance cost in each period is based on the original EIR at inception, the carrying value at the end of each period is adjusted to the present value of the expected cash flows discounted at the original EIR. This gives rise to a further adjustment that is recognised as part of the finance cost in each period.

Amortisation of bond based on AG8

	Opening balance	Finance cost @ 7.408%	Cash flow	Closing balance	AG8 adjustment	Adjusted closing balance (see below)	Total finance cost
31 Dec 20X5	100,000	7,408	5,060	102,348	−297	102,050	7,110
31 Dec 20X6	102,050	7,559	5,181	104,428	−1,305	103,123	6,255
31 Dec 20X7	103,123	7,639	5,181	105,581	−3,720	101,860	3,919
31 Dec 20X8	101,860	7,545	5,358	104,048	3,321	107,369	10,866
31 Dec 20X9	107,369	7,953	115,323	0	0	0	7,953
			136,103				36,103

Present value of expected cash flows based on original discount rate

	31 Dec 20X6	31 Dec 20X7	31 Dec 20X8	31 Dec 20X9	PV @7.408%
31 Dec 20X5	5,131	5,228	5,411	117,615	102,050
31 Dec 20X6		5,270	5,380	115,921	103,123
31 Dec 20X7			5,244	111,878	101,860
31 Dec 20X8				115,323	107,369

Comparison between AG7 and AG8

	AG7 – Method 1		AG7 – Method 2		AG8	
	Finance cost	Loan balance	Finance cost	Loan balance	Finance cost	Loan balance
31 Dec 20X5	6,260	101,200	7,408	102,348	7,110	102,050
31 Dec 20X6	7,610	103,629	7,496	104,662	6,255	103,123
31 Dec 20X7	5,181	103,629	7,172	106,653	3,919	101,860
31 Dec 20X8	8,881	107,152	5,235	106,530	10,866	107,369
	8,171	0	8,793	0	7,953	0
	36,103		36,103		36,103	

The comparisons between the two methods indicate that the finance cost calculated in accordance with AG7 is consistent with the trend in the actual inflation rate.

Perpetual debt instruments

6.7.92 It is not uncommon for entities to issue debt instruments on terms with no redemption date, but on which interest payments are made, usually at a fixed rate or a variable market based rate (for example, a fixed margin over LIBOR) in perpetuity. At initial recognition, assuming there are no transaction costs, the debt instrument will be recorded at its fair value, which is the amount received. The difference between this initial amount and the maturity amount, which is zero if the interest rate at inception is the market rate for that instrument, will never be amortised, as there is no repayment of principal. This means that at each reporting date the debt instrument will be recorded at its principal amount, which is also its amortised cost. This is because the amortised cost, which is the present value of the stream of future cash payments discounted at the effective interest rate (fixed for fixed rate instruments or variable for floating rate instruments) equals the principal amount in each period. [IAS 39 para IG B24]. If, on the other hand, the entity incurs transaction costs, the debt instrument will be recorded in each reporting period at its initial amount, which is the amount received less transaction costs. The result is that the transaction costs are never amortised, but reflected in the carrying amount indefinitely.

6.7.93 Sometimes perpetual debt instruments are repackaged in such a way that the principal amount is effectively repaid. One way of achieving this is to pay a high rate of interest for a number of years (the primary period) which then falls to a negligible amount. If the interest were simply charged to profit or loss, the company would bear an artificially high interest expense during the primary period and little or no interest expense thereafter to perpetuity. Such treatment might reflect the form of the loan agreement, but not its substance. From an economic perspective, some or all of the interest payments are repayment of principal as illustrated in the example below. A similar example is included in IAS 39 paragraph IG B25.

Example – Perpetual debt instrument with decreasing interest

An entity issues a perpetual bond for C100,000 on which interest at 14% is paid annually for the first 10 years and thereafter at a nominal rate of 0.125%.

It is clear that at the end of the ten year period, the bond has little or no value. The principal amount is repaid, in effect, over the initial 10 year primary period. Consequently, the interest payments during the primary period represent a payment for interest and repayment of capital. The effective interest rate calculated on the basis of C14,000 for 10 years followed by C125 to perpetuity is 6.84%.

	Opening amortised cost	Interest expense @ 6.84%	Cash payments	Closing amortised cost
	C	C	C	C
Year 1	100,000	6,840	14,000	92,840
Year 2	92,840	6,350	14,000	85,190
Year 3	85,190	5,827	14,000	77,017
Year 4	77,017	5,268	14,000	68,285
Year 5	68,285	4,671	14,000	58,956
Year 6	58,956	4,033	14,000	48,989
Year 7	48,989	3,351	14,000	38,340
Year 8	38,340	2,622	14,000	26,962
Year 9	26,962	1,844	14,000	14,806
Year 10	14,806	1,013	14,000	1,819
		41,819	140,000	

Although the carrying value at the end of year 10 is small, an amount of C100,000 may fall to be repayable should the entity go into liquidation. In practice, however, there will usually be arrangements to enable the entity to repurchase the debt instrument for a nominal amount and, therefore, extinguish any liability on it.

Fair value measurement considerations

General

6.7.94 The IASB believes that fair value is the most relevant measure for financial instruments and is the only relevant measure for derivative assets and liabilities. As a result, IAS 39 gives entities an option to measure all financial assets and liabilities that meet certain qualifying criteria at fair value. The importance of fair value in the measurement process arises because it is a market-based notion that is unaffected by the history of the asset or liability, the specific entity that holds the asset or the liability and the future use of the asset or the liability. Thus, it represents an unbiased measure that is consistent from year to year, within an entity and between entities. As a result, if an investor knows a financial instrument's fair value and has information about its essential terms and risks, it has all the information it needs to make decisions about that instrument.

IFRS 13 amended IAS 39 and IFRS 9 to remove their guidance on fair value measurement. The guidance below on fair value measurements applies the requirements of IAS 39. Entities that have adopted IFRS 13 should refer to chapter 5 for the relevant fair value measurement guidance.

6.7.95   IAS 39 defines fair value as *"the amount for which an asset could be exchanged, or a liability settled, between knowledgeable, willing parties in an arm's length transaction"*. [IAS 39 para 9]. The price at which an asset could be exchanged is the price an entity would have received if it had sold the asset. Similarly, the price at which a liability is settled is the price an entity would have paid if it had been relieved of the liability. This implies that fair value is an estimate of the market 'exit' price that is determined by reference to a current hypothetical transaction between willing parties. Willing parties are presumed to be market-place participants representing unrelated buyers and sellers that are knowledgeable, having a common level of understanding about factors relevant to the asset or liability and the transaction and willing and able to transact in the same market(s) having the legal and financial ability to do so.

6.7.96   Underlying the definition of fair value is a presumption that an entity is a going concern without any intention or need to liquidate, to curtail materially the scale of its operations or to undertake a transaction on adverse terms. Fair value is not, therefore, the amount that an entity would receive or pay in a forced transaction, involuntary liquidation or distress sale (see from para 6.7.101). However, fair value does reflect the instrument's credit quality. [IAS 39 para AG69]. This means that when a financial liability is measured at fair value, its credit quality must be reflected in the valuation process (see further para 6.7.153 below).

6.7.97   There is a general presumption that fair value can be reliably measured for all financial instruments. Nonetheless, the measurement process can be quite complex and gives rise to numerous issues. It is not surprising, therefore, that IAS 39 provides a significant amount of guidance about how to determine fair values, in particular for financial instruments for which no quoted market prices are available. Therefore, in looking for a reliable measure of fair value, the standard provides a hierarchy for determining an instrument's fair value as shown below:

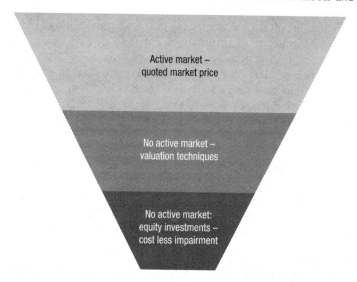

6.7.98 As can be seen from the above, the hierarchy gives the highest priority to quoted prices in active markets. Unfortunately, for many of the financial assets for which fair values are required, there may be no active market. In the absence of an active market, fair value is established by using a valuation technique. Indeed, as financial instruments become more complex in nature, the ability to obtain a quoted market price diminishes and the requirement to derive a fair value using valuation techniques increases. Such valuation techniques include the use of recent market transactions in similar instruments between knowledgeable, willing parties in an arm's length transaction. Hence, recent market transactions and valuation techniques are given equal prominence in the hierarchy. However, as with any valuation, judgement will often be necessary. Only as a last resort, is an entity permitted to use cost and this is limited to unquoted equity instruments whose fair value cannot be measured reliably and derivatives that are linked to and must be settled in such instruments.

Quoted prices in an active market

6.7.99 The existence of published price quotations in an active market *is* the best evidence of fair value and, where available, they *must* be used to measure the financial instrument. The phrase 'quoted in an active market' means that quoted prices are readily and regularly available from an exchange, dealer, broker, industry group, pricing service or regulatory agency and those prices represent actual and regularly occurring market transactions on an arm's length basis. [IAS 39 para AG 71].

6.7.100 Readily available means that the pricing information is currently accessible and regularly available means that transactions occur with sufficient frequency to provide pricing information on an ongoing basis. For example, in an active market, such as the London Stock Exchange, quoted prices that represent actual (observable) transactions that are readily and regularly available.

6.7.101 What is meant in practice by the phrase 'regularly available' is a matter of judgement. An absence of transactions for a short period, or a lower than normal volume of transactions, does not necessarily mean that a market has ceased to be active or that observed transactions are distress sales, nor does it necessarily mean that transactions are motivated other than by normal business considerations. If transactions are occurring frequently enough for an entity to obtain reliable pricing information on an ongoing basis, the market is considered active.

6.7.102 Similar to the above, an imbalance between supply and demand (for example, fewer buyers than sellers) is not always a determinant of a forced transaction. A seller might be under financial pressure to sell but is still able to sell at a market price if there is more than one potential buyer in the market and a reasonable amount of time is available to market the instrument.

6.7.103 Indicators of a forced transaction include the following, as identified in the final report of the IASB's Expert Advisory Panel in October 2008:

- A legal requirement to transact, for example, a regulatory mandate.

- A necessity to dispose of an asset immediately and there is insufficient time to market the asset to be sold.

- The existence of a single potential buyer as a result of the legal or time restrictions imposed.

6.7.104 However, considering the first bullet above, if an entity sells assets to market participants to meet regulatory requirements, the regulator does not establish the transaction price and the entity has a reasonable amount of time to market the assets, the transaction price would still provide evidence of fair value. Similarly, transactions initiated during bankruptcy should not automatically be assumed to be forced. Determining whether a transaction is forced requires a thorough understanding of the facts and circumstances of the transaction.

6.7.105 In determining whether a market is active, the emphasis is on the level of activity for a particular asset or liability. [IAS 39 para AG 71]. For instance, if the market is not well established and only a small volume of a particular instrument is traded relative to the amount of the instrument in issue or trading is infrequent, quoted prices in those markets will not be suitable for determining fair value. In that situation, the entity will have to move down the hierarchy to determine a suitable fair value.

6.7.106 The IASB Expert Advisory Panel report mentioned above discusses the characteristics of an inactive market. It includes a significant decline in the volume and level of trading activity; significant variation in available prices over time or among market participants; and a lack of current prices. However, these factors alone do not necessarily mean that a market is no longer active.

6.7.107 It is not necessary for quoted prices to be obtained from regulated markets. Prices can be obtained from other sources although the available information may vary. For example, some industry groups or pricing services publish price information about certain instruments, while little or no information may be available about prices of other instruments. An entity is not generally required to perform an exhaustive search for price information, but should consider any information that is publicly available, or that can be obtained reasonably from brokers, industry groups, publications of regulatory agencies or similar sources, such as journals and web sites. It should be noted that these prices may be indicative prices only. It should not be assumed that these prices reflect the price in an active market (see para 6.7.133).

6.7.108 The objective of determining fair value for a financial instrument that is traded in an active market is to arrive at the price at which a transaction would occur at the balance sheet date in that instrument (that is, without modifying or repackaging the instrument) in the *most advantageous* active market to which the entity has immediate access. [IAS 39 para AG 71]. This means that if an entity has immediate access to different markets having different prices for essentially the same financial asset, the most advantageous market is the one with the price that maximizes the net amount that would be received in a current transaction for the financial asset. For example, if a trader that originates a derivative instrument with an entity in an active 'retail' market takes out an offsetting derivative in a more advantageously priced active dealers' 'wholesale' market, the trader records the derivative with the entity at the higher value and recognises a profit on initial recognition. However, the price in the more advantageous dealers' market should be adjusted for any differences in counterparty credit risk between the derivative instrument with the entity and that with the dealers' market. [IAS 39 para BC98]. It follows that price can be taken from the most favourable market readily available to the entity, even if that was not the market in which the transaction actually occurred.

6.7.109 For the purpose of determining the most advantageous market, costs to transact in the respective markets should be considered. If such costs are not taken into account, the entity will be unable to determine which market offers the most advantageous price. However, as explained in paragraph 6.7.20 above, the price used to estimate fair value, that is, the price in the most advantageous market, should not be adjusted for transaction costs that may be incurred on sale or disposals.

Example – Quoted prices in different markets

An entity holds financial assets that are traded in markets A and B. The entity has access to both markets. The price in market A is C25 and costs to transact in that market are C5 (the net amount that would be received for the asset in that market is C20). The price in market B is C35 and costs to transact in that market are C20 (the net amount that would be received for the asset in that market is C15). In that case, the most advantageous market is market A. The estimate of fair value would be determined using the price in market A (C25). That price would not be adjusted for costs to transact in that market.

67045

Bid and ask prices

6.7.110 As stated in a paragraph 6.7.99 above, financial instruments may be traded on exchanges, in dealer markets, and in brokered transactions. Closing prices of financial instruments such as stocks, bonds, options, warrants etc, are readily and regularly available on exchange markets and these are used to value instruments identical to those being traded. However, many securities and financial instruments that are not traded on the organised exchanges are traded in dealer markets, such as AIM and NASDAQ. In such markets, dealers stand ready to trade (either buy or sell for their own account), thereby providing liquidity by using their capital to hold an inventory of the securities for which they make a market. Typically, bid and ask prices are more readily and regularly available than closing prices. Similarly, in a brokered market, brokers attempt to match buyers with sellers but do not stand ready to trade for their own account. The broker knows the prices bid and asked by the respective parties, but each party is typically unaware of another party's price requirements. Prices of completed transactions are sometimes available. Brokered markets include electronic communication networks (ECNs), in which buy and sell orders are matched.

6.7.111 In an active dealer market where bid and ask prices are more readily and regularly available than closing prices, fair value should be determined using these prices. However, the price that will normally be appropriate for valuation purposes will depend on whether the relevant financial instrument being valued is an asset or a liability, and whether it is already held or to be acquired. The standard specifies the appropriate quoted market prices that should be used as indicated in the table below. [IAS 39 para AG72].

	Instrument held	Instrument to be acquired
Financial asset	Bid	Ask
Financial liability	Ask	Bid

The bid price represents the price a dealer is willing to pay for the instrument and, therefore, the price the entity would receive if it sold the asset. The ask price represents the amount at which a dealer is willing to sell the instrument and, therefore, the price that the entity would have to pay to acquire the asset. The ask price (also known as the 'offer' price) will almost always be higher than the bid price. The difference represents the dealer's profit, which is called the 'spread'. The standard clarifies that the terms 'bid price' and 'asking (offer) price' should be used in the context of quoted market prices and the 'bid-ask' spread should be interpreted as including only transaction costs. [IAS 39 para AG70].

Example 1 – Treatment of bid-ask spread on initial recognition

An entity purchases an equity financial asset that it classifies as equity available-for-sale, paying the ask (offer) price of C102 and a brokerage commission of C3. At the balance sheet date, the entity uses the bid price to re-measure the financial asset and to recognise changes in fair value in other comprehensive income.

The following data is relevant:

	Acquisition	Balance sheet date
Reference price		
Bid price	C100	C110
Ask or offer price	C102	C113

Financial assets classified as available-for-sale should be initially recognised at fair value, plus transaction costs paid to acquire the asset.

As stated above, the ask price represents the amount at which a dealer is willing to sell and, therefore, the price that the entity would have to pay to acquire the asset. The difference between the bid price that represents the asset's fair value and the ask price (the bid-ask spread) is a transaction cost. The commission paid to the broker is also a transaction cost.

Given the asset is classified as available-for-sale (that is, not at fair value through profit or loss) the transaction costs are included in the initial carrying value of the asset. Therefore, the asset will be recorded at its fair value of C100 (bid price) plus the bid-ask spread (C2) plus commission (C3), a total of C105. At the balance sheet date, the asset will be valued at bid price (C110) at that date and any difference between this price and the amount recognised initially (C5) will be recorded in other comprehensive income.

Therefore, the appropriate accounting entries at initial recognition and at the balance sheet date are as follows:

	Dr C	Cr C
At acquisition		
Available-for-sale asset (bid price inclusive of transaction costs)	105	
Cash		105
At balance sheet date		
Available-for-sale asset	5	
Gain in other comprehensive income		5

If the asset is a debt instrument, the bid-ask spread, brokerage commission, and any premium, discount or other deferred fees and costs, are subsequently amortised and recognised as part of interest income over the asset's life using the effective interest method.

If the market price had not changed since the date of acquisition, the entity would report a loss of the difference between C105 and bid price of C100, that is a loss of C5.

Example 2 – Treatment of bid-ask spread not included in initial carrying value of a financial asset

The facts are the same as in example 1 above, except that the entity classifies the financial asset as at fair value through profit or loss.

Financial assets classified as at fair value through profit or loss should be recognised initially at fair value. As stated in paragraph 6.7.20 above, transaction costs arising on a financial asset classified as at fair value through profit or loss are immediately recognised in profit or loss and do not form part of the initial carrying value of the asset. Hence, the asset is measured on initial recognition using the bid price (C100). At the balance sheet date, the asset will be valued at bid price (C110) at that date and any difference between this price and the amount recognised initially (C10) will be recorded in profit or loss.

The appropriate accounting entries at initial recognition and at the balance sheet date are as follows:

	Dr C	Cr C
At acquisition		
Available-for-sale asset (bid price)	100	
Profit or loss (bid-ask spread of C2 + commission of C3)	5	
Cash		105
At balance sheet date		
Available-for-sale asset	10	
Gain		10

6.7.112 The standard does not permit the use of mid-market price (average of bid and ask prices) for valuation purposes when quoted bid and ask prices are available. This is because applying mid-market prices to an individual instrument would result in entities recognising up-front gains and losses for the difference between the bid-ask price and the mid-market price. [IAS 39 para BC99]. This makes sense as the mid-market price cannot be relied upon to represent the price at which a market transaction would occur. The IASB Expert Advisory Panel report issued in October 2008 clarifies that if a valuation technique is used to estimate fair value and the model calculates a mid-market price, fair value should be adjusted to take into account the relevant bid-offer spread. However, IAS 39 offers a concession in circumstances where an entity holds assets and liabilities with offsetting market risks. In those circumstances, the entity may use mid-market prices as a basis for establishing fair values for the offsetting risk positions and apply the bid or ask price to the net open position as appropriate. [IAS 39 para AG72]. The IASB believes that use of the mid-market price is appropriate because the entity has locked in its cash flows from the asset and liability and potentially could sell the matched position without incurring the bid-ask spread. It is presumed that such matching positions would be settled within a similar time period.

6.7.113 The rules applicable to some investment funds require net asset values to be reported to investors on the basis of mid-market prices. The existence of regulations that require a different measurement basis for specific purposes does not justify a departure from the general requirement to use the current bid price in the absence of a matching liability position. Therefore, in its financial statements, an investment fund should measure its assets at current bid prices. In reporting its net asset value to investors, an investment fund may wish to provide a reconciliation between the fair values recognised on its balance sheet and the prices used for the net asset value calculation. [IAS 39 para IG E2.1].

Unavailability of published prices

6.7.114 Where current prices of financial instruments are unavailable at the reporting date, the price of the most recent transaction should be used adjusted for any changes in conditions between the date of the transaction and the balance sheet date. [IAS 39 para AG 72]. This is essentially a valuation technique that is considered further from paragraph 6.7.118 below.

6.7.115 If a published price quotation in an active market does not exist for a financial instrument in its entirety, but active markets exist for its component parts, fair value is determined on the basis of the relevant market prices for the component parts. [IAS 39 para AG 72]. This is relevant for complex financial instruments, which by their nature are illiquid and prices cannot be obtained as an instrument in their own right. An example might be a commodity-linked debt instrument whose coupon is indexed to the price of crude oil, but where the coupon can never exceed 10% nor be less than 0%. In that situation, as active markets exist for the basic components (the debt instrument and derivatives linked to that commodity), but not for the whole instrument, an overall valuation can be obtained by combining the values of the component parts.

Large blocks of instruments

6.7.116 The fair value of a portfolio of financial instruments is the product of the number of units of the instrument and its quoted market price. [IAS 39 paras AG71 to AG73]. This definition precludes an entity from using a 'blockage' factor (that is, a premium or discount based on the relative size of the position held, such as a large proportion of the total trading units of an instrument) in determining the fair value of a large block of financial instruments. In other words, if an entity holds a large block of a particular instrument and the only available market exit prices come from transactions involving small blocks, no adjustment should be made for the expected effect of selling the large block in a single transaction as illustrated in the following example, taken from the implementation guidance to IAS 39.

Example – Valuation of large holding

Entity A holds 15% of entity B's share capital. The shares are publicly traded in an active market. The currently quoted price is C100. Daily trading volume is 0.1% of outstanding shares. Because entity A believes that the fair value of the entity B shares it owns, if sold as a block, is greater than the quoted market price, entity A obtains several independent estimates of the price it would obtain if it sells its holding. These estimates indicate that entity A would be able to obtain a price of C105, that is, a 5% premium above the quoted price.

The published price quotation in an active market is the best estimate of fair value. Therefore, entity A should use the published price quotation (C100). Entity A cannot depart from the quoted market price solely because independent estimates indicate that entity A would obtain a higher (or lower) price by selling the holding as a block. [IAS 39 IG para E2.2].

6.7.117 Although the converse situation is not dealt with in the standard, it follows that if an entity holds only a small number of instruments and the available market exit prices come from transactions involving large blocks, the entity should not adjust the available price for the potential effect of selling individual instruments.

Valuation techniques in the absence of an active market

6.7.118 The best evidence of fair value is the quoted price in an active market. If the market for a financial instrument is not active, fair value should be determined using a valuation technique. The objective of using a valuation technique is to establish what the transaction price would have been on the measurement date in an arm's length exchange motivated by normal business considerations. This is by no means an easy task and involves the exercise of a significant amount of judgement. Even at the end of the most careful and detailed valuation, there will be uncertainty about the final numbers, coloured by the assumptions of risks and returns and any resulting bias introduced in the process.

6.7.119 As the objective of the valuation process is to arrive at a reasonable estimate of a financial instrument's fair value, the technique used should reasonably reflect how the market could be expected to price the instrument. That expectation is likely to be met if the valuation technique makes maximum use of market inputs and relies as little as possible on entity-specific inputs. Also the inputs should reasonably represent market expectations and measures of the risk-return factors inherent in the financial instrument. In other words, an acceptable valuation technique should incorporate all factors that market participants would consider in setting a price, and be consistent with accepted economic methodologies for pricing financial instruments. [IAS 39 paras AG75 to AG76]. A valuation technique should, therefore, reflect how the market could be expected to price the instrument under the conditions that exist at the measurement date. Even where a market is considered to be inactive, the most recent transaction prices should be considered as an input to a valuation model, provided that these are not forced transactions. Current market conditions cannot be ignored.

6.7.120 Periodically, an entity should calibrate the valuation techniques it uses and test their validity using prices from any observable current market transactions in the same instrument (that is, without modification or repackaging) or based on any available observable market data. [IAS 39 para AG 76]. As market conditions change, it might be necessary either to change the models used or to make additional adjustments to model valuations. Valuation adjustments are appropriate if they result in a better estimate of the price at which an orderly transaction would take place between market participants on the measurement date. Valuation adjustments include, for example, model deficiencies highlighted through calibration of the model, liquidity adjustments and credit adjustments. Adjustments to valuation technique are not appropriate if they adjust the measurement away from fair value, for example, for conservatism. [IASB Expert Advisory Panel report, October 2008].This process is not only important but essential, as the benchmark for comparison in most valuations remains the market price. When a value from the use of a valuation technique is significantly different from market price, there are two possibilities: one is that the valuation is correct and the market is wrong; the other is that the valuation is wrong and the market is correct. The presumption should be that the market is correct.

6.7.121 Valuation techniques that are well established in financial markets include recent market transactions, reference to a transaction that is substantially the same and discounted cash flows and option pricing models. These techniques are considered below. If there is a valuation technique commonly used by market participants to price the instrument and that technique has been demonstrated to provide reliable estimates of prices obtained in actual market transactions, that technique should be used. [IAS 39 para AG 74]. For example, well established external proprietary software packages are available for pricing many types of financial options. An entity that holds or writes one of those options would use the model best suited for the type of option held or written.

6.7.122 Valuation techniques used to estimate fair value should be applied on a consistent basis. A change in the valuation techniques used is appropriate only if the change results in a more reliable estimate of fair value, for example, as new markets develop or as new and improved valuation techniques become available.

Inputs to valuation techniques

6.7.123 As explained above, an appropriate valuation technique should incorporate observable market data about the market conditions and other factors that are likely to affect the instrument's fair value. The technique would be only as robust as the inputs used. Market inputs should be determined based on information that is timely, originated from sources independent of the entity and used by market-place participants in making pricing decisions. Examples of market inputs that may be used, directly or indirectly, as a basis for determining a financial instrument's fair value include the following:

- The time value of money (that is, interest at the basic or risk-free rate).

  Basic interest rates can usually be derived from observable government bond prices and are often quoted in financial publications. These rates typically vary with the expected dates of the projected cash flows along a yield curve of interest rates for different time horizons.

  For practical reasons, an entity may use a well-accepted and readily observable general rate, such as LIBOR or a swap rate, as the benchmark rate. However, as benchmark is not a risk free interest rate, the credit risk adjustment appropriate to the particular financial instrument is determined on the basis of its credit risk in relation to the credit risk in this benchmark rate.

  In some countries, the central government's bonds may carry a significant credit risk and may not provide a stable benchmark basic interest rate for instruments denominated in that currency. Some entities in these countries may have a better credit standing and a lower borrowing rate than the central government. In such a case, basic interest rates may be more appropriately determined by reference to interest rates for the highest rated corporate bonds issued in the currency of that jurisdiction.

- Credit risk.

  The effect on fair value of credit risk (that is, the premium over the basic interest rate for credit risk) may be derived from observable market prices for traded instruments of different credit quality or from observable interest rates charged by lenders for loans of various credit ratings.

- Foreign currency exchange prices.

  Active currency exchange markets exist for most major currencies, and prices are quoted daily in financial publications.

- Commodity prices.

  There are observable market prices for many commodities.

- Equity prices.

  Prices (and indices of prices) of traded equity instruments are readily observable in some markets. Present value based techniques may be used to estimate the current market price of equity instruments for which there are no observable prices.

- Volatility (that is, magnitude of future changes in price of the financial instrument or other item).

  Measures of the volatility of actively traded items can normally be reasonably estimated on the basis of historical market data or by using volatilities implied in current market prices

■ Pre-payment risk and surrender risk.

This is the risk that a financial instrument may be pre-paid or surrendered earlier than its maturity date. Expected pre-payment patterns for financial assets and expected surrender patterns for financial liabilities can be estimated on the basis of historical data. However, the fair value of a financial liability that can be surrendered by the counterparty cannot be less than the present value of the surrender amount (see para 6.7.151 below).

■ Servicing costs for a financial asset or a financial liability.

Costs of servicing can be estimated using comparisons with current fees charged by other market participants. If the costs of servicing a financial asset or financial liability are significant and other market participants would face comparable costs, the issuer would consider them in determining the fair value of that financial asset or financial liability. It is likely that the fair value at inception of a contractual right to future fees equals the origination costs paid for them, unless future fees and related costs are out of line with market comparables.

[IAS 39 para AG 82].

Recent transaction prices

6.7.124 Where, current prices of financial instruments are unavailable at the reporting date, the price of the most recent transaction should be used. [IAS 39 para AG 72]. This is a fairly simple technique and provides a foundation for estimating fair value, as long as there has not been a significant change in economic circumstances since the relevant transaction occurred.

6.7.125 If, however, conditions have changed since the relevant transaction occurred, the fair value should reflect the change in conditions by reference to current prices or rates for similar financial instruments, as appropriate. That means, the most recent market-exit transaction price would be adjusted for changes due to passage of time as long as such an adjustment is capable of producing a reasonable estimate of fair value. It would also be adjusted if changes in market conditions indicate that transactions occurring at the balance sheet date probably would not have occurred at that price. An example would be a change in the risk-free interest rate following the most recent price quote for a corporate bond. That observable price would be adjusted to reflect the interest for the period between the transaction date and the measurement date (to take into account the time value of money), the effect on fair value of the changes in rates and any cash distribution in that period. Similarly, if the entity can demonstrate that the last transaction price is not fair value (for example, because it reflected the amount that an entity would receive or pay in a forced transaction, involuntary liquidation or distress sale), that price should be adjusted. [IAS 39 para AG 72].

6.7.126 However, it may not always be possible to make the adjustment referred to above, because not all the information may be available at each measurement date. For example, at the date that an entity makes (or acquires) a debt instrument that is not actively traded, the transaction price is also a market price. At the next measurement date, although the general level of market interest rates are available, the entity may not have information from recent transactions to determine the appropriate credit spread over the basic interest rate that market participants would consider in pricing the instrument on that date. In that situation, in the absence of evidence to the contrary, it would be reasonable to assume that no changes have taken place in the spread that existed at the date the loan was made. However, the entity would be expected to make reasonable efforts to determine whether there is evidence that there has been a change in such factors. When evidence of a change exists, the entity would consider the effects of the change in determining the financial instrument's fair value. [IAS 39 para AG 78].

Using price information about similar financial instruments

6.7.127 Another market based valuation technique estimates a financial instrument's value by using quoted prices for similar financial instruments in active markets, adjusted as appropriate for differences, whenever that information is available. Instruments are considered to be similar if they have similar remaining maturity, cash flow pattern, currency, credit risk, collateral and interest basis. [IAS 39 para AG77]. Estimating a financial instrument's fair value based on the market price of a similar financial instrument is best explained by an example.

Example – Valuation based on market price of a similar financial instrument

On 1 January 20X5, entity A acquires a bond issued by entity B through a private placement. The consideration paid and, therefore, the bond's fair value at initial recognition is C1 million. The entity classifies the bond as at fair value through profit or loss. The bond has no observable market price. At 31 December 20X5, the entity is able to identify actively traded corporate bonds that are similar to its bond.

In carrying out the evaluation, the major elements of the two bonds that should be compared are as follows:

- The amount and timing of the contractual cash flows, including pre-payment expectations.

- The currency in which the bonds are payable.

- The credit risk rating and the factors on which changes in the credit risk rating are dependent. For example, the fair value of bonds issued by entities with different industry and geographical bases would be expected to respond differently to changes in the market factors.

- Any other term and conditions that could affect the bond's fair value.

6.7.128 By definition, similar financial instruments are not identical and some of the differences will cause the fair value to be different. Therefore, it is necessary to ensure that the effect on fair value of any such differences is reasonably determinable. In the above example, the initial net effects of differences may be discerned by comparing the fair values of the two instruments at the acquisition date of the non-traded bond, assuming that its fair value is equal to the consideration paid. It is likely that the private placement bond's fair value will be less than that of the market-traded bond, because it is less marketable. Therefore, it may be reasonable to assume that any premium for marketability differences between the effective interest rates of the two bonds at the date the entity acquired its bond remains unchanged from period to period, except if an observable event that could be expected to affect marketability takes place.

Other valuation techniques

6.7.129 Where it is not possible to estimate a financial instrument's fair value by reference to market prices, the entity uses other valuation techniques (pricing models and methodologies). Because they require more estimation and assumptions, they are necessarily more subjective than the market price approach. Two valuation techniques that are widely used are the discounted cash flow (present value) approach and option pricing models.

6.7.130 Present value is a technique used to link future amounts (cash flows) to the present through a discount rate. Present value concepts are central to the development of techniques for estimating the fair value of financial instruments because the market exit price of a financial instrument represents market participant's collective estimate of the present value of its expected cash flows. Therefore, cash flows and discount rate should reflect only factors that are specific to the financial instrument being measured and should reflect assumptions that market participants would use in their estimates of fair value. Also, as the cash flows used are estimates rather than known amounts, a fair value estimate, using present value, is made under conditions of uncertainty. As market participants generally seek compensation for bearing the uncertainty inherent in cash flows (risk premium), the effect of variability (risk) in the cash flows should be reflected either in the cash flows or in the discount rate.

6.7.131 In applying discounted cash flow analysis, an entity uses discount rates equal to the prevailing rates of return for financial instruments having substantially the same terms and characteristics, including the credit quality of the instrument, the remaining term over which the contractual interest rate is fixed, the remaining term to the principal's re-payment and the currency in which payments are to be made. Short-term receivables and payables with no stated interest rate may be measured at the original invoice amount if the effect of discounting is immaterial. [IAS 39 para AG 79].

6.7.132 Option pricing models, first developed by Black and Scholes, can be used to value any asset (not just financial instruments) that has the characteristics of an option, with some caveats. For example, an unquoted equity instrument can be valued as a call option on the entity's assets, the exercise price of the call being equal to the value of the entity's debt. Option pricing models are based on the premise that it is possible to create a replicating portfolio using a combination of the underlying asset and risk-free borrowing and lending to create the same cash flows as the option being valued. The principles of arbitrage then apply and the option's value is then equal to the value of the replicating portfolio. Although real markets do not always follow the idealised behaviour of financial models, these portfolios constructed in line with theoretical models have been found to be robust in practice, despite their imperfections.

Broker quotes and pricing services

6.7.133 An entity may not have its own valuation model and may instead rely on broker quotes, third-party pricing services or information from other financial institutions. The existence of such prices doesn't necessarily indicate an active market. In this case, the entity needs to understand how the third party has derived that valuation and whether it is in accordance with the requirements of IAS 39. Factors to consider include:

- Whether and how the valuation incorporates current market events (for example, does it include 'stale' prices).

- How frequently the valuation is updated to reflect changing market conditions.

- The number of sources from which the valuation is derived (a valuation derived from many quotes or data sources generally being preferable to one based on a small number).

- Whether it reflects actual transactions or merely indicative prices.

- Whether it reflects a price at which the entity could be expected to transact (for example, a market to which the entity has access).

- Whether it is consistent with available market information, including any current market transactions in the same or similar assets.

Application to intra-group financial guarantee contracts

6.7.134 The way in which the various valuation techniques discussed above can be applied to determine the fair value of an intra-group financial guarantee contract that is not negotiated in an arm's length transaction is considered in the paragraphs that follow (see from para 6.7.61 for accounting for intra-group financial guarantee contracts).

References to market prices of similar instruments

6.7.135 An entity may be unable to identify a market price for financial guarantees identical to those that either it or a member of its group has issued. However, it may be possible to identify market prices for similar guarantees, credit default swaps or credit insurance products, the price of which could be adjusted. For example, parent P has guaranteed C100 million of five year debt issued by subsidiary S. It may be possible to identify credit insurance products issued by a bank relating to debt of this amount, maturity and credit quality.

However, an adjustment may still be necessary, for example, to reflect liquidity aspects and differences between P's credit rating and that of the bank.

Interest rate differentials

6.7.136   Under this method, the entity calculates the value of the difference between the interest charged on the guaranteed loan and what would have been charged had the loan not been guaranteed. The premise is that the interest that the bank is willing to forego represents a 'price' that it is willing to pay for the guarantee. For example, parent P has guaranteed C100 million of five year debt issued by subsidiary S. Subsidiary S pays interest of X% on the debt. In the absence of the guarantee, the bank would impose an interest rate of Y%. Hence, the fair value of the guarantee represents the difference in the present value of the interest payments over the period of the guarantee.

6.7.137   This model is simple in principle, but presents practical problems when attempting to measure Y%. It is unlikely that the bank would provide a reliable estimate. Determining Y% requires an estimate of the credit spread (for example, above a base index such as LIBOR) appropriate to subsidiary S in isolation. This may prove difficult as, even without the guarantee, subsidiary S's credit rating will benefit from the company being a member of parent P's group. Nevertheless, models based on determining a stand alone credit rating for subsidiary S do exist and these should enable a reliable estimate to be made.

Discounted cash flow analysis (expected value)

6.7.138   Instead of considering the 'price' that a bank would pay for a guarantee, it might be possible to consider the 'price' that the issuer would demand for accepting the guarantee obligation. This can be estimated using a probability-adjusted discounted cash flow analysis. For example, parent P has guaranteed C100 million of five year debt issued by subsidiary S. The probability of default by subsidiary S is estimated at 0.04% (based on historical default rates amongst companies with the same credit rating as subsidiary S) and the loss in the event of default is estimated at 50% (based on subsidiary S's asset base and other collateral available to the bank). The expected value of the liability (its fair value) would, therefore, be C20,000.

6.7.139   Similar to the interest rate differential approach described above, this model is simple in principle, but presents practical problems when attempting to estimate the probability of default and the loss given default. Although data on these points is available, they rely on determining subsidiary S's credit rating as in the interest rate differential approach.

Fair value of derivatives and credit risk

6.7.140   Paragraph AG69 of IAS 39 requires the fair value of a financial instrument to reflect its credit quality. Paragraph AG82(b) adds that where an entity uses a valuation technique to estimate fair value, credit risk would generally be built into the valuation model. Therefore, fair value should incorporate the

67057

impact of credit risk to the extent that credit risk affects the price for which a derivative could be exchanged between willing parties in an arm's length transaction.

6.7.141 Counterparty credit risk typically arises when a derivative is in an asset position at the reporting date. On the other hand, the entity's own credit risk will be incorporated when the derivative is in a liability position at the reporting date. IAS 39 is clear that financial assets measured at fair value need to be valued on an 'exit price' basis, but it is less clear how to estimate the fair value of liabilities. Paragraph BC89 of IAS 39's Basis for Conclusions indicates that credit risk affects the value at which liabilities could be repurchased or settled. In many cases, the only way an entity can settle a derivative liability at the reporting date is through paying the counterparty a 'close-out amount' that does not incorporate changes in the entity's credit risk since the inception of the contract. In other words, an entity often has no practical ability to realise gains by settling liabilities at a lower amount due to deterioration in its own credit risk.

6.7.142 The standard is unclear whether the practical ability to settle a liability in a way that enables the entity to realise gains and losses from changes in its own credit risk should be considered in determining fair value. In our view, either of the following approaches is acceptable for measuring the fair value of liabilities not traded in an active market:

- Fair value based on a presumption that an entity has the practical ability to settle the liability in a way that enables it to realise gains and losses from changes in its own credit risk ('the full own credit risk approach').

- Fair value based on a 'close-out amount' that would be paid to the counterparty. This reflects the amount the entity would pay to settle the liability with the counterparty at the reporting date ('the counterparty close-out approach')

6.7.143 The chosen accounting policy should be applied consistently in both measuring and disclosing fair value. The policy selected should be disclosed where it has a significant effect on either measurement or disclosure.

6.7.144 Depending on the accounting policy chosen, credit risk may have an impact on hedge effectiveness for both cash flow and fair value hedge relationships. When an entity determines fair value for financial liabilities based on the 'counterparty close-out approach', in many cases the entity's own credit risk would not have a significant impact on hedge effectiveness during the period that the derivative is in a liability position. On the other hand, when an entity determines fair value for financial liabilities based on the 'full own credit risk approach', hedge effectiveness would be impacted by changes in the entity's own credit risk. Hedge accounting is covered in chapter 6.8.

Unquoted equity instruments and related derivatives

6.7.145 Normally it is possible to estimate an equity instrument's fair value that does not have a quoted market price in an active market, as well as derivatives that are linked to and must be settled by delivery of such unquoted equity instruments with sufficient reliability by applying valuation techniques based on reasonable assumptions. The fair values of such instruments are deemed to be reliably measurable if:

- the variability in the range of reasonable fair value estimates is not significant for that instrument; or

- the probabilities of the various estimates within the range can be reasonably assessed and used in estimating fair value.

[IAS 39 para AG 80].

6.7.146 There are many situations in which the variability in the range of reasonable fair value estimates is likely not to be significant and, hence, the fair value is reasonably measurable. However, if the range of reasonable fair value estimates is significantly wide and the probabilities of the various estimates cannot be reasonably assessed, an entity is precluded from measuring the instrument at fair value. In that situation, such instruments are measured at cost, less impairment. [IAS 39 paras 46(c), AG81]. It is not permissible for the entity to measure the equity instrument at fair value, for instance, by judgementally picking a fair value estimate within a range.

6.7.147 A similar dispensation applies to derivative financial instruments that can only be settled by physical delivery of such unquoted equity instruments. It does not apply to derivative instruments in any other situations as illustrated in the following example.

> **Example – Reliability of fair value measurement**
>
> An entity acquires a complex stand alone derivative that is based on several underlying variables, including commodity prices, interest rates and credit indices. There is no active market or other price quotation for the derivative and no active markets for some of its underlying variables. The entity contends that the derivative's fair value cannot be reliably measured.
>
> Notwithstanding the entity's contention, there is a presumption that the fair value of derivatives can be determined reliably by reference to appropriate market prices, or prices of similar instruments, or discounted cash flow or other pricing models or by reference to prices/rates for components, with the exception only of derivatives that are linked to and must be settled by delivery of an unquoted equity instrument (see para 6.7.147 above). This is not the situation here and, therefore, the entity cannot measure the derivative at cost or amortised cost.

'Day 1' gain or loss

6.7.148 As noted in paragraph 6.7.98 above, the best evidence of the instrument's fair value on initial recognition is the transaction price. However, it is possible that the instrument's fair value may not be the transaction price. The only exception to using the transaction price is if the fair value is evidenced by comparison with other observable current market transactions in the *same* instrument, or is based on a valuation technique whose variables include *only* data from observable markets. [IAS 39 para AG 76]. In such situations, the entity is required to use this value. Consequently, the difference between the estimated fair value using a valuation technique and the transaction price results in immediate 'day 1' recognition of a gain or loss. The IASB concluded that these conditions were necessary and sufficient to provide reasonable assurance that this fair value was genuine for the purposes of recognising up-front gains or losses. In all other cases, the transaction price gives the best evidence of fair value and 'day 1' gain recognition is precluded, an approach that achieves convergence with US GAAP. [IAS 39 para BC104].

> **Example – Day '1' gain or loss recognition**
>
> Entity A acquires a financial asset for C110, which is not quoted in an active market. The asset's fair value based on the entity's own valuation technique amounted to C115. However, that valuation technique does not solely use observable market date, but relies on some entity-specific factors that market participants would not normally consider in setting a price.
>
> The entity cannot recognise a 'day 1' profit of C5 and record the asset at C115. The use of unobservable entity-specific inputs to calculate a fair value that is different from transaction price on 'day 1' is so subjective that its reliability is called into question. Hence, recognition of a 'day 1' gain or loss is not appropriate. Accordingly, the entity restricts its valuation to the transaction price and the asset is recorded at C110.

6.7.149 A question arises as to whether and how any gain or loss not recognised on 'day 1' should be recognised subsequently, or at all. An unrecognised 'day 1' gain or loss should be recognised after initial recognition only to the extent that it arises from a change in a factor (including time) that market participants would consider in setting a price. [IAS 39 para AG 76A]. It is not clear how the phrase *"a change in a factor (including time) that market participants would consider in setting a price"* should be interpreted. One interpretation is that a gain or loss should remain unrecognised until all market inputs become observable. Another interpretation is that it permits the recognition of 'day 1' gain or loss in profit or loss on a systematic basis over time, even in the absence of any observable transaction data to support such a treatment. Indeed, some constituents asked the Board to clarify whether straight-line amortisation was an appropriate method of recognising the difference. The Board decided not to do this. It concluded that although straight-line amortisation may be an appropriate method in some cases, it will not be appropriate in others. [IAS 39 para BC222(v)(ii)]. This would appear to suggest that an unrecognised 'day 1' gain or loss could be amortised either on a straight line basis or on another rational basis that reflects the nature of the financial instrument (for example, a non-linear amortisation for some option-based derivatives).

6.7.150 It should be noted that an unrecognised 'day 1' gain or loss is not separately identified in the balance sheet. However, IFRS 7 requires disclosure of the unrecognised amount, together with the change in the amount previously deferred, and the entity's accounting policy for determining when amounts deferred are recognised in profit or loss (see chapter 6.9).

Demand deposit liabilities

6.7.151 A demand deposit represents a promise by the deposit-taking institution to deliver cash either to the depositor or to third parties designated by the depositor. It imposes a contractual obligation that is a financial liability. A typical example is a current account in a bank. The current account holder can demand settlement at any time and the bank generally has the right to return the depositor's money at any time (even though that right is seldom exercised). It is often argued that the fair value of the financial liabilities with a demand feature is less than the demand amount, because not all depositors withdraw their money at the earliest opportunity. Often there is a core of deposits (withdrawals replaced by new deposits) that is left outstanding for long periods of time.

6.7.152 However, the IASB was not prepared to concede that demand financial liabilities could have a fair value different from face value until further work had been done, particularly, in respect of insurance contract liabilities. Consequently, IAS 39 makes it clear that the fair value of a financial liability with a demand feature is not less than the amount payable on demand, discounted from the first date that the amount could be required to be paid. [IAS 39 para 49]. This follows from the fact that the maturity date of an item with no contractual repayment terms cannot be later than the earliest date on which payment can be demanded. The Basis for Conclusion section in IAS 39 notes that recognising a financial liability with a demand feature at less than the demand amount would give rise to an immediate gain on the origination of such a deposit, which is not considered appropriate. In substance, the gain represents the benefits of future interest free or low interest use of funds expected to occur as a result of the deposit relationship. Such benefits are not considered to be directly attributable to the rights and obligations that constitute the demand deposit liabilities existing at a measurement date and accordingly should not enter into the estimate of their fair value. The future benefit of the deposit relationship may be recognised as an intangible asset in circumstances where customer relationships are acquired, together with the related portfolio of demand deposits, if the recognition criteria in IAS 38 are met. However, the Basis for Conclusion section in IAS 39 notes that, absent such an acquisition, the market price observed for such financial liabilities is the price at which they are originated between the customer and the deposit-taker, that is, the demand amount. [IAS 39 para BC 94]. In the absence of an acquisition of a portfolio of demand deposits, this customer deposit intangible asset should not be recognised.

Credit risk of liabilities

6.7.153 When financial liabilities are measured at fair value, changes in their credit risk should be reflected in their fair value measurement. Many question whether a liability's credit risk or changes in its credit risk should enter into the measurement of its liabilities. They argue that it is not useful to report lower liabilities when an entity is in financial difficulty precisely because its debt levels are too high and that it would be difficult to explain to users of financial statements the reasons why income would be recognised when a liability's creditworthiness deteriorates. The IASB, however, takes the view that because financial statements are prepared on a going concern basis, credit risk affects the value at which liabilities could be repurchased or settled. Accordingly, a financial liability's fair value reflects the credit risk relating to that liability. Therefore, the IASB decided to include credit risk relating to a financial liability in the fair value measurement of that liability for the following reasons:

- entities realise changes in fair value, including fair value attributable to the liability's credit risk, for example, by renegotiating or repurchasing liabilities or by using derivatives;

- changes in credit risk affect the observed market price of a financial liability and hence its fair value;

- it is difficult from a practical standpoint to exclude changes in credit risk from an observed market price; and

- a financial liability's fair value (that is, the price of that liability in an exchange between a knowledgeable, willing buyer and a knowledgeable, willing seller) on initial recognition reflects its credit risk. Therefore, it is inappropriate to include credit risk in the initial fair value measurement of financial liabilities, but not subsequently.

[IAS 39 para BC89].

6.7.154 It should be noted that the issue relates to the financial liability's credit risk, rather than the entity's creditworthiness. Although the two are closely related, a deterioration of the entity creditworthiness may not, by itself, affect the credit risk of all the entity's liabilities in the same way. For example, the fair value of liabilities secured by valuable collateral, guaranteed by third parties or ranking ahead of virtually all other liabilities is generally unaffected by changes in the entity's creditworthiness. [IAS 39 para BC92]. If an entity designates a financial liability as at fair value through profit or loss, IFRS 7 requires it to disclose the amount of change in the fair value of the financial liability that is attributable to changes in the liability's credit risk (see further chapter 6.9). There is further discussion of how to reflect credit risk into measurement of fair value from paragraph 6.7.140.

6.7.155 In October 2010, the IASB updated IFRS 9. The new requirements retain the classification and measurement requirements of IAS 39 for financial liabilities, including bifurcation of embedded derivatives, except that the effects of changes in the credit risk of liabilities, designated under the fair value option would not affect profit or loss. Changes in fair value of a liability due to an entity's own credit risk will be recognised as a component of 'other comprehensive income'. The new requirements respond to the concern that recognising the effects of changes in the fair value of a liability attributable to the liability's credit risk in profit or loss is counter-intuitive and does not provide useful information, unless the liability is held for trading.

Impairment of financial assets

6.7.156 A financial asset measured at amortised cost is impaired when its carrying value exceeds the present value of the future cash flows discounted at the financial asset's original effective interest rate. A financial asset that is carried at fair value through profit or loss does not give rise to any impairment issues as diminution in value due to impairment is already reflected in the fair value and, hence, in profit or loss. It follows that impairment issues are only relevant to financial assets that are carried at amortised cost and available-for-sale financial assets whose fair value changes are recognised in other comprehensive income.

6.7.157 IAS 39 deals with impairment of financial assets through a two-step process. First, an entity must carry out an impairment review of its financial assets at each balance sheet date. The aim of this review is to determine whether there is objective evidence that impairment exists for a financial asset. [IAS 39 para 58]. This is considered from paragraph 6.7.162 below.

6.7.158 Secondly, if there is objective evidence of impairment, the entity should measure and record the impairment loss in the reporting period. [IAS 39 para 58]. The measurement of impairment losses differs between financial assets carried at amortised cost (see para 6.7.173 below), financial assets carried at cost (see para 6.7.200 below) and available-for-sale financial assets (see para 6.7.201 below). There is also a difference on whether impairment losses can be reversed depending on whether the available-for-sale instrument is debt or equity (see para 6.7.204 below).

Incurred versus expected losses

6.7.159 Under IAS 39, a financial asset or a group of financial assets is impaired and impairment losses are incurred if, and only if, there is objective evidence of impairment as a result of one or more events that occurred after the asset's initial recognition (a 'loss event'). It may not be possible to identify a single, discrete event that caused the impairment. Rather the combined effect of several events may have caused the impairment. In addition, the loss event must have a reliably measurable effect on the present value of estimated future cash flows and be supported by current observable data. [IAS 39 para 59].

6.7.160 Losses expected as a result of future events, no matter how likely, are not recognised. Possible or expected future trends that may lead to a loss in the future (for example, an expectation that unemployment will rise or a recession will occur) are also not taken into account. The standard states that to recognise impairment on the basis of expected future transactions and events would not be consistent with an amortised cost model.

6.7.161 As the impairment model in IAS 39 is based on the 'incurred loss' model and not on an 'expected loss' model, an impairment loss is not recognised at the time an asset is originated, that is, before a loss event can have occurred as illustrated in the following example:

> ### Example – Recognition of an impairment loss on origination
>
> Entity A lends C1,000 to a group of customers. Based on historical experience, entity A expects that 1% of the principal amount of loans given to the customers will not be collected.
>
> Entity A is not permitted to reduce the carrying amount of a loan asset by C10 on initial recognition through the recognition of an immediate impairment loss.
>
> Under the incurred loss model of IAS 39, an impairment loss is recognised only if there is objective evidence of impairment as a result of a past event that occurred after initial recognition. Furthermore, recognition of an immediate impairment loss based on future expectation would be inconsistent with the general rule that a financial asset should be initially measured at fair value. For a loan asset, the fair value is the amount of cash lent adjusted for any fees and costs (unless a portion of the amount lent is compensation for other stated or implied rights or privileges). [IAS 39 para IGE4.2]. In practice, however, the expectation of loss is built in to the credit spread for the customer.

Objective evidence of impairment

6.7.162 IAS 39 provides examples of factors that may, either individually or taken together, provide sufficient objective evidence that an impairment loss has been incurred in a financial asset or group of financial assets. They include observable data that comes to the attention of the holder of the asset about the following loss events:

- Significant financial difficulty of the issuer or obligor.

- A breach of contract, such as a default or delinquency in interest or principal payments.

- The lender, for economic or legal reasons relating to the borrower's financial difficulty, granting to the borrower a concession that the lender would not otherwise consider.

- It becomes probable that the borrower will enter bankruptcy or other financial reorganisation.

- The disappearance of an active market for that financial asset because of financial difficulties.

- Observable data indicating that there is a measurable decrease in the estimated future cash flows from a group of financial assets since the initial recognition of those assets, although the decrease cannot yet be identified with the individual financial assets in the group, including:

  - adverse changes in the payment status of borrowers in the group (for example, an increased number of delayed payments or an increased number of credit card borrowers who have reached their credit limit and are paying the minimum monthly amount); or

  - national or local economic conditions that correlate with defaults on the assets in the group (for example, an increase in the unemployment rate in the geographical area of the borrowers, a decrease in property prices for mortgages in the relevant area, a decrease in oil prices for loan assets to oil producers, or adverse changes in industry conditions that affect the borrowers in the group).

[IAS 39 para 59].

6.7.163 A downgrade of an entity's credit rating is not, of itself, evidence of impairment, although it may be evidence of impairment when considered with other available information. Other factors that an entity considers in determining whether it has objective evidence that an impairment loss has been incurred include information about:

- The debtors' or issuers' liquidity.

- Solvency, business and financial risk exposures.

- Levels of and trends in delinquencies for similar financial assets.

- National and local economic trends and conditions.

- The fair value of collateral and guarantees.

These and other factors may, either individually or taken together, provide sufficient objective evidence that an impairment loss has been incurred in a financial asset or group of financial assets. [IAS 39 para 60, IG para E4.1].

6.7.164 A decline in the fair value of a financial asset below its cost or amortised cost is not necessarily evidence of impairment (for example, a decline in the fair value of an investment in a debt instrument that results from an increase in the risk-free interest rate). Also, in contrast with the fifth bullet point mentioned in paragraph 6.7.162 above, the disappearance of an active market because an entity's financial instruments are no longer publicly traded is not evidence of impairment. [IAS 39 para 60].

Evidence of impairment for equity instruments

6.7.165 The standard provides additional guidance about impairment indicators that are specific to investments in equity instruments. They apply in addition to the impairment indicators described above, which focus on the assessment of impairment in debt instruments.

6.7.166 The additional impairment indicators that may indicate that the equity investment's cost may not be recovered are:

- Significant adverse changes in the technological, market, economic or legal environment in which the issuer operates. For example, such changes include but are not limited to:

  - Structural changes in the industry or industries in which the issuer operates, such as changes in production technology or the number of competitors.

  - Changes in the level of demand for the goods or services sold by the issuer resulting from factors such as changing consumer tastes or product obsolescence.

  - Changes in the political or legal environment affecting the issuer's business, such as enactment of new environment protection, tax or trade laws.

  - Changes in the issuer's financial condition evidenced by changes in factors such as its liquidity, credit rating, profitability, cash flows, debt/equity ratio and level of dividend payments.

- A 'significant' or 'prolonged' decline in the fair value of an investment in an equity instrument below its cost.

[IAS 39 para 61].

6.7.167 In the context of the last bullet point above, the IFRIC confirmed that a significant decline in fair value should be evaluated against the original cost at initial recognition and 'prolonged' should be evaluated against the period in which the fair value of the investment has been below that original cost. In May 2009 the IFRIC tentatively decided, that a significant or prolonged decline cannot be considered only an indicator of possible impairment in determining whether there is objective evidence. When such a decline exists, recognition of an impairment loss is required. Furthermore, any further declines in value after an impairment loss has been recognised in profit or loss should be recognised immediately in profit or loss. [IAS 39 para IG E4.9]. IAS 39 refers to original cost on initial recognition of an equity instrument and does not permit a prior impairment to establish a new deemed cost against which subsequent declines in fair value are evaluated. [IFRIC Update April 2005]. However, no guidance is provided on what is a 'significant' or 'prolonged' decline in the fair value of an equity instrument. Consequently, judgement is required.

6.7.168 Whether a decline in fair value below cost is considered as 'significant' must be assessed on an instrument-by-instrument basis. In our view, the assessment of significant should be based on both qualitative and quantitative factors. An entity should develop an accounting policy for assessing a 'significant' decline in fair value.

6.7.169 The expected level of volatility for an instrument may also be a factor that entities should take into consideration when assessing what is 'significant'. Volatility is a tendency of a stock's value to fluctuate. Stocks with higher volatility are considered riskier because their value changes more from day to day. Stocks will a lower volatility are more stable and, therefore, viewed as less risky. For example, a company may hold listed shares in an established supermarket chain whose share price changes by 3% over a period of time and listed shares in a speculative mining enterprise whose share price fluctuates by 10% over the same period. In this case, a larger decline in the mining company's shares might be tolerated before an entity records an impairment loss, given its greater volatility compared with the supermarket chain. It is also important to note that where volatility is taken into account in a company's assessment of whether a decline is significant, the volatility is considered relative to the instrument's fair value at the date impairment is being considered, not its original cost. In addition, that volatility should be determined over a relatively long period. For example, a market downturn due to decline in the overall economy over a short period of time would not be considered adequate to establish an estimate of expected future volatility.

6.7.170 What is a 'prolonged' decline in fair value will also require judgement and a policy will need to be established. In general, a period of 12 months or greater below original cost is likely to be a 'prolonged' decline. However, the assessment of 'prolonged' should not be compared to the entire period that the investment has been or is expected to be held. For example, if a security's fair value has been below cost for 12 months, whether that security has been held or is intended to be held for two or 20 years is irrelevant. The assessment is whether the period of 12 months accords with the entity's chosen policy.

6.7.171 Following the amendment to IAS 39 described in paragraph 6.7.41, on reclassification of an equity instrument out of a category measured at fair value (that is, held-for-trading or available-for-sale) and into another category, the fair value at the date of reclassification becomes its new cost or amortised cost. [IAS 39 para 50C, F]. This new cost or amortised cost is the basis against which future 'significant' or 'prolonged' declines in fair value should be assessed.

6.7.172 In practice, an entity may have purchased securities in a company on multiple dates and at different prices. IAS 39 does not provide guidance on this point. By analogy to IAS 2, in our view the basis for measuring the cost for calculating impairment could be a specific identification method, weighted average cost or FIFO method. The basis should be the same as the basis for calculating realised gains or losses upon disposal and should remain consistent across periods. This is an accounting policy choice and should be applied consistently.

Financial assets carried at amortised cost

General requirements

6.7.173 Financial assets carried at amortised cost are those that are classified as either loans and receivables or held-to-maturity. If there is objective evidence that an impairment loss on such an asset has been incurred, the amount of the loss should be measured as the difference between the asset's carrying amount and the present value of estimated future cash flows. The expected cash flows should exclude future credit losses that have not been incurred and should be discounted at the financial asset's original effective interest rate (that is, the effective interest rate computed at initial recognition). [IAS 39 para 63].

6.7.174 The standard allows the carrying amount of the asset to be reduced either directly by writing it down or through use of an allowance account such as a loan loss provision or provision for bad and doubtful debts. However, the amount of the loss should be recognised in profit or loss. [IAS 39 para 63]. The asset's carrying amount in the entity's balance sheet is stated net of any related allowance. [IAS 39 para AG 84].

6.7.175 In some circumstances, it may not be practicable to make a reasonably reliable direct estimate of the present value of future cash flows expected from an impaired financial asset measured at amortised cost. As a practical expedient, the carrying amount of the impaired asset may be determined in these circumstances on the basis of an instrument's fair value using an observable market price. [IAS 39 para AG 84].

6.7.176 A loan's observable market price is the loan's quoted price that can be obtained from reliable market sources. For example, loans with an active secondary market could be measured based on the observable market price. Similarly, an entity that has a viable plan to dispose of loans in a bulk sale could measure impairment by comparison to the net proceeds received on similar loan sales. However, it is likely that the use of the observable market price will be infrequent, because either there may not be a market for the loans or the market may be illiquid.

6.7.177 The expected future cash flows that are included in the calculation are the contractual cash of the instrument itself, reduced or delayed based on the current expectations of the amount and timing of these cash flows as a result of losses incurred at the balance sheet date. In circumstances where the amount outstanding is expected to be collected in full, but the collection period is delayed, an impairment loss must still be recognised, unless the creditor receives full compensation (for example, in the form of penalty interest) for the period of the delinquency, as illustrated in the example below.

Example – Impairment arising from changes in the amount and timing of cash flows

Entity A is concerned that, because of financial difficulties, customer B will not be able to make all principal and interest payments due on a loan in a timely manner. It negotiates a restructuring of the loan. Entity A expects that customer B will be able to meet its obligations under the restructured terms in any of the 5 scenarios indicated below.

- Customer B will pay the original loan's full principal amount 5 years after the original due date, but none of the interest due under the original terms.

- Customer B will pay the original loan's full principal amount on the original due date, but none of the interest due under the original terms.

- Customer B will pay the original loan's full principal amount on the original due date with interest only at a lower interest rate than the interest rate inherent in the original loan.

- Customer B will pay the original loan's full principal amount 5 years after the original due date and all interest accrued during the original loan term, but no interest for the extended term.

- Customer B will pay the original loan's full principal amount 5 years after the original due date and all interest, including interest for both the loan's original term and the extended term.

[IAS 39 para IG E4.3].

Given that customer B is in financial difficulties, an impairment loss has been incurred, as there is objective evidence of impairment. The amount of the impairment loss for a loan measured at amortised cost is the difference between the loan's carrying amount and the present value of future principal and interest payments discounted at the loan's original effective interest rate.

In the first four scenarios above, the present value of the future principal and interest payments discounted at the loan's original effective interest rate will be lower than the loan's carrying amount. Therefore, an impairment loss is recognised in those cases.

In the final scenario, even though the timing of payments has changed, the lender will receive interest on interest, and the present value of the future principal and interest payments discounted at the loan's original effective interest rate will equal the carrying amount of the loan. Therefore, there is no impairment loss. However, this fact pattern is unlikely given customer B's financial difficulties.

6.7.178 Where an impaired financial asset is secured by collateral, the calculation of the present value of the estimated future cash flows of the collateralised financial asset should reflect the cash flows that may result from foreclosure less costs for obtaining and selling the collateral, whether or not foreclosure is probable. [IAS 39 para AG 84]. As the measurement of the impaired financial asset reflects the collateral asset's fair value, the collateral is not recognised as an asset separately from the impaired financial asset, unless it meets the recognition criteria for an asset in another standard. [IAS 39 IG para E4.8].

6.7.179 For financial assets reclassified to another category following the amendment to IAS 39 in October 2008, see paragraph 6.7.45.

Appropriate discount rate

6.7.180 As stated above, impairment of a financial asset carried at amortised cost is measured by discounting the expected future cash flows using the financial instrument's original effective interest rate. Since impairment reflects a fall in the asset's carrying amount, which is evidenced by a decrease in the estimate of expected cash flows to be received from the financial asset, discounting at a rate of interest that reflects a current market rate of interest would impose fair value measurement on the financial asset. This would not be appropriate for assets that are measured at amortised cost. [IAS 39 para AG 84]. The historical effective rate should be used as the discount rate even where it is lower or higher than the rate on current loans originated by the entity. In other words, loan impairments are based solely on the reduction in estimated cash flows rather than on changes in interest rates. This approach ensures that a financial asset carried at amortised cost that becomes impaired continues to be carried at an amount that considers the present value of all expected future cash flows, in a manner consistent with the asset's measurement before it became impaired.

> **Example – Impairment of fixed rate loan**
>
> The facts are the same as in example 2 in paragraph 6.7.78 above, except that at 31 December 20X9 it became clear that as a result of structural changes in the industry in which the borrower operates, the borrower was in financial difficulties and its credit rating had been downgraded. At that date, the loan's amortised carrying value, calculated at the original effective rate of 6.7322%, amounted to C583,435.
>
> Faced with this objective evidence, the entity believes that the borrower will be unable to make all the remaining 5 annual scheduled repayments of C142,378. Accordingly, the entity restructures the loan under which the annual payment due on 31 December 20Y0 is waived followed by three annual payments of C175,000 until 31 December 20Y3. The interest on the outstanding loan under the revised payment schedule is reduced to 6.3071%.
>
> The present value of the annual payments of C175,000 due on 31 December 20Y1, Y2 and Y3, discounted at the original effective interest rate of 6.7322% amounts to C432,402. Accordingly, the entity recognises an impairment loss of C151,033 (C583,435 – C432,402) in profit or loss on 31 December 20X9. Therefore, the carrying amount is written down by the amount of the impairment loss.

6.7.181 Even if the terms of a loan, receivable or held-to-maturity investment are renegotiated or otherwise modified because of financial difficulties of the borrower, impairment is measured using the original effective interest rate before the terms were modified. [IAS 39 para AG 84]. However, in some situations, significant modification of the terms may result in derecognition of the existing asset and recognition of a new asset.

6.7.182   There are three specific instances where the original discount rate is not used to measure impairment losses.

- For variable rate loans and variable rate held-to-maturity investments, the discount rate for measuring any impairment loss is the current variable rate determined under the contract. [IAS 39 para AG 84].

Example – Discount rate for loan impairment calculation

Entity A has provided a loan of GBP1m to entity B. In entity A's financial statements, the loan is classified as 'loans and receivables' in accordance with IAS 39. The loan was originally priced at three month GBP Libor + 300bp. However, entity B has run into financial difficulty and following renegotiations the loan has been re-priced at three month GBP Libor + 100bp.

Objective evidence that an impairment loss on the loan has been incurred is provided by the fact that the terms of the loan have been re-negotiated (that is, the price of the loan was reduced) in response to the counterparty being in financial difficulties.

The impairment loss should be measured as the difference between the carrying amount of the loan and the present value of estimated future cash flows. Estimated future cash flows should be based on the revised terms of the loan – that is, GBP three month Libor + 100bp. These estimated future cash flows should then be discounted at the loan's effective interest rate, which in this case is the *current* GBP three month Libor + 300bp, according to the terms of the original loan. The amount of the loss should be recognised in profit and loss. It is the *current* GBP three month Libor plus the *original* spread of 300bp that should be used to measure any impairment loss.

In addition, following any impairment, management should consider whether the contractual rights to the financial asset have in substance expired – that is, whether the terms of the loan have been modified to such a large extent that it is in substance a new loan. If they have, the financial asset is derecognised under paragraph 17(a) of IAS 39, and a new asset is recognised for the new loan at its fair value. Derecognition is considered in chapter 6.6.

- For financial assets reclassified out of held-for-trading or available-for-sale, the effective interest rate will be recalculated using the fair value at the date of reclassification (see para 6.7.43). This new effective interest rate will be used to calculate interest income in future periods and considered as the original effective interest rate when measuring impairment. Subsequent to reclassification, an increase in the recoverability of cash flows would also result in an adjusted effective interest rate (see para 6.7.81).

- For a fixed rate loan that is designated as a hedged item in a fair value hedge of interest rate risk, the loan's carrying amount is adjusted for any changes in its fair value attributable to interest rate movements. The loan's original effective interest rate before the hedge, therefore, becomes irrelevant and the effective interest rate is recalculated using the loan's adjusted carrying amount. The adjusted effective rate is used as the rate for discounting the estimated future cash flows for measuring the impairment loss on the hedged loan. [IAS 39 para IG E4.4]. Hedge accounting is considered in chapter 6.8.

6.7.183 Consistent with the initial measurement requirements set out in paragraph 6.7.9 above, cash flows relating to short-term receivables are not discounted if the effect of discounting is immaterial. [IAS 39 para AG 84].

Evaluation of impairment on a portfolio basis

6.7.184 IAS 39 contains specific guidance for assessing and measuring the impairment losses of a group of financial assets that is carried at amortised cost. The assessment process is as follows:

- First, financial assets that are considered to be individually significant are assessed for impairment individually based on whether objective evidence of impairment exists.

- Secondly, all other assets that are not individually significant are assessed for impairment. They may be assessed either individually or collectively on a group basis as indicated below.

- Thirdly, all assets that have been individually assessed for impairment, whether significant or not, but for which there is no objective evidence of impairment, are included within a group of assets with similar credit risk characteristics and collectively assessed for impairment.

- Fourthly, assets that are individually assessed for impairment and for which an impairment loss is (or continues to be) recognised are not included in a collective assessment for impairment.

[IAS 39 para 64].

6.7.185 It seems perhaps illogical and superfluous to subject individual loans that have been reviewed individually for impairment and found not to be impaired to be included again in a portfolio of similar loans for collective assessment. The Basis for Conclusions sets out in extensive detail the arguments for and against this requirement and concludes that impairment that cannot be identified with an individual loan may be identifiable on a portfolio basis. [IAS 39 paras BC111 to BC117].

6.7.186 There is no guidance in the standard as to what is meant by 'individually significant'. What is significant for one entity may not be significant to another, so each entity should assess what is significant based on its own facts and circumstances.

Example – Individual versus collection assessment

An entity has a portfolio of similar receivables amounting to C100m. The entity considers that within this portfolio are C30m of loans that are individually significant. It assesses these loans for impairment on an individual basis and determines that C20m of loans are impaired. Of the remaining C70m loans that are not significant, the entity selects C15m for individual assessment and finds them all to be individually impaired. The rest of the portfolio is subject to an impairment review on a collective basis.

The result of this assessment means that loans amounting to C35m that have been assessed for impairment on an individual basis, whether significant or not, and found to be impaired will not be included for collective assessment. The remaining C65m of loans (C10m of individually significant loans that are found not to be impaired) and C55m that were not assessed for impairment on an individual basis) are included in the collective assessment.

However, loss probabilities and other loss statistics differ at a portfolio level between the C10m of individually evaluated loans that are found not to be impaired and the C55m of loans that were not individually evaluated for impairment. This means that a different amount of impairment may be required for these sub-portfolios. [IAS 39 AG 87].

6.7.187 For the purpose of a collective evaluation of impairment, financial assets should be grouped on the basis of similar credit risk characteristics that are indicative of the debtors' ability to pay all amounts due according to the contractual terms. This may be done on the basis of a credit risk evaluation or grading process that considers asset type, industry, geographical location, collateral type, past-due status and other relevant factors. If an entity does not have a group of assets with similar risk characteristics, it does not make the additional assessment. [IAS 39 para AG 87]. In that case, such assets are individually assessed for impairment.

6.7.188 It should be noted that as soon as information is available that specifically identifies losses on individually impaired assets in a group, those assets should be removed from the group. [IAS 39 para AG 88].

6.7.189 The Basis for Conclusions in IAS 39 provides detailed guidance on how to perform impairment assessments within groups of financial assets. Most of the detailed guidance will be highly relevant to banks and financial institutions that have large portfolios of loans and receivables. The following elements are critical to an adequate process:

- Future cash flows in a group of financial assets should be estimated on the basis of historical loss experience for assets with credit risk characteristics similar to those in the group.

- Entities that have no entity-specific loss experience or insufficient experience should use peer group experience for comparable groups of financial assets.

- Historical loss experience should be adjusted on the basis of current observable data to reflect the effects of current conditions.

- Changes in estimates of future cash flows should be directionally consistent with changes in underlying observable data (such as changes in unemployment rates, property prices, payment status, or other factors indicative of changes in the probability of losses in the group and their magnitude).

■ The methodology and assumptions used for estimating future cash flows should be reviewed regularly to reduce any differences between loss estimates and actual loss experience.

[IAS 39 para BC124].

6.7.190 Applying the above process ensures that the collective assessment of impairment for a group of financial assets is still an 'incurred' and not an 'expected' loss model that aims to reflect the loss events that have occurred with respect to individual assets in the group, but have not yet been identified on an individual asset basis. IAS 39 provides an example of an entity that determines, on the basis of historical experience, that one of the main causes of default on credit card loans is the death of the borrower. Although the death rate is unchanged from one year to the next, some of the borrowers in the group may have died in that year. This indicates that an impairment loss has occurred on those loans, even if, at the year-end, the entity is not yet aware which specific borrowers have died. It would be appropriate for an impairment loss to be recognised for these 'incurred but not reported' (IBNR) losses. However, it would not be appropriate to recognise an impairment loss for deaths that are expected to occur in a future period, because the necessary loss event (the death of the borrower) has not yet occurred. [IAS 39 para AG 90].

6.7.191 The standard allows the use of formula-based approaches or statistical methods to determine impairment losses in a group of financial assets as long as they:

■ Do not give rise to an impairment loss on a financial asset's initial recognition.

■ Are consistent with the general requirements outlined above.

■ Incorporate the effect of the time value of money.

■ Consider the cash flows for all of the remaining life of an asset (not only the next year).

■ Consider the age of the loans within the portfolio.

[IAS 39 para AG 92].

Measurement difficulties in the absence of observable data

6.7.192 Making a reasonably reliable estimate of the amount and timing of future cash flows from an impaired financial asset is a matter of judgement. The best estimate is based on reasonable and supportable assumptions and observable data concerning the ability of a debtor to make payments in relation to circumstances existing at the impairment measurement date.

6.7.193 However, sometimes observable data required to estimate the amount of an impairment loss on a financial asset may be limited or no longer fully relevant to current circumstances. For example, this may be the case when a borrower is in financial difficulties and there is little available historical data relating to similar borrowers. In such cases, an entity should use its judgement to estimate the amount of any impairment loss and to adjust observable data for a group of financial assets to reflect current circumstances. The use of reasonable estimates is an essential part of the financial statement's preparation and does not undermine their reliability. [IAS 39 para 62].

General provisions for bad and doubtful debts

6.7.194 It has not been uncommon for entities under previous GAAPs to determine bad debt provisions for non-performing loans based on a provision matrix or similar formula that specifies fixed provision rates for the number of days a loan or a debt is overdue. For example, the provisioning rates could be 0% if less than 90 days overdue, 20% if 90-180 days, 50% if 181-365 days and 100% if more than 365 days. Such a method of provisioning would not be acceptable under IAS 39, unless it produces a result that is sufficiently close to the one obtained by following a discounted cash flow methodology required by the standard, which is considered highly unlikely. [IAS 39 para IG E4.5].

6.7.195 Similarly, it was fairly common for entities under previous GAAPs to make a general provision for bad and doubtful debts on the grounds of prudence and set aside sums that are not specifically related to losses in a group of assets, but intended to cover unplanned and unexpected losses. Such provisioning methods are not allowed under IAS 39 as it results in impairment or bad debt losses that are in excess of those that can be attributed to incurred losses. Accordingly, amounts that an entity might want to set aside for additional possible impairment in financial assets, such as reserves that cannot be supported by objective evidence about impairment, are not recognised as impairment or bad debt losses under IAS 39. [IAS 39 para IG E4.6]. This does not prevent an entity designating part of its reserves in equity to cover such 'prudence' or related losses.

Recognition of interest on impaired assets

6.7.196 Once a financial asset or a group of similar financial assets has been written down as a result of an impairment loss, interest income is thereafter recognised using the rate of interest used to discount the future cash flows for the purpose of measuring the impairment loss. [IAS 39 para AG 93]. That is the discount in the carrying amount is unwound. This would be the original effective rate for fixed rate instruments carried at amortised cost and current interest rate for floating rate instruments.

6.7.197 An entity should not stop accruing interest on loans that are non-performing. When non-performing loans are reviewed for impairment, the collection or non-collection of the future interest payments would be taken into account in the estimation of future cash flows for the purposes of the impairment calculation. Interest income would be recognised as the discount unwinds.

Example – Income recognition on impaired loans

The facts are the same as in the example in paragraph 6.7.182 above. Following recognition of the impairment loss at 31 December 20X9, the amortised cost amounted to C432,402.

On the assumption that cash inflows will occur as restructured, the amortisation schedule based on the revised cash flows and the original discount rate is shown below. In accordance with paragraph 6.7.196 above, interest income is recognised at the rate of discount used to the measure the impairment.

	Cash in flows	Interest income @ 6.7322%	Carrying amount
1 Jan 20Y0			432,402
31 Dec 20Y0		29,110	461,512
31 Dec 20Y1	175,000	31,070	317,582
31 Dec 20Y2	175,000	21,380	163,962
31 Dec 20Y3	175,000	11,038	–
	525,000	92,598	

Reversal of impairment losses on assets held at amortised cost

6.7.198   As stated in paragraph 6.7.157 above, an impairment review should be carried out at each reporting date. If, in a subsequent period, the amount of the impairment loss decreases and the decrease can be related objectively to an event occurring after the impairment was recognised (such as an improvement in the debtor's credit rating), the previously recognised impairment loss should be reversed either directly or by adjusting an allowance account. The reversal should not result in a carrying amount of the financial asset that exceeds what the amortised cost would have been had the impairment not been recognised at the date the impairment is reversed. The amount of the reversal should be recognised in profit or loss. [IAS 39 para 65]. This is in contrast with an equity instrument where an impairment loss is specifically not reversed (see para 6.7.204).

6.7.199   If a financial asset has been reclassified out of a category measured at fair value (that is, held-for-trading or available-for-sale) and into a category measured at amortised cost, an increase in cash flows would be a reversal of impairment only if the impairment loss was recognised after the date of reclassification. Any other increase in cash flows will be a change in expected cash flows and adjusted cumulatively in accordance with paragraph AG 8 of IAS 39 (see para 6.7.81).

Financial assets carried at cost

6.7.200 As set out in paragraph 6.7.145 above, an unquoted equity instrument that is not carried at fair value because its fair value cannot be reliably measured, or on a derivative asset that is linked to and must be settled by delivery of such an unquoted equity instrument, are measured at cost. For such instruments, if there is objective evidence that an impairment loss has been incurred, the amount of the impairment loss is measured as the difference between the carrying amount of the financial asset and the present value of estimated future cash flows discounted at the current market rate of return for a similar financial asset. Such impairment losses are not permitted to be reversed. [IAS 39 para 66].

Available-for-sale financial assets

6.7.201 When a decline in the fair value of an available-for-sale financial asset has been recognised directly in other comprehensive income and there is objective evidence that the asset is impaired, the cumulative loss that had been recognised directly in other comprehensive income should be reclassified from equity and recognised in profit or loss even though the financial asset has not been derecognised. [IAS 39 para 67]. It is not appropriate to allocate part of the reduction below cost to impairment and part to a fair value movement through other comprehensive income.

6.7.202 The amount of cumulative loss that is recycled to profit or loss is the difference between the acquisition cost (net of any principal repayment and amortisation) and current fair value, less any impairment loss on that financial asset previously recognised in profit or loss. [IAS 39 para 68]. Any portion of the cumulative net loss that is attributable to foreign currency changes on that asset that had been recognised in equity is also recognised in profit or loss (see para 6.7.213 below). Subsequent losses, including any portion attributable to foreign currency changes, are also recognised in profit or loss until the asset is derecognised. [IAS 39 para IG E4.9].

6.7.203 For financial assets reclassified out of a category measured at fair value (that is, held-for-trading or available-for-sale) and into another category, see paragraph 6.7.41.

> **Example – Impairment of available-for-sale debt security**
>
> On 1 January 20X3, an entity purchased C10 million 5 year bond with semi-annual interest of 5% payable on 30 June and 31 December each year. The bond's purchase price was C10,811,100, which resulted in a bond premium of C811,100 and an effective interest rate of 8% (4% on a semi-annual basis). The entity classified the bond as available-for-sale.
>
> The entity received all the interest due in 20X3 and 20X4 on a timely basis. At 31 December 20X4, the amortised cost of the loan amounted to C10,524,226. The cumulative amount recognised in equity to that date was a loss C266,322.

The entity did not receive the half-yearly interest due on 30 June 20X5 and it soon became clear that the issuer was in financial difficulties. At 31 December 20X5, the entity reviews the issuer's financial condition and prospects for repayment of the loan and determines that the bond is impaired. On the basis of the information available at the time, the entity's best estimate of future cash flows (on a yearly basis) is cash receipts of C2m on 31 December 20X6 and C7m on 31 December 20X7, the scheduled repayment date.

Although the bond is non-performing, the entity recognises the interest income for the period to 31 December 20X5 at the original effective interest rate. On this basis, the bond's amortised cost at 31 December 20X5 amounts to C11,383,002.

As the bond is classified as available-for-sale, it is necessary to determine the bond's fair value at 31 December 20X5. As there is no observable market price for the bond, the bond's fair value, can only be obtained by discounting the expected cash flows at the current market rate. As a market rate for a comparable bond may not exist, it would be necessary to derive a current market rate for the bond. One way of estimating the current rate for a comparable bond with terms and credit risk profiles similar to the existing bond is by reference to a benchmark rate or the risk-free rate, which is part of the bond's effective rate of interest of 8%, and amending that rate by the original credit risk premium of the existing bond.

Assume that when the bond was purchased on 1 January 20X3, the risk-free rate was 6% for a debt instrument with the same terms as the one purchased by the entity. Thus, the credit risk premium of the bond is 200 basis points. At 31 December 20X5, the risk-free rate for a similar type of instrument is 8%. Therefore, using the bond's credit risk premium of 200 basis points, the current interest rate for discounting the expected cash flows is 10% (8% + 200 basis point). Using this rate of 10%, the present value of the expected cash flow of C2m and C7m arising on 31 December 20X6 and 31 December 20X7 amounts to C7,603,305.

Therefore, the impairment loss recognised in profit or loss is as follows:

Amortised cost at 31 December 20X4	10,524,226
Accrual of half-yearly interest to 30 June 20X5 @ 4%	420,969
	10,945,195
Accrual of half-yearly interest to 31 December 20X5 @ 4%	437,808
Amortised cost at 31 December 20X5 before impairment	11,383,003
Fair value of bond at 31 December 20X5	(7,603,305)
Impairment arising during 20X5	3,779,698
Recycling of loss recognised in equity	266,322
Impairment recognised in profit or loss	4,046,020
Bond stated in the balance sheet at 31 December 20X5	7,603,305

On 31 December 20X6, the holder received the expected cash flow of C2m. The amortised cost of the bond at 31 December 20X6 amounts to:

Amortised cost at 31 Dec 20X5	7,603.305
Accrual of interest to 31 Dec 20X6 @10%	760,330
	8,363,635
Less cash received at 31 Dec 20X6	2,000,000
Amortised cost at 31 Dec 20X6	6,363,635

Note that once the bond has been written down as a result of an impairment loss, interest income is thereafter recognised using the rate of interest used to discount the future cash flows for the purpose of measuring the impairment loss. (See para 6.7.196.) This rate is 10% as stated above.

During the year to 31 December 20X6, interest rates increased and as a result the bond's fair value at 31 December 20X6 fell to C6.0m. There was no further change in the credit status/rating of the issuer and there is no evidence of any further credit-related impairment since the original assessment of impairment was made during 20X5. At 31 December 20X6, there is a difference between the bond's amortised cost and its fair value as shown below:

Amortised cost at 31 Dec 20X6 as above	6,363,635
Fair value at 31 Dec 20X6	6,000,000
Further reduction	363,635

The further reduction of C363,635 is also the difference between the fair value of C7,603, 305 at 31 December 20X5 after adjusting for interest income of 10% and the cash of £2m received and the fair value of C6,000,000 at 31 December 20X6.

The question arises as to whether the further decrease of C363,635 should be taken to the AFS reserve in equity or recognised as a further impairment loss in profit or loss for the period to 31 December 20X6.

There are two acceptable views. An entity makes an accounting policy choice as to which view it accepts and applies this view to all similar transactions. If material, an entity discloses this policy in its financial statements.

View A – AFS reserve in equity

Without any further objective evidence of impairment, no further impairment charge is recognised in profit or loss. Hence, the change in fair value is recognised in equity.

This view is consistent with paragraph 58 of IAS 39, which requires an entity to assess at each balance sheet date whether there is any objective evidence that a financial asset is impaired. If such evidence exists, the entity should apply the requirement for available-for-sale financial asset considered in paragraphs 6.7.201 and 6.7.202 above. In this situation, at 31 December 20X6, as there is no new evidence of a further credit impairment, the requirements of those paragraphs do not apply and the further decrease of C363,635 is recognised in equity. In addition, IAS 39 paragraph IG E4.10 acknowledges that the AFS reserve in equity can be negative – for example, because of a decline in the fair value of an investment in a debt instrument that results from an increase in the basic risk free interest rate.

Similarly, had interest rates decreased resulting in an increase in fair value, it would be appropriate to recognise that change in the AFS reserve in equity. This would not be considered a reversal of impairment as for a reversal to occur there should be an increase in fair value attributable to an improvement in the issuer's credit standing.

View B – impairment/reversal of impairment in profit or loss

This view is that, at the reporting date, there is still objective evidence of impairment since acquiring the asset and, therefore, a further decline in fair value is recognised in profit or loss as further impairment. Any changes in fair value (gains or losses) subsequent to impairment are reflected in profit or loss up to the asset's amortised cost and afterwards in equity.

This view interprets paragraph 58 of IAS 39 as referring to evidence of impairment since acquiring the asset. This view is also consistent with the treatment in a period in which objective evidence of impairment first arises on an asset where the entire change in fair value (IAS 39 para 68) is recognised in profit or loss, even if some of that change in fair value is market related (for example, due to an increase in interest rates). This is a broader reading of the term event in paragraph 70 of IAS 39 to mean any event rather than only a credit-related event.

This view is also consistent with paragraph IG E4.9 of IAS 39. It states that for non-monetary AFS financial assets that became impaired in a previous period, any subsequent losses including the portion attributable to foreign exchange losses (that are also not additional impairments) are also recognised in profit or loss until the asset is derecognised.

Similarly, had interest rates decreased resulting in an increase in fair value and the increase can be objectively related to an event occurring after the impairment loss was recognised in profit or loss, it would be appropriate to recognise the change in profit or loss as a reversal of the previous impairment in accordance with IAS 39 paragraph 70.

Reversal of impairment losses

6.7.204   It is possible that after an impairment loss has been recognised for an available-for-sale financial asset circumstances change in a subsequent period such that the fair value of the available-for-sale financial instrument increases. In those circumstances, the treatment required by the standard for reversals of impairment losses on available-for-sale debt instruments is different from those on available-for-sale equity instruments as noted below:

- For available-for-sale debt instruments (monetary assets), past impairment losses should be reversed through the profit or loss when fair value increases and the increase can be objectively related to an event occurring after the impairment loss was recognised in profit or loss. [IAS 39 para 70].

- For available-for-sale equity investments (non-monetary assets), past impairment losses recognised in profit or loss should not be reversed through profit or loss when fair value increases. [IAS 39 para 69]. This means that subsequent increases in fair value including those that have the effect of reversing earlier impairment losses are all recognised in equity. This is a significant change from the previous version of the standard.

6.7.205 The inability to reverse impairment losses recognised in profit or loss on available-for-sale equity instruments raises a particular issue for entities that have recognised such impairment losses in their interim reports. This is because, at the subsequent reporting or balance sheet date, conditions may have changed to such an extent that a loss would not have been recognised, or a smaller loss would have been recognised, if the impairment review were first carried out at that date.

6.7.206 The confusion arises because paragraph 28 of IAS 34 requires an entity to apply the same accounting policies in its interim financial statements as are applied in its annual financial statements. This suggests that an impairment loss recognised in the interim period should not be reversed at the subsequent balance sheet date. On the other hand, the same paragraph states that 'the frequency of an entity's reporting (annual, half-yearly, or quarterly) should not affect the measurement of its annual results. To achieve this objective, measurement for interim reporting purposes should be made on a 'year-to-date' basis. This suggests that an impairment loss recognised in one interim period can be reversed at the subsequent balance sheet date.

6.7.207 The IFRS IC considered the matter and issued IFRIC 10 in July 2006. The IFRS IC concluded that the prohibitions on reversals of recognised impairment losses on investments in equity instruments in IAS 39 should take precedence over the more general statement in IAS 34 regarding the frequency of an entity's reporting not affecting the measurement of its annual results.Therefore, any impairment losses that are recognised in a previous interim period in respect of an investment in an equity instrument may not be reversed in a later interim periods or when preparing the annual financial statements. [IFRIC 10 para 8].

Foreign currency financial instruments

General

6.7.208 Financial instruments are often denominated in foreign currencies. The way in which changes in foreign exchange rates in foreign currency financial assets and liabilities should be dealt with is covered in IAS 21. The measurement principles of IAS 39 generally do not override these rules, except in the area of hedge accounting which is considered in chapter 6.8.

6.7.209 Under IAS 21, all transactions in foreign currencies are initially recognised at the spot exchange rate at the date of the transaction. The spot exchange rate is the exchange rate for immediate delivery. It follows that on initial recognition, all foreign currency financial instruments are translated at the spot rate into the entity's functional currency, irrespective of whether the instrument is carried at cost, amortised cost or fair value.

6.7.210   Gains and losses associated with financial instruments, such as interest income and expense and impairment losses, are recognised at the spot exchange rate at the dates on which they arise. Dividends should be recognised in profit or loss when the shareholder's right to receive payment is established. [IAS 18 para 30(c)]. The exchange rate ruling at that date, which is normally the dividend declaration date, is used to record the income. Entities are permitted to use an average rate where it represents an approximation to the spot rate in that period.

Subsequent measurement

6.7.211   The subsequent measurement of foreign currency financial assets and liabilities will depend on whether the assets and liabilities are monetary or non-monetary in nature. Monetary items are units of currency held and assets and liabilities to be received or paid in a fixed or determinable number of units of currency. [IAS 21 para 8]. It follows that financial assets and liabilities that are debt instruments are monetary items. Derivative financial instruments are also monetary items as they are settled at a future date, even though the underlying may be non-monetary. Non-monetary items are all items other than monetary items. In other words, the right to receive (or an obligation to deliver) a fixed or determinable number of units of currency is absent in a non-monetary item. This is the case for financial assets that are equity instruments.

Monetary financial assets

6.7.212   IAS 21 requires that an entity should translate its foreign currency monetary items outstanding at the balance sheet date using the closing spot rate at that date. [IAS 21 para 23(a)]. Exchange differences arising on translating monetary items or on the settlement of monetary items at rates different from those at which they were translated on initial recognition during the period or in previous financial statements, are recognised in profit or loss in the period in which they arise. [IAS 21 para 28]. However, exchange differences on monetary items that are designated as hedging instruments in cash flow hedges or net investments in foreign entities are recognised in equity. [IAS 39 para AG 83].

6.7.213   For the purpose of recognising foreign exchange gains and losses under IAS 21, a foreign currency monetary available-for-sale financial asset is treated as if it were carried at amortised cost in the foreign currency. Accordingly, for such a financial asset, exchange differences arising from changes in amortised cost, such as interest calculated using the effective interest method and impairment losses are recognised in profit or loss. All other gains and losses are recognised in equity. [IAS 39 para 55(b)]. An example illustrating the above treatment is included as example E3.2 in the Implementation Guidance to IAS 39. A similar example is given below.

Example – Available-for-sale debt security denominated in foreign currency

On 1 January 20X1, an entity whose functional currency is the local currency (LC) purchases a foreign currency (FC) denominated bond for its fair value of FC1,000. The bond has 5 years remaining to maturity and a principal amount of FC1,250. Interest is payable annually at 4.7% (that is, FC59) on 31 December each year. Assuming there are no transaction costs, the effective interest rate is 10%. The entity classifies the bond as available-for-sale.

The relevant foreign exchange rates are as follows:

	Average rate FC =	Closing rate FC =
1 January 20X1		LC 1.50
31 December 20X1	LC 1.75	LC 2.00
31 December 20X2	LC 2.25	LC 2.50
31 December 20X3	LC 2.35	LC 2.20
31 December 20X4	LC 2.05	LC 1.90
31 December 20X5	LC 2.10	LC 2.30

For the purpose of this illustrative example, it is assumed that the use of the average exchange rate provides a reliable approximation of the spot rates applicable to the accrual of interest income during the year.

The cumulative gain or loss that is recognised in equity is the difference between the amortised cost (adjusted for impairment, if any) and the fair value of the available-for-sale financial asset in the entity's functional currency.

At 1 January 20X1, the fair value of the bond (FC1,000) translated in the entity's functional currency is LC1,500 and the entry to record this is as follows:

At 1 January 20X1	Dr LC	Cr LC
Available-for-sale financial asset	1,500	
Cash		1,500

The amortisation schedule in foreign currency (FC) is as follows:

Date	Interest income @ 10%	Cash inflow	Amortised cost
1 Jan 20X1			1,000
31 Dec 20X1	100	59	1,041
31 Dec 20X2	104	59	1,086
31 Dec 20X3	109	59	1,136
31 Dec 20X4	113	59	1,190
31 Dec 20X5	119	59	1,250

67083

As the entity classifies the bond as an available-for-sale investment, the asset is treated as an asset measured at amortised cost in foreign currency for the purposes of applying IAS 21. Therefore, the amortisation schedule in the entity's functional currency (LC) shown below is calculated from the above amounts at the appropriate exchange rates as follows:

	Interest income @ 10% (average rate) LC	Cash inflow @ 4.7% (actual rate) LC	Amortised cost LC
1 Jan 20X1			1,500
31 Dec 20X1	175	118	1,557
31 Dec 20X2	234	148	1,643
31 Dec 20X3	256	130	1,769
31 Dec 20X4	232	112	1,889
31 Dec 20X5	250	136	2,003
	1,147	644	

	Amortised cost as above FC	Amortised cost translated at year end rate LC	Carrying amount as determined above LC	Cumulative exchange difference LC	Exchange difference recognised in profit or loss LC
31 Dec 20X1	1,041	2,082	1,557	525	525
31 Dec 20X2	1,086	2,715	1,643	1,072	547
31 Dec 20X3	1,136	2,498	1,769	729	(342)
31 Dec 20X4	1,190	2,261	1,889	372	(358)
31 Dec 20X5	1,250	2,875	2,003	872	500

As the debt instrument is classified as an available-for-sale investment, it is necessary to determine the bond's fair value at each balance sheet date. The bond's fair value at each balance sheet date is given below. The difference between the amortised cost and asset's fair value is the cumulative gain or loss that is recognised in equity. This difference will include exchange differences that would not be separated out from the overall movement recognised in equity. All other changes in foreign exchange rates are recognised in profit or loss as shown above.

	Fair value FC	Fair value at year end rate LC	Amortised cost at year end rate as above LC	Cumulative difference LC	Gain or loss recognised in equity LC
31 Dec 20X1	1,060	2,120	2,082	38	38
31 Dec 20X2	1,070	2,675	2,715	(40)	(78)
31 Dec 20X3	1,140	2,508	2,499	9	49
31 Dec 20X4	1,200	2,280	2,261	19	10
31 Dec 20X5	1,250	2,875	2,875	0	(19)

The movements in the fair value of the bond can be summarised as follows:

	Fair value at the beginning of the period	Interest income	Cash received	Exchange difference recognised in profit or loss	Gain or loss recognised in equity	Fair value at the end of the period
	LC	LC	LC	LC	LC	LC
31 Dec 20X1	1,500	175	(118)	525	38	2,120
31 Dec 20X2	2,120	234	(148)	547	(78)	2,675
31 Dec 20X3	2,675	256	(130)	(342)	49	2,508
31 Dec 20X4	2,508	232	(112)	(358)	10	2,280
31 Dec 20X5	2,280	250	(136)	500	(19)	2,875

Dual currency bond

6.7.214 Dual currency bonds are bonds that are denominated in one currency, but pay interest in another currency at a fixed exchange rate. For example, an entity with pound sterling as a functional currency may issue a debt instrument that provides for the annual payment of interest in euros and the repayment of principal in pound sterling. Sometimes both the interest payments and the principal repayments may be denominated in currencies that are different from the entity's functional currency. For example, an entity with pound sterling functional currency may issue a euro denominated bond that pays interest in US dollars. Such a foreign currency bond can be viewed as a host debt instrument with principal and interest payments denominated in pound sterling and two embedded swaps that convert the pound sterling interest payments into US dollars and the pound sterling principal payments into euros. However, as explained in chapter 6.3, IAS 39 does not permit such embedded foreign currency derivatives to be separated from the host debt instrument, because IAS 21 requires foreign currency gains and losses to be recognised in profit or loss. [IAS 39 para AG33(c)].

6.7.215 We believe the most appropriate accounting treatment would be to analyse the bond into its two components – the interest component that exposes the entity to US dollar exchange rate risk and the principal component that exposes the entity to euro exchange rate risk. Each component would be recognised at its fair value at initial recognition, being the present value of the future payments to be made on the respective components. This means that the entity would have an instalment bond with annual payments denominated in US dollars for the US dollar interest payments and a zero coupon bond denominated in euros for the euro principal payment. The carrying amount of each component would be translated to pound sterling at each period end using the closing exchange rate and the resulting exchange differences recognised in the income statement in accordance with paragraph 28 of IAS 21.

6.7.216 Analysing the dual currency bond into its two components for measurement purposes reports the foreign currency risk on the principal on a discounted basis, recognising that the euro payment is not due until redemption and also captures the foreign exchange risk associated with the dollar interest cash flows inherent in the bond. The analysis is consistent with the rationale given in paragraph AG 33(c) of IAS 39 for not separating the foreign currency embedded derivative.

Example – Dual currency bond

On 1 January 20X5, an entity with pound sterling functional currency issued a €5m bond repayable in 3 year's time. The bond pays fixed interest at 6% per annum in US dollars, calculated on a notional dollar equivalent of the proceeds raised in euros. There is no issue cost.

The following exchange rates are relevant:

	01 Jan 20X5	31 Dec 20X5	31 Dec 20X6	31 Dec 20X7
£1 = Spot rate	€1.4142	€1.4530	€1.4852	€1.3571
Average rate		€1.4627	€1.4673	€1.4621
£1 = Spot rate	$1.9187	$1.7208	$1.9591	$1.9973
Average rate		$1.8207	$1.8429	$2.0018
€1 = Spot rate	$1.3569			

In accordance with the treatment discussed above, the amounts that should be recognised in the income statement and the balance sheet at the end of each period are shown below:

	£	€	US$
Proceeds received		5,000,000	6,784,500
Interest payable @ 6% pa on USD amount			407,070
Zero Coupon Bond = PV of € principal repayment at the end of year 3 discounted 6%	2,968,531	4,198,096	
Instalment Bond = PV of 3 yearly USD interest payments discounted at 6%	567,104		1,088,103
Proceeds received for the single bond	3,535,635		

Note that the discounting is carried out at 6% assuming a flat yield curve. The actual proceeds of €5,000,000 translated at the spot rate at 1 January 20X5 are actually £3,535,568. The small difference of 67 is due to the effect of discounting and cross exchange rate and is ignored.

Amortisation of instalment bond

	Balance brought forward US$	Finance cost @ 6% US$	Cash Payments US$	Balance carried forward
31/12/20X5	1,088,103	65,286	407,070	746,319
31/12/20X6	746,319	44,779	407,070	384,028
31/12/20X7	384,028	23,042	407,070	0

	Balance brought forward £	Finance cost at average rate £	Payment at spot rate £	Balance carried forward £	Retranslated US$ @ year end rate £	Exchange difference £
31 Dec 20X5	567,104	35,858	236,559	366,403	433,705	67,301
31 Dec 20X6	433,705	24,298	207,784	250,219	196,023	−54,196
31 Dec 20X7	196,023	11,510	203,810	3,723	0	−3,723
		71,666	648,153			9,382

Amortisation of zero coupon bond

	Balance brought forward €	Finance cost@ 6% €	Cash Payments €	Balance carried forward €
31/12/20X5	4,198,096	251,886		4,449,982
31/12/20X6	4,449,982	266,999	0	4,716,981
31/12/20X7	4,716,981	283,019	5,000,000	0

	Balance brought forward £	Finance cost at average rate £	Payment at spot rate £	Balance carried forward £	Translated US$ @ year end rate £	Exchange difference £
31/12/20X5	2,968,531	172,206		3,140,737	3,062,617	−78,120
31/12/20X6	3,062,617	181,966		3,244,583	3,175,991	−68,592
31/12/20X7	3,175,991	193,570	3,684,327	−314,766	0	314,766
		547,742	3,684,327			168,054

Amortisation of single bond				
	Opening balance sheet	Income statement	Cash payments	Finance cost	Exchange gain/(loss)
	£	£	£	£	£
31/12/20X5	3,535,635	208,064	–10,819	236,559	3,496,322
31/12/20X6	3,496,322	206,264	–122,788	207,784	3,372,013
31/12/20X7	3,372,013	205,081	311,043	3,888,137	0
		619,409	177,436	4,332,480	

These amounts are calcultated by adding the bonds two components together.

Non-monetary financial assets

6.7.217   Translation of non-monetary items depends on whether they are recognised at historical cost or at fair value. Items recognised at historical cost are not retranslated at subsequent balance sheet dates. This would apply to foreign currency denominated unquoted equity instruments that are measured at cost, because their fair values cannot be reliably determined. However, most non-monetary financial instruments, such as equity instruments, are measured at fair value. Non-monetary assets that are measured at fair value in a foreign currency are translated using the exchange rates at the date when the fair value was determined. [IAS 21 para 23(c)]. When a gain or loss on a non-monetary item is recognised directly in equity, any exchange component of that gain or loss should also be recognised directly in equity. Therefore, for available-for-sale equity instruments remeasured through equity the entire change in fair value is recognised in equity. [IAS 39 para AG 83].

Impairment of foreign currency financial asset

6.7.218   Although not specifically dealt with in IAS 39, measuring impairment losses on financial assets that are denominated in foreign currency is, in principle, no different from those that are denominated in the entity's functional currency. Thus, for a foreign currency financial asset that is carried at amortised cost, the expected future cash flows denominated in the foreign currency are discounted at the financial asset's original effective interest rate. This amount is then translated into the entity's functional currency using the foreign exchange rate at the date when the impairment is recognised. The difference between the translated present value and the carrying amount in the entity's functional currency is the impairment loss that is recognised in profit or loss. Similarly, if in a subsequent period, circumstances change that result in a reversal of the impairment loss, in whole or in part, the reversal should be measured using the foreign exchange rate at the date when the reversal is recognised.

6.7.219   For foreign currency non-monetary assets that are held as available-for-sale with changes in fair value recognised in equity, the situation is different. In this case, the amount of the loss that is removed from equity and included in profit or loss is the difference between the asset's acquisition cost translated at the rate of exchange ruling at the acquisition's date and its current fair value translated at the rate of exchange ruling at the date of the impairment. [IAS 21 para 25]. This is because an impairment loss may be recognised in the foreign currency, but not in the entity's functional currency and *vice versa* as illustrated below.

Example – Foreign currency equity instrument designated as available-for-sale

On 1 January 20X3, an entity whose functional currency is the local currency (LC) purchases a foreign currency (FC) denominated equity instrument at its fair value of FC1,000. The entity classifies the equity as available-for-sale. The exchange rate at acquisition was FC = LC1.5. The asset's fair value at subsequent balance sheet dates in FC and the closing exchange rates are given below:

Date	Exchange rate	Fair value of asset		Change in fair value recognised in OCI	
	FC	LC	LC	Recognised in the period LC	Cumulative
1 Jan 20X3	1.5	1,000	1,500		
31 Dec 20X3	1.7	900	1,530	30	30
31 Dec 20X4	1.6	800	1,280	–250	–220
31 Dec 20X4 Loss reclassified from equity and recognised in profit or loss					220
31 Dec 20X5	1.8	850	1,530	250	250

As can be seen from the above, even though the asset's fair value measured in FC at 31 December 20X3 is less than the original cost in FC, no impairment loss is recognised in that year because any impairment of an equity AFS asset is determined in terms of an entity's functional currency (as confirmed by an agenda decision published in the IFRIC in July 2009). An impairment loss is recognised in the following year when the fair value measured in the entity's functional currency (LC1,280) is lower than the asset's acquisition price (LC1,500). The impairment loss of C220 is reclassified from equity and recognised in profit or loss. Even if circumstances change, as happens in 31 Dec 20X5, the loss recognised in profit or loss is never reversed. Instead, the change in fair value during the year of LC250 is recognised in equity (see further para 6.7.204 above).

6.7.220 For foreign currency monetary assets that are held as available-for-sale, past impairment losses recognised in profit or loss can be reversed through profit or loss as explained in paragraph 6.7.204 above. Again the exchange rate at the date of the reversal should be used to measure the amount of the reversal. Since, for the purposes of recognising foreign exchange gains and losses under IAS 21, a monetary available-for-sale asset is treated as if it were carried at amortised cost in the foreign currency, all exchange differences arising on the reversal should be recognised in profit or loss.

Financial assets held in foreign operations

6.7.221   An entity may have both financial assets that are classified as at fair value through profit or loss and available-for-sale investments. When such an entity is a foreign operation that is a subsidiary, its financial statements are consolidated with those of its parent. In that situation, IAS 39 applies to the accounting for financial instruments in the financial statements of the foreign operation and IAS 21 applies in translating the financial statements of a foreign operation for incorporation in the reporting entity's consolidated financial statements. Under IAS 21, all exchange differences resulting from translating the financial statements of a foreign operation are recognised in equity until disposal of the net investment. This would include exchange differences arising from financial instruments carried at fair value, which would include both financial assets classified as at fair value through profit or loss and financial assets that are available-for-sale as illustrated in the example below.

> **Example – Financial instruments held in a foreign entity – Interaction of IAS 39 and IAS 21**
>
> Entity A is domiciled in the UK and its functional currency and presentation currency is pound sterling. Entity A has a foreign subsidiary, entity B, in France whose functional currency is the euro. Entity B is the owner of a debt instrument, which is held-for-trading and, therefore, carried at fair value under IAS 39. [IAS 39 para IE 3.3].
>
> In entity B's financial statements for year 20X5, the fair value and carrying amount of the debt instrument is €400. In entity A's consolidated financial statements, the asset is translated into pound sterling at the spot exchange rate applicable at the balance sheet date, say €1 = £0.50. Thus, the carrying amount in the consolidated financial statements is £200.
>
> At the end of year 20X5, the fair value of the debt instrument has increased to €440. Entity B recognises the trading asset at €440 in its balance sheet and recognises a fair value gain of €40 in its income statement. During the year, the spot exchange rate has increased from €1 = £0.50 to €1 = £0.75, resulting in an increase in the instrument's fair value from £200 to £330 (€440 @ 0.75). Therefore, entity A recognises the trading asset at £330 in its consolidated financial statements.
>
> Since entity B is a foreign entity, entity A translates the income statement of entity B in accordance with IAS 21 *"at the exchange rates at the dates of the transactions"*. Since the fair value gain has accrued through the year, entity A uses the average rate of €1 = £0.625 as a practical approximation. Therefore, while the fair value of the trading asset has increased by £130 (£330 – £200), entity A recognises only £25 (€40 @ 0.625) of this increase in consolidated profit or loss. The resulting exchange difference, that is, the remaining increase in the debt instrument's fair value £105 (£130 – £25) is classified as equity until the disposal of the net investment in the foreign operation.

6.8 – Hedge accounting

6.8 – Hedge accounting

Introduction

6.8.1 Some entities are applying IFRS 9 for the classification of their financial assets and financial liabilities while using IAS 39 for hedge accounting. This chapter assumes the application of IAS 39 for both classification and hedge accounting and does not deal with issues that arise from the application of IFRS 9. See Chapter 6.10 for further details of the development of IFRS 9.

What is hedging?

6.8.2 Entities face many types of business risk. One of the most significant is financial risk. Different companies, however, are exposed to different risks. Some may be concerned about commodity prices, such as the price of copper or oil; others about interest rates or exchange rates. Successful entities manage risk by deciding to which risk, and to what extent, they should be exposed, by monitoring the actual exposure and taking steps to reduce risks to within agreed limits, often through the use of derivatives. However, hedging one risk may magnify another. Management has to decide for example whether it is cash flow risk averse, which will mean that it is not concerned with fair value risk.

6.8.3 Entering into a derivative transaction with a counterparty in the expectation that the transaction will eliminate or reduce an entity's exposure to a particular risk is referred to as hedging. Risk is reduced because the derivative's value or cash flows are expected, wholly or partly, to move inversely and, therefore, offset changes in the value or cash flows of the 'hedged position' or item. The hedged position/item can include recognised assets and liabilities, a firm commitment or a forecast transaction. Sometimes an entity can arrange its affairs so as to be naturally hedged. For example, if an entity's portfolio of fixed interest securities is financed by fixed rate borrowings of the same amount and duration, a rise in the general level of interest rates will decrease the value of both asset and liability positions by approximately the same amount, so the entity has no net exposure to interest rate risk. Hedging in an economic sense, therefore, concerns the reduction or elimination of different financial risks such as price risk, interest rate risk, currency risk, etc, associated with the hedged position. It is a risk management activity that is now commonplace in many entities.

What is hedge accounting?

6.8.4 Once an entity has entered into a hedging transaction, it must be reflected in the financial statements of the entity. Accounting for the hedged position should be consistent with the objective of entering into the hedging transaction, which is to eliminate or reduce significantly specific risks that management considers can have an adverse effect on the entity's financial position and results, whilst acknowledging that such strategies can increase other risks with which management is less concerned. This consistency can be achieved if both the hedging instrument and the hedged position are recognised and measured on symmetrical bases and offsetting gains and losses are reported in profit or loss in the same periods. Unfortunately, mismatches occur under existing recognition and measurement standards and practices. Hedge accounting practices have been developed to correct or mitigate these mis-matches.

6.8.5   In simple terms 'hedge accounting' is a technique that modifies the normal basis for recognising gains and losses (or revenues and expenses) on associated hedging instruments and hedged items so that both are recognised in earnings in the same accounting period. Hedge accounting thus allows management to eliminate or reduce the income statement volatility that otherwise would arise if the hedged items and hedging instruments were accounted for under GAAP separately, without regard to the hedge's business purpose.

Hedge accounting under IAS 39

6.8.6   IAS 39 provides a set of strict criteria that must be met before hedge accounting can be used. These require that the hedge relationship is designated and formally documented at inception. There are also requirements to demonstrate both at inception and throughout the life of the hedge that the hedge is 'highly effective'. As a result, not all hedging activities undertaken by entities qualify for hedge accounting. Failure to meet any of the criteria whilst the hedge is in place results in the discontinuance of hedge accounting.

6.8.7   The standard also specifies three methods of hedge accounting that were designed to reflect the standard's requirement to measure all derivatives at fair value. As a result, hedge accounting in IAS 39 can be applied to three types of hedging relationships as indicated below:

■   Where the hedged risk is that the hedged item's *fair value* will change in response to some variable, such as changes in interest rates, foreign exchange rates, or market prices, gains and losses on the hedging instrument and the offsetting losses and gains on the hedged item are both recognised in profit or loss. This is a fair value hedge.

■   Where the hedged risk is that the hedged item's future *cash flows* will change in response to such variables, the gain or loss on the hedging instrument is initially recognised in other comprehensive income and subsequently recycled from equity to profit or loss as the hedged item affects profit or loss. This is a cash flow hedge.

■   Where the hedge risk is that the carrying amount of a *net investment* in a foreign operation will change in response to exchange rate movements, the gain or loss on the hedging instrument is initially recognised in other comprehensive income and subsequently recycled to profit or loss from equity on disposal of that foreign operation. This is a hedge of a net investment in a foreign operation.

6.8.8   IAS 39 does not mandate the use of hedge accounting. It is a privilege not a right. Entities intending to use hedge accounting must have proper systems and procedures to monitor each hedging relationship. Many entities may find these requirements too onerous and decide not to try to hedge account. However, this approach generally comes at a cost – income statement volatility.

Hedged items

6.8.9   Before the hedge accounting principles and methods set out in the standard can be appreciated, it is necessary to understand the basic definitions and concepts that underpin all hedging relationships.

Definition

6.8.10   A hedged item is an asset, liability, firm commitment, highly probable forecast transaction or net investment in a foreign operation that:

■   exposes the entity to risk of changes in fair value or future cash flows; and

■   is designated as being hedged.

[IAS 39 para 9].

6.8.11   In particular, the hedged item can be:

■   a single asset, liability, firm commitment, highly probable forecast transaction or net investment in a foreign operation;

■   a group of assets, liabilities, firm commitments, highly probable forecast transactions or net investments in foreign operations with similar risk characteristics; or

■   in a portfolio hedge of interest rate risk only, a portion of the portfolio of financial assets or financial liabilities that share the risk being hedged.

[IAS 39 para 78].

6.8.12   One of the key aspects of the above definition is that the hedged item must expose the entity to risk of changes in the fair value or future cash flows that could affect profit or loss. [IAS 39 para 86(a)-(b)]. This could be in the current or future periods. As a result, hedge accounting cannot apply to any items included in equity or transactions that directly affect equity (see further para 6.8.46 below).

6.8.13   The assets or liabilities referred to above are assets and liabilities that are recognised in the entity's balance sheet. It could be a financial item or a non-financial item such as inventory. Unrecognised assets cannot qualify as a hedged item except for firm commitments. For example, internally generated core deposit intangibles (for a bank) are not recognised as intangible assets under IAS 38. Because they are not recognised, they cannot be designated as hedged items. [IAS 39 para IG F2.3].

6.8.14 For hedge accounting purposes, only assets, liabilities, firm commitments or highly probable forecast transactions that involve a party external to the entity can be designated as hedged items. It follows that hedge accounting can be applied to transactions between entities in the same group only in the individual or separate financial statements of those entities and not in the consolidated financial statements of the group. [IAS 39 para 80]. However, there are some exceptions to this general rule, which are considered from paragraph 6.8.39 below.

Designation of groups of items as hedged items

6.8.15 The definition of a hedged item in paragraph 6.8.11 above permits similar assets, or similar liabilities to be grouped together and designated as a hedged item. Designating a group/portfolio of items as a hedge requires that:

■ the individual assets or individual liabilities in the group share the risk exposure that is designated as being hedged; and

■ the change in the fair value attributable to the hedged risk for each individual item in the group is expected to be approximately proportional to the overall change in fair value attributable to the hedged risk of the group of items.

[IAS 39 para 83].

6.8.16 In grouping similar assets and liabilities in a portfolio, an entity should consider various factors, including:

■ The type of assets or liabilities.

■ The interest rate (fixed or variable) and, in the case of fixed rate assets or liabilities, the coupon rate.

■ The currency in which the assets or liabilities are denominated.

■ The scheduled maturity date and, in the case of prepayable assets, the prepayment terms, past prepayment history and expected future prepayment performance.

6.8.17 With respect to the first bullet point in paragraph 6.8.15 above, it is not necessary that each item in the group shares all of the same risks, as long as they all share a common risk characteristic that is the subject of the hedge. Sharing the same risk exposure means not only that the hedged items have a common risk (for example, foreign currency risk), but also that the exposure moves in the same direction. For example, forecast foreign currency sales and purchases do not share the same risk exposure, because the risks move in opposite directions.

6.8.18 With respect to the second bullet point in paragraph 6.8.15 above, the standard does not provide any guidance on the meaning of 'approximately proportional'. FAS 133 provides some guidance in the context of US GAAP. It considers that a movement of the fair value of the individual items within a fairly narrow range, such as from 9% to 11%, when the fair value of the portfolio as a whole moves 10%, would be consistent with this requirement, but a move such as from 7% to 13% would not be consistent. A similar approach could be applied in IAS 39. The following two examples demonstrate applications of this second bullet point:

Example 1 – Designating a portfolio of bonds as the hedged item

An entity has a portfolio of fixed rate corporate bonds with different coupons. All the bonds mature within a period of 4-5 years. The entity designates an interest rate swap to hedge the entire portfolio's risk-free interest rate.

The group of bonds may be designated as the hedged item as the risk free rate that is being hedged is common to all the bonds. However, the fair value movement of each individual bond that is attributable to the hedged interest-free rate should be approximately proportional to the portfolio's fair value movement that is attributable to the hedged risk. The entity's management should, therefore, model the changes in fair value of the portfolio relative to the fair values of individual bonds in response to the hedged risk.

Example 2 – Designating a portfolio of shares as the hedged item

Entity A acquires a portfolio of French CAC 40 shares, in the same proportions as are used to calculate the French CAC 40 index and classifies the investments as available-for-sale. At the same time, the entity purchases a put option on the CAC 40 index to hedge changes in the fair value of the portfolio. The option constitutes a near perfect hedge of decreases in the value of the portfolio, in economic terms. Any decline in the portfolio's fair value below the option's strike price will be offset by an increase in the put option's intrinsic value.

The entity cannot designate the portfolio of shares as the hedged item in a hedge of equity price risk. The hedged risk is the total change in value of each share in the portfolio. Some share prices may increase and others may decrease. The relationship will not qualify for hedge accounting, because the change in the fair value attributable to the hedged risk for each individual item in the group (individual share prices) is not expected to be approximately proportional to the overall change in fair value attributable to the hedged risk of the group.

Hedging an overall net position

6.8.19 An entity cannot designate an overall net position as the hedged item. Hedging a common risk in a portfolio of similar assets and liabilities would mean allocating the overall gain or loss on the hedging instrument to the individual items in the portfolio. Furthermore, if some of the items in the portfolio were producing gains and others losses, the entity would have to impute both gains and losses to the single hedging instrument to offset both the gains and the losses on the hedged items. As such an allocation would be inherently arbitrary and produce significant ineffectiveness, designating the hedged item as a net position is not permitted. [IAS 39 para 84]

6.8.20 However, almost the same effect on profit or loss can be achieved by designating some of the underlying gross items as the hedged item equal in amount to the net position. For example, an entity (C functional currency) with a firm commitment to make a purchase in a foreign currency of FC100 and a firm commitment to make a sale in the foreign currency of FC90 can hedge the net amount of FC10 by acquiring a derivative and designating it as a hedging instrument associated with FC10 of the firm purchase commitment of FC100. Similarly, an entity with C100 of fixed rate assets and C90 of fixed rate liabilities with terms of a similar nature could hedge the net C10 exposure by designating as the hedged item C10 of those assets. [IAS 39 para AG 101].

6.8.21 An entity's hedging strategy and risk management practices may assess cash flow risk on a net basis, but the net cash flow exposure cannot be designated as a hedged item for hedge accounting purposes. This is because, as explained above, it would not be possible to identify the net exposure arising from forecast sales and purchases as the exposure being hedged, because forecast sales and purchases are not similar items and the effectiveness test would fail. However, once again hedge accounting can be achieved by designating some of the forecast purchases or sales as the hedged item equal in amount to the net position, as illustrated in the example below.

Example 1 – Hedging a net FX position

Entity A, whose functional currency is the euro, has a global treasury centre that is responsible for collecting and assessing the group's foreign currency risks and offsetting the net position using derivative instruments with an external party. For example, it forecasts sales of US$2.5m and purchases of US$1m in June and has, therefore, entered into a forward contract to sell US$1.5m against euros in that month.

As stated in paragraph 6.8.19 above, the entity is prohibited from designating a net position as the hedged item. It is possible to achieve a similar effect by designating the hedged item as part of one of the gross positions that is equal in amount to the net position. Entity A can, therefore, designate the forward contract as a hedge of highly probable forecast sales of US$1.5m in June.

Example 2 – Hedging a net interest rate position

Entity B has a number of bank loans with different interest rates and terms. The entity also has loans receivable with different interest rates. Management proposes to hedge the net interest-rate risk position in a number of separate maturity bands through the use of interest-rate swaps for the net asset or liability in each maturity band.

Management may allocate the net exposure in each band to a specific asset or liability, so that the net position in each maturity band could qualify as a hedged item. This approach provides management with an interest-rate gap methodology to manage interest-rate risk. [IAS 39 para AG111]. Alternatively, management may choose to apply fair value hedge accounting for a portfolio hedge of interest rate risk and designate an amount of assets or liabilities in given time buckets as hedged items (see para 6.8.104 onwards for definition and examples of fair value hedge accounting and para 6.8.218 for details of portfolio hedging). [IAS 39 para 81A].

Designation of financial items as hedged items

6.8.22 When the hedged item is a financial instrument or a forecast transaction involving a financial instrument, examples of financial risk exposures that can be hedged are described below.

Examples of financial instrument risks that can be hedged

- Market risk – the risk that a financial instrument's fair value or cash flows will fluctuate because of changes in market prices. Market risk embodies not only the potential for loss but also the potential for gain. It comprises three types of risk as follows:

    - Interest rate risk – the risk that a financial instrument's fair value or future cash flows will fluctuate because of changes in market interest rates.

    - Currency risk – the risk that a financial instrument's fair value or future cash flows will fluctuate because of changes in foreign exchange rates.

    - Other price risk – the risk that a financial instrument's fair value or future cash flows will fluctuate because of changes in market prices (other than those arising from interest rate risk or currency risk), whether those changes are caused by factors specific to the individual financial instrument or its issuer, or factors affecting all similar financial instruments traded in the market.

- Credit risk – the risk that one party to a financial instrument will cause a financial loss for the other party by failing to discharge an obligation. However, credit risk is not normally deemed to be a separately identifiable component for hedging purposes – see paragraph 6.8.23-24 below re hedges of portions.

- Liquidity risk – the risk that an entity will encounter difficulty in meeting obligations associated with financial liabilities.

    Other examples of risks that can be hedged in financial items include:

    - Pre-payment risk in mortgages (provided not held-to maturity investments – see para 6.8.47)

    - Credit spread.

    - Closely related embedded derivatives that were not separated from the host financial contract.

[IFRS 7 App A].

Hedges of portions of financial items

6.8.23 For hedges of financial assets and financial liabilities, IAS 39 does not restrict hedge accounting to hedges of the entire risk of change in the fair value or all of the cash flows of a financial instrument, or the entire exposure to interest rate risk, currency risk, credit risk or other risks of changes in a financial instrument's fair value or cash flows. In June 2008 the IASB changed IAS 39 to clarify that provided that effectiveness can be measured, it is possible to designate the risks associated with only a portion of its cash flows or fair value, such as one or more selected contractual cash flows or portions of them or a percentage or a proportion of the fair value. For example :

(a) all of the cash flows of a financial instrument may be designated for cash flow or fair value changes attributable to some (but not all) risks; or

(b) some (but not all) of the cash flows of a financial instrument may be designated for cash flow or fair value changes attributable to all or only some risks (that is, a 'portion' of the cash flows of a financial instrument may be designated for changes attributable to all or only some risks).

6.8.24   To be eligible for hedge accounting, the designated risks and portions must be separately identifiable components of the financial instrument, and changes in the cash flows or fair value of the entire financial instrument arising from changes in the designated risks and portions must be reliably measurable. For example:

(a) For a fixed rate financial instrument hedged for changes in fair value attributable to changes in a risk-free or benchmark interest rate, the risk-free or benchmark rate is normally regarded as both a separately identifiable component of the financial instrument and reliably measurable.

(b) Inflation is not separately identifiable and reliably measurable and cannot be designated as a risk or a portion of a financial instrument unless the requirements in (c) are met.

(c) A contractually specified inflation portion of the cash flows of a recognised inflation-linked bond (assuming there is no requirement to account for an embedded derivative separately) is separately identifiable and reliably measurable as long as other cash flows of the instrument are not affected by the inflation portion.

[IAS 39 paras AG99E-AG99F].

It should be noted that hedges of portions apply only to financial assets and liabilities and not to non-financial assets and liabilities (see para 6.8.34 below).

The variety of different hedgeable risk exposures that may arise on a five year fixed rate bond classified as loans and receivables can be demonstrated in the following table:

	Risk exposure		Contractual cash flows	
	All	**Specific component**	**Principal**	**Interest**
Hedge the fair value of all the cash flows for all risks (100% of fair value of the debt).	✓		✓	✓
Hedge the fair value of all the cash flows for a specific risk, for example, interest rate (100% of fair value of the debt for a specific risk).		✓	✓	✓
Hedge a proportion of the fair value of all the cash flows for all risks (90% of fair value of the debt).	✓		90%	90%
Hedge a proportion of the fair value of all the cash flows for a specific risk, for example, interest rate risk (90% of fair value of the debt for a specific risk).		✓	90%	90%
Hedge the fair value of a specifically identified cash flow for all risk.	✓		✓ or	✓
Hedge the fair value of a specifically identified cash flow for a specific risk (for example, interest rate risk).		✓	✓ or	✓
Hedge the fair value of a portion of a specifically identified cash flow for all risk.	✓		90% or	90%
Hedge the fair value of a portion of a specifically identified cash flow for a specific risk, for example, interest rate risk.		✓	90% or	90%

6.8.25 Consistent with paragraph 6.8.23 above, financial assets or liabilities may be hedged with respect to a specific risk (a component of total risk), provided that the exposure to the specific risk component is identifiable and separately measurable, which is also a pre-requisite for measuring effectiveness. Some examples of situations where component of a risk may be hedged are given below. [IAS 39 para 81].

Example – Hedging a risk component of a fixed rate debt instrument

An entity issues 8% fixed rate debt instrument for C100 that is repayable at par at the end of year 2. At the time of issue the market interest rate is 6%. Therefore, the credit spread on the new issue is 2%.

In this scenario, the entity can designate an identifiable and separately measurable portion of the interest rate exposure as the hedged risk. Such a portion may be a risk-free interest rate or benchmark interest rate component of the debt instrument's total interest rate exposure, that is, the entity's own credit spread of 2% may be excluded. This is subject to the *proviso* that effectiveness can be measured.

So if the entity intends to designate the benchmark LIBOR component of 6% as the hedged risk, it may take out a receive 6% fixed pay floating LIBOR interest rate swap to hedge the changes in the debt's fair value due to changes in LIBOR. The hedge will be expected to be highly effective as the credit spread is not included in the net cash flows relating to the swap.

Note that it is not necessary for the pay leg of the swap to be the same as LIBOR (receive 6% pay LIBOR). The entity could take out a receive 8% pay floating LIBOR + 2% interest rate swap and still designate the benchmark LIBOR component as the hedged risk. This is because the fair value of the swap comprises the net of the present values of both the fixed and the floating legs. Therefore, increasing both sides of the swap by 2% (from receive 6% pay LIBOR to receive 8% pay LIBOR + 2%) will not change the fair value for a given change in interest rates. However, this is only true when the payment frequency of both legs is identical. If the fixed leg pays yearly and the variable leg pays quarterly, there would be a difference.

6.8.26 If a portion of the cash flows of a financial asset or financial liability is designated as the hedged item, that designated portion must be less than the total cash flows of the asset or liability. As a designated portion of the cash flows cannot be greater than the whole, an entity that issues a debt instrument whose effective interest rate at issuance is below LIBOR (such an issuance of debt at below LIBOR rates may be possible by some entities with exceptionally strong credit rating), cannot designate the following components as hedges:

- a portion of the liability equal to the principal amount plus interest at LIBOR; and

- a negative residual portion.

[IAS 39 para AG 99C].

It should be noted, however, that the above prohibition does not feature in the EU carve-out version of IAS 39.

6.8.27 However, the entity may designate all of the cash flows of the entire financial asset or financial liability as the hedged item and hedge them for only one particular risk (for example, only for changes that are attributable to changes in LIBOR) as illustrated in the example below:

Example – Designating a benchmark interest rate as the hedged risk on a fixed rate debt instrument issued at sub-LIBOR rate

An entity issues a 5% fixed rate debt instrument for C100 that is repayable at par at the end of year 2. At the time of issue, the benchmark LIBOR rate is 6%.

The entity can designate the entire financial liability as the hedged item (that is, principal + interest) and hedge the change in the fair value or cash flows of that entire liability that is attributable to changes in LIBOR. Some ineffectiveness will occur. However, the entity may choose a hedge ratio of other than one to one (a proportion of the total cash flow) in order to improve the effectiveness of the hedge. [IAS 39 para AG 99C].

6.8.28 It is also possible to hedge the benchmark interest rate risk portion of a fixed rate financial instrument some time after its origination, by which time interest rates may have changed since the instrument's origination. This is possible if the benchmark rate is higher than the contractual rate paid on the item as illustrated in the example below. [IAS 39 para AG 99D]. It should be noted that the restriction that the hedged benchmark rate is higher than the contractual rate does not feature in the EU carve-out version of IAS 39.

> **Example – Designating a benchmark interest rate as the hedged risk of a fixed rate debt instrument subsequent to its origination**
>
> On 1 April 20X1, an entity issues a 6% fixed rate debt instrument for C100 that is repayable at par at the end of year 5 (31 March 20X6). Interest is payable annually in arrears. At the time of issue, the benchmark LIBOR rate is 5%. On 1 July 20X2, the entity decides to hedge the interest rate risk on the debt instrument with an interest rate swap when LIBOR has increased to 7%. At that time, the fair value of the debt instrument is C93.
>
> The entity calculates that if it had issued the debt instrument on 1 July 20X2 when it first designates it as the hedged item for its fair value of C93, the effective yield on the instrument would have been 8.1%. Because LIBOR on 1 July 20X2 is 7% and is less than this effective yield, the entity can designate a LIBOR portion of 7% that consists partly of the contractual interest cash flows and partly of the discount that is included in the difference between the current fair value of C93 and the amount repayable on maturity of C100.

6.8.29 In the valuation of cross currency interest rate swaps and long term currency forwards, spreads are applied to cash flows in currencies with a perceived higher credit risk or lower liquidity. These spreads – commonly referred to as 'currency basis spreads' – are typically quoted in the market against a USD LIBOR benchmark. In the past, the effect of currency basis spreads was generally immaterial (2-3bp). However, since early 2008 these spreads have widened significantly. The question therefore arises as to whether the increased currency spreads lead to hedge ineffectiveness. It is generally accepted that in the case of a cash flow hedge where effectiveness is measured using a hypothetical derivatives method, currency basis spreads can be included in the hypothetical derivative and hence will not give rise to ineffectiveness. This reflects both that (a) the hedged risk is modelled as a derivative and hence includes all features that a stand-alone derivative would and (b) in a cash flow hedge it can be argued there is an implicit exchange of the foreign currency cash flow being hedged into the entity's functional currency and currency basis is part of the cost the market charges for such an exchange.

6.8.30 However, in a fair value hedge, the currency basis spread cannot be included in the fair value measurement of the hedged item. There is normally a single fair value measure for the hedged item with respect to the hedged risk. As the hedged item is a foreign currency asset or liability, it does not contain the currency basis risk, and hence the hedged risk should not include the currency basis adjustment. Furthermore, fair value is defined in terms of a price in a current transaction. If the hedged item is quoted, IAS 39 requires the quoted price to be used. This will be the price in the foreign currency and, when translated to the entity's functional currency at the spot rate, will not include the currency basis. Finally, were the entity to sell/repay the hedged item and close out the hedge part way through its life (for example, by entering into an offsetting derivative), it would incur a gain or loss from changes in the currency basis. Thus, in a fair value hedge currency basis spreads will cause ineffectiveness.

6.8.31   Under IAS 39, when a gain or loss on a non-monetary available-for-sale equity security is recognised in other comprehensive income, any exchange component of that gain or loss is also recognised directly in other comprehensive income. [IAS 39 para AG 83]. Normally, items taken to other comprehensive income/equity cannot be hedged, however, foreign currency exposure in such an equity security can be hedged provided there is a clear and identifiable exposure to changes in foreign exchange rates and all the other hedge accounting criteria are met. In the case of a fair value hedge, the changes in foreign currency exposure will be recognised in profit or loss. The implementation guidance explains that this would be possible only if:

- the equity instrument is not traded on an exchange (or in another established marketplace) where trades are denominated in the same currency as the entity's functional currency (investor); and

- dividends to the investor are not denominated in the investor's functional currency.

Thus, if a share is traded in multiple currencies and one of those currencies is the reporting entity's functional currency, hedge accounting for the foreign currency component of the share price is not permitted.

[IAS 39 para IG F2.19]

> **Example – Hedging foreign currency risk of an available-for-sale investment**
>
> On 1 April 20X5, entity A, a Swiss company with Swiss Francs as its functional currency, buys equity shares in entity B located in the US. The shares are listed on the New York Stock Exchange and pay dividends in US$. The acquisition cost is US$1m. On that date US$ = CHF1.3 resulting in an investment of CHF1.3m. Entity A classifies the investment as available-for-sale.
>
> At the same time, to protect itself from the exposure to changes in the foreign exchange rate associated with the shares, entity A enters into a forward contract to sell US$1m and buy CHF. Entity A intends to roll over the forward exchange contract for as long as it retains the shares. It is assumed that the hedge is effective and the other conditions for hedge accounting are met.
>
> Entity A could designate the currency exposure relating to the shares' fair value as the hedged risk, because it meets the two conditions set out in the above paragraph. Also, entity A could designate the forward contract as either a fair value hedge of the foreign exchange exposure of US$1m or as a cash flow hedge of a forecast sale of the shares, provided the future sale and its timing are highly probable. For the purposes of this example, it is assumed that the forward contract is designated as a fair value hedge.

At 31 March 20X6, the entity's financial year end, shares increased in value to US$2m. At that date, US$ = CHF1.20.

The change in fair value is calculated as follows:

	CHF m
Value of investment at 31 March 20X6 – US$2m @ 1.2 =	2.4
Value of investment at 1 April 20X5 – US$1m @ 1.3 =	1.3
Fair value change	1.1
Exchange component of change – US 1m (@ 1.2 — @1.3)	(0.1)
Recognised in other comprehensive income – change in fair value US$1m @ 1.2	1.2

In this situation, the gain arising from the changes in the forward contract's fair value is recognised in the income statement. This includes both the spot component (which may be designated as part of the hedging relationship to improve effectiveness) and the forward points component (see further paragraph 6.8.60 below). The entity also recognises the exchange loss of CHF100,000 in profit or loss to offset the gain on the forward contract. [IAS 39 para 89(b)]. The remaining portion of the change in fair value of CHF1.2m is deferred in equity in accordance with the subsequent measurement rules for available-for-sale investments.

Partial term hedging

6.8.32   The ability to hedge a portion of one or more selected cash flows of a financial asset or liability means that an entity will be able to hedge exposures that have a term that is less than the hedged item's term – so called 'partial term' hedges. This is subject to the proviso that effectiveness can be measured and the other hedge accounting criteria are met. This will usually be so if the hedging derivative also has the same term as the selected cash flows, as illustrated in the example below. It should be noted that the notion of 'partial term' does not apply to a hedging instrument as stated in paragraph 6.8.65 below. Note, where a forecasted transaction is designated with a foreign currency derivative of shorter duration, if the hedging relationship is designated on a "forward" basis (that is, as a hedge of changes in forward exchange rates), it will not be fully effective. This is because a time portion of a forecasted transaction is not an eligible portion of a non-financial item and the hypothetical derivative must be based on the full term until the forecasted transaction is expected to occur. However, such a relationship may be designated on a 'spot' basis (that is, as a hedge of changes in spot exchange rates) with minimal ineffectiveness.

Example – Partial term hedging

Entity A acquires a 10% fixed rate government bond with a remaining term to maturity of ten years. Entity A classifies the bond as available for sale. On the same date, to hedge against fair value exposure on the bond associated with the first five year interest payments, the entity acquires a 5 year pay-fixed, receive-floating swap. The swap has a fair value of zero at the inception of the hedge relationship.

The swap may be designated as hedging the fair value exposure of the interest rate payments on the government bond until year 5 and the change in value of the principal payment due at maturity to the extent affected by changes in the yield curve relating to the 5 years of the swap. [IAS 39 para IG F2.17].

The same principle applies if the hedged item had been a financial liability instead of a financial asset with the same terms. In that situation, the entity could designate the fair value exposure of the first 5 years interest payments due to changes in interest rate only and hedge that exposure using a 5 year receive-fixed, pay-floating interest rate swap.

The entity is also able to achieve effective partial term cash flow hedges. For instance, assume an entity issues a 10 year floating rate debt and wish to hedge the variability in the first three year of interest payments. This could be easily done by using a 3 year receive-floating, pay-fixed interest rate swap.

Loans and receivables

6.8.33 Under IAS 39, loans and receivables are carried at amortised cost. An entity may decide to hold such loans and receivables to maturity. Indeed, banking institutions in many countries hold the bulk of their loans and receivables until maturity. Therefore, it would appear that as changes in the fair value of such loans and receivables that are due to changes in market interest rates will not affect profit or loss, fair value hedge accounting for loans and receivables is precluded (see para 6.8.12 above). However, it is always possible that such instruments will be disposed of or extinguished before then, in which case the change in fair values would affect profit or loss. Accordingly, fair value hedge accounting is permitted as such loans and receivables are not designated as held-to-maturity. Financial assets designated as held to maturity cannot be designated as hedged items for interest rate or pre-payment risk (see para 6.8.47). [IAS 39 IG para F2.13].

Designation of non-financial items as hedged items

6.8.34 If the hedged item is a non-financial asset or non-financial liability, it may only be designated as a hedged item:

- for foreign currency risks; or
- in its entirety for all risks.

[IAS 39 para 82].

Hedges of portions of non-financial items

6.8.35 The standard explains that changes in the price of an ingredient or component of a non-financial asset or non-financial liability generally do not have a predictable, separately measurable effect on the item's price that is comparable to the effect of, say, a change in market interest rates on a bond's price. Therefore, because of the difficulty of isolating and measuring the appropriate portion of the cash flows or fair value changes attributable to specific risks other than foreign currency risks, a non-financial asset or non-financial liability is a hedged item only in its entirety or for foreign exchange risk. [IAS 39 para AG 100]. Accordingly, when an entity chooses to hedge the fair value of inventory (a non-financial asset), the inventory cannot be separated into its commodity and other components, regardless of whether the inventory consists of a single commodity component and conversion or rework costs, or is a product comprised of multiple commodities. The standard makes no exception to this rule even though in some cases it may be possible to isolate the changes in cash flows or fair value attributable to a particular risk. In some cases, ineffectiveness can be minimized by designating multiple derivatives as a hedging instrument based on the expected ingredients of the non-financial item (for example, where a metal concentrate containing gold and copper is hedged using a combination of gold and copper forwards) or by designating the quantity of the hedged item expected to contain the quantity of the non-financial item contracted for in the hedging instrument.

Example 1 – Separation of risks in non-financial assets

An entity manufacturers aluminium cans from sheets of aluminium. The entity intends to use aluminium futures as a fair value hedge of the exposure to changes in the aluminium cans' fair value held in inventory.

The entity cannot designate aluminium's market price as the hedged risk, even though the price of aluminium is likely to account for a significant portion of the exposure to changes in the price of aluminium cans held in inventory. Permitting an entity to designate the market price of aluminium as the hedged risk would ignore other components of the price of the cans, such as protective coating materials, labour and production overheads.

However, provided the requirement for effectiveness and other hedge accounting criteria are met (see para 6.8.154 below), the derivative instrument (aluminium futures) could be designated as a hedge of the exposure to changes in the full fair value of the inventory. See also the fair value and cash flow examples in paragraphs 6.8.110 and 6.8.130 below for examples hedging the full fair value of silver inventory.

Example 2 – Forecast purchase of a non-monetary asset in foreign currency

Entity A is planning to buy a large piece of machinery from a foreign supplier. The forecast purchase will be denominated in a foreign currency, so the company enters into a forward contract to hedge the risk of movements in the relevant foreign exchange rate.

The forecast purchase can be designated as a hedged item in a cash flow hedge of foreign currency risk, provided that the forecast purchase is highly probable, the requirements for effectiveness and the other conditions for hedge accounting are met. The hedged risk (movements in exchange rates) will affect the amount paid for the machine and will, therefore, affect profit or loss as the machine is depreciated.

Example 3 – Hedge of foreign currency denominated commodity risk

Entity A plans to purchase a fixed quantity of a commodity in twelve months time in US dollars. The functional currency of entity A is the euro. Entity A wants to reduce the risk of price changes of the commodity and hedges its exposure to that price risk by entering into a twelve-month cash-settled forward contract for this commodity. The price in the forward contract is denominated in US dollars, reflecting that the underlying commodity is commonly traded in US dollars.

The purchase exposes entity A to two risks: price risk regarding the market price of the commodity; and foreign exchange risk of US dollars against the euro. Under IAS 39 it is possible to designate only the market price component as the hedged item. This designation is possible because the market price component is the difference between the total price risk and the foreign currency risk, both of which could be individually designated as the hedged risk as noted in paragraph 6.8.34 above.

6.8.36 As stated in paragraph 6.8.34 above, a non-monetary item can be hedged for foreign currency risk only if it is separately measurable. As the hedged item is remeasured in a fair value hedge (see para 6.8.106 below), a non-monetary financial asset that was purchased in a foreign currency and initially recorded, under IAS 21 in the purchaser's functional currency, at the exchange rate at the date of the transaction cannot be classified as a fair value hedge for foreign currency risk. This is because it is not subsequently remeasured under IAS 21 and, therefore, does not contain any separately measurable foreign currency risk. Nevertheless, if all the hedge accounting conditions are met, an entity could designate as a cash flow hedge the anticipated sale of the non-monetary asset in a foreign currency. This is because, in a cash flow hedge, the non-monetary item is not remeasured. However, in practice, it would be rare for such a hedge to meet all the hedging accounting criteria as illustrated in the example below.

Example 4 – Foreign currency borrowings hedging a ship

A shipping entity in Denmark has a US subsidiary that has the same functional currency (the Danish Krone). In its consolidated financial statements shipping entity measures its ships at historical cost less depreciation. In accordance with paragraph 23(b) of IAS 21 the ships are measured in Danish Krone using the historical exchange rate. To hedge, fully or partly, the potential currency risk on the ships at disposal in US dollars, the shipping entity normally finances its purchases of ships with loans denominated in US dollars.

US dollar borrowings cannot be classified as a fair value hedge of a ship, because ships do not contain any separately measurable foreign currency risk, even though the entity purchases and sells them in US dollars.

US dollar borrowing (or a portion of it) may, however, be designated as a cash flow hedge of the ship's anticipated sale proceeds in US dollars financed by the borrowing provided all the hedging criteria are met. Those conditions are likely to be met if the sale is highly probable because it is expected to occur in the immediate future, the amount of the sales proceeds designated as being hedged is equal to the amount of the foreign currency borrowing designated as the hedging instrument and the timing of the future cash flows on the debt coincides with the timing on the future cash flow from the disposal. [IAS 39 IG para F6.5].

Firm commitments

6.8.37   A firm commitment is a binding agreement for the exchange of a specified quantity of resources at a specified price on a specified future date or dates. [IAS 39 para 9]. Therefore, the key characteristic of a firm commitment is that it must have fixed terms, namely: fixed quantity, fixed price and fixed timing of the transaction. A firm commitment must be with a party that is external to the entity (see para 6.8.14 above). As the firm commitment is a binding agreement, it is usually legally enforceable. Firm commitments are discussed further in paragraph 6.8.114 below.

Forecast transactions

6.8.38   In many cases, entities will not be hedging risk exposures arising from firm commitments but rather those arising from forecast transactions that they expect to happen, but for which there is not a binding contract. Therefore, the definition of a hedged item also includes a forecast transaction. A forecast transaction is an uncommitted but highly probable, anticipated future transaction. [IAS 39 para 9]. Concluding that an uncommitted but anticipated transaction is highly probable and will happen is more difficult than for transactions arising from firm commitments. The qualifying conditions for getting hedge accounting for forecast transactions are considered further from paragraph 6.8.121 below.

Intra-group and intra-entity hedging transactions

6.8.39   It is common for entities in a group to transact with other group members or segments. These transactions may expose the entities to risks that they wish to hedge. The entity exposed to the risk can hedge it by entering into internal derivative contracts with, say, group treasury, or through external derivative contracts. However, as stated in paragraph 6.8.14 above, only assets, liabilities, firm commitments or highly probable forecast transactions that involve a party external to the entity can be designated as hedged items. It follows that such intra group transactions can be designated as hedged items only in the individual or separate financial statements of those entities and not in the consolidated financial statements of the reporting group. This is because the intra-group transactions cancel out on consolidation and do not expose the consolidated group to any risk that affects consolidated profit or loss. There are, however, two exceptions to this general rule involving foreign currency exposures:

- foreign exchange gains and losses on intra group monetary items; and
- forecast intra group transactions.

These are considered in the paragraphs that follow.

6.8.40   Under IAS 21, foreign exchange gains and losses on intra group monetary asset (or liability) between group entities with different functional currencies, whether short-term or long-term, do not fully eliminate in the consolidated profit or loss. This is because a foreign currency monetary item represents a commitment to convert one currency into another and exposes the reporting entity to a gain or loss through currency fluctuations. Accordingly, in the reporting entity's consolidated financial statements, such exchange differences continue to be recognised in profit or loss. For this reason, the foreign currency exposure on such an intra group monetary item can be designated as a hedged item on consolidation. [IAS 39 para 80].

Example – Hedging intra group monetary items

Subsidiary A, whose functional currency is the euro, has an intra group receivable from subsidiary B, whose functional currency is the Swiss franc. The receivable is denominated in Swiss francs and subsidiary A enters into a €/CHF forward contract with an external party to hedge the resulting foreign currency risk.

In its separate financial statements, subsidiary A translates the receivable into euros using the spot rate at the balance sheet date and recognises a foreign currency gain or loss in accordance with IAS 21. Subsidiary B, in its separate financial statements, records the payable to subsidiary A in its own functional currency and does not recognise any gain or loss. On consolidation, the gain or loss recognised by subsidiary A is translated into the group's presentation currency and is recognised in the group's income statement. There is no offsetting loss or gain arising from subsidiary B.

Subsidiary A uses the €/CHF forward contract to hedge the foreign currency exchange risk on the receivable from subsidiary B in its individual financial statements. As the receivable gives rise to an exposure to foreign currency gains or losses that is not fully eliminated on consolidation, the foreign currency exposure on the intra group receivable can be designated as the hedged item in the consolidated financial statements. The group can designate the €/CHF forward contract in subsidiary A as the hedging instrument. The hedge accounting achieved by subsidiary A is reversed on consolidation and replaced with hedge accounting achieved by the group.

For group purposes, it is not necessary for the subsidiary to take out the forward contract for the foreign exchange exposure on the intra group receivable to qualify as a hedged item on consolidation. The parent entity could have taken out the same forward contract hedging the €/CHF exchange risk instead.

6.8.41 IAS 39 permits the foreign currency risk of a highly probable forecast intra group transaction to be designated as a hedged item in the consolidated financial statements, provided the following two conditions are met:

- the highly probable forecast intra group transaction is denominated in a currency other than the functional currency of the group member entering into that transaction; and

- the foreign currency risk will affect the group's consolidated profit or loss.

[IAS 39 para 80].

6.8.42 The group member entering into the transaction can be a parent, subsidiary, associate, joint venture or branch. The first condition is necessary because, under IAS 21, a foreign currency exposure arises only when a transaction is denominated in a currency other than the functional currency of the entity entering into that transaction. The second condition is met if the forecast intra group transaction is related to an external transaction. An example is forecast sales or purchases of inventories between members of the same group if there is an onward sale of the inventory to a party external to the group (see example below). However, if there is no external related transaction, which will often be the case for royalty payments, interest payments or management charges between members of the same group, the foreign currency risk of those forecast intra group transactions would not affect consolidated profit or loss and, so, cannot qualify as hedged items. [IAS 39 para AG 99A]. Intra group foreign currency dividends can never qualify as hedged items (see para 6.8.46 below).

6.8.43 An entity cannot apply hedge accounting to only one part of the foreign currency risk arising on a highly probable forecast intra-group transaction.

> **Example – hedging of inter-company transactions**
>
> Subsidiary A has a functional currency of euro (EUR); subsidiary B has a functional currency of Japanese Yen (JPY); both subsidiaries are part of a group with presentation currency of USD
>
> Subsidiary A sells goods to subsidiary B based on USD-denominated prices, invoicing takes place in USD. USD is used due to the group's global transfer pricing strategy, whereby it has been agreed internally and with relevant tax authorities that all intra-group transactions are priced and invoiced in USD. Subsidiary B will sell the goods in the Japanese market in JPY.
>
> Subsidiary B enters into a USD/JPY derivative to hedge the USD-risk on its purchases; subsidiary A does not enter into any hedge in relation to this transaction.
>
> Paragraph 80 of IAS 39 requires that the foreign currency risk affects consolidated profit and loss. Since the overall profit and loss on this intra-group transaction is ultimately affected by the EUR/JPY exposure, rather than the USD/JPY exposure, hedge accounting cannot be applied.

6.8.44 If a hedge of a forecast intra-group transaction qualifies for hedge accounting, any gain or loss that is recognised directly in equity should be reclassified into profit or loss in the same period or periods during which the foreign currency risk of the hedged transaction affects consolidated profit or loss (see further para 6.8.131 below).

Example 1 – Hedging the foreign currency risk of an intra group forecast transaction

Group A (pound sterling presentation currency) includes entity B with euro functional currency and entity C with US dollar functional currency in the consolidation. Entity B manufactures tyres and incurs production costs in euros. It sells most of the tyres to entity C and those transactions are denominated in US dollars. Entity C markets and sells those tyres to external customers in the US, also in US dollars.

In June 20X6 entity B forecasts that it will sell tyres to entity C in October 20X6 amounting to US$ 10m. These sales are highly probable and all the other conditions in IAS 39 for hedge accounting are met. Entity C expects to sell this inventory to external customers in early 20X7. At the same time in June 20X6, entity B enters into a euro/US$ derivative (buy €/sell US$) to hedge the foreign currency risk of the forecast sale of US$10m to entity C in October 20X6.

Group A intends to designate the forward contract as hedging the foreign currency risk of the forecast intra group sales of US$10m by entity B in a cash flow hedging relationship in the consolidated financial statements. It is able to do so because all the following conditions are met

- The intra group sales are highly probable and all the other conditions for using hedge accounting are met.

- The intra group sales are denominated in a currency (US$) other than entity B's functional currency (€).

- The existence of the expected onwards sale of the inventory in US dollars to third parties outside the group results in the hedged exposure affecting the pound sterling consolidated profit or loss. This is because the intra group profit on sale recognised in entity B is € number that is fixed according to the €/$ rate when the sale takes place in October 20X6. This profit is eliminated on consolidation against the carrying value of tyre inventory in entity C and released to consolidated profit or loss when the onward sale of inventory to third parties take place in 20X7.

Gains/losses on the €/US$ derivative are recognised initially in consolidated equity to the extent the hedge is effective. These amounts are reclassified to consolidated profit or loss in 20X7 when the external sales occur.

The standard notes the difficulty in demonstrating that there is a related external transaction for intra-group royalty and interest payments, but does not preclude the use of hedge accounting for such transactions where a clear link to an external transaction can be demonstrated.

Example 2 – Linkage to an external transaction

A GBP parent obtains a GBP external loan and immediately lends the proceeds in USD to a subsidiary with a USD functional currency. The subsidiary uses the money to make external loans to customers in USD. In the consolidated financial statements including the parent and subsidiary the group proposes to hedge the GBP/USD risk of the loan to the subsidiary with a GBP/USD swap. In considering whether the hedge can be designated under IAS 39 it is necessary to evaluate the linkage between the loan by the parent and the external transaction by considering factors such as whether:

- the stated purpose of the parent lending is to allow the subsidiary to on-lend to external parties;

- there is a short time lag between lending by the parent an on-lending by the subsidiary (ideally simultaneous on-lending);

- similar terms exist between the loan to the parent and the subsidiary. If the loan with the parent is longer in duration than the external loan the parent should demonstrate an intention to rollover the external loans;

- if the loans were repaid early by the subsidiary's external borrowers, there is a requirement to repay the loan to the parent company.

Items that do not qualify as hedged items

6.8.45   There are a number of items that, for various reasons, cannot qualify as a hedged item in a hedging relationship. For such items the normal measurement and recognition rules will apply. These items are as considered below.

Own equity instruments

6.8.46   Hedge accounting cannot be applied for hedges of any items included in equity or transactions that directly affect equity. This is because the hedged item cannot create an exposure to risk that will affect profit or loss. Therefore, hedges of risks relating to the forecast sale, purchase or redemption of an entity's own equity shares cannot qualify as hedged items. Similarly, distributions to holders of an equity instrument are debited by the issuer directly to equity. [IAS 32 para 25]. Therefore, such distributions cannot be designated as a hedged item. However, a dividend that has been approved in a general meeting of members and has not yet been paid and is recognised as a financial liability may qualify as a hedged item, for example, for foreign currency risk if it is denominated in a foreign currency as illustrated in the example below. [IAS 39 IG para F2.7].

Example – Inter-company dividends denominated in foreign currency

Entity A, whose functional currency is the pound sterling, has a subsidiary in the US, whose functional currency is the US dollar. On 1 January 20X6, entity A forecasts that it will receive a US$100m dividend from its US subsidiary in six months. The inter company dividend was approved in general meeting of members (or equivalent) on 30 April 20X6, at which time both entity A and its subsidiary recognised the dividend as a receivable or payable in their respective financial statements.

The foreign currency dividend receivable in entity A's balance sheet was retranslated at the reporting period end, 31 May 20X6, resulting in a foreign currency loss. The subsidiary paid the dividend on 30 June 20X6.

Entity A wanted to designate the foreign currency risk on highly probable inter-company dividend as the hedged item in its group financial statements in a cash flow hedge from 1 January 20X6 to 30 June 20X6, in order to hedge the exposure to changes in the £/US$ exchange rate. However, inter-company dividends are not foreign currency transactions that can be hedged, because they do not affect the consolidated income statement. They are distributions of earnings.

The foreign currency exposure arising from the receivable in US dollars recognised on 30 April 20X6 can be designated as a hedged item because it gives rise to foreign currency gains and losses that do not fully eliminate on consolidation and, therefore, affect the consolidated income statement (see para 6.8.40 above). Entity A can, therefore, apply hedge accounting from that date until 30 June 20X6 when the cash is received in its group financial statements.

Held-to-maturity investments

6.8.47 Unlike loans and receivables (see para 6.8.33 above), a held-to-maturity (HTM) investment (whether it pays fixed or floating interest) cannot be hedged for interest rate risk, because designation of an investment as held-to-maturity requires the holder's positive intent and ability to hold the instrument to maturity. Held-to-maturity classification implies that the net changes in fair value stemming from changes in market interest rates from inception to maturity will not have an impact on profit or loss as the entity has committed itself to retaining the investment to maturity. Similarly, a held-to-maturity investment cannot be hedged for pre-payment risk – risk that an investment will be paid earlier or later than expected. As interest rates fall below rates on existing loans, borrowers may, and commonly do, pre-pay their existing loans and refinance at lower rates. Therefore, as pre-payment risk is primarily a function of interest rates, it is more akin to interest rate risk and, accordingly, cannot be designated as a hedged risk. However, a held-to-maturity investment can be a hedged item with respect to risks from changes in foreign currency exchange rates and credit risk. [IAS 39 para 79].

6.8.48 Although hedge accounting is prohibited for hedging the interest rate risk of a held-to-maturity asset, the prohibition only applies to held-to-maturity assets that have already been recognised on the entity's balance sheet. The prohibition does not apply to a forecast purchase of a held-to-maturity asset as illustrated in the example below.

Example – Forecast purchase of held-to-maturity investment

An entity has a forecast transaction to purchase a financial asset that it intends to classify as held-to-maturity when the forecast transaction occurs. It enters into a derivative contract to lock in the current interest rate and designates the derivative as a hedge of the forecast purchase of the financial asset.

Provided all the hedge accounting criteria are met, the entity can apply cash flow hedge accounting to the forecast purchase of a held-to-maturity security. This is because the investment is not classified as held-to-maturity until the transaction occurs. [IAS 39 IG para F2.10].

6.8.49 The standard also permits cash flow hedge accounting for future interest receipts from a debt instrument that originated from the re-investment of interest receipts from an held-to-maturity investment as illustrated in the example below.

Example – Hedging reinvestment risk of funds obtained from held-to-maturity investments

An entity owns a variable rate asset that it has classified as held-to-maturity. The cash from variable interest receipts is re-invested in debt instruments. The entity enters into a derivative contract to lock in the current interest rate on the reinvestment of variable rate cash flows and designates the derivative as a cash flow hedge of the forecast future interest receipts on debt instruments.

Provided all the hedge accounting criteria are met, the hedging relationship will qualify for cash flow hedge accounting even though the cash from the interest receipts that are being reinvested come from an asset that is classified as held-to-maturity. The source of the funds used to purchase the debt instrument is not relevant in determining whether the reinvestment risk can be hedged. This answer applies also if the source of the funds used to purchase the debt instrument had been a fixed rate held-to-maturity investment. [IAS 39 IG para F2.11].

Equity method investment and investment in consolidated subsidiaries

6.8.50 An equity method investment, such as an associate or joint venture, cannot be a hedged item in a fair value hedge because the equity method recognises in profit or loss the investor's share of the associate's profit or loss, rather than changes in the investment's fair value. [IAS 39 para AG 99]. Although this applies to consolidated financial statements, an entity may be able to designate an investment in an associate as a fair value hedge in its separate financial statements, provided that its fair value can be measured reliably.

6.8.50.1 Additionally, entities that applied proportionate consolidation under IAS 31 and designated hedging relationships for hedged items that were proportionately consolidated (for example, a cash flow hedge of a joint arrangement's variable rate debt), will be required to cease hedge accounting for such relationships from the date of application of IFRS 11, if equity accounting is required for a joint venture under that standard.

6.8.51 The ability of an entity to treat an associate as the hedged item in a cash flow hedge is considered in the following example.

Example – Forecast cash flows in associates

Entity A has a 25% investment in a foreign entity over which it has significant influence. It, therefore, accounts for the foreign entity as an associate using the equity method. The associate's functional currency, in which most of its sales and costs are denominated, differs from entity A's functional currency. In entity A's consolidated financial statements its share of the associate's net results will fluctuate with the changes in the exchange rate. The entity intends to designate a portion of the forecast cash flows in the associate as the hedged item in a hedge of foreign currency risk.

Under the functional currency concept in IAS 21, a cash flow that is denominated in an associate's functional currency does not give rise to a foreign currency (transaction) exposure for the associate in its separate financial statements. The variability in entity A's share of its associate's net results arises only in its consolidated financial statements and arises from the translation of the associate's financial statements into the group's presentation currency. This is a translation rather than a transaction exposure. IAS 39 permits an entity to apply hedge accounting to a hedge of the translation risk on its existing net investment, but this does not extend to the investee's forecast future cash flows or profits.

6.8.52   An investment in a consolidated subsidiary cannot be a hedged item in a fair value hedge, because consolidation recognises in profit or loss the subsidiary's profit or loss, rather than changes in the investment's fair value. If a subsidiary was allowed to be designated as a hedged item, it would result in double counting, as both the income from the investment as well as changes in the fair value would be reported in profit or loss. A hedge of a net investment in a foreign operation is different because it is a hedge of the foreign currency exposure, not a fair value hedge of the change in the investment's value. [IAS 39 para AG 99]. Another example of a transaction undertaken by a foreign subsidiary that cannot be hedged at the consolidation level is considered below

> **Example 1 – Forecast foreign currency transaction undertaken by a foreign subsidiary**
>
> Entity A's functional currency is the euro. It has a US subsidiary, subsidiary B, whose functional currency is the US dollar. Subsidiary B has highly probable forecast sales denominated in Japanese yen.
>
> Entity A wishes to hedge subsidiary B's forecast Japanese yen inflows back into euros (entity A's functional currency) using external foreign currency forward contracts (¥/€). Entity A's management intends to designate, in the consolidated financial statements, the forward contracts as hedging instruments in a cash flow hedge of the forecast transactions denominated in Japanese yen.
>
> The ¥/€ forward contracts taken out by entity A do not qualify for cash flow hedge accounting on consolidation. This is because there is no ¥/€ cash flow exposure that affects consolidated profit or loss. The consolidated income statement will be exposed to ¥/US$ movements, as subsidiary B will translate its ¥ sales into its own functional currency (US$). The exposure to movements in US/€ constitutes a translation risk rather than a cash flow exposure and, therefore, cannot be the subject of a cash flow hedge.
>
> However, it is possible for the subsidiary B to use a ¥/US$ forward contract to designate a cash flow hedge of its ¥/US$ transaction exposure. Alternatively, entity A could use a ¥/US$ forward contract to hedge the exposure since IAS 39 does not require that the operating unit that is exposed to the risk being hedged be a party to the hedging instrument. [IAS 39 para IG F2.14].
>
> Entity A could also hedge its net investment in subsidiary B using a €/US$ forward (see para 6.8.150 below). This would, however, not include the forecast transaction.

Example 2 – Parent hedging forecasted future revenues denominated in the functional currency of a subsidiary which is different from functional currency of the parent

Entity A, based in Germany, whose functional currency is euro, has a subsidiary in the UK, whose functional currency is GBP. The group's presentation currency is also euro. The UK subsidiary sells gas within the UK for GBP to British customers. At the group level, the group's treasury department enters into external GBP/euro forward contract to hedge against movements in GBP *versus* euro on behalf of the group. The group cannot obtain cash flow hedge accounting for the UK subsidiary sales. The sales of the UK subsidiary are made in its functional currency so it has no foreign currency exposure. The consolidated group has a foreign currency exposure, but it will not affect the group's reported net profit or loss. At the consolidated level the foreign currency exposure will be deferred as part of cumulative translation adjustment in equity when the UK subsidiary's financial statements are translated into the group's presentation currency for consolidation [IAS 21 para 39(c)]. Group management may, therefore, consider the possibility of net investment hedge accounting under paragraph 102 of IAS 39. However, the group will not be able to obtain hedge accounting for hedges of forecasted sales – see last sentence of the example 1 above.

Example 3 – Hedging of foreign currency sales of a foreign subsidiary denominated in group's presentation currency by the parent

A European parent entity whose functional currency is euro, has a Chinese subsidiary whose functional currency is RMB. The presentation currency of the group is euro. The Chinese entity has highly probable forecast sales in euro that its management has not hedged. The parent's management enters into EUR/RMB forward contracts and designates these as cash flow hedges of the Chinese subsidiary forecast sales.

The forecast euro sales give rise to a currency risk that will affect the subsidiary's profit or loss in its separate financial statements. This is because the RMB amount at which the sales are reported in the subsidiary's separate financial statements will be affected by the EUR/RMB exchange rate at the time the sales occur.

However, in the consolidated financial statements the sales will be translated into euro using the exchange rates at the dates of the transactions (or an average rate when this approximates the rates at the dates of the transactions) in accordance with paragraph 39(b) of IAS 21. Hence, the amount at which the sales are reported in the group's consolidated financial statements will not be affected by the EUR/RMB exchange rate at the time the sales occur. Even though the exchange rate may not have an impact on the sales expressed in euros, the consolidated profit or loss is affected by the realised margin in the Chinese subsidiary.

The forecast transaction meets the requirements of paragraph 88(c) of IAS 39. The reference in paragraph 88(c) of IAS 39 to 'profit or loss' refers to the subsidiary's profit or loss where the exposure is located and not to the profit or loss of the consolidated entity. This is consistent with the functional currency framework in IAS 21 under which a foreign exchange exposure arises whenever a transaction is denominated in a currency other than the functional currency of the entity entering into the transaction. Paragraph IG F.2.14 of IAS 39 also permits the hedging instrument to be entered into by the parent and states that it need not be entered into by the subsidiary that has the exposure. Hence, provided all the other criteria in paragraph 88 of IAS 39R are met, the group may obtain cash flow hedge accounting in its consolidated financial statements.

Future earnings

6.8.53 Future earnings or future results cannot be designated as hedged items because they are the net effect of various transactions that do not share the same risk characteristic. However, future revenue or future expenditure may be separately designated as hedged items if the underlying risk exposure can be specifically identified and measured (see example in para 6.8.121 below).

Derivative instruments

6.8.54 A derivative instrument (whether a stand-alone or separately recognised embedded derivative) cannot be designated as a hedged item, either individually or as part of a hedged group in a fair value or cash flow hedge. For instance, it is not possible to designate a pay-variable, receive-fixed forward rate agreement (FRA) as a cash flow hedge of a pay-fixed, receive-variable FRA. This is because derivative instruments are always deemed held for trading and measured at fair value with gains and losses recognised in profit or loss unless they are designated and effective hedging instruments. As an exception, IAS 39 permits the designation of a purchased option as the hedged item in a fair value hedge. [IAS 39 paras AG 94, IG F2.1]. A contract to buy or sell a non-financial asset that can be settled net in cash will be accounted for as a derivative under IAS 39, unless it meets the 'own use' exception discussed in chapter 6.1 and so cannot be a hedged item.

General business risk

6.8.55 To qualify for hedge accounting, the hedge must relate to a specific identified and designated risk and not merely to the entity's general business risks and must ultimately affect the entity's profit or loss. For example, a firm commitment to acquire a business in a business combination cannot be a hedged item, except for foreign exchange risk in respect of the purchase consideration, because the other risks being hedged cannot be specifically identified and measured. These other risks are general business risks. [IAS 39 paras AG 98, AG 110]. Similarly, the risk that a transaction will not occur such that it would result in less revenue than expected is an overall business risk that is not eligible as a hedged item. [IAS 39 para IG F2.8]. A hedge of the risk of obsolescence of a physical asset or the risk of expropriation of property by a government is also not eligible for hedge accounting; effectiveness cannot be measured because those risks are not measurable reliably.

Hedging instruments

Definition

6.8.56 A hedging instrument is a designated derivative or, for a hedge of the risk of changes in foreign currency exchange rates only, a designated non-derivative financial asset or non-derivative financial liability, whose fair value or cash flows are expected to offset changes in the fair value or cash flows of a designated hedged item. [IAS 39 para 9].

6.8.57 Only instruments that involve a party external to the reporting entity (that is, external to the group, or individual entity that is being reported on) can be designated as hedging instruments. Therefore, if an entity wishes to achieve hedge accounting in the consolidated financial statements, it must designate a hedging relationship between a qualifying external hedging instrument and a qualifying hedged item. However, internal derivative contracts may qualify for hedge accounting in the individual or separate financial statements of individual entities within the group provided that they are external to the individual entity being reported on (see para 6.8.86 below). [IAS 39 para 73].

Derivative financial instruments

6.8.58 IAS 39 does not restrict the circumstances in which a derivative may be designated as a hedging instrument provided the hedge accounting conditions are met (see para 6.8.156 below), except for some written options. This means that derivative instruments such as forward exchange contracts, futures contracts, interest rate swaps, cross-currency and commodity swaps and purchased options can all be designated as hedging instruments. An embedded derivative that is accounted for separately from its host contract can be used as a hedging instrument. Also, those contracts for purchases or sales of non-financial assets that are accounted for as derivatives under IAS 39 (that is, can be settled net or by exchanging another financial instrument and that are not for own use) may be used as hedging instruments.

> **Example 1 – Hedging with a sales commitment**
>
> Entity J's functional currency is the Japanese yen. It has issued a US$ fixed rate debt instrument with semi-annual interest payments that matures in 2 years with principal due at maturity of 5 million US dollars. It has also entered into a fixed price sales commitment for 5 million US dollars that matures in two years that is not accounted for as a derivative, because it meets the exemption for normal sales. Entity J intends to designate the sales commitment as a hedge of the fair value change of the maturity amount of the debt attributable to foreign currency risk.
>
> In this scenario, the sales commitment is accounted for as a firm commitment and not as a derivative and, therefore, cannot be designated as a hedging instrument. However, if the foreign currency component of the sales commitment is required to be separated as an embedded derivative on the grounds that US dollar is not the customer's functional currency and otherwise not closely related under IAS 39, it could be designated as a hedging instrument in a hedge of the exposure to changes in the fair value of the debt's maturity amount attributable to foreign currency risk. [IAS 39 para IG F1.2]. However, as the exchange difference on the fixed rate debt would, in any event, be reported in profit or loss under IAS 21, a separate hedging relationship is not necessary.

Example 2 – Hedging with fixed to fixed cross currency swaps

Entity X, whose functional currency is the euro, has issued a US dollar fixed rate debt. Entity X's management intends to hedge the foreign exchange cash flow exposure on the debt's interest and principal by entering into a fixed to fixed euro/US dollar cross currency interest rate swap.

Entity X expects the cross currency interest rate swap to be a highly effective hedge of the cash flow exposure, since the critical terms of the hedging instrument and the hedged item match.

IAS 39 does not specify the methodology that should be used for effectiveness testing other than to require this to be consistent with the entity's risk management strategy. One possible method would be to apply the hypothetical derivative method.

The hypothetical derivative method models the hedged item as a derivative (called the 'hypothetical derivative' as it does not exist) and then compares the change in the fair value of the hedging instrument with the change in the fair value of the hypothetical derivative. The USD leg of the hypothetical derivative will have terms that identically match those of the hedged item and the euro leg is set such that the fair value of the hypothetical derivative is zero at the inception of the hedge.

As mentioned in paragraph 6.8.29, it is generally accepted that in the case of a cash flow hedge where effectiveness is measured using a hypothetical derivative method, currency basis spreads can be included in the hypothetical derivative and hence will not give rise to ineffectiveness.

If all the critical terms of the swap exactly match the terms of the underlying bond (as reflected in the hypothetical derivative), this test is likely to give rise to no ineffectiveness. If this is the case and, if all the remaining requirements of paragraph 88 of IAS 39 relating to documentation and designation are met, management could defer the entire change in the fair value of the swap in other comprehensive income.

At each reporting date, the underlying bond will be re-measured through profit or loss using the spot exchange rate in accordance with IAS 21. At the same time an equivalent offsetting portion of the fair value adjustment of the swap should be recycled to profit or loss. The remaining revaluation gain or loss deferred in equity relates to the forward points, that is, the difference between the spot rate and the forward rate. These forward points deferred in equity should be recognised in profit or loss over the period of the hedging relationship (this being the period(s) in which the hedged item affects profit or loss) using the effective interest rate method.

6.8.59 It is not necessary for an entity to enter into a new derivative contract every time it enters into a new hedging relationship. Provided the hedge accounting criteria are met, a pre-existing derivative instrument that has been held for some time and classified as held-for-trading can be designated as a hedging instrument in a new hedging relationship, as can a derivative that has been designated previously as a hedging instrument in a hedge relationship that no longer qualifies for hedge accounting. However, an existing derivative will have a non-zero fair value because of its 'off market terms'. Consequently, it cannot be assumed that the new relationship will be highly effective without performing the necessary analysis of the impact of the 'off market' nature of the derivative on the new relationship, particularly when compared to a new 'on market' hypothetical derivative where the hedge is a cashflow hedge (see paras 6.8.190-6.8.192 for more details of constructing a hypothetical derivative). The 'off market' nature of the derivative can be described as an 'embedded financing' within the derivative. For example, a derivative asset can be thought of as containing an 'embedded loan receivable' and a derivative liability as containing an 'embedded loan payable'. However, it does not change the fact that the instrument is still a derivative and must be carried in its entirety at fair value. This 'embedded' financing can be a source of ineffectiveness. Changing the designation of a derivative from a trading instrument to a hedging instrument occurs at inception of the new hedging relationship.

Portions and proportions of a hedging instrument

6.8.60   There is normally a single fair value measure for a hedging instrument in its entirety and the factors that cause changes in fair value are co-dependent. Thus, a hedging relationship is designated by an entity for a hedging instrument in its entirety. It follows that a derivative instrument cannot be split into components representing different risks with each component designated as the hedging instrument. The only exceptions permitted are:

■   separating the interest element and the spot price of a forward contract; and

■   separating the intrinsic value and time value of an option contract and designating as the hedging instrument only the change in intrinsic value of an option.

These exceptions are permitted because the intrinsic value of the option and the premium or discount on the forward can generally be measured separately.

[IAS 39 para 74].

Example 1 – Definition of a forward contract

For hedging purposes, entity A enters into the following derivative instruments:

■   A fixed to fixed cross-currency swap.

■   A floating to floating cross-currency swap.

■   A floating to fixed cross-currency swap.

Entity A's management wishes to designate only the spot element of these derivatives as hedging instruments in separate hedging relationships.

Paragraph 74 of IAS 39 allows an entity to designate the spot element of a derivative as a hedging instrument provided the derivative is a forward contract. A simple forward contract is a contract to exchange a fixed amount of a financial or non-financial asset on a fixed future value date or dates beyond the spot value date. For the purposes of applying paragraph 74 of IAS 39, the term 'forward contract' should be interpreted as being any derivative instrument that is a simple forward contract or that may be constructed using only a series of simple forward contracts. Forward contracts may be settled by gross delivery of the financial asset in return for cash, or on a net basis at each settlement date.

The fixed to fixed cross-currency swap entered into by entity A constitutes a forward contract under paragraph 74 of IAS 39 provided that the settlements on each leg of the swap occur on the same dates in the future (that is, there is no timing mismatch between the two legs of the swap).

However, the other derivatives (the floating to floating cross-currency swap and the floating to fixed cross-currency swaps) are not forward contracts since they cannot be constructed using only simple forward contracts.

Example 2 – Splitting a written swaption into components

Entity A, whose functional currency is euro, issues 30-year fixed-rate debt. At the same time, entity A enters into an interest rate derivative with a third party with the following terms: entity A receives 7% fixed and pays 5% fixed for 7 years. After 7 years, the counterparty has the option to require entity A to enter into a pay fixed 5%, receive LIBOR interest rate swap with a maturity of 23 years. (Economically, entity A has sold the counterparty a swaption on a 23 year swap with 7 years until exercise date and with premium payments spread over 7 years).

Entity A proposes to split the derivative into separate components, one of which is an on-market receive fixed, pay variable interest rate swap. It would designate this component as a hedge of the first seven years of interest rate exposure under the fixed rate debt. The remaining component would be treated as a trading derivative.

Entity A cannot split the derivative into its components, because of the requirements of paragraph 74 of IAS 39 and paragraph IG F1.8 of IAS 39 so any attempt to designate it as a hedging instrument would be likely to fail the prospective effectiveness requirements.

In addition the combined instrument is a written option and cannot be designated as a hedging instrument under paragraph AG94 of IAS 39 (see para 6.8.75).

6.8.61 The fair value of a foreign exchange forward contract is affected by changes in the spot rate and by changes in the forward points. The latter derives from the interest rate differential between the currencies specified in the forward contract. Changes in the forward points may give rise to ineffectiveness if the hedged item is not similarly affected by interest rate differentials unless only the spot component of the forward is designated as the hedging instrument (see para 6.8.208 below).

6.8.62 The fair value of an option can be divided into two portions: the intrinsic value, which is determined in terms of the difference between the strike price and the current market price of the underlying (as described in more detail below); and the time value, which is the option's remaining value and depends on the volatility of the price of the underlying, interest rates and the time remaining to maturity. When the option is used to hedge the one-sided risk on a non-optional position, changes in the option's time value will not be offset by an equivalent change in the value or cash flows of the hedged item (for more details about hedging of portions see para 6.8.23). IAS 39 does not specify how the intrinsic value of an option is determined. Intrinsic value can be defined based on the spot rate. For example, for an interest rate cap that is used to hedge the exposure to interest rates on floating rate debt, the intrinsic value may be deferred by projecting all future cash flows on the cap at the current spot rate and discounting the result using the zero-coupon curve. If the current spot rate is below the market rate, the cap is 'out of the money' in all periods. Alternatively, the intrinsic value could be defined using the forward rate curve. The projected cash flows would be calculated using the forward rates. In that case the cap may be in the money in some periods, even when the current spot rate is below the strike price.

The intrinsic value of a European option (that is, an option which is settled at the end of its term) may be defined as discounted where the difference between:

- the strike price of the option's underlying specified in the option; and
- the market price of the underlying

is discounted to present value.

The intrinsic value may also be defined as undiscounted – that is, simply as the absolute difference between the strike price and market price of the underlying asset.

The intrinsic value of an American style option may be defined as the difference between the undiscounted spot price on the day when it is determined and the strike price specified in the option contract. This is because the American style option can be exercised at any time.

6.8.63   Generally, it may be advantageous to exclude the forward points and the time value of an option to improve effectiveness. However, this comes at a price as it will most probably increase the volatility in the income statement. This is because as the forward points or time value are not subject to hedge accounting, any changes in their fair value will be recognised as gains or losses in the income statement as they occur. If forward points were included in the hedge relationship then they could generate ineffectiveness for example if the timing of the hedged forecast transaction changed and change in fair value of the forward was higher in absolute terms than change in fair value of the hedged cash flow (see para 6.8.129). [IAS 39 para 96].

6.8.64   A proportion of the entire hedging instrument, such as 50% of the notional amount, may be designated as the hedging instrument. [IAS 39 para 75]. The proportion that is not acting as a hedge is either treated as held-for-trading or designated as a hedging instrument in another hedge relationship.

Example – Proportions of derivatives as hedging instruments

Entity A, whose functional currency is the euro, enters into a US$10m forward contract on 1 June 20X1 to hedge forecast future US$-denominated sales in March 20X2. At the time of entering into the forward contract, only US$8m of forecast sales are considered to be highly probable of occurring in March 20X2.

In this situation, entity A can designated 80% of the forward contract as a hedge of the highly probable future sales of US$8m in March 20X2. The remaining US$2m of the forward contract (20%) may either be designated as trading or as a hedging instrument in another hedge relationship. In other words, 20% of the total change in the fair value of the forward contract would be reported in profit or loss, or used as an offset in another hedge relationship.

6.8.65 A hedging relationship may not be designated for only a portion of the time period during which a hedging instrument remains outstanding as illustrated in the example below. [IAS 39 para 75].

Example – Portion of the outstanding life of a derivative as a hedging instrument

An entity enters into a pay-fixed, receive-variable interest rate swap to hedge the cash flow exposure of a floating rate debt instrument. Both the swap and the debt instrument are entered into on the same date. The floating rate debt instrument has a term of 5 years and the swap has a term of 7 years.

The entity cannot designate the cash flows arising in the first 5 years of the 7 year swap as a hedging instrument. The swap's fair value derives from the present value of the net settlements over the entire 7 year period, not the first 5 years. Furthermore, the fair value of the swap cannot be time apportioned using linear interpolation, as the change in the swap's fair value per unit of time is non-linear.

However, the entity can designate the entire 7 year swap as a hedge of the 5 year debt, but ineffectiveness will arise because of timing mismatches and is likely to be so large (that is, outside the 80%-125% range, see para 6.8.165) as to prohibit hedge accounting.

On the other hand, if the swap's terms and the debt are reversed so that they are 5 years and 7 years respectively, the 5 year swap can be designated as a hedge of the first 5 years of the debt instrument. This is referred to as 'partial-term' hedging and is discussed in paragraph 6.8.32 above.

Hedging more than one risk with a single instrument

6.8.66 A derivative, such as a forward contract, swap or an option, is used as a hedging instrument to hedge a single risk (foreign currency, interest rate or equity price risk). However, entities may often use a single derivative such as a cross-currency swap (combined interest rate and currency swap) to convert a variable rate position in a foreign currency to a fixed rate position in the entity's functional currency. IAS 39 permits a single hedging instrument to be designated as a hedge of more than one type of risk provided that:

- The risks hedged can be identified clearly.

- The effectiveness of the hedge can be demonstrated.

- It is possible to ensure that there is specific designation of the hedging instrument and different risk positions.

[IAS 39 para 76].

6.8.67 If a single hedging instrument is used to hedge different risk exposures and each of these risk exposures are accounted for using different forms of hedge accounting (fair value hedge for one, cash flow hedge for the other), IFRS 7 requires separate disclosures for each type of hedge (see chapter 11). [IAS 39 IG para F1.12].

Example 1 – Dual foreign currency forward exchange contract to hedge currency risk

Entity A's functional currency is the Japanese yen. Entity A has a 5 year floating rate US dollar liability and a 10 year fixed rate pound sterling denominated bond (an asset). The principal amounts of the asset and liability when converted into the Japanese yen are the same. Entity A enters into a single foreign currency forward contract to hedge its foreign currency exposure on both instruments under which it receives US dollars and pays pound sterling at the end of 5 years.

Entity A designates the forward exchange contract as a hedging instrument in a cash flow hedge against the foreign currency exposure on the principal repayments of both instruments. Since entity A's functional currency is Yen, it is exposed to US$/¥ foreign currency risk on the floating rate liability and ¥/£ foreign exchange risk on the fixed rate asset.

IAS 39 permits a single hedging instrument to be designated as a hedge of multiple types of risk if three conditions stated in paragraph 6.8.66 above are met. In this example, the derivative hedging instrument satisfies all of these conditions, as follows:

- The risks hedged can be identified clearly. The risks are the exposures to changes in the forward exchange rates between US dollars and yen and yen and pounds, respectively.

- The effectiveness of the hedge can be demonstrated. For the pound sterling bond, the effectiveness is measured as the degree of offset between the fair value of the principal repayment in pounds sterling and the fair value of the pound sterling payment on the forward exchange contract. For the US dollar liability, the effectiveness is measured as the degree of offset between the fair value of the principal repayment in US dollars and the US dollar receipt on the forward exchange contract. Even though the receivable has a 10-year life and the forward protects it for only the first 5 years, hedge accounting is permitted for only a portion of the exposure as described in paragraph 6.8.32 above.

- It is possible to ensure that there is specific designation of the hedging instrument and different risk positions. The hedged exposures are identified as the principal amounts of the liability and the note receivable in their respective currency of denomination.

[IAS 39 para IG F1.13].

It should be noted that in respect of the second point above, the US $/£ forward is theoretically divided into two different derivatives. The Yen is imputed as the base currency for the two derivatives creating a synthetic US$/Yen (receive US dollar, pay Yen) foreign currency forward and a synthetic ¥/£ (receive Yen, pay sterling) foreign currency forward. The synthetic Yen leg is defined in such a manner that the fair value of each synthetic forward contract is nil at the hedge's inception. This can be pictorially represented as follows:

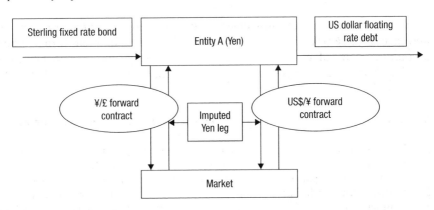

Furthermore, it should be noted that the hedge accounting criteria must be satisfied for both the designated hedged risks. For instance, if effectiveness of the hedge can be demonstrated for US$/¥ risk only and not ¥/£ risk, hedge accounting is not permitted. Similarly, if one of the hedged risks no longer exists or a hedge effectiveness test is failed for that risk during the term of the hedge then both hedges must be discontinued. This is because a derivative instrument must be fair valued and used as a hedging instrument in its entirety apart from the specific exemptions discussed in paragraph 6.8.60.

Example 2 – Hedging a floating rate foreign currency debt with a floating rate cross currency interest rate swap

Entity A's functional currency is sterling. Entity A has issued a floating rate (3 month USD LIBOR) bond denominated in USD and on the same date entered into a cross currency swap to hedge the bond to floating rate (3 month Stg LIBOR) in sterling. So the swap (after the initial exchange of principal amounts) is to receive 3 month USD LIBOR plus USD principal, and to pay 3 month Stg LIBOR plus Stg principal.

Entity A wishes to designate the swap in its entirety as a cash flow hedge of the foreign exchange and interest rate risk on the bond so as to minimise ineffectiveness, including from currency basis. However, the swap can be designated as a cash flow hedge of spot foreign exchange risk only. All variability due to foreign exchange has been eliminated and the foreign exchange movements, including the effect of changes in currency basis, can be recognised in OCI.

As regards interest rate risk, this cannot be designated as being hedged as entity A's exposure to cash flow variability associated with interest rate changes has not been reduced. Rather entity A has merely exchanged one exposure to variable rates (3 month USD LIBOR) for another (3 month Stg LIBOR).

Under paragraph IG F5.5 of IAS 39 the hypothetical derivatives method can be used to measure the effectiveness of cash flow hedges. In the circumstances described, the USD leg of the hypothetical derivative would mirror the hedged debt and hence have a receive leg of receive 3 month USD LIBOR plus USD principal. However the sterling leg should be to pay sterling overnight rates plus sterling principal (that is, with daily resets) to exclude any interest rate risk. As a result of the sterling leg of the hypothetical derivative resetting daily, some ineffectiveness will arise. Entity A will need to assess whether this is so big as to prevent the use of hedge accounting.

6.8.68   It is also possible to use a single derivative instrument to hedge more than one risk in more than one hedged item. In order to do this, the entity should be able to identify the hedged risks in each of the hedged items and split the single derivative into its components in order to allocate those components to each hedged risk identified. As a derivative has only a single fair value, care should be taken in splitting a derivative so that it does not result in the recognition of cash flows in the single hedging instrument that do not contractually exist. Hedging multiple risks in multiple items in this way is complex and the desired effectiveness may not always be achieved. Therefore, expert guidance should always be sought.

Example 1 – Cross currency interest rate swap hedging multiple risks in multiple hedged items

Entity A's functional currency is the euro. On the same date, entity A has issued a 10 year fixed-rate debt denominated in US dollar with an annual 5% coupon and has made a 10 year 6 months LIBOR + 80bp loan to a third party in sterling. Entity A has also entered into on the same date a cross-currency interest rate (CCIR) US\$ fixed/£ floating swap. Under the terms of the swap. Entity A will receive fixed interest in US dollar at 4% and will pay variable 6-month LIBOR interest in sterling. The entity wishes to obtain hedge accounting for the swap.

With regard to the loan asset, entity A is exposed to a £/€ exchange risk, because the loan is denominated in sterling which is not entity A's functional currency. It is also exposed to cash flow interest rate risk (sterling 6 months LIBOR) because entity A will pay variable coupon on the loan. Entity A is also exposed to a credit risk (change in the credit rating of the issuer of the loan).

With regard to the liability, entity A is exposed to a risk of changes in the fair value of the debt due to €/US\$ exchange risk (both the notional amount and the interest on the loan are denominated in US dollars, which is not entity A's functional currency). Entity A is also exposed to fair value interest rate risk (US\$ 6 months LIBOR is defined as the benchmark risk), because it will pay fixed coupon in US\$ on the debt.

Two ways in which entity A could use the CCIR swap as a hedging instrument are described below. A single swap (receive US\$ 4% fixed, pay floating £) may be analysed into its separate risk components for hedging purposes by imputing a notional leg denominated in the entity's functional currency. The additional leg may be either fixed or floating, provided the chosen alternative qualifies for hedge accounting for both of the exposures hedged and effectiveness can be reliably measured for both elements. Prospective and retrospective effectiveness testing must be performed on both elements of the hedge relationship. Both elements must be highly effective in order for the hedge relationship to qualify for hedge accounting.

Therefore, the entity could separate the swap by inserting a euro floating leg (6 month LIBOR) into the CCIR swap, creating a US$ fix/€ float swap and a € float/£ float swap. Entity A will end up with a fair value hedge of both the interest rate and currency risk on the US $ debt and a cash flow hedge of the foreign currency exposure on the sterling floating rate loan. This is shown in the diagram below.

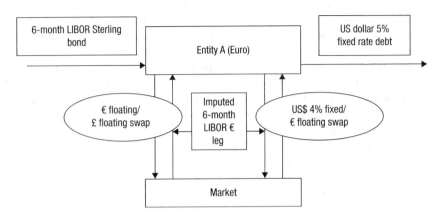

Alternatively, entity A could separate the swap by inserting a € fixed leg into the CCIR swap, creating a US $ fixed/€ fixed swap and a € fixed/£ floating swap. Entity A will end up with a cash flow hedge of the currency risk on the US$ debt and a cash flow hedge of the interest rate and foreign currency risk on the sterling floating rate loan. This is shown in the diagram below.

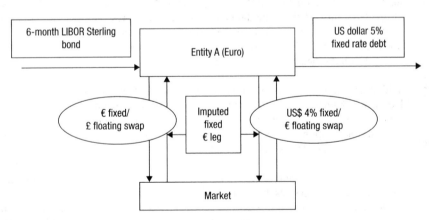

The risks hedged can be identified clearly.

Situation 1 (€ floating leg)

For the US$ denominated debt, the hedging relationship is a fair value hedge of the exposure to changes in the fair value attributable to both changes in the 6 months US LIBOR interest rate (benchmark rate) and US$/€ spot rate movements.

For the sterling floating loan, the hedging relationship is a cash flow hedge of the variability in cash flow attributable to the £/€ spot rate movements.

Situation 2 (€ fixed leg)

For the US$ denominated debt, the hedging relationship is a cash flow hedge of the variability in cash flow on the fixed rate US$-denominated debt attributable to the US$/€ spot rate movements.

For the sterling floating loan, the hedging relationship is a cash flow hedge of the variability in cash flow attributable to both the change in sterling 6 months LIBOR (benchmark rate) and £/€ spot rate movements.

Example 2 – Using a single FX forward to hedge forecast sales in two different currencies

Entity J, whose functional currency is the euro, has highly probable forecast sales in US dollars and highly probable forecast purchases in Japanese yen. Entity J enters into an external foreign currency forward contract to sell US dollars and buy Japanese yen. Entity J's management intends to designate the foreign currency forward contract as a hedge of both the US dollar/euro foreign currency risk associated with the forecast sales and the Japanese yen/euro foreign currency risk associated with the forecast purchases.

For hedge effectiveness testing the Japanese yen/US dollar forward contract is theoretically divided into two different derivatives. The euro is imputed as the base currency for the two derivatives creating a synthetic US dollar/euro foreign currency forward and a synthetic euro/Japanese yen foreign currency forward. The hedged item is designated as two risks:

- The foreign currency cash flow risk associated with the forecast US dollar sales.

- The foreign currency cash flow risk associated with the forecast Japanese yen purchases.

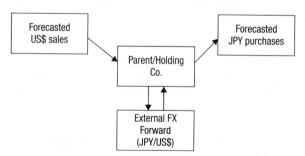

The Japanese yen/US dollar forward may be designated as a cash flow hedge of both the foreign currency cash flow risks associated with the forecast sales in US dollars and the forecasted purchases in Japanese yen, provided all of the conditions in paragraph 76 of IAS 39 are met.

This solution is consistent with paragraph IG F2.18 of IAS 39, which allows a Japanese yen functional currency entity to designate a US dollar/sterling swap as a hedge of both a US dollar liability and sterling asset. However, each hedging relationship must be tested for effectiveness separately and if one of the two hedging relationships becomes ineffective (either because an effectiveness test is failed or because one of the forecast transactions is no longer highly probable to occur), hedge accounting will be discontinued prospectively for both hedge relationships.

Combination of derivative instruments

6.8.69 A derivative may also be designated as the hedging instrument in combination with one or more other derivatives, or even, for a hedge of foreign exchange risk, in combination with groups of non-derivative assets or liabilities. Two or more derivatives or proportions of them may be viewed in combination and jointly designated as the hedging instrument, provided none of them is a written option or a net written option (see further para 6.8.75 below). For hedges of currency risk, two or more non-derivatives, or proportions of them, may be designated as the hedging instrument. [IAS 39 para 77].

6.8.70 Derivative instruments do not have to be similar to be combined, either together or with non-derivative instruments. Even when the risks arising from some derivatives offset(s) those arising from others, the combination can still be designated as a hedging instrument. [IAS 39 para 77].

6.8.71 Multiple derivatives need not be acquired at the same time to be designated as a hedge of the same item. They could be acquired at different times. For instance, an entity can designate two purchased options as a hedge of the same hedged item. Multiple derivatives can be used to hedge the same risk or different risks, provided that all of the other hedge criteria have been met and there is no 'duplicate' hedging of the same risk. For example, assume that two derivatives are designated as a hedge of the risk of a change in the fair value of a foreign currency denominated bond. One derivative hedges interest rate risk and the other hedges currency risk. In assessing an expectation of offsetting changes in fair value that are attributable to the type of risk that is being hedged, an entity would consider the two hedges separately, since the derivatives are hedging two separate risks.

> **Example – Combination of derivatives designated as a hedging instrument**
>
> Entity A's functional currency is pound sterling. On 1 January 20X5, the entity issues a 5 year 5% fixed-rate £100m debt with interest payable annually on 31 December. The debt is classified as other financial liabilities.
>
> The risk management policy of entity A requires it to pay variable rate interest on debt except during the first 2 years. Accordingly, entity A enters into:
>
> - A 5-year £100m notional receive fixed 5%, pay floating (3 month LIBOR) interest swap (swap 1).
>
> - A 2-year £100m notional pay fixed 5%, receive floating (3 month LIBOR) interest swap (swap 2).
>
> IAS 39 permits entity A to designate the combination of swap 1 and swap 2 as a hedge of the fair value exposure relating to interest rate movements in the debt instrument for the cash flows on the bond (principal plus interest) that will occur in period 1 January 20X7 to 31 December 20X9. This is because IAS 39 permits the designation of a portion of the fair value or cash flows of a financial instrument as a hedged item. Therefore, provided that all criteria for hedge accounting are met (in particular the

hedge, as described, is expected to be highly effective and the new hedge relationship is consistent with entity A's risk management policies), fair value hedge accounting can be applied.

As a result of combining the two swaps entity A will achieve its objective of paying fixed interest in the first two years and achieve fair value hedge of the interest rate risk in the remaining 3 years as shown below:

	20X5	20X6	20X7	20X8	20X9
Debt instrument	−5%	−5%	−5%	−5%	−5%
Swap 1 −receive 5%	+5%	+5%	+5%	+5%	+5%
−pay 3 month Libor	Libor	Libor	Libor	Libor	Libor
Swap 2 −receive 3 month Libor	Libor	Libor			
−pay 5%	−5%	−5%			
Net interest	−5%	−5%	Libor	Libor	Libor

Hedging instrument

Changes in the aggregate fair value of swap 1 and swap 2 will be recognised in profit or loss. Similarly changes in the fair value of the debt attributable to interest rate movements relating to the period 1 January 20X7 to 31 December 20X9 will be recognised in profit or loss (see para 6.8.107 below). Some ineffectiveness is likely to arise because of the variable rate leg of swap 1 that is not mirrored in the hedged item. Also, the fair value of swap 2 is based on a different section of the yield curve from the section of the yield curve used for determining swap 1's fair value of (2 year *versus* 5 years).

6.8.72 IAS 39 also permits derivative instruments to be combined with non-derivative instruments, or proportions of them, and the combination designated as the hedging instrument, but only for hedges of foreign currency risk. For example, a Swedish kroner functional currency entity could hedge its net investment in Korea with debt denominated in US dollars combined with a pay Korean won receive US dollar swap (excluding forward points) in its consolidated financial statements. Alternatively, if the entity wanted to minimise ineffectiveness in the profit or loss account, the entity may impute two identical (but offsetting) Swedish kroner pay and receive legs and then designate the resulting pay Swedish kroner receive US dollar swap as a hedge of the US dollar debt and the receive Swedish kroner pay Korean won swap as a hedge of its foreign net investment in Korea. Similarly, an entity could use a combination of a foreign currency cash instrument and a derivative to hedge the foreign currency risk of a firm commitment, provided all the hedge accounting conditions are met. However, a combination of a non-derivative and derivative cannot be the hedged item.

Options as hedging instruments

6.8.73 Options, in contrast to forward and swaps, give the holder the right but not the obligation to exercise the instrument and exchange the underlyings.

Generally, options that have the potential to reduce risk exposure can qualify as hedging instruments. For instance, a purchased option has potential gains equal to or greater than losses and, therefore, has the potential to reduce profit or loss exposure from changes in fair values or cash flows. Therefore, it can qualify as a hedging instrument. [IAS 39 para AG 94].

> **Example 1 – Purchased option as a hedging instrument in cash flow hedges**
>
> Entity A operates a mail-order business. Its functional currency is the euro, but it purchases approximately 20% of its merchandise from the USA.
>
> Entity A issues the mail-order catalogue for the coming year, incorporating its price list, before entering into a firm purchase commitment with US suppliers. Entity A, therefore, sets the prices in the catalogue based on expected exchange rates of €1 = US$1.25. It is highly probable that the entity will make purchases of at least €500,000 from the US in the first six months.
>
> The entity's documented risk management policy requires it to hedge the risk that exchange rates will be higher than expected by purchasing a call option to buy US dollars for euros with a strike price equal to the expected exchange rate. Entity A, therefore, purchased a call option at a rate of €1 = US$1.25, for a maximum of €500,000 in six months' time at a cost of €60,000.
>
> The spot rate at the time of entering into the option contracts was €1 = US$1.1.
>
> Entity A can designate the intrinsic value of the purchased option as a hedge against the movements in the €/$ exchange rate. The exposure being hedged is the variability in cash flows that would arise if the US dollar exchange rate exceeds the expected level of €1 = US$1.25.
>
> **Example 2 – Purchased option as a hedging instrument in fair value hedges**
>
> Entity A has issued a 5 year €100m debt that bears interest at a fixed rate of 3%. It wishes to hedge the risk of increases in the fair value of the debt if interest rates decrease. It enters into a €100m 5 year floor on 3 month EURIBOR with a strike rate of 3%.
>
> The purchased option (the interest rate floor) can be designated as a hedging instrument in a hedge of changes in the fair value of the 5 year debt as a result of changes in interest rates. IAS 39 states that a financial item may be hedged with respect to the risks associated with only a portion of its cash flow or fair value, provided that effectiveness can be measured (see para 6.8.23 above). It is, therefore, possible to designate the hedge as the risk of changes in the fair value if interest rates fall below 3%. The effectiveness of the hedge will be improved if the entity designates only the intrinsic value of the floor as the hedging instrument. In this case, the floor's time value is excluded from the hedge relationship and changes in time value are recognised in the income statement as they occur.

6.8.74 In a hedge of one-sided risk, entities are permitted to designate the hedged risk as the intrinsic value of a purchased option that has the same principal terms as the hedged item, but may not include the time value of the option. For example, an entity can designate the variability of future cash flow outcomes resulting from a price increase of a forecast commodity purchase. [IAS 39 para AG99BA]. Only cash flow losses that result from an increase in the price above the specified level are designated. The inclusion of an option's time value is prohibited in the designated one sided risk on a non-optional hedged item because time value is not a component of a forecast transaction that will affect profit or loss. [IAS 39 para 86(b)]. Greater hedge effectiveness is, therefore, likely to be achieved if the hedging instrument is designated in the same way – that is, to exclude time value. Since hedging a one-sided risk is not a hedge of a portion, this covers financial as well as non-financial items. An option may be in-the-money at the time of designation from an intrinsic value perspective. It may be possible to hedge account in these circumstances as long as only changes in the intrinsic value after the date of designation are deferred in OCI.

6.8.75 A *written* option (as opposed to a purchased option) exposes its writer to the possibility of unlimited loss but limits the gain to the amount of premium received. A written option serves only to reduce the potential for gain in the hedged item or hedged transaction. It leaves the potential for loss on the hedged item or hedged transaction unchanged, except for the amount of the premium received. As a result, a written option generally increase risk exposure because the potential loss on an option that an entity writes could be significantly greater than the potential gain in value of a related hedged item. In other words, a written option is not effective in reducing the profit or loss exposure of a hedged item. Therefore, a written option does not qualify as a hedging instrument, either on its own or in combination with other derivatives, unless it is designated as an offset to a purchased option. In addition, a written option can be designated as an offset to a purchase option that is embedded in another financial instrument. For example, in a callable debt, a written option can be used as a hedging instrument to hedge the callable liability where the issuer can call the debt early. [IAS 39 para AG 94].

6.8.76 An entity may enter into a hedging strategy that involves a written put option and a purchased call option combining to form a collar. The objective of such a hedging strategy is to protect the entity from loss below a certain value (the floor/written put) and also limit the upside potential for gain above a certain value (the cap/purchased call) so as to reduce the cost of the hedging strategy. A typical example is an interest rate collar. Such an interest rate collar or other derivative instrument that combines a written option and a purchased option does not qualify as a hedging instrument if it is, in effect, a net written option (for which a net premium is received). [IAS 39 para 77].

6.8.77 However, an interest rate collar or other derivative instrument that includes a written option may be designated as a hedging instrument, if the combination is a net purchased option or zero cost collar (that is, it is neither a net written or a net purchased option). Such a combination is not a net written option and, therefore, can be designated as a hedging instrument provided all the following conditions are met:

- No net premium is received either at inception or over the life of the combination of options. The distinguishing feature of a written option is the receipt of a premium to compensate the writer for the risk incurred.

- Except for the strike prices, the critical terms and conditions of the written option component and the purchased option component are the same (including underlying variable or variables, currency denomination and maturity date).

- The notional amount of the written option component is not greater than the notional amount of the purchased option component.

[IAS 39 para IG F1.3]

6.8.78 Where a collar whose fair value was zero at inception is designated as a hedging instrument some time into its life, it may have some fair value on the date of designation. If its fair value on the date of designation is negative then the first criteria above would be failed and such a collar would not be allowed for designation as a hedging instrument. If the collar's fair value is zero or positive then, subject to compliance with criteria two and three it could be designated as a hedging instrument.

6.8.79 It should be noted that since a collar combines two options, it is subject to the 2008 amendment to IAS 39 described in paragraph 6.8.74. Hence, it will not be fully effective if the net time value of the written and purchased options is included in the designation of the hedging instrument. That is, ineffectiveness is minimised where the collar is designated on an intrinsic value basis (see para 6.8.207 onwards).

6.8.80 If a combination of a written option and a purchased option (such as an interest rate collar) is transacted as a single instrument with one counterparty, an entity cannot split the derivative instrument into its written option component and purchased option component and designate the purchased option component as a hedging instrument. This is because a hedging relationship is designated by an entity for a hedging instrument in its entirety. The only exceptions permitted are splitting the time value and intrinsic value of an option and splitting the interest element and spot price on a forward (see para 6.8.60 above). [IAS 39 para IG F1.8].

Example 1 – Combination of written and purchased options

Entity A purchases a call option from bank X and sells a put option to bank Y. Bank X and bank Y are not related. The contracts are entered into on the same day, with the purpose of creating a collar. The premium paid on the purchased call equals the premium received on the sold put; no net premium is, therefore, received.

The combination of these two instruments cannot be designated as a hedging instrument, as one of the options is a sold (written) option for which a premium is received. A collar can only be designated as a hedging instrument if the purchased and written option are combined in a single instrument and the collar is not a net written option (that is, no net premium is received).

If the two instruments have the same counterparty and are entered into simultaneously and in contemplation of one another with the intent of creating a collar, the two instruments should be viewed as one transaction.

Example 2 – Combination of written and purchased options

Entity A holds a variable interest rate debt and wishes to hedge the risk of the interest rate increasing above 3%. Entity A's assessment of the risk of the interest rate increasing above 4% is remote and it is prepared to bear that excess risk. It, therefore, enters into a 'cap spread' structure, which is a single instrument, consisting of:

- the purchase of an interest rate cap whose strike rate is 3% (purchased option); and

- the sale of an interest rate cap whose strike rate is 4% (written option).

The cap spread is structured as a single contract entered into with the same counterparty.

Entity A can designate the hedged risk as the risk that the interest rate rises to between 3% and 4%, provided that the cap spread does not constitute a net written option (that is, the entity does not receive a net premium for the cap spread). In this case, the entity is permitted to apply hedge accounting if the strategy is in line with the company's risk management strategy and all other conditions for hedge accounting are met.

If the entity had entered into two separate options (a purchased interest rate cap and a written interest rate cap), it could not designate both options as the hedging instrument. This is because two or more derivatives may be jointly designated as the hedging instrument only when none of them is a written option.

Example 3 – Designating a combination of several derivatives as a hedging instrument in a fair value hedge

Entity A has issued a 7%, 5 year fixed rate bond and at the same time entered into a receive-fixed (7%), pay-floating (LIBOR) 5 year interest rate swap to hedge the bond against changes in fair values resulting from changes in interest rates. The entity has also entered into a zero cost collar (a combination of written floor at 5% and purchased cap at 10%) to limit variability in cash flows arising from the combination of the fixed rate debt and interest rate swap. There is no net premium received for the cap and floor, therefore, there is no net written option.

Entity A's management can designate the combination of the interest rate swap and the zero cost collar as a hedging instrument to hedge the changes in the bond's fair value arising from changes in the risk-free rate, provided all other hedge accounting criteria required by paragraph 88 of IAS 39 are met. Although the zero cost collar contains a written option component, this is written as a single instrument and the combination is not a net written option as no premium is received by entity A at inception or over the contract's life. The hedging documentation could specify that the hedged risk is the risk of changes in the bond's fair value arising from changes in the risk-free rate within the range from 5% to 10%. Specifying the hedge in this way would improve hedge effectiveness.

Dynamic hedging strategies

6.8.81   IAS 39 states that a dynamic hedging strategy that assesses both an optional contract's intrinsic value and time value can qualify for hedge accounting. [IAS 39 para 74]. This allows an entity to apply hedge accounting for a 'delta neutral' hedging strategy and other dynamic hedging strategies under which the quantity of the hedging instrument is constantly adjusted in order to maintain a desired hedge ratio (for example, to achieve a delta neutral position insensitive to changes in the hedged item's fair value). For example, a portfolio insurance strategy that seeks to ensure that the hedged item's fair value item does not drop below a certain level, while allowing the fair value to increase, may qualify for hedge accounting. [IAS 39 para IG F1.9].

6.8.82   To qualify for hedge accounting, the entity must document how it will monitor and update the hedge and measure hedge effectiveness, be able to track properly all terminations and redesignations of the hedging instrument and demonstrate that all other criteria for hedge accounting in IAS 39 are met. Also, it must be able to demonstrate an expectation that the hedge will be highly effective for a specified short period of time during which the hedge is not expected to be adjusted. [IAS 39 para IG F1.9].

Example – Dynamic hedging strategy

Entity A whose functional currency is the euro has an investment in a listed equity security denominated in US dollars. The fair value at acquisition was US$ 70 and entity A hedged it by entering into a sell US$ 70 buy €44 foreign currency forward. Entity A periodically re-assesses the fair value of the equity security and FX revaluation of it is based on such fair value. Entity A also re-assesses the amount of the exposure that should be hedged in accordance with its strategy. For instance, if the fair value of the security reduces from US$ 70 to US$ 40 then the nominal amount of the forward should be adjusted from sell US$ 70 to US$ 40.

When changing the amount of hedged exposure in US$, entity A first:

- de-designates the existing hedge relationship between US$ 70 security vs. sell US$70/buy €44 forward;

- enters into a new foreign currency forward contract (being buy US$ 30 sell €20) with the same maturity date to modify its position; and

- re-designates the new combination of derivative instruments (the previous hedging instrument being buy US$ 70/sell €44 plus the new forward being sell US$ 30 / buy €20) as the hedging instrument.

Entity A is permitted to periodically de-designate and re-designate the cash flow hedge relationship. However the mechanism of de-designation and re-designation must be properly documented and consistent with its risk management policy. Assuming that the other hedge accounting criteria are met, the accounting treatment at the date of de-designation and re-designation is as follows:

- Hedge accounting may be applied to the original hedge relationship until the date of its de-designation.

- Hedge accounting may be applied to the second hedge relationship starting from the date of re-designation.

The strategy described will require a significant amount of documentation to support the de-designation/re-designation process and a detailed monitoring of the accounting entries. Entity A will have to disclose in its financial statements the objective of this hedging strategy and the corresponding policies, together with a discussion of the associated risks and the business objectives pursued.

6.8.83 It follows from the above that there is no prohibition in IAS 39 against terminating one hedge and initiating another with the same hedging instrument. Furthermore, there is no limitation on the frequency of such terminations/designations and re-designations. Provided an entity can properly track all of the terminations and re-designations and demonstrate that all other qualifying criteria, such as high effectiveness, have been met, hedge accounting using the same instrument on a recurring basis is not prohibited. However, initiating new hedging relationships with existing derivatives may not qualify for hedge accounting if the ineffectiveness caused by the derivatives' 'non-zero' fair value is too great to satisfy the 80% – 125% range for effectiveness.

Example – Continuation of hedge accounting where the underlying reference risk is changed and additional hedging instruments are entered into

Entity A borrows money from a bank on 1 January 20X1 by entering into a 5 year floating rate bullet loan with a bank. The loan contract allows entity A to elect at each reset date whether the interest should be based on 3 month LIBOR or 1 month LIBOR. Entity A enters into a 5 year pay fixed (say 4%) receive floating interest rate swap, with the notional terms matching those of the loan. The swap's floating leg prices off 3 month LIBOR, and entity A elects the loan to also price off 3 month LIBOR. The net effect economically is a synthetic fixed rate loan of 4%.

In January 20X3, entity A recognises an opportunity to save 10 bps based on the differential between 1 month LIBOR and 3 month LIBOR. It decides to elect that the loan should be priced off 1 month LIBOR for the next year. Simultaneously, it enters into a basis swap with a bank, paying 3 month LIBOR and receiving 1 month LIBOR (with spreads). The net effect amounts to a synthetic fixed rate loan of 3.9% for the next year, and a synthetic fixed rate loan of 4% for the remainder of the loan term, assuming that entity A will elect the loan interest as 3 month LIBOR for the remaining period.

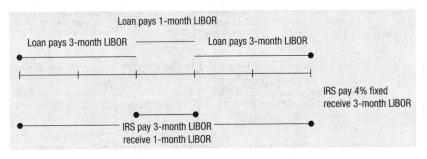

Hedge accounting should be available at inception, and even if the new basis swap is not entered into, providing that the hedged risk is designated to allow for potential variability in the reference rate. That variability will result in some ineffectiveness each time the reference rate changes. Note that the hedging documentation must still document the hedged risk with enough specificity to identify the hedged transaction/risk when it occurs.

If the hedged risk is designated as "*cash flow changes due to changes in the 3 month LIBOR rate*" (being the initial pricing mechanism) and does not anticipate that the reference rate might change, then the hedging relationship would cease when management elect a new reference rate.

However, if a new basis swap is entered into in January 20X3 as proposed then only a partial de-designation of the hedge would be needed in the example where the documentation did not allow for flexibility in the reference rate (and no de-designation where potential variability was documented). The benchmark rate for year three cash flows would be re-assessed based on the 1 month LIBOR rates on the re-designation date. The remaining hedge relationship would continue and the combination of the two interest rate derivatives would be compared to the change in the fair value of the hedged item for effectiveness testing purposes.

All-in-one hedges

6.8.84 Under IAS 39, a derivative can be an instrument which is settled gross by delivery of the underlying asset and the payment of the price specified in the contract rather than by net settlement of the difference between the two legs. The implementation guidance states that such an instrument can be designated as a hedging instrument in a cash flow hedge of the variability of the consideration to be paid or received in the future transaction that will occur on gross settlement of the derivative contract itself, assuming the other cash flow hedge accounting criteria are met. Without the derivative, there would be an exposure to variability in the purchase or sale price. As the derivative eliminates the exposure, it qualifies as a hedging instrument. This applies to all fixed price contracts that are accounted for as derivatives under IAS 39.

> **Example – Gross settled derivative designated as an 'all-in-one hedge'**
>
> An entity enters into a forward contract to purchase a bond that will be settled by delivery. The forward contract is a derivative, because its term exceeds the regular way delivery period in the marketplace.
>
> The entity may designate the forward as a cash flow hedge of the variability of the consideration to be paid to acquire the bond (a future transaction), even though the derivative is the contract under which the bond will be acquired. [IAS 39 para IG F2.5].

6.8.85 Such 'all-in-one hedge' accounting strategy can be beneficial to entities. For instance, if an entity enters into a fixed price contract to buy a commodity that falls to be accounted for as a derivative under IAS 39, the contract would be recognised at fair value with gains and losses recognised in profit or loss. By applying an all-in-one hedge accounting strategy, the entity is able to defer gains and losses on the hedging instrument in equity under cash flow hedge accounting until the hedged transaction occurs. In other words, the entity is able to keep gains and losses from being recognised in profit or loss on what is effectively a fixed price purchase or sale commitment.

Internal hedging instruments

6.8.86 Entities with sophisticated central treasury functions often use internal hedging transactions to 'transfer' interest rate and currency risk to the group treasury. For instance, central treasury may enter into internal derivative contracts such as forward contracts and swaps with subsidiaries and various divisions of a consolidated group with the objective of 'converting' all financial assets and liabilities of those operating units to variable rate instruments in the reporting currency. Central treasury will assess its exposure to various currencies and to interest rate risk and enter into external forward contracts and swaps to manage those risks on a centralised basis, thereby generating economies of scale and pricing efficiency.

6.8.87 Consistent with paragraph 6.8.39 above, internal derivative contracts used to transfer risk exposures between different companies within a group or divisions within a single legal entity cannot be designated as hedging instruments if the derivative contracts are *internal* to the entity being reported on. It follows that internal derivative contracts cannot be designated as hedging instruments in the consolidated financial statements. Nor can they be designated as hedging instruments in the individual or separate financial statements of a legal entity for hedging transactions between divisions in the entity. IAS 39 makes it clear that only instruments that involve a party external to the reporting entity (that is, a group, or an individual entity that is being reported on) can qualify as designated hedging instruments.

6.8.88 However, if an internal contract is offset with an external party, the external contract may be regarded as the hedging instrument and the hedging relationship may qualify for hedge accounting. [IAS 39 para IG F1.4]. In such situations, the hedging relationship consists of the external instrument and the item that was the subject of the internal hedge. The internal derivative is often used as a tracking mechanism to relate the external derivative to the hedged item. Indeed, many entities take advantage of this provision in IAS 39 that allows them to net risk through a central treasury centre and thereafter hedge the net exposure by entering into external contracts with third parties. This avoids the cost of each subsidiary entering into contracts with third parties, some of which may duplicate each other. The following example illustrates the situations described above.

Example – Internal derivative contracts

The banking division of Entity A enters into an internal interest rate swap with the trading division of the same entity. The purpose is to hedge the interest rate risk exposure of a loan (or group of similar loans) in the loan portfolio. Under the swap, the banking division pays fixed interest payments to the trading division and receives variable interest rate payments in return.

If a hedging instrument is not acquired from an external party, IAS 39 does not allow hedge accounting treatment for the hedging transaction undertaken by the banking and trading divisions. This is because only derivatives that involve a party external to the entity can be designated as hedging instruments. [IAS 39 para 73]. Furthermore, any gains or losses on intra-group or intra-entity transactions are eliminated on consolidation. Therefore, transactions between different divisions within entity A do not qualify for hedge accounting treatment in entity A's financial statements. Similarly, transactions between different entities within a group do not qualify for hedge accounting treatment in entity A's consolidated financial statements.

However, if in addition to the internal swap in the above example the trading division enters into an interest rate swap or other contract with an external party that offsets the exposure hedged in the internal swap, hedge accounting is permitted under IAS 39. For the purposes of IAS 39, the hedged item is the loan (or group of similar loans) in the banking division and the hedging instrument is the external interest rate swap or other contract.

The trading division may aggregate several internal swaps or portions of them that are not offsetting each other and enter into a single third party derivative contract that offsets the aggregate exposure. Under IAS 39, such external hedging transactions may qualify for hedge accounting treatment provided that the hedged items in the banking division are identified and the other conditions for hedge accounting are met. It should be noted, however, that hedge accounting is not permitted where the hedged items are held-to-maturity investments and the hedged risk is the exposure to interest rate changes. [IAS 39 para IG F1.4].

6.8.89 IAS 39 provides a very useful summary of its application to internal hedging transactions that is reproduced below.

- The standard does not preclude an entity from using internal derivative contracts for risk management purposes and it does not preclude internal derivatives from being accumulated at the treasury level or some other central location so that risk can be managed on an entity-wide basis or at some higher level than the separate legal entity or division.

■ Internal derivative contracts between two *separate entities* within a consolidated group can qualify for hedge accounting by those entities in their individual or separate financial statements, even though the internal contracts are not offset by derivative contracts with a party external to the consolidated group.

■ Internal derivative contracts between two *separate divisions* within the same legal entity can qualify for hedge accounting in that legal entity's individual or separate financial statements only if those contracts are offset by derivative contracts with a party external to the legal entity.

■ Internal derivative contracts between separate divisions within the same legal entity and between separate entities within the consolidated group can qualify for hedge accounting in the consolidated financial statements only if the internal contracts are offset by derivative contracts with a party external to the consolidated group.

■ If the internal derivative contracts are not offset by derivative contracts with external parties, the use of hedge accounting by group entities and divisions using internal contracts must be reversed on consolidation.

[IAS 39 para IG F1.4].

For segment reporting purposes entities may present financial information including the effects of hedging as reported to management; for that purpose entities do not have to meet the IAS 39 criteria for hedge accounting. This was the subject of an amendment published in 2008 that removed reference to segments from paragraph 73 of IAS 39. Hence, internal derivatives between segments may be freely accounted for as hedges for the purpose of segment reporting if this is the information presented to the chief operating decision maker. Disclosure of intra-group hedging policies may be required.

Offsetting internal hedging instruments

6.8.90 As noted in the example in paragraph 6.8.86 above, central treasury often, before laying off the risk, first nets off internal derivative contracts against each other and then enters into a single third party derivative contract that offsets the net exposure. The circumstances in which such a single external contract can be treated as a hedging instrument on consolidation is considered below in the context of interest rate risk and foreign currency risk management.

Example 1 – Offsetting internal derivative contracts used to manage interest rate risk

Entity A has a number of subsidiaries. All treasury activities of the group are undertaken by entity A. Individual subsidiaries intending to hedge their exposure to interest rate risk are required to enter into separate derivative contracts with entity A.

Entity A aggregates the internal derivative contracts and enters into a single external derivative contract that offsets the internal derivative contracts on a net basis. For instance, Entity A may enter into three internal receive-fixed, pay-variable interest rate swaps (total notional amount of say C100m) that lay off the exposure to variable interest cash flows on variable rate liabilities in the three subsidiaries and one internal receive-variable, pay-fixed interest rate swap (notional amount of C80m) that lays off the exposure to variable interest cash flows on variable rate assets in another subsidiary. It then enters into receive-variable, pay-fixed interest rate swap (notional amount of C20m) with an external counterparty that exactly offsets the four internal swaps. It is assumed that the hedge accounting criteria are met.

In entity A's consolidated financial statements, the single offsetting external derivative would not qualify as a hedging instrument in a hedge of an overall net position, that is, it cannot be used to hedge all of the items that the four internal derivatives are hedging, as explained in paragraph 6.8.31 above.

However, as explained in paragraph 6.8.32 above, designating a part of the underlying items as the hedged position on a gross basis is permitted, that is, the external derivative can hedge C20m of variable rate liabilities totalling C100m. Therefore, even though the purpose of entering into the external derivative was to offset internal derivative contracts on a net basis, hedge accounting is permitted if the hedging relationship is defined and documented as a hedge of a part of the underlying cash inflows or cash outflows on a gross basis. [IAS 39 Para IG F2.15].

Example 2 – Offsetting internal derivative contracts hedging foreign currency fair value risk

An entity has a number of subsidiaries. Subsidiary A has trade receivables in foreign currency (FC) of 100, due in 60 days, which it hedges using a forward contract with the treasury centre (TC) subsidiary. Subsidiary B has payables of FC50, also due in 60 days, which it hedges using a forward contact with TC. TC nets the two internal derivatives and enters into a net external forward contract to pay FC50 and receive LC in 60 days.

At the end of month 1, FC weakens against LC. Subsidiary A incurs a foreign exchange loss of LC10 on its receivables, offset by a gain of LC10 on its forward contract with TC. Subsidiary B makes a foreign exchange gain of LC5 on its payables offset by a loss of LC5 on its forward contract with TC. TC makes a loss of LC10 on its internal forward contract with subsidiary A, a gain of LC5 on its internal forward contract with subsidiary B, and a gain of LC5 on its external forward contract. At the end of month 1, the following entries are made in the individual or separate financial statements of subsidiary A, subsidiary B and TC.

Accounting entries	Dr (Cr)			
	Receivable	Payable	Derivative	P&L
Subsidiary A				
Recognition of loss on receivable	(10)			10
Recognition of gain on internal derivative			10	(10)
Subsidiary B				
Recognition of gain on payable		5		(5)
Recognition of loss on internal derivative			(5)	5
Central Treasury (TC)				
Recognition of loss on internal derivative with A			(10)	10
Recognition of gain on internal derivative with B			5	(5)
Recognition of gain on external derivative			5*	(5)

* External derivative

The above entries are recorded in the individual financial statements of the three entities. In this case, no hedge accounting is required because gains and losses on the internal derivatives and the offsetting losses and gains on the hedged receivables and payables are recognised immediately in the income statements of entity A and entity B without hedge accounting.

In the consolidated financial statements, the internal derivative transactions are eliminated. In economic terms, the payable in B hedges FC50 of the receivables in A. The external forward contract in TC hedges the remaining FC50 of the receivable in A. Hedge accounting is not necessary in the consolidated financial statements, because monetary items are measured at spot foreign exchange rates under IAS 21 irrespective of whether hedge accounting is applied.

The net balances before and after eliminating the accounting entries relating to the internal derivatives are the same, as set out below. Accordingly, there is no need to make any further accounting entries on consolidation to meet the requirements of IAS 39.

	Dr (Cr)			
	Receivable	Payable	Derivative	P&L
Consolidation				
Receivable in A	(10)			
Payable in B		5		
External derivative			5	

[IAS 39 para IG F1.7].

Example 3 – Offsetting internal derivative contracts hedging foreign currency cash flow risk

An entity has a number of subsidiaries. Subsidiary A has highly probable future revenues of FC200 on which it expects to receive cash in 90 days. B has highly probable future expenses of FC500 (advertising cost), also to be paid for in 90 days. Entity A and entity B enter into separate forward contracts with TC to hedge these exposures and TC enters into an external forward contract to receive FC300 in 90 days.

FC weakens at the end of month 1.

A incurs a 'loss' of LC20 on its anticipated revenues because the LC value of these revenues decreases. This is offset by a 'gain' of LC20 on its forward contract with TC.

B incurs a 'gain' of LC50 on its anticipated advertising cost because the LC value of the expense decreases. This is offset by a 'loss' of LC50 on its transaction with TC.

TC incurs a 'gain' of LC50 on its internal transaction with B, a 'loss' of LC20 on its internal transaction with A and a loss of LC30 on its external forward contract.

Entity A and entity B complete the necessary documentation, the hedges are effective, and both entity A and entity B qualify for hedge accounting in their individual financial statements. A defers the gain of LC20 on its internal derivative transaction in a hedging reserve in equity and B defers the loss of LC50 in its hedging reserve in equity. TC does not claim hedge accounting, but measures both its internal and external derivative positions at fair value, which net to zero. At the end of month 1, the following entries are made in the individual or separate financial statements of A, B and TC.

Hedge accounting entries at end of month 1	Derivative	Dr (Cr) Equity	P&L
Subsidiary A			
Recognition of gain on internal derivative with TC	20	(20)	
Subsidiary B			
Recognition of loss on internal derivative with TC	(50)	50	
Subsidiary TC			
Recognition of loss on internal derivative with A	(20)		20
Recognition of gain on internal derivative with B	50		(50)
Recognition of loss on external derivative	(30)*		30

* External derivative

For the consolidated financial statements, TC's external forward contract on FC300 is designated, at the beginning of month 1, as a hedging instrument of the first FC300 of B's highly probable future expenses. IAS 39 requires that in the consolidated financial statements at the end of month 1, the accounting effects of the internal derivative transactions must be eliminated. However, the net balances before and after elimination of the accounting entries relating to the internal derivatives are the same, as set out below. Accordingly, there is no need to make any further accounting entries in order for the requirements of IAS 39 to be met.

Note that only FC300 in costs that were designated in hedge relationships are effectively reported at the hedged foreign currency rate in profit or loss. The revenue and cost of sales that were not designated in hedge relationships are reported at the currency rate ruling on the date of the respective transactions.

Consolidation	Derivative	Equity	P&L
Recognition of loss on external derivative	(30)	30	

[IAS 39 para IG F1.7].

Example 4 – Offsetting internal derivative contracts hedging fair value and cash flow risks

Assume that the exposures and the internal derivative transactions are a combination of the transactions in examples 2 and 3 above. However, instead of entering into two external derivatives to hedge separately the fair value and cash flow exposures, TC enters into a single net external derivative to receive FC250 in exchange for LC in 90 days.

TC has four internal derivatives, two maturing in 60 days and two maturing in 90 days. These are offset by a net external derivative maturing in 90 days. The interest rate differential between FC and LC is minimal and, therefore, the ineffectiveness resulting from the mismatch in maturities is expected to have a minimal effect on profit or loss in TC.

As in examples 2 and 3, subsidiary A and subsidiary B apply hedge accounting for their cash flow hedges and TC measures its derivatives at fair value. Subsidiary A defers a gain of LC20 on its internal derivative transaction in equity and subsidiary B defers a loss of LC50 on its internal derivative transaction in equity.

At the end of month 1, the following entries are made in the individual or separate financial statements of subsidiary A, subsidiary B and TC.

Hedge accounting entries	Receivable	Payable	Dr (Cr) Derivative	Equity	P&L
Subsidiary A					
Loss on receivable	(10)				10
Gain on internal derivative with TC (FV)			10		(10)
Gain on internal derivative with TC (CF)			20	(20)	
	(10)		30	(20)	–
Subsidiary B					
Gain on payable		5			(5)
Loss on internal derivative with TC (FV)			(5)		5
Loss on internal derivative with TC (CF)			(50)	50	
		5	**(55)**	**50**	–

Subsidiary TC

Loss on internal derivative with A (FV)	(10)	10
Loss on internal derivative with A (FV)	(20)	20
Gain on internal derivative with B (CF)	5	(5)
Gain on internal derivative with B (CF)	50	(50)
Loss on external contract (Net)	(25)*	25

* External derivative

The gross amounts relating to fair value of monetary assets and liabilities and the forecast transactions in subsidiary A and subsidiary B are as follows:

	Dr (Cr) Monetary items		Dr (Cr) Forecast transactions
Subsidiary A	100		200
Subsidiary B		50	500

For the consolidated financial statements, the following designations are made at the beginning of month 1:

■ The payable of FC50 in entity B is designated as a hedge of the first FC50 of the highly probable future revenues in entity A (non-derivative financial liability designated as a hedging instrument hedging foreign exchange risk). Therefore, at the end of month 1, the following entries are made in the consolidated financial statements: Dr Payable LC5; Cr Other comprehensive income LC5.

■ The receivable of FC100 in entity A is designated as a hedge of the first FC100 of the highly probable future expenses in entity B (non-derivative financial asset designated as a hedging instrument in hedging foreign exchange risk). Therefore, at the end of month 1, the following entries are made in the consolidated financial statements: Dr Other comprehensive income LC10, Cr Receivable LC10.

■ The external forward contract on FC250 in TC is designated as a hedge of the next FC250 of highly probable future expenses in entity B. Therefore, at the end of month 1, the following entries are made in the consolidated financial statements: Dr Other comprehensive income LC25; Cr External forward contract LC25.

In the consolidated financial statements at the end of month 1, IAS 39 requires the accounting effects of the internal derivative transactions to be eliminated. The effect of the above entries are summarised below:

Consolidation	Receivable	Payable	External derivative	Other comprehensive income/equity
Hedge accounting entries	(10)	5	(25)	30

As can be seen, the total net balances before and after elimination of the accounting entries relating to the internal derivatives are the same, as set out above. Accordingly, there is no need to make any further accounting entries to meet the requirements of IAS 39. [IAS 39 para IG F1.7].

6.8.91 An entity's risk management objectives and strategies may require an entity to enter into a master netting agreement with a counterparty under which the entity is required to settle all external derivative contracts with that counterparty on a net basis. Although netting arrangements imply that an entity is able to set off profitable and loss making contracts against each other, this, in itself, would not preclude the external derivative contracts from being designated as hedging instruments.

> **Example 1 – External derivative contracts that are settled net**
>
> Entity A has a number of subsidiaries. All the group's treasury activities are undertaken by entity A. Individual subsidiaries intending to hedge their exposure to interest rate risk are required to enter into separate derivative contracts with entity A, which in turn enters into a separate offsetting matching derivative contract with a single external counterparty B. For instance, if entity A enters into an intra-group receive 5% fixed, pay LIBOR or interest rate swap, then entity A would also enter into a separate offsetting pay 5% fixed, receive LIBOR interest swap with counterparty B.
>
> Although each of the external derivative contracts is formally documented as a separate contract, only the net of the payments on all of the external derivative contracts is settled by entity A, as there is a netting agreement with the external counterparty B.
>
> The individual external derivative contracts, such as the pay 5% fixed, receive-LIBOR interest rate swap above, can be designated as hedging instruments of underlying gross exposures, such as the exposure to changes in variable interest payments on the pay-LIBOR borrowing above, in the group's consolidated financial statements, even though the external derivatives are settled on a net basis.
>
> External derivative contracts that are legally separate contracts and serve a valid business purpose, such as laying off risk exposures on a gross basis, qualify as hedging instruments even if those external contracts are settled on a net basis with the same external counterparty, provided the hedge accounting criteria in IAS 39 are met. [IAS 39 para IG F2.16] Note that it would not be considered a valid business purpose if the entity entered into the two transactions only to achieve hedge accounting for one of them (that is, if accounting treatment for one of them was the only reason for entering into two transactions and not one).
>
> It may well be that by entering into the external offsetting contracts and including them in the centralised portfolio, entity A is no longer able to evaluate the exposures on a net basis. As a result, it may decide to manage the portfolio of offsetting external derivatives separately from the entity's other exposures. Thus, it enters into an additional, single derivative to offset the portfolio's risk.
>
> In this situation, the individual external derivative contracts in the portfolio can still be designated as hedging instruments of underlying gross exposures. This is so even if the final external derivative is affected with the same counterparty under the same netting arrangement and, as a result, may net to zero.
>
> The purpose of structuring the external derivative contracts in the above manner, which is consistent with the entity's risk management objectives and strategies, constitutes a substantive business purpose. Therefore, external derivative contracts

that are legally separate contracts and serve a valid business purpose qualify as hedging instruments. In other words, hedge accounting is not precluded simply because the entity has entered into a swap that mirrors exactly the terms of another swap with the same counterparty if there is a substantive business purpose for structuring the transactions separately. [IAS 39 paras IG F2.16, IG F1.14].

Non-derivative financial instruments

6.8.92 As stated in paragraph 6.8.56 above, a non-derivative financial asset or liability may only be designated as a hedging instrument for foreign currency risk. This means that foreign currency cash deposits, loans and receivables, available-for-sale monetary items and held-to-maturity investments carried at amortised cost may be designated as a hedging instrument in a hedge of foreign currency risk. Similarly, a contract to purchase the non-controlling interest in a subsidiary which is required to be recognised as a liability under paragraph 23 of IAS 32 is not accounted for as a derivative and, accordingly, could be designated as a hedged item or a hedging instrument in a hedge of foreign currency risk only. The following examples illustrate the type of situations in which a non-derivative financial instrument can be designated as a hedging instrument.

Example 1 – Hedging with a non-derivative the fair value exposure of an available-for-sale bond

Entity J, whose functional currency is the Japanese yen, has issued US$5m 5 year fixed rate debt. It also owns a US$5m 5 year fixed rate bond that it has classified as available-for-sale. Entity J intends to designate its US dollar liability as a hedging instrument in a fair value hedge of the entire fair value exposure of its US dollar bond.

The total change in bond's fair value is a function of interest rate risk, currency risk and credit risk. The debt instrument is a non-derivative that cannot be used to hedge the entire fair value exposure of the bond. However, the debt instrument can be designated as a hedge of the foreign currency component of the bond in either a fair value or cash flow hedge.

In this situation, hedge accounting is unnecessary since the amortised cost of the hedging instrument and the hedged item are both remeasured using closing rates with any differences arising in the period recognised in profit or loss in accordance with IAS 21. In other words, there is a natural offset regardless of whether entity J designates the relationship as a cash flow hedge or a fair value hedge. Any gain or loss on the non-derivative hedging instrument designated as a cash flow hedge is immediately recognised in profit or loss in accordance with paragraph 100 of IAS 39 to correspond with the recognition of the change in spot rate on the hedged item in profit or loss. [IAS 39 para IG F1.1].

Example 2 – Hedging a firm commitment with a non-derivative financial instrument

Entity J's functional currency is the Japanese yen. It has issued a fixed rate debt instrument with semi-annual interest payments that matures in 2 years with principal due at maturity of US$5 million. It has also entered into a fixed price sales commitment for US$5 million that matures in 2 years and is not accounted for as a derivative because it meets the exemption for normal sales. Entity J intends to designate the fixed rate debt instrument as a hedge of the entire fair value change of the firm sales commitment.

The US dollar liability cannot be designated as a fair value hedge of the *entire* fair value exposure of its fixed price sales commitment and qualify for hedge accounting, because it is a non-derivative. However, as IAS 39 permits the designation of a non-derivative asset or liability as a hedging instrument in either a cash flow hedge or a fair value hedge of foreign exchange risk, entity J can designate its US dollar liability as a cash flow hedge of the foreign currency exposure associated with the future receipt of US dollars on the fixed price sales commitment.

Any gain or loss on the non-derivative hedging instrument that is recognised in equity during the period preceding the future sale is recognised in profit or loss when the sale takes place (see further para 6.8.133 below). [IAS 39 para IG F1.2].

Example 3 – Hedging a foreign currency exposure in a net investment with a hedging instrument denominated in a different currency

An entity with a Sing$ functional currency has an investment in a subsidiary in Hong Kong with a HK$ functional currency. Since the HK$ is linked to the US$, management decides to designate a US dollar borrowing as the hedging instrument in a hedge of its net investment.

Management may use a US$ borrowing to hedge a net investment denominated in HK$ if it is highly correlated to that currency, there is qualitative evidence to support the relationship and actual results are in the range of 80-125%. It is possible to designate a borrowing in one foreign currency as a hedge of a net investment in another currency with any ineffectiveness recognised in profit or loss. However, the requirements of paragraph AG105 of IAS 39 – that the hedging instrument is expected to be highly effective – is likely to prevent the use of hedge accounting for most currency pairs. A high degree of correlation between the two currencies would be achieved if one of the currencies was formally pegged to the other, as in this case, but for hedge accounting to be possible, it must be reasonable to assume that this correlation will continue. Some ineffectiveness will arise as a result of inefficiencies in the linking mechanism.

6.8.93 Consistent with paragraph 6.8.64 above, a proportion of a non-derivative financial instrument, such as 50% of the carrying amount of a foreign currency liability, may be designated as the hedging instrument. However, as stated in paragraph 6.8.65 above, an entity cannot treat the cash flows of only a proportion of the period during which a non-derivative instrument designated as a hedge against foreign currency risk remains outstanding and exclude the other cash flows from the designated hedging relationship. For example, the cash flows during the first three years of a ten – year borrowing denominated in a foreign currency cannot qualify as a hedging instrument in a cash flow hedge of the first three years of revenue in the same foreign currency.

Items that do not qualify as hedging instruments

6.8.94 Generally, financial assets and financial liabilities whose fair value cannot be reliably measured cannot be hedging instruments. This means that an investment in an unquoted equity instrument that is not carried at fair value because its fair value cannot be reliably measured, or a derivative that is linked to and must be settled by, delivery of such an unquoted equity instrument cannot be designated as a hedging instrument. [IAS 39 para AG 96].

6.8.95 An entity's own equity instruments are not financial assets or financial liabilities of the entity and, therefore, cannot be designated as hedging instruments. [IAS 39 para AG 97]. Similarly, minority interests in consolidated financial statements are treated as part of equity and, hence, cannot be designated as hedging instruments in the consolidated financial statements.

6.8.96 Firm commitments and forecast transactions cannot be designated as hedging instruments since they are not normally recognised in the financial statements. However, if the foreign currency component of the sales commitment is required to be separated as an embedded derivative under paragraph 11 of IAS 39 and paragraph AG33(d) of IAS 39, it could be designated as a hedging instrument in a hedge of the exposure to changes in the fair value of the maturity amount of the debt attributable to foreign currency risk. [IAS 39 para IG F1.2].

6.8.97 IFRS 3 requires an acquirer entity to re-assess *"designation of a derivative instrument as a hedging instrument in accordance with IAS 39...on the basis of the pertinent conditions as they exist at the acquisition date"*. [IFRS 3 para 16]. In other words the acquirer is required to re-designate all hedge relationships of the acquired entity as if they started at the date of acquisition.

6.8.98 Corporates that are using derivatives for hedging normally take them out at market rate. If the derivatives do not contain option provisions they are expected, therefore, to have fair value of zero at inception. If such derivatives are designated as hedges at inception the underlying hedged risk (modelled as a hypothetical derivative – see para 6.8.192) would be almost a mirror of the actual derivative and such hedge relationships are often highly effective.

6.8.99 As market rates would be likely to have changed from the inception of acquiree's hedges until the date of the business combination the requirement to re-assess designation of derivatives as hedges means that the underlying hypothetical derivative would have to be 're-set' to the market rates current at the time of business combination and, hence, their fair value would then also be 're-set' to zero.

6.8.100 The 'off-market' nature of the hedging derivative at the date of acquisition could be described as an embedded financing within the derivative, representing the amount that would have to be paid to settle a derivative liability (or the amount that would be received to settle a derivative asset) at the date that the entity decides to re-designate the derivative in a new hedge relationship.

6.8.101 The derivative itself will still be recorded at full fair value going forward and this embedded financing does not necessarily keep the new hedge relationship from being within the required range of effectiveness (80%-125%), but it could be a source of ineffectiveness. Specifically, it is the change in fair value of the financing element that represents the hedge ineffectiveness, not the eventual settlements of the embedded financing element. As a result more hedge relationships will be likely to fail, or at least there will be more ineffectiveness.

The hedge accounting models

6.8.102 Hedge accounting recognises the offsetting effects on profit or loss of changes in the fair values of the hedging instrument and the hedged item. Hedge accounting may be applied to three types of hedging relationships:

■ Fair value hedges (see para 6.8.104 below).

■ Cash flow hedges (see para 6.8.119 below).

■ Hedges of a net investment in a foreign operation (see para 6.8.137 below).

[IAS 39 para 86].

Risk reduction and hedge accounting

6.8.103 IAS 39 does not require risk reduction on an entity-wide basis as a condition for hedge accounting. Exposure is assessed on a transaction basis, focusing on the risks inherent in an individual item. For example, an entity may have a fixed rate asset and a fixed rate liability, each having the same principal amount. Under the instrument's terms, interest payments on the asset and liability occur in the same period and the net cash flow is always positive, because the interest rate on the asset exceeds the interest rate on the liability. The entity may decide to enter into an interest rate swap to receive a floating interest rate and pay a fixed interest rate on a notional amount equal to the asset's principal and designate the interest rate swap as a fair value hedge of the fixed rate asset. Although the effect of the interest rate swap on an entity-wide basis is to create an exposure to interest rate changes that did not previously exist, hedge accounting may be applied to this hedge relationship provided that the relevant hedge accounting criteria are met. [IAS 39 para IG F2.6].

Fair value hedges

Definition

6.8.104 A 'fair value hedge' is a hedge of the exposure to changes in fair value of a recognised asset, liability or unrecognised firm commitment, or portion thereof, that is attributable to a particular risk and could affect profit or loss. [IAS 39 para 86(a)].

6.8.105 Examples of fair value hedges that often occur in practice are shown below:

Hedges of market price risk exposure

An entity fixes the value of its commodity inventory by entering into a commodity futures contract.

Fair value exposure

The entity is hedging the risk of changes in the inventory's overall fair value.

An entity purchases a put option to protect the fall in value of its quoted equity investments.

The entity is hedging the risk of fall in the fair value of the equity securities below the option's strike price.

Hedges of interest rate exposures

An entity with fixed rate debt converts the debt into a floating rate using an interest rate swap.

The entity is hedging the risk of changes in the fair value of the debt due to changes in interest rate.

Hedges of foreign currency exposures

An entity enters into a binding contract to purchase machinery for a fixed amount in foreign currency at a future date and hedges the amount in its functional currency by entering into a forward foreign exchange contract.

The entity is hedging the risk of changes in the purchase price of machinery due to changes in foreign exchange rate.

An entity enters into a forward contract to hedge a foreign currency receivable or a payable due for settlement in six months' time.

The entity is hedging the risk of changes in the carrying amount of the receivable or payable due to changes in foreign exchange rate.

Fair value hedge accounting

6.8.106   Under IAS 39, if a fair value hedge meets the hedge accounting conditions discussed in paragraph 6.8.155 below during the period, it should be accounted for as follows:

■   the gain or loss from re-measuring the hedging instrument at fair value (for a derivative hedging instrument) or the foreign currency component of its carrying amount measured in accordance with IAS 21 (for a non-derivative hedging instrument) should be recognised in profit or loss; and

■   the gain or loss on the hedged item attributable to the hedged risk adjusts the carrying amount of the hedged item and is recognised in profit or loss. This applies even if the hedged item is an available-for-sale financial asset or if it is otherwise measured at cost.

[IAS 39 para 89].

6.8.107   As stated in the second bullet point above, where the hedged item is an available-for-sale financial asset, the gain or loss attributable to the risk being hedged is recognised in profit or loss, rather than other comprehensive income, although the remainder of any fair value change is still recognised in other comprehensive income

6.8.108   The standard explains that if only particular risks attributable to a hedged item are hedged, recognised changes in the hedged item's fair value unrelated to the hedged risk are recognised in accordance with paragraph 55 of IAS 39 (see chapter 6.7). This means that changes in fair value of a hedged financial asset or financial liability that is not part of the hedging relationship would generally be accounted as follows:

- For instruments measured at amortised cost, such changes would not be recognised.

- For instruments measured at fair value through profit or loss, such changes would be recognised in profit or loss in any event.

- For available-for-sale financial assets, such changes would be recognised in other comprehensive income as explained above. However, exceptions to this would include foreign currency gains and losses on monetary items and impairment losses, which would be recognised in profit or loss in any event.

6.8.109 If the fair value hedge is fully effective, the gain or loss on the hedging instrument would exactly offset the loss or gain on the hedged item attributable to the risk being hedged and there would be no net effect in profit or loss. However, this would rarely be the case and often some difference would arise. The recognition of this difference in profit or loss is commonly referred to as hedge ineffectiveness. Hedge ineffectiveness is considered further from paragraph 6.8.206 below.

6.8.110 An in-depth application of fair value hedge accounting for a hedge of interest rate risk of a fixed rate debt instrument using an interest rate swap (including full prospective and retrospective hedge effectiveness testing) is illustrated in the comprehensive examples included at the end of this chapter.

> **Example – Fair value hedge of inventory (commodity)**
>
> On 1 October 20X5, a metal refining entity has 1m troy ounces of silver in its inventory. The silver is recorded at an average historical cost of C5.00 per ounce (C5m total value). To protect the inventory from a decline in silver prices, the entity hedges its position by selling 200 silver futures contracts on a specified commodity exchange. Each contract is for 5,000 troy ounces of silver priced at C5.55 per ounce. The futures contracts mature on 31 March 20X6, which is the date that the entity has scheduled delivery of the entire silver inventory to its customer at the spot price at that date.
>
> The entity designates the futures contract as a fair value hedge of its silver inventory (that is, it is hedging changes in the inventory's fair value). Based on historical data, the entity determines and documents that changes in the fair value of the silver futures contracts will be highly effective in offsetting all changes in the fair value of the silver inventory.
>
> On 31 December 20X5 (the entity's financial year end) and on 31 March 20X6, the entity determines that the fair value of its silver inventory has declined cumulatively by C160,000 and C320,000 respectively. The fair value of the silver inventory has declined by more than the spot price of silver, because the fair value of the inventory is influenced by other factors such as changes in expected labour and transport costs.

On 31 March 20X6, the entity closes out its futures. On the same day it also sells the entire silver inventory at the spot price of C5.25 per ounce.

The following data is relevant:

Date	Spot price	Futures price (for delivery on 31 March 20X6)	Fair value of futures contract assuming yield curve is flat at 6% per year*
	C	C	C
1 Oct 20X5	5.40	5.55	–
31 Dec 20X5	5.30	5.40	147,830
31 Mar 20X6	5.25	5.25	300,000

*Fair value $= (1m \text{ ounces} \times (5.55 - 5.40))/1.06^{¼} = $ C147,830
*Fair value $= (1m \text{ ounces} \times (5.55 - 5.25)) = $ C300,000

The entity assesses hedge effectiveness by comparing the entire change in the fair value of the futures contract to the entire change in the fair value of the silver inventory, based on futures prices. A summary of the hedge's effectiveness, calculated using the dollar offset method discussed in paragraph 6.8.186, is shown below.

Date	Change in full fair value of future contracts Gain (loss)	Change in full fair value of inventory Gain (loss)	Effectiveness ratio for the period
	C	C	C
31 Dec 20X5	147,830	160,000	92.39
31 Mar 20X6	152,170	160,000	95.11

Ignoring any margin payments on the futures contract, the accounting entries from inception of the hedge to its termination following closure of the future contracts (which is settled daily) and delivery of inventory are as follows:

Date	Transaction	Cash	Futures contract	Inventory	Profit or loss
		Dr (Cr)			
		C	C	C	C
31 Dec 20X5	Change in fair value of futures contract		147,830		(147.830)
31 Dec 20X5	Change in fair value of silver stock			(160,000)	160,000
31 Dec 20X5	Cumulative cash settlement for period*	147,830	(147,830)	–	–
	Entity A's year end	147,830	–	(160,000)	12,170
31 Mar 20X6	Change in fair value of futures contract		152,170		(152,170)
31 Mar 20X6	Change in fair value of silver stock			(160,000)	160,000
31 Mar 20X6	Sale of silver @ 5.25	5,250,000			(5,250,000)
31 Mar 20X6	Cost of sale			(4,680,000)	4,680,000
31 Mar 20X6	Cumulative cash settlement for period*	152,170	(152,170)	–	–
		5,550,000	–	(5,000,000)	(550,000)

* Futures contracts are settled daily. The entries summarises the daily journals for each day throughout the quarter.

The fair value hedge example illustrates that if the entity had not hedged the change in fair value of the silver stock, it would have made a gain of C250,000 (revenue of C5,250,000 less cost of sales of C5,000,000). By entering into the hedge the company has 'locked in' a net profit of C550,000, that is, gross profit of C570,000 (revenue of C5,250,000 less cost of sales of C4,680,000) less loss of C20,000 on the hedging activity. In this example, the hedge was not 100% effective, which lead to some ineffectiveness being recognised in profit or loss.

At the entity's year end, the derivative asset and the carrying value of the inventory amounted to C147,830 and C4,840,000. The carrying value of C4,840,000 is neither cost nor realisable value nor fair value. It is cost less a hedging adjustment. The gain on the derivative offsets the loss on the inventory in profit or loss, except for ineffectiveness of C12,170. This matching is achieved by accelerating the recognition in the profit or loss of part of the gain or loss on the silver inventory. In other words part of the gain or loss that would normally be recognised only on the sale of the inventory is recorded earlier. Therefore, in the case of a fair value hedge, hedge accounting accelerates income recognition on the hedged item to match the profit or loss effect of the hedging instrument.

Adjustments to hedged items

6.8.111 The adjustment made to the carrying amount of a hedged asset or liability due to fair value changes that are attributable to a specific hedged risk, as stated in the second bullet point in paragraph 6.8.106 above, are dealt with in accordance with the normal accounting treatment for that item. The adjustment is often referred to as a 'basis adjustment', because the hedging gain or loss adjusts the carrying value of the hedged item resulting in an amount that is neither cost nor fair value. Thus, in the above example, changes in fair value of silver are adjusted against the carrying value of silver inventory and the adjusted carrying amount becomes the cost basis for the purposes of applying the lower of cost and net realisable value test under IAS 2. In other words, the basis adjustment remains part of the carrying value of inventory and enters into the determination of earnings when the inventory is sold.

6.8.112 When the hedged item is an interest bearing financial instrument for which the effective interest rate method of accounting is used, any adjustment to the carrying amount of the hedged financial instrument should be amortised to profit or loss. The adjustment should be based on a recalculated effective interest rate at the date the amortisation begins and should be fully amortised by maturity. Amortisation may begin as soon as an adjustment exists and should begin no later than when the hedged item ceases to be adjusted for changes in its fair value attributable to the risk being hedged.

6.8.113 The IASB decided to permit entities to defer amortisation of a basis adjustment until the hedged interest bearing financial instrument ceases to be basis adjusted in order to simplify the accounting and record keeping that an entity might otherwise have to undertake to track and properly account for such adjustments, as explained in the example below.

> **Example – Deferral of amortisation of basis adjustment**
>
> Entity A enters into an interest rate swap contract to hedge changes in the fair value of a fixed rate borrowing of C100m due for settlement in 5 years. The terms of the borrowing and the swap exactly match. Interest rates rise so that the borrowing's fair value falls to C90m and the swap's fair value changes from zero to – C10m.
>
> Under fair value hedge accounting, the swap is carried as a liability of C10m (less any settlement paid). The carrying amount of the borrowing is reduced to C90m. Both the loss and the gain are recognised in the profit or loss. Under the amortised cost method, the C90m carrying amount of the liability would be amortised back up to C100m, giving rise to additional finance cost over the remaining period to maturity.
>
> As explained above, the standard allows amortisation to be deferred until hedge accounting is discontinued. If the swap is in place until the borrowing's maturity date, the debt's carrying amount will be adjusted back to C100m through further hedge accounting adjustments. In other words, any fair value adjustments to the debt's carrying value would be reversed by maturity as the fair value of the liability immediately before settlement must be C100m. Therefore, no amortisation will be necessary.
>
> However, if only the first 2 years of the debt instrument is hedged for interest rate risk and the entity chooses to defer amortisation until end of year 2 when hedge accounting ceases, a significant income statement impact could result in later periods. This is because the entity would need to 'catch up' the basis of the hedged item to its settlement amount of C100m over the remaining 3 years.

Hedges of firm commitments

6.8.114 Hedges of firm commitments are generally treated as fair value hedges except in one situation. If a firm commitment has a price fixed in foreign currency, the standard allows the hedge of the foreign currency risk in the firm commitment to be accounted for as a cash flow hedge of the foreign currency risk. [IAS 39 para 87]. If a firm commitment has a fixed price in the functional currency of the entity rather than a price fixed in a foreign currency, there would be no cash flow variability in the entity's functional currency in the anticipated transaction and cash flow hedging would not be possible. For this reason, hedges of firm commitments, other than those denominated in a foreign currency, are accounted for as fair value hedges because the entity is exposed to changes in fair value of that commitment.

6.8.115 When an unrecognised firm commitment to acquire an asset or assume a liability is designated as a hedged item in a fair value hedge, the accounting treatment is as follows:

■ The subsequent cumulative change in the fair value of the firm commitment attributable to the hedged risk since inception of the hedge is recognised as an asset or a liability with a corresponding gain or loss recognised in profit or loss.

■ The changes in the fair value of the hedging instrument are also recognised in profit or loss.

■ When the firm commitment is fulfilled, the initial carrying amount of the asset or liability is adjusted to include the cumulative change in the firm commitment that was recognised in the balance sheet under point one above.

[IAS 39 paras 93, 94].

> **Example – Measurement of the fair value of a firm commitment**
>
> On 1 January 20X6 entity A enters into a firm commitment to purchase 100,000 widgets for C5 each in 6 month's time. On 31 March 20X6, the entity's year end, the market price of the widgets has increased to C6.
>
> The fair value of a firm commitment represents the amount that an entity would have to pay, or the amount that it would receive, upon terminating the commitment. On 1 January 20X6, the company has an obligation to pay C500,000 in 6 month's time and a right to receive 100,000 widgets in 6 months. The initial value of the obligation and the right are generally equal, resulting in a net fair value of zero.
>
> At 31 March 20X6 when the widget's market price increases to C6, the right's value to receive widgets increases. This is because the widget's value received in three months would be C600,000, while the obligation to pay C500,000 in three months would remain the same, resulting in a fair value that reflects the C100,000 difference adjusted for the discount that is appropriate for the remaining three month duration of the commitment. The present value of the C100,000 represents the amount that the entity

could reasonably expect to receive if the counterparty to the commitment were to terminate the commitment at 31 March 20X6.

Firm commitments represent rights and obligations that are assets and liabilities, even though they are generally not recorded. If entity A designates the firm commitment as a hedged item, it would account for the changes in the fair value of the hedged commitment due to changes in the market price of widgets in a manner similar to how that entity would account for any hedged asset or liability that it records. That is, changes in fair value (that are attributable to the risk that is being hedged) would be recognised in profit or loss and, on the balance sheet, recognised as an adjustment of the hedged item's carrying amount.

Because firm commitments normally are not recorded, accounting for the initial change in the fair value of the firm commitment would result in the entity recognising the firm commitment on the balance sheet. Therefore, in this example, the entity would record the present value of C100,000 as an asset on the balance sheet with a corresponding gain in profit or loss. Recognition of subsequent changes in fair value would adjust that recognised firm-commitment amount. Assuming no further changes in fair value, the widgets would be recognised on the balance sheet on 30 June 20X6 at C600,000 (being C500,000 purchase price plus the C100,000 basis adjustment).

Discontinuing fair value hedge accounting

6.8.116   Fair value hedge accounting should be discontinued prospectively if any of the following occurs:

■   The hedging instrument expires or is sold, terminated or exercised. For this purpose, the replacement or rollover of a hedging instrument into another hedging instrument is not an expiration or termination if such replacement or rollover is part of the entity's documented hedging strategy.

■   The hedge no longer meets the criteria for hedge accounting discussed in paragraph 6.8.155 below.

■   The entity revokes the designation.

[IAS 39 para 91].

6.8.117   When an entity ceases to apply hedge accounting because the hedge does not meet hedge effectiveness criteria, it should discontinue hedge accounting from the last date on which compliance with hedge effectiveness was demonstrated. However, if the event or change in circumstances that caused the hedging relationship to fail the effectiveness criteria can be identified and it can be demonstrated that the hedge was effective before the event or change in circumstances occurred, the entity should discontinue hedge accounting from the date of the event or change in circumstances. [IAS 39 para AG 113].

6.8.118   The table below sets out the accounting treatment to be applied when fair value hedge accounting is discontinued.

Discontinuance of fair value hedges (including firm commitments)

Hedge termination events	Hedging instrument		Hedged item	
	Continue mark-to-market accounting Note 1	Derecognise from the balance sheet	Derecognise from the balance sheet Note 2	Freeze basis adjustments Note 3
Hedging instrument no longer exists (that is, sold, terminated, extinguished, exercised or expired)		✓		✓
The hedge no longer meets the criteria for hedge accounting (effectiveness)	✓			✓
The entity revokes the hedge designation	✓			✓
The hedged item is sold or extinguished	✓		✓	

Note 1 – The hedging instrument will continue to be marked to market, unless it is re-designated as a hedging instrument in a new hedge.

Note 2 – The derecognition of the hedged item occurs through profit or loss (for example, the firm commitment asset or liability or the gain or loss on sale or extinguishment of the hedged item (inclusive of fair value basis adjustments) is recognised in profit or loss).

Note 3 – The hedged item ceases to be adjusted for changes in its fair value attributable to the risk being hedged and continues to be accounted for in a manner that was applicable prior to it being hedged. Once the basis adjustment on the hedged item is frozen, it either:

- Continues as part of the carrying amount of the asset up to the date the carrying value is recovered through use or sale or the asset becomes impaired.

- Is amortised through profit or loss (for interest bearing financial instruments). Amortisation should begin no later than when the hedged item ceases to be adjusted for changes in its fair value attributable to the risk being hedged (see para 6.8.114 above).

Example 1 – Discontinuance of a fair value hedge of a bond

Two years ago, entity A issued at par a C4m, 5 year fixed interest rate bond. At the same time, it entered into a 5-year fixed-to-floating interest rate swap that it designated as a fair value hedge of the bond. After 2 years, the hedge fails a retrospective test and the entity determines it is no longer expected to be highly effective for the remaining 3 years of the hedge. At the date the hedge last passed an effectiveness test, the bond's carrying value included a cumulative adjustment of C0.2m, reflecting the change in the fair value of the hedged risk.

Entity A discontinues hedge accounting prospectively (that is, previous accounting entries are not reversed). If the reason for discontinuance is that the hedge failed an effectiveness test, hedge accounting is discontinued from the last date when the hedge was demonstrated to be effective.

The adjustments to the carrying amount of the hedged item to reflect the changes in fair value that are attributable to the hedged risk remain as part of the item's carrying value, but no further adjustments are made in future periods. When the hedged item is carried at amortised cost, these previous hedging adjustments are amortised over the item's remaining life by recalculating its effective interest rate, or on a straight-line basis if this is not practicable.

The adjusted carrying value of C4.2m will be the basis for calculating a new effective interest rate, starting from the last date the hedge passed an effectiveness test. The hedging adjustment of C0.2m is, therefore, recognised in profit or loss over the bond's remaining life.

Example 2 – Discontinuance of a fair value hedge of an available-for-sale investment

Entity A is a Swiss entity whose functional currency is the Swiss franc (CHF). Entity A buys an equity investment in entity X, which is classified as available-for-sale. Entity X's shares are listed only in the US in US dollars and it pays dividends in US dollars. The fair value at the date of purchase including transaction costs is US$10m.

Entity A does not want to be exposed to the risk of future losses if the US$ weakens against the CHF. It intends to hold the investment for 2 years and enters into a forward contract to sell US$ and receive CHF in 2 years, with a notional amount of US$9m to hedge US$9m of the fair value of the investment in entity X.

Entity A designates the forward contract as a fair value hedge of the currency risk on US$9m of its investment in entity X. This designation allows entity A to take the foreign exchange movements on US$9m of the investment to the income statement to offset the fair value changes in the derivative. The rest of the fair value movements in CHF for the instrument are retained in equity until the instrument is sold.

One year later, entity A believes that the US dollar is not likely to decline further and decides to discontinue the hedge and revoke the hedge designation. The hedge is demonstrated to have been highly effective up to the time it is discontinued.

Entity A discontinues hedge accounting prospectively (that is, previous accounting entries are not reversed). When the hedged item is an equity instrument classified as available-for-sale, all future changes in the instrument's fair value, including all changes related to exchange rate movements, are deferred in equity until the instrument is sold or impaired.

Cash flow hedges

Definition

6.8.119 A 'cash flow hedge' is a hedge of the exposure to variability in cash flows that is attributable to a particular risk associated with a recognised asset or liability or a highly probable forecast transaction and could affect profit or loss. [IAS 39 para 86(b)].

6.8.120 Examples of some cash flow hedges that often occur in practice are shown below:

Hedges of market price risk exposure

An entity that has a highly probable sales of a commodity in the future at the then prevailing market price 'fixes' the selling price of the goods by entering into a futures contract.

Cash flow exposure

The entity is hedging the risk of variability in the cash flows to be received on the sale due to changes in the good's market price.

Hedges of interest rate exposures

An entity with floating rate debt converts the rate on the debt to a fixed rate using an interest rate swap.

The entity is hedging the risk of variability in interest payments due to changes in the interest rate specified for the debt.

An entity that has a highly probable issuance of fixed rate debt in the future at the then coupon rate enters into a forward starting interest rate swap to protect itself from the effects of changes in a specified interest rate that may occur before the debt is issued.

The entity is hedging the variability in the expected interest payments from the issuance of a debt due to changes in a specified interest rate on a debt expected to be issued within a specified period.

Hedges of foreign currency exposures

An entity that has a highly probable sale of goods in foreign currency takes out a forward exchange contract to 'fix' the local (functional) currency price of the goods.

The entity is hedging the risk of changes in local (functional) currency amount of the sale due to changes in foreign exchange rates.

An entity enters into a forward contract to hedge a foreign currency receivable or a payable due to be settled in six months' time.

The entity is hedging the risk of changes in the amount receivable or payable on settlement in six month's time due to changes in the foreign exchange rates.

Forecast transactions

6.8.121 A forecast transaction is an uncommitted but anticipated future transaction. [IAS 39 para 9]. To qualify for cash flow hedge accounting, the forecasted transaction should be specifically identifiable as a single transaction or a group of individual transactions. If the hedged transaction is a group of individual transactions, those individual transactions must share the same risk exposure for which they are designated as being hedged. Thus, a forecast purchase and a forecast sale cannot both be included in the same group of individual transactions that constitute the hedged transaction (see para 6.8.21 above).

6.8.122 The key criterion for hedge accounting purposes is that the forecast transaction that is the subject of a cash flow hedge must be 'highly probable'. In IFRS terminology, probable means 'more likely than not'. Therefore, in the context of forecast transaction, the term 'highly probable' is taken to indicate a much greater likelihood of happening than the term 'more likely than not'. This is consistent with the IASB's use of highly probable in IFRS 5, where 'highly probable' is regarded as implying a significantly higher probability than 'more likely than not'. [IFRS 5 para BC81]. The other conditions are that the forecast transaction must be with a party that is external to the entity (see para 6.8.14 above) and it presents an exposure to variations in cash flows for the hedged risk that could affect profit or loss (see para 6.8.12 above).

6.8.123 IAS 39's implementation guidance explains that a transaction's probability should be supported by observable facts and the attendant circumstances and should not be based solely on management's intentions, because intentions are not verifiable. In assessing the likelihood that a transaction will occur, an entity should consider the following circumstances:

- The frequency of similar past transactions.

- The financial and operational ability of the entity to carry out the transaction.

- Substantial commitments of resources to a particular activity (for example, a manufacturing facility that can be used in the short run only to process a particular type of commodity).

- The extent of loss or disruption of operations that could result if the transaction does not occur.

- The likelihood that transactions with substantially different characteristics might be used to achieve the same business purpose (for example, an entity that intends to raise cash may have several ways of doing so, ranging from a short-term bank loan to an offering of ordinary shares).

- The entity's business plan.

[IAS 39 para IG F3.7].

6.8.124 The length of time until a forecast transaction is projected to occur is also a factor in determining probability. Other factors being equal, the more distant a forecast transaction is, the less likely it is that the transaction would be regarded as highly probable and the stronger the evidence that would be needed to support an assertion that it is highly probable. For example, a transaction forecast to occur in five years may be less likely to occur than a transaction forecast to occur in one year. However, forecast interest payments for the next 20 years on a plain vanilla variable rate debt would typically be highly probable if supported by an existing contractual obligation and it is expected that the debt will not be paid early.

6.8.125 In addition, other factors being equal, the greater a forecast transaction's physical quantity or future value in proportion to the entity's transactions of the same nature, the less likely it is that the transaction would be regarded as highly probable and the stronger the evidence that would be required to support an assertion that it is highly probable. For example, less evidence generally would be needed to support forecast sales of 100,000 units in the next month than 950,000 units in that month when recent sales have averaged 800,000 units per month for the past three months. [IAS 39 para IG F3.7].

6.8.126 A history of having designated hedges of forecast transactions and then determining that the forecast transactions are no longer expected to occur would call into question both an entity's ability to predict forecast transactions accurately and the propriety of using hedge accounting in the future for similar forecast transactions. [IAS 39 para IG F3.7].

6.8.127 The documentation that needs to be put in place before a forecast transaction can be designated as a hedged item is considered further from paragraph 6.8.157 below.

Cash flow hedge accounting

6.8.128 Under IAS 39, if a cash flow hedge meets the hedge accounting conditions discussed in paragraph 6.8.155 below during the period, it should be accounted for as follows:

- the portion of the gain or loss on the hedging instrument that is determined to be an effective hedge should be recognised directly in other comprehensive income; and

- the ineffective portion of the gain or loss on the hedging instrument should be recognised in profit or loss.

[IAS 39 para 95].

6.8.129 In particular:

- the separate component of equity associated with the hedged item is adjusted to the *lesser* of the following (in absolute amounts):

  - the cumulative gain or loss on the hedging instrument from inception of the hedge; and

  - the cumulative change in fair value (present value) of the expected future cash flows on the hedged item from inception of the hedge;

- any remaining gain or loss on the hedging instrument or designated component of it (that is not an effective hedge) is recognised in profit or loss; and

- if an entity's documented risk management strategy for a particular hedging relationship excludes from the assessment of hedge effectiveness a specific component of the gain or loss or related cash flows on the hedging instrument, that excluded component of gain or loss is recognised in accordance with the instrument's normal classification. If the hedging instrument is a derivative, the excluded components can include the time value of an option or the interest element of a forward (see para 6.8.60

above) or a proportion, such as 50% of a derivative (or non-derivative financial instrument for hedges of foreign currency risk) (see para 6.8.64 above). Changes in the value of those excluded components are recognised in profit or loss (unless, in the case a proportion of a derivative, the remaining portion is designated as the hedging instrument in a different cash flow hedge or a net investment hedge).

[IAS 39 para 96].

6.8.130 The way in which an entity accounts for cash flow hedges is illustrated in the examples below. In addition, another more in-depth application of cash flow hedge accounting for a hedge of a highly probable foreign currency purchase of raw materials using a forward contract (including full prospective and retrospective hedge effectiveness testing) is given in illustration 2 at paragraph 6.8.224.

Example 1 – Cash flow hedge of commodity sale

The facts are the same as in the example in paragraph 6.8.110 above, except that the entity decides to designate a silver forward contract as a cash flow hedge of the forecast sale of 1million troy ounces of silver to a customer that is expected to occur on 31 March 20X6. It is highly probable that the sale will occur based on its sales history with the customer. The entity is hedging its exposure to change in cash flows from the highly probable sales. The futures contract entered into on 1 October 20X5 on a specified commodity exchange for 1 million troy ounces of silver at a forward price of C5.55 per ounce matures on 31 March 20X6 and will be settled net in cash. This is the date the entity expects to deliver 1 million troy ounces of silver to its customer at the forward price.

The hedging relationship qualifies for cash flow hedge accounting. The entity determines and documents the entire change in the full fair value of the forward contract will be highly effective in offsetting all the variability in cash flow from the expected sale based on the forward prices.

The entity prepares its financial statements to 31 December each year. The accounting entries from inception of the hedge to its termination following closure of the forward contract (which is settled daily) and the inventory's delivery are as follows:

Date	Transaction	Cash C'000	Forward contract C'000	Equity C'000	Silver stock C'000	Profit and loss C'000
31 Dec 20X5	Change in fair value of fwd contract		147,830	(147,830)		
31 Mar 20X6	Change in fair value of fwd contract		152,170	(152,170)		
31 Mar 20X6	Sale of silver inventory	5,250,000				(5,250,000)
31 Mar 20X6	Cost of sale				(5,000,000)	5,000,000
31 Mar 20X6	Recycle of hedging gain from equity			300,000		(300,000)
31 Mar 20X6	Settlement of fwd contract	300,000	(300,000)			
		5,550,000	–	–	(5,000,000)	(550,000)

As can be seen from the above, through the hedge transaction, the entity has locked in a cash flow of C5.55 per troy ounce of silver, that is, C5,500,000. This is equivalent to the sale at spot rate plus the gain on the derivative.

Example 2 – Cash flow hedge of a variable rate debt

Entity A has a floating rate liability of C10m with 5 years remaining to maturity. It enters into a 5 year pay-fixed, receive-floating interest rate swap in the same currency and with the same principal terms as the liability to hedge the exposure to variable cash flow payments on the floating rate liability attributable to interest rate risk.

At inception, the swap's fair value is zero. Subsequently, there is an increase of C490,000 in the swap's fair value. This increase consists of a change of C500,000 resulting from an increase in market interest rates and a change of minus C10,000 resulting from an increase in the credit risk of the swap counterparty. There is no change in the fair value of the floating rate liability as the interest rate regularly resets to market rates, but the fair value (present value) of the future cash flows needed to offset the change in variable interest cash flows on the liability increases by C500,000. The fair value movement in this hedged risk can be demonstrated using a hypothetical derivative – see paragraph 6.8.190 for an explanation of how the hypothetical derivative method can be used to measure effectiveness.

Entity A determines that although the hedge is not fully effective, because part of the change in the derivative's fair value is attributable to the counterparty's credit risk that is not reflected in the floating rate liability, the hedge is still highly effective. Therefore, entity A credits the effective portion of the change in fair value of the swap, that is, the net change in fair value of C490,000 to other comprehensive income. There is no debit to profit or loss for the change in fair value of the swap attributable to the deterioration in the credit quality of the swap counterparty, because the cumulative change in the present value of the future cash flows needed to offset the exposure to variable interest cash flows on the hedged item, that is the hedged risk, C500,000, exceeds the cumulative change in value of the hedging instrument, C490,000 (see para 6.8.129 above). If entity A concludes that the hedge is no longer highly effective, it discontinues hedge accounting prospectively as from the date the hedge ceased to be highly effective (see para 6.8.134-135 below).

Alternatively, if the change in the fair value of the swap increased to C510,000 of which C500,000 results from the increase in market interest rates and C10,000 from a decrease in the credit risk of the swap counterparty, there would be a credit to profit or loss of C10,000 for the change in the swap's fair value attributable to the improvement in the swap counterparty's credit quality. This is because the cumulative change in the value of the hedging instrument, C510,000 exceeds the cumulative change in the present value of the future cash flows needed to offset the exposure to variable interest cash flows on the hedged item, C500,000. The difference of C10,000 represents the ineffectiveness attributable to the derivative hedging instrument, the swap and is recognised in profit or loss. [IAS 39 para IG F5.2].

Reclassifying gains and losses from equity

6.8.131 If a hedge of a forecast transaction subsequently results in the recognition of a financial asset or liability, the associated gains or losses that were recognised directly in equity (see para 6.8.128 above) should be reclassified into profit or loss in the same period or periods during which the asset acquired or liability assumed affects profit or loss (such as in the periods when interest expense or income is recognised). However, if an entity expects that all or a portion of a loss recognised in other comprehensive income will not be recovered in one or more future periods, it should reclassify into profit or loss the amount that is not expected to be recovered. [IAS 39 para 97]. In addition, in the April 2009 'Improvements to IFRSs', the IASB amended paragraph 97 of IAS 39 to clarify the case when an entity hedges some, but not all, of the cash flows of a forecast transaction that would result in the recognition of a financial asset or liability, for example, the first three years of a highly probable forecast five year fixed debt issuance in six months time. In such a case the associated gains or losses deferred in other comprehensive income should be reclassified from equity to profit or loss as a reclassification adjustment in the same period or periods during which the hedged forecast cash flows affect profit or loss (that is, over the first three years of the debt in the above example).

6.8.132 If a hedge of a forecast transaction subsequently results in recognising a *non-financial* asset or liability (or a forecast transaction for a *non-financial* asset or liability becomes a firm commitment for which fair value hedge accounting is applied), then the entity should adopt either of the following approaches as its accounting policy and apply that policy consistently:

■ It should reclassify the associated gains and losses that were recognised directly in equity into profit or loss in the same period or periods during which the asset acquired or liability assumed affects profit or loss (such as in the periods that depreciation or cost of sales is recognised). However, if an entity expects that all or a portion of a loss recognised directly in equity will not be recovered in one or more future periods, it should reclassify into profit or loss the amount that is not expected to be recovered.

- It should remove the associated gains and losses that were recognised directly in equity and include them in the initial cost or other carrying amount of the asset or liability (often referred to as 'basis adjustment').

[IAS 39 paras 98-99].

6.8.133 For cash flow hedges other than those covered by paragraphs 6.8.131 and 6.8.132 above, amounts that had been recognised directly in equity should be recognised in profit or loss in the same period or periods during which the hedged forecast transaction affects profit or loss (for example, when a forecast sale occurs). [IAS 39 para 100].

Example 1 – Reclassification of derivative loss recorded in equity

Entity A regularly purchases inventory from a foreign supplier and designates a forecast purchase of particular inventory as the hedged item in a cash-flow hedge. At the date the inventory is purchased, a loss on the hedging instrument of C30 has accumulated in equity. In a subsequent period, the purchased inventory has a carrying amount of C100 (without any basis adjustment) and a fair value of C110. The entity expects to sell the inventory at a price equivalent to its fair value.

In this example, the entity determines that the combined value of the loss deferred in equity and the carrying amount of the inventory (that is, C130) exceeds the inventory's fair value of C110, such that a net loss of C20 on the hedged transaction will be recognised in a future period. Therefore, in accordance with the first bullet point in paragraph 6.8.132 above, the loss of C20 should immediately be reclassified into profit or loss since the entity determines that the loss cannot be recovered. The remaining C10 will only be recognised in profit or loss when the inventory is sold or if there is a further decline in its fair value.

The same effect in profit or loss would result had the entity chosen to adjust the inventory's carrying value by the amount of the loss deferred in equity of C30 as noted in the last bullet point in paragraph 6.8.132 above. In that case, the carrying value of the inventory of C130 would be greater than fair value of C110 resulting in the recognition of an immediate loss of C20 in profit or loss in accordance with IAS 2.

Example 2 – Reclassification of derivative gain recorded in equity

Entity A regularly purchases inventory from a foreign supplier and designates a forecast future purchase of particular inventory as the hedged item in a cash-flow hedge. At the date that the inventory is purchased, a gain on the hedging instrument of C30 has accumulated in equity. In a subsequent period, the fair value of the purchased inventory, which has a carrying amount of C100 (no basis adjustment), declines to C80.

In accordance with IAS 2, the entity writes down the inventory to its net realisable value of C80 and recognises an impairment loss of C20. The entity should also reclassify from equity an equivalent amount of gain of C20 (that is, part of the total gain of C30 deferred in equity) to profit or loss. The effect of the above adjustments is that inventory is recorded at its net realisable value of C80, the gain deferred in equity is C10 and there is no net impact in profit or loss. The gain in equity of C10 would continue to be deferred until the hedged forecast transaction impacts profit or loss when the inventory is sold or there is a further reduction in fair value.

The same effect in profit or loss would result had the entity chosen to adjust the inventory's carrying value by the amount of the gain deferred in equity of C30. In that situation, the carrying value of the inventory of C70 would be less than fair value of C80 and there will be no immediate impact on profit or loss. The hedging gain of C10 included in the carrying value will affect profit or loss when the inventory is sold.

Example 3 – Reclassification of derivative gains/losses hedging partial term of forecast debt issuance

Entity A took out a 5 year (pay fix, receive float) forward starting swap 6 months ago to hedge the first 5 years of cashflows on its highly probable forecast issuance of 15 year fixed rate debt. It is assumed that appropriate documentation was in place, that entity A demonstrated the issuance of debt was highly probable and effectiveness tests were passed prospectively and retrospectively. As anticipated at inception, on issuance of the debt, the forward starting swap is terminated. Interest rates have increased since the forward starting swap was transacted, which has resulted in a gain on the swap, but the debt being issued at a higher interest rate. In accordance with the amendment to paragraph 97 referred to in paragraph 6.8.131 above, this gain will be released to the income statement over the first 5 years of the debt as the hedged cash flows affect the income statement.

Discontinuing cash flow hedge accounting

6.8.134 Cash flow hedge accounting should be discontinued prospectively if any of the following occurs:

- The hedging instrument expires or is sold, terminated or exercised.

  For this purpose, the replacement or rollover of a hedging instrument into another hedging instrument is not an expiration or termination if such replacement or rollover is part of the entity's documented hedging strategy.

  In this case, the cumulative gain or loss on the hedging instrument that remains recognised directly in equity from the period when the hedge was effective should remain in equity until the forecast transaction occurs. Thereafter, it should be dealt with in accordance with paragraphs 6.8.131 to 6.8.133 above.

- The hedge no longer meets the criteria for hedge accounting discussed in paragraph 6.8.155 below.

  In this case, unless the next bullet point is also met, the cumulative gain or loss on the hedging instrument that remains recognised directly in equity from the period when the hedge was effective should remain in equity until the forecast transaction occurs. Thereafter, it should be dealt with in accordance with paragraphs 6.8.131 to 6.8.133 above.

- The forecast transaction is no longer expected to occur.

  In this case, the cumulative gain or loss on the hedging instrument that remains recognised directly in equity from the period when the hedge was effective should be recognised in profit or loss. However, a forecast transaction that is no longer highly probable (and, therefore, the hedge no longer meets the criteria for hedge accounting discussed in para 6.8.154 below) may still be expected to occur, in which case, the cumulative gain or loss is treated in the same way as set out in the previous bullet point.

- The entity revokes the designation.

  In this case, the cumulative gain or loss on the hedging instrument that remains recognised directly in equity from the period when the hedge was effective should remain in equity until the forecast transaction occurs. Thereafter, it should be dealt with in accordance with paragraphs 6.8.131 to 6.8.133 above. However, if the transaction is no longer expected to occur, the cumulative gain or loss in equity is dealt with in accordance with the third bullet point above.

[IAS 39 para 101].

6.8.135 The above rules are summarised in the table below:

Discontinuance of cash flow hedges	Hedging instrument		Amount accumulated in equity	
Hedge termination events	Continue mark-to-market accounting	Derecognise from the balance sheet	Reclassify to profit or loss	Retain amounts in equity
	Note 1			Note 2
Hedging instrument no longer exists (that is, sold, terminated, extinguished, exercised, or expired)		✓		✓
The hedge no longer meets the effectiveness criteria for hedge accounting	✓			✓
The entity revokes the hedge designation	✓			✓
The forecast transaction is no longer highly probable, but is still expected to occur	✓			✓
The forecast transaction is no longer expected to occur	✓		✓	
Variability of cash flow ceases (for example, the forecast transaction becomes a fixed price firm commitment)	✓			✓

Note 1 – The hedging instrument will continue to be marked to market, unless it is re-designated as a hedging instrument in a new hedge.

Note 2 – The cumulative gain or loss on the hedging instrument previously recognised directly in other comprehensive income from the period when the hedge was effective remains recognised in equity and is reclassified to profit or loss when profit or loss is impacted by the hedged item.

6.8.136   When an entity ceases to apply hedge accounting because the hedge does not meet hedge effectiveness criteria, it should discontinue hedge accounting from the last date on which compliance with hedge effectiveness was demonstrated. However, if the event or change in circumstances that caused the hedging relationship to fail the effectiveness criteria can be identified and it can be demonstrated that the hedge was effective before the event or change in circumstances occurred, the entity should discontinue hedge accounting from the date of the event or change in circumstances. [IAS 39 para AG113].

> **Example – Discontinuance of cash flow hedge**
>
> On 1 January 20X6, entity A has a highly probable sale that is expected to occur on 31 May 20X6. Entity A expects to collect the cash on 30 June 20X6. Entity A's functional currency is pound sterling and the sale is denominated in US dollars. At the same time on 1 January 20X6, entity A takes out a £/US$ forward contract to hedge the future sale. This forward contract matures on 30 June 20X6. Entity A has put in place all the documentation required to achieve cash flow hedge accounting.
>
> On 1 March 20X6, the transaction is no longer considered to be highly probable, but is still expected to occur. On 1 April 20X6, the transaction is no longer expected to occur. The entity does not close out the forward contract earlier than maturity.
>
> The fair value of the forward contract at each date is as follows:
>
> | | Fair value of forward (maturity 30 June 20X6) £'000 |
> |---|---|
> | 31 January 20X6 | 35,000 |
> | 28 February 20X6 | 30,000 |
> | 31 March 20X6 | 25,000 |
> | 30 April 20X6 | 27,000 |
> | 31 May 20X6 | 28,000 |
> | 30 June 20X6 | 32,000 |
>
> The accounting entries from the inception of the hedge to settlement of the forward contract, assuming perfect effectiveness (that is, the hedged risk is the forward rate and no other mismatches occur), are as follows:

Date	Transaction	Cash £'000	Forward contract £'000	Equity £'000	Profit or loss £'000
			Dr (Cr)		
31 Jan 20X6	Change in fair value of forward		35	(35)	
28 Feb 20X6	Change in fair value of forward		(5)	5	
	Hedge accounting ceases prospectively from 1 March 20X6. Gain deferred in equity remains in equity but the forward is now marked to market through profit or loss				
31 Mar 20X6	Change in fair value of forward		(5)		5
30 Apr 20X6	Change in fair value of forward		2		(2)
30 Apr 20X6	Recycling of gain as hedged transaction is no longer expected to occur			30	(30)
31 May 20X6	Change in fair value of forward		1		(1)
30 Jun 20X6	Change in fair value of forward		4		(4)
30 Jun 20X6	Settlement of forward	32	(32)	–	–
		32	–	–	(32)

Had the transaction continued to be highly probable, the movements on the forward contract to the extent that the hedge was effective would continue to be taken to equity until the sale occurred in May at which date the gain would be recycled from equity to the income statement. Management would then de-designate the forward contract as a hedge and the fair value movements would be recorded through the income statement between May and June and this should offset the gain or loss on the receivable (settlement due on 30 June 20X6) caused by currency fluctuations. There would be some income statement volatility as the interest element (forward points) included in the forward contract's fair value is not present in the undiscounted trade receivable. Alternatively, the forward contract could be re-designated as a hedge of movements in the spot rate on the receivable, but this is not necessary because movements in the receivable and forward will approximately offset as the receivable is measured at spot exchange rates under IAS 21 irrespective of whether hedge accounting is applied.

Net investment hedges

Background

6.8.137 A net investment in a foreign operation is defined as *"the amount of the reporting entity's interest in the net assets of that operation"*. [IAS 21 para 8]. Such foreign operations may be subsidiaries, associates, joint ventures or branches. An entity may decide to hedge against the effects of changes in exchange rates in its net investment in a foreign operation. This may be done with non-derivative financial liabilities or with derivatives. Because the foreign operation's net assets are reported in the reporting entity's consolidated financial statements, hedging a net investment in a foreign operation can only be carried out at the consolidation level. Under IAS 21, the reporting entity's share of the net assets of a foreign operation is translated into the group's presentation currency at the closing exchange rate, and all resulting exchange differences are recognised as a separate component in equity until it disposes of the foreign operation. The hedge of a net investment in a foreign operation at the consolidated level is, therefore, a hedge of the translation foreign currency risk arising on the foreign operation, which is included in the reporting entity.

6.8.138 The IFRS IC recognised that IAS 39 and IAS 21 provided limited guidance on the application of their requirements for hedges of net investments in foreign operations and therefore issued IFRIC 16 on 3 July 2008. IFRIC 16 applies only to hedges of net investments in foreign operations; it should not be applied by analogy to other types of hedge accounting such as fair value or cash flow hedge accounting.

Hedged items

6.8.139 In a hedge of the foreign currency risks arising from a net investment in a foreign operation, the hedged item can be an amount of net assets equal to or less than the carrying amount of the net assets of the foreign operation in the consolidated financial statements of the parent entity. The amount of the net assets that may be designated as the hedged item in the consolidated financial statements of a parent depends on whether any lower level parent of the foreign operation has applied hedge accounting for all or part of the net assets of that foreign operation and that accounting has been maintained in the parent's consolidated financial statements. The hedged risk may be designated as the foreign currency exposure arising between the functional currency of the foreign operation and the functional currency of any parent entity (the immediate, intermediate or ultimate parent entity) of that foreign operation. The fact that the net investment is held through an intermediate parent does not affect the nature of the economic risk arising from the foreign currency exposure to the ultimate parent entity.

6.8.140 However, the hedged risk must relate to the functional currencies of the entities involved (that is, the foreign operation and any of its parents). IFRIC 16 does not permit an entity to hedge a foreign operation to the group's presentation currency. This is because IAS 21 places no restrictions on what presentation currency a group can select, and therefore presentation currency risk is not viewed as a true economic exposure. In practice, this limitation is likely to have little effect as most entities either only hedge functional currency risk or choose a presentation currency that is also the functional currency of a relevant parent.

6.8.141 If the same net assets of a foreign operation are hedged by more than one parent entity within the group (for example, both a direct and an indirect parent entity) for the same risk, only one hedging relationship will qualify for hedge accounting in the consolidated financial statements of the ultimate parent. A hedging relationship designated by one parent entity in its consolidated financial statements need not be maintained by another higher level parent entity. However, if it is not maintained by the higher level parent entity, the hedge accounting applied by the lower level parent should be reversed before the higher level parent's hedge accounting is recognised.

Example

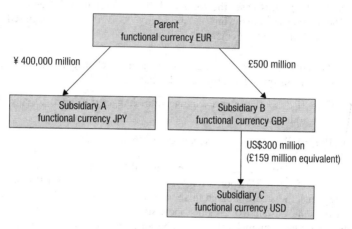

For example, in the group depicted above the parent can hedge its net investment in each of subsidiaries A, B and C for the foreign exchange risk between their respective functional currencies (Japanese yen (JPY), pounds sterling and US dollars) and euro. In addition, parent can hedge the USD/GBP foreign exchange risk between the functional currencies of subsidiary B and subsidiary C. In its consolidated financial statements, subsidiary B can hedge its net investment in subsidiary C for the foreign exchange risk between their functional currencies of US dollars and pounds sterling.

Parent wishes to hedge the foreign exchange risk from its net investment in subsidiary C. Assume that subsidiary A has an external borrowing of US$300m. The net assets of subsidiary A at the start of the reporting period are ¥400,000m including the proceeds of the external borrowing of US$300m. The hedged item can be an amount of net assets equal to or less than the carrying amount of parent's net investment in subsidiary C (US$300m) in its consolidated financial statements. In its consolidated financial statements parent can designate the US$300m external borrowing in subsidiary A as a hedge of the EUR/USD spot foreign exchange risk associated with its net investment in the US$300m net assets of subsidiary C. In this case, both the EUR/USD foreign exchange difference on the US$300m external borrowing in subsidiary A and the EUR/USD foreign exchange difference on the US$300m net investment in subsidiary C are included in the foreign currency translation reserve in parent's consolidated financial statements after the application of hedge accounting.

In the absence of hedge accounting, the total USD/EUR foreign exchange difference on the US$300m external borrowing in subsidiary A would be recognised in parent's consolidated financial statements as follows:

- USD/JPY spot foreign exchange rate change, translated to euro, in profit or loss, and

- JPY/EUR spot foreign exchange rate change in equity.

Instead of designating the US$300m external borrowing as a hedge of the EUR/USD spot foreign exchange risk on the investment in subsidiary C in its consolidated financial statements, the parent could designate the borrowing in subsidiary A as a hedge of the GBP/USD spot foreign exchange risk between subsidiary C and subsidiary B. In this case, the total USD/EUR foreign exchange difference on the US$300m external borrowing in subsidiary A is instead recognised in parent's consolidated financial statements as follows:

- the GBP/USD spot foreign exchange rate change in the foreign currency translation reserve relating to subsidiary C,

- GBP/JPY spot foreign exchange rate change, translated to euro, in profit or loss, and

- JPY/EUR spot foreign exchange rate change in equity.

Parent cannot designate the US$300m external borrowing in subsidiary A as a hedge of both the EUR/USD spot foreign exchange risk and the GBP/USD spot foreign exchange risk in its consolidated financial statements. A single hedging instrument can hedge the same designated risk only once. Subsidiary B cannot apply hedge accounting in its consolidated financial statements because the hedging instrument is held outside the group comprising subsidiary B and subsidiary C.

Hedging instruments

6.8.142 A derivative or a non-derivative instrument (or a combination of derivative and non-derivative instruments) may be designated as a hedging instrument in a hedge of a net investment in a foreign operation. The hedging instrument(s) may be held by any entity or entities within the group, as long as the designation, documentation and effectiveness requirements of IAS 39 paragraph 88 that relate to a net investment hedge are satisfied. In particular, the hedging strategy of the group should be clearly documented because of the possibility of different designations at different levels of the group.

6.8.143 The designated risk may be spot foreign exchange risk if the hedging instruments are not derivatives (for example, a debt instrument). If the hedging instruments are forward contracts, an entity can designate either the spot or the forward foreign exchange risk as the hedged risk.

[IFRIC 16 para 14, AG2]

Effectiveness testing

6.8.144 When determining the effectiveness of a hedging instrument in the hedge of a net investment, an entity calculates the gain or loss on the hedging instrument by reference to the functional currency of the parent entity against whose functional currency the hedged risk is measured, in accordance with the hedge documentation. This is the same regardless of the type of hedging instrument used. This ensures that the effectiveness of the instrument is determined on the basis of changes in fair value or cash flows of the hedging instrument, compared with the changes in the net investment as documented. Any effectiveness test is not therefore dependent on the functional currency of the entity holding the instrument. In other words, the fact that some of the change in the hedging instrument is recognised in profit or loss by one entity within the group and some is recognised in other comprehensive income by another does not affect the assessment of hedge effectiveness.

6.8.145 In our example above, the total change in value in respect of foreign exchange risk of the US$300 million external borrowing in subsidiary A is recorded in both profit or loss (USD/JPY spot risk) and equity (EUR/JPY spot risk) in parent's consolidated financial statements in the absence of hedge accounting. Both amounts are included for the purpose of assessing the effectiveness of the hedge because the change in value of both the hedging instrument and the hedged item are calculated by reference to the euro functional currency of parent against the US dollar functional currency of subsidiary C, in accordance with the hedge documentation. The method of consolidation (that is, direct method or step-by-step method) does not affect the assessment of the effectiveness of the hedge. However, as explained in paragraph 6.8.148 below, it may affect the amounts that are recycled when the hedged foreign operation is disposed of.

Recycling on disposal of foreign operation

6.8.146 When a foreign operation that was hedged is entirely disposed of, the amount reclassified or 'recycled' to profit or loss from the foreign currency translation reserve in respect of the hedging instrument is the effective portion of the revaluation of the hedging instrument calculated in accordance with IAS 39 paragraph 102. The amount reclassified to profit or loss from the foreign currency translation reserve in respect of the net investment in that foreign operation is the amount included in that parent's foreign currency translation reserve in respect of that foreign operation. [IAS 21 para 48]. This latter amount may vary depending on what consolidation method (direct or step-by-step) the entity has chosen.

6.8.147 The direct method of consolidation is the method of consolidation in which the financial statements of the foreign operation are translated directly into the functional currency of the ultimate parent. The step-by-step method is the method of consolidation in which the financial statements of the foreign operation are first translated into the functional currency of any intermediate parent(s) and then translated into the functional currency of the ultimate parent (or the presentation currency if different). IAS 21 does not prescribe which method of consolidation entities should use. In the ultimate parent's consolidated financial statements, the aggregate net amount recognised in the foreign currency translation reserve in respect of all foreign operations is not affected by the consolidation method. However, whether the ultimate parent uses the direct or the step-by-step method of consolidation (see para 6.8.141 above) may affect the amount included in its foreign currency translation reserve in respect of an individual foreign operation. The amount of foreign currency translation reserve for an individual foreign operation determined by the direct method of consolidation reflects the economic risk between the functional currency of the foreign operation and that of the ultimate parent (if the parent's functional and presentation currencies are the same). The use of the step-by-step method of consolidation may result in the reclassification to profit or loss of an amount different from that used to determine hedge effectiveness. This difference may be eliminated by determining the amount relating to that foreign operation that would have been posted if the direct method of consolidation had been used. However, IAS 21 does not require this adjustment. It is, therefore, an accounting policy choice that should be followed consistently for all net investments. Entities with foreign currency net investments will have to disclose their choice of accounting policy for revaluation of the net investments in foreign operations.

6.8.148 The IFRS IC noted that this issue arises also when the net investment disposed of was not hedged and, therefore, is not strictly within the scope of the interpretation. However, because it was a topic of considerable confusion and debate, the IFRS IC decided to include a brief example illustrating its conclusions, which are discussed below.

[IFRIC 16 para 16, 17, BC38, BC39]

> **Example 1 – Choice of consolidation method and effect on recycling**
>
> Using the same facts as in the example of the group in paragraph 6.8.141 above, parent used a USD borrowing in subsidiary A to hedge the EUR/USD risk of the net investment in subsidiary C in Parent's consolidated financial statements. Parent uses the step-by-step method of consolidation. Assume the hedge was fully effective and the full USD/EUR accumulated change in the value of the hedging instrument before disposal of subsidiary C is €24m (gain). This is matched exactly by the fall in value of the net investment in subsidiary C, when measured against the functional currency of Parent (euro). If the direct method of consolidation is used, the fall in the value of parent's net investment in subsidiary C of €24m is reflected totally in the foreign currency translation reserve relating to subsidiary C in parent's consolidated financial statements. However, because parent uses the step-by-step method, this fall in the net investment value in subsidiary C of €24m is reflected both in subsidiary B's foreign currency translation reserve relating to subsidiary C and in parent's foreign currency translation reserve relating to subsidiary B. The aggregate amount recognised in the foreign currency translation reserve in respect of subsidiaries B and C is not affected by the consolidation method. Assume that using the direct method of consolidation, the foreign currency translation reserves for subsidiaries B and C in parent's consolidated financial statements are €62m gain and €24m loss respectively; using the step-by-step method of consolidation those amounts are €49m gain and €11m loss respectively.

IAS 39 requires the full €24m gain on the hedging instrument to be reclassified to profit or loss when the investment in subsidiary C is disposed of. Using the step-by-step method, the amount to be reclassified to profit or loss in respect of the net investment in subsidiary C is only €11m loss. The parent could adjust the foreign currency translation reserves of both subsidiaries B and C by €13m in order to match the amounts reclassified in respect of the hedging instrument and the net investment as would have been the case if the direct method of consolidation had been used, if that was its accounting policy. An entity that had not hedged its net investment could make the same reclassification.

Where a foreign operation is partially disposed of, the amount of the hedging reserves to reclassify to the income statement has changed under IAS 27 as compared to IAS 27 (superseded). In the table below hedging reserves refer to the cash flow hedge reserve in the subsidiary itself and the net investment hedge reserve in the consolidated financial statements. The table below illustrates common situations and the effect on hedging reserves:

Relationship of foreign operation before disposal	Relationship of foreign operation after disposal	Reclassification of hedging reserves
Subsidiary	Subsidiary (with new NCI recognised)	Reattribute share of hedging reserves to non-controlling interest(s). No amount reclassified to profit and loss.
Subsidiary	Associate	Reclassify 100% of hedging reserves related to foreign operation to profit and loss as part of gain or loss on disposal of subsidiary.
Associate	Associate	Reclassify proportionate amount of share of hedging reserves to profit and loss as part of gain or loss on partial disposal of an associate.
Associate or subsidiary	Financial asset (IAS 39)	Reclassify 100% of share of hedging reserve related to foreign operation to profit and loss as above

If a foreign operation that is a subsidiary is contributed to a joint venture, the question of whether to recycle is based on the policy choice. See chapter 26.

It should be noted that reductions of the net investment in a foreign operation through payment of non-liquidating distributions or repayment of quasi-equity loans may no longer trigger reclassification of CTA. Whether such reductions trigger a reclassification of CTA is, in our view, an accounting policy choice as discussed in chapter 7. Where such a payment is made and a policy of reclassifying CTA adopted, then this may also trigger the reclassification of part of the net investment hedge reserve related to that foreign operation.

> ### Example 2 – Recycling of amounts in OCI due to return of capital
>
> Entity A (pound sterling functional currency) owns a net investment of 30 billion USD in a foreign operation (entity B, wholly-owned, with functional currency USD). Entity A hedges the foreign currency risk with derivatives and designates them as hedging the first 15 billion USD of the net investment in entity B. After some time, there is a 20 billion USD return of capital, which represents two thirds of the net investment. In view of the return of capital, the entity de-designates the hedging relationship. The amount to be recycled from the hedging reserve because of the return of capital could be either two thirds, that is, proportionate reclassification based on a two thirds return of capital; or one third, based on the fact that only 5 billion USD of the first 15 billion USD net investment has been returned. This is a policy choice and should be adopted consistently by entity A in any further partial disposals of foreign operations.

Hedging with derivatives

6.8.149   It is also possible to hedge a net investment with derivatives. A derivative that is commonly used is a forward contract. However, in this situation, it would be necessary for the entity to designate at inception whether effectiveness would be measured by reference to changes in spot exchange rates or changes in forward exchange rates. If the spot rate method is used, only the change in the fair value of the forward contract due to changes in spot rates would be reported in other comprehensive income and the balance of the fair value of the forward (due to the forward points) would be included in profit or loss. On the other hand, if the forward rate method is used, the full change in the fair value of the forward would be reported in other comprehensive income. This is explained further in paragraph 6.8.207 below. If the notional amount of a currency forward that swaps the functional currency of the hedged net investment into the investor's functional currency matches the portion of the net investment hedged, it is likely to be an effective hedging instrument.

6.8.150   It is possible to designate a cross-currency interest rate swap as a hedge of a net investment in a foreign operation. However, such cross-currency interest rate swaps (CCIRS), having foreign exchange and interest rates as underlyings may not be effective hedging instruments since the hedged net investment is not affected by changes in interest rates. Nevertheless, cross-currency swaps could be designated as hedging instruments in a net investment hedge, provided both legs of the swap are either floating rates or fixed rates. This is because a cross-currency interest rate swap that has two floating legs has a fair value that is primarily driven by changes in foreign exchange rates rather than changes in interest rates. However, a cross-currency swap interest rate swap with one fixed-leg and one floating-rate leg is unlikely to be effective as a hedging instrument in a net investment hedge.

6.8.151   To designate a fixed-fixed CCIRS as a hedge of net investment, management should bear in mind that hedges of a net investment in a foreign operation are accounted similarly to cash flow hedges. [IAS 39 para 102]. There is no other guidance within IAS 39 or the Basis for Conclusions, regarding the basis for this similarity. One interpretation of this statement could be that a net investment hedge is capable of being viewed as analogous to a cash flow hedge of the foreign currency cash flows that would arise from a sale of the net investment at a (or several) future date(s) for the cash flow variability arising due to foreign currency risk. This interpretation would give a rationale for accounting for net investment hedges in a similar manner to cash flow hedges.

Example

An entity A, with Swiss francs as its functional currency, which has a net investment of US$ 120m. Entity A wishes to eliminate foreign exchange risk associated with the retranslation of part of this net investment into its functional currency and enters into a fixed-fixed CCIRS. The swap has a CHF 100m receive leg receiving interest at 3% and US$80m pay leg paying interest at 5% (assume that CHF100m and US$80m are equivalent based on the spot rate at inception). The swap has annual interest settlements, a five year maturity and has a zero fair value at inception.

In applying paragraph 102 of IAS 39, the cash flow hedge method may be applied to the US dollar net investment by viewing the hedged net investment as a series of cash flows on various 'deemed disposal' dates in the future. In other words, the net investment hedge would be treated in a manner similar to a cash flow hedge of cash flows arising on a deemed sale of US$4m (that is, US$80m × 5%) of the net investment at the end of each of the next 4 years, and a deemed sale of US$84m at the end of year 5. The total net investment of US$ 120m exceeds the aggregate of the deemed disposals (US$4 + US$4 + US$4 + US$4 + US$84 = US$100m) and, hence, this designation is acceptable.

This net investment (series of deemed cash flows) is identical to the profile of cash flows in a US$80m foreign currency debt (which is an asset of entity A) that pays interest annually at 5%, and hence effectiveness may be measured in a manner similar to that used for a cash flow hedge of a fixed rate foreign currency debt.

In a cash flow hedge of a recognised foreign currency fixed rate liability, a fixed-fixed CCIRS can be used to hedge the foreign currency exposure. The most appropriate hypothetical derivative to test effectiveness is a fixed to fixed CCIRS which would ensure little-to-no ineffectiveness.

As hedges of a net investment in a foreign operation are accounted similarly to cash flow hedges, an at-market fixed-fixed CCIRS may be used as a hypothetical derivative to test effectiveness in a net investment hedge. This hypothetical derivative is a CCIRS that is equivalent (and opposite) to the actual hedging instrument. Ineffectiveness is likely to be minimal as the fair value changes in the hedging instrument and hypothetical derivative will offset.

However, this designation requires the net investment to equal or exceed the aggregate of notional principal and interest flows on the CCIRS, in this case US$100m. This approach cannot be adopted where the notional principal in the CCIRS is equal to the net investment balance.

Hedging in individual or separate financial statements

6.8.152 IAS 27 states that in a parent's separate financial statements, investments in subsidiaries, jointly controlled entities and associates that are included in the consolidated financial statements should be carried at cost or accounted for in accordance with IAS 39. This means that the equity investment can be designated as 'available-for-sale' or 'at fair value through profit or loss' (if permitted by IAS 39). However, in some jurisdictions, entities normally record their investments in subsidiaries, associates and joint ventures at cost in their separate financial statements. A question, therefore, arises as to whether a foreign currency borrowing can be designated as a hedge of the entity's foreign equity investment in its separate financial statements where the foreign equity investment is recorded at historical cost.

6.8.153 The answer is that it may be possible to construct a hedging relationship to achieve hedge accounting despite the apparent contradictions with IAS 21 and IAS 39. The rationale for achieving hedge accounting is set out in IG E3.4 of the implementation guidance of IAS 39. In summary, IG E3.4 states that, as an exception, if the financial asset or financial liability is designated as a hedged item in a fair value hedge of the exposure to changes in foreign currency rates under IAS 39, the hedged item is re-measured for changes in foreign currency rates even if it would otherwise have been recognised using a historical rate under IAS 21. This exception applies to non-monetary items that are carried in terms of historical cost in the foreign currency (such as equity investments in foreign subsidiaries) and are hedged against exposure to foreign currency rates. In effect, this exception allows an entity to hedge the change in the historical foreign currency cost of the foreign equity investment due to the movement in the relevant foreign currency rates. In these circumstances, the historical foreign currency cost of the foreign currency investment would be retranslated at each balance sheet date at the closing rate and the exchange difference arising on the retranslation will be recognised in profit or loss to offset the exchange difference recognised in profit or loss arising on the retranslation of the foreign currency borrowings (where these are used as the hedging instrument) or the change in the fair value of the foreign currency derivative, that is used as the hedging instrument. Although this treatment is an exception, nevertheless it is still classified as a fair value hedge. Accordingly, the hedging criteria set out in paragraph 6.8.154 below must still be met in order to achieve fair value hedge accounting in the reporting entity's separate financial statements. Whether, in practice, a parent entity would apply hedge accounting in its separate financial statements may depend on the tax treatment of undertaking such hedging activities.

> **Example – Hedge of a foreign subsidiary in entity's separate financial statements**
>
> Entity A whose functional currency is the pound sterling acquired a subsidiary B in France for €300m in 20X0 when the £/€ exchange rate on the day of the transaction was £1 = €1.50. Entity A, therefore, measures its investment on initial recognition at £200m (€300/1.50). Entity A borrowed €300m to make the purchase and designates the euro borrowing as a hedge of the exposure to the change in £/€ spot rate.

Assuming that the hedging criteria in paragraph 6.8.154 below are met and using the exception discussed above, entity A will retranslate its investment in its French subsidiary at each balance sheet date using the closing £/€ spot rate. Therefore, if at the first balance sheet reporting date following the acquisition, the spot rate has moved to £1 = €1.75, entity A will re-measure the historical euro cost of its investment into £171.43m. The exchange difference of £28.57m is recognised as an exchange loss in profit or loss for the period. At the same time the €300m borrowing is retranslated at the closing rate and the exchange gain of £28.57m is also recognised in profit or loss. Therefore, in this case the net effect as a result of hedge accounting is £nil on profit or loss. This example ignores any tax consequences of such a strategy.

Criteria for obtaining hedge accounting

6.8.154 Hedge accounting is an exception to the normal accounting principles for financial instruments (and sometimes non-financial instruments). IAS 39, therefore, requires hedge relationships to meet certain criteria in order to qualifying for hedge accounting. The three types of hedging relationship set out in paragraph 6.8.102 qualify for hedge accounting only if all of the following conditions are met:

- At the inception of the hedge there is formal designation and documentation of the hedging relationship and the entity's risk management objective and strategy for undertaking the hedge.

- The hedge is expected to be highly effective in achieving offsetting changes in fair value or cash flows attributable to the hedged risk, consistently with the originally documented risk management strategy for that particular hedging relationship.

- A forecast transaction that is the subject of a cash flow hedge must be highly probable and must present an exposure to variations in cash flows that could ultimately affect profit or loss.

- The effectiveness of the hedge can be reliably measured, that is, the hedged item's fair value or cash flows that are attributable to the hedged risk and the hedged instrument's fair value can be reliably measured.

- The hedge is assessed on an ongoing basis and determined actually to have been highly effective throughout the financial reporting periods for which the hedge was designated.

[IAS 39 para 88(a)-(e)].

6.8.155 The criteria for hedge accounting are onerous and have systems implications for all entities. Hedge accounting is optional and management should consider the costs and benefits when deciding whether to use it. Much of the burden and cost associated with hedge accounting arises from the effectiveness testing requirement. These requirements are considered from paragraph 6.8.164 below.

Documentation and designation

6.8.156 Formal hedge documentation in support of the hedge must be prepared at the inception of the hedge and should include the following:

- The entity's risk management objective and strategy for undertaking the hedge.

- The nature of the risk being hedged.

- The hedged item.

- The hedging instrument.

- How the entity will assess the hedging instrument's effectiveness in offsetting the exposure to changes in the hedged item's fair value or cash flows attributable to the hedged risk.

[IAS 39 para 88(a)].

6.8.157 Since there must be formal designation and documentation of the hedging relationship at the inception of the hedge, a hedge relationship cannot be designated retrospectively. However, IAS 39 does not require a hedging relationship to be established at the time the hedging instrument is acquired. For instance, an entity is permitted to designate and formally document a derivative contract as a hedging instrument after entering into the derivative contract. Hedge accounting will apply prospectively from the date all hedge accounting criteria in paragraph 6.8.154 above are met. [IAS 39 paras IG F3.8, F3.9].

6.8.158 Risks associated with assets previously designated at fair value through profit and loss that were not previously designated as a hedged risk can be so designated from the date they are reclassified in accordance with the 'Reclassification of financial assets' amendment.

Documentation relating to forecast transaction

6.8.159 When the entity is hedging a forecast transaction, the hedge relationship documentation should also identify the date on, or time period in, which the forecast transaction is expected to occur. This is because to qualify for hedge accounting:

- the hedge must relate to a specific identified and designated risk;

- it must be possible to measure its effectiveness reliably; and

- the hedged forecast transaction must be highly probable.

[IAS 39 para IG F3.11].

6.8.160 To meet the above criteria, the hedged forecast transaction must be identified and documented with sufficient specificity so that when the transaction occurs, it is clear whether the transaction is or is not the hedged transaction. Therefore, a forecast transaction may be identified as the sale of the first 15,000 units of a specific product during a specified three-month period, but it could not be identified as the last 15,000 units of that product sold during a three-month period, because the last 15,000 units cannot be identified when they are sold. For the same reason, a forecast transaction cannot be specified solely as a percentage of sales or purchases during a period. [IAS 39 para IG F3.10].

6.8.161 An entity is not required to predict and document the exact date a forecast transaction is expected to occur. However, it is required to identify and document the time period during which the forecast transaction is expected to occur within a reasonably specific and generally narrow range, as a basis for assessing hedge effectiveness. To determine that the hedge will be highly effective, it is necessary to ensure that changes in the expected cash flow's fair value are offset by changes in the hedging instrument's fair value and this test may be met only if the cash flows occur within close proximity of each other. [IAS 39 para IG F3.11].

6.8.162 The change in timing of the forecast transaction within the specific and narrow time range does not affect the validity of the designation. For instance, if, subsequent to designating a derivative as a hedging instrument in a cash flow hedge of a forecast transaction such as a commodity sale, the entity expects the forecast sale to occur in an earlier period than originally anticipated, the original designation is not invalidated. Provided the hedging relationship met all the hedge accounting conditions, including the requirement to identify and document the period in which the sale was expected to occur within a reasonably specific and narrow range of time as explained above, the entity can conclude that this transaction is the same as the one that was designated as being hedged. However, this may well affect the assessment of the effectiveness of the hedging relationship since the derivative would need to be designated as a hedging instrument for the whole remaining period of its existence, which will include a period after the forecast sale. [IAS 39 para IG F 5.4].

> **Example – Hedging cash flows in specific time periods**
>
> Entity A manufactures and sells ice cream. Its functional currency is the euro, but 30% of its sales are made in the UK and denominated in pounds sterling. Entity A forecasts highly probable sales in the UK for the next summer season on a monthly basis. Using these forecasts, it enters into forward contracts to sell pounds sterling in exchange for Euros. Due to the nature of its business, entity A is not able to forecast or track individual sales transactions.
>
> Although the forecast transaction should be specifically identifiable as a single transaction or a group of individual transactions in order to qualify for cash flow hedge accounting, Entity A can designate the forecast sales of ice cream as the hedged item. It should do this by designating the hedged item as the first £Xm of highly probable cash flows in specific time periods (for example, in each month). To qualify for hedge accounting, the designation must be sufficiently specific to ensure that when a forecast transaction occurs, it is possible to determine objectively whether that

transaction is or is not the one that is hedged. If the forecasted cash flows are no longer expected to occur in the designated time period, management cannot continue with hedge accounting for the related hedging instruments. It should reclassify the amounts previously deferred in equity to profit or loss at that point.

Example documentation

6.8.163 IAS 39 does not mandate any standard format for documenting the hedging relationship and, therefore, in practice, the nature and style of the documentation may vary from entity to entity. The important thing to note is that the documentation must include all of the basic contents required by IAS 39 paragraph 88 (see para 6.8.156 above) and must be in place at inception of the hedge. Examples of hedge designation and documentation are included in the three comprehensive examples illustrated from paragraph 6.8.223 below.

Hedge effectiveness

6.8.164 The requirement to assess hedge effectiveness is critical for a hedge transaction to qualify for hedge accounting. But this requirement is also the most onerous of the hedge accounting criteria because of the time, cost and effort that it entails. Hedge effectiveness is defined as *"the degree to which changes in the fair value or cash flows of the hedged item that are attributable to a hedged risk are offset by changes in the fair value or cash flows of the hedging instrument"*. [IAS 39 para 9]. Assessing the degree or the extent to which such offset will be effective for hedge accounting purposes is by no means an easy task. The difficulty is also exacerbated by the lack of practical guidance in the standard for undertaking the effectiveness exercise. Often, it will require the use of complex statistical techniques whose output will require careful interpretations. As a result, the approach taken by entities may vary: from electing not to adopt hedge accounting and managing the resulting volatility in the income statement through communications with the market, to putting hedge accounting systems and processes in place and thereby obtaining the benefits of hedge accounting. In practice, most entities are likely to adopt a mixed approach, undertaking hedge accounting only for large material hedges and not electing to adopt hedge accounting for immaterial ones.

Requirements for assessing effectiveness

6.8.165 To qualify for hedge accounting, IAS 39 requires a hedge to be highly effective. A hedge is regarded as highly effective if both of the following two conditions are met:

■ At the inception of the hedge and in subsequent periods, the hedge is expected to be highly effective in achieving offsetting changes in fair value or cash flows attributable to the hedged risk during the period for which the hedge is designated.

■ The actual results of the hedge are within a range of 80%-125%.

[IAS 39 para AG 105].

6.8.166 In order to comply with the first condition above, an entity needs to perform a *prospective hedge effectiveness assessment*. This is a forward looking test that assesses whether the entity expects the hedging relationship to be highly effective in achieving offset in the future. An expectation that the hedging relationship will be highly effective can be demonstrated in various ways, including a comparison of the critical terms of the hedging instrument with those of the hedged item (see para 6.8.182 below), or a comparison of past changes in the fair value or cash flows of the hedged item that are attributable to the hedged risk with past changes in the fair value or cash flows of the hedging instrument (see para 6.8.186 below), or by demonstrating a high statistical correlation between the fair value or cash flows of the hedged item and those of the hedging instrument (see para 6.8.195 below). The entity may choose a hedge ratio of other than one to one in order to improve the effectiveness of the hedge as described in paragraph 6.8.206 below. [IAS 39 para AG 105(a)].

6.8.167 In order to comply with the second condition above, an entity needs to perform a *retrospective hedge effectiveness assessment*. This is a backward looking test that assesses whether the hedging relationship actually has been highly effective in achieving offset. The objective is to demonstrate that the hedging relationship has been highly effective by showing that actual results of the hedge are within a range of 80%-125%. For example, if actual results are such that the loss on the hedging instrument is C120 and the gain on the hedged item is C100, offset can be measured by 120/100, which is 120%, or by 100/120, which is 83%. In this example, assuming the hedge meets the first condition above, the entity would conclude that the hedge has been highly effective. [IAS 39 para AG 105(b)].

6.8.168 An entity is required to perform the prospective test at the inception of the hedging relationship *and* at the beginning of each assessment period to demonstrate that the hedge is expected to be highly effective in the future. If, at any point, the prospective consideration indicates that the hedging instrument is not expected to be highly effective in the future, hedge accounting must be discontinued from that point forward. An entity must also perform the retrospective test at the end of every period to demonstrate that the hedge has been highly effective through the date of the periodic assessment. If the retrospective test indicates that the hedging instrument has not been highly effective, hedge accounting must be discontinued from the point the hedging relationship ceased to be highly effective. Both tests must be met for a particular period of the hedge relationship for hedge accounting to be available. The requirements are illustrated as follows:

Prospective and Retrospective Assessment

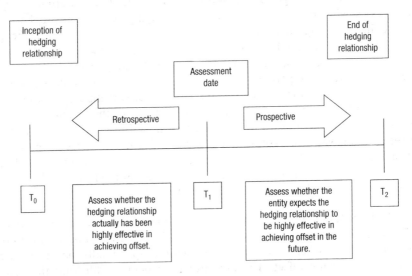

Note: The diagram refers to tests being carried out at time T, (the assessment date). It is assumed that the prospective test at inception of hedge at time T_o has been met.

6.8.169 Given the nature of the two assessments, it is possible for an entity to pass the prospective test at the beginning of the period but fail the retrospective test at the end of the period (for example, due to unexpected market factors). In that situation, hedge accounting would be precluded for the current period in question. However, a new hedge relationship could be designated and hedge accounting applied in future periods for the same hedging instrument and hedged item, provided the prospective test is met for those periods. Similarly, if the entity passes the retrospective test at the end of one period, but fails the prospective test at the beginning of the next period, hedge accounting would be permitted for the period just ended, but could not be applied in the next period. To some degree, these results will be impacted by the manner in which an entity elects to assess hedge effectiveness, because the entity is not required to use the same method for both the prospective and the retrospective assessments.

Example – Failed retrospective test with a successful prospective test

A hedge relationship designated by entity A fails the retrospective test for a given period. Accordingly, entity A ceases to apply hedge accounting from the last date on which it demonstrated effectiveness. Entity A performs a successful prospective effectiveness test with the same hedging instrument and the same hedged item at the start of the following period. It should be noted that this prospective effectiveness testing will need to take account of the fact that the derivative now has a non-zero fair value as discussed in paragraph 6.8.59 above.

In this scenario, entity A can designate a new hedge relationship for the remaining life of the instrument following a successful prospective effectiveness test. IAS 39 does not preclude an entity from designating the same derivative as a hedge of the same item in a subsequent period, provided the hedge relationship meets the criteria for hedge accounting (including effectiveness) in that subsequent period. [IFRIC Update April 2005].

6.8.170 Effectiveness is assessed, at a minimum, at the time an entity prepares its annual or interim financial statements. [IAS 39 para AG 106]. However, the standard does not prevent an entity from undertaking an assessment more frequently. Indeed, an entity may wish to assess effectiveness more frequently say, at the end of each month or other applicable reporting period, in order to minimise the time period during which the hedge may fail due to ineffectiveness and to better manage the hedged risk exposure.

6.8.171 IAS 39 does not specify a single method for assessing hedge effectiveness. The method an entity adopts for assessing hedge effectiveness depends on its risk management strategy. Also the appropriateness of a given method of assessing hedge effectiveness will depend on the nature of the risk being hedged and the type of hedging instrument used. IAS 39, however, does require an entity to document at the inception of the hedge how effectiveness will be assessed. The method of assessing effectiveness must be reasonable and consistent with other similar hedges, unless different methods can be explicitly justified. The defined and documented method should be used on a consistent basis throughout the hedge's duration. [IAS 39 paras 80, IG F4.4]. There is nothing in the standard to prevent an entity from using one method for prospective testing and another different method for retrospective testing as long as the chosen methods are reasonable and properly documented upfront and used on a consistent basis throughout the hedge's duration. Methods normally used for testing hedge effectiveness are considered in paragraph 6.8.181 below.

6.8.172 There is nothing in the standard to prevent an entity from changing its method of assessing hedge effectiveness. However, if an entity wishes to change its method of assessing hedge effectiveness, this will result in a new hedging relationship. Hence, the entity should de-designate the old hedging relationship and then immediately designate a new hedging relationship using the new method of assessing hedge effectiveness. As a result, new documentation would need to be prepared. It should be noted, however, that there is a danger in de-designating and re-designating the hedge relationship. This is because the hedging instrument will have a non-zero fair value and this may well impact the assessment of hedge ineffectiveness due to ineffectiveness caused by the non-zero fair values.

Assessment on a cumulative or a period-by-period basis

6.8.173 IAS 39 permits an entity to assess hedge effectiveness using either a period-by-period approach or a cumulative approach, provided the chosen approach is incorporated into the hedging documentation at inception of the hedge. [IAS 39 para IG F4.2]. The period-by-period approach involves comparing the changes in the hedging instrument's fair values (or cash flows) that have occurred during the period being assessed to the changes in the hedged item's fair value (or hedged transaction's cash flows) attributable to the risk hedged that have occurred during the same period. The cumulative approach involves comparing the cumulative changes (to date from inception of the hedge) in the hedging instrument's fair values (or cash flows) to the cumulative changes in the hedged item's fair value (or hedged transaction's cash flows) attributable to the risk hedged. The two methods can produce significantly different results as illustrated below:

	Cumulative basis			Period-by-period basis		
Assessment period	Hedging instrument	Hedged item	Ratio (%)	Hedging instrument	Hedged item	Ratio (%)
Quarter 1	50	(50)	100%	50	(50)	100%
Quarter 2	105	(107)	98%	55	(57)	96%
Quarter 3	129	(120)	108%	24	(13)	184%
Quarter 4	115	(116)	99%	(14)	4	350%

6.8.174 It is clear from the above table that the period-by-period approach of retrospective assessment results in the disqualification of hedge accounting in quarters 3 and 4. By contrast, had the cumulative method of retrospective assessment been applied, all periods would have been considered highly effective and qualified for hedge accounting. It is, therefore, important to ensure that the chosen method of assessment, in this instance, the cumulative method, is documented at the inception of the hedging relationship. Indeed, in most situations, the cumulative method would be adopted in practice as it results in less ineffectiveness. Another example of assessing expected hedge effectiveness on a cumulative basis is given below.

> **Example – Hedge effectiveness assessment on a cumulative basis**
>
> An entity designates a LIBOR-based interest rate swap as a hedge of a borrowing whose interest rate is a UK base rate plus a margin. The UK base rate changes, perhaps, once each quarter or less, in increments of 25-50 basis points, while LIBOR changes daily. Over a period of 1-2 years, the hedge is expected to be almost perfect. However, there will be quarters when the UK base rate does not change at all, while LIBOR has changed significantly.
>
> Expected hedge effectiveness may be assessed on a cumulative basis if the hedge is so designated and that condition is incorporated into the appropriate hedging documentation. Therefore, even if a hedge is not expected to be highly effective in a particular period, hedge accounting is not precluded if effectiveness is expected to remain sufficiently high over the life of the hedging relationship. However, any ineffectiveness is required to be recognised in profit or loss as it occurs. [IAS 39 para IG F4.2].

Counterparty credit risk

6.8.175 An entity must consider the likelihood of default by the counterparty to the hedging instrument in assessing hedge effectiveness. This is because an entity cannot ignore whether it will be able to collect all amounts due under the contractual provisions of the hedging instrument. When assessing hedge effectiveness, both at the inception of the hedge and on an ongoing basis, the entity should consider the risk that the counterparty to the hedging instrument will default by failing to make any contractual payments to the entity when due (see chapter 6.7 for further guidance). For a cash flow hedge, the fair value of the underlying cash flow (hypothetical derivative) will not be affected by change in credit risk of the hedge counterparty. However, the fair value of the actual hedging instrument will be affected. This will lead to ineffectiveness and may even cause hedge relationship to fail if the effectiveness test result falls outside of the 80%–125% range. Furthermore if it becomes probable that the derivative counterparty bank will default, an entity would be unable to conclude that the hedging relationship is expected to be highly effective in achieving offsetting cash flows. As a result, hedge accounting would be discontinued. For a fair value hedge, if there is a change in the counterparty's creditworthiness, the fair value of the hedging instrument will change, which affects the assessment of whether the hedge relationship is effective and whether it qualifies for continued hedge accounting. [IAS 39 para IG F4.3].

Entity credit risk

6.8.175.1 Entities will be required to adopt IFRS 13 for accounting periods commencing after 1 January 2013 (subject to EU endorsement). This has amended the definition of fair value. Derivative liabilities should be recorded at a settlement price and this includes an adjustment for the entity's own credit risk. Although it is possible to include credit risk in liability valuations under IAS 39 it is not common so this will be a change in estimate for many entities. The updated valuations may affect hedge effectiveness testing in a similar way to the adjustments for counterparty credit risk. See chapter 5 for more details on fair value accounting under IFRS 13.

Transaction costs

6.8.176 Transaction costs are never part of a fair value movement under IAS 39 and, therefore, they should be excluded from hedge effectiveness tests.

Example – transaction costs

Entity A, whose functional currency is the pound sterling, granted a US$ denominated loan to entity B. Entity A measures the loan at amortised cost, which at initial recognition is the amount lent of US$1m plus transaction costs of US$ 5,000. Entity A designates the loan as a hedging instrument for the foreign exchange risk of a forecast purchase of US$1m. The repayment of the loan and the forecast purchase occur on the same date and all other requirements for hedge accounting are met. Since transaction costs of US$5,000 would not be included in the loan's fair value if it had been carried at fair value, entity A's management should exclude transaction costs of US$5,000 from the effectiveness test.

Pre-payment risk

6.8.177   Pre-payment risk will impact the effectiveness of fair value hedges of pre-payable assets, such as mortgage loans and, therefore, should be taken into account when an entity designates the hedge relationship. The hedged mortgage loans' contractual terms include the pre-payment option (for the borrower), which cannot be ignored. Furthermore, pre-payment rates are primarily a function of interest rates and, hence, IAS 39 specifies that pre-payment risk is a component of interest rate risk. Therefore, if an entity intends to hedge a portfolio of mortgage loans for interest rate risk, pre-payment risk cannot be excluded. For instance, an entity may have a portfolio of C500 million of mortgage loans that may be pre-paid at par. The entity may wish to hedge the changes in fair value of this portfolio attributable to interest rate movements by entering into a simple receive-variable, pay-fixed interest rate swap. Such a swap, however, would not be a highly effective hedging instrument, because the hedged item contains a pre-payment option that is not present in the swap. However, if the entity can demonstrate (based on historical data) that C100 million of the portfolio would not pre-pay if interest rate were to decline, it could designate that specific portion of the mortgage portfolio as the hedged item.

6.8.178   Cash flows after the pre-payment date may be designated as the hedged item to the extent it can be demonstrated that they are 'highly probable'. For example, cash flows after the pre-payment date may qualify as highly probable if they result from a group or pool of similar assets (for example, mortgage loans) for which pre-payments can be estimated with a high degree of accuracy or if the pre-payment option is significantly out of the money. In addition, the cash flows after the pre-payment date may be designated as the hedged item if a comparable option exists in the hedging instrument. [IAS 39 para IG F2.12].

6.8.179   Historically, derivative valuations were based on a LIBOR discount rate applied to the derivative's contractual cash flows. The LIBOR discount rate reflected the cost of funding for banks. The use of LIBOR as the standard discount rate, however, ignores the fact that some of derivative transactions are collateralised. Collateralised trades involve a funding rate based off the overnight indexed swap (OIS) curve rather than LIBOR. This discrepancy has always existed, however historically the difference between LIBOR and OIS has been small. This basis differential widened significantly in 2008 and the structural shift in credit pricing following 2008.

6.8.180   As a result, valuing collateralised swaps has been shifting from using a discount rate of LIBOR to using an OIS rate. Companies should assess at each reporting date whether market practice has moved sufficiently that the use of LIBOR as the discount rate to value collateralised derivatives is no longer appropriate. They should also consider the impact on hedge effectiveness. In particular, in a cash flow hedge, it may be possible to avoid additional ineffectiveness by designating the hedge such that the hypothetical derivative is discounted using either LIBOR or OIS as appropriate, given both are used by the market to price swaps (as LIBOR continues to be used to price uncollateralised swaps). However, for a fair value hedge, ineffectiveness may arise where the hedging instrument is a collateralised swap and the appropriate discount rate used to value the swap is determined to be OIS, unless the appropriate benchmark rate for the hedged item is also deemed to be OIS.

Methods used to assess hedge effectiveness

6.8.181 IAS 39 does not specify a single method for assessing hedge effectiveness prospectively or retrospectively. The method an entity adopts for assessing hedge effectiveness depends on its risk management strategy and should be included in the documentation at the inception of the hedge. There are a number of methods that are used in practice ranging from the most simple (qualitative) to the more complex (highly quantitative). Although the particular method selected would depend on the nature and type of the hedging relationship, all of the methods attempt to gauge the relative change in value of the hedged item and the hedging instrument. The methods that are commonly used in practice to assess hedge effectiveness are described in the paragraphs that follow. It should be noted, however, that whatever method is used test the effectiveness of a hedge, a quantitative retrospective test must be performed to determine the amount of ineffectiveness that has occurred and that must be recognised in profit or loss (see para 6.8.211 below).

Critical terms comparison

6.8.182 This method consists of comparing the principal terms of the hedging instrument with those of the hedged item. If the principal terms of the hedging instrument and of the hedged item are the same, the changes in fair value and cash flows attributable to the risk being hedged may be likely to offset each other fully, both when the hedge is entered into and afterwards. [IAS 39 para AG 108]. The principal terms of the hedging instrument and hedged items are those that are critical to the assessment of hedge effectiveness. Further, critical terms are the same if and only if the terms are exactly the same and there are no features (such as optionality) that would invalidate an assumption of perfect effectiveness. Therefore, this method may only be used in limited circumstances, but in such cases it is the simplest way to demonstrate that a hedge is expected to be highly effective on a prospective basis. This method does not require any calculation. For instance, an interest rate swap is likely to be an effective hedge if the notional and principal amounts, term, re-pricing dates, dates of interest and principal receipts and payments and basis for measuring interest rates are the *same* for the hedging instrument and the hedged item. [IAS 39 para AG 108]. A separate assessment is required for the retrospective effectiveness test, as ineffectiveness may arise even when critical terms match; for example, because of a change in the liquidity of a hedging derivative or in the creditworthiness of the derivative counterparty.

6.8.183 Similarly, a hedge of a highly probable forecast purchase of a commodity with a forward contract is likely to be highly effective if:

- the forward contract is for the purchase of the same quantity of the same commodity at the same time and location as the hedged forecast purchase;

- the fair value of the forward contract at inception is zero; and

- either the change in the discount or premium on the forward contract is excluded from the assessment of effectiveness and recognised in profit or loss or the change in expected cash flows on the highly probable forecast transaction is based on the commodity's forward price. [IAS 39 para AG 108].

In these circumstances, the change in the derivative's fair value can be viewed as a proxy for the present value of the change in cash flows attributable to the risk being hedged. The documentation that the critical terms of the hedging instrument and hedged item match must be performed at the inception of the hedging relationship and on an ongoing basis throughout the hedging period.

6.8.184 It should be noted that the critical terms of the hedged item and hedging instrument listed in the above example all pertain to factors that could produce ineffectiveness in a hedging relationship. The fair value of the forward must be zero at the inception of the hedging relationship because forward contracts with a value of other than zero include a 'financing' element that is a source of ineffectiveness (see para 6.8.59 above). Accordingly, the use of this method should be restricted to situations where an entity enters into the derivative at or very close to the same time it establishes the hedging relationship.

6.8.185 Even if all of the critical terms of a hedging relationship match, an entity *cannot assume perfect hedge effectiveness throughout the life of the hedge without further effectiveness testing.* An entity still must assess retrospectively the effectiveness of the relationship, at a minimum, at the time it prepares its annual or interim financial statements. A separate quantitative assessment is required for the retrospective effectiveness test, as ineffectiveness may arise even when critical terms match as illustrated in the following example. [IAS 39 para IG F4.7].

> **Example – Testing effectiveness retrospectively when critical terms match**
>
> Entity A enters into a 5 year fixed-rate borrowing. On the same date, it enters into a receive-fixed/pay-floating interest rate swap on which the floating leg is reset every 3 months. The principal terms of the swap and the debt match (start date, end date, fixed payment dates, calendar basis, principal amount, fixed interest rate) and there are no features or conditions (such as optionality) that would invalidate an assumption of perfect effectiveness.
>
> As the principal terms of the debt and the fixed leg of the swap match and entity A is able to demonstrate and document that the change in the fair value of the floating leg of the swap will not give rise to material ineffectiveness, this is sufficient that the hedge is expected to be highly effective on a prospective basis. Thus, a numerical test is not required to demonstrate prospective effectiveness.

However, even though the critical terms of the fixed rate borrowing and the swap match, hedge effectiveness cannot be assumed throughout the life of the hedge and a retrospective test must be performed. The objective of the retrospective effectiveness test is to determine that the hedge actually has been highly effective throughout the financial reporting period for which it was designated. If the principal terms of the hedging instrument match those of the hedged item, ineffectiveness may still arise, for example if in the case of a fair value hedge:

- there is a change in the swap's liquidity;

- there is a change in the swap counterparty's creditworthiness; or

- the floating rate leg is not reset on the testing date.

Dollar offset method

6.8.186 This is a quantitative method that consists of comparing the change in fair value or cash flows of the hedging instrument with the change in fair value or cash flows of the hedged item attributable to the hedged risk. If this ratio falls within the range of 80%-125% as explained in paragraph 6.8.169, the hedge is regarded as highly effective. Depending on the entity's risk management policies, this test can be performed either on a cumulative basis or on a period-by-period basis as explained in paragraph 6.8.173-6.8.174 above. The formula for assessing hedge effectiveness on cumulative basis under the dollar-offset method can be expressed as follows:

$$0.8 \leq - \left| \frac{\left| \sum_{i=1}^{n} X_i \right|}{\left| \sum_{i=1}^{n} Y_i \right|} \right| \leq 1.25$$

where $\sum_{i=1}^{n} X_i$ is the cumulative sum of the periodic changes in the values of the hedging instrument and

$\sum_{i=1}^{n} Y_i$ is the cumulative sum of the periodic changes in the values of the hedged item and

n = number of periods since inception of the hedge. Since X_i and Y_i are variables that offset each other, the minus sign has been introduced to ensure that the ratio is an absolute number.

For a perfect hedge, the change in the value of the hedging instrument exactly offsets the change in the value of the hedged item. Therefore, the above ratio of the cumulative sum of the periodic changes in value of the hedging instrument and the hedged item would equal one in a perfect hedge.

Example – Dollar-offset method

Entity A has a C1,000 debt at 10% fixed rate with a 2 year term. Interest payments are made annually In order to hedge against future changes in interest rates it enters into a 2 year C1,000 notional interest rate swap requiring interest payments at one year LIBOR in exchange for the receipt of fixed interest at 10% (fair value hedge of interest rate risk).

At inception, LIBOR is expected to be 10% for the following 2 years, but at the end of year 1 LIBOR is expected to be 5% for the second year. At the end of year 1, the retrospective test would be performed as follows:

		C
Hedged item (debt)	Fair value at inception =	1,000
	Fair value at end of year 1 = C1,000 × 1.10/1.05	1,048
	Change in fair value	(48)
Hedging instrument	Fair value at inception	0
	Fair value at end of year 1 = C50 */1.05	48
	Change in fair value	48

* Difference in anticipated swap cash flows = C1,000 × (10% − 5%)

Dollar offset test at end of year 1

$$\frac{\text{Change in fair value of hedging instrument}}{\text{Change in fair value of hedged item}} = \frac{48}{(48)} = 1$$

This hedge is, therefore, currently 100% effective.

If there had been a contractual difference or delay in the timing of the cash flows either on the debt or the swap, or if effectiveness is tested at a date other than the swap re-pricing date, then some ineffectiveness would most likely result. Also no account has been taken here of the credit risk in the swap payments, which could have introduced some ineffectiveness. Note that any credit risk on the debt was not designated as part of the hedging relationship and any impact of this would be booked to the income statement anyway over time, though not on a fair value basis.

Consider the example above, but the cash flows on the debt are anticipated to slip by one month at the end of year 2. The end of year 1 retrospective test would show:

		C
Hedged item (debt)	Fair value at inception =	1,000
	Fair value at end of year 1 = C1,000 × 1.10/(1.05)$^{13/12}$	1,043
	Change in fair value	(43)
Hedging instrument	Fair value at inception	0
	Fair value at end of year 1 = C50 */1.05	48
	Change in fair value	48

* Difference in anticipated swap cash flows = C1m × (10% − 5%)

Dollar offset test at end of year 1

$$\frac{\text{Change in fair value of hedging instrument}}{\text{Change in fair value of hedged item}} = \frac{48}{(43)} = 1.12$$

Due to the cash flow slippage on the debt ineffectiveness of C5 has been introduced. This is still within the 80-125 % range so hedge accounting is still permitted, however, the C5 will need to be recognised in profit or loss as explained further in paragraph 6.8.213 below.

6.8.187 The above examples illustrate that the dollar-offset method has the advantage that the calculation is straightforward and does not rely on maintaining a large population of valuation data. When applied retrospectively to an assessment of actual effectiveness, the dollar-offset method can be applied either on a period-by-period basis or cumulatively from the date of the inception of the hedge as explained in paragraph 6.8.173 above. However, the example in that paragraph also indicated that even though on a cumulative basis the hedge was highly effective, two test ratios were outside the critical range on a period-by-period basis. This is an unfortunate consequence of the 80/125 rule that during periods of market stability virtually any hedge is likely to fail as small changes in the values of either the hedged item or the hedging instrument can produce extreme ratios. This is a general shortcoming of the dollar-offset method and is likely to occur when there are short testing intervals. As a result, the dollar offset method can be unreliable, causing hedges that are, by other reasonable standards, highly effective, to fail the effectiveness test. In practice, however, this short coming is often overcome by performing a cumulative dollar-offset test.

6.8.188 Notwithstanding the above, when the dollar offset method is used for assessing retrospectively the effectiveness of a hedge, it has the advantage of determining the amount of ineffectiveness that has occurred and of generating the numbers required for the accounting entries. For instance, to the extent that the sum of the changes in the value of the hedged item and the hedging instrument is not zero, there is an element of ineffectiveness in the hedge that is included in profit or loss. Thus, even when a hedge is determined to be highly effective, there is an impact on profit or loss when there is not an exact offset of the hedged risk as illustrated in the example in paragraph 6.8.186 above.

6.8.189 The dollar offset method can be performed using different approaches. Three approaches that are generally used in practice are:

- The hypothetical derivative method (see para 6.8.190 below).

- The benchmark rate method (see para 6.8.193 below).

- The sensitivity analysis method (see para 6.8.194 below).

Hypothetical derivative method

6.8.190   The hypothetical derivative method is used under dollar offset method to measure the effectiveness of cash flow hedges. Under the hypothetical derivative method, the hedged risk is modelled as a derivative called a 'hypothetical derivative' (as it does not exist). The hypothetical derivative approach compares the change in the fair value or cash flows of the hedging instrument with the change in the fair value or cash flows of the hypothetical derivative. The hypothetical derivative method is referred to as 'method B' in IAS 39 paragraph IGF5.5. The measurement of hedge ineffectiveness is based on a comparison of the change in fair value of the actual derivative designated as the hedging instrument and the change in fair value of a hypothetical derivative. That hypothetical derivative would have terms that identically match the critical terms of the hedged item. For example, for a cash flow hedge that involves either a variable rate asset or a liability, the hypothetical derivative would be a swap that must have the same notional amount and the same re-pricing dates. Also, the index on which the hypothetical swap's variable rate is based should match the index on which the asset or liability's variable rate is based, and must mirror any caps, floors or any other non-separated embedded derivative features of the hedged item. Thus, the hypothetical swap would be expected to perfectly offset the hedged cash flows. The change in fair value of the 'perfect' hypothetical swap is regarded as a proxy for the present value of the cumulative change in expected future cash flows on the hedged transaction. However, if the hedge starts part way through the life of the hedged item, the hypothetical swap (or benchmark rate in example 1 of para 6.8.193) will not identically match the critical terms of the hedged item as the relevant rate for the fixed leg of the hypothetical derivative or benchmark rate will be the market rate at inception of the hedge, not the rate at inception of the hedged item or hedging instrument. This will give rise to ineffectiveness and may preclude the use of hedge accounting if rates have moved significantly since the hedged item was taken out.

6.8.191   Accordingly, once an entity has determined the change in fair value of the hypothetical swap and the change in the fair value of the actual swap for particular periods, it would use this data to assess the hedging relationship's effectiveness. The actual swap would be recorded at fair value on the balance sheet and the amount reported in equity would be adjusted to a balance that reflects the lesser of either the cumulative change in the actual swap's fair value or the cumulative change in the 'perfect' hypothetical swap's fair value. Determining the fair value of both the 'perfect' hypothetical swap and the actual swap should use discount rates based on the relevant swap curves. Thus, for the hypothetical swap the discount rates used are the spot rates implied by the current yield curve for hypothetical zero coupon bonds due on the date of each future net settlement of the swap. The amount of ineffectiveness, if any, recorded in profit or loss would then be equal to the excess of the cumulative change in the fair value of the actual swap over the cumulative change in the fair value of the 'perfect' hypothetical swap.

6.8.192 The hypothetical derivative method often is useful in evaluating the effectiveness of cash flow hedging relationships involving other derivatives, such as cross-currency swaps, commodity swaps and forward exchange contracts.

Example – Hypothetical derivative method

Entity A hedges the foreign currency risk of highly probable forecast transactions using forward contracts. Entity A intends to measure the effectiveness of the hedge by modelling the hedged risk of the forecast transaction as a hypothetical derivative.

As explained above, this method is specifically mentioned in IAS 39. Entity A would construct a hypothetical derivative whose terms reflect the relevant terms of the hedged item. Since entity A hedges the foreign currency risk of highly probable sales, the relevant hypothetical derivative is a forward foreign currency contract for the hedged amount maturing at the date on which the cash flows are anticipated, at the relevant forward rate *at inception* of the hedge. The change in the fair value of the hypothetical derivative is then compared with the change in the fair value of the hedging instrument to determine effectiveness.

The benchmark rate method

6.8.193 The benchmark rate approach is used under the dollar offset method to measure the effectiveness of cash flow hedges. Although not specifically mentioned in IAS 39, it is a variant of the hypothetical derivative method that is permitted by the standard and discussed in paragraph 6.8.192 above. Under this method, a 'target' rate is established as the benchmark rate for the hedge. For example, in an interest rate hedge of a variable rate debt instrument using an interest rate swap, the benchmark rate is usually the swap's fixed rate at the inception of the hedge. The benchmark rate method first identifies the difference between the hedging item's actual cash flows and the benchmark rate. It then compares the change in the amount or value of this difference with the change in the cash flow or fair value of the hedging instrument as illustrated in the example below.

Example 1 – Cash flow hedge effectiveness testing – 'fixed benchmark method'

Entity A issues a variable rate bond. On the same date, it enters into an interest rate swap under which it will receive variable and pay a fixed rate of interest. An equivalent fixed rate debt instrument with the same maturity could have been issued at 8%. Entity A designates the swap as a cash flow hedge of the bond. All the criteria for hedge accounting in paragraph 6.8.154 are met.

Entity A proposes to test effectiveness both prospectively and retrospectively by comparing:

■ the present value of the cumulative change in expected future cash flows on the swap; with

■ the present value of the cumulative change in the expected future interest cash flows on the variable leg less the fixed rate (8%).

In this situation, entity A can use the 'fixed benchmark method' in a cash flow hedge relationship for both prospective and retrospective effectiveness testing. This method reflects the risk management objective of the hedging relationship – that is, to swap a series of future variable cash flows to a fixed rate and is consistent with the requirements in IAS 39 that the method an entity adopts for assessing hedge effectiveness depends on its risk management strategy. [IAS 39 para AG 107].

Entity A should define the hedged risk as the change in the fair value of the variable cash flows, less the change in the fair value of a fixed rate of interest that could have been achieved at the inception of the underlying debt instrument (8%). It therefore measures the variability against a specified fixed rate. Effectiveness testing should be performed based on the ability of the hedging instrument to deliver that specified set of cash flows and should, therefore, measure variability from that fixed rate.

Example 2 – Cash flow hedge effectiveness testing – 'Change in variable cash flow method'

Using the facts as set out in example 1 above, the entity's management proposes to test effectiveness both prospectively and retrospectively by comparing the present value of the cumulative change in expected future cash flows on the swap's floating rate leg and the present value of the cumulative change in the expected future interest cash flows on the floating rate liability.

This method is sometimes referred to as the 'change in variable cash flow' method. This method is an acceptable method for performing prospective effectiveness testing, but not for retrospective effectiveness testing.

The justification for using this approach for prospective effectiveness testing is that the change in variable cash flows method is consistent with the cash flow hedge objective of effectively offsetting the changes in the hedged cash flows attributable to the hedged risk and that only the floating rate leg of the swap provides the cash flow hedge protection.

With regards to retrospective effectiveness testing, the change in variable cash flow method is *not* permitted for retrospective effectiveness testing since only a portion of the derivative (the floating rate leg only) is used for the test. Paragraph 74 of IAS 39 states that a hedging relationship is designated by an entity for a hedging instrument in its entirety and that the only exceptions are for the split between time value and intrinsic value of an option and the spot and forward points on a foreign exchange forward. Neither of these exceptions applies when the hedging instrument is an interest rate swap. The entire fair value of the hedging instrument must be used in performing retrospective hedge effectiveness testing.

The last paragraph of IAS 39 IG F5.5 explicitly states that this method is not acceptable, as it has the effect of measuring ineffectiveness on only a portion of the derivative. IAS 39 does not permit the bifurcation of a derivative for the purposes of assessing effectiveness.

Sensitivity analysis method

6.8.194 This method is applied to assess the effectiveness of a hedge prospectively. The method consists of measuring the effect of a hypothetical shift in the underlying hedged risk (for example, a 10% shift in the foreign currency exchange rate being hedged) on both the hedging instrument and the hedged item.

Regression analysis

6.8.195 Regression analysis is a statistical technique used to analyse the relationship between one variable (the dependent variable) and one or more other variables (known as independent variables). A common application of regression analysis is to build a model using past information that can be used to predict, say, the value of the dependent variable (for example, current year revenue of a particular retail outlet) for a new observation of the independent variable (for example, local employment). However, in the context of hedge effectiveness test, the method investigates the extent to which changes in the hedged item (the independent variable) and the hedging instrument (the dependent variable) are highly and negatively correlated and, thus, supportive of the assertion that there will be a high degree of offset in fair values or cash flows achieved by the hedge.

6.8.196 For purposes of the hedge accounting effectiveness test, the analysis usually involves a *simple* linear regression that involves determining a 'line of best fit' and then assessing the 'goodness of fit' of this line. *Multiple* linear regression analysis examines the relationship between a dependent variable and two or more independent variables. The linear equation estimated in a simple regression is commonly expressed as:

$$Y = a + bX + e$$

Y: The dependent variable
X: The independent variable
a: The intercept, where the line crosses the Y axis
b: The gradient of the line
e: The random error term

The values of the X and Y variables are plotted and a 'best fit' line is drawn as illustrated below.

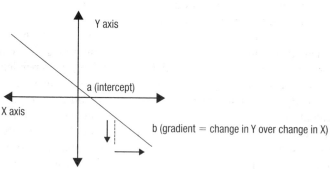

6.8.197   There are three critical test statistics to determine an effective hedge relationship when using regression analysis. These are as follows:

■   Gradient of the line (b) must be negative and in the range -0.8 < b < -1.25.

The gradient that the regression analysis determines 'best fits' the data, is the ratio of the change in Y value over the change in X value (assuming the model is developed using the hedging derivative as Y or the dependent variable and the hedged item as X or the independent variable). The gradient is a very important component when developing a highly effective hedging relationship and represents the variance-minimising hedge ratio. A gradient of -1 means that for a C1 increase (decrease) in the hedged item, the derivative will generally decrease (increase) by C1, which represents a perfect hedge. The gradient should be negative because the derivative is expected to offset changes in the hedged item. Therefore, if the regression analysis is performed using equal units of the hedging instrument and the hedged item, the gradient b can be used to determine the optimal hedge ratio (that is, the optimal volume of derivative that should be transacted to maximise expected effectiveness). This ratio can then be used by the entity to determine how many units of the hedging instrument it should transact to best mitigate the risk for the particular position being hedged. For example, if the gradient = -0.95, a hedge ratio based on 95 units of the hedging instrument to 100 units of the hedged item will maximise expected effectiveness.

Once the hedge ratio has been determined and the hedge transacted, the regression analysis is re-performed using the actual quantities of the hedging instrument and the hedged item. The gradient is used when assessing the effectiveness of the actual hedge relationship. The gradient must be negative and fall within the range of -0.8 to -1.25. If the gradient is positive, there is no hedge relationship (that is, the hedging instrument does not mitigate the hedged risk). If the gradient is negative but outside of the range of -0.8 to -1.25, there is some hedge relationship, but it is not strong enough to pass the effectiveness test. Hedge accounting is not permitted in either case.

■   The co-efficient of determination (R^2) > 0.96

The co-efficient of determination (R^2) measures the degree of explanatory power or correlation between the dependent and independent variable. Best practice is that it should have a value greater than 0.96, since this is equivalent to a dollar offset of between 80% and 125%. R^2 represents the proportion of variability in the hedging derivative (the dependent variable) that can be explained by variation in the hedged item (the independent variable). By way of illustration, an R^2 of .98 indicates that 98% of the movement in the hedging instrument is 'explained' by variation in the hedged item. R^2 values will always be positive (as it is a squared number) and can never exceed 1 (that is, it is not possible to explain more than 100% of the movement in the dependent variable). The square root of R^2 or 'r' is called the co-efficient of correlation. The co-efficient of correlation can be either positive or negative depending on the underlying relationship between the dependent and independent variables. Whereas values of R^2 are easily interpreted, 'r' does not have a clear-cut operational interpretation. It should be noted that although it is best practice to have a value of $R^2 > 0.96$, a value of 0.8 (used under US GAAP) maybe acceptable, provided the other regression statistics are also met. In other words, $R^2 > 0.8$ is not, on its own, sufficient.

■ The statistical validity of the overall regression model (the F-statistic) must be significant.

The F-statistic is a standard output from the statistical model. It is a measure of the statistical significance of the relationship between the dependent variable and the independent variable (that is, whether the derivative relationship, relative to the hedged risk, is a statistically valid relationship). A non-significant F-statistic indicates there is no statistically significant relationship between the dependent and independent variables. The F-statistic varies with the number of data points used. It can be obtained from statistical tables. To be significant, the result of the F-statistic should be less than 5% (sometimes expressed as a whole number, for example, 4.96) at a 95% or greater confidence level.

6.8.198 It is important to note that in order to be deemed highly effective, a regression analysis of a hedging relationship must yield acceptable levels for all three factors as noted above. For example, a regression analysis may produce an $R^2 = 0.96$, but an F-statistic that is not significant at the 95% threshold. In this situation, it is not possible to conclude that there is a statistically significant relationship between the hedged item and the hedging derivative and, therefore, the hedging relationship is not considered effective. Another example is where an entity establishes a 1 for 1 hedge and the regression analysis results in an $R^2 = 0.96$, an F-statistic that is significant at the 95% threshold, but a gradient of only -0.7. In this situation, the hedge relationship would be ineffective, because, on average, it would achieve a dollar offset of only 70% of the hedged item. However, if the entity adjusted its hedge ratio from 1 to 1 to reflect the gradient of -0.7 in order to achieve a higher dollar offset, hedge accounting would be permitted.

6.8.199 When using regression analysis to test the effectiveness of a hedge, it is important to use a sufficient number of matched paired data points to ensure a statistically valid analysis. Generally speaking, the higher the sample size, the more robust will be the analysis and more reliable the conclusion drawn from the model's output. For statistically reliable results, hedge effectiveness should be based on more than 30 observations. However, as a rule of thumb, no less than 12 observations should be used.

6.8.200 In using regression or other statistical analysis, it also will be necessary for an entity to determine the interval between data points – for example, whether to use daily, weekly, monthly, or quarterly changes in prices in assessing effectiveness. Generally, the selection frequency would depend on:

- The nature of the hedged item.

- The nature of the hedging derivative.

- Whether certain data points will most appropriately represent the interaction of the hedged item versus the hedging instrument.

- The availability of the data.

Ideally, the entity should try to incorporate as much *relevant* information as possible. Determining what is relevant requires considerable judgment. For instance, it would not be appropriate to use past data that is no longer representative of the current or future market conditions. In those circumstances, it may be appropriate to use a shorter more recent data set consisting of say, daily or weekly frequency period that more faithfully represents the current hedging relationship. On the other hand, too short a period might be equally problematic. If, say, interest rates remained stable over the past few months, a regression analysis based over this short time span would provide a poor indication of how the hedge will perform when interest rates become more volatile.

6.8.201 When a regression analysis is first performed (at the inception of the hedging relationship), an entity may need to determine that the hedging relationship will be highly effective on a prospective basis. This analysis may use historical data to determine valuations for the proposed derivative and the hedged item. The historical data observation would *typically* (but not necessarily) cover the same period as the length of the hedging relationship. For example, assume an entity issues a three-year fixed rate debt instrument today and enters into an interest rate swap to hedge the fair value exposure to changes in interest rate. The entity should use last three year's data as input for a regression analysis to test whether, at inception, given the terms of the loan and the swap, the hedge is likely to be highly effective on a prospective basis. Conversely, if the last three years' data were not representative of the next three years', use of regression analysis would not be appropriate.

6.8.202 As the standard requires that effectiveness should be assessed at a minimum at the time an entity prepares its annual or interim financial statements, the entity would carry out both prospective and retrospective hedge effectiveness testing at the subsequent measurement date. If one method is being used for both prospective and retrospective analyses, the same number of data points should be used in the subsequent assessment. Assuming that the entity has chosen monthly data points, the regression analysis at the next annual reporting date would also include 36 data points (12 monthly actual data after inception and the 24 monthly data before inception). As such, 12 months of the oldest data is excluded from the regression analysis. Accordingly, the regression analysis will always contain the same number of data points. It should be noted that the method outlined is not the only acceptable method to determine inputs for regression analysis. Instead of using discrete monthly data, the entity could use a cumulative retrospective evaluation as long as the same number of data points is included in the analysis.

6.8.203 From an accounting perspective, regression analysis proves whether or not the relationship is sufficiently effective to qualify for hedge accounting. It does not calculate the amount of any ineffectiveness, nor does it provide the numbers necessary for the accounting entries where the analysis demonstrates that the 'highly effective' test has been passed. The accounting entries are based on the dollar-offset method of measuring the changes in the fair values of the derivative and in the hedged risk of the hedged item, both calculated using actual rates at the test date as explained in paragraph 6.8.211 below.

Comparison between regression analysis and dollar offset method

6.8.204 There may be circumstances where the results from regression analysis support the use of hedge accounting, but the dollar offset measurement indicate that the hedge would not be highly effective if the dollar offset method had been used. Indeed, it would not be unusual for this to happen, as the two methods are very different. Therefore, in a period where the dollar offset accounting measurement indicates that the accounting results are slightly outside of the 80% — 125% range, hedge accounting would still be appropriate assuming that there was a sound statistical regression analysis supporting the use of hedge accounting for that period. However, if the dollar offset accounting measurements indicate that the hedging relationship was significantly outside of the 80% — 125% range, then the validity and soundness of the regression analysis would be called into question. In that situation, the entity should seek to ascertain the causes for such differences. It may be that small changes in the values of either the hedged item or the hedging instrument cause the dollar offset method to be outside the range based on current hedge designation. In that situation, continuation of hedge accounting may be appropriate. However, continual failure to achieve high effectiveness under the dollar offset method for reasons other than small dollar differences may invalidate the use of regression analysis for the hedging relationship. In that situation, hedge accounting should be discontinued prospectively unless the entity is able to correct any known deficiencies in the prior model and demonstrate that the new model produces a sound statistical regression result that is representative of the hedging relationship.

Hedge ineffectiveness

Sources of hedge ineffectiveness

6.8.205 Hedge relationships are seldom perfect. Therefore, ineffectiveness will almost always arise with the result that changes in the fair value or cash flows of the hedged item that are attributable to a hedged risk and the hedging instrument do not offset within a period. Examples of differences that can produce ineffectiveness include:

- Basis differences – the fair value or cash flows of the hedged item depend on a variable that is different from the variable that causes the fair value or cash flows of the hedging instrument to change. For example, an entity designates the benchmark interest rate as the hedged risk when the hedged item uses a different index, such as the prime base rate. The basis difference between those indices would affect the assessment and measurement of hedge ineffectiveness.

- **Location differences** – the fair value or cash flows of the hedged item and hedging instrument both depend on the price of the same commodity, but are based on the price at different locations. The price of a commodity will be different in different locations, because of factors such as regional supply and demand and transportation costs.

- **Timing differences** – the hedged item and hedging instrument occur or are settled at different dates. For example, an entity hedges the forecast purchase of a commodity with a derivative that settles at an earlier or later date than the date of the forecast purchase. Another example is a floating rate debt whose variability is hedged with an interest rate swap where the interest rate reset dates on the two instruments are different.

- **Quantity or notional amount differences** – the hedged item and hedging instrument are based on a different quantities or notional amounts.

- **Changes in the fair value or cash flows of a derivative** hedging instrument or hedged item relating to risks other than the specific risk being hedged. For example, an entity hedges the variability in the price of a forecast purchase of a commodity with a derivative whose cash flows are based on the price of a different commodity and this is the only source of ineffectiveness in the relationship or there is a change in estimated future cashflows following impairment of the hedged item.

- **Use of off market derivatives** – an off market derivative is an existing derivative that has a non-zero fair value. Hedge ineffectiveness can arise when using an off market derivative in a number of common place scenarios such as: documentation of a hedge not completed at inception, attempting to restart hedge accounting following a documentation deficiency, temporary interruption of a hedging strategy, change of method of assessing hedge effectiveness in the middle of a hedge period, hedges acquired in a business combination and renegotiation of terms of the derivative.

- **Currency basis** – as discussed in paragraphs 6.8.29-6.8.30 the different treatment of currency basis in calculating changes in the fair value of the derivative hedging instrument and the hedged item will create ineffectiveness.

Minimising hedge ineffectiveness

6.8.206 The key to minimising hedge ineffectiveness lies in the hedge designation. In many cases, it will be possible to minimise the ineffectiveness in a hedging relationship by the way an entity designates the risk being hedged. This is because under IAS 39 financial assets or liabilities can be hedged with respect to specific risk only (a component of total risk), provided that the exposure to the specific risk component is identifiable and separately measurable (see para 6.8.25 above). Also, it is possible to designate a hedged financial asset or a financial liability with respect to the risks associated with only a portion of its cash flows or fair value (see para 6.8.23 above). For non-financial items only certain risks can be hedged and this is discussed from paragraph 6.8.34. Therefore, considerable ineffectiveness can be eliminated when the risk designated as being hedged matches the risk of the hedging instrument. Consider the following example.

Example – Exclusion of credit risk from interest rate risk

On 1 October 20X5, entity A issues a fixed-interest note at 8% for C1,000. On the same day, entity A enters into an interest rate swap to pay LIBOR and receive interest at 7% based on the same payment terms and with a notional principal of C1,000. At inception entity A designates the swap as a hedge of the variability in fair value of the issued note.

| | Fair values | | |
	1 October 20X5	30 September 20X6	Change
Fixed interest note	(1,000)	(1,048)	(48)
Interest rate swap	–	102	102
Difference			54
The effectiveness of the hedging relationship	= – 102/48 =		213%

Hedge accounting is not permitted, as the results of the effectiveness test are significantly below the minimum required effectiveness of 125%. The main reason for the difference in fair value movements leading to the ineffectiveness is entity A's deteriorating creditworthiness.

IAS 39 permits an entity to designate any portion of risk in a financial asset or liability as the hedged item. Hedge effectiveness is generally significantly easier to achieve if the designated hedged risk matches the hedging instrument as closely as possible. In this case, entity A should re-designate the risk being hedged in order to improve the hedge effectiveness for future periods. As the entity's deteriorating creditworthiness is the major cause of the hedge ineffectiveness, it should exclude this risk going forward and hedge only the changes in the bond's fair value attributable to changes in the risk-free interest rate. The new designation to exclude the bond's credit risk from the hedge relationship will improve hedge effectiveness, because the bond's credit risk is not reflected in the hedge.

6.8.207 There is normally a single fair value measure for a hedging derivative in its entirety. Therefore, a derivative cannot be split into components representing different risks and designating such components as the hedging instruments. However, as stated in paragraph 6.8.60 above, the interest element of a forward contract and the time value of an option may be excluded from the fair value measurement of the hedging derivative. These exclusions can often improve the hedge's effectiveness as they allow the hedging derivative's risk to match that of the hedged item. In that case, changes in the excluded component, for example, interest element portion of the fair value of the forward exchange contract are recognised in profit or loss. The interest element of a forward contract is never amortised to profit or loss under IAS 39. [IAS 39 para IG F6.4].

6.8.208 Similarly, when the hedging instrument is an option rather than a forward contract, the option's time value can be excluded from the option's fair value and hedge effectiveness assessed based on the changes in the option's intrinsic value. However, in such situations, the excluded time value, which is not part of the hedge relationship, will be recognised in profit or loss as explained in paragraph 6.8.63 above and illustrated in the example below.

> **Example – Exclusion of time value of option from hedge effectiveness assessment**
>
> Entity A owns 100,000 equity shares in a quoted entity B, which it has classified as available-for-sale. The current price of the security is C25. To give itself partial protection against decreases in the share price of entity B, Entity A acquires an at-the-money put option on 100,000 shares of entity B at a strike price of C25 for C10,000. Entity A designates the change in the intrinsic value of the put as a hedging instrument in a fair value hedge of changes in the fair value of its share in entity B.
>
> In this situation, IAS 39 permits entity A to designate changes in the intrinsic value of the put option as a hedge of its equity investment that is consistent with entity A's hedging strategy. The hedge relationship is designated only for the price range when the put option is in-the-money (current market price = strike price), that is, the option provides protection against the risk of variability in the fair value of entity B's 100,000 shares below or equal to the strike price of the put of C25.
>
> Effectiveness is measured by comparing the change in the investment's fair value below the strike price of C25 with changes in the option's intrinsic value. Therefore, when the option is out-of-the-money, no effectiveness measurement is necessary, but prospective assessment is still required. This means that gains and losses on entity B's 100,000 shares for prices above C25 are not attributable to the hedged risk for the purposes of assessing hedge effectiveness and for recognising gains and losses on the hedged item. Therefore, entity A reports changes in the shares' fair value in other comprehensive income if it is associated with variation in its price above C25. [IAS 39 paras 55, 90]. Changes in the fair value of the shares associated with price declines below C25 form part of the designated fair value hedge and are recognised in profit or loss. [IAS 39 para 89(b)]. Assuming the hedge is effective, those changes are offset by changes in the intrinsic value of the put, which are also recognised in profit or loss. [IAS 39 para 89(a)].
>
> Since the option is at-the-money at inception, the premium paid of C10,000 is all attributable to the option's time value. Changes in the put option's time value are not included in the assessment of hedge effectiveness and are recognised in profit or loss. [IAS 39 para 55(a)]. The option's fair value may change due to factors such as volatility of the share price, the passage of time and risk free rate. As such factors do not affect the option's intrinsic value (current price – strike price), they form part of the time value component.

6.8.209 Another issue in connection with ineffectiveness arises when assessing the effectiveness of hedging instruments such as interest rate swaps. In an interest rate swap, the payments are usually set at the beginning of a period and paid at the next interest reset date. Where hedge effectiveness assessments are undertaken between two re-pricing dates, the effect of interest accrual will affect the swap's fair value. Accordingly, the corresponding changes in the swap's fair value will not fully offset changes in the bond's fair value. However, it is possible to improve the hedge's effectiveness by using the swap's 'clean' fair value rather than the 'dirty' fair value that includes the accrued interest. Using the clean fair value in effectiveness testing often decreases the ineffectiveness, as it excludes the accrued interest on the swap's variable leg that will not have any offsetting component in the bond. The comparison between 'clean' and 'dirty' fair values and the impact on effectiveness of the hedge can be seen in illustration 1 of the comprehensive examples in paragraph 6.8.223 and onwards.

Measuring hedge ineffectiveness

6.8.210 High effectiveness must be achieved initially and on an ongoing basis in order for a hedging relationship to qualify for hedge accounting. High effectiveness does not guarantee, however, that there will be no earnings volatility resulting from hedge ineffectiveness. Where the hedge is highly effective but not perfectly effective (that is, if a dollar-offset test is used the hedge is between 80% and 125% effective, but it is not 100% effective), there will be some volatility in earnings due to the ineffective portion of the hedge. Equally, the designation of the hedge may be very precise and thus achieves hedge accounting but volatility will be caused by that which has been excluded from the hedge relationship, although this is not 'hedge ineffectiveness'.

6.8.211 Regardless of whether dollar-offset or regression analysis is used to assess prospective and/or retrospective hedge effectiveness, the dollar offset measurements are used to determine the amount of ineffectiveness that has occurred and that must be recognised in profit or loss in each reporting period. Similarly, where hedge effectiveness is assessed using clean prices of an interest rate swap, the spot component of a forward contract, or the intrinsic value of an option to improve hedge effectiveness, the measurement of the hedging instrument for accounting purposes must still be based on the entire fair value of the derivative that will include accrued interest, forward points or time value.

6.8.212 The extent to which hedge ineffectiveness is recognised in profit or loss will depend on whether the hedge is a fair value hedge or a cash flow hedge. In a fair value hedge, any hedge ineffectiveness directly affects profit or loss. This is because the entire change in the fair value of the hedged item (attributable to the hedged risk) and the entire change in the fair value of the hedging instrument are both reflected in profit or loss in each reporting period and the two changes may not perfectly offset each other.

6.8.213 For cash flow hedges, the measurement of hedge effectiveness is different from a fair value hedge. As explained in paragraph 6.8.129 above, the amount recognised in equity for a cash flow hedge is the lower of the cumulative gain or loss on the hedging instrument from inception of the hedge and the cumulative change in fair value (present value) of the expected future cash flows on the hedged item from inception of the hedge. To the extent that the cumulative gain or loss on the hedging instrument exceeds the cumulative change in fair value of the expected cash flows on the hedged item, the excess is recognised in profit or loss. However, if there is a shortfall, there will be no ineffectiveness recognised in profit or loss.

6.8.214 The implementation guidance to IAS 39 provides a very comprehensive example of the dollar offset method for cash flow hedges. [IAS 39 IGF5.5]. The example sets out two practical methods for assessing effectiveness and measuring ineffectiveness for cash flow hedge of a forecast issuance of fixed rate debt. These two methods are known as 'the hypothetical derivative method' and the 'change in fair value method'. Although the example is not reproduced here, the way in which the hypothetical derivative and the change in fair value methods work in practice is explained in paragraphs 6.8.190 and 6.8.215 respectively. Regardless of which method is used for the measurement of cash flow hedge effectiveness, an entity must meet the requirements of paragraph 6.8.154 above for designation of a cash flow hedging relationship. That is, in designating a cash flow hedging relationship, an entity must have the expectation, both at inception of the hedge and ongoing, that the relationship will be highly effective at achieving offsetting changes in cash flows.

Change in fair value method

6.8.215 The 'change in fair value method' is referred to as 'method A' in paragraph IG F5.5 of IAS 39. This is similar to the benchmark rate method (see para 6.8.193). This method is applicable for determining hedge effectiveness for variable rate financial assets and liabilities and forecast issuance of fixed rate debt. Under this method, the measurement of hedge ineffectiveness is based on a calculation that compares the present value of the cumulative change in expected variable future interest cash flows that are designated as the hedged transactions and the cumulative change in the fair value of the swap designated as the hedging instrument. The discount rates applicable to determining the fair value of the swap designated as the hedging instrument should also be applied to the computation of present values of the cumulative changes in the hedged cash flows.

[The next paragraph is 6.8.218.]

Portfolio (or macro) hedging

6.8.218 Portfolio or macro hedging is a technique used to reduce or eliminate the risk of a portfolio of assets and liabilities. Banks and similar financial institutions often use this technique to manage the interest rate risk of a portfolio of assets and liabilities. They do this by hedging the net position (for example, net of fixed rate assets and fixed rate liabilities).

6.8.219 Prior to the issue of the amended version of IAS 39 (see below), the hedging techniques used by banks were not in accordance with the underlying core principles of IAS 39 of not permitting hedges of a net position of assets and liabilities to qualify for hedge accounting. In addition, many of the assets included in a portfolio are typically pre-payable fixed rate assets, that is, the counterparty has the right to pre-pay the item before its contractual maturity. When interest rates change, the resulting change in the fair value of the pre-payable asset differs from the change in fair value of the hedging derivative (which is not pre-payable), with the result that the hedge would often fail the IAS 39 hedge effectiveness test. Furthermore, many of the liabilities included in a portfolio are repayable on demand or after a notice period (often referred to as core deposits). Including them in a portfolio implies that their fair values change with movements in interest rates, which is against the notion in IAS 39 that the fair value of a demand deposit is not less than the amount repayable on demand, because that amount does not change with movements in interest rates.

6.8.220 Therefore, when the exposure draft of proposed improvements to IAS 39 was published in June 2002, it did not contain any substantial changes to the requirements for hedge accounting as they applied to a portfolio hedge of interest rate risk. Banks were concerned that portfolio hedging strategies that they regarded as effective hedges would not qualify for fair value hedge accounting under IAS 39. They would either:

- not qualify for hedge accounting at all, with the result that profit or loss would be volatile; or

- qualify only for cash flow hedge accounting with the result that equity would be volatile. This is could potentially give rise to genuine problems for some banks because of capital adequacy requirements imposed by prudential regulators.

6.8.221 The banks' concerns found considerable political sympathy and the IASB was strongly encouraged to come to an agreement with them. As a result, after much deliberation, in March 2004, the IASB published an amendment to IAS 39. Unfortunately, not all of the banks' concerns were addressed. In particular, significant restrictions for hedging deposits with a demand feature still remained. As a result, the version of IAS 39 that was endorsed by the EU had a carve-out that primarily allows banks to apply fair value hedge accounting to hedges of the interest rate risk in their portfolio of demand or core deposits for interest rate risk, which is prohibited by the full IAS 39 as noted in paragraph 6.8.219 above. It also removed the need for banks to recognise ineffectiveness in the income statement as a result of under hedging that may arise in certain circumstances in fair value hedge accounting for a portfolio hedge of interest rate risk.

6.8.222 IAS 39 sets out in paragraphs AG114-AG132 a series of procedures that an entity would need to comply with for achieving hedge accounting for a fair value hedge of interest rate risk associated with a portfolio of financial assets or financial liabilities. It should be noted, however, that in the EU carve-out version some of the above paragraphs were amended and some deleted. The implementation guidance to IAS 39 also sets out a series of issues that an entity should consider when applying cash flow hedge accounting to a portfolio hedge of interest rate risk. [IAS 39 IG F6.2]. A very comprehensive example of applying the approach discussed in IG F6.2 is also included [IAS 39 IG F6.3]. As the topic of macro hedging is of little interest to entities other than banks and other financial institutions, it is not dealt with in this chapter.

Comprehensive examples

6.8.223 Three detailed illustrations of how hedge accounting can be applied in practice are given below. The objective is to present the mechanics of applying IAS 39 requirements, starting with the entity's risk management and effectiveness testing policies, working through the necessary designation and effectiveness testing and culminating with the accounting entries.

6.8.224 The three examples illustrate some of the most common hedging strategies used in practice. They cover the three types of hedges recognised for accounting purposes by IAS 39 (fair value hedges, cash flow hedges and net investment hedges). The issues addressed are summarised in the table below:

	Type of hedge and hedged risk	Hedged item and hedging instrument	Effectiveness testing		Other key points of the illustration
			Prospective	Retrospective	
Illustration 1 'Conversion' of fixed rate debt into variable rate debt using an interest rate swap	Fair value hedge – Interest rate risk	Fixed rate debt – Interest rate swap	Dollar offset using clean market values, sensitivity analysis approach	Dollar offset on a cumulative basis using clean market values, benchmark approach	Credit risk not hedged
Illustration 2 Hedge of highly probable foreign currency forecast purchases	Cash flow hedge – Foreign exchange risk	Highly probable forecast transaction – Forward contract	Dollar offset, sensitivity analysis approach	Dollar offset on a cumulative basis, hypothetical derivative approach	Spot/spot rate designation – Change in timing of cash flows – Basis adjustment
Illustration 3 Foreign currency hedge of a net investment in a foreign operation	Net investment hedge – Foreign exchange risk	Net investment – Borrowing	Dollar offset using dirty market values, sensitivity analysis approach	Dollar offset on a cumulative basis using dirty market values, benchmark approach	Credit risk in borrowing excluded – Effect of losses

6.8.225 Despite the range of approaches covered, these illustrations do not set out all of the ways of complying with IAS 39's hedging requirements. Other approaches to hedge accounting may meet IAS 39's requirements. One issue not covered in the illustrations is the discontinuance of hedge accounting. This is covered earlier in the chapter. The underlying calculations in some of the illustrations have been performed using more decimal places for interest rates and discount factors than are presented. If the calculations are reperformed using the data presented, some minor differences in the numbers may arise. Finally, at various points 'helpful hint' boxes have been included. These highlight important issues, give additional guidance and contain tips relating to the illustrations.

Fair value hedge of fixed rate debt

Company A is a UK company with a £ functional currency. Company A's reporting dates are 30 June and 31 December.

On 15 March 20X5, company A issues at par a £10m four year debt with the following characteristics:

Type	Issued debt
Principal amount	£10m
Start date	15 March 20X5
Maturity date	15 March 20X9
Interest rate	7%
Settlement date	15 March, 15 June, 15 September and 15 December each year

No transaction costs are incurred relating to the debt issuance. On the date on which the debt was issued, consistent with its risk management policies, company A enters into a four year pay three month £ LIBOR receive 5% interest rate swap. The variable leg of the swap is pre-fixed/post-paid on 15 March, 15 June, 15 September and 15 December each year. The fixing of the variable leg for the first three-month period is 4.641%.

> **Helpful hint**
>
> A pre-fixed/post-paid interest rate swap is an interest rate swap in which the variable coupon is determined based on the market interest rate at the beginning of each period and is paid at the end. The variable coupon on the interest rate swap determined on 15 March is paid on 15 June, and so on.
>
>

The cash flows on the debt and the swap can be represented as follows:

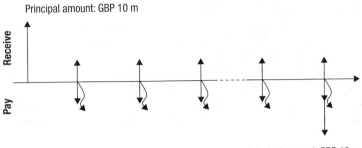

Fixed interest received on the swap (1.25% per quarter) | Fixed interest paid on the debt (1.75% per quarter) | Floating interest paid on the swap (three-month GBP LIBOR)

Three-month £ LIBOR rate at various dates when the swap is reset is as follows:

15 Mar 20X5	4.562%
15 Jun 20X5	5.080%
15 Sep 20X5	5.280%
15 Dec 20X5	5.790%

The forward rates derived from the £ LIBOR swap yield curve and the implied zero coupon rates at the dates of testing effectiveness are as follows:

	Forward rates for testing dates			Zero coupon rates for testing dates		
	15 Mar 20X5 (YC1)	30 Jun 20X5 (YC2)	31 Dec 20X5 (YC3)	15 Mar 20X5 (ZC1)	30 Jun 20X5 (ZC2)	31 Dec 20X5 (ZC3)
15 Jun 20X5	4.562%	–	–	4.641%	–	–
15 Sep 20X5	4.623%	5.069%	–	4.672%	5.172%	–
15 Dec 20X5	4.684%	5.130%	–	4.704%	5.204%	–
15 Mar 20X6	4.744%	5.191%	5.705%	4.735%	5.235%	5.835%
15 Jun 20X6	4.805%	5.251%	5.767%	4.766%	5.266%	5.866%
15 Sep 20X6	4.865%	5.311%	5.827%	4.798%	5.298%	5.898%
15 Dec 20X6	4.926%	5.371%	5.887%	4.829%	5.329%	5.929%
15 Mar 20X7	4.986%	5.432%	5.947%	4.860%	5.360%	5.960%
15 Jun 20X7	5.046%	5.492%	6.007%	4.892%	5.392%	5.992%
15 Sep 20X7	5.107%	5.552%	6.067%	4.923%	5.423%	6.023%
15 Dec 20X7	5.167%	5.612%	6.127%	4.954%	5.454%	6.054%
15 Mar 20X8	5.228%	5.673%	6.187%	4.986%	5.486%	6.086%
15 Jun 20X8	5.288%	5.733%	6.246%	5.017%	5.517%	6.117%
15 Sep 20X8	5.348%	5.793%	6.306%	5.048%	5.548%	6.148%
15 Dec 20X8	5.409%	5.853%	6.366%	5.080%	5.580%	6.180%
15 Mar 20X9	5.469%	5.913%	6.426%	5.111%	5.611%	6.211%

> **Helpful hint**
>
> The forward rates are used to calculate the projected cash flows. The zero-coupon rates are used to discount the projected cash flows to the testing date.

Extracts of risk management policies for interest rate risk

Company A is exposed to market risk, primarily related to foreign exchange, interest rates and the market value of the investments of liquid funds.

Company A manages its exposure to interest rate risk through the proportion of fixed and variable rate net debt in its total net debt portfolio. Such a proportion is determined twice a year by company A's financial risk committee and approved by the board of directors. The benchmark duration for net debt is 12 months.

To manage this mix, company A may enter into a variety of derivative financial instruments, such as interest rate swap contracts.

Extracts of hedge effectiveness testing policies

Strategy 1A Hedges of interest rate risk using interest rate swaps for fair value hedges

Prospective effectiveness testing

Prospective effectiveness testing should be performed at the inception of the hedge and at each reporting date. The hedge relationship is highly effective if the changes in fair value or cash flow of the hedged item that are attributable to the hedged risk are expected to be offset by the changes in fair value or cash flows of the hedging instrument.

Prospective effectiveness testing should be performed by comparing the numerical effects of a shift in the hedged interest rate (£ LIBOR zero coupon curve) on both the fair value of the hedging instrument and the fair value of the hedged item.

This comparison should normally be based on at least three interest rate scenarios. However, for hedges where the critical terms of the hedging instrument perfectly match the critical terms, including reset dates of the hedged item, one scenario is sufficient.

$$\text{Effectiveness} = \frac{\text{Change in clean fair value of hedging instrument when zero coupon curve is shifted}}{\text{Change in clean fair value of hedged item when zero coupon curve is shifted}}$$

Change in the clean fair value of a swap is the difference between the clean fair value of the projected cash flows of the swap discounted using the zero coupon curve derived from the swap yield curve at the date of testing, and the clean fair value of the projected shifted cash flows discounted using the shifted zero-coupon rates.

Change in the clean fair value of a bond is the difference between the clean fair value of the cash flows on the bond excluding the credit spread discounted using the zero coupon curve derived from the swap yield curve at the date of testing, and the clean fair value of the same cash flows discounted using the shifted zero coupon rates.

The scenarios that should be used in the effectiveness test are:

(1) a parallel shift (upwards) of 100 basis points of the zero coupon curve;

(2) a change in the slope of the zero coupon curve of a 5% increase in the rate for one year cash flows, a 10% increase in the rate for two year cash flows, and a 15% increase in the rate for three and more year cash flows; and

(3) a change to a flat zero coupon curve at present three-month LIBOR.

Helpful hint

The number of scenarios needed to assess prospectively the effectiveness of a hedge when using the dollar offset method will vary depending on the terms of the hedge. When the critical terms of the hedging instrument (start date, end date, currency, fixed payment date, interest rate re-set date, fixed interest rate, principal amount) do not match those of the hedged item, or the hedged item contains a feature – such as optionality – that is likely to cause ineffectiveness, several scenarios should be used, including scenarios that reflect the mismatch in terms or optionality.

The pre-fixed/post-paid feature of the swap that is not present in the bond prevents the use of the critical terms method, as there will be some ineffectiveness. Three scenarios should be used to test effectiveness prospectively, consistent with the entity's policy. The example below shows only the first of these three scenarios.

The dirty fair value is the fair value including accrued interest. The clean fair value excludes accrued interest. Using the clean fair value in effectiveness testing often decreases the ineffectiveness, as it excludes the accrued interest on the variable leg of the swap that will not have any offsetting component in the bond.

Retrospective effectiveness testing

Retrospective effectiveness testing should be performed at each reporting date using the dollar offset method on a cumulative basis. Hedge effectiveness is demonstrated by comparing the cumulative change in the clean fair value of the hedging instrument with the cumulative change in the clean fair value of the hedged item attributable to the hedged risk and showing that it falls within the required range of 80%-125%.

$$\text{Effectiveness} = \frac{\text{Cumulative change in clean fair value of hedging instrument}}{\text{Cumulative change in clean fair value of hedged item}}$$

Change in the clean fair value of a swap is the difference between:

(a) the clean fair value of the projected cash flows of the swap based on the original yield curve discounted using the zero coupon curve derived from the yield curve at the beginning of the hedge; and

(b) the clean fair value of the projected cash flows of the swap based on the yield curve at the date of testing discounted using the zero coupon curve derived from the yield curve at the date of testing.

Change in the clean fair value of a bond is the difference between:

(a) the clean fair value of the cash flows on the bond, excluding the credit spread discounted using the zero coupon curve derived from the yield curve at the beginning of the hedge; and

(b) the clean fair value of the same cash flows discounted using the zero coupon curve derived from the yield curve at the date of testing.

> **Helpful hint**
>
> In a fair value hedge, the carrying amount of the hedged item, in this case the debt, is adjusted for changes in value attributable to the hedged risk only. This might not be the same as the total changes in the fair value of the debt. Fair value changes attributable to credit or other risks that are not hedged are not included in the adjustment of the carrying amount of the hedged item.

Hedge designation

Company A's hedge documentation is shown below.

1 Risk management objective and strategy

For the current period, company A's approved strategy in accordance with its risk management policies is to maintain a ratio of fixed:floating rate net debt of between 40:60 and 50:50. In order to achieve this ratio, management has selected this debt to be swapped from fixed to floating.

2 Type of hedging relationship

Fair value hedge: swap of fixed to floating interest rates.

3 Nature of risk being hedged

Interest rate risk: change in the fair value of debt number C426 million attributable to movements in the £ LIBOR zero coupon curve. Credit risk on the debt is not designated as being hedged.

4 Identification of hedged item

Transaction number: reference number C426 million in the treasury management system.

The hedged item is a four-year, £10m, 7% fixed rate debt, which pays interest quarterly.

5 Identification of hedging instrument

Transaction number: reference number L1815E in the treasury management system.

The hedging instrument is a four-year interest rate swap, notional value £10m, under which fixed interest of 5% is received quarterly and actual three-month LIBOR is paid with a three-month reset.

Hedge designation: the fair value movements on the full notional £10m of the swap L1815E is designated as a hedge of fair value movements in the debt C426 million attributable to movements in £ LIBOR zero coupon curve (see point 3 above).

6 Effectiveness testing

Testing shall be performed using hedging effectiveness testing strategy 1A in the effectiveness testing policy.

Description of prospective test

Dollar offset method, being the ratio of the change in the clean fair value of the swap L1815E, divided by the change in clean fair value of the bond C426 million attributable to changes in £ LIBOR zero coupon curve.

The critical terms of the swap do not perfectly match the critical terms of the hedged debt. The prospective tests will therefore, as required by the risk management policies, be performed based on three scenarios. (Only scenario 1, the 100 basis point increase, is illustrated below; all three would be performed in practice.)

Frequency of testing: at inception of the hedge and at each reporting date (30 June and 31 December).

Description of retrospective test

Dollar offset method, being the ratio of the change in the clean fair value of swap L1815E, divided by the change in the clean fair value of the bond C426 million attributable to changes in the £ LIBOR zero coupon curve on a cumulative basis.

Frequency of testing: at every reporting date (30 June and 31 December) after inception of the hedge.

Effectiveness tests and accounting entries

1 Prospective effectiveness test on 15 March 20X5

Company A's management should assess prospectively the effectiveness of the hedge, as required by IAS 39.

Based on the hedge documentation, the prospective effectiveness test consists of comparing the effects of a 100 basis points shift upwards of the zero coupon curve on the clean fair value of the swap and the clean fair value of the hedged item.

A coupon of 7% per annum is paid on the debt (that is, £175,000 per quarter), which can be split into an AA interest rate of 5% and a credit spread of 2%. For effectiveness testing purposes, only the cash flows relating to the AA interest rate (that is, £125,000 per quarter) are taken into account. The credit risk associated with the debt is not part of the hedge relationship; the credit spread of 2% in the coupon is, therefore, excluded from the tests.

Prospective effectiveness test on 15 March 20X5

	15 Jun 20X5	15 Sep 20X5	15 Dec 20X5 ...	15 Dec 20X8	15 Mar 20X9	Total
Cash flows on the swap						
Fixed leg	125,000	125,000	125,000 ...	125,000	125,000	
Variable leg*	(114,059)	(115,573)	(117,088) ...	(135,221)	(136,729)	
Net cash flows	10,941	9,427	7,912 ...	(10,221)	(11,729)	
Discounted CF @ ZC1	10,818	9,214	7,644 ...	(8,488)	(9,609)	0
Shifted zero coupon curve						
Fixed leg	125,000	125,000	125,000 ...	125,000	125,000	
Variable leg + 1%	(114,059)	(139,640)	(141,144) ...	(159,148)	(160,646)	
Net cash flows	10,941	(14,640)	(16,144) ...	(34,148)	(35,646)	
Discounted CF @ ZC1 + 1%	10,792	(14,242)	(15,486) ...	(27,368)	(28,117)	**(315,574)**
						(315,574)

6.8 – Hedge accounting

Cash flows on the debt

Cash flows	(125,000)	(125,000)	(125,000)	...	(125,000)	(10,125,000)
Discounted CF at ZC1**	(123,590)	(122,178)	(120,764)	...	(103,804)	(8,294,694)	**(10,000,000)**
Discounted CF @ ZC1 + 1%	(123,297)	(121,599)	(119,906)	...	(100,182)	(7,986,407)	**(9,660,676)**
							339,324
Effectiveness							**-93.0%**

* The variable leg of the swap is the projected cash flow according to forward rates derived from the swap yield curve. As an example, the 15 Sep 20X5 projected cash flow is calculated as 10 million £* 4.623%/4 = 115,573, as the swap has quarterly reset and settlement.

** The discounted cash flows are calculated using the zero coupon rate for the relevant point on the implied zero coupon curve using the normal discounting formula $cf/(1+r)^{(d/360)}$, where cf is the undiscounted cash flow, r is the relevant zero coupon rate and d is the number of days remaining to the cash flow (on 360 day basis). As an example, the discounted cash flow on 15 Sep 20X5 is calculated as $125,000/(1.0467)^{(180/360)} = 122,178$.

Conclusion: The hedge is expected to be highly effective.

Helpful hint

The ineffectiveness in the prospective test comes from the change in the fair value of the variable leg of the swap that occurs when projected cash flows are changed. The change in fair value of the fixed leg of the swap perfectly offsets changes in the fair value of the bond.

2 Accounting entries on 15 March 20X5

The debt is recognised at the proceeds received by company A, which represents its fair value on the issuance date. The debt is classified as other financial liabilities and will subsequently be measured at amortised cost.

	Dr	Cr
Cash	10,000,000	
Other financial liabilities – debt		10,000,000

Issuance at par of a £10m four-year debt with a fixed coupon of 7%

The swap entered into by company A is recognised at fair value on the balance sheet. The fair value of the swap is nil at inception, as it is issued at market rate. The floating rate for the first period is set to 4.562%, which is the three-month swap rate.

	Dr	Cr
Derivative instruments	nil	
Cash		nil

Recognition of the interest rate swap at fair value (nil)

3 Accounting entries on 15 June 20X5

On 15 June, the first coupon on the loan is paid and the first period of the swap is settled.

Recognition of interest on the debt

	Dr	Cr
Finance costs – interest expense	175,000	
Cash		175,000

Interest on the debt at 7% for three months

Cash settlement of the swap

	DR	CR
Finance costs – interest expense	114,059	
Finance costs – interest expense		125,000
Cash	10,941	

Settlement of the swap: receive 5% and pay 4.562% for three months

These two transactions result in a total charge of £164,059 to finance cost, which is equivalent to 6.562% interest for the period (that is, the rate on the variable leg of the swap of 4.562% + 2% credit spread). The variable rate on the swap for the following quarter is set at the three-month swap rate of 5.080%.

> **Helpful hint**
>
> In order to increase clarity, we have chosen to show the entry gross (that is, with the effects of the pay and receive legs of the swap shown separately). This entry is often made on a net basis.
>
> The charge to interest expense has been made without performing an effectiveness test, as no effectiveness test is required until 30 June. In the event that the next effectiveness test is failed, the entries will have to be reversed out of interest expense, as hedge accounting is not permitted for the period after the last successful test. The entries could be to 'other operating income and expense'.

4 Retrospective effectiveness test on 30 June 20X5

IAS 39 requires the effectiveness of a hedging relationship to be assessed retrospectively as a minimum at each reporting date. Based on company A's risk management policies, the effectiveness of the hedge must be assessed using the dollar offset method.

The dollar offset method consists of comparing the effects of the change in £ LIBOR swap yield curve between 15 March and 30 June (in this case, a parallel shift of 0.5%) on the clean fair values of the hedged item and the hedging instrument.

Retrospective effectiveness test on 30 June 20X5

	15 Sep 20X5	15 Dec 20X5	15 Mar 20X6 ...	15 Dec 20X8	15 Mar 20X9	Total
Cash flows on the swap						
Fixed leg	104,167	125,000	125,000 ...	125,000	125,000	
Variable leg at YC2	(105,833)*	(128,257)	(129,765) ...	(146,327)	(147,830)	
Net cash flows	(1,667)	(3,257)	(4,765) ...	(21,327)	(22,830)	
Discounted CF at ZC2	(1,649)	(3,182)	(4,596) ...	(17,676)	(18,646)	**(161,184)**
Clean fair value at original yield curve						**0**
Change in clean fair value (cumulative)						**(161,184)**
Cash flows on the debt						
Cash flows	(104,167)**	(125,000)	(125,000) ...	(125,000)	(10,125,000)	
Discounted CF at ZC2	(103,078)	(122,127)	(120,563) ...	(103,600)	(8,269,357)	**(9,839,030)**
Clean fair value at original yield curve						**(10,000,000)**
						160,970
Effectiveness						**−100.1%**

* The variable rate for the first period is set to 5.08%. The rest of the variable cash flows are projected according to the forward rates derived from the current swap yield curve (YC2), as they have not yet been set.

** The effect of accruals needs to be removed, as the test is based on the clean fair value. 75 days of the next coupon have not yet been accrued; the amount of the first coupon included in the test is, therefore, the cash flow 125,000*75/90.

Conclusion: The hedge has been highly effective for the period ended 30 June 20X5.

> **Helpful hint**
>
> Based on company A's risk management policies, the retrospective effectiveness test above uses the clean fair values of the swap and the debt. Accrued interest for the current period as well as the fair value changes due to the passage of time on the original swap yield curve are excluded from the tests.
>
> The relationship is ineffective because the variable leg of the swap is pre-fixed/post-paid. As the interest on the variable leg of the swap is determined at the beginning of the period (15 June) it is fixed until the next re-pricing date and, therefore, has an exposure to changes in its fair value. If the variable leg of the swap had been post-fixed/post-paid, then the ineffectiveness would have been lower.

5 Accounting entries on 30 June 20X5

Recognition of accrued interest on the bond

Accrued interest for 15 days on the loan is recognised.

	Dr	Cr
Finance costs – interest expense	29,167	
Accrued interest		29,167

Interest on the debt at 7% for 15 days

Recognition of fair value changes of the swap

The recorded change in dirty fair value of the swap can be reconciled to the clean fair value of the swap as follows:

Clean fair value on 30 Jun 20X5	(161,184)
Accrued interest on receive fixed 5% for 15 days (discounted)	20,617
Accrued interest on pay variable 5.080% for 15 days (discounted)	(20,947)
Dirty fair value	**(161,514)**

The swap is recorded at the dirty fair value (that is, including the accrued interest).

	Dr	Cr
Other operating income and expense – ineffectiveness	161,184	
Finance costs – interest expense	330	
Derivative instruments		161,514

Fair value hedge – change in fair value of the swap including accrued interest

Fair value adjustment to the hedged item

All the criteria for hedge accounting are met for the period ended 30 June 20X5, and fair value hedge accounting can be applied. The carrying amount of the debt is adjusted for the fair value change of the hedged risk (that is, the changes in the clean fair value of the debt attributable to changes in the zero coupon curve). The entry is as follows:

	Dr	Cr
Other operating income and expense – ineffectiveness		160,970
Other financial liabilities – debt	160,970	

Fair value hedge – change in fair value of the debt attributable to the hedged risk

As the hedge is not 100% effective, the ineffectiveness of £214 (£161,184 – £160,970) is recognised in profit or loss. Best practice is to present the ineffectiveness in 'other operating income and expense', as illustrated above.

6 Prospective effectiveness test on 30 June 20X5

The same method is used as at the inception of the hedge.

Prospective effectiveness test on 30 June 20X5

	15 Sep 20X5	15 Dec 20X5	15 Mar 20X6 ...	15 Dec 20X8	15 Mar 20X9	Total
Cash flows on the swap						
Fixed leg	104,167	125,000	125,000 ...	125,000	125,000	
Variable leg @ YC2	(105,833)	(128,257)	(129,765) ...	(146,327)	(147,830)	
Net cash flows	(1,667)	(3,257)	(4,765) ...	(21,327)	(22,830)	
Discounted CF @ ZC2	(1,649)	(3,182)	(4,596) ...	(17,676)	(18,646)	**(161,184)**
Shifted zero coupon curve						
Fixed leg	104,167	125,000	125,000 ...	125,000	125,000	
Variable leg @ YC2 + 1%	(105,833)	(152,234)	(153,731) ...	(170,177)	(171,669)	
Net cash flows	(1,667)	(27,234)	(28,731) ...	(45,177)	(46,669)	
Discounted CF @ ZC2 + 1%	(1,646)	(26,493)	(27,526) ...	(36,241)	(36,807)	**(451,850)**
						(290,666)

Cash flows on the debt

Cash flows	(104,167)	(125,000)	(125,000) ...	(125,000)	(10,125,000)	
Discounted CF @ ZC2	(103,078)	(122,127)	(120,563) ...	(103,600)	(8,269,357)	**(9,839,030)**
Discounted CF @ ZC2 + 1%	(102,875)	(121,599)	(119,758) ...	(100,277)	(7,985,352)	**(9,528,668)**
						310,362
Effectiveness						**-93.7%**

Conclusion: The hedge is expected to be highly effective.

7 Accounting entries on 1 July 20X5

The accrual of the interest on the debt is reversed.

	Dr	Cr
Finance costs – interest expense		29,167
Accrued interest	29,167	

Interest on the debt reversed at 7% for 15 days

The accrual on the swap is reversed.

	Dr	Cr
Finance costs – interest expense		330
Other operating income and expense – ineffectiveness	330	

Accrued interest on the swap reversed for 15 days

8 Accounting entries on 15 September 20X5

On 15 September the coupon on the loan is paid and the second period of the swap is settled.

Recognition of interest on the debt

	Dr	Cr
Finance costs – interest expense	175,000	
Cash		175,000

Interest on the debt at 7% for three months

Cash settlement of the swap

	Dr	Cr
Finance costs – interest expense	127,000	
Finance costs – interest expense		125,000
Cash		2,000

Settlement of the swap: receive 5% and pay 5.080% for three months

These two transactions result in a total charge of £177,000 to finance cost, which is equivalent to 7.08% interest for the period (that is, the variable rate of 5.08% plus 2% credit spread).

The floating rate on the swap for the following quarter is set at the three-month swap rate of 5.28%.

9 Accounting entries on 15 December 20X5

On 15 December the coupon on the loan is paid and the third period of the swap is settled.

Recognition of interest on the debt

	Dr	Cr
Finance costs – interest expense	175,000	
Cash		175,000

Interest on the debt at 7% for three months

Cash settlement of the swap

	Dr	Cr
Finance costs – interest expense	132,000	
Finance costs – interest expense		125,000
Cash		7,000

Settlement of the swap: receive 5% and pay 5.28% for three months

These two transactions result in a total charge of £182,000 to finance cost, which is equivalent to 7.28% interest for the period (that is, the variable rate of 5.28% plus 2% credit spread).

The floating rate on the swap for the following quarter is set at the three-month swap rate of 5.79%.

10 Retrospective effectiveness test on 31 December 20X5

The same method for retrospective testing is used as on 30 June 20X5. As required in company A's risk management policies, the effectiveness test is done using the dollar offset method on a cumulative basis.

Retrospective effectiveness test on 31 December 20X5

	15 Mar 20X6	15 Jun 20X6	15 Sep 20X6	...	15 Dec 20X8	15 Mar 20X9	Total
Cash flows on the swap							
Fixed leg	104,167	125,000	125,000	...	125,000	125,000	
Variable leg at YC3	(120,625)	(144,165)	(145,666)	...	(159,157)	(160,654)	
Net cash flows	(16,458)	(19,165)	(20,666)	...	(34,157)	(35,654)	
Discounted CF at ZC3	(16,265)	(18,671)	(19,844)	...	(28,605)	(29,386)	**(308,922)**
Clean fair value at original yield curve							**0**
Change in clean fair value (cumulative)							
							(308,922)
Cash flows on the debt							
Cash flows	(104,167)	(125,000)	(125,000)	...	(125,000)	(10,125,000)	
Discounted CF at ZC3	(102,943)	(121,776)	(120,028)	...	(104,681)	(8,345,128)	**(9,692,833)**
Clean fair value at original yield curve							**(10,000,000)**
Change in clean fair value (cumulative)							**307,167**
Effectiveness							**-100.6%**

Conclusion: The hedge has been highly effective for the period ended 31 December 20X5.

11 Accounting entries on 31 December 20X5

Recognition of accrued interest on the bond

Accrued interest for 15 days on the loan is recognised.

	Dr	Cr
Finance costs – interest expense	29,167	
Accrued interest		29,167

Interest on the debt at 7% for 15 days

Recognition of fair value changes of the swap

Clean fair value of the swap	(308,922)
Accrued interest on receive fix 5% for 15 days	20,589
Accrued interest on pay variable 5.79% for 15 days	(23,842)
Dirty fair value of the swap on 31 December 20X5	(312,175)
Dirty fair value of the swap on 30 June 20X5	(161,514)
Change in fair value to be recognised on 31 December 20X5	**(150,661)**

The swap is recorded at the dirty fair value (that is, including the accrued interest).

	Dr	Cr
Other operating income and expense – ineffectiveness	147,408	
Finance costs – interest expense	3,253	
Derivative instruments		150,661

Fair value hedge – change in fair value of the swap

Fair value adjustment to the hedged item

All the criteria for hedge accounting are met for the period ended 31 December 20X5, and fair value hedge accounting can be applied.

Fair value adjustment on debt on 30 June 20X5	160,970
Fair value adjustment on debt on 31 December 20X5	307,167
Change in the clean fair value of the debt	**146,197**

As the hedge is not 100% effective, the ineffectiveness of £1,211 (£147,408 – £146,197) is recognised in profit or loss. Best practice is to present the ineffectiveness in 'other operating income and expense', as illustrated above.

12 Prospective effectiveness test on 31 December 20X5

The same method is used as at the inception of the hedge.

Prospective effectiveness test on 31 December 20X5

	15 Mar 20X6	15 Jun 20X6	15 Sep 20X6	...	15 Dec 20X8	15 Mar 20X9	Total
Cash flows on the swap							
Fixed leg	104,167	125,000	125,000	...	125,000	125,000	
Variable leg at YC3	(120,625)	(144,165)	(145,666)	...	(159,157)	(160,654)	
Net cash flows	(16,458)	(19,165)	(20,666)	...	(34,157)	(35,654)	
Discounted CF at ZC3	(16,265)	(18,671)	(19,844)	...	(28,605)	(29,386)	**(308,922)**
Shifted zero coupon curve							
Fixed leg	104,167	125,000	125,000	...	125,000	125,000	
Variable leg at YC3 + 1%	(120,625)	(168,030)	(169,520)	...	(182,917)	(184,403)	
Net cash flows	(16,458)	(43,030)	(44,520)	...	(57,917)	(59,403)	
Discounted CF at ZC3 + 1%	(16,233)	(41,740)	(42,466)	...	(47,176)	(47,511)	**(556,044)**
							(247,122)
Cash flows on the debt							
Cash flows	(104,167)	(125,000)	(125,000)	...	(125,000)	(10,125,000)	
Discounted CF at ZC3	(102,943)	(121,776)	(120,028)	...	(104,681)	(8,345,128)	**(9,692,833)**
Discounted CF at ZC3 + 1%	(102,742)	(121,253)	(119,231)	...	(101,818)	(8,097,959)	**(9,426,135)**
Effectiveness							**266,698** **-92.7%**

Conclusion: The hedge is expected to be highly effective.

The testing and accounting entries are carried out in the same manner throughout the remaining life of the hedge relationship.

6.8 – Hedge accounting

	Balance sheet				Income statement	
	Derivative instruments	Accrued interest	Other financial liabilities – debt	Cash	Finance cost – interest expense	Other operating income and expense – ineffectiveness
15 Mar 20X5						
Debt			(10,000,000)	10,000,000		
Swap						
15 Jun 20X5						
Interest on debt				(175,000)	175,000	
Settlement of swap				10,941	114,059	
					(125,000)	
30 Jun 20X5						
Accrued interest on debt		(29,167)			29,167	
Fair value change of swap	(161,514)				330	161,184
Hedge adjustment to debt			160,970			(160,970)
01 Jul 20X5						
Accruals reversed on debt		29,167			(29,167)	
Accruals reversed on swap					(330)	330
15 Sep 20X5						
Interest				(175,000)	175,000	
Settlement of swap				(2,000)	127,000	
					(125,000)	
15 Dec 20X5						
Interest				(175,000)	175,000	
Settlement of swap				(7,000)	132,000	
					(125,000)	
31 Dec 20X5						
Accrued interest on debt		(29,167)			29,167	
Fair value change of swap	(150,661)				3,253	147,408
Hedge adjustment to debt			146,197			(146,197)

Cash flow hedge of a highly probable forecast purchase in foreign currency

Background and assumptions

Company C is a Swedish company with a SEK functional currency. Its reporting dates are 30 June and 31 December.

Company C produces and sells electronic components for the automotive industry and is planning to launch a new electronic component that it expects to be more reliable and cheaper than the existing alternatives.

Production is scheduled to start in June 20X6. Company C's management expects to purchase a significant amount of raw material in May 20X6 for the start of production. An external company based in Spain will supply the raw material. Based on C's production plans and the prices that the supplier is currently charging, Company C's management forecasts that 500,000 units of raw material will be received and invoiced on 1 May 20X6 at a price of EUR 50 per unit. The invoice is expected to be paid on 31 August 20X6.

On 1 January 20X5, Company C's management decides to hedge the foreign currency risk arising from its highly probable forecast purchase. C enters into a forward contract to buy EUR against SEK. On that date, the forecast purchase is considered as highly probable, as the board of directors has approved the purchase, and negotiations with the Spanish supplier are far advanced.

The foreign currency forward contract entered into as a hedge of the highly probable forecast purchase is as follows:

Type	European forward contract
Amount purchased	EUR 25,000,000
Amount sold	SEK 192,687,500
Forward rate	EUR 1 = SEK 7.7075
Start date	1 January 20X5
Maturity date	31 August 20X6

Exchange rates on various dates during the hedge are as follows:

	1 Jan 20X5	30 Jun 20X5	31/12/20X5	30 Jun 20X6	31 Jul 20X6	31 Aug 20X6	31/10/20X6
SEK/EUR spot rate	7.6900	7.6500	7.7500	7.8100	7.9000	8.1500	8.0500
SEK/EUR forward rate*	7.7075	7.6622	7.7574	7.8118	7.9008	8.1500	
Forward points	**0.0175**	**0.0122**	**0.0074**	**0.0018**	**0.0008**	**0.0000**	

* For a forward maturing on 31 August 20X6.

Annualised interest rates applicable for discounting a cash flow on 31 August 20X6 at various dates during the hedge are as follows:

	1 Jan 20X5	30 Jun 20X5	31/12/20X5	30 Jun 20X6	31 Jul 20X6	31 Aug 20X6
SEK interest rate	1.3550%	1.3850%	1.3670%	1.3850%	1.4240%	1.4030%
EUR interest rate	1.4916%	1.5213%	1.5100%	1.5200%	1.5470%	1.5170%

Extracts of risk management policies for foreign currency risk

Foreign currency risk

Company C's functional and presentation currencies are the SEK (Swedish krona). Company C is exposed to foreign exchange risk because some of its purchases and sales are denominated in currencies other than SEK. It is therefore exposed to the risk that movements in exchange rates will affect both its net income and financial position, as expressed in SEK.

Company C's foreign currency exposure arises from:

- highly probable forecast transactions (sales/purchases) denominated in foreign currencies;

- firm commitments denominated in foreign currencies; and

- monetary items (mainly trade receivables, trade payables and borrowings) denominated in foreign currencies.

Company C is mainly exposed to EUR/SEK and GBP/SEK risks. Transactions denominated in foreign currencies other than EUR and GBP are not material.

Company C's policy is to hedge all material foreign exchange risk associated with highly probable forecast transactions, firm commitments and monetary items denominated in foreign currencies.

Company C's policy is to hedge the risk of changes in the relevant spot exchange rate.

Hedging instruments

Company C uses only forward contracts to hedge foreign exchange risk. All derivatives must be entered into with counterparties with a credit rating of AA or higher.

Extracts of effectiveness testing policies for interest rate risk

Strategy 2A: Cash flow hedges of foreign currency exposure in highly probable forecast transactions

Prospective effectiveness testing for cash flow hedges

Prospective effectiveness testing should be performed at the inception of the hedge and at each reporting date. The hedge relationship is highly effective if the changes in fair value or cash flow of the hedged item that are attributable to the hedged risk are expected to be offset by the changes in fair value or cash flows of the hedging instrument.

Prospective effectiveness testing should be performed by comparing the numerical effects of a shift in the exchange rate (for example, EUR/SEK rate) on: the fair value of the hedged cash flows measured using a hypothetical derivative; and the fair value of the hedging instrument. Consistent with Company C's risk management policy, the hedged risk is defined as the risk of changes in the spot exchange rate. Changes in interest rates are excluded from the hedge relationship (for both the hedging instrument and the hedged forecast transaction) and do not affect the calculations of effectiveness. Only the spot component of the forward contract is included in the hedge relationship (that is, the forward points are excluded).

At least three scenarios should be assessed unless the critical terms of the hedging instrument perfectly match the critical terms of the hedged item, in which case one scenario is sufficient.

Retrospective effectiveness testing for cash flow hedges

Retrospective effectiveness testing must be performed at each reporting date using the dollar offset method on a cumulative basis. The hedge is demonstrated to be effective by comparing the cumulative change in the fair value of the hedged cash flows measured using a hypothetical derivative; and the fair value of the hedging instrument. A hedge is considered to be highly effective if the results of the retrospective effectiveness tests are within the range 80%-125%.

Cumulative change in fair value of hedging instrument

$$\text{Effectiveness} = \frac{\text{Cumulative change in fair value of hedging instrument}}{\substack{\text{Cumulative change in fair value of hedged item} \\ \text{(hypothetical derivative)}}}$$

Cumulative change in fair value of hedged item (hypothetical derivative)

Change in the fair value of the spot component of the hedging instrument (the forward contract) is the difference between the fair value of the spot component at the inception of the hedge, and the end of the testing period based on translating the foreign exchange leg of the forward contract at the current spot rate and discounting the net cash flows on the derivative using the zero-coupon rates curve derived from the swap yield curve.

Change in fair value of the hedged cash flows of the hedged item (hypothetical derivative) is the difference between the value of the hypothetical derivative at the inception of the hedge, and the end of the testing period based on translating the foreign exchange leg of the hypothetical derivative at the current spot rate and discounting the net cash flows on the hypothetical derivative using the zero-coupon rates curve derived from the swap yield curve.

> **Helpful hint**
>
> The fair value of a foreign exchange forward contract is affected by changes in the spot rate and by changes in the forward points. The latter derives from the interest rate differential between the currencies specified in the forward contract. Changes in the forward points may give rise to ineffectiveness if the hedged item is not similarly affected by interest rate differentials.

Hedge designation

Company C's hedge documentation is as follows:

1   Risk management objective and strategy

In order to comply with Company C's foreign exchange risk management strategy, the foreign exchange risk arising from the highly probable forecast purchase detailed in 5 below is hedged.

2   Type of hedging relationship

Cash flow hedge: hedge of the foreign currency risk arising from highly probable forecast purchases.

3   Nature of risk being hedged

EUR/SEK spot exchange rate risk arising from a highly probable forecast purchase denominated in EUR that is expected to occur on 1 May 20X6 and to be settled on 31 August 20X6.

4   Identification of hedged item

Purchase of 500,000 units of raw material for EUR 50 per unit.

5   Forecast transactions

Hedged amount: EUR 25,000,000

Nature of forecast transaction: purchase of 500,000 units of raw material

Expected timescale for forecast transaction to take place:

- delivery: 1 May 20X6
- cash payment: 31 August 20X6

Expected price: EUR 50 per unit.

Rationale for forecast transaction being highly probable to occur:

- production of electronic component is scheduled to start in June 20X6;
- purchase has been approved by the board of directors; and
- negotiations with supplier are far advanced.

Method of reclassifying into profit and loss amounts deferred through equity: in accordance with Company C's chosen accounting policy, the gains or losses recognised in other comprehensive income will be included in the carrying amount of the inventory acquired (that is, basis adjustment).

6   Identification of hedging instrument

Transaction number: reference number K1121W in the treasury management system.

The hedging instrument is a forward contract to buy EUR 25,000,000 with the following characteristics:

Type	European forward contract
Amount purchased	EUR 25,000,000
Amount sold	SEK 192,687,500
Forward rate	EUR 1 = SEK 7.7075
Spot rate at inception	EUR 1 = SEK 7.6900
Spot component of notional amount	SEK 192,250,000
Start date	1 January 20X5
Maturity date	31 August 20X6

Hedge designation: the spot component of forward contract K1121W is designated as a hedge of the change in the present value of the cash flows on the forecast purchase identified in 5 above that is attributable to movements in the EUR/SEK spot rate, measured as a hypothetical derivative.

7   Effectiveness testing

Hedge accounting strategy 2A should be applied (see hedge effectiveness testing policy). The hypothetical derivative that models the hedged cash flows is a forward contract to pay EUR 25,000,000 on 31 August 20X6 in return for SEK. The spot component of this hypothetical derivative is SEK 192,250,000 (that is, EUR 25,000,000 at the spot rate on 1 January 20X5 of 7.6900).

Description of prospective testing

Dollar offset method, being the ratio of the change in the fair value of the spot component of forward contract K1121W, divided by the change in present value of the hedged cash flows (hypothetical derivative) attributable to changes in spot EUR/SEK rate.

Frequency of testing: at inception of the hedge and then at each reporting date (30 June and 31 December).

Description of retrospective testing

Dollar offset method, being the ratio of the change in fair value of the spot component of the forward contract, divided by the change in present value of the hedged cash flows (hypothetical derivative) attributable to changes in spot EUR/SEK rate, on a cumulative basis.

Frequency of testing: at every reporting date (30 June and 31 December) after inception of the hedge.

Effectiveness tests and accounting entries

1   Prospective effectiveness test on 1 January 20X5

On 1 January 20X5, the forward EUR/SEK exchange rate is 7.7075. On that date, the spot EUR/SEK exchange rate is 7.6900. Company C's management should assess prospectively the effectiveness of the hedge, as required in IAS 39.

Based on the hedge documentation, the prospective effectiveness test consists of comparing the effects of a 10% shift of the spot EUR/SEK exchange rate on both the fair value of the spot component of the hedging instrument and on the hedged cash flows (hypothetical derivative).

Hedged item and hedging instrument (spot components)

The EUR leg of both the hypothetical derivative (hedged item) and the forward contract (hedging instrument) are translated into SEK using the shifted spot exchange rate (8.459), then discounted back using the current SEK interest rate (1.3550%) for a cash flow due on 31 August 20X6. The SEK leg is discounted back using the current SEK interest rate. The difference between the present values of each leg represents the fair value of the spot component. As the fair value of this spot component is nil at inception, the change in fair value is equal to its fair value.

Hedged item Hypothetical derivative – spot component			Hedging instrument Spot component	
Notional amount	(25,000,000)	EUR	25,000,000	EUR Notional amount
Spot rate + 10%	8.4590		8.4590	Spot rate + 10%
Notional amount in SEK	(211,475,000)	SEK	211,475,000	SEK Notional amount in SEK
Discount factor*	0.9776		0.9776	Discount factor
FV of the EUR leg (spot) (A)	(206,729,957)	EUR	206,729,957	SEK FV of the EUR leg (spot) (A)
Spot component of notional	192,250,000	SEK	(192,250,000)	Spot component of notional
Discount factor	0.9776		0.9776	Discount factor
FV of SEK leg (spot) (B)	187,936,324	SEK	(187,936,324)	SEK FV of SEK leg (spot) (B)
(A-B) FV of the hypothetical derivative (spot)	**(18,793,632)**	**SEK**	**18,793,632**	**SEK (A-B) FV of the derivative (spot)**
Effectiveness	**-100%**			

* The discount factor has been derived from the annualised SEK interest rate on 1 January for cash flows on 31 August 20X6 and has been calculated as $1/(1.01355)^{(607days/360)}$.

Conclusion: the hedge is expected to be highly effective.

> **Helpful hint**
>
> As the critical terms of the forward perfectly match the critical terms of the forecast purchase, a quantitative test is not necessarily required. A qualitative test consisting of a comparison of the critical terms of the hedging instrument and the hedged item may be used as long as it is consistent with Company C's risk management policies.

2 Accounting entries on 1 January 20X5

No entry, as the fair value of the forward contract is nil, as shown below:

Derivative

Notional amount in EUR	25,000,000	EUR
Forward rate	7.7075	
Notional amount in SEK	192,687,500	SEK
Discount factor	0.9776	
FV of the EUR leg	188,364,007	SEK
Notional amount in SEK	(192,687,500)	SEK
Discount factor	0.9776	
FV of the SEK leg	(188,364,007)	SEK
FV of the derivative	0	SEK

3 Retrospective effectiveness test on 30 June 20X5

IAS 39 requires the effectiveness of a hedging relationship to be assessed retrospectively as a minimum at each reporting date. Based on Company C's risk management policies, the effectiveness of the hedge is assessed using the dollar offset method on a cumulative basis.

The dollar offset method consists of comparing the effects of the change in spot EUR/SEK exchange rate (from 7.69 to 7.65) on the fair value of the spot component of the hedging instrument and the hypothetical derivative (hedged cash flows).

	Hedged item			Hedging instrument	
	Hypothetical derivative – spot component			Spot component	
Notional amount	(25,000,000)	EUR	25,000,000	EUR	Notional amount
Spot rate at test date	7.6500		7.6500		Spot rate at test date
Notional amount in SEK	(191,250,000)	SEK	191,250,000	SEK	Notional amount in SEK
Discount factor	0.9838		0.9838		Discount factor $(1/(1.01385)^{\wedge} (427\text{days}/360))$
FV of the EUR leg (spot) (A)	(188,155,087)	EUR	188,155,087	SEK	FV of the EUR leg (spot) (A)
Spot comp of notional at inception	192,250,000	SEK	(192,250,000)		Spot comp of notional at inception
Discount factor	0.9838		0.9838		Discount factor
FV of SEK leg (spot) (B)	189,138,905	SEK	(189,138,905)	SEK	FV of SEK leg (spot) (B)
(A-B) FV of the derivative (spot)	**983,818**	**SEK**	**(983,818)**	**SEK**	**(B-A) FV of the derivative (spot)**
Effectiveness	**-100%**				

Conclusion: the hedge has been highly effective for the period ended 30 June 20X5.

> **Helpful hint**
>
> Ineffectiveness can arise from a number of causes, including changes in the date of the forecast transaction and changes in the credit risk or liquidity of the forward contract.

4 Accounting entries on 30 June 20X5

All the criteria for hedge accounting are met for the period ended 30 June 20X5. Cash flow hedge accounting can therefore be applied. The hedge is 100% effective; the change in the fair value of the spot component of the hedging instrument is, therefore, recognised in other comprehensive income. The full fair value of the hedging instrument includes the forward points. The change in the fair value of the forward points component is recognised in the income statement.

Derivative

Notional amount in EUR	25,000,000	EUR
Forward rate	7.6622	
Notional amount in SEK	191,554,154	SEK
Discount factor	0.9838	
FV of the EUR leg	188,454,319	SEK
Notional amount in SEK	(192,687,500)	SEK
Discount factor	0.9838	
FV of the SEK leg	(189,565,963)	SEK
FV of the derivative	**(1,111,644)**	**SEK**

The entry is as follows:

	Dr	Cr
Derivative (financial liability)		1,111,644
Cash flow hedge reserve (equity)	983,818	
Interest expense (income statement)	127,826	

Cash flow hedge – change in fair value of the forward contract

---

Helpful hint

The forward points represent the interest rate differential between the currencies of the forward contract. It is common to recognise fair value movements on the forward points component as interest income or expense, although they could also be recognised as 'operating income and expense'.

---

5   Prospective effectiveness test on 30 June 20X5

The same method is used as at the inception of the hedge.

	Hedged item Hypothetical derivative – spot component		Hedging instrument Spot component	
Notional amount	(25,000,000)	EUR	25,000,000	EUR Notional amount
Spot rate + 10%	8.4150		8.4150	Spot rate + 10%
Notional amount in SEK	(211,475,000)	SEK	210,375,000	SEK Notional amount in SEK
Discount factor	0.9838		0.9838	Discount factor
FV of the EUR leg (spot) (A)	(206,970,596)	EUR	206,970,596	SEK FV of the EUR leg (spot) (A)
Spot component of notional	191,250,000	SEK	(191,250,000)	Spot component of notional
Discount factor	0.9838		0.9838	Discount factor
FV of SEK leg (spot) (B)	188,155,087	SEK	(188,155,087)	SEK FV of SEK leg (spot) (B)
(A-B) FV of the hypothetical derivative (spot)	**(18,815,509)**	**SEK**	**18,815,509**	**SEK (A-B) FV of the derivative (spot)**
Effectiveness	**-100%**			

Conclusion: the hedge is expected to be highly effective.

6   Retrospective effectiveness test on 31 December 20X5

Change in timing of expected cash flow

In December 20X5, management decides to delay the start of production by two months, due to the late delivery of an essential machine. The production will now start in August 20X6, and the raw materials will be purchased in July. The invoice for the raw materials is expected to be paid on 31 October 20X6.

Annualised interest rates applicable for discounting a cash flow on 31 October 20X6 at various dates during the hedge are as follows:

	31/12/20X5	30 Jun 20X6	31 Jul 20X6	31 Aug 20X6
SEK interest rate	1.3920%	1.4060%	1.4420%	1.4030%

The dollar offset method consists of comparing the effects of the cumulative change in spot EUR/SEK exchange rate (from 7.69 to 7.75) on the fair value of the spot component of the hedging instrument and the hedged cash flow (hypothetical derivative). As the hedged cash flow has been delayed, it is discounted from the revised payment date. The payment date on the hedging instrument and the associated discount factor remain unchanged.

	Hedged item			Hedging instrument	
	Hypothetical derivative – spot component			Spot component	
Notional amount	(25,000,000)	EUR	25,000,000	EUR	Notional amount
Spot rate at test date	7.7500		7.7500		Spot rate at test date
Notional amount in SEK	(193,750,000)	SEK	193,750,000	SEK	Notional amount in SEK
Discount factor*	0.9884		0.9909		Discount factor**
FV of the EUR leg (spot) (A)	(191,501,389)	EUR	191,982,442	SEK	FV of the EUR leg (spot) (A)
Spot comp of notional at inception	192,250,000	SEK	(192,250,000)	SEK	Spot component of notional at inception
Discount factor*	0.9884		0.9909		Discount factor**
FV of SEK leg (spot) (B)	190,018,798	SEK	(190,496,126)	SEK	FV of SEK leg (spot) (B)
(A-B) FV of the derivative (spot)	**(1,482,591)**	**SEK**	**1,486,316**	**SEK**	**(A-B) FV of the derivative (spot)**
Effectiveness	**-100.25%**				

* Discount factor calculated based on changed timing of cash flows — $(1/(1.01392)\hat{}(304\text{days}/360))$.

** Discount factor calculated based on original timing of cash flows — $(1/(1.01367)\hat{}(243\text{days}/360))$.

Conclusion: the hedge has been highly effective for the period ended 31 December 20X5.

7   Accounting entries on 31 December 20X5

The full fair value of the hedging instrument is as follows:

Derivative

Notional amount in EUR	25,000,000	EUR
Forward rate	7.7574	
Notional amount in SEK	193,935,000	SEK
Discount factor	0.9909	
FV of the EUR leg	192,165,754	SEK
Notional amount in SEK	(192,687,500)	SEK
Discount factor	0.9909	
FV of the SEK leg	(190,929,635)	SEK
FV of the derivative	**1,236,119**	**SEK**

All the criteria for hedge accounting are met for the period ended 31 December 20X5. Cash flow hedge accounting can therefore be applied. The hedge is not, however, 100% effective and, therefore, the amount recognised in other comprehensive income is adjusted to the lesser of (a) the cumulative change in the fair value of the spot component of the hedging instrument, and (b) the cumulative change in the fair value of the spot component of the hypothetical derivative.

	Derivative (full fair value)	Hedging instrument (spot component)	Hedged item hypothetical derivative (spot component)	Effective portion	Ineffective portion
30 Jun 20X5	(1,111,644)	(983,818)	983,818	(983,818)	–
31/12/20X5	1,236,119	1,486,316	(1,482,591)	1,482,591	3,725
Change	2,347,763	2,470,134	(2,466,409)	2,466,409	3,725

The difference between the full fair value of the forward contract and the amount deferred in other comprehensive income is charged to the income statement. The portion relating to the forward points is recognised in 'interest expense' and the ineffectiveness (SEK 1,486,316 – SEK 1,482,591 = SEK 3,725) is recognised in 'other operating income and expense'.

> **Helpful hint**
>
> The forward points reflect an interest element and can therefore be included in interest income and expense. Alternatively all fair value movements in excess of the effective portion may be recognised in 'other operating income and expense'.

The entry is as follows:

	Dr	Cr
Derivative (financial asset)	2,347,763	
Cash flow hedge reserve (equity)		2,466,409
Interest expense (income statement)	122,371	
Other operating income and expense		3,725

Cash flow hedge – change in fair value of the forward contract

8   Prospective effectiveness test on 31 December 20X5

The same method is used as at the inception of the hedge

Hedged item Hypothetical derivative – spot component			Hedging instrument Spot component	
Notional amount	(25,000,000)	EUR	25,000,000	EUR Notional amount
Spot rate + 10%	8.5250		8.5250	Spot rate + 10%
Notional amount in SEK	(213,125,000)	SEK	213,125,000	SEK Notional amount in SEK
Discount factor	0.9884		0.9909	Discount factor
FV of the EUR leg (spot) (A)	(210,651,528)	EUR	211,180,686	SEK FV of the EUR leg (spot) (A)
Spot comp of notional at inception	193,750,000	SEK	(193,750,000)	SEK Spot component of notional
Discount factor	0.9884		0.9909	Discount factor**
FV of SEK leg (spot) (B)	191,501,389	SEK	(191,982,442)	SEK FV of SEK leg (spot) (B)
(A-B) FV of the derivative (spot)	(19,150,139)	SEK	19,198,244	SEK (A-B) FV of the derivative (spot)
Effectiveness	-100.25%			

Conclusion: the hedge is expected to be highly effective.

9   Retrospective effectiveness test on 30 June 20X6

The dollar offset method consists of comparing the effects of the change in spot EUR/SEK exchange rate (from 7.69 to 7.81) on the fair value of the spot component of the hedging instrument, and the hypothetical derivative (hedged cash flows). As the hedged cash flow has been delayed, it is discounted from the revised payment date. The payment date on the hedging instrument and the associated discount factor remain unchanged.

	Hedged item Hypothetical derivative – spot component			**Hedging instrument** Spot component	
Notional amount	(25,000,000)	EUR	25,000,000	EUR	Notional amount
Spot rate at test date	7.8100		7.8100		Spot rate at test date
Notional amount in SEK	(195,250,000)	SEK	195,250,000	SEK	Notional amount in SEK
Discount factor*	0.9952		0.9976		Discount factor**
FV of the EUR leg (spot) (A)	(194,320,802)	EUR	194,788,017	SEK	FV of the EUR leg (spot) (A)
Spot comp of notional at inception	192,250,000	SEK	(192,250,000)	SEK	Spot component of notional at inception
Discount factor	0.9952		0.9976		Discount factor
FV of SEK leg (spot) (B)	191,335,079	SEK	(191,795,116)	SEK	FV of SEK leg (spot) (B)
(A-B) FV of the derivative (spot)	(2,985,723)	SEK	2,992,901	SEK	(A-B) FV of the derivative (spot)
Effectiveness	-100.24%				

* Discount factor calculated based on changed timing of cash flows — $(1/(1.014060)\hat{}(123 days/360))$.

** Discount factor calculated based on original timing of cash flows — $(1/(1.01385)\hat{}(62 days/360))$.

Conclusion: the hedge has been highly effective for the period ended 30 June 20X6.

10   Accounting entries on 30 June 20X6

The full fair value of the hedging instrument is as follows:

Derivative

Notional amount in EUR	25,000,000	EUR
Forward rate	7.8118	
Notional amount in SEK	195,293,907	SEK
Discount factor	0.9976	
FV of the EUR leg	194,831,821	SEK
Notional amount in SEK	192,687,500	SEK
Discount factor	0.9976	
FV of the SEK leg	(192,231,581)	SEK
FV of the derivative	**2,601,240**	**SEK**

All the criteria for hedge accounting are met for the year ended 30 June 20X6. Cash flow hedge accounting can therefore be applied. The hedge is not however 100% effective; the amount recognised in other comprehensive income is, therefore, adjusted to the lesser of (a) the cumulative change in the fair value of the spot component of the hedging instrument, and (b) the cumulative change in the fair value of the spot component of the hypothetical derivative.

	Derivative (full fair value)	Hedging instrument (spot component)	Hedged item hypothetical derivative (spot component)	Effective portion	Ineffective portion
31/12/20X5	1,236,119	1,486,316	(1,482,591)	1,482,591	3,725
30 Jun 20X6	2,601,240	2,992,901	(2,985,723)	2,985,723	7,178
Change	1,365,121	1,506,585	(1,503,132)	1,503,132	3,453

The difference between the full fair value of the forward contract and the amount deferred in equity is charged to the income statement. The portion relating to the forward points is recognised in 'interest income' and the ineffectiveness is recognised in 'other operating income and expense'.

The entry is as follows:

	Dr	Cr
Derivative (financial asset)	1,365,121	
Cash flow hedge reserve (equity)		1,503,132
Interest expense (income statement)	141,464	
Other operating income and expense		3,453

Cash flow hedge – change in fair value of the forward contract

11 Prospective effectiveness test on 30 June 20X6

The same method is used as at the inception of the hedge.

	Hedged item		Hedging instrument	
	Hypothetical derivative – spot component		Spot component	
Notional amount	(25,000,000)	EUR	25,000,000	EUR Notional amount
Spot rate + 10%	8.5910		8.5910	Spot rate + 10%
Notional amount in SEK	(214,775,000)	SEK	214,775,000	SEK Notional amount in SEK
Discount factor	0.9952		0.9976	Discount factor
FV of the EUR leg (spot) (A)	(213,752,882)	EUR	214,266,819	SEK FV of the EUR leg (spot) (A)
Spot comp of notional at inception	195,250,000	SEK	(195,250,000)	SEK Spot component of notional
Discount factor	0.9952		0.9976	Discount factor
FV of SEK leg (spot) (B)	191,335,079	SEK	(191,795,116)	SEK FV of SEK leg (spot) (B)
(A-B) FV of the derivative (spot)	(22,417,803)	SEK	22,471,703	SEK (A-B) FV of the derivative (spot)
Effectiveness	-100.24%			

Conclusion: the hedge is expected to be highly effective.

12 Retrospective effectiveness test on 31 July 20X6

The dollar offset method consists of comparing the effects of the change in spot EUR/SEK exchange rate (from 7.69 to 7.90) on the fair value of the spot component of the hedging instrument, and the hedged cash flows (hypothetical derivative). As the hedged cash flow has been delayed, it is discounted from the revised payment date. The payment date on the hedging instrument and the associated discount factor remain unchanged.

	Hedged item Hypothetical derivative – spot component			Hedging instrument Spot component	
Notional amount	(25,000,000)	EUR	25,000,000	EUR	Notional amount
Spot rate at test date	7.9000		7.9000		Spot rate at test date
Notional amount in SEK	(197,500,000)	SEK	197,500,000	SEK	Notional amount in SEK
Discount factor*	0.9963		0.9988		Discount factor**
FV of the EUR leg (spot) (A)	(196,778,708)	EUR	197,259,676	SEK	FV of the EUR leg (spot) (A)
Spot comp of notional at inception	192,250,000	SEK	(192,250,000)	SEK	Spot component of notional
Discount factor	0.9963		0.9988		Discount factor
FV of SEK leg (spot) (B)	191,547,882	SEK	(192,016,064)	SEK	FV of SEK leg (spot) (B)
(A-B) FV of the derivative (spot)	**(5,230,826)**	**SEK**	**5,243,612**	**SEK**	**(A-B) FV of the derivative (spot)**
Effectiveness	**-100.24%**				

* Discount factor calculated based on changed timing of cash flows — $(1/(1.01442)\hat{\ }(92\,\text{days}/360))$.

** Discount factor calculated based on original timing of cash flows — $(1/(1.01424\hat{\ }(31\,\text{days}/360))$.

Conclusion: the hedge has been highly effective for the period ended 31 July 20X6.

> **Helpful hint**
>
> Although IAS 39 does not explicitly require it, an effectiveness test is performed when the hedged highly probable forecast transaction occurs in order to determine the amount to be reclassified into the carrying amount of the hedged item.

13 Accounting entries on 31 July 20X6

Recognition of the purchase

	Dr	Cr
Inventory	197,500,000	
Trade payable		197,500,000

Purchase of EUR 25m at spot rate of 7.90

As the trade payable is short-term and EUR interest rates are low, Company C has determined that the effect of discounting is not material. The trade payable is therefore recognised at its face value, as permitted in IAS 39.

Recognition of the change in the fair value of the derivative

The full fair value of the hedging instrument is as follows:

Notional amount in EUR	25,000,000	EUR
Forward rate	7.9008	
Notional amount in SEK	197,520,232	SEK
Discount factor	0.99878	
FV of the EUR leg	197,279,883	SEK
Notional amount in SEK	(192,687,500)	SEK
Discount factor	0.99878	
FV of the SEK leg	(192,453,032)	SEK
FV of the derivative	**4,826,851**	**SEK**

All the criteria for hedge accounting are met as at 31 July 20X6. Cash flow hedge accounting can therefore be applied. The hedge is not however 100% effective; the amount recognised in other comprehensive income is, therefore, adjusted to the lesser of (a) the cumulative change in the fair value of the spot component of the hedging item, and (b) the cumulative change in the fair value of the spot component of the hypothetical derivative.

	Derivative (full fair value)	Hedging instrument (spot component)	Hedged item hypothetical derivative (spot component)	Effective portion	Ineffective portion
30 Jun 20X6	2,601,240	2,992,901	(2,985,723)	2,985,723	7,178
31 Jul 20X6	4,826,851	5,243,612	(5,230,826)	5,230,826	12,786
Change	2,225,611	2,250,711	(2,245,103)	2,245,103	5,608

The difference between the full fair value of the forward contract and the amount deferred in equity is charged to the income statement. The portion relating to the forward points is recognised in 'interest expense' and the ineffectiveness is recognised in 'other operating income and expense'.

The entry is as follows:

	Dr	Cr
Derivative (financial asset)	2,225,611	
Cash flow hedge reserve (equity)		2,245,103
Interest expense (income statement)	25,100	
Other operating income and expense		5,608

Cash flow hedge – change in fair value of the forward contract

Basis adjustment

Company C's accounting policy is that the gain on the hedging derivative is included in the carrying amount of the inventory acquired. The gain is reclassified to profit or loss when the inventory affects profit or loss (that is, on sale of the goods containing the hedged components or impairment of the inventory).

	Dr	Cr
Cash flow hedge reserve (equity)	5,230,826	
Inventory		5,230,826

Reclassification of gains recognised in equity into the carrying amount of the inventory acquired by Company C

Helpful hint

The 'basis adjustment' approach is not required. It can be used only if the hedged item is non-financial (for example, a forecast purchase of inventory) and only if its use is consistent with the Company's chosen accounting policy. If Company C's management had chosen not to adjust the carrying amount of the inventory acquired, the amount accumulated in the cash flow hedge reserve would have remained in equity until the inventory affects the income statement (for example, when it is sold or impaired).

---

14 Retrospective effectiveness test on 31 August 20X6

The spot EUR/SEK exchange rate is 8.15. Company C's management assesses the effectiveness of the hedge retrospectively. The same method is used as at 30 June 20X6. As required in Company C's risk management policies, the effectiveness test uses the dollar offset method on a cumulative basis.

	Hedged item Hypothetical derivative – spot component			Hedging instrument Spot component	
Notional amount	(25,000,000)	EUR	25,000,000	EUR	Notional amount
Spot rate at test date	8.1500		8.1500		Spot rate at test date
Notional amount in SEK	(203,750,000)	SEK	203,750,000	SEK	Notional amount in SEK
Discount factor $(1/(1.0403)^{\wedge}$ (61days/360))	0.9976		1.0000		Discount factor
FV of the EUR leg (spot) (A)	(203,269,558)	EUR	203,750,000	SEK	FV of the EUR leg (spot) (A)
Spot comp of notional at inception	192,250,000	SEK	(192,250,000)	SEK	Spot component of notional
Discount factor	0.9976		1.0000		Discount factor
FV of SEK leg (spot) (B)	191,796,675	SEK	(192,250,000)	SEK	FV of SEK leg (spot) (B)
(A-B) FV of the derivative (spot)	**(11,472,883)**	**SEK**	**11,500,000**	**SEK**	**(A-B) FV of the derivative (spot)**
Effectiveness	**-100.24%**				

Conclusion: the hedge has been highly effective for the period ended 31 August 20X6.

15   Accounting entries on 31 August 20X6

Translation of the trade payable at the spot rate

The trade payable is a monetary item denominated in a foreign currency that must be retranslated at the spot rate under IAS 21, with the resulting currency gain or loss recognised in profit or loss.

The calculation of the gain or loss is as follows:

Trade payable translated at 31 July at 7.90	197,500,000
Trade payable translated at 31 August at 8.15	203,750,000
Foreign exchange loss to be recognised in profit or loss	**6,250,000**

The accounting entry is as follows:

	Dr	Cr
Other operating income and expenses – foreign exchange loss	6,250,000	
Trade payable		6,250,000

To recognise the foreign exchange loss on retranslating the trade payable

All the criteria for hedge accounting are met as at 31 August 20X6. Cash flow hedge accounting can, therefore, be applied. The hedge is not however 100% effective; the amount recognised in other comprehensive income is therefore adjusted to the lesser of:

(a)   the cumulative change in the fair value of the spot component of the hedging instrument less the basis adjustment recognised in the previous period; and

(b)   the cumulative change in the fair value of the spot component of the hypothetical derivative (hedged item) less the basis adjustment recognised in the previous period.

	Derivative (full fair value)	Hedging instrument (spot component)	Hedged item hypothetical derivative (spot component)	Effective portion (recognised as basis adjustment)	Ineffective portion
31 Jul 20X6	4,826,851	5,243,612	(5,230,826)	5,230,826	12,786
31 Aug 20X6	11,062,500	11,500,000	(11,472,883)	11,472,883	27,117
Change	6,235,649	6,256,388	(6,242,057)	6,242,057	14,331

The difference between the full fair value of the forward contract and the amount deferred in equity is charged to the income statement.

The entry is as follows:

	Dr	Cr
Derivative (financial asset)	6,235,649	
Cash flow hedge reserve (equity)		6,242,057
Interest expense (income statement)	20,739	
Other operating income and expense		14,331

Cash flow hedge – change in fair value of the forward contract

Settlement of derivative

Under the terms of the forward contract, Company C receives EUR 25m (at 8.15 – SEK 203,750,000) and pays SEK 192,687,500. The difference is the fair value of the derivative (SEK 11,062,842).

The accounting entry is as follows:

	Dr	Cr
Cash in EUR	203,750,000	
Cash in SEK		192,687,500
Derivative (financial asset)		11,062,500

Settlement of the derivative in cash

Reclassification of gains and losses from equity to profit or loss

The amount deferred in equity is recycled to the income statement

	Dr	Cr
Other operating income and expenses – foreign exchange gain		6,242,057
Cash flow hedge reserve (equity)	6,242,057	

Reclassification of gains recognised in equity to profit or loss

Company C decides to keep the euro amount received in a euro account until payment of the invoice.

> **Helpful hint**
>
> Hedge accounting is not always necessary when a company is hedging the foreign currency risk arising from short-term monetary items such as foreign currency payables and receivables.
>
> A similar result to that achieved under hedge accounting would have been achieved had Company C de-designated the hedge relationship when the purchase was recognised, as:
>
> 1   the derivative, not being designated as a hedging instrument, would have been measured at fair value through profit or loss; and
>
> 2   the receivable, which is a monetary item, would have been revalued using the spot exchange rate at the balance sheet date.

16   Accounting entries on 31 October 20X6

The trade payable and the euro bank account are revalued using the closing rate (8.05).

	Dr	Cr
Trade payable	2,500,000	
Other operating income and expenses – foreign exchange gain		2,500,000
Euro bank account		2,500,000
Other operating income and expenses – foreign exchange gain	2,500,000	

Revaluation of trade payable and bank account (both EUR 25m)

Finally the trade payable is settled.

	Dr	Cr
Trade payable	201,250,000	
Euro bank account		201,250,000

Reclassification of gains recognised in equity to profit or loss

Summary of accounting entries

	Balance sheet				Income statement		
	Derivative instrument	Equity	Payable	Inventory	Bank account (SEK and EUR)	Interest expense	Other operating income and expense – foreign exchange gains and losses
1 Jan 20X5 No entry							
30 Jun 20X5 CFH accounting	(1,111,644)	983,818				127,826	
31/12/20X5 CFH accounting	2,347,763	(2,466,409)				122,371	(3,725)
30 Jun 20X6 CFH accounting	1,365,121	(1,503,132)				141,464	(3,453)
31 Jul 20X6 Purchase of inventory			(197,500,000)	197,500,000			
CFH accounting	2,225,611	(2,245,103)				25,100	(5,608)
Basis adjustment		5,230,826		(5,230,826)			
31 Aug 20X6 Foreign currency reval. of payable			(6,250,000)				6,250,000
CFH accounting	6,235,649	(6,242,057)				20,739	(14,331)
Reclassification		6,242,057					(6,242,057)
Settlement of derivative	(11,062,500)				11,062,500		
31/10/20X6 Revaluation			2,500,000				(2,500,000)
Settlement of payable			201,250,000				(201,250,000)

Net investment hedge in a foreign operation

Background and assumptions

Company K, a Swiss company with a CHF functional currency, has an Italian subsidiary, Company D, whose functional currency is EUR. Company K's reporting dates for its consolidated financial statements are 30 June and 31 December. The group's presentation currency is CHF.

On 1 January 20x5, Company K issues a two-year floating rate debt with the following characteristics:

Type	Issued debt
Principal amount	EUR 100m
Start date	1 January 20X5
Maturity date	31 December 20X6
Interest rate	Six-month EURIBOR
Settlement dates	30 June 20X5, 31 December 20X5, 30 June 20X6, 31 December 20X6

No transaction costs are incurred relating to the debt issuance. K's management has chosen to issue euro-denominated debt to hedge K's net investment in Company D. It wishes to reduce the consolidated balance sheet volatility arising from EUR/CHF fluctuations by designating the debt as a hedge of the net investment. On 1 January 20X5, the net investment in Company D is EUR 100m. It is not expected to fall below EUR 100m, as Company D has been a profitable company for many years and its forecasts for the next two years, as approved by Company K's board of directors, show it continuing to make material profits.

Exchange rates on various dates during the hedge relationship are as follows:

> **Helpful hint**
>
> A net investment in a foreign operation is the amount of the reporting entity's interest in the net assets of the operation, including goodwill. If the entity is financed through an inter-company loan that will not be repaid in the foreseeable future (quasi-equity), this loan is included in the net investment.
>
> A hedge of a net investment is a hedge of an accounting exposure (that is, the variability in equity arising from translating the net investment at different exchange rates).

Average exchange rates for the six-month periods during the hedge are as follows:

	1 Jan 20X5	30 Jun 20X5	31 Dec 20X5	30 Jun 20X6	31 Dec 20X6
EUR/CHF spot rate	1.5000	1.5800	1.6000	1.6200	1.6500
EUR/CHF forward rate	1.5667	1.6343	1.6364	1.6383	1.6500
Forward points	**0.0667**	**0.0543**	**0.0364**	**0.0183**	**0.0000**

		30 Jun 20X5	31 Dec 20X5	30 Jun 20X6	31 Dec 20X6
EUR/CHF average rate		1.5400	1.5900	1.6100	1.6400

Annual interest rates on various dates during the hedge are as follows:

	1 Jan 20X5	30 Jun 20X5	31 Dec 20X5	30 Jun 20X6	31 Dec 20X6
CHF interest rate	3.5500%	3.6200%	3.6500%	3.5750%	3.6450%
EUR interest rate	1.3505%	1.3500%	1.3750%	1.3250%	1.3550%

For the purpose of this illustration, the yield curve (that is, interest rate) at each reporting period end is assumed to remain the same through the term of the hedge designation (that is, the yield curve is flat at all times). This simplification does not have any impact on the effectiveness test in this example, as the reset dates of the loan coincide with the effectiveness testing date. With a non-flat yield curve, the calculation of the fair value of the variable rate debt will still give a fair value equal to the face value, as the variable coupons will be at market rate.

Extracts of the risk management policies for foreign currency risk

Background to the group

The group is an international retailer operating around the world, particularly in Western Europe (Switzerland, Italy and the UK) and the US. The biggest subsidiary is based in Italy.

Foreign currency risk

The group's presentation currency is CHF. Foreign currency risk arises from transactions denominated in foreign currencies and net investments in foreign operations.

Investments in foreign operations (translation foreign currency risk)

A foreign currency exposure arises from net investments in group entities whose functional currency differs from the group's presentation currency (CHF). The risk is defined as the risk of fluctuation in spot exchange rates between the functional currency of the net investments and the group's presentation currency. This will cause the amount of the net investment to vary. Such a risk may have a significant impact on the group's financial statements.

This translation risk does not give rise to a cash flow exposure. Its impact arises only from the translation of the net investment into the group's presentation currency. This procedure is required in preparing the group's consolidated financial statements.

Hedging instruments

The group uses derivatives (such as forward contracts and purchased options) and cash instruments (non-derivatives such as foreign currency borrowings) to hedge foreign currency risk. All derivatives must be entered into with counterparties with a credit rating of AA or higher.

Extracts of hedge effectiveness testing policies

Strategy 2C: Hedge of a net investment for foreign currency risk with a debt instrument.

Prospective effectiveness testing for net investment hedges

Prospective effectiveness testing should be performed at the inception of the hedge and at each reporting date. For hedges where the hedging instrument is a cash instrument, the hedge relationship is highly effective if the foreign currency gains and losses on the hedged item (net investment) that are attributable to the hedged risk (changes in spot exchange rates) are expected to be offset by the foreign currency gains and losses on the hedging instrument (cash instrument).

Prospective effectiveness testing must be performed by comparing the numerical effects of an upward shift in the benchmark exchange rate (EUR/CHF spot exchange rate) on both the value of the hedging instrument and the value of the hedged item.

- **The value of the hedging instrument:** when the hedging instrument is a cash instrument (for example, a debt instrument), this value is determined by discounting the future cash flows, including interest payments, on the debt and translating the result at the spot exchange rate. Accrued interest (if any) is excluded from the calculation.

- **The value of the net investment being hedged:** this is determined by translating the amount of the net investment into the group's presentation currency using the spot exchange rate.

This test should normally be performed using at least three currency scenarios. However, for hedges where the critical terms of the hedging instrument perfectly match the critical terms of the hedged item, one scenario is sufficient.

Retrospective effectiveness testing for net investment hedges

Retrospective effectiveness testing should be performed at each reporting date using the dollar offset method on a cumulative basis. The hedge is demonstrated to be effective under this method by comparing the cumulative foreign currency gains and losses on the hedging instrument with the cumulative foreign currency gains and losses on the net investment being hedged, and showing that it falls within the required range of 80%-125%.

- **Foreign currency gains and losses on the hedging instrument:** when the hedging instrument is a cash instrument (for example, a debt instrument), such foreign currency gains and losses are determined by discounting the future cash flows (using the current euro interest rate) on the debt and translating the result at the spot exchange rate. Accrued interest (if any) is excluded from the calculation.

■ **Foreign currency gains and losses on the net investment being hedged:** such gains and losses are determined by translating the amount of the net investment into the group's presentation currency using the spot exchange rate.

Hedge designation

Company K's hedge documentation is as follows:

1 Risk management objective and strategy

In order to comply with Company K's foreign currency risk management strategy, the foreign currency translation risk arising on the net investment in Company D is hedged.

2 Type of hedging relationship

Net investment hedge.

3 Nature of risk being hedged

In accordance with the group's risk management policies, the hedged risk is the risk of changes in the EUR/CHF spot exchange rate that will result in changes in the value of the group's net investment in Company D when translated into CHF. The risk is hedged from 1 January 20X5 to 31 December 20X7.

4 Identification of hedged item

The group's net investment in EUR in Company D on 1 January 20x5 is EUR 100m. EUR 100m of the net investment is designated as the hedged item.

(5) Identification of hedging instrument

Transaction number: reference number G0901Z in the treasury management system.

The hedging instrument is a two-year floating rate debt with the following characteristics:

Type	Issued debt
Principal amount	EUR 100m
Start date	1 January 20X5
Maturity date	31 December 20X6
Interest rate	Six-month EURIBOR
Settlement dates	30 June 20X5, 31 December 20X5, 30 June 20X6, 31 December 20X6

Hedge designation: the foreign currency exposure of debt G0901Z is designated as a hedge of the change in the value of the net investment identified in 4 above that is attributable to movements in the CHF/EUR spot rate.

6   Effectiveness testing

Effectiveness testing strategy 2C will be applied.

Description of prospective effectiveness testing

Dollar offset method, being the comparison of the numerical effects of a shift in the benchmark exchange rate (EUR/CHF spot exchange rate) on both the value of the hedging instrument and the value of the hedged item.

As permitted in the risk management policies, one scenario is used for assessing prospectively the effectiveness of the hedge relationship (a 10% upward shift of the EUR/CHF spot exchange rate), as the critical terms of the hedging instrument perfectly match the critical terms of the hedged item.

Frequency of testing: at inception of the hedge and then at each reporting date (30 June and 31 December).

Description of retrospective effectiveness testing

Dollar offset method, being the ratio of the cumulative foreign currency gains and losses on the debt (G0901Z), divided by the foreign currency gains and losses on the net investment being hedged.

Foreign currency gains and losses on the debt are the change in the present value of cash flows of the debt (interest and principal repayment) attributable to change in the EUR/CHF spot exchange rate.

Foreign currency gains and losses on the net investment being hedged are the change in the value of the net investment being hedged using the EUR/CHF spot exchange rate.

Frequency of testing: at every reporting date (30 June and 31 December) after inception of the hedge.

Effectiveness tests and accounting entries

1   Prospective effectiveness test on 1 January 20X5

At inception of the hedge, the forward EUR/CHF exchange rate is 1.5667 and the six-month EURIBOR is at 1.3505%. On that date, the spot EUR/CHF exchange rate is 1.5000.

Company K's management assesses the effectiveness of the hedge prospectively, as required by IAS 39. Based on the hedge documentation, the prospective effectiveness test consists of comparing the effects of a 10% shift of the EUR/CHF spot exchange rate on the net investment and the debt instrument.

Prospective effectiveness test on 1 January 20X5

Cash flows on the debt	30 Jun 20X5	31 Dec 20X5	30 Jun 20X6	31 Dec 20X6	Total
Expected cash flows at 1.3505% (EUR)	(675,250)	(675,250)	(675,250)	(100,675,250)	
Discount factor	0.99332	0.98653	0.97990	0.97344	
Discounted cash flows (EUR)	(670,736)	(666,153)	(661,675)	(98,001,436)	
EUR/CHF spot exchange rate	1.5000	1.5000	1.5000	1.5000	
Discounted cash flows (CHF)	**(1,006,104)**	**(999,229)**	**(992,513)**	**(147,002,154)**	**(150,000,000)**
Expected cash flows at 1.3505% (EUR)	(675,250)	(675,250)	(675,250)	(100,675,250)	
Discount factor	0.99332	0.98653	0.97990	0.97344	
Discounted cash flows (EUR)	(670,736)	(666,153)	(661,675)	(98,001,436)	
10% shift in EUR/ CHF spot exchange rate	1.6500	1.6500	1.6500	1.6500	
Discounted cash flows (CHF)	**(1,106,714)**	**(1,099,152)**	**(1,091,764)**	**(161,702,370)**	**(165,000,000)**
				Change	**(15,000,000)**
Net investment					
Net investment in EUR				100,000,000	
EUR/CHF spot exchange rate				1.5000	
Net investment in CHF				150,000,000	**150,000,000**
Net investment in EUR				100,000,000	
10% shift in EUR/ CHF spot exchange rate				1.6500	
Net investment in CHF				165,000,000	**165,000,000**
				Change	**15,000,000**
				Effectiveness	**100%**

Conclusion: the hedge is expected to be highly effective.

2   Entries on 1 January 20X5

The debt is recognised at the proceeds received by Company K, which represents its fair value on the issuance date. The debt is classified as other financial liabilities and will subsequently be measured at amortised cost.

	Dr	Cr
Cash	100,000,000	
Other financial liabilities – debt		100,000,000

Issuance at par of a EUR 100m two-year debt

3   Retrospective effectiveness test on 30 June 20X5

IAS 39 requires the effectiveness of a hedging relationship to be assessed retrospectively as a minimum at each reporting date. Based on Company K's risk management policies, the effectiveness of the hedge is assessed using the dollar offset method. The dollar offset method consists of comparing the effects of the change in EUR/CHF spot exchange rate on the hedged item (net investment) and the hedging instrument (cash instrument).

	30 Jun 20X5	31 Dec 20X5	30 Jun 20X6	31 Dec 20X6	Total
Cash flows on the debt					
Expected cash flows at 1.3505% (EUR)	(675,250)	(675,250)	(675,250)	(100,675,250)	
Discount factor	0.99332	0.98653	0.97990	0.97344	
Discounted cash flows (EUR)	(670,736)	(666,153)	(661,675)	(98,001,436)	
EUR/CHF spot exchange rate at inception	1.5000	1.5000	1.5000	1.5000	
Discounted cash flows (CHF)	(1,006,104)	(999,229)	(992,513)	(147,002,154)	**(150,000,000)**
Expected cash flows at 1.3500% (EUR)		(675,000)	(675,000)	(100,675,000)	
Discount factor		0.99317	0.98650	0.98002	
Discounted cash flows (EUR)		(670,389)	(665,885)	(98,663,726)	
EUR/CHF spot exchange rate at testing date		1.5800	1.5800	1.5800	
Discounted cash flows (CHF)		(1,059,215)	(1,052,098)	(155,888,687)	**(158,000,000)**
				Change	**(8,000,000)**

Net investment

Net investment in EUR	100,000,000	
EUR/CHF spot exchange rate at inception	1.5000	
Net investment in CHF at inception	150,000,000	**150,000,000**
Net investment in EUR	100,000,000	
EUR/CHF spot exchange rate at testing date	1.5800	
Net investment in CHF at testing date	158,000,000	**158,000,000**
	Change	**8,000,000**
	Effectiveness	**100%**

Conclusion: the hedge has been highly effective for the period ended 30 June 20X5.

Helpful hint

In practice, both the prospective and retrospective effectiveness tests may be performed by:

1   translating the principal amount of the debt into CHF using the relevant EUR/CHF spot exchange rates (for the retrospective test, the rates at the beginning and end of the period); and

2   comparing the difference with the foreign currency gains and losses on the net investment.

This 'short cut' gives the same results, as shown below.

Principal amount of the debt (in EUR)	EUR 100,000,000
EUR/CHF spot exchange rate at inception	1.5000
	CHF 150,000,000
Principal amount of the debt (in EUR)	EUR 100,000,000
EUR/CHF spot exchange rate at testing date	1.5800
	CHF 158,000,000
Difference (+ gain/-loss):	**CHF (8,000,000)**
Foreign currency gain on the net investment (see table above)	**CHF 8,000,000**
Effectiveness	**100%**

3   Accounting entries on 30 June 20X5

Recognition of interest on the debt

Interest for the first six months (EUR 675,000) is paid on 30 June. The payment is translated using the spot rate on 30 June. The interest expense is translated at the average rate for the six month period as interest accrues over time. The difference in translation rates gives rise to a loss that is recorded as 'other operating income and expense'.

	Dr	Cr
Finance costs – interest expense	1,039,500	
Other operating income and expense	27,000	
Cash		1,066,500

Payment of interest on the debt at 1.35% for six months

Net investment hedge accounting

As the hedge has been fully effective for the period, the entire foreign currency loss on the debt is recognised in other comprehensive income, and there is no ineffectiveness to recognise in profit or loss.

	Dr	Cr
Translation reserve (equity)	8,000,000	
Debt instrument		8,000,000

Net investment hedge

> **Helpful hint**
>
> A gain of CHF 8 million will also be recognised in the translation reserve from the translation of the hedged net investment in the Italian subsidiary. As a result, the net change in the translation reserve for the six months ended 30 June 20X5 is nil.

4   Prospective effectiveness test on 30 June 20X5

The same method is used as at the inception of the hedge.

	30 Jun 20X5	31 Dec 20X5	30 Jun 20X6	31 Dec 20X6	Total
Cash flows on the debt					
Expected cash flows at 1.3505% (EUR)	(675,250)	(675,250)	(675,250)	(100,675,250)	
Discount factor	0.99332	0.98653	0.97990	0.97344	
Discounted cash flows (EUR)	(670,736)	(666,153)	(661,675)	(98,001,436)	
EUR/CHF spot exchange rate	1.5800	1.5800	1.5800	1.5800	
Discounted cash flows (CHF)	(1,059,763)	(1,052,522)	(1,045,447)	(154,842,269)	**(158,000,000)**
Expected cash flows at 1.3500% (EUR)		(675,000)	(675,000)	(100,675,000)	
Discount factor		0.99317	0.98650	0.98002	
Discounted cash flows (EUR)		(670,389)	(665,885)	(98,663,726)	
10% shift in EUR/CHF spot exchange rate		1.7380	1.7380	1.7380	
Discounted cash flows (CHF)		(1,165,137)	(1,157,308)	(171,477,556)	**(173,800,000)**
				Change	**(15,800,000)**
Net investment					
Net investment in EUR				100,000,000	
EUR/CHF spot exchange rate				1.5800	
Net investment in CHF				158,000,000	**158,000,000**
Net investment in EUR				100,000,000	
10% shift in EUR/CHF spot exchange rate				1.7380	
Net investment in CHF				173,800,000	**173,800,000**
				Change	**15,800,000**
				Effectiveness	**100%**

Conclusion: the hedge is expected to be highly effective.

5   Retrospective effectiveness test on 31 December 20X5

The forward EUR/CHF exchange rate is 1.6364 and the six-month EURIBOR is at 1.3750%. On that date, the spot EUR/CHF exchange rate is 1.6000. The method used is the same as at 1 January 20X5.

Retrospective effectiveness test on 31 December 20X5

	30 Jun 20X5	31 Dec 20X5	30 Jun 20X6	31 Dec 20X6	Total
Cash flows on the debt					
Expected cash flows at 1.3505% (EUR)	(675,250)	(675,250)	(675,250)	(100,675,250)	
Discount factor	0.99332	0.98653	0.97990	0.97344	
Discounted cash flows (EUR)	(670,736)	(666,153)	(661,675)	(98,001,436)	
EUR/CHF spot exchange rate at inception	1.5000	1.5000	1.5000	1.5000	
Discounted cash flows clean (CHF)	(1,006,104)	(999,229)	(992,513)	(147,002,154)	**(150,000,000)**
Expected cash flows at 1.3750%			(687,500)	(100,687,500)	
Discount factor			0.99316	0.98639	
Discounted cash flows (EUR)			(682,796)	(99,317,205)	
EUR/CHF spot exchange rate at testing date			1.6000	1.6000	
Discounted cash flows clean (CHF)			(1,092,473)	(158,907,527)	**(160,000,000)**
				Change	**(10,000,000)**
Net investment					
Net investment in EUR				100,000,000	
EUR/CHF spot exchange rate at inception				1.5000	
Net investment in CHF at inception				150,000,000	**150,000,000**
Net investment in EUR				100,000,000	
EUR/CHF spot exchange rate at testing date				1.6000	
Net investment in CHF at testing date				160,000,000	**160,000,000**
				Change	**10,000,000**
				Effectiveness	**100%**

Conclusion: the hedge has been highly effective for the period ended 31 December 20X5.

6 Accounting entries on 31 December 20X5

Recognition of interest on the debt

Interest for six months (EUR 687,500) is paid on 31 December. The payment is translated using the spot rate on 31 December. The interest expense is translated at the average rate for the six-month period as interest accrues over time. The difference in translation rates gives rise to a loss that is recorded as 'other operating income and expense'.

	Dr	Cr
Finance costs – interest expense	1,093,125	
Other operating income and expense	6,875	
Cash		1,100,000

Payment of interest on the debt at 1.375% for six months

Net investment hedge accounting

As the hedge has been fully effective for the period, the entire foreign exchange loss on the debt is recognised in other comprehensive income and there is no ineffectiveness to recognise in profit or loss.

	Dr	Cr
Translation reserve (equity)	2,000,000	
Debt instrument		2,000,000

Net investment hedge

Cumulative foreign exchange loss on the debt on 31 December 20X5	(10,000,000)
Cumulative foreign exchange loss on the debt on 30 June 20X5	(8,000,000)
Foreign exchange loss to be recognised in translation reserve	**(2,000,000)**

7 Prospective effectiveness test on 31 December 20X5

The same method is used as at the inception of the hedge.

Prospective effectiveness test on 31 December 20X5

	30 Jun 20X5	31 Dec 20X5	30 Jun 20X6	31 Dec 20X6	Total
Cash flows on the debt					
Expected cash flows at 1.3505% (EUR)	(675,250)	(675,250)	(675,250)	(100,675,250)	
Discount factor	0.99332	0.98653	0.97990	0.97344	
Discounted cash flows (EUR)	(670,736)	(666,153)	(661,675)	(98,001,436)	
EUR/CHF spot exchange rate	1.6000	1.6000	1.6000	1.6000	
Discounted cash flows (CHF)	(1,073,178)	(1,065,845)	(1,058,680)	(156,802,298)	**(160,000,000)**
Expected cash flows at 1.3750% (EUR)			(687,500)	(100,687,500)	
Discount factor			0.99316	0.98639	
Discounted cash flows (EUR)			(682,796)	(99,317,205)	
10% shift in EUR/CHF spot exchange rate			1.7600	1.7600	
Discounted cash flows (CHF)			(1,201,720)	(174,798,280)	**(176,000,000)**
				Change	**(16,000,000)**
Net investment					
Net investment in EUR				100,000,000	
EUR/CHF spot exchange rate				1.6000	
Net investment in CHF				160,000,000	**160,000,000**
Net investment in EUR				100,000,000	
10% shift in EUR/CHF spot exchange rate				1.7600	
Net investment in CHF				176,000,000	**176,000,000**
				Change	**16,000,000**
				Effectiveness	**100%**

Conclusion: the hedge is expected to be highly effective.

8 Retrospective effectiveness test on 30 June 20X6

On 30 June 20X6, Company K's net investment has decreased to EUR 98.5m because Company D made unexpected losses. The spot EUR/CHF exchange rate on 30 June 20X6 is 1.6200 and the six-month EURIBOR is 1.3250%. Effectiveness is tested using the same method as is described on 31 December 20X5.

Retrospective effectiveness test on 30 June 20X6

	30 Jun 20X5	31 Dec 20X5	30 Jun 20X6	31 Dec 20X6	Total
Cash flows on the debt					
Expected cash flows at 1.3505% (EUR)	(675,250)	(675,250)	(675,250)	(100,675,250)	
Discount factor	0.99332	0.98653	0.97990	0.97344	
Discounted cash flows (EUR)	(670,736)	(666,153)	(661,675)	(98,001,436)	
EUR/CHF spot exchange rate at inception	1.5000	1.5000	1.5000	1.5000	
Discounted cash flows clean (CHF)	(1,006,104)	(999,229)	(992,513)	(147,002,154)	**(150,000,000)**
Expected cash flows at 1.3250%				(100,662,500)	
Discount factor				0.99342	
Discounted cash flows (EUR)				(100,000,000)	
EUR/CHF spot exchange rate at testing date				1.6200	
Discounted cash flows clean (CHF)				(162,000,000)	**(162,000,000)**
				Change	**(12,000,000)**

Net investment

Net investment in EUR	98,500,000	
EUR/CHF spot exchange rate at inception	1.5000	
Net investment in CHF at inception	147,750,000	**147,750,000**
Net investment in EUR	98,500,000	
EUR/CHF spot exchange rate at testing date	1.6200	
Net investment in CHF	159,570,000	**159,570,000**
	Change	**11,820,000**
	Effectiveness	**101.5%**

As illustrated above, the hedge is no longer fully effective because the carrying value of the hedged net investment is lower than the principal amount of the hedging debt instrument. However, the hedge remains highly effective.

Conclusion: the hedge has been highly effective for the period ended 30 June 20X6.

9   Accounting entries on 30 June 20X6

Recognition of interest on the debt

Interest for six months (EUR 662,500) is paid on 30 June. The payment is translated using the spot rate on 30 June. The interest expense is translated at the average rate for the six month period as interest accrues over time. The difference in translation rates gives rise to a loss that is recorded as 'other operating income and expense'.

	Dr	Cr
Finance costs – interest expense	1,066,625	
Other operating income and expense	6,625	
Cash		1,073,250

Payment of interest on the debt at 1.325% for six months

Net investment hedge accounting

As the hedge has not been fully effective for the period, ineffectiveness must be recognised in profit or loss.

Cumulative foreign exchange loss on the debt on 30 June 20X6	(12,000,000)
Cumulative foreign exchange loss on the debt on 31 December 20X5	(10,000,000)
Foreign exchange loss on the debt for the period (A)	**(2,000,000)**
Translation reserve balance on 30 June 20X6	11,820,000
Translation reserve balance on 31 December 20X5	10,000,000
Difference (B)	**1,820,000**

As the change in the hedging instrument (the debt) is greater than the change in the hedged item (the net investment), it is not fully absorbed by the hedged item. The difference must therefore be recognised in the income statement as ineffectiveness.

	Dr	**Cr**
Other operating income and expense (A + B)	180,000	
Translation reserve (equity)	1,820,000	
Debt instrument		2,000,000

Net investment hedge

10   Prospective effectiveness test on 30 June 20X6

The same method is used as at the inception of the hedge. In addition, Company K's management does not expect its Italian subsidiary to make further losses for the remaining life of the hedge (until 31 December 20X6).

Prospective effectiveness test on 30 June 20X6

	30 Jun 20X5	31 Dec 20X5	30 Jun 20X6	31 Dec 20X6	Total
Cash flows on the debt					
Expected cash flows at 1.3505% (EUR)	(675,250)	(675,250)	(675,250)	(100,675,250)	
Discount factor	0.99332	0.98653	0.97990	0.97344	
Discounted cash flows (EUR)	(670,736)	(666,153)	(661,675)	(98,001,436)	
EUR/CHF spot exchange rate	1.6200	1.6200	1.6200	1.6200	
Discounted cash flows (CHF)	(1,086,592)	(1,079,168)	(1,071,914)	(158,762,326)	**(162,000,000)**
Expected cash flows at 1.3250% (EUR)				(100,662,500)	
Discount factor				0.99342	
Discounted cash flows (EUR)				(100,000,000)	
10% shift in EUR/CHF spot exchange rate				1.7820	
Discounted cash flows (CHF)				(178,200,000)	**(178,200,000)**
				Change	**(16,200,000)**
Net investment					
Net investment in EUR				98,500,000	
EUR/CHF spot exchange rate				1.6200	
Net investment in CHF				159,570,000	**159,570,000**
Net investment in EUR				98,500,000	
10% shift in EUR/CHF spot exchange rate				1.7820	
Net investment in CHF				175,527,000	**175,527,000**
				Change	**15,957,000**
				Effectiveness	**101.5%**

Conclusion: the hedge is expected to be highly effective, although some ineffectiveness is expected because the carrying value of the hedged net investment is smaller than the principal amount of the hedging debt instrument.

Helpful hint

This ineffectiveness could be avoided by re-designating the hedge, so that the hedging instrument is designated as 98.5% of the debt instrument (that is, an amount that matches the reduced net investment). In this example, in which the losses are relatively small, such re-designation would make no difference to the accounting entries, as the hedge remains highly effective. However, had the losses been so big as to cause the hedge to fail the effectiveness test, re-designating the hedge in this way may allow the company to apply hedge accounting for future periods.

Helpful hint

What will happen if the hedged net investment is sold? If Company D is sold or otherwise disposed of, the hedging gains or losses on the debt previously accumulated in the translation reserve (equity) will be transferred to profit or loss as part of the gain or loss on disposal.

Summary of accounting entities

	Balance sheet		Income statement		
				Other	
			Translation	operating	
			reserve	income &	
	Debt instrument	Cash	(equity)	expense	Finance cost
01 Jan 20X5					
Recognition of the debt	(100,000,000)	100,000,000			
30 Jun 20X5					
Interest on the debt		(1,066,500)		27,000	1,039,500
Debt re-translation	(8,000,000)		8,000,000		
31 Dec 20X5					
Interest on the debt		(1,100,000)		6,875	1,093,125
Debt re-translation	(2,000,000)		2,000,000		
30 Jun 20X6					
Interest on the debt		(1,073,250)		6,625	1,066,625
Debt re-translation	(2,000,000)		1,820,000	180,000	

6.9 – Presentation and disclosure

6.9 – Presentation and disclosure

Presentation of financial instruments

6.9.1 This chapter deals with two aspects of presentation of financial instruments: presentation of items as current or non-current (IAS 1), and the principles relating to offsetting (IAS 32). It also deals in detail with the disclosure of financial instruments (IFRS 7). Consideration of the IAS 32 requirements to present items as either financial liabilities or equity is in chapter 6.5.

6.9.2 The principles for presenting financial and other assets and liabilities, and any related income and expense, are set out in IAS 1. This standard's requirements are considered in chapter 4. The paragraphs that follow consider only the presentation of financial assets and liabilities as current or non-current.

Presentation as current or non-current

6.9.3 IAS 1 states that an entity should present current and non-current assets, and current and non-current liabilities, as separate classifications on the face of the balance sheet, except when a presentation based on liquidity provides information that is reliable and is more relevant. When that exception applies, all assets and liabilities should be presented broadly in order of liquidity. [IAS 1 para 60].

Current and non-current assets

6.9.4 Where an entity presents assets and liabilities as either current or non-current, it should classify an asset as current when:

- it expects to realise the asset, or intends to sell or consume it in its normal operating cycle;

- it holds the asset primarily for the purpose of trading;

- it expects to realise the asset within 12 months after the reporting period; or

- the asset is cash or a cash equivalent (as defined in IAS 7), unless it is restricted from being exchanged or used to settle a liability for at least 12 months after the reporting period.

[IAS 1 para 66].

6.9.5 Applying the above definition, it could be argued that financial assets classified as held for trading in accordance with IAS 39 should be presented as current assets. Similarly, trading derivative assets should also be presented as current assets.

6.9.6 However, paragraph 68 of IAS 1 clarifies that some rather than all financial assets and liabilities classified as held for trading are current assets and liabilities respectively. Non-hedging derivatives are not required to be classified as current simply because they fall within the 'held for trading' category in IAS 39. Rather, the requirements of IAS 1 referred to above should be applied in determining classification. This means that financial assets, including portions of financial assets expected to be realised within 12 months of the balance sheet date, should only be presented as current assets if realisation within 12 months is expected. Otherwise they should be classified as non-current. Financial liabilities should be presented as current if they meet the criteria in paragraph 69 of IAS 1, see also paragraph 6.9.8 below.

6.9.7 The treatment of hedging derivatives will be similar. Where a portion of a financial asset is expected to be realised within 12 months of the balance sheet date, that portion should be presented as a current asset; the remainder of the financial asset should be shown as a non-current asset. This suggests that hedging derivatives should be split into current and non-current portions. However, as an alternative, the full fair value of hedging derivatives could be classified as current if the hedge relationships are for less than 12 months and as non-current if those relationships are for more than 12 months.

Current and non-current liabilities

6.9.8 Where an entity presents assets and liabilities as either current or non-current, the entity should classify a liability as current when:

■ it expects to settle the liability in its normal operating cycle;

■ it holds the liability primarily for the purpose of trading;

■ the liability is due to be settled within twelve months after the reporting period; or

■ the entity does not have an unconditional right to defer settlement of the liability for at least twelve months after the reporting period.

[IAS 1 para 69].

6.9.9 Under IAS 32, the equity and liability components of financial instruments must be classified separately as financial liabilities, financial assets or equity instruments. [IAS 32 para 28]. The liability component of financial instruments should be classified as current or non-current, depending on the terms of the contract. Similar to financial assets, where a portion of a financial liability (including a hedging derivative) is expected to be settled within 12 months of the balance sheet date, or settlement cannot be deferred for at least 12 months after the balance sheet date, that portion should be presented as a current liability; the remainder should be presented as a non-current liability.

6.9.10 In particular a question arises whether the liability component of a convertible financial instrument should be presented as current or non-current, when the instrument is convertible to equity at any time within the next 12 months, but if not converted, is repayable in cash only beyond 12 months. Such instruments would have an equity component, being the holders' right to convert the instrument into a fixed number of equity instruments of the issuer any time before the maturity date; and a liability component, being the entity's obligation to deliver cash to holders at the maturity date, which is more than one year after the balance sheet date.

6.9.11 The 2009 annual improvements clarified that conversion features that are at the holder's discretion do not impact the classification of the liability component of a convertible instrument. [IAS 1 para 69 (d)]. The liability component of the convertible debt should be classified as non-current when repayable in more than 12 months and the components of an instrument that are classified as equity should be ignored. In the case of a convertible instrument, ignoring the conversion option leaves a debt component that is not re-payable within 12 months. Ignoring any equity components when classifying the liability component reflects that the equity components are not part of the liability for accounting purposes. Any equity components are accounted for in the same way as if they had been issued as separate instruments. It follows that the presentation should be the same as if they had been issued as separate instruments.

6.9.12 In contrast, consider puttable debt that is puttable by the holder within the next 12 months but, if not put, is repayable only beyond 12 months. In this case, the puttable debt should be classified in its entirety as current, irrespective of whether IAS 39 requires the put option to be accounted for as a separated embedded derivative and, if it does, of whether the host debt contract is reported in a separate balance sheet line item from the embedded derivative. This reflects that the put option could cause the entire instrument to be settled in a manner that is regarded as a liability under IAS 32.

6.9.13 The presentation of financial liabilities as current or non-current would take account of similar considerations to financial assets (see para 6.9.5 above). However, IAS 1 provides additional guidance for financial liabilities that have been renegotiated or refinanced. Specifically, the standard requires that a financial liability should be presented as current when it is due to be settled within 12 months after the balance sheet date, even if:

- the original term was for a period longer than 12 months; and

- an agreement to refinance, or to reschedule payments, on a long-term basis is completed after the balance sheet date and before the financial statements are authorised for issue.

[IAS 1 para 72].

6.9.14 The current or non-current classification of financial liabilities is governed by the condition of those liabilities at the balance sheet date. Where rescheduling or refinancing is at the lender's discretion, and it occurs after the balance sheet date, it does not alter the liability's condition at that date. Accordingly, it is regarded as a non-adjusting post balance sheet event and it is not taken into account in determining the current/non-current classification of the debt. On the other hand where the refinancing or rescheduling is at the entity's discretion and the entity can elect to roll over an obligation for at least one year after the balance sheet date, the obligation is classified as non-current, even if it would otherwise be due within a shorter period. [IAS 1 para 73]. However, if the entity expects to settle the obligation within 12 months, despite having the discretion to refinance for a longer period, then the debt should be classified as current.

Example – rolling over bank facilities

A company has entered into a facility arrangement with a bank. It has a committed facility that the bank cannot cancel unilaterally and the scheduled maturity of this facility is 3 years from the balance sheet date. The company has drawn down funds on this facility and these funds are due to be repaid 6 months after the balance sheet date. The company intends to roll over this debt through the three year facility arrangement. How should this borrowing be shown in the company's balance sheet?

Would the answer be different if the facility and existing loan were with different banks?

The borrowing should be shown as non-current. Although the loan is due for repayment within six months of the balance sheet date, the company is entitled to 'rollover' this borrowing into a 'new loan'. The substance is, therefore, that the debt is not repayable until 3 years after the balance sheet date when the committed facility expires. In addition, the entity expects to rollover the debt, so does not expect to repay it within 12 months.

The position would be different if the facility was with a different bank or if the loan was in the form of commercial paper. In the first case, the company would have a loan repayable in six months, but would be entitled to take out a new loan to settle its existing debt. These two loans are separate and the new loan is not, either in substance or in fact, an extension of the existing. Similarly if the loan was in the form of commercial paper, which typically has a maturity of 90 to 180 days, it would be classified as a current liability as it is likely that the backup facility would be provided by a different bank.

6.9.15 It is common practice for financial institutions to include borrowing covenants in the terms of loans. Under these borrowing covenants a loan which would otherwise be long-term in nature becomes immediately repayable if certain items related to the borrower's financial condition are breached. Typically, these items are measures of liquidity or solvency based on ratios derived from the entity's financial statements. Where the borrower has breached the borrowing covenant by the balance sheet date and the lender agrees after the balance sheet date but before authorisation of the financial statements not to require immediate repayment of the loan, the agreement of the lender is regarded as a non-adjusting post balance sheet event. Since, at the year end, the agreement of the lender had not been obtained, the condition of the borrowing at the balance sheet date was that it was immediately repayable and should, therefore, be shown as a current liability. [IAS 1 para 74]. An example of disclosure of a breach of covenant disclosed in an interim report and events subsequent to the interim reporting date is given in Table 6.9.1.

Table 6.9.1 – Breach of covenant resulting in loans restated as current at period end, post the balance sheet refinancing

First Technology plc – Interim report – 31 October 2005

14. Bank overdrafts and loans

	Six months ended 31st October 2005 £'m	Six months ended 31st October 2004 £'m	Year ended 30th April 2005 £'m
Bank overdrafts	0.3	2.8	1.0
Bank loans	112.4	111.4	105.3
	112.7	114.2	106.3
Repayable:			
On demand or within one year	112.7	7.9	6.2
In the second year	–	48.9	47.0
In the third year	–	8.1	7.8
In the fourth year	–	8.1	7.8
In the fifth year	–	41.2	37.5
	112.7	114.2	106.3
Less: Amount due for settlement within 12 months (shown under current liabilities)	(112.7)	(7.9)	(6.2)
Amounts due for settlement after more than 12 months	–	106.3	100.1

The Group's principal source of debt at 31st October 2005 was a multi-currency syndicated bank loan ('the Facilities') entered into with a group of seven banks in May 2004 in connection with the Group's offer for BWT. The Facilities comprised three tranches: a US$75 million revolving credit facility; a term loan of up to US$75 million and a US$100 million revolving credit facility. The Facilities were repayable between May 2006 and May 2009. The Facilities were unsecured and initially carried interest at a margin of 1.5% over LIBOR (or EURIBOR for amounts advanced in Euros), plus mandatory costs. The applicable margin was variable (ranging from a minimum of 0.875% up to a maximum of 1.75%) according to the ratio of consolidated net borrowings to EBITDA.

The Facilities were subject to three financial covenants, which were tested quarterly. On 17th August 2005, First Technology PLC informed its bankers that it had failed to meet one of these covenants with respect to the test for the period ended 26th July 2005. As a result of the covenant breach, the Facilities technically became repayable on demand.

On 12th December 2005, the Group signed an agreement for a new bank loan ('the new Facility') with its two principal bankers, HSBC Bank plc and The Royal Bank of Scotland plc, the proceeds of which are being used to repay the existing Facilities. The new Facility comprises two tranches: a US$80 million revolving credit facility and a US$140 million term loan, each available until December 2006. Both tranches, under certain circumstances, can be extended at the Company's option for a further twelve months to December 2007. The new Facility carries interest at a margin of 1.5% over LIBOR, plus mandatory costs. The new Facility is unsecured, although certain of First Technology PLC's wholly-owned subsidiaries have given guarantees with respect to First Technology PLC's obligations under the agreement. However, in the event that the offer announced on 19th December, or any other offer, for the entire issued share capital of the Company does not become wholly unconditional or that the Company has not completed an equity issue raising proceeds of at least £40 million and used such amount to repay the new Facility, the Company will be required to give security by 30th September 2006. Any net proceeds of an equity issue must be applied to repay the new Facility. If the amount prepaid is more than £40 million, the Company has the option to extend the new Facility for an additional one year term. Under all circumstances, the Company retains the flexibility to re-finance this new Facility.

In July 2004, First Technology PLC entered into an interest rate swap to fix the rate of interest that it would pay under the US$75 million term loan tranche of the syndicated loan. The interest rate swap fixed for the whole term the rate of interest at 3.605% plus the applicable margin for this element of the Group's debt. This swap is now being used to fix the rate of interest payable under a proportion of the new Facility.

6.9.16 However, following a breach of a borrowing covenant, lenders often agree to a period of grace during which the borrower agrees to rectify the breach. The lender agrees not to demand repayment during this time but, if the breach is not rectified, the debt would become immediately repayable at the end of the period of grace. If, before the balance sheet date, the lender has agreed to such a period of grace and that period ends at least 12 months after the balance sheet date, then the liability should be shown as non-current. [IAS 1 para 75]. If the breach of the borrowing covenant occurs after the balance date, then the liability would still be shown as non-current, unless the breach was so serious that the financial statements could no longer be prepared on a going concern basis. However, if the breach occurred before the balance sheet date, but the period of grace was not granted until after the balance sheet date, then the liability would be classified as current. The key to this approach is that the loan's presentation is dictated by the loan's condition as at the balance sheet date. Events after the balance sheet date may give evidence of that condition but they do not change it. This is consistent with IAS 10.

6.9.17 The standard's approach to breaches of borrowing covenants focuses on the legal rights of the entity rather than on the intentions of either of the parties to the loan. In dealing with situations where the entity has the discretion to roll over or refinance loans, the entity's expectations on the timing of settlement play a part in deciding the liability's classification. The liability's classification is, however, unaffected by the entity's intentions in the case of a breach of a loan agreement. If the entity breaches the loan agreement before the balance sheet date and the lender grants a period of grace of more than 12 months from the balance sheet date, then the loan is classified as non-current. In many cases, however, the period of grace will be a matter of negotiation between the borrower and the lender and will match the borrower's intentions in any event. In addition, breaches of loan agreements occur most often in entities that are experiencing financial difficulties and these entities are unlikely to wish to repay the loan earlier than required by the lender.

6.9.18 Although post balance sheet events may not alter the liability's classification, they may require disclosure as a non-adjusting event. IAS 1 paragraph 76 states that, in respect of loans classified as current liabilities, the following events must be disclosed as non-adjusting events in accordance with IAS 10, if they occur between the balance sheet date and the date of authorisation of the financial statements:

■ Refinancing on a long-term basis.

■ Rectification of a breach of a long-term loan agreement.

■ The receipt from the lender of a period of grace to rectify a breach of a long-term loan agreement ending at least 12 months after the balance sheet date.

6.9.19 IAS 1 does not specify any disclosures for non-adjusting post balance sheet events in respect of loans classified as non-current liabilities. However, IAS 10 requires that an entity should disclose the following for each material category of non-adjusting event after the balance sheet date:

■ The nature of the event.

■ An estimate of its financial effect or a statement that such an estimate cannot be made.

[IAS 10 para 21].

6.9.20 Further disclosure of defaults and breaches of loan agreements is required by IFRS 7 (see para 6.9.104 et seq below).

Offsetting a financial asset and a financial liability

General principle

6.9.21 A financial asset and a financial liability should be offset when, and only when, both of the following conditions are satisfied:

■ The entity currently has a legally enforceable right to set off the recognised amounts.

■ The entity intends either to settle on a net basis, or to realise the asset and settle the liability simultaneously.

[IAS 32 para 42].

6.9.22 Where the above offset conditions are satisfied, the entity has the right to receive or pay a single net amount and intends to do so, it has, in effect, only a single financial asset or financial liability. In that situation, the financial asset and the financial liability are presented on the balance sheet on a net basis. Where the offset conditions are not satisfied, the financial asset and the financial liability are presented separately from each other, consistently with their characteristics as the entity's resources or obligations. [IAS 32 para 43].

6.9.23 There can be situations where there are transfers of financial assets that do not qualify for derecognition and in such case the entity has to recognise an associated liability (see chapter 6.6). Such assets and liabilities cannot be offset because offsetting a recognised financial asset and a recognised financial liability and presenting the net amount is different from derecognising that financial asset or financial liability. Derecognising a financial instrument not only results in the removal of the previously recognised item from the balance sheet, but also may result in recognition of a gain or loss. Offsetting does not give rise to recognition of a gain or loss. [IAS 32 paras 42, 44]. In other words, when considering presentation of particular items, recognition, derecognition and measurement need to be considered first.

6.9.24 In December 2011, the IASB issued an amendment to the application guidance in IAS 32 to clarify some of the requirements for offsetting financial assets and financial liabilities in the statement of financial position. These clarifications are to be retrospectively applied, with an effective date for annual periods beginning on or after 1 January 2014. They are discussed in paragraphs 6.9.35 to 6.9.38. Also in this regard the IASB has published an amendment to IFRS 7 to enhance current offsetting disclosures. These additional disclosures, whose effective date is for annual periods beginning on or after 1 January 2013, are discussed from paragraph 6.9.86.

Legal right of set-off

6.9.25 IAS 32 defines a right of offset as *"a debtor's legal right, by contract or otherwise, to settle or otherwise eliminate all or a portion of an amount due to a creditor by applying against that amount an amount due from the creditor"*. Because the right of offset is essentially a legal right, the conditions supporting the right may vary from one legal jurisdiction to another and, therefore, the laws applicable to the relationships between the parties would need to be considered carefully. [IAS 32 para 45]. It follows that instruments such as receivables and payables with the same counterparty would be offset if a legal right of offset is agreed between the parties (and the entity intends to settle net or simultaneously).

6.9.26 In unusual circumstances, a debtor may have a legal right to apply an amount due from a third party against the amount due to a creditor provided that there is an agreement between the three parties that clearly establishes the debtor's right of set-off. [IAS 32 para 45].

Intention to settle on a net basis

6.9.27 It is clear from the general principle in paragraph 42 of IAS 32 (see also para 6.9.21 above) that, in order to achieve offset, an entity must have both the right to set off and the intention to do so. It is not sufficient to have one and not the other. Although the existence of an enforceable legal right of offset affects the entity's rights and obligations associated with a financial asset and a financial liability and may affect its exposure to credit and liquidity risk, it is, by itself, not a sufficient basis for offsetting. This is because, in the absence of an intention to exercise the right or to settle simultaneously, the amount and timing of the entity's future cash flows are not affected. However, if, in addition to the legal right, the entity clearly intends to exercise the right or to settle simultaneously, it is, in effect, exposed to a net amount, which reflects the timing of the expected future cash flows and the risks to which those cash flows are exposed. Similarly, an intention by one or both parties to settle on a net basis without the legal right to do so is not sufficient to justify offsetting because the rights and obligations associated with the individual financial asset and financial liability remain unaltered. [IAS 32 para 46].

6.9.28 An entity's intentions with respect to settlement of particular assets and liabilities may be influenced by its normal business practices, the requirements of the financial markets and other circumstances that may limit the ability to settle net or to settle simultaneously. When an entity has a right of offset, but does not intend to settle net or to realise the asset and settle the liability simultaneously, the effect of the right on the entity's credit risk exposure is disclosed in accordance with paragraph 6.9.141 below.

Simultaneous settlement

6.9.29 IAS 32 states that realisation of a financial asset and settlement of a financial liability are treated as simultaneous only when the transactions occur at the same moment. For example, the operation of a clearing house in an organised financial market or a face-to-face exchange will facilitate simultaneous settlement of two financial instruments. In these circumstances the cash flows are, in effect, equivalent to a single net amount and there is no exposure to credit or liquidity risk. In other circumstances, an entity may settle two instruments by receiving and paying separate amounts, becoming exposed to credit risk for the full amount of the asset or liquidity risk for the full amount of the liability. Such risk exposures, though brief, may be significant and therefore, net presentation is not appropriate. [IAS 32 para 48].

Situations where offset is usually inappropriate

6.9.30 IAS 32 sets out the following specific situations where the offset criteria in paragraph 6.9.21 above are not met.

■ Several different financial instruments are used to emulate the features of a single financial instrument (a 'synthetic instrument'). For example, a floating rate long-term debt combined with an interest rate swap that involves receiving floating payments and making fixed payments synthesises a fixed rate long-term debt. Each of the individual financial instruments that together constitute a 'synthetic instrument':

  ■ represents a contractual right or obligation with its own terms and conditions;

  ■ may be transferred or settled separately;

- is exposed to risks that may differ from the risks to which other financial instruments are exposed.

  Accordingly, when one financial instrument in a 'synthetic instrument' is an asset and another is a liability, they are not offset and presented on an entity's balance sheet on a net basis unless they meet the criteria for offsetting in paragraph 6.9.21 above.

- Financial assets and financial liabilities arise from financial instruments having the same primary risk exposure (for example, assets and liabilities within a portfolio of forward contracts or other derivative instruments), but involve different counterparties.

- Financial or other assets are pledged as collateral for non-recourse financial liabilities.

- Financial assets are set aside in trust by a debtor for the purpose of discharging an obligation without those assets having been accepted by the creditor in settlement of the obligation (for example, a sinking fund arrangement).

- Obligations incurred as a result of events giving rise to losses are expected to be recovered from a third party by virtue of a claim made under an insurance contract.

[IAS 32 para 49].

Master netting agreements

6.9.31　An entity that undertakes a number of financial instrument transactions with a single counterparty may enter into a 'master netting arrangement' with that counterparty. Such an arrangement creates a right of set-off that becomes enforceable and affects the realisation or settlement of individual financial assets and financial liabilities only following a specified event of default or in other circumstances not expected to arise in the normal course of business. These arrangements are commonly used by financial institutions to provide protection against loss in the event of bankruptcy or other circumstances that result in a counterparty being unable to meet its obligations. In the event of default on, or termination of, any one contract, the agreement provides for a single net settlement of all financial instruments covered by the agreement. [IAS 32 para 50].

6.9.32　Where an entity has entered into such an agreement, the agreement does not provide a basis for offsetting unless both of the criteria in paragraph 6.9.21 above are satisfied. This is because the entity's right of set off under such an agreement is conditional and enforceable only on the occurrence of some future event, usually a default of the counterparty. To offset a financial asset and a financial liability, an entity must have a currently legally enforceable right to set off the recognised amounts. Thus, such an arrangement does not meet the conditions for offsetting. [IAS 32 para 50].

Example – Various arrangements in a group for cash management purposes

Group X comprises various subsidiaries, each of which has a separate bank account with bank B. At any time, some of these accounts have a positive cash balance and others a negative (overdraft) balance. Group X operates the following arrangements for cash management purposes:

- Zero balancing (sometimes referred to as a cash sweep), under which the balances on a number of designated accounts are transferred to a single netting account on a regular basis, including at the balance sheet date. In some cases, the amounts transferred are repaid to the relevant subsidiaries shortly afterwards. This may be agreed contractually or at the choice of group management.

- Notional pooling, under which bank B calculates the net balance on a number of designated accounts with interest being earned or paid on the net amount. There may be a transfer of balances into a netting account, but this is not always at the balance sheet date.

Is group X able to offset cash and overdraft balances and hence present net balances in its consolidated balance sheet?

If balances are to be presented net, both of the criteria set out in paragraph 6.9.21 should be satisfied. Group X should have a currently legally enforceable right to set-off, which means that it is enforceable at anytime and not just in stipulated circumstances, such as an event of default or bankruptcy. Also, group X should demonstrate a clear prospect that there will be future settlement of cash flows with the same counterparty. A notional pooling for the purpose of calculating interest that does not involve settlement of the associated balances will not meet the requirements described in paragraph 6.9.27 above.

Assuming the agreement with bank B gives group X the necessary legally enforceable right to set off, its position will be as follows:

- Where there is zero balancing at the balance sheet date and no repayment of funding (reversal of cash flows) takes place, either on the following day or any day thereafter, group X has a single cash balance or overdraft at the balance sheet date and it is presented as such. The IAS 32 offsetting requirements are not relevant in this case.

- Where there is zero balancing at the balance sheet date, but the amounts transferred are repaid to the relevant subsidiaries shortly afterwards as a practice of group X, there would often be a single cash balance or overdraft at the balance sheet date that should be presented as such. Again, the IAS 32 offsetting requirements are not relevant in this case. However, there may be circumstances where group X has separate cash and overdraft balances, for example this might sometimes be the case where it has a contractual obligation to return the balances to the respective subsidiaries the following day. In such circumstances the cash and overdraft balances would generally be considered separately separate assets and liabilities under IFRS and the offsetting requirements of IAS 32 would be relevant. In this case, group X would not be able to demonstrate 'the intention to settle net' and, therefore, would not be able to present net balances in its consolidated balance sheet.

- Where there is zero balancing at the balance sheet date, but the amounts transferred are repaid to the relevant subsidiaries shortly afterwards as a practice of group X and without an existing contractual requirement to do so, group X will need to consider if at the balance sheet date the derecognition criteria on the zero balanced accounts have been met such that a single cash balance or overdraft indeed exists as a result of the zero balancing (similar to the first case above). This will depend on the facts and circumstances. If there is such a single cash balance or overdraft, it is presented as such, and the offsetting requirements are not relevant. If, on the other hand, there remain separate cash and overdraft balances, the offsetting requirements will be relevant. In this case, group X would not be able to demonstrate 'the intention to settle net' and therefore would not be able to present net balances in its consolidated balance sheet.

- Where there is notional pooling, but no physical transfer of balances to one account, group X will not be able to demonstrate 'the intention to settle net', as the arrangement does not actually involve net cash settlement. Accordingly, the balances should be presented gross.

- Where there is notional pooling and there is regular net cash settlement of the accounts, net presentation is appropriate. This will not be affected by the fact that actual settlement of the net position may not coincide with the balance sheet date, as long as group X can clearly demonstrate the intention to settle net through a regular practice of net cash settlement throughout the year.

Note that arrangements such as those described above can be complex; each arrangement should be viewed in light of its specific facts and circumstances. Further disclosure of gross balances may be necessary if the amount at the balance sheet date does not reflect normal cash balances throughout the year.

6.9.33 When financial assets and financial liabilities subject to a master netting arrangement are not offset, the effect of the arrangement on an entity's exposure to credit risk is disclosed in accordance with paragraph 6.9.141 below.

6.9.34 A question might arise whether cash collateral posted (for example, on a derivative) should be netted with a balance sheet position. For example, an entity may have entered into a derivative with a bank or clearing house. To reduce credit risk, the two entities may have agreed to post cash collateral periodically with each other equal to the fair value of the derivative. The posting of the collateral does not result in legal settlement of the outstanding balance. However, the terms of the collateral agreement are that the collateral will be used to settle the derivative as and when payments are due (as well as on a default or bankruptcy of either party) and both entities intend to settle this way. If this is the case, the entity will have a legally enforceable right to set off the derivative and the collateral, and will intend to settle net. If market prices do not change, no further cash flows will arise. Any changes in the collateral balance post balance sheet date arise as a result of future events and are not relevant to the balance sheet date assessment. The offsetting requirements in IAS 32 are therefore met, and the collateral should be offset.

Amendments to offsetting financial assets and financial liabilities

6.9.35   As discussed in paragraph 6.9.24 the IASB has amended IAS 32 to clarify its requirements for offsetting financial instruments. The clarification guidance as discussed below applies to accounting periods beginning on or after 1 January 2014 with retrospective application.

6.9.35.1   The amendments do not change the current offsetting model in IAS 32, which requires an entity to offset a financial asset and financial liability in the statement of financial position only when two conditions are met: first, the entity currently has a legally enforceable right of set-off; and secondly, it intends either to settle the asset and liability on a net basis or to realise the asset and settle the liability simultaneously.

6.9.35.2   While the current offsetting model does not change, the application guidance is now more detailed. This may result in changes for individual entities depending on how they had interpreted the previous guidance. As regards the first condition, the amendments in paragraph AG38B of IAS 32 clarify that the right of set-off:

- must be available today – that is, it is not contingent on a future event;

- must be legally enforceable in all of the normal course of business, in the event of default, and in the event of insolvency or bankruptcy; and

- must be legally enforceable for both entity and all counterparties.

6.9.35.3   The application guidance in paragraph AG38C of IAS 32 explains that the nature and extent of the right of set-off, including any conditions attached to its exercise and whether it would remain in the event of default or bankruptcy, may vary from one legal jurisdiction to another. It cannot therefore be assumed that the right of set-off is automatically available outside of the normal course of business. For example, the bankruptcy or insolvency laws of a jurisdiction might prohibit or restrict the right of set-off in the event of bankruptcy or insolvency. Entities will therefore need to consider the laws that apply to the relationships between the parties (including the laws that govern the contract, defaults or bankruptcies) to ascertain whether the right of set-off is enforceable in the normal course of business, the event of default and the insolvency or bankruptcy of any of the parties (including the entity itself).

6.9.35.4   Paragraph AG38E of IAS 32 clarifies the second condition for offset (that the entity "*intends to either settle on a net basis or to realise the asset and settle the liability simultaneously*") – for example, when balances are cleared through clearing houses or similar settlement systems. The entity might have a right to settle net, but it might still realise the asset and settle the liability separately. If the entity can settle amounts in such a way that the outcome is in effect equivalent to net settlement, the entity will meet the second criterion. Paragraph AG38F of IAS 32 states that this will occur only if the gross settlement mechanism has features that eliminate or result in insignificant credit and liquidity risk, and that will process receivables and payables in a single settlement process or cycle. This would then be effectively equivalent to net settlement and would satisfy the IAS 32 criterion. The standard gives an example of characteristics that a gross settlement system could have to meet a net settlement equivalent in paragraph 42(b) of IAS 32. [IAS 32 para AG 38F].

6.9.35.5   Master netting agreements (as discussed in para 6.9.31) where the legal right of offset is only enforceable on the occurrence of some future event, such as default of the counterparty, continue not to meet the offsetting requirements.

[The next paragraph is 6.9.39.]

Disclosure of financial instruments

6.9.39   There have been significant developments in risk management concepts and practices in recent years. New techniques have evolved for measuring and managing exposures to risks arising from financial instruments. This, coupled with the credit and liquidity crisis experienced recently in the financial markets, has increased the need for more relevant information and greater transparency about an entity's exposures arising from financial instruments and how those risks are managed. In response, the IASB published an amendment to IFRS 7 in March 2009 to enhance the disclosure requirements on fair value measurement (see para 6.9.116) and liquidity risk (see para 6.9.157). Financial statement users and other investors need such information to make more informed judgements about the risk that entities run from the use of financial instruments and their associated returns. IFRS 7 sets out the disclosure requirements for financial instruments. For annual periods beginning on or after 1 January 2013, IFRS 13 amends IFRS 7 to move certain fair value disclosures from IFRS 7 to IFRS 13 (see paragraph 6.9.116).

Scope of IFRS 7

6.9.40   IFRS 7 applies to all types of financial instruments, except those that are specifically covered by another standard such as interests in subsidiaries, associates and joint ventures, acquirer's interest in contracts for contingent consideration in a business combination, employers' rights and obligations arising from employee benefit plans, share based payments and insurance contracts. IFRS 7's scope is similar to IAS 39. chapter 6.1 discusses in detail which instruments are in the scope of IAS 39 and therefore also in IFRS 7's scope. However, although finance leases are mostly outside the scope of IAS 39, they remain within the scope of IFRS 7. Operating leases are not regarded as financial instruments and are not therefore in the scope of either IAS 39 or IFRS 7, except for those individual payments that are currently due and payable. [IAS 32 para AG 9].

6.9.41   Applying IFRS 7 can be challenging for entities that enter into contracts for the purchase, sale or usage of commodities. Commodity contracts that are settled net in cash or through other financial instruments are in IFRS 7's scope; those contracts that meet the 'own use exemption' would be outside IFRS 7's scope, because they are not financial instruments. [IAS 39 para 6]. These terms are discussed in detail in Chapter 6.1. It is likely for internal reporting purposes that management may exclude 'own use' contracts when assessing the company's exposure to financial risks, such as liquidity risk, credit risk and market risk, or they may treat all commodity contracts in the same way. The onus therefore falls on management to determine how to provide disclosures that capture the complete exposure of the risks faced by the reporting entity in connection with its commodity contracts. IFRS 7 does not preclude management from providing additional explanations or details to assist users of the financial statements in interpreting the disclosures or in providing a complete picture.

6.9.42 Receivables and payables arising from application of IAS 11 need to be considered carefully in order to determine whether these items are in IFRS 7's scope or not. The amount due from/to customers is generally the net amount of cost incurred plus recognised profits less progress billings and recognised losses. This amount is 'billable' to customers. It, therefore, represents a contractual right to receive cash and is a financial asset in IFRS 7's scope. Progress billings to customers are also receivables in the IFRS 7's scope. On the other hand, advances received from customers are non-financial liabilities (obligation to perform work) and hence are not in the scope of IFRS 7.

6.9.43 In a similar manner, accruals representing a right to receive cash or an obligation to deliver cash are in IFRS 7's scope. For example, an accrual for goods received but not yet invoiced is within the IFRS 7's scope. On the other hand, a pre-paid expense, which is settled by the future delivery of goods or services, is not a financial instrument and is excluded from IFRS 7's scope.

6.9.44 Provisions as defined in IAS 37 are scoped out of IFRS 7 because they are not financial instruments. [IAS 37 para 2; IFRS 7 paras 3-4; IAS 39 para 2(j)]. Financial guarantee contracts may be measured in accordance with IAS 37's principles if the provision is higher than the unamortised premium amount, but they are financial instruments within IAS 39's scope and so are within IFRS 7's scope. Financial guarantee contracts that are considered insurance contracts and measured in accordance with IFRS 4 are outside the scope of IFRS 7. [IFRS 4 para 4(d)].

6.9.45 IFRS 7 applies to both recognised and unrecognised financial instruments. [IFRS 7 para 4, 5]. For example, some loan commitments are outside IAS 39's scope and may not be recognised, but are within IFRS 7's scope because they expose an entity to financial risks, such as credit and liquidity risk. However, the same is not necessarily true for a firm commitment that is designated as a hedged item in a fair value hedge. The subsequent cumulative change in the fair value of the firm commitment attributable to the hedged risk is recognised as an asset or liability under IAS 39's hedge accounting rules. [IAS 39 para 93]. However, this 'firm commitment' asset or liability does not expose the entity to credit or liquidity risk until it becomes a financial asset or liability. The fact that hedge accounting is applied does not mean that the 'firm commitment' asset or liability is a financial instrument or that IFRS 7's disclosure requirements would apply.

6.9.46 There is no scope exemption in IFRS 7 for financial assets and liabilities within the scope of IFRS 5. However, IFRS 5 specifies the disclosures required in respect of non-current assets (or disposal groups) classified as held for sale and discontinued operations. Paragraph 2 of the standard states that the classification and presentation requirements of IFRS 5 apply to all recognised non-current assets and to all disposal groups of an entity and paragraph 5(c) specifies that the measurement provisions do not apply to financial assets within IAS 39's scope. A question arises as to whether IFRS 7 disclosures are also required for financial assets and financial liabilities classified as held-for-sale or part of disposal groups. This question was addressed by the IASB in an amendment to IFRS 5 issued in April 2009. The amendment clarifies that disclosures required by other standards do not apply to non-current assets or disposal groups held for sale unless they are outside the scope of IFRS 5's measurement requirements. [IFRS 5 para 5B(b)]. As financial instruments measured in accordance with IAS 39 are outside the scope of IFRS 5's measurement requirements, IFRS 7 should be applied. See chapter 26.

6.9.47 Consistent with IAS 32 and IAS 39, the standard applies to all entities, not just those in the financial services sector. This means that it applies to a manufacturing entity whose only financial instruments may be cash, bank loans and overdrafts, trade debtors and creditors as well as to a bank with many and complex financial instruments. It also applies to subsidiaries of a consolidated group, even though in most large groups risks are managed at the consolidated level.

6.9.48 There is no scope exemption for the financial statements of subsidiaries or, as yet, for small and medium-sized companies. The application of IFRS 7 to subsidiaries may present a challenge, as financial risk is often managed at a consolidated or group level.

Objectives of IFRS 7

6.9.49 IFRS 7's objective is to provide information to users of financial statements about an entity's exposure to risks and how the entity manages those risks. To this end, the standard requires an entity to provide disclosures in its financial statements that enable users to evaluate:

- the significance of financial instruments for the entity's financial position and performance; and

- the nature and extent of risks arising from financial instruments to which the entity is exposed (quantitative disclosure) and how the entity manages those risks (qualitative disclosures).

[IFRS 7 paras 1, 7, 31].

6.9.50 The first bullet point above covers disclosures about the figures in the balance sheet and the income statement. IFRS 7 requires disclosures of categories of financial instruments and hedging activities. In addition, it requires various disclosures by 'class' of financial instruments (see para 6.9.54).

6.9.51 The second bullet point covers disclosure of qualitative and quantitative information about an entity's exposure to risks arising from financial instruments. IFRS 7 expands the qualitative disclosure to include information on the process that an entity uses to manage and measure risk. IFRS 7 requires quantitative risk disclosures that should be given 'through the eyes of management', that is, based on information provided internally to key management personnel. Certain minimum disclosures are also required to the extent they are not already covered by the 'through the eyes of management' information. Entities are required to communicate to the market how they perceive, manage and measure risk.

6.9.52 The 'through the eyes of management' approach brings financial reporting more closely into line with the way management run their businesses.

6.9.53 IFRS 7 includes mandatory application guidance that explains how to apply the standard's requirements. It is also accompanied by non-mandatory implementation guidance that describes how an entity might provide the necessary disclosures.

General matters

Classes of financial instruments

6.9.54 IFRS 7 requires certain disclosures to be given by class of financial instruments, including the following:

- financial assets not qualifying for derecognition (see para 6.9.73);

- the reconciliation of an allowance account (see para 6.9.102);

- the amount of impairment loss for financial assets (see para 6.9.108);

- fair values and the methods or assumptions applied in determining those values (see para 6.9.116); and

- specific disclosures relating to credit risk (see para 6.9.149).

The standard itself does not provide a prescriptive list of classes of financial instruments. However, IFRS 7 states that an entity should take into account the characteristics of financial instruments and that the classes selected should be appropriate to the nature of information disclosed. [IFRS 7 para 6].

6.9.55 A 'class' of financial instruments is not the same as a 'category' of financial instruments. Categories are defined in paragraph 9 of IAS 39 as financial assets at fair value through profit or loss (held for trading or designated at initial recognition), held-to-maturity investments, loans and receivables, available-for-sale financial assets, financial liabilities at fair value through profit or loss (held for trading or designated at initial recognition) and financial liabilities measured at amortised cost. [IFRS 7 para 8]. Classes are potentially determined at a lower level than the measurement categories and need to be reconciled back to the balance sheet. [IFRS 7 para 6]. The level of detail for a class should be determined on an entity specific basis and may be defined for each individual disclosure in a different way. In determining classes of financial instrument, an entity should, at a minimum:

- Distinguish instruments measured at amortised cost from those measured at fair value.

- Treat as a separate class or classes those financial instruments outside IFRS 7's scope. IFRS 7's disclosure requirements would not apply to this class.

[IFRS 7 App B para 2].

6.9.56 For example, in the case of banks, the category 'loans and receivables' comprises more than one class, unless the loans have similar characteristics. In this situation, it may be appropriate to group financial instruments into the following classes:

- types of customers – for example, commercial loans and loans to individuals; or

- types of loans – for example, mortgages, credit cards, unsecured loans and overdrafts.

However, in some cases, 'loans to clients' can be one class if all the loans have similar characteristics (for example, a savings bank providing only one type of loan to individuals).

6.9.57 'Available-for-sale' assets could be split into bond and equity investment classes. The equity investments could be further subdivided into those that are listed and those that are unlisted.

Location, level of disclosure and aggregation

6.9.58 An entity is permitted to disclose some of the information required by the standard either in the notes or on the face of the balance sheet or of the income statement. [IFRS 7 paras 8, 20]. Some entities might present some of the information required by IFRS 7, such as the nature and extent of risks arising from financial instruments and the entity's approach to managing those risks, alongside the financial statements in a separate management commentary or business review. This is only permissible where the information is incorporated by cross-reference from the financial statements and is made available to users of the financial statements on the same terms as the financial statements and at the same time. [IFRS 7 App B para 6].

6.9.59 An entity should decide, in the light of its own circumstances, how much detail it should provide, how much emphasis it should place on different aspects of the disclosure requirements and how much aggregation it should undertake to satisfy the standard's requirements. Obviously, a significant amount of judgement is required to display the overall picture without combining information with different characteristics. A balance should be maintained between providing excessive detail that may not assist users of financial statements and obscuring important information as a result of too much aggregation. For example, an entity should not obscure important information by including it amongst a large amount of insignificant detail. Similarly, an entity should not disclose information that is so aggregated that it obscures important differences between individual transactions or associated risks. [IFRS 7 App B para 3].

Risks arising from financial instruments

6.9.60 IFRS 7 requires a significant amount of qualitative and quantitative disclosure about risks associated with financial instruments. In the context of financial instruments, risk arises from the uncertainty in cash flows, which in turn affects the future cash flows and fair values of financial assets and liabilities. The following are the types of financial risk that are related to financial instruments:

- Market risk – the risk that the fair value or cash flows of a financial instrument will fluctuate, because of changes in market prices. Market risk embodies not only the potential for loss, but also the potential for gain. It comprises three types of risk as follows:

    - Interest rate risk – the risk that the fair value or future cash flows of a financial instrument will fluctuate because of changes in market interest rates.

    - Currency risk – the risk that the fair value or future cash flows of a financial instrument will fluctuate because of changes in foreign exchange rates.

    - Other price risk – the risk that the fair value or future cash flows of a financial instrument will fluctuate because of changes in market prices (other than those arising from interest rate risk or currency risk), whether those changes are caused by factors specific to the individual financial instrument or its issuer, or factors affecting all similar financial instruments traded in the market.

- Credit risk – the risk that the counterparty to a financial instrument will cause a financial loss for the entity by failing to discharge an obligation.

- Liquidity risk – the risk that an entity will encounter difficulty in meeting obligations associated with financial liabilities.

[IFRS 7 App A].

6.9.61 Operational risk disclosures, on the other hand, are not within IFRS 7's scope.

Balance sheet disclosures

6.9.62 The carrying amounts of each of the following categories should be disclosed, either on the face of the balance sheet or in the notes:

■ Financial assets at fair value through profit or loss, showing separately:

    ■ those designated as such upon initial recognition; and

    ■ those classified as held for trading in accordance with IAS 39.

■ Held-to-maturity investments.

■ Loans and receivables.

■ Available-for-sale financial assets.

■ Financial liabilities at fair value through profit or loss, showing separately:

    ■ those designated as such upon initial recognition; and

    ■ those classified as held for trading in accordance with IAS 39.

■ Financial liabilities measured at amortised cost.

[IFRS 7 para 8].

6.9.63 Table 6.9.2 shows an example of a group disclosing a matrix analysis of financial assets and financial liabilities by category and by class. The group explained in its accounting policies that all the financial assets at fair value through profit or loss are held for trading assets and that the group has no held-to-maturity investments.

Table 6.9.2 – Analysis of financial assets and financial liabilities by class and by categories

Amer Sports Corporation – Annual Report – 31 December 2011
[Note: comparatives have not been reproduced in this extract]

28 Balance sheet values of financial assets and liabilities by measurement categories

EUR million	Financial assets/ liabilities fair value through income statement	Derivative financial instruments used in hedge accounting	Loans and other receivables	Available-for-sale financial assets	Financial liabilities measured at amortized cost	Carrying amount by balance sheet item	Fair value
Non-current financial assets							
Other non-current financial assts			2.2	0.6		2.8	2.8
Derivative financial instruments							
Foreign exchange derivatives		1.2				1.2	1.2
Interest rate derivatives and cross country swaps	0.7					0.7	0.7
Current financial assets							
Accounts receivables			518.4			518.4	518.4
Loan receivables			0.2			0.2	0.2
Other non-interest yielding receivables			49.3			49.3	49.3
Derivative financial instruments							
Foreign exchange derivatives	0.6	18.5				19.1	19.1
Cash and cash equivalents			78.8			78.8	78.8
Balance sheet values by category at December 31, 2011	1.3	19.7	648.9	0.6		670.5	670.5
Long-term financial liabilities							
Long-term interest bearing liabilities					251.4	251.4	247.1
Other long-term liabilities					13.0	13.0	13.0
Derivative financial instruments							
Foreign exchange derivatives	0.0					0.0	0.0
Interest rate derivatives and cross currency swaps	3.3					3.3	3.3

Current financial liabilities					
Current interest-bearing liabilities			219.0	219.0	219.0
Accounts payable			200.5	200.5	200.5
Other current liabilities			199.3	199.3	199.3
Derivative financial instruments					
Foreign exchange derivatives	12.3	6.2		18.5	18.5
Balance sheet values by category at December 31, 2011	12.3	9.5	883.2	905.0	900.7

Financial assets or liabilities at fair value through profit or loss

6.9.64 If the entity has designated a loan or receivable (or group of loans or receivables) as at fair value through profit or loss, it should disclose:

■ The maximum exposure to credit risk of the loan or receivable (or group of loans or receivables) at the reporting date (see para 6.9.146 below).

■ The amount by which any related credit derivatives or similar instruments mitigate that maximum exposure to credit risk, for example financial guarantees and credit insurance.

■ The amount of change, during the period and cumulatively, in the fair value of the loan or receivable (or group of loans or receivables) that is attributable to changes in the financial asset's credit risk, determined either

■ as the amount of change in its fair value that is not attributable to changes in market conditions that give rise to market risk; or

■ using an alternative method the entity believes more faithfully represents the amount of change in its fair value that is attributable to changes in the asset's credit risk.

Changes in market conditions that give rise to market risk include changes in an observed (benchmark) interest rate, commodity price, foreign exchange rate or index of prices or rates (see para 6.9.66 below).

■ The amount of the change in the fair value of any related credit derivatives or similar instruments that has occurred during the period and cumulatively since the loan or receivable was designated as at fair value through profit or loss.

[IFRS 7 para 9].

6.9.65 The disclosures described above apply only to those loans and receivables (or groups of loans and receivables) that have been designated at fair value through profit and loss ('FVTPL'). They do not apply to all loans and receivables or to all assets designated as FVTPL assets. For example, a quoted financial asset can never be classified as 'loans and receivables'. Therefore, in this case the above disclosures are not required.

6.9.66 Where an entity discloses the information required by the third bullet point in paragraph 6.9.64, it should also disclose the methods used to comply with the disclosure requirements. However, where the entity believes that this disclosure does not faithfully represent the change in the financial asset's fair value attributable to changes in its credit risk, it should disclose the reasons and the factors it believes are relevant in reaching that conclusion. [IFRS 7 para 11].

6.9.67 If the entity has designated a financial liability as at fair value through profit or loss, it should disclose:

- The amount of change, during the period and cumulatively, in the financial liability's fair value that is attributable to changes in the credit risk of that liability determined either:

  - as the amount of change in its fair value that is not attributable to changes in market conditions that give rise to market risk; or

  - using an alternative method the entity believes more faithfully represents the amount of change in its fair value that is attributable to changes in the asset's credit risk.

  Changes in market conditions that give rise to market risk include changes in an observed (benchmark) interest rate, the price of another entity's financial instrument, a commodity price, a foreign exchange rate or an index of prices or rates. For contracts that include a unit-linking feature, changes in market conditions include changes in the performance of the related internal or external investment fund.

- The difference between the financial liability's carrying amount and the amount the entity would be contractually required to pay at maturity to the holder of the obligation.

[IFRS 7 para 10].

6.9.68 As stated in the first bullet point in paragraph 6.9.67 above, an entity is required to disclose the amount of change in a liability's fair value that is attributable to changes in the liability's credit risk. Although quantifying such changes might be difficult in practice, the IASB concluded that disclosure of such information would be useful to users and would help alleviate concerns that users may misinterpret the profit or loss changes in credit risk, especially in the absence of disclosures. Consequently, the standard provides a relatively easy method of computing the amount to be disclosed, as illustrated in the example below. The method assumes that the only relevant change in market condition for the liability is a change in the observed benchmark interest rate. Changes in fair value arising from factors other than changes in the instrument's credit risk or changes in interest rates are assumed not to be significant.

Example – Fair value change attributable to changes in a liability's credit risk

On 1 January 20X1, an entity issues a 10 year bond with a par value of C150,000 and an annual fixed coupon rate of 8%, which is consistent with market rates for bonds with similar characteristics. The entity uses LIBOR as its observable (benchmark) interest rate.

The entity assumes a flat yield curve, all changes in interest rates result from a parallel shift in the yield curve, and the changes in LIBOR are the only relevant changes in market conditions. It is also assumed that changes in the fair value arising from factors other than changes in the bond's credit risk or changes in interest rate are not significant.

At the date of inception of the bond, LIBOR was 5%. At the end of the first year, LIBOR has decreased to 4.75%. The bond's fair value is C153,811, consistent with a market interest rate of 7.6% for the bond. The market rate reflects the bond's credit rating at the end of the first year (see below).

The entity estimates the amount of change in the bond's fair value that is not attributable to changes in market conditions that give rise to market risk as follows:

■ Calculate the instrument-specific component of the bond's internal rate of return:

At inception, the internal rate of return for the 10 year bond is 8%. Since LIBOR at inception was 5%, the instrument-specific component of the internal rate of return is 3% (8% – 5%).

■ Determine the discount rate to be used to calculate the present value of the bond at the end of year 1 using the bond's contractual cash flows:

Since the only relevant change in the market conditions is that LIBOR has decreased to 4.75% at the end of the year, the discount rate for the present value calculation is 7.75% (4.75% + 3%).

■ Calculate the present value at the end of year 1 using the above discount rate and the bond's contractual cash flows as follows:

		C
PV of C12,000 interest payable for 9 years (year 2 -10) =	$\dfrac{12{,}000 \times [1 - (1 + 0.0775)^{-9}]}{0.0775}$	75,748
PV of C150,000 payable in year 10 =	$150{,}000 \times (1 + 0.0775)^{-9}$	76,619
Total PV		152,367

- Calculate the present value at the end of year 1 using the market rate and the bonds contractual cash flows as follows. (Note that this second calculation uses the same cash flows and the same benchmark interest rates as the first calculation – the main difference is that credit spread is adjusted to reflect the current market price.)

		C
PV of C12,000 interest payable for 9 years (year 2 -10) =	$\dfrac{12{,}000 \times [1 - (1 + 0.076)^{-9}]}{0.076}$	76,226
PV of C150,000 payable in year 10 =	$150{,}000 \times (1 + 0.076)^{-9}$	77,585
Observed market value of liability		153,811

- Calculate change in fair value that is not attributable to the change in the benchmark interest rate

	C
Observed market value of bond	153,811
PV of bond as calculated above	152,367
Change in fair value not attributable to changes in the observed benchmark rate	1,444

The change in fair value not attributable to changes in the observed benchmark rate is a reasonably proxy for the change in fair value that is attributable to changes in the liability's credit risk, since the difference in present values calculated at 7.75% and 7.6% is assumed to reflect changes in the instrument's credit risk. Thus, the amount to be disclosed is C1,444. [IFRS 7 para IG 11].

6.9.69 Where an entity discloses the information required by the first bullet point in paragraph 6.9.67 above, it should also disclose the methods used to comply with the disclosure requirements. However, where the entity believes that the disclosure it has given to comply with the requirements does not faithfully represent the change in the fair value of the financial asset attributable to changes in its credit risk, it should disclose the reasons and the factors it believes are relevant in reaching that conclusion. [IFRS 7 para 11].

Other sundry balance sheet disclosure

Re-classification

6.9.70 If the entity has re-classified a financial asset (in accordance with paras 51-54 of IAS 39) as one measured:

- at cost or amortised cost, rather than at fair value; or

- at fair value, rather than at cost or amortised cost,

it should disclose the amount re-classified into and out of each category and the reason for that re-classification (see chapter 6.4). [IFRS 7 para 12].

6.9.71 In addition to the disclosure required by the previous paragraph, if the entity has taken advantage of the amendment to IAS 39 issued in October 2008 (see chapter 6.4) and has reclassified a financial asset out of the fair value through profit or loss category (in accordance with paras 50B or 50D of IAS 39) or out of the available-for-sale category (in accordance with para 50E of IAS 39), it should disclose the following:

- The amount reclassified into and out of each category.

- For each reporting period until derecognition, the carrying amounts and fair values of all financial assets that have been reclassified in the current and previous reporting periods.

- If a financial asset was reclassified in accordance with paragraph 50B of IAS 39, the rare situation, and the facts and circumstances indicating that the situation was rare.

- For the reporting period when the financial asset was reclassified, the fair value gain or loss on the financial asset recognised in profit or loss or other comprehensive income in that reporting period and in the previous reporting period.

- For each reporting period following the reclassification (including the reporting period in which the financial asset was reclassified) until derecognition of the financial asset, the fair value gain or loss that would have been recognised in profit or loss or other comprehensive income if the financial asset had not been reclassified, and the gain, loss, income and expense recognised in profit or loss.

- The effective interest rate and estimated amounts of cash flows the entity expects to recover, as at the date of reclassification of the financial asset.

[IFRS 7 para 12A].

6.9.72 An example of some of this disclosure is provided in the following table.

Table 6.9.3 – Financial assets reclassified from held for trading category in rare circumstances

Royal Bank of Scotland Plc – 2008 annual report Note 11 – Page 208

As discussed in accounting policies, during 2008 the Group reclassified financial assets from the held-for-trading and available-for-sale categories into the loans and receivables category (as permitted by paragraph 50D of IAS 39 as amended) and from the held-for-trading category into the available-for-sale category (as permitted by paragraph 50B of IAS 39 as amended).

The turbulence in the financial markets during the second half of 2008 was regarded by management as rare circumstances in the context of paragraph 50B of IAS 39 as amended.

The balance sheet values of these assets, the effect of the reclassification on the income statement for the period from the date of reclassification to 31 December 2008 and the gains and losses relating to these assets recorded in the income statement for the years ended 31 December 2008, 2007 and 2006 were as follows:

	2008 – on reclassification			31 December 2008		After reclassification (2008)					2007	2006
	Carrying value £m	Effective interest rate %	Expected cash flows £m	Carrying value £m	Fair value £m	Gains/(losses) up to the date of reclassification £m	Income £m	Impairment losses £m	Gains/(losses) in AFS reserves £m	Amount that would have been recognised £m	Gains/(losses) recognised in the income statement in prior periods £m	£m
Reclassified from HFT to LAR:												
Loans:												
Leveraged finance	3,602	10.15	6,083	4,304	2,523	(457)	454	–		(1,206)	(155)	–
Corporate loans	5,040	6.19	7,582	5,827	4,940	(76)	198	–		(681)	(50)	3
	8,642		13,665	10,131	7,463	(533)	652	–		(1,887)	(205)	3
Debt securities:												
CDO of RMBS	215	4.92	259	236	221	4	5	–		(11)	5	6
RMBS	1,765	6.05	2,136	2,011	1,536	(115)	157	–		(302)	(12)	–
CMBS	1	11.11	4	1	1	1	–	–		–	–	–
CLOs	835	6.34	1,141	952	717	(22)	104	–		(130)	(14)	(2)
Other ABS	2,203	5.07	3,202	2,514	2,028	(67)	129	–		(338)	3	(1)
Other	2,538	2.62	2,764	2,602	2,388	72	3			(166)	94	476
	7,557		9,506	8,316	6,891	(127)	398	–		(947)	76	479
Total	16,199		23,171	18,447	14,354	(660)	1,050	–		(2,834)	(129)	482

Reclassified from HFT to AFS: Debt securities:												
CDO of RMBS	6,228	8.14	8,822	5,695	5,695	(1,330)	1,147	(464)	(1,069)	(280)	(400)	–
RMBS	5,205	8.03	8,890	5,171	5,171	(530)	24	–	(162)	(122)	(4)	73
CMBS	32	6.81	85	31	31	(5)	5	–	(3)	2	(4)	–
CLOs	1,457	5.02	1,804	1,288	1,288	(168)	421		(383)	58	(36)	1
Other ABS	2,199	6.02	3,183	1,847	1,847	(356)	(10)	–	(354)	(311)	(42)	72
Other	614	12.55	1,311	698	698	–	130	–	(166)	(5)	(1)	–
	15,735		24,095	14,730	14,730	(2,389)	1,717	(464)	(2,137)	(658)	(487)	146
Reclassified from AFS to LAR: Debt securities	704	1.38	772	1,028	968	(12)[1]	6	–	–	(37)[1]	–	–
Total	32,638		48,038	34,205	30,052	(3,061)	2,773	(464)	(2,137)	(3,529)	(616)	628

Note:

[1] Gains/(losses) recognised in the available-for-sale reserve

Amounts included in the consolidated income statement:

	Group		
	2008 £m	2007 £m	2006 £m
Gains on financial assets/liabilities designated as at fair value through profit or loss	**(901)**	1,074	573
Gains on disposal or settlement of loans and receivables	**4**	3	21

On the initial recognition of financial assets and liabilities valued using valuation techniques incorporating information other than observable market data, any difference between the transaction price and that derived from the valuation technique is deferred. Such amounts are recognised in profit or loss over the life of the transaction; when market data become observable; or when the transaction matures or is closed out as appropriate. At 31 December 2008, net gains of £102 million (2007 – £72 million) were carried forward in the balance sheet. During the year net gains of £89 million (2007 – £67 million) were deferred and £65 million (2007 – £10 million) released to profit or loss.

Derecognition

6.9.73 An entity may have transferred financial assets in such a way that part or all of the financial assets do not qualify for derecognition (see chapter 6.6).

6.9.74 The IASB amended IFRS 7 in October 2010 to enhance the disclosure requirements of transferred financial assets. The amendment is effective for accounting periods beginning on or after 1 July 2011. Comparative information is not required for any periods presented that begin before the date of initial application of the amendment.

6.9.75 Transferred assets are defined in paragraph 42A of IFRS 7 as those where the entity either (a) transfers the contractual rights to receive the cash flows or (b) retains the contractual rights to receive the cash flows but assumes an obligation to pay the cash flows to another party. The amendment has different requirements for the following two categories of transferred asset.

6.9.76 The first category relates to transferred assets that are not derecognised in their entirety, that is where:

- the entity assumes an obligation to pay the cash flows from the financial asset, but the 'pass through' requirements of paragraph 19 of IAS 39 are not met (see paras 6.9.83 and 6.9.84 below); or

- the entity retains substantially all the risks and rewards of ownership of the financial asset [IAS 39 para 20(b)]; or

- the entity neither transfers nor retains substantially all the risks and rewards of ownership, but retains control, in which case it continues to recognise the asset to the extent of its continuing involvement. [IAS 39 para 20(c)(ii)].

6.9.77 Control of the transferred asset depends upon the transferee's ability to sell the asset. The transferor entity has not retained control if the transferee has the practical ability to sell the asset in its entirety to an unrelated third party and is able to exercise that ability unilaterally and without needing to impose additional restrictions on the transfer. Otherwise the transferor entity has retained control. [IAS 39 para 23].

6.9.78 IFRS 7 paragraph 42A defines transferred assets as those where either (a) the entity transfers the contractual rights to receive the cash flows or (b) the entity retains the contractual rights to receive the cash flows and assumes an obligation to pay the cash flows to another party. However unlike the IAS 39 requirements, there is no requirement for the IAS 39 paragraph 19 'pass through' tests to be met in case (b). Therefore the IFRS 7 disclosures in paragraph 42D (including the existing IFRS requirements) are extended to those transferred assets that are not derecognised because they fail the IAS 39 paragraph 19 pass through tests.

6.9.79 For those assets that continue to be recognised under paragraph 6.9.76 above, disclosures should include the following. [IFRS 7 para 42D]:

- the nature of the transferred assets;

- the nature of the risks and rewards of ownership to which the entity is exposed;

- a description of the nature of the relationship between the transferred assets and the associated liabilities, including restrictions arising from the transfer on the reporting entity's use of the transferred assets;

- when the counterparty to the associated liabilities has recourse only to the transferred assets, a schedule must be given that sets out the fair value of the transferred assets, the fair value of the associated liabilities and the net position (the difference between the fair value of the transferred assets and the associated liabilities);

- when the entity continues to recognise all of the transferred assets, the carrying amounts of the transferred assets and the associated liabilities;

- when the entity continues to recognise the assets to the extent of its continuing involvement, the total carrying amount of the original assets before the transfer, the carrying amount of the assets that the entity continues to recognise, and the carrying amount of the associated liabilities.

6.9.80 The second category relates to transferred assets that are derecognised in their entirety, where the entity has a 'continuing involvement' in them. Transferred assets that are derecognised in their entirety are those where the entity (a) transfers the contractual rights to receive the cash flows or (b) retains the contractual rights to receive the cash flows and assumes an obligation to pay the cash flows to another party and the IAS 39 paragraph 19 pass through requirements are met; and (in the case of either (a) or (b)):

- the entity transfers substantially all the risks and rewards of ownership of the financial asset [IAS 39 para 20(a)]; or

- the entity neither transfers nor retains substantially all the risks and rewards of ownership, but does not retain control, in which case any rights and obligations created by the transfer are recognised separately as assets or liabilities. [IAS 39 para 20(c)(i)].

6.9.81 For this second category of transferred assets, the new disclosure requirements are extensive. However, they only apply to derecognised transferred assets where the entity has a 'continuing involvement'. For this purpose paragraph 42C of IFRS 7 states that *"an entity has continuing involvement in a transferred financial asset if, as part of the transfer, the entity retains any of the contractual rights or obligations inherent in the transferred financial asset or obtains any new contractual rights or obligations relating to the transferred financial asset"*. This is not the same as the IAS 39 definition of continuing involvement where the extent of continuing involvement is *"the extent to which the entity is exposed to changes in the value of the transferred asset"*. [IAS 39 para 30]. The new disclosures are mostly in respect of the continuing involvement (as defined in IFRS 7).

6.9.82 Examples of common transactions involving transferred assets and the additional disclosures likely to be required are given in Table 6.9.4 below. Whilst it will depend upon the particular facts and circumstances in each case, it would appear that in practice the majority of common transactions fall into the first category of disclosures above.

Table 6.9.4 – Example disclosures in case of transfer of financial assets

Transaction	Typical accounting treatment	Disclosures requirements
Repos and securities lending (for example a bank repos bonds to third party for cash collateral. Bank will pay a fixed return).	Transferred asset (that is the bonds) remains on bank's balance sheet. Associated liability to repay cash received is recognised.	Description of the nature of the transferred assets (that is the bonds). [IFRS 7 para 42D(a)]. The nature of the risks and rewards of ownership to which the entity is exposed (for example, the credit risk that the bond issuer may not be able to repay the bonds on their maturity date). [IFRS 7 para 42D(b)]. Description of the nature of the relationship between the transferred assets (that, is the bonds) and the associated liabilities (that is, the liability to repay the cash received), including restrictions arising from the transfer on the reporting entity's use of the transferred assets (that is, that the bank cannot use, sell or pledge the transferred assets for the duration of the repo transaction). [IFRS 7 para 42D(c)]. Repos are generally with recourse to assets other than the repo-ed bonds, in which case there is no requirement for a schedule that sets out the fair value of the transferred assets (that is, the bonds), the fair value of the associated liabilities (that is, the liability to repay the cash received) and the net position. [IFRS 7 para 42D(d)]. The transferred assets (that is, the bonds) continue to be recognised on balance sheet. The entity should disclose the carrying amount of the transferred assets (that is, the bonds) and the associated liabilities (that is, the liability to repay the cash received). [IFRS 7 para 42D(e)].

Securitisations (for example mortgage book transferred to SPE with credit enhancement provided by transferor).

Transferred assets (mortgage book) remain on balance sheet of transferor entity and a liability is recognised for the obligation to transfer the cash flows from the mortgage book to the holders of the notes.

SPE is generally consolidated by transferor's group. In the group accounts, the assets remain on balance sheet and the associated liability is the liability to pass cash flows to the SPE noteholders.

Consolidated and transferor's entity accounts:

Description of the nature of the transferred assets (that is, the mortgage book). [IFRS 7 para 42D(a)].

The nature of the risks and rewards of ownership to which the entity is exposed (for example, the credit risk that the borrowers under the mortgage agreements may not be able to repay in accordance with the mortgage terms). [IFRS 7 para 42D(b)].

Description of the nature of the relationship between the transferred assets (that is, the mortgage book) and the associated liabilities (that is, the liability to pass on the cash flows from the mortgage book), including restrictions arising from the transfer on the reporting entity's use of the transferred assets (for example, the transferor cannot use, sell or pledge the mortgage book). [IFRS 7 para 42D(c)].

Where the liability holders (that is, the SPE noteholders from a group perspective) have recourse only to the transferred assets (that is, the mortgages) (for example, if the transferor has a subordinated interest in the SPE through junior tranche notes) then the fair value of the transferred assets, the fair value of the associated liabilities and the net position must be disclosed. [IFRS 7 para 42D(d)].

The transferred assets (that is, the mortgage book) continue to be recognised on balance sheet. The entity should disclose the carrying amount of the transferred assets (that is, the mortgage book) and the associated liabilities (that is, the liability to transfer the cash flows from the mortgage book to the holders of the notes). [IFRS 7 para 42D(e)].

Factoring with recourse, where transferee is unable to sell the transferred asset (for example, the entity factors trade receivables, but retains late payment and credit risk)	Transferred asset remains on balance sheet in its entirety (no derecognition). Associated liability for cash received is recognised.	Description of the nature of the transferred assets (that is the trade receivables). [IFRS 7 para 42D(a)]. The nature of the risks and rewards of ownership to which the entity is exposed (for example, the risk of late payment and credit risk). [IFRS 7 para 42D(b)]. Description of the nature of the relationship between the transferred assets (that is, the trade receivables) and the associated liabilities (that is, the secured borrowing), including restrictions arising from the transfer on the reporting entity's use of the transferred assets (for example, the entity cannot use, sell or pledge the receivables). [IFRS 7 para 42D(c)] Transferred assets (that is, the trade receivables) continue to be recognised on balance sheet. The entity should disclose the carrying amount of the transferred assets (that is, the trade receivables) and the associated liabilities (that is, the secured borrowing). [IFRS 7 para 42D(e)].
Factoring with no recourse for either credit risk or late payment risk	The transferred assets (for example trade receivables) are derecognised in their entirety.	No disclosure required, unless the entity has some continuing involvement as defined in IFRS 7 para 42C, despite transferring substantially all the risks and rewards of the assets. In such cases the disclosures in IFRS 7 paras 42E-42G are required.
Investment fund issues a new class of shares (for example, S shares) over a ring-fenced class of debt assets ('side pocket shares'). The S shares are not redeemable at the option of the holder, but are mandatorily redeemable after the assets are realised. Proceeds from the realisation of the debt assets cannot be reinvested.	The ring fenced debt assets are not derecognised as there is no requirement to remit any cash flows collected from the assets to the S shareholders without material delay and/or as the fund is not prohibited from pledging the assets other than as security to the S shareholders. The S shares are recognised as a financial liability as the fund does not have the ability to hold the assets indefinitely and hence has an obligation to pay the S shareholders when the assets are sold.	The ring fenced debt assets are transferred (for disclosure purposes, see paragraph 6.9.78 above), but are not derecognised as they fail to meet the IAS 39 paragraph 19 'pass through' tests. The disclosure requirements in paragraph 42D of IFRS 7 should be given: The nature of the ring-fenced assets (that, is a ring-fenced class of debt assets). [IFRS 7 para 42D(a)]. The nature of the risks and rewards of ownership to which the entity is exposed (for example, credit risk). [IFRS 7 para 42D(b)]. A description of the nature of the relationship between the ring-fenced assets and the S shares, including

restrictions arising from the transfer on the fund's use of the ring-fenced assets. [IFRS 7 para 42D(c)].

As the S shareholders have recourse only to the ring-fenced assets, a schedule that sets out the fair value of the transferred assets (the ring-fenced assets), the fair value of the associated liabilities (the S shares) and the net position. [IFRS 7 para 42D(d)].

Transferred assets (that is, the ring fenced debt assets) continue to be recognised on balance sheet. The entity should disclose the carrying amount of these assets (that is, the ring fenced debt assets) and the associated liabilities (that is the S shares). [IFRS 7 para 42D(e)].

6.9.83 The IAS 39 derecognition requirements apply to a group of similar financial assets and so the new disclosure requirements also apply to a transferred group of similar assets. Similarly, in certain circumstances the IAS 39 derecognition requirements apply to a part of a financial asset (or group of financial assets). Consistent with paragraph 42A of IFRS 7, if the conditions in paragraph 16 of IAS 39 apply, then the IFRS 7 disclosure requirements apply only to those parts of the financial asset that are transferred. For example for an interest strip of a debt instrument that results in part of the debt instrument being derecognised (that is, the interest strip only), under paragraph 16 of IAS 39 the derecognised 'asset' only relates to the interest cash flows and so, if that part is derecognised in its entirety without a continuing involvement, the above disclosures do not apply.

6.9.84 Some entities (for example SPVs, investment funds, insurance companies) may have a portfolio of similar financial assets that generate cash flows that are used to pay obligations to other instrument holders (for example. to redeem units in an investment fund or to pay out on life insurance policies in a life fund). In most cases the entity (for example, the investment funds or insurance company) will be able to reinvest proceeds from the assets (either interest, dividend or principal contractual cash flows or arising from sale) rather than having an obligation to pay those cash flows to a third party (for example, the unit or policy holders). Hence, such assets are not 'transferred' and the IFRS 7 disclosure requirements are not required. However, there could be some situations where the IFRS 7 disclosure requirements are needed, for example certain side pocket arrangements in the hedge fund industry (see example in Table 6.9.4 above), although this will depend upon the particular terms of the related.

6.9.85 For those transferred assets that are derecognised in their entirety (for example, non-recourse factoring), the transferor may continue to service the assets for a fee, which could be based on a percentage of the asset value. Under paragraph 24 of IAS 39, the transferor will recognise a servicing asset or liability unless the fee adequately compensates the entity for the servicing. Such a servicing asset/liability is not a financial asset or liability as it relates to future services to be provided. Therefore, arguably it falls outside of the IFRS 7's scope and so the disclosure requirements for continuing involvement in paragraphs 42E-42F of IFRS 7 would not apply. However, disclosure of the servicing obligations is encouraged, where useful to an understanding of the transaction.

Offsetting

6.9.86   As discussed in paragraph 6.9.24, in December 2011 the IASB amended IAS 32 to clarify some of the requirements for offsetting financial assets and financial liabilities in the statement of financial position. This is discussed in paragraphs 6.9.35 to 6.9.38. At the same time, the IASB amended IFRS 7 to enhance the current offsetting disclosures. The new disclosure requirements are retrospectively applied, with an effective date of annual periods beginning on or after 1 January 2013.

6.9.87   The new disclosures require quantitative information about recognised financial instruments that are offset in the statement of financial position, as well as those recognised financial instruments that are subject to master netting or similar arrangements irrespective of whether they are offset. [IFRS 7 para 13A]. Similar arrangements include derivative clearing agreements, global master repurchase agreements, global master securities lending agreements and any related rights to financial collateral. Examples of financial instruments that are not within the scope of the new disclosures are loans and customer deposits at the same institution (unless they are set off in the statement of financial position) and financial instruments that are subject only to a collateral agreement. [IFRS 7 para B41].

6.9.88   Paragraph 13B of IFRS 7 sets out the objective for the offsetting disclosures: it requires an entity to disclose information that enables users of its financial statements to evaluate the effect or potential effect of netting arrangements on its financial position.

6.9.89   To meet this objective, paragraph 13C of IFRS 7 requires an entity to disclose at the end of each reporting period the following quantitative information separately for recognised financial assets and recognised financial liabilities that are within the scope:

(a)   the gross amounts of those recognised financial assets and recognised financial liabilities;

(b)   the amounts that are set off in accordance with the criteria in paragraph 42 of IAS 32 when determining the net amounts presented in the statement of financial position;

(c)   the net amounts presented in the statement of financial position;

(d) the amounts subject to an enforceable master netting arrangement or similar agreement that are not otherwise included in paragraph 13C(b) of IFRS 7, including:

   (i) amounts related to recognised financial instruments that do not meet some or all of the offsetting criteria in paragraph 42 of IAS 32; and

   (ii) amounts related to financial collateral (including cash collateral); and

(e) the net amount after deducting the amounts in (d) from the amounts in (c) above.

[IFRS 7 para 13C].

The information set out above should be presented in a tabular format, separately for financial assets and financial liabilities, unless another format is more appropriate. [IFRS 7 para 13C].

6.9.90 It is possible that financial instruments disclosed under the above requirements are measured differently – for example, a payable related to a repurchase agreement may be measured at amortised cost, while a derivative will be at fair value. Entities include financial instruments at recognised amounts and describe resulting measurement differences in the related disclosures.

6.9.91 The 'gross amounts' required by paragraph 13C(a) relate to both:

■ recognised financial instruments that are set off in accordance with paragraph 42 of IAS 32; and

■ recognised financial instruments that are subject to an enforceable master netting arrangement or similar agreement irrespective of whether they meet the offsetting criteria.

However, the 'gross amounts' required by paragraph 13C (a) do not relate to any amounts recognised as a result of collateral agreements that do not meet the offsetting criteria in para 42 of IAS 32. Instead, such amounts are disclosed in accordance with paragraph 13C (d). [IFRS 7 para B43].

6.9.92 With regards to the 'amounts that are set off' when determining the 'net amounts' as required by para 13C (b), the amounts of both the recognised financial assets and the recognised financial liabilities that are subject to set-off under the same arrangement are disclosed in both the financial asset and financial liability disclosures. However, the amounts disclosed (in, for example, a table) are limited to the amounts that are subject to set-off. For example, an entity may have a recognised derivative asset and a recognised derivative liability that meet the offsetting criteria in paragraph 42 of IAS 32. If the gross amount of the derivative asset is larger than the gross amount of the derivative liability, the financial asset disclosure table will include the entire amount of the derivative asset (in accordance with para 13C(a)) and the entire amount of the derivative liability (in accordance with para 13C(b)). However, while the financial liability disclosure table will include the entire amount of the derivative liability (in accordance with para 13C(a)), it will only include the amount of the derivative asset (in accordance with para 13C(b)) that is equal to the amount of the derivative liability. [IFRS 7 para B44].

6.9.93 With regards to the disclosure of 'net amounts' in the statement of financial position as required by paragraph 13C(c), paragraph B45 of IFRS 7 clarifies the following: If an entity has instruments that meet the scope of these disclosures (as specified in para 13A) but that do not meet the offsetting criteria in paragraph 42 of IAS 32, the amounts required to be disclosed by paragraph 13C(c) would equal the amounts required to be disclosed by paragraph 13C(a). Furthermore, the 'net amounts' required to be disclosed by paragraph 13C(c) must be reconciled to the individual line item amounts presented in the statement of financial position. For example, if an entity determines that the aggregation or disaggregation of individual financial statement line item amounts provides more relevant information, it must reconcile the aggregated or disaggregated amounts disclosed in paragraph 13C(c) back to the individual line item amounts presented in the statement of financial position. [IFRS 7 para B45 and B46].

6.9.94 With regards to the disclosure of *"amounts subject to an enforceable master netting arrangement or similar arrangement "*, paragraph 13C(d)(i) refers to amounts related to recognised financial instruments that do not meet some or all of the offsetting criteria in paragraph 42 of IAS 32 (for example, current rights of set-off that do not meet the criterion in paragraph 42(b) of IAS 32, or conditional rights of set-off that are enforceable and exercisable only in the event of default, or only in the event of insolvency or bankruptcy of any of the counterparties). Paragraph 13C(d)(ii) refers to amounts related to financial collateral, including cash collateral, both received and pledged. An entity discloses the fair value of those financial instruments that have been pledged or received as collateral. The amounts disclosed in accordance with paragraph 13C(d)(ii) should relate to the actual collateral received or pledged and not to any resulting payables or receivables recognised to return or receive back such collateral.

6.9.95 Paragraph 13D of IFRS 7 imposes a limit on the total amount disclosed in accordance with paragraph 13C(d) for an instrument to the net amount recognised in the balance sheet for that instrument. When disclosing amounts in accordance with paragraph 13C(d), an entity must take into account the effects of over-collateralisation by financial instruments. To do so, the entity must first deduct the amounts disclosed in accordance with paragraph 13C(d)(i) from the amount disclosed in accordance with paragraph 13C(c). The entity should then limit the amounts disclosed in accordance with paragraph 13C(d)(ii) to the remaining amount in paragraph 13C(c) for the related financial instrument. However, if rights to collateral can be enforced across financial instruments, these rights can be included in the disclosure provided in accordance with paragraph 13D. [IFRS 7 para B49].

6.9.96 Paragraph 13E of IFRS 7 requires an entity to include a description in the disclosures of the rights of set-off associated with its recognised financial assets and recognised financial liabilities subject to enforceable master netting arrangements and similar agreements that are disclosed in accordance with paragraph 13C(d), including the nature of those rights. For example, an entity should describe its conditional rights. For instruments subject to rights of set-off that are not contingent on a future event but do not meet the remaining criteria in paragraph 42 of IAS 32, the entity should describe the reason why the criteria are not met. Also, for any collateral received or pledged, the entity should describe the terms of the collateral agreement – for example, when the collateral is restricted. Finally, paragraph 13F of IFRS 7 requires an entity that discloses the information required by paragraph 13B-E in more than one note to the financial statements to cross-refer between those notes.

6.9.97 With regards to the quantitative offsetting disclosures in paragraph 13C(a)-(c) of IFRS 7, paragraph B51 of IFRS 7 allows grouping by type of financial instrument or by type of transaction – for example, derivatives, repurchase and reverse repurchase agreements or securities borrowing and securities lending agreements. Alternatively, grouping by type of financial instrument for the quantitative disclosures in paragraph 13C(a)-(c) is also allowed with the disclosures required by paragraph 13C(c)(e) by counterparty. In that case, counterparties do not need to be identified by name, but their designation (counterparty A, counterparty B, etc.) should remain consistent from year to year. Individually significant counterparties should be separately disclosed, and remaining ones may be aggregated into one line. Additional qualitative disclosures should be considered about the types of counterparty.

6.9.98 Paragraph B53 of IFRS 7 notes that the disclosures in paragraph 13C-E are minimum requirements to meet the objective stated in paragraph 13B. Depending on facts and circumstances, there may need to be additional disclosures to meet the objective.

Collateral

6.9.99 An entity should disclose:

■ The carrying amount of financial assets it has pledged as collateral for liabilities or contingent liabilities, including amounts that have been re-classified in circumstances where the transferee has the right to sell or pledge the transferred asset. [IAS 39 para 37(a)].

■ The terms and conditions relating to its pledge. [IFRS 7 para 14].

6.9.100 When an entity holds collateral (of financial or non-financial assets) and is permitted to sell or repledge it in the absence of default by the owner of the collateral, it should disclose:

■ The fair value of the collateral held.

■ The fair value of any such collateral sold or repledged, and whether the entity has an obligation to return it.

■ The terms and conditions associated with its use of the collateral.

[IFRS 7 para 15].

6.9.101 An example of how an entity has disclosed the necessary information about assets pledged and held as collateral is given in Table 6.9.5 below.

Table 6.9.5 – Assets pledged and held as collateral

Deutsche Bank AG – Annual Report – 31 December 2011

21 – Assets Pledged and Received as Collateral

The Group pledges assets primarily for repurchase agreements and securities borrowing agreements which are generally conducted under terms that are usual and customary to standard securitized borrowing contracts. In addition, the Group pledges collateral against other borrowing arrangements and for margining purposes on OTC derivative liabilities. The carrying value of the Group's assets pledged as collateral for liabilities or contingent liabilities is as follows.

in € m.	Dec 31, 2011	Dec 31, 2010
Interest-earning deposits with banks	71	930
Financial assets at fair value through profit or loss	83,862	101,109
Financial assets available for sale	11,886	3,362
Loans	17,619	15,867
Other	330	181
Total	**113,768**	**121,449**

Assets transferred where the transferee has the right to sell or repledge are disclosed on the face of the balance sheet. As of December 31, 2011, and December 31, 2010, these amounts were € 99 billion and € 98 billion, respectively.

As of December 31, 2011, and December 31, 2010, the Group had received collateral with a fair value of € 304 billion and € 269 billion, respectively, arising from securities purchased under reverse repurchase agreements, securities borrowed,, derivatives transactions, customer margin loans and other transactions. These transactions were generally conducted under terms that are usual and customary for standard secured lending activities and the other transactions described. The Group, as the secured party, has the right to sell or repledge such collateral, subject to the Group returning equivalent securities upon completion of the transaction. As of December 31, 2011 and December 31, 2010, the Group had resold or repledged € 262 billion and € 249 billion, respectively. This was primarily to cover short sales, securities loaned and securities sold under repurchase agreements.

Allowance amount for credit losses

6.9.102 When financial assets are impaired by credit losses and the entity records the impairment in a separate account (for example, an allowance account used to record individual impairments or a similar account used to record a collective impairment of assets) rather than directly reducing the asset's carrying amount, it should disclose a reconciliation of changes in that account during the period for each class of financial assets. [IFRS 7 para 16].

Compound financial instruments with multiple embedded derivatives

6.9.103   If an entity has issued an instrument that contains both a liability and an equity component (see chapter 6.4) and the instrument has multiple embedded derivatives whose values are interdependent (such as a callable convertible debt instrument), it should disclose the existence of those features. [IFRS 7 para 17].

Defaults and breaches

6.9.104   An entity is required to disclose information on defaults and breaches of loans payable (that is, financial liabilities other than short-term trade payables on normal credit terms) and other loan agreements. Such disclosures provide relevant information about the entity's creditworthiness and its prospects for obtaining future loans. Any defaults or breaches may affect the liability's classification as current or non-current in accordance with IAS 1 (see para 6.9.15 above) and may also require disclosure if the liability is considered as capital by the entity's management. [IAS 1 para 135(e)].

6.9.105   For loans payable recognised at the reporting date, an entity should disclose:

■   Details of any defaults during the period of principal, interest, sinking fund, or redemption terms of those loans payable.

■   The carrying amount of the loans payable in default at the reporting date.

■   Whether the default was remedied, or the terms of the loans payable were renegotiated, before the financial statements were authorised for issue.

[IFRS 7 para 18].

6.9.106   If, during the period, there were breaches of loan agreement terms other than those described in the above paragraph, an entity should disclose the same information as above if those breaches permitted the lender to demand accelerated repayment, unless the breaches were remedied, or the loan's terms were renegotiated, on or before the reporting date. [IFRS 7 para 19].

6.9.107   The above requirements would apply if the terms were renegotiated after the balance sheet date but before the signing of the financial statements. However, the disclosure need not include short-term trade payables on normal credit terms as these do not meet the definition in the standard of loans payable. [IFRS 7 App A].

Income statement and equity disclosures

Items of income, expense, gains or losses

6.9.108   An entity should disclose the following items of income, expense, gains or losses, either on the face of the financial statements or in the notes:

- Net gains or net losses on:

  - Financial assets or financial liabilities at fair value through profit or loss, showing separately those on financial assets or financial liabilities designated as such upon initial recognition and those on financial assets or financial liabilities that are classified as held-for-trading in accordance with IAS 39. Where these financial instruments accrue interest income or expense, the standard allows an accounting policy choice on how to disclose these. The interest income, interest expense and dividend income can be reported as part of net gains or net losses on these financial instruments or can be disclosed separately as part of interest income and expenses. [IFRS 7 App B5(e)]. In addition, it is possible to adopt one treatment for interest income and expense and a different treatment for dividend income as no such prohibition exists in IFRS 7. However, different treatments cannot be adopted for interest income and interest expense.

    Note that if the dividend income is significant, regardless of how it is disclosed here, it will also need to be disclosed separately in the notes. [IAS 18 para 35(b)(v)].

  - Available-for-sale financial assets, showing separately the amount of gain or loss recognised directly in other comprehensive income during the period and the amount reclassified from equity and recognised in profit or loss for the period.

  - Held-to-maturity investments.

  - Loans and receivables.

  - Financial liabilities measured at amortised cost.

- Total interest income and total interest expense (calculated using the effective interest method) for financial assets or financial liabilities that are not at fair value through profit or loss.

- Fee income and expense (other than amounts included in determining the effective interest rate) arising from:

  - Financial assets or financial liabilities that are not at fair value through profit or loss.

  - Trust and other fiduciary activities that result in the holding or investing of assets on behalf of individuals, trusts, retirement benefit plans and other institutions.

- Interest income on impaired financial assets accrued in accordance with paragraph AG93 of IAS 39, which requires an entity to continue to recognise interest income using the rate of interest used to discount the future cash flows for the purposes of measuring the impairment loss (see chapter 6.7).

- The amount of any impairment loss for each class of financial asset.
[IFRS 7 para 20].

6.9.109 Certain of the disclosure requirements described above are illustrated in Table 6.9.6.

Table 6.9.6 – Items of income, expense, gains or losses

EADS N.V. – Annual Report – 31 December 2011

34. Information about Financial Instruments (extract)

e) Net gains or losses

EADS net gains or (losses) recognised in profit or loss in 2009 and 2008 respectively are as follows:

(in €m)	**2011**	2010
Financial assets or financial liabilities at fair value through profit or loss:		
Held for trading	71	35
Designated on initial recognition	4	22
Loans and receivables	19	(123)
Financial liabilities measured at amortised cost	105	97

Interest income from financial assets or financial liabilities through profit or loss is included in net gains or losses.

Net gains or (losses) of loans and receivables contain among others impairment losses.

Net gains or (losses) of € -20 million (2010: € + 12 million) are recognised directly in equity relating to available-for-sale financial assets.

In 2011, the net gains or (losses) of financial liabilities measured at amortised cost include among others the gains from the release of European government refundable advances due to the termination of the A340 programme (see Note 27 "Other financial liabilities").

f) Total interest income and total interest expenses

In 2011, the total interest income amounts to € 372 million (in 2010: € 309 million) for financial assets which are not measured at fair value through profit or loss. For financial liabilities which are not measured at fair value through profit or loss € -364 million (in 2010: € -415 million) are recognised as total interest expenses. Both amounts are calculated by using the effective interest method.

g) Impairment losses

The following impairment losses on financial assets are recognised in profit or loss in 2011 and 2010 respectively:

(in €m)	2011	2010
Available-for-sale financial assets	(12)	(39)
Loans and receivables	(156)	(60)
Other[1]	(2)	(6)
Total	(170)	(105)

[1] Concerns finance lease receivables.

Other disclosures

Accounting policies

6.9.110 IAS 1 requires an entity to disclose, in the summary of significant accounting policies, the measurement basis (or bases) used in preparing the financial statements and the other accounting policies used that are relevant to an understanding of the financial statements. [IAS 1 para 108; IFRS 7 para 21]. For financial instruments such disclosure may include:

- For financial assets or financial liabilities designated as at fair value through profit or loss:

    - The nature of the financial assets or financial liabilities the entity has designated as at fair value through profit or loss.

    - The criteria for so designating such financial assets or financial liabilities on initial recognition.

    - How the entity has satisfied the conditions for such designation, including, where appropriate, a narrative description of the circumstances underlying the measurement or recognition inconsistency that would otherwise arise, or how designation at fair value through profit or loss is consistent with the entity's documented risk management or investment strategy.

- The criteria for designating financial assets as available for sale.

- Whether regular way purchases and sales of financial assets are accounted for at trade date or at settlement date (see chapter 6.7).

- When an allowance account is used to reduce the carrying amount of financial assets impaired by credit losses:

    - The criteria for determining when the carrying amount of impaired financial assets is reduced directly (or, in the case of a reversal of a write-down, increased directly) and when the allowance account is used.

    - The criteria for writing off amounts charged to the allowance account against the carrying amount of impaired financial assets.

- How net gains or net losses on each category of financial instrument are determined, for example, whether the net gains or net losses on items at fair value through profit or loss include interest or dividend income.

- The criteria the entity uses to determine that there is objective evidence that an impairment loss has occurred.

- When the terms of financial assets that would otherwise be past due or impaired have been renegotiated, the accounting policy for financial assets that are the subject of renegotiated terms.

[IFRS 7 App B para 5].

6.9.111   IAS 1 also requires entities to disclose, in the summary of significant accounting policies or other notes, the judgements, apart from those involving estimations, that management has made in the process of applying the entity's accounting policies and that have the most significant effect on the amounts recognised in the financial statements. [IAS 1 para 113].

Hedge accounting

6.9.112   An entity should disclose the following separately for each type of hedge described in IAS 39 (that is, fair value hedges, cash flow hedges and hedges of net investments in foreign operations).

■   A description of each type of hedge.

■   A description of the financial instruments designated as hedging instruments and their fair values at the reporting date.

■   The nature of the risks being hedged.

[IFRS 7 para 22].

6.9.113   In addition, for cash flow hedges, an entity should disclose:

■   The periods when the cash flows are expected to occur and when they are expected to affect profit or loss.

■   A description of any forecast transaction for which hedge accounting had previously been used, but which is no longer expected to occur.

■   The amount that was recognised in other comprehensive income during the period.

■   The amount that was reclassified from equity and included in profit or loss for the period, showing the amount included in each line item in the income statement. This would also apply to hedging instruments with a short maturity that have been acquired and have matured within the same accounting period. As a practical expedient it is common for entities to recognise the gains and losses on such instruments directly in the income statement rather than to recognise the gains and losses initially in the hedging reserve and then recycle to the income statement. Although the accounting entries net off in the same accounting period, there should still be disclosure of the amounts that would have been recycled.

■   The amount that was reclassified from equity during the period and included in the initial cost or other carrying amount of a non-financial asset or non-financial liability whose acquisition or incurrence was a hedged highly probable forecast transaction.

[IFRS 7 para 23].

6.9.114 An entity should disclose separately:

- In fair value hedges, gains or losses on:

  - The hedging instrument.

  - The hedged item attributable to the hedged risk.

  The requirement here relates to the current reporting period only and not to a disclosure on a cumulative basis (since the inception of the hedge designation).

- The ineffectiveness recognised in profit or loss that arises from cash flow hedges.

- The ineffectiveness recognised in profit or loss that arises from hedges of net investments in foreign operations.

[IFRS 7 para 24].

6.9.115 Some of the required disclosures of information on fair value hedges, cash flow hedges and hedges of net investments are given in Table 6.9.7 below.

Table 6.9.7 – Income statement, hedge ineffectiveness, fair value hedges, interest

National Grid plc – Annual Report – 31 March 2012

4. Finance income and costs

	2012 £m	2011 £m	2010 £m
Interest income and similar income			
Expected return on pension and other post-retirement benefit plan assets	1,273	1,256	981
Interest income on financial instruments:			
Bank deposits and other financial assets	19	22	18
Gains on disposal of available-for-sale investments	9	3	6
Interest income and similar income before exceptional items	1,301	1,281	1,005
Exceptional items			
Exceptional interest credit on tax settlement	–	43	–
Interest income and similar income	1,301	1,324	1,005
Interest expense and other finance costs			
Interest on pension and other post-retirement benefit plan obligations	(1,203)	(1,231)	(1,193)
Interest expense on financial liabilities held at amortised cost:			
Bank loans and overdrafts	(84)	(85)	(80)
Other borrowings	(1,105)	(1,184)	(938)
Derivatives	122	84	22
Unwinding of discounts on provisions	(72)	(128)	(70)
Less: Interest capitalised [(i)]	124	129	99
Interest expense and other finance costs before exceptional items and remeasurements	(2,218)	(2,415)	(2,160)

69045

Exceptional items			
Exceptional debt redemption costs	–	(73)	(33)
Remeasurements			
Net gains/(losses) on derivative financial instruments included in remeasurements [(ii)]:			
Ineffectiveness on derivatives designated as:			
Fair value hedges [(iii)]	**9**	40	67
Cash flow hedges	**14**	9	(5)
Net investment hedges	**(15)**	7	(19)
Net investment hedges – undesignated forward rate risk	**39**	(16)	51
Derivatives not designated as hedges or ineligible for hedge accounting	**(117)**	(4)	(13)
Financial element of remeasurements on commodity contracts	–	–	(1)
	(70)	36	80
Exceptional items and remeasurements included within interest expense	**(37)**	(37)	47
Interest expense and other finance costs	**(2,288)**	(2,452)	(2,113)
Net finance costs	**(987)**	(1,128)	(1,108)

(i) Interest on funding attributable to assets in the course of construction was capitalised during the year at a rate of 5.2% (2011: 5.3%; 2010: 2.8%).

(ii)   Includes a net foreign exchange gain on financing activities of £280m (2011: £173m; 2010: £334m) offset by foreign exchange gains and losses on derivative financial instruments measured at fair value.

(iii)   Includes a net gain on instruments designated as fair value hedges of £233m (2011: £86m gain; 2010: £90m loss) offset by a net loss of

Fair value

6.9.116   In May 2011 the IASB issued IFRS 13. The standard provides a single source of fair value measurement guidance. It clarifies the definition of fair value and provides a framework for measuring fair value. The standard does not determine when fair value measurements are required. The measurement guidance in IFRS 13 will apply to all fair value measurements except for those within the scope of IFRS 2 or IAS 17, and certain other measurements that are required by other standards and are similar to, but are not, fair value. Extensive disclosures are required in IFRS 13 for all assets and liabilities measured at fair value, not just for financial instruments, with some exceptions. In addition, IFRS 13 requires entities to disclose the level of the fair value hierarchy as well as certain other disclosures for all assets and liabilities (including financial instruments) not measured at fair value but for which the fair value is disclosed. IFRS 13 amends IAS 39 to remove the guidance on fair value measurement and amends IFRS 7 to relocate most of the disclosures about fair value to IFRS 13 – in particular, the disclosures around the fair value hierarchy. The standard is effective for annual periods beginning on or after 1 January 2013, with earlier application permitted, and it is applied prospectively as of the beginning of the annual period in which it is initially applied. IFRS 13 is dealt with in chapter 5. In the present chapter, guidance on fair value disclosures describes the current requirements of IFRS 7.

Entities looking for guidance on measurement of fair value and disclosures about fair values under IFRS 13 should refer to chapter 5.

6.9.117 Under IFRS 7, except as set out in paragraph 6.9.122 below, for each class of financial assets and financial liabilities (see para 6.9.54 above), an entity should disclose the fair value of that class of assets and liabilities in a way that permits it to be compared with its carrying amount. [IFRS 7 para 25].

6.9.118 Where an entity has issued a convertible bond and has under IAS 32 accounted for it as a compound instrument, the equity component will not need to be fair valued. This is because the above requirement is only for financial assets and financial liabilities and the equity component does not meet the definition of a financial asset or a financial liability.

6.9.119 In disclosing fair values, an entity should group financial assets and financial liabilities into classes, but should offset them only to the extent that their carrying amounts are offset in the balance sheet. [IFRS 7 para 26].

6.9.120 An entity should disclose, for each class of financial instruments measured at fair value, the methods and, when a valuation technique is used, the assumptions applied in determining fair values of each class of financial asset or financial liability. For example, if applicable, an entity should disclose information about the assumptions relating to pre-payment rates, rates of estimated credit losses and interest rates or discount rates. If there has been a change in valuation technique, the entity should disclose that change and the reasons for making it. [IFRS 7 para 27].

6.9.121 If the market for a financial instrument is not active, its fair value is established using a valuation technique. [IAS 39 paras AG 74-79]. The best evidence of fair value at initial recognition is the transaction price (that is, the fair value of the consideration given or received), unless the fair value of that instrument is evidenced by comparison with other observable current market transactions in the same instrument (that is, without modification or repackaging) or based on a valuation technique whose variables include only data from observable markets as described in paragraph AG 76 of IAS 39. There could be a difference between the fair value at initial recognition and the amount that would be determined at that date using the valuation technique. If such a difference exists, an entity should disclose, by class of financial instrument:

- Its accounting policy for recognising that difference in profit or loss to reflect a change in factors (including time) that market participants would consider in setting a price. [IAS 39 para AG 76A].

- The aggregate difference yet to be recognised in profit or loss at the beginning and end of the period, and a reconciliation of changes in the balance of this difference.

[IFRS 7 para 28].

6.9.122 Disclosure of fair values is not required:

- When the carrying amount is a reasonable approximation of fair value – for example, for financial instruments such as short-term trade receivables and payables.

- For an investment in equity instruments that do not have a quoted market price in an active market, or derivatives linked to such equity instruments, that are measured at cost in accordance with IAS 39, because their fair value cannot be measured reliably.

- For a contract containing a discretionary participation feature (as described in IFRS 4) if the fair value of that feature cannot be measured reliably.

[IFRS 7 para 29].

6.9.123 In the cases described in the second and third bullet points above, an entity should disclose information to help users of the financial statements make their own judgements about the extent of possible differences between the carrying amount of those financial assets or financial liabilities and their fair value, including:

- The fact that fair value information has not been disclosed for these instruments because their fair value cannot be measured reliably.

- A description of the financial instruments, their carrying amount and an explanation of why fair value cannot be measured reliably.

- Information about the market for the instruments.

- Information about whether and how the entity intends to dispose of the financial instruments.

- If financial instruments whose fair value previously could not be reliably measured are derecognised, that fact, their carrying amount at the time of derecognition and the amount of gain or loss recognised.

[IFRS 7 para 30].

Fair value hierarchy

6.9.124 The following section on the fair value hierarchy is affected by IFRS 13, as all of the fair value hierarchy guidance and disclosure requirements noted in this section are relocated from IFRS 7 into IFRS 13. IFRS 13 is effective for annual periods beginning on or after 1 January 2013. Entities applying IFRS 13 either early or after the effective date should refer to chapter 5. IFRS 13 amends IFRS 7 in that it moves all of the fair value hierarchy guidance and disclosure requirements noted in this section into IFRS 13 and out of IFRS 7. The guidance that now follows in this section therefore only applies to entities that do not apply IFRS 13.

6.9.125 In order to increase comparability between entities and take one further step towards IFRS and US GAAP convergence, the in 2009 the IASB introduced a requirement to make disclosures according to a 'fair value hierarchy' similar to that required under US GAAP by SFAS 157, 'Fair value measurements'.

6.9.126   The IFRS 7 fair value hierarchy does not apply to financial instruments measured at amortised cost (for example, held-to-maturity investments), or loans and receivables, whereas IFRS 13 fair value hierarchy will also apply to financial instruments measured at amortised cost (see chapter 5 for further guidance).

6.9.127   The hierarchy has three levels that reflect the significance of the inputs used in measuring fair value. These are as follows:

■   Quoted prices (unadjusted) in active markets for identical assets or liabilities (Level 1).

■   Inputs other than quoted prices included within level 1 that are observable for the asset or liability, either directly (that is, as prices) or indirectly (that is, derived from prices) (Level 2).

■   Inputs for the asset or liability that are not based on observable market data (unobservable inputs) (Level 3).

[IFRS 7 para 27A].

6.9.128   The level in the fair value hierarchy within which a financial instrument is categorised in its entirety is determined on the basis of the lowest level input that is significant to the fair value measurement. For this purpose, the significance of an input is assessed against the fair value measurement in its entirety. [IFRS 7 para 27A].

6.9.129   Assessing the significance of a particular input to the fair value measurement in its entirety requires judgement, considering factors specific to the asset or liability. In assessing the significance of unobservable inputs to a financial instrument's fair value, an entity should:

■   consider the sensitivity of the instrument's overall value to changes in the data; and

■   re-assess the likelihood of variability in the data over the instrument's life.

For example, if an interest rate swap with a ten-year life has an observable yield curve for nine years, provided that the extrapolation of the yield curve to ten years is not significant to the fair value measurement of the swap in its entirety, the fair value measurement is considered to be at level 2 in the hierarchy.

6.9.130   Only instruments traded on an exchange or an active index/market can fall within level 1 of the hierarchy. Generally, for a price to qualify as level 1, reporting entities should be able to obtain the price from multiple sources. A market is active for a financial instrument if quotes are regularly available and do not represent forced transactions (see chapter 6.7). The price quote may be a level 2 or level 3 input where there are few transactions for the instrument, where the

69049

price is not current, or where price quotations vary substantially either over time or among market makers, or for which little information is released publicly.

6.9.131 Whether or not an instrument is considered to have a 'price quoted in an active market' for the purposes of the fair value hierarchy is a different assessment from whether it is considered 'quoted in an active market' for the purposes of IAS 39 and the assessment of whether it can be classified as a loan or receivable. In writing the basis of conclusions to IFRS 7 the board acknowledged that some financial instruments that for measurement purposes are considered to have an active market in accordance with paragraphs AG 71 – AG73 of IAS 39 might be in level 2 for disclosure purposes in the fair value hierarchy. [IFRS 7 BC para 39D].

6.9.132 Many reporting entities obtain information from pricing services, broker pricing information and similar sources, for use as inputs in their fair value measurements. The information provided by these sources could be at any level in the fair value hierarchy, depending on the source of the information for a particular security. However, if the information forms an input to a valuation technique that would preclude classification at level 1, the level is determined on the basis of the valuation inputs, not on the methodology or complexity of the model – that is, the use of a model does not automatically result in a level 3 fair value measurement. For example, a standard valuation model using only observable inputs is likely to result in a measurement that is classified as level 2. However, to the extent that adjustments or interpolations are made by management to level 2 inputs in an otherwise standard model, the measurement may fall into level 3, depending on whether the adjusted inputs are significant to the measurement. Furthermore, if a reporting entity uses a valuation model that is proprietary and relies on unobservable inputs, the resulting fair value measurement is likely to be categorised as level 3.

6.9.133 The US standard (SFAS 157) provides examples of inputs and where they would typically lie in the hierarchy. In view of the similarity between SFAS 157 and the amended IFRS 7, the following examples from the former may be relevant.

- As noted in paragraph 6.9.127, level 2 inputs are inputs other than quoted prices included within level 1 that are observable for the asset or liability, either directly (that is, as prices) or indirectly (that is, derived from prices). Examples of level 2 inputs for particular assets and liabilities include the following:

  - Receive-fixed, pay-variable interest rate swap based on the LIBOR swap rate. A level 2 input would include the LIBOR swap rate if that rate is observable at commonly quoted intervals for the swap's full term. However, other inputs will also need to be considered. For example, if credit is a component of the valuation for the pay and receive leg of the swap, its observability and significance to the measurement will need to be evaluated.

- Three-year option on exchange-traded shares. A level 2 input would include the implied volatility for the shares derived through extrapolation to year three if prices for one- and two-year options on the shares are observable, and the extrapolated implied volatility of a three-year option is corroborated by observable market data for substantially the option's full term. In that case, the implied volatility could be derived by extrapolating from the implied volatility of the one- and two-year options on the shares and corroborated by the implied volatility for three-year options on comparable entities' shares, provided that correlation with the one- and two-year implied volatilities is established.

- Equity investment. A level 2 input would include a valuation multiple (for example, a multiple of earnings or revenue or a similar performance measure) derived from observable market data, for example, multiples derived from prices in observed transactions involving comparable businesses, considering operational, market, financial, and non-financial factors.

- As noted in paragraph 6.9.127, level 3 inputs are inputs that are not based on observable market data. They are inputs that reflect the reporting entity's own views about the assumptions market participants would use in pricing the asset or liability (including assumptions about risk), developed based on the best information available in the circumstances. Assumptions about risk include the risk inherent in a particular valuation technique used to measure fair value (such as a pricing model) and/or the risk inherent in the inputs to the valuation technique. Examples of level 3 inputs for particular assets and liabilities include the following:

  - Long-dated currency swap. A level 3 input would include interest rates in a specified currency that are not observable and cannot be corroborated by observable market data at commonly quoted intervals or otherwise for substantially the full term of the currency swap. The interest rates in a currency swap are the swap rates calculated from the respective countries' yield curves.

  - Three-year option on exchange-traded shares. A level 3 input would include historical volatility, that is, the volatility for the shares derived from the shares' historical prices. Historical volatility typically does not represent current market participant expectations about future volatility, even if it is the only information available to price an option.

  - Equity investment. A level 3 input would include a financial forecast (for example, of cash flows or earnings) developed using the reporting entity's own data if there is no information that indicates that market participants would use different assumptions.

6.9.134 For each class of financial instruments measured at fair value, an entity should disclose the following (the quantitative disclosures should be presented in tabular format, unless another format is more appropriate):

- The level in the fair value hierarchy into which the fair value measurements are categorised in their entirety, segregating fair value measurements in accordance with the levels defined in paragraph 6.9.127 above.

- Any significant transfers between level 1 and level 2 of the fair value hierarchy and the reasons for those transfers. Transfers into each level should be disclosed and discussed separately from transfers out of each level. Significance should be judged with respect to profit or loss and total assets or total liabilities.

- For fair value measurements in level 3 of the fair value hierarchy, a reconciliation from the beginning balances to the ending balances, disclosing separately changes during the period attributable to the following:

  - Total gains or losses for the period recognised in profit or loss and a description of where they are presented in the statement of comprehensive income or the separate income statement (if presented).

  - Total gains or losses recognised in other comprehensive income.

  - Purchases, sales, issues and settlements (each type of movement disclosed separately).

  - Transfers into or out of level 3 (for example, transfers attributable to changes in the observability of market data) and the reasons for those transfers. For significant transfers, transfers into level 3 should be disclosed and discussed separately from transfers out of level 3.

- The amount of total gains or losses for the period included in profit or loss resulting from level 3 financial instruments that are attributable to those assets and liabilities held at the end of the reporting period and a description of where those gains or losses are presented in the statement of comprehensive income or the separate income statement (if presented).

- For fair value measurements in level 3, if changing one or more of the inputs to reasonably possible alternative assumptions would change fair value significantly, the entity should state that fact and disclose the effect of those changes. The entity should disclose how the effect of a change to a reasonably possible alternative assumption was calculated. Significance should be judged with respect to profit or loss, and total assets or total liabilities, or, when changes in fair value are recognised in other comprehensive income, total equity.

6.9.135 Examples of the fair value hierarchy are provided in Tables 6.9.8 and 6.9.9. Table 6.9.8 also gives the Level 3 reconciliations and sensitivity analysis required by IFRS 7. It should be noted that the example does not reproduce the company's description of the control framework for financial instruments carried at fair value, its detailed description of valuation techniques used, details of risk related adjustments, model related adjustments and credit risk adjustment methodology.

Table 6.9.8 – Fair value disclosures relating to financial assets and liabilities

HSBC Holdings plc – Annual report – 31 December 2011

Fair values of financial instruments (extract)

16 Fair values of financial instruments carried at fair value (extract 1)

The classification of financial instruments is determined in accordance with the accounting policies set out in Note 2.

The use of assumptions and estimation in valuing financial instruments is described on page 40.

Fair value is the amount for which an asset could be exchanged, or a liability settled, between knowledgeable, willing parties in an arm's length transaction.

The following table sets out the financial instruments carried at fair value.

Bases of valuing financial assets and liabilities measured at fair value

	Quoted market price	Using observable inputs	With significant unobservable inputs	
	Level 1	Level 2	Level 3	Total
At 31 December 2011				
Assets				
Trading assets	**180,043**	**145,628**	**4,780**	**330,451**
Financial assets designated at fair value	**22,496**	**7,644**	**716**	**30,856**
Derivatives	**1,262**	**340,668**	**4,449**	**346,379**
Financial investments: available for sale	**217,788**	**151,936**	**9,121**	**378,845**
Liabilities				
Trading liabilities	**98,208**	**159,157**	**7,827**	**265,192**
Financial liabilities designated at fair value	**27,461**	**57,696**	**567**	**85,724**
Derivatives	**1,991**	**340,260**	**3,129**	**345,380**
At 31 December 2010				
Assets				
Trading assets	224,613	154,750	5,689	385,052
Financial assets designated at fair value	23,641	12,783	587	37,011
Derivatives	2,078	254,718	3,961	260,757
Financial investments: available for sale	214,276	158,743	8,237	381,256
Liabilities				
Trading liabilities	124,874	164,436	11,393	300,703
Financial liabilities designated at fair value	22,193	65,370	570	88,133
Derivatives	1,808	253,051	3,806	258,665

The reduction in Level 1 trading assets and liabilities reflects a decline in listed equity, government and debt security positions and short positions. The rise in Level 2 derivative balances reflects an increase in both derivative assets and liabilities generally, driven by declining yield curves in the second half of 2011.

There were no material transfers between Level 1 and Level 2 in the year. An analysis of the movements of Level 3 financial instruments is provided on page 353.

16 Fair values of financial instruments carried at fair value (extract 2)

Fair value valuation bases

Financial instruments measured at fair value using a valuation technique with significant unobservable inputs – Level 3

| | Assets | | | | Liabilities | | |
| | | | Designated at fair value through | | | Designated at fair value through | |
	Available for sale US$m	Held for trading US$m	profit and loss US$m	Derivatives US$m	Held for trading US$m	profit and loss US$m	Derivatives US$m
At 31 December 2011							
Private equity investments	4,565	88	432	–	–	–	–
Asset-backed securities	2,584	710	–	–	–	–	7
Leveraged finance	–	682	–	–	–	–	7
Loans held for securitisation	–	92	–	–	–	–	–
Structured notes	–	–	–	–	7,340	–	–
Derivatives with monolines	–	–	–	940	–	–	–
Other derivatives	–	–	–	3,509	–	–	3,122
Other portfolios	1,972	3,208	284	–	487	567	–
	9,121	4,780	716	4,449	7,827	567	3,129
At 31 December 2010							
Private equity investments	4,057	278	120	–	–	–	–
Asset-backed securities	1,949	566	–	–	–	–	–
Leveraged finance	–	–	–	–	–	–	11
Loans held for securitisation	–	1,043	–	–	–	–	–
Structured notes	–	–	–	–	10,667	–	–
Derivatives with monolines	–	–	–	1,005	–	–	–
Other derivatives	–	–	–	2,956	–	–	3,787
Other portfolios	2,231	3,802	467	–	726	570	8
	8,237	5,689	587	3,961	11,393	570	3,806

Private equity and strategic investments

HSBC's private equity and strategic investments are generally classified as available for sale and are not traded in active markets. In the absence of an active market, an investment's fair value is estimated on the basis of an analysis of the investee's financial position and results, risk profile, prospects and other factors, as well as by reference to market valuations for similar entities quoted in an active market, or the price at which similar companies have changed ownership.

Asset-backed securities

While quoted market prices are generally used to determine the fair value of these securities, valuation models are used to substantiate the reliability of the limited market data available and to identify whether any adjustments to quoted market prices are required. For ABSs including residential MBSs, the valuation uses an industry standard model and the assumptions relating to prepayment speeds, default rates and loss severity based on collateral type, and performance, as appropriate. The valuations output is benchmarked for consistency against observable data for securities of a similar nature.

Loans, including leveraged finance and loans held for securitisation

Loans held at fair value are valued from broker quotes and/or market data consensus providers when available. In the absence of an observable market, the fair value is determined using valuation techniques. These techniques include discounted cash flow models, which incorporate assumptions regarding an appropriate credit spread for the loan, derived from other market instruments issued by the same or comparable entities.

Structured notes

The fair value of structured notes valued using a valuation technique is derived from the fair value of the underlying debt security, and the fair value of the embedded derivative is determined as described in the paragraph below on derivatives.

Trading liabilities valued using a valuation technique with significant unobservable inputs principally comprised equity-linked structured notes, which are issued by HSBC and provide the counterparty with a return that is linked to the performance of certain equity securities, and other portfolios. The notes are classified as Level 3 due to the unobservability of parameters such as long-dated equity volatilities and correlations between equity prices, between equity prices and interest rates and between interest rates and foreign exchange rates.

Derivatives

OTC (i.e. non-exchange traded) derivatives are valued using valuation models. Valuation models calculate the present value of expected future cash flows, based upon 'no-arbitrage' principles. For many vanilla derivative products, such as interest rate swaps and European options, the modelling approaches used are standard across the industry. For more complex derivative products, there may be some differences in market practice. Inputs to valuation models are determined from observable market data wherever possible, including prices available from exchanges, dealers, brokers or providers of consensus pricing. Certain inputs may not be observable in the market directly, but can be determined from observable prices via model calibration procedures or estimated from historical data or other sources. Examples of inputs that may be unobservable include volatility surfaces, in whole or in part, for less commonly traded option products, and correlations between market factors such as foreign exchange rates, interest rates and equity prices. The valuation of derivatives with monolines is discussed on page 154.

Derivative products valued using valuation techniques with significant unobservable inputs included certain types of correlation products, such as foreign exchange basket options, equity basket options, foreign exchange interest rate hybrid transactions and long-dated option transactions. Examples of the latter are equity options, interest rate and foreign exchange options and certain credit derivatives. Credit derivatives include certain tranched CDS transactions.

Reconciliation of fair value measurements in Level 3 of the fair value hierarchy

The following table provides a reconciliation of the movement between opening and closing balances of Level 3 financial instruments, measured at fair value using a valuation technique with significant unobservable inputs:

Movement in Level 3 financial instruments

	Assets				Liabilities		
	Available for sale	Held for trading	Designated at fair value through profit and loss	Derivatives	Held for trading	Designated at fair value through profit and loss	Derivatives
	US$m	US$m	US$m	US$m	US$m	US$m	US$m
At 1 January 2011	8,237	5,689	587	3,961	11,393	570	3,806
Total gains/(losses) recognised in profit or loss	222	(330)	11	767	36	8	628
Total gains recognised in other comprehensive income[1]	(179)	(12)	(15)	(16)	11	(11)	–
Purchases	1,858	1,483	242	–	(1,843)	–	–
New issuances	–	–	–	–	4,569	–	–
Sales	(756)	(2,578)	(69)	–	–	–	–
Settlements	(1,088)	(199)	(7)	(33)	(1,528)	–	(1,083)
Transfers out	(1,891)	(569)	(173)	(410)	(5,266)	–	(608)
Transfers in	2,718	1,296	140	180	455	–	386
At 31 December 2011	9,121	4,780	716	4,449	7,827	567	3,129
Total gains/(losses) recognised in profit or loss relating to those assets and liabilities held on 31 December:	134	(237)	36	617	101	8	80
– net interest income	105	–	–	–	–	–	–
– trading income excluding net interest income	–	(265)	–	617	119	–	80
– net interest income on trading activities	–	28	–	–	(18)	–	–
– net income/(expense) from other financial instruments designated at fair value	–	–	36	–	–	8	–
– dividend income	29	–	–	–	–	–	–

Movement in Level 3 financial instruments

	Assets				Liabilities		
	Available for sale	Held for trading	Designated at fair value through profit and loss	Derivatives	Held for trading	Designated at fair value through profit and loss	Derivatives
	US$m	US$m	US$m	US$m	US$m	US$m	US$m
At 1 January 2010	10,214	6,420	1,224	4,453	8,774	507	5,192
Total gains/(losses) recognised in profit or loss	345	158	63	(675)	166	(11)	(240)
Total gains recognised in other comprehensive income	618	(101)	(36)	(110)	(157)	74	93
Purchases	3,708	858	81	–	(356)	–	–
New issuances	–	–	–	–	4,025	–	–
Sales	(2,461)	(1,543)	(8)	–	–	–	–
Settlements	(1,032)	1	(22)	64	(948)	–	(820)
Transfers out	(7,065)	(629)	(894)	(669)	(1,750)	–	(1,003)
Transfers in	3,910	525	179	898	1,639	–	584
At 31 December 2010	8,237	5,689	587	3,961	11,393	570	3,806
Total gains/(losses) recognised in profit or loss relating to those assets and liabilities held on 31 December:	113	116	17	268	180	(14)	361
– net interest income	89	–	–	–	–	–	–
– trading income excluding net interest income	–	98	–	268	198	–	361
– net interest income on trading activities	–	18	–	–	(18)	–	–
– net income/(expense) from other financial instruments designated at fair value	–	–	17	–	–	(14)	–
– dividend income	24	–	–	–	–	–	–

[1] *Included in 'Available-for-sale investments: Fair value gains/(losses)' and 'Exchange differences' in the consolidated statement of comprehensive income.*

Available-for-sale securities: Transfers in and out of Level 3 relate principally to assets whose prices have been unobservable during the year and those whose prices have become observable, respectively. Purchases of available-for- sale securities reflects the acquisition of corporate bonds across a range of geographies.

Trading liabilities: Transfers out of Level 3 are driven by certain equity volatilities and correlations becoming observable as the market continues to evolve. Settlement of trading liabilities reflect structured note maturities during the period, including the unwind of a large structured transaction which also impacted sales of assets held for trading.

Effect of changes in significant unobservable assumptions to reasonably possible alternatives

As discussed above, the fair value of financial instruments are, in certain circumstances, measured using valuation techniques that incorporate assumptions that are not evidenced by prices from observable current market transactions in the same instrument and are not based on observable market data. The following table shows the sensitivity of these fair values to reasonably possible alternative assumptions:

Sensitivity of fair values to reasonably possible alternative assumptions

	Reflected in profit or loss		Reflected in equity	
	Favourable changes US$m	Unfavourable changes US$m	Favourable changes US$m	Unfavourable changes US$m
At 31 December 2011	**369**	**(436)**	–	–
Derivatives, trading assets and trading liabilities[1]	**72**	**(72)**	–	–
Financial assets and liabilities designated at fair value	–	–	**814**	**(818)**
Financial investments: available for sale	**441**	**(508)**	**814**	**(818)**
At 31 December 2010				
Derivatives, trading assets and trading liabilities[1]	554	(444)	–	–
Financial assets and liabilities designated at fair value	77	(75)	–	–
Financial investments: available for sale	–	–	763	(744)
For footnote, see page 195.	631	(519)	763	(744)

[1] *Derivatives, trading assets and trading liabilities are presented as one category to reflect the manner in which these financial instruments are risk-managed.*

The decrease in the effect of favourable changes in significant unobservable inputs in relation to derivatives, trading assets and trading liabilities during the year primarily reflects greater pricing certainty in some areas, most notably structured credit and structured rates either as a result of decreased exposures or enhanced analysis. Unfavourable changes in derivatives, trading assets and liabilities has been impacted by similar factors but these have been offset by an increased potential unfavourable impact on monoline exposures, driven by increasing credit default spreads even though exposures have reduced over the period.

Sensitivity of fair values to reasonably possible alternative assumptions by Level 3 instrument type

| | Reflected in profit or loss | | Reflected in equity | |
	Favourable changes US$m	Unfavourable changes US$m	Favourable changes US$m	Unfavourable changes US$m
At 31 December 2011				
Private equity investments	**123**	**(83)**	**451**	**(451)**
Asset-backed securities	**3**	**(3)**	**183**	**(175)**
Leveraged finance	**4**	**(4)**	–	–
Loans held for securitisation	**6**	**(6)**	–	–
Structured notes	**76**	**(178)**	–	–
Derivatives with monolines	**145**	**(154)**	–	–
Other derivatives	**84**	**(80)**	**180**	**(192)**
Other portfolios	**441**	**(508)**	**814**	**(818)**
At 31 December 2010				
Private equity investments	112	(71)	383	(383)
Asset-backed securities	8	(8)	179	(181)
Loans held for securitisation	8	(8)	–	–
Structured notes	18	(16)	–	–
Derivatives with monolines	94	(8)	–	–
Other derivatives	256	(258)	–	–
Other portfolios	135	(150)	201	(180)
	631	(519)	763	(744)

Favourable and unfavourable changes are determined on the basis of changes in the value of the instrument as a result of varying the levels of the unobservable parameters using statistical techniques. When parameters are not amenable to statistical analysis, quantification of uncertainty is judgemental.

When the fair value of a financial instrument is affected by more than one unobservable assumption, the above table reflects the most favourable or most unfavourable change from varying the assumptions individually.

In respect of private equity investments, in many of the methodologies, the principal assumption is the valuation multiple to be applied to the main financial indicators. This may be determined with reference to multiples for comparable listed companies and includes discounts for marketability.

For ABSs, the principal assumptions in the models are based on benchmark information about prepayment speeds, default rates, loss severities and the historical performance of the underlying assets.

For leveraged finance, loans held for securitisation and derivatives with monolines the principal assumption concerns the appropriate value to be attributed to the counterparty credit risk. This requires estimation of exposure at default, probability of default and recovery in the event of default. For loan transactions, assessment of exposure at default is straightforward. For derivative transactions, a future exposure profile is generated on the basis of current market data. Probabilities of default and recovery levels are estimated using available evidence, which may include financial information, historical experience, CDS spreads and consensus recovery levels.

For structured notes and other derivatives, principal assumptions concern the value to be attributed to future volatility of asset values and the future correlation between asset values. These principal assumptions include credit volatilities and correlations used in the valuation of structured credit derivatives (including leveraged credit derivatives). For such unobservable assumptions, estimates are based on available market data, which may include the use of a proxy method to derive a volatility or a correlation from comparable assets for which market data is more readily available, and/or an examination of historical levels.

69059

Table 6.9.9 – Fair value hierarchy

Centrica plc – Annual report – 31 December 2010

29. Fair value of financial instruments (extract)

Fair value hierarchy

Financial assets and financial liabilities measured at fair value are classified into one of three categories:

Level 1
Fair value is determined using observable inputs that reflect unadjusted quoted market prices for identical assets and liabilities, for example exchange-traded commodity contracts valued using close-of-day settlement prices. The adjusted market price used for financial assets held by the Group is the current bid price.

Level 2
Fair value is determined using significant inputs that may be either directly observable inputs or unobservable inputs that are corroborated by market data, for example over-the-counter energy contracts within the active period valued using broker-quotes or third-party pricing services and foreign exchange or interest rate derivatives valued using quotes corroborated with market data.

Level 3
Fair value is determined using significant unobservable inputs that are not corroborated by market data and may be used with internally developed methodologies that result in management's best estimate of fair value, for example energy contracts within the inactive period valued using in-house valuation techniques. The fair value hierarchy of financial assets and liabilities measured at fair value as at 31 December was as follows:

	Level 1 £m	Level 2 £m	Level 3 £m	2010 Total £m	Level 1 £m	Level 2 £m	Level 3 £m	2009 Total £m
Financial assets								
Derivative financial instruments:								
Energy derivatives	–	492	119	**611**	46	550	64	660
Interest rate derivatives	–	108	–	**108**	–	72	–	72
Foreign exchange derivatives	–	71	–	**71**	2	74	–	76
Treasury gilts designated at fair value through profit and loss	164	–	–	**164**	104	–	–	104
Debt instruments	64	–	1	**65**	62	56	–	118
Equity instruments	17	–	11	**28**	17	–	11	28
Total financial assets	**245**	**671**	**131**	**1,047**	231	752	75	1,058

Financial liabilities
Derivative financial instruments:

Energy derivatives	(113)	(849)	(320)	**(1,282)**	(198)	(1,954)	(490)	(2,642)
Interest rate derivatives	–	(16)	–	**(16)**	–	(15)	–	(15)
Foreign exchange derivatives	–	(105)	–	**(105)**	–	(93)	–	(93)
Total financial liabilities	**(113)**	**(970)**	**(320)**	**(1,403)**	**(198)**	**(2,062)**	**(490)**	**(2,750)**

There were no significant transfers out of Level 1 into Level 2 and out of Level 2 into Level 1 during 2010 and 2009.

The reconciliation of the Level 3 fair value measurements during the year is as follows:

	Equity/debt instruments £m	Energy derivatives £m	2010 £m	Equity/debt instruments £m	Energy derivatives £m	2009 £m
Level 3 financial assets						
1 January	11	64	**75**	3	399	402
Total realised and unrealised losses:						
Gains/(losses) recognised in Income Statement	–	60	**60**	–	(247)	(247)
Gains recognised in Other Comprehensive Income	–	2	**2**	–	–	–
Purchases, sales, issuances and settlements (net)	1	37	**38**	–	–	–
Transfers from Level 3 to Level 2	–	(44)	**(44)**	–	(88)	(88)
Acquisitions	–	–	–	8	–	8
31 December	12	119	**131**	11	64	75
Total gains/(losses) for the year for Level 3 financial assets held at the end of the reporting period[i]	–	**74**	**74**	–	64	64

(i) £72 million gains (2009: £258 million losses) for the year for Level 3 financial assets held at the end of the reporting year were recognised within certain re-measurements and £2 million gains (2009: £nil) were recognised in Other Comprehensive Income. The 2009 figures have been restated for comparative purposes.

Energy derivatives	2010 £m	2009 £m
Level 3 financial liabilities		
1 January	**(490)**	(568)
Total realised and unrealised losses:		
Recognised in Income Statement	**(72)**	(54)
Recognised in Other Comprehensive Income	–	(9)
Purchases, sales, issuances and settlements (net)	77	–
Transfers from Level 3 to Level 2	165	141
31 December	**(320)**	**(490)**
Total losses for the year for Level 3 financial liabilities held at the end of the reporting period[i]	**(86)**	(112)

(i) £86 million losses (2009: £103 million losses) for the year for Level 3 financial liabilities held at the end of the reporting year were recognised within certain re-measurements and £nil (2009: £9 million) were recognised in Other Comprehensive Income. The 2009 figures have been restated for comparative purposes.

The impacts of reasonably possible changes to assumed gas, power, coal, emissions and oil prices on the net fair value of the Group's fair value measurements categorised as Level 3 are as follows:

Energy price	2010 Reasonably possible change in variable	2009 Reasonably possible change in variable
UK gas (p/therm)	**+/-11**	+/-10
UK power (£/MWh)	**+/-5**	+/-5
UK coal (US$/tonne)	**+/-21**	+/-20
UK emissions (/tonne)	**+/-2**	+/-3
UK oil (US$/bbl)	**+/-18**	+/-19
Increase/(decrease) in fair value	**2010 £m**	**2009 £m**
UK energy prices - increase/(decrease)	9/12	17/(17)

The impacts disclosed above result from changing the assumptions used for fair valuing energy contracts in relation to gas, power, emissions, coal and oil prices to reasonably possible alternative assumptions at the Balance Sheet date. The fair value impacts only concern those contracts entered into which are within the scope of IAS 39 and are marked-to-market based on valuation models using assumptions that are not currently observable in an active market. The sensitivity analysis provided is hypothetical only and should be used with caution, as the impacts provided are not necessarily indicative of the actual impacts that would be experienced because the Group's actual exposure to market rates is constantly changing as the Group's portfolio of energy contracts changes. Changes in fair values based on a variation in a market variable cannot be extrapolated as the relationship between the change in market variable and the change in fair value will not always be linear. This can be seen in the results from the above 2010 sensitivity analysis. Due to the interaction of various contract price floors and ceilings and optionality in purchase/sales volumes, both scenarios lead to an increase in the total fair value of the Level 3 assets and liabilities.

Financial instrument risk disclosures

6.9.136 An entity should disclose information that enables users of its financial statements to evaluate the nature and extent of risks arising from financial instruments to which the entity is exposed at the reporting date. [IFRS 7 para 31].

6.9.137 The disclosures described from paragraph 6.9.141 onwards focus on the risks that arise from financial instruments and how they have been managed. These risks typically include, but are not limited to, credit risk, liquidity risk and market risk as discussed in paragraph 6.9.60 above. [IFRS 7 para 32].

6.9.138 As part of the improvements to IFRSs issued in May 2010, the IASB emphasised the intended interaction between the qualitative and quantitative disclosures of the nature and extent of risks arising from financial instruments. IFRS 7 clarifies that providing qualitative disclosures in the context of quantitative disclosures enables users to link related disclosures and hence form an overall picture of the nature and extent of risks arising from financial instruments. The IASB concluded that an explicit emphasis on the interaction between qualitative and quantitative disclosures will contribute to disclosure of information in a way that better enables users to evaluate an entity's exposure. [IFRS 7 para 32A].

6.9.139 When an entity uses several methods to manage a risk exposure, it should disclose information using the method or methods that provide the most relevant and reliable information. [IFRS 7 App B para 7].

6.9.140 The disclosures should be given either in the financial statements or incorporated by cross-reference from the financial statements to some other statement, such as a management commentary or risk report, that is available to users of the financial statements on the same terms as the financial statements and at the same time. Without the information incorporated by cross-reference, the financial statements are incomplete. [IFRS 7 App B para 6].

Qualitative disclosures

6.9.141 For each type of risk arising from financial instruments, an entity should disclose:

■ The exposures to risk and how they arise.

  Information about risk exposures might describe exposures both gross and net of risk transfer and other risk-mitigating transactions.

■ Its objectives, policies and processes for managing the risk and the methods used to measure the risk. This might include, but is not limited to:

  ■ The structure and organisation of the entity's risk management functions, including a discussion of independence and accountability.

- The scope and nature of the entity's risk reporting or measurement systems.

- The entity's policies for hedging or mitigating risk, including its policies and procedures for taking collateral.

- The entity's processes for monitoring the continuing effectiveness of such hedges or mitigating devices.

- The entity's policies and procedures for avoiding excessive concentrations of risk.

- Any changes in the above for the period.

  Entities should disclose the reasons for the change. Such changes may result from changes in exposure to risk or from changes in the way those exposures are managed.

[IFRS 7 paras 33, IG 15-16].

6.9.142 An example of a company that has included the above disclosure requirements in its risk management policy is given in Table 6.9.10 below.

Table 6.9.10 – Risk management policy

Diageo plc – Annual Report – 30 June 2011

23. Financial instruments and risk management (extract 1)

Derivative financial instruments are used to hedge exposure to fluctuations in foreign exchange rates, interest rates and commodity price movements that arise in the normal course of the group's business.

The group's funding, liquidity and exposure to foreign exchange rate and interest rate risks are managed by the group's treasury department. The treasury department uses a range of financial instruments to manage these underlying risks.

Treasury operations are conducted within a framework of board-approved policies and guidelines, which are recommended and subsequently monitored by the finance committee. This committee is described in the Corporate governance report. These policies and guidelines include benchmark exposure and/or hedge cover levels for key areas of treasury risk. The benchmarks, hedge cover and overall appropriateness of Diageo's risk management policies are reviewed by the board following, for example, significant business, strategic or accounting changes. The framework provides for limited defined levels of flexibility in execution to allow for the optimal application of the board-approved strategies. Transactions arising on the application of this flexibility may give rise to exposures different from the defined benchmark levels that are separately monitored on a daily basis using value at risk analysis. These transactions are carried at fair value and gains or losses are taken to the income statement as they arise. In the year ended 30 June 2011 gains and losses on these transactions were not material.

The finance committee receives monthly reports on the activities of the treasury department, including any exposures different from the defined benchmarks.

(a) Currency risk
The group publishes its consolidated financial statements in sterling and conducts business in many foreign currencies. As a result, it is subject to foreign currency exchange risk due to exchange rate movements, which will affect the group's transactions and the translation of the results and underlying net assets of its foreign operations. To manage the foreign exchange risk the group's treasury department uses certain financial instruments. Where hedge accounting is

---

applied, hedges are documented and tested for hedge effectiveness on an ongoing basis. Diageo expects hedges entered into to continue to be effective and therefore does not expect the impact of ineffectiveness on the consolidated income statement to be material.

Hedge of net investment in foreign operations
The group hedges a substantial portion of its exposure to fluctuations in the sterling value of its foreign operations by designating net borrowings held in foreign currencies and by using foreign currency spots, forwards, swaps and other financial derivatives. The board reviewed and approved a revised policy, applicable from 3 December 2010, to manage hedging of foreign exchange risk arising from net investment in foreign operations. The group's revised policy is, where a liquid foreign exchange market exists, to seek to hedge currency exposure on its net investment in foreign operations by using gross debt in foreign currencies and foreign currency spots, forwards, swaps and other financial derivatives within the following percentage bands: 80% to 100% for US dollars and euros and, at management's discretion, 0% to 100% for other currencies. The group's previous policy where a liquid foreign exchange market existed, was to aim to hedge currency exposure on its net investment in foreign operations by using net debt in foreign currencies and foreign currency spots, forwards swaps and other financial derivatives and within the following percentage bands: 80% to 100% for US dollars and euros and 50% to 100% for other currencies. As at 30 June 2011, these ratios were 89% and 87% for US dollars and euros, respectively, and 42% for other currencies.

Exchange differences arising on the retranslation of foreign currency borrowings (including foreign currency forwards swaps and other financial derivatives), to the extent that they are in an effective hedge relationship, are recognised in other comprehensive income to offset exchange differences on net investments in foreign operations. Exchange differences on foreign currency borrowings not in a hedge relationship and any ineffectiveness are taken to the income statement.

Transaction exposure hedging
The board reviewed the group's transactional foreign exchange risk management policy and approved a revised policy, on 1 October 2010. The group's revised policy is to aim to hedge 18 months forecast transactional foreign exchange rate risk in the three major currency pairs (US dollar/sterling, euro/sterling and euro/US dollar), up to 100%, with a target range of between 75% and 100% once the relevant annual plan has been approved. In addition, at management's discretion, the group may decide to hedge other currencies for up to 18 months. The group's previous policy was to seek, for currencies in which there was an active market, to hedge between 60% and 100% of forecast transactional foreign exchange rate risk, for up to a maximum of 21 months forward, using foreign currency forward contracts with coverage levels increasing nearer to the forecast transaction date. The effective portion of the gain or loss on the hedge is recognised in other comprehensive income and recycled into the income statement at the same time as the underlying hedged transaction affects the income statement. Any ineffectiveness is taken to the income statement.

Hedge of foreign currency debt
The group uses cross currency interest rate swaps to hedge the foreign currency risk associated with certain foreign currency denominated borrowings. The effective portion of the gain or loss on the hedge is recognised in other comprehensive income and recycled into the income statement at the same time as the underlying hedged transaction affects the income statement. Any ineffectiveness is taken to the income statement.

At 30 June 2011, as a result of the net investment, transaction exposure and foreign currency debt cover outlined above, the group had outstanding gross foreign exchange contracts as disclosed in note 23(g). Further quantitative analysis of the sensitivity to movements in currency rates is reported in the 'Market risk sensitivity analysis' in note 23(d).

(b) Interest rate risk
The group has an exposure to interest rate risk, arising principally on changes in US dollar, euro and sterling interest rates. To manage interest rate risk, the group manages its proportion of fixed to floating rate borrowings within limits approved by the board, primarily through issuing fixed and floating rate borrowing and commercial paper, and by utilising interest rate derivatives. These practices aim to minimise the group's net finance charges with acceptable year on year

volatility. To facilitate operational efficiency and effective hedge accounting, the group's policy is to maintain fixed rate borrowings within a band of 40% to 60% of forecast net borrowings. For these calculations, net borrowings exclude interest rate related fair value adjustments. A template approved by the board specifies different duration guidelines and fixed/floating amortisation periods (time taken for the fixed element of debt to reduce to zero) depending on different interest rate environments. The majority of Diageo's existing interest rate derivatives are designated as hedges and are expected to be effective. Fair value of these derivatives is recognised in the income statement, along with any changes in the relevant fair value of the underlying hedged asset or liability.

(c) Commodity price risk

The group is exposed to commodity price risk. The group primarily uses long term purchase contracts to secure prices with suppliers to protect against volatility in commodity prices.

23. Financial instruments and risk management (extract 2)

(e) Credit risk

Credit risk refers to the risk that a counterparty will default on its contractual obligations resulting in financial loss to the group. Credit risk arises from cash balances (including bank deposits and cash and cash equivalents), derivative financial instruments and credit exposures to customers, including outstanding loans, trade and other receivables, financial guarantees and committed transactions.

Credit risk is managed separately for financial and business related credit exposures.

Financial credit risk

Diageo aims to minimise its financial credit risk through the application of risk management policies approved and monitored by the board. Counterparties are limited to major banks and financial institutions and the policy restricts the exposure to any one counterparty by setting credit limits taking into account the credit quality of the counterparty. The group's policy is designed to ensure that individual counterparty limits are adhered to and that there are no significant concentrations of credit risk. The board also defines the types of financial instruments which may be transacted. Financial instruments are primarily transacted with major international financial institutions with a long term credit rating within the A band or better. The credit risk arising through the use of financial instruments for interest rate and currency risk management is estimated with reference to the fair value of contracts with a positive value, rather than the notional amount of the instruments themselves.

When derivative transactions are undertaken with bank counterparties, Diageo may, where appropriate, enter into certain agreements with such bank counterparties whereby the parties agree to post cash collateral for the benefit of the other if the net valuations of the derivatives are above a pre-determined threshold.

Diageo annually reviews the credit limits applied and regularly monitors the counterparties' credit quality reflecting market credit conditions.

Business related credit risk

Trade and other receivables exposures are managed locally in the operating units where they arise and credit limits are set as deemed appropriate for the customer. There is no concentration of credit risk with respect to trade and other receivables as the group has a large number of customers which are internationally dispersed.

The maximum credit risk exposure of the group's financial assets was as follows:

	2011 £ million	2010 £million
Trade and other receivables (excluding taxes)	1,751	1,825
Accrued income	23	31
Assets held for sale	9	13
Cash and cash equivalents	1,584	1,453
Derivative financial assets	200	334
Other investments	102	117
Total	**3,669**	**3,773**

Derivative financial assets comprise the fair value of derivatives receivable from financial institutions partly offset by cash collateral received.

Cash and cash equivalents comprise cash in hand and deposits which are readily convertible to known amounts of cash and which are subject to insignificant risk of changes in value and have an original maturity of three months or less at acquisition including money market deposits, commercial paper and investments.

At 30 June 2011, approximately 13% and 17% of the group's trade receivables of £1,501 million are due from counterparties based in the United Kingdom and in the United States, respectively.

(f) Liquidity risk
Liquidity risk is the risk that Diageo may encounter in meeting its obligations associated with financial liabilities that are settled by delivering cash or other financial assets. The group's policy with regard to the expected maturity profile of borrowings is to limit the amount of such borrowings maturing within 12 months to 50% of gross borrowings less money market demand deposits, and the level of commercial paper to 30% of gross borrowings less money market demand deposits. In addition, it is group policy to maintain backstop facility terms from relationship banks to support commercial paper obligations.

Quantitative disclosures

6.9.143   For each type of risk arising from financial instruments, an entity should disclose:

- Summary quantitative data about its exposure to that risk at the reporting date. This disclosure should be based on the information provided internally to the entity's key management personnel (as defined in IAS 24), for example, the entity's board of directors or chief executive officer. An entity with two distinct operations (for example, a retail division and a manufacturing division) may be monitored by management separately as two divisions. All disclosures should normally be provided on a consolidated basis. However, those disclosures that are based on management reporting could be presented separately for both the divisions as that is the way management monitors the financial risks, unless there were material transactions between the divisions, in which case separate disclosures could be misleading.

- The items described in paragraphs 6.9.144 to 6.9.201, to the extent not provided in the previous bullet point. [IFRS 7 para 34(b)]. These are

IFRS 7's minimum disclosure requirements, regardless of whether management uses this information to manage the entity's risks.

■ Concentrations of risk if not apparent from the disclosures made in accordance with the previous two bullet points (see para 6.9.144 below).

[IFRS 7 para 34].

6.9.144 Concentrations of risk arise from financial instruments that have similar characteristics and are affected similarly by changes in economic or other conditions. The identification of concentrations of risk requires judgement taking into account the entity's circumstances. Disclosure of concentrations of risk should include:

■ A description of how management determines concentrations (see para 6.9.145 below).

■ A description of the shared characteristic that identifies each concentration (for example, counterparty, geographical area, currency or market).

■ The amount of the risk exposure associated with all financial instruments sharing that characteristic.

[IFRS 7 App B para 8].

6.9.145 Concentrations of credit risk may arise from:

■ Industry sectors.

Thus, if an entity's counterparties are concentrated in one or more industry sectors (such as retail or wholesale), it would disclose separately exposure to risks arising from each concentration of counterparties.

■ Credit rating or other measure of credit quality.

Thus, if an entity's counterparties are concentrated in one or more credit qualities (such as secured loans or unsecured loans) or in one or more credit ratings (such as investment or non-investment grade), it would disclose separately exposure to risks arising from each concentration of counter-parties.

■ Geographical distribution.

Thus, if an entity's counterparties are concentrated in one or more geographical markets (such as Asia or Europe) it would disclose separately exposure to risks arising from each concentration of counterparties.

■ A limited number of individual counterparties or groups of closely related counterparties.

[IFRS 7 para IG18].

6.9.146 Similar principles apply to identifying concentrations of other risks, including liquidity risk and market risk. For example, concentrations of liquidity risk may arise from the repayment terms of financial liabilities, sources of borrowing facilities or reliance on a particular market in which to realise liquid assets. Concentrations of foreign exchange risk may arise if an entity has a significant net open position in a single foreign currency, or aggregate net open positions in several currencies that tend to move together. [IFRS 7 para IG18].

6.9.147 If the quantitative data disclosed as at the reporting date are unrepresentative of an entity's exposure to risk during the period, an entity should provide further information that is representative. [IFRS 7 para 35]. To meet this requirement, an entity might disclose the highest, lowest and average amount of risk to which it was exposed during the period. For example, if an entity typically has a large exposure to a particular currency, but at year-end unwinds the position, the entity might disclose a graph showing the exposure at various times during the period, or disclose the highest, lowest and average exposures. [IFRS 7 para IG20]. In addition consider the following examples:

Example 1 – Year end credit risk exposure unrepresentative due to seasonal fluctuations

Entity Y is producing seeds for the agricultural industry. The main season for planting is the spring. 75% of entity Y's markets are in the northern hemisphere; 25% are in the southern hemisphere. Entity Y's account receivables are approximately C400 million in June and C100 million in December. Entity Y has a December year end. Does entity Y have to disclose additional information about its exposure to credit risk on the receivables that is representative of its exposure to risk during the year?

In this case, the December year end exposure to credit risk is unrepresentative of the entity's exposure during the period. Entity Y should provide further information that is representative, such as a description (with amounts) of how the exposures vary during the year, or the average (or highest) exposure to credit risk during the year.

Example 2 – Year end credit risk exposure unrepresentative due to a major acquisition

On 30 November 20X6, entity A (€ functional currency) acquires a major competitor. Due to the acquisition, the US$ denominated receivables increased from $100 million to $300 million and variable interest rate debt doubled from €200 million to €400 million compared to the balances as at 30 June 20X6. Entity A has a December year end. The balances as of 31 December 20X6 are considered to be representative of the next year(s). Does entity A have to disclose additional information that is representative of its exposure to risk during the year?

In this scenario, entity A should disclose additional information because the quantitative data as at 31 December 20X6 is not representative of the financial period 20X6. A mere statement that the data is not representative is not sufficient. To meet IFRS 7's requirement the entity might disclose the highest, lowest and average amount of risk to which it was exposed during the period. However, a full high/low/average analysis might not be required if the exposure at the year end is representative for future periods and if sufficient explanations of the facts and circumstances are provided.

Credit risk

6.9.148   Activities that give rise to credit risk include, but are not limited to:

- Granting loans and receivables to customers and placing deposits with other entities. In these cases, the maximum exposure to credit risk is the carrying amount of the related financial assets.

- Entering into derivative contracts (for example, foreign exchange contracts, interest rate swaps and credit derivatives). When the resulting asset is measured at fair value, the maximum exposure to credit risk at the reporting date will equal the carrying amount.

- Granting financial guarantees. In this case, the maximum exposure to credit risk is the maximum amount the entity could have to pay if the guarantee is called on, which may be significantly greater than the amount recognised as a liability.

- Making a loan commitment that is irrevocable over the life of the facility or is revocable only in response to a material adverse change. If the issuer cannot settle the loan commitment net in cash or another financial instrument, the maximum credit exposure is the commitment's full amount. This is because it is uncertain whether the amount of any undrawn portion may be drawn upon in the future. This may be significantly greater than the amount recognised as a liability.

[IFRS 7 App B para 10].

6.9.149   IFRS 7 requires an entity to disclose information about its exposure to credit risk by class of financial instrument. Financial instruments in the same class share economic characteristics with respect to the risk being disclosed (in this case, credit risk). For example, an entity might determine that residential mortgages, unsecured consumer loans, and commercial loans each have different economic characteristics. The information an entity should disclose by class of financial instrument is as follows:

- The amount that best represents its maximum exposure to credit risk at the reporting date without taking account of any collateral held or other credit enhancements (for example, netting agreements that do not qualify for offset in accordance with IAS 32 – see para 6.9.33 above). This disclosure is not required for financial instruments whose carrying amount best represents the maximum exposure to credit risk.

- A description of collateral held as security and of other credit enhancements (see para 6.9.152 below). A description is required of the financial effect of collateral held as security and of other credit enhancements (for example, a quantification of the extent to which collateral and other credit enhancements mitigate credit risk) in respect of the amount that best represents the maximum exposure to credit risk (whether disclosed in accordance with the previous bullet point or represented by the carrying amount of a financial instrument).

- Information about the credit quality of financial assets that are neither past due nor impaired (see para 6.9.154 below).

- The disclosure of the carrying amount of financial assets that would have otherwise been past due or impaired but whose terms have been renegotiated has been removed by the changes to IFRS 7 as part of the 2010 annual improvements.

[IFRS 7 para 36].

6.9.150 The above disclosures do not apply to an entity's holdings of equity investments. This is because the definition of equity in IAS 32 requires that the issuer has no obligation to pay cash or transfer other assets. Therefore, such equity investments are subject to price risk, not credit risk. The only exception is where such financial assets have been impaired. They will then require the disclosure discussed in second bullet of paragraph 6.9.155.

6.9.151 In respect of the first bullet point in paragraph 6.9.149 above, the amount that best represents the entity's maximum exposure to credit risk relating to financial assets is typically the gross carrying amount, net of:

- any amounts offset in accordance with IAS 32 (see para 6.9.21 above); and

- any impairment losses recognised in accordance with IAS 39.

[IFRS 7 App B para 9].

Collateral and other credit enhancements

6.9.152 In respect of the second bullet point in paragraph 6.9.149 above, an entity's description about collateral held as security and other credit enhancements might include:

- The policies and processes for valuing and managing collateral and other credit enhancements obtained.

- A description of the main types of collateral and other credit enhancements (examples of the latter being guarantees, credit derivatives and netting agreements that do not qualify for offset in accordance with IAS 32).

- The main types of counterparties to collateral and other credit enhancements and their creditworthiness.

- Information about risk concentrations within the collateral or other credit enhancements.

[IFRS 7 para IG22].

6.9.153 When an entity obtains financial or non-financial assets during the period by taking possession of collateral it holds as security or calling on other credit enhancements, and such assets meet the recognition criteria in other IFRSs, an entity should disclose for such assets held at the reporting date:

- The nature and carrying amount of the assets; and

- when the assets are not readily convertible into cash, its policies for disposing of such assets or for using them in its operations.

[IFRS 7 para 38].

The 2010 annual improvements to IFRS 7 clarified that these disclosures are required only for foreclosed collateral at the balance sheet date. This amendment applies to annual periods beginning on or after 1 January 2011.

Credit quality of financial assets that are neither past due nor impaired

6.9.154   In respect of the third bullet point in paragraph 6.9.149, information about credit quality of financial assets that are neither past due nor impaired might include:

- An analysis of credit exposures using an external or internal credit rating system.

  Where an entity manages its credit exposures using an external credit rating system, an entity might disclose information about:

  - The carrying amounts of credit exposures for each external credit rating.

  - The rating agencies used.

  - The amount of an entity's rated and unrated credit exposures.

  - The relationship between internal and external ratings.

  Where an entity manages its credit exposures using an internal credit rating system, an entity might disclose information about:

  - The internal credit ratings process.

  - The amounts of credit exposures for each internal credit rating.

  - The relationship between internal and external ratings.

- The nature of the counterparty.

- Historical information about counterparty default rates.

- Any other information used to assess credit quality.

[IFRS 7 paras IG23-25].

Financial assets that are either past due or impaired

6.9.155   A financial asset is past due when the counterparty has failed to make a payment when contractually due. As an example, an entity enters into a lending agreement that requires interest to be paid every month. On the first day of the next month, if interest has not been paid, the whole loan is past due, not just the interest. Past due does not mean that a counterparty will never pay, but it can trigger various actions such as renegotiation, enforcement of covenants, or legal proceedings. [IFRS 7 para IG26]. An entity should disclose by class of financial asset:

- An analysis of the age of financial assets that are past due as at the reporting date but not impaired. The purpose of this disclosure is to provide users of the financial statements with information about those financial assets that are more likely to become impaired and to help users to estimate the level of future impairment losses. Thus, the entire balance which relates to the amount past due should be disclosed, rather than only the amount that is past due, as this is the amount that would be disclosed as the amount of the impaired financial assets if impairment crystallises.

  Other associated balances due from the same debtor are not included if the debtor has not yet failed to make a payment on these balances when contractually due.

  In preparing such an age analysis of financial assets, an entity uses its judgement to determine an appropriate number of time bands. For example, an entity might determine that the following time bands are appropriate:

  - Not more than three months.
  - More than three months and not more than six months.
  - More than six months and not more than one year.
  - More than one year.

- An analysis of financial assets that are individually determined to be impaired as at the reporting date, including the factors the entity considered in determining that they are impaired. These disclosures are not only given in the year of impairment, but also in each subsequent reporting period during which the fair value of a financial asset is below its historical cost and, therefore, considered 'impaired'. Such an analysis might include:

  - The carrying amount, before deducting any impairment loss.
  - The amount of any related impairment loss.

  The requirement to include a description of collateral held by the entity as security and other credit enhancements and, unless impracticable, an estimate of their fair value has been removed as part of the 2010 annual improvements to IFRS 7.

Example – Assessment of receivables individually determined to be impaired

Entity M has C300m of receivables which it has analysed as follows:

- C120m has been assessed individually for impairment and are considered to be impaired.

- C40m represents a collection of insignificant receivables that are individually determined to be impaired, but the impairment calculation is performed on the whole C40m amount for efficiency purposes.

- C140m represents a portfolio of receivables for which there is observable data indicating that there is a measurable decrease in the estimated future cash flows, although the decrease cannot be identified with individual balances.

Of these, only the first two amounts have been individually assessed for impairment and so would require disclosure under IFRS 7. [IFRS 7 para 36(b)]. Disclosure would not be required in respect of the third bullet, as the receivables have been assessed on a portfolio basis rather than individually.

[IFRS 7 paras 37, IG28-29].

6.9.156 An example of a company that has given credit risk disclosures (qualitative and quantitative) for a class of its financial assets (trade receivables) is given in Table 6.9.11.

Table 6.9.11 – Trade and other receivables

Adidas AG – Annual report – 31 December 2011

Risk and Opportunity Report (extract)

Financial Risks (extract)

Credit risks

A credit risk arises if a customer or other counterparty to a financial instrument fails to meet its contractual obligations. The adidas Group is exposed to credit risks from its operating activities and from certain financing activities. Credit risks arise principally from accounts receivable and, to a lesser extent, from other third-party contractual financial obligations such as other financial assets, short-term bank deposits and derivative financial instruments see Note 28. Without taking into account any collateral, the carrying amount of financial assets and accounts receivable represents the maximum exposure to credit risk.

At the end of 2011, there was no relevant concentration of credit risk by type of customer or geography. Our credit risk exposure is mainly influenced by individual customer characteristics. Under the Group's credit policy, new customers are analysed for creditworthiness before standard payment and delivery terms and conditions are offered. Tolerance limits for accounts receivable are also established for each customer. Both creditworthiness and accounts receivable limits are monitored on an ongoing basis. Customers that fail to meet the Group's minimum creditworthiness are in general allowed to purchase products only on a prepayment basis.

Other activities to mitigate credit risks include retention of title clauses as well as, on a selective basis, credit insurances, accounts receivable sales without recourse and bank guarantees.

Objective evidence that financial assets are impaired includes, for instance, significant financial difficulty of the issuer or debtor, indications of the potential bankruptcy of the borrower and the

---

disappearance of an active market for a financial asset because of financial difficulties. The Group utilises allowance accounts for impairments that represent our estimate of incurred credit losses with respect to accounts receivable.

Allowance accounts are used as long as the Group is satisfied that recovery of the amount due is possible. Once this is no longer the case, the amounts are considered irrecoverable and are directly written off against the financial asset.

The allowance consists of two components:
(1) an allowance established for all receivables dependent on the ageing structure of receivables past due date and
(2) a specific allowance that relates to individually assessed risk for each specific customer – irrespective of ageing.

At the end of 2011, no Group customer accounted for more than 10% of accounts receivable. We therefore believe that the potential financial impact of our credit risks from customers, particularly smaller retailers, is moderate and we rate the likelihood of occurrence as possible.

The adidas Group Treasury department arranges currency and interest rate hedges, and invests cash, with major banks of a high credit standing throughout the world. adidas Group companies are authorised to work with banks rated BBB+ or higher. Only in exceptional cases are subsidiaries authorised to work with banks rated lower than BBB+. To limit risk in these cases, restrictions are clearly stipulated, such as maximum cash deposit levels. In addition, the credit default swap premiums of our partner banks are monitored on a weekly basis. In the event that the defined threshold is exceeded, credit balances are shifted to banks compliant with the limit.

As financial market conditions remain challenging and highly volatile, our assessment of credit risks from these assets is unchanged. We continue to believe that the potential financial impact is moderate and the likelihood of occurrence is possible. Nevertheless, we believe our risk concentration is limited due to the broad distribution of our investment business with more than 20 banks. At December 31, 2011, no bank accounted for more than 9% of our investments and the average concentration, including subsidiaries' short-term deposits in local banks, was 1%. This leads to a maximum exposure of € 97 million in the event of default of any single bank. We have further diversified our investment exposure by investing into AAA-rated money market funds.

In addition, we held derivatives with a positive fair market value in the amount of € 181 million. The maximum exposure to any single bank resulting from these assets amounted to € 28 million and the average concentration was 4%.

06 Accounts receivable

Accounts receivable consist mainly of the currencies euro, US dollar and Japanese yen and are as follows:

Accounts receivable (€ in millions)

	Dec. 31, 2011	Dec. 31, 2010
Accounts receivable, gross	1,858	1,794
Less: accumulated allowances for doubtful accounts	151	127
Accounts receivable, net	**1,707**	**1,667**

Movement in allowances for doubtful accounts (€ in millions)	2011	2010
Allowances at January 1	**127**	**124**
Additions	81	50
Reversals	(37)	(31)
Write-offs charged against the allowance accounts	(17)	(23)
Currency translation differences	(3)	7
Allowances at December 31	**151**	**127**

Accounts receivable past due but not impaired

(€ in millions)	past due 1 – 30 days	past due 31 – 60 days	past due 61 – 90 days	past due 91 – 180 days	past due > 180 days
Dec. 31, 2011	**158**	**70**	**29**	**6**	**2**
Dec. 31, 2010	118	53	11	9	1

With respect to accounts receivable as at the balance sheet date past due but not impaired, based on credit history and current credit ratings, there are no indications that customers will not be able to meet their obligations.

Further, no indications of default are recognisable for accounts receivable that are neither past due nor impaired.

Liquidity risk

6.9.157 Summary quantitative data about an entity's exposure to liquidity risk should be disclosed on the basis of the information provided internally to key management personnel. An entity should explain how those data are determined. If the outflows of cash (or another financial asset) included in those data could either:

■ occur significantly earlier than indicated in the data; or

■ be for significantly different amounts from those indicated in the data (for example, for a derivative that is included in the data on a net settlement basis, but for which the counterparty has the option to require gross settlement),

the entity should state that fact and provide quantitative information that enables users of its financial statements to evaluate the extent of liquidity risk, unless that information is included in the maturity analyses described in paragraph 6.9.160 below. [IFRS 7 App B para 10A]. An example of a cash outflow that could occur significantly earlier than indicated in the data could be a bond that is callable by the issuer in, say, two years but has a remaining contractual maturity of, say, ten years.

6.9.158 The amendment to IFRS 7 modified the minimum disclosure requirements related to liquidity risk. An entity should disclose:

■ A maturity analysis for non-derivative financial liabilities (including issued financial guarantee contracts) that shows the remaining contractual maturities.

■ A maturity analysis for derivative financial liabilities. The maturity analysis should include the remaining contractual maturities for those derivative financial liabilities for which contractual maturities are essential for an understanding of the timing of the cash flows.

■ A description of how it manages the liquidity risk inherent in the above.

[IFRS 7 para 39].

6.9.159   This information can be summarised in one or several maturity analysis tables. It should be clear for the users of the financial statements whether the disclosure is based on contractual maturities or expected maturities and whether the financial liabilities are derivatives or non-derivatives.

6.9.160   In preparing the contractual maturity analyses described in paragraph 6.9.160, an entity uses its judgement to determine an appropriate number of time bands. For example, an entity might determine that the following time bands are appropriate:

- Not later than one month.

- Later than one month and not later than three months.

- Later than three months and not later than one year.

- Later than one year and not later than five years.

[IFRS 7 App B para 11].

6.9.161   For the maturity analyses based on contractual cash flows, when a counterparty has a choice of when an amount is paid, the liability is included on the basis of the earliest date on which the entity can be required to pay. For example, financial liabilities that an entity can be required to repay on demand (for example, demand deposits) are included in the earliest time band. [IFRS 7 App B para 11C(a)].

6.9.162   When an entity is committed to make amounts available in instalments, each instalment is allocated to the earliest period in which the entity can be required to pay. For example, an undrawn loan commitment is included in the time band containing the earliest date it can be drawn down. [IFRS 7 App B para 11C(b)].

6.9.163   When an entity has issued a financial guarantee contract, the maximum amount of the guarantee is allocated to the earliest period in which the guarantee could be called. [IFRS 7 App B para 11C(c)].

6.9.164   The maximum amount of an undrawn loan commitment should also be included in the maturity analysis, allocated to the earliest period in which the commitment could be called. Once a loan is drawn down, it will be included in the maturity analysis as a non-derivative financial liability.

6.9.165   The amounts disclosed in the maturity analyses on a contractual basis (see para 6.9.157) are the contractual undiscounted cash flows (including principal and interest payments). For example:

- Gross finance lease obligations (before deducting finance charges).

- Prices specified in forward agreements to purchase financial assets for cash.

- Net amounts for pay-floating receive-fixed interest rate swaps for which net cash flows are exchanged.

- Contractual amounts to be exchanged in a derivative financial instrument (for example, a currency swap) for which gross cash flows are exchanged.

- Gross loan commitments.

[IFRS 7 App B para 11D].

6.9.166 The undiscounted cash flows described above differ from the amounts included in the balance sheet, which are based on discounted cash flows. There is no specific requirement to reconcile the amounts disclosed in the maturity analysis to the amounts included in the balance sheet.

6.9.167 When the amount payable is not fixed, the amount disclosed in the maturity analyses is determined by reference to the conditions existing at the end of the reporting period. For example, when the amount payable varies with changes in an index, the amount disclosed may be based on the level of the index at the end of the period. [IFRS 7 App B para 11D]. For floating rate financial liabilities and foreign currency denominated instruments, the use of forward interest rates and forward foreign exchange rates may be conceptually preferable, but the use of a spot rate at the end of the period is also acceptable. Whichever approach is adopted (that is, current/spot rate or forward rate at the reporting date), it should be applied consistently.

6.9.168 As noted in paragraph 6.9.160, the contractual cash flows of derivative financial liabilities for which contractual maturities are essential for an understanding of the cash flows should be included in maturity analysis. For example, this would be the case for the following:

- An interest rate swap with a remaining maturity of five years in a cash flow hedge of a variable rate financial asset or liability.

- All loan commitments.

[IFRS 7 App B para 11B].

6.9.169 Other derivatives are included in a separate maturity analysis on the basis on which they are managed. It may be expected that contractual maturities are essential for an understanding of the timing of cash flows for derivatives, unless the facts and circumstances indicate another basis is appropriate. For example, contractual maturities would not be essential for an understanding of the derivatives in a trading portfolio that are expected to be settled before contractual maturity on a net basis. Disclosure of fair values of such derivatives on an expected maturity basis would, therefore, be appropriate.

6.9.170 An entity should disclosure a maturity analysis of financial assets it holds for managing liquidity risk (for example, financial assets that are readily saleable or expected to generate cash inflows to meet cash outflows on financial liabilities), if that information is necessary to enable users of its financial statements to evaluate the nature and extent of liquidity risk. [IFRS 7 App B para 11E].

6.9.171 IFRS 7 gives as an example of an amount included in the maturity analysis on a contractual undiscounted basis the amounts exchanged in a gross-settled derivative contract). The standard refers only to a maturity analysis for derivative financial liabilities, so it would appear that only disclosure of gross cash outflows (that is, the pay leg) in respect of derivative financial liabilities is required. However, it may be more helpful to also disclose the cash inflows (that is, the receive leg). As explained in paragraph 6.9.170, IFRS 7 requires disclosure of a maturity analysis for financial assets where that information is necessary to enable users of financial statements to evaluate the nature and extent of liquidity risk. By analogy, we consider that disclosure of the receive leg in a gross-settled derivative financial liability will also often be necessary for an understanding of liquidity risk. A maturity analysis of derivative financial assets may also be required.

6.9.172 A similar analysis to the previous paragraph applies in the case of gross-settled commodity contracts. Where such a contract falls within IAS 39's scope, the associated cash outflows should be included in the maturity analysis where the contract is a financial liability at the reporting date (that is, it has a negative fair value) and where it will result in a cash outflow (rather than physical outflows of commodities). It may be helpful to disclose the contractual cash outflows of all commodity contracts, including those with both positive and negative fair values at the balance sheet date. Alternatively, it may be more meaningful to disclose gross-settled commodity contracts in a separate table showing both the cash inflows/outflows and the associated commodity outflows/inflows for all contracts. If this additional disclosure is given, an entity might cross-reference the cash outflows to the maturity analysis. Whichever of these alternative methods of presentation is adopted, the basis of preparation and measurement should be explained.

6.9.173 The liquidity risk disclosures for derivative financial liabilities can be summarised as follows:

	Gross settled deriviatives	Net settled derivatives
Contractual maturity is essential to understanding	■ Disclose pay leg based on contractual maturity. ■ Disclose receive leg	■ Disclose net cash flows based on contractual maturity.
Contractual maturity is not essential to understanding	Disclose how the risk is managed. For example, an entity might disclose: ■ Cash flows based on contractual maturities – pay and receive leg. ■ Fair value in the relevant time band (based on expected maturity (that is, expected settlement date); contractual maturity or in the on demand category).	Disclose how risk is managed. For example, an entity might disclose: ■ Net cash flows based on contractual maturity. ■ Fair value in the relevant time band (based on expected maturity (that is, expected settlement date); contractual maturity or in the on demand category).

6.9.174 For the purpose of the maturity analysis, embedded derivatives included in hybrid (combined) financial instruments should not be separated. A hybrid instrument should be included in the maturity analysis for non-derivative financial liabilities. [IFRS 7 App B para 11A].

6.9.175 Contracts settled in own shares that are not equity instruments of the issuer (for example, a contract that requires an entity to issue a fixed number of its own shares for a variable amount of cash upon the holder's request) are not in the scope of the maturity analysis, as the entity will issue own shares to meet the above obligation and does not, therefore, have an obligation to deliver cash or another financial asset. An obligation to deliver own shares does not give rise to liquidity risk as defined by IFRS 7. [IFRS 7 para BC58A(a)].

6.9.176 The factors that an entity might consider in providing a description of how it manages liquidity risk include, but are not limited to, whether the entity:

■ Has committed borrowing facilities (for example, commercial paper facilities) or other lines of credit (for example, stand-by credit facilities) that it can access to meet liquidity needs.

■ Holds deposits at central banks to meet liquidity needs.

■ Has very diverse funding sources.

■ Has significant concentrations of liquidity risk in either its assets or its funding sources.

■ Has internal control processes and contingency plans for managing liquidity risk.

■ Has instruments that include accelerated repayment terms (for example, on the downgrade of the entity's credit rating).

■ Has instruments that could require the posting of collateral (for example, margin calls for derivatives).

■ Has instruments that allow the entity to choose whether it settles its financial liabilities by delivering cash (or another financial asset) or by delivering its own shares.

■ Has instruments that are subject to master netting agreements.

[IFRS 7 App B para 11F].

6.9.177 Collateral requirements on financial instruments can pose a significant liquidity risk. For example, an entity with a derivative liability may be required to post cash collateral on the derivative should the liability exceed certain limits. As a result, if collateral calls pose significant liquidity risk, entities should provide quantitative disclosures of their collateral arrangements as those cash flows could occur earlier than the contractual maturity (see also para 6.9.157).

6.9.178 Financial institutions typically use financial assets to manage their liquidity risk. A maturity analysis of financial assets is likely to be necessary to enable users of financial statements to evaluate the nature and extent of liquidity risk. However, the disclosure requirements are not only relevant for financial institutions. Certain other types of entities with significant trading activities (such as energy companies) may hold financial assets to manage liquidity risk. Where such activities are a significant part of the entity's business, a maturity analysis of financial assets may be required.

6.9.179   Where an entity presents a maturity analysis of financial assets, it should be prepared on the basis of information provided internally to key management personnel. It may be based either on contractual or expected maturity dates, depending on how the risk is managed. Alternatively, the analysis could be presented on a net basis (that is, fair value).

6.9.180   The examples that follow illustrate how a maturity analysis may be prepared on a contractual basis for some typical financial instruments.

Example 1 – Floating rate notes

On 1 January 20X6 entity A issued two-year, US$30m floating rate notes that pay interest of 6m LIBOR plus 2%. The notes mature on 31 December 20X8.

Principal is redeemable at maturity. The carrying amount at the balance sheet date is US$30m (C21.6m).

The functional currency of the entity is C (currency units).

The spot rate at the balance sheet date is US$ = C0.72

The 6 month LIBOR at the balance sheet date is 5% per annum.

	30 Jun 20X7	31 Dec 20X7	30 Jun 20X8	31 Dec 20X8	Total
Principal (US$)	–	–	–	30,000	**30,000**
Interest payments (LIBOR + 2%)	1,050	1,050	1,050	1,050	**4,200**
Total (in US$)	**1,050**	**1,050**	**1,050**	**31,050**	**34,200**
US/C spot rate as at 31 Dec 20X6	0.72	0.72	0.72	0.72	0.72
Total cash flows (in C)	**756**	**756**	**756**	**22,356**	**24,624**

Scenario 2 – Contractual cash flows of the notes (using forward rates available at the balance sheet date)

6m LIBOR yield curve	5.25%	5.50%	5.75%	5.40%
6m LIBOR yield curve + 2% per annum	7.25%	7.50%	7.75%	7.40%

	30 Jun 20X7	31 Dec 20X7	30 Jun 20X8	31 Dec 20X8	Total
Principal (US$)	–	–	–	30,000	**30,000**
Interest payments (LIBOR + 2%)	1,088	1,125	1,163	1,110	**4,486**
Total (in US$)	**1,088**	**1,125**	**1,163**	**31,110**	**34,486**
US/C forward rate as at 31 Dec 20X6	0.75	0.78	0.79	0.76	
Total cash flows (in C)	**816**	**878**	**919**	**23,644**	**26,257**

Liquidity analysis

Analysis (based on spot rates)

Financial liabilities as at 31 Dec 20X6	Less than 1 month	Between 1 and 3M	Between 3M and 1Y	Between 1 and 5Y	Over 5Y	Balance sheet amounts
Floating rate notes	–	–	1.512	23,112	–	21,600

Alternative answer based on forward rates

Financial liabilities as at 31 Dec 20X6	Less than 1 month	Between 1 and 3 months	Between 3 months and 1 year	Between 1 and 5 years	Over 5 years	Balance sheet amounts
Floating rate notes	–	–	1,694	24,563	–	21,600

Either the spot rate or the forward rate could be used for the interest rate cash outflow calculation. The forward rate would be based on a yield curve (which will show by how much LIBOR is expected to move each quarter/six months).

Both alternatives are acceptable provided they are properly disclosed and applied consistently.

The sum of all the amounts in the maturity analysis does not reconcile to the balance sheet amount. This is because the liquidity analysis is based on the undiscounted cash flows.

Example 2 – Interest rate swap

Entity A entered into a two-year interest rate swap, notional value C10m, under which fixed interest of 5% per annum is received quarterly and actual 3 month LIBOR is paid. The contract is settled on a net basis. The swap has a negative fair value of C0.071m at the balance sheet date.

Estimated cash flows on the swap (C'000)

	31 Mar 20X7	30 Jun 20X7	30 Sept 20X7	31 Dec 20X7	31 Mar 20X8	30 Jun 20X8	30 Sept 20X8	31 Dec 20X8	Total
Fixed leg (receives fixed)	125	125	125	125	125	125	125	125	
Variable leg (pays 3 month LIBOR)	-110	-122	-136	-150	-155	-160	-172	-186	
Undiscounted net cash flows	15	3	-11	-25	-30	-35	-47	-61	-191
Discounted cashflows	13	2	-7	-14	-14	-15	-17	-19	-71

Only derivatives with a negative fair value (financial liabilities) at the balance sheet date need be included in the liquidity analysis. The cash flows to be included are those undiscounted cash flows that result in an outflow for the entity at each reporting date. While the standard only requires the gross cash outflows (that is, the pay leg) to be included in the maturity analysis, separate disclosure of the corresponding inflows (that is, the receive leg) might make the information more meaningful in the case of gross settled derivatives.

Liquidity analysis (based on forward rates)

Financial liabilities as of 31 Dec 20X6

	Less than 1 month	Between 1 and 3 months	Between 3 months and 1 year	Between 1 and 5 years	Over 5 years	Balance sheet amounts
Interest rate swaps		15	-33	-173		-71

6.9.181   For some instruments, such as perpetual bonds and written put options, it is difficult to determine how, if at all, to include amounts in the maturity analysis. In the case of perpetual bonds, where the debtor/issuer has a call option to redeem the bond, the debtor/issuer has discretion over the repayment of the principal. Until the option is exercised, the bond's contractual terms are that it is a non-redeemable perpetual bond. Once the call option is exercised, the bond's contractual terms are changed and the bond has a maturity date. If the call option was not exercised, then the undiscounted cash flows would be paid in perpetuity. This raises the question of what amount should be shown in the last time band. The standard does not deal explicitly with such a situation so a number of alternative approaches could be applied. One would be to include the principal amount in the last time band. Another option would be not to include any cash flows in the last time band, but disclose the principal amount in time band entitled 'no maturity'. Whatever form of disclosure is chosen, this is an area where it will be important to provide a clear narrative description of the instrument's terms.

6.9.182 The inclusion of an 'out of the money' written put option (financial liability) in the maturity analysis will depend on whether the option is settled net or gross. If the option is out of the money and net settled, no liability is required to be disclosed in the maturity table, because there is no obligation to make a payment based on the conditions existing at the balance sheet date. [IFRS 7 App B para 11D]. However, for gross settled derivatives where the counterparty can force the issuer to make a payment, the pay leg is disclosed in the liquidity table in the earliest time bucket irrespective of whether the instrument is in or out of the money. An American style option should be disclosed in the earliest time band, a European style option depending on the exercise date.

6.9.183 A narrative disclosure should explain that written options have been included based on their intrinsic value and that the amount actually payable in the future may vary if the conditions change. This is supported by paragraph 10A(b) of appendix B to IFRS 7, which states that an explanation is required if the outflows of cash included in the maturity analysis could be significantly different from those disclosed in the contractual maturity table.

6.9.184 An entity that has provided a disclosure of its liquidity risk is shown in Table 6.9.12. This company does not have financial guarantees or loan commitments. Such features are more common in banks, although certain industrial companies, particularly in the construction industry do issue financial guarantees and companies in the motor industry often have lending facilities for customers. Note that the examples below include only certain of the potentially extensive disclosures that IFRS 7 requires.

Table 6.9.12 – Liquidity risk

Givaudan Plc – Annual report – 31 December 2011

4.2 Financial risk management (extract)

4.2.3 Liquidity risk

Prudent liquidity risk management implies maintaining sufficient cash and marketable securities, the availability of funds through an adequate amount of committed credit facilities and the ability to close out market positions. Due to the dynamic nature of the underlying businesses, Group Treasury maintains flexibility in funding by maintaining availability under committed and uncommitted credit lines.

Group Treasury monitors and manages cash at the Group level and defines the maximum cash level at affiliate level. If necessary, inter-company loans within the Group provide for short-term cash needs; excess local cash is repatriated in the most appropriate manner.

The following table analyses the Group's remaining contractual maturity for financial liabilities and derivative financial instruments. The table has been drawn up based on the undiscounted cash flows of financial liabilities based on the earliest date on which the Group is obliged to pay. The table includes both interest and principal cash flows:

2011 in millions of Swiss francs	Up to 6 months	6 – 12 months	1 – 5 years	Over 5 years	Total
Short-term debt (excluding bank overdraft)	(427)				(427)
Accounts payable	(299)				(299)
Net settled derivative financial instruments	(14)	(5)	(47)	(4)	(70)
Gross settled derivative financial instruments – outflows	(1,427)	(172)			(1,599)
Gross settled derivative financial instruments – inflows	1,440	162			1,602
Long-term debt	(30)	(16)	(1,208)	(531)	(1,785)
Balance as at 31 December	**(757)**	**(31)**	**(1,255)**	**(535)**	**(2,578)**

2010 in millions of Swiss francs	Up to 6 months	6 – 12 months	1 – 5 years	Over 5 years	Total
Short-term debt (excluding bank overdraft)	(34)	(284)			(318)
Accounts payable – trade and others	(309)				(309)
Net settled derivative financial instruments	(11)	(8)	(35)	(2)	(56)
Gross settled derivative financial instruments – outflows	(866)	(110)			(976)
Gross settled derivative financial instruments – inflows	913	115			1,028
Long-term debt	(30)	(15)	(1,890)	(53)	(1,988)
Balance as at 31 December	**(337)**	**(302)**	**(1,925)**	**(55)**	**(2,619)**

Market risk

Sensitivity analysis

6.9.185 Unless an entity complies with paragraph 6.9.196 below, it should disclose:

- A sensitivity analysis for each type of market risk to which the entity is exposed at the reporting date, showing how profit or loss and equity would have been affected by changes in the relevant risk variable that were reasonably possible at that date. The sensitivity analysis should show the effect of changes over the period until the entity next presents these disclosures, which usually is its next annual report. [IFRS 7 App B para 19(b)]. Note that the standard requires this disclosure based on reasonably possible changes and not on a 'worst case scenario' or 'stress test'. Risk variables that are relevant to disclosing market risk include, but are not limited to:

    - The yield curve of market interest rates. It may be necessary to consider both parallel and non-parallel shifts in the yield curve.

    - Foreign exchange rates.

    - Prices of equity instruments.

    - Market prices of commodities.

- The methods and assumptions used in preparing the sensitivity analysis.

- Changes from the previous period in the methods and assumptions used and the reasons for such changes.

[IFRS 7 para 40].

6.9.186 In providing the sensitivity analysis for each type of market risk, an entity should decide how it aggregates information to display the overall picture without combining information with different characteristics about exposures to risks from significantly different economic environments. Entities are not required to disclose the effect for each change within a range of reasonably possible changes of the relevant risk variable. Disclosure of the effects of the changes at the limits of the reasonably possible range would be sufficient. [IFRS 7 App B paras 18 to 19]. For example, an entity that trades financial instruments might disclose this information separately for financial instruments held for trading and those not held for trading. Similarly, an entity would not aggregate its exposure to market risks from areas of hyperinflation with its exposure to the same market risks from areas of very low inflation. Conversely, if an entity has exposure to only one type of market risk in only one economic environment, it would not show disaggregated information. [IFRS 7 App B para 17].

6.9.187 In addition, where there are changes in volatility, an entity should not restate the prior year disclosures. For example, where the reasonable possible change in an exchange rate changes from 5% in the prior year to 8% in the current year, the prior year disclosures should not be restated. An entity could, however, present additional sensitivity information for the comparative period.

6.9.188 For the purposes of disclosing the effect on profit or loss and equity of reasonably possible changes in the relevant risk variable, for example interest rate risk, as required by the first bullet point of paragraph 6.9.185 above, an entity might show separately the effect of a change in market rates on:

- Interest income and expense.

- Other line items of profit or loss (such as trading gains and losses).

- When applicable, equity.

[IFRS 7 para IG34].

6.9.189 An entity might disclose a sensitivity analysis for interest rate risk for each currency in which the entity has material exposures to interest rate risk. Similarly, a sensitivity analysis is disclosed for each currency to which an entity has significant exposure. [IFRS 7 paras IG34, App B para 24].

6.9.190 This disclosure would also be relevant to those instruments where an entity has effectively hedged the interest rate risk, as illustrated in the following example.

Example – A bond hedged for variable interest rate risk

An entity hedges its exposure to variable interest rate risk on an issued bond. The hedge is designated as a cash flow hedge. The bond and the hedging instrument (interest rate swap) have a five-year remaining life. The variable leg of the swap exactly matches the variable interest of the bond (causing no ineffectiveness).

The high effectiveness of the hedge does not necessarily mean that there would be no impact on equity or profit or loss due to changes in interest rate risk. The accounting for a cash flow hedge means that the fair value movement related to the effective part of the hedging instrument is included in other comprehensive income. Amounts deferred in other comprehensive income are recycled in profit or loss when the hedged transaction occurs. Hence, reasonably possible movements in the interest rate risk exposure have an impact on both profit or loss and equity.

At the same time, reasonably possible movements in the interest rate risk exposure on the outstanding bond would impact profit or loss, as the bond pays variable interest.

If the effects of recycling and ineffectiveness are not material, the entity could consider the following disclosure as an approximation for the sensitivity analysis: *"The movements related to the bond and the swap's variable leg are not reflected as they offset each other. The movements related to the remaining fair value exposure on the swap's fixed leg are shown in the equity part of the analysis".*

6.9.191 It should be noted that for the purposes of disclosing a sensitivity analysis for foreign currency risk, translation related risk is not taken into account. This is because foreign currency risk can only arise on financial instruments that are denominated in a currency other than the functional currency in which they are measured. [IFRS 7 App B para 23]. Translation exposures arise from financial and non-financial items held by an entity (for example, a subsidiary) with a functional currency different from the group's presentation currency. Therefore, translation-related risks are not taken into consideration for the purpose of the sensitivity analysis for foreign currency risks. This also includes quasi-equity loans (foreign currency inter-company loans that are part of the net investment in a foreign operation). On the other hand, any loans or derivatives used as hedges of translation risk should be included within the sensitivity analysis. Also, foreign currency denominated inter-company receivables and payables would be included because, even though they cancel in the consolidated balance sheet, the effect on profit or loss of their revaluation under IAS 21 is not fully eliminated. Although they cannot be included within the analysis of foreign currency risks, additional translation risks can, however, be separately disclosed. This may be appropriate where an entity manages its translation risks together with its foreign currency transaction risks (for example, where a forward contract hedges movements in the retranslation of a foreign operation).

6.9.192 In the same way that translation exposures may have an impact on equity but are not included in the sensitivity analysis, there are other items that may be exposed to market price risk, but which are not necessarily included. For example, consider instruments that expose an entity to changes in its own share price. These include entities that have issued warrants with a foreign currency exercise price, those that have issued convertible debt that fails the 'fixed for fixed' requirement in IAS 32 and those that have issued share based compensation awards that are classified as liabilities. In the first two cases, the entity should disclose information about the effect of reasonably possible changes in its share price on its profit or loss and equity. This is because the first two instruments are in the scope of IAS 39 and, therefore, in the scope of IFRS 7. The third instrument, although classified as a liability, is outside the scope of IAS 39 as it is accounted for under IFRS 2. It, therefore, also falls outside the IFRS 7's scope.

6.9.193 Because the factors affecting market risk vary depending on the specific circumstances of each entity, the appropriate range to be considered in providing a sensitivity analysis of market risk varies for each entity and for each type of market risk. [IFRS 7 para IG35].

6.9.194 However, an entity is not required to determine what the profit or loss for the period would have been if relevant risk variables had been different. Instead, it should disclose the effect on profit or loss and equity at the balance sheet date, assuming that a reasonably possible change in the relevant risk variable had occurred at the balance sheet date and had been applied to the risk exposures in existence at that date. For example, if an entity has a floating rate liability at the end of the year, the entity would disclose the effect on profit or loss (that is, interest expense) for the current year if interest rates had varied by reasonably possible amounts. [IFRS 7 App B para 18(a)].

6.9.195 Furthermore, an entity is not required to disclose the effect on profit or loss and equity for each change within a range of reasonably possible changes of the relevant risk variable. Disclosure of the effects of the changes at the limits of the reasonably possible range would be sufficient. [IFRS 7 App B para 18(b)].

6.9.196 If an entity prepares a sensitivity analysis, such as value-at-risk (VaR), that reflects interdependencies between risk variables (for example, interest rates and exchange rates) and uses it to manage financial risks, it may use that sensitivity analysis in place of the analysis described above. However, a precondition for disclosing sensitivity in such a format (VaR) is that the company uses VaR in managing its financial risks. It cannot choose just to apply VaR for disclosures purposes but continue to manage each risk variable separately. In addition, it is likely that outstanding intercompany foreign currency receivables and payables at the year-end are not considered in the VaR model. If this is the case, the entity will need to prepare additional sensitivity disclosures for these amounts (see para 6.9.191 above). The entity should also disclose:

■ an explanation of the method used in preparing such a sensitivity analysis, and of the main parameters and assumptions underlying the data provided; and

■ an explanation of the objective of the method used and of limitations that may result in the information not fully reflecting the fair value of the assets and liabilities involved.

[IFRS 7 para 41].

6.9.197 In view of the requirement for VaR to be used in managing financial risk, IFRS 7 recognises that the measure used may not reflect the full potential risk over the next reporting period. [IFRS 7 App B para 20]. For example, an entity may use a 10 day VaR, or a measure that recognises only the potential for loss and not the potential for gain.

6.9.198 An example of a company that has provided an analysis of market risk sensitivity and how it manages its market risk is provided in Table 6.9.13 (Note the company had no equity investments and, therefore, price risk sensitivity has not been disclosed.) An example of a company providing a price risk sensitivity is provided in Table 6.9.14.

Table 6.9.13 – Disclosure of market risk management and sensitivity

Glaxosmithkline plc – Annual report – 31 December 2008

Interest rate risk management

The policy on interest rate risk management requires the minimum amount of net borrowings at fixed rates to increase with the ratio of forecast interest payable to trading profit. The fixed to floating ratio is reviewed monthly by the TMG.

We use an interest rate swap to redenominate one of our external borrowings into the interest rate coupon required by GSK. The duration of this swap matches the duration of the principal instrument. Interest rate derivative instruments are accounted for as fair value or cash flow hedges of the relevant assets or liabilities.

Foreign exchange risk management

Foreign currency transaction exposure arising on internal and external trade flows is not hedged. The exposure of overseas operating subsidiaries to transaction risk is minimised by matching local currency income with local currency costs. For this purpose, our internal trading transactions are matched centrally and we manage intercompany payment terms to reduce risk. Exceptional foreign currency cash flows are hedged selectively under the management of Corporate Treasury.

We manage the short-term cash surpluses or borrowing requirements of subsidiary companies centrally using forward contracts to hedge future repayments back into the originating currency. We seek to denominate borrowings in the currencies of our principal assets and cash flows. These are primarily denominated in US dollars, Euros and Sterling. Certain borrowings are swapped into other currencies as required.

Borrowings denominated in, or swapped into, foreign currencies that match investments in overseas Group assets are treated as a hedge against the relevant assets. Forward contracts are also used in major currencies to reduce our exposure to our investment in overseas Group assets (see 'Net Investment Hedges' section of this note for further details). The TMG review the ratio of borrowings to assets for major currencies monthly.

Sensitivity analysis

The sensitivity analysis has been prepared on the assumption that the amount of net debt, the ratio of fixed to floating interest rates of the debt and derivatives portfolio and the proportion of financial instruments in foreign currencies are all constant and on the basis of the hedge designations in place at 31st December. Financial instruments affected by market risk include borrowings, deposits and derivative financial instruments. The following analyses are intended to

---

illustrate the sensitivity of such financial instruments to changes in relevant foreign exchange and interest rates.

Foreign exchange sensitivity

The table below shows the Group's sensitivity to foreign exchange rates on its US dollar, Euro and Yen financial instruments excluding obligations under finance leases and certain non-derivative financial instruments not in net debt and which do not present a material exposure. These three currencies are the major currencies in which GSK's financial instruments are denominated. GSK has considered movements in these currencies over the last three years and has concluded that a 20% movement in rates is a reasonable benchmark. In this table, financial instruments are only considered sensitive to foreign exchange rates where they are not in the functional currency of the entity that holds them. Intercompany loans which are fully hedged to maturity with a currency swap have been excluded from this analysis.

	2008		2007	
	Increase/ (decrease) in income £m	Reduction in equity £m	Increase/ (decrease) in income £m	Reduction in equity £m
20% appreciation (2007 – 10% appreciation) of the US dollar	210	991	38	580
20% appreciation (2007 – 10% appreciation) of the Euro	(20)	1,760	(10)	709
20% appreciation (2007 – 10% appreciation) of the Yen	1	52	–	15

A 20% (2007 – 10%) depreciation of the stated currencies would have an equal and opposite effect. The movements in the income statement relate primarily to hedging instruments for US dollar legal provisions, trade payables and trade receivables. Whilst these are economic hedges, the provisions are not financial instruments and therefore are not included in the table above. The sensitivity of these hedging instruments would be insignificant if the provisions were included. The movements in equity relate to foreign exchange positions used to hedge Group assets denominated in US dollar, Euro and Yen. Therefore, a depreciation on the currency swap would give rise to a corresponding appreciation on the Group asset. Foreign exchange sensitivity on Group assets other than financial instruments is not included above.

The table below shows the Group's sensitivity to interest rates on its floating rate Sterling, US dollar and Euro financial instruments, being the currencies in which GSK has historically issued debt and held investments. GSK has considered movements in these interest rates over the last three years and has concluded that a 2% increase is a reasonable benchmark. Debt with a maturity of less than one year is floating rate for this calculation. A 2% movement in interest rates is not deemed to have a material effect on equity.

	2008 Increase/ (decrease) in income	2007 Increase/ (decrease) in income
2% increase (2007 – 1% increase) in Sterling interest rates	16	1
2% increase (2007 – 1% increase) in US dollar interest rates	13	(16)
2% increase (2007 – 1% increase) in Euro interest rates	4	3

A 2% (2007 – 1%) decrease in these interest rates would have an equal and opposite effect, with the exception of US dollar, where interest rates could not be decreased by 2% as they are currently less than 0.5%. The maximum decrease in income would therefore be limited to £1 million. Interest rate movements on obligations under finance leases, foreign currency and interest rate derivatives, trade payables, trade receivables and other financial instruments not in net debt do not present a material exposure to the Group's balance sheet based on a 2% increase or decrease in these interest rates.

Table 6.9.14 – Disclosure of price risk management and sensitivity

Henderson Group plc – Annual report – 31 December 2011

28. Financial risk management (extract)

Financial risk management objectives and policies

Financial assets principally comprise investments in equity securities, short-term investments, trade and other receivables, and cash and cash equivalents. Financial liabilities comprise borrowings for financing purposes, certain provisions and trade and other payables. The main risks arising from financial instruments are price risk, interest rate risk, liquidity risk, foreign currency risk and credit risk. Each of these risks is examined in detail below. The Group monitors financial risks on a consolidated basis and intra-Group balances are settled when it is deemed appropriate for both parties to the transaction. The Company is not exposed to material financial risk and separate disclosures for the Company have not been included.

The Group has designed a framework to manage the risks of its business and to ensure that the Directors have in place risk management practices appropriate for a listed company. The management of risk within the Group is governed by the Board and overseen by the Board Risk Committee.

28.1 Price risk
Price risk is the risk that a decline in the value of assets adversely impacts on the profitability of the Group.

The Group is exposed to price risk in respect of seed capital investments in Group funds (available-for-sale financial assets). Seed capital investments vary in duration, depending on the nature of the investment, with a typical range of less than one year for Investment Management products and between three and seven years for Private Equity and Property funds. The total market value of seed capital investments at 31 December 2011 was £54.3m (2010: £46.6m).

Management monitors exposures to price risk on an ongoing basis. Significant movements in investment values are monitored on a daily basis. Where appropriate, management will hedge price risk. At 31 December 2011, investments with a carrying value of £1.4m (2010: £2.9m) werehedged against price risk through the use of contracts for difference (CFDs).

A fall in the value of an investment which is prolonged or significant is considered to be objective evidence of impairment under IAS 39 Financial Instruments: Recognition and Measurement. In such an event, an investment is written down to its fair value and cumulative amounts previously recognised in equity, in respect of market value and unhedged foreign exchange movements on the investment, are recognised in the Consolidated Income Statement as an impairment charge.

Price risk sensitivity analysis on available-for-sale financial assets

	2011		2010	
	Consolidated income statement	**Consolidated Statement of Comprehensive Income**	**Consolidated Income Statement**	Consolidated Statement of Comprehensive Income
	£m	**£m**	£m	£m
Market value movement +/- 10%	–	5.2	–	4.4

Other market risk disclosures

6.9.199 When the sensitivity analyses disclosed in accordance with paragraph 6.9.185 above are unrepresentative of a risk inherent in a financial instrument (for example because the year-end exposure does not reflect the exposure during the year), the entity should disclose that fact and the reason it believes the sensitivity analyses are unrepresentative. [IFRS 7 para 42].

6.9.200 As noted above, the sensitivity analysis might be unrepresentative of a risk inherent in a financial instrument where the year-end exposure does not reflect the exposure during the year. Other circumstances include the following:

- A financial instrument contains terms and conditions whose effects are not apparent from the sensitivity analysis, for example options that remain out of (or in) the money for the chosen change in the risk variable. In such a situation, additional disclosure might include:

  - the terms and conditions of the financial instrument (for example, the options);

  - the effect on profit or loss if the term or condition were met (that is, if the options were exercised); and

  - a description of how the risk is hedged.

- Financial assets are illiquid, for example, when there is a low volume of transactions in similar assets and an entity finds it difficult to find a counterparty. In such a situation, additional disclosure might include the reasons for the lack of liquidity and how the entity hedges the risk.

- An entity has a large holding of a financial asset that, if sold in its entirety, would be sold at a discount or premium to the quoted market price for a smaller holding. In such a situation, additional disclosure might include:

  - The nature of the security (for example, entity name).

  - The extent of holding (for example, 15% of the issued shares).

  - The effect on profit or loss.

  - How the entity hedges the risk.

[IFRS 7 para IG37-40].

6.9.201 An entity should provide sensitivity analyses for the whole of its business, but may provide different types of sensitivity analysis for different classes of financial instruments. [IFRS 7 App B para 21].

6.9.202 The sensitivity of profit or loss (that arises, for example, from instruments classified as at fair value through profit or loss and impairments of available-for-sale financial assets) is disclosed separately from the sensitivity of equity (that arises, for example, from instruments classified as available for sale). [IFRS 7 App B para 27]. For example, where the fair value of a non-monetary available-for-sale asset is close to the impairment threshold, an entity should distinguish between profit or loss and equity effects, taking into consideration its impairment policy. In cases where the asset is already impaired, the downward shift (due to the impairment) should be shown as affecting the profit or loss while the upward shift should be shown as affecting equity.

6.9.203 Financial instruments that an entity classifies as equity instruments are not remeasured. Neither profit or loss nor equity will be affected by the equity price risk of those instruments. Accordingly, no sensitivity analysis is required. [IFRS 7 App B para 28].

Disclosures on transition to IFRS 9

6.9.204 IFRS 7 requires certain disclosures when an entity first applies IFRS 9. These requirements are detailed in chapter 6.10.

6.10 – IFRS 9

6.10 – IFRS 9

Introduction

6.10.1   The IASB has been reviewing accounting issues that have emerged as a result of the recent global financial crisis, including those identified by the G20 and other international bodies such as the Financial Stability Board. As part of this, the IASB has accelerated its project to replace IAS 39 and sub-divided it into three main phases (see table below). The IASB completed part of the first phase of this project on classifying and measuring financial assets and issued IFRS 9 in November 2009. It completed the part on classifying and measuring financial liabilities in October 2010. On 15 November 2011, the IASB tentatively decided to consider making limited modifications to the requirements in IFRS 9 for classifying and measuring financial assets to deal with specific application issues and the interaction with the insurance project and to try to achieve convergence with proposals being developed by the FASB. IFRS 13 is effective for annual periods beginning on or after 1 January 2013, entities that have adopted IFRS 13 should refer to chapter 5 for the relevant fair value measurement guidance.

6.10.2   The IASB also considered changes to the guidance that addresses when financial instruments are derecognised (this was in response to concerns over whether off-balance-sheet structures were appropriately treated during the financial crisis). No changes were made to the accounting, but improved disclosures are now required (see chapter 6.9 for the requirements).

6.10.3   IFRS 9 now contains guidance for:

- recognising and derecognising financial instruments;
- classifying and measuring financial assets; and
- classifying and measuring financial liabilities.

6.10.4   The phases and status of the project is shown in the table below.

Phase	Status
Classification and measurement	Financial assets – IFRS 9 published November 2009. Limited modifications to IFRS 9 exposure draft expected Q4 2012. Financial liabilities – IFRS 9 published October 2010.
Impairment	A further exposure draft is expected Q4 2012 on the expected-loss impairment model.
Hedge accounting	General hedging final standard expected Q4 2012. Macro hedging discussion paper expected Q4 2012.

610001

6.10.5 This chapter on IFRS 9 does not yet address impairment, hedge accounting or the limited modifications to IFRS 9 as these are currently under discussion by the Board. However, we expect these to be incorporated into IFRS 9 once the Board has finalised its work in those areas.

Executive summary

6.10.6 IFRS 9 replaces the multiple classification and measurement models for financial assets in IAS 39 with a model that currently has only two classification categories: amortised cost and fair value. Classification under IFRS 9 is driven by the entity's business model for managing the financial assets and the contractual cash flow characteristics of the financial assets. A possible third category of fair value through other comprehensive income may be introduced to IFRS 9 for eligible investments in debt instruments as part of the limited modifications to IFRS 9. This chapter does not address this third category as it is currently under discussion by the Board.

6.10.7 A financial asset is measured at amortised cost if two criteria are met:

- The objective of the business model is to hold the financial asset for the collection of the contractual cash flows.

- The contractual asset's cash flows solely represent payments of principal and interest.

6.10.8 IFRS 9 removes existing IAS 39 categories, notably the held-to-maturity and available-for-sale categories and the tainting rules associated with the former.

6.10.9 The standard also removes the requirement to separate embedded derivatives from financial asset hosts. It requires a hybrid financial asset contract to be classified in its entirety at either amortised cost or fair value.

6.10.10 Two of the existing three fair value option criteria become obsolete under IFRS 9, as a fair value driven business model requires fair value accounting, and most hybrid contracts are classified in their entirety at fair value. The remaining fair value option condition in IAS 39 is carried forward to the standard – that is, management may still designate a financial asset as at fair value through profit or loss on initial recognition if this significantly reduces an accounting mismatch. The designation at fair value through profit or loss continues to be irrevocable.

6.10.11 IFRS 9 prohibits reclassifications between amortised cost and fair value through profit or loss except when the entity's business model changes.

6.10.12 There is specific guidance for contractually linked instruments that create concentrations of credit risk, which is often the case with investment tranches in a securitisation.

6.10.13 IFRS 9's classification principles require all equity investments to be measured at fair value. However, management has an irrevocable option to present in other comprehensive income unrealised and realised fair value gains and losses on equity investments that are not held-for-trading. If this election is used, dividends are nevertheless presented in profit or loss unless they clearly represent recovery of part of the investment's cost. The election is available at initial recognition on an instrument-by-instrument basis, with no recycling to profit or loss.

6.10.14 IFRS 9 removes the cost exemption for unquoted equities and derivatives on unquoted equities, but provides guidance on when cost may be an appropriate estimate of fair value.

6.10.15 The classification and measurement of financial liabilities under IFRS 9 remains the same as in IAS 39 except where an entity has chosen to measure a financial liability at fair value through profit or loss. For such liabilities, changes in fair value related to changes in own credit risk are presented separately in OCI.

6.10.16 Amounts in OCI relating to own credit are not recycled to the income statement even when the liability is derecognised and the amounts are realised. However, the standard does allow transfers within equity.

6.10.17 Entities are still required to separate derivatives embedded in financial liabilities where they are not closely related to the host contract.

6.10.18 In December 2011, the Board amended IFRS 9 to defer the mandatory effective date from 1 January 2013 to annual periods beginning on or after 1 January 2015. Early application of IFRS 9 will continue to be permitted. IFRS 9 has not yet been endorsed for use in the EU. The Board also amended the transitional provisions to provide relief from restating comparative information and introduced new disclosures to help users of financial statements understand the effect of moving to the IFRS 9 classification and measurement model. See paragraph 6.10.82.

Objective

6.10.19 IFRS 9's objective is to establish principles for the financial reporting of financial assets and financial liabilities that will present relevant and useful information to users of financial statements for their assessment of amounts, timing and uncertainty of the entity's future cash flows. [IFRS 9 para 1.1].

Scope

6.10.20 IFRS 9 has to be applied by all entities preparing their financial statements in accordance with IFRS and to all types of financial assets and financial liabilities within the IAS 39's scope, including derivatives. The IAS 39's scope is broad and is addressed in chapter 6.1.

6.10.21 Essentially any financial assets and financial liabilities that are currently accounted for under IAS 39 will fall within the IFRS 9's scope.

Financial assets

Initial recognition

6.10.22 Consistent with IAS 39, all financial assets under IFRS 9 are to be initially recognised at fair value, plus, in the case of a financial asset that is not at fair value through profit or loss, transaction costs that are directly attributable to the acquisition of the financial asset. [IFRS 9 para 5.1.1]. IFRS 13 amended IFRS 9 to remove its guidance on fair value measurement. IFRS 13 is effective for annual periods beginning on or after 1 January 2013. Entities that have adopted IFRS 13 should refer to chapter 5 for the relevant fair value measurement guidance.

Classification and measurement

6.10.23 IFRS 9 has two measurement categories: amortised cost and fair value. In order to determine the financial assets that fall into each measurement category, management should consider whether the financial asset is an investment in an equity instrument as defined in IAS 32. Chapter 6.5 provides further details on this determination. If the financial asset is not an investment in an equity instrument, management should consider the guidance for debt instruments from paragraph 6.10.24 below. If it is an equity instrument, management should consider the guidance for equity instruments from paragraph 6.10.51 below.

Debt instruments

6.10.24 If the financial asset is a debt instrument (or does not meet the definition of an equity instrument in its entirety), management should consider whether both the following tests are met:

- The objective of the entity's business model is to hold the asset to collect the contractual cash flows.

- The asset's contractual cash flows represent only payments of principal and interest. Interest is consideration for the time value of money and the credit risk associated with the principal amount outstanding during a particular period of time.

[IFRS 9 paras 4.1.2-4.1.3].

6.10.25 If both these tests are met, the financial asset falls into the amortised cost measurement category. If the financial asset does not pass either of the above tests, or only one of the above tests, it is measured at fair value through profit or loss. [IFRS 9 para 4.1.4].

6.10.26 Even if both tests are met, management also has the ability to designate a financial asset as at fair value through profit or loss if doing so reduces or eliminates a measurement or recognition inconsistency ('accounting mismatch'). [IFRS 9 para 4.1.5]. IFRS 9 retains only one of the three conditions in IAS 39 to qualify for using the fair value option. It removes the conditions regarding being part of a group of financial assets that is managed and its performance evaluated on a fair value basis and where the financial asset contains one or more embedded derivatives, as the conditions are no longer necessary under the classification model in IFRS 9.

Business model

6.10.27 Financial assets are subsequently measured at amortised cost or fair value based on the entity's business model for managing the financial assets. An entity assesses whether its financial assets meet this condition based on its business model as determined by the entity's key management personnel (as defined in IAS 24). [IFRS 9 App B para B4.1.1].

6.10.28 Management will need to apply judgement to determine at what level the business model condition is applied. That determination is made on the basis of how an entity manages its business; it is not made at the level of an individual asset. Therefore, the entity's business model is not a choice and does not depend on management's intentions for an individual instrument; it is a matter of fact that can be observed by the way an entity is managed and information is provided to its management.

6.10.29 The following are indicators that management may find helpful to consider in assessing the business model for each portfolio it has identified:

- the purpose of the portfolio as assessed by management (for example whether the portfolio is held to collect cash flows, maximise investment return, meet liquidity requirements, etc);

- the composition of the portfolio and its alignment with the declared objectives of the portfolio;

- the mandates granted to managers of the portfolio (for example how broad are the investments that can be made, what are limitations on disposals, etc);

- the metrics used to measure and report on portfolio performance (for example are fair values a important KPI, etc);

- the methodology for the portfolio manager's remuneration (for example is the manager remunerated based on realised profits, unrealised gains and losses, etc); and

- levels of and reasons for any sales of assets in the portfolio (see para 6.10.30 below).

6.10.30 The following are examples of sales before maturity that IFRS 9 states would not be inconsistent with a business model of holding financial assets to collect contractual cash flows:

- an entity may sell a financial asset if it no longer meets the entity's investment policy, because its credit rating has declined below that required by that policy;

- when an insurer adjusts its investment portfolio to reflect a change in the expected duration (that is, payout) for its insurance policies; or

- when an entity needs to fund capital expenditure.

[IFRS 9 App B para B4.3].

6.10.31 Other examples of such sales include disposals:

- so close to maturity or the financial asset's call date that changes in the market rate of interest would not have a significant effect on the financial asset's fair value;

- in response to a change in tax law that significantly affects the tax status of the financial asset or a significant change in regulations, such as a requirement to maintain regulatory capital that directly affects the asset;

- in response to a significant internal restructuring or business combination;

- to execute a liquidity crisis plan; and

- other than the above, due to an isolated event that is beyond the entity's control, is non-recurring and could not have been reasonably anticipated by the entity.

6.10.32 However, if more than an infrequent number of sales are made out of a portfolio, management should assess whether and how such sales are consistent with an objective of collecting contractual cash flows. There is no set rule for how many sales constitutes 'infrequent'; management will need to use judgement based on the facts and circumstances to make its assessment.

6.10.33 For example, an entity manages a portfolio of financial assets with the objective of realising cash flows through selling the assets, it could not be argued that its business model is to hold instruments to collect the contractual cash flows. Another example is when an entity actively manages a portfolio of assets in order to realise fair value changes arising from changes in credit spreads and yield curves, which results in active buying and selling of the portfolio. Based on the above, it is likely that many liquidity portfolios as presently assessed under IAS 39 will not qualify as 'held to collect'. However, management may find that they have multiple liquidity portfolios where some are separately managed on a held to collect basis and, therefore, may be eligible for amortised cost measurement.

Example 1 – Factoring

An entity has a past practice of factoring its receivables. If the significant risks and rewards have transferred from the entity, resulting in the original receivable being derecognised from the balance sheet, the entity is not holding these receivables to collect its cash flows, but intends to sell them and hence should classify such receivable as fair value thought profit or loss.

However, if the significant risks and rewards of these receivables are not transferred from the entity, and the receivables do not qualify for derecognition, the client's business objective may still be to hold the assets in order to collect the contractual cash flows.

Example 2 – Syndicated loans

An entity's business model is to lend to customers and hold the resulting loans for the collection of contractual cash flows. However, sometimes the entity syndicates out portions of loans that exceed their credit approval limits. This means that, at inception, part of such loans will be 'held to collect' and part will be held-for-sale. The entity, therefore, has two business models to apply to the respective portions of the loans.

Example 3 – Portfolio of sub-prime loans

An entity that operates in the sub-prime lending market purchases a portfolio of sub-prime loans from a competitor that has gone out of business. The loans are purchased at a substantial discount from their face value, as most of the loans are not currently performing (that is, no payments are being received, in many cases because the borrower has failed to make payments when due). The entity has a good record of collecting sub-prime loan arrears. It plans to hold the purchased loan balances to recover the outstanding cash amounts relating to the loans that have been purchased. As the business model is to hold the acquired loans and not to sell them, this will qualify as 'held to collect'.

Example 4 – Securitisation

An entity originates loans with a view to later selling them to a securitisation vehicle. On the sale to the vehicle, the loans continue to be recognised in the consolidated financial statements, but are derecognised in the separate financial statements of the originating entity. In the consolidated financial statements the loans may be part of a portfolio managed in order to collect the contractual cash flows since they are not derecognised (that is, are not considered 'sold' for accounting purposes). However, in the separate financial statements of the originating entity, where they will be derecognised, they cannot be considered part of a portfolio that is 'held to collect'.

Contractual cash flows that are 'solely payments of principal and interest'

6.10.34   The other condition that must be met in order for a financial asset to be eligible for amortised cost accounting is that the contractual terms of the financial asset give rise on specified dates to cash flows that are *"solely payments of principal and interest on the principal amount outstanding"*. Interest is defined as consideration for the time value of money and for the credit risk associated with the principal amount outstanding during a particular period of time. [IFRS 9 para 4.1.3].

6.10.35 In order to meet this condition, there can be no leverage of the contractual cash flows. Leverage increases the variability of the contractual cash flows with the result that they do not have the economic characteristics of interest. Leverage is generally viewed as any multiple above one.

6.10.36 However, unlike leverage, certain contractual provisions will not cause the 'solely payments of principal and interest' test to be failed. For example, contractual provisions that permit the issuer to pre-pay a debt instrument or permit the holder to put a debt instrument, back to the issuer before maturity result in contractual cash flows that are 'solely payments of principal and interest' as long as the following certain conditions are met:

- The pre-payment amount substantially represents unpaid amounts of principal and interest on the principal amount outstanding (which may include reasonable additional compensation for the contract's early termination).

- The pre-payment amount is not contingent on future events (other than to protect the holder against the issuer's credit deterioration, or a change of control of the issuer or against changes in tax or law).

[IFRS 9 App B para B4.1.10]

6.10.37 Contractual provisions that permit the issuer or holder to extend the contractual term of a debt instrument are also regarded as being 'solely payments of principal and interest', provided during the term of the extension the contractual cash flows are 'solely payments of principal and interest' (for example, the interest rate does not step up to some leveraged multiple of LIBOR), and the provision is not contingent on future events. [IFRS 9 App B para B4.1.11]

6.10.38 The following are examples of contractual cash flows that are not 'solely payments of principal and interest':

- Bonds where the amount of interest varies inversely to a market rate of interest (inverse floaters).

- Links to equity index, borrower's net income or other non-financial variables.

- Deferrals of interest payments where additional interest does not accrue on those deferred amounts.

- Variable rate loan where at each reset date, the borrower can choose to pay one month LIBOR for a three month term and one month LIBOR is not reset each month.

- Five year constant maturity bond at variable rate, which is reset periodically but always reflects a five year maturity (that is, disconnected with the instrument's term except at origination). See also example 6 below.

- Convertible bond (from the holder's perspective).

6.10.39 If a contractual cash flow characteristic is not genuine, it does not affect the financial asset's classification. In this context, 'not genuine' means the occurrence of an event that is extremely rare, highly abnormal and very unlikely to occur. [IFRS 9 App B para B4.1.18].

Example 1 – Changing credit spread

An entity has a loan agreement that specifies that the interest rate will change depending on the borrower's credit rating, EBITDA or gearing ratio. Such a feature will not fail the 'solely payments of principal and interest' test provided the adjustment is considered to reasonably approximate the credit risk of an instrument with that level of EBITDA, gearing or credit rating. That is, if such a covenant compensates the lender with higher interest when the borrower's credit risk increases then this is consistent with interest being defined as the consideration for the credit risk and the time value of money. However, if the covenant would result in more than just compensation for credit or provides for some level of interest based on the entity's profitability, that will not meet the test.

Example 2 – Average rates

An entity has a loan agreement where interest is based on an average LIBOR rate over a period. That is, the loan has no defined maturity, but rolls every two years with reference to the two year LIBOR rate. The interest rate is reset every two years to equal the average two year LIBOR rate over the last two years. The economic rationale is to allow borrowers to benefit from a floating rate, but with an averaging mechanism to protect them from short-term volatility. Such a feature will not fail the 'solely payments of principal and interest' test provided the average rate represents compensation for only the time value of money and credit risk.

Example 3 – Market disruption clauses

An entity has a variable rate loan contract that contains a market disruption clause. This clause states the mechanism for determining the interest rate when the reference rate is unavailable (for example, LIBOR cannot be determined). In the case when an alternative rate cannot be found the contractual terms require immediate repayment at principal plus accrued interest. The repayment on such a contingent event (market disruption), which is other than those listed in paragraph B4.1.10(a) of appendix B to IFRS 9 will not make a loan fail the 'solely payments of principal and interest' test, provided a market disruption event is considered to be extremely rare, highly abnormal and very unlikely to occur. Therefore, it can be treated as a non-genuine characteristic and should not impact whether the instrument is eligible for amortised cost.

Example 4 – Regulatory capital clauses in debt instruments

An entity holds a debt instrument issued by a bank where there is the ability for the issuer to call the instrument on a capital disqualification event – that is, the instrument is no longer eligible due to a change in regulatory requirements for inclusion in Tier 1 or 2 capital. Although such a feature is not specifically mentioned as an example in IFRS 9, it is reasonable to read into the principle in paragraph B4.1.10(a)(ii) of appendix B to IFRS 9, which covers changes in tax or law, that as long as the repayment when the event happens results in the holder being compensated for principal and interest then the instrument will not fail the 'solely payment of principal and interest' test.

Example 5 – Classification of euro bond linked to inflation in Italy (or another EU county)

An entity has an investment in a euro bond linked to inflation in Italy. That is, the bond has a coupon that is increased or decreased depending on inflation in Italy. Such a feature will not fail the 'solely payments of principal and interest' test as the pricing of the bond inherently reflects the market price for time value of money and credit risk. The adjustment factor applied would vary with the inflation index used, such that different euro denominated bonds each linked to inflation in a different euro country could all meet the 'solely payments of principal and interest' test. However, a euro denominated bond linked to inflation in the UK (or other non-euro zone country) will not meet the test.

In addition, an inflation linked bond need not be principal protected to pass the contractual cash flow test even though the investor might not get back all of its initial recorded investment. The key test is whether the interest is compensation for only the time value of money and credit risk.

Example 6 – Constant maturity interest rate

An entity has a loan whose interest rate is reset periodically to equal the prevailing rate currently applied to new loans with an initial term of 5 years, regardless of the remaining time to maturity of the existing loan. If such a reset represents the only legal pricing basis available in a particular jurisdiction, it does not preclude the loan from having contractual cash flows that are 'solely payments of principal and interest'. This may be the case in jurisdictions where interest rates on loans are extensively regulated by the government and reset based on their original maturity regardless of the remaining time to maturity. However, if in the jurisdiction concerned similar loans are available on other pricing bases (for example, a periodic reset to a rate that reflects the remaining time to maturity of the loan), the constant maturity interest rate will not represent payments of solely principal and interest.

Example 7 – Equity release mortgages

A bank granted a mortgage to a borrower whose terms are that whilst the borrower is still alive they pay interest, but when they die the property is sold and the net proceeds are used to repay the principal on the loan. Where on sale of the property the bank is exposed to a shortfall between the sales proceeds and the amount of the loan, insurance risk will be transferred to the bank. If this insurance risk is significant, the contract will fall within the scope of IFRS 4 (see chapter 8). In such a case, if the deposit element (the mortgage) can be and is subsequently unbundled from the insurance component (see chapter 8), the classification of the separate mortgage component would then be assessed under IFRS 9.

Example 8 – Extension option

A bank has provided a loan with a five year term and a fixed coupon rate of 8%. At the end of the five years, the bank has the option to extend the loan at the initial fixed coupon rate for an additional five years regardless of what the current market rate is at that time for a 5 year instrument. The extension option embedded in the loan is not contingent on any future events other than the passage of time and as such will meet the 'solely payments of principal and interest' test. The commercial effect of the option is no different to a cap or a floor, or to that of an early redemption option at year 5 of a 10 year loan at 8%. Such features also do not fail the 'solely payments of principal and interest' test.

Example 9 – Multi-currency clauses

An entity holds a bond where it has the option to change the denomination of the bond at any time until maturity. For example, in year 1 the bond is denominated in HUF, with a floating interest rate of BUBOR plus a margin. The borrower has the ability to change the denomination to EUR, in which case the loan is converted at the spot rate, and the interest rate is converted to EURIBOR plus a margin from that moment on. However, the margin is fixed and is the same regardless of the currency. The borrower can switch back and forth between HUF and EUR as many times as it wishes. Such a feature does not fail the 'solely payments of principal and interest' test because at any point in time the interest rate corresponds with the currency of the principal. Although the margin is fixed regardless of currency, this is no different to a plain vanilla floating rate loan, whereby at each period the reference rate is reset but the spread is fixed at inception. For such loans there are no subsequent adjustments to the margin for changes in liquidity or credit risk after inception and such loans also meet the 'solely payments of principal and interest' test.

Example 10 – Step up notes

An entity invests in a 10 year note for which the floating interest rate on the note steps-up by 100bp after 5 years unless the issuer redeems the note. Such a feature will not fail the 'solely payments of principal and interest' test. The instrument may be viewed as having an interest margin during the first 5 years that incorporates a credit spread that is at least equal to that of a similar instrument maturing at the end of 5 years and the stepped-up rate represents at least the rate at inception for a similar instrument that starts in year 6 and matures at the end of year 10. Alternatively, if the step-up is higher this may be intended to economically compel the issuer to exercise the call and redeem the notes. If the call is not exercised it may indicate that market conditions have changed since the issuance of the notes (for example, the issuer may have experienced a credit downgrade) and, hence, the step up can be seen as compensating the holder for time value of money and credit risk.

Example 11 – Shareholder loans with no interest

Entity A provides a shareholder loan with no interest and no fixed terms of repayment to its subsidiary entity B. The loan is not deemed to be an investment in entity B. If there are no fixed repayment terms, the loan is deemed to be repayable on demand and classified as a current liability of entity B. The loan, therefore, has a contractual cash flow being the repayment of the principal on demand and, therefore, can be considered for amortised cost measurement. However, if there is no contractual requirement to repay the loan (and, therefore, it is classified as equity from entity B's perspective) then in this case the loan is considered part of entity A's investment in entity B.

Example 12 – Dual currency bonds

An entity invests in a fixed rate dual currency bond. The bond's principal is denominated in JPY and its interest payments are denominated in USD. In this case, the bond may be separated into two components: a zero coupon JPY bond and an USD interest only strip that is equivalent to an amortising bond. However, each component would need to meet the 'solely payments of principal and interest' criteria in order for the entire bond to be measured at amortised cost. This will often not be the case. For example: if a dual currency bond contains an option to prepay at the JPY principal amount, both components will fail the 'solely payments of principal and interest' test. This is because on early repayment the investor in the JPY zero coupon bond is repaid the par amount which is a payment that is considerably in excess of the unpaid amounts of principal and interest. Hence it fails the requirement in paragraph B4.1.10(b) of appendix B to IFRS 9.

Non-recourse

6.10.40 A non-recourse provision is an agreement that, should the debtor default on a secured obligation, the creditor can look only to the securing assets (whether financial or non-financial) to recover its claim. Should the debtor fail to pay and the specific assets fail to satisfy the full claim, the creditor has no legal recourse against the debtor's other assets. The fact that a financial asset is non-recourse does not necessarily preclude the financial asset from meeting the condition to be classified at amortised cost. [IFRS 9 App B para B4.1.17].

6.10.41 If a non-recourse provision exists, the creditor is required to assess (to 'look through to') the particular underlying assets or cash flows to determine whether the financial asset's contractual cash flows are 'solely payments of principal and interest'. If the instrument's terms give rise to any other cash flows or limit the cash flows in a manner inconsistent with the 'solely payments of principal and interest' test, the instrument will be measured in its entirety at fair value through profit or loss. [IFRS 9 App B para B.4.1.17]. Examples are (a) where the amount of the cash flows that are contractually due varies with the asset's performance such as in the case where the number of cars that drive down a toll road determines the amounts to be paid, or (b) a loan that is pre-payable at an amount that varies with the value of an underlying asset.

6.10.42 There is limited guidance as to how the existence of a non-recourse feature may impact the classification of non-recourse loans at amortised cost. Judgement will, therefore, be needed to assess these types of lending relationships.

Example 1 – Non-recourse real estate financing in SPV

A bank has a real estate financing business where its business model is to provide non-recourse financing to customers so as to generate interest income on the resulting loans. The bank's business model is not to participate in the economic performance of the underlying real estate (upside or downside). The bank limits its exposure to the real estate, in several ways, including: (a) by limiting the amount lent to between 60% and 75% of the value of the real estate at the inception of the loan (depending on the term of the loan and the nature of the real estate); (b) by ensuring the cash flows expected to be generated by the customer are more than sufficient to repay the loan (both principal and interest); and (c) by ensuring another party has contributed sufficient equity or subordinated financing to absorb all expected losses. Interest received is determined upfront as floating rate plus a fixed margin (determined primarily based on the credit quality of the borrower) with no reference to the performance of the underlying asset. Such a loan will meet the 'solely payments of principal and interest' test as the amount of cash flows due does not vary with the asset's performance nor is the payment linked to asset risk.

Example 2 – Non-recourse to portfolio of equity instruments

A bank has provided a loan to a borrower with a fixed rate of interest and fixed maturity date. The loan is secured on a non-recourse basis on a portfolio of equity instruments (shares). As such, at the maturity of the loan, the borrower intends to sell the shares and use the proceeds to repay the loan. The borrower would keep any upside in the share price, but the bank would suffer any loss. The pricing in this case is the same as a written put option on the shares. This loan would fail the 'solely payments of principal and interest' test as the amount of cash to be repaid varies with the performance of the equity instruments.

Contractually linked instruments (tranches)

6.10.43 The payments on some financial assets are contractually linked to the payments received on a pool of other instruments. These are referred to as contractually linked instruments. They are often issued by special purpose entities (SPEs) in various tranches, with the more senior tranches being repaid in priority to the more junior ones. Contractually linked instruments are financial assets that create concentrations of credit risk. As the definition focuses on the contractual 'linkage' between cash flows of issued tranches, there needs to be multiple tranches for the contractually linked requirements to apply. The 'contractually linked' test is essentially form driven, that is, there need to be a contractual cash waterfall or similar arrangement and if there is no explicit contractual linkage the guidance within paragraphs B4.1.20-26 of IFRS 9 does not apply. If an adjustment of the investment's cash flows occurs only upon default and liquidation, then this is not contractual linkage. The classification criteria for the holder of such contractually linked instruments (tranches) should be assessed based on the conditions at the date the entity initially recognised the investment using a 'look through' approach. This approach looks at the terms of the instrument itself as well as through to the pool of underlying instruments to assess both the characteristics of these underlying instruments and the tranche's exposure to credit risk relative to the pool of underlying instruments. [IFRS 9 App B para B4.1.20-26].

6.10.44 To measure an individual tranche at amortised cost, the tranche itself (without looking through to the pool of underlying instruments) must give rise to cash flows that are 'solely payments of principal and interest' and the underlying pool must contain one or more instruments that have contractual cash flows that are 'solely payments of principal and interest'.

6.10.45 In this context, the underlying pool is that which creates (rather than passes through) the cash flows. [IFRS 9 App B para B4.1.22].

16.10.46 The underlying pool of instruments may also include instruments that:

■ Reduce the variability of the instruments in the underlying pool (for example, an interest rate cap or floor or a contract that reduces the credit risk of the underlying pool of instruments).

■ Align the cash flows of the tranches with the cash flows of the pool of underlying instruments to address differences in and only in:

  ■ whether the interest rate is fixed or floating;

  ■ the currency in which the cash flows are denominated; or

  ■ the timing of the cash flows.

[IFRS 9 App B para B4.1.24].

6.10.47 Any derivatives in the SPE structure should, therefore, reflect a risk that is present in either the assets or the liabilities or both to achieve amortised cost accounting for the tranche.

6.10.48 In addition, the credit risk of the tranche must be equal to or lower than the weighted average credit risk of the underlying pool of financial instruments. [IFRS 9 App B para B4.1.21c].

6.10.49 The standard does not explicitly address how the weighted average credit risk test should be performed. A simple way might involve comparing the credit rating of the tranche to the average credit rating of the underlying pool of assets if that gives a clear answer. If not, a more complex quantitative assessment may be required that compares the variability of the tranche held based on a variety of probability-weighted outcomes with that of the underlying assets.

6.10.50 Fair value measurement is required if any instrument in the pool does not meet the conditions outlined above, or if the composition of the underlying pool might change after the initial recognition such that it would no longer meet the qualifying conditions, or if it is impracticable to look through. [IFRS 9 App B para B4.1.26]. The only case where a change in the components of the underlying pool might still meet the qualifying conditions is where collateral (for example, property) is seized in connection with the default of the underlying loans (for example, if collateral can be seized only in connection with a default, any collateral seized is required to be sold as soon as practicable thereafter and the overall effect is that no material asset/property risk is taken).

Example 1 – Investments in units issued by close-ended fund

An entity invests in units issued by a close-ended fund. The fund holds only debt instruments that themselves would qualify for amortised cost classification under IFRS 9 had these instruments been directly held by the unit holder. The fund's objective is to hold the assets to maturity rather than to realise fair value changes. Payments made by this fund to the holder may, therefore, represent 'solely payments of principal and interest'. The holder may, therefore, be able to measure its investment at amortised cost. However, if the fund does not hold only debt instruments, the investor will not be able to measure its investment at amortised cost, because the fund will generally pay out changes in the fair value of assets of the fund, which will not be 'solely payments of principal and interest'.

Example 2 – Derivatives in underlying pool of assets

An SPE holds floating rate EUR assets and issued fixed rate GBP notes contractually linked to the assets. The SPE has entered into one swap that is a pay EUR floating and receive GBP floating, and a second swap that is a pay GBP floating and receive GBP fixed. Both these swaps would meet the requirements in paragraph B4.24(b) of appendix B to IFRS 9 of aligning the cash flows of the tranches with the cash flows of the pool of underlying instruments. The holder may, therefore, be able to measure its investment at amortised cost. However, if the SPE were to have a derivative that introduced a third currency – say USD – this would not align the cash flows, and the tranche would have to be measured at fair value through profit or loss.

Example 3 – Derivative with optionality in underlying pool of assets

An SPE holds a fixed-for-floating swap that also hedges pre-payment risk such that if the underlying pool of fixed rate assets pays down early, the derivative is cancelled with no further amounts to pay. This is to ensure there is no excess derivatives and no fair value gains/losses on settlement, as when the assets pre-pay, the notes pre-pay. This feature would not fail the requirements of paragraph B4.1.24 of appendix B to IFRS 9; the holder may, therefore, be able to measure its investment at amortised cost. This could also be achieved by other mechanisms (for example, the SPE could be required to enter into an offsetting derivative as soon as practicable) to ensure there are not any excess derivatives after the prepayment of the notes.

Example 4 – Investments in collateralised debt obligations (CDOs)

An entity has an investment in a cash CDO where the issuing SPE holds the underlying referenced assets. Cash CDOs may qualify for amortised cost accounting as long as the underlying assets qualify for amortised cost accounting and the other requirements of IFRS 9 are met for contractually linked instruments. However, investments in synthetic CDOs (where the SPE has a credit derivative that references particular exposures) would not qualify, as the derivatives on the reference exposures do not have cash flows that are solely payments of principal or interest, nor do they align the cash flows permitted by IFRS 9.

Equity instruments

6.10.51 Investments in equity instruments (as defined in IAS 32 by considering the perspective of the issuer) are always measured at fair value. Equity instruments that are held for trading (including all equity derivative instruments such as warrants and rights issues) are required to be classified as at fair value through profit or loss. [IFRS 9 para 5.7.5]. For all other equities, management has the ability to make an irrevocable election on initial recognition, on an instrument-by-instrument basis, to present changes in fair value in other comprehensive income (OCI) rather than profit or loss. [IFRS 9 para 5.7.5]. If this election is made, all fair value changes, excluding certain dividends, will be reported in OCI. Dividends are recognised in profit and loss unless they clearly represent a recovery of part of the cost of an investment in which case they are recognised in OCI. [IFRS 9 App B para B5.7.1]. There is no recycling of amounts from OCI to profit and loss – for example, on sale of an equity investment – nor are there any impairment requirements. However, the entity may transfer the cumulative gain or loss within equity. [IFRS 9 App B para B5.7.1].

Example 1 – Investment in perpetual note

An entity (the holder) invests in a subordinated perpetual note, redeemable at the issuer's option, with a fixed coupon that can be deferred indefinitely if the issuer does not pay a dividend on its ordinary shares. The issuer classifies this instrument as equity under IAS 32. For the holder, unless the investment is held for trading, the holder has the option to classify it at either fair value through OCI or fair value through profit or loss under IFRS 9, as it is an equity instrument from the perspective of the issuer as defined in IAS 32.

Example 2 – Investment in a puttable share

An entity (the holder) invests in a fund that has puttable shares in issue – that is, the holder has the right to put the shares back to the fund in exchange for its *pro rata* share of the net assets. The puttable shares may meet the requirements to be classified as equity from the issuer's perspective, but this in an exception within IAS 32. Instruments meeting the provisions of paragraphs 16A-16E of IAS 32 do not meet the definition of equity in IAS 32. As a result, the holder does not have the ability to classify this investment as fair value through OCI. This is supported by paragraph 96C of IAS 32 which states that puttable instruments should not be considered an equity instrument under other guidance. Investments in puttable shares are, therefore, required to be classified as fair value through profit or loss, as they cannot be regarded as equity instruments for IFRS 9 and they do not have payments of solely principal and interest.

Example 3 – Special dividend that is clearly recovery of the cost of investment

An entity invests in shares at a cost of C12 and designates these at fair value through OCI. The issuer immediately pays a special dividend of C10. This dividend is not recorded in profit or loss in accordance with IAS 18 and paragraph B5.7.1 of appendix B to IFRS 9, as such a dividend clearly represents a recovery of part of the investment's cost, which is required to remain in OCI.

Example 4 – Special dividend that is not clearly recovery of the cost of investment

An entity invests in shares at a cost of C12 and designates these at fair value through OCI. Over the next five years it receives dividend income, which is recognised in profit or loss. At the end of the five years the fair value of the shares has increased to C22, giving rise to an unrealised gain of C10 in OCI. The issuer then pays a special dividend of C10.

IFRS 9 does not specify how to interpret the phrase 'cost of investment' in a more complex situation. One view is that cost could be interpreted as relating solely to the original cost of C12. Under this view, since the special dividend does not reduce the investment's carrying value below its original cost, the special dividend of C10 is recognised in profit or loss.

Alternatively, paragraph BC 5.25 of IFRS 9 indicates that dividends that represent a return of investment, rather than a return on investment, should be recognised in OCI. If this is viewed as a broader interpretation of cost, then, since the special dividend is a return of approximately half the fair value of the investment, it is a return of investment and should be recognised in OCI.

Other interpretations of cost may also be appropriate depending on the fact pattern. An entity should, therefore, make an accounting policy choice regarding how it interprets 'cost of investment' in the context of the fair value through OCI election. The policy should be applied consistently and disclosed where material.

Example 5 – Investments in associates

A venture capital organisation has an investment in an associate that it has previously designated at fair value through profit or loss in accordance with IAS 39, as is permitted by the scope exclusion in IAS 28. This investment is not permitted to be accounted for at fair value through OCI under IFRS 9, as IAS 28 has not been amended to permit such accounting. However, on adopting IFRS 9, the venture capital organisation could revoke its previous designation and, hence, apply equity accounting.

Example 6 – Convertible bonds – holder and issuer perspective

An entity has an investment in a convertible bond that from the issuer's perspective has both a liability and equity component. From the holder's perspective as the cash flows on the convertible bond are not solely payment of principal and interest the bond cannot be classified as a financial asset measured at amortised cost. [IFRS 9 App B para B4.14]. Convertible bonds that are compound instruments from the issuer's perspective will, therefore, always be classified at fair value through profit or loss by the holder. However, if a convertible bond were to be classified as equity in its entirety from the issuer's perspective (for example, as would be the case if the bond had no interest payments and mandatorily converts into a fixed number of the issuer's equity instruments on a future date), the holder may choose to designate it at fair value through OCI.

6.10.52 The standard removes the requirement in IAS 39 to measure unquoted equity investments at cost when the fair value cannot be determined reliably. However, it indicates that in limited circumstances, cost may be an appropriate estimate of fair value – for example, when insufficient more recent information is available from which to determine fair value; or when there is a wide range of possible fair value measurements and cost represents the best estimate of fair value within that range. However, IFRS 9 includes indicators of when cost might not be representative of fair value. These are:

- A significant change in the investee's performance compared with budgets, plans or milestones.

- Changes in expectation that the investee's technical product milestones will be achieved.

- A significant change in the market for the investee's equity or its products or potential products.

- A significant change in the global economy or the economic environment in which the investee operates.

- A significant change in the performance of comparable entities or in the valuations implied by the overall market.

- Internal matters of the investee such as fraud, commercial disputes, litigation, or changes in management or strategy.

- Evidence from external transactions in the investee's equity, either by the investee (such as a fresh issue of equity) or by transfers of equity instruments between third parties.

[IFRS 9 App B para B5.4.14-15].

6.10.53 Given the indicators above, it is not expected that cost will be representative of fair value for an extended period of time.

Embedded derivatives

6.10.54 The accounting for embedded derivatives in host contracts that are financial assets is simplified by removing the requirement to consider whether or not they are closely related and should, therefore, be separated. The classification approach in the new standard applies to all financial assets, including those with embedded derivatives.

6.10.55 Many embedded derivatives introduce variability to cash flows. That is not consistent with the notion that the instrument's contractual cash flows solely represent the payment of principal and interest. If an embedded derivative was not considered closely related under the existing requirements, this does not automatically mean the instrument will not qualify for amortised cost treatment under the new standard. However, the number of circumstances where such instruments will qualify for amortised cost is limited

6.10.56 The accounting for embedded derivatives in non-financial host contracts and financial liabilities currently remains unchanged.

Reclassifications

6.10.57 An instrument's classification is made at initial recognition and is not changed subsequently, with one exception. Reclassifications between fair value and amortised cost (and *vice versa*) are required only when the entity changes how it manages its financial instruments (that is, changes its business model). [IFRS 9 para 4.4.1]. Such changes are expected to be infrequent. The reclassification must be significant to the entity's operations and demonstrable to external parties. Any reclassification should be accounted for prospectively. Entities are not, therefore, allowed to restate any previously recognised gains or losses. The asset should be remeasured at fair value at the date of a reclassification of a financial asset from amortised cost to fair value; this value will be the new carrying amount. Any difference between the previous carrying amount and the fair value would be recognised in a separate line item in the income statement. At the date of a reclassification of a financial asset from fair value to amortised cost, its fair value at that reclassification date becomes its new carrying amount. [IFRS 9 paras 5.6.1-5.6.3].

6.10.58 Examples of change in the business model that would require reclassification include:

■ An entity has a portfolio of commercial loans that it holds to sell in the short-term. Following an acquisition of an entity whose business model is to hold commercial loans to collect the contractual cash flows, that portfolio is managed together with the acquired portfolio to collect the contractual cash flows.

■ An entity decides to close its retail mortgage business and is actively marketing its mortgage loan portfolio.

[IFRS 9 App B para B4.4.1].

6.10.59 The following are not changes in business model:

■ A change in intention related to particular financial assets.

■ A temporary disappearance of a particular market for financial assets.

■ A transfer of financial assets between parts of the entity with different business models.

[IFRS 9 App B4.4.3].

All other reclassifications are prohibited.

> **Example 1– Leverage feature in an instrument lapses**
>
> An entity holds a convertible bond where the conversion feature lapses after a certain period of time. The lapse of the term does not constitute a reclassification event. Classification is determined on initial recognition. It is only when an entity changes its business model that instruments can be reclassified.

> **Example 2 – Loans transferred to a run-off portfolio**
>
> An entity has a portfolio of loans that are classified as amortised cost. After a period of time, some of the loans become non-performing and are transferred into a run-off portfolio where the entity's intention is to maximise the recovery of the loans, which could be by selling the loans if a good price can be obtained in the market. Such a transfer does not constitute a reclassification event as IFRS 9 is clear that a change of intention or a transfer of financial assets between different portfolios is not a reclassification event. [IFRS 9 App B para B4.4.3].

Financial liabilities

Initial recognition

6.10.60 Consistent with IAS 39, all financial liabilities in IFRS 9 are to be initially recognised at fair value, minus, in the case of a financial liability that is not at fair value through profit or loss, transaction costs that are directly attributable to issuing the financial liability. [IFRS 9 para 5.1.1]. IFRS 13 amended IFRS 9 to remove the guidance on fair value measurement. Entities that have adopted IFRS 13 should refer to chapter 5 for the relevant fair value measurement guidance.

Classification and measurement

6.10.61 Financial liabilities are measured at amortised cost, unless they are required to be measured at fair value through profit or loss or an entity has opted to measure a liability at fair value through profit or loss. [IFRS 9 para 4.2.1].

6.10.62 The main concern in revising IAS 39 for financial liabilities was potentially showing, in an entity's income statement, the impact of 'own credit risk' for liabilities recognised at fair value – that is, fluctuations in value due to changes in the liability's credit risk. This can result in gains being recognised in income when an entity is in financial distress resulting in the liability being downgraded, and losses being recognised when the liability's credit risk improves. Many users found these results counterintuitive, especially when there is no expectation that the change in the liability's credit risk will be realised. This issue would have been problematic if the IASB had adopted an approach similar to the classification and measurement of financial assets in IFRS 9, where hybrid instruments (that is, financial instruments that contain embedded derivatives) are accounted for at fair value through profit or loss as this would have required the full change in the liability's credit risk to be recognised in profit or loss.

6.10.63 In view of this concern, the IASB has retained the existing guidance in IAS 39 for classifying and measuring financial liabilities, except for those liabilities where the fair value option has been elected.

Financial liabilities (except those designated at fair value through profit or loss using the fair value option)

6.10.64 The classification and measurement of financial liabilities under IFRS 9 remains the same except where an entity has chosen to measure a liability at fair value through profit or loss. There continue to be two measurement categories for financial liabilities: fair value and amortised cost. Certain liabilities are required to be at fair value through profit or loss, such as liabilities held for trading and derivatives. Other liabilities are measured at amortised cost, unless the liability has embedded derivatives that require separation or the entity elects the fair value option. [IFRS 9 para 4.2].

6.10.65 The existing guidance in IAS 39 for embedded derivatives has been retained for financial liabilities under IFRS 9. Entities are still required to separate derivatives embedded in financial liabilities where they are not closely related to the host contract (for examples see chapter 6.3). The separated embedded derivative continues to be measured at fair value through profit or loss and the residual debt host is measured at amortised cost.

6.10.66 The treatment of financial assets and liabilities under IFRS 9 is not symmetrical. The existing embedded derivative guidance in IAS 39 is retained in IFRS 9 for financial liabilities and non-financial instruments; this results in some embedded derivatives being separately accounted for at fair value through profit or loss. However, embedded derivatives are no longer separated from financial assets. Instead, they are part of the contractual terms that are considered in determining whether the entire financial asset has 'solely payments of principal and interest' and hence is measured at amortised cost (if the 'held to collect' business model test is also met) or whether it must be measured at fair value through profit or loss. (See para 6.10.54 above.)

Financial liabilities designated at FVTPL using fair value option

6.10.67 IFRS 9 changes the accounting for financial liabilities that an entity chooses to account for at fair value through profit or loss, using the fair value option. For such liabilities, changes in fair value related to changes in own credit risk are presented separately in OCI. [IFRS 9 para 5.7.7].

6.10.68 That is, elements of the fair value movement of the liability are presented in different parts of the performance statement; changes in own credit risk are presented in OCI, and all other fair value changes are presented in the income statement. [IFRS 9 para 5.7.7]. (See also para 6.10.74 below.)

6.10.69 Amounts in OCI relating to own credit are not recycled to the income statement even when the liability is derecognised and the amounts are realised. This is consistent with the requirements in IFRS 9 that prohibit recycling to profit or loss for investments in equity instruments that are measured at fair value through OCI. However, the standard does allow transfers within equity, so entities that wish to transfer realised balances to retained earnings, for example, could do so. [IFRS 9 App B para B5.7.9].

Example – Presentation

Assume a liability that has been designated at FVTPL has a fair value movement of C100 for the period. Of that C100, C10 relates to changes in own credit risk. This would be presented as follows:

	C
Income statement	
Change in fair value other than from own credit risk	90
Other comprehensive income	
Change in fair value from own credit risk	10

6.10.70 The eligibility criteria for the fair value option remain the same and are based on whether:

- the liability is managed on a fair value basis;

- electing fair value will eliminate or reduce an accounting mismatch; or

- the instrument is a hybrid that would require separation of an embedded derivative.

[IFRS 9 para 4.2.2].

6.10.71 A common reason for electing the fair value option is where liabilities have embedded derivatives that the issuer does not wish to separate from the host liability. In addition, entities may elect to use the fair value option where they would otherwise have an accounting mismatch between a financial liability and an asset that is required to be held at fair value through profit or loss.

6.10.72 Financial liabilities that are required to be measured at fair value through profit or loss (as distinct from those that the entity has chosen to measure at fair value through profit or loss) continue to have all fair value movements, including those related to changes in the credit risk of the liability, recognised in profit or loss. This includes all derivatives (such as foreign currency forwards or interest rate swaps), or an entity's own liabilities that it considers as 'held for trading'.

6.10.73 Financial guarantees and loan commitments that entities choose to measure at fair value through profit or loss will have all fair value movements recognised in profit or loss. The IASB decided that financial guarantees and loan commitments are very similar to derivatives and should, therefore, continue to have all changes in fair value recorded in profit and loss where they have been designated at fair value through profit or loss. [IFRS 9 para 5.7.9].

6.10.74 In addition, if presenting the changes in own credit of a financial liability in OCI would create an accounting mismatch in profit or loss, all fair value movements are recognised in profit or loss. The accounting mismatch must arise due to an economic relationship between the financial liability and a financial asset that results in the liability's credit risk being offset by a change in the asset's fair value. The accounting mismatch:

■ is required to be determined when the liability is first recognised;

■ is not re-assessed subsequently; and

■ must not be caused solely by the measurement method that an entity uses to determine the changes in a liability's credit risk.

[IFRS 9 para 5.7.8].

> **Example – Own credit and accounting mismatch**
>
> A mortgage bank provides loans to customers and funds the loans by selling matching bonds in the market. The customer can repay the mortgage by buying the bond and delivering it to the mortgage bank. If the fair value of the bond (the financial liability of the mortgage bank) decreases due to own credit risk, it is offset by changes in the fair value of the mortgage (financial asset). Therefore, recognising the credit risk of the bond in OCI would create an accounting mismatch in profit or loss.

6.10.75 This exemption from the requirement to present movements in the own credit risk of a liability in OCI is expected to be rare. Staff papers prepared for the IASB's discussions in finalising IFRS 9 indicated that the mortgage bank example was the only accounting mismatch they had discovered so far that would meet the criteria in IFRS 9.

Measuring changes in own credit risk of liabilities

6.10.76 For those financial liabilities where changes in fair value related to own credit risk are presented separately in OCI it is necessary to calculate the amount. Prior to the issuance of IFRS 9, IFRS 7 already required disclosure of the amount of fair value changes that are attributable to own credit risk for liabilities designated at fair value through profit or loss. This guidance was retained but has been relocated to IFRS 9, and some aspects have been clarified.

6.10.77 Own credit risk can be determined as either:

■ the amount of fair value change not attributable to changes in market risk (for example, benchmark interest rates). This is often referred to as the default method; or

- an alternative method that the entity believes more faithfully represents the changes in fair value due to 'own credit' (for example, a method that computes credit risk directly based on credit default swap rates).

[IFRS 9 para B5.7.16].

6.10.78 However, if the changes in fair value arising from factors other than changes in the liability's credit risk or changes in observed interest rates (that is, benchmark rates such as LIBOR) are significant, an entity is required to use an alternative method and not the default method. For example, changes in the fair value of a liability may arise due to changes in value of a derivative embedded in that liability rather than changes in benchmark interest rates. In that situation, changes in the value of the embedded derivative must be excluded in determining the amount of own credit risk that is presented in OCI.

6.10.79 The expanded guidance in IFRS 9 confirms that the credit risk of a liability with collateral is likely to be different from the credit risk of an equivalent liability without collateral issued by the same entity. [IFRS 9 para B5.7.13].

6.10.80 It also clarifies that unit-linking features usually contain specific asset performance risk rather than credit risk – that is, the value of the liability changes due to changes in value of the linked asset(s) and not because of changes in the own credit risk of the liability. This means that changes in the fair value of a unit-linked liability due to changes in the fair value of the linked asset will continue to be recognised in the income statement, as they are not regarded as being part of the own credit risk of the liability that is recognised in OCI. [IFRS 9 para B5.7.15].

> **Example 1 – Unit linked liabilities at FVTPL**
>
> An entity issues unit-linked liabilities that it has designated at fair value through profit or loss and it holds the related assets at fair value. At the beginning of the period, the assets and the liabilities both have a fair value C100. During the period, the fair value of the assets decreases by C20. The fair value of the liability also decreases by C20 during the period due to the change in the value of the linked assets. As this change in fair value is attributable to the change in the fair value of the related assets, the entire fair value change of C20 is recognised in profit or loss.

Transition and effective date

6.10.81 The requirements in IFRS 9 are generally applied retrospectively to assets held at the date of initial application with some exceptions. For example, if it is impracticable to retrospectively apply the effective interest method or impairment requirements, the entity should determine the instrument's amortised cost, or any impairment on the financial asset, in each period, by using its fair value at the end of each comparative period. [IFRS 9 para 7.2.10].

6.10.82 In December 2011, the Board amended IFRS 9 to defer the mandatory effective date of IFRS 9 from 1 January 2013 to annual periods beginning on or after 1 January 2015. Early application of IFRS 9 will continue to be permitted. IFRS 9 has not yet been endorsed for use in the EU. The Board also amended the transitional provisions to provide relief from restating comparative information and introduced new disclosures to help users of financial statements understand the effect of moving to the IFRS 9 classification and measurement model. The IFRS as amended supersedes IFRS 9 issued in 2009. However, for annual periods beginning before 1 January 2015, an entity may elect to apply IFRS 9 issued in 2009 instead of applying the amended IFRS. [IFRS 9 para 7.3.2].

6.10.83   The effective date and transition requirements for financial liabilities are consistent with those for financial assets. Entities may choose to adopt early, but it is not possible to adopt the part for financial liabilities without also adopting the requirements for financial assets. However, entities are still permitted to adopt early the requirements for financial assets in IFRS 9 without adopting the requirements for financial liabilities.

6.10.84   Additional disclosures are required by IFRS 7 when the entity adopts the standard. See paragraph 6.10.95 below. As noted above, the standard as amended in December 2011, also provides transition relief and introduced new disclosures to help users of financial statements understand the effect of moving to IFRS 9. These are as follows:

- for reporting periods beginning before 1 January 2012 entities need not restate prior periods and are not required to provide the disclosures set out in paragraphs 44S–44W of IFRS 7;

- for reporting periods beginning on or after 1 January 2012 and before 1 January 2013 entities must elect either to provide the disclosures set out in paragraphs 44S–44W of IFRS 7 or to restate prior periods; and

- for reporting periods beginning on or after 1 January 2013 entities should provide the disclosures set out in paragraphs 44S–44W of IFRS 7. The entity need not restate prior periods.

See further detail on these disclosures in paragraph 6.10.96 below.

6.10.84.1   The implementation guidance on IFRS 9 has also been amended to include an illustration of one possible way to meet the quantitative disclosure requirements in paragraphs 44S-44W of IFRS 7. [IFRS 9 para IE6].

6.10.84.2   If an entity does not restate prior periods, the entity should recognise any difference between the previous carrying amount and the carrying amount at the beginning of the annual reporting period that includes the date of initial application in the opening retained earnings (or other component of equity, as appropriate). [IFRS 9 para 7.2.14].

6.10.85   IFRS 9 introduces the concept of a 'date of initial application'. This date is important for:

- identifying the assets and liabilities to which IFRS 9 should be applied (the standard is not applied to assets derecognised by the date of initial application);

- assessing the business model;

- designations or de-designations for using the fair value option; and

- designations of non-trading equity investments as at FV through other comprehensive income.

However, the date is not relevant for performing a contractually linked credit risk assessment. Such a test is required to be based on circumstances that existed at the date the entity originally invested in the instrument, rather than at the date of initial application. This is because the contractual characteristics test must be applied retrospectively. Any subsequent changes in risk are not relevant for this assessment.

6.10.86 For example, at the date of initial application an entity assesses the business model for holding a particular asset on the basis of the facts and circumstances that exist at that date. The resulting classification is then applied retrospectively, irrespective of the entity's business model in prior reporting periods. Similarly, at the date of initial application, an entity may designate a financial asset or financial liability at fair value through profit or loss or an investment in an equity instrument as at fair value through other comprehensive income on the basis of the facts and circumstances that exist at that date. That classification is then applied retrospectively.

6.10.87 The date of initial application may be any date between the issue of the new standard (November 2009 for the classification and measurement of financial assets) and 31 December 2010 for entities adopting the new IFRS before 1 January 2011. For entities adopting IFRS 9 on or after 1 January 2011, the date of initial application is the beginning of the first reporting period in which the entity adopts. [IFRS 9 para 7.2.2].

6.10.88 The 2011 amendments to IFRS 9 also clarify that the definition of reporting period relates to the annual reporting period that includes the date of initial application. [IFRS 9 para 8.2.12].

> **Example 1 – From AFS to amortised cost under IFRS 9**
>
> Management has decided to apply IFRS 9 on 1 January 2012 (the date of initial application) and not restate its comparatives as is permitted under IFRS 9 but will provide the disclosures as set out in paragraphs 44S-44W of IFRS 7. The entity has a debt instrument that is accounted for as AFS under IAS 39. On the date of initial application of IFRS 9, it is determined that the asset is held to collect the contractual cash flows and those cash flows solely represent payments of principal and interest. It will, therefore, be measured at amortised cost under IFRS 9. On transition, this will require the debt instrument to be measured at amortised cost at 1 January 2012 (as if it had always been measured at amortised cost since it was initially recognised by the entity). Any existing AFS reserve is reclassified against the carrying value at 1 January 2012.

Example 2 – From AFS to FV through profit and loss for equities

Management has decided to apply IFRS 9 on 1 January 2012 (the date of initial application) and not restate its comparatives as is permitted under IFRS 9 but will provide the disclosures as set out in paragraphs 44S-44W of IFRS 7. On the date of initial application, management decides that its holding of equity investments will be classified as FV through profit and loss. The original cost of these equities was C100. At 31 December 2011, fair value was C30, so the AFS reserve was negative C70. It was determined at that date that those equities were impaired; C70 was, therefore, reflected in the income statement. At 31 December 2012, the fair value of the equities is C55. The entity is not restating its comparatives for 2011. Therefore, in 2012, when it first applies IFRS 9 and measures the equities at FV through profit and loss, the increase of C25 in fair value would be reflected in profit or loss for the 2012 year end.

Example 3 – FV through profit and loss to amortised cost

Management has decided to apply IFRS 9 on 1 January 2012 (the date of initial application) and not restate its comparatives as is permitted under IFRS 9 but will provide the disclosures as set out in paragraphs 44S-44W of IFRS 7. The entity has a debt instrument that was held at FV through profit and loss under IAS 39. On the date of initial application of IFRS 9, it is determined that the asset is held to collect its cash flows and that its cash flows solely represent payments of principal and interest. On transition, the debt instrument is measured at amortised cost (as if it had always been measured at amortised cost since it was initially recognised by the entity). Any difference between that amount and its fair value under IAS 39 will be reflected in opening retained earnings at 1 January 2012.

Example 4 – FV through profit and loss to FV through OCI

Management has decided to apply IFRS 9 on 1 January 2012 (the date of initial application) and not restate its comparatives as is permitted under IFRS 9 but will provide the disclosures as set out in paragraphs 44S-44W of IFRS 7. The entity has an equity investment that it currently classifies as FV through profit and loss under IAS 39. On the date of initial application of IFRS 9, management decides that it will classify the equity investment as FV through OCI, as it is not held-for-trading. On transition, as this measurement has to be applied retrospectively, a reserve will be created (that is, reclassified from opening retained earnings at 1 January 2012) in OCI, based on the difference between the instrument's original cost and its fair value at the opening balance sheet date.

Example 5 – AFS instruments disposed of during period prior to adoption

Management has decided to apply IFRS 9 on 1 January 2012 (the date of initial application). On 30 June 2011, the entity disposed of an AFS debt security (original cost C100, and FV on date of disposal of C110) and recognised a gain of C10 as a result of reclassifying the AFS reserve to profit and loss. There are no adjustments to be made for that AFS investment when the entity adopts IFRS 9 in its 2012 financial statements, as IFRS 9 is not applied to financial assets that have already been derecognised by the date of initial application. The entity would apply the same AFS accounting to that debt security as it had under IAS 39 in its 2011 financial statements.

Example 6 – 2008 IAS 39 reclassification amendment

The transition provisions in IFRS 9 require an entity to apply it retrospectively with a few exceptions. The reclassification amendment of October 2008 allowed certain instruments to be reclassified out of held-for-trading and AFS to loans and receivables; upon reclassification, the fair value at the date of reclassification becomes the new amortised cost of the reclassified assets. Upon initial application of IFRS 9, assuming these reclassified assets will continue to be measured at amortised cost, management is required to go back to the asset's initial recognition and measure it as if it had always been measured at amortised cost under IFRS 9. Its amortised cost for IFRS 9 will not, therefore, be the same amortised cost that was determined when these assets were reclassified under IAS 39.

Example 7 – Portfolios in run off

On transition to IFRS 9, an entity has a portfolio in 'run-off' where it has stopped trading in certain products because the market has become illiquid (for example, certain asset backed securities). The entity's intention is to maximise the recovery of the portfolio by either holding the positions and collecting coupons and principal payments, or by selling the positions if a good price can be obtained in the market. As opportunistic sales may be made to liquidate the portfolio in a quicker fashion if advantageous pricing is available, this is not consistent with a held to collect amortised cost business model. Such a portfolio will have to be measured at fair value through profit or loss.

Presentation and disclosure

6.10.89 IFRS 9 made some consequential amendments to IFRS 7. The majority of the changes were to align the disclosure requirements with the new measurement categories; however, some new disclosures are also required.

6.10.90 Entities that have designated a financial asset at fair value through profit or loss that would otherwise be measured at amortised cost are required to disclose:

- The financial asset's maximum exposure to credit risk at the end of the reporting period.

- The amount by which any related credit derivatives or similar instruments mitigate that credit risk and their fair value.

- The amount of change during the period and cumulatively in the financial asset's fair value that is attributable to changes in its credit risk.

6.10.91 Entities that apply IFRS 9 are required to disclose the following in relation to financial assets measured at fair value through OCI:

- Which investments in equity instruments have been designated to be measured at fair value through OCI.

- The reasons for using this presentation alternative.

- The fair value of each such investment at the end of the reporting period.

- Dividends recognised during the period, showing separately those related to investments derecognised during the reporting period and those related to investments held at the end of the reporting period.

- Any transfers of the cumulative gain or loss within equity during the period and the reason for such transfers.

- For any equity investments that were derecognised during the period, the reason for disposing of the investments, the fair value of the investments at the date of derecognition and the cumulative gain or loss on disposal.

[IFRS 7 paras 11A-11B].

6.10.92   In addition, there are new disclosure requirements for assets that are required to be reclassified under IFRS 9 because of the change in business model, as follows:

- The date of reclassification.

- A detailed explanation of the change in business model and a qualitative description of its effect on the entity's financial statements.

- The amount reclassified into and out of each category.

- For each reporting period following reclassification until derecognition, the effective interest rate determined on the date of reclassification and the interest income or expense recognised.

- If the entity has reclassified financial assets so that they are measured at amortised cost since its last annual reporting date, the financial assets' fair value at the end of the reporting period and the fair value gain or loss that would have been recognised in profit or loss during the reporting period if the financial assets had not been reclassified.

[IFRS 7 paras 12B-12D].

6.10.93   An entity is required to disclose an analysis of the gain or loss recognised in the statement of comprehensive income arising from derecognising the financial assets measured at amortised cost showing separately gains and losses arising from derecognition of those financial assets. This disclosure must also include the reasons for derecognising those financial assets. [IFRS 7 para 20A].

6.10.94   The following new disclosure requirements apply to entities that have designated a financial liability at fair value through profit or loss in addition to the requirement to present changes in own credit risk for liabilities separately in OCI:

- Details of transfers of cumulative gains/losses within equity and the reasons for the transfer.

- The amount presented in OCI that was realised on derecognising liabilities during the period.

610029

Although the standard prohibits recycling of cumulative gains/losses relating to own credit risk to profit and loss, the disclosures provide users of the financial statements with the same information that recycling through profit or loss would have provided.

6.10.95 When an entity first applies IFRS 9, there are additional disclosures required for each class of financial assets and financial liabilities on the date of initial application, as follows:

- The original measurement category and carrying amount determined in accordance with IAS 39.

- The new measurement category and carrying amount determined in accordance with IFRS 9.

- The amount of any financial assets and financial liabilities in the statement of financial position that were previously designated as measured at fair value through profit or loss but that are no longer so designated, distinguishing between those that IFRS 9 requires an entity to reclassify and those that an entity elects to reclassify.

- Qualitative information about how it applied the classification requirements in IFRS 9 to those financial assets whose classification has changed as a result of applying IFRS 9.

- Qualitative information about the reasons for any designation or de-designation of financial assets or financial liabilities as measured at fair value through profit or loss.

[IFRS 7 paras 44I-44J].

The quantitative disclosures should be presented in a tabular format.

6.10.96 In December 2011, the Board amended IFRS 7 by adding paragraphs 44S-44W to require additional disclosures on transition from IAS 39 to IFRS 9 as follows:

- At the date of initial application an entity shall disclose the changes in the classifications of instruments, showing separately a) the changes in the carrying amounts on the basis of their measurement categories in accordance with IAS 39 and b) the changes in the carrying amounts arising from a change in measurement attribute on transition to IFRS 9. These need not be made after the annual period in which IFRS 9 is initially applied.

- When IFRS 9 is initially applied, an entity should disclose for instruments that have been reclassified on transition to IFRS 9 to amortised cost:

  (a)   the fair value of the instruments at the end of the reporting period;

(b)   the fair value gain or loss that would have been recognised in profit or loss or other comprehensive income during the reporting period if the financial assets or financial liabilities had not been reclassified;

(c)   the effective interest rate determined on the date of reclassification; and

(d)   the interest income or expense recognised.

If an entity treats the fair value of a financial asset or a financial liability as its amortised cost at the date of initial application the disclosures in (c) and (d) should be made for each reporting period following reclassification until derecognition. Otherwise, the disclosures in this paragraph need not be made after the reporting period containing the date of initial application.

■ The disclosures above and the disclosures in paragraph 28 of IAS 8 must permit reconciliation between:

(a)   the measurement categories in accordance with IAS 39 and IFRS 9; and

(b)   the line items presented in the statements of financial position.

■ The disclosures above and the disclosures in paragraph 25 of IFRS 7 must permit reconciliation between:

(a)   the measurement categories in accordance with IAS 39 and IFRS 9; and

(b)   the class of financial instrument at the date of initial application,

6.10.97   Implementation guidance of IFRS 9 has also been amended to include an illustration of one possible way to meet the quantitative disclosure requirements in paragraphs 44S-44W of IFRS 7. [IFRS 9 para IE6].

Chapter 7

Foreign currencies

Chapter 7

Foreign currencies

Introduction

7.1   Entities conduct businesses that are not confined within national boundaries. The globalisation of markets for goods and services as well as capital means entities have to engage in international trade, cross-border alliances and joint ventures if they are to survive and grow in today's competitive business environment. Entities conduct business in the international market place in a number of ways. First, entities may buy goods and services from overseas suppliers and sell goods and services to overseas customers. Secondly, they may extend their international reach by conducting business through overseas subsidiaries, branches and associates.

7.2   In the first situation, transactions are often expressed in foreign currencies. The results of these transactions are translated into the entity's functional currency for financial reporting purposes. In the second situation, it is usual for the foreign operation to maintain its accounting records in the currency of the primary economic environment in which it operates. It is not possible to combine, add or subtract measurements expressed in different currencies, so management translates the foreign operation's results and financial position into the currency in which the reporting entity presents its consolidated financial statements.

7.3   Accounting for foreign currencies is, therefore, primarily concerned with the translation process whereby financial data denominated in one currency is expressed in terms of another currency. The translation process does not change the essential characteristics of the assets and liabilities measured. It merely restates assets and liabilities, initially expressed in a foreign currency unit, to a common currency unit by applying a rate of exchange factor — a translation rate.

7.4   Different translation rates may be used depending on the circumstances. These are:

- The historical rate — the rate of exchange ruling at the date the transaction or revaluation occurred.

- The closing rate — the rate ruling at the balance sheet date.

- The average rate ruling during the year.

The average rate is generally confined to income and expenditure items. The rates used for balance sheet items (historical or closing) depend on the types of assets and liabilities – monetary or non-monetary. These methods are addressed later in this chapter.

7.5 The treatment of exchange differences that arise on foreign currency transactions is different from those that arise on foreign currency translation. Foreign currency translation also raises a number of questions, such as: the extent to which exchange gains and losses from different sources can be offset; whether some exchange differences should be recognised immediately whilst others should be deferred; and whether the recognition should be through the income statement or in other comprehensive income.

[The next paragraph is 7.23.]

Objectives

7.23 IAS 21 prescribes how to:

■ Include foreign currency transactions and foreign operations in an entity's financial statements.

■ Specify which exchange rates to use and how to report the effects of changes in exchange rates in the financial statements.

■ Translate the financial statements into a presentation currency.

[IAS 21 paras 1, 2].

Applying these requirements in practice can be complex. This chapter provides guidance on the issues commonly encountered.

Scope

7.24 IAS 21 sets out the requirements for foreign currency translation. It applies to any entity that comes within its scope and engages in foreign currency operations. The standard is applied in:

■ Accounting for transactions and balances in foreign currencies, except for those derivative transactions and balances that are within the scope of IAS 39.

■ Translating the results and financial position of foreign operations that are included in the entity's financial statements by consolidation, proportionate consolidation or equity accounting.

■ Translating an entity's results and financial position into a presentation currency.

[IAS 21 para 3].

7.25 Accounting for foreign currency derivatives is scoped out of IAS 21 (and included in IAS 39). Foreign currency derivatives that may be embedded in various contracts and that require separate accounting under IAS 39 are scoped out of IAS 21; embedded foreign currency derivatives that do not require separate accounting under IAS 39 are included in IAS 21. However, IAS 21 applies to translation of foreign currency derivatives from a functional currency to a presentation currency. [IAS 21 para 4].

7.26 The standard does not apply to hedge accounting for foreign currency items, including the hedging of a net investment in a foreign operation. These issues are addressed in IAS 39. [IAS 21 para 5]. See chapter 6.8.

The functional currency approach

Introduction

7.27 IAS 21 requires each individual entity to determine its functional currency and measure its results and financial position in that currency. Each individual entity included in the consolidation therefore has its own functional currency. There is no such thing as a group functional currency.

7.28 The requirement to identify each entity's functional currency is the key feature of IAS 21. The functional currency serves as the basis for determining whether the entity is engaging in foreign currency transactions. This is because IAS 21 defines foreign currency as a currency other than the functional currency. [IAS 21 para 8]. Additionally, identifying the functional currency has a direct impact on the treatment of exchange gains and losses arising from the translation process and, thereby, the reported results, as will be evident later. IAS 21 provides guidance on determining the functional currency, which is considered from paragraph 7.31 below.

> **Example – Identification of foreign currency transactions**
>
> An entity trades in crude oil and has a US dollar functional currency per the assessment required under IAS 21, because substantially all of its sales and purchases are in US dollars. The entity is located in London and has significant transactions in sterling. It has issued euro-denominated share capital to its Dutch parent. Transactions with the parent are denominated in euros.
>
> The sterling transactions and euro transactions are foreign currency transactions because the entity has a US dollar functional currency. The entity's physical location and the denomination of its share capital do not change the treatment of sterling- and euro-denominated transactions.

[The next paragraph is 7.31.]

Determining the functional currency

7.31 An entity's functional currency is a matter of fact. In some cases, the facts will clearly identify the functional currency. In other cases they will not and judgement will be required. IAS 21 provides guidance on how to determine an entity's functional currency.

7.31.1 An entity's functional currency is the currency of the primary economic environment in which it operates. [IAS 21 para 8]. It should, therefore, be determined at the entity level. An entity includes a foreign operation, that is, a subsidiary, associate, branch or joint venture whose activities are based or conducted in a country or currency other than that of the reporting entity.

7.31.2 An individual entity (including a foreign operation) for these purposes may not correspond to a legal entity (for example, a company). For example, a branch that is part of a single legal entity may be a foreign operation. Judgement is required in determining an entity's functional currency based on individual facts and circumstances.

7.31.3 A group comprised of multiple entities identifies the functional currency of each entity for the purpose of defining that entity's foreign currency exposure. Different entities within a multinational group, therefore, often have different functional currencies. The group as a whole does not have a functional currency.

7.32 The primary economic environment in which an entity operates is normally the economic environment in which it primarily generates and expends cash. [IAS 21 para 9].The functional currency is normally the currency of the country in which the entity is located. It may, however, be a different currency. In addition, circumstances might indicate that the foreign operation's functional currency is the same as the reporting entity's functional currency. For this purpose, a foreign operation is defined as an entity that is a subsidiary, associate, joint venture or a branch of the reporting entity, the activities of which are based or conducted in a country or currency other than that of the reporting entity. [IAS 21 para 8].

7.33 IAS 21 requires entities to consider primary and secondary indicators when determining the functional currency. Primary indicators are closely linked to the primary economic environment in which the entity operates and are given more weight. Secondary indicators provide supporting evidence to determine an entity's functional currency. Both of these indicators and the factors needing consideration are shown in the table below.

Primary indicators of functional currency [IAS 21 para 9]	
Indicators	**Factors to be considered by the entity in determining the functional currency**
Sales and cash inflows	(a) The currency that *mainly influences* sales prices for its goods and services. This will often be the currency in which sales prices for goods and services are denominated and settled. [IAS 21 para 9(a)(i)]. In other words, where an active local sales market exists for the entity's products that are also priced in the local currency, and revenues are collected primarily in that local currency, the local currency is the functional currency. However, the standard gives greater emphasis to the currency of the economy that determines the

pricing of transactions than the currency in which transactions are denominated.

(b) The currency of the country whose competitive forces and regulations *mainly determine* the sales prices of its goods and services. [IAS 21 para 9(a)(ii)]. Where sales prices of the entity's products are determined by local competition and local government regulations rather than worldwide competition or by international prices, the local currency is the functional currency. For example, aircraft manufacturers often price aircraft in US dollars or in euros, but the legal and regulatory environment of the country in which the manufacturer is located may inhibit the entity's ability to pass hard currency costs (that is, dollars or euros) to its customers. Therefore, while the business is influenced by the hard currency, its ability to generate revenue is determined by the local environment, which may indicate that the local currency is the functional currency.

Expenses and cash outflows	The currency that *mainly influences* labour, material and other costs of providing goods and services. This is often the currency in which such costs are denominated and settled. [IAS 21 para 9(b)]. For example, where labour, material and other operating costs are primarily sourced and incurred locally, the local currency is likely to be the functional currency, even though there also might be imports from other countries.

Secondary indicators of functional currency [IAS 21 para 10]

Indicators	Factors to be considered by the entity in determining the functional currency
Financing activities	The currency in which funds from financing activities (for example, issuing debt and equity instruments) are generated. [IAS 21 para 10(a)]. For example, where financing is raised in and serviced by funds primarily generated by the entity's local operation, this may indicate that the local currency is the functional currency, in the absence of other indicators to the contrary.
Retention of operating income	The currency in which receipts from operating activities are usually retained. [IAS 21 para 10(b)]. This is the currency in which the entity maintains its excess working capital balance, which would generally be the local currency.

7.34 The above primary and secondary indicators for determining of the functional currency must be considered by all entities. If the entity is a foreign operation, the standard specifies four additional factors that should be considered in determining the functional currency and whether it is the same as that of the reporting entity. These additional factors are shown in the table below. They set out the conditions that point to whether the foreign operation's functional currency is the same as, or different from, the reporting entity (the reporting entity, in this context, being the entity that has the foreign operation as its subsidiary, branch, associate or joint venture).

Additional indicators for foreign operations [IAS 21 para 11]

Indicators	Conditions pointing to functional currency being *different from* that of the reporting entity	Conditions pointing to functional currency being the *same as* that of the reporting entity
Degree of autonomy	Activities are carried out with a significant degree of autonomy. An example is when the operation accumulates cash and other monetary items, incurs expenses, generates income and arranges borrowings, all substantially in its local currency.	No significant degree of autonomy – activities are carried out as an extension of the reporting entity. An example is when the foreign operation only sells goods imported from the reporting entity and remits the proceeds to it. It follows that such an entity (which would be considered an integral foreign operation in the previous version of IAS 21) must have the same currency as the reporting entity. This is because it would be contradictory for an integral foreign operation that *"carries on business as if it were an extension of the reporting entity's operations"* to operate in a primary economic environment different from its parent. [IAS 21 para BC6].
Frequency of transactions with reporting entity	Few inter-company transactions with the reporting entity.	Frequent and extensive inter-company transactions with the reporting entity.
Cash flow impact on reporting entity	Mainly in local currency and do not affect reporting entity's cash flows	Directly impact the reporting entity's cash flows and are readily available for remittance to the reporting entity.
Financing	Primarily in the local currency and serviced by funds generated by the entity's operation.	Significant financing from or reliance on the reporting entity to service existing and normally expected debt obligations.

7.35 The relative importance of the various indicators will vary from entity to entity. For example, the primary and secondary indicators apply to the generality of entities that provide goods and services, but they may not be directly relevant in certain other situations. Examples of situations in which the primary and secondary indicators may be less relevant include treasury entities, structured or special purpose entities, ultimate holding entities and intermediate holding entities. In those situations, management may need to consider the additional indicators stated in paragraph 7.34 above when determining the functional currency.

7.36 In assessing the indicators' relative importance, management may find it useful to consider the following aspects of each indicator:

■ The significance of that indicator to the entity's operation. For example, the existence of sterling denominated debt in a foreign entity of a UK parent may not be significant if the foreign entity is primarily self-financing through retained earnings.

■ How clearly the indicator identifies a particular currency as the functional currency. For example, if the same entity purchases raw materials both from the UK and locally, the 'expenses' indicator may be inconclusive. In contrast, if the majority of sales occur in the host country at prices determined by local conditions, the 'sales' indicator might be regarded as the key determinant in concluding that the local currency is the functional currency.

7.37 After considering all the factors, the functional currency may still not be obvious. The operation may be diverse, with cash flows, financing and transactions occurring in more than a single currency. In these situations, judgement is required in determining the functional currency that most faithfully represents the economic effects of the underlying transactions, events and conditions. In exercising that judgement, management should give priority to the primary indicators before considering the secondary indicators and the additional factors set out above. [IAS 21 para 12].

7.38 The standard gives greater emphasis to the primary indicators because, as stated above, these indicators are closely linked to the primary economic environment in which the entity operates. The currency of the economy in which the entity operates generally determines the pricing of transactions; this is considered to be more influential than the currency in which the transactions are denominated and settled. This is because transactions can be denominated and settled in any currency management chooses, but as the pricing of the transaction is normally done by reference to the economy of the country whose competitive forces and regulations affect the transaction, the currency of that economy becomes the functional currency by definition. In other words, the currency of the country whose economy drives the business and which determines the gains and losses to be recognised in the financial statements most faithfully reflects the economic effects of the underlying transactions, events and conditions.

7.39   The standard's intention that the primary and secondary indicators should be looked at as a hierarchy is intended to avoid practical difficulties in determining an entity's functional currency. For example, if all the primary indicators, which should be considered together, identify a particular currency as the functional currency, there is no need to consider the secondary indicators. Secondary indicators serve to provide additional supporting evidence in determining an entity's functional currency. [IAS 21 para BC9].

7.39.1   The IFRS IC has considered the functional currency of an ultimate holding entity whose only activity is to hold investments in subsidiaries. In its March 2010 update, it noted that the primary indicators in IAS 21 should not be considered in isolation and that judgement is required when the functional currency is determined. In our view, a policy choice exists for an ultimate holding entity as to how to interpret IAS 21 in order to determine its functional currency. The ultimate holding entity may determine that it is acting as an extension of its subsidiaries and, therefore, has the same functional currency as those subsidiaries. Alternatively, as the entity is an ultimate holding entity it may consider that IAS 21's 'foreign operation' indicators do not require it to 'look down' and be a foreign operation of its subsidiaries. It is not required to 'look down' simply because there is no entity for the ultimate holding entity to 'look up' to. Under such a view, an entity looks at all of the primary and secondary indicators and will likely conclude that its functional currency is determined by the currency of its own dividend revenue, its own expenses and the currency of its own financing. See further example 3 in paragraph 7.40 below.

7.39.2   When considering the autonomy indicator in paragraph 11 of IAS 21, (see para 7.34 above) typically a non-autonomous subsidiary or branch derives its functional currency from its parent; 'the look up approach' (see example 5 below). For an intermediate holding entity, the autonomy indicator may also point to the conclusion that the intermediate holding entity is acting as an extension of its subsidiary or group of subsidiaries and, therefore, has the same functional currency as its subsidiary or group of subsidiaries; 'the look down approach'. An intermediate holding entity that is not autonomous does not have a policy choice. Whether it is appropriate for such an entity to look up or down depends on the particular facts and circumstances.

7.39.3   Associates and joint ventures are likely to be autonomous from an individual investor given the lack of control in the relationship and the paragraph 11 additional indicators are not likely to be relevant.

Illustrative examples

7.40   Determining an entity's functional currency depends on the facts and circumstances. The following examples are for illustrative purposes only and should not be used as solutions for specific situations.

Example 1 – Functional currency of an entity with transactions denominated in a stable currency.

Example 2 – Functional currency of an entity with products normally traded in a non-local currency (such as oil and gold).

Example 3 – Functional currency of an offshore ultimate holding entity.

Example 4 – Functional currency of an intermediate parent with some operating activities.

Example 5 – Functional currency of an intermediate parent with no operating or financing activities of its own.

Example 6 – Functional currency of an entity raising finance for the group in a foreign currency compared to the other entities in the group.

Example 7 – Functional currency of separate treasury centres in different geographical areas.

Example 8 – Functional currency of a treasury centre that pools resources in the group.

Example 9 – Functional currency of a foreign subsidiary importing products from parent for local distribution.

Example 10 – Functional currency of a structured entity.

Example 11 – Different functional currencies for stand-alone accounts and for group reporting purposes?

Example 12 – Functional currency after a group restructuring.

Example 1 – Functional currency of an entity with transactions denominated in a stable currency

A real estate entity operates in Russia. It owns several office buildings in Moscow and St Petersburg that are rented to Russian and foreign entities. All lease contracts are denominated in US dollars, but payments can be made in either US dollars or in Russian roubles. However, almost all of the lease payments are settled in roubles. This has also been the historical pattern of payment.

On first analysis, the 'sales and cash inflows' indicators appear to produce a mixed response, because the currency that mainly influences the pricing of the lease contracts is the US dollar, whereas the cash inflows are in roubles. Also, cash outflows such as the principal operating costs, management of properties, insurance, taxes and staff costs are likely to be incurred and settled in roubles, which would indicate that the functional currency is the Russian rouble.

The lease payments are denominated in US dollars, but the US dollar is not considered to be significant to the entity's operation because: (a) most of the collection is in roubles, which is subject to short-term changes in US dollar/rouble exchange rate; and (b) it is the local conditions and circumstances in Russia, not the US, that determine the rental yields of properties in Moscow and St Petersburg that mainly influence the pricing of the lease contracts, which are merely denominated in US dollar.

It is, therefore, the currency of the Russian economy, rather than the currency in which the lease contracts are denominated, that most faithfully represents the economic effects of the real estate activity in Russia. Since the transactions are denominated in a different currency to the entity's functional currency, there is an embedded foreign exchange derivative in the contract that may have to be separated in as explained in paragraph AG33(d) of IAS 39. For further guidance on embedded derivatives refer to chapter 6.3.

Example 2 – Functional currency of an entity with products normally traded in a non-local currency (such as oil and gold)

Entity A operates an oil refinery in Saudi Arabia. All of the entity's income is denominated and settled in US dollars. The oil price is subject to the worldwide supply and demand, and crude oil is routinely traded in US dollars around the world. Around 45% of entity A's cash costs are imports or expatriate salaries denominated in US dollars. The remaining 55% of cash expenses are incurred in Saudi Arabia and denominated and settled in riyal. The non-cash costs (depreciation) are US dollar denominated, as the initial investment was in US dollars.

The functional currency of entity A is the US dollar. The crude oil sales prices are influenced by global demand and supply. Crude oil is globally traded in US dollars around the world. The revenue analysis points to the US dollar. The cost analysis is mixed. Depreciation (or any other non-cash expenses) is not considered, as the primary economic environment is where the entity generates and expends cash. Operating cash expenses are influenced by the riyal (55%) and the US dollar (45%). Management is able to determine the functional currency as the US dollar, as the revenue is clearly influenced by the US dollar and expenses are mixed.

Example 3 – Functional currency of an offshore ultimate holding entity

A group of companies is organised as follows:

Entity A is a reporting entity with three operating subsidiaries (entities B, C and D) that are incorporated in Russia. Management has concluded that the functional currency of each subsidiary should be the local currency (roubles).

Entity A is the holding entity and has been set up by institutional investors in Cyprus (a eurozone country). Entity A has obtained equity and loan financing and has invested in Russian entities B, C and D. It pools cash from all group entities, invests excess cash and obtains external financing, according to the group's needs. The financing is drawn in US dollars, and all of its monetary assets are denominated in US dollars. The entity retains cash in US dollars, its expenses that are not associated with financing are insignificant compared to the investments in the Russian investees or the funding costs and it has no employees. The entity's activities are carried out by employees of its operating subsidiaries. Its shares are denominated in US dollars and it pays dividends to its investors in US dollars.

In January 2010, the IFRS IC received a request for guidance on determining the functional currency of an ultimate holding entity. The IFRS IC was asked whether the underlying economic environment of its subsidiaries should be considered in determining the functional currency of an ultimate holding company. The IFRS IC decided not to issue guidance on this matter, but noted that assessing functional currency requires the exercise of judgement and that the paragraph 9 indicators (sales and expenses) should not be considered in isolation. Our view is that there is an accounting policy choice for determining the functional currency of an ultimate holding entity in this situation:

Option 1: The ultimate holding entity is viewed as having the same functional currency as its operating subsidiaries. Entity A's functional currency is the Russian rouble.

Management is required to use its judgement to determine the functional currency that most faithfully represents the economic effects of the underlying transactions, events and conditions. [IAS 21 para 12]. Entity A has no activity of its own. The currency that reflects the economic substance of the underlying economic events that affect the holding entity is the Russian rouble, as all of the holding entity's subsidiaries operate in Russia and entity A's primary source of income will be dividends obtained from the subsidiaries in Russia. Entity A's ability to service debts and pay dividends to shareholders is dependent on the Russian economy. Although paragraph 11 of IAS 21 explicitly defines a foreign operation as a reporting entity's subsidiary, branch, associate or joint venture, paragraph 11 may be applied by analogy, and viewing an ultimate holding entity as an extension of its subsidiaries is appropriate.

Option 2: The ultimate holding entity's functional currency is not viewed as being dependent on its foreign operations. Entity A's functional currency is the US dollar.

Entity A has no sales or purchases, nor does it incur significant expenses other than in respect of its financing activities. The economic source of dividend revenues is not a key factor in determining the functional currency of a non-operating ultimate parent entity. The primary indicators in paragraph 9 are not directly relevant. It is the currency denomination of the financing activities that drives the functional currency determination (the secondary indicators in paragraph 10). The functional currency is determined based on the primary economic environment in which the entity generates and expends cash, consistent with the secondary indicators. All cash flows associated with financing and dividends are US dollar. Paragraph 11 of IAS 21 explicitly defines a foreign operation as a reporting entity's subsidiary, branch, associate or joint venture. While a foreign operation may be viewed as an extension of its parent, paragraph 11 is not required to be applied by analogy to view an ultimate holding entity as an extension of its subsidiary, because the parent controls the subsidiary and not *vice versa*.

Example 4 – Functional currency of an intermediate parent with some operating activities

Parent (entity P) is a manufacturing business located in the UK with sterling as the functional currency. Entity P invests US dollars in an intermediate parent (entity IP), which then invests in three separate US dollar operating subsidiaries (entity S1, S2 and S3). Entity IP undertakes no 'operating' activities of its own; however, it acts as the holding entity of the US subsidiaries – heading up the US group. It has a dedicated management team and staff that carry out the head office functions, including the US group's payroll, cash management and preparation of a sub-consolidation package. The management team takes finance decisions related to the sub-group and controls the activities of the sub-group. Its management team reports monthly to entity P's board on the results of the US group. Its key cash inflows are the dividends from its subsidiaries (which it remits up directly to entity P), and inter-company balances from its subsidiaries (that are used to settle both entity IP's own administration costs and those costs incurred directly by entity IP on behalf of its subsidiaries — that is payroll costs, computer services, maintenance, etc). All cash inflows and outflows are denominated in US dollar. Entity IP is a US-registered entity.

Entity IP has operating activities, in that it provides local management services to its subsidiaries. It incurs local costs and then either recharges these to its subsidiaries or retains dividend income from its subsidiaries to pay for these costs. All the costs incurred are incurred in US dollar and will be reimbursed in US dollar.

Entity IP does not raise finance; consideration of the currency in which funds from financing activities are generated is not directly applicable. However, the funding of its costs through dividends and inter-company balances is in US dollars. The currency in which receipts from operating activities is usually retained indicates a US dollar functional currency.

Looking to the additional factors in paragraph 11 of IAS 21 revised:

■ Entity IP has a significant degree of autonomy: it has its own management team and staff; a budget for which it is responsible; and discretion over its head office functions.

■ It has a number of transactions with parties outside the group.

■ The cash flows of entity IP do not directly affect the parent; entity IP is not merely acting as a conduit.

Consideration of paragraph 11(d), *"whether cash flows from activities of the foreign operation are sufficient to service existing and normally expected debt obligations without funds being made available by the reporting entity"* is not applicable.

Unlike example 5, entity IP is carrying out operating activities of its own, albeit not in the traditional trading sense. These activities consist of holding and managing the subsidiaries of the sub-group. Under paragraphs 9 and 10 of IAS 21 revised, the costs entity IP incurs and any receipts retained from operating activities are in US dollar. IP in this example is not merely acting as a conduit/'cash box' for entity P. It is carrying out management activities and has a significant degree of autonomy. It has an active management team and exercises discretion over the US group's operations. The US group has been structured in this way for operational as well as tax reasons. This suggests that entity IP's functional currency is not necessarily that of entity P. The functional currency of entity IP would be US dollar.

Example 5 – Functional currency of an intermediate parent with no operating or financing activities of its own

Parent (entity P) is a manufacturing business located in the UK with sterling as the functional currency. P invests US dollar in an intermediate parent (entity IP), which then invests in a US-dollar operating subsidiary (entity S) on behalf of entity P. Entity IP is a shell entity that undertakes no operating or financing activities as it only holds investments. Its key cash inflows are dividends from entity S, which it remits directly to parent entity P. Entity IP is a US-registered entity.

Entity IP undertakes no operating or financing activities. Any investing activity that entity IP undertakes is not carried out as a separate stand-alone activity, but at the behest of its parent. It is not, therefore, relevant to consider the 'sales and cash inflow' indicator. The 'expenses and cash outflow' indicator may be relevant, as it is more likely than not that entity IP will incur some local costs. But that indicator by itself is not considered significant to entity IP's operations, nor does it clearly identify the US dollar as the functional currency.

The secondary indicators do not clearly identify the US dollar as the functional currency, as entity IP does not raise any finance from external local sources – any finance raised is primarily from its parent or from sterling sources. Nor does entity IP retain any funds for own use, which are all remitted to the parent. All the additional factors also point to the US dollar not being the currency that most faithfully represents entity IP's activities of receiving dividend income from entity S in US dollar and remitting these to its parent.

The primary, secondary and additional indicators are mixed and therefore management should exercise judgement in determining the currency that most faithfully represents entity IP's activities.

One analysis might focus on the fact that Entity IP is a 'foreign operation' in relation to its parent, entity P. entity IP does not have autonomy, transacts frequently with its parent and does not retain cash and relies on parent P for financing. It is, therefore, simply a device or a shell corporation for the holding of investments that could have been held by entity P itself. The functional currency of entity IP is the same as its parent: sterling.

An alternative analysis might focus on the fact that the results of entity IP are dependent on the economic activities of its subsidiary whose functional currency is the US dollar. The cash inflow indicator, therefore, suggests that the US dollar is significant to its investing activity.

The facts and circumstances indicate that entity IP is a shell intermediate holding entity that merely holds the investment and receives occasional dividends, passing them on to the parent. Entity IP does not have autonomy as it was set up and operates at the behest of the parent, carrying out a function that the parent could equally carry out itself. Our view is that sterling is entity IP's functional currency.

Example 6 – Functional currency of an entity raising finance for the group in a foreign currency compared to the other entities in the group

A French-listed parent has significant French, UK and US operating subsidiaries, but no Japanese operations. The French parent creates a new subsidiary, Newco SA, incorporated and resident in France. Newco issues in yen 1bn of equity capital to French parent, receiving yen 1bn of cash. Newco also raises yen 100m of external financing and places the yen 1.1bn total cash on deposit with a bank in Japan, earning 0.1% interest per annum. The cash will be reinvested in yen-denominated financial instruments such as bonds and commercial paper. Newco has few staff that manages the entity's investing activities. It incurs sterling operational costs that are insignificant compared to the interest paid on its yen borrowing. Like any wholly-owned subsidiary, the retained profits are under the parent's control.

Newco does not undertake any key operating activities on its own. Consideration of the currency that mainly influences sales and costs is not directly relevant. Newco incurs expenses in euro, but these are not significant enough to suggest that the euro is the functional currency. It is necessary to look at the secondary indicators.

Newco raises finance by issuing its own equity instruments to the parent in a currency that is different from the parent, but the proceeds are invested in yen-denominated assets at the behest of the parent. The external funds raised through the issue of debt instruments are insignificant compared to the issue of equity shares to the parent. The question is silent as to whether the income generated from the investments is reinvested in other yen denominated assets or whether it is wholly passed on to the parent.

Whatever that may be, the decision to reinvest or distribute is under the parent's control.

Consideration of the other additional factors suggests that Newco is a 'cash box' type entity with no independent management/activity. Newco is simply a conduit for the parent entity that could invest the yen directly. It may be that the only reason the parent entity has invested the yen through Newco is in the hope that its exposure to changes in the euro/yen exchange rate is reported in other comprehensive income through the translation of its net investment in Newco, rather than in the income statement, which would be the case if the yen deposits were treated as belonging to the parent. The 'autonomy factor' points to the euro as the functional currency, as Newco appears to be merely an extension of the activities of the parent. This would point to the functional currency being the same as that of its parent — the euro. This would be the answer if Newco carried out only the activities described.

The investing activity could have been done by the parent rather than the subsidiary and, therefore, based on the additional indicators relevant to a foreign operation, the parent's functional currency should determine the foreign entity's functional currency.

Example 7 – Functional currency of separate treasury centres in different geographical areas

A Swiss multi-national entity with Swiss franc as its functional currency has operating subsidiaries in the US and Europe whose functional currencies are the US dollar and the euro respectively. It has established a treasury centre (TC) in each of these geographical regions. The activities of the two TCs are identical in that each provides financial and risk management services to its relevant operating subsidiaries. All transactions (for example, management of liquid funds, borrowings and hedging activities) between a TC and its respective operating subsidiaries are carried out either in US dollars or euros.

Each TC earns dividends and income from cash management activities in US dollars and euros respectively. Each TC charges a monthly fee for providing such financial services to its operating subsidiaries that is denominated either in US dollars or euros, depending on its area of operation. All operating costs — such as staff costs payable to treasury and financial management specialists and other administrative and running costs — are incurred and settled by each TC in US dollars or euros. The TCs' short and long-term financing are provided by the Swiss parent in the form of Swiss franc loans. The TCs do not retain any US dollars or euros generated from their operation for their own use. After meeting local expenses, management either uses US dollars or euros to settle the inter-entity payables to the operating subsidiaries or distributes any surplus to the parent as dividends.

This response addresses only the US dollar TC; the considerations for the euro TC are the same.

The primary factors (currency that influences sales price and the costs of providing goods and services) are arguably irrelevant because TC does not have any third-party sales and purchases. However, the determination of the functional currency is an entity-by-entity question and it is not relevant to whether an entity's fee income comes from inside or outside the group. What is relevant is the nature of the fee income and the manner in which it is earned. In this example, the TC provides financial services to the US operating subsidiaries for which it charges a fee. The fees are invoiced and settled in US dollar. TC also earns investment income in US dollars. As TC earns its revenue and income in US dollar and the underlying US economy determines the pricing of TC's fee income to the US operating subsidiaries, the 'sales and cash inflow' indicator identifies the US dollar as the functional currency of TC. As all administrative and local expenses are incurred and settled in US dollar, the 'expenses and cash outflow' indicator also provides strong evidence that the US dollars is the TC's functional currency. The primary economic environment in which the TC generates and expends cash is the US and, therefore, its functional currency is the US dollar.

The primary indicators are clear, so there is no need to consider the secondary indicators, even if these seem to provide evidence that the Swiss franc is the functional currency (for example, TC's short and long-term financing is primarily in the form of Swiss franc loans from the parent).

Example 8 – Functional currency of a treasury centre that pools resources in the group

A UK multi-national entity with sterling as its functional currency has set up a treasury centre (TC) in Switzerland. TC borrows US dollars, euros and sterling in the euro-market and lends the proceeds to its parent and other operating subsidiaries with the loans denominated in the borrowing entity's functional currency. As part of its cash management operations, it pools the liquid resources of the parent and the operational units and invests them temporarily in the euro-market. It also manages foreign exchange and interest rate risks of operating units by executing derivative contracts with third parties and/or with operating units.

TC earns dividends and income from cash management activities in US dollar, euros and sterling. It charges a monthly fee for providing such financial services to its parent and operating subsidiaries that is denominated in the relevant entity's functional currencies. All operating costs, such as staff costs payable to treasury and financial management specialists and other administrative and running costs are incurred and settled in Swiss francs. TC's short and long-term financing needs are provided by its parent in the form of sterling loans.

TC provides financial services to group companies for which it charges a fee. However, the fees are invoiced in the functional currencies of the group companies and settled in those currencies. This ensures that the risk of non-functional currency transaction gains and losses on all inter-company transactions with the TC are passed on from the operating units to the TC for centralised management and control. TC also earns investment income in US dollar, euro and sterling. As TC earns its revenue and income in different currencies, the 'sales and cash inflow' indicator fails to identify a particular currency that is significant in its own right as the functional currency of TC. Furthermore, there is no explicit or implicit evidence to suggest that the underlying Swiss economy determines the pricing of TC's fee income to the group companies.

On the other hand, as all administrative and local expenses are incurred and settled in Swiss francs, the 'expenses and cash outflow' indicator provides strong evidence that Swiss franc is the functional currency.

Therefore, as the primary indicators are not sufficiently conclusive in identifying the functional currency, it is necessary to consider the secondary indicators.

The secondary indicators provide evidence that sterling is the functional currency. This is because TC does not raise any finance from external local sources for meeting the cost of its operations in excess of its operating income but relies on short- and long-term financing from its parent. Furthermore, since cash inflows from operations occur in various currencies that are used to meet local expenses, retention of cash indicator is not significant in determining TC's functional currency.

The additional factors also support sterling as the functional currency. For example, the 'autonomy indicator' suggests that the UK parent has set up the TC to achieve overall financial efficiency of its international operations through centralised control and effective management of cash and financial risk. The volume of inter-company transactions is large due to the regular transfer of foreign currency cash balances from and to the parent. The cash flows of the TC, therefore, impact the parent's cash flows on a regular basis. The financing indicator also identifies sterling as the functional currency.

This analysis suggests that the primary indicators do not provide conclusive evidence that the local currency of the country in which TC operates is its functional currency. However, the secondary indicators support sterling as the functional currency. Overall, the evidence is mixed. Management should exercise judgement in determining the currency that most faithfully represents the economic effects of TC's activities. There are a number of possible solutions. One indicator may be that TC has been set up primarily as a conduit to undertake the treasury operations of the entire multi-national group headed by the UK parent. The currency of the country that most faithfully represents TC's operations is, therefore, the functional currency of the UK parent: sterling. Another factor to consider is whether any of the three major currencies (dollars, euros, sterling) is dominant. If no clear currency is suggested by the previous factors, and if the TC's operating expenses are significant, the Swiss franc may be the TC's functional currency.

Example 9 – Functional currency of a foreign subsidiary importing products from parent for local distribution

A subsidiary located in Spain imports a product manufactured by its US parent at a price denominated in US dollars. The product is sold throughout Spain at prices denominated in euros, which are determined primarily by competition with similar locally produced products. All selling and operating expenses are incurred locally and paid in euros. The operation's long-term financing is primarily in the form of US dollar loans from the parent. The distribution of profits is under the parent's control.

The 'sales and cash inflows' indicators suggest that the foreign subsidiary's functional currency is the euro, as that is the currency in which the sales prices are denominated and settled. Furthermore, the sales prices for the foreign entity's products do not respond on a short-term basis to changes in exchange rates, but are determined by local competition and local government regulation. This is a strong indicator that the functional currency is the euro.

The 'expenses and cash outflows' indicators provide a mixed response. This is because cost of sales is primarily denominated and settled in US dollars, whereas local expenses, including selling expenses, are denominated and settled in euros. Given that a significant part of the expenses are settled in US dollars, this indicator does not provide conclusive evidence that the euro is the functional currency.

The primary indicators produce a mixed response, although overall they favour the euro. It is, therefore, necessary to look at the secondary indicators.

The secondary indicators provide supporting evidence that US dollar is the functional currency. This is because the foreign subsidiary's long-term financing is primarily in the form of US dollar loans from the parent, and the subsidiary does not raise any finance from external local sources. Furthermore, the foreign subsidiary does not retain any euros generated from its operations for its own use. After meeting local expenses, management either uses the euros to settle the inter-entity payables to the parent, or distributes any surplus to the parent as dividends.

If the 'autonomy' indicator suggests that the foreign subsidiary is simply acting as an agent for its US parent by selling parent-produced goods to customers in Spain, collecting the proceeds and remitting the same to the US parent, the functional currency would be US dollar. The volume of inter-company transactions is large, as the foreign subsidiary imports goods from its US parent and settles the proceeds on a regular basis. The subsidiary's cash flows, therefore, regularly impact the parent's cash flows.

However, if the foreign subsidiary's operations were carried out with a significant degree of autonomy (that is, local management has a significant degree of authority and responsibility, such as to borrow loans, invest excess cash, modify prices or grant discounts and hire and fire staff), the functional currency would be determined independently from the parent. Management would conclude that the functional currency is the euro, as the primary indicators of paragraph 9 of IAS 21 are overall in favour of the euro.

Example 10 – Functional currency of a structured entity

Entity A is a US bank with a US dollar functional currency. Entity A establishes a structured entity in a European country in order to invest in a European bond portfolio. Entity A has funded the structured entity with equity and inter-company debt denominated in euros. The structured entity uses the financing to purchase a portfolio of euro government bonds. There is no intention for the structured entity to perform any activities other than holding the bond portfolio. The directors are all employees of the US parent, and the structured entity has no active management of its own.

The functional currency of the structured entity is the US dollar, as the entity has no operations and does not provide any services. The primary indicators, therefore, do not apply. The 'financing' indicator supports the euro, as all financing is in euros. However, all the financing is inter-company and entity A could denominate the financing in any currency it wanted. Considering the 'autonomy' indicator, it is clear the structured entity is not autonomous. It is a shell entity, has no independent activities and no active management of its own.

Example 11 – Different functional currencies for stand-alone accounts and for group reporting purposes?

Entity A is an autonomous foreign operation of reporting entity Z. Entity A operates in a country where the US dollar is frequently used because the local currency has been inflationary in the past.

Entity A primarily operates in the local market and is requested to prepare statutory standalone financial statements in accordance with IFRS. Local regulations require entity A to use the local currency as presentation currency for the statutory accounts. Management has determined that the local currency should be the functional currency for the standalone financial statements. Entity A is also required to prepare an IFRS reporting package for entity Z. Management believes that entity A should use the US dollar as the functional currency for group reporting purposes, because the US dollar is frequently used in the local economy and because the group presentation currency is the US dollar.

An entity can have only one functional currency. The functional currency is the currency of the primary economic environment. This is the same for standalone financial statements and group reporting purposes. Entity A should use the local currency as its functional currency for both statutory and group reporting purposes.

Example 12 – Functional currency after a group restructuring

Group X is a complex multi-national group with numerous intermediate parent entities. As part of a group restructuring, intermediate parent entity A sold some of its subsidiaries to intermediate parent entity B. Should the functional currency of both entities, A and B, be re-assessed after the group restructuring?

Yes. The functional currency of both companies should be re-assessed to determine whether the previous IAS 21 functional currency determination is impacted by the group restructuring. For example, if the subsidiaries sold to entity B are substantial operating companies and entity B has limited or no other activities, IAS 21 may require entity B to have the same functional currency as that of the newly acquired subsidiaries. On the other hand, entity B may be acting as an extension of its ultimate parent entity X, in which case the functional currency will be the same as that of entity X both before and after the group restructuring. The group restructuring by itself does not trigger a reassessment of the functional currency of the ultimate holding entity X, because nothing has changed as regards to the primary economic environment in which the holding entity operates. The functional currency of entity X would have been determined before by entity X's management according to the policy choice in example 3, and the ultimate holding entity X may or may not have independent activities. The existence or not of such activities does not determine whether an intermediate holding entity is an extension of its parent.

Entity with multiple operations

7.41   The definition of a foreign operation indicates that an operation should have activities. [IAS 21 para 8]. An entity might have more than one distinct and separable operation, such as a division or a branch. In determining whether each operation may be considered a separate entity for the purposes of this standard, the definition of a 'business' per IFRS 3 could be useful. For example, a foreign entity might have one operation that acts as a selling agent, receiving inventories of goods from the parent entity and remitting the proceeds back to the entity, and another operation that manufactures and sells products locally. If those two operations are conducted in different economic environments, they may have different functional currencies.

7.42 Once the number of operations has been determined, each foreign entity should determine its functional currency and measure its results and financial position in that currency before it can be included in the reporting entity when it prepares its financial statements. Once the foreign entity's functional currency is determined, the results and financial position of its branches having different functional currencies will be included in the foreign entity using the translation method set out in paragraph 7.83 below.

Different functional currencies for entities in the same country

7.43 It is also possible for an entity to have two or more foreign operations in one country and determine different functional currencies for those entities. For example, a UK entity could have a sales branch and an operating subsidiary in the same country, which justifies different functional currencies. Another example is where the UK entity has a subsidiary in a foreign country that manufactures and sells goods locally, and another subsidiary in that same country whose operations are fundamentally different. Management should determine for each of these entities the appropriate functional currency using the guidance addressed in paragraph 7.31 above.

Accounting records not maintained in functional currency

7.44 If a foreign operation's books or records are not maintained in its functional currency, management should re-measure into the functional currency. That remeasurement is required at the time the foreign operation prepares its financial statements before they are translated into the presentation currency of the reporting entity. The remeasurement into the functional currency, which should be carried out using the translation method set out in paragraph 7.48 onwards below, would produce the same amounts in the functional currency as would have occurred had all the items been recorded in the functional currency in the first place. For example, monetary items are translated into the functional currency using the closing rate, and non-monetary items that are measured on a historical cost basis are translated using the exchange rate at the date of the transaction that resulted in their recognition. [IAS 21 para 34].

Financial statements in foreign currencies

UK.7.44.1 Although not specifically dealt with in the Companies Act, the Registrar of Companies accepts annual financial statements prepared in a foreign currency (that is, a currency other than sterling), provided that the currency exists legally and the exchange rate to sterling at the balance sheet date is disclosed in the notes to the financial statements.

Change in functional currency

7.45 Once the functional currency of an entity is determined, it should be used consistently, unless significant changes in economic facts, events and conditions indicate that the functional currency has changed. For example, a branch that carried out its operations as an extension of the reporting entity's business may become independent and primarily regional in nature as a result of changed circumstances.

7.46 A change in functional currency should be accounted for *prospectively* from the date of change. In other words, management should translate all items (including balance sheet, income statement and statement of comprehensive income items) into the new functional currency using the exchange rate at the date of change. [IAS 21 para 37]. Because the change was brought about by changed circumstances, it does not represent a change in accounting policy and, therefore, a retrospective adjustment under IAS 8 is not relevant. As all items are translated using the exchange rate at the date of change, the resulting translated amounts for non-monetary items are treated as their historical cost. There is no specific guidance in IAS 21 on what should be done with equity items, but it would be consistent that these are also translated using the exchange rate at the date of the change of functional currency. This means that no additional exchange differences arise on the date of the change.

7.46.1 Entities should also consider presentation currency (see further para 7.76) when there is a change in functional currency. It may be that the presentation currency does not change. For example, a standalone Irish entity previously presented its financial statements in its euro functional currency and its functional currency changes to US dollar. It is based in Ireland and has Irish shareholders. It does not wish to change its presentation currency and so continues to present its financial statements in euros. Alternatively, the entity is part of a group and the presentation currency of the group does not change following the change in functional currency of a foreign operation. In such a case the numbers in the entity's own financial statements for the period up to the change in functional currency do not change in presentational currency terms. From the point that the functional currency changes new foreign exchange differences will arise in the entity's own financial statements when items expressed in the new functional currency are translated into the presentation currency.

7.46.2 An example follows of an entity changing its functional but not its presentation currency.

Example 1 – Change in functional currency

Using the Irish entity example from paragraph 7.46.1, assume that its functional currency changes to US dollars on 1 January 20X8. The entity presented its financial statements for the year to 31 December 20X7 in euros. It will continue to present its 20X8 financial statements in euros. In its 20X8 financial statements, its 20X7 comparatives will be exactly as they were in the 20X7 financial statements. A US dollar loan, for example, will be transalated into euro at the closing rate, with exchange differences between opening and closing rates recorded in the income statement. An item of property, plant and equipment (PP&E) that was purchased in euro will be stated at its euro historical cost less depreciation.

On 1 January 2008 all financial statement items are translated into US dollars at the rate ruling at that date.

In its 20X8 financial statements, no foreign exchange will arise on the US dollar loan in the entity's 20X8 income statement, as it is now an item expressed in the entity's functional currency. Any monetary items that are not denominated in US dollars will be translated at the closing rate with exchange differences recorded in the income statement.

Any items of PPE will have been retranslated into US dollars at 1 January 20X8 and these retranslated amounts become their US dollar historical cost and accumulated depreciation (see further para 7.46.3). The PPE is depreciated in US dollars throughout 20X8.

For the 20X8 financial statements, the US dollar (functional currency) balance sheet amounts are translated into euros (presentation currency) at the closing rate and income statement items are translated into euros at the actual or average rates for the period. Any exchange differences arising from opening to closing rates, and average to closing rates, is recorded in other comprehensive income (following the accounting set out from para 7.76 below).

In the entity's separate financial statements, CTA will be recognised in other comprehensive income and recorded in a separate component of equity. CTA is reclassified to profit or loss on disposal of a foreign operation (see further para 7.106). In the context of the entity's separate financial statements where there is one functional currency and a different presentation currency, the 'foreign operation' is the entire business of the entity. CTA would, therefore, only ever be reclassified if the entire business of the entity were to be sold, leaving a shell.

7.46.3 In the case where a foreign entity such as a subsidiary is translated into a different presentation currency, cumulative translation adjustment (CTA) will arise in the presentation currency consolidated financial statements. When the functional currency of that foreign entity changes, to one that may be the same or different from the group's presentation currency, any CTA previously recorded in equity remains in equity and is only adjusted on disposal or part-disposal of the foreign entity. [IAS 21 para 37]. For disposals and partial disposals see paragraph 7.106.

7.46.4 A change in functional currency may be accompanied by a change in presentation currency, as many entities prefer to present financial statements in their functional currency. Accounting for a change in presentation currency is dealt with from paragraph 7.82 below. A change in presentation currency is accounted for as a change in accounting policy and is applied retrospectively, as if the new presentation currency had always been the presentation currency.

Example 1 – Change in functional currency: impact on a depreciated asset

A UK entity has a branch in France with a sterling functional currency. The UK entity presents its financial statements in sterling. A significant change in trading operations and circumstances occurred during the first quarter of the financial year ended 30 June 20X6. This meant that sterling no longer faithfully represents the underlying transactions, events and conditions of the foreign branch. UK management decided that the euro should be the functional currency of its foreign operation and that all transactions undertaken from the beginning of the financial year 30 June 20X6 (that is, from 1 July 20X5) should be recorded in euros.

The branch purchased, on 1 January 20X0, an asset for €164,000 with a useful life of 10 years; the rate of exchange was £1 = €1.64. Since the branch's functional currency was sterling, the asset is recorded at the sterling equivalent cost of £100,000. At 1 July 20X5, the equipment has a net book value of £50,000.

As a result of the change in functional currency from sterling to euros on 1 July 20X5 (exchange rate at 30 June 20X5 is £1 = €1.45), the functional currency amount of the asset is carried at is €72,500 (£50,000 @ 1.45, presented as cost of €145,000 and accumulated depreciation of €72,500). This becomes its new historical net book value.

If the asset had been expressed in euro since its purchase it would have had a net book value of €82,000 (€164,000 × 5/10). This number is only relevant if, as a result of exchange movements, the new historical net book value exceeded the previous historical euro value at the date of change. In such a case an impairment review could be necessary if the indications are that the recoverable amount is less than €82,000 and the asset is carried at more than €82,000. [IAS 21 para 25].

The financial statements of the euro branch will be retranslated into sterling from the date that its functional currency changed to euro, and CTA will arise from this point on the difference between opening net assets at opening versus closing rates, and profit or loss at average to closing rates, where the UK entity presented, and continues to present, its financial statements in sterling.

If the UK entity decided to change its presentation currency to euro for its 30 June 20X6 financial statements, it would need to go through the process described in paragraph 7.82 below in order to present its sterling functional currency branch in euro for prior periods. This involves translating the assets and liabilities at the closing rate at 30 June 20X4 and translating the income statement at actual or average rates for year to 30 June 20X5. Equity items should be translated at historic or closing rates, and retained earnings and CTA should be restated if practicable to do so. From 1 July 20X5 no retranslation will be required in relation to the euro branch, since the euro branch has the same functional currency as the UK entity's presentation currency. The sterling to euro CTA that is calculated up to 30 June 20X5 will remain in equity until the branch is disposed of or subject to partial disposal.

7.47 It may not be practicable to determine the date of change precisely at a point during the year. It is also likely that the change may have occurred gradually during the year. If so, it may be acceptable to account for the change as of the beginning or end of the accounting period in which the change occurs, whichever more closely approximates the date of change.

Example 1 – Change in functional currency

The facts are the same as in the previous example; a UK entity has a branch in France with sterling as its functional currency. A significant change in trading operations and circumstances occurred during the first quarter of the financial year ended 30 June 20X6. This meant that sterling no longer faithfully represented the underlying transactions, events and conditions of the foreign branch. The UK management decided that the euro should be the functional currency of its foreign operation and that all transactions undertaken from the beginning of the financial year 30 June 20X6 should be recorded in euros.

The foreign branch's financial statements at 30 June 20X5, previously prepared in sterling, are translated to euros at the rate of exchange ruling at the date of change — in this situation, 1 July 20X5, the first day of the current financial year. All items in the balance sheet are translated at the rate of exchange ruling at 30 June 20X5, which approximates to the date of change. Retrospective application is not permitted, as the change in functional currency is accounted for prospectively.

Foreign currency transactions

Introduction

7.48   Foreign currency transactions are transactions denominated in a currency other than the entity's functional currency. Foreign currency transactions may produce receivables or payables that are fixed in terms of the amount of foreign currency that will be received or paid. For example, an entity may buy or sell goods or services in a foreign currency; borrow or lend money in a foreign currency; acquire or dispose of assets; or incur and settle liabilities in a foreign currency.

Initial recognition

7.49   A foreign currency transaction is recorded, on initial recognition in the functional currency, by applying to the foreign currency amount the spot exchange rate between the functional currency and the foreign currency at the date of the transaction. [IAS 21 para 21]. This process is known as 'translation' — financial data denominated in one currency is expressed in terms of another currency. Translation includes not only the expression of individual transactions in terms of another currency, but also the expression of a complete set of financial statements prepared in one currency in terms of another currency (see para 7.76).

7.50   The date of transaction is the date on which the transaction first qualifies for recognition in accordance with IFRS. [IAS 21 para 22]. The spot exchange rate is the exchange rate for immediate delivery. [IAS 21 para 8]. For revenues, expenses, gains and losses, the spot exchange rate at the dates on which those elements are recognised is used. Translation at the actual exchange rate at the dates the numerous revenues, expenses, gains and losses are recognised is generally impractical; management may, therefore, use a rate that approximates to the actual rate — for example, an average rate.

7.51   The above requirements appear straightforward, but their application may create problems. They include: determining the date of transaction, which may not always be obvious; determining an average rate as an approximation to the actual rate; and the selection of an appropriate rate for translating foreign currency transactions where there is more than one rate in operation.

Determining the average rate

7.52   Management may use an average rate for a period for recording foreign currency transactions as a proxy to the actual rate prevailing at the date of each transaction, provided that there is no significant change in rates during that period. An average rate is unlikely to be used by entities undertaking few transactions in a foreign currency. It is also unlikely to be used for translating large, one-off transactions that would be recorded at the actual rate. The flexibility allowed in IAS 21 is likely to be most beneficial to entities that enter into a large number of transactions in different currencies, or that maintain multi-currency ledgers. However, no guidance is provided in the standard as to how such a rate is determined.

7.53   Determining an average rate and its use in practice depends on a number of factors, such as: the frequency and value of transactions undertaken; the period over which the rate will apply; the extent of any seasonal trade variation and the desirability of using a weighting procedure as well as the acceptable level of materiality and the nature of the entity's accounting systems. There are a large number of methods under which an average rate can be calculated. These range from simple monthly or quarterly averages to more sophisticated methods using appropriate weighting that reflects changes both in exchange rates and in the volume of business. The choice of the period to be used for calculating the average rate will depend on the extent to which daily exchange rates fluctuate in the period selected. If exchange rates are relatively stable over a period of one month for example, the average exchange rate for that month can be used as an approximation to the daily rate. If, however, there is volatility of exchange rates, it may be appropriate to calculate an average rate for a shorter period such as a week. Whatever period is chosen, materiality is likely to be an important consideration.

7.54   An entity may use an actual average rate or an estimated average rate, depending on the circumstances. An actual average rate is likely to be used where there is some delay between the date when the transactions occurred and the date when they are recorded. In other situations, it may be necessary for an entity to use an estimated average rate for a period rather than wait for the period to end in order to calculate an actual average rate. This estimate may be based on the average of daily exchange rates for the previous period or the closing rate of the previous period. Whichever basis is used, it will be necessary to ensure than the estimated average rate is a close approximation of the actual rates prevailing during the period. If it is not, the rate should be revised accordingly.

Multiple exchange rates

7.55   Some countries may operate more than one exchange rate. When several exchange rates are available, the rate used to translate and record the foreign currency transactions and balances is that at which the future cash flows represented by the transaction or balance could have been settled if those cash flows had occurred at the measurement date. [IAS 21 para 26]. Chapter 31 contains an example of an entity disclosing the exchange rate it used when several are available (Table 31.2.1). When translating a net investment under IAS 21, the rate used would often be the dividend remittance rate, but another rate may be more appropriate if the proceeds would in practice be remitted in another way. Where a country has multiple exchange rates, judgement is often required to determine which exchange rate qualifies as a spot rate that can be used for translation under IAS 21. In determining whether a rate is a spot rate, an entity should consider whether currency is obtainable at a quoted rate and whether the quoted rate is available for immediate delivery. In practice, a normal administrative delay in obtaining funds would be acceptable.

Suspension of rates

7.56   Countries may experience economic conditions from time to time that affect the free-market convertibility of the local currency. As a result, the exchangeability between two currencies may be temporarily unavailable at the transaction date or a subsequent balance sheet date. IAS 21 requires entities to use the rate on the first subsequent date at which exchanges could be made. [IAS 21 para 26].

7.57   Doubts as to convertibility may arise if, for example, a Canadian entity makes a long-term currency loan to an overseas supplier but restrictions on the remittance of funds are imposed by the overseas country sometime before the balance sheet date. Such restrictions may arise as a result of currency devaluation, political upheaval or severe exchange control regulations in the overseas country. Management should use the rate on the first subsequent date at which exchanges could be made following restoration of normal conditions.

Example – Suspension of foreign exchange rates

In October 20X3, entity A, which is incorporated in the UK, used surplus currency to make a long-term loan of FC 15m to its overseas supplier. The loan was made when the exchange rate was £1 = FC 5.00 and is repayable on 30 September 20X5, entity A's year-end. Initially, the loan is translated and recorded in entity A's books at £3m. The amount that entity A ultimately receives depends on the rate of exchange ruling on the date when the loan is repaid.

On 28 September 20X5, a few days before the due date of the loan's repayment, the exchange rate was £1 = FC 6. On the same date the local government announced that a devaluation would occur on 2 October 20X5 and all foreign exchange transactions would be suspended until 3 October 20X5. On 2 October 20X5, foreign exchange transactions were executed but left unsettled until the following day when a new rate was established. On 3 October 20X5 a new rate of £1 = FC 7.5 was established and was effective for transactions left unsettled the previous day.

An official exchange rate at 30 September 20X5 is temporarily unavailable. In this situation, the exchange rate was temporarily lacking and the rate established on 3 October 20X5, the first subsequent date, is the appropriate rate to use for translating the monetary asset at the balance sheet date of 30 September 20X5. Therefore, entity A would record the loan receivable at £2m and recognise a foreign exchange loss of £1m in profit or loss.

Subsequent measurement

7.58   A foreign currency transaction may give rise to assets and liabilities that are denominated in a foreign currency. The procedure for translating such assets and liabilities into the entity's functional currency at each balance sheet date will depend on whether they are monetary or non-monetary.

Translation of monetary items

7.59   Monetary items are units of currency held and assets and liabilities to be received or paid in fixed or determinable number of units of currency. [IAS 21 para 8]. The essential feature of a monetary item is a right to receive (or an obligation to deliver) a fixed or determinable number of units of currency. Examples are

- Financial assets such as cash, bank balances and receivables.

- Financial liabilities such as debt.

- Provisions that are settled in cash.

- Pensions and other employee benefits to be paid in cash, deferred taxes and cash dividends that are recognised as a liability.

- Derivative financial instruments, such as forward exchange contracts, foreign currency swaps and options are also monetary items as they are settled at a future date.

Short-term monetary items are those that fall due within one year of the balance sheet date; long-term monetary items are those that fall due more than one year after the balance sheet date.

7.60   In some instances, it may not be readily apparent whether an item should be regarded as a monetary or a non-monetary item. Management should consider whether the item represents an amount to be received or paid in money, in which case it would fall to be treated as a monetary item.

7.61   For an item to qualify as a monetary item, it does not need to be recovered or settled in cash. A contract to receive (or deliver) a variable number of an entity's own equity instruments or a variable amount of assets in which the fair value to be received (or delivered) equals a fixed or determinable number of units of currency is also a monetary item. [IAS 21 para 16]. In other words, an entity's own equity instruments can be used 'as currency' in a contract that can be settled at a value equal to a fixed or a determinable amount. Such a contract is not an equity instrument, but a monetary financial asset or a liability. Not all financial assets should be treated as monetary items. For example, an investment in an equity instrument is not a monetary item – there is no right to receive a fixed or determinable amount of cash. [IAS 39 para AG83].

7.62 IAS 21 requires entities to translate foreign currency monetary items outstanding at the end of balance sheet date using the closing rate. [IAS 21 para 23(a)]. The closing rate is the spot exchange rate at the balance sheet date. [IAS 21 para 8]. A rate of exchange that is fixed under the terms of the relevant contract cannot be used to translate monetary assets and liabilities. Translating a monetary item at the contracted rate under the terms of a relevant contract is a form of hedge accounting that is not permitted under IAS 39. The treatment of the exchange differences that arise on translating a monetary item at the balance sheet date is considered from paragraphs 7.67 below.

Translation of non-monetary items

7.63 Non-monetary items are all items other than monetary items. In other words, the right to receive (or an obligation to deliver) a fixed or determinable number of units of currency is absent in a non-monetary item. Typical examples are:

■ Intangible assets.

■ Goodwill.

■ Property, plant and equipment.

■ Inventories.

■ Amounts pre-paid for goods and services (pre-paid rent).

■ Equity investments.

■ Provisions that are to be settled by the delivery of a non-monetary asset.

[IAS 21 para 16].

7.63.1 Advances paid and received (including pre-payments) can be difficult to classify as monetary or non-monetary. An example of a non-monetary item is an advance payment for goods that, absent a default by the counterparty, must be settled by the counterparty delivering the goods. However, if an advance is refundable in circumstances other than a default by either party, this may indicate that it is a monetary item as the item is receivable in units of currency.

7.64 Translation of non-monetary items depends on whether they are recognised at historical cost or at fair value. For example, property, plant and equipment may be measured in terms of historical cost or revalued amounts in accordance with IAS 16.

7.65 Non-monetary items that are measured in terms of historical cost in a foreign currency are translated using the exchange rate at the date of the transaction. [IAS 21 para 23(b)]. This means that such assets are recorded at historical cost, and no retranslation of the asset is required at subsequent balance sheet dates. However, if the asset is impaired, the recoverable amount is translated at the exchange rate ruling at the date when that value was determined (for example, the closing rate at the balance sheet date). Comparing the previously recorded historical cost with the recoverable amount may or may not result in recognising an impairment loss in the functional currency. For example, an entity's functional currency is sterling. A foreign currency asset costing FC 925,000 is recorded at the date of purchase at £500,000 when £1 = FC 1.85. At a subsequent balance sheet date, the asset's recoverable amount in foreign currency is FC 787,500 when £1 = FC 1.5. Although there is impairment loss in foreign currency, no impairment loss is recognised, because the recoverable amount at the balance sheet date of £525,000 is higher than the carrying value.

7.66   Non-monetary assets that are measured at fair value in a foreign currency are translated using the exchange rates at the date when the fair value was determined. [IAS 21 para 23(c)]. For example, a UK entity has a euro-denominated investment property located in France that is carried at fair value with gains and losses from changes in fair value recognised in profit or loss for the period in which they arise, in accordance with IAS 40. The fair values measured initially in euros due to the property's appreciation in value are translated to sterling at the exchange rate ruling at the relevant measurement dates. The resulting change in fair value in sterling includes foreign exchange differences arising on the retranslation of the opening euro carrying value. This exchange difference is recognised as part of the change in fair value in profit or loss for the period.

Recognition of exchange differences

Monetary items

7.67   Exchange differences arising on the settlement of monetary items, or on translating monetary items at rates different from those at which they were translated on initial recognition during the period or in previous financial statements, are recognised in profit or loss in the period in which they arise, except as described in paragraph 7.70 below. [IAS 21 para 28].

7.68   When monetary items arise from a foreign currency transaction and there is a change in exchange rate between the transaction date and the date of settlement, an exchange difference results. Where a transaction is *settled* within the same accounting period at an exchange rate that differs from the rate used when the transaction was initially recorded, the exchange difference is recognised in the income statement of the period in which the settlement takes place. [IAS 21 para 29]. It is appropriate to recognise such exchange differences as part of the profit or loss for that year, as the exchange difference will have been reflected in the cash flow at the time of the settlement.

Example – Treatment of a foreign currency denominated purchase of plant

In March 20X5, a UK entity purchases plant for use in the UK from an overseas entity for FC 1,980,000. At the date the entity purchases the plant, the exchange rate is £1 = FC 1.65. The purchase price is to be settled in three months, although delivery is made immediately. The UK entity records both the plant and the monetary liability at

£1,200,000 (FC 1,980,000/£1.65). The entity will not need to translate the plant again. At the settlement date, the exchange rate is £1 = FC 1.75. The actual amount the UK entity will pay to settle the liability is therefore £1,131,429. The entity should include the gain on exchange of £68,751 (that is, £1,200,000 — £1,131,429) in arriving at its profit or loss.

7.69 Where a monetary item arising from a foreign currency transaction remains *outstanding* at the balance sheet date, an exchange difference arises as a consequence of recording the foreign currency transaction at the rate ruling at the date of the transaction (or when it was translated at a previous balance sheet date) and the subsequent retranslation of the monetary item to the rate ruling at the balance sheet date. Such exchange differences are reported as part of the profit or loss for the year.

7.69.1 Monetary assets classified as available-for-sale in accordance with IAS 39 are carried at fair value but are treated for the purpose of calculating foreign exchange differences as if they were carried at amortised cost. The exchange differences resulting from changes in amortised cost are recognised in the income statement. [IAS 39 AG 83]. Other fair value gains and losses on available-for-sale monetary financial assets are required to be recognised in other comprehensive income. [IAS 39 para 55(b), IG E 3.2]. See chapter 6.7 for an example of the treatment of foreign exchange gains and losses on monetary available-for-sale assets.

7.70 Not all exchange differences on monetary items are reported in the income statement. There are number of exceptions. These are:

■ A monetary item that is designated as a hedging instrument in a cash flow hedge. Any exchange difference that forms part of the gain or loss on the hedging instrument is recognised in other comprehensive income. [IAS 39 para 95].

■ A monetary item that is designated as a hedge of a net investment *in consolidated financial statements*. The exchange difference on the hedging instrument that is considered to be an effective hedge is recognised in other comprehensive income. [IAS 39 para 102]. See from paragraph 7.108 onwards below.

■ A monetary item that forms part of the net investment in a foreign operation in the consolidated financial statements. See from paragraph 7.93 onwards below.

Non-monetary items

7.71 When a gain or loss on a non-monetary item is recognised directly in other comprehensive income, any exchange component of that gain or loss is recognised directly in other comprehensive income. [IAS 39 para 30]. For example, an entity purchases equity securities denominated in a foreign currency that are classified as available for sale. Under IAS 39, the equity securities are carried at fair value. Any changes in fair value that are recognised directly in other comprehensive income also include any related foreign exchange element. [IAS 39 paras 55(b), AG83]. Another example is where a property denominated in a foreign currency is revalued. Any exchange difference arising when the property is translated at the rate of exchange ruling at the valuation date is reported directly in other comprehensive income along with other changes in value.

Example – Translation of a revalued foreign asset

A UK entity with a sterling functional currency has a property located in the US, which it acquired at a cost of US$1.8m when the exchange rate was £1 = US$1.6. The property was revalued to US$2.16m at the balance sheet date. The exchange rate at the balance sheet date was £1 = US$1.8.

Ignoring depreciation, the amount that would be reported directly to equity is:

	£
Value at balance sheet date = US$2,160,000m @ 1.8 =	1,200,000
Value at acquisition date = US$1,800,000 @ 1.6 =	1,125,000
Revaluation surplus recognised in other comprehensive income	75,000
The revaluation surplus may be analysed as follows:	
Change in fair value = US$360,000 @ 1.8 =	200,000
Exchange component of change = US$1,800,000 @ 1.8 –	
US$1,800,000 @ 1.6	(125,000)
Revaluation surplus recognised in other comprehensive income	75,000

7.72 On the other hand, when a gain or loss on a non-monetary item is recognised in profit or loss, any exchange component of that gain or loss is also recognised in profit or loss. [IAS 21 para 38].

Example – Translation of an impaired foreign asset

A UK entity with a sterling functional currency has a property located in the US, which was acquired at a cost of US$1.8m when the exchange rate was £1 = US$1.6. The property is carried at cost. At the balance sheet date the recoverable amount of the property as a result of an impairment review amounted to US$1.62m. The exchange rate at the balance sheet date was £1 = US$1.8.

Ignoring depreciation, the impairment loss that would be reported in the income statement as a result of the impairment is:

	£
Carrying value at balance sheet date – US$1,620,000m @ 1.8 =	900,000
Historical cost – US$1,800,000 @ 1.6 =	1,125,000
Impairment loss recognised in profit or loss	(225,000)
The impairment loss may be analysed as follows:	
Change in value due to impairment = US$180,000 @ 1.8 =	(100,000)
Exchange component of change = US$1,800,000 @ 1.8 –	
US$1,800,000 @ 1.6	(125,000)
Impairment loss recognised in profit or loss	(225,000)

Foreign currency translation of financial statements

Introduction

7.73 Accounting for transactions in foreign currencies that are directly undertaken by an entity and that are measured and expressed in the entity's functional currency is addressed earlier in this chapter. Where foreign activities are undertaken through foreign operations, the financial statements of those foreign operations are translated so that they can be included in the reporting entity's financial statements by consolidation, proportional consolidation or the equity method. The process of translation addresses the appropriate exchange rates to use for translating the income statement and the balance sheet of the foreign operation and how the financial effects of changes in exchange rates are recognised in the reporting entity's financial statements.

7.74 The standard permits an entity to present its financial statements in a currency other than its functional currency. The currency in which the financial statements are presented is referred to as the 'presentation currency'. [IAS 21 para 8]. There is no requirement in the standard for an entity to present its financial statements in its functional currency, which most faithfully portrays the economic effect of transactions and events on the entity. The IASB explains why entities are permitted to present their financial statements in any currency in paragraphs BC10 to BC14 of the Basis for Conclusions of IAS 21.

7.75 Although entities have a free choice in the selection of the presentation currency, they are likely to use the functional currency, the currency used for measurement, as the presentation currency. If management uses an alternative currency, disclosure of the reasons for selecting a different currency is required. There must, therefore, be substantive and valid reasons for choosing an alternative presentation currency. For example, in some countries, an entity may be required by local and legal regulations to present its financial statements in the local currency even if this is not its functional currency.

Translation to the presentation currency

7.76 Selecting a presentation currency that is different from the functional currency requires a translation from the functional currency into the presentation currency. For example, when a group contains individual entities with different functional currencies, the results and financial position of each entity is expressed in a common currency so that consolidated financial statements may be presented. IAS 21 has prescribed a translation methodology for translating from the functional currency to a different presentation currency. This translation methodology seeks to ensure that the financial and operational relationships between underlying amounts established in the entity's primary economic environment and measured in its functional currency are preserved when translated into a different measurement currency. The translation method is described in the next paragraph. A different translation methodology applies to an entity whose functional currency is the currency of a hyper-inflationary economy. This method is described in chapter 31.

7.77   The translation methodology referred to above requires an entity's results and financial position whose functional currency is not the currency of a hyper-inflationary economy to be translated into a different presentation currency using the following procedures:

■   Assets and liabilities for each balance sheet presented (including comparatives) are translated at the closing rate at the date of that balance sheet.

Use of a constant rate of exchange for all items on the balance sheet maintains the relationship in the retranslated financial statements as existed in the foreign operation's financial statements. Therefore, for example, fixed assets are the same proportion of long-term liabilities.

■   Income and expenses for each income statement (including comparatives) is translated at exchange rates at the dates of the transactions. For practical reasons, a rate that approximates the exchange rates at the dates of the transactions — for example, an average rate for the period — is often used to translate income and expense items. However, if exchange rates fluctuate significantly, the use of the average rate for a period is inappropriate (see para 7.81 below).

The use of a closing rate is more likely to preserve the financial results and relationships that existed prior to translation, but the use of an actual or average rate reflects more fairly the profits or losses and cash flows as they accrue to the group throughout the period.

■   All resulting exchange differences are recognised in other comprehensive income and accumulated as a separate component of equity.

[IAS 21 paras 39, 40].

Equity items

7.77.1   The standard is silent on how to translate items that are recognised directly in equity, that is, items that have not been recognised through the performance statements. These will generally be recognised as a result of a transaction with a shareholder, such as share capital, share premium or treasury shares. Management has a choice of using either the historical rate or the closing rate for these items. The chosen policy should be applied consistently. If the historical rate is used, these equity items are not retranslated and the CTA will, therefore, only include the cumulative differences between opening and closing rates on total net assets, and average to closing rates on retained earnings and other performance statement items, such as AFS or hedging reserves. If the closing rate is used, the resulting exchange differences are recognised directly in equity as part of the CTA reserve. This effectively reduces the CTA that arises on retranslating the net assets. Any exchange differences arising on translating equity items are not recognised in the performance statements. They are instead recognised directly in equity, with the result that the CTA movement in equity will not equal the CTA recognised in total comprehensive income. The policy choice has no impact on the amount of total equity. The regulatory framework in some jurisdictions may mandate one treatment.

7.78 The exchange differences referred to in the last bullet point in paragraph 7.77 above comprises:

- Differences arising from translating the income statement at exchange rates at the dates of the transactions or at average rates, and assets and liabilities at the closing rate. Such exchange differences arise on items recognised in the income statement as well as in other comprehensive income.

- Differences arising on the opening net assets' retranslation at a closing rate that differs from the previous closing rate.

[IAS 21 para 41].

CTA may also include differences on retranslation of equity items, depending on the policy choice made, as described in paragraph 7.77 above.

7.79 The above exchange differences are not recognised in the income statement. This would distort the results from trading operations shown in the functional currency financial statements. Such differences, which primarily result from a translation process, are unrelated to the foreign operation's trading performance or financial operations; in particular, they do not represent or measure changes in actual or prospective cash flows. They do have an impact on the net investment that may be realised upon sale or liquidation, but that effect is related to the net investment and not to the investee's operations. It is, therefore, inappropriate to regard them as profits or losses. Hence, they are recognised in a separate component of other comprehensive income.

7.80 The IASB chose the translation method described in paragraph 7.77 because, for a multi-national group comprising operations with a number of functional currencies, it means that the operations can be translated into the presentation currency directly without having to determine a 'functional currency' for the group first. The method also results in the same amounts in the presentation currency regardless of whether the financial statements of a foreign operation are first translated into the functional currency of the parent and then into the presentation currency or translated directly into the presentation currency. [IAS 21 para BC18].

Determining the average rate for translating the income statement

7.81 The standard permits a foreign operation's income statement to be translated at an average rate for the period. IAS 21 does not prescribe any definitive method of calculating the average rate, probably because the appropriate method may justifiably vary between individual entities. For further information refer to paragraphs 7.52 and 7.53 above.

Change in presentation currency

7.82 IAS 21 allows entities a free choice of the currency in which they present their financial statements. [IAS 21 para 38]. The question, therefore, arises how a change in presentation currency should be treated. An entity may choose to change its presentation currency when there is a change in its functional currency, although this is not required (see para 7.46.1). The choice of presentation currency represents an accounting policy and any change should be applied fully retrospectively in accordance with IAS 8, unless impracticable. This means that the change should be treated as if the new presentation currency had always been the entity's presentation currency, with comparative amounts being restated into the new presentation currency. Since using a presentation currency is purely applying a translation method, and does not affect the underlying functional currency of the entity or any entities within a group, it is straightforward to apply a change in presentation currency to assets, liabilities and income statement items. All assets and liabilities are translated from their functional currency into the new presentation currency at the beginning of the comparative period using the opening exchange rate and retranslated at the closing rate. Income statement items are translated at an actual rate or at an average rate approximating the actual rate.

7.82.1 However, for the individual items within equity, the process can be more complex. Management has a choice of translating these equity items from an entity's functional currency into its presentation currency at either the closing rate or at the historical rate, with the balancing amount being reported in CTA (see para 7.77.1). Retained earnings, CTA and similar reserves should be expressed in the new presentation currency as if it had always been the presentation currency, unless it is impracticable to do so (see further para 7.82.4).

7.82.2 A change in presentation currency is less problematic where a stand-alone entity (or a group with no foreign operations) reports equity at the closing rate, as it means that some of the CTA that would have arisen on retranslation of net assets will be offset by CTA on retranslation of equity items. CTA will, however, arise as a result of differences between the historical average and closing exchange rates when applied to profit or loss and other performance statement items.

7.82.3 Where equity items are translated at the historical rate and/or where a group has foreign operations, the individual equity items should also be re-expressed in the new presentation currency on a change of presentation currency as if it had always been the presentation currency. [IAS 8 para 19]. This requires determining the amount of each individual equity balance on each earlier reporting date. For unvarying items of equity such as share capital and premium, this may not be too difficult, although even this may be complicated by share issues and buy-backs in different reporting periods.

7.82.4 However, for retained earnings and other similar reserves, the amounts in functional currencies must be translated at the transaction dates with a resulting impact on the amount recognised in CTA. Calculating the split between retained earnings and CTA may be onerous in practice. How difficult will be influenced by whether average rates can be used as an approximation for actual rates, the period over which these changes are to be calculated as well as the number of transactions. It will usually be relatively straightforward to go back as far as the opening balance sheet of the first period presented. The effect of going back further (which will affect only the relative amounts reported in CTA and retained earnings), may not be material, although this will depend on factors such as:

- The size of assets and liabilities.

- The stability of the relevant exchange rates.

- Legal requirements around distributability of profits.

- The reclassification of the deferred foreign exchange gains and losses on the ultimate disposal of a foreign operation.

7.82.5 Where an entity, on adopting IFRS, took the exemption to reset the CTA to zero, we believe that it would not be necessary to restate beyond its transition date (see chapter 2).

7.82.6 In the case where an entity changes its presentation currency it should present an additional balance sheet in accordance with paragraph 10(f) of IAS 1. See further chapter 4.

Consolidated financial statements

Translation of a foreign operation

7.83 Translating foreign currency financial statements into the presentation currency is necessary so that the foreign operation's financial statements may be included in the reporting entity's financial statements by consolidation, proportional consolidation or the equity method. The method of translation in consolidated financial statements reflects the financial and other operational relationships that exist between the reporting entity and its foreign enterprises. This objective is achieved by following the closing rate/net investment method described in paragraph 7.77. This translation method is illustrated by the example below. Once the foreign operation's financial statements have been translated into the reporting entity's presentation currency, its incorporation into the reporting entity's consolidated financial statement follows normal consolidation procedures.

Example 1 – Translation of a foreign subsidiary

Entity A, a UK entity, whose accounting period ended on 30 September 20X5, has a wholly-owned US subsidiary, S corporation, which was acquired for US$500,000 on 30 September 20X4. The fair value of the net assets at the date of acquisition was US$400,000 giving rise to goodwill of US$100,000. The exchange rate at 30 September 20X4 and 20X5 was £1 = US$2.0 and £1 = US$1.5 respectively. The weighted average rate for the year ended 30 September 20X5 was £1 = US$1.65. During the year, S corporation paid a dividend of US$14,000 when the rate of exchange was £1 = US$1.75.

The foreign currency movements in this example have been exaggerated. In reality, if exchange rates were this volatile, an entity would not be permitted to use average rates for translating the income statement. [IAS 21 para 40].

The summarised income statement of S corporation for the year ended 30 September 20X4, and the summarised balance sheets at 30 September 20X3 and 20X4 in dollars and sterling equivalents, are as follows:

S corporation: Income statement for the year ended 30 September 20X5

	$'000	Exchange rate	£'000
Operating profit	135	1.65	81.8
Interest paid	(15)	1.65	(9.0)
Profit before taxation	120		72.8
Taxation	(30)	1.65	(18.2)
Profit after taxation	90		54.6

Balance sheets of S corporation

	20X5 $'000	20X4 $'000	20X5 £'000	20X4 £'000
Closing exchange rate £1 =			$1.50	$2.00
Property, plant and equipment				
Cost (20X5 additions: $30)	255	225	170.0	112.5
Depreciation (20X5 charge: $53)	98	45	65.3	22.5
Net book value	157	180	104.7	90.0
Current assets:				
Inventories	174	126	116.0	63.0
Debtors	210	145	140.0	72.5
Cash at bank	240	210	160.0	105.0
	624	481	416.0	240.5

Current liabilities:				
Trade creditors	125	113	83.3	57.5
Taxation	30	18	20.0	9.0
	155	131	103.3	65.5
Net current assets	469	350	312.7	175.0
Loan stock	150	130	100.0	65.0
Net assets	476	400	317.4	200.0
Share capital	200	200	100.0	100.0
Retained profits	276	200	217.4	100.0
	476	400	317.4	200.0

Analysis of retained profits

	$'000	£'000
Pre-acquisition profit brought forward	200	100.0
Profit for the year	90	54.6
Dividends paid in the year *	(14)	(8.0)
Exchange difference	–	70.8
Retained profits	276	217.4

* Dividend paid during the year is translated at the actual rate $1 = $1.75

Analysis of exchange difference:

Arising on retranslation of opening net assets (excluding goodwill – see below)	
at opening rate — $400,000 @ $2 = £1	200.0
at closing rate — $400,000 @ $1.5 = £1	266.7
Exchange gain on net assets	66.7
Exchange gain arising from translating retained profits from average to closing rate – $90,000 @1.5 – £54.6	5.4
Exchange loss arising from translating dividend from actual to closing rate – $14,000 @1.5 – £8.0	(1.3)
Total exchange difference arising on translation of S corporation	70.8
Exchange difference on goodwill of US$100,000 treated as a currency asset (see para 7.86 below)	
at opening rate — US$100,000 @ $2 = £1	50.0
at closing rate — US$100,000 @ $1.5 = £1	66.7
Exchange gain on goodwill included in consolidation	16.7
Total exchange difference included in consolidated balance sheet as a separate component of equity (see below)	87.5

It is assumed that parent entity A's functional currency is the pound sterling. It has received a dividend from S corporation during the year. The summarised balance sheets of entity A at 30 September 20X4 and 20X5 are as follows:

Foreign currencies

Entity A — Balance sheets

	20X5 £'000	20X4 £'000
Investments in subsidiary S ($500,000 @ 2.0)	250	250
Cash	208	200
Net assets	458	450
Share capital	450	450
Retained profits (dividend received: $14,000 @ 1.75*)	8	—
	458	450

*actual rate on date dividend received

The summarised consolidated income statement for the year ended 30 September 20X5 and the consolidated balance sheet as at date prepared under the closing rate/net investment method are as follows:

Consolidated income statement for the year ended 30 September 20X5

	£'000
Operating profit of S corporation	81.8
Operating profit of entity A	8.0
	89.8
Elimination of inter-company dividend*	(8.0)
Net operating profit	81.8
Interest paid	(9.0)
Profit before taxation	72.8
Taxation	(18.2)
Retained profit	54.6

Consolidated balance sheet as at 30 September 20X5

	£'000
Goodwill	66.7
Property, plant and equipment	104.7
	171.4
Current assets:	
Inventories	116.0
Debtors	140.0
Cash (S corporation: £160; entity A £208)	368.0
	624.0
Current liabilities:	
Trade creditors	83.3
Taxation	20.0
	103.3
Net current assets	520.7
Loan stock	100.0
Net assets	592.1

Capital and reserves	
Share capital	450.0
Retained profit	54.6
Cumulative translation adjustment	87.5
	592.1

Different reporting dates

7.84 Where a foreign subsidiary's financial statements are drawn up to a date that is different from that of the parent, the foreign subsidiary often prepares additional financial statements as of the same date as the parent for inclusion in the parent's financial statements. Therefore, the foreign subsidiary's financial statements are translated at the exchange rate at the parent's balance sheet date. Where additional financial statements are not prepared, IAS 27 allows the use of a different reporting date that is not more than three months before or three months after the reporting entity's balance sheet date. The foreign subsidiary's financial statements are translated at the exchange rate ruling at the foreign operation's balance sheet date. However, if significant transactions or events occur between the date of the subsidiary's financial statements and the date of the parent's financial statements, adjustments are made. [IAS 27 para 23]. This may include changes to the exchange rate, as shown in the example below.

> **Example – Translation of a foreign subsidiary with a different reporting date to that of the parent**
>
> Entity A prepares its annual financial statements at 31 January. However, local regulations require one of its subsidiaries, entity B, to prepare its financial statements at 31 December. Entity A uses entity B's results for the 12 months to 31 December for consolidation purposes, rather than have a second set of results audited to 31 January.
>
> The exchange rate between the US dollar (used for group reporting) and entity B's local currency was US$1: LC15,000 at 31 December 20X2 and US$1: LC18,000 at 31 January 20X3. There were no significant transactions or other events at entity B during January 20X3. Entity B's net assets at 31 December 20X2 were LC234 million.
>
> The net assets of entity B at 31 December 20X2 using the exchange rate of 31 December 20X2 are US$15,600.
>
> The change in exchange rates between 31 December 20X2 and 31 January 20X3 is significant. Therefore, entity A uses the exchange rate of 31 January 20X3 for consolidation purposes.
>
> Accordingly, management should translate entity B's balance sheet as at 31 December 20X2 using the 31 January 20X3 exchange rate. This results in the consolidation of a balance sheet with net assets of US$13,000.
>
> The same approach is used for foreign associates and joint ventures. [IAS 21 para 46].

Equity Items

7.84.1   The standard is silent on how to translate equity items. Management, therefore, has a choice of using either the historical rate or the closing rate. The chosen policy should be applied consistently. If the closing rate is used, the resulting exchange differences are recognised in equity; the policy choice, therefore, has no impact on the amount of total equity. The regulatory framework in some jurisdictions may mandate one treatment. In this case, the policy choice does not apply.

Non-controlling interest

7.85   Exchange differences arising on the retranslation of a foreign subsidiary's financial statements are recognised in other comprehensive income and accumulated as a separate component of equity. Where the foreign subsidiary is not wholly-owned, the exchange differences that are attributable to the non-controlling interest are allocated to, and reported as part of, the non-controlling interest in the consolidated balance sheet. [IAS 21 para 41].

Goodwill and fair value adjustments arising on an acquisition

7.86   Goodwill arising in a business combination is measured as the excess of the consideration transferred for the combination over the acquirer's interest in the net fair value of the acquiree's identifiable assets and liabilities and any non-controlling interest.

7.87   Goodwill and fair value adjustments form part of the acquired entity's assets and liabilities.

- Any goodwill arising on the acquisition of a foreign operation and any fair value adjustments to the carrying amounts of assets and liabilities arising on a foreign operation's acquisition are treated as the foreign operation's assets and liabilities.

- They are expressed in the foreign operation's functional currency and are translated at the closing rate in accordance with paragraphs 7.77 above, where the functional currency is not the currency of a hyper-inflationary economy, and in accordance with paragraph 7.109 below, where the functional currency is the currency of a hyper-inflationary economy.

[IAS 21 para 47].

7.88   Therefore, where a parent entity acquires a multinational operation comprising businesses with many different functional currencies, the goodwill arising on acquisition is allocated to the level of each functional currency of the acquired foreign operation. This means that the level at which goodwill is allocated for foreign currency translation purposes may be different from the level at which goodwill is tested for impairment in accordance with IAS 36. [IAS 36 para 83].

Example – Translation of goodwill and fair value adjustments

On 30 June 20X5, a UK parent entity with sterling as the functional currency acquired a multinational group with operations in Canada, the US and Europe. All foreign operations are highly profitable. The functional currencies of the foreign operations are their respective local currencies. The total purchase consideration amounted to £3,000m. The UK parent financial year ends on 31 December 20X5.

The fair values of the net assets of the acquired businesses, including fair value adjustments and the relevant exchange rates at the date of acquisition and at the balance sheet date, are given below. The UK parent allocates the purchased goodwill to the acquired businesses on the basis of their relative adjusted fair values of the net assets acquired.

Business acquired	Canada	US	Europe	Total
Exchange rate at acquisition £1 =	2.19	1.66	1.42	
Exchange rate at balance sheet date £1 =	2.29	1.80	1.45	
	C$000	**$'000**	**€'000**	**£'000**
Net assets — book value	1,200	1,500	2,000	
Fair value adjustments	150	50	(100)	
Adjusted fair values	1,350	1,550	1,900	
Allocation of goodwill				
Translated at exchange rate at date of acquisition	£616	£934	£1,338	2,888
Purchase consideration				3,000
Goodwill allocated on the basis of adjusted fair values	£24	£36	£52	112
	C$'000	**$'000**	**€'000**	
Adjusted net assets as above	1,350	1,550	1,900	
Goodwill treated as currency asset	53	60	74	
Adjusted fair value + goodwill	1,403	1,610	1,974	
Translation adjustment on opening net assets	**£'000**	**£'000**	**£'000**	**£'000**
Adjusted net assets + goodwill @ closing rate	613	894	1,361	2,868
Adjusted net assets + goodwill @ opening rate	640	970	1,390	3,000
Exchange loss taken to other comprehensive income on consolidation	(27)	(76)	(29)	(132)

Consolidated balance sheet at 31 December 20X5

Goodwill at closing rate	23	33	51	107
Net assets at closing rate	590	861	1,310	2,761
Cash outlay				(3,000)
Consolidated net assets				(132)
Translation adjustments in equity	(27)	(76)	(29)	(132)

Intra-group trading transactions

7.89 Where normal trading transactions take place between group companies located in different countries, the transactions give rise to monetary assets (liabilities) that may either have been settled during the year or remain unsettled at the balance sheet date. As the transactions will be recorded in the functional currency of one of the companies in question, exchange differences will arise. These are reported in the entity's income statement in the same way as gains or losses on transactions arising with third parties, as explained from paragraph 7.67 above. Where the monetary asset or liability is settled during the year, the exchange gain or loss will have affected group cash flows. It is, therefore, included in consolidated results for the year. The exchange difference arising simply reflects the risk of doing business with a foreign party, even though that party happens to be a group member. Even where the transaction remains unsettled at the balance sheet date and the monetary asset (liability) in one group entity is eliminated against the corresponding liability (asset) in another group entity, the exchange difference reported in the group entity's own income statement continues to be recognised in consolidated profit or loss. This is because the monetary item represents a commitment to convert one currency into another and exposes the reporting entity to gain or loss through currency fluctuations. [IAS 21 para 45].

Example – Elimination of intra-group trading transactions where the inventory is still owned by the group

A UK parent entity has a wholly-owned subsidiary in the US. During the year ended 31 December 20X5, the US entity purchased plant and raw materials to be used in its manufacturing process from the UK parent. Details of the transactions are as follows:

	Exchange rate
Purchased plant costing £500,000 on 30 April 20X5	£1 = US$1.48
Paid for plant on 30 September 20X5	£1 = US$1.54
Purchased raw materials costing £300,000 on 31 October 20X5	£1 = US$1.56
Balance of £300,000 outstanding at 31 December 20X5	£1 = US$1.52
Average rate for the year	£1 = US$1.55

The following exchange gains/losses will be recorded in the US subsidiary's income statement for the year ended 31 December 20X5.

	US$	US$
Plant costing £500,000 @ 1.48	740,000	
Paid £500,000 @ 1.54	770,000	
Exchange loss – settled transaction		(30,000)
Raw materials costing £300,000 @ 1.56	468,000	
Outstanding £300,000 @ 1.52	456,000	
Exchange gain – unsettled transaction		12,000
Net exchange loss recorded in income statement		(18,000)

The exchange loss of US$30,000 that arises as the inter-company payable for plant purchase is settled during the year will flow through on consolidation when the US subsidiary's results are incorporated in the consolidated financial statements. The inter-company payable of US$456,000 in the US subsidiary's balance sheet that remains outstanding will be translated into sterling at the closing rate to £300,000 and will be eliminated against the receivable recorded in the UK parent's inter-company account. However, the exchange gain of US$12,000 will not be eliminated on consolidation and will be reported as part of the consolidated results of the group. The rationale of keeping this gain in the group's result is that to repay the payable balance, the US subsidiary will some day have to expend the amount of its local currency necessary to acquire the required amount of the reporting currency. This exposes the group to a gain or loss on reconversion.

7.90   The same treatment that applies to an unsettled inter-company monetary item arising from trading transactions also applies to intra-group loans made by one group member to another in a currency that is different from the borrower's functional currency. That is, the borrower will initially record the foreign currency loan at the rate of exchange ruling at the date the loan is made. At each balance sheet date thereafter, until it is repaid, the loan will be translated at the closing rate and any exchange difference will be reported in the borrower's income statement. On consolidation, the intra-group loan account will cancel out, but the exchange difference reported in the borrower's income statement continues to be recognised in profit or loss.

Unrealised profit on inventories

7.91   IAS 27 requires intra-group profit arising from the transfer of assets between entities in the group to be eliminated in full in the group accounts where such assets are still held in the undertakings included in the consolidation at the balance sheet date. This is because it does not represent profit to the group (see further chapter 24). No specific guidance is given in IAS 21 as to the exchange rate at which the profit should be eliminated. However, US GAAP requires elimination at the actual rate ruling at the transaction date or at a weighted average rate (Codification para 830-30-45-10).

Example – Elimination of intra-group trading transactions where the inventory had been sold outside the group

The facts are the same as in the example in paragraph 7.89 except that the raw materials purchased for £300,000 by the US subsidiary are still in inventory at 31 December 20X5. These goods cost the UK parent £270,000.

Unrealised profit of £30,000 (£300,000 — £270,000) that the parent entity made on the inter-company sale would, therefore, need to be eliminated on consolidation. However, elimination of this unrealised profit of £30,000 will not necessarily result in the inventories being included in the consolidated balance sheet at cost to the group where the closing rate method is used, as illustrated below.

The amount for raw materials included in inventory in the US entity's balance sheet at the transaction date is US$468,000. Under the closing rate method, the inventory would be retranslated at the year end rate of 1.52 to £307,895. Therefore, the inventory will be recorded in the consolidated balance sheet as follows:

	£
Cost of inventory US$468,000 @ 1.52	307,895
Unrealised profit	(30,000)
Inventory carried in consolidated balance sheet	277,895

The difference of £7,895 represents the exchange difference arising on the retranslation of the inventory in the subsidiary's financial statements to the year end rate under the closing rate/net investment method — that is, £307,895 less the cost to the subsidiary of £300,000.

If the parent has purchased the raw materials from the US subsidiary for US 468,000 at 31 October 20X5, which cost the US subsidiary US$421,200, and these items were still in the parent's inventory at the year end, a problem arises as to what rate the unrealised profit of US$46,800 is eliminated.

As stated above, if the guidance in US GAAP is followed, the profit will be eliminated at the actual rate ruling at the transaction date. The inventory will be recorded in the consolidated balance sheet as follows:

	£
Cost of inventory US$468,000 @ 1.56	300,000
Unrealised profit US$46,800 @ 1.56	(30,000)
Inventory carried in consolidated balance sheet	270,000

The amount of inventory recorded in the balance sheet represents the original cost to the group of US$421,200 translated at the rate ruling at the date of the intra-group transaction – that is, US$421,200 @ 1.56 = £270,000. This is the method required by US GAAP, which can be applied under IAS 21.

In practice, it is likely that the UK parent will use an average rate for translating the results of foreign operations. The amount of profit to be eliminated is calculated using that average rate. Use of an average rate is permissible where it approximates the exchange rate at the date of the transaction.

	£
Cost of inventory US$468,000 @ 1.56	300,000
Unrealised profit US$46,800 @ 1.55	(30,194)
	269,806

The amount of inventory recorded in the consolidated balance sheet under the closing rate/net investment method will not be the same as the actual cost to the group.

7.92 Even if intra-group transactions do not give rise to intra-group profit, there could still be an effect on asset values, as the following example illustrates.

Example – Intra-group trading transaction at cost

A UK parent has a wholly-owned subsidiary in Pololand. The currency is Pol. The net assets of the group at 31 March 20X5 are £54,000, consisting of cash £24,000, held in the UK parent and inventory held in the Pololand subsidiary costing Pol 3m. This was included in the consolidated balance sheet at the closing rate of £1 = Pol 100. On 30 September 20X5, the subsidiary transfers the goods to its UK parent at cost price when the rate of exchange is £1 = Pol 125. The transaction is settled in cash, and the goods are included in the parent's inventory at £24,000. At 31 March 20X6, the goods are still in inventory. The Pol has weakened further against sterling and the exchange rate at the balance sheet date is £1 = Pol 150.

No gain or loss is recorded by either entity on the transfer; there are therefore no interentity profits to be eliminated.

	31 March 20X5
	£
Net assets:	
Inventory 3m @ 100 (held by subsidiary)	30,000
Cash (held by parent)	24,000
	54,000

	31 March 20X6
	£
Net assets:	
Inventory (held by parent)	24,000
Cash 3m @ 150 (held by subsidiary)	20,000
	44,000

Exchange difference on retranslation of opening net assets of foreign subsidiary:		
3m @ 100 =	30,000	
3m @ 150 =	20,000	10,000
		54,000

No exchange difference is included in the consolidated income statement, as there is no trading gain or loss. However the effect of switching inventory around the group affects the asset's carrying value. If the inventory had not been transferred, the net assets would still have decreased by £10,000, but the reduction would have been entirely in the inventory value with the cash balance unchanged. However, the result of moving the inventory and cash around the group is that there is a decrease of £6,000 in the inventory value and a decrease of £4,000 in the group's cash position. This reflects the fact that the group's foreign currency exposure is centred on different assets.

Monetary items forming part of net investment in a foreign operation

7.93 The net investment that a reporting entity has in a foreign operation is its interest in the net assets of that operation. [IAS 21 para 8]. In circumstances described in paragraph 7.95 below, a monetary item that is receivable from or payable to a foreign operation, such as long-term loans and receivables and long-term payables, may be regarded as an extension of, or reduction, in the reporting entity's net investment in that foreign operation. In those situations, it may not be appropriate to include the resulting exchange differences arising on the retranslation of such monetary items in consolidated profit or loss when exchange difference arising on equivalent financing with equity capital would be taken to other comprehensive income on consolidation.

7.94 IAS 21 recognises the above situation and requires exchange differences arising on a monetary item that forms part of a reporting entity's net investment in a foreign operation that is a subsidiary, associate or joint venture to be treated as follows:

■ In the separate financial statements of the reporting entity or the individual financial statements of the foreign operation as appropriate, such exchange differences are recognised in the income statement.

■ In the financial statements that include the foreign operation and the reporting entity (for example, consolidated financial statements when the foreign operation is a subsidiary), such exchange differences are recognised initially in a separate component of other comprehensive income and recognised in the profit or loss on disposal of the net investment (see further para 7.106).

[IAS 21 para 32].

7.95 The inclusion of long-term loans and receivables as part of the net investment in the foreign operation is only permitted where settlement is neither planned nor likely to occur in the foreseeable future. [IAS 21 para 15]. In other words, the parent must regard them as permanent as equity. For example, a loan to a foreign entity that is repayable on demand may seem to be a short-term item, rather than part of capital. However, if there is demonstrably no intent or expectation to demand repayment (for example, the short-term loan is allowed to be continuously rolled over, whether or not the subsidiary is able to repay it), the loan has the same economic effect as a capital contribution. On the other hand, a long-term loan with a specified maturity (say 10 to 15 years) does not automatically qualify to be treated as being part of the net investment simply because it is of a long duration, unless management has expressed its intention to renew the note at maturity. The burden is on management to document its intention to renew by auditable evidence, such as board minutes. Otherwise, absent management's intention to renew, the note's maturity date implies that its settlement is planned in the foreseeable future.

7.96 Some may argue that inter-company accounts of a trading nature should qualify for the same treatment as above because, although individual transactions are settled, the account's aggregate balance never drops below a specified minimum. In other words, as a minimum amount is permanently deferred, an appropriate amount of the resulting exchange difference should also be deferred in equity. This treatment is not permitted; the standard prohibits its application to trade receivables and payables. [IAS 21 para 15]. The rationale is that as each individual transaction included in the overall inter-company balance is settled and replaced by a new transaction; settlement is always contemplated and, therefore, exchange gains and losses arising on such active accounts as described above would not qualify for deferral treatment.

7.97 The example below illustrates a number of scenarios setting out the treatment that management is required to follow on consolidation when inter-company loans are made between various members of a group.

Parent A is the reporting entity that has two subsidiaries B and C, which themselves have subsidiaries D and E. The functional currencies of each of the entities are as noted next to the letters designating the entities.

Group structure

In all the scenarios that follow, loans made between group entities are permanent in nature (that is, settlement is neither planned nor likely to occur).

Scenario 1

Parent A has a loan receivable from or payable to its foreign subsidiary C that is denominated in either sterling or the dollar.

The loan would be regarded as an extension to or a reduction of entity A's net investment in entity C as appropriate. An exchange difference is recognised in entity A's income statement if the loan receivable or payable is denominated in dollars. An exchange difference will be recognised in entity C's income statement if the loan receivable or payable is denominated in sterling. Any exchange difference recognised in either entity's profit or loss is recognised in other comprehensive income on consolidation. The above situation is dealt with in the numerical examples below.

Example — currency loan made by parent A to foreign subsidiary C

Parent A with sterling as its functional currency is preparing its financial statements to 30 September 20X5. It has a loan receivable of US$1m from its foreign subsidiary C that has been outstanding for some time. The parent notified the overseas subsidiary at the beginning of the financial year that no repayment of the amount will be requested for the foreseeable future.

The relevant exchange rates are as follows:

	30 September 20X5	30 September 20X4
£1 =	US$1.82	US $ 1.45

The following exchange differences will arise in the financial statements of the individual entities if the loan is retranslated at the closing rate:

Foreign subsidiary C

No exchange difference arises in the foreign subsidiary as the loan payable is denominated in its functional currency.

UK parent A

	£
Exchange difference on long-term loan receivable	
On closing rate – US$1m @ 1.82	549,450
On opening rate – US$1m @ 1.45	689,655
Exchange loss	140,205

In the parent entity's separate financial statement, the loan is regarded as a monetary item and any exchange difference is taken to the profit or loss in accordance with paragraph 7.94 above. [IAS 21 para 32].

On consolidation, the retranslated long-term loan is regarded as part of the net investment in the foreign subsidiary and, therefore, the related exchange loss is recognised in other comprehensive income and accumulated as a separate component of equity in accordance with paragraph 7.94 above. [IAS 21 para 32]. There would also be a corresponding exchange gain included in other comprehensive income, arising as part of the retranslation of the net assets (which include the US dollar loan creditor) of the overseas subsidiary under the closing rate/net investment method.

Example — sterling loan made by parent A to overseas subsidiary C

The facts are the same as the above example, except that parent A has a loan receivable from its overseas subsidiary of £200,000 that has been outstanding for some time. The loan is treated by the parent entity as forming part of its net investment in the overseas subsidiary.

In the financial statements of the individual entities, the following exchange differences will arise if the loan is retranslated at the closing rate.

UK parent A

There is no exchange difference in the parent's financial statements in respect of the loan as it is denominated in sterling.

Subsidiary C

	US$
Exchange difference on long-term loan payable	
On closing rate – £200,000 @ 1.82	364,000
On opening rate – £200,000 @ 1.45	290,000
Exchange loss	74,000
Exchange loss translated at the closing rate @ 1.82	£40,659

The exchange loss of US$74,000 on the sterling loan is recognised in the foreign subsidiary C's income statement, because the subsidiary is exposed to the foreign currency risk.

On consolidation, the inter-company loan will cancel out. However, as the long-term loan is regarded as part of the net investment in the subsidiary, the exchange loss of £40,659 is recognised in other comprehensive income and accumulated as a separate component of equity in the consolidated financial statements. There is a corresponding exchange gain included in other comprehensive income arising as part of the retranslation of the net assets of the overseas subsidiary. The effect is that the consolidated income statement will not reflect any exchange difference on the loan, which is consistent with the fact that the loan has no impact on group cash flows, unless the investment is sold.

The two examples above consider the accounting implications when a loan is made by the parent entity to an overseas subsidiary. In the case of a foreign currency upstream loan, for example, a borrowing by a parent entity from its subsidiary in the subsidiary's local currency, the treatment of exchange differences in the consolidated financial statements will depend on whether the loan is regarded as part of the net investment in the subsidiary. If that is the case, the treatment will be the same as identified above. That is, the exchange difference arising on the currency loan's retranslation in the parent's income statement is classified to a separate component of equity in the consolidated financial statements. On the other hand, if the loan is not regarded as part of the net investment, the exchange difference will continue to be recognised in consolidated profit or loss.

Scenario 2

Subsidiary B makes a loan denominated in sterling to subsidiary C ('sister-entity loans')

Subsidiary C recognises an exchange difference in its own income statement. The question is whether the exchange difference can be recognised in other comprehensive income and accumulated as a separate component of equity on consolidation.

IAS 21 has been amended to clarify in paragraph 15A that it is not necessary for the lender or the borrower to have the net investment in the foreign operation for the exchange differences on translation of the monetary item to be classified within entity. The entity that has the monetary item receivable from or payable to a foreign operation may be any member of group

7.98 The above examples deal with situations where a monetary item forming part of the net investment was denominated in the functional currency of either the reporting entity or the foreign operation. The question then arises as to whether a similar treatment is permissible in circumstances where a monetary item forming part of the net investment in a foreign operation is denominated in a currency that is different from the functional currency of either the reporting entity or the foreign operation.

7.99 Under IAS 21, a monetary item that meets the criteria to be part of an entity's net investment in a foreign operation is similar to an equity investment in a foreign operation. Hence, the accounting treatment in the consolidated financial statements does not depend on the currency in which the monetary item is denominated. Paragraph 33 of IAS 21 requires exchange differences on translation of such a monetary item to be recognised in other comprehensive income in the consolidated financial statements, irrespective of the currency of the monetary item.

7.99.1 Consider the situation in the group structure set out in paragraph 7.97 above where parent A, whose functional currency is the pound sterling, makes a loan denominated in euros to subsidiary C, whose functional currency is the US dollar. If the euro loan meets the criteria to be regarded by entity A as part of its net investment in entity C, the exchange differences that arise from retranslating the loan receivable in sterling in entity A's income statement and the loan payable in dollars in entity C's income statement are recognised in other comprehensive income in the financial statements that include the foreign operation and the reporting entity (that is, entity A's consolidated financial statements). [IAS 21 para 33].

7.100 Another issue that might arise is the appropriate treatment to be adopted in the year in which the parent decides to designate any long-term loans and receivables as part of its net investment in the foreign operation. Consider the first example in scenario 1 above where the long-term US dollar loan made by parent A was designated as being part of its net investment in the foreign subsidiary C from the beginning of the accounting period. If the parent did this part way through the financial year ended 30 September 20X5, say, at 31 March 20X5, the parent recognises any exchange difference arising in profit or loss up to that date and reclassifies any exchange difference that arises subsequently following the designation to the separate component in other comprehensive income in the consolidated financial statements.

7.101 Although not dealt with in the standard, the designation of an inter-company loan as part of the net investment in a foreign operation is periodically reassessed. This is because management's expectations and intent may change due to a change in circumstances. Such changes in circumstances are carefully evaluated to determine that management's previous assertions for not requiring repayment remain valid. For example, the change in circumstances may be such that it could not have been anticipated at the time of initial designation or the change in circumstances could be outside management's control.

7.102 Where, as a result of a change in circumstance, a previously designated 'net investment' loan is intended to be settled, the loan is de-designated. As the loan is no longer regarded as part of the net investment, a partial disposal of the net investment may have occurred and reclassification of cumulative translation adjustment may be required. See from paragraph 7.106 onwards for discussion of partial disposals.

7.102.1 There is no explicit guidance in IAS 21 about the timing of reclassification in the circumstances described in the previous paragraph. Does it occur when the loan is no longer considered to form part of the net investment in the foreign operation, or when the loan is actually repaid? Either approach may be adopted as an accounting policy choice. The selected policy should be applied consistently to all of the entity's 'net investment' loans and to all of its investments in foreign operations.

Inter-entity dividends

7.103 Where a foreign subsidiary pays a dividend to its parent entity, the dividend is charged directly to equity in its financial statements, and as the dividend is paid in the functional currency of the foreign subsidiary no exchange difference arises. However, if the dividends are payable in a currency that is different from the subsidiary's functional currency, exchange rate fluctuations between the dividend being recognised as an asset and being paid will produce foreign exchange gains or losses impacting profit or loss.

7.104 In the parent entity's financial statements, the dividend is translated at the rate in effect upon declaration (that is, the transaction date). An exchange gain or loss will arise if the rate of exchange moves between the date of declaration and the payment date. This exchange difference is reported in the parent's income statement as a normal inter-company transaction exchange gain or loss that is also reported in the consolidated financial statements. Consider the following example:

Example – Treatment of foreign exchange gains or losses on inter-entity dividends

A subsidiary with a dollar functional currency declared a dividend of $100,000 to its euro functional currency parent on 31 August 20X5 for the year ended 31 December 20X5. The dividend was appropriately authorised and recognised by the subsidiary as a liability at 31 August 20X5. The parent prepares consolidated financial statements for the year ended 31 December 20X5 in its presentation currency of euros. The following exchange rates are relevant:

31 August 20X5	$1.50 = €1
31 December 20X5	$1.75 = €1
15 January 20X6	$1.80 = €1

Dividend paid on 15 January 20X6

The dividend remains outstanding at the balance sheet date. The dividend is recorded in the subsidiary's and parent's separate and consolidated financial statements as follows:

In subsidiary's balance sheet (as translated for consolidation)

	€
Dividend payable – $100,000 @ 1.75	57,142

In parent's income statement

	€
Initially recorded at rate when dividend is declared – $100,000 @ 1.5 (transaction date)	66,667
Exchange loss on receivable recognised in the income statement	(9,525)
In parent's balance sheet – Dividend receivable at year end rate – $100,000 @ 1.75	57,142

In consolidated income statement

In the consolidated financial statements the dividend receivable of €66,667 is reclassified to consolidated retained earnings and offsets the dividend payable in the subsidiary's retained earnings that is translated at the year end rate @ 1.75 = €57,142. The difference of €9,525 (€66,667 — €57,142) comprises a loss recorded in the parent's income statement and no further exchange difference arises. The inter-entity receivable and payable cancel out.

Some may argue that the exchange difference of €9,525 included in the parent's income statement should be removed from consolidated income and reclassified to equity as it relates to dividends that are initially charged to equity. We believe that this treatment is not appropriate, as the exchange difference arises on a monetary asset and would affect group cash flows when it is settled. Such an exchange difference should, therefore, remain in consolidated income.

7.105 Given that exchange differences can arise on any transaction where the settlement date is different from the date when the transaction is recorded, it may be appropriate to ensure that inter-entity dividends are paid on the same date as they are declared as liabilities, particularly where it is likely that an exchange loss will arise. This may not always be possible, so it is not uncommon for a parent entity to mitigate exchange differences arising by taking out appropriate forward contracts so as to hedge the future remittance. Hedge accounting for foreign currency items is dealt with in IAS 39. Hedge accounting is considered in chapter 6.8.

Disposal or partial disposal of a foreign operation

7.106   As discussed in paragraph 7.77, the cumulative amount of exchange differences recognised in other comprehensive income (cumulative translation adjustment, or CTA) is carried forward as a separate component of equity until there is a disposal of the foreign operation. On the foreign operation's disposal, such exchange differences are recognised in profit or loss (that is, reclassified) when the gain or loss on disposal is recognised. [IAS 21 para 48]. Disposal may occur either through sale, liquidation, repayment of share capital or a quasi-equity loan, or abandonment of all, or part of, the entity.

7.106.1   When an entity loses control of a subsidiary that includes a foreign operation this is a disposal that triggers reclassification of the entire amount of CTA that has been recorded in equity attributable to the parent entity, even if the entity retains an interest in that former subsidiary. [IAS 21 para 48, 48A]. This applies, for example, when 80% of a 100% subsidiary is sold and a 20% interest in an associate is retained. The entire amount of CTA in relation to that subsidiary is reclassified to profit or loss. In the case where a foreign operation is partially owned (that is, where a non-controlling interest exists) the amount of the CTA that has been allocated to the non-controlling interest is derecognised, but is not transferred to profit or loss. [IAS 21 para 48B]. De-recognition of the non-controlling interest that includes the non-controlling interest's share of CTA will form part of the journal to calculate the gain or loss on disposal of the foreign operation.

7.106.2   The principle of full reclassification also applies to the loss of joint control or significant influence over a jointly controlled entity or an associate. All CTA that has been accumulated in equity in relation to that jointly controlled entity or associate is reclassified to profit or loss when joint control or significant influence is lost. [IAS 21 para 48A].

7.107   On a partial disposal that does not involve loss of control of a subsidiary that includes a foreign operation, the entity re-attributes the proportionate share of the CTA to the non-controlling interests in that foreign operation. [IAS 21 para 48C].

7.107.1   On the partial disposal of an interest in a jointly controlled entity or an associate, where joint control or significant influence are not lost, a proportionate amount of CTA is reclassified to profit or loss. [IAS 21 para 48C].

7.107.2   A write-down of the carrying amount of a foreign operation does not constitute a partial disposal. No part of the deferred foreign exchange gain or loss is recognised in profit or loss at the time of a write-down. [IAS 21 para 49]. Where the write-down arises from an impairment assessment as a result of a planned sale or liquidation (for example, where the foreign subsidiary is treated as a disposal group in accordance with IFRS 5 the write-down is also not treated as a partial disposal. [IFRS 5 BC 37, 38]. Therefore, any exchange difference attributable to that write down is not recognised in profit or loss. Reclassification will occur when the foreign operation is sold.

7.107.3 The cessation of hedge accounting of a net investment as the hedge no longer meets the criteria for the hedge accounting in IAS 39 is not a disposal. Therefore, the effective portion of the hedge as well as the related CTA previously recognised in other comprehensive income remain in other comprehensive income until the disposal, or partial disposal, of the foreign operation.

7.107.4 The conversion of a 'net investment' loan to an equity instrument as defined in IAS 32 does not result in reclassification. The reason for this is that the conversion of the loan is the swapping of the legal form of an investment from a debt instrument to an equity instrument so no disposal has occurred. No further exchange differences will arise on the equity investment in the parent's separate financial statements, as it is now a non-monetary item. (However, exchange differences would continue to arise on the net assets of the foreign operation.) The re-denomination of a 'net investment' loan into a different currency also does not constitute a disposal or partial disposal of the foreign operation. It does not change the parent's net investment in the foreign operation, there is no cash movement therefore in substance there has been no disposal. Therefore, no gains or losses are reclassified from equity to profit or loss.

7.107.5 A partial disposal is a reduction in an entity's 'ownership interest' in a foreign operation, other than loss of control, significant influence or joint control (see paras 7.106.1, 7.107.1). [IAS 21 para 48D]. Where a subsidiary that is a foreign operation repays a quasi-equity loan or repays/returns share capital but there is no change in the parent's proportionate percentage shareholding there is an accounting policy choice regarding whether the CTA should be reclassified depending on how 'ownership interest' in IAS 21 is interpreted.

Option 1 – No disposal of interest in subsidiary

Since the parent continues to own the same percentage of the subsidiary, and continues to control the foreign operation, there has been no change in its proportionate 'ownership interest' and hence no disposal or partial disposal under paragraphs 48D and 49 of IAS 21. Under this view 'ownership interest' refers only to the proportionate interest. The CTA should not, therefore, be reclassified.

Option 2 – Disposal of interest in subsidiary

The transaction is a partial disposal under paragraph 49 of IAS 21, as there has been a reduction in the parent's absolute ownership interest. Under this view, in addition to a proportionate change in ownership being a partial disposal, 'ownership interest' can also be interpreted as a change in the absolute interest held in a net investment. A *pro rata* share of the CTA should be reclassified.

Entities should make an accounting policy choice between these two methods and apply this policy consistently.

7.107.6 The receipt of a dividend from a foreign operation may only be considered a disposal or partial disposal when it is in substance a repayment/return of capital or liquidation and the parent entity applies the policy of treating such events as partial disposals (see para 7.107.5 and example 3 in para 7.107.7 below). [IAS 21 para 48D].

7.107.7 The rules on disposals and partial disposals and their effect on CTA can be summarised in the following table:

Event	Disposal or partial disposal	Effect on CTA
Subsidiary to Subsidiary (change in non-controlling interest)	Partial disposal	Re-attribute proportionate share of CTA to NCI
Subsidiary to JV or Associate (loss of control)	Disposal	All CTA reclassified to profit or loss
Subsidiary to Investment (loss of control)	Disposal	All CTA reclassified to profit or loss
Associate to Associate (reduction in ownership percentage)	Partial disposal	Proportionate share of CTA reclassified to profit or loss
Associate or JV to Investment	Disposal	All CTA reclassified to profit or loss
Write down of carrying amount of foreign operation	Neither	None
Cessation of hedge accounting for a net investment	Neither	None
Conversion of 'net investment' loan to equity instrument	Neither	None
Repayment of quasi equity loan	Accounting policy choice – disposal or not a disposal	Depends on policy choice
Dividend	Depends on substance and policy choice	If in substance the dividend payment is a return of capital or liquidation there is an accounting policy choice – disposal or non disposal. If in substance it is not a return of capital or liquidation, – it is not a disposal/ partial disposal.

Example 1 – Partial disposal of an associate

An investor owns 40% of the share capital of an entity. It has significant influence over the entity and accounts for the investment as an associate using equity accounting. The associate is a foreign operation. The investor sells half of its total shareholding, retaining a 20% investment. It continues to have significant influence and to account for the investment as an associate.

How much, if any, CTA is reclassified to profit or loss?

The reduction in the investor's ownership interest is a partial disposal per paragraph 48D of IAS 21. Half of the investment in associate has been disposed of, therefore 50% of the CTA relating to the foreign associate is reclassified to profit or loss [IAS 21 para 48C].

Example 2 – Partial disposal of a subsidiary while control is retained

A parent owns 100% of a subsidiary. The subsidiary is a foreign operation. The parent sells 30% of its shareholding, retaining a 70% shareholding and control.

How much, if any, CTA should be re-attributed to the non-controlling interest?

The reduction in the parent's ownership interest is a partial disposal per paragraph 48D of IAS 21. 30% of the subsidiary has been disposed of, therefore 30% of CTA should be re-attributed to the new non-controlling interest. This transfer is accounted for in the statement of changes in equity and is not presented in the performance statements. None of the CTA is reclassified to the income statement. [IAS 21 para 48C].

Example 3 – Repayment of a quasi equity loan

A parent owns 100% of a subsidiary. The subsidiary is a foreign operation. The subsidiary repays a quasi-equity loan by paying cash equal to 10% of its net assets to its parent. Prior to the transaction there had been no intention of repaying the quasi-equity loan. After the transaction the parent continues to own 100% of the subsidiary.

How much, if any, CTA is reclassified to profit or loss?

There are two ways that this transaction might be analysed (para 7.107.5).

Option 1 – No disposal of interest in subsidiary

Since there has been no change in the parent's proportionate 'ownership interest' there is no disposal or partial disposal under paragraphs 48D and 49 of IAS 21. CTA should not, therefore, be reclassified.

Option 2 – Disposal of interest in subsidiary

The transaction is a partial disposal under paragraph 49 of IAS 21, as there has been a 10% reduction in the parent's absolute ownership interest. A pro rata share (10%) of CTA should be reclassified.

The above options would equally apply to a return of capital/repayment of share capital in similar circumstances.

Entities should make an accounting policy choice between these views and apply this policy consistently.

Example 4 – Reclassification of cumulative exchange differences due to a group restructuring

In a group restructuring, a foreign operation is transferred from one intermediate holding entity to another. The group continues to hold a 100% interest in that foreign operation. No third parties are involved with the group restructuring.

Are the cumulative exchange differences reclassified in the group's consolidated financial statements?

The key question is whether the restructuring results in an economic change from the group's perspective that constitutes a partial or full disposal. The foreign operation continues to be part of the consolidated group and the restructuring is not a disposal event from the group's perspective.

However, if the intermediate holding entity that disposes of the foreign operation prepares consolidated financial statements under IFRS, the cumulative translation adjustments deferred in equity (if any) that arise at that intermediate reporting level are reclassified to profit or loss.

7.107.8 The tracking of cumulative exchange differences can be onerous. For a parent with more than one foreign operation, it could be tempting to aggregate these exchange differences related to all the net investments in one currency together, with the reclassification of these exchange differences on the disposal (or partial disposal) of some of those foreign operations being calculated proportionately based on the whole investments portfolio. However, IAS 21 requires reclassification whenever there is a disposal, or partial disposal, of a foreign operation, so the cumulative translation adjustments are required to be tracked on an individual net investment basis.

Hedging a net investment

7.108 A net investment in a foreign operation is defined as *"the amount of the reporting entity's interest in the net assets of that operation"*. [IAS 21 para 8]. Management may decide to hedge against the effects of changes in exchange rates in the entity's net investment in a foreign operation. This may be done by taking out a foreign currency borrowing or a forward contract to hedge the net investment. Hedging a net investment in a foreign operation can only be carried out at the consolidation level, because the net assets of the foreign operation are reported in the reporting entity's consolidated financial statements. However, IAS 21 does not apply to hedge accounting for foreign currency items including the hedging of a net investment in a foreign operation. IAS 39 and IFRIC 16 apply to hedge accounting. Under IAS 39, the hedging documentation and criteria set out in paragraph 88 of IAS 39 must be met, and any exchange differences recognised in equity through other comprehensive income relating to the foreign operation and the related borrowing are recognised in profit or loss on disposal of the foreign operation. IFRIC 16 gives further detailed guidance on hedges of net investments. Hedging of net investments is addressed in greater detail in chapter 6.8.

7.108.1 Where a reporting entity has a foreign currency borrowing that is designated as a hedge of its net investment in a foreign operation and all the conditions in IAS 39 and IFRIC 16 are met, the exchange gain or loss on the foreign currency borrowing reported in the reporting entity's separate income statement is reclassified to other comprehensive income in the reporting entity's consolidated financial statements.

7.108.2 IAS 27 states that in a parent's separate financial statements, investments in subsidiaries, jointly controlled entities and associates that are included in the consolidated financial statements are carried at cost or accounted for in accordance with IAS 39. This means that the equity investment can either be carried at cost less impairment, designated as 'available for sale' or designated as 'at fair value through profit or loss' (if permitted by IAS 39). IAS 27 requires the same accounting to be applied for each category of investment. A question arises as to whether a foreign currency borrowing can be designated as a hedge of the entity's foreign equity investment in its separate financial statements where the foreign equity investment is recorded at cost. IAS 39's rules on net investment hedging apply only to consolidated financial statements. However, we believe that the reporting entity can designate the foreign currency borrowing as a fair value hedge of foreign currency risk attributable to its foreign equity investment. In those circumstances, the foreign equity investment is retranslated at each balance sheet date and exchange difference arising on the retranslation is recognised in profit or loss to offset the exchange difference arising on the retranslation of the foreign currency borrowings. However, the hedging criteria set out in paragraph 88 of IAS 39 must still be met in order to achieve fair value hedge accounting in the reporting entity's separate financial statements. Whether, in practice, such a parent entity would apply hedge accounting in its separate financial statements may well depend on the tax treatment of undertaking such hedging activities.

Foreign operations in hyper-inflationary economies

7.109 Where a foreign entity operates in a country in which a very high rate of inflation exists and its functional currency is the local currency, the closing rate/ net investment method is not suitable for translating the foreign entity's financial statements for inclusion in the consolidated financial statements. This is because an asset acquired in a currency that is the currency of a hyper-inflationary economy may be worth very little at a time of high inflation, when the foreign currency has weakened considerably against the reporting entity's functional currency, leading to a large debit to consolidated reserves. At the same time, the results of the foreign entity are included at an inflated amount in the consolidated income statement (whether from high interest income on deposits in a rapidly depreciating foreign currency or from trading operations that could be considered to reflect unrealistically high profitability). Therefore, as money loses purchasing power in a hyper-inflationary economy, the reporting of operating results and financial position in the local currency without adjustment to reflect current price levels is misleading.

7.110 When an entity's functional currency is the currency of the hyper-inflationary economy, the entity applies IAS 29. For information on the accounting treatment for entities operating in hyper-inflationary economies, refer to chapter 31.

[The next paragraph is 7.115.]

Presentation and disclosure

General

7.115 The paragraphs that follow deal with IAS 21's disclosure requirements that apply to both individual financial statements and consolidated financial statements. IFRS 7 requires significant additional disclosures about foreign currency transactions and activities. The requirements of IFRS 7 are dealt with in chapter 6.9.

Accounting policies

7.116 There is no specific requirement in IAS 21 to disclose accounting policies in respect of foreign currency transactions. This is because IAS 1 requires disclosure of significant policies that are relevant to an entity's financial statements. [IAS 1 para 108]. In respect of foreign currency transactions, the accounting policy note should state, as a minimum, the methods used in translating foreign currency transactions and the financial statements of foreign operations including those operating in hyper-inflationary economies, and the treatment accorded to exchange differences. The following is an example of a foreign currency accounting policy.

Table 7.1 – Accounting policy for foreign currency

Heineken N.V. – Report and accounts – 31 December 2011

2. Basis of preparation (extract)

(c) Functional and presentation currency

These consolidated financial statements are presented in euro, which is the Company's functional currency. All financial information presented in euro has been rounded to the nearest million unless stated otherwise.

3. Significant accounting policies (extract)

(b) Foreign currency

(i) Foreign currency transactions

Transactions in foreign currencies are translated to the respective functional currencies of HEINEKEN entities at the exchange rates at the dates of the transactions. Monetary assets and liabilities denominated in foreign currencies at the reporting date are retranslated to the functional currency at the exchange rate at that date. The foreign currency gain or loss arising on monetary items is the difference between amortised cost in the functional currency at the beginning of the period, adjusted for effective interest and payments during the period, and the amortised cost in foreign currency translated at the exchange rate at the end of the reporting period.

Non-monetary assets and liabilities denominated in foreign currencies that are measured at fair value are retranslated to the functional currency at the exchange rate at the date that the fair value was determined.

Non-monetary items in a foreign currency that are measured in terms of historical cost are translated using the exchange rate at the date of the transaction. Foreign currency differences arising on retranslation are recognised in profit or loss, except for differences arising on the retranslation of available-for-sale (equity) investments and foreign currency differences arising on the retranslation of a financial liability designated as a hedge of a net investment, which are recognised in other comprehensive income.

Non-monetary assets and liabilities denominated in foreign currencies that are measured at cost remain translated into the functional currency at historical exchange rates.

(ii) Foreign operations

The assets and liabilities of foreign operations, including goodwill and fair value adjustments arising on acquisition, are translated to euro at exchange rates at the reporting date. The income and expenses of foreign operations, excluding foreign operations in hyperinflationary economies, are translated to euro at exchange rates approximating the exchange rates ruling at the dates of the transactions. Group entities, with a functional currency being the currency of a hyperinflationary economy, first restate their financial statements in accordance with IAS 29, Financial Reporting in Hyperinflationary Economies (see 'Reporting in hyperinflationary economies' below). The related income, costs and balance sheet amounts are translated at the foreign exchange rate ruling at the balance sheet date.

Foreign currency differences are recognised in other comprehensive income and are presented within equity in the translation reserve. However, if the operation is a non-wholly-owned subsidiary, then the relevant proportionate share of the translation difference is allocated to the non-controlling interests. When a foreign operation is disposed of such that control, significant influence or joint control is lost, the cumulative amount in the translation reserve related to that foreign operation is reclassified to profit or loss as part of the gain or loss on disposal. When HEINEKEN disposes of only part of its interest in a subsidiary that includes a foreign operation while retaining control, the relevant proportion of the cumulative amount is reattributed to non-controlling interests. When HEINEKEN disposes of only part of its investment in an associate or joint venture that includes a foreign operation while retaining significant influence or joint control, the relevant proportion of the cumulative amount is reclassified to profit or loss.

Foreign exchange gains and losses arising from a monetary item receivable from or payable to a foreign operation, the settlement of which is neither planned nor likely in the foreseeable future, are considered to form part of a net investment in a foreign operation and are recognised in other comprehensive income, and are presented within equity in the translation reserve.

The following exchange rates, for the most important countries in which HEINEKEN has operations, were used while preparing these consolidated financial statements:

In EUR	Year-end		Average	
	2011	2010	2011	2010
BRL	0.4139	0.4509	0.4298	0.4289
GBP	1.1972	1.1618	1.1522	1.1657
MXN	0.0554	0.0604	0.0578	0.0598
NGN	0.0049	0.0050	0.0047	0.0051
PLN	0.2243	0.2516	0.2427	0.2503
RUB	0.0239	0.0245	0.0245	0.0248
USD	0.7729	0.7484	0.7184	0.7543

(iii) Hedge of net investments in foreign operations

When the economy of a country in which we operate is deemed hyperinflationary and the functional currency of a Group entity is the currency of that hyperinflationary economy, the financial statements of such Group entities are adjusted so that they are stated in terms of the measuring unit current at the end of the reporting period. This involves restatement of income and expenses to reflect changes in the general price index from the start of the reporting period and, restatement of non-monetary items in the balance sheet, such as P, P & E to reflect current purchasing power as at the period end using a general price index from the date when they were first recognised. Comparative amounts are not adjusted. Any differences arising were recorded in equity on adoption.

(iv) Hedge of net investments in foreign operations

Foreign currency differences arising on the retranslation of a financial liability designated as a hedge of a net investment in a foreign operation are recognised in other comprehensive income to the extent that the hedge is effective and regardless of whether the net investment is held directly or through an intermediate parent. These differences are presented within equity in the translation reserve. To the extent that the hedge is ineffective, such differences are recognised in profit or loss. When the hedged part of a net investment is disposed of, the relevant amount in the translation reserve is transferred to profit or loss as part of the profit or loss on disposal.

Disclosure

7.117 In respect of exchange differences, IAS 21 requires disclosure of:

■ The amount of exchange differences recognised in profit or loss except for those arising on financial instruments measured at 'fair value through profit or loss' in accordance with IAS 39.

■ Net exchange differences recognised in other comprehensive income and classified in a separate component of equity and a reconciliation of the amount of such exchange differences at the beginning and end of the period.

[IAS 21 para 52].

7.118 The disclosure required above is on an aggregate net basis. The total amount of exchange differences recognised in profit or loss include exchange differences recognised on subsequent settlement and retranslation to closing rate on balances arising on foreign currency transactions. However, the standard is silent as to where in profit or loss they should be included. A cue can be taken from IAS 12, which states that exchange differences arising on foreign deferred tax assets and liabilities may be included as part of the deferred tax expense (income) if that presentation is considered to be the most useful to financial statement users. Therefore:

- Foreign exchange differences arising from trading transactions may be included in the results of operating activities.

- Foreign exchange differences arising from financing may be included as a component of finance cost/income.

7.118.1 The following examples illustrate the disclosure of the recognition of exchange differences in profit or loss and as a separate component in equity.

Table 7.2 – Disclosure of exchange differences recognised in profit or loss			
Associated British Foods plc – Report and accounts – 17 September 2011			
2. Operating costs (extract)			
	Note	2011 £m	2010 £m
OPERATING COSTS ARE STATED AFTER CHARGING/(CREDITING):			
Employee benefits expense	3	1,613	1,497
Amortisation of non-operating intangibles	8	83	81
Amortisation of operating intangibles	8	13	8
Profits less losses on disposal of non-current assets		(5)	9
Depreciation of owned property, plant & equipment	9	317	324
Operating lease payments under property leases		110	95
Operating lease payments for hire of plant & equipment		13	11
Other operating income		(19)	(14)
Research and development expenditure		24	22
Fair value gains on financial assets and liabilities held for trading		(29)	(27)
Fair value losses on financial assets and liabilities held for trading		24	31
Foreign exchange gains on operating activities		(35)	(40)
Foreign exchange losses on operating activities		38	38

4. Interest and other finance income and expense

		2011 £m	2010 £m
FINANCE INCOME			
Interest income on financial assets not at fair value through profit or loss:			
– cash and cash equivalents		9	11
– finance leases		–	1
Total finance income		9	12
FINANCE EXPENSE			
Interest expense on financial liabilities not at fair value through profit or loss:			
– bank loans and overdrafts		(48)	(34)
– all other borrowings		(45)	(46)
– finance leases		(1)	(1)
– other payables		(3)	(3)
– unwinding of discount on provisions		(4)	(4)
Total finance expense		(101)	(88)
OTHER FINANCIAL INCOME			
Expected return on employee benefit scheme assets	12	149	188
Interest charge on employee benefit scheme liabilities	12	(142)	(143)
Net financial income in respect of employee benefit schemes		7	(5)
Net foreign exchange gains/(losses) on financing activities		–	(3)
Total other financial income		7	(8)

Table 7.3 – Disclosure of exchange differences recognised in a separate component of equity

Xstrata plc – Report and accounts – 31 December 2011

US$m	Revaluation reserves	Other reserves	Net unrealised gains (losses)	Foreign currency translation	Total
At 31 December 2009	1,440	1,229	188	2,749	5,606
Gains on available-for-sale financial assets	–	–	118	–	118
Realised losses on available-for-sale financial assets	–	–	(73)	–	(73)
Gains on cash flow hedges	–	–	117	–	117
Realised losses on cash flow hedges*	–	–	(131)		(131)
Foreign currency translation differences	–	–	–	2,459	2,459
Deferred tax	–	–	(9)	(48)	(57)
At 31 December 2010	1,440	1,229	210	5,160	8,039
Gains on available-for-sale financial assets	–	–	37)	–	37)
Realised gains on available-for-sale financial assets	–	–	(8)	–	(8)
Gains on cash flow hedges	–	–	26	–	26
Realised gains on cash flow hedges*	–	–	(51)	–	(51)
Foreign currency translation differences	–	–	–	(1,309)	(1,309)
Deferred tax	–	–	19	2	21
At 31 December 2011	**1,440**	**1,229**	**159**	**3,853**	**6,681**

* Recycled gains of US$59 million (2010 US$115 million) are included in Revenue in the income statement, including non-controlling interests.

Revaluation reserves

This reserve principally records the re-measurement from cost of the 19.9% interest held in Falconbridge Limited (Falconbridge) to the fair value of 19.9% of the identifiable net assets of Falconbridge on 15 August 2006, the date the Group obtained control of Falconbridge.

Other reserves

This reserve principally originated during 2002 from the merger of Xstrata AG into Xstrata plc of US$279 million and the issue of shares from the acquisition of the Duiker and Enex Groups of US$935 million.

Net unrealised gains/(losses) reserve

This reserve records the re-measurement of available-for-sale financial assets to fair value (refer to note 22) and the effective portion of the gain or loss on cash flow hedging contracts (refer to notes 23, 29 and 36). Deferred tax is provided on the re-measurement at tax rates enacted or substantively enacted.

Foreign currency translation reserve

This is used to record exchange differences arising from the translation of the financial statements of foreign subsidiaries. It is also used to record the exchange differences from the translation of quasi equity inter-company loans in foreign operations. On disposal or partial disposal of a foreign entity, the deferred accumulated amount recognised in this reserve is transferred to the income statement.

7.119 The standard permits a reporting entity to present its financial statements in a currency that is different from its functional currency. In this situation, the following should be disclosed:

- The fact that the presentation currency is different from the functional currency.

- The disclosure of the functional currency.

- The reasons for using a different presentation currency.

[IAS 21 para 53].

In these cases the entity provides the foreign currency risk disclosures required by IFRS 7 in reference to its functional currency rather than its presentation currency. The entity's exposure to currencies other than the functional currency will affect its future performance, and the details of these exposures are provided in the financial statements.

Table 7.4 – Presentation currency differs from functional currency

DP World Limited – Report and accounts – 31 December 2011

2 Basis of preparation (extract)

(d) Functional and presentation currency

The functional currency of the Company is UAE Dirhams. Each entity in the Group determines its own functional currency and items included in the financial statements of each entity are measured using that functional currency.

These consolidated financial statements are presented in United States Dollars ("USD"), which in the opinion of management is the most appropriate presentation currency in view of the global presence of the Group. All financial information presented in USD is rounded to the nearest thousand.

UAE Dirham is currently pegged to USD and there are no differences on translation from functional to presentation currency.

7.120 When there is a change in the functional currency of either the reporting entity or a significant foreign operation, that fact and the reason for the change in functional currency is disclosed. [IAS 21 para 54]. As changes in functional currency may be due to a number of reasons, it is not possible to say what disclosure might be required in a particular case. However, it will certainly require a more substantial disclosure than, for example, 'this currency was chosen because it gives the most appropriate presentation'. Table 7.5 below is an example where the entity's functional currency is changed, but the presentation currency has remained the same as the latter was already in dollars. Table 7.5.1 is a situation where both the functional currency of the parent (see para 7.46) and the parent and group's presentation currency (see para 7.82) are changed. The parent accounts under UK GAAP, but the relevant standard, FRS 23, is the same as IAS 21 in all material respects.

Table 7.5 – Change of functional currency

Royal Dutch Shell plc – Report and accounts – 31 December 2005

3 Accounting policies (extract)

Change in functional currency

Following Royal Dutch Shell becoming the parent company of Royal Dutch and Shell Transport on July 20, 2005 and through Royal Dutch and Shell Transport, of the rest of the Shell Group, the Directors have concluded that the most appropriate functional currency of the Company is dollars. This reflects the fact that the majority of the Shell Group's business is influenced by pricing in international commodity markets, with a dollar economic environment. The previous functional currency of the Company was the euro.

On the date of the change of functional currency all assets, liabilities, issued capital and other components of equity and income statement items were translated into dollars at the exchange rate on that date. As a result the cumulative currency translation differences which had arisen up to the date of the change of functional currency were reallocated to other components within equity (refer to Note 13).

As a result of the change in functional currency the Company's functional and presentation currency are now the same.

13 Other reserves (extract)

Cumulative currency translation differences

Cumulative currency translation differences represent the currency differences which arose as a result of translating the financial statements from the Company's previous functional currency of euro to the reporting currency of dollars.

The impact of the change in functional currency was the reallocation at that date of the cumulative currency translation differences of $15 million to issued capital.

Table 7.5.1 – Change of functional and presentation currencies

Smith & Nephew plc – Annual report – 31 December 2006

NOTES TO THE PARENT COMPANY ACCOUNTS (extract)

A. General Information (extract)

Presentation of Financial Information

The Company redenominated its share capital into US Dollars on 23 January 2006 and will retain distributable reserves and declare dividends in US Dollars. Consequently its functional currency became the US Dollar. Financial information for prior periods has been restated from Sterling into US Dollars in accordance with FRS 23. As a result the presentational currency of the Company (i.e. US Dollars) in the restated 2005 accounts is different from the functional currency of the Company.

Share capital and share premium in comparative periods was translated at the rate of exchange on the date of redenomination.

NOTES TO THE GROUP ACCOUNTS (extract)

Presentation of financial information

As the Group's principal assets and operations are in the US and the majority of its operations are conducted in US Dollars, the Group changed its presentational currency from Pounds Sterling to US Dollars with effect from 1 January 2006. The Company redenominated its share capital into US Dollars on 23 January 2006 and will retain distributable reserves and declare dividends in US Dollars. Consequently its functional currency became the US Dollar. This lowers the Group's exposure to currency translation risk on its revenue, profits and equity. Financial information for prior periods has been restated from Pounds Sterling into US Dollars in accordance with IAS 21.

The cumulative translation reserve was set to nil at 1 January 2003 (i.e. the transition date to IFRS). All subsequent movements comprising differences on the retranslation of the opening net assets of non US Dollar subsidiaries and hedging instruments have been charged to the cumulative translation reserve included in "Other Reserves". Share capital and share premium was translated at the rate of exchange on the date of redenomination.

As a result of the above the presentational currency of the Group (i.e. US Dollars) in the restated years of 2005 and 2004 is different from the functional currency of the Company (i.e. Pounds sterling).

In previous years the Group protected its equity, as measured in Sterling, by matching non-Sterling assets with non-Sterling liabilities principally by the use of currency swaps. Exchange movements on both the non-Sterling net assets and the hedging instruments were recorded as movements in "Other Reserves". As hedging was effective up to the date of the change in functional currency, the Group has continued to present these as movements in "Other Reserves" as this hedging is regarded as valid in the comparator years. When presenting comparative periods in US Dollars the retranslation of the net Sterling assets results in the large exchange differences shown in the Statement of Recognised Income and Expense.

Table 7.5.2 – Change of functional and presentation currencies

Sibir Energy plc – Annual report – 31 December 2007

NOTES TO THE COMPANY FINANCIAL STATEMENTS (extract)

1 SIGNIFICANT ACCOUNTING POLICIES (extract)

Foreign currencies

Presentational currency

Given that the functional currency of the Company is now US Dollars, management have elected to present for the first time Company financial statements in US Dollars.

This is a change from prior years when the financial statements were presented in pound sterling in line with the previous functional currency of the Company.

Change in presentational currency

For the 2006 comparative period, assets and liabilities were translated into US Dollars using the closing rate ruling at the 2006 balance sheet date ($/£ 1.9572).

Equity and Share capital items were translated using the historic closing rate applicable on 1 January 2005 and were not re translated at each subsequent balance sheet date. All share capital transactions which were effected after 1 January 2005 were recorded using an exchange rate which prevailed at the date of those transactions.

Resulting exchange differences were reflected as currency translation adjustments and included in the cumulative currency translation reserve.

The applicable exchange rates used for 2005 and 2006 were:

	US Dollar to Pound Sterling Exchange Rate ($/£)		
Date	01/01/2005	31/12/2005	31/12/2006
Av Rate	–	1.8188	1.8369
Closing Rate	1.9212	1.7167	1.9572

NOTES TO THE CONSOLIDATED FINANCIAL STATEMENTS (extract)

2 SUMMARY OF SIGNIFICANT ACCOUNTING POLICIES (extract)

Presentational currency

In the 2006 financial statements, the functional currency of Sibir Energy plc (the Company) was Pound Sterling. Although the Company is domiciled in the UK the Group's operations are based in the Russian Federation. The functional currency of the Group's various entities is either the Russian Rouble or US Dollar. This is due to the direct or indirect linkage of oil and oil product prices to the US Dollar, even when some trades are priced and settled in Roubles. As a result the 2006 financial comparatives together with the 2007 financial statements have been presented in US Dollars ($).

This is a change from prior years and the Group's last published interims when the financial statements were presented in Pound Sterling.

Assets and liabilities were translated into US Dollars using the closing rate at the 2006 balance sheet date. Income, expenses and cashflows recognised in the period were translated at an average US Dollar exchange rate for the period. Resulting exchange differences were reflected as currency translation adjustments and included in the cumulative currency translation reserve.

Equity and share capital items were translated using the historic closing rate applicable on 1 January 2005 and were not re translated at each subsequent balance sheet date. All share capital transactions which were effected after 1 January 2005 were recorded using an exchange rate which prevailed at the date of those transactions.

The applicable exchange rates used for 2006 were:

Period Ended	1 January 2006	31 December 2006
Average	0.5498	0.5444
Closing Rate	0.5825	0.5109

7.121   When an entity presents its financial statements in a currency that is different from its functional currency, it describes the financial statements as complying with International Financial Reporting Standards only if they comply with all the requirements of each applicable standard and each applicable interpretation of those standards including the translation method set out in paragraphs 7.77 and 7.109 above.

Convenience translation

7.122   IAS 21 does not prohibit an entity from providing, as supplementary information, a 'convenience translation'. Such a convenience translation may display financial statements or other financial information (such as five year summaries) in a currency that is not its functional currency or its presentation currency, as convenience to some users. Convenience translations are normally prepared by applying a single exchange rate to all amounts appearing in financial statements presented in the entity's functional or presentation currency. The relationships among amounts in the financial statements do not change. Thus, convenience translation fails to account for the effects of changes in foreign exchange rates and, therefore, does not comply with the translation procedures set out in paragraphs 7.77 above. Therefore, where an entity displays its financial statements or other financial information in a currency that is different from either its functional currency or its presentation currency and the requirements of paragraph 7.121 above are not met, it should:

- Clearly identify the information as supplementary information to distinguish it from the information that complies with International Financial Reporting Standards.

- Disclose the currency in which the supplementary information is displayed.

- Disclose the entity's functional currency and the method of translation used to determine the supplementary information.

[IAS 21 para 57].

Table 7.6 – Disclosure for convenience translation

OJSC RBC – Report and accounts – 31 December 2010

2 Basis of preparation (extract)

(c) Functional and presentation currency

The national currency of the Russian Federation is the Russian Rouble ("RUR"), which is the Group's functional currency and the currency in which these consolidated financial statements are presented. All financial information presented in RUR has been rounded to the nearest million.

(d) Convenience translation

In addition to presenting the consolidated financial statements in RUR, supplementary information in the US Dollars ("USD") has been presented for the convenience of users of the financial statements.

All amounts in the consolidated financial statements, including comparatives, are translated from RUR to USD at the closing exchange rate at 31 December 2010 of RUR 30.4769 to USD 1.

Other matters

Tax effects of all exchange differences

7.123   Gains and losses on foreign currency transactions and exchange differences arising on the translating the results and financial position of an entity (including a foreign operation) into a different currency may have tax effects. IAS 12 applies to these tax effects, and the issues are considered in chapter 13.

Cash flow statements

7.124   Cash flows arising from transactions in foreign currency and cash flows of a foreign subsidiary are translated at the exchange rates between the functional currency and the foreign currency at the dates of the cash flows. IAS 7 applies to foreign currency cash flows, which is addressed in chapter 30.

Chapter 8

Insurance contracts

Insurance contracts

Introduction

8.1 IFRS 4 defines insurance contracts and sets out the accounting requirements that apply to issuers of insurance contracts. IFRS 4 is not restricted to insurance companies but applies to all issuers of insurance contracts. Insurance companies and other financial services entities that issue insurance contracts are usually regulated. The accounting for the insurance contracts that financial service companies issue can be complex and differs from country to country. This chapter does not deal in any detail with the specialised accounting that is required by regulated insurance companies or other financial services companies for the insurance contracts they issue. This chapter focuses on how IFRS 4 may impact other entities that issue contracts that meet the definition of insurance contracts. It should be noted that IFRS 4 and this chapter do not deal with the accounting for insurance contracts from a policyholder's point of view.

Objective

8.2 IFRS 4's objective is to specify the accounting for insurance contracts for any entity that issues such contracts. It includes improvements in accounting and disclosure to identify and explain the amounts in financial statements arising from insurance contracts. IFRS 4 is an interim standard, pending the completion of phase II of the IASB's project on insurance contracts. IFRS 4 was developed with the intention of minimising short-term systems changes. It allows entities to continue to use their existing accounting policies for liabilities arising from insurance contracts as long as the existing policies meet certain minimum requirements set out in IFRS 4. In addition to these minimum requirements to achieve some limited improvements to accounting for insurance contracts, the standard introduces significant disclosures for insurance contracts.

Scope

8.3 IFRS 4 applies to insurance and reinsurance contracts that an entity issues and reinsurance contracts that it holds. The standard deems any entity that issues an insurance contract 'an insurer' whether or not the entity is regarded as an insurance company for legal or regulatory purposes. [IFRS 4 App A]. It also covers financial instruments that any entity issues that have a 'discretionary participation feature'. It does not apply to an entity's other assets and liabilities that do not arise from insurance contracts or financial instruments with discretionary participating features.

8.4 IFRS 4 does not apply in the following situations where, although the transaction meets the definition of an insurance contract, another standard applies:

- Product warranties issued directly by the manufacturer, retailer or dealer (IAS 18 and IAS 37).

- Employee benefit plans and retirement benefit obligations (IFRS 2 and IAS 19).

- Rights or obligations that are contingent on the use of non-financial items (IAS 17, IAS 18 and IAS 38).

- Financial guarantees that are within IAS 39's scope. (See chapter 6 – financial guarantees are not discussed in this chapter.)

- Contingent consideration payable on a business combination (IFRS 3).

[IFRS 4 para 4].

Definition of insurance contracts

8.5 IFRS 4 defines an insurance contract as *"a contract under which one party (the insurer) accepts significant insurance risk from another party (the policyholder) by agreeing to compensate the policyholder if a specified uncertain future event (the insured event) adversely affects the policyholder"*. [IFRS 4 App A]. More guidance on the definition of an insurance contract is given in Appendix B of IFRS 4.

8.6 The definition's key principle is that there should be significant insurance risk arising from an uncertain future event that adversely affects the policyholder. To meet this principle there should be:

- a specified uncertain future event that adversely affects the policyholder;

- the event arises from a scenario with commercial substance and from a pre-existing risk; and

- the additional benefits due if the insured event occurs are significant compared to all other scenarios.

This principle is illustrated in the following examples.

Specified uncertain future event

8.7 Uncertainty (or risk) is the essence of an insurance contract. At least one of the following is uncertain at the inception of an insurance contract:

- whether an insured event will occur;

- when it will occur; or

- how much the insurer will need to pay if it occurs.

Example 1

Entity P owns a portfolio of properties. It outsources its property maintenance and repair on all of these properties to entity S, a property management company, for a five year period for a fixed fee. This fee covers both property management and the cost of repair work. All repairs and maintenance required to maintain the property to an agreed standard based on the condition on inception of the contract are now the responsibility of entity S. The contract covers normal wear and tear and certain other conditions, such as dry rot and damp should they be discovered in the course of any remedial work. Repairs required as a result of external events, such as fire or storm damage, continue to be covered by entity P's property insurance arrangements with a regulated insurance company.

When either the number of services to be performed over a period or the nature of those services is not pre-determined, there can be significant insurance risk. There is uncertainty in the situation above in the following areas:

- whether any particular repairs will be required;

- when any particular repairs will be required; and

- how much any particular repair will cost.

There is a specified uncertain event as it is uncertain whether or when any particular repair will be required and how much it may cost. The significance of the insurance risk for entity S is assessed contract by contract under IFRS 4. Insurance risk may be significant, even though there may be a minimal probability of material losses for entity S arising from all its property management contracts, because a significant loss could arise on any one contract, such as the contract with entity P. If the insurance risk is significant, this contract will be an insurance contract and IFRS 4 will apply.

Example 2

Entity G sells photocopiers to small businesses. The photocopiers require servicing after each 100,000 copies are made and break down from time to time. The photocopiers are sold with a one-year manufacturer's warranty. When selling a photocopier, entity G offers its customers an extended fixed period repair and maintenance contract. Under this extended contract, entity G will perform servicing and repairs to the photocopier as necessary for an annual fixed fee.

There can be significant insurance risk where either the number of services to be performed over the term of a contract or the nature of those services is uncertain. This arises as the issuer of the warranty and the extended contract will be compensating the customer if the photocopier breaks down and these additional breakdowns will adversely affect the photocopier's owner. The potential number and extent of any breakdowns are unknown, so the warranty and the extended contract meet the 'uncertain future event' element of the insurance contract definition.

However, paragraph 4(a) of IFRS 4 specifically scopes out product warranties issued directly by a manufacturer, retailer or dealer. These contracts are warranty contracts that have been issued by entity G, the retailer, and fall outside the IFRS 4's scope.

The scope exclusion would not apply if the same repairs and maintenance were to be provided by a party other than the manufacturer, retailer or dealer (such as an entity specialising in photocopy repairs or a competing retailer).

Significant insurance risk

8.8 The risk must be of insurance. Insurance is defined in IFRS 4 Appendix A as any risk other than financial risk. Financial risk is defined as *"the risk of a possible future change in one or more of a specified interest rate, financial instrument price, index of prices or rates, credit rating or credit index or other variable, provided in the case of a non-financial variable that the variable is not specific to a party to the contract"*. [IFRS 4 App A].

8.9 Contracts can contain both financial and insurance risk; such contracts are not excluded from being insurance contracts as long as the insurance risk is significant. IFRS 4 distinguishes contracts issued by insurance companies that do not contain significant insurance risk and refers to them as 'investment contracts'. Investment contracts are accounted for using IAS 39 or IFRS 9 and IAS 18 rather than IFRS 4, even if legally or for regulatory purposes they are called insurance contracts.

8.10 IFRS 4 does not set a numerical range for the level of insurance risk to be 'significant'. Instead it describes insurance risk as *'significant'* if the occurrence of an insured event could result in the payment of "*significant additional benefits in any scenario, excluding scenarios that lack commercial substance (i.e. have no discernible effect on the economics of the transaction)*". This requires identifying a scenario with commercial substance and considering the cash flows that will be paid in that scenario compared to the cash flows that will be paid in all other scenarios. IFRS 4 states that a scenario with commercial substance in which the insured event occurs can also be one with a low probability.

8.11 The entity first needs to identify a scenario with commercial substance where the insured event occurs. If such a scenario exists, the entity needs to consider whether the cash flows under this are greater in that scenario than in any other scenario (resulting in *'additional benefits'*). Once the entity has established that there is a difference between the cash flows under the two scenarios it will have to determine whether this difference is significant. If the answer to those questions is 'yes', the contract is one of insurance. IFRS 4 gives the following example of where insurance risk is not significant.

> **Example**
>
> A contract requires the issuer to pay C1m if an asset suffers physical damage causing an insignificant economic loss of C1 to the holder. The holder transfers to the insurer the insignificant loss of losing C1. The contract also creates the non-insurance risk that the issuer will need to pay C999,999 if the physical damage occurs. Because the issuer does not accept significant insurance risk from the holder, this contract is not an insurance contract. [IFRS 4 App B24C].

8.12 This situation can be contrasted with a scenario where the amount of the potential loss would be high, but the event has a low probability of occurring. For example, the likelihood of a hurricane devastating a building in London is small, but the payment by the insurer in that case would be a substantial amount and there would not be a similar payment in all other scenarios. This would result in the contract being an insurance contract as the insurance risk is significant.

Adversely affects the policyholder

8.13 A contract may require payment to the policyholder if a specified uncertain event occurs. However, the contract is not insurance unless the event arises from a non-financial variable specific to the policyholder and that event adversely affects the policyholder. Gaming or betting contracts depend on the outcome of a specified uncertain event, often the winner of a race or other sporting event. A gambler is not adversely affected by the outcome of a race prior to placing his bet; gaming or betting contracts are not, therefore, insurance contracts. [IFRS 4 App B19(d)].

8.14 Similarly, contracts that require a payment based on climatic variables (sometimes described as weather derivatives) or on other geological or other physical variables are not insurance contracts. Such contracts do not require an adverse effect on the policyholder as a precondition of payment. The risk transferred arises from a variable that is a non-financial variable not specific to either party of the contract. This is not an insurance contract even if the policyholder uses the contract to mitigate an underlying risk exposure. A weather derivative that is triggered by its 'underlying' pays even if the holder has not suffered any damage from the weather. See further chapter 6.1.

8.15 IFRS 4 does not require the insurance contract to exactly compensate the policyholder for the financial impact of the adverse event. The payment under the insurance contract can be predetermined. The payment can also be in excess of the loss suffered as occurs in 'new-for-old' policies where the insurer pays for the replacement cost of a new asset rather than capping the compensation to the value of the old and damaged asset. [IFRS 4 App B para 13].

Another party

8.16 The definition specifies that the insurer must accept risk from another party. Therefore, the insurer must be a separate entity from the policyholder. Groups may self-insure using a captive insurance subsidiary to provide insurance cover to all of the members of the group. This allows the captive insurer to pool the risks of the members of the group. The pooled risk may enable the captive to insure the pooled risks more cheaply with an insurer (or reinsurer) external to the group. If the captive insurance subsidiary presents separate financial statements, it treats the contracts with the other members of the group as insurance contracts under IFRS 4. The transactions between the captive and the other members of the group are eliminated on consolidation as are all other intra-group transactions. [IAS 27 para 20]. If the captive holds a reinsurance contract with a third party reinsurer, the group is the policyholder in that relationship, therefore, IFRS 4 does not apply.

8.17 IAS 37 applies when a group self-insures and a provision will be recognised if there is an obligation at the balance sheet date. This is discussed further in chapter 21.

Existing accounting policies

8.18 IFRS 4 allows entities to continue with their existing accounting policies for insurance contracts if those policies meet certain minimum criteria in IFRS 4. Therefore, applying IFRS 4 may not have a large impact on recognising and measuring insurance contracts. However, IFRS 4 does require extensive disclosures relating to insurance contracts. These are discussed further below.

8.19 For insurance companies, banks and other financial service companies that issue insurance contracts, their existing accounting policies for insurance contracts will often be determined by regulatory accounting requirements or other local accounting standards. The IFRS 4 permission to continue with these policies (subject to the minimum requirements) results in diversity between insurance companies in how they account for insurance contracts. Where the issuer is not an insurance company, the choice of accounting policies for an insurance contract can be complicated by the lack of specific local GAAP standards. Often local GAAP for insurance contracts is directed to insurance companies and may not be suitable for other entities. IAS 37 scopes out insurance contracts, but where the insurer is not an insurance company, accounting policies modelled on IAS 37 are appropriate.

Recognition

8.20 An insurance obligation arises from a contractual relationship between the insurer and the policyholder. This contract must exist at the balance sheet date in order to recognise an insurance liability – IFRS 4 prohibits the creation of liabilities for potential claims that may arise under future contracts. Liabilities of this type are often called catastrophe or equalisation provisions and are created when a liability is built up over time to be used on the occurrence of a future catastrophic loss covered by current or future contracts. They are prohibited as they do not meet the definition of a liability under the Framework.

Derecognition

8.21 An insurer may only remove an insurance liability from its balance sheet when it is discharged, cancelled or expires. This is consistent with the treatment of financial liabilities under IAS 39 and IFRS 9. Some insurance liabilities, for example claim liabilities, are extinguished by payments made in kind or the provision of services rather than by the payment of a monetary amount.

Example

Entity C provides car breakdown services to customers. Customers pay a fixed fee and entity C undertakes to provide roadside assistance or to tow the car to a nearby garage for repair. Entity C has determined there is significant insurance risk and, therefore, IFRS 4 applies.

In this case entity C discharges its obligation by the provision of either assistance at the roadside or by towing the car rather than paying a monetary amount. [IFRS 4 App B para 6].

Measurement

8.22   IFRS 4 allows insurers to continue to use their local GAAP accounting policies to measure insurance liabilities. However, the amount of the insurance liability is subject to a liability adequacy test. The minimum requirement needed for a liability adequacy test to comply with IFRS 4 is that it should consider current estimates of all contractual cash flows and of related cash flows such as claims handling costs, as well as cash flows resulting from embedded options and guarantees. If the recognised liability is inadequate in the light of the estimated future cash flows, the entire deficiency must be recognised in profit or loss. [IFRS 4 para 16].

8.23   Where local GAAP accounting policies used by the insurer do not specify a liability adequacy test, the insurer should compare the insurance liability's carrying amount (less any related deferred acquisition costs and other insurance related intangible assets) with the provision that would be required if it were measured using IAS 37. If the net carrying amount of the liability is insufficient when compared with the IAS 37 measurement, the insurer increases the liability or reduces the related assets and recognises the difference in profit or loss. [IFRS 4 para 17].

8.24   If an insurer's local GAAP accounting policies meet the requirements of the IFRS 4 liability adequacy test, the local GAAP test is applied at the level of aggregation specified by that local GAAP. If the insurer is required to compare the adequacy of its insurance liabilities with the provision that would be required by IAS 37, this comparison should be done for each portfolio of contracts. A portfolio includes all contracts that are managed together and that are subject to broadly similar risks. [IFRS 4 para 18].

Changes in accounting policy

8.25   Insurers are only allowed to change their existing accounting policies for insurance contracts where the change results in presenting information that is more relevant and no less reliable, or more reliable and no less relevant than before. [IFRS 4 para 22]. The criteria in IAS 8 are used to determine whether a change in policy would result in more relevant or more reliable information. IFRS 4 continues to provide relief to insurers from full compliance with IAS 8 as long as the change moves the insurer closer to meeting those criteria.

8.26 IFRS 4 gives specific guidance on changes in accounting policies in the following areas:

- Current interest rates.

- Continuation of certain existing practices.

- Prudence.

- Future investment margins.

- Shadow accounting.

8.27 The final two bullet points above refer to accounting that is usually specific to insurance companies and so are not discussed further here.

Current interest rates

8.28 Insurers may change their local GAAP accounting policies to re-measure insurance liabilities to reflect current market interest rates. However, the insurer may do this for designated liabilities without applying this policy to all similar liabilities. This provides additional relief from IAS 8. [IFRS 4 para 24].

Continuation of certain existing practices

8.29 Paragraph 25 of IFRS 4 clarifies certain policies that are acceptable as existing local GAAP policies that can continue under IFRS. However, because these policies do not satisfy the more relevant and no less reliable, or more reliable and no less relevant criteria of paragraph 22, they cannot be introduced with a change in accounting policy if the entity did not use that policy prior to adopting IFRS 4. These include:

- Measuring insurance liabilities on an undiscounted basis.

- Measuring contractual rights to future investment management fees at an amount that exceeds their fair value (this criterion is likely to impact mainly insurance companies and is outside the scope of this chapter).

- Using non-uniform accounting policies for insurance contracts of subsidiaries.

Prudence

8.30 Local GAAP accounting policies may result in measuring insurance liabilities including excessive prudence. IFRS 4 does not require insurers to eliminate excessive prudence if that was part of their accounting policies prior to the adoption of IFRS 4. However, it does prohibit changes to accounting policies that introduce additional prudence, if the liabilities are already measured with sufficient levels of prudence.

Distinction between insurance and investment contracts

8.31 As discussed above in paragraph 8.8, insurance contracts must contain significant insurance risk. However, there are circumstances where IAS 39 can apply to elements within an insurance contract and where IFRS 4 can apply to investment contracts. These are discussed below.

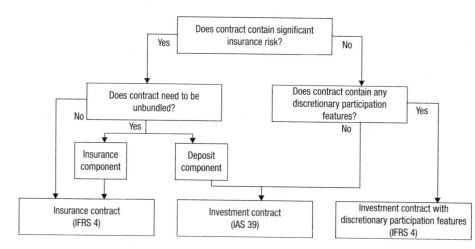

Unbundling insurance contracts

8.32 Some insurance contracts may have a significant deposit component. Paragraph 10 of IFRS 4 sets out criteria when deposit components within insurance contracts should be unbundled as follows:

■ Unbundling is required if:

■ the insurer can measure the deposit component (including any embedded surrender options) separately (that is, without considering the insurance component); and

■ the insurer's accounting policies do not otherwise require it to recognise all obligations and rights arising from the deposit component.

■ Unbundling is permitted (but not required) if the insurer can measure the deposit component separately but its accounting policies require it to recognise all obligations and rights arising from the deposit component, regardless of the basis used to measure those rights and obligations.

■ Unbundling is prohibited if an insurer cannot measure the deposit component separately.

Example

Entity B loans C100,000 to a customer over a period of 10 years. If the customer dies during the period of the loan agreement, the loan's remaining balance will be waived.

The contract between entity B and the customer contains a deposit element (the loan) and an insurance element (waiving the remaining loan balance on death is equivalent to a cash death benefit). Unbundling the deposit component from the insurance contract is required or permitted if the criteria above are met. If the insurance component is not unbundled, the contract is an insurance contract if the insurance component is significant in relation to the whole contract. [IFRS 4 IG example 1 para 1.24].

8.33   The issuer of a contract uses IAS 39 to account for the deposit component when the contract is unbundled into separate deposit and insurance components. It uses local GAAP accounting policies in accordance with IFRS 4 to account for the insurance component. [IFRS 4 para 12].

Discretionary participation features

8.34   IFRS 4 applies to insurance and investment contracts that contain discretionary participation features. These are often called 'with profits' or 'participating' contracts. Discretionary participation features arise where the policyholder has a contractual right to receive additional benefits in excess of guaranteed benefits from the issuer. The additional benefits need to be:

■   Likely to be a significant portion of the total contractual benefits.

■   Contractually at the issuer's discretion regarding their amount or timing.

■   Contractually based on:

■   the performance of a specified pool of contracts or a specified type of contract;

■   realised and/or unrealised investment returns on a specified pool of assets held by the issuer; or

■   the profit or loss of the company, fund or other entity that issues the contract.

[IFRS 4 App A].

8.35   IFRS 4 allows issuers of both insurance and investment contracts containing discretionary participation features to continue with their existing accounting policies. However, some additional requirements apply to such contracts. The issuer has a choice either to treat the whole contract as a liability, or if not, must separate out the guaranteed element and recognise that element as a liability. [IFRS 4 para 34(a)].

8.36   The issuer may recognise the discretionary participation feature (separate from the guaranteed element) as either a liability, a separate component of equity or may split the discretionary participation feature between a liability and equity. IFRS 4 does not stipulate how the issuer should determine the classification of the discretionary participation feature, but does require that this is done consistently. The issuer is restricted to the above choices, either equity, liability or an allocation between the two. It is prohibited from treating the amounts from the discretionary participation feature as an intermediate or mezzanine category that is neither debt nor equity. [IFRS 4 para 34(b)].

8.37   IFRS 4 also specifies how the revenue arising from such contracts and how subsequent changes in the valuation of the guaranteed element and discretionary participation feature should be treated. [IFRS 4 para 34(c)].

8.38   Some further requirements apply to investment contracts with discretionary participation features.

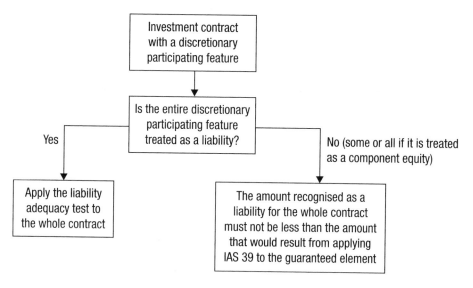

Embedded derivatives

8.39   Insurance contracts can contain embedded derivatives (see further chapter 6.3). IAS 39 applies to embedded derivatives contained in insurance contracts, unless the embedded derivative is itself an insurance contract.

8.40   Payments under an insurance contract can be linked to a price index. This link to a price index can be an embedded derivative, but it may also transfer insurance risk. If the transfer of insurance risk is significant, the embedded derivative will meet the definition of an insurance contract. In this case, the embedded derivative need not be separated and measured at fair value in accordance with IAS 39.

Example

Entity G (who is not the manufacturer, retailer or dealer) offers a repair or replacement service for washing machines and other domestic appliances for a pre-determined fee. If a faulty appliance cannot be repaired, entity G is obliged to make a specified payment to the policyholder for a replacement appliance. This payment is based on a formula that adjusts the appliance's original cost by an inflation index.

The link to the inflation index is an embedded derivative. However, the payment is contingent on an uncertain future event (whether or not the appliance breaks down and needs replacing), which adversely affects the policyholder (by being unable to use the appliance). Therefore, the payment transfers insurance risk and the embedded derivative meets the definition of an insurance contract.

Insurance contracts acquired in a business combination

8.41   Insurance contracts can be transferred as part of a business combination. As with all assets and liabilities acquired in a business combination, the acquirer must measure insurance liabilities assumed and insurance assets so acquired at fair value. The acquirer may (but is not required to) expand the presentation of the insurance liabilities and insurance assets into two components as follows:

- a liability measured in accordance with the insurer's accounting policies for insurance contracts that it issues; and

- an intangible asset, representing the fair value of the contractual insurance rights and obligations acquired to the extent that the liability does not reflect that fair value.

[IFRS 4 para 31].

8.42   The measurement of the intangible asset is consistent with the related liability. The intangible asset is, therefore, excluded from the scope of IAS 36 and IAS 38 and IFRS 4 applies. [IFRS 4 para 33]. However, IAS 36 and IAS 38 will apply to customer lists and customer relationships that are not part of the contractual insurance rights and obligations that existed at the date of the business combination.

Presentation and disclosure

Presentation

8.43   IFRS 4 does not specify how insurance contracts should be presented in the primary statements. Appropriate presentation will depend on the accounting policies the insurer uses under its local GAAP. However, IFRS 4 prohibits the netting of reinsurance amounts against the amounts arising from insurance contracts that are reinsured under those reinsurance contracts. [IFRS 4 para 14(d)].

Disclosure

8.44 One of IFRS 4's objectives is to help users of financial statements understand the impact on the financial statements of amounts arising from insurance contracts. Disclosure is particularly important for information relating to insurance contracts as insurers can continue to use local GAAP accounting policies. The diversity of local GAAP would result in difficulty in comparing the financial performance of insurers without extensive disclosure.

8.45 IFRS 4 has two main principles for disclosure:

- An insurer should disclose information that identifies and explains the amounts in its financial statements arising from insurance contracts. [IFRS 4 para 36].

- An insurer should disclose information that enables users of its financial statements to evaluate the nature and extent of risks arising from insurance contracts. [IFRS 4 para 38].

8.46 The standard expands these principles with implementation guidance. Certain minimal levels of disclosure are included in IFRS 4 supplementing the principles in paragraph 36 and 38. An insurer is required to disclose:

- Its accounting policies for insurance contracts and related assets, liabilities, income and expense.

- The recognised assets, liabilities, income and expense (and if it presents its cash flow statement using the direct method, cash flows) arising from insurance contracts.

- The process used to determine the assumptions that have the greatest effect on the measurement of the recognised amounts described above and, where practicable, quantified disclosures of those assumptions.

- The effect of changes in assumptions used to measure insurance assets and insurance liabilities, showing separately the effect of each change that has a material effect on the financial statements.

- Reconciliations of changes in insurance liabilities, reinsurance assets and, if any, related deferred acquisition costs.

[IFRS 4 para 37].

8.47 An insurer is also required to disclose:

- Its objectives, policies and processes for managing risks arising from insurance contracts and the methods used to manage those risks.

- Information about insurance risk, including information about:

  - sensitivity to insurance risk;

  - concentrations of insurance risk; and

  - actual claims compared with previous estimates.

- Information about credit risk, liquidity risk and market risk that IFRS 7 would require if the insurance contracts were in IFRS 7's scope. However, a maturity analysis is not required if the entity discloses information about estimated timings of the net cash outflows resulting from insurance liabilities.

- Information about exposures to market risk arising from embedded derivatives contained in a host insurance contract if the insurer is not required to, and does not, measure the embedded derivatives at fair value.

[IFRS 4 para 39].

8.48 IFRS 4 has implementation guidance that explains in more detail how an entity may meet the above disclosure requirements. The implementation guidance is aimed at insurance companies and is not discussed further here.

8.49 Table 8.1 shows extracts from the disclosures made by the AA Limited.

Table 8.1 – Insurance disclosures

AA Limited – Annual Report and Financial Statements – 31 December 2006

2 Accounting policies (extract)

Insurance contracts – payables and receivables

Payables and receivables are recognised when they fall due. These include amounts due to and from insurance contract holders to which inward reinsurance contracts have been issued by the Group. At each balance sheet date, liability adequacy tests are performed to ensure the adequacy of the insurance contract liabilities. In performing these tests, current best estimates of future contractual cash flows and claims handling and administration expenses are used. Any deficiency is immediately charged to the income statement by increasing claims accruals.

Revenue recognition

Roadside membership subscriptions and premiums receivable on other insurance products are shown gross of any commission due to intermediaries and are exclusive of insurance premium tax. Premiums are recognised over the period in which the Group is liable for risk cover. The proportion of the premiums written relating to the period of the policy that has not expired at the balance sheet date is shown within deferred income.

Insurance contracts

Insurance contracts are defined as those containing significant insurance risk. Significant insurance risk arises if an insured event could cause an insurer to pay benefits or incur costs at the inception of the contract. Such contracts remain designated as insurance contracts until all rights and obligations are extinguished or expire. Insurance contracts continue to be measured and accounted for under existing accounting practices at the date of transition to IFRS.

Insurance contracts – operating expenses

Commissions and other acquisition costs that vary with, and are related to, securing new and renewing existing insurance contracts are expensed to the income statement at the point they are incurred. Claims incurred comprise claims and related expenses paid in the year and changes in the accruals for outstanding claims, including accruals for claims incurred but not reported and any other adjustments to claims from previous years. Claims incurred include the cost of providing breakdown assistance which is expensed as incurred.

Insurance contracts – claims costs

The estimation of the ultimate liability from claims made under insurance contracts is not considered to be one of the Group's most critical accounting estimates. This is because the principal insurance claims costs for the group relate to the provision of Roadside recovery services. There is a short period of time between the receipt of a claim, i.e. a breakdown, and the settling of that claim. Consequently there are no significant provisions for unsettled claims costs.

33 Insurance Contracts (extract)

The Group's principal insurance contracts are contracts for the provision of Roadside recovery services for a fixed fee, under which insurance risk is assumed by the Group.

Amount, timing and uncertainty of profit and loss and future cashflows

The risk under any one insurance contract is the possibility that the insured event occurs and the uncertainty of the amount of the resulting claim. The nature of the business written by the Group is generally of one year or less in duration, however it is still subject to some unpredictability. The key risks the Group faces are significant fluctuations in the frequency, timing and severity of claims relative to expectations.

The risk and level of service required for Roadside recovery contracts is dependent upon the occurrence of uncertain future events, in particular, the number of breakdowns and the nature of each breakdown. Breakdowns are sensitive to the reliability of cars as well as the impact of weather conditions. The Group employs a patrol force which attends over 90% of all breakdown calls received. In the event that a patrol is unable to attend a breakdown, the Group has built up an extensive network of garages with pre-agreed prices to ensure that all breakdowns are attended on a timely basis. The Group uses historical data and statistical techniques to predict levels of claims and therefore actively manages the size and location of its patrol force. The Group continually invests in its patrol force, for example the introduction of the new Vehicle Recovery System, to improve their efficiency in attending breakdowns. There is no concentration of risk due to the large size of the Group's membership base across the UK and Ireland.

For other insurance contracts, the Group only enters into contracts with insurance risk where it has experience of the market. Claims must be made within a short time of the policy expiring, and most claims are settled within one year. This allows the Group to achieve a high degree of certainty about the estimated cost of claims and therefore future cashflows. The Group manages its insurance risk by constantly monitoring the level of claims for each product and has the ability to adjust prices in the future to reflect any change in claims experience. The Group has a claims handling process which includes the right to review and reject fraudulent claims. There is limited concentration of risk due to the large size of the Group's portfolio.

Income and expenses arising directly from insurance contracts

	2006 £m	2005 £m
Revenue excluding terminated contract	503.5	483.4
Terminated contract*	–	11.0
Revenue – premiums earned	503.5	494.4
Operating expenses		
Claims costs	211.8	252.5
Other expenses	90.5	84.2
	302.3	336.7

* The Group terminated its contract to reinsure a 50% quota share of the Churchill Motor book on 4 May 2004. The impact on operating profit was broadly neutral.

Operating expenses arising directly from insurance contracts primarily relate to breakdown assistance and include employment costs, vehicle depreciation and other operating expenses.

Insurance contracts

Assets and liabilities arising directly from insurance contracts

	2006 £m	2005 £m
Assets		
Receivables arising out of direct insurance operations	26.9	21.1
Prepayments	18.2	14.2
	45.1	35.3

	2006 £m	2005 £m
Liabilities		
Deferred income arising from unearned premiums	250.8	252.5
Claims accruals	51.1	60.4
Other accruals	6.3	5.2
Payables arising out of direct insurance operations	17.6	17.1
Provision for onerous insurance contracts	0.1	0.7
	325.9	335.9

Claims accruals include payables and accruals relating to breakdown assistance expenses.

Reconciliation of movement in insurance liabilities

Deferred income arising from unearned premiums	2006 £m	2005 £m
At 1 January	252.5	262.0
Revenue – premiums earned	(503.5)	(494.4)
Premiums written	501.8	484.9
At 31 December	250.8	252.5

Claims accruals	2006 £m	2005 £m
At 1 January	60.4	59.1
Claims incurred	211.8	252.5
Claims paid	(221.1)	(251.2)
At 31 December	51.1	60.4

Chapter 9

Revenue and construction contracts

Revenue and construction contracts

Introduction

9.1 Revenue is the top line in the income statement and is often considered to be the measure of the size and hence growth of an entity. It is the key variable in a number of calculations and ratios that management and others may consider to be important indicators of its financial performance. Revenue directly impacts the gross margin and operating profit of an entity, as well as the calculation of EPS and a range of non-GAAP measures including EBITDA. As a result, it can be argued that the amount shown as revenue is the single most important item to the users of financial statements.

9.2 The majority of revenue transactions fall within the scope of IAS 18. Linked to this is additional guidance relevant to specific circumstances published by the Interpretations Committee. A specific standard exists in relation to construction contracts – IAS 11. The IAS 11 requirements are addressed from paragraph 9.289.

9.3 It is usually easy to determine whether a transaction falls within the scope of IAS 18 or IAS 11. However, for some transactions, such as certain real estate transactions, the relevant standard may not be obvious. IFRIC 15, clarifies this. This guidance is addressed from paragraph 9.274.

9.3.1 When an entity operates a service concession arrangement that is in the scope of IFRIC 12 it still recognises revenue in accordance with IAS 18 and IAS 11. Chapter 33 covers the related accounting issues, including revenue recognition.

9.4 The FASB and the IASB have issued a joint exposure draft on revenue recognition. The proposal is for a single model for the recognition of revenue that will apply to all contracts with customers.

9.5 Income from government grants is covered by IAS 20. The requirements of IAS 20 are addressed from paragraph 9.350.

Objective and scope of IAS 18

9.6 IAS 18's objective is to provide principles to be applied when accounting for revenue from certain types of transactions and events. The standard distinguishes 'revenue' from 'income' (see para 9.13 below) and sets out criteria to be applied to determine when revenue should be recognised. It also provides detailed guidance on a number of specific transaction types.

9.7 The standard deals only with revenue and not with other forms of income. It sets out criteria to be used in accounting for revenue from:

- The sale of goods.

- The rendering of services.

- Use by others of assets belonging to the entity and giving rise to interest, royalties and dividends.

[IAS 18 para 1].

9.8 The standard excludes from its scope revenue arising from:

- Lease agreements (dealt with by IAS 17).

- Dividends from equity-accounted investments (dealt with by IAS 28).

- Insurance contracts within the scope of IFRS 4 (see further para 9.9).

- Changes in the fair value of financial assets and liabilities or their disposal (dealt with by IAS 39).

- Changes in the fair value of other current assets.

- Initial recognition and changes in the fair value of biological assets related to agricultural activity (dealt with by IAS 41).

- Initial recognition of agricultural produce (also dealt with by IAS 41).

- The extraction of mineral ores.

[IAS 18 para 1].

9.9 Contracts within the scope of IFRS 4 include fixed fee service contracts in which the level of service depends on an uncertain event, but that are not regulated as 'insurance contracts' in some countries. An example is a maintenance contract where the service provider agrees to repair specified equipment when required for a fixed fee. Because it is uncertain whether the machine will break and consequently, whether the service provider will be required to compensate the owner by ensuring that the equipment is repaired, that meets the definition of an insurance contract. [IFRS 4 App B para B6]. Generally, however, IFRS 4 permits such contracts to be accounted for in the same way as if they were accounted for under IAS 18, that is, under the percentage of completion method. [IFRS 4 App B para B7]. The percentage of completion method is discussed in this chapter and, in particular, measurement of the stage of completion (including how this may be applied to maintenance contracts) is discussed from paragraph 9.106.

9.10 Changes in the fair value of investment property are dealt with by IAS 40. IAS 40 refers to IAS 18 in respect of determining the date of disposal of investment property. IAS 40 is dealt with in chapter 17.

9.11 The sale of goods includes goods manufactured for sale by the entity and goods purchased for resale. Services rendered include those provided within a single accounting period and those provided over more than one accounting period. Some contracts for the rendering of services are an element of a construction contract, for example, the services of architects and project managers may be connected to the construction of the related asset. [IAS 18 paras 3, 4]. Such services are accounted for under IAS 11 as addressed from paragraph 9.305.

9.11.1 An increasing number of entities are selling digital versions of products such as books, music and movies. Additionally, some entities are selling entirely new products that exist only in the digital space, for example during an online game a player may buy a virtual sword. It is not always clear whether the sale of non-physical products such as the sword is analogous to the sale of a good or the sale of services. Careful analysis is needed to assess the appropriate pattern of revenue recognition for such products.

9.12 Use by others of an entity's assets in the context of IAS 18 generally relates to financial assets or intangibles, as IAS 17 deals with leasing, which is the most common form of tangible asset use. Charges for the use of financial assets, such as loans in the form of cash or cash equivalents are usually in the form of interest. Charges for the use of intangible assets such as patents, trademarks, copyrights and computer software may be in the form of royalties or licence receipts. Equity investments give rise to revenue in the form of dividends (but note that the standard excludes equity-accounted investments such as associates from its scope). [IAS 18 para 5].

Basic principles

Definition of revenue

9.13 The IASB's Conceptual Framework for the preparation and presentation of financial statements defines 'income' as:

> "...increases in economic benefits during the accounting period in the form of inflows or enhancements of assets or decreases of liabilities that result in increases in equity, other than those relating to contributions from equity participants." [Framework para 4.25(a)].

9.14 Revenue is a subset of income and is defined in IAS 18 as:

> "...the gross inflow of economic benefits during the period arising in the course of the ordinary activities of an entity when those inflows result in increases in equity, other than increases relating to contributions from equity participants." [IAS 18 para 7].

9.15 Both revenue and income exclude contributions from equity participants, which could include subscriptions for share capital and capital contributions.

9.16 'Revenue' includes only economic benefits arising in the ordinary course of an entity's activities, whereas 'income' includes such benefits that arise from all activities whether ordinary or otherwise.

9.17 The Conceptual Framework explains that income encompasses both revenue and gains. Revenue is referred to by various names including sales, fees, interest, dividends, royalties and rent. Gains are other items that meet the definition of income and may or may not arise in the course of the entity's ordinary activities. [Framework paras 4.29, 4.30].

9.18 The reference in the Conceptual Framework to gains being 'other items' suggests that they are not revenue, but the Conceptual Framework notes that such gains may occur, like revenue, in the course of the entity's ordinary activities. The Conceptual Framework gives examples of gains. They include those arising on the disposal of non-current assets, for example, property, plant and equipment or long-term investments. They also include revaluation surpluses arising on revaluation of marketable securities or fixed assets. [Framework para 4.31].

9.19 It is clear that revenue excludes revaluation gains as well as contributions from equity participants and income from non-ordinary activities. Gains from revaluations are not revenue, because the definition of revenue refers to inflows of economic benefits alone as giving rise to revenue. Gains on disposal of tangible fixed assets might be part of an entity's ordinary activities, but often are not revenue. The Conceptual Framework points out: *"When gains are recognised in the income statement, they are usually displayed separately because knowledge of them is useful for the purpose of making economic decisions. Gains are often reported net of related expenses"*. [Framework para 4.31]. The fact that gains may be reported net of related expenses further distinguishes them from revenue. There are also specific requirements, for example, in IAS 1 that ensure that material gains on disposal of fixed assets and other items of an exceptional nature or amount, are disclosed separately from the basic types of revenue.

9.20 Gains from the disposal of fixed assets are not included in revenue as the standard refers to the sale of goods including goods produced by the entity for sale or purchased for resale. Property constructed for sale and held as inventory would therefore be included in the scope, but property held as a fixed asset would not. Paragraph 68 of IAS 16 and paragraph 113 of IAS 38 state that gains arising from the derecognition of non-current assets should not be classified as revenue.

9.21 The distinction between revenue and income is not always clear. Determining whether a transaction should result in the recognition of revenue will depend on the facts surrounding the business and the transaction itself. Consider the following example.

> **Example – Distinction between revenue and income**
>
> A car dealership has demonstration cars available that can be used by potential customers for test drives. The cars are used for more than one year and then sold as used. The dealership sells both new and used cars. Does the sale represent the sale of a fixed asset, as the car was used by the dealership for the purpose of securing sales, or is the sale of the car the sale of an item of inventory resulting in the recording of revenue, as the dealership is in the business of selling new and used cars?
>
> Based upon the circumstances above, the car dealership is in the business of selling new and used cars. As selling used cars is part of the dealership's ordinary revenue generating activities, the sale of the cars would represent revenue.

9.22   It may not be immediately clear whether a transaction should be recorded as revenue or income when an entity sells an asset that it had previously held for rental to third parties or as a display model. This is similar to the example above except that the asset generated direct rental income prior to its sale outside the company. This often occurs in the shipping and automotive industries. The asset is manufactured or acquired with a dual intention in such situations: to rent it out then sell it. The question arises on the asset's sale as to whether any income should be recognised as revenue or, alternatively, as a gain on the asset's disposal.

9.23   The IASB clarified this issue by amending IAS 16 to specify that assets held for rental are to be transferred to inventory at their carrying amount when they become held for sale and that the proceeds from the sale of such assets should be recognised as revenue.

9.24   Similarly, interest receivable may constitute revenue for some entities but not for others. The interest charged by banks on loans made to customers is revenue. The interest represents a gross inflow of economic benefits arising from the bank's ordinary course of business. Interest charged by a manufacturing entity on delinquent customer receivables, for example, is not revenue, if deriving interest income is not part of a manufacturing entity's ordinary activities.

9.25   IAS 18 explains that revenue includes only the economic benefits that are received and receivable by the entity on its own account. It excludes amounts collected by the entity, such as sales taxes, that the entity collects on behalf of a third party. The standard also refers to agency arrangements and states that revenue for an agent excludes amounts that the agent collects on behalf of its principal. The agent's revenue consists of the commission that it earns for carrying out the agency function. Agency arrangements can be complicated and are discussed further from paragraph 9.159.

Distinction between capital and income

9.26   Changes in equity that relate to contributions from or distributions to owners are excluded from the definitions of income and expense. These capital items should, therefore, be excluded from the income statement. [Conceptual Framework para 4.25].

9.27 Contributions from owners are usually in the form of cash, but they may also arise when other assets are transferred into the business or when equity is accepted in satisfaction of a liability. Such transfers of capital amounts are often made by parent companies to their subsidiaries. What constitutes a capital contribution might be difficult to determine in practice. A shareholder transferring an asset to an entity for no consideration is presumed to be acting in its capacity as a shareholder. However, in some circumstances entities might receive assets from shareholders where the shareholder is acting in a different capacity, but where consideration is still not paid. For example, a government that is also a shareholder might award a government grant to an entity. An indicator that they are acting in their capacity of a government rather than as a shareholder could be that a similar grant is awarded to other entities where the government is not a shareholder. On the other hand, entities may receive grants or gifts for no consideration from non-governmental organisations, and in these circumstances the receiving entity may draw an analogy to IAS 20. This would only be appropriate where the gift is genuinely a non-exchange transaction (see para 9.180 for guidance on barter transactions). Further guidance can be found in paragraph 9.350.

9.28 Under IAS 1, capital contributions should be presented in the statement of changes in equity. Such contributions (referred to as equity contributions) are not gains and, therefore, should not be reported in the income statement. The standard states:

> *"Except for changes resulting from transactions with owners acting in their capacity as owners (such as equity contributions, reacquisitions of the entity's own equity instruments and dividends) and transaction costs directly related to such transactions, the overall change in equity during a period represents the total amount of income and expense, including gains and losses, generated by the entity's activities during that period."* [IAS 1 para 109].

An entity receiving a contribution from its owner should consider the transaction's substance and terms under which the contribution is made in order to determine the appropriate treatment. Further guidance is given in chapter 23 and in chapter 6.

Identifying the transaction

9.29 Revenue has a variety of names, such as sales, turnover, fees, interest, dividends, royalties and rents. Many transactions are straightforward, but some can be highly complex. Software arrangements, outsourcing contracts, barter transactions, service contracts, contracts with multiple elements or long-term elements and contracts with milestone payments can be challenging to understand, including what the transaction entails, how much revenue should be recognised and when it should be recorded.

9.30 An entity should look to the substance, not the form, of a transaction to determine when revenue should be recorded. The substance is not based only on the transaction's visible economic effect; it will also have to be analysed based on all the transaction's contractual terms, or the combination of the contractual terms of linked transactions. Contracts, while inherently form-driven, often provide strong evidence of the intent of the parties involved, as parties to a transaction generally protect their interests through the contract. Other factors, such as local legal frameworks and business practices, will need to be taken into consideration as well.

9.31 Understanding a revenue transaction's substance requires more than a high-level knowledge of the business arrangement. It is often a lack of understanding of the details of contracts or of the existence of additional contractual terms, such as side letters or oral agreements, that creates difficulties in assessing revenue recognition. Only once the transaction has been properly understood can the questions of when and how much revenue to recognise be addressed.

Timing of recognition

9.32 IAS 18 distinguishes between revenue from the sale of goods, revenue from the rendering of services and revenue from the use by others of the entity's assets. The principles for recognising revenue for each category are similar and are set out in the following paragraphs.

9.33 For the sale of goods, revenue should be recognised when all the following conditions have been satisfied:

■ The entity has transferred to the buyer the significant risks and rewards of ownership of the goods (see para 9.59).

■ The entity does not retain either continuing managerial involvement to the degree usually associated with ownership or effective control over the goods sold (see para 9.81).

■ The amount of revenue can be measured reliably (see para 9.40).

■ It is probable that the economic benefits associated with the transaction will flow to the entity (see para 9.49).

■ The costs incurred or to be incurred in respect of the sale can be measured reliably (see para 9.43).

[IAS 18 para 14].

9.34 When the outcome of transactions involving the rendering of services can be estimated reliably, revenue should be recognised by reference to the transaction's stage of completion at the balance sheet date. The transaction's outcome can be estimated reliably when all the following conditions are satisfied:

■ The amount of revenue can be measured reliably (see para 9.40).

- It is probable that the economic benefits associated with the transaction will flow to the entity (see para 9.49).

- The transaction's stage of completion at the balance sheet date can be measured reliably (see para 9.106).

- The costs incurred and the costs to complete the transaction can be measured reliably (see para 9.43).

[IAS 18 para 20].

9.35 Revenue arising from the use by others of the entity's assets yielding interest, royalties and dividends should be recognised when:

- It is probable that the economic benefits associated with the transaction will flow to the entity (see para 9.49).

- The amount of the revenue can be measured reliably (see para 9.40).

[IAS 18 para 29].

9.36 The following conditions are common to the sale of goods, rendering of services and the recognition of interest, royalties and dividends:

- Reliable measurement of consideration.

- Probability that the economic benefits from the transaction will flow to the entity.

9.37 Reliable measurement of the costs incurred or to be incurred is common to the sale of goods and rendering of services.

9.38 In addition to the recognition criteria above, a signed contract should normally be in place between the vendor and the customer to support the recognition of revenue. This is because the contract drives key issues such as measurement of consideration, and the probability of economic benefits flowing to the vendor. However, in some cases it may be possible to recognise revenue before the sales contract has been signed if all key terms and conditions are agreed upon by both parties, for example where a master agreement is in place and criteria in paragraph 14 of IAS 18 have been satisfied. Before recognising revenue in such a situation, the entity should consider the likelihood of the contract being amended before it is signed. If the content of any potential amendments is unknown, it becomes difficult to establish whether the recognition criteria have been met. This may be the case even if certain elements of the contract appear to have already been delivered as, without knowing all obligations under the contract, it will not be possible to allocate the appropriate amount of revenue to the elements already performed or to know if delivered items might be returned.

9.39 The three conditions highlighted in paragraphs 9.36 and 9.37 above that are common to both the sale of goods and the rendering of services are discussed in more detail below. Conditions specific to the sale of goods are discussed from paragraph 9.57 onwards and condition specific to the sale of services are discussed from paragraph 9.106 onwards.

Reliable estimate of revenue

9.40   IAS 18 discusses the conditions necessary for a reliable estimate to be made of revenue for the rendering of services, but the three conditions below, suitably adapted, are equally valid for the sale of goods and use by others of the entity's assets. The standard states that the entity should have agreed the following with the other party for the sale of services:

■   Each party's enforceable rights relating to the services to be provided under the contract.

■   The consideration payable and receivable.

■   The manner and terms of settlement.

[IAS 18 para 23].

9.41   To make reliable estimates the entity should normally have an effective system of internal budgeting and reporting. Estimates should be reviewed and, where necessary, revised as the contract for services is performed. However, such revisions do not necessarily indicate that the outcome of the contract cannot be reliably measured. [IAS 18 para 23].

9.42   The seller must also be able to reliably estimate any discounts or rebates offered in conjunction with the product to determine the revenue to be recognised for the sale of goods (see paras 9.84 and 9.85).

Reliable measurement of costs

9.43   Costs incurred for the sale of goods produced by the entity are generally the manufacturing costs, which are calculated in accordance with IAS 2 (see chapter 20). Where goods are purchased for resale the costs generally comprise all costs of purchase. Measurement of each of these types of cost is usually relatively straightforward for an established business that is offering an existing product. It can be more difficult for a new business or an entity selling a new product. Costs such as those associated with setting up internal systems and processes and other start-up costs, must be segregated from the cost of the products to be manufactured. When a new business starts selling products or when an entity offers a new product, estimating the costs associated with returns or warranties (see para 9.84) can be difficult, because there might be no experience upon which to estimate return rates and warranty costs.

9.44   Estimating the cost of providing services may prove challenging in some circumstances, especially where the contract for services spans several accounting periods. Determining the costs incurred to date can be relatively straightforward, but determining the future costs to be incurred in the transaction is subject to uncertainty. Given the difficulty inherent in such judgement, management should consider the need to disclose the judgements made as a key source of estimation uncertainty in the financial statements in accordance with paragraph 125 of IAS 1.

9.45 The standard also states that when the expenses cannot be measured reliably, revenue cannot be recognised and any consideration received should be recognised as a liability. [IAS 18 para 19].

9.46 Paragraphs 9.106 onwards set out the requirements for determining the stage of completion of a contract for services. IAS 18 paragraph 23 states that it is usually necessary for an entity to have an effective budgeting system and that an entity should review the estimates used periodically.

9.47 Pre-contract costs in relation to service contracts and construction contracts are addressed from paragraph 9.264.

9.48 Cost recognition is considered further from paragraph 9.305.

Probability that economic benefits will flow to the entity

9.49 One of the conditions for revenue recognition is that it is probable that the economic benefits relating to the transaction will flow to the entity. In some situations, it may not be probable that the economic benefits will flow to the entity until the consideration is received by the entity or until an uncertainty is removed. An example of the latter is where there is uncertainty as to whether a foreign government will grant permission for the proceeds of a sale in the foreign country to be remitted. When the permission is granted, the uncertainty is removed and the revenue may be recognised. [IAS 18 para 18]. Another example might be where the receipt of consideration is dependent on whether the buyer can obtain funding, in which case recognition of the sale would be delayed until that uncertainty was removed.

9.50 Where uncertainty arises about the collectability of an amount that has already been included in revenue, any provision required as a result of that uncertainty is recognised as an expense and not as a reduction of revenue. [IAS 18 paras 18, 22, 34]. The following example demonstrates the distinction between uncertainty at the time of sale and uncertainty arising subsequent to the sale.

> **Example – Timing of an uncertainty arising**
>
> Entity A has an existing manufacturing customer, entity B, who has recently announced that it expects to have to restructure its debts with current creditors, including entity A, in order to ensure sufficient operating liquidity to avoid bankruptcy. Subsequent to the announcement, entity A ships an order of replacement parts to entity B based on a purchase order received from entity B prior to the announcement.
>
> Entity A should not recognise revenue for the latest shipment to entity B, as it is not probable that the economic benefit related to the products shipped will flow to the entity. Entity A may record revenue when entity B pays for the shipment of

replacement parts, which is when it becomes probable that the economic benefit will flow to entity A and when the amount of revenue can be measured reliably.

In contrast, any allowance recorded against any existing receivable balance as a result of entity B's announcement of its need to restructure debts should be recorded as an expense, not as a reversal of revenue.

Measurement of revenue

9.51 The principle set out in IAS 18 is that revenue should be measured at the fair value of the consideration received or receivable. [IAS 18 para 9].

9.52 The concept of fair value is used in the standard's measurement guidance. The definition of fair value is similar to that used in other standards. The definition is *"the amount for which an asset could be exchanged, or a liability settled, between knowledgeable, willing parties in an arm's length transaction"*. [IAS 18 para 7]. Further detailed discussion of fair value can be found in chapter 5, which covers IFRS 13.

9.53 The fair value is generally the amount receivable where goods are sold or services provided in return for consideration in the form of cash or cash equivalents (as defined in IAS 7) receivable at the time of the transaction. However, even then the following factors, and perhaps others, would require consideration in determining the revenue to be recognised:

■ Whether a principal/agency arrangement exists. If an entity is acting as an agent in a relationship, revenue should only be recognised to the extent that it represents payment for acting as an agent (see further from para 9.159).

■ The existence of trade discounts, volume rebates and other incentives (such as cash settlement discounts) should be taken into account in measuring the fair value of the consideration received or receivable. [IAS 18 para 10].

■ Whether the transaction forms part of a multiple element transaction. When there are multiple elements, the arrangement consideration should be allocated to each separable element of the transaction (see further from para 9.131).

9.54 If there is a significant lag between when the good or services are provided and the consideration is received the time value of money should also be taken into account. That is, deferred payments might indicate that there is both a sale and a financing transaction. If there is a financing element it is necessary to discount the consideration to present value in order to arrive at fair value. IAS 18 requires that the rate of discount should be whichever of the following is the more clearly determinable:

■ the prevailing rate for a similar instrument of an issuer with a similar credit rating; or

■ a rate of interest that discounts the nominal amount of the instrument to the current cash sales price of the goods or services.

[IAS 18 para 11].

This is demonstrated in the following example:

> **Example – Sale on extended credit**
>
> An entity sells goods on extended credit. The goods are sold for C1,200, on 1 January 20X1, receivable on 1 January 20X3. The customer can borrow at 4.5% a year.
>
> Management should determine the fair value of revenue by calculating the present value of the cash flows receivable.
>
> On the transaction date, revenue of C1,099 is recorded, being C1,200 discounted for 2 years. The discounted receivable should be updated at each balance sheet date to reflect the passage of time. The resulting increase in the receivable represents interest income that should be recognised over the period from the date of sale to the expected date of receipt of cash.

9.55 Entities will often sell the same type of goods on a cash or a credit basis. The cash price equivalent will normally be the more readily determinable indicator of fair value in such situations. The difference between the discounted amount (that is, the fair value of the deferred cash payment) and the nominal amount is treated as interest income and accounted for in accordance with the requirements of IAS 18 (and IAS 39).

9.56 The measurement of revenue can be further complicated in barter transactions, when goods or services are exchanged for other goods or services. Barter transactions are considered from paragraph 9.180.

Sale of goods

9.57 The principles set out in paragraph 9.33 provide sufficient guidance to account for most revenue transactions. For example, a contract for the sale of goods will normally give rise to revenue recognition when all the criteria above have been satisfied, which is usually when delivery of the goods to the customer takes place. If payment from a customer is received in advance (or in arrears) of the transfer of goods, the entity will defer revenue as a liability (or record an accrued income asset) on the balance sheet until the recognition criteria have been met.

[The next paragraph is 9.59]

Transfer of significant risks and rewards of ownership

9.59 The transfer of the significant risks and rewards of ownership of goods usually occurs when legal title or possession is transferred to the buyer. [IAS 18 para 15]. IAS 18 notes that in some circumstances the transfer of the significant risks and rewards of ownership may occur before or after delivery. The timing of the transfer will depend on the contract's specific terms and conditions.

9.60 Examples of such situations where the transfer of significant risks and rewards has not taken place include:

■ When the entity retains an obligation for unsatisfactory performance not covered by normal warranty provisions. An example is where an entity supplies a new type of machine and guarantees that it will achieve a certain level of output or a refund will be given and it is uncertain whether the required level of output will be achieved.

■ When the receipt of the revenue from the sale is contingent on the buyer deriving revenue from its sale of the goods. An example is a sale to a distributor where payment is due only if the distributor sells on the goods to a third party (see para 9.80).

■ When the goods are shipped subject to installation and such installation is a significant part of the contract that has yet to be completed by the entity (see also para 9.89). An example is the supply of a turnkey project where the seller is responsible for installing and making sure that the equipment is working to the customer's satisfaction.

■ When the buyer has the right to rescind the purchase for a reason specified in the sales contract and the entity is uncertain as to whether or not that right will be exercised and the goods returned. An example is goods supplied on a sale or return basis (see para 9.75).

[IAS 18 para 16].

9.61 The timing of transfer of the risks and rewards of ownership can be affected if the vendor enters into insurance arrangements during delivery. This is illustrated by the following example. See also the discussion in paragraph 9.93.

> **Example – Goods insured during delivery**
>
> Entity A manufactures and sells transformers. The transformers are shipped to the buyer by sea, but in order to transfer risk related to the shipment of the transformers, entity A purchases insurance coverage for the goods while they are in transit from the factory to the buyer's premises. The insurance policy reimburses the seller for the full market value of the goods in the event of loss or damage from the point when the goods depart from the factory to the point when the goods arrive at the buyer's premises. The legal title passes when the goods arrive at the buyer's premises one month later.
>
> The seller should recognise revenue for the sale when the goods arrive at the buyer's premises. The seller has not transferred the transformers' significant risks and rewards of ownership to the buyer when the goods depart from the factory as evidenced by the fact that any insurance proceeds received from the goods' damage or destruction will be repaid to the seller. Also, legal title does not pass until the goods arrive at the buyer's location. The criteria above for revenue recognition have, therefore, not been met until the goods arrive at the buyer's location.

9.62 If, however, an entity retains only insignificant risks and rewards of ownership, a sale has occurred and revenue is recognised. The standard notes that, in some situations, a seller might retain legal title solely to protect the collectability of the amount due. [IAS 18 para 17]. In fact, retention of legal title is no guarantee of collectability and the retention of title in such circumstances is normally only to ensure that the seller has a claim in the – usually unlikely – event that the buyer becomes insolvent. Whilst in general retention of legal title may well bring in to question whether the significant risks and rewards of ownership have passed, in these narrow circumstances such a clause would not normally affect revenue recognition by the seller as the significant risks and rewards of ownership have been transferred to the buyer.

> **Example – Retention of legal title**
>
> Entity A operates in a country where it is commonplace to retain title to goods sold as protection against non-payment by a buyer. The retention of title will enable entity A to recover the goods if the buyer defaults on payment.
>
> Subsequent to the delivery of the goods to the buyer (entity B), entity A does not have any control over the goods. Entity B makes payments in accordance with the normal credit terms provided by entity A. Product liability is assumed by entity B. Settlement is due 14 days after delivery.
>
> Entity A has sold the goods to entity B. The buyer controls the goods following the delivery and is free to use or dispose of them as it wishes. The most significant risk of ownership, the product risk, has been transferred to entity B. Entity A's retention of legal title does not affect the substance of the transaction, which is the sale of goods from entity A to entity B. Entity A should, therefore, derecognise the inventory and recognise the revenue from the sale.

UK.9.62.1 Retention of title clauses in contracts are often known in the UK as Romalpa clauses. These are addressed in more detail in chapter 20 on inventory.

9.63 Other potential indicators that the risks and rewards of ownership have not passed are:

- The seller retains the risk of physical damage to the product.

- The buyer lacks economic substance apart from that provided by the seller.

- There is significant doubt as to the buyer's intention or ability to take delivery of goods.

- The seller shares in the future revenue of the goods' onward sale (when this is not contingent consideration).

- The seller has a repurchase option at a fixed price.

9.64 The inclusion of any of the above conditions in a sale agreement may indicate that the risks and rewards of ownership have not passed and, hence, preclude revenue recognition.

Bill and hold sales

9.65 Bill and hold (lay away) sales occur where a customer obtains title to goods, but requests that the goods are held by the supplier until the customer requests delivery or collects the goods.

9.66 Normally, revenue on sale of goods is only recognised when all performance conditions have been satisfied, including delivery of the goods to the customer.

9.67 The issue, therefore, arises as to whether, in the absence of delivery, revenue can be recognised in a bill and hold sale or whether inventory should continue to be recognised.

9.68 Revenue recognition depends on whether there has been substantive performance under the contract. Normally, for example, a customer might make an order for goods and then take delivery. This contract is executory and revenue would be recognised when the product is delivered.

9.69 Clearly, it would not reflect the arrangement's substance to advance revenue recognition in the above situation. A key factor to consider is inventory risk. If the seller retains the risk of damage to inventory, it would not be appropriate to recognise the sale. The Appendix to IAS 18 lists some specific conditions that distinguish bill and hold sales from executory contracts. These conditions are that the buyer must have requested the delay in delivery and:

- The buyer must have taken title to the goods and accepted billing.

- It must be probable that delivery will take place.

- The goods must be on hand, identified and be ready for delivery to the buyer at the time the sale is recognised.

- The buyer must specifically acknowledge the deferred delivery instructions.

- The usual payment terms must apply.

[IAS 18 App para 1].

9.70 Revenue is not recognised when there is simply an intention to acquire or manufacture the goods in time for delayed delivery. [IAS 18 App para 1].

UK.9.70.1 As noted above, the goods must be on hand, identified and be ready for delivery. The UK's Application note G to FRS 5 has similar requirements, but emphasises the point that the seller may not use the goods to satisfy other orders. This is implicit in the third bullet point, but is more clearly stated in Application note G, which says *"the goods should be identified* *separately from the seller's other stock and should not be capable of being used to fill other orders that are received between the date of the bill and hold sale and shipment of the goods to the customer".* [FRS 5 App G para G46].

9.71　The reason the goods need to be separately identified from the seller's other inventories is as follows; the passing of economic benefits and risks occurs on delivery in a normal sales contract, when specific goods are appropriated to the contract and passed to the customer. The goods are not specific until then if the goods are of a general sort manufactured by the seller. The seller can still sell inventories that are allocated to the customer and substitute similar items when it comes time for delivery. Only if the goods are separately identified and unable to be used to fill other orders can the customer have secured the inventory's economic benefits on passing of title. Separately identified would include (but would not be confined to) inventories that are so specific to the customer that they are unable to be replaced from the seller's other general inventories.

9.72　Where the conditions listed above are satisfied and the inventory is considered to be the customer's asset, the seller should recognise revenue. Where any of the conditions are not satisfied, the inventory will continue to be the seller's asset and retained on its balance sheet. Any amounts received from the customer should be included as deferred revenue as they represent the seller's liability to fulfil its contractual obligations.

Example – Bill and hold sales

Entity A entered into a contract during 20X6 to supply video game consoles to customer B. The contract is for 100,000 game consoles at C50 each. The contract contains specific instructions from customer B with regard to the timing and location of the delivery. Entity A must deliver the consoles to customer B in 20X7 at a date to be specified by the customer. Usual payment terms apply.

At its year end of 31 December 20X6, entity A has inventory of 120,000 game consoles, including the 100,000 relating to the contract with customer B. However, entity A cannot use the 100,000 game consoles to satisfy other sales orders and at 31 December 20X6 title to the 100,000 consoles has passed to customer B. Delivery is expected to take place in 20X7. When should entity A recognise revenue?

Considering the criteria in IAS 18 for recognition of revenue in a bill and hold sale at 31 December 20X6:

- Delivery has been delayed at the buyer's request. – Yes, customer B has specified delivery in 20X7 in the contract.

- The buyer has taken title. – Yes.

- It is probable that delivery will be made. – Yes.

- The item is on hand, identified and ready for delivery and cannot be used to satisfy other orders. – Yes.

- The buyer specifically acknowledges in writing the deferred delivery instructions. – Yes, this is acknowledged in the contract.

- The seller's usual payment terms apply. – Yes.

Therefore, the conditions for revenue recognition have been met in the year to 31 December 20X6 and entity A can recognise 100,000 game consoles as sold.

Payments in advance of sale of goods

9.73   Payments received in advance of performance do not represent revenue, because they have not been earned. Until the selling entity completes its contractual performance, the increase in cash is matched by an increase in liabilities.

Example – Non-refundable deposit

An entity manufactures and supplies reproduction furniture. Since the choice of the final colouring and polishing of the furniture is left to the customer, the entity takes a large non-refundable deposit from the customer at the time of the initial order. In some situations, the piece ordered is in inventory and only needs finishing before it can be shipped to the customer, in other cases the item needs to be completely manufactured.

At first sight, it might appear as though there are different points along the production process at which revenue could potentially be recognised, when the deposit is received provided the item only needs finishing, or only when the goods have been shipped to the customer and the invoice has been raised.

However, revenue must not be recognised when there is simply an intention to acquire or manufacture the goods in time for delivery regardless of whether payment has been received. Revenue is not earned until the manufacturing process is complete, including the finishing, the goods have been delivered (if not bill and hold or lay away sales) and all significant risks and rewards have been transferred. See further paragraph 9.60 above.

9.74   The appendix to IAS 18 considers the situation where goods are delivered only when the buyer makes the final payment in a series of instalments, sometimes referred to as 'lay away' sales. Revenue from such sales is recognised when the goods are delivered as the supplier, in general, is not certain of the flow of economic benefit. Where experience indicates that the vast majority of such sales are completed, revenue may be recognised when a significant deposit is received, provided that the goods are on hand, identified and ready for delivery to the buyer. [IAS 18 App para 3]. One further condition that we consider should be met before revenue can be recognised is that the seller must not be able to dispose of the goods to any party other than that buyer, unless the buyer defaults.

Example – Partial down payment for sale of goods

Entity A enters into a sale agreement to sell 10 television sets at a total price of C15,000 (C1,500 per television) to a customer. Entity A has only five televisions in inventory and sets them aside in its inventory. Entity A collects a cash deposit of C1,000 from the customer. The television sets are not released to the customer until the full purchase price is paid. The customer has to finalise the purchase in three months or it forfeits the cash deposit. Entity A must either refund the cash deposit to the customer or provide a replacement product if the television sets are damaged or lost prior to delivery. When should revenue be recognised?

Entity A retains the risk of ownership of the television sets held in inventory until they are delivered to the customer. Also, entity A does not have an enforceable right to the remainder of the purchase price prior to delivery as only the cash deposit is forfeited if the purchase is not finalised. Furthermore, not all the goods are on hand, identified and ready for delivery and there is no restriction on entity A selling the goods to another party.

Therefore, entity A should recognise C15,000 as revenue only when the 10 television sets are delivered to the customer or when all 10 are set aside and all other criteria are met. The cash deposit should be recognised as a liability up to that point or the point at which the buyer fails to finalise the purchase contract and forfeits the deposit.

Goods shipped subject to conditions (sale or return/consignment)

9.75 Some contracts may give the customer the right to return goods they have purchased and obtain a refund or release from the obligation to pay. This occurs more often than in the obvious example where goods are held on a sale or return basis. For example, retailers often have a policy of giving refunds on returned goods, whether or not the goods are defective. Rights of returns can be explicit or implicit and can also arise through statutory requirements.

9.76 In some situations, the entity may expect few returns and that the level of returns can be reliably estimated. An example is where a retailer sells goods, but offers to refund the purchase price if the customer is not satisfied. In such a situation, revenue is normally recognised in full and a provision is made against revenue for the expected level of returns, provided that the seller can reliably estimate the level of returns based on an established historical record and other relevant evidence. [IAS 18 para 17].

9.77 Although technically the seller has retained some of the risks and rewards in each of the above situations, the significant risks and rewards of the sales, taken as a whole, have passed in the situation where there will be few returns and the level of returns can be reliably estimated.

9.78 Where the entity can estimate the level of returns reliably, the liability recognised for expected returns will be measured in accordance with IAS 37. The liability is not a financial liability as the contract for return is executory and no cash will be paid unless the goods are returned. The liability should be measured at the best estimate of the expenditure necessary to settle the obligation. [IAS 37 para 36]. The entity has an accounting policy choice as to whether it adjusts revenue for the value of expected returns or whether it adjusts both revenue for the expected value of returns and cost of sales for the value of corresponding goods expected to be returned. The result of this second approach is that the provision for returns is measured as the margin on the sale. Where an adjustment is made to cost of sales, the value of the return goods may be their original cost. However, if a reliable measurement of net realisable value is available and this is lower than the original cost of the goods, net realisable value should be used when determining the liability to be recognised. In assessing the value of the returned goods, management will need to consider whether the returned goods will be impaired for damage or obsolescence.

Example – Expected level of returns

A clothing retailer sells T-shirts. Customers have the right to return T-shirts within 28 days of purchase, provided that the T-shirts are unworn and undamaged. The retailer has sufficient history to reliably estimate the level of T-shirts that will be returned.

Because the retailer can reliably measure the level of returns, revenue should be recognised when the sale is made and adjusted for the expected level of returns. Thus, for each T-shirt sold, a portion of the consideration will be recognised as revenue with the remaining portion being recognised as a provision. It would also be appropriate, if the retailer has made this accounting policy choice, to adjust cost of sales recognised on each sale to reflect the impact of returned goods, with the reduction in inventory partially offsetting the provision for returns. This adjustment reflects the impact of the returned goods in measuring the provision in accordance with IAS 37.

9.79 When goods are returned, an adjustment for the value of the goods is made to the provision, inventory and cash. The entity will need to assess whether the goods are impaired on return. Any remaining provision can be released to revenue when the period for returning goods has passed or the entity has assessed that it is probable that there will not be any further returns. If the original estimate of the provision is too low, returns may continue to be received once the provision has been written back in full. In such a situation, the returned goods would be accounted for as a debit to revenue and credit cash (or deferred income if the refund takes the form of store credit). This is considered in more detail in paragraph 9.215 below.

9.80 IAS 18 states that if there is uncertainty about the possibility of return (and if there are issues relating to the reliability of measurement), revenue is recognised when the shipment has been formally accepted by the buyer or the goods have been delivered and the time period for rejection has expired. [IAS 18 App para 2(b)]. Revenue is not recognised on consignment sales or items shipped on a sale or return basis until performance has taken place. If the purchaser of goods on consignment has undertaken to sell the items on the seller's behalf, then revenue should not be recognised by the seller until the goods are sold to a third party. [IAS 18 App para 2(c)]. This recognition point is the same for goods sold on a sale or return basis or sales to distributors or dealers where the purchaser is acting as an agent for the seller. [IAS 18 App para 6].

Example – Sale with a right of return

An entity imports sports clothing and has a number of distributors. It gives its distributors an extended credit deal whereby it supplies new fashion items worth C10,000 to each distributor for sale to third parties to encourage a market in these items. The distributor does not have to pay for the goods until the goods are sold to a third party. If they are not sold within six months of receipt, the distributor can either return them to the entity or pay for them and keep them.

Revenue should not be recognised by the entity until the earlier of the distributor receiving payment for the sale of the goods to a third party or six months after the distributor receives them, provided that they are not returned. Only then can the entity determine whether performance under the sales contract has occurred and the risks and rewards of ownership have passed to the distributor, because until then the goods may be returned. The goods should continue be treated as the entity's inventory until they are sold.

Continuing managerial involvement

9.81 One of the conditions for revenue recognition is that *"the entity retains neither continuing managerial involvement to the degree usually associated with ownership nor effective control over the goods sold"*. [IAS 18 para 14]. The concept of control is relatively straightforward, since the definition of an asset in the Conceptual Framework is: *"...a resource controlled by the entity as a result of past events and from which future economic benefits are expected to flow to the entity"*. [Conceptual Framework para 4.4]. It follows that if the entity retains effective control over the goods sold, the transaction is not a sale and revenue is not recognised.

9.82 *"Continuing managerial involvement to the degree usually associated with ownership"* is less straightforward, although it is highly unlikely that an entity would retain such involvement without retaining the risks and rewards associated with the asset. Nor is it likely that a buyer would accept continuing involvement where it had acquired the asset for fair consideration. Commercially, continuing involvement to the degree envisaged would not normally occur where a genuine sale has taken place. If it does, it is likely that there are other features of the arrangement that need to be considered.

9.83 Indicators of continuing managerial involvement or retention of effective control might include:

- The seller can control the future onward sale price of the item.

- The seller is responsible for the management of the goods subsequent to the sale (outside of any other separable contract for management services).

- The economics of the transaction make it likely that the buyer will return the goods to the seller.

- The seller guarantees the return of the buyer's investment or a return on that investment for a significant period.

■   The seller has control over the re-sale of the item to third parties (for example, the seller can control the selling price, timing or counterparty of any re-sale transaction or, alternatively, re-sale is entirely prohibited).

Example – Ongoing involvement

Entity A sells a racehorse to entity B. As part of the arrangement entity A continues to house and train the horse, determine which races the horse will enter and set stud fees for the horse. Should entity A recognise revenue on the sale of the horse to entity B?

If a proper training agreement is in place that provides a market fee for the services that entity A provides and any winnings or fees achieved by the horse going to the buyer, it may be appropriate to recognise revenue on the sale. However, it would also be necessary to consider whether entity A had given any guarantees or incurred other obligations that may indicate it had not disposed of the significant risks and rewards of ownership of the horse.

Warranties

9.84   A warranty is often provided in conjunction with the sale of goods. Warranties represent guarantees made by the seller that a product will perform as specified for a period of time. Warranties should not be confused with general rights of return. A warranty only permits a customer to return or exchange a product if the product does not meet the specified performance criteria. Warranty costs represent additional costs that the seller may have to incur in relation to the product it has sold.

9.85   When an entity sells a product subject to warranty, it must first determine whether the warranty represents a separable component of the transaction. (Multiple element arrangements are considered further from para 9.131.)

Initial warranty

9.86   When a warranty is not a separate element, the seller has completed substantially all the required performance and can recognise the full consideration received as revenue on the sale. The expected future cost to be incurred relating to the warranty should not be recorded as a reduction of revenue, but rather should be recorded as a cost of sale, as the warranty does not represent a return of a portion of the purchaser's sales price. The costs of warranties should be determined at the time of the sale, and a corresponding provision for warranty costs recognised. Warranties and similar costs can normally be measured reliably because entities have historical evidence of the costs associated with various products. However, if such costs cannot be measured reliably, revenue should not be recognised until the warranty period has expired and the related warranty costs are identified. [IAS 18 para 19].

Example – Standard warranties

A manufacturer of televisions sells them to retailers for C300 with a one year manufacturer's warranty. The manufacturer does not sell the televisions without this warranty, nor does any manufacturer of a similar product. The manufacturer expects claims to be made on one in every 100 televisions sold, with repairs costing an average of C100.

The warranty is not separable from the sale of the television. As a result, the revenue recognition criteria of IAS 18 are applied to the transaction as a whole. On making the sale to the retailer, the manufacturer has completed substantially all the required performance, retaining only an insignificant interest in the risks of holding the inventory. Thus, on the sale of a television, the manufacturer should recognise revenue of C300 and make a provision of C1 (being C100 for 1 in 100 sales) against cost of sales for the expected cost of repair.

Extended warranty

9.87 An extended warranty is an agreement to provide warranty protection in addition to the scope of coverage of a manufacturer's original warranty, or to extend the period of coverage provided by the manufacturer's warranty. They are often sold separately from the original product but, where warranties included in the price of a product provide protection in excess of that provided by the normal terms and conditions of sale for the relevant product, the transaction's substance is that the entity has sold two products. This might be the case if similar warranties are sold separately by the entity or by competitors of the entity, or if the same product is sold with no equivalent warranty by another entity.

9.88 If an entity sells an extended warranty, the revenue from the sale of the extended warranty should be deferred and recognised over the period covered by the warranty. No costs should be accrued at the inception of the extended warranty agreement.

Example 1 – Extended warranty sold separately

Entity A sells electrical goods. The goods come with a manufacturer's 12 month warranty. Entity A also offers customers the option of purchasing an extended warranty to cover years 2 to 5.

The sales price of the extended warranty is C100 and entity A typically receives valid warranty claims from 4% of customers during the extended warranty period. The average cost of repairing or replacing the goods under the warranty is C600 per valid claim.

As this is an extended warranty, management should defer the revenue and recognise it on a straight-line basis (unless another method is more appropriate) over years 2 to 5, which is the period over which the extended warranty is provided.

The costs incurred under the warranty should be charged to cost of sales as incurred. Management should not recognise a provision for the expected warranty costs, but should monitor the arrangements to ensure that the total warranty cost does not exceed the amount of revenue allocated to the warranty. If this occurs, the warranty contract will be onerous and it may be necessary to recognise an onerous contract provision (see chapter 21).

Example 2 – Extended warranties sold as part of a package

X plc is a retailer of domestic appliances and sells washing machines. Each of a particular model of washing machine is sold with an initial one-year warranty and a three-year extended warranty at no extra cost to the customer. X plc sells this washing machine for C399 in its stores, while its competitor, Y plc, sells an identical washing machine with the one-year initial warranty, but without an extended warranty for C379, and an unrelated insurer offers an equivalent extended warranty for C60.

How should X plc account for its income from the sale of the washing machine, the initial warranty and the extended warranty?

Paragraph 13 of IAS 18 requires that, where a single transaction is made up of two or more separately identifiable components, it may be necessary to recognise the revenue earned in respect of each component of the transaction separately (refer to para 9.131).

Assuming that the sale of the initial one-year warranty cannot be separated (as the circumstances are similar to those discussed in para 9.86 above), the substance of this transaction is that X plc has sold two products: (i) the washing machine with an accompanying one-year warranty and (ii) the extended warranty. Where two or more components of a contractual arrangement operate independently from each other, they should be separated and the revenue earned on the sale of each product recognised separately in accordance with the principles of IAS 18.

X plc will need to attribute a fair value to each component of the transaction. Where the bundle of goods is sold at less than the aggregate of the fair values of each component, the discount should be allocated to the components on a reasonable basis.

For X plc, the fair value of the washing machine is C344 (being 399 × 379 ÷ (379 + 60)). It will be appropriate to recognise this revenue because X plc has fulfilled its contractual performance obligation relating to the supply of the washing machine in full.

The calculated fair value of the extended warranty is C55, that is 399 — 344, or (399 × 60) ÷ (379 + 60). This should be recognised over the three periods over which it is earned by X plc.

Installation fees and shipping and handling charges

Goods sold subject to installation and inspection

9.89 IAS 18 states that revenue relating to goods that are sold subject to installation and inspection is normally recognised when the buyer accepts delivery and the installation and inspection are complete. However, revenue is recognised on delivery when:

- The installation process is simple – for example, external speakers for a computer, where the installation merely requires that the equipment be plugged in.

- The inspection is performed only for the purpose of determining the contract prices – for example shipments of iron ore, sugar or soya beans.

[IAS 18 App para 2(a)].

9.90   IAS 18 states that installation fees are recognised as revenue by reference to the stage of the installation's completion, unless they are incidental to the product's sale in which case they are recognised when the goods are sold. [IAS 18 App para 10].

9.91   Determining whether installation is incidental to the sale of a product is often difficult. In the case of a television receiver, for example, it can be argued that the installation is usually straightforward.

9.92   Where installation is more complicated, for example, in a contract to supply a computer system, the contract may be broken down into separate components one of which could be the installation. However, this approach would only be possible where a reliable fair value could be ascertained for the installation component – see from paragraph 9.131.

Shipping and handling charges

9.93   FOB (free on board) or CIF (cost, insurance, freight) terms may affect the timing of revenue recognition. If the seller is responsible for carriage, insurance and freight until the goods are delivered, these form part of the entity's performance and result in retention of the risks and rewards of the item sold until delivery to the client site has occurred. As a result, the timing of revenue recognition will be different depending upon the terms of delivery. If an item has been sold on an FOB basis, such that the entity has no further performance obligations, recognition on despatch of the item is likely to be acceptable. It should not, however, be assumed that the use of the term 'FOB' leads to the treatments detailed above. Whether the insurance and freight risk is taken on by the customer will depend on the arrangement's terms. The terms should be examined to ensure that the timing of revenue recognition appropriately reflects the transfer of risks and rewards.

Example – Sale of goods on a CIF basis

Entity A sells steel from its factory on a CIF basis to entity B. The contractual terms state that insurance is taken out by entity A for the period the steel is in transit and that:

> *"The seller must pay the costs and freight necessary to bring the goods to the named port of destination, but the risk of loss or of damage to the goods, as well as any additional costs due to events occurring after the goods cross the ship's*

rail, are transferred from the seller to the buyer when the goods pass the ship's rail."

To comply with these terms entity A takes out a bearer insurance document, which means that entity A would claim for any loss or damage to the steel until the steel passes the ship's rail (that is, the steel is officially documented as being loaded as part of the ship's cargo). From this point on, the insurance policy is transferred to entity B (now being the bearer of the insurance document). Entity B will need to make a claim directly to the insurers (that is not *via* entity A) for any steel damaged in transit once the steel crosses the ship's rail.

As the risk of loss is transferred when the steel crosses the ship's rail, revenue should be recognised by entity A at that point and should not be deferred until delivery, presuming all other conditions under paragraph 14 of IAS 18 have been satisfied.

If the risk of loss remains with entity A until the goods are delivered, revenue recognition would be delayed until the steel is delivered to entity B.

9.94 Shipping and handling charges are common in many retail industries. Charges may be levied to customers based on:

- Specific amounts dependent upon the general geographic region of the customer.

- A single specified amount irrespective of the geographic location of the customer.

- The actual amount incurred to ship the item to the specific customer.

9.95 There is no specific guidance within IFRS that addresses accounting for shipping and handling charges. However, IAS 18 is clear that amounts collected on behalf of third parties are not revenue. [IAS 18 para 8]. As such, shipping and handling charges should not be included as part of revenue if the seller is acting as an agent on behalf of the shipper. Where the seller is able to determine the additional margin it will receive from the shipment (or the additional cost it is willing to bear), this would indicate that the entity is not acting as an agent. In such situations, the charges attributed to shipping and handling are included in revenue. Where the seller is acting as an agent on behalf of the shipper, revenue would be recognised net of any shipping or handling charge (see from para 9.159 for further consideration of agency transactions). An example of a policy is given in Table 9.A.1.

Table 9.A.1 – Shipping and handling

Stora Enso Oyj – Annual report – 31 December 2011

Note 1 Accounting Principles (extract)

Shipping and handling costs

When Stora Enso is responsible for arranging transport for its sales, such costs are not billed separately but are included in revenue in the value of the goods billed to customers; the shipping costs incurred are shown in cost of sales.

Sale of property

9.96 Transactions relating to the sale of property are addressed by IFRIC 15. The guidance in IFRIC 15 is considered from paragraph 9.274.

Sale of software

9.97 In the software industry, revenue recognition poses a number of issues. Software houses normally earn their revenue from a combination of the following:

■ Sale of off-the-shelf software where the licensing arrangement gives the customer the right to use the software for a specified period.

■ Sale of customised software developed for a specific application.

■ Sale of software support services.

9.98 Selling software is different from selling a tangible product, since what is being sold is the right to use intellectual property. The delivery of the software may, therefore, appear to be less of an indication that a sale should be recognised than with sales of other types of goods. In fact, recognition may need to be delayed until acceptance by the customer. For example, an off-the-shelf package may require tailoring to meet the customer's specifications. If the arrangement does not qualify as a construction contract, revenue may not be earned until after tailoring, delivery, set up and the subsequent testing and acceptance of the software by the customer. If, however, the contract is for the development of customised software, revenue would be recognised on a percentage of completion basis. [IAS 18 App para 19].

9.99 The sale of a standard software package, such as a word processor package or spreadsheet tools, may be treated differently from software that needs to be customised for each customer. Entities that sell standard off-the-shelf packages generally treat their sales no differently from the sale of a physical product and recognise revenue on delivery.

9.100 Sales of software can be subject to significant levels of customer rejection; reasons include incompatible hardware and software and the length and complexity of software installation. These risks should be considered in determining the appropriate point to recognise revenue relating to software sales. As a result, customer acceptance is often required to give the necessary assurance of a completed sale.

9.101 Where acceptance is subject to installation and inspection and the installation process is simple (for example, involving unpacking and loading the software), revenue can be recognised immediately upon the buyer's acceptance of delivery. However, if, as is often the case, the installation process is more substantial and there is more than an insignificant risk of non-acceptance, revenue recognition should be delayed until the installation and inspection processes are complete and customer acceptance has occurred.

9.102 Fees from the development of customised software are recognised as revenue by reference to the developments' stage of completion, including completion of services provided for post-delivery service support. [IAS 18 App para 19]. The recognition of revenue by reference to the stage of completion is referred to as the percentage of completion method and is dealt with from paragraph 9.106.

9.103 Under this method, revenue is recognised as the contract activity progresses. Revenue and associated costs are recognised in proportion to the work completed. Where the outcome cannot be assessed with reasonable certainty before the contract's conclusion, revenue should be recognised only to the extent that the expenses recognised are recoverable. [IAS 18 para 26].

9.104 When the project involves the provision of hardware as well as software, the contract will need to be carefully reviewed to ensure that revenue is not recognised before the risks and rewards relating to the hardware are transferred and also to determine whether the contract has multiple elements that can be separated (see from para 9.131).

9.105 Where a software house provides maintenance services or other after sales support with the initial contract for hardware and software, it is necessary to determine if there are separable components in the arrangement. If it can, then revenue relating to the maintenance component is recognised as performance of the maintenance service occurs. Maintenance revenue will generally be recognised on a straight-line basis over the period of the maintenance contract, unless another method better reflects the pattern of performance.

9.105.1 The separation of components in software contracts can be complex. Issues associated with multiple element transactions are considered in more detail from paragraph 9.131.

Sale of services

Performance over time

9.106 The 'percentage of completion' method is used to recognise revenue for rendering services in accordance with IAS 18.

9.107 IAS 11 and IAS 18 give similar guidance on determining a transaction's stage of completion, although the guidance in IAS 18 is specific to the rendering of services, whereas IAS 11 relates to the construction of assets. Various methods may be used to determine the stage of completion. The key to determining which method to use is that revenue should relate only to work that has been performed and should not include any element relating to work that has yet to be carried out. The methods set out in IAS 18 are:

- Surveys of work performed. The standard does not give further guidance on, for example, who might carry out such surveys, but normally it should be someone who has relevant experience and knowledge.

- Services performed to date as a percentage of total services to be performed. For example, an entity might have a three year contract to provide environmental inspection and maintenance services on landfill sites and it is expected that over the three year period ten such inspections involving similar amounts of maintenance will be required. If by the end of the first year two inspections have been completed it may, in the absence of other factors, be reasonable to assume that one fifth of the contract revenues have been earned and should be recognised.

- The proportion of the estimated total costs of the contract incurred to date. The standard stresses that only costs that reflect actual services performed to the year end are included in costs incurred and only costs that reflect services performed or to be performed are included in the estimated total costs.

[IAS 18 para 24].

9.108 Where performance of a single service contract takes place over time, revenue should be recognised as performance takes place. For example, under a maintenance contract for six months, revenue should be recognised over the six months as the service is provided over that period. It is not acceptable to record all the revenue upfront and provide for the costs expected to be incurred in providing the services, because to do this would be to recognise revenue before the seller had performed any part of the contract.

9.109 When considering how to account for a service contract, it is essential to understand the contractual terms. By agreeing to the terms in the contract, the buyer specifies at what point the contract has value to them. These terms will indicate when the criteria for revenue recognition are met. If the vendor performs under the contract over the period the services are rendered, the timing of revenue recognition should reflect this. Alternatively, if the vendor has only performed under the contract after the fulfilment of a significant act, no revenue should be recognised until that act has occurred (see para 9.113 onwards). This is illustrated below.

> **Example – Professional services**
>
> Mr A is an accountant who is half way through completing his client's tax return at the end of June (Mr A's year end). The client has agreed to pay Mr A C500 for the completion of the return. The contract specifies that Mr A has the right to receive payment for any work performed and shall be paid for services rendered if the contract is broken off before completion at the client's request. Mr A has accounted for C250 of the revenue.
>
> The criteria for revenue recognition will be met over the period in which Mr A works on his client's tax return. Although it might seem that a half-completed tax return is of little practical use to the client, the client has agreed that Mr A is performing under the contract as he is performing his work. On this basis, revenue would be recognised by reference to the contract's stage of completion and, as such, it would be appropriate to recognise C250 of the revenue at the end of June.

9.110   Determining the stage of completion may, in some situations, be a matter of breaking down a contract into separate stages of completion. For example, in the shipping industry ships may be engaged in journeys to more than one port, which are not completed at the year end.

9.111   Where revenue is recognised in relation to the proportion of total estimated costs incurred to date, paragraph 24(c) of IAS 18 further emphasises that the estimation of costs incurred to the year end should include only costs that reflect performance to that point.

9.112   Where a contract for services involves an indeterminate number of acts over a specified time, IAS 18 states that, for practical purposes, revenue is recognised on a straight line basis, unless there is evidence that some other method gives a better reflection of the stage of completion at each year end. For example, revenue from a contract to provide maintenance services for a six month period would normally be reflected on a straight-line basis over the six months. This is because the timing and amount of maintenance services is indeterminate and the straight-line method of spreading revenue is the best practical method to use. In such situations, costs should be recognised as incurred and neither accrued nor deferred, unless they qualify for recognition as a liability or an asset. See also paragraph 9.108 above.

9.113   However, where there is one specific act during the contract that is more significant than the rest of the acts under the contract (for example, the delivery and acceptance of a report), revenue recognition is postponed until the significant act has been carried out. See further paragraph 9.118 onwards below.

9.113.1   A contract's stage of completion determines the proportion of services delivered (under the contractual terms) and hence the revenue that should be recognised. An entity sometimes receives non-refundable cash payments (as part of the contractual terms) before the related services have been delivered. Paragraph 20 of IAS 18 states that revenue should be recognised for *"the rendering of services"* and, hence, in addition to the recognition criteria covered in paragraph 9.65, there is a requirement for services to be rendered prior to revenue being recognised. Revenue is not recognised solely because a non-refundable cash payment has been received. Such payments are very common in the financial services industry. This is considered further in paragraph 9.247.

9.114 If any of the conditions for reliably estimating a transaction's stage of completion involving the rendering of services are not met, or if the stage of completion cannot be reliably estimated for some other reason, revenue should be recognised only to the extent that costs incurred and recognised are recoverable. [IAS 18 para 26].

9.115 IAS 18 explains that, in the early stages of a transaction, it is often the case that the outcome cannot be estimated reliably, but it may still be probable that the entity will recover the costs incurred to date. It states that, accordingly, the entity should recognise revenue only to the extent of costs incurred that are expected to be recoverable. No profit is recognised as the outcome of the transaction cannot be reliably estimated. [IAS 18 para 27].

9.116 Where the outcome of a transaction cannot be reliably estimated and costs have been incurred that are not expected to be recoverable, IAS 18 states that revenue is not recognised and such costs should be expensed immediately. [IAS 18 para 28].

9.117 If costs have been expensed in the circumstances described in the preceding paragraph and the uncertainties preventing reliable estimation of the outcome of the transaction are subsequently removed, the entity resumes accounting for revenue according to the stage of completion of the transaction at the balance sheet date. [IAS 18 para 28]. Hence there would be a revenue true-up to maintain a position at the balance sheet date as if no uncertainties had occurred. However, costs already expensed would not be reinstated even if they are now considered recoverable.

Contracts containing significant acts

9.118 When a contract contains a specific act that is much more significant than any other acts to be performed under the contract, the recognition of revenue is postponed until the significant act is executed. [IAS 18 para 25]. The existence of a specific act that is much more significant than any other act may indicate that the other acts do not substantively advance the transaction's stage of completion.

9.118.1 IAS 18 provides limited guidance on what may constitute a significant act. The appendix gives three examples:

- commissions on the allotment of shares to a client;
- placement fees for arranging a loan between a borrower and an investor; and

■ loan syndication fees that an entity receives for arranging a loan for which it retains no portion of the loan package for itself.

Financial services fees are considered further from paragraph 9.239.

9.118.2 There are a number of factors that an entity needs to consider to determine whether an arrangement contains a specific act that is much more significant than any other acts. For example, tasks undertaken by a supplier that do not build on one another toward completion of the service may indicate that there is a single significant act since each act is not integral to providing the service. This may be the case when the service is the bringing together of parties in an arrangement or an agreement, as indicated in the examples described above or, perhaps, a travel or estate agent. When the service provider determines the level of work performed and controls whether the service is ultimately delivered, this may indicate there is not a single significant act and that the service is performed over the contract period.

9.118.3 The timing of cash payments should not, by itself, determine whether a single act is much more significant than any other in an arrangement. However, the terms of an arrangement that involve payment only upon completion of a single act should be assessed to determine whether the timing of the payment suggests that one act is more significant than the others. Judgement will be required in many circumstances to determine whether a specific act is much more significant than any others.

9.118.4 In some cases it may not be immediately obvious whether a contract contains a significant act or contingent consideration. Where the contract contains a significant act, the entity has not earned revenue until the specific act is performed. A significant act is something that the entity must do itself. In comparison, where a contract includes contingent consideration an entity will have performed all of its obligations under the contract, but the receipt of the consideration may be determined by events outside of its control. Where a contract contains a significant act no revenue is recognised until this act has occurred, since the entity has not yet performed under the contract. Where the entity has performed but consideration is contingent, revenue will be recognised to the extent that the entity can determine that there is a probable inflow of economic benefits that can be reliably measured. This approach can be used even if there is a further event outside the entity's control that must occur to determine the amount of revenue to be received. See from paragraph 9.179.1 for further discussion of contingent consideration.

[The next paragraph is 9.120.]

Contracts with milestone payments

9.120 Contracts in certain industries, particularly pharmaceutical and biotechnology, are often structured to provide for the payment of cash upon the achievement of certain 'milestones' identified in the contract. Such contracts often relate to research and development of new product offerings. Contract terms often include significant up-front payments or other payments over the course of the contract that in substance represent a form of financing, as opposed to compensation for services provided. Accounting for such contracts can be complex and the appropriate revenue recognition will vary depending on the substance of the arrangements.

9.121 A number of factors should be considered when determining the appropriate accounting for revenue in a milestone payment arrangement, including:

- The reasonableness of the payments compared to the effort, time and cost to achieve the milestones. If payments bear little or no relation to performance under the contracts, then recording revenue based on the payment profile would not be appropriate.

- The nature of royalty or licence agreements relating to the product being developed. Where royalty or licence agreements are in place, a component of the payments made under the contract may relate to the royalty or licence fees rather than the provision of services and should be accounted for accordingly. (See further para 9.223 onwards.)

- The existence of any cancellation clauses that require the repayment of amounts received under the contract upon cancellation by either party. Such cancellation clauses may indicate that recognition of revenue for amounts received is not appropriate as the amounts may be linked to future performance or a reduction in the contractual consideration to which the entity is entitled.

- The risks associated with achievement of milestones. If payments are dependent upon the achievement of certain milestones, and there is doubt as regards the achievement of the milestones, then revenue should not be recognised until the relevant milestone has been achieved (see further from para 9.118).

- Any obligations that must be completed to receive payment under the contract or the existence of penalties for failure to deliver. All obligations under a contract must be considered in assessing the extent to which an entity has performed.

Factors such as the above will impact the timing and recognition of revenue where milestone payments are included in customer contracts. The certainty and substance of related contract provisions should be carefully analysed to determine when recognition is appropriate.

Example – Contract with milestone payments

Entity A, a small pharmaceutical entity, contracts with the much larger entity B to develop a new medical treatment for cancer, which it expects to take five years. Entity A will periodically have to update entity B with the results of its work. Entity B has exclusive rights over any development results. Entity B will make an up-front payment of C1m on contract signature and five equal annual payments of C500,000, provided entity A demonstrates compliance with the development programme. In addition, upon the successful testing of the treatment in clinical trials, entity B will pay a further C1.5m. Entity A's management estimates the total cost of the contract will be C3m.

Entity A incurs costs of C600,000 in year one, in line with its original estimate. Entity A is in compliance with the research agreement, including the provision of updates from the results of its work.

How should entity A recognise the payment it receives in year one from entity B to conduct development?

The contract involves the rendering of pharmaceutical development services. As such, entity A should recognise the revenue for the payments in accordance with the percentage of completion model, using one of the estimation techniques outlined in paragraph 9.107, or on a straight-line basis, whichever method measures reliably the services performed to date.

In applying the percentage of completion model, the C1.5m payment relating to the successful testing of the treatment in clinical trials will be excluded from total contract revenue. This is because the payment depends upon the outcome of the clinical trials. Therefore, recognition of the C1.5m should be postponed until the outcome of the trials is known (or reasonably estimable). This is because, until that point, it cannot be assumed that the company will receive economic benefit (see para 9.118 above).

In year one, entity A has met its obligations, the project is developing in line with the estimates and is forecast to be profitable, so entity A should recognise revenue of C700,000 ((1m + 2.5m) ÷ 5) , costs of C600,000 (3m ÷ 5) and profit of C100,000. The consideration received in excess of the revenue recognised of C800,000 (1.5m — 700,000) will be recognised as a liability on entity A's balance sheet, representing a liability for future performance.

Inception/membership fees

9.122 The appendix to IAS 18 deals with initiation, entrance and membership fees. The guidance states that revenue recognition depends on the nature of the services provided. If the fee covers membership, or joining only and other services or products are paid for separately, or if there is a separate annual subscription, the joining or membership fee is recognised as revenue when there is no significant uncertainty as to its collectability. If the joining or membership fee entitles the member to services or products during the membership period, or to purchase goods or services at prices lower than those charged to non-members, revenue is recognised on a basis that reflects the timing, nature and value of the benefits provided. [IAS 18 App para 17].

9.123 The issue is whether it is possible to separate clearly the membership or joining fee from other goods or services that are provided during the membership period.

9.124 The IAS 18 approach requires an analysis of the arrangement to see whether any part of the joining fee is in fact an advance payment for future goods or services. In practice, the annual subscription might well be discounted if the joining fee covers other services and, thus, the joining fee might not be solely for membership.

9.125 Where, however, it can be demonstrated that the seller has no further obligations in respect of the fee once it has been received, the seller should recognise the fee on the date it becomes entitled to receive it. The seller may have no further obligations in respect of the fee if the customer has to pay the full commercial price for all future goods or services including any access to the organisation. [IAS 18 App A para 17]. See from paragraph 9.247.

Subscriptions

9.126 In respect of subscriptions and similar items, IAS 18 states that revenue should be recognised on a straight-line basis over the period when the items are despatched if they are of a similar nature in each time period, such as a typical magazine subscription. Where the items vary in value from one period to another, such as a 'wine of the month' club, revenue is recognised on the basis of the sales value of the item despatched as a proportion of the total estimated sales value of the items covered by the subscription. [IAS 18 App para 7]. Table 9.1 below gives an example of an accounting policy in respect of subscription revenues.

Table 9.1 – Policy for subscription revenue

Thomson Reuters Corporation – Annual Report – 31 December 2011

NOTE 1: SUMMARY OF BUSINESS AND SIGNIFICANT ACCOUNTING POLICIES (extract)

Revenue recognition (extract)

Subscription-based products, including software term licenses

Subscription revenues from sales of products and services that are delivered under a contract over a period of time are recognized on a straight-line basis over the term of the subscription. Where applicable, usage fees above a base period fee are recognized as services are delivered. Subscription revenue received or receivable in advance of the delivery of services or publications is included in deferred revenue.

Admission fees

9.127 Admission fees from, for example, artistic performances, banquets and other special events are recognised when the event takes place. When a subscription to a number of events is sold, the fee is allocated to each event on a basis that reflects the extent to which services are performed at each event. [IAS 18 App para 15].

9.128 When an event is held at a particular time, cash receipts and payments may occur in advance. For example, exhibitions, conferences and courses may involve delegates paying in advance of attending and certain costs, such as advertising, may also be incurred in advance. Since performance does not occur and revenue is not earned until the exhibition is held or the course is given, the payments received in advance represent deferred revenue, which should be released to the income statement when the event takes place. If income is deferred, a question can arise regarding the treatment of any costs incurred prior to the year end. This issue is considered in paragraph 9.254.

Tuition fees

9.129 Tuition fees should be recognised as revenue over the period of instruction. [IAS 18 App para 16].

9.130 Whilst this deals with the straightforward situation where a single session of tuition is given over a fixed time period, some instruction courses are structured differently. For example, a course may be structured as a number of modules. Students may be able to choose to attend and complete a fixed number of modules at any time within, say, a two-year period. It would be more appropriate to recognise revenue as the modules are attended and completed by the student, that is, as the service is provided to the student, rather than recognising revenue on a straight-line basis as indicated above.

Multiple element transactions

Separation of components

9.131 A transaction may contain separately identifiable components that should be accounted for separately. IAS 18 states that, it is necessary to apply the revenue recognition criteria to each separately identifiable component of a single transaction in order to reflect the transaction's substance. IAS 18 gives an example of a product sold with an obligation for subsequent servicing and states that the amount attributable to the subsequent servicing should be deferred and recognised over the period during which the service is performed. [IAS 18 para 13, App para 11].

9.132 In assessing the transaction's substance, the transaction should be viewed from the perspective of the customer and not the seller: that is, what does the customer believe they are purchasing? If the customer views the purchase as one product, then it is likely that the recognition criteria should be applied to the transaction as a whole. Conversely, if the customer perceives there to be a number of elements to the transaction, then the revenue recognition criteria should be applied to each element separately. When looking at the arrangement's substance, it is possible that the separable components are dealt with under different standards; for example, one component of a contract being a construction contract and the other component being for the sale of goods or rendering of services. In such cases, the guidance in paragraph 13 of IAS 18 should be applied to the contract as a whole to determine the contract's separable elements. [IAS 18 para 13]. For elements within IAS 18's scope, the guidance in IAS 18 would be applied when considering revenue recognition or any further separation of components. Likewise, the guidance in IAS 11 would be applied to elements in IAS 11's scope.

Example 1 – Separation of components within a contract

An entity supplies equipment and provides maintenance service for a year. The entity also sells maintenance services and equipment separately. How should the sale of the equipment and maintenance package be accounted for?

The contract has two separable components, the equipment and the maintenance contract. The revenue for the sale of the equipment would be recognised on delivery, whilst the revenue for the maintenance contract would be taken to the income statement over the contract period. See paragraph 9.138 onwards for further consideration of the allocation of consideration to the separable components of a transaction.

Example 2 – Separation of components within a contract

A mobile phone network packages within a single contract a handset, line rental and pre-paid calls. These three products and services are also available separately and their stand-alone retail prices are a good guide to determine the fair value of the consideration received for each component.

At the start of the contract, the handset is delivered, but provision of the line rental and pre-paid calls will be outstanding. Thus revenue is recognised immediately for the handset, but revenue for the line rental and pre-paid calls is deferred. The revenue from line rental will be recognised over the rental period and revenue from the calls will be recognised on a usage basis.

There is a further consideration in respect of the handset. If the handset can be used on any network, it has value to the customer when separated from the associated line rental, so the customer could reasonably have bought just the handset and the revenue would be recognised upon delivery. However, in the unlikely event that the handset can only be used with the associated line rental, it may have no stand-alone value and no revenue would be recognised in respect of the handset alone. Where a handset is sold with no associated line rental and, instead, cards with pre-paid units are purchased by the user, revenue would be recognised on the sale of the handset. Revenue from the sale of pre-paid units would be deferred and recognised as the units are used.

9.133 If the vendor sells the different components separately (or has done so in the past), this is a strong indicator that separation within a multiple element contract is necessary for the purposes of revenue recognition. If the entity in question does not sell the separate components independently, the transaction's components may be sold separately by other vendors in the market. In such a situation, separation of the components may still be necessary.

9.134 Certain contracts may include elements that the vendor has no legal obligation to deliver. An example is in the software industry where the contract may specify that the vendor will provide upgrades and enhancements to the customers on a 'when and if available' basis. As the vendor has no obligation to develop upgrades, the question arises as to whether the future upgrades to which the customer may become entitled are a separable component of the contract for the purposes of revenue recognition.

9.135 IFRS does not define identifiable components of a single transaction. Elements that the entity has no legal obligation to deliver and immaterial costs to execute might not immediately be considered as separate elements. However, management should also consider the value of each element to the customer. The assessment of components and future obligations is a matter of judgement (regardless of whether the obligation is specifically stated in the contract or to some extent implied). If there is a history of delivering upgrades to clients every six months and the customers, therefore, consider the upgrades to have significant value, these upgrades may be regarded as separate elements. In some situations, it may be considered that much of the contract's value lies in the upgrades (for example, if the goods supplied are anti-virus software, which becomes rapidly obsolete if not upgraded regularly).

9.136 Another situation where the separation of components may not be immediately clear is where goods or services are supplied based on a prepaid amount with a 'ceiling' for the amount that the customer can use within a specified period of time. Examples of such arrangements include the prepayment of monthly fees for mobile phone services (for X minutes per month), gift vouchers sold by a vendor for its services and goods that can be utilised for a specified period of time or take-or-pay arrangements. In such cases, the customer may not end up demanding full performance from the vendor. The question then arises as to when revenue associated with 'undemanded' or 'breakage' services can be recognised.

9.137 IFRS does not prescribe a specific method for recognising breakage and as such there is an accounting policy choice when accounting for breakage. The appropriate model will depend on the specific features of the arrangement to which the entity is party and the entity's ability to reliably estimate breakage. Three possible approaches are summarised below:

■ The entity could choose to recognise revenue when a customer's right to redeem expires. This model might be most appropriate if the entity is not able to reliably estimate breakage. For rights that do not expire, this model may be impractical.

■ Entities that can reliably estimate the pattern of redemptions over time may be able to determine when the likelihood of further redemptions becomes remote. It would be appropriate to recognise breakage at that time, based on the expectation that the holder of the rights will not demand performance. That expectation should be developed using sufficient relevant historical experience; however, this model will never result in immediate revenue recognition.

■ When a reliable, supportable estimate can be made for the expected breakage, revenue recognition can take into account the expected forfeitures prior to the actual expiry date based on when forfeitures are expected to occur. Such a treatment would be dependent on a reliable and evidenced history of breakages. In such a situation, any consideration for the transaction would be allocated amongst the items expected to be redeemed on a consistent basis. See the example in paragraph 9.195.

Allocation of consideration

9.138   The principles in IAS 18 require that the revenue in respect of each separable component of a transaction is measured at its fair value. The price that is regularly charged for an item when sold separately is often the best evidence of its fair value.

9.139   However, sometimes the total revenue arising from a transaction may be different to the aggregate fair value of the transaction's separate components. If it appears that the contract value exceeds the sum of the fair value of the separable elements, this likely indicates that the values being used are inappropriate or additional goods or services provided have not been identified. Entities that find themselves in this situation should re-evaluate the components previously indentified and the associated fair values.

9.140   In other situations, the contract value may be less than the fair value of the transaction's separable elements. When this occurs, the difference should be allocated between the separable components based on the most appropriate method of allocating the separable components. Examples of revenue allocation methods include relative fair values, cost plus a reasonable margin and the residual method (see examples below). Any loss on the overall contract should be recognised at the outset in accordance with IAS 37. However, in general, if the contract is profitable as a whole, the entity should ensure that the revenue allocation policy adopted results in the most appropriate allocation of revenue to the elements of the contract.

Example 1 – Contract value is lower than the fair value of the separable elements

An entity sells boats for C30,000 each. The entity also provides mooring facilities for C2,000 per annum. The entity sells these goods and services separately. If a purchaser of a boat contracts to buy mooring facilities for a year there is a 5% discount on the whole package. Thus the 'package' costs C32,000 less 5% or C30,400. How should revenue be recognised?

The discount in this case is C1,600 (the difference between C32,000 and C30,400). Using the relative fair value approach, the element of the discount attributable to the boat is C1,500 (C1,600 × C30,000/C32,000) and the element of the discount attributable to the mooring facilities is C100 (C1,600 × C2,000/C32,000). The revenue recognised on the sale of the boat should, therefore, be C28,500 (C30,000 — C1,500), which will be recognised on delivery of the boat. The revenue recognised for the mooring facilities is C1,900 (C2,000 — C100), which will be recognised evenly over the year for which the mooring facility is provided.

Example 2 – Contract value is lower than the fair value of the separable elements

Entity A sells a copying machine in December 20X7 and will provide maintenance services for one year. The total consideration received for both the sale and the maintenance activity is C1,200. Costs expected to be incurred to fulfil the contract are C700 for the machine (being the cost of inventory) and C200 for the maintenance activity. The relative fair values are C1,050 and C150, respectively.

If the entity were to apply a relative fair value approach, this would result in a loss on the maintenance component of the contract. The entity therefore needs to consider whether this reflects the economics of the transaction. Where the economic substance of the transaction is that maintenance services are loss making, the entity should record an accrual to the extent that the remaining expected costs exceed the remaining expected revenue. After accruing for the loss, the remaining undelivered items will be at break-even once recognised.

If however this does not match the economics of the transaction, in these limited circumstances, an entity that uses relative fair values might apply cost plus a reasonable margin as an exception to the normal accounting policy. This is illustrated below

Relative fair value policy

The cost of the maintenance activity of C200 exceeds the relative fair value of C150, resulting in a loss of C50. Costs of C750 are calculated as the total cost of the sale of the machine plus the loss of C50 relating to the maintenance contract. Following this allocation the entries on the transaction would be as follows:

December 20X7	Dr C	Cr C
Cash	1,200	
Deferred revenue		150
Revenue		1,050
Cost of sales	700	
Cost for loss on maintenance element accrual	50	
Inventory		700
Accrual for loss on maintenance element		50

Cost plus a reasonable margin policy

The overall profit is C300 (being the difference between the revenue of C1,200 and costs of C900). This profit may be allocated based on a reasonable margin, say for example, C250 on the machine and for C50 on the maintenance service. Following this allocation, the entries on the transaction date would be as follows:

December 20X7	Dr C	Cr C
Cash	1,200	
Deferred revenue (C200 + C50 margin on service)		250
Revenue (C700 + C250 margin on copier machine)		950
Cost of sales	700	
Inventory		700

Linked transactions

9.141 IAS 8 requires accounting policies to reflect the economic substance of transactions, other events and conditions and not merely their legal form. [IAS 8 para 10(b)(ii)]. Therefore, where two or more transactions are linked they should be treated as a single transaction, where it is necessary to understand the transaction's commercial effect. It gives as an example the situation where an entity sells goods but, at the same time, enters into an agreement to repurchase the goods at a later date, so negating the substantive effect of the original sale. It states that, in such a situation, the two transactions should be dealt with as one whole transaction. [IAS 18 para 13].

9.142 When such a sale and repurchase agreement is entered into, the agreement's terms need to be analysed to ascertain whether, in substance, the seller has transferred the significant risks and rewards of ownership to the buyer and whether revenue should, therefore, be recognised. When the seller has retained the risks and rewards of ownership, even though legal title has been transferred, the transaction is a financing arrangement and does not give rise to revenue. [IAS 18 App para 5].

Example – Legal sale linked to a financing arrangement

The management of entity A is considering the following two alternative transactions:

(a) sale of inventory to a bank for C500,000 with an obligation to repurchase the inventory at a later stage; or

(b) sale of inventory to a bank for C500,000 with an option to repurchase the inventory any time up to 12 months from the date of sale.

The repurchase price in both alternatives is C500,000 plus an imputed financing cost. The bank is required to provide substantially the same quality and quantity of inventory as was sold to it (that is, the bank is not required to return precisely the same physical inventory as was originally sold to it). The fair value of the inventory sold to the bank is C1,000,000.

How should management record the transactions?

Management should recognise the transactions as follows:

(a) Sale with repurchase obligation: management should not recognise revenue on the transfer of the inventory to the bank. The inventory should remain on entity A's balance sheet and the proceeds from the bank should be recognised as a collateralised borrowing.

Even though the inventory repurchased from the bank may not be the inventory sold, it is in substance the same asset. The substance of the transaction is that the sale and repurchase are linked transactions and entity A does not transfer the risks and rewards associated with the inventory to the bank.

(b) Sale with repurchase option: management should not recognise revenue unless and until the repurchase option is allowed to lapse. The inventory should remain on entity A's balance sheet and the proceeds recognised as a collateralised borrowing until entity A's right to repurchase the inventory lapses. (Entity A is unlikely to let the repurchase option lapse as the enforced 'sale' was at significantly below fair value.)

UK.9.142.1 The UK standard FRS 5 deals in more detail with such transactions and may provide additional guidance that will be useful in applying the principles of IAS 18.

9.143 Another example is so-called 'two-way trading transactions'. Sometimes an issue can arise, where an entity sells a product to another entity and that other entity sells a different product to the first entity. Provided the two transactions are not connected no problem arises. However, problems may arise where the transactions are connected, for example:

- Entity A may sell a product to entity B, which entity B uses in the manufacture of a product that is then purchased by entity A.

- A retailer may buy goods from a manufacturer and the manufacturer may pay the retailer to promote those products, for example, by displaying advertising material in its stores (see further from para 9.177).

9.144 In the first of these examples, the issue is whether the two transactions should be regarded as two separate contracts or as one larger contract. The latter will be the case if the contracts are legally or economically conditional or dependent on each other; for example, this might be the case where entity A is obliged to purchase the finished product from entity B (especially if the repurchase price is determined other than by reference to the item's fair value). However, if the contracts are genuinely independent of each other they will be treated as two contracts and entity A will recognise profit on the first sale to entity B and record the price paid for the product purchased from entity B as the cost of that purchase. Generally, the individual circumstances of the arrangements will need to be analysed, but signs that the contracts are independent would include:

- Entity B selling the product manufactured from products supplied by entity A to other third parties.

- Entity A having no obligation to purchase the product from entity B.

- Arm's length market prices for each transaction with price risk resting with entity B between the first and second transaction.

Example 1 – Two way trading transactions that are not linked

Entity A sells materials for making door profiles to a manufacturer who assembles the frames and puts glass in the door. Entity A then repurchases the doors and sells them to a house builder for installation in homes. The sale of the profile material and the purchase of the doors are not linked because:

- The manufacturer buys profile material regardless of whether the doors which are assembled can be sold to entity A, as the manufacturer has other markets to which it can and does sell assembled doors.

- Entity A is not committed to buy doors from this manufacturer, as it could and does use other suppliers.

- The price of the door is not fixed at the time the profile material is sold and so the manufacturer bears the risks of price fluctuations and obsolescence.

Should the sale of the materials for the door profiles to the manufacturer be accounted for separately from the purchase of doors from the same manufacturer, or should the transactions be regarded as linked and conditional on each other for accounting purposes?

In this case the details indicate that the transactions are not conditional on each other, because the manufacturer takes the risk of the manufactured doors, both in terms of price and because entity A does not have to buy any doors from that manufacturer. Therefore, the sales and purchases should be accounted for as separate, distinct transactions.

Example 2 – Two way trading transactions that are linked

The facts are the same as example 1, except that entity A sold the materials (which cost it C5) for C10 per profile and at that time agreed to buy back the materials made up into a finished door with glass fitted for C100.

In this case, the two transactions might be linked, because the sale carries a corresponding commitment to repurchase the materials in the future at a fixed price. If after considering price risk and the circumstances of the arrangement entity A believes that a sale did not occur, it should not record a sale of the C10 materials (or a profit on that sale). Instead the cost of the materials should be retained in inventory and the C10 received from the manufacturer should be recorded as a liability. When the door is purchased the additional net C90 paid by entity A will be recorded as inventory, giving an inventory value for the completed door of C95.

[The next paragraph is 9.147.]

9.147   Sometimes, transactions whereby cash is paid by party A to party B are related to transactions that require party B to pay cash to party A. These transactions must be carefully analysed to determine if they should be treated as separate transactions or a single transaction accounted for on a net basis. Factors to consider (in addition to those outlined above) that might lead to a net presentation include:

- The arrangements are entered into in close time proximity to each other and/or their mutual existence is acknowledged in the separate agreements.

- The lack of sufficient evidence to support the assertion that the amount being charged for the product or service in each transaction is its fair value.

- The party to the transactions that receives the greater amount of cash inflows does not have a clear immediate business need for the product or service it is purchasing.

9.148   These types of transactions can be particularly troublesome if they involve what is, in reality, a barter transaction, such as receiving advertising services in consideration for rendering other services to a counterparty, which is discussed from paragraph 9.180.

Lease present in an arrangement

9.149   Entities sometimes enter into arrangements that do not take the legal form of a lease, but which nevertheless convey a right to use an asset in return for a payment or series of payments. Examples include:

- Outsourcing arrangements.
- Rights to use capacity in the telecommunications industry.

9.150   IFRIC 4 sets out criteria for determining whether an arrangement is, or contains, a lease. If it is determined that an arrangement contains a lease, the lease element should be accounted for in accordance with IAS 17.

9.151   If a revenue arrangement contains a lease, this could have a significant impact on the revenue recognised under the arrangement. Furthermore, if a finance lease exists, this will result in the recognition of interest income over the life of the lease. The requirements of IFRIC 4 and IAS 17 are discussed in detail in chapter 19.

9.152   It is also possible that a transaction has the legal form of a lease but the commercial effect of the transaction is not that of a lease. A specific application of this principle is addressed in SIC 27.

9.153   SIC 27 considers transactions that have the legal form of a lease but that may not have the substance of one, in that the primary purpose may not be to convey the right to use the asset. Instead, the transaction or series of transactions may, for example, be intended to secure a tax benefit for one party that is then shared with another party in the form of a fee. In such a situation, although one of the transactions within the series may legally be a lease, the application of lease accounting to this element may not reflect the economic substance.

9.153.1   SIC 27 sets out criteria for determining whether a particular arrangement involves the conveyance of the right to use an asset (accounted for under IAS 17) or whether it does not, in which case SIC 27 applies.

9.153.2   SIC 27 gives some examples of when a transaction may not be a lease arrangement in substance. Examples include where an entity leases an asset to the investor and leases it back on the same terms and conditions. The entity and the investor have a legally enforceable right to set off amounts owing to each other and an intention to settle the amounts on a net basis. A more complicated arrangement might involve the investor paying a sum equal to the discounted amount of the future rentals up-front and the entity placing the money in an investment account, to which it does not have any further access and from which its own obligation to pay lease rentals is met.

> **Example – Lease and leaseback on identical terms**
>
> Entity A is a manufacturer that owns a factory in tax jurisdiction X.
>
> Bank B operates in tax jurisdiction Y. Entity A leases the factory to bank B for a period of five years (the factory has a useful economic life of 25 years). Bank B has the right to (and intends to) prepay all rent at inception of the lease. Bank B simultaneously leases the factory to entity A on a lease with identical terms and duration except that entity A does not have a pre-payment option and pays rent annually in arrears.
>
> Entity A pays bank B a fee for entering into the arrangement, which enables entity A to obtain a favourable tax treatment.

These two (linked) transactions do not convey the right to use the asset to bank B. The transaction's substance is that it is a financing arrangement that enables entity A to obtain tax benefits (although the substance would be no different if there were no tax benefits involved and the only economic objective had been for entity A to obtain a secured loan from bank B).As the transactions do not convey the right to use an asset, paragraph 9 of SIC 27 applies and, therefore, the transactions should be presented based upon their economic substance and nature.

9.154   Where the transaction does not convey the right to use an asset, SIC 27 sets out factors to be considered in determining whether to recognise assets and liabilities for investments made, payment obligations and how any fee receivable by the entity is recognised. The criteria for recognition of revenue from rendering services should be applied to the facts and circumstances of each arrangement to determine when to recognise a fee as income. Management should consider factors such as whether there is continuing involvement in the form of significant future performance obligations necessary to earn the fee, whether there are retained risks, the terms of any guarantees, and the risk of having to repay the fee. [SIC 27 para 8].

9.155   Any one of the following factors will demonstrate that it is not appropriate to recognise the entire fee as income when received (if received at the beginning of the arrangement):

■   Obligations of the entity either to perform or to refrain from certain significant activities are conditions of earning the fee received; entering into a legally binding arrangement is not, therefore, the most significant act required by the arrangement.

■   Limitations are put on the use of the underlying asset that have the practical effect of restricting and significantly changing the entity's ability to use (for example, deplete, sell or pledge as collateral) the asset.

■   The possibility of having to repay any part of the fee and possibly paying some additional amount is not remote. This may occur, for example, when:

   ■   the underlying asset is not a specialised asset that has to be used by the entity in its business and, therefore, there is a possibility that the entity may pay an amount to terminate the arrangement early; or

   ■   the entity is required under the terms of the arrangement, or has discretion, to invest a pre-paid amount in assets that carry more than an insignificant amount of risk (for example, currency, interest rate or credit risk). In these circumstances, the risk that the value of the investment at maturity will be insufficient to satisfy the lease payment obligations is not remote; there is, therefore, a possibility that the entity may be required to pay some amount – for example, under a guarantee.

[SIC 27 para 8].

9.156 If none of the above factors are present, it may be appropriate to recognise the entire fee as income when it is received. Immediate recognition is not, however, appropriate if at least one factor described in paragraph 8 of SIC 27 is present.

9.156.1 SIC 27 gives further guidance on how to judge whether the risk of repaying part of the fee is remote. For example, the risk of repayment is remote when the terms of the arrangement require that an amount prepaid is invested in risk-free assets that are expected to generate sufficient cash flows to satisfy the entity's lease payment obligations. [SIC 27 para 6(b)]. In difficult market circumstances, the assessment of whether the amount put aside on an investment account is invested in risk-free assets should be considered carefully. If the probability is more than remote that the entity will pay some amounts because the investment is not sufficient to meet the lease payment obligations, immediate recognition of the fee would not be appropriate.

> **Example – Recognition of fee income**
>
> Entity A has entered into a sale and leaseback transaction with bank B. As part of the transaction, entity A receives an upfront fee from bank B. The entity has concluded that the transaction does not contain a lease in substance and should, therefore, be accounted for in accordance with SIC 27.
>
> During the period of the leaseback, entity A (as lessee) may not sub-lease the asset concerned without the prior consent of bank B.
>
> It would not be appropriate to recognise the entire fee as income upfront. This is because the arrangement sets out limitations that may restrict entity A's practical ability to use the asset (in this case, by granting a sub-lease). The fee should be recognised in income over the term of the arrangement.

9.157 SIC 27 requires the fee to be presented in the statement of comprehensive income (or income statement where presented) based on its economic substance and nature. [SIC 27 para 9]. SIC 27 requires several disclosures to be made in respect of the transactions and assets involved in such a scheme. It also requires disclosure of the accounting treatment applied to any fee received, the amount recognised in the period and the line item of the statement of comprehensive income in which it is included. [SIC 27 para 10].

9.158 The above discussion of SIC 27 relates mainly to the aspect that concerns revenue recognition; it does not address the consideration in SIC 27 of whether and when amounts payable and receivable under such arrangements should be netted in the balance sheet.

Measurement of revenue — specific issues

Agency arrangements

9.159 The issue concerning agency arrangements is whether the entity is functioning as:

- An agent acting as an intermediary earning a fee or commission in return for arranging the provision of goods or services on behalf of a principal.

- A principal acting on its own account when contracting with customers for the supply of goods or services in return for consideration.

9.160 Whether an entity is acting as a principal or an agent in transactions is dependent on the facts and circumstances of the relationship.

9.161 IAS 18 states that *"…in an agency relationship, the gross inflows of economic benefits include amounts collected on behalf of the principal and which do not result in increases in equity for the entity. The amounts collected on behalf of the principal are not revenue. Instead, revenue is the amount of commission"*. [IAS 18 para 8].

9.162 Additional guidance is provided in the illustrative examples attached to IAS 18, in paragraph 21.

9.163 An entity is acting as a principal when it has exposure to the significant risks and rewards associated with selling goods or rendering services. Indicators that an entity should account for a transaction as a principal include:

- The entity has the primary responsibility for providing the goods or services to the customer or for fulfilling the order, for example by being responsible for the acceptability of the products or services ordered or purchased by the customer.

- The entity has inventory risk before or after the customer order, during shipping or on return.

- The entity has the latitude in establishing prices, either directly or indirectly, for example by providing additional goods or services.

- The entity bears the customer's credit risk for the amount receivable from the customer.

9.164 One of the indicators that management should consider in determining whether an entity is acting as a principal or an agent is which entity retains the credit risk associated with the product. Frequently, this factor is presumed to carry a significant amount of weight as it relates to payment. However, credit risk is determined to be a less significant factor in many cases. Where an entity is acting as an agent but retains the credit risk associated with the transaction, consideration needs to be given as to whether this represents a financial guarantee. Financial guarantees are discussed in detail in chapter 6.

9.164.1 One feature indicating that an entity is acting as an agent is that the amount the entity earns is predetermined, being either a fixed fee transaction or a stated percentage of the amount billed to the customer.

9.165 An increasing number of entities are selling digital versions of their products such as books, music and movies. These are often sold through e-commerce sites, which act as virtual shops for consumers. Assessing the significant risks and rewards to which each entity has exposure in such transactions can be more difficult than for the sale of physical products, since certain of the indicators described above are less relevant. In most cases inventory risk will be low given that the products are digital and there will be limited credit risk as payments are received before digital goods are supplied. Consequently, other indicators will be given more weight and hence the assessment of whether an entity is acting as principal or agent can be less clear.

9.166 When the transaction's substance is that an entity is acting as a principal, the entity should recognise revenue based on the gross amount received or receivable in respect of its performance under the sales contract. When the substance is that the entity is acting as agent, it should recognise as revenue only the commission or other amounts received or receivable in return for its performance under the contract. In this case, the contract in question may be the agency agreement with its principal rather than the sales contract with the customer. Any amounts received from the customer that have to be paid to the principal should not be included in the agent's revenue.

9.167 The example below illustrates the application of revenue recognition to an agency arrangement involving the sale of goods.

> **Example – On-line retailer**
>
> Entity A operates a website selling used books. Entity A enters a contract with entity B, a used bookshop. The terms and conditions of the contract are such that entity A:
>
> - Stores, transports and invoices the goods sold to the customer.
>
> - Earns a fixed margin on the products sold, but has no flexibility in establishing the sales price.
>
> - Has the right to return the goods to entity B without penalty.
>
> - Is responsible for the goods while the goods are stored in entity A's warehouse, but entity B bears the risk of obsolete goods.
>
> The credit risk rests with entity B.
>
> Should entity A recognise revenue on the transfer of the goods to the customer on a gross or net basis?

> Entity A should recognise an agency fee or commission revenue in its income statement for the sales made on entity B's behalf; that is, on a net basis. Entity A is acting as an agent for the principal, entity B. Entity B does not transfer the risks and rewards of ownership of the goods to entity A. Entity A has the option to return the goods and entity B bears the inventory risk. Entity B retains continuing managerial involvement over the goods by being able to set the sales price.

9.168 Depending on the terms of the agreement between interested parties, consideration for the transaction may be received either gross or net. This may provide an indicator to consider when determining whether an entity is acting as agent or principal. However, the key remains to establish which party holds the risks and rewards of the transaction. It is not appropriate to recognise the transactions as agent transactions simply because the cash flows are received net.

Concession agreements

9.169 Retailers, and in particular department stores, frequently operate an element of their business on a 'store-in-store' or concessionary basis. For example, a large department store may have perfume stores from various fragrance companies within its store. If analysis of the arrangement shows that the concessionaires are acting as principals in their dealings with customers, the department store should not include in its revenue the value of sales made by the concessionaires. In such circumstances, only the commission or rent receivable from the concessionaire constitutes a source of revenue for the store and would be recognised as revenue.

Shipping and handling charges

9.170 An entity may sell items either FOB (free on board) or CIF (cost, insurance, freight). The CIF charges should normally be included as part of revenue unless the entity is acting as an agent in respect of these charges. This may be the case where there is no profit element in the insurance and freight charged to the customer, so that these charges are merely the reimbursement of expenses and are not revenue. In this situation, any consideration attributable to these elements should be netted off against carriage costs in the income statement. However, where the entity is able to determine the additional margin on the CIF charges, revenue should include the full CIF selling price, as the recharge of the CIF elements is effectively a revenue-earning part of the transaction. See further paragraph 9.93 above.

Sales taxes

9.171 Sales taxes are a common example of an agency relationship. When an entity sells a product, sales taxes that are collected on behalf of a government body should be excluded from the revenue recognised. These taxes are remitted to the government in full and do not increase equity. Revenue should, therefore, be presented net of sales taxes. [IAS 18 para 8].

9.172 The treatment of sales taxes differs from that of production taxes, which are treated as a cost of sales. It may be necessary to analyse, for each jurisdiction in which the entity operates, whether certain taxes are sales taxes or production taxes to determine the accounting treatment for the tax in each jurisdiction. For example, excise duty payable by manufacturers of tobacco and alcoholic products is a sales tax in some jurisdictions and a production tax in others. In some jurisdictions it may be difficult to determine the exact nature of the tax. The treatment of excise duty in one jurisdiction may, therefore, be different from that in another.

9.173 When determining whether revenue should be presented gross or net of excise tax, the key consideration is whether the entity is acting as agent or principal. There are several indicators that could help in this determination as outlined in paragraph 9.163. Indicators that the entity is acting as principal (and should recognise the excise taxes received gross) include but are not limited to:

- Risks and rewards of the transaction – the entity holds the inventory and credit risk and the entity will not be refunded excise taxes paid to the government even if the inventory is not sold or receivables are not collected.

- Ability to choose the selling price – the entity has no legal or constructive obligation to change prices in order to reflect excise taxes.

- Basis of calculation – the tax is based on the number of units or on the physical quantity (for example number of cigarettes, or alcoholic content) produced by the entity.

- Point of payment – the entity must pay tax to the government when the unit is produced or relatively close to that date.

As circumstances are likely to differ between jurisdictions, this evaluation should be performed for each different jurisdiction as necessary.

Advertising agency commissions

9.174 Revenue should only be recognised on advertising commission transactions when the service is completed. Advertising agency income may consist of media commissions, which relate to the advertisement appearing before the public and production commissions, which relate to production of the advertisement. Recognition should occur for media commissions when the advertisement appears before the public and for production commissions according to the stage of completion of the project. [IAS 18 App para 12].

Insurance agency commissions

9.175 The appendix to IAS 18 states that insurance agency commissions are recognised on the effective date of commencement or renewal of the related policies, if the agent is not required to render further service. However, where it is probable that the agent will be required to render further services during the life of the policy, the commission or part thereof is deferred and recognised as revenue over the period during which the policy is in force. [IAS 18 App para 13]. Whether part or all of the commission is deferred in the latter situation will depend on the extent to which the agent has performed.

Cash payments not directly linked to sales transactions

9.176 Revenue is measured at the fair value of the consideration received or receivable. This is normally the price specified in the contract taking into account the amount of any trade discounts and volume rebates allowed by the entity. [IAS 18 para 10]. Cash consideration given by a vendor to a customer is a reduction of the revenue earned from the customer, unless the vendor is purchasing separately identifiable goods or services from the customer (see 'Linked transactions' from para 9.141 above). Where no separately identifiable goods are supplied or services provided by the customer in consideration for cash, the substance is that the payment of cash is linked to the sale to the customer. It is therefore treated as a discount on the purchase price and is reflected as a reduction in the revenue recognised (see examples from para 9.143).

9.177 Conversely, a customer may make a payment to a supplier at the outset of a contract as illustrated below. Such payments made at the outset of a contract are common, particularly in relation to outsourcing or sole supplier contracts where amounts are paid in an effort to secure a long-term contract.

Example 1 – Upfront payment made by customer

Entity A is a logistics service provider. Entity A enters into a 10 year service contract with entity B under which entity B will outsource all of its procurement activities to entity A. In addition to earning an annual fee for the services, entity A receives a non-refundable upfront cash payment of C1,000. This is intended to compensate entity A for the following costs it is expected to incur, which have been estimated as:

Expected redundancy costs C350

Expected employee salary increases C650

Entity A should not record income for the receipt of the upfront payment. This payment is linked to the outsourcing contract; paragraph 18 of IAS 18 is, therefore, applicable. The amounts received are deferred and recognised over the term of the service contract. A question may arise in relation to the treatment of any costs prior to the inception of the contract. This is considered in paragraph 9.262.

Example 2 – Marketing support contract

A retailer has signed a 12 month contract to purchase inventory from a supplier. On signing the contract, the retailer has received from the supplier a 'marketing support' payment. The contract requires the retailer to display the products prominently in the stores and to make purchases at the same level as in the previous year. If the conditions are not met for the full 12 month period, the amount is refundable to the supplier.

The income should not be treated as revenue. In substance, the income is a discount on purchases (cost of inventory), which is recognised within cost of sales as the inventory is sold.

The reduction in cost of inventory is earned over the period and is subject to certain conditions being satisfied. It could be argued that, until all of these conditions have been satisfied, none of the payment has been earned and, therefore, it ought to be deferred in total until the conditions have been satisfied. However, satisfying the conditions is within the company's control, so it is reasonable to spread the reduction in the cost of inventory over the period as long as it intends to abide by the conditions for the full period. It would not be acceptable to recognise all this reduction on day one.

Volume or settlement discounting

9.178 Suppliers may offer customers discounts for either achieving a minimum threshold of purchases (volume discounts) or for prompt settlement of outstanding receivables (settlement discounts). In either case, the principles of IAS 18 require the amount of revenue recognised under the transaction to be reduced by the amount of the discount at the time of sale.

9.179 Management will need to estimate the volume of sales or the expected settlement discounts to be taken to determine the revenue to be recognised. The sales price is then reduced by this estimate, such that the revenue recognised represents the fair value of the consideration expected to be received. The need to estimate the amount of discounts expected to be taken does not preclude the reduction of revenue for these discounts. However, if no reliable estimate can be made, the revenue recognised on the transaction should not exceed the consideration that would be received if the maximum discounts were taken.

Example 1 – Estimating cash volume discounts

A paint manufacturer with a 31 December year end offers several large customers stepped rebates on sales based on the following volumes:

Up to 100,000 litres: no discount.
Between 100,000 litres and 250,000 litres: 5% discount on all sales.
Over 250,000 litres: 10% discount on all sales.

All rebates are paid to the customers at the end of the customer's contract year.

At 31 December 20X6, a customer has purchased 140,000 litres of paint. That customer has a history of purchasing over 250,000 litres of paint each year, spread evenly during the year. The customer's contract year runs from July to June.

At 31 December 20X6, the manufacturer has a contractual liability to pay the customer a rebate of 5% on all sales to date, because the volume threshold of 100,000 litres has been exceeded. However, based on all the available evidence, it is probable that the customer will also exceed the 250,000 litre threshold and that the manufacturer will pay a rebate of 10% on all sales. The adjustment to revenue (and the resultant provision made) is, therefore, based on 10% of the sales made to date. If the contract were structured such that sales prices were reduced immediately, rather than rebates paid at the end of the year, giving the same commercial effect, revenue would be adjusted in the same way.

Example 2 – Estimating settlement discounts

A food manufacturer sells canned food and has 100 customers. The delivery of the goods is made on the last day of each month. Standard payment terms require settlement within 45 days of delivery. The entity's policy is to grant a settlement discount of 2% to customers who pay within 15 days of delivery. Experience shows that 45% of customers normally pay within 15 days. How much should the food manufacturer recognise as revenue upon a month end delivery with an invoice value of C1,000?

The food manufacturer should recognise revenue of C991. This amount is calculated by deducting from the total invoiced value the expected amount of discounts to be taken of C9 (C1,000 × 45% × 2%).

Contracts with both contingent and non-contingent consideration

9.179.1 Entities in a broad range of industries may enter into a single contract with both contingent and non-contingent revenue streams. For example, an entity may receive part of a contract's total consideration on delivery of a good, with the remainder being received over a future period, based on the outcome of a future event. If upon receipt of the initial consideration the entity has further goods to supply or services to deliver in relation to the remaining consideration, this may indicate that there is a multiple element arrangement for which the consideration should be allocated to each of the elements (see from para 9.131).

9.179.2 However, in some cases, upon receipt of the initial consideration, the seller has supplied all goods or delivered all services but some part of the consideration remains contingent on the outcome of future events.

9.179.3 IAS 18 is not explicit as to whether all elements of consideration must meet the revenue recognition criteria simultaneously in order for any portion of the revenue to be recorded, or if each element of consideration can be assessed separately and meet the revenue recognition criteria at different times. As a result, we believe that a policy choice can be made; either the contingent and non-contingent elements of consideration are considered separately when determining when revenue is recognised or the contract is assessed as a whole. Whichever policy choice is taken, the policy should be applied consistently and, where material, be disclosed as a key accounting policy. The two approaches are considered in turn below.

Approach 1: Separate assessment of each element of consideration

9.179.4 For contracts with both contingent and non-contingent elements of consideration, a separate assessment of each element of consideration is supportable based on IAS 18 and by analogy to the accounting for incentives and for variations and claims in construction accounting (see from para 9.193 and from para 9.315).

9.179.5 For example, an entity might determine that it has met the revenue recognition criteria for the non-contingent portion of the consideration when the goods and services are delivered, but has failed one of the revenue recognition criteria (such as the probable inflow of economic benefit or reliable estimation of revenue to be recognised) for the contingent portion. In such a situation, the entity records revenue for the non-contingent consideration when the goods or services are delivered. Revenue is recorded for the contingent portion of consideration at the point in time when the revenue recognition criteria are met for that portion. In determining when the revenue recognition criteria are met for the contingent portion, an entity should consider, amongst other factors, historical trends and any specific features of the contract.

9.179.6 The revenue recognition criteria may be met for the contingent portion prior to the receipt of the cash. If all the revenue recognition criteria are met for the contingent consideration prior to cash being received, an asset is recorded. Any such receivable should be measured initially at the fair value of the amount to be received, taking into account the time value of money and any related uncertainties.

> **Example 1 – Sales transactions with contingent and non-contingent consideration**
>
> Entity A sells intellectual property relating to an approved drug to entity B. Title to the intellectual property passes to entity B on sale and entity A has no further ownership rights or performance obligations. Entity A receives C15m in non-refundable cash upon transfer of title. It is also entitled to a payment for each drug sold for a period of 20 years.
>
> The two elements of consideration are considered separately for the purposes of revenue recognition. Entity A records revenue for the amount of cash initially received (C15m) when the revenue recognition criteria for the transfer of the intellectual property to entity B are met, which is when the risks and rewards of ownership have passed from entity A to entity B. Revenue for the contingent consideration is recorded when all the revenue recognition criteria in paragraph 14 of IAS 18 are met in relation to that consideration. In this case, the key judgements will be in relation to the expected future payments on drug sales for the next 20 years. Specifically, determining the point in time that it becomes both probable that there will be an inflow of economic benefit and revenue can be reliably measured. To the extent that the revenue recognition criteria are met prior to the contingent consideration being received, an asset is recorded. Any such asset is measured by reference to future cash flows from the expected future drug sales adjusted as necessary for any uncertainty risk associated with the future cash flows and the time value of money.

Example 2 – Sales transactions with contingent and non-contingent consideration

Entity A sells land to a developer for C100,000. Control and the risks and rewards of ownership of the land transfer upon completion of the sale. Entity A has no continuing involvement or obligation under the contract after the sale is complete. Entity A is also entitled to receive 5% of any future onward sales price in excess of C200,000.

As in example 1, entity A records revenue for the amount of initial cash received (C100,000) when control and the risks and rewards associated with the land are transferred to the developer, in this case upon completion of the sale.

Entity A records revenue for the contingent consideration when all the revenue recognition criteria for that element are met. When assessing whether all the criteria are met, entity A needs to consider the reliable measurement of the contingent revenue and the probability of inflow of economic benefits.

To the extent that entity A cannot predict or reliably measure any future sales price upon completion of the sale to the developer, the recognition of revenue for the contingent portion of consideration will occur later than the recognition of revenue for the non-contingent portion.

9.179.7 It is likely that the key judgements in determining when to recognise contingent revenue are the probability of inflow of economic benefit and the reliable measurement of contingent consideration. These two criteria may be difficult to assess given the contingent nature of the revenue. Depending on the facts and circumstances, these criteria may be met either at the contract's inception or subsequently. Nevertheless, in cases where contingent revenue arrangements are routinely part of the vendor's business model and there is appropriate available evidence as to expected future contingent revenue amounts, it is likely that the revenue recognition criteria will be met prior to the receipt of the contingent consideration.

Example – Timing of recognition for contingent revenue

Entity A develops cartoon characters. Entity B develops and sells cartoons and runs theme parks based on the cartoon characters. Entity B contracts with entity A to purchase the intellectual property rights over certain characters. The intellectual property agreement contains the following key terms:

1   The agreement grants entity B full ownership of the cartoon characters and related intellectual property. No further work will be required on the part of entity A, as entity B's in-house animation department will complete the development of all stories and required drawings.

2   Upon signing the agreement and providing all sketches and story ideas, entity A will be paid C1m up-front. This amount is non-refundable.

3   Entity A will also be paid an amount equal to 1% of all revenues generated from the use of the characters.

Based on prior experience in numerous similar situations, entity B shares its projections with entity A. Entity B has estimated that the contingent revenues will be as follows:

Year	Revenues (C)	A's Share (C)
2010	10,000,000	100,000
2011	25,000,000	250,000
2012	50,000,000	500,000
2013	50,000,000	500,000
2014	25,000,000	250,000
Total	**160,000,000**	**1,600,000**

Entity B has entered into hundreds of similar agreements and the creative artist achieved these payment levels in the majority of cases.

Upon signing the agreement, how much revenue should entity A recognise? Would the accounting change if this were the first time that entity B had entered into such an agreement with a creative artist?

In the scenario where entity B has entered into hundreds of similar agreements with other artists, entity A may be satisfied that all of the revenue recognition criteria have been met in relation to the contingent revenue. Specifically with respect to probability of economic benefit and reliable measurement of revenue, entity A may consider that it has sufficient evidence to meet these criteria given entity B's past experience with similar transactions. In that case, both the up-front payment of C1m and the fair value of the total expected future payments of C1.6m are recorded as revenue when the cartoons and related intellectual property are delivered. A corresponding receivable for the fair value of C1.6m is recorded and adjusted each reporting period to the extent that relevant evidence indicates a change in the expected cash flows and to unwind any discount applied. (Note, that the contingent revenue is discounted only to the extent that the impact is material.)

Where entity B has no experience of similar transactions, entity A may not be satisfied that all the revenue recognition criteria have been met in relation to the contingent revenue. Specifically, future payments may not be deemed probable or reliably measurable. For the up-front payment of C1m, revenue is recognised on delivery of the cartoons, as all the recognition criteria have been met for that non-contingent component of consideration. The expected future payments, being the contingent portion, are only recorded as revenue once all the recognition criteria have been met, that is, once it is deemed probable that economic benefits will flow and revenue can be reliably measured.

9.179.8   In some cases (although not in the example above), the contingent portion of consideration may make up a substantial proportion of the total expected consideration under the contract. When the contingent portion of revenue is significant and its recognition is delayed due to certain IAS 18 criteria not being met, the entity should consider whether the significant risks and rewards of ownership have been transferred on delivery of the underlying good or service and payment of the non-contingent consideration. If this is not the case, it may not be appropriate to recognise revenue for the non-contingent portion of consideration until such time as those criteria are met.

Approach 2: Contract considered as a whole

9.179.9   Where the contract is considered as a whole, revenue is recognised in the income statement when the IAS 18 criteria are met for the overall transaction. Following this approach, assuming that all other revenue recognition criteria are met and that the existence of non-contingent consideration means that the inflow of economic benefit from the contract is probable, the key judgment to be made in determining when to recognise revenue will be determining the date upon which the total consideration for the contract can be reliably measured.

9.179.10   The total consideration on the contract includes the contingent portion of consideration. When assessing the date upon which the total contract consideration can be reliably measured, an entity considers historic trends, factors specific to the contract and the uncertainties relating to the contingent consideration. The assessment of these factors is illustrated in the example in paragraph 9.179.7. If all other criteria have been met on the contract's inception, revenue will be recognised on the date the total contract consideration can be reliably measured. This may occur at the contract's inception or subsequently.

9.179.11   As noted above, in cases where contingent revenue arrangements are routinely part of the vendor's business model and there is appropriate available evidence as to expected future contingent revenue amounts, it is likely that the contingent consideration will be reliably measurable prior to its receipt. In such cases, the overall consideration on the contract will also be reliably measurable prior to the receipt of the contingent element and the revenue on the contract will be recognised in the income statement accordingly.

9.179.12   When revenue is recognised in the income statement and consideration (contingent or non-contingent) has not been received, an asset is recognised. Any such receivable is measured initially at fair value, taking into account the time value of money and any related uncertainties.

9.179.13   Under both approaches, any asset recognised for contingent consideration is adjusted each reporting period to the extent that relevant evidence indicates a change in expected cash flows. Depending on the nature of the adjustment, it may be appropriate to recognise the adjustment as revenue, an impairment of a financial asset or, if the adjustment relates to the time value of money, as finance income or expense. The appropriate treatment depends on the factors driving the change in estimate; this should be assessed on a case by case basis. Further guidance is given on distinguishing between adjustments to revenue and the impairment of financial assets from paragraph 9.50.

Barter transactions

9.180   Companies usually trade for cash or the right to receive cash. Sometimes, however, transactions are undertaken that involve the swapping of goods or services. These are known as barter transactions. IAS 18 does not permit revenue to be recognised in an exchange or barter of similar goods or services. [IAS 18 para 12]. The following paragraphs, therefore, deal only with exchanges of goods or services of a dissimilar nature.

9.181 In terms of determining the point at which a sale should be recognised, the accounting for barter transactions is no different from accounting for transactions that are settled in cash. However, measuring the value of, or consideration for, barter transactions is more difficult than measuring the consideration for transactions undertaken for cash or the right to receive cash.

9.182 Where goods or services are exchanged for goods or services of a dissimilar nature, the revenue is measured at the fair value of the goods or services received, adjusted by the amount of any cash or cash equivalents received or paid. If the fair value of the goods or services received cannot be reliably measured, the revenue is measured at the fair value of the goods or services given up, again adjusted by the amount of cash or cash equivalents received. [IAS 18 para 12].

9.183 A particular issue that arose during the 'dotcom' boom of the late nineties, but is of continuing relevance, is the exchange of advertising services by entities. To deal with the issues, SIC 31 was issued.

9.184 SIC 31 notes that the exchange of similar advertising services does not give rise to revenue under IAS 18; it deals only with the exchange of dissimilar advertising services. [SIC 31 para 3]. It deals with advertising on the internet, on poster sites, on television or radio, published in magazines or journals or through some other medium. [SIC 31 para 1].

9.185 SIC 31 concludes that revenue from an exchange involving advertising services cannot be reliably measured by reference to the fair value of the services received. This is because reliable information is not available to the seller to support such measurement. Revenue in such circumstances should, therefore, be measured at the fair value of the services supplied by the selling entity.

> **Example – Measuring revenue in a barter arrangement involving advertising services**
>
> A travel agency sells low-price holidays. The agency has entered into an advertising agreement with a radio broadcaster. The agreement provides for the travel agency to place radio advertisements to the value of C15,000; in return the radio broadcaster advertises on the travel agency's web page. The travel agency has previously sold similar web site advertising space to others for cash of C10,000.
>
> How should the travel agency account for the advertising revenue?
>
> The travel agency should recognise advertising revenue of C10,000 and advertising expenses, also of C10,000. This is calculated by reference to the value of advertising services provided and not by reference to the value of services received.
>
> The medium of the advertising (broadcasting *versus* web site advertisements) is dissimilar in nature. The sale is, therefore, regarded as a transaction that generates revenue.

9.186 However, SIC 31 states that the seller can only reliably measure the fair value of advertising services it provides in the exchange by reference to non-barter transactions. For such evidence to be sufficient for reliable measurement the non-barter transactions must:

- Involve advertising similar to the advertising in the barter transaction.

- Occur frequently.

- Represent a predominant number of transactions and amount when compared to all transactions to provide advertising that is similar to the advertising in the barter transaction.

- Involve cash and/or another form of consideration (for example, marketable securities, non-monetary assets and other services) that has a fair value that is reliably measurable.

- Not involve the same third party as in the barter transaction.

[SIC 31 para 5].

9.187 An exchange of advertising services that includes partial cash payment provides reliable evidence of the fair value of the transaction to the extent of the cash component, but does not provide reliable evidence for the fair value of the entire transaction. Where partial cash payments of equal or substantially equal amounts are swapped between the counterparties, this cash payment does not support such a fair value. [SIC 31 para 9]. An example of an accounting policy for exchanges of goods and sevices involving advertising is given in Table 9.1.A. The example also shows the disclosure of revenue derived from exchanges in accordance with IAS 18 (see para 9.271).

Table 9.1.A – policy for exchange of goods and services involving advertising

Mecom Group plc – Annual report – 31 December 2011

4. Significant accounting policies (extract)

Revenue recognition (extract)

(d) Revenue from the exchange of goods and services

Revenue includes amounts recognised from the exchange of goods and services ("barter transactions"). The majority of the Group's barter transactions involve advertising services. The Group recognises revenue in relation to barter transactions involving advertising services only when the services exchanged are dissimilar in nature and when the fair value of the advertising services it provides in a barter transaction can be reliably measured by reference only to non-barter transactions that:

- involve advertising similar to the advertising in the barter transaction;

- occur frequently;

- represent a predominant number of transactions and amount when compared to all transactions to provide advertising that is similar to the advertising in the barter transaction;

- involve cash and/or another form of consideration that has a reliably measurable fair value; and

- do not involve the same counterparty as in the barter transaction.

If the above criteria are met, the Group recognises revenue, with an equal and opposite cost recognised as a cost of sale, adjusted for any cash payments made from/to the Group.

6. Revenue (extract)

Included within total revenue from continuing operations for the year of €1,109.1m (2010: €1,155.7m) is €6.2m (2010: €11.1m) arising from exchanges of goods or services. The corresponding amount for discontinued operations is €2.5m (2010: €2.7m). For both continuing and discontinued operations, all amounts are included, for both years, within the category "sales of goods".

Capacity transactions

9.188 In some network-based industries, such as telecommunications and electricity, entities enter into transactions for the sale or purchase of network capacity. For example, a telecommunications entity may sell excess capacity on its trans-Atlantic cables. The entity would probably retain ownership of the network assets, but would convey an indefeasible right of use (usually referred to as an IRU) to the buyer for an agreed period of time.

9.189 Occasionally, an entity may sell capacity to another party in exchange for receiving capacity on that other party's network. Where there is no valid commercial purpose, exchange transactions have come to be known as 'hollow swaps' or 'round-tripping'. An example could be where the telecommunications entity described above had exchanged its excess capacity for another entity's excess capacity on the same route.

9.190 The principles of SIC 31 described above can be equally well applied to capacity transactions. The key consideration is whether the capacity swap transaction has substance.

> **Example – Exchange of telecoms capacity**
>
> Entity A has network capacity on a route from London to Frankfurt, but it needs to increase its capacity between London and Paris (a similar route). Entity B, on the other hand, has capacity between London and Paris, but needs to increase its capacity between London and Frankfurt. Entity A agrees to grant a 20 year IRU to entity B over the route from London to Frankfurt in consideration for a one-off payment of C10m. In addition, entity B agrees to grant to entity A an IRU of equivalent term over the route from London to Paris, also for a one-off payment of C10m.
>
> The transaction's commercial substance must be considered. To the extent that the swap does not have substance, entity A and entity B should not record revenue or costs in respect of the capacity exchanged. To the extent that the transaction has substance, it may be appropriate to recognise revenue.

UK.9.190.1 In relation to exchanges of capacity UITF Abstract 36, 'Contracts for sale of capacity', takes a similar line to SIC 31 on advertising services. It concludes:

> *"Turnover or gains in respect of contracts to provide capacity in exchange for receiving capacity should be recognised only if the assets or services provided or*

received have a readily ascertainable market value. The same principle applies to reciprocal transactions to provide capacity entered into wholly or in part for a cash consideration. No accounting recognition should be given to transactions that are artificial or lacking in substance." [UITF 36 para 23].

UK.9.190.2 For this purpose 'readily ascertainable market value' means the value of an asset that is established by reference to a market where:

- the asset belongs to a homogeneous population of assets that are equivalent in all material respects; and

- an active market, evidenced by frequent transactions, exists for that population of assets.

UK.9.190.3 In view of the similarity of the circumstances and conclusions between UITF Abstract 36 and SIC 31, we consider that the approach set out in the Abstract could also be used in applying IAS 18 to such transactions.

[The next paragraph is 9.192.]

Shares for services

9.192 Revenue recognition issues can arise where entities accept shares in consideration for services provided. This most commonly occurs when the services are provided to start-up entities.

> **Example – Consideration paid in shares**
>
> An entity provides corporate finance services (for example, assistance in preparing for eventual flotation) to start-up entities and proposes to take equity stakes in the start-up entities instead of fees.
>
> The benefit for the corporate finance adviser is that they can share in the success of the start-up entities it advises and the benefit for the start-up entity is that it obtains advice without a cash outflow.
>
> As noted in paragraph 9.40, one of the conditions that need to be satisfied before revenue in relation to provision of services is recognised is that the amount of revenue can be measured reliably. The key difficulty with these sorts of arrangements is whether the value of the shares can be reliably measured.

Listed/marketable securities

Where shares are listed/marketable and there is a sufficiently liquid market, the consideration can be reliably measured and the revenue should be recognised.

Non-marketable securities

Whether revenue can be recognised on the receipt of non-marketable securities will depend on whether a reliable basis exists or can be determined for valuing the securities. Paragraphs AG69 to AG82 of the application guidance to IAS 39 give guidance on ways in which the value might be determined. If a basis of valuation exists then the amount of revenue can be reliably measured and should be recognised in the income statement.

Vouchers, coupons and customer loyalty programmes

Vouchers granted for consideration

9.193 IAS 18 does not deal specifically with vouchers that require future performance; however, payment received in advance of future performance should be recognised as revenue only when the future performance to which it relates occurs.

9.194 The sale of a voucher is a contract with a customer in its own right; it should be considered together with the contract that arises if and when the voucher is exercised. IAS 18 states that *"the recognition criteria are applied to two or more transactions together when they are linked in such a way that the commercial effect cannot be understood without reference to the series of transactions as a whole"*. [IAS 18 para 13]. The revenue from the sale of the voucher is generally accounted for when the seller performs under the latter contract, that is when the seller supplies the goods or services on exercise of the voucher.

9.195 A common type of vouchers issued for consideration are gift vouchers issued by retailers. The following example explains the appropriate accounting for gift vouchers.

> **Example – Accounting for gift vouchers**
>
> A retailer has a 31 December year end. While in store, customers may purchase a gift voucher that entitles the holder to purchase goods from the store up to the amount spent on the voucher. The sale of gift vouchers greatly increases in December as customers purchase the vouchers to present as gifts to family and friends. In December, the retailer sold gift vouchers with a face value of C1,000. None of the gift vouchers were redeemed in December, but all of the gift vouchers were redeemed in the following year. The gift vouchers expire one year from the date of purchase.
>
> Where the retailer has only limited historical evidence of voucher redemption rates it should not recognise revenue from the sale of the gift vouchers until the voucher has been redeemed for merchandise, until the vouchers expire or until it can be reliably demonstrated that it is unlikely the voucher will ever be presented. Until this point, consideration received for the voucher should be deferred and recognised as a liability. This determination should be made for each individual voucher (or group of vouchers in an ageing profile) and not to the whole portfolio of vouchers. See from paragraph 9.136.
>
> If, however, the retailer maintains records on redemption rates that have historically been shown to be reliable, then the accounting may differ. With the additional fact that the retailer has a reliable, established pattern of 20% of vouchers not being redeemed before expiry, the retailer may choose to adopt a policy of allocating the consideration for the 20%, the 'breakage', to the remaining 80% of the vouchers that are expected to

be redeemed. The breakage revenue would then be recognised as the other vouchers are redeemed. If the retailer follows this approach, it must apply the policy consistently in future years and should adjust the non-redemption rate if estimates change.

Vouchers granted as part of a sales transaction

9.196 Where vouchers are issued as part of a sales transaction and are redeemable against future purchases from the seller, revenue should be reported at the amount of the consideration received or receivable less the voucher's fair value. In substance, this is a multiple element arrangement, as the customer is purchasing both goods or services and a voucher. The revenue should be allocated based on the fair values of the goods or services and the voucher (taking breakage into consideration). See from paragraph 9.138. This can be differentiated from the situation described in paragraph 9.195, where there is only one element to the sales transaction.

Customer loyalty programmes

9.197 Some companies offer point schemes or award credits. Examples are airlines that offer 'free' air miles and supermarkets that offer loyalty cards that accumulate points that can then be used to reduce the cost of future purchases. A variety of loyalty programmes is currently available in the market place, of which there are three main types:

■ Schemes where points earned through the purchase of goods or services can only be redeemed for goods and services provided by the issuing entity. Such schemes are normally self-administered. The same principles apply to these schemes as apply to the issue of vouchers by the entity as part of a sale transaction.

■ Schemes where points earned through the purchase of goods or services cannot be redeemed for goods or services sold by the issuing entity. The points may, however, be used in other establishments that participate in the loyalty scheme.

■ Schemes whereby points earned through the purchase of goods or services can be redeemed either at the issuing entity or at other entities that participate in the loyalty programme.

9.198 IFRIC 13 was issued in June 2007 which deals with 'award credits' (sometimes known as vouchers or points). Historically, certain entities were accounting for the provision of loyalty award credits as marketing expenses. IFRIC 13 clarified the distinction between items that are adjusted against revenue and arrangements that are treated as a marketing expense. The 'Basis for conclusion' explains that marketing costs are incurred independently of a sale transaction, so any vouchers, allowances and discounts or other incentives offered to a customer as part of a sales transaction are part of a multiple element arrangement resulting in the deferral of some revenue. This clarification may impact discussions beyond accounting for incentives.

9.199 The fair value of the consideration received or receivable in respect of the initial sale is allocated between the award credits and the other components of the sale. IFRIC 13 does not mandate a specific approach for estimating the fair value of an award credit.

9.200 The fair value of award credits is determined based on the fair value to the holder, not the cost of redemption to the issuer. The fair value of award credits may be estimated by reference to the discount that the customer would obtain when redeeming the award credits for goods or services. The nominal value of this discount should be reduced to take into account:

- The discount the customer obtains when redeeming the award credits compared to the discount that could be obtained by customers who do not redeem award credits. This includes consideration of the extent to which the award credits are similar to other vouchers that are distributed to customers free of charge.

- The proportion of award credits not expected to be redeemed.

[IFRIC 13 para AG 2].

9.200.1 In the 'Improvements to IFRSs' issued in May 2010, paragraph AG2 was amended to clarify that when the fair value of award credits is measured on the basis of the value of the awards (that is, goods or services) for which they could be redeemed, the fair value of the award credits should take account of expected forfeitures as well as the discounts or incentives that would otherwise be offered to customers who have not earned award credits from an initial sale. However, the improvement did not specify an approach for ascertaining fair value and as such either a residual or a relative fair value method may be used, dependent on which is deemed most appropriate.

> **Example 1 (the residual method) – Voucher for future money off (100% redemption expected)**
>
> A hotel company operates a loyalty scheme. A customer who stays in one of the company's hotels is given a voucher entitling them to a discount of C10 on a subsequent stay in any of the company's hotels. The price for one night's stay in a hotel is C100. The marginal cost to the hotel of one extra guest is negligible, because most of the hotel's costs are fixed.
>
> The initial stay in the hotel is a multiple element arrangement, the components being the night's accommodation and the voucher. The total consideration (C100) is allocated to the components based on their fair values; C10 is allocated to the voucher, as that is its fair value to the customer. The residual of C90 is allocated to the sale. The fact that the marginal cost of honouring this voucher is negligible is irrelevant.

Example 2 (*the relative fair value method*) – Voucher for future money off (10% redemption expected)

The facts are the same as in example 1 except that the hotel company has reliable evidence that only 10% of vouchers are ever redeemed. No other factors affect the voucher's fair value. The fair value of the voucher is, therefore, C1.

The hotel has sold goods with a fair value (if sold individually) of C101 for consideration of C100.

Allocating the discount between the two components based on their fair values results in C99.01 being allocated to the initial stay in the hotel and C0.99 to the voucher.

9.200.2 An award credit's face value and the expected redemption rate are important factors in determining the award credit's fair value. However, some other factors may also be relevant, as considered below:

- A seller includes with a popular line of goods a voucher giving money off a subsequent purchase of a line of goods that are not popular with customers or that are close to their sell-by date. The fair value of the vouchers will be relatively lower if the seller is likely to offer similar discounts to all customers in order to dispose of the goods.

- A tour operator sells a holiday and offers C50 off the list price of a subsequent holiday taken with the tour operator between certain dates. If the operator has in the past offered or is likely to offer similar discounts on holidays between those dates to all customers, new or returning, the fair value of the C50 offer is most likely an amount below C50. This is because, as the discounts are generally available, the customer who acquires the C50 discount is not C50 better off than other customers.

- A supermarket sells a product with a voucher for money off the next purchase of that item, but at the same time regularly sends customers sheets of free coupons that they can use to purchase those and other goods at the same discounted price. In such a situation, the value of the voucher could again be lower than its face value.

9.201 The estimation of the fair value of a voucher includes consideration of the proportion of vouchers expected to be redeemed. The value released to revenue upon a voucher's redemption also needs to be based on the number of vouchers expected to be redeemed. [IFRIC 13 para AG 2]. When it is expected that only half of all vouchers will be redeemed, this will reduce the fair value allocated to each voucher by half. However, on redemption of a voucher, the fair value of two vouchers will be released to revenue. If this were not the case, the fair value of the vouchers never to be redeemed would be deferred indefinitely. For transactions outside the scope of IFRIC 13, the recognition of vouchers that are never redeemed is considered in the example at paragraph 9.195.

9.202 An example of the accounting for a voucher issued as part of a sales transaction is as follows:

Example – Mechanics of IFRIC 13 accounting

A retailer sells a toy for C10. A voucher entitling the bearer to a discount of C5 on a subsequent purchase of the same type of toy is issued with each sale. The retailer has historical experience that for every two vouchers issued, one is redeemed.

The customer is purchasing both the toy and a voucher. Therefore, part of the consideration received should be allocated to the 'money-off' coupon. There are two ways in which the revenue could be allocated to the coupon; by using a residual method or by using relative fair values. Under the residual method, the revenue allocated to the voucher is based on the fair value of those vouchers, with the residual consideration being allocated to the sale of the toy. Under the relative fair value method, revenue is allocated to each component of a transaction on a relative fair value basis. Both approaches are illustrated below.

The residual method

In the absence of other factors, the fair value of the voucher would appear to be C2.5. This is calculated by comparing the nominal value of the voucher (C5) and adjusting that value for the proportion of vouchers expected to be redeemed (50%), arriving at a fair value of C2.5.

The consideration received is equal to the aggregate fair value of the toy and the voucher.

The accounting entry upon sale of, for example, 10 toys and issue of the vouchers, would be:

	C	C
Dr Cash	100	
Cr Revenue		75
Cr Deferred revenue		25

Given 50% of the vouchers are expected to be redeemed, out of the 10 initial sales made, a further five sales will result in use of a voucher. The aggregate accounting entries for these five sales would be as follows:

	C	C
Dr Deferred revenue	25	
Dr Cash	25	
Cr Revenue		50

The amount of revenue recognised upon redemption of each voucher is based on the number of vouchers redeemed relative to the total number expected to be redeemed. Given that only half of all vouchers are expected to be redeemed, amounting to five vouchers in this case, revenue of C5 (1/5 × 25) is released on the redemption of each voucher.

The relative fair value method

The facts are as in the example above whereby a retailer sells a toy for C10 along with a voucher entitling the bearer to a discount of C5 on a subsequent purchase.

As above, the fair value of the toy is C10 and the fair value of the voucher is C2.5. The revenue attributable to the toy on a relative fair value basis is, therefore, C8 ((C10/C12.5) × C10) and the revenue attributable to the voucher is C2 ((C2.5/C12.5) × C10). The accounting entries for the sale of 10 toys and issue of the vouchers would be:

	C	C
Dr Cash	100	
Cr Revenue		80
Cr Deferred revenue		20

Given 50% of the vouchers are expected to be redeemed, the aggregate accounting entries for these five sales would be as follows:

	C	C
Dr Deferred revenue	20	
Dr Cash	25	
Cr Revenue		45

The amount of revenue recognised upon redemption of each voucher is based on the number of vouchers redeemed relative to the total number expected to be redeemed, so revenue of C4 (1/5 × 20) is released on the redemption of each voucher.

9.203   The estimation of the fair value of a voucher includes considering the proportion of vouchers expected to be redeemed. The expected rates of redemption may change over time as management update its estimates. Further to this, at any balance sheet date, the cumulative actual redemption rates may prove to be different from management's original expectations.

9.203.1   In the illustrative examples to IFRIC 13, it is clear that a balance sheet approach should be used to account for changes in both the ultimate expected and actual redemption rates for customer loyalty arrangements. This results in adjustments being made to revenue as illustrated below.

Example – Adjustments to revenue for changes in expected and actual redemption rates

Entity A grants 100 award credits as part of sale transactions in year 1. The award credits have a three year life. Initial expectations are that 80 credits will be redeemed. The fair value of the award credits is C1.25. C100 of the consideration received is, therefore, deferred at the time of the transaction.

At the end of year 1, 40 points have been redeemed, hence, C50 (being C100 × (40/80)) is recognised as revenue.

Scenario 1

At the end of year 2, 20 points have been redeemed. In addition, the redemption expectations have changed such that management now think that 75 points will ultimately be redeemed. Using the balance sheet approach, the total amount recognised as revenue at the end of year 2 would be:

(40 redeemed in year 1 + 20 redeemed in year 2) / (75 expected to be redeemed in total) × C100 = C80. As C50 was recognised in year 1, the amount to be recognised in year 2 is C30.

If the assumptions remain unchanged, the remaining C20 will be released in year 3.

Scenario 2

At the end of year 2, only 2 additional credits have been redeemed. In addition, the redemption expectations have changed such that management now think that 90 credits will ultimately be redeemed. The total amount recognised at the end of year 2 would be:

(40 redeemed in year 1 + 2 redeemed in year 2) / (90 expected to be redeemed in total) × C100 = C47. As C50 was recognised in year 1, the amount to be recognised in year 2 is a debit of (C3).

If the assumptions remain unchanged, the remaining C43 will be recognised in year 3.

The illustration in scenario 2 is an extreme example and is unlikely to occur if redemption expectations are updated on a regular basis. However, it is included to illustrate how the adjustments made as a result of these revisions in expectations may cause credits or debits to the income statement. As noted from paragraph 9.215, we consider that it is appropriate to recognise any such adjustments (whether debits or credits) in the revenue line of the income statement.

9.204 The provision of money-off coupons might result in a future sale appearing to be made at a loss. However, it is unnecessary to provide for any future loss if when the total consideration is apportioned between the linked transactions, there is no loss. This is illustrated by the following example.

Example – Second transaction appears to be made at a loss

An entity buys a particular product for C5 and normally sells it for C8. It issues a voucher for 50% off a second item if a customer buys one. How should this be accounted for?

If the fair value of the voucher is ignored, there is a gain on the first sale of C3 (C8 — C5) and a loss on the second sale of C1 (C4 — C5). However, part of the consideration from the first sale, representing the fair value of the voucher, should be deferred and recognised as revenue when the second sale is made. If the fair value of the voucher is C2 (nominal value of C4 is adjusted for the discount that could be obtained by customers who do not redeem vouchers and the proportion of vouchers not expected to be redeemed), the revenue on the first sale would be C6; the revenue on the second sale would also be C6 (C4 + C2).

9.205 IFRIC 13 requires an entity issuing award credits to determine whether it is collecting revenue on its own account (as principal in the transaction) or on behalf of the third party (as an agent) when the award credits are redeemed by the third party. When the entity is collecting revenue on behalf of a third party it earns commission income:

■ commission income is the net amount (the difference between the consideration allocated to the incentive and the amount payable to the third party supplying the incentive); and

■ commission income should be deferred until the third party is obliged to supply the awards and is entitled to receive consideration for doing so.

[IFRIC 13 para 8].

When the issuing entity is acting as principal and collecting consideration on its own behalf, revenue is measured as the gross consideration. However, an element of the revenue needs to be deferred.

Example – Loyalty card schemes

Entity A runs a loyalty card scheme independently from any retailers. Entity A has contracts with each retailer and the retailer can take any one of the following different roles:

■ Be an issuer of points,

■ Be a redeemer of points.

■ Both issue and redeem points.

The customer holds a loyalty point card that is issued by entity A and allows the customer to earn points at a given list of retailers and use points at other retailers. The nominal value of the point issued is C1 and for each point issued, the issuing retailers will pay C0.98 to entity A, in doing so earn C0.02 of commission income. Once the issuing retailer has paid entity A, it has no further obligation to the customer. When a redeeming retailer redeems points with a face value of C1, it will receive compensating cash from entity A of C0.91. Entity A's margin is the difference between the redemption price and the issue price. Where a retailer both issues and redeems points, there is no netting of cash flows: cash is paid to entity A for points issued and cash is received from entity A for points redeemed. The benefits for the participating retailers being:

■ There is no need to administer the scheme.

■ There is no obligation in respect of outstanding points and the retailer can exit the scheme.

■ The fair value for the customer will be higher if the points are redeemable at a variety of stores.

The accounting for such a scheme is as follows. When the retailer makes a sale of C10, it issues points with face value of C1:

	C	C
Dr Cash	10.00	
Cr Revenue		9.00
Cr Commission income		0.02
Cr Liability to A		0.98

When the risks and rewards associated with the points are immediately passed to entity A, the liability is offset:

	C	C
Dr Liability	0.98	
Cr Cash		0.98

When the points are redeemed, the redeeming retailers will recognise the revenue made by the points with a face value of C1 at C0.91:

	C	C
Dr		
Receivable from Company A	0.91	
Cr		
Revenue		0.91

9.206 Companies that issue award credits need to collect the information necessary to estimate the individual fair value of the award credits and expected redemptions. Historical information will often provide the best estimate of the redemption rate and where records are computerised there should be sufficient data to make an assessment. The estimate might be more difficult with informal arrangements, for example, where a customer holds a card that is stamped every time a coffee is bought (entitling the holder to the tenth cup of coffee free). It is not clear how entities gather data to support a reliable fair value; however, the interpretation does not provide any exception for this type of scheme.

Vouchers redeemable for cash

9.207 Accounting for the deferral of revenue in respect of vouchers requires further consideration when vouchers may be redeemed for cash. The accounting is complicated by the fact that in most situations, a portion of vouchers will never be redeemed because they are lost, damaged or invalidated over time.

9.208 Vouchers that are redeemable for cash meet the definition of a financial liability under IAS 39. As a result, the financial liability cannot be derecognised until the derecognition criteria of IAS 39 are met (see further chapter 6.6). Furthermore, the liability may not be measured at an amount less than the cash redemption value. [IAS 39 para 49]. As a result, the obligation must be accounted for in full for all outstanding vouchers, until the obligation to deliver cash is extinguished, through the voucher's redemption or, where the voucher has an expiry date, through expiry. [IAS 39 para 39]. For vouchers with no expiry date that are redeemable for cash, the financial liability will remain indefinitely. The liability is not recognised until the entity has an obligation to issue the voucher.

Vouchers granted without consideration

9.209   Some vouchers may be granted for no consideration. An example is where a supermarket, service provider or manufacturer issues money-off coupons or vouchers that can be redeemed in the future for goods or services. These are often included as part of marketing circulars or newspaper advertisements.

9.210   Where vouchers are distributed free of charge and independently of another transaction, such vouchers do not give rise to a liability, except where redemption of the vouchers will result in products (or services) being sold at a loss. Where this is the case, the seller has entered into an onerous contract and provision will need to be made in accordance with IAS 37. When the vouchers are redeemed, the seller should recognise revenue at the amount received for the product, that is, after deducting the discount granted on exercise of the vouchers from the normal selling price. This type of voucher is no different from a reduction in the sales price made during an annual or seasonal sale.

> ### Example – Vouchers granted for no consideration
>
> A clothing retailer has launched a new promotional campaign. It publishes a coupon in a national newspaper giving a discount of 5% off any purchase over C50 in any of the retailer's stores. The retailer's normal gross margin on sales is 60%.
>
> The retailer should not recognise the distribution of coupons in its financial statements at the time the coupons are distributed. Rather, the retailer should treat the coupon as a discount against revenue when the customers redeem them. The discount that results from the customer using the coupon should not be recorded as a marketing expense, as the coupon results in a reduction of the goods' sales price. The cost of the newspaper advertisement should be expensed when the newspaper is published.

Free products

9.211   Some sales promotions are described as 'buy one, get one free' or 'two for the price of one', or a vendor may price products below cost to attract volume. The revenue on such transactions is the actual sales proceeds and the purchase or production cost of the 'free' product and 'loss leader' is a cost of sale.

Example 1 – Buy one get one half price

A retailer is offering a special 'buy one get one half price' deal whereby customers who purchase one box of chocolates are then entitled to purchase another box at the same time and obtain the second box for half the price. How should the retailer record the transaction?

The revenue recognised is the cash consideration received for the two boxes of chocolates. The additional cost from offering the second box at a discount to the normal price is recorded as a cost of sales, not as a marketing expense.

Example 2 – First product is sold for free

A start-up entity retails an electronic product. It is attracting a customer base by allowing the customer to have the first product free. The customer is under no obligation to take further products.

There has been no inflow of economic benefit to the entity as this transaction was undertaken for nil consideration. The transaction is not linked to any other transaction, as the customer can just take the free product and walk away. Neither the customer nor the vendor has any rights or obligations relating to future transactions as a result of giving (or taking) the free product. As a result, the cost of the goods given away is charged as a marketing cost. It is not a cost of sale, as no sale has been made.

Other reward schemes

9.212   Other reward schemes that are similar to points schemes include those where customers become entitled to benefits (such as free products) when they have satisfied certain criteria. Such criteria might be achieving a certain level of purchases or they might be time-based, for example, continuing to be a member of a scheme for a specified period.

9.213   Where benefits are based on achieving a level of purchases, the benefit should be recognised by the supplier as the purchases occur. That is, part of the revenue equal to the fair value of the benefit to the customer should be deferred. This should be deferred until the free products are given (and matched against any costs thereof that are then charged).

9.214   Where a benefit is given in the form of a cash rebate, the payment should be charged against the revenue that has been deferred, so that only the net revenue is recorded.

9.214.1   Where criteria are based on a time factor (for example, on remaining a member for a specified period), consideration needs to be given as to whether the customer needs to complete certain acts or whether the criteria are genuinely time-based. Criteria that are time-based are likely to be rare. There is likely to be some other action by the customer required, such as payment of a membership fee or subscription. Part of the fee or subscription should be treated as deferred revenue and recognised when the free products or other benefits are claimed (and any other associated costs are recognised). Where the benefits are genuinely time-based only, with no further action required by the customer, the obligation arises immediately and provision would need to be made and discounted if necessary to reflect the fact that the cost may not crystallise in the short-term.

Adjustments to revenue

9.215 The adjustments made to revenue for discounts, returns and sale incentives can lead to entries being made that are debits to the revenue line of the income statement. This will often be the result when the actual results differ significantly from estimates originally made. Examples of when this may occur are given in paragraphs 9.79 and 9.203.1.

9.216 The recognition of such an adjustment may seem counter-intuitive. However, to the extent that the adjustment has been generated through the application of the requirements of IAS 18 or IFRIC 13 (to record revenue net of discounts and to make estimates in relation to the level of expected returns and expected redemption of sale incentives), we consider that it is appropriate to present such adjustments in revenue.

[The next paragraph is 9.218.]

Dividends, royalties and other practical applications

Dividends

9.218 Dividend income should be recognised when the shareholder's right to receive payment is established. [IAS 18 para 30]. Determining when a right to receive payment has been established will vary from one jurisdiction to another. However, the accounting for the receipt of dividends should mirror the accounting in the paying entity under IAS 10.

9.219 IAS 10, states that dividends payable to holders of equity instruments (as defined in IAS 32) that are declared (that is, the dividends are appropriately authorised and no longer at the entity's discretion) after the balance sheet date should not be recognised as a liability at the balance sheet date. [IAS 10 para 12]. Similarly, dividends should not be recognised as receivable if they have not been declared by the balance sheet date. IAS 10 is dealt with in chapter 22.

UK.9.219.1 In the UK, directors are normally permitted by the entity's articles of association to pay interim dividends without shareholder approval, but the dividend is not a liability for the entity until it is paid (see chapter 22). Final dividends are usually recommended by the directors and then declared by the shareholders by ordinary resolution. The shareholders cannot declare a dividend that exceeds the amount recommended by the directors. Normally, therefore, the shareholders' right to an interim dividend is established when it is paid and the right to a final dividend is established when it is declared by the shareholders in general meeting. If the right to the dividend cannot be established until the income is received, then recognition should be delayed until then.

Example – Recognition of dividend income

During the year ended 31 December 20X1 entity A made the following investments in entity B (a listed entity):

1 January 2,000 shares, registered on 28 February 20X1
15 June 5,000 shares, registered on 10 July 20X1
5 October 3,000 shares, registered on 20 December 20X1
29 December 1,000 shares, registration outstanding

The directors of entity B declared an interim dividend on 31 July 20X1 of C0.05 per share, with a last registration date of 30 June 20X1. This dividend declaration does not require shareholder approval. The dividend was paid on 30 September 20X1.

At 31 December 20X1 the directors of entity B proposed a final a dividend of C0.15 per share, with a last registration date of 30 November 20X1. The proposed final dividend was approved by shareholders at the annual general meeting on 31 January 20X2 and the dividend was paid on 31 March 20X2.

Entity A and entity B both have December year ends. What should entity A recognise as dividend income in the year ended 31 December 20X1?

Entity A should recognise dividend income at 31 December 20X1 in respect of the interim dividend, but it should not recognise dividend income in respect of the final dividend.

The interim dividend is recognised as income by entity A, as it was paid by entity B in the period. However, entity A is not entitled to receive the final dividend until the shareholders approve it.

Therefore, entity A should recognise a dividend of C100 (2,000 × C0.05) in respect of the interim dividend on the 2,000 shares purchased in January 20X1.

9.220 The situation for parent companies' investments in subsidiaries is no different from that where the shareholding is held as a trade investment.

[The next paragraph is 9.222.]

9.222 Bonus issues of shares by a subsidiary to its parent (or similar transactions such as stock dividends or stock splits) do not transfer any value from the subsidiary to the parent. There are more shares in issue, but there is no economic significance to the transaction. Therefore, a bonus issue does not give the parent a reason to recognise a gain by increasing the carrying value of its investment in the subsidiary. Bonus issues are considered further in chapter 24.

9.222.1 When investors have the right to elect for their dividend payment to be in either cash or shares, there is economic significance to the transaction when the choice between cash or shares is substantive. Revenue would be recognised if the number of shares offered is close to or equals the fair value of the cash offer. However, if the cash offer is priced in such a way that it would be unlikely that it is to be taken, this would be no different from the bonus issue discussed above, and no dividend income would be recorded.

Licensing and royalties

Royalties

9.223 Royalties include other fees for the use of assets such as trademarks, patents, software, copyright, record masters, films and television programmes. IAS 18 requires that royalties should be recognised on an accruals basis in accordance with the relevant agreement's substance. [IAS 18 para 30].

9.224 The terms of an agreement normally indicate when the revenue has been earned. In general, the application of the accruals basis means that revenue is recognised on a straight-line basis over the agreement's life or another systematic basis such as in relation to sales to which the royalty relates.

9.225 For example, if an agreement provides for a 5% royalty to be received on each sale by a third party it would be normal to recognise royalty income on the basis of 5% of total sales made by the third party.

9.226 On the other hand, in a similar situation, an up-front non-refundable payment might be made to the entity by the other party and then a royalty of 1% of sales might be receivable thereafter. In that situation, it would be appropriate to reflect the agreement's substance rather than its form and spread the up-front receipt over the expected number of sales to be made in the future where, in substance, the receipt is an advance royalty.

Licensing

9.227 In general, revenue should not be recognised under licensing agreements until performance under the contract has occurred and the revenue has been earned.

Example 1 – Licence fee with continuing obligation

Entity A grants a licence to a customer to use its web-site, which contains proprietary databases. The licence allows the customer to use the web site for a two year period (1 January 20X1 to 31 December 20X2). The licence fee of C60,000 is payable on 1 January 20X1.

How should entity A account for the licence fee received?

The substance of the agreement is that the customer is paying for a service that is delivered over time. Although entity A will not incur incremental costs in serving the customer, it will incur costs to maintain the web site.

The revenue from the licence fees should be accrued over the period that reflects the provision of the service. The entity has an obligation to provide services for the next 2 years, therefore, the fee of C60,000 received on 1 January 20X1 should be recognised as a liability. Each month for the period January 20X1 to December 20X2, an amount of C2,500 should be released from the liability and recognised as income to reflect the service that is delivered.

Example 2 – Licence fee with a trigger event

A film distributor grants a licence to a cinema operator. The licence entitles the cinema to show the film once on a certain date for consideration of the higher of a non-refundable guarantee or a percentage of the box office receipts.

Based on the facts provided, the film distributor should recognise the revenue on the date the film is shown. It is only when the film is shown that the revenue has been earned (however see also para 9.229, which deals with slightly different facts).

9.228 An assignment of rights for a non-refundable amount under a non-cancellable contract that permits the licensee to use those rights freely and where the licensor has no remaining obligations to perform is, in substance, a sale. [IAS 18 App para 20].

9.229 Another example where a licensing agreement may be recognised as an outright sale is if a non-refundable one-off fee has been received for the foreign exhibition rights to a film that allow the licensee to use the rights at any time in certain countries without restriction. In such a situation, it may be appropriate to recognise the income when the fee is due. Since the licensor has no control over the product's further use or distribution and has no further action to perform under the contract, the licensor has effectively sold the rights detailed in the licensing agreement.

9.230 If a licence is granted for a limited period of time, the question arises as to whether revenue should be recognised at one point in time (for the sale of the license) or spread over the licence term. The appropriate treatment will depend on the facts and circumstances. A fixed license term is an indicator that the revenue should be recognised over the period; however, this is not definitive. The fixed period suggests that all the licence's risks and rewards have not been transferred to the customer. In some situations, there may be no clear performance obligation for the vendor subsequent to the transaction and the asset's risks and rewards may have been transferred for the asset's entire useful life. In such a case, it may be appropriate to recognise the revenue upfront even if the licence rights are sold for a fixed period only.

9.231 Whether it is appropriate to recognise revenue over the period of the license or as a sale of goods will be a matter of judgement. The following additional indicators should be considered when making that judgement (the presence of the indicator implying that treatment as a sale may be appropriate).

- Fixed fee or non-refundable guarantee. The fee is pre-determined in amount. It is non-refundable and is not contingent on the occurrence of a future event.

- The contract is non-cancellable. This will ensure that risks and rewards have been transferred and the inflow of economic benefit to the vendor is probable.

- The customer is able to exploit the rights freely. For this to be possible, the licence rights must be a separable component that can meet the sale of goods criteria on their own. The vendor should not have any significant involvement during the contractual period and should not have the right to control or influence the way the customer uses the rights (as long as the customer acts within the specified contractual terms). The ability to sub-sell the rights or even to stop using the licence at any time, may indicate that the customer is able to exploit the rights freely.

- Vendor has no remaining obligations to perform subsequent to delivery. Such obligations might include significant updating of the product (for example, software upgrades), marketing efforts and fulfilling specified substantive obligations to maintain the reputation of the vendors' business and promote the brand in question.

[The next paragraph is 9.233.]

Franchise fees

9.233 Franchise agreements may provide for the supply of initial services (such as training and assistance to help the franchisee set up and operate the franchise operation), subsequent services and the supply of equipment, inventory and other tangible assets and know-how. Therefore, these agreements may generate different types of revenue such as initial franchise fees, profits and losses from the sale of fixed assets and royalties.

9.234 In general, franchise fees should be recognised on a basis that reflects the purpose for which they were charged. The appendix to IAS 18 states that revenue from the supply of assets should be recognised when the items are delivered or title passes. Fees charged for the use of continuing rights granted by a franchise agreement or for other continuing services provided during the agreement's term should be recognised as the service is provided or the rights are used. [IAS 18 App para 18].

9.235 However, the appendix to IAS 18 goes on to require that, where the franchise agreement provides for the franchisor to supply equipment, inventory or other assets at a price lower than that charged to others, or at a price that does not allow the franchisor to make a reasonable profit on the supplies, part of the initial franchise fee should be deferred. The amount of the initial franchise fee deferred should be sufficient to cover the estimated costs in excess of the price charged to the franchisee for any assets and to allow the franchisor to make a reasonable profit on these sales. This deferred income can then be recognised over the period the goods are likely to be provided. The balance of the initial fee should be recognised when performance of the initial services and other obligations (such as assistance with site selection, staff training, financing and advertising) has been substantially accomplished. This approach is based on the fact that the initial fee in these circumstances is unlikely to be capable of being treated as a separable component.

9.235.1 In some situations, the consideration receivable by an entity will comprise both contingent and non-contingent elements. The accounting for such transactions is considered from paragraph 9.179.1.

9.236 Similarly, if there is no separate fee for the supply of continuing services after the initial fee or if the separate fee is not sufficient to cover the cost of providing any subsequent services together with a reasonable profit, then part of the initial fee should also be deferred and recognised as the subsequent services are provided.

9.237 The initial services and other obligations under an area franchise may be based on the number of outlets established in the area. If so, revenue from franchise fees attributable to the initial services is recognised in proportion to the number of outlets for which the initial services have been substantially completed. [IAS 18 App para 18].

9.238 If the initial fee is collectable over an extended period and there is significant uncertainty as to whether it will be collected in full, revenue should be recognised as collection of the fee is made.

Financial services fees

9.239 Financial service fees arise in many forms, including transactions such as loan origination fees, commitment fees and also management and performance fees in relation to funds and unit trusts.

9.240 Determining the revenue relating to financial services can be challenging because of the interrelationship between IAS 18 and IAS 39. IAS 39 governs the recognition and measurement of financial instruments and IAS 39 is dealt with in detail in chapter 6. Revenue recognition for financial service fees depends on the nature and substance of the services provided as well as the subsequent basis of accounting for any related financial instrument. The description of fees levied for financial services may not be indicative of the nature and substance of the services provided.

9.241 The appendix to IAS 18 provides some guidance on the accounting for such fees. The appropriate accounting for financial service fees is primarily determined by whether the fees are:

■ An integral part of the financial instrument's effective interest rate.

■ Earned as a result of services being provided.

■ Earned upon the execution of a significant act.

9.242 It may be difficult to determine in which of these categories a fee should be included. In addition, a fee may cover more than one service by the financial institution and may, therefore, appear to fit into more than one category. An example of this is structuring fees on the origination of financial instruments.

Fees that are an integral part of the effective interest rate

9.243 Fees that are an integral part of the effective interest rate are normally treated as an adjustment to the effective interest rate. [IAS 18 App para 14(a)]. The standard deals specifically with three types of fees:

■ Origination fees relating to the creation or acquisition of a financial asset other than one that is classified under IAS 39 as 'at fair value through profit or loss'.

 Such fees include fees for assessing the financial position of the borrower, evaluating and recording guarantees, collateral and other security, negotiating the instrument's terms, preparing and processing documentation and finalising the transaction. These activities are an integral part of originating the financial instrument and, together with the related direct costs (transaction costs), are deferred and recognised as an adjustment to the effective interest rate. The application of the effective interest rate method is discussion in detail in chapter 6.

■ Commitment fees received to originate a loan when the loan commitment is outside IAS 39's scope.

 If it is probable that an entity will enter into a specific lending arrangement, and the loan commitment is outside IAS 39's scope, the commitment fee is deferred and, together with the related direct transaction costs, is recognised as an adjustment to the effective interest rate. If, however, the commitment period expires without a loan having been made, the fee is recognised as revenue on expiry of the commitment period. Loan commitments that are within IAS 39's scope are accounted for as derivatives and measured at fair value.

■ Origination fees received on issuing financial liabilities measured at amortised cost.

Such fees are an integral part of generating an involvement with a financial liability. If a financial liability is not classified as 'at fair value through profit or loss' the fees, together with related transaction costs incurred, are included in the initial carrying amount of the financial liability and recognised as an adjustment to the effective interest rate on the instrument. An entity should distinguish fees and costs that are an integral part of the effective interest rate from origination fees and transaction costs that relate to the right to provide services, such as investment management services.

[IAS 18 App para 14(a)].

Example – Loan origination fee

Entity A grants a loan to entity B for C100,000 on 1 January 20X1. The loan is repayable at 31 December 20X5. Interest of 8% that is equal to the market rate is payable annually. The loan origination fees amount to C2,000 and are paid by entity B to entity A on 1 January 20X1.

How should entity A account for the loan origination fees?

Loan origination fees charged by entity A are an integral part of establishing a loan. These fees are deferred and recognised as an adjustment to the effective yield. [IAS 18 App A example 14(a)(i)]. The effective yield is the interest needed to discount all the cash flows (C8,000 for 5 years and the principal amount of C100,000) to the present value of C98,000. In this case the effective yield obtained by a discounted cash flow calculation is approximately 8.51% and, therefore, the entity recognises a finance income at 8.51% on the carrying amount in each period.

9.244 When origination fees relate to financial instruments measured at fair value through profit or loss, these fees may be taken immediately to profit and loss. However, this is only permitted where the instrument's initial fair value excluding the origination fees is evidenced by comparison with other observable current market transactions in the same instrument or based on a valuation technique whose variables include only data from observable markets. Without such evidence, it will not be possible to distinguish between the origination fees and the fair value of the instrument itself and, therefore, it would not be appropriate to treat the origination fees as a separate transaction.

Fees earned as services are provided

9.245 Other types of financial service fees are earned as the service is provided. Three types of such fees are dealt with in the standard.

- Fees charged for servicing a loan. These are recognised as revenue as the services are provided.

- Commitment fees to originate a loan that is outside IAS 39's scope (as opposed to commitments that are within IAS 39's scope as discussed in para 9.243). If it is unlikely that a specific loan will be made and the loan commitment is outside IAS 39's scope, the commitment fee is recognised on a time basis over the commitment period. Loan commitments that are within IAS 39's scope are accounted for as derivatives and measured at fair value.

- Investment management fees. Fees for managing investments are recognised as revenue as the services are provided. Where incremental costs are incurred in acquiring an investment management contract they are recognised as an asset if they can be separately identified and reliably measured and if it is probable that such costs are recoverable. Incremental costs are those that would not have been incurred if the entity had not secured the management contract. The asset represents the entity's contractual right to benefit from providing management services and is amortised as the entity recognises the related revenue. Entities are permitted to assess the recoverability of costs of securing investment management contracts on a portfolio basis where the entity has a portfolio of such contracts.

[IAS 18 App para 14(b)].

9.246 There are some financial services contracts that involve both the origination of one or more financial instruments and the provision of investment management services. The standard gives as an example a long-term monthly savings contract linked to the management of a pool of equity securities. In such cases, the provider of the contract must distinguish between the transaction costs relating to the financial instrument's origination and the costs of securing the right to provide investment management services. [IAS 18 App para 14(b)].

Fees earned upon the execution of a significant act

9.247 A third type of financial service fee relates to performing a particular, significant act. Commissions received on the allotment of shares or placement fees for arranging a loan between a borrower and an investor are examples of such significant acts. Revenue should be recognised when the act has been performed, for example, when the shares have been allotted or the loan arranged. However, fees earned for the completion of a significant act must be distinguished from fees that relate to future performance or to any risk retained. A loan syndication fee, for example, may be earned when the transaction takes place, if the entity that arranges the loan either has no further involvement or retains part of the loan package at the same effective interest rate for comparable risk as the other participants. [IAS 18 App para 14(c)].

9.248 It is common within the investment management industry for a financial broker to receive an upfront payment from a fund manager for signing up a new customer. When the financial broker is also the fund manager, the question arises as to whether a non-refundable upfront fee can be recognised as revenue. The IFRS IC (formerly IFRIC) provided limited guidance (in the form of a rejection) in determining whether an upfront fee could be recognised as revenue (details given below):

- Fees may be recognised as revenue only to the extent that services have been provided.

- Whilst the proportion of costs incurred in delivering services may be used to estimate the stage of completion of the transaction, incurring costs does not by itself imply that a service has been provided.

- The receipt of a non refundable initial fee does not, in itself, give evidence that an upfront service has been provided or that the fair value of the consideration paid in respect of any upfront services is equal to the initial fee received.

- To the extent that:

    - an initial service can be shown to have been provided to a customer;

    - the fair value of the consideration received in respect of that service can be measured reliably; and

    - the conditions for the recognition of revenue in IAS 18 have been met (see para 9.34 above).

upfront and ongoing fees may be recognised as revenue in line with the provision of services to the customer.

9.248.1 The interaction between this Interpretations Committee rejection and the example in paragraph 17 of Appendix A to IAS 18 on membership fees has been a subject of wide debate. We consider that the same theory is being applied in both cases. To the extent that the fee is received upfront and the seller has no further obligations, the seller should recognise the fee on the date it has been received. Before this is possible, however, management should consider whether there is any indication that the fee is linked to other services or obligations. This could be indicated, for example, if the fee was not at fair value or the pricing of other services to be provided in the future could only be commercially understood with reference to the fee received upfront. In order to recognise upfront fees received as revenue upon receipt, management would need to demonstrate the existence of a separate service provided upfront; it would also be necessary to reliably estimate the fair value of the consideration received for that service. See paragraph 9.122 for discussion of membership fees.

9.249 If it is determined that the upfront fee is linked to future services to be provided, the revenue would be deferred on the balance sheet and recognition would occur over the period in which those future services were performed.

Management and performance fees

9.250 An investment manager generally provides a number of services including investment advice, research services and certain administrative services under an investment advisory agreement to an investment fund in return for a fee. The fee is typically a fixed or a reducing percentage of the fund's average net assets. This type of fee is usually called a management fee. Recognition of revenue from management fees that are not dependent on fund's performance would be recognised when the criteria for sale of services are met (see from para 9.106).

9.251 In addition, fees could also be based on performance; these fees are known as incentive or performance fees. A performance fee is paid to the investment manager if it achieves a performance in excess of a specified minimum during a specified period (the performance period). The amount of the performance fee payable to the manager if this condition is met may be an absolute share of the fund's performance or a share of performance in excess of a specified benchmark, such as the FTSE 100 index or Standard and Poor's 500 index. There are numerous permutations of how these fees are calculated including the benchmark used and the performance period. Both the management and performance fees are fees for the provision of services.

9.252 A performance period may not coincide with a reporting period. For example, an investment manager prepares interim financial statements for the 6 month period ended 30 June 20X7, and the performance period is for the 12 months ending 31 December 20X7. In this case, the performance fee will only be received if the investment manager achieves the performance condition at the end of the 12 month period. The fee is contingent upon a future event.

9.252.1 In these situations there will often be issues over the reliable measurement of the revenue as well as a question over whether there is a probable inflow of economic benefits. The recognition of revenue for a performance fee will depend on the facts and circumstances. However, generally, we consider that revenue would not be recognised until a service has been delivered and the recognition criteria in IAS 18 have been met.

9.252.2 In some situations the consideration receivable by an entity will comprise both contingent and non-contingent elements. The accounting for such transactions is considered from paragraph 9.179.1.

Transfers from customers

9.253.1 Historically, there has been diversity in accounting practice where entities have entered into arrangements where assets have been transferred to an entity by its customers. IFRIC 18 was issued in response to this and is specifically relevant for the utilities industry. It considers how an entity should account for assets received from a customer in return for connection to a network and/or ongoing access to goods or services.

9.253.2 The interpretation applies to agreements with a customer for the transfer of property, plant and equipment that must be used to connect the customer to a network or provide the customer with an ongoing supply of goods or services. The same accounting applies if:

- the customer transfers cash to the entity and that cash is to be used only to build an asset that in turn is to be used to connect the customer to a network and/or provide ongoing access to goods or services; or

- the customer pays a third party to provide the connection service, who then transfers the connection asset to the network entity upon completion.

The interpretation does not apply to government grants or service concession arrangements. These are covered in more detail in other standards and interpretations. [IFRIC 18 paras 4-7].

9.253.3 For example, IFRIC 18 applies to the accounting by a utility provider when a house developer installs water mains and pipes to connect the houses being developed to the water network and transfers the mains and pipes to the utility provider. The developer has exchanged the pipes and utilities with the utility entity in order to get a connection to the network and/or receive an ongoing supply of water. Note that paragraph 2 of the interpretation clarifies that *"Transfers of assets from customers may also occur in industries other than utilities"*. The interpretation is, therefore, relevant to similar transactions outside the utilities industry. See paragraph 9.253.8.

9.253.4 The key issues to consider when applying the interpretation are:

- Was an asset received?

- How should the asset be valued?

- How should the related income be recognised?

9.253.5 IFRIC 18 requires:

- A transferred item of property, plant and equipment from a customer to be recognised by the recipient as part of its own property, plant and equipment to the extent that it meets the definition of an asset in the Conceptual Framework from the recipient's perspective. All relevant facts are considered to determine whether the item is controlled by the recipient and whether it is probable there will be future economic benefits. For example, the water utility in the example in paragraph 9.253.3 would consider whether it can: use the pipes and mains to supply other customers; decide when to sell, maintain or replace the assets; and use the assets as security for its borrowings.

- The asset to be recognised initially at fair value, in accordance with the guidance in IAS 16 in respect of measurement on initial recognition of property, plant and equipment acquired as a result of a non-monetary exchange. The corresponding credit is revenue that is recognised in accordance with IAS 18. The application of IAS 18 may require this revenue to be recognised in the income statement immediately or at a later date depending on when the revenue recognition criteria in IAS 18 are met.

■ The entity receiving the asset determines whether the asset has been received in exchange for one or more separately identifiable services — for example, connection to a network, ongoing access to that network or a supply of goods or services. Two features that indicate that connection to a network is a separately identifiable service are:

   ■ The service is delivered to the customer and has stand-alone value for that customer.

   ■ The fair value of the service can be measured reliably.

[IFRIC 18 paras 9-15].

9.253.6 The requirement for stand-alone value means the customer transferring the asset receives value from the connection separate from any other service received subsequently. The houses to be sold by the developer in the above example are likely to be more valuable with access to the water network than without, so it is likely that there is a stand-alone value in the connection. The fair value of the pipes and mains would be recognised as revenue immediately by the water utility if it has no further service obligations resulting from the transaction. If the fair value of the connection service cannot be measured reliably, revenue should be deferred and recognised over the period in which the ongoing access service is provided.

9.253.7 A feature that indicates that providing the customer with ongoing access to a supply of goods or services is a separately identifiable service is that, in the future, the customer making the transfer receives the ongoing access, the goods or services, or both at a price lower than would be charged without the transfer of the item of property, plant and equipment. [IFRIC 18 para 16]. An example of a situation where the service provided to the customer has no stand-alone value is given below.

> **Example – Service delivered to the customer has no stand-alone value**
>
> A real estate company is building a residential development in an area that is not connected to the electricity network. In order to have access to the electricity network, the real estate company is required to construct an electricity substation that is then transferred to the network company responsible for the transmission of electricity. The network company concludes that the transferred substation meets the definition of an asset. The network company then uses the substation to connect each house of the residential development to its electricity network.
>
> In this case, it is the homeowners that will eventually use the network to access the supply of electricity, although they did not initially transfer the substation. By regulation, the network company has an obligation to provide ongoing access to the network to all users of the network at the same price, regardless of whether they

transferred an asset. Therefore, users of the network that transfer an asset to the network company pay the same price for the use of the network as those that do not. Users of the network can choose to purchase their electricity from distributors other than the network company, but must use the company's network to access the supply of electricity.

The fact that users of the network that transfer an asset to the network company pay the same price for the use of the electricity network as those that do not indicates that the obligation to provide ongoing access to the network is not a separately identifiable service of the transaction. Rather, connecting the house to the network is the only service to be delivered in exchange for the substation. The network company should, therefore, recognise revenue from the exchange transaction at the fair value of the substation when the houses are connected to the network in accordance with in paragraph 20 of IAS 18.

9.253.8 Revenue is recognised when each separately identifiable service is delivered. When only one service is provided, revenue is recognised when the service is performed. If there are ongoing services to be delivered as well as a connection, revenue is allocated to each service using an appropriate method and recognised when each service is delivered. [IFRIC 18 paras 18, 19]. It would not, for example, be appropriate to recognise the revenue matched against the depreciation on the asset. The allocation of revenue to multiple elements is considered from paragraph 9.131. Costs associated with connection may be capitalised only to the extent that they meet specific criteria as discussed from paragraph 9.254 onwards.

9.253.9 IFRIC 18 may also apply to transactions outside the utilities industry. An example is given below.

Example – IFRIC 18 and an outsourcing contract

An entity enters into an agreement with a customer involving the outsourcing of the customer's IT functions. As part of the agreement, the customer transfers ownership of its existing IT equipment to the entity. Initially, the entity must use the equipment to provide the service required by the outsourcing agreement. The entity is responsible for maintaining the equipment and for replacing it when the entity decides to do so. The useful life of the equipment is estimated to be three years. The outsourcing agreement requires service to be provided for 10 years for a fixed price that is lower than the price the entity would have charged if the IT equipment had not been transferred.

The facts above indicate that the IT equipment is an asset of the entity. The entity, therefore, recognises the equipment and measures its cost on initial recognition at its fair value in accordance with paragraph 24 of IAS 16. The fact that the price charged for the service to be provided under the outsourcing agreement is lower than the price the entity would charge without the transfer of the IT equipment indicates that this service is a separately identifiable service included in the agreement. The facts also indicate that it is the only service to be provided in exchange for the transfer of the IT equipment. The entity, therefore, recognises revenue arising from the exchange transaction when the service is performed, that is over the 10 year term of the outsourcing agreement.

9.253.10 The interpretation is clear that the guidance applies specifically to transfers of property, plant and equipment. This poses the question of whether the guidance is applicable to situations where assets other than property, plant and equipment are transferred by a customer, for example, intangible assets. The Interpretations Committee clarified in the basis for conclusions that, while the scope of IFRIC 18 should not be extended to include such transfers, the guidance in IFRIC 18 may be applied by analogy in determining the appropriate accounting in other situations.

Recognising costs

9.254 As noted in paragraph 9.43 above, reliable measurement of costs incurred is one of the criteria to be satisfied before revenue can be recognised for the sale of goods or rendering of services. Alongside considering whether costs can be reliably measured, entities must also consider the period in which costs should be recognised in the income statement.

9.254.1 In certain situations, the timing of costs can vary significantly from the profile of revenue recognition. This can happen, for example, in outsourcing contracts where the service provider may incur costs before revenue is recorded (see from para 9.177). When this occurs, the question may arise as to whether it is appropriate to defer recognising these costs in the income statement until revenue recognition begins.

9.255 The IASB's Conceptual Framework is based on a balance sheet approach. This balance sheet approach applies in considering how costs and revenues should be recognised. As a result, balances should only be recognised on the balance sheet to the extent that they meet the Conceptual Framework's definition of an asset or a liability.

9.256 IAS 18 refers to the matching of revenue and expenses, stating that revenue and expenses that relate to the same transaction are recognised at the same time. [IAS 18 para 19]. The reference is made in the context of sale of goods, but applies equally to transactions involving the rendering of services. It is important to note that, whilst IAS 18 does make reference to the matching of revenue and expenses, it does this within the context of the Conceptual Framework as a whole.

[The next paragraph is 9.258.]

9.258 When considering costs in relation to a sales contract — be it for goods, services or a construction contract – it is important to firstly determine which standard is applicable.

9.259 IAS 11 is clear that, for construction contracts, direct costs of the contract can be deferred in the balance sheet when certain criteria are satisfied. In contrast, no specific guidance exists in IAS 18 for recognising costs in relation to selling goods or rendering services. However, paragraph 21 of IAS 18 states that, for the rendering of services, the requirements of IAS 11 generally apply to recognising revenue and associated expenses. This cross-reference clarifies that the principles of percentage of completion accounting, as outlined in IAS 11, are applied to contracts for the rendering of services only to the extent that they do not conflict with the principles of IAS 18. Additionally, it would be inappropriate to delay recognising costs associated with service contracts in the income statement solely on the basis that paragraph 21 of IAS 18 states the requirements of IAS 11 are *"generally applicable"* to service contracts.

9.260 When considering a contract, other than a construction contract, the treatment of costs will be dependent on the nature of the costs and the relevant facts and circumstances. It may be appropriate to capitalise costs if the entity can recognise an asset under IAS 2, IAS 16 or IAS 38. Some costs, while not meeting the recognition criteria in these standards, may be carried forward in accordance with paragraph 27 of IAS 11 provided the costs meet the definition of an asset in the Conceptual Framework. An asset is defined as:

> *"An asset is a resource controlled by the entity as a result of past events and from which future economic benefits are expected to flow to the entity."* [Framework para 4.4(a)]

9.260.1 This could include costs that relate to future activity on the contract (provision of the service). However, as such costs must meet the definition of an asset and also be contract costs as defined in IAS 11, there are limited situations where this is the case. For example, although staff training costs are costs that relate to the future activity of the business, they do not meet the definition of an asset. This is because, as the trained member of staff can leave at any time, the entity does not control any benefit associated with the training.

9.261 The application of this principle to contracts for the provision of a service is considered in the examples below.

Example 1 – Contract for the performance of services to numerous customers

A shipping entity provides specialised transportation services to numerous customers. A ship travels (empty) to the load port where it picks up cargo. It then loads the cargo and transports it to the discharge port. Costs are incurred on the voyage to the load port. The question arises as to whether these costs can be deferred until the vessel reaches the load port so that they are recognised in the income statement in the same period as the revenue?

Management should consider the nature of the costs incurred on a case by case basis. Only costs meeting the definition of inventory, property, plant and equipment or intangible assets under IAS 2, IAS 16 or IAS 38 respectively or otherwise meeting the definition of an asset in the Conceptual Framework would be capitalised (in line with the relevant standard). In all other cases, costs should be expensed as incurred. To illustrate, the cost of fuel used to travel to the load port would be expensed, whereas fuel purchased but not yet utilised would be capitalised as inventory. Other costs, such as staff training costs, would be expensed as incurred.

Example 2 – Contract for the performance of a repetitive service to one customer

Entity C offers outsourced travel booking services to corporate clients. A five-year contract is put in place whereby entity C will undertake all travel bookings on behalf of one specific customer. Entity C allocates separate space within its premises for the provision of services to that customer. Therefore, it is possible to obtain all direct costs for the contract, for example, rent, staff costs, computer and telephone links. Over the period of the contract, entity C will make numerous individual bookings for this specific customer.

The revenue is on a transactional basis — that is, for each individual booking a fee is charged. Often, transaction numbers are relatively low in the first year of the contract. In addition, certain non-recurring costs (such as training costs) are incurred in the early years of the contract. As such, income is expected to be below costs in the early years of the contract. However, the contract is very likely to be profitable overall as, in later years, the number of transactions will increase and fewer non-recurring costs will be incurred. The entity has good historical data when predicting future revenues and costs of the business under each contract based on experience with similar clients.

As above, costs incurred would be capitalised if they meet the definition of inventory, property, plant and equipment or intangible assets. For example, the cost of acquiring equipment such as desks and computers would be capitalised under IAS 16. Other costs would be expensed as incurred.

Revenue associated with each booking would be recognised as each booking is made. If it is not appropriate to capitalise costs and they are expensed as incurred, then based upon the transaction pattern above, this may result in losses being made in the early years of the contract and profits being made in the later years.

9.262   Service contracts may have initiation or pre-contract costs as well as costs incurred during the contract. For construction contracts, paragraph 21 of IAS 11 requires costs incurred to secure a contract to be included as part of contract costs provided they can be separately identified, reliably measured and it is probable that the contract will be obtained. If such costs are expensed in the period they were incurred, they cannot be capitalised and included in contract costs when the contract is obtained in a subsequent period. This guidance specifically applies to construction contracts, but the question arises as to whether the costs of securing a service contract or a contract to deliver goods can be deferred and recognised over the contract period in a similar way. For such contracts, we consider that the principle in paragraph 9.260 above applies. Consequently, such costs may be capitalised only when they meet the definition of inventory, property, plant and equipment, intangible assets or an asset, within the Conceptual Framework, provided such an asset falls within the definition of a contract cost under paragraph 27 of IAS 11.

UK.9.262.1   The UITF issued Abstract 34, 'Pre-contract costs'. It contains some useful guidance on the nature of pre-contract costs, but is stricter than IAS 11 because it allows inclusion of directly related costs only from the point where UITF 34 becomes virtually certain that a contract will be obtained. Like

IAS 11, the abstract prohibits the reinstatement of costs that have already been written off.

Example 1 – Costs of acquiring a service contract

Telecoms operator A pays commissions of C175 to a third-party dealer for the acquisition of a subscriber that has passed the usual credit checks. The subscriber signs a 12 month contract with a minimum revenue guarantee. Operator A has estimated that the expected margin from the minimum contracted revenues will be C250. The subscriber acquisition costs are expected to be recovered in full within the initial contract term. Operator A tracks subscriber acquisition costs on an individual subscriber basis.

In this case, operator A should capitalise the cost of acquiring the service contract (the payment of C175) as these costs meet the definition of an intangible asset. Operator A has acquired an identifiable benefit — namely, the minimum contractual net cash flows from the subscriber – and has a legally enforceable contractual right to receive the minimum net cash flows. Additionally, it is probable that the contract's economic benefits will flow to A.

Example 2 – Pre-contract costs for a service contract

An event organiser runs exhibitions for its clients. Experience shows that each event makes a profit. In some cases, costs are incurred before the year end, but the exhibition takes place after the year end.

The timing of cost recognition in the income statement depends on the types of costs that have been incurred (see from para 9.258). As above, costs may be capitalised if they fall to be inventory, property, plant and equipment or intangible assets. Other costs should be expensed as incurred.

More specifically, it may be appropriate to capitalise costs relating to the pre-payment of space for the exhibition as an intangible asset under IAS 38 — the payment represents the right to use something in the future. It may also be possible to capitalise costs incurred in acquiring tables, chairs and other furnishings for the exhibition as these may meet the definition of property, plant and equipment under IAS 16.

However, costs such as staff training costs do not meet the definition of an asset as noted above in paragraph 9.260.1.

9.263 The same principle can be applied to situations outside of service arrangements. Consider the following examples:

Example 1 – Premium paid for the extension of a contract

An entity has a contract with a supplier that expires in mid 20X8 (a three year contract at C4 million per annum). It has identified a new and cheaper supplier (five year contract at C3 million per annum). The new supplier will not be ready until January 20X9. The current supplier has stated that it will continue services beyond contract expiry until the end of the year, but will charge a premium rate over the rate they would have charged of C1 million, that is C5 million for the year.

It would not be appropriate to carry the premium forward and spread it over the contract term with the new supplier on the basis of the cost savings that will be made.

There are no economic benefits from the payment to the old supplier as this is not a prepayment for services to be received in the future from that old supplier, nor will the payment generate any cash inflow. Hence the C5 million should be expensed in the year which it is incurred.

Example 2 – Payment for termination of a contract

Entity X terminated a contract with a computer supplier that provided entity X with production facilities. The termination payment was C250,000. It has entered into a contract with a new supplier and this will save the entity money in the future.

Entity X may not carry forward the termination payment. There is no benefit from the old contract that has been terminated, so the costs do not meet the definition of an asset. The new contract is a separate agreement, and the costs associated with it should be recognised as incurred.

9.264   As highlighted in the examples above, the key consideration with regards to the treatment of costs relating to sales contracts is whether they meet the definition of an asset at the balance sheet date in line with IAS 2, IAS 16 or IAS 38. This is the case whether the costs have been incurred in relation to a service contract, the sale of goods or prior to the inception of a contract.

[The next paragraph is 9.267.]

Disclosure

9.267   IAS 18 requires disclosure of the accounting policies adopted for the recognition of revenue, which should include a description of the methods used to determine the stage of completion of transactions that involve the rendering of services. [IAS 18 para 35(a)].

9.268   The purpose of the disclosure of accounting policies is to enable users to understand the financial statements. This is discussed further in chapter 4.

9.269   Because IAS 18 does not prescribe any specific accounting policies that must be followed, a detailed description of the policies applied will be required. It is expected that an entity's revenue recognition accounting policy will address as a minimum, for each principal source of revenue:

- The timing of the recognition of revenue.

- The measurement of revenue.

- The treatment of discounts or loyalty plans offered to customers.

- The method of allocation of revenue between different components of the same transaction (where different recognition policies are applied to the components).

UK.9.269.1 The FRRP has noted in the past that several companies' revenue accounting policies were lacking. It noted that this was a particular issue for companies with a range of revenue streams.

9.270 The standard also requires such disclosure of each significant category of revenue that has been recognised in the period, including revenue from:

- Sale of goods.

- Rendering of services.

- Interest.

- Royalties.

- Dividends.

9.271 The amount of revenue derived from exchanges of goods or services, which is included in each of the significant categories of revenue, should also be disclosed. [IAS 18 paras 35(b),(c)]. Table 9.1.A above includes an example of disclosure of revenue derived from exchange transactions involving advertising.

9.272 Revenue is one of the items required to be presented in an income statement under IAS 1.

9.273 In most situations, 'revenue' in the income statement will include revenue from sale of goods and provision of services, and interest will be included under a heading 'finance income'. However, the classification adopted will depend on the nature of an entity's operations and, for example, interest income would generally form part of a bank's 'revenue'. See further chapter 4.

UK.9.273.1 UK company law is more restrictive than IAS 18 in terms of profits that may be included in the profit and loss account. Paragraph 13(a) of Schedule 1 of SI 2008/410, 'The Large and Medium-sized Companies and Groups (Accounts and Reports) Regulations 2008' states: *"...only profits realised at the balance sheet date shall be included in the profit and loss account"*. IAS 18 contains no such restriction and, therefore, there could be instances where revenue that represents an unrealised profit might be included in the profit and loss account under IFRS, which the provisions of the Act would not permit to be included.

UK.9.273.2 However, Schedule 1 of SI 2008/410 does not apply to companies preparing their financial statements under EU-adopted IFRS and so the restriction against taking unrealised profits to the profit and loss account does not apply to those companies.

UK.9.273.3 In any case, whether this difference between the Act's requirements and IAS 18 would have any effect in practice is debatable and examples of the effect are not immediately apparent. This is because IAS 18 itself requires that for revenue to be recognised it should be capable of reliable measurement and it should be probable that the economic benefits associated with the transaction will flow to the entity. It is more likely that the difference will be more important in the context of accounting for revaluation gains such as those on investment property that are covered by IAS 40 (see chapter 17).

UK.9.273.4 However, there is a further effect of the difference that is likely to have a continuing impact where companies prepare their individual financial statements under IFRS. UK rules on distributions require generally that distributions may only be made out of realised profits. Company law states that for the purpose of determining realised profits reference should be made to:

"...principles generally accepted, at the time when the accounts are prepared, with respect to the determination for accounting purposes of realised profits or losses." [CA06 Sec 853(4)].

UK.9.273.5 The effect of the requirement in paragraph UK.9.273.1 above has been that generally the profit and loss account is made up of realised and, therefore, distributable profits. If the income statement under IFRS includes unrealised profits it will be necessary to keep track of such profits and exclude them when considering profits available for distribution.

UK.9.273.6 The Institute of Chartered Accountants in England and Wales (ICAEW) and the Institute of Chartered Accountants of Scotland (ICAS) issued guidance in Tech 02/10, 'Guidance on the determination of realised profits and losses in the context of distributions under the Companies Act 2006'. This is now *de facto* GAAP on what constitutes a realised profit. The concepts of 'realised' and 'distributable' profits' are considered in detail in chapter 23.

Property transactions and IFRIC 15

Background

9.274 This section gives guidance on whether IAS 18 or IAS 11 is applicable to a particular transaction. IAS 11 applies to the construction of an asset whose terms have been specifically negotiated. Thus, if revenue arises from such a contract, revenue will be recognised under IAS 11, otherwise, IAS 18 will apply (see para 9.338 below). [IAS 11 para 3]. In the construction industry it has not always been clear whether a property sale should be accounted for following IAS 18 or IAS 11. The accounting becomes even more complex when a contract involves the acquisition of land for development, construction and related sale of the completed property.

IFRIC 15 — Agreements for the construction of real estate

9.275 Property companies enter into transactions of different types. In some, they build developments, where the properties may be 'pre-sold' so that the contract has been entered into before construction begins and all the terms and conditions of the sale are known. In other cases, they build houses or developments speculatively.

9.276 IFRIC 15 gives guidance as to which standard applies when accounting for the construction of real estate. In addition, paragraph BC6 of the interpretation states that the principles of the interpretation can be used by analogy for other industries, in accordance with IAS 8, as similar issues can arise in many industries.

9.277 Entities most affected will be those that have previously recognised revenue from the sale of real estate (or other significant assets) under IAS 11 where the application of IAS 11 is no longer appropriate. This might apply for example to entities that build residential houses or apartments for sale to individuals 'off plan' and may result in revenue being recognised later than under their existing accounting policy.

9.278 The interpretation also provides further guidance on the separation of a contract into its components to determine the basis for revenue recognition. This may include the delivery of services, such as property management, in addition to the sale of goods and construction services. IAS 18 might apply to one component of a contract and IAS 11 to another.

Scope

9.279 The interpretation applies to accounting for revenue and associated expenses by entities that undertake construction of real estate directly or through sub-contracts. IFRIC 15 is applied to transactions where the entity has concluded that the arrangement will result in the recognition of revenue, but the timing of recognition is unclear.

9.280 A single agreement for the construction of real estate may apply to the delivery of additional goods or services such as the sale of land or provision of property management services. An entity may need to split such an agreement into its separately identifiable components in accordance with paragraph 13 of IAS 18 (see from para 9.131 above). Each component would be considered separately to determine the appropriate guidance and the basis for revenue recognition. To do this, paragraphs 10 to 12 of IFRIC 15 should be applied to each separate construction contract component and then the segmentation criteria of IAS 11 should be applied if the component is within the scope of that standard. The segmentation requirements in IAS 18 would be applied for other revenue components. Any further segmentation of the construction contract element would only take place if the specific segmentation criteria in IAS 11 were met. [IFRIC 15 para 8]. The segmentation criteria in IAS 11 are discussed in paragraph 9.297 onwards below.

Determining whether IAS 11 or IAS 18 applies

9.281   Determining whether an agreement for the construction of real estate is within the scope of IAS 11 or IAS 18 requires the application of judgement. IFRIC 15 interprets the guidance in both IAS 11 and IAS 18 as it relates to agreements for the construction of real estate as follows:

- IAS 11: an agreement meets the definition of a construction contract when the buyer is able to specify the major structural elements of the design of the real estate either before or during construction.

- IAS 18: an agreement is for the sale of goods when the buyer has only a limited ability to influence the design, for example, selecting a design from a range of options that is determined by the entity. [IFRIC 15 para 12].

9.282   The substance of an agreement to manufacture a large volume of similar assets to a buyer's specification should be considered carefully to determine whether the agreement is for the sale of goods within IAS 18's scope or a construction contract within IAS 11's scope. Factors that indicate the contract may be a construction contract include, but are not limited to:

- The complexity in the product's structural design – items being produced are highly complex and the major elements of structural design are specified by the buyer.

- Inter-relationships or inter-dependencies between the items being produced. A construction contract is defined as a contract specifically negotiated for the construction of an asset or combination of assets that are closely interrelated or interdependent. [IAS 11 para 3].

- Transfer of significant risks and rewards associated with each item produced is not restricted to delivery of completed units. Rather, significant risks and rewards of the work in progress transfer to the buyer as construction or manufacture progresses. If each individual item must be delivered in order for the risks and rewards associated with those items to transfer, this is an indicator that the contract is for the sale of goods and not a construction contract. [IFRIC 15 para BC28].

9.283   IFRIC 15 contains a flow chart to help users follow the interpretation. The flow chart (reproduced in an annex to this chapter) considers the nature of the agreement under the following three headings.

Agreement is a construction contract

9.283.1   An entity applies the percentage of completion method in line with the guidance in IAS 11 for an agreement that meets the definition of a construction contract. IAS 11 applies to both construction of real estate and any directly related services. [IFRIC 15 para 11]. The percentage of completion method is discussed from paragraph 9.325.

Agreement is for rendering of services

9.283.2   An entity that is responsible only for the assembly of materials supplied by others but not the provision of materials (that is, it has no inventory risk for the construction materials) applies the guidance in IAS 18 for sale of services and revenue is recognised by reference to the stage of completion. Rendering of services is discussed from paragraph 9.106.

Agreement is for the sale of goods

9.283.3   An entity recognises revenue when the recognition criteria in paragraph 14 of IAS 18 are met for an agreement that is for the sale of goods. The criteria may be met at different times, when control and significant risks and rewards of ownership transfer to the buyer:

■   An entity may continually transfer control and the significant risks and rewards of ownership as construction progresses (referred to as 'continuous transfer'). The revenue recognition criteria may be met and, hence, revenue is recognised continuously throughout the construction period by reference to the stage of completion using the percentage of completion method. [IFRIC 15 para 17]. This is covered from paragraph 9.285.

■   Alternatively, the entity may transfer control and the significant risks and rewards of ownership of the real estate at a single point in time, and the revenue would be recognised at that point. [IFRIC 15 para 18].

9.284   IFRIC 15 recognises that judgement should be applied carefully and notes how the agreement's terms, the surrounding facts and circumstances and the local legal requirements should be considered.

The continuous transfer model

9.285   IFRIC 15 introduces the concept of a continuous transfer model that is applicable to certain contracts for the sale of goods. Agreements with continuous transfer characteristics might not be encountered frequently. [IFRIC 15 para BC26]. This model only applies where the construction of real estate was not to the buyer's specification, but the rights of ownership transfer to the buyer as construction occurs as a result of legal or constructive provisions in the relevant jurisdictions. In other words, the buyer would have control and the significant risks and rewards of ownership of the real estate constructed to date and throughout the construction. This means that the buyer would retain control and the significant risks and rewards of ownership of the work in progress if the construction halted at any time. For example, continuous transfer may occur when the developer is building on land owned by the customer provided the customer controls any part-completed work. If, however, the developer completes work prior to the customer taking control, then continuous transfer would not be available.

Example – Continuous transfer model

Entity B is a construction company and is contracted by entity X to build a property on surplus land that is owned by entity X. As part of the contract's terms, both parties are able to terminate the contract at any time, with the following clauses:

- If entity B terminates, or passes its building responsibility to another party, it is legally obliged to guarantee completion of the work.

- If entity X terminates the contract it will take full control over the partly-completed construction project.

Given the specific terms of the agreement, entity B will be able to recognise revenue under the continuous transfer model as entity X is clearly taking control of the work in process.

In this example, the customer has significant rights over the work in process as a result of the agreement's terms.

9.285.1   Terms and conditions of real estate contracts can be complex. It will be necessary to examine the facts and circumstances of each contract on a case by case basis to consider whether the continuous transfer model can be applied. Agreements with continuous transfer rights might not be encountered frequently. Some more detailed examples are considered below.

Example 1 – Real estate sale with continuous transfer?

A construction company, entity A, constructs and builds developments for private purchasers. A signs a contract with a buyer, under which the buyer purchases and obtains full legal ownership of the land. On the date the contract is signed the buyer may mortgage the land, and the land cannot be reverted to entity A for any reason (even in the event of the construction contract being broken).

The contract is a sale legally; there is no possibility of terminating the sale. However, the buyer may disengage from the contract by selling the contract on to a third party. In such a situation, the buyer would sell his ownership of the land and the uncompleted construction to the third party.

Entity A is legally obliged to guarantee the completion of the construction. This guarantee may take the form of an insurance contract, but it may also be, for example, in the form of a bank deposit.

In the case of entity A going bankrupt, the buyer keeps the partly completed construction and must pay entity A for work performed to date. The construction would be completed by a new developer, financed by the guarantee.

In this situation, it is possible that the continuous transfer model would be applied. However, before applying the continuous transfer model, management would need to ensure that this is appropriate in the light of all other relevant factors, including contractual terms and applicable laws and regulations.

Example 2 – Real estate sale with continuous transfer?

A construction company, entity B, owns a piece of land and designs an office block to be built on this land. Entity B enters into an agreement with a buyer to transfer the land upon signing the contract and to transfer legal ownership of the building upon its completion.

The contract is non-cancellable on both sides. The buyer cannot sell back the land to entity B at any time. As the legal title of the building is not transferred until construction is complete, the buyer can neither sell the property while it is under construction nor pledge the partly constructed building as security.

In case of entity B's inability to complete the work, the buyer will have an obligation to pay for the work performed until that date and to take over the incomplete building.

In this case, it would appear that the buyer has an indirect obligation to pay for the construction on a continuous basis. However, the legal title of the building does not pass until the construction is completed (or entity B goes bankrupt). The buyer has no ability to use the building (sell it, mortgage it or pledge it as security) until such time as legal title has been transferred. On this basis, it would not be appropriate for entity B to use the continuous transfer model.

9.285.3   In the first example above, legal ownership of the land passes on the date the contract is signed. In some jurisdictions there may be legal restrictions relating to the transfer of title on land. In such jurisdictions, the perpetual right of use may be passed on in respect of a piece of land or, alternatively, a long-term right of use may be transferred. In such cases, each situation should be judged based upon the relevant facts and circumstances to determine whether the continuous transfer model should be applied.

9.285.4   IFRIC 15 recognises that judgement should be applied carefully and notes how the agreement's terms, the surrounding facts and circumstances and the local legal requirements should be considered.

Disclosures

9.286   Where an entity recognises revenue using the percentage of completion method and as such revenue is continuously recognised as construction progresses, the following additional disclosures are required:

- The basis for determining which agreements meet all the revenue recognition criteria for the continuous sale of goods as construction progresses.

- Disclosures about the amount of revenue arising in the period.

- The method used to determine the stage of completion.

In addition, all entities should provide the disclosure required by either IAS 11 or IAS 18 as applicable. Disclosures required by IAS 11 are discussed from paragraph 9.349 and those required by IAS 18 from paragraph 9.267.

Practical applications of IFRIC 15

9.287   The following examples illustrate the application of IFRIC 15 both to real estate contracts and, by analogy, to other transactions:

Example 1 – Property development business selling houses 'off-plan'

Entity A operates a property development business. This involves entity A purchasing plots of undeveloped land in residential areas with the intention of building housing complexes on the land.

In order to obtain financing at an early stage of the process, entity A advertises the developments at a discount well in advance of building the housing. Customers who wish to own a property may purchase them 'off plan' before any building has commenced. The customer pays a 15% deposit initially with the remainder payable once the property is completed and transferred into the customer's name, that is the customer takes possession of the property.

When customers purchase the housing 'off plan', they must choose one of three designs specified by entity A. The customer may decide the type of tiling, flooring and wall colour of their property.

Based on these factors, the contracts should be accounted for in accordance with IAS 18. The customers cannot specifically negotiate the significant elements of the structural design and, hence, it would be inappropriate to follow IAS 11.

Example 2 – Components fall within the scope of different standards

Entity A develops and sells tailored computer hardware. It also sells off-the-shelf software for use with the hardware. The software sales take the form of a two year licence to use the software and include both after-sales support and planned upgrades during the period of the licence. These components satisfy the separation criteria of IAS 18. The hardware sales include a significant amount of specific structural design of the basic hardware to meet the customer's needs.

Entity A charges its customers a series of fees during the hardware development period. An additional fee is charged at the start of the period of the licence. No further amounts are payable during the licence period, either for the use of the software or for the maintenance support.

IFRIC 15 may be used here by analogy. [IFRIC 15 para BC6]. Paragraph 8 of IFRIC 15 confirms that different components of the same contract may fall within the scope of either IAS 11 or IAS 18.

Assuming that the development of the hardware meets the definition of a construction contract (see para 9.290 below), it falls within IAS 11's scope. The sale of the software licence and the after-sales support fall within IAS 18's scope. These two elements would, therefore, be unbundled.

The development of the hardware should be accounted on a percentage of completion basis in accordance with the principles of IAS 11. The revenue element of the contract would be further segmented between the sale of the software and the provision of after-sales support services (as the separation criteria of para 13 of IAS 18 are met). Applying the principles of IAS 18 for the sale of services, the fee for the use of the software and that for the maintenance support should both be recognised on a straight-line basis over the period of the licence. Given that the number of calls for support is unknown at inception, the straight-line basis is used since it is the best available method. If the pattern of calls can be reliably estimated at inception, another method could be used, although care should be taken not to recognise revenue too early. For further discussion on revenue recognition for indeterminate number of acts, see paragraph 9.112.

It should be noted that, consistent with this example, paragraph 19 of the appendix to IAS 18 considers fees from the development of computer software and states that such fees are recognised as revenue by reference to the development's stage of completion.

[The next paragraph is 9.289.]

Construction contracts

Objective and scope

9.289   Construction contracts are dealt with in IAS 11. The standard applies to accounting for construction contracts in the financial statements of contractors. [IAS 11 para 1; IAS 18 para 21]. See also the discussions at paragraph 9.274 above in connection with the guidance in IFRIC 15, that offers guidance on when to apply which standard.

Nature of construction contracts

9.290   A construction contract is defined in IAS 11 as "…*a contract specifically negotiated for the construction of an asset or a combination of assets that are closely interrelated or interdependent in terms of their design, technology and function or their ultimate purpose or use*". [IAS 11 para 3]. The standard notes that the key issue in accounting for construction contracts is the allocation of contract revenue and costs to accounting periods in which construction work is carried out. This is because a feature of construction contracts is that the activity usually falls into several accounting periods.

9.291   In addition the standard distinguishes two types of construction contract, fixed price contracts and cost plus contracts and defines each of these as follows:

> *"A fixed price contract is a construction contract in which the contractor agrees to a fixed contract price, or a fixed rate per unit of output, which in some cases is subject to cost escalation clauses.*
>
> *A cost plus contract is a construction contract in which the contractor is reimbursed for allowable or otherwise defined costs, plus a percentage of these costs or a fixed fee."*

[IAS 11 para 3].

9.292   There is no fixed contractual period stated in the definition of a construction contract. Whilst such contracts will in general last for more than a year, some shorter contracts may also fall within the definition. The duration of a contract is unlikely to be relevant when deciding whether to apply IAS 11. The contract needs to be for the construction of an asset or a combination of assets that are interdependent or inter-related. Hence, where a contract is completed wholly within an accounting period, the application of IAS 11 may not be obvious, however, the short duration of the contract does not necessarily eliminate the possibility that IAS 11 should be applied.

9.293   Contracts within IAS 11's scope may be for the construction of a single asset such as a bridge, a building, or a pipeline. A construction contract may be for a number of assets that are closely related or interdependent as to their design, technology and function or their ultimate purpose or use. Examples are the construction of refineries and other complex pieces of plant and equipment. [IAS 11 para 4].

9.294   Other examples might include contracts to supply a large item of manufacturing plant, such as a machine for making corrugated cardboard. IAS 11 notes that for the purpose of the standard the following are treated as construction contracts:

- Contracts for rendering services, which are directly related to the construction of the asset, for example, the services of project managers and architects.

- Contracts for the destruction or restoration of assets and the restoration of the environment following the demolition of assets.

[IAS 11 para 5].

9.295   However, the production of a series of assets would not necessarily meet the definition of a construction contract. For example, an entity entered into a contract with a retailer that sells furniture. The contract will last for a period of two years. The entity is required to manufacture 2,000 sofas over the two-year term to the retailer's specification. In many cases this is simply a contract between a supplier and a purchaser for the production of goods rather than being a construction contract. The contract is for the construction of a series of assets that are not interrelated because one sofa is not connected to or dependent on another sofa. Where the terms of the contract are such that it is not immediately clear as to whether IAS 11 or IAS 18 applies entities should refer to the guidance in IFRIC 15. See paragraph 9.281.

9.296   Although the standard notes that construction contracts are usually formulated as fixed price or as cost plus contracts, some contracts may have features of both types. For example, a contract may be formulated as a cost plus contract, but may also have an agreed maximum price. In such cases, the standard states that, in order to determine when to recognise contract revenue and expenses, the contractor needs to consider all the conditions for both fixed price and cost plus contracts set out in the standard. [IAS 11 para 6].

9.297   Normally, the requirements of IAS 11 are applied separately to each construction contract. However, sometimes it is necessary to break a single contract down into separable elements and apply the standard to each of those elements separately. Conversely, there may be situations where a group of separate contracts should be treated as one contract, because in substance they represent a single contract. [IAS 11 para 7]. The standard sets down the principles for each of these situations as explained in the following paragraphs.

9.298   A single contract may cover the construction of a number of assets. The construction of each asset should be treated as a separate contract where:

- separate proposals have been submitted for each asset;
- each asset has been the subject of separate negotiations and the contractor and customer have each been able to accept or reject that part of the contract relating to each asset; and
- the costs and revenues of each asset can be identified.

[IAS 11 para 8].

Note that these requirements are more onerous than those of IAS 18, as discussed from paragraph 9.131.

9.299   Where a single contract covers several elements of a transaction that need to be 'unbundled' and accounted for separately, some of these elements may be construction contracts and others may not be.

9.300   A group of contracts, whether with a single customer or a number of customers, should be combined where:

- the contracts have been negotiated as a single package;
- the contracts are so closely interrelated that they are in substance part of a single contract with an overall profit margin; and
- the contracts are performed concurrently or in a continuous sequence.

[IAS 11 para 9].

> **Example – Combined contracts**
>
> A contractor is negotiating two contracts with a single customer under IAS 11. The customer must either accept both contracts or reject both. The first contract will be for the design of a chemical plant and the second for the plant's construction. The planned profit margin on the design contract is 20% and the planned profit margin on constructing the plant is 10%.
>
> The two contracts should be accounted for as a single contract. The contracts were negotiated as a single package as the customer must accept both or reject both. The contracts are closely related and will be performed in a continuous sequence. An overall profit margin should be recorded as work is performed on both contracts.

9.301   The combination of contracts or the segregation of a single contract is not optional, but a requirement when the relevant criteria are met.

9.302   Where a contract provides for the construction of an additional asset at the customer's option, or is amended to include construction of an additional asset, the construction of that asset should be accounted for as a separate construction contract where:

■   the asset differs significantly in design, technology or function from the asset or assets covered by the original contract; or

■   the price of the asset is negotiated without regard to the original contract price.

[IAS 11 para 10].

Recognition

9.303   Costs incurred prior to the contract being probable and costs that do not relate to future activities should be recognised as expenses. Costs incurred on a construction contract after the date the contract is probable should be capitalised if they meet the criteria for construction costs in IAS 11. When considering such costs, it is necessary to use judgement to determine whether they relate to a new contract, as opposed to a variation to an existing contract. The treatment of costs for contract variations is considered in paragraph 9.306.

9.304   Costs directly relating to a contract that are incurred in obtaining the contract are recognised as an asset if they can be separately identified and reliably measured and if it is probable that the contract will be obtained (see para 9.307). [IAS 11 para 21]. (See Table 9.4 below, for example.) IAS 11 also deals with a situation where costs of obtaining a contract have been written off in a period prior to that in which the contract is obtained (because at that point it was not probable that the contract would be obtained). It states that the write off of such costs is not reversed and, hence, they are not capitalised when the contract is obtained in the subsequent period.

Measurement

Definition and determination of costs

9.305   Contract costs comprise:

- Costs that relate directly to the specific contract.

- Costs that are attributable to contract activity in general and can be allocated to the contract.

- Such other costs as are specifically chargeable to the customer under the contract's terms.

[IAS 11 para 16].

9.306   Direct costs include:

- Site labour costs, including site supervision.

- Costs of materials used in construction.

- Depreciation of plant and equipment used on the contract.

- Costs of moving plant, equipment and materials to and from the contract site.

- Costs of hiring plant and equipment used on the contract.

- Costs of design and technical assistance that is directly related to the contract.

- Estimated costs of rectification and guarantee work, including expected warranty costs.

- Claims from third parties.

[IAS 11 para 17].

Costs of variations (see para 9.315) should be included in the contract costs where it is appropriate to include the amount of the variation in contract revenue (see para 9.313), but only if and to the extent that such costs are considered to be recoverable. A degree of judgement should be used in assessing the recoverability of such amounts.

9.307   As noted in paragraph 9.304 above, costs of securing the contract that relate directly to the contract are also included as part of contract costs if they can be separately identified and reliably measured. However, they may only be included from the point at which it becomes probable that the contract will be obtained. [IAS 11 para 21]. Costs of securing a contract would normally comprise the direct costs of preparing and presenting the bid for the contract, which could include design costs, external consultancy fees and the costs of preparation and printing of the bid documentation. In some cases a number of bids are submitted for a number of contracts. If only one of those contracts is obtained it is only the costs associated with the contract that is actually obtained that may be included in contract costs and then only if those costs are separately identifiable and able to be reliably measured.

9.308   Costs that are attributable to contract activity in general and which can be allocated to specific contracts include:

■   Insurance.

■   Costs of design and technical assistance that are not directly related to a specific contract.

■   Construction overheads.

[IAS 11 para 18].

9.309   The costs should be allocated to specific contracts on a systematic and rational basis that is applied in a consistent manner to all costs that have similar characteristics. The allocation should be based on the entity's normal level of construction activity. Construction overheads include costs such as the preparation and processing of construction workers' payroll. Where borrowing costs meet the definition of contract costs in paragraph 16 of IAS 11, the borrowing costs will be attributable to a qualifying asset and should be capitalised under IAS 23. It follows that the borrowing costs must then be included as costs of the contract and capitalised accordingly. IAS 23 is dealt with in chapter 16.

9.310   Where the contract specifies particular costs that can be charged to the customer these are included in contract costs. Such costs may sometimes include general administrative overheads and development costs that are specifically reimbursable under the contract. [IAS 11 para 19]. Research and development costs are not normally included in work in progress, but may be allowed where specific costs are rechargeable under the construction contract, as illustrated in the next example. The question is whether the criteria for recognising an asset are met. The existence of future revenue does not mean an asset should be recorded for costs incurred. Accordingly, an entity needs to determine whether or not the costs meet the definition of an asset. Most general contract costs (such as insurance) cannot be capitalised. The more distant the relationship between the contract costs and the asset, the more difficult it becomes to capitalise the costs. Where development costs are not included in work in progress, these costs may meet the definition of an intangible asset in IAS 38 and should be capitalised. IAS 38 is dealt with in chapter 15.

9.310.1   When such costs are specifically referred to in the contract, the question often follows whether the criteria for recognising an asset have been met. As noted above, the existence of future revenue does not automatically mean an asset should be recorded for costs incurred. Accordingly, an entity needs to determine whether the costs meet the definition of an asset. Most general contract costs (such as insurance) cannot be capitalised. The more distant the relationship between the contract costs and the asset, the more difficult it becomes to capitalise the costs. Where development costs are not included in work in progress, these costs may meet the definition of an intangible asset in IAS 38 and should be capitalised. IAS 38 is dealt with in chapter 15.

> **Example – Research and development expenses**
>
> Entity A manufactures sophisticated scientific equipment for its customers. Customer B contracts A to develop lightweight gamma-ray detection equipment for inclusion in a satellite.
>
> Entity A is required to undertake research and development work on new materials in order to meet the required specifications. The contract terms provide for entity B to reimburse entity A with the costs of the research and development work, subject to an agreed budget.
>
> In this instance, research and development expenses should be included in work in progress. Entity A has a specific right to recharge the costs of the research and development work under the construction contract.

9.311 The standard lists categories of costs that cannot be allocated to contracts and which, therefore, are excluded from contract costs. These are:

- General administration costs for which reimbursement is not specified in the contract.

- Selling costs.

- Research and development costs for which reimbursement is not specified in the contract.

- Depreciation of idle plant and equipment that is not used on a particular contract.

[IAS 11 para 20].

9.312 The contract costs may be reduced by incidental income that is not included in contract revenue, for example, from sales of surplus material or the disposal of plant and machinery after the contract has been completed. [IAS 11 para 17].

Definition and determination of revenue

9.313 Contract revenue comprises:

- The initial amount of revenue agreed in the contract.

- Variations in contract work, claims and incentive payments to the extent that it is probable that they will result in revenue and they are capable of being reliably measured (see para 9.315 below).

[IAS 11 para 11].

9.314   Revenue is measured at the fair value of the consideration received or receivable. The amount of revenue and estimates should be revised as events occur and any uncertainties are resolved. The standard notes that contract revenue may increase or decrease from one period to the next and gives the following examples of the potential causes:

- A contractor and a customer may agree variations or claims that increase or decrease contract revenue in a period subsequent to that in which the contract was initially agreed.

- The amount of revenue agreed in a fixed price contract may increase as a result of cost escalation clauses.

- The amount of contract revenue may decrease as a result of penalties arising from delays caused by the contractor in completing the contract.

- When a fixed price contract involves a fixed price per unit of output, contract revenue increases as the number of units is increased.

[IAS 11 para 12].

9.314.1   As stated above, contract revenue is measured at the fair value of the consideration received or receivable. This means that where payment is received in arrears to such an extent that the fair value of the consideration is less than the nominal amount of cash received or receivable, it would be necessary to discount the revenue (and the related receivable, being a contractual right to cash) to fair value, with the unwinding of the discount credited to finance income. [IAS 39 paras 43, AG79].

> **Example – Progress billings**
>
> Entity A entered into a contract with entity B to construct a mobile telecom network. The total revenue from the contract is estimated at C200,000. Entity A will take three years to construct the network.
>
> The contract states that, although progress billings will be made at the end of each year, entity B only has to settle the invoices when the contract is 100% completed.
>
> Progress billings are invoiced at the end of each year to reflect the stage of completion on the contract. The stage of completion is determined by the proportion that the costs incurred to date bear to the estimated total costs of the transaction (considered from para 9.326). Progress billings invoiced by entity A were as follows:
>
> End of year 1:   C50,000.
> End of year 2:   C60,000.
> End of year 3:   C90,000.
>
> The applicable discount rate is 4.5%.
>
> Management should recognise revenue as work is performed throughout the contract life. Discounting the revenue to reflect the delay in receipt of cash from the customer ensures that the revenue is reported at the fair value of consideration to be received.

The difference between the discounted revenue and the payment received should be recognised as interest income. [IAS 18 para 11].

The calculation of the revenue's fair value is given in the following table:

Progress billings invoiced:	Year 1		Year 2		Year 3	
	Discount factor	Discounted value (C)	Discount factor	Discounted Value (C)	Discount factor	Discounted value (C)
Year 1: 50,000	0.91573	45,787	0.95694	47,847	1	50,000
Year 2: 60,000	n/a	n/a	0.95694	57,416	1	60,000
Year 3: 90,000	n/a	n/a	n/a	n/a	1	90,000

The results that management should report are as follows:

	Year 1 (C)	Year 2 (C)	Year 3 (C)
Revenue	45,787	57,416	90,000
Interest income (accretion of discount)	–	2,060[a]	4,737[b]

Notes

(a) Accretion of discount calculated 47,847 — 45,787 = 2,060.
(b) Accretion of discount calculated (50,000 — 47,847) + (60,000 — 57,416) = 4,737.

9.315 A 'variation' is an instruction by the customer for a change in the scope of the work to be performed under the contract. Examples are changes in the specification or design of an asset and changes in the contract's duration. A variation is included in contract revenue when:

■ it is probable that the customer will approve the variation and the amount of revenue arising from the variation; and

■ the amount of revenue can be reliably measured.

[IAS 11 para 13].

9.316 A 'claim' is an amount that the contractor seeks to collect from the customer or another party as reimbursement for costs not included in the contract price. A claim may arise from, for example, errors in the initial specifications, delays caused by the customer or disputed variations. The settlement of claims arising from circumstances not envisaged in the contract or arising as an indirect consequence of approved variations is subject to a high level of uncertainty relating to the outcome of future negotiations. In view of this, claims are included in contract revenue only when:

■ negotiations have reached an advanced stage such that it is probable that the customer will accept the claim; and

■ the amount of the claim that the customer will probably accept can be reliably measured.

[IAS 11 para 14].

9.317 In practice, because of the frequency and large number of disputes that arise on construction contracts and the length of time over which negotiations may stretch, it is often more appropriate to take variations and claims into account only when they have actually been approved by the customer. Examples of accounting policies for claims and variations (sometimes referred to differently as 'change orders' or 'disputes') are given in Tables 9.4 and 9.5. In addition, the following table considers whether contract revenue should be recognised for certain claims and variations.

Variation or claim	Contract revenue recognised?
At the year end the following variations and claims occurred on a contract:	
(a) The customer approved changes to the contract's design specifications with a total cost of C5,000.	Yes, all criteria set out in paragraph 13 of IAS 11 are met. The C5,000 can be included in the contract price (revenue).
(b) Due to poor weather, the contract will overrun by 3 months. This will lead to an increase in costs of C3,000. The customer will probably not approve the amount of revenue arising from the variation.	No, the customer will probably not approve the variation amount. The additional costs already incurred should be included in the calculation of work in progress, if the contract is still profitable. However, a lower expected profit margin should be recognised because of the additional costs incurred. The total expected loss should be recognised immediately if the additional costs will result in a loss on the contract. For recognition of losses on contracts see paragraph 9.333.
(c) Due to unforeseen circumstances the contractor incurred additional costs in the current year on the contract. Negotiations to obtain the customer's acceptance of these claims are in early stages.	No, negotiations have not reached an advanced stage where it is probable that the customer will accept the claim. The contractor should include the additional costs in the work in progress calculation and recognise a lower expected profit margin due to the additional costs incurred.
(d) The customer will probably accept a claim of C2,000 due to delays caused by the customer itself.	Yes, all criteria set out in paragraph 14 of IAS 11 are met. The C2,000 can be included in the contract price (revenue).

9.318 'Incentive payments' are additional amounts that the customer pays to the contractor if certain specified performance targets or standards are met. An example is a payment for completing a contract ahead of schedule. Incentive payments are included in contract revenue when:

- the contract is sufficiently advanced that it is probable that the specified performance standards will be met or exceeded; and

- the amount of the incentive payment can be reliably measured.

[IAS 11 para 15].

Subsequent measurement

Contract revenue and expense

9.319 The subsequent measurement of construction contract work in progress is determined by the way in which contract revenue and expenses are recognised. Where the outcome of a contract can be reliably estimated, contract costs and revenue are recognised by reference to the stage of completion of the contract activity at the balance sheet date. Where the outcome of a contract cannot be reliably estimated, contract costs are recognised as an expense when incurred and revenue is recognised only to the extent of the contract costs incurred and that it is probable the revenue will be recoverable. In both cases, any expected contract loss is recognised immediately. [IAS 11 paras 22, 32].

9.320 Subsequent measurement of contract work in progress as part of inventories represents cost less amounts transferred to cost of sales. The method of accounting for construction contracts according to the stage of completion of the contract is known as the 'percentage of completion' method and involves:

- Estimating the outcome of the contract reliably (see para 9.321 onwards).

- Determining the revenue and costs attributable to the stage of completion of the contract (see para 9.325 onwards).

- Determining the profit attributable to the stage of completion (see para 9.328).

[IAS 11 para 25].

Reliable estimation of contract outcome

9.321 An entity can normally make reliable estimates when it has entered into a contract that sets out:

- Each party's enforceable rights regarding the asset to be constructed.

- The consideration to be received.

- The manner and terms of settlement.

[IAS 11 para 29].

9.322 The entity should also have an effective internal financial budgeting and reporting system so that it can capture and track costs. Such a system will also enable the entity to review and reassess the expected outcome of a contract. The need for such revisions does not necessarily mean that the outcome of a contract cannot be reliably estimated. [IAS 11 para 29].

9.323   In the case of a fixed price contract, the outcome can be reliably estimated when all of the following conditions are satisfied:

- Total contract revenue can be measured reliably.

- It is probable that the economic benefits associated with the contract will flow to the entity.

- Both the contract costs to complete the contract and the stage of contract completion at the balance sheet date can be measured reliably.

- The contract costs attributable to the contract can be clearly identified and measured reliably so that actual contract costs incurred can be compared with prior estimates.

[IAS 11 para 23].

9.324   For cost plus contracts, reliable estimates of the outcome can be made when both of the following conditions are satisfied.

- It is probable that the economic benefits associated with the contract will flow to the entity.

- The contract costs attributable to the contract, whether or not specifically reimbursable, can be clearly identified and measured reliably.

[IAS 11 para 24].

Revenue and costs attributable to the stage of completion

9.325   Under the percentage of completion method, contract revenue is recognised as revenue in the income statement in the accounting periods in which the work is performed. Contract costs are recognised as an expense in the income statement in the accounting periods in which the work to which they relate is performed, unless the contract is expected to result in a loss, which is recognised as an expense immediately. [IAS 11 para 26].

9.326   In order to determine the revenue attributable to the stage of completion of the contract it is necessary to be able to measure the stage of completion. IAS 11 illustrates this by giving the following examples:

- Measuring the proportion that the costs incurred for work performed to date compared to the total estimated costs.

- Carrying out surveys of work performed to date.

- Completing a physical proportion of the contract work.

[IAS 11 para 30].

9.327 Progress payments and advances received usually do not give a reliable basis for measuring the stage of completion. When using the method that compares costs to date to total expected costs, only those costs that reflect work performed to date are included in the costs to date. For example, the following are excluded:

- Contract costs that relate to future activity on the contract, such as costs of materials that have been delivered to a contract site or set aside for use in a contract but not yet installed, used or applied during contract performance, unless the materials have been made specially for the contract.

- Payments made to sub-contractors in advance of work performed under the sub-contract.

Such costs are recognised as an asset provided it is probable that they can be recovered and included in work in progress, but they are not taken into account for the purpose of determining the costs incurred to date for comparison with total expected contract costs. They are, however, included in the estimate of total contract costs. [IAS 11 paras 27, 31].

> **Example – Application of percentage of completion method**
>
> Entity A entered into a contract with entity B to construct a power station. The cost of the station is estimated at C150,000. The total revenue from the contract is estimated at C200,000. Entity A will take three years to construct the power station.
>
> At the end of year 1 entity A incurred costs of C60,000. The customer was invoiced for C50,000 at the end of year 1. Payment of this progress billing is due, early in year 2, in accordance with the normal credit terms that entity A offers.
>
> Using the percentage of completion method to determine the stage of completion, entity A should compare the proportion of costs incurred to date to the total estimated costs.
>
> Based on the relationship between the costs incurred to date and total estimated costs, the contract is 40% (60,000/150,000) completed at the end of year 1. Revenue of 80,000 (40% of 200,000) should be recognised at the end of year 1.

Profit attributable to the stage of completion

9.328 The profit attributable to the stage of completion will represent the difference between the revenue and the costs attributable to the stage of completion.

9.329 Tables 9.4 and 9.5 are examples of accounting policies for contract work in progress applying the percentage of completion basis.

Table 9.4 – Accounting policy for construction contracts

Aker ASA – Annual report and accounts – 31 December 2011

ACCOUNTING PRINCIPLES (extract)
Construction contracts

Revenues related to construction contracts are recognized using the percentage of completion method, based primarily on contract costs incurred to date, compared to estimated overall contract costs.

If the final outcome of a contract cannot be estimated reliably, contract revenue is recognized only to the extent costs incurred are expected to be recovered. Any projected losses on future work done under existing contracts are expensed and classified as accrued costs/provisions in the balance sheet under current provisions.

Losses on contracts are recognized in full when identified. Recognized contract profit includes profit derived from change orders and disputed amounts when, in management's assessment, realization is probable and reasonable estimates can be made. Project costs include costs directly related to the specific contract and indirect costs attributable to the contract.

Project revenue is classified as operating revenue in the profit and loss account. Work in progress is classified as projects under constructions in the balance sheet. Advances from customers are deducted from the value of work in progress for the specific contract or, to the extent advances exceed this value, recorded as customer advances. Customer advances that exceed said contract offsets are classified as trade and other payables.

Use of estimates and assumptions (extract)

(a) Revenue recognition

The group applies the percentage-of-completion method in accounting for its construction contracts.

Use of the percentage-of-completion method requires the group to estimate the construction performed to date as a proportion of the total construction to be performed. Another significant uncertainty is the expected total profit of the projects. See note 19.

Table 9.5 – Accounting policy for construction contracts

Taylor Wimpey plc – Annual report and accounts – 31 December 2010

1. Significant accounting policies (extract)Revenue (extract)

(c) Contracting work
Where the outcome of a construction contract can be estimated reliably, revenue and costs are recognised by reference to the stage of completion of the contract activity at the balance sheet date. This is normally measured by surveys of work performed to date. Variations in contract work, claims and incentive payments are included to the extent that it is probable that they will result in revenue and they are capable of being reliably measured.

Where the outcome of a construction contract cannot be estimated reliably, contract revenue is recognised to the extent of contract costs incurred that it is probable will be recoverable. Contract costs are recognised as expenses in the period in which they are incurred. When it is probable that total contract costs will exceed total contract revenue, the expected loss is recognised as an expense immediately.

Reliable estimation of contract outcome not possible

9.330 Where it is not possible to estimate reliably the outcome of a contract, a different percentage of completion method is applied. Revenue is only recognised to the extent of recoverable contract costs. This approach is necessary to avoid recognising profit on a contract before it is probable that a profit will be earned on the overall contract.

9.331 To the extent that contract costs are not expected to be recoverable, contract revenue is not recognised. As all contract costs are recognised as an expense as incurred, this means that the irrecoverable costs will not be covered by contract revenue and a net loss will be recorded. The standard gives examples of circumstances where contract costs may not be recoverable, including a contract:

■ That is not fully enforceable, that is, its validity is seriously in question.

■ The completion of which is subject to the outcome of pending litigation or legislation.

■ Relating to a property that is likely to be condemned or expropriated.

■ Where the customer is unable to meet its obligations.

■ Where the contractor is unable to complete the contract or otherwise meet its obligations under the contract.

[IAS 11 para 34].

9.332 When uncertainties that have prevented the outcome of a contract from being reliably estimated are removed or no longer exist, the entity should commence accounting for revenue and costs using the percentage of completion method described from paragraph 9.319 onwards above. [IAS 11 para 35]. That is, the entity will recognise revenue according to the stage of completion of the contract with a cumulative catch up, relating to previous years, in the year this occurs.

Recognition of losses

9.333 When it is probable that contract costs will exceed total contract revenue the expected loss should be recognised immediately as an expense. [IAS 11 para 36].

9.334 An expected loss may be identified either when the outcome of a contract can be reliably estimated or even when the outcome is in doubt. In the latter case, although the outcome may not be capable of reliable estimation it may still be probable that a loss will be incurred. An estimate should be made based on the available information and provision made. [IAS 11 para 33]. This provision would then be reviewed and revised as necessary as the contract proceeds. Even when the outcome cannot be reliably estimated, it may still be possible to make reasonable estimates using projected cash flows and budgets similar to those used in an impairment review under IAS 36. Although construction contracts are outside IAS 36's scope, its principles can still be used for this purpose.

9.335 Provision for an expected loss is made irrespective of:

■ Whether or not work has commenced on the contract.

■ The stage of completion of the contract activity.

■ The profitability of other contracts that are separately accounted for in accordance with the standard.

[IAS 11 para 37].

9.336 Provisions for losses are set against the amount 'due from customers' (if an asset) or added to 'due to customers' (if a liability). [IAS 11 para 43 and 44]. Note that these provisions for losses on construction contracts are specifically excluded from the scope of IAS 37 and so the losses should not be included within provisions that an entity makes in accordance with IAS 37. The presentation and disclosure of losses and progress billings is discussed from paragraph 9.339 below.

9.337 Where revenue has been validly recognised on a contract, but an uncertainty subsequently arises about the recoverability of the related amount due from the customer, any provision against the amount due is recognised as an expense, rather than as a reduction of contract revenue. [IAS 11 para 28]. The principles involved are illustrated by the following example.

> **Example – Recognition of loss**
>
> Entity A is constructing a building for its customer. The construction is in its second year of the three year project.
>
> Management had originally assessed the contract to be profitable and recognised a profit in year 1 of C20,000, based on the percentage of the contract that had been completed at that time. Management now believes the contract will incur a loss of C30,000.
>
> Management has proposed that a loss of C30,000 on the contract is recognised in year 2, but has questioned how the profit of C20,000 recognised in year 1 should be treated.
>
> In line with paragraph 32(b) of IAS 11, management should recognise a loss in respect of the contract of C50,000 in year 2. This represents a reversal of the C20,000 profit recognised in year 1 and the C30,000 loss expected on the contract as a whole.
>
> The loss has been assessed through a revision of the estimated costs to completion. The appropriate accounting entry is, therefore, to recognise the adjustment in the current year's results rather than record a prior-period adjustment.
>
> Note that this example illustrates recoverability against agreed contract revenue. It does not illustrate the inability to recover payment against invoices from the customer. If and when management considers that the amount is no longer recoverable, the receivable should be impaired.

9.337.1 The necessary provision may be substantial in situations where it covers a long time period. IAS 11 is silent on whether discounting should be used. We consider that it would be appropriate to apply discounting to provisions against construction contracts to the extent that the impact is material. This would be in line with the guidance in paragraph 15 of IFRIC 12 (which considers the measurement of financial assets in service concession arrangements).

Changes in estimates

9.338 Changes in estimates of contract revenue or contract costs are accounted for as changes in accounting estimates under IAS 8. Accordingly, the effects of such changes are accounted for in the current and future periods, as appropriate, and not as a prior year adjustment. [IAS 11 para 38]. Further guidance is given under 'Practical application' below.

Presentation and disclosure

9.339 The standard defines the gross amount due from customers for contract work as the net amount of:

■ costs incurred plus recognised profits; less

■ the sum of recognised losses and progress billings.

for all contracts in progress for which costs incurred plus recognised profits (less recognised losses) exceeds progress billings.

[IAS 11 para 43].

9.340 For example, assume that under the percentage of completion method, revenue recognised is C100, attributable costs recognised are C60 and amounts billed in respect of work completed at the balance sheet date are C70. In that case, the gross amount due from customers is C30 (costs of C60 plus attributable profit of C40 less amounts billed of C70). This is illustrated in the table below as contract 1. Assume instead that there were two separate contracts, which had costs to date of C60 and C40 respectively, and revenue had been recognised of C100 and C40 and expected losses of C20 had been recognised on the second contract. Progress billings were C70 and C10 respectively. The gross amount due from customers would be C40 as illustrated in the table below.

	Contract 1 C	Contract 2 C	Total C
Costs to date	60	40	100
Profit	40	–	40
Losses	–	(20)	(20)
Billings	(70)	(10)	(80)
Gross amount due from customers	30	10	40

9.341 Where progress billings exceed costs incurred plus recognised profits (less recognised losses), the balance will be a net credit balance and is defined in the standard as the gross amount due to customers. [IAS 11 para 44].

9.342 The gross amount due from customers for contract work should be disclosed as an asset. The gross amount due to customers for contract work should be disclosed as a liability. [IAS 11 para 42]. The standard does not specify the classification of either the asset or the liability. In practice the classification of the amount varies. To ensure clarity for users of the financial statements, we consider that the asset is best disclosed under a separate heading such as 'Construction contract work in progress due from customers'. The liability is normally disclosed in liabilities and described in terms such as 'Amounts due to customers for contract work'.

9.343 Progress billings are amounts billed for work performed on a contract whether or not they have been paid by the customer. The work in progress billings used in the calculation of the gross amounts due from and to customers are the amounts actually invoiced. Amounts invoiced to customers, but for which payment has not been received at the balance sheet date should be included in trade receivables. For example, assume that under the percentage of completion method C100 is recognised as revenue, attributable costs recognised are C60 and progress billings are C70. Of the C70 progress billings C50 has been paid by the customer at the balance sheet date. The balance sheet would then include gross amounts due from customers of C30 (C60 + C40 – C70) and trade receivables of C20 (C70 – C50). There is no specific requirement in the standard to disclose separately the C20 included in trade receivables. Such presentation, however, may be considered beneficial to users.

9.343.1 IAS 11 is unclear whether amounts billed for work not yet performed for which no cash has been received, should be recorded as a separate liability or as part of billings in excess of work performed. In our view, either is acceptable.

> **Example – Progress billings issued in excess of work performed**
>
> Entity A, which has been contracted to build an office block, raises billings of C100 to entity B. The construction to date is 70% complete. In line with IAS 11, C70 has been recorded as revenue. At the end of the reporting period, the entity had collected C80 on the billings raised. How should this be reflected in the financial statements?
>
> C10 of the cash collected should be recorded as an advance, as only C70 of revenue has been earned to date. The C20 of uncollected bills, which represent excess billings over work performed, should be recorded as deferred revenue. The advance and deferred revenue would be released to the income statement as construction progresses. The advance of C10 would be disclosed; however there is no specific disclosure requirement in respect of the deferred revenue of C20.
>
> Alternatively, the C30 could be recorded as an 'amount due to construction customer'. In this view, advances are a subset of progress billings. The advance of C10 should be disclosed.

9.344 Other disclosure requirements of the standard are:

- The methods used to determine the contract revenue recognised in the period.

- The methods used to determine the stage of completion of contracts in progress.

- The amount of contract revenue recognised as revenue in the period.

- In respect of contracts in progress at the balance sheet date:

  - The aggregate amount of contract costs incurred and recognised profits (less recognised losses) to date. There is no requirement to disclose the amount of profits recognised separately as it is the aggregate of costs and profits that has to be given, although some entities do disclose each of the two constituents separately as well as the aggregate amount – see for example Table 9.7 below.

  - The amount of contract advances received. Advances are amounts paid by customers before the related contract work has been carried out.

  - The amount of contract retentions. Retentions are amounts of progress billings that are not paid until the satisfaction of conditions specified in the contract for their payment or until defects have been rectified.

- Contingent liabilities and assets in accordance with IAS 37. These may arise from items such as warranty costs, claims, penalties or possible losses.

[IAS 11 paras 39, 40, 41, 45].

9.345 Tables 9.4 and 9.5 above illustrate the disclosure of the methods used to determine contract revenue and the stage of contract completion. Tables 9.6 and 9.7 illustrate the remaining disclosure requirements.

Table 9.6 – Construction contract disclosures

Invensys plc – Annual report and accounts – 31 March 2012

18 Amounts due from/(to) contract customers

	2012 £m	2011 £m
Amounts due from contract customers:		
Amounts expected to be recovered within 12 months	**273**	**233**
Amounts expected to be recovered after more than 12 months	**11**	—
	284	233
Amounts due to contract customers:		
Amounts expected to be settled within 12 months	**(205)**	(203)
Amounts expected to be settled after more than 12 months	**(23)**	(11)
	(228)	(214)
Net amounts due from/(to) contract customers	**56**	19
Analysed as:	**3,111**	2,790
Contract costs incurred plus recognised profits less recognised losses to date		
Less: progress billings	**(3,055)**	(2,771)
Contracts in progress at balance sheet date	**56**	19
	1,233	1,193
Revenue from construction contracts		

At 31 March 2012, retentions held by customers for contract work amounted to £37 million (2011: £30 million) and advances received from customers for contract work amounted to £8 million (2011: £11 million).

The directors consider that the carrying amount of amounts due from/(to) contract customers is a reasonable approximation of their fair value.

Table 9.7 – Construction contract disclosures

FLSmidth & Co A/S – Annual report and accounts – 31 December 2011

23. Work-in-progress for third parties

Work-in-progress for third parties is measured according to the percentage of completion method at the sales value of the portion of the contract completed less partial invoicing and invoicing on account. The sales value is measured on the basis of the stage of completion at the balance sheet date and the total expected earnings from the individual contract.

DKKm	2011	2010
Total costs defrayed	35,646	33,992
Profit recognised as income, net	6,811	6,450
Work-in-progress for third parties	42,457	40,442
Invoicing on account to customers	(43,584)	(41,168)
	(1,127)	**(726)**
Of which work-in-progress for third parties is stated under assets	3,633	3,120
and under liabilities	(4,760)	(3,846)
	(1,127)	**(726)**

Profit/loss included in the year's financial result is recognised in the gross profit in the income statement.

25. Receivables (extract)

Recognised trade receivables include retentions on contractual terms at DKK 604m (2010: DKK 716m).

4. Revenue

DKKm	2011	2010
Project and product sales	13,294	12,557
Sales of parts and services, etc.	7,244	6,246
Building materials	1,460	1,383
	21,998	**20,186**
Income recognition criteria		
Income recognised when delivered	7,521	6,642
Income recognised according to the percentage-of-completion method	14,477	13,544
	21,998	**20,186**

49. Accounting policies (extract)

Work-in-progress for third parties

Work-in-progress for third parties is measured according to the percentage of completion method at the sales value of the portion of the contract completed less partial invoicing and invoicing on account. The sales value is measured on the basis of the stage of completion at the balance sheet date and the total expected earnings from the individual contract.

The stage of completion for the individual project is, in principle, calculated as the ratio between the resources spent and the total budgeted resource requirements. In some projects, where resource requirements cannot be used as a basis, the ratio between completed subactivities and the total project is used instead.

Work-in-progress for third parties where invoicing on account exceeds the value of the work completed is recognised as Work-in-progress for third parties under Short-term liabilities.

Contractual prepayments are recognised as Prepayments received from customers among Long-term and Short-term liabilities.

Prepayments to subcontractors consist of prepayments to subcontractors in connection with work-in-progress for third parties and are measured at amortised cost.

Write-downs are made for losses on Work-in-progress for third parties. Allowances are based on individual assessment of the estimated loss until the work is completed.

Costs deriving from sales work and winning of contracts are recognised in the income statement in the financial year during which they are incurred.

Revenue (extract)

Revenue is recognised in the income statement on delivery and passing of the risk to the buyer and when the income can be measured reliably.

Work-in-progress for third parties is recognised in revenue based on the value of the work completed at the balance sheet date, whereby the revenue corresponds to the sales value of the year's completed work (production method). The general rule is to base percentage of completion on the costs incurred. The value of Work-in-progress for third parties is based on the costs incurred in percentage of the total budgeted costs.

Consolidated balance sheet (extract)

Assets (extract)

DKKm		2011	2010
Notes			
25	Trade receivables	5,554	4,238
23	Work-in-progress for third parties	3,633	3,120
	Prepayments to subcontractors	467	364
25	Other receivables	1,112	1,046
	Prepayments	181	97
	Receivables	**10,947**	**8,865**

Equity and liabilities (extract)

DKKm		2011	2010
Notes			
27	Deferred tax liabilities	886	813
38	Pension liabilities	207	219
35	Other provisions	530	602
36	Mortgage debt	352	346
36	Bank loans	825	812
36	Finance lease liabilities	10	8
36	Prepayments from customers	435	218
36 + 37	Other liabilities	288	127
	Long-term liabilities	**3,533**	**3,145**
38	Pension liabilities	19	0
35	Other provisions	1,384	1,404
	Bank loans	126	4
36	Finance lease liabilities	8	2
	Prepayments from customers	1,771	1,973
23	Work-in-progress for third parties	4,760	3,846
	Trade payables	2,682	2,192
	Current tax liabilities	398	340
37	Other liabilities	1,917	1,510
	Deferred revenue	35	44
	Short-term liabilities	**13,100**	**11,315**
	Total liabilities	**16,633**	**14,460**

Practical application

Revision of estimates

9.346   The figures to be included in the year's income statement will be both the revenue and the associated costs of achieving that revenue, to the extent that these exceed amounts recognised in previous years. The estimated outcome of a contract that extends over several accounting years will nearly always vary in the light of changes in circumstances and, for this reason, the result of the year will not necessarily represent the profit on the contract that is appropriate to the amount of work carried out in the period. It may also reflect the effect of changes in circumstances during the year that affect the total profit estimated to accrue on completion. This is illustrated in the following example.

Example – Fixed price contract with revised estimates

A construction contractor has a fixed price contract for C11,500. The initial estimate of costs is C7,500 and the contract is expected to take four years. In year two the contractor's estimate of total costs increases to C8,000. Of the C500 increase, C300 is to be incurred in year three and the remainder in year four.

The contractor determines the stage of completion of the contract by comparing the costs of work performed to date with the estimated total costs.

	Year 1	Year 2	Year 3	Year 4
	C	C	C	C
Revenue agreed in contract	11,500	11,500	11,500	11,500
Contract costs incurred to date	3,000	4,500	6,675	8,000
Contract costs to complete	4,500	3,500	1,325	-
Total estimated costs	7,500	8,000	8,000	8,000
Estimated profit	4,000	3,500	3,500	3,500
Stage of completion	40%	56.3%	83.4%	100%

$$(3,000 \div 7,500)(4,500 \div 8,000)(6,675 \div 8,000)$$

The amount of revenue, costs and profit recognised in the profit and loss account in the four years is as follows:

	To date	Prior years	Current year	Profit margins
Year 1				
Revenue (11,500 × 40%)	4,600		4,600	
Costs (7,500 × 40%)	3,000		3,000	
Profit	1,600		1,600	35%
Year 2				
Revenue (11,500 × 56.3%)	6,475	4,600	1,875	
Costs (8,000 × 56.3%)	4,500	3,000	1,500	
Profit	1,975	1,600	375	20%
Year 3				
Revenue (11,500 × 83.4%)	9,591	6,475	3,116	
Costs (8,000 × 83.4%)	6,675	4,500	2,175	
Profit	2,916	1,975	941	30%
Year 4				
Revenue	11,500	9,591	1,909	
Costs	8,000	6,675	1,325	
Profit	3,500	2,916	584	30%

The profit margin in year two (that is, 20%) is lower than in the subsequent years (that is, 30%) because it takes into account the revised estimates.

If the initial cost estimates had been C8,000, then the percentage completion at the end of year one would have been 37.5% (that is, C3,000 as a percentage of C8,000). This means that revenue of C4,313 (C11,500 × 37.5%) would have been attributed to the costs incurred to date of C3,000 giving a profit of C1,313 compared with the reported profit of C1,600. The revenue recognised in year two is that attributed to the total costs incurred to date, calculated on the basis of the revised estimates, less the revenue of C4,600 reported in year one. Therefore, the results in year two reflect the fact that an adjustment is necessary in respect of year one.

Inefficiencies

9.347 Contract costs are usually recognised as an expense in the period in which the work to which they relate is performed. Only if the costs relate to future activity should they be carried forward as work in progress. The way in which inefficiencies are accounted for has an impact on the entity's results.

9.348 The impact of inefficiencies on the percentage of completion calculation must be considered if costs incurred to date are used to determine the stage of completion on a contract. If the contract is partially complete, the percentage of completion calculation should be appropriately updated to reflect the impact of inefficiencies on total estimated contract costs. If this is not undertaken, these additional costs incurred could imply a higher state of completion on a contract than is actually the case. Care should be taken to ensure that revenue attributed to work carried out is not increased to offset additional costs incurred when these costs represent inefficiencies

Contract disclosures

9.349 The following example illustrates how the disclosures required by the standard are derived. The example is based on one given in an appendix to IAS 11.

Example – Disclosures

A contractor has reached the end of its second year of operations. All its contract costs have been paid for in cash and all its progress billings and advances have been received in cash. Contract costs for contracts A and C in year 2 include cost of materials purchased for the contracts that have not yet been used in the contract. The contractor recognised costs of C10,000 and profit of C2,000 in the previous year and had progress billings of C11,000. All amounts had been settled in cash at the previous balance sheet date and the contractor showed amounts recoverable from customers of C1,000 (C10,000 plus C2,000 less C11,000). Advances from customers in year 2 were C300 (year 1: C100). There were retentions of C200 in year 2 (year 1: C200).

The status of the contractor's three contracts at the year end is:

Contract	Contract A		Contract B		Contract C		Total	
	Year 1	Year 2	Year 1	Year 2	Year 1	Year 2	Year 1	Year 2
	C	C	C	C	C	C	C	C
Contract revenue recognised [IAS 11 para 22]	6,000	7,000	4,000	4,000	2,000	3,000	12,000	14,000
Contract expenses recognised [IAS 11 para 22]	5,000	6,000	3,000	3,000	2,000	3,000	10,000	12,000
Expected losses recognised [IAS 11 para 36]	–	–	–	–	–	1,500	–	1,500
	5,000	6,000	3,000	3,000	2,000	4,500	10,000	13,500
Recognised profits less recognised losses	1,000	1,000	1,000	1,000	–	(1,500)	2,000	500
Contract costs incurred in the period	5,000	6,080	3,000	3,000	2,000	3,020	10,000	12,100
Contract costs incurred recognised as contract expenses in the period [IAS 11 para 22]	5,000	6,000	3,000	3,000	2,000	3,000	10,000	12,000
Contract costs that relate to future activity recognised as an asset [IAS 11 para 27]	–	80	–	–	–	20	–	100
Contract revenue (see above)	6,000	7,000	4,000	4,000	2,000	3,000	12,000	14,000
Progress billings [IAS 11 para 41]	5,000	6,300	4,000	3,500	2,000	2,500	11,000	12,300
Unbilled contract revenue	1,000	700	–	500	–	500	1,000	1,700

The amounts to be disclosed in accordance with the standard are:

	Year 1	Year 2
	C	C
Contract revenue recognised in the period. [IAS 11 para 39(a)].	12,000	14,000
Contract costs incurred and recognised profits (less recognised losses) to date. [IAS 11 para 40(a)].	12,000	24,600
(Year 2 = 12,000 (Year 1) plus 12,100 plus profits 2,000, less losses 1,500.)		
Advances received. [IAS 11 para 40(b)].	100	300
(From figures given in the example narrative.)		
Gross amount due from customers for contract work presented as an asset. [IAS 11 para 42(a)].	1,000	1,280
Gross amount due to customers for contract work presented as a liability. [IAS 11 para 42(b)].	–	(980)
Retentions. [IAS 11 para 40(c)].	200	200
(From figures given in the example narrative.)		

Contract	Contract A		Contract B		Contract C		Total	
	Year 1	Year 2	Year 1	Year 2	Year 1	Year 2	Year 1	Year 2
	C	C	C	C	C	C	C	C
Contract costs incurred in the period	5,000	6,080	3,000	3,000	2,000	3,020	10,000	12,100
Recognised profits less recognised losses	1,000	1,000	1,000	1,000	–	(1,500)	2,000	500
	6,000	7,080	4,000	4,000	2,000	1,520	12,000	12,600
Progress billings	5,000	6,300	4,000	3,500	2,000	2,500	11,000	12,300
Due from customers	1,000	780	–	500	–	–	1,000	1,280
Due to customers	–	–	–	–	–	(980)	–	(980)

The net amount due to/from customers above of C300 (C1,280 less C980) includes the C100 of contract costs relating to future activity. Instead of presenting this amount as part of amounts due to/from customers it could be shown as part of contract work in progress. [IAS 11 para 27].

Note that retentions are progress billings that are retained by the customer until certain conditions have been satisfied. As such they will form part of amounts due from customers, but in some cases they are shown separately due to the additional conditions attached to their receipt. In all cases the amount of retentions must be disclosed in accordance with paragraph 40(c) of the standard.

Note also that, the disclosure of contract costs incurred and of recognised profits is in respect only of contracts in progress at the balance sheet date. The example above is not, therefore, necessarily typical, as all the contracts are in progress at both year ends and none has been completed in year 2.

Government grants

9.350   Government grants may be given to an entity to help finance a particular asset or other expenditure. When these grants are given by government, including inter-governmental agencies, guidance on the accounting treatment is contained in IAS 20. This standard differentiates between the treatment for revenue and capital based grants. Payments and assets transferred to entities from sources other than government for no consideration may also be accounted for in accordance with IAS 20. However, before applying IAS 20 in these circumstances, management should consider whether the gift or grant of the asset is genuinely a non-exchange transaction.

9.350.1   If an entity receives an asset from a service provider for no consideration and the asset is essential to other services received from the same provider, then it is clear from paragraph 13 of IAS 18 that the asset and services received are a linked transaction so it would not be appropriate to apply IAS 20. However, if the asset was received from a charitable foundation for the reason that the entity will use it for purposes that are consistent with the foundation's charitable objectives, then the substance of the transaction is similar to a government grant, so applying IAS 20 by analogy would be permissible.

9.351   IAS 20 indicates that government grants should be recognised in the income statement to match them with the expenditure towards which they are intended to compensate. [IAS 20 para 12]. In most situations the periods over which an entity recognises the costs or expenses related to a government grant are readily ascertainable and thus grants in recognition of specific expenses are recognised as income in the same period as the relevant expense. [IAS 20 para 17]. The relationship between the grant and the related expenditure is, therefore, of paramount importance in establishing the accounting treatment.

9.352   Government grants should not be recognised until there is reasonable assurance that the entity will comply with the conditions for their receipt and that the grant will be received. [IAS 20 para 7]. In the event that a grant that has been recognised appears likely to have to be repaid, provision should be made for the estimated liability.

9.353   Difficulties of matching the grant and related expense may arise where the grant's terms do not specify the expenditure towards which it is intended to contribute. For example, grants may be awarded to defray project costs comprising both revenue and capital expenditure. Project grants are normally awarded on this basis and may be related, for example, to the project's capital expenditure costs and the number of jobs created or safeguarded. In such circumstances, the expenditure eligible for grant aid may be all the costs incurred that are directly attributable to the project. The terms of the grant itself often need to be carefully examined to establish whether the intent is to defray costs or to establish a condition relating to the grant's entire amount.

Example — Capital or revenue grant?

An entity obtains a grant from an industrial development agency for an investment project. The project is a building to house a manufacturing plant. The principal terms are that the grant payments relate to the level of capital expenditure and the grant's intention is to help ensure that imports of the product can be replaced with products produced in the country and to safeguard 500 jobs. The grant will have to be repaid if there is an underspend on capital or if the jobs are not safeguarded until 18 months after the date of the last fixed asset purchase.

This grant is related to capital expenditure. The employment condition should be seen as an additional condition to prevent replacement of labour by capital, rather than as the reason for the grant. If the grant were revenue it would be related to revenue expenditure such as a percentage of the payroll cost or a fixed amount per job safeguarded.

9.354   IAS 20 states that grants are sometimes received as part of a package of financial or fiscal aids where a number of conditions are attached. Care is needed in identifying the conditions giving rise to costs and expenses that determine the periods over which the grant will be earned. It will sometimes be appropriate to allocate part of the grant on one basis (capital) and part on another (income). [IAS 20 para 19]. It will then be possible to account for the grant according to the different types of expenditure towards which it is intended to contribute. If the grant is paid when evidence is produced that certain expenditure has been incurred, the grant should be matched with that expenditure.

9.355   Government grants related to assets, including non-monetary grants at fair value, should be presented in the balance sheet either by setting up the grant as deferred income or by deducting the grant in arriving at the asset's carrying amount. [IAS 20 para 24]. In both cases, this will result in the grant income being recognised in the same period in which the asset is depreciated. In this way, the grant income is matched with the expenditure relating to the asset.

Example — Treatment of a capital grant

Entity A is awarded a government grant of C100,000 on 1 January 20X6 towards the construction of a manufacturing plant. The plant's useful life is estimated at 10 years. The entity took two years to construct the plant. At 1 January 20X9 the entity started to use the plant for manufacturing products. The entity has a December year end.

The C100,000 grant relates to the construction of an asset and should be initially recognised as deferred income.

The deferred income should be recognised as income on a systematic and rational basis over the asset's useful life.

The entity should recognise a liability on the balance sheet for the years ending 31 December 20X7 and 31 December 20X8. Once the plant starts being used in the manufacturing process, other operating income of C10,000 should be recognised in each year of the asset's 10 year useful life to match depreciation.

Under the allowed alternative treatment in IAS 20, entity A would also be permitted to set-off the deferred income of C100,000 against the cost of the plant on 1 January 20X9.

9.356 The treatment of a capital grant when the associated asset is impaired is considered in the example below.

Example — Treatment of a capital grant when the associated asset is written down for impairment

Some years ago an entity constructed a factory with the assistance of a government grant. The grant is non-repayable and, following the construction of the factory, cannot be clawed back by the government. There are no further conditions attached to the grant that the entity is required to satisfy. The grant received has been treated as deferred income and is being credited to the income statement over the same period as the factory is being depreciated. Following an adverse change in the line of business the factory serves, the directors have concluded that the factory's carrying value is no longer recoverable in full and that a write-down for impairment is required. The write-down is more than covered by the unamortised deferred income balance relating to the grant. Management would like to match the write-down of the asset to the corresponding release to deferred income.

Paragraph 24 of IAS 20 states that government grants related to assets, including non-monetary grants at fair value, should be presented in the balance sheet either by setting up the grant as deferred income or by deducting the grant in arriving at the asset's carrying amount. Paragraph 12 of IAS 20 also states that government grants should be recognised as income over the periods in which the entity recognises as expenses the related costs that they are intended to compensate, on a systematic basis. As far as the income statement is concerned, we would expect the outcome to be the same regardless of whether grants are netted or deferred.

If the grant had been netted against the cost of the factory, there would be no need for an impairment write-down, as the net carrying value would be less than the recoverable amount. The income statement would continue to be charged with annual depreciation on the net cost.

Therefore, where the grant has been shown as deferred income and the asset is initially recorded at its gross cost, it is reasonable to achieve the same result by releasing an amount of deferred income to the income statement to match the impairment write-down. It is important to note that if there are further conditions attached to the grant beyond construction of the factory, it may not be appropriate to release an amount of deferred income to match the impairment write down. An entity would need to assess those further conditions to determine the amount, if any, of deferred income to release.

Furthermore, the above accounting would also be applied differently in the context of investment tax credits where an entity chooses to apply the guidance in IAS 20 by analogy (see further chapter 13).

9.357   Sometimes the actual expenditure the grant is intended to contribute towards may differ from the expenditure that forms the basis of its payment. For example, the grant may relate to a total project expenditure that may include, in addition to capital expenditure, working capital costs, training costs and removal costs. However, the grant may become receivable in instalments on incurring specific amounts of capital expenditure as the project progresses. It would be wrong to match the grant with the capital expenditure alone. The most appropriate treatment, therefore, would be to match the grant received rateably with the expenditure towards which the grant is assisting, that is, the grant would have to be spread rateably over the constituent parts of the project expenditure. This appropriately allocates part of the grant on one basis and part on another basis. Therefore, where such evidence exists and is sufficiently persuasive, it is appropriate to match grants received with identified expenditure.

9.358   Sometimes grants may be receivable on a different basis, for example, on the achievement of a non-financial objective. In such situations, the grant should be matched with the identifiable costs of achieving that objective. Such costs must be identified or estimated on a reasonable basis. For example, if a grant to support the manufacture of a new product is given on condition that jobs are created and maintained for a minimum period, the grant should be matched with the cost of providing the jobs for that period. As a result, a greater proportion of the grant may fall to be recognised in the project's early stages because of higher non-productive and set-up costs.

Example — Grant payable on achievement of a non-financial goal

Entity A is awarded a government grant of C60,000 receivable over three years (C40,000 in year 1 and C10,000 in each of years 2 and 3), contingent on creating 10 new jobs and maintaining them for three years. The employees are recruited at a cost of C30,000, and the wage bill for the first year is C100,000, rising by C10,000 in each of the subsequent years.

The income of C60,000 should clearly be recognised over the three-year period to match the related costs.

In year 1, C21,667 of the C40,000 received from government will match the related costs of C130,000 incurred during the year, and should, therefore, be recognised as income. The amount of the grant that has not yet been credited to income (that is C18,333, being C40,000 of cash received less C21,667 credited to income) is reflected in the balance sheet.

Year	Labour cost	Grant income	Grant calculations	Deferred income	Calculations
1	130 000	21 667	60 000 × (130/360)	18 333	(40 000 — 21 667)
2	110 000	18 333	60 000 × (110/360)	10 000	(50 000 — 40 000)
3	120 000	20 000	60 000 × (120/360)	–	
	360 000	60 000			

9.359 In certain circumstances, government grants may be awarded unconditionally without regard to the entity's future actions, or requirement to incur further costs. Such grants may be given for the entity's immediate financial support, or assistance, or for the reimbursement of costs previously incurred. They may also be given to finance an entity's general activities over a specified period, or to compensate for a loss of income. In some instances, the extent of these grants may constitute a major source of revenue for the entity. Where grants are awarded on such a basis, they should be recognised in the income statement of the period in which they become receivable. [IAS 20 para 20].

Example – Grant received unconditionally

Entity A incurred expenses of C5,000 that related to training employees during the period May 20X1 to September 20X1. The employee training was required by government. Entity A entered into negotiations with the government for compensation for the training expenses incurred in December 20X1. In February 20X2 the government agreed that it would compensate the entity for the expenses incurred for the year ended 31 December 20X1.

Although entity A incurred the expenses for the year ended 31 December 20X1, it should recognise the income received from the government for the year ended 31 December 20X2. The grant of C5,000 will only become receivable for the year ended 31 December 20X2, that is the year in which the government agreed to compensate entity A for the training expenses.

9.360 IAS 20 offers some flexibility with regards to where grant income is presented in the income statement. Grants related to income (revenue grants) are sometimes presented as a credit in the income statement, either separately or under a general heading such as 'other income'. Alternatively they are deducted in reporting the related expense. [IAS 20 par 29]. Whichever presentation is chosen it should be applied consistently to all grants and year on year.

9.361 Where an entity has recognised government grant income, disclosure should be made of:

- The accounting policy applied for recognising the grant.

- The method of presentation applied in the financial statements.

- The nature and extent of government grants recognised.

- An indication of other forms of government assistance from which the entity has directly benefited.

- Unfulfilled conditions and other contingencies attaching to government assistance that has been recognised.

[IAS 20 para 39].

In this example, the customer has significant rights over the work in process as a result of the agreement's terms.

Annex — IFRIC 15 flow chart

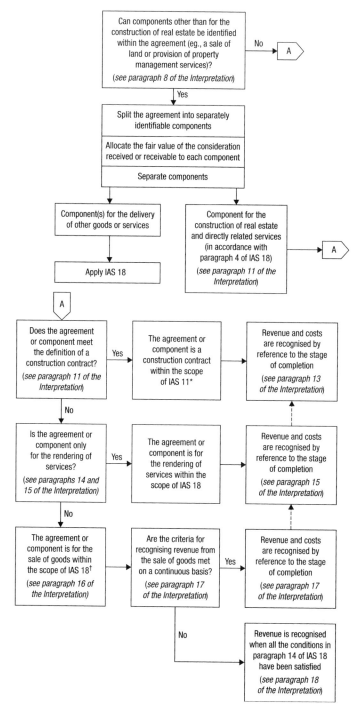

* The construction contract may need to be segmented in accordance with paragraph 8 of IAS 11
† Directly related services may need to be separated in accordance with paragraph 13 of IAS 18

Chapter 10

Segment reporting

Chapter 10

Segment reporting

Introduction

10.1 For entities that operate in a variety of classes of business, geographical locations, regulatory or economic environments or markets, the availability of segmental information is essential for good management. Such information is vital if management is to be able to monitor performance within its specific business and geographical regions and to decide how best to allocate resources to segments. With good segment information, management is better placed to devise strategies and focus actions towards countering adverse trends or exploiting opportunities in specific business lines, geographical areas or market places.

10.2 The form of segmental information that is of use in a particular business depends to a great extent on how the business management is organised. Most businesses are managed on a product or service basis, a geographical basis, or on a mixture of both. Less commonly, a business might be managed on the basis of the markets it serves. If a business is partly regulated (such as a utility) and partly unregulated, management may manage on the basis of those two separate elements. The management structure of the majority of international businesses, however, includes both geographical and product structures. Therefore, segmental information by product or service and by geographical region is relevant to most entities.

10.3 The value of segmental information is not limited to its application as an internal management tool. It also has an important role in external reporting, since by providing segmental information in financial statements, the entity's management can explain to investors and to the market many of the factors that contribute to the result for the year. These factors might be developments introduced by management, such as the expansion of products or markets, or events outside management's control, such as political or economic events.

10.4 Segmental information reported externally is arguably more useful if it corresponds with the information that management uses in making decisions. However, in instances where the segmental information used by management and reported in the notes to the financial statements differs from that which is presented in the primary financial statements, external users need an explanation of the bases used to identify segments and to calculate the measures used by management, together with appropriate reconciliations to figures used in the financial statements.

[The next paragraph is 10.7.]

Objective

10.7 The objective of IFRS 8 is set out in a core principle. This core principle is to require an entity to disclose information that enables users of the financial statements to evaluate the nature and financial effects of the business activities in which the entity engages and the economic environments in which it operates. [IFRS 8 para 1].

10.8 This principle makes it clear that the standard is primarily a disclosure standard. The standard does not prescribe the way management should measure segmental information (it only requires that the disclosure is based on information reported to the chief operating decision maker (CODM)), but the standard does include requirements for reconciliations from segmental information to figures in the income statement or statement of comprehensive income and balance sheet and for disclosure of explanations of how segments are identified and how segmental measures have been determined.

10.9 The fact that the IASB states an overriding principle from which all the other requirements of the standard flow is also an example of the IASB's preferred approach of basing standards on principles rather than solely on detailed rules. The IASB has demonstrated this preferred approach by not including the extensive implementation guidance which supported the US standard ASC 280 (formerly SFAS 131) when it was issued by the FASB in June 1997.

Scope

10.10 IFRS 8 applies to:

- The separate or individual financial statements of an entity:
    - whose debt or equity securities are traded in a public market (that is a domestic or foreign stock exchange or an over-the-counter market, including local or regional markets); or
    - that files, or is in the process of filing, its financial statements with a securities commission or other regulatory organisation for the purpose of issuing any class of instruments in a public market.

- The consolidated financial statements of a group with a parent:
    - whose debt or equity securities are traded in a public market (that is a domestic or foreign stock exchange or an over-the-counter market, including local or regional markets); or
    - That files, or is in the process of filing, the consolidated financial statements with a securities commission or other regulatory organisation for the purpose of issuing any class of instruments in a public market.

[IFRS 8 para 2].

10.11   If an entity that is not required to apply IFRS 8 voluntarily discloses information about segments, but that information does not comply with the IFRS, the entity should not describe the information as segment information. [IFRS 8 para 3]. For example, if such an entity disclosed information about segments, but that information was not the information reported to the CODM, it should not be described as segment information. Similarly, if such an entity voluntarily disclosed only part of the information required by the standard, such as sales information for segments, but did not disclose segment profit or loss or the other information required by the standard, it should not describe the sales information as segment information. [IFRS 8 para BC 22].

10.12   Where a parent's separate financial statements that are required to comply with IFRS 8 are included in a financial report with the consolidated financial statements of the parent and its subsidiaries, segment information need only be given for the consolidated financial statements. [IFRS 8 para 4].

10.12.1   A subsidiary company whose debt or equity securities are traded in a public market or who is in the process of filing its financial statements with a securities commission or regulatory authority for the purpose of issuing its securities in a public market is required to present segment information. The subsidiary would need to analyse its segments separately from the parent's analysis. This would include identifying its own CODM (see further para 10.31.3), determining its own operating segments based on its CODM's review and disclosure of its reportable segments in accordance with IFRS 8. The separate subsidiary's reportable segments will not necessarily be the same as the parent company's disclosures of the activities of the listed subsidiary. It would not be uncommon for the subsidiary's reportable segments to be more detailed than the corresponding segment disclosures in the parent company financial statements.

10.12.2   Where a subsidiary has listed securities but the parent does not, whether the consolidated financial statements are required to comply with IFRS 8 will depend on whether the consolidated financial statements need to be filed with a regulator. Where the consolidated financial statements are required to be filed with a regulator irrespective of the filing requirements of the subsidiary, the consolidated financial statements must comply with IFRS 8.

[The next paragraph is 10.13.1.]

10.13.1   IFRS 8 may apply to entities that issue instruments on a public market where those instruments can only be redeemed by 'putting them back' to the issuer. For example, an entity that is a fund issues a public prospectus whereby members of the public can subscribe for units. Investors can only redeem their units by selling them back to the fund. Since the entity was required to file its financial statements, as part of the public prospectus, for purposes of issuing the instruments and subsequently issued instruments to members of the public, IFRS 8 would apply.

10.13.2   In contrast however, a regulatory requirement to file financial statements is not always linked to the process of issuing instruments to a public market. Therefore, entities that file financial statements will not always be within IFRS 8's scope. Where an entity does not file financial statements for issuing instruments for example, a mutual fund has to file financial statements but not for the purpose of issuing instruments to the public, such an entity would not be required to comply with IFRS 8.

> **UK.10.13.2.1** The term 'traded in a public market' used in IFRS's encompasses both listed companies in the UK and companies quoted on AIM, as AIM meets the definition of an over-the-counter market.

10.14 An entity that is not within the scope of IFRS 8 may still be required to identify its operating segments in accordance with this standard. IAS 36 states that a cash generating unit to which goodwill acquired in a business combination is allocated for the purpose of impairment testing cannot be larger than an operating segment. [IAS 36 para 80(b)]. Therefore, although the entity does not need to comply with the disclosure requirements of IFRS 8, it will still need to comply with the standard's requirements for determining its operating segments.

[The next paragraph is 10.17.]

Operating segments

Context

10.17 IFRS 8 requires an entity to identify its *operating segments*. Once an entity has done that it is required to determine its *reportable segments*. Reportable segments may comprise single operating segments or an aggregation of operating segments that meet certain quantitative thresholds set out in the standard. Reportable segments are dealt with from paragraph 10.43.

Definition

10.18 An operating segment is defined in IFRS 8 as a component of an entity:

- that engages in business activities from which it may earn revenues and incur expenses (including revenues and expenses relating to transactions with other components of the same entity);

- whose operating results are regularly reviewed by the entity's CODM to make decisions about resources to be allocated to the segment and assess its performance; and

- for which discrete financial information is available.

[IFRS 8 para 5]

Revenues and expenses

10.19 Start-up operations may be operating segments as the standard explains that operating segments may engage in business activities from which they have yet to earn revenues. [IFRS 8 para 5]. For example, an entity whose sole activity is the development of a new product may only be incurring research and development expenses and administration expenses without any revenue yet being earned from the product, but it may still need to treat those activities as an operating segment.

10.19.1 Operations that are being run down or liquidated can also meet the definition of operating segments if the results are regularly reviewed by the CODM. Refer to paragraph 10.25 for further discussion.

10.20 Some parts of an entity will not necessarily meet the definition of an operating segment as they may not be in a position to earn revenues or may earn revenues that are only incidental to the entity's activities. [IFRS 8 para 6].

> **Example – Corporate headquarters support function that does not meet the definition of an operating segment**
>
> A corporate headquarters carrying out support functions in the areas of accounting, treasury, information technology, legal, human resource, environmental and internal audit, would generally not be an operating segment since the revenue earned and expenses incurred are only incidental to the entity's business (as these activities only arise to support the main business). This is the case even if discrete, internal financial information about the headquarters' activities is reviewed by the CODM. However, IFRS 8 does not preclude the additional disclosure of any information by management that is consistent with the core principle and contributes to the understanding of the entity. An entity might therefore separate the corporate headquarters results from the 'all other segments' results provided it clearly identified that the corporate headquarters information presented did not represent an operating segment.

10.20.1 An example of a corporate function that does not meet the definition of an operating segment is given in Table 10.1.

> **Table 10.1 – Corporate and other expenses not forming part of operating segments**
>
> **BASF SE – Report and accounts – 31 December 2011**
>
> **4 – Reporting by segment and region (extract)**
>
> Group corporate costs consist of the expenses for steering the BASF Group and are not allocated to the segments, but rather reported under Other.

10.20.2 A research and development function can be an operating segment provided that discrete information is regularly reviewed by the CODM. Although the function does not earn revenues, it differs from a corporate overhead department in that its activities are not incidental activities; rather, its activities serve as an integral component of the entity's business. The research and development business unit is essentially a vertically integrated operation of the entity. (Refer to para 10.24 for further discussion on vertically integrated operations.)

10.21 The standard notes specifically that an entity's post employment benefit plans are not operating segments. [IFRS 8 para 6].

Discrete financial information

10.22 The definition of an operating segment requires discrete financial information to be available. Where the CODM reviews revenue information only for a particular area of business, in most cases this will not meet the definition of an operating segment. For most entities, the review of revenue-only data is not sufficient for decision-making related to resource allocation or performance evaluation of a segment. In cases where product sales or service provisions involve minimal costs, the revenue-only data could be representative of the operating results. In this case, the review of the revenue-only data by the CODM may be sufficient to conclude that the business activity falls within the definition of an operating segment.

10.22.1 A segment balance sheet is not necessary to conclude that discrete financial information is available. The requirement for discrete financial information can be met with operating performance information only, such as gross profit by product line.

Vertically integrated operations

10.23 The definition of an operating segment envisages that part of an entity that earns revenue and incurs expenses relating to transactions with other components of the same entity may still qualify as an operating segment even if all of its revenue and expenses derive from such intra-group transactions.

10.24 Such a situation may occur in a vertically integrated operation. Vertically integrated operations are structures that combine many or all of the production and selling processes within one entity. An example is in the oil industry where the activities of exploration and production (upstream activities) and refining and marketing (downstream activities) are carried out within one entity. Even though most, or all, of the upstream product (crude petroleum) is transferred internally to the entity's refining operations, the standard's requirements mean that the upstream activities could still qualify as an operating segment.

10.24.1 IFRS 8 defines an operating segment as a *"component of an entity that engages in business activities from which it may earn revenues and incur expenses"*. This recognises that not all business activities earn revenues and, therefore, a vertically integrated operation of an entity for which no revenues are allocated can still meet the definition of an operating segment. For example, manufacturing entities that are managed by an operating cost centre may not have revenues allocated to each cost centre. Provided discrete financial information is prepared and reviewed by the CODM, such components would be considered operating segments.

10.24.2 An example of disclosure of vertically integrated operations is given in Table 10.2. In this example, two of the reportable segments (the development and production segments) have sales that are substantially intra-group.

Table 10.2 – Disclosure of vertically integrated operations

Statoil ASA – Annual report – 31 December 2011

4 Segments (extract)

Operating segments (extract)

The composition of Statoil's reportable segments has changed on the basis of the new corporate structure implemented with effect from 1 January 2011. Comparable periods have been restated accordingly.

Statoil's operations are managed through the following operating segments; Development and Production Norway (DPN; previously Exploration and Production Norway); Development and Production North America (DPNA; previously included in International Exploration and Production); Development and Production International (DPI; previously International Exploration and Production); Marketing Processing and Renewable Energy (MPR; previously Natural Gas, Manufacturing and Marketing and parts of Technology and New energy which were included in the Other segment); Fuel and Retail (FR) and Other.

The Development and Production operating segments, which are organised based on a regional model with geographical clusters or units, are responsible for the commercial development of the oil and gas portfolios within their respective geographical areas, DPN on the Norwegian continental shelf, DPNA in North America including offshore and onshore activities in the United States of America and Canada, and DPI worldwide outside of North America and Norway.

Exploration activities are managed by a separate business unit, which has the global responsibility across the group for discovery and appraisal of new resources. Exploration activities are allocated to and presented in the respective Development and Production segments.

The MPR segment is responsible for marketing and trading of oil and gas commodities (crude, condensate, gas liquids, products, natural gas and LNG), electricity and emission rights; as well as transportation, processing and manufacturing of the above mentioned commodities, operations of refineries, terminals, processing and power plants, wind parks and other activities within renewable energy.

The FR segment markets fuel and related products principally to retail consumers.

The Other reporting segment includes activities within Global Strategy and Development, Technology, Projects and Drilling and the Corporate Centre, and Corporate Services.

. . .

The Eliminations section includes elimination of inter-segment sales and related unrealised profits, mainly from the sale of crude oil and products. Intersegment revenues are based upon estimated market prices.

The measurement basis of segment profit is *Net operating income*. Financial items, tax expense and tax assets are not allocated to the operating segments.

Segment data for the years ended 31 December 2011, 2010 and 2009 is presented below:

Segment reporting

(in NOK million) Year ended 31 December 2011	Development and Production Norway	Development and Production International	Marketing, processing and renewable Energy	Fuel and retail	Other	Eliminations	Total
Revenues third party and Other income	7,861	25,158	564,139	70,779	1,004	0	668,941
Revenues inter-segment	204,181	44,810	45,674	2,904	1	(297,570)	0
Net income (loss) from associated companies	60	953	163	3	85	0	1,264
Total revenues and other income	212,102	70,921	609,976	73,686	1,090	(297,570)	670,205
Net operating income	152,713	32,821	24,743	1,869	(256)	(106)	211,784

Discontinued operations and operations being wound down

10.25   A discontinued operation can meet the IFRS 8 definition of an operating segment, if it continues to engage in business activities, the operating results are regularly reviewed by the CODM and there is discrete financial information available to facilitate the review. This might be the case where an operation is being wound down, even if no strategic or long-term planning decisions are being made with respect to the operation. If the CODM continues to review the operation's results for the purpose of short-term management, it could still meet the definition of an operating segment as illustrated in the example below.

> **Example – Insurance company disposing of its workers' compensation business**
>
> An insurance company discontinues its workers' compensation business. The discontinuation meets the criteria for 'discontinued operations' treatment under IFRS 5. For internal purposes, separate financial results are maintained for this business and they are reviewed by the CODM until the discontinuance is complete. The operation is still being managed by the CODM and would continue to meet the definition of an operating segment.

10.25.1   Conversely, if the CODM no longer reviews discrete financial information on the discontinuing operation, it would no longer fall within the definition of an operating segment. However, note that particular disclosures may still need to be presented in accordance with IFRS 5.

Joint ventures

10.26   Joint venture operations can qualify as operating segments provided the entity manages these operations separately and such operations meet the IFRS 8 definition of an operating segment. The financial information (as reported to the CODM) regarding the joint venture activities that comprise the segment would be disclosed. If the results of the whole of the joint venture are reviewed by the CODM such financial amounts must be disclosed and then reconciled to the corresponding amounts (for example, the investors 50% interest) reported in the consolidated financial statements. In addition, appropriate eliminations would need to be reflected in the reconciliation column for amounts reported in excess of those amounts reflected in the consolidated financial statements. For example, since the joint venture's revenue information is not included in the revenue figure reported in the consolidated financial statements (if the joint venture is accounted for under the equity method), an elimination of the revenue amount disclosed for the joint ventures would need to be reflected as a reconciling item.

Management approach

10.27   A condition for identifying an operating segment is that it should be a component of the entity whose operating results are regularly reviewed by the entity's CODM to make decisions about resources to be allocated to the segment and to assess its performance.

10.28   The IASB chose to adopt the 'management approach' to identifying operating segments for several reasons, which include:

- It gives consistency between what is reported to users and what is reported internally to management, that is, it enables the user of the financial statements to review the operations 'through the eyes of management'.

- Segment information is more consistent with information reported elsewhere in the financial report, for example in a management commentary.

- The cost of producing segment information is less than before as the information is the same as that generated internally for management, rather than having to be specially produced for the financial statements.

- The management approach in IFRS 8 is consistent with the US standard ASC 280 and thus the adoption of this approach helps to converge IFRS and US GAAP.

[IFRS 8 para BC 9].

10.29   The IASB also believes that adopting the same approach as in ASC 280 results in some entities reporting more segments and also more segment information in interim financial reports. [IFRS 8 para BC 9].

UK.10.29.1   In the UK the Companies Act requirements for a business review and the ASB's statement on the OFR refer to 'key performance indicators' (KPIs). It is likely that consistency between the KPIs used in the OFR and business review and the measures used in segmental reporting in the financial statements is improved by adopting the management approach for segmental reporting under IFRS 8.

[The next paragraph is 10.31.]

Chief operating decision maker

10.31 The standard explains that the term chief operating decision maker ('CODM') is intended to mean a function rather than a manager with a specific title. The function that the term encompasses is that of allocating resources to operating segments and assessing their performance. This function may be carried out by the person who is the entity's chief executive or chief operating officer but, for example, it could also be a group of executive directors or others. [IFRS 8 para 7]. Deciding who the CODM is can be difficult and judgement is needed to ensure that the right person or persons have been identified. The CODM is responsible for the allocation of resources and assessing the performance of the entity's operating segments. The CODM's identity will not always be clear and will depend on the entity's structure. Hence, the CODM will vary from entity to entity and may be the chief executive officer, chief operating officer, senior management team or the management board.

10.31.1 In some jurisdictions, a supervisory board may have significant oversight responsibilities over the function of the board of directors. However, it is unlikely that a supervisory board is the CODM. The supervisory board would need to act in the same capacity as the typical chief executive officer to be the CODM including, for example, regular reviews and interaction with segment management. Veto rights or rights of approval alone would not constitute the function of allocating resources and assessing performance in the context of IFRS 8. Hence, a supervisory board function that simply approves management's decisions would not constitute the CODM.

10.31.2 Additionally, a committee of non-executive directors is unlikely to be the CODM. Non-executive directors are not usually involved in resource allocation decisions, except at a very high level. Their role is a governance one, rather than a management role. Therefore, they would not meet the definition of the CODM. So care should be taken when non-executives are members of a committee that is deemed to be the CODM.

10.31.3 In some territories, consolidated information relating to several listed entities within a conglomerate organisation may be reviewed by the owner of the conglomerate. Whilst the the owner may be making strategic decisions and resource allocation decisions for the group as a whole, this does not necessarily mean that the owner is the CODM at the individual reporting entity level. The CODM should be identified for and within each reporting entity or group separately.

10.32 Once the CODM has been identified, it is important to reconsider the identification when appropriate and following any business re-organisations, acquisitions or disposals. If there has been a change to the function that is the CODM, this may have an impact on the composition of the operating segments as a different composition or membership of the CODM may well require different information to allocate resources and assess performance.

Identifying operating segments

10.33 In many cases, the operating segments can be clearly identified using the three characteristics of operating segments listed above – engaging in activities that earn revenues and incur costs, review of operating results by the CODM and availability of discrete financial information. In other situations the CODM may receive and review reports giving several different types of segment information that make it more difficult to clearly identify operating segments. For example, the CODM might receive reports on an entity's sales and operating profit both by product and by geographic region. On its own this information might make it unclear as to whether the 'management approach' would result in operating segments based on the type of product (or business unit responsible for the product) or geographic criteria. Refer to paragraph 10.38 for discussion on the matrix form of an organisation.

10.34 In circumstances such as this, other factors may have to be taken into account to identify the operating segments as defined in the standard. IFRS 8 notes that these other factors may include the nature of the business activities, the existence of managers responsible for them and information presented to the board of directors. [IFRS 8 para 8].

10.35 Taking the example above the issue would be fairly easily resolved if, for example:

■ The entity had managers responsible for each product area.

■ The entity had just one sales manager.

■ The CODM also received information regularly on development costs of new products and employee numbers in each product area.

■ Information on each product area was regularly supplied to the whole board.

■ The board only received information on total global sales figures.

In such a situation, the management approach would result in operating segments that were based on the type of product (or business unit responsible for the product), because there are individual managers for each of these business units (product areas), but not for each geographical region and the board receives information on each product area, but does not receive sales figures on individual geographic regions.

10.35.1 The CODM may review multiple sets of information when assessing the entity's overall performance and deciding how to allocate resources. This is an area that requires significant judgement. For example, the CODM may review three levels of reports. Level 3 is the more detailed component level and is represented by 25 individual components. Level 2 contains the level 3 components aggregated into 10 components and level 1 is an aggregation of level 2, yielding three components. In order to determine the operating segments, the following factors should be considered:

- Understanding the regular process that the CODM uses to assess performance and what information is used and with whom the CODM interacts. The presumption would be that any information provided to the CODM on a regular basis is used. An entity should consider whether the receipt of certain specific information (such as ratios) can logically be used to assess performance and allocate resources or whether the CODM could practically perform the function at the low disaggregated level 3.

- Identifying the segment managers and what are they responsible for. Segment managers are usually compensated on the basis of the results of the segment as a whole. However a segment manager can be in charge of more than one operating segment. [IFRS 8 para 9].

- The budgeting process, on the assumption that the operating and capital budget would be approved or modified by the CODM for the segment as a whole.

- The information sent to the board of directors. The board would not usually receive information at a level lower than the operating segments.

- Whether the level of the organisation viewed makes sense as operating segments in the context of the core principle that is, whether the presentation of segments at a lower level contribute significantly to the understanding of the business activities.

Segment managers

10.36 Consistent with the management approach, the standard identifies the existence of segment managers as an important factor in determining operating segments. Segment managers are those who are directly accountable to the CODM and who regularly discuss with that person the operating activities, financial results, forecasts or plans for the segment that they manage. The term 'segment manager' relates to a function and need not be a single person but could, for example, be the executive committee of a subsidiary that constitutes an operating segment. The CODM might also have a dual role, fulfilling both that function and the function of segment manager of one or more operating segments. A single manager might be the segment manager for more than one operating segment, for example a regional manager might have responsibility for several segments within that region. [IFRS 8 para 9].

10.37 The function of segment manager is a key indicator where several components of an entity would meet the criteria for identifying operating segments set out in paragraph 10.18, but segment managers are held responsible for only one of those components. In that situation only the component for which they are held responsible is an operating segment.

Example – Role of segment manager as an indicator of operating segments

An entity manufactures and sells electronic components for the automotive and aerospace industries in three geographic markets, which are Europe, USA and Asia. There is discrete financial information available for each manufacturing location and for the selling activity for each product in each geographic region. This financial information is regularly reviewed by the CODM. There is a sales director who is responsible for all worldwide sales to whom each regional sales manager reports. There are also line managers responsible for each of the automotive and aerospace manufacturing activities worldwide. The line managers report directly to the CODM, which in this case is the group chief executive officer.

In this situation both the geographic sales areas and the product areas may meet the criteria for operating segments set out in paragraph 10.18. However it is likely that, because the automotive and aerospace line managers report directly to the CODM, they would be considered to be 'segment managers'. The regional sales managers do not report directly to the CODM and, therefore, would probably not be regarded as 'segment managers'.

Therefore, it is likely that the entity's operating segments would be identified as being the automotive and aerospace product areas.

10.38   In a matrix form of organisation, components of an entity may overlap with different aspects of components for which managers are responsible, with both being reported to the CODM. For example, some regional managers may be responsible for products and services worldwide and others may be responsible for different geographical areas. The CODM regularly reviews the operating results of both sets of components and financial information is available for both. Where such a situation occurs it is more difficult to determine clearly which set of components should be identified as the entity's operating segments. The standard states that in such circumstances the entity should determine which set of components are the operating segments by reference to the standard's core principle. [IFRS 8 para 10]. The core principle is that the entity should disclose information to enable users to evaluate the nature and financial effects of the types of business activities in which it engages and the economic environments in which it operates. [IFRS 8 para 1]. The entity should also assess whether the identified operating segments could realistically represent the level at which the CODM is assessing performance and allocating resources. Additionally, the identified operating segments are expected to be consistent with other information the entity produces such as press releases, interviews with management, company websites, management discussions and other public information about the entity.

UK.10.38.1   In the UK, the FRRP's annual report for 2011 notes that questions put to companies by the FRRP during the year were often prompted by apparent inconsistencies between the narrative reports and the audited accounts. An example given is where the segmentation of the operating analysis within the chief executive's report did not appear to be reflected in the segmental disclosures in the audited accounts.

10.39 A matrix form of organisation is similar to the example in paragraph 10.37, except that in this scenario the regional sales managers would be responsible for the geographic markets (not just sales) and would report to the CODM. Thus it would be difficult to determine operating segments by reference to the way in which management assesses the business as it does this on both a product and a geographical basis.

10.40 In this situation application of the core principle might depend on the way in which the CODM assigns priorities in making decisions. If, for example, the priority is to increase total sales, market share and geographic spread, application of the principle might mean that the most relevant information for shareholders should be based on geographic markets. If, on the other hand, the priority is to improve the sales of individual products and the CODM believes that improving and maintaining the product quality is the key to this and that different geographic markets are likely to respond uniformly to such measures, then application of the principle might mean that the most relevant information for shareholders should be based on products.

10.41 Although the standard requires a decision to be made as to what the operating segments are, applying if necessary the core principle, there is nothing in the standard to prevent an entity from reporting additional information, to supplement the information required for operating segments. An entity could give such information in the form of a matrix presentation so that, for example, if operating segments were based on products, the additional information would also give geographic information. Although not required by the standard information, a matrix presentation can be very useful to users of the financial statements.

10.42 Where discrete financial information is not available a business activity is not an operating segment. Table 10.3 gives an example where discrete financial information is available for revenues but not for costs of certain activities and as a result they are not treated as operating segments. See paragraph 10.22, which explains the circumstances when a component of the business may meet the definition of an operating segment if revenue-only information is reviewed by the CODM.

Table 10.3 – Activities not treated as operating segments as discrete financial information is not available

ARM Holdings plc – Report and accounts – 31 December 2011

2 Segmental reporting (extract)

At 31 December 2011 the Group was organised on a world-wide basis into three main business segments:

Processor Division (PD), encompassing those resources that are centred around microprocessor cores, including specific functions such as graphics IP, fabric IP, embedded software and configurable digital signal processing IP.

Physical IP Division (PIPD), concerned with the building blocks necessary for translation of a circuit design into actual silicon.

System Design Division (SDD), focused on the tools and models used to create and debug software and system-on-chip (SoC) designs.

This is based upon the Group's internal organisation and management structure and is the primary way in which the CODM is provided with financial information. Whilst revenues are also reported into four main revenue streams (namely licensing, royalties, development systems and services), the costs, operating results and balance sheets are only analysed into these three divisions.

Reportable segments

Context

10.43 IFRS 8 requires an entity to identify its *operating segments*. Once an entity has done that, it is required to determine its *reportable segments*. Reportable segments may comprise single operating segments, or an aggregation of operating segments, that meet certain quantitative thresholds set out in the standard. Reportable segments are the basis for *disclosure of segment information* in the financial statements. Disclosure requirements are dealt with in a separate section below.

Determining reportable segments

10.44 Reportable segments are those operating segments or aggregations of operating segments for which segment information must be separately reported. Aggregation of one or more operating segments into a single reportable segment is permitted (but not required) where certain conditions are met, the principal condition being that the operating segments should have similar economic characteristics. Once aggregation has been considered, single operating segments or aggregations of operating segments (where permitted) must be treated as reportable segments when they exceed certain quantitative thresholds that are based on a comparison of segment revenues, profit or loss and assets with the comparable figures for all segments. (An entity is allowed, however, to report segment information for smaller operating segments or aggregations of operating segments if it wishes to do so.) [IFRS 8 para 11].

[The next paragraph is 10.46.]

10.46 The process for determining reportable segments is not straightforward and the IASB has included a useful flow chart in its 'Guidance on implementing IFRS 8 Operating Segments', which is reproduced as an appendix to this chapter. The sequence of steps may be summarised as follows:

- Identify operating segments.

- Determine whether any operating segments meet *all* the aggregation criteria and if so aggregate them, if desired.

- Review the identified operating segments and aggregated groups of operating segments to see if they individually meet the quantitative thresholds. Those that do are treated as reportable segments.

- For the remainder, check whether any of the identified operating segments or aggregated groups of operating segments meet a *majority* of the aggregation criteria. If they do, aggregate them and treat as reportable segments if desired. Individual operating segments can also be treated as reportable segments even if they are not aggregated with another segment or do not meet the quantitative threshold.

- Test whether the external revenues of reportable segments identified so far represent 75% or more of the entity's external revenue. If they do, then aggregate the remaining segments into a segment called 'All other segments', which is not a reportable segment in the context of IFRS 8. If they do not, then additional reportable segments must be identified, until the total of reportable segments reaches the 75% point.

[The next paragraph is 10.48.]

Aggregation criteria

10.48   Background information on the development of the US standard, ASC 280, is included as an appendix to the Basis for Conclusions on IFRS 8. This explains that the US standard setters believed that segment information would not add significantly to a user's understanding of an entity if its operating segments had characteristics so similar that they could be expected to have essentially the same future prospects. Although information on each similar segment might be available, the benefit would be insufficient to justify disclosure for each segment. It cites the example of an entity with ten stores that individually met the definition of an operating segment, but which all had essentially the same characteristics as each other. [IFRS 8 BC App A para 73].

10.49   The US standard setters also rejected suggestions that the aggregation criteria in the US standard should be treated as indicators rather than tests and that segments need to be similar in only a majority of characteristics. The US standard setters took this strict line partly because they had noted that one of the failures in practice of the previous US standard had been that segments with different characteristics had at times been aggregated. [IFRS 8 BC App A para 74].

10.50   IFRS 8 takes the same strict line as ASC 280, requiring that the aggregation criteria are tests and not indicators and that all the criteria should be satisfied before operating segments may be aggregated.

10.51   The standard notes that operating segments often show the same long-term financial performance if they have similar economic characteristics. Long-term average gross margins would be expected to be similar. Although, IFRS 8 does not provide guidance on what would be considered an acceptable difference in long term average gross margins, any differences should be closely examined as these may come under scrutiny of regulators. In addition to long-term average gross margins, other economic factors such as trends in the growth of products and management's long-term expectations for the product lines may also be considered. Several years of both historical and future expected financial performance should be considered if such information is available. The standard concludes that two or more operating segments may be aggregated if:

- aggregation is consistent with the core principle that the result is to provide information that enables users to evaluate the nature and financial effects of the business activities in which the entity engages and the economic environments in which it operates;

- the segments have similar economic characteristics; *and*

- the segments are similar in each of the following respects:

    - the nature of products and services;

    - the nature of production processes;

    - the type or class of customer for the products and services;

    - the methods used to distribute the products or provide the services; *and*

    - where applicable, the nature of the regulatory environment, for example banking, insurance or public utilities.

[IFRS 8 para 12].

10.51.1   One might therefore assume that a start-up entity could never be aggregated with a mature business as the gross margins are not likely to be similar. However, to the extent that the expected future financial performance (including the competitive and operating risks) of the start-up business is expected to converge and be similar to that of the entity's mature businesses, the economic characteristics requirement for aggregation would be satisfied and hence the operating segments may be aggregated. However, while the standard does not specify the period over which the financial performance should converge, we do not expect it to be in the long-term.

10.51.2   The criteria for aggregating an entity's segments whose management reporting is prepared on a geographical basis are the same as the criteria listed above. However, in order to be aggregated, each of the individual country segments must possess the same economic characteristics. This may present a problem for combining individual countries since, in addition to assessing the financial performance and risks of the underlying products comprising the segment, an entity must also consider the economic conditions, exchange control regulations and underlying currency risks associated with the countries when it is determining whether the economic characteristics are similar. Furthermore, even if individual countries were to be aggregated, the entity-wide disclosures required by IFRS 8 mean that revenues and assets are required to be disclosed for each material foreign country anyway. An example of issues that may occur when aggregating segments is considered below.

Example – Aggregating segments

A retailer of women's coats has the following operating segments: store label – wool coats; other designer brands – wool coats; and fur coats. The following table shows limited financial information for each segment:

	'Store label wool coats	'Other designer brands wool coats	Fur coats
Average gross-margin percentage	25%	30%	33%
Sales volume	500,000 units	375,000 units	20,000 units
Average sales price	175 per unit	265 per unit	4,200 per unit
Growth rate per year	3% (steady)	2% (steady)	-5% (declining)

The entity's fur coats line of business has experienced sales decline in recent years and the rate of decline is expected to continue. Management believes that the sales decrease is principally in response to the growing consumer focus on animal rights. Management expects that it can maintain the profit margin at 33% for at least the next three years. While management views the 'fur coats' line as still favourably contributing to its operations, it has indicated that after a five year period it will consider whether to maintain the line.

The wool for the 'store label' and 'other designer brands' segments is purchased from the same manufacturer. Average margins and gross sales of the two segments differ, but there are lines in the 'other designer brands' segment with margins and sales prices very similar to the 'store label' segment. The growth rates of the two segments have moved in tandem over the past 10 years and management expects this to continue in the future.

The 'store label' and 'other designer brands' segments possess similar economic characteristics despite the difference in average gross margins. The 'fur coats' segment may be viewed as having different economic characteristics because of the ongoing differences in growth and the operating risks, despite the similarity of its average gross margins to that of the 'other designer brands' segment.

Certain regulators may challenge the conclusion above due to the differences in gross margins between 'store label' and 'other designer brands'. Caution should be exercised when aggregating operating segments with disparate gross margins to ensure that they are economically similar despite the differences in margins. As long-term gross margins of operating segments become more divergent, we would expect it to become more difficult to support the assertion that the operating segments are economically similar.

10.52 The IASB has issued an exposure draft proposing disclosures in respect of the factors used to identify the entity's reportable segments when operating segments have been aggregated (see para 10.74.1).

Quantitative thresholds

10.53 After identifying operating segments and aggregating those that met the aggregation criteria an entity should determine which operating segments or aggregations of operating segments meet the quantitative thresholds for separate disclosure as reportable segments.

10.54 Quantitative thresholds are included in the standard so as to limit the amount of disclosures about operating segments to a reasonable level. Without such thresholds some entities might have to disclose information on as many as 25 operating segments. [IFRS 8 BC App. A para 75]. On the other hand, as a safeguard, the standard requires that *external* revenue of reportable segments must constitute at least 75% of total external entity revenue. [IFRS 8 para 15]. An example of reporting individually small segments on an aggregated basis is included in Table 10.4.

Table 10.4 – Aggregation of reportable segments

OJSC Mostotrest – Annual report – 31 December 2010

5 Operating segments (extract)

Information about reportable segments (extract)

At 31 December 2010 the Group had 17 segments (2009: 15 operating segments), as described below which are the Group's strategic business units. During the first half of 2010 the Group acquired two new subsidiaries, OOO Engtransstroy Corporation and OOO Transstroymekhanizaciya, which have become two additional operating segments.

The strategic business units, including the newly acquired subsidiaries, are managed separately as they are located in different regions, operate different construction projects and require different technology strategies. Each segment represents a separate legal entity or branch of the Company. For each of the strategic business units, the Group's CEO reviews internal management reports on at least a quarterly basis.

The information about the location of each reportable segment is summarized below:

Segment	Short name	Management location
Mostotryad -4	MO-4	Moscow
Mostotryad -1	MO-1	Nizhny Novgorod
Mostotryad -6	MO-6	Yaroslavl
Mostotryad -10	MO-10	Rostov-On-Don
Mostotryad -114	MO-114	Moscow
Mostotryad -90	MO-90	Dmitrov
Mostotryad -81	MO-81	Voronezh
Mostotryad -99	MO-99	Serpukhov
OOO Engtransstroy Corporation	ETS	Moscow
OOO Transstroymechanizatsiya	TSM	Moscow
Other segments	Other	–

Other segments include 7 operating segments that were combined into one reportable segment due to their size.

10.55 Information about an operating segment or about a permitted aggregation of operating segments is required to be reported where it meets *any one* of the following quantitative thresholds:

- The operating segment's reported revenue, including both sales to external customers and inter-segment sales or transfers, is 10% or more of the combined revenue, internal and external, of all operating segments.

- The absolute amount of its reported profit or loss is 10% or more of the greater, in absolute amount, of:

  - the combined reported profit of all operating segments that do not report a loss; and

  - the combined reported loss of all operating segments that report a loss.

- Its assets are 10% or more of the combined assets of all operating segments.

[IFRS 8 para 13].

10.56 The application of the quantitative threshold guidance above is illustrated in the examples below.

Example 1 – Revenue threshold

An entity has the following:

	Segment revenue	External revenue	Internal revenue	Total revenue (including inter-segment)
Operating segment A	40	25	15	350

Operating segment A's internal and external revenues exceed 10% of the total revenues, internal and external, of all operating segments (the first condition above) and so it is a reportable segment.

Example 2 – Revenue and results thresholds

After the aggregation criteria have been applied to its operating segments, an entity has the following:

	Segment revenue	Total revenue (including inter-segment)	Segment loss	Total segment loss of loss-making segments	Total segment profit of profit-making segments
Operating segment A	40	500	10	90	200

Operating segment A's assets are less than 10% of the total assets of all operating segments.

In this case segment A is not a reportable segment. It does not satisfy the revenue test as its revenue, internal and external, is less than 10% of the aggregate internal and external revenues of all operating segments. Nor, as stated, does it satisfy the assets test. In relation to the profits test, although its losses of 10 are greater than 10% of the total of all operating segments in loss, they are less than 10% of the total of all segments in profit. The comparison required by the standard is with the total (profit or loss) that is greater in absolute terms. Segment A's loss of 10 must be compared with the total for all operating segments in profit, which is 200. As segment A's result is less than 10% of the total of all operating segments on this basis, it does not meet the results test either and so segment A is not a reportable segment. In this situation, the entity may treat the immaterial non-reportable segment in one of the following ways:

- include the segment in an 'all other' category;

- voluntarily report the segment separately; or

- if applicable, aggregate the segment with other non-reportable segments in accordance with paragraph 14 of IFRS 8 which would then make the combined segments reportable. (See para 10.63 for discussion on the aggregation of non-reportable segments).

(This example illustrates the profits and losses test and highlights the fact that it may be necessary to compare segment losses with total profits rather than merely with total losses, where total profits exceed total losses. This is because the figure for comparison purposes is the greater of total profits or losses.)

Example 3 – All quantitative thresholds

An entity has the following:

	Segment revenue	Total revenue (including inter-segment)	Segment profit	Total segment profits	Segment assets	Total segment assets
Operating segment A	50	600	5	60	200	400

There are no loss making operating segments.

In this case segment A is a reportable segment. This is because it satisfies the assets test, because its assets represent 10% or more of the total assets of all operating segments.

(This example illustrates the fact that an operating segment only has to satisfy one of the tests in order to be a reportable segment. Segment A does not satisfy the revenue test as its internal and external revenue of 50 does not represent 10% or more of total segment revenue of 600. Nor does it satisfy the profits test as its profit of 5 is less than 10% of the total profits of 60. However, it does satisfy the assets test.)

Example 4 – Quantitative thresholds for a number of segments

Entity A has the following operating segments. The revenues (internal and external), profits and assets are as set out below. Entity A needs to determine how many reportable segments it has. The figures are in the same proportions as in the previous year.

Segment	Total revenue	Profit/(loss)	Total assets
A	11,000,000	2,000,000	25,000,000
B	7,500,000	1,000,000	15,500,000
C	3,000,000	(1,000,000)	10,500,000
D	3,500,000	(500,000)	7,000,000
E	4,000,000	600,000	7,000,000
F	1,500,000	400,000	3,500,000
	30,500,000	2,500,000	68,500,000

In this example segments A, B, D and E clearly satisfy the revenue and assets tests (so there is no need to consider the profits test in these cases) and are reportable segments. Segment C does not satisfy the revenue test but does satisfy the assets test (again there is, therefore, no need to consider the profits test) and is also a reportable segment. Segment F does not satisfy the revenue or the assets tests but does satisfy the profits test. This is because its profit of 400,000 is 10% of the greater of the absolute amount of losses of those segments in loss (1,500,000) and those which either break even or make a profit (including segment F this is 4,000,000). Therefore, segment F is also a reportable segment.

(This example illustrates how to apply of the thresholds to each of the relevant measures of revenue, profit and assets for a number of segments. It also illustrates the importance of other information required by the standard, which is described later in the chapter and for interpreting the segment information. Looking at the above figures it would appear that segment C is the weakest. However, other information required by the standard would help to explain its significance to the entity. The standard requires inter-segment revenue to be reported and the basis of inter-segment pricing. If, for example, segment C produced a vital raw material that was essential for the production processes carried out by other segments and its sales were primarily made at cost to other segments, this could explain why its results were poor compared with the other segments.)

10.57 Although the terms 'revenue' and 'assets' are straightforward in the quantitative thresholds, some doubt might arise as to which level of profit or loss should be used in comparing profits and losses. Entities often report 'operating profit' and other measures include 'profit before tax' and 'profit for the period after tax'. Also, for the purpose of reporting segment information to the CODM, an entity might use a measure of profit adjusted to exclude certain unusual items. As this latter figure (the figure reported to the CODM) is the only profit figure that is likely to be identified for reporting of segment information, in our view this is the figure to be used to make the comparisons of profit or loss required in determining whether the quantitative thresholds have been met.

10.58 This may seem counter-intuitive. However, the standard considers issues through the eyes of management and all segment profits would be calculated on this basis.

10.59 Some entities may use different profit measures for each segment, which causes difficulty when performing the 10% test in relation to profit. IFRS 8 does not contain any guidance in the area. When operating segments have different profit measures, management should determine a reasonable and consistent basis to compare segments for the 10% profit test. The basis used by management should be considered with the core principle in IFRS 8 to provide users with information that enables them to evaluate the nature and financial effects of the business activities.

> **Example – Segments use different measures of profitability**
>
> An entity has three operating segments, none of which can be combined under the aggregation criteria. The following is reported to the CODM:
>
> ■ Segment 1 measures profitability based on net profit, with pension amounts reported on the cash basis. (Segment 1 is the only segment for which pension expense is reported, that is, while the other segments do have pension expenses, allocations of pension amounts are not made to the other two segments.) Asset information is limited to the presentation of accounts receivable.
>
> ■ Segment 2 measures profitability based on pre-tax income, which includes an internal cost-of-capital amount charged by 'corporate' that is assessed to segment 2 only. Asset information includes only accounts receivable and fixed assets.
>
> ■ Segment 3 measures profitability based on post-tax income. Asset information is limited to accounts receivable.
>
> Management have concluded that the most appropriate measure for determining the 10% threshold is the lowest level of profitability reported to the chief operating decisions maker. The lowest level of profitability reported to the CODM is the net profit of operating segment 1. This amount should be determined for the remaining segments for the purposes of the 10% profit test. Similarly, accounts receivable would be the most consistent measure of assets on which to perform the 10% test for assets.

Operating segments below the quantitative thresholds

Designation of single segment as a reportable segment

10.60 As well as *requiring* that operating segments that meet the quantitative thresholds should be treated as reportable segments the standard *allows* any other operating segment to be treated as a reportable segment if management believes that information about that segment would be useful to users of the financial statements. [IFRS 8 para 13].

10.61 One reason for treating an operating segment that does not meet the thresholds as a reportable segment might be that the performance of the segment depends more on market forces than all the other segments and is highly volatile. Alternatively, the activity represented by the segment may be a new activity that the entity wishes to highlight, such as a start-up activity that incurs costs, but does not yet generate much revenue. Examples of such activities in the past have been internet and digital television ventures. An example of a reporting segment that has been voluntarily disclosed is given in Table 10.5.

Table 10.5 – Voluntary disclosure of reportable segment not meeting quantitative thresholds

Sasol Limited – Report and accounts – 30 June 2011

Segment information (extract)

The group has formed significant joint ventures to promote Sasol technology and products internationally. The group is promoting and marketing its gas-to-liquids (GTL) technology for converting remote or flared natural gas into new-generation, low-emission GTL diesel, GTL naphtha and other products. It is envisaged that Sasol Synfuels International (SSI) through the recent development of the GTL plants in Qatar and Nigeria will contribute to the growing of a global GTL business in the future.

Whilst Sasol Petroleum International (SPI), like SSI, does not meet the quantitative criteria for disclosure as a separate segment, it is expected to become a significant contributor to the group's performance in future years as the upstream supplier of resources for the group's GTL and coal to liquids (CTL) activities.

Consequently, the GEC has chosen to include SSI and SPI as reportable operating segments even though SSI and SPI do not meet any of the quantitative thresholds as the GEC believes that such information would be useful to the users of the financial statements.

Aggregation of segments with a majority of similar features and disclosure as a reportable segment

10.62 If, alternatively, an operating segment that does not meet the 10% criteria is not designated as a reportable segment, it may be combined into a separately reportable segment with one or more other operating segments. This is acceptable as long as those operating segments are also below all the 10% thresholds, have similar economic characteristics and share a majority of the aggregation criteria listed in detail in paragraph 10.51 and again below in summary for convenience:

- the nature of products and services;

- the nature of production processes;

- the type or class of customer for the products and services;

- the methods used to distribute the products or provide the services; and

- where applicable, the nature of the regulatory environment, for example banking, insurance or public utilities.

[IFRS 8 para 14].

10.63 Note that for the purpose of combining segments in these circumstances, the segments need to be economically similar and only satisfy a *majority* of the aggregation criteria, not necessarily all of them. This is different from the aggregation of segments that may be done *prior to* the initial determination of reportable segments, where *all* the criteria must be satisfied (see para 10.50).

10.64 The distinction between the two stages of aggregation is important and is explained as follows:

■ In the first stage, described in paragraphs 10.50 and 10.51, the aggregation takes place *before* determining the reportable segments. Each of the aggregation criteria is considered to be significant and for that reason they all have to be satisfied.

■ In the second stage, described in paragraph 10.62, the reportable segments have already been identified and the segments that are being aggregated are those that do not meet the thresholds for treatment as reportable segments. Therefore, the aggregation criteria are less important.

10.65 Nevertheless it would be useful, when describing the factors used to identify the entity's reportable segments (a requirement of the standard that is dealt with later in this chapter), to explain that the reportable segment formed as a result of the aggregation process described in paragraph 10.62 is the result of the aggregation of segments that share only a majority of features in common.

Other segments that are not reportable segments

10.66 Information on other business activities and operating segments that are not reportable segments should be combined and disclosed under a heading 'All other segments'. Note that unless all of the aggregation criteria have been met, an immaterial non-reportable segment cannot be aggregated with a reportable segment. The 'all other segments' category should be shown separately from other reconciling items (such as elimination of inter-segment revenue and profits) in the reconciliations to figures reported in the entity's income statement and balance sheet. (These reconciliations are required by the standard and are discussed later in the chapter.) The standard requires that the sources of the revenue included in the 'All other segments' category should be described. [IFRS 8 para 16]. Table 10.6 in paragraph 10.76 below gives such descriptions.

75% test for reportable segments

10.67 If, after determining reportable segments, the total external revenue attributable to those segments amounts to less than 75% of the total consolidated or entity external revenue (depending on whether consolidated or entity financial statements are being prepared), additional segments should be identified as reportable segments, even if they do not meet the 10% thresholds described above, until at least 75% of the consolidated or entity external revenue is included in reportable segments. [IFRS 8 para 15]. Consolidated revenue for the purpose of this comparison would, by definition, mean external revenue, as inter-segment revenue would be eliminated on consolidation. The standard does not prescribe which segments should be included to reach the 75% threshold. We would expect an entity to select the most significant operating segment, however, there is no requirement to do so.

> **Example – 75% test for reportable segments**
>
> An entity has identified three reportable segments. However, the total external revenues generated by these three segments represent only 68% of the entity's total external revenues. The entity's systems also provide for reports to be made to the financial controller on five other activities that are reported to the CODM. None of these five activities is individually large enough to constitute a reportable segment under IFRS 8. The largest such activity accounts for 8% of total entity external revenue. In accordance with the requirement of the standard, the entity designates this activity as a reportable segment, making the total external revenues attributable to reportable segments 76% of total entity revenues. The remaining four activities are aggregated into an 'All other segments' category (see para 10.66).

Prior years

10.68 If a segment was a reportable segment in the prior period, because it met the relevant 10% thresholds, it should continue to be treated as a reportable segment in the current period even if it no longer meets any of the 10% thresholds, if the entity's management considers the segment to be of continuing significance. [IFRS 8 para 17]. However, in the next period, as the comparative would not qualify as a separate segment, this segment would no longer be required to be reported in the current or the prior period, unless it qualified as a separate reportable segment again in the current period.

10.69 If a segment is identified as a reportable segment in the current accounting period, because it meets the relevant 10% thresholds, comparatives should be restated to show the newly reportable segment as a separate segment, even if that segment did not meet the 10% threshold in the comparative period. This comparative information must be given unless the necessary information is not available and the cost to develop it would be excessive. [IFRS 8 para 18]. However, given the management approach to segment identification it would seem difficult to prove that costs would be excessive.

Practical limits on number of reportable segments

10.70 The standard notes that there may be a practical limit to the number of reportable segments that an entity discloses beyond which segment information may become too detailed. The standard suggests that where the number of segments that are reportable in accordance with the criteria set out in the standard (and described above) increases to above ten, the entity should consider whether a practical limit has been reached. [IFRS 8 para 19].

10.71 If an entity has more than ten reportable segments it may not limit the number of operating segments it discloses if all of the quantitative thresholds have not yet been met. In particular, paragraph 15 says that additional operating segments should be identified as reportable segments until at least 75% of the entity's revenue is included in reportable segments (see para 10.67). Accordingly, if an entity has 20 different operating segments, all of which are the same size (that is, each contributes 5% of revenue) and none of which are reportable segments or meet the aggregation criteria in paragraph 17 or paragraph 19, such an entity would be expected to disclose at least 15 operating segments as reportable (that is, 75% of consolidated revenue divided by 5% of revenue per segment equals 15 segments).

Disclosure of information on reportable segments

10.72   The standard requires that an entity should disclose information about reportable segments to enable users of the financial statements to evaluate the nature and financial effects of the business activities in which the entity engages and about the economic environments in which it operates. [IFRS 8 para 20].

10.73   Information to be disclosed about reportable segments falls into four categories:

■   General information on how reportable segments are identified.

■   Detailed disclosures about measures of segment profit or loss, and about measures of assets and liabilities (if these are reported to the CODM – see para 10.77.1).

■   Disclosure of measurement basis.

■   Reconciliations of segment information to corresponding entity amounts (as reported in the financial statements). Balance sheet amounts are required to be reconciled for each date at which a balance sheet is presented.

[IFRS 8 para 21].

10.73.1   Management may be concerned about whether IFRS 8 will require information that they consider commercially sensitive to be presented to the external market. Indeed, IFRS 8 would potentially make more detailed disaggregated information provided to the CODM reportable, which some entities might regard as commercially sensitive. However, IFRS 8 does not include a 'competitive harm' exemption. So, information reported to the CODM will need to be disclosed.

10.73.2   Another consideration is that management accounts may not be supported by the same robust internal processes and control systems as the external reporting systems. Management will need to ensure that there are relevant control systems in place to obtain information that is presented in the management accounts, and hence within the segment information. Furthermore, IFRS 8 requires reconciliation between amounts disclosed for reportable segments and the corresponding amounts in the financial statements.

General information

10.74 The general information that the standard requires is:

- A description of the factors used to identify the entity's reportable segments, which should include the basis of organisation, for example whether the entity is organised around differences in products and services, or geographical areas, or regulatory environments or a combination of factors. The description should also disclose whether operating segments have been aggregated.

- The types of products and services from which each reportable segment earns its revenues.

[IFRS 8 para 22(a)(b)].

10.74.1 IFRS 8 currently contains a requirement to disclose whether operating segments have been aggregated. In May 2012, the IASB issued an exposure draft proposing additional disclosures in respect of the factors used to identify the entity's reportable segments when operating segments have been aggregated. The IASB proposes that where operating segments have been aggregated, disclosure should be given of the judgements made by management in applying the aggregation criteria. In particular, a brief description of the operating segments that have been aggregated and the economic indicators that have been assessed in determining that they share similar economic characteristics (for example, profit margin spreads and sales growth rates) would have to be disclosed under the proposal.

UK.10.74.1.1 In the UK, this aggregation is an area that the FRRP has focused on. In its annual report for 2011, the FRRP notes that it has continued to challenge companies that appeared to have aggregated operating segments where it was difficult from the information provided to appreciate the sense in which the segments were economically similar as required by IFRS 8. The FRRP has been encouraging companies to provide clear explanations in support of any decision to aggregate segments and notes that it hopes to see evidence of significant improvements in this area in future financial reporting.

10.75 In practice many entities give considerable detail on how they are organised and on the composition of segments in a management commentary such as the 'Operating and financial review' or 'Management discussion and analysis'. Therefore, the disclosures required in the financial statements will often be those that meet the minimum requirements above. In most cases there should not be differences between the management commentary and the operating segment information.

10.76 An example of the disclosure of general information is given in Table 10.3 in paragraph 10.42 and another example is given in Table 10.6. Table 10.6 illustrates the relationship between segmental information given in the financial statements and that given in the other sections of the annual report. The first extract is from the 'Review of operations', which includes a description of how the group is structured. It includes extensive segment discussion and analysis (not reproduced in the example below due to its length). The second extract is a description of the constituents of each reportable segment that is given in the financial statements where the detailed figures required by IFRS 8 are given.

Table 10.6 – Description of reportable segments

RWE AG – Report and accounts – 31 December 2011

Review of operations (extract)

1.5 COMMENTARY ON THE SEGMENTS (extract)

Group structure with seven divisions.

Reporting on the financial year that just ended is based on the segment structure used in the 2010 financial statements. The RWE Group is divided into seven divisions based on geographic and functional criteria. The following is an overview of them.

- Germany. This division consists of the Power Generation and Sales/Distribution Networks Business Areas.

- Power Generation: This business area includes the activities of RWE Power, Germany's largest electricity generator. The company mainly produces power from coal, gas and nuclear fuel. Lignite is produced by RWE Power through in-house mining activities.

- Sales/Distribution Networks: Our German sales and distribution network operations are pooled in this business area. They are overseen by RWE Deutschland, which mainly encompasses the network companies Rhein-Ruhr and Westfalen-Weser-Ems, RWE Vertrieb (including eprimo, RWE Energiedienstleistungen and RWE Aqua), RWE Effizienz, RWE Gasspeicher and our German regional utilities. The latter operate their own electricity generation facilities to a small extent, as well as managing network and end-customer operations. The Sales/Distribution Networks Business Area also includes some non-German activities: our minority interests in Austria-based KELAG and Luxembourg-based ENOVOS as well as our water operations in Zagreb, Croatia, which have been assigned to RWE Aqua.

- Netherlands/Belgium: By acquiring Essent with effect from 30 September 2009, we have become a leading energy utility in the Benelux region. In the Netherlands, the business area's core market, Essent generates electricity from gas, hard coal and biomass and holds a minority stake in Borssele, the only nuclear power station in the Netherlands. In addition, the company is active in the electricity and gas sales business and runs gas midstream operations. Since the acquisition, some of Essent's former activities have been transferred to other RWE divisions. Most recently, since 1 January 2011, parts of the gas midstream business of Essent have been transferred to RWE Supply & Trading.

- United Kingdom: This is the division under which we report on RWE npower, one of the country's leading energy utilities. The company generates electricity from gas, hard coal, oil and biomass. Furthermore, RWE npower sells electricity and gas to end-customers.

- Central Eastern and South Eastern Europe: This division contains our companies in the Czech Republic, Hungary, Poland, Slovakia and Turkey. In the Czech Republic, our activities encompass the supply, distribution, supraregional transmission, transit and storage of gas. In 2010, we started marketing electricity there as well. In Hungary, we cover the entire electricity value chain, from production through to the operation of the distribution system and the end-customer business, and are also active in the gas and water supply sector via minority stakes. Our Polish operations consist of the distribution and supply of electricity. In Slovakia, we are active in the electricity network and electricity end-customer businesses via our minority interest in VSE and in the gas supply sector via RWE Gas Slovensko. In

Turkey, we are building a gas-fired power station with a partner. The newly established RWE East, headquartered in Prague, Czech Republic, started overseeing the companies belonging to the Central Eastern and South Eastern Europe Division in 2011. One exception is NET4GAS, the operator of our Czech long-distance gas network. To comply with regulatory requirements, this company is assigned directly to RWE AG. However, it is still part of the Central Eastern and South Eastern Europe Division for accounting purposes.

- Renewables: This division comprises the activities of RWE Innogy, which specialises in electricity and heat production from renewable sources.

- Upstream Gas & Oil: This segment consists of RWE Dea's business. The company produces gas and oil, focusing on Germany, the United Kingdom, Norway and Egypt.

- Trading /Gas Midstream: This is the item under which we report on RWE Supply & Trading, which is responsible for our energy trading activities and most of our gas midstream business. Furthermore, the division supplies major German industrial and corporate customers with electricity and gas. However, parts of these activities were transferred to the Germany Division with effect from 1 January 2011.

We report certain groupwide activities outside the divisions as part of 'other, consolidation.' These are the Group holding company, RWE AG, and our internal service providers, namely RWE Service, RWE IT, RWE Consulting and RWE Technology. This item also encompasses Thyssengas, the long-distance gas network operator we sold on 28 February 2011. The company is considered in the January and February figures for 2011. We also report the electricity transmission system operator Amprion in 'other, consolidation.' However, we started accounting for it using the equity method in September 2011, as we have only held a minority stake in Amprion since then. Revenue and capital expenditure following the change in accounting treatment are no longer considered in the consolidated financial statements. However, Amprion continues to contribute to both RWE's EBITDA and operating result, on the basis of pro-rated income after tax.

Consolidated financial statements (extract)

(31) Segment reporting (extract)

Within the RWE Group segments are defined both in accordance with functional and geographical criteria.

The segment "Power Generation" essentially consists of the power generation business and lignite production in Germany.

For the most part, the segment "Sales /Distribution Networks" encompasses sales and distribution networks in Germany.

The segment "Netherlands /Belgium" comprises the Group's electricity and gas business in this region.

The segment "United Kingdom" consists of almost all of the electricity and gas business in this region.

Central Eastern and South Eastern European power generation and the supply and the distribution activities in this region are included in the segment "Central Eastern and South Eastern Europe".

Activities for the generation of electricity and heat from renewable energy sources are bundled in RWE Innogy and presented in the segment "Renewables".

The segment "Upstream Gas & Oil" covers all of the Group's gas and oil production activities.

The segment "Trading /Gas Midstream" covers energy trading and the commercial optimisation of non-regulated gas activities. The latter aspect comprises procurement, transport and storage contracts in Germany, the UK and the Czech Republic, and the liquefied natural gas (LNG) business. This segment is also responsible for key account business with major German and Dutch industrial and commercial customers, as well as the trading activities of the Essent Group.

"Other, consolidation" covers consolidation effects, the Group Centre and the activities of other Group areas which are not presented separately. Such activities consist primarily of the cross-segment services provided by RWE Service GmbH, RWE IT GmbH, and RWE Consulting GmbH, as well as German transmission grid activities in the electricity and gas business, until such are sold.

Detailed disclosures of measures of profit and loss, assets and liabilities

10.77   Disclosure of the amount of each segment item that is reported should be based on the information provided to the CODM for the purpose of making decisions about allocation of resources to the segment and for assessing its performance. [IFRS 8 para 23]. The standard requires disclosure of a measure of profit or loss for each reportable segment.

10.77.1   In addition, a measure of assets and a measure of liabilities for each reportable segment should also be disclosed if they are regularly provided to the CODM. [IFRS 8 para 23].

10.77.2   Where certain specific asset balances are reviewed by the CODM, only the total of these balances is required to be disclosed as segment assets and not the individual asset balances. This is considered in the following example.

> **Example – Disclosure of assets**
>
> An entity reports the following discrete financial information to its CODM: cash, accounts receivable and inventory. No other information is reported to or used by the CODM in order to assess performance and allocate resources. In this case, the total of cash, accounts receivable and inventory would be disclosed as 'segment assets'. Note that the total of reported segment assets would then have to be reconciled to total assets (either consolidated or entity, as appropriate). Significant reconciling items must be disclosed and an explanation of the measurement of segment assets must also be provided.

10.78   Where the CODM only receives information with respect to the entity's cash flows, that is the CODM receives no profit or asset information, an entity should assume that the net cash flows reported are the measure of profit or loss. Cash flows that are reported as inflows only are likely to be representative of revenue, rather than of profit. Hence, net cash flow would be expected in order to qualify as a measure of profit or loss. This cash flow information would then need to be reconciled to the entity's profit or loss.

10.79   Certain other profit or loss information should also be separately disclosed. This comprises specified amounts for each reportable segment if they are *either* included in the measure of profit or loss that is reported to the CODM *or* they are otherwise provided to the CODM, *even if not included in that measure of profit or loss*. These amounts are:

■   Revenues from external customers.

- Revenues from transactions with other operating segments of the same entity (inter-segment revenue).

- Interest revenue.

- Interest expense.

- Depreciation and amortisation.

- Material items of income and expense disclosed in accordance with paragraph 97 of IAS 1.

- The entity's interest in the profit or loss of associates and joint ventures accounted for by the equity method.

- Income tax expense or income.

- Material non-cash items other than depreciation and amortisation (an example is impairment which is covered by IAS 36, see para 10.139).

[IFRS 8 para 23].

10.79.1 In some entities the information presented to the CODM may include ratios and percentages, for example, working capital or taxation as a percentage. When considering whether such percentages or ratios are required to be disclosed, management should keep in mind the core principle of IFRS 8. The standard requires disclosure of information that is used by the CODM to make decisions about the allocation of resources and assessment of performance.

10.79.2 Where various revenue streams within a segment are reported separately to the CODM, an entity is not required to report these revenue streams separately. IFRS 8 requires revenues from internal and external customers only to be reported separately. However, an entity may choose to voluntarily provide disclosure of the different revenue streams. As illustrated in the example below.

> **Example – Voluntary disclosure of aggregated revenue streams**
>
> Entity A is a magazine publisher of eight different magazines, all of which derive revenue from classified advertising, display advertising, and subscriptions. Entity A manages its business by individual magazine. Separate reports for each magazine are provided to the CODM, and each revenue stream is separately identified in those reports. The magazines meet the aggregation criteria of IFRS 8. Accordingly, entity A is deemed a one-segment entity. Entity A is not required to separately report each revenue stream. However, it can choose to voluntarily provide disclosure of the different revenue streams.

10.80 Interest income should be reported separately from interest expense, unless a majority of the reportable segment's revenues are from interest and the CODM relies primarily on the net interest figure in assessing the segment performance and in making decisions about resources to be allocated to the segment. Where this is the situation an entity may report interest on a net basis, but should disclose that it has done so. [IFRS 8 para 23].

10.81 Other balance sheet information should also be disclosed if the amounts are *either* included in the measure of segment assets reviewed by the CODM *or* are otherwise provided regularly to the CODM, *even if they are not included in the measure of segment assets.* These amounts are:

- The amount of the investment in associates and joint ventures accounted for by the equity method.

- The amount of additions to non-current assets, other than financial instruments, deferred tax assets, post employment benefit assets and rights arising under insurance contracts.

[IFRS 8 para 24].

10.82 The term 'non-current assets' used above includes both intangible and tangible assets. In developing the standard the IASB considered whether to require a subtotal for tangible non-current assets, but decided against doing so. However, they noted that entities could provide such a sub-total voluntarily if they wished. [IFRS 8 BC paras 56, 57].

10.83 For entities that classify assets according to a liquidity presentation, such as many banks, non-current assets are those assets that include amounts expected to be recovered more than twelve months after the balance sheet date. [IFRS 8 para 24(b) footnote].

10.84 An example that illustrates many of the above disclosures is included in Table 10.8. Items not disclosed in this example, either because they are not relevant or are not reported to the CODM, are segment liabilities, investments in joint ventures and associates, material non-cash items and material items of income and expense that are separately disclosed as required by paragraph 97 of IAS 1. For reasons of space only the 2012 figures are reproduced in the example.

Table 10.8 – Segment disclosures

Vodafone Group plc – Reports and accounts – 31 March 2012

3. Segment analysis (extract)

The Group has a single group of related services and products being the supply of communications services and products. Segment information is provided on the basis of geographic areas, being the basis on which the Group manages its worldwide interests. Revenue is attributed to a country or region based on the location of the Group company reporting the revenue. Inter-segment sales are charged at arm's length prices.

	Segment revenue £m	Intra-region revenue £m	Regional revenue £m	Inter-region revenue £m	Group revenue £m	EBITDA[1] £m
31 March 2012						
Germany	8,233	(44)	8,189	(1)	8,188	2,965
Italy	5,658	(28)	5,630	(1)	5,629	2,514
Spain	4,763	(54)	4,709	(3)	4,706	1,193
UK	5,397	(37)	5,360	(6)	5,354	1,294
Other Europe	8,352	(59)	8,293	(5)	8,288	2,479
Europe	**32,403**	**(222)**	**32,181**	**(16)**	**32,165**	**10,445**
India	4,265	–	4,265	(6)	4,259	1,122
Vodacom	5,638	–	5,638	(8)	5,630	1,930
Other Africa, Middle East and Asia Pacific	3,965	–	3,965	(23)	3,942	1,063
Africa, Middle East and Asia Pacific	**13,868**	**–**	**13,868**	**(37)**	**13,831**	**4,115**
Non-Controlled Interests and Common Functions	423	–	423	(2)	421	(85)
Group	**46,694**	**(222)**	**46,472**	**(55)**	**46,417**	**14,475**
Verizon Wireless[2]	*20,187*					*7,689*

Notes:

[1] The Group's measure of segment profit, EBITDA, excludes the Group's share of results in associates. The Group's share of results in associates, by segment, for the year ended 31 March 2012 is Other Europe £3 million (2011: £nil; 2010 £nil), Vodacom £nil (2011: £nil; 2010: £(2) million), Other Africa, Middle East and Asia Pacific £36 million (2011: £51 million; 2010: £56 million) and Non-Controlled Interests and Common Functions £4,924 million (2011: £5,008 million; 2010: £4,688 million).

[2] Values shown for Verizon Wireless, which is an associate, are not included in the calculation of Group revenue or EBITDA.

A reconciliation of EBITDA to operating profit is shown below. For a reconciliation of operating profit to profit before taxation, see the consolidated income statement on page 94.

	2012 £m	2011 £m	2010 £m
EBITDA	**14,475**	**14,670**	**14,735**
Depreciation, amortisation and loss on disposal of fixed assets	(7,906)	(7,967)	(8,011)
Share of results in associates	4,963	5,059	4,742
Impairment losses	(4,050)	(6,150)	(2,100)
Other income and expense	3,705	(16)	114
Operating profit	**11,187**	**5,596**	**9,480**

	Non-current assets [1] £m	Capital expenditure [2] £m	Other expenditure on intangible assets £m	Depreciation and amortisation £m	Impairment loss/ (reversal) £m
31 March 2012					
Germany	19,151	880	4	1,469	–
Italy	13,978	621	875	783	2,450
Spain	8,069	429	71	626	900
UK	6,430	575	–	880	–
Other Europe	10,146	1,092	313	1,389	700
Europe	**57,774**	**3,597**	**1,263**	**5,147**	**4,050**
India	8,431	805	–	1,066	–
Vodacom	6,469	723	–	840	–
Other Africa, Middle East and Asia Pacific	4,735	793	–	771	–
Africa, Middle East and Asia Pacific	**19,635**	**2,321**	**–**	**2,677**	**–**
Non-Controlled Interests and Common Functions	760	447	–	35	
Group	**78,169**	**6,365**	**1,263**	**7,859**	**4,050**

Notes:
[1] Comprises goodwill, other intangible assets and property, plant and equipment.
[2] Includes additions to property, plant and equipment and computer software, reported within intangible assets.

Measurement

Profit or loss measure

10.85   The measure of profit or loss that is required to be disclosed is the measure that is reported to the CODM. The standard is not prescriptive as to how this measure should be calculated, nor does it require that the same accounting policies are used as those used in preparing the financial statements. The measures used are not required to be in accordance or consistent with a measure defined in IFRS. The standard does not establish any boundaries and would only consider whether the core principle of the standard was being followed with regard to the presentation. A non-GAAP presentation will be acceptable so long as the presentation is clear about what constitutes the non-GAAP measures and there is a clear and detailed reconciliation of the disclosed measure to the respective IFRS amount reported in the financial statements. In practice this means that there is inconsistency between the segment information reported by different entities as they do not all report the same measure of profit to the CODM. When a non-GAAP presentation is applied, it is likely that more reconciling items will have to be included in the reconciliation, as illustrated by the following example:

Table 10.9 – Segment disclosures

OAO Gazprom – Report and accounts – 31 December 2011

7 SEGMENT INFORMATION (extract)

The CODM assesses the performance, assets and liabilities of the operating segments based on the internal financial reporting. The effects of certain non-recurring transactions and events, such as business acquisitions, and the effects of some adjustments that may be considered necessary to reconcile the internal financial information to IFRS consolidated financial statements are not included within the operating segments which are reviewed by the CODM on a central basis. Gains and losses on available-for-sale financial assets, and financial income and expenses are also not allocated to the operating segments.

	Production of gas	Transport	Distribution	Gas storage	Production of crude oil and gas condensate	Refining	Electric and heat energy generation and sales	All other segments	Total
Year ended 31 December 2011									
Total segment revenues	388,537	790,629	3,046,082	29,658	553,734	979,981	349,028	224,101	6,361,750
Inter-segment sales	381,481	677,634	238,290	28,583	318,302	6,955	–	–	1,651,245
External sales	7,056	112,995	2,807,792	1,075	235,432	973,026	349,028	224,101	4,710,505
Segment result	31,001	72,496	1,084,551	4,351	116,997	122,811	54,449	(16,556)	1,470,100
Depreciation	87,214	265,694	7,717	9,805	44,521	25,331	19,034	17,369	476,685
Share of net income (loss) of associated undertakings and jointly controlled entities	957	(10,932)	21,553	–	65,511	1,860	–	20,100	99,049
Year ended 31 December 2010									
Total segment revenues	340,918	651,483	2,367,366	25,823	446,507	717,607	295,436	174,962	5,020,102
Inter-segment sales	334,524	558,852	187,555	24,892	250,433	8,545	–	–	1,364,801
External sales	6,394	92,631	2,179,811	931	196,074	709,062	295,436	174,962	3,655,301
Segment result	45,102	37,309	715,260	3,860	77,064	84,901	28,753	(4,928)	987,321
Depreciation	78,349	260,733	5,618	9,153	43,205	22,441	18,631	16,584	454,714
Share of net income (loss) of associated undertakings and jointly controlled entities	7,093	(16,097)	19,390	–	40,226	1,530	–	24,378	76,520

A reconciliation of total operating segment results to total profit before profit tax in the consolidated statement of comprehensive income is provided as follows:

Note		For the year ended 31 December 2011	2010
	Segment result	**1,470,100**	**987,321**
	Difference in depreciation	201,501	205,021
	Income (expenses) associated with pension obligations	3,811	(58,473)
37	Gain from disposal of interest in OAO NOVATEK	–	77,375
27	Finance income (expense), net	(77,335)	2,694
	Gains on disposal of available-for-sale financial assets	1,379	3,292
13	Share of net income (loss) of associated undertakings and jointly controlled entities	99,049	76,520
	Other	(18,569)	(20,047)
	Profit before profit tax	**1,679,936**	**1,273,703**

A reconciliation of reportable segments' external sales to sales in the consolidated statement of comprehensive income is provided as follows:

	For the year ended 31 December 2011	2010
External sales for reportable segments	4,486,404	3,480,339
External sales for other segments	224,101	174,962
Total external segment sales	**4,710,505**	**3,655,301**
Differences in external sales	(73,415)	(58,247)
Total sales per the statement of comprehensive income	**4,637,090**	**3,597,054**

10.86 In developing the US standard ASC 280, on which IFRS 8 is based, the measure of profit or loss to be disclosed was considered at length. It was concluded that whilst segment information based on the management approach might be less reliable than standardised information, it was more relevant. Relevance of the information was considered to be the more important objective. It was accepted, however, that in these circumstances analysts would assume more responsibility for making meaningful comparisons of segment information between entities that were organised differently from each other. [IFRS 8 BC App A para 86].

10.87 In practice, there is a wide range of profit measures that are used by CODMs. Management needs to identify and influence the main elements that make up the profit or loss. In some cases, this leads to a focus on 'normal trading' or 'underlying performance'. These measures sometimes exclude reorganisation costs and other items that may not occur regularly or which introduce volatility into the results, such as fair value movements in financial instruments. For this reason the CODM may use profit figures that exclude certain elements such as these in assessing performance and making decisions on the allocation of resources. Management may also wish to review results on a basis that highlights more closely the cash flows of the segments and, therefore, may monitor EBITDA. Some management bodies, on the other hand, take a less sophisticated view and use the same measures in their management of the business as they report in the financial statements. Examples of measures used are included in the tables in the 'Disclosure of measurement basis' section below. Disclosure of the other measures listed above should also be based on the actual amounts reported to the CODM.

Liabilities

10.88   The disclosure of segment liabilities is another difference from the US standard ASC 280. That standard did not require disclosure of segment liabilities, because many respondents to the exposure draft of ASC 280 commented that usually liabilities were incurred centrally and entities often did not allocate those amounts to segments. [IFRS 8 BC App A para 96]. The IASB, however, considered that if liabilities were reported to the CODM it would be consistent with the management approach to require their disclosure. There was also support for such disclosure from commentators on the exposure draft of IFRS 8, particularly from users of financial statements. [IFRS 8 BC para 38].

More than one measure used

10.89   Sometimes the CODM uses more than one measure of profit, assets or liabilities for the purpose of assessing performance and allocating resources. In these circumstances the segment measures to be reported should be those that are determined in accordance with the measurement principles most consistent with those used in measuring the corresponding amounts in the entity's financial statements. For example, if the CODM uses both net profit excluding unrealised financial instrument gains or losses and net profit before tax, the latter measure would be more consistent with the profit figures used in the financial statements. [IFRS 8 para 26]. If each measure is equally consistent with the measurement principles reflected in the corresponding amount that appears in the consolidated financial statements, the measure to be reported externally would be the measure that is most consistent with the core principle in IFRS 8 (see para 10.7).

Example – Two measures of profit used for each operating segment

Company A provides the CODM with two measures of profitability by operating segment, operating profit and profit before income tax expense. Segment operating profit is determined based on the same measurement principles that are used in the preparation of consolidated operating profit. However, segment profit before income tax expense includes certain internal cost-of-capital charges that are eliminated in determining the consolidated profit before income tax expense. In this situation, segment operating profit would be the measure reported externally because this measure is the most consistent with its corresponding amount in the entity's financial statements.

In addition, a disclosure would need to be made for interest income and expense because that information is included in the profit before income tax expense measure provided to the CODM.

10.90   Although the standard requires this basis to be used to decide which of the two measures should be reported, there does not appear to be anything that prevents the entity from reporting both measures if it wishes to do so. Table 10.10 in paragraph 10.107 shows an example where this has been done.

Adjustments, allocations and accounting policies

10.91   Adjustments and eliminations made in preparing the entity's financial statements and allocations of revenues, expenses, gains and losses are included in determining reported segment profit or loss only if they are included in the measures used by the CODM. Similarly only those assets and liabilities that are included in the measures used by the CODM should be reported as segment assets and liabilities. [IFRS 8 para 25].

10.91.1   When management information is reviewed in a currency other than the presentational currency of the financial statements, the segment disclosures should replicate management information. Presenting segment information in the currency in which the CODM reviews it follows the requirements of IFRS 8. This approach, however, is usually less convenient for the users of the financial statements and requires reconciliation from the currency used by the CODM to that of the presentational currency. Alternative approaches to enhance clarity of the translation to the presentational currency for users of the financial statements are outlined below.

10.91.2   One alternative approach is to translate the information reported to the CODM into the presentational currency of the financial statements in accordance with IAS 21. If translation results in a difference between segment information and that presented in the financial statements, due to, for example, the underlying information being translated using different rates then a reconciliation from the segment information to the primary statements is required.

10.91.3   In cases where translation using IAS 21 results in significant distortion of ratios and trends in the segment information presented, such that it would affect the decisions of either the users of the financial statements or those of the CODM, a second alternative would be a convenience translation. Such a translation would use a single rate for all measures. An additional reconciling item should then be disclosed to explain the difference to the primary financial statements, arising from the use of such a different translation method.

10.91.4   Management information is sometimes reviewed at constant rates of exchange, for instance by reporting current year figures at prior year exchange rates (or by reporting prior year figures at current year exchange rates). In line with paragraph 25 of IFRS 8, the segmental information reported in the financial statements should replicate the management information. In this case, the impact of the constant currency adjustments would be disclosed in the reconciliation to the amounts in the primary statements. An example where segment information is disclosed at constant exchange rates to facilitate comparison of the entity's results had these been translated at the previous year's exchange rate is given in Table 10.9.1.

Table 10.9.1 – Segment information disclosed at constant exchange rates

British American Tobacco p.l.c – Annual Report – 31 December 2011

Financial review (extract)

Non-GAAP measures (extract)

Management reviews current and prior year segmental adjusted profit from operations of subsidiaries and adjusted post-tax results of associates and joint ventures at constant rates of exchange. This allows comparison of the Group's results had they been translated at last year's average rate of exchange. Other than in exceptional circumstances, this does not adjust for the normal transactional gains and losses in operations which are generated by exchange movements.

Note 2 – Segmental analyses (extract)

The Management Board reviews current and prior year segmental revenue, adjusted profit from operations of subsidiaries and adjusted post-tax results of associates and joint ventures at constant rates of exchange. The constant rate comparison provided for reporting segment information is based on a retranslation, at prior year exchange rates, of the current year results of the Group's overseas entities but, other than in exceptional circumstances, does not adjust for transactional gains and losses in operations which are generated by movements in exchange rates. As a result, the 2011 segmental results were translated using the 2010 rates of exchange. The 2010 figures are also stated at the 2010 rates of exchange.

The analyses of revenue for the 12 months to 31 December 2011 and 31 December 2010, based on location of sales, are as follows:

			2011	Restated 2010
	Revenue Constant rates £m	Translation exchange £m	Revenue Current rates £m	Revenue £m
Asia-Pacific	4,150	101	4,251	3,759
Americas	3,574	(16)	3,558	3,498
Western Europe	3,532	68	3,600	3,695
EEMEA	4,206	(216)	3,990	3,931
Revenue	**15,462**	**(63)**	**15,399**	14,883

The analyses of profit from operations and the Group's share of the post-tax results of associates and joint ventures, reconciled to profit before taxation, are as follows:

	2011					Restated 2010		
	Adjusted* segment result Constant rates £m	Translation exchange £m	Adjusted* segment result Current rates £m	Adjusting items £m	Segment result Current rates £m	Adjusted* segment result £m	Adjusting items £m	Segment result £m
Asia-Pacific	1,480	59	1,539	(58)	1,481	1,332	(56)	1,276
Americas	1,440	1	1,441	(15)	1,426	1,382	(36)	1,346
Western Europe	1,204	24	1,228	(153)	1,075	1,103	(236)	867
EEMEA	1,362	(51)	1,311	(298)	1,013	1,167	(338)	829
	5,486	33	5,519	(524)	4,995	4,984	(666)	4,318
Fox River**	–	–	–	(274)	(274)	–	–	–
Profit from operations	5,486	33	5,519	(798)	4,721	4,984	(666)	4,318
Net finance costs	–	–	–	–	(460)	–	–	(480)
Asia-Pacific	238	(13)	225	28	253	208	(9)	199
Americas	448	(16)	432	(17)	415	412	(63)	349
EEMEA	2	–	2	–	2	2	–	2
Share of post-tax results of associates and joint ventures	688	(29)	659	11	670	622	(72)	550
Profit before taxation					4,931			4,388

10.92   Typical adjustments that are included in preparing the entity financial statements would include the elimination of intra-group sales, profits and losses and intra-group receivables and payables. These would normally be eliminated for the purpose of determining segment information, but instead an adjustment would be made in total, separately from the segment information, in order to reconcile the segment information with that reported for the consolidated entity as a whole.

10.93   Often an entity manages its borrowings centrally and does not allocate them to individual segments. In this situation, the borrowings would not be included in segment liabilities. Similarly many entities will not allocate interest cost when reporting the profit or loss of individual segments. For some entities, however, particularly financial institutions, interest income and expense are an integral part of business performance and normally that type of business will include interest in segment profit or loss reported to the CODM.

10.94   The standard does not prescribe how measures should be calculated or how centrally incurred expenses and central assets should be allocated to segments, or indeed which, if any, of such types of costs or assets should be allocated. Allocation of costs and expenses and assets to segments is an area where the basis chosen by an entity can have a significant effect on the segment results.

10.95   However, the standard does require that if amounts are allocated to reported segment profit or loss, assets or liabilities, those amounts should be allocated *on a reasonable basis*. [IFRS 8 para 25].

10.96 An illustration of how the basis of allocation selected for common costs or assets can affect the segmental results is given in the following example.

Example – Allocation of common costs

An entity has three distinct business segments, A, B and C. Prior to the allocation of any common costs to these segments, the financial information on these segments is as follows:

	A	B	C
	Cm	Cm	Cm
Net assets	2,000	300	800
Turnover	5,000	2,000	3,000
Profit before common costs	200	40	100

On the assumption that the common costs total C100m, the allocation of such costs on the basis of the turnover of each segment as a percentage of total turnover would lead to the following depiction of segment results:

	A	B	C
	Cm	Cm	Cm
Profit before common costs	200	40	100
Allocation of common costs	50	20	30
Profit after common costs	150	20	70

This contrasts with the situation where common costs are allocated on the basis of the individual segment's proportion of total net assets. In this instance, the results would be as follows:

	A	B	C
	Cm	Cm	Cm
Profit before common costs	200	40	100
Allocation of common costs	64	10	26
Profit after common costs	136	30	74

Thus, the basis of allocation chosen may have a material effect on the segment result that is reported. However, assuming that both of the bases described in the example are 'reasonable', either could be used.

10.97 Another example is allocation of pension expense which might be allocated on the basis of either the number of employees in a segment or by reference to the total salary expense of each segment. The choice of allocation basis in this situation could give a significantly different measure of segment profit or loss. This is an example given in the basis of conclusions for the US standard ASC 280, which is included as an appendix to the basis for conclusions on IFRS 8. It notes that both bases might be reasonable but that, for example, allocating pension expense to a segment that had no employees eligible for the pension plan would not seem to be 'a reasonable basis'. [IFRS 8 BC App A para 88]. The same could be said for allocation of share based payment expense relating to employee options.

10.98   The standard requires disclosure of differences between the measurement of reportable segments' profit or loss and the profit or loss of the entity before tax. It suggests that such differences could include accounting policies and the policy for allocation of centrally incurred costs that are necessary for understanding the reported segment information (see 'Disclosure of measurement basis' below).

10.99   In practice it may be possible to allocate some costs but not others. For instance, if a group bears the cost of managing properties centrally, it should be possible to allocate such costs reasonably to each segment on a basis that takes account of the type, age and value of properties used by each segment. Similarly, central administrative overheads in respect of personnel might be allocated on the basis of the number of employees in each segment. If different bases are appropriate for different types of common costs it would be reasonable to apply the appropriate basis in allocating each of the types of cost. However, this is only applicable where the CODM requires such allocation in the segment information that is used to assess performance and make decisions on resource allocation.

10.100   The standard does not require allocation of costs, assets and liabilities to a segment to be on a consistent basis. For example, an entity may allocate interest to segment profit or loss but does not then have to allocate the related interest bearing asset or liability to segment assets or liabilities. The standard calls this asymmetrical allocation. It is likely to be fairly uncommon as it would be expected that the CODM would normally require information on profits and assets that was 'symmetrical'. If there are instances of asymmetrical allocation the standard requires disclosure of these (see 'Disclosure of measurement basis' below).

10.101   There is no requirement for segment information to be prepared in conformity with the accounting policies used for preparing and presenting the entity's financial statements (consolidated or individual, as appropriate). However, differences between policies used for the entity financial statements and those used for measuring and presenting the segment disclosures should be explained.

[The next paragraph is 10.105].

Disclosure of measurement basis

10.105   The standard requires an entity to disclose an explanation that enables users to understand the basis on which segmental information is measured. The explanation should cover as a minimum:

- Description of the measurement basis for segment profit or loss and, if reported to the CODM, for each of segment assets and segment liabilities. (See Table 10.10 in para 10.107 and Table 10.11 in para 10.112 for examples.)

■ The basis of accounting for transactions between reportable segments (inter-segment transactions). Such transactions might be, for example, based on market prices or, more unusually, at cost. (See Table 10.10 in para 10.107 for example.)

■ The nature of any differences between the measurement of reportable segments' profits or losses and the profit or loss before tax and discontinued operations that is reported in the entity's income statement. This information is only required if it is not already apparent from the reconciliations that the standard also requires. The requirement for reconciliations is described below under 'Reconciliations'. The reconciliations will pick up many of the numerical differences, so the explanation may focus on a description of other differences such as differences in accounting policies and policies for allocating centrally incurred costs. (See Table 10.10 in para 10.107 and Table 10.11 in para 10.112 for examples.)

■ Similar information to that in the previous bullet point about differences between the segmental measures of assets and segmental liabilities (in both cases, if reported to the CODM) and the assets and liabilities reported in the entity's balance sheet. Again this would exclude differences that are apparent from the reconciliations required by the standard and would focus on differences in accounting policies and policies for allocation of central assets or liabilities. (See Table 10.10 in para 10.107.)

■ The nature of any changes from prior periods in the measurement methods used and the effect of the changes.

■ The nature and effect of any asymmetrical allocations to reportable segments. The standard gives the example of an entity that might allocate depreciation expense to a segment without allocating the related depreciable assets to the segment. Any such asymmetrical allocations should be explained.

[IFRS 8 para 27].

10.106 Examples of disclosure of the measurement basis (first bullet point above) are given in Tables 10.10 and 10.11. Generally these measures would exclude interest, except where interest income and expense is a key part of segment performance.

10.107 An example of an entity that uses several different measures for management purposes and that reports each basis is given in Table 10.10.

Table 10.10 – Use of several profit measures for segmental reporting

NorskHydro ASA – Report and accounts – 31 December 2011

Note 7 — Operating and geographic segment information (extract)

Operating segment information

Hydro uses two measures of segment results, Earnings before financial items and tax — EBIT and EBITDA. EBIT is consistent with the same measure for the group, considering the principles for measuring certain intersegment transactions and contracts described below. Hydro defines EBITDA as Income (loss) before tax, financial income and expense, depreciation, amortization and write-downs, including amortization and impairment of excess values in equity accounted investments. Hydro's definition of EBITDA may be different from other companies.

Because Hydro manages long-term debt and taxes on a Group basis, Net income is presented only for the Group as a whole.

Intersegment sales and transfers reflect arm's length prices as if sold or transferred to third parties at the time of inception of the internal contract, which may cover several years. Transfers of businesses or assets within or between Hydro's segments are reported without recognizing gains or losses. Results of activities not considered part of Hydro's main operations as well as unallocated revenues, expenses, liabilities and assets are reported together with Other under the caption Other and eliminations.

The accounting policies used for segment reporting reflect those used for the Group with the following exceptions: Internal commodity contracts may meet the definition of a financial instrument in IAS 39 or contain embedded derivatives that are required to be bifurcated and valued at fair value under IAS 39. However, Hydro considers these contracts as sourcing of raw materials or sale of own production, and accounts for such contracts as executory contracts. Certain other internal contracts may contain lease arrangements that qualify as a capital lease. However, the segment reporting reflects the responsibility allocated by Hydro's management for those assets. Costs related to certain pension schemes covering more than one segment are allocated to the operating segments based either on the premium charged or the estimated service cost. Any difference between these charges and pension expenses measured in accordance with IFRS, as well as pension assets and liabilities are included in Other and eliminations.

Reconciliations

10.108 In order that analysts and others can understand and interpret the segmental information properly in the context of the overall financial statements, IFRS 8 requires additional disclosures. These additional disclosures include:

- Reconciliations of the segment information to entity totals included in the entity's financial statements. [IFRS 8 para 28].

- Explanations of how segment measures are calculated. [IFRS 8 para 27].

- Details of differences in accounting policies between those used in the entity financial statements and those used in preparing the segment information. [IFRS 8 para 27].

10.109 The standard requires that all material items should be separately identified and described. As an example of a reconciling item, the standard says that the amount of each material adjustment needed to reconcile reportable segment profit or loss to the entity's profit or loss that arises from using different accounting policies for segment and entity profit or loss should be separately identified and described. [IFRS 8 para 28].

10.110   The example quoted above is important as it clarifies that the *amount* of each adjusting item should be disclosed as part of the reconciliation. It is not sufficient just to describe the types of reconciling item without giving the actual amounts of each material adjustment.

10.111   Reconciliations should be given of each of the following:

■   Total reportable segments' revenues to the entity's revenue.

■   Total reportable segments' measures of profit or loss to the entity's profit or loss before tax and discontinued operations. However, if an entity allocates to reportable segments items such as tax expense (tax income), the entity may reconcile the total of the segments' measures of profit or loss to the entity's profit or loss after those items).

■   Total reportable segments' assets to the entity's assets. (The IASB is proposing an amendment in annual improvements to clarify that this reconciliation only needs to be disclosed if the amounts are regularly provided to the CODM. Although this is a proposal, we believe this was what the IASB originally intended in IFRS 8 and entities normally only include a reconciliation if assets are reported to the CODM.)

■   Total reportable segments' liabilities to the entity's liabilities, if segment liabilities are regularly provided to the CODM.

■   Total reportable segments amounts for every other material item of information to the corresponding amount for the entity (for example depreciation and amortisation).

[IFRS 8 para 28].

10.112   An example of a reconciliation of segments' measure of profit or loss to entity profit or loss is given in Table 10.11. The table also includes reconciliations for segment assets and liabilities.

Table 10.11 – Reconciliation of segment profit, assets and liabilities to entity figures

Smith & Nephew plc – Annual report – 31 December 2011

The following tables present revenue, profit, asset and liability information regarding the Group's operating segments. The share of results of associates is segmentally allocated to Orthopaedics.

2 Business segment information (extract 1)

2.2 Trading and operating profit by business segment

Trading profit is a trend measure which presents the long-term profitability of the Group excluding the impact of specific transactions that management considers affects the Group's short-term profitability. The Group presents this measure to assist investors in their understanding of trends. The Group has identified the following items, where material, as those to be excluded from operating profit when arriving at trading profit: acquisition and disposal related items including amortisation of acquisition intangibles and impairments; significant restructuring events; gains and losses arising from legal disputes; and uninsured losses. Operating profit reconciles to trading profit as follows:

	Notes	2011 $ million	2010 $ million	2009 $ million
Operating profit		862	920	723
Acquisition related costs	3	–	–	26
Restructuring and rationalisation expenses	3	40	15	42
Amortisation of acquisition intangibles and impairments	8&9	36	34	66
Legal provision	3	23	–	–
Trading profit		961	969	857
Trading profit by business segment				
Orthopaedics		492	536	508
Endoscopy		222	200	189
Advanced Wound Management		247	233	160
		961	969	857
Operating profit by business segment reconciled to attributable profit for the year				
Orthopaedics		415	503	410
Endoscopy		215	197	169
Advanced Wound Management		232	220	144
Operating profit		862	920	723
Net interest payable		(8)	(15)	(40)
Other finance costs		(6)	(10)	(15)
Share of results of associates		–	–	2
Taxation		(266)	(280)	(198)
Attributable profit for the year		582	615	472

2.3 Assets and liabilities by business segment and geography (extract)

Business segment (extract)

	2011 $ million	2010 $ million	2009 $ million
Balance sheet			
Assets:			
Orthopaedics	2,550	2,778	2,656
Endoscopy	846	769	705
Advanced Wound Management	819	755	810
Operating assets by business segment	4,215	4,302	4,171
Assets held for sale (relating to Orthopaedics business segment)	125	–	–
Unallocated corporate assets	407	431	394
Total assets	4,747	4,733	4,565

Liabilities:			
Orthopaedics	**398**	457	426
Endoscopy	**128**	124	111
Advanced Wound Management	**169**	146	194
Operating liabilities by business segment	**695**	727	731
Liabilities directly associated with assets held for sale (relating to Orthopaedics business segment)	**19**	–	–
Unallocated corporate liabilities	**846**	1,233	1,655
Total liabilities	**1,560**	1,960	2,386

Unallocated corporate assets and liabilities comprise the following:

	2011 **$ million**	2010 $ million	2009 $ million
Deferred tax assets	**223**	224	202
Cash and bank	**184**	207	192
Unallocated corporate assets	**407**	431	394
Long-term borrowings	**16**	642	1,090
Retirement benefit obligations	**287**	262	322
Deferred tax liabilities	**66**	69	31
Bank overdrafts and loans due within one year	**306**	57	45
Current tax payable	**171**	203	167
Unallocated corporate liabilities	**846**	1,233	1,655

[The next paragraph is paragraph 10.114]

Changes in policy and presentation

10.114 An entity should consider at each reporting date whether the current operating segment disclosure continues to be appropriate. If an entity changes its internal organisation, such that the composition of its reportable segments changes, it should restate the corresponding information for prior periods, including interim periods, unless the information is not available and the cost to develop it would be excessive. [IFRS 8 para 29]. Operating segments should be identified based on the internal organisation at the balance sheet date. If management changes the structure of its internal organisation after the balance sheet date but before the financial statements are issued, the new segment structure should not be presented in the financial statements until operating results, managed on the basis of the new segment structure, are reported to the CODM. Similarly, where the composition of an entity's operating segments changes in the interim period and this new segment structure is reported to the CODM, at the interim balance sheet date, the operating segment disclosure should reflect this reorganisation. Refer to Manual of Accounting – Interim financial reporting for further guidance on the disclosure of operating segment information in interim reports.

10.114.1 Determining operating segments is an area of significant judgement and scrutiny, so it is important that entities consider how internal organisation change will impact identifying and measuring of their operating segments. An entity should consider whether any of the following have changed when determining its operating segments:

- The CODM.

- The reporting package reviewed by the CODM.

- The organisational chart. For example, this may have changed due to business acquisitions and disposals.

- The person/people who the CODM meets with.

- The budgeting process or level at which budgets are set.

- Communications to external parties such as investors, creditors and customers.

Scenarios that may impact identified operating segments include entering a new line of business, a change in the internal reporting structure from geographical reporting to product line reporting or implementing a new system that enables the entity to report on and manage its business activities differently.

10.115 An entity should determine whether the information is available and whether the cost to develop it would be excessive for each individual item of disclosure. For example, information might be available for revenue on the new basis, but not for the level of profit reported to the CODM.

10.116 Following a change in the composition of its reportable segments an entity must disclose whether or not it has restated corresponding amounts. [IFRS 8 para 29].

10.117 If an entity changes the composition of its reportable segments, but does not restate corresponding amounts on the new basis for the above reasons, it should report segmental information on both the old and the new bases of segmentation in the year in which it changes the composition of its segments. In other words, whilst it does not alter the comparatives, it gives additional information in the current year, being segmental information on the old basis as well as on the new basis. [IFRS 8 para 30].

10.118 As well as changes in the composition of reportable segments, changes in accounting policies for segmental reporting that have a material effect on measurement of segmental information should be disclosed. An example of such a change might be a change in the basis of allocating revenues or expenses to segments. Whilst such a change will not change the entity's aggregate financial information, it will change the segmental information. As described in paragraph 10.105 details of any such change in the measurement basis should be given, together with the effect of the change on the measure of segment profit or loss. [IFRS 8 para 27].

10.118.1 IFRS 8 does not require segment information to be restated for a change in the measure of segment profit or loss. Restatement is only required when there has been a change in the composition of the segments resulting from changes in the structure of the entity's internal organisation. However, it is preferable to show all segment information on a comparable basis if it is practicable to do so.

10.119 Changes in other accounting policies, that is, policies for matters other than segmental reporting, should be dealt with in accordance with IAS 8, which is dealt with in chapter 3.

Entity-wide disclosures

10.120 The standard requires all entities that report in accordance with IFRS 8 to make certain entity-wide disclosures, that is disclosures for the entity as a whole rather than by segment. This requirement also applies to those entities with only one reportable segment. The reason for requiring this additional information is that some entities' business activities are not organised on the basis of differences in products and services or differences in geographical areas of operations. For example, an entity might be organised around markets and those markets might encompass different types of products or different geographical areas. Similarly several of the entity's reportable segments might provide similar products and services (if the reportable segments are based on geographical areas) or several reportable segments might cover the same geographical areas (if the entity's reportable segments are based on different products and services). [IFRS 8 para 31].

10.121 The type of entity wide disclosures are mainly information on the entity's products and services and information on the entity's geographical areas of operation. These are the types of information that analysts and other users find useful for assessing trends in performance, concentrations of risk or other purposes.

10.121.1 Entity-wide information should be comparable from period to period. Therefore, the guidance on prior year disclosures contained in paragraphs 10.68 and 10.69 should be applied. For example, where a previously material product grouping becomes immaterial, it would continue to be reported in the current period and then reassessed as to whether it is material in the next period.

10.122 The disclosures listed below are not required if they are otherwise provided as part of the reportable segment information required by the standard. [IFRS 8 para 31]. For example, an entity whose operating segments are based on products and services is not required to provide additional information on its products and services. The disclosures are also not required where the necessary information is not available and the cost to develop it would be excessive, but in such a situation that fact must be disclosed. [IFRS 8 paras 32, 33].

Products and services

10.123 Entities whose reportable segments report revenues from a broad range of essentially different products and services are required to disclose the revenues from external customers for each product and service or each group of similar products and services. In order to determine whether an entity's individual segments contain essentially different products and services, one reasonable approach would be to look at the aggregation criteria of IFRS 8. For example, if the products have similar production processes, classes of customers, and economic characteristics as evidenced by similar rates of profitability, similar degrees of risk, and similar opportunities for growth, it may be concluded that the products are essentially similar and no additional disclosure would be required. Furthermore, where an entity is required to provide these additional disclosures, this approach would also be reasonable for determining groups of similar products and services for entities. Revenues should be based on the financial information used to produce the entity's financial statements. [IFRS 8 para 32].

Geographical areas

10.124 The geographical information to be disclosed, based on financial information used to produce the entity's financial statements, is as follows:

- Revenues from external customers attributed as follows:

    - To the entity's country of domicile.

    - To all foreign countries in total from which the entity derives revenues (subject to the next bullet point).

    - If revenues from external customers attributable to an individual foreign country are material, those revenues should be disclosed separately.

    - The basis for attributing revenue from external customers to individual countries should be disclosed. (The standard does not prescribe what basis should be used but does require disclosure of the basis.)

    - Sub-totals *may* be given for groups of countries assuming that none of the countries' revenues are individually material, but these sub-totals are not *required* (see para 10.102).

- Non-current assets, other than financial instruments, deferred tax assets, post employment benefit assets and rights arising under insurance contracts located in:

    - The entity's country of domicile.

    - All other foreign countries in total in which the entity holds assets (subject to the next bullet point).

- If assets in an individual foreign country are material those assets should be separately disclosed.

- Sub-totals *may* be given for groups of countries, but these sub-totals are not *required*.

[IFRS 8 para 33].

10.124.1 IFRS 8 does not prescribe how revenue should be allocated to geographic areas. An entity may choose to allocate revenue on the basis of either the customer's location, the location to which the product is shipped (which may differ from the location in which the customer resides) or the location in which the sale originated. An entity must disclose the basis it has selected for attributing revenue to geographic areas.

10.125 The standard does not define the term 'material' for the purpose of determining whether an individual country's revenue or non-current assets should be separately disclosed. The entity should consider materiality from both quantitative and qualitative perspectives. When considering quantitatively, as the standard uses the threshold of 10% or more in determining whether an operating segment is a reportable segment or not, it seems reasonable to apply the same test to determine whether an individual country's revenue or assets are material for the purpose of separate disclosure. We consider that the materiality test would be applied by comparing the country's revenue or assets to total entity external revenue or assets (including the country of domicile). However entities may determine materiality at a lower level as illustrated in Table 10.14 in paragraph 10.128.

10.126 Non-current assets for the purpose of disclosure include tangible and intangible assets, but exclude those other assets listed above. Where an entity classifies assets in its balance sheet using a liquidity presentation, non-current assets are assets that include amounts expected to be recovered more than 12 months after the balance sheet date. See also paragraph 10.79.

[The next paragraph is 10.128.]

10.128 An example of the disclosure of geographical revenues is given in Table 10.14, which gives a detailed breakdown of individual countries' revenues (the country of domicile is Switzerland).

Table 10.14 – Disclosure of entity revenues by geographical area

Roche Holding Ltd – Reports and accounts – 31 December 2011

2. Operating segment information (extract)

Information by geographical area *in millions of CHF*

| | Revenues from external customers | Royalties and other operating | Non-current assets | |
	Sales	income	Property, plant and equipment	Goodwill and intangible assets
2011				
Switzerland	507	190	3,169	1,912
European Union	12,815	54	4,210	1,913
– of which Germany	*2,595*	*47*	*3,030*	*1,871*
Rest of Europe	1,486	2	47	1
Europe	**14,808**	**246**	**7,426**	**3,826**
United States	14,133	1,283	5,204	8,465
Rest of North America	1,047	2	109	86
North America	**15,180**	**1,285**	**5,313**	**8,551**
Latin America	3,115	1	460	15
Japan	4,314	46	1,872	383
Rest of Asia	3,616	4	1,025	191
Asia	**7,930**	**50**	**2,897**	**574**
Africa, Australia and Oceania	1,498	–	105	3
Total	**42,531**	**1,582**	**16,201**	**12,969**
2010				
Switzerland	464	221	3,032	1,923
European Union	14,596	59	4,261	1,785
– of which Germany	*2,970*	*59*	*3,097*	*1,740*
Rest of Europe	1,630	2	42	1
Europe	**16,690**	**282**	**7,335**	**3,709**
United States	16,446	1,372	5,849	8,394
Rest of North America	1,051	16	118	88
North America	**17,497**	**1,388**	**5,967**	**8,482**
Latin America	3,397	12	476	17
Japan	4,718	7	1,848	427
Rest of Asia	3,591	5	991	218
Asia	**8,309**	**12**	**2,839**	**645**
Africa, Australia and Oceania	1,580	–	112	2
Total	**47,473**	**1,694**	**16,729**	**12,855**

> Supplementary unaudited information on sales by therapeutic areas in the Pharmaceuticals Division and by business areas in the Diagnostics Division are given in the Financial Review. Sales are allocated to geographical areas by destination according to the location of the customer. Royalties and other operating income are allocated according to the location of the Group company that receives the revenue. European Union information is based on members of the EU as at 31 December 2011.

Information not available and cost to develop excessive

10.129 As noted in paragraph 10.121 the entity-wide disclosures of products and services and geographical information need not be given if it is unavailable and the cost to develop it would be excessive. However, because the information is on an entity basis and is not required to be given by segment, which would involve much more detailed disclosure, it seems unlikely that this exemption will need to be invoked often. Most companies are likely to collect and retain information about their geographical operations and products and services.

Information about major customers

10.130 The standard requires disclosure of an entity's reliance on its major customers. If revenues from transactions with a single customer amount to 10% or more of an entity's revenues the entity should disclose:

- The fact that revenue from a customer exceeds 10% or more of the entity's revenues (if this applies to more than one customer, the number of customers should be given).

- The total amount of revenues from each such customer.

- The identity of the segment or segments that report the revenues.

[IFRS 8 para 34].

10.131 There is no need to disclose the identity of the customer or customers or the amount of revenues that each segment reports from that customer or customers. [IFRS 8 para 34].

10.132 For the purpose of disclosure, a group of entities known by the entity to be under common control should be considered to be a single customer. The IASB has recognised that it may not be practicable or meaningful to regard all government-related entities as a single customer. IFRS 8 clarifies that judgement is required when determining whether a government (including government agencies and similar bodies whether local, national or international) and entities known to the reporting entity to be under the control of that government are considered a single customer. The extent of economic integration between the entities should be considered. [IFRS 8 para 34]. This clarification resulted from an amendment to IAS 24, which is dealt with in chapter 29.

10.133 An example of customer disclosure is Table 10.15. The example also gives the names of the customers which would be additional voluntary information under IFRS 8.

Table 10.15 – Disclosure of information on major customers

BAE Systems plc – Report and accounts – 31 December 2011

1. SEGMENTAL ANALYSIS (extract)

Revenue by major customer

Revenue from the Group's three principal customers, which individually represent over 10% of total revenue, is as follows:

	2011	Restated[1] 2010
	£m	£m
UK Ministry of Defence[2]	4,802	5,059
US Department of Defense	5,675	7,696
Kingdom of Saudi Arabia Ministry of Defence and Aviation	2,276	2,870

Revenue from the UK Ministry of Defence and the US Department of Defense was generated by the five principal reporting segments. Revenue from the Kingdom of Saudi Arabia Ministry of Defence and Aviation was generated by the Platforms & Services (UK) and Platforms & Services (International) reporting segments.

1 Restated following the classification of the Regional Aircraft line of business as a discontinued operation (see note 7)

2 Revenue from the UK Ministry of Defence includes £1.3bn (2010 £1.3bn) generated under the Typhoon work share agreement with Eurofighter GmbH. This revenue is included within Rest of Europe in the analysis by customer location above.

Segmental disclosures required or encouraged by other standards

IFRS 5

10.134 IFRS 5 sets out the disclosure requirements where a non-current asset (or disposal group) has either been classified as held for sale or sold (see further in chapter 8). It requires disclosure, where applicable, of the reportable segment in which the non-current asset (or disposal group) is presented in accordance with IFRS 8. [IFRS 5 para 41(d) as amended by IFRS 8].

IFRS 7

10.135 Paragraph 34 of IFRS 7 requires disclosure of information about the entity's exposure to credit risk, including concentrations of credit risk insofar as they are material to the entity or reported internally to the entity's key management personnel. This is in addition to the disclosure required by IFRS 8. An example of segmental disclosure of credit risk relating to receivables is given in Table 10.16.

Table 10.16 – Disclosure of credit risk by segment

Sasol Limited – Report and accounts – 30 June 2011

64 Financial risk management and financial instruments (extract)

Credit risk

Credit risk, or the risk of financial loss due to counterparties not meeting their contractual obligations, is managed by the application of credit approvals, limits and monitoring procedures. Where appropriate, the group obtains security in the form of guarantees to mitigate risk. Counterparty credit limits are in place and are reviewed and approved by the respective subsidiary credit management committees. The central treasury function provides credit risk management for the group-wide exposure in respect of a diversified group of banks and other financial institutions. These are evaluated regularly for financial robustness especially in the current global economic environment. Management has evaluated treasury counterparty risk and does not expect any treasury counterparties to fail in meeting their obligations.

Trade and other receivables consist of a large number of customers spread across diverse industries and geographical areas. The exposure to credit risk is influenced by the individual characteristics, the industry and geographical area of the counterparty with whom we have transacted. Trade and other receivables are carefully monitored for impairment. An allowance for impairment of trade receivables is made where there is an identified loss event, which based on previous experience, is evidence of a reduction in the recoverability of the cash flows. Details of the credit quality of trade receivables and the associated provision for impairment is disclosed in note 13.

No single customer represents more than 10% of the group's total turnover or more than 10% of total trade receivables for the years ended 30 June 2011, 2010 and 2009. Approximately 49% (2010 – 51%; 2009 – 50%) of the group's total turnover is generated from sales within South Africa, while about 23% (2010 – 22%; 2009 – 23%) relates to European sales. Approximately 47% (2010 – 51%; 2009 –53%) of the amount owing in respect of trade receivables is from counterparties in South Africa, while European receivables amount to about 28% (2010 – 24%; 2009 – 25%).

Credit risk exposure in respect of long-term receivables and trade receivables is further analysed in notes 9 and 13, respectively. The carrying value represents the maximum credit risk exposure.

The group has provided guarantees for the financial obligations of subsidiaries, joint-ventures and third parties. The outstanding guarantees at 30 June 2011 are provided in note 57.1.

13 Trade receivables (extract 1)
Credit risk exposure in respect of trade receivables is analysed as follows:
for the year ended 30 June

	2011 Rm	2010 Rm	2009 Rm
Business segmentation			
South African energy cluster	**7 666**	7 038	6 062
Mining	129	47	18
Gas	377	379	268
Synfuels	305	176	152
Oil	6 850	6 434	5 615
Other	5	2	9
International energy cluster	**1 105**	533	651
Synfuels International	970	335	519
Petroleum International	135	198	132
Chemical cluster	**12 852**	10 997	8 435

Polymers	**3 356**	2 543	1 973
Solvents	**2 733**	2 704	1 925
Olefins & Surfactants	**4 939**	4 016	2 962
Other	**1 824**	1 734	1 575
Other businesses	**5**	56	28
Total operations	**21 628**	18 624	15 176

13 Trade receivables (extract 2)
Geographic information of trade receivables

South Africa	**10 119**	9 443	8 028
Rest of Africa	**387**	281	343
Europe	**6 073**	4 455	3 780
North America	**1 770**	1 695	1 019
South America	**352**	296	187
Southeast Asia and Australasia	**663**	526	495
Middle East and India	**1 483**	1 202	678
Far East	**781**	726	646
	21 628	18 624	15 176

IAS 7

10.136 IAS 7 encourages disclosure of the amount of cash flows arising from the operating, investing and financing activities of each reportable segment. [IAS 7 para 50 (d) as revised by IFRS 8]. An example of the disclosure of operating and investing activities is given in Table 10.17. Disclosure of financing activities might be less common as financing is often managed on a central basis.

Table 10.17 – Segmental analysis of cash flows

Deutsche Telekom AG – Annual Report – 31 December 2011

32 Segment reporting. (extract)

		Net cash from operating activities	Net cash (used in) from investing activities	Of which: cash capex*	Net cash (used in) from financing activities
		millions of €	millions of €	millions of €	millions of €
Germany	2011	8,323	(3,617)	(3,644)	(6,272)
	2010	9,167	(4,977)	(4,765)	(10,023)
	2009	9,777	(2,801)	(3,158)	(3,689)
Europe	2011	4,837	(493)	(1,870)	(1,895)
	2010	4.481	(3,045)	(2,012)	(2,839)
	2009	5,034	(1,510)	(2,489)	(6,071)
United States	2011	3,523	(3,013)	(1,963)	(364)
	2010	3,691	(1,870)	(2,121)	(1,920)
	2009	3,929	(3,014)	(2,666)	(1,004)

Systems Solutions	2011	606	(596)	(553)	(23)
	2010	517	(726)	(725)	(373)
	2009	325	(643)	(681)	88
Group Headquarters & Shared Services	2011	6,276	(952)	(493)	(5,457)
	2010	7,486	3,424	(406)	(5,554)
	2009	6,801	(2,995)	(449)	(2,147)
Total	**2011**	**23,565**	**(8,671)**	**(8,523)**	**(14,011)**
	2010	**25,342**	**(7,194)**	**(10,029)**	**(20,709)**
	2009	**25,866**	**(10,963)**	**(9,443)**	**(12,823)**
Reconciliation	2011	(7,351)	(604)	117	8,053
	2010	(10,611)	(3,517)	178	14,340
	2009	(10,071)	2,314	241	7,700
Group	2011	16,214	(9,275)	(8,406)	(5,958)
	2010	14,731	(10,711)	(9,851)	(6,369)
	2009	15,795	(8,649)	(9,202)	(5,123)

* Cash outflows for investments in intangible assets (excluding goodwill) and property, plant and equipment, as shown in the statement of cash flows.

10.137 In addition to the disclosures encouraged by IAS 7, IFRS 8 also requires disclosure of material non-cash items. [IFRS 8 para 23(i)].

IAS 34

10.138 IAS 34 requires segmental disclosures in interim financial statements. Entities should disclose the information listed below, as a minimum, in the notes to their interim financial statements, if material and if not disclosed elsewhere in the interim financial report. The information should normally be on a year-to-date basis, but the entity should also disclose any events or transactions that are material to an understanding of the current interim period (for example if an entity reports on a quarterly basis the segmental information for the second quarter should cover the six months of the financial year to date, but any significant events or transactions in the second quarter should be disclosed). The information is only required if IFRS 8 requires the entity to disclose segment information in the entity's annual financial statements.

- Segment external revenues, if included in the measure of segment profit or loss reviewed by the CODM or if it is otherwise regularly provided to the CODM.

- Inter-segment revenues if included in the measure of profit or loss reviewed by the CODM or is otherwise provided to the CODM.

- A measure of segment profit or loss.

- Total segment assets for which there has been a material change from the amount disclosed in the last annual financial statements (see para 10.138.1).

- Description of any differences from the last annual financial statements in the basis of segmentation or in the basis of measurement of segment profit or loss.

- A reconciliation of total reportable segments' profit or loss to the entity's profit or loss before tax and discontinued operations. A reconciliation to profit or loss after tax and discontinued operations may be substituted if an entity allocates tax or discontinued operations to segments. The reconciliations should identify and describe separately each material reconciling item.

[IAS 34 para 16A(g)].

10.138.1 To be consistent with the requirements in IFRS 8, in May 2012 the IASB amended IAS 34 in its 'Annual improvements to IFRSs'. The amendment clarifies that, in addition to the existing criteria for a material change, the total assets for a particular reportable segment need to be disclosed only if the amounts are regularly provided to the CODM.

10.138.2 In addition, the amendment to IAS 34 requires disclosure in interim financial statements of a measure of total liabilities for a particular reportable segment if such amounts are regularly provided to the CODM and if there has been a material change from the amount disclosed in the last annual financial statements for that reportable segment. The amendment is effective for annual periods beginning on or after 1 January 2013, with early adoption permitted.

IAS 36

10.139 IAS 36 states that a cash generating unit to which goodwill acquired in a business combination is allocated for impairment testing purposes cannot be larger than an operating segment. [IAS 36 para 80(b)]. This applies to all entities irrespective of whether they are within the scope of IFRS 8 or not. Refer to chapter 18 for further guidance on cash generating units and impairment testing.

10.139.1 IAS 36 requires that where an entity applies IFRS 8, it should disclose the following for each reportable segment:

- The amount of impairment losses recognised in profit or loss and comprehensive income during the period.

- The amount of reversals of impairment losses recognised in profit or loss and comprehensive income during the period.

[IAS 36 para 129].

10.140 IAS 36 requires that if an impairment loss on an individual asset is recognised or reversed in the period and is material to the entity's financial statements as a whole, and the entity reports in accordance with IFRS 8, the entity should disclose the nature of the asset and reportable segment to which the asset belongs. [IAS 36 para 130(c)].

10.141 If the material impairment or reversal of an impairment relates to a cash generating unit, the financial statements should give a description of the unit (such as whether it is a product line, a plant, a business operation, a geographical area, or a reportable segment as defined in IFRS 8). It should also disclose the amount of the impairment loss recognised or reversed by class of assets and by reportable segment. [IAS 36 para 130(d)]. Table 10.18 illustrates the disclosure of impairment charges in a segmental analysis (the additional disclosures required by IAS 36 are not reproduced in this example).

Table 10.18 – Disclosure of impairment in a segmental report

Vodafone Group Plc – Report and accounts – 31 March 2012

3. Segment analysis (extract 1)

The Group has a single group of related services and products being the supply of communications services and products. Segment information is provided on the basis of geographic areas, being the basis on which the Group manages its worldwide interests. Revenue is attributed to a country or region based on the location of the Group company reporting the revenue. Inter-segment sales are charged at arm's length prices.

3. Segment analysis (extract 2)

	Non-current assets[1]	Capital expenditure[2]	Other expenditure on intangible assets	Depreciation and amortisation loss/	Impairment (reversal)
	£m	£m	£m	£m	£m
31 March 2012					
Germany	19,151	880	4	1,469	–
Italy	13,978	621	875	783	2,450
Spain	8,069	429	71	626	900
UK	6,430	575	–	880	–
Other Europe	10,146	1,092	313	1,389	700
Europe	**57,774**	**3,597**	**1,263**	**5,147**	**4,050**
India	8,431	805	–	1,066	–
Vodacom	6,469	723	–	840	–
Other Africa, Middle East and Asia Pacific	4,735	793	–	771	–
Africa, Middle East and Asia Pacific	**19,635**	**2,321**	**–**	**2,677**	**–**
Non-Controlled Interests and Common Functions	760	447	–	35	–
Group	**78,169**	**6,365**	**1,263**	**7,859**	**4,050**

Notes:
[1] Comprises goodwill, other intangible assets and property, plant and equipment.
[2] Includes additions to property, plant and equipment and computer software, reported within intangible assets.

Additional voluntary disclosures

10.142   In addition to the required disclosures, many entities provide additional voluntary segmental disclosures. Sometimes, particularly in the case of non-financial disclosures, these are given in the management report rather than in the financial statements. Some of the types of additional disclosure are listed below:

- Employees. (See Table 10.19).

- Sales orders. (See Table 10.20).

- Research and development.

- Environmental expenditure, health and safety and other non-financial segment information.

Table 10.19 – Segmental disclosure for employees

Vodafone Group – Report and accounts – 31 March 2012

32. Employees (extract)

	2012 Employees	2011 Employees	2010 Employees
By segment:			
Germany	12,115	12,594	13,507
Italy	5,838	6,121	6,207
Spain	4,379	4,389	4,326
UK	8,151	8,174	9,766
Other Europe	20,061	18,953	18,582
Europe	**50,544**	**50,231**	**52,388**
India	11,234	10,743	10,132
Vodacom	7,437	7,320	6,833
Other Africa, Middle East and Asia Pacific	10,886	10,896	10,887
Africa, Middle East and Asia Pacific	**29,557**	**28,959**	**27,852**
Non-Controlled Interests and Common Functions	6,272	4,672	4,750
Total	**86,373**	**83,862**	**84,990**

Table 10.20 – Segmental information on new orders

Siemens AG – Report and accounts – 30 September 2011

37 – Segment Information (extract 1)

New orders

New orders are determined principally as estimated revenue of accepted purchase orders and order value changes and adjustments, excluding letters of intent. New orders are supplementary information, provided on a voluntary basis. It is not part of the audited Consolidated Financial Statements.

Segment information (continuing operations) (extract)

As of and for the fiscal years ended September 30, 2011 and 2010

(in millions of €)

	New orders [1]	
	2011	**2010**
Sectors		
Industry	37,594	30,243
Energy	34,765	30,122
Healthcare	13,116	12,872
Total Sectors	**85,476**	**73,237**
Equity Investments	–	–
Financial Services (SFS)	961	787
Reconciliation to		
Consolidated Financial Statements		
Centrally managed portfolio activities	473	760
Siemens Real Estate (SRE)[6]	2,204	1,941
Corporate items and pensions	449	606
Eliminations, Corporate Treasury and other reconciling items	(3,982)	(3,275)
Siemens	**85,582**	**74,055**

[1] This supplementary information on New orders is provided on a voluntary basis. It is not part of the Consolidated Financial Statements subject to the audit opinion.

Combined management's discussion and analysis (extract)

C.12.2 Definitions of other financial performances measures (extract)

Under its policy for the recognition of **new orders**, Siemens generally recognizes a new order when we enter into a contract that we consider legally effective and compulsory based on a number of different criteria. In general, if a contract is considered legally effective and compulsory, Siemens recognizes the total contract value. The contract value is the agreed price or fee for that portion of the contract for which the delivery of goods and / or the provision of services has been irrevocably agreed. Future revenues from service, maintenance and outsourcing contracts are recognized as new orders in the amount of the total contract value only if there is adequate assurance that the contract will remain in effect for its entire duration (e.g., due to high exit barriers for the customer). New orders are generally recognized immediately when the relevant contract becomes legally effective and compulsory.

The only exceptions are orders with short overall contract terms. In this case, a separate reporting of new orders would provide no significant additional information regarding our performance. For orders of this type the recognition of new orders thus occurs when the underlying revenue is recognized.

Future developments

10.143 In July 2012, the IASB published a request for information (RFI) as part of its post-implementation review of IFRS 8. The review seeks feedback on whether the standard is functioning as intended, as well as practical information on the challenges and costs associated with implementing the standard. In particular, the IASB is requesting information on experience of:

- The effect of the IASB's decision to identify and report segments using the management perspective.

- The use of non-IFRS measurements.

- The use of internally-reported line items.

- The impact of IFRS 8 disclosures on managements' role.

- The impact of implementation of IFRS 8.

Appendix

The following chart is reproduced from the 'Guidance on Implementing IFRS 8'. See also paragraph 10.49 of the chapter.

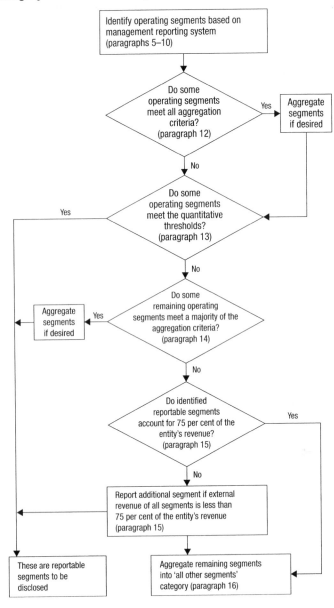

Employee benefits

Employee benefits

Introduction

11.1 The international standard dealing with the accounting for and disclosure of employee benefits is IAS 19. IAS 19 applies to all types of employee benefits, although it is in the area of accounting for defined benefit pension plans that IAS 19 provides most complexity.

Recent developments – Amendments to IAS 19

11.2 The IASB issued IAS 19 (revised 2011) in June 2011. The revised standard makes significant changes to the recognition and measurement of defined benefit expense and to the disclosures for post employment benefits. The amendments are effective for periods beginning on or after 1 January 2013, with early adoption permitted. See chapter 11A for the requirements of IAS 19 (revised) which is included in the IFRS Manual of Accounting.

[The next paragraph is 11.36.]

Objective and scope

11.36 IAS 19 approaches accounting for employee benefits from a balance sheet perspective. The standard's first stated objective is to ensure that an employer's financial statements reflect a liability when an employee has provided service in exchange for employee benefits to be paid in the future. This balance sheet approach reflects the trend in accounting standards to base accounting on the definitions of assets and liabilities and to make more use of fair value measurements.

11.37 The second objective of IAS 19 relates to the recognition of the cost of employee benefits in the performance statements. The objective is to ensure that an expense is recognised when the employer consumes the economic benefit arising from the services provided by the employee in exchange for employee benefits. Nevertheless, this secondary objective can result in balance sheets and performance statements prepared in accordance with IAS 19 giving figures that are smoothed rather than accurately reflecting actuarial gains and losses, where an entity follows the IAS 19's 'corridor approach', which is described from paragraph 11.268.1.

Scope of IAS 19

11.38   IAS 19 applies to all types of employee benefits (except those to which IFRS 2 applies), which are defined as *"all forms of consideration given by an entity in exchange for service rendered by employees"*. [IAS 19 para 7]. Employee benefits (including social security contributions payable in respect of employee benefits), therefore, include the following categories, each of which have different characteristics and, therefore, have separate requirements:

■   Short-term benefits such as wages, salaries, holiday pay, sick leave and bonuses payable within twelve months of the balance sheet date.

■   Long-term benefits such as long-term incentive plans (LTIPs), long-service awards, holiday pay and bonuses payable more than twelve months after the balance sheet date.

■   Termination benefits such as redundancy payments.

■   Post-employment benefits such as pensions and post-retirement medical insurance.

[IAS 19 para 4].

11.39   Share options and other forms of share-based payment that reward employees for services are not dealt with in IAS 19, but are dealt with in IFRS 2 (see chapter 12).

11.40   Although not defined in the standard, the term 'employees' potentially has a broader application under IAS 19 than might normally be assumed, for example under companies legislation of some countries. Paragraph 6 of the standard notes that an employee may provide services to an entity on a full time, part time, permanent, casual or temporary basis. In our view, the scope of the definition 'employees' should be driven by the substance of the relationship between the individual and the 'employer'. Only where the latter is exposed to risks consistent with a contract of employment should the former be considered to be an employee for the purposes of IAS 19. Furthermore, the definition of an employee may also be outlined in national legislation.

UK.11.40.1   Companies legislation in the UK defines employees as those employed under contracts *of service*. [CA06 Sec 411(3) to (5)]. Self-employed people should normally be excluded, because their contracts will be contracts *for services*. No such distinction is drawn in IAS 19. This could be interpreted as requiring all costs of engaging personnel, whether under employment contracts or otherwise, to be dealt with under IAS 19. As noted above, in our view, the scope of the definition 'employees' should be driven by the substance of the relationship between the individual and the 'employer'.

11.41   Employee benefits may be provided to the employees themselves or to their dependants, such as in the case of death-in-service benefit. The standard also applies to benefits that are settled by payment to a third party such as an insurance company or the state. For example, an employer may have a policy of settling its pension obligations by purchasing annuities from an insurance company. Although the employer has not actually provided benefits directly to its employees, this arrangement would fall within IAS 19's scope. [IAS 19 para 5].

Benefits payable during employment

11.42   Benefits payable during employment include the following:

- Wages, salaries and bonuses.

- Social security contributions.

- Holiday pay.

- Paid disability, sick and maternity leave.

- Benefits-in-kind, such as private medical insurance, company cars and accommodation.

- Long-term bonuses such as LTIPs and long-service awards.

[IAS 19 paras 8, 126].

UK.11.42.1   Although FRS 12 has been relevant to the accounting for provisions in respect of bonuses, there have not been any specific UK accounting standards dealing with employee benefits such as those listed above. As a result, differing accounting treatments have developed, for example in respect of the period over which a holiday pay liability is recognised. Reporting entities in the UK may, but are not obliged to, look to IFRS (and in particular to IAS 19) for guidance on how to account for such provisions.

[The next paragraph is 11.45.]

Recognition and measurement

11.45   Different principles are applied to recognising and measuring employee benefits payable during employment depending on whether they are long-term or short-term. Short-term benefits are those amounts due to be settled wholly within 12 months of the end of the period in which the employees render the related service. Naturally, long-term benefits are those amounts due to be settled, at least in part, after 12 months of the end of the period. Accounting for short-term benefits is generally simple, because no actuarial assumptions are required and any obligations are measured on an undiscounted basis.

Wages, salaries and other short-term benefits payable in cash

11.46 Accounting for wages and salaries is generally straightforward. A liability and an expense (unless capitalisation is appropriate) are recognised when an employee has rendered services. Capitalisation of employee benefits as part of the cost of an asset is dealt with in IAS 2 (see chapter 20), IAS 11 (see chapter 9), IAS 16 (see chapter 16), and IAS 38 (see chapter 15).

11.47 Short-term bonuses and other short-term profit sharing arrangements are also straightforward. A liability and an expense (unless capitalisation is permitted as described above) are recognised when the reporting entity has a present legal or constructive obligation to make payments as a result of past events and a reliable estimate can be made of the amount payable. [IAS 19 para 17]. This language is similar to that used in IAS 37 and the considerations are also similar. IAS 37 is dealt with in chapter 21. The only additional guidance regarding recognition is whether a reliable estimate can be made of the amount payable in paragraph 20 of IAS 19. Paragraph 20 of IAS 19 provides that a reliable estimate can be made when, and only when:

- the formal terms of the profit sharing or bonus plan contain a formula for determining the amount payable;

- the amount payable is determined before the financial statements are authorised for issue; or

- past practice gives clear evidence of the amount of the entity's constructive obligation.

[IAS 19 para 20].

11.47.1 The following example illustrates when a change in the terms and conditions of employment should be recognised and when past practice creates a constructive obligation on the entity.

Example 1 – One-off compensation payment associated with future operations

To remain competitive, an entity intends to alter the terms and conditions of employment at one factory in such a way that overtime will be paid in future at 1.5 times the normal rate, rather than twice the normal rate as in the past. The entity intends to compensate employees with a one-off payment and has put this offer to the union. The employees are also aware of this impending change. No agreement has been reached with the union at the year end. However, if the offer is not accepted, the entity is likely to switch overtime work to other factories.

Provision should not be made for the planned expenditure to operate in a particular way in the future, because the entity can avoid that expenditure by changing its method of operation. Therefore, the proposed one-off compensation payment that is associated with the future operations and that could be avoided by switching overtime production to other factories should not be provided for, in advance, at the year end. However, if agreement for the payment had been reached with the unions by the year end and the payment was no longer dependent on future events (that is, the structure and recipients of the payment had been identified), then a liability should be recognised for the payment at the year end.

Example 2 – Performance bonus based on sales target

A car dealer has a practice of paying a performance bonus to its sales staff.

Past evidence indicates that sales staff who meet their sales targets received a bonus of 10% of their current salary package at the year end. Sales staff who were not in service throughout the whole year received a bonus in proportion to their service period. The bonuses are paid, in the first quarter of the following year, to the sales staff who are still employed by the entity at the year end.

At the year end, seven of the sales staff met their sales targets. Two of the seven began their employment halfway through the year and one of them left the entity at the year end.

The car dealer should recognise a liability at the expected cost of the bonuses to be paid in the subsequent year for the following reasons:

- the dealer created a valid expectation among the sales staff that they would receive bonuses if they met their sales targets and were still in the entity's service, that is, there is a constructive obligation; and
- the amount of the payment can be estimated reliably. There are four sales staff who will receive a bonus of 10% of their current salary packages and two who will receive 5% because their employment commenced halfway through the year. No provision should be recognised for the employee who resigned at the year end, because he left the entity before the year end and will, therefore, not receive a payment.

11.48 If a bonus has not been paid by the balance sheet date, the amount recognised as a liability should be based on the expected amount payable. Often an annual bonus is payable some time after the year end and only to those employees who remain in employment until that time. IAS 19 makes it clear in paragraph 18 that if the amount payable has not been determined by the date on which the financial statements are signed, the amount provided at the balance sheet date should take account of the expected number of leavers. However, the standard is unclear as to whether the additional service condition (that is, the requirement to remain in employment until the date on which the bonus is paid) should be taken into account when considering the period over which the bonus expense is recognised. It states that *"employees render service that increases the amount to be paid if they remain in service until the end of the specified period"*. [IAS 19 para 18]. There are two schools of thought as to how this should be interpreted.

11.48.1   The first is that because the amount of the bonus does not increase after the end of the performance period, the full liability should be recognised at the balance sheet date (with appropriate adjustment for expected leavers). Thus the associated expense is recognised over the shorter performance period.

11.48.2   The second is that there is another vesting condition to be fulfilled in addition to the performance condition, namely that the employee must remain in employment until the later date and may still forfeit the right to payment by leaving before that date. By analogy with IAS 19 paragraphs 70 and BC14, for a plan that pays a lump sum of C1,000 on completion of ten years of service, an expense of C100 (adjusted to reflect the probability that the employee might leave and ignoring the time value of money for simplicity) should be recognised each year. Thus the associated expense is recognised over the longer vesting period.

11.48.3   Furthermore, IFRS 2 concludes that a liability and an expense should be recognised in respect of a cash-settled share-based payment arrangement as services are rendered over the entire vesting period. In this context, the vesting period is the period until *all* conditions (both performance and service) are satisfied. Short-term employee benefits within the scope of IAS 19 are outside the scope of IFRS 2, but the IASB considered the standards to be consistent in this area. [IFRS 2 para BC245].

11.48.4   Hence, although a case can be made for an expense to be recognised in respect of a short-term bonus over only the performance period, we believe that the more appropriate and consistent treatment is to recognise an expense over the longer vesting period until the bonus award vests. This is illustrated in the example below.

> **Example – Bonus payable to employees three months after the year-end**
>
> An entity has a December year end. It pays a bonus in respect of each year to employees who have provided services during the year and remain on the payroll at 31 March. The bonus pool is determined as 5% of entity profits and each employee's entitlement is determined as at 31 December. There is no re-allocation of the bonus entitlement of employees who leave before 31 March. On average, 1% of employees leave the entity each month. The financial statements for the year ended 31 December 20X3 showed a profit for the purpose of the bonus plan of C100m and they were signed on 28 February 20X4.

In the period from 1 January to 31 March it is expected that an average of 3% of the employees who worked during the previous year will leave the entity. The bonus pool for the year ended 31 December 20X3 was C5m so the expected amount payable on 31 March 20X4 would be C4.85m (97% of C5m). The actual experience in the period up to the date on which the financial statements were signed should be taken into account when it is a confirmation of expectations at the balance sheet date. If 3% of employees actually left during January and February 20X4, but it is still expected that a further 1% will leave during March through the normal course of business, the total amount recognised as an expense would be C4.8m (96% of C5m). However, if employees left after the balance sheet due to a post balance sheet event such as an acquisition or a loss of a major contract or customer, then this will likely be new information arising after the balance sheet date and should not be taken into account.

As employees are required to provide services until 31 March, although an argument can be made for recognition over the shorter 12 month performance period as discussed above, in our view the expense should be recognised over the longer 15 month vesting period ending on 31 March. Accordingly, a liability of C3.84m (that is, C4.8m × 12/15) should be recognised at 31 December 20X3.

11.49 If the amount payable under a bonus arrangement is determined by reference to the value of the reporting entity's shares, this represents a share-based payment. The accounting for share-based payments is dealt with in chapter 12.

Cash payments to employee trusts

11.50 Sometimes, an entity may establish a trust to act as intermediary in respect of payments to employees. The entity makes a payment to the trust for the benefit of the entity's employees and the trust uses the assets accumulated from those payments to pay the entity's employees for some or all of the services rendered. The key consideration is whether, in such circumstances, the trust should be consolidated.

[The next paragraph is 11.60.]

11.60 SIC 12, 'Consolidation – special purpose entities', concludes that an entity should consolidate a special purpose entity (SPE) when the substance of the relationship between the parties indicates that the SPE is controlled by the entity, unless the SPE meets the definition of a long-term employee benefit fund as defined in paragraph 7 of IAS 19. [SIC 12 paras 6, 8]. The interpretation goes on to give examples of circumstances in which an SPE may be consolidated. These include the following:

- The activities of the SPE are being conducted on behalf of the entity according to its specific business needs so that the entity obtains benefits from the SPE's operation.

- The entity has rights to obtain the majority of the SPE's benefits and, therefore, may be exposed to risks incident to the SPE's activities.

[SIC 12 paras 10(a)(c)].

11.61 If it is determined that an employee benefit trust is controlled by its sponsoring entity SIC 12 would require consolidation in the group financial statements, unless the trust meets the definition of a long term employee benefit fund in which case plan asset accounting would be applied as set out in paragraph 11.132.

UK.11.61.1 The general requirement to aggregate the trust into the sponsoring company's balance sheet set out in UITF 32 does not apply under IFRS.

11.62 Does a sponsoring entity's payment to an employee benefit trust represent an immediate expense? Generally speaking, most expenses are incurred when a liability arises (that is, when services are received), not when they are paid for. An immediate expense to the sponsoring entity will occur only if a payment neither results in the acquisition of another asset nor the settlement of a liability.

11.63 SIC 12 is superseded by IFRS 10 which is effective for annual periods beginning on or after 1 January 2013, with earlier application permitted. There will no longer be specific accounting guidance for special purpose entities because IFRS 10 applies to all types of entities. See chapter 5 for further guidance.

[The next paragraph is 11.65.]

Compensated absences

11.65 Compensated absences are periods during which an employee does not provide services to the employer, but employee benefits continue to be paid. Typical examples include:

- Annual leave.

- Sick leave.

- Maternity leave.

- Jury service.

- Military service.

11.66 IAS 19 distinguishes accumulating absences that may be carried forward and used in future periods, from non-accumulating absences that lapse if not used in full. Accumulating absences are typically earned by employees as they provide services whereas non-accumulating absences are not related to services. Of the examples listed above, sick leave, maternity leave and jury service are usually non-accumulating whereas annual leave entitlements may be accumulating or non-accumulating. Where holiday benefit is accumulating, that is, it is earned over time and capable of being carried forward, a reporting entity should provide for the expected cost of accumulated benefit. On the other hand, where benefit is non-accumulating, a reporting entity should not recognise a liability or expense until the absence occurs. However a non-accumulating benefit may be treated as being accumulating in the context of an interim reporting period. The following examples illustrate the distinction.

Example 1 – Holiday pay carried forward

Employees of entity A are entitled to 20 days of paid leave each year. The entitlement accrues evenly throughout the year and unused leave may be carried forward to future periods. This is an example of an accumulating compensated absence.

Example 2 – Sick leave entitlement not carried forward

Employees of entity B are entitled to 10 days of paid sick leave each year, regardless of how long they have worked for the entity. Unused sick leave may not be carried forward and may not be used as additional annual leave. This is an example of a non-accumulating compensated absence. Although there is an entitlement to 10 days of paid sick leave each year, employees do not earn this entitlement as the year progresses and its use cannot be predicted.

Example 3 – Holiday pay while factory is closed

An entity has made a provision for holiday pay, accruing three weeks pay per worker over the year until the summer holiday when the factory is closed for three weeks. The holiday year runs until the end of this summer holiday. The employees of this entity accumulate benefit throughout the year so provision should be made for the expected cost of the holiday pay. The fact that employees may lose the benefit if they leave the entity does not remove the need for a provision, although it may influence the measurement of the provision. [IAS 19 para 13].

Example 4 – Holiday pay not carried forward

An entity has a 31 December year end and a holiday entitlement that also runs with the calendar year. The entity has a policy that any holiday entitlement not taken at 31 December each year is lost and so cannot be carried forward. Thus, there is no liability for holiday pay at the year end.

However, since the entity is listed it prepares interim accounts. At 30 June each year, each employee will have accumulated half of his or her entitlement to holiday pay. Thus, in each interim set of financial statements, a calculation of accrued holiday pay should be made for every employee.

11.67 Identifying absences as accumulating or non-accumulating is important as it will determine the timing of recognising an expense. The expected cost of compensated absences is recognised as follows:

■   In the case of accumulating compensated absences – when the employees render services that increase their entitlement to future compensated absences.

■   In the case of non-accumulating compensated absences – when the absences occur.

[IAS 19 para 11].

11.68 Accumulating compensated absences are further categorised as either vesting or non-vesting. If the benefits are vesting, employees who leave are entitled to cash payment in respect of any unused entitlement. Non-vesting benefits, on the other hand, are lost if an employee leaves without using them. This distinction will influence measurement. This is because the amount recognised as a liability is the *"additional amount that the entity expects to pay as a result of the unused entitlement that has accumulated at the balance sheet date".* [IAS 19 para 14]. Therefore, if benefits are non-vesting, the amount recognised as a liability will take into account the possibility that employees will leave before they utilise their entitlement.

11.69 The principles described above are summarised in the flow chart below.

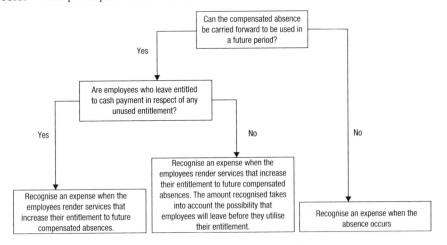

Example – Holiday pay that lapses if employee leaves

Employees of entity A are entitled to 20 days of paid leave each year. The entitlement accrues evenly throughout the year and unused leave may be carried forward to future periods. There is no cash payment in respect of an unused entitlement if an employee leaves the entity.

At 31 December 20X3, entity A has 100 employees and the average unused holiday entitlement per employee is two days. Historically, 10% of employees leave having never taken their unused holiday entitlement and management expect this trend to continue. At the balance sheet date (31 December), entity A should recognise a liability representing the number of days of accumulated entitlement that it expects to have to pay in the future. This will be 180 days (that is, 90% of 200 days).

If entity A was to change its terms and conditions of employment such that a cash payment was made in respect of unused holiday entitlement when an employee leaves the entity, the amount provided would be 200 days. This is because it would be irrelevant that 10% of employees never take all of their holiday entitlement as they would receive a cash payment of equivalent value on leaving the entity.

11.70 The example above considers a simple scenario and ignores the fact that further benefits, some of which will not be utilised, will be earned in the future. This is illustrated in the following example.

Example – Unused holiday carried forward for one year only

The facts are as in the previous example, except that unused holiday entitlements may be carried forward for only one year. Each year, the current year entitlement is used before any balance brought forward from the previous year.

At 31 December 20X3 all 100 employees have 2 days unused holiday entitlement. Management of entity A expects that 75% of employees will take 22 days of holiday in 20X4 (that is, including 2 days each brought forward from 20X3), 15% will take 20 days (that is, lose their 2 days carried forward) and the remainder (10%) will take 18 days (that is, lose their 2 days carried forward from 20X3 and be eligible to carry forward 2 days from 20X4's entitlement at 31 December 20X4). This means that the total expected holiday to be taken in 20X4 is 2,130 days.

How much should be recognised as a liability at 31 December 20X3?

IAS 19 requires a measurement basis whereby the liability is calculated at the level of individual employees and is based on the additional amount that an entity expects to pay as a result of the unused entitlement. On this basis the liability would be based on only the 75% of employees who utilise their brought forward entitlement. So, the liability recognised at 31 December 20X3 would be 150 days (that is, two days for each of 75 employees).

11.71 The previous examples consider the situation where an entity's holiday year corresponds with its financial year. This is not always that case. Similarly, issues arise in respect of the preparation of interim reports at a date that does not correspond with the end of a holiday year. The examples below illustrate these issues.

Example 1 – Financial year different to holiday year

Entity A has a March year end but its holiday year runs to the end of September. Employees of entity A are entitled to 20 days of paid annual leave, all of which must be taken by the end of September or it will be lost. On the basis of past experience, management estimates that staff will take only 95% of their holiday entitlement. Staff do not work at weekends or on national holidays and this means in this case that there are 253 working days per year.

The total annual salary cost for the year ended 31 March 20X4 is C800,000. A pay rise of 4% was awarded with effect from 1 April 20X4 so the total annual salary cost for the year ending 31 March 20X5 will be C832,000.

By 31 March 20X4, staff have earned half of their total annual holiday entitlement (that is, ten days) but have taken only four days. Hence, the amount of holiday earned but not yet taken at 31 March 20X4 is six days. Although this entitlement would be lost if not taken by the end of September, management believe that most will be taken in line with its overall estimates for the year (that is, cumulatively 95%). Four days have been taken so far so a provision should be made in respect of the remaining five and a half days expected to be taken (95% × 10 days less 4 days taken).

The amount provided should be based on the pay rate at which management expects the leave to be taken. The annual salary cost with effect from 1 April 20X4 is C832,000 so the amount provided should be C18,087 (that is, 5½/253 × C832,000).

Example 2 – Non-accumulating sick leave

Entity B has 100 employees, each of whom is entitled to 6 working days of paid sick leave for each year. Unused sick leave may not be carried forward to the next calendar year. Employees are also not entitled to a cash payment for unused entitlement of sick leave on leaving the entity's service.

An entity should not recognise an expense in respect of non-accumulating sick leave until the time of the absence, because employee service does not increase the amount of the benefit. Accordingly, in preparing the interim report for the first half of the year, entity B should not recognise a provision for unused sick leave. The use of sick leave is determined by an unpredictable future event, that is, the illness of the employee and not through the employee's choice. A high or low level of sickness in employees in the first half of the year does not cause a lower or higher level of sickness in the second half.

11.71.1   As a further point, the IFRS IC, in November 2005, considered whether long service leave was in IAS 19's scope or whether it was a financial liability within IAS 32's scope. The IFRS IC noted that IAS 19 indicates that employee benefit plans include a wide range of formal and informal arrangements. [IAS 19 para 3]. The exclusion of employee benefit plans from IAS 32 covers all employee benefits within IAS 39's scope including long-term service leave.

Benefits in kind

11.72   The cost of providing non-monetary benefits (including housing, cars and free or subsidised goods or services) should be recognised according to the same principles as benefits payable in cash. The amount recognised as a liability and an expense should be measured at the cost to the employer of providing the benefit. For example, the cost of a leased company car would be the amount of the lease charges during the year, while the cost of private medical insurance for medical benefits provided in the course of employment would be the amount of premiums paid in the year.

Long-term benefits

11.73   Long-term employee benefits are employee benefits (other than post-employment benefits (see para 11.94) and termination benefits (see para 11.79)) that are due to be settled more than 12 months after the end of the period in which the employees render the related service. [IAS 19 para 7]. This means benefits that are expected to be settled more than 12 months after the balance sheet date for the first annual period in which any of the benefit is earned. For example, a bonus granted with a three-year vesting period is long-term in nature even though the bonus is paid shortly after completion of the three-year vesting period, because the benefit is considered as being earned over three or four annual accounting periods rather than over one three-year period.

11.73.1 Long-term employee benefits, such as long-term bonuses, LTIPs and long service awards, share many of the characteristics of the short-term benefits discussed above. One might expect, therefore, that the same accounting principles would apply, with appropriate adjustment for increased uncertainty and the time value of money. With the exception of the matters set out below, long-term employee benefits are accounted for in the same way as defined benefit pension benefits (see from para 11.127). This includes the use of the projected unit credit method for measuring the obligation arising. Further details on this method are included from paragraph 11.188. The exceptions are as follows:

■ Actuarial gains and losses are recognised immediately through profit or loss. It is not possible to apply either the 'corridor' or the other comprehensive income approach (see from para 11.274.1).

■ All past service costs are recognised immediately (see from para 11.237).

[IAS 19 para 127].

Where other long-term benefits are provided as part of a post-employment benefit plan, it is our view that such a plan should be treated as either a post-employment benefit plan or an other long-term benefit plan in its entirety, depending on the plan's substance.

11.73.1.1 The accounting for long-term benefits involves discounting of future cash flows where the time value of money is material. Also, the complexity and length of some long-term benefit arrangements will require the use of actuarial assumptions such as salary increases and inflation in order to calculate the obligation using the projected unit credit method. The following examples illustrate how the projected unit credit method is applied when considering long-term employee benefits that require the use of actuarial assumptions.

Employee benefits

Example 1 – Bonus on completion of five years service

Entity A operates a long-term bonus scheme, whereby employees receive a bonus on completion of five years service. The bonus is calculated as 1% of each year's salary. Salaries are expected to increase by 5% per annum and the discount rate is 8%.

The following table illustrates how the liability for the bonus would build up over the five years for an employee that joins the company in year 1. It is assumed that the employee will reach five years service and that there are no changes in actuarial assumptions. The employee's salary in year 1 is C40,000.

Year	1	2	3	4	5
Current year benefit (1% of current year salary)	400	420	441	463	486
Cumulative bonus payable	400	820	1,261	1,724	2,210
Opening obligation	–	325	702	1,137	1,637
Interest at 8%	–	26	56	91	131
Current service cost	325	351	379	409	442
Closing obligation	325	702	1,137	1,637	2,210

In the above table, the current service cost is the present value of the benefit attributed to the current year. The benefit attributed to the current year is the overall benefit payable of C2,210 divided by five, being C442 each year. So in year 3, for example, the current service cost is C379 (that is, $C442/1.08^2$).

Example 2 – Non-contractual bonus paid after ten years service

There is a German sub-group of a UK listed plc. The German sub-group has traditionally awarded an anniversary bonus to employees on completion of ten years service. This entitlement is not part of their employment contract, but the payment is established common practice, and accordingly the sub-group will record a provision for the anticipated bonus. Under IFRS, long-term employee benefits, such as long service awards, are recognised and measured in a similar way to pensions (and other post-retirement benefits). Paragraph 128 of IAS 19 requires a provision to be built up, by spreading the charge over the ten years' service using the projected unit credit method.

11.73.2 Under some arrangements employees are awarded specified cash bonuses that are conditional upon additional employment. For example, employees may be awarded specific bonuses based on a performance year, but where terms of the bonus arrangement require the employees to remain in employment for an additional one, two, or three years. We consider that these arrangements are long-term in nature and should be accounted for in the same way as defined benefit pension plans. This means that the benefits should be allocated to periods of service. In these types of plans, significant actuarial calculations would not generally be necessary, as certain assumptions (for example, mortality, life expectancy, asset return, etc) may not be relevant or material. In practice, the liability to be accrued would generally reflect the present value of expected cash outflows, with any unwind in the discount reflected as part of the benefit expense. The liability should be assessed and trued-up at each balance sheet period for any changes in expected cash flows.

11.73.2.1 The presentation of current service cost and interest cost within the income statement would follow the treatment of equivalent income statement items arising from defined benefit pension obligations (see para 11.279).

11.73.3 In some situations long-term benefit plans might vest in instalments over the vesting period. We believe there are two acceptable approaches to recognise the expense.

11.73.4 One approach is to recognise the expense according to the plan's benefit formula based on the principle in paragraph 67 of IAS 19. This means that an entity would attribute an expense to separate periods of service. However, where benefits are materially higher in later years, the expense should be recognised over the vesting period on a straight-line basis (see further from para 11.164).

11.73.5 The second approach is to view the bonus arrangement as multiple awards with different service periods; thus the plan's benefit formula is based on each award's individual service period. This means the expense is recognised for each instalment over the respective service periods in a manner similar to staged-vesting (or tranche vesting) for share-based payment transactions (see further guidance in chapter 12). The period of service is the period the employee is required to be employed by the entity before being unconditionally entitled to the bonus payments.

11.73.6 An entity will need to consider the specific terms and conditions to determine which approach is most appropriate. For example, if an entity grants an annual recurring bonus as part of an employment agreement (for example, C10,000 payable at the end of each year for the next three years), this might indicate the first approach is more appropriate as this arrangement is similar to accounting for wages and salaries. However, if an entity otherwise grants a bonus that vests and is payable in three future instalments, this might indicate that a staged-vesting approach is more appropriate as employees could be viewed as providing services for each instalment of the bonus until payment.

11.73.7 The following examples illustrate these principles.

Example 1– Deferred bonus arrangements with two different instalments

Entity A awards its employees a cash bonus of C100 based on the performance of the employee and the entity in 20X1. 50% of the bonus will be paid in February 20X2 and the remaining 50% will be paid at the end of 20X3 provided the employee remains working for the entity.

An entity could use the staged-vesting approach in this scenario as, in substance, the employee is working for two awards with different service periods. The bonus expense should be recognised for each instalment. This means that 50% of the bonus should be spread from 1 January 20X1 to 28 February 20X2 and the other 50% of the bonus should be spread from 1 January 20X1 to 31 December 20X3.

It might also be appropriate to recognise the expense based on the bonus plan's benefit formula. This means that 50% of the bonus should be spread from 1 January 20X1 to 28 February 20X2 (14 months), and the other 50% of the bonus should be spread from 1 March 20X2 to 31 December 20X3 (22 months).

Example 2 – Deferred bonus arrangements with equal instalments

Entity A awards its employees a cash bonus of C100. A third of the bonus will be paid at the end of year 1, a third paid at the end of year 2, and a third paid at the end of year 3 provided the employee in question is in employment with the entity on each payment date.

An entity could use the staged-vesting approach in this scenario as, in substance, the employee is working for three awards with different service periods. This means that a third of the bonus should be spread over year 1, a third spread over years 1 and 2, and the remaining third spread over years 1, 2, and 3. This will result in a front-loading of the charge.

It might also be appropriate to recognise the expense based on the bonus plan's benefit formula. This means that a third of the bonus expense would be recognised in each year, which is similar to straight-line attribution in this scenario.

Example 3 – Deferred bonus with a material instalment at end of vesting period

The facts are the same as in example 1 above, except that 25% of the bonus will vest and be paid in February 20X2 and the remaining 75% will vest and be paid at the end of 20X3 provided the employee remains working for the entity.

An entity could use the staged-vesting approach in this scenario as, in substance, the employee is working for two awards with different service periods. The bonus expense should be recognised for each instalment. This means that 25% of the bonus should be spread from 1 January 20X1 to 28 February 20X2 and the other 75% of the bonus should be spread from 1 January 20X1 to 31 December 20X3.

It might also be appropriate to recognise the expense based on the bonus plan's benefit formula. However, as mentioned above in paragraph 11.73.4, where benefits are materially higher in later years, the expense should be recognised over the vesting period on a straight-line basis. As the employees will receive 75% of their award at the end of year 3, this is considered materially higher in later years, therefore, the bonus expense should be recognised on a straight-line basis over the vesting period.

Example 4 – Deferred bonus arrangement that is recurring

Entity A grants members of its senior management a bonus of C20,000 payable at the end of each year for three years as part of their annual benefits package and contract of employment. The only condition is that the senior manager remains in employment. New joiners to the senior management may be invited to participate in the bonus arrangement during the period.

In our view, it is more appropriate to recognise the expense according to the plan's benefit formula. This is because the bonus is part of their annual benefits package and should be treated in a similar way to short-term benefits. Therefore, C20,000 should be recognised each year for three years.

However, there is an alternative approach where an entity could recognise a bonus expense based on a staged-vesting approach. This means that C20,000 is recognised in year 1, C20,000 is recognised over years 1 and 2, and the remaining C20,000 is spread over years 1, 2, and 3.

Modifications

11.74 Entities may replace cash bonus arrangements in the scope of IAS 19 with an equity settled share-based payment. For example, an annual bonus plan for 1 January 20X1 to 31 December 20X1 is changed in November 20X1 so that the 100% cash bonus will now be settled 50:50 between cash and shares. There is no clear guidance in IFRS as to how an entity should account for the change from an incentive scheme under IAS 19 to an equity-settled share-based payment arrangement under IFRS 2. This is also further complicated in situations where there is not only a classification change but also a modification of other vesting conditions (that is, extension of the vesting period). We believe three potential approaches are acceptable based on facts and circumstances.

11.74.1 One approach is for the entity to account for the modification to the vesting conditions before accounting for the change from an IAS 19 bonus arrangement to an IFRS 2 equity-settled arrangement. Under this approach, the entity would adjust the liability at the modification date for the new vesting conditions in accordance with IAS 19. This could lead to a negative past-service cost where the expense recognised to date is more than the expense that should be recognised after modifying the vesting conditions. The entity would then account for the change to an equity-settled share-based payment as a 'modification' following the principles of IFRS 2. The entity would immediately reclassify the amount recognised as a liability at the modification date to equity. The expense for the remainder of the vesting period of the share-based payment is based on the award's fair value, measured at the modification date, less amounts already recognised.

11.74.2 A second approach is for the entity to account for the change from an IAS 19 bonus arrangement to an IFRS 2 equity-settled arrangement before the modification of the vesting conditions. As noted above, following the principles of IFRS 2, the entity would immediately reclassify the amount recognised as a liability at the modification date to equity. Then, using the award's fair value measured at the modification date, the remaining expense should be recognised in accordance with IFRS 2's modification accounting. If a modification of vesting conditions is considered non-beneficial (that is, an extension of vesting period), the entity should continue to account for the original grant as if the modification had not occurred (that is, ignore any increase in the vesting period). See further guidance in chapter 12.

\ **11.74.3**   A third approach is to consider the exchange of the IAS 19 entitlement for a right to receive shares similarly to a settlement. In circumstances where the employee has a choice of whether to take cash or shares we consider this to be the most appropriate approach. Furthermore, where the bonus under IAS 19 is already vested it could be argued that this approach better reflects the facts and circumstances than the approaches in paragraphs 11.74.1 and 11.74.2 above. Under this approach, the entity would immediately reclassify the amount recognised as a liability at the modification date to equity and the remaining expense (that is, the balance of the fair value at the modification date) is recognised over the modified vesting period. This approach would include the earned IAS 19 benefit given up as part of the consideration for an IFRS 2 award.

11.74.4   The following example illustrates these principles.

Example – Modification to long-term benefit plan

An entity has an annual bonus scheme in place that pays cash bonuses to employees based on the entity's performance against profit targets. Due to economic conditions, the annual bonus scheme for 20X0 is changed in November 20X0 so that the 100% cash bonus is split 50:50 between cash and shares. Employees do not have a choice, and they would forfeit their shares if they did not continue to work for the entity for an additional three year period after the 20X0 year end.

The fair value of the award was C120,000 at the modification date (that is, 30 November 20X0). On the basis of the original terms as at the end of November 20X0, C110,000 would have been recognised as an expense.

Under one approach, the entity would account for the modification to the vesting period before the change in classification to an equity-settled share-based payment. The following entries would be recorded:

At modification date

Dr Liability	55,000		(reverse 50% of the accrued liability as it will now be accrued over a longer period and settled in shares)
Cr Income statement		41,250	(true up expense based on modified vesting period – 11/48 months × C60,000 less C55,000 already recognised)
Cr Equity		13,750	

The remaining expense of C46,250 (fair value at modification of C60,000 less amount already recognised of C13,750) should be recognised straight-line over the remaining vesting period of 37 months. The entity would, therefore, record the following entry each month for 37 months:

Dr Income statement	1,250	
Cr Equity		1,250

To recognise the share-based payment expense each month (C60,000/48).

A second approach is for the entity to account for the classification change to an equity-settled share-based payment before the extension of the vesting period. In this scenario, the extension of the vesting period would be treated as a non-beneficial modification in accordance with IFRS 2 and, therefore, would be ignored. The following entries would be recorded:

At modification date

Dr Liability	55,000	
Cr Equity		55,000

To reclassify 50% of the accrued liability to equity.

The remaining expense of C5,000 (fair value at modification of C60,000 less amount already recognised of C55,000) should be recognised over the original vesting period of one year. The entity would, therefore, record the following entry for the remaining month:

Dr Income statement	5,000	
Cr Equity		5,000

A third approach is for the entity to account for the classification change to an equity-settled share-based payment as a settlement of the accrued liability. In this scenario, the extended vesting period would be treated as in substance a new award under IFRS 2. The following entries would be recorded:

At modification date

Dr Liability	55,000	
Cr Equity		55,000

To reclassify 50% of the accrued liability to equity.

The remaining expense of C5,000 (fair value at 'grant date' of C60,000 less amount of C55,000 already recognised which is effectively treated as consideration for the share-based payment) should be recognised over the remaining revised vesting period of 37 months. The entity would, therefore, record the following entry each month for 37 months:

Dr Income statement	135	
Cr Equity		135

To recognise the share-based payment expense each month (C5,000/37).

Long-term disability

11.75 Long-term disability is not a termination benefit as defined in paragraph 11.79. IAS 19 is explicit that long-term disability benefits should be accounted for in accordance with the principles used for other long-term employee benefits described in paragraph 11.73 above.

Example 1 – Lump-sum disability payments

Entity A pays, in accordance with a trade union agreement, a lump-sum of C10,000 to an employee who becomes disabled as a result of an accident. This payment is the same regardless of the length of service.

Entity B pays, in accordance with its trade union agreement, a lump-sum of C10,000 to an employee who becomes disabled as a result of an accident within the first 5 years of employment and C20,000 if the employee becomes disabled after 5 years of employment.

The future cash outflow of entity A does not depend on past employee service. In accordance with paragraph 130 of IAS 19, no accruals should be made by entity A until the occurrence of an accident that causes the disability of an employee.

The level of benefits of entity B's employees depends on the length of employee service. An obligation arises when service is rendered. [IAS 19 para 130]. Entity B's obligation should be measured using the projected unit credit method. It should reflect the probability that payments will be required and the length of service (that is amount) for which payments are expected to be made.

Example 2 – Disability payments covered by an insurance policy

Legislation requires an entity to provide compensation to employees whose disability was caused by injuries at work.

Entity A, a construction group, has decided to cover its exposure to disability compensation payments by taking out an insurance policy with one of the world's largest insurance entities. The insurance premium is payable monthly. The amount of disability payment does not vary based on years of service and is paid out to the employee as an annuity rather than a lump sum. The insurance policy can only be used to pay the disability benefits and is not available to the entity's own creditors even in the event of bankruptcy. The proceeds from the policy cannot be paid to the entity unless they represent surplus assets. Entity A recognises the insurance premium as an expense when incurred. When an event occurs that causes a long-term disability, entity A recognises an expense for the disability payments. Since the level of benefit does not vary based on years of service, the obligation only arises when the disability occurs. Entity A also recognises income that reflects the claim due under the insurance policy. The net impact on profit or loss will be the expense related to the insurance premium. Another way of looking at this is to view the insurance premium as purchasing a qualifying insurance policy that, under paragraph 104 is measured as being equal to the insured liability, such that the asset and liability are netted off.

[The next paragraph is paragraph 11.77.]

Disclosure

11.77 IAS 19 does not require specific disclosure in respect of benefits payable during employment. However, other standards may require disclosure, for example:

- IAS 1 requires disclosure of employee benefits expense (see chapter 4).

- IAS 24 requires disclosure of employee benefits payable to key management personnel (see chapter 29).

11.78 Disclosure of the accounting policies for benefits payable during employment is not commonplace. This is to be expected in the case of wages and salaries, but it is surprising that there is not more widespread disclosure of policies for items such as holiday pay and long-term bonuses. Two examples of companies that disclose their policy for benefits payable during employment are given below. The third example below gives extracts that deal with annual leave and bonuses taken from a company that gives comprehensive disclosures on aspects of its employee benefits.

Table 11.2 – Accounting policy for benefits payable during employment

Roche Holding Ltd – annual report & group accounts – 31 December 2011

1. Summary of significant accounting policies (extract)

Employee benefits

Wages, salaries, social security contributions, paid annual leave and sick leave, bonuses, and non-monetary benefits are accrued in the year in which the associated services are rendered by employees of the Group. Where the Group provides long-term employee benefits, the cost is accrued to match the rendering of the services by the employees concerned. Liabilities for long-term employee benefits are discounted to take into account the time value of money, where material.

Table 11.3 – Accounting policy for benefits payable during employment

Barloworld Limited – annual report – 30 September 2011

Accounting policies (extract)

21. Employee benefit costs

The cost of providing employee benefits is accounted for in the period in which the benefits are earned by employees.

The cost of short-term employee benefits is recognised in the period in which the service is rendered and is not discounted. The expected cost of short-term accumulating compensated absences is recognised as an expense as the employees render service that increases their entitlement or, in the case of non-accumulating absences, when the absences occur.

The expected cost of profit-sharing and bonus payments is recognised as an expense when there is a legal or constructive obligation to make such payments as a result of past performance and a reliable estimate of the obligation can be made.

Table 11.4 – Annual leave and bonus policies and disclosure

Telkom SA Limited – annual report – 31 March 2009

2. SIGNFICANT ACCOUNTING POLICIES (extract)

Employee benefits (extract)

Leave benefits
Annual leave entitlement is provided for over the period that the leave accrues and is subject to a cap of 22 days.

Deferred bonus incentives
Employees of the wholly owned subsidiaries of Vodacom, including executive directors, are eligible for compensation benefits in the form of a Deferred Bonus Incentive Scheme. The benefit is recorded at the present value of the expected future cash outflows.

Short-term employee benefits
The cost of all short-term employee benefits is recognised during the year the employees render services, unless the Group uses the services of employees in the construction of an asset and the benefits received meet the recognition criteria of an asset, at which stage it is included as part of the related property, plant and equipment or intangible asset item.

Long-term incentive provision
The Vodacom Group provides long-term incentives to eligible employees payable on termination or retirement. The Group's liability is based on an actuarial valuation. Actuarial gains and losses are recognised as employee expenses.

	2007 Rm	2008 Rm	2009 Rm
29. PROVISIONS (extract)			
Annual leave	413	438	**428**
Balance at beginning of year	356	413	**438**
Transferred to disposal groups	–	–	**(67)**
Charged to employee expenses	66	44	**72**
Leave paid	(9)	(19)	**(15)**
Bonus	1,090	992	**671**
Balance at beginning of year	1,071	1,090	**992**
Transferred to disposal groups	–	–	**(397)**
Charged to employee expenses	965	797	**577**
Payment made	(946)	(895)	**(501)**
Long-term incentive provision	81	113	**–**
Balance at beginning of year	61	81	113
Transferred to disposal groups	–	–	**(113)**
Charged to employee expenses	21	41	–
Payment	(1)	(9)	–

Annual leave
In terms of Telkom's policy, employees are entitled to accumulate vested leave benefits not taken within a leave cycle, to a cap of 22 days which must be taken within an 18 month leave cycle. The leave cycle is reviewed annually and is in accordance with legislation.

Bonus
The Telkom bonus scheme consists of performance bonuses which are dependent on achievement of certain financial and non-financial targets. The bonus is to all qualifying employees payable bi-annually after Telkom's results have been made public.

Termination benefits

11.79   Termination benefits are benefits payable as a result of either:

- an employer's decision to terminate an employee's employment before the normal retirement date; or
- an employee's decision to accept voluntary redundancy in exchange for those benefits.

[IAS 19 para 7].

11.80   In broad terms, termination benefits are amounts payable when an employee ceases to work for an employer. In this context they are similar to post-employment benefits, such as pensions. However, whereas post-employment benefits are earned throughout an employee's working life, termination benefits arise as a result of an event, such as a factory closure. The event that gives rise to an obligation is the termination, rather than employee service. Termination benefits are not earned in a literal sense, although their magnitude may be set by reference to an employee's period of service.

11.81   Typically termination benefits comprise lump sum payments, although they could take other forms such as retention of a company car. Termination benefits also include:

- Pension enhancements.
- 'Gardening leave'. That is, salary until the end of a specified notice period during which the employee renders no further service.

[IAS 19 para 135].

[The next paragraph is 11.83.]

11.83   The excerpts below disclose an accounting policy for termination benefits. It also has other statutory termination benefits (leaving service gratuities) that are earned over employees' working lives, which are treated as post-employment benefits, and jubilee plan benefits, which are treated as other long term benefits. The distinction between termination benefits and post-employment benefits is explored further in the paragraphs that follow.

Table 11.5 – Termination benefits

Coca-Cola Hellenic Bottling Company SA – annual report – 31 December 2011

1. Basis of preparation and accounting policies (extract)

Termination benefits

Termination benefits are payable whenever an employee's employment is terminated before the normal retirement date or whenever an employee accepts voluntary redundancy in exchange for these benefits. The Group recognises termination benefits when it is demonstrably committed to either terminate the employment of current employees or to provide termination benefits as a result of an offer made to encourage voluntary redundancy.

Employee benefits

The Group operates a number of defined benefit and defined contribution pension plans in its territories.

The defined benefit plans are made up of both funded and unfunded pension plans and employee leaving indemnities. The assets of funded plans are generally held in separate trustee-administered funds and are financed by payments from employees and/or the relevant Group companies.

The liability recognised in the balance sheet in respect of defined benefit plans is the present value of the defined benefit obligation at the balance sheet date less the fair value of the plan assets, together with adjustments for unrecognised past service costs. The value of any defined benefit asset recognised is restricted to the sum of any past service costs and the present value of any economic benefits available in the form of refunds from the plan or reductions in the future contributions to the plan.

For defined benefit pension plans, pension costs are assessed using the projected unit credit method. Actuarial gains and losses are recognised in full in the period in which they occur in other comprehensive income. Such actuarial gains and losses are also immediately recognised in retained earnings and are not reclassified to the income statement in subsequent periods. The defined benefit obligations are measured at the present value of the estimated future cash outflows using interest rates of corporate or government bonds, depending on whether or not there is a deep market for corporate bonds in the relevant country, which have terms to maturity approximating the terms of the related liability. Past service cost is recognised immediately to the extent that the benefits are already vested and otherwise are amortised over the remaining vesting period.

A number of the Group's operations have other long service benefits in the form of jubilee plans. These plans are measured at the present value of the estimated future cash outflows with immediate recognition of actuarial gains and losses.

The Group's contributions to the defined contribution pension plans are charged to the income statement in the period to which the contributions relate.

17. Provisions (extract)

Employee benefits

Employee benefits consisted of the following at 31 December:

	2011 € million	2010 € million	2009 € million
Defined benefit plans			
Employee leaving indemnities	**94.6**	99.4	113.4
Pension plans	**41.4**	19.5	25.0
Long service benefits—jubilee plans	**7.9**	7.7	7.0
Total defined benefits plans	**143.9**	**126.6**	**145.4**
Other employee benefits			
Annual leave	**9.2**	9.6	6.7
Stock appreciation rights	**–**	0.1	1.2
Other employee benefits	**17.3**	16.6	20.3
Total other employee benefits	**26.5**	**26.3**	**28.2**
Total employee benefits obligations	**170.4**	**152.9**	**173.6**

Employee benefit obligations at 31 December were split between current and non-current as follows:

	2011 € million	2010 € million	2009 € million
Current	**23.9**	22.4	22.5
Non-current	**146.5**	130.5	151.1
Total employee benefits obligations	**170.4**	**152.9**	**173.6**

Employees of Coca-Cola Hellenic's subsidiaries in Austria, Bulgaria, Croatia, Greece, Italy, Montenegro, Nigeria, Poland, Romania, Serbia and Slovenia are entitled to employee leaving indemnities, generally based on each employee's length of service, employment category and remuneration.

Coca-Cola Hellenic's subsidiaries in Austria, Greece, Northern Ireland, the Republic of Ireland and Switzerland sponsor defined benefit pension plans. Of the three plans in the Republic of Ireland, two have plan assets, as do the two plans in Northern Ireland, one plan in Greece and one plan in Switzerland. The Austrian plans do not have plan assets.

Coca-Cola Hellenic provides long service benefits in the form of jubilee plans to its employees in Austria, Croatia, Nigeria, Poland, Slovenia and Switzerland.

11.84 It will often, but not always, be clear from the facts whether a benefits package represents a termination benefit or a post-employment benefit. Paragraph 136 of IAS 19 acknowledges this potential difficulty and draws a distinction between the two types of benefit. The following examples illustrate the distinction.

> ### Example 1 – Statutory payments to employees leaving after five years service
>
> Entity A operates in country C. Local labour laws require that payments are made to employees leaving the entity for any reason after five years' service. The amounts payable are determined by reference to final salary and length of service. Benefits will, therefore, be payable to the workforce, but these will not be termination benefits as defined in IAS 19. This is because the benefits are earned during an employees' working life and the entity is obliged to pay them regardless of the reason for the employee's departure so, if the employee works for entity A for at least five years, only the timing of the payment is uncertain. Hence, these benefits are treated as post-employment benefits and accounted for as specified from paragraph 11.127 below (see also Table 11.6 above for examples both of statutory termination benefits that are accounted for as a defined benefit plan and of termination payments as defined in IAS 19 that are accounted for as specified in the section 'Recognition' below).

> ### Example 2 – Voluntary redundancy payments
>
> Entity B also operates in country C and is subject to the same labour laws. However, in connection with a voluntary redundancy programme, entity B has agreed to make additional payments to those employees who accept the offer of voluntary redundancy. These additional payments will represent termination benefits as defined in IAS 19 as the entity had no obligation to make the payments until it made the decision to instigate the voluntary redundancy programme.

11.85 Sometimes it can be difficult to decide whether a particular benefit should be classified as a termination benefit or a post-employment benefit. As a guide, termination benefits generally have three characteristics:

- The benefits are offered for a clearly defined period.

- There is no legal or constructive obligation on the employer to extend the closing date, although extensions might be made, at the employer's discretion. Repeated practice of doing this is likely to establish a constructive obligation.

- There is no linking of the amount of the benefit to length of future service.

[The next paragraph is 11.87.]

Recognition

11.87 The principles for recognition of termination benefits are consistent with those of IAS 37 (see chapter 21). A liability should be recognised when an entity has a demonstrable commitment, which may be legal, contractual or constructive, to either:

- terminate the employment of an employee or group of employees before the normal retirement date; or

- provide termination benefits as a result of an offer made in order to encourage voluntary redundancy.

[IAS 19 para 133].

11.88 A demonstrable commitment exists when, and only when, the reporting entity is committed (without realistic possibility of withdrawal) to a detailed formal plan for the termination specifying:

- The location, function and approximate number of employees whose services are to be terminated.

- The termination benefits for each job classification or function.

- The timescale for implementation of the plan. Implementation should begin as soon as possible and the period of time to complete implementation should be such that material changes to the plan are unlikely.

[IAS 19 para 134].

Although there is no explicit requirement in IAS 19 for the plan to be communicated to those affected, (or their representative, union or regulatory body) there is such a requirement in IAS 37 and it should be presumed in order for a demonstrable commitment to exist.

11.89 A pre-requisite for making a provision under IAS 37 is that a reliable estimate of the amount of the obligation can be made. [IAS 37 para 14(c)]. Where this is not possible, and such circumstances are expected to be extremely rare, the obligation is treated as a contingent liability. [IAS 37 para 26]. IAS 19 is silent on this subject, although there is a reference to the disclosure that may be necessary where there is uncertainty about the number of employees who will accept an offer of termination benefits. This implies that the normal IAS 37 principles will apply and a provision for termination benefits should be made only where a reliable estimate can be made.

11.90 The following example illustrates the above principles.

Example – Redundancies following restructuring

The board of an entity has announced two major restructuring plans and, in both cases, has communicated details of the redundancy package to the staff affected:

- Sale of half of the entity's global manufacturing business over a three-year period, starting immediately. This will involve the immediate redundancy of 15% of the machine workers in each factory and 10% of the middle management at each location.

- Re-organisation of the head office over a one-year period, commencing in two years' time. 20% of the head office staff will lose their jobs during the restructuring.

As regards the sale of the manufacturing business, a provision should be recognised for the estimated costs of the disposal and redundancy. The sites and details of the redundancy and other costs, have been identified. The scale and complexity of the disposal requires that it be completed over an extended period. Disposal activities will begin immediately. Three years is the time necessary to complete the disposal and should not prevent the provision from being recognised. See chapter 21, where the requirements of IAS 37 are discussed in more detail. In some cases, chapter 26 on IFRS 5 may also be relevant.

In contrast, the entity should not recognise a provision for the head office's re-organisation. The re-organisation is not due to start for two years. External parties are unlikely to have a valid expectation that management is committed to the restructuring, because the timeframe allows significant opportunities for management to change the details of the plan or even to decide not to continue with it. Additionally, the degree of identification of the staff to lose their jobs is not sufficient to support recognising a redundancy provision. Details of the departments within head office that will be affected should be identified, together with the approximate numbers of staff from each department.

Measurement

11.91 An obligation to pay termination benefits should be measured according to the principles of IAS 19. Accordingly, the amount recognised as a provision should be measured at the expected amount to be paid, subject to discounting, if the amount is due to be paid more than 12 months after the balance sheet date. Discounting in relation to pension plans is discussed from paragraph 11.174. In the case of an offer made to encourage voluntary redundancy, this best estimate will be based on the number of employees expected to accept the offer. [IAS 19 para 140].

11.92 If payment of termination benefits falls due more than 12 months after the balance sheet date, the amount should be discounted using a high-quality corporate bond rate, the currency and term of which are consistent with the obligation to pay benefits. [IAS 19 para 139]. This requirement is different to the principle for measuring other provisions as set out in IAS 37. That standard requires that the discount rate should be a rate that *"reflects current market assessments of the time value of money and the risks specific to the liability"*. [IAS 37 para 47]. This could mean that in measuring the obligations arising from a restructuring programme, a reporting entity will use one discount rate for employee termination benefits and another for other long term obligations that fall within the scope of IAS 37 rather than IAS 19. Furthermore, IAS 19 requires the use of discounting in respect of all payments falling due more than 12 months after the balance sheet date, whereas IAS 37 requires the use of discounting only where the effect of the time value of money is material.

> **Example 1 – Voluntary redundancy payment with a time limit**
>
> Entity A restructures its operations in a particular location. It agrees with trade unions during December 20X3 a plan to reduce staff numbers in that location by 100 by February 20X4. Management communicated an offer of C5,000 for voluntary redundancy by the end of January 20X4. If sufficient staff do not accept the offer, management will terminate the employment of additional staff to reach the target of 100. Employees terminated involuntarily are entitled to a termination payment of C4,000 each.

Management estimate at 31 December 20X3 that 60 employees will accept the voluntary termination within the stated time.

A liability should be recognised at 31 December 20X3. Management should recognise a provision for termination benefits of C460,000 (40 employees x C4,000 plus 60 employees x C5,000). The contingent liability of C40,000 for the additional amount that would be payable if the maximum number of employees accepted the termination voluntarily should also be disclosed.

The measurement of voluntary termination benefits should be based on the number of employees expected to accept the offer.

Example 2 – Use of discount rate

Entity A's management has decided to make 250 staff redundant within the next year. However, the costs of the redundancy will arise over a longer period and are expected to be C20 million, payable as C8 million in one year's time and C12 million in two year's time.

The market yield for high-quality corporate bonds at 31 December 20X1 is 5.5%.

Management should recognise the cost of the redundancy provision at the present value of the future cash flows of C18,364,360:

	Year 1	Year 2	Total
Cash flows	C8,000,000	C12,000,000	C20,000,000
Discount factor (5.5%)	0.94787	0.89845	
Present value of cash flows	C7,582,960	C10,781,400	C18,364,360
Interest expense			C1,635,640

The difference between the undiscounted cash flows and their present value of C1,635,640 will be recognised in the income statement over years 1 and 2 as the discount accretes.

Disclosure

11.93 IAS 19 contains no specific disclosure requirements relating to termination benefits. Instead, reference is made to the requirements of other standards. For example, disclosure may be required:

- In accordance with IAS 37 (see chapter 21) – which requires disclosure of the carrying amount, movement in the period and other information relating to the provision.

- In accordance with IAS 1 (see chapter 4) – where the expense is of such size, nature or incidence that disclosure is relevant to explain performance.

- In accordance with IAS 24 (see chapter 29) – where the termination benefits are payable to key management.

An example of disclosure of a termination programme is given below.

Table 11.7.1 – Early termination plan disclosures

Peugeot S.A. – Report and accounts – 31 December 2005

Note 29 – Early-termination plan

29.1. Internal agreements
Internal agreements have been signed between the Group and employee representatives in France, concerning the implementation of early-termination plans. The plans in question fulfil the criteria laid down in Decree no. 2000-105 dated February 9, 2000 related to the early termination of certain employees over 55 years of age and qualify for government financing covering part of the cost.

A. Automobile Division
An early-termination plan has been set up for Automobile Division employees in France, in application of an internal agreement dated March 4, 1999 and an industry-wide agreement signed on July 26, 1999 by UIMM (the industry federation) with the support of the majority of trade unions represented within the Group.

B. Automotive Equipment Division
Following further negotiations between UIMM and the trade unions in March 2001, the plan was extended to additional companies, including the Faurecia group.

29.2. Estimated liability
A. Calculation method
The estimated cost to be financed by the Group corresponds to the total benefits payable to the employees concerned, net of government funding. The present value of the liability has been calculated by applying a discount rate of 3% and an inflation rate of 2%.

B. Change in estimated liability

(in millions of euros)	Dec 31, 2005	Dec 31, 2004
At January 1	**345**	**423**
Early-termination costs for the year	(108)	(102)
Change in the number of employees concerned	(6)	(8)
Discounting adjustment	2	32
At December 31	**233**	**345**

The €4 million net gain reflects the cumulative effects of headcount restructuring, amounting to €6 million, and a discounting charge of €2 million. The €108 million release from the provision in respect of early-termination costs for the year is offset by a charge corresponding to the Group's contribution to the UNEDIC Fund responsible for paying benefits, less the sums received from the State to help finance early-termination measures.

C. Number of employees concerned
At December 31, 2005, 9,599 employees were concerned by the plans, including 471 Faurecia group employees.

29.3. PROJECTED 2006 BENEFIT PAYMENTS
Benefits payable to employees who are expected to leave the Group in 2006 under the early-termination plan are estimated at €87 million.

Post-employment benefits

11.94 Post-employment benefits are defined in IAS 19 in very simple terms as *"employee benefits (other than termination benefits) which are payable after the completion of employment"*. [IAS 19 para 7]. The most common type of post-employment benefit is a pension, although post-retirement health care is also common in some countries.

Death-in-service benefits

11.95   If a benefit is earned during the employee's working life, the recognition and measurement principles applied to defined benefit pension plans will be appropriate.

11.96   Paragraph 67(b) of IAS 19 requires attribution of the cost of the benefits until the date *"when further service by the employee will lead to no material amount of further benefits under the plan, other than from further salary increases"*. In January 2008 the IFRS IC noted that:

- The anticipated date of death (that is, the date assumed for actuarial purposes) would be the date at which no material amount of further benefit would arise from the plan.

- Using different mortality assumptions for a defined pension plan and an associated death-in-service benefit would not comply with the requirement in paragraph 72 of IAS 19 to use actuarial assumptions that are mutually compatible.

- If the conditions in paragraph 39 of IAS 19 were met, then accounting for death-in-service benefits on a defined contribution basis would be appropriate.

It is our view that, where death-in-service benefits form part of a defined benefit pension plan, they must be measured as part of the actuarial assumptions (and, hence, factored into the valuation of the defined benefit plan liabilities) and attributed to periods of service using the projected unit credit method. They cannot be separated from the plan of which they are a part.

UK.11.96.1   The conclusion in paragraph 11.96 is consistent with the UK GAAP treatment as set out in UITF Abstract 35.

11.97   Sometimes, employers insure their death-in-service and disability obligations. If this is the case, such that the employer has transferred all risks and obligations to the insurer, the cost of providing benefits is represented by the payment of insurance premiums. In substance, such death-in-service and disability arrangements are treated as defined contribution pension plans. Insured pension plans are considered further from paragraph 11.121. However, it is important to note that generally for death benefits the insurance cover is only for a limited period, normally one year, so that the employer (or the plan trustees) have a choice each year whether or not to insure. This means that the decision whether to insure is an investment choice. In addition, when this choice has been made the employer has not transferred all risks and obligations to the insurer.

Types of pension plan

UK.11.97.1 There are three basic types of pension arrangements that are common in many countries:

- The state plan.

- Occupational pension plans.

- Personal pension plans.

UK.11.97.2 The state plan in the UK consists of two elements, the basic pension and the earnings related pension. All employers and employees make contributions towards the state plan through their national insurance payments. Those who are members of the earnings related scheme, known as the State Second Pension (S2P), make additional national insurance contributions. It is possible to 'contract out' of S2P either through an occupational pension plan or through a personal pension.

UK.11.97.3 In a contracted out occupational plan, both employer and employee pay a lower rate of national insurance contributions. The occupational plan is then used to provide employees with benefits that replace part of their state earnings related benefits. The broad intention is that the pension provided by a contracted out plan is at least as good as the pension that would have been available from S2P. On retirement, the employee receives a state basic pension and a pension from the occupational plan.

UK.11.97.4 Occupational pension plans are not required to contract out of S2P and many do not. Where a plan is 'contracted in' to S2P, employer and employee pay the full rate of national insurance contributions. The responsibility for payment of S2P remains with the state. On retirement, the employee receives a state basic and earnings related pension, together with a pension from the occupational plan.

UK.11.97.5 Personal pension plans are pension arrangements available to individuals.

[The next paragraph is 11.100.]

11.100 Accounting for the cost of providing pension benefits is particularly affected by the type of benefits that are promised by a plan and by the way in which the employer's obligations in respect of such benefits are funded. The broad classifications used in pensions terminology are summarised in the following paragraphs. Each involves a cost to the employer wherever it is obliged to contribute towards the cost of the benefits receivable by its employees or their dependants.

Defined contribution plans

11.101　Defined contribution plans (often referred to as money purchase plans) are pension plans where the level of benefits depends on the value of contributions paid in respect of each member and the investment performance achieved on those contributions. Normally, the rate of contribution to be paid by the employer will be specified in the plan's rules. Therefore, the employer's liability is limited to the contributions it has agreed to pay. The employee takes both the actuarial risk (that benefits will be less than expected) and the investment risk – if the investments have performed well the individual will obtain a higher pension than if the investments have performed badly. IAS 19 does not require plan assets to be segregated into individual accounts.

11.102　IAS 19 defines defined contribution plans as *"post-employment benefit plans under which an entity pays fixed contributions into a separate entity (a fund) and will have no legal or constructive obligation to pay further contributions if the fund does not hold sufficient assets to pay all employee benefits relating to employee service in the current and prior periods"*. [IAS 19 para 7].

Defined benefit plans

11.103　Defined benefit plans are pension plans where the rules specify the benefits to be paid and they are financed accordingly. The majority of these plans define benefits in relation to an employee's salary. Often the pension will be based on a percentage of final salary for each year of pensionable service. Another form of defined benefit plan that is becoming increasingly common is the average salary plan where the pension is calculated by reference to average pay over an extended period. In most defined benefit plans the risk of poor investment performance lies fully with the sponsoring company. However, in some circumstances plans will include provisions that call for participants to share in a portion of the potential funding requirements. Such arrangements are discussed later in this chapter (see further para 11.179).

11.104　Under IAS 19, defined benefit plans are the residual category. They are defined as *"post-employment benefit plans other than defined contribution plans"*. [IAS 19 para 7].

Distinguishing defined contribution plans and defined benefit plans

11.105　IAS 19 considers all pension plans to be defined benefit plans, unless the criteria for treatment as defined contribution plans are satisfied. Hence, a plan will be a defined benefit plan unless the employer's legal or constructive obligation is limited to the amount that it agrees to contribute to the plan. The following are examples of situations where the employer's obligation is not limited and the plans are, therefore, defined benefit plans.

■　The plan's benefit formula is not linked solely to the amount of contributions.

Employee benefits

- The entity, either indirectly through a plan or directly, guarantees a specified return on contributions.

- Informal practices give rise to a constructive obligation, for example where the employer has a history of increasing benefits to keep pace with inflation.

[IAS 19 para 26].

Example 1 – Unfunded overseas scheme

Entity E plc has a subsidiary overseas, entity F, in a territory where there is a legal requirement for an employer to provide a 'salary' to retired employees based on the duration of their service to the company and their salary during the period of employment. In accordance with local GAAP, entity F makes an accrual at each year end that is calculated by reference to the employees' service and salaries to date (that is, it represents an estimate of net present value of the amount that entity F would have to pay if all employees retired at the end of the year). Changes in the accrual are reflected in the income statement. Do such schemes fall within IAS 19's scope?

The IAS 19 definition of post-employment benefits includes any consideration given by an employer in exchange for employees' services that is payable after the completion of employment (other than termination benefits). The 'salary' above falls within IAS 19's scope and is a defined benefit pension plan. The defined benefit obligation should be calculated in accordance with IAS 19 using the projected unit credit method: the local GAAP accrual is unlikely to be appropriate.

Example 2 – Voluntary enhancements to state pension benefits

The national pensions authority administers a state pension plan in country X. Mandatory contributions from employers fund the plan on a pay-as-you-go basis. Pension legislation determines the minimum benefits paid to each employee when they retire and the national pensions authority sets annual employer contributions at the level required to meet expected pension obligations in the same period. Employers have no obligation to the state pension plan beyond their annual contributions, but the legislation permits employers to voluntarily enhance the state pension benefits paid to their former employees.

Entity A operates in country X and pays annual contributions to the state pension plan on behalf of all its employees. Entity A has elected to enhance the benefits received by certain classes of employee:

(a) Entity A makes annual payments to an insurance entity equal to 5% of the salary of each employee based overseas. The insurance policy matures when the employee retires and the employee must use the proceeds to purchase additional post-retirement benefits. Entity A has no obligation to the employee or the insurance company beyond the annual payment.

(b) The employment contracts of management grade employees state that their pension will be at least 1% of final salary for each year of service. Entity A will pay to each retired employee each year an amount equal to the difference between the guaranteed benefit and the state pension. Entity A has no obligation if the state pension is greater than the guaranteed benefit.

The arrangement's substance determines the accounting treatment applied to the different components of the pension plan.

Employers fund the basic state pension on a pay-as-you-go basis and entity A has no obligation to pay benefits beyond its annual contribution. The state takes actuarial and investment risk. Therefore, this is a defined contribution plan. [IAS 19 para 38].

Employees based overseas receive additional benefits based on the proceeds of an insurance policy. Entity A has no obligation beyond paying the annual insurance premium. The insurance company takes the investment risk and the employee takes the actuarial risk. This is also a defined contribution arrangement. [IAS 19 para 39].

Management grade employees receive a pension equivalent to 1% of their final salary for each year of service. Entity A has a contractual obligation to make a top-up payment to former employees when the state pension is less than the guaranteed minimum pension. Entity A has the investment risk and the actuarial risk. This is a defined benefit arrangement and the company should recognise a pension liability for the additional benefit, that is, the amount of any shortfall where the guaranteed benefit is greater than the state pension.

The substance of each component of a pension plan determines the accounting treatment. Different components of the same plan might have a different accounting treatment.

Example 3 – Pension plan with guaranteed interest

An entity provides a pension plan with the following characteristics:

- The employees contribute 3% of their salaries to the plan.

- Entity A's contribution matches the employees' contribution.

- The retirement age is 65.

- The employee's account balance consists of accumulated contributions, credited with interest guaranteed by the employer at 4% per year.

Under this arrangement, the entity has the investment risk that the return from assets invested will be less than the guaranteed return. The entity's obligation is not limited to the amount that it agrees to contribute [IAS 19 para 26b]. Although the entity may anticipate that the fund's investment returns will exceed the guaranteed rate of 4%, there is a risk that investment returns will fall short and the employer will be required to make additional contributions. This is, therefore, a defined benefit plan.

11.106 Some plans contain features of both defined contribution and defined benefit plans. IAS 19 requires that such plans are categorised as either defined contribution or defined benefit according to their substance. IAS 19 is clear that all plans fall into one category or the other and default to defined benefit, if they fail to meet the defined contribution definition. The consideration of substance therefore has little impact in practice. For example, a plan may provide money purchase benefits, but with a guaranteed level of benefit based on a proportion of final salary. If investments perform satisfactorily the employer will have no obligation in excess of the contributions it has agreed to make. This would suggest treatment as a defined contribution plan. However, as the employer bears downside investment risk and may be required to make further contributions in order for the plan to fulfil its final salary guarantee, the plan should be accounted for as a defined benefit plan. The promise of a particular level of return means that the sponsoring entity may have to make additional contributions to the plan. Accordingly, the criteria for treatment as defined contribution (see para 11.102) are not met so plans such as these are to be treated as defined benefit plans.

Funded plans

11.107 Funded post-employment benefit plans are plans where the future liabilities for benefits are provided for in advance by the accumulation of assets held externally to the employing company's business, or through a qualifying insurance policy.

> **UK.11.107.1** In the UK, plan assets are usually placed under the control of trustees, who administer the plan in accordance with the provisions of trust law and the terms of the trust deed governing the particular plan. Employer and employee contributions paid to the trust are invested by the trustees; pensions are paid out of the accumulated funds of the trust. Most funded plans in the UK that are established under trusts enjoy considerable tax benefits through Inland Revenue recognition as exempt approved plans. However, the Finance Act 1989 introduced an upper limit on the amount of salary that may be taken into account for pension purposes (the 'earnings cap'). In response, many employers established unapproved plans to run alongside existing exempt approved plans. Unapproved plans can provide unlimited benefits and are mainly used to provide 'top-up' pensions for higher paid employees whose pensionable earnings in the exempt approved plan are capped. Unapproved arrangements, which may be funded or unfunded, do not enjoy the tax benefits that apply to exempt approved plans. For example, investment gains will suffer capital gains tax.

[The next paragraph is 11.109.]

Unfunded plans

11.109 Unfunded post-employment benefit plans are plans where no assets are set aside in advance to provide for future liabilities; instead pension liabilities are met out of the employer's own resources as they fall due.

> **UK.11.109.1** In the UK, unfunded plans are uncommon in the private sector, but are found in the public sector. The 'earnings cap' introduced by the Finance Act 1989 (and removed in April 2006) led to an increase in unfunded plans, particularly for higher paid executives.

Multi-employer and state plans

11.110 Some employers participate in industry-wide pension plans, which provide centralised pension arrangements for identifiable groups of unrelated employers. Similarly, some employers contribute to state or public sector pension plans. Sometimes each employer has its own separate fund within the plan. However, where this is not the case the extent of each individual employer's obligations may not be clear.

11.111 IAS 19 defines a multi-employer plan as a plan, other than a state plan, that:

■ pools the assets contributed by various entities that are not under common control; and

■ uses those assets to provide benefits to employees of more than one entity, on the basis that contribution and benefit levels are determined without regard to the identity of the entity that employs the employees concerned.

[IAS 19 para 7].

11.112 State plans, on the other hand, are established by legislation to cover all entities (or all entities in a particular category, for example a specific industry) and are operated by national or local government or by another body (for example, an autonomous agency created specifically for this purpose) which is not subject to control or influence by the reporting entity. [IAS 19 para 37].

11.113 The distinction between a multi-employer plan and a state plan is somewhat academic as IAS 19 currently requires that they are treated in the same way. [IAS 19 para 36].

11.114 Multi-employer plans are distinct from group administration plans, although in practice the terms may be used together. A group administration plan is merely an aggregation of single employer plans combined to allow participating employers to pool their assets for investment purposes and reduce investment management and administration costs, but the claims of different employers are segregated for the sole benefit of their own employees. Group administration plans pose no particular accounting problems as they do not expose the participating entities to actuarial risks associated with the current and former employees of other entities and information is readily available to treat them in the same way as any other single employer plan.

Example – Industry-wide multi-employer plans

Entity A participates in two trustee-administered pension plans that provide centralised pension arrangements for employees throughout the industry. A large number of unrelated employers participate in the plans to provide pension benefits for their employees. Entity A's employees can be members of either plan, but not both. Entity A contributes to each plan in accordance with the trustees' instructions.

Plan one accumulates the contributions made in respect of each employee in a separate account. The trustees use the accumulated contributions, together with the related investment income, to purchase an annuity for each employee at retirement. Entity A has no obligation to plan one beyond its annual contribution.

Plan two pays benefits based on final salary and years of service. The employers fund plan two's pension obligations by contributing to an independent trust. The trustees estimate the pension funding requirements to set the annual contribution. Entity A has an obligation to fund plan two based on the decisions made by the trustees, which will take into consideration the actual experience of the plan.

Entity A should classify multi-employer plans as defined benefit plans or defined contribution plans by reference to the economic substance of the arrangements. [IAS 19 para 29].

Plan one is a multi-employer plan. The plan pools assets contributed by various unrelated entities and provides benefits to the employees of more than one entity. Entity A has no obligation to plan one or its employees beyond its annual contribution. The employees take the actuarial and investment risk. Plan one is a defined contribution plan.

Plan two is a multi-employer plan. The plan pools assets contributed by various unrelated entities and provides benefits to the employees of more than one entity. Entity A has an obligation to plan two beyond its annual contribution, because as long as entity A continues to participate in the plan, the contributions will vary based on the overall experience of the scheme. Entity A is taking some of the actuarial and investment risk, so plan two is a defined benefit plan. [IAS 19 para 31].

Entity A should account for its proportionate share of the defined benefit obligation, plan assets and costs associated with plan two.

11.115 IAS 19 requires that where an employer participates in a defined benefit multi-employer plan, including a state plan, it should account for its proportionate share of assets, liabilities and costs as for any other defined benefit plan. [IAS 19 para 29]. However, when sufficient information is not available to use defined benefit accounting, an entity should instead account for its participation in the plan as if it were a defined contribution plan. [IAS 19 para 30]. In this context, the term 'is not available' is considered to mean 'cannot be obtained'. Hence, it is expected that an entity will make every practicable effort to obtain the necessary information in order to apply defined benefit accounting. Nevertheless, the standard envisages two situations where individual participating employers would account for a defined benefit multi-employer plan as if it were a defined contribution plan. These are as follows:

- The entity does not have access to sufficient information to enable the employer to use defined benefit accounting.

- The plan exposes the participating employers to actuarial risks associated with the current and former employees of other entities, with the result that there is no consistent and reliable basis for allocating the obligation, plan assets and cost to individual entities participating in the plan.

[IAS 19 para 32].

In both of these circumstances, there will be additional disclosure as described in paragraph 11.285. Note that, in the second point above, we regard the lack of a consistent and reliable basis for allocation as an additional condition. The existence of actuarial risk alone is not sufficient to justify use of defined contribution accounting as it is an automatic consequence of a multi-employer plan.

> **Example 1 – Employers share risks of a multi-employer plan**
>
> Entity A participates in an industry-wide pension plan administered by an insurance company. The plan pays benefits based on years of service and final salary. The participating employers fund the plan's obligations through annual contributions. Entity A must pay a penalty if it withdraws from the plan.
>
> The insurance company does not allocate contributions and employee benefits to separate funds for each participating employer. It does not maintain any detailed records tracking the source of the contributions or which entity employs each member. The employers share the actuarial risks associated with their employees and former employees.
>
> The actuarial valuation of the industry-wide pension shows a small surplus.
>
> Entity A can only describe and make disclosure about the multi-employer plan, because it has insufficient information to account for it.
>
> In theory, entity A should account for its proportionate share of the defined benefit obligation, plan assets and pension cost in the same way as for any other defined benefit plan. The industry-wide plan exposes participating employers to the actuarial risks associated with the current and former employees of other participating employers. Entity A does not have access to the information necessary to apply the defined benefit accounting rules.
>
> Entity A should:
>
> - Account for the pension plan as a defined contribution plan.
>
> - Disclose that the plan is a defined benefit plan and the reasons why insufficient information is available for defined benefit accounting.
>
> - Disclose the extent of any surplus or deficit in the plan that may affect future contributions and any information that is available about the surplus. [IAS 19 para 30].

Example 2 – Plan in which assets are segregated by employer

The facts are the same as example 1, but in this case, the insurance entity segregates the assets contributed by each employer and uses the assets contributed by entity A, plus the related income and capital appreciation, to pay benefits to entity A's employees.

Entity A makes cash contributions to the pension plan each year in accordance with an actuary's recommendations.

Again, entity A has a defined benefit pension plan, as entity A bears the actuarial and investment risk. However, the insurance company segregates the assets contributed by entity A. The pension arrangements do not expose entity A to actuarial risks associated with other entities' employees, so these arrangements are not a multi-employer plan and do not pose any accounting problems. Such plans may be referred to as multiple employer plans in some countries to distinguish them from multi-employer plans.

Entity A should account for its employees' pension arrangements as a defined benefit plan. The information required to apply defined benefit accounting is readily available because the assets are segregated. [IAS 19 para 33].

11.116 The standard acknowledges that there may be a contractual agreement between a multi-employer plan and its participants that determines how a surplus in the plan will be distributed (or a deficit funded). As a result, even if a participant in a multi-employer plan accounts for that plan as a defined contribution plan, as described in paragraph 11.115, it should recognise the asset or liability that arises from the contractual agreement and the resulting income or expense. [IAS 19 para 32A]. This is illustrated below.

Example – Contractual schedule of contributions to a multi-employer plan

Entity A participates in a multi-employer defined benefit plan. It accounts for the plan as if it were a defined contribution plan as described in paragraph 11.115. The trustees of the plan have agreed with its participants that the current deficit in the plan will be eliminated over the next five years. A contract has been drawn up, including a schedule of contributions showing that entity A will contribute C10m in addition to its normal contributions over the next five years. Accordingly, entity A should recognise a liability and an expense equal to the present value of the C10m payable. However, this will not affect the entity's treatment of its normal contributions as if the plan was a defined contribution plan.

[The next paragraph is 11.119.]

Group plans

11.119 Group pension plans could be considered to be a type of multi-employer plan. Contributions from a number of employers (the members of the group) are pooled and pension arrangements are administered centrally. However, IAS 19 states that *"defined benefit plans that share risks between various entities under common control, for example a parent and its subsidiaries, are not multi-employer* *plans"*. [IAS 19 para 34]. Instead, IAS 19 contains specific rules for group pension plans.

11.119.1 An entity that participates in a defined benefit plan that shares risks between various entities under common control should obtain information about the plan as a whole, measured in accordance with IAS 19. The net defined benefit cost should then be allocated among the participating entities as follows:

- If there is a contractual agreement or stated policy for charging the net defined benefit cost for the plan as a whole to participating entities, the entity should, in its separate or individual financial statements, recognise the net defined benefit cost that is charged.

- If there is no such agreement or policy, the net defined benefit cost for the plan as a whole should be recognised in the separate or individual financial statements of the entity that is legally the sponsoring employer for the plan. The other group entities should recognise, in their separate or individual financial statements, a cost equal to their contribution payable for the period.

[IAS 19 para 34A].

11.119.2 It is perhaps surprising that no definition is provided for terms such as 'net defined benefit cost' or 'sponsoring employer'. The latter, in particular, can be interpreted in various ways (see example 1 below). As regards net defined benefit cost, paragraph 61 of IAS 19 provides that, *"an entity shall recognise the net total of the following amounts in profit or loss"*. This might suggest that the net defined benefit cost is the net amount recognised in the income statement, thus ignoring any actuarial gains and losses recognised outside profit or loss as described from paragraph 11.274.1. In our view, the term should not be interpreted in this way. Instead it should be considered more broadly to include the total income or expense recognised in respect of the pension plan, regardless of whether amounts are recognised within or outside profit or loss.

11.119.3 The practical application of these requirements, specifically determining whether a contractual agreement or stated policy exists, and if not, who the sponsoring employer is, is considered in the following examples.

> **Example 1 – No contract nor stated policy for allocation**
>
> Entity A has several subsidiaries. The subsidiaries all trade and are of a similar size. All of the subsidiaries, as well as entity A itself, participate in the 'entity A group defined benefit plan'. The plan rules do not specify how any surplus or deficit should be allocated among participating employers. Furthermore, there is neither a contractual agreement nor a stated policy for allocating the net defined benefit cost to the individual group entities. Accordingly, the net defined benefit cost for the plan as a whole should be recognised in the separate or individual financial statements of the entity that is legally the sponsoring employer for the plan. The other participating entities will recognise a cost equal to their contribution for the period.

As noted above, IAS 19 does not define the term 'sponsoring employer'. The basis for conclusions section of the standard provides a little guidance in paragraph 10I, which states that *"the entity that is the sponsoring employer by default bears the risk relating to the plan"*. Hence, it would appear that any decision as to which entity is the sponsoring employer should be based on a consideration of the risks faced by each participating entity when compared to the others.

Often the identity of the sponsoring employer will be clear from a plan's trust deed and rules. However, in the absence of such clarity we consider that the following factors should be taken into account.

- Which entity's management is responsible for making decisions concerning the plan and negotiating with its trustees (such as agreeing contribution rates)?

- How are responsibilities described in the contribution schedule agreed with the plan trustees? Are contributions the responsibility of one entity, with all other participants making payments to that entity rather than the plan?

- Does one entity guarantee the contributions made by the other group entities?

Example 2 – Stated policy for allocation

Entity B also has several trading subsidiaries of similar size. All of the subsidiaries, as well as entity B itself, participate in the 'entity B group defined benefit plan'. The plan rules do not specify how any surplus or deficit should be allocated amongst participating employers. However, management has defined a policy for allocating the net defined benefit cost to the individual group entities on the basis of pensionable payroll. Hence, the net defined benefit cost (and the resultant asset or liability) should be recognised on this basis in each of the participating entities' separate or individual financial statements.

Example 3 – Schedule of contributions agreed with trustees

Entity C also has several trading subsidiaries of similar size. All of the subsidiaries, as well as entity C itself, participate in the 'entity C group defined benefit plan'. The plan rules do not specify how any surplus or deficit should be allocated among participating employers. However, a schedule of contributions has been agreed with the plan trustees. Although this deals with cash payments rather than the net defined benefit cost, it could be argued that a contribution schedule provides evidence as to how the net defined benefit cost (and, hence, the plan surplus or deficit) should be allocated. Hence, we believe that in this example the net defined benefit cost (and the resultant asset or liability) could be recognised on this basis in each of the participating entities' separate or individual financial statements. Alternatively, the net defined benefit cost for the plan as a whole could be recognised in the separate or individual financial statements of the entity that is legally the sponsoring employer.

UK note – In the UK, the requirements of the Pensions Act 2004 mean that where a defined benefit plan has insufficient assets to cover its liabilities, the trustees must establish a recovery plan setting out how the statutory funding objective (SFO) is to be met and over what period (see para 11.324.10). In detailing the steps to be taken in order to meet the SFO, the recovery plan will specify the contributions sought from each participating entity. Given this requirement, it is likely that a schedule of contributions similar to that described in the above example will be in place for most defined benefit plans in the UK.

Furthermore, for accounting periods ended on or after 6 April 2006 the rules for employers deducting pension contributions for tax purposes changed. The more general tax 'wholly and exclusively' test applies so that deductions are allowed only for contributions made wholly and exclusively for the purposes of the employer's trade or profession. In the context of group plans, where contributions to a group pension plan are made by the holding entity in the group with each employing subsidiary entity in the group being recharged an appropriate amount relating to its employees, the intra-group recharge may be accepted as being a contribution paid by the employer to the registered plan. More importantly, the contribution paid by the holding entity on behalf of each subsidiary entity must be recharged to each subsidiary entity on a reasonable basis (so as to meet the 'wholly and exclusively' test) in order for a tax deduction to be available.

An entity reporting under IFRS has a choice over whether they have an allocation policy as covered in IAS 19 paragraph 34A (see para 11.119.1 above). It, therefore, depends on whether a schedule of contributions is deemed to be a contractual agreement or policy.

Example 4 – 95% of active plan members employed by one entity in the group

Entity D has several trading subsidiaries but one (entity E) is considerably larger than the rest. All of the subsidiaries, as well as entity D itself, participate in the 'D group defined benefit plan' but approximately 95% of active members of the plan are employed by entity E. The plan rules do not specify how any surplus or deficit should be allocated among participating employers and the entity does not have a stated policy for allocation. However, in substance most of the risk in respect of the plan is borne by entity E and it is management of that entity that deals with the plan trustees. In our view, entity E will be considered to be the sponsoring employer so the net defined benefit cost (and the resultant asset or liability) should be recognised in full by that entity. In accordance with paragraph 34A of IAS 19, the other entities in the group (including entity D) should treat their participation in the plan as if it was a defined contribution plan (that is, they should recognise a cost equal to their contributions payable for the period).

Example 5 – Non-trading service company

Entity F, a trading company, has several trading subsidiaries, some of which are overseas. All employees in the 'entity F group' are legally employed by a separate non-trading service company subsidiary, entity G, for administrative reasons, but provide services to the trading entities within the group, not entity G. Entity G recharges staff costs, including pension costs, to entity F and its trading subsidiaries. The existence of a recharge arrangement between the group entities is indicative of a stated policy for allocating costs. Furthermore, the service company is a so-called 'shell company' and would be unable to meet the full costs of the pension plan as it is not trading. The net defined benefit cost (and the resultant asset or liability) should be recognised on the same basis as the costs are recharged in each of the participating trading entities' separate or individual financial statements.

11.120 IAS 19 sets out disclosures that must be made in respect of group pension plans. These requirements are explained in paragraph 11.287.1.

Insured plans

11.121 An employer may pay insurance premiums to fund a pension plan. The employer should treat such a plan as a defined contribution plan unless it has, either directly or indirectly through the plan, a legal or constructive obligation to either:

- pay the employee benefits directly when they fall due; or
- pay further amounts if the insurer does not pay all future benefits relating to employee service in the current and prior periods.

[IAS 19 para 39].

In either of these situations the plan will be treated as defined benefit.

11.122 For example, if the insurance company bears all of the actuarial and investment risk and has sole responsibility for paying the benefits, the plan will be treated as a defined contribution plan. In this situation, the insurance premium costs are, in substance, costs of settling the pension obligation. On the other hand, if the employer, either directly, indirectly through the plan, through a mechanism for setting future premiums, or through a relationship with the insurer, retains a legal or constructive obligation, the payment of the premiums does not settle the pension obligation. Instead, the plan would be treated as defined benefit and the insurance policy would be treated as a plan asset or reimbursement right (see from para 11.132).

11.123 The following example illustrates the above principle.

> **Example – Insurance policy against accident and injury compensation**
>
> Legislation in a particular country requires an entity to provide compensation to employees injured in an accident at work. The legislation allows employers to cover their obligation with an insurance policy, but makes it clear that employers cannot transfer the legal obligation for making compensation payments to a third party.
>
> A construction entity has a large workforce and the nature of its business increases the risk of injuries at work. The entity has decided to cover its exposure to injury compensation payments by taking out an insurance policy. Management believes the risk that the insurance company will default on its obligations is remote.
>
> The entity should treat its obligations as a defined benefit plan. The legislation does not allow the entity to transfer the obligation for making compensation payments to the insurance entity. Should the insurance company fail to make any payment required by legislation, the company would be required to meet the obligation. The probability of being required to make payments in the future does not affect the accounting treatment. The existence of the legal obligation determines the accounting treatment.

11.123.1 In other circumstances, arrangements will be undertaken to insure liabilities, or to transfer legally such liabilities to third parties. An example where individual annuities have been purchased and the assets and liabilities have been derecognised is given in Table 11.7.3. An example where a bulk annuity has been purchased which remains an investment of the pension scheme and is included in the pension scheme assets is given in Table 11.7.2. Insurance of defined benefit obligations is discussed further from paragraph 11.140.

Table 11.7.2 – Insurance policy included in pension scheme assets

Resolution Limited – Annual report – 31 December 2011

8. Staff pension schemes (extract 1)
c) FPPS additional disclosures (extract 1)
vi) Assets in the defined benefit scheme and the expected rate of return

	Expected rate of return	value	Expected rate of return	value
	2011	2011	2010	2010
	%	£m	%	£m
Equities	5	180	7	192
Liability-driven Investment pools	5	398	6	284
Fixed interest (LDI in specie)	5	173	6	148
Insured assets	5	513	5	447
Cash	2	30	3	42
Total market value of assets		**1,294**		1,113
Present value of scheme liabilities		**(1,242)**		(1,047)
Surplus in the Scheme		**52**		66

The expected return on net pension scheme assets is calculated using the assumptions and the market value of pension scheme assets as stated in the table above for the preceding year.

c) FPPS additional disclosures (extract 2)
x) Risk management (extract)

Market risk
The Trustee, with the full support of the Group, has agreed and implemented a strategic asset allocation to return-seeking assets of 25% of the non-insured fund

Longevity risk
The Trustee, with the full support and involvement of the Group, first invested 37% of the scheme's assets in a bulk annuity contract with Aviva Annuity UK Limited as a buy-in investment in 2008 with a further tranches of investment in 2009, 2010 and 2011. The contract between the Trustee and Aviva now reassures benefits for pensioners in payment up to 30 June 2011 and includes a facility for the Trustee to invest further tranches of benefits in 2012 and 2013.

The contract is an investment of the Trustee and includes additional security to that of a standard bulk annuity contract with an insurance company. The ownership of the scheme's assets are being drip fed to Aviva over the duration of the contract. This additional protection has been negotiated by the Trustee to mitigate the risk of any decline in the financial strength of Aviva as the counterparty under the contract. These assets have been set up under a ring-fenced Trustee Investment Plan that is managed by Aviva and with the title to those assets secured in the Trustee's name through a safekeeping custody account set up with Citibank. These ring-fenced assets would only be accessed by the Trustee in the event of Aviva failing to meet its obligations under this long-term contract.

> **Table 11.7.3 – Insurance policy leading to derecognition of pension scheme assets and liabilities**
>
> **Delta plc – Annual report – 31 December 2008**
>
> **Financial Review (extract)**
>
> **INCOME STATEMENT — PRESENTATION**
>
> The Group's Consolidated Income Statement reflects a number of exceptional items that have been separately disclosed in order to provide increased clarity to the performance of the Group. The largest of the exceptional items relates to the pension scheme. As mentioned in the Chief Executive's Review, the completion of the pensioner buyout transaction led to a settlement charge being expensed and shown separately of £48.8 million. The transaction consisted of two stages. The first was the purchase of the bulk annuity policy into the Delta Pension Scheme from PIC. The second stage occurred in the second half and culminated in the individual annuity policy documents being issued by PIC just prior to the year end. The last stage was a key part of the transaction structure as this element allowed the Group to discharge fully the liability of that portion of the pension scheme population and to show a much reduced pension scheme in terms of both assets and liabilities (as detailed in note 40). In order to achieve this outcome a data verification exercise was undertaken in the second half and a further premium adjustment amount of £0.8 million was paid to PIC by the pension scheme.

Defined contribution plans

Recognition and measurement

11.124   Accounting for defined contribution plans is straightforward, as the amount recognised as an expense is the contribution payable. Except for contributions outstanding or prepaid, an employer has no assets or liabilities in respect of a defined contribution plan. [IAS 19 para 44].

11.125   In the unlikely event that contributions are payable more than 12 months after the end of the period to which they relate, they should be discounted using the rate specified in paragraph 11.174. [IAS 19 para 45].

11.125.1   An employer might contribute, or be obliged to contribute, an amount to an employee's defined contribution plan that vests over three years subsequent to the contribution, with the effect that, if the employee leaves within the three-year period, the employer is entitled to a refund of the contribution or its then investment value. In July 2011, the IFRS IC issued an agenda decision that clarifies the effect of vesting conditions on the accounting for such defined contribution arrangements plans (as defined in para 43 of IAS 19). The IFRS IC concluded that each contribution to a defined contribution plan is recognised as an expense or recognised as a liability (accrued expense) over the period of service that obliges the employer to make this pay this contribution to the defined contribution plan. This means that the expense would be recognised once the contribution payment is made (or the obligation to make the contribution arises) rather than over the subsequent vesting period. that employees are providing service to obtain the benefit. In their conclusion, the Committee made a distinction between the period that creates the employer's obligation and the period of service that entitles an employee to receive the benefit from the defined contribution (that is, the vesting period). Refunds are recognised as an asset and income when the entity/employer becomes entitled to them (that is, by the employee failing to meet the vesting condition). The Committee's agenda decision is only applicable in circumstances where employer contributions to a defined contribution plan have vesting conditions; it does not apply to defined benefit plans or to short-term and other long-term benefits. See further guidance related to benefit attribution for defined benefit plans (para 11.164) and other long-term benefits (para 11.73.3).

Disclosure

11.126 The only specific disclosure required by IAS 19 in respect of defined contribution plans is the amount recognised as an expense in the period. [IAS 19 para 46]. Pension plans are related parties and so contributions paid into defined contribution plans are transactions with related parties and should be disclosed as such. Additionally, disclosure of contributions paid and any balances outstanding in respect of key management personnel may also be required by IAS 24 (see chapter 29).

Defined benefit plans

Basic principles

11.127 Accounting for defined benefit plans is complex because actuarial assumptions and valuation methods are required to measure the balance sheet obligation and the income statement expense. The expense recognised is not necessarily the contributions made in the period. IAS 19's first objective is to ensure that an employer's financial statements reflect a liability when employees have provided services in exchange for benefits to be paid in the future. The standard describes how a defined benefit liability should be recognised and measured but, to the extent that this balance may be negative (that is, an asset), the same principles would apply. The plan liabilities (described by IAS 19 as the 'defined benefit obligation') and, in the case of a funded plan, the plan assets, are measured at each balance sheet date. The plan assets are measured at fair value. The defined benefit obligation is measured on an actuarial basis discounted to present value. The difference between the fair value of the plan assets and the present value of the defined benefit obligation is a surplus or deficit that, subject to certain conditions and delayed recognition options, should be recognised as an asset or liability on the employer's balance sheet.

11.128 A surplus is regarded as an asset to the extent that the employer can gain an economic benefit from it. A deficit is regarded as a liability to the extent that the employer has a legal or constructive obligation to make it good – this will nearly always be the case. In an unfunded plan, the employer has a direct obligation to pay the retirement benefits itself, so it recognises as a liability the gross amount of the plan liabilities. In a funded plan, plan assets are held in an entity (fund) that is legally separate from the reporting entity, so it recognises as an asset or liability the *net* surplus or deficit.

UK.11.129.1 The previous paragraphs could be applied to FRS 17 as much as IAS 19. However, there are important differences in the recognition of surpluses or deficits as assets or liabilities under IAS 19. First, in simple terms, IAS 19 does not require all of the movement in a surplus or deficit to be recognised immediately. Some may be deferred and recognised over time according to a mechanism sometimes referred to as the 'corridor' approach.

UK.11.129.2 Secondly, in determining the amount of a surplus that may be recognised as an asset in terms of the amount of economic benefit available as a refund, under FRS 17, the amount would only include refunds that have been agreed with the pension plan trustees as at the balance sheet. However, IAS 19 does not restrict refunds to those already agreed, if, in principle, a refund would be available to the employer on ultimate winding up of the scheme then an asset should be recognised. Hence, the net amount recognised as an asset or liability under IAS 19 is not necessarily the same as under FRS 17.

11.129 IAS 19 avoids implying that a surplus in a defined benefit pension plan is 'owned' by the employer. But conceptually an employer does not have to own a surplus in order to recognise an asset. It is sufficient that the employer has access to future economic benefits that it controls *via*, for example, the ability to reduce future employer contributions. Consequently, a surplus should be recognised as an asset to the extent that the employer is able to recover it through reduced future contributions or refunds, either directly to the employer or indirectly to another plan in deficit. [IAS 19 para 59]. Recoverability of a surplus is considered from paragraph 11.214.

11.130 IAS 19 requires the amount recognised as a defined benefit liability (or asset, if negative) to be the net total of the following amounts:

- The present value of the defined benefit obligation at the balance sheet date (see from para 11.158).

- *Plus* any actuarial gains (less any actuarial losses) not recognised because of the application of the 'corridor' approach (see from para 11.268.1).

- *Minus* any past service cost not yet recognised (see from para 11.237).

- *Minus* the fair value at the balance sheet date of plan assets (if any) out of which the obligations are to be settled directly (see from para 11.132).

[IAS 19 para 54].

11.131 Tables 11.8 and 11.8.1 give examples of companies with a defined benefit liability or asset comprising these components. One of which reflects unrecognised actuarial gains (in determining its recognised deficit) and the other unrecognised actuarial losses (in determining its recognised asset). Paragraph 11.282.2 contains an example of how the defined benefit liability is calculated.

Table 11.8 – Analysis of defined benefit liability using the 'corridor' method

Dexia SA – annual report – 31 December 2010

1.1. BASIS OF ACCOUNTING (extract)

1.1.1. General (extract)

The consolidated financial statements are prepared on a "going-concern basis" and are given in millions of euro (EUR) unless otherwise stated.

8.6. PROVISIONS AND OTHER OBLIGATIONS (extract)

D. Provisions for pensions and other long-term benefits (extract)

c. Amounts recognized in the balance sheet	Dec. 31, 2009	Dec. 31, 2010
Funded plans		
1. Present value of funded obligations	1,390	**1,455**
2. Fair value of plan assets	1,237	**1,284**
3. Deficit/(surplus) for funded plans	153	**171**
4. Present value of unfunded obligations	611	**633**
5. Unrecognized net actuarial gains/(losses)	(16)	**(39)**
6. Unrecognized past service (cost)/benefit	1	**0**
7. Effect of paragraph 58(b) limit	9	**12**
8. NET LIABILITY/(ASSET)	758	**777**
Amounts in the balance sheet		
1. Liabilities	780	**797**
2. Assets	(22)	**(20)**
3. NET LIABILITY/(ASSET)	758	**777**

11.8.1 – Analysis of defined benefit asset using the 'corridor' method

TNT N.V. – Annual report – 31 December 2010

11 Pension assets: 1,153 million (2009: 884) and provisions for pension liabilities: 231 million (2009: 292) (extract)

	2010	2009
Change in benefit obligation		
Benefit obligation at beginning of year	**(4,659)**	(4,215)
Transfer to assets classified for demerger	**9**	1
Service costs	**(102**	(90)
Interest costs	**(256)**	(256)
Curtailments/settlements	**90**	0
Actuarial (loss)/gain	**(1,044)**	(310)
Benefits paid	**217**	212
Benefit obligation at end of year	**(5,663)**	(4,659)
Change in plan assets		
Fair value of plan assets at beginning of year	**4,890**	4,104
Transfer to assets classified for demerger	**(53)**	–
Actual return on plan assets	**635**	716
Express contributions	**27**	24
Contributions	**235**	258
Benefits paid	**(217)**	(212)
Fair value of plan assets at end of year	**5,517**	4,890
Funded status as per 31 December		
Funded status	**(146)**	231
Unrecognised net actuarial loss	**1,076**	398
Unrecognised prior service costs	**4**	6
Pension assets/liabilities	**934**	635
Other employee benefit plans	**(12)**	(43)
Net pension asset/(liability)	**922**	592

Plan assets

Identification and recognition of plan assets

11.132 Identifying plan assets is important because the accounting for them is quite different from the accounting for other investments that are not plan assets. This applies to both the balance sheet and the income statement. In the balance sheet, plan assets are deducted from plan liabilities to give a net item. The income statement is credited each period with the expected long-term rate of return (income plus capital growth) on the plan assets. Differences between the expected and actual return are treated as actuarial gains or losses and may be recognised in one of three ways:

- in full in the income statement (see para 11.274);

- over a longer period when the 'corridor' approach is applied (see para 11.268.1); or

- in full as they arise, outside profit or loss, in other comprehensive income (see para 11.274.1).

> **UK.11.132.1** In the UK, the identity of plan assets should usually be apparent from the way funded pension plans are constituted. The assets are usually placed under the control of trustees, who administer the plan in accordance with the provisions of trust law and the terms of the trust deed governing the particular plan. In some other countries, identifying plan assets may not be so clear cut.

[The next paragraph is 11.134.]

11.134 IAS 19 defines plan assets as either:

- Assets held by a long-term employee benefit fund. These are assets, other than non-transferable financial instruments issued by the reporting entity, that:

  - are held by an entity (a fund) that is legally separate from the reporting entity and exists solely to pay or fund employee benefits; and

  - are available to be used only to pay or fund employee benefits, are not available to the reporting entity's own creditors (even in bankruptcy), and cannot be returned to the reporting entity, unless either:

    - the fund's remaining assets are sufficient to meet all the related employee benefit obligations of the plan or the reporting entity; or

    - the assets are returned to the reporting entity to reimburse it for employee benefits already paid.

- Qualifying insurance policies. These are policies issued by an insurer that is not a related party of the reporting entity where the proceeds of the policy:

  - can be used only to pay or fund employee benefits under a defined benefit plan; and

  - are not available to the reporting entity's own creditors (even in bankruptcy), and cannot be paid to the reporting entity, unless either:

    - the proceeds represent surplus assets that are not needed for the policy to meet all the related employee benefit obligations; or

    - the proceeds are returned to the reporting entity to reimburse it for employee benefits already paid.

[IAS 19 para 7].

11.135 In both cases above, the assets are held solely for the purpose of paying or funding employee benefits and cannot be used by the employer for any other purpose, including settlement of liabilities on the employer's liquidation. This point is important as plans in some countries contain clauses that may give a liquidator access to plan assets. In such circumstances, the assets in question are not plan assets for the purposes of IAS 19.

11.136 The above principles are illustrated in the following examples.

Example 1 – Assets held by the entity

Entity A has a German subsidiary that operates a defined benefit pension plan. The plan is unfunded, but the entity holds a number of investments to fulfil its future pension obligations, which are treated as available-for-sale financial assets as defined in IAS 39 (see chapter 6).

Although the investments may be identified as relating to the defined benefit obligation, the fact that they are not held by a separate legal entity means that they are not plan assets as defined by IAS 19.

Example 2 – Assets available to creditors on a winding up

Entity B has a US subsidiary that provides retirement benefits to its senior executives through a Rabbi Trust. The trust agreement's legal form is such that the assets held to cover the pension liabilities are available to the general creditors of the entity on winding up. Accordingly, the assets held by the trust are not plan assets as defined by IAS 19. Additionally, consolidation of the Rabbi Trust should be considered under IAS 27 or SIC 12 (or superseded by IFRS 10 with effect from 1 January 2013).

Example 3 – Pension plan is controlled by the entity

Entity A established entity B as its subsidiary and is its only shareholder. The articles of incorporation of entity B state that entity B is a pension plan and its only purpose is to collect and invest pension contributions made by entity A and pay pensions to former employees of entity A under specified defined benefit pension plan terms.

All members of the board of directors of entity B are nominated by entity A. There are no laws that would prohibit the controlling shareholder of a pension plan entity from changing the articles of incorporation or the purpose of existence of the subsidiary pension entity. A change in the articles of incorporation could allow the pension assets to revert to entity A prior to satisfying the benefit payments to employees.

Entity B does not satisfy the criteria for pension plan assets in paragraph 7 of IAS 19, because entity A controls entity B and, therefore, can change the articles of incorporation and the purpose of entity B. Entity A can thus require that the assets are returned to it before all pension benefit payments to the current and former employees are satisfied.

Entity A should, therefore, consolidate entity B. The assets held by entity B will be classified as AFS assets in entity A's consolidated balance sheet and the pension obligation will be recognised as a separate liability.

11.137 The following are also not plan assets:

■ Non-transferable financial instruments issued by the reporting entity.

■ Unpaid contributions due from the reporting entity.

[IAS 19 para 103].

11.138 Non-transferable financial instruments issued by the reporting entity include loans and shares subject to restrictive conditions, unlisted corporate bonds that are redeemable but not transferable without the reporting entity's permission, insurance policies which cannot be sold and loans to the reporting entity than cannot be assigned to a third party. The principle underlying the definition of plan assets requires that the assets are moved beyond the reporting entity's control so that they are available to meet employee benefit obligations regardless of the reporting entity's financial position. Non-transferable financial instruments issued by the reporting entity would only ever be available to meet benefit obligations if the reporting entity were to repay or redeem them. Such assets would not be available if the reporting entity were to go into liquidation, so IAS 19 excludes them from plan assets.

11.139 For similar reasons, amounts due from the reporting entity in respect of unpaid contributions are not plan assets, but plan assets do include other current assets and liabilities that do not necessarily relate directly to the payment of benefits, for example rental on property, plant and equipment used by the plan, professional fees incurred by the plan but not yet paid, liabilities (or assets) arising from a derivative financial instrument or other futures contract. [IAS 19 para 103].

11.140 Sometimes, an entity may look to another party, such as an insurance company, to settle all or part of a defined benefit obligation. Qualifying insurance policies, as defined in paragraph 11.134, are plan assets. However, IAS 19 also contains guidance in respect of insurance policies that do not satisfy the definition of qualifying insurance policies. Where it is virtually certain that another party will reimburse some or all of the expenditure required to settle a defined benefit obligation, even though this does not represent a qualifying insurance policy or a plan asset, this right to reimbursement should be recognised as a separate asset. In many respects this requirement may be considered academic as a right to reimbursement that is virtually certain will satisfy the definition of an asset contained within the IASB's Framework. Nevertheless, it is important to identify reimbursement rights as they are not accounted for in the same way as other assets. Reimbursement rights are recognised as separate assets rather than as a deduction in determining the defined benefit liability. In all other respects reimbursement rights, and the income they yield, are treated in exactly the same way as other plan assets. [IAS 19 para 104A]. This means, for example, that:

■ The asset representing the reimbursement right is measured at the same amount as the liability that it reimburses. Although paragraph 104A of IAS 19 uses the term 'fair value', in this context, 'fair value' does not have the same meaning as elsewhere in IFRS. See paragraph 11.151 for the definition of fair value in this context.

■ The expected return on the asset is recognised in the income statement and may be netted off the expense relating to the defined benefit plan.

■ The difference between the expected return and the actual return on the asset is treated as an actuarial gain or loss in the same way as actuarial gains and losses on the defined benefit obligation.

11.140.1 The cost of purchasing an insurance policy will typically be larger than the present value of the defined benefit obligation it is intended to reimburse. Any difference between the cost of purchasing an insurance policy and the present value of the defined benefit obligation to which it relates, should generally be viewed and treated as an actuarial loss. This is independent of whether the insurance policy is purchased by the pension fund or the entity itself provided the policy itself is an asset of the plan, or meets the definition of a qualifying insurance policy or reimbursement right. This is because paragraphs 104C and 104D of IAS 19 stipulate that a reimbursement right is treated in the same way as plan assets except for its recognition as a separate asset rather than deducting it to determine the defined benefit liability.

11.141 The difference between a qualifying insurance policy and a reimbursement right is illustrated in the following examples.

Example 1 – Qualifying insurance policy

Entity A operates a defined benefit pension plan for its senior management. It has decided to cover its pension obligation with an insurance policy taken out with a leading insurance entity. The policy requires the insurer to reimburse entity A in full for all benefit payments. The policy is a qualifying insurance policy as its proceeds can only be used to fund employee benefits and are not available to entity A for any other purpose.

Example 2 – Non-qualifying insurance policy

The facts are the same as in example 1, except that the insurance entity is a related party of entity A.

The definition of plan assets in IAS 19 (see para 11.134) provides that where an insurance policy is issued to a reporting entity by a related party of the reporting entity (as defined in IAS 24) it cannot be treated as a plan asset. Accordingly, in this example the insurance policy is not a plan asset. It will, however, represent a reimbursement right as described in paragraph 11.140.

The definition of plan assets in IAS 19 (see para 11.134) has a hierarchical structure, so that it is only necessary to consider when an insurance policy is a qualifying insurance policy where it is not held by a separate employee benefit fund. This is because policies held by a separate employee benefit fund may be treated as plan assets regardless of whether they are 'qualifying' insurance policies.

In practice, some insurance companies have set up separate legal entities, such as trusts, for their employee benefit arrangements. Insurance policies issued by the employer are then held by these entities. Regardless of whether all the other conditions for treatment as plan assets are met (that is, the assets are available only to pay or fund employee benefits and are not available to the reporting entity's own creditors), such policies that are 'non-transferable financial instruments issued by the reporting entity' (see para 11.138) do not meet the definition of plan assets under IAS 19.

IFRS 4 provides clarity in this area by concluding that where an insurance contract has been issued by an insurer to a defined benefit plan covering the employees of the issuer, or of another entity consolidated within the same financial statements as the issuer, such contracts should generally not be treated as plan assets. [IFRS 4 para IG1.21].

On the other hand, policies held by a long-term employee benefit fund that are freely transferable, or issued by a related party that is not consolidated, may still meet the definition of plan assets under IAS 19.

It is common for a group entity to guarantee to third parties the liabilities of fellow group members, associates and joint ventures. An example is a parent company issuing a contingent guarantee in respect of its subsidiary's defined benefit pension liability. Such a guarantee reduces the risk that the subsidiary will not make payment when due, for example due to cash flow difficulties. In our view, the parent issuing the contingent guarantee should account for it as an insurance contract in accordance with IFRS 4, that is, record a liability. The subsidiary benefiting from the guarantee should disclose it as a contingent asset of the pension plan. It is not a plan asset: the plan's right to receive payment under a guarantee is no different from its right to receive contributions from the employer and unpaid contributions are not plan assets. The plan deficit should not be reduced because a subsidiary is able to secure the support of its parent in making contributions.

Example 3 – Reimbursement right

Entity B operates a similar defined benefit pension plan to entity A and it has also decided to cover its pension obligation with an insurance policy taken out with the same leading insurance entity. The policy is similar to that taken out by entity A except that it also permits entity B to cancel the arrangements, in which case the insurer repays a pre-determined amount to entity B.

The existence of the contractual right to terminate the policy and receive the proceeds means that entity B can apply the proceeds of the policy in its business regardless of the benefit obligation. The use of the proceeds is not restricted to paying employee benefits. Hence, this policy is not a qualifying insurance policy but it does represent a reimbursement right as described in paragraph 11.140.

11.142 The above discussion will only be relevant where a plan is treated as a defined benefit plan. Sometimes, an entity's relationship with an insurance company will be such that the entity pays premiums to the insurer, but has no obligation to make any additional payments. In such circumstances, the plan would be treated as defined contribution.

Measurement of plan assets

11.143 Plan assets should be measured at their fair value at the balance sheet date. [IAS 19 para 54]. Fair value in the context of IAS 19 has the same meaning as in many other accounting standards, so it reflects the amount for which an asset could be exchanged in an arm's length transaction between knowledgeable and willing parties. With the exception of certain insurance policies, there is no specific guidance in IAS 19 on how fair value should be determined, although it is suggested that, where no market price is available, fair value should be estimated, for example by reference to discounted cash flows. [IAS 19 para 102].

UK.11.143.1 FRS 17 gives guidance on determining fair value. Quoted securities are measured at current bid price, the fair value of unquoted securities must be estimated and the fair value of unitised securities is measured at current bid price. Property should be valued at open market value or in accordance with guidance issued by the Royal Institution of Chartered Surveyors. Insurance policies that exactly match the amount and timing of some or all of the benefits payable under a plan should be measured at the same amount as the related obligations. For other insurance policies the best approximation to fair value given the plan's circumstances should be used. [FRS 17 paras 16 to 18].

[The next paragraph is 11.145]

11.145 Although pension and other employee benefit plans are specifically outside the scope of IAS 39 that standard uses the same definition of fair value as IAS 19 and it does provide guidance as to how the fair value of securities should be measured. Paragraph AG71 of IAS 39 states that *"The existence of published price quotations in an active market is the best evidence of fair value…"* and paragraph AG72 goes on to state that *"The appropriate quoted market price for an asset held or liability to be issued is usually the current bid price…"*. Hence, bid price should be used when measuring the fair value of quoted and unitised securities.

11.146 As regards unquoted securities, for which no market price is available, IAS 19 states that fair value should be estimated. Once again, IAS 39 provides guidance as to how this might be achieved. Valuation techniques are described in paragraphs AG74 to AG79 of IAS 39 and include:

- Prices obtained in recent arm's length transactions.

- Comparisons with fair values of similar securities.

- Discounted cash flows.

- Option pricing models.

11.147 Further guidance on the valuation of investments and other financial assets is given in chapter 6.

11.148   For properties, reference should be made to IAS 40 and IAS 16. IAS 40 uses the same definition of fair value as IASs 19 and 39 and it considers the issue in a similar way to the former. The best evidence of fair value is considered to be the current market price of similar property in the same location and condition. [IAS 40 para 45]. If such a price is not available, reference may be made to other measures such as discounted cash flows. [IAS 40 para 46].

11.149   Sometimes, properties owned by a pension fund may be occupied by the sponsoring employer. For such properties, the guidance in IAS 16 may be more appropriate. IAS 16, like IAS 40, requires property valuations to be based on 'fair value', which is usually determined from market based evidence. [IAS 16 para 32]. If there is no market-based evidence of fair value because of the specialised nature of the property, and it is of a type that is rarely sold except as part of a continuing business, an entity may need to estimate fair value using an income or a depreciated replacement cost approach. [IAS 16 para 33].

11.150   Further guidance on the valuation of properties is given in chapter 16.

11.151   Where plan assets include qualifying insurance policies, or there are insurance policies that represent reimbursement rights as defined in paragraph 11.140, that exactly match the amount and timing of some or all of the benefits payable under a plan, the fair value of those insurance policies is deemed to be the present value of the related obligations, subject to any reduction required if the amounts receivable under the insurance policies are not recoverable in full. [IAS 19 paras 104, 104D].

11.152   Where an insurance policy does not exactly match the amount and timing of some or all of the benefits payable under a plan, the determination of fair value is rather more problematic. IAS 19 provides no guidance as to how the fair value of such policies should be determined. The UK SORP, 'The financial reports of pension schemes', discusses a number of the main methods of valuation used in practice. Techniques set out in the SORP that might be useful in estimating an appropriate range in which the fair value may fall are described below. The selection of the appropriate method will depend upon the circumstances of the particular pension plan and is a matter of judgement:

- Actuarial value. This is the value that an actuary places on the policy on a basis that is consistent with the valuation of the liabilities. It is typically derived by discounting the estimated proceeds, allowing for anticipated future bonuses, mortality and other contingencies. In practice, the valuation may be up to three years old, but it can be adjusted in the intervening years for the net cash invested in the policy together with any bonuses declared and/or other adjustments for interest recommended by the actuary.

- Premium value. This method generally applies to contracts where there are underlying guarantees (for example, with-profit contracts). The premium value is the amount that an insurer would charge at the date of valuation to provide the benefits bought to date and can, therefore, be regarded as a measure of replacement cost. It will include an allowance for expenses (including commission) and it may be appropriate to remove this so that the value is not overstated. On the other hand, there may be no allowance for terminal bonus, which can be significant, particularly for older policies. The premium value method (with or without an allowance for expenses) is somewhat artificial in its approach since, in practice, it is unlikely that a pension plan's trustees would seek to replace policies in this way. Nevertheless, the use of this method would generally result in relatively consistent values from year to year, albeit less so where the insurance company has rates or bonuses closely linked to current interest rates and there have been wide swings in these interest rates.

- Surrender value. This is the value at which the insurer is effectively prepared to buy back the contract from the policyholder. The value quoted by the insurance company will depend on many factors, such as market conditions, the willingness of the insurance company to buy back the policy and its need to realise assets to pay the surrender value. Nevertheless, in many cases, insurance companies routinely provide surrender values for policies on the grounds that the plan actuary requires the information in order to carry out the minimum funding requirement valuation. The surrender value may be the most appropriate value for insurance policies held by plans that are being wound up, but it may not provide an appropriate measure of fair value for other plans.

Example – Assets with different risk and maturity profiles

Entity A operates a defined benefit pension plan. Pension legislation requires all pension plans to maintain a range of plan assets. Entity A's pension plan has invested in:

(a) Quoted equity securities.

(b) Unquoted equity securities.

(c) Quoted treasury bonds.

(d) Unquoted high-quality fixed-interest corporate bonds.

(e) Land and buildings.

(f) Qualifying insurance policies that do not exactly match the amount and timing of some or all of the employee benefits.

(g) Qualifying insurance policies that exactly match the amount and timing of some or all of the employee benefits.

Entity A determines the fair value and discount rate for each investment separately due to their different risk and maturity profiles as follows:

(a) Quoted equity securities and treasury bonds at market value (defined as the bid price for securities quoted in an active market).

(b) Unquoted equity securities at fair value estimated using appropriate valuation models, such as discounted cash flow models.

(c) Unquoted fixed-interest bonds by discounting the expected future cash flows using a current interest rate that reflects the risk in the bonds.

(d) Land and buildings by reference to market value, unless there is no market value for the assets. When there is no market value, entity A uses the expected future rental stream, discounted using an appropriate interest rate.

(e) Qualifying insurance policies that do not exactly match the amount and timing of some or all of the employee benefits by discounting the expected cash receipts using a discount rate that reflects the term and risk of the policies. The policy's surrender value may also be considered as a starting point for determining fair value under certain circumstances.

(f) Qualifying insurance policies that exactly match the amount and timing of some or all of the benefits payable will be measured at the IAS 19 value of the related obligation, subject to any reduction required if the reimbursement is not recoverable in full.

11.153 In May 2011, the IASB issued IFRS 13, which defines fair value and sets out a framework for measuring fair value. IFRS 13 defines fair value as *"...the price that would be received to sell an asset or paid to transfer a liability in an orderly transaction between market participants at the measurement date"*. [IFRS 13 para 9]. IFRS 13 will apply to the measurement of plan assets, other than insurance policies that exactly match the amount and timing of some or all of the benefits payable, for annual periods beginning on or after 1 January 2013, with earlier application permitted. See chapter 5 for further guidance.

[The next paragraph is 11.158.]

Defined benefit obligation

Recognition of the defined benefit obligation

11.158 The defined benefit obligation reflects *"expected future payments required to settle the obligation resulting from employee service in the current and prior periods"*. [IAS 19 para 7]. It comprises not only legal obligations under the formal terms of the plan, but also constructive obligations arising from an employer's informal practices. [IAS 19 para 52]. Hence, the components of the defined benefit obligation reflect the characteristics of a 'present obligation' in IAS 37. Furthermore, actuarial techniques allow the obligation to be measured with sufficient reliability to justify recognition of a liability. The recognition of a provision stems from the existence of a present obligation, which may be legal or constructive. IAS 37 defines a constructive obligation as:

"An obligation that derives from an entity's actions where:

(a) by an established pattern of past practice, published policies or a sufficiently specific current statement, the entity has indicated to other parties that it will accept certain responsibilities; and

(b)   as a result, the entity has created a valid expectation on the part of those other parties that it will discharge those responsibilities."

[IAS 37 para 10].

11.159   In practice, a constructive obligation may be more difficult to discern than a legal obligation, as it derives from the employer's actions and it is a question of judgement as to whether an obligation has been established. A constructive obligation would for example arise where a change in an entity's informal practices would cause unacceptable damage to its relationship with employees. [IAS 19 para 52]. The principles are illustrated further in the following examples.

Example 1 – Valid expectation

Entity A has agreed with its trade unions that it will contribute 5% of every employee's salary to a pension plan administered by an insurance company. The employee uses the accumulated contributions, together with the related investment returns, to purchase an annuity at retirement. Entity A has no obligation to make additional payments to its employees after their retirement and, hence, this is treated as a defined contribution plan.

However, in each of the last ten years, entity A has used its active employees' medical plan to meet the medical costs of retired employees. Entity A has met all pensioners' medical expenses and has not made any communications to indicate that this is a limited action on the employer's part without any commitment to continue doing so.

Whilst the entity has no legal obligation to meet its pensioners' medical costs, its actions have created an expectation that it will continue to meet these costs. The entity has, therefore, created a constructive obligation, and should account for the costs of providing medical cover as a defined benefit plan. [IAS 19 para 26(c)]. The 5% salary contributions continue to be treated as a defined contribution plan.

Example 2 – Established practice

An entity has a practice of granting annual increases to pensions in payment and deferred pensions over and above any increases that may be required by law or the pension trust deed. Such increases are granted as a measure of protection against inflation.

Although the entity has no legal or contractual obligation to grant the discretionary increases, it has an established practice and has created a valid expectation that it will continue with this practice in the future. It has no realistic alternative but to pay the increases in order to avoid damaging employee relations. Accordingly, the entity has a constructive obligation to continue to grant annual increases so their cost should be factored into the measurement of the defined benefit obligation.

Example 3 – *Ad hoc* discretionary increases

An entity has, in the past, granted occasional discretionary increases to pensions in payment. These increases have been made on an *ad hoc* basis and have no established pattern. Management considers that the entity has not created an expectation of similar increases in the future. Hence, the entity has not established a constructive obligation so the cost of any increases will result in additional past service liabilities when they are granted (see para 11.237). If the employer's practice changes such that a valid expectation of future increases is created, the cost of future increases should be factored into the measurement of the defined benefit obligation.

Example 4 – Issue of a public statement

Entity A is the parent of a group with subsidiaries in 25 countries. Every subsidiary operates its own benefit plan. Entity A has decided to streamline its pension arrangements and on 30 November 20X1, prior to its year-end the board of directors approved and announced a single uniform pension plan for all its subsidiaries and employees. The relevant trade unions and the trustees of the existing pension plans approved the new arrangements before the announcement.

Entity A's employees must also approve the new arrangements, since they will be required to transfer their pension entitlement to the new plan. The new arrangements provide enhanced benefits for past service for every employee as an incentive to vote in favour of the new arrangements. The employees vote on the new plan on 31 March 20X2 and entity A expects a large margin in favour.

Public statements can create a constructive obligation. However, a public statement in itself may not be sufficient to create a constructive obligation and an entity should consider all of the facts and circumstances relevant to each case.

A constructive obligation is created for entity A by the board's approval and announcement of the amended plan. Approval by the trade union and the trustees provides additional evidence that the entity is committed to provide enhanced benefits. The impact of the benefit enhancement is included in the present value of the defined benefit obligation at 31 December 20X1. The present value of the defined benefit obligation at 31 December 20X1 includes the impact of the past service cost arising from the benefit enhancement.

The prior service cost should be recognised in the income statement over the vesting period (that is, 30 November 20X1 to 31 March 20X2) since the benefits will only vest upon approval of the enhancement by the employees.

Example 5 – Surplus shared with employees

An entity has a substantial surplus in its defined benefit pension plan. The plan rules state that the surplus is to be shared two-thirds to the company and one-third to employees. The surplus attributable to employees must be used in either of two ways – funding past service benefits such as improved death benefits or surviving spouse benefits, or reducing employee contributions in the future, regardless of what the entity does with its share.

> If the plan's formal terms (or a constructive obligation) oblige an entity to use a surplus for the benefit of plan participants, paragraph 85(b) of IAS 19 requires this to be reflected in the measurement of the defined benefit obligation. The amount that will be passed to employees should be treated as increasing the plan liabilities. It is irrelevant how the employees' share of the surplus is to be used up. The resulting, smaller, net surplus is subject to the requirements of IFRIC 14 (see para 11.216).

11.160 Employee service gives rise to an obligation under a defined benefit plan even if the benefits are conditional on future employment (in other words, they are not vested). Employee service before the vesting date gives rise to a constructive obligation because, at each successive balance sheet date, the amount of future service that an employee will have to render before becoming entitled to the benefit is reduced. The probability that some employees may not satisfy vesting conditions is taken into account in the measurement of the defined benefit obligation, but does not determine whether the obligation exists. For example, although certain post-employment medical benefits become payable only if a specified event or illness occurs after retirement, an obligation is created when the employee renders services that provide entitlement to those benefits.

11.161 The formal terms of a defined benefit plan may permit an entity to terminate its obligation under the plan. Nevertheless, it is usually difficult for an entity to cancel a plan if employees are to be retained. Therefore, in the absence of evidence to the contrary, it should be assumed that an entity that is currently promising post-retirement benefits will continue to do so over the remaining working lives of employees. [IAS 19 para 53].

Measurement of the defined benefit obligation

11.162 Paragraph 50 of IAS 19 describes the steps necessary to measure the defined benefit obligation. These include:

- Determine how much benefit is attributable to the current and prior periods.

- Make estimates (actuarial assumptions) about demographic variables (such as employee turnover and mortality) and financial variables (such as future increases in salaries and medical costs) that will influence the cost of the benefit.

- Discount that benefit to present value using the projected unit credit method.

[IAS 19 para 50].

11.163 The objective of this process is to derive the best estimate of the present value of future cash outflows that will arise in respect of the benefits earned by employees at the valuation date. This normally requires the expertise of an actuary although, as discussed in paragraph 11.202, this is not actually required by IAS 19.

Attribution of benefit to periods of service

11.164 Benefit should be attributed to periods of service according to a plan's benefit formula, unless an employee's service in later years will lead to a materially higher level of benefit than in earlier years, in which case a straight-line basis should be used. [IAS 19 para 67]. Benefit is attributed to the current period in order to determine current service cost. Benefit is attributed to the current and prior periods in order to determine the present value of the defined benefit obligation. This is illustrated in the examples below.

Example 1 – Lump-sum benefit

A plan provides a lump-sum benefit of C1,000, payable on retirement, for each year of service. A benefit of C1,000 is attributed to each year.

Example 2 – Annual final salary pension

A plan provides an annual pension of 1/60 of final salary for each year of service. The pension is payable from the age of 65. Benefit equal to the present value, at the expected retirement date, of an annual pension of 1/60 of the estimated final salary, payable from the expected retirement date until the expected date of death, is attributed to each year of service.

11.165 As noted in paragraph 11.160, employee service gives rise to an obligation under a defined benefit plan even if the benefits are not vested. However, when attributing benefit to periods of service, the probability that some employees may not satisfy vesting conditions (which includes performance hurdles) before becoming entitled to benefits is taken into account. [IAS 19 para 69]. For example, if the benefits described in the first example above (a lump-sum benefit of C1,000, payable on retirement, for each year of service) did not vest until an employee had completed ten years of service, the measurement of the defined benefit obligation in each of the first ten years would reflect the probability that some employees may not complete ten years of service.

11.166 A plan's benefit formula may set a point beyond which no further benefit can be earned. For example, a plan may pay a single lump-sum of C1,000 after ten years of service. It is logical, and IAS 19 provides that, a benefit of C100 would be attributed to each of the first ten years of employee service (taking into account the fact that some employees may not complete ten years' service, and ignoring discounting) but no benefit would be attributed to later years. [IAS 19 para 70].

11.167 On the other hand, a plan's benefit formula may result in service in later years giving rise to greater benefit than earlier years (see example below). In circumstances such as this, where service in later years gives rise to a materially higher benefit than in earlier years, IAS 19 requires that the benefit is attributed on a straight-line basis from:

- the date on which employee service first leads to benefits under the plan; until

- the date on which employee service will lead to no material amount of further benefit (other than from further salary increases).

[IAS 19 para 67].

11.168 In summary, paragraph 67 of IAS 19 requires benefits to be allocated to periods of service according to the benefit formula, unless the benefit formula allocates a materially higher level of benefit to later years of service, in which case a straight-line allocation should be made. This principle is illustrated in the following examples.

Example 1 – Benefit increases after 20 years service

A plan provides an annual pension of 1/60 of final salary, but this increases to 1/40 of final salary if an employee leaves after more than 20 years' service.

For those employees expected to remain with the employer for at least 20 years, benefit equal to the present value, at the expected retirement date, of an annual pension of 1/40 of the estimated final salary, payable from the expected retirement date until the expected date of death, is attributed to each year of service.

For all other employees, benefit equal to the present value, at the expected retirement date, of an annual pension of 1/60 of the estimated final salary, payable from the expected retirement date until the expected date of death, is attributed to each year of service.

In all cases, the measurement of the defined benefit obligation will reflect the probability that an employee may leave or die before the normal retirement date.

Example 2 – Benefits are only earned after the age of 25

A plan provides a benefit of C100 for each year of service, excluding service before the age of 25. The benefits vest immediately.

No benefit is attributed to service before the age of 25, because service before that date does not lead to benefits (conditional or unconditional). A benefit of C100 is attributed to each subsequent year.

Example 3 – Benefit increases slightly in later years

A post-employment medical plan reimburses 40% of an employee's post-employment medical costs if the employee leaves after more than 10 and less than 20 years of service, and 50% of those costs if the employee leaves after 20 or more years of service.

Under the plan's benefit formula, the entity attributes 4% of the present value of the expected medical costs (40% divided by ten) to each of the first 10 years and 1% (50% — 40%, divided by ten) to each of the second 10 years. For employees expected to leave within 10 years, no benefit is attributed.

> **Example 4 – Material increase in benefits in later years**
>
> The facts are as in example three, but only 10% of medical costs are reimbursed if the employee leaves between 10 and 20 years of service.
>
> Service in later years leads to a materially higher level of benefit than in earlier years. For employees expected to leave after more than 20 years, benefit is attributed on a straight-line basis under paragraph 67 of IAS 19. Benefit attributed to the first 20 years is 2.5% (50% divided by twenty) of the present value of the expected medical costs. For employees expected to leave between 10 and 20 years, this percentage is reduced to 1% (10% divided by ten) in the first 10 years and zero thereafter. For employees expected to leave within 10 years, no benefit is attributed.

> **Example 5 – Material increase in benefits in later years**
>
> Entity A operates a pension plan that pays a pension of C100 for each of the first 3 years of service; C500 for each of the years of service from years 4 to 6; and C2,400 for each of the years of service from years 7 to 9. An employee will, therefore, be entitled to a pension of C9,000 (C100 x 3 + C500 x 3 + C2400 x 3) after 9 years of service. Further service after 9 years does not give rise to additional pension.
>
> Entity A's employees' services in later years will lead to a materially higher level of benefit than in earlier years. Entity A should, therefore, attribute benefit to years of service on a straight-line basis from the date when service by the employee first leads to benefits under the plan until the date when further service by the employee will lead to no material amount of further benefits under the plan, other than from further salary increases.
>
> Entity A should, therefore, attribute C1,000 to each year of service (C9000/9 years, ignoring discounting) rather than following the attribution formula in the plan.

11.169 Where the amount of benefit is a constant proportion of final salary for each year of service, future salary increases will affect the amount required to settle the obligation that exists for service before the balance sheet date, but do not create an additional obligation. [IAS 19 para 71]. For example, if employees are entitled to a benefit of 1/30 of final salary for each year of service up to a maximum of 20 years, benefit of 1/30 of estimated final salary will be attributed to the first 20 years of service. No benefit is attributed to service beyond that point. A worked example illustrating this point is included in paragraph 11.189. Salary increases do not lead to further benefits, even though the amount of benefit is dependent on final salary. The extent to which actual final salary at the date of retirement is different to that estimated in the calculation of the defined benefit obligation is reflected as an actuarial gain or loss as it derives from a change to an actuarial estimate (see from para 11.266).

11.169.1 In their basis of conclusions to IFRIC D9, 'Employee benefit plans with a promised return on contributions or notional contributions', the IFRS IC concluded that expected increases in salary *should* be taken into account in determining whether a benefit formula expressed in terms of *current* salary (such as a career average plan) allocates a materially higher level of benefit to later years of service. This would mean that if salary increases do not lead to a materially higher benefit in later years, then benefits are allocated to periods of service according to the benefit formula, but if salary increases are significant, then a straight-line allocation should be made. A worked example illustrating this point is included in paragraph 11.189. IFRIC D9 was withdrawn in November 2006; and the specific issue of salary increases was not addressed in the final amendments to IAS 19 (revised) issued in June 2011. Our view is that the practice of including future salary increases in determining whether a benefit formula allocates a materially higher level of benefit to later years is appropriate.

Actuarial assumptions

11.170 Actuarial assumptions reflect an entity's best estimate of the variables that will determine the ultimate cost of providing post-employment benefits. Some defined benefit pension promises are based on achieving specific performance targets. Such targets are also variables that will affect the ultimate cost of providing the benefit and, hence, should be included in the determination of the benefit.

11.171 Demographic assumptions concern the future characteristics of the present and former membership of the plan, such as:

■ Mortality, both during and after employment.

■ Rates of employee turnover, disability and early retirement.

■ Age, sex and marital status of membership.

■ The proportion of plan members with dependants who will be eligible for benefits.

■ Claim rates under medical plans.

11.172 Financial assumptions deal with matters such as:

■ The discount rate (see para 11.174).

■ Future salary and benefit levels (see para 11.177).

■ Rates of return on investments (see para 11.230).

■ Price inflation.

■ Future medical costs, including, where material, the cost of administering claims and benefit payments (see para 11.182).

11.173 Financial assumptions should be determined in nominal terms, unless estimates in real (inflation-adjusted) terms are more reliable, for example, in a hyper-inflationary economy or where benefits are index-linked and there is a deep market in index-linked bonds of the same currency and term. [IAS 19 para 76]. Financial assumptions should be based on market expectations at the balance sheet date. [IAS 19 para 77].

11.173.1 Actuarial assumptions should be both unbiased and mutually compatible. [IAS 19 para 72]. For assumptions to be unbiased, they must be neither imprudent nor excessively conservative. [IAS 19 para 74]. For assumptions to be mutually compatible, they must reflect the economic relationships between factors such as inflation, rates of salary increase, returns on plan assets and discount rates. [IAS 19 para 75]. IAS 19 also requires disclosure of key actuarial assumptions (see para 11.282).

Example – Mutually compatible assumptions

Entity A operates a defined benefit pension plan. It has calculated the net present value of the defined benefit obligation on the assumption that:

- Salary cost will increase in line with general price inflation at 2.5% a year.

- The rate of return on plan assets is 5.0%.

- The discount rate, calculated by reference to the yield on high quality fixed rate corporate bonds, is 4%.

There is a liquid market for fixed interest and inflation linked bonds and the difference between the yield on fixed rate bonds and inflation linked bonds is 3.5%.

The rate of return on plan assets is usually greater than the discount rate, reflecting the difference between the risk profile of plan assets and the risk on high quality corporate bonds. Entity A should demonstrate that the difference between the discount rate and the return on plan assets assumptions is justified based on the mix of plan assets.

The difference between the yield on fixed interest and inflation linked bonds gives an indication of the expected rate of general inflation. Entity A's assumptions about salary inflation and the discount rate appear to be incompatible, because they have a different view of underlying inflation.

Entity A should demonstrate that the discount rate and inflation assumptions are compatible by explaining the reasons for the difference between the inflation assumption and the inflation rate implied by the difference between the yields on fixed and inflation linked bonds.

11.174 The discount rate reflects the time value of money, based on the expected timing of the benefit payments. The discount rate does not reflect investment risk or actuarial risk, since other actuarial assumptions deal with these items. The discount rate does not reflect the specific risk associated with the entity's business, nor does it reflect the risk that future experiences may differ from actuarial assumptions. IAS 19 requires that the discount rate is determined by reference to market yields at the balance sheet date on high quality corporate bonds of equivalent currency and term to the benefit obligations. [IAS 19 para 78]. The bonds' currency should be the currency in which the benefits are to be paid. It may not necessarily be the entity's functional currency. In our opinion, for a bond to be considered 'high quality' for the purposes of IAS 19, it should be rated at least at the level of AA.

> **UK.11.174.1**   In this regard, IAS 19 is less specific than FRS 17, which states that a high quality corporate bond is a bond that has been rated at the level of AA or equivalent status. Hence, our view that a bond should be rated at least at the level of AA for IAS 19 purposes is based on the guidance in FRS 17.

11.175   In countries where there is no deep market in high quality corporate bonds, the market yields (at the balance sheet date) on government bonds of equivalent currency and term should be used. [IAS 19 para 78]. In June 2005, The IFRS IC considered this further and took the view that the wording of this paragraph is clear that a synthetically constructed equivalent to a high quality corporate bond by reference to the bond market in another country may not be used to determine the discount rate. The IFRS IC observed that the reference to 'in a country' could reasonably be read as including high quality corporate bonds that are available in a regional market to which the entity has access, provided that the currency of the regional market and the country were the same (for example, the Euro). This would not apply if the country currency differed from that of the regional market.

11.175.1   A conclusion as to whether a deep market exists will be made on a case by case basis for each country. Corporate and government bond markets develop over time. As a result, a deep corporate or government bond market may develop where one did not previously exist, or the reverse may occur, and such a development may result in a change in the basis or reference for determining the discount rate to be applied. Where a change in the discount rate occurs because of the development of a deep corporate bond market in a country that previously did not have one, this change would be accounted for prospectively. However, where a change in discount rate is made from a country specific government bond rate to a rate in a previously existing broader regional corporate bond market in the same currency, this change would be accounted for as a change in accounting policy in accordance with IAS 8. For example, as a result of recent economic developments in Europe, interest rates in the eurozone regional corporate bond market may become a more relevant basis than interest rates on government bonds of a specific country within the eurozone. An entity may, therefore, elect to change the basis for its discount rate from the local government bond rate to the broader regional corporate bond rate.

11.176   In some cases, there may be no deep market in bonds with a sufficiently long maturity to match the estimated maturity of all the benefit payments. In such cases, the discount rate for longer maturities should be estimated by extrapolating current market rates of shorter term payments along the yield curve (a graphical representation of the relationship between the return on a financial asset and its time to maturity). [IAS 19 para 81].

11.176.1   In times of global market liquidity problems, AA rated corporate bond yields may increase significantly and there may be wide spreads of yields on AA rated bonds. This is likely to lead to both greater volatility and lower defined benefit liabilities as a result of the higher discount rate. At such times it becomes important to consider the following:

- Whether a robust methodology has been used to set the discount rate and whether this methodology has changed since the previous reporting date.

- What allowance has been made for plan specific factors such as age profile. For example, if the yield on an index has been used, how has the yield been adjusted to reflect differences between the term of bonds comprising the index and the term of the plan's liabilities.

- If the yield on an index has been used, what consideration has been given to whether the constituents of the index are appropriate? For instance, if an index contains a larger number of bonds issued by financial institutions which currently have high yields, it may not be appropriate to consider them 'high quality'.

A change in an index or the exclusion of some constituents from an index to reflect current circumstances would be a change in accounting estimate and applied prospectively. The accounting policy to apply a high quality corporate bond yield of appropriate duration has not changed, merely the approach considered appropriate to determine that yield. Additionally, care is needed when considering the impact of changes in the constituents of indices to ensure that such changes are appropriately taken into account at the balance sheet date. For example, if a bond that is a constituent of a particular index is downgraded on 15 December 20X1, but the index is not published until 5 January 20X2, reporting entities should reflect the downgrade as an adjustment in the index yield used to determine liabilities at 31 December 20X1, where material.

11.176.2 Disclosure will be required in accordance with IAS 1 when management concludes that the choice of discount rate is a major source of estimation uncertainty. It is likely that many companies will disclose additional information about the assumptions used to measure the pension obligation, including sensitivity analyses.

11.177 Estimates of future salary increases take account of, for example, inflation, seniority, promotion and supply and demand in the employment market. Assumptions about future salary and benefit levels should reflect an entity's legal and constructive obligations. When the formal terms of a plan (or a constructive obligation that goes beyond those terms) require an entity to change benefits in future periods, the measurement of the obligation reflects those changes. This is the case when, for example:

- the entity has a past history of increasing benefits, for example to mitigate the effects of inflation, and there is no indication that this practice will change in the future; or

- actuarial gains have already been recognised in the financial statements and the entity is obliged, by either the formal terms of a plan (or a constructive obligation that goes beyond those terms) or legislation, to use any surplus in the plan for the benefit of plan participants.

[IAS 19 para 85].

11.178   The latter point is illustrated in the following example.

> **Example – Actuarial gains resulting in a surplus**
>
> An entity operates a defined benefit pension plan, the terms of which provide that any surplus in the plan must be applied towards the enhancement of pension benefits. During 20X5, significant actuarial gains have resulted in the plan having a surplus as at 31 December 20X5 and according to the entity's accounting policy, actuarial gains (and losses) are recognised in other comprehensive income. Paragraph 85B of IAS 19 requires that the measurement of the defined benefit obligation should also take into account the additional benefits that would be payable out of the surplus as a result of the plan terms.

UK.11.178.1   FRS 17 provides that the present value of the additional contributions that the members are required to make should be treated as reducing the liability to be recognised by the employer. [FRS 17 para 40].

11.179   In contrast, some plans provide that members may be required to contribute towards the funding of a deficit. The IFRS IC concluded, in September 2007, that if an employer has a right to increase required employee contributions under cost-sharing provisions, that right should be taken in to account when measuring the obligation.

11.179.1   Some pension plans include provisions that specify employee contributions not as a fixed amount but as a proportion of the total contribution rate, for example a 60:40 split between employer and employees. These arrangements typically call for surpluses to be shared between the employer and its employees and that contributions for both employer and employees are increased proportionally where there is a deficit. The employer's share of any surplus could be used to reduce employer contributions whilst the employee share may be used either to reduce contributions or enhance benefits. Whilst the plan terms may specify a shared cost approach, legally and practically it is often not possible to force employees to pay increased contributions as legislation usually gives employees a statutory right to opt out of employer sponsored pension plans and many might elect to do so where they considered the required contribution level to be onerous.

11.179.2   For such plans, the accounting issue is how to measure the deficit when there is an expectation that employee contribution rates will need to be increased to help meet the deficit, but such increase has not yet been agreed and is not enforceable. In order to determine whether a liability for the full deficit or only a part of the deficit should be recognised, an entity should consider whether or not there is an asset (that is, a reimbursement right) or some other way to avoid the obligation.

11.179.3 If the employer can force employees to fund their share of the deficit, either through payment of additional contributions or a reduction in benefits, then it would seem clear that the employer cannot be obliged to meet the employees' share of the deficit and accordingly, it might be appropriate to recognise only its portion of the deficit (60% in the above example). The wording of the IFRS IC agenda decision supports this treatment as stated above in paragraph 11.179.

11.179.4 However, where the employer cannot enforce a benefit reduction nor force employees to pay future contributions at the pre-specified rate because the employees could choose to leave or opt out of the pension plan, the plan does not include a *"requirement for employees to make contributions to reduce or eliminate an existing deficit"*. The entity would generally record the full deficit. In substance the plan includes a provision that makes it likely employees will help to fund the deficit, but it is clear that future expected employee contributions do not meet the framework definition of an asset and would not be recogniseable as a reimbursement right under IAS19.

11.179.5 An alternative view is to regard the rate of future expected employee contributions as an actuarial assumption. Where this is the case, this assumption should be consistently applied, correlate logically with the plan's assumption about future service, and be appropriately disclosed.

11.180 It follows that the measurement of the defined benefit obligation should not reflect future changes that are not set out in the formal terms of the plan (or a constructive obligation). Such changes, when they occur, will result in:

- past service cost, to the extent that they change benefits for service before the change; and

- current service cost for periods after the change, to the extent that they change benefits for service after the change.

[IAS 19 para 86].

11.181 Some post-employment benefits are linked to variables such as the level of state retirement benefits or state medical care. The measurement of such benefits reflects expected changes in such variables if, and only if, either:

- those changes were enacted before the balance sheet date; or

- past history, or other reliable evidence, indicates that those state benefits will change in some predictable manner, for example in line with future changes in general price levels or general salary levels.

[IAS 19 para 83(c)].

11.182 Assumptions about medical costs consider the effect of technological advances, changes in health care utilisation and changes in health status of plan participants. Medical costs assumptions should take into account the level and frequency of future claims and the cost of meeting those claims, which are affected by, for example, age, gender, geographical locations and health status. Some plans require employees to contribute towards the medical costs covered by the plan and this should also be taken into account in the actuarial assumptions. Changes in employee contributions will be reflected as a past service cost or, where applicable, a curtailment (see paras 11.237 and 11.249 respectively). The cost of meeting claims may also be reduced by benefits from the state or other medical providers, as described in the previous paragraph, and this also should be reflected in the actuarial assumptions.

11.183 The choice of assumptions is a difficult area of judgement, because relatively small changes in certain key assumptions, such as mortality rates and the rate of growth in pensionable earnings, can have a material impact on the amount of the defined benefit obligation. It is not unusual for the assumptions that are made for a funding strategy to differ from an actuary's 'best estimates'. For example, there may be a deliberate policy of funding very conservatively, so that the members' benefits are given a high degree of security. The importance of disclosing key assumptions, including mortality assumptions, is discussed in paragraph 11.284.1.

Actuarial methods

11.184 The third step in the process of measuring the defined benefit obligation is to discount the estimated benefit to present value using an actuarial method. IAS 19 requires the whole amount of the obligation to be discounted to present value, even if part of the obligation falls due within twelve months of the balance sheet date. [IAS 19 para 66].

11.185 There are two principal categories of valuation methods for pension plan liabilities, namely 'accrued benefits methods' and 'prospective benefits methods'.

11.186 As the name suggests, accrued benefits valuation methods measure the present value of pension benefits earned to date. Allowance may be made for future increases in earnings. Prospective benefits valuation methods, on the other hand, estimate the total cost of providing benefits earned and expected to be earned in the future by employees. The total cost is then spread evenly over the service lives of the employees, usually as a level percentage of salaries.

11.187 The important difference between the two types of methods is that prospective benefits methods tend to smooth out changes in the annual cost that may arise under accrued benefits methods. For example, using an accrued benefits method, the cost attributable to an individual employee will increase each year as the employee gets older. This is because the present value of the benefits earned each year increases as retirement approaches and the date of payment of a pension draws nearer. Hence, where there is an ageing workforce, the current service cost under an accrued benefits method will tend to rise as a percentage of salary, whereas under a prospective benefits method it should remain constant as the rise has been anticipated in the cost allocated to the earlier years.

11.188   IAS 19 requires an entity to use the projected unit credit method, which is a type of accrued benefits method, to determine the present value of its defined benefit obligation. [IAS 19 para 64].

Example 1 – Projected unit credit method

An entity has a statutory obligation to operate a termination indemnity scheme under which employees who leave for any reason receive a lump sum based on one month's salary for each year of service. Senior staff receive enhanced benefits. The benefits are not conditional on future employment and vest at the balance sheet date.

The entity has a legal obligation to pay the termination indemnity, calculated by reference to an employee's salary and length of service. The employer has the actuarial risk, so this is a defined benefit arrangement.

The liability for termination indemnities should *not* reflect an assumption that all eligible staff resign at the balance sheet date, instead the employer should calculate the liability using the projected unit method. The calculation of the liability will include a projection of the benefit earned to date to each future point that the benefit could be paid (for example, end of each year), with allowance for salary increases and probabilities of payment. Each payment would then be discounted back to the valuation date using the yield on high quality corporate bonds, to reflect the time value of money based on the expected payment date of benefits. A liability calculated without reference to future salary increases or the expected payment date would misstate the liability. If the effect of discounting the payment exceeded the impact of future salary increases then the accrued liability would be overstated.

11.189   The projected unit credit method views each period of service as giving rise to an additional unit of benefit entitlement, with each unit being measured separately to build up the total obligation. This is illustrated in the examples below.

Example 1 – Final salary

An entity operates a defined benefit plan that pays a lump sum on termination of service of 1% of final salary for each year of service. An employee joins the entity at the beginning of year 1 on a salary of C50,000. Salaries are assumed to increase at 7% per annum and the discount rate is 8%. It is expected that the employee will retire after 5 years of service.

The following table shows how the defined benefit obligation builds up for this employee over the 5 years of service. It is assumed that there are no changes in actuarial assumptions and the possibility that the employee may leave the entity before retiring is ignored.

Year	1	2	3	4	5
Estimated salary (7% growth)	50,000	53,500	57,245	61,252	65,540
Benefit attributed to each period	655	655	655	655	655
Cumulative benefit payable	655	1,311	1,966	2,622	3,277
Opening obligation	0	482	1,041	1,686	2,428
Interest (8% on opening obligation)	0	39	83	135	194
Current service cost (discounted at 8%)	482	520	562	607	655
Closing obligation	482	1,041	1,686	2,428	3,277

At the end of year 5, the employee's final salary is C65,540 (C50,000*1.07^4). The cumulative benefit earned at the end of 5 years is 1% of the final salary times 5 years of service (C3,277). The current year benefit earned in each of the 5 years is one-fifth of this (C655). The current service cost is the present value of the benefit attributed to the current year. So in year 2, for example, the current service cost is C520 (C655/1.08^3).

Example 2 – Career average, materially higher benefits in later periods

An entity operates a defined benefit plan that pays a lump sum on termination of service of 1% of current salary for each year of service. An employee joins the entity at the beginning of year 1 on a salary of C50,000. Salaries are assumed to increase at 30% per annum and the discount rate is 8%. It is expected that the employee will retire after 5 years of service. Because the benefit is materially higher in later years due to the significant salary increases, the benefit attributable to each period is spread on a straight-line basis.

The following table shows how the defined benefit obligation builds up for this employee over the five years of service. It is assumed that there are no changes in actuarial assumptions and the possibility that the employee may leave the entity before retiring is ignored.

Year	1	2	3	4	5
Estimated salary (30% growth)	50,000	65,000	84,500	109,850	142,805
Benefit earned each period	500	650	845	1,099	1,428
Benefit attributed to each period	904	904	904	904	904
Cumulative benefit					4,521
Opening obligation	0	665	1,436	2,326	3,349
Interest (8% on opening obligation)	0	53	115	186	268
Current service cost (discounted at 8%)	665	718	775	837	904
Closing obligation	665	1,436	2,326	3,349	4,521

The current year benefit earned in each year is 1% of the current year salary, but the current year benefit attributed to each period is the cumulative benefit earned spread on a straight-line basis, C904 (C4,521/5). The current service cost is the present value of the benefit attributed to the current year. So in year 2, for example, the current service cost is C718 (C904/1.08^3).

[The next paragraph is 11.194.]

11.194 The projected unit credit method is the only actuarial method permissible under IAS 19. For the purposes of funding other valuations may be used but, where this is the case, a separate valuation of the defined benefit obligation will be required for the purposes of IAS 19.

Employee benefit plans with a promised return on contributions or notional contributions

11.195 The measurement of the defined benefit obligation can be complicated in the case of plans with a promised return on contributions, sometimes known as cash balance plans, which include the following types of plan.

- Plans that promise a fixed return on actual or notional contributions (for example, a plan that provides a benefit equal to specified contributions plus a return of 4% a year over a specified future period).

- Plans that promise a return on actual or notional contributions based on specified assets or indices (for example, a plan that provides a benefit of an amount equal to specified notional contributions plus or minus the return on a notional holding of a basket of shares).

- Plans that combine both of the above features.

11.196 The IFRS IC published a draft interpretation D9, 'Employee benefit plans with a promised return on contributions or notional contributions', in July 2004. The draft interpretation was subsequently withdrawn because the IASB published a discussion paper in March 2008. However, when IAS 19 (revised) was issued in June 2011 it did not include the proposals in the discussion paper, and the IASB is not expected to address this topic in the near future. As such, the discussion paper proposals are not considered further here; however even though D9 was withdrawn, it still contains useful guidance on best practice.

11.197 Most respondents to D9 agreed that such plans are defined benefit plans. This is because the promise of a specified return (whether fixed or variable) means that the employer may have to make additional contributions so the plans cannot be defined contribution plans (in which an entity has no legal or constructive obligation to pay further contributions relating to current or past service). The distinction between defined contribution and defined benefit plans is discussed further from paragraph 11.105.

11.198 As regards the accounting, plans that promise a *fixed* return on actual or notional contributions do not present significant problems. The benefit to be paid in the future is estimated by projecting forward the contributions or notional contributions at the guaranteed fixed rate of return. It is then attributed to periods of service and discounted to present value in the same way as any other defined benefit plan. Plan assets are also treated in the same way as any other defined benefit plan.

11.199 The accounting for plans that promise a *variable* return on actual or notional contributions based on specified assets or indices is more complicated and two approaches are considered acceptable. If the usual methodology for measuring the defined benefit obligation were to be applied, benefits would be projected forward at the expected rate of return on the assets and discounted back to a present value. Hence, if a company established such a plan and immediately contributed C100, the defined benefit obligation on the same day would exceed C100 if the expected return on assets was greater than the discount rate. This method always gives rise to a deficit. An acceptable alternative (as proposed by the IFRS IC in D9) is for the accounting to be based on paragraph 85(b) of IAS 19, which states that the measurement of the defined benefit obligation should reflect actuarial gains that have already been recognised when an entity is obliged to use any resulting surplus for the benefit of plan participants (see further para 11.177). This means that the present value of an obligation for the use of a surplus is the amount of that surplus at the balance sheet date. The same principle could be applied to any benefits that depend on future returns on assets. In other words, the plan liability is measured at the fair value at the balance sheet date of the assets or notional assets upon which the benefit depends, with an adjustment for any margin on asset returns where this is reflected in the benefits. No projection forward of the benefits or discounting is made. If benefits are unvested, the measurement of the plan liability takes into account the probability that some employees may not satisfy vesting conditions. Plan assets (if any) are recognised and measured as normal.

11.200   Plans that provide a combination of a fixed guarantee and benefits that depend on future returns on assets are sometimes described as 'defined contribution plans with a defined benefit underpin'. In our view, such schemes should be accounted for under the higher of the defined benefit obligation relating to the fixed guarantee and the obligation arising from the variable return, where the latter is determined using either of the two approaches set out above for variable schemes (see para 11.199).

[The next paragraph is 11.202.]

Frequency of valuations

11.202   IAS 19 requires an entity to determine the present value of defined benefit obligation with sufficient regularity that the amounts recognised in the financial statements do not differ materially from the amounts that would be determined at the balance sheet date. [IAS 19 para 56]. Annual actuarial valuations are not required as at the balance sheet date. Indeed, IAS 19 does not require an entity to involve a qualified actuary at all in the measurement of the defined benefit obligation. Such a practice is merely encouraged. [IAS 19 para 57]. For practical reasons, however, we consider that an entity is likely to use a qualified actuary.

> **UK11.202.1**   In the UK, FRS 17 requires full actuarial valuations to be carried out by a professionally qualified actuary at least every three years. We would expect this practice to continue under IAS 19.

11.203   The employer's and the pension plan's financial statements often have different accounting periods. In practice, it is likely that at least two full actuarial valuations will be required for funded pension plans: one for IAS 19 accounting and one (on a funding basis) for the pension plan trustees. That is because the funding valuation may use different, possibly more conservative, assumptions in relation to the liabilities. The IAS 19 valuation need not necessarily be done as at the employer's balance sheet date. In fact, a valuation as at an employer company's year end may not be available in time for the completion of the company's financial statements. It could, therefore, be done at an earlier date, or the same date as the valuation required by the trustees, as suits the employer's reporting timetable and then be updated as necessary to the employer's year end. For example, a company with a December year-end may have a pension plan with a March year end and obtain actuarial valuations as at 31 March. The full valuation would then have to be updated to each company year-end for any material transactions and other material changes in circumstances (including changes in market prices and interest rates). [IAS 19 para 57].

11.204 An update is in effect an estimate of a full valuation. IAS 19 indicates that some aspects of the valuation should be updated at each balance sheet date of the reporting employer. For example, the financial assumptions underpinning the valuation of the plan liabilities should be updated to reflect changes in market conditions. Thus the discount rate should always be the current rate of return on an appropriate bond at the employer's balance sheet date. A change in the discount rate may also require other financial assumptions, such as the inflation assumption, to be updated. Other aspects of the valuation of the liabilities can be estimated from the previous full valuation by rolling the valuation forward and updating it for changes to the plan, such as benefit improvements. Assumptions that are not directly affected by changes in market conditions need not be updated annually.

11.205 Individual circumstances will dictate whether a full valuation is required in between the previous full valuation or whether an update is sufficient. If the latest full valuation was a long time ago and many changes have occurred since, the actuary may not be confident that an update will produce a reliable current estimate of the plan liabilities. In such circumstances, a full valuation may be appropriate.

11.206 The following example illustrates the considerations relevant to determining the appropriate frequency of actuarial valuations.

Example – Frequency of actuarial valuations

A UK-based multi-national group operates a large number of defined benefit pension plans in different countries. The pension plans include:

- A group pension plan, which provides generous benefits but is open only to UK employees. The pension cost recorded in respect of this plan is equivalent to 5% of the group's total employee cost and 10% of net profit.

- A US pension plan, which provides benefits only to US-based employees. The group's operations in the US are not significant and investment returns have been stable for a number of years.

- A Latin America pension plan, which provides pension and medical insurance benefits to all employees in Latin America. The operations in Latin America are material to the group and the stock markets in Brazil and Venezuela are extremely volatile. Venezuela is a hyper-inflationary economy.

- An Africa pension plan, which provides limited benefits to expatriate staff in Africa. The plan is unfunded and covers a limited number of employees. The group announced a benefit enhancement in the current year.

- A Benelux pension plan, which provides limited benefits to top up the state pension received by former employees in the Benelux region. The state pensions in these countries are inflation-linked and the group has never been required to make top-up payments.

Deciding on the frequency of valuations requires judgement. Factors to be taken into account include the size of the pension obligation, the volatility of the economic environment in which each plan operates, changes in plan benefits and the overall impact of employee benefit costs on the financial statements. The same frequency does not necessarily apply to all plans.

It will also be necessary to determine the extent of the valuation. Sometimes a full actuarial valuation will be necessary, but often it will be sufficient to update an existing valuation as described in paragraph 11.204.

In this example, management concluded that the following valuation frequency was appropriate for each of its plans:

- The cost of the group pension plan is material to the financial statements. Although both the economic environment in the UK and the benefit package are stable, the income statement is sensitive to changes in the employee benefit cost. Accordingly, the present value of the defined benefit obligation and the fair value of plan assets should be determined each year.

- The US pension arrangements are not significant and the economic environment is stable. The fair value of quoted plan assets and updates to the discount rate for example are determined every year, but a full valuation of the defined benefit obligation is obtained only every three years.

- The Latin America pension plan is significant and it operates against a volatile economic background. The scale of the changes in the economic environment that occur every year might have a profound effect on the actuarial assumptions. Accordingly, the present value of the defined benefit obligation and the fair value of plan assets should be determined every year.

- The pension obligation in Africa is not significant and the liability is unfunded. Hence, there are no plan assets to be valued. The group usually determines the fair value of the defined benefit obligation every three years. However, in view of the announcement of the benefit enhancement, it may be necessary to obtain a valuation in the current year.

- The Benelux pension plan is not significant. The defined benefit obligation exists, but is very small. There are no plan assets. Hence, the present value of the defined benefit obligation is determined every three years, unless there is a change in the state pension arrangements.

Interim reports

11.207 IAS 34 requires that an interim financial report should be prepared for a discrete period (that is, items of income and expenses should be recognised and measured on a basis consistent with that used in preparing the annual financial statements and no adjustments should be made for events expected to occur subsequent to the end of the interim period) and that the entity's assets and liabilities should be measured in the same way as they would be at a year end.

11.208 For a defined contribution pension plan, the expense recognised in a period is equal to the contributions payable in respect of that period. Hence, defined contribution plans are treated in an interim financial report in the same way as in annual financial statements. However, the treatment of defined benefit plans is potentially more complicated.

11.209 Consistent with the discrete period principle, paragraph B9 of Appendix B to IAS 34 states that the pension cost for an interim period should be calculated on a year-to-date basis by using the actuarially determined pension cost rate as at the end of the previous year, as adjusted for significant market fluctuations (for example changes in bond yields, expected market returns, inflation or asset values) since the previous year end and for significant curtailments, settlements, or other significant one-off events.

11.209.1 Paragraph 77 of IAS 19 states that financial assumptions should be based on market expectations at the balance sheet date, paragraph 82 states that interest cost should be calculated using the discount rate at the start of the period and paragraph 106 states that the expected return on plan assets should be based on market expectations at the beginning of the period. IAS 19 is silent on service cost and demographic assumptions such as mortality.

11.209.2 IAS 19 requires opening assumptions to be used and, therefore, appears to contradict the appendix to IAS 34, which states that significant market fluctuations should be adjusted for. If the service cost, interest cost or expected return on plan assets recognised in the income statement were to be updated in each interim period, then the cumulative full year amounts in those primary statements would not be the same as if the opening assumptions had been used throughout the annual period. The difference would depend on how many interim periods there are.

11.209.3 We believe that market fluctuations that have a significant positive or negative impact on the income statement should be adjusted for when they occur and not just at interim reporting dates. Alternatively, on the basis that Appendix B accompanies, but is not part of IAS 34, and IAS 19 is clear that opening assumptions should be used in specific cases, it would also be acceptable, as an accounting policy choice, to always use opening assumptions and not adjust for market fluctuations at all during the reporting period.

11.210 Neither IAS 34 nor IAS 19 specify how frequently the assets and liabilities of a defined benefit plan should be revalued. This will depend on the facts and circumstances specific to the pension plan and requires the exercise of a degree of professional judgement. However, IAS 19 does require an entity to determine the present value of the defined benefit obligation and the fair value of the plan assets with sufficient regularity that the amounts recognised in the financial statements do not differ materially from the amounts that would be determined at the balance sheet date. [IAS 19 para 56]. In other words, the impact of any actuarial gains and losses since the last valuation must be expected to be immaterial. This may be the case where an entity follows the 'corridor approach' described from paragraph 11.268.1 and hence recognises only a small proportion of actuarial gains and losses. However, in a volatile economic environment, it will be more difficult to reach such a conclusion where actuarial gains and losses are recognised immediately and it may be necessary for an entity to obtain a valuation at each interim balance sheet date.

> **Example – Interim remeasurements**
>
> Entity A obtains actuarial valuations of its defined benefit pension obligations at annual intervals. An actuary performs a valuation in January 20X1 to determine, with sufficient reliability, the present value of the defined benefit obligation and the fair value of plan assets at 31 December 20X0, the entity's year-end.
>
> The measurement procedures to be followed in interim reports should be designed to ensure that the resulting information, including the value attributed to the defined benefit obligation and plan assets, is sufficiently reliable. The preparation of interim financial reports may require a greater use of estimates than the preparation of annual reports. Extrapolation (a roll forward) of the latest actuarial valuation as adjusted for significant market fluctuations or other significant one-time events will often provide a reliable measurement for interim reporting purposes.
>
> Entities operating in volatile economic environments in which other actuarial assumptions such as interest rates are significantly changed during interim periods may need to perform an interim remeasurement of their pension obligations.
>
> An interim remeasurement always needs to be performed if a curtailment or settlement occurs.

11.211 Obtaining fair values of certain assets held by the pension plan, such as traded securities, is a low-cost and relatively simple task for an entity to perform at the interim balance sheet date. However, obtaining fair values for other assets such as untraded securities (or securities that are traded so thinly that the most recent trade price is not considered a fair reflection of the fair value of the security) or properties, or obtaining a present valuation of the liabilities of the pension plan are costly and time-consuming tasks. Estimating these values accurately may involve the use of experts such as property surveyors or actuaries.

11.212 IAS 34 recognises that there will be a greater use of estimates by an entity when it is preparing an interim financial report than when it is preparing its annual financial statements. [IAS 34 para 41]. Consequently, it may be appropriate for an entity to extrapolate a valuation that had been previously obtained for the purposes of calculating the appropriate asset/liability for recognition in the interim financial report. [IAS 34 App C para C4]. As discussed in paragraph 11.202, IAS 19 encourages, but does not require, the entity to involve a qualified actuary in the measurement of plan liabilities, so it may sometimes be appropriate at an interim reporting date for the entity's directors to perform this extrapolation exercise without actuarial assistance.

11.213   Interim reports are considered in greater detail in Manual of Accounting – Interim financial reporting.

Restrictions on the amount recognised as a defined benefit asset

11.214   Sometimes, a net balance recognised in respect of a defined benefit pension plan may be an asset. Consistent with the principle that a pension plan surplus is regarded as an asset to the extent that the employer can gain an economic benefit from it, IAS 19 contains a restriction over the amount that may be recognised. In principle, the amount recognised as an asset may not exceed its recoverable amount. However, where applied, the workings of the 'corridor' approach (see from para 11.268.1) mean that the asset ceiling test under IAS 19 is rather more complicated. The amount recognised as an asset is measured as the lower of the amount determined under paragraph 54 of IAS 19 (see para 11.130) and the aggregate of:

■   any cumulative unrecognised net actuarial losses and past service cost; and

■   the present value of any economic benefits available in the form of refunds from the plan or reductions in future contributions to the plan.

[IAS 19 para 58].

11.215   The application of this restriction is considered in the following example.

Example – Amount recognised as an asset

A defined benefit plan has the following characteristics at the balance sheet date.

	C'000
Present value of defined benefit obligation	(1,000)
Fair value of plan assets	1,200
	200
Unrecognised actuarial losses (presented as an asset in the balance sheet)	150
Asset determined in accordance with paragraph 54 of IAS 19 (see para 11.130)	350
Present value of available future refunds and reductions in future contributions	170

The amount that may be recognised as an asset in this example is C320,000, being the aggregate of the cumulative unrecognised net actuarial losses (C150,000) and the present value of available future refunds and reductions in future contributions (C170,000).

11.216   IAS 19 currently contains no specific guidance concerning the measurement of the recoverable amount of a pension plan surplus. However, IFRIC 14 addresses:

- the amount of pension scheme surpluses that entities can include as a defined benefit asset in their balance sheets, in particular when refunds or reductions in future contributions should be regarded as 'available'; and

- when a minimum funding requirement may give rise to additional liabilities.

The reach of IFRIC 14 is wider than this might suggest since it may lead to an increase in liabilities even when a scheme is in deficit under IAS 19. This happens where contributions to reduce an existing deficit under a funding requirement may not be recoverable once they are made.

If a defined benefit plan is in deficit and there is no minimum funding requirement, then IFRIC 14 is not relevant. However, if a plan is in surplus, and the employer has an unconditional right to the surplus, it can recognise an asset, there is no need to consider the impact of any minimum funding requirement.

11.216.1 Statutory minimum funding requirements exist in many countries to improve the security of the post-employment benefit promise made to members of an employee benefit plan. Such requirements normally stipulate a minimum amount or level of contributions that must be made to a plan over a given period. Therefore, a minimum funding requirement may limit the ability of the entity to reduce future contributions. [IFRIC 14 para 2]. IFRIC 14 does not change statutory or contractual funding rules, as these are set by regulators or pension fund trustees. The interpretation does clarify how entities should account for the effect of any such requirements. It is worth noting that minimum funding requirements can result from the revision of a schedule of contributions, where such a schedule creates an obligation on the employer to pay amounts specified. They do not have to be enforced by statute or by a regulator. Note also that where a schedule of contributions constitutes a minimum funding requirement, it is likely to be revised regularly (typically every three years) by the plan's actuary. The contribution schedule cannot be viewed as having a three year duration (on the basis that it will be replaced by a new schedule after three years), but must be extrapolated forward indefinitely (on the basis that it will be replaced by an equivalent schedule at the end of the three years). [IFRIC 14 para 21].

11.216.2 Further, the limit on the measurement of a defined benefit asset may cause a minimum funding requirement to be onerous. Normally, a requirement to make contributions to a plan would not affect the measurement of the defined benefit asset or liability. This is because the contributions, once paid, will become plan assets and so the additional net liability is nil. However, a minimum funding requirement may give rise to a liability if the required contributions will not be available to the entity once they have been paid. [IFRIC 14 para 3]. Such an additional liability arises only if two conditions are satisfied:

- the entity has a statutory or contractual obligation to pay additional amounts to the plan; and

- the entity's ability to recover those amounts in the future is restricted.

11.216.3 IFRIC 14 does not affect an entity's ability to get a refund, as this is determined by statutory requirements in the jurisdiction in question and the plan rules. The interpretation does provide guidance on how to account for any restrictions that may be in place. An economic benefit, in the form of a refund or a reduction in future contributions, is available if the entity can realise it at some point during the life of the plan or when the plan liabilities are settled, even if this is not until some distant time in the future, such as when the last benefit is paid to the last pensioner in the scheme. A surplus does not have to be immediately realisable at the balance sheet date in order to be recognised. [IFRIC 14 para 8]. A refund does not have to have been agreed to be available.

11.216.4 A refund is deemed to be 'available' only if the entity has an unconditional right to a refund, which is a more stringent test than some have applied in the past. If the entity's right to a refund of a surplus depends on the occurrence or non-occurrence of one or more uncertain future events not wholly within its control, the entity does not have an unconditional right and shall not recognise an asset. [IFRIC 14 paras 11, 12]. An asset is not recognised when it is conditional, even if the receipt of the refund is probable.

11.216.5 Interpreting whether an unconditional right exists or not in practice can be difficult. An entity does not have an unconditional right to a refund when the payment of the refund is subject to approval by another party, for example a regulator or governing body of the plan. However, if a regulator's approval is required for a refund, but that approval is perfunctory (for example, for a closed fund with no more members) then this may be treated as an unconditional right because the approval process is not substantive. In establishing whether there is an unconditional right, it will be important to check the scheme rules. In some cases, legal advice may have to be obtained to determine whether an unconditional right exists.

> **UK.11.216.5.1** FRS 17 has a harsher test for recognising surpluses compared to IAS 19. Under FRS 17, there must be either an ability to reduce future contributions or a refund that has been *agreed* by the pension scheme trustees in place. The issue of an unconditional refund, therefore, does not apply. In the cases where there is a surplus in excess of any future contribution reductions, there is likely to be a GAAP difference unless a refund has been agreed by the balance sheet date.

11.216.5.1 Where a third party (for example plan trustees) has a discretionary power but not an obligation to wind up a plan or grant benefit improvements on the occurrence of a particular event, the question arises as to whether the exercise of that power should be anticipated or whether the effects should be recognised only when they occur. We believe that there are two acceptable views:

- Based on paragraph BC10 of IFRIC 14, the existence of an asset at the balance sheet date depends on whether the company has a *right* to obtain a refund or a reduction in future contributions. This *right* is not affected by future acts that could change the amount of the surplus that may ultimately be recovered. The fact that the trustees could choose to wind up the scheme or grant benefit improvements (and thus reduce the surplus) should not be anticipated and would not remove the company's unconditional right to the surplus.

- Based on paragraphs 12 and BC12 of IFRIC 14, if the entity's right to a refund resulting in economic benefit depends on actions by a third party, even if these actions are discretionary, the entity does not have an unconditional right. If the trustees could force the plan to wind up before the last benefit is paid, or grant benefit improvements and thus effectively eliminate any surplus, the company does not have an unconditional right to the surplus.

The policy that a company adopts is likely to represent a critical accounting judgement requiring disclosure in accordance with paragraph 122 of IAS 1.

11.216.6   The economic benefit available as a *refund* is the surplus at the balance sheet date (the fair value of plan assets less the present value of the defined benefit obligation) that the entity has a right to receive as a refund, less any associated costs (for example, a tax other than income tax or professional fees). The refund should not be discounted. [IFRIC 14 para 12-15]. Where a refund would not be available until after a plan is wound up, the costs of winding up the plan should be deducted from the amount included in the balance sheet.

UK.11.216.6.1   Such costs of winding-up may be high in the UK.

11.216.7   The economic benefit available as a *future reduction in contributions*, in the absence of any minimum funding requirement, is the future service cost to the entity for each period over the shorter of the plan's expected life and the entity's expected life. The future service cost, which excludes amounts that will be borne by employees, should be calculated using actuarial assumptions that are consistent with those used to determine the defined benefit obligation. [IFRIC 14 para 16-17].

11.216.8   Minimum funding contributions may be required to cover future service as well as any existing shortfall relating to past service. The two sub-components are treated differently. [IFRIC 14 para 18].

11.216.9   IFRIC 14 concluded that a pre-payment provides an economic benefit to the entity when it relieves the entity of an obligation to pay future minimum funding contributions that exceed future service cost. Therefore, an entity should consider those economic benefits in measuring an asset. For minimum funding contributions relating to future service, the economic benefit available as a reduction in future contributions is the sum of:

- any amount that reduces future minimum funding requirement contributions for future service because the entity made a pre-payment (that is, paid the amount before being required to do so); and

- the estimated future service cost in each period less the estimated minimum funding requirement contributions that would be required for future service in those periods if there were no pre-payment as described in the first bullet point above.

[IFRIC 14 para 20].

11.216.10　If an entity has an obligation to pay contributions to cover an existing shortfall in respect of services already received, and those contributions (or a proportion thereof) will not be available after they are paid, then a liability should be recognised. The liability and its subsequent remeasurement should be recognised immediately, either *via* a charge to the income statement or to other comprehensive income, depending on the entity's policy for recognising actuarial gains and losses. [IFRIC 14 para 23 to 26].

11.216.11　The principles of IFRIC 14 are illustrated in the following examples.

Example 1 – Trustee approval required for a contribution holiday

The trustees of an entity's defined benefit pension plan comprise two employer-nominated representatives and two employee-nominated representatives. The trustees determine the rates of contribution to the plan by unanimous vote on the basis that the employer contributes two thirds of the funding requirement and the employees contribute one third. The terms of the plan do not permit refunds. There are no minimum funding requirements. However, the plan's terms stipulate that the level of contributions must be agreed between the entity and the trustees.

A surplus of C3m has arisen in the year ended 31 December 20X5. As the terms of the plan do not permit a refund, the fact that trustee approval is required is not relevant. The surplus can only be recovered through a future reduction in contributions. Where there is no minimum funding requirement the maximum asset value that can be recognised is the future reduction in contributions (or the present value of the service cost) over the shorter of the expected life of the plan or the entity. As the service cost is, say C0.3m – which, if projected forward over the future service period is in excess of C3m – the amount recognised as an asset by the entity is the full amount of C3m.

Example 2 – Refunds when access to a surplus is limited

Entity A participates in a multi-employer pension plan that provides benefits to employees based on final salary and years of service. Independent trustees administer the plan in accordance with relevant pension legislation. The trustees provide the information each participating employer requires to apply defined benefit accounting.

The most recent actuarial valuation revealed a surplus. Pension legislation permits the trustees to refund surplus contributions to participating employers, subject to a legal maximum. The pension legislation also requires that the plan maintains a solvency margin determined as a percentage of the plan assets. The solvency margin is an insurance for contingencies that is ultimately available for refunds. The trade unions have challenged the trustees in connection with previous refunds and the proposed refunds were subject to litigation. The refunds the participating employers finally received following negotiations with trade unions were significantly less than the legal maximum and were paid in instalments.

Entity A proposes to use its share of the surplus in the plan to calculate the asset limit.

Entity A should take account of the legal maximum ignoring the solvency margin. Local legislation restricts the proportion of the surplus the trustees may refund. Entity A, therefore, restricts the asset limit to the amount of the surplus that is available for refund.

Trade union action might restrict the refund and force the employer to provide additional benefits from the surplus. When the terms of the pension plan change and employees obtain additional benefits for their past service, the entity recognises the past service costs over the vesting period.

The IAS 19 asset ceiling is based on whether a refund is possible and not on whether a refund is likely.

Example 3 – IAS 19 surplus and minimum funding contributions fully refundable

Entity A has a funding level on a minimum funding requirement (MFR) basis (which is measured on a different basis from that required under IAS 19) of 82% in plan B. Under the minimum funding requirements, entity A is required to increase the funding level to 95% immediately and as a result, it has a statutory obligation at the balance sheet date to contribute C200 to plan B immediately. The plan rules permit a full refund of any surplus to entity A at the end of the life of the plan. The year end valuations for plan B are set out below.

	C
Market value of plan assets	1,200
Present value of defined benefit obligation	(1,100)
Surplus	100

The defined benefit asset before consideration of the MFR is C100.

Entity A should recognise a liability to the extent that the contributions payable are not fully available. Payment of the contributions of C200 will increase the IAS 19 surplus from C100 to C300. Under the plan's rules this amount will be fully refundable to the entity with no associated costs. Therefore, no liability is recognised for the obligation to pay the contributions.

Example 4 – IAS 19 deficit and minimum funding contributions not fully available

Entity C has a funding level on a minimum funding requirement basis of 77% in plan D. Under the minimum funding requirements, entity C is required to increase the funding level to 100% immediately and as a result it has a statutory obligation at the balance sheet date to pay additional contributions of C300 to plan D. The plan rules permit a maximum refund of 60% of the IAS 19 surplus to entity C and entity C is not permitted to reduce its contributions below a specified level, which happens to equal the IAS 19 service cost. The year end valuations for plan D are set out below.

	C
Market value of plan assets	1,000
Present value of defined benefit obligation	(1,100)
Deficit	100

The defined benefit liability before consideration of the MFR is C100.

The payment of C300 would change the IAS 19 deficit of C100 to a surplus of C200. Of this C200, 60% (C120) is refundable. Therefore, of the contributions of C300, C100 eliminates the IAS 19 deficit and C120 (60% of C200) is available as an economic benefit. The remaining C80 (40% of C200) of the contributions paid is not available to entity C.

Paragraph 24 of IFRIC 14 requires the entity to recognise a liability to the extent that the additional contributions payable are not available to it. Entity C should increase the defined benefit liability by C80. As required by paragraph 26 of IFRIC 14, C80 is recognised immediately in accordance with entity C's policy for recognising actuarial gains and losses and entity C recognises a net balance sheet liability of C180. No other liability is recognised in respect of the statutory obligation to pay contributions of C300. When the contributions of C300 are paid, the net balance sheet asset will be C120.

11.217 The standard requires that the application of paragraph 58 should not result in a gain being recognised solely as a result of an actuarial loss or past service cost in the current period, or in a loss being recognised solely as a result of an actuarial gain in the current period. [IAS 19 para 58A]. In order for this result to be achieved, the following should be recognised immediately to the extent that they arise while the carrying amount of a defined benefit asset is subject to the restriction described in paragraph 11.214:

■ Net actuarial losses and past service cost of the current period to the extent that they exceed any reduction in the present value of the economic benefits specified in paragraph 11.214. If there is no change, or there is an increase, in the present value of the economic benefits, the entire net actuarial losses and past service cost of the current period should be recognised immediately.

■ Net actuarial gains of the current period, after the deduction of any current period past service cost, to the extent that they exceed any increase in the present value of the economic benefits specified in paragraph 11.214. If there is no change, or there is a decrease, in the present value of the economic benefits, the entire net actuarial gains of the current period, after the deduction of any current period past service cost, should be recognised immediately.

[IAS 19 para 58A].

The effect of paragraph 58A of IAS 19 is that further unrecognised actuarial losses are only deferred on the balance sheet to the extent that they offset decreases in the present value of any economic benefits available, that is they will not lead to an increase in the net pension asset.

11.218 The application of the above principles is illustrated in the following examples.

> **Example 1 – Immediate recognition of actuarial losses in accordance with paragraph 58A of IAS 19**
>
> At the end of 20X1, a defined benefit plan has a surplus of C60m and there are unrecognised actuarial losses of C40m. Were it not for the restrictions imposed by paragraph 58 of IAS 19, the amount recognised as an asset would be C100m. However, the present value of any economic benefits available in the form of refunds from the plan or reductions in future contributions to the plan is only C30m so the amount recognised as an asset is restricted to C70m (that is, C40m plus C30m).
>
> During 20X2, further actuarial losses of C35m arise. Assuming that no losses are amortised in the income statement through the normal operation of the 'corridor' approach, this would increase the cumulative unrecognised actuarial losses to C75m. If the present value of any economic benefits available in the form of refunds from the plan or reductions in future contributions to the plan is reduced to, say, C20m, this would mean that the amount recognised as an asset would increase to C95m (that is, C75m plus C20m). The increase in the asset would be recognised as income.
>
> Paragraph 58A seeks to prevent outcomes such as this. Hence, to the extent that the actuarial loss of C35m exceeds the reduction in the present value of the economic benefits (that is, C10m) it is recognised immediately in the income statement. Therefore, an actuarial loss of C25m is recognised immediately, so the amount recognised as an asset at the end of 20X2 remains at C70m. In effect, the actuarial loss of C25m offsets the reduction in the effect of the asset ceiling.
>
> **Example 2 – Immediate recognition of actuarial gains in accordance with paragraph 58A of IAS 19**
>
> The facts at the end of 20X1 are the same as in example 1.
>
> During 20X2, actuarial gains of C35m arise. Assuming that no actuarial losses are amortised in the income statement through the normal operation of the 'corridor' approach, this would reduce the cumulative unrecognised actuarial losses to C5m. If the present value of any economic benefits available in the form of refunds from the plan or reductions in future contributions to the plan is increased to, say, C40m, this

would mean that the amount recognised as an asset would reduce to C45m (that is, C5m plus C40m). The reduction in the asset would be recognised as an expense.

As in the previous example, paragraph 58A seeks to prevent outcomes such as this. Hence, to the extent that the actuarial gain of C35m exceeds the increase in the present value of the economic benefits (that is, C10m) it is recognised immediately in the income statement. Therefore, an actuarial gain of C25m is recognised immediately so, once again, the amount recognised as an asset at the end of 20X2 remains at C70m (economic benefit of C40m plus unrecognised losses of C30m, brought forward loss of C40m less the C10m of the C35m gain that has not been immediately recognised).

Example 3 – Immediate recognition of actuarial gains when there is a reduction in the present value of economic benefits

The facts are the same as in example 2, except that during 20X2 there is a reduction of C10m in the present value of economic benefits available. This means that the present value of any economic benefits available in the form of refunds from the plan or reductions in future contributions to the plan is C20m.

Were it not for the requirements of paragraph 58A, the amount recognised as an asset at the end of 20X2 would be C25m (that is, C5m plus C20m). The reduction in the asset of C45m would be recognised as an expense. However, paragraph 58A requires that where there is no change, or there is a decrease, in the present value of the economic benefits, the entire net actuarial gains of the current period, after the deduction of any current period past service cost, should be recognised immediately. Hence, in this example, the entire actuarial gain of C35m should be recognised immediately in the income statement. The amount recognised as an asset will be C60m (that is, C40m plus C20m). In effect, the actuarial gain of C35m is more than offset by the increase in the effect of the asset ceiling. This is illustrated below.

Year	Asset before ceiling test	Effect of asset ceiling	Amount recognised
	C	C	C
20X1	100	(30)	70
20X2	135	(75)	60
Gain/(loss)	35	(45)	(10)

11.218.1 Where an entity has a policy of recognising actuarial gains and losses directly through other comprehensive income, rather than profit or loss (see para 11.274.1), any adjustment arising from a restriction in the amount recognised as a defined benefit asset should also be recognised through other comprehensive income. Such amounts should not be recycled through profit or loss in a subsequent period. [IAS 19 paras 93C, 93D].

Recognition in the income statement

11.219 Since the plan assets and liabilities are re-measured at each period end, the income statement reflects the change in the surplus or deficit except, that is, for the following:

- Contributions to the plan.

- Unrecognised actuarial gains and losses (see para 11.266) and past service costs (see para 11.237).

- Actuarial gains and losses if recognised outside profit or loss in accordance with the entity's accounting policy (see para 11.274.1).

- Business combinations.

11.220 The amount of pension expense (income) to be recognised in profit or loss is comprised of the following individual components:

- Current service cost (see para 11.223).

- Interest cost (see para 11.228).

- Expected return on any plan assets and on any reimbursement rights (see para 11.230).

- Actuarial gains and losses as required by the entity's policy (see paras 11.266 and 11.274.1).

- Past service costs (see para 11.237).

- The effect of any settlement or curtailment (see para 11.249).

- The effect of the limit described in paragraph 11.214, unless it is recognised in other comprehensive income (see para 11.218.1).

[IAS 19 para 61].

11.220.1 While IAS 19 analyses the changes in the plan assets and defined benefit obligation into various components and provides guidance in respect of each, the standard does not prescribe how such components be reported within profit or loss. Accordingly, an entity may present the net of all components within a single line item or alternatively to classify the net interest component separately within finance costs (see para 11.279).

UK.11.220.1.1 In the UK, common practice in this area has tended towards companies presenting interest cost and the expected return on plan assets within finance costs with all other costs being presented as an operating expense. This is consistent with paragraph 56 of FRS 17, which prescribes that the net of interest cost and the expected return on plan assets is presented as other finance costs/income.

11.221 If actuarial gains and losses are ignored, the following example illustrates how the above items reflect the change in a surplus or deficit.

Example – Double entry

The actuarial valuation of a company's pension plan at 31 December 20X3 showed a surplus of C39m. The profit and loss charge for 20X4 is C66m (that is, the aggregate of current service cost, interest cost and expected return on assets, which is not analysed here into different components). After consulting with its actuaries, the company decided to reduce its employer contributions for 20X4 to C50m. At 31 December 20X4 the surplus in the plan was measured at C23m. There are no minimum funding requirements and the surplus is fully refundable.

The double-entry for the year 20X4 would be as follows:

	C	C
Dr Profit and loss account (net pension cost)	66	
Cr Defined benefit asset		66
Dr Defined benefit asset	50	
Cr Cash (contributions paid)		50

The movements in the defined benefit asset are as follows:

	C
Asset b/f	39
Pension cost (profit and loss account)	(66)
Contributions paid	50
Asset c/f	23

The asset of C39m at 31 December 20X3 is increased by contributions of C50m during 20X4 and reduced by the pension cost of C66m. At 31 December 20X4 an asset of C23m is recognised reflecting the current surplus of C23m.

11.222 IAS 19 does not overrule the requirements of other accounting standards regarding the recognition of amounts as assets, so employee benefit costs, including appropriate proportions of the above items, may be capitalised within the cost of assets such as inventories or property, plant and equipment. [IAS 19 para 62].

Current service cost

11.223 Current service cost is defined as *"the increase in the present value of the defined benefit obligation resulting from employee service in the current period"*. [IAS 19 para 7]. It represents the actuarially calculated present value of the pension benefits earned by the active employees in each period and is supposed to reflect the true economic cost relating to each period based on current market conditions. This cost is determined independently of the funding of the plan. In principle, therefore, for a given set of employees and benefit formula, the current service cost should be the same irrespective of whether the plan is in surplus, in deficit or unfunded.

11.224   Current service cost is not necessarily a stable percentage of pensionable pay year-on-year. For example, current service cost will vary if the discount rate changes. It will also increase year-on-year as a proportion of pay if the average age of the workforce is increasing, as is likely where a plan is closed to new entrants.

11.225   The valuation of the plan liabilities and, hence, the calculation of current service cost for each year should be based on the plan's benefit formula. An exception is where a disproportionate amount of total benefits relates to later years of service, in which case the benefit should be allocated on a straight-line basis over the period in which it is earned. [IAS 19 para 67]. The attribution of benefit to periods of service is discussed further from paragraph 11.164.

11.226   The mechanics of the projected unit credit method calculations are illustrated in the examples in paragraph 11.189.

11.227   The current service cost should be based on the most recent actuarial valuation at the beginning of the year. The financial assumptions underlying the calculation of the present value of the benefits earned (that is, the rate used to discount liabilities, rate of inflation, rate of salary increase and rates of pension and deferred pension increases) should be current as at the beginning of the year. Although the current service cost for the year is based on the financial assumptions set at the beginning of the year, the financial assumptions should be updated at the end of the year for the purpose of re-measuring the plan liabilities. The adoption of new assumptions at the end of the year does not affect the current service cost for the past year, but it sets the assumptions underlying the current service cost for the next year. Therefore, the financial assumptions on which the current service cost for 20X4 is based (that is, those at the beginning of 20X4) should already have been updated in the valuation of the plan liabilities at the end of financial year 20X3 and will also have been disclosed in the financial statements for 20X3 (see further para 11.282). See paragraph 11.209 for a discussion of whether assumptions should be updated at interim reporting dates.

Interest cost

11.228   Interest cost is defined as *"the increase during a period in the present value of a defined benefit obligation which arises because the benefits are one period closer to settlement"*. [IAS 19 para 7]. The interest cost represents the unwinding of the discount on the plan liabilities. As for the current service cost, the interest cost is determined independently of the plan's funding. The discount rate applicable to any financial year, being the appropriate high quality corporate bond rate (or government bond rate if appropriate) at the beginning of the year, is the same as the rate at which the plan liabilities are measured at the end of the previous year.

11.229   Interest cost is calculated by multiplying the discount rate as determined at the start of the period by the present value of the defined benefit obligation throughout that period, taking account of any material changes in the obligation. [IAS 19 para 82]. For example, the current service cost, past service costs relating to benefit improvements and transfers into the plan will increase the liability during the year; benefits paid to pensioners and transfers out of the plan will reduce the liability during the year.

Expected return on plan assets and reimbursement rights

11.230 The return on plan assets is defined as *"interest, dividends and other revenue derived from the plan assets, together with realised and unrealised gains or losses on the plan assets, less any costs of administering the plan (other than those included in the actuarial assumptions used to measure the defined benefit obligation) and less any tax payable by the plan itself"*. [IAS 19 para 7]. Hence, the return on assets component of the pension cost reflects the plan's funding.

11.231 The amount recognised in the income statement under IAS 19 is the expected return on assets. The difference between the expected return and the actual return achieved in the period is an actuarial gain or loss. [IAS 19 para 105]. The return on reimbursement rights is treated in the same way.

11.232 The expected return on plan assets is based on market expectations, at the beginning of the period, for returns over the entire life of the related obligation. The income statement is credited each period with the expected long-term rate of return on the plan assets, based on their market values at the beginning of the year. Where applicable – for example, equities and properties – the rate of return will include expected capital growth as well as income from dividends and rents. For government bonds and corporate bonds, the expected return should be the gross redemption yield at the beginning of the period. The treatment in the employer entity's income statement is, therefore, unrelated to the realisation of income and capital gains in the pension plan itself. The plan assets are revalued to fair value at each balance sheet date. The difference between the fair value and the 'expected' value of the assets – that is, the value that has accrued by crediting the expected rate of return – is treated as an actuarial gain or loss. Thus the amount credited each year as the expected return on plan assets should be a relatively stable long-term return, whereas short-term volatility in equity and other asset values is dealt with as described from paragraph 11.266.

11.233 For each class of asset, the calculation needs to reflect the market value at the beginning of the year and movements during the year – for example, contributions received, pensions paid and transfers of assets in and out. [IAS 19 para 106]. Assumptions need to be made about where contributions are invested and from where benefit payments are sourced. The standard does not require changes during the year in the portfolio mix or risk profile to be taken into account in the calculations, so the effect of such changes would in general be reflected as an actuarial gain or loss. However, if the pension plan trustees significantly changed the risk profile of the portfolio mid-year (for example, making a significant switch from equities to bonds), it might be appropriate for the calculations to reflect this.

11.234 The following example illustrates the above principles:

Example – Return on plan assets

Entity A has opening plan assets of C10,000, contributes cash of C4,900 and pays out benefits of C1,900 (net cash contributed C3,000) during the year. The expected return on plan assets is 7.5%.

	C
Return on C10,000 held for 12 months at 7.5%	750
Return on C3,000 held for 6 months at 3.68% (equivalent to 7.5% annually, compounded every six months)	110
Expected return on plan assets	860

The actual return on plan assets is calculated as follows:

	C
Fair value of plan assets at 31 December 20X4	15,000
Less fair value of plan assets at 1 January 20X4	(10,000)
Less contributions received	(4,900)
Plus benefits paid	1,900
Actual return on plan assets	2,000

The difference between the expected return on plan assets (C860) and the actual return on plan assets (C2,000) is an actuarial gain of C1,140.

11.235 As noted in paragraph 11.230 above, the return on plan assets should take account of any costs of administering the plan other than those included in the actuarial assumptions used to measure the defined benefit obligation, to avoid double counting. This is further emphasised by paragraph 107 of IAS 19. Expenses will be included in the measurement of the defined benefit obligation where they reflect a present obligation (for example, to administer and pay pension benefits that have already been earned) and not where they reflect future obligations (for example, the production of annual accounts). Invariably questions arise as to whether certain expenses should be included in the measurement of the obligation or deducted from the return on plan assets. In our view, expenses should be accounted for in accordance with their substance. Hence, investment management and similar expenses should be deducted from the return on plan assets, while expenses in respect of commitments to administer the plan should be included in the measurement of the defined benefit obligation. At present, tax payable by the plan should be deducted from the return on plan assets, in accordance with the definition of the return.

11.236 Sometimes administration expenses may be incurred by the sponsoring employer on behalf of a pension plan, with or without a recharge to the plan. The principles described in the previous paragraph will continue to apply, so:

■　If the employer recharges pension administration costs, the plan will be in the same position as where it makes payments to third parties. Hence, the measurement of the defined benefit obligation would take account of administration costs as described above.

■ If the employer does not make a recharge, it should make a provision for future administration expenses and add this to the defined benefit obligation. In substance, the fact that the expenses are incurred by the employer rather than the plan makes no difference to the accounting.

Example 1 – Accounting for expenses

An entity incurs the following administrative expenses:

■ A fee of 0.5% a year paid to a bank for asset management services by an independent trust holding pension plan assets.

■ Salaries of members of the management board of the trust who manage pension plan assets.

■ Salaries of members of the management board of the trust who administer the pension payments.

■ Bank transaction fees paid by the trust for processing payments to pensioners.

■ Administration costs incurred by the entity to administer the pension plan participants' database; the database is not required to satisfy general reporting obligations of the entity.

■ Actuarial valuation costs that relate to financial reporting obligations of the entity rather than to pension obligations incurred by the entity.

■ Income tax payable by the trust holding plan assets.

Expenses should be accounted for in accordance with their substance. Those related to revenue generated by investments held in the pension plan are charged to expected/ actual return on plan assets in the income statement.

Non-investment related expenses that are an integral part of the entity's obligation to administer the pension plan may be included in the actuarial assumptions used to measure the defined benefit obligation. [IAS 19 para 107].

An entity may treat the expenses as follows:

■ A fee paid to a bank for asset management services should be charged to expected return on plan assets.

■ Salaries of members of the board of the trust who manage pension plan assets should be reflected in calculating the expected return on plan assets.

■ Salaries of members of the trust's management board who administer the pension payments should be included in actuarial assumptions as part of the pension obligation; payments of such salaries out of trust's assets reduce pension plan assets and the related pension obligation.

■ Bank transaction fees for payments made by the trust to pensioners should be included in actuarial assumptions as part of the pension obligation.

- Administration costs incurred to administer the pension plan participants' database should be included in actuarial assumptions as part of the pension obligation because the database is not related to the entity's general reporting obligations.

- Actuarial valuation costs that relate to the entity's financial reporting obligations rather than to pension obligations should be charged to administration expenses in the income statement.

- Income tax payable by the trust holding plan assets relating to revenue generated by these assets should be charged to the expected return on plan assets.

Example 2 – Social security and payroll taxes

Entity A incurs social security and payroll tax charges of 10% of its cash contributions to a defined benefit pension plan administered by independent trustees. The taxes are payable in the month following the cash contribution to the trust and pension payments from the trust to retirees are not subject to further social security or payroll taxes.

Non-investment related expenses that are an integral part of the entity's pension contributions obligation should be included in actuarial assumptions used to measure the defined benefit obligation. The social security and payroll tax charges are linked to the pension and do not constitute a separate employee benefit, because they are only payable if the entity provides the pension benefit. Consequently, they should be included in actuarial assumptions used to measure the defined benefit obligation rather than expensed in the year in which the cash contributions are made.

Payments of the social security contributions are recorded against the pension liability.

Past service costs

11.237 Past service costs are defined as *"the change in the present value of the defined benefit obligation for employee service in prior periods, resulting in the current period from the introduction of, or changes to, post-employment benefits or other long-term employee benefits"*. [IAS 19 para 7]. Negative past service costs are discussed in paragraph 11.246 below.

11.238 Benefit changes may produce both an increase in the cost of future service relating to active members (reflected in a higher annual current service cost) and an increased liability for past service relating to current and ex-employees. The cost (that is, the capitalised present value) of benefit changes that relate to past service and that have not previously been allowed for in the valuation of the plan liabilities should be charged to the profit and loss account on a straight-line basis over the vesting period. The vesting period is the period until the pension plan member becomes unconditionally entitled to the benefits. [IAS 19 para 96]. Past service cost is recognised over the vesting period, regardless of the fact that the cost refers to employee service in previous periods. [IAS 19 para 97]. In some territories, the changes will vest immediately upon grant and so the whole cost is recognised immediately as an expense. This treatment applies irrespective of whether the additional past service liability relates to pensioners, ex-employees entitled to benefits that are not yet in payment or current employees, or whether the benefit changes are funded by a surplus or give rise to a deficit.

11.239 Where benefit changes have been awarded but some have not yet vested, IAS 19 requires only the vested portion to be recognised in the reporting employer's financial statements. The unrecognised past service cost (that is, the cost that will be recognised in the future periods over which the benefits vest) should be deducted from the plan liabilities in arriving at the asset or liability to be recognised in the balance sheet. [IAS 19 para 54]. The standard implies, therefore, that the full past service cost (vested and unvested) will be included in the defined benefit obligation and that the existence of unrecognised past service costs will give rise to a difference between the surplus or deficit in the plan and the asset or liability that is recognised in the reporting employer's balance sheet.

11.240 The recognition of past service costs is illustrated in the following example:

Example – Recognition of past service cost

An entity operates a pension plan that provides a pension of 1% of final salary for each year of service, subject to a minimum of 5 years' service. On 1 January 20X4 the entity improves the pension to 1.25% of final salary for each year of service, including prior years. As a consequence, the present value of the defined benefit obligation increased by C500,000 as shown below:

	C
Employees with more than 5 years' service at 1 January 20X4	300,000
Employees with less than 5 years' service at 1 January 20X4 (average of three years of service so two years until vesting)	200,000
Increase in defined benefit obligation	500,000

A past service cost of C300,000 should be recognised immediately as those benefits have already vested. The entity has changed the benefits payable to these employees in connection with services they have already provided, so the past service costs are charged in the income statement immediately. The remaining C200,000 is recognised on a straight-line basis over the two year period from 1 January 20X4. The pension entitlement of these employees has not vested, so the additional benefit is given in return for services to be delivered by the employees over the period until the benefits are vested.

11.241 The schedule for recognising past service costs in the income statement should be established when the benefits are introduced or changed. It is considered impracticable to require entities to maintain the detailed records needed to identify and implement subsequent changes in that amortisation schedule. Moreover, the effect is likely to be material only where there is a curtailment or settlement. Accordingly, IAS 19 requires an entity to amend the amortisation schedule for past service cost only if there is a curtailment or settlement. [IAS 19 para 99].

11.242 It is important to distinguish between past service costs and actuarial losses. A larger than expected increase in pensionable salaries, for example, will increase the plan liabilities relating to past service. This is an actuarial loss rather than a past service cost, since it is a re-measurement of the existing commitment to pay retirement benefits based on final salary. Similarly, the cost of a higher than anticipated increase to pensions in payment will generally be regarded as an actuarial loss, being a re-measurement of the employer's existing commitment to provide cost of living increases. On the other hand, the introduction of a new or additional commitment to protect pensions from inflation, where none previously existed, would give rise to a past service cost, because such pension increases would not previously have been allowed for in the valuation of the plan liabilities.

11.243 In practice, the distinction between past service costs and actuarial losses is often quite blurred. Some transactions do not fit easily into either category, for example the introduction of a government subsidy for the provision of benefits, which gives rise to a change in the cost of the benefit, without a change in the benefit actually received.

11.244 Specifically, IAS 19 states that the following are not past service costs:

- The effect of differences between actual and previously assumed salary increases on the obligation to pay benefits for service in prior years (there is no past service cost, because actuarial assumptions allow for projected salaries).

- Under and over estimates of discretionary pension increases when an entity has a constructive obligation to grant such increases (there is no past service cost, because actuarial assumptions allow for such increases).

- Estimates of benefit improvements that result from actuarial gains that have been recognised in the financial statements if the entity is obliged to use any surplus in the plan for the benefit of plan participants, even if the benefit increase has not yet been formally awarded (the resulting increase in the obligation is an actuarial loss and not past service cost).

- The increase in vested benefits when, in the absence of new or improved benefits, employees satisfy vesting requirements (there is no past service cost, because the entity recognised estimated cost of benefits as current service cost as the service was rendered).

- The effect of plan amendments that reduce benefits for future service (this is a curtailment – see para 11.249).

[IAS 19 para 98].

11.245 Past service costs also exclude benefits that become payable as a result of the early termination of an employee's employment. Therefore, where employees made redundant are granted enhanced pension benefits (say, for early retirement) in lieu of, or in addition to, redundancy payments, the cost of the enhanced pension benefits are in effect treated as termination payments (see para 11.79) rather than past service costs.

11.246　Past service costs may be either expenses (where benefits are introduced or improved) or income (where existing benefits are reduced). [IAS 19 para 7]. For example, past service costs may be positive (expenses) when benefits are introduced or changed so that the present value of the defined benefit obligation increases, or negative (income) when existing benefits are changed so that the present value of the defined benefit obligation decreases. The constitution of many pension funds means that existing benefits are rarely reduced, so negative past service costs are rare.

11.247　Where a 'negative' past service cost (that is, income) does arise, the resulting reduction in the defined benefit obligation is recognised over the average period until the reduced portion of the benefits becomes vested. [IAS 19 para 100]. This is consistent with the normal treatment of past service costs described above.

11.248　If, in a period, an entity increases certain benefits and reduces others available to the same employees, the net impact may be recognised as a single net expense or credit. [IAS 19 para 101].

Settlements and curtailments

11.249　Settlements and curtailments are events that materially change the liabilities relating to a plan and that are not covered by the normal actuarial assumptions.

11.250　A settlement arises when *"an entity enters into a transaction that eliminates all further legal or constructive obligation for part or all of the benefits provided under a defined benefit plan"*. [IAS 19 para 112]. Settlements have the effect of extinguishing a portion of the plan liabilities, usually by transferring plan assets to or on behalf of plan members, for example, when a subsidiary is sold or when assets and liabilities are transferred into a defined contribution plan.

11.251　The purchase of an insurance policy to fund some or all of the employee benefits relating to employee service in the current and prior periods is not a settlement if the entity retains a legal or constructive obligation to pay further amounts should the insurer not pay the employee benefits specified in the insurance policy. [IAS 19 para 113]. Such a policy may, however, be treated as a plan asset or a reimbursement right. See paragraphs 11.140-11.141 above for further guidance on the accounting treatment for qualifying and non-qualifying insurance policies.

Example 1 – Insurance policy

On 1 January 2003, entity A insured its defined benefit pension obligations with a third party insurer (entity B). The insurance policy is in the name of entity A and not in the name of specific plan participants. However, entity B will pay pensions directly to entity A's former employees. Entity A can revoke the insurance policy at any point in time and obtain the policy's cash surrender value. The insurance policy does not form part of entity A's bankruptcy estate under existing legislation. Entity A believes it retains no further legal or constructive obligation towards its employees for the defined benefit pension plan. It is not required to pay further amounts if the insurer does not pay the pension benefits.

The acquisition of the insurance policy is not a settlement of the pension obligation. The insurance policy has eliminated the legal or constructive obligation and entity A is no longer exposed to actuarial risks. However, entity A can revoke the policy at any point in time and obtain the policy's cash surrender value. The transaction cannot be considered a settlement of the existing pension obligation.

The policy is a non-qualifying insurance policy, because the proceeds of the policy can be paid to entity A. It should be recognised as a reimbursement right, if appropriate.

Example 2 – Lump sum payment on retirement

Entity A operates a final salary pension plan that gives a right to a pension of 1% of final salary for each year of service. The terms of the plan allow an employee to choose to receive a lump sum payment at the time of retirement instead of receiving monthly pension payments. The option for the lump sum payment may only be exercised within 3 months prior to retirement.

The *option* for a lump sum is not a settlement. It is a normal employee benefit entitlement. The actuarial valuations should include assumptions about the number of employees that are expected to choose to receive the lump sum payments.

A settlement with the resulting recognition of actuarial gains and losses and past service costs only occurs when an entity enters into a transaction that eliminates all further legal or constructive obligations for part or all of the benefits provided under a defined benefit plan.

11.252   A curtailment occurs when an entity either:

■   is demonstrably committed to make a significant reduction in the number of employees covered by a plan; or

■   amends a defined benefit plan's terms such that a significant element of future service by current employees will no longer qualify for benefits, or will qualify only for reduced benefits.

[IAS 19 para 111].

11.253   A curtailment may arise from an isolated event, such as the closing of a plant, discontinuance of an operation or termination or suspension of a plan, or a reduction in the extent to which future salary increases are linked to the benefits payable for past service. Curtailments are often linked with a restructuring. When this is the case, an entity accounts for a curtailment at the same time as for a related restructuring.

[The next paragraph is 11.255.]

11.255 The accounting for a settlement or a curtailment is in principle the same (see para 11.257). Nevertheless, the following example illustrates the difference between them.

Example 1 – Difference between curtailment and settlement

Management of entity C has decided to restructure one of the entity's three business segments and announce the plan at 31 December 20X5. The terms of the plan are as follows:

- In Germany, they will close three of entity C's six factories and relocate 500 of the 1,000 employees. As part of the relocation package, unions have agreed that in exchange for retraining, the affected employees' benefits will be frozen and new employees will not be covered by the plan.

- In Sweden, they will discontinue all activities. Management has agreed with the unions that it will make a one off payment to all of its employees in exchange for cancelling their pension entitlement.

The negotiated settlement in Germany is a curtailment, since the entity is demonstrably committed to making a significant reduction in the number of employees covered by a plan. The closure of half the factories in Germany is likely to have a material impact on entity C's consolidated financial statements.

The discontinuation in Sweden will be both a curtailment and a settlement, since the entity will enter into a transaction that eliminates all liabilities (both past and future) for the benefits provided under the pension plan. The timing of curtailments and settlements is considered in paragraph 11.261.

11.256 Table 11.11 shows the recognition of both a settlement loss and a curtailment gain from closure of the scheme to future service accrual from February 2008, resulting from the termination of a defined benefit plan.

Table 11.11 – Settlement and curtailment

The Rank Group Plc – Annual report – 31 December 2008

Finance review (extract)

Transfer of the defined benefit pension plan:

The Group transferred its defined benefit pension plan to Rothesay Life Limited on 27 June 2008, receiving proceeds of £29.0m before transaction costs and corporation tax. The defined benefit pension asset at the date of transfer, calculated in accordance with IAS19, was £137.7m. Further details of the £99.2m pre-tax loss on transfer are detailed in note 4 to the financial statements. As a result of the transfer, the Group has no further liabilities in respect of the plan.

2008 exceptional items

Continuing operations

On 27 June 2008, the Group completed the transfer of the assets and liabilities of the Rank Pension Plan ('the Plan'), a defined benefit scheme, to Rothesay Life (an FSA regulated insurance company and wholly owned subsidiary of Goldman Sachs).

The transfer secured the accrued benefits for the members of the Plan and removed all financial risks and liabilities in relation to the Plan from the Group. As a result of the transfer, the Group will no longer make the remaining scheduled contributions of £30.8m, which were part of an ongoing funding agreement made at the time of the sale of Deluxe Film in 2006.

Further details of the exceptional loss arising on the transfer are disclosed in the table below:

	£m
Proceeds	29.0
Costs associated with transfer	(1.0)
Net proceeds from transfer of defined benefit pension asset	28.0
Curtailment gain on closure of scheme to future contributions	10.5
Carrying value of defined benefit pension asset at transfer	(137.7)
Exceptional loss before taxation	(99.2)
Taxation	27.8
Total exceptional loss arising on transfer after taxation	(71.4)

11.257 Calculating the gain or loss arising from a settlement or curtailment event requires a 'before' and 'after' measurement. The gain or loss is in principle the resulting change in the surplus or deficit (that is, the plan assets less the plan liabilities) plus related unrecognised actuarial gains and losses and past service cost attributable to the reporting employer. It comprises:

■ Changes in the present value of the defined benefit obligation.

■ Changes in the fair value of plan assets.

■ Any related actuarial gains and losses and past service cost that had not previously been recognised (see from paras 11.266 and 11.237 respectively).

[IAS 19 para 109].

Example – Restructuring

The facts are the same as in the previous example at paragraph 11.255. Immediately before the announcement of the restructuring plan, the net pension liability in each of the countries affected was as follows:

	Germany	Sweden
	Cm	Cm
Present value of defined benefit obligation	(5.0)	(7.5)
Fair value of plan assets	3.5	5.0
Unrecognised actuarial losses	0.1	0.5
Net pension liability	(1.4)	(2.0)

After the restructuring, the present value of the pension obligation in Germany is reduced to C4m and the unrecognised actuarial loss is C80,000. The one-off payment made to the employees in Sweden was C2.5m.

The settlement/curtailment gain or loss is the aggregate of the change in the present value of the defined benefit obligation, the change in the fair value of plan assets and any related unrecognised actuarial gains and losses. Hence, the entity recognises a curtailment gain of C980,000 in respect of the German curtailment, being the reduction in the present value of the defined benefit obligation (C5m — C4m) less the reduction in the unrecognised actuarial loss (C100,000 — C80,000). It also recognises a loss of C500,000 in respect of the Swedish discontinuance, being the difference between the net pension liability before the settlement (C2m) and the payment made to settle the liability (C2.5m).

11.258 The treatment of actuarial gains and losses can often prove problematic. In particular, it is unclear what is meant in paragraph 109 by the phrase *"related actuarial gains and losses"*. Paragraph 115 of IAS 19 provides some guidance. It requires that where a curtailment relates to only some of the employees covered by a plan, or where only part of an obligation is settled, the gain or loss includes a proportionate share of the previously unrecognised past service cost and actuarial gains and losses. The proportionate share is determined on the basis of the present value of the obligations before and after the curtailment or settlement, unless another basis is more rational in the circumstances. For example, it may be appropriate to apply any gain arising on a curtailment or settlement of a plan to first eliminate any unrecognised past service cost relating to the same plan.

11.259 As a curtailment is defined on the basis of a change in the future accrual of benefits for current active members, the impact of a curtailment on the existing defined benefit obligation will generally be quite small and it would not be unusual for it to have no impact. In such circumstances, it is arguable that none of the unrecognised actuarial gains and losses are 'related'. In contrast, in the event of a total curtailment, it would not be unreasonable to argue that all gains and losses are 'related'. However, where a partial curtailment does have an impact on the defined benefit obligation, for example because benefits are to be based on current rather than future salary, the guidance in paragraph 115 indicates that the 'related gain or loss' should be determined on the basis of the movement in the defined benefit obligation. This is an area in which a number of approaches may be defended as *"rational in the circumstances"* and it will be necessary to exercise judgement. [IAS 19 para 115].

Example 1 – Unrecognised actuarial gains or losses on a fully curtailed plan

In connection with closing a subsidiary and making all of the employees redundant, entity A curtailed one of its defined benefit pension plans. The present value of the defined benefit obligation before the curtailment was C100.

The present value of the pension obligation decreased to C90 as a consequence of the curtailment. The unrecognised actuarial gain was C20. The corridor (see para 11.268.1) was determined to be C9.

The related portion of the actuarial gain that needs to be recognised as part of the curtailment is 10%, that is, the percentage decrease in the defined benefit obligation. The amount recognised is, therefore, 10% of 20 = C2.

The remaining actuarial gains of C18 normally should be recognised over the expected average remaining working lives of the employees participating in the plan. However, the remaining working life is zero where all the employees are made redundant. This is a full curtailment and the entity should, therefore, also recognise the actuarial gain outside the corridor (18 — 9 = C9) as part of the curtailment, because there is no remaining working life over which to spread the gain.

Management alternatively may consider a faster recognition of the actuarial gains and assess that in a full curtailment all of the actuarial gains are related to the curtailment. In this case, all of the unrecognised actuarial gain of C20 would, therefore, be recognised.

Example 2 – Unrecognised actuarial gains or losses on a partially curtailed plan

Entity B curtailed its unfunded defined benefit pension plan. The future service of a portion of the entity's labour force no longer qualifies for pension benefits. The present value of the defined benefit obligation decreased from C100 to C90. Unrecognised past service cost was C20 and unrecognised actuarial losses were C10 before the curtailment.

The gain or loss on curtailment includes a proportionate share of the previously unrecognised past service cost and actuarial gains and losses where a curtailment relates to only some of the employees covered by a plan. The proportionate share is determined on the basis of the present value of the obligations before and after the curtailment or settlement, unless another basis is more rational in the circumstances.

The entity's position before and after the curtailment is as follows:

	Before curtailment	Change	After curtailment
	c		c
Present value of the defined benefit obligation	100	10% decrease	90
Less unrecognised past service costs	(20)	10% × 20	(18)
Less unrecognised actuarial loss	(10)	10% × 10	(9)
Balance sheet liability	70		63

The curtailment gain is C7 (10 — 2 — 1).

11.260 IAS 19 does not specify different measurement dates for settlements and curtailments depending on whether they result in gains or losses. Instead, IAS 19 requires recognition of any gain or loss when the event giving rise to the settlement or curtailment occurs. [IAS 19 para 109].

UK.11.260.1 FRS 17 specifies that losses arising on settlement or curtailment not allowed for in the actuarial assumptions should be measured at the date on which the employer becomes demonstrably committed to the transaction. Gains arising on settlements and curtailments not allowed for in the actuarial assumptions should be measured at the date on which all parties whose consent is required are irrevocably committed to the transaction. [FRS 17 para 64].

Timing

11.261 Determining the period in which a settlement or curtailment occurs can be difficult, especially in cases where there is a curtailment and a settlement, but they are not recognised at the same time. This is illustrated in the following examples.

Example 1 – Involuntary termination of employee service

Entity A announced in December 20X3 that 100 employees will be terminated in February 20X4 as part of a restructuring project that the entity is demonstrably committed to carry out.

Entity A has given the 100 employees an option to have their pensions settled by a lump sum payment of C75,000 per employee payable at the date of termination in February 20X4. 90 employees made an irrevocable decision to accept the payment in December 20X3. Entity A expects that the remaining 10 employees will not accept the offer.

Entity A had a pension liability towards the 90 employees of C6,300,000 at 31 December 20X3 prior to considering the lump sum settlement offer. There are no unrecognised actuarial gains and losses or prior service costs and the plan is wholly unfunded.

Both a curtailment and a past service cost have occurred in December 20X3 as a result of the restructuring. The future service of the 90 employees who exercised the lump sum option will not earn them any additional benefits and the plan is curtailed. The entity entered into a transaction with the 90 employees that changed the pension obligation at the same time. Entity A should recognise in its financial statements for the year ended 31 December 20X3 a liability of C6,750,000 (90 × C75,000) towards the 90 employees that accepted the offer, which will result in the recognition of additional expense of C450,000 (C6,750,000 — C6,300,000). This liability should be adjusted as necessary when final settlement actually occurs *via* payment.

Example 2 – Timing of curtailment due to plan amendment

Entity B announced its intention to curtail a pension plan. Under the current plan, employees earn a pension of 1% for each year worked. The plan will be amended so that the benefit is based on employee's average salary measured over the period from 1 January 20X4 to leaving.

Entity B published amended terms of the pension plan on its web site on 20 December 20X3. The entity's human resource department prepared amended employment contracts in early January 20X4 and sent them to employees for signature. All amended employment contracts were signed by the end of January 20X4. The amendment is not contractually binding under local legislation until signed by the employee.

The curtailment should not be recognised before the amended terms become contractually binding. The terms of a defined benefit plan were amended in January 20X4 when the new terms became contractually binding through signature of the employees. Entity B should account for the effects of the curtailment in January 20X4. The date from which arrangements are contractually binding will vary depending on local legislation.

Example 3 – Timing of curtailment due to replacement by a new defined contribution plan and subsequent settlement *via* a lump sum payment

Entity C operates a non-contributory defined benefit pension plan for its senior employees. Entity C has not funded its benefit obligation. On 1 January 20X3, entity C decides to remove the uncertainty about its future benefit obligation and replace the defined benefit plan with a defined contribution plan. The benefits with respect to services provided up to 1 January 20X3 are not affected.

On 30 June 20X3, entity C agrees with employee representatives to make a lump sum cash payment of C5,000 and introduces a defined contribution plan in exchange for cancelling their pension entitlement.

The pension liability recognised in the balance sheet on 30 June before the agreement was C5,500.

The introduction of the new plan is a curtailment of the old plan. Entity C recognises the change in the defined benefit obligation and the unrecognised actuarial gains and losses related to the curtailment in January 20X3.

Entity C recognises a settlement gain of C500 on 30 June 20X3 when a legally binding agreement has been reached that eliminates all further legal or constructive obligations for the benefits provided under the pension plan in exchange for the lump sum payment. The settlement gain is the difference between the accrued pension liability before the settlement and cash payment to senior management.

Example 4 – Meaning of 'demonstrably committed' when disposing of a major business division (interim period)

Entity E has a December year end. In June 20X3, entity E publicly announced the disposal of a major division D to entity Z. The sale and purchase agreement (SPA) had been signed, but was still subject to shareholder approval at June 20X3. A contractually binding, unconditional sale agreement was in place, and division D sold, in October 20X3.

On completion of the sale, division D employees are no longer able to accrue benefits for future service in entity E's defined benefit pension plan. Entity Z announced in June 20X3 that it intends to offer division D employees membership of its own pension plan and those employees will be able to transfer their benefit (with an enhancement funded by entity E) from entity E's plan to entity Z's plan. Letters to employees setting out the terms and conditions of the offer were sent in October 20X3 and employees have until March 20X4 to accept or decline.

The cessation of the employee's ability to accrue benefits in entity E's plan gives rise to a curtailment gain (as entity E's obligation is reduced).

If employees subsequently choose to transfer to entity Z's plan, this gives rise to a settlement loss, due to the enhancement offered by entity E as an incentive to transfer.

IAS 19 requires that curtailment and settlement losses, as well as gains, should be recognised when the curtailment or settlement occurs. Paragraph BC79 of IAS 19 states that management's intent to curtail or settle a defined benefit plan is not a sufficient basis to recognise such an event.

Even when an entity has taken a decision to sell an operation and announced that decision publicly, it cannot be demonstrably committed to the sale until a purchaser has been identified and there is a binding, unconditional sale agreement. Until there is a binding sale agreement, the entity will be able to change its mind and indeed will have to take another course of action if a purchaser cannot be found on acceptable terms. At the June 20X3 half year, the SPA is still subject to shareholder approval and is not yet contractually binding and, hence, no curtailment should be recognised at this time.

A settlement should be recognised on the date when the entity enters into a transaction that eliminates all further legal or constructive obligations for part or all of the benefits provided under the plan. [IAS 19 para 112]. In the example above, settlement would occur only once the entity E employees concerned have made an irrevocable decision to accept the new offer and the transfer payment has been made. No settlement should be recognised at the June 20X3 half year either.

Example 5 – Timing of settlement and restructuring provision when disposing of a major business division (year end)

The facts are the same as in example 4.

In October 20X3 a contractually binding sale agreement is in place, division D has been sold and division D employees can no longer accrue future benefits in entity E's scheme. A curtailment should be recognised at the December 20X3 year end, with the gain being based on all active members in the scheme on the date of the curtailment.

The settlement should only be recognised when all further legal/constructive obligations for all or part of the defined benefit obligation have been eliminated. This does not occur until the employees concerned have made an irrevocable decision to transfer to the entity Z plan and the transfer payment has been made. If this has not occurred by the year end date, the settlement loss should not be recognised.

Although the settlement cannot be accounted for under IAS 19 until the transfers actually take place, if the offer of the enhanced transfer values can be justified as a restructuring cost of the disposal, then entity E should be able to set up a provision at the year end for the excess amount they expect to pay out as a result of employees accepting the enhanced transfers. The pension obligation is recorded in accordance with IAS 19 at the year end along with an additional restructuring provision. Both the curtailment gain and the restructuring loss would be included within the profit or loss on disposal (see further para 11.263). In the following year, 20X4, the provision would be utilised in settling the transfers with any difference between the expected and actual amounts going to the income statement.

11.262 Before determining the effect of a settlement or curtailment, an entity should re-measure both the defined benefit obligation and any plan assets using current actuarial assumptions (including a current discount rate and other current market prices). [IAS 19 para 110]. The approach required by IAS 19 makes sense as the gain or loss attributed to the settlement or curtailment event is then based on fair values at the date of such event.

Example – Settlement loss on sale of a subsidiary

A wholly-owned subsidiary is sold for C100m. The book value of the subsidiary's net assets on the date of the sale was C70m. The subsidiary participated in the group defined benefit pension plan. There was no contractual agreement or stated policy for charging the net defined benefit cost to individual group entities, and so in accordance with IAS 19 para 34A, the subsidiary, in its individual financial statements, recognised only its contributions payable. At the date of the sale, the plan was in surplus by C35m. The surplus was recognised in full as an asset in the consolidated financial statements (in other words, actuarial gains and losses were recognised immediately). As part of the sale agreement, a bulk transfer of plan assets was made to the purchaser's pension plan. The 'before' and 'after' measurements of the group plan are as follows:

	Before disposal	After disposal	Settlement loss
	Cm	Cm	Cm
Plan assets	160	130	(30)
Plan liabilities	(125)	(100)	25
Plan surplus	35	30	(5)

The profit on sale is as follows:

	Cm	Cm
Sale proceeds		100
Less:		
– subsidiary's net assets at date of sale	(70)	
– settlement loss	(5)	(75)
		25

Introducing unrecognised actuarial gains and losses into the example, the 'before' and 'after' measurements would be as follows:

	Before disposal	After disposal	Settlement loss
	Cm	Cm	Cm
Plan assets	160	130	(30)
Plan liabilities	(125)	(100)	25
Plan surplus	35	30	(5)
Unrecognised actuarial gains	(20)	(16)	4
Defined benefit asset	15	14	(1)

Of the previously unrecognised actuarial gains of C20m, it has been assumed that 20% (that is 25/125) 'relates' to the part of the obligation that was eliminated through the settlement. Accordingly, actuarial gains of C4m are recognised to reduce the settlement loss to only C1m.

11.263 Further complications can arise when a defined benefit plan is in surplus, but the surplus is not recognised because the entity cannot gain economic benefit from it (see further para 11.216). One question that arises is whether the unrecognised surplus should be adjusted through OCI and then included within the calculation of the settlement gain or loss recognised in the income statement. The following example illustrates this.

Example – Settlement with an unrecognised surplus

Entity A has a defined benefit plan and recognises actuarial gains/losses in other comprehensive income. At 31 December 20X1, the following amounts were attributable to the plan:

Fair value of plan assets	135
Defined benefit obligation	(100)
Surplus	35

This surplus has been deemed irrecoverable in accordance with IFRIC 14; the surplus was, therefore, written off through other comprehensive income.

Two years later, entity A settles its defined benefit plan. When the settlement occurs, all plan assets with their fair value of C135 are used to settle the defined benefit obligation of C100. What, if any, impact should this settlement have on the income statement?

A settlement loss of 35 should be recognised in the income statement. When the settlement takes place, the entity should re-assess its original irrecoverability assumption concerning the surplus. When the settlement occurs, the surplus is recoverable, in that the entity does not need to inject additional funds to settle the plan's obligation, which is an economic benefit. Therefore, the entity should first recognise the surplus adjustment through OCI in accordance with paragraph 58(b) of IAS 19 (see further para 11.214) and then calculate the settlement loss of C35 according to paragraph 109 of IAS 19 (see further para 11.257).

Difference between a curtailment and a negative past service cost

11.264 Sometimes, it may prove difficult to distinguish a curtailment from a negative past service cost. The distinction is important as curtailments are recognised immediately, whereas past service costs are spread over the period until the benefits concerned vest. A curtailment relates to benefits to be earned in respect of future service, while a past service cost relates to benefits that have already been earned. However, in practice an amendment to a pension plan may appear to have features of both. If a change to a benefit plan affects the extent to which future salary increases after the reporting date impact benefits payable for past service, the total impact of that change on the present value of the defined benefit obligation should be treated as a curtailment, not a negative past service cost. This is consistent with the treatment of a change related to future service. [IAS 19 para BC62B]. The following example illustrates the difference.

Example – Difference between a curtailment and a past service cost

An entity operates a defined benefit pension plan that provides a benefit of 1% of final salary for each year of service. In December 20X3, management agreed with trade unions to amend the terms of the plan such that employees will be entitled to a pension of 0.5% of final average salary, calculated over a 5 year period, for both past and future service. The plan's actuaries re-measured the defined benefit obligation using current assumptions and determined that:

■ the change in accrual rate from 1% to 0.5% decreased the present value of defined benefit obligation by C1,000; and

■ the change in definition of final salary decreases the present value of defined benefit obligation by C100.

There are no unrecognised actuarial gains and losses.

The change in accrual rate from 1% to 0.5% means that the value of benefits already earned by employees will be reduced so the present value of the defined benefit obligation for employee service in prior periods will decrease. Hence, this appears to satisfy the definition of a 'negative' past service cost (see further para 11.246).

The change in the accrual rate will also represent a curtailment as future service will qualify for reduced benefits. However, this change in future benefits *would* not impact the present value of the defined benefit obligation as at December 20X3. In contrast, the change in definition of final salary is also a curtailment, but this future change *will* impact the present value of the defined benefit obligation as at December 20X3. This is because the level of final salary is an assumption that will impact the measurement of the defined benefit obligation.

The impact of the above analysis is that part of the plan amendment would be treated as a curtailment and part as a negative past service cost. The calculation of the amounts falling into each part and the resulting accounting could be complex, because past service costs are spread over a vesting period, while curtailments are recognised immediately, along with any related unrecognised past service cost or actuarial gain or loss.

Accounting for the closure of a defined benefit pension plan

11.265 The term 'closed' may be used to describe a pension plan at various stages of its life. It may be closed to new members, although existing members continue to earn benefits. Alternatively, there may be no future accrual of benefit, although benefits already earned are preserved. Finally, it may be being wound up. The accounting implications of each stage are considered in the following examples. For simplicity, it is assumed that actuarial gains and losses are recognised immediately.

Example 1 – Plan closed to new employees

Entity A operates a defined benefit plan (which is currently in deficit) for all employees, once they have completed three months' service. Employee turnover is high, but the number of employees covered by the plan has been stable for a number of years.

On 31 December 20X1, entity A decides to close the existing plan to new employees, who will instead be offered a new defined contribution plan. Employee turnover means that the number of employees in the defined benefit plan will diminish as time passes.

Entity A has not committed to reduce the number of employees currently in the defined benefit plan or to change the benefits payable under the plan. Hence, the benefit commitment is unaffected by the closure and the reduction in employees will reflect staff turnover, rather than any action by the entity. Accordingly, the action of closing the plan to new employees does not represent a curtailment and there will be no accounting implications.

Example 2 – Benefit accrual ceased

A year later, on 31 December 20X2, the entity changes the terms of the plan. Defined contribution arrangements will apply to all future service. Hence, no further benefits based on final salary will be earned by employees, although the entity will retain its defined benefit obligation in connection with prior service. With effect from 1 January 20X3, the entity has no liability in respect of service after that date beyond its annual contributions to the defined contribution plan.

However, benefits earned in respect of this prior service will no longer be based on final salary, but will instead be based on salary as at 31 December 20X2.

At 31 December 20X2, the net pension liability was C10m. The plan's actuary has advised that the net pension liability after the plan amendment is C7m.

The cessation of future benefit accrual and the change from final to current salary represent curtailments. Hence, entity A should recognise a gain of C3m when the terms of the plan are amended.

Example 3 – Plan wound up

A year later, on 31 December 20X3, entity A decided to close its defined benefit pension plan. It proposes to make a one off payment which will end its involvement in the plan. The payment will have two elements:

■ An amount to cover the deficit in the plan (which remains at C7m).

■ A 'risk premium' of C1m to an insurance company to take over the pensions liability and risk so that the plan can be wound up as fully paid.

After making the payments, the entity will have no further obligations in respect of the defined benefit plan and contributions to the defined contribution plan will not be related to the defined benefit plan.

There is no curtailment to account for in the current period, as the members of the plan were no longer earning any benefit. However, as the payment of C8m eliminates all further legal or constructive obligation for the benefits provided under the plan it represents a settlement as defined by IAS 19. The amount paid (C8m) exceeds the deficit in the plan so a settlement loss of C1m will be recognised upon the execution of the settlement transaction.

Example 4 – Plan wind up requiring approval

As noted above, as of 31 December 20X3, the entity decides to close its defined benefit pension plan. However, in the entity's jurisdiction, approval from a government agency is required to settle a defined benefit plan. The entity has filed the appropriate paperwork to request approval, which is expected, but not merely a formality. The approval process is expected to take up to 18 months.

IAS 19 is clear that the high quality corporate bond rate should be used for discounting post-employment benefit obligations. It is also clear that the currency and term of the corporate bonds should be consistent with the currency and estimated term of the post-employment benefit obligation. [IAS 19 para 78].

Although the expected timing of benefit payment could be viewed as being in 18 months time, (that is, when the entity expects to settle its obligation), the term of the corporate bonds should be consistent with the estimated term of the post-employment benefit obligation, which is still the length of the expected payment stream to employees as currently required under the plan. While the entity began the process to gain approval required to settle the plan, it is not obligated to settle, even if approval is received. Settlement cannot be anticipated. The entity also cannot accelerate the expense by using a rate for a corporate bond of 18 month duration, which is lower than the rate on a long-term corporate bond, to obtain a higher present value for the defined benefit obligation. Furthermore, as noted above, although entity A anticipates a one off payment of C8m to settle its obligations, a settlement loss would not be recognised until the settlement transaction happens.

11.265.1   Sometimes a pension plan may be wound up and replaced by another plan offering similar benefits. Such a situation is recognised by IAS 19, which says that where a plan is terminated and replaced by a new plan that offers benefits that are, in substance, identical, the termination should be treated as neither a curtailment nor a settlement. [IAS 19 para 114].

Example – Plan replaced by a similar plan

Entity A acquired another entity some years ago. Both entities have defined benefit plans, which pay similar pension benefits based on final salary and years of service. Entity A decided to simplify its pension administration by introducing a new pension plan to replace the two existing plans. Each employee's pension entitlement transfers to the new plan, without any change of entitlement.

The replacement of both plans does not amend the previous plans substantially. Employees retain their benefit entitlement.

Previously unrecognised items should be carried forward and amortised as before.

11.265.2 An example showing both a curtailment and a settlement is given in Table 11.12.

Table 11.12 – Examples of curtailments and settlements

Telkom SA Limited – annual report – 31 March 2007

5.1 Employee expenses (extract)

	2005 Rm	2006 Rm	2007 Rm
Post-retirement pension and retirement fund (refer to note 30)	12	(58)	**33**
Current service cost	3	4	**5**
Interest cost	320	364	**329**
Expected return on plan assets	(360)	(454)	**(508)**
Actuarial loss/(gain)	34	78	**(136)**
Settlement loss	–	–	**21**
Asset limitation	15	(50)	**322**
Post-retirement medical aid (refer to note 29 and 30)	182	361	**330**
Current service cost	27	48	**83**
Interest cost	249	249	**286**
Expected return on plan asset	–	–	**(188)**
Actuarial loss	–	63	**149**
Settlement loss	18	7	**–**
Curtailment gain	(112)	(6)	**–**
Telephone rebates (refer to note 29 and 30)	15	19	**104**
Current service cost	2	3	**4**
Interest cost	16	6	**19**
Past service cost	–	–	**76**
Actuarial gain	–	–	**5**
Curtailment gain	(3)	–	**–**

Post-retirement pension and retirement fund

Settlement loss

The settlement loss in the current year relates to a settlement event that occurred in the Telkom Pension Fund whereby 106 members were transferred to the Telkom Retirement Fund. The portion of unrecognised cumulative actuarial gains and losses that relates to the settlement event has also been recognised in the current financial year.

Post-retirement medical aid and telephone rebates

Expected return on plan asset

During the current year the medical aid cell captive annuity policy qualified as a plan asset.

The expected return on this asset is therefore determined from that date (refer to note 12).

Curtailment gain

The curtailment gain in 2005 resulted from a reduction in the number of participants covered by the post-retirement medical aid and telephone rebates.

Actuarial gains and losses

11.266 IAS 19 defines actuarial gains and losses as:

- experience adjustments (the effects of differences between the previous actuarial assumptions and what has actually occurred); and

- the effects of changes in actuarial assumptions.

[IAS 19 para 7].

11.267 Actuarial gains and losses arise when the values of plan assets and liabilities are re-measured at the balance sheet date. They result from unexpected increases or decreases in the fair value of the plan assets or the present value of the plan liabilities. Examples include the following:

- Experience gains and losses arising where actual events during the year differ from the actuarial assumptions in the previous valuation (for example, unexpectedly high or low rates of employee turnover, early retirement or mortality or of increases in salaries, benefits or medical costs).

- The effects of changes in actuarial assumptions from one period to the next, for example to reflect increased life expectancies.

- The effects of changes in the discount rate, which will alter the net present value of the defined benefit obligation.

- The difference between the expected and actual return on plan assets. The fair value of plan assets will increase or decrease if there are changes in the return on plan assets. The return on plan assets reflects the change in the fair value of plan assets after taking account of contributions received and benefits paid. For example, higher than expected dividend income on plan assets or higher than expected market values will cause an actuarial gain in the return on plan assets.

[IAS 19 para 94].

Example – Events causing actuarial gains and losses

- Actual or estimated mortality rates or the proportion of employees taking early retirement will alter the period for which an entity will be required to make benefit payments. For example, accelerating technological change might cause a manufacturer to reduce its workforce gradually by offering early retirement to a number of employees.

- Estimated salaries or benefits will alter the amount of each benefit payment. For example, a software developer might decide to increase its salaries by more than the rate of inflation to retain its skilled work force.

- Estimated employee turnover may for example alter the number of employees that are expected to transfer their benefits to another pension plan. For example, an unexpected change in tax legislation that makes personal pensions more attractive might lead to a greater number of employees leaving defined benefit plans and making their own pension arrangements.

11.268 There are three permissible methods under IAS 19 for recognising actuarial gains and losses:

- The 'corridor' approach.

- Faster recognition, or recognition in full in the profit and loss account.

- Recognition in other comprehensive income (OCI).

These three methods are outlined in the paragraphs below.

Recognition of actuarial gains and losses using the corridor approach

11.268.1 The first method is accounting for actuarial gains and losses from the perspective that estimates of post-employment benefit obligations may be viewed as a range (or 'corridor') around a best estimate. Hence, if actuarial gains and losses fall within the 'corridor', this provides evidence that estimates and assumptions were reasonably reliable so the actuarial gains and losses need not be recognised in the income statement. In other words, the 'corridor' represents a tolerable margin of uncertainty.

UK.11.268.1.1 The 'corridor' approach to accounting for actuarial gains and losses represents the most significant difference between IAS 19 and FRS 17. The other comprehensive income (OCI) approach allows UK entities adopting IFRS to account for actuarial gains and losses in the same way as they would do under FRS 17. OCI is the equivalent of the statement of total recognised gains and losses (STRGL) under UK GAAP. The majority of UK entities adopting IFRS in 2005 adopted the OCI approach.

11.269 In June 2011, the IASB issued IAS 19 (revised 2011), which eliminates the option for entities to apply the 'corridor' approach. The amendment is effective for periods beginning on or after 1 January 2013, with earlier application permitted. The amendment should be applied retrospectively in accordance with IAS 8. See chapter 11A for further guidance.

11.270 In broad terms, the 'corridor' approach provides that an entity should, as a minimum, recognise actuarial gains and losses in excess of a *de minimis* over the remaining working lives of employees. The *de minimis* amount, which is sometimes referred to as the 'corridor limit', is the greater of:

- 10% of the present value of the defined benefit obligation at the end of the previous reporting period (before deducting plan assets); and

- 10% of the fair value of any plan assets at that date.

[IAS 19 para 92].

These limits should be calculated and applied separately for each defined benefit plan. We would also expect that entities adopting the 'corridor' approach apply this policy consistently to all post-employment defined benefit plans, and to all actuarial gains and losses.

11.271 Having determined the 'corridor limit', the amount recognised in the income statement for each defined benefit plan is determined by reference to the excess over the 10% corridor limit of the net cumulative unrecognised (that is, deferred) actuarial gains and losses at the end of the previous reporting period. This excess is generally recognised in the income statement over the expected average remaining working lives of employees participating in the plan. [IAS 19 para 93]. However, IAS 19 also permits an entity to use any systematic method that results in faster recognition, including immediate recognition, so long as an entity applies the method consistently to both gains and losses. The following extract illustrates the accounting policy of an entity that uses the 'corridor' approach'.

Table 11.13 – Application of the 'corridor' approach

Lloyds Banking Group plc – Report and accounts – 31 December 2011

Note 2: Accounting policies (extract)

(L) Pensions and other post-retirement benefits (extract)

The Group's income statement charge includes the current service cost of providing pension benefits, the expected return on the schemes' assets, net of expected administration costs, and the interest cost on the schemes' liabilities. Actuarial gains and losses arising from experience adjustments and changes in actuarial assumptions are not recognised unless the cumulative unrecognised gain or loss at the end of the previous reporting period exceeds the greater of 10 per cent of the scheme assets or liabilities ('the corridor approach'). In these circumstances the excess is charged or credited to the income statement over the employees' expected average remaining working lives. Past service costs are charged immediately to the income statement, unless the charges are conditional on the employees remaining in service for a specified period of time (the vesting period). In this case, the past service costs are amortised on a straight-line basis over the vesting period.

11.272 The following example illustrates the method using average remaining service lives to recognise gains and losses.

Example – The 'corridor' approach

The following information relates to an entity's defined benefit pension plan at the end of 20X1.

	C'000
Present value of defined benefit obligation	1,500
Fair value of plan assets	1,200
Unrecognised actuarial gains (presented as a liability in the balance sheet)	190
Average remaining working lives of employees participating in the plan	10 years

In order to determine the amount of actuarial gains to be recognised in the income statement in 20X2, three steps should be followed.

Step 1 – Calculate the 'corridor limit'

The 'corridor limit' is the greater of 10% of the present value of the defined benefit obligation and 10% of the fair value of the plan assets at the end of the previous reporting period. In this case, the former is the greater amount, so the 'corridor limit' is C150,000 (that is, 10% of C1.5m).

Step 2 – Calculate the total actuarial gains and losses to be recognised

The total amount to be recognised over the remaining working lives of employees participating in the plan is the excess of the net cumulative unrecognised actuarial gains and losses at the end of the previous reporting over the 'corridor limit'. At the end of 20X1, there were cumulative unrecognised actuarial gains of C190,000 so the excess of this amount over the 'corridor limit' of C150,000 is C40,000.

Step 3 – Determine the amount to be recognised in the year

The amount to be recognised in 20X2 is the total determined in the previous step (that is, C40,000) divided by the average remaining working lives of employees participating in the plan (that is, 10 years). Hence, the amount recognised as a gain in the income statement in 20X2 is C4,000.

11.273 As can be seen from the previous example, the accounting for actuarial gains and losses under the 'corridor' approach takes no account of actuarial gains and losses arising in the year. Both the 'corridor limit' and the amount to be recognised are established by reference to the state of the plan as at the end of the previous reporting period. Accordingly, all actuarial gains and losses that arise in a period are deferred at the end of that period.

Example – Application of the corridor approach (over time)

Entity A has a defined benefit pension plan.

At 31 December 20X0:

- The fair value of plan assets is C5,000.

- The present value of the defined benefit obligation is C4,500.

- There are cumulative unrecognised actuarial gains of C750.

- The average remaining working lives of the employees in the plan is 10 years.

During 20X1:

- The fair value of plan assets increases to C5,500.

- The present value of the defined benefit obligation increases to C4,750.

- The net actuarial gain is C100.

- The average remaining working lives remain 10 years.

Entity A must recognise a portion of the net actuarial gain or loss in excess of 10% of the greater of the defined benefit obligation or the fair value of plan assets. The gain or loss that falls outside the 10% 'corridor' is recognised over the average remaining working lives of the employees participating in the plan.

The actuarial gain recognised in 20X1 is:

	C
Unrecognised actuarial gain at 31 December 20X0	750
Limit of the corridor (10% of the fair value of plan assets)	(500)
	250
Average remaining working lives of employees in the plan	10
Actuarial gain recognised in 20X1 (250/10)	25

The movements in unrecognised actuarial gains during 20X1 are:

	C
Unrecognised actuarial gain at 31 December 20X0	750
Actuarial gain during the year	100
Actuarial gain recognised	(25)
Unrecognised actuarial gain at 31 December 20X1	825

The actuarial gain recognised in 20X2 would be:

	C
Unrecognised actuarial gain at 31 December 20X1	825
Limit of the corridor (10% of the fair value of plan assets)	550
	275
Average remaining working lives of employees in the plan	10
Actuarial gain recognised in 20X2 (275/10)	27.5

Recognition of actuarial gains and losses using a faster recognition method

11.274 As noted above, IAS 19 allows an entity to adopt any systematic method that results in faster recognition of actuarial gains and losses, provided that the same basis is applied to both gains and losses and the basis is applied consistently from period to period. [IAS 19 para 93]. Such methods may be used even if this results in the recognition of gains and losses within the 'corridor limit', so immediate recognition in the income statement of all actuarial gains and losses is permissible, although extremely rare in practice. Nevertheless, an example illustrating a method that results in faster recognition is shown below.

Example – Application of the faster recognition approach

Entity A has a defined benefit pension plan that is closed to new members. There are 400 pension plan members, but only 120 of these are active members with the remainder being retired or deferred members. The average remaining service lives of the 120 active members is 10 years.

Entity A can take account of non-active members in recognising actuarial gains and losses. Using the 'corridor' approach, the minimum rate of recognition of actuarial gains and losses by entity A is 10%. This is based on the average remaining service lives of the 120 active members. Non-active members have an average remaining service life of zero. Hence, when taking non-active members into account, the resulting rate of recognition is 33%, as the collective average remaining service life reduces to 3 years, as illustrated below:

$$\frac{(120*10 \text{ years}) + (280*0 \text{ years})}{400} = 3 \text{ years weighted average}$$

As a result, entity A has the option to recognise actuarial gains and losses at a faster rate of 33%, although should it choose to apply this approach to determining the spreading period, it must apply this consistently to all of its defined benefit schemes.

Recognition of actuarial gains and losses in other comprehensive income

11.274.1 The third approach allows entities to recognise actuarial gains and losses in full as they arise, outside profit or loss, in other comprehensive income. [IAS 19 paras 93A, 93B]. IAS 19 makes it clear that actuarial gains and losses recognised outside profit or loss must be presented in other comprehensive income. [IAS 19 para 93B]. Further explanation of IAS 1's requirements is given in chapter 4.

UK.11.274.1.1 This means that an entity recognising actuarial gains and losses outside profit or loss and, therefore, following an approach similar to UK GAAP, must present a statement equivalent to a UK statement of total recognised gains and losses (STRGL).

[The next paragraph is 11.274.4.]

11.274.4 Most gains and losses under IFRS that are recognised outside profit and loss are reclassified to the income statement in a later period, but not all. For example, revaluation gains and losses on property, plant and equipment are not recycled. IAS 19 is clear that actuarial gains and losses that have been recognised directly in other comprehensive income should not be recognised in the income statement in a subsequent period. [IAS 19 para 93D].

11.274.5 Paragraph 93D of the standard also makes it clear that actuarial gains and losses recognised directly in other comprehensive income should be added to or deducted from retained earnings. They should not be presented in a separate reserve. This is consistent with the treatment of actuarial gains and losses that have flowed through the income statement, either immediately or over time through application of the 'corridor' approach.

11.274.6 An entity adopting a policy of recognising actuarial gains and losses in full as they arise, outside profit or loss, must apply that policy consistently. This means that it must be applied to:

■ all of its defined benefit plans; and

■ all of its actuarial gains and losses.

[IAS 19 para 93A].

11.274.7 An example of a company that has opted to recognise actuarial gains and losses in full outside profit or loss is given in Table 11.14.

Table 11.14 – Recognition of actuarial gains and losses in statement of comprehensive income

HSBC Holdings plc – Report and accounts – 31 December 2011

Consolidated statement of comprehensive income for the year ended 31 December 2011

	2011 US$m	2010 US$m	2009 US$m
Profit for the year	**17,944**	14,191	6,694
Other comprehensive income/(expense)			
Available-for-sale investments	**674**	5,835	10,817
– fair value gains/(losses)	**1,279**	6,368	9,821
– fair value gains transferred to income statement on disposal	**(820)**	(1,174)	(648)
– amounts transferred to the income statement in respect of impairment losses	**583**	1,118	2,391
– income taxes	**(368)**	(477)	(747)
Cash flow hedges:	**187**	(271)	772
– fair value gains/(losses)	**(581)**	(178)	481
– fair value (gains)/losses transferred to income statement	**788**	(164)	808
– income taxes	**(20)**	71	(517)
Actuarial gains/(losses) on defined benefit plans	**1,009**	(61)	(2,608)
– before income taxes	**1,267**	(60)	(3,586)
– income taxes	**(258)**	(1)	978
Share of other comprehensive income/(expense) of associates and joint ventures	**(710)**	107	149
Exchange differences	**(2,865)**	(567)	4,975
Income tax attributable to exchange differences	**165**	–	–
Other comprehensive income/(expense) for the year, net of tax	**(1,540)**	5,043	14,105
Total comprehensive income/(expense) for the year	**16,404**	19,234	20,799
Total comprehensive income/(expense) for the year attributable to:			
– shareholders of the parent company	**15,366**	18,087	19,529
– non-controlling interests	**1,038**	1,147	1,270
	16,404	19,234	20,799

The accompanying notes on pages 291 to 413, 'Critical accounting policies' on pages 38 to 42, the audited sections of 'Risk' on pages 98 to 210 and the audited sections of 'Capital' on pages 211 to 217 form an integral part of these financial statements.

2 Summary of significant accounting policies (extract)

(t) Pension and other post-employment benefits

HSBC operates a number of pension and other post-employment benefit plans throughout the world. These plans include both defined benefit and defined contribution plans and various other post-employment benefits such as post-employment healthcare.

Payments to defined contribution plans and state-managed retirement benefit plans, where HSBC's obligations under the plans are equivalent to a defined contribution plan, are charged as an expense as the employees render service.

The defined benefit pension costs and the present value of defined benefit obligations are calculated at the reporting date by the schemes' actuaries using the Projected Unit Credit Method. The net charge to the income statement mainly comprises the current service cost, plus the unwinding of the discount rate on plan liabilities, less the expected return on plan assets, and is presented in operating expenses. Past service costs are charged immediately to the income statement to the extent that the benefits have vested, and are otherwise recognised on a straight-line basis over the average period until the benefits vest. Actuarial gains and losses comprise experience adjustments (the effects of differences between the previous actuarial assumptions and what has actually occurred), as well as the effects of changes in actuarial assumptions. Actuarial gains and losses are recognised in other comprehensive income in the period in which they arise.

The defined benefit liability recognised in the balance sheet represents the present value of defined benefit obligations adjusted for unrecognised past service costs and reduced by the fair value of plan assets. Any net defined benefit surplus is limited to unrecognised past service costs plus the present value of available refunds and reductions in future contributions to the plan.

The cost of obligations arising from other post-employment defined benefit plans, such as defined benefit healthcare plans, are accounted for on the same basis as defined benefit pension plans.

Deficit reduction schemes

11.274.8 Given the size and volatility of defined benefit obligations, many entities that operate defined benefit plans have explored ways to reduce their exposure to such obligations and volatility. Such actions are typically aimed at reducing the liability on the balance sheet, removing volatility from both the balance sheet and from reported profit or loss, or some combination thereof. Arrangements required to achieve these aims will usually result in a curtailment, settlement or other one-off charge to report through profit or loss.

11.274.8.1 In the UK typical examples of deficit reduction schemes are:

■ Buy-out schemes, where the entire defined benefit obligation, its risks, rewards and costs are eliminated in return for an insurance company or similar entity taking full responsibility for all benefits payable under the plan. Typically, buy-out schemes involve closure of plans to new members and cessation of accrual of future benefits. As a result, there will normally be a settlement gain or loss reported through the income statement.

■ Buy-in schemes, where an insurance company undertakes to 'track' the liability with an insurance policy that exactly matches the liability, thereby enabling full netting of the liability being tracked. [IAS 19, para 104D]. This may result in a curtailment gain or loss depending on the circumstances, but will not be a settlement, since the reporting entity retains ultimate responsibility for funding the plan.

- Schemes where plan members are encouraged to allow assignment of the members' benefits to a third party, which then assumes all the risks and rewards of the plan. Once the risks and rewards have been removed from the reporting entity's balance sheet, the third party will typically seek to limit its exposure by offering a cash incentive to encourage plan members to take out personal pensions, hence putting all future risks on to the members. Depending on the precise arrangements, this is likely to lead to a settlement (or at least a partial settlement) for the reporting entity.

- For pensions in payment, a cash incentive to members to move from an inflation linked pension (such as C1,000 each year, increasing by a percentage linked to an inflation index) to a pension of C1,500 each year, fixed at C1,500 for the remaining life of the member. Since recipients are no longer providing service to the reporting entity, there is no future service being provided, hence the cost of providing the incentive cannot be a curtailment. This is because paragraph 111A of IAS 19 makes clear that curtailments only apply where the effect is to reduce future service costs. It will, therefore, be recognised as a negative past service cost in profit or loss in the period in which it is incurred. The future cost of providing the pension to members will reduce as a result, because the actuarial calculation will no longer include inflation assumptions: the amount is now fixed in monetary terms for the rest of the member's life.

Presentation

11.275 Where an entity operates more than one plan, some plans may be in surplus and some may be in deficit. Where this is the case, aggregate amounts of net defined benefit assets and net defined benefit liabilities (which include any unfunded benefits) should be shown separately on the face of the balance sheet. IAS 19 does not permit a net asset in respect of one plan and a net liability in respect of another to be netted off in arriving at the amounts to be presented on the face of the balance sheet, unless the entity:

- has a legally enforceable right to use a surplus in one plan to settle obligations under the other plan; and

- intends either to settle the obligations on a net basis, or to realise the surplus in one plan and settle its obligation under the other plan simultaneously.

[IAS 19 para 116].

These criteria are similar to those in paragraph 42 of IAS 32 (see chapter 6).

Example – Offset of pension plan balances in different plans

Entity A operates four defined benefit schemes, two in Bermuda and one each in Switzerland and the United States. The plans in each country are separate and administered by independent trustees.

One of the Bermuda plans covers management grade staff and the other is for manufacturing staff. Strong investment performance means that the management plan has a substantial surplus. Benefit enhancements in connection with a redundancy programme caused a deficit in the manufacturing plan. The same trustees administer the two plans. The trustees have agreed that entity A can use the surplus in the management plan to cover the deficit in the manufacturing plan, subject to granting certain benefit enhancements to management. Entity A will arrange for the trustees to transfer assets from one plan to the other.

The balance sheet position under IAS 19 for each scheme at the end of the year is as follows:

Switzerland	Liabilities of C100
Bermuda (manufacturing)	Liabilities of C150
Bermuda (management, after deducting C50 benefit enhancements)	Assets of C300
United States	Assets of C50

Entity A offsets assets of C300 in the Bermuda management plan with liabilities of C150 in the Bermuda manufacturing plan. Entity A has a legally enforceable right of offset because of its agreement with the trustees, and plans to transfer assets from one plan to the other.

Entity A should present a net pension asset of C200 (C50 in the United States plus C150, being the net asset in the Bermuda management plan after deducting the benefit enhancements and the payment to the manufacturing plan) and a net pension liability of C100 in the Swiss plan.

11.276 A consequence of the netting off criterion is that at least some of the footnote disclosures have to be disaggregated into plans that have given rise to assets in the balance sheet and plans that have given rise to liabilities. This is necessary, for example, in order to comply with the requirement to reconcile plan surpluses or deficits to balance sheet assets and liabilities (see para 11.282). To comply with that reconciliation requirement, say where there is an irrecoverable surplus, the following would have to be disclosed as a minimum, but a further breakdown of the total assets and liabilities may also be necessary for a proper understanding of the net position.

	C	C	C
Total plans' assets	400		
Total plans' liabilities	380		
Net surpluses	20		
Comprising:		**Surplus not recoverable**	**Net pension asset (liability)**
Surpluses	50	(10)	40
Deficits	(30)		(30)
	20	(10)	10

[The next paragraph is 11.278.]

11.278 IAS 1 requires that assets and liabilities should be categorised as current or non-current, unless a presentation based on liquidity provides information that is reliable and more relevant. [IAS 1 para 60]. Furthermore, IAS 1 specifies that regardless of which method of presentation is adopted, for each line item that combines amounts expected to be recovered or settled within 12 months and amounts to be recovered or settled after more than 12 months there should be separate disclosure of the latter. [IAS 1 para 61]. IAS 19 does not specifically require an entity to distinguish the current and non-current portions, because the IASB believes that such a distinction may sometimes be arbitrary and far from straightforward to prepare. [IAS 19 paras 118, BC81]. An entity should present the portion of any pension asset or liability expected to be settled within the next year as a current item, if the portion can be reasonably determined. When a reliable distinction is available, for example, because the actuary provides the information, or there is an agreed refund receivable within the next 12 months, separate presentation would be appropriate. When the split into current and non-current is not available, the entire pension asset or liability is presented as a non-current item. This is particularly the case for funded pension plans, where the funded status of the plan to be reflected in the statement of financial position reflects the net of plan assets and liabilities. As a result, for funded plans the net plan asset or liability is generally presented as a single non-current item.

11.279 As regards the income statement, IAS 19 does not specify how items should be presented. Indeed, paragraph 119 explicitly states that IAS 19 *"does not specify whether an entity should present current service cost, interest cost and the expected return on plan assets as components of a single item of income or expense on the face of the income statement"*. This means that an entity may choose, for example, whether the interest cost and the expected return on plan assets should be included as an operating expense or as a component of finance costs, although it is our view that these related items should be presented in the same place. It is more common, however, for the total cost of providing pensions to be included as a component of employee benefit costs, where expenses are analysed by nature, or within the relevant function headings (such as cost of sales or administrative expenses) where expenses are analysed by function.

Disclosure

11.280   IAS 19 contains extensive disclosure requirements in respect of defined benefit pension plans. When an entity has more than one defined benefit plan, disclosures may be made in total, separately for each plan, or in such groupings as are considered to be the most useful. [IAS 19 para 122]. IAS 19 suggests that it may be useful to group plans according to the following criteria, although other groupings are permissible:

- The geographical location of the plans, for example by distinguishing domestic plans from foreign plans.

- Whether plans are subject to materially different risks, for example, by distinguishing average salary plans from final salary plans and from post-employment medical plans.

When an entity provides disclosure for a grouping of plans, disclosure of significant actuarial assumptions is provided in the form of weighted averages or of relatively narrow ranges. [IAS 19 para 122]. It follows that any assumptions outside those narrow ranges should be disclosed separately.

11.281   The tables that follow illustrate some of the types of grouping commonly seen in practice.Table 11.17shows a financial statement extract that distinguishes UK plans, US plans and Netherlands plans, while Table 11.18 shows an extract that makes separate disclosure of pension and health care plans.

Table 11.17 – Grouping of post-employment benefit plans

Elementis plc – consolidated financial statements – 31 December 2011

23 RETIREMENT BENEFIT OBLIGATIONS (extract)

The following amounts have been recognised in the financial statements:

2011	UK pension scheme	US pension schemes	US PRMB scheme	Netherlands pension scheme	Total
	$million	$million	$million	$million	$million
Consolidated income statement					
Current service cost	(0.7)	(0.4)	(0.1)	(0.8)	(2.0)
Expected return on pension scheme assets	39.2	6.6	–	1.9	47.7
Interest on pension scheme liabilities	(36.5)	(6.3)	90.4)	(2.4)	(45.6)
Net finance income/(charge)	2.7	0.3	(0.4)	(0.5)	2.1
Curtailment loss	–	–	–	(7.0)	(7.0)
Net income statement	2.0	(0.1)	(0.5)	(8.3)	(6.9)
Other comprehensive income					
Actual return less expected return on pension scheme assets	17.2	(7.4)	–	0.6	10.4
Experience gains and losses arising on scheme liabilities	(9.8)	(0.7)	(0.4)	0.6	(10.3)
Changes in assumptions underlying the present value of scheme liabilities	(32.1)	(12.3)	–	(0.8)	(45.2)
Actuarial gain/(loss) recognised	(24.7)	(20.4)	(0.4)	0.4	(45.1)

Table 11.18 – Grouping of post-employment benefit plans

Dyckerhoff AG – annual report – 31 December 2011
44. Provisions for pensions and similar obligations (extract)
Recognized net values of provisions for pensions and healthcare costs

in thousands of EUR, December 31 respectively	2011	2010	2009	2008	Pensions 2007
Benefit obligation of funded commitments	309,534	296,069	273,558	294,402	292,013
Fair value of plan assets	-128,201	-122,391	-112,867	-128,042	-147,012
Short-cover (+) / Surplus-cover (–)	**181,333**	**173,678**	**160,691**	**166,360**	**145,001**
Benefit obligation of other commitments	22,184	21,609	18,426	19,150	19,235
Unrecognized actuarial gains (+) / losses (–)	-57,073	-46,488	-33,807	-37,369	-9,453
Unrecognized prior service costs	0	0	0	0	0
Surplus-cover capitalized as assets	20,319	20,313	22,689	23,681	19,192
Total	166,763	169,112	167,999	171,822	173,975

in thousands of EUR, December 31 respectively	2011	2010	2009	2008	Healthcare costs 2007
Benefit obligation of funded commitments	0	0	0	0	0
Fair value of plan assets	0	0	0	0	0
Short-cover (+) / Surplus-cover (–)	**0**	**0**	**0**	**0**	**0**
Benefit obligation of other commitments	52,755	52,084	47,873	48,217	49,626
Unrecognized actuarial gains (+) / losses (–)	3,581	3,162	4,795	6,587	2,830
Unrecognized past service cost	0	0	0	0	0
Surplus-cover capitalized as assets	0	0	0	0	0
Total	**56,336**	**55,246**	**52,668**	**54,804**	**52,456**

in thousands of EUR, December 31 respectively	2011	2010	2009	2008	Total 2007
Benefit obligation of funded commitments	309,534	296,069	273,558	294,402	292,013
Fair value of plan assets	-128,201	-122,391	-112,867	-128,042	-147,012
Short-cover (+) / Surplus-cover (–)	**181,333**	**173,678**	**160,691**	**166,360**	**145,001**
Benefit obligation of other commitments	74,939	73,693	66,299	67,367	68,861
Unrecognized actuarial gains (+) / losses (–)	-53,492	-43,326	-29,012	-30,782	-6,623
Unrecognized prior service costs	0	0	0	0	0
Surplus-cover capitalized as assets	20,319	20,313	22,689	23,681	19,192
Total	**223,099**	**224,358**	**220,667**	**226,626**	**226,431**

11.282 The disclosure required in respect of a defined benefit pension plan comprises the following.

■ A general description of the type of plan. Such a description distinguishes, for example, average salary pension plans from final salary pension plans and from post-employment medical plans. It should also describe the informal practices that give rise to constructive obligations (see further para 11.158).

■ The entity's accounting policy for recognising actuarial gains and losses.

■ The principal actuarial assumptions (in absolute terms, not just as a margin between different percentages or other variables (for example, equity risk premium)) used as at the balance sheet date, including, when applicable:

   ■ Discount rates.

   ■ Expected rates of return on any plan assets, or on any reimbursement right recognised as an asset, for the periods presented in the financial statements.

   ■ Expected rates of salary increases (and of changes in an index or other variable specified in the formal or constructive terms of a plan as the basis for future benefit increases).

   ■ Medical cost trend rates.

   ■ Any other material actuarial assumptions used (that is, mortality).

■ A reconciliation of the opening and closing balance of the present value of the defined benefit obligation, showing separately, if applicable, the effects attributable to each of the following:

   ■ Current service cost.

   ■ Past service cost.

   ■ Interest cost.

   ■ Settlements.

   ■ Curtailments.

   ■ Actuarial gains and losses.

   ■ Foreign currency translation differences.

   ■ Contributions by plan participants.

   ■ Benefits paid.

   ■ Business combinations.

■ An analysis of the defined benefit obligation into amounts arising from plans that are wholly unfunded and amounts arising from plans that are wholly or partly funded.

- A reconciliation of the opening and closing balance of the fair value of plan assets and any reimbursement right recognised as an asset, showing separately, if applicable, the effects attributable to each of the following:

  - Expected return on plan assets.

  - Settlements.

  - Actuarial gains and losses.

  - Foreign currency translation differences.

  - Contributions by the employer.

  - Contributions by plan participants.

  - Benefits paid.

  - Business combinations.

- A reconciliation of the present value of the defined benefit obligation and the fair value of plan assets to the assets and liabilities recognised in the balance sheet, showing at least:

  - The net actuarial gains and losses not recognised in the balance sheet (see para 11.266).

  - The past service cost not recognised in the balance sheet (see para 11.237).

  - Any amount not recognised as an asset, because of the limit described in paragraph 11.214.

  - The fair value at the balance sheet date of any reimbursement right recognised as an asset (with a brief description of the link between the reimbursement right and the related obligation).

  - Any other amounts recognised in the balance sheet.

- The total expense recognised in profit or loss for each of the following and the line item(s) in which they are included:

  - Current service cost.

  - Interest cost.

  - Expected return on plan assets.

  - Expected return on any reimbursement right recognised as an asset.

  - Actuarial gains and losses.

  - Past service cost.

  - The effect of any curtailment or settlement.

  - The effect of the limit described in paragraph 11.214.

- The total amount recognised in other comprehensive income for each of the following:

    - Actuarial gains and losses.

    - The effect of the limit described in paragraph 11.214.

- For entities that recognise actuarial gains and losses in other comprehensive income as described in paragraph 11.274.1, the cumulative amount of actuarial gains and losses recognised in other comprehensive income.

- For each major category of plan assets (which should include, but is not limited to, equity investments, debt instruments, property and all other assets), the percentage or amount that each major category constitutes of the fair value of the total plan assets.

- The amounts included in the fair value of plan assets for:

    - each category of the reporting entity's own financial instruments; and

    - any property occupied by, or other assets used by, the reporting entity.

- A narrative description of the basis used to determine the overall expected rate of return on assets, including the effect of the major categories of plan assets.

- The actual return on plan assets, as well as the actual return on any reimbursement right recognised as an asset.

- The effect of an increase of one percentage point and the effect of a decrease of one percentage point in the assumed medical cost trend rates on the following:

    - The aggregate of the current service cost and interest cost components of net periodic post-employment medical costs.

    - The accumulated post-employment benefit obligation for medical costs.

    For the purposes of this disclosure, all other assumptions should be held constant. For plans operating in a high inflation environment, the disclosure should be the effect of a percentage increase or decrease in the assumed medical cost trend rate of a significance similar to one percentage point in a low inflation environment.

- The amounts for the current annual period and the previous four annual periods of the following (see also para 11.282.1):

    - The present value of the defined benefit obligation, the fair value of the plan assets and the surplus or deficit in the plan.

    - Experience adjustments arising on:

        - the plan liabilities expressed either as an amount or a percentage of the plan liabilities at the balance sheet date; and

- the plan assets expressed either as an amount or a percentage of the plan assets at the balance sheet date.

- The employer's best estimate, as soon as it can reasonably be determined, of contributions expected to be paid to the plan during the annual period beginning after the balance sheet date.

[IAS 19 paras 120A-121].

11.282.1   For entities that adopt IFRS for the first time, IFRS 1 states that the five year history disclosure required in paragraph 120A(p) of IAS 19 may be built up gradually as the amounts are determined for each accounting period prospectively from the transition date. [IFRS 1 App D para D11]. This will mean, for example, that if an entity first adopts IFRS in 20X9, the information presented to satisfy this particular disclosure requirement will start from the first period presented in the 20X9 financial statements: that is, the 20X8 comparative period. In 20Y0 there will be three years of information, in 20Y1 four years and so on. For further discussion on transition to IFRS see chapter 5.

11.282.2   IAS 19 requires the amount recognised as a defined benefit liability (or asset, if negative) to be the net total of the following amounts:

- The present value of the defined benefit obligation at the balance sheet date (see from para 11.158).

- *Plus* any actuarial gains (less any actuarial losses) not recognised because of the application of the 'corridor' approach (see from para 11.268.1).

- *Minus* any past service cost not yet recognised (see from para 11.237).

- *Minus* the fair value at the balance sheet date of plan assets (if any) out of which the obligations are to be settled directly (see from para 11.132).

[IAS 19 para 54].

Example – Calculation of the pension liability

Entity A operates a defined benefit pension plan for all its employees.

At 31 December 20X1, entity A's actuary advises that the present value of the defined benefit obligation is C5,500. An actuarial gain of C500 arose in 20X0 and entity A is recognising the gain over 10 years, being the average remaining working lives of the employees in the plan, without using the corridor. Entity A enhanced the plan benefits in December 20X0, but C1,000 of the cost associated with the enhancement vests in 20X5.

At 31 December 20X0, the pension liability recognised in the balance sheet was C1,100, and there were no unrecognised actuarial gains or losses or unrecognised past service costs. Current service costs for 20X1 are C700, expected return on plan assets is C450 and contributions to the plan are C850.

Entity A determined the fair value of plan assets to be C4,500 at 31 December 20X1.

Entity A's balance sheet at 31 December 20X1 includes a liability calculated as follows:

	C
Present value of benefit obligation	5,500
Unrecognised actuarial gain (C500 x 9/10)	450
Unrecognised past service cost (C1000 x 4/5)	(800)
Fair value of plan assets	(4,500)
Net defined benefit pension liability	650

The closing balance sheet liability can be reconciled to the movements during the period as follows:

	C
Pension liability recognised in the balance sheet at 1 January 20X1	1,100
Plus pension expense:	
– current service costs	700
– past service costs (1/5 × C1,000)	200
– actuarial gains recognised (1/10 × C500)	(50)
– expected return on plan assets	(450)
Less contributions paid by the employer	(850)
Pension liability recognised in the balance sheet at 31 December 20X1	650

11.283 The example below presents the disclosures required by IAS 19 where actuarial gains and losses are recognised immediately in other comprehensive income.

Table 11.19 – IAS 19 disclosures in respect of defined benefit plans

Pearson plc – Report and accounts – 31 December 2011

1. Accounting policies (extract)

o. Employee benefits

1. Pension obligations The retirement benefit asset and obligation recognised in the balance sheet represents the net of the present value of the defined benefit obligation and the fair value of plan assets at the balance sheet date. The defined benefit obligation is calculated annually by independent actuaries using the projected unit credit method. The present value of the defined benefit obligation is determined by discounting estimated future cash flows using yields on high quality corporate bonds which have terms to maturity approximating the terms of the related liability.

The determination of the pension cost and defined benefit obligation of the Group's defined benefit pension schemes depends on the selection of certain assumptions, which include the discount rate, inflation rate, salary growth, longevity and expected return on scheme assets.

Actuarial gains and losses arising from differences between actual and expected returns on plan assets, experience adjustments on liabilities and changes in actuarial assumptions are recognised immediately in other comprehensive income.

The service cost, representing benefits accruing over the year, is included in the income statement as an operating cost. The unwinding of the discount rate on the scheme liabilities and the expected return on scheme assets are presented as finance costs or finance income.

Obligations for contributions to defined contribution pension plans are recognised as an operating expense in the income statement as incurred.

2. Other post-retirement obligations The expected costs of post-retirement healthcare and life assurance benefits are accrued over the period of employment, using a similar accounting methodology as for defined benefit pension obligations. The liabilities and costs relating to significant other post-retirement obligations are assessed annually by independent qualified actuaries.

25. Retirement benefit and other post-retirement obligations

Background

The Group operates a number of defined benefit and defined contribution retirement plans throughout the world. For the defined benefit plans, benefits are based on employees' length of service and final pensionable pay. Defined contribution benefits are based on the amount of contributions paid in respect of an individual member, the investment returns earned and the amount of pension this money will buy when a member retires.

The largest plan is the Pearson Group Pension Plan ('UK Group plan') with both defined benefit and defined contribution sections. From 1 November 2006, all sections of the UK Group plan were closed to new members with the exception of a defined contribution section that was opened in 2003. This section is available to all new employees of participating companies. The other major defined benefit plans are based in the US.

Other defined contribution plans are operated principally overseas with the largest plan being in the US. The specific features of these plans vary in accordance with the regulations of the country in which employees are located.

Pearson also has several post-retirement medical benefit plans (PRMBs), principally in the US. PRMBs are unfunded but are accounted for and valued similarly to defined benefit pension plans.

Employee benefits

Assumptions

The principal assumptions used for the UK Group plan and the US PRMB are shown below. Weighted average assumptions have been shown for the other plans, which primarily relate to US pension plans.

%	UK Group plan	2011 Other plans	PRMB	UK Group plan	2010 Other plans	PRMB
Inflation	3.0	2.5	2.5	3.5	2.5	2.5
Rate used to discount plan liabilities	4.9	4.2	4.2	5.5	5.1	5.1
Expected return on assets	5.7	6.4	–	6.0	6.6	–
Expected rate of increase in salaries	4.0	4.0	–	4.7	4.0	–
Expected rate of increase for pensions in payment and deferred pensions	2.4 to 4.3	–	–	2.6 to 4.4	–	–
Initial rate of increase in healthcare rate	–	–	7.5	–	–	8.0
Ultimate rate of increase in healthcare rate	–	–	5.0	–	–	5.0

The UK discount rate is based on the annualised yield on the iBoxx over 15-year AA-rated corporate bond index, adjusted to reflect the duration of liabilities. The US discount rate is set by reference to a US bond portfolio matching model.

The inflation rate for the UK Group plan of 3.0% reflects the RPI rate. In line with changes to legislation in 2010 certain benefits have been calculated with reference to CPI as the inflationary measure and in these instances a rate of 2.0% has been used. The change from RPI to CPI for deferred revaluation and Post 88 GMP pension increases in payment for 2010 has been included in the prior year results, resulting in a gain of £23m, taken as an actuarial gain on the obligation.

The expected rates of return on categories of plan assets are determined by reference to relevant indices. The overall expected rate of return is calculated by weighting the individual rates in accordance with the anticipated balance in the plan's investment portfolio, plus a diversification premium.

The expected rate of increase in salaries has been set at 4.0% for 2011 with a short-term assumption of 3.3% for three years.

For the UK plan the mortality base table assumptions have been derived from the SAPS 'all pensioners' tables for males and the SAPS 'normal health pensioners' tables for females, adjusted to reflect the observed experience of the plan, with medium cohort improvement factors. A 1.5% improvement floor on the medium cohort is applied for males, and 1.25% for females, with tapering.

For the US plans the RP2000 table is used, reflecting the mortality assumption most prevalent in the US. In 2010 a 10 year projection was added.

Using the above tables, the remaining average life expectancy in years of a pensioner retiring at age 65 on the balance sheet date for the UK Group plan and US plans is as follows:

	UK 2011	UK 2010	US 2011	US 2010
Male	22.6	22.8	19.2	18.4
Female	23.5	23.6	21.1	20.6

The remaining average life expectancy in years of a pensioner retiring at age 65, 20 years after the balance sheet date, for the UK and US Group plans is as follows:

		UK			US
	2011	2010		2011	2010
Male	25.2	25.4		19.2	18.4
Female	25.6	25.7		21.1	20.6

Financial statement information

The amounts recognised in the income statement are as follows:

2011

All figures in £ millions	UK Group plan	Defined benefit other	Sub-total	Defined contribution	PRMB	Total
Current service cost	21	3	24	69	3	**96**
Total operating expense	21	3	24	69	3	**96**
Expected return on plan assets	(107)	(7)	(114)	–	–	**(114)**
Interest on plan liabilities	100	8	108	–	3	**111**
Net finance (income)/expense	(7)	1	(6)	–	3	**(3)**
Net income statement charge	14	4	18	69	6	**93**
Actual return on plan assets	161	5	166	–	–	**166**

2010

All figures in £ millions	UK Group plan	Defined benefit other	Sub-total	Defined contribution	PRMB	Total
Current service cost	21	2	23	68	2	93
Curtailments	(5)	–	(5)	–	–	(5)
Total operating expense	16	2	18	68	2	88
Expected return on plan assets	(93)	(7)	(100)	–	–	(100)
Interest on plan liabilities	100	9	109	–	3	112
Net finance expense	7	2	9	–	3	12
Net income statement charge	23	4	27	68	5	100
Actual return on plan assets	177	13	190	–	–	190

There are no amounts in the 2011 results relating to discontinued operations.

Included within the 2010 results are discontinued operations of £5m relating to the curtailment credit, a £1m charge relating to defined benefit schemes and a £2m charge relating to defined contribution schemes.

Employee benefits

The amounts recognised in the balance sheet are as follows:

All figures in £ millions	UK Group plan	Other funded plans	Other unfunded plans	Total	UK Group plan	Other funded plans	Other unfunded plans	2010 Total
				2011				
Fair value of plan assets	**2,008**	**149**	–	**2,157**	1,847	135	–	1,982
Present value of defined benefit obligation	**(1,983)**	**(173)**	**(24)**	**(2,180)**	(1,852)	(158)	(20)	(2,030)
Net pension asset/(liability)	**25**	**(24)**	**(24)**	**(23)**	(5)	(23)	(20)	(48)
Other post-retirement medical benefit obligation				**(85)**				(72)
Other pension accruals				**(33)**				(28)
Net retirement benefit obligations				**(141)**				(148)
Analysed as:								
Retirement benefit assets				25				–
Retirement benefit obligations				**(166)**				(148)

The following (losses)/gains have been recognised in other comprehensive income:

All figures in £ millions	2011	2010
Amounts recognised for defined benefit plans	**(47)**	75
Amounts recognised for post-retirement medical benefit plans	**(9)**	(5)
Total recognised in year	**(56)**	70
Cumulative amounts recognised	**(232)**	(176)

The fair value of plan assets comprises the following:

%	UK Group plan	Other funded plans	Total	UK Group plan	Other funded plans	Total
		2011				**2010**
Equities	**31.6**	**2.7**	**34.3**	27.0	3.3	30.3
Bonds	**44.7**	**3.4**	**48.1**	49.3	2.7	52.0
Properties	**11.1**	**0.1**	**11.2**	11.2	0.1	11.3
Other	**5.6**	**0.8**	**6.4**	5.6	0.8	6.4

The plan assets do not include any of the Group's own financial instruments, or any property occupied by the Group.

Changes in the values of plan assets and liabilities of the retirement benefit plans are as follows:

All figures in £ millions	2011 UK Group plan	Other plans	Total	2010 UK Group plan	Other plans	Total
Fair value of plan assets						
Opening fair value of plan assets	**1,847**	**135**	**1,982**	1,609	118	1,727
Exchange differences	**–**	**1**	**1**	–	4	4
Expected return on plan assets	**107**	**7**	**114**	93	7	100
Actuarial gains /(losses)	**54**	**(2)**	**52**	84	6	90
Contributions by employer	**71**	**18**	**89**	132	13	145
Contributions by employee	**3**	**–**	**3**	3	–	3
Benefits paid	**(74)**	**(10)**	**(84)**	(74)	(13)	(87)
Closing fair value of plan assets	**2,008**	**149**	**2,157**	1,847	135	1,982
Present value of defined benefit obligation						
Opening defined benefit obligation	**(1,852)**	**(178)**	**(2,030)**	(1,798)	(169)	(1,967)
Exchange differences	**–**	**–**	**–**	–	(5)	(5)
Current service cost	**(21)**	**(3)**	**(24)**	(21)	(2)	(23)
Curtailment	**–**	**–**		5	–	5
Interest cost	**(100)**	**(8)**	**(108)**	(100)	(9)	(109)
Actuarial losses	**(81)**	**(18)**	**(99)**	(9)	(6)	(15)
Contributions by employee	**(3)**	**–**	**(3)**	(3)	–	(3)
Benefits paid	**74**	**10**	**84**	74	13	87
Closing defined benefit obligation	**(1,983)**	**(197)**	**(2,180)**	(1,852)	(178)	(2,030)

Changes in the value of the US PRMB are as follows:

All figures in £ millions

All figures in £ millions	2011	2010
Opening defined benefit obligation	**(72)**	(65)
Exchange differences	**(2)**	(2)
Current service cost	**(3)**	(2)
Interest cost	**(3)**	(3)
Actuarial losses	**(9)**	(5)
Benefits paid	**4**	5
Closing defined benefit obligation	**(85)**	(72)

The history of the defined benefit plans is as follows:

All figures in £ millions	2011	2010	2009	2008	2007
Fair value of plan assets	**2,157**	1,982	1,727	1,578	1,853
Present value of defined benefit obligation	**(2,180)**	(2,030)	(1,967)	(1,594)	(1,811)
Net pension (liability)/asset	**(23)**	(48)	(240)	(16)	42
Experience adjustments on plan assets	**52**	90	56	(268)	29
Experience adjustments on plan liabilities	**(99)**	(15)	(351)	194	50

Funding

The UK Group plan is self-administered with the plan's assets being held independently of the Group. The trustees of the plan are required to act in the best interest of the plan's beneficiaries. The most recent triennial actuarial valuation for funding purposes was completed as at 1 January 2009 and this valuation revealed a funding shortfall. The Group has agreed that the funding shortfall will be eliminated by 31 December 2020. In 2011 the Group contributed £48m (2010: £41m) towards the funding shortfall and has agreed to contribute a similar amount per annum until 2020 in excess of regular contributions. Regular contributions to the plan are estimated to be £22m for 2012.

Under UK law (section 75 debt) a company that participates in a multi-employer defined benefit plan is liable, on withdrawal from that pension plan, for its share of the total deficit in the plan calculated on a 'solvency' or 'buy out' basis. The Interactive Data sale and the termination of Interactive Data Corporation (Europe) Ltd's participation in the UK Group plan triggered this 'section 75' liability. £68m was contributed to the plan in respect of this liability in 2010.

The Group expects to contribute $83m in 2012 and $86m in 2013 to its US pension plans.

Future benefit payments

The following table shows the expected benefit payments from the defined benefit plans over the next 10 years. These use actuarial assumptions as at 31 December 2011. These represent payments from the pension funds to pensioners and others entitled to benefits, and are not an indication of payments from the company. For company funding requirements refer to the prior section.

All figures in £ millions	UK Group plan	Defined benefit other	Total
Expected future benefit payments:			
2012	74	24	98
2013	76	23	99
2014	79	24	103
2015	82	21	103
2016	86	18	104
2017 to 2021 combined	479	80	559

Sensitivities

The net retirement benefit obligations are calculated using a number of assumptions, the most significant being the discount rate used to calculate the defined benefit obligation. The effect of a one percentage point increase and decrease in the discount rate on the defined benefit obligation and the total pension expense is as follows:

	2011	
	1%	1%
All figures in £ millions	increase	decrease
Effect on:		
(Decrease)/increase in defined benefit obligation – UK Group plan	(282.0)	348.5
(Decrease)/increase of aggregate of service cost and interest cost – UK Group plan	(0.7)	(1.2)
(Decrease)/increase in defined benefit obligation – US plan	(11.7)	14.0

The effect of members living one year more or one year less on the defined benefit obligation is as follows:

All figures in £ millions	2011 1 year Increase	1 year Decrease
Effect on:		
Increase/(decrease) in defined benefit obligation – UK Group plan	53.6	(52.1)
Increase/(decrease) in defined benefit obligation – US plan	1.9	(2.0)

The effect of a one percentage point increase and decrease in the assumed medical cost trend rates is as follows:

2011

All figures in £ millions	1% increase	1% decrease
Effect on:		
Increase/(decrease) in post-retirement medical benefit obligation	3.2	(2.8)
Increase/(decrease) of aggregate of service cost and interest cost	0.1	(0.1)

11.284.1 In practice, the disclosure of principal actuarial assumptions normally comprises those assumptions to which IAS 19 makes explicit reference (that is, discount rates, expected rates of return on plan assets, expected rates of salary increases and medical cost trend rates). However, IAS 19 also requires disclosure of *"any other material actuarial assumptions used"*. [IAS 19 para 120A(n)(vi)]. There is increasing pressure from the investor community for companies to provide meaningful information about the volatility of their pension obligations.

Extract from letter dated 1 February 2006 from the Corporate Reporting Users Forum to the Financial Times:

> *"At present most companies disclose nothing about the longevity assumptions they are using when calculating the pension liability. Without this information it is impossible to gain a true understanding of the risks inherent in the scheme, and the likelihood of increased cash contributions (or other actions) being required in the future.*

> *"It is clear that many companies will have to revise their longevity assumptions upwards at the next actuarial review. As professional users of financial reports and members of the Corporate Reporting Users Forum we believe that it is essential that companies begin to disclose information about their current assumptions in terms of life expectancy post retirement and also the sensitivity of the pension liability to changes in these assumptions.*

> *"Similarly, it is essential that companies disclose the sensitivity of the liability to changes in the discount rate used. Many companies merely disclose the discount rate itself.*

> *"These disclosures are not explicitly required by the accounting rules (IAS 19) but paragraph 120 of that standard says "An entity shall disclose information that enables users of financial statements to evaluate the nature of its defined benefit plans and the financial effects of changes in those plans during the period." Without these additional disclosures we find it hard to see how users can undertake such an evaluation."*

11.284.2 Some companies disclose expected rates of pension increases and the average remaining working life of employees, but there are other assumptions that could have a material impact on the measurement of the defined benefit obligation. Examples include mortality rates (almost certainly material for most companies providing pension benefits) and employee turnover. Disclosure would include average life expectancies or the name of the mortality tables used. In addition, IAS 1 requires disclosure of *'the sensitivity of carrying amounts to the methods, assumptions and estimates underlying their calculation, including the reasons for the sensitivity'*. [IAS 1 para 129(b)]. An indication of the sensitivity of the pension obligation to changes in these assumptions would satisfy IAS 1 requirements and enable users to 'evaluate the nature of its defined benefit plans'. [IAS 19 para 120]. Such disclosure is often made in the form of a table and an example is shown in Table 11.20 below. IFRIC 14 further suggests that disclosure should be given of any restrictions on the current realisability of a surplus, as well as the basis used to determine any economic benefit available in the form of a refund or future reduction in contributions. [IFRIC 14 para 10]. Table 11.20 is an actual example of a tabular disclosure of sensitivities.

Table 11.20 – Tabular disclosure of pension assumptions sensitivities

London Stock Exchange Group plc – annual report – 31 March 2012

17. Retirement benefit obligations (extract)

The main actuarial assumptions are set out below:

| | 2012 | | 2011 | |
	UK Pension	Italian plan	UK Pension	Italian plan
Inflation rate — CPI	3.4%	2.0%	3.5%	2.0%
Inflation rate — RPI	2.4%	–	2.5%	–
Rate of increase in salaries	4.4%	3.5%	5.0%	3.5%
Rate of increase in pensions in payment	3.6%	3.0%	3.7%	3.0%
Discount rate	5.0%	4.0%	5.6%	4.1%
Expected return on assets as at the start of the year:				
– equities	7.3%	–	7.6%	–
– bonds	3.8%	–	4.8%	–
– property	6.5%	–	6.8%	–
– pensioner buy in policy	5.0%	–	–	–
Life expectancy from age 60 (years)				
– Non retired male member	27.9	–	27.8	–
– Non retired female member	30.7	–	30.6	–
– Retired male member	26.3	–	26.2	–
– Retired female member	29.2	–	29.1	–

Expected return on equities and property are determined by applying an appropriate risk premium to the risk free rate measured with reference to the return on Government bonds. Expected returns on bonds are derived from returns on Government and corporate bonds of an equivalent term to the investments held

The mortality assumptions are based on the standard tables S1NA published by the Institute and Faculty of Actuaries adjusted to take account of projected future improvements in life expectancy from the Self Administered Pension Scheme (SAPS) mortality survey, which was published in 2008. We have used an allowance for the medium cohort effect and applied a one per cent underpin in respect of future mortality improvements.

Sensitivities

The sensitivities regarding the principal assumptions used to measure the scheme obligations are:

Assumption	Change in assumption	Impact on scheme obligations
Inflation rate	Increase/decrease by 0.5%	Increase/decrease by £4.6m
Rate of increase in pensions payment	Increase/decrease by 0.5%	Increase/decrease by £18.0m
Discount rate	Increase/decrease by 0.5%	Decrease/increase by £21.7m
Mortality rate	Increase by 1 year	Increase by £8.1m

11.285 Where a multi-employer defined benefit plan is accounted for as if it were a defined contribution plan (see para 11.115), IAS 19 requires disclosure of the following:

- The fact that the plan is a defined benefit plan.

- The reason why sufficient information is not available to enable the entity to account for the plan as a defined benefit plan.

- To the extent that a surplus or deficit in the plan may affect the amount of future contributions:

  - any available information about that surplus or deficit;

  - the basis used to determine that surplus or deficit; and

  - the implications, if any, for the entity.

[IAS 19 paras 30, 123].

11.286 An example of disclosure by a company that participates in a multi-employer plan, is presented in Table 11.21 below.

Table 11.21 – Multi-employer plan
Nobel Biocare Holding AG – annual report – 31 December 2011
21 Employee benefits (extract)

The Group has a Swedish multi-employer pension plan that should be accounted for as a defined benefit plan. The Swedish plan primarily covers the following benefits:

- Retirement pension;

- ITPK (complementary occupational pension);

- Disability pension;

- Group family pension.

Virtually every clerical employee in the private sector in Sweden is covered by such a plan. The plan is financed by employers, who determine whether the pension insurance is with Alecta (Alecta Pensionsförsäkring, Ömsesidigt), or alternatively, as regards retirement pension and ITPK, whether a provision is to be made in-house by companies within the framework of the FPG/PRI system. The Group has elected to take out pension insurance with Alecta.

Irrespective of how the plan is financed – via pension insurance with Alecta or through in-house provisions by companies – the plan is a defined benefit scheme with respect to retirement pensions and group family pensions. Paid pensions are related to the employee's final salary and the total employment period covered by the plan. This means that the Group should report its proportional share of the defined benefit commitments, and the assets under management and expenses associated with the plan in the same manner as any other defined benefit plan, and provide the information required for such plans.

Alecta, however, is unable to provide sufficient information to report the Group's proportional share of the defined benefit commitments, the assets under management and expenses associated with the plan. There is also no agreement on how any surplus or deficit should be distributed to the participants in the pension plan. As a result, and in line with the Swedish Financial Accounting Standards Council's Emerging Issues Task Force, the scheme is reported as a defined contribution plan. Accordingly, the Group cannot provide the disclosure requirements with respect to the defined benefit plan in Sweden.

11.287 In addition, IAS 37 may require disclosure of contingent liabilities arising in connection with a multi-employer plan. For example:

- Actuarial losses relating to other participating entities because each entity that participates in a multi-employer plan shares in the actuarial risks of every other participating entity.

- Any responsibility under the terms of a plan to finance any shortfall in the plan if other entities cease to participate.

[IAS 19 para 32B].

The requirements of IAS 37 are discussed further in chapter 21.

11.287.1 Where an entity participates in a defined benefit plan that shares risks between various entities under common control, such as a group plan, the following disclosure should be made in the entity's separate or individual financial statements.

- The contractual agreement or stated policy for charging the net defined benefit cost or the fact that there is no such policy.

- The policy for determining the contribution to be paid by the entity.

- If the entity accounts for an allocation of the net defined benefit cost in accordance with IAS 19 paragraph 34A (see para 11.119.1), all the information about the plan as a whole in accordance with paragraphs 120A-121 of IAS 19 (see para 11.282).

- If the entity accounts for the contribution payable for the period in accordance with IAS 19 paragraph 34A (see para 11.119.1), the following information about the plan as a whole.

  - A general description of the type of plan.

  - Reconciliations of the opening and closing balances of the fair value of plan assets and any reimbursement rights and the present value of the defined benefit obligation.

  - An analysis of the defined benefit obligation into amounts arising from plans that are wholly unfunded and amounts arising from plans that are wholly or partly funded.

  - Further analysis of plan assets, comprising the percentage invested in each major category of plan asset at the balance sheet date.

  - The principal actuarial assumptions used as at the balance sheet date.

  - Sensitivity analysis showing the impact on both the amounts recognised in the income statement and the defined benefit obligation of a 1% change in the assumed medical cost trend rates.

  - The employer's best estimate, as soon as it can reasonably be determined, of contributions expected to be paid to the plan during the annual period beginning after the balance sheet date.

[IAS 19 para 34B].

[The next paragraph is 11.289.]

11.289   IAS 24 provides that a post-employment benefit plan established for the benefit of an entity's employees is a related party of the entity. [IAS 24 para 9]. Hence, transactions between an entity and its pension plan fall within the scope of IAS 24. IAS 24 also contains a requirement to disclose compensation payable to key management personnel, which comprises all employee benefits as defined in IAS 19, together with share based payments as dealt with in IFRS 2. [IAS 24 para 17]. The requirements of IAS 24 are discussed further in chapter 29.

> **UK.11.289.1** IAS 19 does not deal with the disclosure of directors' emoluments. Disclosure requirements for directors' emoluments are contained in Schedule 5 and Schedule 8 to SI 2008/410 of the Companies Act 2006 and in the Listing Rules. Details of these requirements are covered in chapter 5 of the Manual of Accounting – Narrative Reporting.

11.290 In addition to the information disclosed in connection with participation in a multi-employer plan (see para 11.285), IAS 37 may require disclosure of contingent liabilities arising from other post-employment benefit obligations. [IAS 19 para 125]. The requirements of IAS 37 are discussed further in chapter 21.

11.290.1 The adequacy of pension disclosures has been the subject of much comment over the last few years. In December 2006 the UK Accounting Standards Board ('ASB') published a new best practice reporting statement, 'Retirement benefits – disclosures'. It is designed to allow users to obtain a clear view of the cost of providing retirement benefits, the related gains, losses, assets and liabilities, the risks and rewards arising from defined benefit schemes and the entity's future funding obligations. The reporting statement complements the disclosures required by IAS 19 and, in our view, represents best practice guidance applicable to all IFRS reporters.

11.290.2 The reporting statement sets out six principles (rather than requirements) to be considered when providing disclosures for defined benefit schemes, and these are considered below.

Relationship between the reporting entity and the trustees of defined benefit schemes

11.290.3 The relationship between the reporting entity and the trustees (managers) will determine how an entity manages and arranges its affairs with regard to the defined benefit scheme. This includes the investment strategy for the assets held by the scheme and the principles for funding the scheme, including how contribution levels to the scheme are agreed. The management and arrangement of affairs may be affected by the powers vested in the trustees.

11.290.4 In recognition of this, the reporting statement recommends that financial statements disclose the arrangements between the trustees of the scheme and the reporting entity, setting out any powers of the trustees that have a material financial effect on the reporting entity and that are both significant and unusual in relation to the legal and regulatory framework in which the entity operates.

Information about the principal assumptions

11.290.5 The reporting statement recommends that financial statements should include sufficient information about the principal assumptions used to measure scheme liabilities to allow users to understand the inherent uncertainties affecting the measurement of scheme liabilities. These assumptions should include mortality rates. Disclosure should be given of the number of years post retirement it is anticipated pensions will be paid to members of the scheme, as this is often more useful than details of a mortality standard table or cohort factor. Where the number of years assumed alters depending on geographical, demographical or other significant reasons, the different mortality rates should be separately disclosed.

Sensitivity analysis for principal assumptions

11.290.6 Financial statements should disclose a sensitivity analysis for the principal assumptions used to measure the scheme liabilities, showing how the measurement of scheme liabilities would have been affected by changes in the relevant assumption that were reasonably possible at the balance sheet date. For the purposes of this disclosure, all other assumptions would be held constant. No further guidance is provided on how the sensitivity analysis would be undertaken other than an illustrative disclosure example in the appendix to the reporting statement.

How defined benefit liabilities are measured

11.290.7 There are alternative approaches to the projected unit credit method for measuring defined benefit scheme liabilities, as required by IAS 19. One such approach is measuring scheme liabilities on a buy-out basis, that is, the cost of buying out benefits at the balance sheet date with a suitable insurer. Where the cost of buying out benefits is made available to trustees and or members of a scheme, then the reporting statement recommends that it is disclosed. Table 11.22 below shows an example of such disclosure.

Table 11.22 – Buy-out basis disclosure

ITV plc – annual report – 31 December 2009

6 Pension schemes (extract)

An alternative method of valuation to the projected unit method is a solvency basis, often estimated using the cost of buying out benefits at the consolidated statement of financial position date with a suitable insurer. This amount represents the amount that would be required to settle the scheme liabilities at the consolidated statement of financial position date rather than the Group continuing to fund the ongoing liabilities of the scheme. The Group estimates the shortfall in the amount required to settle the scheme's liabilities at the consolidated statement of financial position date is £1,500 million (2008: £1,800 million).

Future funding obligations in relation to defined benefit schemes

11.290.8 IAS 19 requires the employer's best estimate, as soon as it can reasonably be determined, of contributions expected to be paid to the scheme during the annual period beginning after the balance sheet date. Scheme liabilities are, however, often of a long term nature and contributions expected to be paid in the next annual period may not provide sufficient information to allow the users of the financial statements to understand how the scheme liabilities affect the economic resources available to the entity, including its cash flow.

11.290.9 Given this, the reporting statement recommends that the financial statements should disclose the following:

- The rates or amounts of contributions which have been agreed with the trustees (managers) of the scheme and are payable to the scheme by or on behalf of the reporting entity.

- The funding principles the entity has agreed or operates with regard to defined benefit schemes.

- Where a defined benefit scheme is in deficit and the entity has entered into an agreement with the trustees (managers) of the scheme to make additional contributions to reduce or recover the deficit, separate disclosure of such additional contributions, and the number of years over which it is anticipated the additional contributions will be paid.

- The duration of scheme liabilities allowing users to see the period of time over which the liabilities of the defined benefit scheme mature. Table 11.23 below shows an example of such disclosures.

- Information that allows users to understand the projected cash flows of defined benefit schemes.

Table 11.23 – Maturity of schemes

BT Group plc – annual report – 31 March 2011

23. Retirement benefit plans (extract)

The estimated average duration of BTPS liabilities is 15 years (2010: 15 years) and the benefits payable by the BTPS are expected to be paid over more than 60 years as shown in the following graph:

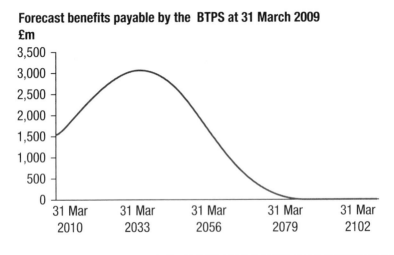

Forecast benefits payable by the BTPS at 31 March 2009

Nature and extent of the risks and rewards arising from financial instruments held by defined benefit schemes

11.290.10   Disclosures should be made to enable users to evaluate the nature and extent of the risks and rewards arising from the financial instruments held by defined benefit schemes. For each type of risk arising from financial instruments held by retirement benefits schemes, the reporting statement recommends the following disclosure:

(a)   the exposures to risk and how they arise;

(b)   the objectives, policies and processes undertaken by the defined benefits scheme or the entity for managing the risk and the methods used to measure the risk; and

(c)   any changes in (a) or (b) from the previous period.

11.290.11   An entity may disclose a sensitivity analysis, such as value-at-risk, for types of risks to which the assets of the defined benefit scheme are exposed. Where an entity discloses such a sensitivity analysis it should also disclose the method and assumptions used in preparing this analysis and any changes from the previous period in the methods and assumptions used.

11.290.12   As well as disclosing the percentage or amount of the fair value of total scheme assets that each major category of assets constitutes. The entity should also disclose the expected rate of return assumed for each category for the period presented.

[The next paragraph is 11.304.]

First-time adoption of IFRS

11.304   There are specific rules in respect of first-time adoption of IFRS, set out in IFRS 1. Under IFRS 1, an entity can apply the 'corridor approach' prospectively from the date of transition to IFRS (that is, recognise all cumulative actuarial gains and losses at the date of transition and then spread post-transition actuarial gains and losses in accordance with IAS 19). The exemption must be applied to all of an entity's pension plans if it is used. This exemption and other implications of IAS 19 for first-time adopters of IFRS are considered in detail in chapter 2.

Companies Acts 2006 requirements

UK.11.305   The Companies Act 2006 contains no specific accounting requirements regarding employee benefits. There are, however, extensive disclosure requirements for salaries, bonuses, pensions and other benefits payable to directors. Details of these requirements are covered in chapter 5 of the Manual of Accounting – Narrative Reporting.

UK.11.306 The Act contains a requirement for disclosure of the following in respect of all persons employed by a company during the financial year:

- Wages and salaries paid or payable in respect of that year to those persons.

- Social security costs incurred by the company on their behalf.

- Other pension costs so incurred.

[CA06 Sec 411(5)].

UK.11.306.1 In addition, a UK company that has securities carrying voting rights admitted to trading on a regulated market at the end of its financial year is required to disclose, in its directors' report, details of any agreement with employees (including directors) of the company providing for compensation for loss of office on the takeover of the company. [SI 2008/410 7 Sch 13(2)(k)]. See further chapter 3 of the Manual of Accounting – Narrative Reporting.

[The next paragraph is UK.11.310.]

Impact on distributable profits

UK.11.310 International Financial Reporting Standards do not concern themselves with the determination of distributable profits. Such matters are dealt with in national law (and are considered in greater detail in chapter 23). The ICAEW and the ICAS guidance on distributable profits, Tech 02/10, 'Guidance on the determination of realised profits and losses in the context of distributions under the Companies Act 2006' includes the impact of retirement benefit plans on distributable reserves. This guidance is considered in more detail below.

UK.11.311 For defined contribution plans, the cost charged to the income statement, which is equal to the contributions payable in the period, is a realised loss. Similarly, where multi-employer plans are treated as defined contribution, the income statement charge is a realised loss.

UK.11.312 The Companies Act defines a company's distributable profits not in terms of its assets and liabilities, but as its accumulated, realised profits less its accumulated, realised losses. [CA06 Sec 830 (2)(3)]. It is the cumulative gain or loss credited or debited to reserves in respect of a pension plan (whether through the income statement or other comprehensive income), rather than the existence of a surplus or deficit, that affects realised profits. The impact on reserves is not usually the same as the pension surplus or deficit due to net contributions paid into the scheme and any asset or liability introduced as the result of a business combination. This is illustrated in the following examples.

Example – Immediate recognition of actuarial gains and losses

Company A established a new defined benefit pension plan at the beginning of 20X5. Its accounting policy is to recognise all actuarial gains and losses in the income statement in the year in which they arise. During 20X5 there is a net pension expense of £4m, but contributions to the plan amount to £5m. Hence, at the end of 20X5 there is a surplus in the plan, and an asset on the balance sheet, of £1m (both taxation and questions over recoverability of the asset are ignored for the purpose of this example). However, the impact on distributable profits is not a credit of £1m, as represented by the surplus in the plan, but a debit of £4m in respect of the net pension expense. Considered another way, the impact on reserves is derived by deducting the contributions to the plan from the surplus.

UK.11.313 It is necessary to determine whether an adjustment to reserves is required to arrive at the amount of distributable profits. Firstly it is necessary to identify the cumulative net gain or loss taken to reserves in respect of the pension surplus or deficit, and secondly to establish the extent to which the gain or loss is realised.

- No adjustment is required if a net cumulative debit or loss has been taken to reserves: this represents a realised loss as it results from the creation of, or increase in a provision for a liability or a loss resulting in an overall reduction in net assets.

- A cumulative net credit or gain in reserves is a realised profit only to the extent that it is represented by an asset to be recovered by agreed refunds in the form of qualifying consideration (as defined in Tech 02/10). Any further cumulative net credit (in excess of agreed refunds) is not qualifying consideration so is treated as unrealised, although it will become realised in subsequent periods to the extent that it offsets subsequent net debits to reserves that are treated as realised losses.

Tech 02/10 Appendix 4 includes a worked example for a company with a surplus at the year-end.

UK.11.314 Although the guidance considers IAS 19 to be within its scope, it was written in the context of FRS 17 and does not consider the application of the 'corridor' approach. The main principle (that is, the impact on distributable profits is determined by the net debit or credit in reserves) remains the same, but should an unrecognised pension plan deficit be taken into account?

UK.11.315 The impact of an unrecognised pension plan deficit on a company's ability to make distributions was considered by the Company Law Committee of the ICAEW in the context of the FRS 17 transitional disclosures. Tech 03/02, 'FRS 17 transitional disclosures and distributions by companies', concluded that a deficit that is disclosed, but not recognised in the financial statements, was not taken into account in determining distributable profits under the Companies Act 1985. However, the position under common law also had to be considered. Under common law, a company cannot lawfully make a distribution out of capital. Thus, regardless of whether a pension plan deficit was recognised in the financial statements, the directors had to consider, both at the time of proposing a distribution and at the time it was made, whether the company had incurred losses that had eroded its profits available for distribution. Applying the principles of this guidance in the context of the 'corridor' approach under IAS 19, this might include considering actuarial losses that are to be recognised in the income statement in future periods. In addition, directors are subject to fiduciary duties, such as to ensure that the company is in a position to settle its debts as they fall due.

> **Example – 'Corridor' approach (see from para 11.270)**
>
> Company B established a new defined benefit pension plan at the beginning of 20X5, but its accounting policy is to recognise a portion of actuarial gains and losses over the average remaining working lives of employees. During 20X5 there is a net pension expense of £4m and at the year end unrecognised actuarial losses amount to £4.5m. Contributions to the plan amount to £5m. Hence, the movements in the plan are as set out below.
>
> | | Plan £m | Income statement £m | Balance sheet £m |
> |---|---|---|---|
> | 1 January 20X5 | | | |
> | Net expense | (4.0) | (4.0) | (4.0) |
> | Contributions | 5.0 | – | 5.0 |
> | Unrecognised actuarial losses | (4.5) | – | – |
> | 31 December 20X5 | (3.5) | (4.0) | 1.0 |
>
> At the end of 20X5 there is a deficit in the plan of £3.5m but a net pension asset of £1m (taxation and questions over recoverability of the asset are ignored). However, the impact on distributable profits is a debit of £4m in respect of the net pension expense. The unrecognised actuarial losses, which, by their nature, are not recognised in the income statement or other comprehensive income, are not taken into account in determining distributable profits (although see also para UK.11.315). Considered another way, the impact on reserves is derived by deducting the contributions to the plan from the deficit in the plan, and adding back the unrecognised actuarial losses.

UK.11.316 Where an entity operates more than one defined benefit plan, it should assess the impact of a surplus or deficit on its distributable profits separately for each plan. In other words, plans should not be aggregated or offset to reach a single net realised profit or loss, unless two plans are to merge and the trustees have irrevocably agreed to the offset of the surplus and deficit.

UK.11.317 The deferred tax impact of pension accounting generally relates to the pension asset or liability and not the cumulative net debit or credit in reserves. A cumulative debit in respect of a deferred tax liability is a realised loss, and a cumulative credit in respect of a deferred tax asset is an unrealised profit. However, where there is an unrealised cumulative net credit in respect of a pension asset, a deferred tax debit is offset against that unrealised profit.

Similarly, where there is a realised cumulative net debit in respect of a pension liability, a deferred tax credit is offset against that realised loss.

First-time adoption of IAS 19

UK.11.318 On first-time adoption of IFRS, the impact of compliance with IAS 19 on distributable profits will be relatively simple to determine. This is because the cumulative net debit or credit to be recognised in reserves under IAS 19 will normally be similar to that determined under FRS 17, adjusted for the effect of applying the 'corridor' approach, where applicable. Subsequent to first-time adoption, the impact on distributable profits of income and expenses in future years will be determined as described from paragraph UK.11.313.

[The next paragraph is UK.11.324.1.]

Pensions Act 2004 implications

UK.11.324.1 The Pensions Act 2004, published in November 2004, is a significant piece of legislation and was followed by a web of supporting regulations, codes of practice and other guidance, much of which came into force from April 2005.

UK.11.324.2 From an accounting perspective, the most significant provisions of the Pensions Act 2004 are in the following areas:

■ The launch of the Pension Protection Fund (see para UK.11.324.4 onwards).

■ Increased powers to the new Pension Regulator (see para UK.11.324.7 onwards).

■ Revised rules for employers ceasing to participate in a pension plan (see para UK.11.324.15 onwards).

UK.11.324.3 The following paragraphs summarise only the main accounting implications of the new legislation and do not attempt to explore the rules in detail.

The Pension Protection Fund (PPF)

UK.11.324.4 The Pension Protection Fund (PPF), which came into force from April 2005, is designed to protect pension plan members in the event that the sponsoring employer becomes insolvent. Broadly, the PPF will fund current pensions in payment as well as up to 90% of the benefits of active and deferred plan members when an 'insolvency event' occurs. The term 'insolvency event' encompasses the administration, administrative receivership or liquidation of the sponsoring employer.

UK.11.324.5   The PPF is funded in part by the assets of the plans it takes over and in part by a levy on all plans covered by the PPF. The pension protection levy is charged annually; the levy year runs from 1 April to 31 March. Initially, the levy was based on factors related to plan size (number of members, value of liabilities, etc). From 2006/7 the PPF levy is divided into two parts: The scheme-based element, which makes up ca 20% of the total levy, is based on a scheme's liabilities to members on a section 179 basis. The risk-based element, which makes up ca 80% of the levy, takes into account funding levels (the worst funded plans pay a higher levy) and the likelihood of the employer's insolvency (the lower a company's Dun & Bradstreet rating, the higher the levy). From 2012/13 the way the PPF levy is calculated will change significantly. It is intended that the revised methodology and levy parameters will be fixed for three years until 2015. Under the new methodology, the funding levels will be assessed on smoothed assumptions (5 year average yields) so that sharp movements in financial markets will have less effect on the risk-based element. The risk-based element will take into account the investment risk of a scheme's portfolio of assets (the riskier the investment strategy the higher the levy). The method for allowing for insolvency risk of employers will change; the measure of insolvency risk will be averaged over 12 months (rather than at a single date) and employers will be divided into 10 rather than 100 risk bands.

UK.11.324.6   The PPF levy can represent a significant cost of maintaining a defined benefit pension plan. Although not literally an administration cost, the levy's accounting treatment should mirror that of other costs incurred by the plan. As noted in paragraph 11.235, IAS 19 is not clear as to whether this means that expenses should be deducted from the return on plan assets or included in the measurement of the defined benefit obligation. Although in the early years the levy was based on plan membership, among other things, that linkage was short-lived. Thus, for the 2006/7 year, 80% of the levy is risk-based with the amount reflecting the level of scheme underfunding (the worst funded plans pay a higher levy) and the viability of the sponsoring employer (the lower a company's Dun & Bradstreet rating, the higher the levy). As a result, it does not seem appropriate to consider the levy to be an additional cost of providing benefit to any plan member or group of members. Rather, the levy relates to the plan as a whole and can be considered analogous to a tax. IAS 19 states that the return on plan assets should be stated net of any taxes payable by the plan itself. [IAS 19 para 7]. Accordingly, we believe that the expected return on plan assets should be stated net of the levy expected to be paid in a period, with the difference between this amount and the actual levy payable being treated as an actuarial gain or loss. However, as with other plan expenses, there is an alternative argument for inclusion of the levy in the measurement of the defined benefit obligation. Whichever approach is followed, the accounting policy should be clearly stated.

The Pensions Regulator

UK.11.324.7 The Pensions Regulator replaced the previous regulator (OPRA), inheriting all of its powers and functions along with several new powers. In our view, there are two areas in which the regulatory regime may influence the financial statements:

- The 'moral hazard' provisions (see para UK.11.324.8 onwards).
- The 'statutory funding objective' (see para UK.11.324.10 onwards).

The 'moral hazard' provisions

UK.11.324.8 The 'moral hazard' provisions in the Pensions Act are designed to prevent employers from re-arranging their affairs so as to avoid their pension obligations. The provisions permit the regulator to impose:

- Contribution notices on people that have been party to an act, or a deliberate failure to act, aimed at avoiding pension obligations.

- Financial support directions on associated or connected parties where the employer is either 'insufficiently resourced' or a service company (that is, a company the turnover of which is solely or principally derived from amounts charged for the provision of employee services to other group members). A financial support direction is a requirement to put financial support in place within a specified time period and to ensure that that support remains in place while the plan is in existence.

- Restoration orders, where the regulator is of the opinion that a transaction has been made at undervalue. Such orders require that a pension plan's financial position is restored to its pre-transaction position.

UK.11.324.9 The existence of these powers could influence the judgement of whether a plan should be treated as defined contribution or defined benefit as they may indicate that an entity could have an obligation to provide funding where one was not thought to exist previously. It will also be necessary to determine whether the risk that the regulator may impose a notice represents a contingent liability (see further chapter 21).

The 'statutory funding objective'

UK.11.324.10 With effect from September 2005, the previous minimum funding requirement (MFR) was replaced by a statutory funding objective (SFO). This means that all defined benefit plans have to have 'sufficient and appropriate assets' to cover their liabilities. Where a plan has insufficient assets to cover its liabilities, the trustees must establish a recovery plan setting out how the SFO is to be met and over what period. Any failure to do this, or to reach agreement with the employer on a funding strategy for the plan, must be reported to the regulator, who may take any of the following courses of action:

- Modify the plan in relation to future accrual of benefits.

- Fix the period over which a shortfall is to be made up.

- Impose a schedule of contributions.

UK.11.324.11 Under the SFO regulations the levels of contributions to defined benefit pension plans have generally increased. However, of greater significance to the financial statements may be the valuation of a plan in wind-up, which is based on the buy-out of all accrued benefits. This makes it more expensive to wind up a pension plan and, taken with the moral hazard provisions described above, almost impossible for a solvent company to walk away from its pension obligations. Employers can become liable to the trustees of a defined benefit plan for a debt if there is a deficit in a defined benefit plan. This can apply on:

- the winding-up of a plan;

- the insolvency of an employer; or

- an employer ceasing participation in a multi-employer plan (which includes 'group pension plans' in IAS 19 terminology – see para UK.11.324.18 onwards).

UK.11.324.12 In situations where a buy-out valuation exceeds the defined benefit liability recognised under IAS 19, there should be consideration as to whether there ought to be disclosure in the financial statements. The ASB's best practice reporting statement on pension disclosures (see para UK.11.290.1 onwards) recommends that where the cost of buying out benefits is made available to trustees (managers) and/or members of defined benefit plans, then the financial statements should also disclose the cost of buying out benefits. [ASB RS para 17].

UK.11.324.13 Where there is a funding plan in place, IAS 19 requires disclosure of future contributions. [IAS 19 para 120A(q)]. However, in the absence of an agreed funding plan, we consider that there should be disclosure of the potential implications of any action by the regulator. Furthermore, where a plan is in wind-up, we consider that there should be disclosure of the fact that the buy-out obligation exceeds amounts recognised under IAS 19. In some circumstances, it may be appropriate to recognise these additional obligations.

UK.11.324.14 Although not arising for the reasons described in paragraph UK.11.324.12 above, Table UK.11.24 shows an example of a company that made disclosure in its 2004 interim statement of a potential requirement to make additional contributions to its pension plan following a failure to equalise properly the retirement ages of men and women. This extract shows the type of disclosure that may be appropriate in the context of obligations arising out of the Pensions Act.

Table UK.11.24 – Obligation to make further contributions

MFI Furniture Group plc – interim report – 12 June 2004

Notes to the financial statements (extract)

12 Pensions (extract)

On 6 May 2004 the Group announced that it had received actuarial and legal advice following a thorough review of an issue arising within its UK pension plans. This issue is liable to result in the Group recognising higher pension obligations than previously identified. The issue has its origins in a failure, back in 1994, effectively to properly equalise the pension age for men and women at age 65 for an employee's service from 17 November 1994. Although announcements to this effect were made at the time to plan members, the relevant trust documentation was not properly amended. This is liable to result in the part of the benefits earned by employee members over a period from 1994 to 2004 having to be calculated using a normal retirement date of age 60 rather than at age 65. Plan rules have now been amended to cap liability in relation to future service.

The Board has sought legal advice on the scope for correction and an independent actuarial assessment of the additional liabilities, which might arise, and of the contributions required to fund them. It appears far from certain that the situation can be corrected, in which case some £40 million of additional liabilities (before tax) will arise. This figure is assessed on the same actuarial assumptions as currently used for funding the UK pension plans and accounting for them under SSAP24 (see note 23 to the Group's 2003 financial statements). Under FRS 17, which the Group has not yet adopted, this figure would be approximately £50 million (before tax).

Under the pensions accounting standard SSAP24, the impact on future profits of the Group will depend on the period over which additional liabilities are recognised. At this stage the funding position has not yet been resolved and is uncertain. Given the current degree of uncertainty in the outcome of the discussions with the Trustees there is no recognition of any additional charge in these interim financial statements.

The Board and the Trustees will be reviewing the funding position in the light of further advice to be received and will then discuss how best to proceed. The Trustees will need to be satisfied both as to the period over which contributions are paid and the date from which contributions commence. The Board expects that the funding position will become clearer in the second half of the financial year and that this would be reflected in the year end accounts.

The Board continues to take advice from leading counsel as to the actions required to obtain recovery from the third parties on whose advice the Group and the Trustees of the plan relied in relation to this issue.

Employers ceasing to participate in a pension scheme

UK.11.324.15 For a single-employer pension scheme, section 75 of the Pensions Act 1995 (as amended by the Pensions Act 2004) ensures that a debt can be placed on the pension scheme's sponsoring employer if the value of the scheme's assets is less than its liabilities. The debt is triggered if:

- the scheme winds-up; or

- on a relevant event (for example, the employer becomes insolvent).

UK.11.324.16 Section 75A was inserted into the Pensions Act 1995 by the Pensions Act 2004 to modify the existing section 75 as it applies to multi-employer schemes (see para UK.11.324.18). For these schemes, the debt is triggered if:

- the scheme winds-up;

- on a relevant event (for example, insolvency) for any one or more companies; or

- on a withdrawal of an individual employer from a multi-employer scheme (referred to as an 'employment-cessation event').

UK.11.324.17 When an employer ceases to participate in a defined benefit multi-employer scheme, whilst other employers continue to participate, the departing employer will normally be liable to pay their 'section 75 debt' – their share of the pension scheme's liabilities calculated on a 'buy-out basis' (that is, the full cost of securing its liabilities with annuities, including an estimate of expenses) (see paragraph 11.324.20 below). There are six prescribed ways in which an employer departing from a multi-employer scheme can have its section 75 debt reduced or removed (see paras 11.324.24 and 11.324.25 below).

UK.11.324.18 A multi-employer scheme is a scheme in relation to which more than one employer is exposed to the scheme. 'Employer' in relation to an occupational pension scheme, means the employer of persons in the description or category of employment to which the scheme in question relates. Multi-employer schemes do not include, for the purposes of the section 75 rules, sectionalised schemes where:

- contributions payable by an employer are allocated to that employer's section;

- a specified part of the scheme's assets is attributable to each section and cannot be used for any other section; and

- there is only one employer in each section.

In such cases, section 75 will apply as if each section of the scheme were a separate scheme.

UK.11.324.19 A liability is triggered when an 'employment-cessation event' occurs. In general, this event takes place when a participating employer ceases to have any employees who are members of the scheme and at least one participating employer remains. This could occur if:

- A company leaves the corporate group and, therefore, ceases to be a participating employer in the pension scheme.

- A company's business is sold, leaving it with no remaining employees.

- A company ceases to be employer of any individuals who are active members of the scheme (for example, a group restructuring).

- A company's employees cease employment through redundancy or resignation.

- Future accruals cease for that company.

This is a complex area and professional advice is likely to be needed.

UK.11.324.20   When an 'employment-cessation event' occurs, part of the total deficit in a multi-employer scheme has to be attributed to the withdrawing employer. The attribution is by reference to the position at the date that the employer ceases to participate in the scheme. The total deficit is calculated on a buy-out basis (that is, based on the full cost of securing the scheme's liabilities with annuities, including an estimate of expenses). The total deficit is attributed according to the participating employers according to the scheme's trust deed and rules, but if the rules are silent then the method for calculating the liability share for each employer is detailed in the Employer Debt Regulations.

UK.11.324.21   Under the legislation, the amount of the employer's debt is:

- the proportion of the buy-out deficit that is attributable to employment with that employer; and

- the expenses attributable to the employer ceasing to participate.

UK.11.324.22   Depending on what is set out in the scheme's own trust deed and rules, the withdrawing employer has to pay not only the buy-out deficit attributable to its own employees, but also a share of the orphan liabilities. 'Orphan liabilities' are material liabilities that are attributable to companies that have already left the scheme, including any liabilities that cannot be attributed specifically to any of the remaining employers. Unless the scheme rules state otherwise, the other employers share any exposure relating to these liabilities.

UK.11.324.23   In simplified terms, the liability of the withdrawing employer is calculated as follows:

$$\frac{\text{buy-out liabilities for withdrawing employer}}{\substack{\text{buy-out liabilities for withdrawing employer} \\ + \text{ remaining employers}}} \times \text{buy-out deficit for the scheme}$$

UK.11.324.24   Under the amendments to the Employer Debt Regulations, from April 2010, there are two mechanisms which allow an employer to depart without becoming liable for the section 75 debt where there is a corporate restructuring event involving one departing and one receiving employer:

- *de minimis restructuring test* – where trustees are satisfied that the amount of the departing employer's liabilities is minimal; and

- *restructuring test* – where trustees are satisfied that there is no weakening of the employer covenant supporting the pension scheme.

UK.11.324.25 There are four mechanisms which allow the employer to depart from the scheme having paid a modified section 75 debt (subject to agreement by the trustees and all the affected employers):

- *Scheme apportionment arrangement* – where the departing employer pays a specified amount that is different from their section 75 debt and, if the amount is lower, the difference is apportioned to one or more of the remaining employers.

- *Withdrawal arrangement* — where the departing employer pays an amount that is less than their section 75 debt (but more than their share of the deficit calculated on the technical provision basis and the difference is guaranteed by one or more guarantors.

- *Approved withdrawal arrangement* – where the departing employer pays an amount that is less than their share of the deficit calculated on the technical provision basis and the difference is guaranteed by one or more guarantors. This type of arrangement must be approved by the Pension Regulator.

- *Regulated apportionment arrangement* – this modifies the departing employer's section 75 debt so that it is greater or less than its liability share. If less, the difference is apportioned to one or more of the remaining employers. This type of arrangement is only available where the scheme is in a PPF assessment period.

[The next paragraph is UK.11.324.30.]

Accounting treatment

UK.11.324.30 As noted in paragraph UK.11.324.16, a situation that will trigger measurement of the defined benefit obligation on a buy-out basis is where a participating employer ceases to participate in a multi-employer scheme. This may typically arise within group pension plans where, for example, a subsidiary within a group is sold. Such an event will trigger a debt on the participating employer, being the amount of the employer's defined benefit pension obligation measured on a buy-out basis, under section 75 of the Pensions Act 1995. In the case where the employer ceases participation in the plan, payment of the section 75 debt equates to a settlement event having the effect of extinguishing the participating employer's share of the plan liabilities (see para 11.250). The examples below illustrate this further. For the purpose of these examples it is assumed that no withdrawal arrangements deferring payment of part of the debt (see para UK.11.324.24) are entered into.

Example 1 – Section 75 payment made by withdrawing employer

Entity B is wholly-owned by entity A. The employees of entity B participate in the group A defined benefit pension plan (other entities owned by entity A, as well as entity A itself also participate in this plan). There is a stated policy for charging the net defined benefit cost for the plan as a whole to the participating entities, such that defined benefit accounting is applied in each entity's financial statements (see para 11.119.1), with actuarial gains and losses recognised in other comprehensive income. Entity A subsequently sells entity B to a third party purchaser.

Following the disposal of entity B, the employees of entity B remain in the group A pension plan as deferred members. Entity A now assumes responsibility for any liabilities arising in respect of these deferred members. Nevertheless, as entity B itself is ceasing to participate in the group A pension plan, this is determined to trigger a section 75 payment.

The group A pension plan is in deficit at the time of the disposal and the share of the deficit relating to entity B's employees (measured on an IAS 19 basis) amounts to £5m. On a buy-out basis, the share of the deficit relating to entity B's employees is £9m (being the value of the section 75 payment). Following the section 75 payment, a surplus of £4m under IAS 19 arises on entity B's share of the plan. All entities in entity A have a year end date of 31 December 20X6 and by this date, the disposal and section 75 payment have occurred.

In entity B's individual financial statements, a settlement loss of £4m is recognised (see para 11.250) as entity B has ceased to participate in the group A pension plan and entity B's liability in respect of the pension plan has been extinguished (through transfer of the obligation to entity A). The settlement loss of £4m reflects the fact that entity B had to make a payment of £9m (being the section 75 payment) in order to exit the group A pension plan where the deficit attributable to entity B's employees, previously recognised and measured on an IAS 19 basis, was £5m.

In entity A's consolidated financial statements, no settlement loss is recognised as, whilst entity B has ceased to participate in the plan, entity B's employees still remain in the plan, albeit as deferred members. Hence, from the perspective of the group, the liabilities associated with entity B's employees (£5m) have not been extinguished and the section 75 payment (£9m) will increase plan assets, resulting in a surplus for this part of the plan of £4m. In addition, a curtailment gain may arise as entity B's employees are now deferred members resulting in a reduction in their future benefit entitlement (see para 11.252).

Furthermore, as defined benefit accounting is applied at an entity level, the surplus of £4m in respect of entity B's employees needs to be allocated to the participating employers. As entity A has assumed responsibility for any liabilities relating to the deferred members, it would appear reasonable for the £4m surplus to be allocated to entity A. It will be recognised in entity A's separate financial statements if it meets the criteria in paragraphs 58 to 59 of IAS 19 (see para 11.214 onwards) and in IFRIC 14. The basic rule is that the amount of surplus recognised as an asset should not exceed the present value of any economic benefits available in the form of refunds from the plan or reductions in future contributions to the plan. If the surplus is recognised in entity A's separate financial statements, it will be included as part of the calculation of profit or loss on disposal of entity B.

The table below summarises the position in respect of entity B's employees (ignoring any curtailment gains):

	entity B (subsidiary) £'m	entity A (parent) £'m	Group £'m
Entity B's deficit as at date of disposal	(5)	–	(5)
Section 75 payment *	9	–	9
Group transfer:			
Settlement loss in entity B	(4)	–	–
Credit (included in profit or loss on disposal of entity B) in entity A	–	4	–
Surplus arising after section 75 payment to group A plan **	–	4	4

* The section 75 payment forms part of the settlement loss calculation in entity B's income statement, but increases plan assets in the group's consolidated financial statements.

** As entity A now assumes responsibility for any liabilities arising in respect of the deferred members, it would recognise the surplus of £4m in its individual financial statements if it meets the recognition criteria in IAS 19 and IFRIC 14.

UK.11.324.31   The above example is based on the situation where defined benefit accounting is applied in each entity's financial statements. In some cases, section 75 payments will become payable by entities that do not have an agreement or policy in place for charging the net defined benefit cost and which have, therefore, used defined contribution accounting in their individual financial statements as permitted by paragraph 34A of IAS 19 (see para 11.119 onwards). In such cases, the settlement loss in the withdrawing employer's individual financial statements will be the amount of the section 75 payment (that is, £9m in the example above). Under defined contribution accounting, there is no deficit previously recognised in the balance sheet and so the loss is recognised on the basis of contributions payable (in this case, the section 75 payment) in the period. Note that where the net defined benefit cost is not allocated to participating entities, the defined benefit obligation is accounted for in full in the sponsoring entity's financial statements. In addition, the consolidated financial statements of entity A will always apply defined benefit accounting.

[The next paragraph is UK.11.324.33.]

UK.11.324.33   The above example in paragraph UK.11.324.30 illustrates a relatively straightforward scenario. However, calculation of the section 75 payment often takes time and it may be the case that calculation of the payment is not completed until after the year end date. The following example illustrates this scenario:

Example 2 – Section 75 payment made by withdrawing employer after the year end

The facts are as for example 1 in paragraph UK.11.324.30 and entity A has taken over responsibility for the deferred members at the balance sheet date, but for administrative reasons entity B has not made the payment at the balance sheet date, as the amount to be paid is only finalised after the balance sheet date (being £9m as in the previous example).

Similar to example 1, in entity B's individual financial statements, a settlement loss of £4m is recognised as entity B has ceased to participate in the group A pension plan (through the transfer of the obligation to entity A). This settlement loss of £4m represents the difference between the section 75 liability of £9m and the deficit, previously recognised and measured on an IAS 19 basis, of £5m. The unpaid section 75 settlement payment is included in creditors in entity B's balance sheet replacing the previously recognised IAS 19 liability. This is consistent with the principles of paragraph 24 of IFRIC 14, which states that to the extent that contributions payable will not be available after they are paid into the plan, the entity should recognise a liability when the obligation arises, which in this case is when entity B leaves the group.

Again, similar to example 1, in entity A's consolidated financial statements, no settlement loss is recognised as, whilst entity B has ceased to participate in the plan, entity B's employees still remain in the plan, albeit as deferred members. Hence, from the perspective of the group, the liabilities associated with entity B's employees (£5m) have not been extinguished. At the balance sheet date, entity B is no longer part of the group and so the creditor for the unpaid section 75 debt (£9m) will not be included in the group's consolidated balance sheet. However, it is taken into account in determining entity B's net assets (which will be net assets excluding pensions less the section 75 creditor) in the calculation of the profit or loss on disposal of entity B and so it has been recognised by the group.

Under paragraph 103 of IAS 19, plan assets exclude unpaid contributions due from the reporting entity to the plan. However, in this case, the section 75 payment is due from entity B, which at the balance sheet date is no longer part of the reporting entity. Further, it is a payment required to be made by legislation and so is an asset receivable by the plan. Therefore, the unpaid section 75 contribution would be shown as part of plan assets, resulting in a surplus of £4m. In addition, a curtailment gain may arise as entity B's employees are now deferred members resulting in a reduction in their future benefit entitlement (see para 11.102).

Furthermore, as defined benefit accounting is applied at an entity level, the surplus of £4m in respect of entity B's employees needs to be allocated to the participating employers. As entity A has assumed responsibility for any liabilities relating to the deferred members, it would appear reasonable for the £4m surplus to be allocated to entity A. It will be recognised in entity A's individual financial statements if it meets the criteria in paragraphs 58 to 59 of IAS 19 and IFRIC 14 (see further example 1). If the surplus is recognised, it will be included as part of the calculation of profit or loss on disposal of entity B.

The table below summarises the position in respect of entity B's employees (ignoring any curtailment gains):

	Entity B (subsidiary) £'m	Entity A (parent) £'m	Group £'m
Entity B's deficit as at date of disposal	(5)	–	(5)
Unpaid section 75 payment *	9	–	9
Group transfer:			
Settlement loss in entity B	(4)	–	–
Credit (included in profit or loss on disposal of entity B) in entity A	–	4	–
Surplus arising after section 75 amount payable to group A plan **	–	4	4

* Note that the unpaid section 75 payment is recognised as a creditor and forms part of the settlement loss calculation in entity B's individual financial statements. In the consolidated financial statements, the section 75 creditor is taken into account in determining entity B's net assets in the calculation of the profit or loss on disposal of entity B and the debit increases plan assets in the group's consolidated financial statements as explained above.

** As entity A now assumes responsibility for any liabilities arising in respect of the deferred members, it would recognise the surplus of £4m in its individual financial statements if it meets the recognition criteria in IAS 19 (see comments in example 1 above).

UK.11.324.34   In the above example, the parent entity has taken over responsibility for the deferred members at the balance sheet date, but the subsidiary has not made the section 75 payment at the balance sheet date for administrative reasons. The situation could be more complicated where the settlement itself has not been finalised at the year end, such that the subsidiary is still responsible for the employees. An entity should recognise gains or losses on the settlement of a defined benefit plan when the settlement occurs. [IAS 19 para 109]. A settlement occurs when an entity enters into a transaction that eliminates all further legal or constructive obligation for part or all of the benefits provided under a defined benefit plan, for example, when a lump-sum cash payment is made to, or on behalf of, plan participants in exchange for their rights to receive specified post-employment benefits. [IAS 19 para 112]. The accounting treatment for settlements that straddle the balance sheet date will depend on the specific circumstances. See further paragraph 11.249 onwards.

UK.11.324.35   The above two examples illustrate the appropriate accounting where the departing employer makes the section 75 payment. Nevertheless, it may be the case that the parent entity agrees to pay the section 75 payment. The accounting impact is considered further in the following example.

Example 3 – Section 75 payment made by the withdrawing employer's parent

The facts are as for example 1 in paragraph UK.11.324.30, but entity A agrees to make the £9m section 75 payment. This amount is not repayable by entity B.

In entity B's individual financial statements, a settlement gain of £5m is recognised. As entity B did not make payments in respect of the section 75 debt, but has ceased participation in the plan, the settlement gain of £5m reflects the release of entity B's share of the deficit (previously recognised and measured on an IAS 19 basis).

Similar to example 1, in entity A's consolidated financial statements, no settlement loss is recognised (although a curtailment gain or loss may arise) as, whilst entity B has ceased to participate in the plan, entity B's employees still remain in the plan, albeit as deferred members. Hence, from the perspective of the group, the liabilities associated with entity B's employees (£5m) have not been extinguished and the section 75 payment (£9m) will increase plan assets, resulting in a surplus for this part of the plan of £4m.

In entity A's separate financial statements, the £5m deficit (measured on an IAS 19 basis) in respect of the liabilities that entity A has taken over should be recognised, with a corresponding loss in respect of the transfer in the income statement (as part of the calculation of profit or loss on disposal of entity B). The payment of £9m into the plan would be treated as a contribution to the pension plan given that entity A participates in the group A pension plan and has taken over the responsibility for funding the obligation for these deferred members. As such, entity A would increase the value of the plan assets it recognises by £9m, resulting in a surplus of £4m (if the recognition criteria in paragraphs 58 to 59 of IAS 19 and IFRIC 14 are met (see further example 1).

The table below summarises the position in respect of entity B's employees (ignoring any curtailment gains):

	Entity B (subsidiary) £'m	Entity A (parent) £'m	Group £'m
Entity B's deficit as at date of disposal	(5)	–	(5)
Section 75 payment *	–	9	9
Group transfer:			
Settlement gain in entity B	5	–	–
Loss (included in profit or loss on disposal of entity B) in respect of liabilities taken over	–	(5)	–
Surplus arising after section 75 payment to group A plan **	–	4	4

* The section 75 payment increases plan assets recognised in both entity A and in the group's consolidated financial statements.

** As entity A now assumes responsibility for any liabilities arising in respect of the deferred members, it would recognise the surplus of £4m in its separate financial statements if it meets the recognition criteria in IAS 19 and IFRIC 14 (see comments in example 1 above).

UK.11.324.36   A further situation that may arise is where there is also a bulk transfer of a subsidiary's share of the scheme into a new scheme. The accounting impact of this situation is considered further in the following examples.

> **Example 4 – Section 75 payment made by withdrawing employer (+ bulk transfer out)**
>
> The facts are as for example 1 in paragraph UK.11.324.30 (that is, entity B makes the section 75 payment), but in addition a bulk transfer is made of the assets and liabilities relating to entity B's employees to the pension plan of entity B's new parent. Following the section 75 payment, a surplus of £4m arises on entity B's share of the plan. For the purposes of the bulk transfer of entity B's share of the plan, it is agreed that the value of the surplus to be transferred into the new parent's pension plan will be £3m. It is decided that any surplus remaining after the bulk transfer will be allocated to entity A.
>
> In entity B's individual financial statements, the section 75 payment of £9m (in respect of a recognised deficit of £5m measured on an IAS 19 basis) initially results in a surplus of £4m. Of this, £3m is transferred to a new pension plan and remains on entity B's balance sheet as an asset. The remaining £1m represents a settlement loss as entity B has ceased to participate in the group A pension plan and entity B's liability in respect of that pension plan has been extinguished.
>
> In entity A's consolidated financial statements, a settlement loss of £3m is recognised in respect of the bulk transfer to the new pension plan (as part of the calculation of profit or loss on disposal of entity B), leaving a surplus of £1m in the group A pension plan.
>
> Furthermore, as defined benefit accounting is also applied at an entity level, the remaining surplus of £1m is recognised in entity A's separate financial statements if it meets the criteria in paragraphs 58 to 59 of IAS 19 and IFRIC 14 (see example 1). If the surplus is recognised, it will be included as part of the calculation of profit or loss on disposal of entity B.

The table below summarises the position in respect of entity B's employees:

	Entity B (subsidiary) £'m	Entity A (parent) £'m	Group £'m
Entity B's deficit as at date of disposal	(5)	–	(5)
Section 75 payment *	9	–	9
	4	–	4
Bulk transfer to new plan (settlement loss)	–	–	(3)
Group transfer:			
Settlement loss in entity B	(1)	–	–
Credit (included in profit or loss on disposal of entity B) in entity A	–	1	–
Surplus arising after section 75 payment to group A plan **	–	1	1
Surplus in new plan	3	–	–

* The section 75 payment initially increases plan assets recognised in both entity B and in the group's consolidated financial statements (prior to the bulk transfer).

** In this example, any surplus remaining after the bulk transfer has been allocated to entity A.

Example 5 – Section 75 payment made by withdrawing employer's parent (+ bulk transfer out)

The facts are as for example 1 in paragraph UK.11.324.30, but entity A agrees to make the £9m section 75 payment (and it is not repayable by entity B). In addition, a bulk transfer is made of the assets and liabilities relating to entity B's employees to the pension plan of entity B's new parent. Following the section 75 payment, a surplus of £4m arises on entity B's share of the plan. For the purposes of the bulk transfer of entity B's share of the plan, it is agreed that the value of the surplus to be transferred into the new parent's pension plan will be £3m. It is decided that any surplus remaining after the bulk transfer will be allocated to entity A.

In entity B's individual financial statements, a total settlement gain of £8m arises. Entity B did not make payments in respect of the section 75 debt, but has ceased to participate in the group A pension plan and entity B's liability in respect of that pension plan has been extinguished. The gain of £8m comprises £5m in respect of the release of entity B's share of the deficit (measured on an IAS 19 basis) and £3m in respect of the surplus (funded by entity A) transferred to a new pension plan (assuming that this is recognised on entity B's balance sheet as an asset).

In entity A's consolidated financial statements, a settlement loss of £3m is recognised in respect of the bulk transfer to the new pension plan (as part of the calculation of profit or loss on disposal of entity B), leaving a surplus of £1m in the group A pension plan.

Similar to example 3 in paragraph UK.11.324.35, in entity A's separate financial statements, the payment of £9m into the plan is treated as a contribution to the pension plan. However, as £8m of this contribution has been transferred out of the plan as a result of the bulk transfer, it represents a loss in entity A's books and it will be included in the profit or loss on disposal of entity B reported in entity A's income statement. The remaining surplus of £1m is recognised in entity A's balance sheet if it meets the criteria in paragraphs 58 to 59 of IAS 19 and IFRIC 14 (see example 1).

The table below summarises the position in respect of entity B's employees:

	Entity B £'m	Entity A £'m	Group £'m
Entity B's deficit as at date of disposal	(5)	–	(5)
Section 75 payment *	–	9	9
			4
Bulk transfer to new plan:			
Settlement gain/(loss)	8	–	(3)
Loss (included in profit or loss on disposal of entity B) in entity A	–	(8)	–
Surplus arising after section 75 payment to group A plan **	–	1	1
Surplus in new plan	3	–	–

* The section 75 payment initially increases plan assets recognised in both entity A and in the group's consolidated financial statements (prior to the bulk transfer).

** The surplus remaining after the bulk transfer is recognised in entity A (if it meets the criteria in IAS 19 and IFRIC 14) as this entity made the section 75 payment.

UK.11.324.37 In the above examples, the settlements and bulk transfers have taken place by the balance sheet date. The situation will be more complicated where the settlement and/or the bulk transfer straddle the balance sheet date. An entity should recognise gains or losses on the settlement of a defined benefit plan when the settlement occurs. [IAS 19 para 109]. A settlement occurs when an entity enters into a transaction that eliminates all further legal or constructive obligation for part or all of the benefits provided under a defined benefit plan, for example, when a lump-sum cash payment is made to, or on behalf of, plan participants in exchange for their rights to receive specified post-employment benefits. [IAS 19 para 112]. The accounting treatment for transactions that straddle the balance sheet date will depend on the specific circumstances. See further paragraph 11.249 onwards.

Employee benefits (IAS 19 revised)

Employee benefits (IAS 19 revised)

Recent developments – Amendments to IAS 19

11A.1 The IASB issued an amended version of IAS 19 in June 2011. The amended standard makes significant changes to the recognition and measurement of defined benefit pension expense and termination benefits, and to the disclosures for all employee benefits.

11A.2 The amended standard is effective for annual periods beginning on or after 1 January 2013, and is to be applied retrospectively in accordance with the general requirements of IAS 8, except for comparative disclosures in respect of the sensitivity analyses that the standard requires and the carrying value of assets, which include capitalised labour costs as at the opening balance sheet date. Early application is permitted. The guidance in IFRIC 14 was not incorporated in the amended IAS 19 so it continues to apply as guidance.

11A.3 The guidance below reflects the standard as revised in 2011 and should be followed from where the standard becomes effective, or when it is adopted early.

Introduction

11A.4 The international standard dealing with the accounting for and disclosure of employee benefits is IAS 19. IAS 19 applies to all types of employee benefits, although it is in the area of accounting for defined benefit pension plans that IAS 19 provides most complexity.

Objective and scope

11A.5 IAS 19 approaches accounting for employee benefits from a balance sheet perspective. The standard's first stated objective is to ensure that an employer's financial statements reflect a liability when an employee has provided service in exchange for employee benefits to be paid in the future. This approach reflects the trend in accounting standards to base accounting on the definitions of assets and liabilities and to make more use of fair value.

11A.6 The second objective of IAS 19 relates to the recognition of the cost of employee benefits in the performance statements. The objective is to ensure that an expense is recognised when the employer consumes the economic benefit arising from the services provided by the employee in exchange for employee benefits.

Scope of IAS 19

11A.7 IAS 19 applies to all types of employee benefits (except those to which IFRS 2 applies), which are defined as *"all forms of consideration given by an entity in exchange for service rendered by employees or for the termination of employment".* [IAS 19 para 8]. Employee benefits (including social security contributions payable in respect of employee benefits), therefore, include the following categories, each of which have different characteristics and, therefore, requirements:

- Short-term benefits such as wages, salaries, holiday pay, sick leave and bonuses payable within twelve months of the balance sheet date.

- Long-term benefits such as long-term incentive plans (LTIPs), long-service awards, holiday pay and bonuses payable more than twelve months after the balance sheet date.

- Termination benefits such as redundancy payments.

- Post-employment benefits such as pensions and post-retirement medical insurance.

[IAS 19 para 5].

11A.8 Share options and other forms of share-based payment that reward employees for services are not dealt with in IAS 19, but are dealt with in IFRS 2 (see chapter 12).

11A.9 Although not defined in the standard, the term 'employees' potentially has a broader application under IAS 19 than might normally be assumed, for example under companies legislation of some countries. Paragraph 7 of the standard notes that an employee may provide services to an entity on a full time, part time, permanent, casual or temporary basis. In our view, the scope of the definition 'employees' should be driven by the substance of the relationship between the individual and the 'employer'. Only where the latter is exposed to risks consistent with a contract of employment should the former be considered to be an employee for the purposes of IAS 19. Furthermore, the definition of an employee may also be outlined in national legislation.

UK.11A.9.1 Companies legislation in the UK defines employees as those employed under contracts *of service*. [CA06 Sec 411(3) to (5)]. Self-employed people should normally be excluded, because their contracts will be contracts *for services*. No such distinction is drawn in IAS 19. This could be interpreted as requiring all costs of engaging personnel, whether under employment contracts or otherwise, to be dealt with under IAS 19. As noted above, in our view, the scope of the definition 'employees' should be driven by the substance of the relationship between the individual and the 'employer'.

11A.10   Employee benefits may be provided to the employees themselves or to their dependants, such as in the case of death-in-service benefit. The standard also applies to benefits that are settled by payment to a third party such as an insurance company or the state. For example, an employer may have a policy of settling its pension obligations by purchasing annuities from an insurance company. Although the employer has not actually provided benefits directly to its employees, this arrangement would fall within IAS 19's scope. [IAS 19 para 6].

Benefits payable during employment

11A.11   Benefits payable during employment include the following:

- Wages, salaries and bonuses.

- Social security contributions.

- Holiday pay.

- Paid disability, sick and maternity leave.

- Benefits-in-kind, such as private medical insurance, company cars and accommodation.

- Long-term bonuses such as LTIPs and long-service awards.

[IAS 19 paras 9, 153].

UK.11A.11.1   Although FRS 12 has been relevant to the accounting for provisions in respect of bonuses, there have not been any specific UK accounting standards dealing with employee benefits such as those listed above. As a result, differing accounting treatments have been applied under UK GAAP, for example in respect of the period over which a holiday pay liability is recognised. Reporting entities in the UK may, but are not obliged to, look to IFRS (and in particular to IAS 19) for guidance on how to account for such provisions.

Recognition and measurement

11A.12   Different principles are applied to recognising and measuring employee benefits payable during employment depending on whether they are long-term or short-term. Short-term benefits are those amounts expected to be settled wholly within 12 months of the end of the annual period in which the employees render the service that gives rise to the benefit. Naturally, long-term benefits are those amounts expected to be settled, at least in part, after 12 months following the end of the period. Accounting for short-term benefits is generally simple, because no actuarial assumptions are required and any obligations are measured on an undiscounted basis.

Wages, salaries and other short-term benefits payable in cash

11A.13 Accounting for wages and salaries is generally straightforward. A liability and an expense (unless capitalisation is appropriate) are recognised when an employee has rendered services. Capitalisation of employee benefits as part of the cost of an asset is dealt with in IAS 2, 'Inventories' (see chapter 20), IAS 11 (see chapter 9), IAS 16 (see chapter 16) and IAS 38 (see chapter 15).

11A.14 Short-term bonuses and other short-term profit sharing arrangements are also straightforward. A liability and an expense (unless capitalisation is appropriate as described above) are recognised when the reporting entity has a present legal or constructive obligation to make payments as a result of past events and a reliable estimate can be made of the amount payable. [IAS 19 para 19]. This language is similar to that used in IAS 37 and the considerations are also similar. IAS 37 is dealt with in chapter 21. The only additional guidance regarding recognition is whether a reliable estimate can be made of the amount payable in paragraph 22 of IAS 19. Paragraph 22 of IAS 19 provides that a reliable estimate can be made when, and only when:

- the formal terms of the profit sharing or bonus plan contain a formula for determining the amount payable;

- the amount payable is determined before the financial statements are authorised for issue; or

- past practice gives clear evidence of the amount of the entity's constructive obligation.

[IAS 19 para 22].

11A.15 The following example illustrates when a change in the terms and conditions of employment should be recognised and when past practice creates a constructive obligation on the entity.

Example 1 – One-off compensation payment associated with future operations

To remain competitive, an entity intends to alter the terms and conditions of employment at one factory in such a way that overtime will be paid in future at 1.5 times the normal rate, rather than twice the normal rate as in the past. The entity intends to compensate employees with a one-off payment and has put this offer to the union. The employees are also aware of this impending change. No agreement has been reached with the union at the year end. However, if the offer is not accepted, the entity is likely to switch overtime work to other factories.

Provision should not be made for the planned expenditure to operate in a particular way in the future, because the entity can avoid that expenditure by changing its method of operation. Therefore, the proposed one-off compensation payment that is associated with the future operations and that could be avoided by switching overtime production to other factories should not be provided for, in advance, at the year end. However, if agreement for the payment had been reached with the unions by the year end and the payment was no longer dependent on future events (that is, the structure and recipients of the payment had been identified), then a liability should be recognised for the payment at the year end.

Example 2 – Performance bonus based on sales target

A car dealer has a practice of paying a performance bonus to its sales staff.

Past evidence indicates that sales staff who meet their sales targets received a bonus of 10% of their current salary package at the year end. Sales staff who were not in service throughout the whole year received a bonus in proportion to their service period. The bonuses are paid, in the first quarter of the following year, to the sales staff who are still employed by the entity at the year end.

At the year end, seven of the sales staff met their sales targets. Two of the seven began their employment halfway through the year and one of them left the entity at the year end.

The car dealer should recognise a liability at the expected cost of the bonuses to be paid in the subsequent year for the following reasons:

■ the dealer created a valid expectation among the sales staff that they would receive bonuses if they met their sales targets and were still in the entity's service, that is, there is a constructive obligation; and

■ the amount of the payment can be estimated reliably. There are four sales staff who will receive a bonus of 10% of their current salary packages and two who will receive 5% because their employment commenced halfway through the year. No provision should be recognised for the employee who resigned at the year end, because he left the entity before the year end and will, therefore, not receive a payment.

11A.16 If a bonus has not been paid by the balance sheet date, the amount recognised as a liability should be based on the expected amount payable. Often an annual bonus is payable some time after the year end and only to those employees who remain in employment until that time. IAS 19 makes it clear in paragraph 18 that if the amount payable has not been determined by the date on which the financial statements are signed, the amount provided at the balance sheet date should take account of the expected number of leavers. However, the standard is unclear as to whether the additional service condition (that is, the requirement to remain in employment until the date on which the bonus is paid) should be taken into account when considering the period over which the bonus expense is recognised. It states that *"employees render service that increases the amount to be paid if they remain in service until the end of the specified period"*. [IAS 19 para 20]. There are two schools of thought as to how this should be interpreted.

11A.17 The first is that because the amount of the bonus does not increase after the end of the performance period, the full liability should be recognised at the balance sheet date (with appropriate adjustment for expected leavers). Thus the associated expense is recognised over the shorter performance period.

11A.18 The second is that there is another vesting condition to be fulfilled in addition to the performance condition, namely that the employee must remain in employment until the later date and may still forfeit the right to payment by leaving before that date. By analogy with IAS 19 paragraphs 73 and BC55, for a plan that pays a lump sum of C1,000 on completion of ten years of service, an expense of C100 (adjusted to reflect the probability that the employee might leave and ignoring the time value of money for simplicity) should be recognised each year. Thus the associated expense is recognised over the longer vesting period.

11A.19 Furthermore, IFRS 2 concludes that a liability and an expense should be recognised in respect of a cash-settled share-based payment arrangement as services are rendered over the entire vesting period. In this context, the vesting period is the period until *all* conditions (both performance and service) are satisfied. Short-term employee benefits within the scope of IAS 19 are outside the scope of IFRS 2, but the IASB considered the standards to be consistent in this area. [IFRS 2 para BC245].

11A.20 Hence, although a case can be made for an expense to be recognised in respect of a short-term bonus over only the performance period, we believe that the more appropriate and consistent treatment is to recognise an expense over the longer vesting period until the bonus award vests. This is illustrated in the example below.

Example – Bonus payable to employees three months after the year-end

An entity has a December year end. It pays a bonus in respect of each year to employees who have provided services during the year and remain on the payroll at 31 March. The bonus pool is determined as 5% of entity profits and each employee's entitlement is determined as at 31 December. There is no re-allocation of the bonus entitlement of employees who leave before 31 March. On average, 1% of employees leave the entity each month. The financial statements for the year ended 31 December 20X3 showed a profit for the purpose of the bonus plan of C100m and they were signed on 28 February 20X4.

In the period from 1 January to 31 March it is expected that an average of 3% of the employees who worked during the previous year will leave the entity. The bonus pool for the year ended 31 December 20X3 was C5m so the expected amount payable on 31 March 20X4 would be C4.85m (97% of C5m). The actual experience in the period up to the date on which the financial statements were signed should be taken into account when it is a confirmation of expectations at the balance sheet date. If 3% of employees actually left during January and February 20X4, but it is still expected that a further 1% will leave during March through the normal course of business, the total amount recognised as an expense would be C4.8m (96% of C5m). However, if employees left after the balance sheet due to a post balance sheet event such as an acquisition or a loss of a major contract or customer, then this will likely be new information arising after the balance sheet date and should not be taken into account.

As employees are required to provide services until 31 March, although an argument can be made for recognition over the shorter 12 month performance period as discussed above, in our view the expense should be recognised over the longer 15 month vesting period ending on 31 March. Accordingly, a liability of C3.84m (that is, C4.8m × 12/15) should be recognised at 31 December 20X3.

11A.21 If the amount payable under a bonus arrangement is determined by reference to the value of the reporting entity's shares, this represents a share-based payment. The accounting for share-based payments is dealt with in chapter 12.

Cash payments to employee trusts

11A.22 Sometimes, an entity may establish a trust to act as intermediary in respect of payments to employees. The entity makes a payment to the trust for the benefit of the entity's employees and the trust uses the assets accumulated from those payments to pay the entity's employees for some or all of the services rendered. The key consideration is whether, in such circumstances, the trust should be consolidated.

11A.23 SIC 12 concludes that an entity should consolidate a special purpose entity (SPE) when the substance of the relationship between the parties indicates that the SPE is controlled by the entity, unless the SPE meets the definition of a long-term employee benefit fund as defined in paragraph 8 of IAS 19. [SIC 12 paras 6, 8]. The interpretation goes on to give examples of circumstances in which an SPE may be consolidated. These include the following:

- The activities of the SPE are being conducted on behalf of the entity according to its specific business needs so that the entity obtains benefits from the SPE's operation.

- The entity has rights to obtain the majority of the SPE's benefits and, therefore, may be exposed to risks incident to the SPE's activities.

[SIC 12 paras 10(a)(c)].

11A.23.1 IFRS 10 supersedes, but incorporates, the concepts set out in SIC 12 and is effective for periods beginning on or after 1 January 2013, with early application permitted. For entities applying IFRS as adopted by the EU, EU endorsement is expected in late 2012; however, endorsement is proposed with an effective date for periods beginning on or after 1 January 2014, with early adoption permitted. IFRS 10 defines the principle of control and establishes control as the basis for determining which entities are consolidated in the consolidated financial statements. The IFRS also sets out the accounting requirements for preparing consolidated financial statements. See chapter 5 for further guidance.

11A.24 If it is determined that an employee benefit trust is controlled by its sponsoring entity SIC 12 and IFRS 10 would require consolidation in the group financial statements, unless the trust meets the definition of a long term employee benefit plan in which case plan asset accounting would be applied as set out in paragraph 11A.101.

UK.11A.24.1 The general requirement to aggregate the trust into the sponsoring company's balance sheet set out in UITF 32 does not apply under IFRS.

11A.25 Does a sponsoring entity's payment to an employee benefit trust represent an immediate expense? Generally speaking, most expenses are incurred when a liability arises (that is, when services are received), not when they are paid for. An immediate expense to the sponsoring entity will occur only if a payment neither results in the acquisition of another asset nor the settlement of a liability.

Short-term compensated absences

11A.26 Compensated absences are periods during which an employee does not provide services to the employer, but employee benefits continue to be paid. Typical examples include:

■ Annual leave.

■ Sick leave.

■ Maternity leave.

■ Jury service.

■ Military service.

11A.27 IAS 19 distinguishes accumulating absences that may be carried forward and used in future periods, from non-accumulating absences that lapse if not used in full. Accumulating absences are typically earned by employees as they provide services whereas non-accumulating absences are not related to services. Of the examples listed above, sick leave, maternity leave and jury service are usually non-accumulating whereas annual leave entitlements may be accumulating or non-accumulating. Where holiday benefit is accumulating, that is, it is earned over time and capable of being carried forward, a reporting entity should provide for the expected cost of accumulated benefit. On the other hand, where benefit is non-accumulating, a reporting entity should not recognise a liability or expense until the absence occurs. However a non-accumulating benefit may be treated as being accumulating in the context of an interim reporting period. The following examples illustrate the distinction.

Example 1 – Holiday pay carried forward

Employees of entity A are entitled to 20 days of paid leave each year. The entitlement accrues evenly throughout the year and unused leave may be carried forward for one calendar year. This is an example of an accumulating compensated absence.

Example 2 – Sick leave entitlement not carried forward

Employees of entity B are entitled to 10 days of paid sick leave each year, regardless of how long they have worked for the entity. Unused sick leave may not be carried forward and may not be used as additional annual leave. This is an example of a non-accumulating compensated absence. Although there is an entitlement to 10 days of paid sick leave each year, employees do not earn this entitlement as the year progresses and its use cannot be predicted.

Example 3 – Holiday pay while factory is closed

An entity has made a provision for holiday pay, accruing three weeks pay per worker over the year until the summer holiday when the factory is closed for three weeks. The holiday year runs until the end of this summer holiday. The employees of this entity accumulate benefit throughout the year so provision should be made for the expected cost of the holiday pay. The fact that employees may lose the benefit if they leave the entity does not remove the need for a provision, although it may influence the measurement of the provision. [IAS 19 para 15].

Example 4 – Holiday pay not carried forward

An entity has a 31 December year end and a holiday entitlement that also runs with the calendar year. The entity has a policy that any holiday entitlement not taken at 31 December each year is lost and so cannot be carried forward. Thus, there is no liability for holiday pay at the year end.

However, since the entity is listed it prepares interim accounts. At 30 June each year, each employee will have accumulated half of his or her entitlement to holiday pay. Thus, in each interim set of financial statements, a calculation of accrued holiday pay should be made for every employee.

11A.28   Identifying absences as accumulating or non-accumulating is important as it will determine the timing of recognising an expense. The expected cost of compensated absences is recognised as follows:

■   In the case of accumulating compensated absences – when the employees render services that increase their entitlement to future compensated absences.

■   In the case of non-accumulating compensated absences – when the absences occur.

[IAS 19 para 13].

11A.29   Accumulating compensated absences are further categorised as either vesting or non-vesting. If the benefits are vesting, employees who leave are entitled to cash payment in respect of any unused entitlement. Non-vesting benefits, on the other hand, are lost if an employee leaves without using them. This distinction will influence measurement. This is because the amount recognised as a liability is the *"additional amount that the entity expects to pay as a result of the unused entitlement that has accumulated at the balance sheet date".* [IAS 19 para 16].

Therefore, if benefits are non-vesting, the amount recognised as a liability will take into account the possibility that employees will leave before they utilise their entitlement.

11A.30   The principles described above are summarised in the flow chart below.

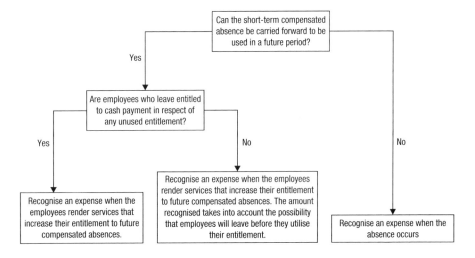

Example – Holiday pay that lapses if employee leaves

Employees of entity A are entitled to 20 days of paid leave each year. The entitlement accrues evenly throughout the year and unused leave may be carried forward to the following year. There is no cash payment in respect of an unused entitlement if an employee leaves the entity.

At 31 December 20X3, entity A has 100 employees and the average unused holiday entitlement per employee is two days. Historically, 10% of employees leave having never taken their unused holiday entitlement and management expect this trend to continue. At the balance sheet date (31 December), entity A should recognise a liability representing the number of days of accumulated entitlement that it expects to have to pay in the future. This will be 180 days (that is, 90% of 200 days).

If entity A was to change its terms and conditions of employment such that a cash payment was made in respect of unused holiday entitlement when an employee leaves the entity, the amount provided would be 200 days. This is because it would be irrelevant that 10% of employees never take all of their holiday entitlement as they would receive a cash payment of equivalent value on leaving the entity.

11A.31   The example above considers a simple scenario and ignores the fact that further benefits, some of which will not be utilised, will be earned in the future. This is illustrated in the following example.

Example – Unused holiday carried forward for one year only

The facts are as in the previous example, unused holiday entitlements may be carried forward for only one year. Each year, the current year entitlement is used before any balance brought forward from the previous year.

At 31 December 20X3 all 100 employees have 2 days unused holiday entitlement. Management of entity A expects that 75% of employees will take 22 days of holiday in 20X4 (that is, including 2 days each brought forward from 20X3), 15% will take 20 days (that is, lose their 2 days carried forward) and the remainder (10%) will take 18 days (that is, lose their 2 days carried forward from 20X3 and be eligible to carry forward 2 days from 20X4's entitlement at 31 December 20X4). This means that the total expected holiday to be taken in 20X4 is 2,130 days.

How much should be recognised as a liability at 31 December 20X3?

IAS 19 requires a measurement basis whereby the liability is calculated at the level of individual employees and is based on the additional amount that an entity expects to pay as a result of the unused entitlement. On this basis the liability would be based on only the 75% of employees who utilise their brought forward entitlement. So, the liability recognised at 31 December 20X3 would be 150 days (that is, two days for each of 75 employees).

11A.32   The previous examples consider the situation where an entity's holiday year corresponds with its financial year. This is not always that case. Similarly, issues arise in respect of the preparation of interim reports at a date that does not correspond with the end of a holiday year. The examples below illustrate these issues.

Example 1 – Financial year different to holiday year

Entity A has a March year end but its holiday year runs to the end of September. Employees of entity A are entitled to 20 days of paid annual leave, all of which must be taken by the end of September or it will be lost. On the basis of past experience, management estimates that staff will take only 95% of their holiday entitlement. Staff do not work at weekends or on national holidays and this means in this case that there are 253 working days per year.

The total annual salary cost for the year ended 31 March 20X4 is C800,000. A pay rise of 4% was awarded with effect from 1 April 20X4 so the total annual salary cost for the year ending 31 March 20X5 will be C832,000.

By 31 March 20X4, staff have earned half of their total annual holiday entitlement (that is, ten days) but have taken only four days. Hence, the amount of holiday earned but not yet taken at 31 March 20X4 is six days. Although this entitlement would be lost if not taken by the end of September, management believe that most will be taken in line with its overall estimates for the year (that is, cumulatively 95%). Four days have been taken so far so a provision should be made in respect of the remaining five and a half days expected to be taken (95% × 10 days less 4 days taken).

The amount provided should be based on the pay rate at which management expects the leave to be taken. The annual salary cost with effect from 1 April 20X4 is C832,000 so the amount provided should be C18,087 (that is, 5½/253 × C832,000).

Example 2 – Non-accumulating sick leave

Entity B has 100 employees, each of whom is entitled to 6 working days of paid sick leave for each year. Unused sick leave may not be carried forward to the next calendar year. Employees are also not entitled to a cash payment for unused entitlement of sick leave on leaving the entity's service.

An entity should not recognise an expense in respect of non-accumulating sick leave until the time of the absence, because employee service does not increase the amount of the benefit. Accordingly, in preparing the interim report for the first half of the year, entity B should not recognise a provision for unused sick leave.

[The next paragraph is 11.34.]

Benefits in kind

11A.34 The cost of providing non-monetary benefits (including housing, cars and free or subsidised goods or services) should be recognised according to the same principles as benefits payable in cash. The amount recognised as a liability and an expense should be measured at the cost to the employer of providing the benefit. For example, the cost of a leased company car would be the amount of the lease charges during the year, while the cost of private medical insurance for medical benefits provided in the course of employment would be the amount of premiums paid in the year.

Long-term benefits

11A.35 Long-term employee benefits are employee benefits (other than post-employment benefits (see para 11A.63) and termination benefits (see para 11A.53)) that are not expected to be settled wholly before 12 months after the end of the annual reporting period in which the employees render the service that gives rise to the benefit. [IAS 19 para 8]. For example, a bonus granted with a three-year vesting period is long-term in nature even though the bonus is paid shortly after completion of the three-year vesting period, because the benefit is considered as being earned over three or four annual accounting periods rather than over one three-year period.

11A.36 Long-term employee benefits, such as long-term bonuses, LTIPs and long service awards, share many of the characteristics of the short-term benefits discussed above. One might expect, therefore, that the same accounting principles would apply, with appropriate adjustment for increased uncertainty and the time value of money. With the exception that actuarial gains and losses are recognised immediately through profit or loss, long-term employee benefits are accounted for in the same way as defined benefit pension benefits (see from para 11A.96). This includes the use of the projected unit credit method for measuring the obligation arising. Further details on this method are included from paragraph 11A.163. Where other long-term benefits are provided as part of a post-employment benefit plan, it is our view that such a plan should be treated as either a post-employment benefit plan or another long-term benefit plan in its entirety, depending on the plan's substance.

11A.36.1 As a further point, IFRS IC, in November 2005, considered whether long service leave was in IAS 19's scope, or whether it was a financial liability within IAS 32's scope. The IFRS IC noted that IAS 19 indicates that employee benefit plans include a wide range of formal and informal arrangements. [IAS 19 para 4]. The exclusion of employee benefit plans from IAS 32 covers all employee benefits within IAS 19's scope of IAS 19 including long-term service leave.

11A.37 The accounting for long-term benefits involves discounting of future cash flows where the time value of money is material. Also, the complexity and length of some long-term benefit arrangements will require the use of actuarial assumptions such as salary increases and inflation in order to calculate the obligation using the projected unit credit method. The following examples illustrate how the projected unit credit method is applied when considering long-term employee benefits that require the use of actuarial assumptions.

Example 1 – Bonus on completion of five years service

Entity A operates a long-term bonus scheme, whereby employees receive a bonus on completion of five years service. The bonus is calculated as 1% of each year's salary. Salaries are expected to increase by 5% per annum and the discount rate is 8%.

The following table illustrates how the liability for the bonus would build up over the five years for an employee that joins the company in year 1. It is assumed that the employee will reach five years service and that there are no changes in actuarial assumptions. The employee's salary in year 1 is C40,000.

Year	1	2	3	4	5
Current year benefit (1% of current year salary)	400	420	441	463	486
Cumulative bonus payable	400	820	1,261	1,724	2,210
Opening obligation	–	325	702	1,137	1,637
Interest at 8%	–	26	56	91	131
Current service cost	325	351	379	409	442
Closing obligation	325	702	1,137	1,637	2,210

In the above table, the current service cost is the present value of the benefit attributed to the current year. The benefit attributed to the current year is the overall benefit payable of C2,210 divided by five, being C442 each year. So in year 3, for example, the current service cost is C379 (that is, $C442/1.08^2$).

> **Example 2 – Non-contractual bonus paid after ten years service**
>
> A German sub-group of a UK listed plc has traditionally awarded an anniversary bonus to employees on completion of ten years service. This entitlement is not part of their employment contract, but the payment is established common practice, and accordingly the sub-group will record a provision for the anticipated bonus. Under IFRS, long-term employee benefits, such as long service awards, are recognised and measured in a similar way to pensions (and other post-retirement benefits). Paragraph 128 of IAS 19 requires a provision to be built up, by spreading the charge over the ten years' service using the projected unit credit method.

11A.38 Under some arrangements employees are awarded specified cash bonuses that are conditional upon additional employment. For example, employees may be awarded specific bonuses based on a performance year, but where terms of the bonus arrangement require the employees to remain in employment for an additional one, two, or three years. We consider these arrangements to be long-term in nature and should be accounted for in the same way as defined benefit pension plans. In these types of plans, significant actuarial calculations would not generally be necessary, as certain assumptions (for example, mortality, life expectancy, asset return, etc) may not be relevant or material. In practice, the liability to be accrued would generally reflect the present value of expected cash outflows, with any unwind in the discount reflected as part of the benefit expense. The liability should be assessed and trued-up at each balance sheet date for any changes in expected cash flows.

11A.39 The presentation of current service cost and interest cost within the income statement would logically follow the treatment of equivalent income statement items arising from defined benefit pension obligations (see para 11A.252).

11A.40 In some situations long-term benefit plans might vest in instalments over the vesting period. We believe there are two acceptable approaches to recognise the expense.

11A.41 One approach is to recognise the expense according to the plan's benefit formula based on the principle in paragraph 67 of IAS 19. This means that an entity would attribute an expense to separate periods of service. However, where benefits are materially higher in later years, the expense should be recognised over the vesting period on a straight-line basis (see further from para 11A.126).

11A.42 The second approach is to view the bonus arrangement as multiple awards with different service periods; thus the plan's benefit formula is based on each award's individual service period. This means the expense is recognised for each instalment over the respective service periods in a manner similar to staged-vesting (or tranche vesting) for share-based payment transactions (see further guidance in chapter 12). The period of service is the period the employee is required to be employed by the entity before being unconditionally entitled to the bonus payments.

11A.43 An entity will need to consider the specific terms and conditions to determine which approach is appropriate. For example, if an entity grants an annual recurring bonus as part of an employment agreement (for example, C10,000 payable at the end of each year for the next three years), this might indicate the first approach is more appropriate as this arrangement is similar to accounting for wages and salaries. However, if an entity otherwise grants a bonus that vests and is payable in three future instalments, this might indicate that a staged-vesting approach is more appropriate as employees could be viewed as providing services for each instalment of the bonus until payment.

11A.44 The following examples illustrate these principles.

> **Example 1 – Deferred bonus arrangements over disproportional service periods**
>
> Entity A awards its employees a cash bonus of C100 based on the performance of the employee and the entity in 20X1. 50% of the bonus will be paid in February 20X2 and the remaining 50% will be paid at the end of 20X3 provided the employee remains working for the entity.
>
> An entity could use the staged-vesting approach in this scenario as, in substance, the employee is working for two awards with different service periods. The bonus expense should be recognised for each instalment. This means that 50% of the bonus should be spread from 1 January 20X1 to 28 February 20X2 and the other 50% of the bonus should be spread from 1 January 20X1 to 31 December 20X3.
>
> It might also be appropriate to recognise the expense based on the bonus plan's benefit formula. This means that 50% of the bonus should be spread from 1 January 20X1 to 28 February 20X2 (14 months), and the other 50% of the bonus should be spread from 1 March 20X2 to 31 December 20X3 (22 months).
>
> **Example 2 – Deferred bonus arrangements with three rateable instalments**
>
> Entity A awards its employees a cash bonus of C100. A third of the bonus will be paid at the end of year 1, a third paid at the end of year 2, and a third paid at the end of year 3 provided the employee in question is in employment with the entity on each payment date.
>
> An entity could use the staged-vesting approach in this scenario as, in substance, the employee is working for three awards with different service periods. This means that a third of the bonus should be spread over year 1, a third spread over years 1 and 2, and the remaining third spread over years 1, 2, and 3. This will result in front-loading the charge.
>
> It might also be appropriate to recognise the expense based on the bonus plan's benefit formula. This means that a third of the bonus expense would be recognised in each year, which is similar to straight-line attribution in this scenario.

Example 3 – Deferred bonus with a material instalment at end of vesting period

The facts are the same as in example 1 above, except that 25% of the bonus will vest and be paid in February 20X2 and the remaining 75% will vest and be paid at the end of 20X3 provided the employee remains working for the entity.

An entity could use the staged-vesting approach in this scenario as, in substance, the employee is working for two awards with different service periods. The bonus expense should be recognised for each instalment. This means that 25% of the bonus should be spread from 1 January 20X1 to 28 February 20X2 and the other 75% of the bonus should be spread from 1 January 20X1 to 31 December 20X3.

It might also be appropriate to recognise the expense based on the bonus plan's benefit formula. However, as mentioned above in paragraph 11A.41, where benefits are materially higher in later years, the expense should be recognised over the vesting period on a straight-line basis. As the employees will receive 75% of their award at the end of year 3, this is considered materially higher in later years, therefore, the bonus expense should be recognised on a straight-line basis over the vesting period.

Example 4 – Deferred bonus arrangement that is recurring

Entity A grants members of its senior management a bonus of C20,000 payable at the end of each year for three years as part of their annual benefits package and contract of employment. The only condition is that the senior manager remains in employment. New joiners to senior management may be invited to participate in the bonus arrangement during the period.

In our view, it is more appropriate to recognise the expense according to the plan's benefit formula. This is because the bonus is part of their annual benefits package and should be treated in a similar way to short-term benefits. Therefore, C20,000 should be recognised each year for three years.

However, there is an alternative approach where an entity could recognise a bonus expense based on a staged-vesting approach. This means that C20,000 is recognised in year 1, C20,000 is recognised over years 1 and 2, and the remaining C20,000 is spread over years 1, 2, and 3.

Modifications

11A.45   Entities may replace cash bonus arrangements in IAS 19's scope with an equity-settled share-based payment. For example, an annual bonus plan for 1 January 20X1 to 31 December 20X1 is changed in November 20X1 so that the 100% cash bonus will now be settled 50:50 between cash and shares. There is no clear guidance in IFRS as to how an entity should account for the change from an incentive scheme under IAS 19 to an equity-settled share-based payment arrangement under IFRS 2. This is also further complicated in situations where there is not only a classification change but also a modification of other vesting conditions (for example, extension of the vesting period). We believe three potential approaches are acceptable based on the facts and circumstances.

11A.46 One approach is for the entity to account for the modification to the vesting conditions before accounting for the change from an IAS 19 bonus arrangement to an IFRS 2 equity-settled arrangement. Under this approach, the entity would adjust the liability at the modification date for the new vesting conditions in accordance with IAS 19. This could lead to a negative past-service cost where the expense recognised to date is more than the expense that should be recognised after modifying the vesting conditions. The entity would then account for the change to an equity-settled share-based payment as a 'modification' following the principles of IFRS 2. The entity would immediately reclassify the amount recognised as a liability at the modification date to equity. The expense for the remainder of the vesting period of the share-based payment is based on the award's fair value, measured at the modification date, less amounts already recognised.

11A.47 A second approach is for the entity to account for the change from an IAS 19 bonus arrangement to an IFRS 2 equity-settled arrangement before the modification of the vesting conditions. As noted above, following the principles of IFRS 2, the entity would immediately reclassify the amount recognised as a liability at the modification date to equity. Then, using the award's fair value measured at the modification date, the remaining expense should be recognised in accordance with IFRS 2's modification accounting. If a modification of vesting conditions is considered non-beneficial (for example, an extension of vesting period), the entity should continue to account for the original grant as if the modification had not occurred (that is, ignore any increase in the vesting period). See further guidance in chapter 12.

11A.48 A third approach is to consider the exchange of the IAS 19 entitlement for a right to receive shares similarly to a settlement. In circumstances where the employee has a choice of whether to take cash or shares we consider this to be the most appropriate approach. Further where the bonus under IAS 19 is already vested it could be argued that this approach better reflects the facts and circumstances than the approaches in paragraphs 11A.46 and 11A.47 above. Under this approach, the entity would immediately reclassify the amount recognised as a liability at the modification date to equity and the remaining expense (that is, the balance of the fair value at the modification date) is recognised over the modified vesting period. This approach would include the earned IAS 19 benefit given up as part of the consideration for an IFRS 2 award.

11A.49 The following example illustrates these principles.

Example – Modification to long-term benefit plan

An entity has an annual bonus scheme in place that pays cash bonuses to employees based on the entity's performance against profit targets. Due to economic conditions, the annual bonus scheme for 20X0 is changed in November 20X0 so that the 100% cash bonus is split 50:50 between cash and shares. Employees do not have a choice and they would forfeit their shares if they did not continue to work for the entity for an additional three year period after the 20X0 year end. The fair value of the award was C120,000 at the modification date (that is, 30 November 20X0). On the basis of the original terms as at the end of November 20X0, C110,000 would have been recognised as an expense.

Under one approach, the entity would account for the modification to the vesting period before the change in classification to an equity-settled share-based payment. The following entries would be recorded:

At modification date

	C	C	
Dr Liability	55,000		(reverse 50% of the accrued liability as it will now be accrued over a longer period and settled in shares)
Cr Income statement		41,250	(true-up expense based on modified vesting period – 11/48 months × C60,000 less C55,000 already recognised)
Cr Equity		13,750	

The remaining expense of C46,250 (fair value at modification of C60,000 less amount already recognised of C13,750) should be recognised straight-line over the remaining vesting period of 37 months. The entity would, therefore, record the following entry each month for 37 months:

	C	C
Dr Income statement	1,250	
Cr Equity		1,250

To recognise the share-based payment expense each month (C60,000/48).

A second approach is for the entity to account for the classification change to an equity-settled share-based payment before the extension of the vesting period. In this scenario, the extension of the vesting period would be treated as a non-beneficial modification in accordance with IFRS 2 and, therefore, would be ignored. The following entries would be recorded:

At modification date

	C	C
Dr Liability	55,000	
Cr Equity		55,000

To reclassify 50% of the accrued liability to equity.

The remaining expense of C5,000 (fair value at modification of C60,000 less amount already recognised of C55,000) should be recognised over the original vesting period of one year. The entity would, therefore, record the following entry for the remaining month:

	C	C
Dr Income statement	5,000	
Cr Equity		5,000

A third approach is for the entity to account for the classification change to an equity-settled share-based payment as a settlement of the accrued liability. In this scenario, the extended vesting period would be treated as in substance a new award under IFRS 2. The following entries would be recorded:

At modification date

	C	C
Dr Liability	55,000	
Cr Equity		55,000

To reclassify 50% of the accrued liability to equity.

The remaining expense of C5,000 (fair value at 'grant date' of C60,000 less amount of C55,000 already recognised, which is effectively treated as consideration for the share-based payment), should be recognised over the remaining revised vesting period of 37 months. The entity would, therefore, record the following entry each month for 37 months:

	C	C
Dr Income statement	135	
Cr Equity		135

To recognise the share-based payment expense each month (C5,000/37).

Long-term disability

11A.50 Long-term disability is not a termination benefit as defined in paragraph 11A.53. IAS 19 is explicit that long-term disability benefits should be accounted for in accordance with the principles used for other long-term employee benefits described in paragraph 11A.35 above.

Example 1 – Lump-sum disability payments

Entity A pays, in accordance with a trade union agreement, a lump-sum of C10,000 to an employee who becomes disabled as a result of an accident. This payment is the same regardless of the length of service.

Entity B pays, in accordance with its trade union agreement, a lump-sum of C10,000 to an employee who becomes disabled as a result of an accident within the first 5 years of employment and C20,000 if the employee becomes disabled after 5 years of employment.

The future cash outflow of entity A does not depend on past employee service. In accordance with paragraph 130 of IAS 19, no accruals should be made by entity A until the occurrence of an accident that causes the disability of an employee.

The level of benefits of entity B's employees depends on the length of employee service. An obligation arises when service is rendered. [IAS 19 para 157]. Entity B's obligation should be measured using the projected unit credit method. It should reflect the probability that payments will be required and the length of service (that is amount) for which payments are expected to be made.

Example 2 – Disability payments covered by an insurance policy

Legislation requires an entity to provide compensation to employees whose disability was caused by injuries at work.

Entity A, a construction group, has decided to cover its exposure to disability compensation payments by taking out an insurance policy with one of the world's largest insurance entities. The insurance premium is payable monthly. The amount of disability payment does not vary based on years of service and is paid out to the employee as an annuity rather than a lump sum. The insurance policy can only be used to pay the disability benefits and is not available to the entity's own creditors even in the event of bankruptcy. The proceeds from the policy cannot be paid to the entity unless they represent surplus assets. Entity A recognises the insurance premium as an expense when incurred. When an event occurs that causes a long-term disability, entity A recognises an expense for the disability payments. Since the level of benefit does not vary based on years of service, the obligation only arises when the disability occurs. Entity A also recognises income that reflects the claim due under the insurance policy. The net impact on profit or loss will be the expense related to the insurance premium. Another way of looking at this is to view the insurance premium as purchasing a qualifying insurance policy that, under paragraph 104 is measured as being equal to the insured liability, such that the asset and liability are netted off.

Disclosure

11A.51 IAS 19 does not require specific disclosure in respect of benefits payable during employment. However, other standards may require disclosure, for example:

- IAS 1 requires disclosure of employee benefits expense (see chapter 4).

- IAS 24 requires disclosure of employee benefits payable to key management personnel (see chapter 29).

11A.52 Disclosure of the accounting policies for benefits payable during employment is not commonplace. This is to be expected in the case of wages and salaries, but it is surprising that there is not more widespread disclosure of policies for items such as holiday pay and long-term bonuses. Two examples of companies that disclose their policy for benefits payable during employment are given below. The third example below gives extracts that deal with annual leave and bonuses taken from a company that gives comprehensive disclosures on aspects of its employee benefits.

Table 11A.1 – Accounting policy for benefits payable during employment

Roche Holding Ltd – annual report & group accounts – 31 December 2011

1. Summary of significant accounting policies (extract)

Employee benefits

Wages, salaries, social security contributions, paid annual leave and sick leave, bonuses, and non-monetary benefits are accrued in the year in which the associated services are rendered by employees of the Group. Where the Group provides long-term employee benefits, the cost is accrued to match the rendering of the services by the employees concerned. Liabilities for long-term employee benefits are discounted to take into account the time value of money, where material.

Table 11A.2 – Accounting policy for benefits payable during employment

Barloworld Limited – annual report – 30 September 2011

Accounting policies (extract)

21. Employee benefit costs

The cost of providing employee benefits is accounted for in the period in which the benefits are earned by employees.

The cost of short-term employee benefits is recognised in the period in which the service is rendered and is not discounted. The expected cost of short-term accumulating compensated absences is recognised as an expense as the employees render service that increases their entitlement or, in the case of non-accumulating absences, when the absences occur.

The expected cost of profit-sharing and bonus payments is recognised as an expense when there is a legal or constructive obligation to make such payments as a result of past performance and a reliable estimate of the obligation can be made.

Table 11A.3 – Annual leave and bonus policies and disclosure

Telkom SA Limited –annual report – 31 March 2009

SIGNFICANT ACCOUNTING POLICIES (extract)

Employee benefits (extract)

Leave benefits

Annual leave entitlement is provided for over the period that the leave accrues and is subject to a cap of 22 days.

Deferred bonus incentives

Employees of the wholly owned subsidiaries of Vodacom, including executive directors, are eligible for compensation benefits in the form of a Deferred Bonus Incentive Scheme. The benefit is recorded at the present value of the expected future cash outflows.

Short-term employee benefits

The cost of all short-term employee benefits is recognised during the year the employees render services, unless the Group uses the services of employees in the construction of an asset and the benefits received meet the recognition criteria of an asset, at which stage it is included as part of the related property, plant and equipment or intangible asset item.

Employee benefits (IAS 19 revised)

Long-term incentive provision

The Vodacom Group provides long-term incentives to eligible employees payable on termination or retirement. The Group's liability is based on an actuarial valuation. Actuarial gains and losses are recognised as employee expenses.

	2007	2008	**2009**
	Rm	Rm	**Rm**
29. PROVISIONS (extract)			
Annual leave	413	438	**428**
Balance at beginning of year	356	413	**438**
Transferred to disposal groups	–	–	**(67)**
Charged to employee expenses	66	44	**72**
Leave paid	(9)	(19)	**(15)**
Bonus	1,090	992	**671**
Balance at beginning of year	1,071	1,090	**992**
Transferred to disposal groups	–	–	**(397)**
Charged to employee expenses	965	797	**577**
Payment made	(946)	(895)	**(501)**
Long-term incentive provision	81	113	**–**
Balance at beginning of year	61	81	**113**
Transferred to disposal groups	–	–	**(113)**
Charged to employee expenses	21	41	**–**
Payment	(1)	(9)	**–**

Annual leave

In terms of Telkom's policy, employees are entitled to accumulate vested leave benefits not taken within a leave cycle, to a cap of 22 days which must be taken within an 18 month leave cycle. The leave cycle is reviewed annually and is in accordance with legislation.

Bonus

The Telkom bonus scheme consists of performance bonuses which are dependent on achievement of certain financial and non-financial targets. The bonus is to all qualifying employees payable bi-annually after Telkom's results have been made public.

Termination benefits

11A.53   Termination benefits result from either:

- an entity's decision to terminate an employee's employment; or
- an employee's decision to accept an offer of voluntary redundancy in exchange for those benefits.

[IAS 19 para 8].

11A.54   Termination benefits do not include employee benefits resulting from the termination of employment at the request of the employee without an entity's offer, or as a result of mandatory retirement requirements, because those benefits are post-employment benefits. [IAS 19, para 160]. In broad terms, termination benefits are amounts payable when an employee ceases to work for an employer. In this context they are similar to post-employment benefits, such as pensions.

However, whereas post-employment benefits are earned throughout an employee's working life, termination benefits arise as a result of an event, such as a factory closure or a decision to reduce the size of the workforce. The event that gives rise to an obligation is the termination, rather than employee service. Termination benefits are not earned, although their magnitude may be set by reference to an employee's period of service.

11A.54.1 Sometimes, the events that give rise to termination benefits will cause the company to award other benefits that do not represent termination benefits. For example, the awarding of a stay bonus that incentivises the employee to remain in service to the company until the end of the period of termination. The cost of the stay bonus should be accrued over this period of service.

11A.55 Typically termination benefits comprise lump sum payments, although they could take other forms such as retention of a company car. Termination benefits also include:

■ Pension enhancements.

■ 'Gardening leave'. That is, salary until the end of a specified notice period during which the employee renders no further service.

[IAS 19 para 161].

11A.55.1 Sometimes, it can be difficult to decide whether a particular benefit should be classified as a termination benefit or a post-employment benefit. As a guide, termination benefits generally have three characteristics:

■ The benefits are offered for a clearly defined period.

■ There is no legal or constructive obligation on the employer to extend the closing date, although extensions might be made, at the employer's discretion. Repeated practice of doing this is likely to establish a constructive obligation.

■ There is no linking of the amount of the benefit to length of future service.

11A.55.2 Paragraph 162 of IAS 19 provides indicators that an employee benefit is provided in exchange for services. The indicators are that the benefit is conditional on future services being provided or the benefit is provided in accordance with the terms of an employee benefit plan.

11A.56 However, paragraph 163 of IAS 19 clarifies that employee benefits provided in accordance with the terms of an employee benefit plan are termination benefits if they both result from an entity's decision to terminate an employee's employment and are not conditional on future service being provided.

11A.57 Where employee benefits are provided regardless of the reason for the employee's departure, the payment of which is certain but the timing uncertain, these are post-employment benefits rather than termination benefits. [IAS 19 para 164]. The following examples illustrate these distinctions:

Example 1 – Statutory payments to employees leaving after five years service

Entity A operates in country C. Local labour laws require that payments are made to employees leaving the entity for any reason after five years' service. The amounts payable are determined by reference to final salary and length of service. Benefits will, therefore, be payable to the workforce, but these will not be termination benefits as defined in IAS 19. This is because the benefits are earned during an employees' working life and the entity is obliged to pay them regardless of the reason for the employee's departure so, if the employee works for entity A for at least five years, only the timing of the payment is uncertain. Hence, these benefits are treated as post-employment benefits and accounted for as specified from paragraph 11A.96 below.

Example 2 – Voluntary redundancy payments

Entity B also operates in country C and is subject to the same labour laws. However, in connection with a voluntary redundancy programme, entity B has agreed to make additional payments to those employees who accept the offer of voluntary redundancy. These additional payments will represent termination benefits as defined in IAS 19 as the entity had no obligation to make the payments until it made the decision to instigate the voluntary redundancy programme.

Recognition

11A.58 An entity should recognise a liability and expense for termination benefits at the earlier of the following dates:

- when the entity can no longer withdraw the offer of those benefits; and

- when the entity recognises costs for a restructuring that is within the scope of IAS 37 (see chapter 21) and involves the payment of termination benefits.

[IAS 19 para 165].

The result of using these two criteria is, in substance, in line with IAS 37's requirements.

11A.59 Where termination benefits are payable as a result of an employee's decision to accept an offer of benefits in exchange for the termination of employment, the time when an entity can no longer withdraw the offer of termination benefits is the earlier of:

- when the employee accepts the offer; and

- when a restriction (for example, a legal, regulatory or contractual requirement or other restriction) on the entity's ability to withdraw the offer takes effect. This would be when the offer is made, if the restriction existed at the time of the offer.

[IAS 19 para 166].

11A.59.1 Where termination benefits are payable as a result of an entity's decision to terminate an employee's employment, the entity can no longer withdraw the offer when the entity has communicated to the affected employees a plan of termination meeting all of the following criteria:

- Actions required to complete the plan indicate that it is unlikely that significant changes to the plan will be made.

- The plan identifies the number of employees whose employment is to be terminated, their job classifications or functions and their locations (but the plan need not identify each individual employee) and the expected completion date.

- The plan establishes the termination benefits that employees will receive in sufficient detail that employees can determine the type and amount of benefits they will receive when their employment is terminated.

[IAS 19 para 167].

11A.59.2 When an entity recognises termination benefits, the entity may also have to account for a plan amendment or a curtailment of other employee benefits. [IAS 19 para 168].

11A.60 The following example illustrates the above principles.

> **Example 1 – Redundancies following restructuring**
>
> The board of an entity has announced two major restructuring plans and, in both cases, has communicated details of the redundancy package to the staff affected:
>
> - Sale of half of the entity's global manufacturing business over a two-year period, starting immediately. This will involve the immediate redundancy of 15% of the machine workers in each factory and 10% of the middle management at each location.
>
> - Re-organisation of the head office over a one-year period, commencing in two years' time. 20% of the head office staff will lose their jobs during the restructuring.
>
> As regards the sale of the manufacturing business, a provision should be recognised for the estimated costs of the disposal and redundancy. The sites and details of the redundancy and other costs, have been identified and communicated. The scale and complexity of the disposal requires that it be completed over an extended period. Disposal activities and recognition of costs for the restructuring will begin immediately. Two years is the time necessary to complete the disposal and should not prevent the provision from being recognised. See chapter 21, where the requirements of IAS 37 are discussed in more detail. In some cases, chapter 26 on IFRS 5 may also be relevant.
>
> In contrast, the entity should not recognise a provision for the head office's re-organisation. The re-organisation is not due to start for two years. External parties are unlikely to have a valid expectation that management is committed to the restructuring, because the timeframe allows significant opportunities for management to change the details of the plan or even to withdraw from the offer of

benefits under the plan. Additionally, the degree of identification of the staff to lose their jobs is not sufficient to support recognising a redundancy provision. Details of the departments within head office that will be affected should be identified, together with the approximate numbers of staff from each department.

Example 2 – Voluntary redundancy payment with a time limit

Entity A restructures its operations in a particular location. It agrees with trade unions during December 20X3 a plan to reduce staff numbers in that location by 100 by February 20X4. Management communicated an offer of C5,000 for voluntary redundancy by the end of January 20X4. The offer for any remaining employees can be withdrawn at any time. If sufficient staff do not accept the offer, management will terminate the employment of additional staff to reach the target of 100. Employees terminated involuntarily are entitled to a termination payment of C4,000 each.

At 31 December 20X3 60 employees have accepted the voluntary termination offer for C300,000 (60 employees x C5000) and for C160,000 (40 employees x C4000). The contingent liability of C40,000 for the additional amount that would be payable if the maximum number of employees accepted the termination voluntarily should also be disclosed.

The voluntary termination benefits of C300,000 are based upon the number of employees that accepted the offer, in accordance with paragraph 166 of IAS 19. The termination benefits of C160,000 are as a result of the company's decision to terminate the remaining 40 employees, and are recorded upon communication of the termination plan, in accordance with paragraph 167 of IAS 19.

Measurement

11A.61 An entity should measure termination benefits on initial recognition, and should measure and recognise subsequent changes, in accordance with the nature of the employee benefit, provided that if the termination benefits are an enhancement to post-employment benefits, the entity should apply the requirements for post-employment benefits. Otherwise:

- If the termination benefits are expected to be settled wholly before 12 months after the end of the annual reporting period in which the termination benefit is recognised, the entity shall apply the requirements for short-term employee benefits.

- If the termination benefits are not expected to be settled wholly before 12 months after the end of the annual reporting period, the entity shall apply the requirements for other long-term employee benefits.

[IAS 19 para 169].

Accordingly, the amounts recognised as a provision should be measured at the expected amounts to be paid and, where long-term, discounted using a high-quality corporate bond rate, the currency and term of which are consistent with the expected payment dates. Discounting in relation to pension plans is discussed from paragraph 11A.137.

Example – Use of discount rate

Entity A's management has decided to make 250 staff redundant within the next year. However, the costs of the redundancy will arise over a longer period and are expected to be C20m, payable as C8m in one year's time and C12m in two year's time.

The market yield for high-quality corporate bonds of both a one year and a two year duration at 31 December 20X1 is 5.5%.

Management should recognise the cost of the redundancy provision at the present value of the future cash flows of C18,364,360:

	Year 1	Year 2	Total
Cash flows	C8,000,000	C12,000,000	C20,000,000
Discount factor (5.5%)	0.94787	0.89845	
Present value of cash flows	C7,582,960	C10,781,400	C18,364,360
Interest expense			C1,635,640

The difference between the undiscounted cash flows and their present value of C1,635,640 will be recognised in the income statement over years 1 and 2 as the discount accretes.

Disclosure

11A.62 IAS 19 contains no specific disclosure requirements relating to termination benefits. Instead, reference is made to the requirements of other standards. For example, disclosure may be required:

- In accordance with IAS 37 (see chapter 21) – which requires disclosure of the carrying amount, movement in the period and other information relating to the provision.

- In accordance with IAS 1 (see chapter 4) – where the expense is of such size, nature or incidence that disclosure is relevant to explain performance.

- In accordance with IAS 24 (see chapter 29) – where the termination benefits are payable to key management.

11A.62.1 An example of disclosure of a termination programme is given in Table 11A.4 below.

Table 11A.4 – Early termination plan disclosures

Peugeot S.A. – Report and accounts – 31 December 2005

Note 29 – Early-termination plan

29.1. Internal agreements

Internal agreements have been signed between the Group and employee representatives in France, concerning the implementation of early-termination plans. The plans in question fulfil the criteria laid down in Decree no. 2000-105 dated February 9, 2000 related to the early termination of certain employees over 55 years of age and qualify for government financing covering part of the cost.

A. Automobile Division

An early-termination plan has been set up for Automobile Division employees in France, in application of an internal agreement dated March 4, 1999 and an industry-wide agreement signed on July 26, 1999 by UIMM (the industry federation) with the support of the majority of trade unions represented within the Group.

B. Automotive Equipment Division

Following further negotiations between UIMM and the trade unions in March 2001, the plan was extended to additional companies, including the Faurecia group.

29.2. Estimated liability

A. Calculation method

The estimated cost to be financed by the Group corresponds to the total benefits payable to the employees concerned, net of government funding. The present value of the liability has been calculated by applying a discount rate of 3% and an inflation rate of 2%.

B. Change in estimated liability

(in millions of euros)	Dec 31, 2005	Dec 31, 2004
At January 1	345	423
Early-termination costs for the year	(108)	(102)
Change in the number of employees concerned	(6)	(8)
Discounting adjustment	2	32
At December 31	233	345

The €4 million net gain reflects the cumulative effects of headcount restructuring, amounting to €6 million, and a discounting charge of €2 million. The €108 million release from the provision in respect of early-termination costs for the year is offset by a charge corresponding to the Group's contribution to the UNEDIC Fund responsible for paying benefits, less the sums received from the State to help finance early-termination measures.

C. Number of employees concerned

At December 31, 2005, 9,599 employees were concerned by the plans, including 471 Faurecia group employees.

Post-employment benefits

11A.63 Post-employment benefits are defined in IAS 19 in very simple terms as *"employee benefits (other than termination benefits and short-term employee* *benefits) that are payable after the completion of employment".* [IAS 19 para 8]. The most common type of post-employment benefit is a pension, although post-retirement health care is also common in some countries.

Death-in-service benefits

11A.64 If a benefit is earned during the employee's working life, the recognition and measurement principles applied to defined benefit pension plans will be appropriate.

11A.65 Paragraph 70(b) of IAS 19 requires attribution of the cost of the benefits until the date *"when further service by the employee will lead to no material amount of further benefits under the plan, other than from further salary increases".* In January 2008 the IFRS IC noted that:

> **UK.11A.65.1** The conclusion in paragraph 11A.65 is consistent with the UK GAAP treatment as set out in UITF Abstract 35.

- The anticipated date of death (that is, the date assumed for actuarial purposes) would be the date at which no material amount of further benefit would arise from the plan.

- Using different mortality assumptions for a defined pension plan and an associated death-in-service benefit would not comply with the requirement in paragraph 75 of IAS 19 to use actuarial assumptions that are mutually compatible.

- If the conditions in paragraph 46 of IAS 19 were met, then accounting for death-in-service benefits on a defined contribution basis would be appropriate.

> It is our view that, where death-in-service benefits form part of a defined benefit pension plan, they must be measured as part of the actuarial assumptions (and, hence, factored into the valuation of the defined benefit plan liabilities) and attributed to periods of service using the projected unit credit method. They cannot be separated from the plan of which they are a part.

11A.66 Sometimes, employers insure their death-in-service and disability obligations. If this is the case, such that the employer has transferred all risks and obligations to the insurer, the cost of providing benefits is represented by the payment of insurance premiums. In substance, such death-in-service and disability arrangements are treated as defined contribution pension plans. Insured pension plans are considered further from paragraph 11A.88. However, it is important to note that generally for death benefits the insurance cover is only for a limited period, normally one year, so that the employer (or the plan trustees) have a choice each year whether or not to insure. This means that the decision whether to insure is an investment choice. In addition, when this choice has been made the employer has not transferred all risks and obligations to the insurer.

UK.11A.66.1 There are three basic types of pension arrangements that are common in many countries:

- The state plan.

- Occupational pension plans.

- Personal pension plans.

UK.11A.66.2 The state plan in the UK consists of two elements, the basic pension and the earnings related pension. All employers and employees make contributions towards the state plan through their national insurance payments. Those who are members of the earnings related scheme, known as the State Second Pension (S2P), make additional national insurance contributions. It is possible to 'contract out' of S2P either through an occupational pension plan or through a personal pension.

UK.11A.66.3 In a contracted out occupational plan, both employer and employee pay a lower rate of national insurance contributions. The occupational plan is then used to provide employees with benefits that replace part of their state earnings related benefits. The broad intention is that the pension provided by a contracted out plan is at least as good as the pension that would have been available from S2P. On retirement, the employee receives a state basic pension and a pension from the occupational plan.

UK.11A.66.4 Occupational pension plans are not required to contract out of S2P and many do not. Where a plan is 'contracted in' to S2P, employer and employee pay the full rate of national insurance contributions. The responsibility for payment of S2P remains with the state. On retirement, the employee receives a state basic and earnings related pension, together with a pension from the occupational plan.

UK.11A.66.5 Personal pension plans are pension arrangements available to individuals.

Types of pension plan

11A.67 Accounting for the cost of providing pension benefits is particularly affected by the type of benefits that are promised by a plan and by the way in which the employer's obligations in respect of such benefits are funded. The broad classifications used in pensions terminology are summarised in the following paragraphs. Each involves a cost to the employer wherever it is obliged to contribute towards the cost of the benefits receivable by its employees or their dependants.

Defined contribution plans

11A.68 Defined contribution plans (often referred to as money purchase plans) are pension plans where the level of benefits depends on the value of contributions paid in respect of each member and the investment performance achieved on those contributions. Normally, the rate of contribution to be paid by the employer will be specified in the plan's rules. Therefore, the employer's liability is limited to the contributions it has agreed to pay. The employee takes both the actuarial risk (that benefits will be less than expected) and the investment risk – if the investments have performed well the individual will obtain a higher pension than if the investments have performed badly. IAS 19 does not require plan assets to be segregated into individual accounts.

11A.69 IAS 19 defines defined contribution plans as *"post-employment benefit plans under which an entity pays fixed contributions into a separate entity (a fund) and will have no legal or constructive obligation to pay further contributions if the fund does not hold sufficient assets to pay all employee benefits relating to employee service in the current and prior periods"*. [IAS 19 para 8].

Defined benefit plans

11A.70 Defined benefit plans are pension plans where the rules specify the benefits to be paid and they are financed accordingly. The majority of these plans define benefits in relation to an employee's salary. Often the pension will be based on a percentage of final salary for each year of pensionable service. Another form of defined benefit plan that is becoming increasingly common is the average salary plan where the pension is calculated by reference to average pay over an extended period. In most defined benefit plans the risk of poor investment performance lies fully with the sponsoring company. However, in some circumstances plans will include provisions that call for participants to share in a portion of the potential funding requirements. Such arrangements are discussed later in this chapter.

11A.71 Under IAS 19, defined benefit plans are the residual category. They are defined as *"post-employment benefit plans other than defined contribution plans"*. [IAS 19 para 8].

Distinguishing defined contribution plans and defined benefit plans

11A.72 IAS 19 considers all pension plans to be defined benefit plans, unless the criteria for treatment as defined contribution plans are satisfied. Hence, a plan will be a defined benefit plan unless the employer's legal or constructive obligation is limited to the amount that it agrees to contribute to the plan. The following are examples of situations where the employer's obligation is not limited and the plans are, therefore, defined benefit plans:

- The plan's benefit formula that is not linked solely to the amount of contributions and requires the entity to provide further contributions if assets are insufficient to meet the benefits in the plan benefit formula.

- The entity, either indirectly through a plan or directly, guarantees a specified return on contributions.

- Informal practices give rise to a constructive obligation, for example where the employer has a history of increasing benefits to keep pace with inflation, even when there is no legal obligation to do so.

[IAS 19 para 29].

Example 1 – Unfunded overseas scheme

Entity E plc has a subsidiary overseas, entity F, in a territory where there is a legal requirement for an employer to provide a 'salary' to retired employees based on the duration of their service to the company and their salary during the period of employment. In accordance with local GAAP, entity F makes an accrual at each year end that is calculated by reference to the employees' service and salaries to date (that is, it represents an estimate of net present value of the amount that entity F would have to pay if all employees retired at the end of the year). Changes in the accrual are reflected in the income statement. Do such schemes fall within IAS 19's scope?

The IAS 19 definition of post-employment benefits includes any consideration given by an employer in exchange for employees' services that is payable after the completion of employment (other than termination benefits). The 'salary' above falls within IAS 19's scope and is a defined benefit pension plan. The defined benefit obligation should be calculated in accordance with IAS 19 using the projected unit credit method: the local GAAP accrual is unlikely to be appropriate.

Example 2 – Voluntary enhancements to state pension benefits

The national pensions authority administers a state pension plan in country X. Mandatory contributions from employers fund the plan on a pay-as-you-go basis. Pension legislation determines the minimum benefits paid to each employee when they retire and the national pensions authority sets annual employer contributions at the level required to meet expected pension obligations in the same period. Employers have no obligation to the state pension plan beyond their annual contributions, but the legislation permits employers to voluntarily enhance the state pension benefits paid to their former employees.

Entity A operates in country X and pays annual contributions to the state pension plan on behalf of all its employees. Entity A has elected to enhance the benefits received by certain classes of employee:

(a) Entity A makes annual payments to an insurance entity equal to 5% of the salary of each employee based overseas. The insurance policy matures when the employee retires and the employee must use the proceeds to purchase additional post-retirement benefits. Entity A has no obligation to the employee or the insurance company beyond the annual payment.

(b) The employment contracts of management grade employees state that their pension will be at least 1% of final salary for each year of service. Entity A will pay to each retired employee each year an amount equal to the difference between the guaranteed benefit and the state pension. Entity A has no obligation if the state pension is greater than the guaranteed benefit.

The arrangement's substance determines the accounting treatment applied to the different components of the pension plan.

Employers fund the basic state pension on a pay-as-you-go basis and entity A has no obligation to pay benefits beyond its annual contribution. The state takes actuarial and investment risk. Therefore, this is a defined contribution plan. [IAS 19 para 45].

Employees based overseas receive additional benefits based on the proceeds of an insurance policy. Entity A has no obligation beyond paying the annual insurance premium. The insurance company takes the investment risk and the employee takes the actuarial risk. This is also a defined contribution arrangement. [IAS 19 para 46].

Management grade employees receive a pension equivalent to 1% of their final salary for each year of service. Entity A has a contractual obligation to make a top-up payment to former employees when the state pension is less than the guaranteed minimum pension. Entity A has the investment risk and the actuarial risk. This is a defined benefit arrangement and the company should recognise a pension liability for the additional benefit, that is, the amount of any shortfall where the guaranteed benefit is greater than the state pension.

The substance of each component of a pension plan determines the accounting treatment. Different components of the same plan might have a different accounting treatment.

Example 3 – Pension plan with guaranteed interest

An entity provides a pension plan with the following characteristics:

- The employees contribute 3% of their salaries to the plan.
- Entity A's contribution matches the employees' contribution.
- The retirement age is 65.
- The employee's account balance consists of accumulated contributions, credited with interest guaranteed by the employer at 4% per year.

Under this arrangement, the entity has the investment risk that the return from assets invested will be less than the guaranteed return. The entity's obligation is not limited to the amount that it agrees to contribute. [IAS 19 para 29b]. Although the entity may anticipate that the fund's investment returns will exceed the guaranteed rate of 4%, there is a risk that investment returns will fall short and the employer will be required to make additional contributions. This is, therefore, a defined benefit plan.

11A.73 Some plans contain features of both defined contribution and defined benefit plans. IAS 19 requires that such plans are categorised as either defined contribution or defined benefit according to their substance. IAS 19 is clear that all plans fall into one category or the other and default to defined benefit, if they fail to meet the defined contribution definition. The consideration of substance therefore has little impact in practice. For example, a plan may provide money purchase benefits, but with a guaranteed level of benefit based on a proportion of final salary. If investments perform satisfactorily the employer will have no obligation in excess of the contributions it has agreed to make. This would suggest treatment as a defined contribution plan. However, as the employer bears downside investment risk and may be required to make further contributions in order for the plan to fulfil its final salary guarantee, the plan should be accounted for as a defined benefit plan. The promise of a particular level of return means that the sponsoring entity may have to make additional contributions to the plan. Accordingly, the criteria for treatment as defined contribution (see para 11A.68) are not met so plans such as these are to be treated as defined benefit plans.

Funded plans

11A.74 Funded post-employment benefit plans are plans where the future liabilities for benefits are provided for in advance by the accumulation of assets held externally to the employing company's business, or through a qualifying insurance policy.

UK.11A.74.1 In the UK, plan assets are usually placed under the control of trustees, who administer the plan in accordance with the provisions of trust law and the terms of the trust deed governing the particular plan. Employer and employee contributions paid to the trust are invested by the trustees; pensions are paid out of the accumulated funds of the trust. Most funded plans in the UK that are established under trusts enjoy considerable tax benefits through Inland Revenue recognition as exempt approved plans. However, the Finance Act 1989 introduced an upper limit on the amount of salary that may be taken into account for pension purposes (the 'earnings cap'). In response, many employers established unapproved plans to run alongside existing exempt approved plans. Unapproved plans can provide unlimited benefits and are mainly used to provide 'top-up' pensions for higher paid employees whose pensionable earnings in the exempt approved plan are capped. Unapproved arrangements, which may be funded or unfunded, do not enjoy the tax benefits that apply to exempt approved plans. For example, investment gains will suffer capital gains tax.

Unfunded plans

11A.75 Unfunded post-employment benefit plans are plans where no assets are set aside in advance to provide for future liabilities; instead pension liabilities are met out of the employer's own resources as they fall due.

UK.11A.75.1 In the UK, unfunded plans are uncommon in the private sector, but are found in the public sector. The 'earnings cap' introduced by the Finance Act 1989 (and removed in April 2006) led to an increase in unfunded plans, particularly for higher paid executives.

Multi-employer and state plans

11A.76 Some employers participate in industry-wide pension plans, which provide centralised pension arrangements for identifiable groups of unrelated employers. Similarly, some employers contribute to state or public sector pension plans. Sometimes each employer has its own separate fund within the plan. However, where this is not the case the extent of each individual employer's obligations may not be clear.

11A.77 IAS 19 defines a multi-employer plan as a plan, other than a state plan, that:

- pools the assets contributed by various entities that are not under common control; and

- uses those assets to provide benefits to employees of more than one entity, on the basis that contribution and benefit levels are determined without regard to the identity of the entity that employs the employees.

[IAS 19 para 8].

11A.78 State plans, on the other hand, are established by legislation to cover all entities (or all entities in a particular category, for example a specific industry) and are operated by national or local government or by another body (for example, an autonomous agency created specifically for this purpose) which is not subject to control or influence by the reporting entity. [IAS 19 para 44].

11A.79 The distinction between a multi-employer plan and a state plan is somewhat academic as IAS 19 currently requires that they are treated in the same way. [IAS 19 para 43].

11A.80 Multi-employer plans are distinct from group administration plans, although in practice the terms may be used together. A group administration plan is merely an aggregation of single employer plans combined to allow participating employers to pool their assets for investment purposes and reduce investment management and administration costs, but the claims of different employers are segregated for the sole benefit of their own employees. Group administration plans pose no particular accounting problems as they do not expose the participating entities to actuarial risks associated with the current and former employees of other entities and information is readily available to treat them in the same way as any other single employer plan.

> **Example – Industry-wide multi-employer plans**
>
> Entity A participates in two trustee-administered pension plans that provide centralised pension arrangements for employees throughout the industry. A large number of unrelated employers participate in the plans to provide pension benefits for their employees. Entity A's employees can be members of either plan, but not both. Entity A contributes to each plan in accordance with the trustees' instructions.

Plan one accumulates the contributions made in respect of each employee in a separate account. The trustees use the accumulated contributions, together with the related investment income, to purchase an annuity for each employee at retirement. Entity A has no obligation to plan one beyond its annual contribution.

Plan two pays benefits based on final salary and years of service. The employers fund plan two's pension obligations by contributing to an independent trust. The trustees estimate the pension funding requirements to set the annual contribution. Entity A has an obligation to fund plan two based on the decisions made by the trustees, which will take into consideration the actual experience of the plan.

Entity A should classify multi-employer plans as defined benefit plans or defined contribution plans by reference to the economic substance of the arrangements. [IAS 19 para 27].

Plan one is a multi-employer plan. The plan pools assets contributed by various unrelated entities and provides benefits to the employees of more than one entity. Entity A has no obligation to plan one or its employees beyond its annual contribution. The employees take the actuarial and investment risk. Plan one is a defined contribution plan.

Plan two is a multi-employer plan. The plan pools assets contributed by various unrelated entities and provides benefits to the employees of more than one entity. Entity A has an obligation to plan two beyond its annual contribution, because as long as entity A continues to participate in the plan, the contributions will vary based on the overall experience of the scheme. Entity A is taking some of the actuarial and investment risk, so plan two is a defined benefit plan. [IAS 19 para 36].

Entity A should account for its proportionate share of the defined benefit obligation, plan assets and costs associated with plan two.

11A.81 IAS 19 requires that where an employer participates in a defined benefit multi-employer plan, including a state plan, it should account for its proportionate share of assets, liabilities and costs as for any other defined benefit plan. [IAS 19 para 33]. However, when sufficient information is not available to use defined benefit accounting, an entity should instead account for its participation in the plan as if it were a defined contribution plan. [IAS 19 para 34]. In this context, the term *'is not available'* is considered to mean *'cannot be obtained'*. Hence, it is expected that an entity will make every practicable effort to obtain the necessary information in order to apply defined benefit accounting. Nevertheless, the standard envisages two situations where individual participating employers would account for a defined benefit multi-employer plan as if it were a defined contribution plan. These are as follows:

- The entity does not have access to sufficient information to enable the employer to use defined benefit accounting.

- The plan exposes the participating employers to actuarial risks associated with the current and former employees of other entities, with the result that there is no consistent and reliable basis for allocating the obligation, plan assets and cost to individual entities participating in the plan.

[IAS 19 para 36].

In both of these circumstances, there will be additional disclosure as described in paragraph 11A.256. Note that, in the second point above, we regard the lack of a consistent and reliable basis for allocation as an additional condition. The existence of actuarial risk alone is not sufficient to justify use of defined contribution accounting as it is an automatic consequence of a multi-employer plan.

Example 1 – Employers share risks of a multi-employer plan

Entity A participates in an industry-wide pension plan administered by an insurance company. The plan pays benefits based on years of service and final salary. The participating employers fund the plan's obligations through annual contributions. Entity A must pay a penalty if it withdraws from the plan.

The insurance company does not allocate contributions and employee benefits to separate funds for each participating employer. It does not maintain any detailed records tracking the source of the contributions or which entity employs each member. The employers share the actuarial risks associated with their employees and former employees.

The actuarial valuation of the industry-wide pension shows a small surplus.

Entity A can only describe and make disclosure about the multi-employer plan, because it has insufficient information to account for it.

In theory, entity A should account for its proportionate share of the defined benefit obligation, plan assets and pension cost in the same way as for any other defined benefit plan. The industry-wide plan exposes participating employers to the actuarial risks associated with the current and former employees of other participating employers. Entity A does not have access to the information necessary to apply the defined benefit accounting rules.

Entity A should:

■   Account for the pension plan as a defined contribution plan.

■   Disclose that the plan is a defined benefit plan and the reasons why insufficient information is available for defined benefit accounting.

■   Disclose the extent of any surplus or deficit in the plan that may affect future contributions and any information that is available about the surplus. [IAS 19 para 36].

Example 2 – Plan in which assets are segregated by employer

The facts are the same as example 1, but in this case, the insurance entity segregates the assets contributed by each employer and uses the assets contributed by entity A, plus the related income and capital appreciation, to pay benefits to entity A's employees.

Entity A makes cash contributions to the pension plan each year in accordance with an actuary's recommendations.

11A037

Again, entity A has a defined benefit pension plan, as entity A bears the actuarial and investment risk. However, the insurance company segregates the assets contributed by entity A. The pension arrangements do not expose entity A to actuarial risks associated with other entities' employees, so these arrangements are not a multi-employer plan and do not pose any accounting problems. Such plans may be referred to as multiple employer plans in some countries to distinguish them from multi-employer plans.

Entity A should account for its employees' pension arrangements as a defined benefit plan. The information required to apply defined benefit accounting is readily available because the assets are segregated. [IAS 19 para 38].

11A.82 The standard acknowledges that there may be a contractual agreement between a multi-employer plan and its participants that determines how a surplus in the plan will be distributed (or a deficit funded). As a result, even if a participant in a multi-employer plan accounts for that plan as a defined contribution plan, as described in paragraph 11A.81, it should recognise the asset or liability that arises from the contractual agreement and the resulting income or expense. [IAS 19 para 37]. This is illustrated below.

Example – Contractual schedule of contributions to a multi-employer plan

Entity A participates in a multi-employer defined benefit plan. It accounts for the plan as if it were a defined contribution plan as described in paragraph 11A.81. The trustees of the plan have agreed with its participants that the current deficit in the plan will be eliminated over the next five years. A contract has been drawn up, including a schedule of contributions showing that entity A will contribute C10m in addition to its normal contributions over the next five years. Accordingly, entity A should recognise a liability and an expense equal to the present value of the C10m payable. However, this will not affect the entity's treatment of its normal contributions as if the plan was a defined contribution plan.

Group plans

11A.83 Group pension plans could be considered to be a type of multi-employer plan. Contributions from a number of employers (the members of the group) are pooled and pension arrangements are administered centrally. However, IAS 19 states that *"defined benefit plans that share risks between entities under common control, for example a parent and its subsidiaries, are not multi-employer plans".* [IAS 19 para 40]. Instead, IAS 19 contains specific rules for group pension plans.

11A.84 An entity that participates in a defined benefit plan that shares risks between various entities under common control should obtain information about the plan as a whole, measured in accordance with IAS 19. The net defined benefit cost should then be allocated among the participating entities as follows:

- If there is a contractual agreement or stated policy for charging the net defined benefit cost for the plan as a whole to participating entities, the entity should, in its separate or individual financial statements, recognise the net defined benefit cost that is charged.

■ If there is no such agreement or policy, the net defined benefit cost for the plan as a whole should be recognised in the separate or individual financial statements of the entity that is legally the sponsoring employer for the plan. The other group entities should recognise, in their separate or individual financial statements, a cost equal to their contribution payable for the period.

[IAS 19 para 41].

11A.85 It is perhaps surprising that no definition is provided for terms such as 'net defined benefit cost' or 'sponsoring employer'. The latter, in particular, can be interpreted in various ways (see example 1 below). As regards net defined benefit cost, paragraph 57(c) of IAS 19 outlines the amounts to be recognised in profit or loss. This might suggest that the net defined benefit cost is the net amount recognised in the income statement, thus ignoring any actuarial gains and losses recognised outside profit or loss. In our view, the term should not be interpreted in this way. Instead it should be considered more broadly to include the total benefit cost recognised in respect of the pension plan, regardless of whether amounts are recognised within or outside profit or loss, for example, remeasurements (see para 11A.242).

11A.86 The practical application of these requirements, specifically determining whether a contractual agreement or stated policy exists, and if not, who the sponsoring employer is, is considered in the following examples.

> **Example 1 – No contract nor stated policy for allocation**
>
> Entity A has several subsidiaries. The subsidiaries all trade and are of a similar size. All of the subsidiaries, as well as entity A itself, participate in the 'entity A group defined benefit plan'. The plan rules do not specify how any surplus or deficit should be allocated among participating employers. Furthermore, there is neither a contractual agreement nor a stated policy for allocating the net defined benefit cost to the individual group entities. Accordingly, the net defined benefit cost for the plan as a whole should be recognised in the separate or individual financial statements of the entity that is legally the sponsoring employer for the plan. The other participating entities will recognise a cost equal to their contribution for the period.
>
> As noted above, IAS 19 does not define the term 'sponsoring employer'. The basis for conclusions section of the standard provides a little guidance in paragraph BC48, which states that *"the entity that is the sponsoring employer bears the risk relating to the plan by default"*. Hence, it would appear that any decision as to which entity is the sponsoring employer should be based on a consideration of the risks faced by each participating entity when compared to the others.
>
> Often the identity of the sponsoring employer will be clear from a plan's trust deed and rules. However, in the absence of such clarity we consider that the following factors should be taken into account:
>
> ■ Which entity's management is responsible for making decisions concerning the plan and negotiating with its trustees (such as agreeing contribution rates)?

- How are responsibilities described in the contribution schedule agreed with the plan trustees? Are contributions the responsibility of one entity, with all other participants making payments to that entity rather than the plan?

- Does one entity guarantee the contributions made by the other group entities?

Example 2 – Stated policy for allocation

Entity B also has several trading subsidiaries of similar size. All of the subsidiaries, as well as entity B itself, participate in the 'entity B group defined benefit plan'. The plan rules do not specify how any surplus or deficit should be allocated amongst participating employers. However, management has defined a policy for allocating the net defined benefit cost to the individual group entities on the basis of pensionable payroll. Hence, the net defined benefit cost (and the resultant asset or liability) should be recognised on this basis in each of the participating entities' separate or individual financial statements.

Example 3 – Schedule of contributions agreed with trustees

Entity C also has several trading subsidiaries of similar size. All of the subsidiaries, as well as entity C itself, participate in the 'entity C group defined benefit plan'. The plan rules do not specify how any surplus or deficit should be allocated among participating employers. However, a schedule of contributions has been agreed with the plan trustees. Although this deals with cash payments rather than the net defined benefit cost, it could be argued that a contribution schedule provides evidence as to how the net defined benefit cost (and, hence, the plan surplus or deficit) should be allocated. Hence, we believe that in this example the net defined benefit cost (and the resultant asset or liability) could be recognised on this basis in each of the participating entities' separate or individual financial statements. Alternatively, the net defined benefit cost for the plan as a whole could be recognised in the separate or individual financial statements of the entity that is legally the sponsoring employer.

UK note – In the UK, the requirements of the Pensions Act 2004 mean that where a defined benefit plan has insufficient assets to cover its liabilities, the trustees must establish a recovery plan setting out how the statutory funding objective (SFO) is to be met and over what period (see para UK.11A.280). In detailing the steps to be taken in order to meet the SFO, the recovery plan will specify the contributions sought from each participating entity. Given this requirement, it is likely that a schedule of contributions similar to that described in the above example will be in place for most defined benefit plans in the UK.

Furthermore, for accounting periods ended on or after 6 April 2006 the rules for employers deducting pension contributions for tax purposes changed. The more general tax 'wholly and exclusively' test applies so that deductions are allowed only for contributions made wholly and exclusively for the purposes of the employer's trade or profession. In the context of group plans, where contributions to a group pension plan are made by the holding entity in the group with each employing subsidiary entity in the group being recharged an appropriate amount relating to its employees, the intra-group recharge may be accepted as being a contribution paid by the employer to the registered plan. More importantly, the contribution paid by the holding entity on behalf of each subsidiary entity must be recharged to each subsidiary entity on a reasonable basis (so as to meet the 'wholly and exclusively' test) in order for a tax deduction to be available.

An entity reporting under IFRS has a choice over whether they have an allocation policy as covered in IAS 19 paragraph 41 (see para 11A.84 above). It, therefore, depends on whether a schedule of contributions is deemed to be a contractual agreement or policy.

Example 4 – 95% of active plan members employed by one entity in the group

Entity D has several trading subsidiaries but one (entity E) is considerably larger than the rest. All of the subsidiaries, as well as entity D itself, participate in the 'D group defined benefit plan' but approximately 95% of active members of the plan are employed by entity E. The plan rules do not specify how any surplus or deficit should be allocated among participating employers and the entity does not have a stated policy for allocation. However, in substance most of the risk in respect of the plan is borne by entity E and it is management of that entity that deals with the plan trustees. In our view, entity E will be considered to be the sponsoring employer so the net defined benefit cost (and the resultant asset or liability) should be recognised in full by that entity. In accordance with paragraph 41 of IAS 19, the other entities in the group (including entity D) should treat their participation in the plan as if it was a defined contribution plan (that is, they should recognise a cost equal to their contributions payable for the period).

Example 5 – Non-trading service company

Entity F, a trading company, has several trading subsidiaries, some of which are overseas. All employees in the 'entity F group' are legally employed by a separate non-trading service company subsidiary, entity G, for administrative reasons, but provide services to the trading entities within the group, not entity G. Entity G recharges staff costs, including pension costs, to entity F and its trading subsidiaries. The existence of a recharge arrangement between the group entities is indicative of a stated policy for allocating costs. Furthermore, the service company is a so-called 'shell company' and would be unable to meet the full costs of the pension plan as it is not trading. The net defined benefit cost (and the resultant asset or liability) should be recognised on the same basis as the costs are recharged in each of the participating trading entities' separate or individual financial statements.

11A.87   IAS 19 sets out disclosures that must be made in respect of group pension plans. These requirements are explained in paragraph 11A.259.

Insured plans

11A.88   An employer may pay insurance premiums to fund a pension plan. The employer should treat such a plan as a defined contribution plan only where it has no legal or constructive obligation, either directly or indirectly through the plan, to either:

■   pay the employee benefits directly when they fall due; or

■ pay further amounts if the insurer does not pay all future benefits relating to employee service in the current and prior periods.

[IAS 19 para 46].

In either of these situations the plan will be treated as defined benefit.

11A.89 For example, if the insurance company bears all of the actuarial and investment risk and has sole responsibility for paying the benefits, the plan will be treated as a defined contribution plan. In this situation, the insurance premium costs are, in substance, costs of settling the pension obligation. On the other hand, if the employer, either directly, indirectly through the plan, through a mechanism for setting future premiums, or through a relationship with the insurer, retains a legal or constructive obligation, the payment of the premiums does not settle the pension obligation. Instead, the plan would be treated as defined benefit and the insurance policy would be treated as a plan asset or reimbursement right (see from para 11A.101).

11A.90 The following example illustrates the above principle.

> **Example – Insurance policy against accident and injury compensation**
>
> Legislation in a particular country requires an entity to provide compensation to employees injured in an accident at work. The legislation allows employers to cover their obligation with an insurance policy, but makes it clear that employers cannot transfer the legal obligation for making compensation payments to a third party.
>
> A construction entity has a large workforce and the nature of its business increases the risk of injuries at work. The entity has decided to cover its exposure to injury compensation payments by taking out an insurance policy. Management believes the risk that the insurance company will default on its obligations is remote.
>
> The entity should treat its obligations as a defined benefit plan. The legislation does not allow the entity to transfer the obligation for making compensation payments to the insurance entity. Should the insurance company fail to make any payment required by legislation, the company would be required to meet the obligation. The probability of being required to make payments in the future does not affect the accounting treatment. The existence of the legal obligation determines the accounting treatment.

11A.91 In other circumstances, arrangements will be undertaken to insure liabilities, or to transfer legally such liabilities to third parties. Insurance of defined benefit obligations is discussed further from paragraph 11A.108.

Defined contribution plans

Recognition and measurement

11A.92 Accounting for defined contribution plans is straightforward, as the amount recognised as an expense is the contribution payable. Except for contributions outstanding or pre-paid, an employer has no assets or liabilities in respect of a defined contribution plan. [IAS 19 para 51].

11A.93 In the unlikely event that contributions are payable more than 12 months after the end of the period to which they relate, they should be discounted using the rate specified in paragraph 11A.138. [IAS 19 para 52].

11A.94 An employer might contribute, or be obliged to contribute, an amount to an employee's defined contribution plan that vests over three years subsequent to the contribution, with the effect that if the employee leaves within the three-year period, the employer is entitled to a refund of the contribution, or its then investment value. In July 2011, the IFRS IC issued an agenda decision that clarifies the effect of vesting conditions on the accounting for such defined contribution arrangements (as defined in para 50 of IAS 19). The IFRS IC concluded that each contribution to a defined contribution plan is recognised as an expense or recognised as a liability (accrued expense) over the period of service that obliges the employer to make the contribution to the plan. This means that the expense would be recognised once the contribution is made (or the obligation to make the contribution arises) rather than over the subsequent vesting period. In their conclusion, the committee made a distinction between the period that creates the employer's obligation and the period of service that entitles an employee to receive the benefit from the defined contribution (that is, the vesting period). Refunds are recognised as an asset and income when the entity/employer becomes entitled to them (that is, by the employee failing to meet the vesting condition). The committee's agenda decision is only applicable in circumstances where employer contributions to a defined contribution plan have vesting conditions; it does not apply to defined benefit plans or to short-term and other long-term benefits. See further guidance related to benefit attribution for defined benefit plans (para 11A.126) and other long-term benefits (para 11A.40).

Disclosure

11A.95 The only specific disclosure required by IAS 19 in respect of defined contribution plans is the amount recognised as an expense in the period. [IAS 19 para 53]. Pension plans are related parties and so contributions paid into defined contribution plans are transactions with related parties and should be disclosed as such. Additionally, disclosure of contributions paid and any balances outstanding in respect of key management personnel may also be required by IAS 24 (see chapter 29).

Defined benefit plans

Basic principles

11A.96 Accounting for defined benefit plans is complex because actuarial assumptions and valuation methods are required to measure the balance sheet obligation and the income statement expense. The expense recognised is not necessarily the contributions made in the period. IAS 19's first objective is to ensure that an employer's financial statements reflect a liability when employees have provided services in exchange for benefits to be paid in the future. The standard describes how a defined benefit liability should be recognised and measured but, to the extent that this balance may be negative (that is, an asset), the same principles would apply. The plan liabilities (described by IAS 19 as the 'defined benefit obligation') and, in the case of a funded plan, the plan assets, are measured at each balance sheet date. The plan assets are measured at fair value. The defined benefit obligation is measured on an actuarial basis discounted to present value. The difference between the fair value of the plan assets and the present value of the defined benefit obligation is a surplus or deficit that, subject to certain conditions, should be recognised as an asset or liability on the employer's balance sheet.

11A.97   A surplus is regarded as an asset to the extent that the employer can gain an economic benefit from it. A deficit is regarded as a liability to the extent that the employer has a legal or constructive obligation to make it good – this will nearly always be the case. In an unfunded plan, the employer has a direct obligation to pay the retirement benefits itself, so it recognises as a liability the gross amount of the plan liabilities. In a funded plan, plan assets are held in an entity (fund) that is legally separate from the reporting entity, so it recognises as an asset or liability the *net* surplus or deficit.

UK.11A.97.1   The previous paragraphs could be applied to FRS 17 as much as IAS 19. However, there is an important difference in the recognition of a net surplus as an asset under IAS 19.

UK.11A.97.2   In determining the amount of a surplus that may be recognised as an asset in terms of the amount of economic benefit available as a refund, under FRS 17, the amount would only include refunds that have been agreed with the pension plan trustees as at the balance sheet date. However, IAS 19 does not restrict refunds to those already agreed, if, in principle, a refund would be available to the employer on ultimate winding up of the scheme then an asset should be recognised. Hence, the net amount recognised as an asset or liability under IAS 19 is not necessarily the same as under FRS 17.

11A.98   IAS 19 avoids implying that a surplus in a defined benefit pension plan is 'owned' by the employer. But conceptually an employer does not have to own a surplus in order to recognise an asset. It is sufficient that the employer has access to future economic benefits that it controls *via*, for example, the ability to reduce future employer contributions. Consequently, a surplus should be recognised as an asset to the extent that the employer is able to recover it through reduced future contributions or refunds, either directly to the employer or indirectly to another plan in deficit. [IAS 19 para 65]. Recoverability of a surplus is considered from paragraph 11A.187.

11A.99   IAS 19 requires the amount recognised as a defined benefit liability (or asset, if negative) to be the net total of the following amounts:

■   The present value of the defined benefit obligation at the balance sheet date (see from para 11A.124).

■   *Minus* the fair value at the balance sheet date of plan assets (if any) out of which the obligations are to be settled directly (see from para 11A.101).

[IAS 19 para 57].

11A.100   Paragraph 11A.164 contains examples of how the defined benefit liability is calculated.

Plan assets

Identification and recognition of plan assets

11A.101   Identifying plan assets is important because the accounting for them is quite different from the accounting for other investments that are not plan assets. This applies to both the balance sheet and the income statement. In the balance sheet, plan assets are deducted from plan liabilities to give a net defined benefit liability (asset). In the income statement, pension expense includes as a component a net interest charge (income) which is based on this net defined benefit liability (asset). Other comprehensive income is also impacted by the actual return on assets.

UK.11A.101.1   In the UK, the identity of plan assets should usually be apparent from the way funded pension plans are constituted. The assets are usually placed under the control of trustees, who administer the plan in accordance with the provisions of trust law and the terms of the trust deed governing the particular plan. In some other countries, identifying plan assets may not be so clear cut.

11A.102   IAS 19 defines plan assets as either:

■   Assets held by a long-term employee benefit fund. These are assets, other than non-transferable financial instruments issued by the reporting entity, that:

    ■   are held by an entity (a fund) that is legally separate from the reporting entity and exists solely to pay or fund employee benefits; and

    ■   are available to be used only to pay or fund employee benefits, are not available to the reporting entity's own creditors (even in bankruptcy), and cannot be returned to the reporting entity, unless either:

- - the fund's remaining assets are sufficient to meet all the related employee benefit obligations of the plan or the reporting entity; or

  - the assets are returned to the reporting entity to reimburse it for employee benefits already paid.

- Qualifying insurance policies. These are policies issued by an insurer that is not a related party of the reporting entity where the proceeds of the policy:

  - can be used only to pay or fund employee benefits under a defined benefit plan; and

  - are not available to the reporting entity's own creditors (even in bankruptcy), and cannot be paid to the reporting entity, unless either:

    - the proceeds represent surplus assets that are not needed for the policy to meet all the related employee benefit obligations; or

    - the proceeds are returned to the reporting entity to reimburse it for employee benefits already paid.

[IAS 19 para 8].

11A.103 In both cases above, the assets are held solely for the purpose of paying or funding employee benefits and cannot be used by the employer for any other purpose, including settlement of liabilities on the employer's liquidation. This point is important as plans in some countries contain clauses that may give a liquidator access to plan assets. In such circumstances, the assets in question are not plan assets for the purposes of IAS 19.

11A.104 The above principles are illustrated in the following examples.

Example 1 – Assets held by the entity

Entity A has a German subsidiary that operates a defined benefit pension plan. The plan is unfunded, but the entity holds a number of investments to fulfil its future pension obligations, which are treated as available-for-sale financial assets as defined in IAS 39 (see chapter 6).

Although the investments may be identified as relating to the defined benefit obligation, the fact that they are not held by a separate legal entity means that they are not plan assets as defined by IAS 19.

Example 2 – Assets available to creditors on a winding up

Entity B has a US subsidiary that provides retirement benefits to its senior executives through a Rabbi Trust. The trust agreement's legal form is such that the assets held to cover the pension liabilities are available to the general creditors of the entity on winding up. Accordingly, the assets held by the trust are not plan assets as defined by IAS 19. Additionally, consolidation of the Rabbi Trust should be considered under IFRS 10 (or IAS 27 or SIC 12 as applicable).

Example 3 – Pension plan is controlled by the entity

Entity A established entity B as its subsidiary and is its only shareholder. The articles of incorporation of entity B state that entity B is a pension plan and its only purpose is to collect and invest pension contributions made by entity A and pay pensions to former employees of entity A under specified defined benefit pension plan terms.

All members of the board of directors of entity B are nominated by entity A. There are no laws that would prohibit the controlling shareholder of a pension plan entity from changing the articles of incorporation or the purpose of existence of the subsidiary pension entity. A change in the articles of incorporation could allow the pension assets to revert to entity A prior to satisfying the benefit payments to employees.

Entity B does not satisfy the criteria for pension plan assets in paragraph 7 of IAS 19, because entity A controls entity B and, therefore, can change the articles of incorporation and the purpose of entity B. Entity A can thus require that the assets are returned to it before all pension benefit payments to the current and former employees are satisfied.

Entity A should, therefore, consolidate entity B. The assets held by entity B will be classified as AFS assets in entity A's consolidated balance sheet and the pension obligation will be recognised as a separate liability.

11A.105   The following are also not plan assets:

■   Non-transferable financial instruments issued by the reporting entity.

■   Unpaidcontributions due from the reporting entity.

[IAS 19 para 114].

11A.106   Non-transferable financial instruments issued by the reporting entity include loans and shares subject to restrictive conditions, unlisted corporate bonds that are redeemable but not transferable without the reporting entity's permission, insurance policies which cannot be sold and loans to the reporting entity that cannot be assigned to a third party. The principle underlying the definition of plan assets requires that the assets are moved beyond the reporting entity's control so that they are available to meet employee benefit obligations regardless of the reporting entity's financial position. Non-transferable financial instruments issued by the reporting entity would only ever be available to meet benefit obligations if the reporting entity were to repay or redeem them. Such assets would not be available if the reporting entity were to go into liquidation, so IAS 19 excludes them from plan assets.

11A.107   For similar reasons, amounts due from the reporting entity in respect of unpaid contributions are not plan assets, but plan assets do include other current assets and liabilities that do not necessarily relate directly to the payment of benefits, for example rental on property, plant and equipment used by the plan, professional fees incurred by the plan but not yet paid, liabilities (or assets) arising from a derivative financial instrument or other futures contract. [IAS 19 para 114].

11A.108 Sometimes, an entity may look to another party, such as an insurance company, to settle all or part of a defined benefit obligation. Qualifying insurance policies, as defined in paragraph 11A.102, are plan assets. However, IAS 19 also contains guidance in respect of insurance policies that do not satisfy the definition of qualifying insurance policies. Where it is virtually certain that another party will reimburse some or all of the expenditure required to settle a defined benefit obligation, even though this does not represent a qualifying insurance policy or a plan asset, this right to reimbursement should be recognised as a separate asset. In many respects this requirement may be considered academic as a right to reimbursement that is virtually certain will satisfy the definition of an asset contained within the IASB's Framework. Nevertheless, it is important to identify reimbursement rights as they are not accounted for in the same way as other assets.

11A.109 Reimbursement rights are recognised as separate assets rather than as a deduction in determining the defined benefit liability. In all other respects reimbursement rights, and the income they yield, are treated in exactly the same way as other plan assets. [IAS 19 para 116]. This means, for example, that the asset representing the reimbursement right is measured at the same amount as the liability that it reimburses. Although paragraph 116 of IAS 19 uses the term 'fair value', in this context, 'fair value' does not have the same meaning as elsewhere in IFRS. See paragraph 11A.118 for the definition of fair value in this context.

11A.109.1 The cost of purchasing an insurance policy will typically be larger than the present value of the defined benefit obligation it is intended to reimburse. Any difference between the cost of purchasing an insurance policy and the present value of the defined benefit obligation to which it relates, should generally be viewed and treated as an actuarial loss. This is independent of whether the insurance policy is purchased by the pension fund or the entity itself provided the policy itself is an asset of the plan, or meets the definition of a qualifying insurance policy or reimbursement right. This is because IAS 19 para 118 and 119 stipulate that a reimbursement right is treated in the same way as plan assets except for its recognition as a separate asset rather than deducting it to determine the defined benefit liability.

11A.110 The difference between a qualifying insurance policy and a reimbursement right is illustrated in the following examples.

Example 1 – Qualifying insurance policy

Entity A operates a defined benefit pension plan for its senior management. It has decided to cover its pension obligation with an insurance policy taken out with a leading insurance entity. The policy requires the insurer to reimburse entity A in full for all benefit payments. The policy is a qualifying insurance policy as its proceeds can only be used to fund employee benefits and are not available to entity A for any other purpose.

Example 2 – Non-qualifying insurance policy

The facts are the same as in example 1, except that the insurance entity is a related party of entity A.

The definition of plan assets in IAS 19 (see para 11A.102) provides that where an insurance policy is issued to a reporting entity by a related party of the reporting entity (as defined in IAS 24) it cannot be treated as a plan asset. Accordingly, in this example the insurance policy is not a plan asset. It will, however, represent a reimbursement right as described in paragraph 11A.108.

The definition of plan assets in IAS 19 (see para 11A.102) has a hierarchical structure, so that it is only necessary to consider when an insurance policy is a qualifying insurance policy where it is not held by a separate employee benefit fund. This is because policies held by a separate employee benefit fund may be treated as plan assets regardless of whether they are 'qualifying' insurance policies.

In practice, some insurance companies have set up separate legal entities, such as trusts, for their employee benefit arrangements. Insurance policies issued by the employer are then held by these entities. Regardless of whether all the other conditions for treatment as plan assets are met (that is, the assets are available only to pay or fund employee benefits and are not available to the reporting entity's own creditors), such policies that are 'non-transferable financial instruments issued by the reporting entity' (see para 11A.106) do not meet the definition of plan assets under IAS 19.

IFRS 4 provides clarity in this area by concluding that where an insurance contract has been issued by an insurer to a defined benefit plan covering the employees of the issuer, or of another entity consolidated within the same financial statements as the issuer, such contracts should generally not be treated as plan assets. [IFRS 4 para IG1.21].

On the other hand, policies held by a long-term employee benefit fund that are freely transferable, or issued by a related party that is not consolidated, may still meet the definition of plan assets under IAS 19.It is common for a group entity to guarantee to third parties the liabilities of fellow group members, associates and joint ventures. An example is a parent company issuing a contingent guarantee in respect of its subsidiary's defined benefit pension liability. Such a guarantee reduces the risk that the subsidiary will not make payment when due, for example due to cash flow difficulties. In our view, the parent issuing the contingent guarantee should account for it as an insurance contract in accordance with IFRS 4 that is, record a liability. The subsidiary benefiting from the guarantee should disclose it as a contingent asset of the pension plan. It is not a plan asset: the plan's right to receive payment under a guarantee is no different from its right to receive contributions from the employer and unpaid contributions are not plan assets. The plan deficit should not be reduced because a subsidiary is able to secure the support of its parent in making contributions.

Example 3 – Reimbursement right

Entity B operates a similar defined benefit pension plan to entity A and it has also decided to cover its pension obligation with an insurance policy taken out with the same leading insurance entity. The policy is similar to that taken out by entity A except that it also permits entity B to cancel the arrangements, in which case the insurer repays a pre-determined amount to entity B.

The existence of the contractual right to terminate the policy and receive the proceeds means that entity B can apply the proceeds of the policy in its business regardless of the benefit obligation. The use of the proceeds is not restricted to paying employee benefits. Hence, this policy is not a qualifying insurance policy but it does represent a reimbursement right as described in paragraph 11A.108.

11A.111 The above discussion will only be relevant where a plan is treated as a defined benefit plan. Sometimes, an entity's relationship with an insurance company will be such that the entity pays premiums to the insurer, but has no obligation to make any additional payments. In such circumstances, the plan would be treated as defined contribution.

Measurement of plan assets

11A.112 Plan assets should be measured at their fair value at the balance sheet date. [IAS 19 para 57(a)(iii)]. With the exception of certain insurance policies as discussed below, 'fair value' in the context of IAS 19 has the same meaning as in many other accounting standards, so it reflects the amount for which an asset could be exchanged in an arm's length transaction between knowledgeable and willing parties. There is no specific guidance in IAS 19 on how fair value should be determined, although it is suggested that, where no market price is available, fair value should be estimated, for example by reference to discounted cash flows. [IAS 19 para 113].

UK.11A.112.1 FRS 17 gives guidance on determining fair value. Quoted securities are measured at current bid price, the fair value of unquoted securities must be estimated and the fair value of unitised securities is measured at current bid price. Property should be valued at open market value or in accordance with guidance issued by the Royal Institution of Chartered Surveyors. Insurance policies that exactly match the amount and timing of some or all of the benefits payable under a plan should be measured at the same amount as the related obligations. For other insurance policies the best approximation to fair value given the plan's circumstances should be used. [FRS 17 paras 16 to 18].

11A.113 IFRS 13 was issued in May 2011 and is to be applied for annual periods beginning on or after 1 January 2013, with early application permitted. Paragraph 18 of IFRS 13 provides the following guidance as to how the fair value of plan assets should be measured: *"If there is a principal market for the asset or liability, the fair value measurement shall represent the price in that market (whether that price is directly observable or estimated using another valuation technique), even if the price in a different market is potentially more advantageous at the measurement date".* Paragraph 70 of IFRS 13 goes on to state that *"If an asset or a liability measured at fair value has a bid price and an ask price (eg an input from a dealer market), the price within the bid-ask spread that is most representative of fair value in the circumstances shall be used to measure fair value...".*

11A.114 As regards unquoted securities, for which no market price is available, IAS 19 states that fair value should be estimated. Once again, IFRS 13 provides guidance as to how this might be achieved. Valuation techniques are described in paragraphs B5 to B30 of IFRS 13 and include:

- Prices obtained in recent arm's length transactions.

- Comparisons with fair values of similar securities.

- Discounted cash flows.

- Option pricing models.

11A.115 Further guidance on the valuation of investments and other financial assets is given in chapter 6.

11A.116 For properties, all measurement guidance previously contained in IAS 16 and IAS 40 is now replaced by IFRS 13. Property is measured using the market approach (comparison with sales/rentals of similar properties), the income approach (discounted future net rental income) or the cost approach.

[The next paragraph is 11A.118.]

11A.118 Where plan assets include qualifying insurance policies, or there are insurance policies that represent reimbursement rights as defined in paragraph 11A.108, that exactly match the amount and timing of some or all of the benefits payable under a plan, the fair value of those insurance policies is deemed to be the present value of the related obligations, subject to any reduction required if the amounts receivable under the insurance policies are not recoverable in full. [IAS 19 paras 115, 119].

11A.119 Where an insurance policy does not exactly match the amount and timing of some or all of the benefits payable under a plan, the determination of fair value should be made following the guidance in IFRS 13 and referenced above.

Defined benefit obligation

Recognition of the defined benefit obligation

11A.120 The defined benefit obligation reflects *"expected future payments required to settle the obligation resulting from employee service in the current and prior periods".* [IAS 19 para 8]. It comprises not only legal obligations under the formal terms of the plan, but also constructive obligations arising from an employer's informal practices. [IAS 19 para 61]. Hence, the components of the defined benefit obligation reflect the characteristics of a 'present obligation' in IAS 37. Furthermore, actuarial techniques allow the obligation to be measured with sufficient reliability to justify recognition of a liability. The recognition of a provision stems from the existence of a present obligation, which may be legal or constructive. IAS 37 defines a constructive obligation as:

> '*An obligation that derives from an entity's actions where:*
>
> *(a)   by an established pattern of past practice, published policies or a sufficiently specific current statement, the entity has indicated to other parties that it will accept certain responsibilities; and*
>
> *(b)   as a result, the entity has created a valid expectation on the part of those other parties that it will discharge those responsibilities.*'

[IAS 37 para 10].

11A.121   In practice, a constructive obligation may be more difficult to discern than a legal obligation, as it derives from the employer's actions and it is a question of judgement as to whether an obligation has been established. A constructive obligation would for example arise where a change in an entity's informal practices would cause unacceptable damage to its relationship with employees. [IAS 19 para 61]. The principles are illustrated further in the following examples.

Example 1 – Valid expectation

Entity A has agreed with its trade unions that it will contribute 5% of every employee's salary to a pension plan administered by an insurance company. The employee uses the accumulated contributions, together with the related investment returns, to purchase an annuity at retirement. Entity A has no obligation to make additional payments to its employees after their retirement and, hence, this is treated as a defined contribution plan.

However, in each of the last ten years, entity A has used its active employees' medical plan to meet the medical costs of retired employees. Entity A has met all pensioners' medical expenses and has not made any communications to indicate that this is a limited action on the employer's part without any commitment to continue doing so.

Whilst the entity has no legal obligation to meet its pensioners' medical costs, its actions have created an expectation that it will continue to meet these costs. The entity has, therefore, created a constructive obligation, and should account for the costs of providing medical cover as a defined benefit plan. [IAS 19 para 29(c)]. The 5% salary contributions continue to be treated as a defined contribution plan.

Example 2 – Established practice

An entity has a practice of granting annual increases to pensions in payment and deferred pensions over and above any increases that may be required by law or the pension trust deed. Such increases are granted as a measure of protection against inflation.

Although the entity has no legal or contractual obligation to grant the discretionary increases, it has an established practice and has created a valid expectation that it will continue with this practice in the future. It has no realistic alternative but to pay the increases in order to avoid damaging employee relations. Accordingly, the entity has a constructive obligation to continue to grant annual increases so their cost should be factored into the measurement of the defined benefit obligation.

Example 3 – *Ad hoc* discretionary increases

An entity has, in the past, granted occasional discretionary increases to pensions in payment. These increases have been made on an *ad hoc* basis and have no established pattern. Management considers that the entity has not created an expectation of similar increases in the future. Hence, the entity has not established a constructive obligation so the cost of any increases will result in additional past service liabilities when they are granted (see para 11A.219). If the employer's practice changes such that a valid expectation of future increases is created, the cost of future increases should be factored into the measurement of the defined benefit obligation.

Example 4 – Issue of a public statement

Entity A is the parent of a group with subsidiaries in 25 countries. Every subsidiary operates its own benefit plan. Entity A has decided to streamline its pension arrangements and on 30 November 20X1, prior to its year-end the board of directors approved and announced a single uniform pension plan for all its subsidiaries and employees. The relevant trade unions and the trustees of the existing pension plans approved the new arrangements before the announcement.

Entity A's employees must also approve the new arrangements, since they will be required to transfer their pension entitlement to the new plan. The new arrangements provide enhanced benefits for past service for every employee as an incentive to vote in favour of the new arrangements. The employees vote on the new plan on 31 March 20X2 and entity A expects a large margin in favour.

Public statements can create a constructive obligation. However, a public statement in itself may not be sufficient to create a constructive obligation and an entity should consider all of the facts and circumstances relevant to each case.

A constructive obligation is created for entity A by the board's approval and announcement of the amended plan. Approval by the trade union and the trustees provides additional evidence that the entity is committed to provide enhanced benefits. The impact of the benefit enhancement is included in the present value of the defined benefit obligation at 31 December 20X1. The present value of the defined benefit obligation at 31 December 20X1 includes the impact of the past-service cost arising from the benefit enhancement.

The prior service cost should be recognised in the income statement for the period ending 31 December 20X1, even though the benefits will only vest upon approval of the enhancement by the employees. IAS 19 requires immediate recognition when the constructive obligation arises on 30 November 20X1.

Example 5 – Surplus shared with employees

An entity has a substantial surplus in its defined benefit pension plan. The plan rules state that the surplus is to be shared two-thirds to the company and one-third to employees. The surplus attributable to employees must be used in either of two ways – funding past service benefits such as improved death benefits or surviving spouse benefits, or reducing employee contributions in the future, regardless of what the entity does with its share.

If the plan's formal terms (or a constructive obligation) oblige an entity to use a surplus for the benefit of plan participants, paragraph 88(b) of IAS 19 requires this to be reflected in the measurement of the defined benefit obligation. The amount that will be passed to employees should be treated as increasing the plan liabilities. It is irrelevant how the employees' share of the surplus is to be used up. The resulting, smaller, net surplus is subject to the requirements of IFRIC 14 (see para 11A.189).

11A.122 Employee service gives rise to an obligation under a defined benefit plan even if the benefits are conditional on future employment (in other words, they are not vested). Employee service before the vesting date gives rise to a constructive obligation because, at each successive balance sheet date, the amount of future service that an employee will have to render before becoming entitled to the benefit is reduced. The probability that some employees may not satisfy vesting conditions is taken into account in the measurement of the defined benefit obligation, but does not determine whether the obligation exists. For example, although certain post-employment medical benefits become payable only if a specified event or illness occurs after retirement, an obligation is created when the employee renders services that provide entitlement to those benefits.

11A.123 The formal terms of a defined benefit plan may permit an entity to terminate its obligation under the plan. Nevertheless, it is usually difficult for an entity to cancel a plan if employees are to be retained. Therefore, in the absence of evidence to the contrary, it should be assumed that an entity that is currently promising post-retirement benefits will continue to do so over the remaining working lives of employees. [IAS 19 para 62].

Measurement of the defined benefit obligation

11A.124 Paragraph 57(a)(i)-(ii) of IAS 19 describes the approach to determining the defined benefit obligation using the projected unit credit method, which involves:

■ Determining how much benefit is attributable to the current and prior periods.

■ Making estimates (actuarial assumptions) about demographic variables (such as employee turnover and mortality) and financial variables (such as future increases in salaries and medical costs) that will influence the cost of the benefit.

- Discounting that benefit to present value using the projected unit credit method.

11A.125   The objective of this process is to derive the best estimate of the present value of future cash outflows that will arise in respect of the benefits earned by employees at the valuation date. This normally requires the expertise of an actuary although, as discussed in paragraph 11A.172, this is not actually required by IAS 19.

Attribution of benefit to periods of service

11A.126   Benefit should be attributed to periods of service according to a plan's benefit formula, unless an employee's service in later years will lead to a materially higher level of benefit than in earlier years, in which case a straight line basis shall be used. [IAS 19 para 70]. Benefit is attributed to the current period in order to determine current service cost. Benefit is attributed to the current and prior periods in order to determine the present value of the defined benefit obligation. This is illustrated in the examples below.

> **Example 1 – Lump-sum benefit**
>
> A plan provides a lump-sum benefit of C1,000, payable on retirement, for each year of service. An expense of C1,000 is attributed to each year (ignoring discounting).
>
> **Example 2 – Annual final salary pension**
>
> A plan provides an annual pension of 1/60 of final salary for each year of service. The pension is payable from the age of 65. Benefit equal to the present value, at the expected retirement date, of an annual pension of 1/60 of the estimated final salary, payable from the expected retirement date until the expected date of death, is attributed to each year of service.

11A.127   As noted in paragraph 11A.121, employee service gives rise to an obligation under a defined benefit plan even if the benefits are not vested. However, when attributing benefit to periods of service, the probability that some employees may not satisfy vesting conditions (which includes performance hurdles) before becoming entitled to benefits is taken into account. [IAS 19 para 72]. Such costs may include fees paid to the bank for asset management services, salaries of the management board who manage the trust, and any tax payable by the plan itself, (other than the tax included in the actuarial assumptions used to measure the defined benefit obligation, for example, social security and payroll tax on contributions).

11A.128   A plan's benefit formula may set a point beyond which no further benefit can be earned. For example, a plan may pay a single lump-sum of C1,000 after ten years of service. It is logical, and IAS 19 provides that, a benefit of C100 would be attributed to each of the first ten years of employee service (taking into account the fact that some employees may not complete ten years' service, and ignoring discounting) but no benefit would be attributed to later years. [IAS 19 para 73].

11A.129 On the other hand, a plan's benefit formula may result in service in later years giving rise to greater benefit than earlier years (see example below). In circumstances such as this, where service in later years gives rise to a materially higher benefit than in earlier years, IAS 19 requires that the benefit is attributed on a straight-line basis from:

■ the date on which employee service first leads to benefits under the plan; until

■ the date on which employee service will lead to no material amount of further benefit (other than from further salary increases).

[IAS 19 para 70].

11A.130 In summary, paragraph 70 of IAS 19 requires benefits to be allocated to periods of service according to the benefit formula, unless the benefit formula allocates a materially higher level of benefit to later years of service, in which case a straight-line allocation should be made. This principle is illustrated in the following examples.

Example 1 – Benefit increases after 20 years service

A plan provides an annual pension of 1/60 of final salary, but this increases to 1/40 of final salary if an employee leaves after more than 20 years' service.

For those employees expected to remain with the employer for at least 20 years, benefit equal to the present value, at the expected retirement date, of an annual pension of 1/40 of the estimated final salary, payable from the expected retirement date until the expected date of death, is attributed to each year of service.

For all other employees, benefit equal to the present value, at the expected retirement date, of an annual pension of 1/60 of the estimated final salary, payable from the expected retirement date until the expected date of death, is attributed to each year of service.

In all cases, the measurement of the defined benefit obligation will reflect the probability that an employee may leave or die before the normal retirement date.

Example 2 – Benefits are only earned after the age of 25

A plan provides a benefit of C100 for each year of service, excluding service before the age of 25. The benefits vest immediately.

No benefit is attributed to service before the age of 25, because service before that date does not lead to benefits (conditional or unconditional). A benefit of C100 is attributed to each subsequent year.

Example 3 – Benefit increases slightly in later years

A post-employment medical plan reimburses 40% of an employee's post-employment medical costs if the employee leaves after more than 10 and less than 20 years of service and 50% of those costs if the employee leaves after 20 or more years of service.

Under the plan's benefit formula, the entity attributes 4% of the present value of the expected medical costs (40% ÷ 10) to each of the first 10 years and 1% (50% — 40% ÷ 10) to each of the second 10 years. For employees expected to leave within 10 years, no benefit is attributed.

Example 4 – Material increase in benefits in later years

The facts are as in example three, but only 10% of medical costs are reimbursed if the employee leaves between 10 and 20 years of service.

Service in later years leads to a materially higher level of benefit than in earlier years. For employees expected to leave after more than 20 years, benefit is attributed on a straight-line basis under paragraph 70 of IAS 19. Benefit attributed to the first 20 years is 2.5% (50% ÷ 20) of the present value of the expected medical costs. For employees expected to leave between 10 and 20 years, this percentage is reduced to 1% (10% ÷ 10) in the first 10 years and zero thereafter. For employees expected to leave within 10 years, no benefit is attributed.

Example 5 – Material increase in benefits in later years

Entity A operates a pension plan that pays a pension of C100 for each of the first 3 years of service; C500 for each of the years of service from years 4 to 6; and C2,400 for each of the years of service from years 7 to 9. An employee will, therefore, be entitled to a pension of C9,000 (C100 × 3 + C500 × 3 + C2400 × 3) after 9 years of service. Further service after 9 years does not give rise to additional pension.

Entity A's employees' services in later years will lead to a materially higher level of benefit than in earlier years. Entity A should, therefore, attribute benefit to years of service on a straight-line basis from the date when service by the employee first leads to benefits under the plan until the date when further service by the employee will lead to no material amount of further benefits under the plan, other than from further salary increases.

Entity A should, therefore, attribute C1,000 to each year of service (C9000 ÷ 9 years, ignoring discounting) rather than following the attribution formula in the plan.

11A.131 Where the amount of benefit is a constant proportion of final salary for each year of service, future salary increases will affect the amount required to settle the obligation that exists for service before the balance sheet date, but do not create an additional obligation. [IAS 19 para 74]. For example, if employees are entitled to a benefit of 1/30 of final salary for each year of service up to a maximum of 20 years, benefit of 1/30 of estimated final salary will be attributed to the first 20 years of service. No benefit is attributed to service beyond that point. A worked example illustrating this point is included in paragraph 11A.164. Salary increases do not lead to further benefits, even though the amount of benefit is dependent on final salary. The extent to which actual final salary at the date of retirement is different to that estimated in the calculation of the defined benefit obligation is reflected as an actuarial gain or loss as it derives from a change to an actuarial estimate (see from para 11A.242).

11A.132   In the basis of conclusions to IFRIC D9, 'Employee benefit plans with a promised return on contributions or notional contributions', the IFRS IC concluded that expected increases in salary *should* be taken into account in determining whether a benefit formula expressed in terms of *current* salary (such as a career average plan) allocates a materially higher level of benefit to later years of service. This would mean that if salary increases do not lead to a materially higher benefit in later years, then benefits are allocated to periods of service according to the benefit formula, but if salary increases are significant, then a straight-line allocation should be made. A worked example illustrating this point is included in paragraph 11A.164. IFRIC D9 was withdrawn in November 2006; and the specific issue of salary increases was not addressed in the final amendments to IAS 19 (revised) issued in June 2011. Our view is that the practice of including future salary increases in determining whether a benefit formula allocates a materially higher level of benefit to later years is appropriate.

Actuarial assumptions

11A.133   Actuarial assumptions reflect an entity's best estimate of the variables that will determine the ultimate cost of providing post-employment benefits. Some defined benefit pension promises are based on achieving specific performance targets. Such targets are also variables that will affect the ultimate cost of providing the benefit and, hence, should be included in the determination of the benefit.

11A.134   Demographic assumptions concern the future characteristics of the present and former membership of the plan, such as:

- Mortality, both during and after employment.
- Rates of employee turnover, disability and early retirement.
- Age, sex and marital status of membership.
- The proportion of plan members with dependants who will be eligible for benefits.
- Claim rates under medical plans.

11A.135   Financial assumptions deal with matters such as:

- The discount rate (see para 11A.137).
- Future salary and benefit levels (see para 11A.144).
- Price inflation.

■ Future medical costs, including, where material, the cost of administering claims and benefit payments (see para 11A.157).

11A.136 Financial assumptions should be determined in nominal terms, unless estimates in real (inflation-adjusted) terms are more reliable, for example, in a hyper-inflationary economy or where benefits are index-linked and there is a deep market in index-linked bonds of the same currency and term. [IAS 19 para 79]. Financial assumptions should be based on market expectations at the balance sheet date. [IAS 19 para 80].

11A.137 Actuarial assumptions should be both unbiased and mutually compatible. [IAS 19 para 75]. For assumptions to be unbiased, they must be neither imprudent nor excessively conservative. [IAS 19 para 77]. For assumptions to be mutually compatible, they must reflect the economic relationships between factors such as inflation, rates of salary increase and discount rates. [IAS 19 para 78]. IAS 19 also requires disclosure of key actuarial assumptions (see paragraph 11A.254).

11A.138 The discount rate reflects the time value of money, based on the expected timing of the benefit payments. The discount rate does not reflect investment risk or actuarial risk, since other actuarial assumptions deal with these items. The discount rate does not reflect the specific risk associated with the entity's business, nor does it reflect the risk that future experiences may differ from actuarial assumptions. IAS 19 requires that the discount rate is determined by reference to market yields at the appropriate balance sheet date on high quality corporate bonds of equivalent currency and term to the benefit obligations. [IAS 19 para 83]. The bonds' currency should be the currency in which the benefits are to be paid. It may not necessarily be the entity's functional currency. In our opinion, for a bond to be considered 'high quality' for the purposes of IAS 19, it should be rated at least at the level of AA.

UK.11A.138.1 In this regard, IAS 19 is less specific than FRS 17, which states that a high quality corporate bond is a bond that has been rated at the level of AA or equivalent status. Hence, our view that a bond should be rated at least at the level of AA for IAS 19 purposes is based on the guidance in FRS 17.

11A.139 In countries where there is no deep market in high quality corporate bonds, the market yields (at the balance sheet date) on government bonds of equivalent currency and term should be used. [IAS 19 para 83]. In June 2005, the IFRS IC considered this further and took the view that the wording of this paragraph is clear that a synthetically constructed equivalent to a high quality corporate bond by reference to the bond market in another country may not be used to determine the discount rate. The IFRS IC observed that the reference to 'in a country' could reasonably be read as including high quality corporate bonds that are available in a regional market to which the entity has access, provided that the currency of the regional market and the country were the same (for example, the Euro). This would not apply if the country currency differed from that of the regional market.

11A.140 A conclusion as to whether a deep market exists will be made on a case-by-case basis for each country. Corporate and government bond markets develop over time. As a result, a deep corporate or government bond market may develop where one did not previously exist, or the reverse may occur, and such a development may result in a change in the basis or reference for determining the discount rate to be applied. Where a change in the discount rate occurs because of the development of a deep corporate bond market in a country that previously did not have one, this change would be accounted for prospectively. However, where a change in the discount rate is made from a country-specific government bond rate to a rate in a previously existing broader regional corporate bond market in the same currency, this change would be accounted for as a change in accounting policy in accordance with IAS 8. For example, as a result of recent economic developments in Europe, interest rates in the eurozone regional corporate bond market may become a more relevant basis than interest rates on government bonds of a specific country within the eurozone. An entity may therefore elect to change the basis for its discount rate from the local government bond rate to the broader regional corporate bond rate.

11A.141 In some cases, there may be no deep market in bonds with a sufficiently long maturity to match the estimated maturity of all the benefit payments. In such cases, the discount rate for longer maturities should be estimated by extrapolating current market rates of shorter term payments along the yield curve (a graphical representation of the relationship between the return on a financial asset and its time to maturity). [IAS 19 para 86].

11A.142 In times of global market liquidity problems, AA rated corporate bond yields may increase significantly and there may be wide spreads of yields on AA rated bonds. This is likely to lead to both greater volatility and lower defined benefit liabilities as a result of the higher discount rate. At such times it becomes important to consider the following:

- Whether a robust methodology has been used to set the discount rate and whether this methodology has changed since the previous reporting date.

- What allowance has been made for plan specific factors such as age profile. For example, if the yield on an index has been used, how has the yield been adjusted to reflect differences between the term of bonds comprising the index and the term of the plan's liabilities.

- If the yield on an index has been used, what consideration has been given to whether the constituents of the index are appropriate? For instance, if an index contains a larger number of bonds issued by financial institutions which currently have high yields, it may not be appropriate to consider them 'high quality'.

A change in an index or the exclusion of some constituents from an index to reflect current circumstances would be a change in accounting estimate and applied prospectively. The accounting policy to apply a high quality corporate bond yield of appropriate duration has not changed, merely the approach considered appropriate to determine that yield. Additionally, care is needed when considering the impact of changes in the constituents of indices to ensure that such changes are appropriately taken into account at the balance sheet date. For example, if a bond that is a constituent of a particular index is downgraded on 15 December 20X1, but the index is not published until 5 January 20X2, reporting entities should reflect the downgrade as an adjustment in the index yield used to determine liabilities at 31 December 20X1, where material.

11A.143 Disclosure will be required in accordance with IAS 1 when management concludes that the choice of discount rate is a major source of estimation uncertainty. It is likely that many companies will disclose additional information about the assumptions used to measure the pension obligation, including sensitivity analyses.

11A.144 Estimates of future salary increases take account of, for example, inflation, seniority, promotion and supply and demand in the employment market. Assumptions about future salary and benefit levels should reflect an entity's legal and constructive obligations. When the formal terms of a plan (or a constructive obligation that goes beyond those terms) require an entity to change benefits in future periods, the measurement of the obligation reflects those changes. This is the case when, for example:

- the entity has a past history of increasing benefits, for example to mitigate the effects of inflation, and there is no indication that this practice will change in the future; or

- the entity is obliged, by either the formal terms of a plan (or a constructive obligation that goes beyond those terms) or legislation, to use any surplus, or a portion of any surplus, in the plan for the benefit of plan participants; or

- the benefits vary in response to a performance target or other criteria. For example, the terms of the plan may state that it will pay reduced benefits or require additional contributions from employees if the plan assets are insufficient. The measurement of the obligation reflects the best estimate of the effect of the performance target or other criteria.

[IAS 19 para 88].

11A.145 Obligations to use a portion of the surplus are illustrated in the following example.

> **Example – Actuarial gains resulting in a surplus**
>
> An entity operates a defined benefit pension plan, the terms of which provide that any surplus in the plan must be applied towards the enhancement of pension benefits. During 20X5, significant actuarial gains have resulted in the plan having a surplus as at 31 December 20X5. IAS 19 requires that the measurement of the defined benefit obligation should also take into account the additional benefits that would be payable out of the surplus as a result of the plan terms. [IAS 19, para 88(b)].

UK.11A.145.1 FRS 17 provides that the present value of the additional contributions that the members are required to make should be treated as reducing the liability to be recognised by the employer. [FRS 17 para 40].

11A.146 Additionally, some defined benefit plans limit the contributions that an entity is required to pay. The ultimate cost of the benefits takes account of the effect of a limit on contributions. The effect of a limit on contributions is determined over the shorter of:

■ the estimated life of the entity; and

■ the estimated life of the plan.

[IAS 19 para 91].

11A.147 Some defined benefit plans require employees or third parties to contribute to the cost of the plan. Contributions by employees reduce the cost of the benefits to the entity. An entity considers whether third-party contributions reduce the cost of the benefits to the entity, or are a reimbursement right as described in paragraph 116 of IAS 19. Contributions by employees or third parties are either set out in the formal terms of the plan (or arise from a constructive obligation that goes beyond those terms), or are discretionary. Discretionary contributions by employees or third parties reduce service cost upon payment of those contributions to the plan. [IAS 19 para 92].

11A.148 Contributions from employees or third parties set out in the formal terms of the plan either reduce the service cost (if they are linked to service), or reduce remeasurements of the net defined benefit liability (asset) (for example, if the contributions are required to reduce a deficit arising from losses on plan assets or actuarial losses). [IAS 19 para 93].

11A.149 Contributions from employees or third parties in respect of service are attributed to periods of service as a negative benefit in accordance with paragraph 70 (that is, the net benefit is attributed in accordance with that paragraph). [IAS 19 para 93].This appears to be a change from the historical practice, where the cost of the benefit for the year is calculated using the benefit plan formula (or straight lined) based on the gross benefit, with contributions deducted to arrive at the service cost. Under the revised guidance above, where contributions are linked to services, entities will have to calculate the benefit this contribution will 'buy'. The balance of the benefit provided by the employer then needs to be attributed over the working life to get to the service cost each year. The guidance does not specify how the benefit paid for by the employee should be derived; it may therefore give rise to differences in the methods used in practice for the calculation and attribution of this amount.

11A.150 Some pension plans include provisions that specify employee contributions not as a fixed amount but as a proportion of the total contribution rate, for example a 60:40 split between employer and employees. These arrangements typically call for surpluses to be shared between the employer and its employees and that contributions for both employer and employees are increased proportionally where there is a deficit. The employer's share of any surplus could be used to reduce employer contributions whilst the employee share may be used either to reduce contributions or enhance benefits. Whilst the plan terms may specify a shared cost approach, legally and practically it is often not possible to force employees to pay increased contributions as legislation usually gives employees a statutory right to opt out of employer sponsored pension plans and many might elect to do so where they considered the required contribution level to be onerous.

11A.151 For such plans, the accounting issue is how to measure the deficit when there is an expectation that employee contribution rates will need to be increased to help meet the deficit. In order to determine whether a liability for the full deficit or only a part of the deficit should be recognised, an entity should consider whether or not there is an asset (that is, a reimbursement right) or some other way to avoid the obligation.

11A.152 If the employer can force employees to fund their share of the deficit, either through payment of additional contributions or a reduction in benefits, then it would seem clear that the employer cannot be obliged to meet the employees' share of the deficit and accordingly, it might be appropriate to recognise only its portion of the deficit (60% in the above example). This is consistent with paragraph 87(c) which specifies that the defined benefit obligation should reflect any limit on the employer's share of the cost of the future benefit.

11A.153 However, where the employer cannot enforce a benefit reduction nor force employees to pay future contributions at the pre-specified rate because the employees could choose to leave or opt out of the pension plan, the plan does not include a *"requirement for employees to make contributions to reduce or eliminate an existing deficit"*. This suggests that the entity would generally record the full deficit. This follows from the view that in substance the plan includes a provision that makes it likely employees will help to fund the deficit, but future expected employee contributions do not meet the framework definition of an asset and would not be recognisable as a reimbursement right under IAS 19.

11A.154 An alternative view is to regard the rate of future expected employee contributions as an actuarial assumption which might lead to recording less than the full deficit. Where this is the case, this assumption should be consistently applied, correlate logically with the plan's assumption about future service, and be appropriately disclosed.

11A.155 It follows that the measurement of the defined benefit obligation should not reflect future changes that are not set out in the formal terms of the plan (or a constructive obligation). Such changes, when they occur, will result in:

- past service cost, to the extent that they change benefits for service before the change; and
- current service cost for periods after the change, to the extent that they change benefits for service after the change.

[IAS 19 para 89].

11A.156 Some post-employment benefits are linked to variables such as the level of state retirement benefits or state medical care. The measurement of such benefits reflects expected changes in such variables if, and only if, either:

- those changes were enacted before the balance sheet date; or
- past history, or other reliable evidence, indicates that those state benefits will change in some predictable manner, for example in line with future changes in general price levels or general salary levels.

[IAS 19 para 87(e)].

11A.157 Assumptions about medical costs consider the effect of technological advances, changes in health care utilisation and changes in health status of plan participants. Medical costs assumptions should take into account the level and frequency of future claims and the cost of meeting those claims, which are affected by, for example, age, gender, geographical locations and health status. Some plans require employees to contribute towards the medical costs covered by the plan and this should also be taken into account in the actuarial assumptions. Changes in employee contributions will be reflected as a past service cost (see paras 11A.219). The cost of meeting claims may also be reduced by benefits from the state or other medical providers, as described in the previous paragraph, and this also should be reflected in the actuarial assumptions.

11A.158 The choice of assumptions is a difficult area of judgement, because relatively small changes in certain key assumptions, such as mortality rates and the rate of growth in pensionable earnings, can have a material impact on the amount of the defined benefit obligation. It is not unusual for the assumptions that are made for a funding strategy to differ from an actuary's 'best estimates'. For example, there may be a deliberate policy of funding very conservatively, so that the members' benefits are given a high degree of security. The importance of disclosing key assumptions, including mortality assumptions, is discussed in paragraph 11A.254.

Actuarial methods

11A.159   The third step in the process of measuring the defined benefit obligation is to discount the estimated benefit to present value using an actuarial method. IAS 19 requires the whole amount of the obligation to be discounted to present value, even if part of the obligation falls due within twelve months of the balance sheet date. [IAS 19 para 69].

11A.160   There are two principal categories of valuation methods for pension plan liabilities, namely 'accrued benefits methods' and 'prospective benefits methods'.

11A.161   As the name suggests, accrued benefits valuation methods measure the present value of pension benefits earned to date. Allowance may be made for future increases in earnings. Prospective benefits valuation methods, on the other hand, estimate the total cost of providing benefits earned and expected to be earned in the future by employees. The total cost is then spread evenly over the service lives of the employees, usually as a level percentage of salaries.

11A.162   The important difference between the two types of methods is that prospective benefits methods tend to smooth out changes in the annual cost that may arise under accrued benefits methods. For example, using an accrued benefits method, the cost attributable to an individual employee will increase each year as the employee gets older. This is because the present value of the benefits earned each year increases as retirement approaches and the date of payment of a pension draws nearer. Hence, where there is an ageing workforce, the current service cost under an accrued benefits method will tend to rise as a percentage of salary, whereas under a prospective benefits method it should remain constant as the rise has been anticipated in the cost allocated to the earlier years.

11A.163   IAS 19 requires an entity to use the projected unit credit method, which is a type of accrued benefits method, to determine the present value of its defined benefit obligation. [IAS 19 para 67].

> **Example – Projected unit credit method**
>
> An entity has a statutory obligation to operate a termination indemnity scheme under which employees who leave for any reason receive a lump sum based on one month's salary for each year of service. Senior staff receives enhanced benefits. The benefits are not conditional on future employment and vest at the balance sheet date.
>
> The entity has a legal obligation to pay the termination indemnity, calculated by reference to an employee's salary and length of service. The employer has the actuarial risk, so this is a defined benefit arrangement.
>
> The liability for termination indemnities should *not* reflect an assumption that all eligible staff resigns at the balance sheet date, instead the employer should calculate the liability using the projected unit method. The calculation of the liability will include a projection of the benefit earned to date to each future point that the benefit could be paid (for example, end of each year), with allowance for salary increases and

probabilities of payment. Each payment would then be discounted back to the valuation date using the yield on high quality corporate bonds, to reflect the time value of money based on the expected payment date of benefits. A liability calculated without reference to future salary increases or the expected payment date would misstate the liability. If the effect of discounting the payment exceeded the impact of future salary increases then the accrued liability would be overstated.

11A.164 The projected unit credit method views each period of service as giving rise to an additional unit of benefit entitlement, with each unit being measured separately to build up the total obligation. This is illustrated in the examples below.

Example 1 – Final salary

An entity operates a defined benefit plan that pays a lump sum on termination of service of 1% of final salary for each year of service. An employee joins the entity at the beginning of year 1 on a salary of C50,000. Salaries are assumed to increase at 7% per annum and the discount rate is 8%. It is expected that the employee will retire after 5 years of service.

The following table shows how the defined benefit obligation builds up for this employee over the 5 years of service. It is assumed that there are no changes in actuarial assumptions and the possibility that the employee may leave the entity before retiring is ignored.

Year	1	2	3	4	5
Estimated salary (7% growth)	50,000	53,500	57,245	61,252	65,540
Benefit attributed to each period	655	655	655	655	655
Cumulative benefit payable	655	1,311	1,966	2,622	3,277
Opening obligation	0	482	1,041	1,686	2,428
Interest (8% on opening obligation)	0	39	83	135	194
Current service cost (discounted at 8%)	482	520	562	607	655
Closing obligation	482	1,041	1,686	2,428	3,277

At the end of year 5, the employee's final salary is C65,540 (C50,000*1.074). The cumulative benefit earned at the end of 5 years is 1% of the final salary times 5 years of service (C3,277). The current year benefit earned in each of the 5 years is one-fifth of this (C655). The current service cost is the present value of the benefit attributed to the current year. So in year 2, for example, the current service cost is C520 (C655/1.08^3).

Example 2 – Career average, materially higher benefits in later periods

An entity operates a defined benefit plan that pays a lump sum on termination of service of 1% of current salary for each year of service. An employee joins the entity at the beginning of year 1 on a salary of C50,000. Salaries are assumed to increase at 30% per annum and the discount rate is 8%. It is expected that the employee will retire after 5 years of service. Because the benefit is materially higher in later years due to the significant salary increases, the benefit attributable to each period is spread on a straight-line basis.

The following table shows how the defined benefit obligation builds up for this employee over the five years of service. It is assumed that there are no changes in actuarial assumptions and the possibility that the employee may leave the entity before retiring is ignored.

Year	1	2	3	4	5
Estimated salary (30% growth)	50,000	65,000	84,500	109,850	142,805
Benefit earned each period	500	650	845	1,099	1,428
Benefit attributed to each period	904	904	904	904	904
Cumulative benefit					4,521
Opening obligation	0	665	1,436	2,326	3,349
Interest (8% on opening obligation)	0	53	115	186	268
Current service cost (discounted at 8%)	665	718	775	837	904
Closing obligation	665	1,436	2,326	3,349	4,521

The current year benefit earned in each year is 1% of the current year salary, but the current year benefit attributed to each period is the cumulative benefit earned spread on a straight-line basis, C904 (C4,521/5). The current service cost is the present value of the benefit attributed to the current year. So in year 2, for example, the current service cost is C718 (C904/1.08^3).

11A.165 The projected unit credit method is the only actuarial method permissible under IAS 19. For the purposes of funding other valuations may be used but, where this is the case, a separate valuation of the defined benefit obligation will be required for the purposes of IAS 19.

Employee benefit plans with a promised return on contributions or notional contributions

11A.166 The measurement of the defined benefit obligation can be complicated in the case of plans with a promised return on contributions, sometimes known as cash balance plans, which include the following types of plan:

- Plans that promise a fixed return on actual or notional contributions (for example, a plan that provides a benefit equal to specified contributions plus a return of 4% a year over a specified future period).

- Plans that promise a return on actual or notional contributions based on specified assets or indices (for example, a plan that provides a benefit of an amount equal to specified notional contributions plus or minus the return on a notional holding of a basket of shares).

- Plans that combine both of the above features.

11A.167 The IFRS IC published a draft interpretation D9, 'Employee benefits with a promised return on contributions or notional contributions', in July 2004. The draft interpretation was subsequently withdrawn because the IASB published a discussion paper in March 2008. However, revised IAS 19 does not include the proposals in the discussion paper, and the IASB is not expected to address this topic in the near future. As such, the discussion paper proposals are not considered further here; however, even though it has been withdrawn, D9 still contains useful guidance.

11A.168 Most respondents to D9 agreed that such plans are defined benefit plans. This is because the promise of a specified return (whether fixed or variable) means that the employer may have to make additional contributions so the plans cannot be defined contribution plans (in which an entity has no legal or constructive obligation to pay further contributions relating to current or past service). The distinction between defined contribution and defined benefit plans is discussed further from paragraph 11A.72.

11A.169 As regards the accounting, plans that promise a *fixed* return on actual or notional contributions do not present significant problems. The benefit to be paid in the future is estimated by projecting forward the contributions or notional contributions at the guaranteed fixed rate of return. It is then attributed to periods of service and discounted to present value in the same way as any other defined benefit plan. Plan assets are also treated in the same way as any other defined benefit plan.

11A.170 The accounting for plans that promise a *variable* return on actual or notional contributions based on specified assets or indices is more complicated. If the usual methodology for measuring the defined benefit obligation is applied, benefits are projected forward at the expected rate of return on the assets and discounted back to a present value. Hence, if a company established such a plan and immediately contributed C100, the defined benefit obligation on the same day would exceed C100 if the expected return on assets was greater than the discount rate. This method always gives rise to a deficit.

11A.171 Plans that provide a combination of a fixed guarantee and benefits that depend on future returns on assets are sometimes described as 'defined contribution plans with a defined benefit underpin'. Such schemes should be accounted for under the higher of the defined benefit obligation relating to the fixed guarantee and the obligation arising from the variable return, where the latter is determined using the approach set out above for variable schemes (see para 11A.170).

Frequency of valuations

11A.172 IAS 19 requires an entity to determine the present value of defined benefit obligation with sufficient regularity that the amounts recognised in the financial statements do not differ materially from the amounts that would be determined at the balance sheet date. [IAS 19 para 58]. Annual actuarial valuations are not required as at the balance sheet date. Indeed, IAS 19 does not require an entity to involve a qualified actuary at all in the measurement of the defined benefit obligation. Such a practice is merely encouraged. [IAS 19 para 59]. For practical reasons, however, we consider that an entity is likely to use a qualified actuary.

UK11A.172.1 In the UK, FRS 17 requires full actuarial valuations to be carried out by a professionally qualified actuary at least every three years. We would expect this practice to continue under IAS 19.

11A.173 The employer's and the pension plan's financial statements often have different accounting periods. In practice, it is likely that at least two full actuarial valuations will be required for funded pension plans: one for IAS 19 accounting and one (on a funding basis) for the pension plan trustees. That is because the funding valuation may use different, possibly more conservative, assumptions in relation to the liabilities. The IAS 19 valuation need not necessarily be done as at the employer's balance sheet date. In fact, a valuation as at an employer company's year end may not be available in time for the completion of the company's financial statements. It could, therefore, be done at an earlier date, or the same date as the valuation required by the trustees, as suits the employer's reporting timetable and then be updated as necessary to the employer's year end. For example, a company with a December year-end may have a pension plan with a March year end and obtain actuarial valuations as at 31 March. The full valuation would then have to be updated to each company year-end for any material transactions and other material changes in circumstances (including changes in market prices and interest rates). [IAS 19 para 59].

11A.174 An update is in effect an estimate of a full valuation. IAS 19 indicates that some aspects of the valuation should be updated at each balance sheet date of the reporting employer. For example, the financial assumptions underpinning the valuation of the plan liabilities should be updated to reflect changes in market conditions. Thus the discount rate should always be the current rate of return on an appropriate bond at the employer's balance sheet date. A change in the discount rate may also require other financial assumptions, such as the inflation assumption, to be updated. Other aspects of the valuation of the liabilities can be estimated from the previous full valuation by rolling the valuation forward and updating it for changes to the plan, such as benefit improvements. Assumptions that are not directly affected by changes in market conditions need not be updated annually.

11A.175 Individual circumstances will dictate whether a full valuation is required in between the previous full valuation or whether an update is sufficient. If the latest full valuation was a long time ago and many changes have occurred since, the actuary may not be confident that an update will produce a reliable current estimate of the plan liabilities. In such circumstances, a full valuation may be appropriate.

11A.176 The following example illustrates the considerations relevant to determining the appropriate frequency of actuarial valuations.

Example – Frequency of actuarial valuations

A UK-based multi-national group operates a large number of defined benefit pension plans in different countries. The pension plans include:

■ A group pension plan, which provides generous benefits but is open only to UK employees. The pension cost recorded in respect of this plan is equivalent to 5% of the group's total employee cost and 10% of net profit.

■ A US pension plan, which provides benefits only to US-based employees. The group's operations in the US are not significant and investment returns have been stable for a number of years.

■ A Latin America pension plan, which provides pension and medical insurance benefits to all employees in Latin America. The operations in Latin America are material to the group and the stock markets in Brazil and Venezuela are extremely volatile. Venezuela is a hyper-inflationary economy.

■ An Africa pension plan, which provides limited benefits to expatriate staff in Africa. The plan is unfunded and covers a limited number of employees. The group announced a benefit enhancement in the current year.

■ A Benelux pension plan, which provides limited benefits to top up the state pension received by former employees in the Benelux region. The state pensions in these countries are inflation-linked and the group has never been required to make top-up payments.

Deciding on the frequency of valuations requires judgement. Factors to be taken into account include the size of the pension obligation, the volatility of the economic environment in which each plan operates, changes in plan benefits and the overall impact of employee benefit costs on the financial statements. The same frequency does not necessarily apply to all plans.

It will also be necessary to determine the extent of the valuation. Sometimes a full actuarial valuation will be necessary, but often it will be sufficient to update an existing valuation as described in paragraph 11A.174.

In this example, management concluded that the following valuation frequency was appropriate for each of its plans:

- The cost of the group pension plan is material to the financial statements. Although both the economic environment in the UK and the benefit package are stable, the income statement is sensitive to changes in the employee benefit cost. Accordingly, the present value of the defined benefit obligation and the fair value of plan assets should be determined each year.

- The US pension arrangements are not significant and the economic environment is stable. The fair value of quoted plan assets and updates to the discount rate for example are determined every year, but a full valuation of the defined benefit obligation is obtained only every three years.

- The Latin America pension plan is significant and it operates against a volatile economic background. The scale of the changes in the economic environment that occur every year might have a profound effect on the actuarial assumptions. Accordingly, the present value of the defined benefit obligation and the fair value of plan assets should be determined every year.

- The pension obligation in Africa is not significant and the liability is unfunded. Hence, there are no plan assets to be valued. The group usually determines the fair value of the defined benefit obligation every three years. However, in view of the announcement of the benefit enhancement, it may be necessary to obtain a valuation in the current year.

- The Benelux pension plan is not significant. The defined benefit obligation exists, but is very small. There are no plan assets. Hence, the present value of the defined benefit obligation is determined every three years, unless there is a change in the state pension arrangements.

Interim reports

11A.177   IAS 34 requires that an interim financial report should be prepared for a discrete period (that is, items of income and expenses should be recognised and measured on a basis consistent with that used in preparing the annual financial statements and no adjustments should be made for events expected to occur subsequent to the end of the interim period) and that the entity's assets and liabilities should be measured in the same way as they would be at a year end.

11A.178   For a defined contribution pension plan, the expense recognised in a period is equal to the contributions payable in respect of that period. Hence, defined contribution plans are treated in an interim financial report in the same way as in annual financial statements. However, the treatment of defined benefit plans is potentially more complicated.

11A.179   Consistent with the discrete period principle, paragraph B9 of Appendix B to IAS 34 states that the pension cost for an interim period should be calculated on a year-to-date basis by using the actuarially determined pension cost rate as at the end of the previous year, as adjusted for significant market fluctuations (for example changes in bond yields, expected market returns, inflation or asset values) since the previous year end and for significant curtailments, settlements, or other significant one-off events.

11A.180 For the measurement of the defined benefit obligation, paragraph 80 of IAS 19 states that financial assumptions should be based on market expectations at the end of the reporting period for the period over which the obligation is to be settled. Furthermore, paragraph 83 states that the rate used to discount post-employment benefit obligations (both funded and unfunded) should be determined by reference to market yields at the end of the reporting period on high quality corporate bonds.

11A.181 The Board noted that there is no requirement to remeasure a net defined benefit liability (asset) for interim reporting purposes under IAS 19 and IAS 34. Both indicate that judgement needs to be exercised. [IAS 19 para BC59].

11A.182 It follows, therefore, that IAS 19 requires opening assumptions to be used for the purpose of calculating current service cost and net interest. Some could see this as a contradiction in that IAS 19 requires amounts to be updated when there is a significant change to the liability and to IAS 34, which states that significant market fluctuations should be adjusted for. However, if the service cost or net interest cost recognised in the income statement were to be updated in each interim period, then the cumulative full year amounts in those primary statements would not be the same as if the opening assumptions had been used throughout the annual period. Updating these amounts would lead to variations in the results based on how many interim periods each entity has, which would conflict with the 'year to date' principle in IAS 34.

11A.183 Neither IAS 34 nor IAS 19 specify how frequently the assets and liabilities of a defined benefit plan should be revalued. This will depend on the facts and circumstances specific to the pension plan and requires the exercise of a degree of professional judgement. However, IAS 19 does require an entity to determine the present value of the net defined liability (asset) with sufficient regularity that the amounts recognised in the financial statements do not differ materially from the amounts that would be determined at the balance sheet date. [IAS 19 para 58]. In other words, the impact of any actuarial gains and losses since the last valuation must be expected to be immaterial. However, in a volatile economic environment, which might impact both asset values and actuarial assumptions underlying the defined benefit obligation, it will be more difficult to reach such a conclusion and it may be necessary for an entity to obtain a valuation at each interim balance sheet date.

> **Example – Interim remeasurements**
>
> Entity A obtains actuarial valuations of its defined benefit pension obligations at annual intervals. An actuary performs a valuation in January 20X1 to determine, with sufficient reliability, the present value of the defined benefit obligation and the fair value of plan assets at 31 December 20X0, the entity's year-end.
>
> The measurement procedures to be followed in interim reports should be designed to ensure that the resulting information, including the value attributed to the defined benefit obligation and plan assets, is sufficiently reliable. The preparation of interim financial reports may require a greater use of estimates than the preparation of annual

reports. Extrapolation (a roll forward) of the latest actuarial valuation as adjusted for significant market fluctuations or other significant one-time events will often provide a reliable measurement for interim reporting purposes.

If entity A operated in volatile economic environments in which other actuarial assumptions such as interest rates are significantly changed during interim periods it may need to perform an interim remeasurement of their pension obligations.

An interim remeasurement of the net pension liability (asset) always needs to be performed if a curtailment or settlement occurs.

11A.184   Obtaining fair values of certain assets held by the pension plan, such as traded securities, is a low-cost and relatively simple task for an entity to perform at the interim balance sheet date. However, obtaining fair values for other assets such as untraded securities (or securities that are traded so thinly that the most recent trade price is not considered a fair reflection of the fair value of the security) or properties, or obtaining a present valuation of the liabilities of the pension plan could be costly and time-consuming tasks. Estimating these values accurately may involve the use of experts such as property surveyors or actuaries.

11A.185   IAS 34 recognises that there will be a greater use of estimates by an entity when it is preparing an interim financial report than when it is preparing its annual financial statements. [IAS 34 para 41]. Consequently, it may be appropriate for an entity to extrapolate a valuation that had been previously obtained for the purposes of calculating the appropriate asset/liability for recognition in the interim financial report. [IAS 34 App C para C4]. As discussed in paragraph 11A.172, IAS 19 encourages, but does not require, the entity to involve a qualified actuary in the measurement of plan liabilities, so it may sometimes be appropriate at an interim reporting date for the entity's directors to perform this extrapolation exercise without actuarial assistance.

11A.186   Interim reports are considered in greater detail in the Manual of Accounting – Interim financial reporting.

Restrictions on the amount recognised as a defined benefit asset

11A.187   Sometimes, a net balance recognised in respect of a defined benefit pension plan may be an asset. Consistent with the principle that a pension plan surplus is regarded as an asset to the extent that the employer can gain an economic benefit from it, IAS 19 contains a restriction over the amount that may be recognised. In principle, the amount recognised as an asset may not exceed its recoverable amount. This amount is measured as the lower of:

■   the surplus in the defined benefit plan; and

■   the asset ceiling, determined using the discount rate specified in paragraph 83 of IAS 19.

[IAS 19 para 64].

11A.188 The application of this restriction is considered in the following example.

> **Example – Amount recognised as an asset**
>
> A defined benefit plan has the following characteristics at the balance sheet date.
>
> | | C'000 |
> |---|---:|
> | Present value of defined benefit obligation | (1,000) |
> | Fair value of plan assets | 1,200 |
> | Asset determined in accordance with paragraph 57 of IAS 19 (see para para 11A.99) | 200 |
> | Present value of available future refunds and reductions in future contributions | 170 |
>
> The amount that may be recognised as an asset in this example is C170,000, being the present value of available future refunds and reductions in future contributions.

11A.189 IAS 19 contains no specific guidance concerning the measurement of the recoverable amount of a pension plan surplus. However, IFRIC 14 addresses:

■ the amount of pension scheme surpluses that entities can include as a defined benefit asset in their balance sheets, in particular when refunds or reductions in future contributions should be regarded as 'available'; and

■ when a minimum funding requirement may give rise to additional liabilities.

The reach of IFRIC 14 is wider than this might suggest since it may lead to an increase in liabilities even when a scheme is in deficit under IAS 19. This happens where contributions to reduce an existing deficit under a funding requirement may not be recoverable once they are made. If a defined benefit plan is in deficit and there is no minimum funding requirement, then IFRIC 14 is not relevant. If a plan is in surplus, and the employer has an unconditional right to the surplus, it can recognise an asset, there is no need to consider the impact of any minimum funding requirement.

11A.190 Statutory minimum funding requirements exist in many countries to improve the security of the post-employment benefit promise made to members of an employee benefit plan. Such requirements normally stipulate a minimum amount or level of contributions that must be made to a plan over a given period. Therefore, a minimum funding requirement may limit the ability of the entity to reduce future contributions. [IFRIC 14 para 2]. IFRIC 14 does not change statutory or contractual funding rules, as these are set by regulators or pension fund trustees. The interpretation does clarify how entities should account for the effect of any such requirements. It is worth noting that minimum funding requirements can result from the revision of a schedule of contributions, where such a schedule creates an obligation on the employer to pay amounts specified.

They do not have to be enforced by statute or by a regulator. Note also that where a schedule of contributions constitutes a minimum funding requirement, it is likely to be revised regularly (typically every three years) by the plan's actuary. The contribution schedule cannot be viewed as having a three year duration (on the basis that it will be replaced by a new schedule after three years), but must be extrapolated forward indefinitely (on the basis that it will be replaced by an equivalent schedule at the end of the three years). [IFRIC 14 para 21].

11A.191 Further, the limit on the measurement of a defined benefit asset may cause a minimum funding requirement to be onerous. Normally, a requirement to make contributions to a plan would not affect the measurement of the defined benefit asset or liability. This is because the contributions, once paid, will become plan assets and so the additional net liability is nil. However, a minimum funding requirement may give rise to a liability if the required contributions will not be available to the entity once they have been paid. [IFRIC 14 para 3]. Such an additional liability arises only if two conditions are satisfied:

■ the entity has a statutory or contractual obligation to pay additional amounts to the plan; and

■ the entity's ability to recover those amounts in the future is restricted.

11A.192 IFRIC 14 does not affect an entity's ability to get a refund, as this is determined by statutory requirements in the jurisdiction in question and the plan rules. The interpretation does provide guidance on how to account for any restrictions that may be in place. An economic benefit, in the form of a refund or a reduction in future contributions, is available if the entity can realise it at some point during the life of the plan or when the plan liabilities are settled, even if this is not until some distant time in the future, such as when the last benefit is paid to the last pensioner in the scheme. A surplus does not have to be immediately realisable at the balance sheet date in order to be recognised. [IFRIC 14 para 8]. A refund does not have to have been agreed to be available.

11A.193 A refund is deemed to be 'available' only if the entity has an unconditional right to a refund, which is a more stringent test than some have applied in the past. If the entity's right to a refund of a surplus depends on the occurrence or non-occurrence of one or more uncertain future events not wholly within its control, the entity does not have an unconditional right and shall not recognise an asset. [IFRIC 14 paras 11, 12]. An asset is not recognised when it is conditional, even if the receipt of the refund is probable.

11A.194 Interpreting whether an unconditional right exists or not in practice can be difficult. An entity does not have an unconditional right to a refund when the payment of the refund is subject to approval by another party, for example a regulator or governing body of the plan. However, if a regulator's approval is required for a refund, but that approval is perfunctory (for example, for a closed fund with no more members) then this may be treated as an unconditional right because the approval process is not substantive. In establishing whether there is an unconditional right, it will be important to check the scheme rules. In some cases, legal advice may have to be obtained to determine whether an unconditional right exists.

UK.11A.194.1 FRS 17 has a harsher test for recognising surpluses compared to IAS 19. Under FRS 17, there must be either an ability to reduce future contributions or a refund that has been *agreed* by the pension scheme trustees in place. The issue of an unconditional refund, therefore, does not apply. In the cases where there is a surplus in excess of any future contribution reductions, there is likely to be a GAAP difference unless a refund has been agreed by the balance sheet date.

11A.195 Where a third party (for example plan trustees) has a discretionary power but not an obligation to wind up a plan or grant benefit improvements on the occurrence of a particular event, the question arises as to whether the exercise of that power should be anticipated or whether the effects should be recognised only when they occur. We believe that there are two acceptable views:

■ Based on paragraph BC10 of IFRIC 14, the existence of an asset at the balance sheet date depends on whether the company has a *right* to obtain a refund or a reduction in future contributions. This *right* is not affected by future acts that could change the amount of the surplus that may ultimately be recovered. The fact that the trustees could choose to wind up the scheme or grant benefit improvements (and thus reduce the surplus) should not be anticipated and would not remove the company's unconditional right to the surplus.

■ Based on paragraphs 12 and BC12 of IFRIC 14, if the entity's right to a refund resulting in economic benefit depends on actions by a third party, even if these actions are discretionary, the entity does not have an unconditional right. If the trustees could force the plan to wind up before the last benefit is paid, or grant benefit improvements and thus effectively eliminate any surplus, the company does not have an unconditional right to the surplus.

The policy that a company adopts is likely to represent a critical accounting judgement requiring disclosure in accordance with paragraph 122 of IAS 1.

11A.196 The economic benefit available as a *refund* is the surplus at the balance sheet date (the fair value of plan assets less the present value of the defined benefit obligation) that the entity has a right to receive as a refund, less any associated costs (for example, a tax other than income tax or professional fees). The refund should not be discounted. [IFRIC 14 para 12-15]. Where a refund would not be available until after a plan is wound up, the costs of winding up the plan should be deducted from the amount included in the balance sheet.

UK.11.196.1 Such costs of winding-up may be high in the UK.

11A.197 The economic benefit available as a *future reduction in contributions*, in the absence of any minimum funding requirement, is the future service cost to the entity for each period over the shorter of the plan's expected life and the entity's expected life. The future service costs, which excludes amounts that will be borne by employees, should be calculated using actuarial assumptions that are consistent with those used to determine the defined benefit obligation. [IFRIC 14 para 16-17].

11A.198 Minimum funding contributions may be required to cover future service as well as any existing shortfall relating to past service. The two sub-components are treated differently. [IFRIC 14 para 18].

11A.199 IFRIC 14 concluded that a pre-payment provides an economic benefit to the entity when it relieves the entity of an obligation to pay future minimum funding contributions that exceed future service cost. Therefore, an entity should consider those economic benefits in measuring an asset. For minimum funding contributions relating to future service, the economic benefit available as a reduction in future contributions is the sum of:

■ any amount that reduces the future minimum funding requirement contributions for future service because the entity made a pre-payment (that is, paid the amount before being required to do so); and

■ the estimated future service cost in each period less the estimated minimum funding requirement contributions that would be required for future service in those periods if there were no pre-payment as described in the first bullet point above.

[IFRIC 14 para 20].

11A.200 If an entity has an obligation to pay contributions to cover an existing shortfall in respect of services already received, and those contributions (or a proportion thereof) will not be available after they are paid, then a liability should be recognised. The liability and its subsequent remeasurement should be recognised immediately, *via* a charge to other comprehensive income,

11A.201 The principles of IFRIC 14 are illustrated in the following examples.

Example 1 – Trustee approval required for a contribution holiday

The trustees of an entity's defined benefit pension plan comprise two employer-nominated representatives and two employee-nominated representatives. The trustees determine the rates of contribution to the plan by unanimous vote on the basis that the employer contributes two thirds of the funding requirement and the employees contribute one third. The terms of the plan do not permit refunds. There are no minimum funding requirements. However, the plan's terms stipulate that the level of contributions must be agreed between the entity and the trustees.

A surplus of C3m has arisen in the year ended 31 December 20X5. As the terms of the plan do not permit a refund, the fact that trustee approval is required is not relevant.

The surplus can only be recovered through a future reduction in contributions. Where there is no minimum funding requirement, the maximum asset value that can be recognised is the future reduction in contributions (or the present value of the service cost) over the shorter of the expected life of the plan or the entity. As the service cost is, say C0.3m — which, if projected forward over the future service period is in excess of C3m — the amount recognised as an asset by the entity is the full amount of C3m.

Example 2 – Refunds when access to a surplus is limited

Entity A participates in a multi-employer pension plan that provides benefits to employees based on final salary and years of service. Independent trustees administer the plan in accordance with relevant pension legislation. The trustees provide the information each participating employer requires to apply defined benefit accounting.

The most recent actuarial valuation revealed a surplus. Pension legislation permits the trustees to refund surplus contributions to participating employers, subject to a legal maximum. The pension legislation also requires that the plan maintains a solvency margin determined as a percentage of the plan assets. The solvency margin is an insurance for contingencies that is ultimately available for refunds. The trade unions have challenged the trustees in connection with previous refunds and the proposed refunds were subject to litigation. The refunds the participating employers finally received following negotiations with trade unions were significantly less than the legal maximum and were paid in instalments.

Entity A proposes to use its share of the surplus in the plan to calculate the asset limit.

Entity A should take account of the legal maximum ignoring the solvency margin. Local legislation restricts the proportion of the surplus the trustees may refund. Entity A, therefore, restricts the asset limit to the amount of the surplus that is available for refund.

Trade union action might restrict the refund and force the employer to provide additional benefits from the surplus. When the terms of the pension plan change and employees obtain additional benefits for their past service, the entity recognises the past service costs.

The IAS 19 asset ceiling is based on whether a refund is possible and not on whether a refund is likely.

Example 3 – IAS 19 surplus and minimum funding contributions fully refundable

Entity A has a funding level on a minimum funding requirement (MFR) basis (which is measured on a different basis from that required under IAS 19) of 82% in plan B. Under the minimum funding requirements, entity A is required to increase the funding level to 95% immediately and as a result, it has a statutory obligation at the balance sheet date to contribute C200 to plan B immediately. The plan rules permit a full refund of any surplus to entity A at the end of the life of the plan. The year end valuations for plan B are set out below.

	C
Market value of plan assets	1,200
Present value of defined benefit obligation	(1,100)
Surplus	100

The defined benefit asset before consideration of the MFR is C100.

Entity A should recognise a liability to the extent that the contributions payable are not fully available. Payment of the contributions of C200 will increase the IAS 19 surplus from C100 to C300. Under the plan's rules this amount will be fully refundable to the entity with no associated costs. Therefore, no liability is recognised for the obligation to pay the contributions.

Example 4 – IAS 19 deficit and minimum funding contributions not fully available

Entity C has a funding level on a minimum funding requirement basis of 77% in plan D. Under the minimum funding requirements, entity C is required to increase the funding level to 100% immediately and as a result it has a statutory obligation at the balance sheet date to pay additional contributions of C300 to plan D. The plan rules permit a maximum refund of 60% of the IAS 19 surplus to entity C and entity C is not permitted to reduce its contributions below a specified level, which happens to equal the IAS 19 service cost. The year end valuations for plan D are set out below.

	C
Market value of plan assets	1,000
Present value of defined benefit obligation	(1,100)
Deficit	100

The defined benefit liability before consideration of the MFR is C100.

The payment of C300 would change the IAS 19 deficit of C100 to a surplus of C200. Of this C200, 60% (C120) is refundable. Therefore, of the contributions of C300, C100 eliminates the IAS 19 deficit and C120 (60% of C200) is available as an economic benefit. The remaining C80 (40% of C200) of the contributions paid is not available to entity C.

Paragraph 24 of IFRIC 14 requires the entity to recognise a liability to the extent that the additional contributions payable are not available to it. Entity C should increase the defined benefit liability by C80. As required by paragraphs 122 and 127 of IAS 19, C80 is recognised immediately in OCI and entity C recognises a net balance sheet liability of C180. No other liability is recognised in respect of the statutory obligation to pay contributions of C300. When the contributions of C300 are paid, the net balance sheet asset will be C120.

11A.202 Any change in the effect of the asset ceiling, excluding amounts included in net interest on the net defined benefit liability (asset), should be recognised through other comprehensive income. Such amounts should not be recycled through profit or loss in a subsequent period. [IAS 19 para 57]. A settlement or curtailment loss that is recognised in the income statement and leads to a reduction in an irrecoverable surplus within other comprehensive income, represent two different, although connected, transactions and does not represent recycling.

Recognition in the income statement

11A.203   Since the plan assets and liabilities are re-measured at each period end, the income statement reflects the change in the surplus or deficit except, that is, for the following:

- Contributions to the plan and benefits paid by the plan.
- Remeasurement gains and losses (see para 11A.242).
- Business combinations.

11A.204   The amount of pension expense (income) to be recognised in profit or loss is comprised of the following individual components:

- Current service cost (see para 11A.207).
- Net interest on the net defined benefit liability (asset) (see para 11A.213).
- Past service costs (including any gain or loss on a curtailment) and gain or loss on settlement (see para 11A.219).

11A.204.1   While IAS 19 analyses the changes in the plan assets and defined benefit obligation into various components and provides guidance in respect of each, the standard does not prescribe how such components be reported within profit or loss. Accordingly, an entity may present the net of all components within a single line item or alternatively to classify the net interest component separately within finance costs (see para 11A.252.1).

UK.11A.204.1.1   In the UK, historic practice in this area has tended towards entities presenting their interest cost within finance costs with all other costs being presented as an operating expense. This is consistent with paragraph 56 of FRS 17, which prescribes that the net of interest cost and the expected return on plan assets is presented as other finance costs/income.

[IAS 19 para 57].

11A.205   If actuarial gains and losses are ignored, the following example illustrates how the above items reflect the change in a surplus or deficit.

Example – Double entry

The actuarial valuation of a company's pension plan at 31 December 20X3 showed a net surplus of C39m. The profit and loss charge for 20X4 is C66m (that is, the aggregate of current service cost, and net interest on the net defined benefit asset, which is not analysed here into different components). After consulting with its actuaries, the company decided to reduce its employer contributions for 20X4 to C50m. At 31 December 20X4 the surplus in the plan was measured at C23m. There are no minimum funding requirements and the surplus is fully refundable.

The double-entry for the year 20X4 would be as follows:

	C	C
Dr Profit and loss account (net pension cost)	66	
Cr Defined benefit asset		66
Dr Defined benefit asset	50	
Cr Cash (contributions paid)		50

The movements in the defined benefit asset are as follows:

	C
Defined benefit asset b/f	39
Pension cost (profit and loss account)	(66)
Contributions paid	50
Defined benefit asset c/f	23

The asset of C39m at 31 December 20X3 is increased by contributions of C50m during 20X4 and reduced by the pension cost of C66m. At 31 December 20X4 an asset of C23m is recognised reflecting the ending net surplus of the plan.

11A.206   IAS 19 does not overrule the requirements of other accounting standards regarding the recognition of amounts as assets, so employee benefit costs, including appropriate proportions of the above items, may be capitalised within the cost of assets such as inventories or property, plant and equipment. [IAS 19 para 121].

Current service cost

11A.207   Current service cost is defined as *"the increase in the present value of the defined benefit obligation resulting from employee service in the current period"*. [IAS 19 para 8]. It represents the actuarially calculated present value of the pension benefits earned by the active employees in each period and is supposed to reflect the true economic cost relating to each period based on current market conditions. This cost is determined independently of the funding of the plan. In principle, therefore, for a given set of employees and benefit formula, the current service cost should be the same irrespective of whether the plan is in surplus, in deficit or unfunded.

11A.208 Current service cost is not necessarily a stable percentage of pensionable pay year-on-year. For example, current service cost will vary if the discount rate changes. It will also increase year-on-year as a proportion of pay if the average age of the workforce is increasing, as is likely where a plan is closed to new entrants.

11A.209 The valuation of the plan liabilities and, hence, the calculation of current service cost for each year should be based on the plan's benefit formula. An exception is where a disproportionate amount of total benefits relates to later years of service, in which case the benefit should be allocated on a straight-line basis over the period in which it is earned. [IAS 19 para 70]. The attribution of benefit to periods of service is discussed further from paragraph 11A.126.

11A.210 The mechanics of the projected unit credit method calculations are illustrated in the examples in paragraph 11A.164.

11A.211 The current service cost should be based on the most recent actuarial valuation that is available at the beginning of the year. The financial assumptions underlying the calculation of the present value of the benefits earned (that is, the rate used to discount liabilities, rate of inflation, rate of salary increase and rates of pension and deferred pension increases) should be current as at the beginning of the year. Although the current service cost for the year is based on the financial assumptions set at the beginning of the year, the financial assumptions should be updated at the end of the year for the purpose of re-measuring the plan liabilities. The adoption of new assumptions at the end of the year does not affect the current service cost for the past year, but it sets the assumptions underlying the current service cost for the next year. Therefore, the financial assumptions on which the current service cost for 20X4 is based (that is, those at the beginning of 20X4) should already have been updated in the valuation of the plan liabilities at the end of financial year 20X3 and will also have been disclosed in the financial statements for 20X3 (see further para 11A.254). See paragraph 11A.179 for a discussion of whether assumptions should be updated at interim reporting dates.

11A.212 However, currently it is unclear as to whether the above approach is acceptable given the wording in paragraphs 92-93 of amended IAS 19, which could lead to diversity in practice. This is an area where further clarity is being sought and careful consideration of the facts and circumstances involved is warranted.

Net interest on the net defined benefit liability (asset)

11A.213 Net interest on the net defined benefit liability (asset) is defined as *"the change during the period in the net defined benefit liability (asset) that arises from the passage of time"*. [IAS 19 para 8]. The net interest cost can be viewed as comprising theoretical interest income on plan assets, interest cost on the defined benefit obligation (that is, representing the unwinding of the discount on the plan obligation) and interest on the effect of the asset ceiling. [IAS 19 para 124].

11A.214 Net interest on the net defined benefit liability (asset) is calculated by multiplying the net defined benefit liability (asset) by the discount rate, both as determined at the start of the annual reporting period, taking account of any changes in the net defined benefit liability (asset) during the period as a result of contribution and benefit payments. [IAS 19 para 123]. The discount rate applicable to any financial year, is an appropriate high quality corporate bond rate (or government bond rate if appropriate). See paragraph 11A.138 for further guidance on the discount rate used.

11A.215 Net interest on the net defined benefit liability (asset) can be viewed as effectively including theoretical interest income on plan assets. Such interest income on plan assets is, in substance, a component of the return on plan assets, which is defined as *"interest, dividends and other income derived from the plan assets, together with realised and unrealised gains or losses on the plan assets, less any costs of managing plan assets and less any tax payable by the plan itself, other than tax included in the actuarial assumptions used to measure the present value of the defined benefit obligation"*. [IAS 19 para 8].

[The next paragraph is 11A.217.]

11A.217 Costs of administering the benefit plan should be expensed in the period the administration services are provided, except for expenses such as, in the case of medical benefit, future medical costs, including claim handling costs, which would also be included in the actuarial assumptions used to measure the defined benefit obligation. [IAS 19 para 76]. Examples of expenses that would be expensed as incurred are:

■ salaries of members of the trust's management board who administer the pension payments.

■ administration costs incurred to administer the pension plan participants' database; and

■ actuarial valuation costs.

Costs of managing the plan assets, are deducted from the return on plan assets (see para 11A.244). Such costs may include fees paid to the bank for asset management services, salaries of the management board who manage the trust, and any tax payable by the plan itself (other than the tax included in the actuarial assumptions used to measure the defined benefit obligation, for example, social security and payroll tax on contributions).

11A.218 The above guidance applies whether or not the cost is paid directly by the sponsoring entity on behalf of the plan or by the plan itself.

> **Example – Social security and payroll taxes**
>
> Entity A incurs social security and payroll tax charges of 10% of its cash contributions to a defined benefit pension plan administered by independent trustees. The taxes are payable in the month following the cash contribution to the trust and pension payments from the trust to retirees are not subject to further social security or payroll taxes.
>
> Social security and payroll tax charges are linked to the pension and do not constitute a separate employee benefit, because they are only payable if the entity provides the pension benefit. Consequently, they should be included in actuarial assumptions used to measure the defined benefit obligation rather than expensed in the year in which the cash contributions are made. [IAS 19 para 76(b)(iv)].
>
> It follows that payments of the social security contributions are recorded against the pension liability because they would have previously been factored into the calculation of the defined benefit obligation.

Past service costs

11A.219   Past service costs are defined as *"the change in the present value of the defined benefit obligation for employee service in prior periods, resulting from a plan amendment (the introduction or withdrawal of, or changes to, a defined benefit plan) or a curtailment (a significant reduction by the entity in the number of employees covered by a plan)'"* [IAS 19 para 8]. Negative past service costs are discussed in paragraph 11A.229 below.

11A.220   Benefit changes may produce both an increase in the cost of future service relating to active members (reflected in a higher annual current service cost) and an increased liability for past service relating to current and ex-employees. The cost (that is, the capitalised present value) of benefit changes that relate to past service and that have not previously been allowed for in the valuation of the plan liabilities, including the unvested portion related to past service, should be recognised in full as an expense in the income statement at the earlier of the following dates:

- when the plan amendment or curtailment occurs; and

- when the entity recognises related restructuring costs or termination benefits.

However, in some circumstances, plan amendments may give rise to a constructive obligation under paragraph 61 of IAS 19, for example, where informal communications made to employees leave the entity with no choice but to pay the benefits. In this situation, any loss associated with the amendment should be accounted for at the point there is a constructive obligation. This treatment applies irrespective of whether the additional past service liability relates to pensioners, ex-employees entitled to benefits that are not yet in payment or current employees, or whether the benefit changes are funded by a surplus or give rise to a deficit.

11A.221   A plan amendment occurs when an entity introduces, or withdraws, a defined benefit plan or changes the benefits payable under an existing defined benefit plan. [IAS 19 para 104]. A curtailment occurs when an entity significantly reduces the number of employees covered by a plan and may arise from an isolated event, such as the closing of a plant, discontinuance or an operation or termination or suspension of a plan. [IAS 19 para 105].

11A.222   The recognition of past service costs is illustrated in the following examples:

Example 1 – Recognition of past service cost

An entity operates a pension plan that provides a pension of 1% of final salary for each year of service, subject to a minimum of 5 years' service. On 1 January 20X4 the entity improves the pension to 1.25% of final salary for each year of service, including prior years. As a consequence, the present value of the defined benefit obligation increased by, say, C500,000 as shown below:

	C
Employees with more than 5 years' service at 1 January 20X4	300,000
Employees with less than 5 years' service at 1 January 20X4 (average of three years of service so two years until vesting)	200,000
Increase in defined benefit obligation	500,000

The entity has changed the present value of the defined benefit obligation as a result of an amendment to the plan, Therefore, a past service cost of C500,000 should be recognised in the income statement immediately. The increase in the defined benefit obligation of C200,000 relating to employees who have not yet vested will include an assumption about how many of them will leave before they complete the 5 year vesting condition and thus forfeit their benefit.

Example 2 – Timing of past service cost due to plan amendment

Entity B announced its intention to amend a pension plan such that benefits are reduced. Under the current plan, employees earn a pension of 1% of final salary for each year worked. The plan will be amended so that the benefit is based on employee's average salary measured over the period from 1 January 20X4 to leaving.

Entity B published amended terms of the pension plan on its web site on 20 December 20X3. The entity's human resource department prepared amended employment contracts in early January 20X4 and sent them to employees for signature. All amended employment contracts were signed by the end of January 20X4. The amendment is not contractually binding under local legislation until signed by the employee.

The past service cost (negative in this case) should not be recognised before the amended terms become contractually binding. The terms of a defined benefit plan were amended in January 20X4 when the new terms became contractually binding through signature of the employees. Entity B should account for the effects of the amendment in January 20X4. The date from which arrangements are contractually binding will vary depending on local legislation.

11A.223   In order to calculate the gain or loss relating to a past service cost arising from a plan amendment or curtailment, an entity shall remeasure the net defined benefit liability (asset) using the current fair value of plan assets and current actuarial assumptions (including current market interest rates and other current market prices) reflecting the benefits offered under the plan before the amendment or curtailment. [IAS 19 para 99]. This remeasured net defined benefit liability (asset) will be compared to the new net defined benefit liability (asset) immediately after the amendment or curtailment with the difference being the gain or loss.

11A.224   It is important to distinguish between past service costs and actuarial losses. A larger than expected increase in pensionable salaries, for example, will increase the plan liabilities relating to past service. This is an actuarial loss rather than a past service cost, since it is a re-measurement of the existing commitment to pay retirement benefits based on final salary. Similarly, the cost of a higher than anticipated increase to pensions in payment will generally be regarded as an actuarial loss, being a re-measurement of the employer's existing commitment to provide cost of living increases. On the other hand, the introduction of a new or additional commitment to protect pensions from inflation, where none previously existed, would give rise to a past service cost, because such pension increases would not previously have been allowed for in the valuation of the plan liabilities.

11A.225   In practice, the distinction between past service costs and actuarial losses is often quite blurred. Some transactions do not fit easily into either category, for example the introduction of a government subsidy for the provision of benefits, which gives rise to a change in the cost of the benefit, without a change in the benefit actually received.

11A.226   Specifically, IAS 19 states that the following are not past service costs:

- The effect of differences between actual and previously assumed salary increases on the obligation to pay benefits for service in prior years (there is no past service cost, because actuarial assumptions allow for projected salaries).

- Under and over estimates of discretionary pension increases when an entity has a constructive obligation to grant such increases (there is no past service cost, because actuarial assumptions allow for such increases).

- Estimates of benefit improvements that result from actuarial gains if the entity is obliged to use any surplus in the plan for the benefit of plan participants, even if the benefit increase has not yet been formally awarded (the resulting increase in the obligation is an actuarial loss and not past service cost).

- The increase in vested benefits when, in the absence of new or improved benefits, employees satisfy vesting requirements (there is no past service cost, because the entity recognised the estimated cost of benefits as current service cost as the service was rendered).

[IAS 19 para 108].

11A.227 Past service costs also exclude benefits that become payable as a result of the early termination of an employee's employment by the employer. Therefore, where employees made redundant are granted enhanced pension benefits (say, for early retirement) in lieu of, or in addition to, redundancy payments, the cost of the enhanced pension benefits are in effect treated as termination payments (see para 11A.53) rather than past service costs. However, if the early retirement benefits were available if the employee had chosen to leave rather than being made redundant, then the increase in the defined benefit obligation would be an actuarial loss.

11A.228 Past service costs may be either expenses or income. [IAS 19 para 106]. More specifically, past service costs may be positive (expenses) when new benefits are introduced or existing benefits changed so that the present value of the defined benefit obligation increases, or negative (income) when existing benefits are changed so that the present value of the defined benefit obligation decreases. The constitution of many pension funds means that existing benefits are rarely reduced, so negative past service costs are rare.

11A.229 Where a 'negative' past service cost (that is, income) arises, the treatment is consistent with the normal treatment of past service costs described above.

11A.230 If, in a period, an entity increases certain benefits and reduces others available to the same employees, the net impact may be recognised as a single net expense or credit. [IAS 19 para 107].

Settlements

11A.231 Like curtailments, settlements are events that materially change the liabilities relating to a plan and that are not covered by the normal actuarial assumptions. A settlement is a payment of benefits not set out in the terms of the plan.

11A.232 A settlement arises when *"an entity enters into a transaction that eliminates all further legal or constructive obligation for part or all of the benefits provided under a defined benefit plan"*. [IAS 19 para 111]. Settlements have the effect of extinguishing a portion of the plan liabilities, usually by transferring plan assets to or on behalf of plan members, for example, when a subsidiary is sold or when assets and liabilities are transferred into a defined contribution plan.

11A.233 An entity recognises a gain or loss on settlement of a defined benefit plan when the settlement occurs, as part of the service cost component recognised in the income statement.

11A.234 The purchase of an insurance policy to fund some or all of the employee benefits relating to employee service in the current and prior periods is not a settlement if the entity retains a legal or constructive obligation to pay further amounts should the insurer not pay the employee benefits specified in the insurance policy. [IAS 19 para 112]. Such a policy may, however, be treated as a plan asset or a reimbursement right. See paragraph 11A.109–11A.109.1 above for further guidance on the accounting treatment for qualifying and non-qualifying insurance policies.

Example 1 – Insurance policy

On 1 January 20X3, entity A insured its defined benefit pension obligations with a third party insurer (entity B). The insurance policy is in the name of entity A and not in the name of specific plan participants. However, entity B will pay pensions directly to entity A's former employees. Entity A can revoke the insurance policy at any point in time and obtain the policy's cash surrender value. The insurance policy does not form part of entity A's bankruptcy estate under existing legislation. Entity A believes it retains no further legal or constructive obligation towards its employees for the defined benefit pension plan. While the policy is in effect, the entity is not required to pay further amounts if the insurer does not pay the pension benefits.

The acquisition of the insurance policy is not a settlement of the pension obligation. The insurance policy has eliminated the legal or constructive obligation and entity A is no longer exposed to actuarial risks. However, entity A can revoke the policy at any point in time and obtain the policy's cash surrender value. The transaction cannot be considered a settlement of the existing pension obligation.

The policy is a non-qualifying insurance policy, because the proceeds of the policy can be paid to entity A. It should be recognised as a reimbursement right, if appropriate.

Example 2 – Lump sum payment on retirement

Entity A operates a final salary pension plan that gives a right to a pension of 1% of final salary for each year of service. The terms of the plan allow an employee to choose to receive a lump sum payment at the time of retirement instead of receiving monthly pension payments. The option for the lump sum payment may only be exercised within 3 months prior to retirement.

The *option* for a lump sum is not a settlement. It is a normal employee benefit entitlement. The actuarial valuations should include assumptions about the number of employees that are expected to choose to receive the lump sum payments.

11A.235   The following examples illustrate the difference between a settlement and a curtailment (which is accounted for as a past service cost (refer to para 11A.219)).

Example 1 – Difference between curtailment and settlement

Management of entity C has decided to restructure one of the entity's three business segments and announce the plan at 31 December 20X5. The terms of the plan are as follows:

- In Germany, they will close three of entity C's six factories and relocate 500 of the 1,000 employees. As part of the relocation package, unions have agreed that in exchange for retraining, the affected employees' benefits will be frozen and new employees will not be covered by the plan.

- In Sweden, they will discontinue all activities. Management has agreed with the unions that it will make a one off payment to all of its employees in exchange for cancelling their pension entitlement.

The negotiated agreement in Germany will trigger a past service cost, since the management is making a significant reduction in the number of employees covered by a plan. The closure of half the factories in Germany is likely to have a material impact on entity C's consolidated financial statements.

The discontinuation in Sweden will be both a curtailment and a settlement, since the entity will enter into a transaction that eliminates all liabilities for the benefits provided under the pension plan and significantly reduce the number of employees in the plan.

11A.236 Similar to the measurement of a gain or loss on a curtailment event, calculating the gain or loss arising from a settlement also requires a 'before' and 'after' measurement. The gain or loss on a settlement is the difference between:

- the present value of the defined benefit obligation being settled, as determined on the date of settlement; and

- the settlement price, including any plan assets transferred and any payments made directly by the entity in connection with the settlement.

[IAS 19 para 109].

Example 1 – Restructuring

The facts are the same as in the previous example at paragraph 11A.235. Immediately before the announcement of the restructuring plan, the net pension liability in each of the countries affected was as follows:

	Germany Cm	Sweden Cm
Present value of defined benefit obligation	(5.0)	(7.5)
Fair value of plan assets	3.5	5.0
Net pension liability	(1.5)	(2.5)

After the restructuring, the present value of the pension obligation in Germany is reduced to C4m. The one-off payment made to the employees in Sweden was C3m.

The gain or loss is the aggregate of the change in the present value of the defined benefit obligations and the change in the fair value of plan assets. Hence, the entity recognises a negative past service cost (gain) of C1,000,000 in respect of Germany, being the reduction in the present value of the defined benefit obligation (C5m — C4m). It recognises a loss of C500,000 in respect of the Swedish discontinuance, being the difference between the net pension liability before the settlement (C2.5m) and the payment made to settle the liability (C3m). In Sweden the curtailment has no net impact on the defined benefit obligation because the curtailment and settlement occur concurrently.

Example 2 – Settlement loss on sale of a subsidiary

A wholly-owned subsidiary is sold for C100m. The book value of the subsidiary's net assets on the date of the sale was C70m. The subsidiary participated in the group defined benefit pension plan. There was no contractual agreement or stated policy for charging the net defined benefit cost to individual group entities, and so in accordance with paragraph 41 of IAS 19, the subsidiary, in its individual financial statements, recognised only its contributions payable. At the date of the sale, the plan was in surplus by C35m. As part of the sale agreement, a bulk transfer of plan assets was made to the purchaser's pension plan. The 'before' and 'after' measurements of the group plan are as follows:

	Before sale	After sale	Settlement loss
	Cm	Cm	Cm
Plan assets	160	130	(30)
Plan liabilities	(125)	(100)	25
Plan surplus	35	30	(5)

The profit on sale is as follows:

	Cm	Cm
Sale proceeds		100
Less:		
– subsidiary's net assets at date of sale	(70)	
– settlement loss	(5)	(75)
		25

11A.237   An entity need not distinguish between past service cost resulting from a plan amendment, past service cost resulting from a curtailment and a gain or loss on settlement if these transactions occur together. In some cases, a plan amendment occurs before a settlement, such as when an entity changes the benefits under the plan and settles the amended benefits later. In those cases an entity recognises past service cost before any gain or loss on settlement. [IAS 19 para 100].

UK.11A.237.1   FRS 17 specifies that losses arising on settlement or curtailment not allowed for in the actuarial assumptions should be measured at the date on which the employer becomes demonstrably committed to the transaction. Gains arising on settlements and curtailments not allowed for in the actuarial assumptions should be measured at the date on which all parties whose consent is required are irrevocably committed to the transaction. [FRS 17 para 64].

Timing

11A.238   Determining the period in which a settlement or curtailment occurs can be difficult, especially in cases where there is both a curtailment and a settlement, but they are not recognised at the same time. This is illustrated in the following examples.

11A.239   Further complications can arise when a defined benefit plan is in surplus, but the surplus is not recognised because the entity cannot gain economic benefit from it (see further para 11A.189). One question that arises is whether the unrecognised surplus should be adjusted through OCI and then included within the calculation of the settlement gain or loss recognised in the income statement. The following example illustrates this.

> **Example 1 – Involuntary termination of employee service**
>
> Entity A announced in December 20X3 that 100 employees will be terminated in February 20X4 as part of a restructuring project that the entity is demonstrably committed to carry out.
>
> Entity A has given the 100 employees an option to have their pensions settled by a lump sum payment of C75,000 per employee payable at the date of termination in February 20X4. 90 employees made an irrevocable decision to accept the payment in December 20X3. Entity A expects that the remaining 10 employees will not accept the offer.
>
> Entity A had a pension liability towards the 90 employees of C6,300,000 at 31 December 20X3 prior to considering the lump sum settlement offer. The plan is wholly unfunded.
>
> A curtailment has occurred giving rise to a past service cost in December 20X3 as a result of the restructuring. The future service of the 90 employees who exercised the lump sum option will not earn them any additional benefits and the plan is curtailed. The entity entered into a transaction with the 90 employees that changed the pension obligation at the same time. Entity A should recognise in its financial statements for the year ended 31 December 20X3 a liability of C6,750,000 (90 × C75,000) towards the 90 employees that accepted the offer, which will result in the recognition of additional expense of C450,000 (C6,750,000 — C6,300,000). This liability should be adjusted as necessary when final settlement actually occurs by way of payment.
>
> **Example 2 – Timing of curtailment due to replacement by a new defined contribution plan and subsequent settlement by way of a lump sum payment**
>
> Entity C operates a non-contributory defined benefit pension plan for its senior employees. Entity C has not funded its benefit obligation. On 1 January 20X3, entity C closes the defined benefit plan to new entrants and benefit accrual and replaces it with a defined contribution plan. The benefits with respect to services provided up to 1 January 20X3 are not affected. The terms of the defined contribution plan are still to be agreed with employees at this stage.

On 30 June 20X3, entity C agrees with employee representatives to make a lump sum cash payment of C5,000 in connection with the introduction of the defined contribution plan in exchange for cancelling their pension entitlement under the previous defined benefit plan.

The pension liability recognised in the balance sheet on 30 June before the agreement was C5,500.

The discontinuation of the old plan is a curtailment event. Entity C recognises any change in the defined benefit obligation related to the curtailment in January 20X3, which is when the curtailment occurs.

Entity C recognises a settlement gain of C500 on 30 June 20X3 when a legally binding agreement has been reached that eliminates all further legal or constructive obligations for the benefits provided under the pension plan in exchange for the lump sum payment. The settlement gain is the difference between the accrued pension liability before the settlement and cash payment to senior management.

Example 3 – Recording a curtailment gain and settlement loss related to the disposal of a major business division

Entity E has a December year end. In June 20X3, entity E publicly announced the disposal of a major division, D, to entity Z. The sale and purchase agreement (SPA) had been signed, but was still subject to shareholder approval. A contractually binding, unconditional sale agreement was in place, and division D sold, in January 20X4.

On completion of the sale, division D employees are no longer able to accrue benefits for future service in entity E's defined benefit pension plan. Entity Z announced in June 20X3 that it intends to offer division D employees membership of its own pension plan and those employees will be able to transfer their benefit (with an enhancement funded by entity E) from entity E's plan to entity Z's plan. Letters to employees setting out the terms and conditions of the offer were sent in October 20X3 and employees have until March 20X4 to accept or decline.

The cessation of the employee's ability to accrue benefits in entity E's plan, upon completion of the sale, gives rise to a curtailment gain (as entity E's obligation is reduced).

If employees subsequently choose to transfer to entity Z's plan, this gives rise to a settlement loss, due to the enhancement offered by entity E as an incentive to transfer.

In the December 20X3 financial statements, under the requirements of IFRS 5 entity E discloses division D as held for sale and records its non-current assets at the lower of their carrying amount and fair value (less costs to sell). This results in a loss in the 20X3 income statement related to the write down of certain assets where fair value (less costs to sell) is less than their carrying amount.

However, IAS 19 requires that curtailment and settlement losses, as well as gains, should be recognised when the curtailment or settlement occurs (unless, for a curtailment, it is related to a restructuring, in which case it may be recorded earlier (see para 11A.220 above)). The curtailment relating to the disposal of division D is recorded upon completion of the sale in January 20X4, when the division D employees are no longer able to accrue for future service in entity E's defined benefit pension plan. Hence, it is possible that when a curtailment occurs in connection with the disposal of a business, any gain or loss arising from adjustments to record the non-current assets as held for sale may be recorded in advance of the recording of the curtailment gain or loss, and could even be in a different accounting period. Practically speaking, generally any anticipated curtailment gain would effectively be offset against any loss on sale.

A settlement should be recognised on the date when the entity enters into a transaction that eliminates all further legal or constructive obligations for part or all of the benefits provided under the plan. [IAS 19 para 111]. In the example above, settlement would occur only once the entity E employees concerned have made an irrevocable decision to accept the new offer and the transfer payment has been made.

Although the settlement cannot be accounted for under IAS 19 until the transfers actually take place, if the offer of the enhanced transfer values can be justified as a cost of the disposal, then entity E should be able to set up a provision at the year end for the excess amount they expect to pay out as a result of employees accepting the enhanced transfers. In the following year, 20X4, the provision would be utilised in settling the transfers with any difference between the expected and actual amounts going to the income statement.

Example 4 – Settlement with an unrecognised surplus

Entity A has a defined benefit plan. At 31 December 20X1, the following amounts were attributable to the plan:

Fair value of plan assets	135
Defined benefit obligation	(100)
Surplus	35

This surplus has been deemed irrecoverable in accordance with IFRIC 14; the surplus was, therefore, written off through other comprehensive income.

Two years later, entity A settles its defined benefit plan. When the settlement occurs, all plan assets with their fair value of C135 are used to settle the defined benefit obligation of C100. What, if any, impact should this settlement have on the income statement?

A settlement loss of C35 should be recognised in the income statement. When the settlement takes place, the entity should re-assess its original irrecoverability assumption concerning the surplus. When the settlement occurs, the surplus is recoverable, in that the entity does not need to inject additional funds to settle the plan's obligation, which is an economic benefit. Therefore, the entity should first recognise the surplus adjustment through OCI in accordance with paragraph 58(b) of IAS 19 (see further para 11A.187) and then calculate the settlement loss of C35 according to paragraph 109 of IAS 19 (see further para 11A.236).

Accounting for the closure of a defined benefit pension plan

11A.240   The term 'closed' may be used to describe a pension plan at various stages of its life. It may be closed to new members, although existing members continue to earn benefits. Alternatively, there may be no future accrual of benefit, although benefits already earned are preserved. Finally, it may be being wound up. The accounting implications of each stage are considered in the following examples:

Example 1 – Plan closed to new employees

Entity A operates a defined benefit plan (which is currently in deficit) for all employees, once they have completed three months' service. Employee turnover is high, but the number of employees covered by the plan has been stable for a number of years.

On 31 December 20X1, entity A decides to close the existing plan to new employees, who will instead be offered a new defined contribution plan. Employee turnover means that the number of employees in the defined benefit plan will diminish as time passes.

Entity A has not committed to reduce the number of employees currently in the defined benefit plan or to change the benefits payable under the plan. Hence, the benefit commitment is unaffected by the closure and the reduction in employees will reflect staff turnover, rather than any action by the entity. Accordingly, the action of closing the plan to new employees does not represent a plan amendment or curtailment as it does not impact the measurement of the defined benefit obligation and, therefore, there will typically be no accounting implications

Example 2 – Benefit accrual ceased

A year later, on 31 December 20X2, the entity changes the terms of the plan. Defined contribution arrangements will apply to all future service. Hence, no further benefits based on final salary will be earned by employees, although the entity will retain its defined benefit obligation in connection with prior service. With effect from 1 January 20X3, the entity has no liability in respect of service after that date beyond its annual contributions to the defined contribution plan.

However, benefits earned in respect of this prior service will no longer be based on final salary, but will instead be based on salary as at 31 December 20X2.

At 31 December 20X2, the net pension liability was C10m. The plan's actuary has advised that the net pension liability after the plan amendment is C7m.

Both the cessation of future benefit accrual and the change from final to current salary represent a negative past service cost. Hence, entity A should recognise a gain of C3m when the terms of the plan are amended.

Example 3 – Plan wound up

A year later, on 31 December 20X3, entity A decided to close its defined benefit pension plan. It proposes to make a one off payment which will end its involvement in the plan. The payment will have two elements:

- An amount to cover the deficit in the plan (which remains at C7m).

- A 'risk premium' of C1m to an insurance company to take over the pensions liability and risk so that the plan can be wound up as fully paid.

After making the payments, the entity will have no further obligations in respect of the defined benefit plan and contributions to the defined contribution plan will not be related to the defined benefit plan.

There is no curtailment to account for in the current period, as the members of the plan were no longer earning any benefit. However, as the payment of C8m eliminates all further legal or constructive obligation for the benefits provided under the plan it represents a settlement as defined by IAS 19. The amount paid (C8m) exceeds the deficit in the plan so a settlement loss of C1m will be recognised when the settlement occurs.

Example 4 – Plan wind up requiring approval

As noted above, as of 31 December 20X3, the entity decides to close its defined benefit pension plan. However, in the entity's jurisdiction, approval from a government agency is required to settle a defined benefit plan. The entity has filed the appropriate paperwork to request approval, which is expected, but not merely a formality. The approval process is expected to take up to 18 months.

IAS 19 is clear that the high quality corporate bond rate should be used for discounting post-employment benefit obligations. It is also clear that the term of the corporate bonds should be consistent with the estimated term of the post-employment benefit obligation. [IAS 19 para 83].

Although the expected timing of benefit payment could be viewed as being in 18 months time, (that is, when the entity expects to settle its obligation), the term of the corporate bonds should be consistent with the estimated term of the post-employment benefit obligation, which is still the length of the expected payment stream to employees as currently required under the plan. While the entity began the process to gain approval required to settle the plan, it is not obligated to settle, even if approval is received. Settlement cannot be anticipated. The entity also cannot accelerate the expense by using a rate for a corporate bond of 18 month duration, which is lower than the rate on a long-term corporate bond, to obtain a higher present value for the defined benefit obligation. Furthermore, as noted above, although entity A anticipates a one off payment of C8m to settle its obligations, a settlement loss would not be recognised until the settlement occurs.

11A.241 Sometimes a pension plan may be wound up and replaced by another plan offering similar benefits. Such a situation is recognised by IAS 19, which says that where a plan is terminated and replaced by a new plan that offers benefits that are, in substance, identical, the termination should be treated as neither a curtailment nor a settlement. [IAS 19 para 101].

Example – Plan replaced by a similar plan

Entity A acquired another entity some years ago. Both entities have defined benefit plans, which pay similar pension benefits based on final salary and years of service. Entity A decided to simplify its pension administration by introducing a new pension plan to replace the two existing plans. Each employee's pension entitlement transfers to the new plan, without any change of entitlement.

The replacement of both plans does not amend the previous plans substantially. Employees retain their benefit entitlement.

Remeasurements of the net defined benefit liability (asset)

11A.242 Remeasurements of the net defined benefit liability (asset) comprise:

■ actuarial gains and losses;

■ the return on plan assets excluding amounts included in net interest on the net defined benefit liability (asset) (see para 11A.213); and

■ any changes in the effect of the asset ceiling, excluding amounts included in net interest on the net defined benefit liability (asset)

[IAS 19 para 127].

11A.243 Actuarial gains and losses result from increases or decreases in the present value of the defined benefit obligation because of changes in actuarial assumptions and experience adjustments. Causes of actuarial gains and losses include for example:

■ Experience gains and losses arising where actual events during the year differ from the actuarial assumptions in the previous valuation (for example, unexpectedly high or low rates of employee turnover, early retirement or mortality or of increases in salaries, benefits or medical costs).

■ The effects of changes in actuarial assumptions from one period to the next, for example to reflect increased life expectancies.

■ The effects of changes in the discount rate.

[IAS 19 para 128].

Actuarial gains and losses do not include changes in the present value of the defined benefit obligations because of the introduction, amendment, curtailment or settlement of the defined benefit plan, or changes to the benefits payable under the defined benefit plan. Such changes result in past service costs or gains or losses on settlement. [IAS 19 para 129].

Example – Events causing actuarial gains and losses

- Actual or estimated mortality rates or the proportion of employees taking early retirement will alter the period for which an entity will be required to make benefit payments. For example, accelerating technological change might cause a manufacturer to reduce its workforce gradually by offering early retirement to a number of employees.

- Estimated salaries or benefits will alter the amount of each benefit payment. For example, a software developer might decide to increase its salaries by more than the rate of inflation to retain its skilled work force.

- Estimated employee turnover may for example alter the number of employees that are expected to transfer their benefits to another pension plan. For example, an unexpected change in tax legislation that makes personal pensions more attractive might lead to a greater number of employees leaving defined benefit plans and making their own pension arrangements.

11A.244 In determining the return on plan assets, an entity deducts the costs of managing the plan assets and any tax payable by the plan itself, other than the tax included in the actuarial assumptions used to measure the defined benefit obligation. Other administration costs are not deducted from the return on plan assets. [IAS 19 para 130].

11A.245 Remeasurements should be recognised immediately in full in other comprehensive income (OCI).

11A.246 Many types of gains and losses under IFRS that are recognised outside profit and loss are reclassified to the income statement in a later period. However, it is not always the case. For example, revaluation gains and losses on property, plant and equipment are not recycled. Similarly, IAS 19 is clear that actuarial gains and losses that have been recognised directly in other comprehensive income should not be recognised in the income statement in a subsequent period. [IAS 19 para 122].

Deficit reduction schemes

11A.247 Given the size and volatility of defined benefit obligations, many entities that operate defined benefit plans have explored ways to reduce their exposure to such obligations and volatility. Such actions are typically aimed at reducing the liability on the balance sheet, removing volatility from both the balance sheet and from reported profit or loss, or some combination thereof. Arrangements required to achieve these aims will usually result in a curtailment, settlement or other one-off charge to report through profit or loss.

UK 11A.247.1 In the UK typical examples of deficit reduction schemes are:

- Buy-out schemes, where the entire defined benefit obligation, its risks, rewards and costs are eliminated in return for an insurance company or similar entity taking full responsibility for all benefits payable under the plan. Typically, buy-out schemes involve closure of plans to new members and cessation of accrual of future benefits. In these types of circumstances, there will normally be a settlement or curtailment gain or loss reported through the income statement.

■ Buy-in schemes, where an insurance company undertakes to 'track' the liability with an insurance policy that exactly matches the liability, thereby enabling full netting of the liability being tracked. [IAS 19, para 119]. This may result in a curtailment gain or loss depending on the circumstances, but will not be a settlement, since the reporting entity retains ultimate responsibility for funding the plan.

■ Schemes where plan members are encouraged to allow assignment of the members' benefits to a third party, which then assumes all the risks and rewards of the plan. Once the risks and rewards have been removed from the reporting entity's balance sheet, the third party will typically seek to limit its exposure by offering a cash incentive to encourage plan members to take out personal pensions, hence putting all future risks on to the members. Depending on the precise arrangements, this is likely to lead to a settlement (or at least a partial settlement) for the reporting entity.

■ For pensions in payment, a cash incentive to members to move from an inflation linked pension (such as C1,000 each year, increasing by a percentage linked to an inflation index) to a pension of C1,500 each year, fixed at C1,500 for the remaining life of the member. The cost of providing the incentive will be recognised as a negative past service cost in profit or loss in the period in which it is incurred. The future cost of providing the pension to members will reduce as a result, because the actuarial calculation will no longer include inflation assumptions: the amount is now fixed in monetary terms for the rest of the member's life.

Presentation

11A.248 Where an entity operates more than one plan, some plans may be in surplus and some may be in deficit. Where this is the case, aggregate amounts of net defined benefit assets and net defined benefit liabilities (which include any unfunded benefits) should be shown separately on the face of the balance sheet. IAS 19 does not permit a net asset in respect of one plan and a net liability in respect of another to be netted off in arriving at the amounts to be presented on the face of the balance sheet, unless the entity:

■ has a legally enforceable right to use a surplus in one plan to settle obligations under the other plan; and

■ intends either to settle the obligations on a net basis, or to realise the surplus in one plan and settle its obligation under the other plan simultaneously.

[IAS 19 para 131].

These criteria are similar to those in paragraph 42 of IAS 32 (see chapter 6).

> **Example – Offset of pension plan balances in different plans**
>
> Entity A operates four defined benefit schemes, two in Bermuda and one each in Switzerland and the United States. The plans in each country are separate and administered by independent trustees.
>
> One of the Bermuda plans covers management grade staff and the other is for manufacturing staff. Strong investment performance means that the management plan has a substantial surplus. Benefit enhancements in connection with a redundancy programme caused a deficit in the manufacturing plan. The same trustees administer the two plans. The trustees have agreed that entity A can use the surplus in the management plan to cover the deficit in the manufacturing plan, subject to granting certain benefit enhancements to management. Entity A will arrange for the trustees to transfer assets from one plan to the other.
>
> The balance sheet position under IAS 19 for each scheme at the end of the year is as follows:
>
> | | |
> |---|---|
> | Switzerland | Liabilities of C100 |
> | Bermuda (manufacturing) | Liabilities of C150 |
> | Bermuda (management, after deducting C50 benefit enhancements) | Assets of C300 |
> | United States | Assets of C50 |
>
> Entity A offsets assets of C300 in the Bermuda management plan with liabilities of C150 in the Bermuda manufacturing plan. Entity A has a legally enforceable right of offset because of its agreement with the trustees, and plans to transfer assets from one plan to the other.
>
> Entity A should present a net pension asset of C200 (C50 in the United States plus C150, being the net asset in the Bermuda management plan after deducting the benefit enhancements and the payment to the manufacturing plan) and a net pension liability of C100 in the Swiss plan.

11A.249　A consequence of the netting off criterion is that at least some of the footnote disclosures have to be disaggregated into plans that have given rise to assets in the balance sheet and plans that have given rise to liabilities. This is necessary, for example, in order to comply with the requirement to reconcile plan surpluses or deficits to balance sheet assets and liabilities (see para 11A.254). To comply with that reconciliation requirement, say where there is an irrecoverable surplus, the following would have to be disclosed as a minimum, but a further breakdown of the total assets and liabilities may also be necessary for a proper understanding of the net position.

	C	C	C
Total plans' assets	400		
Total plans' liabilities	380		
Net surpluses	20		

Comprising:	Surplus not recoverable	Net pension asset (liability)
Surpluses		
	50	(10)	40
Deficits	(30)		(30)
	20	(10)	10

11A.250 IAS 1 requires that assets and liabilities should be categorised as current or non-current, unless a presentation based on liquidity provides information that is reliable and more relevant. [IAS 1 para 60]. IAS 1 specifies that regardless of which method of presentation is adopted, for each line item that combines amounts expected to be recovered or settled within 12 months and amounts to be recovered or settled after more than 12 months there should be separate disclosure of the latter. [IAS 1 para 61]. However, IAS 19 does not specifically require an entity to distinguish the current and non-current portions of the net pension asset or liability, because the IASB believes that such a distinction may sometimes be arbitrary and far from straightforward to prepare. [IAS 19 paras 133, BC200]. This is particularly the case for funded pension plans, where the funded status of the plan to be reflected in the statement of financial position reflects the net of plan assets and liabilities. As a result, for funded plans the net plan asset or liability is generally presented as a single non-current item.

11A.251 In some circumstances, an entity may be able to make a reliable distinction between current and non-current, for example, where the actuary provides the information for an unfunded plan, or where there is an agreed refund receivable within the next 12 months. In such circumstances, separate presentation of these balances would be appropriate.

11A.252 As regards the income statement, IAS 19 specifies that an entity should recognise the following components of defined benefit cost, within profit and loss for the period except to the extent that another IFRS requires or permits their inclusion in the cost of an asset:

■ Service cost

■ Net interest on the net defined benefit liability (asset).

[IAS 19 para 120].

Disclosure

11A.253 IAS 19 contains extensive disclosure requirements in respect of defined benefit pension plans. An entity shall assess whether the disclosures should be disaggregated to distinguish plans or groups of plans with materially different risks. For example, an entity may disaggregate disclosure about plans showing one or more of the following features, although other groupings are permissible:

■ Different geographical locations.

■ Different characteristics such as flat salary pension plans, final salary pension plans or post-employment medical plans.

■ Different regulatory environments.

■ Different reporting segments.

■ Different funding arrangements (for example, wholly unfunded, wholly or partly funded).

[IAS 19 para 138].

When an entity provides disclosure for a grouping of plans, disclosure of significant actuarial assumptions is provided in the form of weighted averages or of relatively narrow ranges. [IAS 19 para 144]. It follows that any assumptions outside those narrow ranges should be disclosed separately.

11A.254 The disclosure required in respect of a defined benefit pension plan includes the following:

■ A general description of the type of plan, including the nature of the benefits provided, a description of the regulatory framework in which the plan operates and a description of any other entity's responsibilities for the plan. Such a description distinguishes, for example, average salary pension plans from final salary pension plans and from post-employment medical plans. It should also describe any informal practices that give rise to constructive obligations (see further para 11A.120). [IAS 19 para 139].

■ A description of the risks to which the plan exposes the entity, focused on any unusual, entity-specific or plan-specific risks, and of any significant concentrations of risk. [IAS 19 para 139].

■ The entity should disclose information that:

  ■ explains the characteristics of its defined benefit plans and risks associated with them;

  ■ identifies and explains the amounts in its financial statements arising from its defined benefit plans; and

  ■ describes how its defined benefit plans may affect the amount, timing and uncertainty of the entity's future cash flows.

[IAS 19 para BC213].

- When disclosing this information, the entity should consider the level of detail and emphasis required for each requirement, how much aggregation or disaggregation to undertake and any further information that may be useful to users of the financial statements. [IAS 19 para 136].

- In order to adequately meet the disclosure requirements above, the entity should disclose additional information as necessary. For example, the entity may present the present value of the defined benefit obligation in a manner that distinguishes the nature, characteristics and risks of the obligation. Such disclosure could distinguish between:

  - amounts owing to active members, deferred members, and pensioners;

  - vested benefits and accrued but not vested benefits; and

  - conditional benefits, amounts attributable to future salary increases and other benefits.

[IAS 19 para 137].

- A description of any plan amendments, curtailments or settlements. However, IAS 19 does not require an entity to distinguish between plan amendments, curtailments and settlements if they occur together.

[IAS 19 para BC220].

- The significant actuarial assumptions (in absolute terms, not just as a margin between different percentages or other variables (for example, equity risk premium)) used as at the balance sheet date to determine the present value of the defined benefit obligation, including, for example:

  - Discount rates.

  - Expected rates of salary increases (and of changes in an index or other variable specified in the formal or constructive terms of a plan as the basis for future benefit increases).

  - Medical cost trend rates.

  - Mortality.

[IAS 19 para 144].

- The effect of changes in demographic assumptions should be disclosed separately from the effect of changes in financial assumptions. [IAS 19 para BC219].

- Reconciliations of the opening and closing balance of the present value of the defined benefit asset or liability, defined benefit obligation, plan assets, the effect of any asset ceiling and any reimbursement rights, showing separately, if applicable, the effects attributable to each of the following:

  - Current service cost.

  - Interest income or expense.

- Remeasurements of the net defined benefit liability (asset), showing separately:

  - The return on plan assets, excluding amounts included in interest income or expense.

  - Actuarial gains and losses arising from changes in demographic or financial assumptions.

  - Changes in the effect of limiting a net defined benefit asset to the asset ceiling, excluding amounts included in interest income or expense,

  Also the entity should disclose how it determined the maximum benefit available.

- Past service cost and gains and losses arising from settlements.

- Foreign currency translation differences.

- Contributions to the plan, showing separately those by the employer and by plan participants.

- Benefits paid, showing separately the amount paid in respect if any settlements.

- Business combinations and disposals.

- Other items, including experience gains and losses (possibly split between those based in demographic assumptions and those based on financial assumptions), contributions from parties other than the employer or participants, for example, governments and plan administration expenses.

[IAS 19 paras 140, 141].

- The entity should disaggregate the fair value of the plan assets into classes that distinguish the nature and risks of those assets, subdividing each class of plan asset into those that have a quoted market price in an active market (as defined in IFRS 13 if adopted, otherwise the entity should refer to paragraph AG71 of IAS 39 or paragraph B.5.4.3 of IFRS 9 if applicable) and those that do not. For example, an entity could distinguish between:

  - cash and cash equivalents;

  - equity instruments (segregated by industry type, company size, geography etc);

  - debt instruments (segregated by type of issuer, credit quality, geography etc);

  - real estate (segregated by geography etc);

  - derivatives (segregated by type of underlying risk in the contract, for example, interest rate contracts, foreign exchange contracts, equity contracts, credit contracts etc);

- investment funds (segregated by type of fund);

- asset-backed securities; and

- structured debt.

[IAS 19 para 142].

- The entity should disclose the fair value of its own transferable financial instruments held as plan assets, and the fair value of plan assets that are property occupied by, or other assets used by, the entity. [IAS 19 para 143].

- The entity should disclose:

  - A sensitivity analysis for each significant actuarial assumption (as disclosed under para 144) as of the end of the reporting period, showing how the defined benefit obligation would have been affected by changes in the relevant actuarial assumption that were reasonably possible at that date.

  - The methods and assumptions used in preparing the sensitivity analyses and the limitations of those methods.

  - Changes from the previous period in the methods and assumptions used in preparing the sensitivity analyses, and the reasons for such changes.

  [IAS 19 para 145].

  For the purposes of this disclosure, all other assumptions should be held constant.

- The entity should disclose a description of any asset-liability matching strategies used by the plan or the entity, including the use of annuities and other techniques, such as longevity swaps, to manage risk.

- The entity should provide an indication of the effect of the defined benefit plan on the entity's future cash flows, disclosing:

  - A description of any funding arrangements and funding policy that affect future contributions.

  - The expected contributions to the plan for the next annual reporting period.

  - Information about the maturity profile of the defined benefit obligation, including the weighted average duration of the defined benefit obligation.

11A.255 Some companies disclose expected rates of pension increases and the average remaining working life of employees, but there are other assumptions that could have a material impact on the measurement of the defined benefit obligation. Examples include mortality rates (almost certainly material for most companies providing pension benefits) and employee turnover. Disclosure would include average life expectancies or the name of the mortality tables used. In addition, IAS 1 requires disclosure of *"the sensitivity of carrying amounts to the methods, assumptions and estimates underlying their calculation, including the reasons for the sensitivity"*. [IAS 1 para 129(b)]. An indication of the sensitivity of the pension obligation to changes in these assumptions would satisfy IAS 1 requirements and enable users to understand *"the characteristics of its defined benefit plans and the risks associated with them"*. [IAS 19 para 135]. IFRIC 14 further suggests that disclosure should be given of any restrictions on the current realisability of a surplus, as well as the basis used to determine any economic benefit available in the form of a refund or future reduction in contributions. [IFRIC 14 para 10].

11A.256   Where a multi-employer defined benefit plan is accounted for as if it were a defined contribution plan (see para 11A.81), IAS 19 requires disclosure of the following:

- The fact that the plan is a defined benefit plan.

- A description of the funding arrangements, including method used to determined the entity's rate of contributions and any minimum funding requirements.

- A description of the extent to which the entity can be liable to the plan for other entities' obligations under the terms and conditions of the multi-employer plan.

- A description of any agreed allocation of a deficit or surplus on:

  - wind-up of the plan; or

  - the entity's withdrawal from the plan

- The reason why sufficient information is not available to enable the entity to account for the plan as a defined benefit plan.

- To the extent that a surplus or deficit in the plan may affect the amount of future contributions:

  - any available information about that surplus or deficit;

  - an indication of the level of participation of the entity in the plan compared with other participating entities;

  - the basis used to determine that surplus or deficit; and

  - the implications, if any, for the entity.

[IAS 19 paras 148].

11A.257   An example of disclosure by a company that participates in a multi-employer plan is presented in Table 11A.5 below.

Table 11A.5 – Multi-employer plan

Nobel Biocare Holding AG – annual report – 31 December 2011

21 Employee benefits (extract)

The Group has a Swedish multi-employer pension plan that should be accounted for as a defined benefit plan. The Swedish plan primarily covers the following benefits:

Retirement pension
– ITPK (complementary occupational pension)
– Disability pension
– Group family pension

Virtually every clerical employee in the private sector in Sweden is covered by such a plan. The plan is financed by employers, who determine whether the pension insurance is with Alecta (Alecta Pensionsförsäkring, Ömsesidigt), or alternatively, as regards retirement pension and ITPK, whether a provision is to be made in-house by companies within the framework of the FPG/PRI system. The Group has elected to take out pension insurance with Alecta.

Irrespective of how the plan is financed – via pension insurance with Alecta or through in-house provisions by companies – the plan is a defined benefit scheme with respect to retirement pensions and group family pensions. Paid pensions are related to the employee's final salary and the total employment period covered by the plan. This means that the Group should report its proportional share of the defined benefit commitments, and the assets under management and expenses associated with the plan in the same manner as any other defined benefit plan, and provide the information required for such plans.

Alecta, however, is unable to provide sufficient information to report the Group's proportional share of the defined benefit commitments, the assets under management and expenses associated with the plan. There is also no agreement on how any surplus or deficit should be distributed to the participants in the pension plan. As a result, and in line with the Swedish Financial Accounting Standards Council's Emerging Issues Task Force, the scheme is reported as a defined contribution plan. Accordingly, the Group cannot provide the disclosure requirements with respect to the defined benefit plan in Sweden.

11A.258   IAS 19 requires that the guidance in IAS 37 regarding the recognition and measurement of contingent liabilities is applied in respect of any withdrawal or winding-up liability that may arise from participation in a multi-employer plan. However, the disclosure requirements in IAS 19 rather than IAS 37 should be followed.

11A.259   Where an entity participates in a defined benefit plan that shares risks between various entities under common control, such as a group plan, the following disclosure should be made in the entity's separate or individual financial statements:

■   The contractual agreement or stated policy for charging the net defined benefit cost or the fact that there is no such policy.

■   The policy for determining the contribution to be paid by the entity.

■   If the entity accounts for the contribution payable for the period in accordance with paragraph 41 of IAS 19 (see para 11A.84), the following information about the plan as a whole. If specified conditions are met, this information may be disclosed by cross-reference to disclosures in another group entity's financial statements.

- A general description of the type of plan, its characteristics and associated risks as outlined in paragraph 11A.254 above.

- Further analysis of plan assets, comprising the percentage invested in each major category of plan asset at the balance sheet date.

- The principal actuarial assumptions used as at the balance sheet date.

- A description of any funding arrangements and funding policy that affect future contributions

- The contributions expected to be paid to the plan during the annual period beginning after the balance sheet date.

[IAS 19 paras 42, 149, 150].

11A.260   IAS 24 provides that a post-employment benefit plan established for the benefit of an entity's employees is a related party of the entity. [IAS 24 para 9]. Hence, transactions between an entity and its pension plan fall within the scope of IAS 24. IAS 24 also contains a requirement to disclose compensation payable to key management personnel, which comprises all employee benefits as defined in IAS 19, together with share-based payments as dealt with in IFRS 2. [IAS 24 para 17]. The requirements of IAS 24 are discussed further in chapter 29.

UK.11A.260.1   IAS 19 does not deal with the disclosure of directors' emoluments. Disclosure requirements for directors' emoluments are contained in Schedule 5 and Schedule 8 to SI 2008/410 of the Companies Act 2006 and in the Listing Rules. Details of these requirements are covered in chapter 5 of the Manual of Accounting – Narrative reporting.

11A.261   In addition to the information disclosed in connection with participation in a multi-employer plan (see para 11A.256), IAS 37 may require disclosure of contingent liabilities arising from other post-employment benefit obligations. [IAS 19 para 152]. The requirements of IAS 37 are discussed further in chapter 21.

Companies Act 2006 requirements

UK.11A.262   The Companies Act 2006 contains no specific accounting requirements regarding employee benefits. There are, however, extensive disclosure requirements for salaries, bonuses, pensions and other benefits payable to directors. Details of these requirements are covered in chapter 5 of the Manual of Accounting – Narrative Reporting.

UK.11A.263   The Act contains a requirement for disclosure of the following in respect of all persons employed by a company during the financial year:

Employee benefits (IAS 19 revised)

- Wages and salaries paid or payable in respect of that year to those persons.

- Social security costs incurred by the company on their behalf.

- Other pension costs so incurred.

[CA06 Sec 411(5)].

UK.11A.264 In addition, a UK company that has securities carrying voting rights admitted to trading on a regulated market at the end of its financial year is required to disclose, in its directors' report, details of any agreement with employees (including directors) of the company providing for compensation for loss of office on the takeover of the company. [SI 2008/410 7 Sch 13(2)(k)]. See further chapter 2 of the Manual of Accounting – Narrative Reporting.

Impact on distributable profits

UK.11A.265 International Financial Reporting Standards do not concern themselves with the determination of distributable profits. Such matters are dealt with in national law (and are considered in greater detail in chapter 23). The ICAEW and the ICAS guidance on distributable profits, Tech 02/10, 'Guidance on the determination of realised profits and losses in the context of distributions under the Companies Act 2006' includes the impact of retirement benefit plans on distributable reserves. This guidance is considered in more detail below.

UK.11A.266 For defined contribution plans, the cost charged to the income statement, which is equal to the contributions payable in the period, is a realised loss. Similarly, where multi-employer plans are treated as defined contribution, the income statement charge is a realised loss.

UK.11A.267 The Companies Act defines a company's distributable profits not in terms of its assets and liabilities, but as its accumulated, realised profits less its accumulated, realised losses. [CA06 Sec 830 (2)(3)]. It is the cumulative gain or loss credited or debited to reserves in respect of a pension plan (whether through the income statement or other comprehensive income), rather than the existence of a surplus or deficit, that affects realised profits. The impact on reserves is not usually the same as the pension surplus or deficit due to net contributions paid into the scheme and any asset or liability introduced as the result of a business combination. This is illustrated in the following examples.

Example – Immediate recognition of actuarial gains and losses

Company A established a new defined benefit pension plan at the beginning of 20X5. Its accounting policy is to recognise all actuarial gains and losses in the income statement in the year in which they arise. During 20X5 there is a net pension expense of £4m, but contributions to the plan amount to £5m. Hence, at the end of 20X5 there is a surplus in the plan, and an asset on the balance sheet, of

£1m (both taxation and questions over recoverability of the asset are ignored for the purpose of this example). However, the impact on distributable profits is not a credit of £1m, as represented by the surplus in the plan, but a debit of £4m in respect of the net pension expense. Considered another way, the impact on reserves is derived by deducting the contributions to the plan from the surplus.

UK.11A.268   It is necessary to determine whether an adjustment to reserves is required to arrive at the amount of distributable profits. Firstly it is necessary to identify the cumulative net gain or loss taken to reserves in respect of the pension surplus or deficit, and secondly to establish the extent to which the gain or loss is realised.

- No adjustment is required if a net cumulative debit or loss has been taken to reserves: this represents a realised loss as it results from the creation of, or increase in a provision for a liability or a loss resulting in an overall reduction in net assets.

- A cumulative net credit or gain in reserves is a realised profit only to the extent that it is represented by an asset to be recovered by agreed refunds in the form of qualifying consideration (as defined in Tech 02/10). Any further cumulative net credit (in excess of agreed refunds) is not qualifying consideration so is treated as unrealised, although it will become realised in subsequent periods to the extent that it offsets subsequent net debits to reserves that are treated as realised losses.

Tech 02/10 Appendix 4 includes a worked example for a company with a surplus at the year-end.

UK.11A.269   Where an entity operates more than one defined benefit plan, it should assess the impact of a surplus or deficit on its distributable profits separately for each plan. In other words, plans should not be aggregated or offset to reach a single net realised profit or loss, unless two plans are to merge and the trustees have irrevocably agreed to the offset of the surplus and deficit.

UK.11A.270   The deferred tax impact of pension accounting generally relates to the pension asset or liability and not the cumulative net debit or credit in reserves. A cumulative debit in respect of a deferred tax liability is a realised loss, and a cumulative credit in respect of a deferred tax asset is an unrealised profit. However, where there is an unrealised cumulative net credit in respect of a pension asset, a deferred tax debit is offset against that unrealised profit. Similarly, where there is a realised cumulative net debit in respect of a pension liability, a deferred tax credit is offset against that realised loss.

Pensions Act 2004 implications

UK.11A.271   The Pensions Act 2004, published in November 2004, is a significant piece of legislation and was followed by a web of supporting regulations, codes of practice and other guidance, much of which came into force from April 2005.

UK.11A.272   From an accounting perspective, the most significant provisions of the Pensions Act 2004 are in the following areas:

- The launch of the Pension Protection Fund (see para UK.11A.274 onwards).

- Increased powers to the new Pension Regulator (see para UK.11A.277 onwards).

- Revised rules for employers ceasing to participate in a pension plan (see para UK.11A.284 onwards).

UK.11A.273   The following paragraphs summarise only the main accounting implications of the new legislation and do not attempt to explore the rules in detail.

The Pension Protection Fund (PPF)

UK.11A.274   The Pension Protection Fund (PPF), which came into force from April 2005, is designed to protect pension plan members in the event that the sponsoring employer becomes insolvent. Broadly, the PPF will fund current pensions in payment as well as up to 90% of the benefits of active and deferred plan members when an 'insolvency event' occurs. The term 'insolvency event' encompasses the administration, administrative receivership or liquidation of the sponsoring employer.

UK.11A.275   The PPF is funded in part by the assets of the plans it takes over and in part by a levy on all plans covered by the PPF. The pension protection levy is charged annually; the levy year runs from 1 April to 31 March. Initially, the levy was based on factors related to plan size (number of members, value of liabilities, etc). From 2006/7 the PPF levy is divided into two parts: The scheme-based element, which makes up 20% of the total levy, is based on a scheme's liabilities to members on a section 179 basis. The risk-based element, which makes up 80% of the levy, takes into account funding levels (the worst funded plans pay a higher levy) and the likelihood of the employer's insolvency (the lower a company's Dun & Bradstreet rating, the higher the levy). From 2012/13 the way the PPF levy is calculated will change significantly. It is intended that the revised methodology and levy parameters will be fixed for three years until 2015. Under the new methodology, the funding levels will be assessed on smoothed assumptions (5 year average yields) so that sharp movements in financial markets will have less effect on the risk-based element. The risk-based element will take into account the investment risk of a scheme's portfolio of assets (the riskier the investment strategy the higher the levy). The method for allowing for insolvency risk of employers will change; the measure of insolvency risk will be averaged over 12 months (rather than at a single date) and employers will be divided into 10 rather than 100 risk bands.

UK.11A.276 The PPF levy can represent a significant cost of maintaining a defined benefit pension plan. It does not seem appropriate to consider the levy to be an additional cost of providing benefit to any plan member or group of members. Rather, the levy relates to the plan as a whole and could be considered analogous to a tax or an administration expense. IAS 19 states that the return on plan assets should be stated net of any taxes payable by the plan itself, whereas, administration expenses are not deducted from the return on plan assets [IAS 19 para 130].

The Pensions Regulator

UK.11A.277 The Pensions Regulator replaced the previous regulator (OPRA), inheriting all of its powers and functions along with several new powers. In our view, there are two areas in which the regulatory regime may influence the financial statements:

- The 'moral hazard' provisions (see para UK.11A.278 onwards).
- The 'statutory funding objective' (see para UK.11A.280 onwards).

The 'moral hazard' provisions

UK.11A.278 The 'moral hazard' provisions in the Pensions Act are designed to prevent employers from re-arranging their affairs so as to avoid their pension obligations. The provisions permit the regulator to impose:

- Contribution notices on people that have been party to an act, or a deliberate failure to act, aimed at avoiding pension obligations.

- Financial support directions on associated or connected parties where the employer is either 'insufficiently resourced' or a service company (that is, a company the turnover of which is solely or principally derived from amounts charged for the provision of employee services to other group members). A financial support direction is a requirement to put financial support in place within a specified time period and to ensure that that support remains in place while the plan is in existence.

- Restoration orders, where the regulator is of the opinion that a transaction has been made at undervalue. Such orders require that a pension plan's financial position is restored to its pre-transaction position.

UK.11A.279 The existence of these powers could influence the judgement of whether a plan should be treated as defined contribution or defined benefit as they may indicate that an entity could have an obligation to provide funding where one was not thought to exist previously. It will also be necessary to determine whether the risk that the regulator may impose a notice represents a contingent liability (see further chapter 21).

The 'statutory funding objective'

UK.11A.280 With effect from September 2005, the previous minimum funding requirement (MFR) was replaced by a statutory funding objective (SFO). This means that all defined benefit plans have to have 'sufficient and appropriate assets' to cover their liabilities. Where a plan has insufficient assets to cover its liabilities, the trustees must establish a recovery plan setting out how the SFO is to be met and over what period. Any failure to do this, or to reach agreement with the employer on a funding strategy for the plan, must be reported to the regulator, who may take any of the following courses of action:

- Modify the plan in relation to future accrual of benefits.
- Fix the period over which a shortfall is to be made up.
- Impose a schedule of contributions.

UK.11A.281 Under the SFO regulations the levels of contributions to defined benefit pension plans have generally increased. However, of greater significance to the financial statements may be the valuation of a plan in wind-up, which is based on the buy-out of all accrued benefits. This makes it more expensive to wind up a pension plan and, taken with the moral hazard provisions described above, almost impossible for a solvent company to walk away from its pension obligations. Employers can become liable to the trustees of a defined benefit plan for a debt if there is a deficit in a defined benefit plan. This can apply on:

- the winding-up of a plan;
- the insolvency of an employer; or
- an employer ceasing participation in a multi-employer plan (which includes 'group pension plans' in IAS 19 terminology – see para UK.11A.287 onwards).

UK.11A.282 In situations where a buy-out valuation exceeds the defined benefit liability recognised under IAS 19, there should be consideration as to whether there ought to be disclosure in the financial statements. The ASB's best practice reporting statement on pension disclosures recommends that where the cost of buying out benefits is made available to trustees (managers) and/or members of defined benefit plans, then the financial statements should also disclose the cost of buying out benefits. [ASB RS para 17].

UK.11A.283 Where there is a funding plan in place, IAS 19 requires disclosure of future contributions. [IAS 19 para 147]. However, in the absence of an agreed funding plan, we consider that there should be disclosure of the potential implications of any action by the regulator. Furthermore, where a plan is in wind-up, we consider that there should be disclosure of the fact that the buy-out obligation exceeds amounts recognised under IAS 19. In some circumstances, it may be appropriate to recognise these additional obligations.

Employers ceasing to participate in a pension scheme

UK.11A.284 For a single-employer pension scheme, section 75 of the Pensions Act 1995 (as amended by the Pensions Act 2004) ensures that a debt can be placed on the pension scheme's sponsoring employer if the value of the scheme's assets is less than its liabilities. The debt is triggered if:

■ the scheme winds-up; or

■ on a relevant event (for example, the employer becomes insolvent).

UK.11A.285 Section 75A was inserted into the Pensions Act 1995 by the Pensions Act 2004 to modify the existing section 75 as it applies to multi-employer schemes (see para UK.11A.287). For these schemes, the debt is triggered if:

■ the scheme winds-up;

■ on a relevant event (for example, insolvency) for any one or more companies; or

■ on a withdrawal of an individual employer from a multi-employer scheme (referred to as an 'employment-cessation event').

UK.11A.286 When an employer ceases to participate in a defined benefit multi-employer scheme, whilst other employers continue to participate, the departing employer will normally be liable to pay their 'section 75 debt' – their share of the pension scheme's liabilities calculated on a 'buy-out basis' (that is, the full cost of securing its liabilities with annuities, including an estimate of expenses) (see para UK.11A.289 below). There six prescribed ways in which an employer departing from a multi-employer scheme can have its section 75 debt reduced or removed (see paras UK.11A.293 and UK.11A.294 below).

UK.11A.287 A multi-employer scheme is a scheme in relation to which more than one employer is exposed to the scheme. 'Employer' in relation to an occupational pension scheme, means the employer of persons in the description or category of employment to which the scheme in question relates. Multi-employer schemes do not include, for the purposes of the section 75 rules, sectionalised schemes where:

■ contributions payable by an employer are allocated to that employer's section;

- a specified part of the scheme's assets is attributable to each section and cannot be used for any other section; and

- there is only one employer in each section.

In such cases, section 75 will apply as if each section of the scheme were a separate scheme.

UK.11A.288 A liability is triggered when an 'employment-cessation event' occurs. In general, this event takes place when a participating employer ceases to have any employees who are members of the scheme and at least one participating employer remains. This could occur if:

- A company leaves the corporate group and, therefore, ceases to be a participating employer in the pension scheme.

- A company's business is sold, leaving it with no remaining employees.

- A company ceases to be employer of any individuals who are active members of the scheme (for example, a group restructuring).

- A company's employees cease employment through redundancy or resignation.

- Future accruals cease for that company.

This is a complex area and professional advice is likely to be needed.

UK.11A.289 When an 'employment-cessation event' occurs, part of the total deficit in a multi-employer scheme has to be attributed to the withdrawing employer. The attribution is by reference to the position at the date that the employer ceases to participate in the scheme. The total deficit is calculated on a buy-out basis (that is, based on the full cost of securing the scheme's liabilities with annuities, including an estimate of expenses). The total deficit is attributed to the participating employers according to the scheme's trust deed and rules, but if the rules are silent then the method for calculating the liability share for each employer is detailed in the Employer Debt Regulations.

UK.11A.290 Under the legislation, the amount of the employer's debt is:

- the proportion of the buy-out deficit that is attributable to employment with that employer; and

- the expenses attributable to the employer ceasing to participate.

UK.11A.291 Depending on what is set out in the scheme's own trust deed and rules, the withdrawing employer has to pay not only the buy-out deficit attributable to its own employees, but also a share of the orphan liabilities. 'Orphan liabilities' are material liabilities that are attributable to companies that have already left the scheme, including any liabilities that cannot be attributed specifically to any of the remaining employers. Unless the scheme rules state otherwise, the other employers share any exposure relating to these liabilities.

UK.11A.292 In simplified terms, the liability of the withdrawing employer is calculated as follows:

buy-out liabilities for withdrawing employer

$$\frac{\text{buy-out liabilities for withdrawing employer}}{\text{buy-out liabilities for withdrawing employer + remaining employers}} \times \text{buy-out deficit for the scheme}$$

UK.11A.293 Under the amendments to the Employer Debt Regulations, from April 2010, there are two mechanisms which allow an employer to depart without becoming liable for the section 75 debt where there is a corporate restructuring event involving one departing and one receiving employer:

■ *de minimis restructuring test* – where trustees are satisfied that the amount of the departing employer's liabilities is minimal; and

■ *restructuring test* – where trustees are satisfied that there is no weakening of the employer covenant supporting the pension scheme.

UK.11A.294 There are four mechanisms that allow the employer to depart from the scheme having paid a modified section 75 debt (subject to agreement by the trustees and all the affected employers):

■ *Scheme apportionment arrangement* – where the departing employer pays a specified amount that is different from their section 75 debt and, if the amount is lower, the difference is apportioned to one or more of the remaining employers.

■ *Withdrawal arrangement* – where the departing employer pays an amount that is less than their section 75 debt (but more than their share of the deficit calculated on the technical provision basis and the difference is guaranteed by one or more guarantors.

■ *Approved withdrawal arrangement* – where the departing employer pays an amount that is less than their share of the deficit calculated on the technical provision basis and the difference is guaranteed by one or more guarantors. This type of arrangement must be approved by the Pension Regulator.

■ *Regulated apportionment arrangement* – this modifies the departing employer's section 75 debt so that it is greater or less than its liability share. If less, the difference is apportioned to one or more of the remaining employers. This type of arrangement is only available where the scheme is in a PPF assessment period.

Accounting treatment

UK.11A.295   As noted in paragraph UK.11A.285, a situation that will trigger measurement of the defined benefit obligation on a buy-out basis is where a participating employer ceases to participate in a multi-employer scheme. This may typically arise within group pension plans where, for example, a subsidiary within a group is sold. Such an event will trigger a debt on the participating employer, being the amount of the employer's defined benefit pension obligation measured on a buy-out basis, under section 75 of the Pensions Act 1995. In the case where the employer ceases participation in the plan, payment of the section 75 debt equates to a settlement event having the effect of extinguishing the participating employer's share of the plan liabilities (see para 11A.232). The examples below illustrate this further. For the purpose of these examples it is assumed that no withdrawal arrangements deferring payment of part of the debt (see para UK.11A.293) are entered into.

> **Example 1 – Section 75 payment made by withdrawing employer**
>
> Entity B is wholly-owned by entity A. The employees of entity B participate in the group A defined benefit pension plan (other entities owned by entity A, as well as entity A itself also participate in this plan). There is a stated policy for charging the net defined benefit cost for the plan as a whole to the participating entities, such that defined benefit accounting is applied in each entity's financial statements (see para UK.11A.84), with actuarial gains and losses recognised in other comprehensive income. Entity A subsequently sells entity B to a third party purchaser.
>
> Following the disposal of entity B, the employees of entity B remain in the group A pension plan as deferred members. Entity A now assumes responsibility for any liabilities arising in respect of these deferred members. Nevertheless, as entity B itself is ceasing to participate in the group A pension plan, this is determined to trigger a section 75 payment.
>
> The group A pension plan is in deficit at the time of the disposal and the share of the deficit relating to entity B's employees (measured on an IAS 19 basis) amounts to £5m. On a buy-out basis, the share of the deficit relating to entity B's employees is £9m (being the value of the section 75 payment). Following the section 75 payment, a surplus of £4m under IAS 19 arises on entity B's share of the plan. All entities in entity A have a year end date of 31 December 20X6 and by this date, the disposal and section 75 payment have occurred.
>
> In entity B's individual financial statements, a settlement loss of £4m is recognised (see para 11A.232) as entity B has ceased to participate in the group A pension plan and entity B's liability in respect of the pension plan has been extinguished (through transfer of the obligation to entity A). The settlement loss of £4m reflects the fact that entity B had to make a payment of £9m (being the section 75 payment) in order to exit the group A pension plan where the deficit attributable to entity B's employees, previously recognised and measured on an IAS 19 basis, was £5m.

In entity A's consolidated financial statements, no settlement loss is recognised as, whilst entity B has ceased to participate in the plan, entity B's employees still remain in the plan, albeit as deferred members. Hence, from the perspective of the group, the liabilities associated with entity B's employees (£5m) have not been extinguished and the section 75 payment (£9m) will increase plan assets, resulting in a surplus for this part of the plan of £4m. In addition, a curtailment gain may arise as entity B's employees are now deferred members resulting in a reduction in their future benefit entitlement (see para 11.252).

Furthermore, as defined benefit accounting is applied at an entity level, the surplus of £4m in respect of entity B's employees needs to be allocated to the participating employers. As entity A has assumed responsibility for any liabilities relating to the deferred members, it would appear reasonable for the £4m surplus to be allocated to entity A. It will be recognised in entity A's separate financial statements if it meets the criteria in paragraphs 64 to 65 of IAS 19 (see para 11A.187 onwards) and in IFRIC 14. The basic rule is that the amount of surplus recognised as an asset should not exceed the present value of any economic benefits available in the form of refunds from the plan or reductions in future contributions to the plan. If the surplus is recognised in entity A's separate financial statements, it will be included as part of the calculation of profit or loss on disposal of entity B.

The table below summarises the position in respect of entity B's employees (ignoring any curtailment gains):

	entity B (subsidiary) £'m	entity A (parent) £'m	Group £'m
Entity B's deficit as at date of disposal	(5)	–	(5)
Section 75 payment *	9	–	9
Group transfer:			
Settlement loss in entity B	(4)	–	–
Credit (included in profit or loss on disposal of entity B) in entity A	–	4	–
Surplus arising after section 75 payment to group A plan **	–	4	4

* The section 75 payment forms part of the settlement loss calculation in entity B's income statement, but increases plan assets in the group's consolidated financial statements.

** As entity A now assumes responsibility for any liabilities arising in respect of the deferred members, it would recognise the surplus of £4m in its individual financial statements if it meets the recognition criteria in IAS 19 and IFRIC 14.

UK.11A.296 The above example is based on the situation where defined benefit accounting is applied in each entity's financial statements. In some cases, section 75 payments will become payable by entities that do not have an agreement or policy in place for charging the net defined benefit cost and which have, therefore, used defined contribution accounting in their individual financial statements as permitted by paragraph 41 of IAS 19 (see para 11A.83

onwards). In such cases, the settlement loss in the withdrawing employer's individual financial statements will be the amount of the section 75 payment (that is, £9m in the example above). Under defined contribution accounting, there is no deficit previously recognised in the balance sheet and so the loss is recognised on the basis of contributions payable (in this case, the section 75 payment) in the period. Note that where the net defined benefit cost is not allocated to participating entities, the defined benefit obligation is accounted for in full in the sponsoring entity's financial statements. In addition, the consolidated financial statements of entity A will always apply defined benefit accounting.

UK.11A.297 The above example in paragraph UK.11.295 illustrates a relatively straightforward scenario. However, calculation of the section 75 payment often takes time and it may be the case that calculation of the payment is not completed until after the year end date. The following example illustrates this scenario:

Example 2 – Section 75 payment made by withdrawing employer after the year end

The facts are as for example 1 in paragraph UK.11.295 and entity A has taken over responsibility for the deferred members at the balance sheet date, but for administrative reasons entity B has not made the payment at the balance sheet date, as the amount to be paid is only finalised after the balance sheet date (being £9m as in the previous example).

Similar to example 1, in entity B's individual financial statements, a settlement loss of £4m is recognised as entity B has ceased to participate in the group A pension plan (through the transfer of the obligation to entity A). This settlement loss of £4m represents the difference between the section 75 liability of £9m and the deficit, previously recognised and measured on an IAS 19 basis, of £5m. The unpaid section 75 settlement payment is included in creditors in entity B's balance sheet replacing the previously recognised IAS 19 liability. This is consistent with the principles of paragraph 24 of IFRIC 14, which states that to the extent that contributions payable will not be available after they are paid into the plan, the entity should recognise a liability when the obligation arises, which in this case is when entity B leaves the group.

Again, similar to example 1, in entity A's consolidated financial statements, no settlement loss is recognised as, whilst entity B has ceased to participate in the plan, entity B's employees still remain in the plan, albeit as deferred members. Hence, from the perspective of the group, the liabilities associated with entity B's employees (£5m) have not been extinguished. At the balance sheet date, entity B is no longer part of the group and so the creditor for the unpaid section 75 debt (£9m) will not be included in the group's consolidated balance sheet. However, it is taken into account in determining entity B's net assets (which will be net assets excluding pensions less the section 75 creditor) in the calculation of the profit or loss on disposal of entity B and so it has been recognised by the group.

Under paragraph 114 of IAS 19, plan assets exclude unpaid contributions due from the reporting entity to the plan. However, in this case, the section 75 payment is due from entity B, which at the balance sheet date is no longer part of the reporting entity. Further, it is a payment required to be made by legislation and so is an asset receivable by the plan. Therefore, the unpaid section 75 contribution would be shown as part of plan assets, resulting in a surplus of £4m. In addition, a curtailment gain may arise as entity B's employees are now deferred members resulting in a reduction in their future benefit entitlement (see para 11A.69).

Furthermore, as defined benefit accounting is applied at an entity level, the surplus of £4m in respect of entity B's employees needs to be allocated to the participating employers. As entity A has assumed responsibility for any liabilities relating to the deferred members, it would appear reasonable for the £4m surplus to be allocated to entity A. It will be recognised in entity A's individual financial statements if it meets the criteria in paragraphs 64 to 65 of IAS 19 and IFRIC 14 (see further example 1). If the surplus is recognised, it will be included as part of the calculation of profit or loss on disposal of entity B.

The table below summarises the position in respect of entity B's employees (ignoring any curtailment gains):

	Entity B (subsidiary) £'m	Entity A (parent) £'m	Group £'m
Entity B's deficit as at date of disposal	(5)	–	(5)
Unpaid section 75 payment *	9	–	9
Group transfer:			
Settlement loss in entity B	(4)	–	–
Credit (included in profit or loss on disposal of entity B) in entity A	–	4	–
Surplus arising after section 75 amount payable to group A plan **	–	4	4

* Note that the unpaid section 75 payment is recognised as a creditor and forms part of the settlement loss calculation in entity B's individual financial statements. In the consolidated financial statements, the section 75 creditor is taken into account in determining entity B's net assets in the calculation of the profit or loss on disposal of entity B and the debit increases plan assets in the group's consolidated financial statements as explained above.

** As entity A now assumes responsibility for any liabilities arising in respect of the deferred members, it would recognise the surplus of £4m in its individual financial statements if it meets the recognition criteria in IAS 19 (see comments in example 1 above).

UK.11A.298 In the above example, the parent entity has taken over responsibility for the deferred members at the balance sheet date, but the subsidiary has not made the section 75 payment at the balance sheet date for administrative reasons. The situation could be more complicated where the settlement itself has not been finalised at the year end, such that the subsidiary is still responsible for the employees. An entity should recognise gains or losses on the settlement of a defined benefit plan when the settlement occurs. [IAS 19 para 110]. A settlement occurs when an entity enters into a transaction that eliminates all further legal or constructive obligation for part or all of the benefits provided under a defined benefit plan, for example, when a lump-sum cash payment is made to, or on behalf of, plan participants in exchange for their rights to receive specified post-employment benefits. [IAS 19 para 111]. The accounting treatment for settlements that straddle the balance sheet date will depend on the specific circumstances. See further paragraph 11A.231 onwards.

UK.11A.299   The above two examples illustrate the appropriate accounting where the departing employer makes the section 75 payment. Nevertheless, it may be the case that the parent entity agrees to pay the section 75 payment. The accounting impact is considered further in the following example.

Example 3 – Section 75 payment made by the withdrawing employer's parent

The facts are as for example 1 in paragraph UK.11A.295, but entity A agrees to make the £9m section 75 payment. This amount is not repayable by entity B.

In entity B's individual financial statements, a settlement gain of £5m is recognised. As entity B did not make payments in respect of the section 75 debt, but has ceased participation in the plan, the settlement gain of £5m reflects the release of entity B's share of the deficit (previously recognised and measured on an IAS 19 basis).

Similar to example 1, in entity A's consolidated financial statements, no settlement loss is recognised as, whilst entity B has ceased to participate in the plan, entity B's employees still remain in the plan, albeit as deferred members. Hence, from the perspective of the group, the liabilities associated with entity B's employees (£5m) have not been extinguished and the section 75 payment (£9m) will increase plan assets, resulting in a surplus for this part of the plan of £4m.

In entity A's separate financial statements, the £5m deficit (measured on an IAS 19 basis) in respect of the liabilities that entity A has taken over should be recognised, with a corresponding loss in respect of the transfer in the income statement (as part of the calculation of profit or loss on disposal of entity B). The payment of £9m into the plan would be treated as a contribution to the pension plan given that entity A participates in the group A pension plan and has taken over the responsibility for funding the obligation for these deferred members. As such, entity A would increase the value of the plan assets it recognises by £9m, resulting in a surplus of £4m (if the recognition criteria in paragraphs 64 to 65 of IAS 19 and IFRIC 14 are met (see further example 1).

The table below summarises the position in respect of entity B's employees (ignoring any curtailment gains):

	Entity B (subsidiary) £m	Entity A (parent) £m	Group £m
Entity B's deficit as at date of disposal	(5)	–	(5)
Section 75 payment*	–	9	9
Group transfer:			
Settlement gain in entity B	5	–	–
Loss (included in profit or loss on disposal of entity B) in respect of liabilities taken over	–	(5)	–
Surplus arising after section 75 payment to group A plan**	–	4	4

* The section 75 payment increases plan assets recognised in both entity A and in the group's consolidated financial statements.

** As entity A now assumes responsibility for any liabilities arising in respect of the deferred members, it would recognise the surplus of £4m in its separate financial statements if it meets the recognition criteria in IAS 19 and IFRIC 14 (see comments in example 1 above).

UK.11A.300 A further situation that may arise is where there is also a bulk transfer of a subsidiary's share of the scheme into a new scheme. The accounting impact of this situation is considered further in the following examples.

Example 4 – Section 75 payment made by withdrawing employer (+ bulk transfer out)

The facts are as for example 1 in paragraph UK.11A.295 (that is, entity B makes the section 75 payment), but in addition a bulk transfer is made of the assets and liabilities relating to entity B's employees to the pension plan of entity B's new parent. Following the section 75 payment, a surplus of £4m arises on entity B's share of the plan. For the purposes of the bulk transfer of entity B's share of the plan, it is agreed that the value of the surplus to be transferred into the new parent's pension plan will be £3m. It is decided that any surplus remaining after the bulk transfer will be allocated to entity A.

In entity B's individual financial statements, the section 75 payment of £9m (in respect of a recognised deficit of £5m measured on an IAS 19 basis) initially results in a surplus of £4m. Of this, £3m is transferred to a new pension plan and remains on entity B's balance sheet as an asset. The remaining £1m represents a settlement loss as entity B has ceased to participate in the group A pension plan and entity B's liability in respect of that pension plan has been extinguished.

In entity A's consolidated financial statements, a settlement loss of £3m is recognised in respect of the bulk transfer to the new pension plan (as part of the calculation of profit or loss on disposal of entity B), leaving a surplus of £1m in the group A pension plan.

Furthermore, as defined benefit accounting is also applied at an entity level, the remaining surplus of £1m is recognised in entity A's separate financial statements if it meets the criteria in paragraphs 64 to 65 of IAS 19 and IFRIC 14 (see example 1). If the surplus is recognised, it will be included as part of the calculation of profit or loss on disposal of entity B.

The table below summarises the position in respect of entity B's employees:

	Entity B (subsidiary) £m	Entity A (parent) £m	Group £m
Entity B's deficit as at date of disposal	(5)	–	(5)
Section 75 payment*	9	–	9
	4	–	4
Bulk transfer to new plan (settlement loss)	–	–	(3)
Group transfer:			
Settlement loss in entity B	(1)	–	–
Credit (included in profit or loss on disposal of entity B) in entity A	–	1	–
Surplus arising after section 75 payment to group A plan**	–	1	1
Surplus in new plan	3	–	–

* The section 75 payment initially increases plan assets recognised in both entity B and in the group's consolidated financial statements (prior to the bulk transfer).

** In this example, any surplus remaining after the bulk transfer has been allocated to entity A.

Example 5 – Section 75 payment made by withdrawing employer's parent (+ bulk transfer out)

The facts are as for example 1 in paragraph UK.11.295, but entity A agrees to make the £9m section 75 payment (and it is not repayable by entity B). In addition, a bulk transfer is made of the assets and liabilities relating to entity B's employees to the pension plan of entity B's new parent. Following the section 75 payment, a surplus of £4m arises on entity B's share of the plan. For the purposes of the bulk transfer of entity B's share of the plan, it is agreed that the value of the surplus to be transferred into the new parent's pension plan will be £3m. It is decided that any surplus remaining after the bulk transfer will be allocated to entity A.

In entity B's individual financial statements, a total settlement gain of £8m arises. Entity B did not make payments in respect of the section 75 debt, but has ceased to participate in the group A pension plan and entity B's liability in respect of that pension plan has been extinguished. The gain of £8m comprises £5m in respect of the release of entity B's share of the deficit (measured on an IAS 19 basis) and

£3m in respect of the surplus (funded by entity A) transferred to a new pension plan (assuming that this is recognised on entity B's balance sheet as an asset).

In entity A's consolidated financial statements, a settlement loss of £3m is recognised in respect of the bulk transfer to the new pension plan (as part of the calculation of profit or loss on disposal of entity B), leaving a surplus of £1m in the group A pension plan.

Similar to example 3 in paragraph UK.11A.299, in entity A's separate financial statements, the payment of £9m into the plan is treated as a contribution to the pension plan. However, as £8m of this contribution has been transferred out of the plan as a result of the bulk transfer, it represents a loss in entity A's books and it will be included in the profit or loss on disposal of entity B reported in entity A's income statement. The remaining surplus of £1m is recognised in entity A's balance sheet if it meets the criteria in paragraphs 64 to 65 of IAS 19 and IFRIC 14 (see example 1).

The table below summarises the position in respect of entity B's employees:

	Entity B (subsidiary) £'m	Entity A (parent) £'m	Group £'m
Entity B's deficit as at date of disposal	(5)	–	(5)
Section 75 payment *	–	9	9
			4
Bulk transfer to new plan:			
Settlement gain/(loss)	8	–	(3)
Loss (included in profit or loss on disposal of entity B) in entity A	–	(8)	–
Surplus arising after section 75 payment to group A plan **	–	1	1
Surplus in new plan	3	–	–

* The section 75 payment initially increases plan assets recognised in both entity A and in the group's consolidated financial statements (prior to the bulk transfer).

** The surplus remaining after the bulk transfer is recognised in entity A (if it meets the criteria in IAS 19 and IFRIC 14) as this entity made the section 75 payment.

UK.11A.301 In the above examples, the settlements and bulk transfers have taken place by the balance sheet date. The situation will be more complicated where the settlement and/or the bulk transfer straddle the balance sheet date. An entity should recognise gains or losses on the settlement of a defined benefit plan when the settlement occurs. [IAS 19 para 110]. A settlement occurs when an entity enters into a transaction that eliminates all further legal or constructive obligation for part or all of the benefits provided under a defined benefit plan, for example, when a lump-sum cash payment is made to, or on behalf of, plan participants in exchange for their rights to receive specified post-employment benefits. [IAS 19 para 111]. The accounting treatment for transactions that straddle the balance sheet date will depend on the specific circumstances. See further paragraph 11A.231 onwards.

Chapter 12

Share-based payment

Share-based payment

Introduction

12.1 For some years, many companies have used share option plans for the purpose of employee remuneration, either as a management incentive or through employee share purchase plans that are available to all employees. A more recent development is the increasing use of share awards, either through annual bonuses or long-term incentive plans (LTIPs) as an alternative, or in addition to share option plans. In such plans the amount of the award is normally based on performance criteria; if these criteria are partially achieved, but not met in full, participants may be entitled to a proportion of the full award. Often, the shares are awarded to employees at nominal value or at nil cost (for instance, where an employee share trust subscribes for shares at nominal value).

12.2 In addition to the employee context, share-based payments are also used as a method by which entities procure other goods or services.

12.3 IFRS 2 applies to accounting periods beginning on or after 1 January 2005. The requirements for first-time adoption are considered in detail in chapter 3.

[The next paragraph is 12.7.]

Objective and scope

12.7 The stated objective of IFRS 2 is *"to specify the financial reporting by an entity when it undertakes a share-based payment transaction. In particular, it requires an entity to reflect in its profit or loss and financial position the effects of share-based payment transactions, including expenses associated with transactions in which share options are granted to employees"*. [IFRS 2 para 1]. Behind this objective is the IASB's strongly held view that an entity should recognise all goods or services it obtains, regardless of the form of consideration. Where goods or services are obtained for cash or other financial assets, the accounting is generally straightforward. IFRS 2 starts from the premise that goods or services obtained in a share-based payment transaction should be recognised and measured in a similar way.

12.8 IFRS 2 applies to all share-based payment arrangements. A share-based payment arrangement is defined as:

"an agreement between the entity (or another group entity or any shareholder of any group entity) and another party (including an employee) that entitles the other party to receive:

(a)   *cash or other assets of the entity for amounts that are based on the price (or value) of equity instruments (including shares or share options) of the entity or another group entity, or*

(b)   *equity instruments (including shares or share options) of the entity or another group entity,*

provided the specified vesting conditions, if any, are met."

[IFRS 2 App A].

12.9   Therefore, the requirements of IFRS 2 apply to any transaction in which an entity receives goods or services in exchange for a transfer of its own equity instruments, even if that transfer is made by an existing shareholder rather than by the entity itself. Only when a transfer is clearly for a purpose other than payment for goods or services would it be outside IFRS 2's scope. Furthermore as mentioned above, IFRS 2 will apply where goods or services are obtained by an entity in exchange for equity instruments of its parent or another member of the group. [IFRS 2 para 3A]. Group situations are considered further from paragraph 12.169.

12.10   The standard applies to all share-based payment transactions whether or not the entity can identify specifically some or all of the goods or services received, including:

■   *Equity-settled share-based payment transactions* – Share-based payment transactions in which the entity (a) receives goods or services as consideration for its own equity instruments (including shares or share options), or (b) receives goods or services but has no obligation to settle the transaction with the supplier. Such transactions include employee share option and share incentive plans.

■   *Cash-settled share-based payment transactions* – Transactions in which the entity acquires goods or services by incurring a liability to transfer cash or other assets to the supplier of those goods or services for amounts that are based on the price (or value) of equity instruments (including shares or share options) of the entity or another group entity. Typical examples include 'phantom' options plans, share appreciation rights and certain long-term incentive awards.

■   Transactions in which the entity receives or acquires goods or services and the terms of the arrangement provide either the entity or the supplier of those goods or services with a *choice* of whether the entity settles the transaction in cash (or other assets) or by issuing equity instruments.

[IFRS 2 para 2].

12.11   There is no exemption from IFRS 2's scope for employee share purchase plans or similar broad-based employee share plans. In drafting IFRS 2, the IASB did consider including an exemption for plans similar to employee share purchase plans (such as save as you earn ('SAYE') plans in the UK and employee share ownership plans ('ESOPs') in the US) and other broad-based employee share plans. However, they concluded that the accounting for such plans should be no different from other employee share plans. The IASB also rejected the suggestion that plans should be exempted if the discount available to employees is small so that its impact is likely to be immaterial.

[The next paragraph is 12.18.]

12.18   Associates and joint ventures are more complicated. For example, in situations where employees of a joint venture are granted the right to equity instruments over one or both joint venturer's equity instruments, such a transaction in the joint venture would be outside IFRS 2's scope. This is because the joint venture is not part of a group as defined by IAS 27 (superseded by IFRS 10). Although the shareholders of the joint venture are transferring equity instruments in exchange for employee services to the joint venture, the fact that the equity instruments are not those of the joint venture or another entity in the same group as the joint venture means the awards are not in the scope of IFRS 2 in the financial statements of the joint venture. [IFRS 2 para 3A]. The position for associates is the same. Note that investors would be within IFRS 2's scope for their own financial statements as they are indeed issuing their own equity in return for services (see further para 12.61).

12.19   In the situation described in the previous paragraph, the associate or joint venture entity would need to apply the hierarchy within IAS 8 to determine the appropriate accounting treatment, and apply the principles of paragraph 11 of IAS 8. In such a situation, the entity is likely to determine that either IFRS 2 or IAS 19 (refer to chapter 11) is the most appropriate standard. This would be a policy choice that the entity would make under IAS 8, and would have to be applied consistently. It is our view that the most appropriate treatment is to apply the principles of IFRS 2 to employee benefits that are settled in equity (our view is explained further in example 4, para 12.22 below). See from paragraph 12.169 for details of how to apply IFRS 2 in this situation.

12.20   There are few exclusions from IFRS 2's scope, namely:

■   Business combinations in the acquirer's financial statements to which IFRS 3 applies, notwithstanding the fact that such a transaction may be equity-settled. However, equity instruments granted to employees of the acquiree in their capacity as employees (for example, to encourage them to remain in the employment of the acquiree after the acquisition) do fall within the scope of IFRS 2. [IFRS 2 para 5]. Similarly, the cancellation, replacement or modification of existing share-based payment arrangements as result of a business combination should be accounted for in accordance with IFRS 2. See from paragraph 12.25 for further discussion of business combinations.

■   Contributions of a business on formation of a joint venture and combinations of businesses or entities under common control. This is illustrated from paragraph 12.25.

■ Contracts for the purchase of goods, such as commodities, to which IAS 32 and IAS 39 apply, because these are to satisfy the reporting entity's own expected purchase or usage requirements. [IFRS 2 para 6]. This is illustrated in example 1 of paragraph 12.22 below.

Transactions within the scope of IFRS 2

12.21   Further examples of transactions within IFRS 2's scope are set out below.

Example 1 – Purchase of non-financial item expected to be used by the entity

Entity A enters into a contract to purchase silver for use in its jewellery manufacturing business, whereby it is required to pay cash to the supplier in an amount equal to the value of 1,000 shares of entity A at the date the silver is delivered. This meets the definition of a cash-settled share-based payment transaction (entity A has acquired goods in exchange for a payment the amount of which will be based on the value of its shares).

IAS 32 and IAS 39 apply to those contracts to buy or sell a non-financial item that can be settled net in cash or another financial instrument, or by exchanging financial instruments, as if the contracts were financial instruments, with the exception of contracts that were entered into and continue to be held for the purpose of the receipt or delivery of the non-financial item in accordance with the entity's expected purchase, sale or usage requirements. [IAS 32 para 8; IAS 39 para 5]. Regardless of whether this contract may be settled net, as it was entered into for the purpose of taking delivery of the silver for use in entity A's business and entity A has a history of doing this, it does not fall within the scope of IASs 32 and 39. Hence, it does fall within the scope of IFRS 2 as a cash-settled share-based payment transaction.

Example 2 – Definition of goods or services

Entity B is developing a new product and purchased a patent from entity C. The parties agreed a purchase price of 1,000 of entity B's shares. These will be issued to entity C within 60 days of finalising the legal documentation that transfers the patent from entity C to entity B.

This is an equity-settled share-based payment. IFRS 2 is applicable to a share-based payment for a patent. The goods to which IFRS 2 applies include inventories, consumables, property, plant and equipment, intangible assets and other non-financial assets.

Example 3 – Business combination and continued employee service

Entity D acquires 90% of the share capital of entity E. As part of the acquisition, entity D grants entity E's employees share options that vest after 2 years if the employees remain in service.

In this transaction, equity instruments are granted to employees of the acquiree in their capacity as employees and so fall within IFRS 2's scope. [IFRS 2 para 5].

Example 4 – Award of parent entity shares by a shareholder

An individual with a 40% shareholding in entity F awards 2% of his shareholding in entity F to a director of entity F's subsidiary, entity G.

The award is within IFRS 2's scope. A shareholder of entity F has transferred equity instruments of entity F (entity G's parent) to a party that has supplied services to the entity. [IFRS 2 para 3A]. The award will be reflected in both entity G's financial statements and entity F's consolidated financial statements.

Example 5 – Services paid for by issuing warrants

During the year, entity K's bank provided services to entity K; entity K agreed to issue warrants to the bank as consideration for this service. The warrants have a fixed subscription price and entity K will settle the warrants in equity – that is, if the bank chooses to exercise the warrants, it will receive one entity K share for each warrant held in return for paying the fixed subscription price.

Entity K has received services as consideration for issuing equity instruments of entity K. This is an equity settled share-based payment, which should be accounted for in accordance with IFRS 2.

Example 6 – Formation of a joint venture

Entities X and Y have formed an incorporated joint venture, entity Z. On formation, in exchange for their equity interests in Z, entity X contributed property, plant and equipment and entity Y contributed intangible assets that do not constitute a business.

The asset contributions by venturers X and Y upon entity Z's formation are equity-settled share-based payment transactions from Z's perspective and fall within IFRS 2's scope. The scope exclusion of paragraph 5 of IFRS 2 does not apply, as the formation of a joint venture does not meet the definition of a business combination and X and Y contributed assets not businesses. See further example 2 in paragraph 12.25 below, where the formation of a joint venture is determined to fall within the scope exclusion because two separate entities are being contributed to the formation of the joint venture. See further chapter 28.

Transactions outside the scope of IFRS 2

12.22   The following are examples of transactions that are outside the scope of IFRS 2.

Example 1 – Commodity contracts

Entity H enters into a contract to purchase 100 tonnes of cocoa beans. The purchase price will be settled in cash at an amount equal to the value of 1,000 of entity H's shares. However, the entity may settle the contract at any time by paying an amount equal to the current market value of 1,000 of its shares less the market value of 100 tonnes of cocoa beans. The entity has entered into the contract as part of its hedging strategy and has no intention of taking physical delivery of the cocoa beans.

As in example 1 in paragraph 12.21 above, the transaction meets the definition of a cash-settled share-based payment transaction (entity H has acquired goods in exchange for a payment of which the amount will be based on the value of its shares). However, unlike example 1 in paragraph 12.21, the contract may be settled net and has not been entered into in order to satisfy entity H's expected purchase, sale or usage requirements. Accordingly, the transaction is outside IFRS 2's scope and is instead dealt with in accordance with the requirements of IASs 32 and 39. See further chapter 6.

Example 2 – Cash payments dependent on earnings multiple

A non-quoted entity issued share appreciation rights (SARs) to its employees. The SARs entitle the employees to a payment equal to any increase in the entity's share price between the grant date and the vesting date. The arrangement's terms and conditions define the share price used to calculate payments to employees as five times EBITDA divided by the number of shares in issue.

IFRS 2 is unlikely to be applicable to this transaction because a fixed multiple of EBITDA is not likely to reflect the fair value of the entity's share price. If it does not, management should apply IAS 19 to this deferred compensation arrangement.

Example 3 – Plan investing in other entity shares

Entity I is implementing an unusual share option incentive plan. Entity I will lend C1m to an employee share trust, which will purchase shares in a number of publicly listed companies (but not shares in entity I or any other entities within the same group as entity I). These companies may be suppliers, customers or competitors. Entity I's employees are granted options over 'units' held by the employee share trust, which are shares in listed companies. The units are an amalgam of the shares held by the trust. The units do not entitle the employees to any equity interest in the trust itself. The options are granted at market value at the date of the grant and held over a three year period. When employees exercise their option over the units, they are paid the difference in cash between the market price of the units at the date of the grant (the exercise price) and the market value at the date of exercise. To fund the cash payment the trust sells the shares relating to the exercised units. It then repays the relevant portion of the loan from entity I and also pays the gain to employees (this assumes the price of the underlying investments has increased in value following the grant).

This transaction is outside IFRS 2's scope as the rights are over shares of companies other than the reporting entity, or companies within the entity's group

Accounting for the changes in value of the assets in the trust will depend on how the assets are classified. If they fall into the definition of a plan asset under paragraph 7 of IAS 19 then they should be accounted for in line with IAS 19. Otherwise, the assets will be included in the consolidated accounts and should be treated as available-for-sale financial assets in line with IAS 39. The related liability will be within IAS 19's scope. See further chapter 11.

Accounting for employee share trusts is considered in detail from paragraph 12.241.

Example 4 – Share options in a joint venture

Entity J is a 50:50 joint venture between entities K and L. Entity K grants senior employees of entity J options over its own shares without making any charge to entity J. Entity L does not provide any contribution to the joint venture to compensate entity K. Entity K applies the equity method to investments in joint ventures in its consolidated financial statements and the cost method in its separate financial statements.

Entity J's financial statements

IFRS 2 includes within its scope transfers of equity instruments of an entity's parent or of an entity in the same group in return for goods or services. [IFRS 2 para 3A]. However, entity K is a joint venture investor and is not entity J's parent, nor is it in the same group (defined in IAS 27 or superseded by IFRS 10 as being 'a parent and all its subsidiaries') as entity J. Therefore, on initial consideration, from entity J's perspective, the award in entity J of share options in entity K is not within IFRS 2's scope.

The arrangement also falls outside IAS 19's scope. IAS 19 applies to all employee benefits, but defines those as *"all forms of consideration given by an entity in exchange for service rendered by employees"*. Because no consideration is given by entity J, this does not meet the definition of an employee benefit.

However, IAS 8 requires entities to apply a hierarchy when determining their accounting policies. Where there is no IFRS governing a transaction, IAS 8 requires management to look first to any IFRS standard or interpretation dealing with similar or related issues. Paragraph 10 of IAS 8 states that in the absence of a standard or interpretation that specifically applies to a transaction, *"management shall use its judgment in developing and applying an accounting policy"*. Furthermore, paragraph 11 of the standard clarifies that in making such a judgement, management should consider *"the requirements and guidance in standards and interpretations dealing with similar and related issues"*. While it is not a formal requirement, it is our view that the most appropriate treatment will be for entity J to apply the principles of IFRS 2 to this equity-settled share-based payment. This is further supported by the treatment where a parent entity grants options over its own shares to those of its subsidiary. In this case, while entity K does not meet the definition of a parent company, in the absence of any other guidance, this is an acceptable approach. (See further para 12.169.)

The disclosure requirements of IAS 24 should be applied by entity J if any of the employees are key management personnel. See further chapter 29.

Note that if compensation was, however, given by entity J for the share-based payment, perhaps in the form of a recharge payment required by entity K, then the transaction would be within IAS 19's scope.

Entity K's financial statements

Entity K has an equity-settled share-based payment arrangement and should measure the goods and services received in accordance with IFRS 2 as appropriate. Thus, in its separate financial statements, entity K would capitalise the IFRS 2 grant date fair value into its cost of the investment in the joint venture and consider whether there were any impairment indicators.

Entity K's consolidated financial statements should apply the principles of IAS 31 (or superseded by IAS 28 (revised)). To the extent that entity J has accounted for the share-based payment, 50% of this would be recorded by entity K when the equity method is applied. In addition, since entity L did not provide an equivalent contribution into the joint venture, entity K would record an additional cost resulting in its consolidated financial statements recording 100% of the share-based payment charge.

Entity L's financial statements

Other than the fact that entity L will need to account for its joint venture in entity J, there will be no impact on entity L's separate financial statements. To the extent that entity J has accounted for the share-based payment the proportional share (that is, 50%) of the charge that is recorded by entity L on consolidation would be eliminated against the gain recorded on application of paragraph 48 of IAS 31 (or paragraph 28 of IAS 28 (revised)), hence, there is no impact on consolidation.

12.23 In some cases, the number of equity instruments to which a counterparty is entitled varies. For example, share appreciation rights may be settled in shares such that the number of shares issued to employees varies according to the appreciation of the employer's share price over a period of time. If the requirements of IAS 32 were applied to transactions such as these, an obligation to issue equity instruments would be classified as a liability (a variable number of shares issued for a fixed amount – see further chapter 6). This would have implications for the basis of measurement of the transaction as discussed later in this chapter. For example, equity-settled transactions involving employees are measured at the date on which awards are granted and are not re-measured, whereas liabilities in respect of cash-settled transactions are re-measured at each balance sheet date. However, employees will ultimately receive equity instruments of the reporting entity; the award is therefore accounted for as an equity-settled share-based payment. The IASB concluded that different considerations applied in developing IFRS 2 and the standard inserts an amendment to IAS 32 that exempts from its scope any transactions to which IFRS 2 applies (except as discussed in para 12.20 above). [IAS 32 para 4(f)].

12.24 The following examples consider some practical issues when determining whether a transaction is within the scope of IFRS 2.

Example 1 – Bonus with past history of cash settlement

An entity agrees to pay its employees a bonus. The entity has a choice of settlement, either cash or shares with a value equivalent to the value of cash payment. The entity has a past practice of settling in cash and is considering whether the transaction should be accounted for under IFRS 2.

It could be argued that by applying the principles of IAS 32, shares issued for a fixed amount would be accounted for as a liability and, hence, this type of award should be in the scope of IAS 19 and not IFRS 2. However, as the entity has a *choice* that allows it to settle the award using equity instruments or cash (and, therefore, could issue equity instruments), the transaction is a share-based payment with a settlement choice (see further from para 12.162). [IFRS 2 para 2c].

Example 2 – Variable number of shares for goods

Entity A signed a contract with a construction entity to acquire a new building for C1m with ownership transferring to entity A when the construction work is complete. The purchase price will be settled by entity A issuing a variable number of its own shares with a total market value of C1m.

As the purchase price is being settled in shares, the transaction is within IFRS 2's scope and is excluded from the scope of IAS 32. See further example 11 of paragraph 12.114.

Example 3 – Non-recourse loan enabling counterparty to purchase shares

An entity lends C100 to an employee to purchase the entity's shares from the market. The loan is interest free and only has recourse to the shares. Dividends paid on the shares must be used to reduce the loan. The employee must pay back the balance of the loan, or return the shares at the earlier of three years or resignation.

In November 2005, the IFRS IC confirmed that this transaction would fall within the scope of IFRS 2. The IFRS IC stated that the loan is considered to be part of a share-based payment transaction, which in substance is an option with a three year exercise window where the exercise price is reduced by any dividends. The employee is not exposed to any downside risk in the movement of the share price over the three year period as he/she can repay the loan or surrender the shares. The 'loan' is, therefore, recognised as a debit in equity. The option would be exercised on the date the loan is repaid. In this example the option would vest immediately as the employee could leave on day one, repay the loan and be fully entitled to the shares. Vesting conditions are considered in detail from paragraph 12.77. See example 2 of paragraph 12.114 for a worked example of the accounting treatment.

Example 4 – Full recourse loan enabling counterparty to purchase shares

The facts are the same as example 3 above, except the entity has recourse to personal assets of the employee as well as the shares. This means that if the employee fails to repay the loan, the entity has the ability to take possession of the employees personal assets such as their car, house, etc.

The employee is unconditionally bound to repay the loan. The entity should record a receivable for the loan balance. Since the terms of the loan with the company are such that a preferential interest rate has been given to employees, a fair value adjustment to the loan balance should be recognised (under IAS 39) as an employee remuneration expense over an appropriate service period in accordance with IAS 19. This is because the fair value of the loan has been reduced through a preferential rate and a benefit has been provided to the employee.

Full recourse loans with employees are rare in practice. Before an entity determines that they have granted a full recourse loan to employees, the following factors should be considered to determine if the loan is, in substance, non-recourse:

■ The employer has legal recourse to the employee's other assets but does not intend to seek repayment beyond the shares issued.

- The employer has a history of not demanding repayment of loan amounts in excess of the fair value of the shares.

- The employee does not have sufficient assets or other means (beyond the shares) to justify the recourse nature of the loan.

- The employer has accepted a recourse note upon exercise and subsequently converted the recourse note to a non-recourse note.

Business combinations, private equity deals and sweet equity

Business combinations

12.25 The scope exclusion in respect of business combinations concerns those combinations as defined by IFRS 3. IFRS 3 defines a business combination as, *"A transaction or other event in which an acquirer obtains control of one or more businesses. Transactions sometimes referred to as 'true mergers' or 'mergers of equals' are also business combinations as that term is used in this IFRS."* [IFRS 3 App A]. In addition to business combinations as defined by IFRS 3, contributions of a business on formation of a joint venture and combinations of businesses or entities under common control are excluded from IFRS 2's scope, as explained in paragraph 12.20 above. This is illustrated in the examples below. Business combinations are considered further in chapter 25.

Example 1 – Common control transactions

A business combination occurs between two entities that are under common control. The transaction is outside IFRS 3's scope.

The primary purpose of the issue of shares in such a common control transaction is likely to be to reorganise the legal or managerial structure of a business or to transfer a business, rather than to acquire goods or services. The shares are issued in exchange for a business that is an integrated set of activities and assets that is capable of being conducted and managed for the purpose of providing a return to investors, or lower costs or other economic benefits directly to investors or other owners, members or participants. [IFRS 3 App A]. As such, the transaction is outside IFRS 2's scope. See further guidance on accounting for a business combination between entities under common control in chapter 25.

Example 2 – Formation of a joint venture

Entity A and entity B are brought together to form a joint venture.

The formation of a joint venture is outside the scope of IFRS 3 (see further example 6 in para 12.21 above). This transaction does not meet the definition of a business combination because two separate entities are being brought together into one reporting entity without either entity gaining control; therefore, the scope exclusion in paragraph 5 of IFRS 2 would apply.

The combination of separate businesses to form a joint venture involves the issue of shares for the purpose of forming a joint venture, not the acquisition of goods or services. The transaction is outside IFRS 2's scope because the broader definition of business combination is used in the scope exclusion. See further guidance on accounting for joint ventures in chapter 28 (to be superseded by chapter 28A).

[The next paragraph is 12.30.]

12.30 IFRS 3 states that if the accounting acquiree is not a business then it is not in the scope of IFRS 3. In some circumstances, for example for a reverse acquisition, it is not always clear whether a business has been acquired and, therefore, the substance of the arrangement should be considered. This is illustrated in the following example.

Example – Reverse acquisition into a shell company

Entity V, a listed entity that does not constitute a business at the time of the transaction, issues shares in exchange for shares in entity W. Although entity V becomes entity W's legal parent, the transaction is not a business combination under IFRS 3, because entity V is not a business and has not gained control over entity W in substance.

IFRS 2 scopes out transactions in which an entity acquires goods as part of the net assets acquired in a business combination as defined in IFRS 3.

We believe that the transaction is within IFRS 2's scope because the substance is that shareholders of private entity W have given shareholders of public entity V an interest in entity W in exchange for any assets sitting within entity V and entity V's listing. Accordingly, entity W should fair value the consideration that entity V's shareholders receive (the shares given out by entity W's shareholders) and the identifiable assets of entity V that entity W's shareholders acquired. Any resulting difference would be unidentifiable goods or services which should be expensed (unless it meets the definition of an asset under other standards). Appropriate disclosure to explain the accounting policy is necessary. See further chapter 25 for a more detailed example.

Transactions with employees and transactions with shareholders

12.31 Transactions with employees in their capacity as holders of equity instruments are also outside IFRS 2's scope. [IFRS 2 para 4]. For example, if an entity makes a bonus issue of shares to all of its shareholders, and these include certain of the entity's employees, this will not represent a share-based payment transaction to be dealt with in accordance with IFRS 2. However, there could be a situation where an employee invests in an entity which is working towards a stock market listing or a trade sale. In these cases there could be a venture capital entity or similar investor involved in the transaction and the employee will subscribe for the shares at the same amount as the other investors. The issue is whether the employee is acting as a shareholder or an employee. Often the interested parties (including directors, management and other shareholders) have acquired shares for a 'fair' value, which may not equate to grant date fair value for the purposes of IFRS 2 and would typically be tax driven. It is important to note that a fair value determined for tax purposes often reflects factors which it would not be appropriate to allow for under IFRS 2 (that is, lack of marketability) and, therefore, may be lower than the IFRS 2 grant date fair value.

12.32 It could be that there are no conditions or incentives attached to the acquired shares and, therefore, the employee is purely acting as a shareholder. However, in the majority of situations there are likely to be service conditions or leaver provisions such that the arrangement would be accounted for as a share-based payment transaction under IFRS 2. The shares in question are often referred to as 'sweet' or 'sweat' equity depending on whether they are offered at an advantageous price or in return for services rather than cash.

Example 1 – Employees acting in capacity as shareholders

Entity A made a rights issue to all of its shareholders, entitling them to purchase one new share for each five shares owned at a price of C10. The shareholders include 20 people who are also employees. No other conditions are attached to the rights issue.

In this example, shares are being issued to employees in their capacity as shareholders, and not in exchange for their services. Furthermore, the employees are not required to complete a period of service in exchange for the new shares. As such the transaction is outside IFRS 2's scope.

Example 2 – Capital contribution of a building in settlement of a rights issue

Entity B made a rights issue to all shareholders. Shareholders are entitled to acquire one new share for each share owned at a fixed price of C4 at the date of the rights issue. Entity C owns 1 million of entity B's shares, that is, 10% of the share capital. Entity C subscribed to 1 million of entity B's new shares. Following the subscription, entity C proposed to entity B to settle the purchase price of the new shares by transferring an office building it owns to entity B. Entity B agreed to accept the building as settlement for the new shares.

IFRS 2 is not applicable to this transaction because it is a rights issue to all shareholders. The method of payment is irrelevant as this is a transaction with shareholders in their capacity as shareholders; the transfer of the building is, therefore, outside IFRS 2's scope. The subscription established a right to receive a fixed payment of C4m from entity C. The transfer of the building was agreed after the receivable was established and is in settlement of the C4m receivable.

Example 3 – In-kind capital contribution by existing shareholder

Entity D needs a new office building and has arranged to acquire it from an existing shareholder. The purchase price will be settled by the entity issuing 1,000 new shares. For legal purposes, the transaction is considered an in-kind capital contribution of a building.

The counterparty did not act in its capacity as shareholder, but as a supplier of the office building. As such, the in-kind capital contribution is within IFRS 2's scope. This would mean that the office building is recognised at its fair value with equity being credited by the same amount for the share issue.

12.33 There are a number of issues that need to be considered before reaching a conclusion that transactions with employees are not within the IFRS 2's scope including:

- Whether the instrument that the employees are entitled to is an equity instrument or linked to an equity instrument, as defined by the standard. [IFRS 2 App A]. If the instrument is an equity instrument or linked to an equity instrument and the value to employees varies depending on the extent to which the employee provides services the transaction would be within IFRS 2's scope as a share-based payment.

- Whether the rights/interests of employee shareholders differ from those of other investor shareholders (for example, venture capitalists). Employees may have the right to additional shares with other investor shareholders giving up their rights – a ratchet mechanism. This ratchet usually depends on the business' performance and hence employees get more shares if the business does well. This would qualify as a performance condition, as services from employees contribute towards the company meeting the performance targets and, hence, the transaction is within IFRS 2's scope.

- Whether holders have different rights following an exit event. Through the articles, employees may be given different rights (cash or shares) if an investor exits through an IPO rather than trade sale. This provides evidence of a performance condition (achieving different rights to cash or shares depending on the exit event that occurs) which could scope the arrangement into IFRS 2.

- Leaver conditions (the articles or terms and conditions may define good leavers and bad leavers). In this situation the employees may lose their right to shares by leaving the entity, either by the shares being repurchased or cancelled. Hence, employees may only earn their right to the shares if they stay with the company or, for example, in the event of an IPO. This would also be considered a service condition and, hence, the arrangement is in IFRS 2's scope.

- Whether additional services are being provided. As noted above, employees will often lose their rights to shares if they leave the company. There is often a service requirement, for example, to stay in employment for a number of years or until a change in control. However, this may not always be the case and some employees may have the right to shares whether they stay or leave. This does not automatically scope the arrangement out of IFRS 2, because the entity would still need to determine whether additional services (whether or not they are identifiable) are being provided by the shareholders in their capacity as employees, by reference to the fair value of the shares at the date of grant (refer to para 12.61 onwards). [IFRS 2 para 2].

- Whether a trust is involved in the arrangement. The existence of an employee benefit trust to buy back and warehouse shares for the benefit of other employees could well imply that shares are being issued as an incentive and, hence, the arrangement is in IFRS 2's scope.

The above list is not exhaustive. However, it highlights some of the areas that should be considered in order to determine if the transaction is within IFRS 2's scope.

> **Example – Purchase of shares at fair value, with service condition**
>
> A CEO is offered the opportunity to buy 100,000 shares in entity A at C1 each, the same price paid by the venture capital investor that holds 40% of entity A's shares. If the CEO resigns within two years he must give the shares back to the entity in return for a payment of the lower of his subscription price and the fair value of the shares.
>
> This transaction is in IFRS 2's scope as the CEO accepts a service condition when purchasing the shares that must be satisfied before he is fully entitled to the risks and rewards of the shares (that is, there is a vesting period of two years).
>
> The CEO might be paying IFRS 2 grant date fair value for the shares on grant date (C1), in which case, provided the award was equity-settled this would result in no IFRS 2 charge. However, since the arrangement is within the scope of IFRS 2, consideration should be given to disclosures prescribed in IFRS 2 (see further para 12.257) and IAS 24 (see further para 12.274).

Leaver provisions

12.34 Some share-based payment arrangements include good and bad leaver provisions. A good leaver is often defined as an individual who leaves the entity due to injury, disability, death, redundancy or on reaching normal retirement age. A bad leaver is usually defined as any other leaver. The following example considers the scope implications in relation to typical leaver provisions.

> **Example – Exit event with good and bad leavers**
>
> Entity A's directors have been given an incentive in the form of share options that will vest when an exit event occurs (the entity is unlisted). Each director has paid an upfront exercise price of C10 per share and will become unconditionally entitled to shares in the entity if he or she is still in service when an exit event occurs.
>
> 'Exit event' is defined in the plan's terms and conditions as a trade sale, a listing or other change in control. An exit event is expected to occur in the form of a trade sale in three years' time.
>
> The terms and conditions also set out provisions for good and bad leavers. For every share option held, a 'bad leaver' will receive cash equal to the lower of the amount paid (C10) and the market value of the share (market value will be determined by independent valuation consultants). A 'good leaver' will receive cash equal to the higher of the amount paid and the market value in respect of each share option held.
>
> As any director can choose to leave the entity at any time triggering a contractual 'bad leaver' cash payment that the entity cannot avoid, entity A has a liability in respect of all directors as part of the share-based payment arrangement, that is, for the total number of share options granted. The liability will be measured at the lower of C10 per

share and the market value of the share. The payments by the directors are in effect an advance payment of an exercise price due when the awards vest.

In addition to the bad leaver liability, the arrangement in respect of good leavers and directors who are still in service at the time of the trade sale falls within the scope of IFRS 2.

The fair value of share options (which will be incremental to the amount that has already been provided in case each individual becomes a bad leaver) awarded to any director expected to be a good leaver before the exit event occurs will be treated as a cash-settled share-based payment (see from para 12.98 in relation to non-market vesting conditions).

The fair value of share options that are expected to vest as a result of the trade sale will be treated as an equity-settled share-based payment (this will be incremental to the amount that has already been provided in case each individual becomes a bad leaver and will not include amounts in respect of any individual who is expected to become a good leaver before the exit event). Note that if the share options do vest as a result of the trade sale, the bad and good leaver liability in respect of each individual for whom the award vests will be transferred into equity.

Drag along and tag along clauses

12.35 Some arrangements include 'drag along' and 'tag along' clauses. For example, if an existing majority shareholder chooses to sell his investment in an entity, a drag along clause in an arrangement's terms and conditions may state that the shareholder can force employee shareholders or share option holders to sell their holdings at the same price/date. Alternatively, in the event of a sale of an entity, a tag along clause may allow employees to force an acquirer to purchase their holdings at the same price/date.

Example – Settlement by an acquirer in cash

Entity A grants its employees restricted shares. The articles state that the shares will remain restricted until entity A is acquired. At the date that the entity is acquired, a drag along clause will be invoked such that the employees will be required to sell their shares to the acquirer.

In entity A's financial statements, the award of restricted shares is an equity-settled share-based payment under IFRS 2 because the entity will settle the award in shares. Although the employees can only receive cash for their shares, the cash will be paid by the acquirer to the employees as shareholders. Under no circumstances will entity A be required to settle in cash.

12.36 In some situations, the acquirer may, in substance, initiate the cash payment by the acquiree or may reimburse the acquiree for any cash payment. Further discussion of this and the interaction between IFRS 2 and IFRS 3, including in relation to the treatment of acquiree awards on an acquisition and the accounting in the acquirer's books, is provided in chapter 25.

[The next paragraph is 12.38.]

Recognition of share-based payment transactions

12.38 The goods or services acquired in a share-based payment transaction should be recognised, either as an expense or as an increase in assets, when they are received. [IFRS 2 paras 7, 8].

12.39 This is the aspect of IFRS 2 that has caused most controversy, primarily in respect of employee share and share option plans. Many respondents to ED 2, and the discussion paper before IFRS 2, argued that it was wrong to recognise an expense in respect of such plans, raising a number of conceptual and practical concerns. For example:

■ The effect of an employee share transaction is that existing shareholders transfer some of their ownership interests to employees. Hence, the reporting entity is not involved in the transaction.

■ Employees do not provide services in consideration for an award of shares or options. They are instead rewarded in cash.

■ There is no cost to the entity in an equity-settled transaction as there is no transfer of cash or other assets. Furthermore, an expense recognised in respect of an equity-settled transaction would not be consistent with the IASB's 'Framework for the preparation and presentation of financial statements', which states in paragraph 70 that *"expenses are decreases in economic benefits during the accounting period in the form of outflows or depletions of assets or incurrences of liabilities that result in decreases in equity, other than those relating to distributions to equity participants"*. It is argued that as there is no outflow or depletion of assets, there can be no expense.

■ By reducing earnings and increasing the number of shares (or potential shares) in issue, the impact of an equity-settled transaction is to 'hit' earnings per share twice.

■ The expense in respect of an employee share or share option plan cannot be measured reliably.

■ To require recognition (or greater recognition) of expenses in respect of employee share and share option plans could have adverse economic consequences as it might discourage entities from introducing or continuing with such plans.

12.40 The basis for conclusions section of IFRS 2 discusses these concerns in detail. The rationale for recognising all types of equity-settled share-based payment transactions, irrespective of whether the equity instrument is a share or a share option, and irrespective of whether the equity instrument is granted to an employee or to some other party, is that the entity has engaged in a transaction that is in essence the same as any other issue of equity instruments. In other words, the entity has received resources (goods or services) as consideration for equity instruments. It should, therefore, account for the inflow of resources (goods or services) and the increase in equity. Subsequently, either at the time of receipt of the goods or services or at some later date, the entity should also account for the expense arising from the consumption of those resources. Hence, the issue of equity instruments and the consumption of resources are to be considered separately. The former results in an increase in equity while the latter is reflected as an expense.

Timing of recognition and vesting period

12.41 As noted above, the goods or services acquired in a share-based payment transaction should be recognised when they are received. Typically it will be a question of fact as to when this occurs. However, sometimes, as in the case of employee services, this will be less obvious. For example, a company may grant share options to its employees. Certain performance conditions need to be satisfied over, say, the next three years for the options to be exercisable and even then they may only be exercised after a further year has elapsed and the employee forfeits the options if he leaves prior to exercise. Should an expense be recognised when the award is granted, over the three-year performance period or over the longer period until the options vest (that is, the employees become unconditionally entitled to exercise the options)?

12.42 IFRS 2 concludes that where equity instruments, such as options awarded to employees, vest immediately, in the absence of evidence to the contrary, an entity should presume that they represent consideration for services already rendered. Accordingly, the entity should recognise the employee services received in full on the date on which the options are granted. [IFRS 2 para 14].

12.43 On the other hand, if the options do not vest until the employees have completed a specified period of service, the entity should presume that services are to be rendered over that period. [IFRS 2 para 15]. This is referred to as the vesting period. IFRS 2 defines the vesting period as *"the period during which all the specified vesting conditions of a share-based payment arrangement are to be satisfied"*. [IFRS 2 App A].

12.44 No distinction is drawn in IFRS 2 between vesting periods during which employees have to satisfy specific performance conditions and vesting periods during which there are no particular requirements other than to remain in the entity's employment. Hence, in the example in paragraph 12.41 above, the period over which employee services should be recognised is the four-year period until the options vest and employees become unconditionally entitled to them and not the shorter period during which the employees must satisfy specific performance conditions.

12.44.1 In some share-based payment plans, awards vest in stages or instalments over the vesting period. For example, an employee is granted 100 options with 25% of the options vesting annually over four years. This is known as staged vesting (also known as tranched or graded vesting). When the share-based payment is subject to different vesting periods, IFRS 2 requires each of these instalments to be accounted for as a separate award. [IFRS 2, para IG11]. For example, 25% of the award is recognised over one year, 25% recognised over two years, 25% recognised over three years, and 25% recognised over four years. An example of staged vesting is provided in paragraph 12.114 (see illustrative example 4). In some arrangements, employees are able to leave employment before the end of the full vesting period and are allowed to keep a proportion of the award (that is, pro-rata vesting). Where employees are entitled to *pro rata* shares when they cease employment, application of staged vesting should be applied.

12.44.2 The accounting for services received in advance of the grant date is considered from paragraph 12.70.

12.45 The treatment of vesting conditions is considered in greater detail from paragraph 12.77.

12.46 The following examples illustrate the period over which all specified vesting conditions are to be satisfied, which could be different for different employees in the same share award plan.

Example 1 – Award exercisable on chosen retirement date

An employee is currently 58 years old and is granted some options that vest over five years if he continues in employment. This employee, however, has the option to retire anytime between 60 and 65 (inclusive) without requiring the employer's consent. If the employee chooses to retire at the age of 60, the employee is able to keep the options, which become exercisable at that date. In this example the vesting period for this individual is two years as he becomes entitled to, and can walk away with, the options at the age of 60, whether he chooses to continue working beyond that date or not.

Example 2 – Options awarded instead of annual bonus

An entity normally awards options annually instead of an annual bonus. The entity grants options representing an annual bonus in 20X4, in respect of the year to December 20X3. The award is not exercisable for three years and the employee must remain with the entity throughout this period or they will forfeit the options.

In this situation, there is an expectation on the part of the employees that they will receive a bonus each year. Consequently, employees are providing services in 20X3 to earn the right to equity instruments. However, there is an additional period of service that the employee is required to complete until the equity instrument vests unconditionally with them. Therefore, the expense should be over the performance period (20X3) and the service period (20X4 to 20X6). The vesting period is a total of four years.

It should be noted that if the employee was not required to remain with the entity for the three year period, the vesting period would not include the three year delay until the award is exercisable. The three year delay until the award is exercisable would simply be a post-vesting restriction. See from paragraph 12.202.

Group situations and location of share-based payment charge

12.47 In certain circumstances it may not be immediately clear which entity or entities within a group should bear the IFRS 2 charge. This may be, for example, where an award has been granted to employees who provide services to a number of entities within a group. It may be that employees are remunerated by a service company for services to a number of operating entities. Alternatively, individuals may be directors of both the parent company and an operating subsidiary. The charge should be borne by the entity that is in substance the employer.

12.48 It will be necessary to assess the facts and circumstances surrounding each situation by considering a range of factors, including the following:

- Which entity obtains the benefits associated with the employee. For example, where an individual is a director of both the parent company and an operating subsidiary, consider whether the director is being rewarded for services to the group as a whole (contributing to strategic decisions for the group, or perhaps implementing a restructuring programme) or whether the director is being rewarded for services to the operating subsidiary's business. The latter would point towards the subsidiary being the employer.

- Whether there is a service company arrangement in place. For example, where an individual performs services for a large number of group operating entities and the time spent at each entity varies (or may change) from time to time, this may indicate that the service company is the employer.

- Which entity ultimately bears the employment cost (either directly or through a management recharge). While one entity may physically pay the employee, the cost may be recharged to another group entity that receives services from the employee. The IFRS 2 charge would generally be expected to follow other employee costs.

- The nature of any management recharges. For example:

  - Whether management costs (such as wages and salaries, overheads and other administrative expenses) are charged back individually (such that the entity's income statement includes each cost as a separate line item) or as part of a larger 'block' management recharge. A larger 'block' of recharges may indicate that the entity receiving the management recharge for the employee is, in substance, the employer.

  - Whether the employee's costs are recharged to another entity at a margin. This may indicate that the entity receiving the management recharge is, in substance, the employer.

- Which entity sets the employee's salary, appraises the employee and determines any bonus. The IFRS 2 charge would generally sit with an entity performing such functions.

- Which entity has issued the employee's contract and which entity the employee considers to be their employer. As in the above bullet point, an entity performing such functions would generally be the employer.

- The nature of the employee's contract. For example, whether the employee's contract states that he/she may be required to work for a number of group entities or whether an employee is temporarily seconded to a specific operating entity. An entity to which an employee is temporarily seconded would be the employer for the period of the secondment.

The credit entry

12.49   The treatment of the credit entry in respect of a share-based payment transaction will depend on whether it is accounted for as an equity-settled or as a cash-settled transaction. In the case of an equity-settled transaction, there is no obligation to transfer economic benefits so the credit entry should be recognised as an increase in equity. A cash-settled transaction, on the other hand, does give rise to an obligation so a liability should be recognised. [IFRS 2 para 7].

12.50   As regards equity-settled transactions, IFRS 2 does not stipulate where in equity the credit entry should be recognised. This is a complicated area and companies may need to take legal advice to comply with local legislation.

UK.12.50.1   In the UK it is acceptable to present the credit in the profit and loss reserve. Indeed, this is where it is commonly seen. The credit could be taken to a separate share-based payment reserve, but not the share premium account, which is determined by the amount of cash subscribed for the shares by the employees (or the employee share trust as the case may be).

12.51   The credit to equity will be presented in the statement of changes in equity. It will not be presented in a statement of other comprehensive income, as it reflects the issue of an equity instrument and does not represent a gain.

12.52   Accounting for recharges from a parent to a subsidiary is discussed in paragraph 12.182.

Equity-settled share-based payment transactions

12.53   Equity-settled share-based payment transactions are transactions in which an entity receives goods or services as consideration for its own equity instruments or receives goods or services but has no obligation to settle the transaction with the supplier. Examples include the following:

- Employee share trusts.

- Employee share plans, including employee share purchase plans and share incentive plans.

- Transactions in which an entity obtains goods or services in exchange for its own equity instruments. For example, start-up companies may obtain consultancy and similar services in exchange for shares, thus preserving scarce cash resources and giving the supplier an opportunity to share in the company's success.

12.54 In each case, IFRS 2 requires an entity to measure the goods or services received and the corresponding increase in equity at fair value. Fair value is defined as *"the amount for which an asset could be exchanged, a liability settled, or an equity instrument granted could be exchanged, between knowledgeable, willing parties in an arm's length transaction"*. [IFRS 2 App A]. The measurement of share-based payment transactions is scoped out of IFRS 13; however, in our view the fair value measurement for liabilities in respect of cash settled awards should be consistent with the principles of IFRS 13.

Measurement of equity-settled share-based payment transactions

12.55 Ideally, the fair value of the goods or services obtained by an entity will be measurable directly. However, if the fair value of the goods or services cannot be measured reliably, the standard requires that it should be measured by reference to the fair value of the equity instruments granted as consideration. [IFRS 2 para 10]. This is sometimes referred to as the 'indirect method'. In these circumstances, the fair value of the equity instruments represents the best surrogate for the price of the goods or services.

12.56 The principle described in the previous paragraph is best illustrated in the context of employee services. Shares and share options are often granted to employees as part of their remuneration package, in addition to a cash salary and other employment benefits. Usually, it is not possible to measure directly the services received for particular components of an employee's remuneration package. Furthermore, options or shares are sometimes granted as part of a bonus arrangement, rather than as an element of basic remuneration. By granting options, in addition to other remuneration, the entity is paying additional remuneration to obtain additional benefits. Estimating the fair value of those additional benefits is likely to be difficult. Therefore, IFRS 2 requires an entity to measure the fair value of the employee services received (employee being as defined in para 12.57 below), by reference to the fair value of the equity instruments granted. [IFRS 2 para 11].

12.57 For this purpose employees are individuals who:

- Render personal services to the entity and are regarded as employees for legal or tax purposes.

- Work for the entity under its direction in the same way as individuals considered employees for legal or tax purposes.

- Render services that are similar to those rendered by employees.

[IFRS 2 App A].

Example – Who are employees?

An oil company hired an external consultant to assess its oil reserves. The service was provided over a five month period and will be settled by the entity issuing 100 shares to the consultant, valued at C40,000 when the contract was awarded. The entity estimated the cash fair value of the service to be C36,000, based on bids from other consultants. The consultant was considered an employee for tax purposes.

The consultant is considered an employee for the purpose of IFRS 2. Management should, therefore, recognise the service at the fair value of the equity instruments granted, that is, C40,000.

12.58   In the case of transactions with parties other than employees (employees being as defined in para 12.57 above), it is presumed that it will be possible to measure the fair value of goods or services reliably. [IFRS 2 para 13]. However, this may not always be possible, in which case the presumption should be rebutted and the fair value should be measured indirectly by reference to the fair value of the equity instrument granted as consideration.

12.59   Where the fair value of goods or services (other than those received from employees) is capable of direct measurement, it should be measured at the date on which the goods are received or the services are rendered. [IFRS 2 para 13]. An entity is required to consider if there are any unidentifiable goods or services received or to be received by the entity. This should be calculated as the fair value of the equity instruments granted, less the fair value of goods or services received. When the fair value of goods or services is measured by reference to the fair value of equity instruments granted, measurement should be at either:

- The date on which the equity instruments are granted, in the case of employee services or where the goods or services are unidentifiable.

- The date on which the goods are received or the services are rendered, in all other cases.

[IFRS 2 paras 11, 13, 13A].

12.60   The measurement of fair value at grant date is considered further from paragraph 12.278. Measurement of fair value when the goods or services are received is illustrated in the following examples:

Example 1 – Measurement of fair value by the direct method

Entity A is a small start-up entity. To assist it in developing its business, it receives consultancy services from entity B. The entities have agreed that, as entity A has scarce cash resources, the consideration for the consultancy services will be in the form of entity A's ordinary shares. The agreed rate is one share for each hour of consultancy services. Entity B has a publicised schedule of scale rates and the amount charged for a project of this nature is normally C100 per hour. Therefore, subject to the guidance noted in paragraphs 12.61 to 12.64 below, an expense and an increase in equity of C100 should be recognised by entity A for each hour of consultancy services received.

Note that the counterparty is an entity that is providing services rather than an individual and, therefore, does not fall within the category of employees or others providing similar services.

Example 2 – Measurement of fair value by the indirect method

The facts are similar to example 1, except that further shares are issued to entity B as it assists entity A in respect of a particular project, with 100 shares being awarded if the project is successful.

In this case, it may not be possible to measure reliably the fair value of the consultancy services themselves. The value of the transaction and shares received may have little to do with the value derived from the time spent by the consultants. Instead, the fair value should be measured as the services are rendered by reference to the fair value of the shares offered as consideration.

Example 3 – Contribution of assets to a joint venture

Entities X and Y have formed an incorporated joint venture, entity Z. On formation, in exchange for their equity interests in Z, entity X contributed property, plant and equipment and entity Y contributed intangible assets that do not constitute a business.

As explained in example 6 of paragraph 12.21, the asset contribution by venturers X and Y upon entity Z's formation is an equity-settled share-based payment transaction within IFRS 2's scope. Since the fair value of the assets contributed can be estimated reliably, entity Z should measure the assets received and the corresponding increase in equity directly, at the fair value of the assets received. In addition, entity Z would have to consider whether or not the fair value of the shares issued exceeded the fair value of the assets contributed as that would indicate there are unidentifiable goods or services. See paragraph 12.61.

12.61   The standard's scope has been expanded to include share-based payment transactions where it is difficult to identify that goods or services have been (or will be) received. For example, an entity may grant shares to a charitable organisation for nil consideration. It is usually not possible to identify the specific goods or services received in return for such a transaction. Additionally, there are some situations where the fair value of goods or services received (if any) appears to be less than the fair value of the equity instruments granted or liability incurred. In such situations, the standard requires the entity to measure the identifiable goods or services received at fair value and then the unidentifiable goods or services received will be measured as the difference between the fair value of the share-based payment and the fair value of any identifiable goods or services received. [IFRS 2 para 13A].

[The next paragraph is 12.64.]

12.64   The standard seems to be an almost generic rebuttal of the presumption for non-employee goods or services that the fair value of the goods or services can be more reliably measured than the fair value of the equity instrument. The argument is that if the goods or services cannot be identified then clearly they cannot be reliably measured. As a result of the change to the standard, far more work is required to determine all aspects of the transaction (that is, the fair value of the equity instrument, the identifiable goods or services acquired and the unidentifiable element), and the appropriate accounting for each aspect. The following examples illustrate the principles above.

Example 1 – Measurement of fair value where services are unidentifiable

An entity granted shares with a total fair value of C100,000 to parties other than employees who are from a particular section of the community (historically disadvantaged individuals), as a means of enhancing its image as a good corporate citizen. The economic benefits derived from enhancing its corporate image could take a variety of forms, such as increasing its customer base, attracting or retaining employees (who may prefer to work for an entity that supports such 'good causes'), or improving or maintaining its ability to tender successfully for business contracts.

The entity cannot identify the specific consideration received. For example, no cash was received and no service conditions were imposed. Therefore, the identifiable consideration (nil) is less than the fair value of the equity instruments granted (C100,000). The circumstances indicate that unidentifiable goods or services have been (or will be) received and, therefore, IFRS 2 applies.

The rebuttable presumption in IFRS 2, that the fair value of the goods or services received can be estimated reliably, does not apply here. The entity should instead measure the goods or services received by reference to the fair value of the equity instruments granted. [IFRS 2 para 13, 13A].

Example 2 – Measurement of fair value where fair value of license cannot be reliably estimated

An entity grants 10% of its shares to the local government for nil consideration in exchange for an indefinite-lived license to operate in that country. The fair value of the license is not determinable.

The entity is expected to receive a benefit from the license and, thus, the transaction would fall within the scope of IFRS 2. As the license is an identifiable good, the share-based payment should be recognised at the date when the license is received. As the fair value of the license received cannot be estimated reliably, the entity should instead measure the license received by reference to the fair value of the equity instruments granted.

Note that if the fair value of the license is determinable and less than the fair value of the shares, there may be unidentifiable goods or services to be accounted for, as discussed above. The unidentifiable goods or services could be a premium paid by the company and, therefore, makes up a part of the license's cost. In this case, the company would need to consider if the carrying amount of the license is impaired and it may be able to support the carrying amount through a value-in-use model.

Example 3 – Services provided where equity value appears to be greater than the value of the services

The facts are the same as those in the example in paragraph 12.57, except that the services are being provided by a large consulting firm.

In this case, although IFRS 2 requires the award to be measured directly, with reference to the value of the services received, the fact that the value of the shares given (C40,000) for the consultancy services are clearly worth more than the value for the services (C36,000) indicates that some unidentifiable goods or services will be received by the company. The oil company should, therefore, record a charge of C40,000.

Example 4 – Issue of shares to existing members and customers on listing

Entity A is a mutual entity and its shares are held by members. However, entity A plans to demutualise and list on the local stock exchange and it will convert the existing 'member' shares to ordinary equity capital in a listed entity. As part of the process, entity A will issue free shares to its customers (those customers that are not members).

The appropriate accounting for the share-based payment is determined by separately considering the shares issued to existing members and customers.

Existing members
This is not a share-based payment arrangement as it is with members in their capacity as existing equity holders.

Customers (that are not members)
The entity will issue shares for nil consideration and it is not possible to identify the specific goods and services received in return for the shares. Entity A will account for this arrangement under IFRS 2. Entity A measures the unidentifiable goods and services that are received in accordance with IFRS 2 by using the fair value of the equity instrument granted and recognises a related expense immediately.

12.65 IFRS 2 envisages that it will normally be possible to estimate the fair value of equity instruments granted. However, it is acknowledged that there may be situations in which it is not possible to estimate fair value reliably. In these circumstances, IFRS 2 requires the following approach.

- The equity instruments granted should be measured at their intrinsic value, both initially and subsequently at each reporting date and at the date on which the award is finally settled. For a grant of share options, the award is finally settled when the options are exercised, forfeited or lapse. Any change in intrinsic value is recognised in the statement of comprehensive income.

- The amount recognised as an expense should be based on the number of equity instruments that ultimately vest or, in the case of options, are ultimately exercised.

[IFRS 2 para 24].

12.66 We believe that it will rarely be the case that the fair value of equity instruments granted cannot be estimated reliably. If in a rare situation it is the case that the fair value cannot be measured, the entity would measure the transaction using an intrinsic value measurement method. However, specialist advice should be sought if this measurement method is to be followed.

Grant date

12.67 Grant date is defined in IFRS 2 as *"the date at which the entity and another party (including an employee) agree to a share-based payment arrangement, being when the entity and the counterparty have a shared understanding of the terms and conditions of the arrangement. At grant date the entity confers on the counterparty the right to cash, other assets, or equity instruments of the entity, provided the specified vesting conditions, if any, are met. If that agreement is subject to an approval process (for example, by shareholders), grant date is the date when that approval is obtained"*. [IFRS 2 App A].

12.68 Often it will be clear as to when the parties involved in a share-based payment arrangement have a shared understanding of the arrangement's terms and conditions. Sometimes, however, certain of the terms may need to be confirmed at a later date. For example, if an entity's board of directors agrees to issue share options to senior management, but the exercise price of those options will be set by the remuneration committee that meets in three months' time, grant date is when the exercise price is set by the remuneration committee even though the service period starts when the awards are offered to senior management.

12.69 Similar questions are raised when equity instruments are granted subject to an approval process. This is considered in the following example.

Example – Grant subject to approval process

Directors of an entity customarily include in letters to new employees the offer of options to subscribe for shares in the entity. In February 20X5 the entity offered new employees options over 10,000 shares at the then market price of C10 per share. The letters stated that the board of directors supported the offer. The awards were approved by the shareholders in June 20X5, by which time the market price of the entity's shares had risen to C15 and the fair value of the options had also increased. What is the grant date for the purposes of IFRS 2? The possibilities are:

■ The date on which the original offers were made – February 20X5.

■ The date on which the awards were approved by shareholders – June 20X5.

The allotment of shares or rights to shares in general has to be authorised by shareholders in general meeting or by the entity's articles. In this case, the award of options was subject to shareholder approval so the grant date is the date on which that approval was obtained (that is, June 20X5).

In practice many companies have in place a pre-existing authorisation from shareholders to cover potential awards of equity instruments to employees before the next AGM. If such pre-authorisation were to exist, in this case, the grant date would generally be considered to have been February 20X5. The situation might differ where the board of directors, as majority shareholders, controls the entity. Where the directors' shareholding gives them the necessary power to authorise the award, for example if there is no shareholders' agreement or similar that requires the consent of the minority, the directors might be able to regard their meeting as being a properly constituted shareholders' meeting for this purpose and should, as a matter of good practice, record themselves as meeting in that form.

12.70   In the previous example, if grant date is considered to be June 20X5, employees may have already begun to provide services to the entity before that date. As IFRS 2 requires the entity to recognise an expense as employee services are received, an expense will sometimes be recognised in respect of a share-based payment arrangement in advance of the grant date. [IFRS 2 IG 4]. In this situation, the grant date fair value of the equity instruments should be estimated, for example, by reference to the fair value of the equity instruments at the balance sheet date. An expense will then be based on an estimated amount until the date of grant has been established. At that point, the entity should revise the earlier estimates so that the amounts recognised for services received in respect of the grant are ultimately based on the grant date fair value of the equity instruments.

12.71   The following examples provide further illustrations in determining the grant date when applying IFRS 2. It is vital that the grant date is correctly established as this is the point at which the fair value of the equity-settled share-based payment is measured.

Example 1 – Award subject to shareholder approval

An award is communicated to individual employees on 1 December 20X5, subject to shareholder approval. The award is then approved by shareholders on 1 February 20X6, with the same terms as had initially been communicated to employees. A letter to formalise the award is sent to individual employees on 1 March 20X6.

As the award is subject to an approval process (in this example, by shareholders), the grant date is the date when that approval is obtained. The letter to formalise the award is mainly administrative, both the employees and the employer have a shared understanding on 1 February 20X6 and, therefore, this is the grant date. The vesting period starts on 1 December 20X5 as this is when employees become aware of the nature of the award and begin providing services.

Example 2 – Individual notification of award

An award is approved by the board/shareholders on 1 December 20X5. The general terms and conditions of the award set out the relevant employee population that will participate in the award, but provide insufficient information to determine each employee's share. The general terms and conditions are posted to the website on 31 December 20X5. The employees are individually informed of their shares on 1 February 20X6.

The grant date is when both parties agree to a share-based payment arrangement. The word 'agree' is used in its usual sense, which means that there must be both an offer and acceptance of that offer. Hence, the date at which one party makes an offer to another party is not always the grant date. In some instances, the counterparty explicitly agrees to the arrangement, for example, by signing a contract. In other instances, agreement might be implicit for example, for many share-based payment arrangements with employees, the employees' agreement is evidenced by their commencing to render services. Therefore, in this example the grant date is 1 February 20X6. The vesting period begins on 31 December 20X5 as this is when employees become aware of the award's general terms and conditions and begin providing services.

Example 3 – Communication to employees following standard communication procedures

On 10 June 20X1, the key terms and conditions of an entity's share-based payment award were discussed with all employees concerned. Employees were also informed that the award was subject to board approval, which was expected to be obtained on 20 June 20X1.

As anticipated, the award was approved by the board on 20 June 20X1. Management subsequently followed the normal process for communications, sending the full terms and conditions of the award to the employees' home addresses, such that employees received them in the following few days.

We believe that the grant date in this example is 20 June 20X1 given the following:

- the key terms and conditions were communicated to employees;

- employees had no opportunity to further negotiate the terms and conditions following board approval;

- the entity followed its normal communication procedures to provide full terms and conditions to employees; and

- there is a very short period of time between board approval and employees receiving the full terms and conditions.

The vesting period starts on 10 June 20X1 as this is when employees become aware of the nature of the award and begin providing services. See next example for services received before the grant date.

Example 4 – Services received before grant date

A new compensation package for key employees is announced on 1 January 20X5. The plan covers the calendar year 20X5, incorporates the results of the year's annual appraisal process and includes a new share option plan. The option plan is subject to approval by shareholders. The shareholders approved the plan on 28 February 20X6.

The fair value of the share options is measured at the grant date, 28 February 20X6. If the agreement between the entity and its employees is subject to an approval process (for example, by shareholders), the grant date cannot be earlier than the date on which that approval is obtained. However, IFRS 2 requires the entity to recognise employee services as they are received. In this case, the expense will be recognised in advance of the grant date, so the vesting period will start on 1 January 20X5. This is the date the employees begin rendering services with an expectation of satisfying the condition attached to the compensation package (the date from which the employees become aware that they are working towards the award). [IFRS 2 paras 7, IG 4]. The entity should estimate the grant date fair value for the purpose of recognising the expense during the period between the service commencement date and the grant date. Management should revise the estimate at each reporting period until the grant date has been established. Once the grant date has been established, the recognised expense is based on the actual grant date fair value of the equity instruments in the period of change.

Example 5 – Bonus plan with services received before grant date and settlement in both cash and shares

Note that this example also illustrates the impact of vesting conditions (see further from para 12.77).

On 1 January 20X5 an entity announced a bonus subject to exceeding the revenue target for 20X5.

C500 of the bonus will be paid in cash on 31 March 20X6 provided that the employee is in service at 31 December 20X5. The other part of the bonus will be settled in share options provided that the employee is still in service on 31 March 20X6. The exercise price and number of options will be approved by management on 31 March 20X6. Management expect that the revenue target will be met and that no employees will leave between 31 December 20X5 and 31 March 20X6. At 31 December 20X5 the estimated grant date fair value is C500.

The entity should accrue a liability of C500 for the cash part of the bonus at 31 December 20X5, because the revenue target was met and employees are entitled to the payment even if they leave by 31 March 20X6.

The entity should also recognise an estimated expense of C400 (12/15ths of C500) and a corresponding increase in equity for the part of the bonus that is to be settled in share options subject to the service vesting condition.

As for example 3 above, the share options did not have a grant date on 31 December 20X5, because the parties did not have a shared understanding of the arrangement's terms and conditions. However, IFRS 2 requires the entity to recognise the services when received and, therefore, the fair value at the grant date, 31 March 20X6, must be estimated.

Once the terms of the options are fixed on the grant date, 31 March 20X6, the actual fair value can be calculated and, if necessary, the cumulative charge should be revised.

Example 6 – Award at the discretion of remuneration committee

Employees have been awarded share options that will vest subject to achieving a total shareholder return (TSR) performance target over a three year period. However, at the end of the three year period, where the remuneration committee is not satisfied that the TSR position achieved is supported by the underlying performance of the business, the committee has discretion to refuse the award.

Where the remuneration committee has discretion to override an award, despite a performance condition being achieved, there is no shared understanding at the date the award is made. The grant date does not occur until the remuneration committee operates its overriding discretion at the end of the vesting period. The fair value of the award would, therefore, be estimated at each reporting date from the date that services are provided and final measurement would occur at the end of the vesting period. As a result, this may give rise to significantly greater charges in the income statement than where the grant date occurs when the award is made.

In certain circumstances it may be possible to conclude that grant date has been achieved when the award is made. For example, where a remuneration committee has discretion to alter the award but only where the value of each individual's award is not adversely affected, grant date may have been achieved for the guaranteed element of the award. Alternatively, where, in practice, the remuneration committee has never exercised its discretion to override and the entity can prove that it will not do so in the future (and employees share this understanding), it may be possible to conclude that grant date has occurred. It should be noted, however, that this is likely to be difficult to achieve where a discretion clause is set out in the articles.

The circumstances surrounding the award should be carefully assessed and the situation explained in the financial statements where it is concluded that the grant date has occurred when the award is made. Where material, it should be disclosed as a significant accounting policy judgement under IAS 1. [IAS 1 para 113].

Example 7 – Market performance condition not met but remuneration committee agrees to continue with award

Employees were awarded share options in entity A subject to entity A's share price increasing by 10% between 1 July 20X0 and 30 June 20X3. The 10% target was not achieved. However, on 30 June 20X3 entity A's remuneration committee decided that all the share options should vest anyway.

Entity A modified the share option award at 30 June 20X3. There is likely to be a cumulative charge for the original award as the likelihood of meeting the share price target, a market performance condition, would have been factored into the original grant date fair value calculation. However, the fair value of the original share option award at the modification date is nil, because the performance condition has not been met. The modified award, therefore, has incremental fair value.

Note that if the vesting condition had been a non-market performance condition, such as achieving a net profit target, there would be no cumulative charge for the original award as this would have been reversed at the time it became clear that the net profit target would not be met. The full incremental fair value of the modified award would, however, be recognised.

In practice, the ability of a remuneration committee to make this kind of 'modification' may be set out in the award's terms and conditions as discussed in example 6 above and may mean that there is no grant date.

See from paragraph 12.96 below for definitions of market and non-market conditions. See also from paragraph 12.115 for guidance on modifications.

[The next paragraph is 12.77.]

Vesting conditions

12.77 As explained in paragraph 12.43, where a counterparty to a share-based payment arrangement is required to complete a specified period of service before its equity instruments vest, the goods or services obtained by the reporting entity are recognised over that period. [IFRS 2 para 15]. For example, an entity grants options to its employees with a grant date fair value of C300,000. These options vest in three years' time with the only condition being that the employees remain in the entity's service for that period. Assuming that all of the options do vest (that is, none of the employees leave the entity), the amount charged as an expense each year will be C100,000. This will be the case regardless of any movements in the price of the entity's shares. So, even if the options have an intrinsic value of, say, C500,000 when they are exercised, the amount charged as an expense will be unchanged. Having determined the 'price' of employee services when the options were granted, this remains fixed.

12.78 In reality, employee share trusts, indeed equity-settled share-based payment transactions generally, are seldom that simple. Typically, there will be performance conditions that must be satisfied before employees are absolutely entitled to the equity instruments. For example, the number of options to which employees are entitled under a bonus plan may depend on a certain increase in profit or growth in the entity's share price. Even in the simple example described in the previous paragraph, the amount charged as an expense in each period will vary depending on the latest estimate of the likely number of employees who will remain for three years and, hence, the number of options that will vest. Although the fair value of equity instruments granted is not re-measured, the estimate of the number of equity instruments that is likely to vest is revised, if necessary, until the instruments actually do vest.

12.79 Conditions that must be satisfied before a counterparty becomes unconditionally entitled to the equity instruments it has been granted are referred to as vesting conditions. IFRS 2 defines vesting conditions as:

> *"the conditions that determine whether the entity receives the services that entitle the counterparty to receive cash, other assets or equity instruments of the entity, under a share-based payment arrangement. Vesting conditions are either service conditions or performance conditions. Service conditions require the counterparty to complete a specified period of service. Performance conditions, require the counterparty to complete a specified period of service and specified performance targets to be met (such as a specified increase in the entity's profit over a specified period of time). A performance condition might include a market condition."* [IFRS 2 App A].

It follows that the vesting period is the period during which all the specified vesting conditions are to be satisfied. Paragraph 12.41 above provides guidance on timing of recognition and the vesting period.

12.80 Vesting conditions include the requirements to be satisfied for an employee to obtain the award. In some circumstances there may be, for example, a restriction on employees selling shares received from an award after they have become entitled to them. This is a post-vesting restriction and not a vesting condition. See further from paragraph 12.202.

12.81 Share-based payment awards may include non-compete provisions either during or after the vesting period. Non-compete provisions can be vesting conditions or post-vesting restrictions, depending on the specific circumstances, which would result in different accounting treatments. This is a complex area, and management should seek specialist advice.

[The next paragraph is 12.83.]

12.83 Any other conditions in a share-based payment transaction, such as a requirement to save or a requirement to hold shares, are 'non-vesting conditions'. Non-vesting conditions are taken into account when determining the award's fair value.

12.84 There is a table summarising the implications of vesting and non-vesting conditions on accounting for share-based payment transactions in appendix 1 to this chapter.

12.85 In summary, service vesting conditions (which are non-market conditions) and non-market performance conditions are not incorporated into the grant date fair value calculation. IFRS 2, however, requires that market performance conditions and non-vesting conditions be incorporated into the grant date fair value calculation. This is discussed in more detail in the following sections.

12.86 The following diagram illustrates the principles discussed in this section.

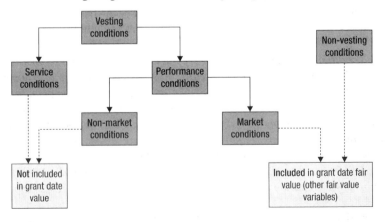

[The next paragraph is 12.88.]

Service conditions

12.88 Identifying a service condition is more straightforward than identifying a performance condition. Service conditions are not explicitly defined by IFRS 2. However, the definition of 'vesting conditions' includes a statement that service conditions require the counterparty to complete a specified period of service.

12.89 Service conditions are non-market conditions (see further from para 12.96 for discussion of market and non-market conditions) and this fact is important in relation to both the measurement and recognition of particular awards. Service conditions are not taken into consideration when determining the grant date fair value of an award. Instead, service conditions are taken into consideration when estimating the number of awards that will vest. On a cumulative basis, therefore, no amount is recognised for goods or services received where an award does not vest because a specified service condition has not been met. [IFRS 2 para 19]. As a result of this, during the vesting period, the IFRS 2 expense can change depending on changes in the service condition expectation.

Performance conditions

12.90 Defining performance conditions is more difficult. As set out in paragraph 12.79 above, the definition of 'vesting conditions' includes a statement that performance conditions require the counterparty to complete a service period and meet specified performance targets.

12.91 We believe that the following principles are appropriate for determining whether a condition is a performance vesting condition.

- The condition occurs during the service period. As explained in paragraph 12.79 above, IFRS 2 defines vesting conditions as the conditions that determine whether the entity receives the services that entitle the counterparty to receive the award. Conversely, if a condition's outcome will only be determined after any required service period, then the condition is not a vesting condition because it does not determine whether the entity receives services in exchange for the award granted. Examples would include where an employee has to work for three years but there is an EPS target based on a longer, say, five year period, or alternatively an employee has to work for three years and will become entitled to an award if the company has listed, whether or not the employee is still working for the company at the time of listing.

- The condition needs to be achievable and either determines the length of period over which the employee has to provide services or in some way reflects a measure of the quality of those services. Achieving the condition, or target, may be partly within the employee's control, but cannot be wholly within their control (see next bullet point).

- The condition is not wholly within the control of either the employee or employer. Where the outcome of a condition (other than whether or not the employee completes the service period related to the performance condition) is wholly within the control of the employee then it is not a performance condition. If the employee can unilaterally decide whether or not the target is achieved, then services are not required. Examples include the requirement to hold a specified number of shares or to continue saving in the context of matching share awards and SAYE plans respectively.

12.92 Performance conditions include performance targets such as revenue targets, EPS growth, total shareholder return (TSR) hurdles and share price growth.

12.93 Performance conditions may be either market or non-market conditions. See further from paragraph 12.96 for discussion of market and non-market conditions.

12.94 Performance conditions that include a market condition (often referred to as market performance conditions) are incorporated into the grant date fair value of an award. An expense will, therefore, be recorded, even if the market performance condition is not met (assuming all other service and non-market performance vesting conditions are met).

12.95 The treatment of performance conditions that include a non-market condition is similar to that of service conditions, that is, they are not included in the grant date fair value. Instead, non-market performance conditions are taken into consideration when estimating the number of awards that will vest. Therefore on a cumulative basis, no amount is recognised for goods or services received where an award does not vest, because a specified non-market performance condition has not been met. [IFRS 2 para 19]. As for service conditions, during the vesting period, the IFRS 2 expense can change as a result of a change in non-market performance vesting conditions expectation.

Market conditions

12.96 The treatment of vesting conditions will vary depending on whether they relate to the market price of the entity's equity instruments. Such conditions, which IFRS 2 calls market conditions, are taken into account when determining the grant date fair value of the equity instruments granted. They are ignored for the purposes of estimating the number of equity instruments that will vest. [IFRS 2 para 21]. The full definition of 'market condition' is:

"A condition upon which the exercise price, vesting or exercisability of an equity instrument depends that is related to the market price of the entity's equity instruments, such as attaining a specified share price or a specified amount of intrinsic value of a share option, or achieving a specified target that is based on the market price of the entity's equity instruments relative to an index of market prices of equity instruments of other entities." [IFRS 2 App A].

12.97 Examples of market conditions include where an entity's share price must out perform the market, achieve a minimum price in a specified period, or achieve a total shareholder return target. Further examples are included in the table in paragraph 12.100. Such conditions are included in the estimate of the fair value of a share-based payment. They should not be taken into account for the purpose of estimating the number of equity instruments that will vest. Market conditions in the context of valuation are considered further from paragraph 12.288.

Non-market conditions

12.98 Vesting conditions other than market conditions are non-market conditions. Examples of non-market conditions are earnings per share or profit targets.

12.99 Unlike market conditions, non-market conditions are not considered when estimating the fair value of a share-based payment. For non-market conditions, an entity should recognise the goods or services it has acquired during the vesting period based on the best available estimate of the number of equity instruments expected to vest. It should revise that estimate, if necessary, when subsequent information indicates that the number of equity instruments expected to vest differs from previous estimates. Finally, on the vesting date, the entity should revise the estimate to equal the number of equity instruments that ultimately vest. [IFRS 2 paras 19-20].

12.100 The following table illustrates some of the more common market and non-market conditions associated with share-based payment arrangements.

Market conditions	Non-market conditions
(Affecting the fair value of the award)	(Affecting the number of awards that vest)
Achieve a minimum share price by a specified date.	Remain in employment for a specified period of time.
Achieve a total shareholder return target.	Achieve earnings per share or profit targets.
Out perform a share price index.	Complete a particular project.
	Successful IPO (see para 12.113.1).

Non-vesting conditions

12.101 Non-vesting conditions are conditions other than service and performance conditions. Non-vesting conditions include the requirement to save or the requirement to hold shares. Although such requirements occur during the vesting period, they are often wholly within the control of the employee and the conditions are not related to duties specified in an employee's employment contract. They, therefore, do not determine whether the entity receives the services linked to shares.

12.102   A typical SAYE (save as you earn) plan, common in the UK, has terms requiring employees to contribute a maximum of £250 per month to an employee share trust. Employees are required to contribute to the SAYE plan for five years, after which they have the choice to either receive their cash back plus accrued interest or use the cash to acquire shares at a 20% discount to the market price on the grant date. An employee that ceases saving receives a reimbursement of all amounts saved to date, plus interest, but must withdraw from the plan and forfeit their right to acquire shares.

12.103   The requirement to hold shares is seen in matching share plans. For example, employees are part of a share award whereby they receive part of their bonus in shares. On becoming entitled to the bonus and shares employees can elect to hold their shares for three years, at which point the entity will give employees an additional share for every share that the employee has not sold, provided that the employees are still in service.

[The next paragraph is 12.105.]

12.105   Non-vesting conditions should be incorporated into the grant date fair value of the award. As a result, the award's grant date fair value may well be lower than awards without such a requirement, because the probability of employees failing to save (and, hence, withdrawing from the plan) or selling their restricted shares (and, hence, losing the matching shares) will be taken into consideration.

12.106   An employee's failure to save or failure to hold restricted shares is treated as a cancellation. This results in the acceleration of any unvested portion of the award on the date that the employee ceases to save or sells the restricted shares (see para 12.234).

[The next paragraph is 12.108.]

12.108   Share awards may vest in instalments or may have more than one vesting period, as illustrated in example 3 of paragraph 12.114 and in example 5 of paragraph 12.161 respectively.

Reload feature

12.109   Some share options contain a reload feature. This provides for an automatic grant of additional options ('reload options') whenever the option holder exercises previously granted options using the entity's shares, rather than cash, to satisfy the exercise price. This is illustrated in the following simple example.

> **Example – Share options with a reload feature**
>
> An entity has issued 100 options to one of its directors. The total exercise price for the options is C100. However, there is a reload feature which means that the exercise price may be satisfied by the option holder surrendering shares in the entity to the value of C100 and, by doing so, becoming eligible for an additional option plan. Like vesting conditions, the existence of a reload feature may influence the value of the option to the holder, but it is not taken into account when estimating fair value. Instead, when a reload option is granted it is accounted for as a new option grant. [IFRS 2 para 22].

Revising estimates due to changes in service or non-market conditions

12.110   Returning to the example set out in paragraph 12.77, management may have estimated at grant date that 10% of employees will leave the entity before the end of three years. Hence, the expense in the first year would be reduced by 10% to C90,000 (that is, C300,000 × 1/3 × 90%). If, during the second year it becomes apparent that fewer employees are leaving, management may revise their estimate of the number of leavers to only 5%. Accordingly, an expense of C100,000 will be recognised in the second year such that the cumulative expense at the end of that second year is C190,000 (that is, C300,000 × 2/3 × 95%). At the end of the third year, 94% of the options do vest. The cumulative expense over the vesting period is C282,000 (that is, C300,000 × 3/3 × 94%) so the expense in the third year is C92,000.

12.111   In a more extreme example, management may estimate in the first year of an employee share option plan that a particular long-term profit target will be met. Accordingly an expense of, say, C100,000 is recognised. During the second year, following a serious downturn in the entity's fortunes, management may consider that there is little chance that targets will be met. If they estimate that no options will vest, the cumulative expense at the end of the second year will be adjusted to zero so the expense to date of C100,000 will be reversed in that second year. Of course, if the vesting condition had been a market condition rather than a profit target, no adjustment would be made. It is interesting to note that if management were to cancel the award in year two on the basis that it will never vest, we believe the application of IFRS 2's cancellation requirements that most align with the principles in the standard would result in accelerated recognition of an expense. See paragraph 12.138 for discussion on accounting for cancellations.

Post-vesting

12.112   In each of the examples above, changes have been made to estimates during the vesting period. However, no further adjustments are made after the vesting date, regardless of whether the equity instruments are later forfeited or, in the case of share options, the options are not exercised. [IFRS 2 para 23]. In drafting IFRS 2, the IASB took the view that the lapse of a share option at the end of the exercise period does not change the fact that the original transaction occurred, that is, goods or services were received as consideration for the issue of an equity instrument. The share option lapsing does not represent a gain to the entity, because there is no change to the entity's net assets. In other words, although some might see such an event as being a benefit to the remaining shareholders, it has no effect on the entity's financial position. In effect, one type of equity interest (the option holders' interest) becomes part of another type of equity interest (the shareholders' interest). So, in the example described in paragraph 12.110 above, after vesting there will be no adjustment to the total expense of C282,000 even if none of the options are exercised.

12.113 The method of revising estimates in each of the examples above is consistent with that applied in the Implementation Guidance to IFRS 2. [IFRS 2 paras IG4, IG12]. Where estimates are revised in a period, the cumulative expense to the end of that period is 'trued up' and the amount recognised in the period is simply the difference between that cumulative expense and the equivalent cumulative expense at the end of the previous period. However, despite the fact that this method is required by IFRS 2, it does not appear to comply with the requirements of IAS 8. A change to the estimate of, for example, the number of share awards that will vest will have an impact on the expense recognised in both the current and future accounting periods. In this scenario (which has some similarity to a change in the useful life or residual value of a fixed asset for the purposes of measuring depreciation) IAS 8 requires that the effect of the change should be recognised prospectively by including it in profit or loss in both the period of the change and future periods. [IAS 8 para 36]. This suggests that when an estimate of the number of share awards that will vest is changed, the revised expense should be recognised over the remainder of the vesting period rather than 'trued up' in the period of change. It can only be assumed that, in drafting the implementation guidance to IFRS 2, the IASB had in mind paragraph 37 of IAS 8, which requires that to the extent that a change in accounting estimate gives rise to changes in assets and liabilities, or relates to an item of equity, it shall be recognised by adjusting the carrying amount of the related asset, liability or equity item in the period of the change. This paragraph would appear to apply if the principle of IFRS 2 was to measure that fair value of the equity instruments granted, but it is less clear why it is invoked when the principle is to measure the fair value of the goods or services received.

Awards conditional on an IPO or change in control

12.113.1 IFRS 2 does not deal explicitly with awards that are conditional on an initial public offering (IPO). As noted above, an expense in respect of an award of, say, options, is recognised immediately if the award vests immediately, or over the vesting period if one exists. [IFRS 2 paras 14, 15]. In the case of an IPO (or similar exit event), the award will generally not vest until the IPO occurs (and employees are still employed by the company at that time). It is therefore reasonable to conclude that the vesting period will commence no later than the grant date and end on the date of the IPO. However, this raises two questions:

- What will the grant date be?
- How can the date of a future IPO be estimated reliably?

12.113.2 As regards grant date, the facts of individual awards will vary. Sometimes, an award will be subject to approval at the time of the IPO, in which case grant date would correspond with the date of the IPO. On other occasions, shareholder approval will have been obtained when the award is made or at some other time in advance of the IPO. Nevertheless, IFRS 2 requires that an expense is recognised as employee services are received, regardless of when grant date is determined to occur. Therefore, where the grant date falls after the employees have begun to provide services, the fair value of the award should be estimated at each reporting period until the grant date is established and then revised once the grant date has been established, as described in paragraph 12.70.

12.113.3 Where an award is conditional upon an IPO occurring but employee service up to the IPO date is not required, or perhaps service is only required for part of the period, the IPO condition becomes a non-vesting condition. Non-vesting conditions are considered from paragraph 12.101.

12.113.4 The more difficult question concerns how the date of a future IPO can be estimated reliably. Paragraph 15(b) of IFRS 2 requires that where the length of the vesting period varies, depending on when a performance condition is satisfied, an estimate is made on the basis of the most likely outcome. Some companies may find it extremely difficult in practice to estimate the date of an IPO. Nevertheless, a reasonable estimate should be made, although this may then be revised if necessary. This is illustrated in the following example.

> **Example – Estimating listing date**
>
> The directors of an entity with a June year end are contemplating a listing of the entity's shares. An award of unvested shares is made to employees on 31 March 20X5, but the shares vest only in the event of an IPO. The company will not pay dividends before an IPO. Employees leaving the entity before the IPO occurs will lose their entitlement to the shares.
>
> When the award is made, the directors estimate that a stock market listing will be achieved in three years' time. However, during the remainder of 20X5 and the first half of 20X6, the entity performs well and, following discussions with the entity's bankers, the directors decide to seek a listing by the end of 20X6. Due to unforeseen circumstances, this target is not achieved, but the shares are finally listed on 31 August 20X7.
>
> Assuming that the directors have the authority to make the award of shares to the employees, grant date will be 31 March 20X5 and the fair value of the award will be measured on that date. If the award is subject to shareholder approval at the date of the IPO, fair value will be estimated (for example, by reference to the fair value of the options at each balance sheet date) and revised at grant date when the shareholder approval is obtained.
>
> When the award is made, the directors estimate that the listing may be achieved in three years' time. An expense in respect of employee services is therefore recognised over this period. By 30 June 20X6, the directors have revised their estimate of the date of listing to the end of 20X6, so the recognition of the expense is accelerated. By

30 June 20X7, the listing has not yet occurred, but the process has commenced, and the directors estimate that it will be achieved within two months. The expense for the year ending 30 June 20X7 will therefore be based on this estimate. So for the three financial years ending 30 June 20X7, the estimated vesting period for the award of shares for the purposes of recognising an expense in accordance with IFRS 2 will be as follows:

Year	Vesting period
30 June 20X5	Three years ending 31 March 20X8
30 June 20X6	One year and nine months ending 31 December 20X6
30 June 20X7	Two years and five months ending 31 August 20X7

The estimated length of the vesting period is not factored into the grant date fair value of the award. This is because the condition to provide employee services until the date of the IPO is a non-market vesting condition. A single best estimate of the grant date fair value is calculated given the interaction of the various components of the fair value calculation. In accordance with the guidance in paragraph 12.110, the estimate of awards expected to vest should be revised at each reporting date, as a result of the change in service period. The accounting for changes in estimates such as these under IFRS 2 is illustrated in example 7 in paragraph 12.114.

12.113.5 Where awards vest only on an exit event such as an IPO, and an exit event is not deemed to be probable, no expense is recognised. It may be determined that some of the awards will vest in another way. These points are illustrated in the following examples.

Example 1 – Vesting linked to a change in control requirement

An entity enters into an equity-settled share-based payment arrangement with employees whereby each employee is entitled to 1,000 free shares provided that:

- There is a change in control of the entity (that is, the majority of shareholders change); and
- The employee is employed by the entity on the date that the change in control occurs.

The change in control requirement is a non-market performance vesting condition. The accounting treatment is to estimate at the grant date and at each reporting date the number of awards that are expected to vest based on:

- the number of employees who are expected to achieve the service period; and
- whether the change in control is probable.

If the change in control condition assessment changes from probable to improbable, the cumulative charge recognised is reversed through the income statement.

Example 2 – Interaction with other vesting conditions

As in the example in paragraph 12.113.4, the directors of an entity are contemplating a listing of the entity's shares. The entity made an award of options to 10 employees on 31 March 20X5. The grant date was achieved on this date.

The award is exercisable in full on an IPO. Alternatively, where an employee who is leaving the entity is determined to be a good leaver before an IPO has occurred, he/she may exercise options on a *pro rata* basis (based on the length of time the employee has served since the award was granted as a proportion of the maximum five-year period that the award may be in existence). The arrangement's terms and conditions define a good leaver as someone who is made redundant, dies or retires on reaching normal retirement age.

There is a cut-off date such that unvested awards will lapse after five years, on 31 March 20Y0.

On 30 June 20X5, the directors estimate that a listing will be achieved on 31 March 20X8. One employee is expected to be a good leaver before 31 March 20X8, reaching normal retirement age on 31 December 20X6. All other employees are expected to remain with the entity beyond 31 March 20X8.

On 30 June 20X6, following a change in the entity's fortunes, the directors are of the view that the entity is unlikely to float before 31 March 20Y0. A restructuring programme is underway; it is anticipated that three employees will be made redundant on 31 December 20X6.

For the entity's 30 June 20X5 year end, the award will be treated in two tranches. Awards are expected to vest on 31 March 20X8 for nine employees. The grant date fair value of their awards will be spread over the three-year vesting period — that is, three out of 36 months of the charge will be taken in the period to 30 June 20X5. The grant date fair value of the award for the good leaver will be spread over the 21-month vesting period to 31 December 20X6 — that is, three out of 21 months' charge will be taken in the period to 30 June 20X5. The calculation for the good leaver will also take into account the fact that vesting will be on a *pro rata* basis — that is, based on 21 out of 60 months' service.

At 30 June 20X6, a reversal of the charge in respect of the nine awards no longer expected to vest on an IPO will be necessary. However, this will only be a partial reversal in respect of the three employees who will be made redundant. The charge in respect of these good leavers will now be spread over the shorter 21-month period from the grant date to 31 December 20X6 and will be adjusted for the fact that it will vest on a *pro rata* basis. A charge will continue to be made for the employee expected to retire on 31 December 20X6.

Illustrative examples

12.114 Having measured the fair value of the goods or services received (either directly or indirectly) and determined the period over which they should be recognised, it is necessary to calculate the amount that should be recognised in each reporting period. This is illustrated in the following examples, which have been categorised according to type of vesting conditions.

Service vesting conditions

Example 1 – Grant of equity instruments with a time-based vesting condition

On 1 January 20X5, entity A made an award of 1,000 options to each of its 60 employees. The only condition associated with the award is that recipients must remain in entity A's employment for three years. The grant date fair value of each option is C5.

At the date of the award, management estimated that 10% of employees (that is, 6 employees) would leave the entity before the end of three years. During 20X6 it became apparent that fewer employees than expected were leaving so management revised its estimate of the number of leavers to only 5% (that is, 3 employees). At the end of 20X7, awards to 55 employees actually vested.

The amount recognised as an expense in each year will be as follows:

Year	Expense for the year	Cumulative expense	Calculation of cumulative expense
	C	C	
31 December 20X5	90,000	90,000	54 (that is, 60 × 90%) × 1,000 × 5 × $^1/_3$
31 December 20X6	100,000	190,000	57 (that is, 60 × 95%) × 1,000 × 5 × $^2/_3$
31 December 20X7	85,000	275,000	55 × 1,000 × 5

Example 2 – Grant of awards with non-recourse loans

On 1 January 20X9, entity S made an award of 1,000 shares to each of its 10 employees. The award was structured as a non-recourse loan whereby the entity 'lends' each employee C50,000 to purchase the shares from entity S and hence there is no cash flow. The only conditions associated with the award are that recipients must remain in entity S's employment for four years and must elect to repay the balance of the loan or return the shares at the conclusion of the required service period. If the employee does not complete the service period, the shares are returned to the company and the loan is forgiven. Any dividends declared during the service period are applied against the loan balance.

As discussed in paragraph 12.24 example 3, the IFRS IC confirmed that non-recourse loan arrangements of this nature are in substance option arrangements with a reducing exercise price (being the notional face value of the loan). The fair value of the services received (by reference to the fair value of the awards), and not the face value of the loan, should therefore be recognised as an expense over the vesting period. At grant date, assume that the fair value of each award is C40. This fair value takes into account that recipients are not entitled to dividends on the underlying shares between the grant date and exercise date, but any dividends declared are used to reduce the exercise price.. Management estimates that all employees will remain employed by the entity over the term of the award. Dividends of C4 were declared each year.

The expense profile would be as follows:

	Expense for the year	Cumulative Expense	Calculation of cumulative expense
	C	C	
31 December 20X9	100,000	100,000	C40 × 1,000 × 10 × ¼
31 December 20Y0	100,000	200,000	C40 × 1,000 × 10 × 2/4
31 December 20Y1	100,000	300,000	C40 × 1,000 × 10 × 3/4
31 December 20Y2	100,000	400,000	C40 × 1,000 × 10

In practice, and separate from the accounting expense, the entity would track the amount receivable from each employee in the event that they satisfy the vesting criteria and elect to exercise the option. This represents the employee's exercise price and, at the conclusion of the vesting period, would be as follows:

	Individual employee option exercise price	Total option exercise prices for all participating employees
	C	C
1 January 20X9 – Opening exercise price	50,000	500,000
31 December 20X9 – 'dividend'	(4,000)	(40,000)
31 December 20Y0 – 'dividend'	(4,000)	(40,000)
31 December 20Y1 – 'dividend'	(4,000)	(40,000)
31 December 20Y2 – 'dividend'	(4,000)	(40,000)
31 December 20Y2 – Exercise price	34,000	340,000

Entity S would record the following:

	C	C
Year ended 31 December 20X9		
Dr Employee expense	100,000	
Cr Equity		100,000
Year ended 31 December 20Y0		
Dr Employee expense	100,000	
Cr Equity		100,000
Year ended 31 December 20Y1		
Dr Employee expense	100,000	
Cr Equity		100,000
Year ended 31 December 20Y2		
Dr Employee expense	100,000	
Cr Equity		100,000
Receipt of exercise price (assuming that all options vest and are exercised)		
Dr Cash	340,000	
Cr Equity		340,000

Example 3 – Staged vesting (also known as tranched or graded vesting)

Entity I grants 1,000 share options to employees on 1 January 20X7. If an exit event (defined in the articles as a listing or change in control) occurs at any time during the period from 1 January 20X7 to 31 December 20Y0, and employees are still in service at the date of exit, the employees will be entitled to exercise all of their outstanding options. Additionally, until the date of exit, 25% of the options vest each year (provided that the employee is in service at that particular year end) as follows:

Tranche	Date	Number of awards that vest	Cumulative number of vested awards
a	31 December 20X7	250	250
b	31 December 20X8	250	500
c	31 December 20X9	250	750
d	31 December 20Y0	250	1,000

At the 31 December 20X7 reporting date, management concluded that a listing was probable and expected to occur after three and a half years, on 30 June 20Y0.

The expense will be calculated in award tranches, resulting in a front-loaded IFRS 2 charge. Assuming that no employees are expected to leave the entity and that the anticipated date of exit does not change, the charge for the first two years of the arrangement will be determined as follows:

Year end	Calculation of expense for year	Cumulative expense to date
31 December 20X7	FV tranche a option × 250 × 1	FV tranche a option × 250 × 1
	FV tranche b option × 250 × 1/2	FV tranche b option × 250 × 1/2
	FV tranche c option × 250 × 1/3	FV tranche c option × 250 × 1/3
	FV tranche d option × 250 × 1/3.5	FV tranche d option × 250 × 1/3.5
31 December 20X8	n/a	FV tranche a option × 250 × 1
	FV tranche b option × 250 × 1/2	FV tranche b option × 250 × 2/2
	FV tranche c option × 250 × 1/3	FV tranche c option × 250 × 2/3
	FV tranche d option × 250 × 1/3.5	FV tranche d option × 250 × 2/3.5

The following diagram illustrates 'front-loading' of the expense in similar circumstances. For simplicity, the grant date fair value of each option within each tranche has been taken as C10, thus the fair value of 250 options is C2,500. While employees would not necessarily be providing more service or be working harder in the first year when the charge is the highest, the reason for the higher charge indicates that the employees are working towards a number of different awards with different vesting periods.

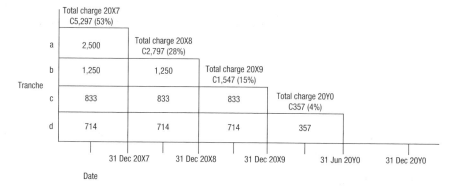

Example 4 – Grant of equity instruments with a specific performance condition (growth in earnings per share)

On 1 January 20X5, entity B made an award of shares to each of its 50 employees. The number of shares to which each employee will become entitled depends on growth in earnings per share (EPS). If EPS increases by an average of 10% over the next three years, each employee will receive 100 shares. If EPS increases by an average of 15%, each employee will receive 200 shares. If EPS increases by an average of 20%, each employee will receive 300 shares. No shares will be awarded if EPS increases by less than 10%. The recipients of the award must also remain in the employment of entity B for three years. The grant date fair value of each share at 1 January 20X5 is C12.

EPS is a non-market performance condition as it is not dependent upon share price. The condition is, therefore, relevant in determining the number of awards that will vest.

In the year ended 31 December 20X5, entity B's EPS increased by 16% and management forecast similar growth for the next two years. Hence, management predicted that each employee would receive 200 shares. However, 20X6 was a comparatively poor year and EPS increased by just 12% resulting in an average for the two-year period of 14%. Management cut back its forecast as a result, predicting growth of 14% for 20X7. On this basis, each employee would receive 100 shares. 20X7 was actually a much better year and EPS increased by 17% resulting in an average for the three-year period of 15% so each employee did, in fact, receive 200 shares.

During 20X5, five employees left the entity and management predicted a similar level of departures for the next two years, so 35 awards would vest. Six employees departed during 20X6, but management maintained its forecast of five departures in 20X7, so 34 awards would vest. However, only three employees left during 20X7, so 36 awards actually vested.

The amount recognised as an expense in each year will be as follows:

Year	Expense for the year C	Cumulative expense C	Calculation of cumulative expense
31 December 20X5	28,000	28,000	$35 \times 200 \times 12 \times \frac{1}{3}$
31 December 20X6	(800)	27,200	$34 \times 100 \times 12 \times \frac{2}{3}$
31 December 20X7	59,200	86,400	$36 \times 200 \times 12$

This example illustrates how the impact of 'truing up' the cumulative expense in each period may result in the reversal of amounts previously charged.

Example 5 – Grant of equity instruments in which the length of the vesting period varies

On 1 January 20X5, entity C granted 1,000 shares to each of its 500 employees, conditional upon the employees remaining in the employment of entity C throughout the vesting period. The shares will vest at the end of 20X5 if the entity's earnings increase by more than 20%; at the end of 20X6 if the entity's earnings increase by more than an average of 15% over the two-year period; and at the end of 20X7 if the entity's earnings increase by more than an average of 10% over the three-year period. If the entity's earnings increase by less than an average of 10% over the three-year period, no shares will vest. The grant date fair value of each share at 1 January 20X5 is C6 (which in this case is assumed to be independent of the length of the vesting period, as no dividends are expected to be paid before 20X8).

During 20X5, earnings increased by 16% and 25 employees left the entity. Management forecast that earnings would grow at a similar rate in 20X6 so the share awards would vest at the end of 20X6. Management also estimated that a further 25 employees would leave the entity, so 450 awards would vest.

During 20X6, earnings increased by only 10% resulting in an average for the two-year period of 13% so the awards did not vest. However, management forecast that earnings growth for 20X7 would be at least 4%, thereby achieving the average of 10% per year. 30 employees left the entity during 20X6 and management estimated a similar level of departures for 20X7, so 415 awards would vest.

During 20X7, earnings increased by 10% (resulting in an average over the three-year period of 12%) and 27 employees left the entity.

The amount recognised as an expense in each year will be as follows:

Year	Expense for the year C	Cumulative expense C	Calculation of cumulative expense
31 December 20X5	1,350,000	1,350,000	$450 \times 1,000 \times 6 \times \frac{1}{2}$*
31 December 20X6	310,000	1,660,000	$415 \times 1,000 \times 6 \times \frac{2}{3}$
31 December 20X7	848,000	2,508,000	$418 \times 1,000 \times 6$

* $\frac{1}{2}$ not $\frac{1}{3}$ as at the end of 20X5 management expected the award to vest at the end of 20X6

Example 6 – Grant of equity instruments in which the exercise price varies

On 1 January 20X5, entity D made an award of 1,000 share options to each of its 50 senior employees. The recipients of the award must remain in entity D's employment for three years. The exercise price of each option is C10, but this will drop to C8 if EPS increases by an average of 10% over the next three years. If EPS increases by an average of 15% or more, the exercise price will drop to C6. The grant date fair value of each option 1 January 20X5 is C6 if the exercise price is C10; C9 if the exercise price is C8; and C12 if the exercise price is C6.

In the year ended 31 December 20X5, entity D's EPS increased by 16% and management forecast similar growth for the next two years. However, 20X6 was a comparatively poor year and EPS increased by just 12% resulting in an average for the two-year period of 14%. Management cut back its forecast as a result, predicting growth of 14% for 20X7. 20X7 was actually a much better year and EPS increased by 17% resulting in an average for the three-year period of 15%, so the options were exercisable at C6.

During 20X5, five employees left the entity and management predicted a similar level of departures for the next two years, so 35 awards would vest. Six employees departed during 20X6, but management maintained its forecast of five departures in 20X7, so 34 awards would vest. However, only three employees left during 20X7, so 36 awards actually vested.

Because the exercise price varies depending on the outcome of a performance condition that is not a market condition, the effect of that performance condition (that is, the possibility that the exercise price might be C10, C8 or C6) is not taken into account when estimating the fair value of the share options at grant date. Instead, the fair value of the options is estimated under each scenario and the accounting in each period reflects the most likely outcome. Hence, the amount recognised as an expense in the first year is based on the assumption that the exercise price will be C6 so the fair value of each option is C12. For 20X6, it is forecast that the exercise price will be C8, so the fair value of each option is C9. In both cases, the fair value is as measured at grant date.

The amount recognised as an expense in each year will be as follows:

Year	Expense for the year	Cumulative expense	Calculation of cumulative expense
	C	C	
31 December 20X5	140,000	140,000	$35 \times 1,000 \times 12 \times {}^1/_3$
31 December 20X6	64,000	204,000	$34 \times 1,000 \times 9 \times {}^2/_3$
31 December 20X7	228,000	432,000	$36 \times 1,000 \times 12$

Example 7 – Expected life of option depends on non-market vesting condition

On 1 January 20X5, entity E granted 1,000 share options to employees. Each option entitles the employee to purchase one share at a fixed price. The options are exercisable between 1 January 20X7 and 31 December 20X7 if the entity meets its EPS target for 20X5 and 20X6, or on 1 January 20X7 if any of the 20X5 and 20X6 EPS targets are not met. The options' grant date fair values are C1.20 if the options are exercisable on 1 January 20X7, and C2 if the options are exercisable between 1 January 20X7 and 31 December 20X7.

Management determined at 31 December 20X5 that the 20X5 EPS target was met and management expected to meet the 20X6 EPS target. However, the 20X6 EPS target was not met. No employees left the entity, and all 1,000 options ultimately vested.

Entity E should recognise an expense of C1,000 for 20X5 (1,000 options × C2 × 50% of the vesting period), because it met its 20X5 EPS target and at the balance sheet date expected to meet the 20X6 target. At 31 December 20X6, management should convert from the grant date fair value of C2 to C1.20 because the non-market EPS condition was not met. It should recognise an expense of C200 for 20X6 (1,000 options × C1.2 × 100% of the vesting period, less C1,000 expensed in 20X5), thus bringing the total expense recognised over the two years to C1,200.

Example 8 – Earnings per share hurdle

Entity G granted share options to employees on 1 January 20X5 in exchange for services through 20X6. The options become exercisable if entity G achieves its earnings per share (EPS) target of C0.23 per share for 20X5 and 20X6. The options' fair value on grant date, ignoring this condition, was C100,000.

Management assessed the probability of meeting the EPS target as 60%. The fair value of the options, including the EPS condition is C65,000. The EPS target was met for 20X5 and management also expects to meet the 20X6 target.

The EPS target is a non-market performance condition and, therefore, the fair value used should *not* include the EPS hurdle. As a result, management should recognise an expense of C50,000 (1/2 × 100,000) in 20X5 based on an expectation that 100% of the options will vest at the end of 20X6.

The outcome of the EPS condition can only be that either all options vest or that no options vest. Management's assessment that it is probable the EPS condition will be met means that management expect 100% of the options to vest.

If employees did not have to remain in service until the EPS target is met, in which case the award has vested, the EPS target is treated as a post-vesting restriction. Therefore, it would be appropriate to use the fair value that includes the EPS hurdle (C65,000) to recognise an expense.

Market performance conditions

Example 9 – Grant of equity instruments with a market condition

On 1 January 20X5, entity F made an award of 10,000 options to each of its 50 senior management employees, conditional upon the employees remaining in the entity's employment until the end of 20X7. However, the share options cannot be exercised unless the share price has increased from C10 at the beginning of 20X5 to at least C17.50 at the vesting date of 31 December 20X7; they can be exercised any time during the next two years.

At grant date, the fair value of each option (which takes into account the possibility that the share price will be at least C17.50 at 31 December 20X7) is C4.

At the date of the award, management estimated that 10% of employees would leave the entity before the end of three years. Hence, 45 awards would vest. During 20X6 it became apparent that more employees than expected were leaving so management revised its estimate of the number of awards that would vest to 42. At the end of 20X7, awards to 40 employees actually vested.

Where awards are granted with market conditions, paragraph 21 of IFRS 2 requires an entity to recognise the services received from a counterparty who satisfies all other vesting conditions, irrespective of whether the market conditions are satisfied. In other words, it makes no difference whether share price targets are achieved – the possibility that a share price target might not be achieved has already been taken into account when estimating the fair value of the options at grant date. Therefore, the amounts recognised as an expense in each year will be the same regardless of whether the share price has reached C17.50 by the end of 20X7.

The amount recognised as an expense in each year will be as follows:

Year	Expense for the year	Cumulative expense	Calculation of cumulative expense
	C	C	
31 December 20X5	C600,000	C600,000	$45 \times 10,000 \times 4 \times \frac{1}{3}$
31 December 20X6	C520,000	C1,120,000	$42 \times 10,000 \times 4 \times \frac{2}{3}$
31 December 20X7	C480,000	C1,600,000	$40 \times 10,000 \times 4$

Example 10 – Vesting conditions relate to share price growth

The facts are the same as in example 5, except that the vesting condition concerns the growth in entity C's share price rather than its earnings. Hence, the shares will vest at the end of 20X5 if the share price increases by more than 20%; at the end of 20X6 if the share price increases by more than an average of 15% over the two-year period; and at the end of 20X7 if the share price increases by more than an average of 10% over the three-year period.

As in example 5 the fair value of each award is C6, but this takes into account the possibility that the share price target will be achieved during the next three years as well as the possibility that it will not be achieved. At grant date, management estimated that the most likely outcome of the market condition was that the share

12049

price target would be reached by the end of 20X6. Management also estimated that 450 awards would vest. However, the target was actually reached in 20X7 and 418 awards vested at 31 December 20X7.

Paragraph 15(b) of IFRS 2 provides that where the length of the vesting period may vary, depending on when a performance condition is satisfied, an entity should base its accounting on an estimate of the expected length of the vesting period, based on the most likely outcome of the performance condition. This is illustrated in example 5. However, if the performance condition is a market condition, the estimate of the length of the expected vesting period should be consistent with the assumptions used in estimating the fair value of the options granted and should not be subsequently revised. Accordingly, in this example entity C should treat the award as if it did vest at the end of 20X6 (when 445 employees remained in employment). The fact that the award actually vested at the end of 20X7, after a further 27 employees had left the entity, is ignored.

The amount recognised as an expense in each year will be as follows:

Year	Expense for the year	Cumulative expense	Calculation of cumulative expense
31 December 20X5	C1,350,000	C1,350,000	$450 \times 1,000 \times 6 \times \frac{1}{2}$
31 December 20X6	C1,320,000	C2,670,000	$445 \times 1,000 \times 6$

If the actual vesting period was shorter than originally estimated, the charge should be accelerated in the period that the entity settles the share-based payment, in line with the general principle of recognising the charge over the vesting period. In accordance with the guidance in paragraph 12.110, the estimate of awards expected to vest should be trued up to the actual as a result of the change in service period.

Example 11 – Grant of a variable number of equity instruments based on a fixed value

On 1 January 20X5, entity H granted a bonus award to employees that entitled them to receive a variable number of shares equivalent to a value of C1,100,000 if they remain in continued employment for three years. The number of shares that the employees will receive will be based on the share price on the vesting date. At the grant date, the share price is C5; at the vesting date, the share price is C10. The risk-free discount rate at grant date is 10%.

This is an equity-settled share-based payment, as employees will receive shares. The fair value is measured at grant date and is not subsequently remeasured. Entity H should recognise an expense of C826,446 (C1,100,000/1.1^3) spread over the vesting period. This is because the grant date fair value is independent of the share price and will be the value of the bonus award discounted.

Modifications, cancellations and settlements

Modifications and re-pricing

12.115 An entity might modify the terms and conditions on which equity instruments were granted. For example, in recent years, during which equity markets have been somewhat volatile and with declining share prices as a result of the global economic crisis, many companies have reduced the exercise price of options to restore some of the perceived value of share option plans to their employees.

12.116 The challenge for management in the current environment is how to modify share option awards where the share price is well below the exercise price ('underwater' options) in order to continue to motivate and reward employees, while managing the financial reporting consequences and shareholder and market expectations.

12.117 There are a number of alternatives for reviving underwater options. For example, in addition to cancelling share option awards, which requires immediate recognition of an expense based on the amount that would otherwise have been recognised over the remainder of the vesting period as discussed from paragraph 12.138 below, entities may reprice the options (lower the exercise price to the current market price) in order to increase the incentive to employees. To counter investor resistance to a straightforward repricing, management may do a combination of repricing share options and reducing the number of options, extending the service period or adding a performance or market condition. Alternatively, management may swap the share options originally awarded for actual shares (in order to avoid the risk of the options going underwater again) or for cash (which would require cash-settled treatment going forward).

12.118 Whichever approach is taken, the decision taken by management will need to carefully balance factors including employee expectations, investor interests, market perception and the financial reporting impacts. Management will also need to be aware of any legal and contractual implications, for example, some option agreements may prohibit the employer from modifying the awards without approval of the option holders. Finally, management should consider the tax consequences, if any, of option repricing in the relevant jurisdiction.

12.119 The accounting for modifications, along with a number of practical examples, is set out below.

12.120 The approach taken in IFRS 2 to the accounting for modifications is to view the new/modified instruments as instruments in their own right. Where a modification increases the fair value of the equity instruments granted (for example, by reducing the exercise price of share options), an entity should include the incremental fair value granted in the measurement of the amount recognised for the services received over the remainder of the vesting period. The incremental fair value is the difference between the fair value of the modified equity instrument and that of the original equity instrument, both estimated as at the date of the modification. An expense based on the incremental fair value is recognised in addition to any amount in respect of the original instrument, which should continue to be recognised over the remainder of the original vesting period (unless there is a failure to satisfy vesting conditions – see from para 12.77). [IFRS 2 para 27].

12.121 Guidance on how to apply the above requirements is given in Appendix B to the standard. In addition to modifications that increase the fair value of equity instruments granted (such as reductions in the exercise price of options), the principles of paragraph 27 of IFRS 2 also apply to other modifications that are otherwise beneficial to the employees. Examples include:

■ An increase in the number of instruments granted.

■ A reduction in the vesting period.

■ The modification or elimination of a performance condition.

12.122 If a modification increases the number of equity instruments granted, the entity should include the fair value of the additional equity instruments, measured at the date of the modification, in the measurement of the amount recognised for services received in a similar way to that described in paragraph 12.120. [IFRS 2 para B43(b)].

12.123 If an entity modifies the vesting conditions associated with an award (for example, by reducing the vesting period or eliminating a performance condition, other than a market condition), this should be taken into account when considering the estimate of the number of equity instruments expected to vest. [IFRS 2 para B43(c)].

12.124 The period over which the impact of a modification is recognised will depend on when it occurs and any vesting conditions it imposes. For example, if the modification described in paragraph 12.120 (reduction in option exercise price) occurs during the vesting period, the incremental fair value granted is included in the measurement of the amount recognised for services received over the period from the modification date until the date when the modified equity instruments vest. IFRS 2 does not, however, specify whether, in the case of a modification that reduces the vesting period, the change in vesting period should be accounted for prospectively or retrospectively. We believe that either approach is acceptable, for the reasons set out in example 4 of paragraph 12.127.

12.125 Sometimes an entity may modify the terms and conditions of a grant of equity instruments in a manner that reduces the arrangement's total fair value or is not otherwise beneficial to the employee. The accounting treatment of such modifications is similar to that described above insofar as the entity should continue to account for the original grant as if the modification had not occurred. However:

■ If the modification reduces the fair value of the equity instruments granted, this should be ignored. The entity should not recognise reduced expense as a consequence of the modification. This prevents an entity from modifying an award simply to reduce the overall income statement charge.

■ If the modification reduces the number of equity instruments granted, this should be accounted for as a cancellation of that portion of the grant (see para 12.138).

- If an entity modifies the vesting conditions associated with an award (for example, by increasing the vesting period or adding a non-market performance condition), this should *not* be taken into account when considering the estimate of the number of equity instruments expected to vest.

[IFRS 2 para B44].

12.126 Entities sometimes 'rebase' share-based payment awards by replacing existing tax inefficient awards with a new award that is more tax efficient. Where the total fair value of an award is the same immediately before and after modification (irrespective of whether there are tax benefits for the entity or employee as a result of the change), this is treated as a non-beneficial modification, that is, the entity should continue to account for the original award as if the modification had not occurred.

12.127 The accounting treatment of modifications to terms and conditions is considered further in the following examples.

Example 1 – Existing options rolled into new award – reduction in exercise price

An entity has previously operated a share option award with an option exercise price of C15, which is equal to the market price of the shares at the date of grant. Management decide to roll the options into a new award. The entity, therefore, cancels the original option plan and issues share options under the new award. The new options are granted at a lower exercise price of C12 because the market price of the shares has fallen to C11 since the date of grant of the initial plan so that the original exercise price is now below the market price of the shares at the date of grant of the new options. The terms of the original options are otherwise the same (that is, they have the same exercise date).

This would not be treated as a cancellation and a new award, but instead as a modification. This is because the entity has indicated that the new award replaces a cancelled award and, therefore, under paragraph 28(c) of IFRS 2 it is treated as if the original award had been modified. Consequently, the entity would be required to account for the incremental fair value of the new award (compared with the existing award) at the date of modification and spread this over the vesting period of the new award. This would be in addition to the entity continuing to charge for the original award over the original vesting period. Note that replacement awards are sometimes structured with similar terms to those of the original award and it may, therefore, be possible that there is no incremental fair value.

It is also worth noting that if the entity had not identified the new award as a replacement award at the same date that the new options were granted, the cancellation and new award would be unrelated and there would be a requirement to accelerate the vesting of the original award and recognise immediately the amount that otherwise would have been recognised for services received over the remainder of the vesting period. (See also example 9 below.) Additionally, there would be a fair value charge for the new award over the new vesting period.

Example 2 – Reduction in option exercise price – worked example

On 1 January 20X5, entity A grants an award of 1,000 options to each of its 60 employees. The only condition associated with the award is that recipients must remain in the employment of entity A for three years. The grant date fair value of each option is C5.

Towards the end of 20X5, entity A's share price dropped so, on 1 January 20X6, management chose to reduce the exercise price of the options. At the date of the re-pricing, the fair value of each of the original share options granted was C1 and the fair value of each re-priced option was C3. Hence, the incremental fair value of each modified option was C2.

At the date of the award, management estimated that 10% of employees would leave the entity before the end of three years (that is, 54 awards would vest). During 20X6 it became apparent that fewer employees than expected were leaving so management revised its estimate of the number of leavers to only 5% (that is, 57 awards would vest). At the end of 20X7, awards to 55 employees actually vested.

The amount recognised as an expense in each year will be as follows:

Year	Expense for the year C	Cumulative expense C	Calculation of cumulative expense
31 December 20X5	90,000	90,000	$54 \times 1,000 \times 5 \times \frac{1}{3}$
31 December 20X6	157,000	247,000	$57 \times 1,000 \times ((5 \times \frac{2}{3}) + (2 \times \frac{1}{2}))$
31 December 20X7	138,000	385,000	$55 \times 1,000 \times (5 + 2)$

Example 3 – Increase in the number of options granted

The facts are similar to example 2, except that instead of reducing the option exercise price on 1 January 20X6, the number of options to which each employee was entitled was increased to 1,500. The fair value of each of these additional options was C1.

The amount recognised as an expense in each year will be as follows:

Year	Expense for the year C	Cumulative expense C	Calculation of cumulative expense
31 December 20X5	90,000	90,000	$54 \times 1,000 \times 5 \times \frac{1}{3}$
31 December 20X6	114,250	204,250	$57 \times ((1,000 \times \frac{2}{3} \times 5) + (500 \times \frac{1}{2} \times 1))$
31 December 20X7	98,250	302,500	$55 \times ((1,000 \times 5) + (500 \times 1))$

Example 4 – Reduction in the vesting period – prospective versus retrospective adjustment

On 1 January 20X6, entity B awarded an employee 100 shares (with no entitlement to dividends during the vesting period) subject only to the employee remaining in service for three years. At 1 January 20X6, the fair value of each share was C6.

On 1 December 20X6, entity B decided to reduce the service requirement from three years to two years, thereby reducing the vesting period to two years.

It is assumed that the employee remains in service beyond 31 December 20X6.

As no dividends are expected to be paid during the vesting period changing the vesting period has no impact on the fair value of the unvested shares.

We believe that entity A has a policy choice for accounting for modifications of equity-settled awards occurring part way through a reporting period that reduce the vesting period by either using a retrospective or a prospective treatment.

Retrospective treatment

The modification may be accounted for retrospectively to reflect the best estimate available as at that date of awards that are expected to vest. This is supported by paragraph 19 of IFRS 2 which states that *"...the amount recognised for goods or services received as consideration for the equity instruments granted shall be based on the number of equity instruments that eventually vest"*. Where there is a change in estimate of the period over which the awards are expected to vest and that change occurs during the year, the cumulative expense may be 'trued up' at the balance sheet date to reflect the best estimate of awards expected to vest as of that date. On this basis, the expense each year as a result of the modification would be as follows:

Year	Expense for the year	Cumulative expense	Calculation of cumulative expense
	C	C	
31 December 20X6	300	300	$100 \times C6 \times \frac{1}{2}$
31 December 20X7	300	600	$100 \times C6$

Prospective treatment

Alternatively, the modification may be accounted for prospectively from the date of modification (1 December 20X6). While paragraph 19 of IFRS 2 states that the expense should be recognised based on the best estimate available, it does not specify the point at which changes in those estimates should be accounted for.

An analogy may be made to IAS 8 and the treatment of changes in estimates where a change in estimate is accounted for prospectively from the date of change. [IAS 8 para 36].

Furthermore, accounting for the change in vesting period prospectively would be consistent with the principle set out in paragraph B43 of IFRS 2, where other types of modifications are accounted for prospectively. In addition, paragraph 15 of IFRS 2 requires that where equity instruments do not vest until the counterparty completes a specified service period, the entity should account for those services as they are rendered by the counterparty over the specified vesting period. Prior to modification, employee services received as consideration were presumed to be received over a three year period and as such, the expense would be recognised on this basis. The presumption changes from three years to two years when the vesting period is modified, hence it would be appropriate to account for the modification prospectively and amend the recognition of expense from the modification date as follows:

Year	Expense for the year C	Cumulative expense C	Calculation of cumulative expense
31 December 20X6	215	215	Original charge, 11 months to 1 December 20X6: $100 \times C6 \times 1/3 \times 11/12 = 183$
			Modification occurs 1 December 20X6. Expense over remaining 13 months to 31 December 20X7: $600 - 183 = 417$
			Expense for December 20X6: $417/13 = 32$ Therefore, total expense for year to 31 December 20X6:
			$183 + 32 = 215$
31 December 20X7	385	600	100 x C6

Whichever approach is followed, the policy should be clearly explained and consistently applied.

It should be noted that where vesting is conditional upon an exit event of some kind such as an IPO, the estimated time until the exit event should be reassessed at each reporting date with adjustments made retrospectively. Prospective treatment would not be appropriate, because any adjustment would be a change in estimate, not a modification.

Example 5 – Reduction in the vesting period before resignation

On 1 January 20X5, entity B granted an award of 1,000 options to its financial director. The only condition associated with the award is that the director must remain employed by entity B for four years. The grant date fair value of each option is C40. The entity expects the director to meet the service condition.

On 1 October of 20X6, the finance director informed the entity that he wished to take early retirement and that after serving his three month notice period, would resign from employment. The remuneration committee, in its ultimate discretion, made a decision in November 20X6 (before he actually failed to meet the service vesting condition by retiring) that entity B would still provide the finance director with his award on termination of his service. This would be accounted for as a beneficial modification, that is, a reduction in the vesting period. The amount recognised as an expense in each year will be as follows:

Year	Expense for the year	Cumulative expense	Calculation of cumulative expense
	C	C	
31 December 20X5	10,000	10,000	1,000 × 40 × 1/4
31 December 20X6	30,000	40,000	1,000 × 40

Example 6 – Modification that is not beneficial to employees

An entity granted 100 share options to employees at an exercise price of C10 per share. The grant date is 1 January 20X4 and the options are subject to a two-year vesting period. The grant date fair value of each option was C50. The entity modified the options at 31 December 20X4 by extending the vesting period to 30 June 20X6. At 31 December 20X4 management expected that the number of options outstanding at 31 December 20X5, the original vesting date, would be 90. The actual number of options outstanding at 31 December 20X5 was 85, of which only 80 vested on 30 June 20X6. The modification did not increase the options' fair value.

The extension of the vesting period should be ignored. Modification of vesting conditions in a manner that is not beneficial to employees should not be taken into account when determining amounts to be recognised.

The expense and corresponding increase in equity recognised for 20X4 is C2,250; C50 × 90 options × 50% of the original two-year vesting period. The expense for 20X5 is C2,000; C50 × 85 options × 100% of the original two-year vesting period less C2,250, the amount expensed in 20X4. No expense is recognised in 20X6 and no adjustment is made to reflect the fact that only 80 awards actually vest as this occurred after the original vesting date.

Example 7 – Modification or cancellation?

Due to an unexpected significant decline in entity C's share price, management reduced the exercise price of an award from C50 to C20. At the same time, the number of options awarded was also reduced from 100 to 17. The 17 remaining options had the same total fair value as the 100 options immediately before the repricing.

The accounting for this can be viewed in two different ways. One view is that for the options that remain, the treatment is the same as for a simple reduction in exercise price described in example 1 above, and the other options are cancelled, so the recognition of the grant date fair value is accelerated in accordance with paragraph B44 of IFRS 2. The alternative view, which we believe better reflects the economics of the situation, is that there is no change in the aggregate fair value of the award so there is neither an incremental fair value nor a cancellation. Therefore, any element of the grant date fair value of the original award will continue to be charged over the original vesting period.

The accounting treatment applied to a reduction in the number of awards and a corresponding, or greater, increase in the fair value of each award is a judgment that will depend on the specific facts of each case and should be applied consistently. Cancellations are discussed further from paragraph 12.138 below.

Example 8 – Re-priced options and extension of vesting period

Management granted 100 share options at an exercise price of C10 per share to employees in exchange for services. The grant date was 1 January 20X4 and the options were subject to a two-year vesting period. The grant date fair value of the options was C5,000 and all options were expected to vest at the end of the vesting period.

The options were modified on 1 January 20X5 by reducing the exercise price to C5 per share (the current market value) and extending the vesting period by six months to 30 June 20X6. The fair value of the options at 1 January 20X5 was C8,000 prior to the modification and C9,500 after the modification. At the modification date, all options were expected to vest.

The original grant date fair value is recognised over the original vesting period. The expense for the year to 31 December 20X4 is C2,500; C5,000 × 50%. The expense for the year to 31 December 20X5 is C3,500; C5,000 × 50% plus the recognised incremental fair value of the modification of C1,500 × 66.7%. The incremental fair value is recognised over the vesting period from 1 January 20X5 to 30 June 20X6; 66.7% of this period passed by the balance sheet date. The incremental fair value is the difference between the fair value of the re-priced options immediately before and after the modification, that is, C9,500 less C8,000. The expense for the six months to 30 June 20X6 is C500; C1,500 × 33.3%.

If an employee leaves during the six month period to 30 June 20X6 and thus fails to meet the revised vesting condition, it is only the repricing impact that is reversed; the original grant date fair value expense of C5,000 is unaffected because the employee satisfied the two-year service condition for the original award.

Example 9 – Impact of rights issue and modification of share schemes

Entity F is planning a rights issue to offer shares at a 30% discount. The entity operates numerous share schemes; it realises that employees in those share schemes will be worse off after the rights issue as the market value of the shares will be reduced. Entity F plans to modify the share schemes at a later date to ensure the awards granted to employees are uplifted to the equivalent value of the original award granted. Management believes that the rights issue and subsequent share-based payment modification are linked. It, therefore, wants to treat the impact of the rights issue and the modification as a single event.

A share-based payment modification occurs when the terms and conditions of the equity instruments change. The modification in this case would, therefore, be later than, not at the date of, the rights issue.

When a modification occurs, an entity will need to compare the fair value of the new and old awards at the modification date and consider whether there is an uplift in fair value. Any uplift will then be expensed, along with the charge for the original awards over the remaining vesting period. As this modification is happening at a later date than the rights issue, then it is likely there will be an increase in fair value as a result of changes in volatility, market value and time value of money (since the date of the rights issue.) If entity F had structured the transaction differently, such that the modification of the awards occurred on the same day as the rights issue, then it is highly likely that the difference between the new and old awards would be nil resulting in no additional charge.

Reclassification — equity-settled to cash-settled

12.128   Reclassification of a share-based payment award may occur because:

■   An entity is de-listing. To provide greater liquidity to employees the entity might change the share-based payment from equity-settled to cash-settled.

■   The entity has changed its settlement practice.

12.129   Where an entity modifies a share-based payment award such that it will be settled in cash as opposed to shares, the entity measures the liability initially using the modification date fair value of the equity-settled award based on the elapsed portion of the vesting period. This amount is then recognised as a credit to liability and a debit to equity, by analogy to paragraph 29 of IFRS 2 which states that the repurchase of vested equity instruments is accounted for as a deduction from equity.

12.130   The entity then re-measures the liability and does so at each subsequent reporting date and recognises any additional expense from increases in the liability. See further paragraph 12.164 below. The example below also illustrates this.

Example – Reclassification from equity-settled to cash-settled

Entity N has an equity-settled share-based payment that will vest when employees provide four years of continuous service. The grant date fair value is C10; the vesting period is four years. At the end of year two, a cumulative charge of C5 has been recognised in the income statement with a corresponding increase in equity.

At the end of year two, entity N decides to change the share-based payment award from equity-settled to cash-settled. The employees will now receive a cash payment based on the fair value of the shares at the end of year four.

When an award is modified to become a cash-settled award, this is accounted for as the repurchase of an equity interest (that is, a deduction from equity). Any excess over the grant date fair value should be treated as a deduction from equity (as opposed to an expense), provided that the deduction is not greater than the fair value of the equity instruments when measured at the modification date.

The accounting is illustrated by two scenarios, in which immediately before the change in classification, the fair value of the grant:

(a) Has increased:
Assume the fair value immediately before modification is C20. At the start of year three, a liability of C10 (20/2) is recognised with a corresponding debit to equity of C10. The subsequent measurement of the liability would follow the requirements for cash-settled share-based payment.

(b) Has decreased:
IFRS 2 requires an entity to recognise a charge in the income statement for services received of at least the grant date fair value, regardless of any modifications to or cancellations of the grant. The only exception to this is where a non-market vesting condition is not satisfied. Assume that the fair value immediately before the modification has decreased to C5 and there are no further movements in the fair value in years three and four. The accounting would be:

- Years one and two: a total expense and increase in equity of C5, is recognised.

- At the start of year three: a liability of C2.5 (5 × 2/4) is recognised with a corresponding decrease to equity.

- Years three and four: an expense of C2.5 is recognised each year with a corresponding increase in the liability of C1.25 and equity of C1.25. The C1.25 expense and increase in equity recognised each year ensures that the income statement expense is at least equal to the grant date fair value.

At the end of the vesting period the total expense is C10 (of which C5 was a credit to equity and C5 a credit to liability). The total expense is equal to the grant date fair value of C10.

If the fair value was to change in years three and four, the entity would need to recalculate the amounts to expense in these years as follows:

- record the expense based on the grant date fair value and allocate this expense between debt and equity based on the ratio of debt to equity on the date of modification; and

- re-measure the value of the liability based on movements in the share price.

To illustrate, assume that at the end of year three, the fair value of the award had decreased to C4. The entity:

- records an expense, based on the grant date fair value, of C2.5 with a corresponding increase in the liability and equity of C1.25 (based on the ratio of equity to cash on the date of modification); and then

- re-measures the value of the liability through the income statement from C3.75 to C3 (representing three-quarters of the fair value of the liability of C4 as it is three years through the four-year vesting period).

12.131 Reclassification from a cash-settled share-based payment to an equity-settled award is discussed in paragraph 12.154 below.

Modifications and IAS 19

12.131.1 Some awards may initially be an employee benefit under IAS 19 and then be modified to a share-based payment arrangement in accordance with IFRS 2. See further guidance provided in chapter 11.

Modifications and business combinations

12.132 IFRS 3 provides detailed guidance on when and how an acquirer should allocate equity instruments between the cost of the business combination and post-combination services for replacement awards granted to employees of the acquiree.

12.133 For situations where the acquiree's employee awards may expire as a consequence of a business combination and the acquirer replaces those awards even though it is not obliged to do so, IFRS 3 requires the entire grant date fair value of the replacement awards to be recognised as remuneration cost in the post-combination financial statements. For all other situations, replacements of share-based payment awards are accounted for as modifications in accordance with IFRS 2. Depending on facts and circumstances, either all or a portion of the IFRS 2 measure of the replacement awards is allocated to the consideration transferred for the purposes of IFRS 3.

12.134 The principle of IFRS 3 is to allocate a portion of a replacement award to the business combination based on the fair value of acquiree awards and the degree to which the acquiree awards have been earned at the date of acquisition. Any excess value in the replacement awards is accounted for as post-combination employee services incorporating any new or amended vesting conditions.

[The next paragraph is 12.136.]

12.136 The requirements set out in IFRS 3 are covered further in chapter 25, along with a number of illustrative examples. Chapter 25 also discusses the employee compensation and contingent consideration guidance in Appendix B to IFRS 3.

An additional example illustrating the modification of a share-based payment award occurring at the same time as an acquisition is set out below.

Example – Modification as a result of acquisition

Entity C granted share options to its employees on 1 May 20X5. The options were exercisable subject to the completion of three years' service from that date. On 30 April 20X7, entity D acquired entity C. Entity D is obliged to replace entity C's share plans. The terms of the share options were modified on acquisition so that employees will be entitled to shares in entity D at the end of the original three year period as opposed to shares in entity C. The modified terms make clear that entity D, the acquirer, has granted, and has the obligation for, the replacement award. The terms of the plan are otherwise unchanged.

Entity C's financial statements

Entity C originally granted an equity-settled share-based payment award to its employees. Immediately upon the acquisition, the plan's terms were modified and the new parent, entity D, had the obligation to settle the award. In accordance with the guidance in IFRS 2 on group settled share-based payments, the award will continue to be treated as equity-settled in entity C's financial statements (see further from para 12.169).

The remainder of the original IFRS 2 charge (measured on 1 May 20X5) will continue to be spread over the vesting period to 30 April 20X8. In addition, if the modification has increased the award's fair value (measured as the difference between the award's fair value immediately before and after the modification), the incremental fair value will be spread over the remaining period to 30 April 20X8. [IFRS 2 App B para B43].

Entity D's separate and consolidated financial statements

From 30 April 20X7, entity D, as the acquirer, has granted an equity-settled award in its own shares to the employees of its subsidiary, entity C. This will be accounted for as a new award in both entity D's separate and consolidated financial statements. Say the award's fair value is C900, measured at the grant date, 30 April 20X7. The terms of the award require employees to provide three years service to entity C, from 1 May 20X5 to 30 April 20X8. Hence, part of the award's fair value relates to pre-combination services and will be taken as part of entity D's cost of investment in entity C.

Management will need to follow the guidance in IFRS 3 to determine the allocation between pre- and post-combination services and in this case, given that two thirds of the vesting period has passed and there is no incremental fair value or change in the vesting period, it would be appropriate to allocate two thirds (C600) of the fair value of entity C's award at the date of acquisition to pre-combination services (this would, therefore, be included as part of entity D's cost of investment in entity C). One third (C300) of the fair value of entity C's award at the date of acquisition, plus any incremental fair value between entity C's and entity D's award at the date of acquisition, would be treated as post-combination services (this would, therefore, be recognised as an expense over the period to 30 April 20X8).

For the year ended 30 April 20X8, the IFRS 2 entries in the consolidated financial statements will be:

		Dr	Cr
		C	C
Dr	Income statement	300 (being one third of the total fair value of the award measured at 30 April 20X7, grant date)	
	Cr Equity		300

Further guidance on the treatment in entity D's separate financial statements is provided from paragraph 12.169. Based on this guidance, the entries in entity D's separate financial statements on 30 April 20X8 will be:

		Dr	Cr
		C	C
Dr	Investment in subsidiary	300 (being the fair value of award measured at 30 April 20X7)	
	Cr Equity		300

Further guidance on the treatment in entity D's separate financial statements is provided from paragraph 12.169. Based on this guidance, the entries in entity D's separate financial statements on 30 April 20X8 will be:

[The next paragraph is 12.138.]

Cancellations and settlements

12.138   All cancellations, whether by the entity or by other parties, are accounted for in the same way. If a grant of equity instruments is cancelled or settled during the vesting period, it should be treated as an acceleration of vesting and should recognise immediately the amount that otherwise would have been recognised for services received over the remainder of the vesting period. Opinions are divided as to the amount that should be recognised at the date of cancellation. Paragraph 28(a) of IFRS 2 states that:

> *"The entity shall account for the cancellation or settlement as an acceleration of vesting, and shall therefore recognise immediately the amount that otherwise would have been recognised for services received over the remainder of the vesting period."*

We believe that the charge should reflect all awards that are outstanding at the date of cancellation, without adjusting for any estimate of the number of awards that are not expected to vest. This is because the cancellation results in early vesting (satisfaction of a non-market vesting condition) and thus accelerated recognition of the grant date fair value. There is an alternative interpretation that focuses on the words *"... the amount that otherwise would have been recognised for services received over the remainder of the vesting period"*. It recognises a charge that reflects the number of awards that were expected to achieve the performance condition just prior to the award being cancelled. Either interpretation could be applied, but we believe that the first is more closely aligned with the principles of IFRS 2.

12.139   Any payment made to a counterparty on the cancellation or settlement of a grant of equity instruments, even if this occurs after the vesting date, should be accounted for as a repurchase of an equity interest (that is, as a deduction from equity), except to the extent that the payment exceeds the fair value of the equity instruments repurchased, measured at the repurchase date. Any such excess should be recognised as an expense. [IFRS 2 paras 28(b), 29].

Example – Cancellation during vesting period

On 1 January 20X5 entity A made an award of 100 shares to an employee. The only condition associated with the award is that the employee must remain in entity A's employment for three years. The award's grant date fair value was C1,200. The employee is expected to remain with the entity for at least three years and, therefore, the award is expected to vest.

The award is cancelled on 1 January 20X6 and entity A settles in cash on a *pro rata* basis. The employee, therefore, receives C400 (C1,200 × 1/3 years). The award's fair value on this date is determined to have fallen from C1,200 to C300.

The amount recognised as an expense during 20X5 before taking account of the cancellation was C400 (C1,200 × 1/3 years). Paragraph 28(a) of IFRS 2 requires the entity to account for the cancellation or settlement as an acceleration of vesting and recognise immediately the amount that otherwise would have been recognised for services received over the remainder of the vesting period. Accordingly, on the basis of the number of awards outstanding at the cancellation date, the amount to be recognised immediately as an expense is C800 (that is, C1,200 – C400), with a credit to equity of C800. Note, if the above award was made to more than one employee, at the date of cancellation, we believe management should accelerate the share-based payment expense based on the actual number of awards on cancellation rather than on the basis of what management had previously expected to vest as discussed above. However, as noted above, an alternative approach based on the number of awards expected to vest may also be considered.

Following the former interpretation, the C400 payment made to the employee on cancellation of the award exceeds the award's fair value of C300 on the date of repurchase. Paragraph 28(b) of IFRS 2 requires an amount equal to the fair value (C300) to be treated as the repurchase of an equity instrument. The excess is recognised as an expense. This means that C300 is deducted from equity while C100 (that is, C300 – C400) is recognised as an expense. In summary the entity would record the following:

Year ended 31 December 20X5

		Dr C	Cr C
Dr	Employee benefits expense	400	
	Cr Equity		400

Year ended 31 December 20X6

		Dr C	Cr C
Dr	Employee benefits expense – cancellation of the award	800	
	Cr Equity		800
Dr	Employee benefits expense – incremental fair value on settlement in cash	100	
Dr	Equity	300	
	Cr Cash		400

12.140   Sometimes an entity may grant new equity instruments as consideration for the cancellation or settlement of an old grant. When this occurs and, on the date when those new equity instruments are granted, the entity identifies the new equity instruments as replacements for the cancelled equity instruments, the entity should treat this as a modification, as described from paragraph 12.115 above. Hence, the incremental fair value granted is the difference between the fair value of the replacement equity instruments and the net fair value of the cancelled equity instruments, at the date the replacement equity instruments are granted. For this purpose, the net fair value of the cancelled equity instruments is their fair value, immediately before the cancellation, less the amount of any payment made to the counterparty that is accounted for as a deduction from equity as described in paragraph 12.139 above. If the entity does not identify the new equity instruments as a replacement for the cancelled instruments, it should account for those new equity instruments as a new grant. [IFRS 2 para 28(c)].

12.141   Where the cancellation of an award has been reported, an entity cannot subsequently identify a replacement award. We believe that the standard is clear that a replacement award should be identified at the same time as the original award is cancelled.

12.142   It may not always be clear whether an award has been cancelled or modified. For example, where the number of share options awarded to an employee is reduced, the question arises as to whether part of the award has been cancelled. This point is illustrated in example 7 of paragraph 12.127.

Forfeitures

12.143   A forfeiture occurs when either a service or a non-market performance condition is not met, as this affects the number of awards that vest. Failures to meet either market conditions or non-vesting conditions are not forfeitures as these are already taken into account when determining the grant date fair value.

12.144 The accounting for forfeitures is different to that of cancellations described from paragraph 12.138 above. The expiry (or lapsing) of a vested award has no accounting implications at the time that the award expires or lapses; if expiry (or lapsing) results from a post-vesting restriction it will have been incorporated into the grant date fair value.

12.145 Where a number of individual awards within a larger portfolio of awards are forfeited, the expense is revised to reflect the best available estimate of the number of equity instruments expected to vest. Hence, on a cumulative basis, no expense is recognised for goods or services received if the equity instruments do not vest as a result of a service or non-market performance condition (for example, if the employee or counterparty fails to complete a specified service period).

> **Example – Employee made redundant**
>
> Entity A granted share option awards to a number of its employees with a three year service requirement. The individuals were required to remain in service with the entity for three years from the date of grant. 18 months into the plan, one employee is made redundant.
>
> Having been made redundant, the employee is unable to satisfy the three-year service condition and, therefore, this should be treated as a forfeiture rather than a cancellation. The expense recognised to date is reversed. If, however, the award was cancelled prior to the employee being made redundant, there would be an accelerated charge.

Cash-settled share-based payment transactions

12.146 Some transactions are 'share-based', even though they do not involve the issue of shares, share options or any other form of equity instrument. Cash-settled share-based payment transactions are defined in IFRS 2 as transactions *"in which the entity acquires goods or services by incurring a liability to transfer cash or other assets to the supplier of those goods or services for amounts that are based on the price (or value) of equity instruments (including shares or share options) of the entity or another group entity"*. [IFRS 2 App A].

12.147 The most common examples of cash-settled share-based payment transactions are employee incentive plans, such as share appreciation rights and 'phantom' share plans. These plans involve the payment of an amount based on the price of the employing entity's shares after a period of time.

12.148 Sometimes, transactions that might appear to be settled in shares will be treated as cash-settled if this is more reflective of their substance. For example, an entity might grant to its employees a right to shares that are redeemable, either mandatorily (such as upon cessation of employment) or at the employee's option. As the entity has an obligation to make a cash payment, the transaction would be treated as cash-settled.

Example 1 – Repurchase of shares on termination of employment

Entity A is the sponsoring entity of a trust that administers an employee share-based compensation plan. Entity A issues new shares to the trust. The trust issues these shares to employees who satisfy the plan's vesting conditions. The shares are non-transferable while employees remain in entity A's employment and each employee has an obligation to sell the shares acquired through the plan back to the trust on termination of employment. The trust buys the shares back at fair value when returned.

Entity A prepares consolidated financial statements and, therefore, under SIC 12, 'Consolidation – special purpose entities', the trust should be consolidated. (SIC 12 is superseded by IFRS 10 'Consolidated financial statements'. See further para 12.246.1). When employment is terminated, the award is settled in cash based on entity A's share price and, therefore, the transaction should be accounted for as a cash-settled award under IFRS 2. [IFRS 2 para 31].

Example 2 – Funding of award – shares purchased by trust

Entity B awarded its employees rights to obtain its shares subject to a three year vesting period. Local legislation does not allow the entity either to issue new shares to employees or to buy its own shares. The entity will establish a trust that will purchase the entity's shares from third parties and transfer those shares to entitled employees. The entity will pay the trust the cash required to purchase those shares.

Entity B prepares consolidated financial statements and, therefore, as in example 1, the trust will be consolidated under SIC 12. (SIC 12 is superseded by IFRS 10. See further para 12.246.1.) The fact that the group, *via* the trust, must buy shares from third parties in order to satisfy the obligation to deliver shares does not change the nature of the award. Employee services will ultimately be settled in shares. As such, the transaction should be treated as an equity-settled transaction under IFRS 2 (and any share purchase would be treated as a treasury share transaction in the consolidation). [IFRS 2 paras B48, B49.]

Measurement of cash-settled share-based payment transactions

12.149   Like share options and other equity instruments, the fair value of share appreciation rights and other cash-settled share-based payment transactions includes both their intrinsic value (the increase in the share price to date) and their time value (the value of the right to participate in future increases in the share price, if any, that may occur between the valuation date and the settlement date). Accordingly, many of the principles described previously for the measurement of equity-settled transactions apply equally to cash-settled transactions. So:

■   The objective is to measure the goods or services acquired and the liability incurred at fair value.

■   Fair value is determined using an option pricing model, taking into account the terms and conditions of the award.

■   The goods or services are recognised as they are received by the entity.

[IFRS 2 paras 30, 32, 33].

12.150 There is, however, an important difference. For cash-settled transactions, the fair value of the liability is re-measured at each reporting date and at the date of settlement. The measurement reflects the impact of all conditions and all possible outcomes on a weighted-average basis, unlike the measurement for an equity-settled award. Any changes in fair value are recognised in profit or loss for the period. [IFRS 2 para 30]. This is illustrated in the following example.

> **Example – Cash-settled award**
>
> On 1 January 20X5, an entity granted 1,000 share appreciation rights (SARs) to each of its 40 management employees. The SARs provide the employees with the right to receive, at the date the rights are exercised, cash equal to the appreciation in the entity's share price since the grant date. All of the rights vest on 31 December 20X6. They can be exercised during 20X7 and 20X8. Management estimates that, at grant date, the fair value of each SAR is C11, and that 10% of the employees will leave evenly during the two-year period. The fair values of the SARs at each year end are shown below.
>
> | Year | Fair value at year end |
> |---|---:|
> | 31 December 20X5 | 12 |
> | 31 December 20X6 | 8 |
> | 31 December 20X7 | 13 |
> | 31 December 20X8 | 12 |
>
> 10% of employees did leave before the end of 20X6. On 31 December 20X7, when the intrinsic value of each SAR was C10, six employees exercise their options, while the remaining 30 employees exercise their options at the end of 20X8 (when the intrinsic value of each SAR was equal to the fair value of C12). The amount recognised as an expense in each year and as a liability at each year end will be as follows:
>
> | Year | Expense | Liability | Calculation of liability |
> |---|---:|---:|---|
> | | C | C | |
> | 31 December 20X5 | 216,000 | 216,000 | $36 \times 1{,}000 \times 12 \times \frac{1}{2}$ |
> | 31 December 20X6 | 72,000 | 288,000 | $36 \times 1{,}000 \times 8$ |
> | 31 December 20X7 | 162,000 | 390,000 | $30 \times 1{,}000 \times 13$. Expense comprises an increase in the liability of C102,000 and cash paid to those exercising their SARs of C60,000 ($6 \times 1{,}000 \times 10$). |
> | 31 December 20X8 | (30,000) | 0 | Liability extinguished. Previous cost reversed as cash paid to those exercising their SARs of C360,000 ($30 \times 1{,}000 \times 12$) was less than the opening liability of C390,000. |

12.151   For cash-settled transactions, it is perhaps more difficult to comprehend the difference between the fair value of a right and its intrinsic value. In the previous example, the fair value of each right at 31 December 20X7 was C13. However, the amount paid to each employee who exercised rights on that day was only C10 (that is, the intrinsic value). The reason for the higher fair value is the same for cash-settled transactions as for equity-settled transactions. The fair value of each SAR at 31 December 20X7 is made up of its intrinsic value (reflected by the current market price of the entity's shares) and its time value. The time value reflects the fact that the holders of the SARs have the right to participate in future gains. At 31 December 20X8, all of the outstanding SARs must be exercised so holders have no right to participate in future gains. Hence, the fair value (C12) at that date is made up entirely of the intrinsic value.

12.152   Prior to applying IFRS 2, some territories may have measured the cash-settled share-based payment using the intrinsic value. Applying IFRS 2 requires measurement at fair value, so for some territories a change to IFRS will necessitate re-measurement of liabilities. Although the IASB did consider the use of intrinsic values to measure cash-settled share-based payment transactions, it concluded that such a method was not consistent with the overall fair value objective of its share-based payment standard.

12.153   As mentioned in example 3 in paragraph 12.161, the fair value of a liability component is determined as the present value of the future cash outflow.

Change in classification — cash-settled to equity-settled

12.154   Where an award is modified such that the classification changes from cash-settled to equity-settled, the entity immediately reclassifies the amount recognised as a liability, up to the modification date, to equity. The expense for the remainder of the vesting period is based on the award's fair value, measured at the modification date and not the original grant date.

12.154.1   In some situations, an award is modified such that the fair value or other vesting conditions are changed in addition to the classification change from cash-settled to equity-settled (for example, additional fair value, extending the vesting period or adding a performance condition). There is no clear guidance in IFRS 2 whether an entity should account for the change in classification or the other modifications first; therefore, we believe either approach is acceptable. The following example illustrates this.

> **Example – Reclassification from cash-settled to equity-settled**
>
> Entity X has a cash-settled share-based payment in the form of share appreciation rights that will vest in three years. At the end of year one, the fair value of the award is estimated to be C300. Therefore, a charge of C100 has been recognised in the income statement with a corresponding liability. At the end of year two, the fair value of the award is C360. As such, a charge of C140 (C240 — C100) has been recognised in the income statement with a corresponding increase in the liability.

Additionally, at the end of year two entity X decides to modify the share-based payment award from cash-settled to equity-settled and extend the vesting period by a year. The employees will now receive equity instruments for the same value after four years. Entity X will provide shares based on the value of the share appreciation rights at the settlement date (that is, C360). However, employees will still need to provide services for two more years.

Under one approach, the entity could account for the change in classification from cash to equity-settled first and then apply modification accounting to the change in vesting period. Therefore, entity X would reclassify the total liability of C240 at the end of year two to equity. The expense for the remaining vesting period will be C120 which is based on the fair value of the award at the modification date of C360, less the amount already recognised in the income statement of C240. However, since the extension of vesting period is not beneficial to employees, it should not be taken into account when determining amounts to be recognised. (See further guidance on modifications in para 12.125.) Therefore, C120 should be expensed over the remaining vesting period of the original grant (that is, one year).

Under an alternative approach, the entity could apply modification accounting to the change in vesting period first and then account for the change in classification. Therefore, the entity would true-up the liability at the end of year two based on a change in vesting period. This would result in a credit of C60 to the income statement since a liability of C180 (C360 ÷ 4 years × 2 years less C240 already recognised) should be recorded at the end of year two. Then, entity X would reclassify the total liability of C180 to equity. An expense of C180, which is based on the fair value of the award at modification date of C360 less the amount already recognised in the income statement of C180, would then be recognised over the remaining vesting period of two years.

Transactions with settlement alternatives

12.155 Some share-based payment transactions give either the entity or the counterparty the choice as to whether to settle in cash or equity instruments. IFRS 2 establishes a principle that an entity should account for such a transaction as cash-settled if, and to the extent that, it has incurred a liability to settle in cash or other assets, or otherwise as equity-settled. [IFRS 2 para 34]. In practice, the accounting is driven by determining which party appears to have the choice of settlement method.

The counterparty may choose the settlement method

12.156 If the counterparty may choose the method of settlement, the entity is considered to have issued a compound financial instrument. This means that it has issued an instrument with a debt component (to the extent that the counterparty has a right to demand cash) and an equity component (to the extent that the counterparty has a right to demand settlement in equity instruments by giving up their right to cash). [IFRS 2 para 35].

12.157 IAS 32 requires that, when valuing a compound financial instrument, an entity first establishes the value of the debt component. The equity component is then measured at the difference between that amount and the value of instrument as a whole. [IAS 32 para 31]. IFRS 2 applies similar measurement principles.

12.158 For transactions in which the fair value of goods or services is measured directly, the fair value of the equity component is measured as the difference between the fair value of the goods or services received and the fair value of the debt component. [IFRS 2 para 35].

12.159 For other transactions in which the fair value of goods or services is measured indirectly by reference to the fair value of the instruments granted, it is necessary to estimate the fair value of the compound instrument as a whole. [IFRS 2 para 36]. To do this, it will be necessary to value the debt and equity components separately, taking into account the fact that the counterparty must forfeit its right to receive cash in order to receive the equity instrument. Transactions are often structured such that the fair value of each settlement alternative is the same. For example, the counterparty might have the choice of receiving either share options or cash-settled share appreciation rights. In order to receive the options, the counterparty would have to 'give up' a cash award of equivalent fair value so, by deduction, the fair value of the equity component will be zero. However, where the fair value of the equity component is greater than zero, it will be necessary to account for each component separately. The debt component will be accounted for as a cash-settled share-based payment transaction as described from paragraph 12.146, while the equity component will be accounted for as an equity-settled share-based payment transaction as described from paragraph 12.53. [IFRS 2 para 38].

12.160 At the date of settlement, the liability in respect of the debt component should be re-measured at fair value. The method of settlement actually chosen by the counterparty will then determine the accounting, as shown in the table below.

Method of settlement	Accounting implications
Cash	The payment is applied to settle the liability in full. Any equity component previously recognised in equity will remain there, although there may be a transfer from one component of equity to another. [IFRS 2 para 40].
Equity	The balance on the liability is transferred to equity as consideration for the equity instrument. [IFRS 2 para 39].

12.161 The above requirements are illustrated in the following examples.

Example 1 – Compound instrument – mutually exclusive alternatives

An entity established a bonus plan on 1 January 20X5. The employees have a right to choose between a cash payment equal to the market value of 100 shares at 31 December 20X5 or to receive 100 shares on the same date. At the grant date, the fair value of the right to cash is C5,000 and the fair value of the right to shares is C5,000. The value of the two alternatives is the same at any point in time.

The equity component is determined as the difference between the fair value of the compound instrument as a whole and the fair value of the liability.

The fair value of the compound instrument as a whole is C5,000, as the cash and share alternatives are mutually exclusive and of equal value. The equity component is, therefore, zero, being the difference between the C5,000 fair value of the compound instrument and the C5,000 fair value of the debt component. This reflects the arrangement's economic substance where there is no benefit to the employee from choosing shares or cash.

Example 2 – Compound instrument – determining the equity component

On 1 January 20X5, an entity granted to its chief executive the right to choose either 10,000 phantom shares (that is, the right to receive a cash payment equal to the value of 10,000 shares) or 15,000 shares. The grant is conditional upon the completion of two years of service. If the chief executive chooses the share alternative, he must keep the shares for a period of five years. The entity's share price at grant date and at subsequent year ends is as follows:

Year	Share price
1 January 20X5	7
31 December 20X5	9
31 December 20X6	15

After taking into account the effects of the post-vesting transfer restrictions (see further para 12.202), management estimates that the grant date fair value of the share alternative is C6.50 per share. Hence, the fair value of the share alternative at grant date is C97,500 (that is, 15,000 × C6.50). The fair value of the cash alternative at grant date is C70,000 (that is, 10,000 × C7) so, by deduction, the fair value of the equity component of the compound financial instrument awarded to the chief executive is C27,500. In order to obtain an equity instrument worth C97,500, the chief executive must surrender a right to C70,000 of cash. In simple terms, the fair value of the equity component is the difference between these amounts. In reality the valuation of a compound instrument can be more complicated and specialist advice may be required. The amount recognised as an expense in each year and as either an increase in equity or a liability at each year end will be as follows:

Year	Expense	Equity	Total liability	Expense calculation
	C	C	C	
31 December 20X5	13,750	13,750		C27,500 × ½
31 December 20X5	45,000		45,000	C10,000 × 9 × ½
31 December 20X6	13,750	27,500		C27,500 × ½
31 December 20X6	105,000		150,000	C10,000 × 15 less C45,000 recognised in 20X5

The chief executive exercises his rights on 1 January 20X7 (on which date the share price is the same as on 31 December 20X6).

If he chooses to receive cash, he will receive a payment of C150,000. This will settle the outstanding liability in full. The amount recognised within equity (C27,500) will remain there, although there may be a transfer from one component of equity to another.

If he chooses the share alternative, the balance on the liability of C150,000 is transferred to equity as consideration for the shares. Once again, the amount already recognised within equity (C27,500) will remain there, although there may be a transfer from one component of equity to another.

Example 3 – Compound instrument – determining the equity component

An entity granted a bonus to its employees on 1 January 20X5. The bonus is due in five years, when each employee will have a right to choose between a cash payment of C1,000 or obtaining 100 shares of the entity. The share price on 1 January 20X5 is C5 per share. There are no vesting conditions. The appropriate discount rate is 5% per year.

The entity should recognise the debt component on 1 January 20X5 at its fair value of C784. Fair value is determined as the present value of the future cash outflow, C1,000/ 1.05^5 (see further para 12.153 above). The entity should then measure the equity alternative, taking into consideration that the employee has to forfeit the right to C1,000 in cash to obtain the shares. The equity alternative is, in substance, a share option with an exercise price of C10 per share and a term of five years. The grant date fair value of the share options was determined as C25 at 1 January 20X5. A corresponding increase in equity should be recognised on 1 January 20X5.

The entity should re-measure the liability component to its fair value at each subsequent balance sheet date and recognise the changes in the fair value in the income statement. The amounts recognised for the equity component are not subject to subsequent re-measurement.

Example 4 – Compound instrument – settlement in shares

Consider the award granted in example 3 if the share price turned out to be C17 on 31 December 20X9.

A rational employee would select settlement in shares because this alternative has a higher fair value (1,700; 17 × 100 shares). The entity should accrete the liability to its fair value of C1,000 on the exercise date through the income statement. Total interest expense of C216 (1,000 – 784) on a cumulative basis is recognised between 1 January 20X5 and 31 December 20X9. The liability of C1,000 is transferred to equity as the shares are issued.

An employee may choose the cash alternative, despite the higher fair value of the settlement in shares. The entity first accretes the liability to its fair value of C1,000 on the exercise date through the income statement. Total interest expense of C216 on a cumulative basis is recognised between 1 January 20X5 and 31 December 20X9. It subsequently records the payment of C1,000 cash against the liability. The charge of C25 recognised in respect of the equity component is not adjusted.

Example 5 – Employee choice of settlement, with different length vesting periods

An entity agreed the details of an award with its employees on 1 January 20X6. Under the terms, employees can choose on 31 March 20X7 either:

■ cash payment of 25%-50% of salary, depending on specified performance measures, at 31 March 20X7; or

■ shares with value equivalent to 150% of the cash payment (based on the 31 March 20X7 share price), but the employee must remain in service for a further three years.

The grant date would be 1 January 20X6, as this is the date both parties involved have a shared understanding of the terms and conditions including the formula that would be used to determine the amount of cash to be paid (or the number of shares to be delivered).

The entity has granted the employee the right to choose whether a share-based payment transaction is settled in cash or by the entity issuing equity instruments. The entity has granted a compound financial instrument, which includes a debt component (that is, the counterparty's right to demand cash payment) and an equity component (that is, the counterparty's right to demand settlement in equity instruments). (See paras 12.156 to 12.161.)

The entity should account separately for the goods or services received or acquired in respect of each of the compound instrument's components. [IFRS 2 para 38]. The vesting period of the equity component and that of the debt component should be determined separately and the vesting period of each component may be different. In the above example, the vesting period for the debt component is 1.25 years (1 January 20X6 – 31 March 20X7) and the vesting period for the equity component is 4.25 years (1 January 20X6 – 31 March 20Y0), because employees are entitled to shares only if they complete a 4.25-year service period.

The entity may choose the settlement method

12.162 If the entity may choose the method of settlement, it should determine whether, in substance, it has created an obligation to settle in cash. This may be, for example, if:

■ The choice of settlement in equity instruments has no commercial substance (for example, because the entity is legally prohibited from issuing shares).

■ The entity has a past practice or stated policy of settling in cash.

■ The entity generally settles in cash whenever the counterparty requests it.

[IFRS 2 para 41].

12.163 If an obligation to settle in cash does exist, the entity should account for the transaction as a cash-settled share-based payment transaction as described from paragraph 12.146. Otherwise, the transaction should be treated as an equity-settled share-based payment transaction as described from paragraph 12.53. [IFRS 2 paras 42, 43].

Settlement choice changes from equity-settled to cash-settled

12.164 In many cases, a company whose equity instruments are not publicly traded will enter into share-based payment arrangements with its employees where the entity has a choice of settlement. For example, the entity may have an option to allow an employee to keep shares when they leave or make a cash payment instead. In these cases, the entity is likely to determine that it will settle in cash for the reason that, in most cases, a private company would not allow employees who leave the company to continue to hold its shares. The entity may reach a different conclusion if it had an expectation of creating a market for the shares by, for example an IPO or sale of the company. Past practice can be the determining factor. The following examples explore this:

> **Example – Employer choice changes from equity-settled to cash-settled**
>
> Entity A is privately owned by a venture capitalist. The entity enters into a share-based payment arrangement with its senior employees whereby:
>
> ■ Each employee will receive 1,000 shares if they remain employed for a period of five years.
>
> ■ If the employee leaves the entity after the five year period, but before the entity is listed, the entity has an option to purchase the shares for fair value from the employee.
>
> ■ The grant date fair value of the award is C2,000.
>
> ■ No employees are expected to leave over the five year period.
>
> ■ On grant date, the entity expects to list in the next three to five years. The entity has no past practice or stated policy of buying back shares from employees

when the employees leave as this is the first such plan to be put in place. Furthermore, the entity does not expect or anticipate that it will settle the awards in cash.

■ At the end of year two, the entity no longer expects to list and employees are informed of this fact. The entity states that, should it not be listed after five years and employees leave the company, it will repurchase the shares. The fair value of the shares is C3,000 on this date.

■ At the end of year three, the fair value of the liability has increased to C4,000.

On grant date, the employer accounts for the arrangement as an equity-settled share-based payment as there is no present obligation to settle in cash. The entries recorded in the first year would be:

	Dr	Cr
	C	C
Dr Employee expense	400	
Cr Equity		400
C2,000 to record the grant date fair value vesting over a period of five years		

At the end of year two, as the entity has stated its intentions the employees would assume that their award will be settled in cash if they work the five-year period. The award would be reclassified at the end of the second year, because the entity has created an obligation to settle in cash through a change in stated policy:

Dr Employee expense	400	
Cr Equity		400
To record the C2,000 vesting over a period of five years which was the expectation until year end		
Dr Equity	1,200	
Cr Liability (C3,000 × 2/5)		1,200

Reclassification of the equity award to cash-settled. Although the cumulative credit to equity to date is C800, it is appropriate to debit equity by more than this amount in order to set up the liability, because IFRS 2 allows the fair value of the resulting liability to be accounted for as a deduction from equity similar to a repurchase of an equity instrument. [IFRS 2 para 43].

At the end of year three, the award is accounted for on a cash-settled basis as follows:

Dr Employee expense	1,200	
Cr Liability (C4,000 × 3/5 − C1,200)		1,200

12.165 Where an entity has a choice of settlement and has classified an award as equity-settled, care should be taken when the entity actually settles the award. In the absence of other factors, an entity settling its first award in cash is a strong indication that a constructive obligation to pay cash has been established through past practice for the remaining awards and hence the other outstanding awards should be reclassified as cash-settled on a prospective basis.

> **Example – Employer choice of settlement where cash option taken**
>
> The facts are the same as in the example in paragraph 12.164, except that at the end of year two the entity does not make a statement to employees that it will repurchase the shares after a five-year period and a listing of the entity's shares is still seen as achievable. At the end of the year six the entity has not yet listed and one of the employees leaves the entity. The entity exercises its settlement choice and buys the leaving employees' shares for fair value.
>
> In the absence of any other evidence, there might be a presumption that the settlement of this award with the employee creates a valid expectation that the remaining employees will also receive cash when they leave. However, judgement will be required in order to determine whether one transaction establishes 'past practice' for which the company has now created an obligation to settle in cash. If this is the case, the entity should treat the remaining awards as cash-settled, since the entity now has a past practice of settling in cash. The entity would also need to revisit the classification of any similar grants it has made and consider whether it should reclassify them to cash-settled.

12.166 If the transaction is accounted for as equity-settled, the entity needs to consider if it has given away further value depending on which alternative has the greater fair value as at the settlement date, as shown in the table below. [IFRS 2 para 43].

Settlement method	Settlement method with the higher fair value	
Cash	**Equity**	
Cash	The amount of payment equal to the fair value of the equity instruments that would otherwise have been issued is accounted for as the repurchase of an equity interest and is deducted from equity. The excess over this amount is recognised as an expense.	The payment is accounted for as the repurchase of an equity interest and is deducted from equity.
Equity	No further accounting is required.	The excess of the fair value of the equity instruments issued over the amount of cash that would otherwise have been paid is recognised as an expense.

12.167 In practice, it is rare for the alternatives to have different values when the entity has the choice of settlement method; however, the example below has been included purely for illustrative purposes.

Example 1 – Entity choice of settlement

A listed entity has granted to its chief executive the right to either 10,000 phantom shares (that is, the right to receive a cash payment equal to the value of 10,000 shares) or 15,000 listed shares in the entity. The entity may choose the settlement method. It has never made an award of this nature and it is free to select either settlement method (that is, there is no restriction over its ability to issue shares). Accordingly, management does not consider that the entity has established an obligation and the transaction is accounted for as equity-settled. An expense is measured on the basis of the fair value of the 15,000 shares at grant date is C80,000. The opposing credit is recognised in equity.

On the settlement date, the entity's share price is C10. Hence, the fair value of the phantom shares is C100,000 while the fair value of the shares themselves is C150,000. If the entity chooses to settle the transaction in cash, being the settlement method with the lower fair value, the payment of C100,000 is deducted from equity. Even though only C80,000 had been recognised as an expense in equity, the additional C20,000 should also be deducted from equity. In substance it represents the re-purchase by the entity of its own shares so no further expense is recognised. However, if the entity chooses to settle the transaction by issuing shares, the excess of the fair value of the shares over the amount of cash that would otherwise have been paid (that is, C50,000) is recognised as an expense.

If the facts were different, such that at settlement date the fair value of the phantom shares was C150,000 while the fair value of the shares was C100,000, the accounting would be as follows. If the entity chose to settle the transaction by issuing shares, being the settlement method with the lower fair value, no further accounting would be required. If the entity chose to settle the transaction in cash, C100,000 (being the fair value of the equity instruments that would otherwise have been issued) would be deducted from equity. The excess of the amount actually paid over the amount deducted from equity (that is, C50,000) is recognised as an expense.

In summary, if the award is treated as equity-settled it should be accounted for in the same way as any other equity-settled transaction until the point of settlement. On settlement, the accounting is straight forward provided the entity chooses the method of settlement with the lower fair value at that date. If, however, it chooses the settlement method with the higher fair value at that date, the excess is treated as an additional expense. In the first scenario described above (settlement in shares when cash settlement has a lower fair value) the double entry on settlement would be as follows:

	Dr	Cr
	C	C
Dr Equity	100,000	
Dr Income statement	50,000	
Cr Share capital/equity		150,000

In the second scenario (settlement in cash when equity settlement has a lower fair value) the double entry on settlement would be as follows:

	Dr C	Cr C
Dr Equity	100,000	
Dr Income statement	50,000	
Cr Cash		150,000

Example 2 – Employer choice of settlement

An entity operates a share plan whereby employees are granted free shares in the company. The employee is, thereafter, entitled to the dividends and may vote. However, if an employee leaves within the first three years, the company may exercise a buy-back option at that time and repurchase all the shares. The price which the entity pays is dependent on when the employee leaves the entity:

- Before the end of year one – nil.

- After year one, but before the end of year two – 30% of the share's fair value.

- After year two, but before the end of year three – 50% of the share's fair value.

In the past, the entity has always exercised the buy back option as there is economic compulsion to do so (the repurchase right is below fair value and, furthermore, the entity does not want to form a non-controlling interest for employees that leave the entity). Although there is no legal obligation on the entity, there is a constructive obligation to buy the shares back on resignation (see para 12.162) through past practice and the fact that, in substance, the call option is a vesting mechanism.

In substance the award consists of three separate components: 30% vests over one year, 20% vests over two years (represented by 50% less the 30% that vests after year one) and 50% vests over three years. The entity has a choice of settlement for the 30% and 20% tranche although past practice indicates that the entity settles in cash. The remaining 50% can only be settled in equity (as the buy back option falls away after three years). Tranche vesting is discussed in more detail in paragraph 12.44.1, and in example 3 in paragraph 12.114, above.

Settlement method contingent on an event outside the control of the entity or employee

12.168   There may be occasions where the conditions of a share-based payment award provide the employee with either cash or equity, but the choice of which option occurs is outside the control of both the employee and the entity. We believe there are two acceptable approaches (covered in paras 12.168.1 and 12.168.2) to account for an award where the manner of settlement (that is, cash or equity) is contingent on an event that is outside the entity's control.

12.168.1   One approach is to account for the award as two mutually exclusive awards, one equity-settled and one cash-settled:

- The cash-settled alternative is a liability. Although this is affected by the probability of being paid, it always has a fair value which is recognised over the vesting period. If the award is ultimately settled in equity the fair value of the liability falls to nil.

■ The equity-settled alternative is only recognised if it is considered probable. If the award is ultimately settled in cash the equity alternative would have become improbable and so no cumulative expense would be recognised for this. The fair value of the liability will have increased to the cash amount ultimately paid.

As can be seen from the above, the factor that determines the settlement method is in effect treated as a vesting condition. Although the charge during the vesting period may appear to be in excess of the total value of the award granted, once the contingent settlement provision resolves, the cumulative charge will represent only the expense actually incurred under the equity settlement option or the cash settlement option.

Example – Equity settlement contingent on a successful listing (IPO)

At 1 January 20X8 an entity enters into a share-based payment arrangement with its employees. The terms of the award are as follows:

■ Employees are required to work for the entity for a period of five years after which time they will receive a cash payment equal to the value of the entity's shares.

■ If the entity engages in a successful IPO before the five year period is met, however, the employees will receive free shares rather than a cash payment. Thus, employees might receive free shares or a cash payment, but not both.

■ No employees are expected to leave the company over the next five years.

■ At the date of the award and the first two year ends thereafter, it was not probable that a successful IPO would occur before year five.

■ At the end of year three, a successful IPO becomes probable and management expect it to occur in year four.

■ At the end of year four, a successful IPO occurs and employees receive free shares.

■ The fair value of the equity-settled award alternative is C1,000 at grant date. The fair value of the cash alternative is C50 at the end of year one, C500 at the end of year two, C100 at the end of year three and C50 at the end of year four.

At the end of the first and second year ends, the entity would not record a charge for the equity-settled award as the vesting conditions are not expected to be met, as there has been no successful IPO. For the cash-settled award, the liability is measured at fair value at each reporting period, which includes the probability of settlement in cash. As such, the entity would record the following entries:

	Dr	Cr
Year end 31 December 20X8	**C**	**C**
Dr Employee expense	10	
Cr Liability		10

Fair value of cash-settled award recognised over the vesting period at the end of year one.

Year end 31 December 20X9		
Dr Employee expense	190	
Cr Liability		190

Cash-settled award recognised over the vesting period ((500 × 2/5) – 10).

At the end of the year three, the entity should start recording a charge for the equity-settled award as a successful IPO is now deemed probable. For the cash-settled award, the liability is measured at fair value at each reporting period, which includes the probability of settlement in cash. As such, the entity would record the following entries:

Year end 31 December 20Y0		
Dr Employee expense	750	
Cr Equity		750

Equity-settled award recognised over the vesting period ((1,000 × 3/4) – 0) as management expect a successful IPO in year four.

Dr Liability	140	
Cr Employee expense		140

Cash-settled award recognised over the vesting period ((100 × 3/5) – 200) which results in a reduction of the previous charge due to a change in fair value.

Year end 31 December 20Y1		
Dr Employee expense	250	
Cr Equity		250

A successful IPO occurs in year four and, therefore, the remaining charge for the equity-settled award is recognised (C1,000 – C750).

Dr Liability	60	
Cr Employee expense		60

The cash-settled share-based payment charge is reversed due to failure to meet the vesting conditions, that is, a successful IPO occurred before five years.

12.168.2 The alternative approach is to look to the principles of IAS 37 in determining whether or not an uncertain future event gives rise to a liability. Under this approach, only a contingent liability exists when the contingency that triggers cash settlement is not probable. The award should be treated as equity-settled, unless cash settlement becomes probable. The classification is an accounting estimate and any change in classification is treated as a change in estimate so that the cumulative expense (and related credit to equity or liability) should be the same as if the new classification had always been applied.

12.168.3 While the cumulative expense over the life of the award will be the same under either approach, the alternative approach of applying the principles of

IAS 37 avoids the issue in the previous approach (see para 12.168.1) that during the vesting period there might be an expense for both the cash and equity-settled alternatives at the same time.

Example – Contingent settlement with alternative approach applying the principles of IAS 37

Using the same facts as in the example in paragraph 12.168.1 above, the amount charged to the income statement in each period will be different under the alternative approach applying the principles of IAS 37 (refer to para 12.168.2).

At the end of the first and second year ends, the entity would not record a charge for the equity-settled award as the vesting conditions are not expected to be met, that is, no successful IPO. A liability is, therefore, recognised as cash settlement is probable until year three.

	Dr	Cr
	C	C
Year end 31 December 20X8		
Dr Employee expense	10	
Cr Liability		10
Cash-settled award recognised over the vesting period.		
Year end 31 December 20X9		
Dr Employee expense	190	
Cr Liability		190
Cash-settled award recognised over the vesting period.		

At the end of year three, a successful IPO becomes probable, therefore, the entity would record a charge for equity-settled award and there should be a reversal of the cash-settled award as it is now deemed not probable.

Year end 31 December 20Y0		
Dr Liability	200	
Cr Employee expense		200
Reversal of cash-settled share-based payment as IPO deemed probable.		
Dr Employee expense	750	
Cr Equity		750
Equity-settled award measured at grant date fair value of C1,000 (C1,000 × 3/4) as IPO is now deemed probable.		
Year end 31 December 20Y1		
Dr Employee expense	250	
Cr Equity		250
Equity-settled award measured at fair value of C1,000. Since all the vesting conditions for this award have been met in year four, the award has vested and the remaining charge of C250 (C1,000 – C750) is recognised in the income statement.		

Practical implications

Group share-based payment arrangements

12.169 As described in paragraph 12.10, the scope of IFRS 2 is broad. Share-based payment transactions include not only transactions settled in an entity's own shares, but also transactions settled in equity instruments of the entity's parent or any other entity in the same group. [IFRS 2 para 3A]. This means that if the employees of a subsidiary are awarded options over the shares of the parent, the subsidiary will recognise an expense in respect of the employee services received.

12.170 The question that arises is how to classify an award in the separate financial statements in the subsidiary and thus how the expense should be measured. IFRS 2 provides a clear basis to determine the classification of awards in both consolidated and separate financial statements by setting out the circumstances in which group share-based payment transactions are treated as equity-settled and cash-settled. The entity receiving goods or services should assess its own rights and obligations as well as the nature of awards granted in order to determine the accounting treatment. The amount recognised by the group entity receiving the goods or services will not necessarily be consistent with the amount recognised in the consolidated financial statements. [IFRS 2 para 43A].

12.171 In group share-based payment transactions, the entity receiving the goods or services should account for awards as equity-settled when:

■   the awards granted are settled with the entity's own equity instruments; or

■   the entity has no obligation to settle the share-based payment transaction.

[IFRS 2 para 43B].

In all other situations, the entity receiving the goods or services should account for the awards as cash-settled.

12.172 For an entity settling a share-based payment transaction when another group entity has received the goods or services, the entity recognises the transaction as an equity-settled share-based payment transaction (and thus recorded in equity) only if it is settled in the entity's own equity instruments. In all other circumstances, the transaction is treated as cash-settled award and a liability is recognised. [IFRS 2 para 43C].

12.173 The accounting treatment described above applies regardless of any intra-group repayment arrangements that may be in place. [IFRS 2 para 43D]. See further paragraph 12.180.

Share-based payment

12.174 The classification of both cash-settled and equity-settled share-based payment transactions in group situations is summarised in the flow chart in appendix 2 to this chapter.

12.174.1 The following examples illustrate the principles.

> **Example 1 – Parent entity grants share awards to subsidiary employees**
>
> A parent grants its shares directly to subsidiary A and subsidiary B employees. The awards will vest immediately, and the parent will issue new shares directly to the employees. The parent will not charge subsidiaries A and B for the transaction.
>
> In the consolidated financial statements, the transaction is treated as an equity-settled share-based payment, as the group has received services in consideration for the group's equity instruments. An expense is recognised in the group income statement for the grant date fair value of the share-based payment over the vesting period, with a credit recognised in equity.
>
> In the subsidiaries' accounts, the award is treated as an equity-settled share-based payment, as the subsidiaries do not have an obligation to settle the award. An expense for the grant date fair value of the award is recognised over the vesting period with a credit recognised in equity. The credit to equity is treated as a capital contribution as the parent is compensating the subsidiaries' employees with no expense to the subsidiaries. In this example, the shares vest immediately, therefore, an expense is recognised in the subsidiaries' income statement in full based on the grant date fair value and a credit to equity.
>
> In the parent's separate financial statements, there is no share-based payment charge as no employees are providing services to the parent. Therefore, the parent would record a debit, recognising an increase in the investment in the subsidiaries as a capital contribution from the parent and a credit to equity (see further para 12.181 below).

> **Example 2 – Subsidiary grants rights over equity instruments of its parent**
>
> Instead of granting rights over its own equity instruments, subsidiary A grants rights over the parent's shares to subsidiary A's employees. The shares vest over two years. When the shares vest, subsidiary A purchases shares from the market and passes them on to its employees. Subsidiary A only makes these purchases when it settles the award with its employees.
>
> The transaction is treated as an equity-settled share-based payment in the consolidated financial statements, as the group has received services in consideration for the group's equity instruments. An expense is recognised in the income statement for the grant date fair value of the share-based payment over the vesting period, with a credit recognised in equity. The purchase of the shares from the market would be treated as a treasury transaction.
>
> IFRS 2 requires the award to be treated in subsidiary A's financial statements as a cash-settled share-based payment, as subsidiary A has the obligation to settle the award (albeit in shares of the parent). An expense would be recognised in the income statement over the vesting period, with a liability being recorded as the other side of

the entry. This liability is re-measured at each reporting date until settlement, in accordance with the accounting for cash-settled awards.

The above transaction has no impact on the parent's financial statements, as the parent is not a party to the transaction.

An arrangement that is similar in substance from an employee's point of view, but results in equity-settled accounting by the subsidiary is where the parent awards its own shares to employees of the subsidiary and makes a cash recharge to the subsidiary for the shares it acquires in the market. This is discussed further from paragraph 12.180.

Example 3 – Parent grants cash-settled awards to employees of its subsidiary

A parent grants share appreciation rights to subsidiary A's employees. At the end of two years, the parent will pay cash to the employees equivalent to the difference between the share price on vesting and the share price at grant date. No intra-group recharge is to be made.

In the consolidated financial statements, the transaction is treated as a cash-settled share-based payment as the group has received services in consideration for cash payments based on the price of the group's equity instruments. An expense is recognised in the group income statement for the fair value of the share-based payment over the vesting period, with a liability being recorded as the other side of the entry. This liability is re-measured at each reporting date until settlement.

In subsidiary A's financial statements, IFRS 2 requires the award to be treated as equity-settled, because the subsidiary does not have an obligation to settle the award. An expense would be recognised in the subsidiary's income statement over the vesting period, with a credit recognised in equity. The credit to equity is treated as a capital contribution from the parent, as the parent is compensating the subsidiary's employees at no expense to the subsidiary.

In the parent's financial statements, there is no share-based payment expense recorded as the employees are not providing services to the parent. Rather, the share-based payment transaction results in a debit to 'investment in subsidiary' with a corresponding liability recorded at fair value at each reporting period end.

Measurement would vary between the two sets of accounts.

12.175   Where an employee receives shares in an unlisted entity, it is important to gain an understanding of how the employee will realise the value in that award. In order to provide an employee with an exit mechanism where there is no market for a subsidiary's shares, it is common for a parent entity to agree to exchange a vested equity award for either cash or for its own shares (where the parent is listed, for example). By providing an exit mechanism, the parent also ensures that its holding in the subsidiary will not be diluted when the shares vest.

12.176   If the employees are provided with an option to convert their award in the subsidiary into the shares of a listed parent, the award would still be equity-settled on a consolidated basis, but the accounting in the individual entities may depend on which entity has the obligation to provide parent shares to the employees. See further the discussion on mandatorily redeemable shares in paragraph 12.148.

> **Example – Options over subsidiary's shares that are convertible into parent's shares**
>
> A group has a fast growing subsidiary and intends to incentivise the subsidiary's employees by granting them options over shares in the subsidiary. The options will be granted by the subsidiary. The grant date fair value of the options from the subsidiary's point of view is C1.
>
> The parent is listed. In order to provide the employees with an 'exit mechanism' the parent has agreed to convert all the vested subsidiary shares into the parent's shares with the same fair value when the employee resigns.
>
> From a consolidated financial statement point of view, this is an equity-settled share-based payment arrangement granted to the subsidiary's employees. The consolidated grant date fair value of C1 would be recorded as an expense in the group income statement over the vesting period.
>
> In the subsidiary's separate financial statements, this would also be an equity-settled share-based payment, as the subsidiary has granted its employees equity instruments of the subsidiary.
>
> In the parent's separate financial statements, there will be no IFRS 2 charge as the parent is only funding the award. The parent has not granted the awards nor have employees provided services to the parent. The parent would, therefore, record a debit, recognising an increase in their investment in subsidiary and a corresponding credit to equity.

12.177   Further implications arise if the subsidiary's employees described in the example above are required to exchange their shares for cash from the parent entity upon vesting. The subsidiary is receiving services and has granted its own equity, but has no obligation to make any payment to its employees. The award would, therefore, be treated as equity-settled in the subsidiary's financial statements. [IFRS 2 para 43A]. The award would be treated as a liability in the parent entity's financial statements, with a corresponding amount recognised as an investment in the subsidiary (see further para 12.181).The award is cash-settled in the group's consolidated financial statements, as the group is obliged to provide employees with a cash payment based on the equity instrument of an entity within the group.

12.177.1   Alternatively, the parent entity may agree to exchange the employees' shares in the subsidiary for its own shares — for example, because the parent entity is listed. In the same way as the situation described in the example above, the subsidiary would account for this as an equity-settled award in its own financial statements. The parent entity would recognise an increase in investment in the subsidiary, with the corresponding amount recognised in equity. [IFRS 2 para 43C]. Additionally, the award is treated as equity-settled in the group's consolidated financial statements.

12.177.1.1 There may be some situations where the entity does not provide an exit mechanism for employees; rather the majority shareholder or other shareholders offer to buy the departing employees' interests. In these circumstances, an entity would still apply the principles of group arrangements as explained above to determine the accounting in the entity's accounts.

Example – Shareholders provide an exit mechanism

Entity T is an unlisted entity and grants restricted shares to key management that will vest in three years. The entity is not planning an exit event, so the terms of the award allow for key management to sell their shares for fair value after the three year vesting period, either to other shareholders or to an approved third party. In addition, there are leaver provisions, even after vesting, which require the employee to sell their shares when they leave the entity. However, in this example, the entity does not have an obligation to purchase the shares because the remaining shareholders are obligated to buy out their fellow shareholders.

The employees will ultimately receive cash as they cannot leave the company with shares and, therefore, do not have unconditional rights to the equity instruments. From their perspective, therefore, this is a group cash-settled arrangement. But in this example, it is the shareholders who have the obligation to settle the cash-settled share-based payment arrangement. Applying the principles in paragraph 43B of IFRS 2, the entity should account for the arrangement as equity-settled in its financial statements as the entity does not have an obligation to settle this arrangement. For equity-settled arrangements, IFRS 2 requires an entity to measure the services received and the corresponding increase in equity (debit expense, credit equity) at modified grant date fair value. The fair value will be measured at grant date and recognised over the vesting period (that is, 3 years).

12.177.2 Another situation that might occur in group share-based payment arrangements is where shares in the parent entity are issued in another currency than the subsidiary's functional currency. The example below considers the interaction between foreign exchange and share-based payment accounting.

Example – Share awards granted in a different functional currency

Employees of a subsidiary are granted the rights to parent shares for services provided to the subsidiary. As the parent granted the award and the subsidiary has no obligation to settle the award, the award is treated as equity-settled by the subsidiary.

The shares in the parent are traded and reported in US dollars (both the presentation and functional currency is US dollars). The subsidiary reports (both functional and reportable) in pounds sterling.

At the grant date, the parent informs the subsidiary of the US dollar grant date fair value of the award for each new participant in the plan. Each year (based on leaver statistics supplied by the subsidiary), the parent informs the subsidiary of the charge to be reflected in the subsidiary's income statement (again in US dollars).

For share-based payment accounting, the fair value is fixed at the grant date for equity-settled awards (deemed to be the best estimate of the services provided where the entity and employee have a shared understanding) and spread over the vesting period to reflect services provided by the employee. The grant date fair value is measured in US dollars, for recognition in the parent entity's financial statements. The grant date fair value of the award for recognition in the subsidiary entity's financial statements is then calculated by translating the US dollar grant date fair value, to pounds sterling, using the spot rate at the grant date. The amount initially translated at grant date would be the amount used in local currency accounts over the vesting period. This is in accordance with the IFRS 2 requirements for each reporting entity.

Employees move between group entities

12.178 IFRS 2 states that where an employee transfers employment from one subsidiary to another during the vesting period (the vesting period could be, for example, a service period), each subsidiary should measure the services received from the employee by reference to the fair value of the equity instrument at grant date, and not re-measure at the date of transfer. If, after transferring between group entities, the employee fails to meet a non-market vesting condition (for example, a service condition) each subsidiary should adjust the amount previously recognised in respect of the services received from the employee.

Intermediate holding companies

12.179 Where a parent grants a share-based payment to a group entity and there are other intermediate subsidiaries within the group between the parent and the entity in which the goods and services are received, a question arises as to whether the intermediate subsidiaries should account for the share-based payment as IFRS 2 is silent in this respect. We believe it would be acceptable to account for the transaction only in the parent and subsidiary which receives the goods and services. The following example illustrates this view:

> **Example – Implications for intermediate holding companies**
>
> Parent entity P owns 100% of an intermediate holding company (entity H1). Entity H1 in turn owns 100% of another intermediate holding company (entity H2), entity H2 owns 100% of trading subsidiary entity S.
>
> Entity P grants, and has the obligation to settle, equity-settled options over P's shares to employees of entity S. The grant date fair value of the award, which has a two year vesting period, is C200,000. Should each intermediate holding company apply IFRS 2 or can entity P recognise an investment in its indirectly held subsidiary, entity S?
>
> The transaction is between entity P and the employees of entity S. Our view is that it is acceptable for entity P to recognise an investment in entity S. There will be no impact on the separate financial statements of entity H1 and entity H2. This is acceptable on the basis that it is possible for an indirectly-held subsidiary and its ultimate parent to transact directly without involving intermediate parent companies. The double entry in parent entity P's separate financial statements at the end of each year would be to recognise a capital contribution to entity S as follows:

		C	C
Dr	Investment in subsidiary entity S	100,000	
	Cr Equity		100,000

Trading subsidiary entity S will recognise the IFRS 2 charge in its separate financial statements:

		C	C
Dr	Income statement	100,000	
	Cr Equity		100,000

Funding arrangements between parent and its subsidiary

12.180   The illustrative example attached to IFRS 2 clarifies that where the parent grants rights over its equity instruments to the employees of its subsidiary (accounted for as an equity-settled share-based payment), the debit would be recognised in the subsidiary's income statement and a credit to equity (as a capital contribution) recognised over the vesting period of the share-based payment arrangement. [IFRS 2 para IG 22A, Example 14].

12.181   The accounting within the parent entity for the capital contribution is not addressed by IFRS 2. The IFRIC exposure draft (IFRIC draft interpretation D17) issued prior to the release of IFRIC 11 indicated that the parent entity would debit its investment in subsidiary and credit equity for the equity instruments it had granted (if the parent entity is satisfying the obligation). When the IFRS IC issued the final interpretation of IFRIC 11, it did not address this issue as the basis for conclusions notes that the IFRS IC *"did not wish to widen the scope of the Interpretation to an issue that relates to the accounting for intra-group payment arrangements"* generally. [IFRIC 11 BC12]. We believe that it was this wider issue that resulted in the deletion of the proposed guidance in the draft interpretation, as opposed to a flaw in the thinking. The only alternatives to the parent debiting its investment in subsidiary would seem to be recognising nothing or recognising an expense, neither of which are attractive. There is no indication in IFRS 2 that the accounting treatment set out in the draft interpretation would be inappropriate and, therefore, we believe it should continue to be applied. The accounting implications are considered in the examples in paragraph 12.187 below.

12.182   Sometimes, a parent company makes a recharge to the subsidiary in respect of share options granted to the subsidiary's employees. IFRS 2 does not address how to account for such intra-group payment arrangements for share-based payment transactions. However, the illustrative example in the draft interpretation did consider the issue. It concluded that an inter-company charge payable by a subsidiary entity should be offset against the capital contribution in the individual or separate financial statements of the subsidiary entity and the parent entity. We believe that this is particularly appropriate where there is a clear link between the recharge and the share-based payment, for example where the recharge is based on the intrinsic value or market value of the shares when they vest. Consistent with the principle of shareholder distributions, if the amount of the inter-company charge exceeded the capital contribution, that excess should be treated as a distribution from the subsidiary to its parent. We consider this to be an appropriate treatment for such a recharge.

12.183 The return of the capital contribution and any excess distribution payment are separate transactions to the credit to equity arising from the equity-settled share-based payment. Therefore, it is necessary to provide separate disclosure of the gross amounts.

UK.12.183.1 If the recharge in excess of the IFRS 2 charge is treated as a distribution, a question arises on whether the distribution would be unlawful if a subsidiary does not have sufficient distributable profits. Tech 02/10, 'Guidance on the determination of realised profits and losses in the context of distributions under the Companies Act 2006', issued in November 2010, clarifies, "...*it will not be unlawful for the subsidiary to make the reimbursement payment, even in the absence of distributable profits, provided that the payment is not a distribution as a matter of law*". [Tech 02/10 para 7.54].

12.184 We believe that it is important that management are able to justify a clear link between the recharge and the share-based payment charge in order to apply the principle of shareholder distributions described in paragraph 12.182. If there is no clear link between the recharge and the share-based payment we believe that the payment between the subsidiary and its parent should be treated in a manner consistent with management recharges. This would result in an expense recognised in the income statement for the amount recharged. Note that this would result in a 'double debit' to the income statement since the subsidiary would have already recorded the services received under IFRS 2.

12.185 Where there is a clear link between the recharge and the share-based payment, the full amount of the recharge would be recorded within equity. It would *not* be acceptable for the subsidiary to split the recharge into two components:

- one equal to the share-based payment expense which is treated as a return of a capital contribution and recorded in equity; and

- the excess of the recharge over the amount above as an additional recharge expense in the income statement.

This would have the effect of creating the same result as if the subsidiary had applied cash-settled accounting. IFRS 2 is clear that this type of arrangement should be treated as an equity-settled award. [IFRS 2 paras 43B, 43D].

Timing of the recharge

12.186 When a subsidiary is recharged by its parent for a share-based payment, the question arises as to when (if at all) a liability should be recorded for the amount that is expected to be recharged in the future, for example, when the award vests or the employees exercise their options. There are two acceptable approaches to account for the recharge. One approach is that when the arrangement can be linked to the IFRS 2 charge, recharges should not be accrued, but should be recognised when paid, for the following reasons:

- IASs 32 and 39 scope out financial instruments, contracts and obligations under share-based payment transactions, except for contracts that can be net settled and in relation to the disclosure of treasury shares. [IAS 32 para 4(f); IAS 39 para 2(i)]. Our view is that these scope exclusions should be read broadly and that recharges clearly related to a share-based payment can be considered outside of the scope of IASs 32 and 39.

- While there is no scope exclusion for share-based payment arrangements under IAS 37, such recharge payments would not generally meet the IAS 37 recognition criteria to be recorded as liabilities until paid because:

  - The subsidiary does not have a present obligation as a result of a past event. In order for there to be a clear link between a share-based payment and a recharge, in most cases the recharge will generally be linked to employees exercising their options. Options cannot be exercised until they have vested and employees are likely to exercise their options once they are in the money. Therefore, there is unlikely to be a present obligation on the entity until all vesting conditions have been satisfied and until it is probable that employees will exercise their options (for example, where the options are in the money). This is further supported by the fact that distributions (such as dividends) are only provided for when an entity has a present obligation and, as discussed above, an analogy may be drawn between such recharges and distributions to shareholders. There is no present obligation since the distribution is conditional upon an uncertain future event (such as employees providing services or choosing to exercise their options) that is not wholly within the control of the entity.

  - It is not probable that an outflow of economic resources will be required. We consider that the point in time at which it becomes probable that there will be an outflow of economic resources would only be reliably known when the options are close to being exercised.

In most cases, we believe that a subsidiary entity would account for a recharge when the payment is made to the parent. The recharge would be disclosed as a contingent liability during the time that the recharge payment is not recognised as a liability. It may be appropriate to recognise a liability for a recharge before the payment is made — for example, once an award has vested and the options to be exercised are deeply in the money.

12.186.1   There is, however, diversity in practice in this area, as there is no specific guidance on recharge arrangements in IFRS. There is an alternative approach in which the subsidiary entity would recognise the recharge over the vesting period as the recharge payment arises from the share-based payment arrangement in which employees are providing services. This approach may also be acceptable in practice.

12.187   Where there is no link between the share-based payment and the future payment by the subsidiary (that is, the double debit treatment discussed in para 12.184), it would be necessary to consider whether the entity has a present obligation in a manner similar to that of a management recharge.

> **Example 1 – Recharge from parent company in respect of share options**
>
> The facts are the same as in example one under paragraph 12.174.1 above, except that the parent makes a recharge to the subsidiary on exercise of the options. The recharge is clearly linked to the share-based payment, being the difference between the option price and the market price of the shares at the date of exercise of the options.
>
> From the subsidiary's perspective, this will still be an equity-settled share-based payment transaction. The requirement for the subsidiary to make a cash payment to the parent does not make this a cash-settled share-based-payment transaction. This is because the subsidiary's obligation is to its parent while the providers of goods or services (that is, the employees) receive equity instruments. Accordingly, the accounting for the share-based payment transaction will be the same as in the previous example. (The subsidiary will recognise an expense and an increase in equity of C100,000.)
>
> Although a recharge such as in this example may be made for a number of reasons, it is often made to enable the parent to acquire shares in the market so as to satisfy the award. In substance, as discussed in paragraph 12.182, the payment by the subsidiary to the parent would be recorded directly in equity for a payment of up to C100,000. Any payment in excess of the amount of capital contribution initially recognised should be treated as a distribution from the subsidiary to its parent. Hence, if the amount of the recharge in this example is C150,000, the double entry in the individual financial statements of the subsidiary would be as follows:
>
> | | C | C |
> |---|---:|---:|
> | Dr   Equity – repurchase of equity instrument | 100,000 | |
> | Dr   Equity – distribution | 50,000 | |
> | Cr   Cash | | 150,000 |
>
> Our view is that the subsidiary should not make a provision for the recharge during the vesting period, because it does not have a present obligation and it is not probable that there will be an outflow of economic resources until the options vest. The subsidiary will, however, disclose a contingent liability. However, as noted above, there are alternative views whereby the provision could be accrued over the vesting period.

It should be noted that certain entities may wish to show the recharge debit entry within the income statement as opposed to equity and we believe that this approach would also be acceptable, provided that it is applied consistently (this does lead to a 'double debit' in the income statement given that the IFRS 2 charge will also be recognised). In addition, where there is no clear link between the share-based payment and the recharge from the parent, we believe that it would be most appropriate to record a second debit through the income statement.

As regards the parent's separate financial statements, the double entry would be as follows:

		C	C
Dr	Cash	150,000	
	Cr Investment in subsidiary		100,000
	Cr Other income		50,000

Some entities may wish to take the full credit entry as other income rather than reducing the parent's investment in subsidiary and we believe that this approach would also be acceptable, provided that the payment is made from the subsidiary's post-acquisition reserves and the policy is applied consistently. Where a credit is taken to other income, the parent entity should ensure that it has considered whether its investment in subsidiary is impaired.

Note that, in certain jurisdictions, the impact of accounting for group share-based payment transactions could impact the ability for an entity to pay dividends. Therefore, legal advice may need to be sought.

Example 2 – Settlement in parent's shares with an advance recharge

Employees of a subsidiary are granted options to acquire 100 shares in the parent entity at a fixed price of C10 per share in exchange for services. The grant date is 1 January 20X6 when the fair value of the total award is C100. The award is subject to a two year vesting period and performance conditions. The options will vest if the total shareholder return exceeds 5% per annum during 20X6 and 20X7.

The parent entity agreed to issue new shares to entitled employees when the options are exercised. At the grant date the subsidiary paid the parent an option premium in exchange for the parent agreeing to satisfy the obligation to employees. The amount paid to the parent is the fair value of the options granted to employees as determined on 1 January 20X6, C100. The 'investment in subsidiary' in the parent entity balance sheet is in excess of C100.

As discussed in paragraph 12.171, the subsidiary should treat the transaction as an equity-settled share-based payment, as the subsidiary does not have an obligation to settle the award. [IFRS 2 para 43B]. The subsidiary should record the following:

Year ended 31 December 20X6

	C	C
Dr Employee benefits expense	50	
Cr Equity		50
Dr Equity	100	
Cr Cash		100

Year ended 31 December 20X7

	C	C
Dr Employee benefits expense	50	
Cr Equity		50

In its separate financial statements, the parent entity will record the following:

Year ended 31 December 20X6

	C	C
Dr Investment in subsidiary	50	
Cr Equity		50
Dr Cash	100	
Cr Investment in subsidiary		100

In its separate financial statements, the parent entity records the exercise price received from employees when the options are exercised on 31 December 20X7 as follows:

Year ended 31 December 20X7

	C	C
Dr Investment in subsidiary	50	
Cr Equity		50
Dr Cash (100 shares at C10 each)	1,000	
Cr Equity		1,000

The payment by the subsidiary is in substance an advance payment on the capital contribution the parent intends to make in the future. Whether the subsidiary makes a payment to its parent in advance or at a later date (such as when employees exercise their awards) does not affect the classification in the subsidiary or the parent accounts. If the upfront recharge is in excess of the 'investment in subsidiary' in the parent's accounts, the excess would be recognised in the income statement.

A subsidiary entity may wish to show the debit side of the cash payment as an additional expense, for example for tax purposes (again, this leads to a double debit). Similarly, a parent entity may wish to show the cash payment as income. We believe that these approaches would also be acceptable, provided that they are applied consistently. In addition, where there is no clear link between the share-based payment and the recharge from the parent, we believe that it would be most appropriate to record a second debit through the income statement in the subsidiary and as a credit through the income statement in the parent.

[The next paragraph is 12.200.]

IFRS 2 disclosures in group arrangements

12.200 Where a subsidiary entity accounts for a share-based payment transaction in group situations such as those described between paragraphs 12.169 and 12.177 above, the disclosures prescribed by IFRS 2 are required in full (see further from para 12.257). The subsidiary entity's financial statements should be stand-alone; it is not possible, for example, to cross-refer to share-based payment disclosures given in the parent's (or group's) financial statements.

Classification issues

Entity purchases own shares from market

12.201 The way in which an entity acquires the shares that will be used to satisfy a share-based payment award is a separate transaction that does not impact the classification of share-based payment awards under IFRS 2. For example, a share-based payment award would not be treated as cash-settled simply because an entity is forced to go to a third party to purchase its equity instruments in order to satisfy the award. If employees will always receive shares on meeting the vesting conditions, they would be treated as equity-settled, because the entity is providing its own equity to employees.

> **Example – Classification following purchase of own shares from the market**
>
> An entity granted employees rights to its shares subject to certain performance conditions. The entity purchases the shares on the market at the date that its employees satisfy those performance conditions.
>
> The entity accounts for the arrangement as an equity-settled share-based payment transaction. When the performance conditions are met and the entity purchases the shares on the market, the transaction is recognised in equity as a treasury share transaction to reflect the purchase of the entity's own shares. This does not affect the share-based payment accounting.

Post-vesting restrictions

12.202 Post-vesting restrictions may affect the classification of share-based payment transactions. IFRS 2 requires entities to consider the post-vesting terms and conditions of a share-based payment. The following example illustrates this point.

> **Example – Post-vesting restriction**
>
> A post-vesting restriction might be a pre-emption right. For example, an employee receives shares in the entity upon vesting, but he or she must offer them for sale to the entity if they resign or otherwise terminate their employment. Where the entity has an intention or established practice of exercising the pre-emption right it would indicate that the award is in fact cash-settled. See further discussion at paragraph 12.146.

12.203 An entity may sometimes act as a broker for its employees by selling their shares to a third party on the employees' behalf. Where the entity is acting as a principal, for example where employees have no choice in the matter or where the employer is the purchaser, the entity having mandated the purchase of shares from the employees, the award would be treated as cash-settled.

12.204 Alternatively, where the entity is acting as agent, for example, selling the shares on the market upon instruction by the employee, the award would be treated as equity-settled as the entity is settling in shares.

12.205 Another situation arises where an entity settles a share option award net, that is, employees receive fewer shares, but pay no exercise price. For example, for an award of 100 shares an employee receives 70 shares. It is not relevant whether the company sells 30 shares on the market to satisfy the exercise price or continues to hold them, since there is no cash outflow or liability for the company. The award should be classified as equity-settled as the entity has settled the full value of the award in shares. See further from paragraph 12.222 for discussion of social security issues.

Deferred tax

12.206 Accounting for deferred tax arising on a share-based payment transaction is addressed in chapter 13.

[The next paragraph is 12.211.]

Equity incentive plans

12.211 Certain equity incentive plans offer organisations an opportunity to widen share ownership as part of their overall reward strategy. These incentive plans may include one or all of the following awards:

- *Free shares* – employers gift shares to employees.

- *Matching shares* – employers match shares which have already been purchased by employees provided the employee continues to provide services for a specified period of time.

- *Dividend shares* – employers offer dividend reinvestment in additional shares with shares held by employees in another plan.

Free shares

12.212 When the award of free shares is not subject to a performance condition and the shares are not forfeitable, an expense will be recognised immediately. This expense will be based on the fair value of the shares at the date that the award is granted. Where the award is subject to vesting conditions, the expense will be recognised over the vesting period.

12.213 In the situation where recipients of an award may retain their entitlements, even if they leave employment, the award would have vested at the point they retain entitlement. At this point, any remaining charge would be accelerated, because there is no further service period. This is considered in the example following paragraph 12.214.

Matching shares

12.214 The accounting for matching shares should be similar to that of a free share award (see para 12.212 above), that is, the expense would be recognised over the vesting period. As discussed in paragraph 12.101, a requirement to hold shares in order to receive matching shares is a non-vesting condition. Failure to hold the required shares results in a cancellation. Where awards are part of an ongoing arrangement under which the employee can purchase shares and, consequently, receive matching shares, the charge should be made over the relevant vesting period. This is considered in example 1.

> **Example 1 – Matching shares with a service condition and good and bad leaver provisions**
>
> An entity operates an equity incentive plan for all of its employees. As part of the arrangement, employees have a right to matching shares when they apply for shares, although they must hold their purchased shares and remain with the entity for three years before the matching shares vest unconditionally. However, 'good' leavers (for example, those leaving due to death, injury, disability, transfer and retirement) will not forfeit their rights to the matching shares.
>
> In the case of good leavers, it is assumed that the matching shares must have vested at the point they become a good leaver (as there are no service conditions to be satisfied for them to receive the shares). Hence, any remaining charge should be accelerated when a good leaver leaves. For an award that will vest on retirement, the vesting period, as anticipated at grant date, ends at the point where the employee is able to retire without requiring the agreement of the employer. For bad leavers, on the other hand, due to the fact they have forfeited their rights to the shares by failing to meet the service condition, there should be a reversal of the related charge to the extent they were not anticipated.
>
> Therefore, at the date the matching shares are granted, it is necessary not only to assess the likely number of leavers and when they are going to leave, but also to split these into good and bad leavers. For those expected to be good leavers the estimated vesting period will be reduced to the likely date of their departure, for example, on retirement. However, it would be difficult to estimate vesting for death and/or disability events and these amounts may not be material. Where such events are unlikely to be material vesting for these conditions might not be adjusted until the event takes place.
>
> What happens if an employee chooses to dispose of their purchased shares without leaving is considered in the next example.

Example 2 – Matching shares with a non-vesting condition (requirement to hold shares)

An entity enters into a share-based payment arrangement with employees whereby each employee is entitled to 1,000 free shares at the end of a three year period provided that:

- The employee completes a three year service period with the entity from the date of the grant of the award.

- The employee elects to take their cash bonus for the year in the form of 1,000 shares on the grant date and then holds them for the three year period ('restricted shares').

However, an employee that leaves the company prior to the end of the three year period or sells their restricted shares within this period will no longer be eligible to receive the matching shares.

IFRS 2 makes it clear that the requirement to hold restricted shares for three years is not a vesting condition. Although the requirement occurs during the service period, it is wholly within the employee's control and does not determine whether the entity receives the services linked to the matching shares. The probability of employees selling their restricted shares (and hence losing the matching shares) will need to be taken into account when calculating the grant date fair value.

An employee's failure to hold the restricted shares is treated as a cancellation. This would result in the acceleration of any unvested portion of the award on the date that the employee sells the restricted shares and receives the cash instead. See further paragraph 12.138.

Dividend shares

12.215 Dividends paid on shares that have vested with employees (perhaps through another plan) accrue to the benefit of the employee. Clearly, these dividends will be included within dividends paid by the company.

12.216 In some situations the shares have not vested (for example, where shares are subject to forfeiture) but dividends on those shares do vest (either by being paid to the employee or by reinvestment in dividend shares that are not forfeitable). This is a complex area and specialist advice may need to be obtained. Refer to paragraph 12.305 below for a discussion on cash dividends.

Deferred bonus plans

12.217 A deferred bonus plan is a type of share incentive plan that is common in some territories. Terms are varied and often complex, but the following are typical features:

- A bonus is awarded to employees based on individual and company performance over one year.

- At the end of the year, employees may elect to receive a portion of their bonus in the form of shares rather than cash.

- If an employee elects to receive shares:

  - the shares are restricted insofar as they cannot be sold for three years; and

  - if the individual is still an employee at the end of the three year period, they receive an allocation of matching shares (see paras 12.211 and 12.214).

12.218   The entitlement to matching shares introduces a degree of complexity as there are, in substance, two awards. The first, which may be settled in cash or shares, vests at the end of the first year. The second (the entitlement to matching shares) does not vest until the end of the fourth year and only then if the employee has chosen shares rather than cash at the end of the first year. This means that an expense should be recognised over one year for the first award and over four years for the second.

12.219   As regards measurement, the grant date value of the cash alternative is the present value of the agreed amount of the bonus. The value of the equity alternative is made up of two components, namely the restricted shares (the value of which may be slightly less than the cash alternative if it is appropriate to reduce the value as a result of the sale restriction – see para 12.279) plus the matching shares.

12.220   If at the end of the first year an employee chooses the cash alternative they will not receive the equity alternative or the matching shares. The accounting treatment is the same as that described in example 2 in paragraph 12.214. If the employee chooses the cash alternative, this would be a cancellation of the second tranche of the grant by the employee which would lead to accelerated expense recognition.

12.221   On the other hand, if the employee chooses the equity alternative, the balance on the liability is transferred to equity and the entity will continue to recognise the balance of the expense in respect of the matching shares over the remaining three years. If, having taken the equity alternative, an employee leaves after, say, two years, this is a forfeiture as the employee has failed to satisfy the service condition, so the expense will be reversed. The expense recognised in the first year in respect of the restricted shares will not be reversed, as the former employee will normally be entitled to retain the shares.

Social security contributions on share options gains

Background

UK.12.221.1   UK employers are required to pay National Insurance Contributions (NIC) (social security contributions) on the exercise of certain share options granted after 5 April 1999. The NIC charge applies to share options issued under unapproved share plans (that is, those not approved by the Inland Revenue) where the shares are 'readily convertible assets', that is, they can be sold on a stock exchange or there are arrangements in place that allow the employees to obtain cash for the shares acquired under the option plan.

UK.12.221.2 The charge is based on the intrinsic value of the options at the date of exercise (that is, the excess of the market price of the shares over the exercise price).

Treatment of social security contributions under IFRS

12.222 There is no specific standard within IFRS that governs the accounting for social security contributions, as there is for income taxes. When considering under which standard social security costs should be accounted for, IAS 19 concludes that in the context of short-term employee benefits, social security contributions (such as NIC in the UK or FICA in the US) are employee benefits and should be considered in the same way as wages, salaries and so on. [IAS 19 para 8(a), IAS 19 (revised) para 9(a)]. Long-term benefits that are part of the entity's obligation should be included in actuarial assumptions used to measure the defined benefit obligation. Social security contributions are, therefore, considered a benefit. (See further chapter 11 or 11A under IAS 19 (revised)). This suggests that the social security contributions payable in connection with a grant of share options should be considered as an integral part of the grant itself. Hence, the accounting for the social security contributions will be dictated by IFRS 2 and the charge will be treated as a cash-settled transaction. Cash-settled share-based payment transactions are discussed in detail from paragraph 12.146.

12.223 The accounting for social security contributions as a cash-settled share-based payment transaction means:

■ A liability should be recognised over the vesting period for social security contributions payable in respect of options to be exercised.

■ The amount of the liability will depend on the number of options that are expected to be exercised (that is, vesting conditions are taken into account).

■ The expense should be allocated over the period from the date of grant to the end of the vesting period. From the end of the vesting period to the date of actual exercise the liability should be adjusted by reference to the current market value of the shares (that is, fair value of the liability at the end of the reporting period).

12.224 The important point is that the liability will be based on an estimate of fair value, as if it represented an element of a cash-settled share-based payment transaction, rather than the market price of the shares at the balance sheet date. This is illustrated in the following example.

Example – Treatment of social security contributions

The facts are the same as example 1 in paragraph 12.114. On 1 January 20X5, entity A made an award of 1,000 options to each of its 60 employees. The only condition associated with the award was that recipients must remain in the employment of entity A for three years. At the date of the award, management estimated that 10% of employees (that is, six employees) would leave the entity before the end of three years. On 31 December 20X6, management revised their estimate of leavers to 5% (that is, three employees). However, awards to 55 employees actually vested on 31 December 20X7. All options must be exercised by the end of 20X9. On 31 December 20X8, when the intrinsic value of each option was C10, ten employees exercised their options. The remaining 45 employees exercised their options on 31 December 20X9 when the intrinsic value of each option was C14. The fair value of an option at each year end is shown below:

Year	Fair value at year end
31 December 20X5	6
31 December 20X6	8
31 December 20X7	9
31 December 20X8	12
31 December 20X9	14

Assuming the rate for employers' social security contributions throughout this period is 12.8%, the amount to be paid by entity A will be 12.8% of the intrinsic value of options exercised. For example, the amount payable at 31 December 20X8 is C12,800 (being 12.8% × C10 × 1,000 × 10). However, the amount recognised as a liability at each period end should be based on an estimate of the fair value of an option at that date. Hence, the amount recognised as an expense in each year and as a liability at each year end will be as follows:

Year	Expense	Liability	Calculation of liability
	C	C	
31 December 20X5	13,824	13,824	$54 \times 1,000 \times 6 \times 12.8\% \times {}^1/_3$
31 December 20X6	25,088	38,912	$57 \times 1,000 \times 8 \times 12.8\% \times {}^2/_3$
31 December 20X7	24,448	63,360	$55 \times 1,000 \times 9 \times 12.8\%$
31 December 20X8	18,560	69,120	$45 \times 1,000 \times 12 \times 12.8\%$ Expense reflects extent to which social security contributions paid (C12,800) exceeds the liability at the previous year end in respect of the ten employees who exercised their options (C11,520) plus an adjustment to the liability of C17,280 (that is, $45 \times 1,000 \times (12\text{-}9) \times 12.8\%$).

| 31 December 20X9 | 11,520 | 0 | Liability extinguished. Expense reflects extent to which social security contributions paid exceeds the liability at the previous year end (45 × 1,000 × 14 × 12.8% = C80,640 less C69,120). |

12.225 The accounting treatment described above differs from that applied when accounting for the corporation tax effects of equity-settled share-based payments, as the accounting for deferred tax is based on the year end intrinsic value rather than an estimate of the fair value of the equity instrument. See further chapter 13.

12.226 A question arises as to how events after the balance sheet date affect the measurement of the liability in respect of social security contributions. This is illustrated in the following example.

Example – Social security contributions on share options — post year end fall in share price

An entity has outstanding employee share options that will attract a social security liability when exercised. The option exercise price is C10 and the market price of the entity's shares at the year end was C50. Since the year end there has been a large fall in share prices in the sector and the entity's share price has dropped to C15. In addition, 30% of the employees to whom options were granted have left and forfeited their options.

Can the entity take those subsequent events into account when calculating the liability at the balance sheet date?

As described from paragraph 12.222 above, a liability is required for the social security contribution on outstanding option grants expected to vest. The liability is derived from the fair value of the equity instrument granted, re-measured at each reporting date and spread over the period from the date the options were granted to the end of the vesting period. It is clear, therefore, that where options are expected to be exercised, the provision recognised at the balance sheet date should not be adjusted for subsequent changes in the market price of the entity's shares. The liability should be calculated at each balance sheet date to reflect the fair value of the liability at that date. Although market prices may fluctuate widely after the year-end, such fluctuations are disregarded, as with movements in foreign exchange rates that occur after the balance sheet date.

At each balance sheet date the entity needs to estimate the number of options that will ultimately be exercised. Where future events will affect the liability that will ultimately be payable, the principles of IFRS 13 require those events to be taken into account in estimating the provision where there is sufficient objective evidence that they will occur. In some cases the estimation necessarily involves a degree of hindsight. We believe the subsequent forfeiture of a substantial number of options should be taken into account when estimating the number of options expected to be exercised if it reflects conditions that existed at the balance sheet date.

Reimbursement or transfer of the liability

12.227 In some countries, such as the UK, it is permissible for employers and employees to agree that the employee can pay the employer's social security contributions on share options. The employee can bear the employer's social security charge arising on share option gains in one of two ways:

- First, the employer and the employee can make an agreement that some or all of the employer's social security liability can be recovered from the employee.

- Secondly, the employer and the employee may make a joint election to legally transfer the liability for the secondary social security contribution to the employee.

12.228 Where there is an agreement between the employer and employee under which the employee agrees to reimburse all or part of the employer's social security contributions, a liability will be recognised by the employer as set out in paragraph 12.223. When considering the presentation of the reimbursement from the employee, IAS 19 would only permit recognition of a separate asset if it is virtually certain that the entity will be reimbursed if the social security contribution expenditure is incurred; a net presentation is permitted in the statement of comprehensive income. [IAS 19 para 104A, IAS 19 (revised) para 116]. Alternatively, as the reimbursement of the social charge by the employee is directly linked to the exercise of the stock option the employer will receive additional cash proceeds from the employee at the time of exercise. Thus, reimbursement from the employee could be treated as an adjustment of the exercise price of the options.

12.229 Where there is a joint election by employer and employee under which the liability is formally transferred to the employee, no liability appears in the employer's financial statements unless the awards are settled net of this liability (see further guidance in para 12.230).

Awards settled net of tax

12.230 Sometimes an entity may agree to pay employee tax on an employee's behalf at the time a share option award is exercised, giving the employee fewer shares in exchange for doing so. While the majority of the share option award will be treated as equity-settled, because the entity has agreed to settle in shares, the portion relating to tax will be treated as a cash-settled share-based payment transaction because the entity has agreed to pay cash to the tax authorities on its employee's behalf. Thus, the entity is acting as a principal in the settlement of the share-based payment using cash and as an agent in remitting that cash to the tax authority on behalf of the employee. In this case, the entity issues a reduced number of shares to the employee and uses its own cash reserves to settle the employee's tax obligation.

12.231 If, instead of only paying cash to the tax authorities, the entity sells a portion of the award on the employee's behalf (thus settling the award using shares and acting as an agent to sell those shares and remit the proceeds) and uses the proceeds to pay the tax authorities, the award would be wholly equity-settled. In this case, all of the shares that are to be issued in accordance with the share-based payment transaction are issued, and the entity sells some of these shares to the market on behalf of the employee and pays the cash received to the tax authority to settle the employee's tax obligation.

Employee share purchase plans

12.232 In some territories, sharesave plans are plans through which employees are given the opportunity to subscribe for shares, often at a discount to the market price. This may be paid for from a reduction of payroll over a period rather than a lump sum payment.

UK.12.232.1 In the UK, save as you earn (SAYE) plans are Inland Revenue approved plans through which employees are given the opportunity to subscribe for shares at a discount of up to 20% of the market price. Typically the plans have a term of three, five or seven years. In the case of three or five year arrangements, employees must make regular savings throughout the term. In the case of a seven-year term, savings made under a five year agreement are left to increase in value for a further two years. The amount that can be invested is up to £250 per month across all plans to which an employee belongs. If an employee ceases saving, they receive a reimbursement of all amounts saved to date, plus interest, but they must withdraw from the plan.

12.233 As described in paragraph 12.11, employee share purchase plans (for instance SAYE plans in the UK) do fall within the scope of IFRS 2. Hence, they should be treated like any other equity-settled share-based payment arrangement. However, unlike many other arrangements, some employee share purchase plans, such as those in the UK, impose a condition on their members that requires regular saving. If an employee ceases saving, they forfeit their right to subscribe for shares.

12.234 As discussed in paragraph 12.101 above, a requirement to save is a non-vesting condition; a failure to save should, therefore, be treated as a cancellation.

Example – Save as you earn (SAYE) plan cancellation

An entity enters into an SAYE plan with its employees. The terms of the plan are that:

- Employees will contribute C250 per month to an employee share trust.

- The employee is required to contribute to the SAYE plan for 5 years, after which the employee has a choice to either receive their cash back plus accrued interest or use this cash to acquire shares at a 20% discount to the market price on the grant date.

- An employee that ceases saving receives a reimbursement of all amounts saved to date, plus interest, but must withdraw from the plan and forfeit their right to acquire shares.

The entity should account for the employee's failure to save as a cancellation. The requirement to save does not meet the definition of a service or performance condition and, therefore, a failure to save cannot be interpreted as the failure to fulfil a service or performance condition.

This results in the acceleration of any unvested portion of the award on the date that the employee stops saving and receives their cash.

The probability of employees ceasing to save (and hence losing the equity option) will need to be taken into account when calculating the grant date fair value.

Employee share trusts

Background

12.235 Share plan trusts are often created by a sponsoring entity for employees. They are designed to facilitate employee shareholding and are often used as a vehicle for distributing shares to employees under remuneration plans.

12.236 Entities usually engage in one of two methods to fund share-based payment arrangements – either they make a new issue of shares or buy their own shares on the market.

12.237 Employee share trusts are usually designed to enable employees to purchase shares in their employing company. The structures of employee share trusts vary, but typically they are arrangements whereby a trust is set up by a sponsoring company to acquire shares in that company for the benefit of its employees, who generally acquire them at a later stage through share option plans, profit sharing arrangements or other share incentive plans. The commercial reasons for establishing an employee share trust include the following:

- It allows a share plan to be extended to new participants without diluting existing shareholders' interests, because it can operate by acquiring and distributing shares that are already in issue rather than by requiring new shares to be issued.

- It can provide a private company with a market in its shares in order to operate an employee share plan, by buying shares from departing employees and other shareholders, warehousing them and then distributing them to new and continuing employees.

- It can facilitate employee participation in connection with a management buyout, privatisation or listing of a private company.

- In cash flow terms, a company can hedge its obligations in respect of options issued under share option plans by avoiding exposure to increases in the market value of shares between the dates of granting the options and the dates of exercising those options.

12.238 The vehicle used to hold the shares in an employee share trust is a discretionary employee benefit trust set up by the sponsoring company for the benefit of all, or most, of its employees. For tax purposes, the trustee may be resident in a different country and a subsidiary of the company will often act as a corporate trustee. The trust buys shares with funds provided by way of cash or loans from the company or by a loan from a third party (which will be guaranteed by the company). The shares held by the trust are typically distributed to employees through an employee share plan. The trust's beneficiaries usually only include the company's or group's employees or former employees and certain of their close relations.

12.239 The legal requirements in some jurisdictions state that entities are not allowed to hold their own shares. Therefore, many entities set up special purpose share plan trusts to hold entity shares on behalf of the plan participants.

12.240 The detailed structures of individual employee share trusts are many and varied. However, the main features are often as follows:

- The trust provides a warehouse for the sponsoring company's shares, for example, by acquiring and holding shares that are to be sold or transferred to employees in the future. The trust will normally purchase the shares with finance provided by the sponsoring company (by way of cash contributions or loans), or by a third party bank loan, or by a combination of the two. Loans from the company are usually interest free.

- Where the trust borrows from a third party, the sponsoring company will often guarantee the loan, that is, it will be responsible for any shortfall if the trust's assets are insufficient to meet its debt repayment obligations. The company will also generally make regular contributions to the trust to enable the trust to meet its interest payments (that is, to make good the shortfall between the dividend income of the trust and the interest payable). As part of this arrangement, the trustees sometimes waive their right to dividends on the shares the trust holds.

- Shares held by the trust are distributed to employees through an employee share plan. There are many different arrangements, which include: the purchase of shares by employees when exercising their share options under an executive share option plan; the purchase of shares by the trustees of plans approved by taxation authorities for allocation to employees under the plan's rules; or the transfer of shares to employees under an incentive plan.

A share nominee company could be used by an entity as opposed to an employee share trust. A share nominee company is used by entities to hold shares and other securities on the entity's behalf to satisfy their obligation for employee share awards.

Accounting for employee share trusts

12.241 IFRS 2 does not deal with the accounting for an entity's shares held by an employee share trust. IFRS 2 also does not deal with funding arrangements between group companies relating to share-based payments.

> **UK.12.241.1** This is similar to the position in the UK, where there has never been an accounting standard on the subject of employee share trusts. However, the UITF issued UITF Abstract 38. For further details, see the Manual of Accounting – UK GAAP.

12.242 SIC 12 concludes that an entity should consolidate a special purpose entity ('SPE') where the substance of the relationship between the parties indicates that the SPE is controlled by the entity. [SIC 12 para 8]. SIC 12 was amended by the IFRS IC in November 2004 to remove the exclusion from its scope of an equity compensation plan, such as an employee share trust and consequentially employee share trusts are now caught by this interpretation. (The amendment does not change the scope exclusion for employee benefit trusts, which continue to be accounted for under IAS 19.) SIC 12 is superseded by IFRS 10; see further paragraph 12.246.1. The interpretation goes on to give examples of circumstances in which an SPE may be consolidated. These include the following:

- The activities of the SPE are being conducted on behalf of the entity according to its specific business needs so that the entity obtains benefits from the SPE's operation.

- The entity has rights to obtain the majority of the benefits of the SPE and, therefore, may be exposed to risks incident to the activities of the SPE.

[SIC 12 paras 10(a)(c)].

12.243 Although the trustees of an employee share trust must act under the trust deed at all times in accordance with the beneficiaries' interests, most employee share trusts (particularly those set up to remunerate employees) are specifically designed to serve an entity's purposes, (otherwise known as the sponsoring entity), and to ensure that there will be minimal risk of any conflict arising between the trustees' duties and the entity's interest. In substance, the sponsoring entity has control of the employee share trust and reaps the benefits or bears the risks associated with its assets and liabilities. In order to determine whether a sponsoring company does control the employee share trust here follows a number of examples where control may occur:

- Where the employee share trust has unallocated shares, the benefit of increases in value of those shares will accrue to the sponsoring entity because, for example, it can pass increased benefits to its employees without using its other resources. Conversely, if the shares fall in value, the sponsoring entity may have to use its other resources to make good the benefits promised to its employees. Therefore, the sponsoring entity benefits from the activities of the trust and will need to make decisions about how many shares, at any point in time, the employee share trust should hold. It is also worth noting that shares in an employee share trust that have been allocated to employees but have not vested unconditionally (for example, where the employee is still required to pay an exercise price), would result in the sponsoring entity retaining the benefits and risks associated with holding the shares. Therefore, the employee share trust would still be controlled by the sponsoring entity and hence consolidated.

■ At the point when shares are conditionally gifted to the employees, the sponsoring entity retains an interest in the shares, because the benefits and risks associated with them remain with the sponsoring entity until the conditions are fulfilled and the shares have been exercised by the employees. Therefore, again by taking the risks with respect to the number of shares the sponsoring company continues to control the employee share trust. The benefits and risks associated with shares that have been allocated to employees that have conditionally vested with the employee could still remain with the sponsoring entity if the employee share trust has ownership of the shares as it could have a liability to the employee to repurchase the shares.

■ In many employee share trusts, dividends on the shares held by the trust are waived until they vest with employees. In other trusts dividends continue to be paid and these will accrue to the trust thereby benefiting the sponsoring entity by either defraying the trust's costs or by reducing the cost of future employee incentive arrangements, which are ultimately borne by the sponsoring entity. Hence, the sponsoring entity has power to govern the financial and operating decisions of the employee share trust by determining how the additional dividend income should be allocated.

■ In many employee share trusts, the sponsoring entity will fund the employee share trust to purchase shares in the market place. These loans are effectively a gift to the trust, which will then be used to satisfy the sponsoring company's employee share remuneration plans. Hence, financing decisions as well as how funds are used are controlled by the sponsoring company.

12.244 Thus, an employee share trust that is controlled by its sponsoring entity should be consolidated into the financial statements with the sponsoring company. If the shares held by the employee share trust are those of the group's parent, then the requirements of IAS 32 relating to treasury shares should be used. [SIC 12 para BC15C].

Example – Treatment of employee share trust

Parent entity P has a subsidiary entity S, which is the sponsoring company of an employee share trust. Entity S does not prepare consolidated financial statements, but prepares separate financial statements.

The employee share trust is required by SIC 12 to be included in the consolidated financial statements of entity P, but not in the separate financial statements of entity S.

12.245 The impact on the consolidated financial statements, in which an employee share trust should be accounted, is as follows:

- Until such time as shares in the sponsoring entity held by an employee share trust vest unconditionally in employees, the consideration paid for those shares should be deducted from consolidated equity. This would be the case even if the shares vest unconditionally with the employee, but the shares are yet to transfer to the employee.

- No gain or loss is recognised in the income statement on the purchase, sale, issue or cancellation of those equity instruments. Instead, any consideration paid or received by the employee share trust is recognised directly in equity.

- Other assets and liabilities, including borrowings, of the employee share trust should be recognised as assets and liabilities of the group.

- External finance costs and administrative expenses should be charged as they become due and not as funding payments are made to the employee share trust.

- Any dividend income arising on own shares held by the employee share trust should be excluded from profit or loss and should not be reported as dividends paid or payable by the sponsoring entity.

- Shares held by the employee share trust should be excluded from the calculation of earnings per share. The calculation of earnings per share is considered in detail in chapter 14.

12.246 In the consolidated financial statements that include the trust, the shares are treated as treasury shares (that is, as a deduction from equity). If the trust prepares separate financial statements, the shares are accounted for as financial assets in accordance with IAS 32 and IAS 39. See chapter 6.

SIC 12 superseded by IFRS 10

12.246.1 IFRS 10 is effective for annual periods beginning on or after 1 January 2013, with earlier application permitted. For entities applying IFRS as adopted by the EU, EU endorsement is expected in late 2012; and endorsement is proposed with an effective date for periods beginning on or after 1 January 2014, with early adoption permitted. IFRS 10 applies to all entities, including employee share trusts used in conjunction with share-based payment arrangements. However, consistent with SIC 12, the new standard has a scope exclusion for trusts or other vehicles used for post-employment benefit plans or other long-term benefit plans that are accounted for in accordance with IAS 19.

12.246.2 IFRS 10 supersedes the guidance in SIC 12 for special purpose entities. IFRS 10 provides a new definition of control that incorporates SIC 12's concept of risks and rewards. Specific guidance for entities that have control over another entity is provided in IFRS 10 paragraph 7. When applying the control principles under IFRS 10, a sponsoring entity has control over an employee share trust, if the following criteria are satisfied:

- The sponsoring entity has power over the relevant activities of the employee share trust;

- The sponsoring entity has exposure, or rights, to variable returns from its involvement with the employee share trust; and

- The sponsoring entity has the ability to use its power over the employee share trust to affect the amount of the sponsoring entity's returns.

See further chapter 24A.

12.246.3 An employee share trust is not controlled by means of equity instruments, so an analysis of control should be performed based on the relationship that exists between the employee share trust and other entities that are involved with the employee share trust. The standard requires the purpose and design of the employee share trust to be used to determine whether the entity has sufficient rights to give it power over the employee share trust and to affect its exposure to returns. [IFRS 10 App B para B3(a)].

12.246.4 When assessing the relationship and contractual arrangements, the sponsoring entity should consider whether it is exposed to the downside risks and upside potential arising from the employee share trust. [IFRS 10 App B para B8]. This analysis will also help to determine whether the sponsoring entity has power over the relevant activities of the employee share trust, which are defined in IFRS 10 as *"the activities of the investee that significantly affect the investee's returns"*. [IFRS 10, App A]. The following examples may provide evidence that the sponsoring entity does control the employee share trust based on its involvement and interest.

- The employee share trust's relevant activities (such as the acquiring and holding of shares under award schemes during the vesting period and the issuing of the shares to employees upon vesting) are conducted on behalf of the entity and for the benefit of the entity's employees For example, an employee share trust is typically used to facilitate the remuneration of the entity's employees through a share incentive plan. The entity makes decisions as to how the employee share trust is designed and operates at inception.

- The trustees of the employee share trust are employees of the entity or another entity within the group. This indicates that the sponsoring entity has the ability to direct the activities of the employee share trust through key management. Although the trustees of an employee share trust must act under the trust deed at all times, most trusts are set up to serve an entity's purpose and to minimise the risk of conflict between the entity and the employee share trust.

- The employee share trust depends on the entity to fund its operations or provide guarantees on behalf of the employee share trust. Often, the employee share trust does not have any assets (other than the shares held under award schemes) to fund employee benefits or support repayment of loans provided by the entity. The financing decisions and how the funds are used are controlled by the sponsoring entity.

- The employee share trust is primarily set up to buy the shares in the entity or another group entity and hold them during the vesting period in order to hedge the entity's cost of providing employee benefits. This mitigates the entity's exposure to changes in the share price during that period.

- If an employee leaves the group during the vesting period, the entity can re-allocate their shares to other employees at no additional cost to the entity. This means that the benefits of the shares are not available to other share option holders unless the entity grants new awards. Additionally, the entity can pass increased benefits to its employees without using its other resources.

- If an employee leaves the group during the vesting period, the entity can re-allocate their shares to other employees at no additional cost to the entity. This means that the benefits of the shares are not available to other share option holders unless the entity grants new awards. Additionally, the entity can pass increased benefits to its employees without using its other resources.

[IFRS 10 App B paras B3(b)-(e), B19, B51, B56, B57].

All criteria listed in paragraph 12.246.2 must be present to evidence control.

12.246.5 Management should assess the specific circumstances for each arrangement against IFRS 10's criteria. An employee share trust that is controlled by its sponsoring entity should be consolidated into the financial statements with the sponsoring entity. IFRS 10 has not changed the consolidation procedures, so the impact on the consolidated financial statements is the same as under SIC 12. See further paragraphs 12.245 and 12.246 above.

> **Example – Accounting for an employee share trust under IFRS 10**
>
> Entity C decides to set up a trust in connection with its employee share option plan. The trust enters into the share-based payment arrangement on behalf of entity C with its employees. On grant date, entity C loans C5,000 to the trust in order for the trust to purchase the same number of shares from the market that have been offered to employees under the plan. The trust has no other assets, and the trust deed states that the trust exists solely to provide remuneration incentives to the employees of entity C.
>
> Entity C demonstrates power through its involvement in the creation and design of the employee share trust at inception. The employee share trust was specifically set up to conduct activities for entity C, as the trust deed stipulates that the relevant activities are to remunerate entity C's employees.

Furthermore, entity C provides funding to the employee share trust and also guarantees its obligations. This is an indicator of entity C having power over the employee share trust and using its power by making financial decisions and determining how the funds are used.

The employee share trust has been set up to buy and hold shares on behalf of entity C, such that entity C manages the exposure to changes in its share price. As a consequence, entity C is using its power over the employee share trust to affect its returns by limiting its exposure to variability. By not using the employee share trust, entity C would have variability in its returns which entity C is able to manage.

Given that all three criteria of control are satisfied, entity C should consolidate the employee share trust.

Separate financial statements of the sponsor

12.247 There is no guidance in IFRS 2 concerning the accounting for an entity's interest in a trust in its separate financial statements. In our view, the appropriate accounting depends on whether:

- The entity has a beneficial interest in the trust's residual assets. If so, the entity would recognise an investment in the trust.

- The employees own the beneficial interest in the residual assets. If they do, and there is no formal loan agreement, the entity would record a debit in equity.

- A formal loan arrangement exists between the entity and the trust. The funding could be treated as a loan to the trust. Entities should be aware that this loan may become impaired.

12.248 If the transfer of cash to the trust is treated as a 'loan and receivable' asset under IAS 39, an impairment charge may often be required, because the asset is not recoverable. The expectation is that the employees will ultimately receive the shares, at which time the trust would no longer have any assets to justify the receivable in the sponsoring entity's accounts and the asset would be impaired. If the transfer of cash to the trust is treated as a capital contribution, any 'investment in trust' balance generated would also be subject to impairment review.

12.249 An impairment may result in a 'double debit', because the entity recognises both the share-based payment charge and an impairment charge. In our view, where it is clear that the sponsor retains the majority of the risks and rewards relating to the funding arrangement, the trust has, in substance, acted as an agent for the sponsor. We believe it would be acceptable in this case for the sponsor to account for the issue of the shares to the trust as the issue of treasury shares, thus eliminating the problem of the 'double debit'.

12.250 Factors that may indicate that the trust has acted merely as an agent and the sponsor retains the risks relating to the funding include:

- the entity bears the ultimate risk of a fall in the price of the shares held by the trust;

- the trust has no other unencumbered assets on which the company could claim should the shares be issued to employees; and

- the entity has guaranteed any portion of a third-party loan the trust has obtained.

Example – Employee trust with loan funding

Entity A has made a decision to set up a trust in connection with its employee share option plan. The trust enters into the share-based payment arrangement on behalf of entity A with its employees. On the date that the terms of the plan are finalised, entity A makes a loan of C2,000 to the trust in order for the trust to purchase the same number of shares from entity A that have been offered to employees under the plan. The trust has no other assets and the trust deed states that the trust exists solely to provide remuneration incentives to employees of entity A.

In this case, it would be acceptable for entity A to account for the loan provided as the issue of treasury shares. The trust is clearly acting as an agent for entity A. Entity A retains the risks relating to the loan. Entity A would record the following entry on the date the loan was provided:

		C	C
Dr	Equity (treasury share reserve)	2,000	
Cr	Share capital and premium		2,000

[The next paragraph is 12.253.]

12.253 The examples that follow illustrate the above principles.

Example 1 – Unallocated shares funded by a bank loan

An employee share trust holds unallocated shares costing C100,000, funded by a bank loan. The trust's sponsoring entity undertakes to make contributions to the trust whenever the loan-to-value ratio falls below a set figure. At the reporting date the market value is at least C100,000. The entity deducts the consideration paid for the shares of C100,000 from equity in its consolidated financial statements. A liability of C100,000 in respect of the bank loan is also recognised. Interest expense is accrued in the usual way.

Example 2 – Reduction in the market value of shares

The facts are the same as in example 1, except that the market value of the shares falls to C80,000 by the entity's year end.

As in example 1, consideration paid for the shares of C100,000 is deducted from equity. The fall in the market value of the shares does not give rise to a recognised loss. Hence, there are no accounting entries to reflect the fall in the market value of the shares.

Example 3 – Market value of shares is in excess of exercise price

The facts are the same as in example 1, but options are granted over the shares at C80,000 when the market value is C100,000.

The entity recognises an expense over the option vesting period in accordance with IFRS 2. As in example 1, consideration paid for the shares of C100,000 is deducted from equity. When the options are exercised, the receipt of C80,000 is credited to equity.

Example 4 – Use of surplus shares for new award

An entity's employee share trust purchased a number of its shares in the market some years ago when the share price was C1. The original share option awards have lapsed and the shares are to be used to satisfy new awards. The shares have been carried at cost. The share price has since risen to C4 and the entity proposes to grant options over those shares to employees at an exercise price of C1.

Under IFRS 2, the share-based payment charge is based on the fair value of the award at the date of grant and, therefore, awarding the options gives rise to an income statement charge. The award's grant date fair value would be charged over the vesting period of the award. In the consolidated financial statements, the own shares held through the trust would be deducted from equity at cost, in line with SIC 12 and, therefore, would not change with the new award. (SIC 12 is superseded by IFRS 10. See further para 12.246.1.)

12.254 An entity could use a share nominee company as opposed to an employee share trust. A share nominee company is used by entities to hold shares and other securities on the entities' behalf to satisfy their obligation for employee share awards. An employee share trust would be acting on behalf of one entity, whereas a share nominee company would be providing a service to a number of entities. In such a situation, the shares are in the possession of the nominee company, but not under its control. Consideration would need to be given as to whether the entity consolidates part of the nominee company applying the principles of SIC 12, or accounts for the holding of shares that the entity has beneficial holding of and not the investment in the nominee company. (SIC 12 is superseded by IFRS 10. See further para 12.246.1.) This is a complex area that requires consideration on a case by case basis.

12.255 It must be remembered that the above principles relate to the accounting for shares (and other assets and liabilities) held by an employee share trust. They have no impact on the recognition or measurement of the expense in respect of a share-based payment arrangement, which is dealt with in accordance with IFRS 2.

UK.12.255.1 Under UK GAAP, this credit arises in the sponsoring company's own equity so there is a question as to whether this is distributable. This is discussed further in paragraph 12.324 onwards.

UK.12.255.2 Consolidation of an employee share trust represents a difference to UK GAAP. Under UITF 38, individual assets and liabilities of such a trust are treated as if they were assets and liabilities of the sponsoring entity itself (that is, they are aggregated with the sponsoring company's own assets and liabilities in its separate financial statements). However, there is no GAAP divergence at a consolidated level: aggregation of a trust's assets and liabilities in consolidated financial statements under UK GAAP gives a similar effect to the consolidation of a trust under SIC 12 under IFRS. (SIC 12 is superseded by IFRS 10. See further para 12.246.1.)

Example – Award investing in other entity shares

Entity I is implementing an unusual share option incentive plan. Entity I will lend C1m to an employee share trust, which will purchase shares in a number of publicly listed companies (but not in entity I). These companies may be suppliers, customers or competitors. Entity I's employees are granted options over 'units' held by the employee share trust. The units are an amalgam of the shares held by the trust. The options are granted at market value at the date of the grant and held over a three year period. When employees exercise their option over the units, they are paid the difference in cash between the market price of the units at the date of the grant (the exercise price) and the market value at the date of exercise. To fund the cash payment the trust sells the shares relating to the exercised units. It then repays the relevant portion of the loan from entity I and also pays the gain to employees.

Under UITF 38 the trust would be considered part of entity I, because there will be an obligation on the trust (and, therefore, entity I) to pay the increase in the value of the units over the market price on the date of grant to the employees in cash. However, the trust will not be holding 'own shares' of the sponsoring entity, and so the shares will be presented as an asset of the entity, rather than as a deduction in arriving at shareholders' funds. [UITF 38 para 10(b)].

Therefore, entity I will be required to provide for the cost (the increase in value of the units) in line with FRS 12. The charge should be based on the difference between the market price of the units at the end of the year and the exercise price of the options.

However, when employees exercise their options and the trust sells the shares a corresponding gain will be recognised in the entity's profit and loss account. The charge under FRS 12 is made each year, but the shares may not be sold until later when the employee exercises the option. Therefore, the charge and the gain may not match in any one year. Assuming that the entity does not apply FRS 26 the only way to achieve such a matching would be for the trust to sell the shares each year to realise a gain that matches the charge (taking market risk so that the gain can be regarded as realised) and then for the trust to repurchase the shares. This could achieve a matching each year in the profit and loss account, but the entity takes market risk.

Trustee company

12.256 The above sections deal with the financial statements of the sponsoring company. In groups of companies, it is common for a non-trading subsidiary company to act as trustee to the employee share trust. The accounting implications for the trustee company are considered in the example below.

> **Example – Treatment of employee share trust by corporate trustee**
>
> A group operates an employee share plan. A subsidiary of the group has been set up to act as a corporate trustee. What should the subsidiary include in its own entity financial statements?
>
> The corporate trustee for an employee share trust normally holds legal title to the trust's assets, but if these are held on trust such that the trustee has no beneficial interest (that is, the trustee's interest is limited to its fiduciary or custodial interest) then they are not, in substance, its assets. Therefore, the trustee company itself does not account for the assets (and likewise, the liabilities and transactions) of the employee share trust. These would be reported in the financial statements of the employee share trust and, as described from paragraph 12.241 above, in the financial statements of the group.
>
> The trustee company may well be a dormant company with a nominal share capital. Even if the trustee company is not dormant (for instance, if it charges the trust a fee for its services), this does not change the fact that its financial statements should not normally include the transactions and balances of the trust.

Disclosure

12.257   IFRS 2 requires extensive disclosure under three broad headings:

- The nature and extent of share-based payment arrangements that existed during the period.

- How the fair value of the goods or services received or the fair value of the equity instruments granted during the period was determined.

- The effect of expenses arising from share-based payment transactions on the entity's profit or loss for the period.

[IFRS 2 paras 44, 46, 50].

12.258   Furthermore, if the information that IFRS 2 requires to be disclosed is insufficient to enable users of the financial statements to understand each of these matters, further information should be provided. [IFRS 2 para 52].

Nature and extent of share-based payments

12.259   Paragraph 44 of IFRS 2 requires disclosure of information that enables users of the financial statements to understand the nature and extent of share-based payment arrangements that existed during the period.

12.260   To satisfy this objective, IFRS 2 requires disclosure of the following:

- A description of each type of share-based payment arrangement that existed at any time during the period, including the general terms and conditions of each arrangement, such as:

  - Vesting requirements.

  - The maximum term of options granted.

  - The method of settlement (for example, whether in cash or equity).

- An entity with substantially similar types of share-based payment arrangements may aggregate this information, unless separate disclosure of each arrangement is necessary for users to understand properly the nature and extent of share-based payment arrangements.

- The number and weighted average exercise prices of share options for each of the following groupings of options:

  - Outstanding at the beginning of the period.

  - Granted during the period.

  - Forfeited during the period.

  - Exercised during the period.

  - Outstanding at the end of the period.

  - Exercisable at the end of the period.

- For share options exercised during the period, the weighted average share price at the date of exercise. If options were exercised on a regular basis throughout the period, the entity may instead disclose the weighted average share price during the period.

- For share options outstanding at the end of the period, the range of exercise prices and weighted average remaining contractual life. If the range of exercise prices is wide, the outstanding options should be divided into ranges that are meaningful for assessing the number and timing of additional shares that may be issued and the cash that may be received upon exercising those options.

[IFRS 2 para 45].

12.261 IFRS 2 requires the above disclosure to be given for share options. However, as share awards are equivalent to share options with a zero exercise price, it would be appropriate to give disclosure consistent with the above requirements for share awards as well as share options.

Disclosures for grants made before 7 November 2002

12.262 IFRS 2 does not require a charge in respect of equity instruments granted before 7 November 2002. However, disclosures are required for such awards.

Determination of fair values

12.263 Paragraph 46 of IFRS 2 requires disclosure of information that enables users of the financial statements to understand how the fair value of the goods or services received, or the fair value of the equity instruments granted, during the period was determined. The level of disclosure will vary depending on whether the fair value of the goods or services was determined directly or indirectly (see from para 12.55).

12.264 In the case of transactions with parties other than employees, there is a rebuttable presumption that the fair value of goods or services will be measured directly. [IFRS 2 para 13]. Where the presumption is rebutted, for example, where unidentifiable goods or services have been provided and the fair value of the goods or services is measured indirectly by reference to the fair value of the equity instruments granted as consideration, the entity should disclose that fact and explain why the presumption has been rebutted. [IFRS 2 para 49].

12.265 Where the fair value of goods or services has been measured directly, the entity should disclose how this fair value was determined. [IFRS 2 para 48]. For example, the fair value may have been determined by reference to a published list of prices or scale rates.

12.266 Where the fair value of goods or services has been measured indirectly by reference to the fair value of the equity instruments granted as consideration, the entity should disclose the number and weighted average fair value of those equity instruments at the relevant measurement date together with information on how the fair value was measured. [IFRS 2 para 45(b)(ii), 47(a)(b)].

12.267 Information on how the fair value was measured will vary depending on the type of equity instruments granted. For share options granted during the period, the information will include the following:

- The option pricing model used and the inputs to that model. These will include, at least on a weighted average basis:
    - Price of the underlying share.
    - Price of the option.
    - Expected volatility of the share price.
    - Life of the option.
    - Dividends expected on the underlying shares.
    - Risk-free interest rate over the life of the option.
    - The method used and the assumptions made to incorporate the effects of early exercise.
- How expected volatility was determined, including an explanation of the extent to which expected volatility was based on historical volatility.

- Whether and how any other features of the option grant were incorporated into the measurement of fair value (for example, market conditions).

[IFRS 2 para 47(a)].

12.268 For other equity instruments granted during the period, information on how fair value was measured will include the following:

- If fair value was not measured on the basis of an observable market price, how it was determined.

- Whether and how expected dividends were incorporated into the measurement of fair value.

- Whether and how any other features of the equity instruments granted were incorporated into the measurement of fair value.

[IFRS 2 para 47(b)].

12.269 Where there has been a modification to a share-based payment arrangement during the period, the following should be disclosed:

- An explanation of the modification.

- The incremental fair value granted.

- Information on how the incremental fair value was measured, consistent with the requirements set out in paragraphs 12.267 or 12.268 as appropriate.

[IFRS 2 para 47(c)].

Impact on profit or loss

12.270 Paragraph 50 of IFRS 2 requires disclosure of information that enables users of the financial statements to understand the effect of share-based payment transactions on the entity's profit or loss for the period and on its financial position.

12.271 To satisfy this objective, IFRS 2 requires disclosure of the following:

- The total expense recognised in the period in respect of share-based payment transactions, with separate disclosure of the portion of the expense that relates to transactions accounted for as equity-settled. In satisfying this requirement, only expenses in respect of goods or services that did not qualify for recognition as an asset are considered. Therefore, depreciation of an asset acquired in a prior-year share-based payment transaction does not need to be disclosed.

- For liabilities arising from share-based payment transactions:

  - the total carrying amount at the end of the period; and

- the total intrinsic value at the end of the period of liabilities for which the counterparty's right to cash or other assets has vested.

[IFRS 2 para 51].

12.272   A question may arise as to whether the expense relating to a cash-settled award should be split between:

- the value of the services received based on the grant date fair value; and
- the movement as a result of changes in the liability's fair value.

Our view is that during the vesting period the full movements in the liability are employee related and the full movement should be employee compensation. Post vesting, since there is no longer a link to employee service, the movements could be either taken to finance costs or continue to be shown as employee costs. This policy choice should be applied consistently.

Example

12.273   Table 12.3 is an example of IFRS 2 disclosures in respect of equity-settled share-based payments.

Table 12.3 – IFRS 2 share-based payment disclosures

British Sky Broadcasting Group plc – Annual Report – 30 June 2011
8. Employee benefits and key management compensation (extract)
a) Group employee benefits

	2011 £m	2010 £m
Wages and salaries	651	631
Social security costs	80	76
Costs of employee share option schemes(i)	67	32
Contributions to the Group's pension schemes(ii)	27	27
	825	766

(i) A £69 million charge relates to equity-settled share-based payments (2010: £35 million charge) and a credit of £2 million relates to cash-settled share-based payments (2010: £3 million credit). At 30 June 2011, there were no liabilities arising from share-based payment transactions (2010: £5 million).

(ii) The Group operates defined contribution pension schemes. The pension charge for the year represents the cost of contributions payable by the Group to the schemes during the year. The amount payable to the schemes by the Group at 30 June 2011 was £4 million (2010: £3 million).

26. Share capital (extract)

Share option and contingent share award schemes

The Company operates various equity-settled share option schemes (the "Schemes") for certain employees.

The number of newly issued shares which may be allocated under the Schemes on any day shall not, when aggregated with the number of newly issued shares which have been allocated in the previous ten years under the Schemes and any other employee share scheme adopted by the

---

Company, exceed such number as represents five percent of the ordinary share capital of the Company in issue immediately prior to that day. In determining this limit no account shall be taken of any newly issued shares where the right to acquire the newly issued shares was released, lapsed, cancelled or otherwise became incapable of exercise. Options and awards which will be satisfied by ESOP shares do not fall within these headroom limits.

The share awards outstanding can be summarised as follows:

	2011 Number of ordinary shares	2010 Number of ordinary shares
Executive Share Option Scheme options(i)	5,583,424	13,803,846
Sharesave Scheme options(ii)	6,554,165	6,175,446
All Employee awards(iii)	1,168,200	1,383,400
Management LTIP awards(iv)	22,326,138	13,447,526
LTIP awards(v)	8,610,930	5,869,560
Management Co-Investment LTIP awards(vi)	1,268,260	599,181
Co-Investment LTIP awards(vii)	1,286,906	728,736
	46,798,023	42,007,695

(i) Executive Share Option Scheme options

All Executive Share Option Scheme options outstanding at 30 June 2011 and 30 June 2010 have vested. No options have been granted under the scheme since 2004.

Grants under the Executive Share Option Scheme were made on an annual basis to selected employees, with the exercise price of options being equal to the Company's share price on the date of grant. For those options with performance conditions, growth in EPS had to exceed growth in the Retail Prices Index plus 3% per annum in order for awards to vest. Options vested on an accelerated basis over a period of up to four years from the date of grant. The contractual life of all Executive Share Option Scheme options is ten years.

(ii) Sharesave Scheme options

All Sharesave Scheme options outstanding at 30 June 2011 and 30 June 2010 have no performance criteria attached, other than the requirement that the employee remains in employment with the Group. Options granted under the Sharesave Scheme must be exercised within six months of the relevant award vesting date.

The Sharesave Scheme is open to all employees. Options are normally exercisable after either three or five years from the date of grant. The price at which options are offered is not less than 80% of the middle-market price on the dealing day immediately preceding the date of invitation. It is the policy of the Group to make an invitation to employees to participate in the scheme following the announcement of the end of year results.

(iii) All Employee awards (20 Year Award Plan)

The All Employee awards outstanding at 30 June 2011 and 30 June 2010 have no performance criteria attached, other than the requirement that the employee remains in employment with the Group. Awards granted under the All Employee award will be exercised upon the award vesting date.

The Company granted the All Employee award to all permanent employees on 5 February 2009. Awards under the scheme are granted in the form of a nil-priced option, and are satisfied using market-purchased shares.

(iv) Management LTIP awards

All Management LTIP awards outstanding at 30 June 2011 and 30 June 2010 vest only if performance conditions are met. Awards granted under the Management LTIP must be exercised within five years of the relevant award vesting date.

The Company grants awards to selected employees under the Management LTIP. Awards under this scheme mirror the LTIP, with the same performance conditions. Awards exercised under the Management LTIP can only be satisfied by the issue of market-purchased shares.

(v) LTIP awards

All LTIP awards outstanding at 30 June 2011 and 30 June 2010 vest only if performance conditions are met. Awards granted under the LTIP must be exercised within five years of the relevant award vesting date.

The Company operates the LTIP for Executive Directors and Senior Executives. Awards under the scheme are granted in the form of a nil-priced option, and are satisfied using market-purchased shares. The awards vest in full or in part dependent on the satisfaction of specified performance targets. For awards made in 2008 and 2009 (i.e. awards which will vest in 2011), 30% of the award vests dependent on TSR performance over a three year performance period, relative to the constituents of the FTSE 100 at the time of grant, and the remaining 70% vests dependent on performance against operational targets. The TSR performance targets are not applicable to awards made since July 2010.

(vi) Management Co-Investment LTIP awards

All Management Co-Investment LTIP awards outstanding at 30 June 2011 and 30 June 2010 vest only if performance conditions are met. Awards granted under the Management Co-Investment LTIP must be exercised within five years of the relevant award vesting date.

The Company grants awards to selected employees under the Management Co-Investment LTIP. Awards under this scheme mirror the Co-Investment LTIP, with the same performance conditions.

(vii) Co-Investment LTIP awards

All Co-Investment LTIP awards outstanding at 30 June 2011 and 30 June 2010 vest only if performance conditions are met. Awards granted under the Co-Investment LTIP must be exercised within five years of the relevant award vesting date.

The Company operates the Co-Investment LTIP award for Executive Directors and Senior Executives. Employees who participate in the plan are granted a conditional award of shares based on the amount they have invested in the Group. The investment will be matched up to a maximum of 1.5 shares for every share invested, subject to a three-year EPS performance condition.

For the purposes of the disclosure below, the Sharesave Scheme options and All Employee awards ("Sharesave Schemes") and the Management LTIP, LTIP, Management Co-Investment LTIP and Co-Investment LTIP awards ("Senior Management Schemes") have been aggregated.

The movement in share awards outstanding is summarised in the following table:

	Executive Scheme		Sharesave Schemes		Senior Management Schemes		Total	
	Weighted average exercise price		Weighted average exercise price		Weighted average exercise price		Weighted average exercise price	
	Number	£	Number	£	Number	£	Number	£
Outstanding at 1 July 2009	17,945,045	7.11	8,110,432	3.40	28,570,198	0.00	54,625,675	2.84
Granted during the year	–	–	2,206,411	4.33	9,143,651	0.00	11,350,062	0.84
Exercised during the year	(2,067,227)	5.22	(1,307,893)	3.97	(12,449,270)	0.00	(15,824,390)	1.00
Forfeited during the year	(702,487)	7.23	(1,109,810)	3.80	(4,619,576)	0.00	(6,431,873)	1.47
Expired during the year	(1,371,485)	6.49	(340,294)	4.71	–	–	(1,711,779)	6.13
Outstanding at 30 June 2010	13,803,846	7.44	7,558,846	3.46	20,645,003	0.00	42,007,695	3.07
Granted during the year	–	–	2,257,055	5.65	14,317,471	0.00	16,574,526	0.77
Exercised during the year	(4,287,534)	6.39	(1,094,690)	4.40	(315,398)	0.00	(5,697,622)	5.65
Forfeited during the year	(383,704)	7.35	(910,357)	4.11	(814,229)	0.00	(2,108,290)	3.12
Expired during the year	(3,549,184)	9.95	(88,489)	4.35	(340,613)	0.00	(3,978,286)	8.98
Outstanding at 30 June 2011	5,583,424	6.65	7,722,365	3.88	33,492,234	0.00	46,798,023	1.43

The weighted average market price of the Group's shares at the date of exercise for share options exercised during the year was £7.85 (2010: £5.50). For those exercised under the Executive Scheme it was £7.99 (2010: £6.27), for those exercised under the Sharesave Schemes it was £7.54 (2010: £5.53), and for those exercised under the Senior Management Schemes it was £7.08 (2010: £5.37).

The middle-market closing price of the Company's shares at 1 July 2011 was £8.49 (25 June 2010: £7.01).

The following table summarises information about share awards outstanding at 30 June 2011:

	Executive Scheme		Sharesave Schemes		Senior Management Schemes		Total	
	Weighted average remaining contractual life		Weighted average remaining contractual life		Weighted average remaining contractual life		Weighted average remaining contractual life	
Range of exercise prices	Number	Years	Number	Years	Number	Years	Number	Years
£0.00 – £1.00	–	–	1,168,200	0.6	33,492,234	1.9	34,660,434	1.9
£3.00 – £4.00	–	–	2,348,795	1.5	–	–	2,348,795	1.5
£4.00 – £5.00	–	–	1,926,019	2.4	–	–	1,926,019	2.4
£5.00 – £6.00	1,802,435	2.5	2,279,351	3.8	–	–	4,081,786	3.2
£6.00 – £7.00	1,537,964	2.1	–	–	–	–	1,537,964	2.1
£7.00 – £8.00	2,243,025	0.3	–	–	–	–	2,243,025	0.3
	5,583,424	1.5	7,722,365	2.3	33,492,234	1.9	46,798,023	2.0

Share-based payment

The following table summarises information about share awards outstanding at 30 June 2010:

| | Executive Scheme | | Sharesave Schemes | | Senior Management Schemes | | Total | |
| | Weighted average remaining contractual life | | Weighted average remaining contractual life | | Weighted average remaining contractual life | | Weighted average remaining contractual life | |
Range of exercise prices	Number	Years	Number	Years	Number	Years	Number	Years
£0.00 – £1.00	–	–	1,383,400	1.6	20,645,003	2.1	22,028,403	2.1
£3.00 – £4.00	–	–	2,720,290	2.5	–	–	2,720,290	2.5
£4.00 – £5.00	–	–	2,579,561	3.1	–	–	2,579,561	3.1
£5.00 – £6.00	3,383,932	3.5	875,595	1.6	–	–	4,259,527	3.1
£6.00 – £7.00	3,296,301	3.2	–	–	–	–	3,296,301	3.2
£7.00 – £8.00	3,574,429	1.3	–	–	–	–	3,574,429	1.3
£9.00 – £10.00	3,448,253	0.4	–	–	–	–	3,448,253	0.4
£12.00 – £13.00	100,931	–	–	–	–	–	100,931	–
	13,803,846	2.1	7,558,846	2.4	20,645,003	2.1	42,007,695	2.1

The range of exercise prices of the awards outstanding at 30 June 2011 was between nil and £7.94 (2010: nil and £12.88). For those awards outstanding under the Executive Scheme it was between £5.03 and £7.94 (2010: £5.03 and £12.88); for those outstanding under the Sharesave Schemes it was between nil and £5.65 (2010: nil and £5.38) and for all awards outstanding under the Senior Management Schemes the exercise price was nil (2010: nil).

The following table summarises additional information about the awards exercisable at 30 June 2011 and 30 June 2010:

	Options exercisable at 30 June 2011	Average remaining contractual life of exercisable options	Weighted average exercise price	Options exercisable at 30 June 2010	Average remaining contractual life of exercisable options	Weighted average exercise price
Executive Scheme	5,583,424	1.5	6.65	13,803,846	2.1	7.44
Sharesave Schemes	72,812	0.1	5.24	204,427	0.1	4.35
Senior Management Schemes	–	–	–	656,011	0.1	–
	5,656,236	1.5	6.64	14,664,284	2.0	7.06

Information for awards granted during the year

The weighted average fair value of equity-settled share options granted during the year, as estimated at the date of grant, was £5.95 (2010: £4.19). This was calculated using the Black-Scholes share option pricing model except for grants of nil-priced options, which were treated as the award of a free share. The fair value of nil-priced options granted during the year was measured on the basis of the market-price of the Company's shares on the date of grant, discounted for expected dividends which would not be received over the vesting period of the options.

Expected volatility was determined by calculating the historical volatility of the Company's share price, over a period equal to the expected life of the options. Expected life was based on the contractual life of the awards and adjusted, based on management's best estimate, for the effects of exercise restrictions and behavioural considerations.

(i) Sharesave Schemes

The weighted average fair value of equity-settled share awards granted during the year under the Sharesave Schemes, as estimated at the date of grant, was £1.91 (2010: £1.65). This was calculated using the Black-Scholes share option pricing model.

The following weighted average assumptions were used in calculating these fair values:

	2011	2010
Share price	£7.09	£5.73
Exercise price	£5.65	£4.33
Expected volatility	28.1%	28.3%
Expected life	4.6 years	4.1 years
Expected dividends	2.7%	3.1%
Risk-free interest rate	1.5%	2.3%

(ii) Senior Management Schemes

The weighted average fair value of equity-settled share awards granted during the year under the Senior Management Schemes, as estimated at the date of grant, was £6.59 (2010: £4.80). The fair value of awards granted as nil-priced options were treated as the award of a free share. For all other awards, fair value was calculated using the Black-Scholes share option pricing model. In the prior year, awards with market-based performance conditions were granted and the fair value of these awards was calculated using a Monte-Carlo simulation model.

The following weighted average assumptions were used in calculating these fair values:

	2011	2010
Share price	£7.11	£5.47
Exercise price	£0.00	£0.00
Expected volatility	–	34.8%
Expected life	3.0 years	2.1 years
Expected dividends	2.5%	3.2%
Risk-free interest rate	–	2.1%

Directors' emoluments disclosure

UK.12.273.1 IFRS 2 does not deal with the disclosure of directors' emoluments. Disclosure requirements for long-term incentive awards and other share-based payment transactions involving directors are contained in sections 412 and 420 of the Companies Act 2006 and in the Listing Rules. Details of these requirements are covered in chapter 5 of the Manual of Accounting – Narrative Reporting.

Related party disclosures

12.274 IAS 24 contains a requirement to disclose compensation payable to key management personnel, which includes share-based payments. [IAS 24 para 16]. This requirement is discussed further in chapter 29.

Voting rights

UK.12.274.1 A UK company that has securities carrying voting rights admitted to trading on a regulated market at the end of its financial year is required to disclose, in its directors' report, details of how the rights regarding the company's control are exercisable where the company has an employees' share plan, but shares relating to that plan have rights regarding the control of the company that are not directly exercisable by the employees. Disclosures in respect of control over a company's shares are dealt with in chapter 3 of the Manual of Accounting – Narrative Reporting.

Cash flow statements

12.275 IAS 7 requires an entity to report cash flows from operating activities. Employee share-based payment transactions that are equity-settled should be adjusted for in reporting the cash flows from operating activities as this represents a non-cash item that is operating in nature. [IAS 7 paras 19, 20]. Cash flow statements are covered in detail in chapter 30.

Materiality

12.276 IAS 8 confirms that accounting policies set out in IFRSs do not need to be applied where the effect of applying them is immaterial. [IAS 8 para 8]. Both the quantitative and qualitative impact of an entity's share-based payment transactions should be assessed in order to determine the impact of applying IFRS 2. It will also be necessary to consider whether the impact of share-based payment transactions is likely to become material in the future. If the impact of applying IFRS 2 is determined to be either quantitatively or qualitatively material, the standard should be applied in full.

12.277 Where IFRS 2 is not applied, certain disclosures in relation to share-based payment transactions may be required under local legislation or listings rules (such as gains on directors' share options or shares receivable under long-term incentive awards). It would be appropriate to explain, particularly in these circumstances, that the standard has not been applied in the financial statements, particularly where disclosures provided under local legislation indicate that the entity has share-based payment transactions in place.

Measuring the fair value of equity instruments

12.278 Under IFRS 2, where the fair value of goods or services is measured by the indirect method (see para 12.55), the fair value of the equity instruments granted should be estimated at the relevant measurement date (see para 12.59). However, the standard also requires entities to measure the fair value of the equity instruments granted for goods or services received. If the fair value of the equity instruments granted is greater than the fair value of the goods or services received or to be received (measured using the direct method as at the grant date), the difference, being the unidentifiable goods or services received, must be recognised by the entity. As with the indirect method, the fair value of the equity instrument granted should be estimated at the relevant measurement date (see para 12.59).

12.279   Fair value should be based on market prices, if available, taking into account any terms and conditions associated with the grant of the equity instruments. [IFRS 2 para 16]. For example, where employees have been granted an award of shares, but they are not entitled to receive dividends during the vesting period, this factor should be taken into account when estimating fair value. Similarly, if the shares are subject to restrictions on transfer after the vesting date, that factor shall be taken into account, but only to the extent that the post-vesting restrictions affect the price that a knowledgeable, willing market participant would pay for that share. If the shares are actively traded in a deep and liquid market, post-vesting transfer restrictions may have little, if any, effect on the price. [IFRS 2 para B3].

> **Example – Fair value implications for options that vest only on an IPO**
>
> An entity grants share options to employees that will vest only if the entity achieves a stock exchange listing within two years.
>
> Management are aware that one of the inputs into the option pricing model to determine the award's grant date fair value is the current price of an entity's shares (see further para 12.284). When determining the current share price for an unlisted entity, a discount to the share price would normally be made to reflect the fact that there is not a market for the shares in the same way that there would be for a comparable entity with listed shares. Should the current share price of the entity's shares be discounted for illiquidity?
>
> The standard requires that the estimated market price of an entity's shares is adjusted to take into account the terms and conditions upon which an award is granted. [IFRS 2 paras B2, B3]. In this case, the award vests only on listing and, therefore, employees will only ever be able to receive a listed share. Therefore, the input to the option pricing model would be the entity's current share price without a discount for lack of marketability which is the entity's current share price as if for a listed share.
>
> Note that this logic would apply similarly if vesting occurred as a result of a trade sale or takeover, as the acquirer would be paying a control premium for the shares.

12.280   Some shares and most share options are not traded on an active market so alternative valuation techniques must be considered. The objective is to derive an estimate of what the price of those equity instruments would have been at the relevant measurement date in an arm's length transaction between knowledgeable, willing parties. [IFRS 2 para 17]. Sometimes, it may be possible to make an estimate of market price based on prices of traded shares or options with similar terms and conditions, although this is unlikely in the case of executive options with specific performance criteria. It is more likely that an alternative valuation technique will need to be applied. Many pricing models are available and IFRS 2 does not specify which should be used. It does, however, describe the factors that should be taken into account when estimating fair value. It also requires the model used to be consistent with generally accepted valuation methodologies for pricing financial instruments.

12.281 It should be remembered that the purpose of deriving a fair value for the equity instruments granted is to measure, indirectly, the fair value of the goods or services acquired by the entity. Accordingly, once the fair value of the equity instruments has been estimated at the relevant measurement date, so the 'price' of the goods or services has been determined, it is not re-measured.

Valuation techniques

12.282 Option pricing models are based on the premise that it is possible to hedge an option exactly by buying (and continually adjusting) a portfolio of the shares over which the option has been granted. Setting up and adjusting the 'hedge portfolio' has a cost. In theory, this hedging cost will be the same, whatever happens to the share price. Given that the option can be hedged precisely at a fixed cost, it follows that this cost will be the market value of the option.

12.283 In practice, real markets do not always follow the idealised behaviour of financial models and there are limits to how frequently a portfolio can be rebalanced. However, investment banks do, as a matter of fact, hedge option contracts using dynamically traded hedge portfolios. These portfolios are constructed in line with the theoretical models, which have proven robust in practice, despite their imperfections.

12.284 All option pricing models take into account, as a minimum, the following factors:

- Exercise price of the option.
- Current price of the underlying share.
- Life of the option.
- Expected volatility of the share price.
- Dividends expected on the underlying shares.
- Risk-free interest rate over the life of the option.

12.285 The first two items define the 'intrinsic value' of the option. The remaining four are relevant to its 'time value'. The time value of an option reflects the right of the holder to participate in future gains, if any. The valuation does not attempt to predict what the future gain will be, only the amount that a buyer would pay at the valuation date to obtain the right to participate in any future gains. In other words, option pricing models estimate the value of the share option at the measurement date, not the value of the underlying share at some future date.

12.286 All other things being equal, a change in the expected volatility of the share price will have the greatest impact of the input assumptions listed in paragraph 12.284 on the option's fair value (an increase in volatility increases the fair value). A change to either the option's exercise price or its life has the next greatest impact on the option's fair value (an increase in the option's exercise price decreases the option's fair value and an increase in the option's expected life increases the option fair value). This will be the case irrespective of the option pricing model used.

12.287 Other factors that knowledgeable, willing market participants would consider in setting the price should also be taken into account. Some of these are described in paragraph 12.279. In addition, many employee options have long lives, are exercisable during specified periods (usually between vesting date and the end of the life) and are often exercised early. Furthermore, the act of exercising the options at a price below the market price at that date might itself reduce the share price. However, vesting conditions (other than market conditions) and reload features are not taken into account in the valuation. Instead, these are dealt with as described from paragraph 12.77.

12.288 Paragraph 21 of IFRS 2 requires that market conditions are taken into account when estimating fair value. Arguably, all conditions associated with a grant of equity instruments will influence the fair value of those instruments. This was the view taken by the IASB in developing ED 2. The exposure draft proposed that all conditions (market related or otherwise) should be taken into account when determining fair value. However, respondents to ED 2 raised a variety of concerns about the practicality and subjectivity of including non-market conditions in a valuation. In response, IFRS 2 draws a distinction between market and non-market conditions, with only the former being taken into account when estimating fair value. Broadly speaking a market condition is one that is dependent on share price.

12.289 Market conditions include target share prices and requirements to achieve a certain level of total shareholder return (that is, the sum of dividends and increases in share price). There are various means by which they may be taken into account when estimating fair value, and some valuation models are better suited to dealing with their effects than others. This is a complex area and specialist advice may need to be obtained.

Inputs to an option pricing model

12.290 The exercise price of the option and the current market price of the underlying share will usually be readily available. However, estimating the other inputs to an option pricing model can be a complex and time consuming exercise.

Life of the option

12.291 Holders of traded options generally have a choice between exercising, keeping or selling their options at any point in time during the option's contractual life. As the sale of options realises both their intrinsic and time value, this will usually be a more attractive proposition than exercising, so the real choice becomes between keeping or selling (it is worthwhile to note that where options are traded in a liquid market, there is no need to use an option pricing model as the traded value of the option in the market is the fair value). A traded option would typically only be exercised (or lapse) at the end of its contractual term. The vast majority of employee options, on the other hand, cannot be traded, so employees only have the choice of either keeping or exercising their options. However, exercising is the only way in which an employee can realise value. In addition, it is common for the contractual life of the option to be cut short if the employee leaves the entity. This means that most employee share options are exercised much earlier than their contractual term. Accordingly, when estimating the fair value of an employee option, it is the expected life rather than the contractual life of the option that is considered.

12.292 Appendix B to IFRS 2 describes a number of factors that should be taken into account when estimating the expected life of an option. These are:

- The length of the vesting period, because the share option typically cannot be exercised until the end of the vesting period. Hence, determining the valuation implications of expected early exercise is based on the assumption that the options will vest.

- The average length of time for which similar options have remained outstanding in the past.

- The price of the underlying shares. Experience may indicate that the employees tend to exercise options when the share price reaches a specified level above the exercise price.

- The employee's level within the organisation. For example, experience might indicate that higher-level employees tend to exercise options later than lower-level employees.

- Expected volatility of the underlying shares. On average, employees might tend to exercise options on highly volatile shares earlier than on shares with low volatility.

[IFRS 2 para B18].

12.293 Other factors that could be considered include the following:

- The general state of the equity market, or the economy. Employees might be more inclined to hold on to their options where markets are climbing, or they might exercise their options once they see a gain if markets are performing poorly.

- The dividend yield on the underlying share. Where no dividend is paid, the option holder does not lose by not exercising. Where the dividend yield is high, the dividends lost by not exercising could outweigh the risk-free return available on the cash thus encouraging early exercise.

■ The tax treatment of the benefits. In some jurisdictions, a tax charge may crystallise on vesting so employees may have to exercise their options to meet their tax liability.

12.294 When estimating the expected life of share options granted to a group of employees, the entity could base that estimate on an appropriately weighted average expected life for the entire employee group, or on appropriately weighted average lives for subgroups of employees, based on more detailed data about employees' exercise behaviour. The distinction is likely to be important. Option value is not a linear function of option term – value increases at a decreasing rate as the term lengthens. For example, although a two-year option is worth more than a one-year option, it is not worth twice as much. That means that calculating estimated option value on the basis of a single weighted average life that includes widely differing individual lives would overstate the total fair value of the share options granted. Separating options granted into several groups, each of which has a relatively narrow range of lives included in its weighted average life, reduces that overstatement.

12.295 For example, the experience of an entity that grants options broadly to all levels of employees might indicate that top-level executives tend to hold their options longer than middle-management employees hold theirs and that lower-level employees tend to exercise their options earlier than any other group. In addition, employees who are encouraged or required to hold a minimum amount of their employer's equity instruments, including options, might on average exercise options later than employees not subject to that provision. In those situations, separating options by groups of recipients with relatively homogeneous exercise behaviour will result in a more accurate estimate of the total fair value of the share options granted.

12.295.1 An increase in an option's expected life will typically increase the option's fair value, as it gives the holder more time to participate in future gains.

Expected volatility

12.296 Expected volatility is a measure of the amount by which the price of the underlying share is expected to fluctuate during the option's life. The measure of volatility used in option pricing models is the annualised standard deviation of the continuously compounded rates of return on the share. Volatility is typically expressed in annualised terms, regardless of the time period used in the calculation, for example, daily, weekly or monthly price observations.

12.297 Standard deviation is a statistical measure of how tightly data are clustered around a mean – the more tightly clustered the data, the smaller the standard deviation. Standard deviation is measured as the square root of the variance, which in turn is measured as the average squared difference between each observation and the mean. This is shown in the following example.

Share-based payment

Example – Calculation of standard deviation

Data	Difference between data and mean	Difference^2
53	(2.2)	4.84
58	2.8	7.84
52	(3.2)	10.24
56	0.8	0.64
57	1.8	3.24
Mean = 55.2		Mean = 5.36

The variance (that is, the average squared difference between each number and the mean) is 5.36 so the standard deviation is 2.32, being the square root of the variance.

12.298 In the previous example, the data represents the entire population. However, the calculation of standard deviation will normally involve a sample of data from a population, in which case the calculation is amended slightly. The formula used in these situations is expressed in one of the ways shown below.

$$\sigma = \sqrt{\frac{n\Sigma x^2 - (\Sigma x)^2}{n(n-1)}} \qquad \sigma = \sqrt{\frac{\Sigma(x - \bar{x})^2}{n-1}}$$

Where: σ = standard deviation
x = an observation
$\bar{x}$ = the mean observation
n = the number of observations

Many spreadsheet packages and scientific calculators are able to calculate the standard deviation for a given series of data.

12.299 An added complication when considering the volatility of rates of return is that the probability distribution of returns is considered to be lognormal rather than normal. This means that it is the logarithm of the returns that is normally distributed, rather than the returns themselves. This implies a smaller probability of significant deviations from the mean than is usually the case in practice. Consider now a more realistic example.

The market price of an entity's shares over a six week period fluctuated as follows:

Date	Share price C
Week 1	5.00
Week 2	5.20
Week 3	5.30
Week 4	5.10
Week 5	5.35
Week 6	5.30

Hence, the return on the entity's shares each week, and the logarithm of those returns, is as shown below:

Date	Weekly return	Relative price change	Logarithm of relative price change
Week 1	–	–	–
Week 2	4.0%	1.040	0.03922
Week 3	1.9%	1.019	0.01882
Week 4	(3.8%)	0.962	(0.03874)
Week 5	4.9%	1.049	0.04784
Week 6	(0.9%)	0.991	(0.00904)

The standard deviation of the logarithm of the weekly return, and hence the weekly volatility, calculated using the formulae above, is 0.036. However, as noted above, the measure of volatility used in option pricing models is the annualised volatility. To derive this figure, it is necessary to multiply the weekly volatility by the square root of 52. This gives an annualised volatility of 0.258, normally expressed as 25.8%.

12.300 So, what does this mean? Statistically, when data are distributed normally, one standard deviation lies within 68% of the mean. Hence, the expected annualised volatility of a share is the range within which the continuously compounded annual rate of return is expected to fall 68% (or approximately two-thirds) of the time. For example, if a share has an expected rate of return of 12% and a volatility of 30%, this means that the probability that the actual rate of return on the share will be between minus 18% (12% — 30%) and 42% (12% + 30%) is approximately two-thirds. This is illustrated in the diagram below.

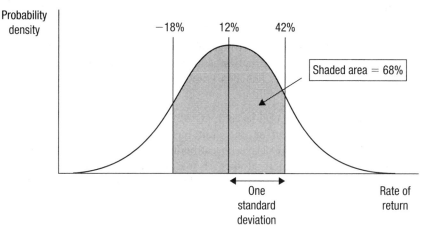

12.301 Appendix B to IFRS 2 describes a number of factors that should be taken into account when estimating expected volatility. These are:

- The implied volatility from traded share options on the company's shares, or other traded instruments that include option features (such as convertible debt).

- The historical volatility of the share price over the most recent period that is generally commensurate with the expected term of the option.

- The length of time a company's shares have been publicly traded. Unlisted and recently listed companies are considered further below.

- The tendency of volatility to revert to its long-term average and other factors indicating that historical volatility may be an unreliable indicator of expected future volatility. For example, if a company's share price was extraordinarily volatile for a short period because of a failed takeover bid or a major restructuring, that period could be disregarded in computing historical average annual volatility.

- Appropriate and regular intervals for price observations. The price observations should be consistent from period to period. For example, a company might use the closing price for each week or the highest price for the week, but it should not use the closing price for some weeks and the highest price for other weeks.

[IFRS 2 para B25].

12.302 An unlisted entity will not have historical data on which to base an estimate of expected future volatility. IFRS 2 suggests alternative methods by which an estimate may be made:

- If the entity regularly issues options or shares to employees (or other parties), it might have set up an internal market for its shares. The volatility of those share prices could be considered.

- The historical or implied volatility of similar listed entities, for which share price or option price information is available, could be used. This would be appropriate if the entity has also based the value of its shares on the share prices of similar listed entities.

- If the entity has not based its estimate of the value of its shares on the share prices of similar listed entities, but has instead used another valuation methodology, it could derive an estimate of expected volatility consistent with that valuation methodology. For example, the entity might value its shares on an earnings basis so it could consider the expected volatility of those earnings.

[IFRS 2 paras B28-B30].

12.303 A newly listed entity may also not have sufficient information on historical volatility on which to base an estimate of expected future volatility. Nevertheless, it should compute historical volatility for the longest period for which trading activity is available. It could also consider the historical volatility of similar entities following a comparable period in their lives. For example, an entity that has been listed for only one year and grants options with an average expected life of five years might consider the pattern and level of historical volatility of entities in the same industry for the first six years in which the shares of those entities were publicly traded.

12.303.1 Expected volatility has the most impact on the option's fair value. The higher the volatility is, the higher the potential gain for the holder, resulting in a higher option value.

Expected dividends

12.304 Whether expected dividends should be taken into account when measuring the fair value of an option depends on whether the counterparty is entitled to dividends on the underlying shares. For example, if employees were granted options, but are not entitled to dividends on the underlying shares between grant date and exercise date, they will have effectively 'lost' those dividends. Hence, the grant date valuation of the options should take expected dividends into account. That is to say, the fair value of the option will be reduced.

12.305 The concept is easier to understand in the case of grants of shares. When estimating the fair value of the shares, the fair value should be reduced by the present value of dividends expected to be paid, and hence 'lost' by the employees, during the vesting period. Conversely, no adjustment is required for expected dividends if the counterparty is entitled to receive dividends during the vesting period. The relatively greater value from receiving dividends during the vesting period is, therefore, included in the award's grant date fair value.

12.306 An alternative method of accounting for dividends during the vesting period is to consider the grant as a compound instrument since the employee will receive both cash over the vesting period and an equity instrument if the award vests. The entity would, therefore, first calculate the value of the debt component (dividends expected to be paid over the vesting period) with the remainder being the equity component. As explained above, the equity component could be valued by estimating the value of the shares excluding the expected dividends to be paid. Once the award has been allocated between the cash and equity components, the entity should account for each element of the grant separately [IFRS 2 para 38].

> **Example – Shares with dividend rights during the vesting period**
>
> Employees of an entity are granted share options in the entity. The employees are required to provide three years service, after which time the options automatically convert into shares (the exercise price of the options is nil). As an added incentive and to align the employees' goals with those of the shareholders, the employees' options have the same rights to dividends as ordinary shares during the vesting period. A valuation shows that the expected value of the dividends over the three year vesting period is C600 and the grant date fair value of the options, excluding the dividends, is C3,000. At the end of the first year, a dividend of C200 is paid out and the entity expects to pay a further C550 in dividends over the remaining vesting period.

The entries required to account for the transaction at the end of the first year would be as follows:

	Dr C	Cr C
Dr Employee expenses	1,000	
Cr Equity		1,000
Equity component recognised straight line over the vesting period		
Dr Employee expense	250	
Cr Share-based payment liability		250
Cash-settled component recognised over the vesting period: 750 total expected liability × 1/3		
Dr Share-based payment liability	200	
Cr Cash		200
Partial settlement of the cash-settled portion of the share-based payment		

Once the options have vested and the employee holds the shares in the capacity as a shareholder, further dividend payments would be recorded as distributions through equity.

12.307 The difference between the two treatments, where dividends are received during the vesting period, can be summarised as follows:

- Where the entity includes the expected dividends to be paid in the calculation of the grant date fair value, any dividends paid during the vesting period are recognised in equity and not in the statement of comprehensive income. Also, if the expected dividends included in the grant date fair value are not equal to the actual dividends paid, no adjustment is made for this, that is, the expected dividends are estimated only once.

- Where the entity treats the expected dividends to be paid as the debt portion of a compound instrument, any dividends paid during the vesting period are recognised in the statement of comprehensive income as an employee expense. In this way, the actual dividends paid are recognised as an expense.

12.308 Option pricing models generally call for expected dividend yield, although they may be modified to use instead an expected dividend amount. If the latter is used, the historical pattern of increases in dividends must be taken into account. For example, if an entity's policy has generally been to increase dividends by around 3% per year, its estimated option value should not assume a fixed dividend amount throughout the option's life, unless there is evidence to support that assumption.

12.309 Generally, expected dividends should be based on publicly available information. An entity that does not pay dividends and has no plans to do so should assume an expected dividend yield of zero. However, an emerging entity with no history of paying dividends might expect to begin paying dividends in the near future. Such an entity could use an average of its past dividend yield (that is, zero) and the dividend yield of an appropriately comparable peer group.

12.309.1 An increase in expected dividend yield will decrease the option's fair value. If the expected dividends are high, this will normally reduce the option's value, because a shareholder receives dividends and an option holder does not. Therefore, giving up the dividends is the opportunity cost of not exercising the option.

Risk-free rate

12.310 Typically, the risk-free interest rate is the yield currently available on zero-coupon government bonds of the country in whose currency the exercise price is expressed, with a remaining term equal to the expected term of the option being valued. It may be necessary to use an appropriate substitute, if no such bonds exist or circumstances indicate that the yield on zero-coupon government bonds is not representative of the risk-free rate (for example, in high inflation economies). Also, an appropriate substitute should be used if market participants would typically determine the risk-free rate by using that substitute.

12.311 All other things being equal, an increase in the risk-free rate would result in an increase in the option's fair value. We typically refer to the risk-free interest rate in terms of discounting future values whereby the higher the rate, the lower the present value. In fact when considering an option, the economics are that the option holder keeps their cash and is able to earn the risk-free interest rate until such time as the option is exercised. On this basis, an increase in the risk-free interest rate makes holding the option more valuable.

12.311.1 The following diagram shows a summary of the impact on fair value when an input is increased (with all other inputs held constant). The more arrows shown, the greater the impact on fair value from changing the input assumptions.

Inputs and assumptions

Increase in:	Impact on fair value
• Current share price	
• Exercise price	
• Expected life	
• Dividends	
• Risk free rate of return	
• Volatility	

Selection of an option pricing model

12.312 As noted above, IFRS 2 does not specify which model should be used to estimate the fair value of an equity instrument. Frequent reference is made to the Black-Scholes-Merton formula (more commonly known as the Black-Scholes formula) but other models such as the binomial model or Monte-Carlo simulation may sometimes be more suitable. Each of these models is described and considered in the following paragraphs.

The Black-Scholes formula

12.313 The most widely used model for valuing straightforward options was published by Fischer Black and Myron Scholes in 1973 and is commonly known as the Black-Scholes formula. This model depends on several assumptions:

- Future returns are independent both of past returns and the current share price.

- Volatility and interest rates both remain constant throughout the option's life.

- The probability distribution of returns is lognormal.

- No transaction costs.

12.314 Based on these assumptions, the price of a European call option (that is, an option that may only be exercised at the end of its life regardless of the country in which it is issued) is estimated by the following formula:

$$C = SN(d_1) - Xe^{(-rt)}N(d_2)$$

Where:

C	=	Price of an option (£)
S	=	Current share price (£)
X	=	Option exercise price (£)
D	=	Dividend yield on underlying share (%)
t	=	Time to expiry
s	=	Expected volatility (%)
r	=	Risk-free rate over the life of the option
$N(d_n)$	=	Value of d found from standard normal distribution curve

And

$$d_1 = \frac{Ln(Se^{rt}/X) + \sigma^2 t/2}{\sigma\sqrt{t}}$$

$$d_2 = \frac{Ln(Se^{rt}/X) - \sigma^2 t/2}{\sigma\sqrt{t}}$$

12.315 Although the Black-Scholes formula is widely used, it has several limitations in the context of employee options. For example:

- It does not allow for market conditions or non-vesting conditions or other terms and conditions that are relevant for determining fair value.

- The option is assumed to be exercised at the end of its life. Early exercise can only be taken into account by use of an expected life rather than a contractual life.

- Inputs (such as expected volatility) cannot be varied over the option's life.

12.316 Nevertheless, for many of the simpler employee options, the Black-Scholes formula can give a reasonably reliable estimate of fair value.

The binomial model

12.317 The binomial model applies the same principles as decision tree analysis to the pricing of an option. At each point, the possible outcomes are simplified to the possibility that prices may increase by a certain percentage or decrease by a certain percentage. On this basis, a 'tree' or 'lattice' is created. Depending on the relative probabilities of each path, an expected outcome may be estimated. This is illustrated in the following simple example.

> **Example – The binomial model**
>
> A entity has granted options that may be exercised in three year's time. The exercise price of the options is C5, which equates to the current market price of the entity's shares.
>
> Management has estimated that there is a probability of p that the market price of the entity's shares will increase by 10% per year and a probability of (1 — p) that it will reduce by 10%. In order to estimate the value of p, management can equate the expected outcome of owning a share to the known outcome of earning a risk-free rate of interest on a cash deposit. If the risk free rate is assumed to be 6%, the value of a C5 investment after one year will be C5.30. Hence, as regards the share, the value of p may be calculated from the following:
>
> $p \times 5.50 + (1 — p) \times 4.50 = 5.30$
>
> Hence, p is 0.8, or 80%.
>
> The current share price of C5 is assumed to be the correct fair value (a present value which already takes into account alternative future outcomes). The deviations from the value of C5.3 (which is expected for t + 1) deemed possible by management (that is, either C5.5 or C4.5) must be assigned probabilities, which average out at a value of C5.3, hence the above equation.
>
> On this basis, the possible outcomes and their relative probabilities for each of the next three years may be estimated as shown below:

Share-based payment

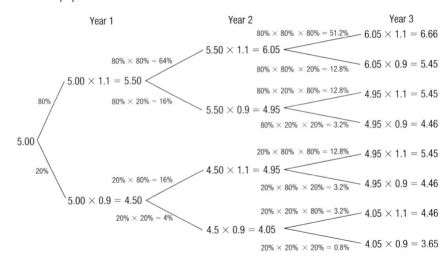

This means, for example, that there is a probability of 51.2% (that is, 80% × 80% × 80%) that the value of a share will be C6.66 in three year's time.

As the exercise price of an option is C5, it will only have value if the market price of the share exceeds C5 at the end of three years. Considering the top path of the tree, if a share is worth C6.66 then the option would be worth C1.66. This represents the intrinsic value of the option. However, considering the bottom path, if the share is worth C3.65 then an option with an exercise price of C5 will be worthless. On this basis, the expected value of the option in three years time may be derived.

Outcome	Option value (A)	Probability (B)	A × B
6.66	1.66 (6.66 − 5)	51.2% (80% × 80% × 80%)	0.85
5.45	0.45 (5.45 − 5)	12.8% (80% × 80% × 20%)	0.06
5.45	0.45 (5.45 − 5)	12.8% (80% × 20% × 80%)	0.06
4.46	0	3.2% (80% × 20% × 20%)	0
5.45	0.45 (5.45 − 5)	12.8% (20% × 80% × 80%)	0.06
4.46	0	3.2% (20% × 80% × 20%)	0
4.46	0	3.2% (20% × 20% × 80%)	0
3.65	0	0.8% (20% × 20% × 20%)	0
Expected value			1.03

If the expected value of an option in three year's time is C1.03, the current price will be the present value of this expected outcome. Hence, the estimated fair value at grant date is C0.865 (that is, $1.03/(1.06)^3$).

12.318 The model sounds simple, but its application can prove complex. For example, the calculation of the probabilities of particular price movements is highly subjective. Nevertheless, the model is widely used and it can often be a more flexible solution than the Black-Scholes formula. However, like the Black-Scholes formula, the binomial model suffers from limitations, including:

- It is difficult, although not impossible, to allow for market conditions or other terms and conditions that are relevant to determining fair value. It is also difficult to allow for turnover or exercise patterns.

- In most cases, the model assumes that options will be sold rather than exercised – only in a few scenarios is early exercise deemed to occur.

12.319 In view of these limitations, the use of the binomial model may not be appropriate for employee options where the probability of early exercise is significant.

Monte-Carlo simulation

12.320 Monte-Carlo simulation takes the binomial model further by undertaking several thousand simulations of future outcomes for key assumptions and calculating the option value under each scenario. As for the binomial model, the expected outcome is then discounted to give an option value.

12.321 Monte-Carlo models can incorporate even the most complex performance conditions, turnover and exercise patterns, such as those that are a function of gain or time since grant date. Consequently, they are generally the most reliable models for valuing employee options. The only drawback is their complexity, although this is rarely a problem with modern computing technology.

[The next paragraph is 12.324.]

Company law requirements

Impact on distributable profits

12.324 International Financial Reporting Standards do not concern themselves with how to determine distributable profits. Such matters are dealt with in national law (and are considered in greater detail in chapter 24). In the case of share-based payment (and the related topic of employee share trusts), several questions are raised:

- Does the expense in respect of an equity-settled share-based payment transaction represent a realised loss?

- Does the opposing credit entry to equity represent a realised profit?

- What is the impact on distributable profits of deducting the cost of acquiring shares through an employee share trust from equity?

- If an employee share trust makes a profit on the sale of surplus shares, is this distributable by the sponsoring entity?

12.325 The answers to the above questions should be dealt with in accordance with national law.

UK.12.326 In the UK, these questions are considered in Tech 02/10 issued by the ICAEW in November 2010. The implications for distributable profits will be similar for entities reporting under IFRS 2 and those reporting under UK GAAP (FRS 20).

Expenses in respect of equity-settled share-based payment transactions

UK.12.327 All expenses and losses should be regarded as realised losses, except to the extent that the law or accounting standards provide otherwise. It is arguable that the expense in respect of an equity-settled share-based payment transaction is not a loss at all because it does not result in a reduction in recorded net assets. However, even if the expense is regarded as a realised loss, Tech 02/10 makes it clear in other contexts (such as revaluation reserves) that an unrealised reserve will be treated as having become realised by the amortisation or writing down of the related asset. Therefore, assuming that the expense has been included in the profit and loss account rather than capitalised as part of the cost of an asset, the credit entry will be treated as a realised profit so there will be no impact on distributable reserves.

Employee share trusts

UK.12.328 Under UK GAAP, the accounting treatment of employee share trusts results in a sponsoring entity including the assets, liabilities and transactions of an employee share trust in its own financial statements as if the trust were an extension of the entity. These financial statements (that is, the combined entity and trust) are the relevant accounts for the purposes of determining profits available for distribution in accordance with section 836 of the Companies Act 2006. It follows, therefore, that transactions entered into by an employee share trust will have an impact on the sponsoring entity's distributable profits in the same way as if they had actually been entered into by the sponsoring entity itself.

UK.12.329 Under IFRS, as described from paragraph 12.241, an employee share trust would be consolidated rather than aggregated with the sponsoring entity's individual assets and liabilities. Accordingly, for a sponsoring entity that has adopted IFRS within its individual financial statements, as the employee share trust's individual transactions, assets and liabilities are not reflected in the sponsoring entity's relevant accounts, they do not affect that sponsoring entity's distributable profits.

UK.12.330 In determining the impact of an employee share trust on a sponsoring entity's distributable profits it will be necessary to consider the nature of transactions and balances between the two parties. An entity may fund an employee share trust by making a gift, a loan or a combination of both. A gift to the trust is clearly an immediate realised loss (as it reduces the net assets of the sponsoring entity). On the other hand a loan, provided it is considered recoverable (that is, sufficient cash is expected when employees exercise their rights to the shares), would not be a realised loss. However, any impairment in the value of the loan (caused by a question over its recoverability) would be an immediate realised loss and, hence, would reduce the sponsoring entity's distributable profits.

UK.12.331 Public companies may face additional problems in respect of the financial assistance rules. Section 682 of the Companies Act 2006 provides that a public company may only give financial assistance for the acquisition of its own shares if the company's net assets are not thereby reduced or, to the extent that net assets are reduced, the company has sufficient distributable profits to cover the full amount of the assistance.

Appendix 1 — Accounting treatment for vesting and non-vesting conditions

The following table, taken from the guidance in IFRS 2, summarises the implications of vesting and non-vesting conditions on accounting for share-based payment transactions.

Summary of conditions that determine whether a counterparty receives an equity instrument granted						
	Vesting conditions			**Non-vesting conditions**		
	Service conditions	**Performance conditions**				
		Performance conditions that are market conditions.	Other performance conditions.	Neither the entity nor the counterparty can choose whether the condition is met.	Counterparty can choose whether to meet the condition.	Entity can choose whether to meet the condition.
Example conditions	Requirement to remain in service for three years.	Target based on the market price of the entity's equity instruments.	Target based on a successful initial public offering with a specified service requirement.	Target based on a commodity index.	Paying contributions towards the exercise price of a share-based payment.	Continuation of the plan by the entity.
Include in grant-date fair value?	No	Yes	No	Yes	Yes	Yes[a]
Accounting treatment if the condition is not met after the grant date and during the vesting period	Forfeiture. The entity revises the expense to reflect the best available estimate of the number of equity instruments expected to vest (paragraph 19).	No change to accounting. The entity continues to recognise the expense over the remainder of the vesting period (paragraph 21).	Forfeiture. The entity revises the expense to reflect the best available estimate of the number of equity instruments expected to vest (paragraph 19).	No change to accounting. The entity continues to recognise the expense over the remainder of the vesting period (paragraph 21A).	Cancellation. The entity recognises immediately the amount of the expense that would otherwise have been recognised over the remainder of the vesting period (paragraph 28A).	Cancellation. The entity recognises immediately the amount of the expense that would otherwise have been recognised over the remainder of the vesting period (paragraph 28A).

[a] In the calculation of the fair value of the share-based payment, the probability of continuation of the plan by the entity is assumed to be 100 per cent.

Appendix 2 — Classification of share-based payment transactions in group arrangements

The flow chart summarises how to determine the classification of awards, in both consolidated and separate financial statements. This flow chart applies specifically to situations where there is either an equity- or cash-settled award in group situations and does not deal with awards where there is a choice of settlement (see further para 12.155).

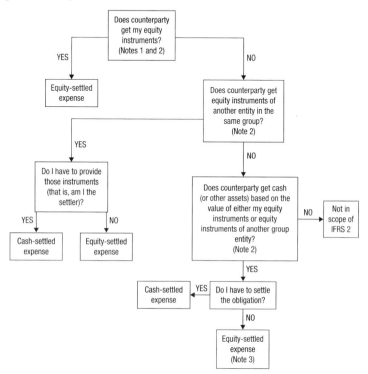

Notes:

1   'My equity instruments', include equity instruments of my subsidiaries (non-controlling interests) in consolidated financial statements, but not when equity instruments are accounted for as an investment in individual financial statements.

2   'Counterparty' includes employees and other suppliers of goods or services even where the goods or services are unidentifiable.

3   For the entity that settles the obligation, treatment will be as equity-settled only if the transaction is settled in equity instruments of that entity (including equity instruments of a subsidiary of that entity). For the entity receiving the goods or services, treatment will be as equity-settled unless there is an obligation to settle in cash or other assets.

Chapter 13

Taxation

Taxation

Introduction

13.1 Tax in financial statements comprises current tax and deferred tax. Current tax is based on the taxable and deductible amounts that are included in the tax return for the current year. Management recognises unpaid current tax expense for the current and prior periods as a liability in the balance sheet. It recognises any overpayment of current tax as an asset.

13.2 The amount of tax payable on taxable profits of a particular period often bears little relationship to the income and expenditure amounts in the financial statements. This is because tax laws and financial accounting standards recognise and measure income, expenditure, assets and liabilities in different ways. For example, some items of income or expenditure in the financial statements might be taxable or tax deductible in a period other than the one in which they were recognised (timing differences). The amount of an asset or liability for tax purposes (tax basis) might be different from the amount recognised in the financial statements; this could result in taxable or deductible amounts in the future when the amount of the asset is recovered or the liability is settled (temporary differences).

13.3 Deferred tax aims to address this mismatch. It is inherent in recognising an asset or liability that a reporting entity expects to recover or settle the carrying amount of the asset or liability. If that carrying amount is recovered or settled, future tax payments will be larger (or smaller) than if this recovery or settlement had no tax consequences. So, if the tax effects of temporary differences resulting from the difference between tax and accounting rules are recognised, the appropriate tax expense will be recognised in the financial statements. The tax charge in the financial statements comprises deferred tax as well as current tax.

UK.13.3.1 This chapter deals with accounting for current and deferred income taxes under IAS 12. The term 'income taxes' in the UK generally applies to taxes payable by individuals. But under the standard it includes all domestic and foreign taxes based on taxable profits. It also includes withholding taxes payable by subsidiaries, associates or joint ventures on distributions to the reporting entity. So, the standard applies to UK corporation tax that is assessed on an entity's profits.

13.4 This chapter contains a number of worked examples, using illustrative tax rates.

Corporation tax

General principles

UK.13.4.1 Corporation tax is based on profits, whether distributed or retained, at the end of each accounting period. Management calculates the tax charge by applying the basic rate of corporation tax to the taxable profit for the period. The taxable profit is calculated by applying relevant tax laws and rules; it is rarely the same as the accounting profit disclosed in the financial statements. Differences between the tax base of assets and liabilities and the amounts reported in the financial statements form the basis of accounting for deferred taxation; this is considered later in this chapter.

UK.13.4.2 The rate of corporation tax is set for a financial year; but management makes its assessments on the basis of the company's actual accounting period. If a company prepares financial statements for a year that straddles 31 March, and the rate of corporation tax is different for different financial years, management calculates an average rate and applies this to the tax calculation (as illustrated in para 13.71.5).

Recent developments

Amendments to IAS 12

13.4.1 The IASB issued 'Deferred tax: recovery of underlying assets (amendments to IAS 12)' in December 2010. The amendments modify the principles in IAS 12 for measuring deferred tax assets or liabilities when investment properties are measured at fair value. The amendments incorporate the previous guidance in SIC 21.

13.4.2 The amendments presume that an investment property measured at fair value is recovered entirely through sale. This presumption is rebutted if the investment property is depreciable and is held within a business model whose objective is to consume substantially all of the investment property's economic benefits over time rather than through sale.

13.4.3 The amendments have retrospective effect, for annual periods beginning on or after 1 January 2012, but can be applied to earlier years. They are discussed further in paragraph 13.219.4 onwards.

IAS 12 — Income taxes

Objective

13.5 IAS 12 sets out the accounting treatment for income taxes. It deals with the accounting for the current and future tax consequences of:

- Transactions and other events of the current period recognised in the financial statements.

- The future recovery (settlement) of the carrying amount of assets (liabilities) recognised in an entity's balance sheet.

13.6 An entity accounts for the tax consequences of transactions and other events in the same way that it accounts for the transactions and other events themselves. So, the tax effects of transactions and other events recognised in profit or loss are also recognised in profit or loss. The tax effects of transactions and other events recognised outside profit or loss (either in other comprehensive income or directly in equity) are also recognised outside profit or loss. See paragraph 13.288 onwards.

13.7 The standard also addresses how to recognise deferred tax assets arising from unused tax losses or unused tax credits, the presentation of income taxes in financial statements, and the disclosure of income tax-related information.

Scope

13.8 IAS 12 applies to accounting for income taxes; that is, taxes based on taxable profit. Income taxes include domestic and foreign income taxes and withholding taxes payable by a subsidiary, associate or joint venture on distributions to the reporting entity. [IAS 12 para 2].

13.9 The standard applies to taxes based on taxable profit. This implies that not all taxes are within IAS 12's scope; but, as taxable profit is not the same as accounting profit, taxes based on a figure that is not exactly accounting profit might be within the standard's scope. This is also implied by the IAS 12 requirement to explain the relationship between tax expense and accounting profit. The IFRS IC discussed this in March 2006 and noted that as 'taxable profit' implies a net rather than gross taxable amount, management might need to exercise judgement to determine whether some taxes are income taxes.

13.10 In some jurisdictions, tax might be assessed using a measure not directly linked to accounting income. Tax might be assessed using a 'taxable margin', which is calculated as revenue less specified costs. Such 'margin taxes' apply a tax rate to income less expenses (an income tax structure); so they differ from systems that assess tax based on sales or gross receipts (a non-income tax structure). In this case, the tax is an income tax in nature, and IAS 12 applies.

13.11 Where a tax is assessed based on the lower of a percentage of revenue and a percentage of revenue less expenses (that is, a 'taxable margin'), it generally has the features of income tax and is within IAS 12's scope. Also, the tax attributes should be assessed based on the overall tax system, not on the basis of the individual tax payers. In other words, the tax classification in an individual entity does not change just because the basis of assessment differs from year to year.

13.12 As well as assessing whether a specific tax payment is based on a measure of net income, management should consider the interaction with overall income tax. If an initial tax payment is not based on net income but represents a payment in advance that is subsequently trued-up to give a tax based on net income, the initial payment forms part of the income tax and falls within IAS 12's scope.

13.13 In some jurisdictions, shipping entities can choose to be taxed on the basis of tonnage transported, tonnage capacity or a notional income, instead of the standard corporate income tax. In some jurisdictions, this choice is irrevocable. The IFRS IC discussed this in May 2009 and noted that taxes on tonnage transported or tonnage capacity are based on gross rather than net amounts; taxes on a notional income derived from tonnage capacity are not based on the entity's actual income and expenses. Such tonnage taxes are not therefore considered income taxes under IAS 12 and are not presented as part of tax expense in the statement of comprehensive income.

13.14 In some jurisdictions, certain items of income are received net of taxes deducted at source. Examples include dividend and royalty income. Because the tax is deducted at source the cash flows of the paying entity are affected. But the tax amount is still payable by (or paid on behalf of) the recipients and hence a tax on income to the receiving entity instead of a tax on income to the paying entity. See further paragraph 13.48.

13.15 Entities in some jurisdictions receive government grants or tax credits. The standard does not address how to account for government grants (see IAS 20) or investment tax credits. But the standard does deal with accounting for temporary differences that arise from such grants or investment tax credits. [IAS 12 para 4]. Investment tax credits are considered in more detail in paragraph 13.275.2.

13.16 An entity does not generally recognise income taxes payable by an entity's shareholders. Shareholders or other group entities might pay income taxes on the entity's behalf in some circumstances – for example, if there is a consolidated tax return, or if relief for one entity's losses is transferred to another group entity. In such circumstances, the appropriate accounting is determined by examining the arrangement's details and considering relevant tax legislation.

UK.13.16.1 In the UK, group relief arrangements might permit management to recognise an accounting impact in relation to arrangements with shareholders and other members of the same tax group. See further guidance in paragraph UK.13.310.1.

13.17 A third party can indemnify an entity for income tax liabilities. Such an indemnity is typically given by a vendor in a business combination, but they can arise in other situations (and does not remove the entity's tax charge in its statement of comprehensive income). In addition to the income relating to the indemnification asset receivable from the third party, there might be subsequent changes in the asset's value. The asset usually changes in line with changes in the indemnified liability, depending on the terms of the arrangement. Income taxes are taxes based on taxable profit (see para 13.8). An indemnification asset receivable from a third party in respect of a tax uncertainty is not within IAS 12's scope. So, movements in a third-party indemnification asset are not included in the income tax line item in the statement of comprehensive income; they are reported as part of pre-tax profits.

13.18 Any taxes not within IAS 12's scope are within the scope of IAS 37. That standard is dealt with in chapter 21.

[The next paragraph is 13.42.]

Accounting for current tax

Introduction

13.42 A number of issues arise in respect of current tax. The following matters are dealt with in this section:

■ Recognition of current tax liabilities and current tax assets on the balance sheet.

■ Presentation of current tax in the performance statements and in equity.

■ The treatment of withholding and underlying taxes in the context of dividends and other interest payable and receivable.

■ The treatment of income and expense subject to non-standard rates of tax.

■ Measurement of current tax liabilities and assets.

■ Uncertain tax positions.

■ Presentation and disclosure of current tax.

Apart from the last item (considered in para 13.276 onwards), these matters are discussed below.

Recognition of current tax liabilities and current tax assets

13.43 Management recognises unpaid current tax expense for the current and prior periods as a liability in the balance sheet. Uncertain tax positions are considered further in paragraph 13.74 onwards. The amount payable in respect of the current tax expense is based on the taxable and deductible amounts that are expected to be reported on the tax return for the current year. The actual tax payable might differ from the tax liability recognised because a tax rule has been applied or interpreted incorrectly or there is a dispute with the tax authorities. Except where the adjustment is caused by a material error (which should be treated under IAS 8), it is treated as a change in accounting estimate and included in tax expense of the period when the adjustment arises. Management should normally disclose a material adjustment resulting from a change in accounting estimate. If the amount paid for current and prior periods exceeds the amount due for those periods, the excess is recognised as an asset. [IAS 12 para 12].

13.44 An entity may incur a tax loss for the current period that can be carried back to set against the profits of an earlier accounting period. As the entity would recover tax paid in a previous period, management should recognise the benefit of the tax loss as an asset in the period in which the tax loss occurs. This is because the asset is reliably measurable and recovery is probable. If the entity cannot carry back the tax loss, it might be able to carry it forward to set against income in a future period. For recognition of a deferred tax asset for carry-forward of unused tax losses, see paragraph 13.144. [IAS 12 paras 13, 14].

Recognition of current tax

Items recognised in profit or loss

13.45 Current tax is generally recognised as income or an expense and is included in profit or loss unless it arises from a transaction or event that is recognised (in the same or a different period), either in other comprehensive income or directly in equity. [IAS 12 para 58].

Items recognised outside profit or loss

13.46 Tax follows the item; so, current tax on items recognised, in the same or a different period in other comprehensive income is recognised in other comprehensive income; and current tax on items recognised, in the same or a different period directly in equity is recognised directly in equity. [IAS 12 para 61A]. The standard gives examples of items recognised in other comprehensive income or credited or charged directly to equity; these are shown in paragraphs 13.288.1 and 13.288.2. [IAS 12 paras 62, 62A].

13.47 Where an entity pays tax on all its profits, including elements recognised outside profit or loss, it can be difficult to determine the amount of current tax attributable to the amounts recognised outside profit or loss, either in other comprehensive income or directly in equity. In those circumstances, the attributable tax is calculated on a reasonable pro rata basis, or other basis that is more appropriate in the circumstances. [IAS 12 para 63].

Example – Allocation of tax on exchange loss

A parent entity made a trading profit of C1,500,000 during the year. The parent has a foreign currency loan receivable from a foreign subsidiary on which a tax deductible exchange loss of C500,000 arose. The loan is regarded by the parent as part of its net investment in the foreign subsidiary; so the exchange loss is reported in the parent's income statement under IAS 21. The tax rate for the year is 30%. Therefore the parent's tax charge for the year is C300,000 (profit before tax of C1,000,000 @ 30%).

On consolidation, the exchange loss of C500,000 is transferred to a separate component in equity under IAS 21 and is recognised in other comprehensive income. The total tax charge of C300,000 to be allocated between the income statement and other comprehensive income is as follows:

	C'000
Tax on trading profit (C1.5m @ 30%)	450
Tax relief on exchange loss (C500,000 @ 30%)	(150)
Total tax charge	300

The income statement would bear a tax charge of C450,000, with C150,000 of tax relief being recognised in other comprehensive income in the consolidated financial statements. (The subsidiary's results have been ignored to keep the example simple.)

Withholding and underlying taxes

13.48   In some jurisdictions, the recipient of a dividend receives a tax credit to acknowledge that the income from which the dividend is paid has been charged to tax in the entity paying the dividend (an imputed credit for underlying tax). This situation differs from one where a withholding tax is deducted at source and paid to the tax authorities on behalf of the recipient by the entity paying the dividend.

13.49   Withholding tax generally means tax on dividends and other income that has been deducted by the payer of the income and paid to the tax authorities on behalf of the recipient. IAS 12 contains no specific definition of withholding tax but includes as an example the portion of a dividend that is paid to the tax authorities on behalf of the shareholders. [IAS 12 para 65A]. This situation is distinct from one where the entity's tax rate depends on the level of profits that are distributed to shareholders (see para 13.175).

13.49.1   Withholding taxes can vary in their characteristics. Some indicators are given below:

■   The recipient of the dividend receives a net amount of income (that is, the amount of dividend received is lower than the amount declared in the paying entity's documentation), instead of the recipient being paid the full amount of the dividend declared and an additional amount being payable to the taxation authorities.

- The correspondence with the tax authorities concerning the tax payment notes that the tax is being paid on the recipient's behalf, rather than being an additional tax on the entity paying the dividend.

- For a dividend received with an imputed tax credit not to be subject to further tax in the recipient, it will have to be subject to specific tax relief. But, where a withholding tax has been charged, this might discharge the liability to the tax authority, so the item is not subject to further tax in the recipient.

13.50 Apart from the fact that withholding tax is paid by or on behalf of the recipient of the dividends, the tax treatment of dividends and other income subject to withholding tax is often different from dividends and other income received with an imputed tax credit.

13.51 The different tax treatments are considered to be sufficiently significant to require different accounting treatments for dividends and other income subject to imputed or underlying tax credits (these are notional and should not be taken into account as income tax of the recipient entity) from those that are subject to withholding tax (these are real and should be taken into account as income tax of the recipient entity).

Outgoing dividends and other interest payable

13.52 Outgoing dividends, interest and similar amounts should be recognised at an amount that includes withholding taxes (that is, gross including the amount of the withholding tax) and excludes any other taxes (such as attributable tax credits) not payable wholly on behalf of the recipient. As distributions to owners are charged to equity under paragraph 107 of IAS 1, any withholding tax should also be charged to equity as part of the dividend. [IAS 12 para 65A].

UK.13.52.1 A UK company does not generally include withholding tax in interest and other similar amounts paid and payable. However, if a UK company is required to deduct UK income tax (being similar in substance to withholding tax) on interest payable to third parties, we believe that interest payable should be shown gross in the income statement, that is, inclusive of the income tax deducted.

[The next paragraph is 13.54.]

Incoming dividends and other interest receivable

13.54 IAS 12 is silent on the treatment of withholding taxes in the recipient's financial statements. As explained in paragraph 13.49, withholding tax is tax actually suffered by the recipient entity; so management should recognise incoming dividends, interest and other income receivable in the income statement at an amount including (that is, gross of) any withholding taxes, but excluding other taxes, such as attributable tax credits, not payable wholly on behalf of the recipient. This treatment mirrors the treatment for outgoing dividends.

UK.13.54.1   As stated in paragraph 13.49, withholding taxes normally arise on dividends received from investments located overseas. Where (as stated in para 13.54) the income is reported gross of the foreign withholding tax, the withholding tax suffered should be shown as part of the tax charge.

13.55   Where tax has been deducted at source on interest income and has been paid by the payer of the interest to the tax authorities on behalf of the recipient, the interest income should be recorded gross of the tax deducted at source. The tax should be shown as part of the tax charge.

[The next paragraph is 13.61.]

Underlying tax

13.61   In some situations, relief is also available for foreign 'underlying tax' (that is, tax on the entity's profits out of which the dividends are paid).

13.62   An entity can claim double tax relief for both withholding and underlying tax, but dividends or other income received should not be grossed up for the underlying rate of tax. This is because the underlying tax is the liability of another entity (the payer of the dividend) and is not tax that has been suffered by the recipient. The underlying tax rate is simply used by the entity's tax authority to calculate the tax due on the dividend income and to work out the total relief that should be given for the double tax suffered. The only tax that the recipient suffers is the withholding tax, which is a 'real tax', as opposed to the underlying tax that, from the perspective of the recipient, is a 'notional tax'.

UK.13.62.1   If a UK company pays tax on its dividend income, it can normally obtain double tax relief on overseas tax paid against UK corporation tax; but this depends on whether the overseas tax rate (withholding and underlying) is less than the UK corporation tax rate. Where the rate of overseas tax exceeds the UK corporation tax rate, a proportion of the overseas tax can remain unrelieved. The unrelieved overseas tax has to be written off in the income statement. This write-off need not be disclosed separately, as it is included with overseas taxation in the income statement taxation charge.

13.63   Consider the following example:

Example – Unrelieved overseas tax

A parent entity has a foreign subsidiary. The foreign subsidiary generated taxable profits equivalent to C100,000, on which it paid tax @ 35% amounting to C35,000. It distributed the remaining after-tax profit of C65,000 to the parent after deducting 5% withholding tax amounting to C3,250. The parent received a cash dividend of C61,750. The parent's rate of tax is 30%. The tax rules in the parent's jurisdiction require it to pay tax on the grossed-up dividend, as illustrated below:

Parent's tax computation	C	C
Cash dividend of C61,750 grossed up for overseas taxes (both underlying and withholding)		100,000
Tax @ 30%		30,000
Less double tax relief:		
Total overseas tax paid (C35,000 + C3,250)	38,250	
Relief restricted to parent's tax payable	(30,000)	(30,000)
Unrelieved overseas tax *	8,250	
Parent's tax liability		nil

* It is assumed that no deferred tax asset can be recognised for the excess foreign tax paid.

Parent's separate income statement	C	C
Dividend received (grossed up for withholding tax)		65,000
Tax charge:		
Parent's tax	–	
Overseas tax paid (withholding tax)	3,250	
Total tax charge		3,250
Profit after tax		61,750

Parent's consolidated income statement	C	C
Profit before tax		100,000
Tax charge:		
Tax	30,000	
Less: double tax relief	30,000	
	–	
Overseas tax paid†	38,250	
Total tax charge		38,250
Profit after tax		61,750

† Total tax charge is effectively tax of C30,000 plus unrelieved overseas tax of C8,250 = C38,250

Income and expenses subject to non-standard rates of tax

13.64   Income received after tax has been deducted is distinguished from income taxable at non-standard rates. Entities often enter into transactions that give rise to income or expense that is not subject to the standard rate of tax. Examples include some leasing transactions, and advances and investments made by financial institutions. In some situations, after taking account of the financing cost, the transaction might result in a pre-tax loss and a post-tax profit. Consider the following example:

> **Example – Income taxed at non-standard rate**
>
> A financial institution borrows C10 million that bears interest at 9% per annum. The proceeds are immediately invested in an instrument that yields 8% per annum, but the income is taxable at 20%. The standard rate of tax is 33%. The entity makes a pre-tax loss of C100,000, but the transaction is profitable, after tax effects are taken into account, as shown below:

Income statement	C'000	C'000
Investment income @ 8%		800
Less: interest expense		(900)
Pre-tax loss		(100)
Taxation:		
On income @ 20%	(160)	
Tax relief on interest @ 33%	297	
Tax credit		137
Post-tax profit		37

13.65   Banks and other institutions enter into such transactions precisely because they are profitable after tax. But they might argue that the presentation above makes it difficult to interpret the income statement and inhibits comparison between different entities, especially since pre-tax profits are an important measure of performance. They might prefer that income subject to the non-standard rate of tax should be presented on a grossed-up basis (as shown below). This would eliminate the distortion between pre- and post-tax profits, by reporting tax at the standard rate.

Income statement (grossed-up)	C'000
Investment income (grossed up): 640/(100% — 33%)*	955
Less: interest expense	(900)
Pre-tax profit *	55
Tax charge @ 33% †	(18)
Post-tax profit	37

*Includes notional income of C155
†Includes notional tax charge of C155

13.66 However, we believe that grossing up, because it is notional, fails to report the transaction's true nature. In our view, if a transaction results in a pre-tax loss and a tax benefit, it is reported as such, to achieve a faithful representation. Grossing up reports a false amount, both as pre-tax profits and as the tax charge for the year. The tax treatment of the transaction should have no bearing on the way it is reported for financial reporting purposes. If grossing up were allowed as a general rule, non-deductible expenditure could be presented on a grossed-up basis. This treatment would be inconsistent with generally accepted practice in accounting for such items, where no adjustments are usually made.

13.67 So, in our view, no adjustment should be made to reflect a notional amount of tax that would have been paid or relieved in respect of the transaction if it had been taxable, or allowable for tax purposes, on a different basis.

13.68 Entities whose results are significantly affected by transactions not at a standard rate of tax should disclose the full effects of such transactions in their financial statements.

Measurement of current tax liabilities and assets

Enacted and substantively enacted tax rates and laws

13.69 Current tax liabilities and assets are measured at the amounts expected to be paid or recovered using the tax rates and laws that have been enacted or substantively enacted by the balance sheet date. [IAS 12 para 46].

13.70 Where the government has announced changes in tax rates and laws at or before the balance sheet date, but the formalities of the enactment process are not yet finalised, management should consider whether the announcement has the effect of substantive enactment. In some tax jurisdictions, such announcements have the effect of substantive enactment; so the announcement of new tax rates and laws should be taken into account in the measurement process. [IAS 12 para 48].

13.71 In 2005, the IASB noted in a board meeting that substantive enactment occurs when any future steps in the enactment process will not change the outcome. This underlying principle should be used to determine if a rate is substantively enacted in a particular territory.

UK.13.71.1 Under FRS 16 in the UK, current tax is measured using the tax rates and laws that have been enacted or substantively enacted by the balance sheet date; so the treatment under IAS 12 will be the same as under FRS 16 in this respect. Under FRS 16, a UK tax rate is taken as 'substantively enacted' if it is included in either:

■ a Bill that has been passed by the House of Commons and is awaiting only passage through the House of Lords and Royal Assent; or

■ a resolution having statutory effect that has been passed under the Provisional Collection of Taxes Act 1968 (PCTA 1968).

UK.13.71.2 The parliamentary resolution under PCTA 1968 is a temporary enactment of tax changes that has statutory force for a limited period. During that period, a permanent statutory provision is made with full parliamentary procedures; the temporary statute falls away when the permanent one is enacted.

UK.13.71.3 In the UK, changes in tax laws and rates are normally announced in a Finance Bill on Budget day. So, where a company's accounting reference period ends on a date that falls between the Budget date and the date when the process of enactment is substantively complete (for instance, when the Bill has been passed by the House of Commons), the substantively enacted rate is the rate in force at the balance sheet date; and current and deferred tax should be measured using that rate.

UK.13.71.4 UK corporation tax rates are set a year in advance by reference to a financial year. For instance, the main rate of corporation tax for the financial year 2008 (the year beginning 1 April 2008) was set at 28% in the 2007 Budget on 21 March 2007. The Finance Bill 2007 was approved by the House of Commons on 26 June 2007; after receiving Royal Assent, it became the Finance Act 2007. So the substantively enacted rate applied for accounting periods ending on or after 26 June 2007 where the tax arose on or after 1 April 2008 (until it was superseded by changes in rate in later Finance Acts).

UK.13.71.5 Where a company prepares financial statements for a period that straddles 31 March, and the enacted or substantively enacted tax rates are different for different financial years, management calculates an effective tax rate. Under UK tax legislation, when a tax rate changes, an entity calculates a pro-rated tax rate for the transitional year, which applies to all profits for that accounting period.

> **Example – Change of tax rate during accounting period**
>
> An entity has an accounting period ending on 30 October 20X8. The rates of corporation tax for the financial years 20X7 and 20X8 are 30% and 28% respectively. The effective rate of tax to be disclosed in the financial statements for the current tax is calculated as follows:
>
> | | | |
> |---|---|---|
> | Period 1 November 20X7 to 31 March 20X8 (FY 20X7) | 5/12 @ 30% | 12.50% |
> | Period 1 April 20X8 to 30 October 20X8 (FY 20X8) | 7/12 @ 28% | 16.33% |
> | Effective rate of corporation tax | | 28.83% |

UK.13.71.6 The accounting period for corporation tax purposes can never exceed 12 months. If the financial statements cover a period of more than 12 months, the first 12 months constitute one accounting period, and the remainder of the period constitutes the second accounting period for tax purposes.

Discounting of current tax assets and liabilities

13.72 Entities might have tax refunds due from or tax liabilities due to the tax authorities that are receivable or payable more than 12 months from the balance sheet date, but are not bearing interest. Deferred tax assets and liabilities cannot be discounted; but the standard is silent on discounting current tax balances. [IAS 12 para 53].

13.73 Current tax assets and liabilities are measured at the amounts expected to be recovered from or paid to the tax authorities. [IAS 12 para 46]. Management does not need to discount long-term current tax balances; but we consider that entities can measure these balances at a discounted value as a matter of accounting policy choice. The impact of unwinding any discount would be presented as finance income or expense.

Uncertain tax positions

13.74 An entity's tax position might be uncertain; for example, where the tax treatment of an item of expense or structured transaction may be challenged by the tax authorities. Uncertainties in income taxes are not addressed specifically in IAS 12. IAS 37 excludes income taxes from its scope and is not used to measure uncertain tax positions. The general measurement principles in IAS 12 should be applied: *"Current tax liabilities (assets) for the current and prior periods shall be measured at the amount expected to be paid to (recovered from) the taxation authorities using the tax rates (and tax laws) that have been enacted or substantively enacted at the balance sheet date"*. [IAS 12 para 46]. The standard does not specify the unit of account and measurement method, so there is diversity in practice.

13.75 We believe the unit of account is an accounting policy choice under IFRS. Management might consider uncertain tax positions individually or grouped together for related uncertainties. Or it might consider tax uncertainties in relation to each taxing authority.

13.76 When management considers uncertain tax positions individually, it should first consider whether each position taken in the tax return is probable of being sustained on examination by the taxing authority. It should recognise a liability for each item that is not probable of being sustained. The liability is measured using either an expected value (weighted average probability) approach or a single best estimate of the most likely outcome. The current tax liability is the total liability for uncertain tax positions.

13.77 When management considers uncertain tax positions in relation to each taxing authority, the key issue is the measurement of the tax liability. It is usually probable that an entity will pay tax, so the recognition threshold has been met. Management should calculate the total amount of current tax it expects to pay, taking into account all the tax uncertainties, using either an expected value (weighted average probability) approach or a single best estimate of the most likely outcome.

13.78 The examples below assume that management considers tax uncertainties individually. They show that the measurement methods referred to in paragraph 13.76 can give rise to different amounts of liability. All the examples assume that it is probable (more likely than not) that tax is payable.

Example 1 – Measuring an uncertain tax position

Entity K has included deductions in a tax return that might be challenged by the tax authorities. Entity K and its tax consultants estimate the probability of additional tax payable as follows:

Potential tax payable	Individual probability	Cumulative probability	Probability-weighted calculation
C			C
800	15%	15%	120
600	30%	45%	180
400	20%	65%	80
200	20%	85%	40
0	15%	100%	–
			420

- Most likely outcome C600.

- Probability weighted outcome C420.

Example 2 – Uncertain tax position with two possible outcomes

Entity K takes a deduction in a tax return that might be challenged by the tax authorities. It estimates a 40% probability that additional tax of C120 will be payable and a 60% probability that additional tax of C80 will be payable.

- Most likely outcome C80.

- Probability weighted outcome C96 (C120 × 40% + C80 × 60%).

Example 3 – Use of probability weighted average method

A deduction of C100 might be challenged. Entity K and its tax consultants estimate the probability of additional tax payable as follows:

Potential tax payable	Individual probability	Cumulative probability	Probability-weighted calculation
C			C
100	45%	45%	45.00
80	10%	55%	8.00
50	25%	80%	12.50
–	20%	100%	–
			65.50

■ Probability weighted outcome C65.5.

■ It would not make sense to use C100 as the most likely outcome in this case, as some of the deductions will probably be accepted by the tax authorities. Although there is a 45% chance that the full amount of C100 will be payable, there is a 55% chance of reduced tax being payable. Here, the probability weighted average would be the appropriate measurement method.

13.79 Where an entity has paid more than the amount payable under the relevant tax legislation, it will estimate the recovery of a tax asset. On the other hand, where an entity has not remitted taxes related to an uncertain tax position, it will evaluate the uncertainty surrounding the potential liability. We believe that the same considerations apply where this evaluation relates to the recovery or payment of taxes (as opposed to interest and penalties, dealt with in para 13.81). Under IAS 12, uncertain tax positions (whether assets or liabilities) are reflected at the amount expected to be recovered from or paid to the taxation authorities. Consistent accounting policies should be applied to uncertain tax assets and liabilities.

13.79.1 An entity discloses tax-related contingent liabilities and contingent assets in accordance with IAS 37 (see para 13.308). [IAS 12 para 88]. So, if IAS 12's recognition threshold is not met, IAS 37's disclosure requirements for contingent liabilities and contingent assets apply to uncertain tax positions. These disclosure requirements are dealt with in chapter 21.

13.80 Once an uncertain tax position is determined, in later periods management need to decide whether a change in the tax estimate is justified. We expect that a change in recognition and measurement is justified where circumstances change or where new facts clarify the probability of estimates previously made. Such changes might be: further judicial developments related to a specific case or to a similar case; substantive communications from the tax authorities; or a change in status of a tax year (for example, moving from open to closed in a particular jurisdiction).

Interest and penalties on uncertain tax positions

13.81 An entity might incur interest or penalties in relation to taxation; for example, where uncertain tax positions have been successfully challenged by the tax authorities. IAS 12 does not specifically address the treatment of uncertain tax positions or associated interest and penalties. The liability for the uncertain tax position is for a tax based on taxable profits, and is therefore an income tax liability. This liability is recognised and measured under IAS 12 (see further para 13.74).

13.82 There is a strong argument that interest and penalties differ from income tax liabilities, because they are not measured and settled by the tax authorities on the basis of taxable profits. This suggests that interest and penalties should be recognised, measured and presented as provisions under IAS 37, and classified as finance or other operating expense, respectively, in the income statement. This is because:

■ such obligations are not based on taxable profits and so they fall outside IAS 12's scope; and

■ the economic substance of reducing or delaying a tax payment is no different from other financing arrangements. Interest that increases with time and is in substance a financing cost of the liability is interest expense; other penalties represent operating costs.

13.83 Practice varies with regard to these items. In some cases, interest and penalties are accounted for as if they are within IAS 12's scope, either because they are rolled up into a lump sum settlement and cannot be separated from the taxes, or as a matter of accounting policy. Any associated charge is normally included within the tax line in the income statement; and the liability is included within the income tax liability on the balance sheet.

13.84 The accounting policy for interest and penalties applies to both interest payable (and any related penalties) and to interest recoverable (and any related damages). For interest and damages recoverable, a contingent asset cannot be recognised under IAS 37 until it is 'virtually certain'; but uncertain tax assets are recorded under IAS 12 on the basis of the amount expected to be recovered. IAS 37 establishes a higher threshold for recognition than IAS 12; so an entity's accounting policy will determine when interest and damages recoverable will be recognised.

13.84.1 Where material amounts are involved, the accounting policy used to recognise, measure and classify interest and tax-related penalties or damages should be disclosed clearly in the financial statements and applied consistently.

Other expenses associated with taxation

Professional fees linked to tax expense

13.85   An entity might incur expenses that are indirectly linked to the income tax expense, such as fees payable to tax consultants that are based on a percentage of savings made under a specific tax scheme. These fees are not 'tax expense' under IAS 1. IAS 1 suggests two formats for analysing expenses charged in arriving at profit before tax: the first is based on the nature of the expense; and the other is based on its function. Using the first format, the appropriate heading under which to charge these expenses would be 'other expenses'; using the other format, 'administrative expenses' would be the appropriate heading. [IAS 1 paras 82, 99 to 103].

Accounting for deferred tax

Introduction

13.86   Most transactions and events recorded in the financial statements have a tax consequence, which can be immediate or deferred. Often, income is taxable and expenses are deductible for tax purposes when incurred. However, the taxation or deduction for tax purposes might be delayed to a later period (for example, when cash flows occur under the transaction). Also, the recovery or settlement of an asset or liability, just at its carrying amount, might have tax consequences.

13.87   Where transactions and events have occurred by the balance sheet date, future tax consequences cannot be avoided; the entity might have to pay less or more tax than if those transactions and events had not happened. Therefore, management recognises the tax effects of all income and expenditure, gains and losses, assets and liabilities in the same period in which they are recognised themselves and not in the period in which they form part of taxable profit. This matching of transactions and events with their tax effects gives rise to current tax; it also gives rise to deferred tax balances that meet the Framework definitions of, and recognition criteria for, assets and liabilities.

13.88   An asset recorded in the financial statements is realised, at least for its carrying amount, in the form of future economic benefits that flow to the entity in future periods; this is the basis for the balance sheet liability method used by IAS 12. When such benefits flow to the entity, they give rise to amounts that may form a part of taxable profits. The asset's tax base (see para 13.111 onwards) can be deducted in determining taxable profits in either the same or a different period. When the asset's carrying amount is greater than its tax base, the amount of the future taxable economic benefits is greater than the amount allowed as a deduction for tax purposes; as a result, it gives rise to a deferred tax liability in respect of taxes payable in future periods. For assets and liabilities within subsidiaries, branches, associates and joint ventures, the principle extends to the tax consequences of recovering the reporting group's investments in those entities, when the reporting group has control over that recovery and expects such recovery to occur in the foreseeable future.

13.89 The balance sheet liability method can instead be viewed as a valuation adjustment approach; under this approach, management needs to provide for deferred tax to ensure that other assets are not valued at more than their economic (that is, post-tax) values to the business. In other words, management should provide for deferred tax to reflect the fact that the economic value to the business of an asset is not the market value of, say, C150. Rather it is the market value of C150 less the present value of the tax that would be payable on selling the asset for C150. In theory, the appropriate method for recognising deferred tax provided for as a valuation adjustment rather than as a liability might be to net the tax provision against the asset's carrying amount. But the IASB considers that an entity's results and position are more clearly communicated if tax effects are shown separately from the items or transactions to which they relate.

General principles

13.90 A deferred tax liability or asset is recognised if the *recovery* of the carrying amount of an asset or the settlement of a liability will result in higher (or lower) tax payments in the future than if that *recovery* or settlement had no tax consequences. [IAS 12 para 10]. So a deferred tax liability or asset is recognised for all such tax consequences that have originated but have not reversed by the balance sheet date. Exceptions to this general principle are discussed later in this chapter.

13.91 The word 'recovery' in italics above is particularly relevant for measuring deferred tax liabilities that arise on assets. An entity generally expects to recover the carrying amount of an asset through use, through sale, or through use and subsequent sale. Tax authorities might levy different rates of tax depending on whether the asset is recovered through use (income tax) or through sale (capital gains tax). Also, some assets are revalued for tax purposes (increase due to indexation to eliminate the effects of inflation) only if the asset is sold. Therefore, the manner in which the entity expects, at the balance sheet date, to recover the asset directly affects the amount of tax that is payable in future; and this should be reflected in the measurement of deferred tax at the balance sheet date. This is an important principle concerning the measurement of deferred tax (see further para 13.170 onwards). Other measurement issues are considered in paragraph 13.165 onwards.

13.92 Deferred tax income or expense should be reported in profit or loss if it relates to items that are themselves reported in profit or loss. For transactions and other events recognised outside profit or loss, any related tax effects are also recognised outside profit or loss. Presentation of deferred tax in performance statements or equity is considered in paragraph 13.286 onwards.

13.92.1 The approach to determining deferred tax can be summarised as follows:

- Consider the entity's structure (for example, a company/corporation or a partnership; a parent or a subsidiary) and the tax jurisdictions that apply to the entity.

- Calculate current income tax.

  Current tax payable to the taxation authorities is calculated based on the tax legislation in the relevant territory. Accounting for current tax is addressed in paragraph 13.42 onwards.

- Determine the tax base.

  The tax base reflects the tax consequences arising from the manner in which management expects, at the balance sheet date, to recover or settle the carrying amount of an asset or liability.

  In simple situations, an asset's tax base equals the future deductible amounts when the asset's carrying amount is recovered. A liability's tax base equals its carrying amount less future deductible amounts. If there are no tax consequences of recovery, there is no deferred tax. Tax bases for assets are addressed in paragraph 13.111 onwards, and for liabilities in paragraph 13.120 onwards.

- Calculate temporary differences.

  Temporary difference is defined as the difference between an asset or liability's carrying amount and its tax base. Temporary differences are addressed in paragraph 13.93 onwards and summarised in paragraph 13.106.

- Consider the exceptions to recognising deferred tax on temporary differences.

  Three exceptions relating to temporary differences arise in the following situations:

  - Initial recognition of goodwill arising in a business combination (for deferred tax liabilities only) (see para 13.158 onwards).

  - Initial recognition of an asset or liability in a transaction that is not a business combination and does not affect accounting profit or taxable profit (see para 13.162 onwards).

  - Investments in subsidiaries, branches, associates and joint ventures, but only where certain criteria apply (see para 13.233 onwards).

- Assess deductible temporary differences, tax losses and tax credits for recoverability.

  A deferred tax asset is recognised to the extent that it is *probable* that taxable profit will be available against which a deductible temporary difference or unused tax losses or tax credits can be utilised (see para 13.128 onwards).

- Determine the tax rate that is expected to apply when the temporary differences reverse; and calculate deferred tax.

  Deferred tax is measured at the tax rates that are expected to apply to the period when the asset is realised or the liability is settled, based on tax rates and tax laws that have been enacted or substantively enacted by the balance sheet date (see para 13.165 onwards).

  Measurement of deferred tax reflects the tax consequences that follow from the manner that management expects, at the balance sheet date, to recover or settle the carrying amount of an asset or liability (see para 13.170 onwards).

- Recognise deferred tax.

  Deferred tax is calculated by multiplying the temporary difference by the tax rate.

- Consider the presentation and offsetting of current and deferred tax.

  The requirements for presenting current and deferred tax are addressed in paragraph 13.278 onwards. The rules for offsetting current and deferred tax assets and liabilities are addressed in paragraph 13.281 onwards.

- Disclose details of current and deferred tax.

  Disclosure requirements relating to current and deferred tax are addressed in paragraph 13.290 onwards.

Temporary differences

13.93   The concept of temporary differences is central to the calculation of deferred taxes under IAS 12. Temporary differences are defined as differences between the carrying amount of an asset or liability and its tax base (see para 13.107 onwards). [IAS 12 para 5]. The term 'temporary difference' is used because ultimately all differences between the carrying amounts of assets and liabilities and their tax bases will reverse. An entity might delay the reversal of temporary differences by delaying the events that give rise to those reversals; for example, it might defer indefinitely the sale of a revalued asset. But the fundamental proposition in the IAS Framework is that the carrying amount of assets and liabilities will always be recovered or settled. So the key questions are when and not whether temporary differences will reverse; and to what extent, on reversal, this will result in taxable or tax deductible amounts in future years. At some point, such tax consequences *will* crystallise. As noted in paragraph 13.111, if the recovery of an asset has no tax consequences, the tax base is equal to the carrying amount and there is no temporary difference.

13.94   The following are examples of temporary differences:

- An item of income or expenditure is included in accounting profit of the period, but recognised in taxable profit in later periods. For example, income receivable might be accrued in the financial statements in one year, but it is taxed in the next year when received. Similarly, management might make provisions for restructuring costs in the financial statements in one period, but those costs would qualify for tax deduction in a later period when the expenditure is incurred.

■ An item of income or expenditure is included in taxable profit of the period, but recognised in accounting profit in later years. For example, development expenditure might be tax deductible in the year in which it is incurred, but it is capitalised and amortised over a period for financial reporting purposes. Similarly, income received in advance might be taxed in the period of receipt, but treated in the financial statements as earned in a later period.

■ Where assets are acquired and liabilities assumed in a business combination, these are generally recognised at their fair values; but no equivalent adjustment is made for tax purposes (see para 13.238).

■ Assets are revalued and no equivalent adjustment is made for tax purposes (see para 13.208).

■ Goodwill arises in a business combination (see para 13.158).

■ An asset or liability's tax base on initial recognition differs from its initial carrying amount; for example, when an entity benefits from non-taxable government grants related to assets (see para 13.162).

■ The carrying amount of investments in subsidiaries, branches and associates or interests in joint ventures differs from the tax base of the investment or interest (see para 13.253).

■ An entity's non-monetary assets and liabilities are measured in its functional currency, but the taxable profit or tax loss (and so the tax base of its non-monetary assets and liabilities) is determined in a different currency (see para 13.274).

[IAS 12 paras IN2, 18].

[The next paragraph is 13.96.]

13.96 Not all of the temporary differences listed above give rise to deferred tax balances. Some are specifically exempted from recognition in the standard (see further para 13.157 onwards).

13.97 The carrying amounts of assets and liabilities used to calculate the temporary differences are determined from the entity's balance sheet. The applicable carrying amount is generally a question of fact; but judgement might be needed to determine the appropriate carrying amounts for use in deferred tax calculations that are based on the dual manner of recovery (see further para 13.172.3). Where applicable, the carrying amounts of assets are included in the computation of temporary differences net of any provision for doubtful debts or impairment losses. Similarly, the carrying amounts of liabilities, such as debts recorded at amortised cost, are included net of any issue costs. The carrying amounts of assets and liabilities in consolidated financial statements are obtained from the consolidated balance sheet. The tax base is determined by reference to a consolidated tax return in jurisdictions that require such a return; and by reference to the tax returns of each individual group entity in other jurisdictions. [IAS 12 para 11].

13.98 The tax base of assets and liabilities is defined so that it equals the carrying amount of the item if reversal will not give rise to taxable or tax deductible amounts. So, temporary differences are either taxable temporary differences or deductible temporary differences. Taxable temporary differences give rise to future taxable amounts, and so to deferred tax liabilities. Deductible temporary differences give rise to future tax deductible amounts, and so to potential deferred tax assets.

Taxable temporary differences

13.99 Taxable temporary differences are temporary differences that will result in taxable amounts in determining taxable profit (tax loss) of future periods when the carrying amount of the asset or liability is recovered or settled. [IAS 12 para 5].

13.100 As stated in paragraph 13.90, the recognition of an asset implies that its carrying amount will be recovered in the form of economic benefits that flow to the entity in future periods. The recovery of the carrying amount of many assets gives rise to taxable and deductible amounts; for example, machinery that produces goods that are in turn sold to generate revenue that enters into the determination of taxable profits and that gives rise to depreciation that is deductible for tax purposes against those taxable profits. When the carrying amount of an asset (the minimum expected future economic benefits) exceeds its tax base (the amount that can be deducted for tax purposes from those future economic benefits – see further para 13.111 onwards), the amount of taxable economic benefits will exceed the amount that is allowed as a deduction for tax purposes. This difference is a taxable temporary difference; and the obligation to settle the resulting income taxes in future periods is a deferred tax liability. The following example (based on the example in IAS 12 para 16) shows how a deferred tax liability can arise.

Example – Deferred tax liability relating to an asset

An asset that cost C150 has a carrying amount of C100. Cumulative depreciation for tax purposes is C90 and the tax rate is 30%.

	Carrying amount C	Tax base C	Temporary difference C
At acquisition	150	150	
Accumulated depreciation	50	90	
Net amount	100	60	40
Tax rate			30%
Deferred tax liability			12

The tax base of the asset is C60 (cost of C150 less cumulative tax depreciation of C90). In recovering the carrying amount of C100, the entity will earn taxable income of C100, but will only be able to deduct tax depreciation of C60. The entity will pay income tax on the excess. The difference between the carrying amount of C100 and the tax base of C60 is a taxable temporary difference of C40. So the entity recognises a deferred tax liability of C12 (C40 × 30%) representing the income tax that it will pay when it recovers the asset's carrying amount.

13.101 When the asset's carrying amount and its tax base are the same, the amount included in taxable profit on the asset's recovery is offset by the amount allowed as a deduction in determining taxable profit. So the recovery of the carrying amount has no net effect on the entity's taxable profit. Hence, no deferred tax arises.

13.102 Similar arguments apply when the carrying amount of a liability is settled through an outflow of resources from the entity in future periods. A taxable temporary difference arises when the carrying amount of a liability is less than its tax base (see further para 13.120 onwards).

Example – Deferred tax liability relating to a liability

An entity has taken out a foreign currency loan of FC1,000 that is recorded at C625. At the reporting date, the carrying amount of the loan is C575. The unrealised exchange gain of C50 is included in profit or loss, but will be taxable when the gain is realised on repayment of the loan.

	Carrying amount C	Tax base C	Temporary difference C
At inception	625	625	
Exchange gain	50	–	
Net amount	575	625	50
Tax rate			30%
Deferred tax liability			15

The tax base of the loan is C625 (carrying amount of C575 plus the C50 of gain that will be taxable in future periods). In settling the liability at its carrying amount of C575, the entity will make a gain of C50; but it will not be able to deduct any amount for tax purposes. The entity will pay income tax of C15 (C50 × 30%) as a result of settling the carrying amount of the liability. The difference between the carrying amount of C575 and the tax base of C625 is a taxable temporary difference of C50. Therefore, the entity recognises a deferred tax liability of C15 (C50 × 30%) representing the income tax to be paid when the carrying amount of the loan is settled at an amount below the original proceeds.

Deductible temporary differences

13.103 Deductible temporary differences are temporary differences that will result in deductible amounts in determining taxable profit (tax loss) of future periods when the carrying amount of the asset or liability is recovered or settled. [IAS 12 para 5].

13.104 The recognition of a liability implies that its carrying amount will be settled through an outflow of economic benefits from the entity in future periods. When such economic benefits flow from the entity, they give rise to amounts that might be deductible when the taxable profits of a later reporting period (that is, after the period when the liability is recognised) are determined. In such situations, there is a difference between the carrying amount of the liability and its tax base (see further para 13.120 onwards). So a deferred tax asset arises in respect of the income taxes that will be reduced or recoverable in the future periods when the settlement amounts are allowed as a deduction in determining taxable profit.

Example – Deferred tax asset relating to a liability

An entity recognises a liability of C1,000 for product warranty costs. For tax purposes, the warranty costs are deductible only when claims are made.

	Carrying amount	Tax base	Temporary difference
	C	C	C
Accrued warranty cost	1,000	–	1,000
Tax rate			30%
Deferred tax asset			300

The tax base of the warranty is nil (carrying amount of C1,000 less the amount of C1,000 that will be deductible in future periods when the claim is made – see further para 13.120). When a claim is made and the liability is settled at its carrying amount of C1,000, the entity obtains a deduction against taxable profits of the period in which the claim is made. So the entity will pay less income tax of C300 (C1,000 × 30%) as a result of settling the carrying amount of the liability. The difference between the carrying amount of C1,000 and the nil tax base is a deductible temporary difference of C1,000. Therefore, the entity recognises a deferred tax asset of C300 (C1,000 × 30%) representing the income tax that will be recoverable (reduced) in the future.

13.105 In the context of assets, a deductible temporary difference arises when an asset's carrying amount is less than its tax base (see further para 13.111 onwards). The difference gives rise to a deferred tax asset to the extent that income taxes will be reduced or recoverable in future periods.

Example – Deferred tax asset relating to an asset

An asset was acquired at a cost of C1,500. It has a carrying amount of C700 after an impairment write-down of C300 was recognised in the year. Cumulative depreciation for tax and accounting purposes amounted to C500 and the tax rate is 30%.

	Carrying amount	Tax base	Temporary difference
	C	C	C
At acquisition	1,500	1,500	
Accumulated depreciation	500	500	
Impairment loss in year	300	–	
Net amount	700	1,000	300
Tax rate			30%
Deferred tax asset			90

The tax base of the asset is C1,000 (cost of C1,500 less cumulative tax depreciation of C500). In recovering the carrying amount of C700, the entity will earn taxable income of C700, but will be able to deduct tax depreciation of C1,000. The entity will recover income tax. The difference between the carrying amount of C700 and the tax base of C1,000 is a deductible temporary difference of C300. So the entity recognises a deferred tax asset of C90 (C300 × 30%) representing the income tax that will be recovered (reduced) when it recovers the asset's carrying amount.

Summary of temporary differences

13.106   The relationship between the carrying amount and tax bases of assets and liabilities on the one hand, and the resulting deferred tax assets and liabilities that arise on the other, can be summarised as follows:

Relationship	For assets	For liabilities
Carrying amount is more than the tax base	**Taxable** temporary difference Deferred tax liability (**DTL**)	**Deductible** temporary difference Deferred tax asset (**DTA**)
Carrying amount is less than the tax base	**Deductible** temporary difference Deferred tax asset (**DTA**)	**Taxable** temporary difference Deferred tax liability (**DTL**)
Carrying amount = tax base	None	None

Tax bases

General

13.107 The tax base of an asset or liability is the amount attributed to that asset or liability for tax purposes. [IAS 12 para 5]. The concept of tax base of an asset or liability is fundamentally important in applying the standard's provisions. This is because the calculation of temporary difference depends on correctly identifying the tax base of each asset and liability in the entity's balance sheet. There is also a specific definition of 'tax base' for assets and liabilities (see paras 13.111 and 13.120 respectively). These definitions modify the general definition so that tax base equals the carrying amount in some circumstances. The standard provides a number of examples for determining the tax bases of assets and liabilities in particular situations.

13.107.1 In many cases, an asset or liability might have more than one tax base; this depends on how the entity intends to recover or settle the asset or liability. See further paragraph 13.170 onwards.

13.108 The tax base as defined in the standard is generally the amount shown as an asset or liability in a tax balance sheet (that is, using tax laws as a basis for accounting). Example 2 of appendix B of the standard shows the preparation of a tax balance sheet. But in some countries there is no requirement or custom to prepare or file a tax balance sheet with the tax authorities. In such cases, the tax bases can be obtained from the tax return or from the working papers for the taxable profit calculation.

13.108.1 The tax base might be different from the amount shown as an asset or liability in a tax balance sheet if there is uncertainty about the tax position. The entity might declare amounts in the tax return that could be subject to challenge by the tax authorities. In this case, management considers what it expects the outcome of any uncertainty will be; and it determines the appropriate tax base on this basis. If it is more likely than not that the uncertain item included in the tax return will be accepted by the tax authorities, the tax base used in the deferred tax calculation will be equal to the amount in the tax return. Otherwise, management calculates the tax base for use in the deferred tax calculation based on its expectations of the future tax consequences.

13.109 In many complex situations, the definitions of tax base are not easy to apply. Fortunately, a number of formulae exist for calculating tax bases; these are shown in the following paragraphs. These formulae can help to determine the tax base and apply the fundamental principle in paragraph 10 of IAS 12; this principle states that, with limited exceptions, an entity recognises a deferred tax liability (asset) whenever recovery or settlement of the carrying amount of an asset or liability would make future tax payments larger (smaller) than if such recovery or settlement had no tax consequences (see para 13.125).

[The next paragraph is 13.111.]

Tax base of an asset

13.111 The tax base of an asset is the amount that will be *deductible for tax purposes* against any *taxable economic benefits* flowing to an entity when it recovers the asset's carrying amount. If those economic benefits will not be taxable, the asset's tax base is equal to its carrying amount. [IAS 12 para 7]. The words in italics are included in the formula below; so their meaning needs to be understood.

13.112 An amount is 'deductible for tax purposes' if the deduction is allowed under the tax laws in determining taxable profits. For example, deductible amounts might include depreciation (or capital allowances) as an allowable deduction for tax purposes, and any indexation benefits for assets subject to tax on disposal. The deduction might be for the full amount, a portion or none of the asset's cost. The deduction might be allowed in the period when the asset is acquired or over a number of periods. If the tax laws allow an asset's full cost on acquisition to be deductible, the asset's tax base on initial acquisition is its cost. But if the asset's cost cannot be deducted in determining taxable profit, either over a number of periods or on disposal, the asset's tax base is nil.

13.113 'Taxable economic benefits' that flow to the entity in future periods are income earned from the asset's use or proceeds arising from its disposal that are included in determining taxable profits. Although an entity often generates economic benefits in excess of an asset's carrying amount through use or sale, the standard does not require an entity to estimate the excess economic benefits that will be generated by the asset. Rather, the standard focuses on the future tax consequences of recovering an asset only to the extent of the asset's carrying amount at the balance sheet date. This is because past transactions and events that affect the entity are recorded in the financial statements through the carrying amount.

13.114 In some circumstances, the economic benefits might not be taxable. Where this is so, the recovery of the asset's carrying amount has no future tax consequences; and so no deferred tax arises. It follows that the temporary difference is zero and the asset's tax base is equal to its carrying amount. This is consistent with the definition in paragraph 13.111. In other circumstances, only a proportion of the asset's carrying amount might be taxable (see example 2 in para 13.163).

13.115 Deferred tax is the future tax consequences of past transactions and events; and so the deductible and taxable amounts referred to above relate to future amounts. The past tax consequences associated with an asset, for example, income generated in prior periods as the carrying amount was realised through the asset's depreciation and capital allowances claimed in those earlier periods as allowable deductions are irrelevant, because they have already been reflected in the calculation of current tax.

13.116   As stated in paragraph 13.109, a formula exists to help determine an asset's tax base.

13.117   The formula can be used at the end of any reporting period; it is as follows:

Tax base of asset = Carrying amount − Future taxable amounts[1] + Future deductible amounts

[1] As noted in paragraph 13.113, IAS 12 focuses on the future tax consequences of recovering an asset only to the extent of the asset's carrying amount at the balance sheet date. So the taxable amount arising from recovery of the asset is limited to the asset's carrying amount.

13.117.1   The temporary difference on an asset is the difference between the asset's carrying amount and tax base. The formula for the temporary difference on an asset is as follows:

Temporary difference = Future taxable amounts — Future deductible amounts

13.118   In connection with the formula for the tax base of an asset, the future taxable amounts at the end of a reporting period will often be the same as the asset's carrying amount; so the first two terms in the formula will net to zero, leaving the future deductible amounts equal to the tax base at the end of the reporting period; this is also the asset's tax written down value. If the income generated by the asset is non-taxable, both the future taxable amounts and the future deductible amounts are nil; so the tax base is equal to the carrying amount (as stated in para 13.114) and there is a nil temporary difference.

13.119   The above formula depends on taxable amounts and deductible amounts for the recovery of an asset's carrying amount, so a number of different scenarios are possible; each scenario below has examples that apply the formula.

Scenario A — Recovery of asset gives rise to both taxable and deductible amounts

Example 1 – Tax base of a machine

A machine cost C1,000. For tax purposes, depreciation of C300 has been deducted in the current and prior periods; and the remaining cost will be deductible in future periods, either as depreciation or through a deduction on disposal. Revenue generated by using the machine is taxable; and any gain or loss on disposal of the machine will be taxable or deductible for tax purposes through a balancing adjustment (such as claw back of capital allowances claimed). For accounting purposes, the machine has been depreciated by C200.

The tax written down value of the asset is C700 (cost of C1,000 less tax depreciation claimed to date of C300), which is also the tax base.

Applying the formula, we have:

Carrying amount of asset	−	Future taxable amount	+	Future deductible amounts	=	Tax base
C800	−	C800	+	C700	=	C700

There is a taxable temporary difference of C100 (C800 — C700).

Example 2 – Tax base of inventory

Inventory at the balance sheet date has a carrying amount of C1,000. The inventory will be deductible for tax purposes when sold.

The amount that will be deductible for tax purposes if the inventory is sold is C1,000, which is its tax base.

Applying the formula, we have:

Carrying amount of asset	−	Future taxable amount	+	Future deductible amounts	=	Tax base
C1,000	−	C1,000	+	C1,000	=	C1,000

The temporary difference is C1,000 – C1,000 = Cnil.

Example 3 – Tax base of revalued land

Land was acquired for C1,000 at the beginning of the financial year. It is revalued to C1,500 at the balance sheet date. The indexed cost of the land at the balance sheet date for tax purposes is C1,100.

If the land is sold at its carrying amount of C1,500, the amount deductible for tax purposes is the indexed cost of C1,100, which is the tax base.

Applying the formula, we have:

Carrying amount of asset	−	Future taxable amount	+	Future deductible amounts	=	Tax base
C1,500	−	C1,500	+	C1,100	=	C1,100

There is a taxable temporary difference of C400 (C1,500 – C1,100).

The deferred tax consequences of the revaluation of land are considered further in paragraph 13.213 onwards.

Example 4 – Tax base of land carried at cost

Land was acquired for C1,000 at the start of the financial year. It is not revalued. The indexed cost of the land at the balance sheet date for tax purposes is C1,100. Under the tax rules applicable to the entity, indexation adjustments cannot create or increase a loss.

If the land is sold for the carrying amount of C1,000, the amount that will be deductible for tax purposes is C1,000 and not the indexed cost of C1,100.

Applying the formula, we have:

Carrying amount of asset	−	Future taxable amount	+	Future deductible amounts	=	Tax base
C1,000	−	C1,000	+	C1,000	=	C1,000

The temporary difference is C1,000 – C1,000 = Cnil.

Example 5 – Tax base of asset held for disposal

An asset costing C500 is carried in the balance sheet at a revalued amount of C700. The asset is held for disposal. For tax purposes, depreciation of C100 has been deducted in the current and prior periods. The gain on disposal will be taxed but limited to the tax allowance previously claimed.

The definition of tax base would suggest that the tax base is the amount that would be deductible in the future; that is, cost of C500 less tax depreciation claimed to date of C100 = C400, which is also the asset's tax written down value. But this is not the case, because not all of the asset's carrying amount of C700 at the balance sheet date would be taxable. The taxable gain is limited to tax allowances previously claimed, so the revaluation surplus of C200 is not taxable. Because the recovery of part of the asset is not taxable, this is equivalent to a tax deduction being available for that same amount. Applying the formula, the tax base becomes:

Carrying amount of asset	−	Future taxable amount	+	Future deductible amounts	=	Tax base
C700	−	C500	+	C400	=	C600

The temporary difference is C700 — C600 = C100 on which deferred tax should be provided. This amount matches the tax that would be payable if the asset was sold at its carrying amount at the balance sheet date (that is, revaluation surplus of C200, but restricted to tax depreciation of C100 previously claimed = C100).

The non-taxable element of the carrying amount (C200) forms part of the tax base (that is, the carrying amount of C700 less the future taxable amount of C500). There is also a deductible amount for the remaining C400 of tax depreciation to be received.

Example 6 – Tax base of asset held for disposal

Facts are the same as in example 5, except that the gain on disposal will be taxed and past tax allowances will be claimed back if the asset is sold at above cost.

The tax base is the amount that would be deductible in the future (that is, cost of C500 less tax depreciation claimed to date of C100 = C400), which is also the asset's tax written down value. Applying the formula, the tax base becomes:

Carrying amount of asset	−	Future taxable amount	+	Future deductible amounts	=	Tax base
C700	−	C700	+	C400	=	C400

Or the tax base can be calculated as the carrying amount of C700 — future taxable amount of C800 (including C100 of tax depreciation that will be clawed back) + future deductible amount of C500 (because C100 of tax depreciation will be clawed back) = C400.

The temporary difference is C700 — C400 = C300 on which deferred tax should be provided. This amount matches the tax that would be payable if the asset was sold at its carrying amount at the balance sheet date (that is, revaluation surplus of C200 + tax depreciation of C100 previously claimed = C300).

Scenario B — Recovery of asset gives rise to taxable amounts but not to deductible amounts

Example 1 – Tax base of interest receivable

Interest receivable has a carrying amount of C1,000. The related interest will be taxed on a cash basis.

The amount of the receivable that will be deductible for tax purposes when the interest is received is Cnil, which is its tax base.

Applying the formula, we have:

Carrying amount of asset	−	Future taxable amount	+	Future deductible amounts	=	Tax base
C1,000	−	C1,000	+	Cnil	=	Cnil

There is a taxable temporary difference of C1,000 (C1,000 – Cnil).

Example 2 – Tax base of foreign currency debtor

Foreign currency debtor has a carrying amount of C1,150 after recognising an exchange gain of C50 in profit or loss. The original amount of C1,100 was included in taxable profit. Exchange gains are taxable only when realised.

Because the original amount of C1,100 has already been included in taxable profit, it will not be taxable in the future when the asset is recovered. So an element of the foreign currency debtor is not taxable. This is similar to scenario A example 5. Where part of the carrying amount is not taxable, it is equivalent to a tax deduction being available for that amount. Applying the formula, we have:

Carrying amount of asset	−	Future taxable amount	+	Future deductible amounts	=	Tax base
C1,150	−	C50	+	Cnil	=	C1,100

There is a taxable temporary difference of C50 (C1,150 — C1,100).

The non-taxable element of the carrying amount (C1,100) forms part of the tax base (that is, the carrying amount of C1,150 less the future taxable amount of C50). Any deductible amounts to be received in the future should also be considered. In this case there are none, so the future deductible amount is Cnil.

Example 3 – Tax base of development expenditure

Development expenditure with a carrying amount of C1,000 is claimed as a deduction when paid. For accounting purposes, the development expenditure is amortised over 5 years.

When the development expenditure's carrying amount is recovered in the future through amortisation, the amount that will be deductible for tax purposes is Cnil, which is its tax base.

Applying the formula, we have:

Carrying amount of asset	−	Future taxable amount	+	Future deductible amounts	=	Tax base
C1,000	−	C1,000	+	Cnil	=	Cnil

There is a taxable temporary difference of C1,000 (C1,000 – Cnil).

Example 4 – Tax base of interest paid

Interest paid of C1,000 is capitalised as part of the asset's carrying amount. Tax deductions were obtained when the interest was paid.

When the asset's carrying amount is recovered in the future through amortisation, the amount of the interest expenditure that will be deductible for tax purposes is Cnil, which is its tax base.

Applying the formula, we have:

Carrying amount of asset	−	Future taxable amount	+	Future deductible amounts	=	Tax base
C1,000	−	C1,000	+	Cnil	=	Cnil

There is a taxable temporary difference of C1,000 (C1,000 − Cnil).

Scenario C — Recovery of asset does not give rise to taxable amounts but gives rise to deductible amounts

Example − Tax base of trade debtors

A portfolio of trade debtors with similar credit risk characteristics has a carrying amount of C5,000 after recognising a bad debt provision of C250. The original amount of C5,250 has already been included in taxable profits. The provision for bad debt is not tax deductible, but would be so when the individual assets are derecognised.

The first part of the definition of tax base would suggest that the debtor's tax base is C250, because that is the amount that will be deductible for tax purposes when the carrying amount of C5,000 is recovered. The second part of the definition would suggest that the tax base is equal to the carrying amount of C5,000, because the economic benefits are not taxable. But that is not the case, as noted in scenario A example 5. Applying the formula, we have:

Carrying amount of asset	−	Future taxable amount	+	Future deductible amounts	=	Tax base
C5,000	−	Cnil	+	C250	=	C5,250

There is a deductible temporary difference of C250 (C5,000 — C5,250).

Scenario D — Recovery of asset does not give rise to either taxable amounts or deductible amounts

Example 1 − Tax base of trade debtors with specific bad debt provision

Trade debtors have a carrying amount of C5,000 after recognising a specific provision of C250. The original amount of C5,250 has already been included in taxable profits. Specific provision of C250 is deductible for tax purposes when it is made.

Applying the formula, we have:

Carrying amount of asset	−	Future taxable amount	+	Future deductible amounts	=	Tax base
C5,000	−	Cnil	+	Cnil	=	C5,000

Example 2 – Tax base of dividend receivable

Management has recognised a dividend receivable of C100,000 from a wholly owned subsidiary in a single-entity set of financial statements. The dividend is not taxable.

Applying the formula, we have:

Carrying amount of asset	−	Future taxable amount	+	Future deductible amounts	=	Tax base
C100,000	−	Cnil	+	Cnil	=	C100,000

The temporary difference is C100,000 — C100,000 = Cnil.

Tax base of a liability

13.120 The tax base of a liability is its carrying amount less any amount that will be deductible for tax purposes in respect of that liability in future periods. For revenue that is received in advance, the tax base of the resulting liability is its carrying amount less any amount of the revenue that will not be taxable in future periods. [IAS 12 para 8].

13.121 The standard focuses on the future tax consequences of settling a liability at its carrying amount, as it does for assets. Management does not need to estimate the amount that might be payable on settlement. For example, where a premium is payable on redemption of a debt instrument, the tax base of the liability is calculated using the premium that has been accrued at the balance sheet date and not the premium that would be payable on redemption. Similarly, where a liability is recorded at a discounted amount under IAS 37, its tax base is determined using that amount and not the gross amount payable in the future; for example, where a tax deduction is available on settlement of a decommissioning liability.

13.122 A formula can be derived from first principles for determining a liability's tax base. But because the settlement of a liability's carrying amount involves the outflow rather than an inflow of economic resources, a liability can be regarded as a negative asset; therefore the equation for a liability's tax base can be obtained simply by changing the sign of each term in the formula for an asset's tax base as follows:

Tax base of liability = Carrying amount − Future deductible amounts + Future taxable amounts

13.122.1 The temporary difference on a liability is the difference between the liability's carrying amount and tax base. The formula is as follows:

Temporary difference = Future deductible amounts − Future taxable amounts

The future taxable amount of a liability is often nil, because no part of a liability's carrying amount (for example, a loan of C1,000) would normally be taxable or deductible when the liability is settled (but see example 3 below). So the formula above is consistent with the standard's definition in paragraph 13.120. Various examples are given below.

Example 1 – Tax base of a loan payable

A loan payable has a carrying amount of C1,000 at the balance sheet date. The repayment of the loan will have no tax consequences.

Applying the formula, we have:

Carrying amount of liability	–	Future deductible amounts	+	Future taxable amount	=	Tax base
C1,000	–	Cnil	+	Cnil	=	C1,000

The temporary difference is C1,000 — C1,000 = Cnil.

Example 2 – Tax base of accrued fines and penalties

Accrued fines and penalties that are not deductible for tax purposes have a carrying amount of C1,000 at the balance sheet date.

Applying the formula, we have:

Carrying amount of liability	–	Future deductible amounts	+	Future taxable amount	=	Tax base
C1,000	–	Cnil	+	Cnil	=	C1,000

The temporary difference is C1,000 — C1,000 = Cnil.

Example 3 – Tax base of foreign currency loan payable

Foreign currency loan payable has a carrying amount of C950 after recognising an exchange gain of C50 in profit or loss. Exchange gains are taxable only when realised.

When the loan is repaid at its carrying amount at the balance sheet date, the amount that would be included in future taxable amount is C50; and no part of the carrying amount would be deductible. Applying the formula, we have:

Carrying amount of liability	–	Future deductible amounts	+	Future taxable amount	=	Tax base
C950	–	Cnil	+	C50	=	C1,000

There is a taxable temporary difference of C50 (C950 — C1,000).

Example 4 – Tax base of accrued wages

Wages payable to employees amounting to C1,000 were accrued at the balance sheet date and allowed as a tax deduction when the expense was recognised.

Because wages have already been allowed as a deduction for tax, no further deductible or taxable amounts would arise in the future when the wages are paid.

Applying the formula, we have:

Carrying amount of liability	−	Future deductible amounts	+	Future taxable amount	=	Tax base
C1,000	−	Cnil	+	Cnil	=	C1,000

The temporary difference is C1,000 — C1,000 = Cnil.

Example 5 – Tax base of accrued long-service leave

A liability of C150,000 for long-service leave has been accrued at the balance sheet date under IAS 19. No deduction will be available for tax until the long-service leave is paid.

Applying the formula, we have:

Carrying amount of liability	−	Future deductible amounts	+	Future taxable amount	=	Tax base
C150,000	−	C150,000	+	Cnil	=	Cnil

There is a deductible temporary difference of C150,000 (C150,000 — Cnil).

Tax base of revenue received in advance

13.123   The formula for the tax base of a liability that is 'revenue received in advance' is consistent with the definition in paragraph 13.120.

> Tax base = Carrying amount − Amount of revenue that will not be taxable in future periods

Where revenue is taxed on a cash basis, amounts recognised in the balance sheet as 'revenue received in advance' will not be taxed in a future period when recognised as revenue for accounting purposes. In this case (or if the revenue is not taxed at all), the tax base of the revenue received in advance is equal to zero. But the tax base of revenue received in advance is equal to its carrying amount if the entire amount is taxed when subsequently recognised as revenue. These situations are dealt with in the following examples.

Example 1 – Tax base of rents received in advance

Rents received in advance amounted to C1,000 at the balance sheet date. The rental income will be taxed in future periods when accommodation is provided to tenants.

Applying the formula, we have:

Carrying amount of revenue received in advance		Amount of revenue that will not be taxable in future periods	=	Tax base
C1,000	–	Cnil	=	C1,000

The temporary difference is C1,000 – C1,000 = Cnil.

Example 2 – Tax base of government grant

A government grant of C1,000 is recognised at the balance sheet date as deferred income rather than being deducted against the cost of the asset. No tax is payable on receipt of the grant or on amortisation. The cost of the asset is fully deductible.

Applying the formula, we have:

Carrying amount of revenue received in advance		Amount of revenue that will not be taxable in future periods	=	Tax base
C1,000	–	C1,000	=	Cnil

There is a deductible temporary difference of C1,000 (C1,000 – Cnil).

Example 3 – Tax base of royalties

Royalties from users of licensed technology for the following financial year amounted to C25,000 at the balance sheet date. Royalties are taxed on a cash receipts basis. The royalty income is deferred in the balance sheet until the period that it relates to.

Applying the formula, we have:

Carrying amount of revenue received in advance		Amount of revenue that will not be taxable in future periods	=	Tax base
C25,000	–	C25,000	=	Cnil

There is a deductible temporary difference of C25,000 (C25,000 – Cnil).

Tax bases with no recognised carrying amounts

13.124 Some items might have a tax base but are not recognised as assets or liabilities on the balance sheet. Where a transaction during the reporting period does not give rise to an asset or liability on the balance sheet but affects taxable profits of future periods, its tax base is calculated using the amount that would affect taxable profits in future periods; for example, expenditure incurred during the year that is written off for accounting purposes but is carried forward in the tax balance sheet at an amount that will be allowable as a deduction in future periods. The difference between the tax base of the costs expensed and the carrying amount of nil is a deductible temporary difference that gives rise to a deferred tax asset. [IAS 12 para 9].

Tax bases not immediately apparent

13.125 The above formulae for determining the tax bases of assets and liabilities should give the correct result in most circumstances. But there could be some rare circumstances where the formulae cannot be readily applied or where the tax base of an asset or liability is not immediately apparent. In those circumstances, an entity should consider the fundamental principle of recognition of deferred tax: that is, with limited exceptions, the entity recognises a deferred tax liability (asset) whenever recovery or settlement of the carrying amount of an asset or liability would make future tax payments larger (smaller) than if such recovery or settlement had no tax consequences. [IAS 12 para 10]. Example C of paragraph 52 of the standard (not reproduced here) illustrates how the fundamental principle is applied where the tax base of an asset or a liability depends on the expected manner of recovery or settlement (see further para 13.170). An example is given in paragraph 13.172.

Recognising deferred tax liabilities

13.126 As explained in paragraph 13.98, all taxable temporary differences give rise to deferred tax liabilities and, with some exceptions, are recognised in the financial statements. A deferred tax liability is recognised even if future tax losses are expected to relieve the liability. A taxable temporary difference might be expected to reverse in a period in which a tax loss arises; this could result in the entity not having to pay any tax for the reversing temporary difference; but the entity will still suffer a sacrifice of future economic benefits, because the benefit derived from the tax loss in future periods will be reduced by the amount of the reversing taxable temporary difference. So IAS 12 requires all deferred tax liabilities to be recognised, except in the limited circumstances described below.

13.127 A deferred tax liability should be recognised for all taxable temporary differences, except where it arises from:

■ The initial recognition of goodwill (see para 13.158 onwards).

■ The initial recognition of an asset or liability in a transaction which:

- is not a business combination; and

- at the time of the transaction, does not affect accounting profit or taxable profit (tax loss) (see para 13.162 onwards).

■ Investment in subsidiaries, branches and associates, and interests in joint ventures, where:

- the parent, investor or venturer is able to control the timing of the reversal of the temporary difference; and

- it is probable that the temporary difference will not reverse in the foreseeable future (see para 13.233.2 onwards).

[IAS 12 paras 15, 39].

13.127.1 The method of accounting for a taxable temporary difference depends on the nature of the transaction that led to the asset or liability being recognised initially. If a transaction is not a business combination (where any adjustment for deferred tax would impact on the amount of goodwill recognised) and does not affect accounting profit or taxable profit, an entity would, in the absence of the exemption described in the second bullet point above, recognise any resulting deferred tax liability (or deferred tax asset – see para 13.128) and adjust the asset or liability's carrying amount by the same amount. The standard states that such adjustments would make the financial statements less transparent. So an entity does not recognise the resulting deferred tax liability (or asset), either on initial recognition or subsequently. Also, an entity does not recognise changes in the unrecognised deferred tax liability or asset as the asset is depreciated. [IAS 12 para 22(c)]. See further paragraph 13.162 onwards.

13.127.2 Tax planning opportunities are not considered in determining the amount of a deferred tax liability to be recognised. For instance, an entity cannot avoid recognising an existing deferred tax liability on the grounds that future tax losses will prevent the transfer of economic benefits, as noted in paragraph 13.126. Tax planning opportunities can only be considered in determining the extent to which an existing deferred tax *asset* will be recovered, as explained in paragraph 13.138.

Recognising deferred tax assets

13.128 An asset is recognised in the balance sheet when it is probable that the future economic benefits will flow to the entity and the asset has a cost or value that can be measured reliably. When deductible temporary differences reverse in future periods, they result in deductions in calculating the taxable profits of those future periods. But economic benefits of the tax deductions can only be realised if the entity earns sufficient taxable profits against which the deductions can be offset. So a deferred tax asset should be recognised for all deductible temporary differences to the extent that it is *probable* that taxable profit will be available against which the deductible temporary difference can be utilised, unless the deferred tax asset arises from:

- The initial recognition of an asset or liability in a transaction which:

    - is not a business combination; and

    - at the time of the transaction, does not affect accounting profit or taxable profit (tax loss).

[IAS 12 para 24].

13.129 In addition, an entity should also recognise a deferred tax asset for all deductible temporary differences associated with investments in subsidiaries, branches and associates, and interests in joint ventures, to the extent that it is probable that:

- the temporary difference will reverse in the foreseeable future; and

- taxable profit will be available against which the temporary difference can be utilised.

[IAS 12 para 44].

13.129.1 Deferred tax assets arising on the initial recognition of goodwill are not included in the exception in paragraph 24 of IAS 12 from recognising deferred tax assets. If the carrying amount of goodwill arising in a business combination is less than its tax base, the difference gives rise to a deferred tax asset. The deferred tax asset arising from the initial recognition of goodwill is recognised as part of the accounting for a business combination; to the extent that it is probable that taxable profit will be available against which the deductible temporary difference could be utilised. [IAS 12 para 32A]. This differs from the situation where a deferred tax liability arises on the initial recognition of goodwill, where an exception does apply (see paras 13.159 and 13.161.1).

13.130 The term 'probable' (referred to in para 13.128) is not defined in IAS 12; but IFRS 5 states: *"For the purposes of IFRSs, probable is defined as 'more likely than not'"*. [IFRS 5 App A, BC 81]. In other words, if it is more likely than not that all or some of the deferred tax asset will be recovered, a deferred tax asset should be recognised for the whole or the part that is more likely than not to be recovered.

13.131 In order to recover a deferred tax asset, an entity would have to do more than simply *not make losses* in future: it would have to *make sufficient taxable profits*.

13.132 All available evidence has to be considered to justify recognising deferred tax assets; this means both favourable and unfavourable evidence. If there is no unfavourable evidence, and the entity has historically been profitable and paid taxes, it may well be concluded that the situation will continue *in the absence of knowledge of facts to the contrary*; and, since there is an expectation of sufficient future taxable profit, that recording a deferred tax asset is appropriate. However, greater care is needed if the losses are very significant relative to expected annual profits. Any unfavourable evidence should also be considered carefully.

Unfavourable evidence can often be objectively verified where it arises from a past event. But it is more difficult to objectively verify positive evidence of future taxable profits. Therefore, evidence of future taxable profits might be assigned lesser weight in assessing whether a deferred tax asset should be recorded when there is other unfavourable evidence. The assessment of future taxable profits, including the period over which such an assessment is made, is considered further in paragraph 13.135.3.

Sources of future taxable profit available to offset deductible temporary differences

13.133 The future realisation of deferred tax assets depends on whether sufficient taxable profit of the appropriate type (trading profit or capital gain) is expected to be available for the utilisation of deductible temporary differences or unused tax losses. The sufficient taxable profit must be available to the 'taxable entity' where those deductible temporary differences or unused tax losses originated, in order for an asset to be recognised by that entity. The meaning of 'taxable entity' is considered further in paragraph 13.156. The following sources of future taxable profit might be available under the tax law to offset deductible temporary differences.

Future reversals of existing taxable temporary differences

13.134 The future reversal of existing taxable temporary differences gives rise to an increase in taxable income. So, to the extent that those profits:

■ relate to the same taxable entity (see para 13.156 onwards);

■ are assessed by the same taxation authority; and

■ arise in the same period in which existing deductible temporary differences are expected to reverse or in a period to which a tax loss arising from the reversal of the deferred tax asset might be carried back or forward;

the asset is regarded as recoverable. [IAS 12 para 28]. In other words, where deferred tax liabilities meeting the above offset criteria exceed deferred tax assets at the balance sheet date and the reversal periods are consistent, a deferred tax asset is recognised.

Example 1 – Recovery of capital tax losses

An entity has a portfolio of properties and has brought forward capital tax losses that can be carried forward indefinitely. In the current year, the entity has revalued its land and buildings; this has resulted in a deferred tax liability for land on a capital gains tax basis being recognised in respect of land and buildings. The entity does not expect to realise the capital gain arising from the revaluation for a number of years. Is the entity required to recognise a deferred tax asset now in respect of the capital losses?

Paragraph 24 of IAS 12 states that deferred tax assets 'shall' be recognised for all deductible temporary differences to the extent that taxable profit will be available against which the deductible temporary differences can be utilised. So the entity is required to recognise a deferred tax asset in respect of the capital losses. If those losses can properly be utilised against the future crystallisation of the capital gains.

If there is no current intention to realise the capital gain by selling the properties, the recognition of the deferred tax liability is not affected. The difference between the tax base (which remains the same despite the revaluation) and the asset's revalued carrying amount is a temporary difference that gives rise to a deferred tax liability.

In terms of presentation, the entity offsets the deferred tax liability arising from the revaluation and the deferred tax asset in respect of the capital losses if they meet the criteria in paragraph 74 of IAS 12 (that is, if there is a legal right to offset the deferred tax assets and liabilities and they relate to the same taxation authority).

Example 2 – Recovery of deferred tax asset against deferred tax liabilities

An entity has taxable temporary differences of C80,000 in respect of deferred tax liabilities; these are expected to be included in taxable income at a rate of C20,000 a year in years 1 to 4. The entity also has a warranty provision of C40,000 that is expected to be deductible for tax purposes as follows: C30,000 in year 2 and C10,000 in year 3. In addition, the entity has unused tax losses of C60,000. A schedule of the reversal of temporary differences and the utilisation of tax losses carried forward is shown below:

	Year 1 C	Year 2 C	Year 3 C	Year 4 C
Taxable temporary differences – expected reversal profile				
Beginning of year	80,000	60,000	40,000	20,000
Recognised in taxable income	(20,000)	(20,000)	(20,000)	(20,000)
End of year	60,000	40,000	20,000	–
Deductible temporary differences – expected reversal profile				
(a) Warranty provisions				
Beginning of year	40,000	40,000	10,000	–
Deducted for tax purposes	–	(30,000)	(10,000)	–
End of year	40,000	10,000	–	–
(b) Tax losses				
Beginning of year	60,000	40,000	50,000	40,000
Increase (utilisation) in year	(20,000)	10,000	(10,000)	(20,000)
End of year	40,000	50,000	40,000	20,000
Total deductible temporary differences	80,000	60,000	40,000	20,000

At the end of year 1, the entity would recognise a deferred tax asset in respect of at least C60,000 of the deductible temporary differences and tax losses at the appropriate tax rate. This is because there are taxable temporary differences in respect of deferred tax liabilities of the same amount that are expected to be included in taxable income; and against which the expected reversal of deductible temporary differences and the tax losses can be utilised.

For similar reasons, a deferred tax asset in respect of at least C40,000 of deductible temporary differences and tax losses would be recognised at the end of year 2, and C20,000 at the end of year 3, if circumstances remained the same at those dates.

However, in order to recognise a deferred tax asset in any of years 1 to 4 with respect to the C20,000 of tax losses that remain unutilised, the entity might need to look for sources of taxable profit other than reversals of temporary differences (see para 13.135).

13.134.1 The implications of existing deferred tax liabilities with regards to recognising a deferred tax asset in relation to a deficit on a defined benefit pension scheme are considered in paragraph 13.203.1.

Future taxable profits

13.135 Where there are insufficient taxable temporary differences against which the deferred tax asset can be offset, management should consider the likelihood that taxable profits will arise in the same period(s) as the reversal of the deductible temporary differences (or in the periods into which a tax loss arising from the deferred tax asset can be carried back or forward). [IAS 12 para 29(a)]. The assessment of taxable profits should take account of the tax rules governing the relief of losses, such as the type of profits permitted to be used (that is, trading profit or capital gain). Also, management needs to consider if the assessment of taxable profits is restricted to the entity with the losses, or whether group relief is available.

13.135.1 In determining future taxable profits, deductible temporary differences that originate in future periods are generally not taken into consideration. The deferred tax asset arising from them will require future taxable profit in order to be utilised. [IAS 12 para 29(a)].

Example – Determining future taxable profits

An entity has tax losses carried forward of C125, which expire after 5 years, and is considering how much of this total can be recognised as a deferred tax asset. Profits before tax allowances for depreciation of plant are expected to be C25 for each of the next 5 years (that is, C125 in total), less tax deductions of C10 per annum; this would result in profits after tax allowances of C15 per annum for the five years (C75 in total). Profits after 5 years are expected to be nil; so, if the tax allowances are deferred, profits will not support their subsequent recovery.

If the tax allowances are claimed in years 1 to 5, the taxable profits will be as follows:

	Years 1 to 5	Years 6 to 10	Total
	C	C	C
Taxable profit before deduction	125	–	125
Tax deduction for plant	(50)	–	(50)
Taxable profit	**75**	**–**	**75**
Loss carry-forwards utilised	(75)	–	(75)

In this situation, C50 of the losses remain unutilised.

If the allowances are disclaimed in years 1 to 5 (so they are available for deduction in years 6 to 10), the taxable profit will be as follows:

	Years 1 to 5	Years 6 to 10	Total
	C	C	C
Taxable profit before deduction	125	–	125
Tax deduction for plant	–	(50)	(50)
Taxable profit	**125**	**(50)**	**75**
Adjustment for disclaimed tax deductions (see below)	(50)	50	–
Taxable profit before utilisation of losses	**75**	**–**	**75**

The result of disclaiming the tax allowances is higher taxable profit in years 1 to 5 of C125 in total. But the overall expected future taxable profits are still C75 in total. So the total tax deductions of C50 should be considered when determining the amount of taxable profit available for utilisation of the brought-forward losses.

Thus, the amount of profit available for recovering the deferred tax asset will be C15 × 5 = C75, rather than C25 × 5 = C125 which would be the amount of profit if the tax deductions were not claimed.

This is because the entity only has an asset if it will gain future economic benefits from the item in question. If it can only gain those future economic benefits by deferring or waiving other future economic benefits due to the entity, in 'net' terms there is no asset.

13.135.1.1 In determining the sufficiency of taxable profits under IAS 12, taxable amounts arising from future deductible temporary differences are generally ignored. But careful analysis is needed where losses cannot be carried forward indefinitely. A deferred tax asset is recognised under IAS 12 where an entity has tax planning opportunities that will create taxable profit in appropriate periods (see para 13.136 onwards). This can mean that unused losses are recoverable out of taxable profits made available by deferring claims for deductions, as this creates a deductible temporary difference. A similar situation arises without tax planning where deductions are given under the relevant tax rules in later periods than the related accounting charge; this also creates a deductible temporary difference.

13.135.1.2 Particular issues arise where profit forecasts include the amounts relevant for tax purposes (rather than the accounting deductions); and where losses that would otherwise expire are only recoverable against taxable profits arising as a result of future deductible temporary differences. In such cases, those taxable profits can only be taken into account if the deferred tax assets relating to the future deductible temporary differences can also be recovered.

> **Example – Interaction of losses and deductible temporary differences**
>
> An entity has unused losses of C300 and is assessing whether it can recognise a deferred tax asset. The losses expire in 5 years' time. The entity is forecasting an accounting loss of C100 in year 1, but this is after charging C400 for a loss on a loan. The tax deduction for the loan can be deferred, and the entity intends to claim this after year 5 (that is, in years 6 to 10).
>
> Accounting profits in years 2 to 5 are forecast to be nil, and in years 6 to 10 to be C600 in total.
>
> | | Years 1 to 5 | Years 6 to 10 | Total |
> |---|---|---|---|
> | | C | C | C |
> | Accounting result before loan loss | 300 | 600 | 900 |
> | Loan loss | (400) | – | (400) |
> | **Accounting result** | **(100)** | **600** | **500** |
> | | | | |
> | Taxable profit before loan loss deduction | 300 | 600 | 900 |
> | Loan loss deduction | – | (400) | (400) |
> | Loss carry-forwards utilised | (300) | – | (300) |
> | **Taxable profit** | **–** | **200** | **200** |
>
> Overall, there are sufficient taxable profits (C900) to recover both the loss carry-forwards (C300) and the loan loss deduction (C400). So a deferred tax asset in respect of the loss carry-forwards is recognised in the current year.

13.135.1.3 The underlying principle in IAS 12 means that a deferred tax asset is not recognised when it is only recoverable through the future creation of, or replacement with, a new unrecoverable deferred tax asset. But a deferred tax asset is recognised where an otherwise profitable entity has expiring unused losses that can be recovered by tax planning (or other deferral of deductions), and those losses create originating deductible temporary differences that are themselves recoverable.

13.135.2 To avoid double counting, taxable profits resulting from the reversal of deferred tax liabilities are excluded from the estimation of future taxable profits where they have been used to support the recognition of deferred tax assets in accordance with paragraph 28 of IAS 12 (see para 13.134).

13.135.3 A strong earnings history will provide the most objective evidence in assuming future profitability when assessing the extent to which a deferred tax asset can be recognised. Hence, there would be less need for profitable entities to consider the pattern and timing of the reversals of existing temporary differences.

13.135.4 Where there is a balance of favourable and unfavourable evidence, careful consideration is given to recoverability of a deferred tax asset based on the entity's projections for taxable profits for each year after the balance sheet date. The amount of taxable profits considered more likely than not for each period is assessed. Management should have regard to any time limit on carry forward of tax losses. The level of taxable profit might be more difficult to predict the longer into the future an assessment is required; but there should be no arbitrary cut-off in the time period over which such an assessment is made. Management should also ensure that the projections on which such assessments are based are broadly consistent with the assumptions made about the future in relation to other aspects of financial accounting (for example, impairment testing), except where relevant standards require a different treatment (for example, impairment testing should not take account of future investment). Also, consideration should be given to the disclosures about key sources of uncertainty required by paragraph 125 of IAS 1 (see para 13.307.1).

13.135.5 Some entities by their nature would not ordinarily recognise deferred tax assets not supported through reversals of existing temporary differences. Examples of such entities are development stage enterprises and start-up businesses. In these cases, the lack of a track record for profits means that a deferred tax asset is unlikely to be recognised. As noted in paragraph 13.132, evidence of future taxable profits might be assigned lesser weight in assessing whether a deferred tax asset should be recorded when there is other unfavourable evidence (such as actual trading losses). An exception might be where the entity has a contract in place that provides a future revenue stream (which exceeds expected costs).

13.135.6 The assessment of the likelihood that taxable profits will arise when there has been a history of trading losses is discussed in paragraph 13.144 onwards.

Tax planning opportunities

13.136 Entities sometimes take advantage of tax planning opportunities to reduce their future tax liabilities. So an entity should consider whether it expects to create suitable taxable profits by undertaking tax planning opportunities. [IAS 12 para 29(b)]. At first sight this might seem at odds with the standard's general thrust that no account should be taken of future events. But putting in place a tax scheme that might reduce future expenses or create additional income is really no different from procuring orders that will result in future sales. Both actions will create future taxable profits to enable a deferred tax asset to be recovered.

13.137 A tax planning opportunity is an action that the entity would not normally take – except to prevent, say, an unused tax loss from expiring. Such actions could include:

- Accelerating taxable amounts or deferring claims for writing-down allowances to recover losses being carried forward (perhaps before they expire) – but see paragraph 13.137.1.

- Changing the character of taxable or deductible amounts from trading gains or losses to capital gains or losses, or vice versa.

- Switching from tax-free to taxable investments.

[IAS 12 para 30].

13.137.1 Where tax planning opportunities bring taxable profit from a later period to an earlier period, a tax loss or tax credit carry-forward can only be utilised where there is future taxable profit from sources other than future originating temporary differences. [IAS 12 para 30]. This is considered further in paragraph 13.135.1.1 onwards.

13.138 Tax planning opportunities should only be considered to determine the extent to which an existing deferred tax asset will be realised. They cannot be used to create a new deferred tax asset or to avoid recognising or reducing a deferred tax liability (see para 13.141). The feasibility of the tax planning opportunity is assessed based on the individual facts and circumstances of each case. Whatever tax planning opportunities are considered, management should be capable of undertaking and implementing them, and should have the expectation that it will implement them.

13.139 An entity might incur various expenses in implementing a tax planning opportunity. A question arises whether the tax benefit of the expenses could be included in the carrying amount of any deferred tax asset recognised as a result of the plan's implementation, or included in current tax expense. We believe that any deferred tax asset recognised as a result of implementing a tax planning opportunity should be recorded net of the tax effects of any expenses or losses expected to be incurred as a result of the opportunity; this is because that is the net amount by which future tax payments will be reduced as a result of implementing it.

Example – Expenses of tax planning opportunity

An entity has gross deductible temporary differences of C1,000 in respect of a deferred tax asset that is not recognised in the balance sheet. The tax rate is 30% and so the unrecognised deferred tax asset is C300. As a result of implementing a tax planning opportunity, the entity expects to generate taxable profits of at least C1,000. But the cost of implementing the opportunity is expected to be C200. Therefore, only C800 of future taxable profits would be available against which the deferred tax asset can be offset. A maximum deferred tax asset of C240 (C800 @ 30%) would qualify for recognition. The remaining C60 will remain unrecognised. In other words, the deferred tax asset of C300 is reduced by C60, which is the tax benefit of the expenses that the entity expects to incur for implementing the tax planning opportunity.

13.140 Where a tax planning opportunity is used to support realisation of unused tax losses in a business combination, the same principles apply; so the benefit of any deferred tax asset recognised should also be reduced by the tax effects of any expenses or losses incurred to implement a tax planning opportunity.

13.141 Tax planning opportunities cannot be taken into account to recognise a reduced deferred tax liability. For instance, an entity cannot avoid recognising an existing deferred tax liability on the grounds that future tax losses will prevent the transfer of economic benefits. See also paragraph 13.126.

13.142 Some examples of tax planning opportunities are considered below:

Example 1 – Sale of appreciated assets when operating losses are projected

An entity has experienced operating losses over the last five years; accumulated tax losses of C20m have given rise to a potential unrecognised deferred tax asset of C6m. Based on its plans to introduce a new product line, management is currently projecting that for the next three years it will experience losses of at least C1m per year (and of approximately C5m in total); it then expects to 'turn the corner' and become profitable. Because of appreciation in the property market, the entity's investment in a shopping centre property is now valued at approximately C500,000 more than the carrying amount in the balance sheet. The entity proposes to recognise a deferred tax asset of C150,000 (C500,000 × 30%) based on a tax planning opportunity to sell the investment. The shopping centre property is not a 'core' asset of the entity; and management says that it would sell the property, if necessary, before it would permit the unused tax losses to expire.

We believe that this tax planning opportunity does not justify recognising a deferred tax asset. A tax planning opportunity to sell appreciated assets constitutes a subset of the broader source of future taxable profit from operations. So a deferred tax asset is not recognised when the tax planning opportunity appears merely to reduce an expected future loss. In the above case, based on (a) the entity's history of losses, (b) an unproved new product line, and (c) the fact that the entity does not anticipate being profitable for at least three years, little weight can be assigned to the projected profitability. Accordingly, there is no incremental tax benefit (at least for the foreseeable future), as the potential gain on the sale of the shopping centre property would only reduce what is otherwise a larger operating loss.

Example 2 – Acquisition of a profitable entity

An entity that has incurred losses for many years proposes a tax planning opportunity to support its deferred tax asset related to unused tax losses. The entity will use a portion of the cash balances it received from a recent public share offering to acquire an entity that generates significant taxable profits. Could such a tax planning opportunity be considered to recognise the deferred tax asset?

No. We believe that a proposed business combination and the accompanying availability of sufficient taxable profits should not be anticipated for the purpose of supporting a deferred tax asset. Until the acquisition of the entity is irrevocable and there are no further statutory or regulatory impediments, the acquirer needs the co-operation of others to make the tax planning opportunity effective. That is, the acquirer does not control an essential part of the tax planning opportunity (the target entity). It would not be appropriate to use future taxable profits in the target entity to support recognising the acquirer's tax losses, as the target entity does not form part of the group holding the tax losses and will not do so until the business combination occurs. As a result, the tax effects of an event such as the acquisition of an entity should not be recognised before the event has occurred. However, once the acquisition has taken place, the acquirer can recognise a deferred tax asset as a credit to the tax charge in the post-acquisition period under paragraph 67 of IAS 12 (see further para 13.250).

Example 3 – Unused tax losses in an acquiree

Entity B has unrecognised deferred tax assets related to unused tax losses. Entity C bought entity B in December 20X3.

Entity C's management intends to integrate entity B's operations into entity C in the first quarter of 20X4 to take advantage of the tax losses. Entity C has a track record of generating taxable profits; and management expects this to continue for the foreseeable future.

In this situation, management should recognise a deferred tax asset in respect of the unused tax losses in the consolidated financial statements for the period ended 31 December 20X3 if it is probable that management will carry out the integration, and also that entity C will generate enough taxable profit to absorb entity B's unused tax losses. This will impact the goodwill calculation in the consolidated financial statements.

This contrasts with the situation in example 2, as both the newly acquired entity holding the losses (entity B) and the profitable entity (entity C) are part of the same group at the balance sheet date.

[The next paragraph is 13.144.]

Unused tax losses and unused tax credits

Trading losses

13.144 Where an entity has tax losses that can be relieved against a tax liability for a previous year, those losses are recognised as an asset, because the tax relief is recoverable by refund of tax previously paid. [IAS 12 para 14]. This asset can be shown separately in the financial statements as a debtor, or it can be offset against an existing current tax balance.

UK.13.144.1 In the UK, where a company incurs a trading loss for tax purposes, that loss is determined after any capital allowances given in that trade have been deducted, and can be offset against other profits (including chargeable gains) made in the same accounting period. If the loss cannot be used against the current period's profits, it can be carried back against the preceding year's profits. Any trading losses of a company that are not offset against current profits or profits of the previous period can be carried forward to be offset against the first available profits of the same trade for later accounting periods.

13.145 Where tax losses can be relieved only by carry-forward against taxable profits of future periods, a deductible temporary difference arises. If an entity maintains a deferred tax account that will result in future tax payable, the tax losses will be recoverable by offset against taxable income that arises when those taxable temporary differences reverse. [IAS 12 para 36(a)]. So losses carried forward can be offset against deferred tax liabilities carried in the balance sheet, as discussed in paragraph 13.134.

13.146 Where the deferred tax liabilities are not sufficient to absorb all the tax losses, management should consider other convincing evidence suggesting that suitable taxable profits will be generated in future (see the example in para 13.134). This consideration becomes difficult, because the very existence of unrelieved tax losses is strong evidence that future taxable profit might not be available. Because of this significant uncertainty about future taxable profits being available, in the absence of profits arising from the reversals of existing temporary differences, the amount of the deferred tax asset and the nature of the evidence supporting its recognition should be disclosed (see para 13.306). [IAS 12 para 35].

13.147 The standard includes criteria that should be considered to determine whether a deferred tax asset in respect of unused tax losses or unused tax credits should be recognised. Some of these criteria are the same as for recognising deferred tax assets in respect of deductible temporary differences, such as the availability of sufficient taxable temporary differences and tax planning opportunities (discussed above).

13.148 For unrelieved trading losses resulting from identifiable causes, it is important to consider whether those losses are likely to recur. Where they are likely to recur, it is unlikely that a deferred tax asset can be recognised. Another criterion considered by the standard is the availability of taxable profits before unused tax losses or unused tax credits expire. [IAS 12 para 36(b)].

UK.13.148.1 This latter criterion is not relevant in the UK, because tax losses can be carried forward indefinitely under UK tax rules.

13.149 As noted in paragraph 13.135.3, a strong earnings history will provide the most objective evidence in assuming future profitability when assessing the extent to which a deferred tax asset can be recognised. This justification becomes stronger if the tax loss arises from identifiable causes that are unlikely to recur, as stated above.

13.150 For entities with no record of profit in recent years, a more rigorous assessment is required of how probable it is that taxable profit will be available against which unrelieved tax losses can be utilised. A history of recent losses creates a level of uncertainty about an entity's future profitability that could be difficult to rebut. If it is not probable that taxable profit will be available, the deferred tax asset is not recognised. [IAS 12 para 35]. See also paragraph 13.135.5 for start-up businesses.

13.150.1 The further into the future it is necessary to look for sufficient taxable profits (the 'look-out' period), the more subjective the projections become. How far an entity should look into the future should be based on the stability and trend in past earnings and on the nature of the business or industry. In the past, one approach has been to project into the future the same number of years as the number of years since the entity has returned to profitability. In those cases, the average annual income for a past period was deemed an indicator of income for a defined number of future years. But it is difficult to reconcile this approach with the requirement to assess the probable future taxable profits.

13.150.2 As noted in paragraph 13.135.4, there should be no arbitrary cut-off in the time period over which an assessment of expected taxable profits is made (for example, the recoverability test should not be limited using an arbitrary look-out period solely because budget information is not available after a certain number of years). The assessment should be broadly consistent with the assumptions used for impairment testing (see further chapter 18), allowing for adjustments for the different time-frame (if the tax losses have expiry dates) and the different methods; these include discounting and the value in use model in IAS 36 (which prohibits inclusion of estimated future cash inflows or outflows from improving or enhancing assets' performance) as compared to a calculation with no discounting and including the impact of future asset improvements under IAS 12.

13.150.3 It could be argued that the probability of taxable profits decreases over time; so there could be a point when taxable profits are no longer probable. However, we consider that management should not generally assume without specific facts (for example, significant contracts or patent rights terminating at a specific date) that no taxable profits are probable after a specified date. The calculation should include the maximum taxable profits that are more probable than not until the expiry of tax losses. This could result in lower estimates for years in the distant future, but it does not mean that those years should not be considered.

13.150.4 Another issue is whether a limited look-out period might be acceptable for industries that historically have profit- and loss-making cycles. Similar to the arguments above, we consider that management cannot generally assume that the entity will not make taxable profits after a limited number of years of industrial upturn. The cyclical downturns should be considered in determining the 'probable' future cash flows, but they should not be used to introduce an arbitrary cut-off date for the recoverability test.

13.150.5 We do not believe that this approach will necessarily lead to recognising only the full or a nil deferred tax asset (that is, an 'all or nothing' approach). Instead, we consider that an assessment should be made of future taxable profits looking forward, with no arbitrary or specified cut-off period. A deferred tax asset is recognised to the extent it is probable that there will be future taxable profits.

13.150.6 In considering whether to provide guidance on how to apply the probability criterion for recognising deferred tax assets arising from unused tax losses, in June 2005 the IFRS IC noted that the criterion should be applied to portions of the total amount of unused tax losses and not just to the amount of unused tax losses taken as a whole. This is consistent with the guidance above.

13.150.7 Where an entity determines its future taxable profits to support recognising a deferred tax asset for trading losses, management should consider a tax planning opportunity that could be undertaken to allow the deferred tax asset to be recovered (see para 13.138). On the other hand, a restructuring or exit plan is normally regarded as an ordinary part of running a business and might be considered, depending on the likelihood of implementing the plan and its expected success.

> **Example – Strategy to implement an exit plan**
>
> An entity has a history of recent losses. Management has developed an exit plan in which a loss-making activity will be discontinued. Management intends to implement the measures from March 20X4. The current date is January 20X4 and the plan has not yet been made public.
>
> Management expects to reverse the losses over the two years following the implementation of the exit plan, and proposes to recognise a deferred tax asset in respect of the losses in the 31 December 20X3 financial statements, using the exit plan to justify the recognition of the deferred tax asset.
>
> A deferred tax asset should be recognised in respect of the losses to the extent that it is probable that future taxable profit will be available against which the unused tax losses can be utilised.

The probability of future taxable profits should be assessed based on circumstances as at the balance sheet date.

The following factors should be considered:

- The probability that management will implement the plan.

- Management's ability to implement the plan (for example, obtaining concessions from labour unions or regulatory approval).

- The level of detailed analysis and sensitivity analysis that management has prepared.

Judgement will be required to establish whether it is probable that the exit plan will go ahead and that taxable profits will be earned. If, at the balance sheet date, management has not finalised its decision to sell, it could be difficult to argue that it is more likely than not that the exit plan will be implemented.

In some cases, management will also need to assess the probability of the disposal at the balance sheet date for the purposes of IFRS 5. If a subsidiary's disposal is considered 'highly probable' for the purposes of IFRS 5 and a taxable profit is expected to be made on the transaction, this would strongly indicate that a deferred tax asset should be recognised in respect of the previously unrecognised losses.

Capital losses

13.151 The offset rules in tax legislation might mean that a deferred tax asset in respect of a capital loss cannot be offset against deferred tax liabilities arising from trading items; in this case, the deferred tax asset will be recognised only if it can be offset against recognised deferred tax liabilities on unrealised capital gains, or there is strong evidence that it will be recoverable against capital gains that are expected to arise in the future. Capital gains might arise in the future as a result of taxable temporary differences in existence at the balance sheet date, from generating future taxable profits, or through tax planning opportunities (see para 13.134 onwards).

UK.13.151.1 In the UK, trading losses can be offset against chargeable capital gains, but capital losses cannot be offset against trading profits. Where a company makes capital losses, those losses can generally be offset only against chargeable capital gains arising in the same period. If those capital losses are greater than the chargeable capital gains, they could be offset against capital gains of a later accounting period.

[The next paragraph is 13.153.]

Effect of a going concern uncertainty

13.153 Disclosure is required when management concludes that there is uncertainty regarding an entity's ability to continue as a going concern for a reasonable period of time (see chapter 4). [IAS 1 para 25]. The inclusion of such disclosure would generally constitute significant unfavourable evidence under

IAS 12; so recognising all or a portion of a deferred tax asset would not be justified, unless realisation is assured by either (a) carry-back to prior tax years or (b) reversals of existing taxable temporary differences. But there could be circumstances where the cause of the going concern uncertainty is not directly related to the entity's profitability. For example, the uncertainty might arise from concerns relating to liquidity or other issues unrelated to profitability (such as uncertainty about the renewal of an operating licence) while it is expected that the entity will continue to generate taxable profits. In these situations, it might be appropriate to recognise a deferred tax asset, provided it is probable (but not certain) that future taxable profits will be available. The specific facts and circumstances giving rise to the uncertainty should be considered in determining whether a deferred tax asset is recoverable. Also, the absence of significant uncertainty regarding an entity's ability to continue as a going concern does not, by itself, constitute favourable evidence that deferred tax assets will be realised.

[The next paragraph is 13.155].

Re-assessment of recoverability

13.155   A deferred tax asset's carrying amount should be reviewed at each balance sheet date. So management needs to assess whether a net deferred tax asset recognised in the balance sheet is still recoverable and has not been impaired. For example, an entity might have recognised a deferred tax asset in respect of tax losses in a previous period based on information available at that time. A year later, circumstances might have changed so that it is no longer probable that the entity would earn sufficient future taxable profits to absorb all the tax benefit. In that situation, the asset has suffered an impairment and should be written down. If circumstances giving rise to the previous write down no longer apply or it is probable that sufficient future taxable profit will be available, the reduction should be reversed. [IAS 12 para 56].

13.155.1   Similarly, where an entity has been unable to recognise a deferred tax asset because sufficient taxable profit is unavailable, management should review the situation at each subsequent balance sheet date to ascertain whether some or all of the unrecognised balance should now be recognised. For example, an improvement in trading conditions or the acquisition of a new subsidiary might make it more likely that a previously unrecognised tax loss in the acquiring entity will be recovered. [IAS 12 para 37]. Where a previously unrecognised deferred tax asset is recognised, this is a change in estimate that should be reflected in the results for the year under IAS 8.

Assessment of the recoverability in a group situation

13.156   In various jurisdictions, entities can form 'tax groups' within which tax losses or other deductible temporary differences could be transferred between entities. This means that tax losses or other deductible temporary differences in an unprofitable entity could be used to reduce the taxable profits of another entity within the tax group, thus benefiting the group as a whole.

13.156.1 The recoverability of deferred tax assets should be assessed with reference to the 'taxable entity'. [IAS 12 paras 28-30, 36]. In our view, it is reasonable to interpret the 'taxable entity' to mean the wider group of entities in the same tax group. In assessing whether a deferred tax asset should be recognised in consolidated financial statements, taxable profits of all entities in the wider tax group could be taken into account. To the extent that tax losses or deductible temporary differences generated can be recovered by a tax group, we consider that it would be appropriate to recognise a deferred tax asset in consolidated financial statements that include the entities of that tax group.

13.156.2 Where tax losses or other deductible temporary differences are transferred within a tax group, the question arises whether a deferred tax asset should be recognised at the entity level. The entity that generated the losses (or where the deductible temporary differences originated) might not itself have sufficient taxable profits to support recognising a deferred tax asset. In such cases, asset recognition at an entity level will depend on whether future economic benefit will flow to the entity; for example, the surrendering entity might have a contract in place to receive payment for transferring its tax benefits. This would indicate that an asset should be recognised at the entity level. In each case, the relevant facts and circumstances should be taken into account to determine the appropriate treatment.

Exceptions to the recognition rules

13.157 Deferred tax liabilities and deferred tax assets (subject to the availability of future taxable profits) should be recognised for all temporary differences, subject to the exceptions in paragraphs 13.127 to 13.129. These exceptions are not based on any conceptual thinking that underpins the balance sheet liability method. Rather they relate to situations where applying the general rule for deferred tax on temporary differences was in the past considered undesirable and meaningless. The specific situations are as follows:

- Initial recognition of goodwill arising in a business combination (for deferred tax liabilities only) (see para 13.158 onwards).

- Initial recognition of an asset or liability in a transaction that is not a business combination and does not affect accounting profit or taxable profit (see para 13.162 onwards).

- Investments in subsidiaries, branches, associates and joint ventures, but only where specified criteria apply (see para 13.233 onwards for separate financial statements and para 13.253 onwards for consolidated financial statements).

Taxable temporary difference on goodwill arising in a business combination

13.158 Under IFRS 3, goodwill arising on a business combination is recognised as an asset and is not amortised. Instead, it is tested annually for impairment. It is tested more frequently if events or changes in circumstances indicate that it is impaired; if it is impaired, it is written down to its recoverable amount. See chapter 25.

13.159 Where the cost of goodwill arising on a business combination is non-deductible for tax purposes (for instance, in some jurisdictions, where the goodwill arises on the acquisition of shares in a company), the goodwill has a tax base of nil. This is the case where reductions in the carrying amount of the goodwill for impairment are not allowed as a deductible expense in determining taxable profits, and the cost of the goodwill is not deductible when the subsidiary is sold. Any difference between the carrying amount of the goodwill and its tax base of nil gives rise to a taxable temporary difference; this would usually result in a deferred tax liability. But such a deferred tax liability is not recognised because goodwill is measured as a residual; and recognition of the deferred tax liability would increase the carrying amount of the goodwill (which would not add to the relevance of financial reporting). [IAS 12 para 21]. Thus, there is an assumption that the carrying amount of the goodwill is recovered on an after-tax basis, while other assets and liabilities are recovered and settled at their carrying amounts.

13.160 If, a few years after an acquisition, an entity recognises an impairment loss on goodwill that is not tax deductible, the amount of the unrecognised taxable temporary difference (and the unrecognised deferred tax liability) on goodwill is reduced. This decrease in the value of the unrecognised deferred tax liability is also regarded as relating to the initial recognition of the goodwill; so it is not permitted to be recognised. [IAS 12 para 21A].

13.161 Where the cost of goodwill arising in a business combination is deductible for tax purposes (for instance, through tax depreciation over a number of years), a taxable temporary difference will arise on which a deferred tax liability should be recognised. This situation is considered further in paragraph 13.240 onwards.

13.161.1 As noted in paragraph 13.129.1, where a *deductible* temporary difference results from the initial recognition of goodwill arising on a business combination, there is no exception. Where sufficient future taxable profits are available, a deferred tax asset is recognised as part of the accounting for the business combination. The initial recognition exception does not apply in this case, as the deferred tax asset reduces, rather than increases, goodwill. The accounting for a deferred tax asset reflects the fact that there will be a tax deduction in future periods, and any tax deduction greater than the goodwill's book value will alter the effective tax rate. This differs from the situation where the goodwill's book value exceeds its tax base. There is no tax attribute associated with the excess goodwill, so the accounting simply determines the residual amount of goodwill; and it would increase this residual amount if a deferred tax liability is recognised (as explained in para 13.159).

Initial recognition of an asset or liability

13.162 Where a temporary difference arises on initial recognition of an asset or liability, other than on a business combination, and the recognition does not affect accounting profit or taxable profit at the time of the transaction, any deferred tax asset or liability in respect of that temporary difference is not recognised [IAS 12 paras 15, 24]. Also, an entity does not recognise subsequent changes in the unrecognised deferred tax liability or asset as the asset is depreciated (see para 13.164). [IAS 12 para 22(c)].

13.163 For example, if an asset's cost is not deductible for tax purposes, either over a number of periods or on disposal, the asset's tax base is nil (as explained in para 13.112). This creates a taxable temporary difference because the recovery of the asset's carrying amount gives rise to taxable profits; but no deduction for the asset's cost is available as the asset has a tax base of nil. The resulting deferred tax liability is not immediately recognised by debiting profit or loss, because that does not allocate the tax expense over the asset's life. Also the deferred tax expense is not added to the asset's cost, because it is difficult to assess whether the consideration paid for the asset takes into account the tax treatment applied by the tax authorities. So the standard does not permit a deferred tax liability to be recognised for the origination or reversal of such temporary difference. This exception is based on pragmatism rather than any conceptual basis. The following flow chart and examples illustrate the application of the above rules.

Temporary difference arising on initial recognition of an asset or liability

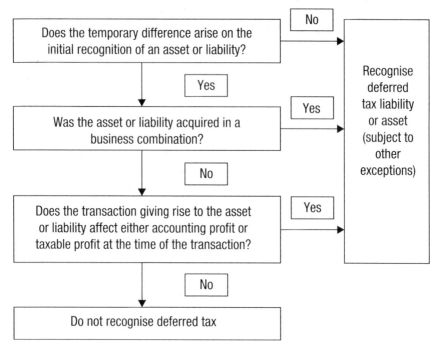

Example 1 – Initial recognition – none of the cost of an asset is deductible for tax purposes

An entity acquired an intangible asset (a licence) for C100,000 that has a life of five years. The asset will be solely recovered through use. No tax deductions can be claimed as the licence is amortised or when it expires. No tax deductions are available on disposal. Trading profits from using the licence will be taxed at 30%.

As the cost of the intangible asset is not deductible for tax purposes (either in use or on disposal), the tax base of the asset is nil. A temporary difference of C100,000 arises; prima facie a deferred tax liability of C30,000 should be recognised on this amount. But no deferred tax is recognised on the asset's initial recognition that arose from a transaction that was not a business combination and did not affect accounting or taxable profit at the time of the recognition (as noted above). At the end of year 1, the asset will have a carrying amount of C80,000. In earning taxable amounts of C80,000, the entity will pay tax of C24,000. The deferred tax liability is not recognised, because it arises from initial recognition of an asset. Similarly, no deferred tax is recognised in later periods.

Although it might appear imprudent not to recognise the deferred tax liability in these circumstances, this can be understood in the following context. If the entity acquired the asset in an arm's length transaction, the price would reflect the asset's non-deductibility for tax purposes. So it would not be appropriate to recognise a loss on the date of purchase.

The above exception does not apply if the intangible asset was acquired in a business combination. In that situation, the recognition of a deferred tax liability on acquisition increases goodwill and does not result in overstating the asset's cost or recognising an expense.

Example 2 – Initial recognition – a proportion of the asset's cost is deductible for tax purposes and book and tax depreciation rates are identical

An entity acquired an asset for C120,000, which it expects to recover solely through use in the business. For tax purposes, only 60% of the asset is deductible when the asset's carrying amount is recovered through use. The asset is depreciated for both tax and accounting purposes at 25% per annum. The tax rate is 30%.

	Carrying amount	Tax base	Temporary difference	Deferred tax
	C	C	C	C
Year 1 – On initial recognition	120,000	72,000	48,000	–
Book/tax depreciation	30,000	18,000		
End of Year 1	90,000	54,000	36,000	–
Book/tax depreciation	30,000	18,000		
End of Year 2	60,000	36,000	24,000	–
Book/tax depreciation	30,000	18,000		
End of Year 3	30,000	18,000	12,000	–
Book/tax depreciation	30,000	18,000		
End of Year 4	nil	nil	–	–

As it recovers the asset's carrying amount, the entity will earn taxable incomes of C120,000, but 60% of C120,000 = C72,000 will be deductible for tax purposes. No deferred tax is recognised on the temporary difference of C48,000 as it arises on initial recognition. At the end of year 1, the entity will be expected to generate C90,000 of taxable income, but 60% of C90,000 = C54,000 will be deductible for tax purposes. No deferred tax is recognised on the temporary difference of C36,000, because it results from the asset's initial recognition

An alternative approach is to consider that the asset effectively consists of two assets: one that is deductible for tax purposes and so should be tax effected; and the other that is not deductible and should be ignored, because it arises on initial recognition. On this basis, 60% of the cost of the asset that is deductible in full (that is, C72,000) would be tax effected in the normal way.

Example 3 – Initial recognition – a proportion of the asset's cost is deductible for tax purposes and book and tax depreciation rates are different

Where an asset is depreciated at a different rate for accounting and tax purposes, a question arises as to how the accounting depreciation should be allocated to the asset. In our view, the accounting depreciation should be allocated pro rata between the deductible and non-deductible portions of the asset.

The facts are the same as in example 2, except that the asset is depreciated at 25% for accounting purposes and $33^1/_3$% per annum for tax purposes. The tax rate is 30%.

	Carrying amount	Tax base	Temporary difference	Unrecognised temporary difference	Recognised temporary difference	Deferred tax
	C	C	C	C	C	C
On initial recognition	120,000	72,000	48,000	48,000	–	–
Book/tax depreciation	30,000	24,000				
End of Year 1	90,000	48,000	42,000	36,000	6,000	1,800
Book/tax depreciation	30,000	24,000				
End of Year 2	60,000	24,000	36,000	24,000	12,000	3,600
Book/tax depreciation	30,000	24,000				
End of Year 3	30,000	nil	30,000	12,000	18,000	5,400
Book/tax depreciation	30,000	–			(18,000)	(5,400)
End of Year 4	nil	nil			Nil	Nil

The asset's carrying amount of C120,000 exceeds the tax base of C72,000; this gives a taxable temporary difference of C48,000. This amount is covered by the initial recognition exception, so no deferred tax is recognised. The asset is consumed at a rate of 25% per year (C30,000 accounting depreciation). So the amount of depreciation that relates to the temporary difference of C48,000 is C12,000 (48,000 × 25%). This amount is treated as a reversal of the temporary difference covered by the initial recognition exception.

In addition, there is a new originating taxable temporary difference of C6,000; this results from the difference in depreciation rates used for book and tax, that is between the remaining book depreciation (C18,000) and the tax deductions (C24,000).

In summary, the overall reduction of C6,000 in the temporary difference comprises:

Reversal of part of the temporary difference covered by the IRE	(12,000)
New originating temporary difference	6,000
Overall reduction in temporary difference	(6,000)

The same result is obtained by carrying out the analysis on the basis that the entity has acquired two assets. As in example 2, no deferred tax is recognised on the part of the asset costing C48,000 with a tax base of nil, because it arises on initial recognition. The other part of the asset costing C72,000 is subject to tax effect accounting. At the end of year 1, the carrying amount of this part of the asset is C54,000 (after book depreciation of C18,000), and the tax base is C48,000 (after tax depreciation of C24,000). To recover the carrying amount of C54,000, the entity will have to earn taxable income of C54,000, but will only be able to deduct tax depreciation of C48,000. The difference between the carrying amount of C54,000 and the tax base of C48,000 gives rise to a taxable temporary difference of C6,000. So the entity recognises a deferred tax liability of C1,800 (C6,000 @ 30%) representing the tax that it would pay when it recovers the asset's carrying amount. Similar reasoning applies in years 2 and 3. At the end of year 4, any deferred tax liability is reversed when the asset is fully depreciated.

Example 4 – Initial recognition – subsequent revaluation of an asset

The facts are the same as in example 2, except that the asset is revalued to C100,000 at the beginning of year 3.

	Carrying amount	Tax base	Temporary difference	Unrecognised temporary difference	Recognised temporary difference	Deferred tax @ 30%
	C	C	C	C	C	C
On initial recognition	120,000	72,000	48,000	48,000	–	–
Book/tax depreciation	30,000	18,000				
End of Year 1	90,000	54,000	36,000	36,000	–	–
Book/tax depreciation	30,000	18,000				
End of year 2	60,000	36,000	24,000	24,000	–	–
Revaluation at beginning of year 3	40,000					
	100,000	36,000	64,000	24,000	40,000	12,000
Book/tax depreciation	50,000	18,000				
End of Year 3	50,000	18,000	32,000	12,000	20,000	6,000
Book/tax depreciation	50,000	18,000			(20,000)	(6,000)
End of year 4	nil	nil	–	–	nil	nil

As in example 2, no deferred tax is recognised on the initial temporary difference of C48,000 or in years 1 and 2. At the beginning of year 3, the asset is revalued to C100,000; but the asset's tax base is C36,000, giving rise to a temporary difference of C64,000. Of this amount, only C24,000 arises on initial recognition. The remaining C40,000 arises on the asset's subsequent revaluation; deferred tax of C12,000 (C40,000 @ 30%) should be provided on this amount. The deferred tax liability that arises on the asset's revaluation is debited direct to the revaluation reserve (see para 13.288.1). By the end of year 3, half of the temporary difference reverses; this results in a corresponding reduction in the deferred tax liability to C6,000. In year 4, the remaining temporary difference reverses when the asset is fully depreciated.

13.163.1 A deferred tax asset can sometimes arise on an asset's initial recognition. For example, a building costing C1 million is constructed in an enterprise zone that attracts 150% tax-deductible allowances on that building. The asset's tax base on initial recognition is C1.5 million. The difference between the carrying amount of C1 million and the tax base of C1.5 million gives rise to a deductible temporary difference of C0.5 million that would reduce future tax payable as the asset is recovered through use. Using a similar argument as in paragraph 13.163, the resulting deferred tax asset is not immediately recognised by crediting profit or loss, because that does not allocate the tax income over the asset's life. Also the deferred tax income is not deducted from the asset's cost, because it is difficult to assess whether the consideration paid for the asset takes into account the tax treatment applied by the tax authorities. And the standard does not permit a deferred tax asset to be recognised for the origination or reversal of such temporary difference. Another example where a deferred tax asset arises on initial recognition is the receipt of a non-taxable government grant. This situation is dealt with in paragraph 13.194 onwards.

13.163.2 In addition to revaluing an asset's carrying amount after initial recognition, it is also possible to 'revalue' the tax base after initial recognition. This can occur if the tax base is subject to an inflation adjustment, such as 'indexation'. Changes such as these (after the initial recognition exception has been applied) are considered in the following paragraphs.

Subsequent changes in an unrecognised deferred tax liability or asset

13.164 The examples in paragraph 13.163 show how subsequent changes in the temporary difference relating to an asset are treated, for instance where the asset is depreciated or revalued upwards. Where a deferred tax liability or asset has not been recognised as a result of the initial recognition exception, an entity does not recognise changes in the unrecognised deferred tax liability or asset as an asset is depreciated. [IAS 12 para 22(c)].

13.164.1 It might not be clear in practice whether subsequent changes in a temporary difference represent (i) a reversal of an amount covered by the initial recognition exception or (ii) a new temporary difference on which deferred tax is recognised. Where changes in a temporary difference (because of subsequent movements in the carrying amount or the tax basis) result from changes in the underlying economics, the general principle is that these should be properly reflected in the deferred tax accounting. The temporary difference on initial recognition arises because one element (carrying amount or tax base) exceeds the other. As a general rule, we consider that a reduction of this excess amount (due to a decrease in the larger element) is treated as a reversal of the unrecognised temporary difference and no deferred tax arises. But an increase of the larger element or a reduction of the other element (that is, the smaller amount) is treated as a new temporary difference; and deferred tax is recognised (subject to the criteria for deferred tax assets in IAS 12). The situation is more complicated where a subsequent change increases the smaller element (and so reduces the temporary difference); and there may be diversity in practice.

13.164.2   The above accounting is illustrated in the following examples for an asset with a carrying amount of C100,000 and a tax base of C90,000 on initial recognition. The resulting taxable temporary difference of C10,000 is subject to the initial recognition exception. Subsequent changes that reduce the carrying amount (up to C10,000) are reversals of the amount covered by the initial recognition exception (see example 1). Changes that increase the temporary difference result in a new temporary difference, and so deferred tax is recognised (see examples 2 and 3). If the temporary difference reduces because of an increase in the tax base (the smaller element), there are alternative acceptable views (as set out in example 4).

Example 1 – Subsequent accounting devaluation

	Carrying amount	Tax base	Temporary difference	Unrecognised temporary difference	Recognised temporary difference	Deferred tax liability/ (asset)@ 30%
	C	C	C	C	C	C
Initial recognition	100,000	90,000	10,000	10,000	–	–
Devaluation	(30,000)	–	(30,000)	(3,000)	(27,000)	(8,100)
	70,000	90,000	(20,000)	7,000	(27,000)	(8,100)

In this case, the accounting devaluation is similar to depreciation and reduces the asset's carrying amount. Consistent with the pro rata approach in example 3 in paragraph 13.163, the amount of devaluation that relates to the temporary difference of C10,000 is C3,000. This amount is treated as a reversal of the temporary difference covered by the initial recognition exception. The remaining devaluation of C27,000 is treated as a new deductible temporary difference; a deferred tax asset is recognised on this amount (provided it meets the recognition criteria).

13063

Example 2 – Subsequent accounting upward revaluation

	Carrying amount	Tax base	Temporary difference	Unrecognised temporary difference	Recognised temporary difference	Deferred tax liability/ (asset)@ 30%
	C	C	C	C	C	C
Initial recognition	100,000	90,000	10,000	10,000	–	–
Revaluation gain	30,000	–	30,000	–	30,000	9,000
	130,000	90,000	40,000	10,000	30,000	9,000

The revaluation of C30,000 increases the asset's carrying amount and the temporary difference. This results in a new taxable temporary difference on which a deferred tax liability is recognised.

Example 3 – Subsequent tax devaluation

	Carrying amount	Tax base	Temporary difference	Unrecognised temporary difference	Recognised temporary difference	Deferred tax liability/ (asset)@ 30%
	C	C	C	C	C	C
Initial recognition	100,000	90,000	10,000	10,000	–	–
Devaluation	–	(30,000)	30,000	–	30,000	9,000
	100,000	60,000	40,000	10,000	30,000	9,000

The change of C30,000 reduces the asset's tax base and increases the temporary difference. This represents a new taxable temporary difference on which a deferred tax liability is recognised.

Example 4 – Subsequent tax upward revaluation

	Carrying amount	Tax base	Temporary difference	Unrecognised temporary difference	Recognised temporary difference	Deferred tax liability/ (asset)@ 30%
	C	C	C	C	C	C
Initial recognition	100,000	90,000	10,000	10,000	–	–
Revaluation gain	–	30,000	(30,000)	–	(30,000)	(9,000)
	100,000	120,000	(20,000)	10,000	(30,000)	(9,000)

The change of C30,000 reduces the taxable temporary difference (and changes it to a deductible temporary difference). But this is because an increase in the tax base rather than a reduction in the carrying amount that gave rise to the unrecognised temporary difference. So, under the general principle in paragraph 13.164.1, the C30,000 represents a new deductible temporary difference on which a deferred tax asset is recognised (provided it meets the recognition criteria).

There is an alternative acceptable view: an increase in the smaller component (in this example, the tax base) reduces the previously unrecognised temporary difference. Under this view, C10,000 is a reversal of the temporary difference covered by the initial recognition exception. The remaining C20,000 is treated as a new deductible temporary difference.

13.164.3 The above examples show the position where the initial recognition exception applies to a taxable temporary difference on an asset. A similar approach applies in relation to a deductible temporary difference. In this case, the temporary difference arises because the asset's tax base is higher than the carrying amount. An entity does not recognise changes in the unrecognised deferred tax liability or asset as an asset is depreciated. [IAS 12 para 22(c)]. In our view, 'depreciation' applies to the tax base (as well as the carrying amount) where this represents a reversal of the unrecognised temporary difference. So, for an unrecognised deductible temporary difference on an asset, depreciation or devaluation of the tax base will represent a reversal of the unrecognised temporary difference (on a pro rata basis, as above).

13.164.4 Changes that increase the deductible temporary difference (such as a tax revaluation or an accounting devaluation or depreciation) are not reversals, but represent new temporary differences on which deferred tax is recognised. The situation is more complicated where the temporary difference is reduced because of an increase in the asset's carrying amount, as illustrated in the following example.

Example – Subsequent accounting upward revaluation

	Carrying amount	Tax base	Temporary difference	Unrecognised temporary difference	Recognised temporary difference	Deferred tax liability/ (asset)@ 30%
	C	C	C	C	C	C
Initial recognition	90,000	100,000	(10,000)	(10,000)	–	–
Revaluation gain	30,000	–	30,000	–	30,000	9,000
	120,000	100,000	20,000	(10,000)	30,000	9,000

The change of C30,000 reduces the deductible temporary difference (and changes it to a taxable temporary difference). But this is because of an increase in the carrying amount rather than a reduction in the tax base that gave rise to the unrecognised temporary difference. So, under the general principle in paragraph 13.164.1, the C30,000 represents a new taxable temporary difference on which a deferred tax liability is recognised.

There is an alternative acceptable view: an increase in the smaller component (in this case, the asset's carrying amount) reduces the previously unrecognised temporary difference. Under this view, C10,000 is a reversal of the temporary difference covered by the initial recognition exception. The remaining C20,000 is treated as a new taxable temporary difference.

13.164.5   The above examples show that where the initial recognition exception applies, any changes in the temporary difference need to be analysed to determine if they represent a reversal of the amount covered by the initial recognition exception or a new temporary difference.

13.164.6   The above examples show the position where a temporary difference on an asset is subject to the initial recognition exception. The principle and approach in paragraph 13.164.1 apply similarly to temporary differences (taxable or deductible) on liabilities that are subject to the initial recognition exception.

Measurement issues

Introduction

13.165   Deferred tax is measured at the tax rates that are expected to apply when the asset is realised or the liability is settled. The tax rates are based on laws that have been enacted or substantively enacted at the balance sheet date. [IAS 12 para 47].

13.166   Realising an asset or settling a liability could take many years. But the tax rate is not normally known in advance. So IAS 12 requires an entity to use a rate that has been enacted or substantively enacted by the balance sheet date. Enacted means that the rate is part of tax law. See paragraph 13.69 onwards for the meaning of 'substantively enacted'.

Change in tax rates

13.166.1   An entity's tax rate might change as a result of new legislation. The impact of changes in rates depends on the nature and timing of the legislative changes. Any impact is recognised in accounting periods ending on or after the date of substantive enactment (and might be disclosable before that date). Changes in tax rates are often prospective, so there will be no impact on current tax assets and liabilities that arose before the change's effective date. But deferred tax balances are likely to be affected.

Example – Change in tax rates

A change in tax rate from 30% to 28% was substantively enacted on 26 June 20X7 with effect from 1 April 20X8. The change has no impact on current tax liabilities arising before its effective date. But the measurement of deferred tax assets and liabilities will be affected for accounting periods (including interim periods) ending on or after 26 June 20X7.

Management needs to determine when the deferred tax balance is expected to reverse and what tax rate will apply in the reversal period. The reduction in tax rate will not affect deferred tax that is expected to reverse before 1 April 20X8, but it will affect later reversals. It will be more complicated for entities with a financial year that straddles 1 April 20X8. They will need to calculate an effective tax rate for reversals in the financial year in which the change takes effect.

The impact of this reduction in tax rate might affect profit or loss, or other comprehensive income or equity (see further para 13.288.7).

The change in tax rate might be disclosable as a non-adjusting post-balance sheet event for accounting periods ending before 26 June 20X7. [IAS 10 para 22(h)].

Average rates

13.167 Management normally needs to calculate an average tax rate only if the enacted or substantively enacted tax rates are graduated; that is, if different rates apply to different levels of taxable income. This average rate is the rate expected to apply to taxable profit (or loss) in the years in which management expects the temporary differences to reverse. [IAS 12 para 49]. Assume the first C5m of profit is taxed at 20%, and profit above that is taxed at 30%. Management needs to estimate the average rate where it expects to earn annual taxable profit in excess of C5m in the future. To determine the rate (which would be between 20% and 30%), management estimates future annual taxable profits, including reversing temporary differences. It is not usually necessary in practice to determine the net reversals of temporary differences for deferred tax assets and liabilities. But management should consider the effect of an abnormal level of taxable profit or any abnormally large temporary difference that could reverse in a single future year and distort the average rate.

> **Example – Different tax rates applicable to different levels of income**
>
> An entity operates in a country where different rates apply to different levels of taxable income. The net deductible temporary differences total C30,000 at 31 December 20X3. The temporary differences are expected to reverse over the next seven years. The average projected profit for the next seven years is C60,000.
>
> A deductible temporary difference relating to impairment of trade receivables of C25,000 is expected to fully reverse in 20X5, when the related expense will be deductible for tax purposes. The taxable profit for 20X5 will be C35,000 (that is, C60,000 – C25,000).
>
> The reversal of this large temporary difference will distort the average tax rate; so management should consider the impact of this separately when calculating the average rate that it will use for deferred tax assets and liabilities.
>
> An example of the calculation of the deferred tax assets and liabilities, assuming graduated tax rates, is:

Taxation

Range	Tax rate	Profit	Average Income tax	Profit	Year 20X5 Income tax
C	%	c	c	c	c
0 – 1,000	18	1,000	180	1,000	180
1,001 – 11,000	25	10,000	2,500	10,000	2,500
11,001 – 36,000	30	25,000	7,500	24,000	7,200
36,001 +	40	24,000	9,600	–	–
		60,000	19,780	35,000	9,880
Average rate			33%		28%

Management uses a 28% tax rate in the 20X3 financial statements for the deferred tax asset relating to impairment of trade receivables; it uses a 33% rate for the remaining temporary differences.

13.168 The requirement to calculate an average tax rate applies to different levels of profit; but it is not used for different rates that are expected to apply to different types of taxable profit or in different tax jurisdictions. If different rates apply to different types of taxable profit (for example, trading profits and capital gains), the rate used will reflect the nature of the temporary difference. The rates used for measuring deferred tax arising in a specific tax jurisdiction will be the rates expected to apply in that jurisdiction. Management should take care when considering tax in countries where state or provincial tax systems apply. Management should apply the appropriate rates for each state or province to the transactions in those states or provinces and avoid using an average rate for the country unless the impact is immaterial.

[The next paragraph is 13.170.]

Expected manner of recovery or settlement of an asset or a liability

13.170 The tax consequences of recovering or settling the carrying amount of assets and liabilities might depend on the manner in which the asset is recovered or the liability is settled. So the tax base might be different depending on how the asset or liability is recovered or settled in practice. The carrying amount of an asset is normally recovered through use, sale, or use and sale. The cumulative amount that is deducted for tax purposes if the asset is recovered through use might be different from the amount that would be deductible on the asset's sale, for example, because of indexing the cost.

13.171 In some jurisdictions, different tax rates apply to income and capital gains. For example, if an entity expects to sell an asset, and the transaction would be subject only to capital gains tax, it should measure the related deferred tax liability at the balance sheet date at the capital gains rate. But if it expects to retain the asset and recover its carrying amount through use, it should measure the deferred tax at the rate applicable to taxable income.

13.172 Entities should measure deferred tax assets and liabilities using the tax rates and tax bases that are consistent with the manner in which the entity expects, at the balance sheet date, to recover or settle the carrying amount of assets and liabilities. [IAS 12 para 52]. See guidance on the expected manner of recovery of investment properties measured at fair value in paragraph 13.219.4 onwards.

13.172.1 There is debate over the deferred tax accounting where a group holds a single asset within a corporate entity (or 'corporate wrapper') and expects to ultimately 'recover' the asset by selling the investment in the corporate entity. In our view, management should determine the asset's expected manner of recovery for the purpose of calculating the related deferred tax on the basis of the asset's recovery within the corporate entity, not by reference to the expected manner of recovery of the investment in the corporate entity. This applies even if the group expects to recover its investment in the corporate entity without an impact on taxable profit (or with a lesser impact than from selling the asset itself). This is because IAS 12 requires that deferred tax is recognised on temporary differences; a temporary difference is defined as the difference between an asset's carrying amount and its tax base (see para 13.93). As it is the asset itself that is recognised in the group's balance sheet (as opposed to the investment in the corporate entity in which the asset resides), the relevant tax base is that of the asset, not that of the investment.

13.172.1.1 Where a group holds assets within a corporate entity (for example, in a subsidiary or a joint venture), it should determine the assets' expected manner of recovery on the basis of their recovery within that corporate entity. The resulting temporary differences are sometimes referred to as 'inside basis' differences. There could be a further temporary difference: the difference between the carrying amount of the investment in the corporate entity and its tax base (sometimes referred to as 'outside basis' difference). See paragraph 13.254 for more guidance on temporary differences arising on investments in subsidiaries, branches, associates and joint ventures.

13.172.1.2 The impact of management expectations on the measurement of deferred tax assets and liabilities is an important principle in the standard. This is true particularly where the tax base of an asset or liability is not immediately apparent.

> **Example – Expected manner of recovery based on use**
>
> A parent entity acquired in a business combination a subsidiary that held a piece of plant. The fair value of the plant was C10m and it will be depreciated over 10 years to its residual value of nil. The accounting depreciation of C1m charged in year 1 and later years is not deductible for tax purposes. If the plant is used in the business for its full 10-year life, it will be fully consumed and will have to be scrapped. No tax deductions will be available for scrapping the asset. But if the asset is sold, the cost of the asset to the subsidiary of, say, C8m (after adjusting for inflation) is deductible on sale. The tax rate is 30% for income and 25% for capital gains.

In this example, the tax base is not immediately apparent. It could be nil if the asset is to be used; or it could be C8m if the asset is to be sold. So management needs to consider how it expects to recover the asset's carrying amount. Management will use the plant for carrying out its business (supported by the fact that the asset is being depreciated to a nil residual value). The plant's full carrying amount is expected to be recovered through use; and there are no tax consequences of scrapping the asset at the end of its life. The tax base that is consistent with the expected manner of recovery through use is nil, as no part of the carrying amount is deductible for tax purposes against the future economic benefits expected to flow from the plant's use. So a temporary difference arises of C10m, which is the difference between the carrying amount on initial recognition and the tax base of nil. This temporary difference reduces to C9m because part of the carrying amount is recovered through depreciation in year 1. On this basis, management would provide a deferred tax liability of C3m at the income tax rate of 30% on the date of the business combination. This deferred tax liability will have reduced to C2.7m at the balance sheet date.

13.172.1.3 The standard has some examples (in para 52) of how this principle is applied. Other examples are considered elsewhere in this chapter; for example, the expected manner of recovery of revalued non-monetary assets is discussed in paragraph 13.211 onwards.

Dual manner of recovery

13.172.2 An entity might plan to use an asset for a number of years and then sell it. In that situation, because the asset's manner of recovery is through use and eventual sale, the deferred tax should reflect this expected 'dual manner of recovery'. It is recognised on the basis of normal income tax rules for the portion of the asset's carrying amount that is expected to be recovered through use; and it is recognised using disposal tax rules for the remainder of the asset's carrying amount that is expected to be recovered through sale.

13.172.3 The 'dual manner of recovery' expectation will often affect assets such as properties and intangible assets. A residual value might indicate that the dual manner of recovery is applicable. Paragraph 6 of SIC 21 supports this. But the dual manner of recovery could still apply even when there is no residual value; for example, where the asset is expected to be disposed of or abandoned (either during or at the end of its useful life) in order to recover any tax base available on disposal or abandonment. This might affect properties or intangibles with nil residual values or other types of asset such as mining assets. The guidance in SIC 21 has been incorporated into IAS 12 by the amendment to IAS 12 issued in December 2010. For guidance on the expected manner of recovery for investment properties measured at fair value, refer to paragraph 13.219.7 onwards; and for guidance on intangible assets with indefinite lives, refer to paragraph 13.225.1 onwards.

13.172.3.1 Where an asset has a nil residual value, it might appear that it will be recovered solely through use. But it is likely that management will take the commercial decision to sell the asset at the end of its useful life if this would recover the asset's tax base. Proceeds are likely to be low (as the asset is at the end of its life), but the asset's cost or indexed cost might be tax deductible. Thus the sale could generate a significant capital loss. If there is a valid expectation that management would sell the asset, a dual manner of recovery expectation would apply.

13.172.4 When a dual manner of recovery expectation applies, deferred tax is calculated as follows:

- Ascertain the expected manner of recovery of the asset's carrying amount.

  For instance, where assets are depreciable (such as buildings), they are expected to be held during their useful life and a portion of the carrying amount recovered through use, with the residual amount (which might be nil) recovered through a disposal at the end of the useful life. Land is not depreciable and it can only be recovered through ultimate disposal (see further para 13.213).

- Split the asset's carrying amount between amounts to be recovered through use and through sale.

  The split might be based on the residual value determined for the purpose of depreciation under the cost model of IAS 16 or IAS 38. This residual value is the estimated value (in present prices at the balance sheet date) of the relevant asset in its expected state at the end of its useful life. But the split could arguably be based on a residual value measured on the same price basis as the carrying amount (that is, based on prices ruling at the date the asset was bought).

  Under the revaluation model in IAS 16, the residual value is likely to be measured on the same price basis as the carrying amount.

- Determine the expected period of recovery through use and the expected date of sale or abandonment.

  For depreciable assets accounted for under the cost or revaluation model, the expected period of recovery through use is normally the asset's useful life as defined in IAS 16 or IAS 38.

- Determine the tax consequences of recovery through use and the temporary differences that will arise.

  The future taxable amount will be the portion of the carrying amount expected to be recovered through use. The tax consequences of recovering this amount through the receipt of operating income (that is, through use) are determined by considering any deductions available during the period of recovery. In a simple situation, this might mean just deducting the expected tax depreciation allowances (if any) from the amount expected to be recovered through use, to determine the resulting temporary difference.

  Where an asset is expected to be recovered through use without any disposal, it might also be necessary to consider any capital gains tax consequences of abandoning the asset and any resulting temporary differences.

Where an asset is expected to be held and used for a period before disposal, it might be necessary to consider the income tax consequences of the disposal; these could affect tax depreciation allowances relating to the carrying amount that is expected to be recovered through use (for example, claw backs of, or additional, tax depreciation allowances based on the disposal proceeds, if applicable).

■ Determine the tax consequences of recovery through sale and the temporary differences that will arise.

The future taxable amount will be the portion of the carrying amount expected to be recovered through disposal. This will be the residual value or adjusted residual value (see the second bullet point above). The tax consequences will be the taxable gain arising on such disposal.

■ Determine which of the temporary differences arising from recovery through use and through sale should be recognised.

The temporary differences arising from the analysis in the above two steps should be considered separately (rather than determining a net temporary difference) if the tax liability (or asset) arising from use and the tax asset (or liability) arising from sale could not be offset. Such offset might not be possible if the amounts are taxed in a different manner (for example, if income tax losses cannot be fully offset against capital gains) or if they are taxed at a different time (for example, a tax loss arising on the reversal of a deductible temporary difference may not be offsettable against taxable income arising from the earlier reversal of a taxable temporary difference).

13.172.5 The impact of the expected manner of recovery and use of residual values is illustrated below:

Example – Impact of expected manner of recovery and residual values

An entity acquired a property during a business combination before transition to IFRS. The total fair value on acquisition of the property was C3.5m (that is, 'cost' to the entity); this was split between land of C1m and buildings of C2.5m.

In accordance with IFRS 1, the property was revalued on transition to IFRS. A revaluation uplift of C2m was recognised; and the revalued amount of C5.5m is used as deemed cost. C800,000 of this revaluation uplift related to the land element, and C1.2m to the building element.

There are no tax deductions for use, but the total cost (plus an adjustment for inflation) is deductible on sale. The tax rate is 30% throughout.

Deferred tax on the land is calculated on a sale basis (see further para 13.213). But the expected manner of recovery for the buildings will have a significant impact on deferred tax.

Expected manner of recovery based on use

If the use basis alone is appropriate for the buildings:

	Land	Building (use)
	C'000	C'000
Carrying amount	1,800	3,700
Tax base		
Cost	1,000	–
Inflation adjustment (say)	200	–
Total tax base	1,200	–
Temporary difference – liability	600	3,700

The entity recognises a deferred tax liability on land for the taxable temporary difference (TTD) of C0.6m and a deferred tax liability on buildings for the TTD of C3.7m; that is a total TTD of C4.3m @ 30%, giving a total deferred tax liability of C1.29m.

Dual manner of recovery with a residual value

If a dual manner of recovery is appropriate for the buildings:

Assume that C1.8m of the buildings will be recovered through sale (residual value) and C1.9m through use.

	Land	Building (sale)	Building (use)
	C'000	C'000	C'000
Carrying amount	1,800	1,800	1,900
Tax base			
Cost	1,000	2,500	–
Inflation adjustment (say)	200	500	–
Total tax base	1,200	3,000	–
Temporary difference – liability (asset)	600	(1,200)	1,900

The deductible temporary difference (DTD) on the sale element of the buildings can be recognised only if it is recoverable under IAS 12's rules. In many jurisdictions, a DTD calculated on a sale element cannot be offset against the TTD on the use element, because capital losses cannot be offset against trading income. It is generally reasonable to assume that the land and buildings will be sold together. So to the extent that the DTD calculated on a capital (that is, sale) basis is covered by a TTD on the related land that is also calculated on a capital basis, it can be offset against it. So the deferred tax liability recognised might relate only to the buildings' use element.

If C0.6m of the DTD is recognised against the C0.6m TTD on the land, the entity recognises a deferred tax liability on the buildings of C1.9m @ 30% = C0.57m.

The remaining deferred tax asset (on DTD of C0.6m) can only be recognised if it meets IAS 12's recognition criteria for assets; this is not possible, unless the entity expects to have suitable taxable profits available to utilise the capital loss.

Dual manner of recovery with a nil residual value

The dual manner of recovery might be appropriate for the buildings even if there is no residual value; for example, if the entity expects to sell the property at the end of its useful life in order to recover the buildings' tax base together with the disposal of the land, or can recover the buildings' tax base at the end of their useful lives in another way. If nearly all of the buildings' carrying amount is expected to be recovered through use, followed by disposal together with the related land:

	Land	Building (sale)	Building (use)
	C'000	C'000	C'000
Carrying amount	1,800	–	3,700
Tax base			
Cost	1,000	2,500	–
Inflation adjustment (say)	200	500	–
Total tax base	1,200	3,000	–
Temporary difference – liability (asset)	600	(3,000)	3,700

There is a DTD on the sale element of the buildings. To the extent it is covered by a TTD (calculated on a capital basis) on the related land, it can be offset against it.

If C0.6m of the DTD is recognised against the C0.6m TTD on the land, the entity recognises a deferred tax liability on the buildings of C3.7m @ 30% = C1.11m.

The remaining deferred tax asset (on DTD of C2.4m) can only be recognised if it meets IAS 12's recognition criteria for assets; this is not possible, unless the entity expects to have suitable taxable profits available to utilise the capital loss.

Comparison of methods

The expected manner of recovery, the useful economic lives and the residual values attributed to the buildings need to reflect management's expectations, as this is the basis of allocating the buildings' carrying amount between the use and sale elements; this allocation, in turn, affects the deferred tax recognised on these elements. Consider the impact of the different manner of recovery expectations in the above scenarios:

	Use only	Dual manner (with residual)	Dual manner (with nil residual)
Deferred tax liability on use element of buildings	1,110	570	1,110
Deferred tax liability on land	180	180	180
Deferred tax asset on sale element of buildings (offset against land)	–	(180)	(180)
Deferred tax liability recognised	1,290	570	1,110
Remaining deferred tax asset on sale element of buildings (available for recognition if IAS 12 criteria are met)	–	(180)	(720)
Reduction in net assets	1,290	390	390

Where there is a residual value, a significant difference arises between the outcome under the single use expectation and the dual manner of recovery expectation.

Even where there is a nil residual value, the outcome under the dual manner of recovery differs from that for single use. This is because some of the deferred tax asset arising on sale of the buildings can be recognised under the dual manner of recovery expectation; this reduces the deferred tax liability on the land by C180,000.

If the TTD on the land was larger, the difference between the outcome under the dual manner of recovery and that for single use would be even greater; this is because more of the deferred tax asset arising on sale of the buildings could be recognised.

[The next paragraph is 13.173.1.]

Dual manner of recovery – implications of the initial recognition exception

13.173.1 Where a temporary difference arises on initial recognition of an asset (other than on a business combination), and the transaction does not affect accounting profit or taxable profit at the time of the transaction, any deferred tax asset or liability in respect of that temporary difference is not permitted to be recognised (see para 13.162 onwards). [IAS 12 paras 15, 24].

Example – Dual manner of recovery and initial recognition exception

Using the example in paragraph 13.172.5, but assuming that the property is separately acquired. On revaluation, the property's residual value was revisited; this resulted in changes to the carrying amounts of the land and both elements of the buildings (that is, sale and use).

	Cost	Revaluation	Carrying amount
	C'000	C'000	C'000
Land	1,000	800	1,800
Buildings – recovered through sale	1,200	600	1,800
Buildings – recovered through use	1,300	600	1,900
Total	**3,500**	**2,000**	**5,500**

Expected manner of recovery for buildings solely through use

The implications of the initial recognition exception (IRE) at the date of the property's acquisition are:

Land: taxable temporary difference of nil – carrying amount (cost of C1m) less tax base (C1m).

Buildings: taxable temporary difference of C2.5m – carrying amount (cost of C2.5m) less tax base (nil) – deferred tax liability not recognised because of the IRE.

After revaluation, if recovery solely through use is appropriate for the buildings:

	Land	Building (use)
	C'000	C'000
Carrying amount	1,800	3,700
Tax base		
Cost	1,000	–
Inflation adjustment (say)	200	–
Total tax base	1,200	–
Temporary difference	600	3,700
Covered by IRE	–	2,500
New temporary difference	600	1,200

To keep this example simple, it ignores depreciation (which reduces the original temporary difference covered by the IRE). The entity recognises a deferred tax liability on the land (TTD of C0.6m) and a deferred tax liability on buildings (TTD of C1.2m); that is a total TTD of C1.8m @ 30%, giving a total deferred tax liability of C0.54m.

Dual manner of recovery with a residual value

The implications of the IRE at the date of the property's acquisition would be:

Land: taxable temporary difference of nil – carrying amount (cost of C1m) less tax base (C1m).

Buildings – sale element: deductible temporary difference of C1.3m – carrying amount (allocated cost of C1.2m) less tax base (C2.5m) – deferred tax asset not recognised because of the IRE.

Buildings – use element: taxable temporary difference of C1.3m – carrying amount (allocated cost of C1.3m) less tax base (nil) – deferred tax liability not recognised because of the IRE.

After revaluation, if a dual manner of recovery is expected for the buildings:

	Land	Building (sale)	Building (use)
	C'000	C'000	C'000
Carrying amount	1,800	1,800	1,900
Tax base			
Cost	1,000	2,500	–
Inflation adjustment (say)	200	500	–
Total tax base	1,200	3,000	–
Temporary difference	600	(1,200)	1,900
Covered by IRE	–	1,300	(1,300)
New temporary difference	600	100	600

Again, to keep the example simple, it ignores depreciation (which reduces the original temporary difference covered by the IRE).

After revaluation, the sale element of the buildings has a carrying amount (C1.8m) that is less than its tax base (C3m); thus a DTD of C1.2m exists at the balance sheet date. On initial recognition, a DTD of C1.3m existed but was not recognised because of the initial recognition exception. So the original DTD has been reduced by C0.1m as a result of the revaluation (C0.6m), partly offset by indexation (C0.5m).

Under the initial recognition exception, the temporary difference resulting from the original carrying amount (and its subsequent depreciation, if applicable) and the original tax base are excluded from recognition. Any increases in the asset's carrying amount or the tax base are considered separately for deferred tax purposes (see further para 13.164.4). In this case, a new revaluation event has occurred, producing an asset with an incremental carrying amount of C0.6m and an incremental tax base of C0.5m. This gives rise to a taxable temporary difference of C0.1m.

So the entity recognises a deferred tax liability on land (TTD of C0.6m), a deferred tax liability on the sale element of the buildings (TTD of C0.1m) and a deferred tax liability on the use element of the buildings (TTD of C0.6m); that is a total TTD of C1.3m @ 30%, giving a total deferred tax liability of C0.39m.

Dual manner of recovery with a nil residual value

If nearly all of the buildings' carrying amount is expected to be recovered through use, followed by disposal together with the related land, the implications of the IRE at the date of the property's acquisition would be:

Land: taxable temporary difference of nil – carrying amount (cost of C1m) less tax base (C1m).

Buildings – sale element: deductible temporary difference of C2.5m – carrying amount (allocated cost of Cnil) less tax base (C2.5m) – deferred tax asset not recognised because of the IRE.

Buildings – use element: taxable temporary difference of C2.5m – carrying amount (allocated cost of C2.5m) less tax base (nil) – deferred tax liability not recognised because of the IRE.

After revaluation, if the dual manner of recovery is used for the buildings:

	Land C'000	Building (sale) C'000	Building (use) C'000
Carrying amount	1,800	–	3,700
Tax base			
Cost	1,000	2,500	–
Inflation adjustment (say)	200	500	–
Total tax base	1,200	3,000	–
Temporary difference	600	(3,000)	3,700
Covered by IRE	–	2,500	(2,500)
New temporary difference	600	(500)	1,200

There is no revaluation of the sale element of the buildings for accounting purposes because this is all attributed to the use element. But there is a revaluation (of C0.5m) of the tax base because of indexation allowance. Assuming there is no restriction of the indexation allowance, the revaluation gives rise to a new DTD (as explained above); to the extent it is covered by a TTD (capital basis) on the related land, it can be offset against this.

If the DTD of C0.5m is recognised against the C0.6m TTD on the land, the entity recognises a deferred tax liability on the land (TTD C0.1m) and buildings (TTD C1.2m); that is a total TTD of C1.3m @ 30%, giving a total deferred tax liability of C0.39m.

Comparison of methods

	Use only C'000	Dual manner (with residual) C'000	Dual manner (with nil residual) C'000
Deferred tax liability on use element of buildings	360	180	360
Deferred tax liability on land	180	180	180
Deferred tax liability/(asset) on sale element of building	–	30	(150)
Deferred tax liability recognised	540	390	390

Comparing this with the scenarios in paragraph 13.172.5, which did not apply the initial recognition exception, the initial recognition exception reduces the difference between the single use and the dual method. But the difference can still be significant.

Under both methods, deferred tax is recognised on the revaluation gains on the buildings. But the dual method also considers the effect of the inflation adjustment on calculating the sale element of the buildings. This reduces the deferred tax liability arising on the revaluation of that element (and could result in a deferred tax asset, subject to any restriction of the inflation adjustment); this might give rise to a smaller overall deferred tax liability than the single use method.

Implications of inflation adjustments

13.173.2 As shown above, inflation adjustments for tax purposes can have a significant impact on the deferred tax calculation where there is a dual manner of recovery expectation. Inflation adjustments are generally an allowance relating to tax on capital gains (as opposed to income tax); so any adjustments to the tax base relating to inflation on the buildings are relevant only to the sale element of the buildings. Inflation adjustments are not allocated to the element of the buildings that will be used in the ongoing business. Instead, inflation adjustments on the buildings' total cost are included in the calculation of deferred tax on the sale element of the property.

13.173.3 Because inflation adjustments are effectively a revaluation of the tax base and arise after initial recognition, they are not subject to the initial recognition exception. The adjustments will increase the asset's tax base and thus reduce the taxable temporary difference relating to the sale element of the buildings.

13.173.3.1 The accounting implications of revaluations for tax purposes are addressed further in paragraph 13.217 onwards.

UK.13.173.3.1.1 In the UK, inflation adjustments (indexation) cannot be used to generate or increase a capital loss. So the impact of indexation can only be recognised where it reduces a taxable temporary difference. Once the taxable temporary difference has been extinguished, any further impact of indexation on the calculation is not recognised. If the land and buildings will be sold together, the overall position of the property should be taken into account when establishing whether indexation should be restricted (on the basis that it is creating or increasing a loss).

UK.13.173.3.1.2 For leasehold properties (that is, where there is no land element), indexation allowance (if available) can be recognised up to the point where the taxable temporary difference (and deferred tax liability) on the sale element of the buildings is nil. For freehold properties, an additional indexation allowance can be recognised; this results in a deferred tax asset on the sale element of the buildings, but only up to the amount of any related deferred tax liability on the land element of the property. Indexation allowance cannot create a deferred tax asset to offset against the deferred tax liability on the use element of the buildings; this is because the latter is not on a capital gains tax basis.

[The next paragraph is 13.173.6.]

Property devaluations

13.173.6 Where the *use* element of a building is revalued downwards below its allocated original cost, this is treated similarly to depreciation of the building (see para 13.212 onwards). Where the initial recognition exception applies, an entity does not recognise later changes in the unrecognised deferred tax liability as the asset is depreciated. [IAS 12 para 22(c)]. In this situation, the downward revaluation is a reversal of the originating temporary difference arising on the asset's initial recognition; so it is not recognised in the deferred tax calculation.

13.173.7 Where the *sale* element of a building is revalued downwards below its allocated original cost, this increases the deductible temporary difference arising on the asset's initial recognition; so it is not a reversal of the originating temporary difference on initial recognition. In this situation, the downward revaluation is a new temporary difference and is recognised in the deferred tax calculation. Any resulting deferred tax asset is recognised only if it can be offset against a deferred tax liability on the related land, or if the IAS 12 recognition criteria are met in some other way.

Change in intention about the expected manner of recovery

13.174 The manner in which management expects to recover an asset's carrying amount or settle a liability's carrying amount might sometimes change. In that situation, the change in the manner of recovery or settlement could affect the deferred tax balances already recognised for that asset or liability. So the deferred tax balances should be remeasured using the tax rates and tax bases that are consistent with the revised expected manner of recovery. Any adjustments resulting from the remeasurement should be recognised in profit or loss or if they relate to items previously recognised outside profit or loss, they should be recognised in other comprehensive income or directly in equity, as appropriate. [IAS 12 para 60(c)]. See the example below and scenario 2 in paragraph 13.211.

Example – Change in intention on expected manner of recovery

An entity acquired a piece of plant in a business combination on 1 January 20X6 at cost of C800,000. The plant is fully deductible in use at a rate of 25% per annum. Accounting depreciation is charged at 10% per annum and the residual value is nil.

If the plant is sold, any chargeable gain will be taxable at 40%. The chargeable gain will be the excess of proceeds over the original cost, adjusted for inflation, less any deductions already claimed (which are clawed back).

The rate for income and capital gains tax is 40%.

Management intended initially to recover the asset in full through use. At the end of its life, the asset would be scrapped and there would be no tax consequences. So deferred tax is calculated on a use basis as at 31 December 20X6.

At the end of 20X7, the intention changes and the plant is expected to be sold. So deferred tax is calculated on a sale basis as at 31 December 20X7.

	NBV	TB	TD	DTL
	C	C	C	C
At 1 January 20X6	800,000	800,000	–	–
Depreciation/tax allowances	(80,000)	(200,000)	120,000	48,000
At 31 December 20X6	720,000	600,000	120,000	48,000
Depreciation/tax allowances	(80,000)	(200,000)	120,000	48,000
At 31 December 20X7	640,000	400,000	240,000	96,000
Change in expected manner of recovery				
Tax cost of plant	–	800,000	800,000	320,000
Inflation adjustment (say)	–	4,000	4,000	1,600
Claw back of allowances claimed	–	(400,000)	(400,000)	(160,000)
New temporary difference at 31 December 20X7	640,000	404,000	236,000	94,400

The adjustment to the deferred tax liability of C1,600 arises from the change in the manner of recovery; and this is credited to the profit or loss. The deferred tax balance of C94,400 reflects the tax consequences if the entity sold the plant at its carrying amount at the balance sheet date. The movement of C1,600 represents the tax effect of the inflation adjustment (C4,000 @ 40%).

Tax consequences of dividends

13.175 Measurement can be more complicated when distributed and undistributed income are taxed at different rates. In some jurisdictions, corporate taxes are payable at a higher or lower rate if part or all of the net profit or retained earnings are distributed as dividends. For example, undistributed profits might be taxed at 45% and distributed profits at 30%. In such situations, deferred tax assets and liabilities should be measured using the tax rates on undistributed profits (45% in the example; that is, with no anticipation of future dividend). [IAS 12 para 52A].

13.175.1 IAS 10 prohibits accrual of a dividend that is proposed or declared after the end of the reporting period but before the financial statements are authorised for issue. So any tax consequences of paying a dividend are recognised when the dividend is subsequently declared and recognised as a liability. [IAS 12 para 52B]. Referring to the example above, assume that tax is recoverable if the entity pays a dividend in the subsequent accounting period. In that case, the entity recognises the refundable part of income taxes (45% – 30% = 15%) as a current tax asset and a reduction of current tax expense when it recognises the dividend. It continues to recognise deferred tax assets and liabilities using the undistributed rate.

13.175.2 In the example above, assume that the tax rate for distributed profits had been higher than that for undistributed profits, say 40% and 30% respectively; in that situation, a current tax liability and increase of current tax expense would be recognised based on the incremental tax rate of 10% when the dividend was recognised.

> **Example – Tax consequences of a dividend**
>
> A dividend of C400 was declared in February 20X4, payable on 31 March 20X4. Under IAS 10, no liability was recognised for the dividend at 31 December 20X3. The profit before tax was C2,000. The tax rate is 30% for undistributed profits and 40% for distributed profits. Should the tax rate applicable to distributed profits be applied for the portion of net profit corresponding to dividends declared after the balance sheet date?
>
> No, the tax rate applicable to undistributed profit should be applied; because the tax rate for distributed profit is used only where the obligation to pay dividends has been recognised. So the current income tax expense is C600 (C2,000 × 30%).
>
> During 20X4 a liability of C400 will be recognised for dividends payable. An additional tax liability of C40 (C400 × 10%) is also recognised as a current tax liability and an increase of the current income tax expense for 20X4.

13.176 The incremental tax effect of the dividend payment (that is, the additional tax @ 10%) is not recognised in equity but in profit or loss, even though the dividend payment is charged to equity. This is because the tax consequences of dividends in such situations are more directly linked to past transactions or events than to distributions to owners. [IAS 12 para 52B]. The past transactions and events in this instance are those that gave rise to profits that were initially taxed at 30% and that were recognised in profit or loss.

13.177 In some jurisdictions, an entity pays tax only when part or all of its net profits or retained earnings are paid out as dividend. In that situation, the tax consequences of dividends are also included as part of the tax charge in profit or loss for the same reasons set out above; that is, the tax payable primarily relates to items recognised in profit or loss and is not different from income taxes generally, even though it arises from paying a dividend. But an exception is made when the amounts payable are in effect a withholding tax for the benefit of the shareholders. The recipients of the dividends would typically be entitled to a tax credit at least equal to the tax paid by the entity. In this case, the subjects of taxation are the shareholders and not the entity. So the tax is charged directly to equity as part of the dividends, as explained further in paragraph 13.52. [IAS 12 paras 52B, 58, 65A]. Finally, the entity should disclose the tax that would result if retained earnings were paid out as dividends (see para 13.304). [IAS 12 para 81(i)].

13.178 Where a parent has a subsidiary in a dual-rate tax jurisdiction and does not expect to re-invest the earnings permanently, it should measure in its consolidated financial statements the temporary differences relating to the investment in the foreign subsidiary at the rate that would apply to distributed profits. This is on the basis that the undistributed earnings are expected to be recovered through their distribution up the group; and the deferred tax should be measured in accordance with the expected manner of recovery. [IAS 12 para 51]. Any future current tax credit that might be received should be recognised when the dividends are paid and the related deferred tax asset released.

Discounting of deferred tax assets and liabilities

13.179 Discounting of deferred tax assets and liabilities is prohibited. [IAS 12 para 53]. Although the balance sheet liability method can lead to the accumulation of large deferred tax assets and liabilities over a prolonged period (particularly for infrastructure entities with large capital expenditure programmes), discounting is not permitted; this is because of its impracticability or complexity in scheduling the timing of reversal of each temporary difference. [IAS 12 para 54].

13.180 But deferred taxes are discounted to some extent, at least implicitly. Temporary differences are calculated by reference to the carrying amount of an asset or liability. Where that carrying amount is already calculated on a discounted basis, as in the case of retirement benefit obligations (see IAS 19), the deferred tax asset or liability is implicitly discounted. In such situations, temporary differences are calculated using the (discounted) carrying amount of assets and liabilities; the implicit effect of discounting should not be reversed. [IAS 12 para 55].

[The next paragraph is 13.186.]

Changes in tax status of an entity or its shareholders

13.186 The tax status of an entity can change because of, say, public listing of its equity instruments, restructuring of its equity or a change in tax jurisdictions of its shareholders; the change could affect current tax assets and liabilities as well as deferred tax assets and liabilities. The entity could be taxed at a different rate in the future or it might lose or gain various tax incentives that affect the tax bases of its assets and liabilities. SIC 25 deals with the resulting change in accounting treatment.

13.187 The current and deferred tax consequences of a change in tax status should be dealt with in profit or loss; unless they relate to transactions and events that result (in the same or a different period) in amounts recognised in other comprehensive income, or in a direct charge or credit to the recognised amount of equity. Tax consequences relating to amounts recognised in other comprehensive income are recognised in other comprehensive income. Tax consequences relating to direct changes in equity are charged or credited directly to equity. [SIC 25 para 4].

13.188 This means that an entity should identify the transactions and events that gave rise to current and deferred tax balances. Where transactions and events are recognised outside profit or loss (for example, asset revaluations), additional current and deferred tax consequences should also be recognised outside profit or loss. So the cumulative amount of tax recognised outside profit or loss would be the same amount that would have been recognised if the new tax status had applied previously. [SIC 25 para 8].

Example – Change in tax status of an entity

On 31 August 20X2, entity A changed its status from one type of entity to another. It became subject to a higher income tax rate (30%) than previously (25%). The change in applicable tax rate applies to taxable income generated from 1 September 20X2. The tax rates applicable to a profit on sale of land also increased from 30% to 40%.

The information below relates to temporary differences that exist at 1 January 20X2 and at 31 December 20X2 (the end of accounting period) and which will all reverse after 1 January 20X3.

	01 Jan X2			31 Dec X2		
	Carrying amount	Tax base	Temporary difference	Carrying amount	Tax base	Temporary difference
Trade receivables	2,200	2,500	(300)	2,500	2,800	(300)
Land (carried at revalued amount)	800	500	300	800	500	300
Plant and machinery	3,000	800	2,200	2,900	600	2,300
Warranty provisions	(1,000)	0	(1,000)	(1,000)	0	(1,000)
Total	5,000	3,800	1,200	5,200	3,900	1,300

The tax consequences of the change in applicable tax rate should be included in profit or loss, unless they relate to items originally recognised outside profit or loss. The deferred tax at the opening and closing balance sheet dates is calculated as follows:

	01 Jan X2		31 Dec X2	
	Temporary difference	Deferred tax	Temporary difference	Deferred tax
Trade receivables	(300)		(300)	
Plant and machinery	2,200		2,300	
Warranty provisions	(1,000)		(1,000)	
Total	900	225 (900 × 25%)	1,000	300 (1,000 × 30%)
Land (carried at revalued amount)	300	90 (300 × 30%)	300	120 (300 × 40%)

The change in deferred tax relating to receivables, the plant and machinery and the warranty provision is included in profit or loss. The change in deferred tax relating to the land is recognised in other comprehensive income, because the revaluation of land itself is recognised in other comprehensive income.

13.189   The deferred tax effects of items recognised outside profit or loss might themselves have been determined pro rata (as discussed in para 13.288.5); in that case, a change in tax status also affects those transactions and events. So the tax effects of the change in tax status should also be allocated in a similar pro rata basis as adopted previously, unless the allocation can be made on a more reasonable basis.

13.190   The tax consequences of a change in tax status could affect deferred tax balances that arose from a previous acquisition. Where the change in tax status arose in the period after acquisition, the tax effects of the change should be dealt with in profit or loss and not as an adjustment against goodwill. But where an entity's tax status is changed because of its acquisition, the tax effects of the business combination should be measured in the acquirer's consolidated financial statements using the revised tax laws and rates; also affecting goodwill. The accounting treatment in the acquired entity's separate financial statements would be as discussed above.

Practical applications

Accelerated capital allowances

13.191   Tax relief for capital expenditure on plant and machinery is given in some jurisdictions by way of capital allowances; these are a form of standardised tax depreciation. Capital allowances are deducted from accounting profit to arrive at taxable profit; the amount of depreciation charged in the financial statements is disallowed in the tax computation. Depreciation for tax and accounting purposes is the same over the asset's life, but differs from year to year; this gives rise to temporary differences under IAS 12, because of differences between the asset's carrying amount and tax base. The capital allowances often depreciate the asset at a faster rate for tax purposes than the rate of depreciation charged in the financial statements; this results in carrying amounts in excess of tax base. So the temporary differences created are referred to as 'accelerated capital allowances'. The following example shows the origination and reversal of a temporary difference on an asset qualifying for capital allowances.

Example – Origination and reversal of temporary differences

An entity buys a machine in 20X1 for C100,000. The asset is expected to be recovered fully through use over five years. Depreciation is charged on a straight line basis for accounting purposes and is C20,000 per annum. The rate of capital allowances is 25% per annum on a reducing balance basis. The machine will be scrapped at the end of its useful life; and the entity will use any unclaimed capital allowances against future trading income.

The temporary difference will arise as follows:

Per financial statements	20X1 C'000	20X2 C'000	20X3 C'000	20X4 C'000	20X5 C'000
Carrying amount of asset	100	80	60	40	20
Depreciation charge	20	20	20	20	20
Book written down value (A)	80	60	40	20	0
Per tax computation					
Carrying amount of asset	100	75	56	42	32
Capital allowance	25	19	14	10	8
Tax written down value = Tax base (B)	75	56	42	32	24
Temporary difference (A) – (B)	5	4	(2)	(12)	(24)
Originating (reversing)					
Capital allowance allowed	25	19	14	10	8
Depreciation charged	20	20	20	20	20
	5	(1)	(6)	(10)	(12)

A temporary difference of C5,000 originates in year 1. This begins to reverse from year 2 onwards. At the end of year 1, the asset's carrying amount is C80,000 and its tax base is C75,000. To recover the carrying amount of C80,000, the entity will have to generate taxable income of at least C80,000; but it will only be able to deduct capital allowances of C75,000. The difference of C5,000 gives rise to a taxable temporary difference on which deferred tax is provided.

This temporary difference unwinds as the benefit of lower current tax in the first year (that is, when capital allowances exceed depreciation) reverses from year 2 onwards; at this point, capital allowances have fallen below depreciation. From year 2 onwards, the current tax assessed and recognised in profit for the period is higher than the total amount due on the profit reported in the financial statements.

The cumulative deductible temporary difference at the end of year 5 will gradually reverse from year 6 onwards as it is utilised against future trading income.

13.191.1   A change in legislation can change the rates at which capital allowances are granted; this could affect the tax base of the asset on which deferred tax is measured. If an entity has taken into account the phasing of the reversal of temporary differences when recognising deferred tax, it will need to take into account changes in the timing of capital allowances. This change is accounted for in the period when the change in rates was substantively enacted (see further para 13.165).

Long-life assets and changes in tax allowances

13.192   On a use basis, an asset's tax base represents the amount that will be deductible for tax purposes against taxable income earned from its use in future periods. For non-current assets (such as property, plant and equipment), accounting depreciation is often recognised at a slower rate than tax depreciation is claimed. As the asset is used, accelerated tax allowances result in the asset's tax base being lower than its carrying amount. This gives rise to a taxable temporary difference on which a deferred tax liability is recognised. After all tax allowances have been claimed, the deferred tax liability unwinds as the asset continues to be used and depreciated for accounting purposes.

13.193   In a number of jurisdictions, legislation has been amended so that tax allowances can no longer be claimed for existing and new assets (that is, to reduce the tax depreciation rate to zero). The removal of future tax depreciation on an existing asset significantly reduces its tax base when deferred tax is measured on a use basis, because future deductions are no longer available. So the deferred tax liability for the existing asset increases; and there is often a tax expense in the income statement in the accounting period when substantive enactment occurs (see para 13.69).

Government grants

13.194   The accounting treatment of government grants and their treatment for tax purposes can give rise to temporary differences. Under IAS 20, government grants relating to assets are presented in the balance sheet in one of two ways: by recognising the grant as deferred income, or by deducting the grant in arriving at the asset's carrying amount. Grants given as a contribution towards an asset's cost of acquisition might be non-taxable; but some are in effect taxed by reducing the cost of fixed assets for capital allowance purposes. Other grants (such as revenue-based grants) are usually taxable on a cash received basis.

13.195 If the grant relating to an asset is not taxable, it has a tax base of nil and gives rise to a deductible temporary difference on initial recognition. This applies in two situations: first, where the grant is deducted from the asset's carrying amount; in this case, a deductible temporary difference arises, because the carrying amount is less than the asset's tax base which is cost; and, secondly, where the grant is set up as deferred income; in this case, the difference between the deferred income and its tax base of nil is a deductible temporary difference. But a deferred tax asset cannot be recognised because of the initial recognition exception noted in paragraph 13.162 and explained in paragraph 13.163.1. It would be irrational to recognise the tax benefit associated with this temporary difference on initial recognition when the income from the grant itself is recognised over a number of periods.

13.195.1 For grants related to assets, there might be a temporary difference relating to the asset as well as the deductible temporary difference relating to the grant. Where the grant is deducted from the asset's cost, any taxable temporary difference relating to the asset (for example, where tax deductions exceed accounting depreciation) needs to be calculated on the difference between the following two amounts: the asset's net book value excluding the grant (that is, gross cost less accumulated depreciation calculated on the gross cost) and its tax written down value also excluding the grant (that is, gross cost less tax allowances claimed).

13.196 Where a grant relating to an asset is taxable, the nature of the deferred tax adjustment depends on how the grant is treated for tax and accounting purposes. If the grant is deducted from the cost of fixed assets for financial reporting and tax purposes, the deferred tax calculation is relatively straightforward where capital allowances for tax purposes are calculated on a reduced cost. If the grant is treated as a deferred credit for financial reporting purposes, but deducted against the asset's cost for capital allowance purposes, the deferred tax calculation consists of two components: a deferred tax asset arises on the unamortised grant; and this is netted off against the deferred tax liability arising on the accelerated capital allowances. In practice, the balance on the deferred income account is netted off against the asset's book value for the purpose of calculating the temporary difference.

Example – Capital allowances restricted by amount of grant

An entity buys a fixed asset for C120,000. The asset qualifies for a grant of C20,000; the grant is treated in the financial statements as a deferred credit. The asset has a useful economic life of five years. The entity claims capital allowances (25% reducing balance), but these are restricted by the amount of the grant. The temporary differences for deferred tax purposes are calculated as follows:

Per financial statements	20X1	20X2	20X3	20X4	20X5
	C	C	C	C	C
Cost of asset	120,000	96,000	72,000	48,000	24,000
Depreciation	(24,000)	(24,000)	(24,000)	(24,000)	(24,000)
Net book value	96,000	72,000	48,000	24,000	–
Unamortised deferred income	16,000	12,000	8,000	4,000	–

Per tax computation	20X1	20X2	20X3	20X4	20X5
	C	C	C	C	C
Cost of asset	120,000				
Less grant	(20,000)				
Cost net of grant	100,000	75,000	56,250	42,187	31,640
Capital allowances @ 25%	(25,000)	(18,750)	(14,063)	(10,547)	(7,910)
Tax base	75,000	56,250	42,187	31,640	23,730

Temporary difference	20X1	20X2	20X3	20X4	20X5
Net book value of fixed asset	96,000	72,000	48,000	24,000	–
Unamortised grant	(16,000)	(12,000)	(8,000)	(4,000)	–
	80,000	60,000	40,000	20,000	–
Tax base	(75,000)	(56,250)	(42,187)	(31,640)	(23,730)
Cumulative temporary difference	5,000	3,750	(2,187)	(11,640)	(23,730)

The temporary difference profile will be the same if the grant is deducted directly from the asset's cost and the net amount is written off over five years.

13.197 Non-taxable revenue-based grants have no deferred tax consequences, because the amortised credit to the income statement does not enter into the determination of taxable profits. If a revenue-based grant is taxable, a temporary difference will arise between its carrying amount and its tax base. Where a revenue-based grant is taxed on receipt but amortised over a period for financial reporting purposes, it gives rise to a deductible temporary difference; this is the difference between the carrying amount of the unamortised balance and a nil tax base. A deferred tax asset is recognised on the deductible temporary difference if it is probable that the entity will earn sufficient taxable profit in later accounting periods (as the deferred credit unwinds through amortisation) so that it will benefit from the reduction in tax payments. A grant that was taxed on receipt might become repayable, and the repayment qualifies for tax relief in the year when the repayment is made; in that case, any deferred tax asset previously carried forward should be immediately written off as part of the tax charge.

Leases

13.198   Many entities enter into lease and hire purchase contracts giving them the right to use or purchase assets. In many jurisdictions, a lease contract does not provide for legal title to the leased asset to pass to the lessee. A hire purchase contract has similar features to a lease, except that the hirer can acquire legal title by exercising an option to purchase the asset on fulfilment of specified conditions (often the payment of a number of instalments).

UK.13.198.1   In the UK, tax legislation provides that capital allowances can be claimed by a lessor under a lease contract in most circumstances, and by a hirer under a hire purchase contract. Capital allowances are claimed by the lessee on longer leases of plant and machinery (whether they are accounted for as finance leases or operating leases) if they meet specified conditions and are essentially financing transactions. Such leases are known as 'long funded leases' for tax purposes.

13.199   Assets acquired under leases and hire purchase contracts give rise to temporary differences between the carrying amount and tax base. Where the asset is bought under a hire purchase agreement, the hirer normally accounts for the fixed asset's acquisition and can claim the capital allowances. So no particular deferred tax problems arise. Similarly, no deferred tax problems normally arise in accounting for an operating lease. This is because the amount that is charged to rentals by the lessee in its income statement is likely to be the same as the amount charged in arriving at the taxable profit. The only exception to this is where accrued rentals give rise to short-term temporary differences.

13.200   Where a lessee enters into a finance lease analysis of the tax effects under the balance sheet liability approach of IAS 12 can be complex. Under IAS 17, an asset acquired under a finance lease is recorded as a fixed asset with a corresponding liability for the obligation to pay future rentals. Management should consider the tax bases of the leased asset and the corresponding liability separately when calculating the respective temporary differences, even though the transaction giving rise to the asset and the liability is a single transaction.

UK.13.200.1   In the UK, the tax treatment of leases usually follows their legal form rather than the economic reality adopted for accounting purposes (except for 'long funded leases' – see para UK.13.198.1). So the lessor and not the lessee is generally entitled to capital allowances on the leased asset that is offset against the gross rental earnings. The lessee (as the user rather than the owner of the leased asset) is granted relief for the rentals payable under the lease agreement. The lease payments specified under the lease contracts are generally deductible for tax purposes; so lessees began to structure their leases in one of two ways: so they could accelerate the tax relief through large initial rentals; or so they could defer it through final balloon rentals. But, for accounting purposes, each period's rentals were apportioned effectively between the finance charge (calculated at a constant periodic rate on the remaining balance of the liability's carrying amount) and depreciation representing the consumption of the leased asset.

UK.13.200.2   To prevent the practice of timing the tax relief to suit the lessees, the Inland Revenue issued a Statement of Practice (SP 3/91) in 1991; this deals with how a lessee should obtain tax relief for its rental obligations. In general terms, SP 3/91 aims to ensure that rental payments (whenever they are due to be paid) are spread so that a finance lessee secures relief for them over the leased asset's estimated useful economic life. To achieve this, the Statement suggests that tax deductions are allowed for the amount of the accounting depreciation plus the finance charge as booked in the income statement in each accounting period. This means that a lessee obtains tax deduction as the asset's carrying amount is recovered through use. The tax deduction obtained in each period is also the same as the depreciation charge; so the carrying amount of the leased asset and its tax base are the same at each balance sheet date. Hence, no temporary difference arises. Similarly, no temporary difference arises on the outstanding lease obligation. This is because tax relief is effectively obtained on the finance charge and not on the reduction of the outstanding obligation. As a result, the tax base of the outstanding lease obligation at the end of any period is the same as its carrying amount.

Example – Tax deductions given on accounting depreciation plus finance charge

A company leases a fixed asset under a finance lease over five years. The annual lease payments are £12,000 per annum. The asset is recorded at the present value of the minimum lease payments of £48,000 and is depreciated at £9,600 per annum. The temporary differences arising are calculated as follows:

	Year 1 £	Year 2 £	Year 3 £	Year 4 £	Year 5 £
Rentals	12,000	12,000	12,000	12,000	12,000
Finance cost @ 7.93%	(3,806)	(3,158)	(2,455)	(1,699)	(882)
Capital repayment	8,194	8,842	9,545	10,301	11,118
Net book value of leased asset					
Opening balance	48,000	38,400	28,800	19,200	9,600
Depreciation	(9,600)	(9,600)	(9,600)	(9,600)	(9,600)
Ending balance	38,400	28,800	19,200	9,600	–
Tax base	38,400	28,800	19,200	9,600	–
Taxable temporary difference	–	–	–	–	–

13091

Outstanding leasing obligations					
Opening balance	48,000	39,806	30,964	21,419	11,118
Capital repayment	(8,194)	(8,842)	(9,545)	(10,301)	(11,118)
Ending balance	39,806	30,964	21,419	11,118	–
Tax base	39,806	30,964	21,419	11,118	–
Deductible temporary difference	–	–	–	–	–
Tax computations – rentals	13,406	12,758	12,055	11,299	10,482
Income statement:					
Finance cost	3,806	3,158	2,455	1,699	882
Depreciation	9,600	9,600	9,600	9,600	9,600
	13,406	12,758	12,055	11,299	10,482
(Origination) and reversal of temporary difference	–	–	–	–	–

No deferred tax arises under SP 3/91 because tax deductions are effectively given over the leased asset's life for finance cost and depreciation charge rather than the rentals payable in each period. Over the leased asset's life, the sum of the finance cost (£12,000) and depreciation charge (£48,000) is equal to cumulative rentals (£60,000).

If tax deductions were given for each period's rentals (as specified under the lease contract), a temporary difference would have arisen on which deferred tax would be recognised. For example, a deductible temporary difference of £1,406 would have arisen in year 1 between the amount recognised in the income statement (£13,406) and the amount of tax deduction allowed in the tax computations (£12,000).

[The next paragraph is 13.202.]

Decommissioning assets and obligations

13.202 Decommissioning costs arise in a number of industries, such as the electricity and nuclear industries; abandonment costs in the mining and extractive industries; and environmental clean-up costs in a number of industries. IAS 37 requires management to recognise a provision at the outset for the obligation to decommission an asset and to capitalise a corresponding decommissioning asset. The decommissioning asset is depreciated over the life of the underlying asset. The accounting for decommissioning obligations (also referred to as 'asset retirement obligations') and the related asset is discussed in chapter 21. In many jurisdictions, the tax deduction for the decommissioning cost is only available when an entity incurs the expenditure; this will have deferred tax implications.

13.202.1 We consider that there are two main approaches for determining the tax bases of decommissioning assets and liabilities. The choice of approach is a matter of accounting policy to be applied on a consistent basis. Under both approaches, the deferred tax accounting applies to discounted carrying amounts for assets and liabilities; so on initial recognition the tax deductions are based on the discounted amounts, rather than the gross amounts payable in the future. This is because IAS 12 focuses on the future tax consequences of recovering an asset or settling a liability at its carrying amount, which is the discounted amount (see paras 13.113 and 13.121).

13.202.2 The first approach allocates the future tax deductions to the asset. On initial recognition, the asset's tax base is the future tax consequence of recovering the asset at its carrying amount. The tax base is thus the discounted amount of deductions, which is the same as the asset's carrying amount; so no temporary difference arises on the asset. There is no deduction associated with the liability; and so its tax base (that is, carrying amount less future deductions) is equal to its carrying amount. As there is no temporary difference on the asset or the liability on initial recognition, the initial recognition exception (see para 13.162) is not relevant.

13.202.3 The alternative approach allocates the future tax deductions to the liability. The asset's tax base is nil because there are no associated tax deductions; so there is a temporary difference equal to the asset's carrying amount on initial recognition. The liability's tax base (that is, carrying amount less future deductions) is also nil; so there is a temporary difference equal to the liability's carrying amount on initial recognition. For decommissioning obligations (and related assets) arising outside a business combination and which do not affect accounting profit or taxable profit on initial recognition, these temporary differences will be covered by the initial recognition exception (see para 13.162); so no deferred tax arises on initial recognition.

13.202.4 For later changes to decommissioning assets and liabilities, management will need to determine how to account for them under the relevant approach. The two approaches will not necessarily give the same results, due to the intricacies of the initial recognition exception. In particular, where the initial recognition exception applies, management will need to analyse the movements in the temporary difference; this is to see if they are due to reversals of the amount that gave rise to the temporary difference or whether they are new temporary differences on which deferred tax is recognised (see para 13.164 onwards).

13.202.5 The accounting implications of the two approaches for determining deferred tax on decommissioning assets and liabilities are shown in the following example.

Example – Deferred tax on decommissioning asset and obligation

An entity will incur decommissioning costs of C1m relating to its plant in 3 years' time. The plant was not acquired as part of a business combination. The applicable discount rate is 8% and the tax rate is 30%.

Expected decommissioning cost in 3 years' time	C1,000,000
Expected decommissioning cost (discounted)	C794,000

Under IAS 37, the decommissioning asset and liability are recorded at C794,000 on initial recognition.

The asset is depreciated on a straight-line basis over 3 years.

It is assumed that there are no changes in estimates.

The decommissioning costs recognised in the balance sheet and income statement are as follows:

	Initial recognition C'000	Year 1 C'000	Year 2 C'000	Year 3 C'000
Balance sheet:				
Asset	794	529	264	–
Liability	(794)	(858)	(926)	(1,000)
Income statement:				
Depreciation (total = 794)		265	265	264
Interest (total = 206)		64	68	74
Total (= 1,000)		329	333	338

Assume that tax deductions will be received when the expenditure is incurred. As noted in paragraph 13.202.1, we consider that there are two main approaches for determining the deferred tax in respect of the decommissioning asset and liability. These approaches are illustrated below.

Approach 1 – Tax deductions allocated to the decommissioning asset

	Initial recognition C'000	Year 1 C'000	Year 2 C'000	Year 3 C'000
Temporary differences:				
Carrying amount of asset	794	529	264	–
Tax base	794	794	794	794
Deductible temporary difference	–	(265)	(529)	(794)
Carrying amount of liability	794	858	926	1,000
Tax base (carrying amount less deductions of nil)	794	858	926	1,000
Temporary difference	–	–	–	–
Deductible temporary difference on cumulative interest charged to income statement	–	(64)	(132)	(206)
Total deductible temporary difference	–	(329)	(661)	(1,000)
Deferred tax asset @ 30%	–	99	198	300

Initial recognition

The asset's tax base is the discounted amount of deductions, which is the same as the asset's carrying amount; so no temporary difference arises on the asset on initial recognition.

There is no deduction associated with the liability; so its tax base (carrying amount less future deductions) is equal to its carrying amount; and no temporary difference arises.

Subsequent changes

As the asset is depreciated, a deductible temporary difference arises on which a deferred tax asset is recognised (subject to IAS 12's recognition criteria).

There is also a deductible temporary difference (and corresponding deferred tax asset) in respect of interest charged to profit or loss for which tax deductions will be received in the future.

13095

Approach 2 – Tax deductions allocated to the decommissioning liability

	Initial recognition C'000	Year 1 C'000	Year 2 C'000	Year 3 C'000
Temporary differences:				
Carrying amount of asset	794	529	264	–
Tax base	–	–	–	–
Taxable temporary difference	794	529	264	–
Covered by initial recognition exception	(794)	(529)	(264)	–
Remaining taxable temporary difference not covered by initial recognition exception	–	–	–	–
Carrying amount of liability	794	858	926	1,000
Tax base (carrying amount less deductions)	–	–	–	–
Deductible temporary difference	(794)	(858)	(926)	(1,000)
Covered by initial recognition exception	794	794	794	794
Remaining deductible temporary difference not covered by initial recognition exception	–	(64)	(132)	(206)
Total deductible temporary difference	–	(64)	(132)	(206)
Deferred tax asset @ 30%	–	19	40	62

Initial recognition

The asset's tax base is nil because there are no associated tax deductions; so there is a temporary difference equal to the asset's carrying amount on initial recognition.

The liability's tax base (carrying amount less future deductions) is also nil; so there is a temporary difference equal to the liability's carrying amount on initial recognition.

Assuming that the decommissioning obligation (and related asset) does not arise from a business combination, these temporary differences will be covered by the initial recognition exception; so no deferred tax arises on initial recognition.

Subsequent changes

As the asset is depreciated, the initial temporary difference that was covered by the initial recognition exception is reversed; the reversal is also covered by the initial recognition exception and so a deferred tax asset is not recognised. [IAS 12 para 22(c)].

The unwinding of the discount on the liability increases the temporary difference; so it is not a reversal of the initial amount but a new temporary difference. Because it affects profit or loss (interest expense), it is not covered by the initial recognition exception and a deferred tax asset is recognised (subject to IAS 12's recognition criteria).

Comparison of the approaches

The impact of depreciation on deferred tax is different under approach 1 (deductions allocated to the asset) and approach 2 (deductions allocated to the liability).

Under approach 1, there are no initial temporary differences and so the initial recognition exception is not applicable. As the asset is depreciated, there is a deductible temporary difference on which a deferred tax asset is recognised (subject to sufficient expected taxable profit).

Under approach 2, there are initial temporary differences covered by the initial recognition exception. As the asset is depreciated, the initial temporary difference is reversed; the reversal is also covered by the initial recognition exception, so a deferred tax asset is not recognised.

Therefore, under approach 1, a deferred tax asset arises in respect of the deductions relating to the depreciation expense and the interest expense. Under approach 2, there is only a deferred tax asset in respect of deductions relating to the interest expense (reflected in the increase in carrying amount of the liability and in its temporary difference).

There is also a third approach, namely a view that the initial recognition exception does not apply under approach 2 (see para 13.202.6).

We consider that all three approaches are acceptable. The choice of approach is a matter of accounting policy to be applied on a consistent basis.

13.202.6   As noted above, there is a view that the initial recognition exception does not apply under approach 2. This is justified by the fact that paragraphs 15 and 24 of IAS 12 refer to 'the initial recognition of an asset *or* liability'; in this case, an asset *and* a liability are recognised at the same time, with equal and opposite temporary differences. Under this view, a deferred tax liability would be recognised in respect of the taxable temporary difference on the decommissioning asset; and (subject to IAS 12's recognition criteria) a deferred tax asset would be recognised in respect of the deductible temporary difference on the decommissioning liability. Later changes to the decommissioning asset and liability would also have a deferred tax impact, because the initial recognition exception has not been applied. Given that different approaches are acceptable, an entity should make clear its accounting policy for deferred tax on decommissioning obligations if this is material.

13.202.7   Changes in estimates (to cash flows or discount rates) impact the carrying amount of the decommissioning asset and decommissioning liability (see chapter 21). Where tax deductions are allocated to the asset (approach 1 in para 13.202.2), no new temporary differences arise. But allocating tax deductions to the liability (approach 2 in para 13.202.3) will result in changes to the initial temporary differences. Increases in the carrying amounts are new temporary differences; but they are covered by the initial recognition exception under approach 2 because they do not affect profit or loss. Decreases in the carrying amount (that is, below the amount on initial recognition) are reversals of the initial temporary difference; so they will be covered by the original initial recognition exception under approach 2.

13.202.8 In some situations, tax deductions are available on some (but not all) of the decommissioning expenditure. Management needs to understand the basis for the tax deductions in order to determine the deferred tax implications. If the tax deduction relates to (or is a proxy for) specific types of expenditure, it might be necessary to treat this expenditure as a separate component of the decommissioning asset and liability for the purpose of allocating the deductions. Or there might be no relationship to specific expenditure, but tax deductions are given instead as a percentage of total expenditure; in this case, the tax base is determined using that percentage figure.

Post-retirement benefits

13.203 Accounting for pension costs and other post-retirement benefits gives rise to a temporary difference for deferred tax purposes. Tax relief on employers' pension contributions is often given in the period when they are paid, rather than when the costs are recognised in the financial statements, with the possible exception of some large contributions, where tax relief might be spread over a period. In an unfunded plan, and in the case of provisions for unfunded benefits (such as post-retirement healthcare), the tax relief is often given when the pensions or other benefits are paid. In the financial statements, on the other hand, pension costs and other post-retirement benefits are recognised under IAS 19 as service is provided by the employee.

UK.13.203.1 In the UK, employer pension contributions are only deductible as an expense if they are incurred *"wholly and exclusively for the purposes of the employer's trade or profession"*; so tax relief is not automatic. Entities should consider this when accounting for tax in respect of pension schemes. Where tax relief is obtained, tax deductions on any significant contributions might also be subject to spreading rules. This will occur when 'relevant excess contributions' (RECs) are made. The implications of spreading tax deductions on RECs are considered in paragraph 13.203.11 . This is a complex area and consultation with a tax specialist is advised.

13.203.1 A deductible temporary difference arises between the carrying amount of the net defined benefit liability and its tax base; the tax base is usually nil, unless tax relief on contributions paid is received in a period subsequent to payment. In most cases, this deductible temporary difference will reverse, but it might take a long time. This is particularly relevant for defined benefit pension plans, unfunded pensions and post-retirement benefit plans. A deferred tax asset is recognised under IAS 12 for these temporary differences if it is recoverable.

UK.13.203.2 Under UK GAAP (FRS 17), a deferred tax balance recognised for a defined benefit asset or liability is offset against the related defined benefit asset or liability. This treatment is not permissible under IAS 12; so deferred tax balances relating to employee benefits are included with other deferred tax assets and liabilities (see also para 13.278 onwards).

13.203.2 A deferred tax asset should be recognised to the extent that it is probable that taxable profit will be available against which the deductible temporary difference can be utilised. [IAS 12 para 24]. The question arises whether deferred tax liabilities resulting from other temporary differences can be taken into account in determining the recoverability of the deferred tax asset relating to pensions. Future reversals of existing taxable temporary differences are dealt with in paragraph 13.134 onwards. A deferred tax asset for a pension obligation cannot be recognised simply because there are sufficient taxable temporary differences at the balance sheet date; the timing of reversal of the taxable temporary differences also needs to be taken into account.

13.203.3 So management might need to schedule the reversal of temporary differences to justify recognising the deferred tax asset. In many jurisdictions, the entity has to have plans in place to eliminate the pension deficit – simply paying the normal regular cost will not eliminate the deficit. Recognising a tax asset in respect of the pension obligations should take into account the expected timing of regular and one-off contributions necessary to eliminate the deficit.

13.203.4 If the entity has incurred losses in the past and also in the current period, this could impact the recognition of tax assets. For example, if the entity continues to make losses in the next few years before a turnaround is anticipated, but the amount of the reversal of the existing taxable temporary differences in those years is not enough to create taxable profits (with the effect that any pension contributions made in those years simply add to the tax loss), the deferred tax asset might not be recoverable. For an assessment of the likelihood that taxable profits will be available when there has been a history of trading losses, see paragraph 13.144 onwards.

13.203.5 Where a net defined benefit asset arises (for example, in respect of a surplus in the pension plan), a taxable temporary difference will arise and a deferred tax liability will be recognised.

13.203.5.1 Guidance on how entities should assess the recoverability of a defined benefit pension surplus is given in IFRIC 14 (see further chapter 11). If a pension surplus refund is subject to a tax other than income tax, an entity measures the amount of the refund net of the tax. [IFRIC 14 para 13]. But if a surplus refund is subject to income tax, the deferred tax liability relating to the pension surplus is determined under IAS 12 and recognised separately from the pension asset.

13.203.5.1.1 IAS 1 requires information to be disclosed about key sources of estimation uncertainty; IFRIC 14 states that such information might include restrictions on the current realisability of the surplus; it might also include the basis used to determine the amount of the economic benefit available. The manner of recovery could also impact deferred tax accounting in jurisdictions where refunds of surplus are subject to income tax at a different rate from the normal corporate income tax rate.

13.203.5.2   Under IFRIC 14, the right to a refund or the right to a reduction of future contributions needs to exist in order to recognise a pension asset; but IAS 12 requires the entity to consider its expected manner of recovery in determining the relevant tax rate and tax base for calculating the deferred tax liability relating to the pension asset. So the entity could have a *right* to a refund from the plan (and immediately pass the IFRIC 14 test), but it might *expect* to realise the economic benefits of the surplus through reductions in future contributions. For instance, this might be the case where a lower tax rate applies to reduced contributions than to a refund.

13.203.5.3   Where the entity expects to recover the surplus through reduced contributions, it will need to confirm that it has sufficient capacity to reduce future contributions over the scheme's remaining life. In some cases, the entity might expect to recover the pension asset in part through reduced contributions and in part through a refund; the appropriate tax rates and tax bases should be used to determine the deferred tax liability for each part of the expected recovery.

UK.13.203.5.3.1   In the UK, pension refunds are 'ring fenced' from the employer's other profits and tax is charged at a special rate. The tax is deducted at source by the pension plan administrators; but it is assessed on the employer company as corporation tax with a set-off for the tax deducted by the pension plan. The special rate is intended to claw back relief on pension plan deductions previously given at a higher rate. In our view, tax on pension refunds in the UK is income tax and should be accounted for under IAS 12.

13.203.6   Under IAS 19, entities currently have a choice of policy in accounting for the net defined benefit cost. They can choose to recognise actuarial gains and losses in full as they arise, outside profit or loss; in that case, various components of pension cost are reported in profit or loss, and actuarial gains and losses are reported in other comprehensive income. Pension cost accounting might give rise to current tax (tax relief on contributions) and deferred tax (on the temporary difference between the net defined benefit asset or liability and its tax base). There is no direct relationship between the components of pension cost reported in the performance statements and the contributions and benefits paid in a period; so current and deferred tax need to be allocated between the performance statements.

13.203.6.1   IAS 19 (revised), issued in June 2011, requires actuarial gains and losses to be recognised as they arise, outside profit or loss; the previously available alternatives have been removed. So all entities will be required to allocate current and deferred tax between the performance statements. The revised standard is effective for annual periods beginning on or after 1 January 2013.

13.203.7 As explained in paragraphs 13.46 and 13.288, current and deferred tax should be recognised outside profit or loss if the tax relates to items that are recognised outside profit or loss. [IAS 12 para 61A]. It can sometimes be difficult to determine the amount of current and deferred tax that relates to items recognised outside profit or loss. In this case, current and deferred tax should be allocated on a reasonable *pro rata* basis, unless another method of allocation is more appropriate in the circumstances. [IAS 12 para 63].

13.203.8 IAS 12 does not specify a method of allocating current and deferred tax relating to defined benefit pensions. It is acceptable for tax relief on pension contributions to be allocated so that the contributions cover profit and loss items first and actuarial losses second (unless some other allocation is more appropriate). If contributions exceed those items, tax relief relating to the excess is credited in profit or loss (unless it is more appropriate to allocate it to other comprehensive income). Where a special contribution is made to fund a deficit arising from an identifiable cause (such as an actuarial loss), an alternative method of allocation might be appropriate; in that case, the tax relief should be allocated to other comprehensive income. But, if there is no clear link between the special contribution and the items recognised in the performance statements, the first method shown above should be used.

UK.13.203.8.1 The above methodology is based on FRS 17. Under FRS 17, actuarial gains and losses are reported in the equivalent to other comprehensive income (that is, the statement of total recognised gains and losses (STRGL)). There is a hierarchy for allocating current and deferred tax between the profit and loss account (the income statement equivalent) and the STRGL. [FRS 17 para 71]. In our view, the hierarchy set out in FRS 17 provides a reasonable basis of allocation as required by IAS 12.

13.203.9 The allocation of current and deferred tax is illustrated in the following simplified examples, which show the movements in the pension balance during the year. A tax rate of 30% is assumed.

Example 1 – Defined benefit asset with an actuarial loss

	Change in defined benefit asset	Current tax relief (30%)	Deferred tax liability (30%)
	C	C	C
Brought forward	120		(36)
Contributions	70	(21)	
Income statement – net pension cost	(60)	18	–
Other comprehensive income – actuarial loss	(20)	3	3
	(80)	21	3
Carried forward	110	–	(33)

Taxation

Current tax relief of C21 arises on contributions paid of C70. This is allocated first to cover pension cost of C60 reported in the income statement (resulting in a credit of C18 in the tax charge). The balance of the contributions paid of C10 is allocated to the actuarial loss; hence, current tax of C3 is credited in other comprehensive income. Deferred tax of C3 is attributable to the balance of the actuarial loss of C10; this is credited in other comprehensive income.

Example 2 – Defined benefit liability with an actuarial loss

	Change in defined benefit liability	Current tax relief (30%)	Deferred tax asset (30%)
	C	C	C
Brought forward	(200)		(60)
Contributions paid	80	(24)	
Income statement – net pension cost	(70)	21	–
Other comprehensive income – actuarial loss	(20)	3	3
	(90)	24	3
Carried forward	(210)	–	63

Current tax relief of C24 arises on contributions paid of C80. This is allocated first to cover pension cost of C70 reported in the income statement (resulting in a credit of C21 in the tax charge). The balance of the contributions paid of C10 is allocated to the actuarial loss; hence, current tax of C3 is credited in other comprehensive income. Deferred tax of C3 is attributable to the balance of the actuarial loss of C10; this is credited in other comprehensive income.

Example 3 – Defined benefit liability with an actuarial gain

If, in the above example, there was an actuarial gain rather than an actuarial loss, the whole of the current tax relief of C24 would be credited in the income statement. None of the current tax can be allocated to other comprehensive income because there is no debit in other comprehensive income. Thus, the initial C21 (30% of C70) is allocated to the income statement, nil is allocated to other comprehensive income, and the excess of C3 is allocated to the income statement. Deferred tax attributable to the actuarial gain would be charged in other comprehensive income, as shown below.

	Change in defined benefit liability	Current tax relief (30%)	Deferred tax asset (30%)
	C	C	C
Brought forward	(200)		60
Contributions	80	(24)	
Income statement – net pension cost	(70)	24	(3)
Other comprehensive income – actuarial gain	20	–	(6)
	(50)	24	(9)
Carried forward	(170)	–	51

13.203.10 The allocation is more complicated if a large contribution is made in the period (for example, to reduce an existing pension deficit). Assume that, in example 2 above, an additional contribution of C100 was paid and tax deductions were received in the period.

Example – Receipt of tax relief on additional contribution

	Change in defined benefit liability	Current tax relief (30%)	Deferred tax asset (30%)
	C	C	C
Brought forward	(200)		(60)
'Normal' contributions paid	80	(24)	
Additional contributions paid	100	(30)	
Income statement – net pension cost	(70)	21	–
Other comprehensive income:			
Current year actuarial loss	(20)	3	3
Relating to previous actuarial losses	–	30	(30)
	(90)	54	(27)
Carried forward	(110)	–	(33)

If tax deductions on the normal contribution of C80 and the additional contribution of C100 are all received in the period (that is, no spreading of deductions), the current tax relief of C24 on the 'normal' contributions is allocated as follows: first, against the pension cost in the income statement; and the balance is allocated against the actuarial loss.

Further current tax deductions of C30 are received on the additional contribution. So there is an excess deduction to be considered. Under the allocation hierarchy in paragraph 13.203.7, this excess would go to the income statement, unless another method of allocation is more appropriate. The treatment of the deferred tax in relation to the additional contribution will depend on the reason for making that contribution. In this case, it is likely that the additional contribution is funding past actuarial losses.

So it is necessary to determine where the underlying items – giving rise to the deficit that is being funded – were originally recognised; this is done by backwards-tracing the items in the performance statement. Thus the tax movement is allocated to other comprehensive income, as illustrated above.

But if the additional contribution was made to fund current year actuarial losses as well as previous actuarial losses, C3 would be allocated to other comprehensive income (to cover the C10 of actuarial loss made in the current year not yet tax affected). There is an excess deduction of C27 after allocating to the net pension cost in the income statement and any actuarial losses in other comprehensive income. Again, this should be allocated to other comprehensive income if the contribution was made to fund the accumulated actuarial losses. Notably, this has the same outcome as the allocation method illustrated in the table above. An element of judgement will be needed when considering why the additional contribution was made.

It will be necessary to backwards-trace further if the deductions received in the year exceed the current and prior year actuarial losses that had not been allocated current tax deductions. If it can be established (using backwards-tracing) that the tax deductions relate to prior year actuarial losses, the excess tax deductions will be recognised in other comprehensive income; and there will be a corresponding reversal of deferred tax (as shown above).

Just because a pension liability recognised on transition to IFRS was charged to equity, current tax deductions or subsequent changes in any related deferred tax asset will not necessarily also be recognised in equity (see further para 13.288.7).

13.203.11 If tax deductions are spread across more than one accounting period, this will impact on the deferred tax calculation because the deduction received in the current year will be lower. Assume that, in the example above, the tax relief for the additional contribution of C100 is spread over three periods; that is, only one-third of the relief on the additional contribution is received in the current period.

Example – Spreading of tax relief on additional contribution

	Change in defined benefit liability	Current tax relief (30%)	Deferred tax asset (30%)
	C	C	C
Brought forward	(200)		(60)
'Normal' contributions paid	80	(24)	
Additional contributions paid	100	(10)	
Income statement – net pension cost	(70)	21	–
Other comprehensive income:			
Current year actuarial loss	(20)	3	3
Relating to previous actuarial losses	–	10	(10)
	(90)	34	(7)
Carried forward	(110)	–	(53)

Note that the deferred tax balance at the period end is not 30% of the pension balance.

Assuming that a deferred tax asset has been recognised in relation to the pension liability at the beginning of the period, part of this deferred tax asset reverses as a result of the tax deductions received in the period. But, if the contributions paid do not receive tax relief in the period, a corresponding portion of the deferred tax asset on the opening pension liability will continue to be carried forward (assuming the recognition criteria are met); and this portion will reverse in the future when the tax deductions are received.

The deferred tax asset can be summarised as:

	C
On pension liability at year end (110 × 30%)	33
Outstanding deductions on contributions made (100 × 30% × 2/3)	20
Total deferred tax asset	53

In terms of the pension liability's tax base, the tax base of a liability is its carrying amount less any amount that will be deductible for tax in future periods (see para 13.122). So the deductible temporary difference will be equal to the future deductible amounts. If, in arriving at the pension liability of C110, contributions of C100 had been paid in the period on which tax relief is spread over 3 years (with tax relief on C33 received in the current year), the tax base will be the carrying amount of the liability (C110) less future deductible amounts (C110 + C67 = C177) = a tax base of – C67. In other words, the carrying amount in the balance sheet is a liability; but the tax base is an asset (of C67), representing the deductions receivable in the future for payments made and payments to be made. This gives a deductible temporary difference of C110 – (– C67) = C177 (that is, equal to the future deductible amounts).

A deferred tax asset of C177 × 30% = C53 should be recognised to the extent that it is probable that the deferred tax asset will be recovered.

Share-based payment transactions

Equity-settled transactions

13.204 IFRS 2 requires entities to recognise the cost of equity-settled share-based awards to employees on the basis of the fair value of the award at the date of grant, spread over the vesting period (see further chapter 12). But any deduction available for tax purposes in the case of equity-settled transactions often does not correspond to the amount charged to profit or loss under IFRS 2.

UK.13.204.1 A tax deduction in connection with an employee share option scheme is generally available under UK tax law at the date of exercise, measured on the basis of the option's intrinsic value at that date (being the difference between the share's market price at the date of exercise and the option's exercise price).

13.205 So there is an impact on deferred tax where a future deduction is available; this is because a deductible temporary difference arises between the tax base of the remuneration expense recognised in profit or loss (that is, the amount permitted by the tax authorities as a deduction in future periods) and its carrying amount of nil on the balance sheet (the credit is against retained earnings). This gives rise to a deferred tax asset. Furthermore, the calculation of the deferred tax asset is complicated by the fact that the future tax deduction will be based on the share price at the date of exercise; and the price cannot be known for certain until that date. So the amount of the tax deduction to be obtained in the future (that is, the tax base) should be estimated on the basis of the information available at the end of the period. Thus, the measurement of the deductible temporary difference should be based on the entity's share price at the balance sheet date. [IAS 12 para 68B].

13.205.1 Management will estimate the future tax deductions available based on the share options' intrinsic value at the balance sheet date (as noted above). The estimate of the tax deduction should be based on the number of options expected to be exercised (as opposed to the number of options outstanding at the balance sheet date); this will give the best estimate of the amount of the future tax deduction.

13.206 But the amount of the future tax deduction (calculated as set out above) is unlikely to be the same as the remuneration expense recognised in profit or loss and credited to equity. If the amount of the estimated future tax deduction exceeds the cumulative amount of the remuneration expense, this indicates that the tax deduction relates to an equity item as well as the remuneration expense. In that situation, the excess deferred tax should be recognised in equity under the principle that the tax should follow the item. This also applies to any excess current tax that arises in the year of exercise. [IAS 12 para 68C]. (See further para 13.288.2.)

[The next paragraph is 13.206.2.]

13.206.2 The accounting for excess deferred tax on an equity-settled share-based award is illustrated in the following example.

> **Example – Excess deferred tax on an equity-settled share-based award**
>
> On 1 January 20X3, 100,000 options are issued with a fair value of C360,000. The vesting period is 3 years and all options are expected to be exercised. All of the share options are exercised in year 4. The tax rate is 30%. The intrinsic value of the share options (that is, market value of the underlying shares less exercise price) at the end of years 1, 2 and 3 and at the date of exercise in year 4 is C330,000, C300,000, C380,000 and C400,000, respectively.
>
> The total staff cost recognised in each of the first 3 years is C120,000. At the end of the first year, the estimated corresponding tax benefit available in the future is C33,000 (30% × $\frac{1}{3}$ × C330,000); this is calculated using the intrinsic value at the balance sheet date. The gross amount giving rise to the tax benefit is C110,000, which is less

than the cumulative remuneration expense of C120,000 recognised to date; so the entire amount of the estimated future tax benefit of C33,000 is recognised in the income statement.

At the end of year 2, the cumulative amount of the estimated tax benefit available in the future is C60,000 (30% × $^2/_3$ × C300,000). The gross amount giving rise to the tax benefit of C200,000 is less than the cumulative remuneration expense of C240,000 recognised to date; so the entire amount is recognised through the income statement. The amount recognised in year 2's income statement is C27,000 (C60,000 — C33,000).

At the end of year 3, the cumulative amount of the estimated tax benefit available in the future is C114,000 (30% × C380,000). The amount giving rise to the benefit of C380,000 exceeds the cumulative remuneration expense of C360,000 recognised to date; so the excess expected future tax benefit of C6,000 (30% × C20,000) is recognised in equity. The cumulative position at the end of year 3 is shown below.

Year	Expense	Income statement Dr (Cr) Current tax	Deferred tax	Equity Dr (Cr) Current tax	Deferred tax	Balance sheet Dr (Cr) Current tax	Deferred tax
	C	C	C	C	C	C	C
1	120,000	–	(33,000)	–	–	–	33,000
2	120,000	–	(27,000)	–	–	–	60,000
3	120,000	–	(48,000)	–	(6,000)	–	114,000
Cumulative position at end of year 3	360,000	–	(108,000)	–	(6,000)		

In year 4, all 100,000 options are exercised. The actual current tax deduction obtained is C120,000 (30% × C400,000 intrinsic value at the date of exercise). This amount exceeds the tax effect of an amount equal to the cumulative remuneration expense of C360,000; so the excess current tax of C12,000 (30% × C40,000) is recognised in equity. The deferred tax asset of C114,000 at the end of year 3 is reversed through the income statement and equity. The double entry is as follows:

			C	C
Dr	Current tax claim (balance sheet)		120,000	
	Cr	Current tax (income statement)		108,000
	Cr	Current tax (equity)		12,000
Dr	Deferred tax (income statement)		108,000	
Dr	Deferred tax (equity)		6,000	
	Cr	Deferred tax (balance sheet)		114,000

The overall position is shown below:

13107

Taxation

| | Income statement Dr (Cr) | | | Equity Dr (Cr) | | Balance sheet Dr (Cr) | |
	Expense	Current tax	Deferred tax	Current tax	Deferred tax	Current tax	Deferred tax
	C	C	C	C	C	C	C
Cumulative position at end of year 3	360,000		– (108,000)	–	(6,000)	–	114,000
Movement in year 4		– (108,000)	108,000	(12,000)	6,000	120,000	(114,000)
Total	360,000	(108,000)	–	(12,000)	–	120,000	–

The tax credit recognised in the income statement of C108,000 is equal to the tax benefit calculated by applying the applicable tax rate of 30% to the remuneration expense of C360,000 recognised in the income statement over the vesting period. Any excess tax deduction received is recognised in equity. A comprehensive example of equity-settled transaction is also included in example 5 of appendix B to the standard.

UK.13.206.2.1 The accounting for deferred tax on equity-settled share-based payments under IFRS differs from the accounting under UK GAAP. Under FRS 19, there is a timing difference between the recognition of the share-based payment charge in the profit and loss account and the related deduction for tax purposes that will be received in the future; this results in a deferred tax asset. But, under UK GAAP, if the tax deduction that will be obtained (based on the share option's intrinsic value at the date of exercise) exceeds the tax asset based on the option's fair value at date of grant, this element is regarded as a permanent difference and is accounted for when it crystallises (that is, when the share options are exercised). A further difference under UK GAAP is that all tax relating to the deduction is recognised in the profit and loss account.

[The next paragraph is 13.206.4.]

13.206.4 The deferred tax in respect of an equity-settled share-based payment award should be calculated for each separate award (or tranche of an award where some options have been exercised and deferred tax is being reversed) and not for all awards in total. Each separate award has its own tax base (that is, the tax deductions that will be received on exercise of the options). This tax base is compared to the carrying amount of each separate award to calculate the temporary difference; and deferred tax should be recognised, where appropriate. The movement on the deferred tax for each grant is allocated between profit or loss and equity based on the cumulative share-based payment charge recognised in profit or loss (as outlined in para 13.206). An appropriate method (for example, weighted average or FIFO) should be used on a consistent basis to identify options that have been exercised or settled.

13.206.5 When the tax is allocated between profit or loss and equity, each award should be considered separately. The allocation should not be done on a total basis, because this could mask underlying movements in relation to specific awards.

Example – Allocation of deferred tax movements on separate awards

An entity has two share-based payment awards. Tax deductions will be received based on the market value of the shares at the date of exercise. The cumulative share-based payment charge under IFRS 2 and the expected tax deductions (measured using the share price at the balance sheet date) for each scheme are given below.

It is assumed that the recognition criteria for deferred tax assets are met and the tax rate is 30%.

	Award 1	Award 2	Total
	C'000	C'000	C'000
Cumulative charge (income statement)	100	100	200
Expected tax deduction	160	80	240
Deferred tax asset (30% of expected tax deduction)	48	24	72

Allocation performed on a grant by grant basis

For Award 1, C100 of the tax deduction relates to the charge recognised in the income statement. The remaining C60 of tax deduction is an equity item.

		C'000	C'000
Dr	Deferred tax asset	48	
Cr	Income statement (100 × 30%)		30
Cr	Equity (60 × 30%)		18

For Award 2, the tax deduction expected is lower than the cumulative charge in the income statement. The full deduction is seen as relating to the charge in the income statement.

		C'000	C'000
Dr	Deferred tax asset	24	
Cr	Income statement (80 × 30%)		24

The total credit recognised in the income statement is C54; and a credit of C18 is taken to equity.

Allocation performed on a total basis

Looking at the awards on a total basis, it appears that C200 of the tax deductions relate to charges recognised in the income statement. The allocation of the tax deduction would credit the income statement with C60 (200 × 30%) and take the balance of C12 directly to equity.

Allocation on a total basis would result in the tax credit in the income statement being overstated; so it is not considered acceptable.

13.206.6 The allocation between profit or loss and equity is also relevant when a deferred tax asset in respect of a share-based payment is reduced because the share price has fallen. When the deferred tax asset has a corresponding portion of tax credit that was previously recorded in equity (under para 68C of IAS 12), the reduction of the deferred tax asset needs to be analysed to determine how much of the reduction should be recognised in equity. This is because the reversal of deferred tax assets and liabilities should be recognised in the statement in which the initial item was recognised (see para 13.288). So, if the share-based payment's tax base reduces, the deferred tax balance needs to be analysed to determine the extent of reversal (if any) from equity.

Example – Allocation of deferred tax when share price has fallen

An equity-settled share-based payment award for employees vests after 4 years of service. An award is made for 2,000 shares. The fair value of the award at the date of grant is C6 (per share).

The entity expects all the shares in the scheme to vest. So, under IFRS 2, the accounting expense is 2,000 shares × C6 = C12,000 × ¼ = C3,000 per annum for 4 years. At the end of year 2, the cumulative IFRS 2 charge is C6,000. The share price at the end of year 2 is C10, but it drops to C7 by the end of year 3. The position at the end of years 2 and 3 is summarised below.

	End of year 2	End of year 3
Number of equity instruments earned for IFRS 2 purposes	1,000	1,500
Cumulative IFRS 2 charge	C6,000	C9,000
Share price (= tax value per share)	C10	C7
Tax base	C10,000	C10,500
Deferred tax (@ 30%)	C3,000	C3,150

The movement in deferred tax in year 3 is analysed as follows:

	Cumulative IFRS 2 charge C'000	Tax base C'000	Deferred tax C'000	Split Income statement C'000	Equity C'000
Opening balance	6,000	10,000	3,000	1,800	1,200
Closing balance	9,000	10,500	3,150	2,700	450
Movement			150	900	(750)

There is a deferred tax credit of C900,000 in the income statement reflecting the deferred tax on the share-based payment charge of C3,000,000 in the period.

Where the share-based payment's tax base reduces, but does not fall below the cumulative accounting charge under IFRS 2, the excess tax deduction is reduced; so it is recognised in equity. The deferred tax charge of C750,000 in equity comprises:

■ A charge of C900,000, being the impact of the drop in share price on the opening deferred tax asset (1,000 shares × (C10 – C7) × 30%).

■ A credit of C150,000, being the excess tax credit on the award earned in the period (500 shares × (C7 – C6) × 30%).

If the share-based payment's tax base falls below the cumulative accounting charge, the full amount that was previously recognised in equity will be fully reversed; the movement in the income statement will comprise a tax credit in respect of the share-based payment charge and a charge in respect of any reduction in the tax base below the cumulative accounting charge.

13.206.7   In jurisdictions where a tax deduction is given when the share options are exercised, there might be no tax deduction where share options lapse after the vesting date and are not exercised. But the share-based payment charge in the income statement for options that lapse after vesting is not reversed. [IFRS 2 para 23]. So, where share options have lapsed after vesting and no tax deduction is available, the total current tax credit in the income statement will be less than the share-based payment charge tax-effected at the standard rate of tax; this reflects the fact that part of the share-based payment charge has not received a tax deduction because the related share options lapsed after vesting.

Example – Share options lapse after vesting

This example uses the facts in the example in paragraph 13.206.2, but assumes that some share options lapse after vesting.

On 1 January 20X3, 100,000 options are issued with a fair value of C360,000. The vesting period is 3 years and all options are initially expected to be exercised. The tax rate is 30%. The intrinsic value of the 100,000 share options (that is, market value of the underlying shares less exercise price) at the date of exercise in year 4 is C400,000. (At the end of years 1, 2 and 3 it is C330,000, C300,000 and C380,000 respectively.)

During years 1, 2 and 3, the expected tax benefit is recognised as explained in the example in paragraph 13.206.2. The cumulative position at the end of year 3 is shown below.

Taxation

Year	Expense	Income statement Dr (Cr)		Equity Dr (Cr)		Balance sheet Dr (Cr)	
		Current tax	Deferred tax	Current tax	Deferred tax	Current tax	Deferred tax
	C	C	C	C	C	C	C
1	120,000	–	(33,000)	–	–	–	33,000
2	120,000	–	(27,000)	–	–	–	60,000
3	120,000	–	(48,000)	–	(6,000)	–	114,000
Cumulative position at end of year 3	360,000	–	(108,000)	–	(6,000)		

In year 4, 85,000 of the share options are exercised and 15,000 lapse without being exercised. The actual current tax deduction obtained is C102,000 (30% × C400,000 total intrinsic value at the date of exercise × 85/100).

The accounting charge in the income statement relating to the 85,000 options that are exercised is C306,000 (360,000 × 85/100); so the tax effect relating to this charge is C91,800 (306,000 × 30%).

The deferred tax asset of C114,000 at the end of year 3 is reversed through the income statement and equity. The double entry is as follows:

			C	C
Dr	Current tax claim (balance sheet)		102,000	
	Cr	Current tax (income statement)		91,800
	Cr	Current tax (equity)		10,200
Dr	Deferred tax (income statement)		108,000	
Dr	Deferred tax (equity)		6,000	
	Cr	Deferred tax (balance sheet)		114,000

The overall position is shown below:

	Expense	Income statement Dr (Cr)		Equity Dr (Cr)		Balance sheet Dr (Cr)	
		Current tax	Deferred tax	Current tax	Deferred tax	Current tax	Deferred tax
	C	C	C	C	C	C	C
Cumulative position at end of year 3	360,000	–	(108,000)	–	(6,000)	–	114,000
Movement in year 4		–	(91,800) 108,000	(10,200)	6,000	102,000	(114,000)
Total	360,000	(91,800)	–	(10,200)	–	102,000	–

In the original example, when all the options were exercised, the overall tax position in year 4 was as follows: nil in the income statement (comprising a current tax credit of C108,000 offset by a deferred tax charge of C108,000); and a net tax credit of C6,000 to equity because of the increase in share price since the end of year 3 (comprising a current tax credit of C12,000 offset by a deferred tax charge of C6,000).

Where only 85,000 options are exercised and the remaining options lapse, the overall tax position in year 4 is:

- A net charge of C16,200 in the income statement. This comprises a current tax credit of C91,800 (360,000 × 85/100 × 30%) and a deferred tax charge of C108,000 reversing the previously recognised asset. This net charge reflects the fact that the expected tax credit on 15,000 options was not received.

- A net credit of C4,200 in equity. This comprises a current tax credit of C10,200, being the excess tax credit on the 85,000 options that were exercised ((400,000 − 360,000) × 85/100 × 30%) and a deferred tax charge of C6,000 reversing the previously recognised asset.

13.206.8 In some jurisdictions, a tax deduction in respect of a share-based payment award is received upfront or part way through the vesting period. The receipt of the tax deduction crystallises the amount; so re-measurement based on share price would not apply after this point, but there are implications for the deferred tax accounting. As explained above, IAS 12 provides guidance on accounting for deferred tax that arises from share-based payment transactions where an entity receives a deduction when the share options are exercised (that is, after the share-based payment expense has been recognised). The standard does not specifically address the situation where the tax deduction is received before the related accounting expense; but similar logic to that in IAS 12 applies. [IFRS 2 paras BC312 to BC314]. In this situation, the receipt of an upfront tax deduction in respect of share-based payments gives rise to a deferred tax liability. [IFRS 2 para BC314].

Example – Tax deduction received upfront

An equity-settled share-based payment award for employees vests after 3 years of service. An award is made for 1,000 shares. The fair value of the award at the date of grant is C120 (per share).

The entity expects all the shares in the scheme to vest. So the accounting expense under IFRS 2 is 1,000 shares × 120 = C120,000 × $\frac{1}{3}$ = C40,000 per annum for 3 years.

Under the tax rules of the entity's jurisdiction, the entity receives a tax deduction upfront (at 30%) for the total number of options based on an amount (C140) that exceeds the fair value of the award at the date of grant. So the amount deductible for tax purposes is C140,000 (1,000 × 140).

A deferred tax liability of C42,000 (140,000 × 30%) is recognised on the tax deduction received upfront; this is unwound over the 3-year vesting period.

A deferred tax credit of C12,000 (40,000 × 30%) is recognised in the income statement each year, in line with the IFRS 2 charge; so a total of C36,000 tax credit is recognised in the income statement.

The excess tax deduction of C6,000 (42,000 – 36,000) is recognised in equity. In our view, this amount is also unwound over the 3-year vesting period (that is, a tax credit of C2,000 per annum is recognised in equity); this is consistent with the unwinding of the deferred tax credit recognised in the income statement.

13.206.9   In group situations, some parent entities recharge their subsidiaries where those subsidiary entities' employees participate in the parent entity's share option schemes. The accounting for share-based payments in a group situation is dealt with in chapter 12. Tax accounting issues arise in the group if the subsidiary receives a tax deduction on the recharge and not when the employee exercises the options. If the tax relief on the recharge is clearly linked to the share-based payment (that is, it is based on an amount derived from the share-based payment, such as the option's intrinsic value or fair value, and there is no other tax relief for the share-based payment), our view is that the tax relief in the consolidated financial statements is treated in accordance with paragraphs 68A to 68C of IAS 12. So, where the tax deductible amount is no greater than the share-based payment expense, the tax relief is reflected in the consolidated income statement. Any excess of the tax relief over the amount of the tax effect of the IFRS 2 charge is reflected in equity. But, if the recharge is not clearly linked to the share-based payment, the tax deduction on the recharge should be credited to the consolidated income statement (like tax deductions on management recharges in general).

13.206.10   Whether or not a deferred tax asset is recognised in the consolidated financial statements for the expected tax deductions on recharges depends on the arrangement between the parent and the subsidiary. If the recharge is made at the parent's discretion, a deferred tax asset is not recognised; this is because a tax deduction will not arise unless there is a recharge. Where a parent agrees to make a recharge when options are exercised, a deferred tax asset should be recognised (subject to meeting IAS 12's criteria) over the period of service in relation to any expected tax deductions that are considered recoverable. This is based on the argument that the expected tax deduction for the recharge can be regarded as a tax deduction in respect of the share-based payment charge to the extent that it is recharged.

UK.13.206.10.1   As noted in paragraph UK.13.204.1, a tax deduction in connection with an employee share option scheme is generally available under UK tax law at the date of exercise of the share options. In a group situation, if a UK parent company recharges a UK subsidiary company for participating in a group share option scheme, a tax deduction is not given on the recharge (because it is given on the exercise of the options instead). But, where a UK parent recharges an overseas subsidiary company, a tax deduction might be available to the subsidiary (depending on local tax rules); in that case, the guidance in paragraphs 13.206.9 and 13.206.10 applies to the parent's consolidated financial statements.

Cash-settled transactions

13.207 Cash-settled share-based payment transactions (such as share appreciation rights issued to employees) give rise to a liability and not a credit to equity. The fair value of the liability is re-measured at each reporting date until the liability is settled. A deductible temporary difference might arise if the liability's carrying amount exceeds the liability's tax base (that is, the carrying amount less any amounts that will be deductible for tax purposes in the future); this would result in a deferred tax asset (subject to IAS 12's recognition criteria). The tax effects of such transactions are always recognised through the income statement.

Revaluation of non-monetary assets

General rule

13.208 Many entities revalue their non-monetary assets such as land and buildings. In some jurisdictions, the revaluation or other restatement (increase or decrease) of an asset to fair value affects taxable profit (loss) for the current period. As a result, the tax base of the asset is adjusted and no temporary difference arises. The resulting current tax that arises on the revaluation is recognised. In other jurisdictions, the revaluation or restatement of an asset does not affect taxable profit in the current period; as a result, the asset's tax base is not adjusted. The increase or decrease does not enter into the determination of taxable profit for the current period; but the future recovery of the carrying amount will result in a taxable flow of economic benefits to the entity, and the amount that is deductible for tax purposes will differ from the amount of those economic benefits. The difference between the carrying amount of a revalued asset and its tax base is a temporary difference; and it gives rise to a deferred tax liability or asset. The resulting deferred tax expense or income arising from the revaluation is recognised in other comprehensive income (see para 13.288.1). This is true even if:

- The entity does not intend to dispose of the asset. In such cases, the asset's revalued carrying amount will be recovered through use; and this will generate taxable income which exceeds the depreciation that will be allowable for tax purposes in future periods.

- Tax on capital gains is deferred where the proceeds of the asset's disposal are invested in similar assets. In such cases, the tax will become payable on sale or use of the similar assets. See further paragraph 13.216 onwards.

[IAS 12 para 20].

UK.13.208.1 The above treatment under IAS 12 is significantly different from the treatment adopted by UK companies under FRS 19. Under FRS 19's incremental liability approach, deferred tax is not generally recognised when non-monetary assets are revalued; the exception is where the reporting entity has entered into a binding agreement (by the balance sheet date) to sell the revalued assets and has recognised the gains and losses expected to arise on sale. Deferred tax liabilities need to be recognised on all non-monetary assets that are carried at a valuation at the date of transition to IFRS (where they were previously unrecognised under FRS 19). This issue is considered further in chapter 2.

13.209 The precise nature of the liability that arises on an asset's revaluation depends on the asset's taxation status. In some jurisdictions, assets that do not attract tax depreciation (such as land) give rise to chargeable gains or losses for tax purposes if they are sold above or below their tax indexed cost (that is, original cost uplifted by an indexation allowance, where applicable). For accounting purposes, such assets are sometimes revalued but rarely depreciated. Depreciable assets, on the other hand, might or might not be revalued. If such an asset is revalued in excess of cost and sold at the revalued amount, a further tax liability – in addition to any liability arising on the capital gain – might arise if the asset was eligible for capital allowances. This further liability (which arises by way of a balancing charge in some jurisdictions) is designed to claw back any tax depreciation previously claimed in respect of the asset.

UK.13.209.1 In the UK, the tax indexed cost of land is original cost uplifted by an indexation allowance calculated using the Retail Price Index, which is intended to exempt purely inflationary gains from taxation.

13.210 Furthermore, as explained in paragraph 13.172, the measurement of the liability also depends on the manner in which the entity expects (at the balance sheet date) to recover the carrying amount of a non-depreciable or depreciable asset that has been revalued in the financial statements – whether through use, sale, or use and sale (that is, 'dual manner of recovery'). The following paragraphs consider the deferred tax consequences of revaluing depreciable and non-depreciable assets and the different ways in which the entity expects to recover the revalued carrying amounts. For guidance relating to the expected manner of recovery for investment properties measured at fair value, refer to paragraph 13.219.4 onwards.

13.210.1 An approach for applying this 'dual manner of recovery' is set out in paragraph 13.172.3. Use of this approach for properties can be summarised as follows:

■ Ascertain the expected manner of recovery of the asset's carrying amount.

■ Split the asset's carrying amount between amounts to be recovered through use and through sale.

■ Determine the expected period of recovery through use and the expected date of sale or abandonment.

- Determine the tax consequences of recovery through use and the temporary differences that will arise.

- Determine the tax consequences of recovery through sale and the temporary differences that will arise.

- Determine which of the temporary differences arising from recovery through use and through sale should be recognised.

Upward revaluation of depreciable assets

13.211 Where a depreciable asset that qualifies for tax depreciation (such as certain buildings or specialised plant in some jurisdictions) is revalued upwards, the revaluation gives rise to a further originating temporary difference; this is in addition to the temporary difference that arises from accelerated tax depreciation. Because the revaluation represents a new originating temporary difference, deferred tax should be provided in a way that reflects how the entity expects (at the balance sheet date) to recover the asset's revalued carrying amount – whether through use, sale, or use and sale. Various scenarios arise.

> **Example – Upward revaluation of depreciable assets**
>
> An entity acquired a building in a business combination at a cost of C1,000,000 on 1 January 20X1. The useful life of the building is 20 years and it will be depreciated to a residual value of C150,000. The building is eligible for allowances of 50% initial allowance and 4% writing down allowance (WDA) each year (up to a total of C500,000) until disposal. On disposal, the proceeds are liable to capital gains tax, subject to a deduction where that cost exceeds capital allowances previously claimed. The tax rate for capital gains and income is 30%. In each of the four years until revaluation, the deferred tax provided is calculated as shown below. Note that the example deals only with the deferred tax on the buildings – a dual manner of recovery expectation is applied, and the residual value is attributed to the carrying amount of the sale element on initial recognition (see further para 13.172.3). There are no changes to the estimated residual value in years 1 to 4. The land element is not a depreciable asset (see further para 13.213).
>
> In the tables: NBV = net book value; TB = tax base; TD = temporary difference; DTL = deferred tax liability; DTA = deferred tax asset.

Use element	NBV	TB	TD	DTL/(DTA)
	C	C	C	C
At 1 January 20X1	850,000	1,000,000	(150,000)	(45,000)
Depreciation/tax allowances – initial + WDA	(42,500)	(540,000)	497,500	149,250
At 31 December 20X1	807,500	460,000	347,500	104,250
Depreciation/tax allowances – WDA	(42,500)	(40,000)	(2,500)	(750)
At 31 December 20X2	765,000	420,000	345,000	103,500
Depreciation/tax allowances – WDA	(42,500)	(40,000)	(2,500)	(750)
At 31 December 20X3	722,500	380,000	342,500	102,750
Depreciation/tax allowances – WDA	(42,500)	(40,000)	(2,500)	(750)
At 31 December 20X4	680,000	340,000	340,000	102,000

Sale element	NBV	TB	TD	DTL
	C	C	C	C
At 1 January 20X1	150,000	0	150,000	45,000
At 31 December 20X1, 20X2, 20X3 and 20X4	150,000	0	150,000	45,000

The tax base on sale is determined using the tax base expected to be available on the sale element at the date of sale. In this case, that is cost of C1,000,000 less tax depreciation claimed while the building is in use (C1,000,000). The tax base on sale is not shown as cost less tax depreciation claimed to date at each balance sheet date because this would result in double counting of the tax base between the use and sale elements. Rather, the tax base in each calculation is based on management's expectation of how tax deductions will be received. The deferred tax liability of C45,000 represents the tax that management expects to pay on recovery of the building's residual value. This deferred tax liability will remain on balance sheet until the building is sold.

Scenario 1 – Entity expects to recover the revaluation uplift of the building through use

At the beginning of 20X5, the building is revalued to C1,400,000; a revaluation gain of C570,000 is recognised. Management still considers the residual value of the building to be C150,000. So the carrying amounts for the use and sale elements are C1,250,000 and C150,000 respectively. As such, the revaluation will affect the use calculation only.

Use element	NBV	TB	TD	DTL
	C	C	C	C
At 31 December 20X4	680,000	340,000	340,000	102,000
Revaluation	570,000	–	570,000	171,000
At 1 January 20X5	1,250,000	340,000	910,000	273,000
Depreciation/tax allowances –				
WDA	(78,125)*	(40,000)	(38,125)	(11,438)
At 31 December 20X5	1,171,875	300,000	871,875	261,562

* The building has a remaining useful life of 16 years at the date of revaluation; so depreciation is C1,250,000/16 = C78,125. This is equal to the annual depreciation on historical cost plus an uplift for the revaluation gain: C42,500 + C570,000/16 = C78,125.

Sale element	NBV	TB	TD	DTL
	C	C	C	C
At 31 December 20X4	150,000	0	150,000	45,000
Revaluation	–	–	–	–
At 1 January 20X5 and 31 December 20X5	150,000	0	150,000	45,000

The journal entries at 1 January 20X5 and 31 December 20X5 are as follows:

		Dr	Cr
1 January 20X5			
Dr	Property, plant and equipment – cost	400,000	
Dr	Property, plant and equipment – accumulated depreciation	170,000	
	Cr Revaluation reserve		570,000
Dr	Revaluation reserve – tax at 30% (income tax rate) on C570,000	171,000	
	Cr Deferred tax liability		171,000
31 December 20X5			
Dr	Depreciation charge	78,125	
	Cr Property, plant and equipment – accumulated depreciation		78,125
Dr	Deferred tax liability – use (B/S)	11,438	
	Cr Deferred tax charge – use (I/S)		11,438

The deferred tax liability of C171,000 arising on the revaluation surplus is added to the opening balance of C102,000 brought forward; this gives the total of C273,000 shown above. In addition, the deferred tax liability is reduced by C11,438 (C273,000 — C261,562) during 20X5 because the temporary difference of C38,125 (C78,125 — C40,000) is reversed; this reduction is credited to the income statement rather than the revaluation reserve because the entity expects to recover through use the carrying amount of the revalued asset of C1,250,000 (C1,400,000 less the residual value of C150,000).

But the entity might decide to transfer an amount from the revaluation reserve to retained earnings, which represents the difference between depreciation based on the asset's revalued amount and depreciation based on the asset's cost. If the entity makes such a transfer, the amount transferred is net of any related deferred tax. [IAS 12 para 64]. In the above example, the entity would transfer C78,125 (depreciation based on revalued amount) — C42,500 (depreciation based on cost) = C35,625 less tax of C10,688 (30% of C35,625) = C24,937.

Scenario 2 – Entity expects to recover the revaluation uplift of the building through use and sale

The building has been revalued as in scenario 1 above. But management now considers the residual value to be C200,000. The entity expects to recover the uplift to the building's carrying amount through use and sale.

The impact of the revaluation and change in residual value is illustrated as follows:

Use element	NBV	TB	TD	DTL
	C	C	C	C
At 31 December 20X4	680,000	340,000	340,000	102,000
Revaluation	520,000	–	520,000	156,000
At 1 January 20X5	1,200,000	340,000	860,000	258,000
Depreciation/tax allowances – WDA	(75,000)*	(40,000)	(35,000)	(10,500)
At 31 December 20X5	1,125,000	300,000	825,000	247,500

* The building has a remaining useful life of 16 years at the date of revaluation; so depreciation is C1,200,000/16 = C75,000. This is equal to the annual depreciation on historical cost plus an uplift for the revaluation gain: C42,500 + C520,000/16 = C75,000.

Sale element	NBV	TB	TD	DTL
	C	C	C	C
At 31 December 20X4	150,000	0	150,000	45,000
Revaluation	50,000	–	50,000	15,000
At 1 January 20X5 and 31 December 20X5	200,000	0	200,000	60,000

The journal entries at 1 January 20X5 and 31 December 20X5 are as follows:

	Dr	Cr
1 January 20X5		
Dr Property, plant and equipment – cost	400,000	
Dr Property, plant and equipment – accumulated depreciation	170,000	
Cr Revaluation reserve		570,000
Dr Revaluation reserve – tax @ 30%	171,000	
Cr Deferred tax liability – use basis		156,000
Cr Deferred tax liability – sale basis		15,000
31 December 20X5		
Dr Depreciation charge	75,000	
Cr Property, plant and equipment – accumulated depreciation		75,000
Dr Deferred tax liability – use (B/S)	10,500	
Cr Deferred tax charge – use (I/S)		10,500

The deferred tax movement of C171,000 arising on the revaluation surplus recognised on 1 January 20X5 impacts both the sale and use calculations as shown above. The reduction in the deferred tax liability during 20X5 that arises from depreciation is recognised in the income statement rather than the revaluation reserve, as discussed in scenario 1 above. To the extent that the asset is recovered through use, a transfer could be made between the revaluation reserve and retained earnings (as discussed in scenario 1). In this case, the transfer is C75,000 (depreciation based on revalued amount) – C42,500 (depreciation based on cost) = C32,500 less tax of C9,750 (30% of C32,500) = C22,750.

Scenario 3 – Entity changes its manner of recovery expectation from dual manner of recovery to sale

Following on from scenario 1, at 31 December 20X6 (two years after revaluation), the entity changes its expectation from recovering the building's carrying amount through the dual manner of recovery (use and sale) to sale. The sale is imminent as at 31 December 20X6; so the building's full carrying amount at that date is expected to be recovered through sale.

Use element	NBV	TB	TD	DTL
	C	C	C	C
At 31 December 20X5	1,171,875	300,000	871,875	261,562
Depreciation/tax allowances – WDA	(78,125)	(40,000)	(38,125)	(11,437)
	1,093,750	260,000	833,750	250,125
Change in expected manner of recovery	(1,093,750)	(260,000)*	(833,750)	(250,125)
At 31 December 20X6	–	–	–	–

*No further capital allowances are available if the building is no longer in use.

Sale element	NBV	TB	TD	DTL
	C	C	C	C
At 31 December 20X5	150,000	0	150,000	45,000
Change in expected manner of recovery	1,093,750	260,000	833,750	250,125
At 31 December 20X6	1,243,750	260,000*	983,750	295,125

* The tax base on sale is equal to cost (C1,000,000) less capital allowances claimed during the period in which the building is in use of C740,000 (that is, initial allowance of C500,000 plus six years' allowance of C40,000).

As in scenario 1, the reduction in the deferred tax liability by C11,437 (C261,562 — C250,125) during 20X6 that arises from depreciation is credited to the income statement; this is because the entity expects to recover the building's carrying amount through use. A transfer could be made between the revaluation reserve and retained earnings, which would be a further C24,937 as in scenario 1. However, at 31 December 20X6, the entity changes its expectation about the manner of the building's recovery from the dual manner of recovery to sale. This gives rise to the following additional journal entry:

		Dr	Cr
Dr	Deferred tax liability – use	250,125	
	Cr Deferred tax liability – sale		250,125

The change in expected manner of recovery has no impact on net assets in this case. But the overall deferred tax liability would be affected if the tax base on sale was subject to adjustments for inflation or if the tax rates for income and capital gains were different. This change would generally be recognised in the income statement; but, where it relates to deferred tax recognised on a previous revaluation gain, it would be recognised in other comprehensive income.

The deferred tax balance of C295,125 reflects the tax consequences that would follow if the entity sold the asset at its carrying amount at the balance sheet date. In other words, if the asset is sold at its carrying amount of C1,243,750, the total taxable profit would be C983,750. This is calculated as proceeds of C1,243,750 less C260,000 (being the original cost of C1,000,000 less capital allowances claimed of C740,000) = C983,750, on which tax @ 30% = C295,125 would be payable.

Scenario 4 – Entity sells revalued building

Following on from scenario 3, suppose the entity sells the building at 1 January 20X7 for C1,500,000 and pays tax at 30% on the taxable profit:

	Taxable profit	Accounting profit
	C	C
Sales proceeds	1,500,000	1,500,000
Tax base/carrying amount before sale	260,000	1,243,750
Taxable/accounting profit	1,240,000	256,250
Tax @ 30% on taxable/accounting profit	372,000	76,875

Current tax is generally included in profit or loss, unless it arises from a transaction or event that is recognised (in the same or a different period) in other comprehensive income or directly in equity (see para 13.45). Under the principle that deferred tax should follow the related item (see para 13.288), the journal entries for the current tax and for the release of the deferred tax liability of C295,125 (see scenario 3) are as follows:

		Dr	Cr
Dr	Current tax (I/S) [1]	201,000	
Dr	Current tax (other comprehensive income) [2]	171,000	
Cr	Current tax (B/S)		372,000
Dr	Deferred tax (B/S)	295,125	
Cr	Deferred tax (I/S) [3]		124,125
Cr	Deferred tax (other comprehensive income) [2]		171,000

1 Current tax recognised in the income statement of C201,000 is the difference between the total current tax payable of C372,000 and the amount recognised in other comprehensive income of C171,000[2].

[2] Current tax recognised in other comprehensive income is calculated as the previously recognised gain of C570,000 × 30% = C171,000, which equals the deferred tax previously recognised in other comprehensive income.

[3] The deferred tax released of C124,125 represents the deferred tax previously recognised in the income statement, being the difference between the total deferred tax liability of C295,125 and the amount previously recognised in other comprehensive income of C171,000.

The tax impact can be summarised as follows:

Tax charge in income statement	
Current tax	201,000
Deferred tax – release	(124,125)
Total tax charge in income statement	76,875
Tax charge in other comprehensive income	
Current tax	171,000
Deferred tax – release	(171,000)
Total tax charge in other comprehensive income	–

The total tax charge of C76,875 in the income statement is the same as tax payable on the accounting profit. In other words, no reconciling difference arises, because the deferred tax liability recorded reflected the manner in which the entity expected to recover the carrying amount of the property (that is, through sale). After the building's sale, the revaluation surplus is realised and the entity will transfer the original surplus of C570,000 net of tax of C171,000 = C399,000 from the revaluation reserve to retained earnings. (This assumes that no annual transfer has been made – see last paragraph of scenario 1). [IAS 12 para 64].

Downward revaluation of depreciable assets

13.212   Where a depreciable asset is revalued downwards, the tax consequence of the impairment loss is similar to depreciation and represents a reversal of an originating temporary difference. This reversal could give rise to a deferred tax asset or a reduction in the deferred tax liability; the treatment will depend on the asset's tax base just before the impairment loss was recognised. Similarly, where a depreciable asset that was revalued upwards is subsequently revalued downwards, the downward revaluation will first reverse the previous upward revaluation; and any excess reversal is recognised in profit or loss.

Example – Downward revaluation of depreciable assets

Facts are generally the same as in scenario 3 in paragraph 13.211; but at 31 December 20X6, two years after revaluation and immediately before sale, the asset is revalued downwards to C600,000. The entity expects to recover the full carrying amount of the building through sale.

There is no use element as at 31 December 20X6 because the expected manner of recovery is solely through sale. The impact of the devaluation on the sale element is shown below.

Sale element	NBV	TB	TD	DTL
	C	C	C	C
At 31 December 20X6 (before impairment)	1,243,750	260,000	983,750	(295,125)
Impairment loss	(643,750)	–	(643,750)	(193,125)
At 31 December 20X6	600,000	260,000	340,000	102,000

Of the impairment loss of C643,750, C570,000 reverses the earlier revaluation surplus and is recognised in other comprehensive income (debited to the revaluation reserve); the balance of C73,750 is debited to the income statement. The corresponding tax credits of C171,000 (30% of C570,000) and C22,125 (30% of C73,750) are similarly recognised in other comprehensive income (credited to the revaluation reserve) and in the income statement.

If the entity has transferred an element of the C570,000 revaluation surplus from the revaluation reserve to retained earnings under paragraph 41 of IAS 16, the amount of the impairment debited directly to the revaluation reserve would be capped at the amount of revaluation surplus remaining in the revaluation reserve at the time of the impairment. [IAS 16 para 40].

Upward revaluation of non-depreciable asset

13.213 Where a non-depreciable asset (such as land having an infinite life) is revalued upwards above the tax deductible amount on sale (including any inflation allowance), the revaluation gives rise to an originating temporary difference on which deferred tax should be provided. The asset is not depreciated, so no part of the asset's carrying amount is expected to be recovered (that is, consumed) through use. It follows that the carrying amount of a non-depreciable asset can only be recovered through sale [SIC 21 para 5; IAS 12 (amended) para 51B].

13.214 The following examples illustrate the tax consequences of revaluing a non-depreciable asset under IAS 16.

Example 1 – Upward revaluation of non-depreciable asset

On transition to IFRS, entity B elected to re-measure its land and buildings at fair value at the date of transition, as permitted by IFRS 1. This fair value was subsequently used as deemed cost for the purpose of historical cost accounting. Entity B does not have a policy of annual revaluations.

One of entity B's assets is a piece of land. The tax base of the land is its original cost when acquired by entity B, increased each year in line with the Retail Price Index.

There is a temporary difference between the revalued accounting base and the tax base of the land. But the temporary difference will reduce over time as the tax base is increased by changes in the Retail Price Index. Management expects to hold the land for the foreseeable future; and it expects that the land's tax base will exceed the accounting base before the land is disposed of.

In this situation, management should recognise deferred tax in respect of the land based on the difference between the accounting base and the tax base at the balance sheet date. Management should not anticipate future changes in the land's tax base arising from changes in the Retail Price Index.

Example 2 – Indexation of tax base on revalued non-depreciable asset

An entity acquired a plot of land for C1,000,000 on 1 January 20X1 when the tax indexed cost was also C1,000,000. On disposal, the proceeds in excess of indexed cost are subject to capital gains tax @ 30%, which is also the rate of tax on income other than capital gains. The price index for calculating indexation allowances increases by 2% in 20X1 and 2.5% in 20X2. But the tax rules state that indexation allowance cannot create or increase a loss. The deferred tax asset recognised in each of those years (if sufficient taxable profits are available) is calculated as follows.

Taxation

	NBV	TB	TD	DTL (A)
	C	C	C	C
At 1 January 20X1	1,000,000	1,000,000	–	–
Increase in tax indexed cost @ 2% (see note below)		–	–	–
At 31 December 20X1	1,000,000	1,000,000	–	–
Increase in tax indexed cost @ 2.5% (see note below)		–	–	–
At 31 December 20X2	1,000,000	1,000,000	–	–

Note that the land is carried at cost during 20X1 and 20X2. If the land is sold at its carrying amount of C1,000,000 at the balance sheet date, the amount deductible for tax purposes is its original cost without the benefit of the indexation allowance. This is because the tax rules applicable to the entity state that indexation allowance cannot create or increase a loss. So the tax base is not increased by indexation of C20,000 (2%) in year 1 and C25,500 (2.5%) in year 2; and a temporary difference does not arise.

During 20X3, the entity revalued the land to C1,500,000 when the indexation allowance has increased by 3%. The tax effect of the revaluation is calculated as follows:

	NBV	TB	TD	DTL (A)
	C	C	C	C
Cost	1,000,000	1,000,000		
Accounting revaluation	500,000			
Increase in tax indexed cost in previous periods*		45,500		
Increase in tax indexed cost in current period @ 3%		31,365		
At 31 December 20X3	1,500,000	1,076,865	423,135	126,940

* The increase in the land's carrying amount as a result of the revaluation means that the tax base is increased by the indexation allowance arising in year 1 (C20,000) and year 2 (C25,500), because this no longer creates a loss.

The revaluation surplus of C500,000 is recognised in other comprehensive income (credited to the revaluation reserve); but the deferred tax liability recognised in other comprehensive income (in the revaluation reserve) is C126,940 (C423,135 @ 30%) because the surplus includes a tax-free amount of C76,865 resulting from inflation since the asset was acquired.

The accounting implications of a revaluation for tax purposes are considered further in paragraph 13.217 onwards.

Example 3 – Sale of revalued non-depreciable asset

Following on from example 2, suppose the land is sold during 20X6 for C2,000,000. There is additional indexation allowance of C23,135 up to the time of sale, so the indexed cost is C1,100,000. Assume the tax effect of the indexation allowance in the period of sale is recognised in other comprehensive income. The entity pays tax at 30% on the taxable profit as follows:

	Taxable profit	Accounting profit
	C	C
Sales proceeds	2,000,000	2,000,000
Tax base/carrying amount before sale	1,100,000	1,500,000
Taxable/accounting profit	900,000	500,000
Tax @ 30%	270,000	150,000

The journal entries for the current tax and for the release of the deferred tax liability of C126,940 (see example 2) are as follows:

		Dr	Cr
Dr	Current tax (I/S) [1]	150,000	
Dr	Current tax (other comprehensive income) [2]	120,000	
Cr	Current tax (B/S)		270,000
Dr	Deferred tax (B/S)	126,940	
Cr	Deferred tax (other comprehensive income) [3]		126,940

[1] Current tax recognised in the income statement of C150,000 is the difference between the total current tax payable of C270,000 and the amount recognised in other comprehensive income of C120,000; and it represents the gain in the income statement of C500,000 @ 30%.

[2] Current tax recognised in other comprehensive income is calculated as the tax on the gain previously recognised in other comprehensive income reduced by indexation; that is, gain of C500,000 less indexation of (C76,865 + C23,135) = gain of C400,000 @ 30% = C120,000.

[3] The reversal of deferred tax of C126,940 represents the deferred tax previously recognised in other comprehensive income. No deferred tax was previously recognised in the income statement; so there is no reversal in the income statement.

Tax charge in income statement

Current tax	150,000
Deferred tax – release	–
Total tax charge in income statement	150,000

Tax charge in other comprehensive income

Current tax	120,000
Deferred tax – release	(126,940)
Total tax credit in other comprehensive income	(6,940)

The tax credit in other comprehensive income of C6,940 arises because of an additional tax-free amount of C23,135 (C1,100,000 — C1,076,865) that has arisen during the year before the disposal date, as a result of indexation (C23,135 @ 30% = C6,940).

IAS 12 does not specify how this additional indexation should be allocated. This example assumes that the indexation is treated consistently with the previous indexation, and is regarded as relating to the accounting gain that has been recognised in other comprehensive income. But other methods of allocation might be appropriate, depending on the entity's accounting policy (for example, allocating the indexation pro rata between the gain recognised in the income statement and the gain previously recognised in other comprehensive income).

Downward revaluation of non-depreciable asset

13.215 Where a non-depreciable asset (that has not been previously revalued) is revalued downwards, an originating temporary difference arises if a capital loss will arise for tax purposes. But, if capital losses can only be offset against chargeable capital gains, a deferred tax asset is not normally recognised unless deferred tax has been provided (in the same or an earlier accounting period) for chargeable gains on upward revaluations of other assets. Where a downward revaluation of a non-depreciable asset simply reverses a previous upward revaluation of the same asset, the tax effect recorded should reverse the tax effect that was previously recorded for the upward revaluation.

Rollover and holdover reliefs

13.216 In some jurisdictions, the tax arising on a taxable gain – when certain assets used for trading purposes (such as properties) are disposed of – might not need to be paid immediately if the sale proceeds are reinvested (within specified time limits) in other qualifying assets. One type of relief ('rollover relief') reduces the 'base cost' of the replacement asset by the taxable gain 'rolled over'; this means that (subject to any tax revaluation in the intervening period) a higher taxable gain will arise on disposal of the replacement asset (and higher tax might become payable) than if the original gain had not been rolled over. It might be possible to claim rollover relief on the gain when the replacement asset is sold, so that tax on that gain again does not need to be paid. This situation can theoretically continue indefinitely and will depend on the specific tax rules.

13.216.1 Another type of relief ('holdover relief') delays payment of tax on the original gain where reinvestment of the proceeds satisfies certain conditions. The taxable gain on disposal of the old asset is not deducted from the new asset's cost; instead, the current tax on the gain is delayed (that is, 'held over') and is payable at a future date, depending on the specific tax rules.

UK.13.216.1.1 In the UK, relief from capital gains tax – when certain assets used for trading purposes are disposed of – can be claimed where the disposal proceeds are reinvested in new qualifying assets; reinvestment should take place in the period beginning 12 months before and ending three years after the original asset's sale. Qualifying assets include goodwill, certain land and buildings used for trading purposes, and fixed plant and machinery. The type of relief available depends on whether the new asset is non-depreciating or depreciating. A depreciating asset is defined in the tax rules as a wasting asset (that is, an asset with a predictable life that does not exceed 50 years) or an asset with a maximum life of 60 years (that is, an asset that will become a wasting asset within 10 years).

UK.13.216.1.2   Where the new asset is non-depreciating, the relief reduces the consideration for disposing of the old asset and reduces the cost of acquiring the new asset ('rollover relief'). Under this relief:

■ The old asset's disposal proceeds equal the allowable expenditure for tax purposes (including any indexation allowance). So the disposal of the old asset does not give rise to a gain or loss.

■ The new asset's acquisition cost for tax purposes is reduced by the same amount as the reduction in the taxable consideration on disposal of the old asset.

Where rollover relief is claimed, the chargeable gain on the old asset is not taxed when realised; instead, for tax purposes, it is deducted from the new asset's acquisition cost. The relief will increase the chargeable gain arising when the new asset is disposed of (subject to any further claim to rollover relief or any other relief available). So the tax base that applies on the new asset's disposal needs to be adjusted where rollover relief is claimed. A claim for rollover relief needs to be made within specified time limits.

UK.13.216.1.3   Where the new asset is a depreciating asset, the chargeable gain on disposal of the old asset is not deducted from the cost of the new asset; instead, the capital gains charge is held over on the old asset ('holdover relief') until the earliest of:

■ disposal of the 'new asset';

■ ceasing to use the 'new asset' for trade; and

■ ten years from the acquisition of the 'new asset'.

13.216.2   Where rollover relief is claimed, the standard might require a deferred tax liability to be recognised on the new asset (often similar in amount to the current tax that did not need to be paid on the old asset). This is because the new asset's tax base has been reduced; so tax might become payable when the new asset is sold or used.

13.216.3   The new asset's reduced tax base is likely to result in a temporary difference when compared with its carrying amount in the financial statements. Where the temporary difference results from rollover relief, it is not covered by the initial recognition exception (see further para 13.162 onwards); this is because it does not arise from the asset's initial recognition, but instead arises as a result of relief given on an asset that was previously disposed of.

13.216.4 The following example considers the deferred tax position on initial recognition of an asset with a tax base reduced by rollover relief – including the interaction with the dual manner of recovery (see further para 13.172.2 onwards) and the initial recognition exception.

Example – Rollover relief

An entity disposes of a building which (without rollover relief) would result in a taxable gain of C400,000. The entity invests in a new building at a cost of C2,500,000; and, under the tax rules in the jurisdiction, it claims rollover relief so that no taxable gain or loss arises on disposal of the old building. Instead, the taxable gain on the old building reduces the acquisition cost of the new building that will be allowable for tax purposes when it is sold. So the new building's tax base (on a sale basis) is as follows:

	C'000
Acquisition cost	2,500
Rolled-over gain	(400)
Tax base (sale basis)	2,100

Tax rate applicable to gain on disposal = 30%.

Assuming there are no tax deductions for use of the building, the deferred tax position on initial recognition (in various scenarios) is as follows:

	Residual value = C1m		Residual value = nil		Residual value = C2.5m	
	Use C'000	Sale C'000	Use C'000	Sale C'000	Use C'000	Sale C'000
Carrying amount	1,500	1,000	2,500	–	–	2,500
Tax base – original cost	–	2,500	–	2,500	–	2,500
Rolled-over gain	–	(400)	–	(400)	–	(400)
New tax base	–	2,100	–	2,100	–	2,100
Taxable/ (deductible) temporary difference	1,500	(1,100)	2,500	(2,100)	–	400
Less: initial temporary difference	(1,500)	1,500	(2,500)	2,500	–	–
Remaining taxable temporary difference not covered by the IRE	–	400	–	400	–	400
Deferred tax liability @ 30%	–	120	–	120	–	120

As noted in paragraph 13.216.3, to the extent that the temporary difference results from rollover relief, it is not covered by the initial recognition exception. So the amount of the temporary difference covered by the initial recognition exception excludes the amount attributable to rollover relief; in other words, it is calculated as the carrying amount less the tax base resulting from original cost (that is, C2.5m).

Management should, therefore, recognise a deferred tax liability of C120,000 on the taxable temporary difference resulting from rollover relief of C400,000. But the resulting taxable temporary difference might enable otherwise unrecognised deferred tax assets on the same (for example, related land) or other assets to be recognised if the criteria in IAS 12 are met.

13.216.5 Where holdover relief is claimed, current tax remains payable in the future (as noted in para 13.216.1). If the entity discounts current taxes (see para 13.73), the carrying amount of the tax payable could be materially reduced if the deferral period is significant.

Revaluation for tax purposes

13.217 An asset can sometimes be revalued for tax purposes; and that revaluation might or might not be reflected for accounting purposes. Where an asset revaluation for tax purposes relates to an accounting revaluation of an earlier period (or to one that is expected to be carried out in a future period), the tax effects of the asset revaluation and the adjustment of the tax base are recognised in other comprehensive income in the periods in which they occur. [IAS 12 para 65]. This is consistent with the general principle that tax follows the item.

13.217.1 Where an asset revaluation for tax purposes does not relate to an accounting revaluation of an earlier period (or to one that is expected to be carried out in a future period), the tax effects of adjusting the tax base are recognised in profit or loss. [IAS 12 para 65].

13.217.2 If an asset is carried at a revaluation ('deemed cost') under the transitional rules of IFRS 1, but the entity has no ongoing accounting policy of revaluation, the effect of changes in the tax base are recognised in profit or loss. This is discussed further in paragraph 13.219 onwards.

13.217.3 The impact of changes in the tax revaluation is only recognised in other comprehensive income if a relationship is established between the accounting revaluation and the tax revaluation; and that relationship does not have to be one of perfect correlation. When a general basis of indexation for tax purposes applies to all entities, the reporting entity needs to establish the relationship. In considering the relationship, it might be helpful to consider how valuations of the relevant class of assets have correlated with the tax index in the past, as well as any indicators that suggest changes in that correlation in the future. Also, where significant amounts are involved, the entity should have regard to the significant judgements disclosure requirements under IAS 1: the financial statements should disclose the judgements that management has made in the process of applying the accounting policies that have the most significant effect on the amounts recognised in those financial statements (see para 13.277.2). [IAS 1 para 122].

13.217.4 If an entity's accounting policy is to revalue an asset (so that a revaluation surplus is taken to reserves in the same or a previous period) – and a relationship between the accounting revaluation and the tax revaluation has been established – then if the tax base is revalued we consider that (to the extent that the tax revaluation is no greater than the cumulative accounting revaluation) the tax revaluation arguably relates to the earlier accounting revaluation; as a result, the effect of the adjusted tax base is recognised in other comprehensive income. But where the tax revaluation exceeds the cumulative accounting revaluation, it is a matter of judgement as to whether the tax revaluation relates to an accounting revaluation expected in the future. If it is judged to be so, the effect of the adjusted tax base is recognised in other comprehensive income; otherwise, it is recognised in profit or loss.

UK.13.217.4.1 In the UK, indexation allowance typically applies to the capital gains tax ('CGT') base cost; this is the asset's tax base when the expected manner of recovery is through sale or will otherwise involve a disposal for CGT purposes. So this impacts on the deferred tax calculation for land and for buildings expected to be recovered wholly or partly (that is, using the dual manner of recovery method) through sale. UK tax indexation is generally considered to 'relate to' accounting revaluations for the purpose of determining whether the tax is recognised in other comprehensive income.

13.217.5 If it is clear that the tax basis revaluation does not relate to the accounting revaluation, the effect of the tax revaluation is taken to profit or loss. This might arise if the basis for the asset's tax revaluation bears no relationship to asset price development in the market (for example, if the tax basis is general inflation but the class of assets has had a reducing fair value in the past – as has been the case for technology products). The tax revaluation might be expected to be upwards, but the accounting revaluation would not be.

13.218 The following paragraphs consider the accounting treatment of changes in deferred tax as a result of tax revaluations.

13.218.1 An entity's accounting policy might be to carry an asset at cost (that is, with no revaluation); if the tax base is revalued for tax purposes, the effect of the tax base's revaluation is recognised in profit or loss because it does not relate to a prior accounting revaluation and none is anticipated in future periods.

Example – Asset carried at cost

Entity A acquires an asset which has an initial tax base equal to its cost.

The asset's tax base is increased each year by an amount based on asset price inflation.

Entity A accounts for the asset using a policy of cost (that is, with no accounting revaluation) under IAS 16.

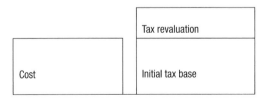

If a tax revaluation is available in this situation (that is, the tax revaluation can create or increase a loss), then the impact of the increase in the tax base as a result of the tax revaluation is recognised in profit or loss; this is because it does not relate to an accounting revaluation that has been recognised in other comprehensive income.

UK note – under the UK tax system, tax indexation given on sale of an asset cannot create or increase a loss; and so the impact of tax indexation would not be recognised in this situation. See example 2 in paragraph 13.214.

13.218.2 Where an entity's accounting policy is to revalue an asset and there is a related tax revaluation, the effect of adjusting the tax base is recognised in other comprehensive income.

Example – Asset carried at revaluation

Entity A acquires an asset which has an initial tax base equal to its cost.

The asset's tax base is increased each year by an amount based on asset price inflation.

Entity A accounts for the asset using a policy of revaluation under IAS 16.

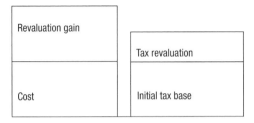

To the extent that the increase in the tax base as a result of the tax revaluation is no greater than the cumulative accounting revaluation surplus recognised in other comprehensive income, the tax revaluation arguably relates to an earlier accounting revaluation; as a result, the effect of the adjusted tax base is recognised in other comprehensive income.

Where the tax revaluation exceeds the cumulative accounting revaluation, the comments in paragraph 13.217.4 apply to the excess amount.

The tax revaluation arising in the period of the asset's disposal is allocated between the income statement and other comprehensive income; see further example 2 in paragraph 13.214.

13.218.3 The situation is more complicated when an acquired asset's tax base has been reduced by rolled-over gains and the tax revaluation is given on the reduced tax base. In summary, the rolled-over gain adjusts the new asset's tax base (that is, the new asset's tax base is initially reduced by the rolled over gain); see further paragraph 13.216 onwards.

Example 1 – Tax base reduced by rolled-over gains, asset carried at cost

Entity A acquires an asset and the initial tax base is reduced by rolled-over gains.

The asset's reduced tax base is increased each year by an amount based on asset price inflation.

Entity A accounts for the asset using a policy of cost (that is, with no accounting revaluation) under IAS 16.

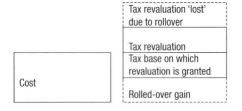

If the tax base of an asset carried at cost has been reduced by rolled-over gains (so that it is lower than the accounting cost) and the tax revaluation is given on the reduced tax base, the increase in the tax base as a result of the tax revaluation is recognised in profit or loss; this is because it does not relate to an accounting revaluation that has been recognised in other comprehensive income.

The tax revaluation reduces the deferred tax arising on the rolled-over gain. But the impact of the change in tax is not 'backwards traced' for accounting purposes to the previously rolled-over gain; this is because it is not related to the rollover, even though it is reversing its effect.

Example 2 – Tax base reduced by rolled-over gains, asset carried at revaluation

Entity A acquires an asset and the initial tax base is reduced by rolled-over gains.

The asset's reduced tax base is increased each year by an amount based on asset price inflation.

Entity A accounts for the asset using a policy of revaluation under IAS 16.

Revaluation gain	Tax revaluation 'lost' due to rollover
	Tax revaluation
Cost	Tax base on which revaluation is granted
	Rollover gain

The accounting is similar to the example in paragraph 13.218.2 (for revalued assets), except that the tax revaluation will be lower; this is because it is given on a lower tax base. As in paragraph 13.218.2, to the extent that the increase in the tax base as a result of the tax revaluation is no greater than the cumulative accounting revaluation surplus recognised in other comprehensive income, the tax revaluation arguably relates to an earlier accounting revaluation; as a result, the effect of the adjusted tax base is recognised in other comprehensive income.

In other words, the accounting in this scenario is similar to that in paragraph 13.218.2; but it will take longer for the tax revaluation to reach the accounting revaluation gain because it is given on a lower tax base.

In this scenario, we do not consider that the impact of the tax revaluation up to the accounting cost of the asset (that is, to the extent of the rolled-over gain) should first be taken to the income statement; because this would suggest that the tax revaluation relates to the reinstatement of the cost (that is, it somehow replaces the impact of the rollover election). We do not believe that this is the case. The rollover reduces the amount of tax revaluation that is available, but otherwise the scenario is similar to the example in paragraph 13.218.2 for revalued assets; and so similar accounting should apply.

The above accounting will apply unless the tax revaluation exceeds the accounting revaluation gain.

Revaluation gain	Tax revaluation
Cost	Tax base on which revaluation is granted
	Rollover gain

To the extent that the increase in the tax base as a result of the tax revaluation exceeds the cumulative accounting revaluation, it is a matter of judgement as to whether the tax revaluation relates to an accounting revaluation expected in the future or whether it is reinstating the tax base back to initial cost and reducing the deferred tax arising on the rolled-over gain; in which case, this element is similar to example 1 above and would be recognised in profit or loss.

13.218.4 Where an asset is acquired in a business combination and the asset's tax base is lower than its fair value at the acquisition date, the accounting in the parent's consolidated financial statements will be the same whether the acquired entity had revalued the property before acquisition by the group or whether the property was revalued on acquisition. In both cases, under IFRS 3, the asset's fair value at the acquisition date is the deemed cost from the acquiring group's perspective; and any deferred tax liability arising as a result of the lower tax base at the acquisition date will form part of the goodwill calculation.

> **Example 1 – Asset carried at a policy of cost (that is, based on fair value at acquisition date)**
>
> Entity A acquires an asset as part of a business combination.
>
> The asset's tax base is lower than its fair value at the acquisition date. The asset's initial tax base is increased each year by an amount based on asset price inflation; and the tax base at acquisition date reflects the tax revaluation to date.
>
> Entity A accounts for the asset using a policy of cost (that is, based on the asset's fair value at the acquisition date, with no subsequent accounting revaluation) under IAS 16.

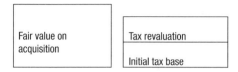

As noted above, if the asset's tax base is lower than its fair value at the acquisition date, the deferred tax liability forms part of the goodwill calculation in the consolidated financial statements. In this situation, any subsequent increase in the tax base as a result of tax revaluation is recognised in profit or loss, because it does not relate to an accounting revaluation that has been recognised in other comprehensive income. In this respect, it does not matter if the acquired entity had revalued the properties before acquisition, because the relevant accounting is in the consolidated financial statements.

> **Example 2 – Asset acquired in business combination subsequently carried at a policy of revaluation**
>
> Entity A acquires an asset as part of a business combination.
>
> The asset's tax base is lower than its fair value at the acquisition date. The asset's initial tax base is increased each year by an amount based on asset price inflation; and the tax base at the acquisition date reflects the tax revaluation to date.
>
> Entity A accounts for the asset using a policy of revaluation under IAS 16.
>
> There are a number of acceptable accounting treatments (described below) for determining how the impact of the tax revaluation is allocated to the performance statements. The accounting treatment selected should be applied on a consistent basis.
>
> (a)   Under this method, the tax revaluation first applies to any shortfall between the asset's 'cost' and tax base at the acquisition date. This might or might not result from a rollover election and/or higher fair value than original cost to the

acquired entity. Either way, from the acquirer's perspective, the asset has a lower tax base. This method reflects the natural order in which the revaluation arises (that is, the fair value revaluation at acquisition arises before any post-acquisition revaluation; and so the tax revaluation is first allocated against the fair value adjustment).

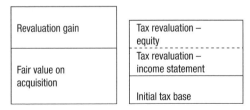

To the extent that the increase in the tax base as a result of tax revaluation builds the tax base up to the fair value at the acquisition date, the accounting treatment is similar to that in example 1 above. The increase in the tax base is recognised in profit or loss, because this element does not relate to an accounting revaluation that has been recognised in other comprehensive income.

Then to the extent that any further increase in the tax base as a result of tax revaluation is no greater than the cumulative post-acquisition accounting revaluation surplus recognised in other comprehensive income, the tax revaluation arguably relates to an earlier accounting revaluation; and so the effect of this adjustment to the tax base is recognised in other comprehensive income.

Note: if the tax indexation exceeds the accounting revaluation, the comments in paragraph 13.217.4 apply.

(b)   Under this method, the tax revaluation is first considered to relate to any post-acquisition revaluation gain; and so the impact is recognised in other comprehensive income (subject to the comments in para 13.217.4). This is consistent with the general principle in example 2 of paragraph 13.218.3 for revalued properties, where the tax revaluation is first considered to relate to the accounting revaluation.

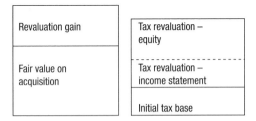

To the extent that the increase in the tax base as a result of the tax revaluation is no greater than the cumulative accounting revaluation surplus recognised in other comprehensive income, the tax revaluation arguably relates to the accounting revaluation that has been recognised in other comprehensive income; and so the effect of the adjusted tax base is recognised in other comprehensive income. This is consistent with the principle in example 2 in paragraph 13.218.3.

To the extent that the increase in the tax base as a result of the tax revaluation exceeds the cumulative accounting revaluation recognised in other comprehensive income, it would be considered to relate to the element of revaluation arising on acquisition (that is, the fair value adjustment); in that case, the increase in the tax base as a result of indexation would be recognised in profit or loss.

To the extent that the tax revaluation exceeds the cumulative accounting revaluation (recognised in other comprehensive income and arising on acquisition), it is a matter of judgement as to whether the tax revaluation relates to an accounting revaluation expected in the future. If it does, the effect of the adjusted tax base would be recognised in other comprehensive income; otherwise, it would be recognised in profit or loss.

(c) Under this method, the tax revaluation would be allocated pro rata, as explained below.

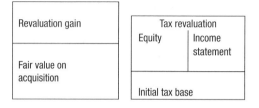

The tax revaluation would be allocated pro rata to the revaluation arising on acquisition (that is, change in tax recognised in profit or loss) and the post-acquisition accounting revaluation (that is, change in tax recognised in other comprehensive income).

13.219 The accounting treatments described above apply regardless of whether a deferred tax liability was recognised on transition to IFRS or later. But the fact that a deferred tax liability recognised on transition to IFRS was charged to equity (as part of the transition adjustment) does not mean that changes in the liability will also be recognised in equity. Instead, management should use the entity's current accounting policies to determine where the items that gave rise to the original deferred tax would have been recognised if IFRS had applied in the earlier periods.

13.219.1 Where it is not possible to assess where the items that gave rise to the original deferred tax would have been recognised if IFRS had applied in the earlier periods, the changes in the deferred tax should, by default, be recognised in profit or loss.

13.219.2 An entity might recognise an asset at a revalued amount ('deemed cost') on transition to IFRS, in lieu of cost, but does not otherwise treat the asset as revalued. Where the entity does not have an accounting policy of revaluing its assets, there is no revaluation surplus shown in the financial statements. In our view, changes in the related deferred tax liability arising as a result of tax revaluation are not regarded as relating to an accounting revaluation recognised in other comprehensive income; and so the impact of the tax revaluation should be recognised in profit or loss.

13.219.3 Similarly, an entity might have recognised deferred tax relating to a business combination on transition to IFRS and taken it (under IFRS 1) to retained earnings. Where the entity does not have an accounting policy of revaluing its assets, this was a one-off entry in lieu of adjusting goodwill (which IFRS 1 only permits in limited circumstances). A later tax revaluation does not relate to an accounting revaluation that has been recognised in other comprehensive income; and so (consistent with example 1 in para 13.218.4) the increase in the tax base as a result of tax revaluation would be recognised in profit or loss.

Investment properties

Recent developments

Amendments to IAS 12

13.219.4 The IASB issued 'Deferred tax: recovery of underlying assets (amendments to IAS 12)' in December 2010. The amendments provide an exception to the principles in IAS 12 for measuring deferred tax assets or liabilities when investment properties are measured at fair value. The amendments incorporate the previous guidance in SIC 21.

13.219.5 The amendments introduce a presumption that an investment property measured at fair value is recovered entirely through sale. This presumption is rebutted if the investment property is depreciable and is held within a business model whose objective is to consume substantially all of the investment property's economic benefits over time rather than through sale.

13.219.6 The amendments are effective for annual periods beginning on or after 1 January 2012, and have retrospective effect. Earlier application is permitted. If the amendments are adopted, the section on investment properties carried at fair value 'post-amendment' (at para 13.219.7 onwards) should be referred to; otherwise, the 'pre-amendment' guidance (at para 13.220 onwards) should be followed.

Carried at fair value – Post-amendment

13.219.7 Investment properties are held to earn rentals or for capital appreciation or both. Under IAS 40, an entity can choose to measure the investment property at cost or at fair value.

13.219.8 In some jurisdictions, an investment property does not qualify for tax depreciation (whatever measurement basis is used); and so no part of the property's cost is deductible against taxable rental income. Instead, the cost of the property (uplifted by an allowance for inflation, where applicable) is allowed as a deduction against sales proceeds for the purpose of computing any chargeable gain arising on sale.

13.219.9   Even in jurisdictions where an investment property might qualify for tax depreciation, there is a presumption that an investment property carried at fair value will be recovered entirely through sale. This presumption is rebutted if the investment property would be considered depreciable if IAS 16 were applied and it is held within a business model whose objective is to consume substantially all of the investment property's economic benefits over time rather than through sale.

13.219.10   Therefore, deferred tax for investment properties carried at fair value should generally be provided using the tax base and the tax rate that are consistent with recovery entirely through sale using capital gains tax rules – or other rules regarding the tax consequences of sale (such as rules designed to claw back any tax depreciation previously claimed in respect of the asset). If the presumption is rebutted, deferred tax should be measured reflecting the tax consequences of the expected manner of recovery. [Amendments to IAS 12, para 51C]. The guidance at paragraph 13.170 (on how to apply the expected manner of recovery approach to assets and liabilities) can also be applied to investment properties carried at fair value.

13.219.11   The presumption also applies where investment property is initially measured at fair value in a business combination and the acquirer uses fair value to measure the investment property later.

13.219.12   The presumption cannot be rebutted for an investment property (or portion of an investment property) that would be considered non-depreciable if IAS 16 were applied (such as freehold land).

Carried at fair value — Pre-amendment

13.220   Investment properties are held to earn rentals or for capital appreciation or both. Under IAS 40, an entity can choose to measure the investment property at cost or at fair value. In some jurisdictions, an investment property does not qualify for tax depreciation (whatever measurement basis is used); and so no part of the property's cost is deductible against taxable rental income. Instead, the cost of the property (uplifted by an allowance for inflation, where applicable) is allowed as a deduction against sales proceeds for the purpose of computing any chargeable gain arising on sale. Deferred tax should be provided using the tax base and tax rate that are consistent with the property's expected manner of recovery; so management needs to determine the appropriate tax base of an investment property that is held for use in the business for its rental yield and not for disposal.

13.221   The investment property is carried at fair value, so it is not depreciated systematically over its useful life. Instead, a gain or loss arising from a change in fair value is recognised in profit or loss. [IAS 40 para 35]. Because the property is not depreciated, it would initially appear logical to provide deferred tax that reflects the tax consequences of selling the asset in line with SIC 21 (as discussed in para 13.214). In other words, deferred tax would be provided on the difference between the property's fair value and its indexed cost for tax purposes at the balance sheet date. But closer scrutiny of the wording of paragraph 4 in SIC 21 would suggest that this is not the case. The interpretation applies to investment properties that are carried at revalued amounts under paragraph 33 of IAS 40 but would be considered non-depreciable if IAS 16 were applied. [SIC 21 para 4]. Under IAS 16, only land is regarded as a non-depreciable asset because it has an infinite life; all other properties (including those that are held for rental and are not depreciated in accordance with IAS 40) would be considered depreciable assets if IAS 16 were applied. SIC 21 concludes that the expected manner of recovery of land can only be through sale; but this is not valid for the buildings element of investment properties that are carried at fair value. The expected manner of recovery for these buildings might be through use, sale, or use and sale. But the conclusion in SIC 21 applies to land elements of investment properties; and so any land element of an investment property will be considered (for the purposes of calculating deferred tax) as recoverable through sale.

13.221.1   In practice, an entity might use an investment property for 5, 10 or 15 years and then sell it. The deferred tax should reflect the fact that the investment property's expected manner of recovery is through rental income and eventual sale. It is provided on the basis of normal income tax rules for the portion of the property's carrying amount expected to be recovered through use; and it is provided using capital gains tax rules for the remainder of the property's carrying amount expected to be recovered through sale. See further paragraph 13.172.2.

13.222   If a dual manner of recovery expectation applies, the asset's carrying amount should be split between use and sale elements. An indicator of the carrying amount to be attributed to the sale element would be the asset's residual value at the balance sheet date. This is the asset's estimated value (in present prices at the balance sheet date) in the state it is expected to be in at the end of its useful life. The two components of the carrying amount are then compared to the relevant tax bases. In some jurisdictions, the tax base relating to use of investment properties might be calculated differently from the tax base on sale; for example, the tax base for use might be cost instead of cost adjusted by allowance for inflation, which only applies to the disposal of assets.

Example – Dual manner of recovery for revalued investment property

An entity acquires an investment property on 1 January 20X7. The building element of this property is valued at C50m. Management expects to use the building for 10 years to generate rental income. At the end of year 10, the expectation is that the building will be sold. The building's estimated residual value at 31 December 20X7 is C20m. For tax purposes, the asset's cost is not deductible against taxable rental income; but any sales proceeds are taxable after deducting cost (not adjusted for inflation) at the date of sale. The tax rate is 30% for taxable income and 40% for chargeable capital gains. The entity's accounting policy is to carry investment property at fair value. At the year end, the property's fair value is C52m. The cost of the building element for tax purposes at that date is C50m.

Following the above guidance, the tax base on the use element of the building is nil on initial recognition and for all later periods. The carrying amount attributed to the use element is C30m (the total cost of the building of C50m less the residual value of C20m expected to be recovered through sale). So a taxable temporary difference of C30m arises in relation to the building's use element on initial recognition; but the initial recognition exception applies (see para 13.162) because the difference does not arise on a business combination and does not affect accounting or taxable profits. Therefore, no deferred tax is provided on the temporary difference.

There is a tax base available on sale. The carrying amount of the sale element of the building is C20m and the tax base is C50m (the building's cost). A deductible temporary difference of C30m exists in relation to the sale element of the building; but, as above, the initial recognition exception applies because the difference does not arise on a business combination and does not affect accounting or taxable profits; so no deferred tax is provided on the temporary difference.

At the end of year 1, the fair value of the building increases to C52m; if there is no change in the tax base in use or on disposal, this will lead to an overall increase in the taxable temporary difference. The C2m increase in fair value arises after initial recognition and affects the accounting profits; so this change in the temporary difference will not be subject to the initial recognition exception. Management needs to revisit its residual value calculation to determine whether the C2m impacts the use or the sale element. If the estimated residual value is still C20m, the C2m increase in carrying amount would impact the calculation of deferred tax in use. The carrying amount of the use element would now be C32m and the tax base nil. A temporary difference of C32m exists, of which C2m has arisen after initial recognition. So the entity would recognise a deferred tax liability of C0.6m (30% of C2m) at the balance sheet date, using the income tax rate (to reflect the fact that this element of the building's carrying amount is expected to be recovered as rental income rather than through sale). The deferred tax expense of C0.6m would be recognised through the income statement in line with the changes in fair value.

On the other hand, if the residual value had increased to C22m, the C2m increase in carrying amount would reduce the deductible temporary difference on disposal by C2m (C22m carrying amount less C50m tax base = C28m deductible temporary difference; this is compared to the original deductible temporary difference of C30m noted above). This change is recognised in deferred tax terms (C2m @ 40% = C0.8m deferred tax liability).

13.222.1 It is common for groups in some jurisdictions to hold an investment property within a corporate entity (or 'corporate wrapper') and expect that the asset will be 'recovered' by selling the investment in the corporate entity. See further paragraph 13.172.1 onwards.

Carried at cost — Post and pre-amendment

13.223 Where an investment property is carried at cost, it would be depreciated in the normal way over its useful economic life for accounting purposes; but (under the tax rules described above) no tax deduction would be obtained, because the asset is consumed through use. The asset's expected manner of recovery might be through use and sale; in that case, the asset's carrying amount is split between the use and sale elements, and these carrying amounts are compared to the relevant tax bases. It follows that the tax base of the building's use element carried at cost would be nil on initial recognition and in all future periods.

13.224 This can be illustrated by changing the circumstances slightly from the example in paragraph 13.222.

Example – Dual manner of recovery for investment property carried at cost

Assume the building purchased on 1 January 20X7 for C50m had a useful life of 25 years and an estimated nil residual value. A carrying amount of nil would be attributed to the sale element of the building on initial recognition, creating a deductible temporary difference of C50m on the sale element. A taxable temporary difference would arise on the use element on initial recognition, being the carrying amount of C50m less the tax base of nil. At the end of year 1, assuming the residual value was still nil, the element of the asset to be recovered through use would have a depreciated cost of C48m (C50m less C2m depreciation charge). The temporary difference on the use element at the balance sheet date is C48m; but no deferred tax is provided because this amount is part of the C50m temporary difference that arose in relation to the use element on initial recognition. It follows that no deferred tax liability will arise on the building's use element where the investment property is carried at depreciated cost. At the end of year 1, the deductible temporary difference for the building's sale element would remain; but, as with the taxable temporary difference above, this will be covered by the initial recognition exception – so no deferred tax is recognised.

Transfers to or from investment property — Post and pre-amendment

13.225 A property might be transferred from investment property carried at fair value to property, plant and equipment following commencement of owner-occupation; or it might be transferred from property, plant and equipment to investment property that will be carried at fair value following end of owner-occupation. This reclassification could have consequences for the deferred tax balances recognised.

Example 1 – Transfer from investment property to property, plant and equipment

An entity acquired an investment property on 1 January 20X7. The building element of the property is valued at C50m and the estimated residual value is nil. Management initially expects to use the building for 10 years to generate rental income, with no residual value. The initial expectation is that the building will be sold at the end of year 10 to recover its tax base.

For tax purposes, the asset's cost is not deductible against rental income; but any sales proceeds are taxable after deducting cost at the date of sale. The tax rate is 30% for taxable income and 40% for chargeable capital gains.

On initial recognition, a taxable temporary difference existed in relation to the building's use element; and a deductible temporary difference existed in relation to the sale element. But no deferred tax was recognised because this was covered by the initial recognition exception. During years 1 to 5, changes in the building's fair value impacted the use element only (because the estimated residual value continued to be nil). These fair value changes arose after initial recognition; so deferred tax was recognised.

Five years after acquisition, the property was transferred from investment property to property, plant and equipment following a change in use. At the date of transfer, the building's fair value and the corresponding deferred tax liability were C60m and C3m respectively; and the building was estimated to have a remaining life of 20 years with a nil residual value.

Where an investment property carried at fair value is transferred to property, plant and equipment, the property's fair value at the date of transfer becomes its deemed cost for subsequent accounting under IAS 16. [IAS 40 para 60]. So no adjustment is made to the carrying amount or to the deferred tax liability at the date of transfer. At the end of the year, the building's use element would have a depreciated carrying amount of C57m; this would give rise to a taxable temporary difference at that date of C57m. Of this amount, C47.5m arose on initial recognition (being the original temporary difference on initial recognition of C50 less a year's depreciation charge of C2.5m). The remaining C9.5m arose after initial recognition; so deferred tax should be provided on this amount. This results from the C10m uplift in the building's valuation (that occurred after initial recognition) less a year's depreciation charge against this (of C0.5m). So the deferred tax balance at the end of the year would be C2.85m (30% of C9.5m). This reduction of C0.15m in the deferred tax balance (from C3m to C2.85m) is recognised through the income statement. The deferred tax liability will continue to reverse at the rate of C0.15m per annum until it has been reversed in full over the building's remaining useful life.

Assuming no change in residual value or tax base for the building's sale element, there would be no impact on the deferred tax calculation for the sale element.

Example 2 – Transfer from property, plant and equipment to investment property

A building was purchased on 1 January 20X7 for C50m, with a useful life of 25 years and an estimated residual value of nil. The building was used in the business; so it was classified as property, plant and equipment. For tax purposes, the asset's cost is not deductible in use, but any sales proceeds are taxable after deducting the cost at the date of sale. The tax rate is 30% for taxable income and 40% for chargeable capital gains.

On initial recognition, a carrying amount of nil was attributable to the building's sale element; this created a deductible temporary difference. A taxable temporary difference existed in relation to the building's use element; but no deferred tax was recognised because this was covered by the initial recognition exception.

Five years after acquisition, the property was transferred from property, plant and equipment to investment property following a change in use. At the date of transfer, the property's depreciated cost was C40m (C50m less five years' annual depreciation of C2m). The property's fair value at the date of transfer amounted to C60m. The entity expects to recover the carrying amount through rentals over the next 25 years. The building's residual value at the date of transfer is estimated as nil.

Where an entity transfers an owner-occupied property to investment property that will be carried at fair value, the difference between the fair value and the property's depreciated cost is treated in the same way as a revaluation under IAS 16. [IAS 40 para 61]. In other words, the difference of C20m (C60m less C40m) is credited to the revaluation reserve and recognised in other comprehensive income. The entity also recognises deferred tax on the revaluation surplus charged to the revaluation reserve in other comprehensive income. Note that deferred tax would be calculated with reference to the full uplift of C20m at the date of transfer (because it arises after initial recognition) and not on C10m (C60m less C50m arising on initial recognition). This is because C10m of the C50m of cost on initial recognition has already reversed through the depreciation charge affecting accounting profit, when the property was held under owner-occupation during the first five years.

As in the example in paragraph 13.224, the entity should determine which element of the building (sale or use) the revaluation gain relates to. If the building's residual value continues to be nil, the revaluation gain will impact the calculation of deferred tax on the building's use element; and a deferred tax liability of C6m (C20m @ 30%) would be recognised.

After the transfer, a gain or loss arising from a change in the investment property's fair value would be recognised in profit or loss for the period in which it arises. Deferred tax should be provided on this change in fair value through profit or loss.

Intangible assets

13.225.1 The amendments to IAS 12 made by 'Deferred tax: Recovery of underlying assets', issued in December 2010, incorporate the guidance in SIC 21, which has been withdrawn for entities applying the amendments.

13.225.2 Paragraph 107 of IAS 38 states that "*an intangible asset with an indefinite useful life shall not be amortised*". This might be the case with, for example, trademarks or brands (see further chapter 15). Non-amortisation of an asset is arguably an indication that the asset is not recovered through use; so the measurement of deferred tax presumes that the asset's carrying amount will be recovered through sale; and the tax base determination follows that presumption.

13.225.3 The carrying amount of a non-depreciable asset (such as land having an unlimited life) will only be recovered through sale. [SIC 21 para 6; IAS 12 (amended) para 51B]. This is because the asset is not depreciated and no part of its carrying amount is expected to be recovered (or consumed) through use. The question arises whether the same conclusion relating to land should be applied to intangible assets with indefinite useful lives.

13.225.4 There are some distinctions to be drawn between land and intangible assets with indefinite lives. The fact that an asset has an indefinite life does not mean that the future economic benefits arising from the asset will not eventually be consumed; it is simply that the timing of that consumption is uncertain. Indeed, the requirement to test intangible assets with indefinite lives for impairment at least annually is an acknowledgement that recovery through use might occur. The intangible asset can be used to generate income on an ongoing basis in the business; so recovery through sale should not be presumed where that is not currently expected.

13.225.5 Consistent with the factors above, we consider that management should use judgement based on individual facts and circumstances to determine the expected manner of recovery of intangible assets with indefinite lives and whether SIC 21 (or IAS 12 (amended) para 51B) should be applied.

13.225.6 In some circumstances, the tax base of an intangible asset with an indefinite life can be determined solely on a sale basis. If revenues generated by intangible assets with indefinite lives are not (and are not expected to be in the future) a recovery of the asset's carrying amount, recovery through sale might be acceptable. But the following factors should be considered:

- Recovery through sale may not be presumed for intangible assets that have been the subject of an impairment write-down – such a write-down is evidence of recovery through use.

- If the asset's carrying amount is subject to impairment in the future, the expected manner of recovery could change to recovery through use; this will have an impact on deferred taxes recognised in current earnings, in addition to the impact of the impairment.

- Management might need to disclose the presumption of recovery through sale to comply with paragraph 122 of IAS 1, which requires disclosure of judgements made by management that have significant effects on amounts recognised.

Financial instruments

Financial assets carried at fair value

13.226 All entities (including non-financial entities) are required or permitted under IAS 39 to measure certain financial assets and liabilities at fair value; and changes in fair values are reported through profit or loss or in other comprehensive income.

13.227 Where financial assets are carried at fair value with adjustments through profit or loss, tax laws might recognise the gains and losses arising from changes in fair value as they accrue; this means that such gains and losses would be subject to current tax when they are recognised and no deferred tax would arise. In other circumstances, the gains and losses might be taxed only when they are realised at a later date. In that case, a temporary difference arises between the asset's fair value and its tax base; so a deferred tax liability or asset (subject to meeting the recognition test) should be recognised through profit or loss.

13.227.1 Where a financial asset is classified as 'available-for-sale' and changes in fair value are recognised in other comprehensive income, the tax effects of such gains and losses should also be recognised in other comprehensive income. In some tax jurisdictions, such gains and losses are taxed in the same period in which they arise; in other tax jurisdictions, they are taxable when the financial asset is sold. In either situation, the related current or deferred tax effects should also be recognised in other comprehensive income.

13.227.2 When an available-for-sale financial asset is derecognised on sale or is impaired, the cumulative gain or loss previously recognised in other comprehensive income is reclassified to profit or loss. [IAS 39 paras 55(b), 67]. A question arises whether the tax on the gain recognised in other comprehensive income should be reclassified to profit or loss. Although IAS 12 is silent on this, we believe that the tax effects of gains and losses recognised in other comprehensive income should be reclassified to profit or loss in the same period as the gains or losses to which they relate. This is a sensible treatment, because reclassifying any cumulative gains or losses to profit or loss ensures that tax on the gain recognised in profit or loss is the same as the tax paid on that gain.

Example – Deferred tax on fair value gains

An entity acquired an equity security for C10,000; the security is classified on initial recognition as 'available-for-sale'. At the year end, the security's fair value increases to C12,000. The tax rate is 30%.

The change in fair value of C2,000 is recognised in other comprehensive income under IAS 39. Ignoring indexation, the tax arising on this gain at the balance sheet date is 30% of (C12,000 – C10,000) = C600. A current or deferred tax liability of C600 will be recognised at the balance sheet date (with a corresponding debit recognised in other comprehensive income), depending on whether the tax on the gain is payable in the current period or deferred until the investment is sold.

The security is sold in the following year at its market value of C11,500. A loss arises for accounting purposes between sales proceeds of C11,500 less carrying amount of C12,000 = C500. Also (under IAS 39) the gain of C2,000 (before tax) previously recognised in other comprehensive income is reclassified to profit or loss; this means that the gain reported in profit or loss is C1,500, which is sales proceeds less original cost.

Ignoring any inflation adjustments for tax purposes, the current tax that arises on sale will depend on whether tax was paid or deferred on the earlier gain.

Scenario 1 – Gains or losses are taxed in the period in which they arise

A taxable loss of C500 arises between sales proceeds of C11,500 and carrying amount for tax purposes of C12,000; this gives rise to a current tax credit of C150 (C500 @ 30%), assuming this is recoverable. The taxable loss of C500 differs from the accounting gain of C1,500; this is because tax on the gain of C2,000 arising in a prior period was paid as current tax. There would have been no deferred tax arising in the previous period; but the current tax of C600 would have been recognised in other comprehensive income.

Where tax on the gain that was previously recognised in other comprehensive income was paid when the gain arose, the reclassification of the tax paid in the current period is regarded as an adjustment of the current tax of prior periods:

	Book profit	Equity*
	C	C
Sales proceeds	11,500	
Carrying amount before sale	12,000	
Loss before reclassification	(500)	–
Reclassification of gain	2,000	(2,000)
Result of sale, as reported	1,500	(2,000)
Current tax – in period	150	–
Current tax – reclassified	(600)	600
Net gain and related tax	1,050	(1,400)

* The amounts shown under 'equity' are recognised in other comprehensive income.

The net loss of C350 (C1,400 loss recognised in other comprehensive income less the C1,050 gain recognised in profit or loss) is the C500 loss for the period less tax at 30% = C150.

The tax credit of C150 would be reported as a current tax credit, and the reclassified tax of C600 would be described as 'prior-year adjustment to current tax' or 'reclassification from equity'. The result is a total tax charge of C450, which is the tax that arises on the net gain of C1,500. A current tax recoverable of C150 would be recognised in the balance sheet.

Scenario 2 – Gains or losses are deferred and taxed in the period in which the investment is sold

In this situation, a taxable gain of C1,500 arises between sales proceeds of C11,500 and carrying amount for tax purposes of C10,000; this gives rise to a current tax charge of C450 = 30% of (C11,500 – C10,000). The taxable and accounting gains are the same, as would be expected; this is because tax on the gain of C2,000 arising in a prior period was deferred. A deferred tax liability of C600 would have been recognised in the previous period (C2,000 @ 30%); and this is released in the current period.

Where tax on the previous gain was deferred, the current tax is recognised in profit or loss; and deferred tax is released through other comprehensive income:

	Book profit	Equity*
	C	C
Sales proceeds	11,500	
Carrying amount before sale	12,000	
Loss before reclassification	(500)	–
Reclassification of gain	2,000	(2,000)
Result of sale, as reported	1,500	(2,000)
Current tax	(450)	–
Deferred tax release	–	600
Net gain/(loss) and related tax	1,050	(1,400)

* The amounts shown under 'equity' are recognised in other comprehensive income.

As in scenario 1, the net loss of C350 (C1,400 loss recognised in other comprehensive income less the C1,050 gain recognised in profit or loss) is the C500 loss for the period less tax at 30% = C150.

The tax payable of C450 would be reported as a current tax charge. A current tax liability of C450 would be recognised in the balance sheet; and the deferred tax liability of C600 that was previously recognised would be credited to other comprehensive income.

UK.13.227.2.1 In the UK, the tax rules for gains and losses on financial instruments are complex. Depending on the elections made under the applicable tax rules, fair value gains and losses are taxable as they accrue for accounting purposes or when they are realised at a later date. Consultation with a tax specialist is recommended in this area.

13.227.3 An equity investment might be recovered through receipt of dividends or through disposal or a combination of both. Where the tax implications differ, the expected manner of recovery needs to be considered.

Example – Expected manner of recovery of available-for-sale investment

An entity holds an available-for-sale investment — that is, shares in a listed entity. The tax base of the shares is C400,000, which was the amount initially paid for the shares. The fair value of the shares at the year end is C1,000,000.

At the balance sheet date, the entity expects to receive dividends of C500,000 over five years and then sell the shares. Dividends are not expected to impair the carrying amount of the investment when paid.

Dividends are non-taxable. Based on current tax legislation, if the shares were sold after five years, capital gains tax at a rate of 10% would be payable on the excess of sales price over cost.

How much deferred tax (if any) should the entity recognise at the balance sheet date?

An entity should recognise deferred tax based on the expected manner of recovery of an asset or liability at the balance sheet date. [IAS 12 para 51].

The entity expects to derive the dividends from the investee's future earnings rather than from its existing resources at the balance sheet date. The entity does not expect the investment's carrying amount at the balance sheet date to be recovered through future dividends, because there is no impairment expectation arising from the dividends. This is important, as the expected manner of recovery will determine the deferred tax treatment.

Therefore the entity expects to recover the investment through sale. The carrying amount of C1,000,000 has a corresponding tax base of C400,000 on sale. There is a taxable temporary difference of C600,000 at the balance sheet date. Tax is payable at the capital gains rate of 10%.

The entity should recognise a deferred tax liability of C60,000 relating to the shares.

But if the entity expects that the dividends or part of the dividends will result in impairment of the investment's carrying amount, applying the dual manner of recovery might be more appropriate.

13.227.4 An entity might use a derivative instrument (for example, a foreign currency forward contract) to hedge its foreign exchange risk exposure on cash flows in connection with a future purchase of an item of property, plant and equipment. The derivative is carried at fair value; and, if it qualifies as a cash flow hedge under IAS 39, gains and losses are initially recognised in other comprehensive income. The entity has an accounting policy choice as to the amount at which to record the hedged asset when it is purchased (see further chapter 6): the entity could record the asset at cost and then reclassify the gain or loss from other comprehensive income to profit or loss gradually as the asset is depreciated. [IAS 39 para 98(a)]. Or the gain or loss on the derivative could be reclassified immediately out of other comprehensive income and added to (or deducted from) the asset's initial cost. [IAS 39 para 98(b)]. If the latter policy is adopted and the asset's cost is adjusted, a temporary difference will arise on the asset's initial recognition. The following example considers the deferred tax implications of this temporary difference and the recognition of tax relating to the derivative in the performance statements.

Example – Cash flow hedge of property, plant and equipment

An entity purchases an item of property, plant and equipment (PPE) in a foreign currency. Before the purchase, it enters into a foreign currency forward contract that meets the criteria for hedge accounting in IAS 39 and is a fully effective cash flow hedge. Under the tax rules of the jurisdiction where the entity is based, the gain or loss on the forward contract is taxed when the forward contract matures (that is, when the asset is purchased). The entity intends to recover the asset entirely through use; the tax authority grants capital allowances over the asset's useful economic life based on its equivalent purchase price in the entity's functional currency on the date of purchase.

The entity's accounting policy for cash flow hedges of this type is to reclassify the gain or loss on the derivative immediately out of other comprehensive income and add it to (or deduct it from) the asset's initial cost. [IAS 39 para 98(b)]. This adjustment to the PPE's cost means that its carrying amount differs from its tax base; so a temporary difference arises on recognising the PPE.

(a) Does the initial recognition exception apply to the temporary difference arising from an asset's cost adjustment for a cash flow hedge?

In our view, the initial recognition exception does not apply; and so deferred tax should be recognised. Any tax on settling the forward contract is inherently linked to the PPE's purchase. This is because the forward contract was a designated hedge for this purchase, and the initial temporary difference on the PPE arises as a result of the hedge accounting. As such, the PPE's purchase cannot be looked at in isolation. So the purchase of the PPE has an impact on accounting profit (that is, the current tax on the derivative) that is inherently linked to the purchase; this means that the criteria for the initial recognition exception in IAS 12 (see para 13.162) are not met.

(b) When should the tax effect of the gain or loss on the forward contract be recognised in profit or loss?

Any deferred tax previously recorded in other comprehensive income should be reclassified out of other comprehensive income and into profit or loss in line with the underlying accounting. This can be achieved by recognising the current tax on the forward contract in profit or loss and unwinding the existing deferred tax asset or liability against other comprehensive income. The net effect to the income tax charge will be nil in this case, because a new deferred tax asset or liability is recognised on initial recognition of the asset (as a result of the temporary difference referred to in (a) above).

Financial assets carried at amortised cost

13.228 Financial instruments carried at amortised cost can also give rise to deferred tax consequences.

> **Example – Deferred tax and financial assets carried at amortised cost**
>
> An entity acquires a 5% bond with a nominal value of C100,000 at a discount of 20% to the nominal value; the bond is repayable in five years' time at a premium of 20% to the nominal value. The costs of acquisition are C5,000, and interest is received annually in arrears. The entity expects to hold the bond to maturity. The costs of acquisition are taxed as part of the cost of the bond; interest is taxed when received; and any profit on redemption (proceeds less cost) is taxed on redemption.
>
> | Net purchase cost of bond | C | Total receivable over life | C |
> |---|---:|---|---:|
> | Nominal value | 100,000 | Nominal value | 100,000 |
> | Discount on issue | (20,000) | Redemption premium | 20,000 |
> | Cost of acquisition | 5,000 | Interest @ 5% for five years | 25,000 |
> | Total | 85,000 | Total | 145,000 |

The total return on the bond over five years is C60,000 (C145,000 – C85,000). This amount should be amortised over the period to maturity using the effective interest method. The effective interest rate is 12.323% that exactly discounts the future cash inflows over the five-year period to the net proceeds received.

Taxation

Year	Amortised cost at beginning of the period	Effective interest @ 12.323 % *	Interest received	Amortised cost at end of the period	Tax Base	Temporary Difference
	C	C	C	C	C	C
1	85,000	10,474	(5,000)	90,474	85,000	5,474
2	90,474	11,149	(5,000)	96,623	85,000	11,623
3	96,623	11,906	(5,000)	103,529	85,000	18,529
4	103,529	12,757	(5,000)	111,286	85,000	26,286
5	111,286	13,714	(5,000)	120,000	85,000	35,000
		60,000	(25,000)			

* Carrying amount of the bond × effective interest rate.

The cost of the bond for tax purposes is C85,000 (C80,000 initial cost plus C5,000 costs) and is deductible against total redemption proceeds. So this is the asset's tax base throughout the bond's ownership. The entity provides deferred tax each year on the taxable temporary difference between the amortised cost and the tax base, as shown above. Just before redemption, the amortised cost will have risen to C120,000; so there will be a taxable temporary difference of C35,000. Current tax payable on the taxable gain of C35,000 (proceeds of C120,000 less tax cost of C85,000) will be offset by the release of deferred tax provided on this taxable temporary difference during the period the bond is held. If the investment also qualifies for indexation allowance, the tax base of C85,000 would change each year; and the temporary difference calculated above would include the effects of indexation.

But if the tax authorities assess tax on the basis of the effective interest (consistent with the manner in which the bond is accounted for each year), the asset's tax base at the end of each year would be equal to its carrying amount; and no deferred tax would arise.

Compound financial instruments

13.229 Compound financial instruments (such as convertible notes) might contain liability and equity components: the liability component represents a borrowing with an obligation to repay; and the equity component represents an embedded option to convert the liability into the entity's equity. Under IAS 32, the issuer is required to present the liability and equity components separately on its balance sheet. First, the carrying amount of the liability component is determined by measuring the fair value of a similar liability that does not have an associated equity component. Secondly, this amount is deducted from the fair value of the instrument as a whole; and the residual amount is assigned to the equity component.

13.230 In some jurisdictions, the tax base of a compound financial instrument that is a simple convertible note (comprising a loan and an equity component) will often be its face value; in other words, the tax base is not split. When such an instrument is split for accounting purposes, the carrying amount of the liability component will initially be less than the face value of the instrument as a whole and less than the tax base; so a taxable temporary difference arises. Even though the tax base of the liability is different from its carrying amount on initial recognition, the initial recognition exception does not apply; this is because the resulting taxable temporary difference arises from the initial recognition of the equity component separately from the liability component. So a deferred tax liability should be recognised on the taxable temporary difference. [IAS 12 para 23].

UK.13.230.1 The tax base of a compound instrument under UK tax rules is likely to be more complicated (see para UK.13.232.1).

13.231 The equity component of the compound instrument is recognised in equity; so the deferred tax liability is also charged directly to equity (as a reduction in the carrying amount of the equity component). But the discount associated with the liability component of the compound instrument unwinds through profit or loss; so the reduction in the associated deferred tax liability in the balance sheet (resulting from the reversal of the temporary difference) is also recognised through profit or loss. This is consistent with the principle that tax follows the item. [IAS 12 para 23]. The following example (based on example 4 of appendix B to IAS 12) illustrates the accounting for the tax effects of a compound financial instrument where the tax base is not split.

Example – Deferred tax on convertible loan where the tax base is not split

An entity issues a non-interest-bearing convertible loan for proceeds with a fair value of C1,000 (which is also the loan's face value) on 31 December 20X4; the loan is repayable at par on 1 January 20X8. Under IAS 32, the entity classifies the instrument's liability component as a liability and the equity component as equity. The entity assigns an initial carrying amount of C751 to the liability component and C249 to the equity component. The entity later recognises imputed discount as an interest expense at an annual rate of 10% on the liability component's carrying amount at the beginning of each year. The tax authorities do not allow the entity to claim any deduction for the imputed discount on the liability component of the convertible loan. The tax rate is 40%.

The temporary differences associated with the liability component (and the resulting deferred tax liability and deferred tax expense and income) are as follows:

Taxation

	Year			
	20X4	20X5	20X6	20X7
	C	C	C	C
Carrying amount of liability component	751	826	909	1,000
Tax base	1,000	1,000	1,000	1,000
Taxable temporary difference	249	174	91	–
Opening deferred tax liability at 40%	0	100	70	37
Deferred tax charged to equity	100	–	–	–
Deferred tax expense (income)	–	(30)	(33)	(37)
Closing deferred tax liability at 40%	100	70	37	–

At 31 December 20X4, the entity recognises the resulting deferred tax liability by adjusting the initial carrying amount of the equity component of the convertible liability (as explained in para 23 of IAS 12). So the amounts recognised at that date are as follows:

	C
Liability component	751
Deferred tax liability	100
Equity component (C249 less C100)	149
	1,000

Later changes in the deferred tax liability are recognised in profit or loss as tax income. [IAS 12 para 23]. So the entity's income statement is as follows:

	Year			
	20X4	20X5	20X6	20X7
	C	C	C	C
Interest expense (imputed discount)	–	75	83	91
Deferred tax (income @ 40%)	–	(30)	(33)	(37)
	–	45	50	54

13.232 The deferred tax balances need to reflect the tax consequences arising from the manner in which the entity expects (at the reporting date) to recover or settle the carrying amount of its assets and liabilities. If there are various settlement options with different tax consequences, the entity needs to assess (at each reporting date) the most likely option that the investors or the issuer will take. For example, management might expect that a convertible instrument will be redeemed or converted early (for instance, in the next accounting period), and the deferred tax liability previously provided does not fully reflect the tax consequences that would follow from conversion or redemption; in that case, the deferred tax liability should be adjusted accordingly. Any adjustment should be made through equity or through profit or loss depending on the tax consequences that would follow from early conversion or redemption. For example, if no tax is payable on early conversion, any outstanding deferred tax liability should be derecognised by crediting equity; this is consistent with the principle that tax follows the item. On conversion, the liability component is transferred directly to equity and no gain or loss arises. It is also consistent with the treatment that the reversal of the deferred tax liability does not arise from the unwinding of the discount. Because the option to convert generally lies with the instrument's holders, the deferred tax balance should only be adjusted for the tax effects of the conversion if there is sufficient evidence that it is probable that the instrument's holders will convert. On the other hand, if early redemption of the convertible instrument would have further tax consequences, any adjustment to the deferred tax liability previously provided should be made through profit or loss.

UK.13.232.1 The above simplified example illustrates the accounting for a compound instrument (with a loan and an equity component) in a jurisdiction where the tax base is not split between the two components. In the UK, the tax rules are more complicated. Generally, where an instrument is split for accounting purposes, it is also split for tax purposes; in this case, the guidance in paragraph 23 of IAS 12 is not applicable. But the tax treatment of the instrument will depend on:

■ when the instrument was issued (the applicable tax rules depend upon whether the instrument was issued in an accounting period beginning pre or post 1 January 2005);

■ whether the option element of the instrument is accounted for as equity or as a derivative liability; and

■ the expected manner of settlement (for example, conversion, redemption at face value, cash settlement at fair value or repurchase in the market).

So, in the UK, the deferred tax accounting will depend on the specific circumstances and terms of the compound instrument.

Investments in subsidiaries, branches, associates and joint ventures

13.233 This section deals with the deferred tax implications of investments in subsidiaries, branches, associates and joint ventures in separate financial statements. When a parent entity or investor acquires such an investment it is accounted for in the separate financial statements of the parent or investor at cost (which is the amount paid for the shares or the business) or under IAS 39. A temporary difference might arise between the investment's carrying amount in the separate financial statements and its tax base (which is often cost or indexed cost).

13.233.1 Where an investment is carried at cost, any increase in the investment's value is not recognised. The investee's post-acquisition profits are not recognised in the parent or investor's separate financial statements; so these are not reflected in the investment's carrying amount in determining the temporary difference.

13.233.2 An entity should recognise a deferred tax liability for all taxable temporary differences associated with investments in subsidiaries, branches and associates, and interests in joint ventures, except to the extent that both of the following conditions are satisfied:

- the parent, investor or venturer is able to control the timing of the reversal of the temporary difference; and

- it is probable that the temporary difference will not reverse in the foreseeable future.

[IAS 12 para 39].

13.233.3 An entity should recognise a deferred tax asset for all deductible temporary differences arising from investments in subsidiaries, branches and associates, and interests in joint ventures, to the extent that it is probable that:

- the temporary difference will reverse in the foreseeable future; and

- taxable profit will be available against which the temporary difference can be utilised.

[IAS 12 para 44].

13.233.4 For guidance on the way in which the above exemptions (for temporary differences relating to investments in subsidiaries, branches, associates, and interests in joint ventures) interact with the initial recognition exceptions in paragraphs 15 and 24 of IAS 12, see paragraph 13.233.10.

13.233.5 The carrying amounts for such investments can be recovered through distributions or disposal or both. Management needs to determine the deferred tax implications based on the manner in which it expects to recover the investment.

13.233.6 The application of the above exceptions from recognising deferred tax in separate financial statements is addressed in the section dealing with deferred tax implications of investments in subsidiaries, associates and joint ventures in consolidated financial statements, from paragraph 13.253 onwards.

Investment in branches

13.233.7 A reporting entity that operates a branch recognises the branch's assets and liabilities in its own financial statements. Where temporary differences arise in relation to those assets and liabilities, deferred tax assets and liabilities are also recognised on those temporary differences in the reporting entity's financial statements under IAS 12. In some jurisdictions, there might be tax consequences where the branch distributes profits or is sold. This is similar to the position for subsidiaries in consolidated financial statements. A temporary difference might arise between the total carrying amount of the reporting entity's net assets in the branch and the tax base of the reporting entity's investment in the branch. Where the reporting entity has determined that the retained profits in the branch will not be distributable in the foreseeable future, and that the branch will not be sold, it does not recognise a deferred tax liability in relation to its investment in the branch. [IAS 12 para 40]. See paragraph 13.274 for foreign branches.

Investments in tax-transparent entities

13.233.8 Around the world, there are a number of entities that do not pay tax but whose profits are taxable in the hands of the investors. Examples of such entities are partnerships, UK limited liability partnerships (LLPs) and US limited liability companies (LLCs). This type of tax structure can give rise to accounting issues in the investor's separate financial statements.

13.233.9 For instance, where an entity invests in a tax-transparent entity ('the investee'), it will initially record its investment at cost in its separate financial statements. But, because the investee is tax transparent, its initial tax base will not necessarily be its cost, but the sum of the tax bases of the underlying assets and liabilities within the investee. As such, there might be an initial taxable temporary difference. A question arises as to whether this is covered by the initial recognition exception (see para 13.162) or whether deferred tax should be provided on initial recognition.

13.233.10 In our view, the initial recognition exception applies, because recognition of the investment in the tax-transparent entity represents the initial recognition of an asset in a transaction that is not a business combination (in the investor's separate financial statements) and which does not affect accounting profit or taxable profit at the time of the transaction. [IAS 12 para 15(b)]. We consider that the reference made in paragraph 15 of IAS 12 to the exemption in paragraph 39 of IAS 12 (see para 13.233.2) – for which different conditions have to be met in order for the exemption to be taken – applies to temporary differences in respect of investments in subsidiaries, branches, associates and joint ventures arising after initial recognition.

13.233.11 Similar logic would apply for the interaction of the exemptions in paragraphs 24 and 44 of IAS 12 if there was an initial deductible temporary difference arising on the investment of the tax-transparent entity.

13.233.12 For the accounting in consolidated financial statements for tax relating to an investment in a tax-transparent entity, see paragraph 13.269 onwards.

Treatment of tax in consolidated financial statements

Introduction

13.234 The treatment of tax in consolidated financial statements involves the same considerations that apply to individual financial statements (that is, deferred tax should be provided on temporary differences that arise between the carrying amounts of assets and liabilities reported in the consolidated balance sheet and their tax bases). The tax base is determined in one of two ways: by reference to a consolidated tax return in jurisdictions that require such a return; or by reference to the tax returns of each individual entity in the group in other jurisdictions. [IAS 12 para 11].

13.234.1 In a group, the tax positions of the individual group members are unlikely to be similar. Some group members might be profitable but others might make a loss; this will lead to different tax considerations. Some group members might operate in the same tax jurisdiction, but others might operate in different tax jurisdictions. Consolidated financial statements are prepared as if the parent entity and its subsidiaries were a single entity; so it follows that the group's tax position needs to be viewed as a whole. A group's total tax liability is determined by adding together the tax liability assessed under local tax laws and borne by individual group members.

13.235 Under IAS 27 and IFRS 10 (effective for accounting periods beginning on or after 1 January 2013), a group should follow uniform accounting policies in preparing consolidated financial statements. Adjustments might be required at the consolidation level where an overseas subsidiary has not followed group accounting policies (for example, because of local requirements) in preparing its own financial statements. These adjustments could result in additional temporary differences in the consolidated financial statements for which deferred tax should be recognised.

13.236 Adjustments are also required to eliminate various intra-group transactions so the group can be treated as a single economic entity. Such adjustments affect the carrying amount of assets and liabilities reported in the consolidated balance sheet; so they give rise to additional temporary differences that defer or accelerate tax (from the perspective of treating the group as a single entity). Such tax effects are recognised as part of the group's deferred tax (see further para 13.252).

13.237 The types of events and transactions that normally give rise to deferred tax adjustments at the group level are as follows:

- Business combinations that are accounted for as acquisitions such as:
  - Fair value adjustments.
  - Tax deductible goodwill.
  - Any additional assets and liabilities that are recognised at the date of acquisition.
  - Deferred tax assets and liabilities that were not recognised by the acquiree as a result of initial recognition exception.
  - Deferred tax asset in respect of unrecognised tax losses or deductible temporary differences of the acquiree.
  - Deferred tax asset in respect of unrecognised tax losses or deductible temporary differences of the acquirer.
- Reverse acquisitions.
- Intra-group transactions eliminated on consolidation.
- Investments in subsidiaries, associates and joint ventures.
- Foreign currency translation.

Business combinations

Fair value adjustments

13.238 In a business combination that is an acquisition, the identifiable assets and liabilities of the acquired business are recognised in the consolidated financial statements at their fair values at the date of acquisition (with limited exceptions). These fair values of the individual assets and liabilities are often different from the book values appearing in the acquired entity's own financial statements at that date. The tax bases of the assets and liabilities generally remain the same; although they sometimes change as a result of the acquisition. So temporary differences arise on consolidation where the tax bases of the related assets and liabilities are not affected by the business combination or are affected differently. For example, a taxable temporary difference arises as a result of the acquisition when the carrying amount of a non-monetary asset (such as a building of the acquired entity) is increased to fair value at the date of acquisition but its tax base remains at cost to the previous owner. The deferred tax liability arising from this taxable temporary difference is recognised in the consolidated financial statements to reflect the future tax consequences of recovering the building's recognised fair value. The resulting deferred tax liability affects goodwill. [IAS 12 para 19].

Example – Deferred tax effects of fair value adjustments

On 1 January 20X5, entity H acquired all the share capital of entity S for C1,500,000. The book values and the fair values of the identifiable assets and liabilities of entity S at the date of acquisition are set out below, together with their tax bases in entity S's tax jurisdictions. Any goodwill arising on the acquisition is not deductible for tax purposes. The tax rates in entity H's and entity S's tax jurisdictions are 30% and 40% respectively.

Net assets acquired	Book values C'000	Tax base C'000	Fair values C'000
Land and buildings	600	500	700
Property, plant and equipment	250	200	270
Inventory	100	100	80
Accounts receivable	150	150	150
Cash and cash equivalents	130	130	130
Total assets	1,230	1,080	1,330
Accounts payable	(160)	(160)	(160)
Retirement benefit obligations	(100)	–	(100)
Net assets before deferred tax liability	970	920	1,070
Deferred tax liability between book and tax basis (50 @ 40%)	(20)		
Net assets at acquisition	950	920	1,070

Calculation of deferred tax arising on acquisition of entity S and goodwill

	C'000	C'000
Fair values of S's identifiable assets and liabilities (excluding deferred tax)		1,070
Less: Tax base		(920)
Temporary difference arising on acquisition		150
Net deferred tax liability arising on acquisition of entity S (C150,000 @ 40%) – replaces book deferred tax		60
Purchase consideration		1,500
Fair values of entity S's identifiable assets and liabilities (excluding deferred tax)	1,070	
Deferred tax	(60)	1,010
Goodwill arising on acquisition		490

The tax base of the goodwill is nil, so a taxable temporary difference of C490,000 arises on the goodwill ; but no deferred tax is recognised on the goodwill (as explained in para 13.159). The deferred tax on other temporary differences arising on acquisition is provided at 40% (not 30%), because taxes will be payable or recoverable in entity S's tax jurisdictions when the temporary differences are reversed.

UK.13.238.1   The above treatment is significantly different from FRS 19. Under FRS 19, no deferred tax is provided on the temporary differences arising on fair value adjustments, unless the acquired entity recognises the tax effect of the revaluation as if it were a timing difference in its own financial statements. That is possible only if the acquired entity had entered into a binding agreement to sell the assets and rollover relief is not available. In other words, where assets are fair valued upwards on acquisition, they were treated in the same way as revaluations and no deferred tax is provided under FRS 19.

[The next paragraph is 13.240.]

Tax deductible goodwill

13.240   Goodwill arising in a business combination is sometimes deductible for tax purposes through amortisation over a number of years rather than against proceeds from sale of the acquired business. The goodwill is carried on the balance sheet without amortisation; so management needs to determine the appropriate tax base of the goodwill that reflects the manner in which it is recovered. If goodwill impairment is not expected in the foreseeable future, there might not appear to be an expectation of imminent recovery through use; and so it might be expected that the goodwill will be recovered solely through sale. The cost of the goodwill is not deductible against sales proceeds; so, if this analysis is appropriate, its tax base is nil and a taxable temporary difference exists between the carrying amount and the tax base. But no deferred tax should be recognised on initial recognition or later – see the exception outlined in paragraph 13.158. But the expected manner of recovery should be considered more closely. When a business is acquired, impairment of the goodwill might not be expected imminently; but it would also be unusual for a sale to be expected imminently. So it might be expected that the asset will be sold a long way in the future; in that case, recovery through use over a long period (that is, before the asset is sold) might be the expected manner of recovery. Management needs to exercise judgement to determine the expected outcome; and this might be a key judgement that should be disclosed (see para 13.307.2).

13.241   Goodwill is not amortised for accounting purposes; but goodwill arising in a business combination is an asset that can be consumed. The goodwill's carrying amount needs to be tested for impairment annually and whenever there is an indication that it might be impaired. Any impairment loss is recognised immediately in profit or loss. Where an entity expects to recover the goodwill's carrying amount at least partially through use (that is, not solely through sale), temporary differences might arise using the tax base that is consistent with recovery through use. Taxable temporary differences arising at the time of the business combination would not be recognised (see the exception outlined in para 13.158). If goodwill is amortised for tax purposes but no impairment is recognised for accounting purposes, any temporary differences arising between the (amortised) tax base and the carrying amount will have arisen after the goodwill's initial recognition; so they should be recognised.

13.242   Referring to the example in paragraph 13.238, assume that goodwill of C490,000 is deductible for tax purposes at the rate of 20% per annum (but there is no tax deduction on sale); the goodwill has a tax base in use of C490,000 on initial recognition, and no temporary difference arises where it is expected to be recovered wholly through use. At the end of the year, following a claim for tax deduction in that year of C98,000 (20% of C490,000), the tax base of the goodwill will reduce to C392,000. The carrying amount remains unchanged at C490,000 without any impairment; so a taxable temporary difference of C98,000 arises (carrying amount of C490,000 less tax base of C392,000). This taxable temporary difference arises during the year and not on initial recognition; so a deferred tax liability is recognised. [IAS 12 para 21B]. The tax deduction that should be recognised on consolidation is C39,200 (40% of C98,000) because the goodwill's carrying amount is recovered against S's taxable profits. By the end of year 5, the deferred tax liability would increase to C196,000, as the cost of the goodwill would have been fully amortised for tax purposes. The temporary difference at that date would be C490,000 (carrying amount of C490,000 less tax base of Cnil). This temporary difference and the corresponding deferred tax liability will remain until a reversal occurs, either on the goodwill's impairment or when the subsidiary is sold.

13.243   In some jurisdictions, the goodwill's cost is deductible (for tax purposes) only against proceeds from sale of the acquired business where the acquiring entity expects to recover the goodwill's carrying amount through use, a temporary difference arises in use; this is because the goodwill's carrying amount exceeds its tax base of nil. But no deferred tax is provided on a taxable temporary difference arising on initial recognition of goodwill (see para 13.158). On the other hand, if (a number of years after acquiring the business) the entity changes its intended method of recovering the goodwill from use to sale, the tax base of the goodwill reverts to its original cost on initial recognition. A deferred tax asset might arise if (after initial recognition) the goodwill has been impaired so that its carrying amount is less than its tax base applicable on sale.

13.243.1   An acquired entity might have tax-deductible goodwill from its own prior acquisitions. For accounting purposes, the existing goodwill is included in the goodwill arising on the new acquisition. But, in some jurisdictions, the tax base in the original goodwill remains available to the acquired entity and will be deductible over the remaining tax life. A question arises as to how the temporary difference (if any) related to the tax-deductible goodwill is determined. We believe that management needs to establish whether some of the goodwill arising in the new acquisition relates to the tax-deductible goodwill from the prior acquisition. If it does, an appropriate proportion of the new goodwill should be allocated to that entity for the purpose of determining the temporary difference. This approach is consistent with the requirement in IAS 36 to allocate goodwill to groups of cash-generating units for impairment testing purposes. The allocation should be made in a manner consistent with the guidance in IAS 36 (that is, allocated to cash-generating units that are expected to benefit from the synergies of the combination). This approach is also consistent with the requirement in IAS 21 to allocate goodwill to the different functional currencies in the acquired entity. The deductible or taxable temporary difference is based on this allocation.

Additional assets and liabilities recognised on acquisition

13.244   In an acquisition, additional assets and liabilities might be recognised (as part of the fair value exercise) that were not recognised in the acquiree's financial statements before the acquisition. Examples of such assets and liabilities include some intangible assets (see para 13.245) and contingent tax liabilities (see para 13.246).

Intangible assets

13.245   Under IFRS 3, an acquirer recognises an acquiree's intangible assets at the acquisition date as assets separately from goodwill; this applies where the assets are identifiable, regardless of whether they were recognised by the acquiree before the business combination. See further chapter 25.

13.245.1   Where such additional assets are recognised, the deferred tax effects should also be recognised. Although the asset is being recognised for the first time (and, like goodwill, the amortisation might not be deductible for tax purposes), the initial recognition exception for deferred tax that applies to goodwill is not extended to such intangible assets arising on a business combination. This is because, unlike goodwill, such intangible assets are not residuals. Also, a reason for not recognising deferred tax on goodwill is to avoid having to gross-up both sides of the balance sheet because goodwill and the related deferred tax are mutually dependent (see para 13.159); such dependency does not exist for other intangible assets.

Example – Deferred tax on intangible assets

The facts are the same as in the example in paragraph 13.238, except that an intangible asset not previously recognised by the acquiree was identified on acquisition and measured at its fair value of C130,000. The intangible asset will be amortised over its useful life of 10 years, but the amortisation will not be deductible for tax purposes.

	C'000	C'000
Fair values of entity S's identifiable assets and liabilities (excluding deferred tax) as before		1,070
Intangible asset identified on acquisition and recognised separately from goodwill		130
Fair value of entity S's identifiable assets and liabilities at acquisition		1,200
Less: Tax base as before		(920)
Temporary difference arising on acquisition		280
Net deferred tax liability arising on acquisition of entity S (C280,000 @ 40%)		112
Purchase consideration		1,500
Fair values of entity S's identifiable assets and liabilities (excluding deferred tax)	1,200	
Deferred tax	(112)	1,088
Goodwill arising on acquisition		412

Note: The goodwill arising on acquisition of C490,000 has been reduced further by the recognition of a previously unrecognised intangible asset of C130,000, net of its deferred tax effect of C52,000; this gives a net reduction of C78,000. In the periods after initial recognition on consolidation, the deferred tax liability of C52,000 will be released to the income statement by C5,200 each year (in line with the intangible asset's recovery through amortisation).

13.245.2 Even if the intangible asset acquired on the business combination has an indefinite useful life (and is not amortised for accounting purposes and is also not deductible for tax purposes), a deferred tax liability should be recognised based on management's expectation of the asset's manner of recovery, for the reasons stated in the previous paragraph. So, in this situation, the goodwill arising on acquisition would be calculated in the same way as indicated above. The only difference is that the deferred tax liability of C52,000 would remain on the balance sheet, but would be released through profit or loss on sale or impairment. See further paragraph 13.225.1.

[The next paragraph is 13.246.2.]

Contingent tax liabilities – IFRS 3

13.246.2 Contingent liabilities are separately recognised in a business combination where fair value can be measured reliably. [IFRS 3 para 23]. Contingent liabilities recognised in acquisition accounting are measured subsequently at the higher of the amount recognised in accordance with IAS 37 and the amount initially recognised less any amortisation recognised under IAS 18. [IFRS 3 para 56]. This differs from IAS 37's requirements, where a provision is recognised only when the outflow of economic resources is probable.

13.246.3 The exceptions to IFRS 3's basic recognition and measurement principles are listed in its introduction. The list of exceptions includes assets and liabilities falling within IAS 12's scope. But the detailed guidance specifies only that deferred tax assets and liabilities in a business combination should be accounted for under IAS 12; and it is silent about current tax assets and liabilities and tax contingencies.

13.246.4 We believe that there are two acceptable approaches to recognising contingent tax liabilities in a business combination. IFRS 3 refers to IAS 37 only in the context of contingent liabilities; and income taxes are listed in the introduction to IFRS 3 as an exception to the recognition and measurement principles. So it can be argued that IFRS 3 does not apply to tax contingencies. Contingent tax liabilities might be recognised when the outflow is probable under IAS 12 (see para 13.74 onwards). Alternatively it could be argued that IFRS 3 applies to all contingent liabilities and that the exception applies only to deferred taxes; so it is also acceptable to recognise and measure contingent tax liabilities at fair value under IFRS 3.

Adjustments arising from initial recognition exception taken by the acquiree

13.247 In some circumstances, the deferred tax effects of temporary differences arising on acquisition might not have been recognised by the acquiree because those differences fell within the initial recognition exception (see para 13.162). The deferred tax effects of such temporary differences should be recognised on consolidation, even though they were not recognised by the acquired entity itself. This is because (from the group's perspective) any additional deferred tax balances are recognised as a result of the business combination and not from an initial recognition of the asset or liability.

> **Example – Impact of initial recognition exception taken by the acquiree**
>
> The facts are the same as in the example in paragraph 13.238, except that entity S purchased a specialised factory in an enterprise zone where such factories are eligible for tax allowances at 150% of their purchase cost. The factory cost C150,000; and that amount was also its fair value at the date of acquisition. The tax base of the property on initial recognition was C225,000, but no deferred tax asset was recognised on the excess tax allowances of C75,000 because of the initial recognition exception.

	C'000	C'000
Fair values of entity S's identifiable assets and liabilities (excluding deferred tax) as before		1,070
Specialised property		150
Fair value of entity S's identifiable assets and liabilities at acquisition		1,220
Less: Tax base (C920,000 as before + C225,000 on specialised property)		(1,145)
Temporary difference arising on acquisition		75
Net deferred tax liability arising on acquisition of S (C75,000 @ 40%)		30
Purchase consideration		1,500
Fair values of entity S's identifiable assets and liabilities (excluding deferred tax)	1,220	
Deferred tax	(30)	1,190
Goodwill arising on acquisition		310

Note: The goodwill arising on acquisition of C490,000 has been reduced by a further C180,000. This reduction relates to the fair value of the specialised property of C150,000 plus a deferred tax asset of C30,000 arising on the excess tax allowances of C75,000 @ 40%; this amount was not recognised by S because of the initial recognition exception. In the periods after acquisition, the deferred tax asset will be released through profit or loss as the excess tax benefit is realised through additional tax allowances.

[The next paragraph is 13.249.3.]

Unrecognised tax losses of acquiree

13.249.3 An acquirer accounts under IAS 12 for the potential tax effects of an acquiree's temporary differences and carry-forwards that exist at the acquisition date or arise as a result of the acquisition. [IFRS 3 para 25]. A deferred tax asset is recognised for the carry-forward of unused tax losses and unused tax credits to the extent that it is probable that future taxable profit will be available against which the unused tax losses and credits can be utilised (see para 13.144 onwards). [IAS 12 para 34].

13.249.4 In some circumstances, the acquiree might not have recognised a deferred tax asset in respect of its past tax losses, because it was uncertain whether future taxable profits would be available. But, as a result of its acquisition, the acquirer might determine that it is probable that other entities within the group will have sufficient taxable profits in the future to realise the tax benefits through transfer of those losses as permitted by the tax laws. So a deferred tax asset attributable to the unrelieved losses should be recognised as a fair value adjustment; and a corresponding reduction should be made in goodwill. As a general rule, the acquired entity's deferred tax assets are included in the fair value exercise (even if they had not been recognised before the acquisition), provided they meet IAS 12's recognition criteria in the context of the enlarged group.

13.249.5 If the potential benefits of the acquiree's unused tax losses or other deferred tax assets do not satisfy the criteria for separate recognition when a business combination is initially accounted for but are subsequently realised, an entity recognises these deferred tax assets as follows:

■ Acquired deferred tax benefits recognised within the measurement period (resulting from new information about facts and circumstances that existed at the acquisition date) are applied to reduce the carrying amount of any goodwill related to that acquisition. If the carrying amount of that goodwill is zero, any remaining deferred tax benefits are recognised in profit or loss.

■ All other acquired deferred tax benefits realised are recognised in profit or loss (or outside profit or loss, if required by IAS 12).

[IAS 12 para 68].

13.249.6 An example of the above is included in Table 13.1.

Table 13.1 – Recognition of tax losses previously not recognised on acquisition

Coca-Cola Hellenic Bottling Company S.A. – Annual report – 31 December 2011

22. Tax (extract)

The income tax charge for the years ended 31 December is as follows:

	2011 € million	2010 € million	2009 € million
Current tax charge	86.6	117.6	119.9
Deferred tax charge (refer to Note 9)	16.1	30.6	24.6
Pre-acquisition deferred tax assets recognised subsequent to acquisition of CCB (refer to Note 20)	–	(10.2)	(1.6)
Total income tax charge	102.7	138.0	142.9

20. Total operating costs (extract)

(b) Adjustments to intangible assets
During 2010 and 2009, the Group recognized deferred tax assets on losses that had previously not been recognised on acquisition of CCB by HBC. Correspondingly, a deferred tax credit of €10.2m (2009: €1.6m) had been included within tax on the income statement. Based on the revised IFRS 3, *Business Combinations*, goodwill is no longer adjusted when deferred tax assets on losses have not been recognised on acquisition and are subsequently recognized. Therefore no charge has been included in the operating expenses of 2010 (2009: €2.2m). For the credit that has been included in taxes please refer to Note 22.

13.249.7 Deferred tax benefits acquired in a business combination might not be recognised at the acquisition date but are recognised later; in that case, a description of the event or change in circumstances that caused the deferred tax benefits to be recognised needs to be disclosed. [IAS 12 para 81(k)]. See paragraph 13.292.2.

Unrecognised tax losses of the acquirer

13.250 As a result of a business combination, an acquirer might consider it probable that it will recover its own unused tax losses against the future taxable profit of the acquiree. In that situation, the standard does not permit a deferred tax asset to be recognised in the fair value exercise or any consequential effect on goodwill arising on the business combination. [IAS 12 para 67]. This is because those losses are not the acquiree's losses; so they would not have met the criteria for separate recognition as an identifiable asset in paragraph 10 of IFRS 3. Instead, the deferred tax asset should be recognised in the separate and consolidated financial statements of the acquirer; and there should be a corresponding credit to the tax charge in profit or loss.

13.250.1 Paragraph 67 of IAS 12 refers to any change in the probability of realising a pre-acquisition deferred tax asset of the acquirer as a result of a business combination. An acquirer might consider it probable that it will recover its own deferred tax asset that was not recognised before the business combination. For example, the acquirer might be able to utilise the benefit of its unused tax losses against the acquiree's future taxable profit. Or the business combination might no longer be probable that the deferred tax asset will be recovered from future taxable profit. In such cases, the acquirer recognises a change in the deferred tax asset in the period of the business combination, but does not include it in the accounting for the business combination. In other words, the acquirer does not take it into account in measuring the goodwill or bargain purchase gain recognised in the business combination. [IAS 12 para 67].

13.250.2 If a business combination changes the amount recognised by the acquirer for its pre-acquisition deferred tax asset, the amount of that change is required to be disclosed. [IAS 12 para 81(j)]. See paragraph 13.292.2.

Reverse acquisitions

13.251 In some business combinations, the acquirer (for accounting purposes) is the entity whose equity interests have been acquired; and the legal parent entity is treated as the acquired entity. These combinations are commonly referred to as 'reverse acquisitions'. [IFRS 3 para B19]. Accounting for reverse acquisitions is dealt with in chapter 25.

13.251.1 For deferred tax accounting, where a temporary difference arises on the initial recognition of an asset or liability in a business combination, the initial recognition exception referred to in paragraph 13.162 does not apply. What does this mean in the case of a reverse acquisition?

13.251.2 Under reverse acquisition accounting, the legal acquired entity is treated (for the purposes of the consolidated financial statements) as the acquirer;

and the legal parent is treated as the acquired entity. So it is the legal parent's assets and liabilities that are fair valued under IFRS 3. In a business combination, the acquired entity's assets and liabilities do not qualify for the initial recognition exception, but the acquirer is unaffected. This is the case, even if the acquirer for accounting purposes is not the legal acquirer. In other words, the entity that is the legal acquired subsidiary (but which, for accounting purposes, is the acquirer) continues to qualify for the initial recognition exception because its net assets are recorded in the consolidated financial statements at existing book values. The entity that is the new legal parent (but which, for accounting purposes, is the acquired entity) does not qualify for the initial recognition exception; so deferred tax is recognised in the consolidated financial statements on any temporary differences on its assets and liabilities.

13.251.3   A similar situation arises where a new parent entity is added to an existing group; this is achieved by setting up a new shell entity (newco) that issues equity shares to the existing shareholders in exchange for shares in the existing group. Such a transaction is accounted for as a 'reorganisation'. Where a reorganisation has occurred, the new entity's consolidated financial statements are prepared using the book values from the previous holding entity's consolidated financial statements. Any previous use of the initial recognition exception by the previous holding entity would be carried forward into the new consolidated financial statements. Accounting for a new entity added to a group is dealt with in chapter 25.

Tax effects of intra-group transactions

13.252   Consolidation adjustments can have tax consequences. Where such adjustments give rise to temporary differences, deferred tax should be provided under IAS 12. A typical consolidation adjustment is where unrealised profits and losses are eliminated on an intra-group transfer of inventories. Such an adjustment gives rise to a temporary difference that will reverse when the inventory is sold outside the group.

> **Example – Deferred tax effects of intra-group transactions**
>
> A subsidiary sells goods costing C60,000 to its parent entity for C70,000; and these goods are still held in inventory at the year end. A consolidation adjustment is required in the financial statements to eliminate the unrealised profit of C10,000 from consolidated income statement and from group inventory. The sale of inventory between the two companies is a taxable event that changes the inventory's tax basis. The difference between the carrying amount of the inventory of C60,000 in the consolidated financial statements and the appropriate tax base of C70,000 (from the parent's perspective) gives rise to a deductible temporary difference.
>
> If the parent and the subsidiary were resident in the same tax jurisdiction and paid income tax at 30%, a deferred tax asset of C3,000 (C10,000 @ 30%) would be recognised in the consolidated financial statements. The resulting credit to income would offset the tax charge on the profit made by the subsidiary. The deferred tax asset would be recovered when the parent sells the inventory to a party outside the group.

But if the parent and subsidiary were resident in different tax jurisdictions and paid income tax at 40% and 30% respectively, a deferred tax asset of C4,000 (C10,000 @ 40%) would be recognised in the consolidated financial statements. The new tax basis of the inventory (C70,000) is deductible on the buyer's tax return when the cost of the inventory (that is, C60,000 after elimination of intra-entity profit) is recovered. Since tax is expected to be paid at 40% when the inventory is sold by the intermediate buyer, it follows (from the expected manner of recovery rule discussed in para 13.170) that the resulting deferred tax asset arising on the deductible temporary difference should be measured at that rate. In the consolidated financial statements, the resulting tax credit of C4,000 would exceed the tax charge of C3,000; and the excess of C1,000 (representing the excess tax benefit attributable to the transferred inventory) would reduce the consolidated tax expense (income) of the period, even though the pre-tax effects of the transaction had been eliminated in full.

UK.13.252.1   Under FRS 19, the deferred tax asset would be provided at the seller's tax rate; so the additional tax of C1,000 attributable to the buyer would not be recognised in the consolidated financial statement.

Investments in subsidiaries, branches, associates and joint ventures

Introduction

13.253   This section deals with the deferred tax implications in consolidated financial statements of investments in subsidiaries, branches, associates and joint ventures. (The deferred tax implications of such investments in the separate financial statements of the parent or investor are dealt with in para 13.233 onwards.) In the consolidated financial statements of the parent or investor, the investment is recorded by consolidating the subsidiary's net assets (line-by-line) or by using the equity method for interests in associates or joint ventures.

13.254   A temporary difference might arise between the investment's carrying amount in the consolidated financial statements and its tax base (which is often cost or indexed cost). This temporary difference is sometimes referred to as 'outside basis' difference. It is additional to the temporary differences relating to the investee's underlying assets and liabilities (sometimes referred to as 'inside basis' difference). The temporary difference relating to the investment might arise in a number of situations. The most common situation is where undistributed profits in the investee increase the parent's investment in the investee to above its tax cost. Other situations include a reduction in the investment's carrying amount to below tax cost due to impairment; and changes in the investment's carrying amount as a result of changes in foreign exchange rates where the investing entity and its investees are based in different countries. [IAS 12 para 38]. The carrying amounts for such investments or interests can be recovered through distributions or disposal. Management needs to determine the deferred tax implications based on the manner in which it expects to recover the investment.

13.255   Accordingly, an entity should recognise a deferred tax liability for all taxable temporary differences associated with investments in subsidiaries, branches and associates, and interests in joint ventures, except to the extent that both of the following conditions are satisfied:

- the parent, investor or venturer is able to control the timing of the reversal of the temporary difference; and

- it is probable that the temporary difference will not reverse in the foreseeable future.

[IAS 12 para 39].

13.255.1 Deferred tax assets arising on investments in subsidiaries, branches and associates, and interests in joint ventures, are addressed in paragraph 13.268 onwards.

Investment in subsidiaries

13.256 In a parent/subsidiary relationship, the parent controls the subsidiary's financial and operating policies (including its dividend policy). So the parent can control the timing of the reversal of the temporary differences arising from that investment (including the temporary differences arising from undistributed profits and from any foreign exchange translation differences). Therefore, where the parent entity (and thus the economic entity – the group) has determined that the subsidiary's profits and reserves will not be distributed in the foreseeable future and that the subsidiary will not be disposed of, it does not recognise a deferred tax liability that arises from the investment in the subsidiary in its separate and consolidated financial statements. [IAS 12 para 40].

13.257 Where no deferred tax is provided, the total amount of taxable temporary difference should still be disclosed (see further para 13.303). But the group continues to recognise (subject to adjustments arising on consolidation) the deferred tax assets and liabilities that are recognised in the subsidiary's own financial statements and those that arise from fair value adjustments on acquisition of that subsidiary.

13.258 The parent's management needs to be able to provide sufficient evidence that the undistributed earnings will continue to be reinvested for the foreseeable future as part of the parent's continuing investment in that subsidiary. This evidence might include documentary resolutions by the parent's management, formal communication to minority shareholders and specific plans for reinvesting the funds. Such plans should take into consideration some or all of the following factors: (a) the financial requirements of the parent and the subsidiary; (b) long-term and short-term operational and fiscal objectives; (c) remittance restrictions imposed by governments, financing agreements or others; and (d) tax consequences of any remittances.

13.259 In practice, most parent entities would not recognise a deferred tax liability in respect of a subsidiary's undistributed profits; exceptions are where profits will be distributed in the foreseeable future, or the subsidiary will be disposed of. It is often difficult to determine the amount of further taxes that would be payable on remittance, as it will depend on the following factors: the tax laws and rates in the countries where the parent and subsidiary are located; the terms of the tax treaties (if any) between the two countries; and/or the time when the profits were earned and the level of the parent entity's local taxable profits at the time of remittance. Difficulties might also arise if the reporting entity has complex structures. For example, a reporting entity with many layers of intermediate holding companies might have several alternative routes for recovering an investment; and each route could have different tax consequences. In such cases, management should judge the manner in which the investment is expected to be recovered; and it should calculate any deferred tax on that basis.

13.260 An example illustrating the above principles is given in example 3 of appendix B to the standard; and it is reproduced here with appropriate adjustments and amendments.

> **Example – Deferred tax on investment in subsidiary**
>
> On 1 January 20X5, entity A acquired 100% of the shares of entity B at a cost of C600,000. At the acquisition date, the tax base (in entity A's tax jurisdiction) of A's investment in entity B is C600,000. Reductions in the carrying amount of goodwill are not deductible for tax purposes; and the goodwill would also not be deductible if entity B disposed of its underlying business. The tax rate in entity A's tax jurisdiction is 30%; and the tax rate in entity B's tax jurisdiction is 40%.
>
> **Goodwill arising on consolidation is calculated as follows:**
>
> | | C'000 | C'000 |
> |---|---:|---:|
> | Fair values of entity B's identifiable assets and liabilities (excluding deferred tax) at 1 January 20X5 | | 504 |
> | Less: Tax base of assets acquired and liabilities assumed | | (369) |
> | Temporary difference arising on acquisition | | 135 |
> | Deferred tax liability arising on acquisition of entity B (C135,000 @ 40%) | | 54 |
> | Purchase consideration | | 600 |
> | Fair values of entity B's identifiable assets and liabilities (excluding deferred tax) | 504 | |
> | Deferred tax liability calculated as above | (54) | 450 |
> | Goodwill arising on acquisition | | 150 |
>
> No deduction is available in entity B's tax jurisdiction for the cost of the goodwill. So the tax base of the goodwill in entity B's jurisdiction is nil. But, under IAS 12, entity A does not recognise any deferred tax liability for the taxable temporary difference associated with the goodwill in entity B's tax jurisdiction (see para 13.159).

During the year ended 31 December 20X5, entity B made a profit of C150,000 and declared a dividend of C80,000. The dividend was appropriately authorised; and it was recognised as a liability by entity B at 31 December 20X5. The net assets of entity B at 31 December 20X5 are as follows:

Net assets at 1 January 20X5 (incorporating the above fair value adjustments)	450
Retained profits (net profit of C150,000 less dividends payable of C80,000)	70
Net assets at 31 December 20X5	520
Entity A's separate financial statements	
Investment in entity B	600
Tax base	600
Temporary difference	Nil

Entity A recognises a liability for any withholding tax or other taxes that it will incur on the accrued dividend receivable of C80,000.

Entity A's consolidated financial statements

At 31 December 20X5, the carrying amount of entity A's underlying investment in entity B (excluding accrued dividend) is as follows:

Net assets of entity B	520
Goodwill	150
Carrying amount	670
Temporary difference associated with entity A's investment in entity B is	
Carrying amount as above	670
Tax base	600
Temporary difference = cumulative retained profits since acquisition	70

If entity A has determined that it will not sell the investment in the foreseeable future and that entity B will not distribute its retained profits in the foreseeable future, no deferred tax liability is recognised in relation to entity A's investment in entity B. But entity A discloses the amount of the temporary difference of C70,000 that is not expected to reverse in the foreseeable future.

On the other hand, if entity A expects to sell the investment in entity B (or that entity B will distribute its retained profits in the foreseeable future), it recognises a deferred tax liability to the extent that the temporary difference is expected to reverse. The tax rate should reflect the manner in which entity A expects to recover the carrying amount of its investment (that is, through dividends or by selling or liquidating the investment). If entity B is dissolved and retained profits are remitted, the realisation of its assets and the remittance of the proceeds could result in capital gains taxes and/or withholding taxes in entity B's tax jurisdictions and capital gains taxes in entity A's tax jurisdictions

Changes in management intentions about a subsidiary's undistributable profits

13.261   A parent's management might decide to recover the carrying amount of its investment in a subsidiary through future distributions. For example, suppose that a parent entity has not previously recognised a deferred tax liability on a subsidiary's undistributed profits amounting to C1,000,000. The subsidiary currently expects to generate earnings of at least C200,000 a year for the foreseeable future. So the parent's management decides to realise earnings (through future dividend payments from the subsidiary) of C200,000 a year. The fact that the subsidiary intends to distribute earnings would initially call into question the 'reinvestment for the foreseeable future' assertion. But, if management can establish that the distributions will be no more than *future* earnings, the 'reinvestment for the foreseeable future' assertion might still be sustainable.

13.262   So, if the parent can provide sufficient corroborating evidence (as discussed in para 13.258) regarding the need to reinvest for the foreseeable future the undistributed profits that have been brought forward – and if it is reasonable to expect the subsidiary to generate annual earnings of at least C200,000 – there is no need to recognise a deferred tax liability relating to the undistributed earnings that have been brought forward. On the other hand, if management intends to distribute C200,000 a year (regardless of the subsidiary's earnings), circumstances will have changed regarding the 'reinvestment for the foreseeable future' assertion; so a deferred tax liability will need to be recognised immediately (at the applicable tax rate) and there should be a corresponding tax charge in profit or loss.

Investment in branches

13.263   A reporting entity that operates a branch will recognise the branch's assets and liabilities and related deferred tax in its own financial statements. In some jurisdictions, tax consequences might arise when the branch distributes profits or is sold. A temporary difference might arise between the carrying amount of the reporting entity's net assets in the branch and the tax base of the reporting entity's investment in the branch (as for subsidiaries). Where the reporting entity has determined that the retained profits in the branch will not be distributable in the foreseeable future, and that the branch will not be sold, it does not recognise a deferred tax liability in relation to its investment in the branch. [IAS 12 para 40]. See further paragraph 13.274.

Investments in associates

13.264   Investments in associates (like subsidiaries) are accounted for at cost or under IAS 39 in the investor's separate financial statements. In the investor's consolidated financial statements, the associate is accounted for using the equity method of accounting under which the carrying amount of the investment is initially cost, adjusted for the post-acquisition change in the investor's share of the associate's net assets. Where the investment is expected to be recovered through sale, the tax base is often the amount paid for the shares in the associate. So a temporary difference arises between the investment's carrying amount and its tax base (for the reasons set out in para 13.254).

13.265 An investor has significant influence over the associate: it has the power to participate in the associate's financial and operating policy decisions; but it does not have control over those policies. So the investor cannot control the associate's dividend payments. Unless there is an agreement that the associate's profits will not be distributed in the foreseeable future, an investor recognises a deferred tax liability in relation to taxable temporary differences arising from the associate's undistributed profits. [IAS 12 para 42]. In practice, such an agreement is unlikely to exist; so a deferred tax liability would be recognised for most associates in respect of post-acquisition earnings. But (for reasons stated in para 13.259) it might not be possible to determine the tax that will be payable when the investment cost is recovered – whether through distribution of the retained profits or through disposal. In that case, the standard suggests that the entity should recognise the minimum amount that can be determined. [IAS 12 para 42].

Example – Deferred tax on investment in associate

On 1 January 20X5, entity A acquired 40% of the shares of a foreign entity B at a cost of FC1m (FC = foreign currency). At the acquisition date, the tax base (in entity A's jurisdiction) of entity A's investment in entity B is C500,000.

During the year ended 31 December 20X5, entity B made a profit of FC240,000. The exchange rate at 1 January 20X5 was C1:FC2; and at 31 December 20X5 it was C1:FC1.6. The tax rate in entity A's jurisdiction is 30%.

	FC'000	C'000
Entity B's net assets		
Book value = Fair values of entity B's identifiable assets and liabilities at 1 Jan 20X5	1,200	
Profit for the year	240	
Net assets at 31 December 20X5	1,440	
Calculation of goodwill on acquisition		
Purchase consideration	1,000	
Share of entity B's net assets at acquisition (40% of FC1,200,000)	(480)	
Goodwill arising on acquisition	520	
Equity carrying amount of investment in entity B at 31 December 20X5		
Share of entity B's net assets at 31 December 20X5 (40% of FC1,440,000 @ 1.6)		360
Goodwill arising on acquisition (FC520,000 @ 1.6)		325
Equity interest at 31 December 20X5		685
Tax base = cost of shares		500
Temporary difference		185

Temporary difference comprises

	C'000
Share of retained profits (40% of FC240,000 @ 1.6*)	60
Share of exchange difference on opening net assets – 40% of (FC1,200,000 × (1/1.6 – 1/2))	60
Exchange difference on goodwill – FC520,000 × (1/1.6 – 1/2)	65
	185

* Under IAS 21, a weighted average exchange rate is used for translating the share of profit (see chapter 7). For simplicity in this example it is assumed that the weighted average exchange rate is the same as the closing rate.

Entity A would recognise a deferred tax liability in its consolidated financial statements as follows:

		C'000	C'000
		Dr	**Cr**
Dr	Deferred tax expense in profit or loss on share of profits @ 30%	18.0	
Dr	Deferred tax expense in other comprehensive income on opening exchange difference on net assets @ 30%	18.0	
Dr	Deferred tax expense in other comprehensive income on exchange difference on goodwill @ 30%	19.5	
	Cr Deferred tax liability @ 30% on C185,000		55.5

Investments in joint ventures

13.266   Under IAS 31, investments in joint ventures could comprise investments in jointly controlled operations, jointly controlled assets or jointly controlled entities. In the case of jointly controlled operations or jointly controlled assets, the investor recognises in its balance sheet the assets that it controls and the liabilities that it has incurred in respect of the joint venture – or its share of such assets and liabilities. The related tax bases would also be included in the investor's tax balance sheet. So any temporary differences arising between the carrying amounts and tax bases of the assets and liabilities should be recognised; and deferred taxes should be provided.

13.267   In the case of jointly controlled entities, the investor's interest in the joint venture entity can currently be reported using proportional consolidation or the equity method. Where the proportionate consolidation method is used, the temporary differences are determined in the same way as for a subsidiary. Where the equity method is used, temporary differences arise between the carrying amount of the investor's interest (that is, the investor's capital contributions plus its share of undistributed profit) and the tax base of the investment. The terms of the contractual arrangement between the venturers on the retention of any profit in the joint venture will determine whether any deferred tax should be provided on the temporary difference (that is, similar to the treatment for associates – see para 13.264 onwards). Where the venturer can control the sharing of profits and it is probable that the profits will not be distributed, a deferred tax liability is not recognised. [IAS 12, para 43]. But the amount of any taxable temporary difference should be disclosed.

13.267.1 The IASB has issued IFRS 11 to replace IAS 31; and the new standard is effective for annual periods beginning on or after 1 January 2013. Under the new standard, joint arrangements could be joint operations or joint ventures. In the case of joint operations, the joint operator recognises in its balance sheet the assets that it holds and the liabilities that it has incurred in respect of the joint operation, including its share of assets held jointly and liabilities incurred jointly. The related tax bases would also be included in the joint operator's tax balance sheet. So any temporary differences arising between the carrying amounts and tax bases of the assets and liabilities should be recognised; and deferred taxes should be provided in the normal way.

13.267.2 In the case of joint ventures, the investor accounts for its investment using the equity method. Temporary differences would arise between the carrying amount of the investor's interest (that is, the investor's capital contributions plus its share of undistributed profit) and the tax base of the investment. The terms of the contractual arrangement between the venturers on the retention of any profit in the joint venture will determine whether any deferred tax should be provided on the temporary difference (that is, similar to the treatment for associates – see para 13.264 onwards). Where the venturer can control the sharing of profits and it is probable that the profits will not be distributed, a deferred tax liability is not recognised. [IAS 12 para 43]. But the amount of any taxable temporary difference should be disclosed.

Deferred tax asset arising on investments in subsidiaries, associates and joint ventures

13.268 An entity should recognise a deferred tax asset for all deductible temporary differences arising from investments in subsidiaries, branches and associates, and interests in joint ventures, to the extent that it is probable that:

- the temporary difference will reverse in the foreseeable future; and

- taxable profit will be available against which the temporary difference can be utilised.

[IAS 12 para 44].

13.268.1 A deferred tax asset might arise in the reporting entity's separate or consolidated financial statements in relation to its investment in a subsidiary, associate or joint venture. For example, the carrying amount of the investment might have been written down to its recoverable amount as a result of impairment, but the tax base remains unaffected. A deferred tax asset that arises should be recognised only if the reporting entity expects that the temporary difference will reverse in the foreseeable future and also expects that taxable profit will be available against which the temporary difference can be utilised. For instance, the temporary difference could be reversed if the investment is sold or if a tax deduction is received for an impairment charge that was previously disallowed. The entity should consider the guidance (set out at para 13.128 onwards) to determine whether the deferred tax asset should be recognised. It should be noted that this deferred tax asset is separate from those that might arise in the financial statements of the subsidiary, associate or joint venture.

Investments in tax-transparent entities (consolidation issues)

13.269 A number of entities around the world do not pay tax (see para 13.233.8); but their profits are taxable in the hands of the investors. Examples of such entities are partnerships, UK limited liability partnerships (LLPs) and US limited liability companies (LLCs). As well as giving rise to accounting issues in the investor's separate financial statements (see para 13.233.8 onwards), this tax structure can give rise to accounting issues in the investor's consolidated financial statements.

13.269.1 One accounting issue relates to the presentation of tax in profit or loss where an investment in a tax-transparent entity is accounted for in consolidated financial statements under the equity method. Consider an investor that has a number of subsidiaries and an investment in an associate. The associate is a limited liability partnership, which is not itself subject to tax; but its investors are taxed on their share of the profits. When the associate is included in the investor's consolidated financial statements, a question arises on the tax impact (current and deferred) of the associate's profits: should they be included within the associate's equity-accounted profits and net assets; or should they be reported within the group's tax charge and as part of the group's current and deferred tax liability?

13.269.2 Our view is that the tax (current and deferred) is reported as part of the group's tax charge; and the corresponding liability is added to the group's current and deferred tax liability. This view is supported by the example in IAS 1, which has a footnote explaining that the equity-accounted profit of an associate is "... *the share of associates' profit attributable to owners of the associates, ie it is after tax and non-controlling interests in the associates*". We consider that the tax (current and deferred) should be reported as part of the group's tax (and not as part of the associate's equity-accounted profit and net assets) because the tax does not arise in the associate but is levied instead on the investor.

13.269.3 Another deferred tax accounting issue arises on acquisition of a tax-transparent associate. If a taxable temporary difference arises, management needs to consider how to account for that temporary difference. We consider that there are two acceptable accounting treatments.

13.269.4 The acquisition of the associate does not give rise to an initial accounting or taxable profit; so it does not logically follow that a deferred tax charge should be recorded in profit or loss. We consider that the initial recognition exception in paragraph 15(b) of IAS 12 applies because the acquisition of an associate is not a business combination (see further para 13.162). So no deferred tax is generally recognised on initial acquisition of a tax-transparent associate.

13.269.5   The alternative acceptable view is that the deferred tax liability arising on acquisition of the associate (for example, on previously unrecognised intangibles or goodwill) is recognised. Any deferred tax liabilities arising on this acquisition are recognised as deferred tax liabilities of the group (as explained in para 13.269.2) – that is, outside the associate's equity-accounted amounts. The question then arises of how to account for the debit relating to this deferred tax liability. We consider that the debit is taken to the associate's equity-accounted share of net assets. This follows from applying business combination principles and adjusting deferred tax against goodwill. But, because goodwill on acquisition of an associate is combined with all the other assets and liabilities for presentation in the consolidated financial statements, it is this single line item that should be debited to allow recognition of deferred tax. IAS 28 requires that an associate is initially recorded at cost. Under the IASB's Framework, cost is the amount of cash or cash equivalents paid or the fair value of other consideration given. It can be argued that the assumption of the tax liability by the investor is part of the consideration for the acquisition, and so increases its cost.

13.269.6   The accounting treatment set out in paragraph 13.269.5 adds the debit to the carrying amount of the equity-accounted investment; so the accounting carrying amount is changed. Any consequential effect on the temporary difference would need to be considered. This accounting treatment could result in an iterative process to arrive at the carrying amount of the equity-accounted investment and the deferred tax liability.

Foreign currency translation

13.270   Gains or losses arising on the translation of an entity's own overseas assets (including investments in subsidiaries and associated companies) and liabilities can give rise to temporary differences; this depends on whether or not the gains or losses have a tax effect. Also, the translation of foreign entities' financial statements can sometimes give rise to temporary differences on which deferred tax might need to be recognised.

> **UK.13.270.1**   In the UK, the tax rules with regard to exchange gains and losses are complex. Depending on the elections made under the applicable tax rules, exchange gains and losses might be taxable as they accrue for accounting purposes; or they might be taxable when they are realised. Consultation with a tax specialist is recommended in this area.

Foreign currency assets and liabilities

13.271   An entity's foreign currency monetary assets and liabilities are translated at the end of each reporting period; and the resulting gain or loss is recognised in profit or loss. Such gains or losses might be taxable (or tax deductible) in the period in which they are realised. So the tax base of the asset or liability is not changed as a result of the change in exchange rate. The difference between the translated carrying amount and its tax base (that is, original carrying amount) might give rise to a taxable or deductible temporary difference.

Example – Foreign currency and deferred tax

Entity A sold goods to overseas customers for FC250,000 on 1 November 20X3. At 31 December 20X3, the receivable was still outstanding. Revenue is recognised on an accrual basis for both accounting and tax purposes. Exchange differences are not assessable for tax purposes in entity A's country until they are realised.

The exchange rates prevailing at the date of sale and at the end of the financial year are as follows:

1 November 20X3	C1:FC1.60
31 December 20X3	C1:FC1.65

Management should calculate the tax base of the receivable balance at 31 December 20X3 as follows:

	C	
Carrying amount	151,515	(FC250,000/1.65)
Future taxable income	–	(Tax was assessed when revenue was recognised)
Future deductible amount	4,735	(Exchange loss deductible when realised)
Tax base	156,250	(FC250,000/1.60)

Entity A has a deductible temporary difference of C4,735 (C151,515 — C156,250); management should recognise a deferred tax asset in respect of this temporary difference. Movements in exchange rates change the taxable or deductible temporary differences of foreign currency-denominated asset or liabilities if the exchange gain or loss is not recognised for tax purposes until it is realised.

13.271.1 The related deferred tax is recognised in profit or loss (see scenario B, example 2 in para 13.119). But, where the exchange differences are recognised outside profit or loss (for example, foreign currency borrowings hedging a net investment in the consolidated financial statements or qualifying as a hedging instrument in a cash flow hedge), the deferred tax is also recognised outside profit or loss.

13.272 Where an entity holds a non-monetary asset in a foreign country, the asset's carrying amount (in the absence of any impairment) is its historical purchase price translated at the exchange rate at the date of purchase. To the extent that the asset's realisation (through use or sale) gives rise to tax consequences in the foreign country, the asset's tax base changes as the exchange rate changes; but the carrying amount remains the same. A deferred tax asset (subject to meeting the recognition test) or a deferred tax liability should be recognised on the temporary difference that arises (see also para 13.274).

Foreign subsidiaries, associates and joint ventures

13.273 Exchange differences arise when the results and financial position of a foreign operation are translated into a presentational currency (for inclusion in the reporting entity's financial statements) by consolidation, proportionate consolidation or the equity method. Such exchange differences arise because the income statement items are translated at the average rate; and balance sheet assets and liabilities are translated at the closing rate. Exchange differences also arise when the opening net assets are translated at a different closing rate to the previous closing rate. All such exchange differences are recognised in a separate component of equity in the consolidated financial statements; and they are shown in other comprehensive income. From a deferred tax perspective, such exchange differences should not give rise to any temporary differences associated with the foreign operation's assets and liabilities. This is because the carrying amounts of the assets and liabilities and their respective tax bases will be measured in the foreign entity's functional currency at the balance sheet date; so any temporary differences arising would have been recognised by the foreign entity as part of its deferred tax balances in its own financial statements. These deferred tax balances (translated at the year-end exchange rate) will simply flow through on consolidation; and no further adjustment is necessary.

13.273.1 Although temporary differences do not arise from translation of the financial statements of a foreign operation, they might arise on consolidation; this occurs as a result of the difference between the translated amount of the reporting entity's net investment in the foreign operation (effectively the group's share of net assets) and the tax base of the investment itself in the reporting entity. See paragraph 13.256 onwards and an example in paragraph 13.265 illustrating the tax effect of exchange differences.

Foreign branches

13.274 Where the activities of a reporting entity's foreign branch are carried out as an extension of the reporting entity (rather than being carried out with any significant degree of autonomy), the foreign branch's functional currency is the same as that of the reporting entity. But changes in exchange rates give rise to temporary differences if the foreign branch's taxable profit or tax loss (and hence the tax base of its non-monetary assets and liabilities) is determined in the foreign currency. This is because the carrying amounts of the foreign branch's non-monetary assets and liabilities (which are translated into the reporting entity's currency at the historical rate) differ from their tax bases (which are translated at exchange rates prevailing at the reporting date). A deferred tax asset (subject to the recognition test) or a deferred liability should be recognised on such temporary differences. The resulting deferred tax is credited or charged to profit or loss. [IAS 12 para 41]. Note that these deferred tax balances relate to the foreign branch; and they are in addition to those that can arise from the reporting entity's investment in the foreign branch (discussed above).

Example – Deferred tax and foreign branch

An entity operates a foreign branch that has the same functional currency as the entity. At 1 January 20X5, the foreign branch acquires a property for FC540,000 (FC = foreign currency) when the exchange rate is C1:FC12. The asset has an expected useful life of 5 years and zero residual value. For tax purposes, the asset is written off over 3 years. The exchange rate at 31 December 20X5 is C1:FC9. The tax rates in the entity's country and the foreign country are 30% and 25% respectively.

At 31 December 20X5, a temporary difference arises in respect of the property as follows:

	Foreign branch FC	Exchange rate C1 = FC	Entity C
Net book value of property			
Cost	540,000	12	45,000
Depreciation charge for the year	(108,000)		(9,000)
Net book value	432,000		36,000
Tax base of property			
Cost	540,000		
Tax depreciation claimed	(180,000)		
	360,000	9	40,000*
Temporary difference	72,000		(4,000)
Deferred tax @ 25%**	18,000		(1,000)

* The tax base is measured at the year-end rate because this rate gives the best measure of the reporting currency amount that will be deductible in future periods.

** The tax rate is 25% (that is, the rate applicable to the foreign country) because the entity will be taxed on the asset's recovery in that jurisdiction.

A taxable temporary difference arises in the foreign entity; but a deductible temporary difference arises in the reporting entity. This is because (following the change in exchange rate from FC12 to FC9) the foreign currency revenue required to recover the asset's reporting currency carrying amount is C36,000 @ 9 = FC324,000; but the tax base of the asset remains at FC360,000. This difference of FC36,000 @ 9 = C4,000 gives rise to a deductible temporary difference; a deferred tax asset @ 25% (that is, C1,000) should be recognised in the entity's financial statements for this temporary difference.

> If the tax base had not been translated at the year-end rate, it would have been recorded at C30,000 (C45,000 less tax depreciation of C15,000) at the year end. This would have given rise to a temporary difference of C6,000 (C36,000 – C30,000); the entity would have provided deferred tax liability of C1,500 (25% of C6,000) on this temporary difference. But translating the tax base at year-end rate resulted in a deferred tax asset of C1,000. The difference of C2,500 is attributable to the tax effect of currency translation on the tax base, that is 25% of (C40,000 – C30,000) = C2,500.

13.274.1 The following extract from the financial statements of Tenaris explains the tax effect of currency translation on the tax base:

Table 13.2 – Tax effect of currency translation on the tax base

Tenaris SA – Annual Report – 31 December 2010

IV. Other notes to the Consolidated financial statements (extract)

8. Income tax

All amounts in thousands of U.S. dollars

Year ended December 31	2010	2009	2008
Current tax	395,183	541,818	1,255,759
Deferred tax	58,848	(32,962)	(244,331)
	454,031	**508,856**	**1,011,428**
Effect of currency translation on tax base (a)	(4,027)	4,297	10,704
	450,004	**513,153**	**1,022,132**
From Discontinued operations	–	58	(6,798)
	450,004	**513,211**	**1,015,334**

The tax on Tenaris' income before tax differs from the theoretical amount that would arise using the tax rate in each country as follows:

All amounts in thousands of U.S. dollars

Year ended December 31	2010	2009	2008
Income before income tax	**1,591,051**	**1,748,948**	**2,984,049**
Tax calculated at the tax rate in each country	440,882	525,844	918,200
Non taxable income / Non deductible expenses (b)	(2,948)	(25,760)	85,950
Changes in the tax rates	(17)	837	(4,476)
Effect of currency translation on tax base (a)	(4,027)	4,297	10,704
Effect of taxable exchange differences	16,185	8,906	8,878
Utilization of previously unrecognized tax losses	(71)	(913)	(3,922)
Tax charge	**450,004**	**513,211**	**1,015,334**

(a) Tenaris applies the liability method to recognize deferred income tax expense on temporary differences between the tax bases of assets and their carrying amounts in the financial statements. By application of this method, Tenaris recognizes gains and losses on deferred income tax due to the effect of the change in the value of the Argentine peso on the tax bases of the fixed assets of its Argentine subsidiaries, which have the U.S. dollar as their functional currency. These gains and losses are required by IFRS even though the devalued tax basis of the relevant assets will result in a reduced dollar value of amortization deductions for tax purposes in future periods throughout the useful life of those assets. As a result, the resulting deferred income tax charge does not represent a separate obligation for Tenaris that is due and payable in any of the relevant periods.

(b) Includes the effect of the impairment charge for 2008.

Tax holidays

13.275   The governments or tax authorities of some jurisdictions offer investment incentives by way of temporary reductions of tax (known as 'tax holidays'). Tax holidays result in tax reductions regardless of an entity's level of taxable profit. A lower tax rate or nil tax rate is normally applied to the taxable profits arising within the tax holiday period. Where deferred tax arises on temporary differences that reverse within the tax holiday period, it is measured at the tax rates that are expected to apply during the tax holiday period (that is, the lower tax rate or nil tax rate). Where deferred tax arises on temporary differences that reverse after the tax holiday period, it is measured at the enacted or substantively enacted tax rates that are expected to apply after the tax holiday period.

13.275.1   The example below considers the deferred tax implications when the start of a tax holiday is delayed until the period when an entity has taxable profits (after using any carried-forward losses).

Example

A jurisdiction grants a tax holiday to specified entities. The tax holiday provides a 0% tax rate for the first two years of the holiday and a tax rate of 20% for the following three years. The normal tax rate is 40%.

The tax holiday does not commence until the year in which an entity generates taxable profits (after use of carried-forward losses). The entity does not expect to generate taxable profits (after use of carried-forward losses) for three years.

An entity's forecast taxable profit is as follows:

	Year 1 C'000	Year 2 C'000	Year 3 C'000	Year 4 C'000
Taxable (losses)/profit in the year	(300)	100	200	250
Use of carried-forward losses	–	(100)	(200)	–
Taxable (losses)/profit after use of carried-forward losses	(300)	0	0	250

In this scenario, the tax holiday begins in year 4.

(a) At the end of year 1, assuming the recoverability criteria in IAS 12 are met, should a deferred tax asset in respect of the taxable losses be recognised?

The entity is receiving a benefit, because the existence of the unused losses effectively delays the start of the tax holiday period. Without these unused losses (and assuming no taxable profit in year 1), the entity would begin paying taxes in year 4 instead of year 6. So a deferred tax asset of C120,000 (C300,000 × 40%) should be recognised.

(b) If the entity does not expect the tax holiday to begin until year 4 (and so it will not pay tax until year 6), should it recognise deferred tax liabilities for any taxable temporary differences on assets or liabilities that will reverse in years 2 to 5?

IAS 12 provides the following exceptions to recognising deferred tax liabilities: for the initial recognition of goodwill; for the initial recognition of assets or liabilities that do not affect accounting or taxable profit; and for some specified investment in subsidiaries. IAS 12 does not provide an exception to recognising deferred tax liabilities based on an expectation of future taxable losses.

So, deferred tax liabilities should be recognised and measured at the rate that will be in effect when the temporary differences reverse. For the temporary differences reversing before the start of the tax holiday (years 2 and 3), the appropriate rate is the normal tax rate (40%). For the temporary differences reversing during the first two years of the tax holiday (years 4 and 5), the appropriate rate is 0%.

Note that deferred tax on temporary differences reversing in the remaining three years of the tax holiday is measured at 20%.

13.275.1.1   A temporary difference might arise on the initial acquisition of an asset or liability during the tax holiday period; and it might appear to be subject to the initial recognition exception. For example, an entity might receive an upfront fee during a tax holiday period; and it would record deferred revenue. The jurisdiction might assess tax on revenue when cash is received; because the tax holiday period provides for a nil tax rate, it might seem that the initial acquisition of the deferred revenue liability does not impact accounting or taxable profit. But the initial recognition exception does not apply because the upfront fee does impact taxable income, even though a nil tax rate is applied as a result of the tax holiday (as opposed to being exempt from tax).

Investment and other tax credits

13.275.2   The governments or tax authorities of some jurisdictions offer investment incentives by way of credits to be applied in determining tax liabilities. In general, tax credits are tax benefits received other than tax deductions that normally arise (at standard rates) from deductible expenditures. Tax credit schemes vary significantly across jurisdictions and can be complex in practice, so each scheme's characteristics warrant careful consideration to determine the appropriate accounting. For example, some tax credits schemes are structured as in substance government grants that are available regardless of the level of an entity's taxable profits, while others offer tax credits that are only recoverable if the entity has sufficient taxable profits against which the credit can be applied.

Tax credit schemes are comprised of (i) investment tax credits and (ii) other tax credits. There is no definition in IFRS of either investment tax credits or other tax credits. While the treatment of unused tax credits is addressed by IAS 12, the standard does not deal with accounting for investment tax credits. [IAS 12 para 4]. Investment tax credits are also outside IAS 20's scope. [IAS 20 para 2].

13.275.3 Therefore, the following questions arise:

■ What differentiates investment tax credits from other tax credits?

■ What is the accounting for investment tax credits and other tax credits?

13.275.4 Other tax credits are within IAS 12's scope. A deferred tax asset is recognised for unused tax credits to the extent that it is probable that future taxable profit will be available against which the unused tax credit can be utilised (see further para 13.144 onwards). [IAS 12 para 34]. The credit entry for the deferred tax asset (and any subsequent adjustment to the asset) will be to the tax line in the income statement in the period the tax credit arises. Where receipt of a tax credit is subject to the entity complying with specific substantive conditions in future periods, the credit is recognised only when the conditions are met.

13.275.5 Investment tax credits are generally tax benefits received for investment in specific qualifying assets (other than tax deductions that are available as part of the asset's tax base in use or on disposal). We believe that this definition should be interpreted narrowly, although in some circumstances, it might also be applied to credits for investments in qualifying but non-capitalised research and development expenditure. When there are substantive additional requirements to be met that are not directly related to the investment, the benefit should not be treated as an investment tax credit, but rather, as an 'other tax credit'. Examples of such requirements would include maintaining a certain number of employees or reaching a certain level of export revenues.

13.275.6 Management needs to use judgement in assessing the substance of each tax credit scheme. Conditions may be attached to a scheme that are perfunctory and do not determine whether the tax benefit will be received; in which case it may still be appropriate to classify the tax benefit as an investment tax credit. For example, if the only additional criterion for receiving a tax credit is to maintain at least 200 employees, but the entity needs at least 2,000 employees to operate the qualifying equipment purchased under the scheme, the additional criterion would be perfunctory and the tax benefit classified as an investment tax credit.

13.275.7 There are three alternative accounting models to account for investment tax credits, which analogise to either IAS 12 or IAS 20. The most appropriate model to apply will depend on the nature of the credit and the specific circumstances of the entity, including previous policy choices.

Tax credit (or flow though) model

13.275.8   This treatment is based on the assumption that investment tax credits are often not substantially different from other tax credits. So it is acceptable to have the same accounting treatment for investment tax credits as previously described for other tax credits (see para 13.144). This model would apply equally to tax credits available as a result of qualifying but non-capitalised research and development expenditure.

Government grant (or deferral) model

13.275.9   This treatment is based on characterising the investment tax credit as being similar to a government grant and recognises the tax benefit in pre-tax profit or loss over the related asset's useful life. The credit results in a reduction to the current tax liability or the recognition of a deferred tax asset (where unused), and under IAS 20 the benefit (that is, the credit entry) is either:

- recognised separately from the related asset as deferred income; in which case the deferred income is amortised over the related asset's life in the income statement as 'other income'; or

- recognised as a reduction of the related asset's carrying amount; in which case, the benefit arises through a lower depreciation charge.

A new temporary difference between the book and tax base of the asset may arise where a non-taxable grant results in adjustment to the asset's carrying value but not its tax base. Alternatively, where such a grant is recognised as deferred income, the difference between the deferred income balance and its tax base of nil will also be a temporary difference. Whichever method of presentation is adopted, the resulting deferred tax asset that arises on the initial recognition of the asset or deferred income is not recognised. [IAS 12 para 33].

In the limited circumstances where this approach is adopted for tax credits on qualifying expenditure that does not result in a capitalised asset, the tax credit entry is generally recognised in pre-tax profit or loss when the related expenditure is incurred.

13.275.10   If an entity is considering adopting this accounting model, it should consider potential consequences for subsequent accounting. For instance, where a deferred tax asset resulting from an investment tax credit cannot be recovered because of unexpected tax losses, should the deferred income (or adjustment to asset carrying amount) be reversed? One view separates the future measurement of the deferred tax asset from the deferred income (or carrying amount of the asset). The recovery of the deferred tax asset depends on future profits and is not linked to the circumstances that gave rise to the grant. Government grants are not adjusted if the granted assets are impaired. An alternative view is that writing off the deferred tax asset is a repayment of government grant, so the deferred income (or adjustment to the carrying amount of the asset) should be reversed. We consider that either approach is acceptable; and the choice of approach is a matter of accounting policy to be applied consistently. However, recognising the complexities that may result from this approach, including the impact of any subsequent reversal of any deferred tax asset, many entities may find it preferable to account for such credits as other tax credits rather than as investment tax credits, unless measurement of the credit is reasonably straightforward, and there is a high expectation of its recovery (for example, where recovery of the tax credit is not dependent on the level of an entity's future taxable profits).

Change of tax base (or IRE) model

13.275.11 Where a related asset is recorded on the balance sheet, in some circumstances it might be acceptable to view the investment tax credit as an increase of the related asset's tax base. Where the asset was not acquired in a business combination (and the related asset's initial recognition does not affect accounting or taxable profit), the deductible temporary difference that arises will qualify for the initial recognition exception in paragraph 15 of IAS 12 (see para 13.162 onwards). Therefore, no deferred tax asset is recognised at the time the tax credit arises, but recognition occurs within tax as the credit is realised.

Presentation and disclosures

General

13.276 It is generally accepted that tax effects (regardless of how they have been calculated) should be shown in the financial statements separately from the items or transactions to which they relate. So it is not surprising that the standard contains a considerable number of disclosure requirements in respect of taxation. Most of the disclosure requirements apply to the financial statements of individual companies as well as to consolidated financial statements. The paragraphs that follow deal with the disclosure requirements of current and deferred tax.

Accounting policies

13.277 There is no specific requirement in IAS 12 to disclose accounting policies in respect of current and deferred tax. This is because IAS 1 requires disclosure of significant accounting policies that are relevant to an understanding of the entity's financial statements. [IAS 1 para 117]. In respect of deferred tax, the policy note should state the measurement basis on which deferred tax has been recognised.

13.277.1 Examples of accounting policies on current and deferred tax under IAS 12 are given in Tables 13.3 and 13.4 below.

13187

Table 13.3 – Tax and deferred tax accounting policies

Koninklijke Philips Electronics N.V. – Report and Accounts – 31 December 2011

12.10 Significant accounting policies (extract)

Income tax (extract)

Income tax comprises current and deferred tax. Income tax is recognized in the Statement of income except to the extent that it relates to items recognized directly within equity or in other comprehensive income. Current tax is the expected tax payable on the taxable income for the year, using tax rates enacted or substantially-enacted at the reporting date, and any adjustment to tax payable in respect of previous years.

Deferred tax assets and liabilities are recognized, using the balance sheet method, for the expected tax consequences of temporary differences between the carrying amounts of assets and liabilities and the amounts used for taxation purposes. Deferred tax is not recognized for the following temporary differences: the initial recognition of goodwill, the initial recognition of assets and liabilities in a transaction that is not a business combination and that affects neither accounting nor taxable profit, and differences relating to investments in subsidiaries to the extent that they probably will not reverse in the foreseeable future. Deferred tax is measured at the tax rates that are expected to be applied to temporary differences when they reverse, based on the laws that have been enacted or substantially-enacted by the reporting date. Deferred tax assets and liabilities are offset if there is a legally-enforceable right to offset current tax liabilities and assets, and they relate to income taxes levied by the same tax authority on the same taxable entity, or on different tax entities, but they intend to settle current tax liabilities and assets on a net basis or their tax assets and liabilities will be realized simultaneously.

A deferred tax asset is recognized for unused tax losses, tax credits and deductible temporary differences, to the extent that it is probable that future taxable profits will be available against which they can be utilized. The ultimate realization of deferred tax assets is dependent upon the generation of future taxable income in the countries where the deferred tax assets originated and during the periods when the deferred tax assets become deductible. Management considers the scheduled reversal of deferred tax liabilities, projected future taxable income, and tax planning strategies in making this assessment.

Table 13.4 – Current and deferred tax

Smith & Nephew plc – Annual report – 31 December 2011

5 Taxation (extract)

Accounting policy

The charge for current taxation is based on the results for the year as adjusted for items which are non-assessable or disallowed. It is calculated using rates that have been enacted or substantively enacted by the balance sheet date. The accounting policy for deferred taxation is set out in Note 17.

17 Deferred taxation (extract)

Accounting policy

Deferred taxation is accounted for using the balance sheet liability method in respect of temporary differences arising between the carrying amount of assets and liabilities in the accounts and the corresponding tax bases used in computation of taxable profit.

Deferred tax liabilities are recognised for all taxable temporary differences except in respect of investments in subsidiaries where the Group is able to control the timing of the reversal of the temporary difference and it is probable that this will not reverse in the foreseeable future; on the initial recognition of non-deductible goodwill; and on the initial recognition of an asset or liability in a transaction that is not a business combination and that, at the time of the transaction, does not affect the accounting or taxable profit.

Deferred tax assets are recognised to the extent that it is probable that future taxable profit will be available against which the temporary difference can be utilised. Their carrying amount is reviewed at each balance sheet date on the same basis.

Deferred tax is measured on an undiscounted basis, and at the tax rates that have been enacted or substantively enacted by the balance sheet date that are expected to apply in the periods in which the asset or liability is settled. It is recognised in the income statement except when it relates to items credited or charged directly to other comprehensive income or equity, in which case the deferred tax is also dealt with in other comprehensive income or equity respectively.

Deferred tax assets and liabilities are offset when they relate to income taxes levied by the same taxation authority, when the Group intends to settle its current tax assets and liabilities on a net basis and that authority permits the Group to make a single net payment.

13.277.2 IAS 1 also requires disclosure in the financial statements of judgements (apart from those involving estimations – see para 13.307.1) that management has made in the process of applying the accounting policies and that have the most significant effect on the amounts recognised in those financial statements. [IAS 1 para 122]. This is discussed in detail in chapter 4.

13.277.3 An example of disclosure of critical judgements in respect of tax is given in Table 13.5 below.

Table 13.5 – Critical judgements in respect of tax

Centrica plc – Annual report – 31 December 2010

3. Critical accounting judgements and key sources of estimation uncertainty (extract)

Petroleum revenue tax (PRT)

The definition of an income tax in IAS 12, Income Taxes, has led management to judge that PRT should be treated consistently with other income taxes. The charge for the year is presented within taxation on profit from continuing operations in the Income Statement. Deferred amounts are included within deferred tax assets and liabilities in the Balance Sheet.

Balance sheet presentation

13.278 Liabilities and assets for current tax should be presented separately on the face of the balance sheet. [IAS 1 para 54(n)]. Similarly, deferred tax liabilities and deferred tax assets should be presented separately on the face of the balance sheet. [IAS 1 para 54(o)]. Where an entity presents current and non-current assets (and current and non-current liabilities) as separate classifications on the face of the balance sheet, it should not classify deferred tax assets (liabilities) as current assets (liabilities). [IAS 1 para 56]. In other words, deferred tax assets and liabilities are always presented as non-current.

13.279 The amount of an asset or liability that is expected to be recovered or settled more than 12 months after the balance sheet date should be disclosed in the following situation: where an entity has a line item that combines (a) amounts expected to be recovered or settled no more than 12 months after the balance sheet date and (b) amounts expected to be recovered or settled more than 12 months after the balance sheet date. [IAS 1 para 61]. This situation might apply to deferred tax assets and liabilities because they are always presented as non-current (see para 13.278); even though they could contain an element expected to be recovered or settled no more than 12 months from the balance sheet date.

13.280 To meet the IAS 1 requirement, an entity should first calculate the amount that becomes due no more than 12 months after the balance sheet date (that is, the 'current' component of the total asset or liability balance). That amount is then deducted from the total balance to give the 'non-current' component. It might be difficult to estimate the current component in practice, because management might need to make subjective judgements on the probable timing of the reversal of taxable and deductible temporary differences and on the probable timing of the reversal of tax losses. Indeed, it is sometimes impossible to obtain a reliable split without making arbitrary assumptions. Nevertheless, it appears that such a split is required to comply with paragraph 61 of IAS 1, even though the entire deferred tax asset or liability balance is presented as non-current in the balance sheet.

UK.13.280.1 UK entities that account under FRS 17 do not include deferred tax assets and liabilities in respect of defined benefit schemes with other deferred tax assets or liabilities. Instead, deferred tax relating to a defined benefit asset or liability is offset against the related asset or liability; and it is presented separately in the balance sheet under paragraph 49 of FRS 17. This treatment is not available under IAS 12. So, deferred tax relating to post-employment benefits should be included (under IFRS) within deferred tax assets and liabilities.

Offset

13.281 Although current tax assets and liabilities are separately measured and recognised, they should be offset for presentation purposes if, and only if, the entity:

■ has a legally enforceable right to set off the recognised amounts; and

■ intends either to settle on a net basis, or to realise the asset and settle the liability simultaneously.

[IAS 12 para 71].

13.282 The above offset criteria are similar to those established for financial instruments in paragraph 42 of IAS 32. The 'legal right of offset' criterion is met only where income taxes are levied by the same tax authority that accepts or requires settlement on a net basis. [IAS 12 para 72].

13.283 In consolidated financial statements, current tax assets of one group member could be offset against a current tax liability of another member if the following conditions are satisfied: there is a legally enforceable right to offset the recognised amounts; and the entities intend to make settlement on a net basis or to recover the asset and settle the liability simultaneously. [IAS 12 para 73]. Simultaneous settlement means that the cash flows are equivalent to a single net amount; this is because the realisation of the current tax asset and the settlement of the current tax liability occur at the same moment.

13.284 Similar conditions apply to offsetting deferred tax assets and liabilities. An entity should offset deferred tax assets and deferred tax liabilities for presentation purposes if, and only if:

■ the entity has a legally enforceable right to set off current tax assets against current tax liabilities; and

■ the deferred tax assets and the deferred tax liabilities relate to income taxes levied by the same taxation authority on either:

  ■ the same taxable entity; or

  ■ different taxable entities which intend either to settle current tax liabilities and assets on a net basis, or to realise the assets and settle the liabilities simultaneously, in each future period in which significant amounts of deferred tax liabilities or assets are expected to be settled or recovered.

[IAS 12 para 74].

13.285 Simultaneous realisation of the asset and settlement of the liability (in the final point above) is particularly relevant to deferred taxes. Without this requirement, offset of specific deferred tax balances could take place only if the temporary differences giving rise to a deferred tax asset reverse before (or at the same time as) those giving rise to a deferred tax liability. If those giving rise to the liability reverse first, there will be a requirement to pay tax before any entitlement to recover tax. The IASB felt that the need to schedule the timings of the reversals of individual temporary differences (to measure the extent to which the balances should be offset for presentation purposes) would be impractical and unnecessarily costly. [IAS 12 para 75].

13.285.1 In rare circumstances, an entity might have a legally enforceable right of offset (and an intention to settle net) for some periods but not for others. Detailed scheduling would be required to establish reliably whether the deferred tax liability of one taxable entity will result in increased tax payments in the same period in which a deferred tax asset of another taxable entity will result in decreased payments by that second taxable entity. [IAS 12 para 76].

13.285.2 The requirement in paragraph 13.284 effectively prohibits offset of deferred tax assets and liabilities relating to different tax jurisdictions in consolidated financial statements. It also means that a net group tax liability cannot be presented by offsetting group tax assets on the grounds of a group tax planning opportunity, unless the opportunity relates to taxes levied by the same tax authority on different group members and the entities are treated as a group for tax purposes.

13.285.3 An entity might have a large number of different temporary differences (giving rise to deferred tax assets and liabilities) that arise during a period. Although these deferred tax assets and liabilities are measured separately, the ability to offset assets against liabilities depends on (a) the nature of the balances (for example, tax rules might not permit deferred tax assets for capital losses to be offset against deferred tax liabilities for trading item tax allowances, such as accelerated capital allowances) and (b) who they are due to or from.

Performance statements and equity

13.286 IAS 12 requires the tax expense (or income) related to profit or loss from ordinary activities to be presented in the statement of comprehensive income. If an entity presents the profit or loss components in a separate income statement (as described in para 81 of IAS 1), it presents the tax expense (or income) related to profit or loss from ordinary activities in that separate statement. [IAS 12 paras 77, 77A].

13.286.1 The treatment of tax in the performance statements is considered further in the following sections.

Items recognised in profit or loss

13.287 Deferred tax is recognised as income or expense and included in profit or loss for the period, except to the extent that the tax arises from:

- A transaction or event that is recognised (in the same period or a different period) outside profit or loss, either in other comprehensive income or directly in equity (see para 13.288).
- A business combination (see para 13.238 onwards).

[IAS 12 para 58].

13.287.1 IAS 12 distinguishes between tax on items recognised in other comprehensive income and tax on items recognised directly in equity; and it requires that the two amounts are presented accordingly and separately disclosed.

Items recognised outside profit or loss

13.288 Under the principle that tax follows the item, deferred tax relating to items that are recognised (in the same or a different period) in other comprehensive income is recognised in other comprehensive income. Similarly, deferred tax relating to items that are recognised (in the same or a different period) directly in equity is recognised directly in equity. [IAS 12 para 61A].

13.288.1 Some examples of items on which deferred tax is recognised in other comprehensive income (including some noted in para 62 of IAS 12) are given below:

■ A change in the carrying amount following revaluation of property, plant and equipment (see para 13.208).

■ The recognition of valuation movements on available-for-sale investments (see para 13.226).

■ The translation of the financial statements of foreign operations (see para 13.273).

13.288.2 Some examples of items on which deferred tax is recognised directly in equity (including some noted in para 62A of IAS 12) are given below:

■ An adjustment to opening retained earnings where a change in accounting policy is applied retrospectively or an error has been corrected.

■ The initial classification of a compound financial instrument where the tax base is not split between the two components (see para 13.229).

■ The amount of the tax deduction (estimated or known) that exceeds the cumulative amount of the expense in an equity-settled share-based payment award (see para 13.206).

13.288.3 The most common type of deferred tax that is recognised in other comprehensive income is on the revaluation of an asset (such as property, plant and equipment). But the deferred tax liability is always released through profit or loss because the revalued asset's carrying amount is recovered through use by way of a depreciation charge. An entity can sometimes make a transfer directly between reserves (from the revaluation reserve to retained earnings) of an amount equal to the difference between depreciation based on the revalued amount and depreciation based on cost. In this case, the transfer should be made net of deferred tax. [IAS 12 para 64]. This issue is addressed in scenario 1 of the example in paragraph 13.211.

13.288.4 IAS 12 does not specify the reserve in which tax charged (or credited) to other comprehensive income or directly to equity should be recognised. But the tax should be recognised in the same reserve as the underlying item (unless such treatment is prohibited by another standard or by the legal requirements relating to that reserve). This is consistent with the general principle in IAS 12 that an entity accounts for the tax consequences of transactions and other events in the same way that it accounts for the transactions and other events themselves. This is supported by paragraph 64 of IAS 12, which requires transfers from revaluation reserve to be made net of tax (see para 13.288.3); this indicates that the tax has been included in that reserve in the first instance.

13.288.5 It can be difficult to determine the amount of deferred tax that relates to items that are recognised outside profit or loss, either in other comprehensive income or directly in equity. For example, this might be the case where:

- There are graduated rates of income tax and it is not possible to determine the rate at which a specific component of taxable profit (tax loss) has been taxed.

- A change in the tax rate or other tax rules affects a deferred tax asset or liability relating (in whole or in part) to an item that was previously recognised outside profit or loss.

- An entity determines that a deferred tax asset should be recognised (or should no longer be recognised in full) and the deferred tax asset relates (in whole or in part) to an item that was previously recognised outside profit or loss.

In such situations, the attributable tax is calculated on a reasonable pro rata basis, or another basis that is more appropriate in the circumstances. [IAS 12 para 63].

> **Example**
>
> An entity was unable to recognise a deferred tax asset of C5m (of which C1m relates to items charged to other comprehensive income) because it was not probable that sufficient taxable profits would be available against which the deductible temporary difference could be utilised. After a few years, circumstances have changed and the entity expects to recover at least C3m of the unrecognised deferred tax asset. Unless the entity cannot analyse the particular categories of deductible temporary differences (which will be rare in practice), some form of apportionment is needed. For example, the entity could allocate part of the C3m (for instance, $1/5 \times 3 = $ C0.6m) to other comprehensive income and the balance of C2.4m to profit or loss.
>
> [The next paragraph is 13.288.7.]

Changes in the carrying amounts of deferred tax assets and liabilities

13.288.7 The carrying amount of deferred tax assets and liabilities can change without a change in the temporary difference. Such changes might arise as a result of:

- A change in tax rates or laws.

- A re-assessment of the recoverability of deferred tax assets (see para 13.155).

- A change in the expected manner of recovery of an asset (see para 13.174).

The resulting change in deferred tax should be recognised in profit or loss except to the extent that it relates to items previously recognised outside profit or loss (see further para 13.288). [IAS 12 para 60]. This is sometimes referred to as 'backwards-tracing'.

Example 1

An entity has a policy of revaluing property under paragraph 31 of IAS 16. As a result of revaluation gains, a taxable temporary difference has arisen between the properties' carrying amount and their tax base; this has led to recognition of a deferred tax liability at the period end.

The revaluation gains were recognised in other comprehensive income under IAS 16; and the related deferred tax liability was also recognised in other comprehensive income (following the principles of paragraph 60 of IAS 12, as noted above).

The corporation tax rate has changed from 40% to 35% with an effective date of 31 May 20X8. This change has been substantively enacted at the balance sheet date and will impact the reversal of the temporary difference from 31 May 20X8 onwards; so the deferred tax liability will be reduced.

Any adjustment to deferred tax resulting from the tax rate change should be traced back to the original transaction recognised in other comprehensive income. As such, the impact of any adjustment to this deferred tax liability would be recognised in other comprehensive income. (This differs from the accounting for reversals of the deferred tax liability resulting from depreciation charged; in that case, the reversal is recognised in profit or loss – see para 13.211.)

Example 2

An entity has a defined benefit pension scheme that is in deficit at the period end. A deferred tax asset has been recognised for the deductible temporary difference in relation to the pension deficit.

The corporation tax rate has changed from 40% to 35% with an effective date of 31 May 20X8. This change has been substantively enacted at the balance sheet date and will impact the reversal of the temporary difference from 31 May 20X8 onwards; so the deferred tax asset will be reduced.

Having identified the transactions that gave rise to the temporary difference, management will need to trace the impact of the tax rate change to the same place. In this case, the pension deficit might have arisen as a result of service costs or other income statement charges, or actuarial losses recognised in other comprehensive income, or both.

Depending on how the pension deficit arose (and thus how the deferred tax asset was originally booked), the reduction in the deferred tax asset will be recognised in profit or loss, in other comprehensive income, or it will be split between the two.

The backwards-tracing for the tax rate change should be consistent with the approach used for allocating tax deductions (see para 13.203.8). The deferred tax asset (which is impacted by the tax rate change) represents the tax on amounts against which tax deductions have not yet been allocated. Where amounts in the performance statements are covered by deductions received on contributions, no deferred tax arises. The deferred tax arises on any excess amounts in the performance statements; and the backwards-tracing should be carried out on that basis.

> If the deferred tax relates to a pension liability recognised on transition to IFRS, management needs to determine where the pension items on which the original deferred tax arose would have been recognised if IFRS had been applied in the prior periods (as explained in para 13.288.8). If this is not possible, the deferred tax would generally be recognised in profit or loss.

13.288.8 In some cases, a deferred tax asset or liability might have been recognised on the initial adoption of IFRS. In our view, the fact that deferred tax was charged to equity (as part of the transition adjustment) does not mean that subsequent changes in the deferred tax asset or liability will also be recognised in equity. Instead, management needs to determine (using the entity's current accounting policies) where the items on which the original deferred tax arose would have been recognised if IFRS had applied in the earlier periods. If it is not possible to assess where those items would have been recognised, the deferred tax changes would generally be recognised in profit or loss (under para 58 of IAS 12).

13.288.9 Where deferred tax arose on the initial adoption of IFRS, the implications of any transitional rules in IFRS 1 for the underlying items will need to be considered; this is for the purpose of backwards-tracing when accounting for deferred tax changes. For instance, if an asset is recognised at 'deemed cost' on the initial adoption of IFRS (with related deferred tax on the transition adjustment), any changes in that deferred tax should be recognised in profit or loss (see para 13.219 onwards). Similarly, where an item or an adjustment is deemed to be nil (for accounting purposes) under the transitional rules in IFRS 1, any subsequent changes in related deferred tax should not be backwards-traced to other comprehensive income or retained earnings, but should instead be recognised in profit or loss. For example, if an entity applies the exemption in para D13 of IFRS 1, cumulative translation differences for all foreign operations are deemed to be nil at the date of transition to IFRS.

13.288.10 A different situation arises where an exemption in IFRS 1 applies for disclosure purposes only; for example, some defined benefit scheme disclosures can be made prospectively from the date of transition to IFRS. [IFRS 1 para D11]. In this case, our view is that backwards-tracing to other comprehensive income should be applied for changes in deferred tax, unless it is not possible to assess where the items on which the original deferred tax arose would have been recognised (see the example in para 13.288.7); this is because the exemption does not apply to the underlying accounting.

Exchange differences on deferred foreign tax liabilities or assets

13.289 IAS 21 is silent on where exchange gains and losses should be shown in the income statement. IAS 12 makes it clear that exchange differences on foreign deferred tax assets and liabilities can be included as part of the deferred tax expense (income) if that presentation is considered to be the most useful to financial statement users. [IAS 12 para 78]. A more usual presentation would be to include the exchange differences on deferred taxes as part of the foreign exchange gains and losses that are credited or charged in arriving at profit before tax.

Disclosures in the notes

13.290   A considerable amount of information about current and deferred tax is disclosed in the notes. In this section, the disclosure requirements are grouped under appropriate headings for ease of reference; and examples from published financial statements are included where relevant.

Analysis of tax expense (income)

13.291   The major components of the tax expense (income) should be identified and disclosed separately. [IAS 12 para 79]. Such components might include:

- In respect of current tax:
    - The current tax expense (income).
    - Any adjustments recognised in the period for current tax of prior periods.
    - The amount of the benefit arising from a previously unrecognised tax loss, tax credit or temporary difference of a prior period that is used to reduce current tax expense.
    - The amount of tax expense (income) relating to changes in accounting policies and errors that are included in profit or loss (under IAS 8) because they cannot be accounted for retrospectively.

- In respect of deferred tax:
    - The amount of deferred tax expense (income) relating to the origination and reversal of temporary differences.
    - The amount of deferred tax expense (income) relating to changes in tax rates or the imposition of new taxes.
    - The amount of the benefit arising from a previously unrecognised tax loss, tax credit or temporary difference of a prior period that is used to reduce deferred tax expense.
    - Deferred tax expense arising from the write-down (or reversal of a previous write-down) of a deferred tax asset that has been reviewed at the balance sheet date.
    - The amount of tax expense (income) relating to changes in accounting policies and errors that are included in profit or loss (under IAS 8) because they cannot be accounted for retrospectively.

[IAS 12 para 80].

13.292   The total current and deferred tax relating to items that are charged or credited directly to equity should be disclosed. [IAS 12 para 81(a)]. An example that shows the amount of tax charged directly to equity is provided in Table 13.5.1.

Table 13.5.1 – Disclosure of tax charged directly to equity

BP p.l.c – Annual report – 31 December 2011

18. Taxation (extract)

Tax on profit

	2011	2010	$ million 2009
Current tax			
Charge for the year	**7,477**	6,766	6,045
Adjustment in respect of prior years	**111**	(74)	(300)
	7,588	6,692	5,745
Deferred tax			
Origination and reversal of temporary differences in the current year	**5,664**	(8,157)	2,131
Adjustment in respect of prior years	**(515)**	(36)	489
	5,149	(8,193)	2,620
Tax charge (credit) on profit (loss)	**12,737**	(1,501)	8,365

Tax included in other comprehensive income[a]

	2011	2010	$ million 2009
Current tax	**(10)**	(107)	–
Deferred tax	**(1,649)**	244	(525)
	(1,659)	137	(525)

a See Note 39 for further information.

Tax included directly in equity

	2011	2010	$ million 2009
Current tax	–	(37)	–
Deferred tax	**(7)**	64	(65)
	(7)	27	(65)

13.292.1 The amount of income tax relating to each component of other comprehensive income (including reclassification adjustments) should be disclosed in the statement of comprehensive income or in the notes. [IAS 12 para 81(ab)]. Components of other comprehensive income can be presented on the face of the statement of comprehensive income net of related tax effects; or they can be presented before related tax effects, with one amount shown for the total amount of income tax relating to those components. [IAS 1 paras 90, 91]. This is considered further in chapter 4.

13.292.1.1 'Amendments to IAS 1' was issued in June 2011; and this alters the disclosure required in the statement of comprehensive income. If an entity presents items of other comprehensive income before related tax effects (with the total tax shown separately), it should allocate the tax between the items that might be reclassified later to profit or loss and those that will not be reclassified. [IAS 1 (revised) para 91]. The amendment is effective for annual periods beginning on or after 1 July 2012. This is considered further in chapter 4.

13.292.2 The following disclosures should be made in the case of business combinations:

■ If a business combination (in which the entity is the acquirer) causes a change in the amount recognised for its pre-acquisition deferred tax asset (see para 13.250.1), the amount of that change.

■ If the deferred tax benefits acquired in a business combination are not recognised at the acquisition date but are recognised after the acquisition date (see para 13.249.5), a description of the event or change in circumstances that caused the deferred tax benefits to be recognised.

[IAS 12 para 81(j), (k)].

13.293 The standard does not require the current tax charge (credit) reported in profit or loss to be analysed further between domestic and foreign tax. Entities with significant amounts of foreign tax might find it useful to give an extra analysis in the tax note as shown below:

	C'000	C'000
Domestic tax		
Current tax on income for the period	X	
Adjustments in respect of prior periods	X	
	X	
Double tax relief	X	
		X
Foreign tax		
Current tax on income for the period	X	
Adjustments in respect of prior periods	X	
		X
Current tax expense		X
Deferred tax expense		X
Tax on profit on ordinary activities		X

A non-mandatory format (including some of the disclosure requirements stated in para 13.291) is given in example 2 of appendix B to IAS 12.

13.294 The originating and reversing temporary differences are disclosed as a single figure within the deferred tax expense in profit or loss; this figure should be further analysed by each type of temporary difference and each type of unused tax losses and tax credits (if this is not apparent from the changes in the amounts recognised in the balance sheet). [IAS 12 para 81(g)(ii)]. These temporary differences are likely to include the tax effects of accelerated capital allowances, fair value gains, material provisions, utilisation of unrelieved tax losses and other temporary differences. In practice, the above disclosure will form part of the balance sheet movements of principal types of deferred tax assets and liabilities. So it will be clear from the changes in balance sheet amounts; and it will not usually need to be disclosed as a separate note to the tax expense or income in profit or loss.

13.294.1 An example of an entity disclosing each type of temporary difference and tax losses is given in Table 13.7 (in para 13.301.1).

Discontinued operations

13.295 The amount of tax attributable to discontinued operations should be disclosed; and it should be analysed between the tax expense relating to:

■   The gain or loss on discontinuance.

■   The profit or loss from the ordinary activities of the discontinued operation for the period, together with the corresponding amounts for each prior period presented.

[IAS 12 para 81(h)].

13.295.1 The presentation of tax on discontinued operations is dealt with in chapter 26.

Explanation of the relationship between tax expense and accounting profit

13.296 The standard requires an explanation of the relationship between tax expense and accounting profit. This relationship can be affected by factors including: significant tax-free income and significant disallowables; tax losses utilised; different tax rates in the locations of foreign-based operations; adjustments related to prior years; unrecognised deferred tax; and tax rate changes. An explanation of these matters enables financial statement users to understand whether the relationship between tax expense and accounting profit is unusual; and it helps the users to understand the significant factors that could affect that relationship in the future. The explanation should be in either or both of the following numerical forms:

■   A reconciliation between tax expense (income) and the product of accounting profit multiplied by the applicable tax rate(s); the basis for computing the applicable tax rate(s) should also be disclosed.

■   A reconciliation between the average effective tax rate (tax expense divided by the accounting profit) and the applicable tax rate; the basis for computing the applicable tax rate should also be disclosed.

[IAS 12 paras 81(c), 84].

13.297 IAS 12 requires the *total tax charge* (current and deferred), rather than the *current* tax charge, to be reconciled to the theoretical tax on accounting profit.

UK.13.297.1 FRS 19 includes a requirement to provide a reconciliation to the current tax charge.

13.298 The starting point for preparing the numerical reconciliation (whether in absolute or in percentage terms) is to determine an applicable tax rate. In the context of a single economic entity (that is, the group), it is important to use an applicable tax rate that provides the most meaningful information to financial statement users. The most relevant rate is often the rate applicable in the reporting entity's country. This rate should be used even if some of the group's operations are conducted in other countries. In that situation, the impact of different tax rates applied to profits earned in other countries would appear as a reconciling item. The basis for computing the applicable tax rate should be disclosed (as well as an explanation of changes in the applicable tax rate(s) compared to the previous accounting period). [IAS 12 para 81(d)]. This is because sometimes it may not be possible to determine a meaningful single applicable tax rate (particularly for multi-national groups).

13.299 Another method is to aggregate separate reconciliations prepared using the applicable tax rate in each individual jurisdiction; and then provide a reconciliation from the aggregation to a single applicable tax rate (that is, the reporting entity's rate). Such information would normally be requested as part of the group reporting packs; and it would greatly simplify the process for presenting the tax reconciliation in the consolidated financial statements.

Example – Reconciliation of tax expense

Entity L is a non-operating holding entity incorporated in Luxembourg. It has subsidiaries in Italy, Finland and Brazil. The following table provides information on the statutory tax rate and profit before tax for each member of the group:

The tax charge in the consolidated financial statements is C520.

Country	Statutory tax rate (A)	Profit before tax (B)	Tax at statutory tax rate (A x B)	Tax at difference between Luxembourg rate and statutory rate (A — 25%) × (B)
Luxembourg	25%	20	5	–
Finland	37%	700	259	84
Italy	29%	400	116	16
Brazil	33%	500	165	40
Total		1,620	545	140

Management would prefer to present a reconciliation of monetary amounts rather than a reconciliation of the tax rates. Management could choose to reconcile the tax charge to the tax rate of the parent (entity L) or to reconcile to an aggregate of separate reconciliations for each country.

The following illustrates the two methods:

Reconciliation of tax expense

	Tax rate of parent C	Average tax rate C
Profit before tax	1,620	1,620
Tax at the domestic rate of 25%	405	n/a
Tax calculated at the domestic rates applicable to profits in the country concerned	n/a	545
Income not subject to tax	(50)	(50)
Expenses not deductible for tax purposes	25	25
Effect of different tax rates in countries in which the group operates	140	n/a
Tax charge	520	520

13.299.1 An example of reconciliation using monetary amounts is shown in Table 13.2 (see para 13.274.1); an example using tax rates is shown in Table 13.6:

Table 13.6 – Reconciliation of tax charge

TeliaSonera AB – Annual Report – 31 December 2011

C11. Income Taxes (extract)

Tax items recognized in comprehensive income and directly in equity
Tax items recognized in comprehensive income and directly in equity were distributed as follows.

SEK in million	Jan-Dec 2011	Jan-Dec 2010
Tax items recognized in net income		
Current tax expense relating to current year	–3,404	–5,867
Underprovided or overprovided current tax expense in prior years	–10	–61
Deferred tax expense originated or reversed in current year	–2,505	–569
Recognition of previously unrecognized deferred taxes	527	124
Effect on deferred tax income (+)/expense (–) from changes in tax rates	–310	–1
Total tax expense recognized in net income	**–5,702**	**–6,374**
Tax items recognized in other comprehensive income		
Current tax relating to current year	–26	–913
Deferred tax originated or reversed in current year	31	–23
Total tax recognized in other comprehensive income	**5**	**–936**
Tax items recognized directly in equity		
Current tax related to treasury share repurchase transaction costs	14	–
Total tax recognized directly in equity	**14**	**–**

Pre-tax income was SEK 26,774 million in 2011 and SEK 29,936 million in 2010. The difference between the nominal Swedish income tax rate and the effective tax rate comprises the following components.

Percent	Jan–Dec 2011	Jan–Dec 2010
Swedish income tax rate	26.3	26.3
Effect of higher or lower tax rates in subsidiaries	–1.0	–1.2
Withholding tax on earnings in subsidiaries, associated companies and joint ventures	2.5	2.6
Underprovided or overprovided current tax expense in prior years	0.0	0.2
Recognition of previously unrecognized deferred taxes	–1.9	–0.4
Effect on deferred tax expense from changes in tax rates	1.2	0.0
Income from associated companies and joint ventures	–5.6	–6.9
Current year losses for which no deferred tax asset was recognized	0.8	1.4
Non-deductible expenses	0.3	0.2
Tax-exempt income	–1.3	–0.9
Effective tax rate in net income	**21.3**	**21.3**
Effective tax rate excluding effects from associated companies and joint ventures	*24.8*	*26.0*

13.300   Where a group operates mainly outside its local territory, a third method is to use an average tax rate (weighted in proportion to accounting profits earned in each geographical territory) as the applicable tax rate. This method is not included in the standard, but it could be used – provided the basis for computing the applicable tax rate is disclosed (under IAS 12, para 81(c)).

Example – Determination of 'applicable rate' for a group with significant overseas subsidiaries

Country	Profit	Tax rate	Weighted average	
UK	100	30%	100/2030 × 30% =	1.48
US	600	40%	600/2030 × 40% =	11.82
France	500	35%	500/2030 × 35% =	8.62
Germany	450	38%	450/2030 × 38% =	8.42
Australia	380	33%	380/2030 × 33% =	6.18
Total	2,030		Average rate =	36.52

The average rate of 36.52% should be used in the tax reconciliation. The basis for calculating the rate should also be disclosed (as stated in para 13.296).

13.300.1   Use of a weighted average tax rate method might be appropriate where all the group entities have made a profit. But this method might not provide a meaningful tax rate where some entities within a group have profits and others have losses. For example, the entity might calculate the weighted average tax rate based on absolute values (that is, making all values positive); in that case, the tax rate obtained might appear meaningful, but there will be a reconciling item in the tax reconciliation. On the other hand, the weighted average rate might be calculated based on actual values; even though the theoretical tax expense will be the correct amount, the weighted average tax rate might not be meaningful because it might be higher than any individual rate. So it might not be appropriate to use the weighted average tax rate method in this situation.

Analysis of deferred tax assets and liabilities (balance sheet)

13.301   Deferred tax assets and liabilities (of the current and previous periods) should be analysed by each type of temporary difference and each type of unused tax losses and tax credits. [IAS 12 para 81(g)(i)]. The significant types of temporary difference that generally need to be disclosed separately include: accelerated capital allowances; revaluation of assets; other short-term taxable temporary differences that affect accounting or taxable profit; provisions; and tax losses carried forward. A format for disclosure is given in example 2 of appendix B to IAS 12. The amount of deferred tax income or expense recognised in profit or loss should be similarly analysed (if this is not apparent from the balance sheet movement of each component – see para 13.294). [IAS 12 para 81(g)(ii)].

13.301.1 An example of an entity disclosing each type of temporary difference and tax losses is given in Table 13.7. (Note that comparatives have not been reproduced.)

Table 13.7 – Disclosure of each type of temporary difference and tax losses

Rolls-Royce Holdings plc – Annual report – 31 December 2011

4 *Taxation* (extract)

The analysis of the deferred tax position is as follows:

	At January 1, 2011 £m	Recognised in income statement £m	Recognised in OCI £m	Recognised in equity £m	Acquisition of businesses £m	Transferred to assets held for sale £m	Exchange differences £m	At December 31, 2011 £m
Intangible assets	(282)	(9)	–	–	–	46	2	(243)
Property, plant and equipment	(150)	16	–	–	–	–	(1)	(135)
Other temporary differences	(64)	(3)	(1)	6	(3)	–	4	(61)
Amounts recoverable on contracts	(229)	(21)	–	–	–	–	–	(250)
Pensions and other post-retirement scheme benefits	263	(111)	(53)	–	–	–	–	99
Foreign exchange and commodity financial assets and liabilities	94	27	–	–	–	–	–	121
Losses	317	11	–	–	–	–	–	328
Advance corporation tax	64	–	–	–	–	–	–	64
	13	(90)	(54)	6	(3)	46	5	(77)

13.301.2 The standard requires an analysis of each type of temporary difference. Where a temporary difference comprises the net amount of deferred tax assets and liabilities that have met the criteria for offset (see para 13.284), we believe that the disclosure applies to the net position for that temporary difference.

Example – Analysis of each type of temporary difference

At its year end, entity A has property, plant and equipment (PPE) with carrying amounts, tax bases and temporary differences outlined below. The differences arise because the assets are deductible for tax purposes in a way that differs from the depreciation recognised for accounting purposes.

Class of PPE	Carrying amount C'000	Tax base C'000	Temporary difference C'000	DT asset/ (liability) @ 30% C'000
Property	100	75	25	(7.5)
Cars	50	65	(15)	4.5
Office equipment	20	10	10	(3.0)
Total	170	150	20	(6.0)

At an effective tax rate of 30%, the property and office equipment give rise to a deferred tax liability of C10,500; and the cars give rise to a deferred tax asset of C4,500. Entity A can use the deferred tax asset to offset the deferred tax liabilities; so the entity discloses the net deferred tax liability position of C6,000 on the face of the balance sheet.

Deferred tax assets and liabilities should be analysed by each type of temporary difference. [IAS 21 para 81(g)].

In respect of the above amounts, we do not believe that IAS 12 requires a gross presentation, because the deferred tax noted in the table above relates to the same type of temporary difference (that is, differences between depreciation for tax and accounting purposes).

Entity A has the right to offset the deferred tax asset and liability (and thus presents the net position in the balance sheet). The amount of the net position relating to the difference between the carrying amount and tax base of PPE is C6,000; that amount should be disclosed as a component of the total deferred tax liability recognised.

Unrecognised temporary differences

13.302 Disclosures are also required in respect of unrecognised temporary differences, such as:

■ The amount (and expiry date, if any) of deductible temporary differences, unused tax losses and unused tax credits for which no deferred tax has been provided. [IAS 12 para 81(e)]. Although not required by the standard, it might be helpful to explain the circumstances in which the deferred tax asset would be recovered.

■ The total amount of temporary differences associated with investments in subsidiaries, branches and associates and interests in joint ventures for which deferred tax liabilities have not been recognised. [IAS 12 para 81(f)].

13.303 For investments in subsidiaries, branches, associates and interests in joint ventures, disclosure is required of the total amount of temporary differences (rather than the deferred tax assets and liabilities associated with such temporary differences). But the standard encourages disclosure of the deferred tax amounts. This is because it might sometimes be difficult (particularly for foreign investments) to quantify the future tax payable in view of a number of factors (for example, the tax laws and tax rates in force, the intended timing of future remittances, and the terms of any tax treaty that might exist between the two countries). [IAS 12 para 87].

13.303.1 For an example of an entity disclosing unrecognised temporary differences on subsidiaries and joint ventures, see Table 13.8. The example also shows the amount of the potential deferred tax (see para 13.303). For an example of disclosure of tax losses and deductible temporary differences for which no deferred tax has been recognised, see Table 13.8.1. That example also shows unrecognised temporary differences on subsidiaries, associates and joint ventures.

Table 13.8 – Disclosure of unrecognised temporary differences on subsidiaries and joint ventures (the group has no significant associates)

MTU Aero Engines Holding AG – Annual report – 31 December 2011

38. DEFERRED TAX LIABILITIES (extract)

DEFERRED TAX LIABILITIES FOR TAXABLE TEMPORARY DIFFERENCES ARISING FROM INVESTMENTS IN SUBSIDIARIES AND JOINT VENTURES

In accordance with IAS 12, deferred tax liabilities were not recognized for temporary differences amounting to € 147.2 million (2010 adjusted: € 109.0 million) that arose in connection with investments in subsidiaries and joint ventures. If these differences were to lead to the creation of deferred tax liabilities, they would result in a tax liability amounting to € 5.1 million (2010 adjusted: € 3.5 million), based on the current provisions of Section 8b of the German Corporate Income Tax Act (KStG).

Table 13.8.1 – Disclosure of unused tax losses and of unrecognised temporary differences on subsidiaries, associates and joint ventures

Anglo American plc – Annual report – 31 December 2011

27. DEFERRED TAX (extract)

The Group has the following balances in respect of which no deferred tax asset has been recognised:

US$ million	2011 Tax losses – revenue	Tax losses – capital	Other temporary differences	Total	2010 Tax losses – revenue	Tax losses – capital	Other temporary differences	Total
Expiry date								
Within one year	–	–	–	–	–	–	–	–
Greater than one year, less than five years	–	–	–	–	15	–	–	15
Greater than five years	111	–	–	111	84	–	–	84
No expiry date	3,082	1,067	403	4,552	3,023	1,252	8	4,283
	3,193	1,067	403	4,663	3,122	1,252	8	4,382

The Group also has unused tax credits of $18 million (2010: $84 million) for which no deferred tax asset is recognised in the balance sheet. None of these credits expire within five years.

No deferred tax has been recognised in respect of temporary differences associated with investments in subsidiaries, branches and associates and interests in joint ventures, where the Group is in a position to control the timing of the reversal of the temporary differences and it is probable that such differences will not reverse in the foreseeable future. The aggregate amount of temporary differences associated with such investments in subsidiaries, branches and associates and interests in joint ventures is represented by the contribution of those investments to the Group's retained earnings and amounted to $25,876 million (2010: $20,277 million).

Tax consequences of dividends

13.304   An entity generally recognises any tax consequences of the payment of a dividend at the time when the dividend is recognised as a liability in the financial statements (see para 13.175 onwards). But the amount of income tax arising on dividends that were proposed or declared before the financial statements were authorised for issue (but are not recognised as a liability in the financial statements) should be disclosed. [IAS 12 para 81(i)].

13.305   Where tax rates vary between distributed and undistributed profits, the nature of the potential tax consequences (that would result from the payment of dividends to shareholders) should also be disclosed. In making this disclosure, an entity should also disclose:

■   The important features of the tax systems and the factors that will affect the amount of the potential income tax consequences of dividends. [IAS 12 para 87A].

■   The amount of the potential tax consequences arising from the payment of dividends to shareholders (where it is practical to determine such amounts).

[IAS 12 para 82A]. For example, in a consolidated group, a parent and some of its subsidiaries might have paid income taxes at a higher rate on undistributed profits; but they are aware of the amount of the tax refund that would arise if future dividends are paid at the lower rate. In that situation, the refundable amount should be disclosed. [IAS 12 para 87B].

■ Whether there are any potential tax consequences that it is not practical to determine. [IAS 12 para 82A]. This could arise where the entity operates a large number of foreign subsidiaries and it would not be practicable to compute the tax consequences arising from the payment of dividends to shareholders. In that situation, an entity simply discloses that fact (as stated above). In the parent's separate financial statements (if any), the disclosure of the potential tax consequences should relate to the parent's retained earnings. [IAS 12 para 87B].

Deferred tax asset of loss-making entities

13.306 Where an entity has incurred a loss in the current or a preceding period and the recovery of the deferred tax asset depends on future taxable profits in excess of those arising from the reversals of existing taxable temporary differences, the amount of the deferred tax asset and the nature of the evidence supporting its recognition should be disclosed. [IAS 12 para 82]. See further paragraph 13.146.

13.307 Recognition of the deferred tax asset should be supported by evidence showing why future profits are likely be available against which the deferred tax assets can be recovered (see further para 13.133 onwards). The evidence might also include tax-planning strategies (see para 13.136 onwards). Any statements made to explain how the asset would be recovered should be balanced, realistic and consistent with the other disclosures made in the financial statements (particularly in the management commentary). References to any profit forecasts etc should be avoided as far as possible.

Estimation uncertainty

613.307.1 *"An entity shall disclose information about the assumptions it makes about the future, and other major sources of estimation uncertainty at the end of the reporting period, that have a significant risk of resulting in a material adjustment to the carrying amounts of assets and liabilities within the next financial year. In respect of those assets and liabilities, the notes shall include details of: (a) their nature, and (b) their carrying amount as at the end of the reporting period."* [IAS 1 para 125].

13.307.2 The disclosures required in respect of estimation uncertainty do not relate to those required in respect of key judgements in applying accounting policies (see further para 13.277.2). The estimation uncertainty disclosures deal with situations where the entity has incomplete or imperfect information (often relating to the future).

13.307.3 Areas that could require disclosure in respect of estimation uncertainty are:

■ Status of negotiations with tax authorities.

■ Assessing the probabilities that sufficient future taxable profits will be available to enable deferred tax assets resulting from deductible temporary differences and tax losses to be recognised.

■ Other assumptions about the recoverability of deferred tax assets (see also para 13.306).

13.307.4 Examples of disclosure in respect of estimation uncertainty on tax are given in Tables 13.9 and 13.10.

Table 13.9 – Estimation uncertainty in respect of tax

Bayer AG – Annual report – 31 December 2011

4. Basic principles, methods and critical accounting estimates (extract 1)

In preparing the consolidated financial statements, the management has to make certain assumptions and estimates that may substantially impact the presentation of the Group's financial position and / or results of operations.

Such estimates, assumptions or the exercise of discretion mainly relate to the useful life of noncurrent assets, the discounted cash flows used for impairment testing and purchase price allocations, and the recognition of provisions, including those for litigation-related expenses, pensions and other benefits, taxes, environmental compliance and remediation costs, sales allowances, product liability and guarantees. Essential estimates and assumptions that may affect reporting in the various item categories of the financial statements are described in the following sections of this note. Estimates are based on historical experience and other assumptions that are considered reasonable under given circumstances. They are continually reviewed but may vary from the actual values.

4. Basic principles, methods and critical accounting estimates (extract 2)

OTHER PROVISIONS (extract)

Uncertainties exist with respect to the interpretation of complex tax regulations and the amount and timing of future taxable income. Given the wide range of international business relationships and the long-term nature and complexity of existing contractual agreements, differences arising between the actual results and the assumptions made, or future changes to such assumptions, could necessitate adjustments to tax income and expense in future periods. The Group establishes provisions for taxes, based on reasonable estimates, for liabilities to the tax authorities of the respective countries that are uncertain as to their amount and the probability of their occurrence. The amount of such provisions is based on various factors, such as experience with previous tax audits and differing legal interpretations by the taxable entity and the responsible tax authority.

Table 13.10 – Estimation uncertainty in respect of tax

Vodafone Group Plc – Annual report – 31 March 2012

Critical accounting estimates (extract)

Taxation

The Group's tax charge on ordinary activities is the sum of the total current and deferred tax charges. The calculation of the Group's total tax charge necessarily involves a degree of estimation and judgement in respect of certain items whose tax treatment cannot be finally determined until resolution has been reached with the relevant tax authority or, as appropriate, through a formal legal process. The final resolution of some of these items may give rise to material profits, losses and/or cash flows.

The complexity of the Group's structure makes the degree of estimation and judgement more challenging. The resolution of issues is not always within the control of the Group and it is often dependent on the efficiency of the legal processes in the relevant taxing jurisdictions in which the Group operates. Issues can, and often do, take many years to resolve. Payments in respect of tax liabilities for an accounting period result from payments on account and on the final resolution of open items. As a result there can be substantial differences between the tax charge in the consolidated income statement and tax payments.

Recognition of deferred tax assets

The recognition of deferred tax assets is based upon whether it is more likely than not that sufficient and suitable taxable profits will be available in the future against which the reversal of temporary differences can be deducted. To determine the future taxable profits, reference is made to the latest available profit forecasts. Where the temporary differences are related to losses, relevant tax law is considered to determine the availability of the losses to offset against the future taxable profits.

Significant items on which the Group has exercised accounting judgement include recognition of a deferred tax asset in respect of losses in Germany (see note 6 of the consolidated financial statements) and the recognition of a deferred tax asset in respect of losses in Luxembourg (see note 6 to the consolidated financial statements). The amounts recognised in the consolidated financial statements in respect of each matter are derived from the Group's best estimation and judgement as described above.

Recognition therefore involves judgement regarding the future financial performance of the particular legal entity or tax group in which the deferred tax asset has been recognised.

Historical differences between forecast and actual taxable profits have not resulted in material adjustments to the recognition of deferred tax assets.

13.307.5 Disclosure of estimation uncertainty is dealt with in chapter 4.

Tax-related contingencies

13.308 It is quite common for an entity to have tax assessments of earlier years still open and disputed by the tax authorities. In those situations, contingent liabilities and assets might well arise. The entity should disclose the following information (consistent with IAS 37) on these tax-related contingencies: the nature of the contingency, an indication of the uncertainty affecting whether the further tax will become payable and an estimate of the financial effect. [IAS 12 para 88].

13.308.1 An example of an entity disclosing contingent liabilities for taxation is given in Table 13.11.

Table 13.11 – Contingent liabilities for taxation

Vodafone Group Plc – Annual report – 31 March 2012

29. Contingent liabilities (extract)

Legal proceedings (extract)

Vodafone India Limited ('VIL') and VIHBV each received notices in August 2007 and September 2007, respectively, from the Indian tax authority alleging potential liability in connection with alleged failure by VIHBV to deduct withholding tax from consideration paid to the Hutchison Telecommunications International Limited group ('HTIL') in respect of HTIL's gain on its disposal to VIHBV of its interests in a wholly-owned subsidiary that indirectly holds interests in VIL. Following the receipt of such notices, VIL and VIHBV each filed writs seeking orders that their respective notices be quashed and that the Indian tax authority take no further steps under the notices. Initial hearings were held before the Bombay High Court and, in the case of VIHBV, the Bombay High Court admitted the writ for final hearing in June 2008. In December 2008, the Bombay High Court dismissed VIHBV's writ. VIHBV subsequently filed a special leave petition to the Supreme Court to appeal the Bombay High Court's dismissal of the writ. On 23 January 2009 the Supreme Court referred the question of the tax authority's jurisdiction to seek to pursue tax back to the tax authority for adjudication on the facts, with permission granted to VIHBV to appeal that decision back to the Bombay High Court should VIHBV disagree with the tax authority's findings. On 30 October 2009 VIHBV received a notice from the tax authority requiring VIHBV to show cause as to why it believed that the Indian tax authority did not have competent jurisdiction to proceed against VIHBV for the default of non-deduction of withholding tax from consideration paid to HTIL. VIHBV provided a response on 29 January 2010. On 31 May 2010 VIHBV received an order from the Indian tax authority confirming their view that they did have jurisdiction to proceed against VIHBV, as well as a further notice alleging that VIHBV should be treated as the agent of HTIL for the purpose of recovering tax on the transaction. VIHBV appealed this ruling to the Bombay High Court, as well as filed a new writ petition against the notice seeking to treat it as an agent of HTIL. On 8 September 2010 the Bombay High Court ruled that the tax authority had jurisdiction to decide whether the transaction or some part of the transaction could be taxable in India. VIHBV appealed this decision to the Supreme Court on 14 September 2010. A hearing before the Supreme Court took place on 27 September 2010 at which time the Supreme Court noted the appeal and asked the Indian tax authority to quantify any liability. On 22 October 2010 the Indian tax authority quantified the alleged tax liability and issued a demand for payment of INR 112.2 billion (£1.6 billion) of tax and interest. VIHBV contested the amount of such demand both on the basis of the calculation and on the basis that no tax was due in any event. On 15 November 2010 VIHBV was asked to make a deposit with the Supreme Court of INR 25 billion (£356 million) and provide a guarantee for INR 85 billion (£1.2 billion) pending final adjudication of the case, which request it duly complied with. On 23 March 2011 the Indian tax authority also initiated proceedings against VIHBV to impose a penalty of 100% of the alleged tax liability. VIHBV challenged this demand to the Indian Commissioner of Income Tax and filed a writ petition in the Bombay High Court. The Supreme Court heard the appeal on the issue of jurisdiction as well as on the challenge to quantification during July and August 2011. In January 2012 the Supreme Court handed down its judgment, holding that VIHBV's interpretation of the Income Tax Act 1961 was correct, that the transaction was not taxable in India and that, consequently, VIHBV had no obligation to withhold tax from consideration paid to HTIL in respect of the transaction. The Supreme Court quashed the relevant notices and demands issued to VIHBV in respect of withholding tax. Separate proceedings taken against VIHBV to seek to treat it as an agent of HTIL in respect of its alleged tax on the same transaction, as well as on the penalties for the alleged failure to have withheld such taxes, are still technically pending and awaiting adjudication by the Supreme Court and the Indian Commissioner of Income Tax, and are expected to be quashed as a result of the Supreme

---

Court decision. Similarly, VEL's writ to quash the relevant notice is also pending, and should be decided upon at the same time as VIHBV's writ. In March 2012 the Indian government introduced proposed legislation (Finance Bill 2012) which seeks to overturn the Supreme Court judgment in VIHBV's favour with retrospective effect. The Finance Bill 2012 has been passed by both Houses of the Indian Parliament and awaits Presidential approval which is expected imminently after which the Bill will become law. VIHBV is considering domestic (Indian) and international remedies available to it. VIHBV believes that neither it nor any other member of the Group is liable for such withholding tax, or is liable to be made an agent of HTIL; however, the Finance Bill 2012 introduces substantial uncertainty, and there can be no assurance that any outcome will be favourable to VIHBV or the Group.

The Group did not carry any provision in respect of this litigation at 31 March 2012 or at previous reporting dates, as it believed it had no obligation to withhold tax on the acquisition under applicable Indian law at the time of the transaction.

Post balance sheet changes in tax rates

13.309 IAS 12 requires the use of tax rates and laws that have been substantively enacted by the balance sheet date (rather than by the date when the financial statements are authorised for issue); this means that information received after the year end about changes in tax rates and laws is not an adjusting post balance sheet event. But changes in tax rates or laws enacted or announced after the balance sheet date that have a significant effect on current and deferred tax assets and liabilities should be disclosed under IAS 10. [IAS 10 para 22(h); IAS 12 para 88].

Table 13.12 – Disclosure of tax rate change, announced but not substantively enacted

Tesco PLC – Annual Report – 25 February 2012

Note 6 Taxation (extract)

The Finance Act 2011 included legislation to reduce the main rate of corporation tax from 27% to 26% from 1 April 2011 and to 25% from 1 April 2012. The reduction from 27% to 25% was substantively enacted at the balance sheet date and has therefore been reflected in these Group financial statements.

In addition to the changes in rates of corporation tax disclosed above, a number of further changes to the UK corporation tax system were announced in both the March 2011 and March 2012 UK Budget Statements. A resolution passed by Parliament on 26 March 2012 reduced the main rate of corporation tax to 24% from 1 April 2012. Legislation to reduce the main rate of corporation tax from 24% to 23% from 1 April 2013 is expected to be included in the Finance Act 2012. Further reductions to the main rate are proposed to reduce the rate to 22% by 1 April 2014. None of these expected rate reductions had been substantively enacted at the balance sheet date and are therefore not reflected in these Group financial statements.

The effect of the changes enacted by Parliament on 26 March 2012 to reduce the corporation tax rate from 25% to 24%, with effect from 1 April 2012, is to reduce the deferred tax liability provided at the balance sheet date by £35m (£53m increase in profit and £18m decrease in other comprehensive income).

The proposed reductions of the main rate of corporation tax by 1% per annum to 22% by 1 April 2014 are expected to be enacted separately each year. The overall effect of the further changes from 24% to 22%, if these applied to the deferred tax balance at the balance sheet date, would be to reduce the deferred tax liability by £70m (being £35m recognised in 2013 and £35m recognised in 2014).

Cash flows relating to taxes on income

13.310 Cash flows from taxes on income should be separately disclosed and classified as cash flows from operating activities (unless they can be specifically identified with financing and investing activities). [IAS 7 para 35]. These issues are considered further in chapter 30.

Groups of entities

Group relief

UK.13.310.1 Trading profits and losses arising in the same accounting period might be offset for tax purposes between companies in the same group by way of group relief (subject to meeting detailed provisions in the UK tax legislation). For example, a subsidiary that incurred a loss during an accounting period might surrender that loss to another group member that made a profit during the same accounting period. The profitable subsidiary (the claimant company) might be able to pay to the loss-making subsidiary (the surrendering company) any amount up to the full amount of the loss surrendered by way of group relief; without any tax impact in either company.

UK.13.310.2 The group can decide whether payment should or should not be made; and its decision does not affect the granting of the relief. However, non-payment or underpayment for group relief received could be undesirable if there are non-controlling interests in the company; this is because non-controlling shareholders' interests will be impaired if a company surrenders its losses (for group relief purposes) without receiving an adequate compensation payment. Likewise, overpayment for group relief could be undesirable if there are non-controlling interests in the receiving company. So it is advisable to make a fair payment where there are non-controlling interests in the surrendering or receiving company.

UK.13.310.3 A payment to the surrendering company might take one of the following forms:

■ The amount of tax saved by reason of group relief. In this situation, the claimant company pays (as group relief) what it would have paid as tax at the applicable rate in force; and the surrendering company receives the benefit of losses relieved at the same time.

■ Any other amount (up to a maximum of the gross amount of the loss surrendered) by way of group relief. For example, it could be less than the amount of tax savings; or it could be more than the amount of tax savings but less than the gross amount of the losses surrendered. Any part of a payment in excess of the tax relief on the loss surrendered by way of group relief (for example, to finance the balance of the underlying loss) is not a payment in respect of group relief; and it should not be dealt with as such in the financial statements.

UK.13.310.4 The decision whether or not to make payment for group relief gives rise to different accounting considerations in the financial statements of the claimant and surrendering companies. The tax computations of two wholly owned fellow subsidiary undertakings, company X and company Y, for the year ended 31 December 20X4 are given below; these show the impact of group relief made with or without payment. The tax rate for both companies is 30% and is expected to remain constant for the foreseeable future.

Tax computations	Company X 31 December 20X4	Company Y 31 December 20X4
	£	£
Profit (loss) before tax	(90,000)	180,000
Temporary differences	(10,000)	(30,000)
	(100,000)	150,000
Group relief	100,000	(100,000)
Taxable profit (loss) chargeable to tax	–	50,000
Tax @ 30%	–	15,000

No payments made for group relief

UK.13.310.5 In surrendering company X's financial statements, no credit can be taken in the income statement; this is because losses surrendered where no payment is received are of no value to the company. But part of the losses surrendered might relate to temporary differences (as shown in the example). In this situation, a deferred tax liability should be set up (with a corresponding debit to the income statement tax charge, even if there is no current tax charge). The surrendering company has lost the benefit of the losses that could otherwise have been utilised against future trading profits created by the reversal of the temporary difference. As a result, the losses cannot be taken into account in the deferred tax calculation.

UK.13.310.6 Where the surrendering company has been advised by its parent to surrender losses without receiving payment, the taxation note to the income statement should disclose this fact and the financial impact. An appropriate note is included in the income statement presentation below.

Company X – The surrendering company		31 December 20X4
		£
Loss on ordinary activities before taxation		(90,000)
Taxation:		
Tax @ 30%		–
Deferred tax	3,000	(3,000)
Loss for the financial year		(93,000)

Note on taxation:
The company has surrendered the benefit of tax losses amounting to £100,000 to a fellow subsidiary undertaking without receiving any payment. Therefore, no tax losses are available for carry-forward and the company has provided deferred tax amounting to £3,000 in respect of temporary differences of £10,000 included in the losses surrendered.

UK.13.310.7 Different considerations apply in the claimant company's financial statements. Group relief received without payment is effectively a gift (as far as the claimant is concerned). Because the relief is included in the claimant's taxable profit, it will reduce (or sometimes completely eliminate) the claimant's liability to current tax. So there could be a significant difference between the actual effective tax rate (tax charge as a percentage of profit before tax) and the prevailing tax rate. In this situation, the difference needs to be explained through the reconciliation of the tax charge (see para 13.296). The presentation in the claimant company's income statement will be as follows:

Company Y – The claimant company		31 December 20X4
	£	£
Profit on ordinary activities before taxation		180,000
Taxation:		
Tax @ 30%	15,000	
Deferred tax	9,000	24,000
Profit on ordinary activities after taxation		156,000
Effective tax rate		13.00%

Note on taxation:
The tax charge for the year has been reduced by £30,000 because of losses surrendered by a fellow subsidiary undertaking. No payment for this surrender is to be made by the company.

The explanation can also be provided by way of a reconciliation between the actual rate of 30% and the effective rate of 13% as follows:

Actual tax rate	30%
Group relief received without payment	(17)%
Effective tax rate	13%

Workings:
Group relief received £30,000 ÷ £180,000 = 17%.

Payments made for group relief

UK.13.310.8 Where a payment passes between the companies concerned, the accounting treatment in the financial statements of the claimant and surrendering companies will depend on the nature of the payment (as shown in the situations discussed below).

Payment represents the amount of tax saving

UK.13.310.9   The payment received or receivable could be credited in the surrendering company's financial statements as part of the tax charge (with a corresponding debit to cash or amounts receivable from group companies). The treatment is similar to tax repaid by the taxation authority. In some situations, it might not be appropriate to take credit until the group's tax affairs have been finalised and the group election has been made. Alternatively, the view can be taken that the payment does not relate to taxation because it has been received from another group company rather than from the taxation authority. In this case, the benefit received is a contribution to the company from another group company on behalf of the parent; and it is reflected as a transaction in equity. This will be a matter of policy choice for the entity. In either case, appropriate wording should be included in the note on taxation (see below).

Example 1 – Payment included within equity

Company X – The surrendering company	31 December 20X4	
	£	£
Loss on ordinary activities before taxation		(90,000)
Taxation	(3,000)	(3,000)
Deferred taxation		
Loss for the financial year		(93,000)

Note on taxation:
The company has surrendered the benefit of tax losses to another group company for a consideration of £30,000, which will be receivable on 30 September 20X5. This contribution has been reflected within equity as a transaction with another group company on behalf of the parent. No tax losses are, therefore, available for carry-forward, and the company has provided deferred tax amounting to £3,000 in respect of temporary differences of £10,000 included in the losses surrendered.

Example 2 – Payment included within taxation credit

	31 December 20X4	
	£	£
Loss on ordinary activities before taxation		(90,000)
Taxation:		
Amount receivable from a fellow subsidiary in respect of group relief	30,000	
Deferred taxation	(3,000)	27,000
Loss for the financial year		(63,000)

Note on taxation:
The company has surrendered the benefit of tax losses to another group company for a consideration of £30,000, which will be receivable on 30 September 20X5. No tax losses are, therefore, available for carry-forward and the company has provided deferred tax amounting to £3,000 in respect of temporary differences of £10,000 included in the losses surrendered.

UK.13.310.10 The claimant company should treat the payment in a similar way to the surrendering company: either as part of the tax charge (to bring this into proper relationship with the profits – but suitably described as payment made for group relief); or in equity as a transaction with a group company (as described above). So the presentation is similar to the example above.

Example 1 – Receipt included within equity

Company Y – The claimant company

	31 December 20X4	
	£	£
Profit on ordinary activities before taxation		180,000
Taxation:	15,000	
Tax @ 30%		
Deferred tax	9,000	24,000
		156,000

Note on taxation:
The taxation payable for the year has been reduced by £30,000 because of group relief received from a fellow subsidiary for which a payment of £30,000 will be made on 30 September 20X5. This payment has been reflected within equity as a transaction with another group company on behalf of the parent.

Example 2 – Receipt included within taxation charge

	31 December 20X4	
	£	£
Profit on ordinary activities before taxation		180,000
Taxation:		
Tax @ 30%	15,000	
Amount payable to a fellow subsidiary in respect of tax saved by group relief	30,000	
Deferred tax	9,000	54,000
Profit on ordinary activities after taxation		126,000

Note on taxation:
The tax payable for the year has been reduced by £30,000, because of group relief received from a fellow subsidiary for which a payment of £30,000 will be made on 30 September 20X5.

Payment is an amount other than the amount of the tax saving

UK.13.310.11 The amount paid by the receiving company to the surrendering company might sometimes be different to the amount of the tax saving. Where the group relief payment is less than the amount of the tax saving, it can be treated in either of the ways noted above (that is, where payment is made for the full amount of the tax saving).

UK.13.310.12 Where the amount paid is more than the amount of the tax saving, the excess amount is not a payment for tax; and so it should not be included in the taxation balance in the income statement. Management can choose (as a matter of policy) to recognise the amount of the tax saving either in the tax charge or in equity (as described above). Any excess payment above the amount of the tax saving should be recognised in equity.

UK.13.310.13 Where the group relief position and group election for the current year are not finalised by the time the financial statements are approved, a payment for group relief can be brought into account in a later year; in this case, the payment should be appropriately described (depending upon its nature) as set out in the examples above; and words should be added to indicate that it relates to previous years. If the tax relief relating to the payment is brought into account at the same time, that also should be appropriately described.

Chapter 14

Earnings per share

Chapter 14

Earnings per share

Introduction

14.1 Earnings per share (EPS) is a ratio that is widely used by financial analysts, investors and others to gauge a company's profitability and to value its shares. Its purpose is to indicate how effective a company has been in using the resources provided by the ordinary shareholders (described as ordinary equity holders in IAS 33). The allocation of earnings accruing to other providers of finance, such as preference shareholders is a prior charge and is often fixed. Therefore, the income remaining after making allocations to those parties is attributable to ordinary shareholders. This amount, when presented on the face of the profit and loss account on a pence per share basis, assists the ordinary shareholders to gauge the company's current net earnings and changes in its net earnings from period to period. It can, therefore, be relevant as a measure of company performance and in evaluating management's effectiveness. Another reason for the popularity of EPS is that it forms the basis for calculating the 'price-earnings ratio', which is a standard stock market indicator. Price-earnings ratios relating to both past and prospective profits are widely used by investors and analysts in valuing shares.

14.2 EPS is simply a ratio of the numerator – earnings measured in terms of profits available to ordinary shareholders – to the denominator – the number of ordinary shares. Therefore, it is very simple in concept, but it is the determination of the numerator and, in particular, the denominator that can make the calculation of this ratio rather complex in practice. Also if the ratio is to be meaningful it must be calculated on a similar basis for every entity so as to facilitate comparisons between different accounting periods for the same entity and between different entities in the same period.

[The next paragraph is 14.40.]

Objectives and scope of IAS 33

Objectives

14.40 IAS 33 specifies the way in which earnings per share data should be calculated, presented and disclosed in the financial statements of entities. In doing so, it focuses primarily on determining the number of shares to be included in the denominator of the earnings per share calculation. [IAS 33 para 1].

14.41 Although it is accepted that earnings per share data may have limitations because of the different accounting policies used for determining 'earnings', a consistently calculated denominator will improve the comparison of the performance of different entities in the same period and of the same entity in different accounting periods. Furthermore, a denominator calculated in accordance with international consensus will go a long way in enhancing global comparison of earnings per share data in spite of different national methods for determining 'earnings'.

Scope

14.42 The standard applies to entities whose ordinary shares or potential ordinary shares (for example, convertible debt, warrants etc) are publicly traded. [IAS 33 para 2]. Therefore, entities whose securities are listed on a recognised stock exchange (for example, London Stock Exchange, Luxembourg Stock Exchange, NASDAQ) or are otherwise publicly traded, will have to calculate earnings per share data in accordance with the standard. Furthermore, entities that file or are in the process of filing financial statements with a securities commission or other regulatory body for purposes of issuing ordinary shares (that is, not private placements) are also required to comply with the standard. [IAS 33 para 2].

14.43 When both the parent's separate and consolidated financial statements are presented, the disclosures are required only on the basis of consolidated information. Users of the financial statements of a parent are normally concerned with, and need information on, the results of operations of the group as a whole. Where an entity chooses voluntarily to present earnings per share based on its entity financial statements as well as earnings per share based on the consolidated financial statements, the entity earnings per share figures may be shown only on the face of the entity statement of comprehensive income (or income statement, if presented). They must not be shown in the consolidated financial statements. [IAS 33 para 4, 4A].

14.44 Entities whose securities are not publicly traded are not required to disclose earnings per share data because, generally, they have a smaller number of ordinary shareholders. However, where such entities choose to disclose earnings per share data, to maintain comparability in financial reporting, they should comply with the standard's provisions. [IAS 33 para 3]. Such entities are likely to be those that intend to establish a track record before seeking entry to the public market at a future date.

[The next paragraph is 14.46.]

Basic earnings per share

Measurement

14.46 Entities that fall within the standard's scope must calculate basic (and diluted) EPS for the profit or loss attributable to the parent entity's ordinary equity holders. Basic (and diluted) EPS should also be calculated for profit or loss from continuing operations if this is presented. [IAS 33 para 9]. Where an entity has no operations that qualify as discontinued under IFRS 5, the profit or loss for the year will all be attributable to continuing operations and so calculation of an additional EPS figure for continuing operations will be unnecessary. Where an entity has operations that qualify as discontinued under IFRS 5, however, it has to give separate disclosure of the results of such operations. IAS 33 then requires the basic (and diluted) EPS for profit or loss attributable to continuing operations to be calculated. The standard requires disclosure of basic and diluted EPS for profit or loss from continuing operations and profit or loss for the year, for each class of ordinary shares that has a different right to share in profit for the period – see 'Presentation and disclosure' from paragraph 14.173 below. The following paragraphs describe the EPS calculation for profit or loss for the period attributable to ordinary equity holders, but the principles are the same for calculating EPS for profit or loss from continuing and discontinued operations.

14.47 Basic EPS should be calculated by dividing the profit or loss for the period attributable to the parent entity's ordinary equity holders by the weighted average number of ordinary shares outstanding during the period. [IAS 33 para 10].

14.48 The term 'ordinary share' is defined as an equity instrument that is subordinate to all other classes of equity instrument. An equity instrument is any contract that evidences a residual interest in the assets of an entity after deducting all of its liabilities. [IAS 33 para 5; IAS 32 para 11].

14.49 Ordinary shares participate in profit only after other types of shares such as preference shares have participated. [IAS 33 para 6]. Indeed preference shares that provide for mandatory redemption by the issuer for a fixed or determinable amount at a fixed or determinable future date or that give the holder the right to require such redemption are treated as liabilities under IAS 32. [IAS 32 para 18(a)]. An entity may have more than one class of ordinary share (see further para 14.59 below). Ordinary shares of the same class will have the same rights to receive dividends. [IAS 33 para 6].

14.50 The computation of the EPS figure requires a calculation of the earnings as the numerator and the relevant number of ordinary shares as the denominator. If no adjustments are required to the numerator or the denominator, the profit or loss attributable to the ordinary equity holders and the relevant number of ordinary shares can be obtained directly from the financial statements and the figure computed. However, in practice the numerator or the denominator or both may need to be adjusted for the reasons discussed in the paragraphs that follow. The circumstances in which such adjustments should be made are considered in the paragraphs that follow.

Computation of earnings

14.51 For the purposes of calculating basic EPS, the profit or loss from continuing operations and the profit or loss for the period attributable to the parent entity's ordinary equity holders are the profit or loss after tax and non-controlling interest and after adjusting for the after tax effects of preference dividends, differences arising on settlement of preference shares and other similar effects of preference shares classified as equity under IAS 32. [IAS 33 paras 12, A1]. In the absence of any preference shares, it is relatively simple to calculate the earnings figure for EPS purposes. However, where the entity has preference shares in issue, some further adjustments as stated above may be necessary. The ways in which such adjustments are likely to affect earnings for the purposes of calculating basic EPS are considered below. There is no requirement to compute 'Comprehensive earnings per share', but this information could be provided as supplementary information (see para 14.187).

Preference dividends

14.52   Where an entity has preference shares in issue, those shares will be classified as financial liabilities or equity under IAS 32, depending on the terms of the shares. Where preference shares are classified as liabilities in accordance with IAS 32 (see para 14.49 above) any dividends or other appropriations in respect of such preference shares (for example, a premium payable on redemption) will be treated as finance costs in arriving at profit or loss for the period. [IAS 32 paras 35, 36]. However, where preference shares are classified as equity, any dividends and other appropriations would be debited directly to equity and an adjustment is, therefore, needed to deduct it from the profit for the period to arrive at the profit attributable to ordinary equity holders for the purpose of calculating EPS. [IAS 33 para 12]. Whether the preference shares are treated as liabilities or as equity, the calculation of amounts of dividend and other appropriations and adjustments attributable to such shares is the same, and in both cases the amounts are deducted to arrive at the profit attributable to ordinary equity holders for the purpose of calculating basic EPS.

14.53   Where preference shares carry the right to a fixed dividend, then those dividends can either be cumulative or non-cumulative. If the preference dividends are cumulative, the dividend for the period should be taken into account, whether or not it has been declared. [IAS 33 para 14(b)]. Thus, in a year in which the company is unable to pay or declare a cumulative preference dividend, because of insufficient distributable profits (for example, the company has accumulated losses), the undeclared amount of the cumulative preference dividend (net of tax, if applicable) should still be deducted in arriving at earnings for the purposes of the EPS calculation. In the year in which these arrears of preference dividends are paid, they should be ignored in the EPS calculation for that year. [IAS 33 para 14(b)]. On the other hand, if the preference dividends are non-cumulative, only the amount of dividends declared in respect of the year should be deducted in arriving at the profit attributable to ordinary shareholders. [IAS 33 para 14(a)].

Other appropriations and adjustments in respect of preference shares

14.54   Under IAS 32 (see para 14.49 above) and IAS 39, the charges made in the profit and loss account in respect of preference shares that are treated as financial liabilities will include not only the preference and/or participating dividends, but also other elements such as the amortisation of transaction costs and accrual for any premium payable on redemption. [IAS 39 paras 47, IAS 32 paras 35, 36]. It follows that these other elements should continue to be deducted in arriving at profit for the financial year and the earnings available to ordinary equity holders. In the year in which the preference shares are redeemed, any premium payable on redemption should be ignored in calculating EPS for that year to the extent that it has been accrued (and, therefore, already taken into account) in earlier years.

14.55 In respect of preference shares classified as equity the following adjustments should also be made:

■ Any original discount or premium that is amortised to retained earnings using the effective interest method is treated as a preference dividend for the purposes of calculating EPS. [IAS 33 para 15]. An example is non-convertible, non-redeemable preference shares that have been issued at a discount to compensate for non-payment of dividends in earlier years, the discount being amortised to retained earnings. Such shares are often referred to as 'increasing rate preference shares'. (See illustrative example 1 in IAS 33.)

■ On the repurchase of preference shares, any excess of the fair value of consideration given over the carrying amount of the shares is a charge to retained earnings and is deducted in determining the profit, or added in determining the loss, available to ordinary equity holders for the purpose of calculating EPS. [IAS 33 para 16].

■ Where preference shares are converted early on favourable terms, the excess of the fair value of ordinary shares or other consideration paid over the fair value of ordinary shares or other consideration payable under the original terms is deducted in determining the profit, or added in determining the loss, available to ordinary equity holders for the purpose of calculating EPS. [IAS 33 para 17].

■ Any excess of the carrying amount of preference shares over the fair value of the consideration paid to settle them is added in determining the profit, or deducted in determining the loss, available to ordinary equity holders for the purpose of calculating EPS. [IAS 33 para 18].

14.56 The treatment of preference shares in the EPS calculation is illustrated in the following example:

Example

An entity has the following preference shares in issue at the end of 20X4:

- 5% Redeemable, non-cumulative preference shares, these shares are classified as liabilities under IAS 32. During the year a dividend was paid on the 5% preference shares. C100,000
- Increasing rate, cumulative, non-redeemable preference shares issued at a discount in 20X0 with a cumulative dividend rate from 20X5 of 10%. The shares were issued at a discount to compensate the holders, as dividend payments will not commence until 20X5. The accrual for the discount in the current year, calculated using the effective interest method amounted to, say, C18,000. These shares are classified as equity under IAS 32. C200,000
- 8% Non-redeemable, non-cumulative preference shares. At the beginning of the year the entity had C100,000 8% preference shares outstanding, but at 30 June 20X4, it repurchased C50,000 of these at a discount of C1,000. C50,000
- 7% Cumulative, convertible preference shares (converted in the year). These shares were classified as equity, until their conversion into ordinary shares at the beginning of the year. No dividend was accrued in respect of the year, although the previous year's dividend was paid immediately prior to conversion. To induce conversion, the terms of conversion of the 7% convertible preference shares were also amended and the revised terms entitled the preference shareholders to an additional 100 ordinary shares on conversion with a fair value of C300. CNil

The profit attributable to ordinary equity holders for the year 20X4 is C150,000. Adjustments for the purpose of calculating EPS are made as follows:

	C	C
Profit for the year attributable to the ordinary equity holders		150,000
Amortisation of discount on issue of increasing rate preference shares	(18,000)[1]	
Discount on repurchase of 8% preference shares	1,000[2]	
		(17,000)
Profit attributable to ordinary equity holders for basic EPS		133,000

Notes

1 The original discount on issue of the increasing rate preference shares has been amortised to retained earnings, so must be treated as preference dividends for EPS purposes and adjusted against profit attributable to the ordinary equity holders. [IAS 33 para 15]. There is no adjustment in respect of dividends as these do not commence until 20X5. Instead, the finance cost is represented by the

amortisation of the discount in the dividend-free period. In future years, the accrual for the dividend of C20,000 will be deducted from profits. [IAS 33 para 14(b)].

2   The discount on repurchase of the 8% preference shares has been credited to equity so must be added to profit. [IAS 33 para 18].

3   The dividend on the 5% preference shares has been charged to the income statement as the preference shares are treated as liabilities, so no adjustment is necessary to profit.

4   No accrual for the dividend on the 8% preference shares is required as they are non-cumulative. Had a dividend been declared for the year it would have been deducted from profit for the purpose of calculating basic EPS as the shares are treated as equity and the dividend would have been charged to equity in the financial statements. [IAS 33 para 14(a)].

5   As the 7% preference shares were converted at the beginning of the year, there is no adjustment in respect of the 7% preference shares as no dividend accrued in respect of the year. The payment of the previous year's cumulative dividend is ignored for EPS purposes as it will have been adjusted for in the prior year. [IAS 33 para 14(b)]. Similarly, the excess of the fair value of additional ordinary shares issued on conversion of the convertible preference shares over fair value of the ordinary shares to which they would have been entitled under the original conversion terms would already have been deducted from profit attributable to the ordinary shareholders and no further adjustment is required.

Participating securities and two-class ordinary shares

14.57 Sometimes, preference shares may be given the right to participate in the profit with ordinary shares according to a predetermined formula, but with an upper limit or cap on the extent of participation by the preference shares. Such participation is usually in addition to a fixed dividend. Participating preference shares would be treated as either financial liabilities or equity instruments under IAS 32, dependent on their terms. Where participating preference shares are classified as liabilities, both the fixed and the participating element would have been charged in arriving at profit or loss attributable to the parent entity and no further adjustments are necessary. Where participating preference shares are classified as equity instruments, IAS 33 contains further guidance that is considered below.

14.58 IAS 33 describes instruments that would include participating preference shares as 'participating equity instruments'. It notes that such instruments include instruments that participate in dividends with ordinary shares according to a predetermined formula (for example, two for one) with, sometimes an upper limit on participation (for example, up to a specified amount per share, but no more). [IAS 33 para A13(a)]. An example might be a participating preference share that receives a fixed dividend of 3% and a variable participation of 20% of the dividend on an ordinary share up to a maximum of 50 pence per participating preference share. Therefore, the total earnings would need to be calculated by reference to the fixed and the participating element in order to calculate the EPS attributable to the participating preference shares.

14.59 In addition to participating equity instruments, an entity could have a class of ordinary shares with a different dividend rate from that of another class of ordinary shares, but without prior or senior rights. [IAS 33 para A13(b)]. IAS 33 describes such instruments as 'two-class ordinary shares'. Where this is the case, the earnings for the period should be apportioned over the different classes of equity shares in issue in accordance with their dividend rights or other rights to participate in undistributed earnings. [IAS 33 para A14]. This means that a company could disclose a number of EPS figures, each attributable to different classes of equity shares and participating equity instruments.

14.60 The steps that should be followed in allocating earnings for the purposes of calculating basic EPS where an entity has different classes of ordinary shares and participating equity instruments that are not convertible into ordinary shares are as follows:

- Profit or loss attributable to ordinary equity holders is adjusted by the amount of dividends declared in the period for each class of shares and by the contractual amount of dividends that must be paid for the period (for example, unpaid cumulative dividends).

- The remaining profit or loss is allocated to ordinary shares and participating equity instruments to the extent that each instrument shares in earnings or losses. The allocation is made as if all the profit or loss has been distributed. The total profit or loss allocated to each class of equity instrument is determined by adding together the amount allocated for dividends and the amount allocated for the participation feature.

- The total amount of profit or loss allocated to each class of equity instrument is divided by the number of outstanding instruments to which the profits or losses are allocated (that is, the instruments in that class) to determine the EPS for that class of instrument.

[IAS 33 para A14].

14.61 Where participating equity instruments (participating preference shares) are convertible into ordinary shares, conversion is assumed if the effect is dilutive. Where this is so, the conversion shares should be included in outstanding ordinary shares for the purposes of calculating diluted EPS (see below under 'Diluted earnings per share'). [IAS 33 para A14].

14.62 The illustrative examples accompanying IAS 33 include a worked example illustrating how the allocation would be done. The following example is based on that example.

Example

An entity has two classes of shares in issue:

5,000 Non-convertible preference shares
10,000 Ordinary shares

The preference shares are entitled to a fixed dividend of C5 per share before any dividends are paid on the ordinary shares. Ordinary dividends are then paid in which the preference shareholders do not participate. Each preference share then participates in any additional ordinary dividend above C2 at a rate of 50% of any additional dividend payable on an ordinary share.

The entity's profit for the year is C100,000 and dividends of C2 per share are declared on the ordinary shares.

The calculation of basic EPS using the allocation method described in the previous paragraph is as follows:

	C	C
Profit		100,000
Less dividends payable for the period:		
Preference (5,000 × C5)	25,000	
Ordinary (10,000 × C2)	20,000	(45,000)
Undistributed earnings		55,000

Allocation of undistributed earnings:

Allocation per ordinary share = A
Allocation per preference share = B where B = 50% of A

$$(A \times 10{,}000) + (50\% \times A \times 5{,}000) = C55{,}000$$

$$A = 55{,}000 / (10{,}000 + 2{,}500)\ A = C4.4$$
$$B = 50\% \text{ of } A$$
$$B = C2.2$$

The basic per share amounts are:

	Preference shares C per share	Ordinary shares C per share
Distributed earnings	5.00	2.00
Undistributed earnings	2.20	4.40
Totals	7.20	6.40

Proof: (5,000 × C7.2) + (10,000 × C6.4) = C100,000

14.63 IAS 33 implies that the EPS attributable to the participating preference shares (participating equity instrument in IAS 33 terminology) should be disclosed even though only one of its two elements (the participating element) is subordinate to all other classes of equity instrument.

14.64   Table 14.1 illustrates disclosure of EPS for different classes of shares – preferred shares and ordinary shares. The equity note describes the respective dividend rights of the shares.

Table 14.1 – EPS for different classes of shares

Volkswagen AG – annual report and accounts – 31 December 2011

Income statement (extract) of the Volkswagen Group for the period January 1 to December 31, 2011

	Note	2011	2010
Basic earnings per ordinary share in €	11	33.10	15.17
Diluted earnings per ordinary share in €	11	33.10	15.17
Basic earnings per preferred share in €	11	33.16	15.23
Diluted earnings per preferred share in €	11	33.16	15.23

11 | Earnings per share

Basic earnings per share are calculated by dividing profit attributable to shareholders of Volkswagen AG by the weighted average number of ordinary and preferred shares outstanding during the reporting period. Earnings per share are diluted by potential shares. These include stock options, although these are only dilutive if they result in the issuance of shares at a value below the average market price of the shares.

A dilutive effect arose in fiscal year 2011 from the eighth tranche of the stock option plan. However, it was so insignificant that it did not affect the reported earnings per share.

	Ordinary		Preferred	
	2011	**2010**	**2011**	**2010**
Weighted average number of shares outstanding – basic	295,068,426	295,024,566	170,142,778	154,905,434
Dilutive potential ordinary shares from the stock option plan	7,508	9,792	0	0
Weighted average number of shares outstanding – diluted	295,075,934	295,034,358	170,142,778	154,905,434

14010

€ million	2011	2010
Profit after tax	15,799	7,226
Non-controlling interests	391	392
Profit attributable to shareholders of Volkswagen AG	15.409	6,835
Basic earnings attributable to ordinary shares	9,767	4,475
Diluted earnings attributable to ordinary shares	9,767	4,476
Basic earnings attributable to preferred shares	5,642	2,359
Diluted earnings attributable to preferred shares	5,642	2,359

€	2011	2010
Basic earnings per ordinary share	33.10	15.17
Diluted earnings per ordinary share	33.10	15.17
Basic earnings per preferred share	33.16	15.23
Diluted earnings per preferred share	33.16	15.23

23 | Equity (extract)

The subscribed capital of Volkswagen AG is composed of no-par value bearer shares with a notional value of €2.56. As well as ordinary shares, there are preferred shares that entitle the bearer to a €0.06 higher dividend than ordinary shares, but do not carry voting rights.

The subscribed capital increased by a total of €0.1 million as a result of the capital increase implemented in the fiscal year due to the exercise of conversion rights from the eighth tranche of the stock option plan. Following the capital increase, the subscribed capital amounted to €1,191 million.

The subscribed capital is composed of 295,089,817 no-par value ordinary shares and 170,142,778 preferred shares.

Authorized capital of up to €110 million, expiring on May 2, 2016, was approved for the issue of new ordinary bearer shares or preferred shares based on the resolution by the Annual General Meeting on May 3, 2011.

Following the capital increase implemented during the previous year, there is still authorized capital of up to €179.4 million, resolved by the Extraordinary General Meeting on December 3, 2009 and expiring on December 2, 2014, to issue up to 70,095,502 new no-par value preferred bearer shares.

The Annual General Meeting on April 22, 2010 resolved to create contingent capital in the amount of up to €102.4 million expiring on April 21, 2015 that can be used to issue up to €5 billion in bonds with warrants and/or convertible bonds.

Earnings per share

CHANGE IN ORDINARY AND PREFERRED SHARES AND SUBSCRIBED CAPITAL

| | | | | Shares € |
	2011	2010	2011	2010
Balance at January 1	465,188,345	400,243,677	1,190,882,163	1,024,623,813
Capital increase	–	64,904,498	–	166,155,515
Stock option plan	44,250	40,170	113,280	102,835
Balance at December 31	465,232,595	465,188,345	1,190,995,443	1,190,882,163

Computation of number of ordinary shares

14.65   The denominator of the basic EPS is calculated using the weighted average number of those ordinary shares that are outstanding during the period under review. [IAS 33 para 19].

14.66   Where there have been no changes in capital structure during the year, the relevant denominator is the number of ordinary shares outstanding at the year end. However, if additional ordinary shares have been issued during the year, it would not give a fair presentation to apportion the earnings for the whole of the year over the larger equity base. This is because the capital invested through the issue of the additional shares was available to the entity to increase its earnings only for part of the year. Similar considerations apply where shares have been bought back during the year. In order to take these factors into account, and to permit comparison of EPS with the previous period when there may have been no such change in the issued equity capital, it is necessary to use an average of the number of shares weighted by the number of days outstanding (a 'weighted average ordinary share capital') in the calculation of the denominator. The time-weighting factor should generally be the number of days that the specific shares are outstanding as a proportion of the total number of days, although a reasonable approximation of the weighted average is adequate in most circumstances. [IAS 33 para 20].

14.67   An example of how the weighted average number of shares should be calculated is given below. The example is derived from the illustrative example in IAS 33.

	Shares issued	Treasury shares	Shares outstanding
1 Jan 20X1 Balance at beginning of year	2,400	–	2,400
31 May 20X1 Issue of new shares for cash	800	–	3,200
1 Dec 20X1 Purchase of shares for cash	–	(200)	3,000
31 Dec 20X1 Balance at end of year	3,200	(200)	3,000

Computation of weighted average:
$(2,400 \times 5/12) + (3,200 \times 6/12) + (3,000 \times 1/12) = 2,850$ shares
or
$(2,400 \times 12/12) + (800 \times 7/12) - (200 \times 1/12) = 2,850$ shares

14.68 The general principle under IAS 33 is that shares should be included in the weighted average calculation from the date the consideration is receivable (which is generally the date of their issue). [IAS 33 para 21]. Therefore, shares issued for cash are brought into the calculation from the date the cash is receivable. Where shares are issued as consideration for the acquisition of an asset or a satisfaction of a liability, the shares are included in the averaging calculation from the date the asset is recognised or the liability is settled. In other situations, the date of inclusion should be determined from the terms and conditions attaching to the issue. The substance of any contract associated with the issue should also be considered. The standard provides a number of examples illustrating the timing of inclusion of ordinary shares in the weighted average calculation. These examples are listed below:

- Ordinary shares issued in exchange for cash are included when cash is receivable.

- Ordinary shares issued on the voluntary reinvestment of dividends on ordinary or preference shares are included when dividends are reinvested.

- Ordinary shares issued as a result of the conversion of a debt instrument to ordinary shares are included as of the date when interest ceases accruing.

- Ordinary shares issued in place of interest or principal on other financial instruments are included as of the date when interest ceases accruing.

- Ordinary shares issued in exchange for the settlement of a liability of the entity are included as of the settlement date.

- Ordinary shares issued as consideration for the acquisition of an asset other than cash are included as of the date on which the acquisition is recognised.

- Ordinary shares issued for the rendering of services to the entity are included as the services are rendered.

- Ordinary shares issued as part of the cost of a business combination are included from the acquisition date (see para 14.78).

[IAS 33 paras 21, 22].

14.69 The general rule that shares should be included in the basic EPS calculation from the date consideration is receivable does not apply to shares that are issued in partly paid form. Partly paid shares are treated as fractions of shares (payments received to date as a proportion of the total subscription price) and included in the averaging calculation only to the extent that they participate in dividends for the period. [IAS 33 para A15]. Partly paid shares that do not participate in dividends are excluded from the basic EPS calculation, but included in the calculation of diluted EPS (see further para 14.110).

Example

A company issues 100,000 ordinary shares of C1 each for a consideration of C2.50 per share. Calls amounting to C1.75 per share were received by the balance sheet date. The partly paid shares are entitled to participate in dividends for the period in proportion to the amount paid. The number of ordinary share equivalents that would be included in the basic EPS calculation on a weighted basis is as follows:

$$100,000 \times \frac{C1.75}{C2.50} = 70,000 \text{ shares}$$

14.70 Whenever changes in ordinary shares occur during the accounting period, an amendment is necessary to the number of shares used in the EPS calculation. In some situations, the EPS in prior periods will also have to be adjusted. Some of the ways in which a company can change its ordinary share capital and the consequential effect on the number of shares used in the EPS calculation are considered below.

Purchase and holding of own shares and ESOPs

14.71 Where a company has purchased its own ordinary shares during the year, there will be a lesser number outstanding after the repurchase. Such repurchases should be reflected in the weighted average number of shares outstanding during the period from the date shares are repurchased as illustrated in paragraph 14.67. Any premium payable on the purchase of a company's own ordinary shares will be charged against reserves and will not affect earnings for the year. No adjustments should be made to the prior year's EPS.

14.72 A company may sometimes hold its own shares in treasury. This situation may arise where it has acquired them in the market, or by forfeiture, or by surrender in lieu of forfeiture, or by way of a gift. Shares held uncancelled in treasury are accounted for as a deduction from shareholders' funds. [IAS 32 para 33; IAS 33 para 20]. Another not uncommon group situation is where a subsidiary continues to hold the shares in the parent that were acquired before it became a group member. Since such shares are no longer available in the market, they are excluded from the weighted average number of ordinary shares for the purpose of calculating EPS. [IAS 33 para 20].

[The next paragraph is 14.75

UK.14.74.1 In the UK, a company may hold its own shares where the shares are held as treasury shares under Chapter 6 of Part 18 of the 2006 Companies Act (sections 724 to 732). Companies with *'qualifying shares'* may purchase such shares out of distributable profits and hold them in treasury for resale, transfer or cancellation at a later date. 'Qualifying shares' are defined as shares that:

■   are included in the official list (that is, listed on the London Stock Exchange);

■   are traded on AIM;

- are officially listed in another EEA State; or
- are traded on a regulated market.

[CA 2006 sec 724(2)].

14.75 Another common situation where a company holds its own shares arises where it operates an Employee Share Ownership Plan (ESOP) for the benefit of its employees. For the purpose of calculating EPS these outstanding shares should also be excluded from the calculation to the extent that they have not vested unconditionally in the employees.

14.76 An example where a company has excluded treasury shares for the purposes of determining the weighted average number of shares for calculating EPS is given in Table 14.2 below. In this example there were no other issues of shares in the year.

Table 14.2 – Treatment of treasury shares in EPS calculation

Telkom SA Limited – annual report and accounts – 31 March 2011

	Restated 2010	2011
12. EARNINGS PER SHARE (extract 1)		
Total operations		
Basic and diluted earnings per share (cents)	7,425.7	**239.9**

The calculation of earnings per share is based on profit attributable to equity holders of Telkom for the year of R1,222 million (2010: R37,458 million) and 509,311,296 (2010: 504,437,832) weighted average number of ordinary shares in issue. ******

12. EARNINGS PER SHARE (extract 2)		
Reconciliation of weighted average number of ordinary shares:		
Ordinary shares in issue (refer to note 24)	520,783,900	**520,783,900**
Weighted average number of treasury shares	(16,346,068)	**(11,472,604)**
Weighted average number of shares outstanding	504,437,832	**509,311,296**
Reconciliation of diluted weighted average number of ordinary shares		
Weighted average number of shares outstanding	504,437,832	**509,311,296**
Expected future vesting of shares	–	**–**
Diluted weighted average number of shares outstanding	504,437,832	**509,311,296**

** *The Telkom Conditional Share Plan was concluded with a final vesting in June 2010, therefore there is no adjustment in the weighted average number of shares as a result of the expected future vesting of shares allocated to employees under this plan. Due to the plan being concluded, there is no further dilutive effect on basic earnings per share.*

Contingently issuable shares

14.77 Contingently issuable shares are ordinary shares that are issuable for little or no cash or other consideration if and when specified conditions in a contingent share agreement have been met. [IAS 33 para 5]. In other words, the consideration for the shares has effectively been received, but the shares remain to be issued – a typical example is contingent consideration on an acquisition payable in shares. Contingently issuable shares are considered to be outstanding and are included in the calculation of basic EPS from the date when all the necessary conditions have been satisfied, that is, the events have occurred. Shares that are issuable solely after the passage of time are not contingently issuable shares, because the passage of time is a certainty and should, therefore, be included in the calculation from inception of the contract. Outstanding ordinary shares that are contingently returnable (that is, subject to recall) are not treated as outstanding, that is they are excluded from the calculation of basic EPS until the date when the shares are no longer subject to recall. [IAS 33 para 24]. Contingently issuable shares are discussed further from paragraph 14.145.

Shares issued as consideration in a business combination

14.78 Where ordinary shares are issued during the financial year as part of the cost of a business combination (for example, in exchange for a majority interest in the equity of another company) – that is, as non-cash consideration, the results of the new subsidiary are included in the consolidation from the acquisition date. Therefore, the shares issued as consideration to obtain those earnings should be included in the EPS calculation on a weighted average basis from the same date. [IAS 33 para 22].

Mandatorily convertible instruments

14.79 An entity may issue a loan note or a preference share that is convertible into ordinary shares of the entity. The instrument may either be mandatorily convertible or convertible at the option of the issuer or holder into a fixed number of shares. Where an instrument is mandatorily convertible, the issue of ordinary shares is solely dependent on the passage of time. Consequently, ordinary shares that are issuable on conversion of a mandatorily convertible instrument should be included in basic EPS from the date that the contract is entered into. [IAS 33 para 23]. On the other hand, debt that is convertible at the option of the holder contains an obligation to issue a fixed number of shares *if* the conversion option is exercised. Such shares are treated as potential ordinary shares as they may never be issued if the conversion option is not exercised. Consequently, such potential shares are not considered outstanding for purposes of calculating basic EPS, but are included in the calculation of diluted EPS (see para 14.114 below).

Example

A company has issued debt that is mandatorily convertible into a fixed number of shares in five years time. Neither the issuer nor the holder has any option to require settlement in cash. Interest is payable (in cash) until conversion. How does it affect EPS?

For the purpose of EPS the potential ordinary shares that would be issued on conversion are included in the weighted average number of ordinary shares used in the calculation of basic EPS (and, therefore, also diluted EPS) from the date of issue of the instrument, since their issue is solely dependent on the passage of time. There is no adjustment to the profit or loss attributable to the ordinary equity holders for consequential interest savings, because the shares are treated as if had already been issued. The interest relates to a separate liability for the interest payments that remain payable.

14.79.1   An entity may have preference shares that are mandatorily convertible when the entity's ordinary share price increases to a specified level. As the conversion is contingent on this uncertain event occuring, the issuable shares are treated in the same ways as an option that is convertible at the option of the issuer or holder. Hence, they are treated as outstanding and are included in the calculation of basic EPS only from the date when all necessary conditions are satisfied (that is, when the ordinary shares have reached the specified share price). [IAS 33 para 24]. Note, that it is still necessary to consider whether these preference shares are themselves participating equity instruments (see para 14.57).

Bonus issue (stock dividends), share split and share consolidation

14.80   The weighted average number of ordinary shares outstanding during the period and for all periods presented should be adjusted for events, other than the conversion of potential ordinary shares, that have changed the number of ordinary shares outstanding, without a corresponding change in resources (see further para 14.169). [IAS 33 para 26]. Where an entity issues new shares by way of a bonus issue or stock dividend during the period, the effect is to increase only the number of shares outstanding after the issue. There is no effect on earnings as there is no flow of funds as a result of the issue. Consequently, the shares should be treated as outstanding as if the issue had occurred at the beginning of the earliest period reported. This means that the earnings for the year should be apportioned over the number of shares after the capitalisation. The EPS figure disclosed for the previous year should be recalculated using the new number of shares in issue. [IAS 33 para 28].

14.81   Similar considerations apply where ordinary shares are split into shares of smaller nominal value (a share of C1 nominal value is divided into four shares of 25c each C1 = 100c) or consolidated into shares of a higher nominal amount (four shares of 25c each are consolidated into one share of C1). In both these situations, the number of shares outstanding before the event is adjusted for the proportionate change in the number of shares outstanding after the event. [IAS 33 para 27].

14.82 The impact on the EPS figure of a bonus issue of shares is illustrated in the following example:

> **Example**
>
> On 31 December 20X7, the issued share capital of a company consisted of C1,000,000 in ordinary shares of 25c each and C500,000 in 10% cumulative preference shares of C1 each. On 1 October 20X8, the company issued 1,000,000 ordinary shares fully paid by way of capitalisation of reserves in the proportion of 1:4 for the year ended 31 December 20X8.
>
> | | 20X8 C'000 | 20X7 C'000 |
> |---|---|---|
> | **Calculation of earnings** | | |
> | Profit for the year | 550 | 450 |
> | Less: preference dividend | (50) | (50) |
> | Earnings | 500 | 400 |
> | **Number of ordinary shares** | No (000) | No (000) |
> | Shares in issue for full year | 4,000 | 4,000 |
> | Capitalisation issue at 1 October 20X8 | 1,000 | 1,000 |
> | Number of shares | 5,000 | 5,000 |
> | **Earnings per ordinary share of 25c** | 10.0c | 8.0c |
>
> The comparative earnings per share for 20X7 can also be calculated by adjusting the previously disclosed EPS in 20X7, in this example 10c, by the following factor:
>
> $$\frac{\text{Number of shares before the bonus issue}}{\text{Number of shares after the bonus issue}}$$
>
> $$\text{Adjusted EPS for 20X7: } 10c \times \frac{4,000}{5,000} = 8.0c$$
>
> The above ratio should also be used to restate previous years' EPS and other financial ratios (for example, dividend per share) disclosed in the historical summary.

Issue of shares at full market price

14.83 Where new ordinary shares are issued during the year for cash at full market price, the earnings should be apportioned over the average number of shares outstanding during the period weighted on a time basis.

> **Example**
>
> On 31 December 20X7, the issued share capital of a company consisted of C1,000,000 in ordinary shares of 25c each and C500,000 in 10% cumulative preference shares of C1 each. On 1 October 20X8, the company issued 1,000,000 ordinary shares at full market price in cash for the year ended 31 December 20X8.

	20X8	20X7
	C'000	C'000
Calculation of earnings		
Profit for the year	550	450
Less: preference dividend	(50)	(50)
Earnings	500	400
Weighted average number of ordinary shares	No (000)	No (000)
Shares in issue for full year	4,000	4,000
Issued on 1 October 20X8 (1,000,000 × 3/12)	250	–
Number of shares	4,250	4,000
Earnings per ordinary share of 25c	11.8c	10.0c

The calculation of earnings per share is based on earnings of C500,000 (20X7: C400,000) and on the weighted average of 4,250,000 ordinary shares in issue during the year (20X7: 4,000,000).

[The next paragraph is 14.85.]

Rights issue

14.85   Companies sometimes raise additional capital during the year by issuing shares to existing shareholders on a *pro rata* basis to their existing holdings in the form of a rights issue. The rights shares may either be offered at the current market price or at a price that is below the current market price. Where shares are issued at full market price, the weighting is carried out on a time basis as discussed in paragraph 14.83 above. However, where ordinary shares are issued during the year by way of a rights issue at a discount to the market price, the weighting calculation must reflect the fact that the discount is effectively a bonus (stock dividend) given to the shareholders in the form of shares for no consideration and must, therefore, be taken into account in calculating the weighted average number of shares. [IAS 33 para A2]. In fact, it can be demonstrated (see example below) that a rights issue is equivalent to a capitalisation issue of part of the shares for no consideration and an issue of the remainder of the shares at full market price. The notional capitalisation issue reflects the bonus element inherent in the rights issue and is measured by the following fraction:

Fair value per share immediately before the exercise of rights
Theoretical ex-rights fair value per share

14.86   The fair value per share immediately before the exercise of rights is the *actual* closing price at which the shares are quoted on the last date inclusive of the right to subscribe for the new shares. This is often referred to as the 'cum-rights price', being the price on the last day of quotation cum-rights. The 'ex-rights price', on the other hand, is the *theoretical* price at which, in a perfect market and without any external influences, the shares would trade after the exercise of the rights. Where the rights themselves are publicly traded separately from the shares themselves, as is the case in some countries, the fair value for the purpose of the above calculation is established at the close of the last day on which the shares are traded together with the rights. [IAS 33 para A2].

14.87 The above factor should be used to adjust the number of shares in issue before the rights issue in order to correct for the bonus (stock dividend) element in the rights issue. This correction should be made both for the current period prior to the rights issue and the previous period. The way in which EPS should be calculated following a rights issue and the adjustment that should be made to the comparative EPS figure are considered in the example below.

> **Example**
>
> At 31 December 20X7, the issued capital of a company consisted of 1.8m ordinary shares of 10c each, fully paid. The profit for the year ended 31 December 20X7 and 20X8 amounted to C630,000 and C875,000 respectively. On 31 March 20X8, the company made a rights issue on a 1 for 4 basis at 30c. The market price of the shares immediately before the rights issue was 60c.
>
> | **Calculation of theoretical ex rights price** | | | |
> |---|---|---|---|
> | | **No** | | **C** |
> | Initial holding | 4 | Market value | 240 |
> | Rights taken up | 1 | Cost | 30 |
> | New holding | 5 | Theoretical price | 270 |
> | Theoretical ex rights price | $\frac{270}{5}$ = 54c | | |
>
> The market price is the fair value of the shares immediately prior to the exercise of rights, that is, the actual cum-rights price of 60c.
>
> Cost is the amount payable for each new share under the rights issue.
>
> **Calculation of bonus element**
> The bonus element of the rights issue is given by the fraction:
>
> $$\frac{\text{Market price before rights issue}}{\text{Theoretical ex-rights price}} \qquad \frac{60}{54} = \frac{10}{9}$$

This corresponds to a bonus issue of 1 for 9. The bonus ratio will usually be greater than 1, that is the market price of the shares immediately prior to the exercise of rights is greater than the theoretical ex-rights price. If the ratio is less than 1 it may indicate that the market price has fallen significantly during the rights period, which was not anticipated when the rights issue was announced. In this situation, the rights issue should be treated as an issue of shares for cash at full market price (see para 14.83 above).

As stated in paragraph 14.85 above, it can be demonstrated, using the figures in the example, that a rights issue of 1 for 4 at 30c is equivalent to a bonus issue of 1 for 9 combined with an issue of shares at full market price of 54c per share. Consider an individual shareholder holding 180 shares.

	No Value	C
Original holding	180 Value at 60c per share	108.00
Rights shares (1:4)	45 Value at 30c per share	13.50
Holding after rights issue	225 Value at 54c per share	121.50

The additional 45 rights shares at 30p can be shown to be equivalent to a bonus issue of 1 for 9 on the original holding followed by an issue of 1:8 at full market price of 54c following the bonus issue as follows:

	No Value	C
Original holding	180 Value at 60c per share	108.00
Bonus issue of 1 for 9	20 Value nil	nil
	200 Value at 54c per share	108.00
Issue of 1 for 8 at full price	25 Value at 54c per share	13.50
Total holding	225 Value at 54c per share	121.50

The shareholder is, therefore, indifferent as to whether the company makes a rights issue of 1 for 4 at 30c per share or a combination of a bonus issue of 1 for 9 followed by a rights issue of 1 for 8 at full market price of 54c per share.

Having calculated the bonus ratio, the ratio should be applied to adjust the number of shares in issue before the rights issue both for the current year and for the previous year. Therefore, the weighted average number of shares in issue for the current and the previous period, adjusted for the bonus element would be:

Weighted average number of shares

	20X8	20X7
Number of actual shares in issue before rights	1,800,000	1,800,000
Correction for bonus issue (1:9)	200,000	200,000
Deemed number of shares in issue before rights issue (1.8m × 10/9)	2,000,000	2,000,000

The number of shares after the rights issue would be:
1.8m × 5/4 = 2,250,000

Therefore, the weighted average number of shares would be:

	20X8	20X7
2.0m for the whole year		2,000,000
2.0m × 3/12 (before rights issue)	500,000	–
2.25m × 9/12 (after rights issue)	1,687,500	–
Weighted average number	2,187,500	2,000,000

Calculation of EPS following a rights issue

	20X8	20X7
		(as previously stated)
Basic EPS	C875,000	C630,000
	2,187,500	1,800,000
	40.0c	35.0c
Basic EPS for 20X7 (as restated)		C630,000
		2,000,000
		31.5c

The restated EPS for 20X7 can also be calculated by adjusting the earnings per share figure of the previous year by the *reciprocal* of the bonus element factor as shown below.

$$35c \times 9/10 = 31.5c$$

In practice, the EPS for the corresponding period can be adjusted directly using the reciprocal of the bonus element factor above.

14.88 A question arises as to whether the averaging calculation in a rights issue made during the year should be performed from the announcement date, or from the last date of acceptance of the subscription price, or from the share issue date following despatch of the share certificates. Depending on the circumstances of each case, there is often a delay of between 60 to 80 days between the date of announcement of the rights issue and the share issue date. Following the principle in paragraph 21 of IAS 33 that shares should generally be included from the date consideration is receivable, it follows that the averaging calculation should be performed from the day following the last date of acceptance of the subscription price, which is also the date when the rights are legally exercised. This is because the company begins to generate income from all the proceeds received from that date, which is often midway between the announcement date and the share issue date. Therefore, the new shares should be included in the EPS calculation from the day following the last date on which proceeds are received and not from the announcement date or from the date when the new shares are actually issued. An example of a rights issue (and a share consolidation – see para 14.81 above) is Table 14.2.A.

Table 14.2.A – Effect of rights issue on earnings per share

SEGRO plc – Annual report – 31 December 2009

14. EARNINGS AND NET ASSETS PER SHARE

The earnings per share calculations use the weighted average number of shares and the net assets per share calculations use the number of shares in issue at year end. Both earnings per share and net assets per share calculations exclude 1.3 million shares held on trust for employee share schemes (2008 1.5 million).

On 7 April 2009, the Company issued 5,240.7 million new ordinary shares (pre-share consolidation) through a rights issue. The rights issue was offered at 10 pence per share and represented a discount to the fair value of the existing shares. The number of shares used for prior year calculations of earnings per share and net assets per share shown below have been adjusted for the discounted rights issue in order to provide a comparable basis for the current year. An adjustment factor of 6.92 has been applied based on the Company's share price of 136.5 pence per share on 20 March 2009, the day before the new shares commenced trading on the London Stock Exchange and the theoretical ex-rights price at that date of 19.73 pence per share. In addition, the impact of the 10 for 1 share consolidation has also resulted in an adjustment to the prior period comparables. Note 25 provides further detail on the rights issue and the share consolidation. As discussed in note 1, these adjustments to comparative earnings per share and net assets per share calculations have not impacted the income statement or balance sheet and therefore, since it has not changed from the previously presented figures, a balance sheet at 31 December 2007 has not been shown.

14(i) – Earnings per ordinary share (extract)

	2009			2008		
	Earnings £m	Shares million	Pence per share	Earnings £m	Shares million	Pence per share
Basic EPS	(233.1)	563.8	(41.3)	(938.1)	300.5	(312.2)
Dilution adjustments:						
Share options and save as you earn schemes	–	0.2	–	–	–	–
Diluted EPS	(233.1)	564.0	(41.3)	(938.1)	300.5	(312.2)

25. SHARE CAPITAL AND SHARE-BASED PAYMENTS (extract 1)
On 7 April 2009, the Company issued 5,240.7 million new ordinary shares (pre share consolidation) at 10 pence per share on the basis of 12 new ordinary shares for every 1 existing ordinary share to raise £500 million (net of expenses).

25. SHARE CAPITAL AND SHARE-BASED PAYMENTS (extract 2)
At the General Meeting held on 28 July 2009;

(a) an ordinary resolution was passed to conduct a share consolidation, consolidating and re-classifying 10 of each existing authorised and existing issued shares of the Company of 1 pence each into 1 share of 10 pence each. The purpose of the share consolidation was to reduce the number of the Company's shares in issue so that the likely share price is appropriate for a Company of SEGRO's size. The share consolidation took effect on 31 July 2009.

Issue of shares at less than market price

14.88.1 Sometimes shares may be issued at a discount to the market price, such as for the acquisition of an asset or the cancellation of a liability. Although the standard does not specifically deal with this situation, it would be appropriate to calculate the inherent bonus element in the issue for the purposes of adjusting the number of shares before the issue. This treatment is implicit in the wording in paragraph 27(b) of IAS 33, which makes reference to a bonus element in *any other issue*.

Dividends payable in shares or cash

14.89 Where a company pays its dividends in the form of shares or gives the shareholder the option to receive a dividend in either cash or shares (sometimes referred to as scrip dividends or enhanced scrip dividends), the shares issued increase the weighted average number of shares used in the EPS calculation.

14.90 Under IAS 33, paragraphs 5 and 7 and paragraphs 58 to 61 'Contracts that may be settled in ordinary shares or cash', scrip dividends may be regarded as potential ordinary shares (see para 14.98 below) that entitle the recipient to ordinary shares. These potential ordinary shares are converted into ordinary shares when the scrip shares are issued, which is after the balance sheet date. Since shares are included in the weighted average from the date consideration is receivable, ordinary shares issued on the voluntary reinvestment of dividends on ordinary or preference shares should be included on a weighted average basis at the date when the dividends are reinvested. [IAS 33 para 21(b)]. In practice, for scrip dividends, this is the dividend payment date.

14.91 Furthermore, the cash dividend foregone by the shareholders electing to take a scrip dividend of shares is taken to be the consideration paid for those shares, which is normally equivalent to the current market value of the shares. The rationale for this is that the cash dividend foregone by the shareholders electing to take shares instead of cash is effectively reinvested in the company as fully paid up shares at market value. As a result, the earnings figure in the numerator already reflects the income generated by the additional cash retained from the dividend payment date. Consequently, for the purposes of the EPS calculation the issue of scrip shares should be treated as an issue at full market price and the relevant number of shares should be included in the denominator on a weighted basis from the dividend reinvestment date.

[The next paragraph is 14.93.]

Special dividend followed by share consolidation

14.93 Companies sometimes return surplus cash to shareholders. This is normally effected by means of a share repurchase or by a synthetic share repurchase that is achieved by the payment of a special dividend to shareholders followed by a consolidation of share capital, for example, changing five 20c shares into four 25c shares.

14.94 IAS 33 deals specifically with the effect on EPS of a special dividend accompanied by a share consolidation. Where a share consolidation is combined with a special dividend and the overall effect of the combined transaction is a share repurchase at fair value the reduction in the number of ordinary shares outstanding is the result of a corresponding reduction in resources. The weighted average number of ordinary shares outstanding for the period in which the combined transaction takes place is adjusted for the reduction in the number of ordinary shares from the date the special dividend is recognised. [IAS 33 para 29].

Example

A company has in issue 10,000 shares with a nominal value of 10c each. At the beginning of 20X8, it decides either to launch a share repurchase of 1,000 shares at the current market price of C1 per share or pay a special dividend of 10c per share (net) followed by a share consolidation of 9 new shares for 10 old shares. The profit after tax for 20X7 and 20X8 (before the effect of the share transactions) is C2,000. Interest rates are 8% per annum and the company pays corporation tax at 31%.

	Balance sheet before transactions	Repurchase of 1,000 shares at c1 per share	Special dividend of 10c per share followed by share consolidation of 10:9
	C	C	C
Net assets	5,000	4,000	4,000
Share capital 10,000 shares at 10c each	1,000		
9,000 shares at 10c each		900	
9,000 shares at 11.1c each			1,000
Capital redemption reserve		100	
Profit and loss account	4,000	3,000	3,000
	5,000	4,000	4,000
Net assets per share	C0.50	C0.44	C0.44

Effect on earnings per share — share repurchase

	20X8	20X7
	C	C
Profit for the year	2,000.00	2,000.00
Loss of interest on cash paid out (£1,000 × 0.08 × 0.69)	55.20	–
Earnings	1,944.80	2,000.00
Number of shares in issue	9,000	10,000
EPS	21.61c	20.00c

Effect on earnings per share – special dividend followed by share consolidation

The total nominal value of the shares remain unchanged, but whereas before there were 10,000 shares of 10c each there are now 9,000 shares of 11.1c each.

	20X8	20X7
	C	C
Profit for the year	2,000.00	2,000.00
Loss of interest on cash paid out	55.20	–
(C1,000 × 0.08 × 0.69)		
Earnings	1,944.48	2,000.00
Number of shares in issue (unadjusted)	9,000	10,000
EPS unadjusted (correct treatment)	21.61c	20.00c
Number of shares in issue (adjusted for consolidation)	9,000	9,000
EPS adjusted (incorrect treatment)	21.61c	22.22c

14.95   As can be seen from the above example, the economic effect, in terms of net asset per share, of an actual share repurchase is identical to a synthetic share repurchase that is achieved by the combination of a special dividend with a share consolidation. It follows that the earnings per share figures for the two transactions should also be identical. If an adjustment were made to the previous year's EPS for the share consolidation as shown above, there would be an apparent dilution of 2.75% ((22.22 — 21.61)/22.22) that would make the share repurchase look significantly more attractive than the special dividend route. But this would be misleading as the economic effect of the two transactions is identical. Therefore, no adjustment to prior year's EPS should be made for the share consolidation. [IAS 33 para 29].

14.96   In the above example, it was assumed for simplicity that the combined transaction took place at the beginning of the year and so the new shares were treated as outstanding for a full year. If the combined transaction takes place part way through the year, the weighted average number of ordinary shares outstanding for the period in which the combined transaction takes place should be adjusted for the reduction in the number of shares from the date the special dividend is paid, that is, when resources leave the entity. [IAS 33 para 29]. An example of a company that has treated the payment of an exceptional dividend and a share consolidation carried out at the same time as equivalent to a share buy-back is given in the Table 14.3 below. The company is an investment company and also shows net assets per share (based on shares in issue at the period end).

Table 14.3 — Effect on EPS of special dividend and share consolidation

Mitchells & Butlers plc —Annual report — 29 September 2007

12. Dividends

	2007 52 weeks £m	2006 52 weeks £m
Amounts paid and recognised in equity		
In respect of the 53 weeks ended 1 October 2005:		
– Final dividend of 7.55p per share	–	38
In respect of the 52 weeks ended 30 September 2006:		
– Interim dividend of 3.65p per share	–	18
– Final dividend of 8.60p per share	35	–
In respect of the 52 weeks ended 29 September 2007:		
– Special interim dividend of 100.0p per share	486	–
– Interim dividend of 4.25p per share	17	–
	538	56
Proposed final dividend of 10.0p (2006 8.60p) per share	40	35

The payment of the special interim dividend amounting to £486m was made on 25 October 2006. The shareholders approved, at an Extraordinary General Meeting on 17 October 2006, the consolidation of the share capital of the Company by the issue of 34 new ordinary shares of 813/24p each for every 41 existing shares of 71/12p each.

The Board recommended on 28 November 2007 the proposed final dividend for the 52 weeks ended 29 September 2007. This did not qualify for recognition in the financial statements at 29 September 2007 as it had not been approved by the shareholders at that date.

13. Earnings per ordinary share

Basic earnings per share (EPS) has been calculated by dividing the profit or loss for the financial period by the weighted average number of ordinary shares in issue during the period, excluding own shares held in treasury and by employee share trusts.

For diluted earnings per share, the weighted average number of ordinary shares is adjusted to assume conversion of all dilutive potential ordinary shares.

Earnings per ordinary share amounts are presented before exceptional items (see note 9) in order to allow a better understanding of the underlying trading performance of the Group.

Earnings per share

	Profit/(loss) £m	Basic EPS pence per ordinary share	Diluted EPS pence per ordinary share
52 weeks ended 29 September 2007			
Loss for the period	(10)	(2.5)p	(2.5)p*
Exceptional items, net of tax	155	38.0p	36.9p
Profit before exceptional items	145	35.5p	34.4p
52 weeks ended 30 September 2006			
Profit for the period	195	39.7p	38.8p
Exceptional items, net of tax	(51)	(10.4)p	(10.2)p
Profit before exceptional items	144	29.3p	28.6p

*The 2007 diluted EPS per ordinary share is unchanged from the basic EPS, as the inclusion of the dilutive potential ordinary shares would reduce the loss per share and is therefore not dilutive.

The weighted average number of ordinary shares used in the calculations above are as follows:

	2007 52 weeks millions	2006 52 weeks millions
For basic EPS calculations	408	491
Effect of dilutive potential ordinary shares:		
Contingently issuable shares	8	7
Other share options	5	5
For diluted EPS calculations	421	503

On 17 October 2006, shareholders approved a share capital consolidation together with a Special Dividend of 100.0p per ordinary share. The overall effect of the transaction was that of a share repurchase at fair value, therefore no adjustment has been made to comparative data.

At 29 September 2007, nil (2006 nil) contingently issuable shares and 1,034,538 (2006 965,822) other share options were outstanding that could potentially dilute basic EPS in the future but were not included in the calculation of diluted EPS as they are antidilutive for the periods presented.

24. Called up share capital
2007 2006

	Number of shares	£m	Number of shares	£m
Authorised				
Ordinary shares of 813/24p each	1,181,130,148	101	–	–
Ordinary shares of 71/12p each	–	–	1,424,304,003	101
	1,181,130,148	101	1,424,304,003	101
Called up, allotted and fully paid				
Ordinary shares of 813/24p each:				
At start of the financial period	486,910,806	34	500,438,040	35
Share capital consolidation	(83,131,113)	–	–	–
Repurchase and cancellation	–	–	(13,527,234)	(1)
At end of the financial period	403,779,693	34	486,910,806	34

All of the ordinary shares rank equally with respect to voting rights and rights to receive ordinary and special dividends. There are no restrictions on the rights to transfer shares.

On 17 October 2006, shareholders approved a share capital consolidation on the basis of 34 new ordinary shares for every 41 existing ordinary shares. This provided for all of the authorised ordinary shares of 71/12p each (whether issued or unissued) to be consolidated into new ordinary shares of 813/24p each, which became effective on 18 October 2006.

Details of options granted under the Group's share schemes are contained in note 7.

Diluted earnings per share

Measurement

14.97 As discussed from paragraph 14.65 above, the basic EPS is calculated on the number of ordinary shares outstanding in respect of the period. Sometimes companies may have 'potential ordinary shares' in issue. The standard defines a 'potential ordinary share' as a financial instrument or other contract that may entitle its holder to ordinary shares. [IAS 33 para 5]. Examples given in the standard are:

- Financial liabilities or equity instruments, including preference shares, that are convertible into ordinary shares.

- Options (including employee share options) and warrants.

- Shares that would be issued on satisfaction of certain conditions that result from contractual arrangements, such as the purchase of a business or other assets.

[IAS 33 para 7].

14.98 In addition IAS 33 clarifies that contracts that may result in the issue of ordinary shares of the entity to the holder of the contract at the option of the issuer or the holder are potential ordinary shares. [IAS 33 paras 58 to 61]. Such contracts are dealt with from paragraph 14.159 below.

14.99 In each of these situations, the effect of the conversion into ordinary shares may be to dilute future EPS. It should be noted that not all potential ordinary shares in issue will have a diluting effect (see further para 14.126). Any potential dilution, however, is of considerable interest to existing ordinary shareholders. This is because it indicates the possible reduction in current earnings that may be distributed to them by way of dividends in the future and the possible increase in the number of shares over which the total market value of the company may be divided.

14.100 The standard, therefore, requires the calculation of diluted EPS, in addition to the basic EPS (see para 14.46), for profit or loss attributable to the parent entity's ordinary equity holders and separately for each of continuing and discontinued operations where these are presented in accordance with IFRS 5.

For the purpose of calculating diluted EPS, the profit or loss for the period attributable to ordinary equity holders adjusted for the effects of all dilutive potential ordinary shares should be divided by the sum of the weighted average number of ordinary shares used in the basic EPS calculation and the weighted average number of shares that would be issued on the conversion of all the dilutive potential ordinary shares into ordinary shares. [IAS 33 paras 30 to 32, 36].

14.101 It should be noted that although existing ordinary shareholders are interested in future dilution, the diluted EPS figure calculated in accordance with the standard is not intended to be a predictor of dilution, or a forward-looking number. It is seen as an additional historical measure. The IASB and the FASB concluded that as the objective of basic EPS is to measure performance over the reporting period, the objective of diluted EPS should be consistent with that objective while giving effect to all dilutive potential ordinary shares that were outstanding during the period. A past performance method of computing diluted EPS will aid comparison between diluted EPS of different periods. In addition, presenting diluted EPS with undiluted EPS that are calculated on a consistent basis will enable users to view the spread between the two figures as representing a reasonable estimate of the potential dilution that exists in the entity's capital structure.

Computation of earnings

14.102 For the purpose of calculating diluted EPS, the profit or loss attributable to the parent entity's ordinary equity holders should be adjusted for the after-tax effect of:

- Dividends or other items related to dilutive potential ordinary shares that have been deducted in arriving at profit attributable to ordinary equity holders for the purpose of calculating basic EPS, such as dividends on dilutive convertible preference shares.

- Interest recognised in the period on dilutive potential ordinary shares, such as interest on dilutive convertible debt.

- Any other changes in income or expense that would result from the conversion of the dilutive potential ordinary shares.

[IAS 33 paras 32(a), 33].

14.103 Once potential ordinary shares are converted into ordinary shares during the period, the dividends, interest and other expense associated with those potential ordinary shares will no longer be incurred. The effect of the conversion, therefore, is to increase profit (or reduce losses) attributable to ordinary equity holders as well as the number of shares in issue. This is illustrated in paragraph 14.114 dealing with convertible securities. Adjustments to profit or loss attributable to ordinary equity holders also include any transaction costs, discounts or premiums on potential ordinary shares that are allocated to periods in accordance with the effective interest method in paragraph 9 of IAS 39, that is, the adjustment to earnings should add back the issue costs (or similar) amortised in the period, in addition to the interest/dividend cost.

14.104 The adjustments to earnings include not only the direct savings in debt servicing cost or dividends and other appropriations and adjustments in respect of convertible preference shares and the related tax effects, but also any other consequential changes in other income or expense arising as a result of the conversion. A situation that often arises in practice is where the equity conversion option in a foreign currency convertible bond, which is treated as a liability, is marked to market through profit or loss. The marked-to-market adjustment needs to be removed from profit or loss for the purposes of calculating diluted EPS. IAS 33 also mentions, as an example, an increase in an employee non-discretionary profit sharing plan as a result of the savings in after-tax interest cost following conversion of convertible debt. [IAS 33 paras 34, 35]. The example given below illustrates such an adjustment. When calculating tax for the purposes of diluted EPS the standard tax rate rather than the entity's effective tax rate should be used. This is because the effective tax rate may be influenced by factors (such as group relief) that affect the entity's results other than the expenses associated with the potential ordinary shares.

Example

Entity A has in issue 25,000 4% debentures with a nominal value of C1. The debentures are convertible to ordinary shares at a rate of 1:1 at any time until 20X9. The entity's management receives a bonus based on 1% of profit before tax.

Entity A's results for 20X2 showed a profit before tax of C80,000 and a profit after tax of C64,000 (for simplicity a tax rate of 20% is assumed in this example).

For the purpose of calculating diluted EPS, the earnings should be adjusted for the reduction in the interest charge that would occur if the debentures were converted and for the increase in the bonus payment that would arise from the increased profit.

This is illustrated below:

	C
Profit after tax	64,000
Add: Reduction in interest cost[1]	
25,000 × 4%	1,000
Less tax expense 1,000 × 20%	(200)
Less: Increase in management bonus	
1,000 × 1%	(10)
Add tax benefit 10 × 20%	2
Earnings for the purposes of diluted EPS	64,792

[1] Note that for simplification, this example does not illustrate the classification of the components of the convertible debenture as liabilities and equity as required by IAS 32.

14.105 It should be noted that the requirement in paragraph 14.102 above refers to adjusting the profit attributable to ordinary equity holders. This figure is after deducting dividends on convertible preference shares and is the figure used for the purpose of calculating basic EPS. In some cases those dividends will be charged as finance costs in arriving at profit for the year (preference shares treated as a financial liability under IAS 32) and no adjustment will be necessary to arrive at profit attributable to ordinary shareholders. In other cases they will be classified in equity (preference shares treated as equity instruments under IAS 32) and an adjustment will be made to profit for the year to arrive at profit attributable to ordinary equity holders. In either case, however, if the convertible preference shares are dilutive, the profit attributable to ordinary shareholders for the purpose of calculating diluted EPS is before deducting the preference dividend.

Computation of number of ordinary shares

14.106 As noted in paragraph 14.100, the denominator of diluted EPS should be calculated as the sum of the weighted average number of ordinary shares used in the basic EPS calculation and the weighted average number of ordinary shares that would be issued on the conversion of all the dilutive potential ordinary shares into ordinary shares. [IAS 33 para 36].

14.107 Entities may have more than one type of potential ordinary share in issue at the reporting date. Whether all these potential ordinary shares actually will be converted into ordinary shares in the future is usually not determinable at the reporting date. The standard requires the assumption that all potential ordinary shares have been converted into ordinary shares at the beginning of the period or, if not in existence at the beginning of the period, the date of the issue of the financial instrument or the granting of the rights by which they are generated. [IAS 33 para 36]. This is sometimes referred to as the 'if converted' method.

14.108 The conversion into ordinary shares should be determined from the terms of the financial instrument or the rights granted and this determination should assume the most advantageous conversion rate or exercise price from the standpoint of the holder of the potential ordinary shares. [IAS 33 para 39]. The effect is to ensure that the diluted EPS is based on the maximum number of new shares that would be issuable under the instrument's terms. In practice, it may be that not all conversion rights or warrants are exercised, in which case the dilutive effect in reality would be less than the diluted figure suggests. Where an instrument has variable conversion terms such that it is convertible at reducing rates over its life (see the example in para 14.115 below), the effect is that the conversion rate at the end of the period is used to determine the number of shares that would be issued on conversion. This is because the maximum number of new shares would not take into consideration the higher conversion rates in previous periods, because the instrument could no longer be converted at those higher rates.

14.109 Potential ordinary shares are included in the diluted EPS calculation on a weighted basis only for the period they were outstanding. Therefore, potential ordinary shares that are issued during the year are included on a weighted basis from the date of issue to the balance sheet date. Where potential ordinary shares that are outstanding at the beginning of the period are converted during the year, they are included on a weighted average basis from the beginning of the year to the date of conversion. This is illustrated in the examples in paragraph 14.115. The new ordinary shares that are issued on conversion are included from the date of conversion in both basic and diluted EPS on a weighted basis. The same principles apply where potential ordinary shares, instead of being converted, are cancelled or allowed to lapse during the reporting period. [IAS 33 para 38].

14.110 In computing diluted EPS, only potential ordinary shares that are dilutive are considered in the calculation. Potential ordinary shares should be treated as dilutive when, and only when, their conversion to ordinary shares would decrease profit per share or increase loss per share from *continuing operations* attributable to ordinary equity holders. [IAS 33 para 41]. The effects of anti-dilutive potential ordinary shares are ignored in calculating diluted EPS. [IAS 33 para 43]. Where a company has a number of different types of potential ordinary shares in issue, each one would need to be considered separately rather than in aggregate. The way in which this should be done is considered further from paragraph 14.126 below.

[The next paragraph is 14.112.]

14.112 As noted in paragraph 14.110, potential ordinary shares are either dilutive or anti-dilutive based on profit or loss from continuing operations attributable to ordinary equity holders. If the potential ordinary shares are dilutive at this level they must be treated as dilutive for all other EPS calculations (that is, total EPS, discontinued operations EPS and any additional EPS given) whether or not they are actually dilutive at the relevant level of profit (see further para 14.126). [IAS 33 para A3].

Partly paid shares

14.113 As stated in paragraph 14.69, partly paid shares are included in the computation of basic EPS to the extent that they rank for dividends during the period. Partly paid shares that do not rank for dividends during the period — for example, they do not rank until they are fully paid — are regarded as the equivalent of share options and warrants. That is, the unpaid balance should be assumed to be the proceeds used to purchase shares under the treasury stock method (see further para 14.117). The number of shares included in diluted EPS is the difference between the number of partly paid shares already in issue and the number of shares assumed to be purchased at average market price during the period. [IAS 33 para A16].

Convertible securities

14.114 Where a company has issued instruments in the form of debentures, loan stocks or preference shares that are convertible into ordinary shares of the entity, the instrument's terms will specify the dates, the number of shares and, in effect, the conversion price or prices at which the new shares will be issued. Convertible preference shares are dilutive when the amount of dividend on such shares declared or accrued in the period per ordinary share obtainable on conversion is below basic EPS for continuing operations (where it exceeds basic EPS, the convertible preference shares are anti-dilutive). Convertible debt is dilutive when the interest, net of tax and other changes in income or expense, per ordinary share obtainable on conversion is lower than basic EPS for continuing operations (where it exceeds basic EPS, the convertible debt is anti-dilutive). [IAS 33 para 50]. However, see paragraph 14.130 for situations where there is more than one class of potential ordinary share.

14.115 A convertible security is a particularly good example to illustrate the application of the principles discussed from paragraphs 14.102 to 14.110 above for calculating diluted EPS.

> **Example 1**
>
> *No conversion during the year*
>
> At 30 June 20X1, the issued share capital of a company consisted of 1,500,000 ordinary shares of C1 each. On 1 October 20X1 the company issued C1,250,000 of 8% convertible loan stock for cash at par. Each C100 nominal of the loan stock may be converted at any time during the years ended 20X6/X9 into the number of ordinary shares set out below:
>
> 30 June 20X6 135 ordinary shares
> 30 June 20X7 130 ordinary shares
> 30 June 20X8 125 ordinary shares
> 30 June 20X9 120 ordinary shares
>
> If the loan stocks are not converted by 20X9, they would be redeemed at par. There are two different ways of assessing these instruments under IAS 32. The conversion option to convert to a number of shares which varies only with time may be viewed as either an option to convert to a variable or fixed number of shares and recognised as either a liability or equity respectively. See chapter 6.5 for more details. This example assumes the written equity conversion option is accounted for as a derivative liability and marked to market through profit or loss. The change in the options' fair value reported in 20X2 and 20X3 amounted to a loss of C2,500 and C2,650 respectively. It is assumed that there are no tax consequences arising from these losses.
>
> The profit before interest and taxation for the year ended 30 June 20X2 and 20X3 amounted to C825,000 and C895,000 respectively and relate wholly to continuing operations. The rate of tax for both periods is 33%.

Trading results	20X3 C	20X2 C
Profit before interest and tax	895,000	825,000
Interest on 8% convertible loan stock (20X2: 9/12 × C100,000)	(100,000)	(75,000)
Change in fair value of embedded option	(2,650)	(2,500)
Profit before tax	792,350	747,500
Taxation @ 33%	(262,350)	(247,500)
Profit after tax	530,000	500,000

Calculation of basic EPS

	20X3	20X2
Number of equity shares outstanding	1,500,000	1,500,000
Basic EPS	C530,000	C500,000
	1,500,000	1,500,000
	35.3c	33.3c

Calculation of diluted EPS

Test whether convertibles are dilutive:
The saving in after-tax earnings resulting from the conversion of C100 nominal of loan stock amounts to C100 × 8% × 67% + C2,650/12,500 = C5.36 + C0.21 = C5.57. There will then be 135 extra shares in issue. Therefore, the incremental earnings per share = 4.12c (that is, C5.57/135). As this incremental earnings per share is less than the basic EPS at the continuing level, it this will have the effect of reducing the basic EPS of 35.3c. Hence the convertibles are dilutive (see further para 14.131).

Adjusted earnings	20X3 C	20X2 C
Profit for basic EPS	530,000	500,000
Add: interest and other charges on earnings saved as a result of the conversion	102,650	77,500
Less: tax relief thereon	(33,000)	(24,750)
Adjusted earnings for equity	599,650	552,750

Adjusted number of shares
From the conversion terms, it is clear that the maximum number of shares issuable on conversion of C1,250,000 loan stock after the end of the financial year would be at the rate of 135 shares per C100 nominal, that is, 1,687,500 shares.

	20X3	20X2
Number of equity shares for basic EPS	1,500,000	1,500,000
Maximum conversion at date of issue 1,687,500 × 9/12	–	1,265,625
Maximum conversion after balance sheet date	1,687,500	–
Adjusted capital	3,187,500	2,765,625
Diluted EPS	C599,650	C552,750
	3,187,500	2,765,625
	18.8c	20.0c

Example 2

Partial conversion during the year

The facts are the same as set out in the previous example, but at 1 January 20X6, the holders of half the loan stock exercised their right of conversion.

	20X6	20X5
Trading results	C	C
Profit before interest and tax	1,220,000	1,000,000
Interest on 8% convertible loan stock	(75,000)*	(100,000)
Change in fair value of embedded option	(2,750)	(5,000)
Profit before tax	1,142,250	895,000
Taxation @ 33%	(377,850)	(297,000)
Profit after tax	764,400	598,000

*Interest $= (C1,250,000 \times 8\% \times \frac{1}{2}) + (C625,000 \times 8\% \times \frac{1}{2}) = C75,000$

Calculation of basic EPS
Adjusted number of shares:		
Number outstanding before conversion	1,500,000	1,500,000
Weighted average shares issued on conversion at 1 January 20X6 = 843,750/2	421,875	–
Adjusted number of shares	1,921,875	1,500,000

Basic EPS	$\dfrac{C764,400}{1,921,875}$	$\dfrac{C598,000}{1,500,000}$
	39.8c	39.9c

Calculation of diluted EPS
Adjusted earnings	C	C
Profit for basic EPS	764,400	598,000
Add: interest and other charges on earnings saved as a result of conversion	77,750	105,000
Less: tax relief thereon	(24,750)	(33,000)
Adjusted earnings	817,400	670,000

Adjusted number of shares

Number of equity shares for basic EPS	1,921,875	1,500,000
Assumed conversion of C1,250,000 loan stock outstanding at the beginning of the year at the maximum rate of 135 shares per C100 of stock up to 1 January 20X6 (6 months)	843,750	–
Assumed conversion of C625,000 of remaining stock outstanding at 30 June 20X6 at the maximum rate of 135 shares per C100 of stock (6 months)	421,875	–
Maximum conversion after balance sheet date at the rate of 135 shares per £100 of stock	–	1,687,500
Adjusted number of shares	3,187,500	3,187,500
Diluted EPS	C817,400	C670,000
	3,187,500	3,187,500
	25.6c	21.0c

Example 3

Final conversion during the year

The facts are the same as set out in the previous example, but the holders of half of the loan stock had exercised their right of conversion on 1 January 20X6 at 135 shares per C100 stock and the remaining stock was converted on 30 June 20X7 at 130 shares per C100 stock.

	20X7	20X6
Trading results	C	C
Profit before interest and tax	1,450,000	1,220,000
Interest on 8% convertible loan stock	(50,000)*	(75,000)
Change in fair value of embedded option	(3,500)	(2,750)
Profit before tax	1,396,500	1,142,250
Taxation @ 33%	(462,000)	(377,850)
Profit after tax	934,500	764,400

*Interest = C625,000 × 8% = C50,000

Calculation of basic EPS

Adjusted number of shares:		
Number outstanding before conversion	1,500,000	1,500,000
Weighted average shares issued on conversion at 1 January 20X6	843,750	421,875
Weighted average shares issued on conversion at 30 June 20X7	–	–
Adjusted number of equity shares	2,343,750	1,921,875

Basic EPS		C934,500	C764,400
		2,343,750	1,921,875
		39.9c	39.8c

Calculation of diluted EPS

Adjusted earnings

	C	C
Profit for basic EPS	934,500	764,400
Add: interest and other charges on earnings saved as a result of conversion	53,500	77,750
Less: tax thereon	(16,500)	(24,750)
Adjusted earnings	971,500	817,400

Adjusted number of shares

Number of equity shares for basic EPS	2,343,750	1,921,875
Assumed conversion of C1,250,000 loan stock outstanding at the beginning of the year at the maximum rate of 135 shares per C100 of stock up to 1 January 20X6 (6 months)	–	843,750
Assumed conversion of £625,000 of remaining stock outstanding at 30 June 20X6 at the maximum rate of 135 shares per C100 of stock (6 months)	–	421,875
Assumed conversion of C625,000 of stock outstanding at the maximum rate of 130 shares per C100 of stock†	812,500	–
Adjusted number of shares	3,156,250	3,187,500

† Deemed to be outstanding for the whole year because the remaining loan stock of C625,000 was redeemed on the last day of the financial year, that is, on 30 June 20X7.

Diluted EPS		C971,500	C817,400
		3,156,250	3,187,500
		30.8c	22.6c

14.116   Table 14.4 shows the presentation of adjustments made for the purpose of diluted EPS that result from dilutive convertible debt. The extract also illustrates disclosure of continuing, total and discontinued EPS, the treatment of own shares held and the effect on diluted EPS of share options issued by a subsidiary, Genentech (see para 14.134).

Table 14.4 – Effect of potential ordinary shares on diluted EPS

Roche Holding Ltd – Annual Report and Accounts – 31 December 2007

29. Earnings per share and non-voting equity security

Basic earnings per share and non-voting equity security
For the calculation of basic earnings per share and non-voting equity security, the number of shares and nonvoting equity securities is reduced by the weighted average number of its own non-voting equity securities held by the Group during the period.

Basic earnings per share and non-voting equity security

	Continuing businesses		Group	
	2007	2006	2007	2006
Net income attributable to Roche shareholders (millions of CHF)	9,761	7,860	9,761	7,880
Number of shares (millions)[28]	160	160	160	160
Number of non-voting equity securities (millions)[28]	703	703	703	703
Weighted average number of own non-voting equity securities held (millions)	(4)	(11)	(4)	(11)
Weighted average number of shares and non-voting equity securities in issue (millions)	859	852	859	852
Basic earnings per share and non-voting equity security (CHF)	11.36	9.22	11.36	9.24

Diluted earnings per share and non-voting equity security
For the calculation of diluted earnings per share and non-voting equity security, the net income and weighted average number of shares and non-voting equity securities outstanding are adjusted for the effects of all dilutive potential shares and non-voting equity securities.

Potential dilutive effects arise from the convertible debt instruments and the employee stock option plans. If the outstanding convertible debt instruments were to be converted then this would lead to a reduction in interest expense and an increase in the number of shares which may have a net dilutive effect on the earnings per share. The exercise of outstanding vested employee stock options would have a dilutive effect. The exercise of the outstanding vested Genentech employee stock options would have a dilutive effect if the net income of Genentech is positive. The diluted earnings per share and non-voting equity security reflects the potential impacts of these dilutive effects on the earnings per share figures.

Diluted earnings per share and non-voting equity security	Continuing businesses		Group	
	2007	2006	2007	2006
Net income attributable to Roche shareholders (millions of CHF)	9,761	7,860	9,761	7,880
Elimination of interest expense, net of tax, of convertible debt instruments, where dilutive (millions of CHF)	4	25	4	25
Increase in minority share of Group net income, net of tax, assuming all outstanding Genentech stock options exercised (millions of CHF)	(141)	(100)	(141)	(100)
Net income used to calculate diluted earnings per share (millions of CHF)	9,624	7,785	9,624	7,805
Weighted average number of shares and non-voting equity securities in issue (millions)	859	852	859	852
Adjustment for assumed conversion of convertible debt instruments, where dilutive (millions)	1	7	1	7
Adjustment for assumed exercise of equity compensation plans, where dilutive (millions)	2	3	2	3
Weighted average number of shares and non-voting equity securities in issue used to calculate diluted earnings per share (millions)	862	862	862	862
Diluted earnings per share and non-voting equity security (CHF)	11.16	9.03	11.16	9.05

28. Equity attributable to Roche shareholders (extract)

Share capital

As of 31 December 2007, the authorised and issued share capital of Roche Holding Ltd, which is the Group's parent company, consisted of 160,000,000 shares with a nominal value of 1.00 Swiss franc each, as in the preceding year. The shares are bearer shares and the Group does not maintain a register of shareholders. Based on information supplied to the Group, a shareholder group with pooled voting rights owns 50.0125% (2006: 50.0125%) of the issued shares. This is further described in Note 33. Based on information supplied to the Group, Novartis International Ltd, Basel, and its affiliates 33.3330% (participation below 331/3%) of the issued shares (2006: 33.3330%).

Non-voting equity securities *(Genussscheine)*

As of 31 December 2007, 702,562,700 non-voting equity securities have been authorised and were in issue as in the preceding year. Under Swiss company law these non-voting equity securities have no nominal value, are not part of the share capital and cannot be issued against a contribution which would be shown as an asset in the balance sheet of Roche Holding Ltd. Each non-voting equity security confers the same rights as any of the shares to participate in the net profit and any remaining proceeds from liquidation following repayment of the nominal value of the shares and, if any, participation certificates. In accordance with the law and the Articles of Incorporation of Roche Holding Ltd, the Company is entitled at all times to exchange all or some of the non-voting equity securities into shares or participation certificates.

Own equity instruments (extract)

Holdings of own equity instruments *in equivalent number of non-voting equity securities*

	31 December 2007 (millions)	31 December 2006 (millions)
Non-voting equity securities	0.4	0.2
Low Exercise Price Options	1.9	6.8
Derivative instruments	9.3	8.2
Total own equity instruments	11.6	15.2

Own equity instruments are recorded within equity at original cost of acquisition.

8. Discontinued businesses (extract)

The 2006 results include 20 million Swiss francs of profit from discontinued businesses. This consisted of income of 28 million Swiss francs relating to the release of certain accruals and provisions that were no longer required less 5 million Swiss francs of expenses for the unwinding of the discounted provisions and 3 million Swiss francs of income tax expenses. This had an impact of 0.02 CHF on earnings per share and non-voting equity security (basic and diluted).

Share warrants, options and other potential ordinary shares

14.117 Where a company has issued warrants to subscribe for shares at fixed prices on specified dates in the future or granted share options to directors and employees, these and other potential ordinary shares should be taken into account in the calculation of diluted EPS if they are dilutive. [IAS 33 para 45]. Warrants or options are defined as financial instruments that give the holder the right to purchase ordinary shares. [IAS 33 para 5]. They are dilutive when they would result in the issue of ordinary shares for less than the average market price of ordinary shares during the period. Under IAS 33, the expected proceeds from the exercise of the dilutive share warrants and options are deemed to be used by the company in purchasing as many of its ordinary shares as possible in the open market, using an average market price for the period. Since these shares are fairly priced and are neither dilutive or anti-dilutive, they are ignored in the diluted EPS calculation. They are, therefore, deducted from the number of shares to be issued under the options or warrants to give the number of shares deemed to be issued at no consideration. As these shares are dilutive, they are added to the number of ordinary shares outstanding in the computation of diluted EPS. [IAS 33 paras 45 to 47].

14.118 The method reflects more dilution as the value of options and warrants increases relative to the value of the underlying share. That is, as the average market price for the underlying share increases, the assumed proceeds from exercise will buy fewer shares, thus increasing the number of shares issued for nil consideration and, hence, the denominator. This method of accounting for share warrants and options and other share purchase agreements is often referred to as 'the treasury stock method'. However, although increases in the share price over a number of periods may increase the dilutive effect, the standard makes it clear that previously reported EPS figures are not retrospectively adjusted to reflect changes in share prices. [IAS 33 para 47].

14.119 It should be noted that the fair value of share options and warrants under the treasury stock method should always be calculated on the basis of the average price of an ordinary share for the period rather than the period end market price. The use of the average stock price is consistent with the objective of diluted EPS to measure earnings per share for the period based on period in formation and that use of end-of-period data or estimates of the future is inconsistent with the objectives as discussed in paragraph 14.101 above. The standard indicates that a pragmatic basis of calculation, such as a simple average of weekly or monthly prices should be adequate for calculating the average price for the period. Also, closing market prices are adequate for calculating the average market price, but where prices fluctuate wildly an average of the high and low prices generally produces a more representative price. The method should be used consistently, unless it becomes unrepresentative due to changed market conditions. For example, an entity that had used closing market prices to calculate the average market price during several years of relatively stable prices might change to using an average of high and low prices, if prices began to fluctuate wildly and closing prices no longer produced a representative average price. [IAS 33 paras A4, A5].

14.120 Paragraph 41 of IAS 33 says that potential shares are treated as dilutive when they decrease profit or increase loss per share from continuing operations attributable to ordinary equity holders. Where an entity is making profits from continuing operations, share options will always be additionally dilutive if the exercise price is below the average of the share price during the period (that is, the options are 'in the money'). However, where an entity has incurred a loss from continuing operations, options that are in the money would only be dilutive if they increased the loss per share from continuing operations, that is, made the loss per share more negative. But as the effect of bringing in more shares will be to increase the denominator and therefore reduce the loss per share, in the money options will be anti-dilutive and so are not included in the diluted EPS.

14.121 An example that illustrates the mechanics of calculating diluted EPS where a company has granted options is given below.

> **Example**
>
> At 31 December 20X7 and 20X8, the issued share capital of a company consisted of 4,000,000 ordinary shares of 25c each. The company has granted options that give holders the right to subscribe for ordinary shares between 20Y6 and 20Y9 at 70c per share. Options outstanding at 31 December 20X7 and 20X8 were 630,000. There were no grants, exercises or lapses of options during the year. The profit after tax attributable to ordinary equity holders for the years ended 31 December 20X7 and 20X8 amounted to C500,000 and C600,000 respectively (wholly relating to continuing operations).

Average market price of share:
Year ended 31 December 20X7 = C1.20
Year ended 31 December 20X8 = C1.60

Calculation of basic EPS		
	20X8	**20X7**
Basic EPS	C600,000	C500,000
	4,000,000	4,000,000
	15.0c	12.5c
Calculation of diluted EPS		
Adjusted number of shares		
Number of shares under option:		
Issued at full market price:		
(630,000 × 0.70) ÷ 1.20		367,500
(630,000 × 0.70) ÷ 1.60	275,625	
Issued at nil consideration — dilutive	354,375	262,500
Total number of shares under option	630,000	630,000
Number of equity shares for basic EPS	4,000,000	4,000,000
Number of dilutive shares under option	354,375	262,500
Adjusted number of shares	4,354,375	4,262,500
Diluted EPS	C600,000	C500,000
	4,354,375	4,262,500
	13.8c	11.7c
Percentage dilution	8.00%	6.40%

Note – If options had been granted or exercised during the period, then the number of 'nil consideration' shares in respect of these options would be included in the diluted EPS calculation on a weighted average basis for the period prior to exercise.

14.122 Table 14.5 illustrates the disclosure of the effect of options on diluted EPS.

Table 14.5 – Effect of share options on diluted EPS

Syngenta AG – Annual Report and Accounts – 31 December 2011

Consolidated Income Statement (extract)
(for the years ended December 31, 2011, 2010 and 2009)

(US$ million, except share and per share amounts)	Notes	2011	2010	2009
Earnings per share (US$):				
Basic earnings per share	8	**17.40**	**15.07**	15.11
Diluted earnings per share	8	**17.31**	**14.99**	15.01
Weighted average number of shares:				
Basic		**91,892,275**	**92,687,903**	93,154,537
Diluted		**92,383,611**	**93,225,303**	93,760,196

8. Earnings per share

Basic earnings per share amounts are calculated by dividing net income for the year attributable to ordinary shareholders of Syngenta AG by the weighted average number of ordinary shares outstanding during the year.

Diluted earnings per share amounts are calculated by dividing the net income attributable to ordinary shareholders of Syngenta AG by the sum of the weighted average number of ordinary shares outstanding during the year plus the weighted average number of ordinary shares that would be issued on the conversion of all the dilutive potential ordinary shares into ordinary shares.

Treasury shares are deducted from total shares in issue for the purposes of calculating earnings per share.

The calculation of diluted earnings per share for the year ended December 31, 2011 excluded 558,727 (2010: 373,365; 2009: 226,897) of Syngenta AG shares and options granted to employees, as their inclusion would have been antidilutive.

(US$ million, except number of shares)	2011	2010	2009
Net income attributable to Syngenta AG shareholders	**1,599**	**1,397**	1,408
Weighted average number of shares			
Weighted average number of shares – basic	**91,892,275**	92,687,903	93,154,537
Adjustments for dilutive potential ordinary shares:			
Grants of options over Syngenta AG shares under employee share participation plans	**261,100**	328,437	396,027
Grants of Syngenta AG shares under employee share participation plans	**230,236**	208,963	209,632
Weighted average number of shares – diluted	**92,383,611**	**93,225,303**	93,760,196

14.123   Although the standard does not specifically say so, it should be assumed that the average price for the period means the average price during the period covered by the financial statements. However, where options are issued during the period the average price should be taken to be the average price during the period for which the options were in issue. This may affect whether the options are dilutive or anti-dilutive.

Example

An entity issued share options on 1 January 20X3. The share options are exercisable upon issue. The exercise price of the share options is 20c. The average share price during the year was as follows:

Average share price 1 January 20X3 to 30 June 20X3	8c
Average share price 1 July 20X3 to 31 December 20X3	22c
Average share price for the year to 31 December 20X3	15c

Management is preparing the financial statements for the year ended 31 December 20X3 and is considering the effect on diluted EPS of the following two scenarios for year-end share prices:

(a)   the share price is 18c at 31 December 20X3; or
(b)   the share price is 23c at 31 December 20X3.

(a)   The fact that the year end share price is less than the exercise price is not relevant because the standard requires the comparison to be made between the exercise price and the average market price of the shares for the period, not with the price at the year end. [IAS 33 para 45]. The share options should not be included in the diluted EPS calculation as they are out-of-the-money, that is, the exercise price (20c) is higher than the average price of the ordinary shares for the period (15c).

(b)   Similarly the fact that the year end share price is more than the exercise price is not relevant. There is no change in the answer from that given in (a) above, because the extent of dilution is calculated by reference to the exercise price and the average share price during the period. The exercise price is 20c and the average fair value of the shares is 15c and, therefore, the options are still out of the money for the purpose of the diluted EPS calculation.

The answer would change, however, if the options had been issued at 1 July 20X3. The average price of the shares during the second half of the year (22c) was above the exercise price of the options (20c), so that the share options would be included in the diluted EPS calculation.

14.124   The basic method of including options or warrants in the EPS computation is the treasury stock method described in paragraph 14.117 above. However, the treasury stock method may not always be applicable for calculating the dilutive effects of options or warrants. Sometimes options or warrants may require or permit the tendering of debt or other securities of the entity in payment of all or part of the exercise price. In computing diluted EPS:

- Those options or warrants are assumed to be exercised and the debt or other securities are assumed to be tendered.

- Interest (net of tax) on any debt assumed to be tendered is added back as an adjustment to the numerator.

- If tendering cash would be more advantageous to the option holder or warrant holder and the contract permits tendering cash, the tendering of cash should be assumed.

[IAS 33 para A7].

Example

An entity issued 50,000 warrants at the beginning of the year. Each warrant may be exercised to purchase 10 ordinary shares by tendering either C100 cash or C100 nominal of outstanding 6% debentures of the entity. The market value of the debentures at the balance sheet date is C92 and the average market price of the entity's share for the period and at the balance sheet date is C9.50 and C9.60 respectively.

In the calculation of diluted EPS, it is first necessary to consider whether the warrants are dilutive. The warrants would be dilutive if either:

(a)   The warrants are exercised for cash and the average market price of the related ordinary shares for the period exceeds the exercise price. This is not the case here as the average share price of C95 (10 shares @ C9.50) is less than the exercise price of C100.

(b)   The warrants are exercised by tendering the entity's debentures and the selling price of the debenture to be tendered is below that at which the debenture may be tendered under the warrant agreement and the resulting discount establishes an effective exercise price below the market price of the ordinary shares obtained upon exercise. This is the case here as the market value of the debentures of C92 (nominal value C100) is less than the market price of the shares obtained of C96 at the balance sheet.

Therefore, the warrants are dilutive, and it is assumed that debentures will be tendered because it will be more advantageous to the warrant holder to surrender the entity's debentures that have a market value of C92 rather than pay cash of C100 to obtain 10 ordinary shares with a market value of C96.

For the purposes of calculating diluted EPS, the company will increase the numerator by the after-tax interest saved of C210,000 (C5m @ 6% less tax @ 30%) on effectively repurchasing C5m (C100 nominal for each 50,000 warrants) of the entity's outstanding debentures. In addition, the full amount of 500,000 shares to be issued following the exercise of warrants, (rather than the number computed under the treasury stock method using an effective exercise price equal to the market value of C92 for the debenture and an average share price of C9.50), is included in the denominator. This treatment reflects the fact that a repurchase of debt with the warrant/option proceeds followed by an issue of shares under the warrant/option agreement is in substance equivalent to a traditional or conventional debt instrument that is convertible into a fixed number of shares.

On the other hand, if the tendering of cash is considered to be more advantageous to the warrant holder, for instance, if cash tendered in the above example was C90 for each warrant, tendering of cash would be considered to be dilutive as the exercise price is less than the average share price. In that situation, the number of dilutive shares included in the denominator would be calculated under the treasury stock method in the normal way for options and warrants.

Furthermore, where both cash and debt instruments are tendered, the number of dilutive shares included in the denominator would be the sum of (a) the amount calculated using the treasury stock method to the cash proceeds and (b) the amount calculated by the treating the debt tendered as a conventional convertible debt.

14.125 In some circumstances, the proceeds from the exercise of options or warrants may be required to be applied to redeem the entity's existing debt instruments. Upon the assumed exercise of such options or warrants, the proceeds are applied to purchase the debt at its market price rather than to purchase ordinary shares under the treasury stock method. The treasury stock method is applied, however, for the excess proceeds received from the assumed exercise of the options or warrants over the amount used for the assumed purchase of debt. Interest, net of income tax, on any debt assumed to be purchased is added back as an adjustment to the numerator. [IAS 33 para A9].

Example

An entity granted 500,000 new options at the beginning of the year to its debenture holders that also own all of the entity's 6% redeemable 20,000 nominal C100 debentures. The exercise price of the option is C6.50. The terms of the options require the company to use the proceeds received from the exercise of options to repurchase the company's outstanding debentures. The average market price of nominal C100 debenture and an ordinary share for the period are C105 and C8 respectively.

For the purposes of calculating diluted EPS, the above options are assumed to be exercised and the proceeds of C3,250,000 (500,000 @ 6.50) are applied to purchase all the outstanding 20,000 nominal debentures at the average price of C105 for C2,100,000. The excess proceeds of C1,150,000 are deemed to be applied to purchase shares in the market at C8 per share, that is, 143,750 shares. Therefore, the number of dilutive shares that are included in the denominator under the treasury stock method is 500,000 – 143,750 = 356,250.

In addition, the entity would increase the numerator by the after-tax interest saved on the assumed repurchase of the debentures, that is, C84,000 (C2m @ 6% less tax @ 30%).

The incremental earnings per share = C84,000 ÷ 356,250 = C0.24.

The options would be included in the diluted EPS calculation if the incremental earnings per share of C0.24 is less than the basic EPS at the continuing operations level.

Calculating diluted EPS

14.126 As stated in paragraph 14.110 above, only potential ordinary shares that are dilutive are considered in the calculation of diluted EPS. Potential ordinary shares should be treated as dilutive when, and only when, their conversion to ordinary shares would decrease profit or increase loss per share from continuing operations attributable to ordinary equity holders. [IAS 33 paras 41, 43]. The profit from continuing operations is the profit for the period after deducting preference dividends (and other appropriations and adjustments in respect of preference shares) and excluding items relating to discontinued operations. This means that the entity would need to calculate a basic earnings per share from continuing operations. A potential ordinary share would be dilutive if its assumed conversion results in reducing this earnings per share from continuing operations below the basic level. On the other hand, if the effect is to increase this earnings per share above the basic level, the security is not dilutive and should be excluded from the diluted EPS calculation. [IAS 33 para 42].

14.127 It follows from the above that on no account should the dilution be tested by reference to whether the conversion of a potential ordinary share reduces the standard basic EPS calculated on the total profit or loss for the period. The reason for choosing, as a control number, the 'profit from continuing operations' is because this level of profit, unaffected by discontinued operations, is likely to remain stable over time and reflect the earnings that will exist in the future when the dilution occurs. This is a sensible approach for the following reason. If there is a loss from discontinued operations and this turns the overall earnings per share attributable to ordinary equity holders into a loss per share, the exercise of, say, an option will increase the denominator and result in a lower overall loss per share. This is because the loss is 'shared' among a higher number of shares. In that situation, the option is anti-dilutive at this level, but may well be dilutive at the continuing operations level.

Example

A company has a profit from continuing activities, but a loss for the year overall because of losses on discontinued operations. Options are dilutive when considered at continuing operations profit level as the diluted EPS at that level decreases profit per share. However, at the overall loss for the year level, applying the dilution caused by the options decreases loss per share. Is it still correct to show the effect of the options in the diluted EPS?

Yes. If the options are dilutive at the profit from continuing operations level then they should be included in the diluted EPS calculation at the loss for the year level. If that reduces loss per share then so be it, but the company should explain the circumstances. A form of explanation might be *"Options are dilutive at the profit from continuing operations level and so, in accordance with IAS 33, have been treated as dilutive for the purpose of diluted earnings per share. The diluted loss per share is lower than basic loss per share because of the effect of losses on discontinued operations"*.

In addition to disclosing basic and diluted EPS for the overall loss for the year, the entity would also be required to disclose basic and diluted EPS at the continuing operations level on the face of the income statement and the basic and diluted EPS for discontinued operations either on the face of the income statement or in the notes (see further para 14.173 onwards). [IAS 33 paras 66, 68].

[The next paragraph is 14.130.]

14.130 In order to determine whether a particular convertible instrument, option or warrant will have a dilutive effect, it is necessary to consider each of them separately rather than in aggregate. This consideration is complicated and involves the following steps:

- The entity first calculates the profit or loss from continuing operations attributable to ordinary equity holders.

- The entity next calculates the earnings per incremental share for each type of potential ordinary share. The earnings per incremental share is the increase in profit or loss (or less commonly the decrease) that would result from the exercise or conversion of the security divided by the weighted average increase in the number of ordinary shares that would result from the conversion.

- The entity next ranks all potential ordinary shares from the most dilutive (lowest earnings per incremental share) to the least dilutive (highest earnings per incremental share). Options and warrants are generally included first because they do not affect the numerator of the calculation and, hence, are most dilutive.

- The entity then calculates a basic EPS using profit or loss from continuing operations attributable to ordinary equity holders as the numerator.

- The most dilutive potential ordinary share with the lowest earnings per incremental share is then included and a new EPS as indicated above is calculated. If this new figure is lower than the previous one, the entity recalculates EPS including the potential shares with the next lowest earnings per incremental share.

- The above process of including increasingly less dilutive shares continues until the resulting EPS figure increases or there are no more potential ordinary shares to consider.

- Any potential ordinary share that has the effect of increasing the cumulative EPS from continuing operations is considered to be anti-dilutive and is excluded from the diluted per share calculation.

- All other potential ordinary shares with higher rankings are considered to be dilutive potential ordinary shares and are included in the diluted EPS calculation in the normal way.

[IAS 33 para 44].

In most instances, where there is a loss from continuing operations, there would be no difference between the basic and diluted EPS as potential ordinary shares would be anti-dilutive.

14.131 The sequence of including each issue or series of potential ordinary shares from the most dilutive to the least dilutive guarantees that the final diluted EPS figure expresses maximum dilution of the basic EPS. A numerical example depicting the above steps is shown below.

Example

The issued share capital of C plc at 31 December 20X7 and 20X8 comprises 2,000,000 ordinary shares of 10c each. The company granted options over 100,000 ordinary shares in 20X6. The options can be exercised between 20X9 and 20Y1 at 60c per share. The average market price of C plc's shares during 20X8 was 75c.

In addition, C plc has 800,000 8% C1 convertible cumulative preference shares (treated as an equity instrument under IAS 32) and C1,000,000 5% convertible bonds in issue throughout 20X8. Each preference share and bond is convertible into 2 ordinary shares.

The company's results for the year ended 31 December 20X8 comprised operating profit from continuing operations of C300,000 and operating profit from discontinued operations of C100,000. Interest and tax at 30% amounted to C100,000 and C90,000 respectively. The profit for the year was C210,000.

The necessary steps to calculate C plc's diluted earnings per share for 20X8 are set out below. Comparative figures for 20X7 have not been included in this example.

1 Calculation of profit from continuing operations

	Total	Continuing operations	Discontinued operations
	C	C	C
Operating profit from continuing operations	300,000	300,000	
Operating profit from discontinued operations *	100,000		100,000
Profit before interest	400,000	300,000	100,000
Interest **	100,000	76,000	24,000
Profit after interest	300,000	224,000	76,000
Tax @ 30% **	90,000	67,200	22,800
Profit	210,000	156,800	53,200
Less: Preference dividend	64,000	64,000	–
Profit attributable to ordinary equity holders	146,000	92,800	53,200

* The above workings are for illustrative purposes and do not show the discontinued operations as they are required to be presented in the income statement by IAS 1 and IFRS 5. The presentation of discontinued operations is dealt with in chapter 26.

** Interest has been allocated to the discontinued operation on the basis of the debt that has been attributed to the discontinued operation. Taxation has been attributed on the basis of the taxation actually payable by the discontinued operation.

2 Determine earnings per incremental share for each class of potential ordinary share and rank them from the most dilutive to least dilutive

Options	Increase in earnings C	Increase in number of ordinary shares	Earnings per incremental share C	Rank (note)
Increase in earnings	nil			
Incremental shares issued for nil consideration 100,000 × (75-60)/75		20,000	nil	1
8% Convertible preference shares				
Increase in earnings 8% × C800,000	64,000			
Incremental shares 2 × 800,000		1,600,000	4.00	3
5% Convertible bonds				
Increase in earnings after taxes 1,000,000 × 5% × 70%	35,000			
Incremental shares 1,000,000 × 2		2,000,000	1.75	2

Note: Ranking is in ascending order of earnings per incremental share.

Since the options, convertible preference shares and convertible bonds have been in issue throughout 20X8, the increase in number of ordinary shares is also their weighted average for the year. If options are granted during the year, they are brought into the averaging calculation from the date of grant.

If there were more than one series, say, of options these would have to be ranked by series.

3 Calculate the cumulative dilution effect on profit per share from continuing operations

	Profit from continuing operations C	Weighted average number of shares	Profit from continuing operations per share (c)	
Profit	92,800	2,000,000	4.64	
Options	–	20,000		
	92,800	2,020,000	4.59	Dilutive
5% Convertible bonds	35,000	2,000,000		
	127,800	4,020,000	3.18	Dilutive
8% Convertible preference shares	64,000	1,600,000		
	191,800	5,620,000	3.41	Anti-dilutive

Since diluted earnings per share from continuing operations is increased when taking the convertible preference shares into account (from 3.18 to 3.41), the convertible preference shares are anti-dilutive and are ignored in the calculation of diluted earnings per share.

4 Calculate diluted earnings per share including only dilutive potential ordinary shares

	Earnings C	Weighted average number of shares	Earnings per share (c)
Profit attributable to ordinary equity holders	146,000	2,000,000	7.30
Options		20,000	–
	146,000	2,020,000	–
5% Convertible bonds	35,000	2,000,000	–
Diluted earnings	181,000	4,020,000	4.50

The final diluted EPS is calculated by reference to profit attributable to ordinary equity holders, but the dilution test is carried out by using the profit from continuing operations as the 'control number' (see para 14.132 below) as set out in step three above.

The above example deals only with the calculation of the diluted EPS for the total profit attributable to ordinary equity holders. However, IAS 33 also requires disclosure of the basic and diluted EPS attributable to continuing and to discontinued operations. The figures to be disclosed would be as follows.

	Basic EPS (c)	Diluted EPS (c)
Profit attributable to ordinary equity holders	7.30	4.50
Profit from continuing operations	4.64[1]	3.18[1]
Profit from discontinued operations	2.66[2]	1.32[2]

Notes:

[1] As per step 3 above, Basic = 92,800/2,000,000 = 4.64 ; Diluted = 127,800/4,020,000 = 3.18

[2] Basic = 53,200/2,000,000 = 2.66; Diluted = 53,200/4,020,000 = 1.32

Note that the income statement effect of the convertible bonds is not adjusted against the discontinued operations results, because it relates to continuing operations. The additional shares are taken into account because the discontinued operation EPS is measured as one element of the EPS for the total entity result. Also, the sum of the continuing operations EPS and discontinued operations EPS (for both basic and diluted) equals the EPS calculated on the profit attributable to ordinary equity holders.

14.132 Paragraph A3 of the standard illustrates the application of the 'control number' with a useful example. The following example is derived from that example.

Example

An entity has a profit from continuing operations of C4m, a loss from discontinued operations of C7m, a loss for the year attributable to equity holders of C3m and C4m ordinary shares and C1m potential ordinary shares outstanding.

The entity's basic EPS for continuing operations is C1 for continuing operations, a (C1.75) loss for discontinued operations and (C0.75) for the loss for the year.

The C1m potential ordinary shares are included in the diluted EPS calculation because (assuming no income statement effect for the potential ordinary shares) their effect on the EPS calculation for continuing operations is dilutive. On that assumption, the resulting diluted EPS for continuing operations is C0.8. Because the profit from continuing operations is the control number, the potential ordinary shares are also included in the calculation of the diluted EPS for loss from discontinued operations and for the total loss for the year attributable to equity holders. The resultant diluted EPS figures are respectively (C1.4) for discontinued operations and (C0.6) for the loss attributable to equity holders. This is despite the fact that these figures are anti-dilutive to their comparable basic EPS figures of (C1.75) and (C0.75).

EPS for interim periods

14.133 IAS 33 states that dilutive potential ordinary shares should be determined independently for each period presented. The number of dilutive potential ordinary shares included in the year to date period should not be a weighted average of the dilutive potential ordinary shares included in each interim computation. [IAS 33 para 37]. In other words, the number of dilutive potential ordinary shares should be determined for each interim period based on the year to date position at the end of the interim period.

Example

An example of this principle might be where an entity made an acquisition in the previous year and entered into an agreement to issue 1,000 additional ordinary shares for each C50,000 of consolidated profit in excess of C1,000,000 in the following year, based on the entity's consolidated financial statements. The entity reports quarterly. The results for each quarter are as follows:

		Cumulative
	C	C
First quarter	600,000	600,000
Second quarter	700,000	1,300,000
Third quarter	(200,000)*	1,100,000
Fourth quarter	400,000	1,500,000

*includes a loss from discontinued operations of C300,000.

The company has 100,000 ordinary shares outstanding during the year.

The EPS and diluted EPS for each quarter are as follows:

	Quarter 1	Quarter 2	Quarter 3	Quarter 4	Year
Numerator C	600,000	700,000	(200,000)	400,000	1,500,000
Denominator:					
Ordinary shares	100,000	100,000	100,000	100,000	100,000
Basic EPS*	C6	C7	(C2)	C4	C15
Potential ordinary shares	–	6,000	2,000**	10,000	10,000
Total denominator for diluted EPS	100,000	106,000	102,000	110,000	110,000
Diluted EPS	C6	C6.6	(C1.96)	C3.64	CC13.64

* The potential ordinary shares are not included in the calculation of the basic EPS, because there is no certainty that the condition will be satisfied until the end of the period.

** In quarter 3 there is a profit from continuing operations of C100,000 and a loss from discontinued operations of C300,000 and as the potential ordinary shares are dilutive at the continuing operations level they are taken into account in the diluted EPS, even though they are anti-dilutive at the total loss level.

The above example demonstrates that the diluted EPS for the year differs from any average or weighted average of the diluted EPS figures reported in the individual quarterly accounts. This is simply because the denominator used in each of the first three quarters differs from the denominator at the year end. Under the rules in the standard the diluted EPS figure for the year should be based on the year to date figures, that is, at the year end the figure should be disclosed as C13.64.

Securities of subsidiaries, joint ventures and associates

14.134 A subsidiary, joint venture or associate may issue potential ordinary shares to parties other than the parent, venturer or investor. These potential ordinary shares may be convertible into either ordinary shares of the subsidiary, joint venture or associate or they may be convertible into shares of the parent, venturer or investor (the reporting entity). If the potential ordinary shares have a dilutive effect on the reporting entity's basic EPS, they should be included in the calculation of the reporting entity's diluted EPS. [IAS 33 para 40].

14.135 If the potential ordinary shares issued by a subsidiary enable their holders to obtain ordinary shares in the subsidiary, then those potential ordinary shares should be included in computing the subsidiary's EPS figures (if indeed the subsidiary is calculating an EPS figure). In any event, those earnings per share amounts would be included in the consolidated EPS based on the group's holdings of the subsidiary's securities. On the other hand, if the potential shares issued by the subsidiary enable their holders to obtain ordinary shares in the parent, then these potential ordinary shares should be considered along with the other potential ordinary shares issued by the parent in the computation of consolidated diluted EPS. The same considerations apply where potential ordinary shares issued by an associate or a joint venture are exchangeable into ordinary shares of the associate or joint venture, or into ordinary shares of the reporting entity. They should be included in the EPS computation of the reporting entity if they are considered to be dilutive. [IAS 33 para A11].

> **Example**
>
> A parent entity has profit attributable to ordinary shareholders of C100,000 (excluding any earnings of the subsidiary). There are 10,000 ordinary shares outstanding. The parent owns 800 ordinary shares in the subsidiary representing 80% of the subsidiary's ordinary share capital. It also owns 200 convertible preference shares in the subsidiary representing 50% of the subsidiary's preference share capital (which is treated as an equity instrument under IAS 32). The parent also has 20 warrants exercisable to purchase ordinary shares in the subsidiary.
>
> The subsidiary has profit attributable to ordinary shareholders of C6,000. Its ordinary share capital consists of 1,000 ordinary shares and it has 400 convertible (one for one) preference shares in issue. It has also issued 150 warrants exercisable to subscribe for ordinary shares of the subsidiary, with an exercise price of C5 per warrant. The average market price of one ordinary share of the subsidiary was C10. Dividends on the preference shares are C1 per share. There were no inter-company transactions or eliminations other than dividends. Tax has been ignored for the purposes of this example.

14055

Subsidiary's earnings per share

$$\text{Basic EPS} \qquad \frac{6{,}000 - 400}{1{,}000} \qquad = \text{C5.6}$$

This is calculated as the subsidiary's profit from which is deducted the preference dividend that had been charged to retained earnings. The result is divided by the number of the subsidiary's ordinary shares.

$$\text{Diluted EPS} \qquad \frac{6{,}000}{1{,}000 + 75 + 400} \qquad = \text{C4.07}$$

This is the subsidiary's profit (preference dividends are not deducted as they would be saved on conversion of the preference shares) divided by the number of ordinary shares plus the ordinary shares that would be issued on conversion of the preference shares on the basis of one for one and the number of ordinary shares that would be issued for nil consideration on exercise of the warrants calculated as follows:

Proceeds of warrants 150 × C5 = C750.
Number of ordinary shares that could be issued at fair value C750 ÷ C10 = 75
Number of ordinary shares that would be issued at nil consideration 150 — 75 = 75

Consolidated earnings per share

$$\text{Basic EPS} \qquad \frac{100{,}000 + 4{,}680}{10{,}000} \qquad = \text{C10.47}$$

The earnings are calculated as the profit attributable to ordinary shareholders, before taking account of the subsidiary's results that are included in the consolidated financial statements, of C100,000, plus the share of the subsidiary's profits calculated as:

6,000 — 400 = 5,600 x 800 ÷ 1000 = 4,480 + 200 (share of preference dividend) = 4,680

$$\text{Diluted EPS} \qquad \frac{100{,}000 + 3{,}256 + 41 + 814}{10{,}000} \qquad = \text{C10.41}$$

The earnings figure comprises:

(a) The profit of parent entity attributable to ordinary shares (excluding dividends from subsidiary) of C100,000.

(b) The share of subsidiary's profit calculated as (800 shares × 4.07) = C3,256 (C4.07 being the diluted EPS of the subsidiary).

(c) The parent's proportionate interest in the subsidiary's earnings attributable to the warrants calculated as (75 shares × 4.07) × 20 ÷ 150 = C40.7.

(d) The parent's proportionate interest in the subsidiary's earnings attributable to the convertible preference shares calculated as (200 shares × 4.07) = C814.

14.136   Table 14.4 above discloses the effect on the group diluted EPS of options in a subsidiary that are convertible into shares of the subsidiary.

14.137   The standard also covers the situation where securities of the reporting entity are issued that are convertible into ordinary shares of a subsidiary, joint venture or associate. In such a situation, the securities are assumed to be converted and the profit or loss attributable to ordinary equity holders of the reporting entity is adjusted, in the normal way, for any changes in dividends, interest or other changes that would result from conversion. The profit or loss is also adjusted for any changes in the reporting entity's share of results of the subsidiary, joint venture or associate that would result from the change in the number of shares in the subsidiary, joint venture or associate held by the reporting entity as a result of conversion. The denominator (number of shares and potential ordinary shares) of the diluted EPS calculation is not adjusted because the number of shares of the reporting entity itself would not change following conversion. [IAS 33 para A12].

Employee share and incentive plans

14.138   Many companies have in place share options and other share award schemes to remunerate officers and other employees. Under some schemes, share options or share purchase rights are granted solely on the basis that the employees continue to render service for a specified period of time, that is, the award does not specify a performance condition for vesting. In other schemes, vesting of the shares depends on both the employee's rendering service to the employer for a specified period of time and the achievement of a specified performance target, for example, attaining a specified growth rate in return on assets or a specified earnings target.

14.139   IAS 33 states that employee share options with fixed or determinable terms and non-vested ordinary shares are treated as options in calculating diluted EPS, even though they may be contingent on vesting. They are treated as outstanding on the grant date. Performance-related employee share options are treated as contingently issuable shares (see para 14.145 below) because their issue is contingent on satisfying specified conditions in addition to the passage of time. [IAS 33 para 48].

14.140   As noted above, performance-related share options are treated as contingently issuable shares and these are dealt with from paragraph 14.145 below. All other awards that do not specify a performance criteria should be regarded as options for the purposes of computing diluted EPS. They should be considered to be outstanding as of the grant date for purposes of computing diluted EPS even though their exercise may be contingent upon vesting. They should be included in the diluted EPS computation even if the employee may not receive (or be able to sell) the stock until some future date. Accordingly, all shares to be issued should be included in computing diluted EPS if the effect is dilutive. The dilutive effect should be computed using the treasury stock method described in paragraph 14.117 above. If the share awards were granted during the period, the shares issuable must be weighted to reflect the portion of the period during which the awards were outstanding. [IAS 33 para 38].

14.141 For share options and other share-based payment arrangements to which IFRS 2 applies, the assumed exercise price should include the fair value (as calculated on the date the options were granted) of any goods or services to be supplied to the entity in the future under the share option or other share-based payment arrangement. [IAS 33 para 47A]. Therefore, in applying the treasury stock method described in paragraph 14.117 above, the assumed exercise price, for the purpose of determining the incremental number of shares issued for nil consideration, would comprise the amount, if any, the employee must pay upon exercise and the balance of any amounts calculated under IFRS 2 that has not yet been charged to the income statement. The assumed proceeds should not include cost attributable to past service. Neither should any adjustments be made to the numerator in respect of the IFRS 2 charge to the income statement as the charge represents the cost of issuing potential ordinary shares that would not be saved on conversion. The treatment of employee share options that are not related to performance is illustrated in the following example (ignoring tax).

Example

Share option scheme not related to performance
Company A has in place an employee share option scheme that awards share options to employees on the basis of period of service with the company.

The provisions of the scheme are as follows at the 20X0 year end.

Date of grant	1 January 20X0
Market price of option at grant date	C2.10
Exercise price of option	C2.50
Date of vesting	31 December 20X2
Number of shares under option	1 million

Applying IFRS 2, the income statement is charged with 70c per option in each of the three years 20X0-20X2 (that is, C2.10/3).

Profit for year 20X0 (after compensation expense) C1,200,000	
Weighted average number of ordinary shares outstanding	5 million
Average market price of an ordinary share during the year	C5.00
Assumed proceeds per option	C3.90 (being the exercise price of C2.50 and IFRS 2 expense attributable to future service, not yet recognised, of C1.40).
	Next year C3.20 (being C2.50 + 70c).

Computation of earnings per share	per share	earnings	shares
Profit for year 20X0		C1,200,000	
Weighted average shares outstanding for 20X0			5,000,000
Basic earnings per share	24.0c		
Number of shares under option			1,000,000
Number of shares that would have been issued at fair value: (1 million × C3.90)/ C5.00			(780,000)
Diluted earnings per share	23.0c	C1,200,000	5,220,000

[The next paragraph is 14.143.]

14.143 Sometimes shares to satisfy the company's obligations under share award schemes have already been purchased by an ESOP trust and are held by the trust as pre-funding for options or other performance-related shares. The trust's holding in the company's shares is treated as treasury shares and deducted from equity. [IAS 32 para 33]. Accordingly, the rules relating to treasury shares would apply and those non-vesting shares should be excluded from both basic and diluted EPS as discussed in paragraph 14.75 above. Instead, the calculation of diluted EPS should include non-performance-related shares in the same way as options as set out from paragraph 14.140 above and performance-related shares in the same way as contingently issuable shares as discussed from paragraph 14.145 below.

14.144 If share based awards are payable in ordinary shares or in cash at the election of either the entity or the employee, the determination of whether such awards are potential ordinary shares should be made in the same way as discussed in paragraph 14.163.

Contingently issuable ordinary shares

14.145 It is not uncommon for acquisition agreements to include a clause under which the purchaser of an acquired entity is required to make an additional consideration payment in the form of ordinary shares in future. The value of such shares may either be known precisely at the time of the acquisition, or may be contingent upon the future performance or future evaluation of the acquired entity. In the first instance, the acquirer has an obligation to issue ordinary shares in future, but the obligation is simply deferred (deferred consideration). In the second instance an obligation may or may not arise depending on whether or not certain earnings conditions are met (contingent consideration). In any event, the need to issue ordinary shares in future could lead to dilution of EPS. The standard refers to these as 'contingently issuable ordinary shares'. [IAS 33 para 52]. Contingently issuable ordinary shares are defined as *"ordinary shares issuable for little or no cash or other consideration upon the satisfaction of specified conditions in a contingent share agreement"* (see also para 14.77 above). [IAS 33 para 5].

14.146 The way in which diluted EPS should be calculated to take account of contingently issuable shares is described below:

■ Contingently issuable shares are considered outstanding and included in the calculation of diluted EPS as if the conditions of the contingency are deemed to have been met, based on the information available, at the end of reporting period. In effect this means that the diluted EPS computation includes those shares that would be issued under the terms of the contingency, based on the current status of conditions, as if the end of the reporting period was the end of the contingency period. An example would be an estimate of the number of shares that would have been issued under an earn-out if that agreement had terminated at the balance sheet date (see further para 14.148). Ordinary shares issuable under such contingent share agreements are included in the diluted EPS calculation as of the beginning of the period or as of the date of the contingent share agreement, if later. Restatement is not permitted if the conditions are not met when the actual contingency period expires. [IAS 33 para 52].

■ Where the conditions relating to the issue have been met (the events occurred) by the end of the period, the relevant shares are included in the computation of both basic and diluted EPS. In effect, this will be when issuing the shares is no longer contingent and when there are no circumstances under which the shares would not be issued. [IAS 33 para 52].

14.147 The criteria under which additional shares are issuable under contingent consideration agreements are many and varied, although in practice most involve either future levels of earnings or the future share price of the issuing company or a mixture of both. It should be noted, however, that such contingently issuable shares should be included in the diluted EPS calculation only if the effect is dilutive.

14.148 Where the number of contingently issuable shares depends upon the level of earnings, the diluted EPS computation should include those shares to the extent that that they would be issuable under the agreement based on the current amount of earnings. However, earnings conditions in earn out agreements come in various forms. Sometimes the terms may specify that further shares will be issued if the average profit earned over a period is a specific amount. Sometimes the maintenance of current earnings levels, or the attainment of specified increased level of earnings of the acquired entity for a specified number of years may be the condition. Other earnings conditions may specify the issue of shares when a minimum earnings target is reached, increasing rateably until the maximum earnings target is reached, with a cap on the maximum number of shares that could be issued.

14.149 IAS 33 deals specifically with one such type of arrangement, where the achievement or maintenance of a specified level of earnings is the condition and that amount has been achieved at the end of the period, but must be maintained for a further period. In such a case the additional ordinary shares are included if dilutive in the *diluted* EPS, because the end of the period is *assumed* to be the end of the contingency period for the purpose of diluted EPS and the level of profit has been achieved at the end of the period. However, the shares are not included in *basic* EPS until the end of the *actual* contingency period, that is, the end of the further period for which the level of earnings must be maintained. This is because there may be losses in that further period that could mean that the contingent condition will not be met at the end of the actual contingency period. [IAS 33 para 53].

14.150 Whatever the earnings criteria, the guiding principle is that the current level of earnings should be used to determine the number of shares that could be issued under the terms, assuming that the contingency period ended on the balance sheet date. They should be included in the diluted EPS calculation only if dilution results. If in the subsequent period, or until the end of the agreement, there is a decline in earnings such that the contingent shares no longer need to be issued, previous period's diluted EPS should not be restated. Hence, basic EPS should not include any contingently issuable shares, because all the necessary conditions have not been satisfied, but the shares would be included in calculating the diluted figure. The following examples illustrate the application of the above principle.

Example 1

Average earnings condition
On 1 January 20X4, company A acquired the whole of the issued share capital of company B. The total consideration payable in respect of the acquisition comprises initial consideration and deferred contingent consideration. Under the terms of the deferred contingent consideration, company A is required to issue 100,000 shares if company B's profit for the year averages C100,000 over a three year period. Any additional shares will be issued on 1 January 20X7 after the end of the three year contingency period. Company B's profit for the year ended 31 December 20X4 amounted to C120,000.

Given that the terms stipulate the achievement of C100,000 of average profit for the three year period, it would appear at first sight that the contingency condition at the balance sheet date has been met as the profit for the year ended 31 December 20X4 exceeds C100,000. This is not the case as it assumes that the company will earn at least C90,000 for each of the next two years ended 31 December 20X6. Projecting future earnings levels in this way is not permitted under the standard because as stated in paragraph 14.101 above, the standard takes a historical approach and not a predictive or forward-looking approach in measuring dilution. The provisions relating to contingently issuable shares in the standard are quite specific and do not allow an entity to consider the probability of a contingent issue occurring.

The correct analysis is to measure whether performance achieved in the current period is deemed to be that achieved over the whole of the contingency period as if the end of the reporting period was the end of the contingency period. On this basis, an average over a period has the same effect as if it were expressed as a cumulative amount over the period. So in this situation, the contingency condition should be expressed in terms of a cumulative target of C300,000 over the three year period. Since the profit for the year ended 31 December 20X4 is only C120,000, which is less than C300,000, the contingency condition is not met at the balance sheet and no additional shares would be brought into the diluted EPS computation.

Similarly, if the profit for the year ended 31 December 20X5 were to increase to C150,000 again the contingency condition is not met in that year, because the cumulative earnings to date amounts to C270,000. So no additional shares would be included in that year. In the final year ended 31 December 20X6 when the contingency period comes to an end, the company will know for certain whether the contingency conditions have been met or not. If the condition is met in that year, the company will include 100,000 shares in both basic and diluted EPS.

Example 2

Attainment of a specified increased level of earnings
The facts are the same as in the previous example except that the deferred contingent consideration agreement provides for the issue of 1,000 shares for each C1,000 of total profit in excess of C250,000 over the three years ending 20X6.

Using the above principles, the company did not earn C250,000 for the year ended 31 December 20X4. Again projecting future earnings levels (C120,000 for 3 years = C360,000) and including 110,000 ((C360,000 — C250,000)/C1,000 × 1,000) contingent shares in the diluted EPS calculation is not permitted by the standard.

For the year ended 31 December 20X5, the cumulative amount earned to that date is C270,000. As this amount exceeds C250,000, the contingency condition is met in that year and the company will include 20,000 contingently issuable shares in the diluted EPS calculation for that year. For the year ended 31 December 20X6, the cumulative amount earned to that date would be known and the actual number of shares issued would be included in both basic and diluted EPS. If the actual number of shares amounts to say 50,000 shares, prior year's diluted EPS, which was based on 20,000 contingent shares, should not be restated.

14.151 Similar considerations apply when computing diluted EPS for interim reports. If at 30 June 20X5, the cumulative amount earned to that date was C245,000 (C120,000 to 31 December 20X4 + C125,000 to 30 June 20X5), the contingency provision is not met. Therefore, no contingently issuable shares would be included in calculating the diluted EPS for the half year, even though at the time of preparing the interim report it is apparent that 20,000 shares will be included in the year end diluted EPS calculation.

14.152 IAS 33 also gives specific guidance for the situation where the number of shares issuable in the future depends on the market price of the shares at the future date. It states that the computation of diluted EPS should reflect the number of shares that would be issued based on the current market price at the end of the reporting period if the effect is dilutive. If the condition is based on an average of market prices over some period of time that extends beyond the end of the reporting period, the average for the period that has elapsed at the period end should be used. Because the market price may change in a future period, basic EPS should not include such contingently issuable shares, because all necessary conditions have not been satisfied. [IAS 33 para 54].

14.153 Where the number of contingently issuable ordinary shares depends on both future earnings and the future market price of ordinary shares, the number of ordinary shares included in the diluted EPS calculation is based on both conditions. Unless both conditions are deemed to be met (using the guidance in the previous paragraphs) the contingently issuable shares are not included in the diluted EPS. [IAS 33 para 55].

14.154 In some deferred consideration agreements, the value of the deferred consideration is known, but the number of shares to be issued when the deferred consideration falls due is not known. IAS 33 does not specifically consider this situation. However, we consider that the number of shares to be included in the calculation should be based on the market price at the balance sheet date as if it were the end of the contingency period.

14.155 IAS 33 also gives guidance for the situation where the contingency is based on a condition other than earnings or market price (for example, opening a certain number of retail stores). It states that the contingent shares should be included in the computation of diluted EPS based on the assumption that the current status (at the period end) of the condition will remain unchanged until the end of the contingency period. So, if during the period only half the required number of new stores that would result in the issue of shares were opened, no contingently issuable shares are included in the diluted EPS computation. [IAS 33 para 56].

14.156 If the contingency is based on a number of different conditions, we consider that the determination of the number of shares included in diluted EPS should be based on the status of all relevant conditions as they exist at the end of each reporting period. If one of the conditions is not met at the end of the reporting period, no contingently issuable shares should be included in diluted EPS. Though not specifically mentioned in IAS 33 it is implicit in the guidance described in paragraph 14.153 above.

14.157 Contingently issuable potential ordinary shares that are not covered by a contingent share agreement, such as contingently issuable convertible instruments, should be included in diluted EPS on the following basis:

■ It is first necessary to determine whether the potential ordinary shares may be assumed to be issued on the basis of the conditions specified for their issue under the contingently issuable share provisions discussed from paragraph 14.145.

■ Depending on the type of those potential ordinary shares, they should be reflected in diluted EPS by following the provisions for convertible securities discussed from paragraph 14.114, the provisions for share options and warrants discussed from paragraph 14.117, and the provisions for contracts that may be settled in ordinary shares or cash discussed from paragraph 14.159.

However, exercise or conversion should not be assumed for purposes of computing diluted EPS, unless exercise or conversion of similar outstanding potential ordinary shares that are not contingently issuable is also assumed. [IAS 33 para 57].

14.158 An example of contingently issuable potential ordinary shares is given in Table 14.6. This relates to contingent consideration for an acquisition that is subject to a lawsuit.

Table 14.6 – Diluted EPS and contingent consideration payable in shares

Altana AG – Annual Report and Accounts – 31 December 2002

Earnings per share

Basic earnings per share are computed by dividing net income by the weighted average number of shares outstanding for the year. Diluted EPS reflects the potential dilution that could occur if securities or other contracts to issue common stock were exercised or converted into common stock. Diluted earnings per share are calculated by adjusting the weighted average number of shares for the effect of the stock option plans as well as the impact of the DAT lawsuit which is payable in the Company's shares (Note 31). No adjustments to net income were necessary for the computation of diluted earnings per share.

The diluted earnings per share were calculated under the assumption that all potential diluting options are exercised.

	2002	2001
Basic earnings per share:		
Net income	**324,408**	327,937
Weighted average common shares outstanding	**136,622,766**	137,533,720
Basic earnings per share in €	**2.37**	**2.38**
Diluted weighted average shares:		
Net income	**324,408**	327,937
Weighted average shares outstanding	**136,622,766**	137,533,720
Dilution from stock options	**604,546**	607,434
Dilution from DAT lawsuit	**306,391**	306,391
Diluted weighted average shares outstanding	**137,533,703**	138,447,545
Diluted earnings per share in €	**2.36**	**2.37**

31 Litigation
Deutsch-Atlantische Telegraphen AG
In 1988, a group of minority shareholders of DAT brought a legal action against the Company in connection with an exchange offer made to these minority shareholders.

After consideration of the case, both the Landesgericht Köln and the Oberlandesgericht Düsseldorf stated that the 1.3 or 1.4 shares offered to the former shareholders was fair consideration. However, in 1999 the Federal Supreme Court of Germany overturned this ruling stating that the fair value should be determined based on a higher market value for DAT shares.

On March 12, 2001, the German Federal Court of Justice (Bundesgerichtshof, BGH) ruled that the exchange ratio must be based on the average market price of the shares to be exchanged during the three months preceding the approval by majority shareholders of DAT to sell its shares to the Company. The BGH referred the appeal back to a lower court (Landgericht Köln).

The expected settlement is recorded as contingent consideration based on the Company's best estimate of the exchange of 3.45 ALTANA shares for one DAT share. However, since all of the assets of DAT were either sold or written off in connection with the Company's restructuring plan in 1995, the additional consideration was expensed immediately as an impairment expense. As of December 31, 2002, consideration expected to be settled by the Company by issuance of shares has been measured at €13.8 million based on the Company's share price at December 31, 2002. The portion of the settlement expected to be paid in cash is €2.3 million. The estimated total settlement of €16.1 million is recorded as an accrual. The final settlement is subject to change based on the final exchange ratio and the market value of ALTANA's stock on the date of the settlement (Note 32).

In 2001, the addition of the accrual was recorded in other operating expenses. In 2002 the reduction of the accrual (€3.4 million) due to the decrease in the ALTANA's share price at the balance sheet date was recorded in other operating income.

32 Subsequent events (extract)
The management board and the supervisory board of ALTANA AG authorized the issuance of the financial statements as of March 17, 2003.

On January 15, 2003, the federal court decided that the consideration of the former DAT shareholders (Note 31) should be based on a conversion ratio of 3.45 shares of ALTANA for one share of DAT. The Company has appealed against that ruling.

Contracts that may be settled in ordinary shares or cash

14.159 IAS 33 deals specifically with contracts that may be settled in ordinary shares or cash. The rules differ depending on whether the option is held by the entity (the issuer) or by the holder of the contract, as set out in the following paragraphs.

14.160 If an entity has issued a contract that may be settled in ordinary shares or in cash at the *entity's option* (but not at the holder's option), IAS 33 lays down the following rules:

■ The entity should presume that the contract will be settled in shares, and the resulting potential ordinary shares should be included in diluted EPS if the effect is dilutive.

■ When such a contract is presented for accounting purposes as an asset or a liability, or when it has both an equity and a liability component under IAS 32, the entity should adjust the numerator (profit or loss attributable to ordinary equity holders) for any changes in the profit or loss that would have resulted during the period if the contract had been classified wholly as an equity instrument. This is similar to the adjustments required in paragraph 33 of IAS 33 (see para 14.102 above).

[IAS 33 paras 58, 59].

14.161 An example of such a contract is a deferred or contingent consideration agreement where the entity has the unrestricted right to settle the consideration in the form of ordinary shares or cash. At the date of acquisition it may not be possible for the entity to determine how the deferred consideration will be settled. It should, therefore, be presumed that the contract will be settled in shares, the more dilutive method, and the resulting potential ordinary shares included in diluted EPS in accordance with the standard's relevant provisions. An example is given in Table 14.7. Another example given in the standard is a debt instrument that, on maturity gives the entity the unrestricted right to settle the liability in cash or in ordinary shares. [IAS 33 para 61].

Table 14.7 – Diluted EPS, contract that can be settled in shares or cash at entity's option

Informa PLC – Interim report – 30 June 2005

9 Earnings per share

Basic

The basic earnings per share calculation is based on a profit on ordinary activities after taxation of £48,769,000 (2004 profit: £15,115,000 six months and £69,836,000 twelve months). This profit (2004: six months profit and twelve months profit) on ordinary activities after taxation is divided by the weighted average number of shares in issue (less those non-vested shares held by employee share ownership trusts) which is 299,335,000 (2004: 193,647,000 six months and 244,928,000 twelve months).

Diluted

The diluted earnings per share calculation is based on the basic earnings per share calculation above except that the weighted average number of shares includes all potentially dilutive options granted by the Balance Sheet date as if those options had been exercised on the first day of the accounting period or the date of the grant, if later, giving a weighted average of 300,900,000 (2004: 195,557,000 six months and 246,713,000. twelve months). In accordance with IAS 33 the weighted average number of shares includes the estimated maximum number of shares payable to the vendors of Routledge Publishing Holdings Limited assuming that there are no claims for compensation by the Group that will reduce this deferred consideration and assuming that the Company does not exercise its option to pay the balance of deferred consideration in cash. The deferred consideration shares are also assumed for the purposes of this calculation to have been issued on 1 January 2005 at the closing mid-market share price on 30 June 2005 of 379p making 335,000 (2004: 314,000 six months and 336,000 twelve months) ordinary shares potentially issued.

The table below sets out the adjustment in respect of diluted potential ordinary shares:

	6 months 2005	6 months 2004	12 months 2004
Weighted average number of shares used in basic earnings per share calculation	299,334,804	193,646,662	244,927,883
Effect of dilutive share options	1,230,032	1,597,198	1,449,594
Shares potentially to be issued or allotted	334,734	313,624	335,629
Weighted average number of shares used in diluted earnings per share calculation	300,899,570	195,557,484	246,713,106

14.161.1 The standard includes an example of the calculation of diluted EPS where the entity has in issue a convertible bond that may be settled in ordinary shares or cash at the issuer's option. The example illustrates also the adjustments that may have to be made to the numerator under the second bullet point in paragraph 14.160 above. The example below is based on the example in the standard.

Example

An entity issues 1,000 convertible bonds at the beginning of 20X5. The bonds have a three-year term and are issued at par with a face value of C1,000 per bond, giving total proceeds of C1,000,000. Interest is payable annually in arrears at a nominal annual interest rate of 4%. Each bond is convertible at any time up to maturity into 150 common shares. The entity has an option to settle the principal amount of the convertible bonds in ordinary shares or in cash.

When the bonds are issued, the prevailing market interest rate for similar debt without a conversion option is 9%. At the issue date, the market price of one common share is C3. Income tax is ignored.

	C
Profit 20X5	
Ordinary shares outstanding	1,000,000
Convertible bonds outstanding	1,200,000
Liability component	873,434[1]
Equity component	126,566
Proceeds of the bond issue	1,000,000

Note 1: Present value of the principal and interest discounted at 9% – C1,000,000 payable at the end of three years; C40,000 payable annually in arrears for three years.

The liability and equity components would be determined in accordance with IAS 32. These amounts would be recognised as the initial carrying amounts of the liability and equity components presented on the balance sheet. The amount assigned to the issuer conversion option equity element is a permanent addition to equity and is not adjusted.

Basic earnings per share 20X5:
$$\frac{C1,000,000}{1,200,000} = C0.83 \text{ per ordinary share}$$

Diluted earnings per share 20X5:

It is presumed that the issuer will settle the contract by the issue of ordinary shares; the dilutive effect is calculated in accordance with paragraph 14.158.

$$\frac{C1,000,000 + C78,609(a)}{1,200,000 + 150,000(b)} = C0.80 \text{ per ordinary share}$$

(a)　The initial carrying amount is adjusted for the accretion of the liability using the effective interest rate – that is, C78,609 (C873,434 × 9%).

(b)　150,000 ordinary shares = 150 ordinary shares × 1,000 convertible bonds

[IAS 33 Example 8].

14.162　For contracts that may be settled in ordinary shares or cash at the *holder's option*, the more dilutive of cash settlement and share settlement should be used in calculating diluted EPS. [IAS 33 para 60]. An example might be an incentive scheme where annual bonuses may be payable in either shares or cash at the election of the employee. In that situation it should be presumed that the contract will be settled by the more dilutive method. Another example given in the standard is a written put option that gives the holder the choice of settling in ordinary shares or cash. [IAS 33 para 61].

14.163 Whilst the standard does not specifically cover the point if a contract may be settled in cash or shares at either the issuer's or the holder's option, the more restrictive of the above rules, that is those where only the issuer has an option should be applied. In practice the rules in the standard recognise that it is likely that only one party will have the option as otherwise there could be a conflict.

[The next paragraph is 14.166.]

Purchased options

14.166 The standard notes that contracts such as purchased put options and purchased call options held by an entity over its own ordinary shares are not included in the calculation of diluted EPS. This is because their inclusion would be anti-dilutive. A put option (defined by IAS 33 as a contract that gives the holder the right to sell ordinary shares at a specified price for a given period) would be exercised only if the option exercise price were higher than the market price and a call option would be exercised only if the option exercise price were lower than the market price. [IAS 33 para 62]. In both instances, the options' effect would be anti-dilutive under the treasury stock method (see para 14.118 above) and the reverse treasury stock method (see para 14.167 below).

Written put options

14.167 The standard also deals with written put options. Contracts that require the entity to repurchase its own shares, such as written put options and forward purchase contracts are reflected in diluted EPS if their effect is dilutive. If the contracts are 'in the money' during the period, that is, if the exercise or settlement price is above the average market price for the period, their dilutive effects should be calculated using the 'reverse treasury stock' method. Under that method:

- It should be assumed that at the beginning of the accounting period sufficient ordinary shares will be issued at the average market price for the period to raise the necessary proceeds to satisfy the contracts.

- It should be assumed that the proceeds from this issue are used to satisfy the contract to buy back ordinary shares.

- The incremental ordinary shares, that is, the difference between the number of shares assumed to be issued and the number of shares received (bought back) on satisfying the contract will be included in the calculation of diluted EPS.

[IAS 33 para 63].

Example

Assume an entity has outstanding 160 written put options on 160 of its ordinary shares with an exercise price of C10 per option. The put obligation is, therefore, C1,600. The average market price of the entity's ordinary shares is C8 for the period. In calculating diluted EPS the entity assumes that it issues 200 ordinary shares at C8 per share to raise the proceeds necessary to satisfy the put option. The difference between the 200 ordinary shares assumed to be issued and the 160 ordinary shares that would have been received on exercise of the option, that is 40 shares is added to the denominator (number of shares) in calculating the diluted EPS. No adjustments are made to the numerator (profit attributable to ordinary shareholders) as the shares are deemed issued for nil proceeds. [IAS 33 para A10].

Restatement of EPS data

14.168 Diluted EPS of any prior period presented should not be restated for changes in the assumptions used (such as for contingently issuable shares) or for the conversion of potential ordinary shares (such as convertible debt) outstanding at the end of the previous period. [IAS 33 para 65]. This is because these factors are already taken into account in calculating the basic and, where applicable, the diluted EPS for the current period. However, in some circumstances, prior period's EPS data should be restated. These circumstances include certain post balance sheet changes in capital (see para 14.169) and prior period adjustments (see para 14.171).

Post balance sheet changes in capital

14.169 As noted in paragraph 14.80 above, the weighted average number of ordinary shares outstanding for all periods presented (and, therefore, both basic and diluted EPS for all periods presented) should be restated for bonus issues, share splits, share consolidations and other similar events occurring during the period that change the number of shares in issue without a corresponding change in the resources of the entity. [IAS 33 para 26]. In addition, if such events occur after the balance sheet date, but before the financial statements are approved for issue, the basic and diluted EPS figures for the current period and for prior periods should be presented on the basis of the new number of shares. [IAS 33 para 64]. Where the EPS figures reflect such post balance sheet date changes, this fact should be disclosed (see further para 14.181 below).

14.170 Other post balance sheet changes in capital should not be adjusted for, but disclosure is required of ordinary share transactions or potential ordinary share transactions that would have changed significantly the number of ordinary shares or potential ordinary shares outstanding at the end of the period if they had occurred before the end of the period (see further para 14.182).

Prior period adjustments

14.171 EPS for all periods presented should be adjusted for the effects of errors and adjustments resulting from changes in accounting policies accounted for retrospectively in accordance with IAS 8. [IAS 33 para 64]. That is, the EPS figure for the prior period should be restated as if the restated profit or loss had been reported originally in the prior period or periods.

14.172 When a change in accounting policy: has an effect on the current period or any prior period; would have such an effect except that it is impracticable to determine the amount of the adjustment; or might have an effect on future periods, an entity should disclose for the current period and each prior period presented, to the extent practicable, the amount of the adjustment for basic and diluted earnings per share. Similarly, for the retrospective correction of material prior period errors, an entity should disclose for each prior period presented, to the extent practicable, the amount of the correction for basic and diluted earnings per share. [IAS 8 paras 28(f)(ii), 29(c)(ii), 49(b)(ii)]. Table 14.8 is an example of disclosure.

Table 14.8 – Effect of changes in accounting policy on EPS

China Mobile Limited – Annual Report and Accounts – 31 December 2009

2 Changes in accounting policies (extract)

(ii) IFRIC/HK(IFRIC) Interpretation 13, *Customer loyalty programmes*

The Group has launched a Reward Program to its customers, which provides customers the option of electing to receive free telecommunications services or other gifts. The level of point reward earned by customers under the Reward Program varies depending on the customers' services consumption, years in services and payment history.

In prior years, the Group accounted for the obligation to provide free or discounted services or goods offered to the customers under the Reward Program using the incremental costs method. The estimated incremental cost to provide free or discounted services or goods was recognized as expenses and accrued as a current liability when customers were entitled to bonus points. When customers redeemed awards or their entitlements expired, the incremental cost liability was reduced accordingly to reflect the outstanding obligations.

With effect from 1 January 2009, as a result of adoption of IFRIC/HK(IFRIC) Interpretation 13, the point reward is accounted for as a separately identifiable component of the sales transactions in which the points are granted. The consideration received in relation to the sales transactions is allocated to points reward by reference to the estimated fair value of the points as revenue and is deferred until such reward is redeemed by the customers or the points expired.

The new accounting policy has been adopted retrospectively and the comparative amounts have been restated.

The effect on the consolidated balance sheet as at 1 January 2008 is an increase in deferred tax assets, an increase in deferred revenue, a decrease in accrued expenses and other payables and a decrease in net assets of RMB676,000,000, RMB6,308,000,000, RMB3,542,000,000 and RMB2,090,000,000, respectively.

The effect on the consolidated balance sheet as at 31 December 2008 is an increase in deferred tax assets, an increase in deferred revenue, a decrease in accrued expenses and other payables and a decrease in net assets of RMB730,000,000, RMB6,841,000,000, RMB3,855,000,000 and RMB2,256,000,000, respectively.

The effect on the Group's consolidated statement of comprehensive income for the year ended 31 December 2008 is an decrease in operating revenue, operating expenses, taxation and profit for the year of RMB533,000,000, RMB313,000,000, RMB54,000,000 and RMB166,000,000, respectively. The effect on the basic earnings per share and diluted earnings per share for the year ended 31 December 2008 is a decrease of RMB0.01 and RMB0.01, respectively.

Presentation and disclosure

Presentation of basic and diluted EPS

14.173 An entity should present both basic and diluted EPS on the face of the statement of comprehensive income or if an entity presents the components of profit or loss in a separate statement, it presents the basic and diluted EPS in that separate statement. The basic and diluted EPS should be presented for profit or loss from continuing operations attributable to the entity's ordinary equity holders and for profit or loss for the period (that is, including both continuing and discontinued operations) attributable to the entity's ordinary equity holders. The basic and diluted EPS should be presented with equal prominence for all periods presented. [IAS 33 paras 66, 67A]. This applies even if the basic and diluted EPS are the same. If they are the same the entity can disclose just one line described as 'Basic and diluted EPS'. [IAS 33 para 67].

14.174 In practice, unless an entity has discontinued operations that it must disclose in accordance with IFRS 5, the EPS from continuing operations is likely to be identical to total EPS. Accordingly, if the basic EPS for continuing and total EPS is the same and the diluted EPS is the same, the entity could disclose the figures as follows:

Basic EPS for profit from continuing operations and for profit for the year	x
Diluted EPS for profit from continuing operations and for profit for the year	y
If the basic and diluted figures are the same the disclosure could be: Basic and diluted EPS for profit from continuing operations and for profit for the year	x

14.175 The standard also requires disclosure either on the face of the statement of comprehensive income (or the income statement, if presented separately) or in the notes of basic and diluted EPS for discontinued operations, where an entity has such operations and is required to disclose them in accordance with IFRS 5. [IAS 33 para 68]. Where an entity has such operations, its EPS from continuing operations will not be the same as its total EPS and so disclosure of three basic and three diluted EPS figures will be required. Assuming that the EPS figures for profit or loss on discontinued operations are disclosed on the face of the statement of comprehensive income the disclosure might be as follows:

	20X5	20X4
Earnings per ordinary share:		
Profit from continuing operations	x	x
Profit from discontinued operations	x	x
Profit for the period	x	x
Diluted earnings per share:		
Profit from continuing operations	x	x
Profit from discontinued operations	x	x
Profit for the period	x	x

An example is also given in Table 14.5 above.

14.176 Where there is more than one class of ordinary shares in issue with different rights to share in the profit for the period, basic and diluted EPS figures must be calculated and disclosed for each such class of ordinary shares. [IAS 33 para 66]. The way in which such calculations should be performed is considered from paragraph 14.57 above.

14.177 If a company incurs a loss or the amount it earns for the ordinary equity holders is a negative figure, basic and diluted EPS should be determined in accordance with the rules set out in the standard and shown as a loss per share. [IAS 33 para 69]. Where the diluted loss per share is the same as the basic loss per share, because the company has incurred a loss from continuing operations and all the company's existing potential ordinary shares are not dilutive as they decrease the loss from continuing operations, the entity can disclose these in one line. An example is given in Table 14.9 below. The example illustrates the basic and diluted EPS figures for the loss attributable to ordinary equity holders only and does not illustrate the disclosure for continuing or discontinued operations.

Table 14.9 – Basic and diluted loss per share

Elan Corporation plc – Annual Report and Accounts – 31 December 2010

Consolidated Income Statement

For the Year Ended 31 December 2010 (extract)

	Notes	2010	2009
Basic and diluted net loss per Ordinary Share	14	$ (0.55)	$ (0.32)
Weighted-average shares outstanding (in millions)	14	584.9	506.8

14. Net Loss Per Share

Basic loss per share is computed by dividing the net loss for the period attributable to ordinary shareholders by the weighted-average number of Ordinary Shares outstanding during the period. Diluted net loss per share is computed by dividing the net loss for the period, by the weighted-average number of Ordinary Shares outstanding and, when dilutive, adjusted for the effect of all potentially dilutive shares, including share options and RSUs.

The following table sets forth the computation for basic and diluted net loss per share for the years ended 31 December:

	2010	2009
Numerator (amounts in $m):		
Basic and diluted net loss	(322.6)	(162.3)
Denominator (amounts in millions):		
Denominator for basic and diluted-weighted-average number of Ordinary Shares outstanding	584.9	506.8
Basic and diluted earnings per share:		
Basic and diluted net loss per share	$ (0.55)	$ (0.32)

For the years ended 31 December 2010 and 2009, there were no differences in the weighted-average number of Ordinary Shares used for basic and diluted net loss per Ordinary Share as the effect of all potentially dilutive Ordinary Shares outstanding was anti-dilutive. As at 31 December 2010, there were 22.9 million (2009: 21.3 million) share options and RSUs outstanding that could potentially have a dilutive impact in the future but were anti-dilutive in 2010 and 2009.

Additional disclosures

14.178 The following additional information should be given for both basic and diluted EPS:

■ The amounts used as the numerators in calculating the basic and diluted EPS figures. These amounts should also be reconciled with the profit or loss for the period. The reconciliation should include the individual effect of each class of instrument that affects EPS, that is, it should describe and list the adjustments arising from each of the types of potential ordinary share that has affected the basic earnings figure.

■ The weighted average number of ordinary shares used as the denominator in calculating the basic and diluted EPS figures. The denominators used in the basic and diluted EPS should also be reconciled to each other. This reconciliation should include the individual effect of each class of instrument that affects EPS, that is, it should list and describe the effects of each of the types of dilutive potential ordinary shares that has affected the basic weighted average number.

[IAS 33 para 70(a)(b)].

14.179 An example of how a company can give the above information in a concise manner is shown in the table below. The example illustrates the basic and diluted EPS figures for the profit attributable to ordinary equity holders only and does not illustrate the disclosure for continuing or discontinued operations.

Earnings per share

Example

	Year ended 31 December 20X5		
	Earnings	Number of shares	Per-share amount
Profit for the year	6,525,000		
Less: preference dividends	75,000		
Basic EPS:			
Earnings available to ordinary shareholders	6,450,000	2,500,000	C2.58
Effect of dilutive securities:			
Options		45,000	
Convertible preferred stock	35,000	255,000	
6% convertible debentures	60,000	60,000	
Diluted EPS:			
Adjusted earnings	6,545,000	2,860,000	C2.29

A further example is given in Table 14.4 above.

14.180 The standard also requires disclosure of instruments, including contingently issuable shares, that could dilute EPS in the future, but that were not included in the computation of diluted EPS in the period (or periods) presented, because they were anti-dilutive in that period (or those periods). [IAS 33 para 70(c)].

14.181 As stated in paragraph 14.80, basic and diluted EPS for all periods presented should be restated for bonus issues, share splits, share consolidations and similar events occurring during the period that change the number of shares in issue without a corresponding change in the resources of the entity. If these events occur after the balance sheet date, but before the financial statements are approved for issue, the EPS figures for the current period, and those of any prior periods, should be based on the new number of shares issued (see para 14.169). As a result, the number of shares used in the EPS calculation will not be consistent with that shown in the balance sheet. Therefore, disclosure should be made to that effect. [IAS 33 para 64]. An example of a share split that occurred in the year is Table 14.10 (only the figures for basic EPS are reproduced in the table).

Table 14.10 – EPS adjusted for share split in the year

STADA Arzneimittel AG – Report and Accounts – 31 December 2004

2.18. Earnings per share (extract)

Earnings per share	2004	Previous year
Net income distributable to shareholders of STADA Arzneimittel AG in € 000s	48,484	43,869
Average number of shares	53,348,910[1,2]	43,327,286[1,2]
Earnings per share in €	0.91[2]	1.01[2]

Basic earnings per share are calculated according to IAS 33.10 by dividing net income distributable to the shareholders of STADA Arzneimittel AG by the average number of shares outstanding, less treasury stock.

[1] Please refer to the notes on shareholders' equity (see note 3.12) regarding the change in the number of shares.

[2] Pursuant to IAS 33.20 in conjunction with IAS 33.22, a capital increase from existing funds changes the average number of shares without any concomitant change in the level of resources. The number of common shares in issue prior to the capital increase is adjusted in accordance with the proportional change in the number of outstanding common shares after the share issue as if the event (the de facto 1:1 stock split) had occurred at the beginning of the period under review. For the purposes of historical comparison, the historical figure for the average number of shares in each fiscal year ending prior to the conversion date will be doubled to adjust for the stock split when calculating the earnings per share.

3.12. Share capital (extract)

As of the balance sheet date, share capital consisted of 53,390,820 common shares, each with an arithmetical par value of € 2.60 (prior year: 26,695,290).

The increase in the number of shares in 2004 is almost entirely due to the de facto 1:1 stock split that took place in the year under review and only to a very small extent due to the increase in shares resulting from the initial exercise of options from STADA warrants 2000/2015. STADA executed the de facto 1:1 stock split resolved by the Annual Shareholders' Meeting on June 15, 2004 after close of trading on Friday, July 30, 2004, once the capital measure had been entered into the commercial register.

STADA shareholders received one bonus share for every registered bearer share of restricted transferability they already held (ISIN DE0007251803, WKN 725180). The Company's share capital thereby increased to €138,816,132.00. As a total of 26,695,410 bonus shares were issued, the number of STADA shares also doubled, arithmetically reducing its share price by half. This capital measure therefore constitutes a de facto 1:1 stock split. The bonus shares created by this capital increase from the Company's own funds were automatically credited to STADA shareholders' custody accounts with a value date of August 2, 2004. Shareholders holding their own shares were requested to effect the credit of the bonus shares to which they were entitled via a bank by submitting profit participation certificate no. 11 as proof of entitlement. The text of the official notification to shareholders was also published on STADA's website, www.stada.de.

14.182 Entities are required to disclose details of all material ordinary share transactions or potential ordinary share transactions entered into after the reporting period, other than those described in the preceding paragraph. Such transactions should be disclosed where they would have significantly changed the number of ordinary or potential ordinary shares outstanding at the end of the reporting period if the transactions had occurred before the end of the reporting period. [IAS 33 para 70(d)]. EPS for the period is not adjusted for such post balance sheet transactions, because they do not affect the amount of capital used to produce the profit or loss for the period. Such transactions include:

- Issue of shares for cash.

- Issue of shares where the proceeds are used to repay debt or preference shares outstanding at the balance sheet date.

- Redemption of ordinary shares.

- Conversion of potential ordinary shares outstanding at the balance sheet date into ordinary shares.

- Issue of warrants, options or convertible securities.

- Achievement of conditions that would result in the issue of contingently issuable shares.

[IAS 33 para 71].

14.183 Most of these transactions would fall to be disclosed anyway as material non-adjusting post balance sheet events under IAS 10. An example of disclosure is Table 14.11.

Table 14.11 – Disclosure of post balance sheet changes in capital

Swisscom AG – Annual Report and Accounts – 31 December 2004

41 Post balance sheet events (extract)

Approval by the Board of Directors

Swisscom Board of Directors approved these consolidated financial statements on March 7, 2005.

Dividend

At the General Meeting of Shareholders on April 26, 2005, a dividend of CHF 14 per share, amounting to a total income distribution of CHF 861 million, is to be proposed for 2004. In these financial this dividend payable is not disclosed as a liability. It is accounted for as a dividend contribution against shareholders' equity in 2005. The dividends declared at the 2004 General Meeting of Shareholders in respect of 2003 was CHF 861 million (previous year: CHF 794 million).

Share buy-back

In 2005 the Board of Directors decided to launch a share buy-back scheme in the amount of around CHF 2 billion in order to distribute the entire equity free cash flow.

Convertible bond of the Swiss Confederation on Swisscom shares

About one third of the convertible bonds of the Swiss Confederation related to Swisscom shares, which mature at the end of February 2005, were exercised by the maturity date. According to the Swiss Confederation authorities, of the 2.67 million shares included in the convertible bond, around 915,000 shares were converted. As a result of the conversion the share of the Confederation in Swisscom fell from 62.7% to 61.4%. On April 26, 2005 the Board of Directors applied to the Shareholders' Meeting for a capital reduction. Taking this into account the share of Confederation in Swisscom is now 66.1%.

14.184 The standard also encourages companies to disclose the terms and conditions of financial instruments and other contracts generating potential ordinary shares if disclosure is not already required by IAS 32 or IFRS 7. Such disclosure may help users to understand the extent to which these instruments are dilutive and, if so, the effect they have on the disclosed diluted EPS data. Disclosure of the terms and conditions are particularly relevant for those anti-dilutive securities that are not included in the computation of diluted EPS. [IAS 33 para 72].

Volatility of published EPS

14.185 The EPS figure, which is based on the profits available to ordinary equity holders, is an 'all inclusive' figure and may be volatile. This is because profits or losses of a period may be affected by certain unusual (exceptional) items, such as: profits or losses on the sale or termination of an operation; reorganisation costs; and profits and losses on the disposal of fixed assets. As a result, the presence or absence of such items will affect the EPS figure from one period to another. The requirement to disclose EPS figures for continuing and discontinued operations goes some way to explaining the volatility caused by disposing of operations. However, many companies prefer also to report an adjusted EPS that removes profits and losses of an unusual nature that do not relate to the entity's trading activities. An adjusted EPS is also popular with analysts.

[The next paragraph is 14.187.]

Additional earnings per share

14.187 IAS 33 recognises that there may be instances where a company would wish to disclose additional EPS figures calculated on a level of earnings other than one required by the standard. It, therefore, permits companies to disclose an additional EPS using a reported component of the statement of comprehensive income other than profit or loss for the period, profit or loss for continuing operations and profit or loss for discontinued operations attributable to ordinary equity holders. Such EPS data should, however, be calculated using the weighted average number of ordinary shares determined in accordance with the standard. This means that the weighted average number of ordinary shares used in the calculation of this additional EPS should be the same as the number used in the basic and diluted EPS figures required by the standard. Entities should indicate the basis on which the numerator, that is, the income statement figure, is determined, including whether amounts per share are before or after tax. In addition, if a component of the income statement is used that is not reported as a line item in the statement of comprehensive income (or income statement if presented), a reconciliation should be provided between the component used and a line item that is reported in the statement of comprehensive income. Additional basic and diluted per share amounts should be disclosed with equal prominence and should be presented in the notes to the financial statements. The requirement that such figures should be presented in the notes means that they should not be shown on the face of the income statement as has often been the practice in the past, before the 2003 revision to IAS 33. [IAS 33 paras 73, 73A].

14.188 In November 2005 the Committee of European Securities Regulators (CESR) issued a recommendation on disclosure of alternative performance measures (APMs), which were defined as including 'operating earnings', 'cash earnings', 'earnings before one-time charges', 'EBITDA – earnings before interest, taxes, depreciation, and amortisation' and similar terms denoting adjustments to line items of income statement, balance sheet or cash flow statement. Thus, for example, they would include additional EPS figures. The recommendation included the following points:

- Under the IAS Framework, there are four qualitative characteristics that make the information provided in financial statements useful to users: understandability, relevance, reliability and comparability. CESR believes that issuers should always follow these principles for preparation and presentation of financial information including the preparation of alternative performance measures.

- Issuers should define the terminology used and the basis of calculation adopted (that is, defining the components included in an alternative performance measure). Clear disclosure is key to the understandability of any alternative performance measure and its relevance. Where relevant, investors should be made aware of the fact that alternative performance measures are not prepared in accordance with the accounting standards applied to audited financial statements. Alternative performance measures should be given meaningful names reflecting their basis of preparation in order to avoid misleading messages.

- Where possible, issuers should present alternative performance measures only in combination with defined measures (for example GAAP measures). Furthermore, issuers should explain the differences between both measures. This might be through a reconciliation of figures to provide investors with enough information to fully understand the company's results and financial position.

- Comparatives should be provided for any alternative performance measure presented.

- Alternative performance measures should be presented consistently over time.

- To ensure that investors are not misled, alternative performance measures should not be presented with greater prominence than defined GAAP measures. Where alternative performance measures are derived from audited financial statements and resemble defined performance measures, but do not actually have the characteristics of the defined measures (such characteristics include being audited, based on an identified reporting framework, consistent and comparable with performance measures of other enterprises), CESR recommends that defined measures should be given greater prominence than the alternative performance measures.

■ Issuers may internally use alternative performance measures for measuring and controlling the company's profitability and financial position. Generally, issuers explain this as the reason for presenting alternative performance measures to investors. CESR expects issuers to give an explanation of the internal use of alternative performance measures in order to make investors understand the relevance of this information. This explanation is useful only when presented in direct relation to the alternative performance measures.

[CESR Recommendation on Alternative Performance Measures].

14.189   In practice, most of these recommendations would normally be observed under IFRS in any case. For example, a requirement for consistency of presentation is contained in IAS 1 and it would normally be logical to explain the reason for presenting additional EPS numbers. The recommendation for a reconciliation is to a large extent covered by the IAS 33 requirement that if components of profit are used that are not reported in the income statement there should be a reconciliation to a line item in the income statement.

14.190   Where a company has disclosed an EPS that is additional to the ones required by IAS 33, the requirements stated in paragraph 14.187 above should be followed. An example where a company has followed the standard's requirements where an additional EPS is presented (as explained in para 14.187) is shown in Table 14.12 below. In this example there are no discontinued operations and basic and diluted continuing and total EPS figures are the same.

Table 14.12 – Disclosure of additional EPS figures

Sappi Limited – Annual Report and Accounts – 2 October 2011

7. (Loss) earnings per share and headline (loss) earnings per share

Basic (loss) earnings per share (EPS)

EPS is based on the group's (loss) profit for the year divided by the weighted average number of shares in issue during the year under review.

| | 2011 | | | 2010 | | | 2009 | | |
	Loss US$ million	Shares millions	Loss per share US cents	Profit US$ million	Shares millions	Earnings per share US cents	Loss US$ million	Shares millions	Loss per share US cents
Basic EPS calculation	(232)	519.9	(45)	66	516.7	13	(177)	482.6	(37)
Share options and performance shares under Sappi Limited Share Trust	–	–	–	–	3.9	–	–	–	–
Share options granted under the Broad-based Black Economic Empowerment transaction	–	–	–	–	0.2	–	–	–	–
Diluted EPS calculation	(232)	519.9	(45)	66	520.8	13	(177)	482.6	(37)

The diluted EPS calculations are based on Sappi Limited's daily average share price of ZAR33.66 (2010: ZAR31.86; 2009: ZAR30.12) and exclude the effect of certain share options granted under the Sappi Share Incentive Scheme as well as share options granted under the Broad-based Black Economic Empowerment transaction as they would be anti-dilutive.

There are 12.0 million (2010: 10.6 million; 2009: 15.6 million) share options that could potentially dilute EPS in the future that are not included in the diluted weighted average number of shares calculation as they are anti-dilutive.

Headline (loss) earnings per share[2]

Headline (loss) earnings per share is based on the group's headline (loss) earnings divided by the weighted average number of shares in issue during the year. This is a JSE Limited listings required measure.

Reconciliation between attributable (loss) earnings to ordinary shareholders and headline (loss) earnings:

| | 2011 | | | 2010 | | | 2009 | | |
	Gross	Tax	Net	Gross	Tax	Net	Gross	Tax	Net
Attributable earnings (loss) to ordinary shareholders	(221)	11	(232)	86	20	66	(218)	(41)	(177)
Profit on sale and write-off of property, plant and equipment	(1)	–	(1)	(4)	–	(4)	(1)	–	(1)
(Impairment reversals) impairment of plant and equipment	167	17	150	(10)	–	(10)	79	–	79
Headline earnings (loss)	(55)	28	(83)	72	20	52	(140)	(41)	(99)

Basic weighted average number of ordinary shares in issue (millions)			519.9			516.7			482.6
Headline earnings (loss) per share (US cents)			(16)			10			(21)
Diluted weighted average number of shares (millions)			519.9			520.8			482.6
Diluted headline earnings (loss) per share (US cents)			(16)			10			(21)

(1) In the 2009 financial year, Sappi conducted a renounceable rights offer of 286,886,270 new ordinary shares of ZAR1.00 each to qualifying Sappi shareholders.

(2) Headline earnings – as defined in circular 3/2009 issued by the South African Institute of Chartered Accountants, separates from earnings all separately identifiable remeasurements. It is not necessarily a measure of sustainable earnings.

14.190.1 Under the IAS 32 amendments, certain puttable financial instruments that would otherwise be presented as liabilities are presented as equity (see chapter 6.5 for further details). The IAS 32 amendment does not extend to IAS 33, so these puttable financial instruments do not meet the definition of ordinary shares for EPS purposes. Entities can, however, elect to provide EPS figures for these instruments, similar to the disclosures for other participating instruments as explained in 14.57 onwards.

14.191 Directors should carefully consider what profit measure to choose when calculating additional EPS figures and what information they would wish those figures to convey. This is because whatever profit measure is chosen it must be used consistently (see para 14.189 above). It is not possible to choose a profit measure to present a particular aspect of a company's performance in one year, because performance at that level is good, and then to ignore that measure in the following year when performance at that level is not so good.

[The next paragraph is 14.200.]

Financial statistics in the historical summary

14.200 Entities often publish a historical summary, usually covering at least five years. IAS 33 does not deal specifically with adjustments to historical summaries, but the following guidance is relevant in such situations. In order to present a fair comparison of EPS figures published in such a summary, the basic EPS figure will need to be adjusted for subsequent changes in capital as set out below:

■ Where a capitalisation issue or share split has taken place during a financial year, all previously published EPS figures should be adjusted by the bonus factor as explained in paragraph 14.80 above.

■ Where a rights issue at less than full market has taken place during a financial year, all previously published EPS figures should be adjusted by the reciprocal of the bonus element inherent in the rights issue as explained from paragraph 14.85 above.

Where there is more than one capitalisation or rights issue during the year, both these factors will operate cumulatively. The cumulative effect of all the above events should be taken into account. The resultant figures should be described as restated EPS and should be set out separately from the other financial data that is not so adjusted.

14.201 Where there has been a bonus or rights issue in the period covered by the summary, the ordinary dividend actually paid in those periods should be set out in the form of pence per share and similarly adjusted by the same factors used in restating EPS. This adjustment is necessary to ensure that the ordinary dividends and EPS data are comparable. The adjusted dividend per share should be described as restated. In practice, the adjusted EPS and the adjusted dividend per share are normally presented next to each other.

14.202 Sometimes companies also disclose a dividend cover, which is the number of times a dividend is covered by current earnings. Some companies even disclose price/earnings ratios, high and low share prices or market capitalisation.

14.203 An example of disclosure in a historical summary is Table 14.13. This example includes adjustment of earlier years for a bonus issue (see para 14.200 above).

14.204 IFRS 1 requires at least one year of comparative information prepared under IFRS in an entity's first IFRS financial statements. [IFRS 1 para 36]. The IFRS does not require earlier years in a historical summary (that is, the years before the current and previous year) to comply with IFRS. However, those earlier years, if not presented in compliance with IFRS, must be clearly labelled as not being prepared under IFRS. In addition the nature of the main adjustments that would make those earlier years comply with IFRS should be disclosed. An entity need not quantify those adjustments. [IFRS 1 para 37]. IFRS 1's requirements are considered in detail in chapter 3.

14.205 In Table 14.13, Huhtamaki Oyj, presents the latest two years of the historical summary in accordance with IFRS and earlier years in accordance with Finnish GAAP, but gives the 2002 figures for the year of transition to IFRS under both Finnish GAAP and IFRS. Elsewhere in the financial statements it includes a detailed description of the differences between accounting policies applied under Finnish GAAP and IFRS (not reproduced in Table 14.13).

Table 14.13 – EPS in historical summaries

Huhtamaki Oyj – Annual Report and Accounts – 31 December 2003

Per share data

Comparison figures (1999-2001) adjusted for the 3:1 bonus issue in August 2002

		1999	FAS 2000	2001	2002	IFRS 2002	2003
Earnings per share	EUR	0.60	0.65	0.74	0.88	0.86	0.38
Earnings per share (diluted)		0.86	0.38				
Dividend, nominal	EUR	0.26	0.28	0.31	0.38	0.38	0.38[1]
Dividend/earnings per share	%	43.3	43.1	41.9	43.2	44.2	100.0[1]
Dividend yield	%	3.1	3.9	3.5	4.0	4.0	4.1[1]
Shareholders' equity per share	EUR	7.61	8.20	8.64	8.79	8.26	7.85
Share price at December 31	EUR	8.40	7.10	8.88	9.55	9.55	9.35
Average number of shares adjusted for share issue		111,856,128	125,903,852	117,117,696	100,769,970	100,769,970	96,292,220
Number of shares adjusted for share issue at year end		125,903,852	125,903,852	101,215,792	97,547,792	97,547,792	96,161,703
P/E ratio		14.0	10.9	12.0	10.9	11.1	24.6
Market capitalization at December 31 EUR million		1,057.6	893.9	898.3	931.6	931.6	899.1

[1] 2003: Board's proposal.